DAY BY DAY

The Forties

DAY BY DAY

The Forties

by Thomas M. Leonard
Associate Professor of History
University of North Florida

Edited by Richard Burbank
and
Steven L. Goulden

Facts On File, Inc.

Day by Day: The Forties

Facts On File, Inc.
132 West 31st Street
New York NY 10001

Library of Congress Cataloging-in-Publication Data

Leonard, Thomas M. 1937–
Day by day, the forties.
p. cm
Includes index.
ISBN 0-87196-375-2
1. History, Modern—20th century—Chronology. I. Burbank, Richard. II. Goulden, Steven L. III. Title.
D427.L4
909.82'4'0202 77-13251

Facts On File books are available at special discounts when purchased in bulk quantities for businesses, associations, institutions or sales promotions. Please call our Special Sales Department in New York at (212) 967-8800 or (800) 322-8755.

You can find Facts On File on the World Wide Web at http://www.factsonfile.com

Cover design by Cathy Rincon

Printed in the United States of America

IBT 10 9 8 7 6

This book is printed on acid-free paper.

CONTENTS

EDITORS' PREFACE

Day by Day: The Forties is a volume designed to provide both quick reference to specific events and a broad overview of the decade. It is intended for the general reader as well as the researcher. This volume is part of the *Day by Day* series, the next volume of which covers the 1950s.

Most of the material in *Day by Day* is based on the *Facts On File Yearbooks*, supplemented by major newspapers and scholarly reference works. The emphasis throughout is on events of public record, reported in the news media, but secret agreements and other nonpublic events (such as the Yalta and Potsdam Conferences) are also included when they are of critical importance. The enormous amount of material in this volume makes it impossible to treat any single event in great detail. Readers interested in more information are advised to consult one of the many excellent reference works on the 1940s, such as Joseph C. Goulden's *The Best Years*, or more specialized works.

One of the main objectives of *Day by Day* is to provide a "feel" for the decade, a sense of what it was like to live during the 1940s. For this reason, the terminology of the period is used whenever it represents common, polite usage. Thus, "Negro" appears in preference to "black" or "African American." The words "German" and "Nazi" are often used interchangeably during the war years, following the practice of newspaper headlines.

The material of *Day by Day* is grouped into 10 categories, designed to facilitate the location and comparison of events. At a glance, the reader can trace a series of similar occurrences down a single column or contrast the events of a single day running across two facing pages. To make this possible, great pains have been taken to group events consistently into broad categories that retain their significance over a long period of time. In general, entries on each left-hand page involve international affairs, while right-hand pages deal almost entirely with U.S. domestic developments. Each year is preceded by a monthly summary of events to include developments that cannot be fixed to a single date.

The end of World War II and the growth of the Cold War brought such profound changes in the international arena that some revision of category columns in the middle of the volume was considered necessary. The third column refers to the Pacific war zone before September 1, 1945, and to the Middle East and Africa after that point. During the war, the fifth column includes all parts of the world (except the United States and Latin America) not directly involved in the fighting. After September 1, 1945, this column contains events in East Asia and the Pacific. Wartime events in North Africa, which had a close relationship to events in Europe, are included in the second column (European war zone); subsequently the area falls under the third column.

Aside from these changes, it is hoped that the meaning of the columns is self-evident. The first column (World Affairs, throughout the volume) includes very important political developments, generally involving more than one country. Significant accidents and weather phenomena are placed in the area in which they occurred, since they often had important political, social and economic consequences for the inhabitants. Accidents and weather reports in the United States are included in the Science and Technology column.

Day by Day: The Forties includes an index designed to facilitate reference to specific events. For this reason, it is keyed to dates and columns rather than page numbers.

The volume's two editors are each responsible for about half of the contents, Richard Burbank handled the war years; Steven L. Goulden, the postwar years. Both editors would like to thank a number of people without whose help the volume would not have been possible. Marjorie Bank and Rachel Rephan Ginsburg devoted great time and effort to compiling the index. Justus Schlichting, James Madsen and Marshall Baron of Commerce Clearing House developed and implemented the computer program originally used in the typesetting of *Day by Day*. Tom Oglesby and Jonathan Heller of the National Archives gave generously of their time to help in photo research for the volume. Patrick Smith designed the photo layouts and many other aspects of the book. Facts On File's former executive editor Edward Knappman originated the concept of *Day by Day* and assisted in innumerable details of the editorial process.

INTRODUCTION

From late summer 1939 until early spring 1940 Europe was engaged in a "Phony War." Britain and France gave the appearance of being removed from a conflict they had come to accept. London was confident in its mastery of the seas, and Paris felt secure behind the Maginot Line. In Berlin, however, Adolf Hitler was plotting. Secure to the east with Poland beaten into submission and Russia tied to a nonagression pact, Hitler looked west. He first decided upon Denmark and Norway, which, in addition to increased food supplies, provided bases for air and sea attacks upon Britain and safeguarded the German flank in an invasion of France.

The blitz of Norway, Denmark, the Low Countries and France began in April and was completed in June. Landing north of the Maginot Line on May 10, German troops moved quickly through Belgium, the Netherlands and Luxembourg, driving into France. Air superiority provided the final German edge, and France capitulated on June 22, after Italy joined the fighting to share in the Axis victory.

Hitler then planned an invasion of the British Isles (Operation Sea Lion). Unable to achieve the air and sea dominance necessary for the assault, Hitler indefinitely postponed the invasion. Britain, however, was not safe from the German Luftwaffe, which carried out intensive air attacks through November 1940, when the Balkan theater heated up.

Russia moved first in the Balkans, forcing Rumania to surrender territory gained at the close of World War I. Hitler determined that Russian expansion had to be checked in order to accelerate Britain's fall. Following Bulgaria's forced adherence to the Axis Pact, German troops invaded Yugoslavia and Greece. By the end of May 1941, both countries surrendered, and German paratroops occupied the strategic island of Crete. Although subsequent Nazi efforts in Iraq and Syria failed, Germany commanded a secure line from the Baltic to the Black Sea.

The vast influx of German forces into Eastern Europe did not go unnoticed, but Soviet premier Stalin refused to heed warnings from the British and Americans, and even from his own intelligence agents. Without provocation, on June 22, 1941, the Germans launched the greatest offensive of World War II. German armored units reached the suburbs of Moscow and Leningrad within a few months, conquering more territory in less time than any army in history. But the Russian winter and the country's vast size stretched the German supply system beyond its limits. When the Red Army launched a counteroffensive in December, Hitler took personal command of the German forces, a move interpreted by many historians to be a major turning point in the German conduct of the war.

Aggression was not confined to Europe. In the name of a "Greater East Asian Co-Prosperity Sphere," Japan intended to establish its economic and political hegemony in the Pacific. At war with China since 1937, Japan controlled most Chinese commercial and population centers, and by March 1940 was secure enough in central China to establish a puppet government in Nanking under Wang Ching-wei. Germany's spring success against France enabled Japan to expand its influence in Indochina and force Britain to close the Burma Road for three months.

In quest of its objectives, Tokyo opened a diplomatic offensive in the fall of 1940. It joined the Axis alliance in the hope of countering U.S. pressure against Japanese Pacific expansion. Tokyo also dictated an end to the Thailand-Indochina border dispute in order to gain access to needed raw materials in both countries. A five-year neutrality pact with Russia in early 1941 secured the northern flank. After Germany's invasion of Russia, a Japanese Imperial Conference on July 2, 1941, approved a thrust into Southeast Asia and the Pacific at the risk of war with the Americans, British and Dutch.

On September 6, 1941, important militarists gave Premier Fumimaro Konoe a month to force American acceptance of Japan's Asian sphere. If diplomacy failed, the U.S. fleet at Pearl Harbor was to be eliminated, enabling Japan to round out an empire stretching from Manchuria southeast to Thailand and south to New Guinea. After October 1941, negotiations in Washington were only a facade. Quietly on the morning of November 26, 1941, a Japanese task force moved out of Hitokappu Bay across the North Pacific toward Pearl Harbor, where a daring and successful attack was carried out on December 7. Japanese forces simultaneously invaded the Philippines, Malaya and Hong Kong. Within four days the world was at war.

The Nazi invasion of the Low Countries and France in the spring of 1940 caused a bitter debate within the United States over the issue of neutrality. Words were used carelessly. Kansas newspaper editor William Allen White chaired the Committee to Defend America by Aiding the Allies, a group favoring assistance short of war. The more outspoken Fight for Freedom Committee wanted a war declaration. The America First Committee presented the anti-involvement side, and drew upon the talents of Charles Lindbergh, General Hugh Johnson and Senators Gerald P. Nye and Burton K. Wheeler. Both Republicans and Democrats were split on the issue. The 1940 presidential candidates Wendell Willkie and Franklin D. Roosevelt issued antiwar statements to placate isolationists, but both favored a stand against the Axis.

Roosevelt pursued a policy that tended toward war in the Atlantic but not in the Pacific. Initially, U.S. aid to Britain flowed secretly through Canada. But the destroyer-for-bases deal of September 1940 and the Burke-Wadsworth bill providing for a peace time army marked a major shift in American policy. After bitter debate, Congress passed the Lend-Lease bill in March 1941, permitting the president to extend $7 billion in aid to the Allies, including Russia after her invasion by Germany in June. Roosevelt went further, extending the hemispheric "safety belt" to Greenland and Iceland, both of which were subsequently occupied by American forces. American and British ships and planes then cooperated in tracking German submarines in the North Atlantic, protecting convoys of supplies destined for England. The Germans responded in kind, sinking the *Robin Moor* in the South Atlantic and the *Kearney* near Iceland. Finally, in the fall of 1941, Roosevelt ordered American ships to "shoot on sight" any Axis raider within the defense perimeter, and Congress partially repealed the 1939 neutrality law to permit U.S. ships to enter the war zones. Thus, as December approached, the United States was engaged in an unofficial but limited war in the Atlantic.

War came, but in the Pacific, where the Americans least expected it. Washington had been troubled for over a decade by Japan's Asian expansion. Committed to the "Open Door," the United States sought to maintain China's territorial sovereignty and political integrity. As 1940 opened, the United States attempted to limit Japanese expansion through economic coercion. First, the 1911 commercial treaty was abrogated, and by the fall of 1940, shipments of oil, scrap iron and other raw materials to Japan were greatly curtailed. After Japan occupied French Indochina in July 1941, all Japanese assets in the United States were frozen. The economic weapon, however, only provoked further Japanese expansion.

In the diplomatic sphere, Admiral Kichisaburo Nomura came to Washington hoping to gain U.S. recognition of Japan's "special relationship" to the Asian mainland. Prince Konoe's proposal for a summit meeting with Roosevelt to settle issues in August 1941 fell upon deaf ears. U.S. officials were convinced that the proposed conference would not bring Japanese militarists to withdraw from China. While proposing a modus vivendi on November 25, 1941, Washington was unaware that the Japanese fleet was assembling that very day for its December 7 attack on Pearl Harbor.

Militarily, the winter of 1942–43 proved to be the war's turning point in Europe. Until this time the Axis had suffered few defeats and retained the strategic initiative. Henceforth, the Allies steadily mobilized their resources and seized the initiative, pressing on to an unconditional victory. The Allied landings in North Africa, British victory in Libya and the Russian success at Stalingrad all took place between November 1942 and March 1943.

In the first step of the new Allied offensive, Gen. Dwight D. Eisenhower directed the U.S. invasion of North Africa (Operation Torch) on November 8, 1942. Thanks to successful negotiations with Vichyite administrators, U.S. forces encountered only slight resistance in their landings at Casablanca, Oran and Algiers. This action caused Hitler to order the occupation of all France, but the Germans failed to seize the French fleet at Toulon. Further east in North Africa, Rommel's Afrika Korps and the British 8th Army were locked in battle. In October 1942 Gen. Bernard L. Montgomery opened an offensive at El Alamein, Egypt. Breaking through the Axis positions, he pursued Rommel's forces through the Libyan Desert to Tripoli. After eventual success in the winter of 1942–43, the Americans and the British attacked Rommel's army from the east and southwest, routing the Germans during April and forcing their surrender in May. North Africa and the Middle East lay securely in Allied hands.

On the Russian front, German troops resumed their offensive in May 1942. By late August, Stalingrad was under siege, but the Russians refused to yield further. Plagued by inadequate logistic support and an early winter, the German 6th Army under Field Marshal Friedrich von Paulus surrendered in January 1943. Only 90,000 of its original 350,000 men remained alive.

To the disappointment of Stalin, the British and Americans were not yet prepared for a cross-Channel invasion of France, selecting Italy as their next target. Sicily was invaded in July 1943 and occupied in 39 days. This was followed in September by an American-British invasion of southern Italy, the overthrow of Mussolini and Italy's surrender. Stiff German resistance, however, slowed the Allies' northward progress. Not until June 1944 did Rome fall, the first Axis capital to so do.

In the meantime, the Allies increased their air assaults upon Germany, hoping to reduce her war-making capabilities. Key targets included the Ploesti oil fields in Rumania, hydroelectric dams in the Ruhr Valley and automotive and munitions plants throughout Germany.

As early as 1942, Allied planners judged that a cross-Channel invasion was the quickest road to victory over Germany. By late 1943, the Americans and British had accumulated adequate men and supplies to conduct the offensive (Operation Overlord). Under Eisenhower's direction, the Allies landed on a 50-mile front along the Normandy coast on June 6, 1944. In late July, U.S. armored forces under Gen. George Patton broke out of the beachhead and penetrated the French interior. Before the German defenses stiffened in September, most of Belgium and France had been liberated. As U.S., British and French forces were regrouping for an assault on Germany, German armies under Gen. Karl von Rundstedt made a sudden drive into the American line in Belgium and Luxembourg. For 10 days in late December 1944 the Battle of the Bulge was waged at heavy cost to the Allies. This proved, however, to be the last major German offensive.

After the last German offensive against Russia in July 1943, the Allied pincers began to close against Germany from the east. Within a year the Soviets had retaken the Ukraine, the Crimea, White Russia and eastern Poland. In a five-month span in 1944, Russia eliminated three Axis satellites protecting Germany's southeastern flank: Rumania, Bulgaria and Hungary. With the opening of 1945, American, British and French forces drove into Germany from the west, meeting the Russian thrust from the Danube valley, Poland and East Prussia. Hitler's suicide on April 30 sealed the collapse of the Third Reich. A seven-day battle for Berlin ended May 7 when German delegates accepted the terms of unconditional surrender in Reims, France.

As the war turned against Germany, the destruction of Jews and other internal "enemies" of Nazism proceeded at an increasing pace. The policy of extermination, decided upon in January 1942, was implemented by Heinrich Himmler's SS in death camps (Auschwitz, Belzec, Sobibor, Maidanek and Treblinka) and through mobile commando units that followed the German Army on the eastern front. Toward the end of the war, as inmates were crowded into fewer and fewer camps, even labor camps not designed for systematic extermination became places of death and destruction. Sixty-seven percent of Europe's Jews, 5.93 million people, fell victim to the SS. The "final solution" came closest to success in Poland and Germany, where scarcely 10 percent of the Jewish population survived the war.

For most of the war's duration, the Allies viewed the Pacific theater as a secondary combat area. Shortly after their successful attack upon Pearl Harbor, the Japanese struck at Allied bases throughout the Pacific. Quickly, the cities of Manila and Cavite in the Philippines and the British Crown colony of Hong Kong were taken, along with the strategic islands of Guam and Wake. Japanese forces moved down the Malay Peninsula, forcing the British to surrender Singapore on February 15, 1942. Japanese troops successfully advanced in the Dutch East Indies, while in the Southeast Pacific they occupied the Admiralty and Solomon Islands. Against stubborn opposition, the Japanese conquered Burma, cutting the Burma Road, the main supply route to Nationalist China. Despite these stunning defeats, however, the Allies did not seek peace as Japan had expected.

U.S. forces checked the Japanese advance during mid-1942 with three important battles. First of these was the Battle of the Coral Sea in May, an air and naval engagement that destroyed 100,000 tons of Japanese shipping. Next came the four-day battle for Midway in June, which cost the Japanese heavily (four aircraft carriers, 250 planes and 2,200 men) and prevented them from securing their outer defense perimeter. The Americans won their third victory in the battle for Guadalcanal, which began in August 1942 and prevented the Japanese from cutting Australia's supply route in the western Pacific. With Guadalcanal secured by February 1943, the Allies put Japan permanently on the defensive.

To move from containment to victory, the Allies began an amphibious offensive with three objectives: (1) recapture the Philippines, (2) cut Japan's lines of communications with her overseas garrisons and (3) establish bases for an attack upon the Japanese home islands.

In the South Pacific, Americans and Australians inched their way up the New Guinea coast toward the major Japanese military installation at Rabaul. U.S. forces in the central Pacific pursued an island-hopping campaign, seizing key islands and bypassing others. In 1943 and 1944 Bougainville, Tarawa, Kwajalein, Guam and Peleliu fell to the Americans. Following successful naval battles in the Philippine Sea and Leyte Gulf, American troops landed on Luzon in January 1945, cutting Japan's southern supply route. The capture of Iwo Jima in March and Okinawa in June 1945 placed U.S. bombers within striking distance of Japanese cities.

On the Asian mainland, Allied strategy called for preserving the war-making capacity of China, where millions of Japanese troops were tied down. As U.S. planes continued to supply Chungking over the Himalayas from India, a campaign began in 1943 to reopen the Burma Road. Completed in January 1945, a new highway connected northwest India with the old road at the Chinese border. In the spring of 1945, British forces recaptured the important cities of Mandalay and Rangoon. Otherwise, progress on the mainland against the Japanese was limited to the struggle for control of central China.

Allied strategists rejected the option of fighting a land war in Asia and chose, instead, to invade Japan as the quickest way of ending the Pacific War. After Germany's defeat, men and material were being gathered in the Pacific for the invasion, when U.S. scientists successfully tested the atomic bomb. To avoid prolonging the fighting for at least another year, President Harry S. Truman ordered the use of atomic bombs against Japan. Hiroshima and Nagasaki were destroyed on August 6 and 9, forcing Japan's surrender on September 2, 1945. The world was at peace after six years of destruction and holocaust.

In the diplomatic field, Allied cooperation began even before U.S. entry into the war. In August 1941, Roosevelt and Churchill conferred aboard the British battleship *Prince of Wales* off the Newfoundland coast. The resulting document, known as the Atlantic Charter, disclaimed territorial gains for Britain and the United States, proposed some form of postwar international organization and called for self-determination in countries liberated from the Axis. Two weeks after the Pearl Harbor attack, Churchill and British foreign secretary Anthony Eden again visited Roosevelt. Joined by Russian ambassador Maxim Litvinov, the Allied statesmen drew up the United Nations Declaration, pledging their countries to use their full resources to defeat the Axis. The conference also agreed to concentrate first on the defeat of Germany and launch a cross-Channel invasion of Europe as quickly as possible. The United States took prime responsibility for keeping China in the war and waging a struggle of attrition against Japan until Hitler was defeated.

Beyond this general agreement, however, the Allied leaders held sharply different (and potentially conflicting) war aims. Stalin's demands on Germany included dismemberment, extensive reparations and reduction to a pastoral state. Stalin also insisted on creating a cordon of "friendly" governments in Eastern Europe to provide a measure of security for Russia. Churchill, who understood balance-of-power politics and feared the expansion of Soviet power, wanted Russia restricted to a limited sphere of influence: at a Moscow conference in October 1944, he actually agreed with Stalin (informally, of course) on the division of Europe into Western and Soviet spheres. Roosevelt refused to participate in such actions. Fearful of the nationalism that had lost the peace after World War I, FDR sought Stalin's trust and wanted to postpone political decisions until the war's end. The Russian leader remained suspicious, however, over the repeated postponement of the cross-Channel invasion; here, it seemed, was a Western plot to let the Nazis and Communists bleed one another white.

The "Big Three" met together for the first time at Teheran in November 1943. Stalin learned that the cross-Channel invasion was definitely scheduled for the spring of 1944. Most other questions raised at the conference were deferred to later meetings, including Stalin's demands on Germany, Soviet absorption of the Baltic states and adjustment of Poland's eastern border. In the Pacific, Operation Overlord meant the scaling down of the anticipated Burma campaign. Russian participation in the war against Japan was also explored, with suggestions for compensation including Russian acquisition of a warm water port and control of the Kuriles and Sakhalin.

In little more than a year, with European victory in sight, the "Big Three" gathered at Yalta. Again, most final decisions were deferred, except for the assignment of German occupation zones. The most troublesome question involved Poland, where the Russians had installed the Communist-dominated Lublin regime at the expense of the official Polish exile government in London. Aside from pressing Stalin to expand participation, Churchill and Roosevelt could do little. Russia also agreed to enter the Pacific War in return for the compensation suggested at Teheran, plus a role in the occupation of Korea and Japan. The meeting ended with an idealistic declaration that did not reveal Allied disunity.

In the spring of 1945, East-West tensions increased. Soviet political interference in Rumania, Bulgaria, Yugoslavia, Albania, Hungary and Poland indicated her definition of "friendly" governments. Her abrasive manner in Germany and pressure upon Turkey and Iran led Truman to terminate Lend-Lease aid to Russia shortly after Germany's defeat. What proved to be the final effort to maintain Allied unity came at Potsdam in July and August 1945. This was Truman's first experience in "summit diplomacy." Churchill was replaced in mid-conference by British Labor Party leader Clement Attlee as a result of British elections. But these changes had little affect on policy. Truman and Attlee were anxious to coordinate Allied German policy and establish the mechanism for free elections in liberated Europe. Stalin, on the other hand, wanted Western acceptance of Poland's new borders, German reparations, and diplomatic recognition of the pro-Soviet governments in Eastern Europe and the Balkans. During the conference, Truman learned of the successful testing of the atomic bomb and directed its use against Japan, possibly to serve notice to the Russians against expansion. After Potsdam, Allied unity was a pipe dream.

Despite diverging Allied war aims, enough unity of purpose remained during the war years to set the groundwork for the international organizations foreseen in the Atlantic Charter. Allied economic experts, meeting in July 1944 at Bretton Woods, New Hampshire, agreed to establish an $8.8 billion international loan fund to help stabilize national currencies and facilitate international payments. Agreement was also reached on the capitalization of a World Bank at $9.1 billion to provide loans for needy nations. The political counterpart to Bretton Woods was a six-week meeting on the Washington estate of Dumbarton Oaks, at which Big Four delegates worked out a tentative draft for the United Nations Organization. In February 1945, a compromise voting procedure was agreed upon at Yalta and invitations went out for a meeting in San Francisco to finalize the organization.

As representatives of 46 nations gathered in San Francisco on April 29, 1945, flags flew at half mast in memory of the late Franklin Roosevelt. Beneath a superficial show of unity, however, four major stumbling blocks indicated prevalent Allied tensions. On the issue of representation, Russian delegates successfully pressed for the admission of the Ukraine and White Russia, but failed in a bid to have Poland seated. Moscow also failed to block the seating of pro-fascist Argentina, which bought admission to the conference with a last-minute declaration of war against the Axis. Another point of friction was colonialism, with Russian demands for thoroughgoing reform clashing with Western attachment to the status quo. A compromise resulted in the creation of a Trusteeship Council, together with a vague promise of eventual independence for colonies. A third disagreement involved regional organizations such as the Pan American Union recently formed at Chapultepec. Although Russia charged that regional pacts would wreck the United Nations, it accepted a charter provision (Article 51) permitting them to function within the organization's framework. Finally, the Soviets insisted that the Big Five (Russia, Britain, France, China and the United States) should have the right to veto any issue before the Security Council and close off debate. Small nations opposed this attempt at a "gag rule." Only after presidential adviser Harry Hopkins appealed personally to Stalin was a compromise reached, permitting the great powers to retain their veto right but allowing small nations to bring any controversial issue before the Security Council for debate.

The United Nations Charter was probably the most satisfactory document attainable at that time. Yet the new organization, like the end of the war, gave only the illusion of peace.

At the war's start, the American government effort to mobilize the nation's resources seemed deficient in many respects and President Roosevelt was widely criticized for inept administration. The partially stagnant economy of 1939 was converted into an all-out war economy in three distinct stages, completed in the summer of 1942. During the first stage, from August 1939 to April 1940, little was accomplished. An economic spurt occurred when fighting began in Europe, but receded during the "Phony War" that followed. The German onslaught in the spring of 1940, however, opened a new stage marked by British orders and vast appropriations for national defense. On May 28, 1940, Roosevelt appointed General Motors president William Knudsen to head the National Defense Advisory Council, which was to balance the conflicting claims of business, labor and agriculture. Torn by constant strife, the NDAC was disbanded in April 1941 and replaced by the Office of Production Management to ensure equal treatment of business and labor, and the Office of Price Administration, charged with preventing inflation and protecting consumer interests.

After Pearl Harbor, mobilization moved into high gear. On January 16, 1942, Roosevelt named Sears Roebuck head Donald M. Nelson chief of the War Production Board with supreme powers over the economy. In October 1942 Supreme Court Justice James F. Byrnes was appointed head of the Office of Economic Stabilization with power to supervise all economic phases of the war effort. Numerous lesser agencies became targets of criticism. Businessmen charged that bureaucrats shunted them from office to board and commission in a web of unending red tape. Yet, most wartime agencies performed creditably. When Japanese success in the Pacific resulted in the loss of America's main rubber supply, a synthetic rubber industry was built from scratch under the guidance of rubber administrator William M. Jeffers. The war shipping administrator, Rear Admiral Emory S. Land, brought the shipbuilding industry up to the incredible level of turning out merchant ships in 10 days from laying a keel to launching. In June 1942, Congress created the Smaller War Plants Corporation, which tapped neglected strata of productive power in small machine shops and parts-fabrication and assembly plants. Finally, Paul V. McNutt was placed in charge of the War Manpower Commission to deal with the sensitive question of rational allocation of personnel to war industry, farm production and the armed forces.

The statistical results of national mobilization were mind-boggling. In dollar value, the national output of goods rose from $97.1 billion in 1940 to $198.7 billion in 1944, of which $31.1 billion represented price increases. The application Of mass-production, assembly-line techniques to the manufacture of airplanes, tanks, ships, guns and other war material brought staggering results. In May 1940 the aircraft industry turned out about 6,000 planes; in 1944 the figure was 96,000. Construction of merchant ships rose from 1 million tons in 1941 to about 18 million tons in 1943 U.S. wartime steel production totaled more than that of the rest of the world combined.

Scientists, too, produced great achievements during the war. In June 1940, the National Defense Research Council was established and reorganized a year later as the Office of Scientific Research and Development. Directed by Vannevar Bush, the agency organized scientists in numerous projects. The highly secret "Manhattan Project" resulted in the successful manufacture of the atomic bomb. Another significant military development was the proximity fuse. Fixed in the nose of a bomb or artillery shell, it detonated upon reaching the target area, markedly increasing the lethal effect. Use of this discovery was especially significant in the naval battles against Japanese aircraft and against the Germans in the Battle of the Bulge. Radar was improved and used widely in fire-control systems for land batteries, on ships and in airplanes. In rocketry, however, the Allies never matched the German advances during the war.

Lifesaving techniques were also perfected. Sulfa drugs, most discovered abroad, were produced in quantity in the United States and used in combating infectious diseases. Among the antibiotics, penicillin was most important. DDT was used by the military abroad to kill disease-bearing vermin.

In the tight labor market created by the war's demands, labor unions grew in strength. In March 1941 Roosevelt attempted to bring together representatives of management, labor and the public by establishing a National Defense Mediation Board. The effort failed in November, when CIO members resigned over the board's refusal to recommend a union shop in the coal mines. In January 1942 Roosevelt replaced it with the National War Labor Board, empowered to set wages, hours and working conditions. In June 1943 Congress overrode Roosevelt's veto to pass the War Labor Disputes Act, which authorized the president to seize plants where labor disputes threatened war production, prohibited strike agitation in seized plants and required 30 days' notice of intention to strike a war plant. Two notable seizures resulting from the act were the nation's railroads in December 1943 and the Montgomery War Company in December 1944. John L. Lewis's coal miners constantly defied the government, threatening strikes and slowdowns. Yet in all there were only 15,000 work stoppages during the war with a loss of 36 million man days, amounting to one-tenth of 1 percent of total working time.

To combat inflation, the Emergency Price Control Act of January 1942 authorized price fixing and rent controls. But scarcity of goods and wage increases under the "Little Steel Formula" created new pressures, and Congress responded with the Anti-Inflation Act of 1942, authorizing the freezing of prices and wages. On April 8, 1943, Roosevelt went further, issuing an executive decree that permitted wage and price increases only to correct substandard living conditions. Rationing of scarce commodities and foods began in 1942. In all, 13 rationing programs were established.

Federal spending during the war (1941–45) amounted to $32.1 billion, while personal income for the same period rose from $92 to $157 billion. To hold down inflationary pressures, the government relied on two methods: (1) raise as much money as possible through taxation and (2) borrow from individuals and from nonbanking institutions. In October 1842 Congress passed the "greatest tax bill in history," raising the total number of taxpayers from 13 to 50 million. In all, about 40 percent of the war costs were paid by current taxes. The Treasury sold some $40 billion worth of series "E" bonds in small denominations and another $60 billion to nonbanking institutions. Despite these efforts, the cost of living rose an estimated 35 percent during the war and the national debt reached $259 billion in 1945.

Party politics revived during the 1942 congressional elections, but only on domestic issues. While the Republicans maintained bipartisan support of the administration's war effort, they campaigned vigorously against the New Deal and alleged government waste and inefficiency. The GOP gained 46 House seats and nine Senate seats, narrowing the Democratic Party margins to 222-209 and 57-38, respectively. The 1944 presidential election caused problems for both parties. Many Democrats did not want FDR to seek a fourth term, but supported him in the absence of another suitable candidate. A party fight prevented the controversial Henry A. Wallace from gaining the vice presidential nod and gave the number-two spot to lesser-known Harry S. Truman. The Republicans rejected Wendell Willkie and instead nominated New York governor Thomas B. Dewey and Ohio governor John W. Bricker for president and vice president. The GOP tried to capitalize on 12 years of New Deal mistakes and rivalries among administration leaders. But voters were attracted by Roosevelt's "Economic Bill of Rights" for postwar reconversion and retained confidence in his foreign policy. The president won the contest by some 3 million votes. The Democrats also gained 20 seats in the House, but lost one in the Senate. Roosevelt did not live to see the war end or have the opportunity to supervise postwar reconversion. He died in Warm Springs, Georgia, on April 12, 1945, and Harry S. Truman became the 32nd U.S. president.

No American escaped the impact of the war effort. Manpower mobilization entailed the greatest reshuffling of population in the nation's history, with an estimated 27.3 million people moving during the war. With the return of prosperity and impending departure of soldiers, marriage and birth rates increased. Young wives and mothers fared badly in crowded housing conditions. More than 2.5 million wives were separated from their husbands due to the war. Because military personnel could not be divorced without their wives' consent, a heavy backlog built up for postwar divorce courts. With mothers forced to work overtime and double shifts, children often suffered neglect. Juvenile delinquency increased by an estimated 56 percent.

The agricultural South was stripped of underprivileged whites and blacks, as approximately 1.6 million people left the region for industrial jobs in the North. Blacks continued to suffer discrimination, and tensions in the North flared into riots, the most serious erupting in Detroit in June 1943. Civil liberties were generally preserved, with one major exception: the relocation of some 117,000 Americans of Japanese descent on the West Coast after Pearl Harbor. Fearful of sabotage and espionage, the government sent these Japanese-Americans to 10 relocation centers in the interior. They suffered financial loss amounting to at least 40 percent of their possessions before being released in 1944.

Shortly after the wartime battles closed, Allied discord developed into a nerve-wracking confrontation. The Cold War took the place of the shooting in both Europe and Asia. By decade's end, East and West were caught in a confrontation short of war. The conflict first became apparent in Europe, as efforts to achieve peace treaties with Germany's partners bogged down in suspicion and recrimination. At Potsdam, the Council of Allied Foreign Ministers was assigned the task of drafting peace treaties for the five secondary Axis powers: Italy, Bulgaria, Rumania, Hungary and Finland. A series of conferences in London, Paris, Moscow and New York finally produced agreement in late 1946 on boundaries, reparations and other questions. The belligerents signed their respective treaties in Paris on February 10, 1947.

In territorial terms, the nations of Europe changed much less after World War II than after World War I. There were no appreciable alterations in the West, where the prewar Franco-German boundary was reestablished. In the East, Hungary and Bulgaria were reduced to their pre-1938 frontiers. Russia legitimized her claims to Bessarabia and northern Bucovina, in addition to territory conquered from Finland in 1940. The Soviets also adjusted the Polish borders westward, retaining the lands that they seized in 1939. The question of Trieste, claimed by both Italy and Yugoslavia, became a major stumbling block in negotiation of the Italian treaty. A final compromise made Trieste a free territory, but the city remained under Allied occupation until 1954 because a governor could not be agreed upon.

In the meantime, disagreements over the occupation of Germany fueled American-Soviet rivalry. The immediate controversy involved reparations. Claiming that Germany owed them $10 billion in war damages, Russian authorities began dismantling industries and rail lines in their occupation zone and sent Germans back to Russia as a labor force. The Russians also failed to provide foodstuffs to the Western zones as previously promised. Reacting to these difficulties in 1946, the Americans and British denied the Russians dismantling rights in western Germany and arranged the economic integration of their occupation zones. France later joined, forming a "Trizonia," which paved the way for creation of the West German state.

Russian actions elsewhere heightened tensions with the West, bringing increased American involvement in European affairs. Controlled Polish elections in 1947 resulted in a Communist victory. Greek guerrillas received Communist aid through Yugoslavia and Bulgaria. Russian pressure in both Turkey and Iran indicated a desire for expansion in the Middle East. By 1948, Communist actions seemed to bear out Winston Churchill's claim that an "Iron Curtain" had descended over Europe from the Baltic to the Adriatic. Compounding the problem was Britain's bleak economic position through the harsh winter of 1947, and her announced military retreat "east of Suez."

Viewing Russian actions as naked aggression, the Truman administration responded forcefully. When economic coercion (interruption of Lend-Lease aid and denial of a reconstruction loan) failed to alter Moscow's policy, Truman and his advisers decided to "contain" Soviet expansion. On March 12, 1947, Truman urged Congress to approve a $400 million economic and military aid package for Greece and Turkey. With this appropriation the United States committed itself to assisting "free peoples" resisting subjugation. The Truman Doctrine also set in motion steps for European economic recovery. Speaking at the 1947 Harvard commencement, Secretary of State George C. Marshall suggested that if the European nations devised long-range plans for their own economic recovery, the United States would supply the necessary assistance. After Russia and other Communist states refused to participate, representatives of 16 Western European nations gathered in Paris from July to September 1947 to discuss their needs. With an initial American outlay of $6.098 billion in 1948, the European Recovery Program was under way.

Russian policy at this time aimed at blunting Western European economic recovery. The Cominform was created in October 1947 with the objective of countering the Marshall Plan. The so-called Molotov Plan tied the nine satellite economies to Russia. Disturbed by the economic revival of western Germany, the Russians blockaded Berlin starting on June 24, 1948, in the hope of driving their former allies from the former German capital. For nearly a year, U.S. and British authorities airlifted the daily needs of 2.5 million people into beleaguered Berlin—a feat known as "Operation Vittles."

Western economic unity was subsequently enhanced by a military alliance. In March 1948 five Western European states—Britain, France, Belgium, Holland and Luxembourg—concluded a 50-year mutual defense pact in Brussels. The U.S. State Department encouraged the agreement, and the Senate's Vandenberg Resolution of June 1948 supported American aid to friendly military pacts. The United States formalized its defense commitment to Western Europe by entering the 12-nation North Atlantic Treaty, the cornerstone of NATO, in April 1949. With the Americans tied militarily to Europe, the organization's strength rested for the time being on U.S. monopoly of the atomic bomb. Containment had been militarized, giving Western Europe a breathing space for economic recovery.

As the European crisis deepened, serious problems arose in China. Before the war's end, China's future appeared promising, and the agreements at Yalta limiting Soviet expansion in the Far East gave hope. The optimism quickly faded. Plagued by eight years of war, China found her trade and transportation disrupted, inflation rampant and agriculture in distress. To the north, Russian occupation forces in Manchuria systematically stripped the territory of factories and carried them off as spoils of war.

More serious was the Russian admission of Chinese Communists into Manchuria, permitting their establishment of a Democratic Unity Army. By early 1946 the Communists controlled all major north-south communication lines and spread throughout Manchuria. Chiang Kai-shek's position was precarious. After taking the Japanese surrender in North and South China, he tried to move his troops into Manchuria in October 1945 for similar purposes. Russian authorities excluded them from the port of Dairen, and elsewhere the Chinese Communists did the same. Chiang had to postpone his intended occupation of Manchuria or risk open conflict on a 1,000-mile supply line.

At this point, Truman sent Gen. George Marshall to China in an effort to bring about a compromise. From December 15, 1945, through March 15, 1946, Marshall's mission appeared successful. Agreement was reached to call a Political Consultative Conference (PCC) for drafting a constitution and establishing a new National Assembly. Chiang seemed willing to cooperate in a coalition government and integrate his armies with those of the Communists. By February 1946 the PCC had made considerable progress toward fusing the Kuomintang and Communist organizations, but pressure within both parties hampered the creation of a new government. In the midst of these difficulties, Marshall returned to the United States for consultation. While he was away, the tentative agreement collapsed. The Kuomintang Central Executive Committee rejected coalition, claiming the sole right to rule China. The Communists struck back with all-out attacks on Manchurian railways, gaining quick control of them. Marshall, when he returned, tried to convince Chiang that war would be useless. But a 15-day truce in June expired without final agreement, and after the summer of 1946 Chiang's only hope rested with American intervention, which was not forthcoming.

The Nationalists reached their peak military effectiveness in July 1947, after which their support rapidly eroded. The population turned against Kuomintang administrators for their harsh and corrupt measures. Nationalist troops were forced to retreat to the cities, but soon found themselves isolated. Chiang resigned as president on January 21, 1949, removing himself to Taiwan. Subsequent peace negotiations failed, and on October 1, 1949, the victorious Communists proclaimed the People's Republic of China. The new government of Mao Tse-tung was quickly recognized by the Soviet Union and its satellites. As in Europe, the lines of Cold War confrontation were firmly drawn in Asia.

In the years that followed World War II, colonial empires began to crumble throughout the world. Most notable was the loss by Britain and France of their overseas possessions.

Among the countries that emerged into independence after the war, the largest and most populous was India. Discontent with British authority in the country was long-standing and increased after the failure of the Cripps mission of 1942. The All-India Congress Party devised a program of noncooperation and nonviolent protest that often erupted into open hostility against the British. The independence problem was complicated by ethnic divisions: Muslim and Sikh minorities demanded either equal status with the Hindu majority or their own states. After the British Labour Party won control of Parliament in 1945, it offered India independence and partition into Hindu and Muslim states. Louis, Lord Mountbatten was sent to New Delhi in 1947 as viceroy and persuaded Congress Party leaders to accept partition and permit Indian Muslims to organize a separate state known as Pakistan. Partition took place on August 15, 1947. Two years later, India accepted membership in the British Commonwealth.

In Burma, British administrators returned after the war with no plans for granting independence. But nationalist aspirations, encouraged by Japanese recognition of Burma's independence in 1943, would not permit restoration of the status quo ante. The country was on the verge of a nationalist rebellion when the British, in January 1947, promised Burma its freedom within a year under its own constitution. As in India, ethnic divisions and civil unrest, some of it Communist-inspired, kept the country in turmoil for several years after independence. Guerrilla warfare also erupted in Malaya, where Communists began a "war of liberation" against British administrators in mid-1948.

For reasons of expediency, the French colonial administration in Indochina remained in office under Japanese control throughout the war. Although the colonial government opposed the Japanese, it also feared that cooperation with Vietnamese resistance groups would strengthen the nationalist cause. Toward the end of the war, the Japanese jailed the French garrison after learning of plans to help the Allies. After Japan declared an end to the colonial status of Indochina in March 1945, nationalist leadership fell to Ho Chi Minh's Vietminh League. After the war, the French reoccupied the cities, while the Vietminh controlled the countryside. Protracted negotiations ended with an agreement on March 6, 1946, whereby France recognized the Republic of Vietnam as a free state linked to a French union, including Cambodia and Laos. Difficulties arose over the extent of French influence within the union and French desire to maintain Cochin China as a separate state. The struggle led to military clashes; when the French created the Bao Dai government in Saigon in 1949 to counter Ho Chi Minh in Hanoi, a civil war erupted.

Nationalist aspirations also flourished under Japanese occupation in the Dutch East Indies. On August 17, 1945, nationalist leader Ahmed Sukarno proclaimed the Indonesian Republic on Java and Sumatra, and the British forces that subsequently arrived to demobilize the Japanese relied upon Sukarno's popular government despite Dutch protests. When Dutch troops arrived in late 1945, Indonesian resistance developed. Over the next four years, Holland made futile efforts to reestablish her authority in the East Indies. By late 1946, the Dutch dominated the outer islands and established friendly regimes there. The Dutch then announced plans to create an Indonesian federation, an effort to ensure the political containment of Sukarno's republic. Not satisfied with a political solution, however, the Dutch launched an all-out attack in December 1948, overrunning republican territory. Sukarno's troops retreated from the cities and began guerrilla activity against the Dutch. Holland's position quickly disintegrated as she found herself diplomatically isolated. The United States, Asian nations and finally the United Nations all supported the Indonesian cause. Within the colony, Dutch officials and businessmen feared that continued warfare would destroy the local economy. Under this pressure the Dutch agreed to negotiate. A round table conference held at The Hague brought an agreement in November 1949 that established the United States of Indonesia.

Stimulated by wartime events, the tide of nationalism also rose during the postwar years in the Middle East. In 1941, Gen. Charles de Gaulle recognized the independence of Syria and Lebanon. When French forces arrived in Beirut in 1945 to reoccupy the Levant, the Arabs resisted and violence resulted. Under Allied and U.N. pressure, the French evacuated in 1946, giving Syria and Lebanon full control over their own affairs.

Britain faced even graver difficulties in Palestine, where it tried to reconcile the conflicting claims of Arabs and Zionists. The situation was complicated by the dislocation of European Jews, thousands of whom sought to migrate to Palestine at the war's end. British efforts to halt the Jewish influx were ineffectual and only increased tensions. In an effort to reach a solution, a joint Anglo-American commission investigated conditions in Palestine, recommending a compromise partition in 1946. Both Jews and Arabs, however, rejected the plan; Zionists demanded a fully independent Jewish state, while the Arabs would not relinquish their claim to a single Palestinian nation with majority rule. In frustration, the British turned the issue over to the United Nations. On November 29, 1947, the General Assembly approved partition of Palestine into Arab and Jewish states. After termination of the British mandate on May 14, 1948, Palestinian Jews proclaimed the state of Israel and managed to defend its territory against Arab onslaughts. U.N.-sponsored armistice talks in 1949 stabilized Israel's borders but failed to bring permanent peace to the Middle East.

Latin America, like Western Europe, fell under the U.S. defense umbrella after World War II. Fearing Communist expansion, the United States sought to create defense machinery against any political danger. In August 1947, the Rio do Janeiro Conference completed a defense pact that provided for action by all contracting nations against an attack on any American republic. This was the first regional agreement to fall under the scope of Article 51 of the U.N. Charter. One year later, the Organization of American States was created at a conference in Bogotá, Colombia. But if the feared Communist aggression was forestalled, the United States failed to help alleviate Latin American poverty or aid significantly in the region's economic development. In the eyes of American policy makers, European recovery had absolute priority during the late 1940s.

Americans after 1945 settled into a life of precarious prosperity at home. The confusion that marked postwar domestic life arose from contradictory fears and desires. Americans wanted immediate demobilization of the armed forces, rapid reconversion of industry and agriculture to peacetime production and an end to wartime controls, priorities and rationing. At the same time, they were haunted by fears of another depression.

After assuming the presidency in 1945, Truman took up FDR's "Economic Bill of Rights." Congressional opposition to administration plans for federal spending resulted in a compromise, the Employment Act of February 1946. This declared a national policy of never again permitting large-scale unemployment. The bill also created a three-man Council of Economic Advisers to make quarterly reports to both Congress and the president, recommending action deemed necessary for prosperity. The measure signaled general agreement that the federal government would take responsibility for the nation's economic welfare.

There was little fear that demobilization would weaken the labor market, partly because the G.I. Bill of Rights gave veterans the opportunity to continue their education at government expense or buy small businesses or farms with guaranteed government loans. Vets seeking jobs received unemployment payments of $20 weekly for up to a year. Contrary to many predictions, veterans as a body did not constitute a political pressure group.

Another unexpected phenomenon was the health of the nation's economy. Instead of falling into a slump, the economy reconverted to peacetime production and entered a long period of prosperity. Employment soared from a wartime high of 54 million to 69 million by 1947, and the GNP reached $225 billion in the same year. Instead of a glut, there were acute problems of scarcity, ranging from homes, automobiles and appliances to men's suits, nylon stockings and beef. Consumers commanded some $129 billion in wartime savings and more in credit. World needs also demanded increased U.S. production and generated inflationary pressures.

Truman conducted his first domestic political battle to prevent inflation and lost. The president wanted price and rationing controls to continue until shortages eased and controls could be relaxed without danger of price rises. On the other hand, businessmen campaigned for an immediate end of all controls, arguing this would encourage maximum production, which in turn would prevent rising prices. Consumers, willing to spend their money for goods in short supply, agreed. Truman had his way until the summer of 1946, when Congress passed a bill reducing the power of the Office of Price Administration and ordering it to end price controls quickly. Truman vetoed the bill and all controls lapsed on June 30, 1946. Prices immediately shot up, and Congress responded with a new control bill signed by Truman, which reimposed rent controls and some price controls. One result of the new bill was a three-way fight between cattlemen, who refused to send their beef to market at controlled prices; consumers, who besieged meat markets; and the administration, which was blamed for both controls and inflation. Admitting defeat, Truman removed meat controls on October 15. After the Republican congressional victories, Truman removed all controls on wages and all price controls except rents, sugar and rice on November 9. The result of all these actions was a 32 percent increase in prices and a 12 percent drop in real earnings below those of July 1945.

As prices increased, so did wage demands. By January 1946 workers had gone on strike in a number of the nation's critical industries—steel, automobiles and electrical manufacturing. The steel strike, starting January 21, 1946, attracted much attention. Steel Workers' union president Philip Murray demanded a 25¢ hourly increase to match the steel workers' wartime take-home pay. Truman sided with labor. Speaking for the industry, United States Steel president Benjamin F. Fairless said the pay increase could be granted only if steel prices were permitted to rise $7 a ton. Ultimately, a settlement provided for an 18 1/2¢ hourly pay increase and $5 a ton price increase. On April 1, 1946, John L. Lewis ordered 400,000 UMW members to strike the bituminous coal mines. In response, Truman ordered federal seizure of the mines while the government negotiated a contract with the union. Mine operators refused to accept compromise proposals, and the government retained control of the mines until the dispute was settled in December 1946.

All signs pointed to a Republican congressional victory in 1946. The administration was blamed for the rampant inflation. Truman had embittered organized labor with his challenge to Lewis and by breaking the railroad strike in the spring of 1946. He lost conservative support by his advocacy of welfare and civil rights. New Dealers were disgruntled over the resignation of Interior Secretary Harold L. Ickes and Commerce Secretary Henry A. Wallace. As a result, few were surprised in November when the GOP won control of both House and Senate for the first time since 1930 and captured governorships in 25 of 32 non-Southern states. What was surprising, however, was the magnitude of the landslide and the sharp decrease in the urban Democratic vote. It was also obvious that the hitherto solid Democratic labor bloc had disintegrated, at least momentarily.

The significance of the Republican victory soon became evident after the 80th Congress convened on January 3, 1947, under an entirely new conservative leadership. Above all, Senator Robert A. Taft (R, Ohio) stood in forceful opposition to the administration's liberal policies. Through 1947 and early 1948 the Republican Congress and the Democratic administration sparred in preparation for the upcoming presidential election.

Congressional Republicans set out to reduce labor union power. Conservatives believed that the unfair labor practices forbidden to employers by the Wagner Act of 1935 should be narrowed and balanced by prohibition of unfair union practices. Passed over Truman's veto on June 22, 1947, the Taft-Hartley Act placed several restrictions on unions, including the prohibition of closed and union shops, secondary boycotts and jurisdictional strikes. Unions were also forced to bend to the public interest with the requirement of a 60-day "cooling off" period before strikes that endangered the national health or safety; the president was empowered to use an injunction against such strikes.

Truman alienated conservative Southern Democrats by appointing a Committee on Civil Rights on December 5, 1946. Consisting of liberal Southerners, Negroes and national liberal leaders, the committee issued a report calling for creation of a permanent Fair Employment Practices Commission, federal laws against lynching and poll taxes, FBI investigations of civil rights violations and prosecution of offenders by the Justice Department. Truman's support of such legislation could not overcome Southern opposition. He did, however, introduce desegregation in the armed forces, appoint Negroes to government posts and prosecute violations of civil rights. This was the background of the "Dixiecrat" rebellion of 1948.

Other confrontations between Truman and the Republican-dominated Congress involved issues of tax reform and inflation. The president argued against further tax reductions as inflationary, but to no avail. Over his veto, Congress adopted a measure giving relief to low- and middle-income taxpayers. As inflation continued into the fall of 1947, Truman called Congress into special session on November 17 to consider a 10-point anti-inflation program. Congress conceded little, other than extension of rent controls and another tax cut. After the nominating conventions of 1948, Truman again called Congress into special session, and again Congress avoided decisive action in the Anti-Inflation Act of August 16.

Not for two decades had the Republicans been so confident of a presidential victory as in 1948. Their most energetic candidate, former Minnesota governor Harold E. Stassen, was not acceptable to the party regulars, who preferred Robert A. Taft. The party, however, rejected Taft, and Gen. Dwight D. Eisenhower rejected the GOP. Only New York governor Thomas B. Dewey remained, with a useful reputation as an internationalist and progressive. On the third ballot in Philadelphia on June 21, 1948, the GOP selected Dewey, who in turn chose California governor Earl Warren as his vice presidential running mate. The brief party platform approved the New Deal reform structure and the postwar bipartisan foreign policy and promised further tax reduction, greater government efficiency and civil rights, welfare and public housing legislation.

Republican confidence could only increase at the sight of growing disarray among Democrats. Former secretary of commerce Henry A. Wallace, dismissed by Truman in 1946 for criticizing administration foreign policy, tried to rally liberal Democrats behind a program emphasizing cooperation with the Soviet Union. On December 29, 1947, Wallace announced he would run for president on the third-party Progressive ticket. Many felt he might poll from 5 million to 8 million votes. Democratic Party chieftains, concerned over Truman's low popularity ratings, tried to force his retirement, while Southerners threatened to bolt the party if a strong civil rights program was adopted. When just this happened at the Democratic National Convention in mid-July, the Southern rebellion erupted. Meeting in Birmingham, Alabama, on July 17, 1948, the "Dixiecrats" nominated South Carolina governor J. Strom Thurmond for president and Mississippi governor Fielding Wright for vice president. Their aim in appealing to the white South was to throw the presidential election to the House of Representatives. Truman, nominated by the Democrats in the absence of any other attractive candidate, seemed isolated.

With the Democrats in rebellion from left and right, Dewey settled on a mild and aloof campaign, repeating old strictures against alleged Democratic incompetence but supporting many aspects of Democratic foreign and domestic policy. Truman, determined to exploit his "underdog" role, conducted an energetic "whistlestop" campaign of more than 30,000 miles and delivered 351 speeches to an estimated 12 million people. Castigating the "do nothing" 80th Congress, he championed liberal causes: civil rights legislation, aid to education, expanded Social Security benefits, national health insurance, repeal of the Taft-Hartley Act and high parity for farm prices. On Election Day, Truman gained 24.1 million votes to Dewey's 21.9 million and an electoral victory of 304 to 189. Thurmond and Wallace each gained a little over 1 million votes. Riding on Truman's coattails, Democrats regained control in both the House and Senate.

Truman determined to take immediate advantage of his victory. In January 1949 he called on Congress to enact a wide-ranging program that included health insurance, repeal of Taft-Hartley, extension of Social Security, minimum wage increase, aid to education and larger appropriations for public housing. In the end, Truman won less than he asked for from the 81st Congress but a good deal more than critics thought he would get. His greatest victory was the 1949 Housing Act, which provided funds to cities for slum clearance and construction of 810,000 low-income housing units. Truman's greatest failure of 1949 was congressional rejection of the Brannan Plan, designed to guarantee farmers an "income standard." For the most part, Truman's struggle for progressive legislation dragged into the 1950s, at which time the nation became embroiled in the Korean War and the "Red Scare" at home.

Domestic concern over Communist influence and controversy over the U.S. response to communism began soon after the war. The chief proponent of a "soft line" toward Russia was Commerce Secretary Henry Wallace, who charged that Soviet truculence was only a response to the rigidity and lack of understanding of U.S. policy makers. On September 12, 1946, at a Madison Square Garden political rally sponsored by leftist political groups, Wallace attacked the emerging postwar world order shaped by U.S.-Soviet antagonism. Truman reacted by ousting Wallace from the administration. Wallace continued his criticism of U.S. foreign policy as editor of the *New Republic.* His effort to mobilize broad support against the Cold War failed in the 1948 presidential election, however, when the Progressive Party proved unable to attract many noncommunist leftists.

Communism was also an important issue in the postwar U.S. labor movement. The American Federation of Labor, despite its long record of opposition to the Soviet Union and domestic Communists, ran into trouble when the Taft-Hartley Act required its officials to sign affidavits certifying they were not Communists. UMW president John L. Lewis refused to comply with this measure, demanding that the act be challenged in court. He immediately clashed with Teamsters Union president Daniel Tobin, who favored compliance with the act and threatened to withdraw the Teamsters from the AFL if Lewis's viewpoint prevailed. The AFL compromised by amending its constitution to designate only the president and secretary-treasurer as officials, which meant that other federation leaders would not have to sign affidavits. The compromise satisfied everyone but Lewis, who in December 1947 withdrew the UMW from its AFL affiliation.

The Communist problem was even more serious for the Congress of Industrial Organizations, which had welcomed Communists since its inception. By the end of the war, many CIO locals and some national unions were Communist-dominated; largest of these was the United Electrical, Radio and Machine Workers of America. After passage of the Taft-Hartley Act, CIO president Philip Murray announced he would not sign the required affidavit but instructed each union to make its own policy on the question. Struggles between Communist and anticommunist factions subsequently erupted in several large CIO unions, notably in the UAW and the United Maritime Workers union, where anticommunists under Walter Reuther and Joseph Curran won control. In 1948 the conflict spilled over into the national CIO; the organization's December convention expelled Communist followers from the Executive Board and passed a resolution condemning the Soviet Union. One year later, the CIO added a provision to its constitution forbidding Communists from serving on the Executive Board and began to take action against its remaining Communist-dominated affiliates. The United Electrical Workers union was expelled in November 1949, and a number of other unions ceased to exist.

Popular fear of Communist infiltration after the war was intensified by two elements—the *Amerasia* case and exposure of a Soviet spy ring in Canada—both of which gave impetus for a full-scale drive to root Communists out of government. On March 11, 1945, U.S. intelligence agents raided the offices of *Amerasia*, a leftist monthly magazine, and unearthed piles of diplomatic and military documents. Knowing it could not make a strong case against the magazine's editor because the FBI had obtained the documents illegally, the Justice Department nevertheless prosecuted in an effort to break up the circle of *Amerasia* contributors. In the end, the group received light sentences for conspiring to receive government property illegally.

Further impetus to the postwar "Red Scare" came from a report issued on March 4, 1946, by a Canadian royal commission appointed to investigate charges of Communist espionage. The commission proved that the Communist Party in Canada was an arm of the Soviet government, exposed the operation of several Soviet spy rings and reported that at least 23 Canadians in "positions of trust" were Communist agents and had sent atomic secrets and samples of uranium to Moscow.

These revelations rattled security officials in Washington and stimulated the work of the House Un-American Activities Committee, which proceeded to turn up material in a variety of widely publicized cases. Some of the most famous involved Hollywood film writers and stars, charged by the committee with systematically indoctrinating the American public with Communist ideas. On May 16, 1947, HUAC chairman J. Parnell Thomas claimed that hundreds of Communists had infiltrated the film industry during the 1930s, occupying 90 percent of the writing positions. Testimony by Communist sympathizers and anticommunists resulted in allegations that several stars were Communists. A number of film personalities, including Humphrey Bogart, Katharine Hepburn and Ava Gardner, responded by organizing a drive to disprove the charges. Intermittent inquiries, continuing for almost a year, could not establish that any crime had been committed or that any subversive material had reached the screen.

Starting on July 30, 1948, former government employee Elizabeth Bentley charged before Congress that she had received wartime documents from top government officials that were passed on to Soviet agents. Among those she accused of providing such information were Lauchlin Currie, Harry Dexter White and William Remington. Her story, completed in August, was inconclusive. It could not stand in court because of its inconsistencies, but the public impact was great. An even more dramatic story was told by former Communist Whittaker Chambers before HUAC beginning August 3, 1948. Chambers charged former high-level State Department official Alger Hiss with belonging to a Communist "underground" in Washington during the 1930s. When Hiss responded with a slander suit in September, Chambers provided microfilm copies of prewar documents Hiss had allegedly passed on to the Communists. Ultimately, Hiss was indicted by a New York grand jury for perjury and convicted in January 1950, after his first trial ended in a hung jury. The statute of limitations prevented prosecution of Hiss for his alleged Communist association. Communist espionage rather than perjury, however, was the real issue of the trial.

As the fear of communism in government began to swell, Truman tried to check the hysteria with an executive order of March 22, 1947, directing a comprehensive investigation of all federal employees by the FBI and Civil Service Commission. When the investigations were completed in early 1951, the Civil Service Commission had cleared more than 3 million federal employees; the FBI had completed investigations of some 14,000 doubtful cases. Over 2,000 employees had resigned, and 212 had been dismissed because of questions about their loyalty. These numbers seemed insignificant compared to the magnitude of the allegations. Yet in February 1950 Senator Joseph McCarthy brought the country to a fever pitch of hysteria with new accusations of communism in government.

The benefits of wartime science and technology reached civilians rapidly after 1945. Inventions and new processes raised productivity to meet growing demand. Innovations such as plastics and petrochemicals, known earlier but kept from production by the depression, developed quickly. The federal government made a concerted postwar effort to promote scientific research and education.

One wartime industry that had great impact on American society was electronics. In 1946 the first electronic computer was put into operation. Called ENIAC (Electronic Numerical Integrator and Calculator), this ancestor of the data-processing industry contained 18,000 electronic tubes and was capable of adding numbers in 1/5000th of a second. During the late 1940s, the computer was refined and reduced in size. Efforts to use atomic power for peaceful purposes also expanded after the war. By 1949, several new cyclotrons were completed or under construction, including one for use in medical research at the University of California, Purdue University and the University of Illinois. Atomic research for military purposes continued in Russia and the United States, fueling the nuclear arms race.

The aeronautics industry was another important beneficiary of wartime innovation. With improved aircraft, speed records were reset every year, including the first breaking of the sound barrier in 1948. Technological advance enabled a pilotless aircraft to cruise the Atlantic and land in England. The application of jet propulsion to military aircraft had taken firm hold by the end of the decade. Advances in rocketry continued, with unmanned vehicles reaching the stratosphere.

Industrial improvements, as always, had their price. Thousands of workers went on unemployment as machines replaced men. Automation in the soft coal industry alone cost 250,000 jobs during the late 1940s. When Bethlehem Steel converted from the open-hearth to the basic oxygen process at its Lackawanna, Pennsylvannia, plant, daily capacity increased from 1.9 to 2.2 million tons, while the number of furnaces fell from 14 to two. In general, unskilled and semiskilled workers suffered most from automation. The full impact of these changes, however, came in later decades.

Wartime research had important postwar applications in medicine and biology. Several new pesticides restricted to military use during the war, including DDT and ANTU, became generally available. Biological warfare research brought peacetime benefits, such as a vaccine against rinderpest and an improved toxoid to fight botulism poisoning in food. The expanded use of the wartime drugs penicillin and streptomycin was also significant. Improved X-ray machines enabled physicians to examine the human anatomy more thoroughly. Throughout the period, research continued into the causes and cure of heart disease, cancer, tuberculosis and infantile paralysis. While progress was reported in all fields, solutions were not discovered. Most tragic was the polio epidemic of 1949, which claimed 33,144 lives in the United States through October 2. As with technological advances, the full effects of wartime medical research had to wait another decade to make their appearance.

The war was over and the depression even further behind. World events had yet to make a strong impression on most Americans or dominate their cultural outlets. Retreat from reality seemed only natural, and in the years immediately following 1945, America's cultural trends revealed a passivity and lack of concern with foreign and domestic problems.

The American retreat from reality was best indicated with the decline of movie popularity. As a form of art, movies have attempted to reflect contemporary events and public moods. Although beset by a cost squeeze, labor disputes and alleged Communist influence, Hollywood sought to capitalize on the war mood. Films like *Pride of the Marines*, *Tomorrow Is Forever*, *Lonely Journey* and *The Best Years of Our Lives* dealt with the problems of veterans' adjustment to civilian life. Only the last succeeded at the box office. Movies about the war, including *They Were Expendable* and *Angel and the Badman*, did just as poorly. By 1950, movie houses were empty on Saturday nights and although the drive-in theater offered a new family outing, the quality of films was not attractive.

The nation's reading habits were perplexing. Despite the pace of world events in 1945–46, the best-selling nonfiction book was Betty MacDonald's *The Egg and I*, a lighthearted story about life on an Oregon chicken farm. Some national problems, however, surfaced in popular fiction. Mary Jane Ward's *The Snake Pit* portrayed the repugnant condition of mental hospitals; Charles Jackson's *The Lost Weekend* illustrated the spree of a business executive; and Frederic Wakeman's *The Hucksters* exposed the intent of Madison Avenue advertisers. Americans apparently wanted to be told off, and many writers did just that. The war provided a number of memoir-type books, typified by *Mr. Roberts* in 1946. Of greater impact in 1948 was Norman Mailer's *The Naked and the Dead*. Set on a Pacific isle, this novel pictured war in its grimmest detail, from disease to death. Sex also made a strong showing in America's postwar reading. Edmund Wilson's *Memoirs of Hecate County* caused a flurry in 1946 for its sexual episodes; some hailed it as a literary piece, while others were shocked by its obscenity. More controversial was Dr. Alfred C. Kinsey's 1948 publication *Sexual Behavior in the Human Male*, a study of the sex habits of some 5,300 males, which became an immediate best-seller. A Gallup Poll indicated that five of six Americans thought the report a "good thing," although clergymen, scientists and sociologists denounced the data on several grounds. As the decade drew to a close with the Cold War raging, the American public still was avoiding books dealing with world events.

Relaxation came in other forms: radio and television. By 1947, 34.8 million households had a radio; 21.6 million receivers were in hotels, stores and institutions and another 8.5 million in automobiles. Programming fell into three broad categories: soap operas, juvenile serials and family shows. The "soaps" were an industry unto themselves. From mid-morning until late afternoon, women could listen to the trials of life, success and failure of others in such series as *Stella Dallas*, *Helen Trent*, *Our Gal Sunday* and *Lora Lawton*. In mid-afternoon, serials for kids took over. Imitating old story-telling traditions, they were devised to make the breakfast food industry profitable, as the soap operas peddled washing powder, bathtub suds and other feminine gimmickry. Youngsters were enthralled by *The Lone Ranger*, *Green Hornet* and *The Shadow*. Cereal sales were also stimulated by the gimmicks available to youngsters for the proper amount of box tops: magnifying glasses, code kits, mock pistols and sundials. In the evenings, an entire family could hope to win, as others did, on *Truth or Consequences*, or listen to the comedy of Jack Benny, the songs of Bing Crosby or the antics of Danny Kaye. Spinning records on radio, disc jockeys became new trendsetters by the decade's end. Attempts to regulate radio were few, although the FCC finally clamped down on giveaway shows in 1948. The American Federation of Musicians could place only temporary roadblocks in the way of the transition from live to recorded music on the airwaves.

By decade's end, however, radio's golden day was passing, as television came into its own. Invented before World War II, television was still a novelty in 1945. By 1947 NBC was on the air 30 hours weekly. In 1948 the three major networks—NBC, CBS and DuMont—covered the presidential nomination conventions. Other coverage included baseball games, old movies and information programs. The cost of a set, however, limited the market. An estimated 325,000 sets dotted the nation, with half located in New York. Finally, Los Angeles car dealer Earl Muntz placed his family name on an 11-tube set selling for under $200. While its quality remained debatable, television became available on a wide scale, so that in 1949, 75 percent of America's viewers watched Milton Berle's *Texaco Star Theater*. Television's impact was just beginning.

Other cultural highlights of the immediate postwar period included chain letters that spread across the country, promising rewards of everything from whiskey to money. Major League baseball enjoyed renewed success with the return of wartime heroes. The sport broke the color barrier in 1947, when Brooklyn Dodger owner Branch Rickey brought Jackie Robinson to Ebbets Field. As veterans flocked to the college campus, football took on a new dimension, marked by the renewed Army–Notre Dame rivalry.

In many respects the decade closed as it had opened. In 1940, the world was at war in Europe and China. Although there was no shooting war in 1949, clear lines of demarcation separated the Western and Communist areas engaged in a struggle known as the Cold War. For different reasons, most Americans tried to ignore the bleak international situation in both 1940 and 1949. Europeans and Americans alike held a false sense of security in 1940. In 1949 they were anxious to recover from the horrors of war and regain some degree of normality. The new decade, however, brought only continued tension and the start of America's frustrating involvement in Asia.

Thomas M. Leonard
Jacksonville, Florida

YEARLY SUMMARIES

	World Affairs	European War Zone	Pacific War Zone	The Americas	Other Countries & Territories
1940	League of Nations winds down operations following the outbreak of the European war.	Germany invades and occupies Denmark, Norway, the low countries, Luxembourg and France. The French Third Republic comes to an end, replaced in unoccupied France by an authoritarian regime under Marshal Henri Petain . . . . London and other British cities suffer severe damage in the Battle of Britain, but the Luftwaffe fails to break British air defenses . . . . Russia forces territorial concessions from Finland and occupies the Baltic states, Bessarabia and Bukovina . . . . Italy attempts unsuccessfully to invade Greece.	Japanese and Nationalist Chinese forces battle indecisively in central and northern China. A Japanese puppet government under Wang Ching-wei begins functioning in Nanking . . . . Japan begins pressuring European colonies in Asia to accept Japanese economic domination.	U.S. strengthens its defense posture in the Western Hemisphere by leasing naval bases in Latin America and sponsoring a conference of American republics to discuss hemispheric solidarity.	Britain grapples with ethnic conflicts and demands for independence in several of its possessions, notably India and Palestine . . . . A territorial dispute between Thailand and Indochina begins when Thailand seizes land from the French colony.
1941	Roosevelt and Churchill meet on the HMS *Prince of Wales* and again in Washington to discuss war aims and aid to Russia . . . . Russia and Japan conclude a four-year non-aggression pact.	German forces overrun Yugoslavia and Greece and invade Russia, advancing to Leningrad, Moscow and Rostov . . . . British and Axis forces battle indecisively in North Africa as the Luftwaffe attempts unsuccessfully to eliminate the British base on Malta . . . . U.S. naval vessels begin patrolling the North Atlantic sea lanes.	Japan occupies French Indochina . . . . New Japanese government of Premier Hideki Tojo takes a more belligerent attitude towards the U.S. . . . . Japanese forces attack the U.S. Pacific Fleet at Pearl Harbor and invade Malaya and the Philippines.	Peru and Ecuador engage in an indecisive border war . . . . Most Latin American states take restrictive measures against Axis diplomats and business interests.	British forces invade Iraq, Syria and Lebanon to prevent establishment of pro-Axis governments . . . . French Indochina cedes territory to Thailand in a Japanese-imposed settlement . . . . Hindu-Moslem clashes continue in India.
1942	Axis conquests reach their greatest extent . . . . Churchill confers with Roosevelt in Washington and Stalin in Moscow on war strategy and military aid . . . . United Nations Declaration commits 26 states to win the war against the Axis.	German advance is turned back by the Russians at Stalingrad and by the British at El Alamein . . . . U.S. forces begin action against the Germans in North Africa (Operation Torch) . . . . SS begins systematic deportation and extermination of European Jews.	Japanese forces complete the conquest of Malaya and the Philippines, capture Singapore and overrun Burma and the Dutch East Indies . . . . U.S. forces turn back the Japanese advance in the Battle of Midway and on Guadalcanal.	Most Latin American states declare war on the Axis . . . . U.S. strengthens its military installations in the Western Hemisphere.	British forces occupy Madagascar to oust the French colony's pro-Vichy governor . . . . British authorities in India intern Congress Party leader Mohandas Gandhi amidst continued controversy over Indian independence.
1943	Allied leaders meet in Casablanca, Washington, Quebec, Cairo, and Teheran to discuss war aims and strategy.	Russian forces drive the Germans back from the Volga and Caucasus . . . . U.S. and British troops eliminate German forces from North Africa, conquer Sicily and invade Italy. Mussolini is overthrown.	U.S. and Australian forces push the Japanese back in the southern Pacific and begin an "island-hopping" campaign aimed at taking strategic positions and isolating Japanese garrisons.	U.S. attempts to strengthen its ties with Latin America through state visits and new commercial agreements . . . . Argentina begins to distance itself from the Axis.	India suffers from famine and continued political unrest over independence.
1944	Plans for a postwar world order take shape at U.N. conferences on food, finance and international security . . . . Roosevelt and Churchill meet again in Quebec to discuss war strategy and the postwar occupation of Germany.	Germany's Eastern Front disintegrates as Russian forces advance across the Ukraine and Poland and enter Germany . . . . British and U.S. forces liberate France and most of Belgium, containing the last German offensive of the war in the Ardennes . . . . Pace of the SS extermination campaign against the Jews accelerates.	U.S. forces continue their island-hopping campaign in the South and Central Pacific, reaching Leyte and Mindoro in the Philippines . . . . U.S. bombers based on Saipan begin massive raids on the Japanese home islands.	Argentina establishes a policy of wartime neutrality, resisting hemispheric pressure to declare war on the Axis . . . . A trend towards military dictatorship develops in several Latin American states.	Three-way conflict between Hindus, Moslems and British authorities continues in India . . . . U.S. oil companies begin commercial penetration of Saudi Arabia.
1945	Allied leaders meet at Yalta and Potsdam in a futile attempt to resolve differences over the postwar international order . . . . Representatives of 38 nations draw up the United Nations Charter in San Francisco. Organization of the U.N. apparatus begins.	Allies complete the conquest of Germany and establish military governments in their occupation zones . . . . Slavic states expel Germans from the Sudetenland, Silesia and other parts of Central Europe . . . . Russia begins to establish friendly governments in Eastern Europe.	U.S. completes the conquest of Japan with two atomic bombs dropped on Hiroshima and Nagasaki . . . . European states clash with Asian nationalists as they attempt to reoccupy their Asian colonies . . . . Civil war between Nationalists and Communists breaks out in China.	American republics negotiate a hemispheric security agreement (the Act of Chapultepec) . . . . Argentina abandons its pro-Axis stance in order to participate in the San Francisco U.N. Conference.	Arab states form a federation as debate over the status of Palestine intensifies . . . . French forces attempting to reoccupy the Levant clash with Syrian and Lebanese nationalists . . . . Indian political leaders reject British independence proposals as inadequate.
	Includes developments that affect more than one world region, international organizations and important meetings of major world leaders.	*Includes all developments in European countries and military engagements between Allied and Axis powers in Africa and at sea.*	*Includes all developments in Japan and China, Japanese foreign policy and military actions in the Pacific region.*	*Includes all domestic and regional developments in Latin America, the Caribbean and Canada.*	*Includes developments in those independent nations and colonial possessions not covered in Columns B, C and D.*

	World Affairs	Europe	Africa & the Middle East	The Americas	Asia & the Pacific
1946	U.N. General Assembly and Security Council hold their first session in London . . . . Allied foreign ministers meet to negotiate European peace treaties.	U.S. and Russia clash over German occupation policy. U.S. also comes into conflict with Yugoslavia, which claims Trieste and parts of Austria . . . . Secondary war criminals go on trial in Germany as trial of major war criminals ends.	Illegal Jewish immigration to Palestine increases, intensifying conflict between Jews and British authorities . . . . Iran and Russia debate the continuing presence of Soviet troops in northern Iran, as a rebellion rages in the Iranian province of Azerbaijan.	Juan Peron takes power in Argentina . . . . Canadian government breaks up a widespread Soviet spy ring attempting to collect atomic secrets.	U.S. attempts unsuccessfully to mediate the Chinese civil war . . . . Fighting between French colonial forces and nationalists under Ho Chi Minh spreads throughout Vietnam . . . . Division of Korea hardens as U.S. and Russia fail to agree on formation of a single government.
1947	Allied representatives negotiate fruitlessly on the German and Austrian peace treaties . . . . U.S. and Russia clash at the U.N. over international atomic control and admission of new members.	Civil war between Communists and royalists intensifies in Greece as Britain begins to withdraw its troops from the country . . . . Communists consolidate their control in Poland, Hungary and Rumania . . . . Labor unrest and food riots break out in France, Italy and western Germany.	Civil strife intensifies in Palestine as Britain prepares to surrender its mandate . . . . French colonial forces suppress a nationalist rising on Madagascar.	American republics negotiate a mutual defense treaty in Rio de Janeiro . . . . Mexican government moves to spur the country's industrialization.	India gains independence amidst widespread Hindu-Moslem violence as the territory is partitioned into two states . . . . Chinese Communists gain ground against Nationalist forces in Manchuria.
1948	First acute crisis of the Cold War emerges as the Russians blockade Berlin.	Communists take power in Czechoslovakia, while Soviet bloc states oust Yugoslavia from the Cominform . . . . Greek government forces gain the upper hand in the civil war.	Proclamation of the state of Israel causes the first Arab-Israeli war, which leaves Palestine partitioned into Jewish and Arab areas.	Representatives of the American republics establish the Organization of American States at a conference in Bogota, Colombia . . . . Civil war in Costa Rica results in the victory of rightist rebels under Col. Jose Figueres.	Chinese Communists gain control over Manchuria and northern China . . . . India consolidates its territory by absorbing most princely states, including Hyderabad . . . . U.S.-Soviet split in Korea results in establishment of separate governments.
1949	U.S. and Western European states negotiate the North Atlantic Treaty . . . . Allied representatives meet again to discuss Germany following the end of the Berlin blockade . . . . Nuclear arms race begins with Russia's first atomic explosion.	Separate states are established in East and West Germany . . . . Eastern European states begin campaigns of repression against potential domestic dissidents, including religious and conservative political leaders.	Peace returns to the Middle East as Israel and its Arab neighbors conclude armistice agreements.	Argentine Pres. Peron increases his power in the government and tightens restrictions on domestic dissent.	Communists complete their conquest of the Chinese mainland . . . . Dutch East Indies becomes the independent state of Indonesia.
	Includes developments that affect more than one world region, international organizations and important meetings of major world leaders.	*Includes all domestic and regional developments in Europe, including the Soviet Union, Turkey, Cyprus and Malta.*	*Includes all domestic and regional developments in Africa and the Middle East, including Iraq and Iran and excluding Cyprus, Turkey and Afghanistan.*	*Includes all domestic and regional developments in Latin America, the Caribbean and Canada.*	*Includes all domestic and regional developments in Asian and Pacific nations, extending from Afghanistan through all the Pacific Islands, except Hawaii.*

U.S. Politics & Social Issues	U.S. Foreign Policy & Defense	U.S. Economy & Environment	Science, Technology & Nature	Culture, Leisure & Life Style	
Roosevelt breaks tradition to win a third presidential term, defeating Republican candidate Willkie and conservative opponents in his own party.	Debate rages in the U.S. between isolationists and advocates of involvement in European and Asian affairs. The U.S. maintains its official neutrality in the European conflict but takes covert steps to support Britain, including conclusion of an agreement to provide destroyers for the Royal Navy in return for use of British bases in the Western Hemisphere.	Economic recession continues despite increased defense spending .... Administration takes steps to raise taxes and increase the federal budget.	Influenza and polio epidemics strike at parts of the U.S. .... University of California constructs a cyclotron in Berkeley capable of producing mesons from atomic nuclei.	World's Fair is held in N.Y.C. .... Duke Ellington gains popularity as a jazz composer and pianist.	1940
Civil rights movement gains momentum with protests against discrimination in defense industries and the armed forces .... N.Y. State legislature conducts extensive investigations of alleged Communist influence in the City College of New York.	U.S. Lend-Lease aid begins flowing to Britain amidst continued controversy between isolationists and internationalists .... Defense spending continues to rise.	Administration takes initial steps to limit production of consumer goods and ration gasoline .... Congress debates whether to permit strikes in defense industries as the Administration attempts unsuccessfully to gain labor-management cooperation on a National Defense Mediation Board.	Intensive research on the military use of atomic energy (the Manhattan Project) begins .... Penicillin is discovered .... A polio epidemic sweeps the U.S.	N.Y. Yankees outfielder Joe DiMaggio sets a major league record by hitting safely in 56 consecutive games .... Music programming of U.S. radio stations is severely restricted by a contract dispute with the American Society of Creative Artists and Performers.	1941
War Relocation Agency evacuates Japanese-Americans from the West Coast and confines them in inland internment camps .... Civil rights protest against military segregation and employment discrimination continues.	Government registers all men 20-65 for military or civilian service .... Coastal shipping losses to German submarines rise rapidly, temporarily exceeding the current rate of ship construction.	U.S. industry converts to war production, causing shortages in a number of consumer items .... Congress takes action to absorb excess domestic spending power through increased taxes.	U.S. scientists develop the first electronic computer .... German scientists launch the world's first successful rocket, called the V-2.	U.S. city-dwellers grow large quantities of vegetables in "Victory gardens." .... "Quick" Nevada divorces become legal throughout the U.S.	1942
Racial tensions in the U.S. erupt in Negro-white clashes in N.Y. and Detroit and white violence against Mexican-Americans in Los Angeles.	Public debate on postwar benefits for military veterans begins.	Strikes of coal miners and railroad workers bring government action to maintain production as the war economy reaches its greatest level of output.	Another polio epidemic strikes the U.S., killing 1,200 children .... Streptomycin is discovered.	Singer Frank Sinatra becomes an American teenage idol.	1943
Roosevelt gains a record-breaking fourth term as President .... Most Japanese-Americans return to their West Coast homes following their release from internment camps.	U.S. armed forces reach their greatest wartime size.	Discussion of postwar economic reconversion begins as production of civilian goods rises.	A synthetic process for the manufacture of quinine is developed .... U.S. atomic researchers construct a uranium pile at Oak Ridge, Tenn.	Television comes into commercial use in the U.S.	1944
Truman becomes President following Roosevelt's death. He quickly reorganizes the cabinet and proposes his own social reform program, called the "Fair Deal."	Armed forces enact their demobilization plans as unrest grows over delayed discharges and alleged inequities .... U.S. refuses to release secret atomic information or place its nuclear weapons under international control.	Economic reconversion begins, accompanied by a wave of price increases and strikes as some government economic controls are lifted .... Truman attempts to improve labor-management relations through creation of fact-finding boards to investigate major disputes.	The Atomic Age begins with detonation of the first atom bomb .... Vitamin A is synthesized.	U.S. divorce rate rises to 31% of all marriages, the highest in the world, as many war marriages disintegrate .... "Bebop" craze sweeps the U.S. .... Horse racing reopens.	1945
Includes elections, federal-state relations, civil rights and liberties, crime, the judiciary, education, health care, poverty, urban affairs and population.	*Includes formation and debate of U.S. foreign and defense policies, veterans affairs and defense spending. (Relations with specific foreign countries are usually found under the region concerned.)*	*Includes business, labor, agriculture, taxation, transportation, consumer affairs, monetary and fiscal policy, natural resources, pollution and accidents.*	*Includes worldwide scientific, medical and technological developments, natural phenomena, U.S. weather and natural disasters.*	*Includes the arts, religion, scholarship, communications media, sports, entertainment, fashions, fads and social life.*	

U.S. Politics & Social Issues	U.S. Foreign Policy & Defense	U.S. Economy & Environment	Science, Technology & Nature	Culture, Leisure & Life Style	
House Un-American Activities Comm. begins investigation of Communist activities in the U.S. .... Tension over civil rights develops in the Democratic Party as Congress debates extension of the Fair Employment Practices Commission .... Crime in the U.S. rises sharply, exceeding the 1945 level by 13%.	Emerging Cold War with Russia becomes a foreign policy issue as Truman dismisses Commerce Secy. Henry Wallace for advocating U.S.-Soviet cooperation .... GIs continue to protest delays in demobilization.	Postwar strike wave continues, with walkouts in trucking, coal mining and other vital industries .... Cost of living rises sharply, exceeding the 1945 level by 18% .... Farmers harvest a record crop, 25% higher than the previous 1942 record.	A polio epidemic strikes the U.S., with infantile paralysis cases nearly double their 1945 level .... Scientists develop color television transmission .... Univ. of Pennsylvania constructs an electronic computer .... Xerography is invented.	U.S. live births rise sharply to 3.44 million, up 19% from the 1945 level, as returning veterans and their wives found families .... Commercial television networks expand along the U.S. East Coast.	1946
House Un-American Activities Comm. investigates alleged Communist influence in the Hollywood film industry .... Loyalty investigation of federal employes begins on Truman's order.	Administration propounds the Truman Doctrine for "containment" of Communism, pledging to help Greece and Turkey resist Communist expansion .... State Secy. George Marshall proposes massive U.S. aid to help in European economic reconstruction .... Armed forces are united under a single Defense Dept.	Congressional concern over the postwar strike wave results in passage of union curbs in the Taft-Hartley Act .... A Bureau of Labor Statistics study reports that Washington, D.C. has the highest cost of living in the nation, and New Orleans the lowest.	U.S. naval expeditions under Adm. Richard Byrd and Commodore Finn Ronne explore Antarctica .... Anthropologist Thor Heyerdahl sails a raft from Peru to Polynesia in 101 days.	U.S. births reach a postwar high of 3.72 million, an annual rate of 25.9 per thousand.	1947
Truman wins the presidency and Democrats regain control of Congress despite a revolt by Southern Democrats and leftist supporters of Henry Wallace .... Alger Hiss case becomes a focus of national debate over Communist influence.	U.S. implements the Marshall Plan as aid dollars flow to Europe.	Congress and the Administration debate conomic policy as the economy enters its first postwar downturn.	A national controversy develops over Dr. Alfred Kinsey's *Sexual Behavior in the Human Male.*	The long-playing record is invented, making possible the marketing of different record sizes .... U.S. baby boom continues with 3.65 million live births, slightly below last year's high.	1948
Domestic debate over Communist activity in the U.S. continues to grow with the perjury trials of Alger Hiss and Harry Bridges, the espionage trial of Judith Coplon and the sedition trial of 11 U.S. Communist leaders.	Armed forces engage in a heated public debate over U.S. defense strategy as Navy officers accuse the Army and Air Force of attempting to dominate the Defense Dept.	Strikes in the mining and steel industries curtail production, but the country's economic recession eases.	Cortisone is developed and produced as a treatment for rheumatism .... Controversy develops over FBI loyalty checks on recipients of Atomic Energy Commission research fellowships.	U.S. television audience expands rapidly with introduction of a low-priced set marketed by Earl Muntz .... Postwar baby boom levels off with 3.58 million live births.	1949
Includes elections, federal-state relations, civil rights and liberties, crime, the judiciary, education, health care, poverty, urban affairs and population.	*Includes formation and debate of U.S. foreign and defense policies, veterans affairs and defense spending. (Relations with specific foreign countries are usually found under the region concerned.)*	*Includes business, labor, agriculture, taxation, transportation, consumer affairs, monetary and fiscal policy, natural resources, pollution and accidents.*	*Includes worldwide scientific, medical and technological developments, natural phenomena, U.S. weather and natural disasters.*	*Includes the arts, religion, scholarship, communications media, sports, entertainment, fashions, fads and social life.*	

1940

A British fighter goes down in an air battle over England, Dec. 18.

Hitler and Spanish dictator Francisco Franco greet each other warmly as they confer at the Franco-Spanish border station of Hendaye on Oct. 29.

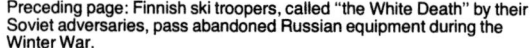

Preceding page: Finnish ski troopers, called "the White Death" by their Soviet adversaries, pass abandoned Russian equipment during the Winter War.

A German U-boat returns to port on the French coast after a raiding expedition against British shipping in the North Atlantic.

Helmets top the grave markers of German soldiers who died during the invasion of Norway in April.

"America First" advocate Charles Lindbergh addresses an isolationist rally in Chicago on Aug. 4, urging that the U.S. cooperate with "a Europe dominated by Germany."

CBS correspondent Edward R. Murrow brought the Battle of Britain home to Americans with daily radio broadcasts from London.

A German officer haughtily gives orders to a Dutch officer after the surrender of Holland on May 14.

German soldiers advance through the ruins of a French border town in May.

GOP presidential candidate Wendell Willkie gets an enthusiastic reception in Elwood, Ind. on his way to deliver a campaign speech Aug. 17.

Reich Propaganda Min. Joseph Goebbels visits a German unit fighting on the Western front in June.

	World Affairs	European War Zone	Pacific War Zone	The Americas	Other Countries & Territories
Jan.		Severe winter weather causes a stalemate in the Soviet-Finnish war.	Japanese and Chinese forces battle indecisively in northern China.		Hindus and Moslems clash throughout India over questions dealing with independence.
Feb.		After making significant military advances, the Russians demand that Finland surrender.	Japanese forces land at several points along the China coast .... War damage closes the Haiphong-Yunnan railroad.	British and German naval vessels skirmish in Brazil's territorial waters.	Britain restricts Jewish immigration and land acquisition in Palestine.
March	League of Nations reports an increase in German trade with neutral nations.	Finland accepts Soviet peace terms, which call for surrender of much Finnish territory to the Russians .... Britain announces it may violate neutral rights in an effort to restrict German aggression.	Japanese officials protest U.S. aid to Nationalist China .... Japanese puppet government in Nanking begins functioning under Wang Ching-wei.	United States expands its defensive posture in Latin America through military agreements and Inter-American Bank loans.	Australia and New Zealand move to improve their defense posture.
Apr.		German troops invade Norway and Denmark, making quick advances in Norway despite the debarkation of Allied forces.	Chinese and Japanese troops engage in heavy fighting in Shansi Province.	Brazilian police move against Communist Party members for alleged efforts to overthrow the government.	Egypt and India press their demands for independence from Britain.
May		German forces invade France and the low countries .... Britain organizes the Home Guard to meet a possible German invasion, while British troops occupy Iceland .... Germans construct the first major ghetto for Polish Jews in Lodz.	Japan, Britain and Holland negotiate fruitlessly on the status of the Dutch East Indies.	Several Latin nations subscribe to the Inter-American Bank. Questions about hemispheric defense and neutrality are raised in several countries.	
June		German troops occupy most of France, as the British Expeditionary Force and some French soldiers are evacuated at Dunkirk .... Russia seizes Bessarabia and Bukovina from Rumania.	Japan increases diplomatic pressure on the Dutch East Indies and French Indochina to join Tokyo's East Asian economic sphere.		
July		Germans begin the Battle of Britain with air attacks on merchant ship convoys in English Channel .... Russia invades and annexes the Baltic states.	Bowing to Japanese demands, Britain closes the Burma supply route to China for three months.	Hemispheric conference in Havana discusses defense and economic cooperation among American states.	
Aug.		Battle of Britain continues with German attacks on airfields in southern England .... Italian forces from Ethiopia overrun British Somaliland.	Chinese Nationalist capital of Chungking endures heavy Japanese air attacks.		France's African colonies declare their allegiance to de Gaulle's Free French movement.
Sept.		Germans begin bombing of London and other British cities .... German submarines intensify their attacks on British merchant shipping in the Atlantic.	Japanese troops operating in China begin using transit routes through French Indochina.	Unsuccessful Mexican presidential candidate General Juan Andreau Almazan organizes support to overthrow the government.	
Oct.		Battle of Britain ends as Germans suspend air raids on British cities.	Japanese forces withdraw from Kwangsi Province in southern China.	United States negotiates leases to naval bases in Latin America.	Thailand seizes territory along its frontier with French Indochina.
Nov.		German authorities establish a Jewish ghetto in Warsaw.		Canadian and U.S. representatives discuss defense cooperation.	
Dec.		British forces under Gen. Archibald Wavell rout the Italians in Libya. Italian forces in Albania withdraw under Greek attack.			

A	B	C	D	E
Includes developments that affect more than one world region, international organizations and important meetings of major world leaders.	*Includes all developments in European countries and military engagements between Allied and Axis powers in Africa and at sea.*	*Includes all developments in Japan and China, Japanese foreign policy and military actions in the Pacific region.*	*Includes all domestic and regional developments in Latin America, the Caribbean and Canada.*	*Includes developments in those independent nations and colonial possessions not covered in Columns B, C and D.*

U.S. Politics & Social Issues	U.S. Foreign Policy & Defense	U.S. Economy & Environment	Science, Technology & Nature	Culture, Leisure & Life Style	
	United States protests alleged British violations of American neutral rights in mail and shipping.	Congressional debate opens on Roosevelt's proposed $8.424-billion budget for fiscal 1941.	A cold wave sweeps across the United States from Canada.	New art showings are presented at the Whitney Museum and Museum of Modern Art in New York.	Jan.
FDR enters several state primaries as a number of surveys indicate he is the presidential choice of most Democrats.	Under State Secy. Sumner Welles begins a European tour to assess the war situation.				Feb.
Vice Pres. John Nance Garner begins campaigning for the Democratic presidential nomination.	Welles completes his European tour, reporting to FDR that there is currently little chance for a European peace treaty.		Adverse weather in the Mississippi River valley and along the East Coast causes property damage and death.		March
Congress acts on reapportionment legislation and the Walter-Logan bill to provide judicial review of federal agencies.	Despite widespread calls for neutrality, government statements indicate steps toward involvement in Greenland, Iceland and the Dutch East Indies.	Despite reports of increased corporate profits, the Commerce Department indicates a continued economic recession.			Apr.
Congress disagrees with FDR's plan to reorganize the CAA and Air Safety Board.	Debate over the extent of American aid to Britain and France rages throughout the U.S.	Government takes action to increase defense spending.	Color television transmission is successfully tested.	World's Fair in New York draws thousands of visitors.	May
GOP convention meets in Philadelphia and nominates Wendell Willkie for president.		FDR signs a tax bill raising the national debt to $49 billion and adding 2.2 million taxpayers to the rolls.		Outdoor track season is highlighted by NCAA and AAU meets.	June
FDR gains a third term nomination from the Democrats .... Willkie organizes his campaign strategy.	Congress approves creation of a two-ocean Navy as political leaders call for increased manpower training.		A heat wave grips the East Coast.		July
	House approves and Senate opens debate on a universal military conscription bill.		Infantile paralysis cases reach epidemic proportions in Indiana and West Virginia.	Agreement is reached to hold inaugural Pan-Am Games in Argentina in 1942.	Aug.
As the presidential campaign gets under way, states begin to challenge the legality of the Communist Party on their ballots.	U.S. and British representatives conclude negotiations on exchange of American destroyers in return for use of British bases in the Western Hemisphere .... Selective Service bill becomes law.		A petroleum-based synthetic rubber is developed.		Sept.
Willkie travels widely in his campaign for the presidency. Roosevelt makes a belated campaign tour in the East.	As FDR orders surveys of available defense stockpiles, production of war material increases.				Oct.
Roosevelt wins an unprecedented third term, and Democrats retain control of Congress.	Construction of naval vessels reaches a new high point.	CIO convention meets in Atlantic City, selecting Philip Murray to succeed John L. Lewis as president.	Tornadoes and blizzards strike large sections of the Midwest.		Nov.
			An influenza epidemic spreads along the West Coast.	Radio stations are locked in labor disputes with the AFM and ASCAP.	Dec.

F	G	H	I	J
Includes elections, federal-state relations, civil rights and liberties, crime, the judiciary, education, health care, poverty, urban affairs and population.	*Includes formation and debate of U.S. foreign and defense policies, veterans affairs and defense spending. (Relations with specific foreign countries are usually found under the region concerned.)*	*Includes business, labor, agriculture, taxation, transportation, consumer affairs, monetary and fiscal policy, natural resources, pollution and accidents.*	*Includes worldwide scientific, medical and technological developments, natural phenomena, U.S. weather and natural disasters.*	*Includes the arts, religion, scholarship, communications media, sports, entertainment, fashions, fads and social life.*

	World Affairs	European War Zone	Pacific War Zone	The Americas	Other Countries & Territories
Jan. 1	Dutch fiscal authorities forecast an increase in the world's gold flow to the U.S. because of the European War .... Vladimir Sokolina is dismissed by the League of Nations as under-secretary general after he refuses to resign as instructed by the Russian government.	Britain's King George VI signs a proclamation providing for the military conscription of all males between the ages of 19 and 28 .... Russian planes bomb Jyvaskyla, Finland .... Floods spread across Turkey from the Aegean to the Black Sea, with nearly 60 towns and villages washed away.	Japanese troops advance in Kwangtung Province in southern China.	The Canadian Army's 1st Division has arrived in Britain, the National Defense Dept. announces in Ottawa.	
Jan. 2		Finnish government claims to have trapped 55,000 Russian troops on the eastern border .... Arrests of disaffected Czechs are reported in German-dominated Bohemia-Moravia.	British officials announce that the Yangtze River patrol flotilla is being reduced from 13 to 3 ships.		Saudi Arabia's King Ibn Saud announces reorganization of his military and civil aviation and the establishment of a new air base at Riyadh.
Jan. 3		Field Marshall Hermann Goering is placed in charge of the German war economy .... Finnish planes drop leaflets over Leningrad depicting ill-equipped and freezing Soviet troops in Finland.			Australia commences military training for 21-year-old males.
Jan. 4		British Amb. Lord Lothian says in Chicago that a federation of European states must follow the war if peace is to be maintained.		Brazil protests French seizure of Brazilian mail addressed to Germany.	
Jan. 5		Oliver Stanley succeeds Leslie Hore-Belisha as secretary of state for war in the British cabinet .... British warn Norway that "illegal" use of Norwegian territorial waters by Germany to ship iron ore will make it necessary for the Royal Navy to enter Norwegian waters .... Swedish government demands that the USSR investigate the shelling of a Swedish steamer in the Gulf of Bothnia.	China Affairs Bd. in Tokyo approves the peace proposals of Wang Ching-wei, who is scheduled to head the Japanese-sponsored China government in Nanking.	U.S. and Canada agree to discuss a possible accord on completion of the St. Lawrence waterway project.	Sir Charles Burnett takes charge of the Royal Australian Air Force.
Jan. 6	FDR says that in the interest of post-war peace protectionist international trade tendencies must be abolished.	Netherlands government announces there can be no negotiation regarding Holland's neutrality.	Japan is reportedly seeking a most-favored-nation treaty with the U.S. when the current trade pact expires on Jan. 26.	Col. Fulgencio Batista, Cuban presidential candidate, urges his nation to maintain strict neutrality in international affairs.	Addressing the National Conference of the United Palestine Appeal in Washington, N.Y. Gov. Herbert H. Lehman says Palestine must become a refuge for the estimated three million Jews in Poland .... Because of the war, the New Zealand government announces postponement of a $25-million steel plant at Onekaka.
Jan. 7			Two hundred and seventy six members of the Japanese Diet sign a declaration of no confidence in the administration of Premier Nobuyuki Abe.		Reports from India indicate that efforts to solve the nation's Hindu-Moslem political rift have broken down .... U.S. and Australia announce establishment of diplomatic relations on the ambassadorial level. Clarence Gauss is appointed minister to Australia.
Jan. 8		Food rationing begins in the United Kingdom.	Japanese cabinet states any Chinese peace treaty must recognize Manchukuo and permit Japanese economic expansion.	Negotiations between government and opposition parties fail to decide when new elections should be held in Cuba.	
Jan. 9	Chase National Bank Pres. Winthrop W. Aldrich urges a free gold market to ease the economic impact on the world of the current flow of gold to the U.S.	Russian 44th Division retreats east of Suomussalmi, Finland after heavy losses. Intense cold (-31 deg.) stops the fighting on all fronts.	Japan and China issue rival claims of victory in the fighting in northern Kwangtung Province.	Negotiations for trade agreements between the U.S. and Argentina and Uruguay are reported to have broken down.	
Jan. 10	There is no celebration in Geneva to commemorate the 20th anniversary of the League of Nations.	A German courier plane crashes in Belgium, and Nazi plans for an invasion of Belgium and France fall into Allied hands provoking immediate troop concentrations .... Finns claim that encirclement and freezing weather has trapped Russian infantry at Kokkamo.	Japanese army and navy officials serve notice to French officials in Shanghai that they must halt the shipment of arms supplies to China over the Haiphong-Yunnan railroad.	Legal experts in Washington say Canadian subsidiaries of U.S. corporations can invest in Canadian war loans without violating U.S. neutrality laws .... Mexican laborers strike in several states, registering opposition to Manual Avila Camacho, the government-sponsored presidential candidate.	Indian Viceroy Lord Linlithgow says feuding between political parties is the only factor detering Britain from granting India dominion status.
	A	B	C	D	E
	Includes developments that affect more than one world region, international organizations and important meetings of major world leaders.	*Includes all developments in European countries and military engagements between Allied and Axis powers in Africa and at sea.*	*Includes all developments in Japan and China, Japanese foreign policy and military actions in the Pacific region.*	*Includes all domestic and regional developments in Latin America, the Caribbean and Canada.*	*Includes developments in those independent nations and colonial possessions not covered in Columns B, C and D.*

U.S. Politics & Social Issues	U.S. Foreign Policy & Defense	U.S. Economy & Environment	Science, Technology & Nature	Culture, Leisure & Life Style	
		In his annual report, Agriculture Secy. Henry A. Wallace says the European War will hinder rather than help U.S. farmers.		Today's major college bowl game scores: Rose: USC 14, Penn. 0; Orange: Ga. Tech. 21, Mo. 7; Cotton: Clemson 6, Boston College 3; Sugar: Texas A&M 14, Tulane 13.	Jan. 1
NAACP announces it will not support John Nance Garner for political office.	U.S. announces its protest to Britain last Dec. 29 for opening U.S. mail to neutral countries in violation of the 11th Hague Convention .... Sen. Robert A. Taft (R.O.) says the Western Hemisphere security zone cannot be enforced short of war.	Supreme Court rules NLRB decisions making unions collective bargaining agents cannot be appealed.			Jan. 2
According to a Gallup Poll, 78% of registered Democrats favor FDR's nomination for a third term in 1940 .... Dies Comm. charges the CP and the German-American Bund are un-American.	FDR urges increased defense expenditures and warns against isolationism in his State-of-the-Union message to the opening session of the 76th Congress .... War Resisters' League charges FDR's policies are aimed at putting the nation on a war footing.	FDR tells the American Farm Bureau Federation that reciprocal trade agreements will not hurt U.S. farmers.		Pope Pius XII appoints the Most Rev. Samuel A. Stritch as Archbishop of Chicago.	Jan. 3
FDR nominates Atty. Gen. Frank Murphy as an associate justice of the Supreme Court .... Solicitor Gen. Robert H. Jackson is nominated by FDR as attorney general.	FDR makes a series of diplomatic nominations: James H.R. Cromwell as minister to Canada, George R. Messersmith as ambassador to Cuba, John Cudahy as ambassador to Belgium and R. Henry Norweb as ambassador to Peru.	FDR asks Congress to approve a $8.424-billion budget for fiscal 1941 and legislate $460 million in new taxes.			Jan. 4
					Jan. 5
Newark (N.J.) Mayor Meyer C. Ellenstein and six others are acquitted of charges of conspiracy in city purchases of meadowlands .... Justice Dept. grants the Bata Shoe Co. a 20-day extension to terminate the employment of 62 Czech nationals illegally in the country.		Sen. Pat Harrison (D, Miss.) says FDR has approved a joint congressional committee to study the proposed 1941 budget.			Jan. 6
Gallup Poll reports 60% of registered Republicans favor Thomas E. Dewey for the 1940 presidential nomination .... Former GOP Rep. John O'Connor hints that a third party, the Andrew Jackson Party, might be formed should FDR seek another term.			Drs. Raymond Pearl and W. Edwin Moffett of Johns Hopkins Univ. report the length of a person's life is probably linked to the heartbeat rate.	Winners of the N.Y. Film Critics Awards are: best picture, *Wuthering Heights*, best actor, James Stewart; best actress, Vivian Leigh; and best director: John Ford.	Jan. 7
Alabama Democratic Executive Comm. adopts a resolution stating a third term for FDR is "unwise" and then endorses House Speaker William B. Bankhead for the Democratic nomination .... An amendment to the Hatch Act is introduced in the Senate aimed at prohibiting employes of state and local governments from influencing elections .... Senate passes and sends to conference an alien bill providing for immediate deportation of spies.	N.Y. Gov. Herbert H. Lehman urges all Americans to support the foreign policy of FDR.	Supreme Court rules that Pierre du Pont is liable for $172,351 for a 1931 tax deficiency and that John T. Smith, vice president of GM, cannot deduct a tax loss resulting from the sale of securities to a corporation owned by himself.			Jan. 8
Sen. Gerald Nye (R, N.D.) declares his support for Sen. Arthur Vandenberg (Mich.) for the GOP presidential nomination.	FDR reveals his peace objectives to leaders of the Baptists, Lutherans and Seventh Day Adventists at the White House after their pledge of secrecy.	Federal Circuit Court of Appeals rules in Chicago that Inland Steel Corp. does not have to recognize the CIO's Steel Workers Organizing Comm. as sole bargaining agent .... Federal Circuit Court of Appeals in San Francisco rules the NLRB must provide equal protection to a worker whether he is a member of a labor union or not.		Joe Burk, the country's outstanding sculler, is named winner of the James E. Sullivan Memorial Trophy for performance and sportsmanship.	Jan. 9
House passes and sends to the Senate the Gavagan anti-lynching bill.				Whitney Museum's annual art show opens in N.Y.	Jan. 10

F	G	H	I	J
Includes elections, federal-state relations, civil rights and liberties, crime, the judiciary, education, health care, poverty, urban affairs and population.	*Includes formation and debate of U.S. foreign and defense policies, veterans affairs and defense spending. (Relations with specific foreign countries are usually found under the region concerned.)*	*Includes business, labor, agriculture, taxation, transportation, consumer affairs, monetary and fiscal policy, natural resources, pollution and accidents.*	*Includes worldwide scientific, medical and technological developments, natural phenomena, U.S. weather and natural disasters.*	*Includes the arts, religion, scholarship, communications media, sports, entertainment, fashions, fads and social life.*

	World Affairs	European War Zone	Pacific War Zone	The Americas	Other Countries & Territories
Jan. 11		A French decree establishes Friday as a meatless day and prohibits the sale of beef, veal and mutton on Monday and Tuesday.	Japanese officials claim a major aerial victory over Kweilin, capital of Kwangsi Province, China.		
Jan. 12		Soviet planes bomb Abo, Lahti, and Helsinki, Finland for the first time since Dec. 25.		Mexican Pres. Lazaro Cardenas asserts the Monroe Doctrine was replaced in 1936 by the "principle of American solidarity." .... A heat wave over Buenos Aires, Argentina takes the lives of 23 people.	
Jan. 13		Russian spokesman claims Finnish troops are not near the Soviet border and that the Murmansk railroad is functioning normally .... British planes scatter propaganda leaflets over Germany.	Sir Stafford Cripps arrives in Chungking, China for a month's stay to study the war situation.	Argentine government openly blames the U.S. for causing the breakdown of recent trade negotiations by being unwilling to make concessions at the expense of American producers.	
Jan. 14		Moscow protests to Sweden and Norway against their material and moral aid to Finland .... A Russian submarine sinks the Finnish armed yacht *Aora* en route to Stockholm.	Japanese Premier Abe and his entire cabinet resign .... Adm. Mitsumasa Yonai accepts the imperial command to form a new cabinet.		
Jan. 15		Russian planes bomb Abo and Viborg, Finland .... British submarines *Starfish* and *Undine* are sunk in a raid on German defenses at Helgoland Bight.	Chinese dispatches claim the Japanese army is falling back towards Canton in Kwangtung Province.	Pan-American Permanent Neutrality Comm., established to serve as the interpreter of American neutrality for the war's duration, begins work in Rio de Janeiro, Brazil .... Cuban Pres. Federico Laredo Bru signs a bill to postpone Cuban elections until March 28.	
Jan. 16		Hitler orders a postponement of the secret planned January offensive against Belgium, Holland and France.	Wang Ching-wei, who is slated to head the Japanese-sponsored government in central China, asks Chiang Kai-shek to make peace with Japan.	Ontario Premier Mitchell Hepburn charges the Canadian government with inefficiency in preparing for war.	British P.M. Chamberlain asserts in London that the German propaganda ministry has failed to inflame the Palestine issue.
Jan. 17	Asst. State Secy Henry Grady tells the House Ways and Means Comm. that the influx of the world's gold supply to the U.S. will continue until other nations are able to pay for American purchases.	With temperatures at their lowest in 20 years, a severe cold wave grips Scandinavia, the Baltic states and Russia .... Intense cold (-54 deg.) at Viborg and (-49 deg.) in Moscow paralyzes war moves on land in Finland and the USSR.		Costa Rica grants permission to the U.S. Navy to protect its territorial waters.	
Jan. 18	Author Clarence K. Streit says in Washington that the way to world peace is through a federal union system.		Chinese forces claim to be within 10 miles of Canton.	Ontario legislature condemns the Ottawa government for the manner in which Canada's war effort is being prosecuted .... Chile, Mexico and Uruguay decline to participate in proposed Latin American protest to the USSR on its invasion of Finland.	
Jan. 19		French legislature bars all CP senators and deputies who did not repudiate their association with the international Communist movement as of Oct. 26, 1939 .... Slovakia adopts military conscription.	Chinese dispatches estimate 3,000 Japanese fatalities in Hupeh Province fighting.		
Jan. 20		Sweden announces it will accept $10 million in RFC credit from the U.S. for purchase of agricultural products.		Canadian Supreme Court rules that the federal parliament can abolish all appeals from Canadian courts to the Privy Council in London.	
Jan. 21		The Netherlands imposes censorship on correspondents of foreign newspapers.	*Ta Kung Pao*, a Hong Kong newspaper, publishes alleged peace terms between Wang Ching-wei and Japan, which would make China a Japanese dependency.	For the first time since 1671 mass is celebrated in the Old Cathedral ruins in Panama City, Panama.	
Jan. 22	International Labor Office in Geneva announces a meeting for Feb. 3 to discuss the effect of the war on labor.	British and French governments agree to combine scientific efforts to expedite development of new weapons systems.	Japanese Army claims the capture of Shaohing, an important Chinese base in Chekiang Province.		Philippine Pres. Manuel L. Quezon tells the national parliament that independence should not be delayed beyond 1946.
	A	B	C	D	E
	Includes developments that affect more than one world region, international organizations and important meetings of major world leaders.	*Includes all developments in European countries and military engagements between Allied and Axis powers in Africa and at sea.*	*Includes all developments in Japan and China, Japanese foreign policy and military actions in the Pacific region.*	*Includes all domestic and regional developments in Latin America, the Caribbean and Canada.*	*Includes developments in those independent nations and colonial possessions not covered in Columns B, C and D.*

U.S. Politics & Social Issues	U.S. Foreign Policy & Defense	U.S. Economy & Environment	Science, Technology & Nature	Culture, Leisure & Life Style	
Rudolph G. Cartier becomes the first candidate to file as an FDR delegate to the national convention, as he registers for the New Hampshire primary race.	Former State Secy. Henry L. Stimson urges the U.S. to halt the shipment of arms and raw materials to Japan .... Senate confirms Charles Edison as secretary of the Navy.			Francis Henry Taylor is chosen director of the Metropolitan Museum of Art by the museum's board of directors.	Jan. 11
FDR writes the chairman of the House Census Comm., Rep. Matthew Dunn (D, Pa.), to push through legislation for congressional reapportionment based on the 1940 census .... Sixty-three percent of the voters approve of FDR's presidential actions, a Gallup Poll indicates.	In collaboration with the *Saturday Review of Literature*, the Gallup Poll reports that 31% of American writers polled believe that the U.S. will enter the European War, while 69% think the U.S. will stay out.	International Brotherhood of Electrical Workers condemns both the AFL and CIO for conducting a "civil war" which is detrimental to the workingman .... Apex Hosiery Co. of Philadelphia appeals directly to the Supreme Court to obtain more than $700,000 in alleged damages from a labor union as a result of a 1937 sit-down strike.		In defending the institution's decision to drop football, Univ. of Chicago Pres. Robert M. Hutchins says the sport is a handicap to education.	Jan. 12
Immigration Commissioner James L. Houghteling reports the admission of 82,998 immigrants into the U.S. during fiscal year 1939, the largest number since 1931.			Prof. Hans Zinsser of the Harvard Medical School announces the development of a method to mass produce a vaccine to combat European typhus.		Jan. 13
FBI Chief J. Edgar Hoover announces the arrest of 18 members of the Christian Front for plotting to overthrow the U.S. government.	Three Democratic senators, Alben Barkley (Ky.), Claude Pepper (Fla.) and Robert Wagner (N.Y.) say that as a neutral nation, the U.S. is in the best position to halt the war .... Dr. Stephen F. Wise, president of the American Jewish Congress, asserts the organization's prime goal is to seek the restoration of Jewish rights in Palestine.			Baseball commissioner Kenesaw M. Landis declares five major league and 87 minor league players free agents as a result of rules violations by the Detroit Tigers management.	Jan. 14
FDR signs a bill to protect witnesses before Congress from intimidation or coercion.	Asst. War Secy. Louis Johnson tells a group of New York bankers that the U.S. should be equipped for a million-man army.	Bonneville Dam authorities reveal plans to establish a steel mill in Oregon to meet local needs.		Trustees of the American Museum of Natural History re-elect F. Trubee Davison as president.	Jan. 15
Senate approves Frank Murphy as an associate justice of the Supreme Court and Robert H. Jackson as attorney general .... Publisher Frank E. Gannett launches his campaign for the GOP presidential nomination in Rochester, N.Y.				Nile Ninnick of the Univ. of Iowa is awarded the Walter Camp Trophy as college football player of the year by the Washington Touchdown Club.	Jan. 16
Sen. Vic Donahey files a declaration of his candidacy for the Democratic presidential nomination in his home state of Ohio.	U.S. protests British interference with American mail destined for Europe.	Gallup Poll reports 53% of the American people think the Wagner Labor Act should be revised.		Carl Sandburg's *Abraham Lincoln - The War Years* and Herman Rauschning's *The Revolution of Nihilism* are chosen by *Current History* as the best non-fiction books of 1939.	Jan. 17
Co-chairman of the Garner for President campaign Maury Hughes announces that a nationwide campaign for delegates will be conducted.					Jan. 18
Dean of the Senate William E. Borah (R, Ida.) dies at 75 in Washington.			AP reports 82 deaths in 24 states due to the cold wave moving across the U.S. from the Canadian northwest.	Pan-American Games Committee of the AAU chooses the U.S. as the best country for the 1940 games, pending formal cancellation of the Olympics in Finland.	Jan. 19
	Britain denies it violated the 11th Hague Convention regarding U.S. mail to the continent in its search for contraband .... Pope Pius XII expresses little hope for FDR's peace effort in a letter released today by the White House.	AFL Pres. William Green issues a plea for unity in the labor movement.		Jane Vaugh retains the women's senior figure skating title in competition at Rye, N.Y.	Jan. 20
Sen. Donahey, withdraws his name form Ohio's Democratic presidential primary to seek re-election to the Senate and casts his support to FDR.		GOP House minority leader Joseph Martin (Mass.) says he sees no reason why FDR's budget cannot be cut at least 6%.		A Gallup Poll reveals 34% of the American people would favor a return to prohibition, while 66% would not.	Jan. 21
CP Gen. Secy. Earl Browder is sentenced to four years in prison for illegally obtaining a U.S. passport; the decision will be appealed.	U.S. demands that Britain modify her treatment of American ships and cargoes in the Mediterranean Sea.			Pierre Caille wins a French literature prize of 10,000 francs for his translation of *Gone With the Wind.*	Jan. 22
F *Includes elections, federal-state relations, civil rights and liberties, crime, the judiciary, education, health care, poverty, urban affairs and population.*	G *Includes formation and debate of U.S. foreign and defense policies, veterans affairs and defense spending. (Relations with specific foreign countries are usually found under the region concerned.)*	H *Includes business, labor, agriculture, taxation, transportation, consumer affairs, monetary and fiscal policy, natural resources, pollution and accidents.*	I *Includes worldwide scientific, medical and technological developments, natural phenomena, U.S. weather and natural disasters.*	J *Includes the arts, religion, scholarship, communications media, sports, entertainment, fashions, fads and social life.*	

	World Affairs	European War Zone	Pacific War Zone	The Americas	Other Countries & Territories
Jan. 23		Ignace Jan Paderewski is chosen president of the Polish National Council in exile in Paris.	Chiang Kai-shek charges that Japan plans the conquest of Malaya and the Philippines . . . . At Tsingtao, China a conference opens between Wang Ching-wei and Japanese representatives . . . . China is hit with its severest cold wave in 20 years, causing 650 deaths in Shanghai alone.		
Jan. 24	League of Nations January bulletin points to an increase in world economic activity owing primarily to the war situation.				
Jan. 25		German planes bomb the Shetland Islands.		Canadian Parliament is dissolved to prepare for a general election over the issue of war preparation.	Mohandas Gandhi begins a 24-hour fast in Bombay, India to draw attention to India's independence demands.
Jan. 26	Dutch Foreign Min. Eduard van Kleffens says that the Netherlands will retain its membership in the League of Nations.	Russians break the Finns' strongest defense, the Mannerheim Line, at Summa on the Karelian Isthmus.	Japanese-American commercial treaty of 1911 expires, but the U.S. refrains from imposing the higher tonnage and import duties permitted under U.S. law.	Mexican CP announces it will purge those members not loyal to Moscow.	
Jan. 27	Japanese diplomats gathering in Budapest, Hungary recommend a reaffirmation of the Anti-Comintern Pact despite the German-Russian Treaty of 1939.			Canadian P.M. W.L. Mackenzie King announces that the general election will be held March 28.	South Africa's House of Assembly, defeats a motion by Gen. T.B.M. Hertzog to halt war with Germany . . . . A Hindu-Moslem clash in Rangoon, Burma results in one death and 46 injuries.
Jan. 28	A Gallup Poll reports that 34% of the American people have given thought to an international peace after the war and favor the creation of a new international organization and complete disarmament . . . . Italian Foreign Min. Count Ciano urges a new Anti-Comintern grouping, omitting Germany from the revised agreement.	Germany denies Vatican charges of persecution against Polish Catholics and the closing of their churches.	Japanese tighten their blockade of Tientsin, China.		Riots between pacifists, Communists and military personnel erupt in Auckland, New Zealand.
Jan. 29	Foreign Office spokesman asserts that Japan must affirm continuation of the Anti-Comintern Pact because Communism is the antithesis of Japan's goals.	German planes bomb targets along 550 miles of Britain's east coast from Shetland to Kent.		Pan-American Neutrality Comm. announces a resolution to standardize treatment of citizens of belligerent countries.	Hindu-Moslem clashes continue in Rangoon despite appeals by civic and religious leaders for harmony.
Jan. 30		Hitler proclaims in Berlin that the second phase of the war, carrying it to the West, is beginning.	Russo-Japanese negotiations to adjust the Outer Mongolian-Manchukuo border break down in Tokyo.		Hindu-Moslem riots in Rangoon claim 12 more lives.
Jan. 31		Chamberlain asks the nations of the world to be tolerant of British interference with their trade because of the war.	Japanese Foreign Min. Arita says his nation does not intend to block the legitimate trading rights of third parties in Asia . . . . North central Japan is racked by a blizzard, causing 78 deaths.		The first of 100 planes ordered from the U.S. arrive in Canberra, Australia.
Feb. 1		Soviets launch a massive assault against Finnish defenses along the Mannerheim Line . . . . Kyosti Kollio, Finnish parliament president, states his country's willingness to reach a peace agreement with Russia.	Japanese Diet receives a record budget request of 10.282 billion yen, of which 4.460 billion are for the military.		
Feb. 2	Japanese Foreign Office explains that its adherence to the Anti-Comintern Pact "involves no question of antagonizing" Russia.	Foreign ministers of the Balkan Entente countries—Greece, Rumania, Turkey and Yugoslavia—meet in Belgrade.	Japanese military sources report the capture of Pinyang, a strategic city in Kwangsi Province.		Civil disorders in the northeast Indian frontier area are reported.
Feb. 3	Robert J. Watt, U.S. delegate to the ILO meeting in Geneva, urges that body to prepare a plan for the world's transition from a war to a peace-time economy.	German planes bomb the British coast from the Tyne to Norfolk, claiming the sinking of 14 ships.	U.S. State Dept. asks both French and Japanese authorities to assure safe passage over the Haiphong-Yunnan railroad.		
Feb. 4	Governing body of the ILO rejects Watt's suggestion for planning a postwar economy.	Balkan Entente conference concludes with comminique that the entente will continue in force until 1949 . . . . Fifteen people are killed and two villages destroyed by an earthquake in the Ersingan area of Turkey.	Japanese planes disrupt traffic on Haiphong-Yunnan rail lines despite U.S. appeals.		*N.Y. Times* reports that because of the European War, Palestine is suffering its worst depression ever.
	A	B	C	D	E
	Includes developments that affect more than one world region, international organizations and important meetings of major world leaders.	*Includes all developments in European countries and military engagements between Allied and Axis powers in Africa and at sea.*	*Includes all developments in Japan and China, Japanese foreign policy and military actions in the Pacific region.*	*Includes all domestic and regional developments in Latin America, the Caribbean and Canada.*	*Includes developments in those independent nations and colonial possessions not covered in Columns B, C and D.*

U.S. Politics & Social Issues	U.S. Foreign Policy & Defense	U.S. Economy & Environment	Science, Technology & Nature	Culture, Leisure & Life Style	
	Joseph E. Davies resigns as ambassador to Belgium to become a special assistant to State Secy. Cordell Hull .... A British-French purchasing board is created with headquarters in New York City .... FDR appoints a three-man interdepartmental commission, chaired by Treasury Secy. Henry Morgenthau, to coordinate the purchase of military supplies in the U.S. by foreign nations.				Jan. 23
UMW Pres. John L. Lewis urges his followers not to endorse FDR for a third term .... Sen. Gerald P. Nye (R, N.D.) is named to fill the vacant seat of Sen. Borah on the Foreign Relations Comm.	British Ministry of Economic Warfare says about 17,000 of the 25,000 U.S. mail packages examined contained contraband.	Postmaster Gen. James A. Farley advocates fair play for business and labor with the government acting as an umpire.			Jan. 24
	U.S. government bans shipment of packages to belligerent countries without an affidavit that the material is being transferred to foreign ownership.				Jan. 25
Sen. Burton K. Wheeler (D, Mont.) demands that FDR state now whether or not he will seek a third term .... Gov. C.A. Bottolfsen (R, Ida.) appoints John W. Thomas to fill the vacant Senate seat of William Borah.		N.Y. Judge Thomas D. Thacher condemns the quasi-judicial authority of the NLRB and urges review of agency decisions by an independent legal authority.		An exhibition of Italian art masterpieces, never shown in N.Y. before, begins at the Museum of Modern Art.	Jan. 26
		Amalgamated Clothing Workers of America Pres. Sidney Hillman praises the New Deal for having improved the standard of living of the American worker.			Jan. 27
					Jan. 28
Supporters of N.Y.C. District Atty. Thomas E. Dewey say they will enter his name in the Illinois presidential primary in April .... Supreme Court upholds the government's contention that a federal appeals court has no right to supervise the FCC.	National Maritime Union expresses its opposition to the granting of U.S. loans to any European belligerent.	Supreme Court upholds a N.Y.C. 2% tax levy on goods moving into the city through interstate commerce.			Jan. 29
	Gen. George C. Marshall tells Congress the Army will need $40 million to give the nation an air raid warning system.	House Appropriations Comm. cuts some $154 million from the Agriculture Dept's. appropriation bill .... AP report indicates a 67% increase in profits for 1939 over 1938 in the top 100 U.S. corporations.		One of Europe's leading historians, Professor Bronislaw Dembjnski, dies at the hands of the Gestapo in Poland.	Jan. 30
Labor Dept. modifies its deportation order against 68 Czech nationals working for the Bata Shoe Co., permitting their stay until June 30.		AFL Exec. Council, meeting in Miami, urges FDR to shorten the work week and continue government efforts to reduce unemployment.		Australia announces that it will retain possession of the Davis Cup Tennis trophy until competition is resumed.	Jan. 31
Sen. Robert F. Wagner (D, N.Y.) and Walter George (D, Ga.) introduce legislation seeking $10 million for rural hospital construction.	U.S. Army tests a new cannon-carrying pursuit plane, traveling up to 400 mph, at Bolling Field .... John L. Lewis claims American labor will oppose any U.S. war participation.	SEC Chmn. Jerome Frank urges the creation of a private agency, federally funded, to make loans for small business expansion .... FDR sends the nominations of Marriner S. Eccles and Chester C. Davis to the Senate for renomination to the Federal Reserve Board.		John Buchan (Lord Tweedsmuir), the novelist and governor general of Canada, dies at 63 in Montreal.	Feb. 1
Vice President Garner announces he will enter the Georgia Democratic primary, if one is held, to challenge FDR's New Deal policies.	Former Pres. Herbert Hoover urges the U.S. to stay out of the European War.	House votes a $66.9 million cut in the Agriculture Dept. bill despite FDR and farm pressure .... A NYSE seat is sold for $48,000, the lowest price since 1918.	Dr. J.B. Collip of McGill Univ. reports the discovery of an oral substance to be used in combating diabetes.	Issac Kashdan wins the international chess tournament in Havana, Cuba.	Feb. 2
Pennsylvania Democratic State Committee announces its endorsement of FDR for a third term.		Senate "farm bloc" moves to restore cuts in the Agriculture bill.		FDR pledges his support to the $1-million drive to save the Metropolitan Opera at its historic New York location.	Feb. 3
					Feb. 4

F	G	H	I	J
Includes elections, federal-state relations, civil rights and liberties, crime, the judiciary, education, health care, poverty, urban affairs and population.	*Includes formation and debate of U.S. foreign and defense policies, veterans affairs and defense spending. (Relations with specific foreign countries are usually found under the region concerned.)*	*Includes business, labor, agriculture, taxation, transportation, consumer affairs, monetary and fiscal policy, natural resources, pollution and accidents.*	*Includes worldwide scientific, medical and technological developments, natural phenomena, U.S. weather and natural disasters.*	*Includes the arts, religion, scholarship, communications media, sports, entertainment, fashions, fads and social life.*

	World Affairs	European War Zone	Pacific War Zone	The Americas	Other Countries & Territories
Feb. 5	ILO declares Russia's permanent seat is now vacant and nominates the Netherlands as successor.	Allied Supreme War Council secretly agrees to prepare to occupy Narvik in Norway and recruit an expeditionary force of "volunteers" to assist Finland.	Japanese Foreign Office says Japanese planes will continue to bomb the Haiphong-Yunnan railroad out of military necessity.	Financial experts of the Western Hemisphere, meeting in Washington, agree upon the establishment of an Inter-American Bank to stimulate trade within the Americas.	Diplomatic relations between the U.S. and Saudi Arabia are established.
Feb. 6	Delegates from 10 League of Nations members meet at The Hague to establish a committee for the study of economic and social problems.	Allied War Council meets in Paris to discuss a French offer to aid Finland.	Sir Stafford Cripps leaves Chungking for Sinkiang on his inspection tour of the Chinese war zone . . . . Japanese spokesmen claim penetration of Ningsia Province in northwest China.		
Feb. 7			Japanese government announces it is considering abrogation of the 1922 Nine Power Naval Pact . . . . The Hague announces plans to build three battle cruisers and modernize the harbor at Surabaya, Java for the defense of the NEI.	The six Radical Party members of the Chilean cabinet resign in a dispute over Jewish immigration.	P.M. Jan Christian Smuts reports widespread support for Germany in the Union of South Africa and Southwest Africa among Germans and people of German extraction.
Feb. 8	League of Nations members meeting at The Hague announce that a 32-member committee on economic and social problems will be created.	Russian forces report the capture of 13 forts on the Mannerheim Line in Finland . . . . Ankara announces it is taking over the German-owned Krupp shipyards in Turkey.		Pan-American Neutrality Comm. resolves that submarines of belligerents should be barred from neutral ports . . . . Chile's Pres. Pedro Aguire Corda announces his new cabinet, which continues as a Popular Front coalition.	
Feb. 9	Japanese Foreign Min. Arita claims that the Anti-Comintern Pact has lost its vitality because of the 1939 Soviet-German accord.		Chinese sources claim Japanese forces failed to encircle and force the surrender of Chinese troops in the Nanning sector.		
Feb. 10		French Chamber of Deputies backs the government's conduct of the war.			New Zealand Labor Min. P.C. Webb is appointed minister of manpower to organize the entire national service.
Feb. 11			Haiphong-Yunnan railroad is closed for several months because of damage by Japanese bombing.	Dr. Rafael Angel Guardia is elected president of Costa Rica.	
Feb. 12		First contingent of Australian troops lands at Suez and is greeted by Dominion Secy. Anthony Eden . . . . A Russo-German economic treaty is signed in Moscow.	Japanese sources report the landing at Fukien Province of a 50,000-man Chinese military force, to be used by Wang Ching-wei against the Chinese Nationalist Army.	British naval ship forces the scuttling of the German freighter *Wakama* in Brazilian waters.	
Feb. 13		Russian forces claim taking a total of 84 forts along the Mannerheim Line in Finland, breaking through at Summa.	Japan announces the abrogation of her arbitration treaty with the Netherlands.		
Feb. 14		Russia reports its forces have made further advances in the Summa sector of Finland.	Japanese government claims control of enough territory to create the Wang Ching-wei regime and asks Chiang Kai-shek to surrender.	Panama receives a German note rejecting the 300-mile security zone plan of the American republic.	British Colonial Secy. Malcolm MacDonald says the Jewish immigration quota for Palestine will not be increased in the foreseeable future.
Feb. 15		Russian military forces reportedly are within 15 miles of Viborg . . . . Britain offers to convoy all neutral vessels regardless of destination.	Chinese claim, and Japan admits, the retreat of Japanese troops in Kwangsi Province and Inner Mongolia.	Brazil orders the German merchant ship *Koenigsberg* to return to Paraguay or sail outside territorial waters.	
Feb. 16		German steamer *Altmark* is seized in Norwegian waters by the British navy and taken to Leith, Scotland.		*Koenigsberg* returns to Paraguay after being challenged by a Brazilian gunboat.	
Feb. 17		Sweden refuses Finland's request for military aid.	Chinese military authorities report the rout of Japanese troops at Nanning.		Afghanistan's minister to Turkey is recalled to Kabul for military discussions dealing with the possible spread of war to western Asia.

A	B	C	D	E
Includes developments that affect more than one world region, international organizations and important meetings of major world leaders.	*Includes all developments in European countries and military engagements between Allied and Axis powers in Africa and at sea.*	*Includes all developments in Japan and China, Japanese foreign policy and military actions in the Pacific region.*	*Includes all domestic and regional developments in Latin America, the Caribbean and Canada.*	*Includes developments in those independent nations and colonial possessions not covered in Columns B, C and D.*

U.S. Politics & Social Issues	U.S. Foreign Policy & Defense	U.S. Economy & Environment	Science, Technology & Nature	Culture, Leisure & Life Style	
At a Hyde Park news conference, FDR refuses to answer questions concerning a third term . . . . American Youth Congress refuses to oust alleged Communists from its organization.					Feb. 5
				Yale swim team sets six American records: four in relay events and two in the breaststroke competition.	Feb. 6
V.P. Garner is reported considering entering the Illinois Democratic primary in an effort to "smoke out" FDR on the third term issue, whose name will be on the ballot . . . . A subcommittee of the Senate Judiciary Comm. conducting hearings on the Gavagan anti-lynching bill is disrupted at its opening session by spectators . . . . House Rules Comm. approves the Walter-Logan bill to limit the power of federal boards and agencies.	FDR appoints three new ministers: George Earle to Bulgaria, David Gray to Ireland and Louis Dreyfus to Afghanistan.		Drs. Sidney O. Levinson, Frank Neuwelt and Heinrich Nicholes announce that blood serum, the colorless liquid part of blood, can be used as the basis of a blood substitute.		Feb. 7
Delegates supporting the nomination of FDR for a third term file for the Wisconsin Democratic primary race.	FDR meets the heads of the State, War and Navy Departments to discuss supplying raw materials to European nations.	Senate Banking Comm. approves FDR's nomination of Eccles and Davis to the Federal Reserve Board . . . . Despite a 54-day strike, the Chrysler Corp. announces a doubling of profits for 1939 to $36,879,829 or $8.47 a share.		Werner Klingsberg of Germany is elected secretary-general of the International Olympic Committee at Lausanne, Switzerland.	Feb. 8
Vice Pres. Garner and N.Y.C. Mayor Fiorello H. La Guardia enter the Democratic and GOP presidential races in the Illinois primary . . . . Senate approves the assignment of isolationist Gerald P. Nye (R, N.D.) to the Foreign Relations Comm.	FDR directs under State Under-Secy. Sumner Welles to visit Italy, France, Germany and Britain for the purpose of assessing the present state of the European War and prospects for peace.	FDR charges that John L. Lewis has refused to resume peace talks with AFL Pres. William Green.		American historian and former ambassador to Germany W.E. Dodd dies.	Feb. 9
Postmaster Gen. James A. Farley announces that he is a candidate for the Democratic presidential nomination . . . . Ivan Poderjay, a former Yugoslav army captain, is deported to Yugoslavia after serving five years in prison for bigamy.	Amb.-to-France William C. Bullitt arrives in Baltimore on his way to Washington to discuss the European War situation with FDR.	Sen. Arthur H. Vandenberg (R, Mich.) calls for an end to reciprocal trade agreements because they are detrimental to farmers . . . . Lewis proposes a labor peace plan in which the CIO would be joined to the AFL.		World Jewish Congress convenes in Washington.	Feb. 10
	Eleanor Roosevelt upholds the American Youth Congress's right not to condemn Russia for its invasion of Finland.	Temporary National Economic Comm. opens hearings on supposed monopolies in the insurance industry . . . . Commerce Dept. reports that nine states maintain restrictive trade barriers against each other.			Feb. 11
Supreme Court saves four Florida Negro youths from the death penalty, when it rules that their 1933 confessions and pleas of guilty on murder and robbery charges were obtained by violation of their civil rights . . . . Fifty-six percent of the Republican voters favor Thomas E. Dewey as the GOP presidential candidate over Arthur Vandenburg and Robert Taft, according to a poll released today.	American Youth Congress, meeting in Washington, adopts a resolution to keep the U.S. out of war . . . . Rep. Hamilton Fish (R, N.Y.) says the most important issue before Americans is keeping out of foreign entanglements . . . . Army announces a new bomber capable of flying 300 mph with a range of 3,000 miles.	Minnesota Gov. Harold Stassen (R) charges the NLRB is responsible for conflict between labor and industry and calls for new legislation limiting its power . . . . Dewey tells a Lincoln's Birthday audience that the New Deal has created a "House Divided" that has shackled enterprise and caused high unemployment.		American Jewish Congress adopts a resolution to safeguard the rights of Jews against anti-Semitism in the U.S. at its Washington meeting.	Feb. 12
FDR begins a 10-day cruise.	House begins debate on a record $966,722,878 navy supply bill.			American Booksellers Assn. announces its awards for 1939: John Steinbeck's *The Grapes of Wrath*, favorite fiction award; Dalton Trumbo's *Johnny Got His Gun*, most original book award; Antoine de St. Exupery's *Wind, Sand and Stars*, favorite non-fiction award.	Feb. 13
		N.Y. Gov. Herbert Lehman signs the Perry bill, making it illegal for labor union officials to engage in any sort of racial or religious discrimination.	Noted British chemist and recognized authority on synthetic chemistry and dyestuffs Sir Gilbert Morgan dies.		Feb. 14
Petitions to put FDR's name in nomination for the Democratic presidential candidacy are filed in Nebraska and Oregon . . . . Garner appoints a five-man committee headed by Sen. Guy Gillette (D, Iowa) to police the presidential primaries.				Despite Russian advances along the Finnish border, the International Olympic Committee continues to plan for the 1940 Summer games in Helsinki.	Feb. 15
	Gallup Poll reports that by a margin of 68% to 32% Americans favor staying out of the European War.			Pan-American Committee of the AAU meets in New York to discuss the possibility of staging Pan-Am Games in the near future.	Feb. 16
Gallup Poll indicates 52% of the American people expect FDR to seek a third term and 60% expect him to win.	Under State Secy. Welles departs for Europe from New York.			John Blozis in the shot put and Allan Tolmich in the 60-yard high hurdles set new world records at the Melrose Games in New York.	Feb. 17
F	G	H	I	J	
Includes elections, federal-state relations, civil rights and liberties, crime, the judiciary, education, health care, poverty, urban affairs and population.	*Includes formation and debate of U.S. foreign and defense policies, veterans affairs and defense spending. (Relations with specific foreign countries are usually found under the region concerned.)*	*Includes business, labor, agriculture, taxation, transportation, consumer affairs, monetary and fiscal policy, natural resources, pollution and accidents.*	*Includes worldwide scientific, medical and technological developments, natural phenomena, U.S. weather and natural disasters.*	*Includes the arts, religion, scholarship, communications media, sports, entertainment, fashions, fads and social life.*	

	World Affairs	European War Zone	Pacific War Zone	The Americas	Other Countries & Territories
Feb. 18		British Treasury takes control of some 60 American stocks held by British citizens.	Shanghai authorities report the landing of Japanese forces at Haiteng and on the Luichow Peninsula in south China.		
Feb. 19		King Gustav publicly announces that Sweden cannot provide Finland with any official assistance . . . . A Moscow communque reports Russian occupation of the Rijonsaari and Revonsaari islands in the Gulf of Finland . . . . French report the loss of 29 men to a German ambush while on a scouting mission east of the Nied River.	Japanese Foreign Office abandons as futile an effort to reopen trade negotiations with the U.S. . . . . Japanese military authorities deny their forces have been routed in Kwangsi Province.		
Feb. 20		French Chamber of Deputies expels 58 CP members who have not denounced Moscow.			Council of the Federated Malay States votes a war gift of $5 million to Britain.
Feb. 21		An earthquake in the Kaysori Province of Turkey takes 40 lives.		Canadian Finance Min. T.L. Ralston announces a $125 million increase to $500 million in war expenditures for fiscal year 1941 . . . . Chilean Foreign Office reaffirms the country's observance of strict neutrality in the European War.	
Feb. 22		A Soviet official hands proposed terms of a settlement with Finland to the Swedish minister, warning that harsher terms will be imposed if these are rejected . . . . Ivan Maisky, Soviet ambassador to London, presents Russia's peace proposals to the British Foreign Office . . . . French socialists abstain in a vote of confidence in the Chamber of Deputies, leaving the Reynaud government with a majority of one.	Chungking dispatches claim the rout of forces of Wang Ching-wei on the Fukien coast.		Gen. Nuri-es Said forms a new Iraqi cabinet, naming himself both premier and foreign minister . . . . La-Mu-Ton-Chu, a 6-year-old boy, is installed as 14th Dalai Lama of Tibet in ceremonies at Lhasa.
Feb. 23		Allies establish a blockade in the Arctic in an effort to halt shipment of high-grade ore to Germany from Scandinavia.	Chinese reject a British offer to settle their dispute over $3.2 million in silver by storing it in a neutral bank.		
Feb. 24		Speaking in Birmingham, British P.M. Chamberlain appeals to all European nations to work together for a new European order. He outlines Britain's peace aims and offers to seek a settlement with any government that subscribes to them . . . . German general staff completes the final secret plan for an offensive in the West . . . . Turkish Supreme Defense Council declares a state of emergency after Soviet troops are reported crossing the Caucasus frontier.			Labor leaders in New Zealand issue a statement supporting the war aims of Britain.
Feb. 25		Foreign ministers of Denmark, Norway and Sweden announce that their countries will act as a unit to gain the belligerents' respect for their neutral rights.	Japan begins constructing extensive fortifications in the Shanghai and Tsingtao areas, indicating her desire to hold the Chinese seacoast.		Francis B. Sayre, high commissioner of the Philippines, says the U.S. will leave the islands as scheduled in 1946.
Feb. 26			U.S. newsman James R. Young is indicted in Tokyo for violating the Japanese army code by disseminating slanderous material about the Japanese military.	Pan-American Neutrality Comm. establishes sharp limitations on auxiliary ships of belligerent nations in American territorial waters.	
Feb. 27		Moscow reports the first Soviet success since Christmas on the Petsamo front in Finland.		Plans for the Inter-American Bank are finally approved by the Inter-American Financial and Economic Advisory Comm. after months of negotiations . . . . Hernan Laborde and Valentin Campa, president and secretary of the Mexican CP, are purged from the party.	
Feb. 28		Soviets give Finland 48 hours to reply to their peace proposal . . . . Russian forces fight to within seven miles of Viborg.			British announce a curb on Jewish land buying in agricultural areas of Palestine.
Feb. 29	Meeting in Philadelphia, representatives of 23 religious denominations urge neutral nations to band together and negotiate an end to the war.	Soviet forces are reported one mile from Viborg . . . . French government revalues its gold stocks to make a 30-billion franc paper profit for the purpose of war finances.	Chinese claim to have repulsed Japanese efforts to clean up guerrilla areas on the Anhwei-Kiangsu border southeast of Nanking.	Brazilian Foreign Min. Oswaldo Aranha protests the British naval action against the German freighter *Wakama* as a violation of Brazilian waters.	League of Nations executive committee adopts a resolution condemning the new British restrictions in land transfers in Palestine . . . . Jews in Jerusalem and Tel Aviv demonstate against the new British restriction . . . . Manuel L. Quezon, president of the Philippine Commonwealth, says he will not be a candidate for re-election in 1941.

A	B	C	D	E
Includes developments that affect more than one world region, international organizations and important meetings of major world leaders.	*Includes all developments in European countries and military engagements between Allied and Axis powers in Africa and at sea.*	*Includes all developments in Japan and China, Japanese foreign policy and military actions in the Pacific region.*	*Includes all domestic and regional developments in Latin America, the Caribbean and Canada.*	*Includes developments in those independent nations and colonial possessions not covered in Columns B, C and D.*

U.S. Politics & Social Issues	U.S. Foreign Policy & Defense	U.S. Economy & Environment	Science, Technology & Nature	Culture, Leisure & Life Style	
Democratic voters favor FDR over Garner as the party's presidential candidate by a 7-1 count, Gallup Poll reports.		To restore prosperity, Sen. Robert Taft proposes the elimination of federal regulatory measures and revision of tax laws to encourage investment.			Feb. 18
Gallup Poll reports 55% of the American people approve of the proposed federal anti-lynching law . . . . Labor Secy. Francis Perkins urges modifications in immigration laws to provide for quicker naturalization of aliens.	State Dept. officials indicate the U.S. will reject Norway's suggestion that FDR arbitrate the *Altmark* incident . . . . House Banking Comm. delays action on the Finnish aid bill pending advice from the State Dept.	Col. Philip B. Fleming is sworn in as wage-hour administrator in Washington.		Ernie Nevers resigns as head football coach of the Chicago Cardinals.	Feb. 19
				Henry Kreis wins the medal of honor from the National Sculpture Society for creative art.	Feb. 20
New York Times reports that Democratic senators and representatives say FDR can have the party's presidential nomination if he wants it . . . . Sen. Nye says FDR should not seek a third term as president but follow George Washington's precedent.			Pasteur Institute in Paris announces development of a vaccine that simultaneously immunizes against smallpox and yellow fever for one year.		Feb. 21
State Dept. reports that applications for immigration doubled last year because of the disturbed conditions in Europe.		Bureau of Labor Statistics reports a five-month low in the wholesale price index as farm products and textiles prices continue to decline . . . . N.Y. Atty. Jacob Javits proposes changes in anti-trust laws to permit industries to form trade associations.			Feb. 22
					Feb. 23
	FCC urges Congress to bring all U.S. cable and radio services overseas under its rule to avoid foreign interference.			Gregory Rice sets a new world record of 13:55.9 for the three-mile run at Madison Square Garden in New York.	Feb. 24
FDR leaves his name on the Illinois Democratic primary ballot to face John Garner. On the GOP side, Dewey becomes the only candidate as Hamilton Fish and Mayor La Guardia withdraw their names.		National Economy League issues a plan for a balanced federal budget of $7.282 billion.			Feb. 25
Bertrand Russell, noted British philosopher, is appointed a professor at CCNY. . . . . NEA legislative committee charges FDR's policies towards public education are meaningless.	Welles delivers confidential message from FDR to Premier Benito Mussolini in Rome.	Supreme Court rules that only the NLRB, not labor unions, can take the initiative in compelling employers to comply with NLRB orders.	Dr. H.J. Corper of the National Jewish Hospital in Denver announces the isolation of a tuberculosis vaccine.		Feb. 26
Through his supporters, V.P. Garner enters the race for the N.Y. delegates to the Democratic National Convention . . . . New York State Assembly passes a resolution petitioning Congress to pass a law prohibiting a third term for any President.				Raymond M. Hand, internationally known architect, is awarded posthumously the Medal of Honor by the American Institute of Architects.	Feb. 27
	House passes and sends to conference a bill providing for a $100 million increase in the lending authority of the Import-Export Bank.		Floods in Northern California from Tehchapi to the Oregon line maroon 4,000 and cause $1 million in damages.		Feb. 28
John W. Studebaker, U.S. commissioner of education, says controversial subjects should be taught in the schools.				Academy Awards are presented to *Gone With The Wind* as best picture, Robert Donat as best actor and Vivien Leigh as best actress in Hollywood, California.	Feb. 29

F	G	H	I	J
Includes elections, federal-state relations, civil rights and liberties, crime, the judiciary, education, health care, poverty, urban affairs and population.	*Includes formation and debate of U.S. foreign and defense policies, veterans affairs and defense spending. (Relations with specific foreign countries are usually found under the region concerned.)*	*Includes business, labor, agriculture, taxation, transportation, consumer affairs, monetary and fiscal policy, natural resources, pollution and accidents.*	*Includes worldwide scientific, medical and technological developments, natural phenomena, U.S. weather and natural disasters.*	*Includes the arts, religion, scholarship, communications media, sports, entertainment, fashions, fads and social life.*

	World Affairs	European War Zone	Pacific War Zone	The Americas	Other Countries & Territories
March 1		Hitler issues secret orders for the occupation of Denmark and Norway .... Russians make headway towards Viborg, reaching the city's outskirts .... British planes scatter propaganda leaflets over Germany as far east as Berlin.	In Chungking, China, the government launches a sweeping evacuation program for the city in anticipation of Japanese air raids.		Leaders of the Indian Congress, meeting at Patna, India, threaten a civil disobedience campaign as the next step towards complete independence from Britain .... Australian P.M. Robert Menzies announces plans for a seven-fold increase in his country's air force.
March 2		Reports from Finland indicate Soviet forces have occupied Tammisuo, north of Viborg, and Lupin Lahti east of the city.			New Zealand government announces it is supplying men to the British Navy, as well as keeping its own at war strength.
March 3		Sweden rejects British and French requests that their troops be permitted to cross Swedish territory to aid Finland .... The island of Tuppuransaari, south of Viborg, falls to the Russians.	Hong Kong sources report Japan will monopolize all Chinese industry under the peace pact with Wang Ching-wei.	Colombia, Panama and Costa Rica agree to permit U.S. military bases on their soil for use in wartime defense of the Panama Canal.	
March 4	Rumanian government rejects the Italian offer to join the Anti-Comintern Pact.	Russian troops cross Viborg Bay on the ice to the Finnish mainland west of Viborg, virtually completing the capture of the city .... Italy protests British orders to seize coal-laden ships leaving German ports.			Meeting in Jerusalem, the National Council of Palestinian Jews adopts a resolution stating that it cannot accept the new British regulations on land sale .... New Zealand Acting P.M. Peter Fraser announces that a $5-million loan by the Bank of New Zealand to the government for war purposes will be interest free for the war's duration.
March 5		British naval forces intercept seven Italian coal-carrying ships from Rotterdam and take them into British ports.		Uruguayan Pres. Alfredo Baldomier says the U.S. should assist Latin American nations to relieve their dependence on European trade markets .... El Salvador's Finance Ministry announces its intention to establish a branch of the Inter-American Bank in San Salvador.	
March 6		Reports from Stockholm indicate that new Soviet peace offers have been made to Finland through the Swedish government .... France and Italy sign a one-year trade agreement.			Australian P.M. Menzies announces plans to recruit an additional 90,000 men for military service by June 1941.
March 7		Russia and Finland agree to armistice negotiations .... Moscow reports the occupation of several islands in Lake Ladoga and the capture of Nautsi on the Arctic front in the Finnish war .... France calls U.S. citizens to military service.	Arrangements are completed for a $20-million American loan to China by the Import-Export Bank.		
March 8		A Finnish delegation headed by Premier Risto Ryti leaves Helsinki for Moscow for peace negotiations.	Japanese foreign office states the $20-million U.S. loans to China through the Import-Export Bank is an unfriendly act .... Japanese forces capture Shekki, the chief town of the Chungshan district.	Dominican Republic President Don Jacinto B. Peynado dies.	
March 9		French and British governments ask Norway and Sweden to permit increased Allied aid to be shipped to Finland .... Britain releases Italian coal ships on Rome's promise not to send any more ships for German coal.			
March 10	International Labor Organization announces the postponement of its annual meeting for one year.			Diplomatic sources in Washington report the scuttling of the German steamer *Hanover* near Puerto Rico, within the American safety zone.	A Hindu-Moslem riot in Calcutta, India claims the lives of six people.
March 11	Britain announces it no longer will submit to the judgment of the Permanent Court of International Justice at The Hague.	Chamberlain tells the British House of Commons that the Allies would immediately help Finland if asked to do so by Helsinki.	Japanese Foreign Min. Hachiro Arita announces he has abandoned the idea that he can alter America's attitude towards Japan's aims in China.	Diplomatic sources in Buenos Aires indicate Japan and Argentina will sign a trade treaty within a month .... Pres. Getulio Vargas of Brazil announces his nation's neutrality in the European War.	

A	B	C	D	E
Includes developments that affect more than one world region, international organizations and important meetings of major world leaders.	*Includes all developments in European countries and military engagements between Allied and Axis powers in Africa and at sea.*	*Includes all developments in Japan and China, Japanese foreign policy and military actions in the Pacific region.*	*Includes all domestic and regional developments in Latin America, the Caribbean and Canada.*	*Includes developments in those independent nations and colonial possessions not covered in Columns B, C and D.*

U.S. Politics & Social Issues	U.S. Foreign Policy & Defense	U.S. Economy & Environment	Science, Technology & Nature	Culture, Leisure & Life Style	
ABA committee on the Bill of Rights appeals to the public to oppose all illegal methods of suppressing civil rights.	State Under Secy. Welles meets German Foreign Min. Joachim von Ribbentrop in Berlin.	House passes and sends to the Senate the Water Pollution Control Act, setting forth a plan for prevention of pollution of navigable waterways.			March 1
Comm. for the Protection of Foreign Born opens its conference in Washington to protest anti-alien legislation before Congress .... Rhode Island House of Representatives adopts a resolution asking Congress to prohibit presidential third terms.	State Under Secy. Welles talks with Hitler in Berlin .... FDR signs a bill increasing Import-Export Bank capital to $200 million, and the U.S. immediately grants credits to Finland, Sweden and Norway.	AFL Pres. William Green, speaking in Atlanta, calls for the elimination of cheap labor in the South.	Tornadoes sweep the lower Ohio and Mississippi river valleys, causing two deaths.	Dartmouth wins the Eastern Intercollegiate Basketball Conference Title, and the Univ. of North Carolina wins the Southern Conference title .... Bobby Riggs wins the national indoor tennis title in Chicago.	March 2
Charles A. McNary (R, Ore.) charges in a radio address that the New Deal has made the hardships of the depression a permanent way of life.					March 3
Speaking at Toledo, O., Wendell Willkie calls for an end to "big government" control of industry.	Gallup Poll reports 55% of Americans favor lending England and France money for arms supplies, should it appear that Germany is going to win the war.	FDR signs a bill extending provisions of the Bankruptcy Act for farmers until March 4, 1944 .... H.L. Mitchell of the Southern Tenant Farmers Union declares nearly one million families have been displaced from Southern cotton farms since 1930 due to mechanization.	An ice storm from eastern Pennsylvania to Boston causes greater damage than the 1938 hurricane.	Purdue Univ. defeats Illinois Univ. to capture the Big Ten basketball title.	March 4
Gallup Poll reports voters now favor political candidates who urge economy over those advocating government spending programs.					March 5
	Charles Rist of France and Frank Ashton-Gwatkin of Britain arrive in Washington for economic conferences with Secy. Hull .... FDR signs a bill providing for increased military plane production by a larger section of industry.			Stanley Modzeleinski of Rhode Island State sets a new national intercollegiate basketball scoring record of 495 points in one season.	March 6
Former federal Judge Martin T. Morton starts a two-year prison term at Lewisburg, Pa. for a bribery conviction.	Welles confers with Pres. Albert LeBrun and Premier Daladier in Paris.			Novelist Hamlin Garland, best known for his books on the American Midwest, dies at 79 .... Maxine Elliott, noted American actress and later a society hostess on the Riviera, dies at 69.	March 7
George M. Spector, convicted of a bribery conspiracy with former Judge Morton, surrenders in federal court in N.Y.C. .... Sen. Prentiss Brown (D, Mich.) proposes that every employe of a company receiving federal grants as benefits be barred from making monetary contributions to political campaigns.		AFL Pres. Green calls for renewed peace talks with the CIO .... A Federal Reserve Board official predicts that unless long-term credit expansion is obtained the Board will not be able to cope with inflation.	American Assn. for the Advancement of Science reports the discovery of pantothenic acid, an essential vitamin for normal growth in animal and plant life.	Yale University relay swim team sets a new world record of 3:54.4 for the 400 meter relays.	March 8
	Senate Foreign Relations Comm. Chmn. Key Pittman (D, Nev.) urges a 30-day truce in Europe to permit neutrals to negotiate a peace settlement.			Bruno Walter makes his last appearance as guest conductor of the NBC radio symphony orchestra .... Patty Aspinwall, 13, sets a new 220-yard breaststroke record of 3:01.1 at Miami Beach, Florida.	March 9
	Dr. Nicholas Murray Butler says that the U.S. should be ready to assume the role of world leader at the end of the war .... Commerce Dept. survey indicates trade with the Netherlands East Indies will increase because of the war.				March 10
Supreme Court overrules an Alabama court decision to put to death David Canty, a Negro, for the murder of a white woman, on the grounds he was coerced into confessing .... Senate defeats the proposed Brown amendment to extend coverage of the Hatch Act .... Postmaster Gen. James A. Farley withdraws his name from the Ohio Democratic presidential primary.	King George and Chamberlain meet with Welles in London.	Supreme Court upholds an NLRB decision ordering the American Mfg. Co. of N.Y. to dissolve a company union.	Doctors at Montefiore Hospital in N.Y. report the development of a hormone to prevent surgical shock.		March 11
F *Includes elections, federal-state relations, civil rights and liberties, crime, the judiciary, education, health care, poverty, urban affairs and population.*	G *Includes formation and debate of U.S. foreign and defense policies, veterans affairs and defense spending. (Relations with specific foreign countries are usually found under the region concerned.)*	H *Includes business, labor, agriculture, taxation, transportation, consumer affairs, monetary and fiscal policy, natural resources, pollution and accidents.*	I *Includes worldwide scientific, medical and technological developments, natural phenomena, U.S. weather and natural disasters.*	J *Includes the arts, religion, scholarship, communications media, sports, entertainment, fashions, fads and social life.*	

	World Affairs	European War Zone	Pacific War Zone	The Americas	Other Countries & Territories
March 12		Soviets and Finns reach a peace agreement in Moscow. Finland agrees to cede the Karelian Isthmus and the shores of Lake Ladoga .... French Premier Daladier states that the Allied War Council agreed on Feb. 6 to send troops to Finland if publicly asked.	Japanese Premier Mitsumasa Yonai announces his government's intention of recognizing and supporting the Wang Ching-wei regime in China.		Country Party in Australia accepts P.M. Menzies' offer to create a coalition cabinet.
March 13		Finnish Foreign Min. Vaino Tanner charges his country lost its war against Russia because no outside nation is willing to help.			Britain announces the suspension of three Hebrew language newspapers in Palestine for violation of censorship guidelines.
March 14		Finland begins evacuation of areas ceded to Russia in the peace treaty.		Brazilian government announces it will finance the development of its own steel industry, rejecting German aid.	Australian P.M. Menzies creates a new coalition cabinet.
March 15		Finnish parliament ratifies the Soviet peace treaty .... In secret session the French Senate severely criticizes the Daladier government for its war policies.	The trial of U.S. newsman James R. Young is concluded in Tokyo without an announced decision .... Japanese forces report a clash with Russian troops on the Sakhalin-Karafuto border.	Argentina and Japan conclude a trade treaty on a most-favored-nation basis.	
March 16				State Dept. announces that 21 nations of the Western Hemisphere have protested to Britain her violation of the safety zone in the *Wakama* affair.	Colonial Secy. Malcolm MacDonald tells the British House of Commons that restricted land sales in Palestine are designed to prevent trouble throughout the Arab world.
March 17		British planes bomb Nazi patrol ships in the Scapa Flow area.	Japanese Army opens a new offensive in Kwangsi Province, China.		
March 18		Hitler and Mussolini confer in a railway station on the Italian side of the Brenner Pass in the Tyrolean Alps .... German sources report optimism that Russia, Italy and Germany will form a new alliance.	Wang Ching-wei assails the U.S. for assisting the Chiang government against Japan.		
March 19	League of Nations reports a marked increase of German trade with neutral nations.	Despite a vote of confidence from the French Chamber of Deputies, Premier Daladier resigns and Paul Reynaud forms a new cabinet .... British airplanes bomb the German air base at Hoernum on the North Sea Isle of Sylt, off the German coast.		Mexican Communist Party charges the U.S. is plotting a revolt by supporters of Gen. Juan Andreu Almazan for purposes of imperialism.	
March 20		Soviet Presidium ratifies the Finnish peace treaty .... According to reports, 40,000 farms and 7,000 estates have been abandoned near Viborg, Finland in territory to be occupied by the Russians .... German planes attack British convoy off Scottish coast, claiming nine ships sunk.		Colombia suggests that all American nations urge the new Spanish government to show mercy towards those supporting the Republican cause during the Civil War.	All-Indian National Congress votes for Mohandas K. Gandhi to direct a program for freedom from Britain .... French authorities in Indochina bar the acquisition of materials for Germany there.
March 21		French Premier Reynaud creates a new five-man war council.	Meeting in Nanking, the Japanese-sponsored Central Political Conference resolves that only Wang Ching-wei will be the ruler of China .... James R. Young is given a six-month suspended sentence when found guilty in Tokyo of spreading rumors about the Japanese Army.		
March 22		British control officers board the Italian liner *Conte Di Savoia* at Gibralter reportedly in search of Hjalmar Schact, Berlin banker.	Japanese War Min. Shunroku Hata says in Tokyo that his country's policies cannot be limited by the Nine Power Pact.	Nicaragua announces it will join the Inter-American Bank.	
March 23					New Zealand Labor Party begins a meeting in Wellington to determine its stand towards the European War.
March 24	In his Easter service message, Pope Piux XII denounces treaty violations and lack of human concern by nations at war .... Guaranty Trust Co. of N.Y. reports that the affects of the war will cause readjustments in the world's economic order, rather than expansion.	German troops observe Easter by dropping flowers inside the French lines.			New South Wales Labor Party votes against any Australian participation in an overseas war .... Indian Moslem League, meeting at Lahore, challenges Britain to provide equal treatment for Arabs in Palestine.

A	B	C	D	E
Includes developments that affect more than one world region, international organizations and important meetings of major world leaders.	*Includes all developments in European countries and military engagements between Allied and Axis powers in Africa and at sea.*	*Includes all developments in Japan and China, Japanese foreign policy and military actions in the Pacific region.*	*Includes all domestic and regional developments in Latin America, the Caribbean and Canada.*	*Includes developments in those independent nations and colonial possessions not covered in Columns B, C and D.*

U.S. Politics & Social Issues	U.S. Foreign Policy & Defense	U.S. Economy & Environment	Science, Technology & Nature	Culture, Leisure & Life Style	
Democratic slate of national convention delegates pledged to FDR wins the New Hampshire primary .... House Census Comm. approves a congressional reapportionment bill which could exclude the counting of alien residents in the determination of the number of House members from each state.	Charles Rist and Frank Ashton-Gwatkin appeal to Americans to understand that France and Britain cannot weaken their blockade of Germany.	Commerce Dept. reports an increase in business inventories and an 8% drop in industrial orders for the first two months of 1940.			March 12
Senate Judiciary Comm. passes and sends to the floor the House-approved Gavagan anti-lynching bill .... By a 53%-47% margin, American voters would not support FDR for a third term, a Gallup Poll indicates .... Sen. Robert Taft announces he will be a candidate in the Ohio primary for the GOP presidential nomination.	FDR issues a statement praising Finnish valor.	FDR expresses his opposition to further funds for flood control navigation and power projects, contending that existing funds are committed for three years.			March 13
	Welles meets Daladier for a second time in Paris.	A House-Senate conference agrees to, and Congress accepts, a $1.032-billion Treasury-Post Office supply bill and sends it to the White House.		Chairman of the Helsinki Olympic Committee Erik von Frenckell says it is too early to decide whether Finland will hold the summer Olympics.	March 14
	Welles returns to Rome for another round of talks with Italian leaders.	AFL says a $10-billion increase in net wealth for 1940 would cut unemployment by 2.7 million .... Twenty one partners are to join Pierce & Co., making it the largest investment firm on Wall St. in terms of numbers.	Drs. Richard Steckal and John Murlin of Rochester Univ. report successful attempts to make cancer cells normal by treating them with insulin.	Univ. of Colorado defeats Duquesne Univ., 51-40, to win basketball's NIT in New York .... Because of the war with China, the Japanese announce they will not send a team to the 1940 Olympics.	March 15
	In an international broadcast, FDR says a European peace must rest on the right of small nations to be free from threats of large nations.			Novelist Selma Lagerlof dies at 63.	March 16
		Sixty-six percent of farmers agree in a Gallup Poll that the Administration's farm policy has helped farmers; 22% say no.			March 17
N.Y.C. Board of Education votes 11 to 1 against the appointment of Bertrand Russell as a professor of philosophy in City College because of his controversial views on sex and marriage .... Senate approves the Hatch bill restricting political activities of state jobholders paid in whole or part by federal funds.		Investment Bankers Association of America passes a resolution calling upon Congress to remove from the SEC unnecessary powers to restrict public investment .... Wage-Hour Administrator Philip Fleming permits a minimum wage increase to 33½¢ per hour for 24,500 workers in the knitwear industry.			March 18
	In a Toronto speech U.S. Minister to Canada James H.R. Cromwell chides American isolationists for being unrealistic.				March 19
Postmaster Gen. James Farley states his name will be entered in nomination as a candidate for President at the Democratic National Convention .... Connecticut's highest court upholds the state's anti-birth control law, which prohibits the use of contraceptives without any exceptions.	Welles leaves Italy to return to Washington .... U.S. Consulate General in Warsaw is closed on German orders, and its staff leaves for Berlin.				March 20
	Hull warns U.S. Minister to Canada Cromwell against making any further strongly pro-Allied speeches.				March 21
	Senate passes and sends to conference a $1 billion defense bill for 1941 .... War Dept. announces a new long-range bomber capable of travelling 6,000 miles with 28 tons of bombs.				March 22
A slate of candidates supporting Vice Pres. Garner is filed in California, challenging a slate filed in favor of FDR.		Treasury Secy. Henry Morgenthau, Jr. rules Allied money advanced to U.S. industry for expansion is a gift and thus is not taxable.		Kilbey Macdonald of the New York Rangers is selected rookie of the year in the NHL by sportswriters.	March 23
Sen. Thomas Connally (D, Tex.) indicates he will lead a Southern filibuster against the Gavagan anti-lynching bill when debate opens on the Senate floor.			American Chemical Society awards the Eli Lilly & Co. prize to Dr. Eric Glendinning of Johns Hopkins Univ. for research in the hormone adrenelin and vitamins.	The earliest Easter Sunday celebration in 27 years is marred by cold weather in many areas of the U.S.	March 24
F	G	H	I	J	
Includes elections, federal-state relations, civil rights and liberties, crime, the judiciary, education, health care, poverty, urban affairs and population.	*Includes formation and debate of U.S. foreign and defense policies, veterans affairs and defense spending. (Relations with specific foreign countries are usually found under the region concerned.)*	*Includes business, labor, agriculture, taxation, transportation, consumer affairs, monetary and fiscal policy, natural resources, pollution and accidents.*	*Includes worldwide scientific, medical and technological developments, natural phenomena, U.S. weather and natural disasters.*	*Includes the arts, religion, scholarship, communications media, sports, entertainment, fashions, fads and social life.*	

	World Affairs	European War Zone	Pacific War Zone	The Americas	Other Countries & Territories
March 25		Britain announces she will use all legal means to harass German ships carrying iron ore from Narvik, Norway to Germany.		Mexico expropriates 1.5 million acres of American-owned land in the state of Chiapas .... Brazil's leading morning newspaper, *O'Estado de Sao Paulo*, is ordered closed by the Brazilian government because of its alleged opposition to Pres. Vargas.	New Zealand Labor Party ousts left-wing leader John Lee.
March 26		In his first address as French premier, Paul Reynaud cautions Hitler not to make advances into the Balkans.	Reports from London indicate Britain will not recognize the Chinese government of Wang Ching-wei.		New Zealand P.M. Michael J. Savage dies in Wellington.
March 27		P.M. Risto Ryti organizes a peacetime cabinet in Finland .... Evacuation of about 100,000 persons from areas ceded to Russia by Finland offically ends at midnight.		Bolivian government suppresses a leftist political revolt in La Paz.	
March 28		Allied War Council in London issues a communique indicating that France and Britain will not conclude a peace treaty without mutual consent. Secret plans to cut the supply of Swedish iron ore to Germany through Norwegian waters are adopted.	Standing Committee of the Nationalist Party in Chungking gives the title of "Father of the Chinese Republic" to Sun Yat-sen.	Liberal Party led by Canadian P.M. Mackenzie King defeats the Conservatives in parliamentary elections after a campaign focused on war policies.	
March 29		German government issues a White Paper of 16 documents, allegedly captured in Warsaw, revealing American promises to prevent the fall of Poland to Germany.			
March 30		Churchill, in a radio broadcast, warns that neutral rights may be violated by Britain in an effort to halt aid to the aggressors.	Japan announces establishment of a pro-Japanese government in the occupied areas of China, to be located in Nanking and headed by Wang Ching-wei .... Japanese Army reports Russia is building a new railroad from the Outer Mongolian capital of Ulan Bator towards Manchukuo's border.		
March 31		French and British governments agree that Jean Monnet be president of the Commission of French-British Cooperation.			Rashid Ali Beg Gailani becomes new premier of Iraq, reshuffling the cabinet, which retains Gen. Nuri-es Said as foreign minister .... Mohammed Ali Jinnah, president of the All-India Moslem League, suggests partitioning India into Hindu and Moslem states.
Apr. 1			Japanese community nominates five members to the Shanghai Council of International Settlement with the express intention of gaining control.		
Apr. 2		Chamberlain warns that Britain cannot accept a legalistic interpretation of neutral rights when Germany threatens neutrals with invasion. He says Britain will enforce an economic blockade against Germany on the high seas .... Rumania drafts four million youths to work on farms to supply grain to Germany.		Police emergency measures in Brazil imposed March 25 to subdue alleged public disorder are lifted.	The president of the Wafd Party in Egypt, Mustapha Nahas Pasha, demands that as soon as the war ends British soldiers leave the country and that London immediately settle all issues with Cairo.
Apr. 3		Winston Churchill is given general supervision over the British Armed Forces; Lord Woolton becomes food minister .... German troops secretly begin to embark for the invasion of Norway .... Severe earthquake shocks are registered throughout Anatolia, in Turkey.		British government announces the appointment of George Augustus Cambridge, the Earl Athlone, as governor-general of Canada.	Acting P.M. Peter Fraser is elected head of the Labor Party in Wellington, New Zealand.
Apr. 4		Supreme Soviet approves a record defense budget and the incorporation of the Karelian-Finnish region as the 12th republic of the Soviet Union.	Representatives of the Communist and Kuomintang parties open conciliatory negotiations in Chungking with the aim of achieving greater Soviet assistance.		

A	B	C	D	E
Includes developments that affect more than one world region, international organizations and important meetings of major world leaders.	*Includes all developments in European countries and military engagements between Allied and Axis powers in Africa and at sea.*	*Includes all developments in Japan and China, Japanese foreign policy and military actions in the Pacific region.*	*Includes all domestic and regional developments in Latin America, the Caribbean and Canada.*	*Includes developments in those independent nations and colonial possessions not covered in Columns B, C and D.*

U.S. Politics & Social Issues	U.S. Foreign Policy & Defense	U.S. Economy & Environment	Science, Technology & Nature	Culture, Leisure & Life Style	
Vice Pres. Garner instructs Oregon Secy. of State Earl Snell to place his name on that state's primary ballot on May 17 .... Speaking in Los Angeles, Harvard Pres. James B. Conant, says equality of opportunity is the prime challenge of education.		Supreme Court finds the Ethyl Gasoline Corp. guilty of violating antitrust laws through its system of licensing jobbers.		Supreme Court rules the FCC need not consider the impact on competition when it issues a new radio license .... Supreme Court awards Edward Sheldon and Margaret Ayre Barnes 20% of MGM's profits from the movie *Letty Lyton* for the latter's violation of copyright laws.	March 25
Seven men from the liner *Uruguay* are indicted by a N.Y.C. federal grand jury for smuggling aliens into the country.	U.S. government decides to sell P-46 pursuit planes to Britain and France .... U.S. Army successfully tests a new means of aerial photography, using bombs exploded above the target area to serve as a light source.				March 26
House approves and sends to FDR the Starnes bill providing for deportation of any alien engaged in espionage or propaganda .... Leaders of the Progressive Republican Clubs in Wisconsin refuse to endorse Dewey's quest for the GOP presidential nomination.	War Secy. Harry J. Woodring reveals the government's plan to sell 2,100 planes to Britain and France that were originally ordered by the U.S. Army .... Senate Foreign Relations Comm. approves an investigation of foreign propaganda in the U.S.				March 27
N.Y. State Senate passes and sends to the governor the McCaffrey bill providing for a Bill of Rights Week in public schools .... Three men plead guilty in N.Y. to smuggling aliens into the U.S. from the liner *Uruguay*.	Welles returns to Washington and reports to FDR on his European fact-finding trip.	SEC announces a 24.4% decrease in total sales on all security exchanges for the month of February .... House passes and sends to the Senate a $1.02-billion Labor-Security appropriations bill.			March 28
Thomas E. Dewey, speaking in Milwaukee, charges that the New Deal has prolonged the Depression.	FDR says Welles's European trip has shown that peace prospects are scant at this time.			Outstanding British rugby player Alexander Obolensky is killed in an accident.	March 29
Sen. Edwin Johnson (D, Colo.) says that FDR's silence on the third term has hurt other Democratic hopefuls and is leading the party into confusion.	Hull announces the U.S. will not recognize the Wang Ching-wei government in China .... War Dept. notifies 175 plane manufacturers they may defer current military building provided they can guarantee superior aircraft at a later date.		Physics department at Toronto Univ. reveals the world's most powerful microscope which forms its images with electrons, not light.	Univ. of Michigan outscores Yale to win the NCAA swimming title in New Haven, Conn. .... Univ., of Indiana defeats Kansas State Univ., 60-42, to capture the NCAA basketball championship in Kansas City.	March 30
	Gallup Poll reports only 1% of the American people favor a German victory in the current war, while 84% favor Britain and France, and 15% offer no opinion.	NAM Pres. H.W. Prentiss, Jr. appeals to every industrialist to mobilize to meet the attacks of "demagogic detractors" and preserve the free enterprise system.	Eduoard Branly, inventor of the "coherer" which enabled Marconi to develop the wireless telegraphy, dies in France at the age of 95 .... Protected behind 37 ft. dikes, Wilkes-Barre, Pa. remains secure from the flooded Susquehanna River.	Helsinki newspaper reports indicate the Olympic games will not be held this year.	March 31
John L. Lewis threatens to form a third party, unless the Democrats nominate a candidate acceptable to "labor and the common people." .... Atty. Gen. Robert H. Jackson in an address to the U.S. Attorneys Conference in Washington says government prosecutors must use extreme care in protecting civil liberties.		Sen. Vandenberg (Mich.), in a radio broadcast to a Nebraska GOP rally, urges an end to New Deal farm policies.		Track Writers' Assn. names Greg Rice as the outstanding athlete of the 1940 indoor season.	Apr. 1
In a key N.Y.C. Democratic primary election, supporters of FDR win over those of John N. Garner for seats to the Democratic National Convention .... FDR and Thomas E. Dewey win the Democratic and GOP primaries in Wisconsin.		House Labor Comm. approves two amendments to the NLRA: one to protect craft unions and another to permit companies to petition for elections where two competing unions exist.			Apr. 2
				St. Louis Post-Dispatch is fined $2,000, and Ralph Coghlon and Daniel R. Fitzpatrick of the paper's staff are given short jail terms when found guilty of contempt for critical articles on an extortion case .... Finnish Education Min. Antti Kukkonen says Finland cannot host the Olympic Games this year.	Apr. 3
House Rules Comm. approves and sends to the floor the House Census Comm. reapportionment bill .... Former presidential candidate Alf Landon charges the Democratic party with being "boss-ridden" and calls for the election of a Republican as President in order to return government to the people.	Hull sharply criticizes Ontario Atty. Gen. Gordon Conant for saying Canada should do all possible to bring the U.S. into the war .... War Dept. announces the sale of munitions to Finland.	Commerce Secy. Harry L. Hopkins announces that the economic recession continued into March but at a slower rate than January and February, offsetting gains registered after the outbreak of the European War in 1939 .... As a means to economic recovery, Wendell Willkie proposes that federal regulatory boards be modified and tax laws altered to encourage investment.		American Museum of Natural History announces its plans to add a wing to house a new Australia and New Zealand collection.	Apr. 4
F	G	H	I	J	
Includes elections, federal-state relations, civil rights and liberties, crime, the judiciary, education, health care, poverty, urban affairs and population.	*Includes formation and debate of U.S. foreign and defense policies, veterans affairs and defense spending. (Relations with specific foreign countries are usually found under the region concerned.)*	*Includes business, labor, agriculture, taxation, transportation, consumer affairs, monetary and fiscal policy, natural resources, pollution and accidents.*	*Includes worldwide scientific, medical and technological developments, natural phenomena, U.S. weather and natural disasters.*	*Includes the arts, religion, scholarship, communications media, sports, entertainment, fashions, fads and social life.*	

	World Affairs	European War Zone	Pacific War Zone	The Americas	Other Countries & Territories
Apr. 5		Chamberlain declares his confidence in victory is growing. The Allies have improved their relative position since the war began, he adds, declaring, Hitler has "missed the bus." .... Germany announces that Cracow will succeed Warsaw as the capital of the Polish government.	Domei news agency reports Portuguese troops are withdrawing from the island of Lappa on Japan's request.	Chile and Argentina agree to submit the Beagle Channel boundary dispute to U.S. arbitration .... State Dept. names 35 educators for service in Latin America under the terms of the 1936 Inter-American Cultural Relations Agreement.	
Apr. 6			Chinese Central News Agency reports 60 Japanese war ships are missing off the coast of Fukien Province.		
Apr. 7		Allies announce the mining of the Norwegian coast, the Stadtlandet Peninsula, Bud, and West Fjord areas to hinder shipping to Germany .... Russia and Finland resume diplomatic relations.	Japanese delegates, negotiating a trade agreement with Russia, abruptly leave Moscow .... Wang Ching-wei decrees that his government will hold invalid any treaties negotiated by the Chungking government.		
Apr. 8		Britain orders an end to commercial air service to northern Europe.	Reports from Chungking indicate that the Kuomintang and the Communist Party have reached an agreement ending their friction.		Iraq and Saudi Arabia reaffirm their 1936 friendship treaty.
Apr. 9		Germany invades Norway and Denmark, claiming it is protecting them against Allied designs to infringe on their neutrality. Berlin warns that resistance will be crushed. Denmark's King Christian orders his subjects not to resist the invasion. The Allied Supreme War Council meets in London to plan countermoves.	Japanese airplanes bomb China near the British colony of Hong Kong.	In an effort to speed its war effort, the Canadian government creates a Department of Munitions and Supply.	
Apr. 10		German advances in Norway are met with continued resistance. British naval forces reportedly win a major victory off Narvik, sinking five German destroyers. Two British destroyers are lost. Luftwaffe bombers sink a British destroyer off Bergen, while British bombers sink a German cruiser in the city's harbor .... Britain and France warn Belgians that a German invasion may be imminent and urge immediate preventative action .... Belgium declares her continued neutrality in European affairs.	Chiang Kai-shek appoints a 10-man commission to propose solutions to rapid inflation in China.		
Apr. 11		Churchill tells the House of Commons Hitler "has committed a grave strategic error" by invading Norway and Denmark and says Britain will seize control of the Norwegian coast.	Japanese effort to gain control of the Shanghai Council of International Settlement fails, as election results give Britain five seats and Japan and the U.S. each two.		
Apr. 12	Pro. James T. Shotwell urges that a "Grand Alliance" of democratic nations be formed to bring world peace and security.	European Allies declare the Danish merchant marine the property of the enemy and begin seizing Danish vessels in foreign ports.	Domei announces Japan will reopen the Pearl River, closed since 1938, to world commercial traffic on April 20th.	Foreign Min. Jose Maria Castillo says Argentina will not recognize the German occupation of Norway and Denmark.	
Apr. 13		Commodore Fritz Bonte, chief of the German destroyer flotilla, is killed in battle with British ships at Narvik. Five more German destroyers and a U-boat are sunk .... German radio broadcasts from Oslo threaten death to Norwegians resisting the German occupation.		FDR says in Washington that 50 years of Pan Americanism has resulted in the Western Hemisphere's rejection of the world's "arrogant forces."	
Apr. 14		Allied troops land at Namsos, north of Trondheim, initiating a two-pronged attack on that key city in central Norway.	Reports in Tokyo claim Japan will use force to prevent the NEI from falling into the hands of a third power.		
Apr. 15		German troops repulse attempted Allied landing at Narvik, Norway .... Maj. Vidkun Quisling resigns as premier of the German-sponsored Norwegian cabinet and is succeeded by Ingolf E. Christensen.	Japanese Foreign Min. Arita warns against any change in the status of the Netherlands East Indies in view of developments in Europe and Japan's economic ties to the Indies.	Rio de Janeiro police arrest 51 Communists for allegedly plotting a nationwide revolt.	

A
Includes developments that affect more than one world region, international organizations and important meetings of major world leaders.

B
Includes all developments in European countries and military engagements between Allied and Axis powers in Africa and at sea.

C
Includes all developments in Japan and China, Japanese foreign policy and military actions in the Pacific region.

D
Includes all domestic and regional developments in Latin America, the Caribbean and Canada.

E
Includes developments in those independent nations and colonial possessions not covered in Columns B, C and D.

U.S. Politics & Social Issues	U.S. Foreign Policy & Defense	U.S. Economy & Environment	Science, Technology & Nature	Culture, Leisure & Life Style	
FDR indicates his opposition to the Walter-Logan bill, which would permit the court review of rulings by federal quasi-judicial agencies.	Senate approves and sends to FDR a bill authorizing the President to negotiate reciprocal trade agreements for the next two years.			Theatre Club, Inc. awards *Life With Father* its annual prize as the best play written by an American .... Bogakar wins the Great Britain Grand National Steeplechase at Aintree.	Apr. 5
Backers of FDR start a Texas campaign to force the state Democratic convention, meeting in May, to send an FDR delegation to the national convention.	A resolution opposing American entry into the war is adopted by a Socialist Party convention in Washington.		At 5 p.m. EST a solar eclipse is visible in the northeastern U.S.		Apr. 6
Rejecting the advice of John L. Lewis, Labor's Non-Partisan League of New Jersey supports a third term for FDR .... Chmn. Martin Dies of the House un-American Activities Comm. demands FDR's support of his plan to expose and curb foreign affiliated organizations .... Norman Thomas is nominated as the presidential candidate of the Socialist Party.			Rockefeller Foundation provides $150,000 to the Univ. of California for the construction of a 4,900-ton cyclotron under the direction of Pro. E.O. Lawrence .... A Gallup Poll reports Americans feel the following to be the most serious public health problems: syphilis, 46%; cancer, 29%; tuberculosis, 16%; and infantile paralysis, 9%.		Apr. 7
FDR vetoes the Starnes bill, which provided for the mandatory deportation of alien drug users.	Reports in Washington indicate that the U.S. would undertake the protection of the Netherland East Indies should the Dutch become involved in the war.	FDR signs a law classifying the bald eagle as an endangered species and placing it under federal protection .... In its campaign platform the Socialist Party calls for a truce between the AFL and CIO as the means to halt "reactionary" tendencies in the U.S.	A fissure four to five miles long opens on the side of Mauna Loa near Hilo, Hawaii.		Apr. 8
FDR and Thomas E. Dewey supporters win easily in the Democratic and GOP primary elections in Illinois .... Dewey defeats Vanderberg in the Nebraska GOP primary.	Sen. Rush D. Holt (D, W.Va.) charges the U.S. is slipping slowly into war.		Bell Laboratories stages the first public demonstration of stereophonic sound at Carnegie Hall in New York.	N.Y. Gov. Herbert Lehman signs the McLaughlin bill, which permits public school children to be absent for religious observance and education .... Famous British actress and demimonde Mrs. Patrick Campbell dies at 75 .... Archbishop of Paris and Primate of France Jean Cardinal Verdier dies at 76.	Apr. 9
Oren Root Jr. announces a drive to gain nationwide popular support for Willkie's GOP nomination.	FDR meets with Danish Min. Henrik de Kauffmann to discuss the fate of Greenland .... FDR freezes the assets of the Danish and Norwegian governments in the U.S.	Agriculture Dept. predicts a winter wheat crop of 426 million bushels, the smallest since 1933.			Apr. 10
House approves a bill for reapportionment based upon the current census .... FDR proposes the merger of the CAA and the Air Safety Bd. and the transfer of the agency to the Commerce Dept.	FDR issues a proclamation barring all U.S. shipping from the expanded European war theater in Norway and Denmark.		Dr. Simon Ruskin tells the American Chemical Society meeting in Cincinnati that vitamin C is useful in combating allergies .... Dr. Mary E. Pennington receives the ACS 1940 Garvan Medal for distinguished work in chemistry.		Apr. 11
Senate passes and sends to FDR the reapportionment bill .... Dewey forces gain control of the New York State GOP Committee, naming Edwin G. Jaeckle as chairman and taking the first step to oust Kenneth F. Simpson as the state's national committeeman.	FDR signs the Reciprocal Trade Agreement Act extending the original act of 1937 for another three years .... FDR confers with Chief of Naval Operations Adm. Harold D. Stark on methods to speed up naval construction.		Dr. Paul Ehrlich of Mount Sinai Hospital in New York reports finding a five-day chemical treatment for syphilis.		Apr. 12
Dies Comm. reports the U.S. CP has a central role in the Soviet-German plan to sponsor a revolution in Mexico.	FDR calls the invasion of Denmark and Norway an "unlawful exercise of force." .... Asst. State Secy. A.A. Berle says that as long as FDR is president of the U.S., America will stay out of war.			Cornelius Warmerdam sets a new world pole vault record of 15 feet in Berkeley, California.	Apr. 13
Kenneth Simpson, GOP national committeeman from New York, says he will fight to keep his position in face of the Dewey challenge and will campaign statewide himself.	Because of Germany's quick success in Norway, U.S. defense officials are reportedly concerned about Britain's ability to defend the Atlantic.				Apr. 14
House opens debate on the Walter-Logan bill .... A Gallup Poll indicates that 53% of the voters would support FDR over Arthur Vandenburg in a presidential election .... Herbert Hoover says it would be "a sign of degeneration" if the American people permit the federal government to control the training of youth.	Herbert Hoover calls for political and military isolation from world affairs.			FDR tosses out first ball at Griffith Stadium in Washington to open the major league baseball season.	Apr. 15

F	G	H	I	J
Includes elections, federal-state relations, civil rights and liberties, crime, the judiciary, education, health care, poverty, urban affairs and population.	*Includes formation and debate of U.S. foreign and defense policies, veterans affairs and defense spending. (Relations with specific foreign countries are usually found under the region concerned.)*	*Includes business, labor, agriculture, taxation, transportation, consumer affairs, monetary and fiscal policy, natural resources, pollution and accidents.*	*Includes worldwide scientific, medical and technological developments, natural phenomena, U.S. weather and natural disasters.*	*Includes the arts, religion, scholarship, communications media, sports, entertainment, fashions, fads and social life.*

	World Affairs	European War Zone	Pacific War Zone	The Americas	Other Countries & Territories
Apr. 16			Shao Li-Tse is appointed Nationalist China's new ambassador to Russia	Election results give the Argentine Radical Party control of the Chamber of Deputies for the first time since 1930.	Egyptian cabinet drafts a law making espionage or treason punishable by death.
Apr. 17		From their newly acquired bases in Norway, German planes raid Scapa Flow.	Japanese embassy in Shanghai reveals a proposal designed to provide Japan with control of the International Settlement Council.		Australian Gov.-Gen., Lord Gowrie announces Communist publications will be censored and those opposing the war effort will be prosecuted.
Apr. 18		German troops take the Norwegian fortresses of Oskarborg and Drobak in Oslo Fjord.	Japanese Army claims the rout of Chinese forces in Shangsi Province in northeast China.	Pres. Roberto M. Ortez recalls the Argentine military mission to Berlin.	All-India National Congress directs its committees to prepare for a declaration of civil disobedience.
Apr. 19		German government expels Norwegian Min. Arne Scheel. First French forces are landed in northern Norway.			
Apr. 20		In an effort to prevent German troops from being air lifted to Norway, British planes bomb Stavanger, Aalborg and Kristiansand .... The Netherlands government declares a state of siege for the entire country.	Japan opens the Pearl River in China to commercial traffic, making Canton accessible to world trade.		
Apr. 21		Allied forces land at Andalsnes, Norway in an effort to prevent the German army in the south from joining units at Trondheim.			Clashes between Hindus and Moslems in Rangoon, Burma result in 11 deaths and 69 injuries.
Apr. 22		Germans introduce aerial Blitzkreig tactics to the Norway fighting, raiding the city of Dombas .... In an effort to maintain her neutrality, Sweden protests to Berlin the flight of Nazi bombers over her territory.	Japanese bombers attack Chungking .... Chinese Central News Agency reports military successes in Kiangsi Province.		
Apr. 23		Canadian and French troops seize from the Germans the town of Gratangen, 25 miles north of Narvik, Norway .... Poland and Norway are represented for the first time at the Allied War Council in Paris.	U.S. Amb. Joseph C. Grew asks the Japanese Foreign Office to alleviate the blockade of Tientsin to relieve Americans there.	Chile and the U.S. agree that an American military aviation mission will be sent to Santiago to advise Chile's air force.	Egyptian Premier Aly Maher Pasha reaffirms his country's stand on the Allied side in the European War.
Apr. 24		Germany claims unrestricted control over areas of occupied Norway and declares war on the Norwegian government .... Berlin responds in a conciliatory manner to the Swedish protest over violations of air rights, but does not promise to end the practice .... Pope Pius sends a message to Mussolini urging him to keep Italy out of the European war.			
Apr. 25			Japanese are reportedly sending 60,000 men into southern Shansi Province to halt a Chinese advance.		
Apr. 26		German forces break Allied defenses at Roeros, Norway .... Allies and Switzerland agree that the latter may obtain supplies for her own use under guarantee that they will not go to Germany.	Terrorists bomb the office of the American-owned *Shanghai Evening Post and Mercury* .... British sources in Hong Kong report that Japan has taken full control of Lappa Island, a Portuguese possession.	Brazilian government sentences 64 persons to prison for being Communist propagandists.	
Apr. 27		Von Ribbentrop reveals allegedly captured British documents indicating British and French military designs on Norway prior to German invasion.		Inter-American Neutrality Comm. announces in Rio de Janeiro that it has agreed upon a 300 mile-wide security belt around the Americas.	

A	B	C	D	E
Includes developments that affect more than one world region, international organizations and important meetings of major world leaders.	*Includes all developments in European countries and military engagements between Allied and Axis powers in Africa and at sea.*	*Includes all developments in Japan and China, Japanese foreign policy and military actions in the Pacific region.*	*Includes all domestic and regional developments in Latin America, the Caribbean and Canada.*	*Includes developments in those independent nations and colonial possessions not covered in Columns B, C and D.*

U.S. Politics & Social Issues	U.S. Foreign Policy & Defense	U.S. Economy & Environment	Science, Technology & Nature	Culture, Leisure & Life Style	
FDR meets with Postmaster Gen. Farley, a candidate for the Democratic presidential nomination, at the White House.	State Dept. announces that diplomatic relations with Iceland will be established shortly.		A freak hailstorm strikes the Los Angeles area.		Apr. 16
	Secy. Hull issues a strong U.S. reply to the Japanese warning of two days ago about the Netherlands East Indies. Hull says any intervention in the affairs of the Indies "would be prejudicial to the cause of stability, peace and security ... in the entire Pacific area."	SEC Pres. William M. Martin says the broad scope of government power hinders industry-government cooperation.			Apr. 17
House passes and sends to the Senate the Walter-Logan bill, which provides court review for rulings of 130 federal bureaus and agencies .... Sen. Taft declines to enter the GOP primary in Maryland, leaving Dewey the only Republican candidate there.					Apr. 18
N.Y.C. members of the state GOP Committee endorse National Committeeman Simpson in his struggle with Dewey forces.				Taitso Maki of Finland sets a new U.S. record for the 3 mile run in 13:42.4 minutes at New Orleans.	Apr. 19
		AFL Pres. William Green opens a union organizing drive in the Southwest with a Dallas, Texas speech calling for the unity of all economic groups.	First public test of the electron microscope is held at the Radio Corporation of America laboratories in Camden, N.J. .... Goodyear-Zeppelin Corp. announces the production of a dirigible capable of resisting storms while airborne.		Apr. 20
A Gallup Poll indicates that if the presidential election were held today, the Democrats would capture 31 states out of 48 and 317 of the 531 electoral votes .... Oren Root, leading a Willkie nomination drive, claims he has 35,000 declarations of support for Willkie.		CIO Pres. John L. Lewis calls upon his union members to support the LaFollette Oppressive Labor Practices Bill .... Justice Dept. announces it is dropping antitrust actions against five major typewriter companies because they will sign decrees promising never again to violate antitrust laws.		George A. Heitzler is elected president of the American Professional Football League.	Apr. 21
	Rear Adm. J.K. Taussig says that unless the U.S. takes a firm stand on the Philippines, the country will be drawn into a Pacific War .... Prof. James T. Shotwell claims the failure of the U.S. to support liberal policies after W.W.I. has been responsible for the weakening of world peace forces.	Anti-picketing laws of California and Alabama are declared unconstitutional by the Supreme Court as violations of free speech .... House approves the creation of an investigation committee to study the problems of migratory labor in the U.S.	Prof. E.A. Doisy, St. Louis Univ., reports the synthetic re-creation of Vitamin K, essential for the prevention of hemorrhaging.		Apr. 22
Delegates opposing a third term for FDR gain victories in the Pennsylvania primary .... Eleanor Roosevelt says the U.S. must guard against hasty defense legislation that would curtail civil liberties.					Apr. 23
N.Y. Gov. Herbert H. Lehman signs the McCaffrey bill, providing for a Bill of Rights Week in the state's public schools.				First general conference of the Methodist Church opens in Atlantic City, New Jersey.	Apr. 24
	FDR declares Norway a belligerent, making Norwegian purchases in the U.S. subject to the cash and carry provisions of the Neutrality Law and prohibits Americans from travelling on Norwegian ships .... State Dept. announces Bertel E. Kuniholm will be the U.S. representative to Iceland.	Bureau of Labor Statistics reports a ½ of 1% rise in the wholesale price index for the first time this year .... Senate passes and sends to conference a $150-million omnibus river bill.			Apr. 25
Senate opposition maps plans to oppose FDR's proposed merger of the CAA and Air Safety Bd.	France and Britain accede to U.S. pressure to keep the inconveniences of their blockade to a minimum.	Senate passes and sends to conference a $1.025-billion Labor and Security Appropriations Bill.		Mrs. Harlow Estes wins $10,000 for her *Hildreth-Her Story* as the best first novel by any author in 1939, from Dodd, Mead & Co. and *Redbook* Magazine.	Apr. 26
Harvard Univ. says its appointment of Bertrand Russell to a lectureship will not be affected by the dispute over his appointment at New York Univ. .... Missouri GOP Convention leaves its 30 national convention votes uninstructed, while endorsing the state's only GOP congressman, Rep. Dewey Short, for vice president.	Frank Ashton-Gwatkim, British economic adviser, says Allied purchase of U.S. goods will leap enormously during the next year.	An AP survey indicates that the top 250 U.S. corporations show a 50% profit increase for the first quarter of 1940 over the same period in 1939.			Apr. 27

F	G	H	I	J
Includes elections, federal-state relations, civil rights and liberties, crime, the judiciary, education, health care, poverty, urban affairs and population.	*Includes formation and debate of U.S. foreign and defense policies, veterans affairs and defense spending. (Relations with specific foreign countries are usually found under the region concerned.)*	*Includes business, labor, agriculture, taxation, transportation, consumer affairs, monetary and fiscal policy, natural resources, pollution and accidents.*	*Includes worldwide scientific, medical and technological developments, natural phenomena, U.S. weather and natural disasters.*	*Includes the arts, religion, scholarship, communications media, sports, entertainment, fashions, fads and social life.*

	World Affairs	European War Zone	Pacific War Zone	The Americas	Other Countries & Territories
Apr. 28		The town of Namsos, the Allied troop landing area in central Norway, is leveled by German air attacks. Allied commanders are ordered to withdraw from Namsos and Andalsnes, thus abandoning the attempt to take Trondheim.	Conflicting reports of success are issued by Tokyo and Chungking concerning the heavy fighting in Shansi Province.		
Apr. 29	Former Belgian P.M. Paul Van Zeeland says in Washington that the U.S. must play the decisive role in the social and economic reorganization of the world after the war.	German troops advance up Gudbrands and Oester valleys in Norway in their drive against the Dombas-Saoeren rail lines.	Chungking reports its troops have stopped a new Japanese offensive in Shansi Province.		
Apr. 30	Communist International issues a statement from Moscow warning that the current war will spread to the Balkans, Near East and Pacific regions.	German troops occupy Dombas and Opdal, thus gaining control of the Oslo-Trondheim rail line.			
May 1		Mussolini receives a strong message from FDR warning him of the dangers to Italy if it enters the war on Germany's side . . . . French steamship *Ile de France* leaves New York City with war material.	U.S. Amb. Grew and British Amb. Robert C. Craigie cancel vacations to remain in Tokyo, hoping to improve relations with Japan . . . . Chou En-lai charges that the U.S., Britain and France want to end the war in China only to bring the country's resources into the war against Germany.	Panama announces it cannot afford to buy its $1 million allotted shares in the Inter-American Bank.	New Zealand P.M. Peter Fraser reshuffles his cabinet, retaining all ministers, but reassigning duties.
May 2		Allies abandon their landing ports in southern and central Norway, thereby giving Germany possession of all Norway south of Steinkjer . . . . King Haakon of Norway and his family flee via the port of Molde.		Mexican newspapers revive a 1911 claim that parts of El Paso, Texas belong to Mexico.	
May 3		Allies evacuate Namsos and abandon the Steinkjer line to the Norwegian troops under Col. O.B. Getz, who asks the German High Command for an armistice . . . . More than 200 French Communists are sent to islands in the Atlantic off the French coast for internment.		Mexican Petroleum Distribution Agency announces a $54-million contract with three U.S. companies for the purchase of Mexican oil.	
May 4			Domei announces the launching of a Japanese drive against an estimated 500,000 Chinese troops in Hupeh Province.		
May 5		Three Allied destroyers, convoying disembarking troops from Norway, are destroyed by German aircraft.	Dr. T.F. Tsiang appeals to the U.S. to help support the Nationalist Chinese currency . . . . Japanese Foreign Min. Arita states his government will sign an agreement soon with Britain and France to end the Tientsin controversy.		
May 6		German troops capture the Hegre fortress and Varnes airport in Norway . . . . Reports in Rome indicate Pope Pius XII is making overtures to FDR to play the role of mediator in bringing peace to Europe.			
May 7		Clement R. Atlee, Labor opposition leader in Britain, decries the ineffective foreign policies of Chamberlain as debate opens on a motion of no-confidence. Adm. Sir Roger Keyes, a Conservative, scores the government's handling of Norwegian campaign. Conservative Leo Amery tells Chamberlain, "In the name of God, go!"	Home Min. Hideo Kodama forbids the formation of a labor party in Japan on the grounds that it would foster class consciousness and impair national unity in wartime.	Acting State Secy. Summer Welles announces in Washington that the U.S. will sign the agreement establishing the Inter-American Bank.	

A	B	C	D	E
Includes developments that affect more than one world region, international organizations and important meetings of major world leaders.	*Includes all developments in European countries and military engagements between Allied and Axis powers in Africa and at sea.*	*Includes all developments in Japan and China, Japanese foreign policy and military actions in the Pacific region.*	*Includes all domestic and regional developments in Latin America, the Caribbean and Canada.*	*Includes developments in those independent nations and colonial possessions not covered in Columns B, C and D.*

U.S. Politics & Social Issues	U.S. Foreign Policy & Defense	U.S. Economy & Environment	Science, Technology & Nature	Culture, Leisure & Life Style	
	Justice Dept. announces the establishment of a Neutrality Laws Unit to centralize control of all alleged violations .... In response to Germany's invasion of Norway, a Gallup Poll reports 93% of the Americans think it unjustified, but 96% do not feel the U.S. should declare war on Germany.			Don Budge defeats Bruce Barnes at White Sulphur Springs, West Virginia to win the national open tennis title .... Famous Italian operatic soprano Signora Luisa Tetrazzini dies in Milan at 68.	Apr. 28
In a joint telegram to the Texas State Democratic Committee, Sam Rayburn and Lyndon Johnson ask that the delegates sent to the national convention endorse Garner only as a "favorite son." .... Florida GOP committee is split when a rump group elects 12 delegates to the national convention, understood to be anti-Dewey, thus challenging the full state committee's choice.	S.H. Church of the Carnegie Institute announces a $1-million reward for the deliverance of Adolf Hitler, alive, to the League of Nations.	Supreme Court upholds Labor Secy. Frances Perkins' determination of wages in steel companies holding government contracts under the Walsh-Henley Law.			Apr. 29
GOP voters reject a Dewey delegate slate in favor of an unpledged one, while Democratic voters favor Farley over FDR in the Massachusetts primary.		Senate passes and sends to the House a bill providing revenue payments, in lieu of taxes, by the TVA to states and counties .... House defeats the proposed amendments to the Wage-Hour Law and then votes to reopen the entire question.		New York Architectural League awards prizes to Constance Ortmayer and Adlai S. Hardin for their exhibits at the Whitney Museum of American Art .... American Football Coaches Assocaition awards the first Amos Alonzo Stagg Award to Donald Grant Herring, Jr.	Apr. 30
FDR confers at the White House with five members of House Comm. on Government Reorganization in an effort to gain support for his proposed merger of the CAA and the Air Safety Bd.	House passes a Senate-approved bill giving FDR the authority to "freeze" assets of belligerents held in the U.S.	House approves an amendment to the Wage-Hour Law, excluding farm and farm-process workers from its provisions.			May 1
U.S. Chamber of Commerce passes a resolution against the proposed merger of the CAA and the Air Safety Bd.	U.S. Chamber of Commerce, meeting in Washington, adopts a resolution asking Congress to keep America out of war.	U.S. Chamber of Commerce asks Congress to do away with the NLRA and the Wage-Hour Law, alleging they inhibit economic growth.	Paris office of Press Wireless, Inc. puts into operation a new method of transmitting photographs by radio.	Maria Euphrasia Pelletier and Gemma Galgani are cannonized by Pope Pius XII	May 2
In a Washington speech FDR challenges would-be Democratic candidates to stop criticizing the New Deal and offer constructive alternatives.				Twenty-seven of the 85 women on the advisory committee for the New York World's Fair resign in protest against the chosen Fair theme: "For Peace and Freedom."	May 3
FDR nominates Robert H. Hinkley as assistant secretary of commerce in a move designed to placate opponents of his CAA reorganization plan .... Atty. Gen. Jackson absolves FBI agents of using "third degree" methods in their arrest of 12 persons recruiting for the Spanish Loyalist Army .... Wendell Willkie says the deficit spending of the New Deal will lead the country to bankruptcy and political chaos.		FDR vetoes a bill extending the provisions of the Federal Crop Insurance Act to cotton and tobacco.		Gallahadion, a 35-1 long shot, wins the Kentucky Derby .... Greg Rice sets a new U.S. record of 8:18.9 for the 3,000-meter run.	May 4
Gallup Poll presidential trial heat reveals FDR would defeat Robert H. Taft by a 58%-42% ratio.					May 5
		Senate approves and sends to FDR a $110-million rivers and harbors bill.		John Steinbeck's *Grapes of Wrath* wins the Pulitzer Prize as the most distinguished novel in 1939 by a U.S. author.	May 6
FDR forces win a landslide victory in the California Democratic primary race .... Sen. Millard E. Tydings and his followers win Maryland Democratic primary, campaigning against a third term for FDR .... Alabama Democrats elect 22 delegates to the National Convention to support a "favorite son", House Speaker William Bankhead.	FDR signs a bill authorizing him to "freeze" assets of belligerents in the U.S.				May 7

F	G	H	I	J
Includes elections, federal-state relations, civil rights and liberties, crime, the judiciary, education, health care, poverty, urban affairs and population.	*Includes formation and debate of U.S. foreign and defense policies, veterans affairs and defense spending. (Relations with specific foreign countries are usually found under the region concerned.)*	*Includes business, labor, agriculture, taxation, transportation, consumer affairs, monetary and fiscal policy, natural resources, pollution and accidents.*	*Includes worldwide scientific, medical and technological developments, natural phenomena, U.S. weather and natural disasters.*	*Includes the arts, religion, scholarship, communications media, sports, entertainment, fashions, fads and social life.*

	World Affairs	European War Zone	Pacific War Zone	The Americas	Other Countries & Territories
May 8	Meeting at International House in N.Y.C. delegates representing 40 peace organizations urge the creation of some form of international government.	Chamberlain wins narrow vote of confidence in the British House of Commons amid Laborite demands he resign. Many Conservative backbenchers join the demand for his resignation. The vote is seen as making his resignation inevitable.	Japanese forces break the Chinese Hupeh-Honan defense lines.	Dr. Rafael Angel Caldron Guardia is inaugurated as president of Costa Rica.	
May 9		British troops land in Iceland to "protect" the island .... Hitler orders amnesty for Norwegian POWs.		U.S., Mexico, Bolivia, Colombia, Equador and the Dominican Republic sign an agreement in Washington to establish the Inter-American Bank.	
May 10		German troops cross the Dutch, Belgian and Luxembourg borders at 5:30 a.m. in a surprise attack with the main thrust spearheaded by the panzers striking through Luxembourg and the Ardennes. German glider troops capture the Belgian Fort Eben Emael, the key to the Albert Canal defense line .... Chamberlain resigns as prime minister of Britain and is replaced by Winston Churchill.	Netherlands East Indies government interns Germans and imposes martial law upon receiving news of the invasion of Holland.		Britain announces plans to permit 1,600 Jewish refugee children to emigrate to Palestine by October.
May 11		German panzers drive the Belgians back from the Albert Canal to the Dyle Line, where British and French units have advanced to form a new defense line. Germans continue to advance almost unopposed through the Andennes toward Sedan and Dinant.	Foreign Min. Arita says Japan will not permit the NEI to change hands.	British and French forces land on Dutch Caribbean islands of Curacao and Aruba at the request of the Dutch to avert any attempted German takeover .... Dutch West Indies authorities intern Germans of military age and seize German ships in port.	President of the Jewish Agency for Palestine, Dr. Chaim Weizmann confers in London with British officials on the future of Palestine.
May 12		German forces cross the Albert Canal and take the city of Wareem in Belgium. Holland is virtually cut in two by advancing German forces. Guderian's panzers strike across the Semois and occupy Sedan. Rommel's forces reach the Meuse near Dinant .... Vatican newspaper, *Osservatore Romano*, agrees to cease publication of political news at the request of the Italian government.		Argentine Foreign Min. Cantillo says the Americas should adpot a non-belligerent attitude towards the European War.	
May 13	Bank of International Settlements relocates from Basel to the interior Swiss town of Chateau d' Oex.	Churchill presents his new coalition government, offering Britain nothing but "blood, toil, tears and sweat" in a war to the finish .... Rommel and Guderian lead their panzer divisions across the Meuse in force near Dinant and Sedan .... Allied forces successfully land near Narvik, Norway .... Queen Wilhelmina, Princess Juliana and her two children flee The Hague to Britain, where they are lodged in Buckingham Palace.	Britain and Holland assure Japan that they have no intention of altering the status of NEI .... China claims, but Tokyo denies, a major victory on the Hupeh-Honan frontier.	Uruguay proposes that all American republics join in a strong protest against German aggression in Europe .... Brazil subscribes to the Inter-American Bank.	
May 14	British Amb. Lord Lothian, in a N.Y.C. speech, says that the free world must mobilize its resources to defeat Hitler.	Luftwaffe bombers level the center of Rotterdam. Gen. Henri Gerard Winkelman, commander-in-chief of the Dutch army, directs his troops to lay down their arms .... In France, German troops consolidate their bridgeheads on the west bank of the Meuse. RAF suffers heavy losses over Sedan.	British authorities in Hong Kong ask all women and children to register for possible evacuation.		
May 15		German forces advance south and west of Sedan. The French Ninth Army is routed along a 50-mile front from Philippeville to Liart. Germans capture Stonne .... Churchill flies to Paris for talks with Reynaud after the French premier calls and tells him the battle is lost .... The official capitulation of the Netherlands army is signed at 11 a.m.		Ottawa court declares the Canadian CP illegal in an effort to curb fifth column activities .... Colombia's oil pipelines are destroyed, allegedly by German fifth columnists in the country.	
May 16		Reynaud addresses the French Assembly promising "revolutionary" steps to deal with the German breakthrough. Churchill meets with French leaders in Paris and promises more fighter squadrons will be thrown into the battle. French foreign office begins burning its secret papers. German units advance beyond Montcornet and Auesnes.	Japanese Amb. Kensuki Horinouchi indicates after a meeting with State Secy. Hull that Japan, Britain, France and the U.S. are in agreement that the status quo of the NEI should be maintained .... Batavia, capital of the NEI, becomes the headquarters for Dutch corporations for the war's duration.	American and Canadian officials join in ground-breaking ceremonies for a bridge across Niagara Falls gorge.	

	A	B	C	D	E
	Includes developments that affect more than one world region, international organizations and important meetings of major world leaders.	*Includes all developments in European countries and military engagements between Allied and Axis powers in Africa and at sea.*	*Includes all developments in Japan and China, Japanese foreign policy and military actions in the Pacific region.*	*Includes all domestic and regional developments in Latin America, the Caribbean and Canada.*	*Includes developments in those independent nations and colonial possessions not covered in Columns B, C and D.*

U.S. Politics & Social Issues	U.S. Foreign Policy & Defense	U.S. Economy & Environment	Science, Technology & Nature	Culture, Leisure & Life Style	
House rejects FDR's proposal for shifting the CAA and Air Safety Bd. to the Commerce Dept. . . . . Sixty-seven percent of GOP voters favor Thomas E. Dewey as their candidate over Arthur Vandenberg and Robert Taft, according to a poll released today.	Wendell Willkie calls for more aid to the democracies.	Commerce Dept. announces the formation of an Interstate Trade Barriers Comm. to study federal legislation needs against trade restrictions.	Drs. Philip Polatin, Hyman Spotnitz and Benjamin Wiesel of N.Y. State Psychiatric Inst. report successful use of insulin in the shock treatment of mental patients.		May 8
Republicans are reportedly planning to place the name of their governor, Raymond E. Baldwin, in nomination for the GOP presidential race at next month's national convention . . . . Prohibition Party adopts a resolution at its Chicago convention that it become the nucleus of a new party coalition opposing the GOP and Democrats.	White House denies a Rome report that FDR offered through Mussolini to mediate the European War.	U.S. Wholesale Grocers' Assn. adopts a resolution at its Savannah convention charging that Agriculture Secy. Henry A. Wallace favors big business.	Monsanto Chemical Corp. opens a new laboratory in Springfield, Mass. devoted solely to research in plastics.		May 9
	FDR condemns the German invasion of the Low Countries as unwarranted aggression . . . . Gallup Poll reports 66% of the American voters would vote for a presidential candidate who would give all help necessary to Britain and France, except U.S. troops.	Senate passes and sends to the House a bill providing that total soil conservation and allotment payments to individuals shall not exceed $10,000 annually.			May 10
Four senators—Norris, Nebraska; Thomas, Oklahoma; Minton, Indiana; and Lucas, Illinois say Germany's invasion of the Low Countries will aid in the renomination of FDR.	Willkie urges all aid to the Allies in Europe short of U.S. entrance into the war . . . . State Dept. announces application of the Neutrality Laws to Belgium, Holland and Luxembourg.			New York World's Fair opens . . . . Bimelech wins the Preakness Race by two lengths in Baltimore, Md.	May 11
Gallup Poll presidential survey reports FDR would gain 52% of the votes, Thomas E. Dewey 48%.				Leo Durocher, manager of the Brooklyn Dodgers, receives the Sporting News Award as the outstanding major league manager in 1939.	May 12
	In an address to the American Society of International Law in Washington, State Secy. Hull says U.S. isolation is futile . . . . Rep. Alfred L. Bulwinkle (D, N.C.) introduces a proposal in Congress seeking to provide U.S. loans to the Allies.				May 13
Senate nullifies House action on the CAA, permitting FDR to transfer the agency to the Commerce Dept. and abolish the Air Safety Bd.	FDR again appeals to Mussolini to keep Italy out of the war.			Museum of Modern Art opens its exhibit of Mexican art spanning 2,000 years.	May 14
Vice Pres. Garner says FDR will win the party's presidential nomination and claims he has no interest in being a candidate for the vice presidency again . . . . In an unprecedented move, the House Immigration Comm. approves a bill to deport Harry Bridges to Australia.			Prof. Albert Einstein tells the American Scientific Congress that man is capable of solving the riddle of the universe's origin.		May 15
	Rome sources indicate Mussolini is cool to FDR's suggestion that Italy stay out of the European war . . . . FDR asks Congress for appropriations to lift airplane production to 50,000 a year . . . . James H.R. Cromwell resigns as U.S. minister to Canada.	FDR signs a bill permitting the RFC to make direct loans to individuals developing any strategic material in war time.	Dr. H.J. Spinden reports that recent dicipherment of Mayan relics in Mexico indicate a civilization 1,250 years in advance of Europe in astronomy and mathematics.		May 16

F	G	H	I	J
Includes elections, federal-state relations, civil rights and liberties, crime, the judiciary, education, health care, poverty, urban affairs and population.	*Includes formation and debate of U.S. foreign and defense policies, veterans affairs and defense spending. (Relations with specific foreign countries are usually found under the region concerned.)*	*Includes business, labor, agriculture, taxation, transportation, consumer affairs, monetary and fiscal policy, natural resources, pollution and accidents.*	*Includes worldwide scientific, medical and technological developments, natural phenomena, U.S. weather and natural disasters.*	*Includes the arts, religion, scholarship, communications media, sports, entertainment, fashions, fads and social life.*

	World Affairs	European War Zone	Pacific War Zone	The Americas	Other Countries & Territories
May 17		German armored forces occupy Louvain and Brussels, forcing the Belgian government to relocate to Ostend on the Channel coast. Hitler orders Guderian to check his advance until the German infantry catches up with him. A counterattack by Gen. Charles de Gaulle's tank units is thrown back near Montcornet. Germans reach the Oise.	Chinese forces report inflicting 7,000 casualties on Japanese troops in an attack on the city of Tsaoyang, Hupeh Province.		
May 18		French Premier Reynaud appoints Marshall Henri Phillippe Petain as vice premier and military adviser.		Under Panama's leadership the 21 American republics issue a declaration stating Germany's invasion of the Low Countries is "unjustified and cruel."	
May 19		Rommel's panzer units reach Cambrai. De Gaulle's tank units attempt a counterattack on the German flank but are repulsed with heavy losses. In the north, British forces fall back to the Escaut line. Lord Gort warns London the evacuation of the BEF must be considered. Gen. Henri Giraud surrenders to German troops after being cut off . . . . Gen. Maxim Weygand is appointed chief of the French general staff and commander-in-chief of all theaters of operation. Daladier is moved from the war office to the foreign ministry . . . . German forces in Belgium push west of Antwerp and Brussels towards the channel ports.	Chiang Kai-shek announces his government will not reduce its war effort against Japan because of lessened foreign aid due to the European war.	The American republics publish a collective protest against German aggression . . . . Brazil's Pres. Vargas extends his country's neutrality laws to Norway, the Netherlands, Belgium and Luxembourg.	New Zealand P.M. Peter Fraser, an0nounces acceleration of military training.
May 20		German forces in France advance south and west, seizing Laon and Amiens. Advance units reach Abbeville.	Rumors in Chungking indicate Germany has offered to mediate the Sino-Japanese War.	Canadian P.M. Mackenzie King reports the acceleration of Canadian troop shipments to Britain.	Supreme commander of the French defense forces in North Africa, Gen. Auguste Nogues, orders the creation of a territorial guard to help protect the interior of Morocco for the war's duration.
May 21		German forces are within 60 miles of Paris and only a few miles from the French coast. The evacuation of Paris begins. British forces begin a counterattack south from Arras to try to cut off the spearhead of the German attack, but are stopped after an advance of 10 miles. Weygand meets with Belgian King Leopold at Ypres.			
May 22		Churchill confers with Reynaud and Weygand in Paris. Guderian's panzers reach the outskirts of Boulogne and Calais on the Channel coast. A French counterattack towards Cambrai is repulsed . . . . British Parliament extends the Emergency Powers Defense Bill, putting the country's war industries under direct government contract.	German Amb. Eugen Ott informs Japanese Foreign Min. Arita that his country is not interested in the NEI.		
May 23		Belgians are pushed out of key points at Ghent and Terneuzen. British abandon Arras . . . . German planes bomb port facilities at Dunkirk and Dover.	Japanese troops commence a counterattack at Tsaoyang, Hupeh Province.	U.S. directs its Latin American envoys to propose secret joint defense talks between army and navy representatives of all the Western Hemisphere nations in view of the German successes in Europe . . . . Col. Fulgencio Batista, Cuban presidential candidate, pledges full cooperation with the U.S. should war come to the Western Hemisphere.	Leopold S. Amery, British secretary for India, asserts that Britain wants the equal partnership of India in the Commonwealth . . . . Australian P.M. Menzies announces the creation of a third army division for service abroad.
May 24		Hitler orders a halt to the German advance around the trapped British-French force in Flanders. German forces capture Calais.		The 21 American republics formally protest to Britain that the sinking of the *Hannover* on March 9 was a violation of the American security belt . . . . Violent earthquakes in Peru cause 249 deaths.	
May 25		German forces tighten their grip on the pocket of Allied troops in Flanders . . . . Belgians try to form a new defense line along the Lys . . . . Turkish government declares a state of emergency.			

A	B	C	D	E
Includes developments that affect more than one world region, international organizations and important meetings of major world leaders.	*Includes all developments in European countries and military engagements between Allied and Axis powers in Africa and at sea.*	*Includes all developments in Japan and China, Japanese foreign policy and military actions in the Pacific region.*	*Includes all domestic and regional developments in Latin America, the Caribbean and Canada.*	*Includes developments in those independent nations and colonial possessions not covered in Columns B, C and D.*

U.S. Politics & Social Issues	U.S. Foreign Policy & Defense	U.S. Economy & Environment	Science, Technology & Nature	Culture, Leisure & Life Style	
	House Military Affairs Comm. opens hearings on FDR's proposal for equipping and training one million fighting men by June 1941 .... With FDR's approval Frank Knox, Chicago newspaper publisher, announces plans to help train 10,000 civilian air pilots this summer.	John L. Lewis asks that the government grant labor a voice in formulating defense policies.			May 17
FDR followers capture the Oregon Democratic primary, putting the President 45 votes short of the party's nomination .... Fifty-six aliens are deported from N.Y.C. to Italy, France, Yugoslavia, Hungary and Rumania.			Earthquakes in Imperial Valley, Calif. take five lives .... Robert Lorenzon developes a TV system capable of broadcasting and receiving in natural color.	Corydon wins the Withers Stakes at Belmont Park, New York.	May 18
Sources in Washington indicate that FDR plans to bring several Republicans into his cabinet for the purpose of defense unity in case of war.	Col. Charles A. Lindbergh says the American people have nothing to fear concerning possible invasion of this continent.			Samuel Reshevsky defeats Reuben Fine to retain the U.S. Chess Federation championship.	May 19
	FDR says in Washington that only liberal trade policies after the war will being world peace and prosperity .... Carl Beck organizes the American Defenders of Freedom to promote an adequate defense posture in the U.S.	FDR asks Congress for $35 million to purchase strategic materials such as manganese, tin and chrome .... William McC. Martin is reappointed governor of the NYSE for one year .... The regulatory provisions of the Bituminous Coal Act are declared constitutional by the Supreme Court.	Igor Sikorsky makes the first successful fully controlled helicopter flight in Bridgeport, Conn.	Sportswriter Grantland Rice receives the Sportsmanship Brotherhood Award in recognition of his service to sports.	May 20
Although Dewey wins the New Jersey GOP presidential primary, Willkie wins nearly 14,000 writein votes .... FDR asks that the Bureau of Naturalization and Immigration be moved to the Justice Dept. in order to better deal with fifth column activities.	FDR appeals to all political groups for unity in defense policy.	FDR vetoes the Rivers and Harbors Bill and asks Congress to appropriate those funds for defense .... American Institute of Architects issues a report claiming improved relations between labor and employers in the construction industry during the last year.	Howard Hughes is designated the winner of the Octave Chanute Award of the Institute of Aeronautical Sciences in recognition of his contribution to air science.	Northern Baptist Convention directs a collection from church members for the immediate emergency relief of war torn countries .... National Poetry Center's golden scroll and medal of honor for the outstanding national poet of the year is presented to Jessie B. Rittenhouse.	May 21
FDR evades Alf Landon's request that he refuse a third term as a price for GOP cooperation in an emergency cabinet.	Senate approves and sends to the House a $1.823 billion defense appropriation bill .... Sen. James F. Byrnes (D. S.C.) accuses Col. Charles Lindbergh of fifth column activities.		Council on Foods of the AMA gives its first seal of approval to the Bird's Eye Corp. for its quick frozen foods.		May 22
By gaining the support of Vermont's delegates to the National Democratic Convention, FDR is assured of nomination for a third term with at least 547 ½ pledged delegates.	Gallup Poll reveals that 51% of Americans favor granting war credits to the Allies.				May 23
	House passes and sends to the Senate a defense bill to permit unlimited expansion of the Army Air Force.			Paris reports claim that priceless art treasures from the Brussels Museum were spirited out of the country to an unknown destination during the German invasion .... First night baseball game in the Polo Grounds, New York is witnessed by 22,260.	May 24
	U.S. opens a consulate in Godthaab, Greenland as an observation post and counter against possible German intervention there .... Brig. Gen. George V. Strong reports the development of a secret device capable of detecting aircraft up to 15 minutes away.	AFL Pres. Green tells a Hartford, Conn. labor meeting the American people should "not underestimate Communist" influence in the CIO.			May 25

F	G	H	I	J
Includes elections, federal-state relations, civil rights and liberties, crime, the judiciary, education, health care, poverty, urban affairs and population.	*Includes formation and debate of U.S. foreign and defense policies, veterans affairs and defense spending. (Relations with specific foreign countries are usually found under the region concerned.)*	*Includes business, labor, agriculture, taxation, transportation, consumer affairs, monetary and fiscal policy, natural resources, pollution and accidents.*	*Includes worldwide scientific, medical and technological developments, natural phenomena, U.S. weather and natural disasters.*	*Includes the arts, religion, scholarship, communications media, sports, entertainment, fashions, fads and social life.*

	World Affairs	European War Zone	Pacific War Zone	The Americas	Other Countries & Territories
May 26		Hitler orders the panzers to resume the advance against Dunkirk .... Lord Gort is told to fall back on the Channel coast and prepare for evacuation at Dunkirk. In the evening, the British war cabinet orders the evacuation to begin.	Heaviest Japanese air assault to date upon Chungking causes 200 deaths.		New Zealand P.M. Peter Fraser announces the creation of a National War Council.
May 27		German planes inflict heavy losses on British forces evacuating from Dunkirk .... Rommel cuts off nearly half the French forces in Flanders in small pockets around Lille.		Mexican Pres. Lazaro Cardenas reaffirms his nation's neutrality in international affairs.	
May 28		Belgium's King Leopold surrenders his troops unconditionally to German forces at 3 a.m. .... Belgian cabinet, under Premier Habort Pierlot, in exile in Paris, delcares the King's surrender illegal and unconstitutional and resolves to continue the war .... British, French and Polish forces drive the Germans out of Narvik and occupy the Norwegian port.	Japanese bombers again inflict heavy damage on Chungking.		
May 29		French warships arrive at Dunkirk and help evacuate 47,310 Allied soldiers .... German forces occupy the continental coast except for 54 miles north and south of Dunkirk.	Shao Li-tsi, the new Chinese ambassador to Russia, leaves Chungking for Moscow.	Canadian Parliament approves a $700-million defense expenditure bill, which receives quick royal assent.	
May 30		Allied forces continue their escape from Dunkirk to Dover under harassment by the Germans .... Belgian government in exile approves an order depriving King Leopold III of his throne .... Civil administration of the Netherlands is turned over to Arthur Seyss-Inquart, the Reich commissioner.			
May 31	U.S. liner *Exeter* docks at Jersey City, N.J. with $4 million in gold bullion assigned to the N.Y. Federal Reserve Bank by the Bank of International Settlements.	A record 68,000 Allied soldiers are evacuated from Dunkirk .... Churchill and Reynaud again meet in Paris. The French are critical of the failure to evacuate more of their troops from Dunkirk.	Tokyo announces near agreement on peace terms with the Wang Ching-wei government in central China.		
June 1		Because of heavy losses to German aircraft, British Admiralty orders that all embarkations from Dunkirk must take place after dark .... Germans carry the war to Southern France with bombing raids in the Rhone Valley .... Hitler orders Dutch POWs released.	Communist Party leader Chou En-lai arrives in Chungking from Moscow.		New Zealand legislature passes a law granting the government full power over all persons and property for the war's duration.
June 2	Chile withdraws from the League of Nations.	German bombers destroy Narvik, Norway.		Germany warns Mexico and Panama that Britain has sent secret service agents to Central America for disruptive purposes.	
June 3		For the first time German planes drop bombs on Paris, which Berlin officials claim were intended for airports near the city .... British Admiralty claims over 335,000 men have been rescued from Dunkirk.	Premier Yonai reaffirms in a Tokyo press conference Japan's commitment to settle the China conflict, recognize the government of Wang Ching-wei, accept the status quo in NEI and keep out of the European war.		
June 4		Churchill addresses Parliament, reporting on the evacuation from Dunkirk. He promises Britain will "go on to the end .... We shall fight on the beaches, we shall fight on the landing-grounds, we shall fight in the fields, and in the streets ... we shall never surrender." .... French Vice Adm. Jean Marie Abrial, leaves Dunkirk, officially concluding the Allied evacuation effort .... German planes bomb the French port of Le Havre.	Chinese Nationalist government claims the recapture of Siangyang in northern Hupeh Province.	P.M. Mackenzie King places all Canadian military forces at the disposal of the British government.	

A	B	C	D	E
Includes developments that affect more than one world region, international organizations and important meetings of major world leaders.	*Includes all developments in European countries and military engagements between Allied and Axis powers in Africa and at sea.*	*Includes all developments in Japan and China, Japanese foreign policy and military actions in the Pacific region.*	*Includes all domestic and regional developments in Latin America, the Caribbean and Canada.*	*Includes developments in those independent nations and colonial possessions not covered in Columns B, C and D.*

U.S. Politics & Social Issues	U.S. Foreign Policy & Defense	U.S. Economy & Environment	Science, Technology & Nature	Culture, Leisure & Life Style	
	FDR castigates isolationists in a fireside radio chat and defends his plan for a massive increase in defense spending .... Gallup Poll reports 86% of Americans support FDR's request for an additional $1 billion in military spending from Congress.	Brookings Institute reports as a result of a two-year study that New Deal economic policies are responsible for the lag in capital investment.			May 26
	FDR appoints Jay Pierpoint Moffat as minister to Canada.	Senate passes and sends to the House a LaFollette civil liberties bill which will bar use of certain tactics, such as employment of strikebreakers, against labor .... House Ways and Means Comm. begins preparation of new tax measures for defense purposes.		Joe DiMaggio receives the Golden Laurel as the outstanding U.S. athlete in 1939.	May 27
New Jersey delegates to the GOP National Convention reportedly are split in their support for Dewey's nomination as the party's presidential candidate .... Senate passes and sends to the House a bill authorizing the attorney general to appoint a five-member commission to prepare a new code of law for the District of Columbia.	FDR names a seven-member National Defense Advisory Commission headed by William Knudsen and Edward R. Stettinus .... Although war sentiment is rising the U.S., the Gallup Poll reveals that Americans oppose entrance into the conflict by a 13-1 margin.	The White House and congressional leaders reportedly are in agreement on a $700-million defense tax measure .... The sale of a NYSE seat falls to the lowest price ($38,000) since 1915.			May 28
		Donald M. Nelson is named by Secy. Morgenthau as director of the Treasury's Procurement Division .... Board of directors of NAM announces its members will meet defense production requirements without profiteering.			May 29
Senate passes and sends to the House the Hospital Construction Act, appropriating $10 million annually for rural hospital construction.					May 30
Senate approves the transfer of the Bureau of Naturalization and Immigration from the Labor to the Justice Dept..... Fifty-six percent of the GOP voters favor Thomas E. Dewey as the party's candidate over Robert Taft and Arthur Vandenburg, according to the Gallup Poll.	FDR asks Congress for $1 billion in supplemental defense funds and authority to call the National Guard and Army reserves to active duty.	Secy. Morgenthau tells the House Ways and Means Comm. it is essential to raise the national debt limit to $45 billion to help finance the defense effort.			May 31
	Because of defense developments, Gen. George C. Marshall suggests U.S. troops may have to be stationed outside the country .... U.S. Communist Party platform condemns FDR's foreign policy as imperialistic.	At its annual meeting in N.Y., the National Lawyers Guild adopts a resolution opposing any change or amendment to the NLRA.	Paul Schlack receives a patent on a process that makes wool mothproof by treatment with alkyline oxide and imine.	Univ. of Pittsburgh captures the IC-4A track championship at Cambridge, Mass.	June 1
Despite the prospect of a four-year prison term, Earl Browder is nominated as the CP's presidential candidate at the party's N.Y.C. convention.	Gallup Poll reports 85% of the American people believe that the U.S. military is now strong enough to thwart a foreign attack.	N.Y. National City Bank's monthly report says that although the arms build-up will spur business, it will not result in permanent prosperity in the U.S.			June 2
A *New York Times* survey indicates that unless there is a sudden shift, Dewey does not have votes to capture the GOP presidential nomination on the first ballot .... House Un-American Activities Comm. Chmn. Martin Dies says he has evidence of espionage activity in the TVA.	House and Senate committees begin consideration of a resolution warning that the U.S. will refuse to recognize or acquiesce in any transfer of territory in the Western Hemisphere from one non-American power to another non-American power.	GM grants William Knudsen an indefinite leave of absence so he may give full attention to the National Defense Council .... Secy. Morgenthau charges Knudsen with the task of coordinating the machine tool industry.			June 3
Originator of the Willkie-for-President movement, Oren Root, Jr., claims Willkie will receive the nomination on the second ballot.	Senate approves the House version of a Navy bill calling for 10,000 airplanes and 16,000 aviators .... Asst. War Secy. Louis Johnson tells a group of 1,200 business executives that it will take two years until the defense program is fully prepared.	House Ways and Means Comm. votes to increase the national debt limit by $4 billion and new tax measures by $1 billion.		Mrs. Simon Guggenheim, Mrs. David M. Leary, Archibald MacLeish and Dr. Carlton Sprague Smith are added to the board of trustees of the Museum of Modern Art.	June 4

F	G	H	I	J
Includes elections, federal-state relations, civil rights and liberties, crime, the judiciary, education, health care, poverty, urban affairs and population.	*Includes formation and debate of U.S. foreign and defense policies, veterans affairs and defense spending. (Relations with specific foreign countries are usually found under the region concerned.)*	*Includes business, labor, agriculture, taxation, transportation, consumer affairs, monetary and fiscal policy, natural resources, pollution and accidents.*	*Includes worldwide scientific, medical and technological developments, natural phenomena, U.S. weather and natural disasters.*	*Includes the arts, religion, scholarship, communications media, sports, entertainment, fashions, fads and social life.*

	World Affairs	European War Zone	Pacific War Zone	The Americas	Other Countries & Territories
June 5	Reports state the only regular work being performed by the League's skeleton staff are the studies and reports of the Economic Section.	At 4 a.m. the Germans launch a new battle of the Somme, striking south along a wide front but encountering stiff French resistance .... Reynaud reshuffles the French cabinet, dropping Daladier and bringing in Paul Baudouin and Charles de Gaulle.	Japanese troops cross the Han River to assault the Yangtze River port city of Ichang.	A Canadian Order in Council outlaws many politically suspect groups, including the CP.	
June 6		French forces hold up the German advance south of Amiens and Peronne .... Italian officials warn the U.S. to stay out of the European war or face the possibility of an invasion.		Chilean government restricts radio broadcasts and newspapers from publishing accounts of the European war.	
June 7			Extremist Fusanosuke Kuharu resigns as Japanese cabinet counselor and challenges the government to take a firm stand against the U.S. and Britain.		
June 8		In a naval battle off the Norwegian coast, the British carrier *Glorious* is sunk and the German battle cruiser *Scharnhorst* is severely damaged .... German army northeast of Paris launches a full-scale offensive.		Cuban Constituent Assembly completes work on a new constitution, including all policies favored by president-elect Batista, to take effect Sept. 15.	
June 9		German tanks are reported 35 miles from Paris.	Chinese Amb. Shao Li-tse arrives in Moscow.	Constituent Assembly completes the new Cuban constitution, which provides for a parliamentary system with a premier appointed by the president.	
June 10		Count Ciano informs the French and British ambassadors that as of tomorrow Italy will consider herself at war with both nations .... French radio announces the government is leaving Paris .... Allies abandon Narvik in Norway. King Haakon and his family flee to Britain as an armistice ends the fighting in Norway.	Japan and the Soviet Union reach an agreement settling their dispute over the Manchurian frontier .... Japanese military dispatches claim the capture of Shasi on the Yangtze River in Hupeh Province.		
June 11		Churchill visits Reynaud at Tours to urge that Paris be defended .... Gen. Weygand declares Paris an open city as German troops reach the suburbs .... Italian planes bomb British bases at Malta and Aden.	Japan and Thailand sign a pact in Tokyo to respect each other's territorial integrity .... Hong Kong government interns resident Italians.	Pres. Vargas reaffirms Brazil's neutrality but also denounces "the sterile demagogy of political democracy." The speech is widely interpreted as a rebuke to FDR's Charlottesville address .... The minister of the interior states Mexico's foreign policy is pro-Allied and one seeking cooperation with the U.S.	Australian government begins arresting some 7,000 Italian nationals in that country.
June 12		Rommel's panzer force captures 40,000 prisoners along the French coast in a single day .... Italian government announces the mining of waters around Malta and Sicily and the French naval base at Bizerta, Tunisia.	Despite stubborn Chinese resistance, Japanese troops capture Ichang .... British and Japanese officials reach an accord on the law and order and currency differences in Tientsin that have strained relations for a year.		
June 13		Churchill again flies to Tours where the French ask if Britain will release them from the pledge not to seek a separate peace. He says he cannot but adds that he understands France's predicament .... Sir Stafford Cripps arrives in Moscow for talks with Soviet leaders.		In response to threatened government action, German Min.-to-Uruguay Otto Longmann says the Nazi Party there has been dissolved .... Princess Juliana of the Netherlands and her two children take refuge near Ottawa, Canada.	Public and private air raid shelters are under construction in Jerusalem.
June 14		French government relocates from Tours to Bordeaux .... Reynaud sends an appeal to FDR to enter the war, warning him that the fall of France is imminent .... German troops enter Paris .... Spanish troops take control of Tangiers, North Africa with the consent of France, England and Italy.	Wang Ching-wei government in China issues a demand that all French, British and Italian warships leave the country.		
June 15					

A	B	C	D	E
Includes developments that affect more than one world region, international organizations and important meetings of major world leaders.	*Includes all developments in European countries and military engagements between Allied and Axis powers in Africa and at sea.*	*Includes all developments in Japan and China, Japanese foreign policy and military actions in the Pacific region.*	*Includes all domestic and regional developments in Latin America, the Caribbean and Canada.*	*Includes developments in those independent nations and colonial possessions not covered in Columns B, C and D.*

U.S. Politics & Social Issues	U.S. Foreign Policy & Defense	U.S. Economy & Environment	Science, Technology & Nature	Culture, Leisure & Life Style	
Charles Edison resigns as secretary of the Navy to run for the governorship of New Jersey.		John L. Lewis expresses little hope of a labor truce between the AFL and the CIO .... International Ladies Garment Workers Union adopts a resolution to reaffiliate itself with the AFL .... New York State Chamber of Commerce calls on Congress to defeat the LaFollette Oppressive Labor Practices Bill, charging it will be detrimental to the national defense program.			June 5
Speaking to the House Appropriations Comm., Atty. Gen. Jackson explains the need for additional funds to help combat fifth column activities .... Speaking in New York, Dewey claims he has a minimum of 400 to 450 delegates pledged to him at the GOP convention.		WPA chief F.C. Harrington gives priority to 73 military orders.		FDR signs bill providing funds for the Library of Congress to purchase sound recordings for the blind.	June 6
Speaking in Chattanooga, Tennessee, Sen. Taft claims that FDR should renounce third term for the sake of the nation's unity.	FDR puts into operation a plan whereby old military equipment will be made available to the Allies immediately .... FDR signs a bill freezing the securities of all invaded countries and blocking importation of any securities held by the governments or nationals of the invaded countries.	House votes to abolish the Labor Board under the NLRA and replace it with a new three-man panel .... Commerce Dept. reports April was the first month since November 1939 in which manufacturers' new orders exceeded shipments.			June 7
In his home town of Palo Alto, Calif., Herbert Hoover supporters start a drive to have him drafted at the GOP convention for the presidential nomination.			Dr. Robert A. Milliken of Cal Tech reports rapid progress in the treatment of cancerous tumors.	Bimelech wins the Belmont Stakes .... Fred Wolcott sets new world record of 22.5 seconds for the 220-yard low hurdles at Princeton Univ.	June 8
Dies Comm. demands that FDR dismiss 563 persons in government service who are members of the League for Peace and Democracy, allegedly a Communist organization.				Lawson Little defeats Gene Sarazan in an 18-hole playoff for the U.S. Open Golf Title at Cleveland, Ohio.	June 9
Gallup Poll reports 95% of Americans favor the registration of all aliens.	Speaking at Charlottesville, Va., FDR denounces Italy's entrance into the war, declaring, "The hand that held the dagger has stuck it into the back of its neighbor." He calls for "full speed ahead" in the defense effort .... Sen. Claude Pepper (D, Fla.) urges Congress to repeal neutrality legislation so FDR can give all possible aid to the Allies.	Agriculture Dept. increases its forecast of anticipated winter wheat production to 488.458 million bushels.	Dr. Chevalier Jackson is voted the AMA's Distinguished Service Award for his work in bronchoscopy.		June 10
Atty. Gen. Jackson opposes formation of volunteer counter-espionage groups in the U.S.	FDR declares the Mediterranean Sea a combat zone from which U.S. ships, planes and civilians are barred .... ACLU Chmn. Justin Haynes Holmes tells a Newark, N.J. audience that universal conscription is a violation of civil liberties.	House passes and sends to the Senate a $1.004 billion defense tax bill, which also authorizes an increase in the national debt to $49 billion .... Congress approves the establishment of Cumberland Gap Historical Park in Tenn., Ky. and Va.		A day-long interfaith conference on the world's current religious crisis is held in Washington.	June 11
		Federal Reserve Board Chmn. Marriner Eccles asks Congress to broaden the board's power to grant loans to small businesses dealing in war contracts.	Dr. Bayard T. Horton of the Mayo Clinic reports that the drug histamine is effective in combating severe headaches.	Vatican newspaper *Osservatore Romano* fails to appear for the first time since 1870 .... American artists vote to withdraw from the biennial Venice Art Exhibit because of Italy's war declaration.	June 12
	Hull condemns "ruthless bombings of civilian population" in a comment on Japanese attacks on Chungking .... FDR signs a $1.308-billion Navy appropriations bill, providing for construction of 22 new warships.				June 13
In welcoming the Naturalization Service into the Justice Dept., Atty. Gen. Jackson says only aliens who can benefit the U.S. will be admitted.	Rear Adm. Joseph K. Taussig says that the "bankrupt" U.S. policy in the Far East will result in war.				June 14
Michigan Democratic State Convention endorses FDR a third term .... House approves and sends to the Senate a bill authorizing increased border patrols to help curb alien entry into the U.S.	Col. Charles Lindbergh urges the U.S. to stay out of the European war, although he says he favors hemispheric defense and universal military service .... FDR signs a Navy bill expanding its air corps by 10,000 planes and 16,000 aviators.	Senate approves the House bill authorizing the RFC to purchase par value stock in Federal Home Loan Banks .... FDR signs a bill limiting federal credit union loans to $100 unless adequate security is provided.	FDR decides to set up a National Defense Research Comm. to plan, coordinate and organize all scientific work on new weapons.		June 15
F	G	H	I	J	
Includes elections, federal-state relations, civil rights and liberties, crime, the judiciary, education, health care, poverty, urban affairs and population.	*Includes formation and debate of U.S. foreign and defense policies, veterans affairs and defense spending. (Relations with specific foreign countries are usually found under the region concerned.)*	*Includes business, labor, agriculture, taxation, transportation, consumer affairs, monetary and fiscal policy, natural resources, pollution and accidents.*	*Includes worldwide scientific, medical and technological developments, natural phenomena, U.S. weather and natural disasters.*	*Includes the arts, religion, scholarship, communications media, sports, entertainment, fashions, fads and social life.*	

	World Affairs	European War Zone	Pacific War Zone	The Americas	Other Countries & Territories
June 16		Churchill offers France a declaration of permanent union with Britain. When the French cabinet shows no interest in the idea, Reynaud resigns and Petain is asked to form a government .... A message arrives from FDR ending Reynaud's hopes for American intervention .... Soviets demand that the Baltic states—Latvia, Estonia and Lithuania—put themselves under Russian military protection .... Italian planes bomb British air bases at Salum and Sidi Barrani, Egypt.	Japanese bombers inflict heavy damage on Chungking.		Communist and Fascist parties are declared illegal in Australia.
June 17	Capt. Francis P. Walters of Britain resigns his post as under-secretary of the League of Nations.	Petain asks the Spanish ambassador to approach the Germans about an armistice .... Russia begins military occupation and political reorganization of Latvia, Estonia and Lithuania.	Japanese military authorities demand French Indochina halt arms shipments to Chiang Kai-shek.	Uruguayan Senate votes wide powers to the government to repress pro-Axis activities and ban all secret societies.	
June 18		French Adm. Jean Darlan promises Britain that under no circumstances will the French fleet fall into German hands. Hitler and Mussolini meet in Munich to hammer out the terms for the French armistice .... The remnants of the British force in France embark for England.		P.M. Mackenzie King reorganizes his cabinet with the creation of a War Services Dept. to aid Canada's war effort.	
June 19		Franco secretly offers to join the war on Germany's side if Spain is given Gibraltar, French Morocco and other territory in Africa .... Gen. de Gaulle urges the French commander in North Africa, Gen. Auguste Nogues, to place himself at the head of a colonial resistance movement .... Advancing German forces occupy Cherbourg, and Brest.	Japanese military authorities demand that Britain close the Burma Road to China and the Hong Kong frontier.		
June 20		Germans occupy Nantes, Vichy and Lyons.	Japanese Navy masses off the Indochina coast near Haiphong .... Japanese Army blockade of Tientsin is lifted.	Canadian Parliament authorizes conscription of the dominion's manpower for defense of economic and industrial resources.	
June 21		Germans read the terms of the proposed armistice to French representatives at Compiegne, in the same railroad car in which the Germans had signed the armistice ending W.W. I. .... King Carol assumes dictatorial powers in Rumania.			
June 22	Albert Einstein urges the creation of a world federation with military power.	French representatives sign an armistice with the Germans at Compiegne. Most of southern France and French overseas possessions are to be left unoccupied.	Japan demands that the French government close the Indochina frontier with China and permit a Japanese control commission to supervise the application of this regulation on the scene.		
June 23		Britain withdraws diplomatic recognition of the French government under Petain .... French delegates consider Italy's peace proposals near Rome at the Villa Incisa.			Egyptian cabinet of Premier Aly Maher Pasha submits its resignation to King Farouk.
June 24	Guaranty Trust Co. of N.Y. predicts the U.S. dollar will replace the British pound as the chief international currency.	French delegates sign a separate peace treaty with Italy .... In London, Charles de Gaulle claims that the French empire will continue to fight against the Axis .... Hitler orders that German flags fly for 10 days in celebration of the "most glorious victory of all times."	French authorities turn over French-held territory in Shanghai to the Japanese .... Japanese naval ships enter Haiphong harbor to observe ships suspected of carrying supplies destined for Chiang Kai-shek.	Panamanian government institutes tighter regulation of radio broadcasting in order to curtail the dissemination of false information.	King Farouk confers with representatives of all Egyptian political factions in an effort to form a new cabinet.
June 25	League of Nations Secy. Gen. Avenol instructs the 89 remaining League employes to resign.	Shortly after midnight, the ceasefire takes effect in France .... France observes a day of national mourning.	Japan says it will not permit any foreign power interference in East Asia, including Indochina and the NEI.		Britain grants India and Burma the right to govern themselves as a step towards dominion status.
June 26		Russia demands the return of Bessarabia and the cession of northern Bukovina from Rumania .... Churchill warns the Soviets of the dangers to Russia of German hegemony in Europe in a personal message to Stalin.		Export-Import Bank extends a $20 million loan to Argentina.	French commander in North Africa, Gen. Auguste Nogues, announces his Moroccan forces will support Vichy.
	A *Includes developments that affect more than one world region, international organizations and important meetings of major world leaders.*	B *Includes all developments in European countries and military engagements between Allied and Axis powers in Africa and at sea.*	C *Includes all developments in Japan and China, Japanese foreign policy and military actions in the Pacific region.*	D *Includes all domestic and regional developments in Latin America, the Caribbean and Canada.*	E *Includes developments in those independent nations and colonial possessions not covered in Columns B, C and D.*

U.S. Politics & Social Issues	U.S. Foreign Policy & Defense	U.S. Economy & Environment	Science, Technology & Nature	Culture, Leisure & Life Style	
GOP National Convention opens in Philadelphia.	Alf Landon warns that FDR is "choosing a course in the direction of war."	Secy. Harold Ickes forms a defense resources commission within the Interior Dept.		Bill Watson amasses 7,523 points to win the national decathlon championship in Cleveland, Ohio.	June 16
	State Dept. cautions Germany and Italy to stay away from British, French and Dutch possessions in the Western Hemisphere .... FDR asks Congress to appropriate $1.2 billion more for naval construction.				June 17
	Congress completes action on a resolution warning European powers against any transfer of territory in the Western Hemisphere .... FDR says a bill for universal government service for all young men and women will soon be introduced.				June 18
	Calling for a conference of the foreign ministers of the American republics, the U.S. again warns the Axis powers to stay out of the Western Hemisphere.	Senate approves and sends to conference the $1-billion tax bill, which also authorizes an increase in the national debt to $49 billion.			June 19
GOP National Comm. approves contested delegations from Louisiana and Mississippi which favor Taft's nomination.	FDR nominates Republicans Henry L. Stimson as secretary of war and Frank Knox as secretary of the navy .... FDR signs a bill creating the Bureau of Ships combining the Navy's Bureau of Construction and Repair and Bureau of Engineering.	FDR nominates Robert M. Hinckley to be an assistant secretary of commerce .... Connally war tax bill, providing for income and excess profits taxes as soon as war breaks out, passes the Senate as a rider to the defense tax bill.			June 20
GOP National Comm. rejects the seating of a South Carolina delegation headed by Joseph W. Tolbert, which supports Sen. Taft .... AP reports that FDR has $707\frac{1}{2}$ pledged delegates giving him a wide lead over Garner and Farley .... Senate passes and sends to the House a bill granting U.S. citizenship to residents of the Virgin Islands.	Dewey charges, in a nationwide broadcast, that FDR is plotting U.S. entry into the war in order to hide his failures .... In separate statements the National Editorial Assn. and the U.S. Junior Chamber of Commerce endorse universal military training.		Geologist Halbert P. Gillette tells the American Assn. for the Advancement of Science convention at Seattle that the worst droughts in 20 centuries are about to start, based on his study of rock strata.		June 21
GOP presidential hopefuls—Dewey, Taft and Willkie—arrive in Philadelphia and begin meeting with delegates.	Gallup Poll reveals that 67% of Americansfavor universal military training.			USC wins the NCAA track and field championship in Minneapolis, Minn. for the sixth year in a row.	June 22
					June 23
Minn. Gov. Harold Stassen gives the keynote address at the opening session of the GOP convention in Philadelphia.	GOP platform committee adopts the position that the U.S. should avoid war.			Don McNeill wins the men's U.S. Clay Court Championship and Alice Marble, the women's in Chicago.	June 24
Charging the New Deal has been a disaster, Herbert Hoover appeals to the GOP convention to make him their standard bearer .... Delegates force changes in the GOP platform, making it more isolationist.		FDR signs the massive tax bill raising the national debt to $49 billion and adding some 2.2 million persons to the tax rolls .... FDR signs a bill permitting RFC to purchase stock of Federal Home Loan Banks.			June 25
GOP convention adopts a platform calling for non-intervention in foreign wars.		FDR approves a graduated excess war profits tax, ranging from 10% to 75%.			June 26

F	G	H	I	J
Includes elections, federal-state relations, civil rights and liberties, crime, the judiciary, education, health care, poverty, urban affairs and population.	*Includes formation and debate of U.S. foreign and defense policies, veterans affairs and defense spending. (Relations with specific foreign countries are usually found under the region concerned.)*	*Includes business, labor, agriculture, taxation, transportation, consumer affairs, monetary and fiscal policy, natural resources, pollution and accidents.*	*Includes worldwide scientific, medical and technological developments, natural phenomena, U.S. weather and natural disasters.*	*Includes the arts, religion, scholarship, communications media, sports, entertainment, fashions, fads and social life.*

	World Affairs	European War Zone	Pacific War Zone	The Americas	Other Countries & Territories
June 27		De Gaulle announces that a French volunteer legion will be formed in Britain .... German radio says Berlin has no interest in the Russian demands on Rumania.			King Farouk entrusts Haasan Sabry Pasha to form a new Egyptian cabinet.
June 28		Russian troops march into the ceded districts of Bessarabia and Bukovina after Rumania accepts the Soviet demands unconditionally .... Britain officially recognizes de Gaulle as "leader of all free Frenchmen, wherever they may be."	Japanese military mission arrives in Indochina and demands the right to supply Japanese forces in China by way of the French railroad .... Japanese government demands that the NEI permit an increased Japanese economic role.		French Gen. Eugene Mittlehauser orders cessation of hostilities by troops under his command in Syria.
June 29		Italian Gov. Gen. of Libya, Air Marshall Italo Balbo, is killed during a British attack on Tobruk, Libya.		Mexico presents the U.S. government with $1 million as partial payment for American lands expropriated since Aug. 30, 1927.	Hassan Sabry Pasha forms a coalition Egyptian cabinet which includes all parties except the Wafdists.
June 30		French government moves from Bordeaux to Clermont-Ferrand .... German decrees published in Paris provide the death penalty for any act of violence against the occupation forces.			
July 1		Stalin meets with Sir Stafford Cripps, who trys to convince him that Soviet interests coincide with Britain's .... Rumanian Council of Ministers rejects the British-French guarantee of its territory and announces Rumania will follow Europe's new direction .... Germans occupy the Channel Islands .... Germany advises the U.S. to discontinue all diplomatic missions in Norway, Belgium, Luxembourg and the Netherlands by July 15.	Governor-general of Hong Kong, the French army commander in Indochina and the high command of the French fleet agree on a common defense against Japanese aggression .... Japanese military forces capture the walled city of Lungchow, China close to the Indochina border.	Work begins on a third set of locks for the Panama Canal. The new Miraflores Locks will cost $227 million and take six years to build.	
July 2		Marshal Rodolfo Graziani is appointed governor general of Libya by the Italian government .... British government notifies Pope Pius XII that so far as possible it will not bomb or shell Rome.	Two shiploads of American citizens and British women and children are evacuated from Hong Kong.	All intercollegiate sports are halted in Canada for the war's duration in order to further military training .... New Cuban constitution is promulgated.	Gandhi appeals to all Britons to cease hostilities with Germany and settle their differences with "non-violent" methods.
July 3	John G. Winant, American director of International Labor Office, leaves Geneva for Lisbon, reportedly to prepare for the relocation of the staff.	British forces attack the French fleet off Mers-el-Kebir to prevent it from being turned over to the Germans. French ships in British ports are seized .... Soviets complete their occupation of ceded Rumanian provinces.	Japanese troops close virtually all land communication between Hong Kong and mainland China.	The first group of German POWs arrive in Canada.	
July 4		In a speech to the House of Commons, Churchill defends the attack on the French fleet and vows to "prosecute the war with the utmost vigor." .... A pro-German, anti-Semitic cabinet is established in Rumania.		Vice President Ramon Castillo is named acting president of Argentina to replace ailing Pres. Roberto Ortiz.	British government promises to consider dominion status for Burma after the war .... Reports from India suggest the formation of a coalition government for the purpose of defense.
July 5	FDR says five freedoms must be achieved to establish world peace: Freedom from fear, freedom of information, freedom of religion, freedom of expression and freedom from want.	French government of Marshal Petain severs diplomatic relations with Britain because of the British attack on the French fleet .... Germany publishes secret Allied documents from earlier this year detailing plans for an attack on the Soviet oil fields in the Caucasus .... Italian forces occupy Kassola and Gallabat in Anglo-Egyptian Sudan .... Sweden grants Germany the right to transport war material and troops over Swedish railroads to Norway.	About 2,000 more British women and children are evacuated from Hong Kong.	British Admiralty establishes a loose blockade of the French island of Martinique to prevent the removal of French warships.	
July 6		Italy proposes a law to encourage repatriated Italians from abroad to colonize the nation's African possessions.	Japanese government issues a decree prohibiting the manufacture and sale of luxuries because of defense needs .... British authorities temporarily suspend air and sea traffic to Indochina.		
July 7		Rumanian Culture Min. Horia Sima prohibits Jewish actors and musicians from performing in public.	U.S. Marines arrest 16 armed Japanese gendarmes for tresspassing on U.S. property in Shanghai .... Reports from London indicate Russia has told Japan it desire that the Burma Road be kept open.	Argentine police allegedly uncover plans for a pro-Nazi insurrection .... Mexican voters go to the polls to choose either Manuel Avila Camacho or Juan Andreu Almazan as president.	All-India National Congress demands that Britain state unequivocally that she will grant India total independence.

A	B	C	D	E
Includes developments that affect more than one world region, international organizations and important meetings of major world leaders.	*Includes all developments in European countries and military engagements between Allied and Axis powers in Africa and at sea.*	*Includes all developments in Japan and China, Japanese foreign policy and military actions in the Pacific region.*	*Includes all domestic and regional developments in Latin America, the Caribbean and Canada.*	*Includes developments in those independent nations and colonial possessions not covered in Columns B, C and D.*

U.S. Politics & Social Issues	U.S. Foreign Policy & Defense	U.S. Economy & Environment	Science, Technology & Nature	Culture, Leisure & Life Style	
		FDR appoints Donald M. Nelson to supervise all government purchases of war supplies and to coordinate U.S. and British defense needs.		Mrs. Antonia Riasanovsky receives the $10,000 Atlantic Novel Award for her work *The Family.*	June 27
GOP nominates Wendell Willkie on the sixth ballot as its presidential candidate with 654 votes to Taft's 318.	FDR signs a bill making it a crime to encourage insubordination or disloyalty among the military, or to distribute literature to that end.	N.Y. Federal Reserve Bank establishes a Foreign Property Control Division to scrutinize the volume of securities pouring into this country from Europe.			June 28
FDR signs the Alien Registration Act providing for the compulsory registration and fingerprinting of all aliens . . . . FDR signs a law granting the Supreme Court the authority to prescribe rules of pleading, practice and procedure with respect to criminal cases in the district courts . . . . Sen. Edwin C. Johnson (D, Colo.) says that only Sen. Wheeler can defeat Willkie in the presidential race.		FDR signs a bill extending the 3½% interest rates charged under the Federal Farm Loan Act and Emergency Farm Mortgage Act through June 1942 . . . . he also signs a bill authorizing the Maritime Commission to insure shipping during wartime when domestic private insurance is not available.	Westinghouse Laboratories announces the discovery that gamma rays (highly penetrating X-rays) can release atomic energy from uranium.		June 29
Sen. Charles McNary (Ore.) is nominated as Willkie's vice presidential running mate at closing session of the GOP convention in Philadelphia.				Cornelius Warmerdam sets world pole vault record of 15 feet 1⅛ inches at the National AAU track meet in Fresno, Calif.	June 30
	U.S. Army strength reaches a total of 257,730 officers and men . . . . FDR signs a Navy bill providing for construction of 45 vessels costing $550 million.	Donald Nelson, acting director of the procurement division of the Treasury Dept., resigns and is replaced by Owen D. Young . . . . CAA and Weather Bureau become units of the Commerce Dept.			July 1
Willkie appoints a 12-man campaign advisory committee headed by Minnesota Gov. Harold E. Stassen and instructs them not to accept corporate contributions . . . . In the first preliminary 1940 Census report, the cities of Newark, Pittsburgh, Philadelphia and St. Louis show population declines since 1930.	Congress passes a bill authorizing FDR to impose controls on exports of all vital materials.		Lake Washington Floating Bridge opens to traffic at Seattle, Washington. The $8-million bridge is the largest floating structure ever built.		July 2
A county court in Detroit, Mich., rules that, in the absence of specific legislation to the contrary, the CP must be allowed a place on the state electoral ballot.	FDR prepares legislation requesting $5 billion more for national defense.	On the 50th anniversary of the Sherman Antitrust Act, Asst. Atty. Gen. Thurman W. Arnold states the law is intended primarily as a consumer aid.			July 3
	American Youth Congress adopts a report asking that U.S. youth not be forced to fight against Hitler.				July 4
Supporters of Sen. Burton K. Wheeler (D, Mont.) open a Chicago headquarters in their drive for his presidential nomination.	State Dept. warns Germany not to permit its representatives in the U.S. to publicly comment on U.S. policies.			World Congress of Faiths, including representatives of Christianity, Hinduism, Buddhism, Confucianism, Judaism and Islam, opens in London.	July 5
At a Hyde Park meeting lasting three hours, FDR reveals his third-term plans to James A. Farley under a pledge of secrecy . . . . Justice Dept. orders an examination of some 18,000 aliens in the U.S. to determine how many may be agents of foreign governments.	FDR urges a Monroe Doctrine for the European and Asiatic continents so that all nations can determine their own fate . . . . Gallup Poll reveals a 5% drop of U.S. voters who favor entering the European War since June 14.		Enrico Fermi obtains a patent for a method of transforming one chemical element into another by bombardment of atoms with neutrons . . . . Charles L. Kee reports the invention of a control and bombing device which improves the accuracy of bombers.	Adolf Kiefer sets three different backstroke records at the National AAU swim meet in Santa Barbara, Calif.	July 6
				With 41 points the Hawaiian team captures the National AAU swim title for the second year in a row.	July 7

F	G	H	I	J
Includes elections, federal-state relations, civil rights and liberties, crime, the judiciary, education, health care, poverty, urban affairs and population.	*Includes formation and debate of U.S. foreign and defense policies, veterans affairs and defense spending. (Relations with specific foreign countries are usually found under the region concerned.)*	*Includes business, labor, agriculture, taxation, transportation, consumer affairs, monetary and fiscal policy, natural resources, pollution and accidents.*	*Includes worldwide scientific, medical and technological developments, natural phenomena, U.S. weather and natural disasters.*	*Includes the arts, religion, scholarship, communications media, sports, entertainment, fashions, fads and social life.*

	World Affairs	European War Zone	Pacific War Zone	The Americas	Other Countries & Territories
July 8		British ships attack the French battleship *Richelieu* at Dakar, severely damaging it with torpedoes and depth charges .... Rome reports successful air raids on British bases at Malta and Alexandria .... King Haakon announces his refusal to resign as requested by the Norwegian parliament.	Over 100 Japanese planes attack Chungking, inflicting heavy damage.		
July 9		Naval warfare between Italian and British warships in the Mediterranean (near Crete and east of Malta) enters second day. The Italian battleship *Cavour* is severely damaged .... Tea is rationed in Britain.	Japan reiterates its demand that Britain close the Burma Road .... Japanese government demands that the U.S. apologize for the arrest of the 16 gendarmes in Shanghai.	Duke of Windsor is appointed governor of the Bahamas by the British Colonial Office.	*N.Y. Times* reports a growing sentiment for creation of a Union of Arab States as a result of the French capitulation to Germany.
July 10	Rumania announces its withdrawal from the League of Nations.	Luftwaffe begins a systematic assault on the ports of southern England and on British shipping in the Channel .... French parliament passes a resolution giving total power to Marshal Petain.			
July 11		British Board of Trade issues an order declaring all French territory, including Corsica, Morocco, Tunisia and Algeria, enemy territory under the "trading with the enemy act."	Tokyo demands that Britain halt all aid to China or "suffer the consequences." .... U.S. authorities in Shanghai deliver a conciliatory, but unpublished note to the Japanese embassy concerning the arrest of the gendarmes.		
July 12		Britain recognizes the Ethiopian Kingdom with Haile Selassie as emperor, promising arms to those who will fight against Italy .... Polish government in exile shifts to London from France .... Nazi occupation in Paris takes all French art treasures under its protection.	Britain secretly agrees to suspend traffic of certain war materials on the Burma Road for the next three months.		Philippine National Assembly begins consideration of a bill providing for compulsory military service .... Fifty-two people are killed as a typhoon hits Seoul, Korea.
July 13			A government spokesman in Chungking explains that U.S. aid is necessary to prevent Britain from surrendering to Japan's Burma Road demands .... Malaya's acting governor says Britain is attempting to mediate the Sino-Japanese War.	Official vote count in Mexico's Presidential election gives Avila Camacho a victory by a wide margin over Almazan. The latter's supporters, who refused to register their votes with the official ballot boards, claim Almazan has won the election.	
July 14		P.M. Churchill, in a London radio broadcast, promises Germany unending resistance if it invades Britain .... Marshal Petain begins a purge of government officials who have taken a pro-British position .... Under the "protection" of the Red Army, the citizens of Estonia, Latvia and Lithuania elect Communist parliaments.		Amid violence which results in six deaths, Fulgencio Batista is elected Cuban president .... German and Italian newspapers charge FDR's intention to purchase surplus Latin American products is designed to control those countries.	
July 15	Instiitute for Advanced Study at Princeton Univ. invites the League of Nations to establish its non-political and technical sections there for the war's duration.	Germany demands that Vichy France permit German forces use of French bases in North Africa .... British commandos raid Guernsey in the Channel Islands .... Italian troops occupy the ruins of Fort Moyale on the Kenya-Ethiopian border .... Italian airplanes raid the Haifa area in the first air attack upon Palestine.	London publicly says it will close the Burma Road to war supplies for three months if Japan would consider it a step towards a Far Eastern peace settlement .... Japanese announce the Chinese coast south of Shanghai will be mined to tighten the blockade of China.		
July 16		Hitler orders the invasion of Britain to be prepared for mid-August and directs the Luftwaffe to secure air superiority over the Channel .... Gen. Francisco Franco says Spanish control of Gibraltar and expansion in Africa is Spain's prime mission .... Finland announces the complete demilitarization of the Aland Islands.	Japanese cabinet of Premier Mitsumasa Yonai resigns under pressure from the military .... Chiang Kaishek spurns British proposal to mediate the Sino-Japanese War.	Spain severs diplomatic relations with Chile for allegedly tolerating anti-Nationalist propaganda.	
July 17		Britain names Sir Roger Keyes as director of combined operations to plan and execute commando raids.	Japan promises an attempt to reach a peace agreement with Chiang Kaishek in return for a British promise to close the Burma Road to war supplies for 3 months starting today.	German chemist Dr. Emil Wolff is held in the Panama Canal Zone on charges of failing to register as a German agent.	Bagdad Railway is inaugurated when the first train leaves the Iraqi capital for Haidar Pasha on the Bosphorus opposite Istanbul.
July 18	Danish government withdraws from the League.	Germans occupy the French island of Quessant, 120 miles south of Land's End, England.	Prince Fumimaro Konoye organizes a new Japanese cabinet .... Churchill says he approves of the Burma Road closing if it will bring peace in the Pacific.	Hull and his staff leave Washington to attend the Inter-American Conference in Havana.	Gen. Smuts reiterates South Africa's resolve to stand by Britain in the war.

A	B	C	D	E
Includes developments that affect more than one world region, international organizations and important meetings of major world leaders.	*Includes all developments in European countries and military engagements between Allied and Axis powers in Africa and at sea.*	*Includes all developments in Japan and China, Japanese foreign policy and military actions in the Pacific region.*	*Includes all domestic and regional developments in Latin America, the Caribbean and Canada.*	*Includes developments in those independent nations and colonial possessions not covered in Columns B, C and D.*

U.S. Politics & Social Issues	U.S. Foreign Policy & Defense	U.S. Economy & Environment	Science, Technology & Nature	Culture, Leisure & Life Style	
Willkie names House minority leader Joseph W. Martin as GOP national chairman.	Marshall Field announces formation of a National Child Refugee Comm. to coordinate the reception of refugee children from Europe .... Chief of the Fleet Adm. James Richardson arrives in Washington from Hawaii for conferences with FDR.	Two British ships arrive in New York with a reported $124.2 million in gold bullion to be used for British war credits.			July 8
	Senate confirms Henry L. Stimson as secretary of war .... U.S. Amb. William C. Bullitt establishes a legation in Vichy, France.			National League defeats the American League 4-0, the first shutout of the All Star Classic, in St. Louis.	July 9
	Asking Congress for $4.8 billion in additional defense funds, FDR promises, "We will not send our men to take part in European wars." .... Senate passes and sends to conference a $75-billion two-ocean navy bill .... Senate approves Frank Knox as secretary of the navy.			Outstanding woman golfer, Patty Berg signs a pro contract to run six years.	July 10
Democratic party leaders in Chicago are told FDR will accept a draft at the national convention to run for a third term.		Federal attorneys file an antitrust suit in Philadelphia against the Pullman Co., which operates all sleeping cars in the U.S. .... Members of NYSE brokerage firms ask Congress to clarify their status under the Fair Labor Standards Act.		Reknowned British musical theorist Sir Donald Tovey dies in London.	July 11
Sen. James Byrnes (D, S.C.) and FDR aide Harry Hopkins arrive in Chicago to organize plans for FDR's nomination as the Democratic presidential candidate .... In a Gallup Poll presidential trial heat, FDR gains 53% of the vote, Willkie 47%.					July 12
Farley, Garner and Wheeler refuse to quit the race for the Democratic presidential nomination in face of pressure to make FDR's renomination unanimous.	To facilitate the entrance of refugee children, State Dept. announces they will be admitted on visitors visas without reference to national quotas.		RCA receives a patent for a TV system to be used in detecting approaching aircraft .... Charles H. Cartwright and Arthur F. Turner announce the invention of non-reflecting glass for use in microscopes, periscopes and other optical devices.	A new American Professional Football League is formed with six teams.	July 13
	Sen. Burton K. Wheeler (D, Mont.) demands that the Democratic Party adopt a platform more anti-war than FDR's position.				July 14
Democratic National Convention opens in Chicago with Sen. William Bankhead (Ala.) giving the keynote address .... With FDR's nomination almost assured, convention focus has centered on the vice presidency, with the favorite choices reported to be Sen. Byrnes, Gov. Stark, Rep. Rayburn and Supreme Court Justice William O. Douglas.	FDR freezes assets of Latvia, Lithuania and Estonia in the U.S.				July 15
Through Sen. Alben W. Barkley, FDR announces he does not wish a third term, and releases all convention delegates committed to him. But the statement, which clearly leaves FDR open to a draft, touches off a long floor demonstration virtually assuring him of the nomination.	State Secy. Cordell Hull issues a statement opposing the closing of the Burma Road.	FDR signs a bill transferring 6,450 acres of the Hawaii National Park to the War Dept. for use as a bombing target range.			July 16
FDR is nominated by acclamation to run for the third term as the Democratic nominee for the presidency.	Democratic platform calls for non-intervention in foreign wars .... Gen. George C. Marshall says two million men are needed for the adequate defense of the U.S.				July 17
Democrats accept, after a floor fight, Henry A. Wallace as their vice presidential candidate.	FDR says in his acceptance speech that he opposes both dictators and appeasers .... Stimson announces that an experiment with parachute troops will be conducted to determine their effectiveness.	FDR signs a bill extending the provisions of the Grain Standards Act to soybeans.	Trans-Pacific mail service on a weekly basis is inaugurated with the arrival of a Pan American Airways clipper in New Zealand after a flight from San Francisco.		July 18

F	G	H	I	J
Includes elections, federal-state relations, civil rights and liberties, crime, the judiciary, education, health care, poverty, urban affairs and population.	*Includes formation and debate of U.S. foreign and defense policies, veterans affairs and defense spending. (Relations with specific foreign countries are usually found under the region concerned.)*	*Includes business, labor, agriculture, taxation, transportation, consumer affairs, monetary and fiscal policy, natural resources, pollution and accidents.*	*Includes worldwide scientific, medical and technological developments, natural phenomena, U.S. weather and natural disasters.*	*Includes the arts, religion, scholarship, communications media, sports, entertainment, fashions, fads and social life.*

	World Affairs	European War Zone	Pacific War Zone	The Americas	Other Countries & Territories
July 19		Hitler says before the Reichstag that Churchill should recognize that Germany cannot be stopped in her creation of a great empire. He declares "reason and common sense" should compell Britain to agree to open peace negotiations .... Italian cruiser *Bartolomeo Colleloni* is sunk off Crete by the Australian cruiser *Sydney* and five destroyers .... RAF suffers serious losses in dogfights with German bombers and fighters over Dover.		In response to notes from the German and British legations, the Costa Rican government appeals to its citizens to curb propaganda.	Adm. Jean Marie Abrial is appointed by the French government as governor-general of Algeria.
July 20		French and Polish troops march from Syria into Palestine to continue the war against Germany and Italy.	Adm. Jean Decoux is appointed governor of Indochina by Marshal Petain.		
July 21		Britain announces the bombing of Bremen and Nazi positions in the Ruhr Valley, Netherlands and northern France .... Parliaments of Estonia, Latvia and Lithuania adopt resolutions declaring themselves to be Soviet Republics.	Japanese Prince Fumimaro Konoye completes his cabinet organization with the exclusion of all political parties.	Pan-American Consultative Conference opens in Havana, Cuba .... Luiz Munoz Marin organizes the Popular Democratic Party in Puerto Rico with the ultimate goal of independence from the U.S.	Meeting in Cairo, leaders of six Arab states adopt plans for a postwar federation in the Middle East.
July 22		Foreign Secy. Lord Halifax answers Hitler's speech, saying that Great Britain will not succumb to force .... Britain reinforces its Gibraltar garrison and evacuates civilians to Morocco and Madeira.		At the Havana Conference, State Secy. Hull suggests a "collective trusteeship" for European territories in the Western Hemisphere.	A system of conscription of all single men goes into effect in New Zealand .... Gov.-Gen. Pierre Ryckmans declares in Elizabethville that the Belgian Congo will support the British against the Axis.
July 23		Czecho-Slovak National Committee, headed by Eduard Benes, says in London that Britain recognizes it as the Czechoslovakian government in exile .... Gen. Wladislaw Sikorski, commander-in-chief of the Polish Army in London, announces a new Polish-British military convention .... Britain provides shelter for Haile Selassie in Khartoum, capital of the Sudan, until his return to Ethiopia.	Japanese residents in the city of Hungchow, China issue a demand that the U.S., leave Asia.		Bengali government in India announces it will remove the "Black Hole" monuments, site of recent protest demonstrations.
July 24		Italian planes shell the city and port of Haifa .... Soviet Union announces the introduction of anti-religious courses throughout the high school and university systems.		Havana Conference considers protective measures against fifth column activities.	Egyptian Premier Hasan Sabry Pasha orders that cotton be shipped to world markets via the Red Sea due to difficulties encountered in the Mediterranean.
July 25		Turkey signs a new trade agreement with Germany.	Tokyo newspapers report Japanese troops are securing their positions along the Indochina border.		
July 26	Joseph A.C. Avenol resigns as secretary general of the League of Nations, stating current realities make his office unnecessary .... League of Nations announces it will transfer its economic and financial departments to Princeton Univ.	Italian planes bomb Gibraltar .... British naval forces seize three Rumanian vessels at Port Said.	Japanese government adopts a document giving top priority to solving the "China incident" by blocking supplies reaching China through Indochina and other routes and to securing its own raw materials by pursuing a more agressive policy in the Netherlands East Indies .... Chungking government announces a new trade treaty agreement with Russia.	Canadian Parliament passes a bill imposing the death penalty for acts commited with intent to help the enemy.	
July 27			Without releasing details, the Konoye cabinet announces plans to increase Japanese defense preparedness .... Japanese naval forces seize the Chinese coastal city of Honghai.	Havana Conference delegates reach agreement on colonies, trade and 5th column activities. A Declaration of Havana, to take effect upon ratification by two-thirds of the American republics, bars direct or indirect transfer of sovereignty of territory in the hemisphere from one non-American power to another. An attempt to do so will result in an inter-American trusteeship over the affected territory.	Indian Congress Party, meeting at Poona, ratifies the Working Committee resolutions declaring it is unable to extend the principle of non-violence to the defense of India at this time and pledging cooperation in the war effort if a provisional national government is established as a first step toward independence.
July 28		Nazi planes intensify their assault on Britain. British sources interpret this as a prelude to invasion .... Germany announces the partition of France into five administrative divisions.	Japanese authorities arrest 11 British subjects on espionage charges.		Afghanistan and the Soviet Union complete a commercial agreement.

A	B	C	D	E
Includes developments that affect more than one world region, international organizations and important meetings of major world leaders.	*Includes all developments in European countries and military engagements between Allied and Axis powers in Africa and at sea.*	*Includes all developments in Japan and China, Japanese foreign policy and military actions in the Pacific region.*	*Includes all domestic and regional developments in Latin America, the Caribbean and Canada.*	*Includes developments in those independent nations and colonial possessions not covered in Columns B, C and D.*

U.S. Politics & Social Issues	U.S. Foreign Policy & Defense	U.S. Economy & Environment	Science, Technology & Nature	Culture, Leisure & Life Style	
Sen. Edward Burke (D, Neb.) announces he will lead an organization of anti-third term Democrats to support Willkie's presidential campaign .... James A. Farley will resign as Democratic national chairman within a month, he announces in Chicago.	Gallup Poll reports 53% of the American people favor giving more aid to England, short of going to war .... Speaking in Quebec, AFL Pres. William Green says his union favors aid to Britain "short of war."	AFL Pres. Green claims the rank and file of the CIO desire a labor truce and only John L. Lewis stands in the way.			July 19
FDR signs a bill extending provisions of Hatch Act to curb political activity by state and local government employes.	FDR signs the "Two-Ocean Navy" act, which calls for a build-up in naval forces to 35 battleships, 20 carriers and 88 cruisers.	A *N.Y. Times* report shows that the top 100 corporations in the U.S. increased their profits by 60.5% for the first half of 1940 over the same period in 1939.	Eli Lilly & Co. announces the development of a simple test doctors can administer to patients to determine if an overdose of sulfa drugs has been given.	The $50,570 Arlington Classic in Chicago is won by Sirocco .... A three day track and field meet opens in Helsinki, Finland to honor athletes killed in the Russian War.	July 20
		UMW Pres. Lewis opens a campaign to have all companies receiving government contracts adhere to the collective bargaining rights contained in the NLRA.			July 21
Eighteen Democratic Senators indicate they will not actively campaign for the party this fall in protest against FDR's third term candidacy and his choice of Wallace as his running mate.	FDR announces he has asked Congress to increase the capital and lending power of the Export-Import Bank to $700 million and to make it easier for the bank to issue credits to Latin American countries.				July 22
FDR says such former supporters as Sen. Edward Burke (Neb.), Lewis Douglas, John W. Hanes and James A. Reed did not "bolt" the party, but that the party has "bolted" them.	War Dept. receives reports that Japanese purchasing agents are trying to corner aviation gasoline supplies on the West Coast .... House passes and sends to the Senate a resolution extending for three years executive authority to negotiate reciprocal trade agreements .... Sumner Welles publicly attacks the "devious processes" by which the Soviets "deliberately annihilated" the independence of the Baltic states.	British Purchasing Mission and U.S. officials agree on allocation of the output from U.S. defense industry. British are to receive some 40% of all aircraft produced.			July 23
FDR's son Elliott says that Willkie will present the American people with a clear alternative to the New Deal .... Sen. Byrnes declines an offer to become Democratic national chairman .... Grandal MacKay announces the creation of the Southern Committee for Jeffersonian Democracy to conduct a radio campaign in 12 Southeastern states against the New Deal.	Asst. War Secy. Louis Johnson says the U.S. should aim to reach the capacity to equip one million men every three months.		British Health Ministry announces a discovery through which blood may be kept for transfusion indefinitely by separating the plasma.		July 24
	State Dept. announces the prohibition of petroleum, petroleum products and scrap metal exports from the U.S. without a specific license. Britain and Americas will not be affected. The measure is seen as aimed directly at Japan, which relies heavily on U.S. oil exports.	Treasury Secy. Henry Morgenthau Jr. announces a plan whereby corporations engaged in defense contracts can accelerate depreciation tax write-offs.	National Academy of Science announces it will study the possibility of recovering of manganese from low-grade ores.		July 25
Wallace announces that he will resign or take a leave of absence without pay from his cabinet post once the campaign begins.		Gallup Poll reports that only 33% of the American people favor increased federal government regulation of business and that 75% feel there should be greater control of labor unions.			July 26
			Chemical Marketing Co. in N.Y. announces it will produce synthetic tooth fillings to replace gold and mercury amalgams.		July 27
National Small Businessmen's Assn. asserts Labor Secy. Frances Perkins has halted the deportation of about 700 undesirable aliens.			N.Y.C. residents swelter through the third day of a severe heat wave.		July 28
F	G	H	I	J	
Includes elections, federal-state relations, civil rights and liberties, crime, the judiciary, education, health care, poverty, urban affairs and population.	*Includes formation and debate of U.S. foreign and defense policies, veterans affairs and defense spending. (Relations with specific foreign countries are usually found under the region concerned.)*	*Includes business, labor, agriculture, taxation, transportation, consumer affairs, monetary and fiscal policy, natural resources, pollution and accidents.*	*Includes worldwide scientific, medical and technological developments, natural phenomena, U.S. weather and natural disasters.*	*Includes the arts, religion, scholarship, communications media, sports, entertainment, fashions, fads and social life.*	

	World Affairs	European War Zone	Pacific War Zone	The Americas	Other Countries & Territories
July 29		Spain and Portugal sign a protocal pledging neutral consultation in case of war threats.	Chinese sources admit that Japanese coastal activity off Fukien and Kwangtung is effectively blockading those regions.		Cairo reports German agents are attempting instigate a coup d'etat to dethrone Afghanistan's king, Mohammed Zahir Shah.
July 30		Hugh Dalton, British minister of economic warfare, announces that all ships going to the Continent without navicerts will be subject to prize court action .... An earthquake inflicts heavy damage on the Anatolian sector of Turkey.		Foreign ministers of the American Republics meeting at Havana sign the final accord dealing with economic and defense cooperation.	
July 31		Britain announces the full application of its blocakade to continental France .... After telling the House of Commons a crisis may soon be imminent, Churchill writes to FDR urgently requesting destroyers and seaplanes to beat back a German invasion.	Chou En-lai leaves Chungking for Yenan with a reported agreement to end the dispute between the Kouminfang and Communist parties in China .... Japanese planes bomb Chungking for four hours, killing 80 persons .... Japanese Foreign Office announces it will arrest all foreigners suspected of espionage.		
Aug. 1		Death toll in Turkey's July 30 earthquake tops 1,000.	Japanese demand transit rights for their forces through Indochina to attack the Chinese .... Japanese government issues statement hinting at the introduction of totalitarianism at home and at the construction of "a new order in Greater East Asia."	FDR approves a priority aid program to bolster the defenses of Latin American countries against possible German aggression .... Montreal Mayor Camillien Houde is arrested following his announcement that he will not comply with the conscription law.	
Aug. 2		Hermann Goering orders Luftwaffe to destroy RAF fighter defenses in southern England within four days .... Italians invade British Somaliland .... Gen. Charles de Gaulle, leader of French forces fighting with England, is condemned to death by a French military court in Clermont-Ferrand.	Japan protests the U.S. ban on the sale of aviation fuel outside the Western Hemisphere .... Japan cancels shipping permits on the Yangtze River on the grounds that U.S. military goods are reaching Chungking via the river.	Chilean plans to purchase military planes from the U.S. are revealed.	
Aug. 3			Japan protests the arrest in London today of two Japanese on charges of threatening British national security.		
Aug. 4			London announces it will deport the two Japanese aliens seized yesterday.		Vichy asserts, and Britain denies, the landing of British troops in Madagascar and the Cameroons to incite insurrection.
Aug. 5		Hitler authorizes a stepped-up air offensive against Britain .... Both the Italians and the British claim success after the largest reported air battle over Libya to date.	Japanese forces take control of Kwangchowan, an important Chinese port city.		
Aug. 6		Italian drive into British Somaliland widens to a 300-mile front.			Kenya, Uganda, Tanganyika, Zanzibar, Rhodesia and Nyasaland form the East Africa Economic Council to coordinate economic policies for war purposes .... New Caldonia, a French colony, refuses to accept the armistice with Germany.
Aug. 7	Officials of the International Labor Office leave Geneva for Lisbon, Portugal.	Striking in three columns, Italian forces drive 50 miles inside British Somaliland.			Philippine National Assembly votes full powers over the country to Gov. Manuel Quezon .... Singapore authorities begin intensive training of a civilian volunteer military force.
Aug. 8		German U-boats break up a British convoy in the Channel. Bombers follow up the attack, sinking six British ships.			Britain reiterates her pledge to India of "equal partnership" in the Commonwealth and invites Indian participation on the war advisory council.
Aug. 9		Britain announces it will consider Algiers, Tunisia, French Morocco and the unoccupied French continental territory as war zones.	More than 90 Japanese planes bomb Chungking causing heavy damage, including destruction of Chiang Kaishek's home .... British troops stationed in Shanghai and north China are reassigned for use elsewhere in the British Empire.		

A	B	C	D	E
Includes developments that affect more than one world region, international organizations and important meetings of major world leaders.	*Includes all developments in European countries and military engagements between Allied and Axis powers in Africa and at sea.*	*Includes all developments in Japan and China, Japanese foreign policy and military actions in the Pacific region.*	*Includes all domestic and regional developments in Latin America, the Caribbean and Canada.*	*Includes developments in those independent nations and colonial possessions not covered in Columns B, C and D.*

U.S. Politics & Social Issues	U.S. Foreign Policy & Defense	U.S. Economy & Environment	Science, Technology & Nature	Culture, Leisure & Life Style	
Willkie claims the election will create political re-alignment centering around acceptance or rejection of the New Deal.	FDR asks Congress for authority to call up the National Guard for extensive training . . . . Gallup Poll reports that 67% of the American people favor universal military training, a 3% increase in the last month.				July 29
Alfred E. Smith, the Democratic presidential candidate in 1928, announces he will support Willkie over FDR in this year's election.					July 30
Preliminary Census data indicates that the District of Columbia registered the largest population gains of any major city in the decade 1930-1940.	State Dept. announces a flat ban on the export of aviation gasoline outside the Western Hemisphere . . . . House passes and sends to the Senate a $4,963,151,957 national defense appropriations bill for rearmament.	Arthur J. Edwards charges that the system of recruiting Southern Negroes to harvest summer crops in N.J. amounts to a form of peonage.			July 31
FDR chooses Edward J. Flynn to succeed James A. Farley as chairman of the Democratic National Committee and also to direct his campaign.	FDR meets with a delegation from the Century Group who urge immediate executive action to transfer U.S. destroyers to British control.	Pan-Am Airways's first stratoplane, flying at 17,000 feet, completes its maiden voyage from Miami, Florida, to San Juan, Puerto Rico.			Aug. 1
A U.S. immigration official in Detroit, John L. Zurbrick, orders an investigation into a possible "underground railroad" from Canada aiding European aliens to enter the U.S.	FDR endorses a compulsory selective service act as vital to the nation's defense . . . . U.S. cabinet agrees in principle to provide destroyers to Britain if Republican support can be lined up in Congress.	House Ways and Means Comm. approves deductions from the taxable income of industry for construction of defense plants.			Aug. 2
After an all-day conference with GOP leaders at Colorado Springs, Willkie says his campaign expenditures will be limited to $2.5-$3 million.			Lewin B. Borringer sets a new altitude record for gliders of 10,400 feet in Sun Valley, Idaho.		Aug. 3
Willkie announces the support of more anti-third term Democrats, including Stephen L. Pinckney, Elizabeth B. Howry, C. Eubank Tucker and golfer Bobby Jones . . . . At their St. Louis convention, UAW delegates pass a resolution endorsing FDR for a third term.	Gen. Pershing in a nationwide radio addresss warns that unless Britain recieves immediate aid the U.S. will soon be involved in the war . . . . Lindbergh says that "if we desire to keep America out of war, we must take a lead in offering a plan of peace."				Aug. 4
If the presidential election were today, the Gallup Poll reports, FDR would defeat Willkie by a 51%-49% margin . . . . FDR asks Congress and state legislatures to enact additional laws dealing with subversive and seditious acts . . . . NEA issues a statement urging all educators to aid the defense program by instilling new faith in democracy.	Senate Military Affairs Comm. approves the Burke-Wadsworth Selective Service Bill and sends it to the full Senate . . . . War Dept. gives approval to construction of future munitions plants between the Allegheny and Rocky Mountains . . . . Willkie urges that industrial plants be decentralized and relocated in smaller communities.	Treasury Dept. announces that, as of July 31, the national debt was $44,034,571,710.	Regular trans-Atlantic airmail service between Britain and the U.S. begins with the landing of the first flight in N.Y.		Aug. 5
Oscar O. Wheeler, CP candidate for governor of West Virginia, is found guilty of fraudulent solicitation of names for a Communist nominating petition.	U.S.-Soviet trade agreement is renewed for another year.		First meeting of the National Inventors Council, formed to encourage inventions useful for national defense, is held in Washington.		Aug. 6
					Aug. 7
American Labor Party leaders announce they will support the election of FDR . . . . Postmaster Gen. James A. Farley announces his resignation effective Aug. 31.		SEC orders Vernon Walton of Walton & Co. suspended from the NYSE for giving false information to the SEC.			Aug. 8
	As the Senate opens debate on the Burke-Wadsworth bill, Sen. Burton K. Wheeler (D, Mont.) asks those who fear Germany to propose a declaration of war . . . . FDR orders the transfer of land on St. Croix, the Virgin Islands from the Interior Dept. to the War Dept. for the construction of a military airfield.	FDR signs a bill increasing to $1.4 billion the amount of obligations the Commodity Credit Corp. may incur.			Aug. 9
F	G	H	I	J	
Includes elections, federal-state relations, civil rights and liberties, crime, the judiciary, education, health care, poverty, urban affairs and population.	*Includes formation and debate of U.S. foreign and defense policies, veterans affairs and defense spending. (Relations with specific foreign countries are usually found under the region concerned.)*	*Includes business, labor, agriculture, taxation, transportation, consumer affairs, monetary and fiscal policy, natural resources, pollution and accidents.*	*Includes worldwide scientific, medical and technological developments, natural phenomena, U.S. weather and natural disasters.*	*Includes the arts, religion, scholarship, communications media, sports, entertainment, fashions, fads and social life.*	

	World Affairs	European War Zone	Pacific War Zone	The Americas	Other Countries & Territories
Aug. 10		Britain announces it will purchase 4,000 U.S.-made tanks at a cost exceeding $200 million .... French Fine Arts Ministry reports little damage to cathedrals and other architectural monuments during the war with Germany.		Argentina announces the arrest of 26 Nazi leaders for fifth column activities.	
Aug. 11		Several hundred German planes bomb the English coast from Dover to Portland .... British headquarters in Cairo issues a communique indicating its troops will fight a war of attrition in Somaliland.			
Aug. 12	Governments of Australia, New Zealand, South Africa, Burma, Hong Kong, Ceylon and the territories of East Africa agree to attend a meeting called by Britain for October in New Delhi to discuss war supplies.	Goering orders German bombers to switch from attacks on British radar bases to airfields .... Moscow announces the abolition of the political commissar system in the Red Army .... Epidemics of smallpox, diptheria, typhoid fever and paratyphoid spread over occupied France.		Mexican Pres. Cardenas asks the federal congress to determine the victor in the July 7 presidential election.	An air crash near Canberra, Australia takes the lives of four cabinet members: Army Min. G.A. Street, Air Min. J.V. Fairbairn, Executive Council Vice Pres. Sir Henry Gulletit and Chief of the General Staff Sir Brudenell White.
Aug. 13		German bombers launch all-out attack on RAF bases but fail to put any out of commission because of heavy cloud cover .... French Supreme Court of Justice opens at Riom to review evidence in secret for the purposes of indicting political criminals and determining who was responsible for France's defeat.	Nobufumi Ito is appointed to the Japanese cabinet as minister of propaganda.		
Aug. 14		British planes fly 1,600 miles to bomb the Italian industrial centers of Milan and Turin.	U.S. and Japanese officials agree to split jurisdiction over the former British sectors in Shanghai .... Travelers reaching Chungking from Rangoon report British fortification of the Burma-China border.	Colombia claims it has eliminated German fifth column activities in the Scadta airline industry.	
Aug. 15		Luftwaffe flies 1,800 sorties over Britain, the highest in the war so far, attacking RAF bases all over southern England. Germans lose 76 planes .... An Italian submarine sinks the Greek cruiser *Helle*.	Minseito Party, the last remaining Japanese political party, voluntarily dissolves itself.	British and French announce agreement on the demobilization of the French fleet in West Indian waters, including the aircraft carrier *Bearn* .... Mexican Congress establishes an electoral college favoring Avila Camacho for the presidency.	
Aug. 16	International Labor Office announces it will establish its headquarters for the war's duration at McGill Univ. in Canada.	German planes bomb and machine-gun the London suburbs on both sides of the Thames.	French cabinet decides to capitulate to Japanese demands for military transit rights across Indochina .... *New York Times* reports that Tokyo will not accept the Shanghai compromise reached Aug. 14 .... U.S. Marines assume responsibility for the British sector in Shanghai.		
Aug. 17		Germany orders a total blockade of Britain.	The last of the British troops in northern China depart from Peking and Tientsin.	FDR and Canadian P.M. Mackenzie King meet in Ogdensburg, N.Y. and agree upon formation of a Joint Board of Defense to plan the defense of North America.	
Aug. 18		British planes bomb German military posts and shipping along the French coast from Boulogne to Calais .... Italian forces claim the capture of Zeila and Bulhar on the British Somaliland coast.	Adm. Thomas Hart says in Shanghai that the dispute with Japan over control of the British sector is deadlocked and is to be negotiated between Washington and Tokyo .... Australian Premier Robert Menzies appoints his country's first minister to Japan, Sir John G. Latham.	A Nazi political party is established in Colombia .... Duke of Windsor is sworn in as governor of the Bahama Islands.	
Aug. 19		British forces evacuate Somaliland, giving the Italians possession of a wedge from Eritrea in the north to Kenya in the south.	More than 200 Japanese bombers attack Chungking, inflicting heavy damage.		
Aug. 20		Praising the RAF, Churchill tells the Commons, "Never in the field of human conflict has so much been owed by so many to so few." He reiterates British determination to enforce a strict blockade against all countries under German control, including France .... Churchill announces in Commons that Britain is willing to lease the U.S. defense facilities in the West Indies and Newfoundland .... Mussolini announces a "total blockade" of all British possessions in the Mediterranean and Africa.	Japanese incendiary bombs destroy an estimated 25,000 homes in Chungking.		

	A	B	C	D	E
	Includes developments that affect more than one world region, international organizations and important meetings of major world leaders.	*Includes all developments in European countries and military engagements between Allied and Axis powers in Africa and at sea.*	*Includes all developments in Japan and China, Japanese foreign policy and military actions in the Pacific region.*	*Includes all domestic and regional developments in Latin America, the Caribbean and Canada.*	*Includes developments in those independent nations and colonial possessions not covered in Columns B, C and D.*

U.S. Politics & Social Issues	U.S. Foreign Policy & Defense	U.S. Economy & Environment	Science, Technology & Nature	Culture, Leisure & Life Style	
	Gallup Poll reports 66% of the American people favor compulsory military service .... Sen. Wheeler calls for a national referendum on the universal conscription issue .... Former Pres. Hoover declares 18 million people face starvation in occupied Europe this winter. He urges immediate U.S. action to send food to Belgium, the Netherlands, Poland and Norway. The U.S. government is reportedly opposed to the plan because it believes the food would help the German occupation.			At its 66th annual meeting in Chicago, the WCTU adopts a resolution opposing the drinking of alcoholic beverages in motion pictures.	Aug. 10
					Aug. 11
John Hanes, Lewis Douglas, Alan Valentine and Mrs. Roberta Lawson open a "Democrats for Willkie" headquarters in N.Y.C. .... Arizona officials ban the CP from the ballot in primary and general elections on the grounds that the party advocates overthrow of the U.S. government.	Sens. Norris and Vandenberg charge that a universal military conscription law is unnecessary at this time.				Aug. 12
FDR signs a bill requiring all government agencies to report to the Bureau of the Budget.	Senate Naval Comm. Chmn. David Walsh (D, Mass.) says any transfer of ships to Britain would be an act of war.				Aug. 13
Willkie says he favors creation of a permanent impartial board to enforce the Hatch and Corrupt Practices Acts.	Navy Secy. Frank Knox tells Senate Military Affairs Comm. compulsory conscription is necessary in face of the Nazi danger.		Dr. Milicent W. Shinn, authority on child psychology and first woman to receive a Ph.D. from the Univ. of California, dies in Alameda County, Calif.		Aug. 14
Wallace meets FDR at the White House to present his letter of resignation as secretary of agriculture, to be effective at a date still to be determined.	House approves a bill granting the President power to call the National Guard to active duty.				Aug. 15
	FDR tells reporters the U.S. and Britain are holding conversations about the acquisition of bases for the defense of the Western Hemisphere .... Construction of a new tank arsenal in Detroit under a $20-million defense order is announced by the Chrysler Corp.			Mary Ryan sets a new U.S. women's mile free style swim record of 23:15 minutes in Portland, Oregon.	Aug. 16
Willkie challenges FDR to a personal debate on the election issues.	Willkie comes out for selective service as "the only democratic way in which to assure the trained and competent manpower we need."				Aug. 17
	U.S. Amb.-to-France William C. Bullitt tells a Philadelphia audience that the war is coming to the Americas.		Carbide and Carbon Chemicals Corp. announces it will introduce the insulation of electrical wires and furniture coverings with plastic vinylite in the spring of 1941.		Aug. 18
AFL Pres. Green endorses the re-election of FDR for a third term.	Gallup Poll indicates 61% of Americans approve the proposal that the U.S. sell Britain 50 destroyers.	Federal Reserve Board increases its loans to member institutions by $15 billion, indicating an expanding economy.		Sam Snead edges Harold McSpaden to capture the Canadian Open Golf Tournament at Toronto.	Aug. 19
Cleveland Plain Dealer and the *Chicago Daily News* announce their support of Willkie's presidential candidacy .... FDR claims he is too busy to engage Willkie in a series of public debates as part of the presidential campaign.	Gen. George C. Marshall says a U.S. army of four million is required for adequate defense of the Western Hemisphere .... House Military Affairs Comm. approves the registration procedures of the Burke-Wadsworth bill.	A joint statement issued by Douglas, Lockheed, Consolidated, Boeing and Vultee aircraft companies asks the government to discuss excess profits at a later time.			Aug. 20

F	G	H	I	J
Includes elections, federal-state relations, civil rights and liberties, crime, the judiciary, education, health care, poverty, urban affairs and population.	*Includes formation and debate of U.S. foreign and defense policies, veterans affairs and defense spending. (Relations with specific foreign countries are usually found under the region concerned.)*	*Includes business, labor, agriculture, taxation, transportation, consumer affairs, monetary and fiscal policy, natural resources, pollution and accidents.*	*Includes worldwide scientific, medical and technological developments, natural phenomena, U.S. weather and natural disasters.*	*Includes the arts, religion, scholarship, communications media, sports, entertainment, fashions, fads and social life.*

	World Affairs	European War Zone	Pacific War Zone	The Americas	Other Countries & Territories
Aug. 21		Rumania and Bulgaria announce agreement that Rumania will cede Southern Dobruja to Bulgaria .... Italian planes bomb Malta and Gibraltar.		Russian revolutionary Leon Trotsky, 61, is murdered in his home in Mexico City, allegedly by an agent of Joseph Stalin.	Australian P.M. Menzies dissolves Parliament to prepare for general elections Sept. 21.
Aug. 22		Greek Premier John Metaxas convenes a special cabinet meeting to deal with Italian troop movements considered threatening to Greece .... Defense Min. Mahmoud Fahmy el Kiessy Pasha declares Egyptian forces will fight with the British.	In a purge of pro-U.S. and pro-British personnel, Tokyo recalls 40 of its diplomats, including its ambassador to the U.S., Kensuki Horinouchi .... Thirteen hundred British troops leave Shanghai, ending nearly a century's influence there.		
Aug. 23		Germany completes its first mass night air raid on London.	Ending an eight-month lull in fighting in northern China, Nationalist forces attack Japanese troops at three points, severing railroad lines.	Roberto M. Ortiz resigns as president of Argentina.	
Aug. 24		German bombers launch 24-hour attack against RAF bases, causing severe damage .... Italians bomb British military installations at Alexandria, Sidi Barrani and Matrouh in Egypt .... Hungary breaks off negotiations with Rumania over the former's demands for the cession of Transylvania.			
Aug. 25		German air attacks on London damage historic St. Giles Church and the Old Roman Wall .... Duke of Guise, pretender to the French throne, dies in Spanish Morocco.		Argentine Congress refuses to accept the resignation of Pres. Ortiz.	
Aug. 26			Japanese newspapers report their government's demand for favorable tariffs and greater supplies of raw materials from the NEI .... A joint Russian-Japanese communique announces the settlement of the Manchukuo-Outer Mongolian border dispute.	U.S.-Canadian Joint Defense Bd. meets in Ottawa, electing as co-chairmen Fiorello La Guardia and Col. O.M. Baggar.	
Aug. 27		Churchill cables FDR that the British cabinet has agreed in principle to the proposed destroyers-for-bases deal .... Under a heavy cloud cover German planes attack London for the fifth consecutive night .... Fighting between Rumanians and Russians and Rumanians and Hungarians breaks out in disputed border areas.			French forces in the Chad area of Equatorial Africa declare their allegiance to Gen. Charles de Gaulle.
Aug. 28		RAF bombers strike Berlin, killing civilians in the German capital for the first time .... Italian planes bomb, for the first time, Port Said at the northern entrance of the Suez Canal .... Hitler presides over an Axis conference at Berchtesgaden to plan a settlement of the dispute between Hungary and Rumania.	Chungking government announces it will send troops into Indochina should Japanese forces enter the country under any pretext .... Chou En-lai returns to Chungking from Yenan to continue negotiations for cooperation between the Kuomintang and Communist parties .... Prince Konoye announces the basic principles of the new national totalitarian structure aimed at solidifying the control of the present regime.	Argentine cabinet of Pres. Ortiz resigns to facilitate a government reorganization.	Australia reports widespread drought, which threatens the country's entire agricultural economy.
Aug. 29	League of Nations Council Pres. Alberto Costa Durelo announces that Secy. Gen. Avenel will resign on Sept. 1.	German air attacks continue over Great Britain, hitting London, Liverpool, Bristol, Cardiff and Birkenhead.	Japanese and French sign a political accord in which France recognizes special Japanese rights in Asia and Japan concedes a "permanent French interest in Indochina."	Argentine Pres. Ortiz turns his responsibilities over to Vice Pres. Castillo.	Most of French Equatorial Africa declares its support of de Gaulle's Free French movement .... Vichy bans the calling of colonial assemblies in an effort to curb discussion of political issues in the French empire.
Aug. 30		Acting as arbiters, von Ribbentrop and Ciano grant Hungary about half of the Rumanian province of Transylvania. In return, the Axis guarantees Rumania's borders.			
Aug. 31			After four months of negotiations, a peace treaty is announced in Nanking between Japan and its puppet Wang Ching-wei government.	Mexican courts reach a final decision fixing total compensation for expropriated U.S. oil properties at about $35.5 million.	Rebellion breaks out in French West Africa, following the action of Equatorial Africa in support of the Free French movement .... French government reports rebellion has broken out in Indochina in support of the Allied effort.
Sept. 1	League of Nations Associate Gen. Secy. Sean Lister replaces Joseph Avenel as secretary general.	A ship carrying 875 persons, including 320 children, is torpedoed off the British coast, but only one life is lost.		Argentina's acting Pres. Castillo appoints his cabinet, ending the country's political crisis.	Governor of Gabon declares his colony's support of de Gaulle, bringing all of French Equatorial Africa into the Free French movement.

A	B	C	D	E
Includes developments that affect more than one world region, international organizations and important meetings of major world leaders.	*Includes all developments in European countries and military engagements between Allied and Axis powers in Africa and at sea.*	*Includes all developments in Japan and China, Japanese foreign policy and military actions in the Pacific region.*	*Includes all domestic and regional developments in Latin America, the Caribbean and Canada.*	*Includes developments in those independent nations and colonial possessions not covered in Columns B, C and D.*

U.S. Politics & Social Issues	U.S. Foreign Policy & Defense	U.S. Economy & Environment	Science, Technology & Nature	Culture, Leisure & Life Style	
		Economists Arthur E. Burns and Donald S. Watson claim the current war expenditures will not bring long-term relief to the U.S. economy . . . . RFC agrees to loan $78.5 million to Curtiss-Wright, Boeing and Bendix aircraft companies for military plane construction . . . . A NYSE seat is sold for $35,000, the lowest price paid since 1914.			Aug. 21
	Gen. Henry H. Arnold releases the first information about the Lockheed Interceptor, describing it as the world's fastest plane, capable of reaching 500 mph.	FDR signs the Investment Company Act of 1940, providing for the regulation and registration of investment companies.	One of the most distinguished scientists of the Victorian era, Sir Oliver Lodge, dies at 89 in London.	Isidore Cardinal Goma y Thomas, primate of Spain, dies in Madrid.	Aug. 22
	U.S. State Dept. delivers a note warning Japan to halt its agression in Asia . . . . FDR asks that Congress enact a military conscription bill within two weeks.		British *Medical Journal* reports successful experimentation with a bacillus for anti-TB vaccination.		Aug. 23
Harry Hopkins resigns as secretary of commerce. FDR nominates Jesse H. Jones to replace him.	Britain and Bermuda announce the leasing of the Great Sound of Bermuda to the U.S. for an airplane base . . . . Willkie calls for the creation of an air force cabinet post.				Aug. 24
					Aug. 25
Willkie says he would agree to a campaign debate with Socialist Party candidate Norman Thomas if FDR would also appear.			Schools in three southern West Virginia counties are closed due to an infantile paralysis epidemic that has already claimed 10 lives.	Sports officials from the Western Hemisphere gather in Buenos Aires to discuss the possible establishment of a Pan-Am Olympiad.	Aug. 26
Willkie rejects the support of Father Charles E. Coughlin and his supporters because of their alleged religious and racial bigotry.	Atty. Gen. Robert Jackson informs FDR there is no constitutional requirement for congressional approval of the destroyers-for-bases deal with Britain . . . . Congress approves FDR's plan to call up the National Guard for a year's training . . . . FDR authorizes the transportation of refugee children in American vessels under a safe conduct pass by all the states named in the 1939 Neutrality Act.				Aug. 27
	FDR signs a bill authorizing the mobilization of the National Guard and other Army reserve units for one year.		National Foundation for Infantile Paralysis rushes all available aid to Indiana to help combat a serious outbreak of poliomyelitis.	Reuben Fine defeats J.C. Thompson in 15 moves to win the U.S. Chess Federation's open championship at Dallas, Tex.	Aug. 28
Wallace asks voters to support FDR as the best way to thwart Hitler's designs on the Western Hemisphere.	Senate approves and sends to conference a $5-billion defense bill to start the "Two-Ocean Navy" program and equip 1.2 million men.	An excess profits tax bill is approved by the House and sent to the Senate.			Aug. 29
	War Dept. orders 410 intercepter pursuit planes from Lockheed and 270 heavy bombers from Boeing.		Sir J.J. Thomson, 83, master of Trinity College, Cambridge and a pioneer in the study of atomic physics, dies.		Aug. 30
Democratic National Chairman Edward J. Flynn supports Wallace's charge that the GOP is a party of appeasement . . . . James A. Farley resigns as postmaster general, and FDR nominates Frank C. Walker as his successor.	FDR orders 26 units of the National Guard, mostly dealing with coastal defense, on active duty for one year.			Pan-Am Sports Congress announces that the first Pan-Am Olympic Games will be held in Buenos Aires, Argentina in 1942.	Aug. 31
Willkie pledges, if elected, to enlist the cooperation of labor, industry, and agriculture to overcome the nation's economic woes.	Transport Union Pres. Michael Quill says labor will defend America but not participate in foreign wars.				Sept. 1
F	G	H	I	J	
Includes elections, federal-state relations, civil rights and liberties, crime, the judiciary, education, health care, poverty, urban affairs and population.	*Includes formation and debate of U.S. foreign and defense policies, veterans affairs and defense spending. (Relations with specific foreign countries are usually found under the region concerned.)*	*Includes business, labor, agriculture, taxation, transportation, consumer affairs, monetary and fiscal policy, natural resources, pollution and accidents.*	*Includes worldwide scientific, medical and technological developments, natural phenomena, U.S. weather and natural disasters.*	*Includes the arts, religion, scholarship, communications media, sports, entertainment, fashions, fads and social life.*	

	World Affairs	European War Zone	Pacific War Zone	The Americas	Other Countries & Territories
Sept. 2		British Air Ministry estimates Germany used 700 planes in attacks upon London today.	French Gov. Gen. Jean Decoux rejects a Japanese ultimatum demanding concessions in Indochina.	Gen. Juan Andreu Almazan, unsuccessful candidate for the Mexican presidency is reported organizing a junta to overthrow Avila Camacho administration.	Egyptian cabinet is reshuffled, but the Sadist and Independent parties continue to dominate the government.
Sept. 3		German planes bomb London continuously all day .... A group of French pilots desert from Morocco to Gibraltar, declaring they wish to fight against the Germans and with the British .... Rumanian cabinet of Premier Ion Gigurtu resigns. Gen. Ion Antonescu is named to form a new government.		Argentine Vice Pres. Ramon Castillo swears in a new cabinet, which pledges itself to democratic rule.	Anti-German uprisings are reported in Chad in French Equatorial Africa and in French New Caledonia.
Sept. 4		Hitler threatens to raze British cities unless the RAF halts its attacks upon Germany .... British planes bomb concentrations of German war material concealed in the Black Forest, the Oberharz Mtns. and the forests of Thuringia.	French authorities in Indochina officially reject the Japanese request for passage of troops en route to China.		Gen. Auguste Nogues announces the reorganization of the Moroccan government in an effort to control dissidents .... Tahiti, capital of the French Society Islands, declares support for de Gaulle.
Sept. 5		Hungarian troops occupy the ceded portion of Transylvania, Rumania .... Italian planes bomb port of Suez, Egypt .... British Ministry of Home Security reports 1,075 deaths were caused by German air raids in August.	Sources in Hanoi report French and Japanese officials there have agreed on a pact permitting Japanese use of Indochina for transit of troops to China .... Chinese warn U.S. government that the situation is rapidly deteriorating and that further U.S. aid is imperative.		Britain and Thailand agree to a non-aggression pact.
Sept. 6		King Carol of Rumania abdicates the throne to his 18-year-old son, who is sworn in as King Michael. Before his abdication, King Carol appoints Iron Guard leader Gen. Ion Antonescu as premier with dictatorial powers.		Some 1,200 Panamanians and West Indian laborers in the Canal Zone strike over pay and food issues.	Marshal Petain reorganizes the French cabinet, giving Gen. Maxime Weygand authority to suppress all separatist movements in the French African colonies.
Sept. 7		German planes renew their bombing offensive against London .... An "invasion imminent" alert is issued along the eastern and southern coasts of Britain .... Rumania agrees to the cession of Southern Dobruja to Bulgaria, restoring the countries' 1912 borders.		Supporters of Gen. Almazan begin leaving Mexico to confer in the U.S. on possible courses of action.	Burmese Premier U Pu resigns after losing a vote of confidence in the House of Representatives.
Sept. 8		Goering announces he has taken personal control over the German air assault on England.		Paraguayan Pres. Jose F. Estigarribia is killed in an airplane crash .... Bolivian Chamber of Deputies approves a bill denying Jews the right to emigrate into the country.	
Sept. 9		A reported 350 German planes make a mass attack on London, killing an estimated 400 people.	Japanese sources in Tokyo indicate there is no agreement with Hanoi on troop transit through Indochina.		
Sept. 10		German planes drop bombs on London for 8 hours and 24 minutes, causing heavy damage to St. Paul's Cathedral and Old Bailey .... Swedish government concludes trade agreements with Nazi-controlled Belgium and Holland.			
Sept. 11		Churchill warns Britain that an invasion may be imminent .... Acting on a report that German troops are about to invade England, British forces launch air and sea attacks upon French and Norwegian coastal ports .... Norwegian Parliament names Ingold Ilster Christensen as regent.	Gov. Gen. Jean Decoux sends a plea to FDR to assist in curbing the Japanese demands upon Indochina .... A Chinese military spokesman states in Chungking that Chinese troops are destroying the Yunnan railway bridge over the Red River to prevent its use by the Japanese.		
Sept. 12		In anticipation of a German invasion, two million British troops are reportedly dispersed along the coastline .... German bombs hit Buckingham Palace, but the royal family is uninjured.	Japanese diplomatic and trade mission, seeking greater access to raw materials, especially oil, arrives in the Netherlands East Indies.	U.S. Senate approves its version of the bill to create an Inter-American Bank and sends it to joint conference with the House.	
Sept. 13	Japanese Foreign Min. Matsuoka predicts a postwar world of great economic blocs, with trade between the blocs on a barter base.	Italian troops attack from Libya across the Egyptian border .... Italian forces based in Ethiopia penetrate some 120 miles into British Kenya.	Under a new decree, cable and radio stations in Japanese-controlled China refuse to accept messages from belligerent countries .... In a daylight attack on Chungking, Japanese bombers destroy the German embassy.	U.S. Treasury Dept. bars the Panamanian ship *Norseland* from American waters for 3 months because its captain flew the American flag in the war zone.	

A	B	C	D	E
Includes developments that affect more than one world region, international organizations and important meetings of major world leaders.	*Includes all developments in European countries and military engagements between Allied and Axis powers in Africa and at sea.*	*Includes all developments in Japan and China, Japanese foreign policy and military actions in the Pacific region.*	*Includes all domestic and regional developments in Latin America, the Caribbean and Canada.*	*Includes developments in those independent nations and colonial possessions not covered in Columns B, C and D.*

U.S. Politics & Social Issues	U.S. Foreign Policy & Defense	U.S. Economy & Environment	Science, Technology & Nature	Culture, Leisure & Life Style	
	In his Labor Day address from Great Smokey Mountains National Park, FDR asks Americans to unite for the total defense of the nation.	AFL Pres. Green asserts that John L. Lewis is the only obstruction to peace with the CIO .... Labor Secy. Frances Perkins announces an increase of more that one million workers in non-agricultural employment during the past year.		Byron Nelson rallies to defeat Sam Snead and win the PGA championship at Hershey, Pa.	Sept. 2
	FDR publicly notifies Congress of the destroyers-for-bases agreement with Britain .... Atty. Gen. Jackson rules FDR has the power to complete deals such as the destroyer-trade by executive agreement.				Sept. 3
Office of Education announces approximately a quarter of the U.S. population, or 32,580,000 million children, will attend school this year.	Hull advises Japan that if it upsets the status quo in Indochina and the NEI the effect on U.S. opinion would be unfortunate.	National Defense Advisory Commission tells Congress it should not extend government control over private industry beyond the defense emergency period.	Dr. Hans Zinsser, world's leading authority on typhus, dies in New York.	Eastern College All-Stars upset the New York Giants in an exhibition football game in New York.	Sept. 4
At a conference with GOP leaders from 21 states in Rushville, Indiana, Willkie formally opens his presidential campaign.	FDR establishes a new National Defense Research Comm. under the chairmanship of Dr. Vannevar Bush to coordinate scientific research for the defense effort.	FDR signs the Federal Highway Act, authorizing nearly $135 million for various highway projects through 1943 .... N.Y. Federal Reserve Bank announces it is now handling the deposits of the British and French governments.			Sept. 5
	National Defense Advisory Commission urges the government to ban the export of all scrap steel .... FDR scores Congress for delays in passing a selective service law.				Sept. 6
Willkie declares he would never lead the U.S. into a European War .... Former GOP Michigan Gov. Charles S. Osborn announces his support for FDR because he claims Willkie is "unfit" for the presidency .... Democratic National Comm. official Charles Michelson says the GOP is supported by groups preaching racial and religious intolerance.	House passes and sends to conference the Burke-Wadsworth selective service bill .... Bowing to Soviet pressure, the State Dept. announces the closing of its legations in Lithuania, Estonia and Latvia.		American Assn. of Scientific Workers offers to take charge of British research threatened by the war.		Sept. 7
Federal Judge John C. Knux bars Communist Party presidential condidate Earl Browder from campaigning and making public speeches.	Historian Charles A. Beard endorses the America First Comm. position on non-intervention in the European War.	Due to action taken by the Federal Crop Insurance Corp., wheat sells for its highest price in two months on the Chicago Board of Trade.		Baltimore Elite Giants defeat the New York Cubans, 3-0, in New York to win the Ruppert Memorial Cup, symbol of supremacy in Negro baseball.	Sept. 8
House passes and sends to the Senate a resolution permitting Jesse H. Jones to serve both as federal loan administrator and secretary of commerce.	Navy Dept. announces contracts for the building of 201 ships, including seven battleships .... FDR signs the $5.251-billion Second Supplemental National Defense Appropriations Act.	President of the Investment Bankers Assn., Emmett F. Connely, says any government loans to small business would only serve as a deterrent to the employment of private capital.	Dr. Per K. Frolich reports the development by Standard Oil Laboratories of a synthetic rubber based upon petroleum.		Sept. 9
National Youth Foundation Chmn. Gene Tunney announces the creation of a Young Voter's Exchange designed to bring out an estimated 9 million first voters in November.			Albert Einstein urges the development of a religion of good and the abandonment of a "personal God" in a paper read before a conference of scientists, philosophers and religious leaders in N.Y.		Sept. 10
Willkie asserts that the third term is a key issue in this campaign, for if FDR and his people stay in power, it will be "destructive of democracy." .... FDR officially opens his presidential campaign with a speech in Washington hailing the success of labor in America. He reasserts his desire to avoid a "foreign war." .... NAACP leader William Pickens establishes a Negro citizens committee to support Willkie.	Senate approves a House bill increasing the Import-Export Bank's lending capacity to $700 million and limiting the amount loaned to a single country at one time to $500 million.	In a Washington speech, FDR says that the nation, having adopted military conscription, cannot deny the government the right to seize and operate reluctant industries in case of national defense .... Ford Motor Co. begins construction of an $11-million plant for the production of airplane engines.	Jacqueline Cochrane wins the annual trophy of the International League of Aviators as the world's outstanding woman pilot.		Sept. 11
In a N.Y.C. radio speech, Mayor La Guardia endorses FDR for a third term, describing the President as a man who has made America the hope of the world.	Amb.-to-Japan Joseph Grew urges the State Dept. to apply greater economic pressure on Japan, calling her "one of the predatory powers."				Sept. 12
					Sept. 13

F	G	H	I	J
Includes elections, federal-state relations, civil rights and liberties, crime, the judiciary, education, health care, poverty, urban affairs and population.	*Includes formation and debate of U.S. foreign and defense policies, veterans affairs and defense spending. (Relations with specific foreign countries are usually found under the region concerned.)*	*Includes business, labor, agriculture, taxation, transportation, consumer affairs, monetary and fiscal policy, natural resources, pollution and accidents.*	*Includes worldwide scientific, medical and technological developments, natural phenomena, U.S. weather and natural disasters.*	*Includes the arts, religion, scholarship, communications media, sports, entertainment, fashions, fads and social life.*

	World Affairs	European War Zone	Pacific War Zone	The Americas	Other Countries & Territories
Sept. 14		Italians report driving a 10-mile wedge in the British defense line in Egypt .... A new international conference of Danube states called by Germany, meeting in Vienna, declares that the International Danube Commission set up by the Versailles Treaty "no longer exists" and appoints a consultative commission with a German chairman in its place.		Reports in Rio de Janeiro indicate that propaganda from the U.S. is increasing in Brazil.	Premier Gen. Luang Bipul Songgram states that negotiations are under way with Indochina for the return of territory allegedly belonging to Thailand .... Gandhi addresses the Working Comm. of the Indian Congress Party, declaring that the Poona Resolution is a departure from previous party policy and that now, since the British rejected its conditions, a direct action policy should be adopted.
Sept. 15		Germans suffer heaviest losses yet in an air battle over Britain. East Enders in London seize the ballroom of the Savoy Hotel as a shelter .... Gen. Antonescu resolves a conflict between his cabinet and the Iron Guard by the formation of a new cabinet. Simultaneously, a royal decree states Rumania is now a "Legionary State." .... Soviets announce the conscription of 19- and 20-year olds for military service.		All single men in Canada, between 21 and 24, are called for military service .... A hurricane lashes the Canadian provinces of Nova Scotia, New Brunswick and Prince Edward Island, cutting the port of Halifax off from outside contact.	British announce the recruitment of Arabs and Jews in Palestine to serve as guardsmen there.
Sept. 16		Italian forces push 25 miles beyond Solum, Egypt to Sidi Barrani .... For the 10th consecutive night, London is attacked by German planes .... Spanish Foreign Min. Serrano Suner arrives in Berlin for talks with Hitler and Ribbentrop about Spanish conditions for entering the war.			
Sept. 17		British refugee ship *The Ellesman*, destined for Canada, is torpedoed and sunk 600 miles west of the British Isles, with 159 survivors out of the 406 persons aboard .... Republic of San Marino declares war on Britain.	A Japanese government committee proposes reorganizing the state along lines similar to Italian Fascism.		All-India Congress elects Mohandas Gandhi as its leader .... Reports from Tangier indicate rioting against Vichy authorities has broken out in French Morocco .... Philippine Finance Min. Manuel Potas asks for U.S. arms aid to prepare the islands' defense.
Sept. 18	Chancellor of the Exchequer Sir Kingsley Wood tells the House of Commons that Britain will keep its tie to the Bank of International Settlement despite the war.	British Air Ministry reports air attacks on French, Belgian and Netherlands coastal ports.	Japan refuses to say when it will fulfill its promise to open the Yangtze River to foreign trade.		
Sept. 19		Hitler formally orders the assembly of the "Sea Lion" invasion fleet halted, pending further developments .... The 13th consecutive nightly German raid on London is made from the northwest, a new direction .... British ships and planes shell the Italian stronghold of Sidi Barrani in Egypt.	Japan gives France two days to accede to her demands in Indochina.		
Sept. 20		Upon his return from Britain, Brig. Gen. George Strong of the U.S. Army says that German bombing has not done any serious military damage .... RAF bombers attack German invasion positions along the Channel coast.		Costa Rica becomes the first nation to approve the defense and cooperation agreements of the Havana Conference.	
Sept. 21		British open London tube stations as bomb shelters for the first time .... British planes bomb the Norwegian coast from Trondheim to Namsos .... Bulgarian forces occupy Southern Dobruja.	French authorities refuse Japan the right to military bases in the state of Tonkin.	Mexican government sends federal troops into the Chihuahua state to crush a rebel uprising.	Congo, Togoland and Dahomey report their opposition to the Petain government in France .... Robert Menzies is re-elected premier in Australia .... Four members of the Saadist Party resign their positions in the Egyptian cabinet.
Sept. 22		Germans torpedo a refugee ship on its way to Canada, killing 293 persons, including 83 children .... Finland agrees to let German troops transport troops to northern Norway across its territory in exchange for arms .... Ribbontrop and Mussolini confer in Rome on postwar plans for the disposition of Africa and the Near East.	Japanese and French finally sign an accord in Hanoi granting the Japanese permission to station 6,000 troops in Indochina and transit rights for larger forces.	Eight Nazi Party leaders are arrested in Uruguay and charged with conspiracy.	
Sept. 23		Anglo-French forces bombard Dakar in French West Africa and attempt a landing but are beaten back by Vichy forces .... RAF bombers blast Berlin for four hours .... Hitler warns Egypt to disavow its ties to Britain or face severe consequences .... British warships shell Sidi Barrani, Egypt, where the Italians are reportedly massing for a push on the Suez Canal.	Japanese troops enter Indochina, crossing the Chinese frontier at Lang Son .... French forces abandon Dong Dang near Hanoi.		U.S. State Dept. figures released today indicate Thailand purchased $480,000 worth of arms in August.

A	B	C	D	E
Includes developments that affect more than one world region, international organizations and important meetings of major world leaders.	*Includes all developments in European countries and military engagements between Allied and Axis powers in Africa and at sea.*	*Includes all developments in Japan and China, Japanese foreign policy and military actions in the Pacific region.*	*Includes all domestic and regional developments in Latin America, the Caribbean and Canada.*	*Includes developments in those independent nations and colonial possessions not covered in Columns B, C and D.*

U.S. Politics & Social Issues	U.S. Foreign Policy & Defense	U.S. Economy & Environment	Science, Technology & Nature	Culture, Leisure & Life Style	
House speaker William B. Bankhead (D, Ala.) dies in Washington . . . . Senate confirms Jesse H. Jones as secretary of commerce.	Both houses of Congress pass the Burke-Wadsworth selective service bill, permitting the induction of all males aged 21 to 35 . . . . Willkie charges FDR has bungled American foreign affairs in recent years and says he bears partial responsibility for the 1938 Munich Pact.			Goncourt Academy in Paris announces it will not award its annual prize for the best French novel of 1940 due to the war.	Sept. 14
	Gen. Douglas MacArthur urges increased aid to Britain.				Sept. 15
Sam Rayburn (D, Tex.) is chosen speaker of the House . . . . Hull, speaking in defense of FDR, says Willkie is "grossly ignorant" of recent foreign affairs and that FDR did not sell "the Czechs down the river."	FDR signs the Selective Service Act and sets Oct. 16 as registration day . . . . National Guardsmen begin to report for induction into federal service for a year's training.			Playwright William A. McGuire, long associated with Flo Ziegfield, dies in Beverly Hills . . . . Vatican radio states its opposition to all those who wish to create a new world order.	Sept. 16
Justice Dept. announces that all 6,000 aliens here on student visas must register and be fingerprinted before Dec. 26.		Local 802 of the American Federation of Musicians and the Manhattan General Hospital agree to a complete hospital care plan for the members of the musicians' union and their families.			Sept. 17
GOP leaders meet in N.Y.C. to map plans for a nationwide speaking campaign in support of Willkie's candidacy.	FDR signs a bill authorizing over $23 million for the construction of drydocks in New York, Boston and the Caribbean.	FDR signs bill enlarging the power of the ICC to approve the pooling or division of routes by multiple carriers.		In defeating Philadelphia 4-3, the Cincinnati Reds clinch their second consecutive National League pennant.	Sept. 18
Willkie asks Los Angeles voters for their support to rescue the country from the New Deal, which he says has brought only economic stagnation.	Hull, the British ambassador and Australian minister confer on joint use of naval and air bases for mutual defense.	Senate passes the excess profits tax bill by a vote of 46 to 23 . . . . Amalgamated Clothing Workers of America demands its parent organization, the CIO, bar all Communists from its N.Y. state offices.			Sept. 19
Father Charles E. Coughlin announces that he "could not in good conscience" support either presidential candidate.					Sept. 20
The three-year-old son of Count and Countess Marc de Tristan is kidnapped in Hillsborough, Calif. and a $100,000 ransom is asked. . . . Socialist presidential candidate Norman Thomas says that both FDR and Willkie will put the nation closer to war.			Dr. Edward H. Armstrong receives a patent for a new FM transmitting system which increases fidelity to new peak levels.		Sept. 21
FBI finds three-year-old Marc de Tristan Jr. unharmed and capture the abductor, Wilhelm J. Muhlenbrotch . . . . California legislature passes, and Gov. Culbert L. Olson endorses, a bill prohibiting the CP from putting its name on any state election ballot.	Reports in London claim U.S. Amb. Joseph P. Kennedy will resign his post in two or three months.		Carnegie Institute of Technology reveals a new method of converting coal into liquid organic chemicals to be used for dyes, explosives and medicines.	AAU selects swimmer Gloria Callen as this year's outstanding woman athlete.	Sept. 22
U.S. Census reports U.S. population in the 1940 census was 131,409,881, a 7% increase in the last decade . . . . Illinois state electoral board takes the CP off the state ballot on the grounds that its nominating petitions are invalid.	Hull denounces the Japanese attack on Indochina . . . . FDR tells the American Legion convention in Boston that the U.S. must take steps to keep war from the country's shores . . . . Gallup Poll reports that 52% of American voters favor aid to England at the risk of war; 48% feel the U.S. should stay out of the war.				Sept. 23

F
Includes elections, federal-state relations, civil rights and liberties, crime, the judiciary, education, health care, poverty, urban affairs and population.

G
Includes formation and debate of U.S. foreign and defense policies, veterans affairs and defense spending. (Relations with specific foreign countries are usually found under the region concerned.)

H
Includes business, labor, agriculture, taxation, transportation, consumer affairs, monetary and fiscal policy, natural resources, pollution and accidents.

I
Includes worldwide scientific, medical and technological developments, natural phenomena, U.S. weather and natural disasters.

J
Includes the arts, religion, scholarship, communications media, sports, entertainment, fashions, fads and social life.

	World Affairs	European War Zone	Pacific War Zone	The Americas	Other Countries & Territories
Sept. 24	Through a private emissary Hitler pressures the Japanese to join the war against Britain.	French planes from North Africa bomb Gibraltar in retaliation for Dakar bombardment.	French forces in Indochina prepare for a Japanese siege of Hanoi and a naval assault on the coast.		Reports from Switzerland claim Italy is plotting a Pan-Arab revolt against Britain's dominance in the Middle East.
Sept. 25		British and Free French abandon Dakar operation after meeting expectedly stiff resistence .... Planes from Morocco renew their attack upon Gibraltar .... Josef Terboven, Reich commissioner in Norway, establishes Vidkun Quisling as the head of government of the country.	U.S. announces a new loan to China.	U.S. and Dominican Republic sign an agreement in Washington, whereby the U.S. gives up its control of the Republic's customs.	
Sept. 26		Reliable sources in Berlin predict a German-Italian-Spanish treaty will be signed in the near future.	Japanese forces land unopposed at Haiphong, Indochina.	Brazil is granted a $20-million U.S. loan for the development of her steel industry.	
Sept. 27	Germany, Italy, and Japan sign, in Berlin, a 10-year mutual assistance pact providing for all-out military aid if one country is attacked by another power not currently involved in war. Germany and Italy also recognize Japan's leadership in Asia. The Tripartite Pact is widely seen as aimed specifically at the U.S.	Rumanian government expropriates all Jewish agricultural land.			
Sept. 28	Berlin sources report the Axis partners agree to Russian participation in the alliance if the Soviets desire .... *N.Y. Times* reports the French press views the Axis Pact as aimed at the U.S. and at creating a Monroe Doctrine for Europe and the Far East.		Prince Konoye tells the Japanese people in a radio broadcast that they now must abandon their personal interests in favor of the state.	Mexican Pres. Cardenas offers safe conduct to Gen. Almazon if he returns to Mexico .... Reports from Chile and Panama indicate that the U.S. will construct naval facilities in those countries.	
Sept. 29		British Air Ministry claims 2,167 German planes and an estimated 5,148 pilots and crewmen were downed by British defenders during August and September .... Italy reports a British air attack on Addis Ababa.			Council of the All-India Moslem League refuses to participate in the new War Advisory Council.
Sept. 30		British planes pound German war industrial centers at Magdeburg, Hanover, Stuttgart and Bitterfeld.	Japanese planes bomb Kunming, China, the northern terminus of the railroad from Haiphong .... A typhoon strikes the southern edge of Formosa, killing 50 people.		
Oct. 1		British announce that London's mothers and children are being evacuated to the country at the rate of 2,000 per day .... German invasion ports on the English Channel coast are bombed by the RAF.		FDR tells visiting Latin American military mission in Washington that hemispheric defense is a common problem.	Gov. Gen. Pierre Ryckmans announces the arrival of a British military unit in the Belgian Congo.
Oct. 2		*Empress of Britain* is sunk by a submarine in the Atlantic. Many British children being evacuated to Canada are lost .... British government announces appointment of a scientific advisory committee to be chaired by Lord Hankey.	Japanese newspapers claim the price of Tokyo's friendship with Russia is the halting of Soviet support of China .... French authorities in Indochina instruct British and American oil companies to remove their stocks from the Hanoi airfield in two days to make room for Japanese supplies.	Panamanian Pres. Arnulfo Arias protests the U.S. has occupied the Rio Hata airfield and other defense sites in the Republic without concluding a binding agreement with his government.	Recruitment of Palestinian Jews to train as territorial guardsmen is completed. British authorities say no further applications will be processed.
Oct. 3		Neville Chamberlain resigns from the British cabinet and is succeeded by Sir John Anderson as home secretary and by Herbert Morrison as lord president of the council .... Finnish government announces an agreement with Russia for the permanent demilitarization of the Aaland Islands.		Buenos Aires sources report the U.S. is conducting discussions with several Latin American nations for the establishment of defense bases.	Local government officials in Dakar, capital of French West Africa, place the city under martial law in an effort to prevent its fall to pro-German elements.
Oct. 4	Bank for International Settlements returns to Basel, Switzerland from Chateau d'Oeux.	Hitler and Mussolini meet at the Brenner Pass, presumably to discuss the relationship of Russia to the Axis Pact .... Yugoslav government bars Jews from the food trade.	In a message to FDR, Churchill proposes staff talks at Singapore between British, Dutch and U.S. naval authorities .... British cabinet decides to reopen the Burma Road into China on Oct. 17 .... Prince Konoye says the question of a Pacific conflict will hinge on American understanding and respect for Japan's position there.		
	A *Includes developments that affect more than one world region, international organizations and important meetings of major world leaders.*	B *Includes all developments in European countries and military engagements between Allied and Axis powers in Africa and at sea.*	C *Includes all developments in Japan and China, Japanese foreign policy and military actions in the Pacific region.*	D *Includes all domestic and regional developments in Latin America, the Caribbean and Canada.*	E *Includes developments in those independent nations and colonial possessions not covered in Columns B, C and D.*

U.S. Politics & Social Issues	U.S. Foreign Policy & Defense	U.S. Economy & Environment	Science, Technology & Nature	Culture, Leisure & Life Style	
Gallup Poll reports 68% of the voters think FDR will be elected President again in November.	FDR establishes the Defense Communications Board charged with coordinating all communications systems for national defense.			Jerome Jones, editor of the *Journal of Labor* and a Southern champion of organized labor, dies in Atlanta.	Sept. 24
House Democrats choose John W. McCormick (Mass.) as their new floor leader.	Army General Staff warns FDR that Germany might invade the Western Hemisphere through northeastern Brazil .... Douglas Aircraft in Santa Monica, Calif. begins construction on $20 million worth of military aircraft, the largest single contract in U.S. history.				Sept. 25
Justice Dept. orders 59 alien employes of the Bata Shoe Co. to leave the country within a reasonable time or face deportation.	U.S. announces a complete embargo on export of all types of steel and iron scrap except to Britain and the Western Hemisphere, cutting off Japan from a principal source of war material .... At its annual convention in Boston, the American Legion votes against a strict U.S. policy of neutrality.				Sept. 26
	FDR says the signing of the Tripartite Pact has, for the moment, no effect on U.S. policies .... Hull says the Tripartite Pact only confirms what has been public knowledge for some time .... U.S. Senate ratifies the Havana Convention by a unanimous vote.			Detroit Tigers clinch the American League pennant by beating Cleveland 2-0.	Sept. 27
	FDR appoints Lt. Col. Lewis B. Hershey as temporary chief administrator of the Selective Service Act.			Joe DiMaggio, New York Yankees, with a .350 average, and Debs Garms, Pittsburgh Pirates, with a .355 average, win the AL and NL batting average titles .... Betty Jameson retains the women's national golf championship with a victory over Jane Cothran at Del Monte, Calif.	Sept. 28
					Sept. 29
Sen. Robert LaFollette (Prog, Wisc.) endorses FDR for a third term .... Willkie opens a five-day campaign swing through Indiana, Michigan, Ohio and Pennsylvania .... House passes and sends to the Senate the McLeod resolution urging the states to bar from the ballot candidates of any party or group that advocates the overthrow of the U.S. government.	Public opinion poll reports 57% of those asked favor U.S. action to keep Japan from becoming more powerful, even at the risk of war.				Sept. 30
	Sen. Claude Pepper (D, Fla.) urges Congress to give all aid to Britain to stop Hitler, whom he calls a threat to the U.S.			Leland Stowe, Hallett Abend and Edward Murrow receive Overseas Press Club awards for their reporting of the war.	Oct. 1
John W. Davis, Democratic standard bearer in 1924, endorses Willkie for President and speaks against FDR's bid for a 3rd term .... Willkie charges FDR with playing "politics" with American defense.		Temporary National Economic Comm. Chmn. Sen. Joseph O'Maheney (D. Wyo.) says the Rockefellers, du Ponts and Morgans own almost $1.4 billion worth of shareholdings, "which gives them considerable influence if not control," of 15 of the top 200 corporations in America.			Oct. 2
Columbia Univ. Pres. Dr. Nicholas M. Butler tells his faculty members to resign voluntarily if thet cannot support the pro-Allied position of the university.	U.S. arsenal at Rock Island, Illinois sends 105 tanks to Canada.				Oct. 3
Speaking to 25,000 people in Philadelphia, Willkie calls the New Dealers incompetent when faced with the necessities of both national defense and economic recovery.		Atty. Gen. Jackson rules NLRB decisions must be regarded as binding in the allotment of defense contracts until overturned by the courts.		Balkan Olympics with teams from Turkey, Greece, Yugoslavia, Rumania and Bulgaria open in Istanbul.	Oct. 4
F *Includes elections, federal-state relations, civil rights and liberties, crime, the judiciary, education, health care, poverty, urban affairs and population.*	G *Includes formation and debate of U.S. foreign and defense policies, veterans affairs and defense spending. (Relations with specific foreign countries are usually found under the region concerned.)*	H *Includes business, labor, agriculture, taxation, transportation, consumer affairs, monetary and fiscal policy, natural resources, pollution and accidents.*	I *Includes worldwide scientific, medical and technological developments, natural phenomena, U.S. weather and natural disasters.*	J *Includes the arts, religion, scholarship, communications media, sports, entertainment, fashions, fads and social life.*	

	World Affairs	European War Zone	Pacific War Zone	The Americas	Other Countries & Territories
Oct. 5		Germans abandon daylight bombing of London because of heavy losses .... In night raids, the RAF bombs the French Channel coast from Dunkirk to Boulogne, setting massive fires.		Mexican Pres.-elect Avila Camacho predicts closer ties with the U.S.	New Zealand Finance Min. Walter Nash announces that individuals and corporations will pay the government $40 million as a war loan without interest for three years.
Oct. 6		Premier Ion Antonescu assumes command of the Iron Guard, making him undisputed dictator of Rumania .... In what is now termed as a systematic assault on Germany's war machine, RAF bombers attack 200 military targets, including the Krupp works at Essen.			
Oct. 7		German military mission arrives in Rumania, taking control of the oil fields at Ploesti .... German authorities in occupied France order all Jews to register within the next 18 days .... In night raids on London, 450 German planes drop explosive and incendiary bombs.	Japanese official spokesman says there is "no room for a basic readjustment of relations" with the U.S.	Cuban Pres. Federico Laredo Bru orders the Superior Electoral Tribunal to clear the legal path for Pres.-elect Fulgencio Batista to be inaugurated.	
Oct. 8	Churchill denounces the Tripartite Pact and announces the British decision to reopen the Burma Road.		American consuls in the Far East advise all Americans there to return to the U.S. as soon as possible .... Official Japanese recognition of Wang Ching-Wei, scheduled for tomorrow, is temporarily postponed by Tokyo.		
Oct. 9		A Vichy government decree establishes a new French army on a volunteer basis.		Cuban Supreme Court rejects the opposition parties' petition to postpone the inauguration of Pres.-elect Batista.	British fleet commences a "starvation blockade" of the French colony of Madagascar .... Gen. de Gaulle raises the flag of the "Free French" at Dirala, Cameroons.
Oct. 10	Japanese Foreign Min. Matsuoka denies the Tripartite Pact is aimed against the U.S.	Germans begin moving troops and supplies down the Danube River.	Japanese mayor of Shanghai Fu Hsiao-en is murdered at his home.	In his inaugural address, Cuban Pres. Batista calls for the American Republics to join together for common defense.	Ten military aircraft destined for Thailand are stopped at Manila to be returned to the U.S. for defense purposes .... Gen. Maxime Weygand arrives in French West Africa in an effort to organize resistance to Gen. de Gaulle in the French African colonies.
Oct. 11		Marshal Petain broadcasts a message to the French people that France is ready to seek collaboration in all fields with all its neighbors .... British War Secy. Eden leaves London for an inspection trip to the front in Egypt .... British warships and planes make a joint attack on Cherbourg.	An unnamed Japanese diplomat says in Tokyo that "Japan has not committed her destiny into Adolf Hitler's hands."		
Oct. 12		Hitler cancels plans for the invasion of Britain because of the failure of the Luftwaffe to establish air superiority and the approach of winter.	U.S. oil companies begin to move their petroleum supplies from Shanghai to the British naval base at Singapore.		Commissioner Francis B. Sayre, Pres. Manuel Quezon, Rear Adm. John M. Smeallie and Major Gen. George Gruneat confer in Manila on possible emergency situations in the Philippines.
Oct. 13		Rippentrop sends a message to Stalin urging him to join the Tripartite Pact .... In a naval battle off Malta the Italians sink one British cruiser and damage two others.	Foreign Min. Matsuoka says Japan has joined the Axis because it shares with Italy and Germany the aim of establishing economic, political and military spheres throughout the world .... Chinese forces claim the capture of Mafang, an important city on the Yangtze River.	Brazil and Chile agree to lease the U.S. naval and air bases.	Working Comm. of the Indian Congress Party promises Gandhi full-cooperation for his direct action program at a meeting in Wardha. The decision stems from the failure of negotiations with the British to establish a national government.
Oct. 14		Germany demands that Yugoslavia submit to the "new European order" as defined by the Axis .... In the heaviest night raid to date on London, German bombers score hits on 63 city districts.	Japanese Air Force is ordered to bomb the Burma Road before it is reopened on Oct. 17.	United Kingdom, U.S. and Canada agree to begin construction of defense bases in the Western Hemisphere despite lack of a formal agreement .... U.S. and Canada agree as a defense measure to permit the Ontario hydro-electric system to take more water from the Niagara River.	Prices are frozen in Syria and Lebanon at June 10 levels with threats of harsh reprisals for those who violate the government decree.
Oct. 15		Mussolini decides to launch an attack on Greece from Albania .... German bombers drop 70,000 incendiary bombs on London, starting huge fires .... British announce air attacks on Berlin, Hamburg, Hanover, Goettingen, Lingen and Bothlen.		FDR warns the American republics to be prepared to answer with force if the Hemisphere's peace is threatened.	Street demonstrations in Bangkok support the Thai demand for the return of territory from Indochina.
	A *Includes developments that affect more than one world region, international organizations and important meetings of major world leaders.*	B *Includes all developments in European countries and military engagements between Allied and Axis powers in Africa and at sea.*	C *Includes all developments in Japan and China, Japanese foreign policy and military actions in the Pacific region.*	D *Includes all domestic and regional developments in Latin America, the Caribbean and Canada.*	E *Includes developments in those independent nations and colonial possessions not covered in Columns B, C and D.*

U.S. Politics & Social Issues	U.S. Foreign Policy & Defense	U.S. Economy & Environment	Science, Technology & Nature	Culture, Leisure & Life Style	
	Knox delivers a strong speech condemning the Tripartite Pact as aimed directly at the U.S. He orders all of the Navy's reserves, 27,591 men, to active duty.	Wage-Hour Division of the Labor Dept. announces the 40-hour work-week will take affect Oct. 24.			Oct. 5
Ill. Gov. Henry Horner dies at his home in Chicago . . . . Willkie confers with AFL President Wm. Green in N.Y., but no announcement of what they discuss is made.					Oct. 6
Willkie charges FDR is perpetuating his power "through petty Hitlers" who control Democratic city machines, such as Mayor Frank Hague of Jersey City . . . . Jesse H. Jones denies any conflict of interest in his positions as federal loan administrator and secretary of commerce.					Oct. 7
Senate majority leader Alben Barkley says that the Gavagan anti-lynching bill will not be called for Senate consideration because of an anticipated filibuster . . . . Speaking in N.Y.C., Willkie demands FDR tell the American people whether he has made secret commitments to drag the nation into war.	FDR signs the $1.3 billion Third Supplemental National Defense Appropriations Act.	FDR signs the Excess Profits Tax Bill.		Cincinnati Reds beat the Detroit Tigers 2-1 in the 7th game to win the World Series.	Oct. 8
In a presidential trial heat, the Gallup Poll gives FDR 54.5% and Willkie 45.5% of the votes . . . . National Federation of Constitutional Liberties adopts a protest resolution against the barring of minority parties from election ballots.		FDR signs a bill extending state taxing power to federal areas within the states.			Oct. 9
FDR begins a two-day tour of Ohio and Pennsylvania to confer with political leaders and inspect defense preparations.	Congress authorizes FDR to requisition any material necessary for national defense . . . . State Dept. announces the freezing of Rumanian assets in the U.S., estimated at $100 million . . . . War Secy. Stimson says U.S. defenses in Hawaii will be strengthened in the near future due to the Far Eastern crisis.	FDR suspends the 8-hour workday for the duration of the national emergency for those engaged in work under contracts with the Maritime Commission.	The medical faculty at Stockholm Univ. announces it will not award the Nobel Prize for medicine this year because of the war.	Sir Wilfred Grenfell, who became one of the world's most famous doctors through his autobiographical books about his experiences in Labrador, dies at 75.	Oct. 10
	In an Akron, Ohio speech, FDR expresses confidence that the U.S. will not be brought into the war by an attack on the U.S.		Glenn L. Martin, pioneer plane designer, is named recepient of the 1940 Daniel Guggenheim Medal for notable achievements in aeronautics.		Oct. 11
Willkie charges that the Democrats have made racial and religious slurs against him and his family . . . . Citizens' Committee for Democracy claims to have 10,000 signatures in support of Willkie and FDR debating the campaign issues.	FDR says in Dayton, Ohio that U.S. policy will be total defense of the Western Hemisphere, continued aid to Britain, insistence on the right of peaceful commerce in the Atlantic and the Pacific and no appeasement of dictators . . . . State Dept. ends the suspension of machine tool shipments to the Soviets.		Dr. Robert H. Goddard announces development of a lightweight combustion chamber for use in rockets.	Tom Mix, cowboy and actor in Western movies, is killed in an automobile accident outside of Florence, Arizona.	Oct. 12
		Commerce Dept. reports crude rubber imports in September (78,792 long tons) set a U.S.record.		Benny Goodman signs a contract to play with the New York Philharmonic Symphony Orchestra.	Oct. 13
In a Washington radio address, Col. Charles Lindbergh fails to endorse either candidate but is critical of FDR's policies.	Clarence A. Dykstra, president of the Univ. of Wisconsin, accepts a post as director of the Selective Service System.	Supreme Court upholds the NLRB ruling in the Link-Belt Co. case in favor of the CIO's Amalgamated Assn. of Iron, Tin and Steel Workers . . . . FDR signs a bill prohibiting the entry of convict-made goods into interstate commerce . . . . FDR signs the Wool Products Labelling Act, banning mislabeled wool from interstate and foreign commerce.			Oct. 14
Atty. Gen. Jackson appoints Maurice M. Milligan to conduct a nationwide investigation into frauds in connection with the national elections.	FDR denies Amb. to Britain Joseph P. Kennedy is planning to resign . . . . FDR instructs the Army and Navy Munitions Boards to survey their needs regarding materiel, machinery and other supplies essential for national defense.			Protestant Episcopal Church requires its bishops to retire at 72.	Oct. 15
F *Includes elections, federal-state relations, civil rights and liberties, crime, the judiciary, education, health care, poverty, urban affairs and population.*	G *Includes formation and debate of U.S. foreign and defense policies, veterans affairs and defense spending. (Relations with specific foreign countries are usually found under the region concerned.)*	H *Includes business, labor, agriculture, taxation, transportation, consumer affairs, monetary and fiscal policy, natural resources, pollution and accidents.*	I *Includes worldwide scientific, medical and technological developments, natural phenomena, U.S. weather and natural disasters.*	J *Includes the arts, religion, scholarship, communications media, sports, entertainment, fashions, fads and social life.*	

	World Affairs	European War Zone	Pacific War Zone	The Americas	Other Countries & Territories
Oct. 16		England announces its heaviest bomb attacks yet directed against Kiel and other German fuel storage depots.	Japanese and Dutch reach the outline of an agreement on oil trade after a month of negotiations in the Netherlands East Indies. Japan will get 40% of its oil for the next six months from the NEI.		Vichy government orders authorities in Indochina to resist Thai incursions into Cambodia or Laos . . . . Australian P.M. Robert Menzies meets with leaders of all parties to determine coordination of defense strategy . . . . A cyclone hits Bombay, India, causing extensive damage and 12 deaths.
Oct. 17		Ramon Serrano Suner, who recently returned from visits to Germany and Italy, is named to replace Juan Beigbeder as Spanish foreign minister. Beigbeder has been regarded as pro-British . . . . Tobruk, Libya and Alexandria, Egypt are attacked by German planes.	The Burma Road supply route to China is reopened in defiance of the Japanese.	Panamanian National Assembly receives for consideration a new charter of government based upon unitarian rule from Pres. Arias . . . . Nelson Rockefeller is appointed chairman of the Inter-American Development Commission.	
Oct. 18		Vichy government bars Jews from the press and radio, from teaching professions and from the armed forces . . . . British announce 489,000 children have been evacuated from the London area . . . . German planes bomb Aden at the southern entrance to the Red Sea.	Japanese military authorities claim to have made the Burma Road useless by destruction of a bridge on the Mekong River.		
Oct. 19		German, Russian and Turkish troops are reported massing at strategic positions in the Balkans . . . . Count Victor Karolyi and former premier M. Imredy announce formation of a new party to promote fascist government in Hungary . . . . German high command claims sinking 26 merchant ships in one convoy in the Atlantic.	Britain contracts to purchase all high octane fuel from the NEI in a move to hinder Japanese demands for oil.		
Oct. 20		British and German guns exchange long-range shells in the heaviest cross-channel bombardment of the war . . . . Italian planes attack U.S. and British oilfields and refineries on Bahrein and in Saudi Arabia.			Gen. Hertzog publishes his draft program for the South African Nationalist Party, calling for a republican form of government which will ensure that South Africa will not "again be drawn into Britain's wars."
Oct. 21		Churchill appeals in a radio broadcast to the French not to take up arms against Great Britain . . . . Yugoslavia announces it has concluded a new trade agreement with Germany, providing for large increases in trade.	Japanese Commerce Secy. Ichizo Kobayashi leaves the NEI oil conference for Tokyo.	Mexican government cancels its oil concession to Japan.	
Oct. 22		Hitler confers with French Vice Premier Pierre Laval at Montoire. He promises French interests will be protected at the end of the war, if France collaborates as Laval has promised . . . . German planes concentrate attacks upon Bristol, Glasgow and Liverpool where U.S. war supplies are landed . . . . Italian government justifies its air attack on the island of Bahrein and damage to American oil company property on the grounds that the island supports the British war effort.	Chinese regular and guerrilla forces attack Japanese positions over a 1,500-mile front in northern China . . . . Japan begins a census of all its nationals abroad.	Military talks between U.S. and Uruguayan officers open, sparking charges by nationalists that the Uruguayan government is planning to lease bases to the U.S.	An Advisory National War Council is established by the Australian government . . . . French High Commissioner in Syria Gabriel Puaux promulgates regulations barring Jews from government positions.
Oct. 23		Meeting with Franco at Hendaye on the French-Spanish border, Hitler urges Spain to enter the war and attack Gibraltar. The meeting ends without any firm commitments.	Chinese Army launches a major offensive south of Shanghai . . . . Japanese government places rice under its control, effective Nov. 1.	Honduran government announces the thwarting of a plot to assassinate Pres. Tiburcio Carias Andios.	War Dept. announces dispatch of two squadrons of pursuit planes to the Philippines.
Oct. 24		Hitler meets with Laval and Petain at Montoire. Petain agrees that "the Axis powers and France have an identical interest is seeing the defeat of England accomplished as soon as possible." . . . . Belgian government in exile is re-established in London by Camille Gutt, Hubert Pierlot, and Paul-Henri Spaak.	Chinese sources claim that the Japanese "autumn offensive" in central China has failed with the loss of 10,000 men.		
Oct. 25		Germans advance in northern Norway as Nazi bombers sever Allied supply lines.			New Zealand government bans the Jehovah Witnesses on the grounds that the sect is conducting subversive propaganda.

A	B	C	D	E
Includes developments that affect more than one world region, international organizations and important meetings of major world leaders.	*Includes all developments in European countries and military engagements between Allied and Axis powers in Africa and at sea.*	*Includes all developments in Japan and China, Japanese foreign policy and military actions in the Pacific region.*	*Includes all domestic and regional developments in Latin America, the Caribbean and Canada.*	*Includes developments in those independent nations and colonial possessions not covered in Columns B, C and D.*

U.S. Politics & Social Issues	U.S. Foreign Policy & Defense	U.S. Economy & Environment	Science, Technology & Nature	Culture, Leisure & Life Style	
	All men between 21 and 35 begin to register for the first peactime conscription in U.S. history .... State Dept. announces plans to establish diplomatic relations with Iceland in the near future.			Democratic National Chmn. Flynn charges newspapers throughout the country are controlled by their advertisers and stockholders, a charge quickly refuted by the *New York Times*, *New York Tribune* and *Seattle Times*.	Oct. 16
FDR abandons his "quiet campaign" and announces plans for a tour through five Eastern states beginning Oct. 23.	U.S. requisitions some 100 planes on order from American factories by the Swedish government.				Oct. 17
Sen. Hiram Johnson (Progressive, Calif.) announces his support of the Willkie-McNary ticket, opposing FDR's third term effort .... Willkie tells a Springfiled, Ill. audience that the election of FDR would result in a furtherance of state socialism.	State Secy. Hull issues a statement to all concerned nations that it is best to maintain the status quo in the NEI.				Oct. 18
In a Minneapolis campaign speech, Willkie indicates he would lift crop restrictions imposed by the AAA .... Meeting in Chicago, the national Planning Board of Colored Voters adopts a resolution endorsing Willkie for president.	FDR and Canadian Gov.-Gen. the Earl of Athlone confer at Hyde Park on defense measures .... DAR adopts a resolution asking Congress to take appropriate measures to improve the U.S. defense posture.			C.V. Whitney pays a reported $100,000 for Mahmoud, winner of the English Derby.	Oct. 19
Willkie proposes that FDR debate campaign issues with him on Oct. 30 in Baltimore.	Gallup Poll reports that 90% of Americans favor a ban on the sale of war materials to Japan.				Oct. 20
FDR declines Willkie's bid for a political debate .... Speaking on behalf of FDR in Detroit, Mich., Mayor La Guardia charges that the social security system would be endangered if Willkie is elected president.	State Dept. requests that the Vichy government state its intentions regarding possible involvement in the war against Britain.	A priorities board is established within the National Defense Advisory Commission. FDR appoints Donald Nelson to administer it .... FDR nominates Rep. John J. Dempsey (D, N.M.) to be a member of the Maritime Commission.	Clinical Congress of the American College of Surgeons recommends a detailed plan for having doctors serve in the military without causing hardships at home .... Rockefeller Foundation announces it will make available to Britain a recently developed vaccine to fight influenza in the war zone.		Oct. 21
Although he opposes FDR's campaign for a third term, the former postmaster general and Democratic national chairman, James A. Farley, announces in Chicago he will vote a straight Democratic ticket .... Willkie asserts FDR is "short on the truth" when he tells the American people he will keep the U.S. out of war.		FDR issues an executive order decreeing priority for defense orders within private industry .... A group of 25 growers, shippers and officials of farmers' cooperatives meet with Agriculture Secy. Claude Wickard and officials of the A & P Co. to discuss a proposal for a national farm cooperative to improve food distribution.	A record low temperature of 21 degrees for the day is recorded in N.Y.C.		Oct. 22
FDR delivers a scathing attack on Willkie in a Philadelphia campaign speech, accusing him of at least 32 deliberate distortions of fact .... Speaking at The Herald Forum in N.Y., Willkie declares the New Deal is following the same path that brought destruction to European democracies .... Former Pres. Hoover accuses the New Deal of creating a system which "drifts down the suicide road of national socialism."	Boeing Aircraft delivers the first lot of new Flying Fortresses to the Army Air Force at Dayton, Ohio .... Knox states categorically that the U.S. Navy is "ready to defend" the Philippines.			Walt Disney receives the Progress Medal of the Society of Motion Picture Engineers for his achievements in cartoon movies.	Oct. 23
Communist Party is ruled off the New York State November election ballot for failing to have sufficient valid signatures.		House Appropriations Comm. Chmn. Edward Taylor (D, Colo.) reports Congress has broken a peacetime record by appropriating $25,572,819,337 this session .... National Council of Farmer Cooperatives attack the A & P Co. for attempting to form a "super cooperative" among growers.			Oct. 24
Charging that FDR will create a dictatorship if re-elected, John L. Lewis announces his support of Wendell Willkie.	FDR warns Petain that if the French fleet is allowed to fall into German hands, the U.S. will regard it as a "flagrant and deliberate breach of faith" .... Britain requests U.S. permission to place orders for some 12,000 additional planes with American factories.				Oct. 25
F	G	H	I	J	
Includes elections, federal-state relations, civil rights and liberties, crime, the judiciary, education, health care, poverty, urban affairs and population.	*Includes formation and debate of U.S. foreign and defense policies, veterans affairs and defense spending. (Relations with specific foreign countries are usually found under the region concerned.)*	*Includes business, labor, agriculture, taxation, transportation, consumer affairs, monetary and fiscal policy, natural resources, pollution and accidents.*	*Includes worldwide scientific, medical and technological developments, natural phenomena, U.S. weather and natural disasters.*	*Includes the arts, religion, scholarship, communications media, sports, entertainment, fashions, fads and social life.*	

	World Affairs	European War Zone	Pacific War Zone	The Americas	Other Countries & Territories
Oct. 26		Italian government accuses Greece of sponsoring armed attacks on the Albanian border and terrorist plots in Porto Edda . . . . Marshal Petain announces Vichy's support, in principle, of Hitler's aims in a European peace . . . . Count Ciano and Laval confer at Vichy to discuss Hitler's "Pan-European bloc" and plans to force Britain to make peace.	Tokyo reports indicate Japan is willing to make many concessions to Russia in order to remove Russian pressure from the Far East.		Government of India announces a ban on the publication of any statements opposing the British war effort.
Oct. 27				Gen. Juan Andrew Almazon, in exile in New York, declares he will take the Mexican presidency by Dec. 1.	
Oct. 28		Italian troops invade Greece across the Albanian border. Athens is bombed . . . . Hitler confers with Mussolini and Ciano at Florence to report on his his meetings with Franco and Petain . . . . In their longest flight to date, RAF bombers hit German munitions plants in the Bohemian-Moravian Protectorate.	Chinese forces retake Nanning, former capital of Kwangsi Province.	Mexican federal troops engage Almazanista rebel forces in the state of Chiapas.	
Oct. 29	Japanese cabinet explains it is not responsible under the Axis Pact terms to commit itself to the Near Eastern theater of war.	Rome radio reports the Italian Army has moved 40 miles inside the Greek border. Other reports claim Greek troops are offering stubborn resistance.		Mexican Pres. Cardenas says that any accord with the U.S. will provide for naval and air bases in Mexico.	Australian War Council is sworn in at Melbourne.
Oct. 30		Athens claims the Italian advance is making little progress, but Italy announces the capture of the town of Breznica, opening the main route to Salonika on the Aegean Sea . . . . Greek Premier John Metaxas says British help has been better than expected, with British marines landing in Greece, the British fleet mining the coast and RAF pilots reportedly landing in northern Greece . . . . Franz von Papen, German ambassador to Turkey, suddenly leaves Ankara for Berlin after a long conversation with Dr. Refik Saydam, the Turkish premier.		Brazil is reported to have banned the export of beef because of a meat shortage in Rio de Janeiro due to a long drought and large beef exports to Europe.	
Oct. 31		Pierre Laval, French vice premier, declares democracy is dead all over the world and expresses hope for Britain's defeat.	Japanese troops abandon the whole of Kwangsi Province in southern China.		Nehru is arrested and charged with violating the Defense of India Rules by making speeches intended to hinder prosecution of the war.
Nov. 1		British forces land at Suda Bay on Crete to aid the Greek resistance to Italy . . . . Conflicting British and Italian communiques indicate a fierce air battle is in progress in Egypt . . . . Pres. Ismet Inonu declares Turkey will remain neutral in the Greco-Italian conflict, follow the lead of Russia and hold fast to her mutual defense treaty with Britain.	More than 200 Americans leave Shanghai on the *S.S. President Pierce* at the request of the U.S. government.		
Nov. 2		According to unconfirmed reports from Bucharest, Soviet Russia has massed 31 divisions, or 558,000 men, and mechanized equipment in Bessarabia and Northern Bukovina . . . . Greek troops are reported driving through the mountains into Albania, threatening the Italians in the rear, while British and Greek fliers bomb Albania's capital, Tirana.		Mexican rebels and their leaders, including the self-styled slayer of Pancho Villa, surrender in the state of Chihuahua, ending all rebellious activities, according to an official military announcement.	
	A *Includes developments that affect more than one world region, international organizations and important meetings of major world leaders.*	B *Includes all developments in European countries and military engagements between Allied and Axis powers in Africa and at sea.*	C *Includes all developments in Japan and China, Japanese foreign policy and military actions in the Pacific region.*	D *Includes all domestic and regional developments in Latin America, the Caribbean and Canada.*	E *Includes developments in those independent nations and colonial possessions not covered in Columns B, C and D.*

U.S. Politics & Social Issues	U.S. Foreign Policy & Defense	U.S. Economy & Environment	Science, Technology & Nature	Culture, Leisure & Life Style	
	Speaking to the National Press Club in Washington, State Secy. Hull says the world's dictators do not intend to stop with conquests in Europe and Asia.				Oct. 26
Wilkie offers a 6-point housing program calling for government and private industry cooperation in slum clearance and housing projects and elimination of duplicity in government agencies dealing with the problem.		*New York Times* reports 150 industrial companies have increased earnings by 31.9% in the first nine months of 1940 from the same period in 1939.		New York World's Fair closes.	Oct. 27
FDR castigates the GOP as the party of "Martin, Barton and Fish" before an enthusiastic crowd of supporters at Madison Square Garden in N.Y. He charges the GOP has tried to sabotage his plans for national defense.		Supreme Court orders Montgomery Ward to give to the Wage-Hour Division of the Labor Dept. records of some 2,000 of its Kansas City employes.			Oct. 28
Amb.-to-Britain Joseph P. Kennedy calls for the re-election of FDR in an N.Y. radio speech.	First U.S. peacetime compulsory service is inaugurated when War Secy. Henry L. Stimson draws numbers at the War Dept. auditorium.			American Olympic Comm. officially disbands with over $110,000 in unspent funds.	Oct. 29
Willkie predicts that if FDR is elected "on the basis of his past performance with pledges to the people, you may expect war by April 1941." Replying in a Boston speech, FDR promises, "Your boys are not going to be sent into any foreign wars." .... Henry Wallace, Democratic vice presidential candidate, tells an American Labor Party rally in New York that "millions of Americans know from personal observation that there is Nazi propaganda and Nazi pressure for the election of the Republican candidate." .... John L. Lewis says the New Deal "is as dead as a dodo." .... Joe Louis, heavyweight boxing champion, urges the election of Willkie because he "will help my people."	The draft lottery in Washington ends at 5:47 a.m. after 17½ hours of drawing .... A fire of unknown origin destroys the top floor of the four-story War Dept. building in Washington, but Army code books and other secret records are saved.	It is revealed that carpenters must pay an $80 union "initiation fee" to work at Fort Dix, N.J., a $75 fee at Fort Edwards, Mass., and $55 at Fort Meade, Md. with no refunds in case of dismissal.		Harvey D. Gibson, chairman of the N.Y. World's Fair board of directors, announces that 3,000 bondholders will get 39.2 cents on the dollar.	Oct. 30
Mrs. Earl Browder, wife of the Communist presidential candidate, is ordered by Atty. Gen. Robert Jackson to be deported to Russia because of her "surreptitious entry" into the U.S. in 1933 .... Dedicating the $4-million National Health Institute in Bethesda, Md., FDR says that the government does not intend to socialize medical practice.	Treasury Secy. Morgenthau discloses Great Britain has ordered "a large number" of freighters from United States shipyards to offset U-boat losses.		Sulfaguanidine, a derivative of sulfanilamide, devised by Dr. E. Kennerly Marshall, is announced as a cure for bacterial dysentery, a common disease among troops in the tropics.	Hollywood film industry pledges its entire facilities to the Army for the production of movies to be used in training draftees.	Oct. 31
Roosevelt charges that "the extreme reactionary and the extreme radical elements of this country" have formed an "unholy alliance" to elect Willkie. He also alleges that "something evil is happening in this country" when a full-page Republican advertisement appears in the Communist *Daily Worker* .... Willkie, campaigning in New Jersey, says "we should stop fooling ourselves with talk about rapidly reaching a goal of fifty thousand planes annually." .... Final figures for the Willkie personal campaign tour of the nation show that he traveled nearly 30,000 miles by train, plane and auto, visited 31 states and made 540 speeches, making it the longest tour in the history of U.S. politics.				Ken Overlin retains the middleweight championship by winning a 15-round decision over Steve Belloise in N.Y.	Nov. 1
Willkie declares in his final major campaign speech in N.Y. that the greatest issue of the election is "the preservation of the free way of life in America."	FDR says his foreign policy is to keep the U.S. out of war and give all possible material aid to the nations that resist aggression.		G.T. Baker, president of National Airlines, flies a Lockheed-Lodestar plane with five passengers from Burbank, Calif., to Jacksonville, Fla., in nine hours, 29 minutes, 30½ seconds, claiming a transcontinental speed record for transport planes with passengers .... Alexander P. de Seversky obtains a patent for a new type of pursuit plane having a tricycle landing gear, four propellers, a sealed cabin, an engine in the rear and mounting six machine guns and one cannon.	Robert Woods Bliss donates his Dumbarton Oaks Research Library and Collection, containing medieval and Byzantine treasures, to Harvard Univ.	Nov. 2

F	G	H	I	J
Includes elections, federal-state relations, civil rights and liberties, crime, the judiciary, education, health care, poverty, urban affairs and population.	*Includes formation and debate of U.S. foreign and defense policies, veterans affairs and defense spending. (Relations with specific foreign countries are usually found under the region concerned.)*	*Includes business, labor, agriculture, taxation, transportation, consumer affairs, monetary and fiscal policy, natural resources, pollution and accidents.*	*Includes worldwide scientific, medical and technological developments, natural phenomena, U.S. weather and natural disasters.*	*Includes the arts, religion, scholarship, communications media, sports, entertainment, fashions, fads and social life.*

	World Affairs	European War Zone	Pacific War Zone	The Americas	Other Countries & Territories
Nov. 3		Greek troops advance towards the Italian base of Koritza in Albania .... A looting epidemic stirs London to action with newspapers suggesting that looters be hanged.			A typhoon strikes Guam, causing heavy property and crop damage.
Nov. 4		Vichy government reportedly informs the U.S. that France will not go to war against Britain, give up her fleet to Germany or yield her West Indies colonies .... Manuel Azana, 60, ex-president of Spain, dies at Montauban, France, where he fled when Franco's troops closed in on Madrid.	According to reports from Hong Kong, Kwangsi Province has been entirely abandoned and Chinese troops are said to be approaching Yamchow, the Kwantung Province port through which the Japanese in Kwangsi were supplied.	The body of Richard von Heynitz, German charge d'affaires to San Salvador, El Salvador, is found dead with a bullet in the right temple. Authorities believe it a suicide .... Five U.S. Army and civil technicians arrive in Hamilton, Bermuda, to survey sites for American naval and air bases.	
Nov. 5		Greeks claim to have taken the Albanian town of Koritza and to have surrounded an Italian division that is being supplied with food dropped from Italian planes .... Highly reliable sources, according to a UP dispatch, report Axis powers have lined up Bulgaria on their side with the promise of a corridor to the Aegean Sea and other territorial concessions .... British Admirality learns the German battleship *Admiral Scheer* is loose in the Atlantic when it sinks the merchant cruiser *Jervis Bay*.	Japanese government outlines a 10-year program to make Japan self-sufficient.		Japan decides to back Thailand's claims on French territory in Indochina on condition that Thailand cooperates with Tokyo in the creation of a New Order in East Asia .... Nehru is sentenced in Gorakhpur, India, to "four years of rigorous imprisonment" under the Defense of India Act.
Nov. 6		London has its 300th alarm and suffers one of the most destructive bombings of the war, lasting for nearly 14 hours .... British bomber squadrons begin arriving in Greece .... Yugoslav reports say Greek troops have surrounded five Italian regiments and are attempting to force their surrender.		Reports indicate accords have been reached with virtually all Latin American republics for the use of naval and air bases .... U.S. forms a committee on communications, chaired by Nelson A. Rockefeller, to spend more than $3 million from the President's special defense fund for cultural activities in Latin America to fight Nazi propaganda .... Chile claims all Antarctic territory between 53 and 90 degrees West Longtitude, including the base established by Adm. Richard E. Byrd.	Gen. J.B.M. Hertzog, former South African premier and opposition leader who advocated a separate peace with Germany, resigns as leader of the reunited Nationalist Party.
Nov. 7		Reports from the 100-mile-long mountainous front on the Greek-Albanian border indicate that the Italians have started their main attack after stemming the Greek advance in the north and south, while Greek troops have beaten back an Italian column in the middle sector near Yanina.	Japanese military mission in Indochina protests to the French governor general against "increasing activities of anti-Japanese elements." .... According to London reports, an understanding has been reached in principle by the U.S., Britain and Australia regarding defense cooperation in the Pacific and possible U.S. use of the British naval base at Singapore.		
Nov. 8		Eden returns from Cairo and presents Gen. Wavell's plans for a major offensive against the Italians to Churchill .... Speaking in Munich, Hitler emphasizes his "unalterable determination to continue the struggle to a clear decision .... [and] .... reject any compromise." .... Germany claims the sinking of an entire British convoy of 15 to 20 ships .... Yugoslavia makes representations to the British, Italian and Greek governments regarding the bombing of Bitolj in southern Macedonia by "unknown planes" on Nov. 5.			
Nov. 9		Neville Chamberlain, 71, former British prime minister, dies in Odiham, England .... A Greek report says that Italy's famous Centaur Division of 15,000 men, trapped by Greek troops in the Pindus Mountain region, has surrendered.	Japanese authorities take over the head office of the Central Bank of China in Shanghai.	Uruguay reaches an agreement with the U.S. for the establishment of naval and air bases on the Uruguayan coast.	After conquering Lambarene in the interior of Gabon, French Equatorial Africa, Free French forces headed by Gen. Charles de Gaulle land near Libreville, Gabon's most important seaport.
Nov. 10		Rumania suffers the worst earthquake in its history, which results in a thousand deaths and extensive property damage .... Italian Under-Secy. of War Gen. Ubaldo Soddu, replaces Gen. Prasca as commander-in-chief of Italian troops in Albania.	China Aid Council, composed of American groups, protests to Roosevelt against the shipment of "war supplies, including finished steel and machine tools, to Japan, contrary to the principles implied in the embargo."		

A	B	C	D	E
Includes developments that affect more than one world region, international organizations and important meetings of major world leaders.	*Includes all developments in European countries and military engagements between Allied and Axis powers in Africa and at sea.*	*Includes all developments in Japan and China, Japanese foreign policy and military actions in the Pacific region.*	*Includes all domestic and regional developments in Latin America, the Caribbean and Canada.*	*Includes developments in those independent nations and colonial possessions not covered in Columns B, C and D.*

U.S. Politics & Social Issues	U.S. Foreign Policy & Defense	U.S. Economy & Environment	Science, Technology & Nature	Culture, Leisure & Life Style	
Willkie announces that if elected president he will recommend a Constitutional Amendment limiting the time any one president may serve to eight years or less . . . . Justice Dept. announces 2,559,706 of the 3.6 million aliens believed to be in the U.S. have registered.		Bureau of Agricultural Economics reports that prices of farm products are higher than in 1939 and estimates 1940 cash farm income at $9 billion, the second highest since 1929.	Harvard zoologists exhibit a mounted specimen of the kouprey, a kind of wild ox from Indochina, said to be the first new genus of large living mammals discovered in 40 years.		Nov. 3
A federal grand jury investigating the election campaign in the Philadelphia area subpoenas the records of 20 banks . . . . Willkie declares in a N.Y. broadcast to "the women of America" that as president he will keep the country out of foreign wars.					Nov. 4
FDR is elected president of the U.S. for a third term, defeating the GOP candidate, Wendell L. Willkie, by a 10% margin in the popular vote, shattering the two-term tradition. Democrats lose four Senate seats but gain eight House seats.	Navy allots $23 million in contracts for construction of naval and air bases in the U.S., Cuba, Puerto Rico, Alaska and the Philippines.	Gates W. McGarrah, 77, known on Wall Street as Silent Gates McGarrah, one of America's greatest financial diagnosticians, dies in New York of pneumonia.		Baseball Writers Assn. chooses Hank Greenberg, Detroit outfielder, as the AL's most valuable player of 1940.	Nov. 5
Willkie concedes defeat in the presidential election and says "I extend my thanks to the thousands who . . . . worked for my election . . . . and supported me. I know that they will continue, as I shall, to work for the unity of our people in the completion of our defense effort, in sending aid to Britain and in insistence upon removal of antagonisms in America."	Selective Service reports that several hundred thousand men have volunteered for a year's military service, making it unlikely that conscription will be needed to fill the first quota.	War Dept. awards a $122,323,020 contract for more than 4,000 Pratt & Whitney airplane engines to the Ford Motor Co. at Dearborn, Mich. It is the first defense contract given to Ford and one of the largest yet made.			Nov. 6
		Treasury Secy. Morgenthau announces FDR will soon ask Congress to adopt a financial program that will include raising the debt limit to $60-65 billion and passage of new defense taxes . . . . Following Morgenthau's statement on the national debt limit, prices jump one to eight points on the NYSE as Wall Street talks of inflation.	The $6-million Tacoma Narrows Bridge, nicknamed "Galloping Gertie," completed last July, collapses in a 42-mile-an-hour wind and falls into Puget Sound 190 feet below. No one is injured.		Nov. 7
Dr. George Gallup notes a reduction of the Democratic majority throughout the nation from 62.5% in 1936 to 54.5% in 1940, with the Midwest becoming the new GOP stronghold . . . . Oren Root Jr., head of the Associated Willkie Clubs of America, indicates that Willkie is laying plans for the creation of a strong opposition party to act as a check on the New Deal.	FDR discloses that he has established a rule of thumb under which Britain and Canada will get 50% of all new American warplanes and war materials. He denies any arrangements have been made with the British for use of the naval base at Singapore . . . . War Dept. announces that about 400,000 men, who will be called into service by March 15, 1941, will be sent directly to regular Army or National Guard units.	CIO N.Y. State Industrial Union Council describes the national election as a "complete repudiation" of John L. Lewis and demands that he resign as president of the CIO.	Agriculture Dept. announces a 23-year campaign has practically eradicated bovine tuberculosis in the U.S.		Nov. 8
	War Dept. discloses that new dive bombers are being delivered to the Army Air Corps by the Douglas Aircraft Co.	California State Supreme Court denies a rehearing in the Howard automobile case decision, which held the closed shop to be legal, upheld the secondary boycott and declared that courts have no right to enjoin peaceful picketing . . . . Samuel J. Mustain, former president of the Continental Securities Corp., is found guilty by a federal jury of having defrauded investors of more than $1 million through the sale of oil royalties and securities.		An overflow audience in Carnegie Hall, N.Y. refuses to leave after Serge Rachmaninoff completes his piano recital and applauds so vociferously that the Russian maestro returns to play for another half hour . . . . Mexican Army team wins the International Low-Score Challenge Trophy at the National Horse Show in N.Y.	Nov. 9
Sen. Key Pittman (D, Nev.), chairman of the Senate Foreign Relations Comm., dies in Reno at 68. He was first elected to the Senate in 1912.		Chairman of the New York Triborough Bridge Authority Robert Moses proposes construction of four major highways in the metroploitan area at a cost of $65,000,000 to facilitate the defense of the city in wartime.		Gerard Cote wins the 6th annual Yonkers Marathon for the National A.A.U. championship, covering the 26 miles 385 yards in 2:34:06.2.	Nov. 10
F *Includes elections, federal-state relations, civil rights and liberties, crime, the judiciary, education, health care, poverty, urban affairs and population.*	G *Includes formation and debate of U.S. foreign and defense policies, veterans affairs and defense spending. (Relations with specific foreign countries are usually found under the region concerned.)*	H *Includes business, labor, agriculture, taxation, transportation, consumer affairs, monetary and fiscal policy, natural resources, pollution and accidents.*	I *Includes worldwide scientific, medical and technological developments, natural phenomena, U.S. weather and natural disasters.*	J *Includes the arts, religion, scholarship, communications media, sports, entertainment, fashions, fads and social life.*	

	World Affairs	European War Zone	Pacific War Zone	The Americas	Other Countries & Territories
Nov. 11	Several countries pause for the customary two-minute observance of the anniversary of the ending of W.W. I.	British carrier planes cripple half the Italian fleet in an attack on Taranto.			Thailand agrees to moderate its demands on French Indochina in exchange for Japanese promise of mediation .... Japanese reports from Indochina say Rear Adm. Jean Decoux has resigned as governor general of the French colony.
Nov. 12		USSR Premier Molotov and Hitler have a 3-hour conference in Berlin although no official announcement is made .... According to Greek reports, the Italians are being routed all along the front.	Japanese and Dutch NEI officials sign contracts to assure supply of oil and other raw materials to Japan.	Gen. Manuel Avila Camacho, president-elect of Mexico, is formally recognized by the U.S. when FDR designates Vice Pres.-elect Henry A. Wallace to represent him at Camacho's inaugural in Mexico City on Dec. 1 .... Restrictions placed in September on the export of wheat and wheat flour are lifted by Argentina now that a surplus of 74 million bushels appears probable .... U.S. and Canadian authorities complete a two-day conference at Ottawa, Ont. on the simplification of border crossing for citizens of both countries.	
Nov. 13			Royal Dutch, Japanese Mitsui and American Standard-Vacuum oil companies sign an agreement in Batavia, NEI, under which Japan will receive 1.8 million tons of oil annually .... Japanese troops are reported standing by at Hainan, Haiphong and Kwangchow awaiting orders for new war operations in Southern Asia, presumably in French Indochina or the NEI.	Gen. Juan Almazan, self-styled president-elect of Mexico, denies in N.Y. receiving Axis support in his attempts to obtain the presidency of Mexico .... Government of Martinique announces the "consolidation of good relations" with the U.S. following Rear Adm. John W. Greenslade's visit from Nov. 2 to Nov. 5.	
Nov. 14		German bombers subject the city of Coventry to a 10-hour blitz, setting most of the city afire, destroying its 500-year-old cathedral and causing more than 600 casualties .... Soviet Premier Molotov leaves Berlin with his entire staff 48 hours after his arrival, reportedly without signing any agreement .... War communiques claim the Greek Army has begun a general advance along the entire Italian front, with British and Greek fliers supporting Greek infantry.	The naval base at Surabaya, NEI is reportedly being enlarged to hold capital ships.		Premier Hassan Sabry Pasha of Egypt collapses and dies at the opening session of Parliament at Cairo .... British announce the appointment of Air Chief Sir Robert Brooks-Popham as supreme commander of British forces in the Far East with headquarters at Singapore.
Nov. 15			The people of the NEI donate 650,000 pounds for bombers and fighters for Britain.	Turibio Olasso, Uruguay's minister of public instruction and social welfare, resigns in Montevideo in protest against the negotiations with the U.S. on naval bases.	King Farouk of Egypt names Hussein Sirry Pasha, former minister of communications and public works, as premier.
Nov. 16		Reports from the front say that the Italian troops are abandoning Koritza in Albania .... Moscow papers publish the two-year-old treaty between Germany and Slovakia, indicating recognition of the German protectorate over this segment of former Czechoslovakia.			
Nov. 17		Britain's Air Chief Marshal Sir Hugh C.T. Dowding is relieved of his duties and assigned to Lord Beaverbrook, minister of aircraft production, for special service in the U.S. .... Gen. Maurice Gustave Gamelin and former Premiers Leon Blum and Edouard Daladier are arrested and brought to the detention center at Bourrasol. They are charged with responsibility for the French defeat .... Hitler confers with King Boris of Bulgaria at Berchtesgaden in an attempt to bring Bulgaria into the Tripartite Pact.		Twenty-one twin-engine Douglas bombers, comprising the 9th Bombardment Group, leave for the Panama Canal Zone.	Japanese press charges a secret pact between Thailand, Britain and the U.S. was signed or is about to be signed, which offers Thailand economic assistance if she retains her neutrality, and help in regaining lost territory in Indochina .... A "United National Front" is formed in Tel Aviv by Pinchas Rutenberg, with the purpose of securing the unity of Palestine Jewry.
	A *Includes developments that affect more than one world region, international organizations and important meetings of major world leaders.*	B *Includes all developments in European countries and military engagements between Allied and Axis powers in Africa and at sea.*	C *Includes all developments in Japan and China, Japanese foreign policy and military actions in the Pacific region.*	D *Includes all domestic and regional developments in Latin America, the Caribbean and Canada.*	E *Includes developments in those independent nations and colonial possessions not covered in Columns B, C and D.*

U.S. Politics & Social Issues	U.S. Foreign Policy & Defense	U.S. Economy & Environment	Science, Technology & Nature	Culture, Leisure & Life Style	
Eleven men die and 52 others become seriously ill after eating pancakes containing roach powder at a Salvation Army Social Service Center in Pittsburgh, Pa., believed to be the revenge of a discharged cook who threatened to get even .... Willkie says that people should support FDR but a "vital element in the balanced operation of democracy is a strong, alert and watchful opposition."	Amb. Kennedy repudiates an interview published in the *Boston Globe* Nov. 9 which quoted him as having said that democracy is finished in Britain.	John L. Lewis appoints the resolutions, credentials, constitution, appeals, and rules committees for the annual CIO convention in Atlantic City assuring that he will control the Nov. 18 meeting.	Twenty-two persons are killed by tornadoes and blizzards that sweep eastward from the Rocky Mountains to the Appalachians and from Canada to the Gulf of Mexico.	Dr. Frank W. Taussig, 80, noted political economist, a founder of the Harvard Graduate School of Business Administration, dies at Cambridge, Mass.	Nov. 11
Oren Root Jr., head of the 10,000 Associated Willkie Clubs, announces that the Clubs will be continued as a part of the "loyal opposition."		U.S. Supreme Court rules 6 to 2 that the NLRB has no power to force the Republic Steel Corp. to reimburse work relief agencies for wages paid to strikers in the 1937 "Little Steel" strike .... Fourteen persons are killed and 23 injured in three separate power plant explosions in the East. Sabotage is suspected.		Alice Marble, women's amateur tennis champion unbeaten in three years, signs a $25,000 professional contract.	Nov. 12
N.Y.C. Board of Education adopts the Coudert-McLaughlin Law, which permits principals to release public school children from their classrooms an hour a week for outside religious instruction at their parents' request.	State Under Secy. Welles states the U.S. "has never sought directly or indirectly" to obtain bases in Uruguay .... U.S. Amb.-to-France William C. Bullitt submits his resignation.			*Fantasia*, a full-length musical cartoon produced by Walt Disney, opens in N.Y. with Leopold Stokowski conducting the score, and Mickey Mouse in the starring role .... Frank McCormick, 1st baseman of the Cincinnati Reds, is chosen by the Baseball Writers Assn. as the most valuable player in the NL for 1940 .... For the second year in succession, the U.S. Army team wins the International Military Perpetual Challenge Trophy in the final event at the National Horse Show in N.Y.	Nov. 13
	In a Boston speech, Knox describes the war as "an irreconcilable conflict which must be fought out to a finish." He urges "every possible degree of aid" to Britain. He says Hitler is "a fanatic, greedy for world domination."			American Academy of Arts and Letters awards the Howells Medal for Fiction to Ellen Glasgow for the most distinguished work of American fiction in the past five years .... Joe McCarthy, N.Y. Yankees manager, signs a three-year contract for a reported $35,000 a year.	Nov. 14
Edward DeRoulhac Blount, former Census Bureau employe who threatened FDR's life, is sentenced in Washington to two to six years in jail.	FDR formally proclaims the existence of a state of war between Greece and Italy and applies the neutrality statutes .... Former Pres. Hoover urges immediate aid to "the five little democracies" of Finland, Norway, the Netherlands, Belgium and central Poland in order to prevent famine and epidemic diseases.	FDR names Dr. Harry A. Millis to succeed J. Warren Madden as chairman of the NLRB .... United Auto Workers union calls a strike at the Vultee Aircraft Company plant at Downey, Calif., halting work on $80,000,000 worth of military aircraft .... SEC announces two new rules under the Securities Exchange Act of 1934, prohibiting members of national securities exchanges and other brokers and dealers from pledging customers' securities as collateral effective Feb. 17, 1941.		Ethel Merman, Broadway singer, marries William B. Smith, manager of a film actors agency, in Elkton, Md.	Nov. 15
CP votes to dissolve its affiliation with the Communist International in order to remove itself from the terms of the so-called Voorhis Act, which requires groups under foreign control to register with the Justice Dept.	Navy officials disclose that the new 35,000-ton dreadnoughts *North Carolina* and *Washington* will be completed several months early, giving the Navy 17 battleships or the strongest battle line in the world .... An official compilation shows the War Dept. since July 1 has awarded contracts totaling more than $4.5 billion.		FCC approves the expenditure of $3 million on research and experimentation in 10 television projects.	Delegates to the 17th annual convention of the National Board of Review of Motion Pictures in N.Y. unanimously recommend films to stress the "social behavior and idealism of our youth."	Nov. 16
		Army pilots drive through a picket line without disturbance at the struck Vultee Aircraft plant at Downey, Calif. and fly 17 completed BT-13 basic training planes to Moffett Field, Sunnyvale .... CIO Pres. John L. Lewis warns that "the whole economy of the United States has been changed from a peace economy to a war economy" and that the economy may collapse when the war period comes to an end.		Eric Gill, the world-famous British writer on aesthetics and designer of type fonts, dies at 58 .... NBC announces the extension of rebroadcasting rights to include 20 Latin American republics "to speed the development of Pan-American solidarity."	Nov. 17
F *Includes elections, federal-state relations, civil rights and liberties, crime, the judiciary, education, health care, poverty, urban affairs and population.*	G *Includes formation and debate of U.S. foreign and defense policies, veterans affairs and defense spending. (Relations with specific foreign countries are usually found under the region concerned.)*	H *Includes business, labor, agriculture, taxation, transportation, consumer affairs, monetary and fiscal policy, natural resources, pollution and accidents.*	I *Includes worldwide scientific, medical and technological developments, natural phenomena, U.S. weather and natural disasters.*	J *Includes the arts, religion, scholarship, communications media, sports, entertainment, fashions, fads and social life.*	

	World Affairs	European War Zone	Pacific War Zone	The Americas	Other Countries & Territories
Nov. 18		Italy admits bombing Bitolj (Monastir) in Yugoslavia by mistake on Nov. 5 and agrees to pay indemnity for the 19 persons killed and 33 wounded .... Italian Premier Mussolini states the "Greeks hate Italy as no other people" and that Italy "will break Greece's back." .... British government orders British holders of 140 major U.S. stocks and bonds issues to sell them to the Treasury at once in order to help pay for war orders in the U.S.		Chilean Chamber of Deputies adjourns in an uproar, refusing to approve the agenda, after Conservative Deputy Sergei Fernandez presents a bill to suppress the CP.	Alleged secret British-U.S. pact with Thailand announced by Japan is denied in London and Washington.
Nov. 19		Swiss government orders dissolution of the Swiss National Movement and two other pro-Nazi groups.		Joint Canadian-American Defense Board opposes U.S. acquisition of bases in Canada but urges Canada to build facilities at once that could be used by U.S. forces in the event of an attack on Canada.	
Nov. 20		Hungary joins the Tripartite Pact .... Hungary's export trade, seriously affected by the war, causes the country to stop the transfer of interest payments on its foreign debts, effective Oct. 15.	Chinese reports indicate China will reject any Japanese peace proposals that would alter its alignment with Britain and the U.S. against Axis aggression.	More than 200,000 Puerto Ricans register for U.S. military service despite an appeal from the Nationalist Party not to do so.	
Nov. 21		Roosevelt denies that the Norden bomb sight, America's best, has been released to Great Britain but confirms that the Sperry bomb sight has been released as more or less obsolete .... Rome announces the capture of British Air Marshal Owen Tudor Boyd when his plane, en route to Cairo, was forced down in Sicily.	Removal of American women and children from the NEI is reported almost completed.		Nearly 1,800 Jewish immigrants who arrived in Palestine without legal status are being held on two ships and will be sent by the British to a British colony since military interests preclude "illegal entry" in that country .... The war budget introduced in the House of Representatives in Canberra shows that 20% of Australia's national income will be devoted to the war effort.
Nov. 22		Greek troops pursuing Italians take the town of Koritza, 12 miles inside Albania, after 10 days of sustained fighting .... Yugoslavia, encouraged by the Greek successes, will not consider joining the Axis, a semi-official source states in Belgrade.		After the Uruguayan Senate passes a resolution opposing the cession of bases to any foreign countries, Pres. Alfredo Baldemir says that the executive will continue to conduct its own foreign policy.	
Nov. 23		Rumania formally joins the Axis.	Chinese dispatches claim 20,000 Japanese troops are moving out of the Yangtze River valley to Shanghai, allegedly for transportation to Formosa, while Japan orders mobilization of her naval reservists.		
Nov. 24		A German semi-official publication warns Greece that it is playing a dangerous game by "spreading the war" in the Balkans as a tool of Britain .... Slovakia signs a protocol of allegiance to the Axis powers .... Viscount Craigavon, 69, premier of Northern Ireland since 1921, dies at Glencraig, near Belfast. He had consistently opposed home rule and the establishment of a United Irish Republic.	Prince Kimmochi Saioji, last of the Genro, or "Elder Statesmen" associated with Emperor Meiji, dies in Okitsu, Japan.	Some 25,000 Cuban workers demand that Pres. Fulgencio Batista accord the Confederation of Cuban Workers legal status in the new constitution.	
	A *Includes developments that affect more than one world region, international organizations and important meetings of major world leaders.*	B *Includes all developments in European countries and military engagements between Allied and Axis powers in Africa and at sea.*	C *Includes all developments in Japan and China, Japanese foreign policy and military actions in the Pacific region.*	D *Includes all domestic and regional developments in Latin America, the Caribbean and Canada.*	E *Includes developments in those independent nations and colonial possessions not covered in Columns B, C and D.*

U.S. Politics & Social Issues	U.S. Foreign Policy & Defense	U.S. Economy & Environment	Science, Technology & Nature	Culture, Leisure & Life Style	
Chmn. Martin Dies of the House Committee on Un-American Activities announces in Chicago his agents have raided the offices of "Italian and German organizations" in Chicago, New York and other cities, seizing their files.	Navy announces that Britain and the U.S. have agreed upon the exact sites for American air and naval bases at Newfoundland, Bermuda, the Bahamas, Jamaica, Antigua, St. Lucia and British Guiana, traded to the U.S. in exchange for destroyers in September.	Lewis tells the CIO convention in Atlantic City that he will resign as president .... Supreme Court rules unanimously that federal courts have no power to grant injunctions against picketing in labor disputes .... RFC announces it will finance defense plant construction or expansion at a $1\frac{1}{2}$% interest rate.		Wm. Henderson (Red) Friesell, referee of the Dartmouth-Cornell game at Hanover, N.H., on Nov. 16, admits he gave Cornell a fifth down on which the previously undefeated and united team scored a touchdown with a foward pass with seconds to play to win 7-3.	Nov. 18
House of Representatives rejects Majority Leader John W. McCormack's resolution to adjourn.	Gallup Poll reports 54% of voters interviewed in a survey favor amending the Johnson Act to make loans available to Britain.	Lewis tells the CIO convention labor unity is impossible until the CIO has strength comparable with the AFL .... FDR appeals for labor unity in a message to the AFL convention in New Orleans.	Dr. Richard B. Goldschmidt, professor of zoology at the Univ. of California, announces a new theory of evolution contending that organic changes occur by rapid "leaps," or mutations rather than by a gradual process, as Darwin had maintained.		Nov. 19
Harriet Stanton Blatch, former leader of the radical wing of the women's suffrage movement in the U.S., dies at Greenwich, Conn.	U.S. and Britain agree on a partial standardization of weapons and a pool of technical knowledge .... Navy Secy. Frank Knox announces U.S. patrol planes are now operating from Bermuda .... Dies Comm. on Un-American Activities releases a White Paper alleging that German agents in the U.S. engaged in propaganda, espionage, economic penetration and activities designed to strain U.S.-Japanese relations.	Sidney Hillman, president of the Amalgamated Clothing Workers of America, tells the CIO convention that his union will remain in the congress .... Rep. Robert L. Doughton, chairman of the House Ways and Means Comm., says after a conference with Roosevelt that the next Congress will be asked to pass new taxes "at least to meet the regular expenses of the government."			Nov. 20
		Lewis resigns as head of the CIO, as he said he would if FDR won reelection. He is succeeded by Philip Murray .... CIO convention, with only a few delegates refusing to vote, unanimously approves a resolution which denounces Nazism, Communism and Fascism .... David Dubinsky, president of the ILGWU, engages in a protracted fistfight with Joseph S. Fay, vice-president of the International Union of Operating Engineers, in New Orleans during the AFL convention .... Gallup Poll reports a majority of voters questioned favor more regulation of labor unions and fewer restrictions on business.		Thirty-two states celebrate Thanksgiving Day and give thanks "for our preservation," in accordance with FDR's proclmation .... Ernest Hemingway, author, and Martha Gellhorn are married by a justice of the peace in Cheyenne, Wyo.	Nov. 21
Rep. Martin Dies says that six million persons in the U.S. are members of "foreign organizations" controlled by Russia, Germany and Italy .... Senate Comm. on Campaign Expenditures charges that ballot-box stuffing and other violations of the election laws occured in Harlan, Bell and Pike Counties, Ky.	FDR indicates that U.S. aid to Britain has reached its peak and that additional aid must wait for increased industrial expansion .... FDR confirms that Gen. John J. Pershing, 80, has refused to accept the post of ambassador to the Vichy regime because of his health. Washington reports indicate Rear Adm. William D. Leahy, has been selected for the post.	AFL Pres. William Green says he will ask CIO Pres. Murray next week to renew unity negotiations but adds that Lewis stands in the way .... Rep. E.E. Cox (D, Ga.) says in Washington that the strike at the Vultee Aircraft plant in California is "treason" against the government in time of emergency and urges that Congress outlaw strikes in national defense industries.		Lew Jenkins, world lightweight champion, retains his title by scoring a TKO over Pete Lello in the 2nd round of a scheduled 15-round bout in N.Y.	Nov. 22
Senate Steering Comm. picks Sen. Walter F. George (D, Ga.) as head of the Foreign Relations Comm.	Marquess of Lothian, Britain's new ambassador to the U.S., arriving in N.Y. states Britain is near the end of her fiscal resources and will need financial aid in 1941. But he says Britain "does not need men." .... Rep. Hamilton Fish (R, N.Y.) urges the U.S. take possession of the British and French islands off the East coast and in the Caribbean in payment of their war debts .... Brooklyn Navy Yard officials disclose that six of the Navy's new 72-mph PT boats have been successfully tested off the N.J. coast.	Atty. Gen. Jackson states that the FBI has investigated the Vultee Aircraft strike at Downey, Calif., and that the investigation shows that Communist influence has caused and is prolonging the strike .... Resolutions committee of the AFL convention agrees on a proposal to curb union racketeers .... CIO Pres. Murray announces plans for an intensive organization drive directed especially at national defense industries.		Tom Harmon of the Univ. of Michigan scores three touchdowns against Ohio State to run his three-year scoring record to 33 touchdowns, breaking Red Grange's record of 31.	Nov. 23
NYA estimates its student aid program is enabling 150,000 undergraduates and graduates to continue their college education.		Antitrust division of the Justice Dept. announces a nationwide investigation into the control of food prices .... U.S. Maritime Commission announces that it has awarded contracts for 179 ships as of Nov. 1 in its 10-year program to rehabilitate the American merchant marine with 500 new vessels.	Record rains flood East Central Texas while ice destroys communication lines in the isolated Texas Panhandle.		Nov. 24

F	G	H	I	J
Includes elections, federal-state relations, civil rights and liberties, crime, the judiciary, education, health care, poverty, urban affairs and population.	*Includes formation and debate of U.S. foreign and defense policies, veterans affairs and defense spending. (Relations with specific foreign countries are usually found under the region concerned.)*	*Includes business, labor, agriculture, taxation, transportation, consumer affairs, monetary and fiscal policy, natural resources, pollution and accidents.*	*Includes worldwide scientific, medical and technological developments, natural phenomena, U.S. weather and natural disasters.*	*Includes the arts, religion, scholarship, communications media, sports, entertainment, fashions, fads and social life.*

	World Affairs	European War Zone	Pacific War Zone	The Americas	Other Countries & Territories
Nov. 25		Soviets inform the Germans Russia is ready to join Tripartite Pact only if German troops withdraw from Finland, if Germany concedes Bulgaria is within the Soviet sphere of influence and if Japan makes concessions in Sakhalin . . . . Informed Nazi sources in Berlin say that Bulgaria will not join the Axis "at present." . . . . Warsaw dispatches report that effective Nov. 26 approximately 500,000 Warsaw Jews will be forced to live in a ghetto district surrounded by a 8-foot concrete wall built by the Germans as a "health measure."		First Inter-American Maritime Conference opens in Washington for the purpose of promoting shipping and trade facilities in the Western Hemisphere . . . . Pres. Morinigo of Paraguay tightens his rule by ousting several opponents from his cabinet and key army positions.	The 11,885-ton French freighter and passenger ship *Patria,* at anchor in Haifa harbor with 1,771 homeless Jewish refugees on board, explodes and sinks. The refugees were awaiting transportation to some colony after having been refused admittance to Jerusalem by the British under the immigration quota law . . . . Rufo Romero, head of the Philippine Boy Scouts, is convicted by a general court martial in Manila of conspiring to sell military information and is sentenced to 15 years in prison.
Nov. 26		Lord Rothermere (Harold Harmsworth), the powerful owner of the *Daily Mirror* and other British newspapers, dies at 72 in Bermuda . . . . Governor general of the Belgian Congo announces Italy has committed hostile acts against the Congo and that he considers National Assembly at war with Italy.	Adm. Kichisaburo Nomura, ambassador-designate to the United States, says "the fate of the world hangs on American actions just now. If the United States becomes involved in conflict either in Europe or in the Pacific, civilization will go up in flames ..." He states that there is no issue between Japan and the United States that cannot be solved peacefully . . . . Japan is making new demands for bases in Indochina, according to the *N.Y. Times*' correspondent in London, asking for control of Saigon, Tonkin and Indochina's South China Sea coast.	Gen. Almazan returns by plane to Mexico City after a voluntary exile of four months in the U.S. . . . . Panamanian Pres. Arnulfo Arias decrees a referendum on Dec. 15 to decide whether the new constitution approved recently by the National Assembly shall become effective in 1941.	
Nov. 27		British claim victory in a battle off Sardinia, damaging a 35,000-ton Italian battleship, three cruisers and two destroyers, while only one of their own cruisers was hit. Italians claim they hit a British battleship, three cruisers and an aircraft carrier . . . . Pro-Nazi Rumanian Iron Guardists execute 64 former high government officials in Bucharest's Jihlava military prison to avenge the slaying of hundreds of Iron Guardists killed during the last years of King Carol's regime . . . . Greek reports claim a steady advance against the southern Albanian bases of Argyrokastron and Tepeleni . . . . Australian Naval Ministry reports two British freighters were sunk in the Indian Ocean by a Nazi surface raider during the last five days.		Uruguayan Chamber of Deputies approves an arrangement with the United States regarding construction of naval and air bases for mutual hemisphere defense by a vote of 53 to 21 . . . . FDR appoints Dr. Jose Miguel Gallardo as governor of Puerto Rico.	Jean Chiappe, newly appointed high commissioner in Syria, is killed when his plane flying to Beirut is shot down by a British plane between Sardinia and the African coast.
Nov. 28		German soldiers in or near Bucharest are mobilized and ordered to stand ready for immediate action to intervene in the conflict between Antonescu's government and Iron Guardists . . . . British report a methodical and relentless bombing of Cologne by the RAF.		U.S. signs a three-year agreement with 14 Latin American nations to stabilize the coffee industry. American import quotas are set for each country . . . . A hostile crowd mars the Mexico City welcome for U.S. Vice President-elect Henry A. Wallace.	Reports from Thailand announce the bombing of Indochina areas after the alleged bombing of Thai positions around Nankorn Panom by French planes.
Nov. 29		Fighting between the Rumanian army and Iron Guards is verging on civil war, according to a Hungarian dispatch.	Chinese guerrillas dynamite a Shanghai-Nanking express, bearing Japanese and Chinese officials to Nanking for the signing of the "peace treaty" between Japan and the Japanese-sponsored Wang Ching-wei government.		Thailand orders French nationals to evacuate frontier provinces within 24 hours, after Thai patrols clash with Indochinese border guards at the Cambodian frontier.
Nov. 30		Greek army announces the capture of the Italian base of Pogradec in northeast Albania . . . . Mussolini's newspaper, *Il Popole d'Italia,* states Italy will settle her quarrel with Greece alone and without the military help of Germany . . . . Rome radio announces the Axis powers have abandoned their plans for the defeat of Britain through actual invasion.	Japan officially recognizes the Chinese Nanking government in a treaty signed by Lieut. Gen. Nobuyuki Abe and "President" Wang Ching-wei in Nanking.	Pres. Morinigo establishes a virtual dictatorship in Paraguay by signing a decree granting him full power to carry out "the Paraguayan revolution."	Thailand announces the occupation of the French Indochina districts of Banongkien, Bankokekrabang and Patruchai, as well as reprisal air raids on Thakhek and Savannakhet in the undeclared war.
Dec. 1		Elizabeth Deegan, clerk of the U.S. embassy in Paris, is arrested by the German Gestapo.		Gen. Manuel Avila Camacho is sworn in as president of Mexico and pledges Mexican-U.S. amity . . . . A Brazilian report says a British cruiser halted the Brazilian coastal ship *Itape* near Cape Sao Thome 18 miles off Brazil and took off 22 passengers as German nationals.	More than 100 followers of Gandhi, including four former prime ministers of Indian provinces, are reported to have been arrested throughout India for "individual civil disobedience."

A	B	C	D	E
Includes developments that affect more than one world region, international organizations and important meetings of major world leaders.	*Includes all developments in European countries and military engagements between Allied and Axis powers in Africa and at sea.*	*Includes all developments in Japan and China, Japanese foreign policy and military actions in the Pacific region.*	*Includes all domestic and regional developments in Latin America, the Caribbean and Canada.*	*Includes developments in those independent nations and colonial possessions not covered in Columns B, C and D.*

U.S. Politics & Social Issues	U.S. Foreign Policy & Defense	U.S. Economy & Environment	Science, Technology & Nature	Culture, Leisure & Life Style	
Supreme Court unanimously rules that the exclusion of Negroes from a Texas grand jury violates the 14th Amendment .... Fifteen Democratic Senators join 19 Republicans in a vote to take up the Logan-Walter Bill, which would increase the authority of the courts to review and set aside the decisions of government boards and agencies.	British Amb. Lothian confers with FDR and Hull, later telling reporters that Britain expects substantial aid from the U.S. next year in the form of credits, warplanes, ships and munitions.	Pres. Green says at the AFL Convention that no strike "for any reason" should be permitted to interrupt the production of war materials for national defense or for Britain.			Nov. 25
Senate passes the Logan-Walter bill, and sends it back to the House with amendments .... Atty. Gen. Jackson orders an investigation of alleged violations of the Hatch Act by the national political parties.	Comm. to Defend America by Aiding the Allies issues statement calling for all-out aid for Britain, revision of American neutrality laws and the use of American sea power to protect shipping in the Atlantic .... Alfred M. Landon tells the Cooperative Club in Kansas City: "If we modify the Neutrality Act to permit our ships to enter the war zones, then it will be a case of 'Johnnie, get your gun' ...."	The 12-day old strike at the Vultee Aircraft plant at Downey, Calif. ends when the company and CIO United Automobile Workers union negotiators sign a 16-month contract .... AFL convention adopts a resolution condemning racketeering in labor unions and authorizes the executive council to apply "all of its influence" to force action should unions evade their "responsibilities." .... Allan A. Ryan, 60, who cornered the Stutz Motor stock in 1920 and went bankrupt as a result, dies in San Francisco, Calif.		Elaine Barrie divorces John Barrymore in Los Angeles on grounds of cruelty.	Nov. 26
Dies Comm. makes public a "Red Paper" containing 281 instances in which violence to overthrow capitalism was advocated by Communist groups.	Navy Secy. Knox announces FDR has allocated $50 million for the construction of eight U.S. air and naval bases from Newfoundland to Trinidad on sites leased from Britain .... Senate Foreign Relations Comm. votes to defer consideration of legislation for financial aid to Britain until the next session of Congress.	AT&T announces the largest single "private placement" deal ever negotiated: the sale of $140 million of $2\frac{3}{4}$% debentures due in 30 years to 14 insurance companies. The money is to pay for plant expansion .... U.S. Treasury calls on the 12 Federal Reserve Banks for $107 million of Treasury deposits to replenish cash in the general fund.	Evidence corroborating Dr. Albert Einstein's theory that time is slowed for a fast-moving object is reported at the Univ. of Chicago by scientists after their research on the life span of the mesotron, or "hard" component of cosmic rays.	Tom Harmon, Univ. of Michigan back, is chosen as the nation's outstanding football player for 1940 in a national sportswriters' and broadcasters' poll .... William Allen White, chairman of the Comm. to Defend America by Aiding the Allies, receives the 4th annual award of the National Association of Accredited Publicity Directors, Inc. for outstanding service in publicity.	Nov. 27
Rep. John J. Cochran (D, Mo.) blocks House action on the Walter-Logan bill by refusing to agree to Senate amendments .... Justice Dept. denies parole to Martin T. Manton, former 10th-ranking federal judge, who was sentenced on March 7 to two years in the Lewisburg, Pa. prison for "conspiracy to obstruct justice and defraud the United States."	John Cudahy resigns as U.S. ambassador to Belgium to devote his time to writing .... Treasury Secy. Morgenthau discloses in Washington that Britain and the U.S. will make joint use of some of the Caribbean naval bases recently leased from Britain .... Rep. Howard W. Smith, (D, Va.) introduces a bill providing up to life imprisonment for persons convicted of sabotage.	AFL convention re-elects Pres. Green .... Atty. Gen. Jackson receives a 1,000-page secret report from the FBI on Harry Bridges, Australian-born West Coast CIO leader .... Jesse Lauriston Livermore, 63, speculator who was known for 25 years as the "Boy Plunger" of Wall Street, shoots himself to death in a New York hotel, leaving a suicide note saying he was "tired of fighting."	American Chemical Society reports the wartime shortage of Indian monkeys may hamper medical research in human diseases.		Nov. 28
FDR confers with Rep. Martin Dies on the coordination of the work of the State and Justice Depts with the House Comm. on Un-American Activities.	Under State Secretary Sumner Welles reports that understandings have been reached in principle on aid to Greece .... FDR reappoints Maj. Gen. Thomas Holcomb as commandant of the Marine Corps for another four years.	FDR holds a conference on fiscal policy with Treasury officials and Senate and House tax experts .... A seat on the NYSE is sold for $33,000, the lowest price since 1899.			Nov. 29
Census Bureau reports that the excess of males over females in the United States is being reduced by nearly 100,000 a year and that in about five years there will be a female majority .... Col. George Brinton McClellan, 75, son of the Civil War general, former member of Congress, former N.Y. City mayor, and professor at Princeton Univ., dies in Washington.	White House announces that a $50 million credit has been given to China and that an additional $50 million loan will be made soon.			Navy defeats Army, 14-0, at the annual Army-Navy game in Philadelphia.	Nov. 30
	Joseph P. Kennedy announces that he submitted his resignation as U.S. ambassador to Britain on Nov. 6 so that he might devote his time to help FDR keep the U.S. out of war.	Sen. Walter George of the Senate Finance Comm. says the corporate income tax may be increased from the present 24% on corporations with annual net incomes of $25,000 or more to 30% before the national defense program is completed.		Charles Richman, one of the most popular stage actors a generation ago and one-time leading man for Ada Rehan and Lily Langtry, dies in N.Y.	Dec. 1
F *Includes elections, federal-state relations, civil rights and liberties, crime, the judiciary, education, health care, poverty, urban affairs and population.*	G *Includes formation and debate of U.S. foreign and defense policies, veterans affairs and defense spending. (Relations with specific foreign countries are usually found under the region concerned.)*	H *Includes business, labor, agriculture, taxation, transportation, consumer affairs, monetary and fiscal policy, natural resources, pollution and accidents.*	I *Includes worldwide scientific, medical and technological developments, natural phenomena, U.S. weather and natural disasters.*	J *Includes the arts, religion, scholarship, communications media, sports, entertainment, fashions, fads and social life.*	

	World Affairs	European War Zone	Pacific War Zone	The Americas	Other Countries & Territories
Dec. 2		German bombers attack Bristol, while Southampton digs itself out after a destructive three-day raid .... An estimated 60,000 more German soldiers join the approximately half million already in Rumania, crossing Slovakia and Hungary in troop trains .... Britain and Spain sign a commercial agreement releasing several hundred thousand pounds of Spanish credits frozen in London for purchases in the sterling area.		Inter-American Maritime Conference ends after resolutions are adopted urging the creation of a permanent body to watch over hemisphere shipping and the establishment of a permanent conference .... Finance Min. J.L. Ilsley introduces in the Canadian Parliament a wartime measure designed to save $5 to $6 million a month in foreign exchange for war material purchases in the U.S. by banning selected imports, mostly luxuries, from the U.S.	
Dec. 3		Assured of Nazi support, the Rumanian Army orders the seizure of arms from "irresponsible persons" and clamps down on the Iron Guards .... King George of Greece asks FDR to provide a loan for purchase of munitions and planes.	Japanese newspaper *Miyako* says the new U.S. loan to China brings Japan and the U.S. closer to "the final test."		
Dec. 4		Athens claims that Premedi, an Italian stronghold, has been captured and that Italian troops are retreating from Porto Edda to Khimara and from Argyrokastron to Tepelini and Klisura in Albania .... Rumania seizes all pipelines and accessories belonging to oil companies, including U.S. concerns, and announces that it will pay for the property with 3% bonds maturing in 25 years.		Chilean Chamber of Deputies approves a bill outlawing Communism and sends it to the senate .... Panama Canal administration opens bids in Washington for the excavation of the third set of locks designed to strengthen the canal against attack.	Indochina reports say 20 native policemen were killed in new native uprising in western Cochin China during a lull in the fighting on the French Indochina-Thai border.
Dec. 5		Dissatisfied with the Soviet refusal to join the Tripartite Pact, Hitler instructs his generals to prepare for an invasion of Russia in the spring .... British Commons votes against any criticism of the King's opening address to Parliament, in which he precluded peace talks with the Axis.	Russia's Amb. Constantin Smetanin advises Japan that Russia has not changed her policy with regard to China despite Japan's recognition of Wang Ching-wei's Nanking regime.	Morgenthau announces that a $50-million loan will be made to Argentina from the Treasury's gold stabilization fund to stabilize her currency .... FDR says in a statement read to the Great Lakes-St. Lawrence Seaway and Power Conference he will seek Senate approval for a treaty with Canada to complete the seaway project.	
Dec. 6		Marshal Pietro Badoglio resigns as chief of the Italian general staff and is succeeded by Gen. Count Ugo Cavallero .... Greek troops occupy Porto Edda on the Albanian coastal front and drive on towards Elbasan, Italian army headquarters in central Albania .... British troops advance toward Italian positions in Egypt in preparation for a major attack.		Leonard Brockington, counselor to the war committee of the Canadian cabinet, says in New York that 10,000 American citizens have volunteered to serve in Royal Air Force in Canada since last May and that 2,520 of the 36,000 airmen now being trained in Canada are Americans.	
Dec. 7		Council of Ministers of the Vichy government announces that Gen. de Gaulle will be deprived of French citizenship.		Pres. Getulio Vargas tells officers of the Brazilian army reserve in Rio de Janeiro that the security and sovereignty of the Americas "demand strict solidarity."	

A	B	C	D	E
Includes developments that affect more than one world region, international organizations and important meetings of major world leaders.	*Includes all developments in European countries and military engagements between Allied and Axis powers in Africa and at sea.*	*Includes all developments in Japan and China, Japanese foreign policy and military actions in the Pacific region.*	*Includes all domestic and regional developments in Latin America, the Caribbean and Canada.*	*Includes developments in those independent nations and colonial possessions not covered in Columns B, C and D.*

U.S. Politics & Social Issues	U.S. Foreign Policy & Defense	U.S. Economy & Environment	Science, Technology & Nature	Culture, Leisure & Life Style	
House passes the Walter-Logan bill, subjecting rules and regulations of federal agencies to judicial reveiw, and sends the bill to the White House .... Rep. Martin Dies declares his committee's disclosures of 5th column activities have not been "premature" as FDR indicated, but should have been made by the government long ago.	House and Senate monetary committees give a unanimous "vote of confidence" to the administration on its proposal to extend a $100 million credit to China .... *Priorities* board of the National Defense Advisory Commission announces that commercial airlines have agreed to restrict their demand for engines and parts.		Sir Henry Hallett Dale, world authority on pharmacology and Nobel Prize winner, is elected president of the Royal Society.	Lou Salica, world bantamweight champion, defends his title in Toronto by scoring a TKO, over Small Montana, in the 3rd round .... Ettore Panizza opens the 58th N.Y. Metropolitan Opera season before a capacity audience of 4,400 by conducting Verdi's *Un Ballo in Maschera.*	Dec. 2
FDR embarks on the cruiser *Tuscaloosa* for a vacation cruise in the Caribbean.	Britain announces it has placed a "first order" with U.S. shipbuilders for 60 new freighters .... Secretaries of the Treasury, War, Navy and Commerce hold an inter-departmental conference in Washington to discuss the defense program and aid to Britain .... War Dept. discloses FDR has allotted $25 million of emergency funds for Army garrisons at the eight naval and air bases acquired from Britain.		Health officials estimate 50,000 cases of influenza in Los Angeles in an epidemic sweeping California.	Pope Pius XII issues an appeal to warring nations to keep a Christmas truce "so that the clash of arms may not drown the angelic concert of peace."	Dec. 3
N.Y. State joint legislative committee investigating subversive activitites in public schools authorizes contempt charges against 25 teachers, 18 of them from Brooklyn College, for refusal to testify.	Russell L. Maxwell, administrator of export control, announces that 41 additional types of machine tools will be put under the export licensing control system as of Dec. 10 because of the "increased pace of the national defense program."	Federal Loan Admin. Jesse H. Jones declares "Britain is a good risk for a loan," but says he will not suggest the repeal of the Johnson Act "now." .... Eleven corporations, including DuPont and Allied Chemical, are revealed to have been indicted on Sept. 1, 1939, by a federal grand jury in N.Y. on a charge of conspiring to control the supply and prices of nitrate products in violation of the antitrust laws.	Germany announces plans for construction of the world's largest research institute on biological immunity in Marburg.		Dec. 4
Rep. J.E. Rankin (D, Miss.) introduces a bill to prevent the loss of seats by eight states under the 1942 reapportionment by increasing membership of the House to 450.			California influenza epidemic spreads to Oregon, Washington, New Mexico, Arizona and Idaho.	Sacred Congregation of the Holy Office, the Catholic Church's highest organ on faith and morals, condemns euthanasia, execution practiced for reasons of race improvement or for economic reasons, as "contrary to natural and positive divine law." .... Jan Kubelik, 60, famous Czech violinist who made his American debut in 1901 and earned more than $1,500,000 during his professional career only to become bankrupt, dies in Prague .... Pittsburgh Pirates announce the unconditional release of outfielder Paul Waner.	Dec. 5
Rep. Martin Dies announces his committee has reached a "complete agreement" with the FBI and has worked out "a formula to avoid possible friction and disagreement" in investigating subversive activities. Atty. Gen. Jackson says Dies statement is "premature" and that "no agreement has been made that the FBI .... would be placed at the disposal of Congressman Dies." .... Solicitor General Francis Biddle declares that the U.S. government will be "embarassed and impeded" in its administration of the federal alien registration law if states are permitted to pass their own registration laws .... Robert Boltz, 53, financial adviser, is indicted by a federal grand jury in Philadelphia on charges of violating three federal laws and defrauding a score of clients of more than $750,000.	Col. Wm. J. Donovan leaves for Europe under an assumed name on an fact-finding mission for the U.S. government.	Senate Finance Comm. approves Treasury Secy. Morgenthau's proposal to issue $500 million in additional five-year defense notes .... Strike by AFL Lumber and Sawmill Workers Union for higher wages, which began in Tacoma two months ago, spreads to Seattle and other Washington districts.		Lily Pons, French-born singer and movie star, becomes an American citizen before the U.S. District Court in New Haven, Conn.	Dec. 6
	FDR says in a message to King George II of Greece that it is the policy of the U.S. to extend aid to those peoples who defend themselves against aggression .... Secy. Knox asks the House Naval Comm. for authorization to spend $300 million for major improvements in the antiaircraft defenses aboard warships as a result of lessons learned in the European war .... Hull states Franco has assured the U.S. that Spain will stay neutral in the European war if it gets a U.S. credit of $100,000,000 with which to buy foodstuffs.	Commerce Secy. Jesse H. Jones reports a 14% rise in new private construction is due more to general prosperity than to the defense program .... Circuit Court Judge James E. Chenot enjoins the city of Dearborn, Mich. from enforcing a ban on the distribution of union handbills by the CIO-UAW near the Ford Motor Co.'s River Rouge plant.			Dec. 7

F	G	H	I	J
Includes elections, federal-state relations, civil rights and liberties, crime, the judiciary, education, health care, poverty, urban affairs and population.	*Includes formation and debate of U.S. foreign and defense policies, veterans affairs and defense spending. (Relations with specific foreign countries are usually found under the region concerned.)*	*Includes business, labor, agriculture, taxation, transportation, consumer affairs, monetary and fiscal policy, natural resources, pollution and accidents.*	*Includes worldwide scientific, medical and technological developments, natural phenomena, U.S. weather and natural disasters.*	*Includes the arts, religion, scholarship, communications media, sports, entertainment, fashions, fads and social life.*

	World Affairs	European War Zone	Pacific War Zone	The Americas	Other Countries & Territories
Dec. 8		A Churchill letter delivered to FDR warns that the loss of British shipping in the Atlantic is reaching the crisis stage. He adds that "the moment approaches when we shall no longer be able to pay cash" for military supplies and equipment . . . . Adm. Domenico Cavagnari resigns as chief of staff of the Italian Navy and is succeeded by Adm. Arturo Riccardi.		German freighter *Idarwald* is reported captured by the British cruiser *Diomede* off the coast of Cuba inside the American neutrality zone.	
Dec. 9		British troops begin an attack on the Italians in Egypt, striking toward Sidi Barrani . . . . Anti-Nazi demonstrations and riots are reported from the south Jutland town of Hadersleben, Denmark.	Foreign Min. Matsuoka says in Tokyo that if Japan and the U.S. "keep their heads cool" there will be no serious clash between them.		Gen. Henri Dentz is appointed French high commissioner to Syria and Lebanon to succeed the late Jean Chiappe.
Dec. 10		Sidi Barrani falls to the British, who capture some 38,000 Italian prisoners . . . . Hitler terms the war a struggle between the world of totalitarianism and democracy and predicts a German victory.	Japanese cabinet approves a budget that will exceed 10 billion yen, or more than the entire national debt in 1936 when the war with China began.		
Dec. 11				Commerce Secy. Jones, announces an Export-Import Bank credit of $60 million to Argentina and another credit of $7,5000,000 to Uruguay for purchases in the U.S. . . . . State Dept. announces a formal agreement between the U.S. and Canada regarding reciprocal treatment in the operation of air services between the two countries . . . . Dutch destroyer *Van Kingsbergen* captures the Nazi freighter *Rhein*, which left Mexico on Nov. 29.	
Dec. 12		Yugoslav Foreign Min. Alexander Cincar-Markovitch and Hungarian Foreign Min. Count Stephen Csaky sign a treaty of "constant peace and perpetual friendship" in Belgrade.		Three Uruguayan ministers and Herrerista Party members resign in protest on the eve of the signing of the Argentine-Uruguayan defense pact . . . . U.S. and Ecuador sign a four-year agreement under which the U.S. will furnish a military aviation and naval commission to advise the Ecuadorian defense ministry . . . . Pres. Avila Camacho orders that Mexican agricultural workers on communal farms be given full title to the lands they till . . . . Executive committee of Chile's Popular Front refuses to oust the CP as recommended by the Socialist Party.	Gen. J.B.M. Hertzog, former antiwar prime minister of South Africa, and N.C. Havenga, former finance minister, resign from Parliament at Cape Town because of the Nationalist Party's "lack of confidence" in them.
Dec. 13		Petain dismisses Laval, shifting French government policy away from its strongly pro-German orientation . . . . British claim capturing 20,000 Italian soldiers and two more generals in the Egyptian offensive and state that "the remnants of the beaten Italian Army" are falling back on Libya.			More than 200 Jewish refugees from Bulgaria on their way to Palestine are drowned when their ship, the 60-ton *Salvator*, sinks in a storm in the Sea of Marmara.
Dec. 14				Argentina and Uruguay reach an agreement for joint defense of the River Plate zone against any non-American aggression.	

A	B	C	D	E
Includes developments that affect more than one world region, international organizations and important meetings of major world leaders.	*Includes all developments in European countries and military engagements between Allied and Axis powers in Africa and at sea.*	*Includes all developments in Japan and China, Japanese foreign policy and military actions in the Pacific region.*	*Includes all domestic and regional developments in Latin America, the Caribbean and Canada.*	*Includes developments in those independent nations and colonial possessions not covered in Columns B, C and D.*

U.S. Politics & Social Issues	U.S. Foreign Policy & Defense	U.S. Economy & Environment	Science, Technology & Nature	Culture, Leisure & Life Style	
National Woman's Party meeting in Washington adopts resolutions to fight legal discrimination against women and to conduct an extensive campaign to have Congress pass an equal rights amendment to the Constitution.	Sen. Elbert D. Thomas (D, Utah) proposes that the U.S. cancel Britain's $5-billion war debt in exchange for U.S. control of all British colonies in the Western Hemisphere except Canada, to be effective until two years after the European war ends.	Labor Policy Advisory Committee of the National Defense Advisory Commission pledges labor's cooperation with the national defense program and promises not to impede production before all conciliation facilities of the federal government have been exhausted.		Chicago Bears crush the Washington Redskins, 73 to 0, in Washington to win the NFL championship and set a new scoring record for pro football.	Dec. 8
	Hull says the U.S. will not make a $100,000,000 loan to Spain but that this country may send food shipments, which would stop if Spain entered the European War .... FDR visits the British island of Antigua and confers with Sir Gordon J. Lethem, governor of the British Leeward Islands.	Morgenthau declares tax-exempt bonds are "slacker money" and announces that a $5-billion series of "national defense notes," to be issued on Dec. 11, will be wholly taxable .... AFL carpenters strike at the $4.5-million War Dept. building in Washington .... Wright Aeronautical Corporation and the Independent Wright Aeronautical Employes Association sign a contract providing for a 7% wage increase and banning strikes.		ASCAP announces it has signed new 10-year agreements with 135 music publishers who control more than 200,000 songs .... Tom Harmon of the Univ. of Michigan is awarded the Heisman Trophy by the Downtown Athletic Club of New York as the outstanding football player of the year.	Dec. 9
National Association of Manufacturers announces it is analyzing 800 public school textbooks for teachings subversive of the government or the system of free enterprise .... Atty. Gen. Jackson writes to Rep. Jerry Voorhis of the Dies Comm. that the two bodies can cooperate in their investigation of fifth column activities.	FDR announces that iron ore, pig iron, ferro alloys and certain iron and steel manufactures will be placed under export licensing control on Dec. 30. The action is seen as a major blow to Japan, which is heavily dependent on U.S. exports of these items .... Duke and Duchess of Windsor are greeted by 12,000 persons when they arrive in Maimi, Fla. from the Bahamas for their first visit to the U.S. since their marriage in 1937.			National and American baseball leagues, meeting separately in Chicago, re-elect Kenesaw Mountain Landis as commissioner for another five-year term.	Dec. 10
	In a speech read for British Amb. Lord Lothian at Baltimore, he says the outcome of the war "now depends largely on" American aid .... Hull indicates the U.S. will not attempt to send food to Nazi-occupied countries but will aid the destitute in unoccupied France, Spain and "other free states."	Treasury issues $500 million in five-year "national defense notes" bearing ¾% and subject to federal taxation .... NYSE rejects a request by the SEC that it rescind its order prohibiting members from multiple trading on outside or regional exchanges.		Challedon is named the "horse of the year" for the second time in the *Turf and Sports Digest*'s annual poll .... Lambert Trophy, symbolic of Eastern football supremacy, is presented to Boston College representatives at a dinner in N.Y.	Dec. 11
John W. Studebaker, U.S. education commissioner, announces a $9 million program to train 25,000 students as defense industry technicians in 65 engineering institutions.	British Amb.-to-U.S. Lord Lothian (Philip Henry Kerr) dies at 58 at the British embassy in Washington .... Army's 2nd Armored Division, composed of 10,000 men in 1,102 vehicles, including 400 tanks, goes 90 miles from Fort Benning, Ga., to Blakely and Abbeville in the first cross country test of a full armored division in the Western Hemisphere.	I.A. Capizzi, chief counsel for the Ford Motor Co., says the company will not consent to a bargaining election among 100,000 production workers because the CIO-UAW does not represent even a small portion of Ford employes .... Rep. Leland M. Ford, (R, Calif.) charges some CIO leaders have "done everything they possibly could do to disturb, disrupt and destroy the defense program." .... Charles A. Pace, 71, co-founder of the Pace Institute in N.Y. and of similar business schools in other cities, dies in N.Y.			Dec. 12
	Duke of Windsor confers with FDR aboard the *U.S.S. Tuscaloosa* on U.S. naval bases in the West Indies and tells newsmen: "We are ready to do what the President wants when he gives the word."	Labor circles in Washington report that Sidney Hillman of the National Defense Advisory Commission protested to the War Dept. against the awarding of $2 million in defense contracts to the Ford Motor Co. because no stipulation was made for compliance with the labor laws .... Federal grand jury in Chicago indicts nine persons associated with the Resources Corp. International of Chicago on charges of defrauding hundreds of investors of $7 million by the fraudulent sale of stock in a Mexican timber deal.	Production of a light ray with a wave length that does not vary by more than one fifty-billionth of an inch is reported by Jacob Wiens and Dr. Luis W. Alvarez. The light beam was generated from mercury made from gold in an atom-smashing cyclotron and is said to make the measurement of length more accurate.	Ken Overlin, middleweight champion, retains his title by outpointing Steve Belloise, Bronx challenger, in 15 rounds in N.Y.	Dec. 13
FDR completes an 11-day defense inspection trip in the Caribbean aboard the *Tuscaloosa* and arrives in Charleston, S.C.	The $31-million aircraft carrier *Hornet* is launched at the navy yard in Newport News, Va.	Morgenthau reports the Treasury's $500 million 5-year taxable defense notes were oversubscribed by more than 8 times .... The 6th Avenue Subway, the newest and most expensive link in the N.Y.C.'s transportation system that cost between $700 and $800 million is officially opened just before midnight by Mayor F.H. La Guardia.		Pres. James Petrillo of the American Federation of Musicians announces that Army bands will not be permitted to broadcast from Army posts until he has an opportunity to confer with the War Dept.	Dec. 14

F	G	H	I	J
Includes elections, federal-state relations, civil rights and liberties, crime, the judiciary, education, health care, poverty, urban affairs and population.	*Includes formation and debate of U.S. foreign and defense policies, veterans affairs and defense spending. (Relations with specific foreign countries are usually found under the region concerned.)*	*Includes business, labor, agriculture, taxation, transportation, consumer affairs, monetary and fiscal policy, natural resources, pollution and accidents.*	*Includes worldwide scientific, medical and technological developments, natural phenomena, U.S. weather and natural disasters.*	*Includes the arts, religion, scholarship, communications media, sports, entertainment, fashions, fads and social life.*

	World Affairs	European War Zone	Pacific War Zone	The Americas	Other Countries & Territories
Dec. 15					French Gov.-Gen. of Indochina Vice Adm. Jean Decoux stresses his desire for peace by saying he is ready "at any moment" to open negotiations with Thailand .... James G. McDonald, chairman of FDR's advisory committee on refugees, predicts an Arab-Jewish federation will be formed in Palestine for mutual defense against Germany and Italy.
Dec. 16	Oslo announces that no Nobel Peace Prize will be awarded this year.	RAF bombers blast military and civilian targets in Mannheim, Germany .... Scotland Yard claims the discovery of a Communist plot to spread discontent among British workers by planting agents in subway air-raid shelters.		Arthur G. McKee and Co. of Cleveland announces the receipt of a Brazilian contract to design and supervise the construction of a $36-million iron and steel plant near Rio de Janeiro.	
Dec. 17		A communique says Marshal Petain "talked over the general situation" with Pierre Laval after Otto Abetz, German ambassador, conferred with Petain and reportedly demanded Laval's release from detention.			
Dec. 18		London reports two Italian Army divisions and thousands of Blackshirt militiamen have been bottled up in Bardia, Libya .... British warships sail through the Strait of Otranto and bombard Valona .... Ousted Vichy Vice Premier Laval is reported to be with Otto Abetz in Paris.	A Japanese delegation headed by Kenkichi Yoshizawa is reported en route to Batavia, NEI, to seek an economic accord between the two countries.	Jesse Jones announces the Export-Import Bank's approval of a $10 million credit to Peru to cover purchases in the U.S.	
Dec. 19		Churchill tells Parliament that British successes in Egypt are due not only to the superiority of British plans and troops but also to the fact that the Italians have no heart in the war and their morale is low .... German bombers resume night raids over Britain after a lull of almost three days, the longest period of quiet since September .... Kyosti Kallio, 67, president of Finland during the war against Russia, dies in a Helsinki railroad station a few hours after Risto Ryti is elected to succeed him. Kallio resigned on Nov. 28 because of ill health.			
Dec. 20	Germany, Italy and Japan establish a military and economic commission to implement their alliance.	Bulgarian Parliament passes a new law limiting the rights of Bulgaria's 50,000 Jews, banning Free Masons and other secret societies and making anti-nationalist propaganda illegal.			
Dec. 21		Germany charges British Shipping Min. Ronald H. Cross is "inciting America to commit a warlike act" against the Axis.			
	A *Includes developments that affect more than one world region, international organizations and important meetings of major world leaders.*	B *Includes all developments in European countries and military engagements between Allied and Axis powers in Africa and at sea.*	C *Includes all developments in Japan and China, Japanese foreign policy and military actions in the Pacific region.*	D *Includes all domestic and regional developments in Latin America, the Caribbean and Canada.*	E *Includes developments in those independent nations and colonial possessions not covered in Columns B, C and D.*

U.S. Politics & Social Issues	U.S. Foreign Policy & Defense	U.S. Economy & Environment	Science, Technology & Nature	Culture, Leisure & Life Style	
	Southern Regional Conference meeting in Southern Pines, N.C., declares that the U.S. faces an unimaginable crisis and calls upon FDR and Congress for mobilization of all necessary resources and all-out aid to Britain.			Byron Nelson wins the Miami Open Golf Tournament with a 271, nine strokes under par for 72 holes.	Dec. 15
The 531 members of the Electoral College, meeting in their respective state capitals, cast 449 ballots for Franklin D. Roosevelt and 82 for Wendell L. Willkie for President.	Sen. Gerald P. Nye opposes immediate financial aid to Britain.	FBI Director J. Edgar Hoover says the 2,500-page FBI report on Harry Bridges, West Coast CIO leader, "confirms the belief that Bridges is a Communist" and urges that Bridges be deported and that the CP be outlawed .... AFL Pres. Green declares that in a great emergency such as now faced, it becomes "our solemn duty to avoid strikes." .... Supreme Court sustains the licensing authority of the Federal Power Commission in the 15-year-old New River case, ruling that a river may be classified as navigable if it can be made so by "reasonable improvements."		American Federation of Musicians reaches an agreement with the Columbia, National and Mutual broadcasting systems under which they are permitted to broadcast Army band music on condition that they do not dismiss their own studio musicians .... Joe Louis, world heavyweight champion, defends his title for the twelfth time by scoring a six-round TKO over Al McCoy in Boston .... National Football League announces that Byron (Whizzer) White of the Detroit Lions led the league in ground-gaining in 1940.	Dec. 16
Justice Dept. refuses to renew the temporary visitor's permit of Princess Stefanie Hohenlohe-Waldenburg-Schillingfurst of Hungary and orders her to leave the country by Dec. 21.	FDR describes his plans to aid Britain at his press conference. Outlining a program to be known as Lend-Lease, he says it is analogous to lending a neighbor whose house is burning your "garden hose." .... Verne the formation of the No Foreign War Committee to combat war propaganda in the U.S. and fight against the influence of William A. White's Committee to Defend America by Aiding the Allies.		The world's largest industrial X-ray unit, with a potential of one million volts, more than twice the energy of previous machines, and capable of peering into metals and detecting their inner structure 40 times faster than hitherto possible, is demonstrated at the research laboratories of G.E. in Schenectady, N.Y.		Dec. 17
FDR vetoes the Walter-Logan bill, providing court review of the rulings of government agencies, stating that the bill is "an invitation to endless .... controversies at a moment when we can least afford" it .... A motion in the House to override FDR's veto of the Walter-Logan bill fails by 153 to 127.	Washington reports that FDR has advised British officials to go ahead with their plan to order about $3 million of additional war materiel without waiting for the completion of financial arrangements .... Rep. Everett M. Dirksen (R, Ill.) criticizes the President's plan to lend guns and munitions to Britain as a "plain effort to circumvent" the Neutrality and Johnson Acts.	CIO Pres. Philip Murray sends FDR a plan proposing the creation of a new National Defense Board, with industry-labor-government councils in every basic industry .... Agriculture Dept. reports that 1940 crop production was the largest for any year except 1937 due to favorable weather, increased farm labor and improvements.			Dec. 18
Papers and records of the Chicago office of the German-American Bund are seized by Illinois authorities. An investigator reports one of the books taken contains the names of 1,500 to 2,000 members supposed to be in the U.S. Army or Navy .... Alan Shaw, 22-year-old Communist convicted of criminal syndicalism although no specific act of violence was charged, is sentenced in Oklahoma City to 10 years in prison and fined $5,000. Shaw claims his case has been a "mockery" from the beginning.	British officials present a list of war orders to Morganthau said to total between $2 and $3 billion and to include 12,000 combat planes.	Allan Sproul, 44, is elected president of the Federal Reserve Bank of N.Y., succeeding George L. Harrison.			Dec. 19
Census Bureau announces American families are shrinking, with the average family now having 3.8 members, vs. 4.9 persons in 1890 and 4.1 in 1930.		FDR announces the creation of the Office of Production Management for Defense, with William S. Knudsen as director and Sidney Hillman as associate director .... U.S. Chamber of Commerce announces that exports and imports in the first nine months of 1940 totaled $4,901,400,000, about 29% above 1939, with exports exceeding imports by about $1 billion.		Connie Mack, manager of the Philadelphia Athletics baseball team for 40 years, acquires financial control of the club by buying stock held by Mrs. Ethel M. Shibe.	Dec. 20
	Army-Navy Joint Board endorses secret defense plan calling for a strong offensive in the European and Atlantic war and a defensive strategy in the Pacific if the U.S. enters the war .... Regular Army strength passes 400,000 men for the first time since W.W. I .... Former President Hoover urges "complete" national unity in a speech in New York. Referring to William White and Charles Lindbergh, he says, "It is a sign of a dangerously irresponsible mind in a nation when patriotic men are fiercely denounced as being tools of Great Britain or the tools of Germany."	OPM Dir. Knudsen says the most important thing now is "the swiftest possible production of the means of defense."		Hal Kemp, 36, one of the most popular orchestra leaders in the country, dies in Madera, Calif. of injuries suffered in an auto accident Dec. 18.	Dec. 21
F *Includes elections, federal-state relations, civil rights and liberties, crime, the judiciary, education, health care, poverty, urban affairs and population.*	G *Includes formation and debate of U.S. foreign and defense policies, veterans affairs and defense spending. (Relations with specific foreign countries are usually found under the region concerned.)*	H *Includes business, labor, agriculture, taxation, transportation, consumer affairs, monetary and fiscal policy, natural resources, pollution and accidents.*	I *Includes worldwide scientific, medical and technological developments, natural phenomena, U.S. weather and natural disasters.*	J *Includes the arts, religion, scholarship, communications media, sports, entertainment, fashions, fads and social life.*	

	World Affairs	European War Zone	Pacific War Zone	The Americas	Other Countries & Territories
Dec. 22		British Foreign Secy. Viscount Halifax is appointed ambassador to the U.S. and Anthony Eden is named to succeed him. David Margesson is named secretary for war . . . . Athens reports that 3 Italian divisions, numbering approximately 45,000 men are being hemmed in around Tepelini and Kisura.		British good will mission leaves Uruguay after a week of the most enthusiastic demonstrations the Uruguayan public has ever accorded to a foreign mission, according to a Montevideo report.	
Dec. 23		Churchill denounces Mussolini as a "criminal." . . . . Greek troops seize the Italian coastal base of Khimara in Albania.		Sylvia Ageloff, a N.Y. woman, held in connection with the slaying of Leon Trotsky in Mexico City last August, is given her freedom . . . . William S. Paley, president of CBS, announces plans for a radio network covering 18 of the 20 Latin American countries to begin operation about Sept. 1, 1941.	
Dec. 24		British planes bomb Tripoli in Libya and report sinking two Italian ships of 3,000 and 6,000 tons.	A pact between Japan and Thailand in which both countries agree to respect each other's territorial integrity and to consult on all questions of common interest, signed Dec. 6, is formally announced in Tokyo.	Ecuador decrees that military and naval forces must learn English in connection with hemisphere defense measures.	
Dec. 25	Official estimates place the world's present combatant naval strength at 1,600 units, exceeding five million tons, with the U.S. building 329 craft or more than Germany, Italy, and Japan combined.	Reports from Hungary indicate that more than 150,000 Nazi troops have been transported by train through Hungary to Rumania during the past two days . . . . British officials estimate Malta has withstood 203 Italian air attacks and that 35 Italian bombers have been shot down there since Italy entered the war last June.		Pres. Arnulfo Arias of Panama issues a decree abrogating the 1904 constitution and replacing it with the new one adopted last month by the National Assembly and accepted in a plebiscite on Dec. 15.	
Dec. 26		According to Belgrade reports, three German divisions have moved into Italy on troop trains from Austria.	Emperor Hirohito opens the Japanese Imperial Diet with the customary one-minute speech.	Mexican Senate passes a bill permitting U.S. Army planes to use either the Tejeria or the Minatitlan airports for stopovers on flights between the Panama Canal Zone and the U.S. . . . . Torrential rains cause a flood in the industrial center of Juiz de Fora, Brazil killing 30 people, making 5,000 homeless and causing $5 million damage.	
Dec. 27		The unofficial three-day Christmas air truce ends when German bombers raid London. Berlin accuses England of violating the truce by bombing French and German cities on Dec. 26 . . . . British report a captured Italian officer claims Mussolini has ordered the 20,000 Italians surrounded in Bardia, Libya to defend the base "at all costs".	P.M. Robert G. Menzies of Australia announces that a sea raider flying the Japanese colors recently shelled the island of Nauru in the western Pacific. The island, undefended under the terms of the League of Nations mandate, is jointly administered by Britain, Australia and New Zealand . . . . Japanese cabinet approves an expanded domestic steel production scheme to meet the U.S. scrap iron embargo.	Pres. Avila Camacho's program to establish government management of Mexico's railroads is completed when the Senate unanimously endorses the legislation . . . . Showing of Charlie Chaplin's picture *The Great Dictator* is forbidden in Buenos Aires after a protest by the Italian Amb. Raffaele Boscarelli.	British High Commissioner Sir Harold MacMichael announces that no quota for immigration to Palestine will be set for the period of October 1940 through March 1941.
Dec. 28		Germany has massed more than a division of troops in Rumania within 13 miles of the Yugoslav border, according to frontier reports.	Japanese government denies that one of its ships shelled Nauru. Australian sources speculate that the ship concerned was a disguised German raider.	Guatemala announces 12 persons who tried to start a rebellion at Fort Metamoros on Christmas eve were executed today by firing squads . . . . Universal military training is established in Ecuador, beginning next month with pre-military instruction in all schools, colleges and universities.	A vote of confidence in the present cabinet by Egypt's Parliament bars the way to active participation of Egypt in the war.
Dec. 29		German planes drop incendiary bombs on the financial district of London, starting 1,500 fires, destroying the medieval Guildhall and burning down or damaging seven churches built by Sir Christopher Wren . . . . British announce that an unidentified German "powerful surface warship" was routed in the North Atlantic on Christmas morning by the British cruiser *Berwick*.		Mexican Pres. Camacho sends a bill to the Chamber of Deputies granting amnesty for political offenders during the presidential campaign.	
	A	B	C	D	E
	Includes developments that affect more than one world region, international organizations and important meetings of major world leaders.	*Includes all developments in European countries and military engagements between Allied and Axis powers in Africa and at sea.*	*Includes all developments in Japan and China, Japanese foreign policy and military actions in the Pacific region.*	*Includes all domestic and regional developments in Latin America, the Caribbean and Canada.*	*Includes developments in those independent nations and colonial possessions not covered in Columns B, C and D.*

U.S. Politics & Social Issues	U.S. Foreign Policy & Defense	U.S. Economy & Environment	Science, Technology & Nature	Culture, Leisure & Life Style	
	No Foreign War Committee publishes full-page advertisements in 50 newspapers appealing for public support.	CIO Pres. Murray urges affiliates and members to lobby against a "sabotage bill" and a "model state home guard bill," saying the first would give local authorities the right to suppress strikes and the second would exempt state guard units "from any civil responsibility for their acts by making them subject to military law only."		Novelist F. Scott Fitzgerald, 44, dies in Hollywood, Calif. .... National Board of Review of Motion Pictures picks *The Grapes of Wrath*, as the best Hollywood picture of 1940.	Dec. 22
	Sen. Warren R. Austin (R, Vt.) tells reporters in Washington that he is in favor of amending the Neutrality Act to restore "freedom of the seas to U.S. shipping." .... Rear Adm. Wm. D. Leahy, accompanied by his wife, sails from Norfolk, Va., aboard the cruiser *Tuscaloosa* en route to Vichy, where he will assume his new post as ambassador to France.	CIO Pres. Murray gives FDR a plan for the mass production of 500 all-metal pursuit planes daily by utilizing idle facilities of automobile plants.		NBC drops all music controlled by the ASCAP, following the lead of CBS and MBS.	Dec. 23
	Sen. Tydings (D, Md.) urges that the U.S. ask the warring powers for a statement on the conditions under which they would be willing to end the war.		An earthquake with its epicenter near Ossipee or Tamworth, N.H., rocks the northeast United States and southern Canada at 8:34 a.m., lasting 20 minutes but causing little damage.	ASCAP is declared an illegal combination in restraint of trade and in violation of the Sherman Antitrust Act by a three-judge Federal Court in Tacoma, Wash.	Dec. 24
	Sen. Burton K. Wheeler (D, Mont.) says FDR should make a determined effort to bring peace to Europe before additional aid is granted to Britain. He criticizes plans to send equipment to Britain as "an evasion of our Neutrality Act." .... Verne Marshall of the No Foreign Wars Committee says that war would not have broken out in Europe were it not for "unwritten" foreign commitments made by the U.S.	American Magnesium Corp. denies that the German I.G. Farbenindustrie A.G. controls magnesium patents in this country and is thus able to restrict production.		Earl (Red) Blaik, Dartmouth football coach since 1934, is appointed coach of the U.S. Military Academy team.	Dec. 25
The four month period for the registration of aliens in the U.S. ends at midnight with total registrations reported in excess of 4.5 million.	White House releases a telegram from 169 prominent educators, clergymen, industrialists, writers, newspapermen and others pledging "unqualified support" of FDR's proposal to send munitions to Great Britain .... Sen. Arthur H. Vandenberg (R, Mich.) urges the government to send an "inquiry" to belligerents regarding the possibilities of peace.	Augustus Eugene Staley Sr., 73, founder of the $20-million A.E. Staley Mfg. Co. of Decatur, Ill. and a pioneer in the corn and soy bean processing industries, dies in Miami, Fla.		Atty. Gen. Jackson authorizes criminal proceedings under the Sherman Antitrust Act against ASCAP, NBC, and CBS charging them with the illegal pooling of copyright music to eliminate competition, illegal discrimination against non-member composers, illegal price fixing and mutual boycotts .... *My Sister Eileen* by Ruth McKenney opens in New York .... Daniel Frohman, 89, dean of American theatrical producers and president of the Actors Fund of America for 34 years, dies in N.Y. .... *Ring Magazine* names Billy Conn, lightheavyweight champion, as "the fighter of the year."	Dec. 26
Chief Justice Charles Evans Hughes says in Washington upon receiving the Inter-Faith Award of the National Conference of Christians and Jews that the sacred basic individual rights must be upheld regardless of race or creed to preserve liberty.	Sen. Wheeler defines the "just" peace he urged FDR to try to bring about as one whose terms the belligerents would be willing to accept in preference to continuing the war .... Numbering 16,000 members, the N.Y. chapter of the Committee to Defend America by Aiding the Allies says in a statement, "Peace is possible for us only if Britain wins." .... Federal Register discloses FDR has ordered an additional 42,000 National Guardsmen into active service between Jan. 6 and Jan. 17.	FDR says he has turned over the CIO proposal to produce 500 planes daily by utilizing unused automobile plant space and equipment to the new defense council.			Dec. 27
	According to a preliminary audit by the U.S. Treasury, Great Britain will have no cash left to pay for U.S. arms and munitions by early autumn of 1941 .... Gallup Poll reports that 60% of American voters now favor aiding Britain even at the risk of war as compared with 36% last May .... The American Student Union in N.Y. charges the Roosevelt Administration with attempting to sabotage progressive legislation and civil liberties under the guise of national defense.	A House committee which spent 17 months investigating the NLRB urges its complete reorganization of to eliminate those employes who have shown bias and a partisan attitude as well as those who have indicated opposition to "the American system of government." .... Edward R. Stettinius of the National Defense Advisory Commission reports there are no serious shortages in aluminum supplies.	Dr. Christian Deetjan, 77, a pioneer in X-ray treatment who lost his fingers and forearm in 1930 as a result of his work, dies from research burns in Baltimore .... Prof. Joseph Kaplan and Dr. S.M. Ruben of the Univ. of California describe a new device called a "cosmic Jacob's ladder," which provides them with evidence that the upper atmosphere contains helium.	Northern All-Stars beat the Southern All-Stars, 14-12, in their third annual football game in Alabama.	Dec. 28
	FDR declares in a "fireside chat" broadcast that the U.S. must become the "arsenal of democracy" and that full aid must be given Britain on a war basis. He adds that no threats by dictators can weaken American determination to give Britain all the aid it needs.	R.J. Thomas, president of the CIO United Auto Workers, says the War Dept. contract for 1,500 scout cars awarded to the Ford Motor Co. will "seriously undermine the morale of labor engaged in defense work."		N.Y. Film Critics name *The Grapes of Wrath* as the best motion picture of the year; Charlie Chaplin as the best male performer, and Katherine Hepburn as the best female performer; and Walt Disney and Leopold Stokowski for a "special award" for their production of *Fantasia* .... The champion Chicago Bears defeat the National League All-Stars, 28-14, in Los Angeles with Sid Luckman starring for the winners and Sammy Baugh for the losers.	Dec. 29

F	G	H	I	J
Includes elections, federal-state relations, civil rights and liberties, crime, the judiciary, education, health care, poverty, urban affairs and population.	*Includes formation and debate of U.S. foreign and defense policies, veterans affairs and defense spending. (Relations with specific foreign countries are usually found under the region concerned.)*	*Includes business, labor, agriculture, taxation, transportation, consumer affairs, monetary and fiscal policy, natural resources, pollution and accidents.*	*Includes worldwide scientific, medical and technological developments, natural phenomena, U.S. weather and natural disasters.*	*Includes the arts, religion, scholarship, communications media, sports, entertainment, fashions, fads and social life.*

	World Affairs	European War Zone	Pacific War Zone	The Americas	Other Countries & Territories
Dec. 30		For the first 15 months of the war in Europe, the total of dead, wounded and missing is estimated by the AP at three to four million.		Rep. Ramon Vina of the National Herrerista Party, which opposes the establishment of Pan-American bases in Uruguay, tries to shoot Emilio Frugoni, a Socialist member, on the floor of the Chamber of Representatives in Montevideo during a debate on the bases.	
Dec. 31		Hitler declares in his New Year's proclamation to the army: "The year 1941 will bring consummation of the greatest victory in our history."	New Year messages of the Japanese government are gloomy, particularly Foreign Min. Matsuoka's, which says, "I fear the coming year will prove most tragic and unfortunate for all mankind."		

A	B	C	D	E
Includes developments that affect more than one world region, international organizations and important meetings of major world leaders.	*Includes all developments in European countries and military engagements between Allied and Axis powers in Africa and at sea.*	*Includes all developments in Japan and China, Japanese foreign policy and military actions in the Pacific region.*	*Includes all domestic and regional developments in Latin America, the Caribbean and Canada.*	*Includes developments in those independent nations and colonial possessions not covered in Columns B, C and D.*

U.S. Politics & Social Issues	U.S. Foreign Policy & Defense	U.S. Economy & Environment	Science, Technology & Nature	Culture, Leisure & Life Style	
National Student Federation of America votes to withdraw from the American Youth Congress, which it helped to found, because of the Youth Congress's alleged radical tendencies.	White House says Roosevelt is "tremendously pleased" by the response to his radio address urging complete aid to Britain .... Sen. D. Worth Clark (D. Ida.) says FDR's address yesterday was "a trick speech, calculated to lead the American people into war and ruin." .... Sen. Wheeler criticizes "warmongers," opposes aid to Great Britain that might involve the U.S. in war and offers an eight-point peace program.				Dec. 30
	FDR characterizes as "silly" a suggestion that this country accept British islands in the Atlantic in exchange for material aid.	Ford Motor Co. appeals to the Supreme Court from a lower court ruling upholding a NLRB order that the company cease "unfair" labor practices. The company accuses the board of "bias and prejudice." .... Howard Hopson, 58, who obtained control of the Associated Gas and Electric Co. in 1922 for $48,000 and built it into a billion-dollar utilities empire, is convicted by a federal jury in New York on 17 counts of defrauding investors of nearly $20,000,000.		Bette Davis, motion-picture star, and Arthur Farnsworth, Boston business man, are married on a ranch in Rimrock, Ariz.	Dec. 31

F	G	H	I	J
Includes elections, federal-state relations, civil rights and liberties, crime, the judiciary, education, health care, poverty, urban affairs and population.	*Includes formation and debate of U.S. foreign and defense policies, veterans affairs and defense spending. (Relations with specific foreign countries are usually found under the region concerned.)*	*Includes business, labor, agriculture, taxation, transportation, consumer affairs, monetary and fiscal policy, natural resources, pollution and accidents.*	*Includes worldwide scientific, medical and technological developments, natural phenomena, U.S. weather and natural disasters.*	*Includes the arts, religion, scholarship, communications media, sports, entertainment, fashions, fads and social life.*

1941

Civil rights leader A. Philip Randolph organized the March on Washington Committee in January to press for an end to segregation in the armed forces and employment discrimination in defense industries.

German mountain troops rest during the invasion of Greece, April 12.

Preceding page: U.S. battleship *Arizona* casts a huge pall of smoke as it burns and sinks after the Japanese attack on Pearl Harbor, Dec. 7.

A Japanese pilot took this picture of battleship row in Pearl Harbor as he prepared to attack one of the vessels. The oil storage tanks and warehouse facilities in the background were also targets of the Japanese raid.

German trucks cross the border into Russia. The sign above them reads: "Welcome workers of the West [to the] USSR."

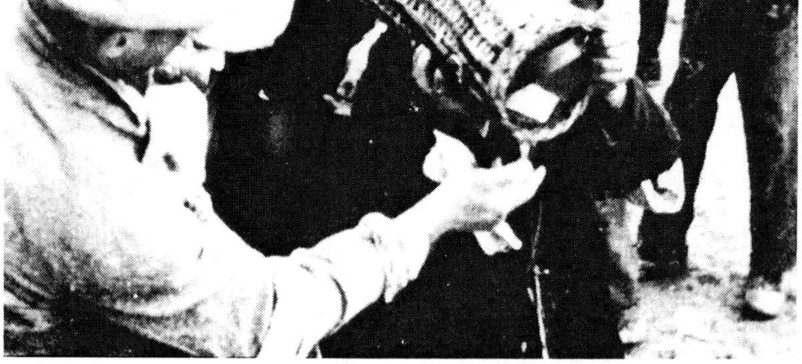

Jews at forced labor load munitions for the German Army near Zamosc, Poland on July 3.

A stalwart Red Army soldier repels the Nazi menace in this Soviet poster, issued after the German invasion of Russia. Legend reads: "Death to the fascist serpent!"

Soldiers of the German Afrika Korps fire an 8.8 cm. anti-tank gun near Sidi Rezegh, Libya in December.

FDR and Churchill confer aboard the British battleship *Prince of Wales* off the coast of Newfoundland, a meeting which produced the Atlantic Charter. Standing behind Churchill are Adm. Ernest King and Gen. George Marshall.

German armored forces enter the White Russian city of Minsk on June 28, one week after the invasion of Russia.

Italian dictator Mussolini strikes a characteristic pose as he confers with Hitler and Field Marshal Wilhelm Keitel (right) at Hitler's Russian headquarters on Aug. 29.

Secretary of State Cordell Hull negotiated with Japanese envoys in a vain effort to reach a modus vivendi in the Pacific. The talks ended with the attack on Pearl Harbor.

	World Affairs	European War Zone	Pacific War Zone	The Americas	Other Countries & Territories
Jan.			Japanese officials affirm Tokyo's intention to establish a "new order" in East Asia.		
Feb.		First German troops under Gen. Erwin Rommel land in Libya .... Germans begin an air offensive against British positions on Malta .... Vichy government in France moves towards closer collaboration with Germany.	British defense measures in Singapore and Malaya draw Japanese protests.		Japan mediates the Thai-Indochinese border dispute, ordering French authorities to cede territory demanded by Thailand.
March	Japanese Foreign Minister Yosuke Matsuoka visits Moscow, Berlin and Rome.	British forces based in the Sudan clear Italians from Eritrea .... German planes resume bombing raids on Britain.		Brazil becomes the leading Latin American spokesman for hemispheric defense.	
Apr.	Matsuoka completes his European tour after signing a five-year neutrality pact with the Russians.	German forces overrun Yugoslavia and Greece as British forces are evacuated to Crete .... Rommel leads a renewed German-Italian drive against the British in North Africa.		Several Latin American nations seize Axis merchant ships in their harbors.	Hindu-Moslem clashes break out again in several Indian cities.
May		German paratroops overrun Crete, forcing evacuation of British forces to Egypt .... German air attacks on Malta reach their greatest intensity .... British forces clear Italians from most of Ethiopia.	Japanese and Chinese forces battle indecisively in central China.	Chilean authorities arrest pro-Nazis for an alleged attempt to overthrow the government.	British troops invade Iraq to suppress the government of pro-Axis Premier Rashid Ali el-Gailani.
June		German invasion of Russia wipes out most post-1939 Soviet territorial gains.	Japanese diplomats negotiate fruitlessly for a favorable trade treaty with the Dutch East Indies.		Free French and British forces invade Syria and Lebanon to prevent pro-Vichy authorities from permitting establishment of German bases.
July		German forces occupy White Russia, advancing to Smolensk .... U.S. Marines arrive in Iceland to reinforce the British.	Japanese troops occupy French Indochina "for defense purposes."	Peru and Ecuador fight indecisively over a disputed boundary region.	Armistice negotiations result in the British occupation of the French-controlled Levant states.
Aug.	FDR and Churchill complete their Atlantic Conference, agreeing to a plan for eventual world peace.	German forces advance in the Ukraine .... U.S. destroyers begin anti-submarine patrols along the North Atlantic sea routes.	Several Japanese government officials charge that western powers are trying to "encircle" their nation.	Peru and Ecuador reject hemispheric requests to end their continuing border war.	British and Russian troops advance into Iran following its refusal to oust Germans.
Sept.	U.S. and British representatives meet in Moscow to discuss Russia's military aid needs.	German forces in the Ukraine eliminate a large Russian salient around Kiev, taking 665,000 prisoners .... Germans overrun the Crimean Peninsula, isolating the Russian garrison in Sevastopol .... German authorities in Western and Central Europe institute repressive measures to halt alleged subversion.		Argentine and Chilean authorities charge German diplomats with subversive activities.	
Oct.		A successful offensive on the central Russian front brings German troops within striking distance of Moscow .... German Army Group North besieges Leningrad.	New Japanese government of Gen. Hideki Tojo takes a more belligerent stance toward the U.S.		
Nov.		German forces eliminate Russian resistance on the Crimean Peninsula and drive on Moscow.	Japanese formally push for diplomatic agreement with the U.S. while secretly preparing for an attack at Pearl Harbor.		
Dec.	Following Japan's attack on Pearl Harbor, American and British representatives meet in Washington to plan war strategy.	A Russian counteroffensive stalls the German drive on Moscow .... Rommel's troops retreat in Libya after British forces break the siege at Tobruk .... First SS extermination camp begins operating at Chelmno, Poland.	Japanese forces overrun Luzon in the Philippines and much of Malaya after immobilizing the U.S. Pacific Fleet at Pearl Harbor.	Canada and several Latin American states declare war on the Axis following Japan's attack on Pearl Harbor. Chile and Argentina maintain their neutrality.	

A	B	C	D	E
Includes developments that affect more than one world region, international organizations and important meetings of major world leaders.	*Includes all developments in European countries and military engagements between Allied and Axis powers in Africa and at sea.*	*Includes all developments in Japan and China, Japanese foreign policy and military actions in the Pacific region.*	*Includes all domestic and regional developments in Latin America, the Caribbean and Canada.*	*Includes developments in those independent nations and colonial possessions not covered in Columns B, C and D.*

U.S. Politics & Social Issues	U.S. Foreign Policy & Defense	U.S. Economy & Environment	Science, Technology & Nature	Culture, Leisure & Life Style	
Negro leaders begin to protest discrimination in defense industries.	Congress opens debate on FDR's Lend-Lease bill. Isolationist groups are organized to speak out against "internationalist" government policies.	Labor's right to strike defense plants is widely debated.	Medical researchers report progress in the fight against pnuemonia and infantile paralysis.	ASCAP's contract with broadcasters expires, severely limiting radio stations' music programs.	Jan.
		FDR signs legislation raising the national debt to $65 billion.	A blizzard sweeps the Eastern seaboard.		Feb.
Several CCNY faculty members come under attack in the N.Y. State legislature for their alleged Communist associations.	Senate Special Comm. to Investigate the National Defense Program, a watchdog group headed by Sen. Harry Truman (D, Mo.), begins functioning.	After much debate, FDR creates a National Defense Mediation Board to settle labor disputes in defense industries.	Northern states are blanketed with heavy snows.		March
	American Lend-Lease aid begins flowing to Britain following congressional approval of the Administration bill.	Labor strikes disrupt several important industries, including Northern soft coal mines.	Forest fires cause extensive destruction in several Eastern states.		Apr.
FBI and Justice Department open drives against fifth columnists and illegal aliens.	Airplane and ship production increases, as FDR seeks additional defense funds from Congress.	Congress completes action on a bill empowering the government to establish priority needs for defense production.	Dr. Martin H. Dawson reports the discovery of penicillin.		May
	Government takes steps to restrict Axis activities in the U.S., including the freezing of German and Italian assets.	As labor unrest spreads, Congress considers legislation banning strikes at defense plants.			June
		Government agencies take initial steps to limit production of several consumer items.		Joe DiMaggio's record-setting 56-game hitting streak ends.	July
Georgia political leaders attack the state's educational system for teaching racial equality.		Because of short supplies the sale of gasoline along the East Coast is restricted.		Rationing of silk stockings begins.	Aug.
	U.S. introduces a convoy system to protect lend-lease supplies en route to Britain from German submarines .... Construction begins in Washington on the Pentagon, headquarters of the War and Navy departments.	Congress completes action and FDR signs a $3.5-billion defense tax bill.	An infantile paralysis epidemic kills 87 persons throughout the country.	Debate over hemline length begins in the women's garment industry, with government agencies pressing for shorter garments to save material.	Sept.
	Congress debates FDR's proposal to repeal the 1939 Neutrality Act.	Labor strikes halt production in several key industries: shipbuilding, aeronautics and coal.	Tornadoes cause heavy damage and death in several states.		Oct.
		FDR appoints special commissions to resolve labor-management disputes in the coal and steel industries.		*Reader's Digest* reports it has reached record monthly circulation sales.	Nov.
	Demand grows in Congress and the nation for an investigation to fix blame for lack of U.S. readiness at Pearl Harbor and other Pacific bases under attack by the Japanese .... Congress completes action on selective service legislation and increased defense appropriations.	Following the outbreak of war, the government moves to restrict labor unrest and further limit production of consumer goods.	The medical profession debates the value of Elizabeth Kenny's massage treatment of infantile paralysis.	Movie critics salute Orson Welles' *Citizen Kane* as the best film in 1941.	Dec.

F	G	H	I	J
Includes elections, federal-state relations, civil rights and liberties, crime, the judiciary, education, health care, poverty, urban affairs and population.	*Includes formation and debate of U.S. foreign and defense policies, veterans affairs and defense spending. (Relations with specific foreign countries are usually found under the region concerned.)*	*Includes business, labor, agriculture, taxation, transportation, consumer affairs, monetary and fiscal policy, natural resources, pollution and accidents.*	*Includes worldwide scientific, medical and technological developments, natural phenomena, U.S. weather and natural disasters.*	*Includes the arts, religion, scholarship, communications media, sports, entertainment, fashions, fads and social life.*

	World Affairs	European War Zone	Pacific War Zone	The Americas	Other Countries & Territories
Jan. 1		RAF bombs Bremen for 3½ hours .... Vichy government announces provisional French budget of approximately 40 billion francs for next four months.		National Herrerista Party withdraws opposition to construction of Pan-American defense base in Uruguay.	South African P.M. Jan Christiaan Smuts predicts U.S. will enter war in order to save Britain from defeat.
Jan. 2		Protectorate of Bohemia-Moravia agrees to double its tribute to Germany as "guarantor of the Protectorate's security and sovereignty."		Pres. Arnulfo Arias says Panama cannot accept U.S. sovereignty or jurisdiction over any segment of his country but is ready to cooperate with U.S. military forces.	
Jan. 3		Australian troops launch attack on Bardia, Libya .... Irish government protests German bombing of Curragh, Julianstown, Duleck, and Burris and demands reparations. Germans deny charge.			
Jan. 4		Johann Wilhelm Rangell forms new Finnish Cabinet.		Ecuadorians and Peruvians clash at Carrol Viejo in a border dispute.	Vichy appoints Gen. Henri Dentz high commissioner for Syria .... Vichy decrees dominion status for Indochina.
Jan. 5		British report capture of Bardia, Libya from Italians .... British Air Ministry reports bombing of Hamburg, Germany, and Brest, France. German bombers hit Bristol.	Foreign Min. Yosuke Matsuoka says Japan must establish "Greater East Asia Sphere" as step towards peace.	*La Razon*, a newspaper in Bogota, says Germany has smuggled counterfeit pesos and dollars into Colombia.	
Jan. 6			Japanese-controled government in Nanking opens Central Reserve Bank and declares its notes must be used for customs duties in central China.	Chile and Argentina agree to confer on territorial rights in Antarctic regions.	
Jan. 7	Foreign Min. Matsuoka protests seizure of Japanese funds in Bermuda by the British.	British troops capture El Adem airport, 15 miles south of Tobruk, Libya.			
Jan. 8		British announce that basic food ration will be cut or raised week-by-week as the situation demands.		Nelson A. Rockefeller, coordinator of commercial and cultural relations within the Americas, reports that anti-American firms frequently represent U.S. business in Latin America.	Thailand imposes martial law in 24 provinces bordering Indochina.
Jan. 9					French military authorities claim destruction of at least 40 Thai war planes on Indochina border, but acknowledge a general withdrawal of five to 10 miles from the frontier.
Jan. 10		Russia and Germany sign an economic agreement to run until Aug. 1, 1942, under which Germany will receive food and raw materials in exchange for indistrial equipment .... Italian and German dive bombers attack British convoy off Sicily. Cruiser *Southhampton* is sunk by British ships after sustaining severe damage.	Kenkicki Yoshizawa, head of Japanese trade mission in Netherlands East Indies, says his country has no improper designs on Dutch colonies.	Federal employes protest in Mexico City against dismissals and reported government intention to reform civil service by barring strikes .... James N. Rosenberg, president of Dominican Republic Settlement Assn., announces that Gen. Rafael L. Trujillo is donating 50,000 acres for European refugees.	
	A *Includes developments that affect more than one world region, international organizations and important meetings of major world leaders.*	B *Includes all developments in European countries and military engagements between Allied and Axis powers in Africa and at sea.*	C *Includes all developments in Japan and China, Japanese foreign policy and military actions in the Pacific region.*	D *Includes all domestic and regional developments in Latin America, the Caribbean and Canada.*	E *Includes developments in those independent nations and colonial possessions not covered in Columns B, C and D.*

U.S. Politics & Social Issues	U.S. Foreign Policy & Defense	U.S. Economy & Environment	Science, Technology & Nature	Culture, Leisure & Life Style	
Jersey City Mayor Frank Hague announces he will run for a seventh term in May .... Census Bureau announces the 1940 U.S. population was 131,669,275, a gain of nearly nine million since 1930.	Sen Arthur Vandenberg (R, Mich.) is quoted as saying he would back Roosevelt's policies, "even though I know it is bound to lead us into war," if the U.S. first exhausted all avenues of peace.	Federal Reserve presents Congress with monetary plan to forestall inflation and improve monetary organization.		ASCAP contract with National Association of Broadcasters expires, forcing 674 radio stations to stop broadcasting 1,500,000 ASCAP-controlled songs, including the nation's most popular hits .... Stanford tops Nebraska 21-13 in Rose Bowl. Boston College wins Sugar Bowl 19-13 over Tennessee. Cotton Bowl is captured by Texas A&M over Fordham, 13-12. Mississippi State defeats Georgetown 14-7 in Orange Bowl.	Jan. 1
Last five of 17 Christian Front members charged with conspiracy to overthrow the government are freed in Brooklyn as prosecution drops the case.	William A. White announces his resignation as chairman of the Comm. to Defend America by Aiding the Allies, complaining that the group is controlled by a pro-war faction .... Gallup Poll reports 85% of voters believe Britain would lose the war if U.S. war shipments stopped.	FDR announces a program to build 200 standardized 7,500-ton freighters for war effort .... Wage and Hour Administrator Phillip B. Fleming orders increase in minimum wages for railroad employes.			Jan. 2
Dies Committee urges Congress to outlaw all political organizations under foreign control and deport aliens advocating "any basic change in the form of our government." .... 77th Congress convenes and re-elects Sam Rayburn (D, Tex.) speaker of the House.	FDR appoints Harry Hopkins as his personal representative to Britain.	FDR suspends eight-hour day for workers constructing army and navy bases in Atlantic and Caribbean.	Dr. Norman Plummer reports dramatic decrease in death rate of pnuemonia victims by using sulfanilamide family of drugs .... William J. Lane, 100, who introduced Lane Steamer automobile in 1901 dies.	Shirley Temple comes out of one-year retirement to star in new Andy Hardy series with Mickey Rooney.	Jan. 3
House Un-American Activities Comm. asks Congress to bar foreign anti-American propaganda from benefit of reduced postage rates.	Sen. Carter Glass (D, Va.) urges U.S. Navy to act against Germany .... Sino-Korean Peoples League in Los Angeles accuses Japanese consulates of conscripting Japanese descendents on Pacific Coast and in Hawaii.	AFL metal unions adopt a no-strike policy to speed national defense effort.		Henri Louis Bergson, world famous French philosopher and Nobel Prize winner, dies in Paris at 81 .... Charles Chaplin declines N.Y. Film Critics Award as best male actor of 1940 because it implies that actors compete with each other.	Jan. 4
	Oil magnate William R. Davis denies funding Verne Marshall's No Foreign War Comm.	Ford Motor Co. blames outside agitators for labor disturbances at its plants .... Executive board of CIO Industrial Union of Marine and Shipbuilders bars Nazis, Communists and Fascists from national or local office.			Jan. 5
	FDR outlines "four essential freedoms"—freedom of speech and worship and freedom from fear and want—in his State of the Union message calling for U.S. to become an arsenal for the democracies. Sen. Burton K. Wheeler (D, Mont.) denounces speech as an attempt to frighten Americans into "a war-time dictatorship" .... Keel of the battleship *Missouri* is laid at the Brooklyn Navy Yard.	Charles E. Wilson is elected president of General Motors.			Jan. 6
N.J. judge uphold state's "race hatred" statutes by overruling objections of nine convicted German-American Bund leaders .... Eleanor Roosevelt says she is "shocked" that GOP Congressmen did not applaud FDR's State of the Union message.		FDR creates Office of Production Management (OPM), with William Knudsen as director general. Sidney Hillman is appointed associate director general with equal powers .... Nineteen national unions affiliated with AFL's Building Trades Department adopt no-strike policy on defense construction.			Jan. 7
		FDR presents his budget to Congress, providing for expenditures of nearly $17.5 billion. $10.8 billion is earmarked for national defense .... CIO Pres. Philip Murray refuses to yield on workers' right to strike despite national emergency.		Long distance runner Gregory Rice receives the AAU's James E. Sullivan Memorial Trophy as outstanding amateur athlete of 1940 .... Sir Robert Baden-Powell, 83, founder of Boy Scouts movement, dies in Nyeri, Kenya.	Jan. 8
GOP Reps. Edith Rogers (Mass.), John Taber (N.Y.), Clare Hoffman (Mich.) and Noah Mason (Ill.) criticize Eleanor Roosevelt's remarks about their failure to applaud FDR's State of the Union speech.	State Dept. reports U.S. denial of French request for aid in solving problem of German-Jewish refugees in France .... Ernest W. Gibson is elected chairman of the Comm. to Defend America by Aiding the Allies .... Hopkins arrives in London in the midst of a German bombing attack.	Several thousand city employes strike for six hours in Chicago to protest wage cuts.		John Hay Whitney is elected president of the Museum of Modern Art in N.Y., succeeding Nelson A. Rockefeller.	Jan. 9
Democratic-controlled Missouri General Assembly refuses to certify election of Gov.-elect Forrest C. Donnell (R), who official returns show won by 3,613 votes .... R.J. Reynolds, of N.C. tobacco family and newly-appointed treasurer of the Democratic National Comm., testifies before a Senate committee probing campaign financing that he loaned Democratic organizations $300,000.	FDR's Lend-Lease bill (H.R. 1776) is introduced to both houses of Congress .... Opposition to Lend-Lease comes from Sens. Hiram W. Johnson (D, Cal.) Patrick A. McCarren (D, Nev.) Robert Taft (R, Ohio) and Rep. Hamilton Fish (R, N.Y.).		Drs. Edwin W. Schultz and Hubert Loring of Stanford Univ. announce extraction of the infantile paralysis virus almost free of impurities and ready for examination.		Jan. 10

F	G	H	I	J
Includes elections, federal-state relations, civil rights and liberties, crime, the judiciary, education, health care, poverty, urban affairs and population.	*Includes formation and debate of U.S. foreign and defense policies, veterans affairs and defense spending. (Relations with specific foreign countries are usually found under the region concerned.)*	*Includes business, labor, agriculture, taxation, transportation, consumer affairs, monetary and fiscal policy, natural resources, pollution and accidents.*	*Includes worldwide scientific, medical and technological developments, natural phenomena, U.S. weather and natural disasters.*	*Includes the arts, religion, scholarship, communications media, sports, entertainment, fashions, fads and social life.*

	World Affairs	European War Zone	Pacific War Zone	The Americas	Other Countries & Territories
Jan. 11		Swedish papers say Vidkun Quisling, head of the Norwegian Nazi regime, has appealed for German help to quell opposition.		Brazilian government says newspaper attacks against U.S. will not be tolerated . . . . State Dept. announces the legation in Uruguay has been raised to embassy status, with Min. Edwin C. Wilson named ambassador.	
Jan. 12		Bulgarian Premier Bogdan Philov reaffirms that his country will remain neutral . . . . Premier Count Paul Teleki of Hungary declares that his country must prepare for anything but will remain independent of outside world.		Chilean CP secy. Carlos Contreras says nitrate and copper purchases by U.S. are bribes by American imperialism.	
Jan. 13		Gen. Ugo Cavallero is appointed commander in chief of Italian forces in Albania.			
Jan. 14		Adam Reiss, leader of German Volksbund, the official German minority organization in Hungary, is ousted from the party on charges of working against the interest of the German minority.		Argentine Finance Min. Dr. Federico Pinedo resigns when government rejects his plan for mobilizing nation against depression . . . . Masked men wreck the German-operated transocean radio station in Quito, Ecuador.	Gen. Mordant arrives in Saigon from France to take command of Indochina army.
Jan. 15	Japanese Foreign Min. Matsuoka stresses the unity in friendship of Japan and Germany in Tokyo speech.				
Jan. 16				Bolivia and Chile sign a non-aggression pact, agree to study a new commercial and financial accord and arrange for "intellectual cooperation."	
Jan. 17		Churchill says Britain needs U.S. weapons, ships and airplanes to defeat Axis powers.	Chungking national military council arrests Gen. Yeh Ting, commander of the Communist 4th route army, for allegedly planning a revolt.	Panamanian Amb. Carlos W. Brin denies Pres. Arnufo Arias is a dictator and declares Panama is ready to aid in the defense of the canal . . . . Chilean Radical, Democratic and Radical Socialist parties, excluding the Communists, sign a pact to uphold democratic and republican ideals.	
Jan. 18		Marshal Petain and Pierre Laval meet and reportedly resolve their differences on Vichy policies . . . . Two former Spanish Republican premiers, Francisco Largo Caballero and Diego Martinez Barrio, lose their Spanish citizenship.		Foreign Min. Ezequiel Padilla says the Mexican government will not lease any property to any foreign country in connection with any bases built on Mexican soil with U.S. aid.	
Jan. 19		Mussolini visits Hitler at Berghof. Hitler outlines his secret plans to invade Greece . . . . Malta reports the second German air attack on Valetta in the last two days.			
Jan. 20		A new German tax effective Jan. 1 levies a 15% additional gross income tax on Jews to "compensate" for their "social inferiority."			
Jan. 21		British and Australian troops begin assault on Italian stronghold of Tobruk, Libya . . . . Fatal shooting of a German Army major by a Greek sets off riots in Bucharest, Rumania.	Premier Prince Fumimaro Konoye tells the Japanese Diet that the creation of "a new order in East Asia" is the backbone of Japan's foreign policy.		Britain signs trade pacts with the Belgian exile government regarding the Congo and with Gen. Charles de Gaulle's Free French Council of Defense regarding the French Cameroons.

A	B	C	D	E
Includes developments that affect more than one world region, international organizations and important meetings of major world leaders.	*Includes all developments in European countries and military engagements between Allied and Axis powers in Africa and at sea.*	*Includes all developments in Japan and China, Japanese foreign policy and military actions in the Pacific region.*	*Includes all domestic and regional developments in Latin America, the Caribbean and Canada.*	*Includes developments in those independent nations and colonial possessions not covered in Columns B, C and D.*

U.S. Politics & Social Issues	U.S. Foreign Policy & Defense	U.S. Economy & Environment	Science, Technology & Nature	Culture, Leisure & Life Style	
Sen. Guy M. Gillette (D, Iowa) says both Democrats and GOP evaded $3-million limit on 1940 campaign expenditures.	Secy. of State Cordell Hull announces a final agreement has been reached with Britain on sites for eight U.S. naval and air bases in the Atlantic and Caribbean under the destroyers-for-bases trade . . . . Sen. W. Warren Austin (R, Vt.) says he favors Lend-Lease bill, but urges two-year limit on presidential authority under the bill.			Former world chess champion Emanuel Lasker dies at 72 in N.Y.	Jan. 11
Clarence A. Hathaway, former editor of the *Daily Worker*, is expelled from the CP for failing to meet his responsibilities and "refusing to take steps to rehabilitate himself."	Wendell L. Willkie supports FDR's Lend-Lease plan with a time limit.				Jan. 12
Mathew M. Neely, sworn in as governor of W. Va. at a secret midnight ceremony, appoints Joseph Rosier to his unexpired Senate term.	Treasury Secy. Henry Morgenthau says Britain is ready to negotiate sale of direct British investments in U.S. to pay for war purchases until Lend-Lease is passed . . . . Kenneth F. Simpson (R, N.Y.) introduces to House substitute Lend-Lease bill, placing a two-year limit on presidential powers . . . . A meeting of 20,000 Communists and sympathizers in N.Y. passes resolution denouncing Lend-Lease.	CIO-UAW strikers clash with non-strikers at Wilcox-Rich plant of Eaton Mfg. Co. in Saginaw, Mich.		Irish novelist James Joyce, whose work was the subject of the century's greatest literary controversy, dies at 58 in Zurich . . . . Anton Christoforidis of Greece wins National Boxing Assn. recognition as world light-heavyweight champion by defeating Melio Bettina in Cleveland.	Jan. 13
Senate refuses to seat either Joseph Rosier, appointed by the new W. Va. governor, or Clarence E. Martin, appointed by the retiring governor.	FDR denounces Sen. Wheeler's statement that Lend-Lease policy would "plow under every fourth American boy."	Federal labor mediator James F. Dewey warns Eaton Mfg. Co. and CIO-UAW to settle their dispute as "an urgent matter of national defense."			Jan. 14
Negro union leader A. Philip Randolph calls for 10,000 Negroes to march on Washington to demand an end to discrimination in defense employment.	Secy. of State Cordell Hull and Treasury Secy. Morgenthau defend Lend-Lease as necessary for national defense and urge quick congressional action . . . . N.Y. Dist. Atty. Thomas E. Dewey says Lend-Lease aid to Britain would end free government in the U.S.	James Dewey announces the CIO-UAW strike against the Eaton Mfg. Co. has been settled.		Van Wyck Brooks' book *New England: Indian Summer, 1865-1915*, is chosen the most important non-fiction book published in 1940 by *Current History and Forum*.	Jan. 15
	Former Pres. Herbert Hoover asks the House Foreign Affairs Comm. to clearly define the powers granted to the President in the Lend-Lease bill . . . . Rep. George H. Pinkham (R, Mass.) accuses FDR of plotting of plotting to get the U.S. into war. Rep. Hamilton Fish (R, N.Y.) describes Lend-Lease as "the President's dictator bill."		Dr. Charles Thurston Holland, British radiologist and a pioneer in the use of X-rays in medicine and surgery, dies in Liverpool.	Will H. Hays, president of the Motion Pictures Producers and Distributers of America, Inc., denies Sen. Wheeler's charge that the motion picture industry is inciting the American people to war.	Jan. 16
	War Secy. Henry L. Stimson says Lend-Lease is "very probably" necessary to prevent a British defeat . . . . Secy. Hull announces Britain has agreed to U.S. establishment of an airbase on the island of St. Lucia in British West Indies.	CIO-Farm Equipment Workers strike at the E. Moline, Ill. plant of the International Harvester Co. protesting what they call a lockout.		Fritizie Zivic, world's welterweight champion, scores a TKO in the 12th round over Henry Armstrong, who later announces his retirement from the ring . . . . Delores del Rio, Mexican film star, divorces Cedric Gibbons, movie art director, in Hollywood.	Jan. 17
Sen. Arthur Capper (R, Kan.) urges the adoption of federal and state health insurance laws.	Retiring American Amb. to Britain Joseph P. Kennedy declares that England is not fighting our battle in Europe, and opposes Lend-Lease bill . . . . OPM Director William S. Knudsen testifies in favor of Lend-Lease even if the money is never repaid, for by helping Britain America helps herself.	NLRB charges Ford Motor Co. with discrimination against 1,021 union workers and orders their reinstatement at Ford's Kansas City plant.	Russian balloonists claim new world's record for their ascent in an open gondola to 36,300 feet.	Professional Football Writers Assn. of America picks quarterback Clarence Parker as the most valuable player in the NFL for 1940.	Jan. 18
	Willkie confers with FDR and Hull in Washington . . . . Treasury Dept. is reported to have drafted an executive order ready for FDR's signature to freeze all foreign assets in the U.S.	Secretary-Treasurer Thomas Kennedy says United Mine Workers union is for labor and Americanism and condemns Communism Nazism, and Fascism.		Bob Feller, Cleveland Indians' pitcher, signs a $30,000 contract, reportedly becoming the highest paid pitcher in baseball's history.	Jan. 19
FDR is inaugurated President for a record-breaking third term . . . . Supreme Court rules Pennsylvania's alien registration law is an illegal infringement on federal authority.		Federal grand jury investigating defense industries indicts three corporations, seven individuals and four foreign companies on charges of creating a monopoly to control magnesite.			Jan. 20
	FDR tells press conference that he is not considering using the U.S. Navy for convoys of ships to Britain . . . . State Dept. announces that the "moral embargo" on shipment of planes to Russia dating from Dec. 2, 1939 has been lifted . . . . Former Amb. Kennedy opposes Lend-Lease bill "in its present form" in testimony before House Foreign Affairs Comm. He doubts Britain will be able to defeat the Axis.				Jan. 21

F	G	H	I	J
Includes elections, federal-state relations, civil rights and liberties, crime, the judiciary, education, health care, poverty, urban affairs and population.	*Includes formation and debate of U.S. foreign and defense policies, veterans affairs and defense spending. (Relations with specific foreign countries are usually found under the region concerned.)*	*Includes business, labor, agriculture, taxation, transportation, consumer affairs, monetary and fiscal policy, natural resources, pollution and accidents.*	*Includes worldwide scientific, medical and technological developments, natural phenomena, U.S. weather and natural disasters.*	*Includes the arts, religion, scholarship, communications media, sports, entertainment, fashions, fads and social life.*

	World Affairs	European War Zone	Pacific War Zone	The Americas	Other Countries & Territories
Jan. 22		Australian troops aided by Free French forces capture Tobruk after a 20-day siege, taking some 14,000 additional Italian prisoners .... Codreanists revolting against Rumanian Premier Ion Antonescu seize the Bucharest radio station and claim control of government buildings and naval stations in Constanza.	Japanese Diet surrenders its right to publicly examine the policies of the cabinet in exchange for a government promise not to amend the election law.	Chilean Chamber of Deputies passes a bill outlawing the Communist Party.	
Jan. 23		German battle cruisers *Scharnhorst* and *Gneisenau* leave Kiel .... Bucharest radio station broadcasts that the Rumanian rebels have agreed to end hostilities.			Vichy announces that France accepted Japan's offer to mediate the conflict between Indochina and Thailand.
Jan. 24		Premier Antonescu blames Vice Premier Horia Sima, chief of the Iron Guard, for the four-day revolt in Rumania and says the German army lent its "moral support" in crushing the rebellion .... Marshal Henri Philippe Petain creates a 188-man advisory National Council in France.		Argentine Foreign Min. Julio Roca tenders his resignation to acting Pres. Ramon Castillo.	
Jan. 25				Cuba's Secy. of State Jose Manuel Cortina repudiates U.S. Sen. George Smather's (D, Fla.) resolution to admit Cuba as a state of the union.	
Jan. 26			Japanese Foreign Min. Matsuoka accuses Secy. Hull of distorting the truth about the "Manchurian Affair," which he blames on "Anglo-Saxon interference in the Far East."		India League meeting in London declares British rule has "ruined" India.
Jan. 27		Petain promulgates a new law requiring all Vichy ministers and high officials to personally swear allegiance to him in his presence .... Italian Foreign Min. Count Galeazzo Ciano has returned to active military duty in the Air Force, according to a Rome communique.	Premier Konoye tells the Japanese Diet that there is no sign of a solution to the conflict in China.	Regional conference on the River Plate opens in Montevideo, Uruguay.	
Jan. 28		Gen. George C. Marshall, U.S. chief of staff, says there are growing indications that Germany will attempt to invade Britain this spring .... Gen. Francisco Franco nationalizes the Spanish transportation systems in order to ease the food situation.	Japanese Finance Ministry announces that about $4.1 billion has been spent on the war in China.	Edward W. Scott, correspondent for Reuters and the UP in Panama, is ordered deported by Pres. Arias for writing that Arias sympathizes with the Axis.	
Jan. 29		Greek Premier John Metaxas, 69, dies after more than five years as virtual dictator of the country. Alexander Korizis is named to replace him .... Vichy government announces the creation of a 40-man national committee called Rassemblement National to replace the old political parties.	Foreign Min. Matsuoka states his hope that the appointment of Nobumasa Nomura as Japanese ambassador to the U.S. will improve relations.	Pres. Fulgencio Batista signs a decree making totalitarian propaganda in Cuba illegal.	Japanese, French and Thai representatives start armistice negotiations to stop border hostilities between Thailand and Indochina.
Jan. 30		Hitler warns that American ships carrying aid to Britain will be sunk .... Derna, Libya falls to British.		Brazilian Pres. Vargas signs a decree creating the National Steel Corp.	
Jan. 31		Free French commander Gen. Charles de Gaulle appeals to Gen Maxime Weygand's African army to help complete the conquest of Italian Libya.	Pres. Manuel Quezon of the Philippines states the defense of the country rests primarily with the U.S.		Thai and French officials sign a Japanese-mediated armistice terminating Indochina border disputes.
Feb. 1		French Gen. Weygand rejects de Gaulle's appeal to liberate Libya .... Berlin reports the creation of the National Popular Assembly in Paris for the reconstruction of France in collaboration with Germany.	Japan announces that rice will be rationed.	Pres. Anastasio Somoza invites the U.S. to establish air and naval bases in Nicaragua.	Mohammed Mahmoud Pasha, Egyptian minister of defense and nationalist movement leader, dies in Cairo at the age of 58.

A	B	C	D	E
Includes developments that affect more than one world region, international organizations and important meetings of major world leaders.	*Includes all developments in European countries and military engagements between Allied and Axis powers in Africa and at sea.*	*Includes all developments in Japan and China, Japanese foreign policy and military actions in the Pacific region.*	*Includes all domestic and regional developments in Latin America, the Caribbean and Canada.*	*Includes developments in those independent nations and colonial possessions not covered in Columns B, C and D.*

U.S. Politics & Social Issues	U.S. Foreign Policy & Defense	U.S. Economy & Environment	Science, Technology & Nature	Culture, Leisure & Life Style	
James Clark McReynolds, associate justice of the Supreme Court since 1914, submits his resignation to FDR, effective Feb. 1.	Sen. George W. Norris (Ind, Neb.), who voted against war in 1917, says he favors Lend-Lease bill but that it should be limited to two years .... Norman Thomas testifies before the House Foreign Affairs Comm. that the Lend-Lease bill amounts to undeclared war .... Willkie leaves N.Y. on Lisbon-bound *Yankee Clipper* en route to England.	More than 9,000 UAW members at Allis-Chalmers Mfg. Co. in West Allis, Wis. strike for a closed shop and higher wages. The company is working on $26-million worth of defense orders.		Detroit Tigers reveal pitcher Buck Newsom received a $30,000 salary last year and will get more in 1941.	Jan. 22
	Charles Lindbergh tells House committee the U.S. does not require a British victory, opposing Lend-Lease and predicting a British defeat .... Judge William Bondy of the U.S. District Court in N.Y. rules that the 1940 Draft Act is constitutional .... FDR nominates Dean G. Acheson to be assistant secretary of state.				Jan. 23
	FDR breaks diplomatic precedent by welcoming Viscount Halifax, the new British ambassador, when he arrives aboard the new battleship *King George V* in Chesapeake Bay.	Labor Secy. Frances Perkins reports the largest employment rise in 11 years, bringing the total number of workers to 37.1 million in December 1940.		Leopold Stokowski, director of the Philadelphia Symphony Orchestra, will train an 85-piece Army band in California in an experiment to develop more "typically American music" and "modernize" Army bands.	Jan. 24
	William C. Bullitt, former ambassador to France, supports Lend-Lease and warns House Foreign Affairs Comm. of German invasion through Latin America if Britain falls.				Jan. 25
NAACP sponsors meetings in 23 states to protest employment discrimination in defense plants.	Sens. Wheeler and Nye and Rep. Fish reiterate their opposition to the Lend-Lease bill.				Jan. 26
Senate confirms the appointment of Frank C. Walker as postmaster general.	Willkie visits Churchill in London .... Senate passes without dissent a House-passed $300-million appropriation to modernize Navy ships against air attack.	U.S. Atty. William F. Smith files a civil antitrust action in Trenton, N.J. against General Electric, Westinghouse Electric and 10 other concerns on charges of monopolizing the electric light bulb industry.	Dr. Alex Hardlisha of the Smithsonian Institute claims that larger and broader skulls, lower cheekbones and dark hair are the physical characteristics that distinguish the nation's "best minds."	William Randolph Hearst's art collection goes on private display in N.Y. Over 10,000 items are included.	Jan. 27
Census Bureau reports the nation's population is growing older, with a median age of 28.9 years in 1940.	Treasury Secy. Morgenthau testifies before the Senate Foreign Relations Comm. that Congress must pass the Lend-Lease bill if the Allies are to continue to fight.	A U.S. Chamber of Commerce committee announces its opposition to anti-strike laws as contrary to fundamental rights of citizens .... CIO Pres. Murray makes public a plan to increase steel output by coordinating the steel industry as a single production unit.			Jan. 28
	House Foreign Affairs Comm. adopts amendments to the Lend-Lease bill, limiting the bill to June 30, 1943 and barring convoying by U.S. Navy. Fifteen other amendments are defeated .... Senate passes the $909-million authorization for Navy expansion and sends it to FDR .... Secret U.S.-British military staff talks begin in Washington.	A third International Harvester Co. plant working on defense orders is closed by the CIO Farm Equipment Workers union strike .... Rep. Carl Vinson (D, Ga.) introduces a bill to bar strikes and closed shop on naval defense projects.			Jan. 29
	House Foreign Affairs Comm. approves amended Lend-Lease bill, 17-8.	War Dept. awards $10 million truck contract to Chrysler affiliate despite a lower bid from Ford Motor Co. because Ford refused to comply with federal, state and local labor laws .... Federal grand jury indicts six companies and nine officials for operating an international magnesium trust since 1927. Two German firms are included.	RCA officials describe a new and simplified electron microscope that magnifies objects up to 100,000 times.	Nation celebrates FDR's 59th birthday with thousands of parties and other festivities to raise money for the Nat. Foundation for Infantile Paralysis.	Jan. 30
Nine German-American Bund leaders are sentenced to 12 to 14 months imprisonment for violating N.J. "race hatred" law.	Eight of 10 GOP members of House Foreign Affairs Comm. issue dissenting report on Lend-Lease, urging a $2-billion loan for Britain instead.	FDR says government is prepared to take over any plant in the country considered necessary in the national defense .... Four major N.Y. banks disclose a cooperative plan to speed up financing of defense contracts.		Richard Wright, 32, author of *Native Son*, wins the Joel Springarn Medal awarded by the NAACP for the highest achievement "in any honorable field of endeavor."	Jan. 31
Former Treasury secretary and California Sen. William McAdoo, 77, dies.	Navy Secy. Frank Knox tells Senate Foreign Relations Comm. he is worried that Britain may be defeated and that he is "positive" that the Axis would then invade the Western Hemisphere .... U.S. Conference of Mayors urges development of a civil defense program for cities that may be exposed to attack.				Feb. 1
F *Includes elections, federal-state relations, civil rights and liberties, crime, the judiciary, education, health care, poverty, urban affairs and population.*	G *Includes formation and debate of U.S. foreign and defense policies, veterans affairs and defense spending. (Relations with specific foreign countries are usually found under the region concerned.)*	H *Includes business, labor, agriculture, taxation, transportation, consumer affairs, monetary and fiscal policy, natural resources, pollution and accidents.*	I *Includes worldwide scientific, medical and technological developments, natural phenomena, U.S. weather and natural disasters.*	J *Includes the arts, religion, scholarship, communications media, sports, entertainment, fashions, fads and social life.*	

	World Affairs	European War Zone	Pacific War Zone	The Americas	Other Countries & Territories
Feb. 2				P.M. W.L. Mackenzie King announces Canada will double her overseas armed forces.	Peace is restored in Johannesburg, South Africa after three days of rioting between soldiers and anti-British civilians.
Feb. 3		Hitler approves final version of the secret "Barbarossa" plan for the invasion of Russia.	Officials say Japan will not abandon her program of economic penetration of the Netherlands East Indies despite Dutch protests.	Pres. Batista takes over personal command of Cuba's armed forces and suspends civil rights for 15 days.	
Feb. 4			Japanese troops make a surprise landing in Kwangtung Province in an effort to cut supply lines into free China.		
Feb. 5		British bombers hit Brest, Dunkerque, Dieppe, Ostend, Bordeaux and Duesseldorf in their heaviest raids in two weeks.			
Feb. 6		Benghazi, Libya falls to British and Australian troops under Lt. Gen. Sir Archibald Wavell .... Rumanian government decrees a new criminal code which doubles prison terms for Communists, Jews, and non-Rumanians.		River Plate Conference ends in Montevideo, Uruguay with the five Latin American nations agreeing on economic matters and signing 26 regional pacts.	
Feb. 7		Gen. Weygand announces that he will not allow German troops to land in Bizerte, Tunisia.		Chile and Peru sign a pact in Lima providing for joint defense of their Pacific coast line .... Pres. Vargas of Brazil suppresses all foreign language publications, granting them 6 months to change to the Portuguese language.	Peace conference between Thailand and French Indochina opens in Tokyo.
Feb. 8		German and Bulgarian general staffs reach secret agreement for permitting passage of German troops to attack Greece .... Greek government asks British aid if Germans attack .... French government reports Laval has rejected Petain's offer to be readmitted into the Vichy cabinet as a minister of state. Laval reportedly demanded the premiership with a cabinet of his own choosing.	Adm. Baron Mineo Osumi, Japanese supreme war councilor, and six naval officers are killed in airplane crash en route to Hainan.	Pres. Vargas decrees that export permits will be required for Brazilian raw materials, chemical products, machinery and tools to all countries outside the Americas .... Malcolm McDonald is appointed British high commissioner to Canada.	
Feb. 9		Churchill says in a London broadcast that Britain doesn't need American armies. "Give us the tools and we will finish the job," he promises .... British fleet shells Genoa, Italy .... Adm. Jean Darlan is appointed foreign minister and vice premier of the Vichy government.			
Feb. 10		British colonial forces cross Kenyan border into Italian Somaliland .... Britain announces it has broken diplomatic relations with Rumania because her territory is being used by Germany as a military base.	RAF bombers leave Singapore for bases in northern Malaya.		
Feb. 11		Vichy publishes a constitutional act announcing the appointment of Admiral Darlan as next in line of succession to Marshal Petain as chief of state.		Paraguayan government takes control of the foreign exchange held in the Bank of the Republic.	

A	B	C	D	E
Includes developments that affect more than one world region, international organizations and important meetings of major world leaders.	*Includes all developments in European countries and military engagements between Allied and Axis powers in Africa and at sea.*	*Includes all developments in Japan and China, Japanese foreign policy and military actions in the Pacific region.*	*Includes all domestic and regional developments in Latin America, the Caribbean and Canada.*	*Includes developments in those independent nations and colonial possessions not covered in Columns B, C and D.*

U.S. Politics & Social Issues	U.S. Foreign Policy & Defense	U.S. Economy & Environment	Science, Technology & Nature	Culture, Leisure & Life Style	
		AFL Pres. William Green claims majority of workers at the River Rouge and Lincoln plants of the Ford Motor Co. want to join the AFL. The CIO disputes the claim and appeals to the NLRB.		Ken Bartholomew captures the 1941 North American speed skating championship.	Feb. 2
Eleanor Roosevelt refuses to speak to the American Youth Congress because of its opposition to the draft and aid to Britain.		Supreme Court unanimously upholds the constitutionality of the 1938 Fair Labors Standards Act, the wage-hour law . . . . Third Federal Court of Appeals rules the NLRB lacks the legal right to police relations between an employer and his employes under a collective bargaining agreement.		Elmer Layden resigns as head football coach of Notre Dame to accept a 5-year contract as commissioner of professional football.	Feb. 3
	FDR announces extention of export licensing system to Russia in an effort to prevent shipments from reaching Germany through Russia . . . . Gen. Robert E. Wood, acting chmn. of the America First Committee, claims Britain has enough assets in the U.S. to finance war orders for another year to 18 months.				Feb. 4
Federal antitrust suit against the AMA, the Medical Society of Washington, the Washington Academy of Surgery and the Harris County (Texas) Medical Society begins in Washington.	House ends the three-day debate on the Lend-Lease bill in an unusual night session . . . . State Supreme Court Justice Morris Eder signs a writ of attachment in N.Y., tying up $260 million in funds of the Bank of France in the U.S. . . . . Willkie leaves Britain for N.Y. after recording an anti-Nazi radio message for broadcast to Germany.	Eleanor Roosevelt tells strikers at Leviton Manufacturing Co. in Brooklyn that every worker "should join a labor organization."		Justice Dept. files suit against the American Society of Authors, Composers and Publishers (ASCAP), charging it is an unlawful conbination in restraint of trade . . . . Three NFL club owners protest appointment of Elmer Layden as "illegal."	Feb. 5
	House votes 148-141 for amendment to Lend-Lease bill giving Congress the power to repeal it by a simple majority . . . . FDR nominates John G. Winant as ambassador to Britain . . . . Japanese Amb. Nomura arrives in San Francisco.	Navy Secy. Knox lists 127 strikes in defense industries during 1940, with 100 now settled.	W.G. Campbell, commissioner of food and drugs, reports there is no known substance which can be relied on to cure colds.		Feb. 6
Helen Keller announces her resignation as honorary national chairman of the American Rescue Ship Mission for Spanish refugees, which has been denounced as Communist-dominated.	House votes down six Lend-Lease amendments that would exclude Russia from receiving any U.S. aid.				Feb. 7
NEA Pres. Dr. Donald DuShane proposes formation of a teachers' defense commission to prevent threatened attacks on public schools.	House passes the Lend-Lease bill by a vote of 260 to 165 after rejecting 13 additional amendments . . . . Gallup Poll reports that 54% of the voters questioned in a recent survey support Lend-Lease bill, while 22% were opposed . . . . Hopkins has last meeting with Churchill at Chequers.	NLRB orders the International Harvester Co. to abolish company-dominated unions in its six Midwestern plants.			Feb. 8
	American Youth Congress denounces the European war as an "imperialist exploitation of the masses."			Book of the Month Club critics' poll selects Ernest Hemingway's *For Whom the Bell Tolls* as the outstanding book of 1940.	Feb. 9
Gen. Walter G. Krivitsky, a fomer Red Army intelligence chief who broke with Stalin in 1937, is found shot to death in his Washington hotel room. His lawyer charges he was murdered by Soviet secret police, but the coroner tentatively lists the death as a suicide.	Sen. Harry S. Truman (D, Mo.) demands a Senate probe of irregularities in the awarding of defense contracts . . . . Senate confirms Winant as ambassador to Britain . . . . Treasury reveals that about $4.369-billion worth of foreign assets have been frozen in the U.S. since last April.	House passes by voice vote the Public Debt Act of 1941, raising the national debt to $65 billion, and sends it to the Senate.		Paramount Pictures purchases the screen rights to the Broadway play *Lady in the Dark* for the record price of $283,000.	Feb. 10
Secret Service begins fingerprinting and photographing reporters and other persons who regularly visit the White House . . . . House votes to extend the Dies Committee probing of "un-American activities" for 15 months.	Wendell L. Willkie testifies before the Senate Foreign Relations Comm. for Lend-Lease, predicting war if Britain falls.	AFL executive council denounces all anti-strike legislation now before Congress.			Feb. 11

F	G	H	I	J
Includes elections, federal-state relations, civil rights and liberties, crime, the judiciary, education, health care, poverty, urban affairs and population.	*Includes formation and debate of U.S. foreign and defense policies, veterans affairs and defense spending. (Relations with specific foreign countries are usually found under the region concerned.)*	*Includes business, labor, agriculture, taxation, transportation, consumer affairs, monetary and fiscal policy, natural resources, pollution and accidents.*	*Includes worldwide scientific, medical and technological developments, natural phenomena, U.S. weather and natural disasters.*	*Includes the arts, religion, scholarship, communications media, sports, entertainment, fashions, fads and social life.*

	World Affairs	European War Zone	Pacific War Zone	The Americas	Other Countries & Territories
Feb. 12		Maj. Gen. Erwin Rommel arrives in Tripoli to take command of German-Italian front in Libya .... German heavy cruiser *Hipper* sinks seven British ships between the Azores and Portugal .... Gen. Francisco Franco, Spanish chief of state, and Mussolini meet at Bordighera, Italy .... Gen. Gregory K. Zhukov is appointed chief of the Red Army's general staff and vice commissar of defense.			
Feb. 13		Marshal Petain and Gen. Franco confer at Montpellier, France .... Alfonso XIII renounces all claims to the throne of Spain in favor of his son, Don Juan.			
Feb. 14		Hitler has a three-hour conference with the Yugoslav premier and foreign minister at Berchtesgaden, after which the visitors leave for Belgrade .... British Board of Trade applies the Trading with the Enemy Act to Rumania, effective tomorrow .... Greece claims its troops have broken through the Italian lines along the entire front in Albania.		U.S. Senate ratifies a revision of the 1924 treaty with the Dominican Republic under which the President will cease to appoint the collector of customs there.	
Feb. 15				Chilean government takes possession of three Danish ships tied up in Talcahuano harbor since the occupation of Denmark.	
Feb. 16		French press announces Adm. Darlan now holds the office of vice premier, foreign minister, minister of interior, commander of the fleet and head of the department of information.	British announce a sea area of 50 by 80 miles north of Singapore has been mined as a precautionary measure.		
Feb. 17		Bulgaria and Turkey sign a declaration of friendship and non-agression.		Brazilian Communist leader Juvenal Viegas Silva is killed in Porto Alegre by police while resisting arrest.	
Feb. 18	Japanese spokesman Koh Ishii says Japan is ready to mediate both the European and Far Eastern wars.		Australian troops land in Singapore and man already-prepared defense positions on the Malayan peninsula.	Miguel Aleman, Mexico's minister of the interior, announces that after the settlement of the expropriation question foreign capital will be permitted to "participate" in the development of new oil fields.	
Feb. 19	British reveal they received a formal Japanese offer on Feb. 17 to mediate the war and that the offer is now being studied.	A Berlin report states 10,000 Jews were rounded up in Vienna last week for transportation to east Poland .... Fifty thousand acres are flooded and 1,000 people are made homeless in Yugoslavia when the Danube overflows in the northern Bachka and Banat districts.			
Feb. 20	Foreign Min. Matsuoka denies that Japan made a formal offer to mediate the war, as announced in London.	British Foreign Secy. Anthony Eden and Gen. Sir John Dill arrive in Cairo to plan the next steps involving the Near East military and political situation.	Tokyo newspaper says Japan has warned Britain that a continuation of military activity in Southeast Asia may compel Japan to take countermeasures.		
Feb. 21		Soviets announce that Maxim Litvinov, Paulina Semyonovana Zhemchuzhina, N.M. Antselovich, F.A. Merkulov and I.A. Likhachev have been dismissed from the Central Committee of the Communist Party.	Japanese newspaper *Chugai* asserts the U.S. "is preparing to resort to economic blockage operations against Japan."	U.S. discloses it has backed Brazil's protest to Britain against the seizure of a French ship within the 300-mile safety zone off the Brazilian coast .... Pres. Pedro Aguirre Cerda of Chile vetoes a bill outlawing the CP.	
Feb. 22		*Scharnhorst* and *Gneisenau* sink five ships in North Atlantic .... British Admiralty announces that 150,000 square miles of the mid-Mediterranean have been mined .... U.S. Minister to Bulgaria George Earle is involved in a cafe fight with a German Army major.		R. Medina Ramirez, acting president of the Nationalist Party in Puerto Rico, is indicted in San Juan on a charge of obstructing registration for the draft.	A Vichy report says France has rejected a Japanese-sponsored proposal whereby Thailand would receive approximately one-third of Laos and Cambodia.
	A *Includes developments that affect more than one world region, international organizations and important meetings of major world leaders.*	B *Includes all developments in European countries and military engagements between Allied and Axis powers in Africa and at sea.*	C *Includes all developments in Japan and China, Japanese foreign policy and military actions in the Pacific region.*	D *Includes all domestic and regional developments in Latin America, the Caribbean and Canada.*	E *Includes developments in those independent nations and colonial possessions not covered in Columns B, C and D.*

U.S. Politics & Social Issues	U.S. Foreign Policy & Defense	U.S. Economy & Environment	Science, Technology & Nature	Culture, Leisure & Life Style	
	Senate Foreign Relations Comm. approves seven House amendments to the Lend-Lease bill, and adds amendment requiring authorizations and appropriations from Congress before giving aid to foreign nations . . . . Sen. Gerald P. Nye (R, N.D.) attacks Willkie's support for Lend-Lease. Thomas Dewey backs passage.	Atty. Gen. Robert H. Jackson announces approval of new deportation proceedings against Harry Bridges, CIO leader, under the new provisions of the Alien Registration Act of 1940.	Standard Oil Company (N.J.) announces it has developed a new process for cracking petroleum, employing the fluid instead of the intermittent type of catalytic cracking, which simplifies and lowers the cost of operation and improves the quality of the gasoline.		Feb. 12
Robert J. Boltz, Philadelphia investment counselor, is arrested in Rochester, N.Y. on charges of embezzling more than $2.5 million . . . . FDR nominates SEC chairman Jerome N. Frank judge of the Second Circuit Court of Appeals.	Senate Foreign Relations Comm. approves Lend-Lease by a vote of 15 to 8.	NYSE declines to extend trading hours after a survey shows more than half of the members opposed the change.			Feb. 13
	Defense authorities estimate 1,002 military planes were manufactured in January, compared with 799 in December and about 500 a year ago . . . . New Japanese Amb. Adm. Nomura presents his credentials to FDR.	Senate passes and sends back to the House a slightly amended version of the Public Debt Act of 1941, raising the debt limit from $49 to $65 billion . . . . Harry Bridges is arrested in San Francisco on a charge of having been a member of an organization advocating the violent overthrow of the U.S. government.		Frank Leahy is named head football coach and director of athletics at Notre Dame . . . . Willie Hoppe wins the world three-cushion billiard title for the second consecutive time.	Feb. 14
	State Dept. reveals Italy has requested the U.S. to close its consulates in Naples and Palermo . . . . House Naval Comm. approves legislation authorizing expenditures of $400,000,000 on naval bases, including Guam and Samoa in the Pacific.	OPM announces the CIO-UAW strike at Allis-Chalmers has been settled . . . . Civil Aeronautics Administrator Donald H. Connolly says over 100,000 certified pilots will have been trained under CAA's program by June 30.		Greg Rice sets a world record of 8:53.4 in winning the two-mile run in the N.Y. Athletic Club games.	Feb. 15
	Herbert Hoover reveals that a plan to feed three million Belgians has been submitted to British and German governments . . . . Hopkins returns to N.Y. from Britain and declares British need U.S. help "desperately" but "they don't need our men."	National Economy League, headed by Ernest Angell, urges a 10% defense tax on all personal incomes.	U.S. Indian Service physicians report that trachoma, a sight-destroying disease, is a virus and can be successfully treated with sulfanilamide within three weeks.	Printing unions urge Congress to limit commercial radio time to 25% of programs, charging that the switch from newspapers to radio by advertisers has cost 25,000 jobs in printing trades.	Feb. 16
Supreme Court rejects CP Gen. Secy. Earl R. Browder's appeal of his four-year prison sentence and $2,000 fine for using a falsely obtained passport.	Under State Secy. Sumner Welles rejects Hoover's food plan for Belgium, saying it is Germany's obligation to feed the population she has conquered . . . . Sen. Alben W. Barkley (D, Ky.), beginning debate on Lend-Lease bill in the Senate, says the only way to stop Hitler is to defeat him.	AFT executive council urges charters of teachers' locals in N.Y. and Philadelphia be revoked because of Communist influence.		Joe Louis knocks out Gus Dorazio in 1:30 of the second round of the scheduled 15-round bout in Philadelphia in his 14th defense of the world's heavyweight title.	Feb. 17
House votes 210 to 143 to reapportion itself in accordance with the 1940 census using the "equal proportions" formula instead of the "major fractions" method . . . . Robert Boltz pleads guilty in Philadelphia to charges of embezzlement and fraud.	Sen. Hiram Johnson (R, Calif.) submits the minority report of the Senate Foreign Relations Comm., listing seven objections to Lend-Lease . . . . FDR appoints W. Averell Harriman as special defense "expediter" in London.				Feb. 18
Missouri Supreme Court orders the Democratic-controlled legislature to seat Forrest C. Donnell (R) as governor . . . . Justice Dept. reports serious crimes rose by 2.2% in 1940 to a total of 1,517,026.		FDR signs bill raising the federal debt limit from $49 to $65 billion . . . . Federal grand jury in Philadelphia indicts American Surgical Trade Assn. on charges of violating the Sherman Antitrust Act by controlling the sale of 95% of all surgical supplies.		ASCAP accepts a consent decree ending the government's antitrust suits and providing that users of ASCAP-controlled music will pay only for the songs they actually use.	Feb. 19
Missouri General Assembly declares Donnell governor.	Washington sources report Gen. George Marshall told a secret meeting of a Senate committee that new planes are being rushed to reinforce the air force in the Pacific . . . . Sen. Robert R. Reynolds (D, N.C.) denounces Lend-Lease as a step toward war.	Associate OPM Dir. Sidney Hillman tells House Judiciary Comm. that anti-strike legislation in defense industries is unwise and may be harmful . . . . Treasury Secy. Henry Morgenthau Jr. says he plans to issue about $2 billion in new taxable federal securities to finance the defense program within the next two months.		Film version of *Tobacco Road* premiers in N.Y.	Feb. 20
Dr. Ralph West Robey, who led a National Manufacturers Association-sponsored survey, declares a "substantial proportion" of social science textbooks are critical of the American form of government and free enterprise.	FDR tells press conference reports of Marshall's testimony are inaccurate and injurious to national defense. Sen. Wheeler charges FDR "wants to muzzle the press."	NLRB orders Ford Motor Co. to reinstate 142 employes with back pay from Jan. 3, 1938, at its Richmond, Calif. plant and to cease discouraging membership in the CIO-UAW.	Sir Frederick Grant Banting, 49, codiscoverer of insulin and Nobel Prize winner, is killed with two other men in a military plane crash near Musgrave Harbor, Newfoundland.	Tony Zale successfully defends his middleweight title in Chicago by knocking out Steve Mamakos in the 14th round.	Feb. 21
NAM textbook survey is assailed by committee of 10 social scientists who see a "censorship threat inherent" in the investigation.	FBI Director J. Edgar Hoover asks the House for about $970,000 to pay for 700 additional special agents to protect the defense program against spies and saboteurs.			J. Gregory Rice wins the three-mile run in the Natl. AAU championships in N.Y., setting a new world indoor record of 13:51.	Feb. 22

F	G	H	I	J
Includes elections, federal-state relations, civil rights and liberties, crime, the judiciary, education, health care, poverty, urban affairs and population.	*Includes formation and debate of U.S. foreign and defense policies, veterans affairs and defense spending. (Relations with specific foreign countries are usually found under the region concerned.)*	*Includes business, labor, agriculture, taxation, transportation, consumer affairs, monetary and fiscal policy, natural resources, pollution and accidents.*	*Includes worldwide scientific, medical and technological developments, natural phenomena, U.S. weather and natural disasters.*	*Includes the arts, religion, scholarship, communications media, sports, entertainment, fashions, fads and social life.*

	World Affairs	European War Zone	Pacific War Zone	The Americas	Other Countries & Territories
Feb. 23	Herbert Claiborne Pell, recently named minister to Hungary, says either the U.S. or Germany will lead the world during the next epoch of history.	Mussolini promises a spring offensive in Greece and predicts a German victory in a 45-minute radio broadcast .... Turkish Foreign Min. Shukru Saracoglu declares Turkey will oppose with force any and all aggression that might be directed against her territorial integrity.			
Feb. 24	Winston Churchill reportedly has rejected Japanese mediation in the war.	Hitler warns of a gigantic spring offensive against British shipping with newly trained crews and new submarines.			Thailand-Indochina armistice is extended for 10 days at Japan's request since no agreement could be reached within the original time limit, expiring Feb. 25.
Feb. 25		British forces capture Mogadishu in Italian Somaliland .... Eden and Sir John Dill arrive in Turkey for discussions on a possible German attack on Greece .... Supreme Soviet votes a 26% increase in Russia's military budget and doubles the peasants' income tax to pay for arms production and defense measures.	Japanese Foreign Min. Matsuoka says he believes that the white race must cede Oceania to the Asiatics.	Canadian P.M. W.L. Mackenzie King announces Leighton McCarthy has been appointed Canadian minister to the U.S.	
Feb. 26		British announce the first clash between German and British motorized patrols in Libya.			Japan presents a "final mediation plan" for the settlement of the border dispute between French Indochina and Thailand.
Feb. 27		Challenging his opponents in the House of Commons Churchill demands a vote of confidence and receives unanimous support .... German businessman in Sofia says he has filed legal charges against U.S. Minister Earle, who he claims hit him with a bottle.		Venezuelan police raid a secret Communist radio station near Caracas.	
Feb. 28		Exiled King Alfonso XIII of Spain dies in Rome .... U.S. consulates in Naples and Palermo, Italy, are closed at the Italian government's request and their staffs are transferred to the Rome consulate general.			Japanese spokesman says France must accept Japan's mediation proposal in the Thailand-Indochina dispute today or face the consequences.
March 1		Premier Bogdan Philov of Bulgaria signs the Tripartite Pact in Vienna, joining his nation to the Axis. German troops occupy Varna and Sofia .... U.S. Amb. John Winant arrives in Bristol, England, where he is greeted by King George VI .... German military authorities fine the city of Amsterdam $8 million as a penalty for disorders against the Nazi occupation.	Soviet Navy newspaper *Red Fleet* reports that Japan has been secretly building a fleet to be used in event of a war with the U.S.		
March 2		Advance units of the German Army reach the Greek border through Bulgaria .... UK Foreign Secy. Anthony Eden arrives in Athens to confer with Greek leaders .... British shipping losses for last week total 29 ships and 148,038 tons, the third highest for any week of the war.		Rightist parties are defeated in the Chilean election as government wins a majority in both houses of congress.	French Amb. to Japan Charles Arsene-Henry indicates that Vichy accepts virtually all the Japanese demands for the cession of Indochinese territory to Thailand.
March 3		Soviets rebuke Bulgaria over German occupation. Turkey is reported to have "nullified" non-agression and friendship pact with Bulgaria.	Japanese troops land along 240 miles of the Kwangtung coast in south China.		
March 4	Dr. Robert M. Hutchins, president of the Univ. of Chicago, declares the world is probably nearer disintegration than at any time since the fall of the Roman Empire .... Gallup-Poll estimates eight million American voters support some sort of post-war international federation of countries.	British raid Lofoten Islands off Norway, destroying fish and whale oil processing plants, sinking 10 ships and capturing 215 Germans .... Nazi mission arrives in Turkey .... Greek leaders say they will fight to the end even if Germany invades Greece .... Yugoslavian Prince Regent Paul secretly visits Hitler.		State Dept. announces that Mexico and U.S. are discussing mutual defense assistance.	

A	B	C	D	E
Includes developments that affect more than one world region, international organizations and important meetings of major world leaders.	*Includes all developments in European countries and military engagements between Allied and Axis powers in Africa and at sea.*	*Includes all developments in Japan and China, Japanese foreign policy and military actions in the Pacific region.*	*Includes all domestic and regional developments in Latin America, the Caribbean and Canada.*	*Includes developments in those independent nations and colonial possessions not covered in Columns B, C and D.*

U.S. Politics & Social Issues	U.S. Foreign Policy & Defense	U.S. Economy & Environment	Science, Technology & Nature	Culture, Leisure & Life Style	
					Feb. 23
Earl Browder announces Robert Minor will become CP general secretary .... Financial operator Robert Boltz receives a 20-to-40-year prison term.	Administration leaders in the Senate abandon plans to limit debate to speed passage of Lend-Lease after isolationists threaten a filibuster.	OPM invokes mandatory priorities for the first time in placing aluminum and machine tools on the priority list in order to ensure an adequate supply for the defense program.		Violinist Efrem Zimbalist is named as the new director of the Curtis Institute of Music in Philadelphia.	Feb. 24
FDR says the pending Hobbs bill to permit wire tapping by federal officials in felony cases "goes entirely too far" .... Protestant Digest Associates award citations for combating racial and religious intolerance to Interior Secy. Harold L. Ickes, Ralph Ingersoll, Dr. Ruth Benedict, the Rev. Dr. Samuel E. Howie and Lester Granger.	Sen. Wheeler declares the British expect the U.S. to get into the war between April and June through the "back door" of the Orient.			N.Y. Rangers defeat the Boston Bruins 2-0 in a NHL game in Boston, ending the Bruins' unbeaten streak at 23 games, a league record.	Feb. 25
Justice Dept. official Maurice M. Milligan reports the special Washington grand jury investigating alleged violations of the federal election laws during the 1940 campaign returned no indictments.	Sen. Wheeler challenges the Administration to let the people vote on the issue of entering the European War.	Gerhard A. Gesell and Ernest J. Howe, members of the SEC insurance section, report that the tremendous assets of life insurance companies are only available for big business.		*L'Osservatore Romano* reports that the Congregation of the Holy Office has placed the German book *Race, Culture and Christianity* by P. Koltz on the list of forbidden works for advocating compulsory sterilization and euthanasia for the unfit.	Feb. 26
Pittsburgh grand jury indicts 71 under the postal law on charges of operating a lottery ring with a total income of millions of dollars in eight Eastern states.	Sen. Taft declares FDR is "deliberately holding back aid to England in order to put pressure on Congress" to pass Lend-Lease .... William C. Bullitt, former ambassador to France and Russia, tells the Overseas Press Club in N.Y. that a national emergency should be proclaimed, if necessary, to speed up defense preparations.	RFC buys $136,330,557 worth of state of Arkansas tax-exempt highway refunding bonds, because the 3½% interest rate demanded by a bank syndicate was considered too high.		Academy of Motion Picture Arts and Sciences in Hollywood votes Ginger Rogers best actress, James Stewart best actor and *Rebecca* best picture of 1940.	Feb. 27
	Federal grand jury in Honolulu indicts 80 persons, most of them Japanese, for conspiring to violate laws on registration of sampans, which are frequently seen in the area when the U.S. fleet is maneuvering.	OPM Director Knudsen submits a three-point plan to curb defense strikes, providing for federal mediation, 60% strike vote and 40-day delay for OPM to investigate and report .... Gesell and SEC commissioner Sumner T. Pike recommend to the Temporary National Economic Comm. (TNEC) that a federal insurance advisory council be created.	A blizzard, which piles up 12-foot snowdrifts, sweeps the Eastern seaboard from Maine to Virginia.	Lew Jenkens, world lightweight champion, scores a technical knockout over Lou Ambers in the seventh round in N.Y.	Feb. 28
	Senate approves $15,000 appropriation for a seven-man committee to be led by Sen. Harry S. Truman (D, Mo.) to probe defense spending program.		Overseas and transcontinental shortwave circuits and telephone communications are disrupted by sunspot activity in the worst magnetic storm since April 1940.	Francisco Goya protrait of Victor Guye sells for $34,000 at Parke-Bernet Galleries in N.Y. .... Mrs. Anthony Pelleteri's Bay View, a 58-1 shot, wins the $100,000 added Santa Anita Handicap, earning $89,360.	March 1
After Delaware legislature refuses to abolish Sunday blue laws, State Atty. Gen. James R. Morford orders the arrest of every person violating them to prove the laws are unenforcable.			Drs. Emilio Segre and Glenn Seaborg announce that they have split uranium and thorium atoms into equal parts, using the Univ. of California's cyclotron.	Torger Tokle wins the national ski-jumping championship on Olympian Hill near Hyak, Wash. with a 288-foot leap, breaking the North American record by 31 feet.	March 2
	Sen. Champ Clark (D, Mo.) blocks a move to close Senate debate on Lend-Lease bill.	War Under Secy. Robert P. Patterson urges in testimony before the House Judiciary Comm. that an agency similar to the National War Labor Board of 1918 be created to mediate labor disputes in defense industries .... Executive council of the AFT reports that the N.Y. teachers union, Local 5, follows the Communist Party line.		Noted German conductor Otto Klemperer is released from Morristown, N.J., jail after being detained overnight following a Rye, N.Y. police broadcast charging he was "dangerous and insane."	March 3
Federal grand jury indicts Dr. Friedrich Ernst Auhagen, founder of the American Fellowship Forum, for failing to register as a paid publicity agent for the German government.	Sen. Gerald Nye, (R, N.D.) makes the last set speech against the Lend-Lease bill, urging its defeat and attacking Britain as the greatest aggressor in all modern history.	CIO Pres. Murray protests proposed creation of labor mediation board for defense industries.			March 4

F	G	H	I	J
Includes elections, federal-state relations, civil rights and liberties, crime, the judiciary, education, health care, poverty, urban affairs and population.	*Includes formation and debate of U.S. foreign and defense policies, veterans affairs and defense spending. (Relations with specific foreign countries are usually found under the region concerned.)*	*Includes business, labor, agriculture, taxation, transportation, consumer affairs, monetary and fiscal policy, natural resources, pollution and accidents.*	*Includes worldwide scientific, medical and technological developments, natural phenomena, U.S. weather and natural disasters.*	*Includes the arts, religion, scholarship, communications media, sports, entertainment, fashions, fads and social life.*

	World Affairs	European War Zone	Pacific War Zone	The Americas	Other Countries & Territories
March 5		Britain breaks off diplomatic relations with Bulgaria .... British announce that Ethiopians have routed an Italian army of 20,000 in Gojjam Province and captured the fort of Burye .... German court martial in Amsterdam sentences 18 Dutch to death and 19 others to prison for espionage and sabotage.		Pres. Arnulfo Arias announces the U.S. has been given permission to establish air and anti-aircraft bases on Panamanian soil to protect the Panama Canal .... Canadian P.M. W.L. Mackenzie King announces that Bulgaria and Hungary will be subject to "trading with the enemy" regulations.	
March 6		Regent Prince Paul of Yugoslavia, calls a conference to decide Yugoslavia's course which, Belgrade says, will be to try to compromise with the Axis .... Church properties confiscated at the time of the separation between church and state in France will be restored by 1943, according to a law promulgated in Vichy.			
March 7		First contingent of a British force of 50,000 lands in Greece .... British announce final conquest of Italian Somaliland.		Foreign Min. Ezequiel Padilla says Mexico will not hesitate to sign a military pact with the U.S. in an emergency.	
March 8		London undergoes its heaviest bombing in weeks, suffering great damage and many casualties .... Greek government spurns any armistice with Axis. Turkish sources say Turkey may not fight if Germany attacks Greece .... Yugoslavia is reported to have reached agreement with Germany on a non-aggression pact.			
March 9		British government again rejects Herbert Hoover's plan to feed Belgians, stating it would only "prolong the war."	Japanese announce their forces withdrew from the entire south Kwangtung coast, having achieved their objective .... Chinese Nationalists report Communists have requested more political power in China. Chiang Kaishek accuses Communists of fomenting disunion.		Vichy announces peace conference in Tokyo has reached a full accord on the Indochina-Thailand frontier dispute .... Vichy says France will defend her African colonies alone and in conformity with armistice agreements with Germany .... Food riots in Damascus and Aleppo, Syria cost four lives.
March 10		French Vice Premier Darlan threatens to use fleet to convoy food ships "so that France can eat." .... Antanas Smetona, former president of Lithuania, arrives in N.Y. declaring that he is still the legal head of his country because he never authorized Russian annexation in June 1940.			
March 11		Vyacheslav Molotov, Russian Premier, is reported by Turkish sources to have promised that Russia will not attack Turkey should the Turks enter the war .... Bombs planted in the luggage of George W. Rendel, British minister to Bulgaria, explode in the lobby of his Istanbul hotel, killing six.			France yields 25,000 square miles of Indochina to Thailand under the Japanese-mediated peace, ending the border dispute.
March 12		The *Diplomatisch-Politische Korrespondenz* in Berlin denounces the Lend-Lease bill as "flagrant meddling" in the war .... Speaking in Parliament, Churchill thanks America for passing Lend-Lease bill.	Chinese engineers leave Chungking to survey a route for a 1,000-mile highway from Ningyuan, China, to Sadiya, Assam, India.		Japanese newspaper *Asahi* says that Indochina and Thailand have pledged they will not enter into any agreement with a third power inimical to Japanese interests.
March 13		Hitler issues secret directive giving the SS administrative control over all territory captured by German Army in the planned attack on Russia .... RAF carries out heaviest British raids of the war on Berlin, Hamburg and Bremen .... Germans execute 15 Dutchmen convicted of espionage and sabotage.		Acting Argentine Pres. Dr. Ramon S. Castillo appoints Dr. Enrique Ruiz Guinazu as foreign minister and Dr. Carlos Alberto Acevedo as finance minister .... Pres. Vargas of Brazil ratifies the Act of Havana approved at the Pan-American Conference of Foreign Ministers in Havana last July.	
March 14		At the end of a two-day German bombing attack on Clydesdale, 1,100 persons are dead and 1,050 injured .... Churchill announces Sir Arthur Salter will go to the U.S. to discuss urgent shipping needs to transport Lend-Lease material.		Representatives of Chile and Argentina begin conferences in Santiago to determine their boundaries in the Antarctic.	

A	B	C	D	E
Includes developments that affect more than one world region, international organizations and important meetings of major world leaders.	*Includes all developments in European countries and military engagements between Allied and Axis powers in Africa and at sea.*	*Includes all developments in Japan and China, Japanese foreign policy and military actions in the Pacific region.*	*Includes all domestic and regional developments in Latin America, the Caribbean and Canada.*	*Includes developments in those independent nations and colonial possessions not covered in Columns B, C and D.*

U.S. Politics & Social Issues	U.S. Foreign Policy & Defense	U.S. Economy & Environment	Science, Technology & Nature	Culture, Leisure & Life Style	
	Senate passes seven amendments to the Lend-Lease bill, ending powers conferred on the President on June 30, 1943 and requiring congressional appropriations for additional aid.	N.Y. Stock Exchange Pres. William McChesney Martin attacks SEC members as "ignorant" and partially responsible for decline in exchange business.		Betty Compton Walker's divorce proceedings against former N.Y. Mayor James J. Walker are dismissed in Key West, Fla.	March 5
National Refugee Service estimates that about 130,000 European refugees are in the U.S. . . . . William M. Canning, history instructor at the CCNY, testifies before the Rapp-Coudert state legislative committee that 40 to 50 faculty members are present or former members of the CP.	Five thousand left-wing CIO members at an anti-war rally in N.Y. hear Lend-Lease denounced as "imperialistic." . . . . Secy. Hull asks Italian government to close its consulates in Detroit and Newark, N.J. for national policy reasons.	National Industrial Conference Board estimates January unemployment was 7,664,000, up more than 700,000 from December 1940 . . . . House passes and sends to the Senate the $1,420,977,559 Agriculture Dept. Supply Bill . . . . House votes to establish a committee to probe civil airline crashes, which have cost 55 lives in eight months.		Gutzon Borglum, 69, the sculptor who spent 14 years carving the heads of Washington, Jefferson, Lincoln and Theodore Roosevelt on Mount Rushmore, dies in Chicago. His son Lincoln says he will finish the carvings . . . . New York Yankee Joe DiMaggio ends holdout, signing $35,000 contract, a $2,500 raise over his 1940 contract.	March 6
Delaware General Assembly repeals 200-year-old Sunday blue laws.	Senate defeats O'Mahoney amendment to Lend-Lease bill to bar convoying and other restrictive amendments by a wide margin.			Historian Worthington Chauncey Ford, 83, dies at sea, returning from Lisbon to the U.S.	March 7
	Senate passes, 60-31, the Lend-Lease bill, after defeating, 56-33, the Walsh amendment to prohibit the transfer of any Navy ships without congressional authorization.	AFL Pres. William Green appeals to the membership of the AFT to vote for the expulsion of three locals charged with undemocratic practices.	Worst snowstorm in six years sweeps the Eastern states from Virginia north, depositing 11.6 inches of snow in N.Y. in 24 hours and 17 inches in other areas.	Sherwood Anderson, 64, author of *Winesburg, Ohio* and other novels of Midwestern life, dies in Cristobal, Canal Zone.	March 8
Thirty-three faculty members of City College and Brooklyn College accused of Communism denounce Rapp-Coudert inquiry as unfair and part of a drive to "plunge" the U.S. into "the imperialist war."	Dr. Nicholas Murray Butler denounces isolationism as "childish" and "suicidal." . . . . Paul Porter, Arthur C. McDowell and Leonard Woodcock resign from the Socialist Party's national executive committee in protest against Norman Thomas's opposition to Lend-Lease.			Toni Matt wins the national combined ski championship at Aspen, Colo.	March 9
	W. Averell Harriman, special representative of FDR, leaves N.Y. for London to expedite material aid for Britain under the Lend-Lease program . . . . Senate passes resolution declaring that the U.S. will not recognize the transfer of any territory in the Western Hemisphere from one non-American power to another.	Acting Commissioner of Works Projects Howard O. Hunter authorizes a 48-hour work week on WPA-certified defense projects affecting about 200,000 workers . . . . N.Y. bus drivers strike for higher wages idling the city's 1305 buses.			March 10
City Councilman Joseph Clark Baldwin (R) is elected to Congress from the 17th district in N.Y. by 23,252 votes to 16,690 for Dean A. Alfange (D) to succeed the late Kenneth F. Simpson (R).	FDR signs the Lend-Lease bill at 3:50 P.M., less than two hours after the House accepts the Senate-amended measure by a vote of 317 to 71. He reveals he will ask Congress for $7 billion for Lend-Lease . . . . About 15 senators who opposed Lend-Lease meet in office of Sen. Hiram W. Johnson to discuss a nationwide anti-war speaking campaign.	CIO-UMW demands a $1 a day wage increase to $7 a day for 450,000 soft-coal miners when the present two-year contract expires April 1 . . . . Sen. Joseph C. O'Mahoney (D, Wyo.) urges Congress to call a national conference to draft a "national economic constitution" to "abolish the economic uncertainties" threatening the U.S. political system.		Broadway producers seek a temporary injunction against the Dramatists Guild, charging the "entire legitimate theatrical industry" is under its domination.	March 11
CCNY Pres. Harry N. Wright tells 3,000 students Communists cannot be tolerated in the schools and supports the Rapp-Coudert investigation of subversive activities.	Secy. Knox dedicates the Navy's largest air training base in Corpus Christi, Tex. . . . . FDR formally asks Congress for $7 billion for Lend-Lease arms aid.	TNEC lists nearly 400 organizations which maintain staffs of lobbyists in Washington and urges that they be periodically registered.			March 12
	FDR signs an order freezing Hungarian funds in the U.S. . . . . House Deficiency Appropriations subcommittee begins secret hearings on the $7-billion Lend-Lease bill.	FDR receives a plan for the creation of an 11-member board to mediate defense strikes from Labor Secy. Frances Perkins and William S. Knudsen and Sidney Hillman of OPM . . . . Soft coal operators reject the CIO-UMW demand for $1-a-day wage increase.		Federal Judge F. Ryan Duffy imposes fines totalling $35,250 in the antitrust suit against ASCAP . . . . Boston Bruins beat the N.Y. Americans in N.Y. to win the NHL championship for the third consecutive year.	March 13
Bureau of Internal Revenue begins a test action to determine whether the federal government has the right to tax income from state and municipal securities.	House passes and sends to the Senate the $3,446,685,144 Navy supply bill for 1942 . . . . Curtiss-Wright Corp. announces a new dive bomber for the Navy said to exceed the German Stuka in performance.	AFL Pres. William Green says he supports the mediation board plan; CIO Pres. Philip Murray describes it as detrimental to labor . . . . Pennsylvania Gov. Arthur James orders state police to protect workers who will remove finished defense goods at a strike-bound Vanadium Steel Corp. plant in Bridgeville.			March 14
F *Includes elections, federal-state relations, civil rights and liberties, crime, the judiciary, education, health care, poverty, urban affairs and population.*	G *Includes formation and debate of U.S. foreign and defense policies, veterans affairs and defense spending. (Relations with specific foreign countries are usually found under the region concerned.)*	H *Includes business, labor, agriculture, taxation, transportation, consumer affairs, monetary and fiscal policy, natural resources, pollution and accidents.*	I *Includes worldwide scientific, medical and technological developments, natural phenomena, U.S. weather and natural disasters.*	J *Includes the arts, religion, scholarship, communications media, sports, entertainment, fashions, fads and social life.*	

	World Affairs	European War Zone	Pacific War Zone	The Americas	Other Countries & Territories
March 15		UP's Berlin reporter Richard C. Hottelet is arrested by the Gestapo on "suspicion of espionage." . . . . Ankara newspaper *Aksam* says Turkey will adhere firmly to her military alliance with Britain. Turkish Pres. Ismet Inonu informs Germany his country has no territorial ambitions but is determined to maintain its independence and integrity . . . . Field Marshal Alexander Papagos, Greek chief of staff, proclaims that his troops have smashed the Italian spring offensive in Albania that began seven days ago.		Brazilian Foreign Min. Oswaldo Aranha says that in defense of American territorial integrity Brazil stands firm in her obligations assumed with other American republics . . . . Bolivia refuses to consider the claims of the Standard Oil Co. (N.J.) for properties confiscated in 1937.	
March 16		German raiders *Scharnhorst* and *Gneisenau* sink 16 ships in two days . . . . Hitler says in a speech that "no power or aid in the world" can save Britain from defeat.			Navy Dept. announces that two American light cruisers and four destroyers are paying a three-day goodwill visit to Auchland, N.Z.
March 17		Yugoslavian Regent Prince Paul receives ultimatum from Hitler to join Tripartite Pact or face occupation . . . . Jijiga, Ethiopia falls to British colonial troops . . . . British announce that their troops have recaptured the British Somaliland port of Berbera, lost to the Italians last Aug. 19.			
March 18		Official British figures disclose that German bombers have killed more than 25,000 and wounded at least 35,000 since the mass air raids started last September . . . . Belgrade reports excessive German demands have postponed the signing of a nonagression pact between Germany and Yugoslavia . . . . Hitler rejects a secret request by Adm. Raeder to attack U.S. warships escorting British convoys west of Iceland.	Japanese bombers and pursuit planes raid Chungking for the first time since last October . . . . Japan's new Imperial Rule Assistance Assoc., a Fascist-like party, receives army support.		
March 19				U.S. and Canada sign an agreement for the immediate development of a $266,170,000 Great Lakes-St. Lawrence River seaway and power project.	French authorities in Indochina protest to Japanese military officials that Thailand has violated the peace agreement of March 11.
March 20		German bombers subject Plymouth, on the south coast of England, to its worst raid of the war . . . . British battleship *Malaya* is struck by a German torpedo in the mid-Atlantic, but there are reportedly no injuries.		Rep. Joseph J. Mansfield (D, Tex.) urges the Panama Canal be converted to a sea-level canal to lessen the danger of air raids.	Seven U.S. warships arrive in Sydney, Australia, on a goodwill visit.
March 21		Three Yugoslavian cabinet members resign in protest against signing a non-aggression pact with Germany.		Colombian government announces that Colombia and Venezuela will sign a treaty on April 5 ending their century-old border dispute.	
March 22		*Scharnhorst* and *Gneisenau* dock at Brest, France . . . . Vichy reveals that the Bank of France's non-interest loan to the government covering the German occupation cost has been raised to $2 billion.	Lt. Gen. Korechika Anami tells a Diet committee that Japan will proceed with a "settlement of the China affair under the firm conviction that we are not an aggressor nation."		
March 23	Japanese Foreign Min. Matsuoka arrives in Moscow for a stopover on his way to Berlin.	Malta is bombed by German aircraft for third straight day . . . . Italy celebrates the 22nd anniversary of the Fascist Party.			Vichy government announces authorization to construct a railroad across 1,500 miles of the Sahara desert to link France's North and Equatorial African possessions.

A	B	C	D	E
Includes developments that affect more than one world region, international organizations and important meetings of major world leaders.	*Includes all developments in European countries and military engagements between Allied and Axis powers in Africa and at sea.*	*Includes all developments in Japan and China, Japanese foreign policy and military actions in the Pacific region.*	*Includes all domestic and regional developments in Latin America, the Caribbean and Canada.*	*Includes developments in those independent nations and colonial possessions not covered in Columns B, C and D.*

U.S. Politics & Social Issues	U.S. Foreign Policy & Defense	U.S. Economy & Environment	Science, Technology & Nature	Culture, Leisure & Life Style	
Atty. Gen. Robert H. Jackson says 8,091 warrants of deportation have been issued against aliens, but 6,249 of them cannot be executed because of the war.	FDR declares in a radio address that aid to the Allies will be increased until total victory has been won.			Betty Compton Walker wins a divorce from former N.Y. Mayor James J. Walker in Key West, Fla. after testifying he flew into "insane tempers for the most commonplace things."	March 15
		CIO Pres. Murray, after conferring with FDR, agrees to a mediation board to settle defense strikes.	Sixty-two persons die in a blizzard that sweeps N.D., Minn., Wis., and Mich. . . . . Pennsylvania Railroad passenger train plunges into the Ohio River near Baden, Pa., killing five persons and injuring 114.		March 16
National Comm. for Planned Parenthood, sponsored by the Birth Control Fed. of America%, begins a nationwide campaign to have birth control included in state and national public health programs . . . . N.Y. Board of Higher Education votes to make membership in a Communist, Fascist, or Nazi group sufficient cause for dismissal of faculty members in any city college.	House Republicans decide to abandon opposition to FDR's $7-billion Lend-Lease appropriation bill at a three-hour conference . . . . Comm. to Defend America by Aiding the Allies urges American navy ships be used to convoy goods to Britain and recommends American volunteers be permitted to join Allied armies.	OPM Dir. Gen. Knudsen says that defense production must rise 60% to handle the Lend-Lease program.		FDR opens the $15-million National Gallery of Art in Washington, which includes the Andrew W. Mellon and Samuel H. Kress collections of paintings and sculptures.	March 17
N.Y. Dist. Atty. Thomas E. Dewey arrests Morris U. Schappes, suspended CCNY English tutor, on a grand jury indictment on four counts of perjury growing out of his alleged misstatements before the Rapp-Coudert committee.	House begins debate on the $7 billion Lend-Lease appropriations bill . . . . Col. William J. Donovan, personal representative of FDR, returns to N.Y. after a 25,000-mile, 14-week tour of Europe and the Near East.				March 18
FDR and Hopkins leave on the yacht *Potomac* for a cruise in the Bahamas.	Navy Secy. Knox reveals Britain has asked the U.S. to repair an undisclosed number of British warships . . . . House passes the $7-billion Lend-Lease appropriation bill by a vote of 336 to 55 and sends it to the Senate.	FDR creates an 11-man National Defense Mediation Board (NDMB) "to assure that all work necessary for national defense shall proceed without interruption." Dr. Clarence A. Dykstra is named chairman . . . . CIO Amalgamated Clothing Workers win 10-13% pay increases for 135,000 garment workers.			March 19
Atty. Gen. Jackson asks Congress to legalize the use of wire-tapping evidence against spies, saboteurs, kidnappers and extortionists.	Col. Charles A. Lindbergh says in an article in *Collier's* that U.S. is being led toward war "with ever-increasing rapidity and with every conceivable deception."	City fact-finding board settles an 11-day strike of 3,500 N.Y. City bus drivers.		Sam Snead wins the North-South open golf championship at Pinehurst, N.C.	March 20
	Army calls for volunteers for the first Negro unit of the Air Corp, the 99th Pursuit Squadron.	NLRB cites the Ford Motor Co. on charges of continued unfair labor practices at its River Rouge, Lincoln, and Highland Park plants. Ford is accused of dismissing 253 workers for CIO-UAW union activities . . . . AFL construction strike at Wright Field, Dayton ends with four CIO electricians, whose hiring led to the strike, allowed to continue on the job . . . . Dykstra resigns as director of Selective Service to assume his new duties as chairman of the NDMB.		In the 15th defense of his heavyweight title, Joe Louis scores a TKO over Abe Simon at 1:20 of the 13th round.	March 21
Census Bureau announces the number of family units in the U.S. increased by about one-sixth from 1930 to 1940, but the average number of persons to a family declined from 4.1 to 3.8.	Senate Appropriations Comm. unanimously approves the $7 billion Lend-Lease bill.	Following a plea from OPM Assoc. Dir. Gen. Sidney Hillman, 3,000 CIO aluminum workers vote to call off their 10-day strike at the Edgewater, N.J. plant of Alcoa and return to work March 24 . . . . Grand Coulee Dam on the Columbia River, 100 miles northwest of Spokane, begins producing electricity two years ahead of schedule.	American Chemical Society awards the $1,000 Eli Lilly prize in biological chemistry to Dr. David Rittenberg of Columbia Univ. for his work on isotopes as tracers in chemical reactions.	Gregory Rice sets a world indoor record of 8:51.1 in winning the two-mile race in the Chicago relays.	March 22
Rapp-Coudert Comm. reports to the N.Y. state legislature that the N.Y. college system should not be judged on the basis of the Communist activities exposed in recent weeks.		Eight-day CIO strike at the Harvill Aircraft Die Casting Corp. plant in Los Angeles is settled.			March 23

F	G	H	I	J
Includes elections, federal-state relations, civil rights and liberties, crime, the judiciary, education, health care, poverty, urban affairs and population.	*Includes formation and debate of U.S. foreign and defense policies, veterans affairs and defense spending. (Relations with specific foreign countries are usually found under the region concerned.)*	*Includes business, labor, agriculture, taxation, transportation, consumer affairs, monetary and fiscal policy, natural resources, pollution and accidents.*	*Includes worldwide scientific, medical and technological developments, natural phenomena, U.S. weather and natural disasters.*	*Includes the arts, religion, scholarship, communications media, sports, entertainment, fashions, fads and social life.*

	World Affairs	European War Zone	Pacific War Zone	The Americas	Other Countries & Territories
March 24		Rommel's forces attack and capture El Aghella, Libya . . . . London suffers its heaviest air attack of the year when Nazi bombers pound it for six hours.	Chinese and Japanese reports announce bitter fighting on the island of Hainan with the Chinese claiming a victory . . . . Japanese claim to have occupied Swabue on Honghai Bay near Hong Kong, while other Japanese forces crossed the Tathow Channel and captured Chaoyang in moves designed to close the remaining coastal route into free China.	Six U.S. B-18 bombers arrive in Belem, Brazil with rubber seedlings sent by the U.S. Dept. of Agriculture for experimental planting in the Amazon Valley . . . . Publications of correspondence between the U.S. State Dept. and Canada reveals that for the first time since 1817 the two countries will construct naval vessels on the Great Lakes for ocean use.	
March 25		Yugoslavia is brought into the Axis alliance when Premier Dragisha Cvetkovitch and Foreign Min. Alexander Cincar-Markovitch sign the Tripartite Pact in Vienna. Anti-Nazi demonstrations break out in Yugoslavia . . . . Germany extends its war zone westward to within three miles of Greenland, including British-occupied Iceland.			
March 26	Japanese Foreign Min. Matsuoka arrives in Berlin.	Riots break out in Yugoslavian cities against the signing of the Axis pact. British radio broadcasts an appeal to Yugoslavs to resist "the betrayal of your honor and independence." . . . . World Zionist Organization Pres. Dr. Chaim Weizmann urges British to permit Palestine Jews to form their own army "for service against the common enemy of mankind."		Bolivian Senate passes a resolution authorizing the government to seek an agreement with the Standard Oil Co. (N.J.) regarding its confiscated properties.	Gen. Henri Fernand Dentz imposes martial law in several Syrian cities after two days of riots caused by food shortages and nationalist agitation.
March 27	Hitler meets Japanese Foreign Min. Matsuoka in Berlin and secretly urges attack on Singapore.	Yugoslav Air Corps Chief Dusan Simovitch overthrows the regency and the pro-Axis Cvetkovitch government in a bloodless coup d'etat and restores King Peter to the throne . . . . Churchill promises aid for the new Yugoslav government.	Japanese government announces that beginning in April the country will have one meatless day a week.		
March 28		King Peter II takes the oath as monarch of Yugoslavia, pledging to defend the independence of the state and the integrity of the nation. Germany reportedly demands the new government state its position on the Axis pact . . . . British and Italian fleets begin Battle of Cape Matapan off the coast of Crete.		Mexico announces it has approved entry applications for former King Carol of Rumania and Madame Magda Lupescu.	
March 29		Battle of Cape Matapan ends after British ships sink three Italian cruisers and two destroyers . . . . Germany orders her nationals to leave the Yugoslavian province of Serbia. New government moves to end Croatian opposition . . . . Polish sources in London report the Gestapo has started a new wave of terror in Poland. They report 3,000 prisoners have died in Oswiecim concentration camp and that 85% of Cracow's Jews have been forced to leave the city.		In accordance with the North American Regional Broadcast Agreement, more than 1,000 of the 1,300 radio stations in the U.S., Canada, Mexico, Cuba, Haiti and the Dominican Republic shift their broadcasting frequency channels at 3 a.m. to eliminate interference and improve reception.	Syrian Arabs demand immediate elections or the creation of a representative governing council and call a general strike.
March 30		French shore batteries in Algeria open fire on a British naval squadron after it halts a French convoy of four merchant ships proceeding from Casablanca to Oran.		Local press in Guayaquil, Ecuador charges that Japanese who control petroleum concessions near Esmeraldas are engaging in anti-government activities and interfering in local politics.	
March 31	Japanese Foreign Min. Matsuoka arrives in Rome to exchange personal greetings with Italian leaders.	German Min. to Yugoslavia Viktor von Heeren leaves Belgrade for Berlin; the Italian diplomatic colony also leaves.		Cuban government seizes an Italian freighter as a "precautionary measure." The crews of a German freighter and an Italian liner set fire to their ships in Costa Rican ports.	

A	B	C	D	E
Includes developments that affect more than one world region, international organizations and important meetings of major world leaders.	*Includes all developments in European countries and military engagements between Allied and Axis powers in Africa and at sea.*	*Includes all developments in Japan and China, Japanese foreign policy and military actions in the Pacific region.*	*Includes all domestic and regional developments in Latin America, the Caribbean and Canada.*	*Includes developments in those independent nations and colonial possessions not covered in Columns B, C and D.*

U.S. Politics & Social Issues	U.S. Foreign Policy & Defense	U.S. Economy & Environment	Science, Technology & Nature	Culture, Leisure & Life Style	
GOP National Committee unanimously rejects Rep. Joseph W. Martin Jr.'s resignation as chairman.	Senate passes, 67 to 9, the $7-billion Lend-Lease appropriation bill after less than two hours of debate .... Navy Secy. Knox urges press to refrain from reporting on or photographing damaged British warships coming to the U.S. for repairs.	CIO Steel Workers Organizing Comm. (SWOC) calls a strike at Bethlehem, Pa. plant of the Bethlehem Steel Corp. to protest against a company union .... Rep. Martin Dies tells the House he has "indisputable evidence" that the CP through its members in the SWOC "is working toward a complete tie-up in the steel industry."		Long Island Univ. defeats Ohio Univ., 56 to 42, to win the National Invitation basketball tournament (NIT) in N.Y.	March 24
CP Secy. Earl R. Browder surrenders to federal authorities in N.Y. to begin serving his four-year prison term for passport fraud.	FDR issues an executive order freezing Yugoslavian assets in the U.S. amounting to $50 million.	Rep. Dies tells the House that the National Maritime Union is a Communist-dominated organization. CIO Pres. Murray denies Communists are employed by SWOC .... State police rout CIO pickets in the Bethlehem steel strike. Violence also flares at Chicago works of International Harvester Co. when CIO strikers clash with police and AFL employes.	U.S. Public Health Service announces that the most serious outbreak of measles in seven years is active along the Eastern seaboard and spreading westward.	Warner Bros. buys Edna Ferber's unpublished novel *Saratoga Trunk* for the record price of $175,000.	March 25
	Wendell Willkie says in a N.Y. address at the opening of the United China Relief drive that the U.S. must help China because "she is standing up against an aggressor." .... Col. William J. Donovan declares that the U.S. must now consider the question of convoying war shipments to Britain.	International Harvester Co. rejects a CIO proposal to have the NDMB settle the strike at the Chicago-McCormick works .... Knudsen and Knox order Allis-Chalmers "to notify your entire work force to report for work and start operations immediately."			March 26
Group Health Assn. Inc., a non-profit organization chartered by N.Y. State, offers preventive medical care as well as treatment during illness to state residents for $24 a year or less.	FDR signs the $7 billion Lend-Lease appropriations bill .... Sen. Robert F. Wagner (D, N.Y.) announces the formation of the American Palestine Comm. to support the movement to develop and colonize Palestine with Jewish refugees.	NDMB gets its first defense strikes to settle at: International Harvester Co., Vanadium Steel Corp., Universal Cyclops Steel Co. and Condenser Corp. of America.Rep. Hatton W. Summers (D. Tex.) declares the Judiciary Committee would not hesitate "one split second" to recommend "the electric chair" for enemies of the defense program "in factories or elsewhere."			March 27
J. Warren Davis, a 74-year-old retired federal circuit court judge, is indicted in Philadelphia on charges of accepting bribes from former film producer William Fox and Fox's attorney in a 1936 bankruptcy proceeding.	FDR sends congratulations to King Peter II of Yugoslavia, expressing the hope that U.S.-Yugoslav relations may be mutually beneficial.	Under the protection of 500 policemen and special deputies, 2,000 men return to work in the Allis-Chalmers plant in answer to a government appeal .... Bethlehem Steel strike is settled after the company promises to continue negotiations with the SWOC, but a new strike begins at the company's Johnstown, Pa. plant.	U.S. Antarctic Expedition leaves for the U.S. after nearly two years in the South Pole region.	English novelist Virginia Woolf, 58, drowns herself near her home in Lewes, Sussex .... British-born actor Cary Grant announces he will donate his entire salary from his next picture, *The Man Who Came to Dinner*, to British war relief.	March 28
Dr. Edwin Nicholson, a scouting camp master, declares that through the method of emotional conditioning and indoctrination Boy Scout training tends to encourage youths to accept the status quo and become subservient to the will of others.	Secret British-American military staff talks end in Washington after producing a war plan for concentrating on Germany in the event of war with Japan.	Five thousand CIO-UAW members vote to continue their 67-day strike at Allis-Chalmers despite the government's appeal.		Wisconsin beats Washington State, 39 to 34, to win the NCAA basketball championship .... Michigan Univ. wins its 8th consecutive NCAA swimming championship.	March 29
FDR leaves his yacht *Potomac* at Port Everglades, Fla. and boards his special train for Washington after an eight-day vacation cruise.	Armed Coast Guardsmen seize 35 Danish, 28 Italian and 2 German merchant vessels in Atlantic, Pacific, Gulf and Caribbean ports under the 1917 Espionage Act after 26 of the Italian ships and one of German vessels are sabatoged by their crews .... Willkie warns in a radio address that if the Axis wins the war in U.S. would become an armed camp and lose its own liberties.	Members of the CIO Farm Equipment Workers union vote in Chicago to end their two-month old strike at four International Harvester Co. plants and submit their dispute to the NDMB .... Bethlehem Steel strike in Johnstown is settled.	Dr. Frank E. Adair, chairman of the executive comm. of the American Society for the Control of Cancer, reports a 30% increase in cures of operable breast cancer from 1920 to 1935.		March 30
John Kenneth Ackley, registrar of CCNY, is suspended pending a trial before the Board of Higher Education on charges that he is a member of the CP.	Germany and Italy protest to the State Dept. against the seizure of their merchant ships.	NDMB announces settlement of the SWOC strike at the Vanadium Steel Corp.'s plant in Bridgeville, Pa. .... TNEC urges a "permanent decentralization" of economic and political power to safeguard democracy in a report to Congress based on its two-year investigation of corporations .... Deportation proceedings against Australian-born CIO leader Harry Bridges are begun in San Francisco .... Justice Dept. announces a grand jury has indicted three of the country's largest drug manufacturers on charges of violating the Sherman Antitrust Act by fixing the price of insulin.			March 31

F	G	H	I	J
Includes elections, federal-state relations, civil rights and liberties, crime, the judiciary, education, health care, poverty, urban affairs and population.	*Includes formation and debate of U.S. foreign and defense policies, veterans affairs and defense spending. (Relations with specific foreign countries are usually found under the region concerned.)*	*Includes business, labor, agriculture, taxation, transportation, consumer affairs, monetary and fiscal policy, natural resources, pollution and accidents.*	*Includes worldwide scientific, medical and technological developments, natural phenomena, U.S. weather and natural disasters.*	*Includes the arts, religion, scholarship, communications media, sports, entertainment, fashions, fads and social life.*

	World Affairs	European War Zone	Pacific War Zone	The Americas	Other Countries & Territories
Apr. 1		Belgrade reports Mussolini has offered to mediate the German-Yugoslavian dispute. German radio charges atrocities against German nationals in Yugoslavia .... Asmara, capital of Eritrea, surrenders to British troops. British claim 130,000 to 150,000 Italian troops and civilians are trapped in central Ethiopia.		Mexico, Venezuela, Peru and Ecuador seize 23 Axis merchant ships (16 Italian and 7 German). Seven of the ships are set afire by their crews .... State Under Secy. Sumner Welles and Mexican Amb. Francisco Castillo Najera sign an agreement providing for reciprocal use of air fields to strengthen hemisphere defense plans.	
Apr. 2	Pope Pius XII receives Japanese Foreign Min. Matsuoka in a conference lasting over an hour.	Yugoslavia rejects Italian offer to mediate its dispute with Germany. German troops mass on Hungarian and Rumanian borders with Yugoslavia.	Chinese government names Kuo Tai-chi as as foreign minister to replace Wang Chung-hui, who becomes secretary general of the Supreme National Defense Council .... Air Chief Marshal Sir Robert Brooke-Popham, British C.O. in East Asia, arrives in Manila to confer with U.S. Adm. Thomas C. Hart and Maj. Gen. Douglas MacArthur on defense plans for the Philippines.	Peruvian Navy announces German freighters that fled Peru March 31 have been found aflame and sinking several hundred miles off the coast .... Mexican marines seize 10 German ships at Tampico to prevent their scuttling.	
Apr. 3		Hungarian government announces that Premier Count Paul Teleki shot himself to death, apparently because of new German demands on Hungary .... British troops evacuate Bengazi, Libya before Rommel's advancing German-Italian forces .... RAF bombers attack German battleships *Gneisenau* and *Scharnhorst* at Brest, France .... Churchill sends a message warning Stalin that Germany is preparing an invasion of Russia.		Gabriel Avila Camacho, brother of Pres. Manuel Avila Camacho, is arrested in Mexico City on a charge of shooting and killing Manuel Cacho in a political argument.	
Apr. 4	Hitler promises Japanese Foreign Min. Matsuoka that if Japan gets into a war with the U.S. Germany will declare war at once.	King Peter II releases a royal proclamation, dated April 1, ordering the mobilization of Yugoslavia's "entire military might." .... Germany and France sign an agreement for the exchange of food surpluses.	Japanese Premier Konoye appoints Vice Adm. Tijero Toyoda as minister of commerce and industry and Lt. Gen. Teiichi Suzuki as president of the planning board.	Mexican Senate ratifies the air pact with the U.S., permitting reciprocal use of airfields.	Iraqi government of Seyid Taha al-Hashimi is reportedly overthrown by nationalist extremists aided by military elements.
Apr. 5		British Imperial forces capture Adowa while South African troops in Ethiopia cross the Awash River and strike to within 80 miles of Addis Ababa .... Soviet news agancy Tass announces that Russia has signed a five-year non-aggression and friendship pact with Yugoslavia.	Chinese claim they won "the greatest victory of the war" last week in a battle near Nanchang, Japan's main army base in central China.	Uruguay takes possession of two Italian and two Danish ships in her ports .... Venezuelan Foreign Min. Dr. Gil Borges and Colombian For. Min. Dr. Luis Lopez de Mesa sign a treaty defining the borders between the two countries, ending a 100-year border dispute.	New regime of Rashid Ali-Bey Gailani pledges Iraq will respect all international treaties, "especially the Anglo-Iraq treaty."
Apr. 6		German troops march into Yugoslavia and Greece at dawn as Nazi planes bomb Belgrade .... Addis Ababa, capital of Ethiopia, is taken by British-South African forces after an 11-week drive .... Lt. Gen. Richard O'Connor and Lt. Gen. Philip Neame are captured by a German patrol in Libya.		Brazilian Pres. Vargas signs a decree modifing the immigration ruling of last February allowing nationals of American nations to enter Brazil and remain for six months without having to register.	
Apr. 7		German troops driving from Bulgaria reach the Aegean Sea through eastern Thrace after the Greeks abandon part of the area. German bombers raid Belgrade for the fifth time .... Britain breaks diplomatic relations with Hungary, charging it has become a base of operations for German forces.			
Apr. 8	Premier Konoye says Japan's foreign policy continues to be based on the three-power pact with Germany and Italy .... Japanese Foreign Min. Matsuoka, en route home from Rome and Berlin, extends his stay in Moscow for three days.	German troops advance to within 23 miles of Salonika, Greece and capture Skopeje in southern Yugoslavia .... Italian communique says Italian and German motorized columns have reoccupied Dernia, Libya.		Mexican Pres. Avila Camacho issues a decree expropriating the 12 German and Italian merchant ships taken into custody at Tampico and Veracruz.	

A	B	C	D	E
Includes developments that affect more than one world region, international organizations and important meetings of major world leaders.	*Includes all developments in European countries and military engagements between Allied and Axis powers in Africa and at sea.*	*Includes all developments in Japan and China, Japanese foreign policy and military actions in the Pacific region.*	*Includes all domestic and regional developments in Latin America, the Caribbean and Canada.*	*Includes developments in those independent nations and colonial possessions not covered in Columns B, C and D.*

U.S. Politics & Social Issues	U.S. Foreign Policy & Defense	U.S. Economy & Environment	Science, Technology & Nature	Culture, Leisure & Life Style	
	Hull defends seizure of 69 Italian, German and Danish ships as entirely legal. Atty. Gen. Jackson announces 875 Axis seamen will be prosecuted on sabotage charges .... House completes congressional action on a Senate resolution opposing the transfer of Western Hemisphere possessions to non-American powers.	Ford Motor Co.'s River Rouge plant is closed by a sit-down strike of some 8,000 CIO-UAW members, who claim several union men were discharged .... Wis. Gov. Julius P. Heil orders Allis-Chalmers to close its Milwaukee plant after 32 workers are injured in a battle between police and 3,500 strikers .... Despite an appeal from FDR, 400,000 soft-coal miners strike in 12 states.			Apr. 1
	German and Italian embassies protest for second time to State Dept. over the seizure of their merchant ships .... FDR orders Navy to prepare secret Hemispheric Defense Plan No. 1, calling for aggressive action by U.S. warship against German submarines in the Western Atlantic .... House passes a resolution, 324 to 1, authorizing its Military and Naval Affairs Comm. to investigate the progress of the defense program, including effects of strikes.	Some 200 CIO-UAW strikers and nonstrikers are injured in clashes at Ford's River Rouge plant. State police are ordered to the scene. Ford personnel director Harry Bennett wires FDR describing the incident as "a Communistic demonstration of violent terrorism." .... Labor Secy. Perkins sends the 71-day Allis-Chalmers strike in Milwaukee to the NDMB .... UMW Pres. John L. Lewis says he will oppose any move to submit the coal strike to the NDMB. Four striking miners are shot to death in a coal company commissary near Harlan, Ky.	Sir Lawrence Bragg and Charles Darwin, two of Britain's outstanding scientists, arrive in Ottawa, Canada to do war research.		Apr. 2
N.Y. state legislature approves a $247,000 appropriation for the expenses of the Rapp-Coudert joint legislative committee investigating subversive activities in the schools.	Secy. Hull again rejects German and and Italian protests against the ship seizures. He asks Italy to recall Italian naval attache in Washington because of his connection with the sabotage of Italian ships in American waters .... Sen. Wheeler names 10 senators and representatives to the executive committee of a congressional group of some 75 members who intend to campaign against U.S. entry into the war.	Federal Judge Arthur J. Tuttle issues an injunction restraining CIO-UAW from barring non-strikers from Ford's River Rouge plant .... Texas Senate passes and sends to Gov. W.L. O'Daniel a bill making it a felony for any person to engage in violence during a strike or to try to stop any employe from going to work.	FDA announces that a heatless permanent hair-waving preparation, known as the Willat method, contains the poison ammonium hydrogen sulfide. All stocks are ordered seized.	All 11 first-string players of the Boston Univ. football team volunteer for service in the U.S. Naval Air Corps.	Apr. 3
A federal jury convicts the AMA and the Medical Society of Washington of Sherman Antitrust Act violations, but acquits 18 individual defendants.	Federal grand jury in New Orleans indicts 64 Italian seamen for sabotaging their two ships.	FDR warns that direct federal action may be taken if the Allis-Chalmers strike in Milwaukee continues much longer .... Senate passes and sends to the White House a bill extending the Bituminous Coal Act, or Guffey Act, for two years from April 26, its expiration date, a move designed to speed settlement of the coal strike .... Ford closes 34 plants on the grounds they lack parts.			Apr. 4
		OPM Dir. Gen. Knudsen assails "organizational and jurisdictional strikes" and urges government supervised bargaining elections and cooling-off periods.		Elmer Layden is elected commissioner-president of the NFL at a meeting of the club owners in Chicago.	Apr. 5
	British battleship *Malaya* arrives in N.Y. for repairs after being torpedoed by a German submarine .... Hull denounces the German invasion of Yugoslavia and "the attempt to annihilate that country by brute force."	NDMB concludes an agreement for the settlement of the 75-day strike at Allis-Chalmers. Company and CIO-UAW agree to arbitrate disputes and bar strikes.		Craig Wood wins the Masters' golf tournament at Augusta, Ga.	Apr. 6
N.J. Assembly passes, 52 to 2, a bill barring Communists or persons advocating the violent overthrow of the government from the election ballot.		NLRB orders collective bargaining elections at Ford's River Rouge and Lincoln plants near Detroit and the Bethlehem Steel Co. near Lackawanna, N.Y.	Dr. George C. Andrews of N.Y. Presbyterian Hospital says so-called "smoker's cancer" of the lower lip is not due to smoking but is the result of a chronic inflammation of the lower lip from habitual sunburn.		Apr. 7
	FDR sends a message to King Peter denouncing Germany's "criminal assault" on Yugoslavia and promising "all material assistance possible." He also denies he favors press censorship but criticizes newspapers that published news of arrival of British battleship *Malaya* in N.Y.	OPM Assoc. Dir. Gen. Sidney Hillman and NDMB Vice Chrmn. William H. Davis tell the House Military Affairs Comm. they oppose legislation to ban strikes .... Breaking a 38-year precedent in which the Ford Motor Co. refused to negotiate with any union official, Ford official Harry H. Bennet and CIO Pres. Philip Murray confer on a settlement of the strike at the River Rouge plant .... CIO Longshoremen's and Warehousemen's Union denounces deportation proceedings against its president, Harry Bridges, and adopts a constitution excluding political affiliation as a qualification for membership.		Joe Louis defeats Tony Musto in the 16th defense of his world heavyweight title in St. Louis.	Apr. 8

F	G	H	I	J
Includes elections, federal-state relations, civil rights and liberties, crime, the judiciary, education, health care, poverty, urban affairs and population.	*Includes formation and debate of U.S. foreign and defense policies, veterans affairs and defense spending. (Relations with specific foreign countries are usually found under the region concerned.)*	*Includes business, labor, agriculture, taxation, transportation, consumer affairs, monetary and fiscal policy, natural resources, pollution and accidents.*	*Includes worldwide scientific, medical and technological developments, natural phenomena, U.S. weather and natural disasters.*	*Includes the arts, religion, scholarship, communications media, sports, entertainment, fashions, fads and social life.*

	World Affairs	European War Zone	Pacific War Zone	The Americas	Other Countries & Territories
Apr. 9		German troops capture Salonika, Greece . . . . Speaking to the House of Commons, Churchill appeals for more U.S. merchant ships, declaring only more escorts for convoys can win the Battle of the Atlantic . . . . RAF makes a heavy night raid on Berlin, while German bombers pound Birmingham.		Ecuadorian government wires all other governments that Ecuador is willing to settle its boundary controversy with Peru by arbitration . . . . Brazilian Pres. Vargas issues a decree forbidding foreign-owned banks from accepting deposits after July 1, 1946.	
Apr. 10		German news agency reports Ljubljana and Zagreb have been captured and that an independent Croatian state has been proclaimed . . . . Regent Nicholas Horthy orders the Hungarian Army to take those territories which the Yugoslavs captured in 1918 from Hungary . . . . Vichy military court condemns Free French Gen. Georges Catroux to death in absentia.			
Apr. 11		German panzer units break through the Yugoslav line at Bitolj, menacing the British-Greek left flank . . . . Hungarian Army marches into the Bacza area between the Danube and Tisa Rivers to take over the sections lost by Hungary in WW 1 . . . . German bombers attack Bristol and Coventry, England.			Iraqi government announces a counter-coup led by former Regent Emir Abdul Illah has been put down by the Basra garrison.
Apr. 12		Italian and German troops capture Bardia, Libya . . . . German bombers hit Piraeus, Greece, damaging British troop transports and harbor facilities . . . . Soviet Union scores Hungarian invasion of Yugoslavia.			
Apr. 13	Soviet Premier Viacheslav M. Molotov and Japanese Foreign Min. Matsuoka sign a five-year neutrality pact in Moscow. Soviets pledge to respect sovereignty of Japanese-controlled Manchukuo. Stalin sees Matsuoka off at the train.	German command announces that Belgrade has been occupied.		Pan Am Airways announces new express air schedules effective April 14, linking all 21 American republics by an 8-day, 15,000-mile air route between Washington and Buenos Aires.	
Apr. 14	Japanese, German, and Italian press hail the Russo-Japanese neutrality pact as a diplomatic victory for the Axis and a blow to Britain and the U.S. . . . . Chinese Amb. to the U.S. Dr. Hu Shih says the Soviet-Japanese treaty was a grave disappointment to his country . . . . Hull says the significance of the Soviet-Japanese pact "could be overestimated."	Axis forces under Maj. Gen. Erwin Rommel attack the town of Solum in Egypt.		American republics and Canada celebrate Pan-American Day with special programs and radio broadcasts.	
Apr. 15		German command claims panzer units have advanced more than 50 miles into northern Greece . . . . Hitler and Mussolini formally recognize independent Croatia . . . . Reports from Sofia indicate Bulgaria has broken off diplomatic relations with Yugoslavia.		Two Puerto Rican nationalists are found guilty of hindering the draft in San Juan and are sentenced to two-year prison terms . . . . Haitian Min. to the U.S. Elie Lescot is elected president of Haiti by members of the National Assembly . . . . An earthquake rocks southern Mexico for five minutes, damaging the city of Colima and leaving half its population of 15,000 homeless.	
Apr. 16		German command says 2nd Serbian Army has capitulated. British concede organized Serbian resistance has ended . . . . Zagreb radio reports that the new government of Croatia has been sworn in with Ante Pavelitch as premier and foreign minister . . . . An estimated 400 German planes pound London for eight hours in the heaviest "reprisal" raid of the war.		P.M. W.L. Mackenzie King of Canada confers with FDR on U.S. aid to the dominion and hemispheric defense problems.	

A	B	C	D	E
Includes developments that affect more than one world region, international organizations and important meetings of major world leaders.	*Includes all developments in European countries and military engagements between Allied and Axis powers in Africa and at sea.*	*Includes all developments in Japan and China, Japanese foreign policy and military actions in the Pacific region.*	*Includes all domestic and regional developments in Latin America, the Caribbean and Canada.*	*Includes developments in those independent nations and colonial possessions not covered in Columns B, C and D.*

U.S. Politics & Social Issues	U.S. Foreign Policy & Defense	U.S. Economy & Environment	Science, Technology & Nature	Culture, Leisure & Life Style	
Eight more members of the CCNY staff deny in testimony before the Rapp-Coudert committee that they were ever Communists .... Sen. Morris Sheppard (D, Tex.), chairman of the Senate Military Affairs Comm., an author of the 18th (Prohibition) Amendment and a member of Congress for 39 years, dies in Washington.	FDR authorizes the transfer of 10 U.S. Coast Guard cutters to Britain for convoy purposes .... State Dept. discloses Italy has requested the recall of an assistant military attache at the U.S. embassy in Rome, apparently in retaliation for the ouster of the Italian naval attache in Washington. Fifty more Italian seamen are indicted in Tampa on charges of sabotage.	Labor Secy. Frances Perkins and OPM Dir. Gen. Knudsen oppose anti-strike legislation in testimony before the House Military Affairs Comm. .... Edward Clayton Eicher, member of the SEC since 1938, is elected chairman to succeed Jerome N. Frank .... William McChesney Martin Jr. resigns as president of the New York Stock Exchange, effective April 16.		Tom Walsh, president of the PGA, announces the creation of a golf Hall of Fame with Bobby Jones, Francis Ouimet, Walter Hagen and Gene Sarazen as the first members.	Apr. 9
	FDR announces that Greenland has been placed under U.S. protection by agreement of the Danish government. The U.S. gets the right to establish air and naval bases on the island .... FDR asks Congress for legislation authorizing him to requisition all foreign ships in American waters considered necessary for the defense program .... U.S. destroyer *Niblack* depth-charges what is believed to be a German submarine while on convoy duty near Iceland.	Eighteen thousand CIO-UAW strikers at the Ford Motor Co.'s River Rouge plant vote to accept a peace formula drawn up by Gov. Murray D. Van Wagoner to end their nine-day walkout.	A report by Mayo Clinic doctors describes a new drug related to sulfanilamide, known as promin, which has proved effective in curbing tuberculosis in guinea pigs.		Apr. 10
	FDR issues a proclamation, signed April 10, opening the Red Sea to U.S. ships on the grounds that it is no longer in the combat zone .... FDR signs a joint Congressional Monroe Doctrine Resolution stating that the U.S. will not recognize the transfer of any Western Hemisphere territory to a non-American power .... FDR cables Churchill that the U.S. is extending its neutral "security zone" 1,000 miles into the Atlantic, barring German U-boat attacks west of 26 degrees longitude.	FDR creates an Office of Price Administration (OPA) under Leon Henderson to prevent runaway prices, profiteering, inflation and speculative hoarding of materials and commodities and to coordinate civilian consumption with defense needs .... Southern coal operators representing 13 associations bolt the N.Y. wage conference to form a new organization known as the Southern Coal Operators' Wage Conference, and appeal for federal mediation in the 11-day soft coal strike.			Apr. 11
	Government in occupied Denmark declares void the agreement between the U.S. and the Danish Min. Hendrick de Kauffmann, placing Greenland under U.S. protection.	Vice Pres. Henry Wallace charges "foreign agents" are "sabotaging our labor organizations to the great disadvantage of labor itself." .... NDMB announces a settlement of the 76-day strike of 650 CIO-UAW members at the Standard Tool Co., Cleveland.		Boston Bruins beat the Detroit Red Wings, 3-2, in Detroit to win the Stanley Cup in four straight games.	Apr. 12
	Interior Secy. Harold Ickes denounces Lindbergh, Gen. Robert E. Wood, Henry Ford and others opposed to aid for Britain as "Hitler's unconscious tools."		Dr. Annie Jump Cannon, 77, the world's most famous woman astronomer, who classified more than 400,000 stars, dies.		Apr. 13
Two lawmen and two prisoners die in Sing Sing's (N.Y.) worst prison break. Two other convicts are captured after seven hours of freedom.	Secret negotiations open in Washington between U.S. officials and Icelandic consul general, resulting in an Icelandic invitation for U.S. Marine occupation of the island .... Hull informs Danish Min. Henrik de Kauffmann that despite his recall by the government of occupied Denmark the U.S. will continue to recognize him as the duly authorized minister, since the Danish government "is acting under duress."	Six steel companies raise wages 10 cents an hour (to $5.80 a day) for more than 400,000 workers, averting a strike scheduled to begin at midnight April 15 against U.S. Steel Corp.		FDR throws out the ball in Washington's Griffith Stadium to open the 1941 baseball season.	Apr. 14
John F. Arena, 43, Italian-born editor of the Chicago newspaper *La Tribuna* is slain by 2 gunmen in Chicago a few hours after testifying before the Dies Committee on Fascist activity in the U.S.	FDR formally entrusts Harry L. Hopkins with the administration of the Lend-Lease program .... Senate passes and sends to the White House a House bill authorizing the Navy to increase its enlisted strength to 232,000 men and empowering FDR to raise this number to 300,000.	Four men, including the president of a coal company, are killed and 25 miners are wounded in a gun battle near Middlesboro, Ky. .... Strikers at Phelps-Dodge Copper Products plant in Elizabeth, N.J. reject an NDMB settlement and vote to continue their walkout .... Dr. J.B. Matthews, a Dies Comm. staff member, testifies before the House Military Affairs Comm. that Communists were active in at least six major defense strikes, including Allis-Chalmers and Ford.			Apr. 15
Wendell L. Willkie announces he will return to law practice early in May as senior member of the firm of Miller, Owen, Otis & Bailey of N.Y.	FDR invokes the Neutrality Act against Hungary for "having without justification attacked Yugoslavia." .... Under a new order released by the Adjutant General's Office all soldiers will be subject to overseas duty, if necessary, whether they volunteered specifically for such service or not.	OPM Dir. Gen. Knudsen calls jurisdictional strikes "plain stupid" and denounces strikes that take advantage of the defense program as "criminal." .... Fed. Price Admin. Leon Henderson freezes iron and steel prices at their first-quarter levels following a general 10¢ hourly wage increase granted to more than 525,000 steel workers.			Apr. 16

F	G	H	I	J
Includes elections, federal-state relations, civil rights and liberties, crime, the judiciary, education, health care, poverty, urban affairs and population.	*Includes formation and debate of U.S. foreign and defense policies, veterans affairs and defense spending. (Relations with specific foreign countries are usually found under the region concerned.)*	*Includes business, labor, agriculture, taxation, transportation, consumer affairs, monetary and fiscal policy, natural resources, pollution and accidents.*	*Includes worldwide scientific, medical and technological developments, natural phenomena, U.S. weather and natural disasters.*	*Includes the arts, religion, scholarship, communications media, sports, entertainment, fashions, fads and social life.*

	World Affairs	European War Zone	Pacific War Zone	The Americas	Other Countries & Territories
Apr. 17		German high command announces that the entire Yugoslavian Army surrendered unconditionally today .... RAF bombers deliver the heaviest attack on Berlin yet made during the war .... German surface raider shells Egyptian liner *Zamzam* 750 miles southwest of St. Helena, wounding two Americans, and then sinks her after the passengers and crew are removed. The ships is carrying 148 American passengers.		Mexican artist David Alfaro Siqueiros is acquitted of a charge of directing the machine-gun attack on Leon Trotsky's home on May 24, 1940, three months before the Russian exile was assassinated .... Casualties in the Mexican earthquake April 15 are placed at 90 dead, 300 injured and 50,000 homeless, most of them in Colima, Tuxpan and Ciudad Guzman.	
Apr. 18		Greek Premier Alexander Korizis commits suicide in Athens as German units advance toward the capital .... British warn Italians that if German planes bomb Athens and Cairo the RAF will begin "systematic" bombing of Rome .... Spanish Falangist Party newspaper *Arriba* warns Portugal that she must choose between Britain and Spain.	RAF in Singapore reveals that U.S. pursuit planes have arrived to strengthen the naval and air base's defenses.	Paraguayan government states in a communique that an attempted revolt against Pres. Higinio Morinigo on April 17 has been suppressed.	
Apr. 19		German command claims capture of Mount Olympus and the town of Larissa in Greece .... London suffers another heavy bombing raid by German planes .... Soviet newspaper *Pravda* says the Russo-Japanese neutrality pact foiled a U.S.-British plan to draw Russia into the war.		Venezuelan Pres. Eleazar Lopez Contreras tells Congress that Britain and Venezuela will soon sign a convention under which two islands in the Gulf of Paria will be ceded to Venezuela.	Britain announces that a strong armed force has been landed at Basra, Iraq, presumably to protect the oil regions.
Apr. 20		King George II of Greece proclaims himself premier of a new military dictatorship 48 hours after the suicide of Premier Alexander Korizis .... Italy claims that its 9th and 11th Armies have reached the Albanian-Greek border in nearly every sector .... Hitler names Alfred Rosenberg commissioner for East European territories.		FDR and Mackenzie King announce a defense production agreement under which the U.S. and Canada will mobilize their resources for hemispheric defense and aid to the Allies .... Pres.-elect Elie Lescot of Haiti announces that the island plans to undertake extensive rubber plantings by agreement with the U.S.	Casualties in Hindu-Moslem roits at Ahmadabad, India which began on April 18, rise to 56 dead and 318 wounded after police fire on a crowd for the second time.
Apr. 21		Germans claim to have destroyed five British troop transports in seas off Greece. Emmanuel Tsouderos become Greek premier and promises a "fight to the end." .... Ankara radio announces that King Peter II of Yugoslavia has arrived in Jerusalem by plane .... British battleships shell Tripoli, chief port of Libya, for 40 minutes at daybreak.	Japanese newspapers report that the U.S., Britain, China, India, Australia and the NEI have concluded a secret military and naval pact to strengthen their Far East defenses and to oppose Japanese expansion southward.	Gen. Isaias Medina Angarita and Romulo Gallegos, candidates for the Venezuelan presidency, agree to drop their election campaigns and let the congress choose between them.	
Apr. 22		King George II of Greece abandons Athens for Crete after the Greek Army of Epirus surrenders. German troops are less than 100 miles from Athens .... Soviets formally protest to Germany over 80 alleged border violations by Nazi planes between March 27 and April 18.	Two thousand American soldiers are landed at Manila from the transport *Republic* to augment the Philippine defense forces.		India Secy. L.S. Amery tells the British House of Commons that an army of 500,000 is rapidly being formed in India.
Apr. 23		Germans admit British rear guard is still holding the pass at Thermopylae. Waves of German bombers pound Greek ports and waiting evacuation ships.	Japanese Army spokesman in Shanghai states that all of Chekiang Province south of Shanghai has been occupied.	N.Y. Mayor Fiorello H. La Guardia, chairman of the American section of the Canada-U.S. Joint Defense Bd., says the two countries plan to defend their shores 1,000 miles into the Atlantic .... Argentine Senate approves a defense bill authorizing the expenditure of 646 million pesos.	Laborities gain a majority of 36 to 35 in the Australian Parliament with the death of a government supporter.
Apr. 24		Heavy fighting at Thermopylae and German aerial attacks on evacuation ships continue. Churchill postpones a debate in the House of Commons on the situation in the eastern Mediterranean until the situation clarifies .... Hitler receives Hungarian Regent Adm. Nicholas Horthy at his Balkan field headquarters.	Emperor Hirohito formally ratifies the Soviet-Japanese neutrality pact after it is unanimously approved by the Privy Council.	Radical Party orders its members in Chilean cabinet to resign after the government orders the suppression of a newspaper for criticizing the government. The cabinet members refuse and are expelled from the party .... Mexico City newspaper *Excelsior* reports the government has approved an initial expenditure of $14 million for improving the harbors on the Gulf and Pacific coasts as naval bases.	

A	B	C	D	E
Includes developments that affect more than one world region, international organizations and important meetings of major world leaders.	*Includes all developments in European countries and military engagements between Allied and Axis powers in Africa and at sea.*	*Includes all developments in Japan and China, Japanese foreign policy and military actions in the Pacific region.*	*Includes all domestic and regional developments in Latin America, the Caribbean and Canada.*	*Includes developments in those independent nations and colonial possessions not covered in Columns B, C and D.*

U.S. Politics & Social Issues	U.S. Foreign Policy & Defense	U.S. Economy & Environment	Science, Technology & Nature	Culture, Leisure & Life Style	
	Lindbergh tells an America First rally in Chicago that Britain has already lost the war . . . . Sen. Charles W. Tobey (R, N.H.) telegraphs FDR asking for a "frank, unequivocal" statement of his attitude on convoys.	U.S. Third Circuit Court of Appeals in Philadelphia reverses a previous opinion and rules the NLRB has the power to police employe-employer relations after a collective bargaining contract is signed . . . . Treasury and congressional leaders agree to increase taxes by one-third to raise $3.444 billion in new revenue . . . . House rejects the Senate-amended $1,340,610,744 agriculture appropriation bill because of the increase of parity payments.			Apr. 17
	Sen. Alben W. Barkley (D, Ky.) tells the Senate he has been authorized by Secy. Knox and Naval Operations Chief Adm. Harold R. Stark to deny categorically that the Navy is secretly engaged in convoying supply ships to Britain.	Sen. Robert A. Taft (R, Ohio) says in Senate that Price Admn. Leon Henderson's price-fixing orders "are absolutely illegal and represent a usurpation of the authority which only Congress may exercise."			Apr. 18
	Formation of a Fight for Freedom Comm. is announced, with Sen. Carter Glass (D, Va.) as honorary chairman and Bishop Henry W. Hobson of Cincinnati as the active chairman . . . . American Palestine Comm., headed by Sen. Robert F. Wagner, issues a declaration signed by 68 senators, urging that the restoration of the Jews to Palestine be adopted as the "declared policy" of the U.S.	UMW and Northern coal operators reject a plea by Labor Secy. Perkins that soft-coal mines be reopened April 22 because of a growing shortage in defense industries.	Dr. Albert Claude of the Rockefeller Inst. for Medical Research says that the mitochondria, or extra-nuclear part of the cell, may be the cause of cancer.		Apr. 19
	A Gallup Poll reports 79% of voters questioned opposed sending part of the Army to Europe; 69% opposed sending any part of the Air Force and 67% were against sending any warships.		Forest fires aided by unseasonably dry weather sweep thousands of acres and cause extensive damage in N.Y., N.J., Mass., Md., W. Va. and Pa.	New England syndicate headed by Bob Quinn buys the controlling interest in the Boston Bees baseball team . . . . Spain's Fine Arts Academy announces a national campaign for donations to buy a painting of Christ signed by Velasquez and dated 1631 which was placed on sale in Madrid recently.	Apr. 20
Texas Gov. W. Lee O'Daniel appoints Andrew Jackson Houston, 87, son of Gen. Sam Houston, to serve in the Senate until June 28 when a successor will be elected to fill the late Morris Sheppard's unexpired term.	Bishop Henry W. Hobson, head of the Fight for Freedom Comm., says the U.S. should send troops to Europe to defeat Hitler, if they are needed.	Treasury officials present their recommendations to the House Ways and Means Comm. for raising $3.6 billion in additional revenue in 1942 . . . . FDR appeals to soft coal operators and the UMW to reopen mines closed since April 1.			Apr. 21
N.Y. Board of Higher Education suspends eight instructors and three administrative assistants of CCNY charged with being members of the CP and obstructing the Rapp-Coudert investigation of subversive activities.		Southern soft coal operators resume negotiations in N.Y. with northern operators and the UMW . . . . CIO Textile Workers Union votes at its convention to bar members of Nazi, Fascist or Communist organizations from holding union office.		N.Y. Drama Critics Circle chooses Lillian Hellman's *Watch on the Rhine* as the best American play produced in N.Y. during the 1940-41 season.	Apr. 22
N.Y. Board of Education votes against a resolution to require teachers and clerks in the school system to state under oath whether they were or are members of Communist, Nazi or Fascist parties.	Students hold peace rallies and "strikes" at many colleges throughout the U.S. American Youth Congress claims 500,000 students took part . . . . Lindbergh tells America First rally in N.Y. that Britain's "last desparate plan" is to get an American expeditionary force into the war . . . . Secy. Knox announces that 20 of the Navy's "mosquito" boats are being shipped to Britain under the Lend-Lease program.	Mich. Gov. Murray D. Van Wagoner names a three-man mediation commission to try to settle the GM-UAW dispute . . . . Southern coal operators break off negotiations with the UMW for the second time . . . . Colin B. Stam, chief tax consultant of the Joint Comm. on Internal Revenue, submits a counter-proposal to raise $3.5 billion in additional revenue in 1942 to the House Ways and Means Comm.	Prof. Russell M. Wilder of the Mayo Foundation reports that two-thirds of the nation suffers from serious malnutrition because of improper diet lacking in vitamins, minerals, and proteins.	The 110-year-old *Boston Evening Transcript* announces that it will suspend publication on April 30 because of lack of funds.	Apr. 23
Senate Comm. on Privileges and Elections votes to seat Joseph Rosier (D) from W. Va., rejecting Clarence Martin's claim to membership.	FDR orders American warships to report movements of German vessels west of Iceland but not to fire unless fired upon . . . . Navy Secy. Knox says in a N.Y. speech, "We cannot allow our goods to be sunk in the Atlantic—we shall be beaten if they do." He says "we must see the job through" by delivering war materials to Britain.	Labor Secy. Perkins certifies the 24-day coal strike to the NDMB . . . . Treasury Secy. Morgenthau urges a cut of $1 billion in ordinary expenditures by reducing agriculture, CCC, NYA and soil conservation appropriations.	Prof. Ernest A. Hooton, Harvard anthropologist, says medical science must regenerate mankind biologically by checking human degeneration through birth control, sterilization and euthansia.	New School for Social Research of N.Y. receives a permanent charter from the Board of Regents. The school is popularly known as the "University in Exile."	Apr. 24

	World Affairs	European War Zone	Pacific War Zone	The Americas	Other Countries & Territories
Apr. 25		German command announces the capture of Thermopylae after an intense three-day battle. German bombers continue attacks on British evacuation from Greek ports.		Julio Ayala, leader of the Cuban Realist Revolutionary Party supporting Pres. Fulgencio Batista, is shot and seriously wounded in a Havana suburb . . . . Acting Pres. Ramon S. Castillo of Argentina announces that he will temporarily govern "by decree" because of the Radical Party's refusal to vote on any bills in Congress.	
Apr. 26		German troops take Thebes and advance southward to within 25 miles of Athens . . . . An Axis advance begins south of Solum on the Egyptian-Libyan frontier . . . . British troops occupy Dessye, Ethiopia.		Inter-American Economic Advisory Comm., representing the 21 American republics, passes a resolution in Washington stating that they have a right to seize immobilized foreign ships with compensation.	Mohandas K. Gandhi says in Bombay that his All-India Congress Party has dropped demands for the independence of India for the time being and wants only "freedom of speech and pen."
Apr. 27		Churchill hails the extension of the U.S. neutrality patrol in a London broadcast, declaring that now the "eventual defeat of Hitler and Mussolini is certain." He admits the seriousness of the Allied defeat in Greece and predicts a German attack on Russia or another country . . . . German troops enter Athens at 9:25 a.m. and hoist the Nazi swastika over the Acropolis, three weeks after the invasion of the Balkans began. The last of the British Imperial forces have withdrawn into the Peloponnesus or evacuated to Egypt or Crete.			
Apr. 28		German advances continue in Greece.		Gen. Isaias Medina Angarita is elected president of Venezuela by the Congress for a five-year term.	Ten people are wounded when police fire into crowds of Hindu and Moslem rioters at Cawnpore, India.
Apr. 29	*The Japan Times Advertiser* publishes exploratory peace terms to end the present war and establish a new world order with Germany dominating Europe; Germany and Italy controlling Africa; the U.S. dominating the Western Hemisphere; Japan ruling Asia; and the British Empire continuing in restricted form.	Berlin sources claim that German troops have reached the southern end of the Peloponnesus peninsula . . . . Cairo reports state that British Imperial troops aided by a furious sandstorm have halted an Axis advance from Libya just inside Egypt.		Costa Rica expels Karl Bayer as the first move of a government campaign to end Nazi propaganda . . . . Mexico reveals Italy has seized three Mexican-owned tankers built in Italy as a reprisal for the Mexican seizure of 10 Italian ships.	
Apr. 30		Churchill reports 45,000 of the 60,000 men of the British expeditionary force have successfully evacuated Greece . . . . Hitler fixes the date for invasion of Russia.			
May 1	Chinese Foreign Min. Dr. Kuo Tai-chi says America, Britain and China should form an ABC combination, pooling their economic and natural resources to crush totalitarianism.	British command in Cairo announces that German and Italian troops have broken through the outer defense of Tobruk, Libya . . . . British Ministry of Economic Warfare urges U.S. to boycott Axis and freeze Axis funds in the U.S.		FDR asks Congress for funds to complete a 1,500-mile stretch of the Inter-American highway from the southern border of Mexico across Guatemala, El Salvador, Honduras, Nicaragua, Costa Rica and Panama to the Panama Canal at a cost estimated at $20 million.	London reports state that additional troops have been landed at Basra, Iraq over the protest of the Iraqi government. Iraqi Premier Rashid Ali Beg Gailani asserts the new arrival of British troops violates the Anglo-Iraqi treaty.
May 2					Iraqi troops attack the British airport of Habbania. British broadcast appeals to people of Iraq to oust the pro-German government.

U.S. Politics & Social Issues	U.S. Foreign Policy & Defense	U.S. Economy & Environment	Science, Technology & Nature	Culture, Leisure & Life Style	
	FDR says at his press conference that the U.S. Navy will extend its neutrality patrol to the seven seas, if necessary, for the protection of the Western Hemisphere. He compares Lindbergh to the "Copperhead" defeatists in the Civil War . . . . Willkie urges using convoys to "protect those shipments" to Britain.	Secy. Perkins certifies the CIO-UAW dispute with GM to the NDMB . . . . Sen. Harry F. Byrd (D, Va.) demands Labor Secy. Perkins resign for failing to certify the coal strike to the NDMB for three weeks.	Dr. J.S.L. Browne of McGill Univ. says that intramuscular injections of the synthetic male hormone, testosterone propionate, have added several inches to the height of 10 dwarfed youths.	Lou Salica, bantamweight champion, outpoints Lew Transparenti in a 15-round title bout in Baltimore.	Apr. 25
	Gallup Poll reports 68% of the persons questioned in a recent survey said they would favor U.S. entrance into the war if there were no other way to defeat the Axis.		Civil Aeronautics Authority experts demonstrate an automatic loop-antennae direction finder that enables a pilot to fly on a straight line by tuning in simultaneously on broadcasting stations at two points.	Violinist Fritz Kreisler, 66, suffers a fractured skull when he is hit by a truck in N.Y.	Apr. 26
	William C. Bullitt tells a United China Relief rally the U.S. should aid China and Britain even at the cost of war . . . . Sen. Wheeler, addressing 9,000 persons at an America First Comm. rally in Chicago, charges that FDR is preparing the nation for a declaration of war.	General Electric Co. announces that 1941-42 radio models will be virtually frozen and the company's resources for research and development will be turned over to defense production.		Stockholders of the Boston Bees agree to change the NL baseball team's name to the Boston Braves.	Apr. 27
Supreme Court rules unanimously that Negroes are entitled to Pullman accommodations and other first-class services equal to those white passengers receive on passenger trains in a case brought by Rep. Arthur D. Mitchell (D, Ill.), the only Negro member of Congress.	Lindbergh writes to FDR that in view of the President's remarks "concerning my loyalty" he is resigning his commission as a colonel in the Army Air Corps.	Southern coal operators accept FDR's request to reopen the mines and continue wage discussions, ending the 28-day Appalachian coal strike of 400,000 miners . . . . NAM condemns strikes as "a major bottleneck" in defense production, claiming over three million man-days were lost during the first three months of 1941 as a result of strikes, more than half of them in defense industries.			Apr. 28
	FDR says he has full authority to send the U.S. Navy on neutrality patrol into any war zone, including that around Britain if he deems it necessary for the defense of the Western Hemisphere . . . . Sen. Gerald P. Nye (R, N.D.) introduces a resolution requiring the President to obtain congressional permission before using the Navy to convoy ships to Britain . . . . War Secy. Stimson accepts Lindbergh's resignation without comment.	Commerce Secy. Jesse H. Jones predicts a national debt of at least $90 million.	Dr. Ernest Witebsky of the Univ. of Buffalo Medical School reports a new test for diagnosing trichinosis in human beings.		Apr. 29
	Senate Foreign Relations Comm. defeats two anti-convoy measures by 13-10 votes . . . . FDR asks Rear Adm. Emory S. Land, chairman of the Maritime Commission, to procure 2 million tons of shipping, domestic and foreign, to carry supplies to Britain.	Northern soft coal operators reopen their mines following a settlement of their 29-day strike, and Southern operators order their mines reopened May 1 after signing a temporary agreement with the CIO-UMW.			Apr. 30
N.Y. Gov. Herbert H. Lehman signs a bill providing for the suspension of the license of an automobile driver involved in an accident unless he carries insurance to cover liability.	Sen. Joseph F. Guffey (D, Pa.) urges that the Navy convoy merchant ships to Britain. Sen. Tobey claims White House "pressure" defeated his anti-convoy resolution and tells FDR to "keep your hands off the Congress." . . . . U.S. defense bonds and stamps ranging from 10¢ to $10,000 go on sale at post offices and banks . . . . Senate passes and sends to the White House the $3,415,521,750 naval appropriations bill.	Workers at Phelps-Dodge plant in Elizabeth, N.J. vote to end three-week-old strike . . . . Albert W. Hawkes of Congoleum-Nairn, Inc. is elected president of the Chamber of Commerce of the U.S.	Dr. Robley D. Evans of M.I.T. reports that new methods of determining geological ages indicate that life has existed on the earth much longer than previous estimates of 500 million years and that man may be much older than the million years now commonly accepted.		May 1
	Willkie, in an article in *Collier's*, urges America to give Britain ships "until it hurts" and to "see that those ships . . . . deliver their cargoes safely." . . . . American Legion's executive committee urges convoys to deliver war material to Britain.	FDR urges in a letter to OPM chiefs Knudsen and Hillman that the machine tool industry go on 24-hour day, 7-day workweek. In a letter to House Ways and Means Comm. Chmn. Robert L. Doughton (D, N.C.), FDR urges a "minimum" $3.5-billion tax increase to cover defense costs . . . . Fed. Price Admin. Leon Henderson says that the government is prepared to fix prices for staple commodities, food and clothing to prevent unwarranted price inflation.	Dr. Rubby Sherr and Prof. Kenneth T. Bainbridge of Harvard Univ. report the transmutation of mercury into radioactive gold and platinum.	FCC authorizes the full commercialization of television broadcasting beginning July 1.	May 2

F	G	H	I	J
Includes elections, federal-state relations, civil rights and liberties, crime, the judiciary, education, health care, poverty, urban affairs and population.	*Includes formation and debate of U.S. foreign and defense policies, veterans affairs and defense spending. (Relations with specific foreign countries are usually found under the region concerned.)*	*Includes business, labor, agriculture, taxation, transportation, consumer affairs, monetary and fiscal policy, natural resources, pollution and accidents.*	*Includes worldwide scientific, medical and technological developments, natural phenomena, U.S. weather and natural disasters.*	*Includes the arts, religion, scholarship, communications media, sports, entertainment, fashions, fads and social life.*

	World Affairs	European War Zone	Pacific War Zone	The Americas	Other Countries & Territories
May 3		Italian government announces the annexation of part of Slovenia in Yugoslavia, comprising the city of Ljubljana and surrounding territory.			Fighting in Iraq spreads to the Basra area where, London reports state, Iraqi attacks on British troops recently landed at Basra were repulsed. The battle at the Habbania airport continues into its second day . . . . Sources in Beirut, Lebanon report that anti-Semitic riots have broken out in Palestine and that Arab nationalists have kidnapped Zionist leaders in reaction to disturbances in Iraq and the arrival of Jewish refugees from the Balkans.
May 4		Vice Premier Darlan returns to Vichy from Paris with Hitler's purported demands for political collaboration with Germany as well as industrial and economic cooperation . . . . Hitler, addressing the Reichstag, declares that Germany and her allies represent power which is superior to any possible coalition in the world . . . . British command in Cairo claims the German-Italian attack on Tobruk, Libya has been brought to a "standstill."	Japanese Foreign Min. Matsuoka rejects a proposal that he visit the U.S.	Sixty-thousand persons are made homeless in Porto Alegre, Brazil, by the worst floods ever recorded in the state of Rio Grande do Sul . . . . A Bolivian spokesman in La Paz says that the government will not consider a Japanese proposal to buy tungsten.	
May 5		Emperor Haile Selassie returns to his throne in Addis Ababa, Ethiopia, after five years in exile . . . . RAF claims its bombers scored direct hits on the German battleships *Scharnhorst* and *Gneisenau* in a raid on Brest.	British and U.S. oil companies in the NEI renew their contracts to supply Japan with 1.8 million tons of oil a year.	Gen. Isaias Medina Angarita takes the oath of office as president of Venezuela in Caracas.	London reports state that Britain has declined a Turkish offer to mediate the Iraqi dispute.
May 6		Stalin replaces Viacheslav M. Molotov as Soviet premier . . . . Germans announce that the Aegean Sea has been closed to British ships with the seizure of eight islands.		The Congressional bloc of the Radical Party in Argentina votes to end its three-month legislative boycott, thus permitting Congress to resume its normal functions.	British troops break the siege of Habbania air base in Iraq . . . . Japan and France sign two agreements in Tokyo for economic collaboration between Japan and Indochina.
May 7		Churchill wins a vote of confidence in the House of Commons, 447 to 3.			Gen. Henri Dentz, French high commissioner in Syria, is reported to have received demands that German troops be permitted to pass through Syria in a drive on Suez.
May 8		British claim that 48 Nazi planes were destroyed within 30 hrs. on May 7 and 8 during raids on Britain . . . . Egypt announces that Axis planes bombed the Suez Canal area for two hours during the night of May 7-8.		Hull, welcoming the naval chiefs of 10 Latin American countries to Washington, says the American republics must collaborate to increase their common defense against the common danger.	
May 9	Japan announces that conferences have started in Tokyo with Germany and Italy to discuss questions relating to cooperation under the Axis Pact.	Between 300 and 400 RAF planes attack Bremen and Hamburg on the night of May 8-9 . . . . Nazi authorities extend the Nuremberg laws to France, forbidding Jews to engage in any business that would bring them into contact with "Aryans."	Japanese fliers raid the Chungking district in China in the second major air attack of the year.		French-Thai peace conference ends in Tokyo with a treaty stating that any future dispute between Thailand and French Indochina will be mediated by Japan.
	A *Includes developments that affect more than one world region, international organizations and important meetings of major world leaders.*	B *Includes all developments in European countries and military engagements between Allied and Axis powers in Africa and at sea.*	C *Includes all developments in Japan and China, Japanese foreign policy and military actions in the Pacific region.*	D *Includes all domestic and regional developments in Latin America, the Caribbean and Canada.*	E *Includes developments in those independent nations and colonial possessions not covered in Columns B, C and D.*

U.S. Politics & Social Issues	U.S. Foreign Policy & Defense	U.S. Economy & Environment	Science, Technology & Nature	Culture, Leisure & Life Style	
	Herbert Agar, editor of the *Louisville Courier-Journal*, urges war against dictatorships abroad.	Bethlehem Steel Corp. signs its first contract with a CIO union, the Industrial Union of Marine and Shipbuilding Workers, covering 1,700 workers in its Hoboken, N.J. shipyard . . . . OPM limits the automobile industry to 4,224,152 vehicles in the model year beginning Aug. 1.		FCC approves regulations to foster free competition among radio stations and strengthen network broadcasting . . . . Warren Wright's Whirlaway with Eddie Arcaro up wins the Kentucky Derby by eight lengths in a field of 11 and sets a new track record of 2:01 for the mile and a quarter race at Churchill Downs.	May 3
	Seventeen military, naval, defense production, economic and political experts release a statement in N.Y. stating that Britain can win the war with U.S. aid . . . . Harvard Pres. James B. Conant says in a Boston broadcast: "I believe we should fight now . . . . I believe the nation is ready to join the fight for freedom."	Pennsylvania Greyhound Lines are struck by 1,400 AFL drivers and other employes.	Dr. Emil Haury, Univ. of Ariz. anthropologist, reports that excavations in a cave on Castle Mt. in Arizona prove that the southwestern U.S. was inhabited by man 5,000 years before Christ.	N.Y. Public Library announces the acquisition of the Owen D. Young collection of 10,000 to 15,000 rare books and manuscripts, valued at more than $1 million.	May 4
	House debate on alien-ship seizure bill precipitates dispute over prospect of convoying . . . . FDR orders "a substantial increase in heavy bomber construction."	Supreme Court unanimously upholds the constitutionality of the Indiana gross income tax law of 1933 as applied to interstate transactions of state residents . . . . The Sheffield Farms Co., Inc., the Borden Co. and four of their affiliates are indicted on charges of violating the Sherman Antitrust Act by selling milk at higher prices than those charged by their affiliates.	Dr. Martin H. Dawson of Columbia Univ. describes a new chemical substance known as penicillin to a medical meeting in Atlantic City, N.J. He says the substance, developed from a special strain of mold in bread and Roquefort cheese, may prove more useful than the sulfanilamides.	Columbia Univ. announces the Pulitzer Prizes for 1940 in literature and journalism include: drama, Robert E. Sherwood; U.S. history, Marcus Lee Hansen; American biography, Ola Elizabeth Winslow; poetry, Leonard Bacon; meritorious public service by a newspaper, *St. Louis Post-Dispatch;* reporting, Westbrook Pegler.	May 5
Dr. Heinrich Simon, 61, a German Jewish refugee and former anti-Nazi editorial writer in Germany, dies in Washington after being beaten by unknown assailants.	War Secy. Stimson urges that the U.S. Navy be used to insure Lend-Lease aid reaches Britain . . . . House votes 161 to 131 to reject an amendment to ship seizure bill that would have barred the President from turning the confiscated vessels over to Britain . . . . Sen. Claude Pepper (D, Fla.) urges the country to get tough with the Axis and occupy, with Britain, Dakar, the Azores, the Canary and Cape Verde Islands, Greenland and Iceland.	Third Federal Circuit Court of Appeals rules that merchant seamen have the right to strike aboard ship when it is in a safe domestic port . . . . RFC Chmn. Emil Schram announces he will accept the presidency of the N.Y. Stock Exchange.	Igor Sikorsky sets a new world record of 1 hr. $32\frac{1}{2}$ min. for sustained flight in a helicopter at Bridgeport, Conn.		May 6
	House passes the alien-ship seizure bill and sends it to the Senate . . . . Immigration officials, acting under orders from Atty. Gen. Jackson, begin a round-up of more than 200 German seamen in a dozen cities who overstayed their leaves . . . . Secy. Knox says that the Navy is "readier than ever," if called upon, to insure the delivery of war supplies to Britain.			Sir James George Frazer, 87, author of *The Golden Bough*, a study of folk customs and beliefs, dies in Cambridge, England . . . . Detroit Tigers star outfielder Hank Greenberg is inducted into the Army . . . . Outfielder Lloyd Waner is traded to the Boston Braves after 14 seasons with the Pittsburgh Pirates.	May 7
	Atty. Gen. Jackson instructs U.S. attorneys to urge uniform sentences of seven years for German and Italian officers and five years for seamen convicted of sabotage aboard the seized Axis ships . . . . John Maynard Keynes arrives in N.Y. to confer with U.S. and British officials regarding the Lend-Lease program . . . . Treasury Secy. Morganthau announces the first week's sale of defense savings bonds and stamps totaled $114,880,000.	House passes the Vinson priorities bill conferring statutory authority on the OPM to administer priorities in defense materials and industries . . . . Treasury Dept. reports that Louis B. Mayer earned $697,048 as managing director of production for Loew's, Inc. in 1940, which made him the highest paid executive in the country.	Dr. H.L. Friedell and Dr. L.M. Rosenthal of the Chicago Tumor Inst. report in the *Journal of the AMA* that observation of eight patients supports the opinion that tobacco chewing is a causative factor in the development of cancer of the mouth.		May 8
Sen. George D. Aiken (R, Vt.) predicts that some form of state socialism will grow out of FDR's emergency powers.	Maritime Commission announces that U.S. merchant ships will begin operating to the Red Sea area soon and that service to China will be increased . . . . Atty. Gen. Jackson orders seizure of the I.G. Farbenindustrie's funds held by National City Bank of N.Y. to force the German chemical trust's appearance in court in answer to an antitrust indictment.	Agriculture Dept. estimates that 1941 winter wheat production will total 653,105,000 bushels.		Drama League of N.Y. awards the Delia Austrian Medal for the most distinguished performance to Paul Lukas, star of Lillian Hellman's play *Watch on the Rhine* . . . . Billy Soose outpoints Ken Overlin to win the world's middleweight championship in a 15-round bout.	May 9
F *Includes elections, federal-state relations, civil rights and liberties, crime, the judiciary, education, health care, poverty, urban affairs and population.*	G *Includes formation and debate of U.S. foreign and defense policies, veterans affairs and defense spending. (Relations with specific foreign countries are usually found under the region concerned.)*	H *Includes business, labor, agriculture, taxation, transportation, consumer affairs, monetary and fiscal policy, natural resources, pollution and accidents.*	I *Includes worldwide scientific, medical and technological developments, natural phenomena, U.S. weather and natural disasters.*	J *Includes the arts, religion, scholarship, communications media, sports, entertainment, fashions, fads and social life.*	

	World Affairs	European War Zone	Pacific War Zone	The Americas	Other Countries & Territories
May 10		Rudolf Hess, 47, deputy leader of the Nazi Party, parachutes to earth near Glasgow, Scotland carrying unauthorized proposals for an Anglo-German peace. Germany claims Hess had become the "victim of hallucinations." .... About 300 German planes bomb London throughout the night of May 10-11 in one of the worst raids the capital has yet undergone. Chamber of the House of Commons and other historic monuments are destroyed.	Gen. Chiang Kai-shek says in Chungking that China can defeat Japan alone and prevent a major Pacific war if the U.S. furnishes her with arms and money.	Argentine Marine Min. Rear Adm. Mario Fincati announces the government is planning to take over all available ships now lying idle in Argentine ports as the first step in the creation of a merchant fleet .... U.S. Interior Dept. announces that final steps are being taken to settle a 158-year-old Minnesota-Canadian border problem with Ottawa.	
May 11			Reports from Chungking say that the Japanese have thrown 10,000 troops into an offensive on the Honan-Hupeh border in central China.		Iraqi Premier Rashid Ali Beg Gailani's attempts to gain Moslem support have been rebuffed by both Saudi Arabia and Iran, according to Cairo sources .... Soviets report Russia has accepted an Iraqi proposal to establish diplomatic relations between the two countries.
May 12	South African P.M. Jan Christian Smuts says in a Capetown broadcast that the U.S. helped pave the way for the present war by abandoning the League of Nations.	Hitler meets Vichy Vice Premier Darlan at Berchtesgaden and presents German demands .... British convoy "Tiger" reaches Alexandria with 238 tanks needed for the defense of Egypt after running an Axis bomber gauntlet in the Mediterranean .... Bucharest military tribunal sentences 206 Iron Guardists to prison terms for attempting to overthrow the government.	Philippine National Assembly passes a bill requiring the registration and fingerprinting of all aliens in the islands.		
May 13		Berlin proclaims the northern area of the Red Sea to be a zone of military operations and warns neutral shipping against sailing in this area.		Ecuador and Peru notify the U.S. State Dept. that they are willing to accept the services of Argentina, Brazil and the U.S. in ending their century-old boundary dispute.	Haj Amin el Husseini, exiled Mufti of Jerusalem, leader of a million Moslems, broadcasts a proclamation from Baghdad summoning all Islam to join Iraqi forces in armed revolt against Britain.
May 14		Berlin sources state Rudolf Hess flew to Britain with the "illusion" that he could promote peace before Britain is "destroyed" and that he expected the British to permit him to return within two days. British reports confirm Hess hoped to arrange a peace through the Duke of Hamilton .... German Amb. Franz von Papen delivers a personal message of friendship from Hitler to Turkish Pres. Ismet Inonu.	Foreign Secy. Eden says Britain has rejected Japanese complaints of economic restrictions in British territories.	Argentine Radical Party convention meeting in Buenos Aires adopts a resolution affirming Argentina's neutrality, denouncing totalitarian ideologies and expressing sympathy for the Allies .... OPM Dir. Gen. Knudsen announces the creation of the Material Coordinating Comm. for the U.S. and Canada to exchange information on their supplies of strategic raw materials.	Cairo sources report German planes are beginning to land in Vichy-occupied Syria.
May 15		Petain says in a radio address that he has approved Darlan's meeting with Hitler "in principle." The Vichy cabinet has reportedly approved a policy of submitting to German demands .... A Rome communique announces that the restoration of the Kingdom of Croatia under the legendary Crown of Zvonimir was proclaimed in Zagreb on May 14.		Bolivian government expropriates German-owned airline Lloyd Aereo Boliviano, which held an exclusive franchise for service within the country .... Elie Lescot is inaugurated in Port-au-Prince as the 30th president of the Republic of Haiti.	Foreign Secy. Eden tells the House of Commons that French authorities are allowing German aircraft to use Syrian airports as staging posts for flights to Iraq.
May 16		British forces occupy Solum and Halfaya Pass in Egypt and Musaid in Libya.	Chinese sources report that the Japanese suffered a severe defeat in a 10-day battle in Hupeh Province.	Bolivian Finance Min. Joaquin Espada announces in La Paz that Bolivia has agreed to sell her entire production of wolframite, a source of tungsten, to the U.S.	Iraq protests to Emir Abdullah of Trans-Jordon over hostilities on the frontier, where British troops are massed under the command of Gen. Sir Henry Maitland Wilson .... British command in Cairo announces that the RAF attacked German aircraft at three Syrian airports on May 15.
May 17		Vichy announces that it will defend Dakar against all aggression and denies that Hitler mentioned Nazi occupation of Dakar in conversations with Adm. Darlan .... Germany announces the recapture of Solum on the Egyptian-Libyan border.	Chungking communique states Chinese troops recaptured Tsaoyang, strategic base in northern Hupeh Province, and Suchi in Chekiang Province. Japanese claim they hold Tsaoyang.	Members of pro-Nazi Chilean Vanguardia Popular Socialista break up Radical Party's national convention in Santiago. Radical Party leader Fernando Pinto Sepulveda is killed.	Air warfare between British and German forces intensifies in Iraq and Syria .... Russian news agency Tass announces the establishment of trade, diplomatic and consular relations between the USSR and Iraq .... British authorities proclaim a state of emergency in the Malay state of Selangor after three rubber plantation strikers are killed in a clash with soldiers.
	A	B	C	D	E
	Includes developments that affect more than one world region, international organizations and important meetings of major world leaders.	*Includes all developments in European countries and military engagements between Allied and Axis powers in Africa and at sea.*	*Includes all developments in Japan and China, Japanese foreign policy and military actions in the Pacific region.*	*Includes all domestic and regional developments in Latin America, the Caribbean and Canada.*	*Includes developments in those independent nations and colonial possessions not covered in Columns B, C and D.*

U.S. Politics & Social Issues	U.S. Foreign Policy & Defense	U.S. Economy & Environment	Science, Technology & Nature	Culture, Leisure & Life Style	
		San Francisco area shipyards are struck by 1,200 AFL and 700 CIO members, tying up $500 million worth of government contracts.		Warren Wright's Whirlaway with Eddie Arcaro up wins the Preakness by 5 lengths in a field of 11.	May 10
	Herbert Hoover opposes convoys in a radio broadcast .... Rep. George H. Tinkham (R, Mass.) issues a statement challenging FDR to ask Congress for a declaration of war and abide by the decision.			Mutual Broadcasting System signs a nine-year contract with ASCAP under which ASCAP will receive 3% of the network's gross receipts for the next four years and 3½% thereafter. ASCAP's 1,250,000 songs have been off the major networks since Jan. 1 .... Peggy Shannon, former screen actress and Ziegfeld Follies star, is found dead in her Hollywood, Calif. home.	May 11
	Senate Commerce Comm. approves the alien ship seizure bill after defeating an amendment to prohibit the transfer of seized ships to belligerents .... Brig. Gen. Lewis B. Hershey, acting draft chief, urges Congress to revise the Selective Service Act so that the President may defer older men.	British economist John Maynard Keynes says in Washington that the best way to block inflation is to withhold personal salaries at the source, as Britain is doing.		Alice Faye, Hollywood screen star, and Phil Harris, band leader, are married by a justice of the peace in Ensenada, Mexico.	May 12
Senate approves Dr. Joseph Rosier's appointment as Senator from W. Va. .... Frank Hague is re-elected mayor of Jersey City, N.J. for his seventh consecutive four-year term.		House passes a bill to raise the crop loan rate from 75 to 85% of parity on cotton, wheat, corn, tobacco and rice and sends it to the Senate .... Most employes of Colt Fire Arms Mfg. Co. in Hartford, Conn. strike for 20-cent-an-hour wage increase. The company has $30 million in defense contracts.			May 13
Census Bureau reports that 62,958,703 persons, or 47.8% of the total population, live in 140 metropolitan areas, an increase of more than eight million since 1930.	War Dept. announces that 214 four-engine flying fortresses have been flown from California to Hawaii during the past 24 hrs. to reinforce the heavy concentration of medium bombers and pursuit planes already there.	CIO strikers at Colt Fire Arms Co. accept 5-8 cents an hour increases and end two-day walkout .... Senate passes a bill authorizing government loans up to 85% of 1909-1914 parity prices to growers of five basic crops and sends it to FDR. Farm commodity prices soar on the Chicago markets.		Mark F. Ethridge, former president of the National Association of Broadcasters, resigns from a federal commission surveying the radio industry and denounces the FCC for its recent anti-monopoly regulations .... Dizzy Dean is given an unconditional release as a pitcher for the Chicago Cubs and becomes a coach for the club.	May 14
	Following Petain's speech on collaboration, FDR warns Vichy against any "voluntary alliance" to "deliver up France and its colonial empire .... with the menace which that involves to the peace and safety of the Western Hemisphere." .... Coast Guard places guards on 11 French ships in U.S. ports, including the liner *Normandie* .... Senate votes, 59 to 20, to pass the alien-ship seizure bill and sends it to conference with minor amendments.	NLRB reports employes of Bethlehem Steel's Lackawanna, N.Y. plant voted overwhelmingly to be represented by the CIO's SWOC.	Dr. Henry G. Poncher of the Univ. of Illinois reports that the recently discovered Vitamin K is proving to be of great value in preventing hemorrhages in babies during the first week of life.		May 15
Wis. Gov. J.P. Heil signs a bill barring the CP from the state primary and general election ballots .... Senate approves the selection of Sen. Robert R. Reynolds (D, N.C.) as chairman of the Military Affairs Comm.	Navy Secy. Knox tells graduates of Naval War College that France has apparently fallen under the "complete subjugation" of Germany and that "it is impossible to exaggerate the mortal danger of our country in this moment of history."	NDMB announces a settlement of the GM dispute with the CIO-UAW. GM agrees to 10-sent-anhour wage increase. Ford announces 5-to-15-cents-an-hour increase for 53,000 workers at River Rouge plant .... Senate unanimously passes the priorities bill after striking out the Cox amendment which would have established an independent priorities director.		NAB Board of directors demands the removal of James L. Fly as chairman of the FCC .... NHL governors elect Frank Calder league president for the 25th consecutive season.	May 16
Justice Dept. begins a nationwide round-up of aliens illegally in the country.	Four Democratic members of the Senate Foreign Relations Comm. urge that the U.S. take over French island possessions in the Western Hemisphere.			Indiana wins the Big Ten outdoor track and field championship in Minneapolis.	May 17

F	G	H	I	J
Includes elections, federal-state relations, civil rights and liberties, crime, the judiciary, education, health care, poverty, urban affairs and population.	*Includes formation and debate of U.S. foreign and defense policies, veterans affairs and defense spending. (Relations with specific foreign countries are usually found under the region concerned.)*	*Includes business, labor, agriculture, taxation, transportation, consumer affairs, monetary and fiscal policy, natural resources, pollution and accidents.*	*Includes worldwide scientific, medical and technological developments, natural phenomena, U.S. weather and natural disasters.*	*Includes the arts, religion, scholarship, communications media, sports, entertainment, fashions, fads and social life.*

	World Affairs	European War Zone	Pacific War Zone	The Americas	Other Countries & Territories
May 18	State Secy. Hull outlines a five-point postwar world reconstruction program based on free trade.	King Victor Emmanuel III of Italy crowns his cousin, the Duke of Spoleto, King Aimone of Croatia in a 10-minute ceremony in Rome.			French High Commissioner for Syria and Lebanon Gen. Henri Fernand Dentz broadcasts from Beirut that the French armies in the mandated territories are ready to defend themselves against British attack.
May 19		Italian commander in Ethiopia, the Duke of Aosta, surrenders to British forces, ending the British conquest of Ethiopia and bringing the total of Italian prisoners to 230,000 . . . . Danish sources report the Iceland Althing (Parliament) has canceled Iceland's personal union with Denmark and declared the island's independence.		U.S. Navy Dept. announces that Capt. William Quigley of the U.S. Navy has been appointed chief of staff of the Peruvian Navy.	Iraq claims that 30 British armored cars and trucks have been destroyed and 2 British gunboats damaged in the Tigris River south of Basra.
May 20		German paratroopers attack British forces on Crete.		Chilean government arrests 32 members of the Socialist Vanguard (Nazi) Party on charges of plotting a second putsch against the government.	British troops in Iraq seize Feluja, important bridgehead on the Euphrates River, about 35 miles west of Baghdad.
May 21		British patrol planes spot German battleship *Bismarck* and cruiser *Prinz Eugen* off Norway . . . . American freighter *Robin Moor* is torpedoed by a German U-boat in the South Atlantic, after crew is first evacuated in lifeboats . . . . Sharp fighting is reported on Crete as German airborne units continue to pour into the island.			
May 22		Churchill discloses that the RAF was forced to abandon its Cretan airports because they were badly damaged. German troops continue to land . . . . British Foreign Secy. Eden declares that if Vichy actively assists Germany, "we shall naturally hold ourselves free to attack the enemy wherever he may be found."			Ankara sources report British troops have advanced from Feluja to within 20 miles of Baghdad, driving 10,000 to 12,000 Iraqi troops before them.
May 23		British cruisers make contact with *Bismarck* and *Prinz Eugen* in the Denmark Strait between Iceland and Greenland. In the battle, the battle-cruiser *Hood* is sunk with the lose of some 1,400 men. The German ships escape . . . . In a Vichy broadcast, Darlan says collaboration with Germany is a matter of "life or death" for France, but adds that Hitler has not demanded the French fleet or colonial territory.	Japanese spokesman admits Chinese troops recaptured Chuki, a railhead in northern Chekiang Province.	CAB authorizes Pan Am-Grace Airways, Inc. to establish commercial air transportation to and from Oruro, Bolivia. FDR allocates $8 million in defense funds to aid airline service in Latin America in competition with Axis-controlled companies.	RAF reports British bombers broke up an Iraqi counterattack at Feluja, 30 miles west of Baghdad, after native troops had gained positions in the town's outskirts.
May 24		German communique claims German troops have occupied the western part of Crete . . . . Vatican officials say German authorities have issued a decree banning all Catholic periodicals and newspapers after June 1.			Ankara sources report that Emir Abdul Illah, deposed regent of Iraq and uncle of King Feisal, has returned to Iraq under British protection and is planning to establish a new government in opposition to Premier Rashid Ali Beg Gailani . . . . P.M. R.G. Menzies returns to Australia after a four-month, 42,000 mile journey to Britain and the U.S.
May 25		King George II of Greece, accompanied by Prince Peter and members of the Greek government, arrives in Cairo after fleeing Crete . . . . German Grand Adm. Erich Raeder is reported by a Japanese news agency to have stated that U.S. convoys or naval aid to Britain would be "a plain act of war and unprovoked aggression" which Germany will meet with force.			An estimated 5,000 persons drown when a storm strikes a large number of villages in the Ganges Delta in India.
May 26		A Berlin spokesman says that the British fleet in the eastern Mediterranean may be considered destroyed . . . . German troops advance on Suda Bay as the fighting on Crete continues.		Nationalist Party of Uruguay adopts a resolution urging Uruguayan neutrality in the present war and opposing the cession of bases to foreign powers.	Six persons are killed in rioting in Bombay, India, bringing the total casualties for five days to 40 dead and 140 injured.

A	B	C	D	E
Includes developments that affect more than one world region, international organizations and important meetings of major world leaders.	*Includes all developments in European countries and military engagements between Allied and Axis powers in Africa and at sea.*	*Includes all developments in Japan and China, Japanese foreign policy and military actions in the Pacific region.*	*Includes all domestic and regional developments in Latin America, the Caribbean and Canada.*	*Includes developments in those independent nations and colonial possessions not covered in Columns B, C and D.*

U.S. Politics & Social Issues	U.S. Foreign Policy & Defense	U.S. Economy & Environment	Science, Technology & Nature	Culture, Leisure & Life Style	
		San Francisco area AFL Metal Trades Council votes to cross CIO and AFL machinist picket lines at 11 shipyards.			May 18
N.Y. Bd. of Higher Education announces the suspension of five more teachers and seven clerks at CCNY on charges of Communist Party membership and refusal to cooperate with the Rapp-Coudert committee investigations.	Rep. Francis Case (R, S.D.) introduces a bill in the House authorizing Hull to negotiate for the purchase of French islands in the Western Hemisphere.	CIO-UMW and hard coal operators agree to a two-year contract in N.Y. providing wage increases for 91,000 miners who will return to their jobs on May 20, ending a one-day strike .... Treasury Asst. Secy. John L. Sullivan urges before the House Ways and Means Comm. that the Excess Profits Tax Act of 1940 be revised to raise at least $1.096 billion in excess profits from the defense programs.		Economic historian Werner Sombart, 78, dies in Berlin.	May 19
FDR announces that Thanksgiving will be restored to its traditional date, the last Thursday in November, because moving it up a week has not improved business.	FDR appoints N.Y. Mayor Fiorello La Guardia as director of the Office of Civilian Defense .... *Saturday Evening Post* drops its isolationist editorial policy and backs FDR's policy on Europe .... Gallup Poll reports that 52% of voters questioned in a survey said they favor convoys for ships carrying war materials to Britain, as compared to 41% in April.				May 20
Dies Committee undercover agent Mary Spargo claims the Coal Division of the Interior Dept. is "loaded from top to bottom with Communists."	Navy Secy. Knox says the Neutrality Act is a blunder and should be repealed.	CIO-UAW wins NLRB elections at the Ford Motor Co.'s River Rouge and Lincoln plants in Detroit .... OPM Dir. Gen. Knudsen reveals plans to raise heavy bomber production to 500 a month by September 1942.			May 21
FBI Dir. J. Edgar Hoover discloses the FBI is mobilizing 150,000 local and state law enforcement officers on a voluntary basis to aid in the drive against fifth column agents.	Stimson denounces the Neutrality Act as a violation of our most important tradition of foreign policy, freedom of the seas .... Hull says rumors that the U.S. plans to seize French Martinique is propaganda .... One hundred American writers issue a manifesto urging "all aid and at once—whatever that may have to mean" to Britain. Signers include Stephen Vincent Benet, Edna Ferber, Thomas Mann, Upton Sinclair and Hendrik William Van Loon.	Navy trucks driven by sailors and Marines carry non-striking AFL shipyard workers through picket lines at two San Francisco yards. Local CIO protests to FDR.	American Social Hygiene Assoc. reports that tests administered to 1,897,599 persons over a five-year period indicate three out of every 100 adults in the U.S. have syphilis.		May 22
William Bioff and George E. Browne are indicted by a grand jury in N.Y. on charges of extorting $550,000 during the past six years from the 20th Century-Fox Film Corp., Loew's Inc., Paramount Pictures, Inc. and Warner Brothers Pictures, Inc.	FDR appoints Maj. Gen. George H. Brett chief of the air corps, Brig. Gen. Courtney Hodges chief of infantry and Col. William N. Porter chief of the Chemical Warfare Service .... Lindbergh and Wheeler denounce interventionists before a crowd of 22,000 attending an America First rally in N.Y.	A conference report on a bill empowering the government to impose priorities on industry to aid defense is passed by the Senate and sent to the White House .... AFL strikers reach agreement to end a walkout at Ravenna, Ohio ammunition loading plant.		Joe Louis successfully defends his heavyweight crown for the 17th time when referee Arthur Donovan disqualifies Buddy Baer at the start of the seventh round of a 15-round bout in Washington because Baer's manager refuses to leave the ring.	May 23
	Battle of Oahu, involving 35,000 troops and army bombers, ends in Hawaii after the enemy invaders are theoretically destroyed .... Sen. James M. Mead (D, N.Y.) urges that the U.S. negotiate with France for temporary bases on French islands in the Western Hemisphere or seize them if necessary.	CIO members at North American Aviation Inc. of Inglewood, Calif. vote 5,829 to 210 to strike to back their wage demands. The company has over $120 million in defense contracts .... Federal Price Admin. Leon Henderson sets a maximum price schedule for ordinary commercial-quality combed cotton yarns.		Les Steers of Oregon breaks the world high-jump record by jumping 6' 10⅞" in the Los Angeles Coliseum Relays.	May 24
					May 25
Supreme Court rules, 4 to 3, that Congress has the power to regulate primary elections for the nomination of candidates for federal office.	FDR orders all men not previously registered who become 21 by July 1 to register on that date under the Selective Service Act.	Sen. Harry F. Byrd (D,Va.) introduces a joint resolution in Congress condemning defense strikes and demands that Labor Secy. Perkins resign .... FDR signs the farm loan bill providing for federal loans at up to 85% of parity prices on five basic crops.			May 26

F	G	H	I	J
Includes elections, federal-state relations, civil rights and liberties, crime, the judiciary, education, health care, poverty, urban affairs and population.	*Includes formation and debate of U.S. foreign and defense policies, veterans affairs and defense spending. (Relations with specific foreign countries are usually found under the region concerned.)*	*Includes business, labor, agriculture, taxation, transportation, consumer affairs, monetary and fiscal policy, natural resources, pollution and accidents.*	*Includes worldwide scientific, medical and technological developments, natural phenomena, U.S. weather and natural disasters.*	*Includes the arts, religion, scholarship, communications media, sports, entertainment, fashions, fads and social life.*

	World Affairs	European War Zone	Pacific War Zone	The Americas	Other Countries & Territories
May 27		British ships reestablish contact with the *Bismarck* 500 miles west of Brest, France and sink her with bombs, torpedoes and shellfire .... German troops capture Canea, capital of Crete.	Japanese official says in a Tokyo broadcast that Japan has 500 warships and 4,000 naval planes in fighting order.		
May 28		British forces begin the evacuation of Crete under heavy German pressure .... German command announces the capture of Halfaya Pass in Egypt southeast of Solum by German and Italian troops.			
May 29		Eden declares in a London speech that FDR's "four freedoms" are the "keystone" of British war aims .... Candia, second largest city of Crete, falls to German troops.	Japanese reveal they have made formal representations to the Netherlands and Britain in an attempt to break the deadlock in the trade negotiations between Japan and the Netherlands East Indies.		
May 30		German command announces that Anglo-Greek resistance has collasped everywhere on Crete.	Foreign Min. Matsuoka says Japan will carry out her obligations under the Tripartite Pact.	Former King Carol of Rumania and Mme. Magda Lupescu arrive in Havana, Cuba, aboard the U.S. liner *America* from the Virgin Islands after fleeing from Europe.	London announces that Premier Rashid Ali el Gailani of Iraq has fled to Iran, while British forces advance to the outskirts of Baghdad .... Vichy announces that French troops have crossed the Sahara to the western shore of Lake Chad, base of Gen. Charles de Gaulle's Free French forces, in an attempt to recover French Equatorial Africa.
May 31		British complete the evacuation of Crete, sustaining heavy casualties .... Darlan denounces Britain for waging a "war of piracy" against France on the high seas and for bombing Sfax, Tunisia.	Kenkichi Yoshizawa, head of the Japanese trade mission in Batavia, NEI, declares that the note submitted to the Netherlands government pertaining to the purchase of raw materials from the Indies is "final."	Pres. Manuel Avila Camacho declares that Mexico will take whatever measures are necessary to assure its independence should the U.S. declare war on the Axis.	British troops enter Baghdad and the Iraqi army sues for an armistice, ending the month-old war of Premier Rashid Ali el Gailani. German and Italian officials begin to flee the country.
June 1					Emir Abdul Illah, ousted regent of Iraq, returns to Baghdad as fighting between British and Iraqi troops ceases at 8 a.m. under the terms of the armistice.
June 2		Hitler and Mussolini meet at the Brenner Pass. The Germans withhold information from the Italians about their secret plan to attack Russia .... King George II of Greece accepts the resignation of his cabinet in exile in Cairo and forms a new one in which Emmanuel Tsouderos remains premier.	Twenty-seven Japanese planes kill 100 and wound 200 persons in Chungking, China.	Former Argentine Foreign Min. Dr. Carlos Saavedra Lamas and former Pres. Augustin P. Justo urge hemispheric defense talks sponsored by the U.S.	British officials in Cairo state German forces have abandoned the Mosul oil region 250 miles north of Baghdad.
June 3		Soviets notify Greek Min. Christoff Diamantopoulos that Russia has withdrawn diplomatic recognition of Greece in view of Greece's "loss of sovereignty."			Ankara reports state Gen. Henri Fernad Dentz, French high commissioner for Syria, has declared a state of siege in the eastern part of the territory .... Iraqi Regent Emir Abdul Illah appoints former Premier Jamil al-Midfai as the new premier.
June 4		Former German Kaiser Wilhelm II, 82, dies in exile in Doorn, Holland. Hitler wires condolences to his family .... Axis planes stage a night raid on Alexandria, Egypt, killing 147 persons and injuring 92.	Japanese Imperial Headquarters in Tokyo announce that a great battle is underway in the Chungtiao (Shansi) area of China.	U.S. State Dept. official Thomas Burke says a new plan for the common defense of the 21 American republics has been completed.	Vichy issues a statement denying that the Nazis will get the use of bases in Syria or that they have any troops there .... Airborne British troops occupy Mosul, and employes of the Iraqi Petroleum Co. resume their work in the area.

A	B	C	D	E
Includes developments that affect more than one world region, international organizations and important meetings of major world leaders.	*Includes all developments in European countries and military engagements between Allied and Axis powers in Africa and at sea.*	*Includes all developments in Japan and China, Japanese foreign policy and military actions in the Pacific region.*	*Includes all domestic and regional developments in Latin America, the Caribbean and Canada.*	*Includes developments in those independent nations and colonial possessions not covered in Columns B, C and D.*

U.S. Politics & Social Issues	U.S. Foreign Policy & Defense	U.S. Economy & Environment	Science, Technology & Nature	Culture, Leisure & Life Style	
	FDR proclaims that "an unlimited national emergency confronts this country, which requires that its military, naval, air and civilian defenses be put on the basis of readiness to repel any and all acts or threats of aggression directed toward any part of the Western Hemisphere." He reasserts doctrine of freedom of the seas .... FDR asks Congress for additional appropriations of over $3.3 billion for aircraft construction.	AFL Pres. Green denounces San Francisco shipyard strike .... House passes a bill extending for two years FDR's power to operate the $2-billion Exchange Stabilization Fund and to alter the gold content of the dollar.		With two games to play, Samuel Reshevsky, U.S. Chess champion, retains his title by drawing the 14th game with Israel A. Horowitz in N.Y.	May 27
Former Kansas City Democratic boss T.J. Pendergast and two other men are found guilty of contempt for deceiving a federal court in a $10 million fire insurance settlement.	FDR tells a special press conference that he has no intention of asking Congress to repeal or modify the Neutrality Act and that he does not plan to institute convoys for war material being shipped to Britain .... Maritime Commission requisitions the 26,454-ton liner *America*, the largest merchant ship ever built in this country, which will be turned over to the Navy.	AFL Executive Council pledges its support of FDR's plea for labor peace and calls upon its unions to refrain from striking defense industries without first seeking mediation .... Harry Bridges denies at his deportation hearing that he is now or ever was a CP member .... Interior Secy. Harold L. Ickes urges priorities on gasoline, oil and electric power on the Eastern seaboard because of the increasing shortage.	A spinproof private plane designed by Dr. Otto C. Koppen for the General Aircraft Corp. is demonstrated in Newark, N.J.	Tony Zale, recognized as world middleweight champion by the National Boxing Assn., KOs Al Hostak in the second round of their scheduled 15-round fight in Chicago.	May 28
Federal Judge James M. Proctor fines the AMA $2,500 and the Medical Society of Washington $1,500 for antitrust law violations.	Maritime Commission announces it is requisitioning 13 more merchant vessels for the Navy .... Dr. Kurt Heinrich Rieth, former German minister to Austria, is arrested in N.Y. pending deportation proceedings .... War Dept. announces 8,000 British pilots will be trained annually in the U.S. beginning June 7.	OPM Priorities Dir. E.R. Stettinius, Jr. signs a general preference order placing steel on a limited priorities basis to curb non-essential civilian consumption.			May 29
Sen. George W. Norris (Ind, Neb.) urges that presidential and vice presidential candidates be nominated by nationwide primary elections instead of by the present convention method.	Guards are increased around defense installations and factories after the FBI receives reports that sabotage is planned for the Memorial Day weekend .... U.S. Amb. to Britain John G. Winant returns to report to FDR and Hull.			Mauri Rose and Floyd Davis win the 500-mile Indianapolis Speedway Race with an average speed of 115.117 mph.	May 30
	Gallup Poll reports that 62% of the persons questioned in a recent survey said that they would rather have the U.S. enter the war than see Britain surrender .... Sen. Hiram W. Johnson says in a radio address that the trend of FDR's administration is toward "dictatorship and war." .... FDR names Interior Secy. Harold L. Ickes as "Petroleum Coordinator for National Defense."	Budget Bureau Dir. Harold D. Smith estimates the net budgetary deficit for the next fiscal year will be $12.767 billion, an increase of $3.577 billion over the deficit estimated in January.		World Peace Commission of the Methodist Church ends a four-day conference in Chicago with a report urging a crusade for Protestant unity as a step toward a just and lasting world peace.	May 31
	National Anti-War Congress, meeting in Washington, passes resolutions urging an immediate U.S. offer to mediate the European and Asiatic wars.			Broadcasting officials meet in Washington to organize their fight against the FCC radio regulations .... Fred Perry regains the world professional single tennis championship by defeating Dick Skeen in Chicago.	June 1
U.S. Solicitor Gen. Francis Biddle says the government will curb all subversive activities in the present emergency but will protect essential civil rights .... Charles Evans Hughes, 79, chief justice of the Supreme Court since his appointment by Pres. Hoover in February 1930, announces his resignation, effective July 1.	War Dept. asks Congress to pass a bill authorizing the President during the national emergency to requisition any property he deems necessary for national defense in return for fair compensation.	FDR signs the mandatory priorities bill .... Labor Secy. Perkins certifies the machinists' strike at the Bethlehem Shipbuilding Corp. in San Francisco to the NDMB .... Treasury Secy. Henry Morgenthau says that the Axis countries have withdrawn virtually all of their funds from the U.S.		Former New York Yankee Lou Gehrig, 37, the "Iron Man" of baseball, dies in N.Y. of amyotrophic lateral sclerosis, a form of spinal paralysis.	June 2
	FDR supports the War Dept.'s property requistion bill, indicating it is designed to ensure the delivery of vital defense material.	NDMB demands that 12,000 striking Washington State lumbermen ratify a back-to-work agreement and calls on CIO leaders to give "a full explanation" of their failure to submit a previous NDMB recommendation to the strikers.			June 3
Four state leaders of the CP, including state chairman Israel Amter, testify before the Rapp-Coudert committee in N.Y. that all CP records of members and dues payments have been destroyed by direct order of national headquarters.	Rep. E.E. Cox (D, Ga.) denounces the property requisition bill as "the kiss of death to free government" and "the most astounding measure of dictatorial powers ever introduced in this country."	O.M. Orton, president of the CIO International Woodworkers of America, rejects the NDMB's request that striking loggers return to work.			June 4

F	G	H	I	J
Includes elections, federal-state relations, civil rights and liberties, crime, the judiciary, education, health care, poverty, urban affairs and population.	*Includes formation and debate of U.S. foreign and defense policies, veterans affairs and defense spending. (Relations with specific foreign countries are usually found under the region concerned.)*	*Includes business, labor, agriculture, taxation, transportation, consumer affairs, monetary and fiscal policy, natural resources, pollution and accidents.*	*Includes worldwide scientific, medical and technological developments, natural phenomena, U.S. weather and natural disasters.*	*Includes the arts, religion, scholarship, communications media, sports, entertainment, fashions, fads and social life.*

	World Affairs	European War Zone	Pacific War Zone	The Americas	Other Countries & Territories
June 5		Turkish sources report 144 German and Rumanian divisions have been concentrated on the Russian frontier to back up demands for food, oil and ore concessions in the Ukraine.	U.S. Amb. Joseph C. Grew protests against the Japanese seizure of U.S. goods in French Indochina and the bombing of American property in Chungking, China . . . . Seven hundred Chinese are suffocated or killed in a stampede at the entrances of one of Chungking's largest air raid shelters during a Japanese bombing attack.	Reports from Costa Rica indicate that considerable quantities of of modern arms have been received from the U.S. and that a U.S. military mission will train the Costa Rican Army how to use the new weapons.	Ankara reports that French planes crossed the Syrian border and bombed Amman, capital of Trans-Jordan, and that German troops continue to move into Syria.
June 6			A Japanese military spokesman says 50,000 Chinese troops were killed and 25,000 taken prisoner during the Japanese spring offensive in south Shansi Province . . . . Netherlands East Indies government delivers a generally unfavorable reply to Japanese trade demands.	Radical Party member of the Argentine Chamber of Deputies Manubens Calvet attacks Nazi propaganda activities in the country and charges the Nazis have recruited a "strong military organization" in Argentina.	Former Egyptian Army chief of staff Gen. Aziz el Masri Pasha is arrested in a Cairo suburb. He reportedly tried to escape to Iraq three weeks ago.
June 7	Gallup Poll reports that 49% of the persons questioned in a recent survey said they would like to see the U.S. join a new league of nations.			Pres. Alfredo Baldomir tells a Chilean journalist in Montevideo that Uruguay is prepared to offer bases for the defense of the Western Hemisphere.	British press dispatches from Cairo state that large German troop-carrying and supply planes are landing in Syria . . . . Vichy is reported to have decided not to fight the French colonies held by the Free French forces of Gen. Charles de Gaulle.
June 8					About 20,000 Australian, Indian and Free French troops commanded by Gen. Sir Henry Maitland Wilson invade Syria in three columns.
June 9		Brazilian ship *Osorio* radios that the U.S. ship *Robin Moore* was torpedoed and sunk by a German submarine on May 21 in the mid-Atlantic south of the Cape Verde Islands.			British and Free French forces, aided by aircraft and naval bombardments along the Mediterranean shore, advance into Syria, taking Tyre along the coast and crossing the Leontes River. Only scattered resistance by Vichy forces is reported.
June 10		Adm. Darlan appeals to the French people in a Vichy broadcast to help him conciliate Germany and thus obtain better peace terms . . . . In a Rome speech, Mussolini says the U.S. is at war with the Axis and declares that U.S. aid will arrive too late to save Britain.			British headquarters announces that British and Free French forces have advanced to within 15 miles of Damascus.
June 11		London and Stockholm sources report Nazi troops are concentrated along the long Soviet frontier with three army corps on the Bessarabian border.		Pres. Pedro Aguirre Cerda of Chile names five new ministers to replace Radical Party members who resigned yesterday . . . . Bolivian Pres. Enrique Penaranda accepts the resignation of his entire cabinet, which quit after receiving reports that Nazis were planning general strikes.	British and Free French forces continue their advance into Syria.
June 12		Representatives of 15 Allied governments meeting in London adopt a resolution declaring "they will continue the struggle against German and Italian aggression until victory is won and will mututually assist each other to the utmost."	Tokyo announces the signing of a Russian-Japanese commercial agreement providing for mutual most-favored-nation treatment and a barter exchange of goods amounting to 30 million yen the first year.		
June 13		Vichy discloses at least 12,000 Jews in unoccupied France have been arrested and interned in concentration camps because of the discovery of an alleged "Jewish plot" to hinder Franco-German collaboration.		A new coalition Bolivian cabinet takes office in La Paz.	

A	B	C	D	E
Includes developments that affect more than one world region, international organizations and important meetings of major world leaders.	*Includes all developments in European countries and military engagements between Allied and Axis powers in Africa and at sea.*	*Includes all developments in Japan and China, Japanese foreign policy and military actions in the Pacific region.*	*Includes all domestic and regional developments in Latin America, the Caribbean and Canada.*	*Includes developments in those independent nations and colonial possessions not covered in Columns B, C and D.*

U.S. Politics & Social Issues	U.S. Foreign Policy & Defense	U.S. Economy & Environment	Science, Technology & Nature	Culture, Leisure & Life Style	
	Hull issues a statement to the press warning Vichy against collaborating with the Axis for the purpose of aggression .... John Cudahy, former U.S. ambassador to Belgium, says Hitler told him on May 23 at Berchtesgaden that "convoy means war."	CIO-UAW strikes the Inglewood, Calif. plant of North American Aviation, halting work on $200 million worth of defense orders and affecting more than 11,000 workers .... CIO Pres. Murray appeals to loggers to accept the NDMB's recommendations and return to work .... House passes a bill authorizing the construction of oil pipelines to the Atlantic Coast to prevent an oil shortage because of lack of transportation facilities.	Dr. Louis I. Dublin, statistician of the Metropolitan Life Insurance Co., says infant mortality in the U.S. has declined by 45% in the last 20 years.		June 5
	FDR signs alien ship seizure bill and issues an executive order authorizing the Maritime Commission to commandeer such vessels in U.S. ports for national defense purposes.	OPM's Labor Policy Advisory Comm., made up of labor leaders, condemns defense strikes in San Francisco shipyards, Puget Sound lumber camps and North American Aviation plant .... Membership of the AFT votes to revoke the charters of the N.Y. Teachers Union, the N.Y. College Teachers Union and the Philadelphia Teachers Union on charges of being Communist-controlled.		American Writers Congress in N.Y. presents the Randolph Bourne Memorial Award for "distinguished service to the cause of culture and peace" to Theodore Dreiser.	June 6
Former Democratic boss of Kansas City Tom Pendergast and former Missouri insurance superintendent R. Emmet O'Malley are sentenced to two-year prison terms for contempt growing out of a bribe case.		White House reveals FDR is ready to commandeer the strike-bound North American Aviation plant and use the Army to run it unless the strike ends. UAW's aviation division chief Richard Frankensteen says in a radio address that the walkout is a "wildcat strike" caused by Communists.		Warren Wright's Whirlaway, winner of the Kentucky Derby and the Preakness, wins the $52,270 Belmont Stakes .... Craig Wood wins the national open golf championship in Fort Worth, Tex. .... American Writers Congress chooses Richard Wright's *Native Son* as the best American novel published since 1939.	June 7
		Hecklers at a local UAW rally in the Inglewood, Calif. strike shout down Richard Frankensteen when he appeals for a return to work.	Eight persons, including five asleep in a farmhouse, are killed by a tornado north of Wichita, Kan.		June 8
	Itaru Tatibana, a Japanese Navy officer, and Torachi Kono, a Japanese servant in the home of Charles Chaplin, are arrested on spying charges in Los Angeles.	Under direct order of FDR, 2,500 regular troops take over the strike-bound plant of North American Aviation, Inc. in Inglewood, Calif. FDR announces the takeover was necessary for national defense. Atty. Gen. Jackson says the strike leaders follow "the Communist Party line." .... Representatives of 5,000 AFL teamsters in Minneapolis, led by Niles B. Dunn, vote to secede from the parent union and seek a charter from the CIO.			June 9
Charles Workman is sentenced to life imprisonment after pleading guilty to the 1935 murder of Arthur (Dutch Schultz) Flegenheimer in Newark, N.J.	Interior Secy. Harold Ickes describes former U.S. Amb. to Belgium John Cudahy as "merely a megaphone through which Hitler is graciously permitted to shout his obscenities into the ears of Americans."	North American Aviation plant strikers vote at a mass meeting to return to work. More than 5,000 of the day shift's 7,000 workers return to their jobs .... Gallup Poll reports 76% of persons questioned in a survey said defense strikes should be forbidden .... Alcoa and CIO officials accept the NDMB's proposals to settle a one-day strike at the company's Cleveland plants. But 4,000 CIO-UAW members begin a strike at the Bohn Aluminum and Brass Corp. in Detroit.			June 10
House passes and sends to the Senate a bill requiring all persons entering or leaving the U.S. to get special permits.	FDR informs Congress that $4,277,412,879 of the $7-billion Lend-Lease appropriation has been allocated for aid to the Allies in the 90 days since the act was passed.	Navy Secy. Knox urges manufacturers to make "superhuman efforts" to speed airplane production. Referring to the North American Aviation strike, he says the government accepted the challenge of "subversive and communistic elements" and would proceed against them "as enemies of the country." .... Federal mediators settle the one-day CIO strike at the Bohn Aluminum and Brass Corp. in Detroit.		Daniel Beard, 90, one of the founders of the Boy Scouts of America, dies .... Cleveland Rams of the NFL are sold to Dan Reeves and Fred Levy Jr. for a reported $140,000.	June 11
FDR nominates Harlan F. Stone as chief justice of the Supreme Court and Sen. James F. Byrnes (D. S.C.) and Atty. Gen. Robert H. Jackson as associate justices.		Senate adopts the Connolly plant-seizure amendment to the Selective Service bill, giving the President power to take over any strike-bound defense plant when mediation efforts have failed .... CIO Pres. Murray denounces the use of troops in strikes and any attempt by a "mediation board" to "impose compulsory arbitration."			June 12
Negro leaders meet in N.Y. with Mrs. Roosevelt and Mayor Fiorello La Guardia, who seek, at FDR's request, to get the Negro march on Washington for fair employment called off. When this is rejected, FDR agrees to meet with the Negro leaders.	Hull denounces "the Darlan-Laval group" in Vichy for seeking to "deliver France politically, economically, socially and militarily to Hitler" and for resisting British forces in Syria .... Sumner Welles charges Germany violated an international agreement by not assuring the safety of the 35 passengers and crew of the American freighter *Robin Moor.*	FDR issues an appeal asking unions to refrain from jurisdictional disputes. The White House reveals AFL Teamsters Pres. Daniel Tobin has complained to the President that "subversive organizations" are trying to damage his union .... It is disclosed that OPM will soon begin a nationwide collection of aluminum to avert a threatened shortage.			June 13

F	G	H	I	J
Includes elections, federal-state relations, civil rights and liberties, crime, the judiciary, education, health care, poverty, urban affairs and population.	*Includes formation and debate of U.S. foreign and defense policies, veterans affairs and defense spending. (Relations with specific foreign countries are usually found under the region concerned.)*	*Includes business, labor, agriculture, taxation, transportation, consumer affairs, monetary and fiscal policy, natural resources, pollution and accidents.*	*Includes worldwide scientific, medical and technological developments, natural phenomena, U.S. weather and natural disasters.*	*Includes the arts, religion, scholarship, communications media, sports, entertainment, fashions, fads and social life.*

	World Affairs	European War Zone	Pacific War Zone	The Americas	Other Countries & Territories
June 14		Soviet news agency Tass belittles rumors in the Western press of a war between Russia and Germany as an "obvious absurdity .... a clumsy propaganda maneuver of the forces arrayed against the Soviet Union and Germany." .... Hitler outlines the final secret plans for the invasion of Russia to his generals in a Berlin meeting. He orders them to use "brutal means" against the Communists.		City Council of Buenos Aires votes to permit the showing of Charles Chaplin's film *The Great Dictator* after it was banned for six months at the request of the Italian ambassador.	
June 15		Neutral diplomats in Ankara say a German attack on Russia is inevitable unless Russia agrees to help feed Nazi-occupied countries. Finland calls up reservists for "military exercises." .... Croatia joins the Axis when its leader, Ante Pavelitch, signs the Tripartite Pact in Vienna.		Reports from San Jose, Costa Rica, state that Guatemala, Costa Rica, El Salvador, Nicaragua and Honduras have agreed to inform Germany that they endorse FDR's May 27th speech.	Allied forces take the Lebanese port of Saida and capture Abu Kemal in the interior after French forces withdraw.
June 16		British command in Cairo announces that an offensive was begun against Axis positions along the Egyptian-Libyan frontier on June 15.		A Brazilian embassy official in Washington says the U.S. and Brazil are negotiating in Rio de Janeiro for the construction of air bases on the Brazilian coast.	Allied forces drive north on the Lebanese coats to within 10 miles of Beirut. Naval battles off the coast are reported.
June 17		British planes attack Nazi air bases in the Boulogne area of France and bomb the German Rhineland area for the seventh successive night .... British forces withdraw from the Fort Capuzzo-Solum area of Libya .... Catholic Church regains virtually all of its former power to appoint the hierarchy and lower clergy under an agreement between Spain and the Vatican, published in Madrid.	Japanese-Dutch trade negotiations in Batavia break down.	Paraguayan Foreign Min. Luis Argana and Brazilian Foreign Min. Dr. Oswaldo Aranha sign 10 treaties in Rio de Janeiro covering commerce, transport and cultural relations between the two countries.	Australian P.M. Robert G. Menzies says strikes and lockouts in war industries will be forbidden.
June 18		German Amb. Franz von Papen and Turkish Foreign Min. Shukru Saracoglu sign a 10-year friendship pact in Ankara.	Japanese spokesman reveals that Japan demanded a right to share in the economic exploitation of the NEI and says that the Dutch reply was "very unsatisfactory."	Brazilian exporters in Rio de Janeiro disclose the government has banned the export of rubber, manganese ore, industrial diamonds, quartz, crystal, mica and other vital defense materials to all countries except the U.S. .... The new Chilean Foreign Min. Juan Bautista Rossetti, says in an interview in Santiago that he is neutral in his attitude towards the war.	Allied troops attack Damascus, Syria after the French reject an ultimatum to surrender the city.
June 19				Argentine Chamber of Deputies votes to appoint a seven-man committee to investigate Nazi activities in the country.	Pres. Manuel Quezon declares in a Loyalty Day celebration in Manila that if the U.S. gets into the European war she will find the people of the Philippines on her side.
June 20		Finland orders general mobilization, calling up all reservists under 45.			RAF bombs Damascus, Syria for the first time.
June 21		Russian Army completes the removal of civilians from the border zone 60 miles deep along the Polish demarcation line and withdraws its main forces from 12 to 30 miles behind their original line, leaving small garrisons facing the German armies.			Gen. Dentz orders French forces to withdraw from Damascus to avoid street fighting. British forces immediately occupy the city.
	A	B	C	D	E
	Includes developments that affect more than one world region, international organizations and important meetings of major world leaders.	*Includes all developments in European countries and military engagements between Allied and Axis powers in Africa and at sea.*	*Includes all developments in Japan and China. Japanese foreign policy and military actions in the Pacific region.*	*Includes all domestic and regional developments in Latin America, the Caribbean and Canada.*	*Includes developments in those independent nations and colonial possessions not covered in Columns B, C and D.*

U.S. Politics & Social Issues	U.S. Foreign Policy & Defense	U.S. Economy & Environment	Science, Technology & Nature	Culture, Leisure & Life Style	
	Gallup Poll reports 55% of persons questioned after FDR's May 27th speech said they approved of naval convoys for ships carrying war material to Britain .... FDR issues an executive order freezing the assets of Germany and Italy.	John L. Lewis' Labor's Nonpartisan League issues a bulletin charging the Administration with responsibility for "the blackest week" in American labor history .... O.M. Orton, leader of the striking loggers in Washington, urges union delegates to accept CIO Pres. Murray's peace plan and return to work.		Albert H. Wiggin, N.Y. financier, presents his $2 million art collection of more than 5,000 items to the Boston Public Library.	June 14
FDR criticizes discrimination against workers in defense industries solely because of race, religion or national origin and asks the OPM to deal with the situation.		AFL and CIO machinists striking San Francisco shipyards vote to continue their five-week strike .... Representatives of 50,000 CIO-Industrial Union of Marine and Shipbuilding Workers members vote in Camden, N.J. to accept a two-year, no-strike agreement proposed by the OPM .... Labor Dept. rules commercial establishments must show that 75% of their sales are retail to qualify for exemption from the Wage-Hour Law.			June 15
Treasury Dept. reveals that the funds of the German-American Bund and other Fascist organizations have been frozen at FDR's order.	U.S. orders Germany to close all 24 of her consulates here as well as the German Library of Information in N.Y., the German Railway and Tourist Agencies and the Transocean News Service by July 10 because they allegedly engaged in activities "of an improper and unwarranted character." .... Sen. Patrick McCarran (D, Nev.) introduces a bill providing for a separate air force.	Because of the oil shortage, Defense Oil Coordinator Harold Ickes prevents the shipment of 252,000 gals. of lubricating oil to Japan .... Ickes declares that if the war is lost "it may be because of the recalcitrance of the Aluminum Company of America." He accuses Alcoa of seeking absolute control of all aluminum sources in the country.		NBC applies to the FCC for permission to establish commercial television stations in N.Y., Washington, D.C. and Philadelphia .... Lou Salica wins a 15-round decision over Tommy Forte to retain his bantamweight title.	June 16
	Germany reports it has protested the closing of German consulates in the U.S. and says "necessary measures" have been ordered against $450 million in American property in Germany .... Justice Dept. and the Treasury order customs officials to prevent any of the 330,000 German nationals in the U.S. from leaving the country "pending further instructions."	Ickes advises 32 Atlantic Coast shippers to halt all shipments of petroleum products abroad without first consulting his office.			June 17
At a White House meeting with A. Philip Randolph and other Negro leaders, FDR agrees to have an executive order drafted barring discrimination in defense plants .... N.Y. State Parole Board refuses to release Fritz Kuhn, former leader of the German-American Bund, from prison because he is "a hazard to the public peace and security."	War Dept.'s bill to requisition property for defense purposes is opposed by Sens. Downey, Kilgore, Reynolds, Johnson, and Lodge of the Senate Military Affairs Comm. as it opens hearings on the measure.	House Military Affairs Comm., declaring Communists are chiefly responsible for the "widespread stoppages and delays" in the defense program, recommends giving the President additional authority to seize strike-bound plants.		Joe Louis successfully defends his world heavy-weight title for the 18th time by knocking out Billy Conn in 2:58 of the 13th round of their scheduled 15-round bout at the Polo Grounds, N.Y.	June 18
	Germany and Italy order the U.S. to close all her 31 consulates in the Axis and Axis-dominated countries and remove their personnel by July 15 .... Gallup Poll reports that 56% of persons recently surveyed said a vote of the people should be required before Congress could send men to fight overseas.	Northern soft-coal operators sign a two-year wage contract with the CIO-UMW covering 250,000 coal miners .... FDR accepts Clarence Dykstra's resignation as chairman of the NDMB .... Lumber operators reject the NDMB's proposals to settle the Washington lumber strike .... OPM orders the rationing of rubber in an effort to reduce consumption from the present rate of 817,000 tons to 600,000 tons annually.		Viscount Halifax, chancellor of the Univ. of Oxford, confers an honorary degree in absentia upon FDR in a special convocation at Harvard commencement exercises in Cambridge, Mass. .... Paul W. Morency, vice chairman of the Independent Radio Network Affiliates, says his organization voted 205 to 18 to denounce the FCC's new radio rules.	June 19
	FDR sends a special message to Congress accusing Germany of acting as an "international outlaw" engaged in "piracy" in the sinking of the American freighter *Robin Moor* .... U.S. submarine 0-9 fails to surface from a dive off Portsmouth, N.H. Thirty-three men are lost .... U.S. asks Italy to close all 47 of her consulates and 7 Italian agencies in this country and remove all their employes by July 15.	Harry H. Bennett, personnel head of Ford Motor Co., and Philip Murray, CIO president, sign a contract covering 130,000 employes in Ford plants throughout the country. The UAW wins a union shop, wage increases and dues check-off .... FDR bans shipment of all petroleum products from the Atlantic Coast to any countries except the British Empire, Egypt, Ireland and the Western Hemisphere.	Soviet archaeologists in Samarkand open the tomb of Tamerlane, Mongol warrior who died in 1405, and find the skeleton well preserved. The body was embalmed with musk and rose water.	Hoover Library on War, Peace and Revolution, containing many rare documents of World War I is dedicated in Palo Alto,Calif. .... Archie Harris of the Univ. of Indiana breaks the world discus record with a throw of 175' 8¾" in the trials for the NCAA championships in Palo Alto, Calif.	June 20
	War Secy. Stimson discloses the War Dept. has reorganized its air arm into an autonomous unit called "the Army Air Forces" under Maj. Gen. Henry H. Arnold .... FDR backs the War Department's property requisition bill.	FDR names William H. Davis to succeed Dykstra as chairman of the NDMB .... ICC votes to reject an application of the Colorado & Southern Railway to lease the Ft. Worth & Denver City Railway and the Wichita Valley Railway on the grounds that many workers would lose their jobs.		Univ. of Southern California wins the NCAA track and field team championship in Palo Alto, Calif.	June 21
F *Includes elections, federal-state relations, civil rights and liberties, crime, the judiciary, education, health care, poverty, urban affairs and population.*	G *Includes formation and debate of U.S. foreign and defense policies, veterans affairs and defense spending. (Relations with specific foreign countries are usually found under the region concerned.)*	H *Includes business, labor, agriculture, taxation, transportation, consumer affairs, monetary and fiscal policy, natural resources, pollution and accidents.*	I *Includes worldwide scientific, medical and technological developments, natural phenomena, U.S. weather and natural disasters.*	J *Includes the arts, religion, scholarship, communications media, sports, entertainment, fashions, fads and social life.*	

	World Affairs	European War Zone	Pacific War Zone	The Americas	Other Countries & Territories
June 22		Germany and Italy declare war on Russia as German armies, aided by Rumanians on the Bessarabian front, smash into Russia in half a dozen columns from the Baltic to the Black Sea. Nazi planes bomb Kiev, Kaunas, Sebastopol, Odessa, Zhitomir and Minsk. Churchill promises full aid to Russia; Turkey proclaims her neutrality. Hitler charges Russian "betrayal" of 1939 pact caused the war . . . . U.S. Marines secretly sail for Iceland.			
June 23		German forces capture Brest-Litovsk as well as the towns of Kovno and Lomza in Soviet-annexed Poland. Leningrad is bombed by Axis planes . . . . Polish Premier Wladyslaw Sikorski offers to resume friendly relations with Russia in a London broadcast if the Russians reinstate the Treaty of Riga boundary.			
June 24		German troops capture Kaunas, capital of Lithuania, Vilna and Shavli in northern Lithuania, while other German forces drive into Soviet-occupied western Ukraine and White Russia. Soviet bombers hit Rumanian cities . . . . Spanish Foreign Min. Ramon Serrano Suner tells a Falangist rally in Madrid that "history and the future of Europe demand the extermination of Russia."		Ignoring the Communists, Chilean leftist parties sign an agreement to strengthen the groups behind Pres. Pedro Aguirre Cerda and speed up the reform program.	
June 25		Turkish National Assembly ratifies the Turko-German friendship pact . . . . English writer P.G. Wodehouse discloses in Berlin that he has been released after a year in an internment camp. He says he will broadcast once a week to the U.S. on non-political subjects over German radio.		Cuban cabinet passes a resolution reiterating Cuba's moral indentification with FDR's statements toward the defense of America . . . . Argentina bans the Chaplin film *The Great Dictator* throughout the country upon the request of the German and Italian ambassadors.	British command announces its troops have reoccupied Merdiayoun and Inbales Saki in the central sector of Syria.
June 26		Finland formally enters the war against Russia, although fighting between the two has proceeded for several days . . . . German motorized units are reported within 50 miles of Minsk . . . . Spanish Falangists begins recruiting volunteers for a legion to fight against Russia.			Australian P.M. R.G. Menzies announces a reorganization and enlargement of his cabinet . . . . A 2-hour earthquake described as one of the most violent in years hits Morocco.
June 27		Soviets admit major retreats in White Russia. British Amb. Sir Stafford Cripps arrives in Moscow with a British military mission . . . . Hungarian Premier Ladislaus de Bardossy announces that there is a state of war between Hungary and Russia.	Japanese trade mission headed by Kenkichi Yoshizawa, which failed to reach a trade agreement with the NEI, sails from Batavia for Japan.		
June 28		Soviets claim 4,000 Russian and German tanks are engaged in a great battle in the western Ukraine.	Chinese government names American Asia expert Owen Lattimore as a special political adviser.	Peru bans the dissemination of propaganda by foreign diplomatic and consular officials in favor of any belligerent country.	

A	B	C	D	E
Includes developments that affect more than one world region, international organizations and important meetings of major world leaders.	*Includes all developments in European countries and military engagements between Allied and Axis powers in Africa and at sea.*	*Includes all developments in Japan and China, Japanese foreign policy and military actions in the Pacific region.*	*Includes all domestic and regional developments in Latin America, the Caribbean and Canada.*	*Includes developments in those independent nations and colonial possessions not covered in Columns B, C and D.*

U.S. Politics & Social Issues	U.S. Foreign Policy & Defense	U.S. Economy & Environment	Science, Technology & Nature	Culture, Leisure & Life Style	
Sen. Pat Harrison (D, Miss.), president pro tempore of the Senate and chairman of the Senate Finance Committee, dies in Washington at 59.	Reacting to the German attack on Russia, America Firster John T. Flynn asks, "Are we going to fight to make Europe safe for Communism?" Alexander Kerensky, leader of the provisional Russian government in 1917, tells reporters all Russians should unite to save their country.			Frank Parker beats Bobby Riggs in Chicago to win the national clay court tennis championship.	June 22
	Under State Secy. Sumner Welles states Hitler's attack upon Soviet Union is further proof of his plans for world domination. Sen. Harry S. Truman (D, Mo.) urges the U.S. to help whichever side seems to be losing and thus "let them kill as many as possible." Rep. Martin Dies (D, Tex.) predicts Russia will be defeated in 30 days .... War Dept. modifies the property seizure bill, limiting the President's requisitioning authority to military or naval equipment and material and machinery needed for their manufacture.	U.S. Navy orders striking CIO and AFL machinists to be signed on civil service rolls in an effort to end the San Francisco shipyards strike.			June 23
	FDR announces at his press conference that the U.S. is going to give all the aid it possibly can to Russia.	CIO-UMW orders 150,000 Southern soft-coal miners to strike unless the Harlan County Coal Operators Association agrees to sign the union contract accepted by 12 other Southern operators' groups .... N.Y.C. Board of Transportation posts notices warning CIO-TWU members they will be subject to dismissal if they strike on subways and other transit lines.		Dennis Cardinal Dougherty, legate of the Pope Pius XII, formally opens the Eighth National Eucharistic Congress in St. Paul with a solemn pontifical mass attended by 50,000 Catholic worshippers.	June 24
FDR issues Executive Order 8802, establishing a Comm. on Fair Employment Practices and barring racial discrimination in defense industries .... A trial committee of the N.Y.C. Board of Higher Education finds John K. Ackley, registrar of City College, guilty of Communist activity and interference with the Rapp-Coudert committee's work and recommends his dismissal.	Sen. Robert A. Taft (R, Ohio) opposes aid to Russia, saying a Communist victory "would be far more dangerous to the United States than the victory of Fascism." .... Sumner Welles announces that FDR will not invoke the Neutrality Act against Russia, thus permitting American ships to carry war material to Vladivostok.	AFL machinists vote 5 to 1 to end their strike at San Francisco shipyards .... Leon Henderson announces the Chrysler Corp. has refused to rescind price increases on new cars and that therefore the OPA will be forced to fix prices for the entire industry.			June 25
Gallup Poll reports that 76% of the persons questioned said they approved of FDR's policies.	Welles informs Soviet Amb. Constantine A. Oumansky, that any Soviet request for material assistance in her defense against Germany will receive favorable consideration .... Interior Secy. Ickes declares in a Hartford speech that it is the right moment for the U.S. "to strike hard and harder, fast and faster" against Hitler. He denounces Lindbergh as a "Hitler stooge."	CIO machinists vote to end their strike and return to work at San Francisco shipyards .... U.S. airlines say they will have to restrict service because of FDR's request that domestic airlines surrender 24 more transport planes for British use, bringing the total to 115 of the 358 planes available .... Senate Defense Investigating Comm. warns of an aluminum shortage and places responsibility on the OPM and Alcoa.		Pope Pius XII, speaking in English from the Vatican, declares in a radio address to the Eucharistic Congress in St. Paul that a current of "black paganism" is sweeping the world today.	June 26
Federal agents raid the offices of the Trotskyite Socialist Workers Party in Minneapolis and St. Paul, seizing records and other materials. Acting Atty. Gen. Francis Biddle accuses party leaders of seditious conspiracy and says they gained control of a Teamsters Union local "to use it for illegitimate purposes." .... Senate confirms the appointment of Harlan Fiske Stone as Chief justice of the Supreme Court.		American Newspaper Guild convention gives its executive vice president, Milton Kaufman, a vote of confidence by a narrow majority after he denies being a Communist .... NLRB rules that the Weirton Steel Co. has violated the Wagner Act by discouraging membership in the CIO Steel Workers Organizing Comm. through intimidation, beatings and labor espionage.			June 27
CCNY faculty member Morris U. Schappes is convicted in N.Y. on four counts of perjury during his testimony on the Communist movement before the Rapp-Coudert committee .... U.S. CP leader William Z. Foster urges an "international front" of Russia, Britain and the U.S. against "Hitler fascism." .... Texas Gov. W. Lee O'Daniel defeats Rep. Lyndon Johnson (D) in a special U.S. Senate election by a little over 1,000 votes.	Chmn. Walter George (D, Ga.) of the Senate Foreign Relations Comm. criticizes the Administration's "totalitarian methods" in its defense policies .... Senate and House pass and send to the White House the $10,384,821,624 Army appropriation bill for 1942, the largest single appropriations measure in history.	Federal Power Commission declares an electric power emergency exsits in the Southeast and orders that the use of electricity for all non-essential and non-defense purposes be curtailed .... CIO-TWU calls off its strike scheduled for July 1 on N.Y.C. transit lines after Mayor Fiorello La Guardia and CIO Pres. Murray agree on a temporary peace formula.	War Dept. discloses that the Army has developed a secret radio beam device for spotting approaching enemy aircraft similar to a British device already in use.	The first revision of the 1891 Baltimore Catechism of the Roman Catholic Church is published with simplified and modernized answers.	June 28

F	G	H	I	J
Includes elections, federal-state relations, civil rights and liberties, crime, the judiciary, education, health care, poverty, urban affairs and population.	*Includes formation and debate of U.S. foreign and defense policies, veterans affairs and defense spending. (Relations with specific foreign countries are usually found under the region concerned.)*	*Includes business, labor, agriculture, taxation, transportation, consumer affairs, monetary and fiscal policy, natural resources, pollution and accidents.*	*Includes worldwide scientific, medical and technological developments, natural phenomena, U.S. weather and natural disasters.*	*Includes the arts, religion, scholarship, communications media, sports, entertainment, fashions, fads and social life.*

	World Affairs	European War Zone	Pacific War Zone	The Americas	Other Countries & Territories
June 29		Churchill names Lord Beaverbrook minister of supply in his war cabinet .... Acting Patriarch Sergei of the Russian Orthodox Church prays for Russia's victory over Germany.	Japanese Premier Konoye says in a Tokyo interview that he "can see no reason why the Japanese and American people cannot remain friendly" and asserts that the Tripartite Pact is purely defensive.	Two persons are killed and eight wounded when armed Italian Fascists clash with opponents in Durazno, Uruguay.	
June 30		German command announces the capture of Lwow, capital of western Ukraine, and Libau on the Latvian coast. Nazi columns are reportedly encircling Minsk .... Stalin is named chairman of a Russian Defense Council "to accelerate mobilization." .... Vichy government breaks off diplomatic relations with Russia.	Chinese Foreign Min. Dr. Kuo Tai-Chi states in Chungking that China will not consider any "specious offer of peace terms or a negotiated peace" which would involve the sacrifice of her "essential rights and interests."	Mexican Amb. Francisco Catillo Najera gives a check to Sumner Welles for $1 million as part payment on the claims of American citizens whose property in Mexico has been expropriated since 1927 .... Argentina rejects Uruguay's proposal that any American republic engaged in a foreign war be regarded as a non-belligerent.	
July 1		Soviets claim Finnish and German attacks against Murmansk and on the Karelian Isthmus toward Kexholm (Kaekisalmi) have been repulsed .... German command announces the capture of Riga, Lithuanian capital.	Japanese government announces that Germany, Italy, Slovakia, Rumania, Croatia, Spain and Bulgaria have recognized the Nanking government of Wang Ching-wei.	Argentine Senate votes unanimously to approve the Havana Congress plan for the American republics to take over and administer any European possession in the Western Hemisphere that might become a target of aggression.	Britain announces that Gen. Sir Archibald Percival Wavell has been made commander in chief in India.
July 2		Pilots of the American Eagle Squadron shoot down three German fighters and damage two others during an RAF raid near Lille, France.		Sumner Welles declares the U.S. welcomes Uruguay's proposal that any American republic engaged in a foreign war be regarded as a non belligerent .... Several persons are injured when police break-up an anti-Fascist demonstration in Trinidad, Uruguay.	Sir Henry John Delves is acquitted in Nairobi, Kenya of a charge of killing the Earl of Erroll.
July 3		Stalin broadcasts to the Russian people urging total "scorched earth" resistance to the German invasion. Guerrilla units, he adds, must be formed behind enemy lines.	Chinese government notifies Germany and Italy that it has broken off diplomatic relations with them as of July 2 because of their recognition of the Wang Ching-wei regime in Nanking.	Following the policy of the U.S., the Costa Rican government declares its non-belligerency rather than neutrality in the European War .... At least three persons are killed in an earthquake in the Andean provinces of Mendoza and San Juan, Argentina.	British and Free French forces capture Tadmur in central Syria after a 13-day seige.
July 4		Both sides report that Russian forces are withdrawing slowly to the Stalin Line in the central Russian sector .... Britain announces that Gen. Pietro Gazzera, supreme Italian commander in Ethiopia, has surrendered with all his forces in Galla Sidamo Province.		An attempted revolt by the garrison of Pilar, led by Capt. Heriberto dos Santos, is crushed by Paraguayan authorities .... Foreign Min. Alberto Ostria Gutierrez says Bolivia supports Uruguay's proposal that any American nation engaged in a foreign war be regarded as a non-belligerent.	Ankara reports rioting has broken out among troops and civilians in Beirut, Lebanon, as the British continuing bombing the city.
July 5		British Foreign Secy. Anthony Eden says he anticipates a peace offer from Hitler, but that Britain is "not, in any circumstances, prepared to negotiate with him at any time on any subject." .... German troops reach the Dnieper River .... Soviets claim successful counterattacks in the Ostrov sector east of Estonia.	Japan announces that 109,250 Japanese soldiers have been killed in the war with China, as against 2,015,000 Chinese killed.		
July 6		A pastoral letter read in the Catholic churches of Germany criticizes Nazi actions against the church and the closing of Catholic schools .... RAF planes bomb the Siclian port of Palermo in their first raid on Italian soil in several months.	Chungking officials disclose that Russia has given China assurances of continued help in return for raw materials.	Ecuador announces Peruvian frontier guards invaded Ecuadorean territory between Huaquillas and Chacras on July 5th and that fighting then broke out along its Peruvian boundary.	
July 7		In the heaviest raids yet carried out over France, RAF planes attack Calais, Boulogne, Mealt and Bethune.		Ecuador announces Peruvian planes bombed Hauquillas in the disputed border province of El Oro on the third day of the undeclared war, Peru charges Ecuadorian troops attacked its border posts July 5 .... Dispatches from Rio de Janeiro state the U.S. and Brazil have concluded a trade pact under which the U.S. will buy Brazil's entire surplus of certain strategic materials such as rubber and manganese for the next two years.	

A	B	C	D	E
Includes developments that affect more than one world region, international organizations and important meetings of major world leaders.	*Includes all developments in European countries and military engagements between Allied and Axis powers in Africa and at sea.*	*Includes all developments in Japan and China, Japanese foreign policy and military actions in the Pacific region.*	*Includes all domestic and regional developments in Latin America, the Caribbean and Canada.*	*Includes developments in those independent nations and colonial possessions not covered in Columns B, C and D.*

U.S. Politics & Social Issues	U.S. Foreign Policy & Defense	U.S. Economy & Environment	Science, Technology & Nature	Culture, Leisure & Life Style	
A bill to permit wiretapping to trap spies and sabateurs is defeated by a House vote of 154 to 146 . . . . Sen. Robert A. Taft (R, Ohio) tells the NEA meeting in Boston that federal control of education "would abandon one of the real safeguards of freedom in the U.S."	FBI Dir. J. Edgar Hoover announces that 26 men and 3 women have been arrested during the past 48 hrs. on charges of espionage . . . . FDR orders the induction of 900,00 new men into the Army in the year beginning July 1 . . . . Former Pres. Hoover declares he is opposed to helping Russia, which he describes as "one of the bloodiest tyrannies ... in human history."	Charles B. Henderson is elected chairman of the RFC.	In the worst sea disaster off Maine in 50 years, 36 passenger and crew are missing after the explosion of the 44-foot cabin cruiser *Don*.	Ignace Jan Paderewski, 80, world famous pianist and former premier of Poland, dies in N.Y. . . . . Joe DiMaggio, New York Yankee outfielder, breaks George Sisler's hitting record set in 1922 when he gets a hit in his 42nd consecutive game.	June 29
N.Y.C. Board of Higher Education votes unanimously to dismiss John Kenneth Ackley, suspended City College registrar found guilty of conduct unbecoming a college instructor.	Knox tells the governors conference in Boston that "the time to use our navy to clear the Atlantic of the German menace is at hand. ... Now is the time to strike." . . . . Seven of 29 persons arested by FBI agents plead guilty to espionage charges in Brooklyn, N.Y.	Two AFL Teamsters officials and five alleged racketeers are arrested in N.Y. on charges of extorting $2.5 million from trucking concerns and wholesale milk dealers . . . . House Ways and Means Comm. tentatively approves $733.2 million in direct consumers' taxes.		FDR dedicates a library of six million items bearing his name and housing his private papers in Hyde Park, N.Y.	June 30
	FDR says at a press conference in Hyde Park that he still hopes the U.S. can avoid war . . . . Sen. Wheeler scores Knox's statement and says he "should resign or be thrown out of office."	Emil Schram assumes his new duties as president of the NYSE . . . . Federal Power Commission orders the immediate construction of seven new interconnections between electric power plants in six Southern states.		Wilbur J. Cash, editor and author of *The Mind of the South*, commits suicide in a Mexico City hotel room.	July 1
	Twenty-eight governors meeting in Boston adopt a resolution pledging full support to FDR in his effort "to preserve the freedom of men and the institutions of free men." . . . . American Peace Mobilization and the CIO-National Maritime Union announce in N.Y. that they now support aid to Britain and Russia. Both had opposed Lend-Lease.	FDR directs War Secy. Stimson to return control of the North American Aviation plant at Inglewood, Calif. to the owners . . . . House Ways and Means Comm. tentatively approves new and additional taxes designed to raise $3.5 billion in additional revenue to help pay for the defense program.		Joe DiMaggio extends his hitting streak to 45 consecutive games, breaking the all-time record of 44 games set by Wee Willie Keeler in 1897 . . . . Joe Louis' wife Marva sues him for divorce in Chicago, charging that he struck her twice.	July 2
The NEA adopts a resolution opposing the employment of any teacher who advocates the changing of the form of government of the U.S. by unconstitutional means.	Army Chief of Staff Gen. George C. Marshall submits a semi-annual report recommending that Congress remove restrictions on sending troops overseas and empower the Army to retain draftees, National Guardsmen and reserve officers indefinitely . . . . The Comm. to Defend America by Aiding the Allies shortens its name to the Comm. to Defend America.	A federal grand jury indicts Wilson & Co., Armour & Co., Swift & Co., two trade associations and seven individuals for conspiring to fix the prices of slaughtered hogs . . . . Sweden sues the Vultee Aircraft Corp. in N.Y. for failure to deliver 144 Vultee pursuit planes ordered in 1940.		More than 4,500 persons attend funeral services in St. Patrick's Cathedral, N.Y., for Ignace Jan Paderewski, the great Polish pianist. . . . . Sam Harris, 69, one of Broadway's most successful producers, dies in N.Y.	July 3
	FDR declares in a holiday broadcast to the nation that the U.S. can "never survive as a happy and fertile oasis of liberty surrounded by a cruel desert of dictatorship." . . . . Willkie asserts in a worldwide broadcast that he is "quite sure that before long now the great force of the American Navy will be brought into play" to ensure delivery of aid to Britain.	OPM Dir. Gen. William S. Knudsen reports the TVA has approved the development of the Fontana (N.C.) hydroelectric project on the Little Tennessee River under an agreement with Alcoa.			July 4
Dr. F.A. Hermens of the Univ. of Notre Dame states in a study of the proportional representation system of voting in the U.S. and abroad that it has failed in practice and actually retards reform in municipal administration.	American Youth Congress passes a resolution pledging cooperation "with the people of Britain and the Soviet Union" in their fight against Hitler, thus reversing the organization's isolationist stand of last year.			Without using a score, 11-year-old Loren Maazell conducts the NBC Summer Symphony in a program of Mendelssohn and Wagner . . . . Dizzy Dean announces he will become a radio announcer for a St. Louis brewing company.	July 5
Dr. Minnie L. Maffet, president of the Nat. Fed. of Business and Professional Women's Clubs, tells the federation women should take steps against their economic exploitation and demand equal pay for equal labor.		Southern bituminous coal mine operators sign a two-year contract with the UMW, thereby averting a strike of 150,000 miners scheduled for July 8 . . . . NAM announces that war production is on schedule or ahead of government requirements in 16 major defense industry areas.		N.Y. Yankees dedicate a monument to Lou Gehrig at Yankee Stadium . . . . White Sox manager Jimmy Dykes is indefinitely suspended by AL Pres. William Harridge for using "obscene and abusive language" to an umpire July 5.	July 6
Senate confirms by voice vote the nomination of Atty. Gen. Robert H. Jackson as associate justice of the Supreme Court . . . . Eleven hundred convicts in Leavenworth Federal Penitentiary agree to call off their five-day strike after a dozen ringleaders are sent to Alcatraz Prison.	FDR informs Congress that U.S. naval forces have landed in Iceland with full agreement of the Iceland government as a measure of self-defense to protect the North Atlantic sea lanes. He says U.S. forces will "eventually" replace the British forces there.	John L. Lewis assails FDR for using the Army to break the CIO strike at North American Aviation. He also criticizes Sidney Hillman for certifying the coal strike to the NDMB . . . . Stettinius places chromium under full priority control in order to build up a stockpile.		William Church Osborn is elected president of the Metropolitan Museum of Art in N.Y. . . . . American League officials vote to rescind the two-year rule which bans trading by the league's pennant winner except by waiver.	July 7

F	G	H	I	J
Includes elections, federal-state relations, civil rights and liberties, crime, the judiciary, education, health care, poverty, urban affairs and population.	*Includes formation and debate of U.S. foreign and defense policies, veterans affairs and defense spending. (Relations with specific foreign countries are usually found under the region concerned.)*	*Includes business, labor, agriculture, taxation, transportation, consumer affairs, monetary and fiscal policy, natural resources, pollution and accidents.*	*Includes worldwide scientific, medical and technological developments, natural phenomena, U.S. weather and natural disasters.*	*Includes the arts, religion, scholarship, communications media, sports, entertainment, fashions, fads and social life.*

	World Affairs	European War Zone	Pacific War Zone	The Americas	Other Countries & Territories
July 8				Sumner Welles, Argentine Amb. Felipe A. Espil and Brazilian Amb. Dr. Carlos Martins confer in Washington on means to settle the border dispute between Ecuador and Peru . . . . Panamanian government reveals 10 persons were killed and eight wounded yesterday in a clash between police and a colony of Swiss German nudists who had refused to register with immigration authorities.	
July 9		Churchill tells the House of Commons British troops will remain in Iceland and cooperate with U.S. forces.		Welles discloses that the U.S., Argentina and Brazil have urged Peru and Ecuador to establish a "no-man's-land" about nine miles wide on each side of their disputed border as a step toward ending their undeclared war.	Gen. Henri Fernand Dentz, French High Commissioner in Syria, asks Britain for armistice terms through the U.S. consul general in Beirut.
July 10		Icelandic parliament votes, 139 to 3, to approve the government's agreement with the U.S. for stationing of occupation forces . . . . Soviets claim the Nazi offensive has been stalled.		Foreign Min. Ezequiel Padilla announces that Mexico supports Uruguay's suggestion that any American nation engaged in a foreign war be considered a non-belligerent.	
July 11		Russia's three ranking marshals—Klementy E. Voroshilov, Semyon K. Timoshenko and Semyon Budenny—are placed in command of the Leningrad, Moscow and Kiev fronts respectively.	Japanese government announces its decision to assume control of the nation's financial system, making private financial institutions virtual subsidaries of the Bank of Japan.	Argentina announces that Peru has accepted "in principle" the offer of the U.S., Brazil and Argentina to mediate the Peruvian-Ecuadorean border dispute . . . . U.S. Office for the Coordination of Commercial and Cultural Relations between the American Republics announces that approximately 1,800 Latin American firms and individuals with Axis connections have been put on a trade "blacklist".	Vichy rejects British armistice terms in Syria and fighting is continued on all fronts.
July 12		Anglo-Soviet agreement for "joint action" is signed in Moscow by Molotov and Sir Stafford Cripps, barring any separate peace with Germany . . . . Germans claim "the Stalin Line has been broken at all decisive points." The Soviets deny a breakthrough.	Japanese news agency says Britain and Gen. Chiang Kai-shek have agreed on, but not yet signed, a military alliance, to become effective when Japan starts a southward drive in the Pacific.	Ecuador announces its acceptance of a mediation proposal made by the U.S., Brazil and Argentina to settle the border conflict with Peru.	Armistice documents between the British-Free French allies and the Vichy command in Syria are initialed in Acre, Palestine.
July 13		The first units of the Spanish Blue Division pass through Bordeaux, France on their way to fight against the Russians on the Eastern Front.			
July 14		Churchill declares the British have achieved equality in the air with the Germans and can bomb Germany "month after month, year after year."		Washington and Mexico City announce that the U.S. has agreed to buy all of Mexico's surplus war commodities for 18 months, while Mexico will limit the export of such products to the Western Hemisphere.	French government ratifies the armistice ending the war in Syria, recognizing Britain's right to occupy the Levant states.
July 15			Chinese War Min. Gen. Ho Ying-chin says China now has an army of 15.8 million men.	Ecuador claims Peruvian Army units twice tried to cross the Zaramilla River today along the disputed boundary but were beaten back . . . . G.R. Cottrelle, Canadian oil controller, issues an order banning the sale of gasoline and lubricants from 7 p.m. to 7 a.m. weekdays and throughout Sunday for all Canada.	
July 16		Moscow Soviet orders the rationing of foodstuffs and manufactured goods for the 4.2 million residents of the capital, effective July 17 . . . . German units capture Smolensk, only 200 miles from Moscow . . . . Vichy government names Gen. Maxime Weygand governor-general of Algeria.	Japanese cabinet of Prince Fumimaro Konoye, submits its resignation to Emperor Hirohito . . . . U.S. Navy begins to mine the entrances to Manila Bay and nearby Subic Bay.	Cuban Pres. Fulgencio Batista's cabinet resigns in Havana over a dispute between the ministers and Congress regarding patronage.	

U.S. Politics & Social Issues	U.S. Foreign Policy & Defense	U.S. Economy & Environment	Science, Technology & Nature	Culture, Leisure & Life Style	
N.Y. State Board of Pardons announces that Richard Whitney, former president of the N.Y. Stock Exchange, will be paroled Aug. 11 after serving three years and four months in Sing Sing of his 1938 sentence for grand larceny.	FDR says at his press conference that the U.S. will defend those areas where its vital interests lie whether they are in the Western Hemisphere or not.			American League beats the National League, 7 to 5, in the 9th annual All-Star game played before 54,674 fans in Detroit, Mich.	July 8
	Knox says FDR's new orders to the Navy to guard the sea lanes indicate "the policy goes further than the original orders ... to report sightings of hostile craft."	FDR accepts Leon Henderson's resignation as commissioner of the SEC so that the latter can devote all his time as administrator of the OPA .... OPM announces 1,476 military planes were produced in June, an all-time record.			July 9
South Carolina Gov. Burnet R. Maybank appoints Alva M. Lumpkin to the U.S. Senate to take Supreme Court Justice James F. Byrnes' seat until an election can be held .... Senate unanimously elects Sen. Carter Glass as president pro tempore.	Sen. Robert R. Reynolds (D, N.C.) introduces three resolutions to permit the President to induct more than 900,000 draftees annually; to keep all soldiers in service until six months after the emergency ends; and to employ the Army "within or beyond the limits of the Western Hemisphere." .... House passes May amendment to the draft act raising the draft age to 28 and requiring draft boards to publicize their reasons for granting deferments.	FDR nominates Edmund Burke Jr. to the SEC to succeed Leon Henderson .... Senate unanimously passes a House bill appropriating $40 million to the TVA to expand its power-generating facilities, chiefly for aluminum production purposes.			July 10
CCNY tutor Morris U. Schappes is sentenced to 18 months to 2 years in Sing Sing after his conviction for perjury.	Morgenthau orders customs officials to seize 18 Axis ships under the Espionage Act of 1917 .... FDR appoints William J. Donovan as head of a new civilian intelligence agency with the title of coordinator of defense information .... Friedrich Ernst Auhagen, former Columbia Univ. professor, is convicted in Washington of failing to register as a German propaganda agent and is sentenced to eight months to two years in prison and a $1,000 fine.	Eleven men are killed in a mine explosion in Acmar, Ala.		Sir Arthur Evans, 90, world-renowned archaeologist who rediscovered and restored the palace of King Minos at Knossos on Crete, dies in Oxford .... James C. Petrillo, president of the American Fed. of Musicians, orders the 138,000 members of the federation to play *The Star-Spangled Banner* at the beginning and end of every musical program.	July 11
	Maritime Commission takes over 16 more Danish cargo ships in U.S. ports .... Gallup Poll reports 72% of persons recently questioned said they would prefer to see Russia win the war with Germany, but 47% thought Germany would win.	National Maritime Union rejects a resolution by Joseph J. Doyle for an outside trial board to investigate charges of Communism against Pres. Joseph Curran. Only two votes are cast for the resolution.		Finnish composer Jan Sibelius appeals to U.S. to understand Finland's fight against Russia. "Bolshevization of Europe," he says, "would annihilate freedom and civilization on this continent."	July 12
	Delegates to a Chicago meeting of the America First Comm. adopt a resolution demanding that Secy. Knox be removed from office for his outright advocacy of undeclared war.	Joe Doyle resigns from the NMU after Curran denounces him as one of "the stooges ... for hire by those elements who seek to destroy progressive unions." .... Following protests by farmers against the 49-cent a bushel penalty on excess wheat, the Agriculture Dept. extends the period during which growers can store such grain and avoid the penalty from April 30, 1942 to April 30, 1943.		Victor Ghezzi beats Byron Nelson to win the PGA championship in Denver.	July 13
Accused by Gov. Eugene Talmadge of advocating racial equality in education, Dr. Walter D. Cocking, dean of the Univ. of Georgia School of Education, and Dr. Marvin S. Pittman, president of Georgia Teachers College, are dismissed by the Board of Regents.	Administration and congressional leaders agree to support a resolution to extend the service of draftees for more than a year of service. They also agree to drop a resolution authorizing the President to send draftees outside the Western Hemisphere .... Ickes denounces Lindbergh in a N.Y. speech as a mouthpiece for the Nazi party line in the U.S.				July 14
A federal grand jury in St. Paul indicts 29 officers and members of the Socialist Workers Party on charges of advocating the overthrow of the U.S. government by revolution.	A federal grand jury in Brooklyn indicts 33 persons on charges of violating the espionage laws by sending defense information to the German government .... FDR warns that unless Congress extends the one-year service of draftees, National Guardsmen and reserve officers, two-thirds of the Army will have to be disbanded in the next few months.	Republic Steel Corp. ends its 4½-year fight with the CIO's Steel Workers Organizing Comm. and the NLRB by agreeing to sign a CIO contract if the NLRB certifies that the CIO has a majority.			July 15
N.Y.C. Democratic leaders announce their slate for the coming campaign, with William O'Dwyer as candidate for mayor .... Prof. Carle C. Zimmerman of Harvard tells a conference on "Tomorrow's Children" that "we need to encourage parents to have their third and fourth children right away" as an aid to defense.	Lindbergh demands Ickes apologize for implying he has connections with the German government .... Navy transport *West Point* sails from N.Y. for Lisbon with 464 Axis nationals .... Knox orders 37,647 enlisted naval reservists now on active duty to be held in service until the emergency ends.	FPC Chmn. Leland Olds says a defense electric power expansion program costing up to $470 million annually for the duration of the emergency is planned.	Karl Fenning, editor of *U.S. Patents Quarterly*, says nearly 30,000 inventions and ideas bearing on defense have been submitted to the National Inventors Council under the Commerce Dept.		July 16

F	G	H	I	J
Includes elections, federal-state relations, civil rights and liberties, crime, the judiciary, education, health care, poverty, urban affairs and population.	*Includes formation and debate of U.S. foreign and defense policies, veterans affairs and defense spending. (Relations with specific foreign countries are usually found under the region concerned.)*	*Includes business, labor, agriculture, taxation, transportation, consumer affairs, monetary and fiscal policy, natural resources, pollution and accidents.*	*Includes worldwide scientific, medical and technological developments, natural phenomena, U.S. weather and natural disasters.*	*Includes the arts, religion, scholarship, communications media, sports, entertainment, fashions, fads and social life.*

	World Affairs	European War Zone	Pacific War Zone	The Americas	Other Countries & Territories
July 17		Supreme Soviet announces political commissars are being restored to Red Army units under the title of "war commissars."		FDR issues a "Proclaimed list of Certain Blocked Nationals," including 1,800 Latin American firms and individuals acting in the interests of Germany and Italy. All U.S. trade with these firms is prohibited .... Pres. Batista forms a new Cuban cabinet.	
July 18		Stalin writes to Churchill urging the establishment of a second front in France and Norway .... Czech Foreign Min. Jan Masaryk and Soviet Amb. Ivan Maisky sign an agreement in London under which both governments agree to exchange ministers and give mutual aid against Hitler.	Prince Konoye forms a new cabinet containing four generals and three admirals. He drops Foreign Min. Matsuoka, who is replaced by Baron Kiichiro Hiranuma.		
July 19		Hitler issues specific secret orders to the German Navy not to attack U.S. merchant ships except within the internationally-accepted blockade zone around the British Isles.	Chinese authorities announce Communist army units attacked Nationalist troops at three places in Shantung Province and two places in southeast Shansi.	Pres. Enrique Penaranda de Castillo of Bolivia proclaims a nationwide state of siege because of the discovery of subversive activities directed by the German legation .... Vincente Lombardo Toledano, Mexican labor leader, urges that all Latin American governments nationalize the 1,800 firms blacklisted by the U.S.	
July 20		V-for-Victory day, proclaimed by the British, is marked as Vs are chalked on walls and streets in much of occupied Europe .... British cabinet is reorganized, with Information Min. Alfred Duff Cooper becoming Chancellor of the Duchy of Lancaster. Brendan Bracken replaces him .... Lavrenti P. Beria, Soviet vice premier, is placed in charge of the NKVD, the Soviet secret police.		Pres. Eduardo Santos, declares Colombia will make certain that the Panama Canal will never be attacked "from our territory." .... Former Bolivian Finance Min. Victor Paz Estenssoro is arrested in Tarija on a charge of being connected with a proposed "Nazi putsch." Several newspapers are suspended. The government claims it has proof the German embassy sought to interfer in Bolivia's internal affairs.	
July 21		German bombers pound Moscow for the first time .... Soviets announce Stalin is "now officially the commander-in-chief of the Red Army."		Bolivian government announces Germany has given the Bolivian charge d'affaires 72 hours to leave Germany in retaliation for the ouster of German Min. Ernst Wendler.	
July 22		Reports reaching Turkey allege that Germans and Croats have executed at least 80,000 Serbians because of guerrilla activity since the Axis occupied Yugoslavia.	A typhoon sweeps portions of Japan, causing extensive damage in the prefecture of Shizuoka and other regions.		
July 23			Vichy agrees to the establishment of Japanese military bases in Indochina to "protect" that possession against Britain, China and the Free French.	Peruvian and Equadorian troops clash between Huaquillas and Matalpo in the disputed border zone.	
July 24		British government announces an additional three million must register for the armed forces or for war work .... Soviets claim the 5th German Infantry Division has been destroyed at Smolensk.	Japanese warships and transports are reported off Cam Rahn Bay in French Indochina.	Bolivian government dismisses Maj. Elias Belmonte Pabon, the military attache to Berlin, for allegedly plotting with Germany against Bolivia .... Ecuador claims one of its military officers saw more than 3,000 Japanese officers and soldiers in the Peruvian front line as border fighting continues .... Argentina approves Havana Convention of 1940.	
July 25		Russian Air Force attacks Rumanian ports of Constante and Sulina.	British Foreign Secy. Eden says "certain defense measures in Malaya have already been enforced in view of the threat to our territories" implied by Japanese actions in Indochina.	Sumner Welles wires the foreign ministers of Peru and Ecuador urging them to stop their border conflict so the U.S., Brazil and Argentina can aid in mediating the dispute .... Over 3000 Panamanian and Latin American workers in the Gatun area of Canal Zone fight with laborers imported from the West Indies.	

A	B	C	D	E
Includes developments that affect more than one world region, international organizations and important meetings of major world leaders.	*Includes all developments in European countries and military engagements between Allied and Axis powers in Africa and at sea.*	*Includes all developments in Japan and China, Japanese foreign policy and military actions in the Pacific region.*	*Includes all domestic and regional developments in Latin America, the Caribbean and Canada.*	*Includes developments in those independent nations and colonial possessions not covered in Columns B, C and D.*

U.S. Politics & Social Issues	U.S. Foreign Policy & Defense	U.S. Economy & Environment	Science, Technology & Nature	Culture, Leisure & Life Style	
	Second draft lottery is held in Washington to determine the order of conscription for 750,000 men.	Leon Henderson requests Gulf Coast petroleum refiners to maintain a basic price of six cents per gallon for Gulf Coast gasoline.		Joe DiMaggio's 56-game hitting streak, which ran from May 15 to July 16, is snapped in Cleveland by the Indians.	July 17
Pennsylvania legislature adjourns its 193-day session, the longest in 99 years, without passing a congressional reapportionment bill.	FDR says the U.S. will keep the sea lanes open against attack or threat of attack not only to Iceland but to all other U.S. bases in the Atlantic and Caribbean .... Five alleged spies plead guilty in Brooklyn for conspiring to transmit defense information to Germany. Twenty-three others plead not guilty.				July 18
FDR names a six-man committee chaired by Mark F. Etherridge to investigate complaints of discrimination against Negroes seeking defense and government employment .... Census Bureau reports the average American lives 62.5 years.	Gallup Poll reports 45% of a cross-section of persons in *Who's Who in America* questioned in a survey said they favored war against the Axis, as compared with 21% of the general public who held a similar opinion.	Henderson tentatively orders reductions of up to 50% in the output of automobiles, light trucks, mechanical refrigerators and washing machines during the next 12 months.			July 19
Eleanor Nelson, secretary-treasurer of the CIO United Federal Workers, charges government employes are undergoing a "virtual reign of terror in which Gestapo methods are being used" to ferret out suspected subversives.	Alf Landon declares he supports the proposal to extend the service of draftees and National Guardsmen because it would be "unsafe" to release them now. He warns that FDR may throw "the finest untrained and unequipped army in the world into a shooting war."	CIO-UAW official Loren Houser urges FDR in a letter to seize the strike-bound Bendix, N.J. plant of Air Associates, Inc.		Will H. Hays, president of the Motion Picture Producers and Distributors of America, says that "the great function of the entertainment screen is to entertain" and not to spread propaganda .... Lew Fields, 74, vaudeville partner of of Joe Weber for 60 years, dies in Los Angeles.	July 20
Mayor Fiorello H. La Guardia of N.Y. announces that he will run for a third successive four-year term.	FDR asks Congress in a special message to extend the one-year service of draftees, National Guardsmen and reserve officers. He says demobilization "would be a tragic error."	Senate passes the modified version of the property seizure bill approved by its Military Affairs Comm. .... Office for Civilian Defense reports a highly successful opening day in its nine-day aluminum collection drive .... House Ways and Means Comm. votes to retain the joint income tax return for husbands and wives in the defense tax bill rather than impose higher surtaxes.			July 21
J.C. Capt, director of the Census Bureau, estimates that the country's population will grow at a steadily decreasing rate until about 1985, after which a decline will set in. He predicts a population peak of 153 million in 1980.	Federal Loan Admin. Jesse H. Jones says the U.S. has offered to buy raw materials from Russia in exchange for Soviet purchases of war material .... RFC announces a $425-million loan at 3% interest per year to Britain to pay for war purchases contracted before Lend-Lease was passed.				July 22
	Gen. George C. Marshall tells the Senate Military Affairs Comm. that efforts by "countless outside sources" and "politicians" to get draftees to protest to Congress against the proposed extension of their service is "sabotage of the most dangerous character."	OPM Dir. Gen. Knudsen, CIO-UAW Pres. R.J. Thomas and Michigan Gov. Murray D. Van Wagoner say an immediate 50% cut in auto production would throw thousands out of work .... House Ways and Means Comm. completes $3.5-billion tax bill for defense for full House consideration.			July 23
Willis C. Hawley, 77, member of Congress from 1906 to 1932 and co-author of the Smoot-Hawley Tariff Act, dies in Salem, Ore.	War. Secy. Stimson asks Senate to declare an emergency and authorize the President to extend indefinitely military service terms .... Stimson charges Sen. Wheeler has sent cards to soldiers urging them to write to the President "against our entry into the European war." He adds that this action "comes very near the line of subversive activities ... if not treason." .... FDR hints the U.S. may stop shipping oil to Japan in view of "what looks like an act of aggression." .... War Dept. announces plans to erect a $35-million office building in Arlington, Va.	OPM Assoc. Dir. Hillman announces the AFL building trades unions have agreed not to strike defense projects .... Merrill Lynch, E.A. Pierce & Cassett and Fenner & Beane, the two largest brokers on the N.Y. Stock Exchange, announce they will merge .... Interior Secy. Ickes says the FPC's five-year electric power expansion program is "ill-advised" and "carelessly prepared."		Bill Smith, 17, sets 800-meter, free-style swimming record of 9 min., 50.9 sec. in Honolulu .... Rexford G. Tugwell is elected chancellor of Univ. of Puerto Rico.	July 24
Mayor Frank Hague of Jersey City, N.J. turns the state Democratic leadership over to Gov. Charles Edison, in order not to "distract the attention of the people from the outrageous railroad tax scandal for which he, alone, is responsible." .... Enoch L. Johnson, GOP leader of Atlantic County, N.J. is found guilty of evading payment of $38,716 in federal income taxes on money he received from the numbers racket.	FDR by executive order freezes Japanese assets in the U.S. Chinese assets are also frozen, at Chiang Kai-shek's request, "to prevent the liquidation .... of assets obtained by duress or conquest." .... Wheeler says probably less than 100 of a million cards he sent out reached soldiers .... The German Transocean Press Service is convicted of failing to register as an agent of the German government and is fined $1,000.		RCA announces development of a high voltage electron microscope, making it possible to magnify objects 100,000 times.	Robert (Lefty) Grove wins his 300th baseball game .... Reuben Fine retains U.S. Chess Federation open title, defeating George Sturgis in St. Louis .... John Ford, 79, founder of the Clean Books League, dies in N.Y.	July 25

F	G	H	I	J
Includes elections, federal-state relations, civil rights and liberties, crime, the judiciary, education, health care, poverty, urban affairs and population.	*Includes formation and debate of U.S. foreign and defense policies, veterans affairs and defense spending. (Relations with specific foreign countries are usually found under the region concerned.)*	*Includes business, labor, agriculture, taxation, transportation, consumer affairs, monetary and fiscal policy, natural resources, pollution and accidents.*	*Includes worldwide scientific, medical and technological developments, natural phenomena, U.S. weather and natural disasters.*	*Includes the arts, religion, scholarship, communications media, sports, entertainment, fashions, fads and social life.*

	World Affairs	European War Zone	Pacific War Zone	The Americas	Other Countries & Territories
July 26			FDR orders Philippine military forces into U.S. Army for duration of emergency. War Dept. appoints Gen. Douglas MacArthur to command the troops .... France and Japan announce agreement on "the joint defense" of Indochina .... Britain freezes Japanese assets, and Japan freezes American and British assets.	Peru and Ecuador are reported to have agreed on a truce in their border dispute .... Brazilian Foreign Min. Oswaldo Aranha says his country supports U.S. foreign policies.	
July 27			China urges a formal U.S. and British embargo on shipment of oil and other war material to Japan.	Peru reports a major battle in the Zaramilla River basin. Peruvian Foreign Office says it has not yet replied to the truce proposal.	
July 28		Finland severs diplomatic relations with Britain.	Japanese forces commence occupation of their new bases in French Indochina .... NEI government cancels trade agreements, under which Japan was to receive about 1.8 million tons of oil, and freezes Japanese banking assets.	Gen. Francisco Franco of Spain asks Latin American countries to support Germany's "holy war" against Russia .... Unarmed Canadian soldiers disperse pickets at National Steel Car Co. in Hamilton, Ont. after CIO calls a strike to obtain bargaining rights.	
July 29		Churchill tells the House of Commons the U.S. "is advancing in rising wrath and conviction to the very verge of war." .... Soviets claim to have begun an offensive at Smolensk.	Japan freezes assets of Netherlands and NEI.	Paraguayan Pres. Higinio Morinigo decrees the death penalty for revolutionaries .... Sen. D. Worth Clark (D, Ida.) says that the U.S. "should take over control" of all Latin America and Canada and set up "puppet governments" because "the Good Neighbor Policy has been a failure."	
July 30		Soviet Amb. Ivan Maisky and Polish Premier Gen. Wladyslaw Sikorski sign an agreement in London ending the state of war between Russia and Poland.	Fourteen Japanese transports carrying 13,000 soldiers land at Saigon, French Indochina .... Queen Wilhelmina says in London the Dutch will defend the NEI.	FDR nominates Dr. Rexford Guy Tugwell to be governor of Puerto Rico.	
July 31		Soviets report their forces have driven the Germans back in the Smolensk area .... Berlin news commentary *Dienst aus Deutschland* reports that Adolf Hitler has banned Christian Science in Germany.	Premier Konoye says Japan must move ahead to create a "Greater East Asia co-prosperity sphere" and prepare for war .... Japan announces that Australian, Burmese and Malayan assets will be frozen, effective Aug. 1.	Reports from Peru and Ecuador state that border hostilities ceased at 6 p.m. after Ecuador agreed to cancel a previous order for general mobilization.	Egyptian Premier Hussein Sirry Pasha forms a new cabinet including five pro-British Saadist Party members, five Liberals and five independents.
Aug. 1		Britain breaks off diplomatic relations with Finland.	London dispatches state Japan has demanded naval, military and air bases in Thailand and control of the Thai rubber, rice and tin production in exchange for Laos and the ancient city of Angkor .... Japanese government announces a Thai-Japanese economic agreement under which Thailand will extend credits worth about $3.6 million to Japan for Thai purchases.	Peruvian Army announces its parachute troops captured the Ecuadorean towns of Puerto Bolivar and Machala a few hours before the 6 p.m. truce in the border fighting yesterday.	India Secy. Leopold S. Amery says India should end internal strife and promises it an "equal partnership" in the British Commonwealth.
Aug. 2		Oslo announces Reich Commissioner Josef Terboven has been given authority to declare a state of emergency to preserve the peace in Norway .... Soviets report fighting in the Byelaya Tserkov sector of Ukraine for the first time, indicating that the Nazis have broken through the Stalin Line southwest of Kiev.	Semi-official Japanese newspaper declares Japan will get rubber, tin and oil in the south Orient regardless of a "de facto embargo" against her in Malaya by the U.S. and Britain .... Pres. Manuel L. Quezon orders up 10 Philippine infantry reserve regiments totaling 15,000 men to be inducted into the U.S. army Sept. 1.	Peru announces sporadic fighting occurred at two points on the Peruvian-Ecuadorean border during the day despite the truce .... Peruvian government informs German legation that German diplomatic pouches will be subject to customs registry because Nazi officials have used them for carrying non-official correspondence.	
Aug. 3	FDR embarks at New London, Conn. for what is described as a cruise but actually for the Argentia conference with Churchill.	Several hundred British planes bomb Berlin, Hamburg and Kiel during the night of Aug. 2-3.	Saigon dispatches report Australian and Indian troops are massing on the Malayan-Thai border and that strong Thai forces are concentrating on the Indochinese frontier as Japanese troops move into Cambodia.		

A	B	C	D	E
Includes developments that affect more than one world region, international organizations and important meetings of major world leaders.	*Includes all developments in European countries and military engagements between Allied and Axis powers in Africa and at sea.*	*Includes all developments in Japan and China, Japanese foreign policy and military actions in the Pacific region.*	*Includes all domestic and regional developments in Latin America, the Caribbean and Canada.*	*Includes developments in those independent nations and colonial possessions not covered in Columns B, C and D.*

U.S. Politics & Social Issues	U.S. Foreign Policy & Defense	U.S. Economy & Environment	Science, Technology & Nature	Culture, Leisure & Life Style	
	Lt. Gen. Philip Golikov and Engineer Gen. Alexander Repin of the Soviet Army arrive in Washington to confer with Gen. George C. Marshall and coordinate Russian military orders in the U.S. . . . . Senate Military Affairs Comm. approves a resolution permitting the President to extend military service.	Edward R. Stettinius, Jr. orders freezing of raw silk stocks due to an anticipated Far East shortage.			July 26
Robert F. Wagner, Jr. is named president of an anti-Nazi organization, the Loyal Americans of German Descent.	Sen. Robert Reynolds (D, N.C.) opposes extension of service for draftees . . . . Harry Hopkins, U.S. Lend-Lease coordinator, pledges continued aid to Russia in a London radio speech.			Edward Beale McLean, 58, former publisher of The *Washington Post* and purchaser of the Hope Diamond, dies in Baltimore.	July 27
James R. Davies says he will enter the GOP primary race against Mayor Fiorello H. La Guardia in N.Y.C. . . . . Rep. Joseph W. Martin, Jr. (R, Mass.) warns the U.S. might become a dictatorship after W.W. II unless it prepares now for the postwar crisis.	Wheeler denounces Stimson's "treason" remarks as part of "a well-organized and carefully planned smear campaign by warmongers to silence opposition to war." Eleven senators defend Wheeler . . . . Sumner Welles pledges the Treasury Dept. "will grant prompt clearance for Japanese vessels clearing from U.S. ports." . . . . House approves the first supplemental defense appropriations bill for $8 billion and sends it to the Senate.	Harold Ickes warns rationing of gasoline is probable.		Screen star Judy Garland, 19, marries composer David Rose, 31, in Las Vegas, Nev.	July 28
Arthur Klein (D) defeats George A. Hastings (R) in special congressional election in the 14th District of N.Y.	Stimson apologizes to Wheeler but says "at least several hundred" cards reached soldiers.	A stike of 8,000 AFL electrical workers ties up construction jobs in N.Y. and stops work on defense projects at the Brooklyn Navy Yard.		Freddie Cochrane beats Fritzie Zivic for the world welterweight title in Newark, N.J.	July 29
Senate Democratic Steering Comm. elects Tom Connally (D, Tex.) chairman of the Foreign Relations Comm., succeeding Walter F. George (D, Ga.), who becomes chairman of the Finance Comm.	Treasury grants a license permitting the Japanese liner *Tatuta Maru* to withdraw frozen funds to refuel. The vessel then docks in San Francisco with 100 American passengers . . . . U.S. protests to Japan over the bombing of the U.S. gunboat *Tutuila* and American embassy property near Chungking, China . . . . Hopkins arrives in Moscow and meets with Stalin to discuss U.S. Lend-Lease aid for the Soviet Union.	FDR asks Congress in a special message for power to establish ceilings for prices and rents to prevent "the disaster of unchecked inflation." . . . . SEC orders the United Gas Improvement Co. to drop 13 non-utility subsidiaries.		Michael (Smiling Mickey) Welch, N.Y. pitching star in the '80s and '90s and one of 12 pitchers ever to win 300 major league baseball games, dies in Nashua, N.H.	July 30
	Several American importers file suits against the Japanese liner *Tatuta Maru* seeking possession of goods aboard the vessel . . . . Welles says the bombing of the *Tutuila* is a closed incident after the Japanese express their regret and offer to pay for damages . . . . Brig. Gen. Lewis Blaine Hershey, deputy director of Selective Service, is named director and is immediately confirmed by the Senate.	FDR creates an Economic Defense Board with Vice Pres. Henry A. Wallace as chairman to advise him on economic defense measures and prepare for postwar economic reconstruction . . . . Harold Ickes recommends that 100,000 gasoline and oil filling stations on the Eastern seaboard close from 7 p.m. to 7 a.m. daily, beginning Aug. 3, to alleviate the growing oil and gasoline shortage.			July 31
Gov. Eugene Talmadge says he will recommend to the next legislature that all books in Georgia schools and libraries that adovcate racial co-education be burned . . . . Enoch L. Johnson, GOP leader in Atlantic County, N.J., is sentenced to 10 years in prison and a $20,000 fine for income tax evasion.	FDR issues an order banning the export of motor fuels and oils suitable for use in aircraft to destinations other than the Western Hemisphere, the British Empire and the unoccupied territories of other countries resisting aggression. The most immediate impact will be on Japan . . . . Hopkins leaves Moscow after completing discussions with Soviet leaders.	Emergency Price Control Act is introduced in the Senate and House, lacking curbs on installment buying and ceilings on wages . . . . OPM Priorities Dir. Edward R. Stettinius Jr. orders that all processing of raw silk for civilian use be stopped at midnight Aug. 2 because of military requirements, mainly for parachutes.			Aug. 1
	Acting State Secy. Welles issues a formal statement denouncing the Vichy government for signing an agreement with Japan for the "joint defense" of Indochina . . . . Gallup Poll reports 51% of the persons recently questioned favored a U.S. check on Japanese expansion even at the risk of war . . . . Welles pledges Russia economic assistance in the interest of U.S. national defense in a note to the Soviet ambassador.	Stettinius places copper under 100% priority control . . . . AFL construction employes at two government munitions plants at Weldon Springs, Mo. fail to report for work in a dispute over overtime pay.			Aug. 2
	Japanese ships in American harbors surrender $4 million worth of silk as a bond for importers' claims and are allowed to sail for home . . . . Hopkins returns by plane to London from Moscow.	Gasoline filling stations stop selling gas at 7 p.m. throughout the Eastern seaboard, with only isolated instances of refusal to comply . . . . UAW Pres. R.J. Thomas urges that the government sponsor a conference of industry, labor and government representatives to draw up a plan for keeping auto employes at work if production is curtailed.			Aug. 3

F	G	H	I	J
Includes elections, federal-state relations, civil rights and liberties, crime, the judiciary, education, health care, poverty, urban affairs and population.	*Includes formation and debate of U.S. foreign and defense policies, veterans affairs and defense spending. (Relations with specific foreign countries are usually found under the region concerned.)*	*Includes business, labor, agriculture, taxation, transportation, consumer affairs, monetary and fiscal policy, natural resources, pollution and accidents.*	*Includes worldwide scientific, medical and technological developments, natural phenomena, U.S. weather and natural disasters.*	*Includes the arts, religion, scholarship, communications media, sports, entertainment, fashions, fads and social life.*

	World Affairs	European War Zone	Pacific War Zone	The Americas	Other Countries & Territories
Aug. 4		Hitler orders that Leningrad be the primary objective of the German attack .... Soviets report fighting in the Kholm sector between Pskov and Polotsk, indicating a 65-mile Nazi advance eastward from Novorzhev.	Japan suspends all steamship service to the U.S., stranding 654 Americans in in the Japanese Empire. In San Francisco the Japanese liner *Tatuta Maru* sails for home .... Vichy asserts France signed the agreement with Japan because "enemy concentrations were threatening" Indochina.	Colombian War Min. Jose J. Castro Martinez announces a number of persons have been arrested on charges of attempting to incite non-commissioned army officers to revolt .... Ecuadorian Pres. Carlos A. Arroyo del Rio says Peruvian troops yesterday occupied the town of Pasaje despite the truce.	
Aug. 5	Washington hears rumors that FDR and Churchill have met or plan to meet in the North Atlantic.	Russia establishes diplomatic relations with the exiled government of Norway and Greece in London.	Japanese Army spokesman says that several Japanese and Russian border troops exchanged shots near Manchuli about two weeks ago after the Russians crossed into Manchukuo.		Ankara dispatches state the British have warned the Afghan government against permitting German tourists into the country and urged that those already there be ousted.
Aug. 6		German command claims the battle of Smolensk on the Moscow front has been "victoriously concluded" and that a German wedge has been driven "to the gates of Kiev" in the south .... Gen. Wladyslaw Anders, who has been released from a Russian prison camp, is appointed commander of a Polish army to be raised in Russia .... Two Germans, who were allegedly landed by seaplane off the British coast, are executed as spies in Wandsworth Prison in London.	Japanese spokesman says the U.S. is threatening Japan by seeking Russian support for an encirclement plan .... Eden tells the House of Commons that any Japanese action against Thailand "would be a matter of concern" to Britain "as a threat to the security of Singapore."	Ecuadorean Congress votes unlimited economic and military powers, including censorship, to Pres. Carlos Arroyo del Rio for the period of the present extraordinary and the next ordinary session of Congress .... Vatican newspaper claims Pope Pius XII helped bring about an armistice in the border fighting between Peru and Ecuador.	
Aug. 7		German troops reach Kunda on the Gulf of Finland, cutting off Russian troops in western Estonia .... Stalin becomes commander in chief of Soviet armies .... Capt. Bruno Mussolini, 23, son of Italian dictator Mussolini, is killed with two other fliers in an airplane crash.	Australian Navy Min. W.M. Hughes says that the question of peace or war in the Pacific depends on Japan .... A Japanese spokesman in Tokyo asserts that U.S. and British warnings concerning Thailand are "unwarrented."	Pres. Manuel Prado of Peru telegraphs FDR that his government will attempt to re-establish normal relations with Ecuador.	
Aug. 8		Germans begin "final" offensive against Russians .... German command claims the Soviet 6th and 12th Armies and parts of the 18th Army in the Ukraine have been destroyed.	Japanese cabinet spokesman Koh Ishii says in Tokyo that the U.S., Britain, the NEI and China are attempting to encircle Japan.	Berlin press publishes a statement accusing the U.S. of employing "dollar imperialism," political threats and aggression to obtain air, naval and military bases in Latin America.	British authorities in Beirut, Lebanon announce that Gen. Henri Fernand Dentz and 35 French officers have been interned and will be held until British prisoners sent to France are released under the terms of the armistice.
Aug. 9	Churchill arrives aboard the *Prince of Wales* at Argentia, Newfoundland for his conference with FDR .... Willkie is quoted as saying that out of this war will come a league of all nations with an international police force to maintain order.			Colombian Pres. Eduardo Santos orders the strict enforcement of a 1940 decree under which aliens engaged in propaganda activities on behalf of belligerent countries may be expelled.	
Aug. 10		Soviets report stubborn fighting at Soltsy, 120 miles south of Leningrad, and at Uman, 130 miles south of Kiev .... Queen Elizabeth in a London broadcast to the women of America thanks the U.S. for its aid to Britain.	Australian External Affairs Min. Sir Frederick Stewart says Japan is using the cry of "encirclement" to justify action against Thailand.		
Aug. 11	FDR and Churchill discuss war aims aboard U.S. crusier *Augusta* at Argentia. The two leaders agree on an eight-point freedom of the seas, self-determination, free trade and post-war disarmament.		Japanese government applies four new imperial ordinances under the National Mobilization Act of 1938 to control minimum prices on the stock exchanges, regulate marine transport, appraise corporation-owned stocks and fix prices for more than 7,000 articles.	Ecuadorean government announces that Peruvian forces attacked the border town of Zapotillo in Loja Province Aug. 9 and again Aug. 10 .... Argentine Foreign Office receives written promises from the British and German ambassadors to eliminate their propaganda in Argentina.	Ankara diplomatic sources report Stalin has warned Iran that unless German agents in the country are expelled Russia may send troops into Iran under the 1921 Soviet-Iranian treaty.
	A *Includes developments that affect more than one world region, international organizations and important meetings of major world leaders.*	B *Includes all developments in European countries and military engagements between Allied and Axis powers in Africa and at sea.*	C *Includes all developments in Japan and China, Japanese foreign policy and military actions in the Pacific region.*	D *Includes all domestic and regional developments in Latin America, the Caribbean and Canada.*	E *Includes developments in those independent nations and colonial possessions not covered in Columns B, C and D.*

U.S. Politics & Social Issues	U.S. Foreign Policy & Defense	U.S. Economy & Environment	Science, Technology & Nature	Culture, Leisure & Life Style	
		Justice Dept. and FBI begin an investigation of possible violations of the antitrust laws in the iron and steel scrap industry .... House passes and sends to the Senate the $3,206,200,000 defense tax bill.			Aug. 4
Gov. Burnet R. Maybank (S.C.) appoints Roger C. Peace, 42, to serve in the Senate until Oct. 15, succeeding Alva M. Lumpkin, who died Aug. 1.	Both Houses accept and send to the White House a conference-approved bill deferring the drafting of men 28 or over and permitting 28-year-old draftees to resign .... Senate defeats Sen. Robert A. Taft's amendment extending army service for draftees to a total of 18 months, instead of 30 months, as desired by the Administration.	House passes the Senate-approved property requisitioning bill after amending it to prevent the seizure of machinery or equipment that is "in use" at the time .... Price Control Admin. Leon Henderson tells a House committee that higher prices are inevitable and that the nation stands "at the brink of inflation." He urges immediate passage of the price and rent control bill.		FCC issues a proposed order prohibiting anyone from owning more than one radio station in the same area.	Aug. 5
Georgia Gov. Eugene Talmadge appoints a five-man committee to weed out all public school textbooks that advocate racial equality, Nazism, Communism, Fascism or Socialism.	Senate votes against extending the service of draftees to a total of two years. Interventionists argue the draftees may have to be in the Army for five years .... Hull says Japanese occupation of Thailand would bear directly upon the problem of American security .... Sgt. Elwyn L. Hargraves and Ned Turman, a Negro draftee, are killed and three military policeman are wounded in a gun battle at Ft. Bragg, N.C. .... Senate votes, 57 to 19, to override FDR's veto of the $320 million defense highway bill, which would apportion the money among states instead of according to military needs.				Aug. 6
Arthur R. Braunlich Jr., CCNY tutor, is found guilty of Communist activities by a trial committee of the Board of Higher Education, which recommends his dissmissal.	Senate passes a resolution declaring that "the national interest is imperiled" and authorizing FDR to extend military service of draftees, reservists and National Guardsmen to a total of 30 months.	Members of the CIO-Industrial Union of Marine and Shipbuilding Workers of America strike the Kearny, N.J. shipyards of the Federal Shipbuilding and Drydock Co., affecting 16,000 workers and tying up work on $450 million worth of defense contracts .... House fails by two votes to override FDR's veto of the $320 million defense highway bill.		Sir Rabindranath Tagore, 80, one of India's greatest poets and winner of the Nobel Prize for literature in 1913, dies in Calcutta.	Aug. 7
	Hull says Japan is in no danger of encirclement except by itself .... Rep. Daniel A. Reed (R, N.Y.) denounces the Senate-approved draft extension bill as "evidence" that another American expeditionary force is being planned.	AFL machinists strike the Curtiss-Wright propeller plant near Caldwell, N.J. .... Interior Secy. Ickes announces 82 insurance companies have agreed to modify automobile liability insurance policies permitting drivers to carry passengers to and from work on a pro-rata cost basis in order to save gasoline.			Aug. 8
		AFL Executive Council urges FDR to set up a planning agency composed of government, industry, labor and agriculture to draw up a program for a rapid shift from war to peace production to avoid a depression at the end of the conflict .... Stettinius places steel under 100% priority control to ensure deliveries for defense.		Sam Snead wins the Canadian Open Golf Championship in Toronto for the third time.	Aug. 9
Warden Jess Dunn of Oklahoma State Prison, Tab Ford, a county jailer, and Claude Beavers and Roy Magee, both convicts, are killed in a gun battle during an attempted prison break in McAlester, Okla.				Dr. Robert D. Leigh, president of Bennington College for women, resigns his post, which he has held since the progressive school was first organized in 1928 .... Mrs. Cordelia Howard MacDonald, 93, the original Little Eva in Harriet Beecher Stowe's *Uncle Tom's Cabin*, dies in Belmont, Mass. She first appeared in the play in 1852 when she was 4.	Aug. 10
Dies sub-committee offers the N.Y. Labor Dept. evidence purporting to prove that Nancy Reed, dismissed on July 11 as an investigator for the department, has been a member of the CP for years .... Richard Whitney, former president of the NYSE, is released on parole from Sing Sing Prison after serving 40 months of his five-to-10 year sentence for grand larceny.	Hull says the U.S. will discuss a restoration of amicable relations with Japan only if Japan adheres closely to international law.	FDR issues an executive order empowering the Federal Reserve Board to curb installment buying of consumers goods made of needed defense materials .... CIO-UAW convention votes, 1,558 to 1,460, to bar Lew Michener, suspended West Coast regional director, because of his connection with the North American Aviation strike.			Aug. 11

F
Includes elections, federal-state relations, civil rights and liberties, crime, the judiciary, education, health care, poverty, urban affairs and population.

G
Includes formation and debate of U.S. foreign and defense policies, veterans affairs and defense spending. (Relations with specific foreign countries are usually found under the region concerned.)

H
Includes business, labor, agriculture, taxation, transportation, consumer affairs, monetary and fiscal policy, natural resources, pollution and accidents.

I
Includes worldwide scientific, medical and technological developments, natural phenomena, U.S. weather and natural disasters.

J
Includes the arts, religion, scholarship, communications media, sports, entertainment, fashions, fads and social life.

	World Affairs	European War Zone	Pacific War Zone	The Americas	Other Countries & Territories
Aug. 12	Argentia conference ends. FDR and Churchill leave for home.	Marshal Petain declares France must collaborate with Germany and appoints Darlan minister of national defense. He adds that Germany is fighting "in defense of civilization" in the east .... Berlin spokesmen assert German troops have pushed southward east of Odessa to the Black Sea, indicating that the seaport has been partially encircled.	A Japanese spokesman says Japan is "urgently concerned" over the shipment of U.S. supplies to Russia via Vladivostok.	Peruvian government claims Ecuadorean troops attacked a Peruvian border post at Pantoja on the Napo River Aug. 11.	
Aug. 13		Six persons are reported killed when Paris police break up a food riot, which is blamed on the Communists .... Soviet government decrees a general amnesty for all Polish war prisoners, who are expected to fight the Nazis .... Russian command reports fighting 140 miles south of Leningrad, indicating a Nazi advance.		Peru reports that three Peruvians and 11 Ecuadoreans were killed Aug. 11 in renewed border warfare at Zapotillo and Roca Fuerte .... Santiago reports at least 60 persons have been killed in storms in central Chile during the past eight days.	
Aug. 14	Washington, London and Ottawa announce that FDR and Churchill have met "at sea" to discuss the war and agreed on an eight-point plan (later known as the Atlantic Charter) for world peace to follow the conflict.		Baron Kiichiro Hiranuma, Japanese vice premier, is shot and seriously wounded in his home in Tokyo by Naohiko Nishiyama, who posed as an autograph seeker.		
Aug. 15	FDR and Churchill send a message to Stalin urging a conference in Moscow at which "high representatives" would discuss the use of joint resources to end war .... Japanese news agency says that the FDR-Churchill declararion is a plot by which the U.S. and Britain intend to establish their own world order.	German command in Paris warns that any person engaging in Communist agitation or aiding the Communists will be regarded as "Germany's enemy" and be liable to the death penalty .... Josef Jacobs, who landed near London by parachute, is executed in the Tower of London as a German spy.	Tokyo announces Japan and Thailand have decided to raise their ministers to the rank of ambassador in order to enhance their friendly relations.	Cuba announces five German consular officials have been ordered to leave the country by Sept. 5 .... Ecuadorean cabinet resigns to give Pres. Carlos Arroyo del Rio freedom to reorganize his administration.	
Aug. 16	German Propaganda Min. Joseph Goebbels says that the FDR-Churchill eight-point program is "an outrage against common sense."	Russia and Britain sign a trade treaty under which Britain will give the USSR a credit of 10 million pounds with which to buy strategic British materials.	Japanese military authorities announce that foreigners in Manchukuo must leave before Aug. 18 and that all Manchurians in North China must return by the same date.	Cuba reveals that Germany has order Cuban consular officials in occupied European countries to leave by Sept. 1 .... Ecuador says Peruvian troops have again attacked in the disputed border zone.	Pres. Manuel Quezon and Vice Pres. Sergio Osmena are renominated by the Nacionalista Party as sole candidates for the Philippine elections in November, assuring them of another two-year term.
Aug. 17		German troops cross the Dnieper River .... U.S.-owned former Danish steamship *Sessa*, carrying food and non-military supplies to the Icelandic government, is torpedoed and sunk with the loss of 24 of its 27-man crew.			London reveals a joint British-Russian warning was delivered to Iran to oust some 3,000 German tourists and technicians in the country.
Aug. 18		Finnish command reports the capture of Kurkijoki, 95 miles north of Leningrad .... Moscow announces Kingisepp, 70 miles southwest of Leningrad, has been evacuated, indicating the Germans have crossed the Luga River.	Japanese news agency reports that Denmark has granted diplomatic recognition to the Japanese-sponsored Nanking government.	Three bombs explode in Havana, injuring at least 12 persons. Four youths are arrested on charges of throwing the bombs in a labor dispute.	
Aug. 19		German command announces that German troops, aided by Rumanian, Hungarian and Italian units, have captured all of the Ukraine west of the Dnieper River and that the attack on Odessa has begun .... Germans launch all-out attack on Tallinn, Estonia.		Canadian P.M. Mackenzie King leaves Montreal aboard a bomber en route to Britain, where he is expected to confer with Churchill .... After the deadlocked Colombian Liberal Party convention adjourns without choosing a presidential candidate, 62 of the 120 delegates name former Pres. Alfonso Lopez to head their ticket in the election next February.	
Aug. 20		Marshal Klementy E. Voroshilov issues an appeal to the people of Leningrad, urging them to prepare to defend the city at all costs against the advancing Nazi army.	New Japanese maps sold in Tokyo show Japan has annexed all the islands and coral reefs bounded by the Spratly Islands in the west, the Half Moon Shoal in the east, North Danger Reef in the north and Swallow Reef in the south.	German Propaganda Min. Joseph Goebbels warns Latin American countries they will become U.S. colonies unless they oppose continued American intervention .... Ecuadorian Pres. Arroyo del Rio completes the appointment of a new cabinet.	

A	B	C	D	E
Includes developments that affect more than one world region, international organizations and important meetings of major world leaders.	*Includes all developments in European countries and military engagements between Allied and Axis powers in Africa and at sea.*	*Includes all developments in Japan and China, Japanese foreign policy and military actions in the Pacific region.*	*Includes all domestic and regional developments in Latin America, the Caribbean and Canada.*	*Includes developments in those independent nations and colonial possessions not covered in Columns B, C and D.*

U.S. Politics & Social Issues	U.S. Foreign Policy & Defense	U.S. Economy & Environment	Science, Technology & Nature	Culture, Leisure & Life Style	
	House votes, 203 to 202, to extend army service for draftees, reserve officers and National Guardsmen to 30 months .... In a letter made public by Agriculture Secy. Claude R. Wickard, FDR says "food is a weapon against Hitlerism just as much as munitions."	Leon Henderson fixes a ceiling of 3½ cents a pound on 96 degree raw sugar, effective Aug. 14.	California Institute of Technology reports that Drs. Clyde K. Emery, S.R. Baker and Melville Jacobs have completed the world's most powerful X-ray tube, expected to generate between two and three million volts, for cancer treatment and research.		Aug. 12
	FDR suspends the eight-hour day for nearly 100,000 workers emloyed directly by the War Dept. on defense projects.	CIO-UAW convention seats 10 delegates from Allis-Chalmers local after it is announced they were re-elected by a 3-to-1 margin in a convention-supervised election .... House votes to reject a conference report on the property seizure bill and sends it back to conference.	John J. O'Neill, president of the Nat. Assoc. of Science Writers, claims the government has "clapped a censorship" on scientists who have discovered the method of releasing the energy of uranium 235 and is "driving them to develop it for war uses." He says the element converted into a bomb "would wreck every structure within 100 miles."		Aug. 13
Price Control Admin. Henderson says he will not accept a report from the Dies Comm. about any employe of his office because Rep. Martin Dies "is not a responsible member of Congress."	Senate passes the House-amended bill extending Army service by 18 months .... British Supply Min. Lord Beaverbrook says in Washington that Britain will end the "menace to democracy" if the U.S. will provide "the largest possible" quantities of planes, tanks and food.	Several hundred AFL machinists vote to end their strike at the Caldwell (N.J.) propeller plant of Curtiss-Wright .... CIO-UAW convention votes to amend its constitution to bar from union office members of any "Communist, Fascist or Nazi organization which owes its allegiance to any foreign government, directly or indirectly."			Aug. 14
	Senate and House pass a conference-approved $7.55-million supplemental defense appropriation bill.	Henderson orders a 10% reduction in the amount of gasoline that may be delivered to filling stations in 17 Eastern states .... Federal Reserve Board issues tentative regulations restricting installment purchases as a curb on inflation.			Aug. 15
	N.Y. State American Legion convention adopts a resolution opposing any U.S. aid to Russia .... CIO-UAW convention adopts a resolution urging U.S. aid to those who fight against Hitler but oposing U.S. entrance into foreign wars.				Aug. 16
Three women are killed when 3,000 persons riot in an attempt to get aboard a Hudson River excursion steamer in N.Y.	FDR returns to Washington from his meeting with Churchill .... FDR warns Amb. Kichisaburo Nomura against further Japanese expansion in the southwestern Pacific .... Rep. John D. Dingell (D, Mich.) says that if Japan refuses to permit Americans to leave peacefully, the U.S. should place 10,000 Japanese in Hawaii in concentration camps.	NDMB, the Navy Dept., the Maritime Commission and OPM urge FDR to seize the strike-bound Kearny, N.J. yard of the Federal Shipbuilding & Drydock Co. because of the company's refusal to accept mediation board recommendations.			Aug. 17
	U.S. Amb. to Japan Joseph Grew protests against restrictions placed upon Americans who wish to leave Japan .... FDR announces agreements have been concluded under which the Pan Am Airways system will ferry warplanes from the U.S. to British forces in the Middle East via West Africa .... FDR signs the 18-month draft extension bill.	At least 13 men are killed when a fire destroys the freighter *Panuco* and its pier in Brooklyn, N.Y.	Dr. C.E. Kenneth Mees of the Eastman Kodak Co. announces that the company has perfected Kodachrome color prints for use by the general public in taking still color pictures.		Aug. 18
	Sen. Hiram Johnson (R, Calif.) charges FDR "violated the Constitution" in making an alliance with Churchill to destroy Hitler and establish a new world order.	FDR urges union and company leaders to settle their differences in the interest of national defense and end the Kearny shipyard strike.		Rev. Hubert Beller, spritual director of the N.Y. branch of the Nat. Catholic Women's Union, says birth control threatens the country with "physical and moral decay" .... Joe Louis and his wife Marva are reconciled in Chicago, and she agrees to drop her divorce suit.	Aug. 19
		Several thousand AFL street car and bus drivers tie up all transportation facilities of the Detroit Street Railways in a strike for exclusive collective bargaining rights .... OPM Dir. Gen. Knudsen says the country is not showing the "proper spirit" in the defense program.		National Catholic Women's Union adopts a resolution opposing Eleanor Roosevelt's proposal for complusory government service for women as an example of the rising tide of bureaucracy.	Aug. 20

F	G	H	I	J
Includes elections, federal-state relations, civil rights and liberties, crime, the judiciary, education, health care, poverty, urban affairs and population.	*Includes formation and debate of U.S. foreign and defense policies, veterans affairs and defense spending. (Relations with specific foreign countries are usually found under the region concerned.)*	*Includes business, labor, agriculture, taxation, transportation, consumer affairs, monetary and fiscal policy, natural resources, pollution and accidents.*	*Includes worldwide scientific, medical and technological developments, natural phenomena, U.S. weather and natural disasters.*	*Includes the arts, religion, scholarship, communications media, sports, entertainment, fashions, fads and social life.*

	World Affairs	European War Zone	Pacific War Zone	The Americas	Other Countries & Territories
Aug. 21		German troops capture Chudovo, cutting the Moscow-Leningrad railroad line .... Moscow radio urges "all God-loving inhabitants of the occupied countries" to rise in defense of religious freedom against the Germans who, it says, are "menacing the very existence of Christianity." .... Paris press announces 7,000 Jews have been arrested within the 48 hours and two Jews have been executed in reprisal for "Communist" demonstrations against the Germans.	Japanese spokesman says it is necessary to blockade supply routes to China.	Fifteen hundred telephone workers strike throughout Mexico for higher wages and reinstatement of a dismissed employee.	
Aug. 22		German commander in Paris announces that as the result of the assassination of a German officer Aug. 21 all Frenchmen arrested by the Germans will he held as hostages, a number of whom will be shot in reprisals "corresponding to the gravity of the act commited."	Daniel Arnstein, U.S. trucking expert, discloses in Chungking that Burma has imposed a 1% ad valorem tax on U.S. Lend-Lease material moving over the Burma Road to China.	Warrants are issued in Buenos Aires for the arrest of 36 Germans described as "the general staff of Nazi penetration in Argentina." .... Mexican government orders all German consulates in Mexico to close by Sept. 1 and recalls its consuls from Germany.	Iranian government formally replies to British-Russian demands that German tourists and technicians be ousted from Iran, indicating that it has refused to expel the Germans.
Aug. 23		Marshal Klementy E. Voroshilov, commander of the Leningrad front, declares "a terrible danger now is hanging over Leningrad" and orders preparations for all-out defense .... Hitler secretly orders that the attack on the Ukraine and Crimea be given priority over the drive on Moscow.	Britain urges Burma to abolish its ad valorem tax on U.S. Lend-Lease and British goods moving to China over the Burma Road .... Japanese Amb. Nomura says after conferring with Hull that the gap between Japan and the U.S. "must be bridged."		
Aug. 24	Churchill says he and FDR in their Atlantic Charter have pledged their countries to the final destruction of the Nazi tyranny. He warns that Japanese aggression in the Far East "has got to stop," but if it does not the British will "range ourselves unhesitatingly at the side of the United States."				
Aug. 25	Japanese press denounces Churchill for his London broadcast.	Soviets announce Novgorod, 100 miles from Leningrad, has been abandoned.		Argentine Foreign Min. Enrique de Ruiz-Guinazu announces an agreement with Italy for the purchase of 16 ships interned in Argentine ports .... Under State Secy. Sumner Welles says the U.S. will increase supplies of defense materials urgently needed by Latin American countries.	British and Russian troops invade Iran at five points "for purposes of self-defense" to thwart "attempts by the Axis powers to establish control" over the country.
Aug. 26		Berlin announces Field Marshal Ewald von Kleist's troops captured Dniepropetrovsk yesterday, eliminating the last bridgehead the Russians held on the west bank of the Dnieper River below Kiev .... German troops break into Tallinn.	Soviets announce Japanese Amb. Yoshitsugu Tatekawa was informed last night that hinderance of normal trade relations of the Soviet Union and the U.S. would be considered an unfriendly act.		British and Russian forces advance in northern and western Iran, meeting little resistance.
Aug. 27		Pierre Laval and Marcel Deat, both ardent advocates of Franco-German collaboration, are shot and seriously wounded by Paul Colette, 21, at Versailles.		Viscount Knollys is named governor of Bermuda.	Iranian cabinet of Premier Ali Khan Mansur resigns as the Anglo-Russian occupation of Iran continues with little opposition.
Aug. 28		Soviets confirm that the Dnieper River power plant near Zaporozhe has been destroyed to cover the Russian retreat in the Ukraine.		Inter-American Financial and Economic Comm. announces an agreement has been reached to utilize between 80 and 100 Danish, German and Italian ships immobilized in Latin American ports.	Premier Ali Furanghi, named head of the new Iranian government by Reza Shah Pahlevi, orders the Iranian Army to cease fire on the fourth day of the Anglo-Russian invasion .... P.M. Robert Menzies of Australia resigns and is replaced by Arthur W. Fadden, leader of the Country Party.
Aug. 29	FDR announces that W. Averell Harriman will head the the U.S. mission to the three-power conference in Moscow.	Berlin and Rome announce that Hitler and Mussolini have conferred for five days from Aug. 25 to 29 at Hitler's headquarters on the Russian front, discussing military and political questions that affect the war .... Eight more persons are executed in Paris, three on charges of espionage and five for "activity against the occupying power."	Chungking spokesman says Chinese troops began a general offensive against the Japanese in Fukien, Chekiang, Kiangsi, Kiangsu and Anhwei provinces on Aug. 25.	A Chamber of Deputies committee investigating anti-Argentine activities reports there are 64,319 Germans in semi-military groups in the country organized by the German embassy.	Despite an Iranian ceasefire order, Anglo-Russian forces continue their advance in Iran.
	A	B	C	D	E
	Includes developments that affect more than one world region, international organizations and important meetings of major world leaders.	*Includes all developments in European countries and military engagements between Allied and Axis powers in Africa and at sea.*	*Includes all developments in Japan and China, Japanese foreign policy and military actions in the Pacific region.*	*Includes all domestic and regional developments in Latin America, the Caribbean and Canada.*	*Includes developments in those independent nations and colonial possessions not covered in Columns B, C and D.*

U.S. Politics & Social Issues	U.S. Foreign Policy & Defense	U.S. Economy & Environment	Science, Technology & Nature	Culture, Leisure & Life Style	
	British make public an official denial that U.S. Lend-Lease aid has been re-exported . . . . FDR sends a message to Congress explaining and defending the eight-point plan with Churchill . . . . Hull announces Russia has been granted a general license to buy chemicals, machinery, iron and steel products, nonferrous metals, rubber, wood, paper and other materials in this country.	OPM orders a 26.6% cut in automobile production to 816,801 cars during the four-month period ending Nov. 30.			Aug. 21
GOP Mayor Robert Lamberton of Philadelphia dies at 54.	FDR orders extensions of military service for all draftees, National Guardsmen, reservists and regulars for 18 months under the recent law.	Federal Reserve Board issues regulations limiting installment credit to 18 months and requiring a cash payment ranging from 10% to $33\frac{1}{3}$% on a wide variety of goods to lessen consumer demand . . . . FDR denies Sen. Harry F. Byrd's charge that defense production has been "appallingly ineffective."	FDR signs a bill barring the filing of applications for patents in foreign countries without a license from the government. The measure is designed to prevent the leakage of patent secrets abroad.		Aug. 22
	Young Democratic Clubs of America, meeting in Louisville, adopt a resolution supporting full and complete aid to Britain, China and Russia.	FDR issues an executive order directing the Navy to take over and operate the Kearny N.J., yard of the Federal Shipbuilding & Drydock Co., which has been closed by a CIO strike since Aug. 7 . . . . AFT convention in Detroit votes to complete the explusion of locals 5 and 537 of N.Y. and 192 of Philadelphia on charges of being Communist-controlled.			Aug. 23
FDR nominates Solicitor Gen. Francis Biddle as attorney general.	FDR authorizes the operation of foreign ships seized in U.S. ports under British masters and crews flying the American flag.	Kearny shipyard strikers vote to end their 17-day strike after Rear Adm. Harold G. Bowen formally takes over the plant for the Navy . . . . AFL members vote to end their strike against Detroit's street car and bus lines.		John Kramer and Ted Schroeder retain the men's national doubles tennis title in Brookline, Mass. by beating Gardnar Mulloy and Wayne Sobin.	Aug. 24
N.Y.C. Board of Higher Education dismisses Arthur R. Braunlich, Dr. Walter Scott Neff and Seymour A. Copstein, CCNY instructors found guilty of Communist activities . . . . Senate confirms the nomination of Rexford Guy Tugwell as governor of Puerto Rico in a close vote.	FDR signs the $7.55-billion supplemental defense appropriations bill.	FDR vetoes a bill to freeze the government's stock of cotton and wheat for the duration of the emergency . . . . AFT votes to bar membership to anyone "whose actions are subject to totalitarian control" such as Communists, Nazis or Fascists.			Aug. 25
City council of Oklahoma City refuses to permit Lindbergh to use the municipal auditorium for an address sponsored by the America First Comm. . . . . AFT meeting scores the N.Y. Rapp-Coudert committee for its treatment of defendants and vows to protect Georgia teachers against any infringement of academic freedom.	FDR announces a U.S. military mission headed by Brig. Gen. John Magruder will go to Chungking to arrange for increased Lend-Lease supplies and advise Gen. Chiang Kai-shek . . . . FDR says reports that British are misusing U.S. aid are dirty falsehoods and vicious rumors.	Senate Commerce Comm. approves a motion to investigate the East Coast gasoline shortage.		Gus Lesnevich, NBA light-heavyweight champion, wins a split decision over Tami Mauriello to gain the undisputed world light-heavyweight title.	Aug. 26
Veterans of Foreign Wars convention urges FDR to dismiss Labor Secy. Frances Perkins because of "lack of ability." Delegates also urge Congress to bar the Communist Party from the ballot.	Sen. Wheeler charges some members of the Administration "have been anxious for a war with Japan for some time." He declares that in such a war "we will be preserving the British domination of Asia rather than helping the United States." . . . . Hull indirectly warns Japan not to interfere with U.S. aid shipments to Vladivostok when he remarks that the U.S. will insist upon the policy of the freedom of the seas in the Pacific.	Stettinius issues a regulation requiring companies to accept all defense orders for the U.S. and foreign countries and to complete them before private non-defense orders . . . . Henderson issues a schedule of fair maximum retail service station prices for regular gasoline in 40 Eastern cities ranging from 16.5 to 20.1 cents a gallon . . . . AFL union defeats a CIO rival in an election for exclusive bargaining rights on the Detroit Street Railway System.			Aug. 27
N.Y. Acting Gov. Charles Poletti says that he has barred a proposed birth control exhibit at the state fair because state law describes the dissemination of information on birth control as "detrimental to the state." . . . . A special Senate committee headed by Sen. Sheridan Downey (D, Calif.) recommends a minimum $30-a-month pension for all unemployed persons past 60.	Japanese Amb. Nomura hands FDR a message from Premier Konoye proposing a mid-Pacific meeting with the President to settle outstanding differences.	FDR appoints a seven-man Supply Priorities and Allocations Bd., headed by Vice Pres. Wallace, as the supreme agency for allocating the available supply of materials among military needs, defense-aid needs, economic warfare needs and civilian needs . . . . Federal official announces deliveries of gasoline to filling stations on the East Coast will be 15% less in September than in July.		Chicago Bears, pro football champs, defeat the College All-Stars, 37 to 13, before 98,200 in Soldiers Field, Chicago, for their third successive victory in the eight-year-old series.	Aug. 28
VFW announces that Earl Southard, suspended commander of the Illinois department, has been found guilty of disloyalty by a court-martial for his activities in the Keep America Out of War Comm. . . . . Lawrence H. Smith, a Republican isolationist, is elected in the First Congressional District of Wisconsin, defeating Thomas R. Amlie (D).	Maritime Commission Chmn. Emory Land says the U.S. will obtain the use of about 26 Axis tankers immobilized in Latin America.	NDMB announces CIO Chemical Workers Union has agreed to end its strike in 17 plants of the U.S. Gypsum Co. pending an investigation of union demands.			Aug. 29

F	G	H	I	J
Includes elections, federal-state relations, civil rights and liberties, crime, the judiciary, education, health care, poverty, urban affairs and population.	*Includes formation and debate of U.S. foreign and defense policies, veterans affairs and defense spending. (Relations with specific foreign countries are usually found under the region concerned.)*	*Includes business, labor, agriculture, taxation, transportation, consumer affairs, monetary and fiscal policy, natural resources, pollution and accidents.*	*Includes worldwide scientific, medical and technological developments, natural phenomena, U.S. weather and natural disasters.*	*Includes the arts, religion, scholarship, communications media, sports, entertainment, fashions, fads and social life.*

	World Affairs	European War Zone	Pacific War Zone	The Americas	Other Countries & Territories
Aug. 30		Finnish command announces the capture of Viborg, capital of Karelia, which had been lost to Russia in the war of 1939-40.	British embassy announces in Tokyo that a ship will be sent to Japan soon to remove all British subjects who wish to leave.	Four Buenos Aires newspapers urge the administration to discard its policy of strict neutrality in the war and crush the Nazi movement in Argentina uncovered by the Chamber of Deputies investigation . . . . Pres. Fulgencio Batista issues a decree placing private shipyards and drydocks in Cuba under virtual control of the Navy to aid defense.	Anglo-Iranian Oil Co. reports in Teheran that Soviet bombers destroyed thousands of gallons of gasoline at Kazvin yesterday after the Iranian Army ceased resistance.
Aug. 31		Marshal Petain announces in Vichy that the French Legion of War Veterans of Two Wars will become the "French Legion of War Veterans and Volunteers of the National Revolution" to include all supporters of his regime . . . . London newspapers publish Stockholm reports that Russo-Finnish peace negotiations are under way.			
Sept. 1		Vichy official in Paris announces Germans have dropped plans for "mass execution" of Jewish hostages after the Petain government "proved" a Communist, and not a Jew, assassinated a German naval officer Aug. 21.	Col. Hayto Mabuchi, Japanese Army press chief, says that if Japan cannot reach a peaceful settlement through diplomatic negotiations she must break her encirclement by force.	Pres. Avila Camacho tells the opening session of Congress in Mexico City that the long-standing problems between the U.S. and Mexico are about to reach a satisfactory conclusion.	A British communique announces that British and Russian forces met at Sinneh in western Iran yesterday, cutting off Iran from Turkey.
Sept. 2		Germans claim to have advanced to within 20 miles of Leningrad . . . . RAF bombers carry out one of their heaviest attacks in several months on Berlin.	*N.Y. Herald Tribune* reports that Prince Konoye has invited FDR to confer with him aboard a Japanese warship in the Pacific on improving U.S.-Japanese relations.		
Sept. 3	FDR appoints the following four men to accompany W. Averell Harriman to the three-power conference in Moscow: Maj. Gen. James H. Burns, Maj. Gen. George H. Brett, Adm. William H. Standley and William L. Batt.	Soviets claim counter-attacks in the Smolensk-Gomel area on the central front have driven the Nazis back more than 30 miles and recaptured 22 towns and villages during the past 10 days.	Imperial Rule Assistance Assn., meeting in Tokyo, adopts a resolution stating Japan must speedily complete "the wartime structure in order to force the establishment of the greater East Asia co-prosperity sphere." . . . . Chungking claims Chinese forces have driven the Japanese out of the Fukien Province port of Foochow. Japanese claim they evacuated the port voluntarily.		
Sept. 4		German U-boat fires two torpedoes at U.S. destroyer *Greer*, whose captain counterattacks with depth charges before losing sonar contact . . . . German artillery begins shelling of Leningrad . . . . Italian government bans all foreign newspapers from Italy.		Canadian P.M. William L. Mackenzie King urges the U.S. to take a more active role in the war in a London speech.	
Sept. 5		American freighter *Steel Seafarer* is sunk in the Red Sea by a bomb. The nationality of the plane is not known.	Iichi Kishi, a Japanese cabinet spokesman, says that if Wang Ching-wei and Gen. Chiang Kai-shek were to negotiate a peace settlement, "that would be an affair between two Chinese regimes." . . . . Japan creates an Air Defense Bureau to rush the construction of air-raid shelters throughout the country.	Argentine Chamber of Deputies investigating committee declares that the German embassy finances Nazi propaganda in Argentina . . . . Argentine minister of the interior bans the U.S. anti-Nazi film *A Voice in the Night* on the ground that it is offensive toward a friendly nation.	
Sept. 6		Reinhard Heydrich issues an order requiring all Jews over six years old throughout Germany to wear a large yellow Star of David with the black inscription "Jew" over the left breast . . . . Three French hostages are executed in Paris in reprisal for the wounding of a German sergeant Sept. 3.			
Sept. 7		Soviets issue a decree ordering the exile of the entire population of the autonomous German Volga Republic, some 600,000, to Siberia on the grounds that "tens of thousands of diversionists and spies" among them are prepared for sabotage at a signal from Germany . . . . Finland announces its forces have advanced 47 miles to the Svir River, further tightening the blockade around Leningrad.		Pres. Getulio Vargas of Brazil declares that any aggression upon the Western Hemisphere "will find us the greatest block of varied nationalities [that] ever got together in any defensive alliance."	
	A *Includes developments that affect more than one world region, international organizations and important meetings of major world leaders.*	B *Includes all developments in European countries and military engagements between Allied and Axis powers in Africa and at sea.*	C *Includes all developments in Japan and China, Japanese foreign policy and military actions in the Pacific region.*	D *Includes all domestic and regional developments in Latin America, the Caribbean and Canada.*	E *Includes developments in those independent nations and colonial possessions not covered in Columns B, C and D.*

U.S. Politics & Social Issues	U.S. Foreign Policy & Defense	U.S. Economy & Environment	Science, Technology & Nature	Culture, Leisure & Life Style	
	Hans Pagel and Frederick Edward Schlosser, both ex-members of the German American Youth Movement, are held in N.Y. in default of $25,000 bail each on charges of having used the mails in espionage activities.	Minnesota Gov. Harold E. Stassen (R) criticizes "the overlapping and confusion" of defense boards and agencies and suggests appointment of a "director of defense." .... OPM gives truck manufacturers an A-3 priority rating to enable them to obtain supplies needed to turn out some 1,189,000 units in the model year ending July 31.		Lon Warneke of the St. Louis Cardinals pitches the first no-hit game of the season when he blanks the Cincinnati Reds in Cincinnati.	Aug. 30
	FDR signs a certificate under his unlimited emergency powers revoking a 1904 ban on shipping gasoline and fuel oil in foreign vessels, permitting British and Dutch tankers operating from the NEI to supply U.S. troops in the Philippines with vital lubricants.			Ben Hogan posts a 72-hole total of 275, 17 under par and 5 under Henry Picard's 1937 record, to win the $5,000 Hershey, Pa. open golf championship.	Aug. 31
	FDR declares, in a world-wide Labor Day broadcast from Hyde Park, that "we shall do everything in our power to crush Hitler and his Nazi forces."	Pres. William Green asserts the AFL disclaims all responsibility for continuation of the civil war within organized labor and charges the CIO with excesses .... Asst. Atty. Gen. Thurman Arnold announces the creation of a small business section within the Justice Dept. to help small businesses in their relations with the government.		Wendell L. Willkie reveals that the Motion Picture Producers and Distributors of America have retained him as counsel in the forthcoming Senate subcommittee investigation of war propaganda films.	Sept. 1
Univ. of Denver announces the establishment of a non-profit National Opinion Research Center, sponsored jointly by the university and the Field Foundation, Inc. of N.Y.					Sept. 2
Federal government sues Al Capone and 14 officers of his former gang in Chicago for $250,000 in taxes and penalties on beer confiscated during prohibition .... Rep. Edward T. Taylor (D, Colo.), oldest member of the House, dies at 83 in Denver.	Three defendants plead guilty to being unregistered foreign agents just before German spy ring trial opens in Brooklyn.	Anti-Communist James B. Carey is defeated, 539 to 635, by Albert J. Fitzgerald for the presidency of the CIO United Electrical, Radio and Machine Workers at the union's convention .... Five hundred delegates to the Eastern Filling Station Proprietors' Conference in Philadelphia adopt a resolution urging the government to permit gasoline price increases to compensate for the diminished amount sold.			Sept. 3
	U.S. ships begin escorting British convoys for a part of the trip across the Atlantic .... State Dept. reveals the first cargo of aviation gasoline for the Russian Air Force has reached Vladivostok aboard the U.S. tanker *L.P. St. Clair.*	Senate votes to lower the individual income tax exemption in the pending tax bill to $1,500 for married persons and $750 for single persons .... Eleven major oil companies agree to make maximum use of all available railroad tank cars to end the gasoline and oil shortage along the East Coast.		N.Y. Yankees beat the Boston Red Sox, 6 to 3, in Boston to win their 12th AL pennant, their fifth in the last six years. It is the earliest a pennant has ever been won in the AL.	Sept. 4
Senate confirms the appointment of Francis Biddle as attorney general without opposition.	FDR says at his press conference that the submarine attack on the *Greer* yesterday was deliberate and that U.S. warships will "eliminate" the U-boat if they find it.	Senate passes the $3,583,900,000 defense tax bill and and sends the measure to conference with the House .... National Railway Mediation Bd. announces it has failed to mediate the wage dispute between the railroads and 19 unions representing 1,250,000 workers .... Federal judge rules market-sharing and patent-pooling agreements between the German dye trust I.G. Farbenindustrie and four U.S. drug manufacturers violate the Sherman Antitrust Act.			Sept. 5
FDR, informed by Mark Ethridge of OPM that discrimination against Negroes is continuing in federal departments, writes to heads of all departments and independent federal establishments to make certain that the practice stops.		War Dept. announces the award of a $337,447,057 contract to the Boeing Aircraft Co. and a $9,709,616 contract to the Douglas Aircraft Co. for 1,000 new 30-ton, four-engined B-17E bombers.		Rosemary Laplanche of Los Angeles is chosen Miss America of 1941 at the Atlantic City pageant.	Sept. 6
Chmn. Martin Dies of the House Un-American Activities Comm. urges that OPM Price Control Admin. Henderson be dismissed on the grounds that he sympathized with Communism. He also urges four of Henderson's aides be fired on similar grounds .... Mrs. Sara Delano Roosevelt, the President's mother, dies at 86 in Hyde Park, N.Y.		N.Y. Mayor La Guardia says "there is no real necessity for closing gasoline stations any part of the day or night" and expresses hope that the curfew order "will be rescinded very soon."	Dr. Walter Granger, paleontologist and curator of fossil mammals at the American Museum of Natural History in N.Y., who took part in 28 scientific expeditions, dies in Lusk, Wyo.	Bobby Riggs beats Frank Kovacs in Forest Hills, N.Y. to regain the national tennis singles championship. Sarah Palfrey Cooke defeats Pauline Betz to take the women's title .... Byron Nelson posts a 72-hole total of 278, 10 under par, to win the $11,000 Tam O'Shanter open golf championship in Chicago.	Sept. 7

F	G	H	I	J
Includes elections, federal-state relations, civil rights and liberties, crime, the judiciary, education, health care, poverty, urban affairs and population.	*Includes formation and debate of U.S. foreign and defense policies, veterans affairs and defense spending. (Relations with specific foreign countries are usually found under the region concerned.)*	*Includes business, labor, agriculture, taxation, transportation, consumer affairs, monetary and fiscal policy, natural resources, pollution and accidents.*	*Includes worldwide scientific, medical and technological developments, natural phenomena, U.S. weather and natural disasters.*	*Includes the arts, religion, scholarship, communications media, sports, entertainment, fashions, fads and social life.*

	World Affairs	European War Zone	Pacific War Zone	The Americas	Other Countries & Territories
Sept. 8		German capture of Schlusselberg completes the blockade of Leningrad .... Canadian, Norwegian and British forces raid Spitsbergen, set fire to coal stocks and destroy mines to prevent the Germans from using them .... A large force of RAF bombers pounds Berlin during the night.		Chilean Interior Min. Arturo Olavarria approves the banning of the U.S. anti-Nazi film *Pastor Hall* by the governor of Santiago Province.	
Sept. 9		Moscow reports state Russian troops have mopped up 250 square miles of territory and recaptured 50 villages around Elnya, 50 miles southeast of Smolensk.	British embassy in Chungking announces the 1% transit duty on U.S. Lend-Lease goods moving through Burma to China was abolished Sept. 3 .... Japanese news agency reports three passenger ships will be sent to Britain, Malaya, India and the Near East to bring about 1,600 nationals back to Japan.	German Amb. Edmund von Thermann protests to the Argentine Foreign Office against a report by a Chamber of Deputies committee accusing his embassy of financing subversive activities.	Iranian government agrees to close the German, Italian, Rumanian and Hungarian legations and establish British and Russian occupation zones according to the terms of an agreement announced in London and Teheran.
Sept. 10		German authorities in Norway declare a state of "civilian emergency" in Oslo and proclaim martial law in the city after several strikes break out .... Moscow dispatches state Soviet troops have smashed to Ryabtsevo, only 11 miles southeast of the ruined city of Smolensk.		Argentine Chamber of Deputies investigating committee introduces a resolution asserting that German Amb. Baron Edmund von Thermann has "abused his diplomatic privileges." .... Chile and Canada sign a trade pact in Santiago under which Chile will obtain most-favored-nation treatment.	
Sept. 11		American-owned cargo ship *Montana*, under Panamanian registry, is torpedoed and sunk midway between Greenland and Iceland .... King Leopold III of Belgium secretly marries Marie Lilian Baels, the daughter of a former agriculture minister, near Brussels. The marriage is morganatic.		Nine more Germans and one German-born Chilean are arrested in Santiago for questioning in the investigation of Nazi activities.	
Sept. 12		Reports reaching Stockholm state German authorities are carrying out mass arrests in Norway to crush spreading opposition .... Reports in Istanbul state 500 persons are missing in the earthquake that struck the Van area of Turkey yesterday.		Ecuador claims Peruvian troops were repulsed with losses in an attack on an Ecuadorean port at Porotillo in the Jubones River section of the border yesterday.	
Sept. 13		German command in Paris decrees that unauthorized Frenchmen possessing arms or war material "of any kind" will be liable to the death penalty .... Moscow reports claim Russian forces have smashed a German offensive near Bryansk, 220 miles southwest of the capital.		Pan Am-Grace Airways announces that two years of diplomatic pressure have "effectively eliminated" German-controlled airlines from western South America.	Eighty Germans leave Teheran on special trains to be interned in India and Siberia for the duration of the war.
Sept. 14		Soviets announce Kremenchug, an industrial city on the east bank of the Dnieper River 165 miles southeast of Kiev, has been abandoned. Germans are reported 15 miles from Leningrad .... Stockholm reports state 2,000 Norwegians have been arrested in four days of martial law in the Oslo area.		Shipping officials in the Canal Zone report an Axis surface raider is believed to be operating in the Pacific on the approaches to the Panama Canal.	A revolt against Riza Shah Pahlevi is reported spreading among tribes in southwestern Iran.
Sept. 15	W. Averell Harriman, head of the U.S. mission to Moscow, arrives in London and confers with Churchill.	Supply Min. Lord Beaverbrook wires all tank factories urging them to speed up output next week, when every tank produced in Britain will be send directly to the Russian frontlines .... German authorities in Olso announce the state of emergency proclaimed Sept. 10 will be lifted at 5 a.m. tomorrow.	Chinese authorities in Chungking claim 30,000 Chinese troops of the Japanese-sponsored Nanking government mutinied during an inspection last week, proclaiming their allegiance to Gen. Chiang Kai-shek.	Peruvian planes bomb and machine-gun the Ecuadorean settlements of Tendales, Pagua and Tenguel .... Argentine Chamber of Deputies passes, 78 to 1, a resolution censuring German Amb. von Thermann for directing Nazi activities in the country.	
Sept. 16		German troops seal off Kiev, trapping four Soviet armies .... Dispatches from Rome report Pope Pius XII politely rejected an alleged request from FDR, delivered by Myron C. Taylor, to declare the war against Nazism a "just war." .... German authorities in Paris execute 10 French hostages in reprisal for attacks on German officers.			Riza Shah Pahlevi of Iran abdicates in favor of his 21-year-old son, Crown Prince Mohammed Riza Pahlevi, and leaves Teheran after Russian and British troops begin moving on the capital. The Allies are said to have forced the resignation .... Gen. George Catroux, Free French commander in Syria, proclaims the independence of the former French mandate, and Sheik Tajeddine Hassani is named the first president of the republic.
	A *Includes developments that affect more than one world region, international organizations and important meetings of major world leaders.*	B *Includes all developments in European countries and military engagements between Allied and Axis powers in Africa and at sea.*	C *Includes all developments in Japan and China, Japanese foreign policy and military actions in the Pacific region.*	D *Includes all domestic and regional developments in Latin America, the Caribbean and Canada.*	E *Includes developments in those independent nations and colonial possessions not covered in Columns B, C and D.*

U.S. Politics & Social Issues	U.S. Foreign Policy & Defense	U.S. Economy & Environment	Science, Technology & Nature	Culture, Leisure & Life Style	
	Prosecution opens the trial of alleged German spies in Brooklyn with charge that one of the defendants, Hermann Lang, sold information on the Norden bombsight to the German government in 1938.		Dr. Roy K. Marshall of the Fels Planetarium in Philadelphia tells the American Astronomical Society that the thousands of craters on the moon were caused by volcanic action and not the impact of great meteors.		Sept. 8
	William G. Sebold testifies at the German spy trial that he was forced to become a Nazi spy in 1939 on a visit to Germany, but turned over his instructions to the FBI, which built a radio station to pass harmless defense information to Germany in exchange for information on espionage in the U.S.	Five major railroad brotherhoods set Sept. 15 as their strike date following the collapse of mediation attempts.		Sen. Gerald P. Nye (R, N.D.) testifies before the Senate subcommittee investigating the motion picture industry that a small group of movie producers, "all born abroad and animated by the persecutions and hatreds of the Old World," are injecting war propaganda into their films.	Sept. 9
N.Y.C. Board of Education fires high school history teacher Ingram Bander on charges of being a Communist.	State Dept. releases a note from British Foreign Secy. Eden stating no Lend-Lease material will be diverted to private interests or used for export.	FDR issues an executive order setting up a fact-finding board to investigate the railway wage dispute, thus delaying the strike of 1,250,000 union members for a least 60 days.	Chattanooga, Tenn. health authorities ban all unnecessary public gatherings because of an infantile paralysis epidemic which has stricken 60 persons in the city and 27 in the rest of the country.	Sen. Bennett Champ Clark (D, Mo.) charges in testimony before the Senate subcommittee investigating the film industry that "a handful of men" are spreading pro-war propaganda through film and radio . . . . NBC announces that Leopold Stokowski will lead the NBC Symphony Orchestra for the 1941-42 season, succeeding Arturo Toscanini.	Sept. 10
	FDR announces he has ordered the Navy to destroy on sight any Axis submarines or surface raiders found "in the waters which we deem necessary for our defense." He declares "when you see a rattlesnake poised to strike, you do not wait until he has struck before you crush him." . . . . Lindbergh tells an America First rally in Des Moines that "the three most important groups which have been pressing this country toward war are the British, the Jews and the Roosevelt Administration."	Special Senate oil investigating committee reports there is no shortage of oil or gasoline in the East and urges that restrictions on sales be removed.		John T. Flynn, America First Comm. leader, charges motion pictures are loaded with "pro-war propaganda" because they are "controlled by four or five men who cannot possibly have an American point of view." . . . . Chalky Wright knocks out Joey Archibald in the 11th round of their scheduled 15-round bout in Washington to win the world featherweight title.	Sept. 11
A Spanish freighter built to carry 28 passengers arrives in Brooklyn with 769 refugees from Nazi-occupied Europe.	White House press secy. Stephen Early says "there is a striking similarity" between Lindbergh's speech and the "outpourings of Berlin."	More members of the CIO-UMW strike in eastern Pennsylvania in protest against an increase in union dues and assessments, bringing the total of men idle to 20,000 . . . . Leon Henderson fixes ceiling prices on anthracite coal to prevent a 15-cent-a-ton increase Sept. 15.			Sept. 12
Dist. Atty. Thomas E. Dewey (R) announces he will support Mayor La Guardia for renomination in the N.Y.C. Republican primary election Sept. 16.	Willkie says Lindbergh's speech was "the most un-American talk made in my time by any person of national reputation."			H.G. Wells is elected international president of the PEN (Poets, Editors and Novelists) Club in London but declines on the grounds that a non-Briton should hold the office.	Sept. 13
Dr. Godfrey P. Schmidt, N.Y. State deputy industrial commissioner, begins an investigation of 4,000 employes in the state labor department to remove persons engaging in subversive activities.	Gen. Robert E. Wood of the America First Comm. announces that 58 "prominent Americans" have joined in denouncing FDR's "shoot-on-sight" speech Sept. 11 as a "grave threat to democratic principles of majority rule."	Members of the AFL Seafarers International Union extend their strike for increased war bonuses to nine more vessels, seven of which are loaded with cargoes for U.S. bases in the West Indies . . . . About 400,000 spectators witness an air show marking the official reopening of the Newark (N.J.) Airport.			Sept. 14
	FDR tells Congress that "planes, tanks, guns and ships have begun to flow from our factories and yards, and the flow will accelerate . . . . until the stream becomes a river and the river a torrent, engulfing the totalitarian tyranny which seeks to dominate the world." . . . . Knox tells the American Legion convention in Milwaukee that, beginning tomorrow, the U.S. Navy will provide protection for ships of every flag carrying Lend-Lease supplies between U.S. waters and Iceland.	Forty thousand CIO coal miners strike in Pa., W.Va., Ky., and Tenn. for a union shop . . . . OPM orders a cut of 48.4% in the December output of passenger automobiles, limiting production to 204,848 units.		FDR appoints Solon J. Buck archivist of the U.S., succeeding Dr. R.D.W. Connor who resigned. Buck will direct the National Archives.	Sept. 15
Mayor La Guardia defeats John R. Davies for the Republican nomination for a third term as N.Y.C. mayor in the GOP primary election . . . . Acting Pres. Harry N. Wright of CCNY suspends instructor Francis J. Thompson, accused by the Rapp-Coudert committee of Communist activity.	Herbert Hoover predicts Hitler will "be crushed by the vicious forces within his own regime" and urges that "no warlike step be taken and no agreement be made that is not submitted to Congress."	House passes and sends to the Senate the conference-approved $3.553-billion defense tax bill . . . . Navy Dept. announces all contracts for the 2,831 ships authorized under its $7,234,262,178 two-ocean program have been awarded.		Abe J. Green is elected president of the National Boxing Assn.	Sept. 16

F	G	H	I	J
Includes elections, federal-state relations, civil rights and liberties, crime, the judiciary, education, health care, poverty, urban affairs and population.	*Includes formation and debate of U.S. foreign and defense policies, veterans affairs and defense spending. (Relations with specific foreign countries are usually found under the region concerned.)*	*Includes business, labor, agriculture, taxation, transportation, consumer affairs, monetary and fiscal policy, natural resources, pollution and accidents.*	*Includes worldwide scientific, medical and technological developments, natural phenomena, U.S. weather and natural disasters.*	*Includes the arts, religion, scholarship, communications media, sports, entertainment, fashions, fads and social life.*

	World Affairs	European War Zone	Pacific War Zone	The Americas	Other Countries & Territories
Sept. 17		German authorities in Paris warn that if attacks on German soldiers continue they will shoot "increasing numbers of hostages." . . . . Myron Taylor denies FDR asked Pope Pius XII to declare the war against Germany a "just war."		Chilean police announce 28 alleged Nazis have been arrested so far as a result of an investigation of subversive activities in southern Chile . . . . Canadian Labor Min. Norman McLarty announces that the cabinet has outlawed all strikes in war industries unless a majority of the workers vote to strike in a government-supervised poll.	Russian and British troops enter the outskirts of Teheran following the abdication of Riza Shah Pahlevi.
Sept. 18		Stalin orders the conscription of male workers between 16 and 60 for military training after hours to build up a reserve estimated at nearly 25 million men.			Iranian government announces that Mohammed Shah Pahlevi has decided to give his father's many possessions to the nation and to release the abdicated Shah's political prisoners.
Sept. 19		Kiev falls to German troops. Other units have already penetrated 150 miles beyond the Ukrainian city . . . . Eight "Communists" are executed in Paris for anti-German activities . . . . U.S. government-owned S.S. *Pink Star* is sunk by a German submarine off Iceland.	Mrs. Constantin Smetanin, wife of the Soviet ambassador, and 50 other relatives of embassy staff members leave Tokyo for Russia, presumably because of deteriorating Russo-Japanese relations.	Peruvian Army announces 100 Ecuadorean troops attacked 20 Peruvian soldiers at Panupali along the border yesterday.	Following revelations by John Curtin, leader of the opposition Labor Party, Australian Atty Gen. W.M. Hughes admits the existence of a secret government fund to combat "subversive activities" but denies it has been used improperly.
Sept. 20		Martial law is declared in Bulgaria amid reports in Ankara and London that King Boris III is ready to take his nation into war on the side of Germany . . . . Twelve more French hostages are executed in Paris by the Germans for the slaying of a German officer.		Pres. Avila Camacho of Mexico orders the nation's 80,000 school teachers to abandon all political activity as of Sept. 30.	Mohammed Shah Pahlevi of Iran issues a declaration in Teheran pledging "the closest cooperation" with Britain and Russia and urging an immediate program of constitutional reform.
Sept. 21		Soviet Amb. Ivan Maisky appeals to British workers on the eve of "Tanks for Russia Week" for "tanks, more tanks and yet more tanks." . . . . German command announces that German troops have broken through from Berislav to the Sea of Azov, isolating the Crimea . . . . Stockholm reports state German authorities have extended martial law to all Norway.		Thirteen Liberal members of the Colombian Senate, together with the minority Conservatives, resign in protest against the Liberal Party's choice of former Pres. Alfonso Lopez-Pumareio as its presidential candidate for the 1942 elections.	
Sept. 22	An official Moscow report says the British and U.S. aid missions have arrived by plane together in Russia.	Germans announce 23 hostages in Tournai, Belgium will he shot in reprisal for the killing of two German police officials unless those responsible are discovered within 10 days. Berlin dispatches estimate 295 persons have been executed in Nazi-occupied countries since Aug. 1, most of them in Yugoslavia.			
Sept. 23		German command claims 50 Soviet divisions have been "completely destroyed" and 380,000 prisoners have been taken in the "trap" east of Kiev . . . . Italian press reports 50 "Communists and Jews" have been executed in Zagreb, Yugoslavia for recent bomb explosions in the telephone exchange.		Eight persons are killed and 24 wounded when soldiers guarding the home of Mexican Pres. Manuel Avila Camacho fire on demonstrating members of the Union of Munition Workers who refuse to disperse . . . . Raul Damonte Taborda, chairman of the Chamber of Deputies investigating committee, announces that Argentine troops thwarted a Nazi plot to overthrow the government yesterday.	
Sept. 24	Representatives of 11 Allied nations at the second meeting of the Inter-Allied Conference in London adopt a resolution pledging adherence to the eight-point Roosevelt-Churchill Atlantic Charter.	Leningrad radio broadcasts an appeal to "every citizen" to aid in the defense of the city, saying that "the enemy is at the gates." . . . . Budapest newspaper *Magyar Nemzet* reports that 12,000 Serbian Chetnik guerrillas attacked a German garrison at an unidentified Serbian town during the day.		Radical deputies, who control the Argentine Chamber, refuse to approve a proposed $110 million U.S. loan recommended by acting Pres. Castillo.	A censure motion against the government is defeated in the Australian House of Representatives by one vote.

A	B	C	D	E
Includes developments that affect more than one world region, international organizations and important meetings of major world leaders.	*Includes all developments in European countries and military engagements between Allied and Axis powers in Africa and at sea.*	*Includes all developments in Japan and China, Japanese foreign policy and military actions in the Pacific region.*	*Includes all domestic and regional developments in Latin America, the Caribbean and Canada.*	*Includes developments in those independent nations and colonial possessions not covered in Columns B, C and D.*

U.S. Politics & Social Issues	U.S. Foreign Policy & Defense	U.S. Economy & Environment	Science, Technology & Nature	Culture, Leisure & Life Style	
	Knox tells his press conference that the escort of convoys by war vessels is "being used in all our defensive areas." .... American Legion convention in Milwaukee adopts a resolution backing FDR's foreign policy, urging repeal of the Neutrality Act and the removal of restrictions on the sending of troops abroad.	Senate passes and sends to the White House the House-approved $3,553,400,000 defense tax bill, the largest in the nation's history .... FDR issues an executive order authorizing the Economic Defense Board, headed by Vice Pres. Henry A. Wallace, to absorb the Office of Export Control.			Sept. 17
Lower house of the Texas legislature adopts a resolution stating that any purpose Charles A. Lindbergh has in opposing FDR's policies will not be served by visiting Texas.	FDR asks Congress for an additional $5.985 billion with which to continue the Lend-Lease program through June 30, 1943.	Petroleum Coordinator Harold L. Ickes says East Coast gasoline rationing will continue despite a Senate committee report that no shortage exists .... Maritime Commission seizes three freighters tied up by the ALF Seafarers' strike.	The aurora borealis produces an unusually colorful display of lights in the Eastern skies from Buffalo to Virginia and as far west as Denver.	Sonja Henie, Norwegian-born ice skating star and wife of Dan Topping, Greenwich sportsman, takes the oath of allegiance in a Stamford, Conn. naturalization court to become a U.S. citizen.	Sept. 18
	Knox announces at least 12 British warships are being repaired in U.S. shipyards under the Lend-Lease program .... Hull tells his press conference the U.S. is planning greater and swifter aid to Russia.	NDMB Chmn. William H. Davis announces a 30-day truce in the "union shop" dispute between the CIO-UMW and operators of mines in Pa., W.Va., and Ky. .... Bernard M. Baruch, testifying before the House Banking and Currency Comm. on the price-fixing bill, urges a blanket ceiling "over the whole price structure, including wages, rents, and farm prices."		Brooklyn Dodger manager Leo Durocher punches and knocks down AP reporter Ted Meier in a street fight in Philadelphia after being asked a "tactless" question.	Sept. 19
Rep. Martin Dies says he has deferred an inquiry by his House Comm. on Un-American Activities into Japanese espionage on the West Coast at FDR's request.	The Keep America Out of War Congress announces it "deeply regrets and disagrees with Mr. Lindbergh's implication" that all Jews back U.S. intervention in the war .... Sen. Gerald P. Nye (R, N.D.) urges "all loyal Americans" to oppose FDR's foreign policy as a deliberate "war" program.	FDR signs the record $3.5 billion defense tax bill in Hyde Park, N.Y. .... Chamber of Commerce officials denounce the price control bill as too "sweeping."			Sept. 20
	Sen. Walter F. George (D, Ga.) says in Washington that "it would be a fatal mistake" for Congress to bar Russia from receiving aid under the pending Lend-Lease appropriations bill.	Juan T. Trippe, president of Pan Am Airways system, wins the 1941 Daniel Guggenheim Medal "for the development and successful operation of oceanic air transport."		The Pennsylvania Homestead Grays defeat the N.Y. Cuban Stars, 20-0 and 5-0, in a double-header at Yankee Stadium to win the Negro National Baseball League championship .... Sam Snead posts a 72-hole total of 272, eight under par, to win the $7,000 Hurst invitation golf tournament at Philadelphia.	Sept. 21
	Congressional leaders meeting with FDR at the White House pledge to give the new $5.985-billion Lend-Lease appropriation bill top priority .... Knox declares in a Hartford speech that American sailors "are today at sea fighting dictatorships. They are keeping watch on the high seas." .... Hull indicates he would favor modification of the Neutrality Act to permit the arming of U.S. merchant ships and allow them to enter war zones.	Henderson testifies before the House Banking and Currency Comm. that Bernard M. Baruch's plan for a blanket price ceiling is impracticable because of the tremendous administrative problem it would create .... Maritime Commission appeals to AFL Seafarers Union and ship operators to end the strike that has spread to 23 ships since it began Sept. 13.	William W. Bishop, librarian of the Univ. of Michigan, says the highly perishable nature of woodpulp threatens the preservation of valuable research documents and suggests the use of microfilms as the most feasible substitute.	FCC Chmn. James L. Fly says the Commission is primarily concerned with the diversification of the radio industry and the "weeding out of monopolistic tendencies in broadcasting."	Sept. 22
Rep. Wall Doxey is elected by less than 1,000 votes to fill the 15-month unexpired term of the late Sen. Pat Harrison in a special Mississippi election.	Knox declares "the time has come to do away with the neutrality law .... It must be repealed." .... FDR says at his press conference that the country is headed toward the arming of its merchant ships .... Agriculture Secy. Wickard says the U.S. must send a billion dollars worth of food to Britain by Feb. 28 "unless the British are to lose to Nazi Germany."	FDR says the ships tied up by striking seamen must be moved and warns that strikes freezing vital defense materials will not be tolerated .... Federal Reserve increases reserve requirements for member banks by about one-seventh, to the present statutory limit, in a further attempt to check inflation.			Sept. 23
	Sen. Tom Connally (D, Tex.), chairman of the Foreign Relations Comm., says he will sponsor amendments to the Neutrality Act to permit the arming of U.S. merchant ships and to allow them to enter the combat zones .... Bales of unused franked envelopes of seven members of Congress are seized in the offices of two isolationist groups in Washington .... Judge Mortimer W. Byers bars the introduction of detailed testimony on the Norden bombsight at the espionage trial of 16 alleged spies in Brooklyn.	Members of the AFL Seafarers International Union vote to end their 12-day strike affecting 26 ships and submit their demand for increased war bonuses to the NDMB .... Morgenthau testifies before the House Banking and Currency Comm. in favor of a 100% tax on all corporate profits over 6% on invested capital for the duration of the emergency .... CIO-UAW Pres. R.J. Thomas charges the auto industry has pursued a "business as usual" policy and delayed switching over to bomber production.	A hurricane that has been lashing the Texas coast for three days moves inland after killing three persons and causing extensive damage.		Sept. 24
F ***Includes elections, federal-state relations, civil rights and liberties, crime, the judiciary, education, health care, poverty, urban affairs and population.***	G *Includes formation and debate of U.S. foreign and defense policies, veterans affairs and defense spending. (Relations with specific foreign countries are usually found under the region concerned.)*	H *Includes business, labor, agriculture, taxation, transportation, consumer affairs, monetary and fiscal policy, natural resources, pollution and accidents.*	I *Includes worldwide scientific, medical and technological developments, natural phenomena, U.S. weather and natural disasters.*	J *Includes the arts, religion, scholarship, communications media, sports, entertainment, fashions, fads and social life.*	

	World Affairs	European War Zone	Pacific War Zone	The Americas	Other Countries & Territories
Sept. 25		Gen. Vittorio Ambrosio, commander of the Italian 2nd Army, reports the reoccupation of the demilitarized Dalmatian coast of Yugoslavia has been completed.		As a result of a seditions movement uncovered in the Argentine Air Corps, Gen. Angel Maria Zyloaga is removed as corps commander . . . . Hull announces that 300 more names have been added to the trade blacklist of pro-Axis firms and individuals in Latin America.	
Sept. 26	Japanese Foreign Min. Teijiro Toyoda says the aim of the Axis Tripartite Pact is not only to establish a "new world order" but also to prevent the spread of hostilities.	Lieut Gen. A.G.L. McNaughton, commander of the Canadian Corps in Britain, says "there will have to be an invasion of the continent."	Authorities in French Indochina protest to Japan against the arrest of more than 100 Annamites and pro-Chungking Chinese by Japanese troops in Hanoi and Haiphong Sept. 25-26.	Twenty thousand Mexicans march in a funeral procession for nine munition workers killed by soldiers Sept. 23.	
Sept. 27		Reinhard Heydrich is appointed by Hitler as Reich Protector in Bohemia-Moravia . . . . American-owned tanker *I.C. White*, flying the Panamanian flag, is torpedoed and sunk in the South Atlantic . . . . Budapest reports German dive bombers destroyed the Yugoslav town of Uzice in a battle with Serbian guerrillas.		Marshal Oscar Benavides, Peruvian ambassador to Argentina, says Peru will not cede any territory in the boundary dispute with Ecuador . . . . At least 100 persons are killed in a hurricane that strikes the Cabo Gracias area of Nicaragua.	
Sept. 28	W. Averell Harriman and Lord Beaverbrook arrive in Moscow for aid talks and are received by Stalin in the Kremlin.	German authorities in Prague arrest Premier Alois Elias of the Nazi-created Protectorate of Bohemia-Moravia on a charge of "preparation for high treason."			
Sept. 29		German news agency announces 24 persons have been shot in Bohemia-Moravia for trying "to separate the protectorate from the Reich." . . . . Britain announces that heavy bombers flew over the Alps from England and bombed Genoa, Turin and other points in Northern Italy.			
Sept. 30		Churchill tells the House of Commons Hitler "still retains the initiative."	Both Japanese and Chinese forces claim possession of Changsha, capital of Hunan Province.		
Oct. 1	Harriman and Beaverbrook, at the end of their three-day aid conference in Moscow, state Russia will receive all war material needed from the U.S. and Britain	Finnish command announces that Petrozavodsk, capital of Soviet Karelia, was captured today by Finnish forces . . . . Thirty-nine persons are executed in Bohemia-Moravia for "preparation for treason," bringing the total in three days to 123.	Chinese military dispatches to Shanghai report Japanese forces are retreating northward from Changsha, Hunan Province capital.	A new Bolivian cabinet is appointed by Pres. Enrique Penaranda del Castillo to succeed one that resigned Sept. 27 following the discovery of an alleged Nazi plot . . . . Hull and Brazilian Amb. Carlos Martins sign an agreement under which Brazil will get a loan in return for strategic products.	
Oct. 2		Germany's central army group resumes its advance on Moscow after a halt of two months . . . . Paul Colette, convicted of attempting to assassinate Pierre Laval and Marcel Deat at Versailles Aug. 27, is sentenced to death in Paris. His sentence is commuted to life imprisonment Oct. 3.	Japan claims its forces have begun a new offensive in Hunan Province toward Chengchow, north of Hankow.		
Oct. 3		Adolf Hitler declares in a speech in Berlin that Russia is broken and will never rise again . . . . German dispatches report Prague Mayor Otakar Klapka has been sentenced to death for allegedly participating in a plot against Germany . . . . Six Paris synagogues are wrecked by bombs.	Japanese government announces its protest to Britain and Iran Sept. 30 against the suspension of diplomatic immunity for the mails and code messages of the Japanese legation in Teheran.	Peruvian government announces that Peru and Ecuador have agreed to create a neutral zone in the area of their border dispute . . . . Argentine Radical Party charges the government of Pres. Ramon S. Castillo with "conspiring against our institutional organization."	Australian P.M Arthur W. Fadden resigns after 37 days in office when the House adopts a vote of no-confidence, 36 to 33.

A	B	C	D	E
Includes developments that affect more than one world region, international organizations and important meetings of major world leaders.	*Includes all developments in European countries and military engagements between Allied and Axis powers in Africa and at sea.*	*Includes all developments in Japan and China, Japanese foreign policy and military actions in the Pacific region.*	*Includes all domestic and regional developments in Latin America, the Caribbean and Canada.*	*Includes developments in those independent nations and colonial possessions not covered in Columns B, C and D.*

U.S. Politics & Social Issues	U.S. Foreign Policy & Defense	U.S. Economy & Environment	Science, Technology & Nature	Culture, Leisure & Life Style	
	Sen. Kenneth McKellar (D. Tenn.) introduces a resolution in the Senate to repeal the Neutrality Act of 1939, saying it was a "mistake" to begin with and that it is "at war with our age-old policy of freedom of the seas." .... The Duke and Duchess of Windsor arrive in Washington for their first visit together and are greeted by FDR and cheering crowds.	Ickes announces plans are under way to build 50 refineries to triple the output of 100-octane aviation gasoline because of the increasing demand .... CIO State, County and Municipal Workers Union meeting rejects a motion disclaiming sympathy with Communism. A resolution urging aid to Britain, Russia and China passes, 183 to 7. The union opposed aid before the Russo-German war.		Brooklyn Dodgers win their first pennant since 1920 .... Gertrude Battles Lane, dean of American magazine editors and editor of the *Woman's Home Companion* since 1912, dies in N.Y.	Sept. 25
	Protestant Digest publishes a statement signed by 700 Protestant leaders scoring Lindbergh's Des Moines speech and declaring "anti-Semitism is anti-Christianity."	OPM Priorities Dir. Donald M. Nelson testifies before the House Banking and Currency Comm. that he is opposed to the Treasury plan to limit corporate profits to 6% on invested capital because it would take away incentive .... CIO Transport Workers Union re-elects Michael J. Quill to his third term as president. Quill promises to "do everthing in my power" to free Earl Browder from prison.	Prof. Ernest O. Lawrence of the Univ. of California describes the creation of "man-made" cosmic rays in a cyclotron.		Sept. 26
		Sen. Walter George (D, Ga.) charges the plan to limit corporate profits to 6% would ruin small business and "disrupt production vital to national defense." .... CIO-TWU meeting in N.Y. votes to organize utility companies other than transit lines throughout the country, subject to the approval of the CIO convention in November.	Dr. Frank Barr Mallory, 78, world-famous pathologist who discovered and isolated the scarlet fever bacillus and also discovered the cause of cirrhosis of the liver, dies in Brookline, Mass.		Sept. 27
	The largest war games in the history of the U.S., involving some 400,000 troops, end after 10 days of mock battle in northern Louisiana .... Eleanor Roosevelt begins a new radio series by scoring isolationists, charging their policies "would destroy us as a nation."	A Brookings Institution survey urges that farm prices and wages be controlled to prevent drastic price increases .... CIO ends its two-day general strike of 16,000 men against the Tennessee Coal, Iron & Railroad Co. in Birmingham, Ala., after Gov. Frank Dixon withdraws guardsmen from the Ensley plant.	British Assn. for the Advancement of Science adopts a seven-point charter of postwar principles at its London meeting.	Ted Williams of the Boston Red Sox wins the AL batting crown with an unofficial batting average of .4057.	Sept. 28
		Judge Charles B. Sears reports to Atty. Gen. Biddle on the basis of an 11-week hearing that Harry R. Bridges has been a member of the CP and therefore should be deported .... Federal Reserve Board Chmn. Marriner S. Eccles says the pending price control bill should be broadened to include farm prices and wage.		A million persons turn out for a gigantic victory parade through Brooklyn streets celebrating the Dodger pennant victory .... Joe Louis successfully defends his world heavyweight title for the 19th time when he scores a TKO over Lou Nova in the sixth round in N.Y.	Sept. 29
FDR says at his press conference that he will soon ask Congress to extend the social security program to include a much greater number of persons than are now covered.	FDR says at his press conference that the Russian constitution guarantees freedom of religion in virtually the same manner as in the U.S. .... Gallup Poll reports 46% of voters questioned now favor changing the Neutrality Act to permit U.S. merchant ships to carry war materials to Britain.	CIO Pres. Murray denounces Judge Charles B. Sears' report recommending the deportation of Harry Bridges .... OPM orders the 10% cut in gasoline deliveries in the East to be continued in October.			Sept. 30
Former Georgia Gov. E.D. Rivers and his wife are attacked and beaten in their home by H.W. Bikle, who then shoots and kills himself as police close in.	FDR's comments on religion in Russia are protested by Rep. Martin Dies, who writes that "freedom of religious worship is, and always has been, ... non-existent in Soviet Russia." Several religious leaders also criticize the President's remarks .... Knox says the U.S. "must provide both the major power and the dominant leadership" to police the world together with Britain after Hitler is defeated.	Ickes appears before the Senate oil investigating committee to denounce it for denying that there is an oil shortage in the East .... CIO strikers vote to end their two-day walkout against the Briggs Mfg. Co.'s plant in Detroit.			Oct. 1
	Gallup Poll reports final returns in a nationwide survey show 62% of voters favor FDR's orders to shoot at German warships on sight.	Morgenthau urges bankers to postpone loans for civilian projects that would require materials needed for defense.		Sen. Joseph P. Guffey (D, Pa.) denounces newspaper chains, declaring "venal, power-mad, money-mad, traitorous newspaper publishers" were responsible for France's defeat and that "we have the same brand of journalism right here in this country."	Oct. 2
Lindbergh tells an America First rally that the suspension of 1942 congressional elections "may be a step ahead on the road our President is taking us." .... American Bar Association elects Walter P. Armstrong of Memphis, Tenn. president.	FDR expresses alarm over the general health of the nation in light of the high ratio of draft rejections because of physical disability. Reports indicate 50% of the men examined are being rejected.	P.J. Currier of the Currier Lumber Co. in Detroit complains to the Justice Dept. that OPM Associate Dir. Gen. Hillman has granted a virtual monopoly of defense construction to AFL trade unions. He claims his bids are rejected because his employes are CIO members .... GM and UAW sign a seven-point agreement to help alleviate unemployment in the auto industry.		Pope Pius XII attacks the present "mania for divorce that contracts and dissolves marriages with greater ease than leases between landlords and tenants."	Oct. 3

F	G	H	I	J
Includes elections, federal-state relations, civil rights and liberties, crime, the judiciary, education, health care, poverty, urban affairs and population.	*Includes formation and debate of U.S. foreign and defense policies, veterans affairs and defense spending. (Relations with specific foreign countries are usually found under the region concerned.)*	*Includes business, labor, agriculture, taxation, transportation, consumer affairs, monetary and fiscal policy, natural resources, pollution and accidents.*	*Includes worldwide scientific, medical and technological developments, natural phenomena, U.S. weather and natural disasters.*	*Includes the arts, religion, scholarship, communications media, sports, entertainment, fashions, fads and social life.*

	World Affairs	European War Zone	Pacific War Zone	The Americas	Other Countries & Territories
Oct. 4		Russian dispatches state Soviet troops have begun a counter-offensive in the southern Ukraine in an attempt to crush the German forces attacking the Crimea.	Japanese Army announces in Shanghai that it has occupied Chengchow, Hunan Province.		New Zealand House of Representatives passes a bill providing free medical treatment beginning Nov. 1.
Oct. 5		Moscow radio claims Russian bombers have flown missions over Yugoslavia to aid Serbian guerrillas fighting the Germans. Swedish reports state a radical socialist government has been created in Montenegro to organize anti-Nazi resistance.	Japan breaks off diplomatic relations with the Polish government in London.	Women vote in Panama for the first time in the election of provincial council members under the new constitution .... A 102-mph hurricane sweeps Bermuda.	
Oct. 6		Moscow radio reports three million German troops have begun a two-pronged drive on Moscow along a 300-mile front .... Soviet officials disclose the bi-monthly magazine *Anti-Religioznik*, publication of the League of Militant Atheists, has been suspended because of a paper shortage.		Panamanian cabinet refuses to authorize the arming of ships as protection against Axis raiders on the grounds that the country's neutrality does not justify such a procedure .... A new Chilean cabinet is formed under Dr. Leonardo Guzman. Radical Party members return to the government.	Australian P.M. John Curtin announces his new Labor cabinet.
Oct. 7		Finnish government rejects Britain's warning that Finland will be regarded as an enemy if it continues its invasion of Russia .... Secret Yugoslav radio broadcast claims 300 Italians were killed in a battle with guerrillas at Plevlje.	Japanese military authorities in Shanghai admit that the Chinese have recaptured Ichang, northwest of Hankow in Hupeh Province.	An 11-man Chamber of Deputies committee is appointed in Montevideo to investigate subversive German activities in Uruguay.	
Oct. 8		German troops capture Orel on the central Russian front .... Press reports to Budapest and Berlin state heavy fighting is continuing in Yugoslavia between Serbian guerrillas and German and Italian troops.	Japanese military authorities in Shanghai state that the Chinese have launched an offensive along the middle Yangtze River and are threatening Shasi in Hupeh Province.		
Oct. 9		Reich Press Chief Otto Dietrich declares the war in the East is essentially over. "For all military purposes, Soviet Russia is done with," he declares .... Turkish Foreign Min. Shukru Saracoglu and German Amb. Franz von Papen sign a new trade pact in Ankara expiring March 31, 1943, providing for chromium ore shipments to Germany.		Ricardo Adolfo de la Guardia is elected president by the Panamanian cabinet following the disclosure that Pres. Arnulfo Arias fled by plane to Cuba on Oct. 7 after his government barred the arming of U.S. merchant ships under Panamanian registry .... W.S. Farish, president of the Standard Oil Co. of N.J., announces the company has rejected Mexico's offer of $9 million for oil properties confiscated in 1938.	
Oct. 10		Moscow dispatches admit Russian forces are withdrawing in the Bryansk sector to a new line of defense on the central front .... British disclose that a secret invasion force is being trained for possible action on the continent.		Pres. Ricardo Adolfo de la Guardia of Panama issues a statement pledging collaboration in the defense of the continent and observance of its obligations to the U.S. .... Argentine cabinet dissolves the elected municipal council of Buenos Aires and replaces it with 21 appointees.	Gen. Nuri es-Said prepares to form a new Iraqi cabinet in Bagdad, following his arrival from Cairo.
Oct. 11		Russian government announces that all women and children not engaged in war industries will be removed from Moscow.	Chungking military spokesman charges Japanese bombers dropped 300 gas bombs on Chinese troops attacking Ichang.	Ecuador announces a Peruvian patrol has seized 12 Ecuadorean farmers in the newly established "demilitarized zone" on the Peruvian-Ecuadorean frontier .... Canadian government moves to curb "inflationary tendencies" by restricting credit buying.	
Oct. 12		German dispatches say a column has reached a point 98 miles west of Moscow.			Mohandas K. Gandhi, Indian leader, says that the U.S. should withdraw help to Britain "unless there are guarantees of human liberties" for India and other British possessions.

A	B	C	D	E
Includes developments that affect more than one world region, international organizations and important meetings of major world leaders.	*Includes all developments in European countries and military engagements between Allied and Axis powers in Africa and at sea.*	*Includes all developments in Japan and China, Japanese foreign policy and military actions in the Pacific region.*	*Includes all domestic and regional developments in Latin America, the Caribbean and Canada.*	*Includes developments in those independent nations and colonial possessions not covered in Columns B, C and D.*

U.S. Politics & Social Issues	U.S. Foreign Policy & Defense	U.S. Economy & Environment	Science, Technology & Nature	Culture, Leisure & Life Style	
		Thirty-two out of 40 locals in District 7 of the UMW in Pennsylvania vote to end their revolt against union dues and return to work Oct. 6 . . . . James J. McEntee, CCC director, announces that 200 CCC camps will be closed by Nov. 1 because of the large number of enrollees getting jobs.	Prof. C.C. Furnas of Yale declares "this generation may very well feel the pinch of partial depletion" of petroleum reserves and urges the development of a system to convert sunlight to charge electric storage batteries.	Fenelon wins the $58,000 N.Y. Handicap at Belmont Park, N.Y.	Oct. 4
Louis Brandeis, 84, associate justice of the Supreme Court from 1916 to 1939, dies in Washington.	Executive Council of the AFL declares the U.S. should aid Russia . . . . A "Fun to be Free" rally, sponsored by Fight for Freedom in N.Y., draws over 17,000. Bill Robinson tap-dances on Hitler's coffin to the tune of *When That Man Is Dead and Gone.*			Yankees defeat the Dodgers, 7-4, to take a 3-to-1 lead in the World Series after Dodger catcher Mickey Owen drops a third strike pitch on Tommy Henrich which should have ended the game in a 4-3 Dodger victory . . . . David O. Selznick, Hollywood motion picture producer, buys a 25% interest in United Artists.	Oct. 5
	Stimson warns that the present dual citizenship provisions of the U.S. immigration laws facilitate espionage and proposes a bill to eliminate the possibility of dual allegiance . . . . House completes congressional action on the conference-approved property seizure bill and sends it to the White House.	Asst. Atty. Gen. Thurman Arnold says the defense program has been retarded by "powerful groups" of both capital and labor "who fear expansion may destroy their domination of industry." . . . . Federal Judge Francis Caffey rules the Justice Dept. failed to prove that Alcoa is an illegal monopoly.	Three persons are killed and 40 injured when a tornado strikes suburban Kansas City, Mo., causing heavy property damage.	N.Y. Yankees win their ninth World Series, 4 games to 1, by beating the Dodgers 3 to 1 behind the four-hit pitching of Ernie Bonham . . . . Attorneys for broadcasting companies protest to the FCC that the commission's plan to prohibit the multiple ownership of radio stations is illegal and undesirable.	Oct. 6
	House votes, 69 to 25, against an amendment to bar Russia from receiving any aid under the bill to increase the lending authority of the RFC . . . . Sumner Welles declares America's postwar high tariff policy helped bring "disaster and despair to countless people," paving the way for the rise of dictatorships. After the present war, he says, America must adopt a free trade policy.	FDR calls upon labor and management to avert strikes and lockouts in a message to the AFL convention in Seattle . . . . Rep. Carl Vinson (D, Ga.) introduces a bill in the House to limit defense profits to 7% of the manufacturing cost.	Six are reported killed as a hurricane moves across Florida and into Georgia.	Joe Gordon, Yankees star second baseman, is voted the outstanding player of the World Series by N.Y. baseball writers.	Oct. 7
Atty. Gen. Biddle states at his first press conference that he approves the use of wire-tapping in cases involving espionage, sabotage or kidnapping.	George Sylvester Viereck is arrested by the FBI in N.Y. on a five-count indictment charging him with withholding information concerning his German propaganda activity . . . . House Appropriations Comm. approves a second supplemental national defense appropriation bill, including $5.985 billion in Lend-Lease funds.	John Santo, former CIO-TWU official, is arrested in N.Y. on charges of illegally entering the country and falsely claiming U.S. citizenship.	Dr. Norman Plummer of Cornell Univ. Medical College says sulfadiazine has cured a case of subacute bacterial endocarditis, an infectious heart disease previously regarded as 100% fatal.	Frederick Lewis Allen is appointed editor of *Harper's Magazine* . . . . Torch singer Helen Morgan, 41, dies in Chicago of a liver ailment . . . . Lorenzo Cardinal Lauri, 76, chamberlain of the Catholic Church, the highest administrative office in the church under the Pope, dies in Vatican City.	Oct. 8
Atty. Gen. Biddle announces the government will drop its prosecution of J. Warren Davis and Morgan S. Kaufman on charges of conspiring to obstruct justice.	FDR urges Congress to repeal Section 6 of the 1939 Neutrality Act, which prohibits arming American-flag ships engaged in foreign commerce, and to modify the provision barring U.S. vessels from war zones. He declares, "It is time for this country to stop playing into Hitler's hands and to unshackle our own."	UMW Pres. Lewis revokes the charter of the District 7 local in Hazleton, Pa. because of its 27-day strike against higher union dues and assessments . . . . Pres. Nicholas Schenck of Loew's, Inc. testifies at the trial of George E. Browne, president of the International Alliance of Theatrical Stage Employes, that Loew's had to pay Browne and an associate $100,000 to call off a projectionists' strike in N.Y. in 1935 . . . . Supply Priorities and Allocation Board (SPAB) announces no priority ratings will be issued from now on for non-essential private or public construction projects requiring "appreciable quantities of critical materials."	Charles Lorenzo Clarke, 88, oldest surviving associate of Thomas A. Edison and original chief engineer of the Edison Electric Light Company, dies in Newton, Mass.	Jockey Alfred (Robby) Robertson wins six out of seven horse races in Jamaica, N.Y., the first time this has been done at a N.Y. track.	Oct. 9
Communist Party withdraws its candidate for mayor and other city offices in the N.Y.C. elections, apparently to strenthen Mayor La Guardia, who promptly repudiates Communist support.	FDR announces the government plans to rehabilitate 200,000 of the one million youths rejected for Army service because of physical or mental defects . . . . House passes the $5.985 billion Lend-Lease bill and sends it to the Senate.	CIO-UAW members vote to end their 11-day strike against Air Associates, Inc. of Bendix, N.J.	Dr. Ernest O. Lawrence, Univ. of California physicist, says that the element strontium can be made artificially radioactive and that it then can be used to destroy cancer cells in the manner of radium.	Robert McGowan Barrington-Ward succeeds Geoffrey Dawson as editor of the *London Times.*	Oct. 10
GOP Chmn. Rep. Joseph W. Martin says the party must regain control of the House in 1942 in order to curb the New Deal.	Japanese embassy announces that under an agreement with the State Dept. three Japanese ships will repatriate nearly 2,000 Japanese from the West Coast and Hawaii . . . . Navy Dept. announces a radio "manned by an agent of the German Gestapo and two Norwegians" was discovered in Greenland and "disposed of."	NDMB Chmn. William Davis announces that Air Associates, Inc. has refused to reinstate CIO strikers . . . . Atty. Gen. Biddle says factories and plants may pool their production facilities to obtain arms orders without fear of prosecution under the anti-trust laws.		FCC suspends indefinitely its ruling that NBC must dispose of one of its two major networks.	Oct. 11
Harry M. Daugherty, 81, U.S. attorney general from 1921 to 1924, dies in Columbus, Ohio.	GOP representatives protest the decision to limit hearings on amending the Neutrality Act before the House Foreign Affairs Comm. to two days as an "unprecedented gag rule."			NAB Pres. Neville Miller declares the FCC's new modified rules constitute as great a peril to broadcasting as the previous regulations.	Oct. 12
F	G	H	I	J	
Includes elections, federal-state relations, civil rights and liberties, crime, the judiciary, education, health care, poverty, urban affairs and population.	*Includes formation and debate of U.S. foreign and defense policies, veterans affairs and defense spending. (Relations with specific foreign countries are usually found under the region concerned.)*	*Includes business, labor, agriculture, taxation, transportation, consumer affairs, monetary and fiscal policy, natural resources, pollution and accidents.*	*Includes worldwide scientific, medical and technological developments, natural phenomena, U.S. weather and natural disasters.*	*Includes the arts, religion, scholarship, communications media, sports, entertainment, fashions, fads and social life.*	

	World Affairs	European War Zone	Pacific War Zone	The Americas	Other Countries & Territories
Oct. 13		Soviet government decides to evacuate many government offices from Moscow to Kuibyshev .... Soviets admit Russian troops have retreated from Vyazma, about 130 miles west of Moscow .... Eight Czechs are executed in Prague for "preparation for treason," economic sabotage and illegal possession of arms.	Chinese admit their forces have evacuated Ichang after occupying the city for three days.	Argentine Radical Party issues a manifesto denouncing Acting Pres. Ramon Castillo's dissolution of the Buenos Aires council as an unconstitutional and "dictatorial" act.	
Oct. 14		Moscow radio admits that the Germans have smashed to Mozhaisk, 60 miles west of Moscow, and to Kalinin, 100 miles to the northwest.		Dr. Arnulfo Arias, deposed president of Panama, arrives at Cristobal from Cuba and surrenders to the Panamanian police .... U.S. Amb. Norman Armour and Argentine Foreign Min. Enrique Ruiz Guinzau sign a three-year treaty in Buenos Aires.	
Oct. 15		Moscow radio reports that Russian troops have abandoned Kalinin. Barricades are erected in Moscow.	Capt. Hideo Hiraide, director of Japanese naval intelligence, says in Tokyo that U.S.-Japanese relations "are now approaching the final parting of the ways," and declares, "the Imperial Navy is itching for action."	Cuban Senate sends to the House a bill passed yesterday to postpone until March 15 the congressional elections for 57 representatives and one senator scheduled for Dec. 1.	
Oct. 16		Near panic reigns in Moscow as residents, fearing German troops are about to capture the city, flee to the east .... German command announces that Odessa was captured today after a two-month siege .... Petain announces the imprisonment of seven former French political and military leaders on charges of responsibility for France's military defeat. They include former premiers Edouard Daladier, Paul Reynaud and Leon Blum.	Premier Konoye submits his resignation to Emperor Hirohito and is replaced by War Min. Hideki Tojo amid reports that U.S.-Japanese relations have reached a new low.	All members of the Colombian cabinet except Foreign Min. Luis Lopez de Mesa resign in order to let Pres. Eduardo Santos reorganize the cabinet.	
Oct. 17		U.S. destroyer *Kearny* is damaged by a torpedo while on patrol duty about 350 miles south of Iceland. Eleven crew members are reported missing .... State Dept. reveals U.S. Amb. Laurence A. Steinhardt, members of his staff and foreign correspondents "have left Moscow for a point eastward of the capital at the request of the Soviet government." A new threat to the city is reported from a German column approaching from the southeast .... Seeking to stem the panic, Moscow radio reports Stalin is still in the city.		Pres. Enrique Penaranda de Castillo of Bolivia signs a decree mobilizing all railroad workers in order to avert a nationwide strike.	British government announces former Shah Riza Pahlevi of Iran has been taken to the Indian Ocean island of Mauritius "owing to the war situation."
Oct. 18		Soviet troops slow down German attack on Moscow .... German command announces the 17-day battle of Bryansk and Vyazma on the central front has ended with the destruction of eight Soviet armies.	Lt. Gen. Hideki Tojo forms a new Japanese cabinet with himself as premier, war minister and home minister.	P.M. Mackenzie King announces the Canadian government has decided to control prices and wages, effective Nov. 15, to avert inflation.	British and Russian troops evacuate Teheran.
Oct. 19		Stalin decrees a state of siege in Moscow and surrounding districts as the Nazi armies continue to move closer to the city .... A meeting of 1,500 British shop stewards in London "demands the opening up of a Western Front as quickly as possible" to help the Soviet Union .... The 4,983-ton, American-owned freighter *Lehigh* is torpedoed and sunk off Freetown, Sierra Leone.		Peru expresses concern to the State Dept. over the U.S. seizure of Douglas bombers consigned to Peru.	Kabul radio announces the government of King Mohammed Zahir Shah has ordered German and Italian nationals to leave Afghanistan.
	A *Includes developments that affect more than one world region, international organizations and important meetings of major world leaders.*	B *Includes all developments in European countries and military engagements between Allied and Axis powers in Africa and at sea.*	C *Includes all developments in Japan and China, Japanese foreign policy and military actions in the Pacific region.*	D *Includes all domestic and regional developments in Latin America, the Caribbean and Canada.*	E *Includes developments in those independent nations and colonial possessions not covered in Columns B, C and D.*

U.S. Politics & Social Issues	U.S. Foreign Policy & Defense	U.S. Economy & Environment	Science, Technology & Nature	Culture, Leisure & Life Style	
Southern University Conference votes unanimously to drop the Univ. of Georgia from its ranks because of the dismissal of Walter D. Cocking .... Philadelphia school superintendent Alexander J. Stoddard tells a meeting of school officials that Americans should replace their critical attitude toward history with one of loyalty for the nation's founders. "There has been too much tinkering with respect to our great leaders who gave us this country," he says.	FDR announces that "within the past few days large amounts of supplies have been sent to Russia." He adds that "everything possible is being done to send material to Russia to help the brave defense which continues to be made." .... Hull, Knox, and Stimson testify before the House Foreign Affairs Comm. that the Neutrality Act should be amended to permit the arming of U.S. merchant ships and allow them to enter war zones.	District 19 of the CIO-UMW and the Harlan County (Ky.) Coal Operators Assn. sign a contract for a union shop after 20 years of violent labor disputes .... Sen. John H. Bankhead (D, Ala.) assails Treasury Secy. Morgenthau as "public enemy No. 1 of the farmer" because of his proposal to put government loan stocks of agricultural products on the market to check rising prices .... Senate passes and sends to the White House the House-approved bill increasing the RFC's borrowing power by $1.5 billion.			Oct. 13
	Eleven isolationist senators meet in the office of Sen. Hiram W. Johnson (R, Calif.) to plan their strategy in opposing a Neutrality Act amendment.	NLRB orders collective bargaining elections among employes of 14 Ford Motor Co. plants in Michigan as the result of an AFL protest against Ford's signing an exclusive contract with the CIO last June 20 .... AFL convention adopts a resolution denouncing Thurman Arnold as "the most articulate and effective spokesman now representing the reactionary, anti-labor forces in this country."		New Opera Co., founded by Mrs. Lytle Hull, opens its first season at the 44th St. Theater in N.Y. with Mozart's *Cosi fan Tutte*, conducted by Dr. Fritz Busch.	Oct. 14
Some 1,000 Univ. of Georgia students parade before the state capitol in Atlanta in protest against Gov. Eugene Talmadge, whom they accuse of responsibility for the expulsion of the university from the Southern University Conference.	Knox discloses the Navy is completing plans for the censorship of outgoing communications from the U.S. .... Alfred E. Smith says in a N.Y. speech that the American people should "stand together" behind the Administration "on all of its foreign policies."	OPM Civilian Supply Dir. Leon Henderson orders automobile production in January reduced by "at least 51%" to 204,848 cars .... AFL convention in Seattle ousts George Browne, on trial in N.Y. on charges of extorting $550,000 from the motion picture industry, from his position as 11th vice president of the federation .... AFL welders agree to return to work at the Ingalls Shipbuilding Corp. yard in Pascagoula, Miss. after a two-day strike.		Jo Davidson, sculptor, says upon his return to N.Y. from South America, where he made busts of nine presidents, that this country is on the verge of an art renaissance, partly because of WPA art projects .... Nicola Cardinal Canali is appointed Grand Penitentiary by Pope Pius XII to succeed the late Lorenzo Cardinal Lauri.	Oct. 15
	Rep. Vito Marcantonio, the radical Congressman from N.Y. who voted against the draft and Lend-Lease, urges that an American expeditionary force be used if necessary "to open up a western front against Hitler." .... War Secy. Stimson says U.S. forces in Iceland are commanded by Maj. Gen. Charles H. Bonesteel and are not under British command.	Morgenthau says the federal debt limit will have to be raised "considerably" above the present statutory limit of $65 billion.	Drs. John R. Paul and James D. Trask of the Yale Univ. School of Medicine say they have caught flies that were found to be carrying the virus of infantile paralysis after feeding in sewage systems.		Oct. 16
Alfred M. Landon declares "a little group" of New Dealers are using national defense as a smoke screen to establish, "beyond repeal, their collective state."	House passes, 259 to 138, and sends to the Senate an amendment to the Neutrality Act to permit the arming of U.S. merchant ships .... Brig. Gen. Irving J. Phillipson admits that a concentration camp for aliens with a capacity of about 700 persons is being completed at Camp Upton on Long Island.	Thirty persons are injured in a clash of 1,000 protesting miners and police and guards in Mohonoy City, Pa. caused by the closing of a bootleg mine.	Dr. John Stanley Plaskett, 75, internationally famous astronomer, dies in Victoria, B.C.		Oct. 17
Dr. Ruth Kotinsky estimates, in a survey made for the American Assn. for Adult Education, that at least 16 million persons in the U.S over 10 years old are functionally illiterate.	Sens. Carter Glass (D, Va.) and Claude Pepper (D, Fla.) urge the entire Neutrality Act be repealed .... Gallup Poll reports 72% of the voters asked said they favored amending the Neutrality Act to permit the arming of U.S. merchant ships.	Wayne L. Morse, chairman of FDR's fact-finding board, announces in Chicago that the board is ready to mediate or arbitrate the demands of 1,250,000 railroad employes for wage increases.			Oct. 18
Chmn. Martin Dies of the House Comm. on Un-American Activities sends Atty. Gen. Francis Biddle a list of 1,124 federal employes whom he calls Communists or fellow travelers.	Navy Dept. announces that the destroyer *Kearny* has reached an undisclosed port with 11 crew members missing and 10 others injured .... Herbert Hoover appeals to the U.S. government to use "every influence in its power" to arrange for the shipment of food to children in Nazi-occupied Europe.	NDMB refers the three-month strike by CIO workers against Air Associates to FDR.		Twenty-five thousand persons at Yankee Stadium see Tom Harmon and John Kimbrough make their professional football debut with the N.Y. Americans against the Columbus Bulls.	Oct. 19
F	G	H	I	J	
Includes elections, federal-state relations, civil rights and liberties, crime, the judiciary, education, health care, poverty, urban affairs and population.	*Includes formation and debate of U.S. foreign and defense policies, veterans affairs and defense spending. (Relations with specific foreign countries are usually found under the region concerned.)*	*Includes business, labor, agriculture, taxation, transportation, consumer affairs, monetary and fiscal policy, natural resources, pollution and accidents.*	*Includes worldwide scientific, medical and technological developments, natural phenomena, U.S. weather and natural disasters.*	*Includes the arts, religion, scholarship, communications media, sports, entertainment, fashions, fads and social life.*	

	World Affairs	European War Zone	Pacific War Zone	The Americas	Other Countries & Territories
Oct. 20		German armored spearheads are within 40 miles of Moscow .... Soviet government sets up a temporary capital at Kuibyshev on the Volga River, 540 miles southeast of Moscow .... Lt. Col. Paul Friedrich Hotz, commander of German forces in the Nantes district of France, is shot and killed by two assailants.		The new Panamanian government revokes the decree which banned the arming of merchant ships sailing under Panamanian registry .... Hull informs the Peruvian ambassador that Peru will be given "full and immediate compensation" for 18 bombers seized in N.Y.	
Oct. 21		Gen. Heinrich von Stulpnagel, German commander in occupied France, orders the execution of 50 French hostages in Nantes for the assassination of Lt. Col. Hotz .... German command announces the capture of Stalino, a Ukrainian industrial city, and of the Estonian island of Dagoe in the Baltic.		Mexican Foreign Office announces that Mexico and Britain have agreed to resume diplomatic relations, which were broken off in 1938 .... Former Panamanian Pres. Arias arrives in Nicaragua after being deported.	
Oct. 22		German authorities seize 100 more French hostages following last night's slaying of Maj. Hans Gottfried Reimers in Bordeaux. Fifty French hostages are shot in reprisal for the slaying of Lt. Col. Hotz in Nantes .... The British announce RAF raids on Germany, Italy, the Netherlands, Denmark, France and North Africa last night and today.		Jesse H. Jones announces that the Export-Import Bank has granted Mexico a $30-million credit for road improvement and the completion of an international highway to Central and South America.	
Oct. 23		Dispatches from Kuibyshev report Gen. Gregory K. Zhukov, chief of the Russian general staff, has replaced Marshal Semyon K. Timoshenko as commander of the central front around Moscow and that Timoshenko has been made commander of the southern front .... British Labor MPs demand an invasion of the continent to take advantage of the Russo-German war.			Gen. J.B.M. Hertzog, leader of the Afrikaaner Party and former premier of the Union of South Africa, announces his support of Nazism at a party congress.
Oct. 24		Kharkov falls to German troops .... Fifty French hostages are executed by German authorities for the slaying of Maj. Reimers.	New Japanese cabinet announces it will convoke the Diet in an extraordinary five-day session beginning Nov. 15 to approve war expenditures and taxation.	Dominican Republic buys the Cuidad Trujillo branch of the National City Bank of N.Y.	Afrikaaner Party of the Union of South Africa issues a statement repudiating Gen. J.B.M. Hertzog for his support of Nazism and reaffirming its belief in democratic principles.
Oct. 25		Adolf Hitler confers with Italian Foreign Min. Count Ciano at the German headquarters in Russia.		Transportation and newspaper employes end their five-day strike in La Paz, Bolivia after being granted a 20% wage increase .... Costa Rica announces that foreigners who attack friendly nations or democratic principles will be expelled.	
Oct. 26		German troops drive on Rostov, the gateway to the Caucasus .... "Aid to Russia" rally in London draws 10,000 to demand an invasion of the Continent to help Russia.	Japanese Premier Tojo declares that "Japan must go on and develop in ever-expanding progress—there is no retreat!"		
Oct. 27	U.S. Labor Secy. Frances Perkins is elected president of the conference of the ILO at Columbia Univ.	Gen. Zhukov, commander of the Moscow front, issues an order of the day commanding his army not to retreat a single step .... Vichy announces the Germans have postponed the execution of 100 hostages to give the people more time to find the guilty.	Soviet news agency reports 20 Japanese soldiers crossed the Soviet-Japanese Far Eastern frontier Oct. 23 but were forced to withdraw after clashing with Russian troops near the village of Raskino. Japan denies the incident took place.		Arabic World Agency reports from Rome that Haj Amin el Husseini, exiled Mufti of Jerusalem, is now in Rome.

A	B	C	D	E
Includes developments that affect more than one world region, international organizations and important meetings of major world leaders.	*Includes all developments in European countries and military engagements between Allied and Axis powers in Africa and at sea.*	*Includes all developments in Japan and China, Japanese foreign policy and military actions in the Pacific region.*	*Includes all domestic and regional developments in Latin America, the Caribbean and Canada.*	*Includes developments in those independent nations and colonial possessions not covered in Columns B, C and D.*

U.S. Politics & Social Issues	U.S. Foreign Policy & Defense	U.S. Economy & Environment	Science, Technology & Nature	Culture, Leisure & Life Style	
	Three GOP senators—Styles Bridges (N.H.), Warren R. Austin (Vt.) and Chan Gurney (S.D.)—introduce an amendment to the House-approved ship-arming resolution to repeal the entire Neutrality Act .... Morgenthau announces the government has advanced $30 million more to Russia against future gold deliveries to help pay for war materials bought here.	OPM priorities division issues an order curtailing the use of copper in more than 100 specific civilian articles by 40% for the rest of 1941 and entirely prohibiting it after Jan. 1, 1942.		*L'Osservatore Romano*, Vatican newspaper, urges Italians not to read "Russian, Hungarian, English, American and French novels" because they are immoral and lead to sensuality and decadence.	Oct. 20
William Fox, bankrupt former motion picture producer, is sentenced to a year in federal prison and a $3,000 fine on a charge of conspiracy to obstruct justice and defraud the government.	Wendell L. Willkie and more than 100 prominent Republicans in 40 states send a message to members of Congress urging them to repeal the Neutrality Act.	Fourteen non-operating railroad unions with 900,000 members reject the offer of FDR's fact-finding board to arbitrate demands for higher wages .... CIO workers vote to end a six-day strike at the Great Lakes Steel Corp. in Ecorse, Mich. after they are warned by the union that the Army is ready to take over the plant .... U.S. officials disclose Britain has released 15 oil tankers to their American owners to relieve the oil shortage on the East Coast.	Paul H. Merriman of the Glenn L. Martin Co. says aircraft production will be increased 30% after spot welding of aluminium alloys has been fully developed.	Mrs. Eleanor Roosevelt announces that all formal White House social entertainments scheduled for this winter have been canceled "because conditions are so serious."	Oct. 21
	Hull calls the attack on the *Lehigh* "in harmony with all the definitions of piracy and assassination." .... Gen. Robert E. Wood of the America First Comm. challenges FDR to ask Congress for a declaration of war .... Maritime Commision announces that beginning Oct. 28 all shipments of war materials to Russia will be routed through Boston, probably to Archangel, instead of across the Pacific to Vladivostok.	CIO-UMW orders a strike at midnight, Oct. 25, in soft coal mines owned by seven steel companies to back up its demand for a closed shop .... Hillman testifies before a Senate committee investigating defense contracts that he recommended rejection of the Currier Lumber Co.'s low bid for a defense housing project in Detroit to avoid "industrial warfare" between the AFL and the CIO.			Oct. 22
	Senate passes the $5.985-billion supplemental Lend-Lease bill and returns it to the House for approval of amendments.	Harold L. Ickes announces Britain is releasing 25 more oil tankers to their American owners, raising the total to 40, and that as a result gasoline rationing in 17 Eastern states is no longer necessary .... A welders' strike in six Seattle shipyards spreads to Tacoma when 500 men walk out at the Seattle-Tacoma Shipbuilding Corp.		Mrs. Florence Maybrick, 80, who in 1889 was sentenced to death in Liverpool for poisoning her husband, is found dead in her home in Connecticut. (Her sentences was commuted and she was released in 1905.)	Oct. 23
FDR endorses Mayor Fiorello H. La Guardia of N.Y. for re-election on the GOP and Labor Party tickets over Dist. Atty. William O'Dwyer, the Democratic candidate .... A grand jury in Washington indicts George Hill, aide to Rep. Hamilton Fish (R, N.Y.), on charges of giving false testimony in its investigation of Nazi activities.	Knox says "the Japanese have no intention of giving up their plans for expansion" in the Far East. "If they pursue that course, a collision there is inevitable," he adds .... FDR says Congress will be asked soon for funds with which to double the present tank program because of military lessons learned from the British-Axis fighting in North Africa.	FDR appeals to John L. Lewis to prevent the strike of 53,000 coal miners scheduled to begin midnight, Oct. 25 .... Mine operators and CIO officials reach an agreement in Birmingham to provide 15,000 striking miners with a $5.25 basic daily wage .... U.S. officials announce Air Associates has agreed to rehire all the CIO strikers at its Bendix, N.J. plant.	Dr. Vannevar Bush, director of the Office of Scientific Research and Development, says 2,000 scientists working under the sponsorship of the National Defense Research Comm. are turning "ideas into copper and iron" three times faster than in peace time.	Arthur H. Starns of Calumet City, Ill. jumps from a plane at an altitude of 30,800 feet near Chicago and falls 29,300 feet in 116 seconds before opening his parachute at 1,500 feet to set a new record for the longest delayed leap.	Oct. 24
	Senate Foreign Relations Comm. votes, 12 to 11, to permit U.S. merchant ships to enter war zones as well as to arm themselves .... FDR officially establishes the new Office of Facts and Figures, with Archibald MacLeish as unpaid director.	Lewis writes to FDR that he will not delay the scheduled strike of 53,000 coal miners.		Henri G. Marceau, curator of the Philadelphia Museum of Art, announces that an 18 by 30-inch painting entitled *Crucifixion* attributed for two centuries to the famous Dutch artist Rembrandt van Rijn, has been proved to be spurious.	Oct. 25
National Women's Party adopts a resolution urging the ILO to recommend that "all laws and regulations governing industry shall apply to the nature of the work and not to the sex of the worker."		FDR again appeals to Lewis to keep the UMW from striking mines owned by steel firms..... SPAB Exec. Dir. Donald M. Nelson issues an order barring the use of bright finish, bright work, metal finish or body trim containing aluminum, chrome, copper or nickel in the manufacture of passenger automobiles beginning Dec. 15.	Two tornadoes strike the towns of Dardanelle and Hamburg in Arkansas, killing 17 persons and injuring more than 200.	Corliss Lamont sues the Bobbs-Merrill Co. of N.Y., publishers of Eugene Lyon's *The Red Decade*, for $100,000 damages on the grounds that the book portrayed him as a Communist.	Oct. 26
	FDR declares in a Navy Day address, "We have wished to avoid shooting, but the shooting has started. And history has recorded who fired the first shot." He says the attack on the *Kearny* was an attempt "to frighten the American people off the high seas." .... Knox urges that the Neutrality Act be completely repealed.	UMW strikes mines owned by steel companies as Lewis rejects FDR's appeal to permit more time for a settlement .... A jury in Lexington, Ky. convicts the R.J. Reynolds, Liggett & Myers and American Tobacco companies, American Suppliers, Inc., an American Tobacco Co. subsidiary, and 13 individuals on charges of monopoly and price fixing in violation of the Sherman Antitrust Act .... FDR proposes to merge the CCC into National Youth Administration.			Oct. 27

F	G	H	I	J
Includes elections, federal-state relations, civil rights and liberties, crime, the judiciary, education, health care, poverty, urban affairs and population.	*Includes formation and debate of U.S. foreign and defense policies, veterans affairs and defense spending. (Relations with specific foreign countries are usually found under the region concerned.)*	*Includes business, labor, agriculture, taxation, transportation, consumer affairs, monetary and fiscal policy, natural resources, pollution and accidents.*	*Includes worldwide scientific, medical and technological developments, natural phenomena, U.S. weather and natural disasters.*	*Includes the arts, religion, scholarship, communications media, sports, entertainment, fashions, fads and social life.*

	World Affairs	European War Zone	Pacific War Zone	The Americas	Other Countries & Territories
Oct. 28		Aided by bad weather, Russian troops counter-attack west of Moscow.		A shot is fired in the air as acting Argentine Pres. Ramon Castillo boards a train in Buenos Aires. One person is arrested.	
Oct. 29	Clement R. Attlee, Britain's Lord Privy Seal, declares in an address to the ILO conference in N.Y., "This fight is not just a fight between nations.. It is a fight for the future of civilization."	German command announces its forces have broken through Soviet defenses and entered the Crimean Peninsula after a battle lasting from Oct. 18 to Oct. 28.		Export-Import Bank announces it will offer more than $70 million monthly in credits to Latin American importers to finance purchases in the U.S.	
Oct. 30		U.S. destroyer *Reuben James* is torpedoed and sunk west of Iceland while on convoy duty .... Soviets claim they have beaten off German attacks on Tula, 110 miles south of Moscow.		Bolivian defense ministry announces it will not renew the Italian military mission's contract at the end of the year.	Vichy announces that French Somaliland authorities have agreed to discuss British requests for the use of the port of Djibuti and the railroad to Addis Ababa, Ethiopia.
Oct. 31		Reports from London say German troops have broken through the outer defenses of Tula, 110 miles south of Moscow, and are also driving forward in the Crimea .... A Berlin spokesman says that the sinking of the U.S. destroyer *Reuben James* was justifiable under international law if it was escorting a British convoy .... A Yugoslav spokesman in London claims 80,000 Serbian guerrillas are fighting German and Italian troops along a 125-mile front in Serbia.	Soviets announce that delegations of the Mongolian People's Republic and Manchukuo fixed the new frontier in the disputed Bor Nor region during a Oct. 16 conference in Harbin, Manchukuo.	Twenty-seven miners are killed in an explosion in the Brazeau Collieries near Nordegg, Alberta in Canada .... FDR announces that Josephus Daniels has resigned as U.S. ambassador to Mexico because of his wife's illness.	
Nov. 1	U.S. delegation to the ILO conference presents a resolution for postwar world reconstruction, including the feeding of hungry nations, economic rebuilding, the revival of international trade, resettlement of workers and the improvement of living conditions.	A statement issued from Hitler's headquarters charges the *Greer* and *Kearny* attacked German submarines and "therefore the United States attacked Germany."	Secret Japanese cabinet meeting decides for war with the U.S. if negotiations do not produce an agreement with the U.S. by Dec. 1 for Japan to receive oil from the East Indies and to be left free to settle the China incident without intervention .... Japanese news agency says that unless the U.S. halts its economic blockade, Japan must seek supply sources for vital goods and materials as a measure of self-defense.	FDR confers with Canadian P.M. Mackenzie King at Hyde Park, N.Y. .... The new international Rainbow Bridge over the Niagara River at Niagara Falls is formally opened to traffic .... Pres. Ricardo Adolfo de la Guardia says Panama's policy of neutrality will have to be revised because peace is now endangered.	Sen. Alben W. Barkley urges in a speech to Zionist organizations in N.Y. that a Jewish homeland be created in Palestine.
Nov. 2		Pres. Risto Ryti of Finland tells Henry J. Taylor of the North American Newspaper Alliance in Helsinki that "there are no German officers or soldiers in the Finnish units" battling against Russia .... German command reports that German and Rumanian troops have captured Simferopol, the Crimean capital.	Gen. Sir Archibald P. Wavell, commander of the British Indian Army, arrives in Singapore to confer on the Far Eastern situation.	Canadian government issues an order in council imposing a ceiling on prices, effective Nov. 17, based on maximum prices between Sept. 15 and Oct. 11.	
Nov. 3		German command announces the splitting of the Russian forces in the Crimea into two groups, both attempting to escape .... Reich Protector Reinhard Heydrich announces in Prague that he has "completed" his campaign to end Czech resistance, during which about 300 Czechs were executed.		Uruguayan Chamber of Deputies adopts a resolution urging other American nations to protest jointly to Germany against the killing of civilians in occupied countries.	
Nov. 4	The U.S. resolution declaring that "the victory of the free peoples in war against totalitarian aggression is an indispensable condition of the attainment of the ideals" of the ILO is unanimously adopted .... Delegates of Czechoslovakia, Poland, Greece and Yugoslavia to the ILO conference sign a declaration for joint post-war action for common economic, social and political aims without affecting each nation's sovereignty.	British announce five French merchant ships attempting "to run contraband for the Germans" to France have been seized off South Africa .... Finnish command announces the occupation of the Koivisto Islands in the Gulf of Finland .... German command announces the capture of Theodosia on the southeastern coast of Crimea.			Dominions Secy. Leopold S. Amery says in London that Britain will help Burma achieve dominion status after the war .... Haj Amin el Husseini, exiled Grand Mufti of Jerusalem, leaves Rome for Berlin after denouncing "British propaganda" in the Near East.
	A *Includes developments that affect more than one world region, international organizations and important meetings of major world leaders.*	B *Includes all developments in European countries and military engagements between Allied and Axis powers in Africa and at sea.*	C *Includes all developments in Japan and China, Japanese foreign policy and military actions in the Pacific region.*	D *Includes all domestic and regional developments in Latin America, the Caribbean and Canada.*	E *Includes developments in those independent nations and colonial possessions not covered in Columns B, C and D.*

U.S. Politics & Social Issues	U.S. Foreign Policy & Defense	U.S. Economy & Environment	Science, Technology & Nature	Culture, Leisure & Life Style	
Joseph E. McWilliams, leader of the American Destiny Party, is ordered to complete a 60-day workhouse term for violating his probation by making anti-Semitic speeches.	FDR signs the $5.985-billion Lend-Lease bill and issues an executive order creating the Office of Lend-Lease Administration in the Office of Emergency Management, with Edward R. Stettinius Jr. in charge.	U.S. Steel Corp., the Weirton Steel Co. and the Wheeling Steel Corp. accept the NDMB's offer to arbitrate the coal mine strike .... UAW threatens to use its "large-scale economic strength" in five Eastern states to force a settlement at Air Associates after returning strikers are assigned to menial work .... Fifteen men are killed in a coal mine explosion near Nortonville, Ky.			Oct. 28
FDR appoints Charles Fahy to be solicitor general, succeeding Francis Biddle.	Knox announces the *Kearny* was struck by one of three torpedoes Oct. 17 after she dropped depth bombs on a submarine attacking a convoy southwest of Iceland .... Justice Dept. announces the arrest of William Michael Etzel, of German descent, by federal agents in Baltimore on charges of sabotaging bombers at the Glenn L. Martin Co.	War Dept. says two Army officers will go to Air Associates to supervise the reinstatement of strikers at the Bendix, N.J. plant .... FDR confers with Lewis at the White House and asks him to reopen the struck coal mines pending consideration of the UMW's union shop demand by the NDMB.		ASCAP signs contracts in N.Y. permitting NBC and CBS to use its songs for the first time since Jan. 1.	Oct. 29
	Lindbergh tells a N.Y. America First rally that FDR is practicing "dictatorship and subterfuge" to lead the U.S. into war .... Hadassah, Women's Zionist Organization of America, adopts resolutions urging the formation of an armed Jewish corps in the Near East and attacking Britain's curtailment of Jewish immigration to Palestine.	Lewis calls off the four-day coal mine strike until Nov. 15 to give the NDMB time to settle the union shop dispute .... FDR orders the Army to take over the Air Associates plant after nonstrikers clash with returning strikers .... Twenty persons are killed aboard an American Airlines plane that crashes near St. Thomas, Ont. Fourteen persons are killed when a Northwest Airlines plane crashes near Moorhead, Minn.		NBC and CBS file suit in N.Y. to restrain the FCC from putting into effect its "anti-monopoly" rules Nov. 15 .... Filisteo, a seven-year-old bay from Argentina, sets a new world record of 3 minutes 30:4.5 seconds for two miles and 70 yards at Pimlico, Baltimore.	Oct. 30
	Sen. George Aiken (R, Vt.), opposing amendments to the Neutrality Act, declares that "by ordering convoys .... President Roosevelt is personally responsible for whatever lives may have been lost" in the sinking of the *Reuben James*. Sen. Connally demands Congress "avenge" this "dastardly act of aggression."	Soldiers occupy the Air Associates plant. By midafternoon every shop is back in operation .... Sen. Harry S. Truman (D, Mo.) scores the government's contract with Alcoa to build and operate four aluminum plants for national defense as "just about the worst contract the government signed."	A severe snow and rain storm sweeps parts of Nebraska, Kansas, Iowa and Wisconsin, causing heavy property damage and disrupting communications .... Eight persons are dead in an Oklahoma flood which leaves 2,000 homeless and ruins $10 million worth of crops.	Welterweight Ray Robinson defeats Fritzie Zivic in N.Y. for his 26th pro victory with no defeats.	Oct. 31
	Knox declares "we are in this fight to the finish." He calls the sinking of U.S. ships "worse than piracy." .... Former U.S. Amb. to Russia Joseph E. Davies states that the "treason trials and purges from 1935 to 1938 .... indicates the amazing far-sightedness of Stalin .... There can be no doubt that these defendants were .... in the employ of the German and Japanese high commands."	House Banking Comm. approves a commodity price-control bill after rejecting an amendment to include wages, and sends it to the House floor.			Nov. 1
	FDR issues an executive order placing the entire Coast Guard under the orders of Navy Secy. Knox .... CP Chmn. William Z. Foster declares the U.S. should "scrap the Neutrality Act and enter into a full military alliance" with the USSR and Britain.	Brig. Gen. Philip B. Fleming, wage and hour administrator, signs five orders increasing the minimum wage rates for about 320,000 workers in the shoe, furniture, jewelry, gray iron foundry and lumber industries.			Nov. 2
James Mulloy, a former associate of of Sen. William Langer (R, N.D.), testifies before the Senate Elections Comm. that he acted as Langer's intermediary in a 1935 attempt to bribe a federal judge .... Howard C. Hopson, former president of Associated Gas & Electric System, pleads guilty in N.Y. to income tax evasion and is sentenced to a two-year prison term	Hull says that if Finland wishes to maintain U.S. friendship it must halt its invasion of Russia and withdraw its troops from Russian soil .... Navy Dept. announces it will build 50 convoy-escort warships in Navy yards for Britain out of Lend-Lease funds at a total cost of $300 million .... Sens. Francis Maloney (D, Conn.) and Theodore Bilbo (D, Miss.) announce their opposition to amending the Neutrality Act.				Nov. 3
Mayor Fiorello H. La Guardia of N.Y.C. is reelected for a third term, defeating Dist. Atty. William O'Dwyer .... Communist Peter V. Cacchione of Brooklyn is elected under the proportional representation system to the N.Y. City Council, its first CP member in history .... Colgate W. Darden, Jr. (D) is elected governor of Virginia, defeating GOP, Socialist and Communist candidates.	Sen. Taft scores the U.S. warning to Finland to cease "a war which is essentially a defensive war for democracy." .... Gallup Poll reports 81% of voters questioned said they favor amending the Neutrality Act to permit American merchant ships to be armed .... British Amb. Halifax is hit by an egg in Detroit during a demonstration by "The American Mothers."	A dispute between the AFL iron workers and boilermakers unions halts construction at the Navy's destroyer base in San Diego. A welders' strike curtails operations at shipyards in Los Angeles.	Dr. Carl Voegtlin, director of the National Cancer Institute, and Dr. C.P. Rhoads of the Memorial Hospital, N.Y. report that their discoveries of significant respiratory differences between cancer cells and normal cells may lead to a new chemical approach in the fight against cancer.	Women writers win all four O. Henry Memorial Awards for the best short stories from August 1940 to July 1941. Kay Boyle and Eudora Welty are the two top prize winners .... Dolph Camilli, first baseman of the Brooklyn Dodgers, is chosen by the Baseball Writers Assn. as the most valuable NL player of 1941.	Nov. 4
F *Includes elections, federal-state relations, civil rights and liberties, crime, the judiciary, education, health care, poverty, urban affairs and population.*	G *Includes formation and debate of U.S. foreign and defense policies, veterans affairs and defense spending. (Relations with specific foreign countries are usually found under the region concerned.)*	H *Includes business, labor, agriculture, taxation, transportation, consumer affairs, monetary and fiscal policy, natural resources, pollution and accidents.*	I *Includes worldwide scientific, medical and technological developments, natural phenomena, U.S. weather and natural disasters.*	J *Includes the arts, religion, scholarship, communications media, sports, entertainment, fashions, fads and social life.*	

	World Affairs	European War Zone	Pacific War Zone	The Americas	Other Countries & Territories
Nov. 5		German command announces its forces have penetrated the Crimean Mountains in Southern Crimea and reached the Black Sea between Yalta and Theodosia.	Japanese government announces that Saburo Kurusu has been ordered to Washington to assist Amb. Kichisaburo Nomura in an effort to reach a settlement with the U.S.	White House announces FDR and Canadian P.M. William Mackenzie King agreed at their recent Hyde Park conference to set up a Joint Defense Production Comm. to coordinate the production of defense material .... Chile announces that so far 11 Latin American governments have agreed to make a joint protest to Germany against the execution of hostages in occupied countries.	
Nov. 6	FDR tells 250 delegates from 33 nations at the final session of the ILO that "the American people have made an unlimited commitment that there shall be a free world." He scores the few industrialists and labor leaders "who place their little victories over one another above triumph against Hitlerism."	Stalin, addressing the Supreme Soviet in Moscow, declares that a second front will "undoubtedly" be created on the European continent soon. He calls for "the extermination to the last man of all Germans who have penetrated the territory of our native land .... Death to the German invaders!" .... Maxim Litvinov is appointed Soviet ambassador to the U.S. to succeed Constantine A. Oumansky.		Panamanian government bans Japanese commercial establishments.	Grand Mufti of Jeruslaem, Haj Amin el Husseini, arrives in Berlin from Rome and is hailed by a government spokesman as a "great man."
Nov. 7		In a speech at Hull, Churchill declares America "is straining every nerve to equip us with all we need to carry on the struggle regardless of the cost to them or the risks to their sailors or ships." .... Helsinki radio rejects U.S. and British demands that Finland end its invasion of Russia.		Cuban Pres. Fulgencio Batista signs decrees granting workers a general wage increase of 10 to 25% .... Secy. Hull and Cuban Amb. Aurelio F. Concheso sign a Lend-Lease agreement for an unspecified amount of defense materials.	
Nov. 8		Hitler says in a Munich speech that he has ordered German warships to fire on American ships only if attacked. He declares, "The German officer who does not defend himself I will place before a court martial." .... British announce their bombers carried out the greatest aerial offensive of the war last night and today, ranging from Oslo, Norway to the Italian air base at Brindisi. Five hundred planes took part in raids on Germany.		Japan announces it has protested to Panama against "discriminatory racial treatment" in the closing of Japanese businesses there.	
Nov. 9		British claim that two Italian convoys comprising 10 merchant ships and a destroyer were sunk today south of Taranto by British surface vessels after a battle with Italian warships .... For the first time since the invasion of Russia June 22, many German Catholic clergymen denounce Bolshevism in sermons and uphold the war as a drive against Bolshevist ideology .... Vichy announces new laws granting subsidies to church primary schools.		Hull announces that 519 pro-Axis firms and individuals in Latin America have been added to the U.S. trade blacklist and that 59 names have been deleted.	Reuters reports that Fakhri Bey Nashashibi, pro-British Arab leader in Palestine, has been assassinated in Baghdad, Iraq.
Nov. 10		Churchill says that "should the U.S. become involved in war with Japan, a British declaration of war will follow within the hour." He adds that the "Lend-Lease bill must be regarded without question as the most unsordid act in the whole of recorded history." .... Gen. Sir Archibald Wavell says in New Delhi that he was fully responsible for the British retreat in Libya last spring when "the enemy attacked at least a month before I had expected it possible."	Finance Min. Okinori Kaya tells the National Financial Council that Japan aims "to force Britain and the United States to retreat from East Asia." .... T.T. Tsiang, Chinese government spokesman, says the U.S., Britain, China and the Netherlands have agreed on measures to meet "Japan's next move in the Pacific."	Pres. Pedro Aguirre Cerda of Chile temporarily resigns his office because of ill health and turns over his executive powers to Vice Pres. Geronimo Mendez, Radical Party leader.	Indian government announces that Subhas Chandra Bose, left-wing leader of Mohandas K. Gandhi's All-India Congress Party, is now believed to be in Berlin or Rome.
Nov. 11		Finnish government sends a note to Washington rejecting the U.S. warning to halt the invasion of Russia or lose American friendship .... British claim seven more Italian ships were sunk by British submarines in the Mediterranean following the sinking of two convoys Nov. 9.	Japanese press denounces Churchill's warning as a British plot to involve the U.S. in a war in the Pacific.		Early returns indicate that Pres. Manuel L. Quezon of the Philippines was re-elected by a wide margin for another four-year term on the Nacionalista Party ticket in today's election.

	A	B	C	D	E
	Includes developments that affect more than one world region, international organizations and important meetings of major world leaders.	*Includes all developments in European countries and military engagements between Allied and Axis powers in Africa and at sea.*	*Includes all developments in Japan and China, Japanese foreign policy and military actions in the Pacific region.*	*Includes all domestic and regional developments in Latin America, the Caribbean and Canada.*	*Includes developments in those independent nations and colonial possessions not covered in Columns B, C and D.*

U.S. Politics & Social Issues	U.S. Foreign Policy & Defense	U.S. Economy & Environment	Science, Technology & Nature	Culture, Leisure & Life Style	
	N.Y. Herald Tribune reports the naval government of Guam has ordered the families of U.S. naval personnel stationed there to return home because of growing tension in the Far East .... Sen. Wheeler attacks the proposal to amend the Neutrality Act in a five-hour Senate speech.	FDR's fact-finding board, headed by Wayne L. Morse, recommends that the railroads increase the wages of 1,150,000 employes by a total of $270 million from Sept. 1, 1941 to Dec. 31, 1942 .... A dispute between the independent United Aircraft Welders Assn. and the AFL International Association of Machinists halts work at Lockheed Aircraft Corp. plants in southern California .... War Dept. announces it will take over the branches and warehouses of Air Associates Inc.	Edwin H. Land of the Polaroid Corp. reports he has perfected a new secret material that permits the photographing of two superimposed pictures on the same film. He says it makes three-dimensional still and motion pictures practical .... Drs. Charles H. Rammelkamp and Chester S. Keefer of the Boston Univ. School of Medicine report on experiments with a powerful new healing substance, called tyrothrycin or gramicidin, which may be used in healing local infections without harming the tissues.		Nov. 5
Rep. Dewey Short (R, Mo.) denounces Willkie as a "bellicose, bombinating blowhard unfit to lead any party." He says Willkie "is seeking to split the Republican Party wide open."	State Dept. discloses the text of FDR's Oct. 30th letter to Stalin, pledging Russia $1 billion in Lend-Lease aid. Stalin accepted Nov. 4 .... Navy Dept. announces that 100 men were lost aboard the destroyer *Reuben James* on Oct. 30 .... Rep. Hamilton Fish (R, N.Y.) introduces a resolution stating that Congress should decide a state of war between the U.S. and Germany should be formally declared. The move is intended to force a congressional vote on the war issue.	Hillman denounces the welders' strike at the Lockheed, Vega and Consolidated aviation plants in California as "an outlaw, wildcat proposition and a definite interference with national defense." .... George E. Browne and Willie Bioff, leaders of the International Alliance of Theatrical Stage Employes, are found guilty in N.Y. on three counts of extorting $1.2 million from the movie industry.		Richard Dana Skinner, writer and economist who was the founder and former dramatic editor of *The Commonweal*, dies in Norwalk, Conn. .... Aldo (Buff) Donelli resigns as coach of the Pittsburgh Steelers professional football team.	Nov. 6
Mayor John F. Aszkler and four councilmen of Lackawanna, N.Y. resign before they receive one-year suspended prison sentences in Buffalo for conspiracy to defraud the city by padding WPA payrolls.	Senate votes, 50 to 37, to amend the Neutrality Act and permit American merchant ships to arm themselves and enter belligerent ports.	Executives of the "Big Five" operating brotherhoods with 350,000 members announce they have rejected the recommendations of FDR's fact-finding board for a temporary 7½% wage increase and will call a railroad strike Dec. 7 .... FDR names a fact-finding board to investigate the Detroit dispute between the Teamsters and the Railway Clerks over jurisdiction in the Railway Express Agency .... Navy informs striking AFL workers at San Diego base that, if they do not return to work, contractors will be permitted to hire other workers and, if necessary, the government "will take over the entire work."	Bette Davis is elected first woman president of the Academy of Motion Picture Arts and Sciences in Hollywood	Elmer Rice is re-elected president of the Dramatists Guild for a two-year term.	Nov. 7
Atty. Gen. Francis Biddle asks the House Judiciary Comm. to impeach J. Warren Davis, retired Federal judge, on charges of misconduct.	Knox announces that a Navy base has been established on Iceland with Rear Adm. James L. Kauffman as commandant.	AFL Teamsters Pres. Daniel Tobin rejects FDR's appeal that he call off the union's strike in Detroit.		U.S. Army team posts a perfect score in the international military jumping event to win the Intra-American Trophy at the National Horse Show in N.Y.	Nov. 8
		Pennsylvania Railroad's luxury *Pennsylvanian* passenger train crashes at Dunkirk, Ohio. Twelve are killed and 42 injured.		Italian Sen. Gaetano Mosca, 83, world-renowned political scientist, dies in Rome.	Nov. 9
The House unanimously adopts a resolution instructing Rep. Hamilton Fish to ignore a summons to appear before a federal grand jury investigating Nazi propaganda until the House Judiciary Comm. rules on whether it "invades the rights and privileges of the House." .... Supreme Court rules unanimously, in its first decision under Chief Justice Harlan F. Stone, that Alabama has the right to impose 2% sales and use taxes on materials bought for government defense projects by contractors.		NDMB votes, 9 to 2, to reject the CIO-UMW's demand for a closed shop in mines struck Oct. 27-30 .... More than 2,000 AFL construction workers strike in San Diego for a $1-a-day wage increase, tying up work on $23 million worth of Navy and Marine Corps projects .... Tobin orders striking Teamsters to return to work at the Detroit Railway Express Agency.			Nov. 10
	Knox says that although the U.S. has sought to avoid war with Japan "there comes a time ... when vital and essential rights can no longer be ignored ... The hour of decision is here."	CIO Pres. Philip Murray and UMW Secretary-Treasurer Thomas Kennedy resign from the NDMB in protest over the mines decision .... AFL building craftsmen are ordered by their leaders to return to work at noon tomorrow after striking on $23 million worth of Navy and Marine construction in San Diego yesterday.		Joe DiMaggio, center fielder of the N.Y. Yankees, is chosen by the Baseball Writers Assn. as the most valuable AL player of 1941.	Nov. 11
F *Includes elections, federal-state relations, civil rights and liberties, crime, the judiciary, education, health care, poverty, urban affairs and population.*	G *Includes formation and debate of U.S. foreign and defense policies, veterans affairs and defense spending. (Relations with specific foreign countries are usually found under the region concerned.)*	H *Includes business, labor, agriculture, taxation, transportation, consumer affairs, monetary and fiscal policy, natural resources, pollution and accidents.*	I *Includes worldwide scientific, medical and technological developments, natural phenomena, U.S. weather and natural disasters.*	J *Includes the arts, religion, scholarship, communications media, sports, entertainment, fashions, fads and social life.*	

	World Affairs	European War Zone	Pacific War Zone	The Americas	Other Countries & Territories
Nov. 12		German U-boat torpedoes the British carrier *Ark Royal*, which later sinks in the Mediterranean . . . . Churchill tells the House of Commons that the Allies will be possessed of large quantities of ships in 1943, which will enable overseas operations to take place.		Arthur Meighen accepts the position of Conservative Party leader in Canada. He urges that conscripts be used for service overseas. P.M. Mackenzie King opposes the idea . . . . Cuban Confederation of Workers votes to accept the government's wage offer and call off the strike of sugar mill workers.	
Nov. 13		German Propaganda Min. Goebbels says the Jews "are suffering no injustice in the treatment we bestow on them—they more than earned it." He adds, "In this historical showdown, every Jew is our enemy." . . . . German command announces its troops are attacking the Kerch fortifications on the eastern tip of Crimea.	A Chinese spokesman says in Chungking that 130 to 140 Japanese warships and more than 100 troop transports have been massed at Hainan Island, presumably for an attack on Indochina.		Premier U Maung Saw of Burma, arriving in N.Y., says that he was disappointed at having failed to obtain postwar dominion status for his country while in London.
Nov. 14				Chilean Radical, Socialist, Democratic and Communist parties agree to give the Popular Front government of Pres. Geronimo Mendez their full support.	Sir Girjz Shankar Bajpzi, the first agent general of India to visit the U.S., arrives in N.Y.
Nov. 15	Professor James T. Shotwell of Columbia Univ. urges the postwar establishment of a worldwide organization for cultural and intellectual cooperation.	Moscow radio reports 20 boatloads of German troops attempting a surprise landing on the Murmansk coast in the far North were sunk.	Saburo Kurusu, special Japanese envoy, says upon his arrival in Washington, "I think I have a fighting chance to make a success of my mission." . . . . P.M. Mackenzie King announces in Ottawa that a Canadian force commanded by Brigadier J.K. Lawson has arrived in Hong Kong.		Pres. Manuel L. Quezon say in Manila that the Philippines will fully cooperate with the U.S. to "save democracy and banish the totalitarians from the face of the earth."
Nov. 16		Russian press reports that U.S. P-40 fighters have gone into action on the Moscow front. Berlin admits winter weather is bogging down the German drive on Moscow and Leningrad.	Emperor Hirohito formally opens the extraordinary session of the Diet in Toyko with a message urging cooperation with Premier Gen. Hideki Tojo's government.	German Foreign Office refuses to accept a protest by the Mexican government against the reprisal executions of French hostages.	Israel M. Sieff, British philanthropist, says the Palestinian Arabs should be resettled in Iraq or anywhere else within the Middle East to clear the way for Jewish immigrants after the war.
Nov. 17		German command announces the capture of Kerch, on the eastern coast of Crimea . . . . Dr. Alfred Rosenberg's appointment as minister for the East or chief civilian administrator of occupied Russian territory is confirmed in Berlin.	Premier Tojo outlines a three-point program before the Japanese Diet, indicating that the success of U.S.-Japanese peace talks depends on its fulfillment. He calls for a free hand in China, an end to the "economic blockade" of Japan and efforts to prevent the spread of the European war to East Asia . . . . FDR receives special Japanese envoy Kurusu at the White House.		
Nov. 18		Lt. Gen. Sir Alan Brooke is named to replace Chief of the Imperial General Staff Gen. Sir John G. Dill when the latter retires on his 60th birthday Dec. 25.	Japanese Diet adopts a resolution stating that the nation's policy has been fixed in support of the creation of an "East Asia cooperative sphere".	About 100 persons are reported killed when a landslide wipes out the village of Mongua in northern Colombia . . . . Inter-American Conference of the Comm. on Intellectual Cooperation in Havana adopts a resolution protesting against Nazi mistreatment of civilians in conquered countries.	

A	B	C	D	E
Includes developments that affect more than one world region, international organizations and important meetings of major world leaders.	*Includes all developments in European countries and military engagements between Allied and Axis powers in Africa and at sea.*	*Includes all developments in Japan and China, Japanese foreign policy and military actions in the Pacific region.*	*Includes all domestic and regional developments in Latin America, the Caribbean and Canada.*	*Includes developments in those independent nations and colonial possessions not covered in Columns B, C and D.*

U.S. Politics & Social Issues	U.S. Foreign Policy & Defense	U.S. Economy & Environment	Science, Technology & Nature	Culture, Leisure & Life Style	
	Atty. Gen. Biddle says that the Depts. of War and Justice have prepared plans for the control of aliens in time of war. He says the situation among the Japanese on the Pacific Coast is "very serious." .... Curtiss-Wright Corp. announces it has developed a new pursuit plane, known as the P-40-F, with fire power equivalent to 12 to 14 machine guns, and a top speed of nearly 400 mph .... Southern Democrats announce their opposition in the House to the Senate resolution amending the Neutrality Act unless the Administration takes firmer steps to curb defense strikes.	CIO leaders James B. Carey and John Brophy resign from the NDMB in protest against the mines decision. Other CIO unions withdraw their cases before the board .... Striking welders at the Lockheed, Vega and Consolidated aviation plants in southern California vote to return to work after the NLRB refuses to order an election .... Willie Bioff and George E. Browne are sentenced to 10 and eight-year prison terms, respectively, for extortion. In San Diego 2,000 AFL construction workers resume work.		National Women's Party dedicates the world's first feminist library in Washington on the 126th anniversary of the birth of Elizabeth Cady Stanton, pioneer campaigner for equal rights .... U.S. Army team wins the International Military Perpetual Challenge Trophy for the third successive year in a jump-off with the Cuban team at the National Horse Show in N.Y.	Nov. 12
N.Y. Gov. Herbert H. Lehman appoints Michael A. Hughes (D) as mayor of Lackawanna following the resignation of Mayor John Aszkler, convicted of conspiring to defraud the city.	House votes, 212 to 194, to accept the Senate's amendments to the Neutrality Act, permiting U.S. merchant ships to be armed and to enter combat zones or belligerent ports .... Knox says the Navy is ready to supply guns and trained crews for arming merchant ships .... Gen. George C. Marshall announces that the Army is seeking 10,000 regular troops to relieve U.S. Marines and British soldiers in Iceland.	Reps. E.E. Cox (D, Ga.) and Howard W. Smith (D. Va.), members of the House Rules Comm., announce they will block further Administration legislation unless an antistrike bill is introduced.		NBC and MBS cancel the broadcasts of their Berlin correspondents on the grounds that undue Nazi censorship deprives their news reports of any value.	Nov. 13
House Judiciary Comm. reports the grand jury summons to Rep. Fish invades the rights and privileges of the House, but that the House may waive its privileges if it desires .... State Dept. announces a series of regulations requiring aliens to obtain exit permits to leave the country and tightening the procedure for the issuance of entrance visas.	FDR announces the 970 U.S. Marines in Shanghai, Tientsin and Peking will be withdrawn at once in view of the serious Far East situation.	FDR declares to John L. Lewis and other CIO and steel company leaders that the government "will not order, nor will Congress pass legislation ordering a so-called closed shop." .... NDMB rejects AFL demands for union shops or strong union security clauses in cases involving the Pascagoula yard of the Ingalls Shipbuilding Corp. and the International Harvester Co. .... Morgenthau urges a billion dollars be cut from non-defense spending for 1944.	Drs. Christian T. Elvey, Polydore Swings and Horace W. Babcock, Univ. of Chicago astronomers, announce they have discovered and identified two new cosmic gases in the tail of the Cunningham Comet by means of ultra-violet spectroscopy .... A severe earthquake shakes Torrance and Gardena, suburbs of Los Angeles, causing an estimated $300,000 worth of damage.	Germany bans reporters for NBC, CBS and MBS from broadcasting because they "submitted to their home companies unjustified complaints" without stating their grievances to Nazi authorities .... Gus Lesnevich, world light-heavyweight champion, defeats Tami Mauriello in a 15-round title bout in N.Y.	Nov. 14
	Five GOP congressmen leave N.Y. for Britain to study war conditions.	A conference of 100 congressmen and highway experts, meeting in Atlantic City, N.J., authorizes the appointment of a 10-man committee to consider plans for the construction of a $50-billion federal coast-to-coast super-highway after the war .... West Coast and Southern welders refuse to take part in an OPM mediation conference until discrimination against returning strikers is ended .... Morgenthau tells the National Grange that American farmers will have to feed "hundreds of millions throughout the continents of Europe and Asia" after Hitler is defeated.	The cornerstone for the $1 million RCA Laboritories, expected to be the world's largest radio-electronic research center, is laid on a 300-acre site three miles southeast of Princeton Univ.		Nov. 15
	Federal Security Admin. Paul V. McNutt says at a N.Y. anti-Nazi rally that "the showdown is daily nearer" between the U.S. and the Axis .... The attacking 1st Army of 200,000 men and the defending 4th Army of 110,000 men begin two weeks of war games in North and South Carolina.	The coal conference in Washington between UMW officials and three steel executives fails to reach an agreement on the union's demand for a union shop in coal mines owned by steel firms.			Nov. 16
House "authorizes" Rep. Fish to appear before the grand jury if he desires when the House is not in session .... Sen. George W. Norris (Ind, Neb.), 80, announces he will retire when his present term expires in January 1943.	FDR signs the congressional resolution repealing sections of the Neutrality Act which have prohibited American merchant ships from mounting guns or entering war zones .... Michael Wiliam Etzel is sentenced by Federal Judge William C. Coleman in Baltimore to a 15-year prison term for sabotaging bombers at the Glenn L. Martin Co.	For the third time since Sept. 15, 53,000 UMW members strke for a union shop in coal mines owned by steel companies in Pa., W.Va., Ala., Ky., and Ill. .... Sen. Tom Connally introduces a bill to give the President increased power to take over defense plants or mines tied up by strikes and to freeze open or closed shops for the duration of the emergency.		Lawrence Di Benedette is re-elected national president of the AAU.	Nov. 17
House rejects, 167 to 141, the alien detention bill, which would have enabled the Justice Dept. to hold non-deportable aliens for 150 days and criminal aliens for life.	Knox announces that merchant ships sailing to Britain and Russia will be the first to be armed by the Navy.	FDR says in a message to the CIO convention meeting in Detroit that war material must be produced "without delay and without interruption." The convention passes a resolution backing all-out aid to the Allies .... Willkie warns labor unions against "bringing down the wrath of the people upon you" and urges that the closed shop issue be settled after the emergency is over.		Tommy Manville Jr., 47, millionaire asbestos heir, and Bonita Francine Edwards, 22, are married in Ridgefield, Conn. It is his fifth marriage.	Nov. 18
F *Includes elections, federal-state relations, civil rights and liberties, crime, the judiciary, education, health care, poverty, urban affairs and population.*	G *Includes formation and debate of U.S. foreign and defense policies, veterans affairs and defense spending. (Relations with specific foreign countries are usually found under the region concerned.)*	H *Includes business, labor, agriculture, taxation, transportation, consumer affairs, monetary and fiscal policy, natural resources, pollution and accidents.*	I *Includes worldwide scientific, medical and technological developments, natural phenomena, U.S. weather and natural disasters.*	J *Includes the arts, religion, scholarship, communications media, sports, entertainment, fashions, fads and social life.*	

	World Affairs	European War Zone	Pacific War Zone	The Americas	Other Countries & Territories
Nov. 19		British command in Cairo announces that British forces began a general offensive into Libya at dawn yesterday, advancing more than 50 miles the first day .... German forces, which began large-scale offensives against Moscow and Rostov yesterday, are today reported to have made some progress on both fronts.	Japan reports one Russian soldier was killed and two were captured Nov. 16 when they crossed the Soviet-Japanese frontier about 30 miles from Manchuli in Manchukuo.	Hull and Mexican Amb. Francisco Castillo Najera sign an economic agreement providing for compensation for U.S. oil property expropriated in 1938.	
Nov. 20		Vichy announces that Gen. Maxime Weygand has "retired." U.S. sources say Weygand's ouster had been demanded by Hitler .... British command announces that the British 8th Army has driven 80 miles into Libya and captured Rezegh, 10 miles from the outer Tobruk forts.	Nineteen members resign from the Japanese Imperial Rule Assistance League in protest against its curb on debate of domestic policy in the Diet.	U.S. Amb. Claude G. Bowers tells Chilean Interior Min. Leonardo Guzman that he repudiates as an "outrage" *Time* Magazine's derogatory article on Pres. Aguirre Cerda .... Brazilian government prohibits the circulation of German newspapers from abroad in Rio Grande do Sul, Santa Catharina and Parano states.	
Nov. 21		Rostov at the mouth of the Don is captured by the Germans.	Japanese Diet adjourns by order of Emperor Hirohito after passing all 13 government bills.	W.S. Farish, president of the Standard Oil Co. of N.J., announces that the U.S. oil companies whose properties were expropriated by Mexico in 1938 have rejected the U.S.-Mexican oil pact.	
Nov. 22				Chilean Interior Min. Leonardo Guzman and Defense Min. Carlos Valdovinos resign .... Panamanian government bans the circulation of anti-democratic propaganda.	
Nov. 23	German news agency announces 13 powers will attend a conference in Berlin beginning Nov. 25 to discuss the renewal and extension of the Anti-Comintern Pact.	Russian dispatches concede Soviet troops are giving ground at Tula, Mozhaisk and Kiln before the all-out German offensive .... The British announce the capture of Bardia and Sidi Omar Nuovo in Libya.		Pres. Batista of Cuba predicts in Havana that the U.S. will declare war by next spring and that "Cuba will be the first nation to enter the war on her side."	Emanuel Neumann, Zionist leader, charges that "conspiring and intriguing British bureaucrats" have "sabotaged" plans to create a Jewish army in Palestine.
Nov. 24		Germans claim to have captured a village 31 miles from Moscow .... British announce that New Zealand forces have captured Gambut, an Axis supply base midway between Bardia and Tobruk on the Libyan coast.	U.S. consulate in Saigon, French Indochina is wrecked by a bomb but no one is injured.	The White House announces U.S. troops have been sent to Dutch Guiana to help Dutch troops protect the bauxite mines .... Ecuadorian government announces Ecuador and Peru will free all prisoners captured during the recent border conflict .... Panama City police arrest nine persons on charges of preparing to overthrow the government of President Ricardo Adolfo de la Guardia.	
Nov. 25	Representatives of 12 nations sign a protocol in Berlin renewing the Anti-Comintern Pact of 1936 for five years.	Moscow radio reports that counter-attacking Russian troops have driven the Germans back 62 miles at some points in the Rostov sector of the Donets Basin .... Adm. Sir Roger Keyes, recently removed as commander of British commandos, says in the House of Commons that the War Office blocked "every worthwhile offensive action I tried to undertake." .... An earthquake described by the director of the Lisbon Observatory as "the most violent recorded since 1755" rocks the Portuguese and Spanish coasts and Madeira and the Azores.	Japanese carrier task force sails from home waters to launch the attack on Pearl Harbor.	Pedro Aguirre Cerda, 62, Chile's former "New Deal" president, dies two weeks after he resigned because of ill health .... FDR apologizes to Chile for *Time* Magazine's derogatory article on the resignation of Pres. Aguirre Cerda.	
	A	B	C	D	E
	Includes developments that affect more than one world region, international organizations and important meetings of major world leaders.	*Includes all developments in European countries and military engagements between Allied and Axis powers in Africa and at sea.*	*Includes all developments in Japan and China, Japanese foreign policy and military actions in the Pacific region.*	*Includes all domestic and regional developments in Latin America, the Caribbean and Canada.*	*Includes developments in those independent nations and colonial possessions not covered in Columns B, C and D.*

U.S. Politics & Social Issues	U.S. Foreign Policy & Defense	U.S. Economy & Environment	Science, Technology & Nature	Culture, Leisure & Life Style	
Seven members of the Georgia Board of Regents meeting in Atlanta vote to reinstate 10 university educators ousted by Gov. Eugene Talmadge .... The Workers Alliance announces that it has disbanded as a national organization.	*N.Y. Herald Tribune* reports Hull told Adm. Nomura and Saburo Kurusu that Japan must withdraw from the Axis and renounce further aggression as a basis for a general settlement of Pacific problems.	FDR urges the steel companies and UMW to immediately settle the coal mine strike, either by allowing the matter of the closed shop to remain in status quo during the national emergency or submitting this point to arbitration. The steel companies offer to accept either proposal, but John L. Lewis rejects both .... About 92,000 miners halt work in the Eastern coal regions in sympathy with strikers in mines owned by steel firms .... Supporters of Pres. Murray are involved in fistfights with backers of Lewis at the CIO convention.		Silliman Evans, publisher, announces that Marshall Field's new Chicago paper will be known as the *Chicago Sun*.... Jackie Wilson defeats Richie Lemos in a 12-round bout in Los Angeles to win the National Boxing Assn. featherweight title.	Nov. 19
		CIO convention passes a resolution denouncing the OPM for its "vicious abuse of authority" in rejecting the Currier Lumber Co.'s housing bid and urging FDR to nullify the "discriminatory" no-strike building stabilization agreement with the AFL.	Dr. Adrian Van Maanen of Mount Wilson Observatory, Pasadena, Calif., reports the discovery of 24 small stars, some of them 1,000 times as faint as the sun, in the Pleiades constellation, raising the total to 211.	*Reader's Digest* reports its monthly circulation has reached five million, the highest ever attained by a magazine .... Lincoln Borglum announces that work on the heads of Washington, Jefferson, Lincoln and Theodore Roosevelt carved into Mount Rushmore has been completed.	Nov. 20
J. Warren Davis, retired federal judge, submits his resignation to FDR.	Secy. Hull and Thor Thors, Icelandic minister to the U.S., sign a Lend-Lease agreement. The U.S. will assume Britain's financial obligations to Iceland, amounting to some $20 million a year .... The 35,000-ton battleship *Indiana*, the third to be launched this year and the 20th in the Navy, is launched six months ahead of schedule at Newport News, Va.	Philip Murray is unanimously re-elected president of the CIO. He declares labor will fight any legislative attempt to bar strikes or freeze wages .... Eleven pickets are wounded when non-strikers open fire on 150 strikers at a coal mine in Edenborn, Pa..... FDR reluctantly signs the $587-million defense highway bill despite his earlier veto of a very similar bill.			Nov. 21
	Hull confers in Washington with Viscount Halifax (Britain), Dr. Hu Shih (China), Richard G. Casey (Australia) and Dr. A. Loudon (Netherlands) concerning the Far Eastern situation.	Lewis and the UMW policy committee accept FDR's appointment of a three-man commission to arbitrate the UMW's demand for a union shop, and order miners to return to work immediately .... CIO convention adjourns after adopting resolutions scoring the FBI as "political police" and the NLRB as biased against CIO unions .... OPM is authorized by an executive order signed by FDR to seize property required for national defense.	Dr. Leslie A. Chambers and Werner Henle of the Univ. of Pennsylvania show the first photographs ever made of the influenza virus type A, which were taken with an electron microscope and show the virus to be four ten-millionths of an inch in diameter.		Nov. 22
		Sen. Robert F. Wagner (D, N.Y.), sponsor of the NLRA, warns labor in a N.Y. broadcast that public opinion will not tolerate defense strikes.		New York Giants defeat the Washington Redskins, 20 to 13, in N.Y. to win their sixth championship in the Eastern Division of the NFL.	Nov. 23
Supreme Court rules unanimously that the California Anti-Migrant Act, which bars indigent migrants, "is an unconstitutional barrier to interstate commerce." .... Federal Judge Guy Bard dismisses the indictments of former Judge J. Warren Davis and Morgan S. Kaufman on charges of conspiring to obstruct justice.	*Time* Magazine reports U.S. officials believe the chances are "nine-to-ten that Japan and the U.S. will go to war." .... U.S. Circuit Court of Appeals rules members of the Iroquois delegation Confederacy are citizens and subject to military service .... Free French delegation announces in N.Y. that the U.S. has agreed to extend Lend-Lease aid to the armies of Gen. de Gaulle in Africa and Syria.	Reps. E.E. Cox (D, Ga.) and Jesse P. Wolcott (R, Mich.) denounce the Steagall price control bill, claiming it would make Leon Henderson a one-man "dictatorship-plus." .... FDR discusses possible antistrike legislation with GOP and Democratic congressional leaders at the White House.			Nov. 24
	FDR announces he is sending William C. Bullitt to the Near East as his special representative.	FDR requests his emergency fact-finding board, headed by Wayne L. Morse, to meet again in an attempt to settle the railroad wage dispute.		Providence, R.I. bans the showing of *Two-Faced Woman*, starring Greta Garbo, after the Legion of Decency denounces it as "immoral." .... Lou Boudreau, 24-year-old shortstop, signs a two-year contract as playing manager of the Cleveland Indians.	Nov. 25

F	G	H	I	J
Includes elections, federal-state relations, civil rights and liberties, crime, the judiciary, education, health care, poverty, urban affairs and population.	*Includes formation and debate of U.S. foreign and defense policies, veterans affairs and defense spending. (Relations with specific foreign countries are usually found under the region concerned.)*	*Includes business, labor, agriculture, taxation, transportation, consumer affairs, monetary and fiscal policy, natural resources, pollution and accidents.*	*Includes worldwide scientific, medical and technological developments, natural phenomena, U.S. weather and natural disasters.*	*Includes the arts, religion, scholarship, communications media, sports, entertainment, fashions, fads and social life.*

	World Affairs	European War Zone	Pacific War Zone	The Americas	Other Countries & Territories
Nov. 26		Russians recapture Rostov and drive the German troops on the southern front back 50 miles to the Mius River .... Dispatches report German forces are driving toward Stalinogorsk, 120 miles southeast of Moscow, in an apparent attempt to encircle the capital.		Canadian Justice Min. Ernest Lapointe, 65, dies in Montreal .... Panama orders the arrest of Third Vice Pres. Anibal Rios, now in Colombia, on charges of peculation while he was minister of education.	Lebanese government issues a proclamation in Beirut declaring the independence of Lebanon under Free French and British protection.
Nov. 27		Berlin spokesmen claim German forces have broken through Russian lines in the Tula-Stalinogorsk sector south of Moscow .... British command announces New Zealand forces in Libya joined with British troops from Tobruk at Ed Duda today after recapturing Rezegh .... Three senators and nine deputies lose their parliamentary seats in France because of a Vichy decree barring Jews from elective assemblies.	Premier Luang Bipul Songgram of Thailand says Japan has given assurances that its troop concentrations in Indochina do not indicate an imminent attack on Thailand.	Argentine Foreign Min. Enrique Ruiz-Guinazu and U.S. Amb. Norman Armour reach an agreement in Buenos Aires under which the U.S. Metals Reserve Co. will buy all of Argentina's production of tungsten for three years .... FDR nominates George S. Messersmith to succeed Josephus Daniels as ambassador to Mexico.	
Nov. 28		Rome and Cairo announce that Gondar in northern Ethiopia, the last outpost of Italy's East African Empire, surrendered at 2 p.m. yesterday after 7½ months of siege .... Turkish reports state the Germans have destroyed more than 40 Serbian towns in an attempt to quell guerrilla warfare.	Reports from Shanghai state that 70 transports bearing 30,000 Japanese troops from central China are sailing southward, probably for Haiphong, French Indochina .... Pres. Manuel Quezon says in Manila that, although given emergency powers by the Phillipine Assembly to prepare for civil defense seven months ago, he was asked not to invoke his powers by FDR.	Argentine government bans 3,000 public meetings scheduled for tomorrow by the pro-British Accion Argentina to protest the government's isolationist policies .... Three U.S. ships arrive at Paramaribo, Dutch Guiana with American troops and equipment under the command of Col. Parley D. Parkinson.	
Nov. 29			Domei reports that Japanese planes bombed the Burma Road at Kunming yesterday.		
Nov. 30		British command announces that mechanized patrols have advanced nearly 300 miles across the Libyan desert to the Gulf of Sidra.	Gen. Kisaburo Ando of the Imperial Rule Assistance Assn. declares that Chungking will collapse when the Burma Road is cut.	Acting Pres. Ramon S. Castillo of Argentina reaffirms the government's policy of strict neutrality.	
Dec. 1		Berlin admits the Germans have withdrawn from Rostov in the face of "reckless" attacks by superior Russian forces .... Petain confers with Hermann Goering near Paris .... British admit Gen. Rommel's forces have succeeded in penetrating British defenses at Rezegh and Ed Duda, Libya.	Japanese Foreign Min. Togo says the U.S. is "trying forcibly to apply to East Asiatic countries fantastic principles and rules .... tending to obstruct the construction of the New Order." .... Sir Shenton Thomas proclaims a state of emergency in Singapore and calls out the volunteer land, sea and air force .... A dispatch from Manila says that an American air unit under the Chinese flag will protect the Burma Road supply line to China from Japanese air attacks.		
Dec. 2		British report the Germans yesterday seized Rezegh and Bir el-Hamed and fought their way to Zaafran, cutting the corridor between Rezegh and Tobruk .... Three German divisions reportedly launch a general offensive against guerrilla forces in the western Morava Valley of Yugoslavia .... Sixty persons go on trial in Trieste, Italy on charges of plotting to kill Mussolini in 1938	The first units of the new British Far Eastern Fleet, led by the new battleship *Prince of Wales*, arrive in Singapore .... Japanese cabinet is shuffled, with Foreign Min. Togo turning over his post to Agricultural Min. Miroyasu Ino.		
	A *Includes developments that affect more than one world region, international organizations and important meetings of major world leaders.*	B *Includes all developments in European countries and military engagements between Allied and Axis powers in Africa and at sea.*	C *Includes all developments in Japan and China, Japanese foreign policy and military actions in the Pacific region.*	D *Includes all domestic and regional developments in Latin America, the Caribbean and Canada.*	E *Includes developments in those independent nations and colonial possessions not covered in Columns B, C and D.*

U.S. Politics & Social Issues	U.S. Foreign Policy & Defense	U.S. Economy & Environment	Science, Technology & Nature	Culture, Leisure & Life Style	
	Hull presents the American terms for settlement of U.S.-Japanese problems to Amb. Nomura and Special Envoy Kurusu in Washington .... Senate committee investigating defense contracts hears testimony that waste and nepotism were extensive in the building of a shell-loading plant in Milan, Tenn. Chmn. Harry S. Truman says the evidence is "shocking." .... House defeats Rep. Albert D. Gore's (D, Tenn.) amendment to the price control bill freezing wages, prices, and rents by a vote of 218 to 63 .... AFL Pres. Green, CIO Pres. Murray, CIO Secy. Carey and Norman Thomas express opposition to anti-strike legislation now being considered by the House Labor Comm.			Limited Editions Club awards its gold medal to Ernest Hemingway for his novel *For Whom the Bell Tolls*, chosen as the book published in the previous three years that is most likely to become a classic .... Archbishop Francis J. Spellman of N.Y. issues a pastoral letter denouncing Garbo's *Two-Faced Woman* as "dangerous to public morals." .... Bobby Riggs and Frank Kovacs sign contracts to appear in 80 pro tennis matches.	Nov. 26
	FDR and Hull confer with Amb. Nomura and Saburo Kurusu at the White House.	Treasury Asst. Secy. John A. Sullivan announces that the Treasury does not "intend to suggest to the Congress any further taxes on income earned during the calendar year 1941." .... FDR rejects the resignations of CIO leaders Murray and Kennedy from the NDMB .... NAM Pres. Charles R. Hook opposes compulsory arbitration of defense strikes in testimony before the House Labor Comm.		Boston censor bans Garbo's *Two-Faced Woman*.	Nov. 27
Willkie confirms he will represent William Schneiderman, Russian-born secretary of the California CP, in a deportation case before the Supreme Court during its January term.	A U.S. government spokesman states unofficially that the U.S. will not compromise with Japan on the issue of aiding China and that fresh Japanese aggression in the Pacific will not be tolerated.	Attorneys for the 19 railroad unions announce the unions will call off their nationwide strike scheduled to begin Dec. 7 if the one million railway employes get $1 a day, or 15%, wage increases .... House passes, 224 to 161, and sends to the Senate the price control bill after rejecting most of the changes desired by the Administration .... House Labor Comm. and Senate Judiciary Comm. approve separate bills to control defense strikes. Both provide for government seizure of plants tied up by labor strife.		Bruce Smith of the Univ. of Minnesota wins the Heisman Trophy as the outstanding college football player in the U.S. .... Tony Zale defeats Georgie Abrams in a 15-round bout in N.Y. to win the undisputed world middleweight championship.	Nov. 28
Federal Circuit Court of Appeals in Philadelphia appoints Thomas Raeburn White to investigate an opinion written six years ago by Federal Judge J. Warren Davis in the Universal Oil Products Co. case.	Rep. Andrew J. May (D, Ky.), chairman of the House Military Affairs Comm., orders public hearings to begin Dec. 3 on the activities of so-called "defense brokers" who obtain defense contracts on a commission basis.	Crucible Steel Co. says it cannot accept in advance any decision which may force its employes to join the UMW. Other steel companies have agreed to accept the coal arbitration board's decision as final.		Gennaro Papi, 53, noted conductor of the Italian repertoire at the Metropolitan Opera in N.Y., dies a few hours before he is to conduct Verdi's *La Traviata*.	Nov. 29
Louis (Lepke) Buchalter and two associates, Emanuel (Mendy) Weiss and Louis Capone, are convicted by a jury in Brooklyn of killing Joseph Rosen, former garment trucker, on Sept. 13, 1936.	Following a telephone conversation with Secy. Hull, FDR cuts short his vacation at Warm Springs to return to Washington.			More than 16,000 attend ceremonies marking the opening of the Cathedral of St. John the Divine in N.Y. .... Jan Valtin, author of *Out of the Night*, is unconditionally released by California Gov. Culbert Olson from a 1926 prison sentence for assault, thus preventing Valtin's deportation .... Don Hutson, Green Bay end, scores 20 points to break six league records and tie two in an NFL game with the Washington Redskins.	Nov. 30
A jury in Minneapolis convicts 18 members of the Socialist (Trotzskyist) Workers Party on charges of conspiracy to create insubordination in the U.S. Army .... Rep. Thomas D. Winter (R, Kan.) charges the Rural Electrification Administration "is teeming with Communists." .... Nick Dean, sought on a charge of extorting $1 million from the movie industry, is arrested by federal agents in Chicago.	FDR returns to Washington from Warm Springs, Ga. as Hull continues talks with Japanese Amb. Kichisaburo and special envoy Saburo Kurusu.	Wayne L. Morse, chairman of FDR's emergency fact-finding board, announces a settlement of the threatened railroad strike scheduled for Dec. 7. Under the agreement reached by 19 unions and railroad representatives, 1.2 million workers will get 10¢ hourly wage increases.	Dr. E.R. Witwer says the formation of cancer in brain cells can be detected in its earliest stages by means of a petrographic microscope.	Minnesota is selected as the country's leading college team for the second successive year, with Duke second and Notre Dame third in the final AP poll of football experts.	Dec. 1
Rapp-Coudert committee charges the Young Communist League has branches in four colleges, high schools and various teachers groups in N.Y. .... In simultaneous raids, FBI agents arrest 30 persons in N.Y., Detroit and Chicago accused of engaging in the interstate traiffic of several million dollars' worth of Ford auto parts stolen from Michigan factories.	FDR announces he formally asked Japan today to explain why it is pouring troops into French Indochina and that he hopes to get a reply "very shortly." .... Navy reports 33 warships were launched in November.	Federal Price Admin. Leon Henderson tells the Economic Club of N.Y. the cost of living has gone up 11% since the war began and will be up 20% by spring .... Chmn. Dies of the House Un-American Activities Comm. charges 2,000 CIO leaders have or had affiliations with the CP or "auxiliary organizations."		Mel Ott, 32-year-old third baseman, signs a two-year contract as playing manager of New York Giants.	Dec. 2

F	G	H	I	J
Includes elections, federal-state relations, civil rights and liberties, crime, the judiciary, education, health care, poverty, urban affairs and population.	*Includes formation and debate of U.S. foreign and defense policies, veterans affairs and defense spending. (Relations with specific foreign countries are usually found under the region concerned.)*	*Includes business, labor, agriculture, taxation, transportation, consumer affairs, monetary and fiscal policy, natural resources, pollution and accidents.*	*Includes worldwide scientific, medical and technological developments, natural phenomena, U.S. weather and natural disasters.*	*Includes the arts, religion, scholarship, communications media, sports, entertainment, fashions, fads and social life.*

	World Affairs	European War Zone	Pacific War Zone	The Americas	Other Countries & Territories
Dec. 3		German command reports the "bulk of a New Zealand division" encircled southeast of Tobruk in Libya has been partly destroyed and partly captured .... Tula is encircled by German troops .... Moscow radio reports that Russian forces have driven the Germans to Taganrog, 40 miles west of Rostov.			Government of India announces in New Delhi that all civil disobedience prisoners "whose offenses have been formal or symbolic in character" will be freed immediately.
Dec. 4		Premier Stalin and Premier Wladyslaw Sikorski sign a declaration in Moscow stating that both Russia and Poland will continue the war until Germany is defeated .... A bill to empower the British government to conscript all men and women between 18½ and 51 passes its first test in the House of Commons after a Labor amendment urging the government to seize transport, coal mining and munitions industries is defeated 336 to 40.	Japanese news agency scores Hull's stand and declares, "It is utterly impossible for Japan to accept the stipulations of the American document [of Nov. 26]."		Five hundred members of the Congress Party are released from prisons in India in line with the government's new policy .... A conference in Washington adopts resolution urging the creation of a 200,000-man Jewish army, to be recruited in the U.S. and Palestine to fight Hitler.
Dec. 5	Germany agrees to a secret treaty with Japan for a war against the U.S. and barring any separate peace.	Hungary, Rumania and Finland reject a British ultimatum to halt their attacks on Russia .... Germans troops are stopped along a 200-mile semicircular front around Moscow .... British command announces that three German attacks against Ed Duda southeast of Tobruk were repulsed yesterday.	Japanese government informs FDR its troops have been reinforced in northern French Indochina "with the object of taking precautionary measures" against Chinese troops along the border.		
Dec. 6		Gen. Zhukov strikes with 100 divisions in a massive counter-attack against the German force investing Moscow .... British Foreign Office announces shortly after 1 a.m. that a state of war exists with Finland, Hungary and Rumania.		U.S. Navy authorities in the Canal Zone report that they are investigating rumors that Axis raiders disguised as Japanese merchant ships are using Port Callao, Peru as a base.	
Dec. 7		Moscow radio claims that Russian troops have broken through Nazi lines at two points on the Moscow front, annihilating two divisions and recapturing a village near Kalinin .... Britain, Canada, New Zealand and India go to war with Finland, Hungary and Rumania at 12:01 a.m. following rejection of the British ultimatum to end their conflict with Russia.	Japan strikes suddenly in the Pacific, bombing U.S. air and naval bases in Hawaii, the Philippines, Guam and Wake islands and British possessions of Singapore and Hong Kong. Japanese troops invade Thailand and Malaya by land and sea. Pearl Harbor attack severly damages the U.S. battleship fleet. Three hours later Japan declares war on the U.S. .... While Japanese bombs fall on Hawaii, Amb. Nomura and special envoy Saburo Kurusu meet with Hull to present Japan's reply to the U.S. note of Nov. 26, stating Japan's justification for war. Hull declares, "In all my 50 years of public service, I have never seen a document that was more crowded with infamous falsehoods and distortions."	Canada, Costa Rica, Nicaragua and Guatemala declare war on Japan.	
Dec. 8		A Berlin spokesman says winter weather has halted the German offensive against Moscow and that its capture is not expected this year	The governments of Britain, the Netherlands and Greece and the Free French Comm. declare war on Japan.	Six more Latin American nations declare war on Japan—Nicaragua, Honduras, El Salvador, Haiti, the Dominican Republic and Panama.	

U.S. Politics & Social Issues	U.S. Foreign Policy & Defense	U.S. Economy & Environment	Science, Technology & Nature	Culture, Leisure & Life Style	
An extraordinary grand jury in Brooklyn recommends the disbarment of Alfred E. Smith, Jr., son of the former governor, on 11 charges of "professional misconduct, fraud, deceit, crime and misdemeanor."	Hull says Japan's policy is based on force while that of the U.S. rests on law, justice, morals, and equality of treatment among nations .... FDR orders Lend-Lease aid be extended to Turkey "as fast as possible." .... House Appropriations Comm. approves the $8,243,839,031 third supplemental defense appropriation bill for the current fiscal year.	House passes and sends to the Senate a defense antistrike bill sponsored by Rep. Howard W. Smith (D, Va.) by a record vote of 252 to 136, despite the opposition of Administration leaders .... Meeting in N.Y., the NAM adopts resolutions pledging "its utmost energies to the production of defense materials" and urging antistrike legislation.	*AMA Journal* announces that a new method of treating infantile paralysis has been developed by Elizabeth Kenny, consisting of massage, movement and re-education of paralyzed muscles as soon as possible after the disease is discovered .... Dr. John C. Larkin reports "encouraging results" have been achieved in the treatment of cancer during the past three years through the use of neutron rays created in the Univ. of California's cyclotron.	Lambert Trophy is awarded in N.Y. to Fordham as the outstanding football team in the East .... Karl Decker, 73, correspondent for the Hearst newspapers in the Spanish-American War, who was widely acclaimed for rescuing the daughter of a Cuban revolutionary leader, dies in N.Y.	Dec. 3
Southern Association of Colleges and Secondary Schools drops 10 state colleges of Georgia from its credited list, effective Sept. 1, because of "unprecedented and unjustifiable political interference" by Gov. Eugene Talmadge.	Chesley Manly of the *Chicago Tribune* reports the Army and Navy Joint Board has prepared a confidential report for FDR on how the U.S. could defeat Germany and her allies. He says it envisions an expeditionary force of five million men.	AFL Pres. William Green and CIO Pres. Philip Murray denounce the antistrike bill passed by the House .... NAM urges that a single agency with a single head be created to supervise defense production .... A bomb wrecks the Detroit home of Patrick J. Currier, head of a lumber company involved in a labor dispute.	National Foundation for Infantile Paralysis announces its approval of the polio treatment developed by Elizabeth Kenny.	*Chicago Sun*, owned by Marshall Field, with Silliman Evans as publisher, publishes its first issue.	Dec. 4
N.J. Supreme Court rules the state's 1935 "race hatred" law violates the free speech provisions of the federal and state constitutions, reversing the convictions of nine German-American Bund leaders.	Stimson, referring to the war plans story in the *Chicago Tribune*, denounces persons "so wanting in loyalty and patriotism" as to publish "unfinished studies of our production requirements for national defense." .... House passes the $8,243,839,031 third supplemental national defense appropriation bill and sends it to the Senate.			Detroit Tigers outfielder Hank Greenberg is released from the Army after six months of service.	Dec. 5
	FDR sends a personal message appealing for peace to Emperor Hirohito of Japan amid reports that Japanese troops are sailing toward Thailand .... Knox says in his annual report that the Navy is "second to none" .... Navy orders six Finnish ships in U.S. ports put under protective custody.	United Brotherhood of Welders, Cutters and Helpers threatens to call a nationwide strike of its 75,000 members unless FDR halts alleged AFL discrimination against the union, which is seeking autonomy .... Two Pan-Am Airways Clippers leave Miami, Fla. with a total of 30 passengers to inaugurate air service to Africa.		MGM Pictures Corp. suspends showing of *Two-Faced Woman*, starring Greta Garbo, after Dec. 16 pending revision of the film .... Big Ten athletic conference in Chicago abolishes the javelin throwing event as harmful because it frequently causes back and shoulder injuries among contestants.	Dec. 6
	FDR orders the Army, Navy and the entire country on a war footing. In the evening he confers with the cabinet and congressional leaders on his war message. He also talks with Churchill by transatlantic telephone. Censorship is established on all messages leaving the U.S. by radio and cable .... Sen. Gerald P. Nye (R, N.D.) says the Japanese attack was "just what Britain planned for us" and that the U.S. has been "doing its utmost to provoke a quarrel with Japan."	FDR's Coal Arbitration Board rules that all coal mine workers must join the UMW as a condition of employment, thus reversing a decision of the NDMB .... United Brotherhood of Welders, Cutters and Helpers order strikers to return to work at an ordnance plant in Morgantown, W. Va. because of the Japanese attack. The strike began Nov. 24 .... New Jersey CIO pledges support for FDR in light of Pearl Harbor and denounces John L. Lewis for his membership in the America First Comm.			Dec. 7
Fed. Judge M.M. Joyce in Minneapolis sentences 12 of the 18 Socialist Workers Party members convicted in the sedition trial to 16-month prison terms and the other six to terms of a year and a day.	In his call for a declaration of war before a joint session of Congress, FDR declares, "Yesterday, Dec. 7, 1941—a date which will live in infamy—the United States of America was suddenly and deliberately attacked by naval and air forces of the Empire of Japan." .... Congress declares war at 1:10 p.m. on Japan with only one dissenting vote, Rep Jeannette Rankin (R, Mont.) .... Rep. John D. Dingell (D, Mich.) demands that the Army and Navy court martial Adm. Husband E. Kimmel, commander-in-chief of the U.S. Fleet, and four generals for the "naval debacle" at Pearl Harbor .... San Francisco undergoes a 2½-hour blackout upon a report that two formations of enemy planes flew in to within 20 miles of the city.	By a 6-3 vote, the Supreme Court reverses the contempt of court convictions of Harry Bridges and the *Los Angeles Times*.		Warren Wright's three-year-old Whirlaway is chosen by the nation's racing experts as the horse of the year in the *Turf & Sports Digest*'s annual poll.	Dec. 8

F	G	H	I	J
Includes elections, federal-state relations, civil rights and liberties, crime, the judiciary, education, health care, poverty, urban affairs and population.	*Includes formation and debate of U.S. foreign and defense policies, veterans affairs and defense spending. (Relations with specific foreign countries are usually found under the region concerned.)*	*Includes business, labor, agriculture, taxation, transportation, consumer affairs, monetary and fiscal policy, natural resources, pollution and accidents.*	*Includes worldwide scientific, medical and technological developments, natural phenomena, U.S. weather and natural disasters.*	*Includes the arts, religion, scholarship, communications media, sports, entertainment, fashions, fads and social life.*

	World Affairs	European War Zone	Pacific War Zone	The Americas	Other Countries & Territories
Dec. 9	China, Australia, New Zealand and South Africa declare war on Japan. China declares war on Germany and Italy.	Vichy discloses 1,850 Communists have been arrested in unoccupied France during the past three days, bringing the total arrested in the past six weeks to 12,850 .... Russian forces recapture Tikhvin, near Leningrad.	Japanese troops supported by warships and planes land on the northern and western coast of Luzon, main island of the Philippines .... Japan lands reinforcements in the Kota Bharu area of northeastern Malaya and in the Singora-Patani area of Thailand.	Cuban Senate and House vote for a declaration of war against Japan .... Argentina and Chile announce that they will grant non-belligerent status to the U.S. as an act of solidarity.	
Dec. 10		British command claims British and Imperial troops have broken the siege of Tobruk, Libya .... A Russian communique reports that Elets, 225 miles south of Moscow in the Orel sector, has been recaptured.	The new 35,000-ton British battleship *Prince of Wales* and the 32,000-ton battle cruiser *Repulse* are sunk in the South China Sea by Japanese war planes .... Japanese troops gain footholds along the northern coast of Luzon. U.S. bases and Manila suburbs are bombed .... According to the War Dept., Army bombers sink the Japanese battleship *Haruna* off northern Luzon .... Japanese capture Kota Bharu, an air base on the east coast of northern Malaya.	Hull proposes before the governing board of the Pan American Union that a meeting of foreign ministers of the American republics be held in Rio de Janeiro in January to discuss hemispheric defense .... Louis S. St. Laurent is appointed minister of justice in the Canadian cabinet.	
Dec. 11	The text of the Axis pact between Germany, Italy and Japan is disclosed by Hitler. It commits them to a joint war against the U.S. and Britain and precludes a separate peace.	Hitler announces the German declaration of war against the U.S. in an address to the Reichstag. He declares Roosevelt is "insane" and a "gangster." .... Mussolini tells 150,000 persons in the Piazza Venezia in Rome that Italy is at war with the U.S.	P.M. John Curtin of Australia announces in Melbourne that all single men from 18 to 45 and married men from 18 to 35 will be required to register for military service under the new draft laws.	Cuba, Costa Rica, Nicaragua, Guatemala and the Dominican Republic declare war on Germany and Italy.	
Dec. 12	State Dept. makes public messages pledging cooperation and victory exchanged between FDR, King George VI of Britain, Chiang Kai-shek of China and Pres. Manuel Quezon of the Philippines during the week.	Soviets claim the Nazi armies besieging Moscow have been routed .... British command reports its troops have pushed 40 miles west of Tobruk, Libya and surrounded El Gazala.	War Dept. claims Japanese landings at several points on the island of Luzon have been repulsed. Japanese bombers raid Clark Field and other Philippine bases .... Japanese troops advance in northwest Malaya. Japanese bombers raid Penang.	Panama, Honduras, Haiti and El Salvador declare war on Germany and Italy.	
Dec. 13		Premiers of Hungary and Bulgaria announce that a state of war exists between their countries and the U.S. .... Russian armies reportedly continue their advance as foreign correspondents return to Moscow .... Soviet Amb. Maxim Litvinov says in Washington that Russia intends to concentrate on defeating Hitler and will not join in the war against Japan at present .... German authorities in Paris announce that 100 "Jews, Communists and anarchists" will be immediately executed as a result of attacks on German soldiers.	The Navy concedes Guam has apparently been captured by the Japanese .... Lt. Gen. MacArthur's headquarters claims Philippine troops have wiped out a Japanese landing party in the Lingayen area of Luzon .... Premier Tojo says Japan must be prepared for a long, hard war, warning against "intoxication by initial victories."	Venezuelan embassy in Washington announces Venezuela has opened its ports to ships of all American nations fighting the Axis .... Argentina issues a decree recognizing the U.S. as a non-belligerent and declaring Argentine neutrality toward Germany and Italy .... More than 500 persons are killed in a mud and rock slide in Huaraz, Peru.	
Dec. 14		Ireland and Turkey announce their neutrality .... Swiss sources report nine of the 60 persons on trial in Trieste have been sentenced to death. Forty-eight others receive long prison terms.	Japanese troops begin a general land and air offensive against Hong Kong at dawn after their ultimatum for surrender is rejected.		
Dec. 15		Soviets announce that Klin, northwest of Moscow, has been recaptured together with Yasnaya Polyana and Bogoroditsk, south of Tula.	British forces are retreating slowly in northeastern Malaya, inflicting heavy casualties on Japanese mechanized troops, according to a communique in Singapore.		

A	B	C	D	E
Includes developments that affect more than one world region, international organizations and important meetings of major world leaders.	*Includes all developments in European countries and military engagements between Allied and Axis powers in Africa and at sea.*	*Includes all developments in Japan and China, Japanese foreign policy and military actions in the Pacific region.*	*Includes all domestic and regional developments in Latin America, the Caribbean and Canada.*	*Includes developments in those independent nations and colonial possessions not covered in Columns B, C and D.*

U.S. Politics & Social Issues	U.S. Foreign Policy & Defense	U.S. Economy & Environment	Science, Technology & Nature	Culture, Leisure & Life Style	
Robert F. Rockwell (R) defeats Frank Delaney (D) in a special congressional election in Denver, Colo. to fill the seat of the late Rep. Edward T. Taylor (D).	FDR says in a broadcast from the White House that the war with Japan will be long and hard but that the U.S. will win. He concedes that "So far, the news has been all bad. We have suffered a serious setback in Hawaii." He declares the U.S. "can accept no result save victory, final and complete." .... FDR invokes "enemy alien" regulations and orders federal agents to round up dangerous German, Italian and Japanese nationals .... N.Y., Boston and other East Coast cities have their first aid raid alarms.		Hart O. Berg, 76, noted engineer and arms expert who helped to develop automobiles, airplanes and submarines and the Browning pistol and machine gun, dies in N.Y.		Dec. 9
	Washington state police report fires in the form of arrows pointing toward Seattle were found and extinguished last night .... FDR authorizes the Defense Communications Board to take over or close any private radio facilities if deemed necessary by the Army or Navy .... Atty. Gen. Biddle reports 2,303 "enemy aliens"—1,291 Japanese, 865 Germans, and 147 Italians—have been arrested for internment.	OPM Dir. Gen. Knudsen calls for a 24-hour-day, seven-day-week in war industries in announcing a victory program in Washington .... OPM bans the sale of new tires for civilian use through Dec. 22 .... The new freighter *Oregon* sinks after colliding with a U.S. Navy ship south of Cape Cod. Nine men drown and eight are missing.		A Motion Picture Industry Conference Comm. is organized in Chicago by film producers, distributors and exhibitors to coordinate action on taxation, advertising and general practices .... Boxing Writers Assn. of N.Y. awards the Edward J. Neil Memorial Plaque to Joe Louis as the outstanding boxer of the year .... Cleveland pitching ace Bob Feller enlists in the U.S. Naval Reserve.	Dec. 10
Democratic National Chmn. Edward J. Flynn and GOP National Chmn. Joseph W. Martin Jr. pledge to call off politics for the duration of the war.	Congress unanimously declares war on Germany and Italy .... Congress amends the Selective Service Act to permit the sending of troops outside the Western Hemisphere and to extend the terms of all soldiers until six months after the war ends .... Sen. Charles Tobey (R, N.H.) demands Knox be removed after the "unspeakable disaster" at Pearl Harbor .... America First Comm. announces it is dissolving and urges its supporters "to give their full support to the war effort .... until peace is attained."	Trading in German, Italian and Japanese securities is suspended "until further notice" on the NYSE.		A plan to merge eight of the largest Protestant interdenominational agencies in the U.S. and Canada is presented at the Conference on the Cooperation of Interdenominational Agencies.	Dec. 11
	Fourteen men are found guilty by a federal jury in N.Y. on charges of espionage and failure to register as agents of Germany. Nineteen others have pleaded guilty .... Senate passes and sends to conference a $10,572,350,705 supplemental defense appropriation bill, increasing the House measure by $2,328,511,774 .... Coast Guardsmen seize 14 French ships in U.S. ports, including the luxury liner *Normandie*.	Ford Motor Co. inaugurates a 24-hour, seven-day week on all defense projects.	Prof. Emil Picard, 85, world-famous French mathematician and permanent secretary to the French Academy of Sciences since 1917, dies in Paris.	Three Protestant women's organizations merge under a single constitution as the National Council of Churchwomen in a meeting in Atlantic City, N.J.	Dec. 12
		White House announces the selection of 12 indrustry representatives and 12 labor leaders to draft a basic war labor policy .... OPM freezes sugar stocks and limits new deliveries by importers and refiners to 1940 levels in a move to prevent hoarding or speculation.		USLTA announces its annual men's and women's national rankings, with Bobby Riggs and Sarah Palfrey Cooke heading each division.	Dec. 13
Univ. of Cincinnati estimates on the basis of a nationwide survey there has been a 9.16% drop below last year's figures in college and university enrollment.				Robert E. Sherwood orders his Pulitzer prize-winning play, *There Shall Be No Night*, based on the Russian invasion of Finland in 1939, to close in Rochester, Minn. .... Chicago Bears beat the Green Bay Packers, 33 to 14, in Chicago in a playoff to win the Western championship of the NFL.	Dec. 14
Pres. Charles Seymour of Yale announces the university will operate on a year-round basis so that students may complete their studies in less than three years, instead of four.	Knox reports on the losses at Pearl Harbor, conceding six warships were lost and several others damaged. He reports almost 3,000 men were killed. He says U.S. forces were "not on the alert against the surprise air attack" and adds that "a formal investigation" will be initiated immediately .... Congress completes action on the conference-approved $10,000,077,005 supplemental defense appropriation bill and sends it to FDR .... FDR reports to Congress that Lend-Lease aid to the Allies during the past nine months has reached $1.202 billion.	AFL Executive Council adopts a no-strike policy in all defense industries.		Rose Bowl is transferred to Durham, N.C. The West Coast classic in Pasadena had been cancelled at the request of the Army.	Dec. 15

F	G	H	I	J
Includes elections, federal-state relations, civil rights and liberties, crime, the judiciary, education, health care, poverty, urban affairs and population.	*Includes formation and debate of U.S. foreign and defense policies, veterans affairs and defense spending. (Relations with specific foreign countries are usually found under the region concerned.)*	*Includes business, labor, agriculture, taxation, transportation, consumer affairs, monetary and fiscal policy, natural resources, pollution and accidents.*	*Includes worldwide scientific, medical and technological developments, natural phenomena, U.S. weather and natural disasters.*	*Includes the arts, religion, scholarship, communications media, sports, entertainment, fashions, fads and social life.*

	World Affairs	European War Zone	Pacific War Zone	The Americas	Other Countries & Territories
Dec. 16		Russians announce the recapture of Kalinin, 90 miles northwest of Moscow .... Six Gestapo agents are killed by a bomb near Paris .... Czech government in London declares a state of war exists between Czechoslovakia and all countries at war with Britain, the U.S. and Russia.	Japanese troops drive toward Panang in northwestern Malaya .... Navy Dept. announces that Japanese warships bombarded the U.S. naval outpost of Johnston Island and a submarine shelled the shipping center of Kahului on Maui Island during the past 24 hours.	Argentine cabinet declares a state of siege throughout the country. All constitutional guarantees are suspended .... Pres. Manuel Avila Camacho asks the Senate for authority to permit troops, warships and planes of American nations fighting the Axis to use Mexican territory, waters and ports for the duration of the war.	
Dec. 17		A Russian communique reports that Alexin and Zukino south of Moscow have been recaptured.	The inter-island passenger vessel *Corregidor* sinks after hitting a mine in Manila Bay. Several hundred persons are reported missing .... British report Japanese troops have landed in the state of Sarawak on the northwestern coast of Borneo .... Chinese troops attack at Tamshui, Shawan and Shumchun, to the rear of the Japanese forces besieging Hong Kong .... Japanese announce that 319 persons were killed and 437 injured in an earthquake in southern Formosa today.	The governing board of the Pan-American Union sets Jan. 15 as the date of the Pan American Conference in Rio de Janeiro, at which hemispheric defense will be discussed .... Argentina bans a pro-Roosevelt demonstration by Accion Argentina .... FDR nominates Spruille Braden as ambassador to Cuba to succeed George S. Messersmith.	
Dec. 18		British command announces Axis forces in Libya "are now in full retreat." .... Italian "human torpedoes," launched from a submarine that had penetrated the harbor at Alexandria, Egypt, attach mines to the hulls of the British battleships *Queen Elizabeth* and *Valiant*. Both ships are severely damaged when the mines detonate the next morning.	The Netherlands government announces in London that Dutch and Australian forces have occupied the Portuguese section of the island of Timor .... Japanese command claims its troops landed on Hong Kong at 10 p.m. and are mopping up "all resistance." .... British authorities in Malaya concede Imperial troops have fallen back about 100 miles in northern Malaya during the past 11 days.	State Dept. officials report an agreement has been reached for neutralizing the French possessions in the Caribbean area, including Martinique, Guadeloupe and French Guiana.	
Dec. 19		British command announces that the Derna airport, 170 miles inside Libya, was captured yesterday.	The entire Philippine Army is inducted into the U.S. Far Eastern Army under Lt. Gen. Douglas A. MacArthur .... Japanese radio broadcasts claim Hong Kong fell to Japanese troops at 11 a.m. .... British abandon their base on Penang Island as Japanese forces press forward .... Portuguese Premier Antonio de Oliveria Salazar demands Britain and the Netherlands withdraw their occupation forces from Portuguese Timor immediately.	Pres. Fulgencio Batista of Cuba signs a congressional resolution declaring a state of national emergency and granting him special war powers .... Nicaragua declares war on Hungary, Rumania, and Bulgaria.	
Dec. 20	White House announces steps are under way to extend the "joint planning for unity of action" between the U.S. and Britain to include Russia, China, the Netherlands and other countries fighting in Asia.	Goebbels reads an appeal from Hitler for the German people to contribute winter clothing for soldiers on the Russian front .... A Russian communique reports the recapture of Volokolamsk on the central front and Voibokala on the northern front.	Japanese troops land from four transports at Davao on the Philippine Island of Mindanao, 600 miles southeast of Manila. Heavy fighting is reported .... British forces continue to resist on Hong Kong.	Cuban government orders internment of all Japanese in Cuba.	
Dec. 21		Berlin radio announces that Hitler removed Field Marshal Walther von Brauchitsch as commander-inchief of the German Army on Dec. 19 and assumed the post himself .... Reports from Stockholm state that an epidemic of spotted typhus has broken out in Lithuania and other German-occupied territory in East Europe.	Japan announces that Thailand Premier Luang Bipul Songgram and Japanese Amb. Teije Tsubogami have signed a 10-year military alliance pledging each country not to make a separate peace .... War Dept. reports planes bombed the islands of Luzon, Cebu and Mindanao in the Philippines during the past 24 hours.		
Dec. 22	Churchill arrives in Washington with an 86-man delegation to discuss with FDR all questions relevant to the concerted war effort.	Marshal Klementy Voroshilov is named commander of Soviet troops in the Far East.	Wake island, 2,000 miles west of Honolulu, falls to the Japanese after two weeks of attacks. The island was garrisoned by less than 400 U.S. Marines .... Eighty to 100,000 Japanese troops attempt to land on Luzon Island around Lingayen at dawn under strong naval and air escort.		
	A *Includes developments that affect more than one world region, international organizations and important meetings of major world leaders.*	B *Includes all developments in European countries and military engagements between Allied and Axis powers in Africa and at sea.*	C *Includes all developments in Japan and China, Japanese foreign policy and military actions in the Pacific region.*	D *Includes all domestic and regional developments in Latin America, the Caribbean and Canada.*	E *Includes developments in those independent nations and colonial possessions not covered in Columns B, C and D.*

U.S. Politics & Social Issues	U.S. Foreign Policy & Defense	U.S. Economy & Environment	Science, Technology & Nature	Culture, Leisure & Life Style	
Atty. Gen. Biddle notifies U.S. attorneys not to prosecute persons arrested on charges of seditious speech without the consent of the Justice Dept.	FDR appoints a five-man board, headed by Supreme Court Justice Owen J. Roberts, to investigate whether there was any negligence by the Army and Navy in the Japanese attack on Pearl Harbor .... FDR appoints Byron Price, AP executive news editor, to be director of the new censorship office .... Former White House aide Thomas G. Corcoran testifies before the Senate defense investigating committee that he has received $100,000 in fees for legal counsel on four defense contracts and not for the sale of contracts .... House and Senate pass legislation giving FDR wartime powers similar to those held by Pres. Wilson during W.W. I.	AFL issues a declaration of war labor policy renewing its request to the CIO "for unity in the labor movement."	U.S. Weather Bureau announces that publication of long-range weather forecasts will be banned for the duration of the war as a defense measure .... National Aeronautics Assn. awards the Collier Trophy, aviation's highest honor, to Dr. Sanford A. Moss for "outstanding success in high altitude flying through the development of the turbo-supercharger."		Dec. 16
Census Bureau reveals the foreign-born white population of N.Y.C. on April 1, 1940 totaled 2,080,020, of whom 62.4% were naturalized citizens.	House amends the Selective Service Act by voice vote to provide for the registration of all men 18-64 and make those 21-44 subject to military service .... Navy, Army and Air Force commanders in Hawaii who were in charge at Pearl Harbor on Dec. 7 are ousted. Adm. Husband Kimmel is replaced by Adm. Chester W. Nimitz as commander of the Pacific fleet. Lt. Gen. Walter Short is replaced by Lt. Gen. Delos Emmons as Army commander in Hawaii .... FDR writes a letter "to the President of the United States in 1956," urging a West Point appointment for Colin Kelly 3rd, the 18-month-old son of Capt. Colin Kelly Jr., a Navy flier killed in the successful bombing of the Japanese battleship *Haruna*.	FDR tells 24 labor and management representatives that "you must reach an agreement" on war labor policy under which all work stoppages will be eliminated .... Henderson places all tire sales under a consumer coupon rationing system, effective Jan. 4, 1942 .... Dr. Fritz J. Hansgirg, the German-born inventor of a new method of manufacturing metallic magnesium, is arrested as an enemy in the offices of the Permanente Corp. in Los Altos, Calif., despite company protests that he is needed for defense work.	Eastman Kodak announces a new film process named Kodacolor, enabling anyone to get full color prints from negatives in the shades of the original object. The film will be offered to the public in six sizes in January.	Roman Catholic Nat. Legion of Decency announces its approval in N.Y. of MGM's film *Two-faced Woman*, starring Greta Garbo, after the elimination of "objectionable scenes." .... Joe DiMaggio, Yankee baseball star, is named the athlete of the year in the annual Associated Press poll of sports writers.	Dec. 17
Senate Elections Comm. votes, 13 to 3, to recommend that the Senate bar William Langer (R, N.D.) from taking his seat on the grounds of moral turpitude. Langer has been accused of attempting to bribe a federal judge .... Dr. Willard C. Rappleye of the Assn. of American Medical Colleges announces 76 medical schools are planning to reduce their present four-year courses to three years by operating on a year-round basis because of war needs for doctors.	Senate passes its own draft bill, 79 to 2, making all men from 19 to 44 subject to military service .... One hundred enemy aliens seized in the San Francisco area are sent to a concentration camp in Montana .... Laura Ingalls, noted woman flier, is arraigned in Washington on a charge of failing to register as a paid agent of the German government.	OPM fixes price ceilings on raw wool, wool tops and wool yarns at the levels prevailing between Oct. 1 and Dec. 6.			Dec. 18
FDR orders 12 federal non-defense agencies or departments with 10,000 employes to move to other cities because of a shortage of office space in Washington.	Both houses of Congress quickly pass a conference-approved draft bill requiring all men between 18 and 64 to register and making those from 20 to 44 subject to military service .... House passes a bill requiring the CP and the German-American Bund to register with the Justice Dept. as agents of foreign governments.	OPM directs industrial branches now reporting to Leon Henderson to report directly to William S. Knudsen and Sidney Hillman, OPM chiefs .... House and Senate pass bills appropriating $300 million for 75,000 new dwellings and continuing the present sugar quotas for three years.		Sammy Angott gains a 15-round decision over Lew Jenkins in N.Y. to win the undisputed lightweight title.	Dec. 19
	FDR appoints Adm. Ernest J. King, current commander of the Atlantic Fleet, as commander-in-chief of the U.S. Fleet .... The DSC is awarded posthumously to Capt. Colin P. Kelly Jr. for sinking the Japanese battleship *Haruna*. .... Two American tankers are attacked by submarines off the Pacific Coast. One ship escapes, but the 6,912-ton *Emidio* is abandoned off Cape Mendocino after being shelled and torpedoed.	Willkie urges the Administration to cut non-defense expenditures "to the bone" and end "bickering" between labor and capital .... Scores of welders strike in shipyards and defense plants in the San Francisco and Los Angeles areas in protest against alleged AFL discrimination.		The Chicago Bears set eight NFL records, according to final figures. They include: the most first downs (181), the most yardage (4,265), the most touchdowns (56), the most points (396) and the most penalty yardage (676.5).	Dec. 20
American Council on Education recommends that the high school and college education of talented students be speeded up to permit them to graduate from college at 20 to meet the new draft requirements.	Knox claims U.S. Navy ships "have up to the present time probably sunk or damaged at least 14 enemy submarines" in the Atlantic.	Marines and Army troops are called out to protect workers going to their jobs at shipyards and other defense plants in the San Francisco Bay area.		Chicago Bears crush the N.Y. Giants, 37 to 9, in the playoff in Chicago to win the NFL title for the second successive year .... National Board of Review of Motion Pictures chooses Orson Welles's *Citizen Kane* as the the best Hollywood motion picture made in 1941.	Dec. 21
	FDR signs the amended Selective Service bill under which men from 20 through 44 will be subject to military service .... War Dept. reports 273 fifth columnists have been arrested among the 35,000 Japanese aliens in Hawaii.	Supreme Court rules, 7 to 0, that an employer has the right to express his views on labor unions so long as he does not attempt to coerce his employes .... Troops are withdrawn from strike duty in San Francisco. About 495 out of 3,000 welders on the day shift continue picketing.			Dec. 22

F	G	H	I	J
Includes elections, federal-state relations, civil rights and liberties, crime, the judiciary, education, health care, poverty, urban affairs and population.	*Includes formation and debate of U.S. foreign and defense policies, veterans affairs and defense spending. (Relations with specific foreign countries are usually found under the region concerned.)*	*Includes business, labor, agriculture, taxation, transportation, consumer affairs, monetary and fiscal policy, natural resources, pollution and accidents.*	*Includes worldwide scientific, medical and technological developments, natural phenomena, U.S. weather and natural disasters.*	*Includes the arts, religion, scholarship, communications media, sports, entertainment, fashions, fads and social life.*

	World Affairs	European War Zone	Pacific War Zone	The Americas	Other Countries & Territories
Dec. 23	At a joint press conference with Churchill, FDR announces that their meetings are being devoted to the immediate question of achieving complete unanimity of action in the Pacific .... The first meeting of the U.S.-British War Council is held in the White House.	British command announces that Imperial forces in Libya reached the coastal plain of the Gulf of Sidra south of Bengazi yesterday.	Gen. Chiang Kai-shek appoints T.V. Soong to be Chinese foreign minister .... The battle of Lingayen continues "with increasing intensity" on Luzon .... Japanese planes carry out a heavy raid on Rangoon, Burma.		
Dec. 24	Pope Pius XII outlines a five-point peace plan based on the "integrity and security" of all states.	British command announces the capture of Barce and Benina in Libya.	Japanese land in force at three points on Luzon—Atimonan, Mauban and Nasugbu .... Japanese forces reportedly land at Kuching, capital of Sarawak, Borneo.	A Free French naval force occupies the Vichy-governed island of St. Pierre and Miquelon off Newfoundland .... Brazilian police close the Japanese newspaper *Brasil Asahi* and a German publication in Sao Paulo and another German paper in Santa Catharina.	
Dec. 25		British command reports devastated Bengazi, capital of Cyrenaica, was captured yesterday by Royal Dragoons, apparently without opposition.	Japan announces the Hong Kong garrison surrendered today after a 16-day siege .... Manila and Tokyo dispatches report that Japanese troops have advanced at three points on Luzon in the Philippines despite strong resistance .... FDR and Australian P.M. John Curtin formally open a 7,420 mile direct radio-telegraph communications system between the U.S. and Australia.	The male population of St. Pierre votes by better than 98% for association with Free French forces, as opposed to collaboration with the Axis.	Reuters reports from Bhagalpur, India that 320 Hindu leaders, including Dr. Syamprosad Mookerjee, finance minister of the Bengal government, have been arrested for trying to attend a conference that had been banned.
Dec. 26	Churchill tells Congress that the Allies should be able to assume the offensive "upon an ample scale" in 1943 .... Canadian P.M. Mackenzie King arrives in Washington to participate in the British-U.S. military and naval conferences.	Soviets announce Naro Fominsk, about 50 miles southeast of Moscow, has been recaptured together with other towns.	Gen. Douglas MacArthur declares Manila to be an open city and orders all troops and anti-aircraft guns to be withdrawn .... British war office announces Lt. Gen. Sir. Henry Pownall has arrived in Singapore to assume command of British forces in the Far East, replacing Air Chief Marshal Sir Robert Brooke-Popham .... British embassy in Chungking announces an American-British-Chinese Military Council has been created there.		
Dec. 27	FDR announces that "excellent progress" has been made during the conferences of 26 Allied governments in Washington to prosecute the war on a worldwide scale .... FDR and Churchill assure representatives of Axis-occupied countries that the U.S. and Britain will do everything possible to restore their independence after the war.	Soviets announce the capture of Likhvin, Vysokinichi, Novosil and Tim on the front southwest of Moscow .... Lisbon, Portugal is rocked by a severe earthquake at 6:25 p.m.	Japanese planes bomb the undefended open city of Manila for 40 minutes in the morning and three hours 22 minutes in the afternoon, starting huge fires .... Australian P.M. John Curtin says, "Australia looks to America, free from any pangs about our traditional links of friendship to Britain." He adds, "We refuse to accept the dictum that the Pacific struggle is a subordinate segment of the general conflict."		
Dec. 28		Britain announces that Foreign Secy. Anthony Eden has been in Moscow since mid-December conferring with Premier Joseph Stalin regarding conduct of the war .... Reports state German troops are retreating in Serbia following a series of defeats by guerrillas.	Japanese pressure increases southeast of Manila. FDR pledges that "the entire resources, in men and in material, of the United States stand behind" the Philippines .... Japanese planes, unchallenged by anti-aircraft batteries or pursuit craft, bomb Manila for two hours in the afternoon.		
Dec. 29		A London communique reports a successful six-hour raid Dec. 27 on the German-occupied islands of Vaagsoe and Maaloy, off the Norwegian coast.	Tokyo reports claim Japanese troops yesterday captured Ipoh, the great tin mining center 290 miles north of Singapore .... Japanese planes bomb the island fortress of Corregidor about 30 miles south of Manila guarding the entrance to Manila Bay.	Churchill and Mackenzie King of Canada arrive in Ottawa .... Argentine Foreign Ministry announces that the Argentine ambassador to Berlin has been recalled.	Mohandas K. Gandhi resigns as leader of the All-India Congress Party because, he says, the party's working committee has abandoned his principles of civil disobedience and non-violence.
Dec. 30		Churchill tells the Canadian Parliament has turned against the Hun." He declares, "These gangs of bandits .... have asked for total war. Let us make sure that they get it." He says that after the French defeat, the French generals said: "In three weeks England will have her neck wrung like a chicken." Churchill adds: "Some chicken! Some neck!" .... Foreign Secy. Eden returns to London from his Moscow conference with Stalin .... Moscow annouces Soviet troops on the Caucasian front landed on the Crimean peninsula, occupying the town and fortress of Kerch.	Manila dispatches report the Japanese are within 30 miles of the city .... Pres. Manuel L. Quezon and Vice Pres. Sergio Osmena of the Philippines are inaugurated for their second terms in a wartime ceremony near Gen. MacArthur's headquarters. .... Lt. Gen. A.E. Percival declares martial law in Singapore following four Japanese air raids last night.		
	A *Includes developments that affect more than one world region, international organizations and important meetings of major world leaders.*	B *Includes all developments in European countries and military engagements between Allied and Axis powers in Africa and at sea.*	C *Includes all developments in Japan and China, Japanese foreign policy and military actions in the Pacific region.*	D *Includes all domestic and regional developments in Latin America, the Caribbean and Canada.*	E *Includes developments in those independent nations and colonial possessions not covered in Columns B, C and D.*

U.S. Politics & Social Issues	U.S. Foreign Policy & Defense	U.S. Economy & Environment	Science, Technology & Nature	Culture, Leisure & Life Style	
	The 8,272-ton U.S. tanker *Montebello* is sunk by a submarine off the California coast . . . . A federal grand jury in Washington indicts Laura Ingalls on a charge of failing to register as a German agent.	FDR accepts a three-point war labor peace plan agreed upon by the 24-man labor-industry conference board in Washington. The plan calls for "no strikes or lockouts," settlement of all disputes "by peaceful means" and establishment of "a proper War Labor Board to handle these disputes."		Pope Pius XII authorized Roman Catholic bishops throughout the world to permit Catholics in their dioceses to eat meat on Fridays and omit certain fast days for the duration of the war.	Dec. 23
Brown Univ. and Pembroke College announce that they will admit to the next freshman class outstanding students who have completed their third year of high school.	FDR and Churchill make brief Christmas Eve addresses at the lighting of the Christmas tree on the lawn of the White House. FDR says Americans must prepare "our hearts . . . . for the labor and sacrifice which lie ahead."	Federal Price Admin. Henderson fixes prices for leather of all types, grades and qualities at levels which prevailed between Nov. 6 and Dec. 6 . . . . Ford Motor Co. announces that it is ready to begin producing about 1,000 pounds daily of synthetic fiber developed from soybeans, to be used principally in upholstery.			Dec. 24
Richard Steere Aldrich, 57, Republican congressman from 1923 to 1933, dies in Providence, R.I.	State Dept. announces that the Free French occupation of St. Pierre and Miquelon off Newfoundland yesterday "was an arbitrary action . . . . without the prior knowledge or consent of the U.S. government."	Congressional-Executive Joint Comm. on Non-Essential Expenditures, headed by Sen. Harry F. Byrd (D. Va.), recommends a total savings of $1.7 billion in non-defense expenditures . . . . Representatives of Air Associates, Inc. and the CIO-UAW reach an agreement in Bendix, N.J. on a one-year contract, providing wage increases and a modified union shop . . . . Jesse Jones announces the creation of a Small Business Unit in the Commerce Dept. under William Shepardson.			Dec. 25
		A minority report written by Sen. Robert M. La Follette Jr. condemns the majority proposals of the joint economic committee, saying they would affect "the very lowest income groups among our population." . . . . Striking welders withdraw their picket lines at defense plants and shipyards in the San Francisco area.	Dr. Paul J. Kolachov reports that the Russian dandelion plant known as kok-sagyz can produce crude rubber and may be grown virtually in any soil.		Dec. 26
	Hull scores Japanese over their bombing of Manila. Sen. Wheeler declares the Japanese are "an inhuman and half-civilized race and in the future will be treated as such." Sen. Norris asserts "their cities are open to attack, when we are ready, [we] . . . . will burn them off the face of the earth." . . . . Atty. Gen. Biddle issues an order requiring all Japanese, German and Italian aliens in seven Pacific Coast states to surrender their short-wave radio sets and cameras to local police.	Federal spokesman announces the AFL Amalgamated Association of Street, Electric Railway and Motor Coach Employes has agreed to end the six-day strike by 1,500 Greyhound drivers and submit the dispute to arbitration . . . . OPM issues an order, effective immediately, restricting the manufacture of new farm machinery in the 12-month period beginning last Nov. 1 to 83% of 1940 production.		Southern All-Stars defeat the North, 16-0, in the fourth annual college football classic in Montgomery, Ala.	Dec. 27
AAUP issues a formal statement assailing Georgia Gov. Eugene Talmadge for "political interference" in ousting Dean Walter D. Cocking of the Univ. of Georgia on charges of advocating racial equality in education.		Brookings Institution issues a report urging the reduction of federal non-defense expenditures by $2,085 billion without curtailing essential social services.		Nat Fleischer, editor of the *Ring*, boxing publication, names Joe Louis, world heavyweight champion, as "the fighter of the year" for the fourth time.	Dec. 28
		Army formally returns the Bendix (N.J.) plant of Air Associates, Inc. to private management after operating it since Oct. 31 . . . . AFL boilermakers rout picketing welders at the California Ship Building Corp. in Los Angeles.	Portland, Ore. is shaken at 10:30 a.m. by a short, sharp eathquake.	Leslie MacMitchell, NYU miler, wins the James E. Sullivan Memorial Trophy of the AAU as the outstanding amateur athlete of 1941.	Dec. 29
	Seven persons are indicted in N.Y. on charges of sending vital defense information to Germany . . . . Lindbergh is revealed to have volunteered for active service in the Air Force . . . . Census Bureau reports there are 25,829,788 men in the continental U.S. between the ages of 20 and 44, inclusive, who can be drafted for military service.	FDR announces plans are underway to boost U.S. war production to 50% of the national income, or about $50 billion in the fiscal year beginning next July 1 . . . . Greyhound companies agree to arbitrate the strike of 1,800 bus drivers . . . . Henderson freezes wholesale cigarette prices at the levels prevailing Dec. 26 and fixes maximum retail prices for automobile tires and tubes at the level in effect Nov. 25.	Dr. Edwin P. Hubble of the Mount Wilson Observatory says that as a result of six years of observation through the observatory's 100-inch telescope he doubts the theory that the universe is exploding.	N.Y. Film Critics choose Orson Welles's *Citizen Kane* as the outstanding film of 1941.	Dec. 30
F	G	H	I	J	
Includes elections, federal-state relations, civil rights and liberties, crime, the judiciary, education, health care, poverty, urban affairs and population.	*Includes formation and debate of U.S. foreign and defense policies, veterans affairs and defense spending. (Relations with specific foreign countries are usually found under the region concerned.)*	*Includes business, labor, agriculture, taxation, transportation, consumer affairs, monetary and fiscal policy, natural resources, pollution and accidents.*	*Includes worldwide scientific, medical and technological developments, natural phenomena, U.S. weather and natural disasters.*	*Includes the arts, religion, scholarship, communications media, sports, entertainment, fashions, fads and social life.*	

	World Affairs	European War Zone	Pacific War Zone	The Americas	Other Countries & Territories
Dec. 31		Hitler declares in Berlin that there will be "still harder battles for 1942 if we are to circumscribe the powerful foe which confronts us" and make the world safe for National Socialism.	Japan demands U.S. forces in the Philippines surrender and rejects the designation of Manila as an open city .... Gen. MacArthur reports his forces are consistently falling back in the face of heavy Japanese assaults.	Berlin announces that the German ambassador to Argentina, Baron Edmund von Thermann, has been recalled .... Venezuala breaks diplomatic relations with Germany, Italy and Japan.	

U.S. Politics & Social Issues	U.S. Foreign Policy & Defense	U.S. Economy & Environment	Science, Technology & Nature	Culture, Leisure & Life Style	
	Justice Dept. extends its ban on the possession of short-wave wireless sets and hand cameras by enemy aliens to cover the entire country, including Puerto Rico and the Virgin Islands .... Adm. Chester W. Nimitz assumes command of the Pacific Fleet in a simple ceremony at Pearl Harbor, Hawaii.	FDR appoints Jesse H. Jones as a member of the Supply Priorities and Allocations Board.		Justice Dept. files civil suits in Chicago against NBC and CBS, charging that through their ownership of key stations and the use of exclusive contracts the two chains almost completely dominate the country's broadcasting industry .... Sol Hess, cartoonist and creator of the comic strip *The Nebbs* syndicated in more than 250 newspapers, dies in Chicago.	Dec. 31

1942

Cheerful U.S. soldiers flash victory signs as they sail from England to North Africa in Operation Torch, Nov. 14.

Adm. William (Bull) Halsey commanded U.S. naval forces during the sea battle of Guadalcanal, Nov. 12-15.

Women assemble a bomber wing section at the Douglas Aircraft plant in Long Beach, Calif. The number of women employed in U.S. factories increased by five million between 1940 and 1943.

A grisly caricature of Japan's Emperor Hirohito grins at workers of the Douglas Aircraft plant in Santa Monica, Calif., where this poster was displayed.

Preceding page: Seattle residents rush to buy buffalo steaks, sold in limited quantities by a meat market. Meat rationing and other restrictions on consumption had a severe impact by late 1942.

Physicist Enrico Fermi supervised construction of the world's first operational atomic pile under the bleachers of the University of Chicago's Stagg Field.

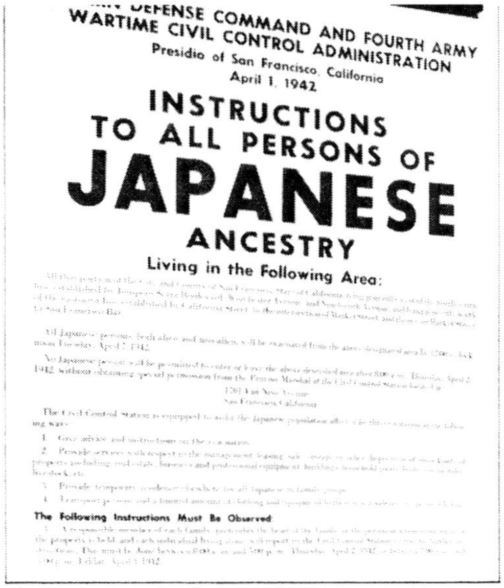

DEFENSE COMMAND AND FOURTH ARMY
WARTIME CIVIL CONTROL ADMINISTRATION
Presidio of San Francisco, California
April 1, 1942

INSTRUCTIONS
TO ALL PERSONS OF
JAPANESE
ANCESTRY
Living in the Following Area:

The Following Instructions Must Be Observed:

An Army poster orders the evacuation of Japanese-Americans from the San Francisco area. Evacuees were sent to dreary relocation centers in Colorado, Utah and Wyoming.

German Field Marshal Erwin Rommel, commander of the Afrika Korps, poses for a picture in Libya on March 20.

World heavyweight champion Joe Louis, who joined the Army in January, promotes the war effort in this recruiting poster.

Japanese planes attack the aircraft carrier *Hornet* during the Battle of the Santa Cruz Islands near Guadalcanal, Oct. 26. The plane diving from above crashed the ship's forecastle seconds after the picture was taken.

New York Yankees outfielder Joe DiMaggio lines a single to left field in a game against the Washington Senators June 29, setting a new major league record by hitting safely in 42 consecutive games.

Hitler greets Finland's Field Marshal Carl Gustav Mannerheim on June 6 during a visit to the Finnish front.

	World Affairs	European War Zone	Pacific War Zone	The Americas	Other Countries & Territories
Jan.	Twenty-six nations become charter members of the United Nations, pledging their full resources to defeat the Axis.	Russian winter offensive pushes the Germans back southwest of Moscow, while British and German forces battle indecisively in Libya .... German administrative officials meet at Wannsee near Berlin to plan the deportation and extermination of European Jews.	Japanese forces invade Burma and the Dutch East Indies, overrunning Borneo and Celebes.	Most Latin American countries sever diplomatic relations with the Axis.	
Feb.		Germans halt the Russian winter offensive .... British forces hold the Afrika Korps at Egypt's western border.	Japanese complete the conquest of Malaya by invading Singapore.	U.S. bolsters its defense facilities in Latin America, notably in the Panama Canal Zone and on the Dutch possessions of Curacao and Aruba.	Free French representatives take charge of the French Somaliland government.
March		SS begins mass deportation of European Jews to extermination camps.	Japanese overrun Java in the Dutch East Indies .... Japanese advances in Burma force the British to evacuate Rangoon.	German submarines begin sinking Brazilian ships in the South Atlantic.	Sir Stafford Cripps, leader of the British House of Commons, confers in New Delhi with Indian leaders on possible self-government arrangements for India.
Apr.	Presidential aide Harry Hopkins and Gen. George Marshall, U.S. Army Chief of Staff, confer in London with British military leaders on Allied war strategy.	Luftwaffe begins "Baedecker raids" against Coventry and other British cathedral cities.	American and Philippine survivors of Bataan make a forced "death march" to prison in Camp McDonnell.		Indian political leaders reject British compromise proposals for limited Indian self-government.
May		Germans halt an attempted Russian summer offensive in the Kharkov area.	Japanese complete the conquest of Burma and gain uncontested control over the Philippines with the capture of Corregidor Island in Manila Bay .... U.S. and Japanese naval forces skirmish indecisively in the Battle of the Coral Sea.	Several Latin American nations increase their restrictive measures against pro-Nazi groups.	
June	Roosevelt and Churchill confer in Washington on war strategy, confirming the "Europe First" policy of the Allies and discussing plans for U.S. action in North Africa.	German Afrika Korps under Rommel drives British forces from Libya, capturing Tobruk .... Luftwaffe ends "Baedecker raids" on British cathedral cities.			
July		German summer offensive sweeps across southern Russia, while the Afrika Korps invades Egypt .... SS begins deportation of Warsaw Jews to Treblinka; Jews from Western Europe are sent to Auschwitz.	Chinese and Japanese forces battle indecisively for control of Central China .... U.S. naval units force the Japanese to withdraw for the first time in the Battle of Midway.	U.S. concludes agreements for acquisition of natural rubber from Bolivia and five Central American states, replacing supplies lost to the Japanese in the Dutch East Indies.	
Aug.	Churchill meets with Stalin in Moscow to discuss prospects for opening a "second front" against Germany in the West.	German forces invade the Caucasus and reach the Volga .... U.S. 8th Air Force arrives in Britain to prepare for the bombing offensive against Germany.	Japanese and U.S. land and sea forces begin a struggle for control of Guadalcanal in the Solomon Islands.		Widespread political demonstrations break out in India following the arrest of Mohandas Gandhi and British refusal to grant full Indian autonomy.
Sept.		Russian forces halt the German advance at Stalingrad.	U.S. and Australian forces begin to advance against the Japanese on New Guinea.		
Oct.		Germans and Russians continue positional warfare in Stalingrad .... Battle for El Alamein begins in Egypt.	U.S. Marines contain a Japanese land offensive on Guadalcanal.	U.S. concludes further rubber acquisition agreements with several Latin American states.	British forces invade Madagascar to depose Vichy French authorities.
Nov.	Axis advance reaches its greatest extent in Europe, Africa, Asia and the Pacific.	Afrika Corps retreats from Egypt following its defeat at El Alamein, as U.S. forces under Gen. Eisenhower invade Morocco and Algeria (Operation Torch) .... Russians encircle the German 6th Army in Stalingrad .... German forces occupy southern France.	U.S. and Japanese naval forces continue fighting for control of the sea in the Guadalcanal area, with the advantage going to the Americans.	Most Latin American states sever diplomatic relations with Vichy France.	British forces complete the occupation of Madagascar.
Dec.		Germans attempt unsuccessfully to break the Russian encirclement of Stalingrad.		FDR discusses hemispheric defense in Washington with Canadian P.M. Mackenzie King and Cuban Pres. Batista.	

A	B	C	D	E
Includes developments that affect more than one world region, international organizations and important meetings of major world leaders.	*Includes all developments in European countries and military engagements between Allied and Axis powers in Africa and at sea.*	*Includes all developments in Japan and China, Japanese foreign policy and military actions in the Pacific region.*	*Includes all domestic and regional developments in Latin America, the Caribbean and Canada.*	*Includes developments in those independent nations and colonial possessions not covered in Columns B, C and D.*

U.S. Politics & Social Issues	U.S. Foreign Policy & Defense	U.S. Economy & Environment	Science, Technology & Nature	Culture, Leisure & Life Style	
	Government begins registration of all men between 20 and 40 for military service.	Harvard economist Alvin Hansen advocates tax reform and a greater economic role for the government in his pamphlet *After the War-Full Employment.*			Jan.
Invasion fears and demands for restrictive measures against Japanese-Americans grow on the West Coast.	National debate grows over Roosevelt's "Germany First" war strategy.	Auto industry begins conversion to war production, primarily aircraft .... The stock market plummets as news of American military reverses comes in.			Feb.
War Relocation Agency begins deportation of 100,000 Japanese-Americans from their West Coast homes to internment camps in Utah, Colorado and other Western states.	Government agencies register all men aged 45-64 for non-military service, while the War Dept. conducts a third draft lottery for men 20-40.	Wartime shortages limit sales of sugar, gasoline and rubber tires.	Radar comes into operational use in ship and airplane navigation .... Snow and tornadoes cause disruption in several Southern and Midwestern states.	Victory Garden fad sweeps the U.S. under the slogan "An Acre for a Soldier."	March
Justice Dept. begins a crackdown on Father Coughlin's *Social Justice* and other anti-war publications.	Coastal shipping losses to German submarines rise to two vessels per day, greater than the current rate of ship construction .... Blackouts are imposed in N.Y. and other East Coast cities.			Government restrictions on the use of fabrics force introduction of the cuffless style in men's trousers. Slacks for women grow in popularity.	Apr.
Evacuation of Japanese-Americans from the West Coast reaches its greatest pace and extent .... Post Office restricts the mailing privileges of pro-Axis publications.	Coastal shipping losses to German submarines rise to three vessels per day .... Army assumes responsibility for East Coast defense.	House Ways and Means Comm. discusses a variety of tax measures aimed at reducing inflation.	Medical researchers report progress in the immunization of babies against whooping cough.	Demands for renewal of Prohibition rise as temperance groups begin an anti-alcohol drive.	May
A. Philip Randolph's March on Washington Movement begins holding rallies across the country to protest continuing racial discrimination in the armed forces and defense industries.	Germans attempt unsuccessfully to infiltrate eight agents into the U.S. (Operation Pastorius).			Lengthy negotiations result in agreement on the basic principles of union between the Episcopal and Presbyterian churches.	June
Federal authorities in N.Y. take legal action against leaders of the German-American Bund.	German agents captured by the FBI in Operation Pastorius are tried for treason in Washington.	Congress prepares the largest tax measure in history in an effort to absorb excess civilian spending power.			July
		Stock market rises sharply in response to improving war news.		Irving Berlin's *White Christmas* sweeps the country, becoming the best-selling song in history.	Aug.
War Relocation Agency completes the internment of Japanese-Americans .... Federal authorities charge several Negro groups with planning pro-Japanese activities.	Wendell Willkie begins a tour of the war zones on behalf of FDR, visiting the Middle East and Russia.	War Production Board begins a drive to expand artificial rubber production following the loss of natural rubber sources in the East Indies to the Japanese.			Sept.
Racial discrimination becomes a focus of national attention as Congress debates prohibition of poll taxes in federal elections.	Willkie concludes his tour of the war zones with a visit to China.	U.S. merchant ship production reaches three vessels per week, offsetting losses to German submarines.	Floods cause heavy damage along the James, Rappahannock and Potomac Rivers in the Washington-Virginia area.	Evangelical Reformed and Congregational Christian churches in America negotiate a merger agreement.	Oct.
	Physicists under the direction of Enrico Fermi construct the world's first operational atomic pile at the University of Chicago.	Government takes action against monopolistic practices in the insurance business and several other industries.			Nov.
	Army begins construction of a nuclear testing facility at Los Alamos, N.M.	War Production Board reaches its greatest extent of operation, with 20,000 employes in its Washington headquarters and 5,000 field workers .... Food Admin. Claude Wickard orders the rationing of several items.	Cold and heavy snow disrupts transportation in Ohio and western Pennsylvania.		Dec.
F *Includes elections, federal-state relations, civil rights and liberties, crime, the judiciary, education, health care, poverty, urban affairs and population.*	G *Includes formation and debate of U.S. foreign and defense policies, veterans affairs and defense spending. (Relations with specific foreign countries are usually found under the region concerned.)*	H *Includes business, labor, agriculture, taxation, transportation, consumer affairs, monetary and fiscal policy, natural resources, pollution and accidents.*	I *Includes worldwide scientific, medical and technological developments, natural phenomena, U.S. weather and natural disasters.*	J *Includes the arts, religion, scholarship, communications media, sports, entertainment, fashions, fads and social life.*	

	World Affairs	European War Zone	Pacific War Zone	The Americas	Other Countries & Territories
Jan. 1		Marshall Henri Philippe Petain appeals for German rapprochement so French "dignity will be restored and our economy relieved."	American and Philippine troops north and southeast of Manila join forces to form a ring around the capital .... Gen. Chiang Kai-shek promises the Chinese people that the Allies will inflict "overwhelming punishment" on Japan.		
Jan. 2	White House makes public the Declaration of United Nations signed by 26 nations at war with the Axis, each pledging not to make a separate peace and to employ its full resources against the common enemy.	South African troops aided by British tanks capture Bardia, Axis coastal stronghold near the Libyan-Egyptian frontier .... Russian troops recapture Maloyaroslavets southwest of Moscow, threatening an estimated 150,000 Germans at Mozhaisk with entrapment .... Yugoslav legation in London publishes document prepared by Serbian Orthodox Church charging 180,000 persons were massacred up to early August by the Nazi puppet state of Croatia.	Manila and Cavite, a nearby naval base, fall to Japanese without resistance .... At the request of Allies, Chinese troops enter Burma, placing themselves under British control in fight against Japanese .... British repulse Japanese attempt to land forces in lower Perak, western Malaya.	Chilean Foreign Office issues a decree declaring nation's neutrality in war between Japan and every Allied nation except the U.S. and Latin American countries, which have been granted non-belligerent status.	
Jan. 3		British announce capture of 5,000 German and Italian prisoners in Bardia.	FDR and Churchill announce appointment of Sir Archibald F. Wavell as supreme commander of American, British, Dutch and Dominion forces in southwest Pacific .... Japanese planes attack Corregidor Island in Manila Bay, causing minor damage and few casualties. Japanese forces land in Borneo.		
Jan. 4	State Dept. announces all nations "silenced by military force" may join the U.N. Declaration; Latvian Min. Alfred Bilmanis immediately pledges his country's support.	Russia announces capture of Borovsk, 50 miles southwest of Moscow, in Red Army's drive on Mozhaisk .... RAF claims destruction of 44 Axis planes in series of attacks on Castelvetrano airdrome in Sicily.	British Imperial forces withdraw to positions further south in Perak, northern Malaya .... Gen. Douglas MacArthur reports Japanese discrimination against all white residents of Manila.	Cuban government orders internment of 4,084 registered German aliens, but only those regarded as dangerous are expected to be detained.	Led by Sir Tej Bahadur Sapru, 15 veteran Indian leaders appeal to Churchill to give India dominion status immediately.
Jan. 5		German Foreign Min. Joachim von Ribbontrop arrives in Budapest to confer on "Hungary's position in the new Europe." .... Soviets capture Bieliv, southwest of Moscow, in which 2,300 Germans are reportedly killed or wounded.	Japanese forces land near Kuala Selangor, a port city some 240 miles northwest of Singapore .... Japanese planes bomb fortifications in Manila Bay, including Corregidor Island and Mariveles, for four hours .... Tokyo radio broadcast issues denial of mistreatment of whites in Manila but says actions are being taken against "white fifth columnists."	State Dept. announces elevation of its legations in Paraguay, Ecuador and Bolivia to embassies.	
Jan. 6		Soviet troops land at two points in Crimea—Eupatoria on west coast and Yalta on southern coast .... Egypt severs diplomatic relations with Vichy France and recalls its minister.	British command in Singapore announces further withdrawals in Perak, northern Malaya, in some areas to points 190 miles north of Singapore.	Brazilian government seizes German-controlled Condor airlines, which it will operate.	
Jan. 7		Former Rumanian King Carol, speaking in Mexico City, denounces Premier Ion Antonescu as a "traitor."	Japanese forces resume heavy fighting along all fronts north of Manila .... Japanese news agency Domei reports that Japanese forces are withdrawing from Changsha in Hunan Province because they "accomplished their objectives."	Argentine Foreign Min. Enrique de Ruiz-Guinazu says in Buenos Aires his country will oppose military action against Axis but may support economic measures.	
Jan. 8		After strong Russian attacks on three sides, German siege of Sevastopol is lifted .... Axis troops retreat westward from Agedabia, Libya under cover of heavy sand storm.			
Jan. 9		Soviet troops reportedly capture towns of Serpeisk, Mozhaisk and Vetchino about 130 miles southwest of Moscow.	After three days of intensive fighting Chinese troops penetrate north and northeast suburbs of Canton .... American President liner *Ruth Alexander* is abandoned after an attack by a Japanese plane in NEI waters.		

A	B	C	D	E
Includes developments that affect more than one world region, international organizations and important meetings of major world leaders.	*Includes all developments in European countries and military engagements between Allied and Axis powers in Africa and at sea.*	*Includes all developments in Japan and China, Japanese foreign policy and military actions in the Pacific region.*	*Includes all domestic and regional developments in Latin America, the Caribbean and Canada.*	*Includes developments in those independent nations and colonial possessions not covered in Columns B, C and D.*

U.S. Politics & Social Issues	U.S. Foreign Policy & Defense	U.S. Economy & Environment	Science, Technology & Nature	Culture, Leisure & Life Style	
Atty. Gen. Francis Biddle orders German, Italian and Japanese nationals in the U.S., Puerto Rico and Virgin Islands to surrender all firearms in their possession to local police.	Returning to Washington from Ottawa, P.M. Churchill greets New Year with a toast: "Here's to 1942, a year of toil, a year of struggle, a year of peril, but a long step forward to victory."	OPM bans retail sale of automobiles and trucks until Jan. 15 .... With unofficial figures of 170,603,671 shares sold in 1941, NYSE reports smallest volume year since 1918.	At its Dallas meeting the American Assn. for the Advancement of Science presents its annual $1,000 prize for outstanding contribution to science to Dugald E.S. Brown and Douglas A. Marsland of NYU and Frank H. Johnson of Princeton Univ., for their studies of luciferase, an enzyme which enables glow worms, fire flies and luminescent bacteria to give off light.	Bowl Game Scores: Rose, Ore. State 20 -Duke 16; Sugar, Fordham 2 - Missouri 0; Cotton, Ala. 29 - Tex. A&M 21; Orange, Georgia 40 - TCU 26.	Jan. 1
First session of the 77th Congress adjourns after meeting for 365 days .... Dr. Guy E. Snavely, executive director of American Assn. of Colleges, urges one year each to be cut from high school and college education so students may complete their work at age 20.	Federal Judge Mortimer W. Byers sentences 33 members of a Nazi spy ring to total of 310 years in prison and fines them $18,000.	Leon Henderson, head of the Office of Civilian Supply, announces new passenger auto production will be banned "for the duration" probably on Jan. 31.		Dorothy Thompson is granted divorce from Sinclair Lewis in Woodstock, Vt. on grounds of willful desertion.	Jan. 2
Former Georgia Gov. E.D. Rivers and 19 others are indicted in Atlanta on charges of defrauding the state of $201,368.		OPM announces it is planning to double present war production .... Chrysler Corp. announces plans to triple its tank capacity and double its anti-aircraft gun production.		East and West tie at 6-6 in the 17th annual All Star Game, played in New Orleans rather than San Francisco because of the war.	Jan. 3
An emergency conference of Nat. Comm. on Education and Defense and U.S. Office of Education issues 15-point declaration which urges acceleration of college programs to three years.				Otis Skinner, 83, dean of American stage, dies in N.Y. .... Chicago Bears defeat NFL all stars, 35-24, at Polo Grounds in N.Y.C.	Jan. 4
Second session of 77th Congress convenes in Washington .... Senate subcommittee investigating motion picture propaganda dissolves in view of war and "in the interest of national unity." .... Housing Admin. Nathan Strauss submits his resignation to FDR because of congressional opposition to his projects.	FDR orders all men between 20 and 44 who did not register before to do so on Feb. 16 for active military service .... At CP rally in Madison Square Garden in N.Y.C. 20,000 pledge to support U.S. in war against Axis.	Auto industry appoints 10-man committee to draw up plans for converting into a war industry capable of turning out $5 billion or more in arms this year .... Immigration Appeals Bd. unanimously reverses deportation order of West Coast CIO leader Harry Bridges.		Federal district court in Philadelphia orders liquidation of the *Evening Public Ledger* for failing to present a plan of satisfactory financial reorganization.	Jan. 5
	In State-of-the-Union message FDR says all-out victory program will cost $56 billion in fiscal 1943.	Capt. Robert Ford lands Pan Am Airways Pacific Clipper in N.Y. after flying westward around world because of war.	Drs. Harold H. Lefft and J. Arthur MacLean report new method of taking brain X-rays which involves replacing serous fluid with di-iodo-tyrosine mixed with gelatine.	Emma Calve, 83, one of foremost opera singers of her day, dies in Millau, France.	Jan. 6
George Hill, 45, second secretary of Rep. Hamilton Fish, (R, N.Y.) is accused by government of having worked with German propagandists and of having distributed pro-Axis literature under congressional frank .... Former Mayor of Detroit Richard W. Reading is sentenced to four to eight years in prison for accepting thousands of dollars to protect gambling rackets .... Atty. Gen. Francis Biddle announces 3,234 Axis nationals have been arrested in U.S.	Laurence A. Steinhardt is appointed by FDR as ambassador to Turkey, replacing John Van Antwerp MacMurray, who has resigned.	FDR submits to Congress a $59.027-billion war budget for fiscal 1943 .... OPM scraps 10-man auto industry committee to create a labor-management group to plan for conversion of auto industry to wartime production.	Drs. Herbert D. Adams and Leo V. Hand of Boston announce the revival of a man whose heart had stopped beating for 20 minutes during a lung operation.		Jan. 7
	House votes to shift Office of Civilian Defense from directorship of N.Y. Mayor Fiorello H. La Guardia to War Dept.	Writing to Sen. Alben Barkley (D,Ky.), FDR urges a single price adminstrator rather than a board as urged by Sen. Robert Taft (R,O.), in Senate price control bill .... OPM orders distilling industry to divert 60% of its capacity from whiskey to ethyl alcohol in a move to increase smokeless powder production.			Jan. 8
	FDR appoints James M. Landis as executive head of OCD.	Senate adopts Bankhead amendment to price control bill, which gives secretary of agriculture veto power over all farm crop ceilings imposed by price administrator .... Price Admin. Leon Henderson allows price of refined sugar to rise 20% to compensate for recent price rises in raw sugar.	House votes and sends to conference daylight savings time bill.	Joe Louis scores knockout over Buddy Baer in first round of a scheduled 15-round bout in N.Y. for his 20th defense of his heavyweight title .... Founder of the Jehovah's Witnesses, Judge Joseph Rutherford, dies in San Diego .... RCA Pres. David Sarnoff announces NBC's Blue Network has been formed into the Blue Network Co., comprising WJZ in N.Y., WENR in Chicago and KGO in San Francisco.	Jan. 9
F	G	H	I	J	
Includes elections, federal-state relations, civil rights and liberties, crime, the judiciary, education, health care, poverty, urban affairs and population.	*Includes formation and debate of U.S. foreign and defense policies, veterans affairs and defense spending. (Relations with specific foreign countries are usually found under the region concerned.)*	*Includes business, labor, agriculture, taxation, transportation, consumer affairs, monetary and fiscal policy, natural resources, pollution and accidents.*	*Includes worldwide scientific, medical and technological developments, natural phenomena, U.S. weather and natural disasters.*	*Includes the arts, religion, scholarship, communications media, sports, entertainment, fashions, fads and social life.*	

	World Affairs	European War Zone	Pacific War Zone	The Americas	Other Countries & Territories
Jan. 10			Japanese commence NEI invasion with landings at Tarakan and Minahassa .... British government announces Alfred Duff Cooper has been recalled as resident minister of cabinet rank at Singapore .... Under heavy pressure from Japanese forces, British troops retreat from Slim River area, some 220 northwest of Singapore.	Argentina orders censorship of all foreign reports that "express contempt for or insult other countries, their peoples or authorities."	
Jan. 11		British announce total prisoners taken in Libyan campaign includes 19,000 Italians and 7,000 Germans .... Soviet forces break Nazi-held north-south Rzhev-Bryansk railroad line by capturing Lyudinovo, about 40 miles from Bryansk.	Japanese troops enter Kuala Lumpur, capital of Federated Malay States .... Japan claims capture of Olangapo, a U.S. naval base at Subic Bay near Manila.	Mexican government announces plans to give military training to male students from grammar school through college, effective Feb. 15 .... Bolivian government declares state of seige in order to suppress violence over tax dispute in mining areas of Potosi, Sucre and Oruro.	
Jan. 12		Yugoslav government in London appoints Dr. Slobodan Yovanovich to succeed Gen. Dusan Simovich as premier. Gen. Draja Mikhailovich, commanding the Serbian Army against Nazis in Yugoslavia, becomes minister of war .... At opening of Swedish Parliament, King Gustav says he is determined on "preserving the peace and freedom of our country uninfringed."	British confirm loss of Kuala Lumpur and announce establishment of a new defense line 35 miles south of the city at Seremban.	Joint Mexican-U.S. Defense Commission is created to study and recommend measures to be adopted for the defense of the two countries.	
Jan. 13		Russian troops capture Gorokhovo, eight miles west of Mozhaisk, and seize Kirov, 100 miles southeast of Smolensk .... Nine exiled governments in London—Belgium, Czechoslovakia, Free France, Greece, Luxembourg, Netherlands, Norway, Poland and Yugoslavia—sign resolution promising vengeance upon Nazi officials responsible for civilian oppression in occupied countries.	Japanese overwhelm defenders and complete occupation of oil island of Tarakan off northeast coast of Borneo.	Under terms of an agreement signed in Washington, Uruguay will receive Lend-Lease aid.	
Jan. 14		Soviet forces take city of Medyn, a railway junction on the southern Podolsk-Vyazma line, in the continuing southern Russian offensive .... A 9,577-ton armed tanker, the *Norness* of Panama, is torpedoed and sunk about 60 miles southeast of Montauk Point, L.I.	Japanese forces occupy eight of nine Malay states, with only Johore remaining under British control.	Canadian Finance Min. J.L. Ilsley announces provinces and municipalities will not collect income taxes until one year after the war.	
Jan. 15		Russian troops take Selizharovo south of Seliger Lake between Leningrad and Moscow.	Australian troops join British in defense of Johore state in Malaya .... British and Japanese troops clash at Myitta, Burma, some 15 miles from Thai border.	Under State Secy. Sumner Welles tells Inter-American Conference every Axis diplomat is a spy and urges the seven republics who have not broken with Axis to do so .... Mexican Foreign Min. Ezequiel Padilla says the "attack by Japan was not on the United States, but on America."	Pandit Jawaharlal Nehru succeeds Mohandas K. Ghandi as leader of All-India Congress Comm. in Bombay.
Jan. 16		British Foreign Office announces appointment of Sir Archibald Clark Kerr, ambassador to China, to succeed Sir Stafford Cripps as ambassador to Soviet Russia .... British planes bomb Hamburg and Emden, Germany for second consecutive night.	British and Australian forces inflict heavy casualties upon Japanese troops in eastern part of Negri Sembilan in Malaya.	Colombia, Mexico and Venezuela offer resolution to Inter-American Conference calling on American Republics to break diplomatic relations with Axis.	Gen. Sir Alan Fleming Hartley is appointed successor of Sir Archibald Wavell as commander-in-chief in India.
Jan. 17		About 5,500 Axis troops in Halfaya, Egypt, last Axis outpost there, surrender to British .... Russian troops begin their assault on German salient at Mozhaisk .... Churchill arrives in London after completing a 3,287-mile flight from Bermuda.	War Dept. states a "heavy Japanese attack" against right flank of American and Philippine troops on Bataan Peninsula of Luzon Island is now in progress .... Japanese troops cross River Muar, establishing a foothold some 90 miles from Singapore.		
Jan. 18		Soviet troops fight their way into Mozhaisk, 60 miles west of Moscow.	British detain Burmese Premier U Maung Saw in London for his alleged contacts with Japanese.	Reports in Rio de Janeiro say German and Italian ambassadors have warned Brazil that severing diplomatic relations with Axis will result in war.	
	A *Includes developments that affect more than one world region, international organizations and important meetings of major world leaders.*	B *Includes all developments in European countries and military engagements between Allied and Axis powers in Africa and at sea.*	C *Includes all developments in Japan and China, Japanese foreign policy and military actions in the Pacific region.*	D *Includes all domestic and regional developments in Latin America, the Caribbean and Canada.*	E *Includes developments in those independent nations and colonial possessions not covered in Columns B, C and D.*

U.S. Politics & Social Issues	U.S. Foreign Policy & Defense	U.S. Economy & Environment	Science, Technology & Nature	Culture, Leisure & Life Style	
		Senate passes House-approved price control bill after adopting amendment to raise parity level at which farm prices can be fixed by 10% to 120% . . . . Actor's Equity Assn. defeats proposed amendment to its constitution to bar Nazis, Fascists and Communists from holding union office . . . . GM Pres. Charles Wilson announces the company has $3.758 billion worth of war contracts and is ready to turn out 10% of the national arms program.		Mutual Broadcasting System files suit in Chicago against RCA and NBC on charges they are freezing out Mutual in certain cities . . . . U.S. Golf Assn. cancels the open, the amateur, the women's amateur and the amateur public links championships for 1942 because of war . . . . Hollywood screen star Mickey Rooney, 21, marries actress Ava Gardner, 19.	Jan. 10
Mrs. Mildred Amelia Carr, 66, well known in Newark, N.J., for her numerous charities, is arrested on charge of defrauding a fellow church member of $4,700; her background includes having been an ex-convict with a career as swindler dating back to 1901.					Jan. 11
Supreme Court invalidates Georgia's Contract Labor Law, under which a debtor can 'work out' his debt, as a violation of 13th Amendment to the Constitution and federal anti-peonage laws.		FDR issues an executive order abolishing National Defense Mediation Bd. and replacing it with a 12-man National War Labor Bd., chaired by William H. Davis, charged with settling all labor disputes . . . . Federal Loan Admin. Jesse H. Jones announces $400 million will be spent to increase synthetic rubber output by 400,000 tons this year.			Jan. 12
House passes and sends to Senate amendment to Nationality Law whereby citizenship of a naturalized citizen can be revoked if he or she is convicted of subversive activities.		FDR assails Senate version of price control law as unsound and inflationary . . . . FDR announces his intention to create War Production Bd., chaired by Donald Nelson and charged with general supervision of all production . . . . As a result of a government, labor and industry conference in San Francisco, 19 Pacific Coast shipyards adopt a 24-hour-day, seven-day-week schedule.			Jan. 13
N.Y.C. Mayor La Guardia is re-elected president of U.S. Conference of Mayors for sixth consecutive year.		National Resources Planning Bd. states in report to Congress "we may have at the end of the war sufficient accumulated shortages" in consumer goods "to give us a vigorous private investment boom" producing more than $100 billion worth of goods a year . . . . Leon Henderson tells U.S. Mayors' Conference in Washington that Senate version of price control bill will cause rampant inflation.		U.S. Censorship Dir. Byron Price issues code to guide press in covering war and at same time avoid giving information to enemy . . . . Boston Red Sox catcher and noted linguist Morris (Moe) Berg is granted an unconditional release by the club to enable him to accept government appointment as "goodwill ambassador" to Latin America.	Jan. 14
Rep. Martin Dies charges Leon Henderson used to be a member of Comm. on Technocracy and Archibald MacLeish's Office of Facts and Figures has employed known Communist Malcolm Cowley . . . . George Hill is convicted by federal jury in Washington of committing perjury before grand jury investigating Nazi activities in U.S.	Sen. Harry S. Truman's committee investigating defense program issues report denouncing the Administration, the Army and Navy, big business, labor and other groups for lag in war production . . . . Stimson announces Army will be expanded from 1.7 million to 3.6 million men during 1942.				Jan. 15
		FDR issues executive order giving Donald Nelson wide powers as chairman of WPB, and transfers OPM Dir. Gen. Knudsen to the War Dept.		TWA transport carrying screen actress Carole Lombard, her mother and 20 others, crashes near Las Vegas, Nev., killing all aboard . . . . Byron Price issues special wartime code for radio stations, which bans quiz programs where audience participation is uncontrolled and participants' backgrounds cannot be checked . . . . In a letter to Commissioner Kenesaw Mountain Landis, FDR urges baseball continue to be played despite war.	Jan. 16
	Treasury Dept. announces it has closed more than 100 Axis firms in U.S. but is allowing 98 others to operate under strict surveillance.	John L. Lewis proposes CIO and AFL resume peace negotiations immediately owing to war conditions.		Original bronze entitled *Le Penseur* (The Thinker), famous work by noted French sculptor Auguste Rodin, is sold to a private collector for $9,500 . . . . Library of a Congress announces appointment of Nobel Prize winner Thomas Mann to its staff as consultant in German literature.	Jan. 17
		Agriculture Secy. Claude R. Wickard says the country is facing probable shortages of sugar, fats and oils because of war . . . . AFL City Employes Union in Detroit votes to strike Jan. 23 for 15% wage increase.		N.Y. Baseball Writers Assn. name Joe DiMaggio "player of the year" for 1941.	Jan. 18
F	G	H	I	J	
Includes elections, federal-state relations, civil rights and liberties, crime, the judiciary, education, health care, poverty, urban affairs and population.	*Includes formation and debate of U.S. foreign and defense policies, veterans affairs and defense spending. (Relations with specific foreign countries are usually found under the region concerned.)*	*Includes business, labor, agriculture, taxation, transportation, consumer affairs, monetary and fiscal policy, natural resources, pollution and accidents.*	*Includes worldwide scientific, medical and technological developments, natural phenomena, U.S. weather and natural disasters.*	*Includes the arts, religion, scholarship, communications media, sports, entertainment, fashions, fads and social life.*	

	World Affairs	European War Zone	Pacific War Zone	The Americas	Other Countries & Territories
Jan. 19	Berlin radio announces Germany, Italy and Japan have signed a new military pact for "common operations against all enemies."	The 7,988-ton passenger liner *Lady Hawkins* is torpedoed and sunk, with loss of 245 lives, off Cape Hatteras, N.C.	Tokyo reports claim Japanese troops are only 25 miles from Johore Bahru, just north of Singapore.		Great Britain and Ethiopia reach accord whereby full sovereignty is restored to Haile Selassie. Economic aid to his country is also promised.
Jan. 20			Thai soldiers invade Burma at Miyawaddi in apparent drive on Moulmein, across Gulf of Martaban .... Japanese troops advance along a 30-mile sector from Muar River to Batu Pahat, 65 miles northwest of Singapore.	Acting Pres. Ramon S. Castillo says Argentina will not break relations with Axis.	
Jan. 21		Three columns of German soldiers penetrate and force British to retreat at Agedabia, Libya as Rommel advances to the Gazala line.	Alliance between Japan and Thailand is concluded .... British troops withdraw from Endau, 85 miles north of Singapore .... American and Filipino troops drive Japanese forces back in heavy fighting on Bataan Peninsula .... Heavy fighting between British and Japanese forces is reported in Kawkareik area, 20 miles inside Burma-Thai border.	Delegations of 21 republics agree at Rio de Janerio to accept resolution pledging their countries to sever diplomatic relations with Axis.	
Jan. 22			Batavia announces firing of oil fields and refineries at Balik Papan, East Borneo to keep them from falling into Japanese hands .... Melbourne, Australia reports loss of radio communications with Rabaul, New Britain .... Japanese reinforcements land at Lingayen Gulf and Subic Bay in the Philippines.	Argentine Acting Pres. Castillo says in Buenos Aires that, while agreeing to solidarity with Americas, he cannot accept thesis that an attack upon one is an attack upon all .... Brazil places foreign societies under surveillance and warns death penalty will be invoked for acts against state.	
Jan. 23		Germans occupy Agedabia, Libya as British forces withdraw .... After 12 days of fighting, Soviets claim 62-mile advance south of Lake Ilmen on the northern front.	War Dept. reports Japanese are continuing to launch heavy attacks on Gen. Douglas MacArthur's positions on Bataan Peninsula but that they are being repulsed with heavy losses .... Japanese forces land at Rabaul, New Britain and in New Guinea.	Stripped of all attempts to satisfy Argentina, a resolution recommending 21 American republics sever diplomatic relations with Axis is adopted unanimously by Inter-American Conference's defense committee in Rio de Janeiro.	
Jan. 24				Acting Pres. Castillo reaffirms Argentina's refusal to sever diplomatic relations with the Axis, despite Rio resolution .... Peru and Uruguay bring total to 15 American republics that have several diplomatic relations with Axis.	
Jan. 25		German columns advance 45 miles northeast from Antelat to Msus, Libya .... RAF reports success in daylong attack upon an Axis convoy in the Mediterranean.	Netherlands Indies command announces in Batavia that Japanese troops have landed at Kendari, southern Celebes, and at Balik Papan, Borneo, and that "our troops are offering strong resistance." .... Lae, capital of Australian New Guinea, is evacuated .... Tokyo radio announces Thailand has declared war on Great Britain .... MacArthur's forces in Philippines claim a "smashing success" against Japanese on Bataan Peninsula.	Paraguay and Bolivia break diplomatic relations with Axis.	
Jan. 26		First U.S. AEF of this war lands in Northern Ireland under command of Maj. Gen. Russell P. Hartle.	Batu Pahat, western Malaya, 60 miles north of Singapore, is abandoned to Japanese.	Canadian P.M. Mackenzie King tells House of Commons an additional corps of troops will be created.	
Jan. 27	FDR and Churchill simultaneously announce three U.S.-U.K. committees to administer shipping, munitions and raw materials of the two countries .... Churchill says he and FDR have agreed to a Combined Chiefs of Staff Comm. in Washington.	Churchill says U.S. planes will take part in "the ever increasing offensive against Germany." .... P.M. Eamon de Valera protests in Dublin that Irish government was not consulted by either Britain or U.S. regarding sending of American troops to Northern Ireland.		Brazil's Foreign Min. Oswaldo Aranha announces agreement between Peru and Ecuador on settlement of their 125-year-old border dispute.	
Jan. 28			British order civilians to evacuate mile-wide strip along northern shore of Singapore Island as Japanese advance to within 40 miles of city.	Inter-American Conference in Rio de Janeiro adopts several resolutions including severance of commerical relations with Axis, creation of an inter-American military headquarters in Washington and adherence to Atlantic Charter .... Brazil severs diplomatic relations with Germany, Italy and Japan.	

A	B	C	D	E
Includes developments that affect more than one world region, international organizations and important meetings of major world leaders.	*Includes all developments in European countries and military engagements between Allied and Axis powers in Africa and at sea.*	*Includes all developments in Japan and China, Japanese foreign policy and military actions in the Pacific region.*	*Includes all domestic and regional developments in Latin America, the Caribbean and Canada.*	*Includes developments in those independent nations and colonial possessions not covered in Columns B, C and D.*

U.S. Politics & Social Issues	U.S. Foreign Policy & Defense	U.S. Economy & Environment	Science, Technology & Nature	Culture, Leisure & Life Style	
Senate passes and sends to the President a House-approved bill giving FDR wartime control of telephone, telegraph and cable facilities.	Both Houses approve conference report leaving Office of Civilian Defense under control of Mayor La Guardia and send it on to FDR . . . . FDR asks Congress for a record $28.5 billion in supplemental war appropriations and contract authorizations.	CIO Pres. Philip Murray says in N.Y. that John L. Lewis's one-man negotiations with the AFL for labor unity are undemocratic.		Metropolitan Museum of Art Pres. Wm. C. Osborn says the museum has leased a concrete and steel vault in N.Y. State as a wartime repository for its most treasured pieces.	Jan. 19
	At a press conference FDR indicates U.S. war efforts are underway in almost all parts of the world.	With FDR's approval, OPM head Donald Nelson orders all passenger car and light truck production to halt by Feb. 1 . . . . Commissioner Ganson Purcell is elected chairman of the SEC, succeeding Edward C. Eicher . . . . House Naval Affairs Comm. charges in majority report "excessive and unconscionable" profits were made under the expanding naval program during past year.	FDR signs daylight savings bill to become effective at 2 a.m. Feb. 9.	Baseball Writers Assn. of America names former St. Louis Cardinal second baseman Rogers Hornsby to Hall of Fame.	Jan. 20
House completes congressional action on bill revising Civil Service pension system to include the president, vice president and congressmen.		WPB Chmn. Nelson abolishes OPM and establishes six new interim divisions in its place: Purchases, Production, Materials, Industry Operations, Labor and Civilian Supply . . . . ICC authorizes a 10% increase in railroad passenger fares to match increased operating costs.		Most Rev. Cosmo Gordon Lang, Archbishop of Canterbury, announces in London he will retire on March 31 . . . . N.Y. Boxing Writers Assn. presents its Edward J. Neil Memorial Plaque to Joe Louis for his contributions to boxing.	Jan. 21
	War Dept. announces plans for organization of two Negro air units: the 93rd Infantry Division and 100th Pursuit Squadron of the Army Air Corps.	House and Senate conferees agree to Bankhead amendment, giving the secretary of agriculture veto power over price ceilings set by the price administrator under the price control bill.		Curator Maurice Block of Henry E. Huntington Art Gallery reports X-rays disclose Gainsborough's famous painting *The Blue Boy* has hidden an incomplete painting of an unknown man's head under the surface paint for two centuries.	Jan. 22
	House approves and sends to Senate $12.556-billion military appropriations bill.	Lewis declines Murray's invitation to meet with CIO executive board to discuss peace with AFL . . . . WPB orders rationing of rubber and latex available for civilian goods to begin Feb. 1.		Walter Richard Sickert, 81, famous British artist who resigned from Royal Academy in 1935 in defense of sculptor Jacob Epstein, dies in Bathampton, Somerset.	Jan. 23
	Roberts Commission reports to FDR that Pearl Harbor disaster was due chiefly to "dereliction of duty" and "errors in judgment" by Adm. Husband E. Kimmel and Gen. Walter C. Short.	Executive boards of AFL and CIO accept FDR's six-man labor committee to preserve labor peace without effecting a formal merger between the two unions . . . . Henderson announces plans to ration sugar to about 50 pounds per capita in 1942.	Dr. John M. Kenney of N.Y. reports progress against certain types of cancer with phosphorus made radioactive by giant atom-smashing cyclotron.		Jan. 24
A crowd of 300 persons takes Cleo Wright, 30, Negro, from the Sikeston (Mo.) jail, where he was held under suspicion of attempting to attack a white woman, drags him through the Negro district, kills him and then burns his body.					Jan. 25
FDR signs Civil Service bill requiring retirement at age 70.	Reps. Melvin J. Maas (R, Minn.) and Andrew J. May (D, Ky.) call for fuller inquiries into Pearl Harbor disaster.	House passes conference-approved price control bill.			Jan. 26
	House approves and sends to Senate largest Navy appropriations bill in history, amounting to $19.977 billion.	FDR approves OPA Dir. Henderson's power to "ration all goods and commodities sold on the retail market." . . . . Senate approves and sends price control bill to FDR.			Jan. 27
	Senate passes and sends to White House $12.556-billion supplemental defense bill, most of which is for 33,000 Army planes . . . . FDR nominates Patrick Hurley as first U.S. minister to New Zealand.	Senate approves second war powers bill, which expands government's authority to expedite production, seize property, control profits and money markets and conserve precious metals.			Jan. 28
F	G	H	I	J	
Includes elections, federal-state relations, civil rights and liberties, crime, the judiciary, education, health care, poverty, urban affairs and population.	*Includes formation and debate of U.S. foreign and defense policies, veterans affairs and defense spending. (Relations with specific foreign countries are usually found under the region concerned.)*	*Includes business, labor, agriculture, taxation, transportation, consumer affairs, monetary and fiscal policy, natural resources, pollution and accidents.*	*Includes worldwide scientific, medical and technological developments, natural phenomena, U.S. weather and natural disasters.*	*Includes the arts, religion, scholarship, communications media, sports, entertainment, fashions, fads and social life.*	

	World Affairs	European War Zone	Pacific War Zone	The Americas	Other Countries & Territories
Jan. 29		Moscow communique announces that in last 10 days Marshal Semyon Timoshenko's troops in the Ukraine have retaken more than 400 towns and several hundred villages encompassing some 5,800 square kilometers . . . . After three days of debate, House of Commons gives Churchill a 464-1 vote of confidence with only James Maxton of the antiwar Independent Labor Party voting no.	Japanese troops land at Pemangkat, West Borneo, 525 miles from Java.	Ecuador breaks diplomatic relations with Germany, Italy and Japan, leaving only Chile and Argentina among Latin American countries not to do so . . . . Foreign ministers of Peru and Ecuador sign treaty in Rio de Janeiro, ending 125-year-old border dispute between the two countries . . . . Senate ratifies treaty settling about 4,300 claims by nationals of Mexico and U.S. against the government of the other and providing for Mexican payment to U.S. of $40 million.	
Jan. 30	Iran, Britain and Russia sign agreement in Teheran based upon Atlantic Charter and providing for military use of Iran "for not longer than six months after the end of the war."	Adolf Hitler, on ninth anniversary of his regime, dismisses FDR as a "fool" and predicts U.S. will soon see "how our submarines operate." . . . . The 6,836-ton American-owned oil tanker *Rochester* is sunk off Virginia coast, with three men killed.	Singapore is placed on a 9 p.m. curfew as Japanese reach Kulai, 18 miles north of the city.	Brazilian police are ordered to imprison all Axis adherents and to prohibit speaking of German, Japanese and Italian in public places.	
Jan. 31		British troops in Libya retreat from Jebel el-Achdar to Maraua, about 80 miles northeast of Bengazi . . . . In a new offensive in southern Ukraine, Soviet troops capture Berestovoya, 30 miles north of Sea of Azov.	British Lt. Gen. A.E. Percival announces "The Battle of Malaya has come to an end," as British troops abandon Malaya and retreat to Singapore . . . . Japanese troops attack Dutch naval base of Amboina between Celebes and New Guinea.		Britain and Ethiopia sign agreement in Addis Ababa restoring Ethiopia's independence, abolishing slavery there and providing for a British loan of 2.5 million pounds.
Feb. 1		Reich Commissar Josef Terboven proclaims Major Vidkun Quisling to be premier of Norway.	Singapore's big guns shell Japanese troops for first time across Strait of Johore, while Japanese bombers continue their raids . . . . Navy Dept. reports 16 Japanese ships, 41 planes and a number of hangars, ammunition dumps, fuel storage tanks, and other shore establishments were destroyed in raid on Marshall and Gilbert Islands in the Pacific . . . . Japanese troops capture Pontianak, the chief city on west coast of Dutch Borneo.	Juan Antonio Rios, Popular Front candidate and U.S. supporter, is elected president of Chile.	
Feb. 2		The 15,355-ton Swedish motorship *Amerikaland* is torpedoed and sunk 30 miles off Cape Hatteras—the 13th sinking off East Coast since Jan. 14.	War Dept. reports two Japanese attempts to land troops on west coast of Bataan were "broken up" with "heavy Japanese casualties in men and boats."	Bolivia announces it has accepted a proposal to pay Standard Oil Co. of Bolivia (a Standard Oil Co. of New Jersey subsidiary) $1,000,000 for claims against the government, thus settling a five-year-old dispute.	Egyptian Premier Hussein Sirry Pasha resigns with his coalition cabinet, giving ill health as reason.
Feb. 3		British announce they are abandoning Derna, Libya, 160 miles from the Egyptian border.	Japanese bombers attack Singapore for fourth consecutive day, causing heavy damage.		Free French officials announce completion of two military supply roads from Atlantic Coast of French Equatorial Africa to Khartum in Anglo-Egyptian Sudan.
Feb. 4		Lord Beaverbrook, British minister of supply, is appointed to new war cabinet post of minister of war production . . . . Reports from Ankara say 700 to 800 children daily are dying of diphtheria in Athens because of a lack of antitoxin.	Japanese forces are again repulsed in their assault on MacArthur's positions on Bataan . . . . Japanese forces capture Poklo, 75 miles east of Canton, and drive within 40 miles north of Hong Kong.		
Feb. 5		Under State Secy. Welles says Germans have taken all food reserves from Greeks and left them to starve . . . . German troops advance to Tmimi, 55 miles west of Tobruk, Libya . . . . Iran notifies Vichy government it is severing diplomatic relations, following action of Iraq and Egypt.	The 16,909-ton luxury liner *Empress of Asia* of Canadian Pacific Steamships Ltd. is destroyed by Japanese dive bombers near Sumatra en route to Singapore with 2,500 Imperial troops; the wrecked ship runs aground . . . . Japanese forces capture Paan, 30 miles north of Martaban and cross Salween River in Burma.	Uruguayan Defense Min. Juio Roletti announces the Uruguayan Navy will be provided with U.S. vessels to patrol River Plate estuary.	Mustafa Nahas Pasha, head of Wafd Party, forms new cabinet in Egypt, with himself as premier.

U.S. Politics & Social Issues	U.S. Foreign Policy & Defense	U.S. Economy & Environment	Science, Technology & Nature	Culture, Leisure & Life Style	
Senate Privileges and Elections Comm. says in its majority report that Sen. Wm. L. Langer (R, N.D.) should be expelled for gross impropriety, violation of oath and civil disobedience .... Atty. Gen. Francis Biddle announces all Japanese, German and Italian enemy aliens must leave special vital areas in San Francisco and Los Angeles by Feb. 24.	House Naval Affairs Comm. votes to table motion calling for access to testimony and documentary evidence used in Roberts Commission report on Pearl Harbor .... Major Gen. Millard F. Harmon is apponted chief of air staff, Army Air Force, succeeding Brig. Gen. Carl Spaatz, who is made chief of air force combat command.		Col. Bion K. Arnold, "father of the third rail" and consulting engineer who devised N.Y.'s Grand Central Terminal electrification plan, dies in Chicago.		Jan. 29
FDR celebrates his 60th birthday, marked by Birthday Balls for Infantile Paralysis Fund, special dinners and a nationwide broadcast to American people .... Gov. Culbert L. Olson announces revocation of professional and business licenses held by about 5,000 enemy aliens in California.		FDR signs Emergency Price Control Act of 1942, although he doubts the wisdom of permitting farm prices to rise to 110% of parity.	Dr. Alan F. Guttmacher of Johns Hopkins Univ. Medical School tells Birth Control Federation of America in N.Y. medical profession should change its view on theraputic abortion for the health and safety of mothers.		Jan. 30
		Total of 1,654 welders strike at three shipyards in Seattle and Tacoma after WPB refuses to recognize them as an independent organization in their dispute with AFL Metal Trades Union .... Labor Secy. Frances Perkins reports non-agricultural employment in December totaled record 40,940,000, an increase of 2.8 million over December 1940.		Leo Durocher signs contract to manage Brooklyn Dodgers.	Jan. 31
		CIO-UAW Pres. R.J. Thomas appeals to WPB to intervene in dispute with auto manufacturers over issue of double pay for Sunday work when the industry converts to war production.			Feb. 1
	FDR asks Congress to approve a $500-million loan to China to strengthen "her internal economy and her capacity in general to function with great military effectiveness in our common effort." .... Senate passes and returns to House record $26.495-billion naval appropriations bill.	Pres. Roosevelt nominates Leon Henderson to be Federal Price Administrator under new price control act .... WPB heads issue joint statement in Washington calling on Seattle-Tacoma striking welders to return to work.			Feb. 2
	House Foreign Affairs Comm. approves FDR's $500-million loan request for China.			Book-of-the-Month Club announces *Berlin Diary* by William L. Shirer and *Keys of the Kingdom* by A.J. Cronin have been chosen by 155 book critics in nationwide poll as 1941's best nonfiction and fiction books .... American and National Baseball Leagues agree to permit each club to play 14 home night games this year except for the Washington Senators, who will be permitted to play 7.	Feb. 3
Atty. Gen. Biddle announces 31 zones in Washington and Oregon will be barred to Japanese, Germans and Italians commencing Feb. 15.	House passes conference-approved $26.495-billion Navy appropriations bill.	Commerce Dept. reports record high retail sales for 1940 of $53.613 billion, a 17% increase over 1940.		Joe Cook, noted comedian, announces his retirement from stage in full page advertisement in *Variety*, because of paralysis in his left arm.	Feb. 4
	Senate passes and sends to White House $26.495-billion Navy appropriations bill.	SEC rejects application of Standard Oil Co. of N.J. for exemption from Holding Co. Act.			Feb. 5

F	G	H	I	J
Includes elections, federal-state relations, civil rights and liberties, crime, the judiciary, education, health care, poverty, urban affairs and population.	*Includes formation and debate of U.S. foreign and defense policies, veterans affairs and defense spending. (Relations with specific foreign countries are usually found under the region concerned.)*	*Includes business, labor, agriculture, taxation, transportation, consumer affairs, monetary and fiscal policy, natural resources, pollution and accidents.*	*Includes worldwide scientific, medical and technological developments, natural phenomena, U.S. weather and natural disasters.*	*Includes the arts, religion, scholarship, communications media, sports, entertainment, fashions, fads and social life.*

	World Affairs	European War Zone	Pacific War Zone	The Americas	Other Countries & Territories
Feb. 6	U.S.-British Combined Chiefs of Staff is established in Washington.	Organizations for Greek relief in Jerusalem report 2,000 Greeks are dying daily in Athens and Piraeus from starvation.	NEI reports Borneo town of Samarinda, 60 miles north of Balik Papan, apparantly has fallen to Japanese.		
Feb. 7		In Rouen, France 200 persons are arrested following an attempt to bomb a German Army building.	Japanese troops invade western coast of Singapore Island after occupying unopposed Ubin Island in the eastern entrance to Johore Strait.	German Transocean, Italian Stefani and Japanese Domei news agencies are closed in Paraguay, and the government instructs all media to cease using news from Axis countries.	King Farouk dissolves Egyptian Parliament, announces general elections will be held before March 30 and appoints Mustafa Nahos Pasha military governor of the country . . . . Martial law is proclaimed in Tangier, Spanish Morocco after anti-British riots break out as result of 25 deaths due to a time bomb explosion.
Feb. 8		British still claim to hold El Gazala, 40 miles west of Tobruk, and to have stopped Rommel's drive 150 miles west of Egyptian border . . . . Red Army reports Russian calvary and fresh infantry have driven a wedge into outer German lines below Leningrad . . . . Berlin announces Maj. Gen. Fritz Todt, 50, Reich minister for armament and ammunition, power and water and builder of Germany's Westwall forts and super-highways, was killed in plane crash today while on "an official mission to the East."		In Costa Rica's congressional elections, Pres. Rafael Calderon Guardia's National Republican Party wins 19 of 22 seats.	
Feb. 9	Pacific Council is formed in London with following members: U.K., Churchill; Australia, Sir Earle C.G. Page; Netherlands, Pieter S. Gerbrandy and E.F. M.J. van Verduynen; and N.Z., W.J. Jordan.	Bank of France estimates $4.2 billion has been paid for German occupation through end of 1941.	MacArthur's troops reportedly repulse all Japanese attempts to penetrate Bataan Peninsula . . . . Japanese troops drive British forces back at several points on west and northwest coasts of Singapore.		
Feb. 10	Gen. Chiang Kai-shek confers with India's Viceroy, the Marquess of Linlithgow, and Pandit Jawaharlal Nehru in New Dehli.		An estimated 100,000 Japanese forces on and around Singapore Island drive British, Australian and Indian troops to within 10 miles of Singapore proper . . . . Japanese command hurls six divisions against Allied forces on Bataan.		
Feb. 11			Japanese demand immediate surrender of Singapore in a note to British Commander Lt. Gen. Arthur E. Percival . . . . Japanese troops land in southern Celebes at Jeneponto and Macassar.	U.S. troops are sent to Netherlands West Indies islands of Curacao and Aruba to assist in their defense and protect important oil refineries.	
Feb. 12		The 26,000-ton German battleships *Scharnhorst* and *Gneisenau* and 10,000-ton cruiser *Prinz Eugen* sail out of Brest, France past Dover and into North Sea, apparantly towards the naval base at Kiel . . . . Leslie Hore-Belisha, Edgar L. Granville and Sir John Henry Morris-Jones resign from Liberal National Party after Granville and Morris-Jones are censured for failing to vote confidence in Churchill's government.	Despite four British counter-attacks, Japanese troops drive to Tanglin, two miles northwest of Singapore City . . . . Japanese claim occupation of Macassar, capital of Celebes, and Banjermassin, capital of Dutch Borneo.		British government invites India to send representatives to British and Pacific War Councils.
Feb. 13					

A	B	C	D	E
Includes developments that affect more than one world region, international organizations and important meetings of major world leaders.	*Includes all developments in European countries and military engagements between Allied and Axis powers in Africa and at sea.*	*Includes all developments in Japan and China, Japanese foreign policy and military actions in the Pacific region.*	*Includes all domestic and regional developments in Latin America, the Caribbean and Canada.*	*Includes developments in those independent nations and colonial possessions not covered in Columns B, C and D.*

U.S. Politics & Social Issues	U.S. Foreign Policy & Defense	U.S. Economy & Environment	Science, Technology & Nature	Culture, Leisure & Life Style	
Commenting on radio address by Edward J. Flynn, Democratic national chairman (who said on Feb. 2 that no "misfortune except a major military defeat could befall this country to the extent involved in the election of a Congress hostile to the President"), Pres. Roosevelt says that when the country is at war, it wants congressmen, regardless of party, who will back up the government of the U.S. . . . . George Hill, secretary to Rep. Hamilton Fish (R, N.Y.), is sentenced to two to six years for perjury before federal grand jury investigating Nazi propaganda . . . . N.Y. County Democratic Comm. (Tammany) ousts Christopher D. Sullivan as its leader.		Nat. Wholesale Druggists Assn. is charged by a Newark, N.J. federal grand jury with conspiring to violate Sherman Antitrust Act by fixing wholesale profit margins on drug products . . . . Federal Security Admin. Paul V. McNutt announces that as of March 1 200 of 800 CCC camps will be closed.	Tornadoes sweep throuh Arkansas, Alabama, Mississippi and Georgia, killing 18 persons . . . . At least four persons are killed in mud avalanches caused by heavy rains in northern California.	Dean Emeritus of Harvard Law School Roscoe Pound says preventing newspapers from owning radio stations would be a movement towards denial of free speech.	Feb. 6
Southern Assn. of Colleges and Secondary Schools passes resolution in Atlanta deploring any proposal to grant a bachelor's degree after two years of study because it would cheapen the degree.	Stimson says Army plans to increase its air force to one million men this year, and double it later, making it the world's largest.			Cornelius Warmerdam pole vaults to a new world's record of 15 ft. ⅜ in. at 35th annual Melrose Games in N.Y.C.	Feb. 7
Dies Comm. recommends all Japanese on West Coast be removed and interned at least 500 miles inland.				Selective Service Dir. Lewis B. Hershey declares motion picture industry "is an activity essential in certain instances to the national health" and orders deferments for its workers.	Feb. 8
Pres. Roosevelt vetoes measure strengthening foreign agent registration law on grounds its present wording would hinder free movement of Allied representatives to and from U.S. . . . . N.Y. Chapter of the Nat. Lawyer's Guild and Nat. Fed. for Constitutional Liberties ask House to disband Dies Comm. because of its "pro Axis leanings."	House passes and sends to Senate deficiency appropriations bill, including $100 million for civil defense . . . . FDR nominates Adm. William H. Standley as ambassador to Russia.	Fire on 83,423-ton French luxury liner *Normandie* starts with sparks from worker's acetylene torch, destroying ship's three upper decks . . . . By voice vote Senate confirms Leon Henderson as federal price administrator under new price control bill.	Clocks are advanced one hour at 2 a.m. as nation goes on War Time to conserve electricity . . . . WPB limits use of Vitamin A to doses prescribed by medical authorities for specified purposes.		Feb. 9
		Senate Agricultural Comm. reports bill forbidding government to sell its cotton, wheat and corn stocks below parity levels.		Jacob Epstein unveils his newest sculpture in London, a four-ton, seven-foot-high group depicting the Biblical story of Jacob wrestling with the angel.	Feb. 10
The New School of Social Research of N.Y. announces organization of a complete French university, staffed by former Belgian and French professors, to be known as Free School of Advanced Studies. Its certificates will be recognized by the Belgian and Free French governments.	Senate and House vote a $500-million loan to China.	Almost 10,000 men strike when Ford Motor Co. refuses to dismiss Horace Merrill as a "troublemaker" at River Rouge plant, as demanded by CIO-UAW . . . . Henderson announces that beginning Feb. 19 recapped and retreaded tires will be rationed . . . . Agriculture Secy. Wickard warns the farm bill before Senate will cost consumers $1 billion a year.		Green Bay Packer end Don Hutson is named MVP in NFL for 1941 by a newspapermen's committee in N.Y. . . . . After 48 years of operation the cooperative news gathering agency N.Y.C. News Assn. disbands due to decrease in membership.	Feb. 11
	Wendell L. Willkie says in Lincoln Day speech in Boston that Gen. Douglas MacArthur should be brought to Washington from Philippines and made supreme commander of U.S. armed forces.		Stimson announces that in addition to routine injections all men will be vaccinated against yellow fever, so that every man will be available for service in the tropics.	Painter of *American Gothic* Grant Wood dies in Iowa City . . . . Leslie MacMitchell of NYU runs 4:08 mile in N.Y., which is fastest ever run in college competition.	Feb. 12
Federal District Court in Washington convicts famous woman speed flier Laura Ingalls on charge of being an unregistered paid agent of Germany . . . . Sen. Millard E. Tydings (D, Md.) attacks government's conduct of war in Senate speech, asks that Wendell L. Willkie be appointed to a responsible "war post," condemns Administration for not stopping all strikes, says James M. Landis is not fitted to be director of OCD and urges an AEF be sent to Bataan or Singapore.	FDR signs $500-million loan to China . . . . Sumner Welles says government will not permit Rumanian King Carol to enter U.S. because his visit would not aid national unity or the war effort.			Charles Boyer, French actor, becomes an American citizen in Hollywood.	Feb. 13
F	G	H	I	J	
Includes elections, federal-state relations, civil rights and liberties, crime, the judiciary, education, health care, poverty, urban affairs and population.	*Includes formation and debate of U.S. foreign and defense policies, veterans affairs and defense spending. (Relations with specific foreign countries are usually found under the region concerned.)*	*Includes business, labor, agriculture, taxation, transportation, consumer affairs, monetary and fiscal policy, natural resources, pollution and accidents.*	*Includes worldwide scientific, medical and technological developments, natural phenomena, U.S. weather and natural disasters.*	*Includes the arts, religion, scholarship, communications media, sports, entertainment, fashions, fads and social life.*	

	World Affairs	European War Zone	Pacific War Zone	The Americas	Other Countries & Territories
Feb. 14		British officials in Ankara announce the chartering of two Swedish ships to carry wheat and medicine to Athens and Piraeus and return with Greek refugee children .... Using U.S. planes, British fliers down 20 and damage 15 of 35 Axis aircraft in Acroma, Libya area, according to British sources.	Japanese paratroopers are dropped at three different points in rich oil refining area around Palembang, Sumatra.		
Feb. 15			Singapore surrenders to the Japanese at 10 p.m., seven days after island was invaded and 70 days after invasion of Malaya began .... In a London radio broadcast, Churchill says Singapore's surrender will not weaken the purpose of the United Nations .... Japanese troops land on Sumatra near mouth of Musi River despite Allied air assaults.		
Feb. 16		RAF pilots based in Cairo score hits on two Italian cruisers and two destroyers in central Mediterranean.	Premier Hideki Tojo tells Japanese Diet Japan will dispose of Burma, China, India, Netherlands Indies, Australia and N.Z., in that order, now that Singapore is eliminated .... MacArthur's forces on Bataan are subjected to Japanese artillery and intermittent infantry attacks .... After two days of intense fighting, Japanese forces occupy Palembang, oil center and capital of Sumatra.	German submarines attack Aruba, sinking three oil tankers and shelling but not damaging Standard Oil Co. refinery there .... Bolivian government agrees to pay $1.5 million to Standard Oil Co. of N.J. in final settlement of all claims.	
Feb. 17			Battle of the Sittang River begins in Burma .... Japanese rename Singapore Shonan, meaning "Light of the South."		
Feb. 18				U.S. bombers drive off enemy submarines near Aruba in Netherlands West Indies .... Mexico bans export of raw rubber and rubber goods unless authorized by the government.	Gen. Chiang Kai-shek and Mohandas K. Ghandi meet in Calcutta for first time and discuss Indian-Chinese relations.
Feb. 19		Churchill bows to popular demand and reorganizes his war cabinet, trimming it from nine to seven positions and dropping Kingsley Wood and Arthur Greenwood .... French "war guilt" trial opens in Riom, with defendants Leon Blum and Edouard Daladier assailing the constitutionality of the Supreme Court specially created to try them.	Australia is bombed for first time when two flights of Japanese bombers raid Darwin on north coast .... Japanese force British back on west side of the Bilin River on South Burma front .... Battle of the Sittang River ends with 17th Indian Division losing heavily after being attacked by two Japanese divisions.		
Feb. 20			Japanese troops invade Bali, one mile off eastern tip of Java, while other forces on Sumatra reach Sunda Strait, facing western end of Java .... Japanese troops land near Deli, capital of Portuguese Timor, and near Kupang, captial of Dutch part of the island.	Recalled by his government seven weeks ago, German Amb. to Argentina Edmund von Thermann leaves Buenos Aires on a Spanish freighter.	
Feb. 21		Vice Premier Adm. Jean Francois Darlan announces in Vichy the 26,500-ton battleship *Dunkerque*, under repair for 18 months at Oran, Algeria, where British fleet damaged her in July 1940, has returned to Toulon naval base.	Japanese claim 73,000 British troops captured while losing only about 3,000 in battle for Singapore.	Uruguayan Pres. Alfredo Baldomir dissolves Congress, postpones the March 29 elections indefinitely, and stations troops in Montevideo after pro-Axis Herreristas vote resolutions censuring the government.	Chiang Kai-shek says in Bombay that Britain should give Indian people "real political power" as speedily as possible.
Feb. 22		Churchill reorganizes his cabinet for second time in four days, dropping four men and adding two new members: Sir James Grigg as war secretary and Viscount Wolmer as minister of economic warfare.	Land communications between Rangoon, Burma and outside points are cut as British troops attempt to slow Japanese drive between Bilin and Sittang Rivers .... Official Chinese Central Daily News in Chungking urges Russia to attack Japan before Tokyo makes the decision for war against Soviets.	Pres. Baldomir signs decree creating Council of State to take place of dissolved Uruguayan Congress, with the power to name his successor in case he abandons office.	Mohandas Ali Jinnah, president of All-India Moslem League, declares India should be partitioned into four separate Moslem and Hindu states .... Sir Tej Bahadur Sapru leads a non-party Indian conference which adopts resolution in New Delhi urging home rule for India.

A	B	C	D	E
Includes developments that affect more than one world region, international organizations and important meetings of major world leaders.	*Includes all developments in European countries and military engagements between Allied and Axis powers in Africa and at sea.*	*Includes all developments in Japan and China, Japanese foreign policy and military actions in the Pacific region.*	*Includes all domestic and regional developments in Latin America, the Caribbean and Canada.*	*Includes developments in those independent nations and colonial possessions not covered in Columns B, C and D.*

U.S. Politics & Social Issues	U.S. Foreign Policy & Defense	U.S. Economy & Environment	Science, Technology & Nature	Culture, Leisure & Life Style	
Progressive Education Assn., meeting in Atlantic City, adopts resolution calling for colleges to liberalize their entrance requirements and thus enable secondary schools to set up a more flexible curriculum.		WPB Chmn. Nelson announces no new tires will be sold for passenger cars until war is over.		Cornelius Warmerdam pole vaults 15 ft. 7¼ in. at Boston A.A. track meet to break all indoor and outdoor records for the event.	Feb. 14
AMA's council on medical education and hospitals votes to drop Univ. of Georgia from its approved list because of Gov. Eugene Talmadge's dismissal of faculty members for urging "racial equality."					Feb. 15
Mayor La Guardia testifies before Comm. on Fair Employment Practices meeting in N.Y.C. that many labor unions do not admit Negroes and urges legislation to end the practice .... Atty. Gen. Biddle recommends Congress enact legislation making it a criminal offense for unauthorized persons to disclose confidential government information.	An estimated nine million men register today in the third draft since October 1940, bringing total to 26.5 million registrants.	Supreme Court rules, 4 to 2, against government in latter's suit to recover $8,000,000 from Bethlehem Shipbuilding Corp. as excess profits on contracts for 86 ships during World War I.			Feb. 16
	House passes a $32.070-billion defense appropriation bill and sends it to the Senate .... FDR says it is possible for enemy ships to shell N.Y.C. or for their planes to bomb Detroit .... Sen. David I. Walsh (D, Mass.) tells Senate Appropriations Comm. that Atlantic and Gulf coasts are "almost defenseless."	FDR vetoes bill to promote growing of guayule and other rubber-producing plants because a House amendment limits expenditure of funds for the purpose to the U.S.			Feb. 17
		Senate and House pass resolutions for separate inquiries to determine whether sabotage or negligence caused fire aboard former French liner *Normandie* .... Bethlehem and Republic Steel Corps. issue statements denouncing maintenance of union membership clause in union contracts as a camouflaged closed shop.		Albert Payson Terhune, 69, famous writer of dog stories, dies at Sunnybank, his home in Pompton Lakes, N.J.	Feb. 18
Following nationwide protests, Senate repeals congressional pension provision of Civil Service Retirement Act .... California State Atty. Gen. Earl Warren rules Gov. Culbert L. Olson cannot revoke all business and professional licences of aliens in California until FDR declares they are "enemies."	War Dept. assigns Brig. Gen. Dwight D. Eisenhower to be chief of War Plans Division, completing reorganization of Army general staff .... Stimson says the Army will not be dispersed to protect U.S. coastlines and industrial centers but is being prepared for offensive action against the Axis.				Feb. 19
United Citizens League is organized by 1,500 American-born Japanese in Los Angeles to oppose evacuation of "loyal aliens" and citizens of Japanese decent .... Laura Ingalls, 40, well-known woman pilot, is sentenced in Washington to eight months to two years in prison for failure to register as paid agent of Germany .... N.Y. federal grand jury indicts 69 persons for operating what is described as the largest bootleg liquor organization ever uncovered by U.S. Alcohol Tax Unit agents.	FDR issues executive order authorizing Stimson to designate military areas from which "any or all persons may be excluded" for purposes of protection against sabotage.			Gian Carlo Menotti's opera *The Island God* premieres at the New York Metropolitan Opera .... Ray Robinson wins his 28th straight fight with a TKO over Maxie Berger in second round of their welterweight battle in N.Y.C.	Feb. 20
Earl Warren tells a congressional committee the Pacific Coast is "approaching an invisible deadline" of organized sabotage.		NWLB denies $1-a-day increase and a union shop sought by CIO International Union of Mine, Mill and Smelter Workers for Phelps Dodge Corp. plant in Douglas, Ariz.			Feb. 21
Census Bureau reports there were over 2.5 million births in U.S. and a record 1.565 million marriages last year.		A federal jury in St. Louis finds Union Electric Co. of Mo. guilty of violating Holding Company Act for its $591,000 "slush fund" used for political favors.		King George nominates Dr. William Temple, Archbishop of York, to succeed Dr. Cosmo Gordon Lang as Archbishop of Canterbury.	Feb. 22
F	G	H	I	J	
Includes elections, federal-state relations, civil rights and liberties, crime, the judiciary, education, health care, poverty, urban affairs and population.	*Includes formation and debate of U.S. foreign and defense policies, veterans affairs and defense spending. (Relations with specific foreign countries are usually found under the region concerned.)*	*Includes business, labor, agriculture, taxation, transportation, consumer affairs, monetary and fiscal policy, natural resources, pollution and accidents.*	*Includes worldwide scientific, medical and technological developments, natural phenomena, U.S. weather and natural disasters.*	*Includes the arts, religion, scholarship, communications media, sports, entertainment, fashions, fads and social life.*	

	World Affairs	European War Zone	Pacific War Zone	The Americas	Other Countries & Territories
Feb. 23	British and Americans sign agreement under which British payment for Lend-Lease supplies is indefinitely postponed and the framework for a post-war economic order based upon Atlantic Charter is established.	Soviet forces capture Dorogobuzh, about 50 miles east of Smolensk, in continuing Russian counter offensive on central front.	In first attack of war on American mainland, a Japanese submarine fires about 25 shells at Bankline Oil Refinery at edge of Ellwood Oil Field, 12 miles west of Santa Barbara . . . . Reports from Bandung claim all ships of the Japanese invasion fleet off Bali are sunk, damaged or dispersed, with only one escaping.		
Feb. 24		German Amb. to Turkey Franz von Papen and his wife escape injury in Ankara when an assassin explodes a bomb near them in street . . . . Churchill tells the House of Commons that during last two months Britain has suffered a "most serious increase in shipping losses" . . . . Russia claims the German 16th Army is defeated around Staraya Russa, south of Lake Ilmen on northern front . . . . Vichy assures U.S. that it will not lend any military aid to Axis "beyond the terms of the armistice agreements."	British troops retreat to west bank of Sittang River, last natural defense line before Rangoon, some 60 miles away.		Colonial Secy. Lord Cranborne tells House of Lords that British government favors India's freedom but Indian leaders must "devise some scheme that would be satisfactory to all."
Feb. 25			Los Angeles area is blacked out from 2:25 to 7:21 a.m. Anti-aircraft guns throw up barrages for first time in war when reports of unidentified flying planes are received by Army . . . . NEI command claims sinking of three Japanese transports near Macassar, Southern Celebes.		Sir Stafford Cripps tells Commons the British government will soon decide on India's political status.
Feb. 26		First Lord of the Admiralty A.V. Alexander says the 26,000-ton German battleships *Scharnhorst* and *Gneisenau* have been hit and that one is in drydock at Kiel . . . . Soviet Amb. to U.S. Maxim M. Litvinov says in N.Y. that Hitler "could be destroyed by summer" if the Allies open a secnd front.	In surprise assaults against Japanese forces on Bataan, MacArthur's troops reportedly capture "a number of the enemy's advance positions." . . . . Stimson says 15 unidentified planes flew over Los Angeles this morning, causing anti-aircraft batteries to go into action.	Peruvian and Ecuadorian Parliaments ratify Rio de Janeiro agreement settling their boundary dispute . . . . Britain signs treaty in Caracas ceding its claim to Patos Island, based on its occupation of island since 1799, to Venezuela . . . . FDR raises U.S. legations in Bolivia, Ecuador and Paraguay to status of embassies.	Jewish population in Palestine stops all activity to mourn for the more than 700 passengers lost in the sinking of the refugee ship *Struma* in a Black Sea minefield.
Feb. 27		In "war guilt" trial at Riom, Edouard Daladier says French Army had more mechanized equipment than Germans in 1940, but military leaders did not use it.	Battle of the Java Sea results in Japanese victory and survival of four American destroyers . . . . 11,050-ton aircraft carrier tender *Langley* is sunk between Australia and Java, most of her crew being transferred to the *Pecos* . . . . Japanese bombers raid Port Blair, capital of Andaman Islands in Bay of Bengal, about 420 miles southwest of Rangoon.	Tresaury Secy. Morgenthau and Ecuadorian ambassador to U.S. sign agreement in Washington whereby Ecuador gets a $5-million U.S. loan for stabilization of exchange rates.	
Feb. 28		At Riom, Daladier accuses Marshal Petain of being responsible for French unpreparedness, negligence and defeat by Germany . . . . British parachutists land at Bruneval, 12 miles north of Havre, and destroy German radio aircraft unit there.	Japanese troops land at two points on Java, beginning the long-expected battle for last Allied bastion in the NEI.		
March 1		Moscow reports continued Russian advances on all fronts and claims the German effort to relieve the trapped army at Staraya Russa with airborne infantry has been frustrated . . . . All seven bishops of Norwegian State Church resign following the invasion of Trondheim Cathedral by Nazi troops and a decree ordering all children from 10 to 18 to join Quisling youth movement.	Japanese troops in Java advance 40 miles in northwest sector to capture Subang, about 30 miles from Dutch Army headquarters in Bandung . . . . Japanese troops cross Sittang River and advance towards main Burma-China highway north of Pegu, 45 miles northwest of Rangoon.		
March 2		Berlin admits Russian attacks of increasing ferocity are taking place in Donets Basin, Crimea and Kursk area, north of Kharkov.	U.N. command of forces in NEI is turned over to Dutch, and Supreme Commander of Southwest Pacific Sir Archibald Wavell resumes his appointment as commander-in-chief in India . . . . Dutch, American and British troops counter-attack against three Japanese columns, halting their inland advance in Java.	Puerto Rican Gov. Rexford G. Tugwell reports NYA camp on Mona Island was shelled by enemy vessel, presumably a submarine.	

U.S. Politics & Social Issues	U.S. Foreign Policy & Defense	U.S. Economy & Environment	Science, Technology & Nature	Culture, Leisure & Life Style	
Atty. Gen. Biddle orders that German, Italian and Japanese aliens who enlisted in U.S. armed forces prior to Dec. 7 and all persons of Greek and Turkish extraction who emigrated from the Aegean or Dodecanese Islands be no longer classified as enemy aliens.	Speaking from White House, FDR tells the American people that "soon, we and not our enemies will have the offensive; we, not they, will win the final battles." . . . . Senate Appropriations Comm. reports $32.762-billion war supply bill, $691,836,000 more than House version.	Thirty-five hundred employes walk out after working eight hours at the Bethlehem Shipbuilding Corp. yards in San Pedro, Calif., in a protest against a 10-hour workday which began Feb. 12.	Major August von Parseval, a pioneer designer and builder of non-rigid dirigibles whose balloons were used by Germans during World War I, dies in Berlin.	Stefan Zweig, 60, world-famous author and biographer, and his wife Elizabeth, 30, commit suicide by taking poison near Petropolis, Brazil.	Feb. 23
House votes to repeal its own pension benefits in Civil Service Retirement Act . . . . FDR merges 16 federal housing agencies into a single National Housing Agency under John B. Blandford, Jr.					Feb. 24
Atty. Gen. Biddle announces 448 enemy aliens have been ordered interned for war's duration.		Senate overrides FDR's veto and votes to prohibit Commodity Credit Corp. from selling government-owned farm products below parity prices . . . . Combined Labor Bd., including representatives from CIO and AFL, asks FDR to oppose any plan to prohibit general wage increases . . . . WPB bars use of rubber for thread in manufacture of corsets, girdles, brassieres and foundation garments for general use.	Harvard Observatory Dir. Dr. Harlow Shapley reports census of the galaxies he is now conducting is two-thirds complete and will include all the galaxies up to 100,000 light years away, involving a thousand milion stars.		Feb. 25
		Standard Oil Co. of N.J. says the oil supply situation on Atlantic Coast is serious because of submarine attacks and transfer of tankers to Navy.		Overseas Press Club presents its 1941 awards for outstanding war coverage to Cyrus L. Sulzberger and Otto D. Tolischus (newspaper) and Cecil Brown (radio).	Feb. 26
S.C. Gov. Joseph Emile Harley dies in the executive mansion in Columbia.	OCD Dir. James M. Landis tells regional directors to request states and communities to black out all signs, window displays and lighting which cannot be put out immediately . . . . Dies Comm. submits 285-page report to House contending Japanese carried out espionage in U.S. for years.	CIO workers at Bethlehem Shipbuilding Corp.'s San Pedro, Calif. plant vote for two 10-hour shifts with overtime pay . . . . House defeats an amendment to second war powers bill to suspend for war's duration laws prescribing a maximum 40-hour work week and extra pay for overtime . . . . Rep. Robert L. Doughton (D, N.C.) introduces bill to House to raise debt limit from $65 billion to $125 billion.		Joan Fontaine and Gary Cooper are named best actors of 1941, John Ford best director and *How Green Was My Valley* best picture by Academy of Motion Picture Arts . . . . Presidential appeals board orders Ted Williams, last year's American League batting champion and Boston Red Sox outfielder, placed in class 3-A and deferred from military service because of a dependent.	Feb. 27
Scores of persons are injured when 1,200 armed whites prevent Negro tenants from moving into a 200-unit federal defense housing project in Detroit.	War and Navy Depts. announce Adm. Husband E. Kimmel and Major Gen. Walter Short will be tried by courts-martial for "dereliction of duty" at such time "as public interest and safety" permits . . . . House passes by voice vote second war powers bill and returns it to the Senate.	FDR orders WPB Chmn. Donald Nelson to "take every step to raise production now, to bring home . . . . the supreme importance of war production this crucial spring."		Gregory Rice sets new world indoor three-mile record of 13:45.7 at National AAU meet in N.Y.	Feb. 28
					March 1
	Senate and House pass $32.762 billion war appropriations bill and send it to White House . . . . FDR issues an executive order reorganizing the Army into three branches: a ground force, an air force and a service of supply command, all under leadership of Chief of Staff Gen. George C. Marshall.				March 2
F	G	H	I	J	
Includes elections, federal-state relations, civil rights and liberties, crime, the judiciary, education, health care, poverty, urban affairs and population.	*Includes formation and debate of U.S. foreign and defense policies, veterans affairs and defense spending. (Relations with specific foreign countries are usually found under the region concerned.)*	*Includes business, labor, agriculture, taxation, transportation, consumer affairs, monetary and fiscal policy, natural resources, pollution and accidents.*	*Includes worldwide scientific, medical and technological developments, natural phenomena, U.S. weather and natural disasters.*	*Includes the arts, religion, scholarship, communications media, sports, entertainment, fashions, fads and social life.*	

	World Affairs	European War Zone	Pacific War Zone	The Americas	Other Countries & Territories
March 3		An estimated 500 civilians are killed and 2,000 injured in RAF air attacks on Paris suburbs of Boulogne-sur-Seine, Villejuif, Clamart, Issy-les-Moulineaux, Montrouge, Neuilly, Le Vesinet, Le Pecq and Sevres.	More Japanese troops land in the Philippines, while other units shell Cebu and Negros islands .... Dutch report Japanese advance in Java has been checked.	U.S. and Brazil reach several accords providing for a $100-million loan to Brazil through Import-Export Bank, development of Itabarra iron mines, expanded Lend-Lease aid to Brazil and a $5-million fund to develop Brazil's raw rubber production.	
March 4		Several thousand additional U.S. forces arrive in Northern Ireland.	Netherlands command in Bandung admits Japanese troops have made advances since their landing on Java Feb. 28 .... Dutch government in London is reportedly permitting NEI companies to transfer their main offices from Batavia to the Dutch West Indies.		
March 5		Polish government in London receives report that 100 Poles were executed in Warsaw yesterday for the recent killing of one German policeman and wounding of another .... Soviets claim capture of Yukhnov, 130 miles southwest of Moscow, in their continuing advance on central front.	Japan claims capture of Batavia, capital of NEI, while Dutch command says the battle is still raging.	Ortiz Rubio is charged with fatal shooting of Mexican State Gov. Alfredo Zarate Albarran in state captial of Tolucca.	Pandit Jawaharlal Nehru says in Allahabad an independent national government should be immediately established in India. He predicts that Hindus and Moslems will reach an agreement "or ultimately the problem will be solved by conflict."
March 6			Dutch command admits fall of Batavia and reports that Jakarta near the southern coast of Java has been abandoned, slicing the island in two and isolating naval base of Surabaya in eastern Java .... Numerically superior Japanese troops, aided by air power, break through Dutch defenses on northern side of volcano of Tangkuban Prahu, 10 miles north of Bandung.	*N.Y. Times* reports three men and a woman described as "top ranking Nazis" have been arrested in Mexico on charges of violating the country's new Espionage Act .... Canadian P.M. W.L. Mackenzie King tells the House of Commons a highway from British Columbia to Fairbanks, Alaska has approval of both the U.S. and Canada.	
March 7		Marshal Petain sends message to families and survivors of RAF raid on Paris stating: "History has already judged the criminal aggression of a former ally who left our soldiers to die alone only to return two years later to spread death among our innocent civilians." .... Ankara reports 50 persons have been arrested in connection with attempt to bomb German Amb. Franz von Papen on Feb. 24 .... Traveling 1,200 miles from Lake Chad in French Equatorial Africa, Free French forces attack three fortified Italian positions in Fezzan, southwest Libya, capturing prisoners and weapons.	AP reports that a Japanese military, naval and air mission is making a survey of Madagascar.	Brazilian government says that, because its embassy and officials in Japan are being treated like prisoners of war, retaliatory steps against Japanese diplomats in Brazil will be taken.	Moslem League of India sends Churchill message asking that "no declaration be made which may prejudice, prejudge or militate against the Moslem demand for Pakistan."
March 8		AP reports Russian capture of Sychevka on central front after two days of fighting in which the German 48th Division was virtually destroyed.	Netherlands government in London denies Axis reports that Java has surrendered .... Japan claims occupation of Rangoon, Burma, but British communiques admit only to the fall of Payagyi north of capital.	Fourth Brazilian ship is sunk in Atlantic since Feb. 15 when 5,152-ton passenger liner *Cayru* is torpedoed off N.Y., with 26 known survivors .... Uruguayan Pres. Alfredo Baldomir appoints 28-man Council of State to replace Congress, which he dissolved Feb. 21.	
March 9		The 35,000 to 50,000-ton German battleship *Tirpitz* is attacked by British naval torpedo planes and retires under cover of heavy smoke screen toward Norwegian coast .... Foreign Secy. Anthony Eden and Greek Premier Emmanuel Tsouderos sign agreement in London under which Britain will equip Greek forces in return for Greek naval aid in Mediterranean .... RAF planes carry out heavy raid on Essen, Germany, starting 22 large fires.	After 10 days of fighting, Japanese forces end conquest of Java, claiming 93,000 Dutch and 5,000 British prisoners .... British admit evacuation of Rangoon, Burma to Japanese forces.	Six-man Anglo-American Caribbean Commission is created to make a study of American and British islands in West Indies area and recommend improvements in their standards of living.	

A	B	C	D	E
Includes developments that affect more than one world region, international organizations and important meetings of major world leaders.	*Includes all developments in European countries and military engagements between Allied and Axis powers in Africa and at sea.*	*Includes all developments in Japan and China, Japanese foreign policy and military actions in the Pacific region.*	*Includes all domestic and regional developments in Latin America, the Caribbean and Canada.*	*Includes developments in those independent nations and colonial possessions not covered in Columns B, C and D.*

U.S. Politics & Social Issues	U.S. Foreign Policy & Defense	U.S. Economy & Environment	Science, Technology & Nature	Culture, Leisure & Life Style	
Lt. Gen. John L. De Witt designates a Pacific Coast military area extending 95 to 250 miles inland in Washington, Oregon, California and southern Arizona, from which all enemy aliens and American-Japanese may be excluded or their movements restricted .... FBI arrests 30 Germans and three Italians in raids on 350 locations in Yorkville, N.Y.C.'s main German-American community.	Office of Lend-Lease Administration announces authorized dollar limit on aid which President may provide to U.N. countries is now $47.410 billion, one-third of all money voted for war program.	WPB Chmn. Nelson issues directive requiring all contracts for military supplies to be placed by negotiation .... WPB issues order effective March 30, imposing 25 restrictions on manufacture of men's and boys' clothing, eliminating extra trousers, trouser cuffs and pleats, patch-pockets and vests for double-breasted suits .... Treasury Secy. Morgenthau presents his tax recommendations to House Ways and Means Comm., calling for $9.610 billion in increased taxes next year.			March 3
					March 4
A federal jury in Washington convicts George S. Viereck, German-born U.S. citizen, of violating Foreign Agents Registration Act by withholding essential information when he registered with State Dept. as agent of German interests.	Vichy's Amb. to U.S. Gaston Henri-Haye protests to State Dept. over U.S. recognition of Free French on Pacific island of New Caledonia.	Price Admin. Henderson tells Senate Defense Investigating Comm. there is little chance of tires for passenger autos being available through 1944 due to growing rubber shortage.		*Saturday Evening Post* and *Liberty Magazine* announce price increases from 5 to 10 cents a copy in April .... Appellate Division of N.Y. State Supreme Court dismisses damage suit of Rep. Edwin Arthur Hall against Binghamton Press Co. for criticizing his vote against Lend-Lease bill, explaining that a newspaper has the right to hold "national legislators .... to the strictest accountability."	March 5
Thomas J. Mooney, 59, labor leader who served more than 22 years in prison for the San Fransisco Preparedness Day bombing of July 22, 1916, a crime he did not commit, dies in San Francisco after his fourth abdominal operation in three years .... Washington, D.C. school board is asked to ban from the schools seven songs, including *My Old Kentucky Home* and *Carry Me Back to Old Virginny*, because they contain certain phrases offensive to Negroes.	Five German-born Americans are found guilty of peacetime espionage by a federal jury in N.Y.	CIO Pres. Philip Murray urges labor in radio address to "support your country and your unions by seeing that not an hour of production time is lost from any cause until we win the war." .... House Ways and Means Comm. reports out a bill to increase national debt limit from $65 to $125 billion.			March 6
U.S. government takes over nearly 5,800 acres of land in Owens Valley, Southern California for "largely self-sustaining" reception center for American-born and alien Japanese to be excluded from the Pacific Coast military areas.		WPB orders manufacture of radios and phonographs for civilian use be discontinued after April 22 so that plants may be converted to full war production .... Commerce Dept. reports record national income of $94.5 billion in 1941, an increase of $17.3 billion from 1940.		Penn State dethrones Fordham as champion of I.C. 4-A indoor track and field championship at Madison Square Garden in N.Y.C. .... Baseball Commissioner Kenesaw Mountain Landis rules secret baseball contracts giving college players financial assistance are legally worthless.	March 7
		Federal Reserve Bd. issues new restrictions reducing standard maturity for most installment credits from 18 to 15 months and raising down payment on many articles from 20% to 33⅓% in an anti-inflation move.		Jose Raoul Capablanca, 53, who became Cuban chess champion at age of 12 and held world title from 1921 to 1927, dies in N.Y. of a cerebral hemorrhage.	March 8
	State Dept. appoints Louis Johnson as chairman of U.S. advisory mission going to India to aid war effort there .... Navy Secy. Knox announces Adm. Ernest J. King will be chief of naval operations, succeeding Adm. Harold R. Stark, who will command U.S. naval forces in European waters.			Greg Rice sets new world record of 11:32.6 in the 2¾ mile run at the ninth annual Catholic Univ. games in Washington.	March 9

F	G	H	I	J
Includes elections, federal-state relations, civil rights and liberties, crime, the judiciary, education, health care, poverty, urban affairs and population.	*Includes formation and debate of U.S. foreign and defense policies, veterans affairs and defense spending. (Relations with specific foreign countries are usually found under the region concerned.)*	*Includes business, labor, agriculture, taxation, transportation, consumer affairs, monetary and fiscal policy, natural resources, pollution and accidents.*	*Includes worldwide scientific, medical and technological developments, natural phenomena, U.S. weather and natural disasters.*	*Includes the arts, religion, scholarship, communications media, sports, entertainment, fashions, fads and social life.*

	World Affairs	European War Zone	Pacific War Zone	The Americas	Other Countries & Territories
March 10		Nicholas von Kallay succeeds Dr. Ladislaus de Bardossy as premier of Hungary and forms new cabinet.	Chungking announces appointment of U.S. Lt. Gen. Joseph W. Stilwell as chief of staff under Chiang Kai-shek and dispatch of a military mission to Washington .... Eden tells Commons that Japanese have committed atrocities in Hong Kong, including bayonetting British officers, rape and murder of European women and refusal of water, food and medical aid to prisoners.		
March 11		Lord Woolton, minister of foods, announces in House of Lords that after March 23 Britain will cease production of white flour and adopt a "national wheat-meal loaf" to conserve shipping space.	MacArthur and his party of 20 leave Bataan Peninsula in the Philippines in four motor torpedo boats to begin their trip to Australia.	Brazilian Pres. Getulio Vargas issues decree that allows him to declare war without vote of parliament and to seize Axis property.	Churchill tells the House of Commons the British government has agreed to a "just and final solution" of India's demands for independence and that Sir Stafford Cripps will go to India to confer with Indian leaders.
March 12			Tojo warns Australians that if they do not submit to Japanese demands their fate will be the same as that of the NEI.	Brazilian citizens in Rio de Janeiro wreck German stores and burn German books in retaliation for sinking of four Brazilian ships.	Refusing to comment on Cripps' mission, Mohandas K. Gandhi says in Wardha that British imperialism "has been the greatest crime against India."
March 13			Australian P.M. John Curtin broadcasts warning to U.S. that "Australia is the last bastion between the West Coast of America and the Japanese."		Ceylon Gov. Sir Andrew Caldecott orders that the United Socialist Party and Lanka Samasamaj be dissolved, presumably to avoid political friction during war crisis.
March 14		Russian troops attack Staraya Russa, the encircled German army base on the northern front.	Joint U.S.-U.K. communique admits 13 U.N. warships were lost in a series of naval battles in the Java Sea from Feb. 27 to March 1 .... New Zealand raises draft age for men from 46 to 50 and mobilizes women for war service; a normal 54-hour work week is established in defense industries.	Spain and Argentina sign a barter trade agreement in Madrid involving about $40-million worth of goods.	
March 15		German high command claims to have repulsed heavy Russian assaults on Kerch Peninsula in Crimea, and on the Donets sector of southern front .... Hitler says in Berlin that the "Bolsheviks .... will be annihilatingly defeated by us in the coming summer."	Tokyo radio broadcast claims all resistance in Sumatra has ceased and that 50,000 American, Australian and British prisoners were taken in Bandung area of Java .... First official Japanese list of Americans interned is published containing 219 names.		
March 16		Marshal Semyon Timoshenko launches large-scale Russian offensive against German lines from Orel through Kursk to Kharkov on southern front .... Swiss police arrest 19 members of outlawed Swiss National Socialist Workers Party on charges of attempting to spread propaganda under direction of Franz Burri, its exiled leader, who is now in Vienna.	War Dept. announces U.S. air and ground troops in considerable numbers are now in Australia.		Sir Stafford Cripps leaves London for India with British plan to settle the Indian problem.
March 17		Germany closes all Norwegian ports and mines waters between North Cape and Aalesund.	MacArthur arrives in Australia by plane to assume supreme command of all U.N. forces in southwest Pacific.	In retaliation for sinking of merchant ship *Montevideo* off Jeremie, Haiti, Uruguay seizes German ship *Tacoma* .... Chilean youths, forbidden to hold protest meeting over sinking of freighter *Tolten*, smash windows of several Axis firms in Santiago.	
March 18		Navy Secy. Knox announces in N.Y. that ships along Atlantic coast will be required to travel in north and southbound lanes, which will be kept clear of submarines by air and sea patrols.	Navy Dept. claims that in recent raids upon Salamaua and Lae, New Guinea, U.S. and Australian bombers sank or damaged 23 Japanese ships, including 12 warships .... British claim 25 Japanese planes are destroyed in raid on Moulmein, Burma, by American Volunteer Group.	Chilean Pres.-elect Juan Antonio Rios says in Santiago "the purpose of my government will be frank and open cooperation with all the American nations, especially the United States."	
March 19		Fernand de Brinon, French envoy to German authorities in Paris, says Riom trial should be ended since it is detrimental to French interests.	Lieut. Gen. Joseph Stilwell assumes command of 5th and 6th Chinese Armies in Burma by appointment of Chiang Kai-shek .... Dispatches from Melbourne state Japanese columns guided by German Lutheran missionaries and Nazi-trained natives are advancing along Markham River valley in northeastern New Guinea, possibly to attack Port Moresby from the rear.	Guatemala discloses establishment of U.S. air base to help protect Central America and Panama Canal.	All-India Congress Pres. Maulana Abul Kalam Azad says in Wardha that Japanese menace has not lessened his party's interest in freedom before it will help in the war.

A	B	C	D	E
Includes developments that affect more than one world region, international organizations and important meetings of major world leaders.	*Includes all developments in European countries and military engagements between Allied and Axis powers in Africa and at sea.*	*Includes all developments in Japan and China, Japanese foreign policy and military actions in the Pacific region.*	*Includes all domestic and regional developments in Latin America, the Caribbean and Canada.*	*Includes developments in those independent nations and colonial possessions not covered in Columns B, C and D.*

U.S. Politics & Social Issues	U.S. Foreign Policy & Defense	U.S. Economy & Environment	Science, Technology & Nature	Culture, Leisure & Life Style	
		House votes to increase national debt limit from $65 to $125 billion.			March 10
House votes to continue Dies Comm. on Un-American Activities until Jan. 3, 1943.	FDR reports to Congress the U.S. has spent $2,570,452,441 on Lend-Lease to aid United Nations, of which $1.1 billion worth of materials was actually exported during the year ending Feb. 28.	House rejects amendment to agriculture appropriations bill prohibiting Commodity Credit Corp. from selling government-owned crops below parity prices . . . . WPA reports number of employed persons in U.S. rose by 400,000 to total of 48 million in February.			March 11
William B. Herlands, N.Y.C. commissioner of investigation, makes public his 3,000-word report to Mayor La Guardia, dated Feb. 20, confirming that Edward J. Flynn's antique Belgian courtyard at Lake Mahopac was paved by Bronx employes with city-owned paving blocks.		NWLB rejects a demand by CIO-UAW for closed shop of 1,540 employes at the Bower Roller Bearing Co. in Detroit . . . . WPB Chmn. Nelson sends an "official plan book" of directions to speed up war production to labor-management committees in war plants throughout U.S.	Sir William Henry Bragg, 79, noted physicist who shared the 1915 Nobel Prize with his son, William Lawrence Bragg, for their work on X-rays and crystals, dies in London.	Ezio Pinza, Italian-born Metropolitan Opera basso, is held by FBI on Ellis Island as an enemy alien . . . . N.Y. Yankee outfielder Joe DiMaggio ends his holdout by signing 1942 contract with the club at a reported $42,500 salary.	March 12
George Viereck, German-born American citizen, is sentenced in Washington to serve two to six years and fined $1,500 for withholding information from State Dept. when registering as a German agent.		House passes $673,225,000 agriculture bill, which prohibits government from selling crops at below parity prices.			March 13
		WPB issues an order effective March 19 curtailing gasoline deliveries to service stations by 20% in 17 Eastern states and Washington, D.C., and imposing a maximum 72-hour-week on stations.			March 14
		Tom Girdler, chairman of Consolidated Aircraft Corp., announces in San Diego, Calif. that B-24 bomber, called the Liberator by the British, is being manufactured on moving production line inaugurated today but that a more regularized production of accessories is needed.		N.Y. Rangers defeat Chicago Blackhawks, 5-1, in Chicago to win NHL championship with total of 60 points.	March 15
		Maritime Commission orders 234 more Liberty cargo ships, each of 10,500 deadweight tons, raising total ordered since February 1941 to 1,456 . . . . Supreme Court upholds constitutionality of 1938 Natural Gas Act and sustains rate regulation of Federal Power Commission.	Tornadoes kill an estimated 150 persons and cause at least $3 million damage in Miss., Mo., Ky., Tenn., Ill., Ind., and Ala. . . . . Research chemist Francis Irenee du Pont, noted for his discoveries in smokeless powder, dies in N.Y.		March 16
	War Secy. Stimson opens third draft lottery since October 1940, which will determine conscription order of some nine million men between ages of 20 and 44.	FRD expresses opposition to any anti-strike legislation for war industries or abolition of 40-hour work week.			March 17
FDR creates War Relocation Authority, headed by Milton S. Eisenhower, under which enemy aliens forced to move from West Coast military areas may voluntarily enlist in "war relocation work corps."	FDR asks Congress for supplemental War Dept. appropriation of $17.579 billion, including some $8.5 billion for Air Corps . . . . Brig. Gen. Mark Clark announces that a corps of troops will soon be in training for desert warfare.	Acting Price Admin. John E. Hamm announces that, effective March 23, gasoline prices will be frozen at March 13 level in 17 Eastern states and Oregon and Washington . . . . Chicago federal grand jury indicts 101 cheese dealers, processors and distributors, charging 45 corporations and 56 individuals with conspiring to fix American cheese and cheese products prices through the medium of Wisconsin Cheese Exchange at Plymouth.		Rockefeller Foundation Pres. Raymond B. Fosdick reports the foundation spent $9,313,964 in 1941, 74% of which was spent in U.S.	March 18
Wendell Willkie says in N.Y. the Navy's racial bias in excluding Negroes from enlisting except as mess attendants is a "mockery" of American ideals . . . . James Wheeler-Hill, former national secretary of German-American Bund, is interned as an enemy alien.	FDR orders all men between 45 and 64, estimated to number 13 million, to register April 27 for non-military service.	WPB Chmn. Nelson and Under Secy. of War Robert Patterson testify before Senate and House committees that they oppose Smith bill to suspend 40-hour-week, overtime pay and closed shop restrictions . . . . Robert R. Guthrie tells House Military Affairs subcommittee investigating his resignation from WPB that government should use $1-a-year men only as consultants on industry problems.			March 19
F *Includes elections, federal-state relations, civil rights and liberties, crime, the judiciary, education, health care, poverty, urban affairs and population.*	G *Includes formation and debate of U.S. foreign and defense policies, veterans affairs and defense spending. (Relations with specific foreign countries are usually found under the region concerned.)*	H *Includes business, labor, agriculture, taxation, transportation, consumer affairs, monetary and fiscal policy, natural resources, pollution and accidents.*	I *Includes worldwide scientific, medical and technological developments, natural phenomena, U.S. weather and natural disasters.*	J *Includes the arts, religion, scholarship, communications media, sports, entertainment, fashions, fads and social life.*	

	World Affairs	European War Zone	Pacific War Zone	The Americas	Other Countries & Territories
March 20			Speaking in Adelaide, Australia, MacArthur announces FDR has ordered him to organize an American offensive against Japan . . . . Australian External Affairs Min. Dr. Herbert V. Evatt says upon arrival in Washington that Australia and New Zealand should be given full partnership in war councils.		
March 21		British report shooting down eight German bombers and two fighters by Malta's anti-aircraft guns.	Lieut. Gen. Jonathan M. Wainwritht's U.S. and Philippine troops make surprise raid on Japanese forces near Zamboanga, Mindanao Island, inflicting "heavy casualties."		
March 22		Swiss sources report Germany has offered Turkey the following in exchange for bases for military operations against southern Caucasus: 50% of Mosul oil output, 15-year mandate over Syria, cession of Lemnos, Mytilene and Chios islands and rectification of Turkey's western frontier in Europe . . . . All Norwegian ministers, except a few Quislings, announce their decision to resign unless the Quisling regime stops trying to control youth.	Japanese Gen. Tomoyuki Yamashita demands that Wainwright surrender his troops on Bataan by noon today or "suffer the consequences."		Cripps arrives in Karachi, India with British plan for Indian independence.
March 23			Japanese forces occupy Andaman Islands in Bay of Bengal . . . . Japanese carry out their heaviest air raid of war on Port Moresby, New Guinea.	AP reports from Buenos Aires that the Argentine military mission to Washington is returning home because it is unable to purchase any arms.	Upon arriving in New Delhi, Cripps says he will stay for only two weeks and wants "quick decision" on British self-government proposals for India.
March 24		In heaviest raids since 1941, German dive bombers attack Dover, Portland and Newhaven on southeastern English coast.	Japanese use 54 new bombers in attacking Allied positions on Corregidor and Bataan, but cause only slight damage . . . . Japanese Navy spokesman Capt. Hideo Hiraide says "Japan seems to be on the defensive while the Anglo-American camp is on the offensive."	Canadian P.M. W.L. Mackenzie King announces new regulations raising draft age limit from 24 to 30 and closing non-war occupations to men of military age who are physically fit.	
March 25		Russian Amb. Ivan Maisky says in London the "initiative has been forced from Hitler" on the Russian front and that is the place to strike with everything the Allies have.	Japanese troops cut the Toungoo-Mandalay road at Kyungon, Burma . . . . Japanese bombers raid harbor defenses of Manila Bay, including Corregidor and Bataan.		Cripps presents secret British plan to settle Indian problem to Maulana Abul Kalam Azad and Mohammed Ali Jinnah in New Delhi.
March 26		In address to Conservative Party in London, Churchill admits "for the time being" the battle of the Atlantic has "worsened again." . . . . RAF conducts heavy raids on Ruhr industrial center of Germany and on docks of St. Nazaire, France . . . . German bombers subject Malta to heaviest mass raid in a week, losing four planes.	Japanese planes subject Corregidor in Manila Bay to "almost continuous" bombardment . . . . Chinese defenders throw back Japanese assault troops attacking Toungoo from all sides.	Rio de Janeiro police smash German spy ring with arrest of more than 200 persons and capture of four secret radio stations.	
March 27			Pres. Manuel L. Quezon and members of his Philippine war cabinet join MacArthur in Australia.	U.S. and Mexico sign new Lend-Lease agreement by which Mexico will receive planes, anti-aircraft guns, trucks and locomotives.	Cripps in New Delhi confers with Gandhi and two other Indian representatives of some four million Hindu Sikhs.
March 28		British commandos aided by planes and warships raid German-held submarine base at St. Nazaire on northwest coast of France. The only dry dock large enough to accomodate German battleship Tirpitz is permanently put out of action.			
March 29		Red Army claims victory in a five-day battle against Germans in Kalinin sector northwest of Moscow, inflicting 2,400 casaulties.			Cripps announces in New Delhi that Britain is prepared to give India dominion status after the war with right of secession.
	A *Includes developments that affect more than one world region, international organizations and important meetings of major world leaders.*	B *Includes all developments in European countries and military engagements between Allied and Axis powers in Africa and at sea.*	C *Includes all developments in Japan and China, Japanese foreign policy and military actions in the Pacific region.*	D *Includes all domestic and regional developments in Latin America, the Caribbean and Canada.*	E *Includes developments in those independent nations and colonial possessions not covered in Columns B, C and D.*

U.S. Politics & Social Issues	U.S. Foreign Policy & Defense	U.S. Economy & Environment	Science, Technology & Nature	Culture, Leisure & Life Style	
		Rear Adm. Charles W. Fisher estimates before House Naval Affairs Comm. that overtime pay for work is costing current Navy construction program $4 billion.			March 20
	Treasury Secy. Morgenthau and Chinese Foreign Min. T.V. Soong sign agreement in Washington completing action on $500-million loan to China voted by Congress.	FDR places 239-mile Toledo, Peoria & Western Railroad under federal control after the line refuses six government appeals to arbitrate wage dispute dating from Dec. 28, 1941 . . . . OPA declares sugar sales will be halted throughout country on April 27 for about one week to permit consumers to register for coupon books.		Darmouth defeats Kentucky to win Eastern Division, and Stanford stops Colorado to capture Western Division of NCAA basketball tournament.	March 21
Army orders about 300 Japanese living on Bainbridge Island in Puget Sound, Washington near Bremerton Navy Yard to leave before March 10 or face forcible evacuation to Owens River Valley reservation in California.					March 22
One thousand Japanese men, part of 112,000 alien and American-born Japanese who must leave the West Coast combat zone, arrive at Owens Valley, Calif.		The federal manager of the Toledo, Peoria & Western Railroad reaches agreement with railroad brotherhoods to end strike against the line . . . . OPA freezes retail prices on refrigerators, vacuum cleaners, stoves, washing and ironing machines, radio sets, phonographs and typewriters effective March 30.	FDR deeds his Georgia properties, except the "Little White House," to Warm Springs Foundation for Infantile Paralysis.		March 23
		CIO Executive Board recommends that its affiliated unions give up double pay for work on Saturdays, Sundays and holidays.			March 24
Atty. Gen. Biddle announces Justice Dept. will take steps to cancel U.S. citizenship of foreign-born persons on clear proof they were disloyal at time they took their oath of allegiance.	MacArthur is awarded Congressional Medal of Honor for "conspicuous gallantry and intrepidity above and beyond call of duty" in defending Philippine Islands against the Japanese.	All patents of Standard Oil Co. of N.J. for manufacture of synthetic rubber and gasoline are made available to American industry for war's duration without payment of royalties in a consent agreement filed in U.S. District Court in Newark, N.J.		West Va. Univ. defeats Western Ky., 47-45, to win NIT basketball tournament in N.Y. . . . . Six world records are set at a Bronx track meet: two-mile relay, Seton Hall; one-mile relay; Georgetown Univ.; 880-yard run and 800-meters, John Borican; and 440-yard run and 400 meters, Ray Cochran.	March 25
		AFL Pres. Green and CIO Pres. Murray pledge they will oppose all strikes for any cause for war's duration . . . . FDR issues executive order giving Army, Navy and Maritime Commission power to make or guarantee loans to small businesses to increase war production.			March 26
After three weeks of debate, Senate votes to permit Sen. William D. Langer (R, N.D.) to retain his seat, rejecting Privileges and Elections Comm. charges that he was guilty of moral turpitude.	FDR orders War and Navy Depts. to bring war shipments to Russia up to schedule so that the total pledged can be completed by June 30.	Asst. Atty. Gen. Arnold tells Senate Defense Investigating Comm. that Standard Oil Co. sought to deal in occupied France in 1941 and to establish Japanese connections in 1939 in case of U.S.-Japanese trade breakdowns . . . . WPB orders tea packers and retailers to ship and receive only 50% of amount of tea sold in first quarter of 1941.		Heavyweight Champion Joe Louis, now a private in the U.S. Army and weighing 207¼ lbs., knocks out Abe Simon, 255¼ lbs., of New York, in 0:16 of the sixth round of their scheduled 15-round bout in Madison Square Garden, New York.	March 27
	FDR signs second war powers bill, which extends executive seizure power, establishes penalties for priority violations and provides free postage for armed forces.	House passes and sends to Senate sixth supplemental appropriations bill for $18.301 billion after adopting amendment to limit profits on war material to 6% . . . . White House discloses Pres. Roosevelt, in letter dated March 20, accepted recommendations that antitrust suits that may interfere with war production be dropped for war's duration.		Stanford routs Dartmouth, 53-38, in Kansas City to win NCAA basketball title . . . . Yale wins National Collegiate A.A. swimming team championship in Cambridge, Mass. with 71 points.	March 28
Vice Pres. Wallace charges Rep. Martin Dies and his committee are "seeking to inflame the public mind by a malicious distortion of facts."			A heavy snow fall, unofficially estimated at 15 to 18 inches, disrupts traffic and communications in Washington in worst storm in 20 years.		March 29
F	G	H	I	J	
Includes elections, federal-state relations, civil rights and liberties, crime, the judiciary, education, health care, poverty, urban affairs and population.	*Includes formation and debate of U.S. foreign and defense policies, veterans affairs and defense spending. (Relations with specific foreign countries are usually found under the region concerned.)*	*Includes business, labor, agriculture, taxation, transportation, consumer affairs, monetary and fiscal policy, natural resources, pollution and accidents.*	*Includes worldwide scientific, medical and technological developments, natural phenomena, U.S. weather and natural disasters.*	*Includes the arts, religion, scholarship, communications media, sports, entertainment, fashions, fads and social life.*	

	World Affairs	European War Zone	Pacific War Zone	The Americas	Other Countries & Territories
March 30		A report from Vichy says Riom "war guilt" trial will be suspended from April 2 to 15.	FDR announces creation of Pacific War Council to meet in Washington, composed of U.S., N.Z., Australian, Chinese, Netherlands, Canadian and British representatives .... Chinese claim Japanese are using poison gas in battle around Toungoo, Burma .... British and Indian troops trapped below Shwedaung in southern Burma cut their way through Japanese lines and rejoin main British force south of Prome.		Appealing to people of India in a radio broadcast, Cripps says if British offer is refused by India's leaders "there will be neither the time nor the opportunity to reconsider this matter till after the war."
March 31			Heavy Japanese assaults against Bataan force Allied troops to retreat .... Japanese troops take Toungoo, which Chinese abandon, and cross Irrawaddy River west of city to attack Shwedaung, blocking British from the south.	Washington reports state that no military or naval equipment will be sold to Argentina, which has failed to break off diplomatic relations with Axis.	Dispatches from New Delhi and London indicate both All India Congress and Moslem League oppose British plan for India because Britain will maintain control over country's defense and the Moslems fear that Hindus will dominate the nation.
Apr. 1		Malta's anti-aircraft defense claim heavy enemy losses today as German bombers pound the island .... Free French leader Charles de Gaulle criticizes continued Allied recognition of the Vichy government in France.	New Pacific War Council meets for first time in Washington with FDR presiding .... Australian Government calls all single men between 18 and 35 for immediate war service on recommendation of Gen. Sir Thomas Blamey, chief of Allied ground forces .... British troops abandon Prome, 150 miles north of Rangoon, to Japanese.		Subhas Chandra Bose, Indian nationalist leader, is quoted by Berlin radio as having broadcast appeal to Indian people not to accept British independence plan but to put their faith in Axis .... Working committees representing the 4.5 million Sikhs in Punjab and the extremist Hindu Mahasabha group reject British plan for Indian independence.
Apr. 2		RAF planes bomb Matford truck plant in Poisey and docks and shipping in Le Havre, France.	Allied forces on Bataan successfully counter-attack, restoring their defense lines and halting Japanese advance.	Juan Antonio Rios is inaugurated in Santiago, Chile as president for four-year term.	Working committee of All-India Congress rejects British plan for Indian independence.
Apr. 3		German bombers raid Dover and Portland in southern England, while RAF planes bomb northern France.	U.S. Flying Fortresses attack Rangoon, starting several fires, and Port Blair in the Japanese-held Andaman Islands .... Approximately two-thirds of city of Mandalay is destroyed by Japanese air assaults.		
Apr. 4			Fierce fighting rages on Bataan as Japanese attack center of Allied defense line, registering small gains.	Gov. G.J.J. Wouters of Curacao announces all Dutch forces in and around Curacao and Aruba are placed under command of Rear Adm. J.B. Oldendorf, U.S.N.	Gen. Sir Archibald Wavell confers with Maulan Abul Kalam Azad and Jawaharlal Nehru in New Delhi regarding postwar independence for India.
Apr. 5		*N.Y. Times* reports Rumania, Slovakia and Croatia have established a "de facto military alliance" to prevent further Hungarian territorial expansion .... Soviets announce 40,000 Germans were killed and 161 localities recaptured on central front between March 21 and April 3.	British 10,000-ton cruiser *Cornwall* and 9,975-ton cruiser *Dorsetshire* are sunk by Japanese planes in Indian Ocean .... Seventy-five Japanese planes raid Colombo, capital of Ceylon, for first time.		
Apr. 6			In third day of their attack upon Allied lines on Bataan, Japanese troops make "some gains but at a heavy cost in casualties." .... Only slight damage results from first Japanese air assaults on Indian ports of Vizagapatan and Cocanada.	U.S. and Haiti sign defense and economic agreement under which U.S. will supply artillery, airplanes and a patrol boat to Haiti, buy Haiti's cotton, extend credit to strengthen dollar exchange and assist in increasing Haiti's sisal hemp production.	FDR's special representative Louis Johnson confers with Nehru and Abul Kalan Azad in New Delhi in an effort to save British-Indian negotiations from collapsing .... Tojo warns India to rebel against Britain or "suffer great calamities" in course of Japanese subjugation of British troops there.
Apr. 7		German planes attack Malta and Alexandria, Egypt while RAF bombers assault Ruhr and Rhineland .... Stockholm report says virtually all Norwegian ministers, except Quislings, have resigned as state officials "for reasons of conscience" but will continue to serve their congregations in an unofficial capacity.	Center of American-Philippine defense line is forced back by Japanese, with heavy casualties on both sides .... British troops retreat more than 40 miles north of Prome after destroying oil and cement installations at Thayetmyo and Allanmyo.	Acting State Secy. Sumner Welles and Mexican Foreign Min. Dr. Ezequiel Padilla issue joint statement in Washington announcing U.S. will aid development of Mexican industries to speed war production.	Reports from New Delhi indicate Cripps has made concessions to Indian leaders, including promise that an Indian will hold key defense post, if the rest of Indian Union plan is accepted.

A	B	C	D	E
Includes developments that affect more than one world region, international organizations and important meetings of major world leaders.	*Includes all developments in European countries and military engagements between Allied and Axis powers in Africa and at sea.*	*Includes all developments in Japan and China, Japanese foreign policy and military actions in the Pacific region.*	*Includes all domestic and regional developments in Latin America, the Caribbean and Canada.*	*Includes developments in those independent nations and colonial possessions not covered in Columns B, C and D.*

U.S. Politics & Social Issues	U.S. Foreign Policy & Defense	U.S. Economy & Environment	Science, Technology & Nature	Culture, Leisure & Life Style	
		U.S. Supreme Court rules in four cases affecting labor that: (1) N.Y. State cannot enjoin peaceful picketing since it is the only method of expression for the union; (2) Texas can constitutionally bar one man-secondary picketing; (3) NLRA was not contravened when a Milwaukee union was found guilty of unfair labor practices in using mass picketing; and (4) under NLRA a closed-shop contract cannot be allowed if the company has aided one union against another with "unfair labor practices." .... WPB orders production of toasters, table stoves, electric razors and other electrical appliances to stop on May 31.		Lew Ayres, 33, movie actor whose outstanding performance was in anti-war film *All Quiet on the Western Front*, leaves Hollywood for a conscientious objectors' camp after refusing to bear arms.	March 30
		Senate rejects two motions to attach amendments to smaller war plants corporation bill which would abolish overtime payments, the closed shop and picketing and outlaw violence in strikes .... Standard Oil Co. of N.J. Pres. William S. Farish denies charges made by Asst. Atty. Gen. Arnold before Senate Defense Investigating Comm.			March 31
		Commerce Secy. Jesse Jones announces in Washington that 25 companies have signed contracts to raise U.S. synthetic rubber production to 700,000 tons by end of 1943 .... Standard Oil of N.J. Pres. William S. Farish admits his company did not reveal its synthethic rubber process to Army and Navy but maintains that they did not request the information prior to the war.	Dr. David R. Climenko of Winthrop Chemical Co. reports a synthetic non-habit forming substitute for morphine named demerol has been successfully tested on 800 persons.	All motion pictures in which Lew Ayres appears are banned by Balaban & Katz in 100 Chicago theaters which the company operates; Ayres is in conscientious objectors' camp for refusing to bear arms in Army.	Apr. 1
One white soldier and two Negroes are shot to death and five Negroes are wounded in fight over use of telephone near Fort Dix, N.J.		President of the Illinois UMW, Ray S. Edmundson, resigns as regional CIO director because its policies "do not contribute to necessary unity within the labor movement or the nation." .... WPB Labor Dir. Sidney Hillman proposes to Senate Labor Comm. that all federal work-training agencies be consolidated under a unified command.			Apr. 2
		Asst. State Secy. Adolf A. Berle tells Senate committee Standard Oil of N.J. supplied gasoline to German-controlled Condor airline in South America until State Dept. threatened to blacklist Standard's Brazilian subsidiary last October.			Apr. 3
	State Dept. announces recognition of Free French control over Cameroon and French Equatorial Africa and appointment of Maynard Barnes as U.S. consul general at Brazzaville.	Senate Appropriations Comm. reports $19-billion sixth supplemental appropriations bill with amendments limiting maximum profits on war contracts from 2 to 10%.		Yale wins National AAU swimming championship in New Haven, Conn.	Apr. 4
		Aircraft War Production Council is created in Los Angeles by eight Pacific Coast plane manufacturers to coordinate and exchange information and pool facilities and plans for war plane production.			Apr. 5
		Upsetting an NLRB decision, Supreme Court rules, 5 to 4, that so long as sailors have signed shipping articles and promised to obey the captain, a strike is mutiny in any waters within admiralty and maritime jurisdiction of U.S., as well as on high seas.		N.Y. Metropolitan Track Writers Assn. names Cornelius Warmerdam as outstanding indoor track and field performer of 1942.	Apr. 6
	Knox announces Navy will soon accept Negro volunteers, heretofore employed only as messmen, in "reserve components" of Navy, Coast Guard and Marine Corps for general service in ranks as non-commissioned officers .... Vichy government announces it has "ordered Amb. Gaston Henry-Haye to protest to State Dept. against creation of an American consulate at Brazzaville without obtaining the consent of the legal government of France."	WPB Chmn. Nelson announces production of virtually all consumer goods will be halted within three months to speed up conversion to war production .... CIO Pres. Murray and AFL Pres. Green pledge in Pittsburgh that labor will give its undivided attention to war effort with program of cooperation, maximum production and no strikes .... Senate passes and sends to conference $19-billion sixth supplemental appropriations bill, after eliminating war profits amendment.			Apr. 7

F	G	H	I	J
Includes elections, federal-state relations, civil rights and liberties, crime, the judiciary, education, health care, poverty, urban affairs and population.	*Includes formation and debate of U.S. foreign and defense policies, veterans affairs and defense spending. (Relations with specific foreign countries are usually found under the region concerned.)*	*Includes business, labor, agriculture, taxation, transportation, consumer affairs, monetary and fiscal policy, natural resources, pollution and accidents.*	*Includes worldwide scientific, medical and technological developments, natural phenomena, U.S. weather and natural disasters.*	*Includes the arts, religion, scholarship, communications media, sports, entertainment, fashions, fads and social life.*

	World Affairs	European War Zone	Pacific War Zone	The Americas	Other Countries & Territories
Apr. 8	U.S. Army Chief of Staff George Marshall and FDR aide Harry Hopkins arrive in London to discuss future war strategy with British officials.	Two or three columns of Rommel's reinforced army begin to move eastward in Tmini-Mekili area of Libya .... Norwegian government in London reports Bishop Eivind J. Berggrav of Oslo, Primate of Norwegian Evangelical Lutheran Church, and Bishops Indreboe, I.B. Carlsen and H.E. Wisloeff have been arrested and placed in Bretvedt concentration camp near Oslo in reprisal for resignations of Norwegian clergy.	Japanese bombers attack rear of Wainwright's position on Bataan in effort to cut supplies, while Japanese Army continues assault on the defense lines, making progress although suffering heavy casualties.	Brazilian Pres. Getulio Vargas authorizes War Min. Encrio G. Dutra to increase army to one million men.	Aly Maher Pasha, premier of Egypt at start of European war, is arrested in Cairo "for reasons relating to the safety and security of the state."
Apr. 9		Stockholm report says Norwegian people observed a complete "silence" strike today as German soldiers and Quisling storm troopers marched in observance of second anniversary of German invasion.	After three months of heavy fighting, Bataan falls to Japanese troops at 5:15 a.m. .... An estimated 35,000 American and Filipino combat troops, 16 generals and about 25,000 civilians are left on Bataan when it falls .... British aircraft carrier *Hermes* is sunk by Japanese dive bombers in Bay of Bengal.		Nehru says in New Delhi that U.S. news stories about Indian-British relations can only be understood "on the basis of American ignorance of India."
Apr. 10		*N.Y. Times* reports that Marshall and Hopkins are in London to determine if British are still adamant against an invasion of Europe this summer because of the lack of shipping .... Speaking in Philadelphia, Soviet Amb. Maxim Litvinoff says defeat of Hitler requires maximum British and Russian efforts, with supplementary U.S. aid.	Navy Dept. reports about 3,500 sailors and Marines escaped to Corregidor before fall of Bataan.		Nehru issues statement in New Delhi asking every Indian to defend his country whatever the outcome of Indian-British negotiations.
Apr. 11		RAF bombers inflict heavy damage on Ruhr and Havre .... Bulgarian cabinet resigns when majority of its members refuse to approve Hitler's war program.	About 12,000 Japanese troops land on Cebu Island in Philippines and establish beachheads at Cebu City, Toledo, Argao, Pinamungajan, Naga and Talisay.	Argentina's Acting Pres. Castillo signs decree ordering 27 citizens to be exiled or interned and 32 aliens to be exiled as alleged "Communist agitators."	Cripps announces in New Delhi that both All-India Congress and Moslem League reject British plan for postwar India.
Apr. 12		Rommel withdraws his column on southern flank of Libya, apparently to Mekili.	Japanese troops, under strong air support, advance on wide front along Irrawaddy River south of Magwe, 100 miles north of Prome, Burma .... Japanese bombers attack Corregidor 12 times but inflict little damage because of stiff anti-aircraft fire.		Cripps leaves for London after the failure of his mission.
Apr. 13		Demarcation line between occupied and unoccupied France is reported closed while Marshal Petain confers with former Vice Premier Pierre Laval for third time since Saturday; Berne reports state Germany has demanded reorganization of French cabinet and "cooperation" instead of "collaboration." .... RAF bombers raid Genoa and Turin, Italy, the Ruhr and Rhineland centers in Germany and Havre, France.	Japanese forces advance towards Burmese oil fields by moving northward from Sinbaungwe, 20 miles south of Magwe .... Churchill discloses that a large Japanese flotilla has been operating in Bay of Bengal since April 4.		
Apr. 14		Laval, leading pro-Nazi collaborationist, is reinstated in Vichy government by Petain and Adm. Darlan after a meeting in Vichy .... Marshal Timoshenko's forces reportedly smash hole 12 miles wide in the German line 25 miles north of Kharkov in Russian Ukraine .... Germans claim to sink two American transports and one tanker of a convoy in Arctic Ocean.	Heavy fighting on Cebu Island continues between U.S.-Philippine forces and Japanese troops .... Japanese occupy Migyaugye, due south of Magwe, on their march towards Burmese oil fields.	AP reports that 30 Axis agents, including Jorge Nicolaus, reputed Gestapo chief in Mexico, have been sent to penal islands for internment.	Iranian government severs diplomatic relations with Japan and orders Min. Hikotaro Ichikawa and his staff to leave country within a week.
Apr. 15		Russian troops claim to have broken through German defense lines around Bryansk, 200 miles southwest of Moscow .... U.S. consulates in Lyon and Marseille urge all Americans in unoccupied France to leave for U.S. as soon as possible .... U.S. bombers attack Ploesti oilfields in Rumania, causing extensive damage.			

A	B	C	D	E
Includes developments that affect more than one world region, international organizations and important meetings of major world leaders.	*Includes all developments in European countries and military engagements between Allied and Axis powers in Africa and at sea.*	*Includes all developments in Japan and China, Japanese foreign policy and military actions in the Pacific region.*	*Includes all domestic and regional developments in Latin America, the Caribbean and Canada.*	*Includes developments in those independent nations and colonial possessions not covered in Columns B, C and D.*

U.S. Politics & Social Issues	U.S. Foreign Policy & Defense	U.S. Economy & Environment	Science, Technology & Nature	Culture, Leisure & Life Style	
		CIO-UAW in Detroit warns that delay by the NWLB in settling disputed cases is driving workers into strike action . . . . In executive order Roosevelt authorizes Nelson to delegate to Price Admin. Leon Henderson such powers with respect to priorities or rationing as he may deem necessary for effective prosecution of war . . . . WPB issues an order restricting use of wool in women's apparel and restricting garments of cotton, rayon and other materials . . . . WPB bans all new non-essential construction in move to conserve iron, steel and copper.			Apr. 8
		WPB orders cutting of deliveries of gasoline to filling stations and bulk consumers from 80% to 66⅔% in 17 Eastern states, District of Columbia and Oregon and Washington . . . . House Speaker Sam Rayburn (D, Tex.) says plane production exceeds 3,300 a month, as compared with 1,914 last September.		ASCAP is accused of misusing its control of almost 100% of the copyrighted musical compositions in suit filed in N.Y. federal court by 157 operators of 235 motion picture theaters.	Apr. 9
					Apr. 10
	War Dept. announces 25% of nation's 340 domestic airliners will be taken over by the Army Air Force to transport supplies and personnel.	Judge Vincent L. Leibell in U.S. District Court in New York directs one former and seven present executives of General Motors Corp., including Alfred P. Sloan, Jr., chairman of the board, to repay $4,348,044 plus interest charges estimated at over $2,000,000 to the company, after ruling they managed the corporation's bonus funds improperly . . . . WPB orders all production of medium and heavy trucks for civilian use halted after existing orders have been completed.			Apr. 11
Comm. on Fair Employment Practice orders 10 industrial plants in the Chicago and Milwaukee areas to cease discrimination against Negroes and Jews.					Apr. 12
	State Dept. rejects Vichy's protest against U.S. establishment of consulate general in Brazzaville, French Equatorial Africa on grounds that Free French, not Vichy, control the area.			Supreme Court holds false charge of racial intolerance against a public official is libelous under N.Y. State law in connection with suit brought by Rep. Martin L. Sweeney (D.) against the *Schenectady Union Star* . . . . Byron Nelson defeats Ben Hogan by one stroke in an 18-hole play-off to win Masters' Golf Tournament in Augusta, Ga.	Apr. 13
Magazine *Social Justice*, founded and formerly edited by Rev. Charles E. Coughlin in Royal Oak, Mich., is barred from mails on charges of violating Espionage Act of 1917 by attacking national war effort along lines closely paralleling Axis propaganda.		Special Asst. Atty. Gen. John H. Lewin charges a prewar monopolistic patent-pooling arrangement between GE and Krupp Works is responsible for current shortage of tungsten in U.S.		Annual baseball season opens in Washington, with Yankees defeating Senators, 7-0, and in N.Y., where Dodgers beat Giants, 7-5 . . . . Opera *Solomon and Balkis* by Randall Thompson is given a radio premiere from Harvard Univ.	Apr. 14
Brig. Gen. Hugh S. Johnson, 59, administrator of National Recovery Act of 1933-34, dies of pneumonia in Washington.		After two months of investigation, House Naval Affairs Comm. reports fire that swept French liner *Normandie* on Feb. 9 was caused by gross carelessness and confusion, not sabotage.			Apr. 15
F	G	H	I	J	
Includes elections, federal-state relations, civil rights and liberties, crime, the judiciary, education, health care, poverty, urban affairs and population.	*Includes formation and debate of U.S. foreign and defense policies, veterans affairs and defense spending. (Relations with specific foreign countries are usually found under the region concerned.)*	*Includes business, labor, agriculture, taxation, transportation, consumer affairs, monetary and fiscal policy, natural resources, pollution and accidents.*	*Includes worldwide scientific, medical and technological developments, natural phenomena, U.S. weather and natural disasters.*	*Includes the arts, religion, scholarship, communications media, sports, entertainment, fashions, fads and social life.*	

	World Affairs	European War Zone	Pacific War Zone	The Americas	Other Countries & Territories
Apr. 16		Thirty German counter-attacks fail to stop Russian assault on central front in first major battle of the spring .... King George VI of England awards George Cross to the island of Malta, which has withstood more than 2,000 Axis air raids; it is first such award in British history .... More than 400 Spitfire fighter planes and medium bombers sweep over Nazi-occupied northern France in almost continuous raids.	Japanese troops land on Panay, fourth island of Philippine archipelago, from eight transports and meet U.S.-Philippine opposition .... Japanese are reportedly sending 5½ divisions as reinforcements on Burma front.		
Apr. 17		Vichy cabinet of Adm. Darlan resigns as Laval attempts to form new government .... U.S. Amb. Adm. William D. Leahy is directed to return to U.S. for consultations in view of Laval's restoration to power in Vichy .... In largest daylight attack of war, an estimated 600 RAF fighters and bombers raid northern France for sixth consecutive day.	British destroy oil fields at Yenangyuang, Burma and retreat on Irrawaddy front under severe Japanese pressure.		
Apr. 18		Laval forms his new cabinet in Vichy, assuming for himself title of chief of government .... Seven of 12 new four-engine Lancaster bombers are shot down in low altitude raids over Augsburg, Germany, but the factory there, which manufactures half of the diesel engines used by German submarine fleet, is reported damaged.	Brig. Gen. James H. Doolittle, famous speed flier, leads squadron of North American B-25s in "highly destructive raid on Japanese mainland," including bombings of Tokyo, Yokohama, Kobe, and Nagoya. It is the first time Japan proper has been bombed .... Cebu City on Cebu Island falls to Japanese troops after fierce fighting.	Cuban Pres. Fulgencio Batista signs decree barring all nationals of Axis powers from his country .... U.S. and Mexico agree to value U.S. oil properties seized by Mexico in 1938 at $23,995,991.	
Apr. 19		Quisling government orders all Norwegian teachers to join new teachers' association before May 1 or be dismissed.	MacArthur's Southwest Pacific Command is formally established with approval of U.S., Britain, Australia, N.Z. and Netherlands .... Chinese troops reinforce battered British forces on Irrawaddy front in Burma as Japanese continue to attack.	An enemy submarine shells Royal Dutch Shell refineries in Bullen Bay, Curacao, Dutch West Indies without causing any damage.	
Apr. 20		Both sides report increased ground and aerial fighting along entire Russian front from Murmansk to Crimea .... Laval pledges in Vichy broadcast that he will seek entente and reconciliation with Germany .... Germans order evacuation of farms in entire Sambre et Meuse district of Belgium, and mines are laid at Lausprelle, Gerpinne, Fleurus, Farcienne and Walcourt against possible invasion.	Combined British-Chinese force recaptures the Burmese oil town of Yenangyaung, freeing several thousand British troops .... Japanese 240 millimeter guns on Bataan and Cavite shell Corregidor, Forts Hughes and Drum in Manila Bay.		
Apr. 21			MacArthur names Maj. Gen. Richard K. Sutherland and Brig. Gen. Richard J. Marshall of U.S. Army as his chief and deputy chief of the Southwest Pacific Command.		
Apr. 22		In fifth commando raid of war, British troops attack Germans near Boulogne on French coast and withdraw after two hours, reportedly without losing a man .... Malta dispatches report 37 Axis planes were destroyed or damaged over the island yesterday and today, raising total since April 1 to 117 shot down, 38 probably destroyed and 100 damaged .... Five members of French embassy in Washington resign because of Laval's assumption of control of French government.	Japanese troops attack U.S.-Philippine positions near San Remingo and Valderrama on Panay Island, forcing defenders to withdraw .... Japanese forces take Pyinmana, Burma, 155 miles south of Mandalay, and attack Loikaw near Thai frontier.		
Apr. 23		Speaking in N.Y., British Lend-Lease official says a second front is needed in support of Russia, claiming "a Russian victory may settle the war for us in 1942." .... *N.Y. Times* reports 1,100 Norwegian teachers who refused to join Quisling teachers' association are being sent to labor camps.	Tass, Russian news agency, reports that an American plane landed in Siberia the day four Japanese cities were bombed (April 18) and the crew was interned "in accordance with international law."	U.S. and Peru reach agreement in Washington whereby U.S. will advance a $1,125,000 credit for Peruvian rubber production increase, establish a $25-million credit for Peruvian public works and agree to buy all Peruvian rubber surplus for five years.	
Apr. 24		RAF bombers carry out attack on German Baltic port of Rostock and Heinkel aircraft factories nearby.	Chinese Command in Chungking announces Japanese mechanized units aided by aircraft have reached Hopong near Taunggyi, 100 miles southeast of Mandalay, indicating an 80-mile advance northward from Loikaw.	Mexican officials arrest reported Nazi Party chief Ewald Bork and three other officials of the party in Mexico City.	Madras section of Hindu Congress Party recommends in resolution to All-India Congress that "it has become necessary to acknowledge the Moslem League's" claim for a separate Moslem state.
	A *Includes developments that affect more than one world region, international organizations and important meetings of major world leaders.*	B *Includes all developments in European countries and military engagements between Allied and Axis powers in Africa and at sea.*	C *Includes all developments in Japan and China, Japanese foreign policy and military actions in the Pacific region.*	D *Includes all domestic and regional developments in Latin America, the Caribbean and Canada.*	E *Includes developments in those independent nations and colonial possessions not covered in Columns B, C and D.*

U.S. Politics & Social Issues	U.S. Foreign Policy & Defense	U.S. Economy & Environment	Science, Technology & Nature	Culture, Leisure & Life Style	
	House passes and sends to Senate bill to create women's Navy auxiliary reserve with age limits of 20 to 50 years .... Col. Claire L. Chennault, commander of the American Volunteer Group in Burma, is recalled to active duty in U.S. Army and nominated by FDR to be a brigadier general.	Carboloy Inc. Chmn. Dr. Zay Jeffries tells Senate Patents Comm. that his company's patent-pooling with Krupp Steel Works prevented Germany from stopping U.S. supplies of tungsten carbide and aided development of economic methods of using the alloy .... OPA announces that an allowance of one-half pound of sugar per person a week will be standard for first eight weeks of sugar rationing program.		Censorship Dir. Byron Price tells American Society of Newspaper Editors meeting in N.Y. that voluntary censorship will remain in effect as long as newspapers and publishers live up to their responsibilities .... Newbold Noyes, 50, poet, associate editor of *Washington Evening Star* since 1919 and former president of North American Newspaper Alliance, dies in Washington .... N.Y. Drama Critics Circle, for second time since 1935, makes no award for best American play of the current season.	Apr. 16
		WPB Chmn. Nelson says combined war production of U.S., Britain and Russia is greater than that of Axis.		First issue of new *Stars and Stripes*, U.S. Army weekly newspaper, is published in London.	Apr. 17
	U.S. Army Chief of Staff Gen. Marshall says U.S. bombers and pilots will soon be assisting RAF and that "inevitably there will be American troops in commando raids."	FDR creates War Manpower Commission of nine members under chairmanship of Paul V. McNutt "to bring about effective mobilization and the maximum use of the nation's manpower" in the war's prosecution.		Toronto Maple Leafs defeat Detroit Red Wings, 3-1, in Toronto to win NHL championship and Stanley Cup, four games to three .... Adolph Kiefer wins 100-meter backstroke event in 1:2.8 to set a new world record in a match held in Detroit.	Apr. 18
	Gen. George C. Marshall, Harry L. Hopkins and British officials arrive in N.Y. from London.	Treasury Secy Morgenthau announces he will start campaign asking public to spend 10% of its income on war savings bonds.			Apr. 19
	GOP National Comm. adopts anti-isolation resolution which demands "the prosecution of an offensive war" until total victory is gained.	Under executive order from Pres. Roosevelt, Navy seizes four plants of Brewster Aeronautical Corp. because of "dissatisfaction with the management," which is blamed for present low rate of production of combat planes.			Apr. 20
		FDR orders Alien Property Custodian Leo T. Crowley to seize all enemy-controlled patents including those ostensibly owned by U.S. citizens, neutral or allied nations.			Apr. 21
Rapp-Coudert committee reports it found 503 pro-Communists in N.Y.C. education system and that most of them have yet to be removed due to administrative indifference.		Rayford W. Alley tells Truman committee that former Mass. Gov. James M. Curley was president of Engineers Group Inc., accused by four contractors of swindling them of $21,000 they paid as bribes for defense housing contracts .... OPA says gas rationing will begin on May 15 in 17 Eastern states and Washington, with each motorist restricted to 21.4 gallons per week .... OPA sets May 5 as the date for sugar rationing to commence.			Apr. 22
Wendell L. Willkie tells University of Rochester's conference on Far Eastern Front the "day is gone when men and woman, of whatever color or creed, can consider themselves the superiors of other creeds or colors."		Senate passes and sends to FDR an excess profits bill whereby U.S. government contracts can be renegotiated to recover excess profits .... Federal jury in Illinois acquits Toledo, Peoria & Western Railroad Pres. George P. McNair and two other officials of violating National Railway Labor Act by coercing union employes.		Most Rev. Dr. William Temple is installed as 96th Archbishop and Primate of All England at Canterbury Cathedral.	Apr. 23
		Budget Dir. Harold D. Smith tells House Ways and Means Comm. that war costs will be $70 billion for fiscal 1943, some $14.214 billion more than orignally estimated.		Jack (Chappie) Blackburn, 58, Negro trainer of heavyweight champion Joe Louis and an outstanding lightweight from about 1900 to 1923, dies in Chicago after apparent recovery from pneumonia.	Apr. 24
F *Includes elections, federal-state relations, civil rights and liberties, crime, the judiciary, education, health care, poverty, urban affairs and population.*	G *Includes formation and debate of U.S. foreign and defense policies, veterans affairs and defense spending. (Relations with specific foreign countries are usually found under the region concerned.)*	H *Includes business, labor, agriculture, taxation, transportation, consumer affairs, monetary and fiscal policy, natural resources, pollution and accidents.*	I *Includes worldwide scientific, medical and technological developments, natural phenomena, U.S. weather and natural disasters.*	J *Includes the arts, religion, scholarship, communications media, sports, entertainment, fashions, fads and social life.*	

	World Affairs	European War Zone	Pacific War Zone	The Americas	Other Countries & Territories
Apr. 25		Berlin radio announces Gen. Henri Honore Giraud, 63, French Army commander who was captured in May 1940, has escaped from fortress of Koenigstein .... RAF planes bomb Rostock for second night in a row.	American troops arrive at New Caledonia, about 800 miles east of Australia, to assist in defending the island .... Japanese columns drive west and northeast of Taunggyi in Burma.	Paraguayan Pres. Higinio Morinigo orders dissolution of Liberal Party on charges of "high treason." .... U.S. and Nicaragua reach agreement whereby Nicaragua will get a $500,000 credit through Import-Export Bank and U.S. will build Nicaraguan portion of Inter-American Highway and purchase the country's rubber.	
Apr. 26		In Reichstag speech, Hitler says war will be decided in Russia with destruction of Communism.	Japanese advance along Rangoon-Mandalay railroad, capturing Yamethin and reaching Pyawbwe, 85 miles south of Mandalay.		
Apr. 27		For fourth consecutive night RAF bombers attack Rostock, Nazi supply base for north Russian front.	Two Japanese mechanized columns drive 67 miles southwest of Lashio, terminus of Burma Road .... Japanese Premier Tojo warns nation in a Tokyo address that the "war's coming stage will be a real test for the Japanese nation," demanding utmost unity.	Canadian voters approve drafting men for overseas service by nearly two to one in nationwide plebiscite.	Gandhi asserts in Ahmedabad that he does not approve of U.S. soldiers coming to India because of the American influence it could lead to. He questions why India's soldiers cannot be trained.
Apr. 28		Strong force of RAF bombers raids new German naval base at Trondheim, Norway.	Lt. Gen. Joe Stilwell's Chinese troops and supporting British forces are driven back on all fronts in Burma, while mechanized Japanese columns drive closer to Burma Road.		Cripps tells the House of Commons that the real reason for his failure in India was the issue of secession from the Indian nation for dissenting native states.
Apr. 29		RAF bombers carry out heavy attacks on Kiel, Germany and Trondheim, Norway .... An Axis air raid on Alexandria, Egypt kills 102 and injures another 111.		Although maintaining official relations with Vichy, Cuba announces its recognition of Free French control over Pacific Islands of Tahiti, New Hebrides, New Caledonia, Equatorial Africa and Cameroons.	
Apr. 30		Hitler and Mussolini, meeting for seventh time, conclude two days of conferences at Castle Fuschl near Salzburg.	Japanese caputre Burma Road terminus of Lashio and railroad town of Hsipaw.		Leader of Madras sector of All-India Congress, C.R. Rajagopalanchari, resigns from the party's working committee in dispute over recognition of Moslem separatist claims.
May 1		In May Day address Stalin says Russia has "no aims of seizing foreign territory or conquering foreign peoples," but only to rid Soviet Union of Nazis .... Rome radio announces additional Gestapo agents have arrived in Italy to study organization of Italian police force.			
May 2		Chief of U.S. military mission in North Africa, Maj. Gen. Russell L. Maxwell, discloses U.S. troops are arriving to support British combat troops and RAF.	Mandalay, Burma is captured by Japanese ground forces.		All-India Congress working committee adopts resolution at its meeting in Allahabad stating that if India is invaded, resistence should only be in the form of non-violence because the British "have prevented the organization of national defense by the people in any other way."
May 3		Russian troops reportedly have advanced 100 miles past Kharkov to a point between Poltava and Dniepropetrovsk.	Japanese take Tulagi in the Solomon Islands unopposed .... Japanese forces on Burma Road are reported to be 30 miles from Burma-Chinese border.	Dr. Alfonso Lopez Pumarejo is elected president of Colombia over Dr. Carlos Arango Velez.	
May 4		RAF bombers attack Hamburg and Nazi submarine bases at St. Nazaire, France and Kristiansand, southern Norway .... German-controlled Dutch radio announces execution of 72 Netherlanders and sentencing of seven to life in prison on charges of espionage and possession of arms.	Seven light Japanese warships are sunk, two Japanese destroyers damaged and six Japanese planes destroyed in Coral Sea naval battle near Solomon Islands .... Corregidor is bombed 13 times and shelled along with other island forts for five hours by Japanese .... *U.S.S. Yorktown*'s aircraft bomb Tulagi.		State Dept. informs French Amb. Gaston Henry-Haye that U.S. endorses British occupation of Madagascar and that the island will be returned to France after war.
May 5			Shortly after midnight, Japanese troops begin landing on north coast of Corregidor Island .... Japanese troops, marching north on Burma Road, cross Nam Mao River and enter Yunnan Province, China.		In an effort to forestall a Japanese advance on the island, British forces begin landing on Madagascar. Laval presents a note of protest against the British occupation to U.S. charge de affaires in Vichy, S. Pinkney Tuck.

A	B	C	D	E
Includes developments that affect more than one world region, international organizations and important meetings of major world leaders.	*Includes all developments in European countries and military engagements between Allied and Axis powers in Africa and at sea.*	*Includes all developments in Japan and China, Japanese foreign policy and military actions in the Pacific region.*	*Includes all domestic and regional developments in Latin America, the Caribbean and Canada.*	*Includes developments in those independent nations and colonial possessions not covered in Columns B, C and D.*

U.S. Politics & Social Issues	U.S. Foreign Policy & Defense	U.S. Economy & Environment	Science, Technology & Nature	Culture, Leisure & Life Style	
		NWLB votes, 8-4, to order Federal Shipbuilding and Dry Dock Co., a U.S. Steel Corp. subsidiary, to grant CIO Industrial Union of Marine and Shipbuilding Workers of America a "maintenance of membership" clause covering 11,500 workers at its Kearney, N.J. plant.		Roy Cochran of Great Lakes Naval Training Station, former Indiana star, sets world record of 0:52.2 in special 440-hurdles event at 33rd annual Drake Relays at Des Moines, Iowa.	Apr. 25
	Eastern Defense Command announces plans to control dimming of shorelights and regulate activities of aliens in 16 Eastern states and Washington.	Five persons are killed and 222 injured when Hudson & Manhattan Railroad train travelling at high speed is wrecked in underground tube in Jersey City, N.J.			Apr. 26
Supreme Court upholds power of law enforcement officers to use information acquired by wiretapping and detectaphone as court evidence.	More than 13 million men aged 45-64 register throughout U.S. in fourth draft registration since October 1940.	FDR sends seven-point plan to Congress to fight inflationary trends produced by wartime .... Federal Reserve Bank of New York announces admission of J.P. Morgan & Co., Inc., to membership in Federal Reserve System.	Eighty to 100 persons are killed by a tornado in Pryor, Okla.		Apr. 27
House votes to grant Un-American Activities Comm. an additional $110,000 to carry on its work.	In a radio broadcast FDR says that since Pearl Harbor U.S. troops have been dispersed world-wide, that U.N. forces will take necessary action to prevent Axis from using French territory anywhere as bases, and that the Japanese advance towards New Zealand is being checked.	OPA issues most drastic price control regulations in nation's history in effort to combat inflation, which has sent cost of living up 15% since September 1939.		Twentieth Century-Fox Film Corp. pays record price of $300,000 for screen rights to John Steinbeck's play *The Moon is Down* .... Emil von Sauer, German pianist acclaimed as one of world's greatest virtuosos over 30 years ago, dies in Vienna.	Apr. 28
Two thousand home guardsmen, state troopers and city police guard 14 Negro families moving into Sojourner Truth Homes in Detroit, a $1-million federal project which 300 families will occupy eventually.		NWLB Chmn. William H. Davis announces that AFL Pres. Green and CIO Pres. Murray have agreed on a formula for settling jurisdictional labor disputes during wartime .... WPB and FPC reach agreement for dividing authority over nation's power supply, with WPB controlling war-related functions only.			Apr. 29
Dr. Hermann Rauschning, who was forced to flee Danzig for opposing Hitler, receives U.S. citizenship papers in N.Y.		House Naval Affairs Comm. votes to table legislation to freeze existing union shop conditions, raise basic work week to 48 hours and place percentage limitation on profits.	Four tornadoes in as many days kill 89 people in Okla., Tex., Kan. and Colo.	Issac I. Kashdan and Samuel Reshevsy, national chess champion, tie for first place in U.S. Chess Federation Championship match in N.Y.	Apr. 30
Postmaster Gen. Frank C. Walker announces Muncie, Ind. weekly newspaper *X-Ray* is seditious under 1917 Espionage Act and asks that it show cause why its second class mailing privileges should not be revoked.	FDR temporarily abandons plans for registering women for war service because there are more women than jobs currently available.	House Ways and Means Comm. tentatively approves 94% excess profits tax and 40% income tax on firms making net profit of over $25,000 a year.			May 1
	FDR announces Lend-Lease aid will be extended to Iraq and Iran because their defense is "vital to the defense of the United States."		Tornadoes sweep Midwest, killing 22 persons in northwest Oklahoma, three in eastern Kansas and one in central Missouri and injuring over 100, including 11 in central Illinois.	Mrs. Payne Whitney's Shut Out with Wayne Wright in saddle wins the 68th running of the Kentucky Derby.	May 2
					May 3
Second class mailing privileges of *Social Justice* are revoked when its representatives fail to appear in Washington to show cause why it should not be barred from mails.		WPB issues an order barring use of iron and steel in more than 400 common items ranging from bathtubs to pie plates .... FDR gives Office of Defense Transportation wartime control of all motor transport in an effort to conserve gasoline .... FDR sends Congress a message asking for $102 million to continue CCC and NYA for fiscal 1943.		Pulitzer Prizes for literature are: fiction, Ellen Glasgow's *In This Our Life;* U.S. history, Margaret Leech's *Reveille in Washington;* biography, Forrest Wilson's *Crusader in Crinoline;* poetry, William Rose Benet's *The Dust Which Is God.* No award for drama is made.	May 4
Bronx County grand jury clears Edward J. Flynn, chairman of Democratic National Committee, of charges that he used New York City-owned building materials and city workers to pave his Lake Mahopac estate courtyard.		WPB announces that beginning May 16 gasoline and light oil consumption in 17 Eastern states and Washington must be cut 50% .... Federal Reserve Bd. issues new credit regulations to help curtail inflation, requiring payment of all retail charge accounts within 40 days after purchase and a 33⅓% down payment on all installment purchases with balance due in 12 months.			May 5
F	G	H	I	J	
Includes elections, federal-state relations, civil rights and liberties, crime, the judiciary, education, health care, poverty, urban affairs and population.	*Includes formation and debate of U.S. foreign and defense policies, veterans affairs and defense spending. (Relations with specific foreign countries are usually found under the region concerned.)*	*Includes business, labor, agriculture, taxation, transportation, consumer affairs, monetary and fiscal policy, natural resources, pollution and accidents.*	*Includes worldwide scientific, medical and technological developments, natural phenomena, U.S. weather and natural disasters.*	*Includes the arts, religion, scholarship, communications media, sports, entertainment, fashions, fads and social life.*	

	World Affairs	European War Zone	Pacific War Zone	The Americas	Other Countries & Territories
May 6		RAF planes bomb Stuttgart, Germany for second consecutive day .... UP report says German authorities executed 30 French civilians at Caen for an attack upon a train and 10 at Romorantin for an attack on a German soldier.	Lt. Gen. Jonathan M. Wainwright surrenders Corregidor and Forts Drum, Hughes and Frank in Manila Bay to Japanese at 11 p.m. .... Advance Japanese troops drive deeper into China along Burma Road, bypassing city of Wangting.	Argentine government suspends the pro-Nazi Buenos Aires newspaper *Pampero.*	British forces continue to advance towards city of Diego Suarez and naval base of Antsirane on east coast of northern Madagascar in spite of stiff French opposition.
May 7		Yugoslav government in London charges Axis powers have killed 465,000 persons throughout Yugoslavia.	Chinese report halting Japanese advance into southern China over Burma Road at Chefang, about 25 miles inside China.	Pres. Roosevelt greets Pres. Manuel Prado y Ugarteche of Peru at Bolling Field, Washington, when the first South American president ever to visit U.S. arrives from Miami by plane .... Cordell Hull and Peruvian Min. David Dasso sign reciprocal trade agreement in Washington calling for lower tariffs on specified goods.	French forces surrender to British on Madagascar after two days of fighting.
May 8	In Edinburgh, Scotland, British Foreign Secy. Anthony Eden says at the end of the war "we have to aim at a state of affairs in which the four great powers of the world [Britain, the U.S. Russia and China] will together sustain the peace system to be established."	German and Italian forces launch an attack against guerrilla army of Yugoslavian Gen. Draja Mikhailovich in Bosnia, Serbia and Montenegro.	Navy Dept. explains the battle of Coral Sea is continuing, with sinking of Japanese aircraft carrier, heavy transport and cargo vessel .... Chinese forces smash two Japanese columns attempting to outflank them near Chefang. .... Philippine Pres. Manuel L. Quezon arrives in San Francisco on his way to Washington where he will establish a government in exile.		
May 9		RAF bombers lose seven planes in heavy attacks on Warnemunde, German Baltic port, and an aircraft plant seven miles down Warne River.	Battle of Coral Sea "temporarily ceases" with U.S. Navy reporting sinking or damaging 178 Japanese ships, as against 36 losses .... Chinese forces recapture Taunggyi behind Japanese lines in Burma, then march northward Maymyo on Laisho-Mandalay railway.	Official U.S. talks open with the high commissioner of French Western Hemisphere possessions, Adm. Georges Robert, for the U.S. to safeguard Martinique, Guadeloupe and French Guiana from Axis forces.	Speaking in N.Y., Zionist leader Chaim Weizmann says Palestine is the only possible postwar home for two to four million Jews who are part of the displaced population of Europe.
May 10	World Women's Council, meeting in Washington, approves a special message to the U.N. council demanding immediate establishment of equality and freedom for all women.	Churchill warns Hitler in London radio broadcast not to use poison gas against the Russians, or Britain will drop gas on Germany in massive air assaults.	MacArthur's headquarters in Australia says the battle of the Coral Sea has ended today .... Retreating British troops turn on advancing Japanese and drive them back several miles at Shwegyin on the Chindwin River in northwest Burma.		
May 11		Malta announces reinforced British fighter planes together with anti-aircraft batteries shot down 31 Axis planes, probably destroyed 20 others and damaged 41 in three days of intense fighting over the island fortress .... German forces launch an offensive attack on Kerch Peninsula at eastern end of Crimea .... Nazi submarine sinks freighter in St. Lawrence River, the first such attack within the river's gulf.	Japanese troops land from several ships on Nan-jisu Island off Fukien Province.	Canadian P.M. Mackenzie King introduces a bill to amend mobilization act and remove ban on conscription for overseas service .... Speaking to U.S. Senate, Peru's Pres. Manuel Prado reaffirms his country's "adherence to the international policy of Pres. Roosevelt."	U.S. and foreign delegates to N.Y. conference on Zionist affairs adopt resolution calling for full Arab-Jewish cooperation in Palestine and a Jewish military force to fight under its own flag.
May 12		British Agriculture Min. Lord Woolton announces in the House of Commons that after June 1 restaurants may not charge more than five shillings (about $1) or serve more than three courses per meal; music, entertainment and cover charges will be extra .... Russian Army sources report their forces are successfully holding German assault on Kerch Peninsula .... As a result of the bombing of five Nazi-occupied hotels and the famous Marguery Restaurant, large sections of Paris are isolated by German and French police.			
May 13		German forces reportedly break through Russian lines on Kerch Peninsula around Parpach in eastern Crimea on sixth day of fighting.	Chinese report Japanese forces are using Lunglin, 50 miles inside China, as their base in a northeastward advance along Burma Road toward Yungchang.	Two-minute earthquake rocks Guayaquil, Portoviejo and nearby towns in Ecuador, killing an estimated 53 persons.	
May 14		Russians report continued advances towards Kharkov and claim that 150 German tanks have been destroyed in last two days.		U.S.-French agreement in Martinique provides for disarming of French aircraft carrier *Bearn* and two cruisers there.	

A	B	C	D	E
Includes developments that affect more than one world region, international organizations and important meetings of major world leaders.	*Includes all developments in European countries and military engagements between Allied and Axis powers in Africa and at sea.*	*Includes all developments in Japan and China, Japanese foreign policy and military actions in the Pacific region.*	*Includes all domestic and regional developments in Latin America, the Caribbean and Canada.*	*Includes developments in those independent nations and colonial possessions not covered in Columns B, C and D.*

U.S. Politics & Social Issues	U.S. Foreign Policy & Defense	U.S. Economy & Environment	Science, Technology & Nature	Culture, Leisure & Life Style	
DAR, meeting in Chicago, adopts resolution endorsing Dies committee investigations of un-American activities.		Senate passes and returns to House the $12.125-billion independent offices appropriations bill with amendment abolishing TVA's revolving fund and requiring congressional approval for future TVA expenditures.			May 6
N.Y. Gov. Herbert H. Lehman (D) announces in Albany he will not be candidate for re-election .... Lehman signs Washburn bill, making it a crime for a war industry in the state to discriminate in hiring personnel, and the Schwartzwald bill, authorizing the state industrial commissioner to investigate charges of discrimination.	Swedish-American liner *Drottningholm* sails from Jersey City with 948 Axis officials, including ambassadors and ministers of Germany, Italy, Rumania, Bulgaria and Hungary, for Lisbon, where they will be exchanged for American officials, newspapermen, and others from Axis countries .... Senate passes and sends to FDR a bill authorizing construction of 200,000 tons of new submarines.	Treasury Secy. Morgenthau proposes raising an additional $1.1 billion in war revenues by lowering personal exemptions under individual income tax to $600 for single persons, $1,200 for married couples and $300 for each dependent .... GM agrees to abide by NWLB directive to continue double time pay for Sunday and holiday work.			May 7
		Commerce Secy. Jesse H. Jones tells Senate Banking Comm. that the RFC needs an additional $5 billion for loans for war plant expansion.			May 8
		OPA announces temporary maximum weekly gasoline ration for non-essential automobiles in 17 Eastern states will be three gallons from May 15 to July 1.	Honorary memberships in the Russian Academy of Sciences are awarded to foreigners for the first time: three Americans (Dr. Walter B. Cannon, Dr. Gilbert Newton Lewis, and Dr. Ernest Orlando Lawrence) and two Britons (Sir Henry Dale and J.B.S. Haldane).	Mrs. Albert Sabath's Alsab wins the Preakness Stakes in record time of 1:57 for the $1\frac{3}{16}$-mile race .... Noted NBC sports announcer Graham McNamee dies in N.Y.	May 9
			Army bombing of the lava flows from Mauna Loa, which erupted on April 26, finally halts flows that have endangered city of Hilo, Hawaii.	Billy Conn, heavyweight contender now in the Army, fractures his left hand, delaying a return match with champion Joe Louis unofficially scheduled for next month .... Joseph M. (Joe) Weber, 74, of Weber and Fields, classic Dutch stage comedians who were originators of elaborate musical comedy revues before 1900, dies in Los Angeles; Lew Fields died last July.	May 10
Senate Justice Comm. approves proposed constitutional amendment granting equal rights to women.	Speaking to graduating class at Union College in Schenectady, N.Y., Wendell L. Willkie charges that "leaders without conviction" betrayed this nation into confused isolation after W.W. I.	Supreme Court rules that the holder of a patent cannot control resale price of patented articles by stipulating price arrangements or licenses without violating Sherman Antitrust Act.			May 11
	Bill to establish volunteer Woman's Auxiliary Army Corps of 150,000 is passed by Senate and sent to the White House.	Drivers throughout the East begin to register for gasoline ration cards.			May 12
	House reaffirms its May 12 vote to increase monthly service pay for privates and apprentice seaman to $50.	House Ways and Means Comm. votes to lower income tax exemptions from $1,500 to $1,200 for married couples and from $750 to $500 for single persons.			May 13
Sen. Sheridan Downey (D, Calif.) introduces resolution stating that senators should waive any special privileges in gasoline rationing .... *Philadelphia Herold*, German-English weekly, surrenders its second-class mailing privilege when its representatives appear in Washington to answer sedition charges.	War Dept. announces Army will soon take control of all commercial airlines.	House passes and sends to Senate a bill to increase RFC's borrowing power by $5 billion for lending operations to expand war production and acquire raw materials .... Federal grand jury in Trenton, N.J. indicts eight corporations and 20 officers for conspiring to monopolize manufacture and sale of dyestuffs on an international scale through an I.G. Farbenindustrie cartel agreement.		Internationally famous comedian Joe Jackson dies after completion of his act in wings of the Roxy Theatre in N.Y. .... Censorship Office reveals that there are 900 translators in N.Y. post office examining foreign mail ranging from Arabic to Urdu.	May 14

F	G	H	I	J
Includes elections, federal-state relations, civil rights and liberties, crime, the judiciary, education, health care, poverty, urban affairs and population.	*Includes formation and debate of U.S. foreign and defense policies, veterans affairs and defense spending. (Relations with specific foreign countries are usually found under the region concerned.)*	*Includes business, labor, agriculture, taxation, transportation, consumer affairs, monetary and fiscal policy, natural resources, pollution and accidents.*	*Includes worldwide scientific, medical and technological developments, natural phenomena, U.S. weather and natural disasters.*	*Includes the arts, religion, scholarship, communications media, sports, entertainment, fashions, fads and social life.*

	World Affairs	European War Zone	Pacific War Zone	The Americas	Other Countries & Territories
May 15		Germans assert their forces are at gates of Kerch, having broken the Russian defense perimeters.	China admits loss of Tengyueh to Japanese forces.		
May 16		German troops capture Kerch in the Crimea after eight days of fighting.	Japanese columns from Thailand attack Mong Lin on Mekong River and Keng Tung and Mong Hai in northwest Burma.	Venezuelan Education Ministry announces closing of Humboldt College on charges that it is center for totalitarian propaganda .... Gen. Rafael Trujillo Molina, the only candidate, is elected president of the Dominican Republic for a five-year term. Women vote in the elections for the first time .... Laval denounces U.S.-Martinique agreement as an example of American interference in French internal affairs.	
May 17		Special Moscow communique announces 12,000 Germans were killed between May 12 and 16 and 300 places liberated in Russian drive on Kharkov which has carried 12 to 37 miles .... RAF Spitfires and bombers carry out four sweeps over French coast, attacking German bases, especially in the Boulogne area.	Chinese troops defeat two Japanese columns advancing north of Burma Road on west side of Salween River in western Yunnan Province.		
May 18		Russians continue to advance along 100 mile front in Kharkov area despite heavy German counterattacks .... Third and largest contingent of U.S. troops together with tank units arrives in British Isles .... British Admiralty announces in London that Rear Adm. Sir Henry Harwood, who commanded British cruisers in battle with German pocket-battleship *Graf Spee* off Uruguay, has succeeded Adm. Andrew Browne Cunningham in command of the Mediterranean fleet.		U.S. and Panama reach agreement in Panama for U.S. to lease land outside Canal Zone for military forces .... Confederation of Mexican Workers formally petitions Pres. Manuel Avila Camacho to delcare war on the Axis.	American Jewish Congress adopts resolution calling for creation of Jewish army in Palestine and of a Jewish commonwealth in that country after the war.
May 19	U.N. Air Training Conference opens in Ottawa with 14 nations represented.	German Field Marshal Fedor von Bock's troops begin counter-offensive in Izyum-Barvenkova sector, southeast of Kharkov.	Chinese spokesman T.F. Tsiang says Japan's current offensive is an effort to knock China out of the war.		
May 20	United Steel Workers of America approve resolution at their Cleveland meeting urging closer cooperation among trade unions of United Nations.	Soviets report halting von Bock's offensive .... Sir Stafford Cripps tells the House of Commons the best way to aid Russia is to bomb Germany until Britain is prepared for an invasion of the Continent, "which we intend to do." .... Several hundred RAF planes drop more than 40,000 incendiary bombs on chemical, armament and other works in Mannheim.		In a move to curb activities of Axis propagandists in Brazil, the Bank of Brazil calls in all U.S. dollars, which will not be legal tender in the country after May 22.	
May 21		Russians report Timoshenko's tanks and troops have broken Nazi lines guarding Kharkov and advanced into an open battlefield .... Duke of Bedford, called Britain's foremost pacifist, defends Hitler in House of Lords, claiming that "if you had shared his experience, you would at least understand why he is ruthless in protecting his country."	Thousands of Japanese troops land in Min River near Fukien Province capital of Foochow and meet heavy Chinese resistence.	In his inaugural speech, Pres.-elect Juan Antonio Rios pledges that Chile's land and territorial waters will not be used for action against American nations.	
May 22		Greek guerrillas reportedly cut the Salonika railroad over which Nazis have been moving troops through Bulgaria to the Russian front.	Chinese troops force Japanese to retreat to their ships after landing at mouth of Min River near Foochow.	Special session of Mexican Congress is called for purpose of declaring war on the Axis countries.	
May 23		Russian troops abandon Kerch Peninsula in the Crimea.	Japanese forces occupy Chuanshih Island at mouth of Min River below Foochow, and 21 Japanese warships shell Santu, Pingtan and Nanjisu islands nearby.		
May 24		Germans encircle a large Russian force south of Kharkov .... Resolutions demanding second front against Hitler are adopted at two mass meetings in London, one sponsored by the CP, the other by Lord Beaverbrook's *Daily Express.*	Japanese troops continue to advance in several columns in Chekiang Province, driving close to Kinhwa, the provincial capital.		

A
Includes developments that affect more than one world region, international organizations and important meetings of major world leaders.

B
Includes all developments in European countries and military engagements between Allied and Axis powers in Africa and at sea.

C
Includes all developments in Japan and China, Japanese foreign policy and military actions in the Pacific region.

D
Includes all domestic and regional developments in Latin America, the Caribbean and Canada.

E
Includes developments in those independent nations and colonial possessions not covered in Columns B, C and D.

U.S. Politics & Social Issues	U.S. Foreign Policy & Defense	U.S. Economy & Environment	Science, Technology & Nature	Culture, Leisure & Life Style	
Senate votes against Downey resolution opposing special gasoline privileges for senators.	FDR signs bill creating the WACS and names Mrs. Oveta Culp Hobby director of the Corps.			Sammy Angott wins split decision over Allie Stolz in Madison Square Garden to retain his light heavyweight championship.	May 15
FDR commutes the four-year sentence of former CP Secy. Earl Browder and orders his release from Atlanta Federal Prison.	Lt. Gen. Hugh A. Drum issues proclamation in N.Y. designating the East Coast as Eastern Military Area, in which the Army will control all artificial lighting along the coast and nearby inland areas to protect shipping.			Dr. Bronislaw K. Malinowski of Yale University, internationally famous Polish anthropologist whose most famous works deal with cultures of the Southwest Pacific area, dies at 58 of a heart attack in New Haven, Conn. .... OSU takes first Big Ten track and field championship in Evanston, Ill.	May 16
N.Y. State Republican Clubs adopt a resolution in Hamilton, N.Y. endorsing Thomas E. Dewey for the GOP gubernatorial nomination.					May 17
Democratic House Whip Patrick J. Boland (Pa.) dies in Scranton of a heart attack.		OPA's price ceillings for retail goods, based on highest March prices, go into effect throughout the nation.		Lew Ayres, screen actor, joins Army as non-combattant at Hood River, Ore., after six weeks in conscientious objectors' camp .... N.Y. Police Commissioner Lewis J. Valentine ends night baseball in city for the war's duration because sky glow from lights endangers shipping.	May 18
	FDR personally awards Congressional Medal of Honor to Brig. Gen. James H. Doolittle for leading American attack upon Japanese cities April 18.	FDR says at his press conference that extension of gasoline rationing throughout the country is being discussed.			May 19
Sen. Alben W. Barkley (D, Ky.) declares in the Senate the FBI has reported there is no "foundation" for stories published in *New York Post* recently that Sen. David I. Walsh (D, Mass.), Senate Naval Affairs Comm. chairman, had visited a "house of degradation" in Brooklyn where Nazi agents congregated .... Atty. Gen. Biddle announces Justice Dept. will group all of its war activities under a new War Division, temporarily headed by Charles Fahy.	Former Pres. Herbert Hoover says in N.Y. that to win the war FDR must have dictatorial powers: "The economic measures necessary to win total war are just plain Fascist economics." .... Navy Dept. announces that on June 1 it will begin recruiting 1,000 Negroes a month for high seas duty and that in June and July the Marine Corps will form a Negro batalion of 900 men.	House Ways and Means Comm. tentatively approves an income surtax ranging from 6% to 81%, which is expected to yield an additional $2.750 billion in revenues .... Senate passes and returns to House $680-million agriculture appropriation bill with an amendment permitting Commodity Credit Corp. to sell government-owned wheat at 85% parity price.	John Lyle Harrington, designer of more than 200 bridges and developer of the vertical lift bridge, dies in Kansas City, Mo.		May 20
	Knox reports to Roosevelt that the Navy can and will salvage former French liner *Normandie*, with the job taking about one year.	Commerce Secy. Jesse H. Jones tells a Senate Agricultural subcommittee he has recommended that the rate of synthetic rubber production be raised from 800,000 tons to 1,000,000 tons in 1943 and indicates grain alcohol will be used more than before.	Standard Oil of N.J. announces new methods of producing synthetic rubber and 100% octane aviation fuel.	Boston Red Sox star Ted Williams joins the Navy with plans to become a flier.	May 21
David B. Vaughan, a member of the Board of Economic Warfare, files a $75,000 libel suit against Rep. Martin Dies, who linked him with Communist front organizations.	Although confident of victory, FDR deplores current over-optimism in the U.S. and says the war will be long .... FDR orders registration of every male who will be 18 or 19 by June 30 in the fifth registration since October 1940 .... Swedish-American liner *Drottningholm* leaves Lisbon, carrying 875 North and South American diplomats, newspaper correspondents and other civilians to the Americas in exchange for Axis officials and correspondents.	AFL Executive Council urges CIO to resume peace talks immediately because of the war needs .... FDR authorizes creation of nine-man National Railway Labor Panel for adjustment of disputes between railways and employes before disputes reach strike votes .... WPB Chmn. Nelson states there will be no new auto tires for the next two years due to the war.			May 22
	House and Senate conferees agree on permanent $42 monthly wage minimum for Army and Marine Corps privates and Navy apprentice seaman.	WPB orders halt in construction of new race tracks, theaters, baseball parks and other public amusement projects costing $5,000 or more by June 6.	British CP National Conference announces in London that Professor J.B.S. Haldane, 49, noted biologist, has applied for membership in the Party .... Flash floods in eastern and central Pennsylvania kill 32 persons.	Princeton Univ. clinches Eastern Intercollegiate Baseball League championship for second straight year by defeating Harvard, 6-5.	May 23
					May 24

F	G	H	I	J
Includes elections, federal-state relations, civil rights and liberties, crime, the judiciary, education, health care, poverty, urban affairs and population.	*Includes formation and debate of U.S. foreign and defense policies, veterans affairs and defense spending. (Relations with specific foreign countries are usually found under the region concerned.)*	*Includes business, labor, agriculture, taxation, transportation, consumer affairs, monetary and fiscal policy, natural resources, pollution and accidents.*	*Includes worldwide scientific, medical and technological developments, natural phenomena, U.S. weather and natural disasters.*	*Includes the arts, religion, scholarship, communications media, sports, entertainment, fashions, fads and social life.*

	World Affairs	European War Zone	Pacific War Zone	The Americas	Other Countries & Territories
May 25		Berlin announces three large Russian armies, including tank forces, have failed to break the German encirclement near Kharkov.	Twenty-three persons allegedly connected with Australia First movement are arrested on charges of treason and conspiracy to aid Japanese invasion of the continent.		
May 26		Under command of Field Marshal Rommel, large German forces begin to advance eastward toward British positions near Bir Hacheim, Libya .... Eden and Molotov sign a 20-year Anglo-Russian mutual assistance pact reaffirming principles of Roosevelt-Churchill Atlantic Charter and replacing the agreement signed July 12, 1941 .... Labor Party convention in London adopts Harold Laski's resolution which demands "socialization of the basic industries and services of the country and the planning of production for community consumption."	Chinese claim to have killed 3,000 Japanese soldiers in their attack upon Kinhwa, Chekiang Province. They claim three of the five Japanese drives on the capital have been stemmed.		
May 27		Head of U.S. Army Air Forces Lt. Gen. Henry H. Arnold and Chief of Naval Bureau of Aeronautics Rear Adm. John H. Towers arrive in London to confer with British officials on an Allied air offensive.	Tojo says in Tokyo that Japan will continue to fight until "the influence of Britain and America and their dreams of world domination" are ended .... Despite heavy Japanese assaults Kinhwa, Chekiang provincial capital, remains in Chinese hands.	First Inter-American Conference on Coordination of Police and Judicial Measures opens in Buenos Aires, with only Honduras, Guatemala and Costa Rica not represented.	
May 28		German High Command announces "battle of encirclement south of Kharkov has resulted in an outstanding victory," with 165,000 prisoners counted .... German forces in Libya split into two columns, attacking British troops at Bir Hacheim and El Gazala.	Chinese forces abandon provincial capital of Kinhwa to Japanese.	Acting Pres. Ramon Castillo indicates in Buenos Aires that Argentina will continue its policy of strict neutrality and not break with Axis .... Pres. Manuel Avila Camacho asks Mexican Congress to declare state of war on Germany, Italy and Japan.	
May 29		German Protector of Bohemia-Moravia Reinhard Heydrich is wounded by a bomb and gunfire while driving through streets of Rotkitzen .... German tanks break through British lines at Sidi Rezegh, Libya, some 50 miles west of Egyptian border.	Japanese forces enter city of Lungyu, west of Kinhwa, and engage Chinese troops in street fighting .... Chinese command claims its troops have been forced to retreat from Kinhwa and Lanchi in Chekiang Province because of Japanese use of poison gas.	Mexican Chamber of Deputies votes unanimously for declaration of war against Germany, Italy and Japan.	
May 30	In a Memorial Day speech at Arlington National Cemetary, Under State Secy. Sumner Welles presents a five-point postwar peace plan calling for the U.N. to maintain world peace.	Battle for Kharkov ends in a major German victory with the capture of an estimated 200,000 Russian troops .... British tank and motorized forces mount a counterattack against Germans southwest of Tobruk, Libya.		Mexican Senate votes unanimously for declaration of war against Germany, Italy, and Japan.	
May 31		In greatest air raid in history, 1,000 RAF bombers assault Cologne, Germany, reportedly killing 20,000 and wounding another 54,000 persons .... Luftwaffe heavily bombs famous cathedral city of Canterbury as reprisal for RAF raid on Cologne.			
June 1		British troops sweep northwest of Bir Hacheim and occupy Segnali, an Axis military base .... Twenty-seven more Czechs are executed in Prague and Brunn, bringing total to 108, for the attack upon Reinhard Heydrich .... Lt. Gen. Arnold says in London that U.S. fliers and planes will soon join RAF in attacks upon the Axis "which they cannot meet, defeat or survive."	Japanese troops advance northward from Tsengshing and Sinkai in Kwangtung Province, China.	Mexican Pres. Avila Camacho signs declaration of war recognizing that war has existed between Mexico and Germany, Italy and Japan since May 22.	
June 2		British armored forces drive Axis units out of Tamar, a strong point southwest of Tobruk, Libya .... A total of 1,036 RAF planes bomb giant Krupp Works at Essen and other points in Ruhr section of Germany.			

A	B	C	D	E
Includes developments that affect more than one world region, international organizations and important meetings of major world leaders.	*Includes all developments in European countries and military engagements between Allied and Axis powers in Africa and at sea.*	*Includes all developments in Japan and China, Japanese foreign policy and military actions in the Pacific region.*	*Includes all domestic and regional developments in Latin America, the Caribbean and Canada.*	*Includes developments in those independent nations and colonial possessions not covered in Columns B, C and D.*

U.S. Politics & Social Issues	U.S. Foreign Policy & Defense	U.S. Economy & Environment	Science, Technology & Nature	Culture, Leisure & Life Style	
		NAM issues 65-page brochure refuting charges of profiteering in war industries.		Eva Chamberlain-Wagner, 75, daughter of composer Richard Wagner and widow of Houston Stewart Chamberlain, who renounced his British citizenship in 1914, dies in Bayreuth, Germany.	May 25
Comm. on Fair Employment Practice orders eight N.Y. and N.J. companies holding war contracts to cease discrimination against Negroes, Jews, and aliens.	Hull presents Soviet Amb. Maxim Litvinov with terms for new Lend-Lease agreement, which would require Russia to liberalize postwar economic relations.	FDR signs a bill increasing the amount of private loans for defense housing which may be guaranteed by FHA from $300 million to $800 million .... Price Admin. Leon Henderson orders rent in 20 war production and military training areas in 13 states reduced to maximum levels prevailing in 1941, except in hotels and rooming houses.			May 26
Harry R. Bridges, president of CIO Longshoremen's and Warehousemen's Union, tells California legislative investigating committee in San Francisco, "I have always thought that Mayor Rossi was a Fascist." He charges that Rossi attended celebration of occupation of Sudetenland, Czechoslavakia, held by visiting Nazi "storm troopers" in Ocotober 1938.	House rejects House-Senate conferees agreement to set minimum base pay for Army and Marine Corps privates and Navy and Coast Guard seamen at $42 monthly .... FDR discusses problems with Pacific War Council and then confers with Louis Johnson, his personal envoy to India .... More than 13,600 women volunteer for the WAACs on the first day of recruiting.	War Manpower Comm. reveals plans are near completion to "freeze" workers in critical war industries, aimed at halting "pirating" of workers by employers .... District 50 of UMW accuses CIO of conducting campaign of intimidation and slander against it.		General Assembly of the Presbyterian Church in the U.S. votes to ask FDR to close all distilleries, breweries, wholesale and retail outlets of liquors and beer for the war's duration.	May 27
		John L. Lewis removes CIO Pres. Philip Murray as a vice president of the UMW and names John A. O'Leary to the post .... Atty. Gen. Biddle overrules Immigration Appeals Bd. and orders deportation of Harry Bridges on grounds he had been a member of the CP since his arrival in the U.S. in 1920 .... SEC reveals names of America's highest salaried persons in 1941 according to corporate reports. The top three are: Louis B. Mayer, managing director of Loew's Inc., with annual income of $704,425.60; James Cagney, $362,500; and Clark Gable, $357,000.		Italian-born opera singer Ezio Pinza is released from Ellis Island, N.Y., where he has been held since March for investigation as an enemy alien.	May 28
		Assn. of American Railroads adopts general war measures which include reduction in luxury passenger accommodations, elimination of non-essential trains and an increase in passenger capacity .... FDR approves Treasury Dept. plan to curb tax evasion by disallowing excessive salaries and war bonuses as "ordinary and necessary" business expenses.		Famous star of stage, screen and radio John B. Barrymore dies at 60 in Hollywood.	May 29
				Penn State Univ. captures IC 4-A track title in N.Y., becoming the first team ever to capture both indoor and outdoor titles in same year.	May 30
				Sam Snead beats Jimmy Turnesa to win PGA championship in Atlantic City, N.J.	May 31
Supreme Court votes to invalidate a 1935 Oklahoma law providing for sterilization of criminals with three felony convictions .... Dr. Maynard C. Kruger is elected national chairman of the Socialist Party to succeed Norman Thomas, who declines to serve again.	Swedish-American liner *Drottningholm* arrives in Jersey City, N.J., from Lisbon with 908 passengers, including Adm. William D. Leahy, U.S. ambassador to France, and U.S. and Latin American diplomats exchanged for Axis officials.	Supreme Court rules building service employes are subject to the Wage and Hour Law when working in buildings in which companies engaged in interstate commerce have their offices.		Supreme Court rules CBS and NBC are entitled to judicial review of FCC's anti-chain regulations issued in 1941 .... Chicago Cubs buy Jimmy Foxx, 34, Boston Red Sox first baseman who was named American League's most valuable player three times.	June 1
	Chinese Foreign Min. T.V. Soong and State Secy. Cordell Hull sign Lend-Lease pact in Washington .... FDR asks Congress to recognize that a state of war exists between U.S. and Bulgaria, Hungary and Rumania.	WPB announces it will assume control of civilian imports beginning July 2 in a move to conserve shipping space.	Alien Property Custodian Leo T. Crowley seizes 600 enemy-owned patents, most of which are in the fields of aviation and science.		June 2

F	G	H	I	J
Includes elections, federal-state relations, civil rights and liberties, crime, the judiciary, education, health care, poverty, urban affairs and population.	*Includes formation and debate of U.S. foreign and defense policies, veterans affairs and defense spending. (Relations with specific foreign countries are usually found under the region concerned.)*	*Includes business, labor, agriculture, taxation, transportation, consumer affairs, monetary and fiscal policy, natural resources, pollution and accidents.*	*Includes worldwide scientific, medical and technological developments, natural phenomena, U.S. weather and natural disasters.*	*Includes the arts, religion, scholarship, communications media, sports, entertainment, fashions, fads and social life.*

	World Affairs	European War Zone	Pacific War Zone	The Americas	Other Countries & Territories
June 3	Viscount Samuel tells House of Lords that a system of collective security, not a balance of power, must prevail after war, and that U.S. participation is vital to any peace.	Several hundred RAF planes bomb Essen and other Ruhr objectives . . . . British government issues White Paper announcing nationalization of all coal mines and control of coal distribution.	Four Japanese bombers and 15 fighters attack Dutch Harbor, Alaska, causing few casualties and setting several warehouses on fire . . . . Chinese expeditionary force arrives in India from Burma under the command of Gen. Stilwell . . . . Japanese troops move towards Chuhsien in western Chekiang Province.	Venezuelan Foreign Min. Dr. C. Parra Perez says his country is on side of U.S. and is "cooperating to the limit of our capacity in the defense of the continent."	
June 4		Adolf Hitler flies to Finland with other German officers to present Finnish Field Marshal Carl Gustav Mannerheim with German medal on his 75th birthday . . . . FDR and Russian Foreign Min. Molotov reach an understanding on need for a second front in 1942 in Europe . . . . Reinhard Heydrich, Reich protector of Bohemia-Moravia, dies in Prague, eight days after being wounded by two Czechs at Rotkitzen . . . . Free French forces repulse another Axis attack on Bir Hacheim, while British and Indian troops attack rear lines.	At 9 a.m. Japanese carry out their sixth assault upon Midway Island, some 1,300 miles northwest of Hawaii . . . . Chinese Chief of Staff Lt. Gen. Stilwell, Commander of U.S. Army Air Force in India Major Gen. Lewis Brereton and American Volunteer Group Commander Brig. Gen. Claire Chennault arrive in Chungking for conferences with Chiang Kai-shek.	Mexican unions agree to ban jurisdictional conflicts and strikes for the war's duration and to set up a National Labor Council to cooperate with the government.	
June 5	Canadian, British, Australian and New Zealand representatives sign an agreement in Ottawa for expansion and extension of the Commonwealth air training program in Canada through March 1945.		In the continuing naval battle off Midway Island, U.S. Navy claims to have inflicted "heavy damage" upon the Japanese.		
June 6	U.S. Amb. John G. Winant says in London that after the war the U.N. must convert war drives to social drives for food, housing and other needs of peoples of all nations.		Admiral Chester W. Nimitz announces that in Midway battle beginning June 4 two or three Japanese aircraft carriers were sunk and 11 or 12 other warships damaged . . . . Japanese forces capture Chuhsien airfield, while heavy fighting continues in center of the walled city in Chekiang Province.	Cuban Office of Price and Supply Control freezes all prices of foodstuffs, clothing and other commodities and limits profits in an anti-inflation decree.	
June 7		Soviet forces repel German assaults on Sevastopol for third day in a row . . . . *N.Y. Times* reports German Catholic bishops have charged the Nazi government with systematically oppressing the Church in an effort to destroy Christianity.	The 19,900-ton aircraft carrier *Yorktown* sinks in the Pacific after being damaged June 4 by Japanese bombs in battle of Midway.		
June 8		In French language broadcast from London, BBC urges French people to evacuate coastal areas of the country, as that area is more likely to become involved in war operations.	Sydney, Australia is shelled for about 15 minutes by Japanese submarines, but little damage is reported.		
June 9	FDR and Churchill announce creation of a Combined Production and Resources Bd., to be chaired by Donald Nelson and Oliver Lyttelton, and a Combined Food Bd. chaired by Claude Wickard and R.H. Brand.	Czech village of Lidice is exterminated by the Germans because its population allegedly "gave shelter and assisted the murderers" of Heydrich . . . . Tank battle in Libya around Knightsbridge and Bir Hacheim continues.	Chinese still claim to hold Chuhsien in Chekiang Province and to have inflicted 7,000 casualties upon Japanese forces there.	Inter-American Conference on the Coordination of Police and Judicial Measures closes in Buenos Aires after adopting resolutions aimed at curbing alien, especially Axis, activities.	
June 10		German Army begins an offensive in Kharkov sector of the Ukraine.	Chinese troops evacuate Chuhsien, Chekiang Province after nine days of battle, claiming to have inflicted 18,000 casualties upon Japanese . . . . Japanese command admits loss of an aircraft carrier, 35 planes and damage to another carrier and one cruiser in Midway battle.	Canadian P.M. Wm. Mackenzie King proposes a bill to amend the National Mobilization Act to permit sending drafted men abroad.	After a conference with Gandhi in Bombay, Nehru says he supports the former's view that Britain should leave India.
June 11		Free French garrison at Bir Hacheim, Libya abandons city to Axis forces.			

A	B	C	D	E
Includes developments that affect more than one world region, international organizations and important meetings of major world leaders.	*Includes all developments in European countries and military engagements between Allied and Axis powers in Africa and at sea.*	*Includes all developments in Japan and China, Japanese foreign policy and military actions in the Pacific region.*	*Includes all domestic and regional developments in Latin America, the Caribbean and Canada.*	*Includes developments in those independent nations and colonial possessions not covered in Columns B, C and D.*

U.S. Politics & Social Issues	U.S. Foreign Policy & Defense	U.S. Economy & Environment	Science, Technology & Nature	Culture, Leisure & Life Style	
Moses L. Annenberg, Philadelphia newspaper publisher, is released on parole from Northeastern Federal Penitentiary at Lewisburg, Pa., because of ill health after serving 23 months of a three-year sentence for income tax evasion.	House passes and sends to Senate formal declarations of war against Bulgaria, Hungary and Rumania .... Navy bill for $8.3 billion for construction of aircraft carriers, cruisers, destroyers and escort ships is introduced into House.	Morgenthau says in a Washington broadcast that no one will be permitted "to amass riches out of this war," adding that the $8.7 billion additional revenue asked of Congress by the Administration is the very least necessary at present and reporting that May war bond sales reached $634,000,000 .... CIO Pres. Murray tells CIO Executive Board that John L. Lewis is "hell bent on creating national confusion and national disunity."			June 3
Census Bureau reports more than half of the 74,775,836 persons 25 years of age or older completed at least eight years of elementary school.	Senate unanimously approves three resolutions declaring war on Bulgaria, Hungary and Rumania.	Philadelphia grand jury indicts E.I. du Pont, Hercules Powder, Atlas Powder, Austin Powder, Illinois Powder and King Powder companies for conspiring to fix prices of commerical explosives and blasting supplies in violation of Sherman Antitrust Act .... UMW policy committee adopts resolution in Washington, 26 to 2, demanding CIO Pres. Murray "publicly renounce his allegiance to and support of Communism; that he discharge from the employment of the CIO those Communists now on the payroll, and that he cease to employ Communists as agents and representatives of the CIO." Murray denies any connection with Communism.	American Meat Institute announces in Chicago development of processes for dehydration of meat to save shipping space.	Actress Paulette Goddard and Charles Chaplin recieve mutual consent divorce decree from Mexican civil court in Juarez, Mexico.	June 4
National professional educational fraternity Phi Delta Kappa votes to eliminate its constitutional clause limiting membership to white males .... Frederick V. Williams and David W. Ryder are sentenced to 16 months to four years in Washington for violating the Foreign Agents Registration Act by serving as Japanese propaganda agents.	FDR signs congressional resolutions declaring war on Bulgaria, Hungary and Rumania.	House abolishes CCC and refuses to fund NYA war worker training program .... WPB sets up nine-man Foods Requirement Comm., to be chaired by Agriculture Secy. Claude Wickard.			June 5
In their first meeting since April 1941, FDR and James A. Farley confer at the White House on N.Y. gubernatorial nominees.				Kentucky Derby winner Shut Out captures the $53,020 Belmont Handicap.	June 6
Wartime Civil Control Administration announces virtually the entire Japanese population of the West Coast has been removed inland .... Francis Lewis Wellman, 87, famous New York Corporation Counsel and trial lawyer who prosecuted many notorious criminals between 1883 and 1894, dies in New York.					June 7
Supreme Court upholds right of municipalities to impose reasonable license fees on Jehovah Witnesses when they distribute literature for which they ask contributions.	FDR asks Congress for record War Dept. appropriation of $39.417 billion for fiscal 1943 .... Hull extends an offer to Belgium, Poland and Greece to become parties to the master Lend-Lease agreement.	OPA announces plans to increase basic gasoline rationing from three to four gallons per week along the East Coast effective July 1.			June 8
		House defeats motion to concur with Senate amendment to the agriculture appropriation bill which would authorize below parity sale of government owned wheat.			June 9
	Federal grand jury in Hartford, Conn. indicts five persons on charges of conspiring to send military information about U.S. to Germany and Japan during 1941 .... House approves and sends to Senate a $50 minimum service pay bill.	WPB approves immediate construction of 550-mile, 24-inch steel pipeline from Longview, Tex. to Salem, Ill. to deliver 350,000 barrels of oil a day to Salem for distribution in the East .... AFL weekly newsletter assails CIO's suggestions for a unified approach to labor peace as fantastic proposals not worthy of consideration.	Drs. Philip Cohen and Samuel J. Scadron report to AMA that they apparently have immunized babies against whooping cough by vaccinating the mothers three months before the babies' birth.		June 10
	Hull and Russian Amb. Maxim Litvinov sign master Lend-Lease agreement in Washington, providing for reciprocal defense aid during the war and economic cooperation designed to create "a new and better world" after the war is won .... Senate passes and sends to the White House the $50 minimum service pay bill.	House Ways and Means Comm. votes to double present 5% transportation tax and also approves increases in cigar, cigarette and tobacco taxes .... Rep. Warren G. Magnuson (D, Wash.) says present Alaskan Highway east of the Rockies is a fantastic error.			June 11
F *Includes elections, federal-state relations, civil rights and liberties, crime, the judiciary, education, health care, poverty, urban affairs and population.*	G *Includes formation and debate of U.S. foreign and defense policies, veterans affairs and defense spending. (Relations with specific foreign countries are usually found under the region concerned.)*	H *Includes business, labor, agriculture, taxation, transportation, consumer affairs, monetary and fiscal policy, natural resources, pollution and accidents.*	I *Includes worldwide scientific, medical and technological developments, natural phenomena, U.S. weather and natural disasters.*	J *Includes the arts, religion, scholarship, communications media, sports, entertainment, fashions, fads and social life.*	

	World Affairs	European War Zone	Pacific War Zone	The Americas	Other Countries & Territories
June 12		Field Marshal Rommel's forces attack El Adem, 18 miles south of Tobruk, while the main body circles eastward through Ed Duda-Rezegh area in a drive to the Mediterranean .... German Propaganda Min. Joseph Goebbels says "Jewish press" in N.Y. and London instigated bombing of German cities, and in reprisal Germany will exterminate European Jews and "perhaps even beyond Europe."	A small contingent of Japanese troops land on Attu Island at westernmost end of Aleutian archipelago and is subjected to U.S. air assaults .... Japanese troops take Nancheng, Kiangsi Province, after Chinese forces evacuate the city .... Navy Dept. says 37 Japanese ships were sunk or damanged and more than 100 planes destroyed in separate actions in the Coral Sea in March and May, as compared to three U.S. ships lost.	Argentine Senate ratifies commercial treaty with U.S., which had been signed Oct. 14, 1941 .... Mexican Treasury orders confiscation of all properties of Axis subjects.	
June 13			Darwin, Australia airfield is attacked by 27 Japanese bombers, escorted by 12 to 15 Zero fighters.	CCC purchases entire Peruvian cotton crop totaling 400,000 bales for $44 million.	
June 14	Mexico and Philippines become 27th and 28th members of U.N. when their representatives sign the U.N. pact of Jan. 1 at the White House.	Lord Louis Mountbatten, chief of British commandos, returns to London after completing conferences in Washington.			
June 15		At the end of three days of attacks, British and U.S. bombers set two Italian battleships afire, sink a 10,000-ton cruiser and two destroyers and damage two other cruisers and possibly two destroyers while protecting two Mediterranean convoys .... Axis forces bypass Acroma, Libya and plunge northward towards Mediterranean coast, isolating El Gazala garrison, 40 miles west of Tobruk.	U.S. Navy announces six Japanese ships — "at least" three cruisers, one destroyer, one gunboat and one transport — have been damaged by Army and Navy planes in western Aleutian Islands .... Two Japanese columns moving along Hangchow-Nanchang railroad and through Kiangsi Province form a giant pincer in eastern China.		Gandhi says in Wardha that he will soon launch a movement against British rule in India that "will be felt by the whole world."
June 16		Axis forces attack in semi-circle stretching from west to south of Tobruk with Acroma, El Adem and Sidi Rezegh as anchors. British and South African troops abandon El Gazala.			
June 17			Japanese bombers attack Port Moresby, New Guinea.	Argentine Foreign Min. Enrique Ruiz Guinazu refuses to answer questions about foreign policy unless Chamber of Deputies stenographers are removed.	
June 18	Churchill arrives in Washington with his staff to confer with FDR on the war's conduct.	British forces withdraw from El Adem, 18 miles south of Tobruk, and Sidi Rezegh, 20 miles southeast of Tobruk .... German-controlled Prague radio announces alleged killers of Heydrich "were discovered in a Prague church" early this morning and "shot immediately on arrest." .... Supreme Soviet approves British-Soviet mutual aid treaty during its first wartime session in Moscow.	Japanese forces land from six small warships at Siaohsiungshih, north of Taichow Bay in eastern Chekiang.		
June 19		Berlin and Rome dispatches claim that Axis troops have surrounded Tobruk .... Alois Elias, the former premier of Protectorate of Bohemia-Moravia, is executed by the Nazis.	Allied bombers attack Japanese at Rabaul, New Britain.	Cuban government grants U.S. the right to anti-submarine facilities in Cuba and an air training center near Havana.	Bey of Tunis, Sidi Ahmed II, nominal ruler of 2.5 million people under French protectorate, dies in Tunis.
June 20		German high command says 20,000 prisoners have been taken in Libya, where the British have been driven back to the Egyptian border or surrounded at Tobruk .... Nazi troops smash through Russian defense lines north of Sevastopol and reach Syevernaya Harbor opposite naval base after 12 days of heavy fighting .... Sir Stafford Cripps says at a London rally that the British and Americans will "launch a great and successful attack upon Hitler in the West."	An Axis submarine attacks telegraph station at Estevan Point, Vancouver Island without causing any damage.		

A	B	C	D	E
Includes developments that affect more than one world region, international organizations and important meetings of major world leaders.	*Includes all developments in European countries and military engagements between Allied and Axis powers in Africa and at sea.*	*Includes all developments in Japan and China, Japanese foreign policy and military actions in the Pacific region.*	*Includes all domestic and regional developments in Latin America, the Caribbean and Canada.*	*Includes developments in those independent nations and colonial possessions not covered in Columns B, C and D.*

U.S. Politics & Social Issues	U.S. Foreign Policy & Defense	U.S. Economy & Environment	Science, Technology & Nature	Culture, Leisure & Life Style	
	FDR creates an eight-man Alaska War Council, headed by Gov. Ernest Gruening.	CIO-USWA wins collective bargaining elections held by NWLB at 23 Carnegie-Illinois Steel Corp. plants .... FDR calls upon every American to turn in every bit of scrap rubber they can to the government for the war effort.	At least 29 persons are killed and more than 50 injured when a tornado strikes southwest section of Oklahoma City .... Danish astronomer Kaj A. Strand reports to American Astronomical Society his discovery of a new red dwarf star accompanying a pair of double stars in Mu Draconis group.		June 12
	Coast Guardsman John C. Cullen, 21, spots four German saboteurs as they land from a U-boat at Amagansett, Long Island .... FDR issues an executive order naming Elmer Davis as director of newly created Office of War Information .... About 2,500,000 spectators line New York City's Fifth Avenue to watch more than 500,000 U.S. and Allied armed forces march for 11 hours starting at 10 a.m. in "New York at War Parade."			USC compiles 85½ points to win NCAA track and field championship for eighth consecutive time in Lincoln, Neb. .... New U.S. Army publication *Yank* appears, to be sold only to soldiers overseas.	June 13
Commission on Fair Employment Practices rules that two Chicago locals of AFL Steamfitters Protective Assn. and Chicago Journeymen Plumbers Union have prevented Negroes from working on defense contracts.					June 14
Federal Court of Appeals upholds conviction of AMA and Medical Society of the District of Columbia on charges of conspiring to violate the Sherman Antitrust Law.	FDR tells Congress in his Lend-Lease report that $1.9 billion in aid was dispersed to allies in three months ending May 31, and that in 15 months since March 1941 over $4.497 billion in aid has been given.	Randolph E. Paul, an assistant to the secretary of the treasury, urges House Ways and Means Comm. to enact a 100% tax on all net income over $25,000 left after regular income tax.			June 15
	House Naval Affairs Comm. approves a $8.550 billion naval expansion program bill.			Big Ten All Stars defeat Pacific Coast Conference track team in Evanston, Ill.	June 16
Rep. Samuel Dickstein (D, N.Y.) charges House Appropriations Comm. failed to allocate money to student loans because of racial and social discrimination at Columbia Univ. Medical School.	FDR signs $50 minimum pay bill for servicemen.			Jessie Bond Ransome, 89, one of last of original Savoyards, leading singer of famous D'Oyly Carte Opera Co., dies in Worthing, Sussex.	June 17
Several thousand CIO-UAW workers stage an unauthorized strike at Hudson Naval Ordnance Arsenal in Detroit when eight Negro workers take over machines formerly operated by whites .... FDR nominates Abe Fortas to succeed John J. Dempsey as under secretary of the Interior.	Japanese Amb. Kichisaburo Nomura, special envoy Saburo Kurusu and 1,095 other Japanese nationals leave N.Y.C. for Lourenco Marques, Portuguese East Africa to be exchanged for 1,500 Americans interned in Japan since Dec. 7, 1941 .... House passes $8.550-billion naval expansion program bill.	Senate's Truman defense investigating committee denounces dollar-a-year men on grounds that they delayed conversion of plants to war work.	Northrop Aircraft Corp. reveals a new method of welding for magnesium sheets, extrusions and tubing called the "heliarc" method, which may eliminate riveted aircraft.		June 18
					June 19
Price Admin. Leon Henderson says he is willing to resign if that is what is necessary to have Congress move to stabilize prices.		House Ways and Means Comm. approves Treasury Dept. plan to collect a 10% withholding tax on individual incomes at the source.	Armour Research Foundation in Chicago announces development and patenting of a device about the size of a portable radio which records sound magnetically on steel wires as thin as a human hair.	NYAC wins National AAU track and field championships at Triborough Stadium, N.Y.	June 20

F	G	H	I	J
Includes elections, federal-state relations, civil rights and liberties, crime, the judiciary, education, health care, poverty, urban affairs and population.	*Includes formation and debate of U.S. foreign and defense policies, veterans affairs and defense spending. (Relations with specific foreign countries are usually found under the region concerned.)*	*Includes business, labor, agriculture, taxation, transportation, consumer affairs, monetary and fiscal policy, natural resources, pollution and accidents.*	*Includes worldwide scientific, medical and technological developments, natural phenomena, U.S. weather and natural disasters.*	*Includes the arts, religion, scholarship, communications media, sports, entertainment, fashions, fads and social life.*

	World Affairs	European War Zone	Pacific War Zone	The Americas	Other Countries & Territories
June 21		Tobruk, Libya falls to Axis after violent 26-hour assault, with Germans claiming 25,000 prisoners .... Lord Beaverbrook says in Birmingham that the British government is now committed to a second front .... German forces drive wedge in Russian defenses at Sevastopol.	U.S. Navy Dept. announces that despite bad weather long-range bombers have sunk a Japanese transport and hit a Japanese cruiser at Kiska in the western Aleutian Islands 650 miles west of Dutch Harbor .... An unidentified craft fires six to nine shells at the coast north of Seaside, Ore. without causing any damage.		
June 22	FDR and Churchill issue a joint statement in Washington saying that the objective of their conferences "is the earliest maximum concentration of Allied war power upon the enemy." .... Minn. Gov. Harold Stassen proposes that a postwar "world association" be established.	British and Axis forces battle at Azeiz, about 12 miles northwest of Fort Capuzzo on Libyan-Egyptian border .... Three U.S. merchant ships are sunk in Gulf of Mexico with 72 men lost.			
June 23		Rommel's Axis forces attempt to flank British defense line on Libyan-Egyptian border .... German forces continue heavy assaults in Sevastopol and Kharkov areas of Russia .... U.S. Navy reports 13 Allied ships were sunk in Caribbean Sea between June 4 and 13.	Chinese recapture important Japanese base at Linhsien in northern Honan near Shansi border.		British government in India outlaws All India Forward Bloc, extremist national group founded by Subhas Chandra Bose in 1939.
June 24		Moscow reports German assaults on Kharkov and Sevastopol fronts are continuing despite heavy Nazi losses .... Germans destroy Czech village Levzsaky and execute entire adult population for allegedly "sheltering parachutists."	Chinese troops recapture Kweiki on Hangchow-Nanchang railway in Kiangsi Province and Lishui, the last important Japanese-held air base in southern Chekiang Province .... New Zealand P.M. Peter Fraser announces in Wellington creation of 13-member war administration combining government and opposition leaders.	Argentine Pres. Roberto M. Ortiz resigns due to poor health and failing eyesight.	
June 25	FDR and Churchill confer with Pacific War Council in Washington.	Major Gen. Dwight D. Eisenhower is appointed head of newly established European theater of operations for U.S. forces .... Rommel's forces drive 60 miles inside Egypt to a point southeast of Sidi Barrani .... Red Army withdraws from Kupyansk, a railway junction on the Oskol River southeast of Kharkov.	Tokyo announces Kiska will now be called Narukami Island and Attu will be Atitu.	With only its two CP members voting no, Chilean Senate votes to continue a foreign policy of maintaining diplomatic relations with the Axis.	
June 26		More than 1,000 RAF bombers raid Bremen, Germany for 75 minutes .... Three Axis armored columns drive at Matruh in the north and the Quattara Depression in the south on the Egyptian front.	U.S. authorities announce removal of 550 natives from Pribilof Islands, a Bering Sea group, and Atka Island in the Aleutians to points in southern Alaska .... Japanese bombers and fighters bomb airfield at Port Moresby, New Guinea but cause little damage.		
June 27	FDR and Churchill issue joint statement concerning their conferences, indicating that efforts will be made to divert Germany's strength from Russia and means to relieve China from Japanese pressure will be found .... U.S., Canada, Argentina, Australia and Britain sign an international agreement to pool 100 million bushels of wheat and flour for relief purposes in war-stricken areas.		U.S. planes from Hawaiian command attack Japanese-occupied Wake Island, reportedly damaging airfield and shore batteries without loss of any planes.	Argentine Congress accepts Pres. Ortiz's resignation and permits Vice Pres. Ramon S. Castillo to complete term which ends Feb. 20, 1944.	
June 28		Moscow reports start of third major German offensive in Kursk area some 280 miles south of Moscow.	U.S. Navy reports four Japanese aircraft carriers—the *Akagi, Kaga, Soryu* and *Hiryu*— were sunk during Battle of Midway.	Foreign Min. Oswaldo Aranha announces all of Brazil's ocean-going merchant marine will be placed under jurisdiction of Allied Shipping Control Bd.	
June 29		Rommel's forces capture Matruh, British base in Egypt, taking 6,000 prisoners, knocking out 36 tanks and shooting down 17 planes .... Soviets admit loss of 10,000 men and report that another 10,000 are missing in Volkhov River area.			

A	B	C	D	E
Includes developments that affect more than one world region, international organizations and important meetings of major world leaders.	*Includes all developments in European countries and military engagements between Allied and Axis powers in Africa and at sea.*	*Includes all developments in Japan and China, Japanese foreign policy and military actions in the Pacific region.*	*Includes all domestic and regional developments in Latin America, the Caribbean and Canada.*	*Includes developments in those independent nations and colonial possessions not covered in Columns B, C and D.*

U.S. Politics & Social Issues	U.S. Foreign Policy & Defense	U.S. Economy & Environment	Science, Technology & Nature	Culture, Leisure & Life Style	
	Yugoslav King Peter II arrives in Washington to discuss anti-Axis opposition and Lend-Lease aid for Yugoslavian guerrillas.			Ben Hogan scores a record low of 271 to win Hale America golf tournament in Chicago.	June 21
	White Russian Fascist leader Anastase A. Vonsiatsky pleads guilty in Hartford, Conn. to conspiracy to send U.S. military information to Germany and Japan before Dec. 7, 1941.				June 22
Dies Committee charges that a Union for Democratic Action is leading a campaign to discredit and obliterate Congress.	House passes and sends to the Senate largest Army supply bill in history, totaling $42.820 billion.	House Military Affairs Comm. says in report on war production program "there has been evidence of widespread and inexcusable waste of public funds."			June 23
Wendell L. Willkie says in a *Saturday Evening Post* article that anti-Semitism and discrimination against all other minorities must be eliminated .... Dissenting from latest Dies Committee report, Rep. Jerry Voorhis (D, Calif.), a committee member, says in Washington the committee is guilty of "name-calling" and every loyal American has the right "to disagree politically with [it] without being branded as subversive and un-American."	Selective Service establishes the order by which men with dependents will be drafted, placing married men with children in the last category.	House Ways and Means Comm. completes work on 1943 tax by eliminating mandatory requirement of joint returns by husband and wife .... Senate Appropriations Comm. votes to end CCC.		Sir Edwin Cooper, reputed to have designed more important buildings in London than any other architect, dies in London.	June 24
Atty. Gen. Biddle announces all persons representing foreign principals must register with Justice Dept. by July 9.	Office of Censorship revises the Code of Wartime Practices, placing further restrictions on reports of ship movements, cargoes, air raids and diplomatic moves or negotiations .... Sen. Allen J. Ellender (D, La.) demands that FDR take over U.N. leadership, charging Britain with inactivity and apathy.	WPB Chmn. Nelson tells Senate's Truman investigating committee that supply of raw materials, especially scrap iron and steel and copper, has become the chief problem in war production.		Dr. William B. Pugh says the committee which has studied the proposal to merge Presbyterian and Protestant Episcopal Churches has reached an accord on the basic principles of union.	June 25
	Senate passes and sends to the White House $8.550-billion naval expansion bill.	FDR reports that during May the U.S. produced nearly 4,000 planes, over 1,500 tanks, nearly 2,000 artillery and anti-tank guns and over 100,000 machine guns .... Senate passes and returns to House $1.157-billion Labor Dept.-FSA appropriation bill with an amendment to continue CCC and NYA .... NAM presents a nine-point postwar program denying that "a postwar depression" and "fundamental changes in the social order are inevitable."			June 26
Supreme Court denies a stay of execution to Negro sharecropper Odell Waller, whose case was appealed on grounds that his jury failed to contain non-payers of poll taxes.	FBI chief J. Edgar Hoover announces arrest of eight highly trained saboteurs who landed on Long Island and Florida coasts .... Navy calls for 1,000 owners of small boats capable of ocean travel to volunteer themselves and ships for service with Coast Guard anti-submarine patrols.				June 27
Federal Security Admin. Paul V. McNutt says in N.Y. that discrimination against Negroes must be eliminated .... Western Defense Command announces German and Italian aliens will be permitted to return to their homes in that area .... NEA proposes creation of a nationwide teachers placement service to be established and controlled by U.S. Employment Service.					June 28
					June 29

F	G	H	I	J
Includes elections, federal-state relations, civil rights and liberties, crime, the judiciary, education, health care, poverty, urban affairs and population.	*Includes formation and debate of U.S. foreign and defense policies, veterans affairs and defense spending. (Relations with specific foreign countries are usually found under the region concerned.)*	*Includes business, labor, agriculture, taxation, transportation, consumer affairs, monetary and fiscal policy, natural resources, pollution and accidents.*	*Includes worldwide scientific, medical and technological developments, natural phenomena, U.S. weather and natural disasters.*	*Includes the arts, religion, scholarship, communications media, sports, entertainment, fashions, fads and social life.*

	World Affairs	European War Zone	Pacific War Zone	The Americas	Other Countries & Territories
June 30		British forces withdraw from coastal point of El Daba (100 miles west of Alexandria naval base) under pressure from Axis armored columns.			
July 1		Rommel's troops attack El Alamein, last British strongpoint east of Alexandria.	Japanese troops complete occupation of 403-mile Hangchow-Nanchang railroad, the last line in Chinese hands.	Argentine Chamber of Deputies refuses to approve Pres. Ramon S. Castillo's state of siege proclamation.	
July 2		General Axis attack on El Alamein is repulsed and counter-attacking Imperial troops force enemy to withdraw to west .... German forces begin new attacks between Kharkov and Kursk in Russia .... House of Commons defeats motion of no-confidence in P.M.Churchill's conduct of war after a two-day debate by a 476-25 vote.	An official Chungking review of the American Volunteer Group record claims that it shot down 284 Japanese planes from Dec. 7, 1941 to June 30, 1942.	U-boat sinks U.S. merchant ship *San Pablo* in Costa Rican harbor of San Jose .... Panama Canal employe and 19 others in British Honduras are arrested by Caribbean Defense Command for allegedly supplying fuel and information to Nazi submarines in Caribbean .... Mexican Ministry of the Interior announces dissolution of Mexican Falange Party.	Sir A. Ramaswami Mudaliar, Hindu member of the executive council of the governor general of India, and Maharaja Jam Saheb, member of Indian Chamber of Princes, are appointed to British war cabinet in London .... British forces occupy French island of Mayotta in Mozambique Channel with no resistance or casualties on either side.
July 3		Germans capture Soviet naval base Sevastopol in southwestern Crimea .... Prague radio announces execution of 123 more persons, bringing total to 1,174 since May 27.	U.S. Army bombers complete four days of air attacks on Japanese installations and ships on Japanese-occupied Kiska in the Aleutians and surrounding waters .... In its last battle, American Volunteer Group drives away eight Japanese bombers trying to raid Hengyang on Canton-Hankow railroad line.		
July 4		Russian troops fall back before a heavy German tank assault in Kursk area .... British claim success in their counter attacks on Rommel's forces west of El Alamein.	U.S. Navy submarines torpedo four and sink three Japanese destroyers in Aleutian Islands.	Sixty person are injured and Axis-owned stores are wrecked in San Jose, Costa Rica during anti-Axis riots.	Gandhi writes in weekly publication *Harijan* that "foreign troops are necessary for the defense of India" and that Anglo-American troops are welcome provided they leave at war's end.
July 5		German troops reportedly reach Don River after breaking Russian defense lines between Kharkov and Kursk.			
July 6		Soviet Information Bureau in Moscow reports German troops have driven 120 miles eastward from Kursk to point west of Voronezh, an important industrial and rail city on Moscow-Rostov railway just east of Don River.	Maj. Gen. Chu Shihming, Chinese military attache, says China's military situation is worse than before U.S. and Britain entered war and that China needs more help.	Puerto Rican Resident Commissioner Bolivar Pagan introduces a bill to the House authorizing Puerto Ricans to elect their own government.	
July 7		German troops capture Voronezh in an offensive that has carried them 60 miles beyond their farthest point of 1941 .... Maj. Gen. Carl A. Spaatz is appointed commander of U.S. Air Force in Europe, under direction of Maj. Gen. Eisenhower.		With 45 Quebec Liberals opposing, Canadian House of Commons votes in favor of bill to send conscripted men overseas if necessary .... Argentine Navy Ministry orders Argentine merchant vessels to avoid U.S. East Coast, presumably due to the German blockade.	
July 8		Polish Vice Premier Mikolajcyk reads report to Polish National Council that 3,000,000 Poles and Jews have become victims of Nazi campaign of extermination in Poland .... Russian troops abandon Staryi Oskol, 100 miles northeast of Kharkov.	Japanese forces are checked at Fengchang and Changshu in their drive towards Hunan Province.	Cuba begins training 100,000 men for military service.	
July 9		British Imperial forces drive Axis troops northward in battle around El Alamein .... Germans reach Rossosh on Rostov-Moscow railroad line, some 150 miles east of Kharkov .... Turkish Pres. Ismet Inonu appoints Foreign Min. Suku Saracoglu premier.	Chungking claims its troops recapture Changshu, Nancheng, Iwang and Poyang in Kiangsi Province.		

A	B	C	D	E
Includes developments that affect more than one world region, international organizations and important meetings of major world leaders.	*Includes all developments in European countries and military engagements between Allied and Axis powers in Africa and at sea.*	*Includes all developments in Japan and China, Japanese foreign policy and military actions in the Pacific region.*	*Includes all domestic and regional developments in Latin America, the Caribbean and Canada.*	*Includes developments in those independent nations and colonial possessions not covered in Columns B, C and D.*

U.S. Politics & Social Issues	U.S. Foreign Policy & Defense	U.S. Economy & Environment	Science, Technology & Nature	Culture, Leisure & Life Style	
	An estimated three million youths from 18 to 20 register in fifth draft call, raising total to 43 million registrants.	Congress votes appropriations bills totaling over $44.804 billion to beat fiscal year deadline . . . . NWLB rules unanimously that it has jurisdiction deriving from President's war powers in wage dispute involving Montgomery Ward & Co., Chicago mail order firm, even though the company produces no war materials.			June 30
Wendell Willkie says he has no intention of becoming a candidate in N.Y. gubernatorial race . . . . Senate confirms appointment of Thomas F. Meaney as federal district judge in N.J. after two days of hearings in which he is accused of being a "pawn" of Mayor Frank Hague of Jersey City.			Monsanto Chemical Corp. announces development of shatter-proof window pane made of transparent cellulose acetate sheeting laminated with wire mesh.		July 1
Odell Waller, 25, Negro sharecropper, is executed in electric chair at Virginia Penitentiary in Richmond for killing his white employer, Oscar Davis, on July 15, 1940.	FDR signs proclamation denying enemies entering U.S. for sabotage and espionage access to civil courts and then appoints a seven-man military commission to try eight Nazi spies who entered the country June 27 . . . . Max Stephan, German-born Detroit restaurant owner, is convicted of treason by federal jury in Detroit for aiding Hans Peter Krug, a German flier who escaped to U.S. from a Canadian prison camp.	House passes and sends to the Senate an Agriculture Dept. funding bill, with an amendment prohibiting sale of government-owned stocks at below parity prices.			July 2
		FDR asserts "certain selfish and power hungry groups" are urging Congress to prohibit sale of government-held grain at 85% of parity.	World's largest flying boat, *Mars*, capable of traveling over 7,000 miles at 200 mph, is tested over Chesapeake Bay, Md.		July 3
Leader of German-American Bund, Gerhard Wilhelm Kunze, is turned over to U.S. officials in Brownsville, Tex. after his capture in Mexico.		Government report indicates 507 Axis-owned or controlled firms in U.S. have been liquidated and over 2,000 patents seized.		Don Budge beats Bobby Riggs in final round of professional national tennis championship in Forest Hills, N.Y. . . . . *This Is the Army*, a soldier revue with a cast of 300 Army men, opens at Broadway Theatre in New York.	July 4
	War Dept. announces new regulations by which foreign governments will supply U.S. troops abroad with facilities, supplies, and equipment without payment of cash, but will receive credits for Lend-Lease supplies.	Arthur B. Newhall, WPB rubber coordinator, announces Goodyear Tire & Rubber Co. started production in a government-financed synthetic rubber plant in May and Firestone Tire & Rubber Co. began in June . . . . UMW regional director Bernard Borah says in Chattanooga, Tenn. that 30 locals are quitting UMW because John L. Lewis is hindering the war effort.			July 5
FDR vetoes bill to deprive all persons guilty of war fraud of their U.S. citizenship on grounds that even a misdemeanor could cause revocation.				AL All-Stars beat NL All-Stars, 3-1, in N.Y. to raise $95,000 for Bat and Ball Fund for armed services.	July 6
Federal grand jury in N.Y. indicts 29 members of German-American Bund for conspiracy to violate the Selective Service Law and Alien Registration Act.					July 7
FBI in N.Y. arrests 72 relatives and associates of the 29 Bund members arrested yesterday . . . . OPA sets new regulations whereby congressmen and other bona fide candidates for political office will receive additional gasoline for their campaigns in the East.		Donald Nelson reorganizes WPB, with Wm. L. Batt becoming chairman of materials requirements committee and James S. Knowles becoming vice chairman.		James C. Petrillo, president of AFL American Federation of Musicians, announces in N.Y. that his 140,000 members will not make any records after July 31 in a campaign to force radio stations, bars and restaurants to employ union musicians . . . . Barbara Hutton, Woolworth heiress, and actor Cary Grant are married at Lake Arrowhead, Calif.	July 8
U.S. Office of Education announces loans will be made to 10,000 students pursuing engineering, physics, chemistry, medicine, dentistry and pharmacy degrees, who can complete the courses in two years and aid war effort . . . . Martin Dies apologizes to David Vaughan for mistakingly naming him a sponsor of the now defunct CP American League for Peace and Democracy.		Pres. Roosevelt again rebukes House farm bloc for seeking to prevent government from selling surplus crops below parity prices.	Bureau of Agricultural Chemistry in Peoria, Ill. announces production of a substance from soy bean and corn oil which looks, smells and feels much like rubber.		July 9
F *Includes elections, federal-state relations, civil rights and liberties, crime, the judiciary, education, health care, poverty, urban affairs and population.*	G *Includes formation and debate of U.S. foreign and defense policies, veterans affairs and defense spending. (Relations with specific foreign countries are usually found under the region concerned.)*	H *Includes business, labor, agriculture, taxation, transportation, consumer affairs, monetary and fiscal policy, natural resources, pollution and accidents.*	I *Includes worldwide scientific, medical and technological developments, natural phenomena, U.S. weather and natural disasters.*	J *Includes the arts, religion, scholarship, communications media, sports, entertainment, fashions, fads and social life.*	

	World Affairs	European War Zone	Pacific War Zone	The Americas	Other Countries & Territories
July 10		Russian troops abandon Rossosh, permitting Germans to cut Moscow-Rostov railway line .... Dutch Amb. to Britain E.F.M.J. Michiels van Verduynen and Soviet Amb. Ivan M. Maisky sign agreement in London to resume diplomatic relations between their countries.		U.S. and Peru reach agreement whereby U.S. will pay 1½% more for future Peruvian cotton crops with each 1% reduction in acreage.	
July 11		AP reports from Istanbul that 250,000 Yugoslavian troops are battling Axis forces in south Serbia and Croatia .... British Imperial forces consolidate their positions at Tel-el Eisa, west of El Alamein.	U.S. forces reach Port Moresby in southeastern New Guinea .... Chinese troops reoccupy Futuoy Island near Fukien seaport of Foochow .... After a five-day drive southeastward from Lishui, Japanese troops occupy the Chekiang port of Wenchow.	Brazil announces that except for high officials and diplomats all private citizens will be barred from private auto use beginning July 17 because of a gasoline shortage.	
July 12		Red Army abandons Kantemirovka and Lisichansk near the Don River, permitting Germans to penetrate to their deepest point inside Russia.		U.S. and Bolivian officials reach an agreement for purchase of Bolivia's entire rubber crop by U.S.	
July 13		Following outbreak of sabotage in occupied zone, Gestapo authorities in Paris announce they will execute all male relatives over 18 of any French saboteur who does not surrender himself within 10 days .... Soviets concede German advances at Rzhev, 130 miles northwest of Moscow, and at Voronezh, Boguchar and Lisichansk on southern front.	Chinese troops recapture Tsingtien, 23 miles up Wu River from Wenchow.		
July 14		Russian troops again withdraw in face of advancing Nazi forces on south Russian front .... Vichy rejects U.S. offer to move nine French warships at Alexandria to an American, neutral or Martinique port to prevent their seizure by Axis.	Chinese director of military training, Gen. Cheng Cheh-yuen announces Chinese Army will be increased to 26 million men.		All-Indian Congress Party working committee adopts resolution demanding British withdrawal from India but denying any intention of embarrassing U.N. war effort.
July 15		Axis forces attack British position at Tel el-Eisa, 10 miles west of El Alamein .... Moscow radio announces famous Peterhof Palace on Gulf of Finland has been destroyed by Germans .... Russian troops abandon Boguchar and Millerovo on southern front.		Former Argentine Pres. Roberto M. Ortiz dies in Buenos Aires.	
July 16		Axis forces counter-attack in central and northern sectors of 35-mile line stretching from El Alamein southward to Quattara Depression .... Soviet communique claims Germans lost 900,000 men, including 350,000 killed from May 15 to July 15.	FDR's administrative assistant Lauchlin Currie arrives in Chungking to confer with Chiang Kai-shek.		
July 17		German troops occupy Ukranian industrial city of Voroshilovgrad, about 100 miles north of Rostov.			
July 18		German armored divisions cross Donets River and advance on wide front east of Rostov, gateway to Caucasus .... Gen. Francisco Franco announces in Madrid that a new Cortes, modeled after the Italian corporative system, will convene in October.	Chinese troops retake Wenchow, Chekiang port, and are pursuing Japanese forces toward Juian, 16 miles away.		Moslem League charges All-India Congress has not done everything to find a solution to India's independence demand.
July 19		Russian troops slow down German advance towards Stalingrad and Rostov.	Chinese troops retake Juian, Kienteh and Iyang and Hengfeng, the latter two towns 15 miles apart on Hangchow-Nanchang railway.	United Fruit Co. announces development plan to supply U.S. with rubber, hemp, quinine and palm oil from Guatemala, Honduras, Nicaragua, Costa Rica and Panama.	
July 20		Russian forces claim they have secured Don River bridgeheads 10 miles west of Voronezh .... RAF planes attack Axis airfield near Fuka, reportedly setting at least 30 planes afire, and also setting fire to enemy barges off Sidi Barrani.		Pres. Eduardo Santos presides over opening session of Colombian Congress, stating that nation's cause is tied to Allies.	

A	B	C	D	E
Includes developments that affect more than one world region, international organizations and important meetings of major world leaders.	*Includes all developments in European countries and military engagements between Allied and Axis powers in Africa and at sea.*	*Includes all developments in Japan and China, Japanese foreign policy and military actions in the Pacific region.*	*Includes all domestic and regional developments in Latin America, the Caribbean and Canada.*	*Includes developments in those independent nations and colonial possessions not covered in Columns B, C and D.*

U.S. Politics & Social Issues	U.S. Foreign Policy & Defense	U.S. Economy & Environment	Science, Technology & Nature	Culture, Leisure & Life Style	
	OWI chief Elmer Davis appoints three assistant directors: Archibald MacLeish, policy development branch; Gardner Cowles, Jr., domestic information; and Robert Sherwood, overseas information . . . . Secy. Hull and Greek P.M. Emmanuel Tsouderos sign master Lend-Lease agreement in Washington . . . . FDR signs legislation providing for construction of 1.9 million tons of Navy combat ships and 1.2 million tons of auxiliary ships.	Senate Appropriations Comm. approves $120 million for OPA, but restricts the money's use.			July 10
California Supreme Court rules that a 1940 law barring the CP from the state ballot is unconstitutional and discriminatory . . . . FBI arrests 158 German aliens in N.Y. on grounds of endangering U.S. security. They are taken to Ellis Island.	Hull signs Lend-Lease agreements with Norwegian Amb. Wilhelm Morgenstierne and Czech Min. Vladimir S. Hurban.	House Ways and Means Comm. approves 1943 tax bill which will raise an estimated additional $7 billion.			July 11
Stern Park Gardens, Ill. public housing project of about 100 Czeckoslovak families is renamed after Bohemian village of Lidice, which the Nazis wiped out.					July 12
	Atty. Gen. Biddle announces arrest of 14 persons as direct contacts with Nazi saboteurs landed in Florida and Long Island.	Sen. Alben Barkley (D, Ky.) opens Administration's fight in Senate against restrictions on OPA.			July 13
Jean Leonard Musa is arraigned in N.Y. on charge of failing to register with State Dept. as agent of French government.					July 14
	FBI announces in Washington it is seeking three German saboteurs: Walter Kappe, Rheinhold Rudolf Barth and Joseph Schmidt.	Senate approves $125 million for OPA and drops two crippling provisions: (1) that OPA get approval to set ceiling prices on farm prices and (2) that Senate approve all appointees making over $4,500 a year . . . . Ending a two-month deadlock, House accepts Senate amendment to Agriculture Dept. appropriations bill to permit government sale of surplus grains at 85% parity . . . . NWLB awards increase of 5.5 cents per hour to 157,000 employes of "Little Steel" companies—Republic, Bethlehem, Inland and Youngstown.		Whirlaway with George Woolf up wins the 1$\frac{1}{8}$ mile, $62,600 Mass. Handicap at Suffolk Downs, setting new track record of 1:48 $\frac{1}{5}$.	July 15
	Atty. Gen. Biddle announces 10 of 14 accomplices of eight Nazi saboteurs will be prosecuted as accessories after the fact . . . . State Dept. announces closing of its consulate in Helsinki and requests Finland to close its consulates in U.S. because of the "untenable situation."	Senate passes and returns to House $1.861-billion war agencies appropriations bill . . . . NWLB announces it is using cost of living index as of Jan. 1, 1941 as yardstick in determining whether any labor group should get a wage increase.	International College of Surgeons, meeting in Denver, admits its first woman member, Dr. Margaret Hie Ding Lin, who has practiced medicine for 22 years in Foochow, China.	Eight-point plan for organic union of of Presbyterian Church in U.S. and Protestant Episcopal Church is announced.	July 16
Federal Judge William F. Smith signs order revoking citiizenship of four leaders of German-American Bund: August Klapprott, Matthias Kohler, William Drexler and Arno Friedrich.		Senate approves and returns to House $93-million Florida barge canal and pipeline bill.		Maury Henry Biddle Paul, 52, society editor and columnist of *New York Journal-American* under name of Cholly Knickerbocker for 25 years, dies in New York.	July 17
George Sutherland, 80, English-born associate justice of U.S. Supreme Court, dies in Stockbridge, Mass. . . . . Senate appropriations subcommittee headed by Sen. Millard E. Tydings (D, Md.) assails Bureau of Budget in report urging thorough investigation of alleged failure to reduce nondefense expenditures.	FDR declares that a state of war exists between U.S. and Bulgaria, Hungary and Rumania.	Unauthorized three-day strike of about 1,000 members of United Mine Workers at American Magnesium Corp.'s plant in Buffalo ends when strikers vote to submit wage dispute to NWLB.		Garden State Park race track in Delaware Township, N.J. opens with first legal horse races in N.J. in more than 50 years . . . . Occupation with Leslie Balaski up wins six-furlong, $62,000 Arlington Futurity in Chicago, setting new track record of 1:10 $\frac{2}{5}$.	July 18
Speaking to NAACP in Los Angeles, Wendell Willkie says that because of war pressures in U.S. "long-standing barriers and prejudice are breaking down."			Professor Marcellin Boule, 72, French paleontologist who specialized in study of Neanderthal and other primitive men, dies at Montsalvy, France.	Seventh Symphony of Dmitri Shostakovich, Russian composer, is played for first time in U.S. by NBC Symphony Orchestra.	July 19
	Swedish liner *Grispholm* arrives in Portuguese East Africa with Thai and Japanese nationals from U.S.	House passes and sends to Senate highest tax bill in history, designed to bring $6.271 billion more into Treasury during fiscal 1943 . . . . House approves and sends to Senate bill to outlaw payment of commissions in negotiation of government contracts.		Robert Garrett donates his collection of 6,000 Arabic and Islamic manuscripts, said to be largest and best in the world, to Princeton Univ.	July 20

F	G	H	I	J
Includes elections, federal-state relations, civil rights and liberties, crime, the judiciary, education, health care, poverty, urban affairs and population.	*Includes formation and debate of U.S. foreign and defense policies, veterans affairs and defense spending. (Relations with specific foreign countries are usually found under the region concerned.)*	*Includes business, labor, agriculture, taxation, transportation, consumer affairs, monetary and fiscal policy, natural resources, pollution and accidents.*	*Includes worldwide scientific, medical and technological developments, natural phenomena, U.S. weather and natural disasters.*	*Includes the arts, religion, scholarship, communications media, sports, entertainment, fashions, fads and social life.*

	World Affairs	European War Zone	Pacific War Zone	The Americas	Other Countries & Territories
July 21		German sources report continued advances towards Rostov, which is reportedly set afire by Axis bombers.			
July 22		British forces extend their offensive along central sector on El Alamein front .... RAF planes bomb Duisburg, Europe's largest inland port, at confluence of Rhine and Ruhr Rivers .... German forces march to Novocherkassk, 20 miles northeast of Rostov.	Japanese troops land from a convoy at Gona Mission, Buna on north coast of New Guinea.		Gandhi wires UP that he would not cooperate with Japanese under any circumstances: "I would rather be shot than cooperate with the Japanese or any other power." .... Government removes ban on Indian CP and its two publications, *The National Front* and *The New Age*.
July 23	In a worldwide broadcast, Secy. Hull says United Nations should create an international agency to maintain peace after this war is won.		Allied bombers make five attacks on new Japanese base near Buna, in southeastern New Guinea .... American correspondents who arrived in Portuguese East Africa from Japan report Japanese atrocities and torture.	Canadian House of Commons approves the third reading of the amendment to the National Mobilization Act authorizing overseas service for conscripts.	
July 24		Heavy fighting continues on 120-mile front stretching along Don River from Rostov through Novocherkassk to Tsimlyansk.	Allied dive bombers and fighters drop 45,000 pounds of bombs on Japanese at Gona, Papua.		
July 25		Germans claim Rostov is being cleared of scattered Russian troops .... American planes complete seven operations against Tobruk and Bengazi in Libya and Suda Bay in Crete, reportedly causing heavy damage to dock installations .... Reports in London state Germans are arresting and deporting Jews in occupied France and Netherlands to Poland.			
July 26		German troops cross Don River south and east of Rostov, while Rumanian troops reach Don west of Stalingrad .... British Labor Min. Ernest Bevin warns against second front creating a division in the country, while a crowd of 50,000 to 60,000 demand a second front at Communist rally in Trafalgar Square.		Mexican Pres. Manuel Avila Camacho orders cancellation of naturalization papers of all former Axis nationals "whose conduct casts doubt on their loyalty to Mexico."	Sir Stafford Cripps says in London it is unthinkable that Gandhi should be allowed to thwart U.N. efforts for sake of political maneuvering.
July 27		An estimated 600 RAF planes drop 175,000 fire and explosive bombs on Hamburg, Germany .... German Gestapo destroys Norwegian village of Televaag, on Sotra Island, in reprisal for shooting of two agents.	Allied patrols make contact with advancing Japanese troops near Oivi, 55 miles inland from Gona Mission on New Guinea .... Tojo says "Japan is determined to destroy the United States and Great Britain."		
July 28		Moscow announces Germans have crossed Don River to south bank at Tsimlyansk, 120 miles northeast of Rostov, despite heavy losses.	Allied patrols reportedly drive Japanese back halfway along 120-mile road to Allied base at Port Moresby .... Chinese troops rout Japanese near Kiangshan in Chekiang Province and widen their hold to 50 miles on Hangchow-Nanchang railway.		
July 29	Henry Ford says in Detroit that unless world federation comes out of this present war, a more tragic conflict will come in a generation.	Despite stiffening Russian resistance, German troops continue to advance into Caucasus south of Rostov .... Yugoslavian Gen. Draja Mikhailovich's forces capture village of Ugrugora on Dalmatian coast and destroy harbor installations at Port Selekhin.	Navy Dept. creates unified command in Aleutian Islands off Alaska to supervise joint naval and air operations.	Canadian Senate passes draft amendment permitting overseas service for conscripted men.	
July 30		Russian troops fall back at many points south and southeast of Bataisk, 15 miles below Rostov on Don River.	Japanese troops occupy Kai, Tanimbar and Aroe groups of islands between Australia and New Guinea .... Allied fighters reportedly shoot down nine of 49 Japanese raiders on Port Darwin on north Australian coast.		British State Secy. for India Leopold Amery says British government will meet situation if All-India Congress Party decides to carry out Gandhi's civil disobedience program.
July 31		Germans, Rumanians and Slovaks cross lower Don River on 155-mile front.	U.S. Navy announces approximately 10,000 Japanese troops are in three occupied Aleutian islands.		

A	B	C	D	E
Includes developments that affect more than one world region, international organizations and important meetings of major world leaders.	*Includes all developments in European countries and military engagements between Allied and Axis powers in Africa and at sea.*	*Includes all developments in Japan and China, Japanese foreign policy and military actions in the Pacific region.*	*Includes all domestic and regional developments in Latin America, the Caribbean and Canada.*	*Includes developments in those independent nations and colonial possessions not covered in Columns B, C and D.*

U.S. Politics & Social Issues	U.S. Foreign Policy & Defense	U.S. Economy & Environment	Science, Technology & Nature	Culture, Leisure & Life Style	
Adm. William D. Leahy is made FDR's chief of staff.	FDR says in a message read in N.Y. that U.S. will hold perpetrators of Nazi war crimes to strict accountability . . . . House approves and sends to White House bill creating the Women's Naval Reserve Corps. . . . . Bund leader Gerhard W. Kunze pleads guilty in Hartford, Conn. to charges of conspiracy to commit espionage.	Wayne L. Morse, public member of WLB, warns labor that "drastic action will be taken" against any labor organization that tries to bring about work stoppages.		Swedish track star Gunder Haegg sets new world record of 5:16.4 for 2,000 meters in Malmoe, Sweden.	July 21
N.Y. Sen. James M. Mead announces he has FDR's endorsement over John J. Bennett for N.Y. Democratic gubernatorial nomination . . . . N.Y.C. Asst. Supt. of Schools Benjamin Greenberg says 20 elementary schools will experiment with "continuous progress system" whereby no grading separates children during the first three years of school.	Liners *Asama Maru* and *Conte Verde* arrive at Lourenco Marques, Portuguese East Africa with 1,500 U.S. and Allied nationals for exchange for Japanese and Thai nationals.	With only nine members present, Senate votes to establish separate war agency to handle manufacture of synthetic rubber from grain alcohol . . . . Bethlehem Pres. Eugene C. Grace writes NWLB that the company accepts under protest the board's 44¢ daily wage increase for steel workers.		Abe J. Greene becomes the first president of National Boxing Assn. to succeed himself.	July 22
Ala. Gov. Frank M. Dixon charges federal agencies are trying "to break down the principle of race segregation" under which the South has lived since Reconstruction . . . . OWI chief Elmer Davis asks Civil Service Commission to check its employe lists to see that no Communists are on OWI payroll.		Democratic Sens. Walter F. George (Ga.) and Joseph C. O'Mahoney (Wyo.) demand legislation to regulate all wages, prices, profits and rents as means of controlling inflation.		Atty. Gen. Biddle authorizes filing of injunction against American Fed. of Musicians Pres. Petrillo's attempt to prevent musicians from making recordings for radio and commerical use.	July 23
	Yugoslavian Foreign Min. Momcilo Nincich signs U.S. master Lend-Lease agreement in Washington which has been signed by nine other nations.	Although lacking a quorum, House passes and sends to White House farm bloc's bill to create a rubber agency separate from WPB.			July 24
		With four labor representatives dissenting, NWLB adopts resolution warning AFL and CIO to settle their jurisdictional disputes or the board will settle them through compulsory arbitration.		Shut Out wins $88,250 1¼ mile Arlington Classic in Chicago in record-tying time of 2:01 ⅖.	July 25
					July 26
		NWLB refuses to permit wage increase for workers at Remington Rand plants in N.Y. on grounds that they had already received increases beyond the cost-of-living index.		Byron Nelson wins Tam O'Shanter golf classic in Chicago with a five-under-par 67.	July 27
Virtually all Negroes are turned away from polls in today's Arkansas Democratic primary.	Swedish liner *Gripsholm* leaves Portuguese East Africa with American nationals for U.S.	Officials of War, Navy, Commerce and Labor Depts., Maritime Commission, War Manpower Commission, WPB and Public Health Service sign a statement in Washington recommending an eight-hour day, 48-hour workweek industry schedule.		Elmer Davis, director of OWI, urges James C. Petrillo of Amer. Federation of Musicians to withdraw his order barring musicians from making recordings for radio or commercial use after July 31.	July 28
Commissioner of Immigration and Naturalization Earl G. Harrison reports a total of 934,100 German, Italian and Japanese aliens have registered.	Supreme Court hears appeal for writ of habeas corpus so that seven of eight German saboteurs may be tried in civil court rather than by military commission.	WPB suspends deliveries of fuel oil for heating and cooling in 12 Eastern states from Aug. 3 to Sept. 15 in order to increase reserve stocks for winter.	Dr. Grinnell Jones of Harvard Univ. announces in Cambridge that he and Dr. Walter Juda have perfected new fire-resisting chemical known as "F.A.M.," which can be sprayed on wood to make it virtually fireproof.		July 29
	FDR signs bill creating Women's Reserve in the Navy, to be known as the Waves . . . . Seven of 28 indicted for sedition on July 21 enter pleas of innocence in Washington . . . . Senate completes action on $974,634,000 bill authorizing naval aviation and shore facilities.	Henry Kaiser tells Senate committees his shipyards could build 70-ton cargo planes in 10 months and 200-toners in 14 months.			July 30
	Supreme Court unanimously refuses writ of habeas corpus to Nazi saboteurs, declaring charges against them within purview of military authorities . . . . The 25,000-ton U.S. aircraft carrier *Essex* is launched in Newport News, Va.			Ray Robinson wins his 33rd consecutive pro fight when he out-points light heavyweight champion Sammy Angott in 10-round fight in N.Y.C.	July 31
F *Includes elections, federal-state relations, civil rights and liberties, crime, the judiciary, education, health care, poverty, urban affairs and population.*	G *Includes formation and debate of U.S. foreign and defense policies, veterans affairs and defense spending. (Relations with specific foreign countries are usually found under the region concerned.)*	H *Includes business, labor, agriculture, taxation, transportation, consumer affairs, monetary and fiscal policy, natural resources, pollution and accidents.*	I *Includes worldwide scientific, medical and technological developments, natural phenomena, U.S. weather and natural disasters.*	J *Includes the arts, religion, scholarship, communications media, sports, entertainment, fashions, fads and social life.*	

	World Affairs	European War Zone	Pacific War Zone	The Americas	Other Countries & Territories
Aug. 1		German forces claim capture of Salsk, railroad junction on Stalingrad-Caucasus line . . . . Allied bombers attack Axis-held Tobruk, Libya for sixth time in a week . . . . One person is killed and nine wounded in Paris food riot.		Argentine government announces American author Waldo Frank will be expelled for his remark that Argentina is in the midst of moral decay . . . . U.S. Amb. Jefferson Caffery signs agreement in Rio de Janeiro whereby U.S. will purchase six Brazilian products at cost of $32,490,000 over next four years.	
Aug. 2		Aided by strong tank and air support, German forces continue to attack at Kletskaya, Tsimlyansk, Kushchevka and Salsk on Don River front.		Waldo Frank is beaten by six men posing as detectives who force their way into his room in Buenos Aires apartment building.	Gandhi says that India's discontent might result in "welcome for the Japanese" should they land in India.
Aug. 3		Moscow radio reports Russia, Great Britain and U.S. have come to agreement regarding a second front this year . . . . German troops are reported driving steadily toward Kuban River, 50 miles above Maikop oil center.	U.S. planes attack Japanese headquaters and other installations in Linchwan, Kiangsi Province, while Chinese ground troops attack city at several points.		
Aug. 4		Russian troops withdraw from Kushchevka-Salsk area below Rostov and at Kletskaya in Don River bend in face of continuous German attacks.	For fifth time since July 1, American bombers attack Japanese-held port of Hankow.		British government in New Delhi publishes documents purporting to support its assertion that Gandhi and majority of All-India Congress Party are seeking to appease Japan.
Aug. 5		In new breakthrough on southern end of Don River, German forces cross river and reach Kotelnikov, 95 miles southwest of Stalingrad . . . . British government issues White Paper denouncing 1938 Munich Pact and saying it will not be guided by it at the war's end in adjusting Czech borders . . . . After four-day battle in northeastern Bosnia, Gen. Mikhailovich's forces drive Bulgarian and Croatian troops back.			Working Comm. of All-India Congress Party adopts a resolution calling for British withdrawal so that India can take its place within United Nations . . . . Sir Stafford Cripps says in London that if Britain were to withdraw from India now, there would be complete anarchy.
Aug. 6		German troops capture Tikhoretsk, at junction of the Krasnodar-Stalingrad and Rostov-Baku railroads . . . . Addressing U.S. Congress, Dutch Queen Wilhelmina says despite German cruelties in Holland, the motto of her people remains: "No Surrender."		U.S. and Mexico sign agreement whereby Mexican farm workers will be brought into U.S. to work where domestic labor is not available.	British War Office announces a Palestine volunteer regiment consisting of separate Arab and Jewish battalions will be created immediately for British Army in the Middle East.
Aug. 7		Germans drive southward from Byeloglina to point 60 miles above Maikop oil fields.	American forces land on Guadalcanal and its satellite islands—Tulagi, Florida and Gavatu—and encounter heavy opposition . . . . Heaviest Allied bombing is carried out against Japanese base at Rabaul, New Britain.	Alfonso Lopez is inaugurated as president of Colombia for a four-year term.	Gandhi calls upon his followers to support his campaign of non-violent non-cooperation against British.
Aug. 8		Germans claim capture of Armavir on Rostov-Baku oil pipeline.	U.S. Marines improve positions on Tulagi, Florida and Guadalcanal islands and capture Japanese air base on Guadalcanal, renaming it Henderson Field . . . . U.S. cruisers and destroyers silence shore batteries and start fires in a surface raid on Japanese-held Kiska in Aleutians.		All-India Congress Party adopts resolution calling for immediate British withdrawal from India and sanctioning non-violent civil disobedience.
Aug. 9	Philippine Pres. Manuel Quezon says in Washington broadcast that Atlantic Charter "applies to the nations and peoples of all the world."	Germans capture Maikop oil center and Krasnodar, capital of Kuban region.	Battle of Savo Island begins with first phase lasting 32 minutes and resulting in three American and one Australian cruisers sunk or put out of action and a Japanese victory. U.S. Marines take Japanese prisoners on the island and destroy land-based planes on Guadalcanal . . . . U.S. planes carry out surprise attack on big invasion port of Haiphong, Indochina without any loss.		India Congress Party leaders Gandhi, Nehru and Maulana Abul Kalam Azad are arrested in Bombay under Defense of India Act. Rioting follows later in the day.
Aug. 10		In their drive to cut Caucasus in half the Germans capture Pyatigorsk, 260 miles southwest of Rostov on Don River . . . . Premier Vidkun Quisling of Norway issues decree dissolving Provisional Church Council created by dissenting clergymen.			Riots continue for the second day in Bombay, Poona, Lucknow and Ahmedabad as British Imperial troops are called out.

	A	B	C	D	E
	Includes developments that affect more than one world region, international organizations and important meetings of major world leaders.	*Includes all developments in European countries and military engagements between Allied and Axis powers in Africa and at sea.*	*Includes all developments in Japan and China, Japanese foreign policy and military actions in the Pacific region.*	*Includes all domestic and regional developments in Latin America, the Caribbean and Canada.*	*Includes developments in those independent nations and colonial possessions not covered in Columns B, C and D.*

U.S. Politics & Social Issues	U.S. Foreign Policy & Defense	U.S. Economy & Environment	Science, Technology & Nature	Culture, Leisure & Life Style	
FBI arrests 66 German, 15 Italian and six Japanese enemy aliens in N.Y.C.					Aug. 1
Sen. John H. Bankhead (D, Ala.) asks Army Chief of Staff George C. Marshall not to permit Negro soldiers to train in the South to prevent possible race conflicts.	U.S. Army reveals first public information about Republic's P-47 Thunderbolt fighter plane, which can reach over 400 mph and 40,000 feet.	CIO Pres. Philip Murray proposes in letter to AFL Pres. William Green that negotiations for unity be reopened.		Roosevelt Memorial Assn. announces its annual awards for public service to War Secy. Henry L. Stimson, author Booth Tarkington and Rufus M. Jones of American Friends Service Comm.	Aug. 2
Rep. Elmer J. Hollander (D, Pa.) says *N.Y. Daily News* and *Washington Times Herald* are "America's No. 1 and No. 2 exponents of the Nazi propaganda line" and should be investigated.				Justice Dept. files suit in Chicago against American Fed. of Musicians Pres. Petrillo for violating Sherman Antitrust Law.	Aug. 3
		Three panels report to NWLB that wages of some 48,000 New England and 13,000 Southern textile workers are substandard and recommend 7½ cent-an-hour increase.			Aug. 4
Leader of now disbanded anti-Semitic Fascist Silver Shirts, William Dudley Pelley, is convicted of 11 counts of sedition by federal jury in Indianapolis, Ind.		Commerce Dept. estimates that wage, salary, dividend and other income payments reached a total of $52.071 billion in first half of 1942.			Aug. 5
	For aiding an escaped Nazi prisoner, Max Stephan is sentenced by Federal Judge Arthur Tuttle to be hanged for treason on Nov. 13 .... Army forms two new airborne units: 82nd commanded by Brig. Gen. Matthew Ridgway and 101st commanded by Brig. Gen. William C. Lee.	FDR vetoes bill to create separate rubber agency and then appoints a three-man panel—Bernard Baruch, James Conant and Karl Compton—to investigate rubber situation .... Reese H. Taylor of WPB tells Truman Comm. that only 5,690,000 tons of steel were delivered in June although there were orders for 11,074,725 tons .... Agriculture Dept. announces plans for selling 125 million bushels of government surplus wheat to livestock and poultry producers at not less than 85% parity.			Aug. 6
	Atty. Gen. Biddle announces a federal grand jury will investigate a news dispatch by Stanley Johnson, published in *N.Y. Daily News, Chicago Tribune* and *Washington Times Herald*, for possible unlawful communication of vital defense information. The dispatch concerns Japanese ship movements in the Battle of Midway.				Aug. 7
	Six of eight Nazi saboteurs are executed in Washington. FDR accepts military commission's recommendation that Ernst Berger be sentenced to life imprisonment at hard labor and George Dasch to 30 years.			Craig Wood wins Canadian open golf championship at the Mississauga Club in Toronto.	Aug. 8
	FDR says in prepared statement that "We have only begun to get in our stride" as far as the war effort is concerned .... *Chicago Tribune* denies it violated national security in publishing the Johnson dispatch concerning Japanese ship movements.			Three-day National A.A.U. men's outdoor swimming championships end today with three world records: Aug. 7: one-mile free-style—Keo Nakama of Ohio State Univ. 20:29.0; Aug. 8: 440-yard free-style—William Smith, 4:39.6; Aug. 9: 880-yard free-style—William Smith, 9:54.6.	Aug. 9
Sen. C. Wayland Brooks (R, Ill.) charges in Senate that "purge and smear campaign" directed at members of Congress and the *Chicago Tribune* has been started by Administration.					Aug. 10

F	G	H	I	J
Includes elections, federal-state relations, civil rights and liberties, crime, the judiciary, education, health care, poverty, urban affairs and population.	*Includes formation and debate of U.S. foreign and defense policies, veterans affairs and defense spending. (Relations with specific foreign countries are usually found under the region concerned.)*	*Includes business, labor, agriculture, taxation, transportation, consumer affairs, monetary and fiscal policy, natural resources, pollution and accidents.*	*Includes worldwide scientific, medical and technological developments, natural phenomena, U.S. weather and natural disasters.*	*Includes the arts, religion, scholarship, communications media, sports, entertainment, fashions, fads and social life.*

	World Affairs	European War Zone	Pacific War Zone	The Americas	Other Countries & Territories
Aug. 11		Russian troops fall back from Armavir along Caucasian foothills across frontier of Circassia to Cherkessk.			More Indians are killed in rioting in Bombay and other cities.
Aug. 12	Churchill flies to Moscow to meet with Stalin and FDR's personal representative Averill Harriman.	Germans claim 62nd Russian Army has been virtually destroyed in a trap on Don River.	U.S. Marines consolidate their positions on the Solomon Islands as U.S. bombers again strike at Rabaul, New Britain.	Chilean government orders censorship of all communications with Axis nations.	Police fire on mobs in Bombay, Tenali Patna and Poona, raising casualty toll in four-day rioting to at least 56 dead and 300 injured . . . . U.S. troops in India are instructed not to interfere at all in internal problems of the country.
Aug. 13		German column drives 50 miles along Rostov-Baku rail line to Mineralnye Vody, which is 140 miles from Grozny oil center . . . . German authorities in Yugoslavia announce Serbia will be annihilated if they are compelled to use one additional soldier above the present occupying force to suppress disorders.		Mexico bars importation of all U.S. currency save $2 bills and coins to prevent Axis agents from dumping dollars seized in Europe.	
Aug. 14	On first anniversary of the Atlantic Charter, FDR writes Churchill that the United Nations are dedicated to put into practice the Charter's principles.	Gen. Sir Harold R.L.G. Alexander is appointed commander of British troops in Middle East, replacing Gen. Sir Claude J.E. Auchinlek, who has failed to drive Rommel out of Egypt . . . . German troops advance to west bank of Don River south of Kletskaya, 80 miles northwest of Stalingrad.	Allied planes attack a Japanese convoy off New Britain and shoot down two Japanese Zeros. U.S. Marines consolidate shore positions in Solomon Islands.		
Aug. 15		Germans capture Georgievsk, 120 miles northwest of Grozny oil fields in Causcasus . . . . Gen. Wladyslaw Sikorski announces in London establishment of Polish armored motor corps for use on Continent.	Chinese forces recapture Wenchow, Chekiang port some 250 miles south of Shanghai.		
Aug. 16		P.M. Churchill, Premier Stalin, W. Averell Harriman and others conclude Allied talks in Moscow, reaching a number of decisions covering the war against Hitler and pledging to carry on the war with all available resources . . . . Russian sources say all oil supplies and equipment were removed from Maikop before abandoning it to Germans.			
Aug. 17		Flying Fortresses strike Dunkirk and Cherbourg in first all U.S. bombing attack in Western Europe . . . . German troops cross Kuban River at two points near Krasnodar in Caucasus.	U.S. Navy Dept. claims shore positions taken by U.S. Marines in Guadalcanal-Tulagi area of Soloman Islands early Aug. 7 "have since been developed and are now well established."	U.S. and Brazilian bombers sink two German submarines in Atlantic off Brazilian coast . . . . Brazilian government announces loss of five ships to Axis submarines in past few days off coast of Brazil.	
Aug. 18		Russian troops retire southeast of Kletskaya and Germans resume offensive northeast of Kotelnikov in their two-pronged attack on Stalingrad.		Brazilian Pres. Getulio Vargas says sinking of Brazil's ships will be avenged and announces Axis ships and property will be seized as compensation.	Armed reserves kill at least six persons in Madras, India as rioting continues.
Aug. 19		An estimated 10,000 Allied troops carry out a nine-hour daylight raid on German-occupied port of Dieppe. Of the 5,000 Canadian troops participating in the raid, 3,350 are casualties (67%), while the Germans lose only about 600 men . . . . Germans continue their advance towards Grozny oil fields while Russians stall German attack at Kletskaya and Kotelnikov on Stalingrad front.	The 10,000-ton Australian cruiser *Canberra* is sunk in the Solomons, but most of crew is saved.		Devadas Gandhi (son of Mohandas K. Gandhi) is arrested in New Delhi for publishing article on civil disobedience campaign, which is a violation of Defense of India Act.
Aug. 20		In one of biggest daylight raids of war, an estimated 500 Allied planes sweep northern France from Le Havre to Furnes, Belgium . . . . German troops advance southeast of Pyatigorsk on Caucasian front and cross Don River southeast of Kletskaya on Stalingrad front.	U.S. Navy Dept. announces U.S. Marines are "mopping up" remnants of Japanese forces on islands in Solomon Archipelago . . . . Chinese troops recapture Kwangfeng and Kweiki, Kiangsi Province, thus placing them in control of more than 50 miles of Hangchow-Nanchang railway.	Brazilian Pres. Vargas issues decree prohibiting all Germans except those with diplomatic passports from leaving the country.	

A	B	C	D	E
Includes developments that affect more than one world region, international organizations and important meetings of major world leaders.	*Includes all developments in European countries and military engagements between Allied and Axis powers in Africa and at sea.*	*Includes all developments in Japan and China, Japanese foreign policy and military actions in the Pacific region.*	*Includes all domestic and regional developments in Latin America, the Caribbean and Canada.*	*Includes developments in those independent nations and colonial possessions not covered in Columns B, C and D.*

U.S. Politics & Social Issues	U.S. Foreign Policy & Defense	U.S. Economy & Environment	Science, Technology & Nature	Culture, Leisure & Life Style	
Rep. Hamilton Fish is renominated in N.Y. Republican primary although Wendell L. Willkie and Thomas E. Dewey came out against him.			Navy Dept. announces Commander Malcolm M. Hanson, 47, who was chief wireless operator on Rear Adm. Richard E. Byrd's first Antarctic expedition, was killed in plane crash "somewhere in the North."		Aug. 11
William Dudley Pelley is sentenced to 15 years in prison for sedition by Federal Judge Robert C. Baltzell.		Richard H. Dearborn, testifying before Senate Patents Comm., denies that he and Frank A. Howard of Standard Oil Development Co. conspired to maintain a Standard Oil-I.G. Farben synthetic rubber cartel . . . . Ellsworth C. Alvord of U.S. Chamber of Commerce urges that a 10% retail sales tax and a 5% withholding tax on compensation be imposed to prevent inflation and raise $10 billion in new revenue.		Clark Gable, 41, Hollywood film star, enlists in Army in Los Angeles as a private.	Aug. 12
Gen. Marshall denies Sen. John H. Bankhead's request to keep Negro troops out of South.	With only 28 members present, House passes Rankin bill authorizing payment of allowances to dependents of enlisted men in armed forces.	Roosevelt orders Navy Secy. Frank Knox to seize and operate Bayonne, N.J., plant of General Cable Corp., idled by a three-day wildcat strike of AFL electrical workers . . . . NLRB directs Standard Oil Co. to disestablish three company-dominated N.J. employe associations at refineries in Linden, Bayonne and Jersey City.		Interior Secy. Harold Ickes says the *Chicago Tribune* not only has given aid and comfort to enemy "but is continuing to do it" and should be prosecuted . . . . A son is born to Anne Morrow Lindbergh, wife of Charles A. Lindbergh, in Detroit.	Aug. 13
		NWLB panel recommends GM increase employe wages by five cents-an-hour to cover cost of living rise.		Serge Koussevitsky and Berkshire Music Center Orchestra present first American concert performance of Dmitri Shostakovich's Seventh Symphony in Lenox, Mass.	Aug. 14
House Un-American Activities Comm. Chmn. Martin Dies submits to FDR names of 17,000 alleged pro-Nazi sympathizers.					Aug. 15
		Sen. Harry Byrd (D, Va.) urges Senate Finance Comm. to adopt tax bill that would remain unchanged for three to four years but include a sales tax to increase revenues by $5 billion annually.		Prince Alexis Alexandrovitch Obolensky, 59, former Czarist officer of royal ancestry, prominent socialite and concert singer, dies in Butler, N.J.	Aug. 16
FDR defends transfer of Comm. on Fair Employment Practices to the War Manpower Commission on grounds that the move strengthens the committee.	Senate passes and sends to White House the House-approved bill authorizing immediate payment of war dependency allowances.		Sen. Harley M. Kilgore, Jr. (D, W. Va.) introduces bill to create an Office of Technological Mobilization to draft technical personnel, patents, secret processes and research facilities.		Aug. 17
		NWLB denies 10¢ hourly wage increase to 21,000 employes at Western Electric in Kearney, N.J. . . . . U.S. Atty. John W. Walker charges more than 100 public utility companies, including GE and Westinghouse, conspired to retard development of flourescent lighting because it uses less electricity than incandescent lighting.			Aug. 18
	Selective Service Commission drops its 1-B classification for registrants fit for limited military service and indicates those registrants will be reclassified either 1-A or 4-F . . . . Federal grand jury in Chicago refuses to indict the *Chicago Tribune* on grounds of violating espionage act in publishing Johnson dispatch on Japanese ship strength.	U.S. troops take possession of S.A. Woods Co. in Boston after company refuses NWLB ruling granting workers maintenance of membership clause in their CIO contract . . . . William S. Farish, president of Standard Oil Co. of N.J., tells Senate Patents Comm. that as result of agreements with I.G. Farbenindustrie of Germany the U.S. "got more from Germany than Germany ever received from us."			Aug. 19
Atty. Gen. James Bennett wins N.Y. Democratic gubernatorial nomination over FDR's choice, Sen. James Mead.	Navy announces recruiting for Waves will begin Sept. 11.				Aug. 20

F	G	H	I	J
Includes elections, federal-state relations, civil rights and liberties, crime, the judiciary, education, health care, poverty, urban affairs and population.	*Includes formation and debate of U.S. foreign and defense policies, veterans affairs and defense spending. (Relations with specific foreign countries are usually found under the region concerned.)*	*Includes business, labor, agriculture, taxation, transportation, consumer affairs, monetary and fiscal policy, natural resources, pollution and accidents.*	*Includes worldwide scientific, medical and technological developments, natural phenomena, U.S. weather and natural disasters.*	*Includes the arts, religion, scholarship, communications media, sports, entertainment, fashions, fads and social life.*

	World Affairs	European War Zone	Pacific War Zone	The Americas	Other Countries & Territories
Aug. 21					
Aug. 22		German troops drive new wedge into Soviet defense positions on Stalingrad front.	Chinese retake Yintan and Yushan, thus gaining control of 100 miles of Hangchow-Nanchang rail line.	Brazilian government announces a state of war exists between Brazil and Germany and Italy.	
Aug. 23		"Largest American convoy" to cross Atlantic in this war reportedly arrives in British ports .... German forces cross Don River souteast of Kletskaya.	Chinese retake Fuchow, a Japanese base on Fu River, after 23-day siege, and Changshan in western Chekiang Province.	Uruguayan government grants all rights of non-belligerency to Brazil.	Gen. Sir Henry Maitland Wilson is appointed commander of new British force in Iran and Iraq .... Chiang Kai-shek orders Chinese troops stationed in India to refrain from discussing that country's internal political problems.
Aug. 24		Germans drive to within 85 miles of Grozny oil center.	U.S. Navy bombers sink Japanese light carrier *Ryujo* in the battle of the Eastern Solomons, while Japanese bombers attack the *U.S.S. Enterprise* and the *U.S.S. North Carolina.*	Governments of Argentina, Bolivia, Chile, Paraguay and Peru declare Brazil non-belligerent in its war with Germany and Italy.	
Aug. 25		Moscow communique mentions fighting northwest of Stalingrad for first time, indicating Germans have driven closer to the Volga River city .... New Zealand troops raid Italian lines in El Mireir area of El Alamein front .... Prince George Edward Alexander Edmund, Air Commodore the Duke of Kent, 39, is killed in flying boat crash in Scotland.	U.S. Marine air group from Henderson Field, Guadalcanal, attacks and badly damages Japanese flagship *Jintsu* and a transport, while B-17 bombers sink a Japanese destroyer .... Chinese troops retake Sankiangkou, Juihung and Tunghsiang in their drive on chief Japanese base in Kiangsi Province at Nanchang.	Pres. Vargas signs decree cancelling Brazilian debt to Germany for expropriation of Condor Airline last year.	
Aug. 26		Soviets claim rout of German troops in a counter-offensive on the central front 120 miles west of Moscow .... Britsh government lifts its ban on CP paper *The Daily Worker*, but warns it not to oppose the war in future.	Japanese troops land from small convoy at Milne Bay, at southeastern tip of New Guinea, and are engaged by Australian troops.	More than 1,000 Germans and Italians are reported to have been arrested in Rio de Janeiro since Aug. 22.	
Aug. 27		AP reports from Berne that 25,000 Jews have been arrested in unoccupied France and deported to German territory in the east .... Russian planes strike at several German cities, including Berlin, Danzig, Tilsit and Stettin.	U.S. planes based at Guadalcanal sink one Japanese destroyer, severely damage another and set fire to a third in the Solomons. The Japanese fleet withdraws from positions near Tulagi .... Chinese vanguard enters outskirts of burning Chuhsien, from which Japan, 800 miles away, can be bombed.	Havana announces Cuban Navy and Air Force are on convoy service.	
Aug. 28		Between 500 and 600 RAF planes raid Baltic port of of Gdynia, Poland and German industrial city of Kassel .... Death of Archduke Joseph Ferdinand, head of Tuscany branch of House of Hapsburg, is announced in Vienna.	Chinese columns recapture Chuhsien and Lishui in Chekiang Province.	Because of gasoline shortage, Chilean government bans use of all private autos and 90% of government-operated vehicles as of Sept. 30.	
Aug. 29		Russian troops defeat Italian troops in an engagement near Kletskaya, northwest of Stalingrad .... Another 500-600 British bombers attack Nuremberg and Saarbruecken, Germany.	Chinese forces open an offensive along Canton-Hankow railroad, 40 miles north of Canton in South China.		
Aug. 30		Russian troops are reportedly holding Germans at Stalingrad.	Australian troops trap Japanese in Milne Bay fighting .... In their drive on Japanese base at Nanchang, Chinese capture Lungyu.		
Aug. 31		Rommel's forces push British back on southern flank near Quaret el Himeimat and near edge of Quattara Depression .... Germans drive from southwest to within 15½ miles of Stalingrad .... Hitler opens fourth Winter Help Campaign, calling for sacrifices by German people since Nazi soldiers have suffered great privations.	Australian troops are reportedly mopping up remainder of Japanese force at Milne Bay, New Guinea.	Brazilian government orders mobilization of country's resources and signs a supplementary decree granting Brazilians the right to cancel contracts with Germans, Italians and Japanese .... Canadian government announces new regulation restricting movement and dismissal of Canadian workers.	British troops leave Addis Ababa in accordance with military convention signed with Ethiopia.

A	B	C	D	E
Includes developments that affect more than one world region, international organizations and important meetings of major world leaders.	*Includes all developments in European countries and military engagements between Allied and Axis powers in Africa and at sea.*	*Includes all developments in Japan and China, Japanese foreign policy and military actions in the Pacific region.*	*Includes all domestic and regional developments in Latin America, the Caribbean and Canada.*	*Includes developments in those independent nations and colonial possessions not covered in Columns B, C and D.*

U.S. Politics & Social Issues	U.S. Foreign Policy & Defense	U.S. Economy & Environment	Science, Technology & Nature	Culture, Leisure & Life Style	
	FDR anounces Axis leaders responsible for war atrocities will have to answer for their acts in court after the war .... Selective Service Dir. Lewis B. Hershey says married men will be reclassified and 18 and 19 year olds will eventually be drafted .... Rev. Kurt E.B. Molzahn is convicted in Connecticut on charges of conspiring to aid the Germans.	Price Admin. Leon Henderson says if food prices remain unchecked, there will be a 30% rise next year.			Aug. 21
Sen. W. Lee O'Daniel wins Democratic nomination for a full term in Senate by defeating James V. Allred in Texas run-off primary .... American Labor Party nominates Dean Alfange for governorship of N.Y.	U.S. aircraft carrier *Independence* is launched in Camden, N.J.			Michel Fokine, 62, Russian-born choreographer known as "father of modern ballet" and creator of *The Dying Swan* for Anna Pavlova, dies in New York.	Aug. 22
				Francisco Segura of Ecuador defeats Gardnar Mulloy to take Longwood Bowl, becoming first South American to win a major U.S. men's tennis tournament.	Aug. 23
Thomas E. Dewey is nominated by N.Y. GOP for governorship.	Herbert Karl Friedrich Bahr is found guilty in Newark, N.J. of espionage for Germany.	NWLB orders Norma-Hoffman Bearings Co. to give women equal pay when they replace men .... Atty. Gen. Francis Biddle announces nine corporations and six officers were indicted on Aug. 17 on charges of "conspiring to make identical bids at unreasonably high prices."			Aug. 24
Senate passes bill permitting 4,000,000 members of U.S. armed forces to vote by mail in November federal elections.	Swedish liner *Gripsholm* arrives in Jersey City with approximately 1,450 Western nationals from Japan.	FDR says government will soon stabilize wage and farm prices at their present level .... NWLB approves 5½¢ hourly increase for 250,000 employes of U.S. Steel Corp.	Total eclipse of moon visible in every continent but Australia begins at 11:09 pm.		Aug. 25
	New Zealand P.M. Peter Fraser confers with FDR at White House.	AFL Pres. Green and CIO Pres. Murray confer with FDR and urge wage stabilization authority be left with NWLB only.			Aug. 26
FBI arrests 100 German aliens on presidential warrants in N.J.	Stimson announces men between 45 and 50 who have special skills may now enlist in Army for general service or special duty .... The 45,000-ton battleship *Iowa*, largest of its class ever built, is launched at Brooklyn Navy Yard.	OPA obtains a temporary writ enjoining Kaiser Co. from paying "black market" prices for steel to Builders Structural Steel Co.	Oxford Univ. scientists announce development of new chemical known as penicillin, produced from cultures of common fungus and more fatal to bacteria than sulfa drugs.		Aug. 27
	FDR suggests people of U.S. and Latin America aid Spain after war with gifts to repair damaged art treasures and by building up tourist trade.	FDR says adoption of meatless day each week is possible because of war demands .... Reese H. Taylor and R.C. Allen resign their positions as iron and steel heads for WPB .... Senate Finance Comm. votes to repeal capital stock and declared-value excess profits tax on corporations, as requested by Treasury.		Justice Dept. files complaint in N.Y. District Court seeking injunction to force AP to supply its news service to any newspaper that can pay the cost .... Chicago Bears beat College All-Stars, 21-0, before 101,200 fans at Soldiers Field, Chicago.	Aug. 28
		Federal government issues an order, effective Sept. 1, drastically restricting taxi cab industry in an effort to save gasoline and rubber.			Aug. 29
				Newark Bears win their seventh International League pennant in 11 years as they divide a double-header with Baltimore Orioles in Newark.	Aug. 30
	In speech at Bethesda, Md., FDR praises war efforts of U.S. Navy, claiming enemy is beginning to know its capabilities.	Agriculture Secy. Claude Wickard says in about four months meat rationing will go into effect to cut down civilian meat consumption .... NLRB certifies AFL International Assn. of Machinists as collective bargaining agent for about 20,000 employes of two Curtiss-Wright plants near Buffalo, N.Y.		Rep. Elmer J. Holland (D, Pa.) tells House several newspapers "tipped off" Japanese high command that U.S. Navy had broken secret Japanese code .... Gypsy Rose Lee is wed to Alexander Kirkland, actor and producer, in Highland Mills, N.Y.	Aug. 31

F	G	H	I	J
Includes elections, federal-state relations, civil rights and liberties, crime, the judiciary, education, health care, poverty, urban affairs and population.	*Includes formation and debate of U.S. foreign and defense policies, veterans affairs and defense spending. (Relations with specific foreign countries are usually found under the region concerned.)*	*Includes business, labor, agriculture, taxation, transportation, consumer affairs, monetary and fiscal policy, natural resources, pollution and accidents.*	*Includes worldwide scientific, medical and technological developments, natural phenomena, U.S. weather and natural disasters.*	*Includes the arts, religion, scholarship, communications media, sports, entertainment, fashions, fads and social life.*

	World Affairs	European War Zone	Pacific War Zone	The Americas	Other Countries & Territories
Sept. 1		Russian sources concede the Germans have penetrated the Stalingrad line southwest of the city and that Russian troops have withdrawn south of Krasnodar on the Caucasian front .... German troops cross Strait of Kerch, separating Crimea and Caucasus.	Japanese Foreign Min. Shigenori Togo resigns and his place is taken by Premier Tojo .... Japanese troops press forward at Kokoda, 60 miles across Owen Stanley Mountain range from Port Moresby in New Guinea.		
Sept. 2	International Student Assembly with 350 representatives from 53 countries opens in Washington.	Russians report Germans have broken defense lines around Stalingrad in both southwest and northwest .... Strong force of RAF bombers attacks German industrial city of Saarbruecken.	Two more Japanese Foreign Office officials—Haruhiko Nishi and Shigeru Kawagoe—resign .... Allied bombers attack Japanese at Lae and Kokoda in New Guinea and Buka in Solomons.	FDR names Morris L. Cooke to head special technical mission of industrial engineers to assist Brazil's industrial and war expansion.	
Sept. 3	U.S., U.K., N.Z., Australia and Free French agree to reciprocal Lend-Lease aid .... FDR addresses international Student Assembly, declaring "that the cause of the United Nations is youth itself."	Russian troops make further retreats on northwest Stalingrad defense line in face of heavy German assaults .... Rommel's troops make slight withdrawal on southern El Alamein front under heavy Allied air and artillery bombardment .... Gen. Francisco Franco ousts three fanatically Falangist cabinet members and assumes presidency of Falange himself.	U.S. Navy Dept. announces Japanese have made several new attempts to land small detachments on various islands in southeastern Solomon group .... Chinese troops drive to within 15 miles north and 25 miles south of Canton.		
Sept. 4		British and New Zealand troops repulse German counterattacks in center of El Alamein line .... *The Black Book of Poland* is published in N.Y., detailing Nazi atrocities in Poland .... Police arrest 144 persons throughout Ulster in a day marked by a gun battle between the IRA and police.			Willkie visits with Egyptian King Farouk in Cairo.
Sept. 5	International Student Assembly closes in Washington after calling for resumption of British-Indian independence negotiations and opening of second front in Europe.	Rommel's troops retreat to their starting point for the attack on El Alamein under heavy Allied pressure .... Russian planes bomb Budapest, Hungary for the first time, starting 33 fires.	U.S. destroyer tenders *Little* and *Gregory* are sunk in the Solomons by Japanese destroyers.	Pres. Ramon Castillo receives 14 albums containing one million signatures supporting Argentina's foreign policy of neutrality .... Argentine and Spanish governments sign barter agreement in Buenos Aires for goods and services valued between $30 and $38 million.	
Sept. 6	Columbia Univ. Pres. Dr. Nicholas M. Butler says an international government should be established to solve postwar problems.	German and Rumanian troops capture Novorossiisk, former Russian Black Sea naval base in Caucasus.	U.S. planes bomb and strafe Japanese installations on Gizo Island in New Georgia group some 215 miles northwest of Guadalcanal.		
Sept. 7		Repulsed or held by the Russians on the northwest and southwest, German forces drive at Stalingrad from the west.	Despite heavy casualties, Japanese forces drive Allies back to a point less than 60 miles from Port Moresby, New Guinea.	U.S. Amb. Spruille Braden and Cuba's Minister of State Jose Agustin Martinez sign military and naval agreement in Havana under which naval and military facilities will be provided on a reciprocal basis.	
Sept. 8	Churchill tells the House of Commons that as a result of Allied discussions in July in London and Moscow complete agreement on war aims has been reached.				
Sept. 9		In 74th day of German offensive, Red Army is again forced back on the front west of Stalingrad .... UP reports in copyrighted dispatch that Edouard Herriot and Jules Jeanneney, former presidents of French Senate and Chamber of Deputies, have written strong letter to Marshal Petain and Laval condemning Petain's assumption of dictatorial powers and virtual abolition of parliament.	Japanese launch heavy attack and outflank Allied positions in Owen Stanley Mountains in New Guinea.		Police use tear gas and fire shots to disperse hundreds of Indians who squat or lie in Bombay streets to commemorate Gandhi's arrest one month ago.
Sept. 10		Russia admits further withdrawals on Stalingrad front.		U.S. and Mexican officials sign agreement in Mexico City whereby U.S. is entitled to buy Mexico's entire guayule crop until 1946 and will supply Mexico free rubber for her internal needs .... National committee of Argentine Radical Party votes to demand a break with Axis powers.	After negotiations with Gov. Gen. Armand Annet of Madagascar fail, British sea, land and air forces attack three ports on west coast of Madagascar simultaneously .... Churchill tells Commons that Indian situation is improving since arrest of Gandhi Aug. 9 .... FDR's special envoy Wendell Willkie arrives in Beirut, Lebanon.

A	B	C	D	E
Includes developments that affect more than one world region, international organizations and important meetings of major world leaders.	*Includes all developments in European countries and military engagements between Allied and Axis powers in Africa and at sea.*	*Includes all developments in Japan and China, Japanese foreign policy and military actions in the Pacific region.*	*Includes all domestic and regional developments in Latin America, the Caribbean and Canada.*	*Includes developments in those independent nations and colonial possessions not covered in Columns B, C and D.*

U.S. Politics & Social Issues	U.S. Foreign Policy & Defense	U.S. Economy & Environment	Science, Technology & Nature	Culture, Leisure & Life Style	
Judge Martin I. Welsh rules in Sacramento, Calif. that FDR's order vesting in military commanders the right to exclude Japanese-Americans from military areas is constitutional.		NWLB orders maintenance of membership clause and voluntary check-off in contracts for 50,000 CIO Industrial Union of Marine and Shipbuilding Workers members in eight East Coast Bethlehem Steel Co. shipyards.			Sept. 1
Atty. Gen. Biddle reports to Congress only 36 federal employes were discharged and 13 disciplined as result of FBI loyalty investigations of 2,095 workers.	Herbert Karl Friedrich Bahr is sentenced to 30 years in prison by Judge Wm. F. Smith for conspiring with Germans to commit espionage . . . . Asst. War Secy. John J. McCloy tells VFW in Cincinnati 500,000 American fighting men and technicians are now abroad.			Presbyterian Church in the United States of America reports record membership of 2,040,492.	Sept. 2
	U.S. Army creates four new armored divisions, bringing total to 14.	OPA orders general licensing of meat packers, wholesalers and custom slaughterers, effective Sept. 8, in move to prevent widespread evasion of price regulations . . . . Morgenthau reveals before Senate Finance Comm. a new tax plan to raise an additional $6.5 billion.		*The World At War*, a film survey of last 10 years written for OWI, begins pre-release run in N.Y.	Sept. 3
		WPB Chmn. Nelson announces a plan has been approved to regulate wholesale and retail inventories of consumer goods to help eliminate hoarding.		Gunder Haegg, Swedish track star, breaks his own unofficial mile record, running the distance in 4:04.6 in Stockholm.	Sept. 4
Joseph Hilton Smyth and Irvine Harvey Williams are arrested in N.Y. by FBI on charges they acted as unregistered Japanese agents since 1937.		Federal Judge Robert N. Wilkin issues consent decree permanently enjoining Kaiser Co. from paying prices for steel above OPA ceilings.			Sept. 5
				Pauline Betz defeats Louise Brough in national women's singles tennis championship in Forest Hills, N.Y. . . . . Western Army All-Stars defeat Chicago Cardinals, 16-10, in Denver.	Sept. 6
		FDR asks Congress to pass legislation by Oct. 1 to stabilize cost of living, including price of farm commodities . . . . Maritime Commission and Navy Dept. launch 174 ships today—Labor Day—at nearly 60 shipyards throughout the country.		Ted Schroeder defeats Frank Parker to win national singles tennis title in Forest Hills, N.Y.	Sept. 7
		Senate Finance Comm. rejects Treasury's tax spending plan.			Sept. 8
Gov. Eugene Talmadge loses Georgia Democratic gubernatorial primary race to Atty. Gen. Ellis G. Arnall . . . . House passes and sends to FDR conference-approved serviceman's absentee voting bill.	Speaking in N.Y.C. Averell Harriman declares immediate aid must be sent to Russia for the battle against Germany.	Senate Finance Comm. confirms tentative approval yesterday of 5%-of-income "Victory Tax" plan, to begin operating by Jan. 1.	AMA assails article in September issue of *Reader's Digest* by Paul de Kruif entitled: "Found: A One-Day Cure for Syphilis" as unwarranted, premature "effusion."	Western Army All-Stars defeat Detroit Lions, 12-0, in Detroit.	Sept. 9
	Stimson says in Washington that student members of enlisted reserve will face active service as soon as they are of age.	Bernard Baruch's report on rubber situation to FDR indicates shortage is so dangerous that nation faces a "military and civilian collapse." . . . . Senate Finance Comm. votes to raise income surtaxes in middle brackets and lower them in lowest brackets for net revenue gain of $33 million . . . . Federal grand jury in Newark, N.J. indicts five companies for conspiring to monopolize world production of plastic materials vital to military needs.	Dr. Kurt A. Oster and Dr. Harry Sobotka of Mount Sinai Hospital, New York, report to American Chemical Society meeting in Buffalo, N.Y., that injections of adrenocrome, an adrenalin derivative, have successfully reduced high blood pressure to normal in experiments on rats and dogs.		Sept. 10

F	G	H	I	J
Includes elections, federal-state relations, civil rights and liberties, crime, the judiciary, education, health care, poverty, urban affairs and population.	*Includes formation and debate of U.S. foreign and defense policies, veterans affairs and defense spending. (Relations with specific foreign countries are usually found under the region concerned.)*	*Includes business, labor, agriculture, taxation, transportation, consumer affairs, monetary and fiscal policy, natural resources, pollution and accidents.*	*Includes worldwide scientific, medical and technological developments, natural phenomena, U.S. weather and natural disasters.*	*Includes the arts, religion, scholarship, communications media, sports, entertainment, fashions, fads and social life.*

	World Affairs	European War Zone	Pacific War Zone	The Americas	Other Countries & Territories
Sept. 11			U.S. Navy claims 20 Japanese planes have been shot down after three days of attacks upon Guadalcanal.	Seven persons, including five policemen, are injured and 97 alleged rioters are arrested in Buenos Aires when police break up pro-democratic Radical Party youth rally held in tribute to Brazil.	Willkie arrives in Jerusalem to determine needs of people in Middle East .... Sheik Taj Eddin Hassani, president of Republic of Syria, says Syrians have right to expect early recognition of independent national status in the spirit of the Atlantic Charter .... Cripps says Gandhi intervened to reverse previously accepted British proposals for postwar independence in India .... Madagascar Gov. Gen. Armand Annet denies British claim of Japanese activity on the island.
Sept. 12		Russian troops break through German defenses near Sinyavino on the Volkhov front below Leningrad and repulse German counterattacks.			British columns advance to within 70 miles of Tananarive, capital of Madagascar .... Indian leaders dispute British claim that All-India Congress Party reversed its decision on Britain's postwar plan .... Willkie arrives in Baghdad, Iraq and confers with Premier Nuri Pasha esSaid.
Sept. 13		German troops enter Stalingrad from the south despite stubborn Russian resistance .... Vichy decrees all Frenchmen between ages of 18 and 50 and women between 21 and 35 must perform any work assigned them by government for good of the nation.	Japanese disarm all Chinese troops of Nanking puppet regime in Nanchang and execute Gen. Chien Yayuan, leader of the troops .... Chinese troops take Pukiang, 30 miles northeast, and Kufang, six miles west of Kinhwa, the Chekiang provincial capital.	UP reports from Managua that Nicaraguan government has evidence of Axis-inspired revolutionary movement and that 13 persons, including some army generals, are being held for investigation.	Speaking in Baghdad, Willkie says peoples of Middle East favor the cause of the U.N. .... Mohammed Ali Jinnah says Britain is ignoring rights of 90 million Moslems in India.
Sept. 14		British mobile columns raid Bengazi in Libya, about 500 miles behind Axis lines, reportedly inflicting heavy damage on Axis supplies and men .... Russian troops retreat to new lines in Mozdok area deep in Caucasus.	Army B-25's heavily bomb and strafe Japanese ships, planes and shore installations at Kiska harbor in the Aleutians .... U.S. fliers report downing 21 Japanese planes over Solomons in air battles since Sept. 11.	Argentine Interior Ministry orders dissolution of Federation of German Welfare and Cultural Clubs.	
Sept. 15			The 14,700-ton aircraft carrier *Wasp* is sunk after three Japanese torpedoes set her afire. Nearly 90% of her 1,800-man crew are rescued .... Adm. Chester Nimitz says at Pearl Harbor that despite success in Solomons "do not think for one minute that we have the Japanese on the run."		
Sept. 16		Russians recapture Mamai Hill and wipe out German tank forces that drove into outer defenses of Stalingrad in the northwest sector.	Japanese troops reach Ioribaiwa, New Guinea, only 32 miles from Allied base at Port Moresby.	Forty thousand Mexican troops parade in Mexico City in celebration of country's 132nd independence anniversary.	Gov. Gen. Annet asks British Lt. Gen. Sir William Platt for armistice terms on island of Madagascar.
Sept. 17		Hand-to-hand fighting breaks out between Russian and German troops in streets of Stalingrad's northwest sector .... Wendell L. Willkie arrives in Kuibyshev, Russia, by plane from Teheran, Iran.	Allied bombers and fighters make their ninth attack upon Japanese base at Buna, New Guinea .... Flying Fortresses complete three days of attacks on Rekata Bay, Santa Isabel Island, and on ship and shore installations at Gizo Island in New Georgia group.	Italian, Hungarian and German diplomats in Brazil leave for Lisbon, Portugal .... Argentine Pres. Castillo and Bolivian Pres. Enrique Penaranda del Castillo meet in Yacuiba, Bolivia for conference on trade and transportation.	Vichy government says British armistice terms for Madagascar are unacceptable and French forces will continue the fight.
Sept. 18		German infantry and tank forces reportedly make further advances in northwest sector of Stalingrad and penetrate to the Volga north of city .... General Otto von Stulpnagel, German commander in Paris, announces execution of 116 "Communist terrorists" in reprisal for attacks on German occupation troops .... Australian and RAF bombers attack Tobruk, Libya, while U.S. bombers hit Bengazi.	State Secy. Cordell Hull sends note to Japanese through Swiss government saying Red Cross is caring for Japanese held in U.S. territory and asking whether or not Japanese will reciprocate.		British troops land and occupy east coast city of Tamatave, Madagascar's principal port.
Sept. 19		Russians troops drive German forces out of streets in Stalingrad, and claim to repulse German troops in Mozdok sector deep in Caucasus .... British War Office announces all inhabitants will be cleared from coastal area across the North Sea from German naval stronghold of Helgoland Bight.	In his dispatch to *N.Y. Times*, Hanson Baldwin reports U.S. Marines hold a six or seven-mile stretch of beach on Guadalcanal.	Ten thousand people at anti-Axis rally in Buenos Aires hear spekers demand war against Germany and Italy.	British troops take city of Brickaville on east coast of Madagascar.

A	B	C	D	E
Includes developments that affect more than one world region, international organizations and important meetings of major world leaders.	*Includes all developments in European countries and military engagements between Allied and Axis powers in Africa and at sea.*	*Includes all developments in Japan and China, Japanese foreign policy and military actions in the Pacific region.*	*Includes all domestic and regional developments in Latin America, the Caribbean and Canada.*	*Includes developments in those independent nations and colonial possessions not covered in Columns B, C and D.*

U.S. Politics & Social Issues	U.S. Foreign Policy & Defense	U.S. Economy & Environment	Science, Technology & Nature	Culture, Leisure & Life Style	
				Gunder Haegg runs three miles in 13:35.4 in Stockholm to set new world record.	Sept. 11
					Sept. 12
					Sept. 13
U.S. Sen. Wallace H. White Jr. and Gov. Sumner Sewall, both Republicans, are reelected in Maine .... Federal grand jury in N.Y. indicts one white and four Negro leaders of Ethiopian Pacific Movement in Harlem on charges of conspiracy to help Japan establish a "dark skinned" empire.	Sen. Harry S. Truman (D, Mo.), chairman of special defense investigating committee, assails Army and Navy in Senate because there is no "workable unity of command."	House and Senate bills are introduced in response to FDR's demand for statutory powers to control inflation .... Senate Finance Comm. approves new tax bill designed to raise additional $6.774 billion in revenue .... Paul V. McNutt, chairman of War Manpower Commission, is given complete control over transfer of any federal employe to other departments or war jobs; McNutt delegates his power to the Civil Service Commission.		New York Yankees beat Cleveland Indians, 8 to 3, in Cleveland to win their 13th American League pennant and their sixth in past seven years.	Sept. 14
Henry Cabot Lodge (R) wins renomination for the Senate in Massachusetts. James O. Eastland wins Missisissippi run-off election for Democratic Senate nomination.		WPB Chmn. Nelson orders rationing of fuel oil in 17 Eastern states, Washington and 13 Midwestern states starting Oct. 1.			Sept. 15
N.Y. State Appellate Division reverses State Supreme Court order barring CP from Nov. 3 election ballot.		War Manpower Commission Chmn. McNutt says in Washington that government control over labor resources is inevitable .... NWLB panel recommends a $1-a-day increase for 10,000 copper, lead and zinc miners in Idaho and Utah.			Sept. 16
	Senate votes $100,000 to Truman investigating committee for its defense probe.	GE Pres. Charles E. Wilson is appointed as WPB vice chairman as a $1-a-year man .... NWLB orders 4 cent-an-hour increase for GM workers and a maintenance of membership provision in their contract.		OWI Dir. Elmer Davis says the proposed musicians ban on making records threatens the morale of the nation by stopping entertainment.	Sept. 17
		Senate and House Banking and Currency committees approve two measures directing the President to stabilize farm prices, wages and salaries at either Aug. 15 or Sept. 15 levels.		FCC Chmn. James L. Fly tells Senate subcommittee that Amer. Fed. of Musicians ban against making recordings for commercial use hurts war effort and calls for legislative action.	Sept. 18
				Conde Nast, 68, president of Conde Nast Publications, Inc., publisher of *Vogue* and *House and Gardens* magazines and the old *Vanity Fair*, dies in New York.	Sept. 19

F	G	H	I	J
Includes elections, federal-state relations, civil rights and liberties, crime, the judiciary, education, health care, poverty, urban affairs and population.	*Includes formation and debate of U.S. foreign and defense policies, veterans affairs and defense spending. (Relations with specific foreign countries are usually found under the region concerned.)*	*Includes business, labor, agriculture, taxation, transportation, consumer affairs, monetary and fiscal policy, natural resources, pollution and accidents.*	*Includes worldwide scientific, medical and technological developments, natural phenomena, U.S. weather and natural disasters.*	*Includes the arts, religion, scholarship, communications media, sports, entertainment, fashions, fads and social life.*

	World Affairs	European War Zone	Pacific War Zone	The Americas	Other Countries & Territories
Sept. 20				Mexico City newspaper *Novedades* says troops are being sent to Villa Cardel in Veracruz following assassination of Federal Deputy Salvador Gonzales on Sept. 15.	
Sept. 21		Moscow reports claim Soviet troops are holding in face of heavy German assaults on Stalingrad .... Willkie tells Moscow press conference he personally favors second front if it is militarily feasible .... Canadian destroyer *Ottawa* is sunk in Atlantic with 112 men lost and 76 rescued.			Indian Council of State convenes in New Delhi with 32 of 56 members present.
Sept. 22		Gen. Walther von Luttwitz, 84, German World War I commander and military leader of the unsuccessful putsch of Wolfgang von Kapp in 1920, dies in Breslau, Germany.			British troops penetrate to within 19 miles of Tananarive, capital of Madagascar.
Sept. 23		Russians make further progress on northwest sector of Stalingrad, having been reinforced by troops that crossed Volga River .... Willkie confers with Stalin and Molotov for two hours in Moscow .... Rumanian government issues decree centralizing all power in Chief of State Marshal Ion Antonescu.			British troops occupy Tananarive and establish military government.
Sept. 24		Counterattacking Russian troops continue to make progress northwest of Stalingrad, while fighting in the city continues for eighth day.	Allied bombers and fighters attack Japanese bases at Mubo and Bun-Kokoda in New Guinea, Rabaul in New Britain and Buka in Solomons.	Pres. Manuel Avila Camacho inaugurates newly-created Council of National Defense in Mexico City.	
Sept. 25		Largest convoy to date reaches Russia's Arctic ports with supplies from England.	Australian troops force Japanese to withdraw from their outposts in Owen Stanley Mountains, some 32 miles from Port Moresby .... Transportation experts in Chungking reveal that two 3,500 to 4,500-mile supply routes to China are now in full readiness for shipments.		Gen. Sir Alan F. Hartley reveals planes have been used to machine gun mobs in eastern Indian frontier area to clear railroad lines.
Sept. 26		Speaking in Moscow, Willkie says U.S. can help Russia by establishing a second front in Europe at earliest possible date .... French Premier Pierre Laval ousts Jacques Benoist-Mechin on grounds he has been plotting to overthrow the government.	Chinese troops advance 40 to 60 miles to attack Chuki and Chenghsien in Chekiang Province .... Japanese Foreign Min. Masayuki Tani says there is no change in Japan's foreign policy towards Russia.		
Sept. 27	Second anniversary of Tripartite Pact is celebrated in Rome, Berlin and Tokyo with speeches by government leaders.	Germany launches nine new assaults against Stalingrad, employing hundreds of dive bombers and advancing through Russian minefields.		Nelson Rockefeller arrives in Miami after a four-week tour of Central and South America, where he discussed with Latin American officials the possibility of aid to Spain.	
Sept. 28		Germans attack Volga shipping, inflicting heavy casualties on Russians.	Navy, Army and Marine fliers claim to have shot down 42 Japanese planes and to have damaged two cruisers, a seaplane tender and a large transport in the Solomons during past four days .... In two days of air assaults, Army bombers reportedly sink Japanese transport and submarine at Kiska and Attu.		Premier of Indian's Sind Province, Allah Baksh, says he is starting a campaign to fight British imperialism.
Sept. 29		P.M. Winston Churchill emphasizes in Commons "the undesireability of public statements or of speculation as to the time or place of future Allied offensive operations."	Allied troops capture Ioribaiwa Ridge in Owen Stanley Mountains, forcing Japanese retreat .... BBC reports Wendell L. Willkie arrived today in Chungking by plane after a temporary stop in western China on way from Moscow.	By vote of 67-64, the Argentine Chamber of Deputies passes a resolution urging a break in diplomatic relations with Axis.	British troops land at Tulear on southwest coast of Madagascar without opposition.
Sept. 30		Heavy fighting continues in northwest sector of Stalingrad, with Germans pouring in new tank units .... Canadian Navy Min. Angus MacDonald claims Canadian Navy recently sank four submarines in St. Lawrence and Atlantic area.	Australian forces advance another 10 miles in Owen Stanley Mountains to jungle village of Naoro.	Canada applies its military conscription law to include 19-year-olds and every male of military age, except enemy aliens .... Under government decree, Brazilian banks commence eight-day holiday to overcome currency shortage .... Paraguayan Pres. Higinio Morinigo announces he will remain in office until 1948, as requested by military leaders.	
	A *Includes developments that affect more than one world region, international organizations and important meetings of major world leaders.*	B *Includes all developments in European countries and military engagements between Allied and Axis powers in Africa and at sea.*	C *Includes all developments in Japan and China, Japanese foreign policy and military actions in the Pacific region.*	D *Includes all domestic and regional developments in Latin America, the Caribbean and Canada.*	E *Includes developments in those independent nations and colonial possessions not covered in Columns B, C and D.*

U.S. Politics & Social Issues	U.S. Foreign Policy & Defense	U.S. Economy & Environment	Science, Technology & Nature	Culture, Leisure & Life Style	
				Post Office bars *National Police Gazette* from mails for publishing lewd and lascivious material .... Gunder Haegg sets a new world mark of 13:58.2 for 5,000-meter run in Goteborg, Sweden .... Chicago Bears defeat the Army Eastern All-Stars, 14-7, in Boston.	Sept. 20
FBI and police arrest 84 Negroes and one white woman in Chicago on charges of draft evasion and conspiracy in Japanese-sponsored disobedience movement.	Sen. Lister Hill (D, Ala.) introduces amendment to Selective Service Act in Senate which would give FDR unlimited presidential power in waging war.			Justice Min. Louis St. Laurent issues order in Ottawa barring Theodore Dreiser, 71, American novelist, from making speeches in Canada after he tells *Toronto Telegram* "I would rather see Germans in England than those damn, aristocratic horse-riding snobs there now."	Sept. 21
					Sept. 22
Judge John C. Knox sets aside charges against Jean Leonard Musa of acting as unregistered agent for Vichy because of lack of evidence.		House passes bill to raise farm prices to 112% of parity, which OPA estimates will boost food prices by $3.5 billion and the cost of living 4-5% .... Henry J. Kaiser's Oregon Shipbuilding Co. at Portland, Ore., launches 10,500-ton Liberty ship *Joseph N. Teal* 10 days after keel was laid.		Senate Interstate Commerce Comm. approves resolution asking for investigation of James C. Petrillo's order that musicians not make recordings for commercial use .... In poll conducted by Dial Press to determine "the greatest living American writers," Carl Sandburg leads over Ernest Hemingway and Willa Cather.	Sept. 23
	The 25,000-ton aircraft carrier *Lexington* is launched at Fore River, Mass.	Administration supporters in Senate agree to the Tydings-Reed compromise to let FDR raise farm prices, but not to raise parity as House bill permits .... Twenty persons are killed when two Washington-bound Baltimore & Ohio passenger trains crash near Dickerson, Md.			Sept. 24
		Rubber Admin. William M. Jeffers orders OPA to institute nationwide gas rationing and directs ODT to fix a nationwide speed limit of 35 mph.			Sept. 25
				Townsend B. Martin's Bolingbroke with jockey Herb Lindberg up beats Whirlaway in the $11,675 mile-and-a-half Manhattan Handicap at Belmont Park, N.Y., setting new American record of 2:27 3/5 .... Bucky Harris resigns after 13 years as manager of Washington Senators.	Sept. 26
				By beating Chicago Cubs, 9-2, St. Louis Cardinals win NL pennant on last day of season.	Sept. 27
Sen. George Norris (Ind, Neb.) accepts nomination to run for re-election after 16,000 Nebraskans sign petitions urging him to run.					Sept. 28
	FDR asks Congress to appropriate an additional $2.862 billion for naval aircraft.	As a concession to farm bloc, Senate accepts Thomas-Hatch amendment to raise farm parity prices by 12%.		Kansas City Monarchs defeat Homestead Grays to win Negro World Series.	Sept. 29
		Senate passes Stabilization of Cost of Living Act, authorizing FDR to fix wages, salaries and farm prices by Nov. 1 .... Senate Finance Comm. tables proposals to limit war profits in current tax legislation because of objections from Army, Navy, Maritime Commission and Treasury.		New York Yankees beat Cardinals, 7 to 4, in opening game of the World Series.	Sept. 30
F *Includes elections, federal-state relations, civil rights and liberties, crime, the judiciary, education, health care, poverty, urban affairs and population.*	G *Includes formation and debate of U.S. foreign and defense policies, veterans affairs and defense spending. (Relations with specific foreign countries are usually found under the region concerned.)*	H *Includes business, labor, agriculture, taxation, transportation, consumer affairs, monetary and fiscal policy, natural resources, pollution and accidents.*	I *Includes worldwide scientific, medical and technological developments, natural phenomena, U.S. weather and natural disasters.*	J *Includes the arts, religion, scholarship, communications media, sports, entertainment, fashions, fads and social life.*	

	World Affairs	European War Zone	Pacific War Zone	The Americas	Other Countries & Territories
Oct. 1		Breaking three-week lull, British Army attacks the center of the Axis line at El Alamein.			French West Africa Gov. Gen. Pierre Boisson orders excess women and children to evacuate Dakar becasue of congestion.
Oct. 2		Stalingrad suburb of Orlovka is claimed by the Germans; Russians deny the claim .... More than 80 Flying Fortresses and 400 Allied fighters sweep occupied coast of France, losing six planes.	Australian troops take and pass Menari, 38 miles from Port Moresby, without catching up with retreating Japanese .... Wendell Willkie arrives in Chungking to confer with Chiang Kai-shek .... In completing two days of air assaults on Kiska, U.S. pilots down five Japanese seaplanes and hit two cargo ships.	Cuba and Mexico sign agreement whereby they will exchange air and naval facilities and information in fighting Axis submarines in Gulf of Mexico.	Police break up demonstrations in New Delhi, India marking 73rd birthday of imprisoned leader Gandhi.
Oct. 3	Speaking in Chungking, Willkie says people everywhere are ahead of the leaders and that the time has come for a unified U.N. offensive.		Australian troops continue their push up Owen Stanley Mountains on New Guinea, reaching Efogi without opposition.		
Oct. 4	Speaking in Chungking, Willkie advocates a free postwar world and an end to imperialistic spheres of influence.	Premier Joseph Stalin says in written statement that Allied aid to Russia has been little in comparison to Russia's aid to the Allied cause .... German troops report capture of Elkhotovo, 70 miles west of Grozny oil center, and Verchniykurp in the same region of Caucasus.			Zionist Organization of America executive council issues statement opposing a reported proposal that a binational state of Jews and Arabs be established in Palestine .... British occupy railway town Antsirabe, 70 miles southwest of Tananarive, Madagascar.
Oct. 5		Three German divisions and 100 tanks supported by aircraft begin new offensive on northern front of Stalingrad.	U.S. Navy carrier-based aircraft attack a Japanese ship concentration in Shortland Islands, but the Japanese sustain no losses.	Argentine Pres. Ramon S. Castillo names Francisco Galindez as federal intervener (commissioner) for province of Corrientes to end administrative disorganization.	
Oct. 6	U.S. Acting State Secy. Welles, Russian Amb. Maxim Litvinov and British Amb. Sir Ronald Campbell sign protocol in Washington formalizing method of shipping war material to Russia.			Brazil issues $150 million in war bonds at 6% interest, to be paid after the war.	
Oct. 7	FDR in Washington and Viscount Simon in London announce that a U.N. commission will be established to investigate Axis crimes against civilians and that "war criminals" will be punished.	Moscow reports Russian troops have repelled several Nazi assaults on Stalingrad.	U.S. Navy announces American reconnaissance planes have discovered that Japanese forces have abandoned Attu and Agattu islands in Aleutians during September and have now relocated to Kiska.		
Oct. 8		Berlin reports its tactics at Stalingrad will be changed from storming the city to systematically destroying it by artillery fire .... German authorities issue decree mandating registration for labor of all Belgian men aged 18-50 and unmarried women 21-35.		Argentine cabinet orders strict supervision of outgoing communications "to prevent the transmission of news prejudicial to the national interests."	While House of Commons votes to support current British policy toward India, Leopold Amery bars any negotiations with All-India Congress Party until it abandons its illegal efforts to seize power.
Oct. 9	Ethiopia becomes 30th nation to adhere to U.N. pact.	U.S. Army headquarters in London reports that 115 Flying Fortresses and Liberators, accompanied by 500 Allied fighters, bombed German-held industrial plants in Lille, France, today in greatest raid on German-occupied territory of war .... German Gestapo Chief Heinrich Himmler begins three-day inspection tour of "German services" in Rome, Milan, Turin, Genoa and Naples, conferring with Premier Benito Mussolini.	Three U.S. cruisers—*Quincy, Vincennes* and *Astoria*—are sunk by a Japanese naval force in Solomon Islands .... Allied bombers carry out biggest raid on Rabaul, New Britain, dropping 60 tons of bombs .... U.S. and Britain announce willingness to begin negotiating immediately with China for an end to their extraterritorial rights, dating to the 19th century.	FDR says St. Lawrence Seaway Project will be delayed until after war because of material shortage.	
Oct. 10	Chinese Foreign Min. Dr. T.V. Soong states in N.Y. an executive council of the U.N. should be set up immediately to enforce order among all nations.	Stalin orders abolition of Red Army political commissars in a decree designed to unify command and eliminate delays in action .... Russian troops begin digging in at Stalingrad as German long-range artillery takes aim on the city .... Canadian and American troops begin to disembark in the British Isles.	Australian troops make contact with Japanese forces in Owen Stanley Mountains in Myola-Templeton Crossings area for first time in several days .... For last three days Army heavy bombers have attacked Japanese at Kiska, without losing a plane or encountering opposition.	Twelve Latin American nations, along with British Guiana, Honduras and Trinidad-Tabago, agree to sell all their rubber above essential needs to the U.S. and to expand production.	

	A	B	C	D	E
	Includes developments that affect more than one world region, international organizations and important meetings of major world leaders.	*Includes all developments in European countries and military engagements between Allied and Axis powers in Africa and at sea.*	*Includes all developments in Japan and China, Japanese foreign policy and military actions in the Pacific region.*	*Includes all domestic and regional developments in Latin America, the Caribbean and Canada.*	*Includes developments in those independent nations and colonial possessions not covered in Columns B, C and D.*

U.S. Politics & Social Issues	U.S. Foreign Policy & Defense	U.S. Economy & Environment	Science, Technology & Nature	Culture, Leisure & Life Style	
	In a Senate speech, James M. Mead (D, N.Y.) says U.S. should sever diplomatic relations with Vichy and occupy French possessions in Western Hemisphere and Africa .... Brown Instrument Co. publicly demonstrates its electronic flight recorder instrument, used to measure temperature and pressure changes of military planes in flight.	FDR completes a 8,754-mile trip to 24 states, visiting industrial and military centers, and says morale of the people throughout country is better than in Washington .... WPB begins drive to gather scrap metal as part of program to raise 17 million tons of iron and steel scrap by year's end.			Oct. 1
Senate Judiciary Comm. rejects Pepper-Geyer bill to abolish payment of poll tax as a prerequisite to voting in congressional and presidential elections.	Lt. Gen. Henry Arnold, returning from a tour of Pacific War Zone, completes flight from Brisbane, Australia to San Francisco in record time of 35 hours and 53 minutes.	Congress passes and FDR signs anti-inflation bill, authorizing the President to fix wages and prices and putting a parity floor of 90% under several farm products .... Senate Finance Comm. reports to floor a tax bill designed to raise an estimated $8 billion in 1943.		Ray Robinson scores his 36th straight win as a professional boxer, outpointing Jake LaMotta in N.Y.	Oct. 2
Atty. Gen. Biddle announces proceedings will begin for all former officials and members of the German-American Bund on charges of obtaining citizenship papers falsely.		Under new legislative authority, FDR orders immediate stabilization of farm prices, rents, wages and salaries and creates an Office of Economic Stabilization headed by James F. Byrnes .... NWLB allows 4 cents-an-hour increase for 90,000 Chrysler Corp. employes.			Oct. 3
	War Dept. announces Army Transport Command will handle ferrying of Lend-Lease and other supplies to Middles East after Oct. 31.	Confederated Unions of America, a newly organized independent labor federation, adopts constitution in Chicago and elects Donald F. Cameron as secretary-treasurer.	Dr. Herman Besser, inventor of Besser X-ray tube, dies in N.Y.		Oct. 4
Negro contralto Marian Anderson accepts the Sept. 29 invitation from the DAR to sing at their war benefit concert, provided that no racial segregation be permitted in seating arrangements .... Special sedition grand jury in Chicago indicts Newell Mercartney on charges of sedition and conspiracy.		Treasury Secy. Morgenthau says he will present new $6-billion tax bill to Congress for action .... Henry J. Kaiser announces launching in California of a new 3,500-ton "secret tank landing ship." .... OPA orders rent ceilings established at March levels in 45 states effective Dec. 5.		St. Louis Cardinals defeat Yankees, 4-2, before 69,052 fans in Yankee Stadium to win the World Series.	Oct. 5
House approves and returns to Senate a bill amending Hatch Act to permit teachers and editors in federal employ to participate in politics.				Pope Pius XII confers upon the apostolic delegate in Washington the authority to settle pending matrimonial cases in U.S. because of communications difficulties with the Vatican.	Oct. 6
		UMW delegates vote overwhelmingly in Cincinnati to withdraw from the CIO .... NWLB reaffirms its "Little Steel" decision to raise wages 15% between Jan. 1, 1941 and May 1942 to compensate for cost-of-living increases .... Labor Secy. Perkins announces that FDR's order banning double-time pay for Sunday work, except when it is seventh consecutive work day, applies only to war industries.		Plans to merge Evangelical and Reformed Churches of America and Congregational Christian Churches are announced in Chicago by Rev. Dr. Louis W. Goebel.	Oct. 7
	House passes and sends to Senate second supplemental national defense appropriation bill for 1943, including $5.595 billion for Navy.	WPB orders domestic gold mines to cease ore production by Oct. 15, except very small mines and those needed for war production .... Senate rejects amendment to tax bill providing for taxation of all state and municipal securities.			Oct. 8
Seven life-term convicts, including Roger Touhy and Basil (The Owl) Banghart, both former members of the notorious Touhy gang, escape from Stateville Prison near Joliet, Ill.	Wendell L. Willkie leaves Chengtu for his return to the U.S., completing a special tour for FDR.	Roane Waring, newly-elected national commander of American Legion, says at AFL convention in Toronto he would shoot strikers in war industries if he had the power .... Senate approves 5% "Victory Tax" on gross incomes over $12-a-week commencing Jan. 1 .... OPA announces new pricing formula for 11 groups of food products under which wholesalers and retailers may raise prices by 15%.		Dr. Ernest E. Loewenstein, 73, prominent German jurist before the rise of Hitler, is killed by a truck in New York.	Oct. 9
		Senate passes and sends to conference largest tax bill in nation's history, designed to raise $8.525 billion.			Oct. 10

F	G	H	I	J
Includes elections, federal-state relations, civil rights and liberties, crime, the judiciary, education, health care, poverty, urban affairs and population.	*Includes formation and debate of U.S. foreign and defense policies, veterans affairs and defense spending. (Relations with specific foreign countries are usually found under the region concerned.)*	*Includes business, labor, agriculture, taxation, transportation, consumer affairs, monetary and fiscal policy, natural resources, pollution and accidents.*	*Includes worldwide scientific, medical and technological developments, natural phenomena, U.S. weather and natural disasters.*	*Includes the arts, religion, scholarship, communications media, sports, entertainment, fashions, fads and social life.*

	World Affairs	European War Zone	Pacific War Zone	The Americas	Other Countries & Territories
Oct. 11		German and Russian infantry remain stationary on Stalingrad front as both sides exchange artillery fire.	Battle of Cape Esperance begins, with about 65 Japanese planes raiding Guadalcanal and losing 12 aircraft compared to the loss of two U.S. fighters. The Japanese also lose one light cruiser and one destroyer.	Pres. Juan Antonio Rios of Chile postpones his visit to the U.S. and tells FDR a in message that the "latest official information circulated in the United States about my country's international policy has created an unpleasant atmosphere."	
Oct. 12		In air battles near Malta during the past two days, Allied planes reportedly have shot down 39 Axis planes, set an enemy cargo ship afire and hit an Italian destroyer .... Churchill strikes a note of optimism in speech at Edinburgh and says that Hitler's latest speeches reveal "a dull low whining note of fear."	In night battle U.S. Navy sinks six Japanese ships west of Savo Island, and a Japanese effort to land more troops on Guadalcanal is repulsed.		
Oct. 13		As steadily worsening weather hinders German operations, Russian troops retake two strategic positions in Stalingrad .... Vichy bans all American and British motion pictures from France and French West Africa.	In heavy fighting on Guadalcanal, Japanese bombers attack U.S. airfield twice, losing three planes; U.S. reinforcements land on island, and during the night Japanese warships bombard American positions.	Brazilian Navy vessels are placed under supervision of U.S. Adm. Jonas A. Ingram.	
Oct. 14	Russia and Australia announce they will exchange envoys for the first time.	Some 4,000 Croatian followers of interned leader Dr. Vladimir Matchek revolt against government of Ante Pavelich.	Japanese ships bombard Marine-occupied installations on Guadalcanal during the night and begin to land troops .... Army planes drop incendiary bombs on Japanese camp at Kiska, starting several large fires.	FDR appeals to Pres. Juan Antonio Rios of Chile to come to Washington a "little later" to discuss matters of common defense.	
Oct. 15		Two German divisions supported by tanks and planes attack Russian positions on northern Stalingrad sector .... Russian Foreign Min. Molotov declares in a message to nine Allied nations that the leaders of Nazi Germany and perpetrators of atrocities should be prosecuted at the war's end.	Japanese execute three U.S. fliers captured during Doolittle's raid on Tokyo April 18 .... *U.S.S. Meredith* is sunk by a 27-plane raid from Japanese carrier *Zuikaku*. Japanese land 4,500 troops on Guadalcanal.		
Oct. 16		Vichy armed forces reportedly kill 50 Frenchmen at Lyon and 15 at Amberieu and wound a total of 400 when crowds riot to protest sending workers to Germany .... In air battles which began over Malta on Oct. 10, the British claim to have shot down 97 Axis planes, with 19 losses .... Polish government in London indicts 10 Nazi leaders for murder of 400,000 Poles and demands they be tried after war.	Japan continues to land troops on Guadalcanal and bombard American positions heavily .... Army bombers set fire to Japanese cargo ship off Kiska and score two hits on destroyers northeast of the island.	Cuban government establishes diplomatic relations with Russia, becoming the only Latin American country to have official relations with the Soviet Union .... U.S. and Venezuela sign agreement whereby U.S. will buy all Venezuelan rubber not required for domestic use.	Nearly 11,000 people are killed in Bengal Province, India when cyclone strikes Calcutta and sweeps inland .... British troops capture Ambositra, Madagascar, 142 miles south of Tananarive, taking 170 French military prisoners.
Oct. 17		RAF and U.S. Army heavy bombers raid Bengazi, Libya.	Allied bombers raid Buka and Buin in the Solomons, Rabaul in New Britain, Japanese-occupied areas in New Guinea and a large transport off Shortland Island. U.S. surface vessels shell Japanese positions on northwestern Guadalcanal, causing heavy explosions and fires in ammunition dumps .... U.S. Southeast Asian commander, Lt. Gen. Stilwell, arrives in New Delhi for conferences with British Commander in India, Sir Archibald Wavell.		Women's Zionist group Hadassah and Zionist Organization of America, meeting in N.Y., adopt resolution rejecting creation of binational Palestine.
Oct. 18		Moscow claims 45 Nazi tanks are destroyed and 3,000 troops disabled as Soviet forces hold off German attacks in Stalingrad.	Australian government creates special Ministry of Shipping, to be headed by John A. Beasley.		
Oct. 19		Supported by tanks and aircraft, German troops occupy one block of buildings in Stalingrad during night assault; 26 tanks are destroyed and two villages southeast of Novorossiisk are captured by the Germans.			
Oct. 20		Moscow communique reports two German attacks, one by 40 tanks and the second by 30, were repulsed inside Stalingrad today, with German prisoners admitting that they have lost 70% of their men in past few days .... Laval tells workers of France to obey his orders to "volunteer" for labor in Germany, otherwise Germans will mobilize all the French workers they want .... U.S. Navy Dept. announces loss of 11 Allied merchant ships in the Atlantic recently, with 212 people missing.		Entire Chilean cabinet resigns to give Pres. Juan Antonio Rios "freedom of action so he can resolve the present political crisis."	

A	B	C	D	E
Includes developments that affect more than one world region, international organizations and important meetings of major world leaders.	*Includes all developments in European countries and military engagements between Allied and Axis powers in Africa and at sea.*	*Includes all developments in Japan and China, Japanese foreign policy and military actions in the Pacific region.*	*Includes all domestic and regional developments in Latin America, the Caribbean and Canada.*	*Includes developments in those independent nations and colonial possessions not covered in Columns B, C and D.*

U.S. Politics & Social Issues	U.S. Foreign Policy & Defense	U.S. Economy & Environment	Science, Technology & Nature	Culture, Leisure & Life Style	
		AFL Pres. William Green bars John L. Lewis from any peace talks between the AFL and CIO, since the UMW has left its parent organization.		*New York Herald Tribune* reports that best-selling books include: *The Song of Bernadette*, by Franz Werfel, and *See Here, Private Hargrove*, by Marion Hargrove.	Oct. 11
Atty. Gen. Biddle says as of Oct. 19 some 600,000 Italian aliens will no longer be classified as enemy aliens.	In fireside chat, FDR says that the draft age will be lowered to 18 and that the country must learn how to ration manpower.			Chicago Federal Judge John P. Barnes dismisses goverment's suit against Pres. James C. Petrillo of the American Federation of Musicians on grounds that it involves a labor dispute and not an antitrust law violation.	Oct. 12
House passes and sends to Senate Geyer bill outlawing payment of poll taxes as prerequisite for voting in federal elections.					Oct. 13
	Testifying before House Military Affairs Comm., Stimson says that by the end of 1943 U.S. will have 7.5 million men in military service . . . . Willkie reports to FDR on results of his 31,000-mile trip which took him to 14 countries and expresses confidence in eventual Allied victory.	UMW accepts government request for six-day week in bituminous coal mines provided workers are paid time-and-one-half for the sixth day . . . . AFL re-elects William Green president and George Meany secretary-treasurer at convention in Toronto . . . . OPA establishes special Food Price Division under A.C. Hoffman to formulate and administer food price regulations.			Oct. 14
	House Military Affairs Comm. approves Wadsworth Amendment to Selective Service Act, lowering draft age from 20 to 18.	House passes and sends to Senate bill authorizing government to control all rents, including hotel and rooming house rates.			Oct. 15
		Economic Stabilization Dir. James F. Byrnes explains he has arranged with the Treasury Dept. to bring all salaries under control.	Georgia health officials order all venereal cases quarantined and the detention and treatment of all victims of the disease who are not receiving medical care. Venereal disease has reportedly grown to epidemic proportions in the state.	Aaron Copland's ballet *Rodeo* is performed in New York for the first time by the Ballet Russe de Monte Carlo.	Oct. 16
Negro Howard Wash is lynched in Laurel, Miss., after being convicted of killing his employer.	House votes to lower draft age from 20 to 18.	Senate and House conferees reach complete agreement on new tax bill which Treasury now estimates will yield $6.881 billion . . . . NWLB orders its mediation panels and investigators to report fully on all union and company activities regarding "wildcat strikes."	Flood waters recede in Va., W. Va., Md. and Washington, D.C. along the James, Rappahannock and Potomac Rivers, leaving five persons dead and extensive damage.	Boysy, with Darrell Clingman up, wins $12,100 Continental Handicap in Jamaica, N.Y., when winner Riverland is disqualified and jockey Wayne Wright is suspended for grabbing Clingman's leg . . . . United Church in America authorizes its president, Dr. F.H. Knubel, to implement a working agreement with American Lutheran Church.	Oct. 17
	U.S. aircraft carrier *Princeton* is launched at Camden, N.J.				Oct. 18
Supreme Court refuses to review Georgia court decision which permits Atlanta taxi cabs to carry signs designating them specifically for Negro or white passengers.	Federal grand jury in N.Y. indicts 24 former leaders of German-American Bund of conspiracy to evade the Selective Service Act.				Oct. 19
	Senate passes and returns to House second supplemental war appropriations bill providing for naval expansion.	Congress passes largest tax bill in the nation's history and sends it to White House.			Oct. 20

F	G	H	I	J
Includes elections, federal-state relations, civil rights and liberties, crime, the judiciary, education, health care, poverty, urban affairs and population.	*Includes formation and debate of U.S. foreign and defense policies, veterans affairs and defense spending. (Relations with specific foreign countries are usually found under the region concerned.)*	*Includes business, labor, agriculture, taxation, transportation, consumer affairs, monetary and fiscal policy, natural resources, pollution and accidents.*	*Includes worldwide scientific, medical and technological developments, natural phenomena, U.S. weather and natural disasters.*	*Includes the arts, religion, scholarship, communications media, sports, entertainment, fashions, fads and social life.*

	World Affairs	European War Zone	Pacific War Zone	The Americas	Other Countries & Territories
Oct. 21		Russian troops repulse Nazi attacks in Stalingrad and in Mozdok area of the Caucasus .... South African P.M. Jan Christian Smuts tells British Parliament that the German Army is being bled to death by the Russians and that Russia is bearing "more than her share of the common burden." .... Maj. Gen. Mark V. Clark and seven other officers leave on secret trip to North African coast to gather political and military information to prepare for Allied landings .... Foreign Secy. Eden says Rudolf Hess is considered a POW and his immediate trial as a war criminal is not contemplated.	Attacking for the first time since landing reinforcements, the Japanese are repulsed on the western flank of the American line on Guadalcanal .... Capt. E.V. (Eddie) Rickenbacker is lost at sea while returning to Hawaii when his plane runs out of fuel.	Ontario Premier Frederick Hepburn, a sharp critic of the present Canadian government, resigns in Toronto.	
Oct. 22		Chief of French armed forces Admiral Jean Francois Darlan broadcasts message from Marshal Petain over Dakar radio, stating "you will meet any aggression with same responses as that of September 1940," when British and Free French attacked and were repulsed by Vichy forces.		Chilean Pres. Rios completes organization of his new cabinet with one major change: Joaquin Fernandez y Fernandez is named foreign minister.	
Oct. 23	FDR says Japan's threat to punish American aviators and German shackling of prisoners are violations of the Geneva Convention for humanitarian teatment of captives.	Battle of El Alamein begins .... Russian troops reportedly capture two points northwest of Stalingrad and repulse three German counterattacks .... Mrs. Eleanor Roosevelt arrives in London after transatlantic flight and is welcomed by King George VI and Queen Elizabeth.	Heavy Allied bombers sink or damage 10 Japanese ships, totaling 50,000 tons, in a pre-dawn attack on Rabaul, New Britain.		
Oct. 24		Gen. Montgomery's British forces attack Rommel's heavily fortified line at El Alamein after four days of intense air pounding .... Russian troops launch offensive in Caucasus, advancing 12½ miles southeast of Nalchik and capturing four cities. Two German infantry divisions and 80 tanks attack inside Stalingrad but are driven back after losing 1,500 men and 17 tanks.	U.S. troops and Marines repulse four Japanese assaults on their western defense lines on Guadalcanal .... Vice Adm. William F. Halsey replaces Vice Adm. Robert L. Ghormley as commander of all American forces in Southwest Pacific .... Hull submits draft treaty relinquishing U.S. extraterritorial privileges in China to Ambassador Dr. Wei Tao-ming in Washington.		
Oct. 25		British troops hold advance lines at El Alamein, despite heavy German counterattacks.	Japanese launch coordinated air, land and sea battle against American positions on Guadalcanal .... Foreign Min. T.V. Soong arrives in Chungking from the U.S. and confers with Chiang Kaishek .... In their first raid upon Hong Kong, American planes damage Kowloon docks and report shooting down 10 Japanese planes.		
Oct. 26		German and Rumanian troops drive closer to Black Sea port of Tuapse.	Eight Japanese warships, including two aircraft carriers and one battleship, are hit by bombs or torpedoes in naval air battle east of Stewart Islands. Badly damaged in two Japanese air attacks near Santa Cruz Islands, the U.S. aircraft carrier *Hornet* is taken in tow but sinks later. American troops repulse Japanese attacks on Guadalcanal.	Street fights between pro-Axis and pro-Allied civilians erupt in Santiago, Chile.	
Oct. 27		British and Allied troops continue their advance into enemy lines at El Alamein .... Germans strike blow at "Red October" plant near Stalingrad and capture northwest part of the factory's territory.	American troops repulse several small-scale Japanese attacks upon their positions on Guadalcanal.		
Oct. 28		British forces defeat attacking German units in major clash of armored units at El Alamein .... On 68th day of Stalingrad battle, the Germans reportedly take 200 yards and two streets, with a reported loss of 2,400 men.	Allied planes raid Buka Island in northern Solomons and Rabaul, New Britain.		
Oct. 29		German counterattacks upon Allied positions at El Alamein are repulsed while Allied planes continue to assault enemy positions.		Stimson announces completion of Alcan Highway from Dawson Creek, Alberta to Fairbanks, Alaska .... Mexican Pres. Avila Camacho signs decree establishing censorship over mail and telegrams effective Nov. 1.	

A	B	C	D	E
Includes developments that affect more than one world region, international organizations and important meetings of major world leaders.	*Includes all developments in European countries and military engagements between Allied and Axis powers in Africa and at sea.*	*Includes all developments in Japan and China, Japanese foreign policy and military actions in the Pacific region.*	*Includes all domestic and regional developments in Latin America, the Caribbean and Canada.*	*Includes developments in those independent nations and colonial possessions not covered in Columns B, C and D.*

U.S. Politics & Social Issues	U.S. Foreign Policy & Defense	U.S. Economy & Environment	Science, Technology & Nature	Culture, Leisure & Life Style	
	U.S. Amb. to Moscow William H. Standley confers with FDR .... Judge Alfred D. Barksdale imposes maximum prison terms of five years each for draft evasion conspiracy on 24 members of German-American Bund in N.Y.	FDR signs record tax bill which will raise federal taxes to about $25 billion yearly.		William Cardinal O'Connell, Archbishop of Boston, says Catholic Church unequivocally opposes birth control and views it as "the decadence of pagan license."	Oct. 21
	Senate passes and sends to FDR the second supplemental war appropriations bill for $15.851 billion, mostly for the Navy .... Senate defeats proposal to ban sale of alcoholic beverages in or near military reservations.				Oct. 22
		NWLB approves pay increase for copper, lead and zinc workers in Idaho and Utah of $1-a-day.			Oct. 23
	Senate passes its own bill lowering draft age from 20 to 18 and returns it to House.		Smithsonian Institution Secy. Dr. Charles G. Abbot credits Wilbur and Orville Wright with having made the first sustained flights in a heavier-than-air machine in 1903, over claims that it was either Samuel P. Langley or Alberto Santos-Dumont.		Oct. 24
		Supreme Court refuses to review its June 8th decision upholding validity of Wage and Hour Law.			Oct. 25
Princeton Univ. Pres. Harold W. Dodds says American colleges must prepare themselves to immediately suspend liberal arts edcuation and convert their facilities to meet military needs.		OPA announces coffee will be rationed to civilians beginning Nov. 28 at rate of one pound every five weeks for each person over 15.	Six N.Y. hospitals announce they will teach the Kenny treatment of infantile paralysis, which includes hot applications, massage and exercise.		Oct. 26
		Economic Stabilization Dir. Byrnes issues regulations limiting individual salaries in 1943 to $25,000 after payment of federal income taxes, customary charitable contributions and fixed obligations .... War Manpower Dir. Paul V. McNutt announces plan to freeze all "necessary" skilled dairy, livestock and poultry workers.		AP charges that the government suit against it is really an attack upon freedom of the press, claiming that the membership system has fostered competition with UP and INS .... Mort Cooper, St. Louis Cardinal pitcher with 22-7 record, is voted NL's MVP by baseball writers.	Oct. 27
	Former State Dept. Latin American specialist William Ray Manning, 70, dies in Washington, D.C.	WPB Chmn. Nelson approves allocation of 224,000 tons of steel piping to complete the gas line between Longview, Tex. and Norris City, Ill.		Effective Nov. 2, *The Stars and Stripes* will become a daily publication, the first in U.S. Army history.	Oct. 28
				Branch Rickey becomes president and general manager of Brooklyn Dodgers, replacing Larry MacPhail, who has entered the Army.	Oct. 29

F	G	H	I	J
Includes elections, federal-state relations, civil rights and liberties, crime, the judiciary, education, health care, poverty, urban affairs and population.	*Includes formation and debate of U.S. foreign and defense policies, veterans affairs and defense spending. (Relations with specific foreign countries are usually found under the region concerned.)*	*Includes business, labor, agriculture, taxation, transportation, consumer affairs, monetary and fiscal policy, natural resources, pollution and accidents.*	*Includes worldwide scientific, medical and technological developments, natural phenomena, U.S. weather and natural disasters.*	*Includes the arts, religion, scholarship, communications media, sports, entertainment, fashions, fads and social life.*

	World Affairs	European War Zone	Pacific War Zone	The Americas	Other Countries & Territories
Oct. 30		British 8th Army makes further advance through El Alamein line under intense artillery barrage .... Anthony Eden says in London that war's defensive phase is waning and Great Britain is beginning to take the offensive .... Adm. Darlan reports to Premier Laval and his cabinet in Vichy on defense measures taken in French North and West Africa .... German and Rumanian ground forces split Russian lines in Nalchik area of Caucasus.	Australian troops capture Alola, eight miles from Japanese base of Kokoda in Owen Stanley Mountains on New Guinea.	Mexico City report claims U.S. will buy 10-15 million barrels of oil annually from Mexico.	British troops capture Fianarantoso, the most important town in southern Madagascar.
Oct. 31		About 30 German planes bomb Canterbury this afternoon in one of the most severe raids on England in two years.	American fliers cause heavy damage to several Japanese ships in a night attack on Buin, Bougainville Island.		
Nov. 1		Turkish Pres. Ismet Inonu says his country is in graver danger of aggression than ever before, but will remain neutral.	Tojo names Kazuo Aoki as head of new Japanese Ministry of Greater East Asiatic Affairs, giving the Army both military and economic control over conquered territory .... Small force of U.S. Marines supported by aircraft cross Matanikau River on Guadalcanal and attack the retreating Japanese.		Willkie urges that Palestine be opened "to the homeless Jews of Central and Eastern Europe who survive the war." .... Sen. Elbert D. Thomas (D, Utah) says establishment of a Jewish national state should not wait until the end of the war.
Nov. 2		An estimated 2,500 Axis troops are reported trapped between El Alamein and Sidi Abd el Rahman on Mediterranean coast by Australian infantrymen .... German troops in the Caucasus capture Alagir, 25 miles west of Orjonikidze, blocking the important Ossetian military highway to Kutais.	After two nights of attacks upon the Buin-Faisi area in the northern Solomons, Allied bombers claim to have sunk or seriously damaged seven Japanese warships.		Gandhi says in message published in *India Today* that the U.S. has "made common cause with Great Britain" and therefore bears responsibility for what happens in India.
Nov. 3		British tanks break through Axis lines in Egypt and sweep into open country .... Stalingrad's defenders claim throwing off two German attacks, killing 2,000 of the enemy.	In an apparent flanking move, the Japanese land troops east of American forces on north coast of Guadalcanal. U.S. forces on Guadalcanal continue to attack and advance west of their positions .... Australian troops recaputre Kokoda, 60 miles from Port Moresby, and are driving the Japanese south toward Oivi.	Inter-American Emergency Advisory Comm. for Political Defense of the Continent, meeting in Montevideo, makes public evidence of a Chilean Nazi spy-ring which sent military and political data to Berlin.	
Nov. 4		After 12 days of ceaseless Allied land and air attacks, Axis forces in western desert are in full retreat from El Alamein .... Russian forces hold German-Rumanian troops southeast of Nalchik in the Caucasus for second day .... Soviet government appoints an investigative board to determine the cost of damage caused by the German occupation of the country.	Japanese troops land on north coast of Guadalcanal despite Allied air efforts to force their withdrawal.		
Nov. 5		Commander of British forces Lt. Gen. Montgomery tells reporters his 8th Army has won a complete victory, with the Axis in full retreat.	U.S. forces repulse several night counterattacks by Japanese on Guadalcanal, west of Matanikau River.	Cordell Hull praises Pres. Juan Antonio Rios of Chile and his government for taking vigorous steps to combat Axis espionage.	
Nov. 6	Speaking in N.Y., Willkie demands an end to current emphasis on the Anglo-American world, claiming that the Atlantic Charter applies to the whole world.	British forces push Rommel's Afrika Korps to the Matruh region, 104 miles west of El Alamein, and attempt to cut the Germans off from Libya .... Speaking in Moscow, Stalin says there will be a second front sooner or later because "our allies need it no less than we do."	U.S. forces advance to Metapono River, four miles east of Koli Point, Guadalcanal, without making contact with Japanese.	Brazilian Pres. Getulio Vargas establishes an economic defense commission to devise new economic war measures and manage all Axis-owned commercial properties.	An armistice is reached on Madagascar between the British and the Vichy-controlled government.
Nov. 7		British forces push retreating Afrika Korps well west of Matruh. Some 20,000 Axis prisoners are reported taken.		Argentine Interior Min. Miguel Culaciati forbids newspapers to refer to activities of Chamber of Deputies committee investigating anti-Argentine activities.	

A	B	C	D	E
Includes developments that affect more than one world region, international organizations and important meetings of major world leaders.	*Includes all developments in European countries and military engagements between Allied and Axis powers in Africa and at sea.*	*Includes all developments in Japan and China, Japanese foreign policy and military actions in the Pacific region.*	*Includes all domestic and regional developments in Latin America, the Caribbean and Canada.*	*Includes developments in those independent nations and colonial possessions not covered in Columns B, C and D.*

U.S. Politics & Social Issues	U.S. Foreign Policy & Defense	U.S. Economy & Environment	Science, Technology & Nature	Culture, Leisure & Life Style	
		FDR announces compulsory registration of women aged 18 to 65 is being studied to ascertain the number of war workers . . . . WPB orders work on $81,000,000 Brooklyn-Battery vehicular tunnel in New York halted to conserve critical materials.	Dr. Henry R. McCarroll tells American Public Health Assn. that the Kenny method of treating infantile paralysis is hopeless for controlling the "after-effects" of the disease and suggests that the answer lies in immunology.	Interpretation of modern American prose literature, *On Native Grounds*, by Alfred Kazin, is published by Reynal & Hitchcock.	Oct. 30
Gallup Poll reports Democratic Party will win 256 to 276 and the GOP 158 to 178 seats in Nov. 3 congressional elections.		Labor Secy. Frances Perkins says at least three million more women and 1.5 million more men must be employed during next year to avert serious labor shortage.		Fritz Kreisler, violinist, receives prolonged ovation when he returns to Carnegie Hall, for his first appearance since April 1941, when he was injured in a traffic accident.	Oct. 31
		Agriculture Dept. announces there will be adequate food in 1943 but predicts shortages in dairy products and canned goods and continued meat rationing.			Nov. 1
FDR asks Congress for wartime authority to suspend any laws hampering the movement of persons, property and information to and from the U.S.		WPB Chmn. Nelson announces new plan to coordinate supply and demand of critical materials in order to increase war production output . . . . Treasury Secy. Morgenthau announces the Department raised a record of $6.836 billion in October . . . . UMW Executive Council authorizes seven-day work week in seven Western states to relieve the growing coal shortage through the area.			Nov. 2
GOP wins major victory in senatorial and gubernatorial races but fails to gain control of the House: Republicans gain nine Senate seats, 42 House seats and four governorships.				Baseball writers picks N.Y. Yankee Joe Gordon as mvp in the AL for 1942.	Nov. 3
	British Production Min. Oliver Lyttelton arrives in Washington for conferences with U.S. military production officials, including Lend-Lease expediter W. Averell Harriman.	In the wake of GOP election victories, the NYSE sales totaled 771,830, the largest volume in three weeks.		*Variety* reports most popular songs to be (1) *White Christmas;* (2) *Praise the Lord and Pass the Ammunition;* (3) *When the Lights go on Again* and (4) *My Devotion.*	Nov. 4
Incomplete returns in New York State election show Republican Thomas E. Dewey defeated John J. Bennett, Jr., Democrat, for governor by more than 63,000 votes.	War Secy. Stimson announces creation of a new military and naval decoration, the Legion of Merit, as an award for "extraordinary fidelity and essential service."	Conservatives in Congress renew their attacks on Administration's labor policies, suggesting an end to the NLRA and the Wage and Hour Law and demanding an increase in the work week . . . . NWLB decides its wage control yardstick will be based on its "Little Steel" principle, permitting wage increases up to 15% to cover the rise in the cost of living between January 1941 and May 1942.		George M. Cohan, famous playwright, producer and songwriter, dies in N.Y. . . . . Museum of Modern Art announces that beginning Nov. 11 it will exhibit about 80 paintings and drawings brought from China by Wendell Willkie.	Nov. 5
U.S. Office of Education reports 50 small colleges have been forced to close because of financial difficulties resulting from nationwide drop in student enrollment . . . . Marian Anderson agrees to sing at an Army benefit program in Washington sponsored by the DAR, stipulating that there will be no segregation of Negroes in the audience.		FDR expresses opposition to the extension of the 40-hour work week, although WPB Chmn. Nelson tells the Senate that such action would increase productive efficiency . . . . American Iron and Steel Institute reports steel ingot production in October totaled 7,584,864 net tons at 100.1% of rated capacity, a new record.		Ray Robinson scores his 38th straight professional boxing victory with a win over Victor Dellicurti in N.Y.	Nov. 6
Rep. Joseph W. Martin (R, Mass.) announces he will resign as GOP National Comm. chairman at a Dec. 7 meeting of the committee in St. Louis.			AMA council on foods and nutrition suggests consumption of sugar in candy and soft drinks, which are low in nutrional value, be limited.		Nov. 7

F	G	H	I	J
Includes elections, federal-state relations, civil rights and liberties, crime, the judiciary, education, health care, poverty, urban affairs and population.	*Includes formation and debate of U.S. foreign and defense policies, veterans affairs and defense spending. (Relations with specific foreign countries are usually found under the region concerned.)*	*Includes business, labor, agriculture, taxation, transportation, consumer affairs, monetary and fiscal policy, natural resources, pollution and accidents.*	*Includes worldwide scientific, medical and technological developments, natural phenomena, U.S. weather and natural disasters.*	*Includes the arts, religion, scholarship, communications media, sports, entertainment, fashions, fads and social life.*

	World Affairs	European War Zone	Pacific War Zone	The Americas	Other Countries & Territories
Nov. 8		An American landing force commanded by Lt. Gen. Dwight D. Eisenhower is put ashore in French North Africa with the object of seizing the widely separated ports of Casablanca, Oran and Algiers and trapping Rommel. Landing at Safi, Fedhala and Mehedia, the troops encounter shore battery resistance. By nightfall, Algiers surrenders to the Americans .... French Gen. Henri Honore Giraud turns up in Algiers, appealing to Frenchmen to fight with the Allies, stating that this "is our chance for revival." .... Vichy breaks diplomatic relations with Washington .... Surrounded Axis forces at Matruh surrender to the British as the Allied chase of Germans and Italians into Libya continues .... U.S. and Britain assure Spain and Portugal that North African invasion is no way intended as preparation for a move into the Iberian Peninsula.	American ground troops penetrate central and northern Papua to the vicinity of Buna.		
Nov. 9		Eisenhower announces Gen. Giraud is the leader of French movement to prevent Axis aggression in North Africa and will organize a French North African army .... U.S. troops penetrate east and west of Oran, Algeria.	U.S. torpedo boats attack three Japanese destroyers in Indispensable Strait and score a hit on one, while U.S. planes destroy six Japanese landing craft west of the American positions on Guadalcanal.	Pres. Avila Camacho announces the breaking of Mexican diplomatic relations with Vichy .... P.M. Mackenzie King announces Canada has ended diplomatic relations with Vichy.	
Nov. 10		Hitler, Laval and Ciano meet in Munich to discuss military alliance between Axis and France and countermeasures against U.S. invasion of North Africa .... U.S. forces capture Algerian port of Oran, with its Mer el Kebir naval base, and proceed to attack Casablanca .... Speaking in London, Churchill says British offensive in Egypt and U.S. invasion of North Africa have opened a new front against Hitler.	Allied forces envelop Japanese position at Gorari, near Oivi, in Owen Stanley Mountains.	Pres. Juan Antonio Rios, in a message to FDR, says Chile will aid U.S. in its North African campaign by increasing war production and suppressing Nazi propaganda and espionage .... Cuban Pres. Fulgencio Batista announces breaking of diplomatic relations with Vichy France.	Gen. Paul Le Gentilhomme, a member of de Gaulle's Free French government, is named high commissioner of Madagascar.
Nov. 11	In a speech at tomb of Unknown Soldier in observance of Armistice Day, FDR says Allied nations are growing towards full strength while Axis faces "inevitable final defeat."	Vichy commander of French armed forces, Adm. Jean Francois Darlan, issues an order from Algiers for all resistance to American occupation to cease .... Hitler orders German troops into unoccupied France .... Eisenhower appeals to French admirals in Toulon, France to bring their ships to the Allied side .... British take Sidi Barrani and move towards Babbag, 35 miles from Libyan border.	Navy planes intercept two Japanese dive bomber formations over Guadalcanal and shoot down 17 enemy planes, losing only seven.	Dominican Republic severs diplomatic relations with Vichy.	
Nov. 12		U.S.-British force lands at Bone, Algeria some 60 miles west of Tunisia, where Axis forces are trying to build up their strength at Tunis and Bizerte airfields .... Three German panzer divisions occupy French Mediterranean coast, while anti-aircraft units take over all airfields in southern France.	During a 10-hour naval bombardment of Japanese positions on Guadalcanal, enemy planes attempting to interrupt the attack sustain heavy losses .... Australian forces report trapping the remaining Japanese forces in the Owen Stanley Mountains of New Guinea.	Argentine government begins censorship of all telegraphic and telephone communications and declares all ports are military zones.	
Nov. 13		As American and British forces advance towards Tunis, reports indicate that French forces there are resisting Germans landing by sea and air .... Adm. Darlan, in a broadcast from Algiers, announces he has assumed responsibility for French interests in North Africa .... British take Bardia, Libya and Tobruk while advance guards close in on El Gazala, west of Tobruk .... German battleship *Tirpitz* is sunk by British bombers in harbor of Tromso, Norway.	Naval battle breaks out in Solomons between U.S. and Japanese ships.	Costa Rican coast guards reportedly repulse a landing attempt from German submarine in the Limon area .... Based on U.S.-supplied information, Argentine government launches an investigation of Axis espionage .... Panama and Honduras sever diplomatic relations with Vichy.	
Nov. 14		British take El Gazala, west of Tobruk, and continue to pursue Rommel's Afrika Korps toward Derna.		El Salvador severs diplomatic relations with Vichy.	
Nov. 15		British, reinforced by U.S. armored columns, drive into Tunisia from Algeria for battle with an estimated 10,000 German and Italian troops believed to have been rushed from Italy .... Adm. Darlan appoints Gen. Giraud "military chief" of French Africa .... Regent of Iceland Sveinn Bjornsson announces British have left Iceland, giving place to "the American Army which is here at our request."	Solomon Islands naval battle ends with two American light cruisers and four destroyers sunk; two Japanese destroyers and a battleship are sunk. .... Australian troops take Ilimow and Wairopi and advance towards Japanese base of Buna, 40 miles away in northeastern New Guinea, while American troops close in from south .... In a worldwide broadcast, FDR praises Filipino effort, and expresses confidence that the Japanese will be driven from the islands.		

A	B	C	D	E
Includes developments that affect more than one world region, international organizations and important meetings of major world leaders.	*Includes all developments in European countries and military engagements between Allied and Axis powers in Africa and at sea.*	*Includes all developments in Japan and China, Japanese foreign policy and military actions in the Pacific region.*	*Includes all domestic and regional developments in Latin America, the Caribbean and Canada.*	*Includes developments in those independent nations and colonial possessions not covered in Columns B, C and D.*

U.S. Politics & Social Issues	U.S. Foreign Policy & Defense	U.S. Economy & Environment	Science, Technology & Nature	Culture, Leisure & Life Style	
				OWI and FCC announce U.S. government has seized radio station WRUL in Boston after negotiations for leasing facilities failed.	Nov. 8
In his first case as a lawyer before the Supreme Court, Willkie defends California CP leader William Schneiderman against lower court ruling cancelling his naturalization papers.	In reacting to Vichy's break in diplomatic relations, FDR says of Laval's act that "no act of Hitler, or any of his puppets, can sever relations" between the French and American people.	Supreme Court upholds constitutionality of 1941 congressional act penalizing farmers 49 cents a bushel for all wheat grown in excess of their marketing quotas.		Stage and screen character comedienne Edna May Oliver dies in Hollywood.	Nov. 9
	House ratifies conference agreement on lowering draft age to 18 . . . . FDR estimates U.S. armed forces will total 9.7 million men by end of 1943.	FDR releases report of War Manpower Commission's Management-Labor Policy Comm., opposing legislation to draft labor and calling for greater cooperation between labor and management.			Nov. 10
		Federal Shipbuilding and Drydock Co. sets new record by launching four destroyers, two at a time, within 50 miles at Kearny and Port Newark, N.J.		*And Keep Your Powder Dry: An Anthropologist Looks at America*, by Margaret Mead, is published.	Nov. 11
Joseph H. Smyth, Walker G. Matheson and Irvine H. Williams are each sentenced to seven years in prison by Judge Marcus B. Campbell for acting as unregistered Japanese agents.	By voice vote, Senate approves conference-approved draft bill lowering draft age to 18 and sends it to FDR.	Sen. Truman's special Senate Investigating Comm. recommends basic 48-hour work week with appropriate overtime pay for war industries . . . . Petroleum Coordinator Harold Ickes asks WPB to reduce crude oil allotments to 17 Eastern states by 11% to compensate for Allied demand in North Africa.			Nov. 12
	FDR orders immediate shipment of weapons, supplies and food through Lend-Lease to civilians of North Africa occupied by Allied forces.	James F. Byrnes outlines program whereby all Americans will be able to acquire life's essentials and asks that WPB promote "simplification and standardization" of production and distribution . . . . Pacific Bridge Co.'s shipyard in Alameda, Calif. launches 4,000-ton freighter *Samuel Very* three days, 8½ hours after the keel was laid . . . . Philip Murray is reelected president and James B. Carey secretary-treasurer of CIO at a convention in Boston.		Eudora Welty wins the $300 O. Henry Memorial prize for her short story "The Wide Net," published by *Harper's Magazine* . . . . World lightweight champion Sammy Angott announces his retirement from the ring due to injuries.	Nov. 13
Chicago federal jury finds six German-Americans guilty of treason for aiding and sheltering Herbert Hans Haupt, Nazi sabotuer executed Aug. 8.	Navy announces Eddie Rickenbacker and two fellow crew members missing at sea since Oct. 21 have been found in a rubber raft 600 miles north of Somoa.				Nov. 14
					Nov. 15
F	G	H	I	J	
Includes elections, federal-state relations, civil rights and liberties, crime, the judiciary, education, health care, poverty, urban affairs and population.	*Includes formation and debate of U.S. foreign and defense policies, veterans affairs and defense spending. (Relations with specific foreign countries are usually found under the region concerned.)*	*Includes business, labor, agriculture, taxation, transportation, consumer affairs, monetary and fiscal policy, natural resources, pollution and accidents.*	*Includes worldwide scientific, medical and technological developments, natural phenomena, U.S. weather and natural disasters.*	*Includes the arts, religion, scholarship, communications media, sports, entertainment, fashions, fads and social life.*	

	World Affairs	European War Zone	Pacific War Zone	The Americas	Other Countries & Territories
Nov. 16		British forces and U.S. armored columns continue to move towards Tunis unopposed . . . . Gen. de Gaulle refuses to deal with Adm. Darlan in North Africa, charging him with being "the No. 2 traitor of France." . . . . British take Martuba, 15 miles southeast of Derna in Libya.	American and Australian troops link up at Kumusi River and are moving in to attack Japanese base at Buna.		
Nov. 17	FDR says "the turning point of the war has at last been reached," but victory is still a way off.	British occupy Derna on Mediterranean coast and Mikili, 50 miles south, and are advancing toward Bengazi, 130 miles westward . . . . Pres. Roosevelt calls for recognition of Admiral Darlan as head of French North African possessions "a temporary expedient" designed to save lives . . . . Gen. Francisco Franco decrees partial mobilization of Spain's military branches "to assure maintenance of peace in our territories." . . . . German troops break into outskirts of populated area on Volkhov front and advance slightly in Stalingrad fighting.			
Nov. 18		British drive to within 70 miles of Bengazi, Libya, while main Axis force continues its retreat towards El Agheila . . . . U.S., British and French troops enter Tunisia from several points . . . . Marshal Petain appoints Pierre Laval dictator of Nazi-occupied France . . . . Moscow claims Germans have lost 1,000 to 4,000 men daily in their three-week offensive at Stalingrad.		Argentine Interior Min. Miguel Culaciati instructs governments of all provinces to prevent dissemination of totalitarian propaganda by Axis agents . . . . U.S. and Mexico agree they will jointly rehabilitate key lines of the Mexican National Railways to facilitate transportation of war materials.	
Nov. 19		British overtake fleeing Axis forces south of Bengazi . . . . Marshal Petain broadcasts appeal from Vichy for French officers in North Africa not to obey Darlan and Giraud but to "resist Anglo-Saxon aggression." . . . . Amidst reports of mobilizing one million men, Gen. Franco warns both Allies and Axis not to seize any Spanish military bases. If one side does, he says he will call for help from the other . . . . Russian forces take an estimated 5,000 prisoners and large quantity of supplies at approaches to Orjonikidze in central Caucasus.		Mexico and Russia resume diplomatic relations.	
Nov. 20		Laval says in Vichy broadcast that Germany will win war and that if Allies win, "we would have to submit to domination of Communists and Jews." . . . . Allied troops claim to drive back Nazi mechanized columns in their first engagement in Tunisia . . . . Rumanian government bans Christian Science activities as "contrary to the interests of the Rumanian state."	U.S. Flying Fortresses sink Japanese cruiser and one destroyer and damage a third ship trying to land troops off Gona . . . . Largest U.S. formation of planes to operate from an Indian air base bombs Japanese-held railway center of Mandalay, Burma.	The 1,671-mile Alcan Highway is formally opened in ceremonies held at Kluane Lake, Yukon Territory, Canada . . . . Argentine Interior Ministry suppresses Fascist, Nazi and Communist propaganda.	
Nov. 21		Russia begins a large offensive supported by tanks south of Stalingrad and on the Kalmuck Steppe . . . . While British armored units continue to repulse German attacks in Tunisia, U.S. Flying Fortresses bomb Tunis . . . . Several hundred RAF bombers attack Turin in heaviest raid on any Italian city in the war so far . . . . Leopold Anthony Johann Sigmund, Count von Berchtold, 79, Austrian minister of foreign affairs who drafted ultimatum to Serbia in 1914 which led to WW 1, dies in Hungary.			Gen. James Barry Munnik Hertzog, 76, prime minister of Union of South Africa from 1924 to 1939 who recently became a supporter of Nazism, dies in Pretoria . . . . Premier of Iraq, Gen. Pasha Nuri es Said, writes FDR that people of the Near East and North Africa are grateful for U.S. actions in North Africa . . . . Indian Liberal leader Sir Tej Bahadur Sapru says situation in India is worsening due to British actions.
Nov. 22		Russians capture Don River stronghold of Kalach in their winter offensive northwest and southwest of Stalingrad . . . . Sir Stafford Cripps relinquishes his posts as Lord Privy Seal in British war cabinet and leader of the House of Commons to become minister of aircraft production.	U.S. planes raid Haiphong, major Japanese base in Indochina.		
Nov. 23		Russia claims that in its five-day Stalingrad offensive 24,000 German prisoners have been taken and 26,000 slain . . . . Adm. Darlan announces over Algiers radio that French West Africa, including the port of Dakar, has placed itself completely under his command.		Hull announces agreement with Martinique ensuring American security in French Caribbean possessions and providing for continued immobilization of French planes and ships at Fort de France . . . . FDR greets Ecuadorian Pres. Carlos Arroyo del Rio on a visit to Washington.	

A	B	C	D	E
Includes developments that affect more than one world region, international organizations and important meetings of major world leaders.	*Includes all developments in European countries and military engagements between Allied and Axis powers in Africa and at sea.*	*Includes all developments in Japan and China, Japanese foreign policy and military actions in the Pacific region.*	*Includes all domestic and regional developments in Latin America, the Caribbean and Canada.*	*Includes developments in those independent nations and colonial possessions not covered in Columns B, C and D.*

U.S. Politics & Social Issues	U.S. Foreign Policy & Defense	U.S. Economy & Environment	Science, Technology & Nature	Culture, Leisure & Life Style	
	Wendell Willkie calls for frank discussion among all Allied peoples concerning war aims and scores State Dept.'s collaboration with Vichy.			Twentieth Century Fox buys Maxwell Anderson's current Broadway play *The Eve of St. Mark* for $300,000.	Nov. 16
	U.S. Army officials announce expanding Army Air Forces Technical Training Command will make barracks out of more than 300 hotels in Miami Beach and Surfside, Fla. . . . . Mrs. Eleanor Roosevelt returns to Washington from her tour of England.	OPA announces as of Dec. 1 the "A" sticker will enable holder to three, instead of the current four gallons of gasoline weekly.			Nov. 17
	House Ways and Means Comm. rejects FDR's request for wartime powers to suspend trade laws which hamper war effort . . . . A N.Y. federal jury declares German-born U.S. citizen Anthony Cramer guilty of treason for having aided Werner Thiel, Nazi saboteur executed Aug. 8.			Thornton Wilder's *The Skin of Our Teeth* opens in New York.	Nov. 18
		NLRB charges that three of Kaiser Co.'s West Coast shipyards made illegal closed shop contracts with AFL unions which excluded CIO . . . . Montgomery Ward Pres. Sewell Avery says company will comply with NWLB order to include membership and dues checkoff in its contract with CIO . . . . A hundred Western congressmen authorize drafting of legislation to postpone nationwide gasoline rationing, scheduled to begin Dec. 1 . . . . Justice Dept. charges Bendix Aviation Corp. conspired with German, Italian, Japanese and other foreign governments to divide world markets and fix prices of aviation equipment dating from 1935.			Nov. 19
	FDR nominates Vice Adm. William F. Halsey to be the Navy's fifth full admiral . . . . Vice Admiral R.R. Waesche, commandant of Coast Guard, accepts "Spars" as name for Woman's Auxiliary Reserve in Coast Guard . . . . Lt. Gen. John A. Lejeune, 75, commander of the 2nd Division composed of Army and Marine troops in WW 1, dies in Baltimore.	An Atlanta federal grand jury indicts five southeastern insurance companies on a charge of conspiracy to suppress competition and fix non-competitive premium rates in six Southern states.		Willie Pep wins recognition by N.Y. State Athletic Commission as world featherweight champion when he outpoints Chalky Wright in N.Y.	Nov. 20
	House Ways and Means Comm. approves bill granting FDR power to suspend laws hampering "free movement of persons, property and information" to and from U.S. but restricting immigration of aliens to those necessary for the war effort . . . . FDR appoints N.Y. Gov. Herbert H. Lehman director of foreign relief and rehabilitation to furnish aid to war victims in areas reoccupied by U.N. forces.				Nov. 21
			Petroleum Industry War Council Chmn. William R. Boyd Jr. says tubeless tires have been successfully tested.		Nov. 22
Senate rejects motion to impose cloture on debate on the anti-poll tax bill, ending consideration of the measure.				Metropolitan Opera opens its 60th season with Donizetti's *Daughter of the Regiment*, staring Lily Pons.	Nov. 23

F	G	H	I	J
Includes elections, federal-state relations, civil rights and liberties, crime, the judiciary, education, health care, poverty, urban affairs and population.	*Includes formation and debate of U.S. foreign and defense policies, veterans affairs and defense spending. (Relations with specific foreign countries are usually found under the region concerned.)*	*Includes business, labor, agriculture, taxation, transportation, consumer affairs, monetary and fiscal policy, natural resources, pollution and accidents.*	*Includes worldwide scientific, medical and technological developments, natural phenomena, U.S. weather and natural disasters.*	*Includes the arts, religion, scholarship, communications media, sports, entertainment, fashions, fads and social life.*

	World Affairs	European War Zone	Pacific War Zone	The Americas	Other Countries & Territories
Nov. 24		Dr. Stephen S. Wise, World Jewish Congress chairman, says in Washington that half of Europe's 4,000,000 Jews have been slain this year by the Nazis, and that Hitler has ordered extermination of all Jews in German-dominated territory by year's end .... Russians claim Germans are retreating so fast they are leaving their Rumanian allies behind along with undamaged tanks and planes .... British forces capture Agedabia and occupy Gialo Oasis, while the main Axis force falls back another 70 miles to El Agheila.	Navy Secy. Knox says in Washington that the U.S. air and sea patrol of Guadalcanal makes it "very unlikely" Japanese on the island can be reinforced or resupplied.		
Nov. 25		Charles de Gaulle halts his broadcasts to the French people from London for as long as Darlan is recognized by the Allies as the leader of the French in North Africa .... Moscow claims an additional 6,000 Germans were killed today and another 15,000 prisoners taken in the Russian Stalingrad offensive.		Addressing the U.S. Senate, Ecuadorian Pres. Arroyo del Rio says his country is doing all it can to facilitate an Allied victory .... Bolivian Pres. Enrique Penaranda del Castillo announces a new cabinet which includes representatives of Liberal and Republican-Socialist parties.	Sultan of Morocco Sidi Mohommed says in message to FDR that Morocco "has no disagreement" with the U.S.
Nov. 26		British drive Germans from Medjez el Bab, 30 miles southwest of Tunis .... Russians claim to have retaken several towns on northwestern Stalingrad front, including Krasnoye Selo and Generalov on Don River bend.	Allied bombers sink two Japanese destroyers and heavily damage a third, all apparently loaded with reinforcements, 150 miles north of the Buna-Gona area, where bitter hand-to-hand fighting enters its 13th day .... Nine U.S. bombers fly 1,500 miles round trip to bomb Japanese-held oil refinery at Bangkok in first American attack on Thailand.	Chmn. Thomas Lamont of International Comm. of Bankers on Mexico announces agreement with Mexico whereby the committee will resume service on Mexico's external debt of $236 million.	
Nov. 27		Main part of French fleet at Toulon, consisting of 60 warships, is scuttled or blown up to prevent seizure by Germans .... British take Tebourba, 15 miles west of Tunis, while another column drives to Mateur, 25 miles south of Bizerte .... Vice Premier Stanislaw Mikolajczyk reports to Polish National Council in London that Nazis seek to exterminate all Jews in Poland now and "kill all Poles tomorrow."	Despite heavy ship losses since Nov. 1, Japanese are reported to have landed shock troops to reinforce their nearly surrounded forces in the Buna-Gona area .... U.S. fliers report downing 23 Japanese planes, sinking two freighters and 100 barges and starting huge fires in an attack on Canton.	Senate approves a $5,000 investigation of economic and social conditions in Puerto Rico after rejecting a proposal that Gov. Rexford Tugwell's administration be investigated .... Mexican Ambassador Dr. Francisco Castillo Najera gives Secy. Hull a check for $2.5 million to pay property claims by U.S. citizens against Mexico .... Colombia and Venezuela end diplomatic relations with Vichy.	
Nov. 28		British submarines sink nine Axis supply ships and damage three others which attempt to cross the Mediterranean from Italy to Africa .... New Russian offensive in Velikiye Luki-Rzhev front northwest of Moscow has reportedly smashed through several points of the German defense line and liberated some 300 villages.			French island of Reunion, 400 miles east of Madagascar in Indian Ocean, is occupied by Free French forces with little resistence.
Nov. 29		Red Army breaks through German defense lines on east bank of Don River northwest of Stalingrad .... In a London broadcast, Churchill warns the Italians that they must choose between an Allied attack from North Africa and a revolt against Mussolini .... British occupy Djedeida on Tunis-Bizerte railroad and aim their guns at Tunis, 12 miles away.		Dr. Juan Jose Amezaga is elected to succeed Gen. Alfredo Baldomir as president of Uruguay for a four-year term.	
Nov. 30		Twin Russian offensives on central and Stalingrad fronts continue amidst snowstorms .... Allied forces drive eastward from Djedeida to split Axis forces holding Tunis and Bizerte .... Italian Socialist manifesto calls for "civil disobedience" and urges workers to "sabotage war production."			
Dec. 1	Hull and Canadian Min. Leighton McCarthy agree to series of conferences on postwar economic settlements and reduction of trade barriers with other U.N. members.	Sir William Beveridge, economist and government planner, submits a plan to the House of Commons to abolish want in Great Britain after the war .... Adm. Darlan takes over authority as chief of state in North Africa on grounds that Petain is a prisoner of Nazis at Vichy .... Allied forces repulse German counter-attack at Tebourba, 20 miles west of Tunis .... Stiffening Nazi resistance slows Russian offensives west of Stalingrad and northwest of Moscow.	U.S. Navy frustrates a Japanese attempt to land reinforcements on Guadalcanal, sinking several transports .... U.S. heavy bombers raid Rangoon, Burma and Adaman Islands.		Jewish Nat. Assembly, meeting in Jerusalem, appeals to the U.N. to rescue European Jews threatened with death by Nazis.
	A	B	C	D	E
	Includes developments that affect more than one world region, international organizations and important meetings of major world leaders.	*Includes all developments in European countries and military engagements between Allied and Axis powers in Africa and at sea.*	*Includes all developments in Japan and China, Japanese foreign policy and military actions in the Pacific region.*	*Includes all domestic and regional developments in Latin America, the Caribbean and Canada.*	*Includes developments in those independent nations and colonial possessions not covered in Columns B, C and D.*

U.S. Politics & Social Issues	U.S. Foreign Policy & Defense	U.S. Economy & Environment	Science, Technology & Nature	Culture, Leisure & Life Style	
Richard Julius Krebs (Jan Valtin), 37, former German Communist and Nazi agent and author of *Out of the Night*, is arrested at his home in Bethel, Conn., by agents of Immigration and Naturalization Service and sent to Ellis Island.	Three naturalized German citizens, Walter W. Froehling, Otto W. Wergin and Herbert Haupt Sr., who aided executed Nazi saboteur Herbert Hans Haupt are sentenced to death by Judge William J. Campbell in Chicago.				Nov. 24
				Boston Symphony Orchestra (the only non-union major symphony) signs agreement with AFL Federation of Musicians.	Nov. 25
		FDR orders nationwide gasoline rationing effective Dec. 1, as scheduled, in order to save rubber.	Formation of the Engineering College Research Assn. to coordinate the war research activities of 73 engineering schools is announced in N.Y.		Nov. 26
	House Ways and Means Comm. fails to act on bill granting FDR power to suspend trade and immigration laws. Sen. Alben Barkley (D. Ky.) indicates Senate will not discuss the bill until House passes it.				Nov. 27
		OWI says 4,000,000 women are now in war industry.	International Harvester Co. Pres. Fowler McCormick announces development of mechanical cotton-picker which does the work of 50 to 80 handpickers . . . . *AMA* Journal reports albumin in human blood can be injected or transfused in a highly concentrated form, providing an effective method for relieving shock.	Fire in Coconut Grove, Boston night club, kills 491 in nation's worst fire disaster since 1903.	Nov. 28
Committee of federal judges recommends to Judicial Conference of Senior Circuit Judges of the U.S. that women be required to serve on all federal juries . . . . History teachers from 25 California junior colleges recommend all U.S. colleges require a U.S. history course for graduation.					Nov. 29
		Economic Stabilization Dir. Byrnes lifts ceiling on agricultural wages and issues order transferring control of farm labor pay rates under $2,400-a-year to Agriculture Secy. Wickard.		Bill Terry announces his resignation as general manager of New York Giants' farm system.	Nov. 30
U.S. Office of Education reports college and university enrollment has dropped 13.7% since October and predicts a sharper drop when 18-19 year olds are drafted.		Nationwide gas rationing begins . . . . Roosevelt says the question of limiting income from sources other than salaries to $25,000 after taxes must be decided by Congress . . . . War Manpower Commission Chmn. Paul V. McNutt reports WMC and Agriculture Dept. are preparing a plan to ensure adequate agricultural labor in 1943.			Dec. 1
F *Includes elections, federal-state relations, civil rights and liberties, crime, the judiciary, education, health care, poverty, urban affairs and population.*	G *Includes formation and debate of U.S. foreign and defense policies, veterans affairs and defense spending. (Relations with specific foreign countries are usually found under the region concerned.)*	H *Includes business, labor, agriculture, taxation, transportation, consumer affairs, monetary and fiscal policy, natural resources, pollution and accidents.*	I *Includes worldwide scientific, medical and technological developments, natural phenomena, U.S. weather and natural disasters.*	J *Includes the arts, religion, scholarship, communications media, sports, entertainment, fashions, fads and social life.*	

	World Affairs	European War Zone	Pacific War Zone	The Americas	Other Countries & Territories
Dec. 2	Speaking in N.Y., Canadian P.M. Mackenzie King pleads for a world order based on human rights and not on "rights of property, privilege or position."	In an 80-minute address to Italian people, Mussolini says that "in the end victory can not fail but come to the Axis," and calls FDR a "hyena."	Allied planes shoot down 23 Japanese Zeros and drive off a naval convoy attempting to reinforce their trapped forces at Buna . . . . In a Tokyo broadcast, Japanese Army claims the mopping-up operation in the Philippines has been completed.	Four Axis spies receive 14-year prison terms for espionage and propaganda in Brazil.	
Dec. 3		Foreign Secy. Eden tells the House of Commons Britain is not bound to support Adm. Darlan, whose assumption of new powers was a "unilateral inspiration of himself." . . . . Germans recapture Tebourba, 20 miles west of Tunis, and still hold Mateur and part of Djedeida.	American planes sink a Japanese warship and set another afire in an attack on 10 warships 150 miles northwest of and headed for Guadalcanal.		U.S. and Liberia agree to a defense pact, giving U.S. full control of airports and defense areas.
Dec. 4		U.S. bombers raid Naples in their first attack on Italy proper in the war . . . . Russian troops continue to retake villages in their Stalingrad offensive . . . . Swiss reports say either Gestapo or Vichy French government has imprisoned Edouard Herriot, former premier and speaker of Chamber of Deputies.	In a surprise attack on Japanese-held Kupang in Timor, Allied planes destroy 21 enemy planes on the ground.	Canadian P.M. Mackenzie King arrives at the White House to confer with FDR on war and postwar cooperation . . . . Argentine government prosecutor prefers formal charges of espionage against unnamed members of German embassy, who are interned to await trial . . . . Senate approves joint resolution authorizing transfer of land in Panama City and Colon to Panama and canceling $2.7 million debt in return for bases in defense areas . . . . Ecuadorian Foreign Ministry recalls its diplomatic staff from Vichy.	Joint resolution signed by 63 Senators and 181 Representatives calling for a national Jewish home in Palestine is sent to FDR.
Dec. 5		Allied North African headquarters, confirming that German mechanized and infantry units have entered Tebourba, reports they are now attacking with infantry supported by tanks and dive bombers.	Navy Dept. reveals for first time the extent of losses after Japan's Pearl Harbor attack, which left Hawaii virtually helpless: 10 ships sunk or damaged greatly; 247 of 475 planes destroyed or disabled; and 4,575 casualties, including 2,117 dead.		
Dec. 6	Under State Secy. Welles says that an association of free peoples at the war's end will be essential to the future security of the U.S.	Allied planes attack France and the Netherlands in one of the biggest daylight raids of the war . . . . German counter-attacks are made northwest and southwest of Stalingrad and west of Rzhev on the central front.	Japanese Foreign Min. Masayuki Tani says Japan must aim at the "annihilation of America" which is essential to creation of the Greater East Asia sphere . . . . U.S. Marine raiders destroy five Japanese bases and kill about 400 enemy soldiers in the mountainous jungle of Guadalcanal.		
Dec. 7		French Delegate General Gen. Georges Catroux says in London that Darlan is a menace to Allies and urges Washington to sever ties with him . . . . Allied planes attack Tunisian points, while Axis planes attack Bone and Philippeville.	In a Tokyo broadcast, government spokesmen announce Japan's losses during first year of the war: 40 warships, 65 merchant ships and 556 aircraft lost and 21,166 killed . . . . Japanese naval force attempting to land reinforcements for fifth time on New Guinea is routed by heavy Allied bombers . . . . Allied planes shoot down Japanese fighters attempting to attack Allied rear positions in Buna-Gona area. Allied troops penetrate to the beach east of Buna village . . . . Maj. Gen. Alexander A. Vandegrift says about 6,640 Japanese have been killed on Guadalcanal since the Marines landed Aug. 7.		
Dec. 8		Although slowed by German counter-offensives and winter weather, Russian offensives continue southwest of Stalingrad and on the central front . . . . British House of Commons passes bill lowering draft age from 18½ to 18 years of age . . . . Gen. Franco states that the liberal world is going down, a victim of its own errors, and with it are disappearing capitalism and mass unemployment.		Cuban Pres. Fulgencio Batista arrives in Washington to discuss Cuba's war effort with FDR.	
Dec. 9		Rain slows up ground fighting but air activity continues in Tunisia and Libya . . . . French West African Gov. Gen. Boisson pledges the support of Dakar to Allied cause against Germany . . . . Most Rev. Cyril F. Garbett, Archbishop of York, demands in House of Lords that British government "deal out" retribution for deaths of Polish Jews.			
	A	B	C	D	E
	Includes developments that affect more than one world region, international organizations and important meetings of major world leaders.	*Includes all developments in European countries and military engagements between Allied and Axis powers in Africa and at sea.*	*Includes all developments in Japan and China, Japanese foreign policy and military actions in the Pacific region.*	*Includes all domestic and regional developments in Latin America, the Caribbean and Canada.*	*Includes developments in those independent nations and colonial possessions not covered in Columns B, C and D.*

U.S. Politics & Social Issues	U.S. Foreign Policy & Defense	U.S. Economy & Environment	Science, Technology & Nature	Culture, Leisure & Life Style	
N.Y. Gov. Lehman resigns his post to become director of foreign relief and rehabilitation; Lt. Gov. Charles Poletti will serve as acting governor until the inauguration of Thomas E. Dewey on Jan. 1 .... German-born Anthony Cramer, convicted Nov. 18 of treason, is sentenced to a 45-year prison term and fined $10,000 by federal Judge Henry W. Goddard in N.Y.	Republic Aviation Corp. announces the new U.S. P-47 (Thunderbolt) reaches a speed of 725 mph in complete power dives from 35,000 feet.		A Lake Eire storm sinks the 94-ton tug *Admiral* near Cleveland, drowning her crew of 14.	*Variety* reports most popular songs are: (1) *White Christmas*, (2) *Praise the Lord and Pass the Ammunition*, (3) *When the Lights go on Again*, (4) *Mr. Five by Five* and (5) *Dearly Beloved*.	Dec. 2
		House unanimously passes bill forcing government to include farm labor costs in its parity levels, and sends it to Senate.		Judge Owen W. Bohan bans further performances of the N.Y. play *Wine, Women and Song*, after a jury finds it to be an indecent performance.	Dec. 3
		FDR orders the liquidation of WPA as of Feb. 1, 1943 or as soon thereafter as feasible because of rising war employment .... Navy Secy. Knox and WPB Chmn. Nelson announce a full agreement to end a long-standing dispute between them, which gives the WPB vice chairman full control over scheduling of all arms output and production of aircraft, radio and detection equipment and escort vessels.			Dec. 4
Atty. Gen. Biddle reports that since Pearl Harbor 12,071 aliens have been arrested with 3,646 interned .... FDR signs an executive order giving WMC Chmn. McNutt full control over all government manpower operations, including the Selective Service System.		OWI reports 1942 war production will total $47 billion, including 49,000 planes, 32,000 tanks and 8.2 million tons of merchant shipping .... Senate Agriculture Comm. approves House bill to force inclusion of farm labor costs in parity formula.		Willie Mosconi regains pocket billiard championship by winning nine of ten matches in national tournament played in Detroit.	Dec. 5
Called under martial law, U.S. soldiers fire at pro-Axis mob in Japanese relocation center at Manzanar, Calif., killing one person and wounding nine. The anti-American group Kibei had called a Pearl Harbor anniversary rally the night before.	U.S. aircraft carrier *Belleau Wood* is launched at Camden, N.J., the fifth since Pearl Harbor.	FDR appoints Agriculture Secy. Wickard national food administrator with full responsibility for nation's food supply, including production and distribution.		Major 1942 conference football champions include: Western, Ohio State; Southwest, Texas; Big Six, Missouri; Southern, Georgia; and Big Seven, Colorado.	Dec. 6
Governor-elect Orland S. Loomis, 49, of Wisconsin dies in Madison .... GOP National Comm. elects Harrison E. Spangler as its chairman to replace Joseph Martin, who resigned.	Battleship *New Jersey*, 25,000-ton aircraft carrier *Bunker Hill* and 14 other Navy ships are launched throughout the nation.			American painters, sculptors and printmakers receive $52,000 in prizes at opening of Artists for Victory Exhibition at the Metropolitan Museum of Art, N.Y. .... American historian Gustavus Myers, 70, author of *History of the Great American Fortunes*, dies in New York.	Dec. 7
			Albert Kahn, architect and engineer who revolutionized construction of industrial plants, dies in Detroit.		Dec. 8
Sen. Frederick Van Nuys (D, Ind.) charges Censorship Dir. Byron Price has been illegally censoring mail between the U.S and its territories.		Justice Dept. charges in Trenton, N.J. that 10 companies are guilty of monopolistic practices in the flourescent lighting industry.		Green Bay Packer back Cecil Isbell wins the NFL forward passing championship with 146 completions out of 268 attempts for 2,021 yards and 24 touchdowns.	Dec. 9

F	G	H	I	J
Includes elections, federal-state relations, civil rights and liberties, crime, the judiciary, education, health care, poverty, urban affairs and population.	*Includes formation and debate of U.S. foreign and defense policies, veterans affairs and defense spending. (Relations with specific foreign countries are usually found under the region concerned.)*	*Includes business, labor, agriculture, taxation, transportation, consumer affairs, monetary and fiscal policy, natural resources, pollution and accidents.*	*Includes worldwide scientific, medical and technological developments, natural phenomena, U.S. weather and natural disasters.*	*Includes the arts, religion, scholarship, communications media, sports, entertainment, fashions, fads and social life.*

	World Affairs	European War Zone	Pacific War Zone	The Americas	Other Countries & Territories
Dec. 10		Hitler shakes up his high command, appointing younger and lesser known men: Gen. Kurt Zeitzler to be chief of the army general staff; Col. Gen. Hans Jesschonnek as chief of the air force general staff; and Adm. Kurt Fricke as chief of the naval general staff .... British Foreign Office announces about 1,400 German prisoners "shackled" in October in reprisal for similar German action, will be "unshackled" Dec. 12 .... German forces spearheaded by 60 tanks attack the Russian lines between Rzhev and Velikiye Luki and make a slight advance.	Allied forces complete the occupation of Gona, New Guinea.		
Dec. 11		Montgomery's 8th Army begins a new drive against the Axis line at El Agheila after a three-week lull. Two German columns supported by infantry are repulsed in drives on Medjez el Bab, 28 miles southwest of Tunis.	U.S. dive bombers score two hits on 11 Japanese destroyers headed for Guadalcanal .... U.S. bombers hit a Japanese ship off Kiska and strafe shore installations .... U.S. heavy bombers hit Japanese installations at Rangoon, Burma and Port Blair in Andaman Islands.	Canadian National Party elects John Bracken as leader and changes the party's name to Progressive-Conservative Party.	
Dec. 12		Soviets claim that 169,000 German soldiers have been killed and 74,500 taken prisoner in the Russian offensive around Stalingrad.		One hundred are killed and 104 injured when fire sweeps Knights of Columbus Hostel in St. John's, Newfoundland during a servicemen's dance.	
Dec. 13		U.S. planes sink ship and start fires in heavy raids on the three main Tunisian ports of Bizerte, Tunis, and Sousse.	Chinese claim to repulse Japanese forces attempting to cross Salween River from the west in Yunnan Province.		
Dec. 14	OWI announces that Britain, Canada and U.S. have formed a joint committee to make recommendations to assure an adequate supply of Allied steel.	Rommel moves back to a position near Buerat, 250 miles west of Mersa Brega, countering a British plan to trap his forces.	Allied troops, mostly American, occupy Buna Village on northeastern New Guinea coast .... U.S. bombers attack Myohaung railroad junction near Mandalay.	Argentine Pres. Castillo decrees an indefinite state of siege under which public discussion of the international situation is banned and press is censored .... Bolivia declares a nationwide state of siege after tin miners strike for a 100% pay increase plus a bonus.	Ethiopia declares war on Germany, Japan, and Italy .... Foreign Secy. Eden and Gen. de Gaulle sign agreement in London whereby Britain turns over the administration of pacified Madagascar to Free French.
Dec. 15		Moscow reports German counterattacks southwest and northwest of Stalingrad and on the central front were repulsed today .... British reports indicate that Rommel's troops in their retreat from El Agheila have mined the roads, hampering British pursuit.	In two days of air attacks on Buin, Bougainville Island and Munda, New Georgia Island, U.S. planes encounter no Japanese resistance.		
Dec. 16		Russians begin their third offensive against Germans west of the Don River between Voronezh and Stalingrad. Russians also score two victories over Nazi forces west of Surovikino, about 80 miles west of Stalingrad, and near Verkhni Kunsky, southwest of Stalingrad .... British column breaks through to Mediterranean at Wadi Matratin, then turns southward, splitting retreating Axis forces in two .... Darlan tells reporters he has no ambitions but to free France and then retire to private life.		Dominican Republic-Haiti boundary commission reaches agreement in Ciudad Trujillo on their nations' frontier dispute .... Five of the six accused German spies in Buenos Aires are released on bail.	Willkie says in a N.Y. speech that British colonial policy is unsatisfactory and leads to a world "half free and half slave."
Dec. 17		Eleven Allied nations and Free French Nat. Comm. denounce Germany's "bestial policy of cold-blooded war extermination" of Jews and call for postwar punishment of those responsible .... U.S. bombers pound Tunis, Gabes and other Axis bases in Tunisia for sixth consecutive day.			
Dec. 18		British Eighth Army takes Nofilia, pursuing fleeing Axis forces toward Sultan, 45 miles west of Nofilia. Some Axis forces break the British trap at Wadi Matratin and join the main retreat westward.	Allied forces capture Cape Endaiadere, east of Buna Village, New Guinea .... Chinese forces retake Yangtze River port of Hoshueh in Hupeh Province .... Atty. Gen. Herbert V. Evatt announces revocation of Australia's ban on CP and its press after Communist central committee agrees to assist in the war effort.	Caribbean Commission Chairmen Sir Frank Arthur Stockdale and Charles W. Taussig agree on tentative formula for economic rehabilatation of British West Indies over the next two years.	
Dec. 19		Inter-Allied Information Comm. states five million European Jews face extermination in Poland .... Hitler confers with German and Italian military commanders and French Premier Laval on war strategy.	British headquarters in New Delhi announces that in the past few days British troops have occupied Maungdaw-Buthidaung area, about 60 miles northwest of Akyab, Burma, without encountering opposition .... Allied headquarters in Australia announces U.S. and Australian planes are now dropping fragmentation bombs via parachute on the Japanese.	Bolivian government announces foiling of Nazi-fostered plot to overthrow the La Paz government using the Revolutionary Party.	
	A	B	C	D	E
	Includes developments that affect more than one world region, international organizations and important meetings of major world leaders.	*Includes all developments in European countries and military engagements between Allied and Axis powers in Africa and at sea.*	*Includes all developments in Japan and China, Japanese foreign policy and military actions in the Pacific region.*	*Includes all domestic and regional developments in Latin America, the Caribbean and Canada.*	*Includes developments in those independent nations and colonial possessions not covered in Columns B, C and D.*

U.S. Politics & Social Issues	U.S. Foreign Policy & Defense	U.S. Economy & Environment	Science, Technology & Nature	Culture, Leisure & Life Style	
	House Ways and Means Comm. agrees to postpone action on second war powers bill, permitting the president to suspend trade and immigration laws until new Congress convenes .... FDR says Ethiopia is now eligible for Lend-Lease aid since it has pledged itself to the U.N. Declaration.		Chemists of Berwind White Coal Mining Co. demonstrate a "colloidal fuel" of 55% fuel oil and 45% pulverized bituminous coal, which they claim gives the same heat as pure fuel oil.	Federal Council of Churches of Christ in America approves a plan in Cleveland for establishment of a North American Council of Churches to include Canada.	Dec. 10
	FDR tells Congress America's expeditionary forces will total one million men by Jan. 1 .... FDR appoints William Phillips as his personal representative to India with rank of ambassador.				Dec. 11
		For second time Pres. Roosevelt directs Montgomery Ward & Co. of Chicago to obey an NWLB order and sign maintenance-of-membership contract with CIO.		Whirlaway with Wendell Eads up wins the $15,000 Louisiana Handicap in New Orleans .... Frederick R. Schroeder and Pauline Betz head annual rankings of U.S. Lawn Tennis Assn.	Dec. 12
				Washington Redskins upset Chicago Bears, 14-6, to win NFL championship.	Dec. 13
				Supreme Court agrees to review the 1941 FCC order barring any company from owning more than one radio network and forbidding exclusive network contracts for affiliated stations.	Dec. 14
		Roosevelt denies Price Admin. Leon Henderson has asked to resign .... Senate and House pass bill extending overtime pay or a 10% bonus to the 1.5 million government workers not previously covered and sends it to FDR.			Dec. 15
77th Congress, which met for a record 711 days from Jan. 3, 1941 through today, finally adjourns.		A long-standing dispute between RFC Administrator Jesse H. Jones and the Board of Economic Warfare over RFC loans for purchases of strategic materials abroad is revealed in the Senate .... OPA virtually suspends sale of oil heaters and reveals plans to ration coal stoves and heaters beginning Dec. 18.		Playwright and author Erskine Caldwell marries 20-year-old June Johnson in Arizona.	Dec. 16
	War Dept. announces plan to contract for facilities of 200 to 300 colleges and universities to train 250,000 men for the armed services .... OWI reports a U.S. economic mission is in North Africa to assit Robert D. Murphy's survey of requirements for non-military supplies.	Price Admin. Leon Henderson resigns due to health reasons. FDR says he will accept the resignation as soon as a successor is found.		OWI announces plans to publish bimonthly magazine *Victory* in several languages to counter Axis propaganda.	Dec. 17
		OPA suspends sale of gasoline to holders of "A" "B" and "C" books in 17 Eastern states except for emergency use.		Nation's sports writers polled by AP choose St. Louis Cardinals as year's outstanding team; Frank Sinkwich, Univ. of Ga. football player, as outstanding male athlete; and swimmer Gloria Callen as best woman athlete .... Beau Jack (Sidney Walker) knocks out Tippy Larkin in third round at N.Y. to win the world's lightweight championship.	Dec. 18
Mrs. Frances Stevens Hall, 68, acquitted in 1926 of a charge of murdering her husband and a choir singer, dies in New Brunswick, N.J.					Dec. 19
F	G	H	I	J	
Includes elections, federal-state relations, civil rights and liberties, crime, the judiciary, education, health care, poverty, urban affairs and population.	*Includes formation and debate of U.S. foreign and defense policies, veterans affairs and defense spending. (Relations with specific foreign countries are usually found under the region concerned.)*	*Includes business, labor, agriculture, taxation, transportation, consumer affairs, monetary and fiscal policy, natural resources, pollution and accidents.*	*Includes worldwide scientific, medical and technological developments, natural phenomena, U.S. weather and natural disasters.*	*Includes the arts, religion, scholarship, communications media, sports, entertainment, fashions, fads and social life.*	

	World Affairs	European War Zone	Pacific War Zone	The Americas	Other Countries & Territories
Dec. 20		Spain and Portugal agree to maintain their neutrality in the current war .... Red Army reportedly drives to within 20 miles of Millerovo on Moscow-Rostov front .... An earthquake in north central Anatolia, Turkey kills 474 and injures 605.		Brazil announces all income tax payers must subscribe to war bond issue starting Jan. 1.	
Dec. 21		Russian troops advance 12-15 miles on Voronezh front, while Germans retreat in disorder, abandoning equipment and supplies on battlefield.	British push 11 miles through the jungle to occupy Alethangyaw, 45 miles from Akyab.	Bolivian Revolutionary Party leader denies his party has any responsibility for the recent plot to overthrow the government.	Ceylon National Congress passes resolution demanding postwar freedom from Britain and asking guarantees from the U.N.
Dec. 22		French forces with Allied air support attack toward Tunisian coast, southeast of Pont du Fahs .... Russian troops continue to pursue Nazi forces in middle of Don sector, liberating several towns including Kamensky, Popovka, Morozovsk, Nikolskoe and Fyodorovka.	While RAF planes attack Akyab, Japanese planes counter with an assault on Calcutta.	U.S. and Brazil sign agreement setting up travel bases for workers being sent to Amazon Valley to increase rubber production.	
Dec. 23		Moscow reports capture of an additional 16,400 German troops and killing of 8,000 more in the offensive on the middle Don River front.	British troops occupy another district just over the Burma border from Bengal Province in their drive into Burma.	Hull and Mexican Amb. Dr. Francisco Castillo Najera sign trade pact in Washington abolishing quota systems on U.S. imports of crude and fuel oils.	
Dec. 24	American Institute of Judaism advocates establishment of a federation of nations with a court of international justice to try war criminals .... FDR sends a Christmas message to all U.N. forces, including the Free French, expressing gratitude for their efforts to bring about peace, freedom and "the advancement of human welfare."	Adm. Darlan is shot in his office at 3 p.m. Later identified as Bonnier de la Chapelle, the assassin belonged to the royalist and Gaullist circle which has been pressing for Darlan's removal.	Allied forces breach Japanese defenses around the Buna Mission on New Guinea .... U.S. planes bomb Japanese airfield and shore installations at Munda on New Georgia Island .... Japanese forces are repulsed in two attempts to retake two positions in the Chin Hills, 100 miles north of Aykab, Burma.		
Dec. 25		French military tribunal convicts de la Chapelle as Darlan's murderer and sentences him to death .... British 8th Army occupies Sirte, 225 miles east of Tripoli, and continues to pursue German troops to the west.	Army bombers from Guadalcanal fly 560 miles to Rabaul, New Britain and score several hits on Japanese cargo ships.		
Dec. 26		Gen. Henri Honore Giraud is elected French high commissioner in Africa by the French Imperial Council in Algiers .... Darlan's assassin is shot to death by firing squad in Algiers .... Russian troops drive to within 105 miles of Rostov on the central Don River front and to within 20 miles of Kotelnikovo, southwest of Stalingrad .... Swedish sources report Germany plans to draft an auxiliary army of more than 2.5 million men the from occupied countries.			
Dec. 27		Soviets continue to advance on the middle Don River front, the Stalingrad front and in the Nalchik area.	Tojo says Allied counter offensives are in progress, and tells Japanese Diet that "the real war is starting now." .... U.S. heavy bombers make night raids on Bangkok, Thailand, hitting the airfield and naval dock area.		
Dec. 28	Speaking with FDR's approval, Henry A. Wallace calls for international postwar cooperation and asks that the U.N. "back up military disarmament with psychological disarmament."	Advancing nearly 16 miles, Soviet forces take towns on both sides of the southern anchor of the Nazis' Stalingrad line .... Vichy radio broadcasts speech by Petain denouncing French African leaders "who have betrayed French Africa to the British and Americans." .... Nevile Henderson, 60, British diplomat and ambassador to Germany from 1937 until the war, dies in London.	In a night attack on Rabaul, New Britain, Allied bombers sink or set fire to four Japanese ships.		
Dec. 29		Russian troops recapture Kotelnikovo, 90 miles southwest of Stalingrad, and occupy Torgovaya, 57 miles southeast of Kotelnikovo.			French Somaliland joins Free French and the U.N. under an agreement signed in Nairobi, Kenya Colony.
	A *Includes developments that affect more than one world region, international organizations and important meetings of major world leaders.*	B *Includes all developments in European countries and military engagements between Allied and Axis powers in Africa and at sea.*	C *Includes all developments in Japan and China, Japanese foreign policy and military actions in the Pacific region.*	D *Includes all domestic and regional developments in Latin America, the Caribbean and Canada.*	E *Includes developments in those independent nations and colonial possessions not covered in Columns B, C and D.*

U.S. Politics & Social Issues	U.S. Foreign Policy & Defense	U.S. Economy & Environment	Science, Technology & Nature	Culture, Leisure & Life Style	
	Eisenhower announces that Robert D. Murphy, his civil affairs administrator, has been raised to rank of minister by FDR.	Treasury Secy. Morgenthau says the December Victory Fund Drive has passed the $9-billion goal and resets the figure at $11 billion.			Dec. 20
Supreme Court rules Nevada divorces are valid and must be recognized by other states .... Supreme Court upsets N.Y. Circuit Court ruling that an accused man cannot waive a jury trial upon advice of his lawyer.			Dr. Fred L. Whipple of Harvard Univ. announces discovery of a new bright comet, which will come within 40 million miles of earth in January.	Dr. Franz Boas, 84, professor emeritus of anthropology at Columbia Univ. and debunker of Nazi race theories, dies in New York.	Dec. 21
					Dec. 22
	Brig. Gen. Claire Chennault is awarded the Distinguished Service Medal.	WPB Chmn. Nelson reports U.S. steel production is at an annual rate of 89 million tons and will rise to 97 million by next summer .... Congressional leaders begin studying a bill drawn up by Granville Clark which would enable the government to order compulsory war work for men 18-65 and women 18-50.			Dec. 23
	A military supply mission for French forces in North Africa, headed by Gen. Emile Bethouart, arrives in Washington.	NWLB orders 18,000 workers of Brewster Aeronautical Corp.'s plants in Long Island City and other plants to stop "slowdown" begun Dec. 18 .... FDR signs bill extending overtime pay to all government employes and asks all departments to establish a six-day, 48-hour work week.		Pope Pius XII in his Christmas message calls for a crusade for a just social order based on the "supreme domination of God."	Dec. 24
				Ring Magazine names Ray Robinson as "fighter of the year." .... In a poll conducted by the *Motion Picture Herald*, the comedy team of Bud Abbott and Lou Costello is voted the leading motion picture box office attraction of 1942 .... National Board of Review of Motion Pictures selects the Noel Coward production *In Which We Serve* as the most important film of the year.	Dec. 25
		Gov. Robert A. Hurley says Connecticut is suffering from a fuel oil shortage due to inadequate transportation .... Sen. Guy M. Gillette (D, Iowa) charges that complacency has caused synthetic rubber production to run behind schedule.	William Slocum Barstow, 76, inventor and associate of Thomas Edison, dies on Long Island, N.Y.	Southern College All-Stars defeat the North, 24 to 0, in fifth annual Blue-Grey game.	Dec. 26
Dr. John E. Wade, New York superintendent of schools, announces a program to counteract rapidly increasing juvenile delinquency and lack of classroom discipline.		Food Admin. Wickard orders Price Admin. Henderson to institute rationing of virtually all canned, dried, frozen and dehydrated vegetables, fruits and soups in February.		NFL All-Stars defeat champion Washington Redskins, 17-14, in Philadelphia.	Dec. 27
		Rubber Dir. William M. Jeffers says the first four government butadiene rubber factories will begin production in January with a potential output of 80,000 tons annually.			Dec. 28
FBI agents account for all seven members of the Touhy gang who escaped from prison Oct. 9.				N.Y. Film Critics select *In Which We Serve* as the top film for 1942, and George M. Cohan and Agnes Moorehead as best actor and actress.	Dec. 29

F	G	H	I	J
Includes elections, federal-state relations, civil rights and liberties, crime, the judiciary, education, health care, poverty, urban affairs and population.	*Includes formation and debate of U.S. foreign and defense policies, veterans affairs and defense spending. (Relations with specific foreign countries are usually found under the region concerned.)*	*Includes business, labor, agriculture, taxation, transportation, consumer affairs, monetary and fiscal policy, natural resources, pollution and accidents.*	*Includes worldwide scientific, medical and technological developments, natural phenomena, U.S. weather and natural disasters.*	*Includes the arts, religion, scholarship, communications media, sports, entertainment, fashions, fads and social life.*

	World Affairs	European War Zone	Pacific War Zone	The Americas	Other Countries & Territories
Dec. 30		Gen. Giraud announces in Algiers arrest of 12 persons for plotting to assassinate high French officials . . . . Parliamentary Colonial Under Secy. Harold Macmillan is named resident minister at Allied headquarters in French North Africa by the British government . . . . Russian troops capture Remontnoe, 40 miles southwest of Elista, Kalmuck provincial capital.		At the request of Pres. Juan Antonio Rios, the Chilean Senate postpones voting on a motion recommending a break with the Axis.	
Dec. 31	Vice Pres. Wallace says an international air force must be built up after the war to guard the peace.	Hitler tells his troops in the order of the day that 1943 "will perhaps be hard, but certainly not harder than last year." . . . . Russians take Oblivskaya, 90 miles west of Stalingrad; and Nizhne-Chirskaya, 30 miles to the east . . . . Gen. Sir Archibald P. Wavell, commander in India, and Gen. Viscount Gort, Malta commander, are made field marshals, the highest rank in British Army.	Allied heavy bombers set two large Japanese ships afire and hit a transport at Rabaul.		

U.S. Politics & Social Issues	U.S. Foreign Policy & Defense	U.S. Economy & Environment	Science, Technology & Nature	Culture, Leisure & Life Style	
N.Y. federal jury convicts four Negro leaders of the Ethiopian Pacific Movement of sedition for advocating a revolt against the U.S..		Henry J. Kaiser opens the Pacific Coast's first integrated iron and steel plant at Fontana, Calif.	A sudden thaw and a three-day storm cause the Mononghahela and Allegheny Rivers to rise above flood levels, closing many plants and driving 5,000 people from their homes.		Dec. 30
				Suffolk County (Mass.) grand jury indicts 10 Boston men on charges stemming from Coconut Grove fire on Nov. 28.	Dec. 31

1943

A Russian soldier flushes two Germans from a Stalingrad building during the death throes of the Nazi 6th Army in January.

Nona Feid, Bambi Linn and Diana Adams dance a scene from *Oklahoma!* at the start of the musical's record-breaking run on Broadway.

A column of Yugoslavian partisans passes through a Bosnian village in late 1943.

Preceding page: Marines advance into a pall of smoke covering the Japanese-held airfield on Tarawa. One of the bloodiest battles of the Pacific war, Tarawa cost the Marines 3,000 casualties in five days.

The first victory celebration: New York's Italian-Americans rejoice on Sept. 8 at news of the U.S.—Italian armistice.

Peasant laborers smooth the runway of a U.S. airfield in China as a Liberator bomber approaches.

Jewish fighters captured after the destruction of the Warsaw Ghetto in May are marched away by SS troops.

The Swedish liner *Gripsholm* enters New York harbor with Americans repatriated from Axis countries. The ship subsequently returned Axis nationals to their homelands from the U.S.

Perched on a ladder, Frank Sinatra happily signs autographs for fans in Pasadena, Calif. on Aug. 11.

Dooley Wilson tries to comfort a distraught Humphrey Bogart after Ingrid Bergman reawakens a painful love affair in *Casablanca*.

The Big Three: FDR, Churchill and Stalin pose for photographers at the Teheran conference in December.

Stamp Out
A
BLACK MARKETS
...WITH YOUR RATION STAMPS
PAY NO MORE THAN LEGAL PRICES

An Office of Price Administration poster urges Americans to adhere to the rationing system.

A U.S. Liberator bomber swoops low over burning Rumanian oil refineries during the raid on Ploesti, Aug. 1.

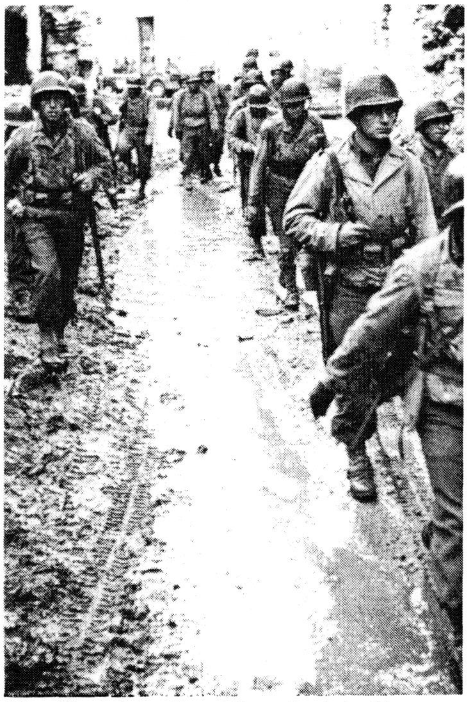

U.S. soldiers advance through the mud and rain of the Italian winter, a scene that became familiar to thousands of GIs in western Europe.

	World Affairs	European War Zone	Pacific War Zone	The Americas	Other Countries & Territories
Jan.	Churchill and FDR discuss Allied war strategy at Casablanca and demand Germany's unconditional surrender.	Soviet forces drive the Germans back in the Caucasus . . . . British and U.S. military leaders complete plans for the invasion of southern Europe.			
Feb.		Russian forces mop up German resistance in Stalingrad and make further progress in the Caucasus . . . . Germans check the American advance toward Tunis at the Kasserine Pass.	U.S. forces complete the occupation of Guadalcanal . . . . Allied forces enter Burma, while the Japanese open offensives in China.	Chile and Brazil move against Axis spies and saboteurs.	Gandhi stirs political unrest in India with another fast.
March	FDR and British Foreign Secy. Anthony Eden confer in Washington on war and postwar problems.	British and U.S. air forces begin a concentrated attack on the Ruhr industrial area . . . . British forces breach the Mareth Line in Tunisia . . . . Germans begin deportation of Greek Jews to Auschwitz.	Chinese forces report victories over the Japanese in Hunan, Hupeh and Yunnan Provinces.	U.S. Vice Pres. Henry A. Wallace tours Latin America, urging postwar cooperation.	
Apr.		British and U.S. forces tighten the ring around German positions in Tunis and Bizerta . . . . Jews of the Warsaw ghetto revolt against the Germans.		FDR meets with Mexican President Avila Camacho at Corpus Christi, Texas.	United States strengthens its ties with Iran and Saudi Arabia.
May	FDR and Churchill hold the "Trident" conference in Washington and agree to a 1944 invasion of France.	British and U.S. forces complete the conquest of Tunisia, forcing the surrender of the Afrika Korps . . . . Germans suppress Jewish resistance in Warsaw.		Political unrest is reported in Cuba, Martinque and Venezuela.	
June			Chinese troops gain several victories along the Yangtze River.		
July		Russians turn back a limited German summer offensive in the Kursk area . . . . Gens. Patton and Montgomery lead an Allied invasion of Sicily.	U.S. forces clear Japanese from the central Solomon Islands.	U.S. concludes economic agreements with several Latin American nations.	
Aug.	Churchill and FDR meet again with their military chiefs in Quebec and agree to target May 1944 for a cross-channel invasion of Europe.	Axis resistance collapses on Sicily . . . . Russian armies begin their summer offensive in White Russia and the Ukraine.	After the capture of New Georgia Island, American forces attack other Japanese positions in the Solomons.		British internment of Gandhi in the palace of the Aga Khan causes further unrest in India.
Sept.		Allied forces invade Italy, forcing the Badaglio government to capitulate. German forces continue to fight in Italy.	Japanese bases at Lae and Salamaua on New Guinea fall to Australian and U.S. forces.		
Oct.	U.S. State Secy. Hull, British Foreign Secy. Eden and Russian Foreign Commissar Molotov meet in Moscow to discuss plans for a second front against Germany and postwar Allied cooperation.	Russian advance reaches the Dnieper River . . . . Germans begin deporting the Jews of Rome to Auschwitz.	Japanese forces win a series of victories in Yunnan Province . . . . Britain's Lord Moutbatten discusses war strategy with Chiang Kai-shek in Chungking . . . . U.S. planes conduct heavy air raids on the Japanese base at Rabaul, New Guinea.	Brazilian and Guatemalan governments seize Axis property.	Famine conditions continue in India, with 2,000 deaths from starvation reported since August in Calcutta.
Nov.	Churchill and FDR meet with Chiang Kai-shek in Cairo to discuss military priorities in Asia and Europe.		Japanese troops open a drive to remove the Chinese threat from the Yangtze River area . . . . U.S. forces invade the Gilbert Islands, taking Tarawa with 3,000 casualties.	Bolivia declares war on the Axis, while Argentine President Ramirez expresses sympathy with the Allied cause.	
Dec.	FDR, Churchill and Stalin discuss European territorial questions and Allied postwar cooperation in Teheran.		Chinese win the battle for Changteh . . . . Americans and Australians continue their island campaigns, landing at Cape Gloucester on New Britain.	New Bolivian revolutionary government nationalizes Axis businesses.	Syrian and Lebanese administrators gain increased authority from the Free French government.

A	B	C	D	E
Includes developments that affect more than one world region, international organizations and important meetings of major world leaders.	*Includes all developments in European countries and military engagements between Allied and Axis powers in Africa and at sea.*	*Includes all developments in Japan and China, Japanese foreign policy and military actions in the Pacific region.*	*Includes all domestic and regional developments in Latin America, the Caribbean and Canada.*	*Includes developments in those independent nations and colonial possessions not covered in Columns B, C and D.*

U.S. Politics & Social Issues	U.S. Foreign Policy & Defense	U.S. Economy & Environment	Science, Technology & Nature	Culture, Leisure & Life Style	
Educational groups question the soundness of shortened high school and college curriculum developed for the war's duration.	Army begins induction of Japanese-Americans willing to "swear unqualified allegiance to the United States."	FDR orders anthracite coal miners back to work after the NWLB fails to mediate their dispute with mine operators.	American, British, Canadian and Norwegian physicians meet to share knowledge on means of dealing with fatigue.	Frank Sinatra's singing popularity spreads rapidly among American teenagers.	Jan.
	FDR promises increased aid to China after meeting with Mme. Chiang Kai-shek in Washington.	WPB and OPA place further restrictions on production and distribution of consumer goods, including foodstuffs.			Feb.
	U.S. Jewish groups begin a campaign for special Administration action to rescue Jews in occupied Europe .... Political debate begins over U.S. participation in a postwar United Nations organization.			Greer Garson and James Cagney win Academy Awards respectively as best actress and actor of the year.	March
Republican Party begins plans for the 1944 presidential election, expressing concern over FDR's reported fourth-term ambitions.		FDR introduces several anti-inflation measures, including price-freezing and restrictions on job mobility.			Apr.
		Federal authorities order coal and rubber workers not to strike as their current contracts expire.	Floods cause heavy damage and death in several Midwestern states.		May
Negro-white riots break out in Detroit, causing 34 deaths, while whites clash with Mexican-Americans in Los Angeles.	Armed Forces Committee on Postwar Educational Opportunities for Service Personnel compiles its first report to the President, urging educational benefits for returning GIs .... Congress completes action on a record military budget.	Government efforts fail to avert a strike of coal miners.		Count Fleet wins the Belmont Stakes, thus capturing racing's famed "triple crown."	June
	Congress begins discussion of postwar benefits for veterans.				July
Racial violence in N.Y. causes six deaths and $5 million in damage.			Anheuser-Busch develops a yeast-based foodstuff, resembling meat but with more protein.		Aug.
Government officials begin to release Japanese-Americans from relocation centers.			American Chemical Society reports the development of "Penicillin B," 10 times more powerful than current penicillin.	Revival of Great Russian nationalism in the Soviet Union results in the crowning of the Archbishop of Moscow as Patriarch of All Russia.	Sept.
Congress begins action to repeal the 1882 Chinese Exclusion Act.		Congress debates the Treasury Department's tax proposals, intended to increase war revenues.	Sulfa drugs are credited with saving numerous lives in army hospitals.		Oct.
Sen. John W. Bricker of Ohio begins campaigning for the 1944 GOP presidential nomination.	Congress debates a proposal to exempt pre-Pearl Harbor fathers from the draft, agreeing on a compromise measure which places them at the bottom of the draft list.	U.S. war production peaks at a monthly rate of $6 billion.			Nov.
		Federal government takes over the nation's railroads in the face of a union strike.			Dec.

F	G	H	I	J
Includes elections, federal-state relations, civil rights and liberties, crime, the judiciary, education, health care, poverty, urban affairs and population.	*Includes formation and debate of U.S. foreign and defense policies, veterans affairs and defense spending. (Relations with specific foreign countries are usually found under the region concerned.)*	*Includes business, labor, agriculture, taxation, transportation, consumer affairs, monetary and fiscal policy, natural resources, pollution and accidents.*	*Includes worldwide scientific, medical and technological developments, natural phenomena, U.S. weather and natural disasters.*	*Includes the arts, religion, scholarship, communications media, sports, entertainment, fashions, fads and social life.*

	World Affairs	European War Zone	Pacific War Zone	The Americas	Other Countries & Territories
Jan. 1	On the first anniversary of the U.N. pact, FDR calls for the "supreme necessity of planning what is to come after" the war.	Soviet forces capture Velikiye Luki, northwest of Moscow, and Elista, captial of Kalmuck Republic, 170 miles south of Stalingrad.		Dr. Afranio de Mello Franco, former judge on the International Court of Justice at the Hague, twice acting president of the League of Nations and Brazilian foreign minister, dies at 72 in Rio de Janeiro.	
Jan. 2	Wendell L. Willkie says in a Washington broadcast that the U.N. must become a common council not only for the war effort but for postwar economic cooperation.	Gen. Charles de Gaulle suggests to Gen. Henri Giraud that "we meet immediately on French soil in order to study the means of attaining" unity among the French forces fighting the Axis .... Red Army drives to within 60 miles of the Latvian border .... A new Yugoslav cabinet is announced with Slobodan Yovanovich as premier and minister of interior and foreign affairs.			
Jan. 3		Russian troops recapture key rail city of Mozdok, 60 miles northwest of the Grozny oil center, and Malgobek, some 15 miles southeast of Mozdok .... British Air Ministry reports the RAF shot down 738 German planes over the British Isles and the Continent in 1942, while losing 593 of its own aircraft.	Allied troops reportedly "break the back" of enemy troops in the Buna area.	Sen. Arthur Vandenburg (R,Mich.) says Puerto Rican Gov. Rexford Tugwell is swiftly expanding his bureaucracy and it should be curtailed.	
Jan. 4		Russians recapture German airbase of Chernishkovsky and the railway station of Chernishkov, 100 miles west of Stalingrad.	U.S. troops attack Japanese on Guadalcanal and gain high ground near Mount Aesten..... Australian-American forces complete the destruction of Japanese forces in the Buna Mission area.	Panama National Assembly votes to continue Pres. Ricardo Adolfo de la Guardia in office for the next two years.	
Jan. 5		British troops capture Djebel Azzag and other points 15 miles west of Mateur in Tunisia .... Russians take six more towns, including Nalchik, in the central Caucasus. .... Allied North African headquarters announces the activation of the U.S. 5th Army under Lt. Gen. Mark W. Clark.	Allied bombers destroy nine Japanese ships at Rabaul, New Britain, including a destroyer tender and a destroyer.		
Jan. 6		A threatened revolt against Ion Antonescu's government is crushed with the arrest of Iron Guard leaders throughout Rumania.		Mexico reports that increased production of farm products in 1942 makes the nation self-sufficient in all major crops except wheat.	
Jan. 7	In his State of the Union message, FDR says U.N. Allies must remain united after the war to maintain peace .... Gov. Harold E. Stassen (R, Minn.) proposes the U.N. be continued after the war with a single-house parliament and with representation based upon literate populations.	In an offensive converging on Rostov, the Russians capture 16 more towns in the lower Don sector and five more in the northern Caucasus .... Allied planes bomb Gabes and Kairouan in Tunisia and Palermo Harbor and Licata in Sicily.	Allied bombers sink two troop transports and down 18 Japanese fighters in repeated attacks on a 10-ship convoy approaching Lae in Huon Gulf.	Peru announces its adherence to the U.N. declaration invalidating Axis seizure of property in occupied countries .... Sen. Arthur Vandenburg introduces a bill to terminate Gov. Tugwell's tenure in Puerto Rico and fixing two-year terms for future governors.	
Jan. 8		Russians recapture some 24 more towns and villages in the Don, Stalingrad and Caucasus sectors.	Allied bombers sink a third Japanese transport and destroy 24 enemy planes in their attacks on the Japanese convoy at Lae .... Allies claim the Japanese force of about 15,000 men which tried to seize Southeastern New Guinea from Buna has been annihilated except for a remnant surrounded at Sanananda Point .... Chinese recapture the provisional Anhwei Province capital of Lihuang.	Bermuda Assembly repeals the ban on general use of automobiles on the island which had been in effect since cars were invented.	
Jan. 9		Russian troops retake 12 more points in the lower Don offensive, six southwest of Stalingrad and four in the Caucasus .... Major Gen. Carl A. Spaatz assumes command of the Allied Air Force in French North Africa.	Wang Ching-wei's Nanking government declares war on the U.S. and Great Britain.	Brazil extends military conscription to all 18-year-olds and naturalized citizens.	Jamai Ulshi succeeds Husni Bey Barazzi as Syrian premier.

A	B	C	D	E
Includes developments that affect more than one world region, international organizations and important meetings of major world leaders.	*Includes all developments in European countries and military engagements between Allied and Axis powers in Africa and at sea.*	*Includes all developments in Japan and China, Japanese foreign policy and military actions in the Pacific region.*	*Includes all domestic and regional developments in Latin America, the Caribbean and Canada.*	*Includes developments in those independent nations and colonial possessions not covered in Columns B, C and D.*

U.S. Politics & Social Issues	U.S. Foreign Policy & Defense	U.S. Economy & Environment	Science, Technology & Nature	Culture, Leisure & Life Style	
Thomas E. Dewey is inaugurated in Albany as New York's first GOP governor in 20 years .... N.Y. State Education Dept. withdraws recognition of the bachelor's degree awarded by the Univ. of Chicago for two years of college work.	AP reports the Army has a compact mechanism which directs anti-aircraft fire by almost instant determination of the horizontal and vertical distance and speed of planes.			*Time* Magazine selects Stalin as its Man of the Year for 1942 .... Major Bowl game scores: Rose: Georgia 9, UCLA 0; Sugar: Tennessee 14, Tulsa 7; Orange: Alabama 37, Boston College 21; Cotton: Texas 14, Georgia Tech 7.	Jan. 1
		Army, Navy and WPB set the 1943 war output goal at "double that of 1942." Quotas call for about 100,000 aircraft .... Morgenthau announces $12.906 billion was subscribed in the December Victory Fund Drive, some $2 billion more than the goal.		Samuel Reshevsky regains full possession of the U.S. chess championship by defeating former co-holder Isaac I. Kashdan .... FDR supports the observance of the Universal Week of Prayer, Jan. 3-10, sponsored by the Federal Council of Churches of Christ in America.	Jan. 2
Rep. Jerry Voorhis (D, Calif.) refuses to sign the annual report of the Dies Committee and submits a minority report that says no opportunity was given for discussion or amendment.				*New York Herald Tribune* reports that *The Robe* by Lloyd C. Douglas is the best-selling fiction book, and *See Here, Private Hargrove* by Marion Hargrove the best-selling non-fiction work.	Jan. 3
Supreme Court rules the three-year limitation statute nullifies the 1941 conviction of former Kansas City Democratic boss Thomas Pendergast for contempt because of bribes he received in 1936.	A District of Columbia grand jury indicts 33 persons and the *New York Evening Enquirer* for sedition, charging them with conspiring to impair the morale and loyalty of the armed forces.	Petroleum Admin. Harold L. Ickes says only one million barrels of oil can be delivered to the East Coast daily despite a demand for 1.5 million .... Chase Manhattan Bank of New York reports assets of over $4.5 billion, the first time a bank has listed assets above $4 billion.			Jan. 4
House Democratic and GOP members hold closed meetings in the House chamber in preparation for the convening of the 78th Congress tomorrow.		Food Admin. Claude Wickard orders 30% of all butter production reserved for military and Lend-Lease purposes effective Feb. 1.	Dr. George Washington Carver, Negro scientist and director of the Tuskegee Institute's Agricultural Research Dept. since 1896, dies at 78 in Tuskegee, Ala.		Jan. 5
The 78th Congress convenes in Washington, with Sam Rayburn elected Speaker of the House for his third term.		A N.Y. federal grand jury indicts 29 corporations which produce 80% of the nation's anthracite coal for price-fixing .... OPA bans pleasure driving and orders a 25% cut in fuel oil rations for heating non-dwelling buildings on the East Coast.	Drs. Walter Minder and Alice Leigh-Smith report discovery of a method of isolating small amounts of radioactive chemical element 85 (anglo-helvetium), the last of the 92 primary components of matter to be identified .... G.A. Petzoldt and his son G.E. Petzoldt report development of a formula for fireproofing aviation uniforms, making them invulnerable to gasoline fires.	Dr. Abbott Lawrence Lowell, 86, president emeritus of Harvard Univ., dies in Boston. The Harvard Graduate School of Business Administration was founded during his tenure.	Jan. 6
Sen. Alben W. Barkley (D, Ky.), Senate majority leader, retains his power to fill steering committee vacancies by a 34-20 party caucus vote.	Rep. Karl Mundt (R, S.D.) introduces legislation to create a postwar planning committee of 32 members chosen by State Secy. Hull and former Pres. Herbert Hoover.		Dr. Nikola Tesla, 86, inventor of the Tesla coil, the induction motor and discoverer of cosmic rays, dies in N.Y. .... Dr. George W. Crile, 78, clinical research specialist and surgeon who performed the first direct blood transfusion in 1905 and developed the nerve-block system of anesthesia, dies in Cleveland.	Negro soprano Marian Anderson breaks the DAR segregation policy when she sings to a full house at Constitution Hall in Washington .... N.Y. State Court of Appeals in Albany reverses the conviction of a member of the Jehovah's Witnesses on a charge of selling Bibles and religious tracts without a license and rules that it "is not bound by a decision of the" U.S. Supreme Court which upheld a similar decision.	Jan. 7
		FDR endorses "pay-as-you-go" taxation in principle, but says the plan to drop a tax year and advance the payment calendar would reduce Treasury revenue .... Price Admin. Henderson orders fuel oil dealers to "sell any amount of their supply to any purchaser who presents the necessary coupons," scoring the chaotic rationing conditions on the East Coast.			Jan. 8
			Lockheed Constellation, giant cargo and transport plane driven by four 2,000-horsepower engines and capable of speeds above 300 mph, makes its first flight at Burbank, Calif.		Jan. 9

	World Affairs	European War Zone	Pacific War Zone	The Americas	Other Countries & Territories
Jan. 10		Hitler and Rumanian Premier Marshal Ion Antonescu meet at Hitler's field headquarters .... Russian forces recapture 13 more points in the Caucasus, further hemming in the railroad junction of Georgievsk .... Eisenhower announces creation of a committee headed by Col. William T. Gardiner to coordinate and plan the rearmament of the French forces in North Africa.	Remnants of the Japanese convoy at Lae withdraw during the night after being bombed incessantly for three days.	Gen. Augustin P. Justo, 66, president of Argentina (1932-1938) and U.N. supporter, dies in Buenos Aires.	
Jan. 11		Soviet forces retake Georgievsk, Piatigorsk, Mineralnye Vodi and 12 other points in the central Caucasus.	U.S. and Britain relinquish their extraterritorial and other special rights in China.	Argentina asks that Capt. Dietrich Niebuhr, attache to the German embassy in Buenos Aires, be recalled.	Prof. J.P. Bhansali, a follower of Gandhi, halts his fast after 61 days in protest against the alleged raping of village women by Indian troops.
Jan. 12		Allies capture Fezzan in southern Libya with the conquest of Murzuk, the capital, and Sebha, the chief military center .... A French Imperial Council spokesman announces at Allied North African headquarters that a small number of persons were arrested Jan. 10 in connection with the murder of Adm. Jean Francois Darlan .... Adhesion of the French Communists to Gen. de Gaulle's French National Comm. is announced upon the arrival in London of Ferdinand Grenier, former Communist deputy from St. Dennis.	U.S. forces occupy Amchitka, one of the Rat Islands in the western Aleutians.		
Jan. 13		Soviets launch their sixth major offensive since November, striking southwest from Shchuche and Seliavnoye and north and northwest from Kantemirovka .... Russian Army advances 50 miles northward from the Georgievsk-Mineralnye Vodi area to Zhurakskoye in the Caucasus .... Fighting French report in London that seven Frenchmen have been executed in Tours by the Germans for attempting to kill Marcel Deat, pro-Nazi editor.	Allied bombers hit the Japanese airfield and harbor installations at Lae, reportedly causing heavy damage.		
Jan. 14	FDR, Churchill and members of their military staffs open a conference in Casablanca, French Morocco, to plan for 1943 war strategy.	Russian Army advances another 26 miles northward in the Caucasus to capture Sotnikovsk.	After capturing Kwangshan and Loshan in Honan Province, Chinese troops break into the Japanese base at Sinyang.		
Jan. 15		British resume their advance on Tripoli, driving northwestward 40 miles from the Buerat el Hsun-Wadi Zemzem area to the Sedada Bir Tala area .... French National Comm. in London invites all Frenchmen except Vichy collaborators to join them in unity .... Soviet troops recapture 30 more localities—six in the Caucasus, eight in the Northern Donets and 16 in the Zimovniki areas .... Chief of staff of the illegal IRA Hugh McAteer escapes with three others from Belfast prison in Northern Ireland.	Allied ground forces break through and destroy enemy forward positions at Sanananda Point in New Guinea .... U.S. planes in the Solomons damage three Japanese destroyers, set a cargo ship afire and shoot down 30 planes, losing only seven of their own.	Nearly 800 Japanese living near Lima, Peru are taken into custody as the first step in a plan to deport 22,000 to the U.S. for internment .... Cuba announces that between 8,000 and 10,000 persons will be drafted for military service by April .... German officials in Buenos Aires ask the Argentine government to provide a safe-conduct return for Capt. Dietrich Niebuhr to Germany.	
Jan. 16			U.S. bombers strike at Japanese positions at Kahili on Bougainville Island, Munda on New Georgia Island and Ballale Island in the Shortland area.		Iraq declares war on Germany, Italy and Japan.
Jan. 17		A large force of RAF bombers dropped four and two-ton bombs and thousands of incendiaries on Berlin last night in the first air raid on the German capital since Nov. 7, 1941. Nazi bombers raid the greater London area today in reprisal .... Soviet forces recapture the railroad junction of Millerovo on the Rostov-Moscow line, some 130 miles north of Rostov.	In fighting since Jan. 13, U.S. forces claim to have killed 1,032 Japanese on Guadalcanal.		
	A *Includes developments that affect more than one world region, international organizations and important meetings of major world leaders.*	B *Includes all developments in European countries and military engagements between Allied and Axis powers in Africa and at sea.*	C *Includes all developments in Japan and China, Japanese foreign policy and military actions in the Pacific region.*	D *Includes all domestic and regional developments in Latin America, the Caribbean and Canada.*	E *Includes developments in those independent nations and colonial possessions not covered in Columns B, C and D.*

U.S. Politics & Social Issues	U.S. Foreign Policy & Defense	U.S. Economy & Environment	Science, Technology & Nature	Culture, Leisure & Life Style	
National Assn. of Secondary School Principals opposes college admission of 17-year-olds who have completed three years of high school .... Harvard Univ. holds the first winter commencement in its 307-year history.		Gov. Stassen outlines a three-point postwar economic policy for the GOP, providing for maximum production through private enterprise .... The Tolan Committee in the House states its opposition to labor draft legislation in its final report, saying "the drift in the direction of compulsion" parallels "the drift in the direction of control over our war effort by a limited number of large corporations."		Francisco Segura of Ecuador wins the Pan-Am tennis singles title in Mexico City by defeating William Talbert of the U.S.	Jan. 10
FDR nominates Wiley Blount Rutledge Jr. to fill the Supreme Court vacancy caused by the resignation of James F. Byrnes .... Carlo Tresca, 68, Italian anti-Fascist leader and revolutionary writer, is shot to death by an unknown assassin on Fifth Ave. in N.Y.	FDR nominates Edward J. Flynn as U.S. minister to Australia.	FDR submits to Congress a war budget of $108.903 billion for fiscal 1944 .... FDR nominates Sen. Prentiss M. Brown (D, Mich.) to succeed Price Admin. Leon Henderson .... Supreme Court rules that witnesses testifying under subpoena before federal grand juries investigating Sherman Antitrust Law violations are entitled to immunity from prosecution.			Jan. 11
		About 8,000 of the estimated 18,000 striking Pennsylvania anthracite coal miners return to work following a joint appeal by the UMW and mine operators yesterday .... OPA orders the price of corn frozen for 60 days at approximately $1 a bushel.			Jan. 12
Sen. Styles Bridges (R, N.H.) charges that Democratic National Comm. Chmn. Edward Flynn acted as counsel for Serge Rubinstein, a representative of Japanese interests in N.Y.	Justice Dept. discloses that six Americans who broadcast for the Axis from Germany and Italy may soon be indicted for treason.	U.S. Circuit Court of Appeals in N.Y. upholds the constitutionality of the "death sentence" clause in the Public Utility Company Act in sustaining an SEC order that the North American Co. divest itself of all but Union Electric Co.		*Variety* reports the most popular current songs are: (1) *Had the Craziest Dream;* (2) *There Are Such Things;* and (3) *Moonlight Becomes You* .... Joe DiMaggio, N.Y. Yankee outfielder, says in Reno, Nev., that he plans to join the armed forces and discloses that he and his wife, the former Dorothy Arnold, who has been in Reno to obtain a divorce, have settled their marital differences .... Musicians union Pres. James Petrillo promises a Senate Interstate Commerce subcommittee that he will open negotiations with the record and radio industries in an effort to remove the ban on recordings and transcriptions by his union's 138,000 members.	Jan. 13
Judge Clarence G. Galston sentences five leaders of the Ethiopian Pacific Movement (Harlem pro-Japanese group), including Leonard Robert O. Jordan, to jail terms of 4 to 10 years.	Army Chief of Ordnance Maj. Gen. Levin H. Campbell reports the production of a 240 mm. howitzer which fires a 350 lb. TNT shell 25,000 yards.	NWLB Chmn. Davis orders a public hearing tomorrow to determine why 15,000 to 18,000 Pennsylvania anthracite miners are still on strike "against the welfare of the nation."	Discovery of pre-Inca ruins is reported atop a 13,000-foot mountain near Arequipa, Peru .... Two earthquakes are felt throughout New England at 5:33 p.m. but cause no damage.		Jan. 14
Jarvis Roosevelt Catoe, who confessed to assaulting and killing seven women, is executed at the District of Columbia jail for the murder of Mrs. Rose Abramowitz on March 8, 1941.	Eighteen Army officers, eight civilians and nine crew members are killed when a U.S. Army transport plane crashes in a Surinam jungle. They were on their way to the Casablanca conference.	NWLB orders striking coal miners to return to work, and 32 officers of the UMW in Washington agree to advise strikers to end their unofficial walkout.			Jan. 15
FBI seizes 18 German enemy aliens in N.J. and 15 more in N.Y.C.		A walkout of 8,000 anthracite coal miners closes seven more mines in the Wilkes-Barre, Pa. area .... Agriculture Secy. Wickard directs 43 dollar-a-year men in the department be given full-time jobs and relinquish their private employment or become unpaid consultants.			Jan. 16
	U.S. aircraft carrier *Cowpens* is launched at Camden, N.J., the sixth since Pearl Harbor.		Eugene Houdry announces an adiabiatic catalytic refining process to procure aviation gasoline from heavy naphtha.	N.Y. Baseball Writers name Boston Red Sox outfielder Ted Williams player of the year for 1942.	Jan. 17
F *Includes elections, federal-state relations, civil rights and liberties, crime, the judiciary, education, health care, poverty, urban affairs and population.*	G *Includes formation and debate of U.S. foreign and defense policies, veterans affairs and defense spending. (Relations with specific foreign countries are usually found under the region concerned.)*	H *Includes business, labor, agriculture, taxation, transportation, consumer affairs, monetary and fiscal policy, natural resources, pollution and accidents.*	I *Includes worldwide scientific, medical and technological developments, natural phenomena, U.S. weather and natural disasters.*	J *Includes the arts, religion, scholarship, communications media, sports, entertainment, fashions, fads and social life.*	

	World Affairs	European War Zone	Pacific War Zone	The Americas	Other Countries & Territories
Jan. 18		Soviets break the Leningrad siege with the recapture of Schlusselburg, 25 miles eastward on Lake Ladoga .... An estimated 500 RAF planes attack Berlin, leaving large fires raging.	Australian troops take Sanananada Village, Sanananada Point, Cape Killerton and Wye Point on New Guinea.		
Jan. 19		British move within 40 miles of Tripoli, while RAF and U.S. planes bomb the retreating Afrika Korps .... Marcel B. Peyrouton is appointed governor-general of Algeria by Gen. Giraud .... After three days of attacks British and Greek destroyers sink 13 Axis ships in the central Mediterranean .... Soviets capture Urazova and Valuiki, some 80 miles east of Kharkov, in their offensive below Voronezh.			
Jan. 20	Germany, Italy and Japan sign pact pledging economic, financial and technical cooperation.	British troops take Homs and Tarhuna in their drive on Tripoli, while the Afrika Korps is evacuating Tripoli by sea and land .... Marcel B. Peyrouton, assuming his new post as governor general of Algeria, says an agreement among all Frenchmen everywhere is the hope of France but maintains that the anti-Jewish laws and liberation of political prisoners are matters for the Algerian high commissariat. A London Fighting French spokesman scores Peyrouton as "one of the first and most brutal of the Vichy leaders."	Philippine Pres. Manuel Quezon announces his government's adherence to the U.N. declaration invalidating property seizures in occupied countries by the Axis.	Supporters of Venezuelan Pres. Isaias Medina Angarita win a majority in the congressional elections .... Chilean Pres. Juan Antonio Rios signs a decree ending diplomatic relations with Germany, Itay and Japan.	
Jan. 21		U.S. Naval Commander for the South Atlantic, Rear Adm. Jonas H. Ingram, announces U.S. and Brazilian naval units sank five Axis submarines during the last month.	Maj. Gen. Alexander M. Patch assumes command of U.S. forces stationed on Guadalcanal, relieving Maj. Gen. Alexander A. Vandegrift.		
Jan. 22	Iraq becomes the 30th member of the U.N. pact.	Russian Army occupies Salsk, 100 miles southeast of Rostov, threatening to trap Nazi troops in the Caucasus.		Inter-American Advisory Comm. for Political Defense of the Continent makes public a U.S. memorandum charging that a spy ring directed by German diplomats in Argentina is operating throughout South America.	
Jan. 23		British move into Tripoli, Libyan capital, at 5 a.m., completing a 1,200-mile drive from El Alamein in exactly three months. The fleeing Afrika Korps continues retreating westward into Tunisia .... Russian troops capture Armavir, key to the Maikop oil fields in the Caucasus, Volokonovka, northeast of Kharkov, and Gigant, 75 miles from Rostov .... Nazi and Croatian troops open a drive against the Yugoslavian force of Gen. Draja Mikhailovich south of Zagreb .... Fighting reaches its height today when German troops supported by tanks move into the Old Harbor district of Marseille, where Frenchmen have defied Nazi and Vichy authorities who ordered the evacuation and razing of the area for military purposes.	Enemy resistance in Papua, New Guinea comes to an end, prompting MacArthur to state that air power is the most effective weapon against Japan .... Australians report the crushing of all organized Japanese resistance at Sanananda .... U.S. troops capture Kokumbona, seven miles west of Henderson Field on Guadalcanal.		
Jan. 24	Casablanca Conference closes after FDR and Churchill secretly agree (1) to bomb German industrial centers 24 hours a day, (2) to invade Sicily after North Africa is secured and (3) to prepare for a cross-channel invasion of the Continent. FDR says the Allies will accept nothing less than "unconditional surrender" by the Axis powers.	Russian troops take 13 more towns on the eastern Ukraine and northern Caucasian fronts .... John Burns, British laborite and first workingman member of a British cabinet who resigned in August 1914 to protest the war, dies at 84 in London.		Joint Economic Comm. of the U.S. and Canada agrees to peacetime development of one million acres of land in Alaska, British Columbia and Yukon territories.	More than 100,000 Polish troops arrive in Iran from Russia to reinforce the Polish Army in the Near East under the command of Gen. Wladyslaw Anders.
	A *Includes developments that affect more than one world region, international organizations and important meetings of major world leaders.*	B *Includes all developments in European countries and military engagements between Allied and Axis powers in Africa and at sea.*	C *Includes all developments in Japan and China, Japanese foreign policy and military actions in the Pacific region.*	D *Includes all domestic and regional developments in Latin America, the Caribbean and Canada.*	E *Includes developments in those independent nations and colonial possessions not covered in Columns B, C and D.*

U.S. Politics & Social Issues	U.S. Foreign Policy & Defense	U.S. Economy & Environment	Science, Technology & Nature	Culture, Leisure & Life Style	
Democratic National Comm. elects Postmaster General Frank Walker to succeed Edward Flynn as its chairman . . . . Supreme Court affirms the conviction of the AMA and the Medical Society of the District of Columbia on charges of conspiring to block the operation of Washington medical co-op Group Health Inc.		Claiming its mediation efforts have failed, the NWLB turns the anthracite coal miners strike over to FDR . . . . Senate confirms Prentiss Brown to succeed Leon Henderson as head of OPA . . . . Supreme Court rules the Federal Wage Hour Law does not affect warehousemen and wholesalers who sell and distribute products entirely in one state.		It is announced in N.Y. that the Whitney Museum of American Art will be consolidated with the Metropolitan Museum of Art.	Jan. 18
Democratic House caucus refuses to confirm Rep. Vito Marcantonio, (American Labor Party, N.Y.) for membership on the Judiciary Committee.		FDR orders the striking coal miners to return to work in 48 hours or, he says, the federal government will take the necessary measures for the safety of the nation . . . . White House announces appointment of Robert Johnson as director of the Smaller War Plants Corp. and as vice chairman of the WPB.		After 866 performances the Broadway play *My Sister Eileen*, by Joseph Fields and Jerome Chodorov, closes in N.Y.	Jan. 19
Edward J. Flynn denies charges made by Sen. Styles Bridges (R, N.H.) at an open hearing of the Senate Foreign Relations Comm., saying he appointed Dutch Schultz a special deputy sheriff under the name of Arthur Flegenheimer before he knew of the racketeer's criminal record.		Brown replaces Henderson as head of the OPA and says a slow price rise is inevitable.	*Journal of the AMA* reports Drs. Robert A. Hingson and Waldo B. Edwards of the Marine Hospital, Staten Island have evolved a new painless childbirth technique called "continuous caudal analgesia."	Sears, Roebuck & Co. gives the 175-year-old Encyclopaedia Brittanica, Inc., to the Univ. of Chicago.	Jan. 20
Sen. Guy M. Gillette, (D, Iowa) introduces a joint resolution calling for a constitutional amendment providing equal rights for women . . . . Mrs. Eleanor Roosevelt says in her daily syndicated newspaper column that young men of 18 and 19 who "are old enough to be trained to fight" are also "old enough to take part in the political life of their country and to be full citizens with voting powers."	U.S. aircraft carrier *Yorktown* is launched at Newport News, Va.	Price Admin. Brown announces consumption of canned and processed foods will be cut more than 50% under point rationing which begins March 1.			Jan. 21
		Persistent strikers in the unauthorized coal miners' strike in the Wilkes-Barre, Pa. area return to work, ending the strike which began Dec. 30 . . . . AFL Executive Committee ratifies a pact for arbitrating jurisdictional disputes with the CIO by a joint committee which will also consider merger plans.		International Amateur Athletic Federation announces in Stockholm it has approved 38 track and field records set in 1942, 11 by Gunder Haegg, Swedish runner.	Jan. 22
House minority leader Joseph Martin advocates the creation of a permanent House committee on aviation to deal with future problems of air transportation.		Commodity Credit Corp. places 235 million bushels of government-owned wheat on the market at parity prices in an effort to check rising prices.		Author and literary critic Alexander Woollcott dies in N.Y. at 56 after suffering a heart attack during a radio broadcast.	Jan. 23
Vice Pres. Henry Wallace says he believes that postwar America will provide for all to become members of the middle class and enjoy its benefits.	Jay Pierrepont Moffat, U.S. minister to Canada since June 1940, dies at 46 in Ottawa.	Agriculture Secy. Wickard predicts drastic food rationing will be necessary in 1943 even if crop production goals are attained.			Jan. 24

	World Affairs	European War Zone	Pacific War Zone	The Americas	Other Countries & Territories
Jan. 25		American tanks and infantry sweep 35 miles eastward to Maknassy near the Gulf of Gabes in Tunisia . . . . German and Italian troops are reported massing along the Mareth line, stretching some 40 miles from Mareth near the Tunisian coast southward to Foum Tatahouine.			
Jan. 26		Russian troops drive German forces out of Voronezh, 10 miles east of the Don River . . . . Russian sources claim 40,000 Germans were killed and 28,000 captured since Jan. 10 in fighting around Stalingrad . . . . French troops take Fort Saint, Tunisia and march across the border and occupy Gadames, Libya.			
Jan. 27	Stalin receives a joint FDR- Churchill note on the results of the Casablanca Conference, pledging maintenance and extension of the initiative won late in 1942 and all possible aid to Russia and assistance for the Chinese armies.	Flying Fortresses carry out the first American attack upon Germany when they bomb Wilhelmshaven and Emden . . . . Soviet troops recapture 15 points on the south Russian and Caucasian fronts and take 3,350 German prisoners on the Stalingrad front.			
Jan. 28		British and American military leaders confer at North African headquarters to finalize plans to drive the Germans out of Tunisia and attack southern Europe . . . . British drive close to Zuara, 60 miles west of Tripoli and only 30 miles from the Libyan border . . . . Russian Army takes Kastornoye, 83 miles east of German-held Kursk on the Voronezh front. German and Rumanian troops are reported surrendering en masse.	Japanese Foreign Min. Masayuki Tani says the neutrality pact with the Soviet Union has not been nor will be modified . . . . U.S. planes bomb two Japanese destroyers, a cargo ship and a tanker off Kolombangara and shoot down nine enemy planes approaching Guadalcanal.	FDR confers with Brazilian Pres. Vargas at Natal after crossing the Atlantic by clipper, to discuss war problems in general and Axis submarine attacks in particular . . . . Plans for Bolivian Pres. Enrique Penaranda del Castillo to visit the U.S. in April at the request of FDR are announced . . . . Chile bans the use of codes in foreign or domestic communications and prohibits the publication or broadcasting of weather reports.	
Jan. 29		Red Army routs the Germans on the Voronezh front and captures Kropotkin in the Caucasus . . . . Berlin reports that Austrian Nazi Ernst Kaltenbrunner has been appointed head of the German security police (Gestapo) and special secret service as successor to the assassinated Reinhard Heydrich . . . . Gen. Henri Giraud, French African high commissioner, says "there is no question of a single united French movement throughout the world at the present time."	Australia says the Japanese are massing troops to the north for a large-scale invasion of the continent.	Russia and Uruguay reveal they will resume diplomatic relations, which were severed in 1934.	
Jan. 30		Germans break through French lines at Faid Pass, Tunisia and advance 6½ miles . . . . Soviets occupy Maikop, the oil-center in northwest Caucasus, and Tikhoretsk, an important railroad junction 85 miles south of Rostov . . . . Adm. Karl Doenitz, commander of the German submarine fleet, replaces Grand Adm. Erich Raeder as commander of all German naval forces.	U.S. cruiser *Chicago* is torpedoed and sunk in the Solomon Islands . . . . Japanese attacks upon Australian troops west of Mubo, in northeast New Guinea, are repulsed and the Japanese are pursued.	FDR stops briefly at Trinidad, British West Indies and inspects U.S. defense installations there.	
Jan. 31		Russians claim the virtual destruction of the German 6th Army and 4th Tank Army at Stalingrad and the capture of 14 German generals . . . . Gen. Vittorio Ambrosio replaces Marshal Ugo Cavallero as chief of the Italian general staff.		Chile detains Japanese Min. Kiyoshi Yamagata and 27 staff members in Santiago in reprisal for the detention of the Chilean minister in Tokyo.	
Feb. 1		U.S. forces drive the Germans from Senad between Gafsa and Makneassy and then retire while other U.S. troops are thrown at the Germans in an effort to regain Faid Pass in Tunisia . . . . Russian Army recaptures Mechetinsk, 45 miles southeast of Rostov, and Kshen, 65 miles east of Kursk on the Voronezh front . . . . Churchill and Turkish Premier Ismet Inonu complete talks at Adana, Turkey on the war's progress, particularly in the East.	Wife of the Chinese ambassador to Britain, Mme. Wellington Koo, says only 2% of U.S. Lend-Lease aid is shipped to China.	Chile orders imprisonment of 168 German and 74 Japanese nationals suspected of espionage.	
Feb. 2		Russians claim victory in the battle of Stalingrad, which has cost the Germans an estimated 503,650 men since Aug. 22.	Japanese Premier Tojo denies any territorial ambitions towards the U.S. or South America.		

A	B	C	D	E
Includes developments that affect more than one world region, international organizations and important meetings of major world leaders.	*Includes all developments in European countries and military engagements between Allied and Axis powers in Africa and at sea.*	*Includes all developments in Japan and China, Japanese foreign policy and military actions in the Pacific region.*	*Includes all domestic and regional developments in Latin America, the Caribbean and Canada.*	*Includes developments in those independent nations and colonial possessions not covered in Columns B, C and D.*

U.S. Politics & Social Issues	U.S. Foreign Policy & Defense	U.S. Economy & Environment	Science, Technology & Nature	Culture, Leisure & Life Style	
	Land-Lease Admin. Edward Stettinius reports to Congress that aid from March 1941 through December 1942 totaled $8.253 billion.	A Treasury-sponsored bill to increase the national debt from $125 billion to $210 billion is introduced into the House.			Jan. 25
	Sen. Albert Chandler (D, Ky.) reports service plans call for 10,420,000 men and women in the armed services by the end of 1943.	Fifteen thousand members of the ILGWU walk off their jobs in N.Y. after wage negotiations break down.		Vernon (Lefty) Gomez, New York Yankee pitcher since 1931, is sold to the Boston Braves.	Jan. 26
	FDR flies from Casablanca to Liberia .... Senate Foreign Relations Comm. votes 13-10 to confirm Edward J. Flynn as minister to Australia.	Assn. of American Railroads Pres. John J. Pelley says the railroads will be able to increase the supply of oil shipped to the East Coast to 900,000 barrels a day within a month.	OWI announces 13 hospitals have been established by the U.S. Public Health Service to treat women for veneral disease and to reduce infection among military men.	Green Bay Packer end Don Hutson is voted the NFL's mvp by Chicago sportswriters.	Jan. 27
	War Secy. Henry L. Stimson announces the Army will accept enlistments by American-born Japanese, many of whom are now in concentration camps, and train them as a separate Army unit .... Selective Service System announces a joint system of drafting men for the Army, Navy, Marine Corps and Coast Guard.	House Judiciary Comm. reports out the Hobbs Bill to make labor unions subject to the Anti-Racketeering Act of 1934, which bans interference with interstate commerce through violence or intimidation.	Sixty-eight physicians from U.K., U.S., Canada and Norway meet in N.Y. to pool their knowledge on combat fatigue.	Don Hutson announces his retirement from pro football after 14 years because of chest injuries.	Jan. 28
	Capt. Nelson of the liner *President Coolidge*, which struck two mines and sank with the loss of all but four of 4,000 troops aboard while entering a South Pacific harbor last December, reveals in San Francisco that a Navy court-martial has acquitted him of any blame.	House Agricultural Comm. approves the Pace bill to include all farm labor costs in computing parity prices for farm products.		Farrar & Rinehart receive the Carey-Thomas Award for "good publishing" for its series of books *The Rivers of America*, edited by Carl Carmer and Stephen Vincent Benet.	Jan. 29
Archibald MacLeish, librarian of Congress, quits his post as assistant director of the OWI "to devote full time to his duties as a librarian." .... The nation celebrates FDR's 61st birthday, which ends the 1943 fund drive for the National Foundation for Infantile Paralysis.		*New York Herald Tribune* reports that Economic Stabilization Dir. James Byrnes has given Rubber Admin. William Jeffers top priority ratings for the completion of plants to produce 452,000 tons of synthetic rubber a year.			Jan. 30
	FDR returns to Washington tonight by special train from Miami after completing a 13,823-mile trip in 23 days .... Navy Secy. Frank Knox returns from a two-week trip inspecting U.S. bases in the Pacific.			In a N.Y. broadcast Arturo Toscanini, conductor of the NBC Symphony Orchestra, substitutes *Italy Betrayed* for *Italy My Country* in the score of Verdi's *Hymn of Nations* .... Alan Ford of Yale Univ. sets new world record for the 100-yard freestyle of 0:50.7 in New Haven.	Jan. 31
Tennessee State Senate votes to repeal the state's 50-year-old poll tax .... Supreme Court dismisses Dr. Wilder Tileston's appeal against the Connecticut birth control law and rules he cannot question the law's alleged illegal deprivation of life since his own life is not involved .... Rep. Martin Dies (D, Tex.), chairman of the Un-American Activities Comm., asks Congress to purge 38 "crackpot and radical bureaucrats" by withholding funds from agencies employing them.	FDR withdraws Flynn's name from nomination as minister to Australia at his own request because he is "unwilling to be made the excuse for partisan political debate."				Feb. 1
		Treasury Dept. counsel Randolph E. Paul asks the House Ways and Means Comm. to adopt a pay-as-you-go income tax, to become operative not later than July 1 .... OPA announces that effective March 1, canned dried, frozen and dehydrated fruits, vegetables and soups will be rationed.			Feb. 2

F	G	H	I	J
Includes elections, federal-state relations, civil rights and liberties, crime, the judiciary, education, health care, poverty, urban affairs and population.	*Includes formation and debate of U.S. foreign and defense policies, veterans affairs and defense spending. (Relations with specific foreign countries are usually found under the region concerned.)*	*Includes business, labor, agriculture, taxation, transportation, consumer affairs, monetary and fiscal policy, natural resources, pollution and accidents.*	*Includes worldwide scientific, medical and technological developments, natural phenomena, U.S. weather and natural disasters.*	*Includes the arts, religion, scholarship, communications media, sports, entertainment, fashions, fads and social life.*

	World Affairs	European War Zone	Pacific War Zone	The Americas	Other Countries & Territories
Feb. 3		Axis forces check the U.S. assault on Faid Pass in Tunisia . . . . Gen. Giraud, French North African high commissioner, has reportedly released 11 of the 14 persons arrested Dec. 29 following the assassination of Adm. Darlan . . . . Soviet forces drive to within 22 miles of Kursk, severing the Kursk-Orel railroad and capturing Zolotukhino and Vozi.		Brazilian security court indicts six Germans and five Brazilians for transmitting shipping information to Berlin.	
Feb. 4		Congratulating Stalin on the Russian victory at Stalingrad, FDR says the joint Allied effort will soon bring victory over the Axis . . . . In fighting since Jan. 27 the Russians report killing 17,000 Axis troops and taking 27,000 prisoners on the Voronezh front . . . . RAF bombers strike at Hamburg, Germany for the 95th time, starting large fires . . . . German Economy Min. Walther Funk orders the retail trade, arts and crafts professions and hotel and eating establishments to release all dispensable labor for war or military work service.		Cuba announces that about 200 Japanese suspected of sabotage have been arrested and are being sent to the Isle of Pines concentration camp.	House of Assembly of the Union of South Africa approves motion for voluntary military service abroad.
Feb. 5		Mussolini names a new cabinet and removes his son-in-law Count Ciano as minister of foreign affairs, assuming the position himself and also assuming full responsibility for military affairs . . . . Russians drive into the Ukraine, recapturing Izyum, a railroad center on the Donets River some 70 miles southeast of Kharkov . . . . Churchill arrives in Tripoli to greet the victorious British 8th Army and discuss future strategy with Gen. Sir Bernard L. Montgomery . . . . Lt. Gen. Hendrik Alexander Seyffardt, 70, Netherlands chief of staff (1929-1934) who was appointed Feb. 1 by the Dutch Nazi leader Anton Mussert to raise an army for the Russian front, is fatally wounded in The Hague by an assassin.			
Feb. 6	Brazil becomes the 31st nation to announce its adherence to the U.N. charter.	Soviets recapture Bataisk, five miles south of Rostov, and Yeisk on the Azov Sea, blocking Axis forces in the Krasnodar area of the Caucasus from escape to the north . . . . Gen. Draja Mikhailovich appeals to the Allies through the Yugoslavian government in London to try to stop the Axis "mass murder" of Serbs.	U.S. forces continue their advance on Guadalcanal, reaching points 1½ miles beyond Tassafaronga . . . . In repeated Japanese attempts to attack the Allied airdrome at Wau, New Guinea, American fighters shoot down 41 Japanese planes.		
Feb. 7	Peru announces its adherence to the U.N. charter.	Churchill returns to London after his North African and Turkish tours. He conferred with Lt. Gen. Dwight D. Eisenhower, Gen. Henri Giraud and Gen. Georges Catroux in North Africa . . . . Russian forces recapture Azov on the Don River and Olginsk, clearing the entire southern bank of the Don and bringing Rostov within artillery distance.			
Feb. 8		Russians retake Kursk, the German stronghold 275 miles south of Moscow.		About 5,000 people are reported to have died of malaria in the Uribia area of northern Colombia.	
Feb. 9			Japanese withdraw their forces from Guadalcanal and Buna, New Guinea, after admitting defeat. They put their troop losses at 16,734 for the entire Battle of Guadalcanal. U.S. Navy puts Japanese troop losses somewhere between 30,000 and 50,000.	Colombia and Russia reach an diplomatic in Washington to exchange diplomatic envoys.	
Feb. 10	CIO Pres. Murray urges creation of a world federation of labor organizations.	British advance into Libya towards the Mareth line . . . . Russian troops occupy Volchansk, 36 miles northeast of Kharkov, and Chuguyev, 22 miles southeast of Kharkov.	U.S. Commander on Guadalcanal Maj. Gen. Alexander Patch states "there is no longer any vestige of any Japanese organized forces" on the island.	Argentine Pres. Ramon Castillo announces he will not be a candidate for re-election when his term expires next February . . . . Puerto Rican House and Senate pass joint resolution petitioning the U.S. Congress to permit an election on the island to determine its own fate . . . . Brazil reveals that a Nazi plot to overthrow the government was crushed some four months ago.	Gandhi commences a 21-day fast, his ninth in 25 years, to protest his confinement in the Aga Khan's palace at Poona.

A	B	C	D	E
Includes developments that affect more than one world region, international organizations and important meetings of major world leaders.	*Includes all developments in European countries and military engagements between Allied and Axis powers in Africa and at sea.*	*Includes all developments in Japan and China, Japanese foreign policy and military actions in the Pacific region.*	*Includes all domestic and regional developments in Latin America, the Caribbean and Canada.*	*Includes developments in those independent nations and colonial possessions not covered in Columns B, C and D.*

U.S. Politics & Social Issues	U.S. Foreign Policy & Defense	U.S. Economy & Environment	Science, Technology & Nature	Culture, Leisure & Life Style	
House Rules Comm. approves the extension of the Dies Un-American Activities Comm. for two more years.		AFL Pres. William Green and CIO Pres. Phillip Murray report to FDR that living costs have outdated the NWLB's formula prohibiting wage increases greater than 15% of the January 1941 level .... Judge James Fee rules in Portland, Ore. that the NLRB has jurisdiction over labor disputes subject to review by the Circuit Court of Appeals .... Sen. John H. Bankhead (D, Ala.) says one million men must be released from the armed forces if an acute food shortage is to be averted.			Feb. 3
Labor Dept. reports juvenile delinquency increased 31% among girls and 7.5% among boys in 1942.		Chmn. Paul McNutt of the War Manpower Commission announces plans to supply labor in 32 shortage areas on a priority basis .... Chmn. Beardsley Ruml of the Federal Reserve Bank in N.Y. defends the pay-as-you-go tax plan for five hours before the House Ways and Means Comm.		Pres. Frank Calder of the NHL dies in Montreal.	Feb. 4
	FDR asks Congress for an additional $4 billion in cash and $210 million in contract authorizations for the Navy.	Phillip Murray announces the CIO, AFL, the railroad brotherhoods and the National Farmers Union have united to fight anti-labor legislation.		Ray Robinson, 144½-pound N.Y. welterweight hitherto undeafeated in 130 bouts, drops a 10-round decision to Jacob (Jack) La Motta in Olympia Stadium, Detroit.	Feb. 5
FDR orders the establishment of a five-man committee within the Justice Dept. to handle cases based on subversive activities of government agency employes .... Federal Judge Ben Hicks denies the appeal of Max Stephan, German-born Detroit restaurant owner, from his death sentence for treason for harboring an escaped German prisoner.		CIO Executive Board demands wage increases to conform with the rise in living costs, an end to substandard wages, elimination of unequal pay for women and a 40-hour work week.		Motion picture actor Errol Flynn, 33, is aquitted of three charges of statutory rape by a jury in Los Angeles Superior Court .... Director of the Office of Defense Transportation Joseph B. Eastman asks that the 1943 Kentucky Derby be canceled because of transportation difficulties.	Feb. 6
		OPA orders suspension of shoe sales until Feb. 9, at which time they will be rationed to three pairs per person for the remainder of 1943.			Feb. 7
Senate confirms nomination of Wiley Blount Rutledge as associate justice of the Supreme Court.	Sen. Warren Austin (R, Vt.) and Rep. James W. Wadsworth (R, N.Y.) introduce to both houses a national war service bill authorizing the drafting of men 18 to 65 and women 18 to 50 for war work.	Federal Judge Martin Welsh denies a petition for a writ of habeas corpus to block deportation of labor leader Harry Bridges.	Ollie W. Reed of the Agriculture Dept. says the process of extracting riboflavin (vitamin B) from milk is being perfected so that it may be used in bread and other foods.	Daniel M. Casey, who claimed he was the original *Casey at the Bat*, dies at 80 in Washington.	Feb. 8
	Navy Secy. Knox recommends the U.S. acquire bases in the Pacific to keep Japan from rising again after the war.	FDR orders a 48-hour minimum workweek for all full-time workers in labor shortage areas.		National League completes the purchase of stock in the Philadelphia Phillies so that the team can be resold to a businessman's syndicate.	Feb. 9
House votes to continue the Dies Un-American Activities Comm. for two years .... Sen. Harry Flood Byrd (D, Va.) announces the Joint Comm. on Reduction of Nonessential Federal Expenditures will investigate *Victory*, the OWI foreign circulation magazine.		Federal Judge Philip Forman adjourns the antitrust trial against GE, Corning Glass Works and nine other producers of electric light bulbs to avoid impairment of their current war production.	Dr. William A. Holla reports that mice are probably carriers of poliomyelitis and spread it by contaminating food.	*Variety* reports the most popular songs to be (1) *There Are Such Things*, (2) *I Had the Craziest Dream*; (3) *I've Heard that Song Before*; and (4) *Why Don't You Fall in Love with Me?*	Feb. 10
F	G	H	I	J	
Includes elections, federal-state relations, civil rights and liberties, crime, the judiciary, education, health care, poverty, urban affairs and population.	*Includes formation and debate of U.S. foreign and defense policies, veterans affairs and defense spending. (Relations with specific foreign countries are usually found under the region concerned.)*	*Includes business, labor, agriculture, taxation, transportation, consumer affairs, monetary and fiscal policy, natural resources, pollution and accidents.*	*Includes worldwide scientific, medical and technological developments, natural phenomena, U.S. weather and natural disasters.*	*Includes the arts, religion, scholarship, communications media, sports, entertainment, fashions, fads and social life.*	

	World Affairs	European War Zone	Pacific War Zone	The Americas	Other Countries & Territories
Feb. 11		British make contact with Rommel's forces east of Ben Gardane in southeastern Tunisia . . . . Churchill reports to the House of Commons on the Casablanca Conference and promises a massive offensive in the next nine months . . . . Russian forces capture Lozovaya in the Ukraine, cutting the Kharkov-Crimea railroad.	U.S. and British military commanders meet with Chiang Kai-shek in New Delhi, reaching agreement on military operations in Southeast Asia . . . . Allied forces push Japanese back some six miles in the Wau-Mubo area of New Guinea.		
Feb. 12	In a Washington radio address, FDR says that victory in Tunisia is a prelude to an invasion of Europe and that the Japanese will be driven from China.	Soviet troops recapture Krasnodar, Kuban Cossack capital in the western Caucasus.	Allied forces repell Japanese counterattacks in the Donbaik and Rathedaung areas of Burma . . . . Japanese lose 1,000 men in their continued retreat in the Wau-Mubo area of New Guinea.		
Feb. 13		Soviets retake Novocherkassk, 19 miles northeast of Rostov . . . . Russian Army comes within 11 miles of Kharkov . . . . U.S. planes bomb Naples and Crotone in southern Italy.	Japanese capture Mafand and Lupao near Canton in China.		
Feb. 14		Rommel's troops, reinforced by 150 tanks, break the American lines in central Tunisia . . . . Russian forces commanded by Col. Gen. Rodion I. Malinovsky recapture Rostov, gateway to the Caucasus . . . . Swiss sources report Hitler plans a new defense line in the east, running from Riga through Smolensk and Kiev to Odessa . . . . Reich Sports Leader Hans von Tshammer und Osten bans all local athletic competition in Germany.	Thai Premier Luang Pibul Songgram and his entire cabinet resign amid rumors of graft and corruption.	Pres. Higinio Morinigo (the only candidate) is re-elected for the 1943-48 term of president in Paraguay.	
Feb. 15		German troops occupy Gafsa, Tunisia, some 36 miles east of the Algerian border . . . . Soviet troops occupy seven more towns in the Ukraine, including the railroad junction of Kuteynikov, 50 miles north of the Sea of Azov . . . . Finnish Pres. Risto Ryti is re-elected by presidential electors.			Ali Soheily becomes premier of Iran, replacing Ahmed Qavan Sultaneh, who resigned.
Feb. 16		Russian troops under the command of Col.Gen. Filip I. Golikov recapture Kharkov, the Ukraine's leading industrial city . . . . SS Chief Himmler orders the liquidation of the Warsaw ghetto.	Allied forces led by Brig O.C. Wingate crosses into Burma and advance eastward in columns, penetrating as far as 200 miles.		
Feb. 17		German forces drive 22 miles west from Sidi bou Zid to the vicinity of Sbeitla, and other Axis units advance 40 miles towards Feriana in Tunisia . . . . Virginio Gayda, editor of *Giornale d' Italia*, hints that Italy would consider making peace with the U.S. and Britain, but not Russia.	Japanese troops land in Kwangchowan on the Luichow Peninsula, 260 miles west-southwest of Hong Kong.		Three Indian members of the Viceroy's Council resign because of the Viceroy's refusal to release Gandhi.
Feb. 18	Mme. Chiang, the first private citizen to address Congress, says defeat of the Japanese is "of relative unimportance and that Hitler is our first concern."	British House of Commons votes against a Labor amendment demanding immediate action on the Beveridge report by creation of a Social Security Ministry . . . . German mechanized forces seize Sbeitla, Kasserine, and Feriana and come within 15 miles of the Algerian border . . . . British occupy Foum Tatahouine, near the southern end of the Mareth line.	Japanese troops open offensive drives on seven fronts in China: along the Grand Canal in Kiangsu Province, east of Suchow, west of Nanchang, the Yochow area in Hunan Province, the Shasi-Ichang area of Hupeh Province, the Luichow Peninsula and northeast of Lungling along the Burma Road . . . . For the first time since last August, U.S. warships attack Japanese positions at Holtz Bay and Chichagof Harbor on Attu Island in the Aleutians.	Argentine Pres. Castillo says he will support Sen. Robustiano Patron Costas as his successor.	
Feb. 19		Germans halt their central Tunisian drive on a line running southwest of Pechon to Feriana . . . . Russians capture seven towns west of Kharkov and 10 more in the Orel Sea area . . . . British Labor Party's National Executive Committee rejects the CP's application for affiliation on the grounds that it is out of harmony with the philosophy and objectives of the Labor Party.		Puerto Rican legislature narrowly endorses Gov. Rexford G. Tugwell and asks FDR not to remove him until the Puerto Ricans can elect their own chief executive.	
Feb. 20		U.S. troops abandon the Ousselat Valley in central Tunisia to straighten their defense lines . . . . Soviet troops take Krasnograd, 60 miles southwest of Kharkov, and Pavlograd, 100 miles south of Kharkov.	Japanese troops make advances in Hupeh Province, Luichow Peninsula and Kiangsu Province.		In appeals to Churchill and U.S. representative in India William Phillips, 200 Indian political leaders ask for Gandhi's immediate release.

A	B	C	D	E
Includes developments that affect more than one world region, international organizations and important meetings of major world leaders.	*Includes all developments in European countries and military engagements between Allied and Axis powers in Africa and at sea.*	*Includes all developments in Japan and China, Japanese foreign policy and military actions in the Pacific region.*	*Includes all domestic and regional developments in Latin America, the Caribbean and Canada.*	*Includes developments in those independent nations and colonial possessions not covered in Columns B, C and D.*

U.S. Politics & Social Issues	U.S. Foreign Policy & Defense	U.S. Economy & Environment	Science, Technology & Nature	Culture, Leisure & Life Style	
FDR nominates Thurman Arnold to be an associate justice of the U.S. Court of Appeals in the District of Columbia.	Eisenhower is nominated to the rank of general by FDR as he assumes command of the British 8th Army.	Florida Circuit Court Judge J.L. Parks voids the closed shop agreement between the Tampa Shipbuilding Co. and 14 AFL unions because the company is doing war work.			Feb. 11
		WPB restricts shoe colors to black, white, army russet and town brown and puts limits on heel heights for women' shoes.	Viscount Nuffield gives about $40 million to create the Nuffield Foundation for scientific research in Britain.		Feb. 12
	WMC Chmn. McNutt and SSS Dir. Lewis B. Hershey announce four million more men must be inducted into the service in 1943.	House Ways and Means Comm. reports the Disney bill to repeal the presidential executive order limiting salaries to $25,000 net by amending the Emergency Price Control Act of 1942 .... Rubber Dir. William Jeffers says the rubber stockpile at the end of 1942 was 420,000 tons, slightly higher than predicted.		Alan Ford, 19, Yale freshman, swims the first leg of a 400-yard free-style relay exhibition race in New Haven in 0:50.6 seconds to lower his own 100-yard free-style world record of 0:50.7 set Jan. 31.	Feb. 13
		Capt. Edward V. (Eddie) Rickenbacker says he personally opposes overtime pay for the 48-hour week because "those back home" should "expend every effort" to support the troops. He says he is also against FDR's order limiting net salaries to $25,000 because it will curb initiative .... House Comm. on Small Business reports small business faces extinction because of lack of sympathetic consideration in the war program.		American Society of Newspaper Editors demands a postwar guarantee of freedom of the press.	Feb. 14
Supreme Court directs rehearing of the undecided case in which Wendell Willkie argued against cancelation of the naturalization of California Communist William Schneiderman .... Supreme Court upholds the conviction of Enoch L. Johnson (N.J. GOP leader) for income tax evasion.				Supreme Court upholds dismissal of the government's antitrust suit against the AFL American Federation of Musicians and James C. Petrillo for banning recordings by union members.	Feb. 15
					Feb. 16
	Mme. Chiang Kai-shek visits FDR at the White House .... Vought F4U-1 Corsair, Navy carrier-based 400 mph fighter with a 2,000 horsepower engine, is demonstrated in East Hartford, Conn.	FDR writes Chmn. Robert L. Doughton, (D, N.C.) of the House Ways and Means Comm. that he wants individual net incomes limited to $25,000 for single people and $50,000 for married couples for the war's duration .... OPA freezes the sale of canned meat and fish to halt hoarding pending rationing scheduled for April 1.	Dr. W.W. Rubey of the U.S. Geological Survey reports that a new vanadium mine, rich enough to meet the current deficit, has been discovered in southwestern Wyoming.		Feb. 17
House votes $75,000 to the Dies Un-American Activities Comm., $100,000 to the Smith Comm. to investigate charges of subversion among government employes and $60,000 to the Cox Comm. to investigate the FCC.	War Dept. activates the 6th Army in Australia and New Guinea under the command of Lt. Gen. Walter Krueger .... Lend-Lease Admin. Edward Stettinius creates the China Division in the Lend-Lease Administration under J. Franklin Ray Jr.	House Ways and Means Comm. reports the Disney rider to repeal FDR's $25,000 net salary limit and instead peg salaries to their Dec. 7, 1941 levels.			Feb. 18
	At a press conference with Mme. Chiang, FDR says the U.S. will speed war goods to China as fast as possible to establish a base of operations against Japan .... Lend-Lease Admin. reports the U.S. has shipped more than 2.9 million tons of war supplies to Russia under Lend-Lease.	House Ways and Means Comm., unable to agree on any of four tax proposals, appoints a subcommittee to draft pay-as-you-go tax legislation.		*The Witness,* an Episcopalian publication, reports 25 Bishops favor union with the Presbyterian Church .... Metropolitan Opera Co. general manager Edward Johnson announces the Met will give 14 performances in Chicago, its first engagement there in 33 years.	Feb. 19
				N.Y. sportsman William D. Cox and a syndicate of 10 unidentified associates purchase the Philadelphia Phillies for $230,000.	Feb. 20
F *Includes elections, federal-state relations, civil rights and liberties, crime, the judiciary, education, health care, poverty, urban affairs and population.*	G *Includes formation and debate of U.S. foreign and defense policies, veterans affairs and defense spending. (Relations with specific foreign countries are usually found under the region concerned.)*	H *Includes business, labor, agriculture, taxation, transportation, consumer affairs, monetary and fiscal policy, natural resources, pollution and accidents.*	I *Includes worldwide scientific, medical and technological developments, natural phenomena, U.S. weather and natural disasters.*	J *Includes the arts, religion, scholarship, communications media, sports, entertainment, fashions, fads and social life.*	

	World Affairs	European War Zone	Pacific War Zone	The Americas	Other Countries & Territories
Feb. 21		German tank units supported by infantry take the Kasserine Pass, 12 miles from the Algerian border .... Russian forces take four towns in the Donets Basin and make further gains near Orel and Krasnodar.	Japanese efforts to cross the Salween River north of Lungling on the Burma Road are repulsed by the Chinese .... Navy reports the loss of the 2,710-ton mine-laying submarine *Argonaut*, believed to be the world's largest, off New Britain Island with the loss of 102 men.	Pres. Manuel Avila Camacho says Mexico will not send troops overseas.	U.S. and British officials in both New Delhi and Washington discuss Indian problems and the release of Gandhi.
Feb. 22		A column of 40 German tanks drives within four miles of Thala in central Tunisia .... Stalin celebrates the 25th anniversary of the Red Army in an order calling for doubling of efforts against Germany because in the absence of a second front "the Red Army is bearing the whole weight of the war." .... *N.Y. Times* correspondent George Axelsson reports Finland will "sue for a separate peace at the first opportunity."		Eric Johnson says hundreds of U.S. war factories will be dismantled and shipped to Latin America after the war.	British authorities in India issue a "white paper" charging that Gandhi instigated uprisings and sabotage during last summer's disturbances .... King Saud of Saudi Arabia severs diplomatic relations with Italy.
Feb. 23	FDR says plans are being discussed for a U.N. conference on postwar food problems.	British tanks and U.S. artillery repulse the German armored attack upon Thala, central Tunisia.			
Feb. 24	British Home Secy. Herbert Morrison urges a world association to control commerce, commodities and currency after the war.	Axis offensive in central Tunisia is halted and turned around, as Axis forces retreat under the heaviest Allied air assault of the Tunisian campaign .... Although the Russians continue to make gains in the Rostov, Kramatorsk, Kharkov, Malo Archangelsk and Krasnodar sectors, German resistance begins to stiffen in the Ukraine .... In commemorating the 23rd anniversary of the National Socialist Party, Hitler promises to revitalize the spiritual and material values of Europe.			Churchill says the reasons for Gandhi's detention still exist and therefore he cannot be released at this time.
Feb. 25		U.S. and British troops reoccupy the Kasserine Pass in Tunisia with little Axis resistence .... Soviet forces recapture Mingrelsk, 30 miles west of Krasnodar, in their drive on the German Black Sea base at Novorossiisk.	Japanese columns are repulsed in their attempt to cross the Yangtze River in Hupeh Province.	U.S. Vice Pres. Henry A. Wallace accepts invitations to visit Peru and Chile next month.	
Feb. 26		Under continued air bombardment, Axis troops retreat along the entire central Tunisian front .... Soviet forces advance west of the Kharkov-Kursk line and capture Angelinsk and Staronizhe-Stebliesvk .... Praising the Franco regime, U.S. Ambassador to Spain Carlton J.H. Hayes says the U.S. has been supplying Spain with foodstuffs, textiles and oil.			Ruler of Yemen, Imam Yahya, orders the arrest of 40 Italians and two Germans, effectively silencing two pro-Axis radio stations.
Feb. 27	Comm. to Study the Organization of Peace, headed by James T. Shotwell, advocates a permanent "Conference of the United Nations" to coordinate war activities.	German troops open several attacks against British positions in northern Tunisia while continuing to retreat in the central sector .... In heavy fighting, Russian troops make advances west of Rostov, southwest of Voroshilovgrad, southwest of Kramatorsk and west of Kharkov.			
Feb. 28		British forces repulse Axis assaults in northern Tunisia and recapture Fort McGregor and Tally-Ho-Corner .... German forces recapture Lozovaya and Kramatorsk south of Kharkov.			
March 1		At the end of an eight-day offensive, Gen. Semyon Timoshenko's forces rout the Germans near Leningrad, freeing 302 localities in a 900-square-mile area .... German tanks and troops drive three miles beyond Sidi Nsir, after the British repulsed five attacks.	Australia announces the Japanese are continuing to reinforce their island positions north of Australia.	Juan Jose Amezaga takes office for a four-year term as president of Uruguay.	
March 2	In a N.Y. speech Mme. Chiang Kai-shek advocates letting the U.N. build a postwar world "resting on the pillars of justice, co-existence, cooperation and mutual respect."	RAF planes subject Berlin to its heaviest raid yet, dropping 900 tons of bombs on the city in 30 minutes .... American troops retake Sbeitla and their advance patrols enter Feriana in central Tunisia, while the British continue to repulse German assaults in the north .... Russians claim the capture of localities of the Kuban area of the Caucasus, while Germans claim successes in the Izyum area of the Ukraine.	U.S. bombers disperse a 14-ship Japanese convoy in the Bismarck Sea bound from New Britain for Lae, New Guinea .... Japanese troops capture Tachupa and Mengting in western Yunnan Province, while Chinese forces retake Fengsin in Kiangsi Province.	In submitting the 1943-44 budget to the House of Commons, Canadian Finance Min. J.L. Ilsley announces a pay-as-you-go tax plan to be effective April 1 .... Acting State Secy. Welles and Chilean Amb. Rodolfo Michels sign a Lend-Lease agreement in Washington.	

A	B	C	D	E
Includes developments that affect more than one world region, international organizations and important meetings of major world leaders.	*Includes all developments in European countries and military engagements between Allied and Axis powers in Africa and at sea.*	*Includes all developments in Japan and China, Japanese foreign policy and military actions in the Pacific region.*	*Includes all domestic and regional developments in Latin America, the Caribbean and Canada.*	*Includes developments in those independent nations and colonial possessions not covered in Columns B, C and D.*

U.S. Politics & Social Issues	U.S. Foreign Policy & Defense	U.S. Economy & Environment	Science, Technology & Nature	Culture, Leisure & Life Style	
			The last lunar eclipse until 1945 is visible along the East Coast beginning at 12:03 a.m.		Feb. 21
		OPA places emergency price ceilings on fresh tomatos, peas, snap beans, carrots and cabbage to halt rising prices resulting from the rationing of canned goods . . . . Senate approves and sends to FDR the bill permitting the Western Union and Postal Telegraph Co. to merge.			Feb. 22
	House approves and sends to the Senate a Navy bill for $1.256 billion for construction of shore bases.				Feb. 23
Rep. Adolf J. Sabath (D, Ill.) says FDR "owes it to the country and to the world" to run again for the presidency.	House Foreign Affairs Comm. approves the extension of the Lend-Lease Act until July 1944.			*The Human Comedy* by William Saroyan is published in N.Y.	Feb. 24
National Education Association's Dept. of Higher Ed. is organized and asks Congress to appropriate $100 million to "save scores of educational institutions from bankruptcy because of the war."	Asst. Chief of Staff Maj. Gen. Idwal H. Edwards says the Army Air Force will total 900 squadrons and 2,450,000 men by the end of 1943.	Members of the AFL International Association of Machinists halt work on Flying Fortresses in the Boeing Aircraft Corp. plants in Seattle and Renton, Wash., for three hours to demand NWLB action on wage increases.			Feb. 25
		House Banking and Currency Comm. approves a bill to prohibit the inclusion of farm benefit payments in establishing parity prices . . . . FDR orders WPB Chmn. Nelson to undertake a program to stimulate the sagging production of lumber.			Feb. 26
Gallup Poll reports that 51% of the voters questioned said they would vote for FDR in 1944 if the war is still going on, but that 50% said they would oppose him if the war were over.		WMC releases regulations for enforcing the 48-hour work-week in 32 local labor shortage areas and extends their provisions to the lumber and nonferrous metal mining industries . . . . Treasury issues a zinc-coated steel penny to save 4,600 tons of copper.		Msgr. John A. Ryan, National Catholic Welfare Conference director, says Axis leaders "should not be permitted to go free after the war" and adds that "the most responsible among them should be put to death." . . . . An all-male jury in Miami, Fla., acquits Ursula Parrott, 40, novelist, of charges of aiding Pvt. Michael W. Bryan to desert . . . . NYU wins the team title at the 55th AAU indoor track championships held at Madison Square Garden.	Feb. 27
New York Herald Tribune reports Willkie has decided to become a candidate for the GOP presidential nomination in 1944.				Pole vault record-holder Cornelius Warmerdam is awarded the James E. Sullivan Memorial Trophy for sportsmanship.	Feb. 28
Supreme Court reverses the conviction of George Sylvester Viereck, Nazi propagandist, ruling he was not obligated to report his activities to the State Dept. except while acting as a foreign agent.					March 1
GOP-backed move to form a standing committee on civil and commercial aviation is defeated in the House.		Senate Military Affairs Comm. approves the Bankhead bill deferring farm workers and reports it to the full Senate.			March 2

F	G	H	I	J
Includes elections, federal-state relations, civil rights and liberties, crime, the judiciary, education, health care, poverty, urban affairs and population.	*Includes formation and debate of U.S. foreign and defense policies, veterans affairs and defense spending. (Relations with specific foreign countries are usually found under the region concerned.)*	*Includes business, labor, agriculture, taxation, transportation, consumer affairs, monetary and fiscal policy, natural resources, pollution and accidents.*	*Includes worldwide scientific, medical and technological developments, natural phenomena, U.S. weather and natural disasters.*	*Includes the arts, religion, scholarship, communications media, sports, entertainment, fashions, fads and social life.*

	World Affairs	European War Zone	Pacific War Zone	The Americas	Other Countries & Territories
March 3		Soviet forces recapture Rzhev, Nazi stronghold 130 miles northwest of Moscow .... Soviet embassy in Washington confirms the execution by Russia of Henryk Erlich and Victor Alter, Polish labor leaders, saying they were convicted in December of urging Red Army troops not to fight .... Capt. Edward Algernon FitzRoy, 73, speaker of the British House of Commons since 1928 and Conservative member from Daventry (1900-1906, 1910-1943), dies in London.	Allied planes attack a Japanese convoy and sink seven of eight transports and two of eight destroyers in the Battle of the Bismarck Sea.		Gandhi ends his 21-day fast with a religious ceremony and a glass of orange juice in the Aga Kahn's palace in Poona, India.
March 4		On the northwestern front the Russians capture the railroad towns of Olenino, Chertolino and Manchalovo.		Pres. Rafael Angel Calderon Guardia of Costa Rica arrives in Mexico City.	
March 5		British troops retake Sedjenane from the Germans in the north, while French units drive from Nefta to Mides in Tunisia.		A military court in Rio de Janeiro acquits Dr. Cauby de Araujo of charges that he obtained military secrets for the Germans.	
March 6		Rommel's reinforced troops launch a dawn attack against the British south of the Mareth Line in southeastern Tunisia .... Presidium of the Supreme Soviet confers the military title of Marshal of the Soviet Union upon Joseph Stalin .... Russians capture German stronghold of Gzhatsk, 100 miles west of Moscow.	Two Japanese destroyers are sunk while trying to drive off a U.S. Navy bombardment force at Vila and Munda in the central Solomons .... Chiang issues a new book, *China's Destiny*, proposing a 10-year economic development plan for the country after the war.		
March 7		Russians claim capture of a total of 94 localities in drives on Vyazma .... French North African Civil and Military Commander Gen. Henri Honore Giraud abolishes Vichy laws affecting Jews.	Chinese repulse a Japanese force striking north from Tachupa on the Yunnan-Burma border.		
March 8	Vice Pres. Wallace says unless the Allies come to a satisfactory agreement on the postwar world before this war ends the seeds for WW III will have been planted.	Axis forces, after losing 33 tanks, retreat toward the hills north of Medenine near the Mareth Line in Tunisia .... Russian troops recapture Sychevka, 34 miles northwest of Gzhatsk, claiming 8,000 Germans killed .... Turkish National Assembly unanimously re-elects Pres. Ismet Inonu to a second four-year term.			
March 9		German-Italian forces continue to retreat to high ground near Hallouf on the Mareth Line, and further north are repulsed in their attack upon Tamera .... French collaborationist Marcel Deat escapes unharmed when gunmen attempt to assassinate him at his home in Arbouse, southeast of Paris.		FDR asks Congress to amend the organic law of Puerto Rico to permit the people there to elect their own government.	
March 10		Russians repulse German counterattacks south and west of Kharkov .... U.S. Amb. to Russia William Standley confers with Foreign Commissar Viacheslav Molotov about charges that U.S. aid to Russia is insufficiently publicized.	Chinese troops recapture Chiakungfang, Kiangchuchieh and other points on the west bank of the Salween River in Yunnan Province .... The 14th U.S. Air Force is created in China under Brig. Gen. Claire L. Chennault, replacing the China Air Task Force.	Pres. Avila Camacho accepts a plan of the Mexican railroad workers whereby they agree to let the government manage the roads and discipline workers for the war's duration.	
March 11		British and Free French forces drive around the southern end of the Mareth Line to Ksar Rhilane .... Germans claim to drive the Russians back in fierce fighting around Kharkov.	A 70,000-man Japanese force attacks southward across the Yangtze River, capturing Hwajung in northern Hunan Province.	Argentine Postmaster Gen. Horacio Rivarola bans five U.S. short-wave radio broadcasts on the ground that they are political propaganda.	Sydney R. Leibrandt is sentenced to death in Pretoria, South Africa for sabotage.

	A	B	C	D	E
	Includes developments that affect more than one world region, international organizations and important meetings of major world leaders.	*Includes all developments in European countries and military engagements between Allied and Axis powers in Africa and at sea.*	*Includes all developments in Japan and China, Japanese foreign policy and military actions in the Pacific region.*	*Includes all domestic and regional developments in Latin America, the Caribbean and Canada.*	*Includes developments in those independent nations and colonial possessions not covered in Columns B, C and D.*

U.S. Politics & Social Issues	U.S. Foreign Policy & Defense	U.S. Economy & Environment	Science, Technology & Nature	Culture, Leisure & Life Style	
Senate Judiciary Comm. approves the McKellar bill to require Senate confirmation of between 25,000-30,000 federal employes earning $4,500 or more a year .... Princeton Univ. announces it will commence a four equal quarter academic year for the war's duration, replacing the semester system now in use.	State Dept. announces it will intern Axis diplomats captured in North Africa, to be exchanged for American diplomats in Vichy held by Germany.	OPA Chief Brown ends police enforcement of the ban on pleasure driving in 17 Eastern states, asking drivers to obey the ban on a voluntary basis .... NWLB grants a general wage increase of $4\frac{1}{2}$¢-an-hour plus a wage adjustment bonus to 30,000 Boeing Aircraft Corp. workers .... WPB Chmn. Nelson names Julius Krug as vice chairman in charge of materials and Donald Davis vice chairman for operations.		Museum of Modern Art purchases the anti-Fascist painting *The Eternal City* by Peter Blume, which had been banned by the Corcoran Gallery of Art of Washington in 1939.	March 3
Rep. John Taber (R, N.Y.) assails an OWI cartoon booklet, *The Life of FDR*, as propaganda designed to promote a fourth term.	Stettinius announces that $295,501,494 worth of Lend-Lease goods have been sent to India since March 1941.	Maritime Commission Chmn. Rear Adm. Emory S. Land tells House Naval Affairs Comm. "illegitimate absenteeism" among shipyard workers is costing the construction program 100 Liberty ships a year .... Texas Gov. Coke R. Stevenson announces state union leaders have signed a pact outlawing strikes, slowdowns and lockouts for the war's duration.			March 4
Lt. Col. Elliot Roosevelt, son of the President, scores criticism of his service record and those of his three brothers by Rep. William P. Lambertson (R, Kan.).		A House Ways and Means subcommittee approves a 20% withholding tax on wages effective July 1.		Academy of Motion Picture Arts and Science names *Mrs. Minever* as the year's best picture; Greer Garson, best actress; and James Cagney, best actor .... Beau Jack (Sidney Walker), $135\frac{1}{2}$-pound Georgia Negro and world lightweight champion, outpoints Fritzie Zivic of Pittsburgh, 146 pounds, in a 12-round non-title bout in Madison Square Garden, New York.	March 5
Postmaster Gen. Frank Walker bars the magazine *The Militant* from the mails on grounds that it openly discourages participation in the war.		FDR appoints a special committee to report on manpower, including James F. Byrnes, Bernard Baruch, Adm. William Leahy, Harry L. Hopkins and Samuel I. Rosenman.		NYU captures the IC 4-A track meet in N.Y.	March 6
		About 1,000 AFL Consolidated Aircraft Corp. workers meet in San Diego, Calif. to protest an NWLB decision granting them a $7\frac{1}{2}$-cent-an-hour wage increase and urge that the Army and Navy take over the plant.			March 7
Mrs. Eleanor Roosevelt says the President's election to a third term was due to a "world situation" rather than politics and that fourth-term talk is premature.		Federal government announces it was unable to obtain sufficient meat to cover the requirements of the armed forces and the Lend-Lease program during the last two months .... FDR signs a bill permitting the merger of Western Union and Postal Telegraph and Cable System.		Supreme Court rules the conviction of two Jehovah's Witnesses in Texas for distributing tracts without a license violates the constitutional rights of freedom of speech and religion.	March 8
		AFL and CIO peace committees, which agreed Dec. 2 to arbitrate jurisdictional disputes, are reported to have signed a secret clause stating that the pact would not interfere with the legal rights of union affiliates.	Harold G. Suggars, pioneer X-ray technician, dies at 65 in London.		March 9
	House approves the extension of Lend-Lease through June 1944.	UMW Pres. John L. Lewis demands a $2-a-day wage increase and a minimum wage of $8 for 200,000 northern Appalachian coal miners .... House Ways and Means Comm. approves a plan for a 20% withholding tax on wages beginning July 1 .... FDR sends to Congress two National Resource Planning Board reports outlining a national social security program and proposing postwar economic adjustments and reforms.	Socony-Vacuum Oil Co. announces a new "bead catalyst" refining method to break down crude oil molecules to produce high octane aviation fuel.	Manuel Ortiz defeats Lou Salica by a TKO in the 11th round to retain his world bantamweight title in Oakland, Calif. .... Dartmouth routs Penn, 70-34, to win its sixth consecutive Eastern Intercollegiate League Basketball Championship.	March 10
	FDR promotes Maj. Gen. George S. Patton, Jr., commander of the 1st Armored Corps in North Africa, and Maj. Gen. Carl W. Spaatz, commander of the U.S. Army Air Force in Northwest Africa, to lieutenant generals .... Congressional resolution extending Lend-Lease for another year is passed by the Senate and signed by FDR .... Lend-Lease Admin. Stettinius reports to Congress that U.S. aid during the two years ended Feb. 28 totaled $9,632,000,000.	Treasury Secy. Morgenthau announces the department will borrow a record $13 billion in April.		Detroit Red Wings defeat Toronto Maple Leafs to clinch their fourth NHL title in 10 years.	March 11
F *Includes elections, federal-state relations, civil rights and liberties, crime, the judiciary, education, health care, poverty, urban affairs and population.*	G *Includes formation and debate of U.S. foreign and defense policies, veterans affairs and defense spending. (Relations with specific foreign countries are usually found under the region concerned.)*	H *Includes business, labor, agriculture, taxation, transportation, consumer affairs, monetary and fiscal policy, natural resources, pollution and accidents.*	I *Includes worldwide scientific, medical and technological developments, natural phenomena, U.S. weather and natural disasters.*	J *Includes the arts, religion, scholarship, communications media, sports, entertainment, fashions, fads and social life.*	

	World Affairs	European War Zone	Pacific War Zone	The Americas	Other Countries & Territories
March 12	British Foreign Secy. Anthony Eden arrives in Washington for conferences on war and postwar problems.	Soviet forces recapture Vyazma, 130 miles southwest of Moscow, claiming 9,000 Germans killed .... RAF planes heavily bomb Stuttgart and other industrial and communication centers in southwest Germany.			
March 13	Eden and FDR begin war discussions at the White House.	RAF and RCAF drop 1,000 tons of bombs on Essen in the worst raid the German industrial city has yet to experience .... German forces make another gain west of Kharkov and increase their pressure in other sectors of the city.			
March 14		Germans retake the Ukrainian industrial center of Kharkov, which the Russians had captured on Feb. 16 .... French North African Civil and Military Commander Gen. Henri Giraud promises cooperation with all Frenchmen "who are participating in the battle against the enemy" and restoration of "the French tradition of human liberty to North Africa." .... Axis guns and British artillery begin a long-range duel along the Mareth Line in Tunisia.	Chinese troops recapture Huiyaochieh and Hsiangyangchiao along the west bank of the Salween River near Burma.		
March 15		Gen. Giraud says the "moment for the union of all Frenchmen of good will has come. I am ready to receive Gen. de Gaulle."	Chinese claim to stop the eight pronged Japanese assault upon the Hupeh - Hunan border south of the Yangtze River.	Import-Export Bank grants Brazil $150 million in credits for mining developments and railroad electrification .... Eric A. Johnson, president of the U.S. Chamber of Commerce, leaves Panama after completing his South American tour.	
March 16		Russian forces drive to within 50 miles of Smolensk on the central front .... U.S. and Canadian naval officials meet in Washington to discuss anti-U-boat warfare.	Chinese troops recapture Shanghachang and Yanglingshih, south of the Yangtze River, reaching the outskirts of Hwajung.	Canadian government presents the House of Commons with a social security plan calling for $30 monthly pensions for single persons and $45 for married couples.	
March 17		Churchill says in London the responsibility for Britain's Empire must remain solely that of the British .... French North African Commander Giraud formerly restores the laws of the French Republic and issues five ordinances to enact reforms which he announced March 14 .... U.S. 1st Division retakes Gafsa and advances towards El Guettar in Tunisia .... Russian troops claim destruction of two German battalions in driving them back at Chuguyev, 22 miles east of Kharkov.	Chinese troops recapture five towns in the Hwajung area and attack Hwajung itself.	Hans Borchers and three other Nazi diplomats leave Buenos Aires for Spain under an Allied safe conduct pass.	
March 18	British Foreign Secy. Eden says in Washington that the U.K., U.S., Russia and China are working in harmony and predicts an agreement on postwar aims.	Soviet troops repulse German counterattacks at Chuguyev, southeast of Kharkov, with heavy losses .... U.S. patrols occupy El Guettar, Tunisia without opposition.	Allied bombers raid 14 Japanese bases along a 2,200-mile front from Amboina to New Ireland and the Solomons .... British troops east of the Mayu River fall back north of Rathedaung, Burma in the face of Japanese attacks.	Import-Export Bank grants $20 million in credits for the development of the Volta Redona steel mill and $14 million for development of the Itabira iron mines in Brazil.	
March 19	FDR announces that within two months U.N. members will gather in the U.S. to discuss postwar food problems.	Nazi Elite Guards capture Belgorod, 46 miles northeast of Kharkov, which the Russians had taken Feb. 9 .... Completing a 10-day cruise in the Mediterranean, two British subs claim sinking six Axis supply ships.	Japanese reinforcements are sent south of the Yangtze River in the Hupeh-Hunan border region to aid in counterattacks at Hwajung, Owchihkow and Mitoushih.		
March 20		After four days of assaults, the Germans report sinking 32 Allied ships in a convoy across the North Atlantic .... In their successes on the Kharkov front, the Germans claim 50,000 Russians killed and 19,594 prisoners taken .... Polish exile government in London reports the Germans have killed 35,000 Jews in Radomsko, Radzymin, Sobolew, Szczerzec and Ujazd.	With the aid of air cover, the Chinese repulse the Japanese counterattacks in the Hupeh-Hunan area.		Sayed Sibghatullah Shah, leader of the Moslem Hur sect of Sind Province, India, is executed in Hyderabad for pillaging, wrecking trains and other terrorist acts.
	A *Includes developments that affect more than one world region, international organizations and important meetings of major world leaders.*	B *Includes all developments in European countries and military engagements between Allied and Axis powers in Africa and at sea.*	C *Includes all developments in Japan and China, Japanese foreign policy and military actions in the Pacific region.*	D *Includes all domestic and regional developments in Latin America, the Caribbean and Canada.*	E *Includes developments in those independent nations and colonial possessions not covered in Columns B, C and D.*

U.S. Politics & Social Issues	U.S. Foreign Policy & Defense	U.S. Economy & Environment	Science, Technology & Nature	Culture, Leisure & Life Style	
Wendell L. Willkie appeals to the Supreme Court against the cancellation of citizenship of William Schneiderman, a Communist, for the second time. Willkie states that conviction on the basis of seditious statements in CP literature is preposterous, since guilt in America is personal.		OPA announces that rationing of meats, canned fish and edible fats and oils, including butter and most cheeses, will begin March 29 . . . . A bill to raise the national debt to $210 billion with a rider to repeal FDR's executive order limiting net salaries to $25,000 is passed by the House and sent to the Senate.			March 12
	Sen. Carl A. Hatch (D, N.M.) reports that he and Sens. Joseph H. Ball (R, Minn.), Harold H. Burton (R, Ohio) and Lister Hill (D, Ala.) have drawn up a resolution calling for a permanent United Nations organization.	John L. Lewis is re-elected by the UMW for his 12th term as international president . . . . Financier J.P. Morgan dies at 75 in Boca Grande, Fla.	Capt. James Loveless and Col. William Denton of the U.S. Army Medical Corps report that sulfathiazole may be a gonorrhea and chancroid preventive. Tests conducted on 1,400 Negro soldiers resulted in a gonorrhea rate of 8 per 1,000, as compared with a rate of 171 per 1,000 in a control group of 4,000 men.	Stephen Vincent Benet, poet and author who won the 1928 Pulitzer Prize for *John Brown's Body*, a 100,000-word narrative poem, and the 1937 O. Henry Award for *The Devil and Daniel Webster*, a short story later made into a motion picture, dies at 44 in New York . . . . Greg Rice runs the season's fastest two-mile race, winning the event at the Knights of Columbus Meet in Madison Square Garden, New York, in 8:52.7.	March 13
	FDR confers with four senators concerning their resolution proposing a U.N. organization, while Sen. Wheeler charges the U.S. should avoid such entangling alliances.				March 14
Supreme Court agrees to review the convictions of Louis Buchalter, Emanuel Weiss and Louis Capone on charges of murdering Joseph Rosen in Brooklyn in 1936.		Lewis threatens a strike of 450,000 miners on April 1 unless a satisfactory wage agreement is signed by then . . . . Herbert Hoover says unless immediate steps are taken to stop a "dangerously degenerating agriculture," this country will face a food disaster which may lose the war . . . . Supreme Court upholds reorganization plans drafted by the ICC for the Western Pacific Railroad and the Chicago, Milwaukee, St. Paul & Pacific Railroad.			March 15
FDR nominates Tom C. Clark to succeed Thurmond Arnold as an assistant attorney general in the Justice Dept.					March 16
	Senate passes the Bankhead-Johnson bill, deferring essential farm labor from military service.	OPA announces its ban on pleasure driving in the East will end March 22.			March 17
Federal Judge John Bright deprives Fritz Kuhn and 10 other members of the German-American Bund of their citizenship . . . . William H. Hastie is awarded the Springarn Award of the NAACP as the outstanding American Negro for 1942. A former federal judge and law school dean, Hastie accused the Army Air Forces of "reactionary policies against Negroes."		Republicans caucus in the House to organize opposition to the Ways and Means Comm. tax bill and support the Carlson proposal.		John Foster Dulles, chairman of a commisssion established by the Federal Council of the Churches of Christ in America, outlines in New York a statement of "political principles" based on six "pillars of peace."	March 18
Frank Nitti shoots himself to death in Riverside, Ill. after being indicted by a N.Y. grand jury on charges of extorting $2.5 million from the AFL International Alliance of Theatrical Stage Employes.	Under War Secy. Robert P. Patterson tells the Senate Military Affairs Comm. that passage of the Austin-Wadsworth national war service bill is needed to utilize manpower now wasted in non-essential jobs.	Commerce Secy. Jesse H. Jones reports the national income rose 26% in 1942 to $119.8 billion . . . . House adopts the Pace bill to include labor costs in parity levels for farm products and sends it to the Senate.			March 19
Frank O. Lowden, governor of Illinois from 1917 to 1921 and candidate for the GOP presidential nomination in 1920 and 1924, dies in Tucson, Arizona at 82.		Appalachian coal mine operators appeal to FDR for government intervention to ward off a UMW strike threatened for April 1 . . . . House Ways and Means Comm. says the Ruml plan will force those in lower brackets to assume the forgiven tax debts of the wealthy.		Ensign Cornelius Warmerdam pole-vaults 15 feet 8½ inches at the Chicago Relays to better his own world record of 15 feet 7¾ inches.	March 20

F	G	H	I	J
Includes elections, federal-state relations, civil rights and liberties, crime, the judiciary, education, health care, poverty, urban affairs and population.	*Includes formation and debate of U.S. foreign and defense policies, veterans affairs and defense spending. (Relations with specific foreign countries are usually found under the region concerned.)*	*Includes business, labor, agriculture, taxation, transportation, consumer affairs, monetary and fiscal policy, natural resources, pollution and accidents.*	*Includes worldwide scientific, medical and technological developments, natural phenomena, U.S. weather and natural disasters.*	*Includes the arts, religion, scholarship, communications media, sports, entertainment, fashions, fads and social life.*

	World Affairs	European War Zone	Pacific War Zone	The Americas	Other Countries & Territories
March 21	Churchill says after the war the U.S., Britain and Russia should work through an international agency to safeguard against future wars.	Allies commence a pincer drive to trap Rommel's Afrika Korps in southeastern Tunisia . . . . Moscow announces the Red Army today abandoned Belgorod, north of Kharkov, and lost another town southeast of Kharkov . . . . Hitler assails the "satanic rage of destruction from the so-called West," which is allied to "the world of barbarism that is threatening from the East."	Japanese troops take Hwajung and Kiangpotu in heavy fighting south of the Yangtze River and destroy dikes, flooding the rice paddies which sustain the population.		
March 22	Axis radio broadcasts announce that representatives in Tokyo under provisions of the Tripartite Pact have reached complete agreement on building a "new world order based on justice and eternal world peace."	British and American forces make gains along the Mareth Line against Rommel's forces . . . . Russian troops capture Durove, 60 miles northeast of Smolensk, and 40 populated places to the north below Byelyi.		Liberals capture 71 seats, the Conservatives 50 and the Communists one in elections to the Colombian Chamber of Representatives.	
March 23		Russia claims 7,000 Germans slain and 140 tanks destroyed in an abortive four-day counteroffensive against the Moscow-Bryansk railroad north of Zhizdra . . . . British take German strongholds between Zarat and Arram on the northern end of the Mareth Line.	Three formations of U.S. planes bomb 250 Japanese planes at airfields at Lakunai, Vunakanau and Rapopo in New Britain.		
March 24		Tunisian battle rages in four sectors: (1) northern end of the Mareth Line. (2) 20 miles beyond the line near El Hamma, (3) northwest near El Guettar and (4) east of Maknassy . . . . Russian troops capture Abinsk, 20 miles northeast of the German-held Black Sea port of Novorossiisk.	Three downed U.S. fliers are rescued by Australians after surviving for 10 months and 12 days in the jungles of New Britain.	Vice Pres. Wallace addresses the Panamanian National Assembly, urging resumption of Latin American relations with Russia.	
March 25			Tojo announces in Tokyo the creation of "the new independent State of Burma," which includes all of Burma except the Shan States that border China and Thailand . . . . Russian Foreign Affairs Vice Commissar S.A. Lozovsky and Japanese Amb. Naotake Sato sign in Kuibyshev a one-year extension of the Japanese-Russian fisheries agreement . . . . American planes drop 2,000-pound bombs for two hours on Rabaul, New Britain, causing large fires and heavy explosions.		
March 26		De Gaulle announces he will be going to North Africa shortly to confer with Giraud . . . . British troops make slight gains against the Mareth Line, while U.S. forces repulse German attacks in the Garsa and Maknassy sectors.	A U.S. Navy light surface force drives off a Japanese flotilla composed of four cruisers, four destroyers and two cargo ships west of Attu Island.		
March 27	FDR and Eden conclude their talks on war and postwar strategy in Washington.	American troops begin a new assault toward Fondouk in central Tunisia . . . . Russian forces wipe out a German wedge driven into their Donets River line.	Chinese troops retake Chuchiachuan in the Ichang section of Hupeh Province.	Brazil announces it will send 500 aviators to train in the U.S.	
March 28		American troops capture Fondouk. 52 miles from the Mediterranean coast at Sousse, while to the south, British forces smash the Axis defenses at El Hamma . . . . In their 59th raid of the war on Berlin, RAF planes drop a record 900 tons of bombs.			Sen. Alben Barkley (D, Ky.) says in N.Y. that postwar settlement "must and will include the establishment of Palestine as a Jewish homeland."
March 29	British economist John Maynard Keynes proposes a plan for an international currency based on international bank money to be known as "bancor," designed to increase postwar trade.	British overrun the Mareth Line in southern Tunisia and drive Rommel's troops towards Gabes in the northwest.	Chinese troops recapture Tiaoyenkow and Hwangchangchiawan, south of the Yangtze River.		
	A *Includes developments that affect more than one world region, international organizations and important meetings of major world leaders.*	B *Includes all developments in European countries and military engagements between Allied and Axis powers in Africa and at sea.*	C *Includes all developments in Japan and China, Japanese foreign policy and military actions in the Pacific region.*	D *Includes all domestic and regional developments in Latin America, the Caribbean and Canada.*	E *Includes developments in those independent nations and colonial possessions not covered in Columns B, C and D.*

U.S. Politics & Social Issues	U.S. Foreign Policy & Defense	U.S. Economy & Environment	Science, Technology & Nature	Culture, Leisure & Life Style	
		OPA announces the suspension of sales of butter, margarine, lard, shortening and cooking and salad oils effective 12:01 a.m. tomorrow to conserve supplies.	Flood waters spread oveer a wide area in Georgia, Mississippi, Alabama and Louisiana.		March 21
Census Bureau reports the population of the continental U.S. increased 1.2% in 1942 to a total of 135, 604,000.		FDR telegraphs John L. Lewis and Appalachian coal mine operators to continue work under their present contract after April 1 until an agreement is reached .... Rep. Frank Carlson (R, Kan.) introduces a new tax bill to erase 1942 taxes and place 1943 taxes on a pay-as-you-go basis.	Prof. L.C. Martin of the Imperial College of Science reports inventing a microscope using beams of electrons instead of light.	Metropolitan Opera Co. plays its first local engagement in Chicago in 33 years, presenting *The Marriage of Figaro* under the baton of Bruno Walter.	March 22
	FDR accepts Patrick Hurley's resignation as minister to New Zealand and names him as his personal representative to the Near and Middle East war theaters .... FDR asks Congress to raise the rank of U.S. envoys in Haiti, Dominican Republic, Ecuador, Guatemala and Costa Rica from ministers to ambassadors.	Senate passes a revised version of the Disney House bill raising the national debt to $210 billion and repealing FDR's salary limitation order .... Employes at the Irvin, Pa. plant of the Carnegie-Illinois Steel Corp., U.S. Steel Corp. subsidiary, admit at a hearing of the Senate (Truman) war program investigating committee that analyses of about 5% of the steel plate manufactured by the plant for naval and other shipyards were faked to circumvent specifications.		*The Year of Decision: 1846* by Bernard de Voto is published.	March 23
		Northern Appalachian coal mine operators and the UMW sign an agreement extending wage negotiations one month beyond the April 1 deadline of the present contract .... House approves the Senate version of a bill fixing the national debt at $210 billion and modifying FDR's order limiting net incomes to $25,000 .... House passes the Bankhead bill to forbid the inclusion of farm benefit payments in fixing parity prices and returns it to the Senate.			March 24
	Senate Foreign Relations Comm. establishes a subcommittee to study all pending resolutions concerning cooperation with the U.N. during and after the war.	FDR appoints Chester C. Davis, 55, president of the Federal Reserve Bank of the St. Louis district, as food administrator to serve in the Agriculture Dept. under Secy. Claude R. Wickard .... Senate approves a conference report on the bill to raise the national debt limit and modify salary limitations and sends it to FDR.		Pauline Betz wins the national indoors singles tennis title in Chestnut Hill, Mass. With Mrs. George Wightman she wins the indoors doubles and with Al Stitt the national mixed doubles.	March 25
		FDR orders the amalgamation of the Commodity Credit Corp., the Extension Service and the Food Distribution and Production Administration into an "Administration of Food Production and Distribution" within the Agriculture Dept.		Gregory Rice breaks his own world record for the two-mile run, winning a Cleveland track meet with a time of 8:51.	March 26
Boston Police Commissioner Joseph F. Timilty and six of his chief subordinates are indicted by a Suffolk County (Mass.) grand jury on charges of conspiracy to permit the operation of gambling houses and the registration of bets.	Chief of Ordnance Maj. Gen. Levin H. Campbell reports the Army is now using a new short-range anti-tank gun called a bazooka.			Ohio State University's swimming team wins the NCAA title with 81 points at Columbus.	March 27
				World-famous pianist, composer and conductor Sergei Rachmaninoff dies at 69 in Beverly Hills, Calif.	March 28
FDR appoints son of former Navy Secy. Josephus Daniels, Jonathan W. Daniels, as a White House administrative assistant.	More than 2,600 Japanese-American volunteers leave Hawaii to train at Camp Shelby in Hattiesburg, Miss., after ceremonies yesterday attended by nearly 20,000 persons in Honolulu.			St. John's Univ. wins the NIT Basketball Tournament defeating Toledo, 48-27, at Madison Square Garden.	March 29
F *Includes elections, federal-state relations, civil rights and liberties, crime, the judiciary, education, health care, poverty, urban affairs and population.*	G *Includes formation and debate of U.S. foreign and defense policies, veterans affairs and defense spending. (Relations with specific foreign countries are usually found under the region concerned.)*	H *Includes business, labor, agriculture, taxation, transportation, consumer affairs, monetary and fiscal policy, natural resources, pollution and accidents.*	I *Includes worldwide scientific, medical and technological developments, natural phenomena, U.S. weather and natural disasters.*	J *Includes the arts, religion, scholarship, communications media, sports, entertainment, fashions, fads and social life.*	

	World Affairs	European War Zone	Pacific War Zone	The Americas	Other Countries & Territories
March 30	Delegates of 38 U.N. countries are invited to meet in the U.S. April 27 to discuss food and other postwar agricultural problems.	British occupy Metouia and Oudref, eight and twelve miles northwest of Gabes in southeastern Tunisia, while in the north British and French troops take Sedjenane, 35 miles southwest of the Bizerte naval base .... Stockholm reports that Lithuanian and Latvian peasants and students are waging guerrilla warfare against the Germans.			
March 31		Berne reports that at least 400 persons were killed and 2,000 injured on March 28 in Naples when an ammunition dump exploded in the harbor area .... Russians capture Anastasevsk, an important German defense base north of Novorossiisk on the Black Sea.		Vice Pres. Wallace says in Chile postwar U.S. investments in Latin America should be supervised by an international board.	
Apr. 1	Speaking in Ottawa, Eden says the U.N. should maintain sufficient force after the war to ensure a lasting peace .... Under State Secy. Sumner Welles says in N.Y. that unless the U.S. is willing to play an active role in the postwar world, peace cannot be kept.	Rommel's forces dig in around Wadi el Akarit, about 20 miles north of Gabes, Tunisia .... In the greatest single raid of the North African campaign, nearly 100 Flying Fortresses bomb Cagliari harbor and south Sardinian airfields.	Japanese forces attempting to invade Yunnan Province are driven back into Burma by Chinese troops who pursue them to Mongwa and Mongtsui .... Chinese sources claim have ambushed several thousand Japanese troops northeast of Kingmen in central Hupeh.		Viceroy of India bans all Indian political leaders from visiting Gandhi, who is interned at Poona.
Apr. 2	British Labor Party calls for a postwar international colonial commission to guarantee equal access for all nations to colonial markets and eliminate enonomic monopolies.	British and French troops advance through El Aouna toward Mateur in the north, while Allied bombers attack Bizerte docks and airfields in the Sfax area.		Sen. Millard Tydings (D, Md.) introduces a bill to give independence to Puerto Rico.	
Apr. 3		Patton's infantry attack is checked by the Germans east of El Guettar in Tunisia .... Soviets release a map of their war position for the first time, indicating a 1,500-mile front from Leningrad to the Caucasus.		Brazilian Foreign Min. Oswaldo Aranha denies Brazil is preparing an army to send to Africa.	
Apr. 4		RAF drops an estimated 900 tons of bombs on the Krupp Works in Essen with the reported loss of 21 heavy bombers .... Allied forces capture Cap Serrat on the Mediterranean, 35 miles west of Bizerte.			
Apr. 5		Russian troops capture more territory in the Kuban area in their drive on the German base of Novorossiisk on the Black Sea.	A Honan Province famine, affecting between three and seven million persons, is called China's worst disaster since the start of war with Japan .... Supported by fighter planes, 10,000 Japanese troops attack east of Shaokwang in central Shantung Province.	Bolivian Council of National Defense asks Pres. Enrique Penaranda del Castillo to declare war on the Axis.	
Apr. 6		After an intense artillery bombardment, the British resume their attack upon the Axis line along Wadi el Akarit .... Alexandre Millerand, first Socialist member of a French cabinet and president of the French Republic (1920-1924), dies in Versailles at 84.		Bolivia declares war on the Axis, becoming the 33rd member of the United Nations.	
Apr. 7	British government publishes a White Paper by John Maynard Keynes announcing its postwar currency stabilization plan, designed to provide an international banking system.	Advance patrols of the U.S. and British armies meet on the Gafsa-Gabes road just south of Djebel Chemsi, Tunisia .... British open an attack between Beja and Medjez-el-Bab in northern Tunisia .... After five days of attacks the Germans cease their effort to destroy the Russian bridgehead south of Izyum on the Donets River.	U.S. planes intercept a Japanese strike force of 50 bombers and 48 Zeros attempting to attack U.S. shipping in the Guadalcanal area, reportedly shooting down 39, while losing only six.	Bolivia orders the mobilization of troops for use in mining, oil and agricultural areas .... Russian Amb. to U.S. Maxim Litvinov arrives in Havana to present his credentials to Pres. Batista as the first Soviet minister to Cuba.	
Apr. 8	U.S. Comm. on Educational Reconstruction approves a plan drafted by Alonzo F. Myers to create a U.N. International Education Office to supervise postwar education in Axis and Axis-occupied countries .... Foreign Secy. Eden tells Commons he has invited Secy. Hull to visit England this summer.	German troops transfer their pressure on the Russians from Izyum to the Balakleya area, 25 miles to the north.	Japanese offensive north of Akyab, Burma is halted by British troops.		Secy. Hull and Iranian Min. Mohammed Shayestoh sign a three-year reciprocal trade agreement providing for tariff reductions.

A	B	C	D	E
Includes developments that affect more than one world region, international organizations and important meetings of major world leaders.	*Includes all developments in European countries and military engagements between Allied and Axis powers in Africa and at sea.*	*Includes all developments in Japan and China, Japanese foreign policy and military actions in the Pacific region.*	*Includes all domestic and regional developments in Latin America, the Caribbean and Canada.*	*Includes developments in those independent nations and colonial possessions not covered in Columns B, C and D.*

U.S. Politics & Social Issues	U.S. Foreign Policy & Defense	U.S. Economy & Environment	Science, Technology & Nature	Culture, Leisure & Life Style	
		House rejects the Carlson bill, which incorporates a modified version of the Ruml Plan; it then recommits the Ways and Means Comm. tax bill to the committee.		The musical *Oklahoma* by Lynn Riggs opens on Broadway, with music by Richard Rodgers and book and lyrics by Oscar Hammerstein II . . . . Wyoming Univ. downs Georgetown, 46-34, to win the NCAA Basketball Championship at Madison Square Garden.	March 30
		AFL and CIO leaders resume peace negotiations begun six years ago, discussing the 1942 proposed agreement covering jurisdictional disputes and "no raiding." . . . . Combined Shipping Adjustment Bd. discloses that the 1943 goal of 18.9 million tons dead weight of merchant vessels will give the U.S. the world's largest merchant fleet . . . . OPA places ceiling prices on all used commercial motor vehicles to curb speculators.	Bendix Aviation Pres. Ernest R. Breech says a revolutionary device has been developed that will conquer the hazards of blind flying and fog in commercial aviation.	Detroit defeats Toronto and Boston beats Montreal to meet for the NHL Stanley Cup . . . . Erich Leinsdorf, 32, a conductor of the Metropolitan Opera Company Orchestra, is appointed to succeed Artur Rodzinski as conductor of the Cleveland Orchestra for three years.	March 31
Postmaster Gen. Walker says there should be an agreement with the GOP for late 1944 Presidential conventions and a short campaign.	CP Secy. Earl Browder charges that Henryk Ehrlich and Victor Alter, Polish Socialists executed in Russia, were agents of "American conspirators" and the Polish government in a plot to overthrow the Soviet government.	House majority leader John McCormack (D, Mass.) urges the Ways and Means Comm. to report a compromise tax bill incorporating partial forgiveness and pay-as-you-go.			Apr. 1
Sens. William D. Langer (R, N.D.) and Pat McCarren (D, Nev.) introduce a bill to give statehood to Alaska.	House passes and sends to the Senate the war security bill designed to stiffen the penalties against spies, saboteurs and others convicted of hostile acts against the U.S.	FDR vetoes the Bankhead bill to exclude farm benefit and subsidy payments from parity ceilings, charging the bill is too inflationary . . . . Truman Investigating committee denounces Lewis for asserting that his no-strike promise to FDR is not necessarily binding.			Apr. 2
	SSS Dir. Lewis B. Hershey says men between 18 and 45 who are in nondeferrable occupations may be inducted after May 1.	House GOP leader Joseph Martin demands immediate action by the Ways and Means Comm. on the pay-as-you-go tax plan.		Ohio State Univ. wins the National AAU swimming championship in N.Y. with 46 points.	Apr. 3
A *N.Y. Times* survey given to 7,000 college freshman indicates that a large majority have little knowledge of elementary U.S. history.					Apr. 4
	Morgenthau lays before the Senate a $5-billion U.N. postwar currency stabilization plan based on a gold-backed international exchange bookkeeping currency called "Unitas," worth $10.			Supreme Court rules the Copyright Law does not nullify agreements by authors to assign their renewal interests.	Apr. 5
Democratic mayor of Chicago since 1933, Edward J. Kelly, wins re-election over GOP candidate George McKibbin for another four-year term.		A Newark, N.J. grand jury indicts 11 individuals and seven corporations on a charge of mulcting consumers of $2 million in a nationwide black market meat conspiracy.		Cleveland Rams announce their withdrawal from the NFL for the duration of the war.	Apr. 6
	FDR requests a record $24,551,070,000 Navy appropriation from Congress for fiscal 1944.	Forty Democratic representatives send Ways and Means Comm. Chmn. Robert Doughton a letter asking the committee to report a new pay-as-you-go tax bill immediately . . . . Senate votes to return the vetoed Bankhead bill to the Agriculture Comm.	Dow Chemical Co. Pres. Willard H. Dow is named winner of the Charles Frederick Chandler Medal, given annually by Columbia Univ. for achievements in chemistry.	Dorothy Lamour is married to Capt. William R. Howard in Beverly Hills, Calif.	Apr. 7
War Secy. Henry L. Stimson says Mayor Fiorello H. La Guardia of New York will not receive an Army commission "at least for the present" because of his "usefulness" as mayor.		In an effort to check inflation, FDR orders the freezing of wages and prices, prohibits workers from changing jobs unless the war effort would be aided and bars increases to common carriers and public utilities . . . . Senate approves a $40-million mobile labor farm bill for the use of Mexican and Bahaman workers to meet critical labor shortage area needs in the U.S.	Rockefeller Foundation reveals that MIT is using a mechanical brain that was built with $130,500 of the Foundation's funds.	Detroit Red Wings defeat Boston Bruins, 2-0, to win the NHL Stanley Cup in four straight games . . . . Lili Damita is awarded a divorce from actor Errol Flynn in Hollywood.	Apr. 8

	World Affairs	European War Zone	Pacific War Zone	The Americas	Other Countries & Territories
Apr. 9		British capture Mahares, 50 miles north of Gabes, as Axis forces continue to retreat towards Sfax.	U.S. bombers the Japanese stronghold in Kwangchowan, former French territory on the South China coast.		
Apr. 10	It is announced in Washington that the U.N. food conference will open May 18 at The Homestead Hotel in Hot Springs, Va.	Hitler and Mussolini complete their 12th wartime conference at the Brenner Pass, discussing defense efforts in case Italy is invaded .... British capture Sfax, central Tunisian port, as Axis troops withdraw towards Enfidaville, above Sousse.			
Apr. 11		British take LaHencha, and with French and American troops drive to wihin 10 miles of the city of Kairouan, Tunisia.		Peru orders the expropriation of all Axis-owned or controlled businesses effective May 1.	
Apr. 12		British capture Sousse, the last Axis port below Tunis.	In a raid on Port Moresby, New Guinea, the Japanese reportedly lose 31 of 100 planes.		
Apr. 13		British and French troops move to hem in an estimated 150,000 Germans and 60,000 Italians in the northeastern corner of Tunisia .... Allied planes report destroying 84 Axis craft at two Sicilian airfields, with a loss of three .... Russian troops beat back continuous German attacks on the Leningrad front.	American intelligence intercepts a top-secret message from the Japanese concerning an inspection tour of Buin on Bougainville by Japanese Admiral Yamamoto .... Japanese troops advance east and northeast of Hwajung in northern Hunan Province.		
Apr. 14		British troops take Djebel el Ang and Heidous, 26 miles west of Tunis, while French take Djebel Sefsouf .... Hitler and Rumanian Premier Ion Antonescu confer at Hitler's headquarters on "Eastern European" problems.	MacArthur says despite Allied submarine efforts the Japanese "have complete control of the sea lanes in the Western Pacific."	Secy. Hull cites American hemispheric unity and cooperation as an example to the rest of the world in a Pan-Am Day address in Washington.	
Apr. 15			Allied bombers attack a Japanese convoy off Wewak, New Guinea, sinking one and damaging two other merchant ships .... U.S. planes bomb Munda, New Georgia Island and Vila on Kolombangara Island in the Solomons.	In a N.Y. broadcast, Under State Secy. Welles says a "regional understanding" exists between the 20 American republics and Canada for postwar collaboration.	
Apr. 16		Polish government in exile asks the International Red Cross to investigate the disappearance of 15,000 Polish officers, soldiers, and civilians from three Russian prison camps from 1939 to 1941 .... Foreign Min. Count Fransisco Gomez de Jordana of Spain offers to mediate the war along with the Vatican and other neutrals .... In fierce fighting the British hold to the 2,204-foot mountain Djebel el Ang while the French repulse German counterattacks on Djebel Sefsouf .... Russian troops repel several German counterattacks in the Kuban-Novorossiisk area.	Remaining ships of the Japanese convoy off Wewak, New Guinea flee under heavy Allied plane assaults.	Jacques Mornard, who killed Leon Trotsky in 1940, is sentenced to 20 years in prison in Mexico City .... Martinique High Commissioner Adm. Georges Robert says he would join the Allies if France were united under one head and the interests of the Antilles safeguarded.	
Apr. 17		Allied planes carry out their greatest series of raids, attacking armament works and chemical plants in Pilsen, Czechoslovakia and Mannheim and Ludwigshafen in Germany.		Brazilian Pres. Vargas issues a decree prohibiting industrial workers from deserting their jobs.	
Apr. 18		In response to German protests about the Katyn Massacre, Moscow radio claims "the Polish prisoners were murdered by the Germans" and "that is why the bodies are still unidentifiable." .... Russians repell Nazi attacks near Novorossiisk.	Japanese Adm. Yamamoto is killed when American planes successfully intercept his flight group, concluding one of the most important American intelligence operations of the war.		
	A *Includes developments that affect more than one world region, international organizations and important meetings of major world leaders.*	B *Includes all developments in European countries and military engagements between Allied and Axis powers in Africa and at sea.*	C *Includes all developments in Japan and China, Japanese foreign policy and military actions in the Pacific region.*	D *Includes all domestic and regional developments in Latin America, the Caribbean and Canada.*	E *Includes developments in those independent nations and colonial possessions not covered in Columns B, C and D.*

U.S. Politics & Social Issues	U.S. Foreign Policy & Defense	U.S. Economy & Environment	Science, Technology & Nature	Culture, Leisure & Life Style	
N.Y. Gov. Thomas E. Dewey calls for a postwar return of state authority to deal with essential local problems and reverse the trend toward national authority.		FDR tells his news conference that retail ceiling prices are being planned for all consumer goods except clothing . . . . House passes and sends to the Senate the Hobbs anti-labor racketeering bill, which heavily penalizes interference with interstate commerce.			Apr. 9
			C.E.H. Hall reports success with growing silkworms on a N.J. farm, expressing confidence that the U.S. could become independent of Japanese silk after the war.	Barnett Welansky, owner of the Coconut Grove nightclub in Boston, is convicted of manslaughter for the fire that swept the club last November killing 491 persons.	Apr. 10
GOP National Chmn. Harrison E. Spangler says the Republicans will accept a short campaign and late conventions in 1944 if given assurances that FDR will not run . . . . Daniel Calhoun Roper, U.S. tariff commissioner (1917), commissioner of internal revenue and first prohibition enforcement chief (1917-1920) and minister to Canada (1938-1939), dies at 76 in Washington.	WPC Chmn. Paul McNutt and SSS Dir. Hershey issue new regulations under which all remaining able-bodied men between 18 and 38 will be inducted in 1943.	FDR permits the bill raising the national debt to $210 billion and repealing his order on salary limitations to become law without his signature.			Apr. 11
	Army reveals some statistical data on the Norden bombsight, which is adjustable for altitude and airspeed.	Secy. Morgenthau opens the Second War Loan Drive for $13 billion and announces that the Treasury plans to borrow $70 billion in 1943.			Apr. 12
	FDR begins a 16-day, 7,600-mile inspection tour of training camps and war factories.		Omaha Municipal Airport and the village of Carter Lake, Iowa are under six feet of water after the Missouri River dikes break.	FDR dedicates the Jefferson Memorial in Washington on the 200th anniversary of Jefferson's birth . . . . Sidney Kingsley's *The Patriots* wins the N.Y. Dramatic Circle's award as the best play of the season.	Apr. 13
	OWI Dir. Elmer Davis says in Washington that 35 psychological warfare experts are in North Africa directing propaganda at enemy troops and populations behind the lines.	WMC says it will meet the need for 6.4 million workers in 1943 by drafting two million women, calling older workers from retirement and shifting three million others from non-essential jobs.		*Variety* reports the most popular songs are (1) *I've Heard That Song Before*, (2) *Old Black Magic*, and (3) *Don't Get Around Much Anymore*.	Apr. 14
	War Secy. Stimson says in reply to MacArthur's request for more planes that "we have had similar pleas from other parts of the world," resulting in allocation difficulties, but he promises to counter increasing enemy air strength . . . . Senate Agricultural Comm. votes to request representation at the U.N. Food Conference in May.	Dun and Bradstreet executive Arthur D. Whiteside is appointed WPB vice-chairman in charge of civilian requirements.	American Chemical Society reveals that a chemical compound known as 2,3,5 tri-iode-benzoic acid checks the growth of tuberculosis bacilli.		Apr. 15
	Senate approves and sends to the House the Wagner bill, extending the $2-billion currency stabilization fund for two years but eliminating the right of the President to devalue the dollar.	FBI arrests eight Baltimore shipyard welders for doing faulty welding to earn money faster. Two others are seized later.	Dallas engineer David Pfeiffer describes five methods (direct vacuum pump, steam jet, cold surface, chemical dessication and physical absorbent) of drying liquid blood plasma to preserve its essential elements.	Book of the Month Club reveals pressure by *The Daily Worker*, a Communist newspaper, and "fellow travellers" to suppress publication April 19 of the English translation of Mark Aldanov's Russian novel *The Fifth Seal* as "subtly and viciously anti-Soviet." . . . . *The World of Yesterday*, by Stephan Zweig, a posthumous autobiography, is published.	Apr. 16
		WMC Chmn. Paul V. McNutt, in conformity with President Roosevelt's anti-inflation order, issues regulations "freezing" 27,000,000 government, railroad, farm and industrial workers in their jobs.			Apr. 17
	An AP poll reveals 32 senators oppose committing the U.S. at this time to participate in the postwar international police force, with 32 others undecided and 24 in favor.			Gerard Cote wins the 47th Boston Marathon, running the 26-mile course in 2:28. 25⅘.	Apr. 18

F	G	H	I	J
Includes elections, federal-state relations, civil rights and liberties, crime, the judiciary, education, health care, poverty, urban affairs and population.	*Includes formation and debate of U.S. foreign and defense policies, veterans affairs and defense spending. (Relations with specific foreign countries are usually found under the region concerned.)*	*Includes business, labor, agriculture, taxation, transportation, consumer affairs, monetary and fiscal policy, natural resources, pollution and accidents.*	*Includes worldwide scientific, medical and technological developments, natural phenomena, U.S. weather and natural disasters.*	*Includes the arts, religion, scholarship, communications media, sports, entertainment, fashions, fads and social life.*

	World Affairs	European War Zone	Pacific War Zone	The Americas	Other Countries & Territories
Apr. 19	Bermuda Refugee Conference opens in Hamilton with the statement that victory is essential to effective refugee aid.	Armed Jews in Warsaw begin to resist German units preparing to liquidate the city's ghetto .... Gen. Giraud proposes to de Gaulle that a "French Council of Overseas Territories" be established, including administrators from Martinique, Algiers and metropolitan France, until provisional governments can be created .... RAF planes make a concentrated raid on the Italian naval base of Spezia in northern Italy.		Spanish refugee leaders agree at a Montevideo, Uruguay conference to meet in Mexico City soon to discuss the formation of a Spanish republican government in exile.	FDR authorizes extension of Lend-Lease aid to Saudi Arabia.
Apr. 20		British sieze Enfidaville and Takrouna near the Tunisian coast .... A U.S. Navy report discloses that ship-based helicopters are patrolling the 500-mile Atlantic gap beyond airplane range.	Tojo realigns his cabinet, with Mamoru Shigemitsu becoming Japanese foreign minister.	FDR and Pres. Avila Camacho meet in Monterrey, Mexico and pledge the extension of the Good Neighbor Policy in the postwar period.	
Apr. 21		British repulse a strong German counterattack by 60 to 80 tanks and five battalions in the Medjez el Bab sector in Tunisia .... Russian troops again repell Nazi assaults in the Novorossiisk area of the Kuban valley .... Turkey and Germany conclude a new commercial agreement to exchange $30 million worth of goods during the next year.	FDR announces with a "feeling of deepest horror" the barbarous execution of some U.S. fliers by the Japanese and says that these efforts of intimidation will make Americans more determined "to blot out the shameless militarism of Japan."	FDR and Avila Camacho inspect the naval air training station at Corpus Christi, Tex., where U.S. and Latin American officers are training.	
Apr. 22			A Tokyo broadcast to the U.S. warns that every U.S. flier who bombs Japan in the future will be given a "one-way ticket to hell."		New Delhi federal court declares invalid the Defense of India Rule No. 26, under which more than 8,000 All-India Congress leaders, including Gandhi and Nehru, have been interned.
Apr. 23		Patton's tank corps moves to within 15 miles of Mateur in a strong offensive, repulsing German counterattacks, and taking some 100 prisoners .... Allied planes fly a record 1,500 sorties over Tunisia, reporting heavy damage .... Red Cross International Comm. in Geneva accepts "in principle" Polish government and German Red Cross demands to identify the bodies of 10,000 Polish officers reported found near Smolensk, but says it will proceed only if asked to do so "by all parties concerned." .... British report sinking six U-boats during an attack upon an Allied convoy in the North Atlantic.	British officials in New Delhi charge that the Japanese bayoneted to death prisoners captured in Burma who were unfit for work .... U.S. Liberators bomb the Japanese base on Tarawa in the northern Gilbert Islands without loss, causing extensive damage.		
Apr. 24		Armed Irish Republican Army members seize a theater in Belfast. IRA chief Hugh McAteer protests the presence of U.S. troops and warns that they may become involved in British-Irish strife.	Nearly 40,000 Japanese troops launch converging offensives from northern Honan and southeastern Shansi Provinces.	Upon his return from a seven-nation Latin American tour, Vice Pres. Wallace says leaders there asked for more machinery to turn out war goods and farm products.	Mohammed Ali Jinnah is re-elected president of the All-India Moslem League and warns Britain against "its shabby treatment of Moslem India."
Apr. 25		French and American troops advance slowly along a wide Tunisian front, as the British press on towards Hallout on the Tunisian coast .... Russian troops occupy the hills surrounding Novorossiisk on the Black Sea.			FDR's personal representative to India, William Phillips, says at his final New Delhi press conference that the Indian government has refused him permission to interview Gandhi and Nehru.
Apr. 26	American and British delegates to the Refugee Conference in Bermuda agree to relocate refugees in French North Africa, Libya and Ethiopia.	Allied North African headquarters announces Axis forces in North Africa have suffered 66,000 casualties, including 36,000 captured .... Russia suspends diplomatic relations with the exiled Polish government in London for its attacks upon the Soviets in connection with the Katyn Massacre.	Japanese troops attack in the Mayu Peninsula area south of Buthedaung, one of the few remaining Allied bases in western Burma.		Moslem League adopts a resolution demanding a separate state and warns of bloodshed if forced into a union with the Hindus.
	A	B	C	D	E
	Includes developments that affect more than one world region, international organizations and important meetings of major world leaders.	*Includes all developments in European countries and military engagements between Allied and Axis powers in Africa and at sea.*	*Includes all developments in Japan and China, Japanese foreign policy and military actions in the Pacific region.*	*Includes all domestic and regional developments in Latin America, the Caribbean and Canada.*	*Includes developments in those independent nations and colonial possessions not covered in Columns B, C and D.*

U.S. Politics & Social Issues	U.S. Foreign Policy & Defense	U.S. Economy & Environment	Science, Technology & Nature	Culture, Leisure & Life Style	
					Apr. 19
		House votes to amend the 1943-44 Agriculture Dept. budget by prohibiting incentive payments to farmers and sends it to the Senate . . . . The Third Circuit Court of Appeals in Philadelphia finds the Pullman companies and 31 officers and directors guilty of violating the Sherman Antitrust Act.		Washington defeats Philadelphia, 7-5, in Washington to open the 1943 baseball season.	Apr. 20
A House subcommittee investigating the Dies Committee charges against federal employes reports that Goodwin B. Watson and William E. Dodd of the FCC are "unfit" for government employment because of their pro-Communist connections.	House passes and sends to the Senate a bill authorizing one million more tons of Navy auxiliary vessels.	CIO Pres. Murray attacks the WMC's order freezing jobs and suggests that labor-management agreements be substituted to stabilize employment . . . . House votes to extend the Guffy Bituminous Coal Act, which sets minimum prices, to Aug. 24 . . . . Economic Stabilization Dir. James F. Byrnes approves wage increases for 26,000 pine lumber workers because the NWLB recommended the raise before FDR ordered wage freezes April 18.		Chas. C. Willoughby, anthropologist and director emeritus of the Peabody Museum, Harvard Univ., dies at 85 in Watertown, Mass.	Apr. 21
		Labor Secy. Frances Perkins certifies the bituminous coal dispute to the NWLB after negotiations collapse in N.Y. . . . . OPA sets maximum wholesale prices for poultry and permits retailers an 18-20% markup.	British Ministry of Health says after experiments with war workers and school children that vitamin pills make no difference in health records when diets are well balanced.		Apr. 22
	Six members of the American legation in Helsinki depart, leaving only Robert M. McClintock, charge d'affaires, and a small clerical staff behind.			Archbishop Francis J. Spellman leads hundreds of U.S. Catholics from the armed forces and thousands of others in a Good Friday procession along the Calvary route of Via Dolorosa in Jerusalem.	Apr. 23
A federal jury in Hattiesburg, Miss. acquits three men of lynching Howard Wash, a Negro: it was the first such trial in 40 years.	An AP poll reveals that at least 40 senators favor continuation of the Administration's reciprocal trade policy. Nineteen were opposed, demanding changes.	House Ways and Means Comm. reports a new tax bill which would "forgive" about 40% of 1942 taxes, apply a 20% withholding tax on wages and salaries July 1 and automatically place taxpayers on a pay-as-you-go basis by March 1946 . . . . NWLB orders operators and miners of the Appalachian region to continue uninterrupted production of coal . . . . As commander-in-chief, FDR orders several hundred striking members of the UMW District 50 to return to work at the Celanese Corp.'s Newark, N.J. plant by noon, April 26 or face government action.			Apr. 24
The GOP forms a committee headed by Rep. Charles Wolverton (N.J.) to study postwar domestic problems.				Vladimir Nemirovich-Dantchenko, cofounder of the Moscow Art Theater with Constantine Stanislavsky in 1898 and its director since, dies at 85 in Moscow.	Apr. 25
	Army releases details of its M-12 tank destroyer or gun motor carriage, a 155 mm. gun mounted on an M-3 tank chassis, capable of shooting a five-pound shell 10 miles . . . . The aircraft carrier *Intrepid* is launched at the Newport News, Va. shipyards.	NWLB Chmn. Davis appoints a three-man panel to hear the coal dispute after Lewis refuses to name a member.		U.S. Jews begin a six-week period of "mourning and intercession" on behalf of European Jews "exterminated by Hitler."	Apr. 26
F	G	H	I	J	
Includes elections, federal-state relations, civil rights and liberties, crime, the judiciary, education, health care, poverty, urban affairs and population.	*Includes formation and debate of U.S. foreign and defense policies, veterans affairs and defense spending. (Relations with specific foreign countries are usually found under the region concerned.)*	*Includes business, labor, agriculture, taxation, transportation, consumer affairs, monetary and fiscal policy, natural resources, pollution and accidents.*	*Includes worldwide scientific, medical and technological developments, natural phenomena, U.S. weather and natural disasters.*	*Includes the arts, religion, scholarship, communications media, sports, entertainment, fashions, fads and social life.*	

	World Affairs	European War Zone	Pacific War Zone	The Americas	Other Countries & Territories
Apr. 27		Allied troops continue to advance along the entire Tunisian front, while Allied planes blast the Axis forces with little opposition . . . . Gen. Giraud proposes that he and Gen. de Gaulle form a government together with a council of department heads . . . . P.M. Churchill, Foreign Secy. Anthony Eden and U.S. ambassadors Biddle and Winant confer with Polish Premier Sikorski and Foreign Min. Count Raczynski in London in an effort to mend the Polish-Soviet breach.	Japanese troops capture Linhsien and reach Chenchiaotsun and Yukiakwan in their offensive in Honan and Shansi Provinces.		
Apr. 28		*Pravda* accuses the Sikorski government of "treacherous behavior" in asking for an investigation of the alleged slaying of 10,000 Polish officers at Katyn Forest and says Russo-Polish relations have been "broken," not suspended . . . . Polish government denies Russian charges of "collaboration" with the Germans and says its policy aims at "a friendly understanding between Poland and Soviet Russia on the basis of integrity and full sovereignty of the Polish Republic." . . . . Counterattacking Germans with the support of 30 tanks drive the British off Djebel bou Aoukaz southwest of Tebourba, Tunisia.			Marquess of Linlithgow, viceroy of India, decrees the arrest of Gandhi and other Indian leaders to be valid and issues an ordinance permitting the arrest and internment of persons thought likely to hamper the war effort.
Apr. 29	Bermuda Refugee Conference closes with a declaration that a "substantial" number of refugees will receive help as a result of the meeting.	Soviets open an offensive against German positions in the Kuban Valley near Novorossiisk.		State Dept. announces a joint U.S.-Mexican committee will make a study of the Mexican wartime economy . . . . Alfredo Michelson is appointed Colombia's first minister to Russia.	
Apr. 30	FDR asserts that the alternative to the present reign of lawlessness is a definite body of laws adhered to by nations in their relations with each other.	German troops with heavy tank support again counterattack along the entire Tunisian front, but are repulsed with heavy losses . . . . U.S. and Canadian naval officials announce Allied planes will provide a protective umbrella over the North Atlantic shipping lanes in an effort to combat German U-boats . . . . A Yugoslav government spokesman in London says Gen. Draja Mikhailovich "fought the Soviet partisans [in Yugoslavia] only because they refused to take orders from anyone but Russia." . . . . Mrs. Beatrice Webb (Lady Passfield), wife of Sidney Webb, one of Britain's leading woman socialists, Fabian Society member, Labor Party leader and author, dies at 85 in Hampshire, England.		Secy. Hull announces severance of political relations and termination of all agreements with Martinique because of its close association with Vichy and Nazi Germany.	
May 1	Bolivia announces its adherence to the U.N. Pact.	American troops clear Djebel Tahent and with Moroccans capture part of Djebel Hazemat in a two-pronged attack on Mateur . . . . The Netherlands are placed under martial law by Nazi Commissioner Arthur Seyss-Inquart.			
May 2		At a Polish rally in London, Churchill predicts "that a great and independent Poland" will be restored after the war.	Allied fighters report destroying or damaging 13 of the 21 Japanese bombers and 30 fighters attacking Darwin, Australia.		U.S. National Conference for Palestine adopts a resolution in Philadelphia denouncing the British 1939 White Paper restricting Jewish settlement in Palestine.

U.S. Politics & Social Issues	U.S. Foreign Policy & Defense	U.S. Economy & Environment	Science, Technology & Nature	Culture, Leisure & Life Style	
	House Ways and Means Comm. approves a three-year extension of the Reciprocal Trade Agreements Act.	Lewis says miners will not report to work May 1 without a wage contract.			Apr. 27
Minn. Gov. Harold Stassen (R) resigns to enter the Navy and Lt. Gov. Ed Thye takes over.	Gen. Joseph W. Stilwell and Maj. Gen. Claire Chennault arrive in Washington from Chungking to confer with FDR on the Pacific Theater.	NWLB refers the soft-coal miners' dispute to FDR.	Four tornadoes sweep northern Ohio, killing three, injuring 150 and destroying $4 million worth of property.		Apr. 28
	FDR returns from his inspection tour of training camps and factories, praising the war effort and saying that a year of military training might benefit the nation's young men in peacetime . . . . Henry J. Kaiser will build two helicopters for the British capable of taking off from merchant ships to attack submarines, Cargoes, Inc., a Lend-Lease Admin. subsidiary, announces in Washington.	FDR warns Lewis that all necssary government power will be used should the miners strike on May 1 . . . . Secy. Morgenthau approves the House Ways and Means Comm.'s new tax bill, which would add an estimated $2.7 to $5.6 billion to government revenues . . . . Sen. Walter George (D, Ga.) says he opposes further increases in corporate and individual income taxes and compulsory savings and favors a reasonable pay-as-you-go tax plan.	Six Parke, Davis & Co. scientists announce the isolation of a 14th vitamin, Bc, in crystalline form from liver.		Apr. 29
		UMW rejects FDR's ultimatum not to strike when its contract expires at midnight tonight.		Count Fleet, ridden by Johnny Longden, wins the 69th Kentucky Derby in a 10-horse field.	Apr. 30
	A Gallup Poll reports 74% of people questioned favor a postwar international police force with 12% undecided and 14% against.	FDR directs Interior Secy. Harold Ickes to take over all bituminous and anthracite mines after 10 a.m. . . . . WMC Chmn. McNutt decrees a 48-hour week for the steel industry and sets July 1 as the final date for compliance . . . . WPB Chmn. Nelson sets up the Office of Civilian Requirements to replace the Office of Civilian Supply within the WPB.	RCA demonstrates in Princeton, N.J. a radio-electronic sewing machine that stitches thermoplastics with radio frequency current instead of thread.		May 1
	GOP Post War Policy Assn. calls for a postwar council of nations based on the U.N. to maintain world order.	Lewis announces an agreement with Secy. Ickes for a two-week truce in the coal strike.			May 2

F	G	H	I	J
Includes elections, federal-state relations, civil rights and liberties, crime, the judiciary, education, health care, poverty, urban affairs and population.	*Includes formation and debate of U.S. foreign and defense policies, veterans affairs and defense spending. (Relations with specific foreign countries are usually found under the region concerned.)*	*Includes business, labor, agriculture, taxation, transportation, consumer affairs, monetary and fiscal policy, natural resources, pollution and accidents.*	*Includes worldwide scientific, medical and technological developments, natural phenomena, U.S. weather and natural disasters.*	*Includes the arts, religion, scholarship, communications media, sports, entertainment, fashions, fads and social life.*

	World Affairs	European War Zone	Pacific War Zone	The Americas	Other Countries & Territories
May 3		Allied troops continue to advance along the entire Tunisian front, with French forces attacking Pont du Fahs in the southwest sector and American troops occupying Mateur, 19 miles south of Bizerte . . . . Berlin radio announces that a German-selected commission drawn from 11 Axis-dominated countries and Switzerland held an "inquest" on 982 corpses dug up near Smolensk and found they were bodies of Polish officers shot in March and April of 1940 by the Russians . . . . U.S. European Commander Lt. Gen. Frank Andrews and 13 other persons are killed in a plane crash on Iceland after attempting to land in bad weather. Andrews is the eighth U.S. general lost in the war.			
May 4		American and French Moroccan forces capture Eddekhila and drive to within 10 miles of Bizerte . . . . Nazis abandon Krymsk after four days of Soviet assaults.	U.S. Liberators participate in the heaviest raid of the Pacific war from China, bombing Hainan Island and Indochina.		William V. Tubman is elected president of Liberia to succeed Edwin J. Barclay, president since 1931.
May 5		Martial law is imposed in Sofia, Bulgaria following widespread rioting . . . . In the war's largest raid by four-engine planes, RAF and RCAF aircraft drop 1,500 tons of bombs on the German manufacturing city of Dortmund . . . . Mussolini says "Italy must and will return" to its African empire, whose loss he describes as only a "pause" in its development . . . . Soviet troops recapture Krymsk and advance on a 15-mile front towards Novorossiisk.		Brazilian Pres. Vargas cancels Paraguay's war indemnity debt dating from 1870 . . . . Venezuelan Pres. Isaias Medina Angarita forms a new cabinet which includes five new ministers.	
May 6		In an all-out attack the British take Massicault in the central Tunisian area . . . . At least four and probably 10 German U-boats are sunk after an eight-day battle ends between an east-bound Atlantic convoy and about 25 Axis submarines . . . . Stalin tells *N.Y. Times* reporter Ralph Parker that he favors a strong and independent Poland after the war.	On the first anniversary of the fall of Corregidor, MacArthur says, "Until we lift our flag from its dust we stand unredeemed before mankind."	Bolivian Pres. Enrique Penaranda del Castillo says Bolivia will use its army in the war if necessary.	
May 7		British drive 16 miles from Massicault to take Tunis at 4:20 p.m., five minutes after U.S. and French troops take the Bizerte naval base.			
May 8	Office of Foreign Relief and Rehabilitation Operations Dir. Herbert H. Lehman says negotiations are proceeding to form a U.N. relief organization.	British, French and U.S. troops drive the remnants of Axis troops toward the Cap Bon Peninsula and mop up thousands of trapped men behind the lines.			
May 9	Gen. Francisco Franco appeals for world peace because the war has reached a point where neither belligerent has the power to destroy his opponent.	Allies take 50,000 German and Italian prisoners, including four German generals, as Allied troops encircle the Cap Bon Peninsula . . . . More than 400 American planes carry out the biggest raid of the campaign against Palermo, Sicily at noon, smashing the industrial and dock area.	Indian and British troops abandon Buthedaung, their Mayu River base 15 miles northeast of Maungdaw on the Bengal border.		
May 10		British troops advance 12 miles south of Creteville and hammer at the German rearguard southeast of Hamman Lif in an effort to close the Cap Bon Peninsula. French troops drive up from the southwest to Djebel Oust. Germans accept Allied demand for unconditional surrender at Cap Bon, surrendering 25,000 additional troops.		Fire destroys the National Library of Peru in Lima, which contained more than 100,000 rare volumes and 40,000 manuscripts.	
May 11	Churchill and advisers arrive in Washington to confer with FDR on the war's progress.	Allied planes from Tunisia, Libya and Malta heavily bomb Marsala and Catania, Sicily, and Pantelleria Island.		British send troops from Barbados to Dominica Island in the West Indies "in connection with the Martinique situation."	
	A	B	C	D	E
	Includes developments that affect more than one world region, international organizations and important meetings of major world leaders.	*Includes all developments in European countries and military engagements between Allied and Axis powers in Africa and at sea.*	*Includes all developments in Japan and China, Japanese foreign policy and military actions in the Pacific region.*	*Includes all domestic and regional developments in Latin America, the Caribbean and Canada.*	*Includes developments in those independent nations and colonial possessions not covered in Columns B, C and D.*

U.S. Politics & Social Issues	U.S. Foreign Policy & Defense	U.S. Economy & Environment	Science, Technology & Nature	Culture, Leisure & Life Style	
		McNutt reveals that plans for a nationwide job-freezing order have been canceled because regulations barring essential-industry workers from changing jobs have already been issued in nine of the 12 WMC regions by local offices.	Harvard Observatory Dir. Dr. Harlow Shapley announces the discovery of 75,000 new galaxies averaging more than one billion suns each.	Columbia Univ. announces the following Pulitzer Prizes: drama, *The Skin of Our Teeth* by Thornton Wilder; novel, *Dragon's Teeth* by Upton Sinclair; history, *Paul Revere and the World He Lived In*, by Esther Forbes; biography, *Admiral of the Ocean Sea* by Samuel E. Morison; and poetry, *A Witness Tree* by Robert Frost .... Supreme Court reverses itself in two 5-4 decisions, invalidating municipal ordinances that compel Jehovah's Witnesses to pay license fees for the distribution of religious tracts in Texas.	May 3
Theodore R. McKeldin (R) is elected mayor of Baltimore, defeating Mayor Howard W. Jackson (D).		Ickes orders all coal miners to a six-day work week and denies he made any promise to Lewis regarding the strike settlement .... House passes the Robertson-Forand tax bill to cancel that part of the 1942 individual income tax liability covered by the 6% normal tax and 13% first surtax.			May 4
	War Dept. announces the promotion of 63 generals, giving the Army more than 600.	Postmaster Gen. Walker announces a system of zoned numbers will be added after the name of the city on all mailed matter in 178 large cities to facilitate delivery .... Senate passes, 63-16, and sends to the House the Connally bill to expand the President's power to seize strike-bound plants.	It is announced that Capt. G.R. Buxton, 37, British Overseas Airway Corp. pilot, has flown a Liberator from Newfoundland to Great Britain in six hours and 12 minutes for a new North Atlantic flying record.	Howard L. Walls, curator of the Library of Congress' new film collection, says the Library plans to restore to celluloid 5,000 motion pictures made from 1897 to 1917.	May 5
Sen. Edward Robertson (R, Wyo.) says Japanese internees in Western camps are exempt from rationing restrictions and are "pampered" by the Relocation Administration .... Committee on American History urges that freshman high school students get a full year of U.S. history.	Lt. Gen. Jacob L. Devers is named U.S. commander in the European theater to succed the late Lt. Gen. Frank M. Andrews .... OWI Dir. Elmer Davis says there is "no question but that there will be Allied operations on Continental Europe this summer."	Senate's Truman committee asserts, in reporting on priorities conflicts in synthetic rubber, aviation gasoline and destroyer escort ship programs to the Senate, that independent "czars" with specified objectives in particular fields encroach on and weaken WPB authority .... Ten GOP members of the House Ways and Means Comm. file a minority report denouncing the Reciprocal Trade Agreements as inadequate to solve postwar foreign trade problems.	Navy reports discovery of a repellant that will keep sharks away from men adrift at sea.		May 6
		FDR says coal miners are now employes of the government and have no right to strike .... Price Admin. Prentiss Brown announces a 10% reduction in the retail prices of meat, coffee and butter effective June 1, to be subsidized by the RFC.	Igor Sikorsky is granted two helicopter patents, one to prevent slewing of the fuselage by the torque of the rotor and the other to control pitching and rolling.	National Federation of Music Clubs announces Nan Merriman is the winner of a $1,000 award in the Young Artists Auditions in N.Y. Nikolai Lopatnikoff wins the Cleveland Orchestra's $1,000 prize for his composition *Opus Sinfonicum*.	May 7
Mrs. Eleanor Roosevelt denounces Young Communist League methods as "intolerable in this country."		Senate Finance Comm. approves the Ruml Plan but modifies its anti-windfall withholding and service relief provisions.	Dr. Nabor Carrillo predicts in Puebla, Mexico that Mexico City will sink into the earth this century unless its continued subsidance into the soft ground is stopped.	Count Fleet, with Johnny Longden riding, wins the 53rd running of the Preakness Stakes at Pimlico, Md. .... Twentieth-Century Fox release of *The Ox-Bow Incident*, directed by William Wellman, starring Henry Fonda and based on the novel by Walter Van Tilburg, premiers in New York.	May 8
U.S. Student Assembly meeting in N.Y. adopts a constitution barring Communist groups from membership.	Duke and Duchess of Windsor arrive in N.Y. from Miami, Fla.				May 9
	FDR asks Congress to appropriate an additional $4.934 billion for naval aviation.	Commerce Dept. reports March exports broke the June 1919 record of $928 million and reached $931 million.		Supreme Court upholds the power of the FCC to prohibit ownership of more than one radio network by a company and to bar exclusive network contracts.	May 10
		House Military Affairs Comm. votes to revise the Connally bill forbidding war plant strikes until workers are polled, banning jurisdictional strikes and making it illegal to prevent workers from accepting jobs in strike-bound plants.		Episcopal Bishop William Manning says that a merger of the Episcopal and Presbyterian Churches would be a union "of organization and not faith" and would "create division and disruption." .... *Four Quartets*, by T.S. Eliot, is published in N.Y.	May 11
F *Includes elections, federal-state relations, civil rights and liberties, crime, the judiciary, education, health care, poverty, urban affairs and population.*	G *Includes formation and debate of U.S. foreign and defense policies, veterans affairs and defense spending. (Relations with specific foreign countries are usually found under the region concerned.)*	H *Includes business, labor, agriculture, taxation, transportation, consumer affairs, monetary and fiscal policy, natural resources, pollution and accidents.*	I *Includes worldwide scientific, medical and technological developments, natural phenomena, U.S. weather and natural disasters.*	J *Includes the arts, religion, scholarship, communications media, sports, entertainment, fashions, fads and social life.*	

	World Affairs	European War Zone	Pacific War Zone	The Americas	Other Countries & Territories
May 12	The Third Anglo - American Conference (Trident) opens in Washington with FDR, Churchill and their staffs. Churchill opposes any diversion of strength to the Pacific.	With the exception of isolated pockets of resistance the Allies claim that hostilities have stopped in Tunisia .... The secret German radio station Gustav Siegfried I says Marion Badoglio, son of Italian Marshal Badoglio, has discussed plans for a separate Italian peace with U.S. representatives in Tangier and Madrid .... *Gazette de Lausanne* reports that 150 Frenchmen, including many government officials and Adm. Rene Platon, former secretary of state, have been arrested in Vichy for plotting against Pierre Laval, Vichy chief of government.	British troops retreat from Maungdaw, Burma without interference from the Japanese and move north towards the Indian border .... Japanese troops establish a foothold on the southern end of Lake Tungting, 50 miles north of Changsha, capital of Hunan Province.	Bolivian Pres. Enrique Penaranda del Castillo arrives in Ottawa for a visit, becoming the first Latin American president ever to visit Canada .... Senate passes and sends to the White House a bill authorizing the appropriation of $25 million for the next two years to continue federal works in Puerto Rico and the Virgin Islands after the WPA expires July 31 .... Uruguay ends relations with the Vichy French government.	
May 13	FDR, Churchill and Czech Pres. Eduard Benes confer on the European theater of operations.	An Allied military spokesman says the total number of Axis prisoners taken in the Tunisian campaign since May 5 will approach 175,000, and Gen. Sir Harold R.L.G. Alexander hails the victory as "one of the most complete and decisive in history." .... RAF and RCAF bombers drop nearly 2,000 tons of bombs on the German industrial center of Duisburg.	Gen. MacArthur and Adm. William F. Halsey meet in Australia to discuss the coordination of Allied commands in the south and southwest Pacific areas.	Gustavo Cuervo Rubio, Paul Menocal, 11 senators and seven representatives withdraw from the National Democratic Party to organize a new conservative group in Cuba.	
May 14		During the past 10 days the Nazis are reported to have liquidated the remaining 70,000 Jews in the Warsaw Ghetto. Of the 56,065 who surrendered, some 7,000 were shot immediately and the remainder sent to concentration camps .... In a Washington broadcast, Churchill claims that British and U.S. troops will soon be fighting on the continent .... With the surrender of the German 90th Light Division, the Allies claim to have taken all enemy prisoners in Tunisia .... Dutch government in London reports 70 Dutchmen have been slain in riots against Nazi storm troopers in Amsterdam and Rotterdam.	A Japanese submarine torpedoes the Australian Red Cross ship *Centaur* off the Queensland coast, with 64 persons saved and 268 missing .... Chinese troops recapture Linhsien and Hochieh in the Taihang Mountain region.	FDR and Bolivian Pres. Penaranda del Castillo issue a joint statement announcing an agreement to strengthen cooperation between the U.S. and Bolivia.	Kan Bahadur Allah Baksh, former president of the All-India Azad Moslem Conference, is killed by a gunman in Shikarpur, near the Baluchistan frontier.
May 15	At a Moscow meeting the Presidium of the Executive Committee of the Third International (Comintern), founded in 1919 to promote world revolution decrees its own dissolution, subject to ratification by the separate Comintern sections.	Russians repel a German attack at Leningrad and an attempt to cross the northern Donets River south of Krasny Liman .... U.S. planes bomb the Italian military base of Civitavecchia, and Sardinian bases and factories at Olbia, Alghero, Porto Torres, Abbasanta and Porto Ponte Romano.	Chinese claim recapture of 12 towns and the killing of 3,000 Japanese in the Taihang Mountains.	Mexican Pres. Avila Camacho decrees that prices of all staple foodstuffs be fixed and their distribution controlled to combat inflation.	Gen. Giraud deposes Sidi Moncef Pasha as Bey of Tunis and replaces him with Sidi Lamine Bey, a member of the Hussein family .... Mohammed Chouaib, the first Afghan consul to the U.S., arrives in Miami, Fla.
May 16		German planes make their heaviest raid on London since February and bomb the shipyards at Sunderland.			
May 17		RAF mine-carrying Lancasters bomb three western German dams—the Mohne, the Eder and the Sorpe—causing heavy flooding, killing 4,000 and leaving an estimated 120,000 homeless .... German troops reportedly suffer "heavy losses" in several attacks upon Soviet positions northwest of Novorossiisk .... RAF planes bomb the Italian seaplane base at Lido di Roma and then drop pamphlets over Rome indicating Italian cities scheduled to be bombed.	About 30,000 Japanese open a drive east of Laiwu in southern Shantung Province.		
May 18	With 45 nations represented, the U.N. Food Conference opens in Hot Springs, Va. with U.S. delegation Chmn. Marvin Jones elected conference president .... FDR confers with Churchill, the Duke of Windsor and Chinese Foreign Min. Dr. T.V. Soong about war strategy.	U.S. Flying Fortresses bomb the Deutsche Werke submarine yard at Kiel and the Flensburg shipyard and power station in northwest Germany, at a cost of six bombers.	U.S. forces on Attu Island in the Aleutians drive inland from their original landing points at Holtz Bay on the northeast shore and Massacre Bay on the southeast shore in a pincers movement against the Japanese.	Chile severs consular relations with the Vichy, Bulgarian and Rumanian governments.	
	A	B	C	D	E
	Includes developments that affect more than one world region, international organizations and important meetings of major world leaders.	*Includes all developments in European countries and military engagements between Allied and Axis powers in Africa and at sea.*	*Includes all developments in Japan and China, Japanese foreign policy and military actions in the Pacific region.*	*Includes all domestic and regional developments in Latin America, the Caribbean and Canada.*	*Includes developments in those independent nations and colonial possessions not covered in Columns B, C and D.*

U.S. Politics & Social Issues	U.S. Foreign Policy & Defense	U.S. Economy & Environment	Science, Technology & Nature	Culture, Leisure & Life Style	
	FDR nominates Anthony J. Drexel Biddle as ambassador to the Czechoslovak government in London.	WPB announces that ample plant and machine facilities now exist in the U.S. to defeat the Axis.		Albert Stoessel, violinist, conductor and composer, dies at 48 shortly after collapsing on stage in N.Y. while conducting an orchestra . . . . *Variety* lists the most popular songs as: (1) *As Time Goes By*, (2) *Don't Get Around Much Anymore* and (3) *It Can't Be Wrong.*	May 12
		House votes to extend the Reciprocal Trade Agreements Act for two years . . . . Ickes returns 94 Illinois coal companies to their owners after receiving a no-strike pledge from 40,000 AFL coal miners.			May 13
		Senate passes the Carlson (Ruml Plan) pay-as-you-go tax bill as approved by its Finance Committee.	*Science* reports that Merck & Co. Laboratories in N.J. have developed Biotin, the rare and powerful vitamin essential to man's life functions.		May 14
		Lewis announces in New York that the UMW will ignore the NWLB's order to send representatives to its bituminous coal hearing tomorrow.	A tornado injures 200 men and destroys or damages 41 buildings valued at $175,000 at the Fort Riley, Kan. cavalry replacement center.		May 15
Vice Pres. Wallace states that the future of the Americas lies in applying the Four Freedoms to bring about "complete productivity of labor in terms of better living conditions" for "the plain people." . . . . GOP Nat. Comm. Asst. Chmn. Marion Martin announces GOP women everywhere are organizing drives to curb the misuse of government propaganda in supporting FDR's fourth term schemes.	Twentieth Century Fund discloses that at least 137 U.S. government and private agencies are engaged in research or public education on a national scale on postwar problems.	War Food Administration and the OPA establish a nine-man War Meat Bd. to combat black market operations.	Authority and pioneer in cancer radium treatments, Dr. James Ewing, dies at 76 in N.Y.		May 16
		Lewis announces the extension of the UMW no-strike agreement to midnight May 31, following an appeal by Ickes . . . . FDR asserts his opposition to the Ruml Plan because it would benefit the taxpayers in the upper income groups.		Council on Books in Wartime announces that 35,000,000 copies of new pocket-size American books will be printed and shipped abroad to the U.S. armed forces in the coming year . . . . Supreme Court rules that a radio station whose interests would be affected by an FCC grant of additional privileges to another station may be represented in hearings on the case.	May 17
		House votes against instructing its conferees on the joint House and Senate committee to accept the Senate version of the Ruml pay-as-you-go tax plan.	Three persons drown, millions of dollars worth of crops are destroyed and hundreds are made homeless in floods in Illinois and Indiana.		May 18
F	G	H	I	J	
Includes elections, federal-state relations, civil rights and liberties, crime, the judiciary, education, health care, poverty, urban affairs and population.	*Includes formation and debate of U.S. foreign and defense policies, veterans affairs and defense spending. (Relations with specific foreign countries are usually found under the region concerned.)*	*Includes business, labor, agriculture, taxation, transportation, consumer affairs, monetary and fiscal policy, natural resources, pollution and accidents.*	*Includes worldwide scientific, medical and technological developments, natural phenomena, U.S. weather and natural disasters.*	*Includes the arts, religion, scholarship, communications media, sports, entertainment, fashions, fads and social life.*	

	World Affairs	European War Zone	Pacific War Zone	The Americas	Other Countries & Territories
May 19	Addressing Congress, Churchill says there will be total war against Japan and that he, FDR, Stalin and Chiang Kai-shek will meet together soon.	Czech Pres. Eduard Benes proposes that his government and that of Poland should lead in the creation of a Central European Federation with the approval of Russia after the war.			Gen. Jean Emile Rene Chadebec de Lavalade arrives in Beirut, Syria to become acting chief of Fighting French Forces in the absence of Gen. Georges Catroux.
May 20	New Zealand delegates present a seven-point program to the U.N. Food Conference calling for international food distribution based upon need rather than ability to pay.	Sources in London report that Gens. Giraud and de Gaulle have agreed to meet concerning the future of France .... Soviet troops reportedly repulse an attack by 12,000 Germans east of Novorossiisk .... U.S. planes destroy 91 Axis planes in bombing raids on airfields in Italy, Sicily, Sardinia and Pantellaria.	Three columns of Japanese troops numbering 60,000 attack toward Enshih, wartime capital of Hupeh Province.		
May 21	Dean Acheson, assistant secretary of state, tells the U.N. Food Conference that an international conference will be held soon to discuss relief for occupied nations as they are freed from the Axis.		Japanese troops continue towards Enshih, capturing Tseliangping and claiming to have annihilated nine Chinese divisions.	In a joint congressional meeting, the Mexican Senate and Chamber of Deputies demand that the semi-fascist Union Sinarquista be dissolved as a threat to national security.	
May 22		RAF planes bomb Berlin for the third straight night and attack railroad installations in northern France .... U.S. planes bomb Sardinia, Sicily and Italy, destroying 93 Axis planes, including 66 on the ground.	U.S. Navy announces the battle for Attu is in its final phase, with the Japanese forces split into three separate groups on the eastern peninusula.	Chmn. Dr. Jose Antonio Arze of the Bolivian Left Revolutionary Party discloses he has reached a political truce with Pres. Enrique Penaranda del Castillo.	
May 23	British delegation to the World Food Conference advocates expanded production and consumption through an international food bank to stabilize supplies .... Berlin radio says the Anti-Comintern Pact will remain in effect despite Russia's dissolution of the Comintern.	Istanbul reports guerrilla warfare is speading in Greece, Albania, Yugoslavia, Bulgaria and Crete, with the attacks being directed by Allied Middle Eastern headquarters.			Egyptian Chamber of Deputies votes confidence in Premier Mustafa Nahas Pasha after a five-day debate over charges he used his official position to gain personal benefits.
May 24	Hull says the dissolution of the Comintern in Moscow is certain to promote greater trust among the U.N. members.	De Gaulle announces his acceptance of Giraud's proposal for a nine-man council and says he will leave for Algiers soon .... RAF makes its heaviest and most concentrated attack of the war, dropping more than 2,000 tons of bombs on Dortmund, Germany.	Japanese move almost 260 miles east of Chungking, capturing Yuyangkwan and moving on Wufeng.		
May 25	Trident (Washington) Conference closes after FDR and Churchill secretly agree to fix the target date for a cross-Channel invasion of Europe (Overlord) for May 1944 .... P.M. Churchill, appearing at a press conference with FDR, calls on the Italian people to discard their leaders and throw themselves upon the justice of the Allies .... U.S. delegation to the U.N. Food Conference proposes the establishment of a U.N. interim commission to further the work of the conference and to deal with food and agricultural problems pending the formation of a permanent international body.	Because of Allied bombing, Rome announces that Cagliari, Sardinian capital, has been abandoned and places all war workers in Sicily and Sardinia under military control.	Japanese forces take Changyang on the central Yangtze front.		
May 26	Russian delegation to the U.N. Food Conference gives its approval to the U.S. proposal that an interim food commission be established .... Henri La Fontaine, president since 1907 of the International Bureau of Peace in Brussels and Nobel Peace Prize winner in 1913, dies at 89 in Brussels.	An RAF bomber fleet numbering 500 makes a heavy raid on the German munitions center of Duesseldorf .... More than 400 Allied planes bomb airfields, railroads, ports and factories in Sicily, Sardinia and Pantelleria.	U.S. Army troops attack a Japanese force on a ridge to the northwest of Chichagof Valley on Attu Island.		Moslem League forms a ministry in the Northwest Frontier Province of India with Mohammed Aurangzeb Khan as premier .... FDR appoints Vice Adm. William Glassford as his representive to French West Africa with the rank of minister.
May 27	U.S. and British military leaders complete their conference in Washington on future war operations.	A Russian force of about 150,000 attacks and drives the Germans back northwest of Krymsk in the Kuban Valley .... U.S. planes continue their attack on Sardinia, Sicily, and Pantelleria, striking at airfields, power stations, railways and dams.	Chinese planes attack the Japanese base of Ichang without loss and also Enshih, 200 miles northeast of Chungking.		
	A *Includes developments that affect more than one world region, international organizations and important meetings of major world leaders.*	B *Includes all developments in European countries and military engagements between Allied and Axis powers in Africa and at sea.*	C *Includes all developments in Japan and China, Japanese foreign policy and military actions in the Pacific region.*	D *Includes all domestic and regional developments in Latin America, the Caribbean and Canada.*	E *Includes developments in those independent nations and colonial possessions not covered in Columns B, C and D.*

U.S. Politics & Social Issues	U.S. Foreign Policy & Defense	U.S. Economy & Environment	Science, Technology & Nature	Culture, Leisure & Life Style	
		AFL Pres. William Green says that the UMW has applied for reaffiliation with the AFL .... OPA again bans pleasure driving in 12 Eastern states as of tomorrow because of a lack of gasoline .... Joseph F. Fay and James Bove, vice presidents of AFL construction workers unions, are held on $25,000 bail each in N.Y. after pleading not guilty to indictments charging them with extorting over $1 million from N.Y. and Delaware contractors.	National Academy of Sciences in N.Y. gives the first $2,000 Charles L. Mayer award to Dr. Charles Huggins of the Univ. of Chicago for his cancer research.	Bob Montgomery outpoints Beau Jack in 15 rounds at Madison Square Garden to win the lightweight championship.	May 19
	FDR asks Congress to appropriate $71.898 billion for the Army, some $6 billion more than he requested in his January budget message.	AFL Pres. Green charges labor-restricting laws of Ark., Colo., Ida., Kan., S.D. and Tex. are an attempt "by the Fascist movement in America to tear the trade movement apart."	A group of Swedish scientists at Upsala Univ. isolate and photograph a virus thought to be the cause of infantile paralysis.		May 20
	House passes and sends to the Senate a supplemental Lend-Lease appropriation to meet requirements to June 30, 1944.	Nearly 40,000 United Rubber Workers Union members strike in Akron in protest against the NWLB wage decision granting them a three-cent instead of an eight-cent-an-hour increase.	Twelve persons die and 108,000 are made homeless as the Mississippi, Illinois, Wabash, Arkansas and other Midwestern rivers break their levees and flood more than a million acres in Ind., Ill., Mo., Ark., Kan. and Okla.		May 21
		AFL Pres. Green names Teamsters Union Pres. Daniel J. Tobin, Railway Clerks Union Pres. George M. Harrison and AFL Vice Pres. Matthew Woll to confer with John L. Lewis concerning reaffiliation.			May 22
		Morgenthau announces subscriptions to the Second War Loan totaled $18.5 billion but states an additional $45 billion will be needed for the war this year.			May 23
		Supreme Court dismisses a "friendly" action to test the Federal Rent Control Law as "collusive" and against the public interest.	Army assigns 10,000 soldiers to flood relief work in the Midwest as the Mississippi River rises to 40.5 feet at Cape Girardeau, Mo., a 100-year record; the death toll reaches 17 and 160,000 persons are reported homeless.		May 24
Gov. Sparks of Alabama orders State Guardsmen to patrol Mobile after race riots at the Alabama Drydock & Shipbuilding Co., in which eight men are injured .... House passes the Marcantonio bill to outlaw the levying of a poll tax by any state as a prerequisite for voting in federal elections.		House and Senate conferees adopt a compromise pay-as-you-go tax plan which would cancel 75% of one year's taxes for most people .... NWLB appeals to striking rubber workers in Akron, Ohio to "honor their no-strike pledge" and return to work.	Mississippi River bursts its levees on the Illinois shore from Columbia to Gale, a distance of 90 miles, putting more than three million acres in six states under water.	Antitrust Division of the Justice Dept. asks the U.S. District Court in N.Y. for a summary judgment against the AP as a news monopoly.	May 25
	FDR is host to Pres. Edwin Barclay and Pres.-elect William Tubman of Liberia; Barclay is the the first Negro to stay in the White House as a guest.	FDR orders 52,000 striking Akron rubber workers to return to their jobs by noon tomorrow .... A National Railway Labor Panel board recommends an eight-cent-an-hour wage increase for more than one million nonoperating railroad emloyes but rejects demands for a union shop.		Manuel Ortiz outpoints Joe Robleto in 15 rounds in Long Beach, Calif. to retain the world bantamweight title.	May 26
Richard Julius Krebs (alias Jan Valtin), author of *Out of The Night* interned on Ellis Island as an undesirable alien, is released on parole.		Striking rubber workers in Akron obey FDR's order and return to work .... International Assn. of Machinists Pres. Harvey W. Brown announces the union's withdrawal from the AFL .... House and Senate conferees amend the pay-as-you-go plan to permit application of a $50 credit against tax liabilities up to $66.67.			May 27

F	G	H	I	J
Includes elections, federal-state relations, civil rights and liberties, crime, the judiciary, education, health care, poverty, urban affairs and population.	*Includes formation and debate of U.S. foreign and defense policies, veterans affairs and defense spending. (Relations with specific foreign countries are usually found under the region concerned.)*	*Includes business, labor, agriculture, taxation, transportation, consumer affairs, monetary and fiscal policy, natural resources, pollution and accidents.*	*Includes worldwide scientific, medical and technological developments, natural phenomena, U.S. weather and natural disasters.*	*Includes the arts, religion, scholarship, communications media, sports, entertainment, fashions, fads and social life.*

	World Affairs	European War Zone	Pacific War Zone	The Americas	Other Countries & Territories
May 28		Germans claim to repulse Russian forces attacking in the lower Kuban Valley .... IRA leader James Steele is captured by police in Belfast, Northern Ireland .... British Labor Party Executive Committee announces in London it will oppose affiliation with the British CP at the annual convention June 14 despite the Comintern's dissolution.	U.S. forces continue their advance along the ridges southeast and northwest of Chichagof Harbor, Attu Island and drive Japanese troops from the Lake Cories area.	Mexican Pres. Avila Camacho marks the first anniversary of the declaration of war against the Axis by declaring that Mexico is ready to send troops abroad.	
May 29	Stalin says the Comintern's dissolution exposes the lies of Hitlerites and indicates Russia's intention not to interfere in the internal affairs of other countries.	Nearly 100 U.S. Flying Fortresses bomb the Italian port and oil refining center of Livorno, 160 miles northwest of Rome, without a loss .... The largest air strike by U.S. planes during the war is made on three Nazi bases in France: St. Nazaire, Rennes and La Pallice.	Chinese troops recapture Yuyangkwan, 35 miles southwest of Ichang, and inflict more than 2,000 casualties on the Japanese.		
May 30	U.N. Food Conference production section predicts an acute postwar shortage of food and food producing machinery and outlines a program to meet it.	De Gaulle arrives in Algiers from London with Rene Massigli and Andre Philip for conferences with Gen. Giraud .... Units of the British Mediterranean Fleet begin shelling Pantelleria Island .... More than 100 U.S. Flying Fortresses bomb Naples and an airplane factory in Pomigliano.	Japan issues a comunique stating that resistance on Attu Island has stopped after a final suicidal attack by Japanese soldiers.		
May 31	Under State Secy. Welles asserts the need for a postwar world court to settle international disputes and an international police force to enforce the peace.	De Gaulle and Giraud set up an executive committee in Algiers to govern the French Empire and to represent the French people until France is liberated .... Nine French warships and several small auxiliary craft commanded by Vice Adm. Rene-Emile Godfroy, which have been immobilized in Alexandria since the fall of France, join the Allied fleet.	Chinese forces rout five Japanese divisions and drive them back to Changyang, 15 miles south of Ichang .... Chinese forces in southeastern Shansi Province recapture Tuohuochen, Fushui and Laohuaishuling.		Egyptian cabinet votes to establish diplomatic relations with Russia, provisional to an agreement not to interfere in each other's internal affairs.
June 1	U.N. Food Conference asserts in a 500-word declaration that freedom from want can be achieved and includes freedom from fear, expanded food production and elimination of poverty among the goals urged.	Marcel Peytrouton, governor general of Algeria, resigns in a letter to Gen. de Gaulle to further "union among Frenchmen."	Chinese forces drive Japanese troops back in northern Hunan and Hupeh provinces along a 300-mile arc extending from Lake Tungting to Suihsien .... Chinese claim the Japanese suffered 30,000 casualties in their unsuccesful Yangtze River Valley offensive.		
June 2			Chinese troops capture Changyang and Chihkiang on the Yangtze River.		
June 3	U.N. Food Conference concludes after confirming the recommendations of its different sections calling for a new world order based on lasting peace and freedom from want.	French Comm. of National Liberation is formed in Algiers as the de facto government of all unoccupied French territories after three days of controversy .... In an effort to split the German Army, Russian forces attack near Temryuk on the Sea of Azov.		Mexican and U.S. representatives sign an agreement in Washington to extend until June 30, 1945 the 1941 stabilization pact under which the U.S. Treasury holds $40 million in Mexican pesos.	
June 4		Gens. Giraud and de Gaulle tell the people of occupied France in a joint broadcast over Algiers radio that all free Frenchmen are now united .... Right Rev. Edward S. Woods, Bishop of Lichfield, urges Rome be spared from bombing because any military advantage "would be more than offset by the moral damage to our cause in the eyes of the world."	Chinese troops recapture Itu and Yangchi, Yangtze River ports in western Hupeh Province, and occupy Nanhsien and Ansiang north of Tungting Lake .... Maj. Kermit Roosevelt, son of the late President Theodore Roosevelt, dies at 53 while on active duty in Alaska.	Argentine Army troops, led by Gen. Arturo Rawson, 58, and Gen. Pedro Ramirez, 59, war minister, overthrow the conservative and isolationist government of President Ramon Castillo, who flees aboard a minesweeper. About 100 soldiers and 15 civilians are killed in isolated clashes and martial law is invoked.	
June 5		Churchill returns to London after two days of talks at the Allied North African headquarters .... Vichy Premier Laval broadcasts from Paris that 200,000 Frenchmen must go to work in Germany by July 1.	Chinese forces recapture Kungan, Japanese base 67 miles south of Ichang, killing more than half of the defending troops.	Gen. Arturo Rawson assumes the presidency of Argentina as head of a military government after Castillo surrenders to Gen. Diego Mason at the La Plata naval base.	Gen. Charles Nogues resigns as resident general of French Morocco.

A	B	C	D	E
Includes developments that affect more than one world region, international organizations and important meetings of major world leaders.	*Includes all developments in European countries and military engagements between Allied and Axis powers in Africa and at sea.*	*Includes all developments in Japan and China, Japanese foreign policy and military actions in the Pacific region.*	*Includes all domestic and regional developments in Latin America, the Caribbean and Canada.*	*Includes developments in those independent nations and colonial possessions not covered in Columns B, C and D.*

U.S. Politics & Social Issues	U.S. Foreign Policy & Defense	U.S. Economy & Environment	Science, Technology & Nature	Culture, Leisure & Life Style	
		FDR issues an executive order naming James F. Byrnes director of an Office of War Mobilization to unify the work of all war agencies.	Mississippi River rises to 42.4 feet at Cape Girardeau, Mo., the highest in its history.	Violinist Fritz Kreisler becomes a U.S. citizen in ceremonies in the Naturalization Court in N.Y.	May 28
		OPA announces that 5¢-a-pound subsidies to butter producers will enable them to roll back prices about 6¢-a-pound, effective June 10.	Madrid reports German scientists in Potsdam have discovered North America is moving away from Europe at the rate of about one foot per year.		May 29
				Step by Step wins the $20,000 Handicap of the Americas, earning $15,000.	May 30
GOP National Chmn. Harrison E. Spangler announces the appointment of a 49-man committee to develop a "realistic peacetime program" for the postwar period.	War Mobilization Dir. Byrnes asserts the U.S. is now girding itself for many attacks on several fronts against the Axis.				May 31
		Approximately 530,000 coal miners strike as the mine operators reject a compromise offered by Lewis for a $1.50 temporary raise pending further study .... House passes the compromise pay-as-you-go tax bill and sends it to the Senate.		Actor Leslie Howard and 16 others are lost on an overseas airliner en route from Lisbon to England after being attacked by an enemy plane.	June 1
	Lend-Lease Admin. Stettinius reports Lend-Lease exports of food in the first four months of 1943 totaled 1,350,200 tons, nearly all of which went to Britain and Russia.	Senate passes the pay-as-you-go tax bill and sends it to FDR .... Senate votes to extend the Reciprocal Trade Agreements Act for two years .... NWLB orders the Appalachian Joint Conference and the UMW to halt negotiations for a new wage contract until the miners return to work.			June 2
	Senate passes and returns to the House a $6.273-billion supplemental Lend-Lease appropriation bill .... Du Pont electrochemical plant at Perth Amboy, N.J. demonstrates how the basic ingredient for a secret new explosive used in "block busters" is formed by mixing synthetic wood alcohol molecules with ammonia molecules.	FDR orders striking coal miners to return to work by June 7 and says that negotiations will continue only after work resumes .... Combined War Labor Board members, headed by AFL Pres. Green and CIO Pres. Murray, urge FDR to set up a $2-billion subsidy program to roll back prices to the May 15, 1942 level.		Charles S. Chaplin, 54, film comedian, is charged with being the father of the unborn child of Joan (Barry) Berry, 23, movie aspirant, in a paternity suit filed in Superior Court in Los Angeles.	June 3
	FDR tells his press conference that understanding and accord between himself and Stalin are excellent and denies that Adm. Standley has resigned as ambassador to Russia .... FDR promotes Maj. Gen. Omar N. Bradley, commander of the U.S. 2nd Army Corps which captured Bizerte, to lieutenant general.	UMW Policy Comm. votes to end the five-day coal strike June 7 after Lewis recommends the move at the request of Harold Ickes .... House approves and returns to the Senate the Smith-Connally anti-strike bill after radically revising it from the floor to make instigation of strikes or lockouts in government-operated plants or mines a crime.			June 4
Federal Judge Arthur J. Tuttle imposes the death sentence for the third time on Max Stephan, convicted of aiding an escaped Nazi flier .... A London, Ky. federal grand jury indicts 99 persons on charges of conspiracy and corruption in the election of Sen. Albert Chandler (D.) last November .... Superior Court Judge James C. Donnelly quashes indictments charging Boston Police Commissioner Joseph F. Timilty and six other police officials with conspiracy to permit gambling.		Policy Comm. of the UMW authorizes miners to return to work until June 20, indicating another strike will be called if wage talks are not completed by then.		After 650 performances, Noel Coward's *Blithe Spirit* closes in New York .... Ensign Hugh S. Cannon sets a world record for the discus throw with 174 feet 10⅛ inches in the Metropolitan A.A.U. senior championships in N.Y. .... *Count Fleet*, with Johnny Longden riding, wins the 1½-mile Belmont Stakes in Belmont, N.Y. by 30 lengths, earning $35,340.	June 5

F	G	H	I	J
Includes elections, federal-state relations, civil rights and liberties, crime, the judiciary, education, health care, poverty, urban affairs and population.	*Includes formation and debate of U.S. foreign and defense policies, veterans affairs and defense spending. (Relations with specific foreign countries are usually found under the region concerned.)*	*Includes business, labor, agriculture, taxation, transportation, consumer affairs, monetary and fiscal policy, natural resources, pollution and accidents.*	*Includes worldwide scientific, medical and technological developments, natural phenomena, U.S. weather and natural disasters.*	*Includes the arts, religion, scholarship, communications media, sports, entertainment, fashions, fads and social life.*

	World Affairs	European War Zone	Pacific War Zone	The Americas	Other Countries & Territories
June 6		British warships shell Pantelleria Island for the fifth time, while U.S. planes bomb the island and attack the Monserrato and Capoterra airfields in Sardinia.	U.S. planes attack Japanese troops and bases in the Yangtze River Valley between Ichang and Shasi, while Chinese troops reportedly kill or wound 1,000 Japanese fleeing from Itu.	Rawson dissolves the Argentine Congress, scheduled to meet tomorrow, and promises a new Congress when the time is "opportune." . . . . Author Waldo Frank says in N.Y. that the revolt in Argentina was "engineered by a military junta whose sole purpose was to get U.S. military supplies in return for a break with the Axis."	
June 7	FDR pledges the better use of human and natural resources "without exploitation by any nation" after the war.	French Comm. for National Liberation in Algiers appoints a cabinet of 14 to govern the French Empire with De Gaulle and Giraud as cochairmen.		Unable to form a new Argentine cabinet, Rawson resigns and turns over the government to Gen. Pablo Ramirez . . . . Chilean cabinet resigns after attacks by Radical Party members upon Interior Min. Dr. Raul Morales Beltrami.	
June 8		Churchill tells Commons that Allied amphibious operations of a very complex nature are approaching as the Allies are about to bring their full force down on the Axis . . . . British fail to land units on the Mediterranean island of Lamand as Axis forces repel the effort . . . . Russian forces repulse a German attempt to cross the Donets River in the Lisichansk area and throw back an attack in the Volkhov sector east of Leningrad.	Chinese troops complete the occupation of Itu, Yangtze River port 18 miles below Ichang.	Argentine government of Gen. Ramirez announces it has been recognized by the Supreme Court and ends martial law.	
June 9		Russian troops establish a bridgehead on the west bank of the Mius River (west of Rostov) and repulse a German effort to dislodge them . . . . Waves of Allied planes bomb Pantelleria, reportedly bringing down 12 Axis planes.		Brazil, Paraguay, Bolivia and Chile recognize the Argentine government of Gen. Pedro Pablo Ramirez . . . . Uruguay recognizes the French Comm. of National Liberation in Algiers as the official French government.	Sultan of Morocco from 1894-1908, Muley Abd-el-Azziz (Al-Hasan IV), dies in Tetuan, Spanish Morocco.
June 10	U.S., U.K., Russian and Chinese governments offer a program to set up a U.N. Relief and Rehabilitation Administration.		Australian P.M. John Curtin says the danger of a Japanese invasion of Australia has passed and the pressure will now be applied to the enemy.	In an address to a joint session of the U.S. Congress, Paraguayan Pres. Higinio Morinigo says his country "will continue to keep faithfully . . . . all international agreements."	
June 11		De Gaulle threatens to resign from the French Comm. of National Liberation and refuses to attend meetings until it agrees to a purge of Vichy army officers . . . . After 1,000 Allied planes subject Pantelleria to its heaviest raid in 20 straight days, the island surrenders to the Allies . . . . In its "most shattering blow" of the war, the RAF destroys more than two square miles of Duesseldorf, Rhineland industrial center . . . . In the first major raid since May 29, more than 200 U.S. heavy bombers attack the U-boat yards and harbors at Wilhemshaven and Cuxhaven, Germany.	Chinese troops take Wangchiachang, northeast of Ichang, while other units advance toward Sungtze on the south bank of the Yangtze.	U.S., Britain and 18 other countries recognize the Ramirez government in ceremonies at the Argentine Foreign Ministry in Buenos Aires . . . . Honduras establishes press and mail censorship to prevent attacks on friendly and Allied governments.	
June 12		Italian island of Lampedusa, 85 miles southeast of Pantelleria, surrenders after being attacked by Allied planes and warships for 24 straight hours . . . . King George VI arrives in North Africa by plane from England to present the insignia of Knight Grand Cross of the Order of the Bath to Gen. Dwight D. Eisenhower . . . . A record number of RAF, RCAF and Polish bombers drop more than 2,000 tons of bombs on Duesseldorf, Muenster and other western German cities.			

	A	B	C	D	E
	Includes developments that affect more than one world region, international organizations and important meetings of major world leaders.	*Includes all developments in European countries and military engagements between Allied and Axis powers in Africa and at sea.*	*Includes all developments in Japan and China, Japanese foreign policy and military actions in the Pacific region.*	*Includes all domestic and regional developments in Latin America, the Caribbean and Canada.*	*Includes developments in those independent nations and colonial possessions not covered in Columns B, C and D.*

U.S. Politics & Social Issues	U.S. Foreign Policy & Defense	U.S. Economy & Environment	Science, Technology & Nature	Culture, Leisure & Life Style	
A. Lewis Hutchinson, 11, is killed by a bullet from a rifle accidentally kicked over by William Donner Roosevelt, 10, grandson of President Roosevelt .... NWLB orders the Southport Petroleum Co. of Texas City, Tex. to abolish pay differentials between white and Negro workers engaged in equal work.		OWI reports that expected 1943 U.S. production of combat and cargo planes will total $20,100,000,000 in value, a fourth of the annual war budget.			June 6
McKellar Bill to require confirmation of virtually all government employes earning above $4,500 a year wins a 43-22 Senate test vote .... Rep. Ed Gossett (D.Tex.) introduces a new bill to repeal the Chinese exclusion acts after the House Immigration Comm. shelves the previous one.	Senate passes by voice vote and sends to conference the largest Navy supply bill in history, over $29 billion starting July 1 .... Gen. Marshall returns to Washington from North Africa.	UMW officials and coal mine operators resume negotiations in Washington as most of the 530,000 striking coal miners return to work.		Christian Science board of directors announces that Mrs. Daisette D.S. McKenzie is elected president of the Mother Church, First Church of Christ, Scientist.	June 7
	Navy authorities declare the entire area of Los Angeles out-of-bounds for sailors on liberty after four nights of street fighting between men of the armed services and "zoot-suited" youths, mostly Mexicans and Negroes, accused of attacking them .... FDR warns the Axis that use of poison gas would bring "full and swift retaliation" in kind .... U.S. and Liberian representatives sign a Lend-Lease agreement at a N.Y. ceremony attended by Liberian Pres. Barclay.	Herbert Hoover urges a complete reorganization of the U.S. food control system to clear up "this muddle of uncontrolled food prices, local famines, profiteering, black markets and stifled farm production."		World featherweight champion Willie Pep defeats Sal Bartolo in 15 rounds in Boston to retain the title.	June 8
	Gov. Earl Warren orders an investigation of the Los Angeles "zoot-suit" riots as fighting between service men and teen-age youths continues in the suburbs.	Lewis and Charles O'Neill, head of the Central Pa. Coal Operators Assn., announce an oral agreement covering 65,000 miners and calling for a $1.30-a-day travel allowance.	Lewis Brown McFarlane, who helped Alexander Graham Bell make the world's first long distance call in 1876, dies at 91 in Montreal.	A New York Supreme Court jury fails to reach a verdict in Dr. Jerome Davis' $250,000 libel suit against the Curtis Publishing Co. and Benjamin Stolberg, author of an article in *The Saturday Evening Post* that characterized Davis as a "Communist and Stalinist." .... Paul Creston's *Symphony No. 1*, Opus 20 is chosen by the N.Y. Music Critics Circle as the best symphonic work by an American composer to be premiered in the current season.	June 9
	U.S. 8th Air Force Commander Maj. Gen. Ira C. Eaker says the unit has doubled its strength since March and will double it again by October.	FDR signs the pay-as-you-go tax bill, making wage and salary earners starting July 1 subject to a 20% withholding tax .... Senate votes to retain the Farm Security Administration despite opposition by the Farm Bureau Federation and appropriates $29.6 million for its operation.		Charlie Chaplin agrees to pay Joan Berry, who is suing him on paternity charges in Los Angeles, $2,500 immediately, $100 weekly and $4,600 for medical attention. He denies he is the father of her expected child and agrees to take a blood test when the child is four months old.	June 10
Senate Labor subcommittee approves legislation to authorize $300 million in federal aid to education annually.	Commenting on Pantelleria's surrender, FDR urges the Italian people oust Mussolini and the Fascist Party, expell the Germans and get out of the war. He states that in such event they would be permitted to set up their own non-Fascist government.	House passes the compromise Connally-Harness-Smith strike and labor control bill outlawing strikes in government-operated plants and prohibiting them in other war industries without 30-day notice and a secret ballot.		Ralph B. Chandler, publisher of *The Mobile* (Ala.) *Press and Register*, is sentenced to six hours in jail and fined $10 for contempt of court by Judge Tisdale J. Touart, who took exception to an editorial criticizing him in connection with the recent racial disorders at the Alabama Drydock & Shipbuilding Co.	June 11
	A Citizen's Committee appointed by Gov. Earl Warren, demands that those guilty of violence in Los Angeles, whether they wore "zoot-suits, police, Army or Navy uniforms," be punished.	Senate passes the Connally-Harness-Smith labor control bill and sends it to FDR .... A nationwide shoe-buying wave of record proportions is reported as shoppers, mostly women, seek to beat the June 15 deadline for the Nov. 17 ration coupon.		USC wins the NCAA track and field championship at Evanston, Ill. for the ninth consecutive year.	June 12

F	G	H	I	J
Includes elections, federal-state relations, civil rights and liberties, crime, the judiciary, education, health care, poverty, urban affairs and population.	*Includes formation and debate of U.S. foreign and defense policies, veterans affairs and defense spending. (Relations with specific foreign countries are usually found under the region concerned.)*	*Includes business, labor, agriculture, taxation, transportation, consumer affairs, monetary and fiscal policy, natural resources, pollution and accidents.*	*Includes worldwide scientific, medical and technological developments, natural phenomena, U.S. weather and natural disasters.*	*Includes the arts, religion, scholarship, communications media, sports, entertainment, fashions, fads and social life.*

	World Affairs	European War Zone	Pacific War Zone	The Americas	Other Countries & Territories
June 13		Two large formations of U.S. Flying Fortresses bomb the Nazi U-boat bases at Bremen and Kiel without escort, losing a record 26 bombers, mostly over Kiel. It is "the greatest air battle in which 8th Air Force heavy bombers have yet participated." .... Algiers radio declares that Rommel is reorganizing Axis Mediterranean defenses and has established headquarters at Perpignan, France .... Small Italian island of Linosa, 25 miles north of Lampedusa, and its garrison of 140 soldiers and sailors surrenders to the British destroyer *Nubian.*			
June 14	Thirty-one Allied nations join the U.S. for the second year in celebrating U.N. Flag Day.	Swiss dispatches state a mass evacuation has begun from the bombed cities of the Ruhr Valley and that German authorities have asked people in the country's interior to open their homes to the refugees.			
June 15		RAF heavy bombers attack Oberhausen, a Ruhr Valley steel and coal center, with the loss of 18 aircraft .... U.S. planes from North Africa bomb Sicilian airfields at Bocca di Falco, Castelvetran, Borizzo, Milo and Sciacca.		Gen. Pedro Pablo Ramirez, Argentine president, promises to re-establish the constitution and says his regime will "clean and restore" rather than "perpetuate itself." .... Dr. Rafael Calderon Guardia y Munoz, first vice president of Costa Rica, dies at 82 in San Jose.	British close the Turkish-Syrian border in an effort to halt military leaks to the Axis.
June 16	WPB Chmn. Donald Nelson tells House Appropriations Comm. the Allies are outproducing the Axis—$125 billion in war goods a year to $65 billion.	Ankara dispatches state Premier Ion Antonescu of Rumania is making peace offers through a neutral ambassador.	In an address to the Japanese Diet, Tojo states new Allied offensives can be expected in Burma, and that Japan will be subjected to air attacks .... Allies claim 1,337 Japanese planes have been destroyed in the South Pacific area since July 31, 1942.	Argentine War Min. Gen. Edelmiro Farrell urges friendship with the U.S.	
June 17		RAF bombers attack Cologne in the Ruhr Valley for the 116th time, while fighters strike at transport facilities in Belgium and the Netherlands .... RAF planes bomb Naples, while U.S. Liberators attack the airfields at Comise and Biscari in southern Sicily .... British Labor Party conclave in London votes to blame the "overwhelming mass" of the German people for the war.			
June 18		U.S. planes make their heaviest raids on Sardinia since the fall of Pantelleria, attacking airfields and railraod installations.	Allied planes bomb Madang, Hopoi and Ceram, New Guinea; Cape Gloucester and Marien Harbor, New Britain; and Langgur in the Kai Islands.	Argentina suspends the Sept. 5 elections and decrees any future elections "must be conditioned to a fulfillment of the aims that motivated the military movement" in its successful revolt.	British Foreign Office appoints Sir Archibald P. Wavell as viceroy and governor general of India to succeed the Marquess of Linlithgow .... London announces the reopening of the Turkish-Syrian border.
June 19			Chinese troops recapture four towns in the Ichang area: Changtien, Tiencheng, Huiliu and Chaohu.		
June 20		De Gaulle's Fighting French group in Algiers says he may leave for Brazzaville or Beirut unless the French Comm. of National Liberation meets his demands for supreme military power and reorganization of the French Army .... RAF planes from Britain strike heavily at the Schneider armament work at Le Creusot, 170 miles south of Paris. Paris radio states 250 persons are killed.	A Japanese force of about 28 bombers and 20 fighters is driven off in an attempted attack on Darwin, Australia by the largest force of Spitfires ever used in the area.		
June 21		Himmler orders the liquidation of Jewish ghettos in occupied Russia .... In a special Russian communique commemorating the second anniversary of the war, Moscow says "everything now depends upon the manner in which our allies will exploit the favorable situation by creating a second front." .... Allied broadcasts from North Africa tell the Italians to demonstrate for peace and to leave industrial areas which will be heavily bombed .... A severe earthquake destroys about 1,000 buildings in Adapazari, Turkey and causes severe damage in Hendek, Geyve and Arifiye, killing 1,304 persons.		British Colonial Office names Sir Bernard H. Bourdillon as governor of Jamaica.	British Colonial Office appoints Sir Arthur F. Richards as governor of Nigeria.

	A	B	C	D	E
	Includes developments that affect more than one world region, international organizations and important meetings of major world leaders.	*Includes all developments in European countries and military engagements between Allied and Axis powers in Africa and at sea.*	*Includes all developments in Japan and China, Japanese foreign policy and military actions in the Pacific region.*	*Includes all domestic and regional developments in Latin America, the Caribbean and Canada.*	*Includes developments in those independent nations and colonial possessions not covered in Columns B, C and D.*

U.S. Politics & Social Issues	U.S. Foreign Policy & Defense	U.S. Economy & Environment	Science, Technology & Nature	Culture, Leisure & Life Style	
Senate passes the McKellar bill which requires Senate confirmation of federal employes receiving $4,500 a year or more who are not under the Civil Service Act.	Supreme Court Justice Owen J. Roberts says he favors a postwar international federation of limited but supreme power and jurisdiction in international affairs .... U.S. Amb. to Britain John G. Winant says more than two million U.S. troops are now in overseas combat zones.				June 13
Supreme Court reverses a 1940 decision and rules that compulsory flag salute is a violation of the Bill of Rights. The verdict upholds the challenge of Jehovah's Witnesses to the flag-salute rule of the West Virginia Board of Education.	SSS Dir. Hershey says the drafting of fathers, scheduled to begin Aug. 1, may be delayed until Oct. 1.	House Appropriations Comm. calls for the liquidation of the National Youth Administration.			June 14
State Executive Comm. of the South Carolina Democratic Party refuses a Democratic National Comm. request for funds to support the 1944 campaign.	House Foreign Affairs Comm. endorses a resolution to put Congress on record as favoring an international organization to keep peace after the war .... Navy reopens Los Angeles to enlisted men as a county grand jury investigation of the "zoot-suit" clashes continues.	Congressional tax leaders agree at a meeting with Morgenthau to draw up a new tax bill by Jan. 1 .... Roosevelt rejects congressional demands for a "food czar" at his press conference and reiterates that food subsidies are the best plan found so far to keep prices down.			June 15
Martial law is declared in Beaumont, Tex. after two persons are killed and 11 injured as a result of a race riot allegedly set off by an attack on a white woman by a Negro .... House votes to pass the Labor and FSA bill after refusing WMC Chmn. Paul McNutt a raise in salary to $15,000.		OPA Chmn. Prentiss Brown tells the Senate Banking and Currency Comm. he will be unable to roll back agricultural prices without federal subsidies.		Charlie Chaplin, 54, is married to Oona O'Neill, 18, daughter of the playwright Eugene O'Neill, in California. It is his fourth marriage. Joan Berry, 23, who claims Chaplin is the father of her unborn child, says: "He can't do this to us." .... Dr. Albert Bushnell Hart, historian, author and professor emeritus of history at Harvard, dies at 88 in Boston.	June 16
Georgia and Louisiana state Democratic committee leaders announce they will refuse to contribute to the Democratic National Comm. unless its leaders "straighten out their policies respecting the South."	House approves and sends to the Senate a revised bill providing for $27.6 billion in Navy appropriations.	Treasury Secy. Morgenthau revises the goal for new 1974 tax revenues from $16 billion to $12 billion.		American Newspaper Guild, meeting in Boston, votes to assume "responsibility for exposing actions of the press destructive to the war effort" through local and national committee action.	June 17
	House Appropriations Comm. adopts a record $71.5-billion War Dept. bill, while Senate approves and sends to FDR $27.6-billion Naval appropriations bill.	NWLB refuses to grant the UMW a wage increase based on travel allowance and directs miners and operators to write a new contract .... House votes to slash 20% from the OPA budget and decides to end the OPA food subsidy program July 1.	National Patent Planning Commission recommends to Roosevelt that the patent term be shortened to 20 years from the application date and that any invention vital to the national welfare be opened to manufacture.		June 18
A Dies subcommittee reports administrators of Japanese relocation camps have allowed internees to decide policy and failed to protect loyal Japanese-Americans.	Sen. Robert Taft (R,O.) says he favors a U.S. postwar commitment to the use of military force "where aggression has been found to exist."	About 58,000 soft coal miners go on strike.			June 19
Race riots between white and Negro mobs begin at 10:45 p.m. in Detroit after a fight on the Belle Isle Bridge sparks the outburst. White mobs invade the Negro section, beating Negroes and smashing stores and homes as Negro snipers fire from apartment houses.	Capt. Edward Rickenbacker arrives in Moscow to represent U.S. War Secy. Stimson and to study Russia's use of U.S. planes.	Conference in Washington between coal operators and UMW officials collapses at noon, and at 5 p.m. UMW policy officials telegraph Harold Ickes offering to work for the government .... Commerce Dept. reports that first quarter corporate profits totaled $1.821 billion, or 18% above the same period for 1942.		Gunder Haegg of Sweden outruns Greg Rice by 35 yards and beats eight other Americans to win the 5,000-meter title at the National AAU track and field championships, New York, in 14:48.5 .... NFL grants Ted Collins a Boston football franchise for 1944.	June 20
Supreme Court holds that agitation for peaceful change in the form of government "is not reprehensible" and rules that California Communist William Schneidermann cannot be denied citizenship.	House passes and sends to the Senate the $71.5 billion War Dept. appropriations bill.	For the third time since May 1, about 530,000 soft coal miners strike. Lewis confers with Ickes, who "freezes" 3,000,000 tons of soft coal in transit, while WPB restricts deliveries.	Goodyear Tire and Rubber Co. and the Chrysler Corp. announce the development of a "cycleweld adhesive process" using plastic glues to cement metal, wood, plastics and rubber.		June 21

F	G	H	I	J
Includes elections, federal-state relations, civil rights and liberties, crime, the judiciary, education, health care, poverty, urban affairs and population.	*Includes formation and debate of U.S. foreign and defense policies, veterans affairs and defense spending. (Relations with specific foreign countries are usually found under the region concerned.)*	*Includes business, labor, agriculture, taxation, transportation, consumer affairs, monetary and fiscal policy, natural resources, pollution and accidents.*	*Includes worldwide scientific, medical and technological developments, natural phenomena, U.S. weather and natural disasters.*	*Includes the arts, religion, scholarship, communications media, sports, entertainment, fashions, fads and social life.*

	World Affairs	European War Zone	Pacific War Zone	The Americas	Other Countries & Territories
June 22		French Comm. of National Liberation reaches a compromise under which Gen. Giraud will retain command of the French armies in Morocco, Algeria, Tunisia and French West Africa and Gen. de Gaulle will continue as commander of all forces in the rest of the empire .... About 700 RAF and RCAF heavy bombers drop more than 2,000 tons of bombs on the steel and chemical center of Krefeld at the western end of the Ruhr Valley.			
June 23		Nearly 700 RAF and RCAF bombers strike twice at the Ruhr steel center of Muelheim for the first time since 1940.		Brazilian Pres. Vargas assures Bolivian Pres. Penaranda del Castillo that Bolivia may have free use of Santo, a southern Brazilian port.	
June 24		Nearly 500 Allied planes bomb oil depots and airfields in France, Belgium and the Netherlands.	Australian Prime Minister John Curtin wins a vote of confidence from the House of Commons.		
June 25		More than 100 Flying Fortresses, the largest formation of heavy bombers ever sent over a single target from North Africa, attack Messina in eastern Sicily .... French Comm. of National Liberation establishes an eight-man military commission to unify the Giraud-de Gaulle forces, and invalidates the acts of Vichy courts against patriots .... King George VI returns by plane to England after a 14-day, 5,800-mile trip to Algiers, Oran, Tunis, Cap Bon, Tripoli and Malta.		Buenos Aires police close volunteer organizations aiding the Allies.	
June 26		King Peter II announces in London that Miles Trifunovich will head the new cabinet of the Yugoslavian government in exile .... RAF heavy bombers attack the Ruhr coal and steel centers of Bochum and Gelsenkirchen.			
June 27		Red Army troops repell repeated Nazi counterattacks on the Orel front and make advances, taking 50 more villages.			
June 28		Paris radio claims 96 German divisions, about 1.7 million troops, are ready to meet an invasion of the continent.	Japanese troops move from Nanking, Hankow and Sinyang to the central Yangtze front.	Three Brazilians and 10 persons now in Germany are given 20-30 year prison terms in Rio de Janeiro on charges of giving shipping information to Berlin before Brazil entered the war.	
June 29	U.N. Education Conference advocates the compulsory teaching of English in non-English-speaking nations and of French in English-speaking nations.	Yugoslavian government in London reveals that Gen. Mikhailovich's forces are counterattacking against eight Nazi divisions in Herzegovina, Montenegro and eastern Bosnia after absorbing a 40-day German offensive .... RAF and RCAF complete the 117th air assault upon Cologne, while other units attack Hanover for the 97th time .... More than 100 Flying Fortresses strike Livorno, 200 miles northwest of Rome.			
June 30	Churchill says the "future of the world" depends on the alignment of U.S. and British policy.	Russian troops repulse Nazi attacks on the Leningrad, Smolensk and Kursk fronts and capture a German position on the Velikie Luki front .... U.S. Flying Fortresses bomb Palermo and the Bocca di Falco airfield in Sicily while other Allied planes attack airfields at Sciacca, Borizzo and Milo.	At dawn, U.S. forces land on Rendova Island in the central Solomons, 195 miles north of Guadalcanal .... U.S. forces land at Nassau Bay, 11 miles southwest of Salamaua, New Guinea, under an umbrella of fighter planes.	Martinique High Commissioner Georges Robert asks the U.S. to send an envoy to "fix terms for a change of French authority" over the island.	

	A	B	C	D	E
	Includes developments that affect more than one world region, international organizations and important meetings of major world leaders.	*Includes all developments in European countries and military engagements between Allied and Axis powers in Africa and at sea.*	*Includes all developments in Japan and China, Japanese foreign policy and military actions in the Pacific region.*	*Includes all domestic and regional developments in Latin America, the Caribbean and Canada.*	*Includes developments in those independent nations and colonial possessions not covered in Columns B, C and D.*

U.S. Politics & Social Issues	U.S. Foreign Policy & Defense	U.S. Economy & Environment	Science, Technology & Nature	Culture, Leisure & Life Style	
FDR orders federal troops to maintain order in Detroit after racial violence results in 1,300 arrests and more than 20 deaths.		Lewis and the UMW Policy Comm. order 530,000 soft coal miners to suspend their two-day strike until midnight Oct. 31, pending a wage agreement.			June 22
Michigan Gov. Harry F. Kelly names a committee to investigate the Detroit race riots as 119 whites and Negroes are sentenced to 90-day jail terms, and the death toll rises to 31 .... District Judge Bolitha Laws declares a mistrial in Washington trial of George Viereck, charged with failing to register as a German agent, because a women juror was seen talking to a Justice Dept. attorney .... The 32 governors at the Governor's Conference in Columbus, O. adopt two resolutions to oppose further encroachments by the federal government on states' rights.	U.S. Ordnance Dept. discloses a 4.7-inch anti-aircraft gun has been invented that can fire 60,000 feet, more than 11 miles, into the air.	Calling the recent miners strike "intolerable," FDR indicates machinery is in motion to conscript the strikers .... Economic Stabilization Dir. Vinson vetoes an 8¢-an-hour wage increase for 1.1 million nonoperating railroad workers reccommended by a presidential emergency board.			June 23
Senate rejects a House-approved conference report on the $150,000,000 deficiency appropriation bill denying funds to pay salaries of Robert Morss Lovett, Goodwin B. Watson and William E. Dodd Jr., all accused of subversive activities.	State Dept. creates an Office of Foreign Economic Coordination, headed by Asst. Secy. Dean Acheson, to coordinate economic activities of civilian economic agencies in liberated areas.	About 40% of the 530,000 striking coal miners remain out, and Secy. Ickes warns rationing may be necessary.	Lt. Col. Wm. R. Lovelace makes a 40,200-foot parachute jump near Ephrata, Wash. to test oxygen equipment, setting a new U.S. record.		June 24
Michigan Gov. Kelly says his committee's investigation of the Detroit race riots indicates there was no plot and that no grand jury investigation is necessary.		Congress quickly overrides FDR's vote of the Connally-Smith antistrike bill .... FDR says he will not recognize the Oct. 31 deadline set by the UMW policy committee.		Central Conference of American Rabbis adopts resolutions in N.Y. declaring there is no essential incompatibility between Reform Judaism and Zionism and urging an end to the fight over Zionism.	June 25
		About 210,000 coal miners, most of them in Pennsylvania, remain out on strike .... Senate approves and sends to joint conference a bill to continue the Commodity Credit Corp. for two years and increase its capital.	Improved technique in administering caudal anesthesia to provide painless childbirth is credited by the *Journal of the AMA* to Drs. Nathan Block and Morris Rotstein of Sinai Hospital, Baltimore.	Francisco (Pancho) Segura of the Univ. of Miami wins the NCAA tennis title, defeating Tom Brown, Jr. of the Univ. of California .... The *Encyclopedia Brittanica* reportedly will be translated into Chinese by Chinese scholars for universities and colleges in China.	June 26
A report to the NEA states two million children aged 14 to 18 have left school for work.	Rep. Claire Boothe Luce says the New Deal is dead because it cannot convince the people of its foreign policy.			Bill Watson retains the National AAU decathlon championship in Elizabeth, N.J. with 5,994 points.	June 27
	Sperry Corp. announces its new automatic computing sight has been installed on Flying Fortresses, which can aim and fire 50-caliber machine guns automatically.	FDR names Judge Marvin Jones to replace Chester C. Davis as war food administrator.		Calumet Stables retires Whirlaway, five-year-old bay who won 32 races and a record $561,161.	June 28
Vice Pres. Henry Wallace charges that Commerce Secy. Jones, as Reconstruction Finance Corp. head, has impeded the war effort by blocking Bd. of Economic Warfare contracts.	Federal Court of Appeals in Chicago grants new trials to six persons convicted of aiding Herbert Haupt, executed Nazi spy, because confessions obtained by the FBI were improperly used at the trial of Hans and Erna Haupt, the spy's parents, Walter and Lucille Froeling, his uncle and aunt, and Otto and Kate Wergin.	Congressional conferees agree on a bill to extend the Commodity Credit Corp. for two more years, adding $750 million to its $2.6-billion lending authority.			June 29
Vice Pres. Wallace and Commerce Secy. Jones confer with War Mobilization Dir. James Byrnes but fail to settle their differences.	Senate Democratic leader Alben W. Barkley appoints a five-man committee to make a world-wide tour in an Army bomber to inspect the equipment of U.S. fighting forces .... N.Y. area has its first test of barrage balloons "somewhere on Long Island" when 34 are sent aloft over an industrial area.	Ickes urges the continuous mining of coal with or without a contract, as about 130,000 coal miners continue to strike .... Both houses of Congress adopt the conference report banning subsidies to hold down retail food prices, ordering the meat and butter price rollback ended by Aug. 1 and extending the Commodity Credit Corp. .... NWLB asks labor and management to strengthen the no-strike, no-lockout agreement by naming plant arbitrators with final authority in disputes .... Favorable war news sends NYSE prices to their highest levels in three years.			June 30
F	G	H	I	J	
Includes elections, federal-state relations, civil rights and liberties, crime, the judiciary, education, health care, poverty, urban affairs and population.	*Includes formation and debate of U.S. foreign and defense policies, veterans affairs and defense spending. (Relations with specific foreign countries are usually found under the region concerned.)*	*Includes business, labor, agriculture, taxation, transportation, consumer affairs, monetary and fiscal policy, natural resources, pollution and accidents.*	*Includes worldwide scientific, medical and technological developments, natural phenomena, U.S. weather and natural disasters.*	*Includes the arts, religion, scholarship, communications media, sports, entertainment, fashions, fads and social life.*	

	World Affairs	European War Zone	Pacific War Zone	The Americas	Other Countries & Territories
July 1		Churchill tells the House of Commons he and FDR support Gen. Giraud, the French military leader in Africa .... RAF bombers from the Middle East make a heavy raid on Catania, Sicily with the loss of five planes, while other British planes from North Africa bomb Palermo in Sicily and Cagliari, Sardinia.	U.S. troops consolidate their positions at Nassau Bay, while Australian forces attack Japanese patrols in the Muba and Malolo areas of Salamaua .... U.S. forces claim Rendova Island after repelling Japanese air assaults.	Treasury Secy. Morgenthau announces extension of monetary stabilization agreements with Cuba and Ecuador.	French Comm. of National Liberation names Pierre Cournarie as governor of French West Africa.
July 2		RAF planes bomb Trapani in Sicily and Olbia, Sardinia.	U.S. troops, who landed yesterday at Viru Harbor on New Georgia Island, complete its occupation .... Australian troops clear the district south of the Bitoi River of Japanese patrols and join U.S. forces at Nassau Bay, Salamaua.	Nicaraguan Senate approves changes in the constitution to permit Pres. Anastasio Somoza to succeed himself .... U.S. Vice Adm. John Howard Hoover is named to confer with Adm. Robert on Martinique about the proposal to end Vichy authority there.	
July 3			Allied troops extend their control in the Nassau Bay-Bitoi River area of New Guinea .... U.S. warships drive off three Japanese light cruisers and four destroyers attempting to attack U.S. positions on Rendova Island.	French Comm. of National Liberation appoints Henri-Etienne Hoppenot as an envoy to neogtiate with Adm. Robert on Martinique.	
July 4		A large force of RAF heavy bombers make their 118th raid on the Kalk and Deutz industrial districts of Cologne in the Rhineland and attack Hamburg for the 98th time .... Allied planes bomb five Axis airfields in Sicily: Catania, Gerbini, Sciacca, Comiso and Milo.	Chaing Kai-shek says "the offensive phase of our war definitely is beginning" and promises democracy for China after the war.	Mexican Revolutionary Party retains control of the lower chamber of Congress and the governorships of seven states in national elections.	
July 5		Polish Premier Wladyslaw Sikorski and 15 others die in a plane crash near Gibraltar; Stanislaw Mikolajzyk is named temporary premier in London .... German troops commence a heavy offensive on a 160-mile front from Belgorod to Orel.	Japan cedes six states of Malaya and Burma, totaling some 38,770 square miles, to Thailand for cooperating with Japan in the Pacific War.		
July 6		Spearheaded by a force of tanks, Nazi troops break the Russian lines at two points in the Belgorod sector.	Five Japanese destroyers and four light cruisers are sunk or beached in the Kula Gulf naval battle off northwest New Georgia .... Chiang predicts victory over Japan will come in two years.		
July 7	Gen. Giraud arrives in Washington to confer with FDR and military leaders.	Nazi offensive on the Belgorod-Orel front continues as thousands of fresh troops are hurled into action.	Chungking ceremonies mark China's sixth anniversary of war with Japan, while "Salute to China" rallies are held in N.Y., San Francisco, London and Moscow.	French Comm. of National Liberation appoints Brig. Gen. Henri-Paul Jacomy military commander of French Guiana and the Antilles, including Martinique.	A record number of votes are cast in parliamentary elections held today in the Union of South Africa .... British Commonwealth Party issues a manifesto demanding common ownership of land, independence for India, self-government for colonies and a post-war world economic council.
July 8		Nazi troops and tanks drive a new wedge into Russian lines in the Belgorod area while a Red Army counterattack in the Orel sector dislodges the Germans in a number of inhabited places.	British and Indian troops seize Maungdaw in Burma, holding it for several hours before withdrawing as planned.	Sir Harry Oakes, 69, American-born mining engineer and prospector who struck the second richest gold vein in the world near Kirkland Lake, Ont., is found dead in bed in Nassau, Bahamas. Police say he was beaten to death .... Argentine Foreign Min. Rear. Adm. Segundo Storni announces an interministerial committee will study the Rio Conference resolutions dealing with subversive activities and recommending a break with the Axis .... Colombia and the U.S. complete arrangements for a public works loan of $18 million.	
July 9	Gen. Giraud reports FDR has agreed to the U.S. rearming some 300,000 French soldiers.	Allied forces seize Ponte Grande on Sicily near Syracuse tonight .... Moscow reports fighting on the Orel-Belgorod front continues with undiminished ferocity .... British Air Ministry announces the RAF made its 119th raid on Cologne in the Rhine valley last night, dropping more than 1,000 tons of explosives.		Count Alfred de Marigny is arrested in Nassau and charged with the murder of his father-in-law, Sir Harry Oakes.	

A	B	C	D	E
Includes developments that affect more than one world region, international organizations and important meetings of major world leaders.	*Includes all developments in European countries and military engagements between Allied and Axis powers in Africa and at sea.*	*Includes all developments in Japan and China, Japanese foreign policy and military actions in the Pacific region.*	*Includes all domestic and regional developments in Latin America, the Caribbean and Canada.*	*Includes developments in those independent nations and colonial possessions not covered in Columns B, C and D.*

U.S. Politics & Social Issues	U.S. Foreign Policy & Defense	U.S. Economy & Environment	Science, Technology & Nature	Culture, Leisure & Life Style	
FDR names six persons to the reorganized Comm. on Fair Employment Practices: John Brophy, Boris Shishkin, Milton P. Webster, Sara Southall, P.B. Young and Samuel Zemurray.	FDR commutes the death sentence of Max Stephen to life imprisonment. He was convicted for treason in aiding an escaped Nazi flier.		Federal Court of Appeals in San Francisco holds patents for producing Vitamin D by ultra-violet radiation invalid, claiming it is a "discovery and not an invention."	Arne Andersson runs the mile in 4:02.6, two seconds under Gunder Haegg's world record, at a meet in Gothenburg, Sweden.	July 1
	Senate Military Affairs Comm. approves the Wheeler bill to postpone the induction of fathers from Oct. 1 until Jan. 1, 1944.	FDR vetoes the Commodity Credit Corp. bill, charging it would "black out the program to reduce the cost of living." .... Senate accepts a House provision in the Labor-Federal Security appropriations bill, forbidding the NLRB to order elections in plants where a labor contract has been in force for three months without an appeal.		Gene Krupa, orchestra leader who was convicted June 30 of employing a minor to transport marijuana cigarettes, is sentenced in San Francisco to serve one to six years in San Quentin prison .... Patty Berg defeats Dorothy Kirby to win the Women's Western Open Golf Championship in Chicago.	July 2
Tennessee State Supreme Court rules that a law abolishing the state's poll tax is unconstitutional .... Senate votes to liquidate the NYA and returns the Labor-Federal Security supply bill to conference.	Truman Investigating Comm. names Senators James M. Mead and Ralph O. Brewster to investigate U.S. rights to "airfields and other properties built and paid for by us" in foreign countries.			Chop Chop with Johnny Longden up wins the $28,100 Empire State Handicap at Jamaica, N.Y., setting a track record of 1:57.2 for the mile and 3/16 run.	July 3
NYA is ordered liquidated by Dir. Aubrey Williams.			A fully loaded Waco CG 4-A Glider is towed across the Atlantic from Montreal to England in 28 hours.	FCC Chmn. James Lawrence Fly charges that Rep. Edward Eugene Cox (D, Ga.) is "conspiring with the radio monopoly and Wall Street interests on the one hand and the military on the other" to "wreck" the FCC.	July 4
	Mrs. Oveta Culp Hobby, Women's Air Auxilliary Corps director, is sworn in as an Army colonel, becoming the first member of the WACS.	Senate approves House revisions in the war agencies supply bill, reducing appropriations for the OWI's domestic branch to $2,750,000 and OPA funds to $155,000,000 .... House Ways and Means Comm. rejects a two-year extension of the Guffey Coal Act setting minimum coal prices at the mines .... FDR says the Florida barge canal will be built when manpower, material and equipment are available.		Orchestra leader Harry James and screen actress Betty Grable are married in Las Vegas, Nev.	July 5
		Officials of the UMW report all but 9,000 coal miners are now at work and all mines are in production .... House Ways and Means Comm. tables a resolution to continue the Guffey Coal Act after its Aug. 23 expiration date, ending congressional consideration of extension .... Senate passes an amendment to the House Commodity Credit Corp. bill to prohibit the use of subsidies to roll back food prices.			July 6
Fair Employment Practices Comm. Chmn. Msgr. Francis J. Haas reports "inadequate housing, recreation and public transportation" were responsible for the recent race riots in Detroit.		CIO Marine and Shipbuilding Workers of America asks the NWLB for a 9% salary increase.		Sen. Robert Taft (R,O.) says the FCC has imposed controls on broadcasting far beyond the intent of Congress and asks Congress to redefine the agency's authority .... Lt. Comdr. William Harrison (Jack) Dempsey, former heavyweight champion, is granted a divorce from Hannah Williams Dempsey, a former actress, in White Plains, N.Y.	July 7
Edward Haight, 17, youngest criminal to be executed in N.Y., is electrocuted at Sing Sing Prison for the murder of the Lynch sisters .... Both houses of Congress adjourn until Sept. 14, the longest recess since 1938 .... *New York Daily News* copy editor Frederick Wright is indicted by a federal grand jury on charges of failing to register as an agent of the Japanese government.	Army Surgeon Gen. Norman Thomas says the Army's death rate from disease is the lowest "of any army at any time."	OPA announces a fixed mark-up price program, effective Aug. 5, for most groceries at wholesale and retail distribution levels to maintain April 8 prices .... Senate votes to eliminate its ban on food price rollback subsidies in the bill to continue the Commodity Credit Corp. to Dec. 31 with $350,000,000 additional borrowing authority.	Prof. Leonid K. Ramzin receives the 150,000-ruble Stalin prize and the Order of Lenin for his invention of a turbo-generator.		July 8
	FDR says the increasing Allied successes are hastening "the hour of deliverance" for Europe.	FDR tells his press conference he cannot force John L. Lewis to sign an NWLB-approved contract.		John Foster Dulles, chairman of a planning commission established by the Federal Council of the Churches of Christ in America, tells the International Conference of Christian Leaders, a council of 68 churchmen from 14 nations, that Protestant churches will sponsor a program in the fall to promote international collaboration.	July 9
F	G	H	I	J	
Includes elections, federal-state relations, civil rights and liberties, crime, the judiciary, education, health care, poverty, urban affairs and population.	*Includes formation and debate of U.S. foreign and defense policies, veterans affairs and defense spending. (Relations with specific foreign countries are usually found under the region concerned.)*	*Includes business, labor, agriculture, taxation, transportation, consumer affairs, monetary and fiscal policy, natural resources, pollution and accidents.*	*Includes worldwide scientific, medical and technological developments, natural phenomena, U.S. weather and natural disasters.*	*Includes the arts, religion, scholarship, communications media, sports, entertainment, fashions, fads and social life.*	

	World Affairs	European War Zone	Pacific War Zone	The Americas	Other Countries & Territories
July 10		Allied troops invade southern Sicily; forces consist of U.S. Seventh Army (Gen. Patton) and the British Eighth Army (Gen. Montgomery). Allied convoys consisting of some 2,700 ships approach Sicily from nearly every port between Gibraltar and Port Said. Americans take Gela and Licata; British take Syracuse.			
July 11		U.S. forces capture two airports near Gela, Sicily, while British and Canadian troops advance inland from both sides of Cape Passero. U.S. planes bomb Catania .... Russian troops counterattack and recapture two towns in the Orel sector after repulsing an attack by 400 Nazi tanks.			
July 12	Canadian Finance Min. J.L. Ilsey reports a postwar currency plan to facilitate international trade which calls for an initial capital exchange fund of $8 billion and a monetary unit valued at about $10.00.				
July 13		British troops in Sicily take the port of Augusta and push north towards Catania; U.S. troops on the southern Sicilian coast take the Axis airfields at Comiso and Ponte Olivo .... A strong force of RAF bombers makes a concentrated attack on the manufacturing center of Turin, Italy — the heaviest Allied attack on any Italian town.	U.S. warships sink a Japanese light cruiser and three destroyers in the Kula Gulf north of New Georgia Island.	U.S. State Dept. announces Adm. Georges Robert has terminated his regime in Martinique and that Henri-Etienne Hoppenot, representing the French Comm. of National Liberation, has been recognized as governor general .... Argentine Interior Ministry orders German culture and welfare organizations closed within 48 hours and also bans Communist groups.	British Colonial Secy. Col. Oliver Stanley reports that plans have been made to establish regional commissions to consult with other nations on colonial problems.
July 14	Churchill tells the House of Commons that the Atlantic Charter is not a treaty requiring ratification but a statement of broad principles common to each country.	U.S. troops on the Sicilian west flank capture the Biscari airport and occupy Campobello and Riesi .... Polish Pres. Wladyslaw Raczkiewicz announces a new cabinet in London with Stanislaw Mikolajzyk as premier .... Soviet forces recapture several villages in the Belgorod sector, killing about 2,000 Germans and destroying many tanks and planes.	Chinese troops repulse Japanese drives in the Tahihang Mountains and on the Burma border.		
July 15	Sixteen airlines notify the CAB that they will apply for international peacetime routes using foreign airports built by the Army.	Allies take four more Sicilian towns, bringing the total to 36, but report that Axis resistance is stiffening .... Soviets announce the recapture of 110 towns and the killing of 12,000 Nazi troops east of Orel.	Mubo, the Japanese base southwest of Salamaua, New Guinea, is captured by Allied forces.	Martinique Gov. Gen. Hoppenot abrogates all laws decreed during the pro-Vichy administration .... Dispatches from Montevideo report that the Argentine government has banned four groups because they are anti-Nazi. They include a women's organization and a labor union.	
July 16		FDR and Churchill deliver an ultimatum to the Italian people calling on them to decide "whether Italians shall die for Mussolini and Hitler or live for Italy and civilization." .... U.S. troops capture Agrigento, Canadians take Caltagirone and Grammichele and the British occupy Scordia on Sicily .... Russian forces advance from six to ten miles north and east of Orel, killing 2,000 Nazi soldiers, destroying 168 tanks and 106 airplanes .... Dmitri Ulyanov, younger brother of Lenin who retired from revolutionary poiltics in 1921 to devote himself to medical research, dies at 69 in Gorki, Russia.	U.S. bombers hit Vila and also attack Bairoki in the Solomons, while ground forces continue their advance towards Munda.	Costan Rican Congress elects Teodore Picado as first designate for the national presidency to succeed the late Dr. Rafael Calderon Guardia y Munoz.	

U.S. Politics & Social Issues	U.S. Foreign Policy & Defense	U.S. Economy & Environment	Science, Technology & Nature	Culture, Leisure & Life Style	
	Truman's Senate committee charges the Wright Aeronautical Corp. with delivery of defective airplane motors to the Army and Navy; the Justice Dept. files suit in Trenton, N.J. against the company .... Foreign Relief and Rehabilitation Dir. Herbert H. Lehman says seed, fertilizer and farm tools will be supplied to liberated nations.			Brooklyn Dodger players, angered by the suspension of pitcher Louis (Bobo) Newsom by manager Leo Durocher, refuse to take the field until pacified a minute before gametime .... Gunder Haegg establishes an American record of 8:53.9 for two miles, beating Gil Dodds in Los Angeles.	July 10
	War Secy. Stimson arrives in London to confer with British military leaders.			*The New York Herald Tribune* reveals that best-selling books include *The Robe*, by Lloyd C. Douglas; *The Valley of Decision*, by Marcia Davenport; *The Human Comedy*, by William Saroyan; and *One World*, by Wendell L. Willkie .... Eulace Peacock wins the AAU pentathlon championship in Elizabeth, N.J. with 3,225 points.	July 11
	Under War Secy. Robert P. Patterson says the Army has removed its resident representative and chief inspection officer at the Wright Aeronautical Corp. plant in Lockland, O., as a result of Truman committee charges.			Random House publishes *Thirty Seconds Over Tokyo*, by Capt. Ted W. Lawson (edited by Robert Considine) .... Marie Cecilia (Cissie) Loftus, Scottish-born actress and mimic who made her stage debut in 1892 in Belfast and became a featured motion picture player, dies at 66 in New York.	July 12
			U.S. Navy announces a "mist-like inhalable" serum has been developed at the Univ. of California which is 90% effective in preventing influenza.	AL wins the annual All Star game from the NL, 5-3, before 31,938 in Philadelphia.	July 13
	FDR signs the omnibus war veterans' bill, increasing compensation for widows and children of men killed in action to $50 monthly for widows, $65 for those with one child and $13 for each additional dependent.	WFA announces 213 million cases of canned vegetables will be allocated for civilian use in the next 12 months, 22% below the 1942 consumption level .... AFL Longshoremen's Assn. elects Pres. Joseph Ryan and second Vice Pres. George Millner to life tenures.	Alien Property Custodian's Office demonstrates a ship propeller that can move a ship forward, backward or sideways.	*For Whom The Bells Tolls*, featuring Gary Cooper and Ingrid Bergman, is released in N.Y. .... Brooklyn Dodgers trade pitcher Louis (Bobo) Newsom to the St. Louis Browns for pitchers Archie McKain and Fritz Ostermueller .... Jules Bledsoe, baritone, who sang *Ol'Man River* in *Show Boat* in 1927, dies at 44 in Hollywood .... *Variety* reports the most popular songs to be (1) *Comin' In On A Wing And A Prayer*, (2) *You'll Never Know*, and (3) *Don't Get Around Much Anymore*.	July 14
War Relocation Authority Dir. Dillion S. Myer says disloyal Japanese will be segregated in a single center.	SSS discloses there are now 9.3 million men and women in uniform and estimates the number will reach 11.3 million by July 1944.	FDR issues an executive order abolishing Vice Pres. Wallace's Board of Economic Warfare and transfers its functions, together with the war financing powers of Commerce Secy. Jesse Jones' RFC, to an Office of Economic Warfare headed by Leo T. Crowley .... Price Admin. Prentiss M. Brown names Chester Bowles, New York advertising executive, as OPA general manager.			July 15
Chicago Tribune publisher Robert McCormick refuses Wendell Willkie's challenge that both enter the Illinois presidential primary .... George Viereck is convicted for a second time by a federal court jury in Washington of failing to register as a German agent. The Supreme Court reversed his first conviction.		FDR signs the bill extending the Commodity Credit Corp. until Jan. 1 and says he does not believe it prohibits grading of commodities for price control purposes .... Governors of Mass., Maine, Vt., R.I. and Conn. close a two-day conference in New London with demands for immediate federal action to end shortages of grain, gasoline, meat and coal.			July 16

F	G	H	I	J
Includes elections, federal-state relations, civil rights and liberties, crime, the judiciary, education, health care, poverty, urban affairs and population.	*Includes formation and debate of U.S. foreign and defense policies, veterans affairs and defense spending. (Relations with specific foreign countries are usually found under the region concerned.)*	*Includes business, labor, agriculture, taxation, transportation, consumer affairs, monetary and fiscal policy, natural resources, pollution and accidents.*	*Includes worldwide scientific, medical and technological developments, natural phenomena, U.S. weather and natural disasters.*	*Includes the arts, religion, scholarship, communications media, sports, entertainment, fashions, fads and social life.*

	World Affairs	European War Zone	Pacific War Zone	The Americas	Other Countries & Territories
July 17		British advance towards the key port of Catania despite increased opposition from German elite divisions .... Eisenhower orders the Allied Military Govt. of Occupied Territories (AMGOT) to abolish the Fascist party, disband Fascist militia and youth organizations, set up military courts to try civilians accused of crimes, annul racial laws and supervise rationing and relief .... Red Army advances up to six miles on the Orel front, occupying several towns, killing 3,000 Nazi soldiers and destroying 78 tanks and 137 planes.	For nine hours U.S. heavy bombers assault the Kahili airfield in the Buin-Faisi area of Bougainville Island.	Mexico and the U.S. continue their economic agreement whereby Mexico will continue to produce strategic war materials and will receive U.S. aid into the postwar period for agriculture, transportation, power and general industrial development .... A Puerto Rican committee asks Congress for independence after an eight-year commonwealth period and a U.S. guarantee to import a million tons of sugar annually.	
July 18		U.S. troops capture the Sicilian communications center of Caltanissetta, while Canadian units take Piazza Armerina .... In operations on the northern, eastern and southern Orel front, Soviet troops retake a total of 130 more villages .... Eight Russians convicted of high treason are hanged in the Krasnodar public square before a crowd of 30,000.		Brazilian Aeronautics Min. Joaquim Pedro Salgado announces Brazil is building U.S. war planes in former German-controlled plants.	
July 19		Allied planes, mostly American, bomb Rome for the first time, blasting railroad yards and airports east and south of the city's center .... British engage German troops in the Catania plains in the greatest battle of the Sicilian campaign.	U.S. forces make a limited advance and enlarge their beachhead at Lilio, east of Munda, New Georgia Island .... Allied forces drive Japanese troops back in a series of skirmishes on the slopes of Mt. Tanbu in the Komiatum sector of New Guinea.	American-Puerto Rican commission begins consideration of home rule for the island.	
July 20		Russian troops attack on a 450-mile front from Orel to Taganrog, capturing 50 villages, killing 4,700 Nazi soldiers and destroying 143 tanks and 117 planes .... Enna, the Axis communications center in central Sicily, is taken by U.S. and Canadian troops on the 11th day of the invasion .... It is reported from Switzerland that German authorities executed 50 Frenchmen in Paris last week for the shooting of a Nazi officer.	U.S. planes sink a Japanese light cruiser and two destroyers north of Vila in the northern Solomons.		
July 21		Vatican radio broadcasts a letter from Pope Pius XII deploring the bombing of Rome and recalling his hope that its "immense historical importance" and "precious documents and relics" would guarantee inviolability .... U.S. troops capture Sciacca, Menfi and Castelvetrano and advance to the outskirts of Marsala on the western tip of Sicily .... Allied Cairo headquarters reveals the British now have a military liaison with the Yugoslav partisans and will aid this resistance group as well as Gen. Draja Mikhailovich's Chetniks .... Sir Kingsley Wood, British chancellor of the exchequer since May 1940 and a member of Parliament for the last 20 years, dies at 62 in London.	More than 150 U.S. planes bomb Bairoko Harbor, New Georgia Island, in the heaviest Allied raid yet in the Southwest Pacific.	Mexican Pres. Avila Camacho authorizes the Ministry of National Economy to seize corn hoarded by speculators.	
July 22		U.S. Army units drive 30 to 35 miles across Sicily, splitting the island and capturing Palermo, its capital and principal port .... Under War Secy. Patterson says the bombing of Rome was caused by Mussolini's refusal to "declare it an open city." .... Russian troops advance three to five miles on the Orel front and capture a number of villages, including the Nazi stronghold of Bolkhov.	U.S. planes blast Japanese positions on Munda, New Georgia and attack three more enemy warships in the Bougainville Strait.		
July 23		U.S. completes the occupation of western Sicily, capturing the port of Marsala and the naval base of Trapani .... Italian War Ministry orders all men from 21 to 36 into the army before Aug. 15 to double Italy's present three-million man force .... FDR tells his press conference the bombing of Rome was necessary to save lives of Allied troops because of Italy's refusal to declare it an open city.		Cuban dispatches report epidemics of typhoid and malaria in Oriente, Santa Clara and Habana provinces.	
	A *Includes developments that affect more than one world region, international organizations and important meetings of major world leaders.*	B *Includes all developments in European countries and military engagements between Allied and Axis powers in Africa and at sea.*	C *Includes all developments in Japan and China, Japanese foreign policy and military actions in the Pacific region.*	D *Includes all domestic and regional developments in Latin America, the Caribbean and Canada.*	E *Includes developments in those independent nations and colonial possessions not covered in Columns B, C and D.*

U.S. Politics & Social Issues	U.S. Foreign Policy & Defense	U.S. Economy & Environment	Science, Technology & Nature	Culture, Leisure & Life Style	
Thomas W. Wallace, lieutenant governor of New York since Jan. 1 and one of the most successful Republican vote-getters despite his father's leadership of the state Democrats, dies at 43 in Schenectady.				Marian Anderson, Negro contralto, is married to Orpheus H. Fisher, a draftsman in a Danbury, Conn. war plant . . . . *Jezrahel* and *Occupy* finish 1-2 in the $60,050 Arlington Futurity at Washington Park, Chicago.	July 17
American Labor Party charges Communists are planning to take over the organization under cover of a "support FDR" campaign.			Two Army tow gliders make a record 1,243-mile flight from Sheppard Field, Tex. to Maxon Field, N.C. in nine hrs. 45 min.		July 18
	An Eastern conference of the GOP Postwar Policy Assn. warns the party that narrow nationalism is dead and that "isolationist stuffed shirts" must be purged.	The world's biggest pipeline is completed, extending from Longview, Tex. to Phoenixville, Pa., and providing the East Coast with 300,000 barrels of oil daily.	General Electric Laboratory in Schenectady announces the development of photographic equipment with an exposure of one-millionth of a second which can photograph rifle bullets in flight.		July 19
Louis (Lepke) Buchalter, Emanuel Weiss and Louis Capone, whose appeal of their conviction for the murder of Samuel Rosen was denied by the U.S. Supreme Court, are sentenced by the State Supreme Court in Albany to die the week of Sept. 13 . . . . Interior Secy. Ickes declares in New York that businessmen "like Knudsen, Nelson and Stettinius" run the war . . . . FDR asks the attorney general to give special attention to the problem of race riots, which endanger "our national unity and comfort our enemies."	Vice Chief of Naval Operations Frederick Horne says the Navy is planning for a war that will last at least until 1949 in the Pacific.			Simon & Schuster, Inc. announces 20th Century Fox has purchased the film rights to Willkie's *One World* for about $100,000.	July 20
		Treasury Secy. Morgenthau says the $15-billion third war loan starting Sept. 9 will be the largest financing program in the history of the world . . . . Lewis signs a two-year contract with the Illinois Coal Operators Assn., affecting 30,500 miners . . . . OPA inspectors and state police seize poultry trucks on Army requisition orders in the Delaware-Maryland-Virginia area, where black markets prevented Army purchases at the 29½¢-a-pound ceiling price.		N.Y. Mayor Fiorello La Guardia announces organization of the City Center of Music and Drama, a private group to sponsor low-priced performances in N.Y.C.	July 21
	War Dept. discloses 65,058 Axis prisoners are interned in the U.S.	AFL Pres. Green, CIO Pres. Murray and Combined Labor War Bd. members tell FDR organized labor cannot be held to account for labor conflict if prices are not rolled back to Sept. 15, 1942 levels.		Alfred Wallenstein, 44, is elected permanent conductor and musical director of the Los Angeles Philharmonic Orchestra, the first native-born conductor to direct a major American orchestra.	July 22
District Judge Lewis V. Trueman, 53, of Ogden, Utah, and four other persons are shot to death by Austin Cox, 38, whose wife got a divorce in the judge's court recently.		NWLB officially denies a wage increase to Los Angeles transit workers and calls labor demands for raises above the Little Steel formula because of increased living costs "specious reasoning," which will be denied as inflationary . . . . FDR reports a new plan to keep down living costs is being drafted for presentation to Congress.			July 23

F	G	H	I	J
Includes elections, federal-state relations, civil rights and liberties, crime, the judiciary, education, health care, poverty, urban affairs and population.	*Includes formation and debate of U.S. foreign and defense policies, veterans affairs and defense spending. (Relations with specific foreign countries are usually found under the region concerned.)*	*Includes business, labor, agriculture, taxation, transportation, consumer affairs, monetary and fiscal policy, natural resources, pollution and accidents.*	*Includes worldwide scientific, medical and technological developments, natural phenomena, U.S. weather and natural disasters.*	*Includes the arts, religion, scholarship, communications media, sports, entertainment, fashions, fads and social life.*

	World Affairs	European War Zone	Pacific War Zone	The Americas	Other Countries & Territories
July 24		U.S. forces mop up in western Sicily and pursue retreating Axis troops toward their new defense line south and west of Mt. Etna . . . . Vatican radio broadcasts in German a denial by Pope Pius XII of a German assertion that he had protested the bombing of Rome to President Roosevelt . . . . Istanbul reports Yugoslavian partisans and Greek patriots are battling Axis troops in the Ibar River disctrict of Macedonia and that Gen. Mikhailovich's troops are in control of large parts of the Vardar and Morava Valleys.		Buenos Aires police burn copies of Joseph E. Davies' *Mission to Moscow* as "objectionable propaganda."	
July 25		Mussolini resigns as Italian premier and King Victor Emmanuel III appoints Marshal Pietro Badoglio as "head of government, premier and state secretary."		Argentina rescinds police restrictions on the British Community Council, a war aid group.	
July 26		Marshal Badoglio names his cabinet, declares martial law and incorporates the Fascist militia into the army . . . . U.S. and Canadian troops turn back a counterattack by German forces on the central Sicilian front . . . . Allied planes bomb Reggio Calabria in southern Italy and airfields at Capodichino and Montecorvino Rovella in the Naples area.	Liberators, Warhawks and Lightnings drop a record 104 tons of bombs in 13 raids on Japanese-occupied Kiska in the Aleutians.		
July 27		Preliminary peace negotiations are reported under way in Vatican City between U.S. and British representatives and delegates of the Badoglio government . . . . Churchill hails the downfall of Italian Premier Mussolini and says Italy must now decide whether it will enjoy "relief from war, freedom from servitude and, after an interval, a respectable place in a new and rescued Europe" or "be seared and scared and blackened from one end to the other." . . . . Allied troops advance toward the northern sector of the Etna line and capture Collesano, Polizzi, Petralia and Alimena in northeastern Sicily.	Allied planes bomb Japanese positions in the Salamaua sector of New Guinea.	Argentina assumes supervision of eight foreign firms accused of violating price laws, including Ford and General Motors, Goodyear, Firestone and Michelin tire companies and International Harvester Co.	
July 28		U.S. 7th Army drives towards the northern flank of the German line in Sicily, capturing Pollina, Castelbuono and Gangi . . . . Italian cabinet orders the dissolution of the National Fascist Party and abolishes the Fascist Grand Council and the special tribunals for national defense . . . . Dispatches from Berne tell of rioting and demonstrations in several Italian cities, with the rioters demanding peace and Italian socialists in Milan beginning a general strike . . . . FDR hails the downfall of Mussolini as "the first crack in the Axis."		Uruguay renews diplomatic relations with the Soviet Union . . . . A delegation of the Inter-American Emergency Advisory Comm. for Political Defense of the Continent arrives in Washington for consultation on Axis activities in the Americas.	
July 29		American troops capture Nicosia, an advance German position in the center of the Etna line, as Canadian troops occupy Agira . . . . Eisenhower, in a message to the Italian people, asks for the immediate cessation of military activities and offers in return the release of all Italian prisoners captured in Africa and Sicily . . . . Soviet troops advance three to six miles on the Orel front, taking 40 villages and occupying a Nazi base containing 16 ammunition dumps.	Navy reveals the sinking of 10 Japanese ships — two transports, six cargo and two tankers — by submarines in the Pacific.	Mexican Foreign Min. Ezequiel Padilla makes public his protest to Texas Gov. Coke R. Stephenson (D) concerning discrimination against Mexican farm laborers.	
July 30		British drive into German defenses south of Catania in Sicily, while Canadians and Americans also make advances . . . . Thousands of Italian workers storm the Cellari jail in Milan and release 200 political prisoners as Italian troops disobey orders to fire on the demonstrators . . . . RAF planes drop 2,300 tons of bombs on Hamburg, with the loss of 28 bombers.	U.S. troops on New Georgia Island repulse a Japanese counterattack in the northern sector of the Munda front . . . . Australian External Affairs Min. Herbert V. Evatt reports that Britain and the U.S. have made "substantial allocation" of planes for Australia.		

A	B	C	D	E
Includes developments that affect more than one world region, international organizations and important meetings of major world leaders.	*Includes all developments in European countries and military engagements between Allied and Axis powers in Africa and at sea.*	*Includes all developments in Japan and China, Japanese foreign policy and military actions in the Pacific region.*	*Includes all domestic and regional developments in Latin America, the Caribbean and Canada.*	*Includes developments in those independent nations and colonial possessions not covered in Columns B, C and D.*

U.S. Politics & Social Issues	U.S. Foreign Policy & Defense	U.S. Economy & Environment	Science, Technology & Nature	Culture, Leisure & Life Style	
Willkie urges political parties to reappraise their obligation to Negro citizens now denied equality in economic opportunities, social benefits, suffrage and military status .... Vice Pres. Wallace says in Detroit he is a "practical" idealist and denounces as "Fascists" big businessmen who oppose FDR.				Gunder Haeg runs the mile in 4:05.3, a new American record, to beat Gil Dodds by eight yards in Cambridge, Mass. .... Slide Rule with Ferril Zufelt up wins the $72,000 Arlington Classic in Chicago's Washington Park.	July 24
Gov. Dwight H. Green (R, Ill.) signs bills making the teaching of history and the principles of representative government compulsory in public schools.	FDR pledges that government efforts will be made to give all possible aid to the Jewish people affected by Nazism .... Wallace calls on the nation to take the initiative now in planning a war-proof postwar world based on world cooperation.				July 25
	Eight American expatriots who have broadcast propaganda for Axis governments are indicted on treason charges by a federal grand jury in Washington. They are: Ezra Pound, Frederick Kaltenback, Robert Best, Douglas Chandler, Edward Delaney, Constance Drexel, Jane Anderson and Max Koischwitz.	A Pittsburgh federal grand jury indicts 30 leaders of unauthorized coal strikes in southwestern Pennsylvania on charges of violating the Smith-Connally War Labor Disputes Law, the first such action under the new statute .... President's Comm. on Fair Employment Practices orders West Coast shipyards to rehire 300 Negroes, discharged under a closed-shop contract when they refused to join an "auxiliary" Negro union set up by the AFL Boilermakers Union.			July 26
	Representing the GOP Postwar Policy Assn., Deneen Watson presents GOP National Chmn. Harrison Spangler with a demand that the party advocate U.S. participation in postwar world affairs.			Bishop Ernest Lynn Waldorf, head of the Methodist Church in the Chicago area since 1932 and leader of the move to unite all Methodists, dies at 67 in Alexandria Bay., N.Y.	July 27
NAACP assails Detroit prosecutor William Dowling for charging that Negro groups and the Negro press helped to instigate recent race riots there.	FDR says he will ask Congress to approve a program providing returning servicemen with "mustering out" pay, unemployment insurance, credit allowances and free training for jobs.	FDR announces an end of coffee rationing and promises early increases in sugar allowances.	Thirteen persons die in a hurricane on the Texas Gulf Coast. The storm causes an estimated $10 million in damages.		July 28
FDR nominates Amos Taylor as director of the Bureau of Foreign and Domestic Commerce.	Army announces officers who have passed age limits of 64 for ranks above brigadier general, 62 for brigadier generals and 60 for lower ranks will be retired Sept. 1, with some exceptions.				July 29
	FDR warns neutral nations not to provide refuge for Mussolini or his followers, and asserts that "war criminals" will be tried and punished.	FDR makes public the report of the Conference on Postwar Adjustment of Civilian and Military Personnel, which advocates government aid in expanding peacetime industry.	Public Health Service reports infantile paralysis is spreading in Tex., Calif., Wash., Kan. and N.Y. .... London reports that because of the work of the Rockefeller Foundation control program there has not been a case of yellow fever among Allied personnel in East Africa since 1939.	Radio Corp. of America announces an agreement to sell the Blue Network for $8,000,000 to Edward J. Noble, owner of station WMCA .... Pope Pius XII directs that $40,000 of Holy See funds be used to restore Catholic churches in Britain damanged in Nazi air raids .... Benjamin J. Dale, British composer and warden of the Royal Academy of Music, dies at 58 in London.	July 30
F *Includes elections, federal-state relations, civil rights and liberties, crime, the judiciary, education, health care, poverty, urban affairs and population.*	G *Includes formation and debate of U.S. foreign and defense policies, veterans affairs and defense spending. (Relations with specific foreign countries are usually found under the region concerned.)*	H *Includes business, labor, agriculture, taxation, transportation, consumer affairs, monetary and fiscal policy, natural resources, pollution and accidents.*	I *Includes worldwide scientific, medical and technological developments, natural phenomena, U.S. weather and natural disasters.*	J *Includes the arts, religion, scholarship, communications media, sports, entertainment, fashions, fads and social life.*	

	World Affairs	European War Zone	Pacific War Zone	The Americas	Other Countries & Territories
July 31	Executive committee of the Latin American Confederation of Workers authorizes its president, Vincente Lombardo Toledano, to visit labor leaders elsewhere with the aim of organizing a U.N. conference on post-war labor.	Allied radio stations broadcast a "solemn warning" to Italy stating that air raids on Italian cities will be resumed since there has been no sign of German withdrawal .... Yugoslavian troops under Gen. Mikhailovich fight their way through Axis lines into the Udine district of northeastern Italy .... Berne states soldiers are joining workers in peace demonstrations throughout northern Italy and that the Fascists in the *Popolo d'Italia* building in Milan surrendered today after Vito Mussolini, nephew of the dictator, was seriously injured .... French Comm. of National Liberation names Giraud military commander subject to committee decisions and appoints a National Defense Comm. headed by de Gaulle.			
Aug. 1		More than 175 U.S. Liberators drop 300 tons of bombs on the Ploesti oil refineries in Rumania with the loss of 20 bombers. This is their second raid on the refineries, which produce 90% of the Luftwaffe's gasoline .... Rioting dies down in northern Italy as Italians begin evacuation from cities to escape Allied air raids .... American troops take Mistretta, Sicily, capturing 10,000 prisoners.	Tokyo grants independence to Burma, which then declares war on the U.S. and Britain .... China severs diplomatic relations with Vichy .... Lin Sen, president of China since 1931, scholar and artist, dies at 79 in Chungking.		
Aug. 2		Allied troops move forward on all sectors of the 120-mile Sicilian front .... Red Army forces advance northwest and southwest of Orel, killing 1,600 Nazi troops and occupying 70 villages, including Znamenskoye.	*PT 109* is cut in two by a Japanese destroyer. Among the crew members missing is Lt. (j.g.) John F. Kennedy, son of Joseph P. Kennedy, former ambassador to Britain.		In a farewell address to the Council and Assembly in New Delhi, Lord Linlithgow says a lack of trust and unwillingness to "accept legitimate claims of minorities" block solution of the Indian problem.
Aug. 3		Lt. Gen. George S. Patton Jr., strikes American Private Charles Herman Kuhl, after charging that Kuhl has no business being in hospital. It is later revealed that Kuhl is suffering from malaria, chronic diarrhea, and a 102.2 degree temperature .... U.S. forces advance on the northern flank of the Sicilian front and capture Caronia, as Canadian and British forces continue their advances .... Russian troops break into Orel, the German stronghold on the Russian front, engaging in street fighting with Nazi defenders.	American troops drive to the eastern end of Munda airfield on New Georgia Island and occupy the northeastern slope of Bibolo Hill.		
Aug. 4		Italian press and radio assail Allied demands for unconditional surrender.	Chinese Foreign Min. T.V. Soong declares China will develop postwar heavy industry "with Western capital under our terms."		Pretoria reports Jan Christiaan Smuts's pro-war coalition won the July 7 election in the Union of South Africa .... Bombay announces more than 2,000 persons died in recent floods which inundated Vijainagar and six other villages in Rajputana.
Aug. 5		Stockholm announces abrogation of the agreement whereby German soldiers on leave and war material have been crossing Sweden to Norway and Finland since June 1940 .... Soviet troops capture the Nazi strongholds of Orel and Belgorod, as the Germans retreat towards Karacheva and Bryansk and the Sumy-Kharkov line.			
Aug. 6		Russian forces break into the Ukraine on a 43-mile front and outflank the Nazi base of Kharkov .... German Foreign Min. von Ribbentrop arrives in Italy for discussions with the Badoglio government at Verona .... British troops take the abandoned German positions in Catania, Sicily .... RAF planes drop pamphlets on Berlin warning civilians the city will suffer the same fate as Hamburg in the near future.	Japanese resistance in the Munda area of New Georgia Island in the Solomons ends at 3 p.m. today and mopping-up operations begin after 38 days of fighting.	Dr. Raul Damonte Taborda, former Argentine deputy and liberal leader, and Santiago Diaz Vieyra, pro-Axis editor, fight a duel with sabers in Buenos Aires. It ends after 30 seconds when Taborda suffers slight wounds.	

U.S. Politics & Social Issues	U.S. Foreign Policy & Defense	U.S. Economy & Environment	Science, Technology & Nature	Culture, Leisure & Life Style	
Alfred Landon charges Vice Pres. Wallace "declared civil war" July 25 in his Detroit speech with the approval of FDR, whom he accuses of "life-term ambition." . . . . George S. Viereck is sentenced in a Washington federal court to one to five years for violation of the Foreign Registration Act.	State Dept. instructs its representatives to call on the governments of Sweden, Turkey, Spain, Portugal, Switzerland, Argentina and Vatican City not to give asylum to Axis leaders.	In his revised budget statement, FDR calls for additional stiff taxation on savings to help meet war costs . . . . Atty. Gen. Biddle rules any group can call for a strike vote in a war plant under the Connally-Harness-Smith Act.		Marriage, with George Burns up, wins the $59,300 Arlington Handicap in Chicago.	July 31
			A system that de-ices planes by circulating heated air through the motor exhaust pipes is revealed by the Consolidated - Vultee Aircraft Corp.		Aug. 1
In Harlem rioting lasting 12 hours, five Negroes are killed, 500 are injured and 500 are jailed with damage and theft loss estimated at $5 million.	WMC Chmn. McNutt instructs draft boards to prepare to draft fathers on or after Oct. 1.		Lt. Col. Cass S. Hough, in 25,000 and 18,000 foot dives with Lightning and Thunderbolt fighters, travels faster than the speed of sound, or more than 780 miles an hour.		Aug. 2
Georgia votes approval of a constitutional amendment lowering the voting age to 18.		Interior Secy. Ickes announces coal mines operated by the government will be returned when the mine managers submit evidence of a return to capacity operation . . . . OPA reports wages in manufacturing industries are up 28.9% over January 1941.			Aug. 3
		Appalachian Joint Wage Conference of Northern coal operators announces it will stand by the NWLB's June 18 decision refusing underground travel pay for miners regardless of the board's disposition of the UMW's proposed contract with Illinois operators providing such pay . . . . In the first election under the Connally-Smith Act, employes of two Allis-Chalmers plants vote to strike in an AFL-CIO jurisdictional dispute.			Aug. 4
WRA Dir. Dillon S. Myer says only 10% of 6,500 Japanese whose repatriation Japan demands in an exchange deal are willing to return there.		Treasury announces 15 million Americans whose income exceeds $2,700 for single persons and $3,500 for married persons must file "a declaration of estimated income and Victory Tax" on short forms by Sept. 15 . . . . WPB Chmn. Nelson announces 80% of the $20,000,000,000 war-plant construction program was completed by the end of June.	Fourteen persons are drowned and nine are missing as a "flash" flood sweeps central West Virginia, causing $2 million in property damage . . . . Anheuser-Busch Inc. announces it is producing a new food for the Army from yeast that resembles meat in taste and is twice as rich as natural meat in protein.	Doplh Camilli, Giant first baseman, announces he will retire from baseball and return to his ranch near Laytonville, Calif.	Aug. 5
Sen. Carter Glass (D,Va.) calls on America to "adjourn politics," deploring the name-calling and cut-throat acts against FDR, so the nation can get on with the war effort.	WMC instructs local draft boards not to call fathers with children born before Sept. 15, 1942 until other eligible men are taken.	WMC orders a minimum 48-hour work week in the Newark, N.J. area to meet labor shortages.			Aug. 6

	World Affairs	European War Zone	Pacific War Zone	The Americas	Other Countries & Territories
Aug. 7		British capture Bronte and occupy Adrano and Belpasso, as American troops advance toward Cesaro. The Americans capture Troina .... German Chief of Staff Field Marshal Wilhelm Keitel arrives in Verona to join Ribbentrop in conference with Italian leaders .... Closing in on Kharkov, Russian troops retake 70 villages, including Graivoron, Mezenovka and Sennoye .... *Polish Labor Fights*, published in London, declares the Nazis have massacred 2,000,000 Jews by suffocation with steam in a death house in Treblinka, Poland.		Second conference of the Inter-American Bar Assn. opens in Rio de Janeiro to discuss postwar problems.	
Aug. 8		Russians advance from seven to nine miles in the Kharkov sector, claiming the capture of 60 more villages .... U.S. troops make an "unopposed landing" behind Axis lines near Torrenova on the northern coast of Sicily and take 300 prisoners.	Eleven members of *PT 109*, including Lt. John F. Kennedy, are rescued by naval units .... Three Japanese destroyers are sunk and one escapes in an hour-long battle with U.S. fleet units in Vella Gulf, central Solomons.	Gen. Pedro P. Ramirez declares in Buenos Aires his military regime has no plans for a permanent dictatorship and adds "freedom is too precious to abandon." .... Canadian P.M. W.L. Mackenzie King's Liberal Party loses four seats in House of Commons by-elections.	
Aug. 9		Berne reports the Verona conferences have ended with Badoglio agreeing to continue the war .... British and U.S. troops join near Maletto as they advance towards Randozzo in the center of the Sicilian line .... With the capture of Slatino, Soviet troops move to within 12 miles of the German base at Kharkov.	Gen. MacArthur announces that recent Allied victories "have been decisive of the final result in the Pacific" and that Japan is on the defensive after the failure of the most "concentrated attack" of which it is capable.		Police arrest hundreds of demonstrators in India on the anniversary of Gandhi's arrest and break up a march on the villa of the Aga Khan in Poona where Gandhi is interned .... A Lend-Lease agreement is signed in Washington by State Secy. Hull and Ethiopian Vice Finance Min. Yilma Deressa.
Aug. 10	Churchill arrives in Quebec for a series of conferences with the Allied High Command and later with FDR.	Lt. Gen. Patton for the second time strikes an American soldier being treated for shell-shock and subsequently apologizes after being reprimanded by his superiors .... British take Guardia on the Sicilian eastern coast and are within sight of the Italian mainland .... Moving forward towards Kharkov, the Red Army claims the capture of another 70 villages .... Yugoslavian cabinet in London resigns over Croat-Serb disputes on postwar policy; a new government is formed immediately headed by Dr. Bojidar Pourich.	U.S. troops reach the Bairoke River, two miles south of Bairoke Harbor, New Georgia Island .... Chinese executive cabinet approves the drafting of legislation for protection of foreign capital in China after the war.		
Aug. 11	Allied war strategy discussions open at the Chateau-Frontenac Hotel in Quebec, with Churchill conferring with members of the Canadian war cabinet.	Italy orders a temporary halt in the shipment of war materials to Germany and food shipments to Nazi forces in northern Italy .... Driving nine to 12 miles further into the Ukraine, Soviet forces pass the peak point of last winter's campaign by capturing Krasnokutsk and Parkhomovka .... RAF planes bomb Nuremberg for the sixth time, dropping 1,680 tons of explosives on industrial targets.	U.S. heavy bombers make their second raid on the Kurile Islands, making numerous hits on the Kataoka Bay naval base on Shimushu and the Kashiabara Bay military base on Paramushiru.		
Aug. 12	Churchill arrives at Hyde Park, N.Y. for strategy conferences with FDR .... Tass reports that the Soviet Union did not receive an invitation to the current Allied conferences at Quebec .... House Speaker Sam Rayburn says the U.S. should contribute to a world army to aid in keeping Germany, Italy and Japan disarmed.	Nazi troops flee Sicily across the Messina Strait to the Italian mainland .... Red Army moves to within five miles of Kharkov and also captures the Nazi stronghold at Chuguyev.	FDR promises the Republic of the Philippines will be established the moment the Japanese forces are destroyed.	Argentine Interior Ministry instructs provincial governors and army and navy officials to stamp out Communism.	
Aug. 13	American delegation to the Quebec Conference, headed by Adm. William D. Leahy, Gen. George C. Marshall, Adm. Ernest King, Gen. Henry H. Arnold and Lt. Gen. Brehon B. Somervell, arrives in Canada.	Two large waves of U.S. planes bomb Rome for the second time, dropping more than 500 tons of explosives on the San Lorenzo and Littorio railroad yards .... RAF planes make their heaviest attack of the war on northern Italy, bombing Turin and Milan, with more than 500 bombers making the 1,300-mile round trip .... Berne reports large crowds demonstrated for peace in Rome, Milan, and Turin after Allied raids shattered their cities .... Allied troops occupy Randazzo, communications center in northeast Sicily.	Allied planes bomb Salamaua, New Guinea and airfields and supply dumps on New Britain.	Cuba recognizes the French Comm. of National Liberation.	

A	B	C	D	E
Includes developments that affect more than one world region, international organizations and important meetings of major world leaders.	*Includes all developments in European countries and military engagements between Allied and Axis powers in Africa and at sea.*	*Includes all developments in Japan and China, Japanese foreign policy and military actions in the Pacific region.*	*Includes all domestic and regional developments in Latin America, the Caribbean and Canada.*	*Includes developments in those independent nations and colonial possessions not covered in Columns B, C and D.*

U.S. Politics & Social Issues	U.S. Foreign Policy & Defense	U.S. Economy & Environment	Science, Technology & Nature	Culture, Leisure & Life Style	
		Western Railroad Assn. Exec. Secy. D.P. Loomis and Railroad Clerks Brotherhood Pres. George M. Harrison announce an agreement on a wage increase for 1.1 million operating employes . . . . CIO Pres. Murray writes FDR protesting Atty. Gen. Biddle's ruling that any group can call for a strike vote under the Smith-Connally Act.		Gunder Haegg sets a new American outdoor mark of 8:51.3 for two miles in Cincinnati.	Aug. 7
	The former French liner *Normandie*, now the U.S. transport *Lafayette*, on its side in a N.Y. Hudson River slip since Feb. 10, 1942, rises to 43.6 feet and is reported "essentially afloat." . . . . Lt. Gen. Hugh A. Drum announces an extension of restricted and prohibited defense zones in 16 Atlantic Coast states.		Patents for a new type of cargo plane, which can be loaded as easily as a motor van, are granted to the Glenn L. Martin Co. of Baltimore.	Karl Krueger, conductor of the Kansas City Philharmonic Orchestra, is named conductor of the Detroit Symphony Orchestra.	Aug. 8
OWI announces 777 employes have been dropped from its domestic branch, reducing personnel from 1,269 to 492 to meet the $5,500,000 budget cut by Congress.				*Burma Surgeon*, by Dr. Gordon S. Seagrave, is published . . . . Howard Schenken wins the contract bridge masters team-of-four championship in N.Y. for the fifth time.	Aug. 9
		OPA Labor Policy Comm. charges Petroleum Admin. Ickes is aiding oil companies to put over a $1.25 billion "steal" through a crude oil price rise.		*The Spanish Labyrinth* by Gerald Brenan is published in New York.	Aug. 10
Gov. Harry F. Kelly's fact-finding committee reports the Detroit race riots were caused by "false rumors and irresponsible leadership." . . . . Senate Majority Leader Alben Barkley refuses to reconvene Congress prior to Sept. 14 to consider draft legislation.		Maritime Commission sets up a committee to plan postwar shipping needs and programs.	Public Health Service officials report 2,753 cases of infantile paralysis through Aug. 7, compared to 1,148 last year. They say the epidemic is limited to California and Texas.	Bertrand Russell, British educator and philosopher, says he will return to England because he has been unable to find employment in the U.S. Russell is suing the Barnes Foundation for $24,000 for breach of contract . . . . Swedish runner Gunder Haegg wins the mile race at Randalls Island in 4:06.9 in the final appearance of his U.S. tour.	Aug. 11
		AFL executive council rejects a CIO proposal for joint political action in the coming elections, affirming its policy of "nonpartisanship."			Aug. 12
		OPA announces the value of gasoline ration coupons will be cut from four to three gallons in the Midwest and Southwest on Aug. 16.			Aug. 13
F	G	H	I	J	
Includes elections, federal-state relations, civil rights and liberties, crime, the judiciary, education, health care, poverty, urban affairs and population.	*Includes formation and debate of U.S. foreign and defense policies, veterans affairs and defense spending. (Relations with specific foreign countries are usually found under the region concerned.)*	*Includes business, labor, agriculture, taxation, transportation, consumer affairs, monetary and fiscal policy, natural resources, pollution and accidents.*	*Includes worldwide scientific, medical and technological developments, natural phenomena, U.S. weather and natural disasters.*	*Includes the arts, religion, scholarship, communications media, sports, entertainment, fashions, fads and social life.*	

	World Affairs	European War Zone	Pacific War Zone	The Americas	Other Countries & Territories
Aug. 14		Soviet forces repulse strong Nazi counterattacks in the Kharkov sector, battling their way into the northern outskirts of the city .... Allied planes bomb the Axis embarkation ports on Sicily and the debarkation points on the mainland .... Italian news agency claims Badoglio has declared Rome an open city .... A joint statement by FDR and Churchill calls the Allied effort in July against the U-boats "our most successful month."		Canadian Labor Min. Humphrey Mitchell announces married men 27 to 30 years of age will be drafted .... Office of the Coordinator of Inter-American Affairs announces plans to train medical and health experts, engineers and agriculturalists from South American countries.	
Aug. 15	Churchill returns to Ottawa after completing his visit to FDR at Hyde Park.	Allies capture Taormina, Kaggi and Castiglione on the east coast of Sicily, and the Americans reach the vicinity of Milazzo on the north coast .... Red Army fights its way into Karachev, last German outpost east of Bryansk.	U.S. and Canadian troops land on Kiska, last Japanese-held island in the Aleutians, only to find it evacuated .... U.S. troops occupy Vella Lavella Island in the central Solomons, bypassing Japanese garrisons at Vila and Bairoko Harbor.	More than 8,000 Independentistas rally in San Juan and approve a message to FDR asking for Puerto Rican independence .... Gen. Higinio Morinigo is inaugurated for a five-year term as president of Paraguay.	
Aug. 16		U.S. and British forces advance against dwindling opposition on Sicily .... Soviet troops gain up to nine miles east of Bryansk, capturing more than 130 towns including Malye Luki, only 18 miles from the Nazi base at Bryansk.	Allied bombers attack Japanese airports at Wewak, New Guinea, destroying 120 grounded enemy aircraft .... Japan announces an "autonomy program" for Java, with native advisers assisting military authorities.		
Aug. 17	Quebec Conference opens in Ottawa, with FDR arriving at Wolf's Cove, Canada by train to meet with Churchill and Canadian officals on war strategy.	British and Canadian bombers drop 1,500 tons of explosives on a secret German rocket research and development plant hidden in a woods at Peenemuende, 60 miles northwest of Stettin, on the Baltic coast .... On the 38th day of the Sicilian campaign U.S. troops take Messina, ending all resistance on the island, save isolated pockets .... Italian islands of Lipari and Stromboli, largest of the Aeolian group in the Tyrrhenian Sea, surrender to a U.S. naval expedition.		Fernando Ortiz Rubio, son of former Mexican President Pascual Ortiz Rubio, is sentenced to 14 years imprisonment in Toluca for the fatal shooting of Gov. Alfredo Zarate Albarran of Mexico State in March 1942.	
Aug. 18	British Foreign Secy. Eden arrives in Quebec to attend the Allied war conferences.	Allied North African headquarters announces all resistance on Sicily has stopped and that through Aug. 10 135,000 Axis prisoners were taken and 32,000 enemy soldiers were killed or wounded .... U.S. warships make their first direct attacks on the Italian mainland, shelling bridges and power stations at Gioia Tauro and Palmi on the southwest coast .... Russian Army resumes its offensive in the Ukraine, capturing more than 50 villages and killing some 3,500 Germans.	A second series of attacks on the Japanese airfield at Wewak completes its destruction, wiping out 215 of the original 225 planes there.		
Aug. 19	U.S. Treasury announces a revised postwar economic stabilization plan, which excludes U.S. veto power but enhances the value of gold.	Russians hurl back German counterattacks on three sides of Kharkov, killing a reported 2,400 German troops and advancing three to seven miles, taking more than 30 villages .... Foggia, a railway junction in southeast Italy, undergoes the heaviest raid of the war in the Mediterranean theater.		Colombian Foreign Office proposes a seven-nation — Chile, Colombia, Ecuador, Paraguay, Peru, Uruguay and Venezuela — conference to study postwar problems, including their role in the U.N.	Two directors of the State Bank of Morocco are arrested in Rabat on orders of the French Comm. of National Liberation for exporting gold to Germany.
Aug. 20	State Secy. Hull arrives in Quebec to attend the Allied war conferences.	Lebedin, most westerly point occupied by the Russians in their winter offensive, is again captured by Soviet troops as they sweep deep into the Ukraine .... Sir Samuel Hoare, British ambassador to Spain, flies from Madrid to La Coruna for conferences with Generalissimo Francisco Franco and Gen. Count Francisco Gomez Jordana, Spanish foreign minister. London dispatches say Hoare has been instructed to protest Spanish propaganda in Latin America.	Allied troops seize Bobdubi Ridge, four miles southwest of the Japanese base at Salamaua, New Guinea.		British government's India Office reports India's population was 388,997,955 in 1941, a 10-year increase of 50 million.
Aug. 21	British War Transport Min. Lord Leathers and U.S. Deputy War Shipping Admin. Lewis W. Douglas confer in Quebec with FDR and Churchill on Allied shipping and supply problems.	About 40,000 German troops are rushed to Copenhagen from Norway to check riots, strikes and sabotage .... Maxim Litvinov is relieved as Russian ambassador to the U.S. and will be succeeded by Andrei Gromyko.	Labor Party of P.M. John Curtin wins Australia's election, claiming 48 seats in the House of Representatives.	British Food Ministry announces an agreement with Argentina on behalf of the U.N. to purchase meat surplus from Argentina for two years.	
	A	B	C	D	E
	Includes developments that affect more than one world region, international organizations and important meetings of major world leaders.	*Includes all developments in European countries and military engagements between Allied and Axis powers in Africa and at sea.*	*Includes all developments in Japan and China, Japanese foreign policy and military actions in the Pacific region.*	*Includes all domestic and regional developments in Latin America, the Caribbean and Canada.*	*Includes developments in those independent nations and colonial possessions not covered in Columns B, C and D.*

U.S. Politics & Social Issues	U.S. Foreign Policy & Defense	U.S. Economy & Environment	Science, Technology & Nature	Culture, Leisure & Life Style	
	WMC sets up a new list of 149 critical occupations for first priority on draft deferments and announces that occupation and not dependency will be the deciding factor in future deferments.				Aug. 14
		A food advisory subcommittee reports to Agriculture Secy. Claude Wickard that the government has failed to develop an adequate food program . . . . SEC orders United Corp. to recapitalize with a single class of stock and cease functioning as a holding company.		Stella Walsh wins three events in the women's national AAU track and field championships in Cleveland. Her Polish Olympic Women's A.C. of Cleveland takes the team title.	Aug. 15
	War Mobilization Dir. Byrnes warns against over-confidence and declares British and U.S. forces have met and defeated "less than 7% of the enemy's combat divisions" in the European area, while 40% have been engaged by Russia.	AFL Pres. Green declares there is no possiblity of reunion with the CIO unless it accepts the AFL formula for merging first and leaving jurisdictional questions for later settlement . . . . FDR issues an executive order empowering the NWLB to withhold dues of unions which refuse to comply with its decisions and to cancel draft deferments of strikers.			Aug. 16
	Capt. Edward Rickenbacker declares Germany will not crack until before late 1944 and that an additional year will be needed to defeat Japan.	SEC orders the Cities Service Power & Light Co. and its subsidiary holding company, Federal Light & Traction Co., to relinquish control of 53 subsidiaries.			Aug. 17
		Anthracite Coal Operators Assn. asks the NWLB to resume jurisdiction over wage negotiations with the UMW.		Betty Smith's novel *A Tree Grows in Brooklyn,* concerning life in the Brooklyn slums, is published.	Aug. 18
N.Y. State Appeals Court orders an election Nov. 2 to fill the vacancy caused by the death of Lt. Gov. Thomas W. Wallace.	WMC sets an October draft quota of 312,000 recruits and says pre-Pearl Harbor fathers in war jobs may be deferred.	Twelve persons are killed and 11 injured in an explosion which wrecks a Congoleum-Nairn, Inc. war plant in Kearny, N.J.			Aug. 19
	State Dept. announces the Swedish liner *Gripsholm* will sail from N.Y. about Sept. 1 with Japanese internees, to be exchanged for Americans at Mormugao, Goa, Portuguese India . . . . Navy Secy. Knox discloses Vice Adm. John S. McCain will serve under Fleet Commander Ernest J. King and will direct combat and training functions.		Western Union Telegraph Co. Vice Pres. F.E. D'Humy tells the FCC a method of sending facsimile telegrams by light waves may be adopted after the war.		Aug. 20
President-elect of the American Federation of Teachers Joseph F. Landes assails "political interference" in public school systems throughout the nation.	Senate Military Affairs Comm. Chmn. Robert R. Reynolds (D, N.C.) says manpower officials should be required to give a definite and final statement regarding the drafting of fathers.	Northwest Airlines, Inc. files an application with the CAB in Washington to operate a commercial air route from Seattle or Alaska to Tokyo via the Aleutian Islands after the war.	GE officials report the development of a machine which produces 100 million-volt X-rays.	Southern Conference college members vote to drop all athletic eligibility rules for the duration of the war.	Aug. 21

F	G	H	I	J
Includes elections, federal-state relations, civil rights and liberties, crime, the judiciary, education, health care, poverty, urban affairs and population.	*Includes formation and debate of U.S. foreign and defense policies, veterans affairs and defense spending. (Relations with specific foreign countries are usually found under the region concerned.)*	*Includes business, labor, agriculture, taxation, transportation, consumer affairs, monetary and fiscal policy, natural resources, pollution and accidents.*	*Includes worldwide scientific, medical and technological developments, natural phenomena, U.S. weather and natural disasters.*	*Includes the arts, religion, scholarship, communications media, sports, entertainment, fashions, fads and social life.*

	World Affairs	European War Zone	Pacific War Zone	The Americas	Other Countries & Territories
Aug. 22		Russian troops advance north of Kharkov, taking 30 villages.	Allied forces capture a ridge dominating the airdrome at Salamaua, New Guinea, as aircraft bomb the base.	FDR and Canadian P.M. William Mackenzie King announce the creation of a Joint War Aid Comm. to study problems arising from Lend-Lease and mutual aid programs.	About 12,000 Polish refugees are established in Uganda with another 8,000 in the British colonies of Tanganyika, Kenya and Northern Rhodesia.
Aug. 23	Chinese Foreign Min. T.V. Soong confers with FDR and Churchill in Quebec.	Russian forces take Kharkov by storm as 10 divisions drive into the city .... In its fourth summer offensive, Soviet troops drive into the Donets Basin south of Izyum.	Japanese bombers attack Chungking this morning for the first time since Aug. 31, 1941.	A brief revolt by Ecuadorian sailors against Pres. Carlos Arroyo del Rio is quelled at Puna .... Lord Burghley, 38, former Olympic hurdler, is named governor of Bermuda.	
Aug. 24	Quebec Conference ends after Churchill and FDR agree that an American will command the cross-Channel invasion still scheduled for May 1944 and that every effort will be made to have Japan surrender unconditionally within 12 months after the defeat of Germany.	Hitler names Heinrich Himmler Reich minister of the interior .... RAF and RCAF bombers drop 1,800 tons of explosives on Berlin in their 74th attack upon the city.		Colombian Pres. Alfonso Lopez Pumarejo names a new cabinet.	Members of a U.S. Senate committee inspecting U.S. war fronts end a visit in Iran and leave Teheran by plane for India.
Aug. 25		Red Army takes the flour-milling center of Zenkov, 85 miles northwest of Kharkov.	Acting Vice Adm. Lord Louis Mountbatten is appointed head of the new Allied Southeast Asia Command to conduct operations in India and Ceylon .... U.S. planes attack the Kowloon dock area at Hong Kong, destroying about 25,000 tons of Japanese shipping.		
Aug. 26		U.S., U.K. and Canada give limited recognition to the French Comm. of National Liberation, stating this does not give recognition to a government of France or of the French Empire .... A report of the American and World Jewish Congresses declares 3,030,050 Jews have died from Hitler's persecution policies in Europe .... RAF bombers attack Berlin for the third straight night, while other planes lay mines in German waters.	For the second consecutive day, U.S. planes hit Japanese targets at Hong Kong and airports at Canton.		
Aug. 27		Russian troops continue their advance on the Kharkov front in the Ukraine .... China, Ecuador, Dominican Republic, Brazil, Venezuela, Nicaragua and Peru grant recognition to the French Comm. of National Liberation.		Bolivian cabinet of Pres. Enrique Penaranda del Castillo resigns in protest against attacks on Labor Min. Juan Manuel Balcazar and Interior Min. Pedro Zilveti Arce by the Chamber of Deputies for suppressing strikes at the Catavi tin mines.	
Aug. 28		Danish cabinet, after receiving King Christian's threat to abdicate if it caves in, rejects German demands for complete control of the country .... King Boris III of Bulgaria dies after a brief illness, and Crown Prince Simeon of Tironovo is named King Simeon II .... Soviet troops advance to nearly five miles west of the Bryansk-Kiev railroad west of Sevsk.	Allies announce all organized Japanese resistance on New Georgia Island has ceased.		
Aug. 29		Some 20 of Denmark's 60 naval vessels are scuttled in Copenhagen harbor, and military installations are destroyed after Germany declares martial law in the country .... Red Army takes 40 more villages southwest of Kharkov, including the rail junction of Lyubotin .... British Foreign Secy. Eden returns to England by plane from Quebec.			
Aug. 30		Stockholm reports the Danish royal family has been interned by the Germans at Amalienborg Castle in Copenhagen .... Russian forces take Taganrog, southern anchor of the German line since Oct. 19, 1941 .... Speakers at the American Jewish Congress Conference in N.Y. call on Allied leaders for immediate action to rescue Jews from Nazi-controlled nations.	U.S. forces occupy Arundel Island in the central Solomons, further closing the trap on the Japanese garrison at Vila, Kolombangara Island.	About 60,000 members of the Mexican Confederation of Workers hold a mass meeting in Mexico City to protest rising living costs and to demand wage increases.	

U.S. Politics & Social Issues	U.S. Foreign Policy & Defense	U.S. Economy & Environment	Science, Technology & Nature	Culture, Leisure & Life Style	
		Livestock and Meat Council declares the nation faces its worst beef shortage in history unless the government restores confidence of cattle producers in its future pricing policies . . . . N.Y. State Federation of Labor Executive Council scores the Smith-Connally anti-strike act as "injurious to worker morale" and urges its repeal.			Aug. 22
		Lewis tells the NWLB the nation faces a coal crisis unless 77,000 anthracite miners are granted a $1.30-a-day wage increase.			Aug. 23
	FBI arrests Grace Buchanan-Dineen, Theresa Behrens and Dr. William Thomas in Detroit and Bertrand Hoffman in N.Y., all on charges of sending war information to Germany . . . . War Dept. announces East Coast Defense Commander Lt. Gen. Hugh A. Drum will be chairman of the Inter-American Defense Bd.				Aug. 24
Federal Judge Delbert Metzger fines Hawaii military governor Lt. Gen. Robert Richardson, Jr. $5,000 for contempt for refusing to produce two interned aliens on habeas corpus writs . . . . Sen. Robert Taft says Gov. John W. Bricker of Ohio is "definitely" a presidential candidate.	FDR reports Lend-Lease aid to July 31 totaled $13,973,339,000 . . . . Supreme Court Justice Wiley B. Rutledge, Jr. tells the ABA a world court must be established after the war and eventually Germany and Japan should be given membership . . . . Columbia Univ. announces courses to train civilians for social, economic and relief administration in foreign countries will begin next month.	NWLB rejects the UMW contract with the Illinois Operators Assn., holding that the $1.25-a-day payment to cover portal-to-portal travel is a hidden wage increase.	A National Research Council report declares penicillin is a "remarkably potent anti-bacterial agent" when injected or applied locally but is ineffective by mouth.	Tommy Manville, asbestos heir, is married to Macie Marie Ainsworth in N.Y.; it is his seventh and her third marriage.	Aug. 25
		Members of the CIO-UAW end their four-day walkout at the Johnsville, Pa. plant of the Brewster Aeronautical Corp., but vote to give the NWLB a 30-day strike notice.			Aug. 26
ABA admits its board of governors has acted on membership applications of two N.Y. Negroes, accepting James S. Watson and rejecting Francis S. Rivers.			American Institute of Chemists Pres. Dr. Gustav Egloff announces Triptane, a "supergas" 50% more powerful than high octane fuel, is now being produced in mass volume for use in military planes.	Ray Robinson, 145 pounds, easily outpoints Henry Armstrong, 140 pounds, in a 10-round bout at Madison Square Garden, N.Y. Armstrong announces he will retire.	Aug. 27
Immigration and Naturalization Service announces that alien travel to and from the U.S. during the year ending June 30 was the lowest in 80 years.		Fuel Admin. Ickes warns U.S. oil reserves total only about 20 billion barrels, sufficient for 14 or 15 years . . . . NLRB charges unions are using high-pressure tactics by filing and withdrawing strike vote notices under the Smith-Connally Act . . . . OPA limits immediate deliveries of anthracite coal in 12 Eastern states to 50% of the 1942 purchases of domestic users.			Aug. 28
		A Brookings Institution report made public in Washington praises Canada's control of living costs as being better than similar programs in the U.S. The report adds that costs have increased 17% in Canada since the outbreak of the war as opposed to a 26% increase in the U.S.	WPB discloses it has granted permission to nine concerns to build facilities for the manufacture of penicillin.	Five hundred delegates representing 65 Jewish organizations attend the opening session of the American Jewish Conference in New York and hold memorial services for Jewish victims of Nazi persecution.	Aug. 29
	State Secy. Hull says charges that the State Dept. is anti-Russian are "monstrous and diabolical falsehoods," and assails columnist Drew Pearson for his assertion that Hull and other State Dept. officials "actually wished the Soviet Union to be bled white." . . . . FDR returns to Washington and confers with Chinese Foreign Min. Dr. T.V. Soong . . . . The new aircraft carrier *Hornet*, successor to the vessel lost off Guadalcanal and previously used as a base for the Tokyo raid, is launched at the Newport News, Va. Shipbuilding and Drydock Co. yards.	Federal Judge Bascon S. Deaver rules rent ceiling prices of the Emergency Price Control Act are unconstitutional; the OPA says it will appeal the decision . . . . Fuel Admin. Ickes and the OPA announce in Washington the ban on pleasure driving on the Atlantic seaboard in effect since May 20 will be lifted Sept. 1 . . . . Twenty-seven persons are killed and 150 injured when the Lackawanna Limited, crack Delaware, Lackawanna & Western Railroad express, collides with a freight locomotive near Wayland, N.Y. and is wrecked. All but one of the fatalities are caused by live steam from the boiler of the freight locomotive.			Aug. 30

F	G	H	I	J
Includes elections, federal-state relations, civil rights and liberties, crime, the judiciary, education, health care, poverty, urban affairs and population.	*Includes formation and debate of U.S. foreign and defense policies, veterans affairs and defense spending. (Relations with specific foreign countries are usually found under the region concerned.)*	*Includes business, labor, agriculture, taxation, transportation, consumer affairs, monetary and fiscal policy, natural resources, pollution and accidents.*	*Includes worldwide scientific, medical and technological developments, natural phenomena, U.S. weather and natural disasters.*	*Includes the arts, religion, scholarship, communications media, sports, entertainment, fashions, fads and social life.*

	World Affairs	European War Zone	Pacific War Zone	The Americas	Other Countries & Territories
Aug. 31	Speaking from Quebec, Churchill states he and FDR are anxious to meet with Stalin.	Red Army opens a drive on Smolensk, 220 miles south of Moscow.		Pres. Juan Antonio Rios of Chile revises his cabinet to give more posts to Radical Party members.	India's highest tribunal upholds the right of the British viceroy to hold Gandhi and other political prisoners without trial.
Sept. 1	Churchill arrives in Washington by train from Canada to confer with FDR.	As the European war enters its fifth year, Russian troops complete the liquidation of the German forces driven from Taganrog, killing more than 35,000 men and capturing 5,100 .... Stockholm reports Gen. Hermann von Hanneken, Nazi commander of Denmark, has modified censorship and curfew restrictions and permitted limited telephone and mail service to be resumed.	Allied Australian headquarters discloses the Japanese have been forced to move their main New Guinea air base to Hollandia, 550 miles northwest of Salamaua, because of their heavy losses at Wewak .... Employing many planes, a U.S. Navy task force bombs and shells Marcus Island, 1,185 miles southeast of Tokyo.	Argentina tells the U.S. and Britain it will continue to grant asylum to persons accused of political crimes, but will consider each case on its individual merits .... A U.S.-Mexican industrial commission is established to deal with postwar economic cooperation between the two countries.	
Sept. 2	Churchill confers with FDR, Army Chief-of-Staff Marshall and British military and supply mission members.	Russian forces capture Sumy, 87 miles northwest of Kharkov, and cut the Bryansk-Kiev railroad by taking Krolevets and Yampol .... On the coast of the Sea of Azov, the Russians capture Budennovka, 20 miles east of Mariupol .... Soviets charge Turkey's neutrality is prolonging the war by protecting Germany's Balkan flank.	Allied troops overrun Japanese positions south and southeast of the airport at Salamaua, New Guinea and are closing in from the coast.	Cuban Maritme Union officers resign from the Confederation of Cuban Workers, charging it is controlled by the CP.	
Sept. 3	Former President Hoover urges a "cooling off" period of several years between the end of the war and a peace conference so that "war passions can subside."	The invasion of the Italian mainland begins at 4:30 a.m. by British and Canadian troops, who cross the straits of Messina and land at Reggio Calabria against light resistance .... French Comm. of National Liberation announces Marshal Henri Petain, members of his Vichy government and other collaborationists will be tried as soon as possible .... Premier Joseph Stalin approves the reestablishment of the Russian Orthodox Church throughout the Soviet Union.	Navy Secy. Knox says Japan has lost 2.5 million tons of shipping, a third of its cargo fleet, since Pearl Harbor .... Japan's worst earthquake in 10 years kills 1,400 persons in the town of Tottori .... U.S. Liberators make a 2,000-mile round-trip to bomb the Japanese-held island of Car Nicobar in the Indian Ocean.		
Sept. 4	Washington reports a Big Three Foreign Ministers conference will be held in the near future.	Italian troops evacuate the Melito district on the south coast of Calabria as well as the Reggio Calabria and San Giovanni areas on the west coast .... Russian troops driving toward Stalino, a steel center in the Donets Basin, caputre Ilovask and take key railway lines.	A large Allied force lands on the north shore of Huon Gulf, east of Lae, New Guinea, and isolates the Japanese bases at Lae and Salamaua.		
Sept. 5		British and Canadian troops seize 38 miles of Italian coastline from Melito in the south to Bagnara on the north and push steadily inland.	Using U.S. paratroopers for the first time, Allied forces close the last escape route for 20,000 Japanese troops in the Lae-Salamaua area.		
Sept. 6		Rome radio states the Italians are "prepared to face stark reality" if their independence and unity are respected .... British capture Palmi and push inland to take Delianova, Italy .... Soviet forces continue their advances on the Donets Basin iron center .... RAF planes drop 1,500 tons of bombs on the twin cities of Mannheim and Ludwigshafen and other Rhineland targets.			
Sept. 7	FDR tells his press conference progress is being made towards a meeting of himself, Churchill and Stalin.			State Secy. Hull assails Argentina's relations with the Axis powers and its failure to join in the defense of the Americas.	

A	B	C	D	E
Includes developments that affect more than one world region, international organizations and important meetings of major world leaders.	*Includes all developments in European countries and military engagements between Allied and Axis powers in Africa and at sea.*	*Includes all developments in Japan and China, Japanese foreign policy and military actions in the Pacific region.*	*Includes all domestic and regional developments in Latin America, the Caribbean and Canada.*	*Includes developments in those independent nations and colonial possessions not covered in Columns B, C and D.*

U.S. Politics & Social Issues	U.S. Foreign Policy & Defense	U.S. Economy & Environment	Science, Technology & Nature	Culture, Leisure & Life Style	
	Without mentioning Drew Pearson's name, FDR assails the columnist as a chronic liar and says his charge that State Secy. Hull is anti-Russian was a lie from beginning to end .... FDR renews his pledges of "justice and liberation" for subjected nations of Europe in a message to Polish Pres. Raczkiewicz in London.	OPA announces plans for new gasoline ration coupon centers to check thefts and permit stricter investigation of requests for extra supplies after Rep. Fred Hartley Jr. (R, N.J.) charges fuel saved by reducing Midwest allotments is going to black markets.			Aug. 31
N.Y. Gov. Thomas E. Dewey demands that Louis Buchalter, now serving a 14-year term in federal prison for narcotics sales, be surrendered to N.Y. State, where he has been sentenced to die for the murder of Samuel Rosen .... State Sen. Clair A. Engle of Red Bluff, Calif. is elected to the U.S. House to succeed the late Harry L. Englebright.	Harry L. Hopkins, writing in *American Magazine*, predicts at "least two more years of hard fighting" to defeat the Axis.	WFA lifts quota restrictions on the slaughtering of livestock to increase civilian supplies.		Lee and J.J. Schubert, theatrical producers, bar Louis Kronenberger, dramatic critic of *PM*, New York newspaper, from their theaters for "unfair, unjust and cruel" reviews. *Variety* discloses the Shuberts are suing it for $300,000 for unfavorable reviews.	Sept. 1
	War and Navy Depts. announce there have been 104,658 U.S. war casualties since Pearl Harbor, including 19,875 dead.				Sept. 2
	Winchester Repeating Arms. Co. announces the development and use of a new carbine, half the weight of the Garand rifle but equal to its speed and fire.				Sept. 3
		FDR accepts the resignation of Rubber Dir. William M. Jeffers, who declares "the big job" of organizing synthetic rubber production "is done." .... Fuel Admin. Ickes orders 369 more soft-coal mines returned to their owners, raisng to 549 those restored to private operations .... War Mobilization Dir. James F. Byrnes announces the WMC and other federal agencies will undertake a program Sept. 15 to balance West Coast production with the labor supply.			Sept. 4
	Gov. Dewey says he favors a postwar military alliance with Britain and hopes Russia and China might be included.		Dr. Max A. Lauffer of the Rockefeller Institute says the tobacco mosaic protein molecule is probably itself a virus which causes plant disease.	Yale Univ., with 58 points, wins the team National AAU swimming championship in Columbus, Ohio.	Sept. 5
	John Clarence Cudahy, former ambassador to Poland and Belgium, dies at 55 when thrown from his horse near Milwaukee, Wisc.	War plants remain open on Labor Day as CIO Pres. Murray and AFL Pres. Green pledge labor to continue its war efforts "come hell or high water." .... NWLB approves an increase in the present 67¢-to-$1.45 hourly wage scale at the Seattle and Renton, Washington plants of the Boeing Aircraft Co. to 82.5¢-to-$1.60 in order to counteract a labor shortage by attracting some of the 14,000 workers to be released by Seattle shipyards .... At least 79 persons are killed and 117 injured when nine cars of the Pennsylvania's Railroad's 16-car Washington-to-New York *Congressional Limited* are derailed at Frankfurt Junction, Philadelphia.		Joseph R. Hunt defeats John A. Kramer at Forest Hills, N.Y. to win the national amateur tennis championship.	Sept. 6
	GOP Postwar Advisory Council unanimously approves U.S. cooperation in organizing nations to preserve the peace after the war.	Fifty men are burned to death and 32 injured when fire destroys the Gulf Hotel in midtown Houston, Tex.		Orson Welles and Rita Hayworth are married in Santa Monica, Calif.	Sept. 7

F	G	H	I	J
Includes elections, federal-state relations, civil rights and liberties, crime, the judiciary, education, health care, poverty, urban affairs and population.	*Includes formation and debate of U.S. foreign and defense policies, veterans affairs and defense spending. (Relations with specific foreign countries are usually found under the region concerned.)*	*Includes business, labor, agriculture, taxation, transportation, consumer affairs, monetary and fiscal policy, natural resources, pollution and accidents.*	*Includes worldwide scientific, medical and technological developments, natural phenomena, U.S. weather and natural disasters.*	*Includes the arts, religion, scholarship, communications media, sports, entertainment, fashions, fads and social life.*

	World Affairs	European War Zone	Pacific War Zone	The Americas	Other Countries & Territories
Sept. 8		Eisenhower announces the Italian acceptance of the Allied demand for unconditional surrender .... In a radio broadcast Badoglio says he asked for an armistice because it was impossible to continue the "unequal struggle." .... Red Army captures Stalino and frees the Donets Basin.	Australian troops defeat a Japanese force at Saingaua Plantation, eight miles from Lae, and are approaching the Busu River, three miles east of the besieged base.		
Sept. 9	U.N. Interim Commission on Food and Agriculture completes the draft of a plan to improve nutrition standards.	U.S. and British troops land under cover of naval shelling at Salerno, 35 miles southeast of Naples, against heavy German opposition .... Italian battleship *Roma* is sunk by German planes in the strait between Corsica and Sardinia .... Strikes at 14 important military targets in France are made by the greatest formation of U.S. and British aircraft ever sent against Europe .... Soviet forces take the important railway center of Bakhmach, 115 miles east of Kiev.	U.S. planes bomb wharves, docks, airports, shipping and railways in China at Canton , Kuikiang, Wusueh, Puchi, Changanyi, Tsingkiachen and Shihweiyao.	Foreign Min. Vice Adm. Segundo Storni resigns as a result of U.S. refusal to sell Argentina arms while she maintains relations with the Axis.	
Sept. 10		Allies disclose their forces in the Salerno area have repulsed five German counterattacks and are extending their beachheads .... Nazi troops under Field Marshal Gen. Albert Kesselring seize Rome and assume "protection of Vatican City." .... In a broadcast to the German people, Hitler says Italy's "betrayal" means little in the "military sense" and hails Mussolini as "the greatest son of Italian soil." .... The Sea of Azov port of Mariupol falls to the Russian Army and the westward drive from the Donets Basin carries to Chaplino, only 60 miles east of the Dnieper River.	Australian troops reach the Busu River, four miles east of Lae, and advance elements of the forces on the west are pushing forward to the main defense outpost at Heath's Plantation.		Iran becomes the 32nd member of the U.N. — 24 hours after declaring war on Germany.
Sept. 11		U.S. and British units capture the port city of Salerno in the face of fierce German counterattacks .... The bulk of the Italian fleet arrives at Malta, surrendering under the terms of the armistice .... Stockholm reports Finnish Premier Edwin Linkomies desires peace with Russia if 1939 territorial status and independence are assured.	Australian troops capture the airport at Salamaua, New Guinea, after swimming the Francisco River.	Mexico City newspaper *Novedades* reports police have broken a plot to overthrow the government of Pres. Manuel Avila Camacho.	
Sept. 12		German S.S. special commando leader Otto Skorzeny recaptures Mussolini from his Italian captors at San Grasso, "frustrating" efforts to deliver him to the Allies. He is taken to Vienna .... Allied forces in southeastern Italy advance from Taranto to capture the important Adriatic port of Brindisi .... Red Army advances to within artillery range of Bryansk by capturing Belye Berega, 12 miles to the east .... Newly-elected Patriarch Sergius, 78-year-old primate of the Russian Orthodox Church, is installed in office in Moscow.	Australian and American troops capture Salamaua air naval base, sending the Japanese northward towards Lae, 22 miles away.		
Sept. 13		U.S. forces encounter the heaviest fighting of the Mediterranean campaign around Salerno, facing repeated German counterattacks .... Russian troops storm through German defenses in the Bryansk area and reach the east bank of the Desna River.	The central executive committee of the Kuomintang, the Chinese government party, names Chiang Kai-shek to a three-year term as president, succeeding President Lin Sen, who died Aug. 1.	Brazilian War Min. Gen. Eurico Gaspar Dutra declares Brazil's active participation in the European War is "only a question of more preparation and more equipment from the United States."	
Sept. 14		Germans regain some ground in and around the Allied beachheads at Salerno .... German news agency DNB reports Finance Min. Bojilov has been named premier of Bulgaria, succeeding Bogdan Filov, who resigned to join the regency with Prince Kyril, brother of the late King Boris, and ex-War Min. Lt. Gen. Mihov.	Foreign Min. T.V. Soong says in Washington China has rejected a Japanese peace offer to withdraw all troops from China, save Manchuria, in return for Chinese collaboration .... Allied troops drive to within two miles of Lae, New Guinea on the northeast and five miles on the west.		

A	B	C	D	E
Includes developments that affect more than one world region, international organizations and important meetings of major world leaders.	*Includes all developments in European countries and military engagements between Allied and Axis powers in Africa and at sea.*	*Includes all developments in Japan and China, Japanese foreign policy and military actions in the Pacific region.*	*Includes all domestic and regional developments in Latin America, the Caribbean and Canada.*	*Includes developments in those independent nations and colonial possessions not covered in Columns B, C and D.*

U.S. Politics & Social Issues	U.S. Foreign Policy & Defense	U.S. Economy & Environment	Science, Technology & Nature	Culture, Leisure & Life Style	
	Americans react calmly to the fall of Italy; the State Dept. issues no statement.	Italy's surrender causes nervous selling, with losses of around two points on the NYSE and sales of 797,600, the largest in more than a month .... FDR opens the $15-billion Third War Loan drive in a nationwide radio broadcast .... OPA obtains temporary restraining orders forbidding F.W. Woolworth Co., J.C. Penny Co., J.J. Newberry Co. and McCrory Stores Corp. from selling women's clothes above ceiling prices.	American Chemical Society announces development by the St. Louis Univ. Laboratory of "Penicillin B," which is 10 times more powerful than current penicillin.	N.Y. Giant pitcher Ace Adams plays in his 62nd game and sets a new major league record for games worked by a pitcher in one year.	Sept. 8
	Lt. Col. Francis V. Keesling Jr. tells the Senate Military Affairs Comm. the Wheeler bill to defer drafting of fathers until Jan. 1 may "hinder" Allied battle plans.				Sept. 9
	Vice Pres. Wallace says FDR is the most magic name in the world today and that he should be named permanent chairman of any peace conference to ensure a workable world .... Sen. Sheridan Downey (D, Calif.) and Rep. Andrew J. May (D, Ky.) say they favor an immediate halt in military inductions until manpower needs on the home front are adjusted to the fighting front .... State Secy. Hull pledges the U.S. will do everything it can to ameliorate "the wretched plight of the Jews" in Europe .... FDR names James M. Landis minister to the Middle East in charge of U.S. economic operations there.				Sept. 10
					Sept. 11
	State Secy. Hull advocates "organized international cooperation" with the use of force, if necessary, to maintain world peace after the war.			Columnist Drew Pearson charges "government Gestapo agents" have tapped his telephone and Naval intelligence officers "shadow" him .... Mrs. George Bernard Shaw, the former Charlotte Frances Payne-Townsend, who married the playwright in 1898, dies in London.	Sept. 12
	SSS orders state directors to induct all available non-fathers before calling pre-Pearl Harbor fathers regardless of local board October quotas.				Sept. 13
Congress reconvenes at noon after a 61-day recess .... FDR reports to the Senate that disloyal Japanese-Americans are being relocated to the Tule Lake Relocation Center in California and that loyal Japanese are being sent from other centers to homes and jobs outside restricted areas .... FDR sends a message to Congress assailing an urgent deficiency bill rider prohibiting Virgin Islands Secy. Robert Morss Lovett and two FCC officials from holding federal office without presidential appointment and Senate confirmation.					Sept. 14
F *Includes elections, federal-state relations, civil rights and liberties, crime, the judiciary, education, health care, poverty, urban affairs and population.*	G *Includes formation and debate of U.S. foreign and defense policies, veterans affairs and defense spending. (Relations with specific foreign countries are usually found under the region concerned.)*	H *Includes business, labor, agriculture, taxation, transportation, consumer affairs, monetary and fiscal policy, natural resources, pollution and accidents.*	I *Includes worldwide scientific, medical and technological developments, natural phenomena, U.S. weather and natural disasters.*	J *Includes the arts, religion, scholarship, communications media, sports, entertainment, fashions, fads and social life.*	

	World Affairs	European War Zone	Pacific War Zone	The Americas	Other Countries & Territories
Sept. 15		A proclamation over German-controlled "Fascist" radio establishes a "Republican Fascist Party" regime, with Mussolini at its head .... Nazi assaults on the Allied positions from Salerno to Agropoli in southern Italy force the U.S. forces to retreat and consolidate.	Allied headquarters reports the Japanese forces at Salamaua have been "completely routed" and only a few isolated units remain in nearby jungles .... Allied planes blast the two remaining usable Japanese airports at Wewak, New Guinea.	Cuba begins induction of 1,780 draftees into the army, the first called under the obligatory military service law.	
Sept. 16		The reinforced Allied lines begin an offensive against the Germans at the Salerno beachhead, driving the Germans back towards Serre .... British drive to a point 25 miles from Foggia .... Soviets capture Novorossiisk, Russia's second most important naval base on the Black Sea.	Allied airmen strike at the Japanese air base on Bougainville Island for the fourth straight day, destroying at least 83 craft at a loss of 16.	Mexico celebrates its 133rd anniversary of independence with a parade of 25,000 troops in Mexico City.	
Sept. 17	Reporting to Congress on the Quebec Conference, FDR says decisions were made to bring definite blows against both Germany and Japan.	Allies link up to form a 225-mile line from the east to the west coast of Italy .... "Free Milan" radio declares Italian troops have seized a stretch of railway track 35 miles south of the Brenner Pass.	Chungking sources claim the Japanese have sent 5,000 - 8,000 troops to the Arakan district of Burma in anticipation of an Allied offensive .... Secy. Hull praises China's refusal "to be conquered" and expresses confidence that the Japanese will be "swept from Chinese soil."		
Sept. 18		Over Radio Munich Mussolini asks the Italians to resume fighting beside Germany .... German resistance on the Salerno front is reported weaker as the Allies recapture Battipaglia and Altavilla .... Russian troops advance in 10 important sectors along a 600-mile front.	Chiang Kai-shek observes the 12th anniversary of the Japanese attack on Mukden, Manchuria with a pledge to recover all lost territory..... Gen. MacArthur announces his Australian and U.S. forces now occupy the important Japanese base of Lae, New Guinea.		
Sept. 19		A U-boat attack sinks eight or more Allied vessels, including three warships, of a 70-ship Allied convoy in the Atlantic .... Russian troops capture more than 1,200 settlements as they sweep westward along the entire front, particularly menacing the Germans at Smolensk and Kiev .... Italian troops collaborating with the Allies attack the Germans on Sardinia, forcing a German retreat towards Corsica.	Allied forces conduct heavy raids on Japanese bases on Tarawa island in the north Gilbert group and on Nauru, 780 miles northeast of Guadalcanal.		
Sept. 20		Premier Badoglio calls on Italians to take up arms against Germany beside the "Anglo-Americans." .... Yugoslavian spokesmen in London say 2,000 Germans have been killed in eight days of fighting for the Adriatic port of Split, which Yugoslavian partisans claim to hold .... French commandos from North Africa are reported in Corsica assisting the patriots opposing Nazi occupation forces on the French island.	Australian airborne troops seize Kaiapit, New Guinea and its airstrip, which outflanks the Japanese at Finschhafen.		
Sept. 21		Crossing the Desna River for the third time in five days, the Russians pull to within 78 miles of Kiev, thus freeing about half of the 580,000 square miles the Germans had taken since their 1941 invasion .... Churchill tells the House of Commons that Britain and the U.S. will launch an offensive against Germany through Western Europe "on the day .... we judge to be the right time." .... German forces retreating from Naples set the city afire.	Gen. MacArthur says an "island hopping" campaign to defeat the Japanese is too costly, preferring his own strategy of massive strokes against strategic objectives.	Mexican Pres. Avila Camacho issues a decree freezing prices of basic foodstuffs including corn, meat, sugar, beans and milk.	
Sept. 22		British midget submarines penetrate the Alten Fjord at the northern tip of Norway and cripple the German battleship *Tirpitz* with torpedoes .... Allied forces occupy San Cipriano, Montecorvino Rovella and Campagna east of Salerno .... Soviet troops occupy Letki, 18 miles east of Kiev .... In the Smolensk area the Soviets take Demidov, 42 miles northwest of the city.	Allied troops land six miles north of Finschhafen, New Guinea and begin a drive on that base, 60 miles north of Lae .... U.S. and RAF planes complete three days of raids in Burma, principally on communications sites at Nabar Junction, Indaw, Saigang, Monywa, Maungdaw, Ye-U and Ningbyen .... Japanese broadcasts announce plans for evacuating unnecessary government offices, factories and civilians from Tokyo and other large cities to perfect aerial defenses.	Argentine government announces it is recalling several of its diplomats in line with a diplomatic corps shake-up designed to eliminate those "who have not displayed the required degree of dignity and capacity."	

U.S. Politics & Social Issues	U.S. Foreign Policy & Defense	U.S. Economy & Environment	Science, Technology & Nature	Culture, Leisure & Life Style	
	The bazooka anti-tank rocket gun is exhibited for the first time by the Army . . . . John da Silva Purvis, a Portuguese citizen, is arrested in Newark, N.J. by FBI agents on charges of acting as a Nazi spy.	FDR confers with leaders of four farm organizations, presenting a tentative 1944 food production program calling for increased support prices for farmers . . . . WPB bans the distillation of alcohol for beverage purposes through 1943 because of additional requirements for industrial alcohol to make synthetic rubber . . . . Office of Defense Transportation announces restrictions on the retail delivery of packages by motor truck, now in effect in 12 Eastern states, will be made nationwide effective Oct. 11.			Sept. 15
Rep. James M. Curley (D, Mass.) and five other members of the Engineers Group Inc. are indicted on charges of using the mails to defraud . . . . Institute for Propaganda Analysis official Clyde E. Miller says Axis propaganda advocating racial superiority has been "effective, dynamic and dangerous" in the U.S.	WMC Chmn. McNutt and Selective Service Dir. Hershey tell the Senate Military Affairs Comm. that pre-Pearl Harbor fathers must be drafted this year to meet armed forces requirements.				Sept. 16
					Sept. 17
		Interior Secy. Ickes warns the public to conserve coal because production has been unable to meet expanding war needs.		St. Louis Cardinals, beating the Chicago Cubs, 2-1, clinch their seventh NL pennant.	Sept. 18
	U.S. Navy claims it now has the "greatest sea-air power on earth," consisting of 14,072 vessels totalling almost five million tons.			Decca Records, Inc. and its transcription subsidiary World Broadcasting System reach an an agreement with the American Fed. of Musicians to resume making records and transcriptions.	Sept. 19
Willkie declares in a *Look Magazine* article he would accept the GOP nomination for the Presidency in 1944.	Army Chief-of-Staff Marshall and Navy Commander-in-Chief Adm. Ernest King warn a joint House-Senate Military Affairs Comm. session that delay in drafting fathers will prolong the war and increase losses . . . . Army Air Force officials disclose an electronically controlled autopilot holds U.S. planes on a steady course during bombing runs, providing a "steady platform" required for high-level precision bombing.				Sept. 20
	Marshall tells the American Legion's national convention in Omaha that American forces are "at last" prepared to launch powerful offensives in Europe and in the Pacific and that "this phase is just about to begin." . . . . House passes the Fulbright resolution advocating U.S. participation in postwar machinery to maintain the international peace and sends it to the Senate.				Sept. 21
	State Dept. annnounces the appointment of Charles Taft as chairman of two committees which will assist in the economic rehabilitation of the East Indies and Malaya.	WPB announces the production of war materials rose 4% in August, the best record since April; plane output rose 3% in numbers and 7% in weight.		Cecil Brown resigns as CBS correspondent because the network's news director Paul W. White criticizes his broadcast statement that "a good deal of enthusiasm for this war is evaporating into thin air."	Sept. 22

F	G	H	I	J
Includes elections, federal-state relations, civil rights and liberties, crime, the judiciary, education, health care, poverty, urban affairs and population.	*Includes formation and debate of U.S. foreign and defense policies, veterans affairs and defense spending. (Relations with specific foreign countries are usually found under the region concerned.)*	*Includes business, labor, agriculture, taxation, transportation, consumer affairs, monetary and fiscal policy, natural resources, pollution and accidents.*	*Includes worldwide scientific, medical and technological developments, natural phenomena, U.S. weather and natural disasters.*	*Includes the arts, religion, scholarship, communications media, sports, entertainment, fashions, fads and social life.*

	World Affairs	European War Zone	Pacific War Zone	The Americas	Other Countries & Territories
Sept. 23	U.K., U.S., Russia and China agree on the creation of a U.N. Relief and Rehabilitation Administration to function in liberated areas when the military asks for assistance.	Swiss border reports say Fascists are conducting a reign of terror in northern Italy in the name of the new Mussolini puppet government .... Russian troops capture Poltava, last major German base in southern Ukraine.	Finschhafen airdrome is taken by Australian troops, placing them within three-quarters of a mile of the Japanese-held town .... American troops destroy all remaining Japanese forces on the north shore of Arundel Island and on nearby Sagakarasa Island.	Chilean Foreign Min. Joaquin Fernandez discloses he has discussed a permanent trade agreement with the U.S.	
Sept. 24		Allies begin their drive for Naples, inaugurating a wide flanking movement eastward from the Sorrentine Peninsula and Salerno .... Churchill names Sir John Anderson as chancellor of the exchequer, replacing the late Sir Kingsley Wood, and Lord Beaverbrook to become lord privy seal .... Archbishop of York declares the fullest freedom of worship exists in Russia and that anti-religious propaganda has been discontinued .... Finnish Finance Min. Vaino Tanner declares Finland is ready to establish normal relations with Russia if it "could get a guarantee that we will not be threatened with permanent danger."	Three Allied columns close in on Finschhafen.	Argentine Pres. Ramirez states the country will adhere to its policy of "fraternal love" for American republics and "peace and friendship" for all free peoples.	Indian food minister announces in Calcutta that 1,292 persons died of starvation in Bengal the week ending Sept. 11.
Sept. 25		Smolensk, Germany's greatest Russian base, and Roslavl are captured by Soviet troops .... In hard fighting U.S. forces in Italy push the Germans back, reaching some mountain positions guarding the plain of Naples.	Japan recognizes the incorporation of the northern territory of the Shan States into Burma.		
Sept. 26	Sir Stafford Cripps declares it would be disastrous for Britain to regard "friendship with the United States as an alternative to friendship with the Soviet Union."	Russians are reported at or near the east bank of Dnieper River along a 300-mile line from Kiev in the south to Dniepropetrovsk.		British Foreign Office, commenting on the signing of "non-political" food purchase agreements with Argentina, says Britain has never understood why Argentina alone of the western republics retains diplomatic ties with Axis countries .... Puerto Rican Gov. Rexford G. Tugwell charges the U.S. has no policy towards the island, keeping the people in "humiliating suspense."	
Sept. 27	Axis radio broadcasts professing belief in eventual victory celebrate the third anniversary of the Tripartite Pact.	British occupy Foggia, southeast Italy air and rail center, without opposition .... Yogoslavian government in London claims Yugoslavian guerrillas now hold one-third of the country .... Russians capture the Nizhne-Dneprovsk suburb of Dnepropetrovsk on the east bank of the Dnieper River.		Argentine Foreign Office announces that closer relations with Britain will be sought.	
Sept. 28	Churchill says the war may last through the autumn of 1944 or even 1945.	Allied forces break through the German mountain defenses southeast of Naples, taking the naval base of Castellemmare di Stabia.			
Sept. 29		Eisenhower and Italian Premier Badoglio confer aboard the British battleship *Nelson* at Malta on means of "making the most effective military effort by the Italians against the common enemy." .... Russian forces take the Ukrainian German stronghold of Kremenchug on the east bank of the Dnieper River .... King Peter of Yugoslavia and his government-in-exile arrive in Cairo from London to establish a new headquarters.	Australian forces tighten their grip on the Japanese base at Finschhafen, New Guinea by seizing Kakakog Spur.	U.S. and Mexico reach an agreement for recompensation of Americans affected by Mexico's expropriation of the oil industry in 1938.	
Sept. 30		Allied troops reach the outskirts of Naples as the Nazis evacuate the city .... Stockholm reports claim Hitler has ordered the German forces at the Dnieper River to hold at all costs, saying the "Stalingrad psychosis must disappear."			
Oct. 1	FDR says he and Churchill are in agreement to support postwar air freedom for aviation.	Lt. Gen. Mark Clark's 5th Army enters a ruined and evacuated Naples .... FDR says Rome is the next big Allied objective and that the campaign will be regarded as a crusade aimed at freeing Pope Pius XII .... For the first time heavy bombers from North Africa strike at Germany, making the 1,800-mile round-trip to Munich.	Japanese open offensives in Chekiang, Kiangsu and Anhwei provinces, as the Chinese rush reinforcements to the area .... In one of the heaviest attacks in the China war theater, Allied planes report shooting down 26 Japanese fighter planes in a raid on Haiphong, French Indochina .... Australian P.M. John Curtin says his country will provide "her share" of troops to recover the Philippines.		

A	B	C	D	E
Includes developments that affect more than one world region, international organizations and important meetings of major world leaders.	*Includes all developments in European countries and military engagements between Allied and Axis powers in Africa and at sea.*	*Includes all developments in Japan and China, Japanese foreign policy and military actions in the Pacific region.*	*Includes all domestic and regional developments in Latin America, the Caribbean and Canada.*	*Includes developments in those independent nations and colonial possessions not covered in Columns B, C and D.*

U.S. Politics & Social Issues	U.S. Foreign Policy & Defense	U.S. Economy & Environment	Science, Technology & Nature	Culture, Leisure & Life Style	
	At its annual convention in Omaha, the American Legion adopts a resolution approving postwar U.S. cooperation for international peace . . . . SSS Dir. Hershey says fathers of children born after Sept. 14, 1943 will be inducted after Oct. 1 unless he is stopped by law . . . . Mrs. Eleanor Roosevelt arrives in San Francisco after a 23,000-mile trip through the Pacific war zone and declares American troops have "no doubt" about defeating Japan and have "very strong feelings" on strikes and absenteeism.	CIO-UAW President R.J.Thomas and three CIO organizers are arrested in Pelly, Tex., after addressing a meeting of the CIO without a license . . . . Robert W. Johnson resigns as chairman of the WPB Smaller War Plants Corp., charging his agency has been a "political football."		Elinor Glynn, English novelist who popularized "It" as a synonym for sex allure, dies at 78 in London . . . . Cincinnati Reds sign William McKechnie to his seventh year as manager.	Sept. 23
	Sen. Millard E. Tydings (D, Md.) offers a resolution to give the Philippine Islands independence now rather than as scheduled in 1946.	WPB Dir. Nelson says U.S. war production this year will be one-and-a-half times the combined output of Germany and Japan and "probably twice as great" next year . . . . *Banking Encyclopedia* reports that bank deposits on June 30 totaled $108,444,940,000 — an increase of $24 billion in a year.			Sept. 24
	FDR announces the resignation of Under State Secy. Sumner Welles and the appointment of Edward Stettinius as his successor.	Brotherhood of Railroad Trainmen ends a two-day strike on the Pacific Electric Railway and Bus Lines in Los Angeles after union chief W. Nutter expresses confidence that a 13¢ wage increase will be approved by the NWLB.		N.Y. Yankees win the AL championship for the 14th time with a 2-1 victory over the Detroit Tigers . . . . *The Skin of Our Teeth* by Thornton Wilder closes in N.Y. after 355 performances.	Sept. 25
	CP Gen. Secy. Earl Browder tells a Chicago rally it is just an illusion for the U.S. to expect the Soviet Union to fight Japan.				Sept. 26
	FDR asks Congress to appropriate an additional $750 million for the Navy.	President Joseph Curran of the NMU-CIO charges upon returning from a six-week trip abroad to investigate conditions facing seamen that the State Dept. ordered he be prevented from going ashore in North Africa and that he was told he would be shot by the military if he did so.	Pres. of the Nat. Foundation for Infantile Paralysis Basil O'Connor announces $5,527,590 was raised in the 1943 campaign.		Sept. 27
	Ernest F. Lehnitz and Erwin H. De Spretter receive 30-year sentences in Brooklyn federal court for espionage on behalf of Germany.				Sept. 28
	Senate Foreign Relations subcommittee considering the U.S. postwar role says it will write its own resolution rather than accept those submitted to it.	OWI reports excess purchasing power has reached a new high of $51.4 billion, creating a dangerous inflationary threat.			Sept. 29
	War Secy. Stimson denies rumors that Army Chief of Staff Marshall will be shifted for political or other ulterior motives.	Commerce Secy. Jones says the "government should get out of industry after the war" although the private sector will need government aid to meet reconstruction problems . . . . WMC orders a 48-hour week in Los Angeles.		*Variety* reports the most popular songs to be: (1) *Sunday, Monday or Always*, (2) *Paper Doll* and (3) *Put Your Arms Around Me* . . . . Harper & Bros. announces Martin Flavin is the winner of a $10,000 prize for his novel *Journey Into the Dark*.	Sept. 30
House GOP leader Joseph Martin (Mass.) says government bureaucrats must be eliminated to avoid a "domestic struggle for survival of the American way of life." . . . . Laura Ingalls, the flier sentenced for failing to register as a German agent, is released from the Alderson Women's Reformatory.	FDR announces the resignation of William H. Standley as ambassador to Russia and names W. Averell Harriman as his successor.	NWLB approves Grumman Aircraft Corp. plan to increase pay rates 5% when production increases 10%.			Oct. 1
F	G	H	I	J	
Includes elections, federal-state relations, civil rights and liberties, crime, the judiciary, education, health care, poverty, urban affairs and population.	*Includes formation and debate of U.S. foreign and defense policies, veterans affairs and defense spending. (Relations with specific foreign countries are usually found under the region concerned.)*	*Includes business, labor, agriculture, taxation, transportation, consumer affairs, monetary and fiscal policy, natural resources, pollution and accidents.*	*Includes worldwide scientific, medical and technological developments, natural phenomena, U.S. weather and natural disasters.*	*Includes the arts, religion, scholarship, communications media, sports, entertainment, fashions, fads and social life.*	

	World Affairs	European War Zone	Pacific War Zone	The Americas	Other Countries & Territories
Oct. 2		Allied forces enter Benevento, 35 miles northeast of Naples .... Russian forces advance some nine miles in their drive toward Gomel and Mogilev in White Russia .... Stockholm announces the Swedish minister to Berlin has notified German authorities Sweden will provide asylum for 7,000 Jews arrested in Denmark Sept. 30 during Jewish New Year festivities.	Australian troops capture the Japanese base at Finschhafen, New Guinea.		
Oct. 3		Stockholm reports more than 1,000 Danish Jews have escaped across the Oeresund Strait to Sweden.	U.S. troops on Vella Lavella Island in the central Solomons close in on Japanese remnants on the north coast.	Brazilian Pres. Vargas orders liquidation of 34 firms found to be of German ownership or under German control.	
Oct. 4		An Allied amphibious landing outflanks the Germans on Italy's east coast and brings the seizure of Termoli. After repulsing a Nazi counterattack British forces continue their advance along the Italian east coast .... Yugoslav army of liberation announces the capture of the Montenegrin towns of Bjelo Polge and Kolasin and the fortified base of Tuzla in eastern Bosnia.	MacArthur says the victories at Salamaua, Lae and Finschhafen have broken the Japanese grip on Australian New Guinea .... Australian troops continue their drive through the Ramu River Valley, occupying Dumpu, New Guinea.		
Oct. 5		Russians clear Nazi forces from the east bank of the Dnieper River along a 400-mile stretch from Dnepropetrovsk north to the confluence of the Dnieper and Sozh Rivers .... Allies capture Aversa and Maddaloni north of Naples and cross the Calore River.	A U.S. Navy task force attacks the Japanese-held island of Wake at dawn .... FDR says in Washington that too little attention has been paid the setbacks the Japanese are suffering in New Guinea and that their retirement from the Solomons was a significant defeat.	The will of the slain Sir Harry Oakes is filed in Nassau, Bahamas today and provides that a full share go to his daughter, Nancy Oakes de Marigny, wife of Alfred de Marigny, who is charged with the millionaire's murder.	
Oct. 6	A resolution by 144 prominent members of the Catholic, Protestant and Jewish faiths call for international bodies empowered to enforce international law through "adequate sanctions" after the war.	Soviet troops in White Russia improve their positions in the Gomel area and repulse Nazi counterattacks around Vitebsk and Mogilev.			
Oct. 7		Allies seize Capua, 20 miles north of Naples, reaching the Volturno River along a 17-mile front .... The reinforced British 8th Army makes gains in fierce fighting near Termoli on the Adriatic coast .... Russian units cross the Volkhov River and capture Kirishi, 60 miles southeast of Leningrad .... Red Army establishes three bridgeheads on the west bank of the Dnieper River: north of Kiev, south of Pereyaslav and southeast of Kremenchug.	Adm. Lord Louis Mountbatten arrives in New Delhi to assume his post as Allied commander-in-chief in Southeast Asia.	Niels Christensen, leader of a German spy ring that radioed news of ship departures from Brazil to Axis subs, and 13 associates are sentenced to prison in Rio de Janeiro.	
Oct. 8	Treasury advises Congress of a proposal to be submitted to U.N. members for a world bank to supplement the International Stabilization Fund in postwar reconstruction.	Russian bridgeheads on the west bank of the Dnieper River are widened, and Russian tank units converge on Kiev from the rear .... Yugoslavian radio says U.S. and British army officers are at partisan headquarters in Yugoslavia .... Cairo reports fighting between Greek guerrillas and German troops on Crete at Vianno and Hierapetra.	Allied Southwest Pacific Headquarters announces the Japanese have abandoned their base at Vila on the southern shore of Kolombangara Island in the central Solomons.		
Oct. 9		Moscow announces the Red Army today completed mopping up in the Caucasus, where the Germans left more than 20,000 dead and 3,000 prisoners .... Allies cross to the north side of the Volturno River between Capua and the sea.	American troops take over the entire island of Kolombangara .... Chinese Foregin Min. Soong arrives in New Delhi to join in military conferences with Lord Mountbatten .... U.S. Liberators in their fourth 2,400-mile-round trip flight from Australia bomb docks, warehouses and fuel depots at Macassar, Celebes Island.	The death penalty, dropped in 1928, is restored by Mexican Pres. Manuel Avila Camacho for highway robbery and kidnapping .... A hurricane strikes a 150-mile stretch of Mexico's Pacific coast, killing 52 persons and injuring 102.	
Oct. 10		Russian forces strengthen their bridgeheads on the west bank of the Dnieper River in face of heavy German counterattacks .... Allies punch a new salient into the front near the center of Italy by taking Pontelandolfo, 11 miles northwest of Benevento .... Yugoslavian partisans attack Trieste, Italy, forcing the Germans back into the city's center.	Chiang Kai-shek takes the oath as president of China on the 32nd anniversary of the founding of the republic.		

A	B	C	D	E
Includes developments that affect more than one world region, international organizations and important meetings of major world leaders.	*Includes all developments in European countries and military engagements between Allied and Axis powers in Africa and at sea.*	*Includes all developments in Japan and China, Japanese foreign policy and military actions in the Pacific region.*	*Includes all domestic and regional developments in Latin America, the Caribbean and Canada.*	*Includes developments in those independent nations and colonial possessions not covered in Columns B, C and D.*

U.S. Politics & Social Issues	U.S. Foreign Policy & Defense	U.S. Economy & Environment	Science, Technology & Nature	Culture, Leisure & Life Style	
Dem. National Comm. Chmn. Frank C. Walker announces each of the 38 states which voted for FDR in 1940 will have two additional delegates-at-large for the 1944 convention.				Army cancels a tour by major league baseball teams of Pacific war areas because of transportation shortages.	Oct. 2
				Archbishop Spellman asks 75,000 at a Holy Name Society rally in N.Y. to pray that Rome be spared from destruction.	Oct. 3
	In presenting his credentials at the White House, Russian Amb. Andrei A. Gromyko says that "friendly relations and closest collaboration" with America is desired by Russia.	Treasury's program to raise $10.560 billion in new taxes is presented to the House Ways and Means Comm.			Oct. 4
A federal grand jury in Newark, N.J. indicts the German-American Vocational League, Inc., its subsidiary, the Recreation Resort of Pompton Lakes, N.J., and its officers and members as Nazi agents.		FDR says his Administration "anticipates a good deal of success in the rollback of prices which will stabilize and reduce the cost of living." .... NWLB orders the striking Milk Wagon Drivers Union of the AFL to return to work in the N.Y. metropolitan area by Oct. 6.	The Martin Mars, the world's largest flying boat, successfully completes an endurance test in a flight of 32 hours and 17 minutes.		Oct. 5
Senate confirms the nomination of Robert E. Hannegan as commissioner of internal revenue.	FDR asks Congress to authorize him to "proclaim the independence of the Philippines as soon as feasible." .... Senate passes and sends to the House a substitute for the fathers' draft deferment bill, which provides that draft boards shall induct able-bodied men not certified by government agencies and industry as indispensable before taking parents.	War Food Admin. Marvin Jones reveals the 1944 food program will cut civilian allotments from 86% to 75% of available foodstuffs.		U.S. District Court in N.Y. orders the AP to amend its by-laws to prevent a member newspaper from barring the news service to a direct competitor in the same city.	Oct. 6
Former Minn. Gov. Harold E. Stassen, now in the Navy, becomes the first candidate formally to seek the 1944 GOP presidential nomination when he enters his name in the Nebraska primary .... House Immigration Comm. votes to report a bill repealing the Chinese Exclusion Act and granting China a quota.		International Assn. of Machinists, which left the AFL May 27, returns to the organization at the Boston convention, raising AFL membership to 6,564,141 .... Petroleum Admin. Ickes ends his regulation of the operating hours of gasoline stations.		It is announced that 42 paintings of the estate of J.P. Morgan, valued at $2 million, will be sold through M. Knoedler & Co. Galleries.	Oct. 7
		American Legion Commander Warren L. Atherton tells AFL convention delegates wartime strikes are "treason."		Columbus American Assn. baseball team wins its third consecutive "Little World Series," defeating Syracuse of the International League, 4-2, taking the series 4-1.	Oct. 8
FBI reports that in 12 months ending June 30 there were 28 convictions for espionage and failure to register as foreign agents, 29 sedition convictions and 3,071 for violation of the Selective Service Act .... Louisiana Gov. Sam Jones declares martial law in Plaquemines Parish. State Guardsmen occupy the courthouse at Pointe a la Hache and install William J. Blaize as sheriff.	WPB Chmn. Nelson arrives in Moscow for conferences en route to Iran.	The right-wing faction of the UAW-CIO, led by Pres. R.J. Thomas, retains control of the union's executive board .... Sen. Walter George (D, Ga.) urges a sales tax "as the only way" to cover nine million persons who would be exempt by repeal of the Victory Tax.			Oct. 9
		Rep. A. Willis Robertson (D, Va.) declares he is in favor of a sales tax in the new revenue bill and estimates that $6 billion can be raised by a 10% tax.	AMA Exec. Dr. Morris Fishbein says U.S. Army hospitals are saving 99% of the wounded and credits use of sulfa drugs as "reducing fatalities to an amazing degree."		Oct. 10

F	G	H	I	J
Includes elections, federal-state relations, civil rights and liberties, crime, the judiciary, education, health care, poverty, urban affairs and population.	*Includes formation and debate of U.S. foreign and defense policies, veterans affairs and defense spending. (Relations with specific foreign countries are usually found under the region concerned.)*	*Includes business, labor, agriculture, taxation, transportation, consumer affairs, monetary and fiscal policy, natural resources, pollution and accidents.*	*Includes worldwide scientific, medical and technological developments, natural phenomena, U.S. weather and natural disasters.*	*Includes the arts, religion, scholarship, communications media, sports, entertainment, fashions, fads and social life.*

	World Affairs	European War Zone	Pacific War Zone	The Americas	Other Countries & Territories
Oct. 11		Yugoslavian partisans report they are within 23 miles of Belgrade and are in the suburbs of the Croatian capital of Zagreb.	P.M. Curtin reveals in Canberra that the Allied flier reported beheaded by Japanese in New Guinea was an Australian. He says such atrocities are being examined "with a view of full retribution against responsible persons."	Venezuelan Pres. Isaias Medina Angarita accepts an invitation from FDR to visit the U.S.	
Oct. 12		London and Lisbon announce implementation of a 570-year-old British-Portuguese treaty to give the U.N. the use of bases in Portugal's Azores for the war's duration.			
Oct. 13		In declaring existence of a state of war between Italy and Germany 35 days after Italy surrendered to the Allies, Premier Badoglio says King Victor Emmanuel III ordered the action because of repeated and intensified acts of war committed against the Italians by Germany .... Russian troops in the southern Ukraine fight inside of Melitopol, 10 miles inland from the north shore of the Sea of Azov.	MacArthur reports Allied attacks on the Japanese airbase of Rabaul, New Britain inflicted a "disastrous" defeat at the cost of five planes .... Allied planes bomb Manokwari, Bira, Ambon and Fak Fak in Dutch New Guinea .... Japanese units make thrusts from Burma into China's Yunnan Province.	Three Argentine cabinet members, reputed to favor a break with the Axis, resign, indicating no change in government policy.	Indian central government takes control of the country's food supply and forbids the export of grain as an anti-famine measure.
Oct. 14		After two days of fighting, the Allies force the main German defense line on the Volturno River and establish bridgeheads on the north bank .... A heavy raid by U.S. Flying Fortresses on the ball and roller bearing works at Schweinfurt, Germany costs 60 bombers, the largest Fortress loss of the war to date .... Soviet units storm and capture Zaporozhie, Ukraine, killing 3,000 Germans.	Tokyo announces the installation of Jose P. Laurel as president of the Philippines and issues a declaration of independence for the Republic .... Allied planes raid airports and shipping at Cape Hoskins, Gasmata and Cape Gloucester in New Britain.		
Oct. 15		Russian forces push closer to the Ukrainian capital of Kiev in fierce fighting as the Germans begin to evacuate the city.	London and Washington announce the appointments of British Lt. Gen. Sir Henry Pownall and U.S. Maj. Gen. Albert C. Wedemeyer as chief of staff and deputy chief of staff respectively for Adm. Lord Louis Mountbatten, Allied Southeast Asia commander .... Japanese troops capture Pienma and several nearby villages in Yunnan Province.	Argentina lifts its decree banning publication of Jewish newspapers with the proviso that editorials be printed in both Yiddish and Spanish.	
Oct. 16		Gen. Draja Mikhailovich pledges to King Peter II of Yugoslavia to refrain from clashing with the rival guerrilla forces of Gen. Josip Brozovich (Tito) .... British Air Under Secy. Lord Sherwood says Germany has lost more than 10,000 planes in Western Europe and at least another 5,000 in the Mediterranean theater .... Driving south from Zaporozhe, Russian units advance six miles, occupying six towns.	Japanese troops invading China's Yunnan Province reach the southern approaches to Mamienkwan, strongest Chinese position west of the Salween River .... British troops successfully attack Maungdaw, 56 miles northwest of Akyab, Burma.	Mexico lifts wage ceilings established last month and admits inability to control the cost of living.	
Oct. 17	Swedish liner *Gripsholm*, carrying Japanese nationals from America, arrives at Mormugao, Portuguese India.	Russian forces break through German defenses on the west bank of the Dnieper River below Kremenchug to get behind the Nazi forces in Dnepropetrovsk.			
Oct. 18	Secy. Hull and Foreign Secy. Eden arrive in Moscow from Teheran, Iran and discuss with Soviet Foreign Commissar Viacheslav M. Molotov plans for a three-power conference.	An exchange of disabled prisoners of war is reported under way between the Allies and Germany at Goteborg, Sweden and Barcelona, Spain .... The Allies advance along the whole Italian front, occupying 23 towns including the last German position on the north bank of the Volturno River, Brezza .... Russian units fight their way into the center of Melitopol, but Nazi forces still hold other portions of the south Ukrainian city .... Yugoslavian partisans begin a new offensive along a 140-mile front in Slovenia, with the aim of pushing south to capture the Croatian captial of Zagreb.	The assembly of the "independent" Philippines government ratifies the alliance with Japan, which commits it to Tokyo's war effort .... In a surprise raid on Rabaul, New Britain, Allied craft destroy 60 enemy planes on the ground and aloft and sink three vessels.		
	A	B	C	D	E
	Includes developments that affect more than one world region, international organizations and important meetings of major world leaders.	*Includes all developments in European countries and military engagements between Allied and Axis powers in Africa and at sea.*	*Includes all developments in Japan and China, Japanese foreign policy and military actions in the Pacific region.*	*Includes all domestic and regional developments in Latin America, the Caribbean and Canada.*	*Includes developments in those independent nations and colonial possessions not covered in Columns B, C and D.*

U.S. Politics & Social Issues	U.S. Foreign Policy & Defense	U.S. Economy & Environment	Science, Technology & Nature	Culture, Leisure & Life Style	
FDR sends a message to Congress asking "prompt repeal" of the Chinese Exclusion Act "as important in the cause of winning the war and of establishing a secure peace."			Office of Censorship lifts restrictions on publication and broadcasting of weather forecasts because of improved defense and other "war conditions."	N.Y. Yankees defeat the St. Louis Cardinals, 2-0, to win the World Series, 4 games to 1.	Oct. 11
		Interior Secy. Ickes announces all government-operated coal mines have been returned to private owners.			Oct. 12
GOP announces its 1944 National Convention will have 1,058 delegates, an increase of 58.	A Senate Foreign Relations subcommittee approves a resolution calling for U.S. cooperation in establishing international machinery to "prevent aggression and preserve peace."	Navy Under Secy. James V. Forrestal tells the House Naval Affairs subcommittee "weak management, labor troubles and high costs" are responsible for the Brewster Aeronautical Corp. being 18 months behind on bomber schedules and 10 months on fighters.	*Science* reports development of a vaccine from dead tuberculosis germs which protects animals against innoculation with live bacilli .... Bendix Aviation Corp. announces a new compass has been developed which overcomes magnetic disturbances and keeps planes on a true course.	Film actor Errol Flynn is sued in Los Angeles by Shirley Evans Hassau, 20, who charges he is the father of a daughter born to her Nov. 13, 1940 .... Macie Marie Ainsworth Manville, seventh wife of Tommy Manville, obtains a divorce in Reno, Nev. and a reported settlement of $75,000.	Oct. 13
		AFL re-elects William Green as president at the closing convention session in Boston .... House Banking and Currency Comm. votes to bar food subsidies after Dec. 31.		Carnegie Institute awards Wayman Adams, the N.Y. artist, the $1,000 first prize for his painting of Gregor Piatigorsky.	Oct. 14
FDR accepts the resignation of Msgr. Francis J. Haas as chairman of the FEPC and names Deputy Chmn. Malcolm Ross as his successor .... Wendell Willkie "dedicates" himself in a St. Louis speech to "the removal from office of the man and group now in Washington."		NWLB asks UMW Pres. Lewis to appeal to 22,000 striking coal miners in Alabama to return to work because the strike is interfering with the war effort .... Some 10,000 employes of the Federal Shipbuilding and Drydock Company's Kearny, N.J. plant, who began a wildcat strike two days ago, return to work at the urging of five discharged shop committeemen, whose dismissal set off the walkout by members of the CIO Industrial Union of Marine and Shipbuilding Workers of America .... FDR says he hopes his successor will veto any legislation to impose a tariff on natural rubber in order to protect the synthetic production because natural rubber is cheaper.			Oct. 15
Young Communist League of the U.S. is dissolved at a meeting in N.Y. The 400 delegates form a new organization called American Youth for Democracy, which will take in non-Communist youth.	Sumner Welles says the U.S. must join a postwar world organization to maintain peace, using "force, if necessary, against lawbreakers." .... Remington Arms Co. announces it is manufacturing a new type of incendiary ammunition that pierces the self-sealing tanks of airplanes.	UMW Pres. Lewis and the NWLB order striking coal miners in Alabama and Indiana to return to work.	Chicago's first subway system, built at a cost of $34,000,000, goes into operation.	The art collection of the late Grenville L. Winthrop, including 4,000 objects valued at several million dollars, is left to the Fogg Art Museum of Harvard Univ.	Oct. 16
		Most of Alabama's 22,000 striking coal miners ignore pleas from Lewis and the NWLB to return to work.		Francisco Segura of Ecuador retains his Pan-Am tennis singles title by defeating William Talbert in Mexico City.	Oct. 17
					Oct. 18

F	G	H	I	J
Includes elections, federal-state relations, civil rights and liberties, crime, the judiciary, education, health care, poverty, urban affairs and population.	*Includes formation and debate of U.S. foreign and defense policies, veterans affairs and defense spending. (Relations with specific foreign countries are usually found under the region concerned.)*	*Includes business, labor, agriculture, taxation, transportation, consumer affairs, monetary and fiscal policy, natural resources, pollution and accidents.*	*Includes worldwide scientific, medical and technological developments, natural phenomena, U.S. weather and natural disasters.*	*Includes the arts, religion, scholarship, communications media, sports, entertainment, fashions, fads and social life.*

	World Affairs	European War Zone	Pacific War Zone	The Americas	Other Countries & Territories
Oct. 19	Moscow Foreign Ministers Conference opens with U.S. State Secy. Hull, British Foreign Secy. Eden and Russian Foreign Commissar Molotov discussing "frankly and freely what is on one another's minds."	Russian troops capture Pyatikhatka, 60 miles west of Dnepropetrovsk, cutting the Germans' main escape route from that city.	Navy Secy. Knox announces American subs have sunk 319 Japanese ships since Pearl Harbor.		
Oct. 20	Military representatives of Russia, Britain and the U.S. hold conferences in Moscow.	Allies report the battle for crossings of the Volturno River is over and the Germans are forming a new 28-mile north-south defense line in high terrain between Mondragone and Venafro .... In a seven-mile advance the British capture Busso and Oratino in central Italy .... Russian units push three to six miles farther in the salient at Kremenchug that threatens to cut off the Germans in Dnepropetrovsk to the east.	Lord Mountbatten completes four days of talks in Chungking with Chaing Kai-shek, Lt. Gen. Joseph Stillwell and Lt. Gen. Brehon B. Somervell .... Renewed Japanese efforts to reach the coast from Satelberg on the New Guinea coast are met with Australian resistance.	Argentina orders the Univ. of Cordoba closed until Oct. 23 because of protests over President Ramirez's dismissal of professors and employes who signed a declaration for "effective democracy and fulfilment of international pledges" .... Brazilian Army begins physical examinations of troops for an expeditionary force.	Viscount Wavell is sworn in at New Delhi as the 19th viceroy and governor general of India.
Oct. 21		Allies seize Alife and Piedimonte d'Alife as they push nearer the northern end of the Germans' Mondragone-Venafro line .... Russian offensive in the Dnieper River bend carries to within 23 miles of Krivoi Rog.	Japanese units make slight gains in the Satelberg-Song River area northwest and north of Finschhafen, New Guinea, infiltrating the Australian lines at night.	Argentine Pres. Ramirez names Gen. Alberto Gilbert as foreign minister and Gen. Luis Perlinger as interior minister.	
Oct. 22	Swedish liner *Gripsholm* with 1,500 Allied repatriates, including 1,236 Americans, sails from Mormugao, Portuguese India.	Soviets gain three to six miles, cutting the Dnepropetrovsk-Krivoi Rog railway, and reach Iskrovka, 18 miles north of Krivoi Rog.	Allied troops and air assaults break the Japanese effort to reach the coast north of Finschaffen, New Guinea.	The first Pan-Am Demographic Congress ends its session in Mexico City and announces establishment of a permanent committee to study immigration problems.	An official announcement of the Indian government says 8,667 persons have died in Calcutta of starvation since Aug. 1.
Oct. 23		British cruiser *Charybdis* and the destroyer *Limbourne* are lost to enemy action in the English Channel off the French coast .... After 11 days of street fighting the Russians take the key city of Melitopol in the southern Ukraine .... British force the Germans to retreat at the Trigno River, taking three towns along a 50-mile front .... Lloyd George, 80, weds Frances L. Stevenson, 55, his secretary since 1911.	The airports at Kahili and Kara on Bougainville Island are put out of commission, at least temporarily, when 230 Allied planes drop 130 tons of bombs.	Charters of Jewish and Masonic societies are withdrawn in Entre Province, Argentina, and the Argentine student organization, *Federacion Universitaria Argentina*, is outlawed as "communistic" in Buenos Aires.	
Oct. 24		Marshal Badoglio tells a press conference in Italy that Mussolini took Italy into the war in 1940 against the advice of his military aides .... Allies take Sparanise on the west flank of the German defense line in Italy .... Soviets enlarge their bridgehead on the west bank of the Dnieper River south of Rechitsa.			
Oct. 25	State Secy. Hull and Amb. Harriman confer with Stalin and Molotov in Moscow.	British take Baranello, Spineto and Bojano in a vital sector of central Italy .... Soviet troops capture Dnepropetrovsk, the Ukriane's third largest city, the nearby industrial center of Dneprodzerzhinsk and 40 other towns in the area.			
Oct. 26		Russian troops capture Karnavatka, a railroad station within the limits of Krivoi Rog.	Emperor Hirohito tells a special session of the Japanese Diet the war situation is "truly grave" and Premier Hideki Tojo says "the United States, defeated at the beginning, is overcoming many difficulties and the war is growing in intensity."		
Oct. 27		British push a wedge within 11 miles of the strategic mid-Italy communications center of Isernia .... Soviets gain up to 18 miles in a westward push from Melitopol into the Nogaisk Steppe .... Germans close the Norway-Sweden border after moving up additional troops .... Yugoslavian partisans report fierce battles at Brcko on the Sava River, 80 miles west of Belgrade, and along both the Hungarian and Albanian borders.	U.S. and New Zealand troops land against light resistance on Mono and Stirling Islands in the northern Solomons.		

A	B	C	D	E
Includes developments that affect more than one world region, international organizations and important meetings of major world leaders.	*Includes all developments in European countries and military engagements between Allied and Axis powers in Africa and at sea.*	*Includes all developments in Japan and China, Japanese foreign policy and military actions in the Pacific region.*	*Includes all domestic and regional developments in Latin America, the Caribbean and Canada.*	*Includes developments in those independent nations and colonial possessions not covered in Columns B, C and D.*

U.S. Politics & Social Issues	U.S. Foreign Policy & Defense	U.S. Economy & Environment	Science, Technology & Nature	Culture, Leisure & Life Style	
		National Planning Assn. urges establishment of a single government agency to deal with postwar reconversion of industry .... GOP members of the House Ways and Means Comm. unite in opposing the increase in income tax rates proposed in the Treasury tax program.		Joe Gordon, star second baseman of the New York Yankees, says he is quitting baseball because he is "just tired" of it, "tired of living conditions that go with baseball in the East."	Oct. 19
Senate sends back to the Comm. on Education and Labor the $300-million, school-aid program.	Medical services of the Army and Navy disclose 7,000 additional doctors are needed to meet personnel expansions planned for the remainder of the year.	WMC orders a 48-hour week to take in effect in 30 more areas by Nov. 15 .... Officials of the Alabama locals of the UMW vote in district meetings to do everything possible to get the state's 22,000 striking coal miners back to work .... Vice Pres. Wallace says "financial exploitation" and "monopolies" in railroads and other transportation fields are the source of many of the nation's ills.		Juilliard School of Music in N.Y. announces that Benny Goodman will conduct a five-week clarinet course in both popular and classical music.	Oct. 20
House votes to repeal the Chinese exclusion laws in effect since 1882 and passes a bill giving China an immigration quota of 105 yearly.	FDR announces Lincoln McVeagh will be in Egypt to serve as ambassador to the Greek and Yugoslavian governments in exile.	FDR accepts the resignation of Prentiss Brown as OPA director .... Pres. John Pelley of the Assn. of American Railroads accuses Vice Pres. Wallace of repeating "old and discredited statements" in his attack on railroads.			Oct. 21
Two Detroit Negroes, Charles Lyon and Leon Tipton, are convicted as the principal inciters of the race riots in that city that began June 20 .... Justice Dept. official Edward J. Ennis announces the ban on issuance of writs of habeas corpus for persons held by the military in Hawaii must stand.	Navy announces three 45,000-ton aircraft carriers, 12,000 tons larger than any previously built, are to be contracted.	Treasury announces it will cease coining the zinc-steel pennies, which when new are confused with dimes .... House Ways and Means Comm. votes to abolish the 5% Victory Tax, substituting a 3% tax on low incomes now reached only through the Victory Tax, and to raise the normal income levy from 6% to 10%.		American-Swedish News Exchange reports the Nobel prizes will not be awarded again this year .... National Assn. of Broadcasters issues a statement condemining the AFM offer to permit recordings on payment of fees to the union.	Oct. 22
	House Military Affairs Comm. approves an amendment to a Senate bill on draft deferments ending War Manpower Commissioner Paul V. McNutt's authority over Selective Service and increasing the power of Lewis B. Hershey.	WPB Acting Chmn. Wilson reports September war production was "disappointing" except for a 6% increase in four-motored bombers .... Representatives of the four railroad brotherhoods and the switchmen's union unanimously reject a 4¢-an-hour wage increase offer at their Chicago meeting and order that the 350,000 members of the operating unions take a strike vote as a protest.			Oct. 23
	The executive committee of the American Jewish Comm. votes to quit the American Jewish Conference because of the Conference's emphasis on the establishment of a Jewish commonwealth in Palestine.			Washington Senators sign Ossie Bluege to manage the team for two more years.	Oct. 24
	Navy discloses the new Grumman "Hellcat" fighter has a speed of 400 mph, a range of 1,500 miles and a ceiling of more than 35,000 feet.	FDR nominates Chester Bowles to be director of the OPA .... About 3,000 of the 22,000 striking coal miners return to work in Alabama, but wildcat strikes spread to six other states.		Leo Durocher signs to manage the Brooklyn Dodgers in 1944.	Oct. 25
	U.S. establishes the Foreign Economic Administration, which will include the Lend-Lease Administration, the Offices of Economic Warfare and Foreign Relief and Rehabilitation and the foreign procurement division of the CCC and State Dept. agencies dealing with foreign economies .... House rewrites the Senate draft deferment bill, providing that pre-Pearl Harbor fathers cannot be drafted until all other eligibles are inducted.	NWLB rejects the contract between the UMW and the Illinois Coal Operators Assn. providing for a basic daily wage of $8.50 and proposes a substitute scale of $8.12½ .... Officials of 15 non-operating railroad unions representing one million workers authorize a strike vote because government agencies have refused to approve an 8¢-an-hour wage increase.		Joseph E. Widener, financier, art collector and turfman who gave a $50,000,000 art collection to the National Gallery of Art in Washington, dies at 71.	Oct. 26
FDR asks Congress for action on a federal aid to education program for service personnel returning from war.	Navy Secy. Knox urges the GOP and Democratic parties make substantially identical declarations on international policy in their 1944 platforms .... Senate refuses to accept House amendments to the draft deferment bill exempting prewar fathers until all eligible non-fathers are inducted.	The former French liner *Normandie*, now the U.S. transport *Lafayette*, is turned back to the Navy after salvage work costing $4,500,000 placed her back on an even keel in the Hudson River .... The carriers' conference committee of the nation's railroads advises immediate payment of a 4¢-an-hour increase to operating employes granted by an NWLB panel.	AMA *Journal* reports a new sulfa drug, desoxyephedronium sulfathiazole, brings prompt relief from colds and seems to shorten their duration.	Director of the Museum of Modern Art since its establishment in 1929, Alfred H. Barr, retires. James T. Soby will succeed him .... Joseph C. Grew, Jay N. Darling and Mrs. August Belmont receive the Theodore Roosevelt Distinguished Service Medals for 1943 in N.Y.	Oct. 27

F	G	H	I	J
Includes elections, federal-state relations, civil rights and liberties, crime, the judiciary, education, health care, poverty, urban affairs and population.	*Includes formation and debate of U.S. foreign and defense policies, veterans affairs and defense spending. (Relations with specific foreign countries are usually found under the region concerned.)*	*Includes business, labor, agriculture, taxation, transportation, consumer affairs, monetary and fiscal policy, natural resources, pollution and accidents.*	*Includes worldwide scientific, medical and technological developments, natural phenomena, U.S. weather and natural disasters.*	*Includes the arts, religion, scholarship, communications media, sports, entertainment, fashions, fads and social life.*

	World Affairs	European War Zone	Pacific War Zone	The Americas	Other Countries & Territories
Oct. 28		Allies continue to advance despite heavy rains in Italy .... The westward drive of Soviet forces reaches a point 26 miles east of the lower Dnieper River .... Soviet troops take Anastasyevka and Blagodatnoye on the northwestern front.	U.S. paratroops land on the south coast of Choiseul Island in the northern Solomons, with the enemy retreating northwards .... Chinese troops in eastern China capture Sioafeng, Chekiang Province, one of the main points seized in the Japanese effort to wipe out guerrillas.	As a result of strikes by more than 10,000 workers, 45 Argentine labor leaders are arrested and sent to concentration camps .... Brazil liquidates 45 Axis-owned concerns, including 25 Japanese operations.	
Oct. 29	FDR tells his press conference the Moscow Conference is a tremendous success, with only document-signing left .... Canada becomes a member of the Combined Food Bd., which controls allocation of food produced by the U.N.	Allies take Mandragone, the Tyrrhenian Sea anchor of the German defense line .... Soviet forces driving northwest from Melitopol seize Bolshaya Belozerka, 25 miles southeast of the Dnieper River.	Tojo tells the closing session of the Diet that Japan has built "an invincible fortification against invasion." .... Japanese troops in the Treasury Islands continue to withdraw northward toward Malsi on Mono Island.	Chilean Pres. Juan Antonio Rios accepts FDR's invitaton to visit the U.S. sometime in the future.	
Oct. 30	The three foreign ministers agree secretly in Moscow that Germany will be stripped of all territory acquired since 1938.	Red Army reaches the northeastern entrance to the Crimea by capturing Genichesk in a rapid sweep through the Nogaisk Steppe that threatens to bottle up the German forces in the Crimea .... Allies advance up to three miles at several points on the southwestern German line in Italy, taking Nocelleto.		Guatemalan Pres. Jorge Ubico orders seizure of the German-owned Verapaz Railway.	
Oct. 31	Moscow Foreign Ministers Conference ends with five basic agreements: (1) establishment of European Advisory Commission to make recommendations regarding enemy countries; (2) a promise to Italy of a non-Fascist democratic government; (3) freedom for Austria independent of Germany; (4) creation of an international organization as soon as possible; (5) agreement that trials will be held for Axis war criminals.	Mussolini orders the death penalty for King Victor Emmanuel, Premier Badoglio, Gen. Vittorio Ambrosio and Gen. Vittorio Roatta .... Allies capture the road center of Teano, 15 miles inland from the Gulf of Gaeta .... Russians capture Chaplinka, eight miles east of the last rail line open to German troops in the Crimea.	Exiled Philippine Pres. Manuel Quezon creates a postwar planning board with Vice Pres. Sergio Osmena as chairman.		
Nov. 1	Moscow Conference ends with the U.S., U.K., Russia and China agreeing to collaborate more closely, achieve unconditional surrender and establish a postwar organization to keep world peace. U.S. and U.K. agree to open a massive second front in the summer of 1944. Russians state Poland's borders "are no more to be discussed than California's."	Russians cut the last line of German retreat from the Crimea by taking Perekop and Armyansk.	U.S. Marines land at Empress Augusta Bay on the west coast of Bougainville Island.		
Nov. 2		Allies crack the German lines between Mt. Massico and the Matese Ridge to bring the Nazi strongpoints of Venafro and Isernia within artillery range .... Red Army takes the historic city of Kakhovka.			
Nov. 3		The largest number of U.S. heavy bombers yet used in a daytime raid bomb targets in northwestern Germany, concentrating on the Wilhelmshaven naval base .... Russian Army advances 10 more miles westward in the Nogaisk Steppe area on the lower reaches of the Dnieper River and Karkinit Bay.	Allies announce all organized resistance on Mono Island in the northern Solomons has ceased.		
Nov. 4		Allies make important gains in Italy on the southwestern half of the front, reaching the south bank of the Garigliano River at the Gulf of Gaeta .... Russians claim they now hold the entire east bank of the Dnieper River from its confluence with the Sozh River to its mouth on the Black Sea.			
Nov. 5		British troops crack the Adriatic end of the Germans' trans-peninsular line by capturing the port of Vasto, while the 5th Army takes Venafro, former interior anchor of the Nazi right wing .... Russian Army closes in on Kiev from the north, northwest and west, cutting rail and highway escape routes .... French Comm. of National Liberation announces it is not bound by "decisions concerning Germany in which it has not participated."	Japanese use 30,000 troops in a central China offensive aimed at removing the Chinese threat to the Yangtze River .... U.S. planes dump more than 250 tons of bombs on targets at Akyab, Burma in the heaviest Allied attack yet on the Asiatic mainland.	Brazil announces food rationing for hotels, restaurants and boarding houses in Rio de Janeiro.	
	A *Includes developments that affect more than one world region, international organizations and important meetings of major world leaders.*	B *Includes all developments in European countries and military engagements between Allied and Axis powers in Africa and at sea.*	C *Includes all developments in Japan and China, Japanese foreign policy and military actions in the Pacific region.*	D *Includes all domestic and regional developments in Latin America, the Caribbean and Canada.*	E *Includes developments in those independent nations and colonial possessions not covered in Columns B, C and D.*

U.S. Politics & Social Issues	U.S. Foreign Policy & Defense	U.S. Economy & Environment	Science, Technology & Nature	Culture, Leisure & Life Style	
		NWLB refers "wildcat" coal mine strikes in seven states to FDR.			Oct. 28
		FDR tells the NWLB he will "take decisive action to see that coal is mined" if an estimated 90,000 striking miners do not return to work by Nov. 1 .... Federal Reserve Bd. Chmn. Marriner S. Eccles tells the House Ways and Means Comm. a tax bill of $13.8 billion is needed to soak up excess buying power and stop inflation.			Oct. 29
					Oct. 30
		Pres. Murray's annual report to the national convention of the Congress of Industrial Organizations scores labor leaders who encourage strikes and work stoppages in war industries and declares such tactics may "weary and discourage" the people, causing them to wish for a negotiated peace.	Marcus Hook of the Sun Oil Co. announces the discovery of a process to extract a new aviation fuel from crude oil formerly used as low-grade fuel; the new fuel is 50% more powerful than 100 octane gasoline.	Max Reinhardt, master of the German theater before Hitler, dies at 70 in N.Y.	Oct. 31
District Court in Washington voids the indictments of Rep. James M. Curley (D, Mass.) and five others on mail fraud charges because the grand jury was illegally summoned.	Treasury Secy. Morgenthau returns to Washington from Europe.	FDR orders Solid Fuels Admin. Ickes to take over operation of the nation's 3,000 coal mines in 26 states in the name of the government as an estimated 530,000 miners refuse to work without a contract .... FDR sends Congress a message urging food subsidies be continued to spur production and check inflation.			Nov. 1
Scattered off-year elections show a GOP trend in N.Y., N.J. and Ky.	Army discloses the development of a 120 mm. anti-aircraft gun with a range of 12 miles.	CIO national convention adopts a resolution calling for ending the Little Steel wage formula.		St. Louis Cardinal outfielder Stan Musial is named MVP of the NL by the Baseball Writers Assn. .... Joe Gordon of the Yankees says in Eugene, Ore. that he will not quit baseball as he recently indicated.	Nov. 2
N.Y. Gov. Dewey says he is not and will not become a candidate for the 1944 GOP Presidential nomination.		UMW Pres. Lewis orders coal miners to return to work after agreeing with Ickes on a wage contract that gives miners a wage rate of $8.50 per day.	Census Bureau reports U.S. cancer deaths totaled 163,400 in 1942.		Nov. 3
A final tabulation of Kentucky votes reveals Simeon S. Willis (R) beat J. Lyter Donaldson (D) to become the first elected GOP governor in the state since 1927.		Senate confirms Chester Bowles as director of the OPA.		Eighth Symphony of Dmitri Shostakovich is given its world premiere at the Moscow Conservatory by the State Symphony Orchestra conducted by Eugeni Mravinski .... W.C. Tuttle resigns as president of the Pacific Coast Baseball League.	Nov. 4
	Senate adopts a revised postwar collaboration resolution which includes the Moscow Conference declaration of an international organization to maintain the peace .... Senate's Truman Committee asks the government to demand postwar prepayment of Lend-Lease advances to reduce peacetime reconversion costs to a minimum.	CIO national convention in Philadelphia reelects Philip Murray as president .... FDR names a five-man committee in the NWLB to investigate living costs and report within 60 days.			Nov. 5

F	G	H	I	J
Includes elections, federal-state relations, civil rights and liberties, crime, the judiciary, education, health care, poverty, urban affairs and population.	*Includes formation and debate of U.S. foreign and defense policies, veterans affairs and defense spending. (Relations with specific foreign countries are usually found under the region concerned.)*	*Includes business, labor, agriculture, taxation, transportation, consumer affairs, monetary and fiscal policy, natural resources, pollution and accidents.*	*Includes worldwide scientific, medical and technological developments, natural phenomena, U.S. weather and natural disasters.*	*Includes the arts, religion, scholarship, communications media, sports, entertainment, fashions, fads and social life.*

	World Affairs	European War Zone	Pacific War Zone	The Americas	Other Countries & Territories
Nov. 6		At dawn the Russian Army storms Kiev, ending a German occupation that began Sept. 19, 1941 .... Stalin, in a Moscow radio address, pays tribute to the Allied efforts in North Africa, the Mediterranean and southern Italy, the bombing of Germany and the shipment of war goods to Russia .... British sweep across the Trigno River on a 20-mile front from the Adriatic coast and take nine towns.	Japanese troops make a general advance along a 90-mile front from the Yangtze River to Tungting Lake in central China.	A decree places all Argentina's wire and radio communications services under the control of the War Ministry for reasons of national defense.	
Nov. 8		Hitler tells Nazi Party leaders Germany will fight on, "come what may," and warns "defeatist criminals" he "would not hesitate to destroy them." .... British cross the Sinello River above Vasto on the Adriatic coast and capture Casalbordino and Scerni near the coast .... Russian Army advances northwest and southwest of Kiev, capturing 70 villages, including Fastov and Nemeshayevo .... Yugoslavian Gen. Mikhailovich's forces report the destruction of a large section of the Belgrade-Skoplje-Salonika railroad between Presevo and Bujanovac.	A large U.S. Army force lands at Empress Augusta Bay, Bougainville to reinforce Marines there.		
Nov. 9	FDR and representatives of 42 U.N. and associated countries sign a pact at the White House establishing the U.N. Relief and Rehabilitation Administration.	Gen. Henri Honore Giraud and four supporters on the French Comm. of National Liberation resign, but he stays on as head of the French armed forces .... Churchill warns Allied nations to expect no early victory and not to count on a German collapse .... Nine German counterattacks are repulsed in Italy along the southwestern half of the Allies' trans-peninsular line.			
Nov. 10	UNRRA conference opens in Atlantic City, N.J. with U.S. Asst. State Secy. Dean Acheson as temporary chairman.	The Soviet drive west of Kiev moves quickly with the taking of more than 60 localities; in a 70-mile arc around the Ukrainian capital .... A survey by U.N. agencies in London reports 21,567,203 persons in Europe are homeless or "displaced." .... De Gaulle says the French Comm. of National Liberation is the only authority of any value in France.		Brazilian Pres. Vargas pledges political reforms when the war ends.	
Nov. 11	Herbert H. Lehman is elected director general of UNRRA at the Atlantic City conference .... Secy. Hull reports to FDR on the Moscow Conference.		U.S. Navy carrier-based planes raid on Rabaul, sinking three Japanese warships and damaging 12 .... Chinese troops in central China take more than 10 points across the Yangtze River from Ichang, forcing a Japanese withdrawal .... Japan opens a drive to mobilize women to aid the war effort, as Tojo warns the nation it faces "an extremely grave situation."	Count Alfred de Marigny is acquitted in the Nassau, Bahamas Supreme Court on a charge of mudering his father-in-law, multi-millionaire Sir Harry Oakes (his trial began Oct. 18) .... Argentine Pres. Ramirez says his people favor an Allied victory but his country has "no directly affecting reasons" for ending diplomatic relations with any country .... State Dept. raises its legation in Canada to the status of embassy.	Lebanese Pres. Bechara el Khoury and Premier Riad Solh are arrested at Beirut by French Senegalese troops on the orders of De Gaulle, reportedly for favoring immediate independence.
Nov. 12		German forces begin an invasion of the Dodecanese island of Lero, gaining "footing" in some places .... Allies drive a two-mile salient into the German lines between Montaquilo and Venafro, seizing Pozzilli and Filignano .... Russians establish a bridgehead across the Sangro and retake Zhitomir.	U.S. Army and Marine forces secure the six-mile long beachhead on Empress Augusta Bay, Bougainville.		French Comm. of National Liberation announces Gen. Georges Catroux will go to Lebanon to settle the dispute growing out of the demand for immediate independence.
Nov. 13		British take Atessa along the Sangro River, 15 miles inland from the Adriatic .... Soviet Amb.-to-Mexico Constantine Oumansky says the new Russian-Polish border will be fixed 180 miles into former Polish territory.		A Mexican parliamentary committee begins investigation of the *Accion Nacional* and *Sinarquist Union* parties, branded as "traitors and outlaws" by authorities.	
Nov. 14	UNRRA council agrees on a tentative budget of $2.5 billion for its postwar relief program.	Badoglio says he plans to quit as head of the Italian government when Rome is captured by the Allies .... Russian units push north from Zhitomir along the Odessa-Leningrad railway to take Chepovichi.	U.S. troops on the west coast of Bougainville extend their defense perimeter in all directions from Cape Torokina .... FDR's special envoy Patrick Hurley leaves Chungking after three days of conferences with Chiang Kai-shek and Allied military leaders.		British Middle East Min. Richard Casey arrives in Beirut for conferences on the Lebanon situation .... Egyptian Premier Mustafa Nahas Pasha says his government will open negotiations for inclusion in the U.N.

A	B	C	D	E
Includes developments that affect more than one world region, international organizations and important meetings of major world leaders.	*Includes all developments in European countries and military engagements between Allied and Axis powers in Africa and at sea.*	*Includes all developments in Japan and China, Japanese foreign policy and military actions in the Pacific region.*	*Includes all domestic and regional developments in Latin America, the Caribbean and Canada.*	*Includes developments in those independent nations and colonial possessions not covered in Columns B, C and D.*

U.S. Politics & Social Issues	U.S. Foreign Policy & Defense	U.S. Economy & Environment	Science, Technology & Nature	Culture, Leisure & Life Style	
FDR directs that all government contracts must carry an anti-race discrimination clause . . . . Sen. Edwin C. Johnson (D, Colo.) urges the Democratic party to draft Army Chief of Staff George C. Marshall as a presidential candidate and declares "the New Deal is through."		War Mobilization Dir. Byrnes announces the appointment of Bernard M. Baruch to head a new unit within the OWM to deal with war and post-war adjustment programs . . . . Price Admin. Bowles says the cost of living "cannot be held at anything like the present levels" if Congress refuses to sanction further subsidies.			Nov. 6
	Interior Secy. Ickes says the "well-being of future generations" depends on relations between the Soviet Union and the United States and charges "powerful and active forces" [Hearst press and and the Patterson-McCormick newspapers] are "deliberately fostering ill-will against Russia."	Spokesman for 15 non-operating railroad unions reject the wage increase formula of a special board raising hourly rates 4-to-10¢.		Dr. Francis E. McMahon, an associate professor of philosophy at the Univ. of Notre Dame, says in South Bend, Ind. that he was fired for refusing to submit manuscripts of speeches to university authorities . . . . Patrice Munsel signs a three-year contract with Sol Hurok in N.Y. for concert apperances which guarantees her $120,000.	Nov. 8
	Roberto Llanas Vallecilla is convicted in N.Y. of espionage on behalf of Germany and is sentenced to 10 years imprisonment.	A spokesman for the railroads tells the Senate Interstate Commerce Comm. that the roads want to pay non-operating employes an 8¢-an-hour wage increase and favor passage of the Truman resolution directing that the vetoed Aug. 7 railroad-union agreement be accepted.		Baseball Writers Assn. of America chooses Spud Chandler, N.Y. Yankee pitcher, as the MVP in the AL for 1943.	Nov. 9
Senate Military Affairs Comm. Chmn. Robert Reynolds (D, N.C.) announces he will not be a candidate for reelection in 1944.	House passes the bill adopted by the Senate extending the terms of office for Pres. Quezon and Vice Pres. Osmena of the Philippine government in exile until the islands are freed of Japanese control.				Nov. 10
	FDR reveals that in return for about $5.5 billion in aid given to the British under Lend-Lease, the U.S. has received $1.174 billion worth of reverse aid through June 30.				Nov. 11
Senate Judiciary Comm. approves the House poll tax repeal bill.		N.Y. Federal Reserve Bank Chmn. Beardsley Ruml proposes a nine-point federal fiscal program based on high employment and lowered taxes to create buying power at the war's end.	Canadian Royal Navy annouces it has developed a pill which is a preventative and cure for sea sickness and air sickness in 75% of the cases treated.	Justice Dept. asks the N.Y. District Court to declare certain AP by-laws illegal, including those giving members power to exclude applicants in their field.	Nov. 12
About 1,000 Japanese demonstrate at Tule Lake, Calif. internee center, causing the imposition of martial law for 15 hours.					Nov. 13
Democratic Sens. James O. Eastland (Miss.) and John L. McClellan (Ark.) announce they will offer "several hundred amendments" to the anti-poll tax bill.		Commerce Dept. reports a decline of $6 million in dividend payments by companies for the first 10 months of 1943 to $2.690 billion.			Nov. 14

F	G	H	I	J
Includes elections, federal-state relations, civil rights and liberties, crime, the judiciary, education, health care, poverty, urban affairs and population.	*Includes formation and debate of U.S. foreign and defense policies, veterans affairs and defense spending. (Relations with specific foreign countries are usually found under the region concerned.)*	*Includes business, labor, agriculture, taxation, transportation, consumer affairs, monetary and fiscal policy, natural resources, pollution and accidents.*	*Includes worldwide scientific, medical and technological developments, natural phenomena, U.S. weather and natural disasters.*	*Includes the arts, religion, scholarship, communications media, sports, entertainment, fashions, fads and social life.*

	World Affairs	European War Zone	Pacific War Zone	The Americas	Other Countries & Territories
Nov. 15		Yugoslavian partisans report the Germans have opened a major drive to recapture all of the Dalmatian coast and the offshore islands .... British warships shell German positions on Lero and make successful attacks upon enemy shipping in the area .... Russian Army narrows the German escape corridor from Gomel, their southern White Russia base, to 40 miles.	The Duke of Gloucester (brother of King George VI) is appointed governor-general of Australia.		
Nov. 16		Marshal Badoglio announces he will act as premier and foreign minister in a new Italian cabinet, with Adm. Raffaele de Doutren and Gen. Renato Sandalli as navy and army ministers .... Rain and mud virtually halt Allied ground operations in Italy .... German troops capture the Dodecanese Island of Lero .... French CP accepts two posts on the French Comm. of National Liberation.	Japanese troops in central China capture Lihsien, west of Tungting Lake, and are attempting to cross the Li River to push toward Changteh.		
Nov. 17	Chinese delegate T.F. Tsiang at the UNRRA meeting in Atlantic City says China will need relief for 84 million inhabitants costing nearly $500 million.	Soviets retreat for the first time since the start of their summer offensive, abandoning several places in the Zhitomir-Korostyshev sector.		Mexican Pres. Avila Camacho says his nation's army is ready to fight for the U.N. cause.	British warn the French Comm. of National Liberation that they will keep their pledges to the Lebanese and maintain British honor in the Arab world.
Nov. 18	Secy. Hull tells a joint congressional session the Moscow Conference decisions will eliminate "old systems of alliance and balance of power." .... *Izvestia* reports Russian Foreign Commisar Molotov told the Moscow Conference that Russia is opposed to unions of small states which might be used as a "cordon sanitaire."	Soviet forces take the Nazi base at Rechitsa in White Russia and the rail junction of Korosten, 90 miles northwest of Kiev.	Chinese troops penetrate 30 miles deeper into Burma, ahead of American units building the Ledo Road .... Australian troops move to within a mile of Satelberg, the last Japanese stronghold in northeastern New Guinea.	A special commission appointed by Pres. Vargas to draft new Brazilian immigration law recommends that Japanese and Negroes be barred as unassimilable.	
Nov. 19		Red Army abandons Zhitomir in the face of an overwhelming Nazi force. This is the first major setback for the Russians in four months .... The greatest force of RAF heavy bombers ever used, estimated to number nearly 1,000, bombs Berlin and Ludwigshafen .... British gain four to five miles on the Sangro River front and capture Perano, 12 miles inland from the Adriatic.	U.S. aircraft continue their assault on Japanese positions in the Marshall and Gilbert Islands.	Ray Atherton presents his credentials to the Canadian government as the first U.S. ambassador to Ottawa.	Gen. Georges Catroux, French Comm. of National Liberation representative, declares in Beirut that Great Britain "should confine its interest in Lebanon to purely military matters and leave the French to deal with political affairs."
Nov. 20	Dir. Gen. Herbert H. Lehman wins a battle to retain for UNRRA control of food allocations regardless of whether they are paid for by the recipients.	Allied forces make their greatest gains in two weeks as the British take Archi on the south bank of the Sangro River near the Adriatic .... Russian troops turn back German attacks near Korostyshev, checking the enemy drive into the Zhitomir salient west of Kiev .... Sir Oswald E. Mosley and Lady Diana Mosley are released from Holloway Prison on order of British Home Secy. Herbert Morrison. Mosley, a prewar Fascist leader, had been imprisoned since May 1940 .... IRA leader Hugh McAteer is captured near Belfast by police.	U.S. Army and Marine troops invade the Makin and Tarawa atolls in the Japanese-held Gilbert Islands at dawn.	Brazilian Adm. Jose Maria Neivas says air bases and other installations constructed for U.S. war use will revert to Brazil after the war.	Riots in Tel Aviv follow the British suspension of two Jewish newspapers.
Nov. 21	A UNRRA subcommittee adopts and submits to the finance committee a plan calling on each member nation able to do so to contribute 1% of its national income as of June 30, 1943 .... Postwar U.N. plans are in conflict and lack coordination for international social and economic organization, the 20th Century Fund says in a report.		A Japanese force of 80,000 makes progress towards Changteh in China.	Honduras thwarts a plot to assasinate President Gen. Tiburcio Carias Andino.	French release Lebanese President Bechara el Khoury, Premier Riad Solh and two other ministers to relieve tension there.
Nov. 22	Cairo Conference opens with FDR, Churchill and Chiang Kai-shek in attendence with their staffs .... A UNRRA subcommittee agrees any relief supplied to the Axis or satellite nations must be paid for by the "exenemy."	Dr. Eduard Benes, president of the Czechoslovak government-in-exile, arrives in Moscow to sign a treaty with Russia for a 20-year defensive alliance .... Russian troops repulse new heavy German attacks in the Zhitomir-Korostyshev sector west of Kiev .... Soviet troops north of Gomel in White Russia deepen their bridgehead across the Sozh River, taking Sherstin and Staroye .... State Dept. places Robert D. Murphy on the Allied Control Commission for Italy.	U.S. troops land on Abemama atoll, the third of the Gilbert Island group, while fighting on Makin and Tarawa atolls continues.		

A	B	C	D	E
Includes developments that affect more than one world region, international organizations and important meetings of major world leaders.	*Includes all developments in European countries and military engagements between Allied and Axis powers in Africa and at sea.*	*Includes all developments in Japan and China, Japanese foreign policy and military actions in the Pacific region.*	*Includes all domestic and regional developments in Latin America, the Caribbean and Canada.*	*Includes developments in those independent nations and colonial possessions not covered in Columns B, C and D.*

U.S. Politics & Social Issues	U.S. Foreign Policy & Defense	U.S. Economy & Environment	Science, Technology & Nature	Culture, Leisure & Life Style	
Sen. Robert Reynolds (D, N.C.) receives an invitation from Gerald Smith to become the presidential candidate of his America First Party .... Senate Judiciary Comm. approves an investigation of the national liquor shortage and names a subcommittee headed by Sen. Frederick Van Nuys (D, Ind.) to conduct the probe.	FDR asks Congress to make an initial appropriation to the UNRRA postwar fund of $1 to 1.5 billion.				Nov. 15
	Senate and House conferees agree on a draft bill putting pre-Pearl Harbor fathers at the bottom of the list of registrants and denying the WMC the power to establish non-deferrable occupations.			Bertrand Russell is awarded $20,000 damages in federal court in Philadelphia in his suit against the Barnes Foundation of Merion, Pa., which discharged him from the faculty.	Nov. 16
Ohio GOP congressional delegation backs the presidential candidacy of Gov. John W. Bricker.	US. aircraft carrier *Bataan* is commissioned in Philadelphia.	OPA warns that congressional legislation eliminating subsidies will mean a 3% increase in living costs and a 7% increase in retail food prices .... Executive council of the CIO Textile Workers Union announces it will seek an increase of 10¢-an-hour for the union's 1,250,000 members.		*Variety* reports the most popular songs to be: (1) *Pistol Packin' Mama*, (2) *Paper Doll* and (3) *Sunday, Monday or Always*.	Nov. 17
		Senate Interstate Commerce subcommittee approves a resolution giving an 8¢-an-hour wage raise to non-operating railroad workers.	Prof. W.E. Gye of the Imperial Cancer Research Fund Lab. in London reports a new substance called patulin has given promising results when used in treating common colds.		Nov. 18
	Socialist Party leader Norman Thomas says the Moscow conference agreements will "Balkanize" Europe and cause a third world war, permitting Russia to draw its own boundaries and allowing Britain to continue its imperialist policy .... John da Silva Purvis, convicted of spying for the Axis, is sentenced to 10 years imprisonment on each of two counts, with the terms to be concurrent.	Coal mine operators send a memo to Economic Stabilization Dir. Fred M. Vinson stating 40% of the nation's coal mines will fold up unless there is an increase in coal prices.		Beau Jack outpoints Bob Montgomery in 15 rounds at Madison Sq. Garden to regain the lightweight title.	Nov. 19
		NWLB approves a pact between the UMW and Solid Fuels Admin. Ickes, cutting weekly wages by 30½¢ to $57.07.			Nov. 20
					Nov. 21
Sen. W. Warren Barbour (R, N.J.), Rep. Henry Steagall (D, Ala.) and Rep. J. William Ditter (R, Pa.) die today, the first two of heart ailments and the third in a plane crash.		Supreme Court rules the National Railway Mediation Bd. and not the courts has the authority to settle jurisdictional disputes and select voting groups among employes for collective bargaining.		Song writer Lorenz Hart, who with Richard Rodgers wrote scores for many musical comedy and motion picture hits for the past 20 years, dies at 47 .... Metropolitan Opera opens its 1943-44 season with Mussorgsky's *Boris Godunov*.	Nov. 22

F	G	H	I	J
Includes elections, federal-state relations, civil rights and liberties, crime, the judiciary, education, health care, poverty, urban affairs and population.	*Includes formation and debate of U.S. foreign and defense policies, veterans affairs and defense spending. (Relations with specific foreign countries are usually found under the region concerned.)*	*Includes business, labor, agriculture, taxation, transportation, consumer affairs, monetary and fiscal policy, natural resources, pollution and accidents.*	*Includes worldwide scientific, medical and technological developments, natural phenomena, U.S. weather and natural disasters.*	*Includes the arts, religion, scholarship, communications media, sports, entertainment, fashions, fads and social life.*

	World Affairs	European War Zone	Pacific War Zone	The Americas	Other Countries & Territories
Nov. 23		RAF bombs Berlin, making a heavy and concentrated attack, starting huge fires and reportedly leaving elephants and other animals at large with the destruction of the Berlin Zoo .... Russian troops in the face of concentrated German attacks fall back in the sector west of Kiev .... British forces capture Alfedena, Italy in the center of the trans-peninsular line and a nearby road junction .... More than 1,000 labor delegates demonstrate outside Parliament, demanding the removal of Home Secy. Morrison for releasing Sir Oswald Mosley.	U.S. command announces the capture of Makin Island in the Gilberts; American dead number 5,500 .... Chinese defenders at Changteh in central China repulse a Japanese assault, killing more than 5,000 enemy troops.		Acting French delegate to Lebanon Yves Chataigneau announces the Chamber of Deputies has repealed the ordinance suspending the French mandate.
Nov. 24	A UNRRA subcommittee report barring use of relief supplies as a political weapon is adopted at the Atlantic City conference.			Brazilian Pres. Vargas orders the seizure of the Farm Mortgage Bank following reports it was under German control.	
Nov. 25		Despite bad weather British units establish and hold a bridgehead against German counterattacks on the west bank of the Sangro River at the Adriatic end of the Italian front .... After three days of driving, Soviet forces advance 60 miles north of Gomel, White Russia, and capture 180 localities.	Four of five Japanese destroyers are sunk and a fifth damaged in a battle with U.S. naval units between Buka, northern Solomons and Rabaul, New Britain .... Chinese planes raid the Japanese-held island of Formosa, bombing and strafing the airport at Shinchiku.	Colombian Pres. Alfonzo Lopez Pumarejo arrives in Miami on the start of a 60-day visit to the U.S.	
Nov. 26	Cairo Conference ends with an Allied commitment to invade Burma in the near future, and at the war's end to strip Japan of all Pacific islands occupied since 1914 and the territories "stolen" from China such as the Pescadores, Formosa and Manchuria.	Russian troops capture Gomel, southern White Russia, the last German bastion east of the Dnieper River .... Earthquakes in Turkey kill 4,000 and injure at least 3,000 persons .... Andre Marty (former Communist deputy from Paris) criticizes Gen. de Gaulle, the French Comm. of National Liberation and the Assembly at a conference in Algiers for failure to send more arms to patriots in France and to open a land front against Germany.	Australian troops capture Satelberg, the last Japanese forward base in northeastern New Guinea .... U.S. Navy announces 745 Japanese ships of all types have been sunk since Pearl Harbor.	Bolivia declares war on the Axis and indicates its adherence to the Atlantic Charter .... Sen. Hugh S. Butler (R, Neb.) files a report with the Senate on a trip he made through 20 Latin American countries in which he charges the government is "lavishing" more than $6,000,000,000 in "wasteful and unneccessary projects which are breeding hate, suspicion and contempt for this country."	U.S. State Dept. approves recent French action to ease tension in Lebanon and expresses sympathy with the independence aspirations of both Lebanon and Syria .... UNRRA conference Chmn. Dean Acheson rejects an Indian request for aid, saying the aid is for liberated countries only.
Nov. 27				Colombia declares a state of belligerency with Germany because of the sinking of its schooner *Ruby* in the Caribbean by a German U-boat.	
Nov. 28	Teheran Conference opens with FDR, Churchill and Stalin meeting personally for the first time.	British troops begin a new drive from the west bank of the Sangro River, advancing six miles .... Russian forces further hem in retreating Germans with the capture of Sharybovka, 18 miles southeast of the rail junction of Zhlobin.	Against stiff enemy opposition, U.S. troops on Bougainville Island advance 800 yards .... Australian troops moving up the New Guinea coast with tank and plane support advance to within a mile of the important rail junction of Bonga .... Japanese radio reports a new plan providing for substantial increases in war material production and food supplies and better use of facilities and people in conquered territories.	Mexican Supreme Court refuses to intervene in the conviction of Jacques Mornard for the murder of Leon Trotzky.	
Nov. 29		British merge their two bridgeheads on the west bank of the Sangro River at the Adriatic end of the front to form a 14-mile line .... Russians drive northwest from Gomel, reaching a point 11 miles south of Zhlobin .... State Secy. Hull denies reports that Germany has made peace moves "through the Vatican or other channels" when asked about Berne dispatches that Franz von Papen, German ambassador to Turkey, is in Rome to seek an audience with Pope Pius XII.	Australian troops occupy Bonga, seaward anchor of the principal Japanese supply line on the northeast New Guinea coast .... Japanese break into Changteh in northern Hunan Province after 10 days of fighting.	Buenos Aires police announce all anti-government propagandists will be sent to concentration camps in Patagonia.	
Nov. 30		In the face of heavy German counterattacks, British units give ground on the west bank of the Sangro River .... In their second important setback on this front, the Russians abandon Korosten rail junction, 90 miles northwest of Kiev.	U.S. naval forces shell Gasmata, New Britain and Madang in the first attacks of this type against these Japanese bases.		

	A	B	C	D	E
	Includes developments that affect more than one world region, international organizations and important meetings of major world leaders.	*Includes all developments in European countries and military engagements between Allied and Axis powers in Africa and at sea.*	*Includes all developments in Japan and China, Japanese foreign policy and military actions in the Pacific region.*	*Includes all domestic and regional developments in Latin America, the Caribbean and Canada.*	*Includes developments in those independent nations and colonial possessions not covered in Columns B, C and D.*

U.S. Politics & Social Issues	U.S. Foreign Policy & Defense	U.S. Economy & Environment	Science, Technology & Nature	Culture, Leisure & Life Style	
		House passes the CCC bill with provisions killing extensions of consumer subsidies after Dec. 31.		Baseball Commissioner Kenesaw Mountain Landis bars the president and chief stockholder of the Philadelphia Phillies, William Cox, from organized baseball for betting on his own team.	Nov. 23
FCC member T.A.M. Craven says the commission has taken powers not granted by Congress and is undertaking "social reforms."	Senate Military Affairs Comm. votes to ask War Secy. Stimson for a full report of the soldier-slapping incident involving Lt. Gen. Patton . . . . Senate Naval Affairs Comm. approves a $5.3-billion naval construction program for 2.5 million tons of auxiliary vessels and one million tons of landing craft.	House passes and sends to the Senate a $2,139,300,000 tax bill, a cut of more than $8 million from the Administration's request . . . . OPA increases the maximum prices of anthracite by 35-to-70¢ a ton to meet increased labor costs.			Nov. 24
	United Aircraft Corp. discloses the development of a supercharger device using a jet of water which gives quick bursts of speed to fighter planes.		Schenley Distillers Corp. announces in N.Y. it has developed a new method of manufacturing penicillin and will begin large-scale production in February 1944.	Thanksgiving Day passes without organized national observance and with most war plants remaining in operation . . . . Army weekly *Yank* wins the *Saturday Review of Literature* Award for distinguished service to American letters.	Nov. 25
Office of Education reports enrollment in colleges and other institutions of higher learning is down 8% since last year.	A detailed report on the conduct of Lt. Gen. Patton by Gen. Eisenhower, read to the Senate, discloses that Patton "dealt roughly" with two hospitalized soldier victims of "battle anxiety" during the Sicilian campaign. Eisenhower describes Patton's conduct as "unseemly and indefensible." . . . . Senate passes and sends to FDR a bill repealing the Chinese Exclusion Act.	The regional office of the WMC orders a 48-hour week in the Chicago area effective Dec. 1.			Nov. 26
William J. Fahy, former postal inspector who served 13 years in prison for a $2,000,000 mail robbery and refused a commutation in return for admission of guilt, dies in Chicago.				Notre Dame quarterback Angelo Bertelli is the winner of the 1943 Heisman Trophy as the outstanding college football player for 1943.	Nov. 27
		CIO Pres. Murray assails the House tax bill as an effort to destroy labor unions by requiring tax-exempt organizations to file income returns.			Nov. 28
Ohio Gov. Bricker names Roy D. Moore to direct his campaign for the 1944 GOP presidential nomination.		Treasury Secy. Morgenthau asks the Senate Finance Comm. to substitute the Treasury's $10.5-billion tax program for the House version.			Nov. 29
GOP's Chester Carrier is elected to Congress from the fourth district of Kentucky to fill the vacancy left by E.W. Creel (D), who died Oct. 13.	Navy Secy. Frank Knox announces Lt. Gen. Alexander A. Vandegrift will become Marine Corps commandant Jan. 1, succeeding Lt. Gen. Thomas Holcomb, who has passed the mandatory retirement age of 64.	Chmn. Ross of the Committee on Fair Employment Practices notifies 20 railroads and seven unions they must cease discrimination "on grounds of race, creed, or color" and directs 10 railroads operating in the Southeast to cancel an agreement with unions which limits employment of Negroes . . . . President R.J. Thomas of the CIO-UAW is acquitted by a Houston, Tex. court of violating the state law forbidding solicitation of union members without a license on technical grounds that the complaint was improperly drawn.		N.Y. Yankee manager Joe McCarthy signs a new three-year contract at a reported salary of $35,000 annually.	Nov. 30

F	G	H	I	J
Includes elections, federal-state relations, civil rights and liberties, crime, the judiciary, education, health care, poverty, urban affairs and population.	*Includes formation and debate of U.S. foreign and defense policies, veterans affairs and defense spending. (Relations with specific foreign countries are usually found under the region concerned.)*	*Includes business, labor, agriculture, taxation, transportation, consumer affairs, monetary and fiscal policy, natural resources, pollution and accidents.*	*Includes worldwide scientific, medical and technological developments, natural phenomena, U.S. weather and natural disasters.*	*Includes the arts, religion, scholarship, communications media, sports, entertainment, fashions, fads and social life.*

	World Affairs	European War Zone	Pacific War Zone	The Americas	Other Countries & Territories
Dec. 1	Teheran Conference ends with these secret agreements: (1) Russia is to launch an eastern offensive at the time of Overlord, May or June 1944, (2) Russia will enter the Pacific War after Germany's defeat, (3) Germany will be divided into occupation zones after the war, pending reunification, (4) the first basic design of the U.N., as proposed by FDR, will consist of members, an Executive Comm. (Big Four) and four policemen (U.S., U.K., USSR, China) to settle disputes, and (5) no resolution on Polish borders .... UNRRA Conference in Atlantic City ends after indicating steps will be taken to relieve the famine in Bengal, India .... The *Gripsholm* reaches Jersey City, N.J. with 1,222 American and 217 Canadian civilian repatriates from Japan.	Strong German counterattacks on all sectors hold the Russians to small gains.	After 40 hours of street fighting, Chinese troops drive the Japanese from Changteh, Hunan Province .... U.S. planes continue their attacks on Japanese targets in the Marshall Islands, northwest of the Gilberts.		
Dec. 2	Second Cairo Conference is opened, with Turkish Pres. Ismet Inonu present for discussions with FDR and Churchill.	A German air raid on Bari, Italy, results in severe damage to Allied shipping, leaving some 1,000 casualties, including 37 U.S. naval personnel .... British breach German positions on the west side of the Sangro River at the Adriatic end of the line, putting the Nazis in full retreat .... Red Army takes 80 towns and villages in its drive northwest of Gomel toward Zhlobin.		Argentine Public Instruction Min. Gustavo Martinez Zuviria announces university professors and students participating in Communist propaganda will be dismissed and subject to other sanctions.	
Dec. 3		Russian forces reach Staraya Rudnya, only nine miles southeast of the rail junction at Zhlobin.	Australian P.M. Curtin reveals MacArthur told him the Big Three agreed at Cairo that final victory against Japan must await the outcome of the European war .... The vital "rice bowl" city of Changteh falls to the Japanese after a 15-day defense of the city fails .... Japanese bombers strike at Tarawa atoll in the Gilberts, causing light damage.		
Dec. 4		Yugoslavian partisans under Gen. Josip Brozovich (Tito) form a government rivalling that of King Peter .... Allies crack the German line at Mt. Camino, 15 miles inland from the Gulf of Gaeta .... British yield the town of Orsogna in the face of strong German counterattacks .... FDR names John G. Winant as the American member of the U.N. European Advisory Commission.	Australians repulse three Japanese counterattacks near Wareo, New Guniea in their drive to expel the enemy from the Huon peninsula .... A U.S. carrier task force carries out the heaviest Allied assault on Japan's Marshall Islands.		Tel Aviv, Palestine newspapers suspended by the British during recent riots resume publication.
Dec. 5		Yugoslavian government in exile calls the Tito partisan group a movement of "terroristic violence" and accuses "certain Allied institutions" of aiding the partisans through propaganda .... New German attacks in the bulge west of Kiev force the Russians to abandon several populated places.	In their first daylight attack and the first raid in 11 months on Calcutta, Japanese bombers inflict 500 civilian casualties.		
Dec. 6		British make a limited crossing of the Moro River at the Adriatic end of the Italian front at San Leonardo .... Red Army troops cut the Znamenka-Smela railway between Krasnoselye and Tsybulevo, southwest of Kremenchug .... An earthquake in the Erbaa region near the Black Sea coast of north-central Turkey takes 550 lives.		Pres. Avila Camacho of Mexico tells the Mexican Senate that the country will be able to meet its foreign debt of $40,000,000.	
Dec. 7	The second Cairo Conference ends with a Turkish affirmation of friendship with the Big Three and a secret agreement that the major offensive originally planned for Burma will be scaled down due to Overlord. Turks agree to complete preparations for Allied air bases by Feb. 15, 1944, but a final decision on Turkey's entrance into the war is postponed until February 1944.	Allies gain new ground in Italy, ousting German forces from positions around Mt. Camino.			

A	B	C	D	E
Includes developments that affect more than one world region, international organizations and important meetings of major world leaders.	*Includes all developments in European countries and military engagements between Allied and Axis powers in Africa and at sea.*	*Includes all developments in Japan and China, Japanese foreign policy and military actions in the Pacific region.*	*Includes all domestic and regional developments in Latin America, the Caribbean and Canada.*	*Includes developments in those independent nations and colonial possessions not covered in Columns B, C and D.*

U.S. Politics & Social Issues	U.S. Foreign Policy & Defense	U.S. Economy & Environment	Science, Technology & Nature	Culture, Leisure & Life Style	
Representatives of 25 Negro groups announce through the NAACP a political code pledging support for a party that works for full Negro rights .... James W. Johnson, a Negro, is sworn in as collector of internal revenue for the third New York district. It is one of the highest federal positions held by a Negro.		Ration point values for beef and 15 processed foods are lowered and citrus juices and soups are made point-free effective Dec. 5 .... CIO United Steel Workers of America policy committee votes to demand a 17¢-an-hour wage increase for its 750,000 members working on 30-day contracts.	AT&T Vice Pres. Dr. Frank B. Jewett says wartime scientific discoveries will have little peacetime value because of "military secrecy" which prevents free exchange of scientific developments.	U.S. Naval Academy wins the 1943 Lambert Trophy, symbolic of football supremacy on the East Coast .... William G. Bramham is reelected president of the National Assn. of Professional Baseball Leagues for a five-year term.	Dec. 1
Rep. Everett M. Dirksen (R, Ill.) announces his candidacy for the GOP presidential nomination in 1944.	Army and Navy report 126,969 U.S. casualties up to Nov. 15, including 27,481 killed in action .... U.S. Navy announces acceptance for the Naval Air Transport Service of the world's largest flying boat, the 70-ton Martin Mars.	OPA Dir. Bowles tells the Senate Banking and Currency Comm. living costs will rise 10% if Congress abolishes subsidies.		Rudy Vallee and actress Bettejane Greer are married in Hollywood.	Dec. 2
Robert M. Lovett, William E. Dodd, Jr. and Goodwin Watson file suit in Washington questioning the right of Congress to remove them from their government jobs because of alleged Communist sympathies.		WPB announces that November plane production totaled 7,789 craft, including "more than 1,000" four-engined bombers, and that "about a dozen" aircraft carriers were among 250,000 tons of warships completed during the month.		Houghton Mifflin Co. announces its $2,500 Life in America award has been given to Dixon Lecter for his book *When Johnny Comes Marching Home.*	Dec. 3
	Army advises the House Military Affairs Comm. that the number of officers will be reduced by 25,000 to a total of 625,000.				Dec. 4
	American Jewish Joint Distribution Comm., meeting in N.Y., sets a 1944 budget of $16 million for relief work among European Jews.				Dec. 5
		WMC reports an increase in manpower needs to a peak of 66,300,000 by July, 1944, sharply revising earlier estimates.		Herman Lohr, British composer of *Little Grey Home in the West,* dies at 72 in Kent, England.	Dec. 6
	U.S. Navy celebrates the Pearl Harbor anniversary with the launching of the super-battleship *Wisconsin,* said to be the world's largest and most powerful warship.	War Mobilization Dir. James F. Byrnes says subsidies are essential to check inflation.		*Carmen Jones,* a musical comedy with lyrics by Oscar Hammerstein II and music by Georges Bizet, opens in New York with an all-Negro cast.	Dec. 7

F	G	H	I	J
Includes elections, federal-state relations, civil rights and liberties, crime, the judiciary, education, health care, poverty, urban affairs and population.	*Includes formation and debate of U.S. foreign and defense policies, veterans affairs and defense spending. (Relations with specific foreign countries are usually found under the region concerned.)*	*Includes business, labor, agriculture, taxation, transportation, consumer affairs, monetary and fiscal policy, natural resources, pollution and accidents.*	*Includes worldwide scientific, medical and technological developments, natural phenomena, U.S. weather and natural disasters.*	*Includes the arts, religion, scholarship, communications media, sports, entertainment, fashions, fads and social life.*

	World Affairs	European War Zone	Pacific War Zone	The Americas	Other Countries & Territories
Dec. 8	Asst. State Secy. Acheson tells the House Foreign Affairs Comm. about 90% of the $1.3 billion which the U.S. plans to contribute to UNRRA work will be spent in the U.S.	Turkish Foreign Min. Numan Menemencioglu states Turkey's "foreign policy remains unchanged," describing President Inonu's conference in Cairo with FDR and Churchill as "one of the most important events in this phase of the war." .... Turkey militarizes three-mile strips on each side of the Dardanelles and intensifies other security precautions, including the arrest of suspected German spies .... Italian forces go into battle alongside the Allies for the first time, attacking German positions on the U.S. 5th Army front .... Minister of State Richard Law tells the House of Commons that Britain is giving "more support" to the partisans of Marshal Josip Brozovich (Tito) in Yugoslavia than to Gen. Mikhailovich "for the simple reason that the resistance of the partisan forces to the Germans is very much greater."	Australian forces capture the Japanese chief defense anchor of Wareo, New Guinea.		
Dec. 9		Soviet forces, after giving ground for two days to German counterattacks, finally hold west of Kiev near Chernyakhov.	Chinese troops recapture Changteh from the Japanese at dawn .... Australian troops mop up on the Huon Peninsula of New Guinea and take Bazuluo, 1½ miles west of Wareo.	Canada orders a ban on wage raises for the war's duration except in cases of "gross inequality or gross injustice."	
Dec. 10		The twin junctions of Znamenk and Khirovka southeast of Kremenchug are captured by Soviet forces.	French Comm. of National Liberation pledges a "more liberal" political status for Indochina .... Chinese forces move out from Changteh, advancing some 13 miles northwest of the city and some 20 miles to the southwest.		
Dec. 11		Secy. Hull warns Bulgaria, Hungary and Rumania they "must share the consequences of the terrible defeat that United Nations' arms are surely bringing to Nazi Germany." .... Mignano, gateway to the Liri Valley, is abandon by German troops to the Allies .... Cairo reveals that in a letter to Greek Premier Tsouderos Nov. 8 King George of Greece said: " .... in in my desire to contribute to the timely clarification of the political atmos phere .... I wish you to know that .... I shall examine the question anew of my return to Greece."	Australian troops moving up the coast from Bonga, New Guinea reach the mouth of the Sowi River.	Gen. Pedro de Goes Monteiro announces his resignation as chief of the Brazilian army general staff.	
Dec. 12		Soviet Union and Czechoslovakia sign a 20-year friendship agreement in Moscow, pledging postwar collaboration and mutual assistance in the war against Germany .... Russian troops force the first real German withdrawal in the area of west of Kiev since the Germans began their counter-offensive a month ago.	Chinese troops capture Niupitan, a strategic point east of Changteh, seizing another 10 villages north of the city.	An "advance reconnaissance party" of the Brazilian expeditionary force arrives in North Africa .... Rep. Eduardo Chibas of the Cuban Revolutionary Party introduces a motion to try Pres. Batista for disbursing funds capriciously and usurping congressional power.	
Dec. 13		Zurich dispatches claim Germany is experimenting with a 12-ton rocket shell, 45 feet long, with a 160-mile range and a destructive force of over 20 square miles .... Allied planes hit the oil depot at Split and the railway yards at Sebenico, Yugoslavia.	Japanese troops north of Changteh are routed and are reportedly fleeing to the northeast.	Sen. Kenneth McKellar (D, Tenn.) says in a Senate speech that charges by Sen. Butler (R, Neb.) that the government has spent $6,000,000,000 in Latin America are "95% wrong" and that actual expenditures in the past three years totalled $324,185,000, which would shrink to $178,593,000 if allowances are made for military and naval expenditures and reciprocal Lend-Lease transfers.	
Dec. 14		British units with bridgeheads on the Moro River join forces to establish a combined holding about five miles long .... Soviet forces storm and take the last major German stronghold on the middle Dnieper River, Cherkassy .... U.S. planes bomb Eleusis, Kalamaki and Tatoi airfields and shipping at Piraeus, the port of Athens, Greece.	Navy Secy. Knox says Pacific preliminaries are out of the way and preparations are being made for major blows against Japan.		

A	B	C	D	E
Includes developments that affect more than one world region, international organizations and important meetings of major world leaders.	*Includes all developments in European countries and military engagements between Allied and Axis powers in Africa and at sea.*	*Includes all developments in Japan and China, Japanese foreign policy and military actions in the Pacific region.*	*Includes all domestic and regional developments in Latin America, the Caribbean and Canada.*	*Includes developments in those independent nations and colonial possessions not covered in Columns B, C and D.*

U.S. Politics & Social Issues	U.S. Foreign Policy & Defense	U.S. Economy & Environment	Science, Technology & Nature	Culture, Leisure & Life Style	
Alfred M. Landon and Herbert Hoover confer in N.Y. and predict a GOP victory in 1944, because FDR does not have the Democratic Party's support.		U.S. Navy takes over the shipyard of the Los Angeles Shipbuilding & Drydock Corp. under an FDR executive order, after saying "the yard's inability to control its costs and its slow production convinced the Navy that satisfactory operation could not be obtained without a change of management."			Dec. 8
Sen. Ellison D. Smith (D, S.C.) "nominates" Sen. Harry F. Byrd (D, Va.) as a presidential candidate and advises the South to organize a Democratic Party of its own.		Senate passes a resolution approving a wage increase of 8¢-an-hour for 1.1 million non-operating railroad employes .... NAM adopts a 1944 platform at its Second War Congress of American Industry in N.Y., pledging a new postwar program for a "better America" whereby everything within the power of NAM will be done "to produce and distribute better goods, in greater volume, at lower prices, to more people."		Frank Sinatra, "swoon singer" of radio, stage and screen, is classified 4-F in Newark, N.J.	Dec. 9
	FDR signs the draft bill which puts pre-Pearl Harbor fathers at the bottom of the induction list.			Censorship Dir. Byron Price issues revised codes for press and radio which give his agency fuller control and larger powers to clear news hitherto released only "by appropriate authority." .... *N.Y. World Telegram*'s annual poll to designate the football coach of the year awards the honor to Amos Alonzo Stagg, 81-year-old coach at the College of the Pacific.	Dec. 10
Wisconsin Democratic convention in Milwaukee endorses FDR for a fourth term.				N.Y.C. Center of Music and Drama is opened with a concert by the N.Y. Philharmonic Symphony Orchestra .... Don Hutson, Green Bay Packer football star and holder of most pass catching and scoring records, announces his retirement .... U.S. Lawn Tennis Assn. ranks Joseph R. Hunt and Pauline Betz as national champions for 1943.	Dec. 11
				New York Giants defeat the Washington Redskins, 31 to 7, and the two teams are tied for the eastern championship of the NFL.	Dec. 12
Marvin H. McIntyre, one of President Roosevelt's secretaries since 1933, dies at 65.		Sixteen Southern railroads and terminal companies notify the FEPC they will not obey its order to abandon agreements with railroad unions which limit employment of Negroes.			Dec. 13
		WPB reports war production in November reached an all-time high: an overall munitions gain of 3% in dollar value over October; the production index reached 665, a gain of 18 points over the previous month.	Courtland Prof. of Biochemistry at London Univ. Dr. E.C. Dodds reports the use of diethylstibestrol, a synthetic female sex hormone, makes it possible to completely control cancer of the prostate gland.		Dec. 14

F	G	H	I	J
Includes elections, federal-state relations, civil rights and liberties, crime, the judiciary, education, health care, poverty, urban affairs and population.	*Includes formation and debate of U.S. foreign and defense policies, veterans affairs and defense spending. (Relations with specific foreign countries are usually found under the region concerned.)*	*Includes business, labor, agriculture, taxation, transportation, consumer affairs, monetary and fiscal policy, natural resources, pollution and accidents.*	*Includes worldwide scientific, medical and technological developments, natural phenomena, U.S. weather and natural disasters.*	*Includes the arts, religion, scholarship, communications media, sports, entertainment, fashions, fads and social life.*

	World Affairs	European War Zone	Pacific War Zone	The Americas	Other Countries & Territories
Dec. 15	British Foreign Secy. Eden says military plans laid down at the Teheran Conference will "take all our energies in the very near future."	Russian troops dislodge the Germans from several settlements south of Malin and northwest of Radomysl in the Kiev bulge . . . . Red Army establishes control of a 250-mile stretch of the west bank of the Dnieper River from Nikopol north to Cherkassy.	U.S. troops invade the Arawe Peninsula of southwestern New Britain Island and establish a firm bridgehead . . . . U.S. and Chinese fliers complete three days of attacks on Kungan, Wuchang, Lichow, Shasi, Yochow, Owchihkow and Shishow in central China.	Argentina and Paraguay sign a trade treaty which gives Paraguay free port facilities at Buenos Aires and sets up a commission to study a possible customs union.	A U.S. military mission visits Saudi Arabia upon the invitation of King Ibn Saud . . . . A third daughter is born to King Farouk of Egypt.
Dec. 16					Premier Ali Soheily of Iran announces the formation of a new government "adapted to new conditions" prevailing after the Big Three conference.
Dec. 17	FDR returns to Washington from Allied conferences in the Middle East, which he says "were in every way a success."	*Army and Navy Register* says Gen. Eisenhower will be transferred to London to head the Allied invasion of Western Europe . . . . Allies make important gains in Italy in their effort to break through the strong German opposition to the important road junction of Cassino.		Brazilian Pres. Vargas names Gen. Mauricio Gardozo army staff chief.	
Dec. 18		U.S. forces take San Pietro Infine, key to the Cassino road . . . . Yugoslavian partisan radio broadcasts a demand for Allied recognition of its government and withdrawal of recognition from King Peter . . . . Russian units make new gains in the Kirovograd area of the Ukraine, capturing several key points.			
Dec. 19		A Soviet offensive in northern White Russia drives a wedge almost 19 miles deep and 50 miles wide into the German line guarding the Baltic states.	Commander of Southeast Asia Lord Mountbatten merges the American and British air forces under Air Chief Marshal Sir Richard Pierse . . . . Japanese radio says "war has turned from one of self-existence to one of self-defense."		
Dec. 20		U.S. planes bomb Bremen, Germany while RAF aircraft attack in northern France.	American troops clear the Arawe Peninsula of New Britain Island of all Japanese troops.	Maj. Gualbert Villarroel leads a coup to depose Pres. Gen. Enrique Penaranda of Bolivia.	
Dec. 21		British fight their way into Ortona on the Adriatic and begin street fighting against a last-ditch Nazi defense . . . . Frankfurt is blasted by some 800 RAF bombers, which drop nearly 2,000 tons of explosives on the city . . . . Russian offensive south of Nevel in White Russia engulfs 100 more inhabited places.	A Chinese offensive in the central China "rice bowl" captures the towns of Lihsien, Nanhsien, Ansiang and Tsingshih in three days of fighting.	Bolivian Foreign Min. Jose Tamayo sends a note to all foreign diplomats in La Paz stating the new government intends to abide by all international obligations.	Saudi Arabian Foreign Min. Emir Feisal says it is no longer the business of Europe to act as guardian of Arab peoples, who "should look after their own affairs."
Dec. 22		Yugoslavian partisan leader Marshall Tito announces the government in exile in Cairo and King Peter are "deprived of all rights" and are to stay out of the country after its liberation . . . . Soviet offensive below Nevel, White Russia gains new ground with more than 20 localities being captured . . . . Soviet magazine *War and the Working Class* says that Latvia, Lithuania and Estonia "joined the Soviet Union with enthusiasm and intend to remain in it."	Chinese troops in northern Hunan Province continue to make progress after clearing the Japanese from both banks of the Lin River.	Secy. Hull says uncertainty exists as to whether the revolt in Bolivia was Axis-inspired and that U.S. recognition will not be given until all doubts are resolved . . . . Five convicted German spies are sentenced to 30 years imprisonment in Rio de Janeiro.	
Dec. 23		Soviet Baltic Army fights its way to a point 12 miles north of Vitebsk.	Chinese forces recapture the city of Sungtze, mopping up the Japanese west of the Sungtze River, which connects the Yangtze with Tungting Lake . . . . British and American heavy bombers assault Bangkok, setting fires visible for 100 miles.		
	A *Includes developments that affect more than one world region, international organizations and important meetings of major world leaders.*	B *Includes all developments in European countries and military engagements between Allied and Axis powers in Africa and at sea.*	C *Includes all developments in Japan and China, Japanese foreign policy and military actions in the Pacific region.*	D *Includes all domestic and regional developments in Latin America, the Caribbean and Canada.*	E *Includes developments in those independent nations and colonial possessions not covered in Columns B, C and D.*

U.S. Politics & Social Issues	U.S. Foreign Policy & Defense	U.S. Economy & Environment	Science, Technology & Nature	Culture, Leisure & Life Style	
	Senate Military Affairs Comm. votes to temporarily hold up action on the promotion of Lt. Gen. Patton from the permanent rank of Colonel to Maj. General.	Leaders of the five railway unions of operating employes announce a nationwide strike has been called for Dec. 30 to enforce demands for a 30% wage increase .... WPB announces U.S. war expenditures in November were $7.794 billion, the highest to date, bringing the total since July 1940 to $146 billion.		Thomas W. (Fats) Waller, Negro composer, pianist and band leader, dies at 39 in Kansas City, Mo. .... Sir Alexander Korda announces he will head a new motion picture producing firm to be called Metro-Goldwyn-Mayer-London Films Ltd. and will undertake a 10-year, $140 million program .... Twentieth Century Fox and the Army Air Force sign a contract for the filming of the Air Forces' production of Moss Hart's play *Winged Victory*.	Dec. 15
		Senate Finance Comm. reports out a tax bill estimated to yield $2.284 billion, $144 million more than the House bill .... Atlantic Coast Line's southbound *Tamiami West Coast Champion* is derailed near Buie, N.C., throwing wreckage across parallel tracks used by northbound trains into which the *Tamiami East Coast Champion* crashes a half hour later; 73 persons are killed and more than 100 are injured.			Dec. 16
	Senate approves a bill providing $200 to $500 mustering-out pay for discharged service veterans.	UMW Pres. Lewis signs a wage contract with operators' associations representing two-thirds of the soft coal industry on terms approximating the contract with Solid Fuel Admin. Ickes.	British government reports it will return to the U.S. Smithsonian Institute the Wright brothers' plane used at Kitty Hawk, N.C.	Count Fleet is named "the horse of the year" in a poll by *Turf & Sport Digest* .... The last surviving original Daughter of the American Revolution, Mrs. Annie Knight Gregory, dies at 100 in Williamsport, Pa.	Dec. 17
Alaska Democrats vote to instruct territorial delegates to favor a fourth term for FDR.				Swedish athelete and track star Gunder Haegg is named the athelete of the year in an AP poll .... National Institute of Arts and Letters announces the election of three new members: W.E.B. DuBois, the first Negro ever elected, Carl Van Doren and Upton Sinclair, both authors.	Dec. 18
		A White House conference with five operating railroad brotherhood leaders and a committee representing the carriers adjourns after several hours without an agreement.		Washington Redskins defeat the N.Y. Giants, 28-0, to win the Eastern title of the NFL .... Doubleday, Doran announces the establishment of the George Washington Carver Memorial Award of $2,500 to be given for any book dealing with American Negroes "which seems to be worthy of this special recognition."	Dec. 19
		FDR summons the leaders of the railroad brotherhoods to the White House and urges them to accept the carriers' offer of an additional 4¢-an-hour increase — a total of 8¢ as compared with their demands for raises of $3-a-day .... Treasury Secy. Morgenthau assails Congress for reducing revenue in the tax bill from $10.5 billion to approximately $2.3 billion.			Dec. 20
Senate and House adjourn until the opening of the new session on Jan. 10, 1944.	Army Chief of Staff Marshall returns to Washington after attending the Cairo conference and stop-offs in the Pacific area for meetings with military leaders.	B.M. Jewell, chairman of a joint committee representing 1,100,000 workers of 15 non-operating railroad unions, announces they will join the strike called for Dec. 30 by the five operating brotherhoods as Congress recesses without approving an 8¢-an-hour pay increase.		Paul Lukas in *Watch on the Rhine*, and Greer Garson in *Random Harvest* are winners of the *Film Daily* poll to name the best film performances of 1943.	Dec. 21
		A committee of the five railroad brotherhoods submits a counter-proposal to the wage offers of carriers, asking a 64¢-a-day increase, two weeks paid vacation and time-and-one-half for overtime.		A federal court in N.Y. finds seven men guilty of extorting one million dollars from the motion picture industry through strike threats .... National Institute of Arts and Letters announces additional new members, including: Roy Harris, Quincy Porter, Louis Ayres, Isobel Bishop, Jo Davidson, Charles D. Maginnis and Benjamin W. Morris, 3d.	Dec. 22
ICC rules the Interstate Commerce Act was not violated by the Atlantic Coast Line's failure to serve 18 Negro seamen meals in a dining car, as the service to the Negroes in their seats was the same as diner service.		FDR instructs Atty. Gen. Biddle to take necessary legal steps to seize the nation's railroads if negotiations collapse.			Dec. 23

F	G	H	I	J
Includes elections, federal-state relations, civil rights and liberties, crime, the judiciary, education, health care, poverty, urban affairs and population.	*Includes formation and debate of U.S. foreign and defense policies, veterans affairs and defense spending. (Relations with specific foreign countries are usually found under the region concerned.)*	*Includes business, labor, agriculture, taxation, transportation, consumer affairs, monetary and fiscal policy, natural resources, pollution and accidents.*	*Includes worldwide scientific, medical and technological developments, natural phenomena, U.S. weather and natural disasters.*	*Includes the arts, religion, scholarship, communications media, sports, entertainment, fashions, fads and social life.*

	World Affairs	European War Zone	Pacific War Zone	The Americas	Other Countries & Territories
Dec. 24	In a radio address FDR says the U.S., U.K., Russia and China have agreed to maintain the postwar peace as long as necessary.	FDR announces Eisenhower will command the Allied forces to invade Western Europe .... In daylight nearly 3,000 Allied planes engage in record operations across the English Channel .... British units continue heavy street fighting against the Germans in Ortona .... Russian offensive aimed at Vitebsk, White Russia nets more than 60 inhabited places, including the large fortified center and rail station of Gorodok.	Chinese troops cross the Sungtze River.		Gen. Georges Catroux, representing the French National Comm. of Liberation, turns over government responsibility to Lebanese and Syrian administrations.
Dec. 25		Allies capture Mt. Sammucro, six miles east of Cassino .... Soviet troops capture 200 more inhabited places in their drive on Vitebsk.	U.S. Marines make two landings at points east and west of Cape Gloucester, New Britain Island .... Chinese troops occupy Kungan, forcing the Japanese across the Hutu River in an eastward retreat.	Ecuador orders several German and Italian nationals held incommunicado and notifies all Axis subjects to leave the country.	Leader of the All-India Moslem League Mohammed Ali Jinnah charges Britain has rejected the League's offer of aid after the war.
Dec. 26		British naval units attack and sink the German battleship *Scharnhorst* in Arctic waters off North Cape, Norway. The sinking leaves Germany with two known battleships, the *Tirptiz* and *Gneisenau* .... Russia resumes the offensive and rolls back the Germans 25 miles on a 50-mile front in the Ukraine .... Street-by-street fighting continues in Ortona, as the Allies slowly clear the northwestern part of the Adriatic port.	Emperor Hirohito tells the Japanese Diet "the war situation is serious," while Tokyo radio says Pacific fighting has reached the point where "the rise or fall of our nation will be decided."	Bolivia announces Axis firms there will be nationalized and their operations transferred to Bolivians.	
Dec. 27		Eisenhower tells an Algiers press conference that an Allied victory in Europe will come in 1944 .... German news agency reports Field Marshals Rommel and von Rundstedt have concluded conferences on measures to meet an Allied invasion and indicates that Rommel is satisfied with the strength of the German defenses .... German units evacuate Ortona on the Adriatic, taking new positions northwest of the town .... Russian troops occupy 30 places near Vitebsk and cut the Vitebsk-Polotsk railway near Dvorishche.	Marines consolidate their beachheads on both sides of Cape Gloucester and advance inland.	Inter-American Emergency Comm. for the Political Defense of the Continent adopts a resolution not to recognize regimes established by force without prior investigation and consultation by all American governments.	
Dec. 28	Union of South Africa P.M. Jan Christiaan Smuts states the future peace of the world depends upon a postwar organization including the U.S., U.K., Russia and China.	In their drive west of Kiev, Soviet units advance on a 65-mile front reaching Behji, five miles northeast of Korosten .... In the Italian mountains in the center of the trans-peninsular front, French Moroccan troops make short advances west of Castel San Vincenzo.			
Dec. 29		Adm. Sir Bertram Ramsay and Air Chief Marshal Trafford L. Leigh-Mallory are named to command Allied sea and air forces under Eisenhower .... Russian Army captures Korosten, an important rail center 90 miles northwest of Kiev .... American troops break into San Vittore, Italy, five miles east of Cassino .... Yugoslavian partisan units penetrate the Yugoslav-Italian border, attacking the German garrisons at Castelnuovo and Gouiza.	U.S. Marines advance to within a half mile of the Japanese airstrip on Cape Gloucester, New Britain.	Cuba and Costa Rica announce they will withhold recognition of the Bolivian revolutionary government .... Pres. Vargas is elected to the Brazilian academy of letters. He is the first chief exective to be named.	
Dec. 30		After a week-old counterattack by the Russians west of Kiev, 22 German divisions flee along a 186-mile front .... Yugoslavian partisans report driving the Germans from the Croatian provinces of Banija and Kordun .... Allies proceed across the Garigliano River at the Tyrrhenian end of the Italian front .... British troops push a mile beyond Ortona along the Adriatic coast on the route to Pescara.	U.S. Marines seize control of the Cape Gloucester air strips as the surviving Japanese flee to the surrounding hills.		
Dec. 31		Russians recapture the rail center of Zhitomir, 87 miles west of Kiev, as Russian penetration of the German lines reaches 200 miles .... Throughout his New Year's message, Hitler finds reasons for German military setbacks and warns that life for the German people will be worse if the war is lost .... AMG orders the removal from public office in Italy of all members of organizations of a Fascist tinge.		Argentine government dissolves all political parties.	

A	B	C	D	E
Includes developments that affect more than one world region, international organizations and important meetings of major world leaders.	*Includes all developments in European countries and military engagements between Allied and Axis powers in Africa and at sea.*	*Includes all developments in Japan and China, Japanese foreign policy and military actions in the Pacific region.*	*Includes all domestic and regional developments in Latin America, the Caribbean and Canada.*	*Includes developments in those independent nations and colonial possessions not covered in Columns B, C and D.*

U.S. Politics & Social Issues	U.S. Foreign Policy & Defense	U.S. Economy & Environment	Science, Technology & Nature	Culture, Leisure & Life Style	
	Rep. James W. Wadsworth (R, N.Y.) outlines a five-point program to maintain U.S. military strength as "peace insurance."	Brotherhood of Locomotive Engineers and Brotherhood of Railroad Trainmen call off the strike scheduled for Dec. 31, but the conductors, firemen and switchmen leave their strike call in effect .... NWLB Dir. William Davis telegraphs CIO Pres. Murray offering to reconvene the board and reconsider its vote rejecting the demand of the United Steel Workers of America that any new wage contracts carry a retroactive clause .... FDR signs the bill extending the CCC through Feb. 17, 1944.		*Motion Picture Herald* survey finds that Betty Grable is the number one box office attraction with Bob Hope second.	Dec. 24
		A $1,000,000 fire razes the waterfront area of Wildwood, N.J., destroying three theaters, an amusement pier, and other buildings.			Dec. 25
			American Institute of Electrical Engineers announces the 1943 Edison Medal goes to Dr. Vannevar Bush for "development of new applications of mathematics to engineering problems."	Chicago Bears beat the Washington Redskins, 41-12, to win the NFL championship .... American Library Assn. reports a survey of 110 libraries reveals a decrease in public reading but an improvement in taste, with entertainment reading suffering a heavy decline in favor of works dealing with international politics, aviation and postwar planning.	Dec. 26
		FDR orders War Secy. Henry L. Stimson to take over all railroads as of 7 p.m. today as three operating unions continue their refusal to accept his arbitration .... FEPC asks FDR to enforce its order to 16 Southeastern railroads and seven unions to end discrimination against Negroes.			Dec. 27
FDR says the "New Deal" cured the nation's "internal injuries" but that an expert surgeon, "Dr. Win-the-War," is needed to heal the broken bones suffered beginning Dec. 7, 1941.		Bureau of Labor Statistics reports 300 strikes in November involving 500,000 workers cost 2,285,000 man-days of idleness, amounting to one-third of 1% of available working time.		N.Y. Film Critics select the anti-Nazi film *Watch on the Rhine* as the best of 1943, Paul Lukas as the best actor and Ida Lupino, the best actress.	Dec. 28
The MacArthur for President Club enters the general's name in the Illinois presidential primary .... Sen. Edward V. Robertson (R, Wyo.) calls on FDR to state his 1944 political intentions.	*Time* Magazine names Army Chief of Staff Marshall as "man of the year" for transforming the U.S. into the world's most effective military power.	Leaders of the railway conductors, firemen's and switchmen's unions tell their members not to strike Dec. 30, but they refuse to accept FDR as an arbiter in the wage dispute.		The play *South Pacific* by Howard Rigsby and Dorothy Heyward opens in New York .... Gil Dodds, middle distance runner, is named winner of the John E. Sullivan Memorial Trophy for sportsmanship.	Dec. 29
		War Dept. announces it will retain control of the nation's railroads because the threatened strike has been "postponed" and not "cancelled." .... Treasury reports expenditures for 1943 at $87,932,000,000, of which $82,142,000,000 was for war costs .... OPA takes a number of canned vegetables and fruits off the ration list.		After a long series of Washington hearings in which Post Office lawyers sought to prove *Esquire* magazine was "lewd and lascivious," Postmaster Gen. Walker orders second class mailing privileges withdrawn effective Feb. 28, 1944 .... Dr. George Fisher is named National Scout Commissioner of the Boy Scouts of America, succeeding the late Daniel C. Beard .... Metropolitan Opera reveals it has obtained rights to the first performance outside of Russia of Sergei Prokofiev's *War and Peace.*	Dec. 30
		CIO Pres. Murray says his organization will make an annual minimum wage a 1944 political issue.		Louis Kaufman is fined $10,000 and sentenced to seven years' imprisonment. Six others convicted with him receive 10-year prison terms and $10,000 fines for extortion in the motion picture industry.	Dec. 31

F	G	H	I	J
Includes elections, federal-state relations, civil rights and liberties, crime, the judiciary, education, health care, poverty, urban affairs and population.	*Includes formation and debate of U.S. foreign and defense policies, veterans affairs and defense spending. (Relations with specific foreign countries are usually found under the region concerned.)*	*Includes business, labor, agriculture, taxation, transportation, consumer affairs, monetary and fiscal policy, natural resources, pollution and accidents.*	*Includes worldwide scientific, medical and technological developments, natural phenomena, U.S. weather and natural disasters.*	*Includes the arts, religion, scholarship, communications media, sports, entertainment, fashions, fads and social life.*

1944

U. S. Marines hit the beach during the invasion of Saipan in June. The strategic Marianas island became the base for the first U.S. bombing raids on Japan.

Soldiers of the U.S. 1st Army move through the Krinkelter Woods in Belgium just before the start of the Battle of the Bulge.

Delegates at the 1944 Democratic National Convention demonstrate for FDR. Many Democrats, uneasy about a fourth term for the President, supported Roosevelt in the absence of any other unifying candidate.

A German soldier, standing in front of a disabled U.S. halftrack, orders his unit to advance during the Battle of the Bulge.

U.S. tanks cautiously enter the ruined Italian village of Cosma E' Damiano on the German Gustav Line in May.

Economist John Maynard Keynes, whose theories largely supplanted the conventional wisdom of bankers during the Depression, represents Britain at the International Monetary Conference in Bretton Woods, N.H.

Preceding page: Exhausted survivors of the smashed German Army Group Center go into captivity in White Russia. Few survived the rigors of Russian POW camps.

A Negro Army unit lands near Hollandia, New Guinea in May. This fighting unit was not typical of the wartime military role of Negroes, who usually filled service and support positions in the segregated Army.

Women didn't fight, but some aspects of Army life were the same for both sexes. These WACs clean their mess kits in a British camp as a male comrade looks on grinning.

Invasion of France: Lines of U.S. troops and equipment move up the Normandy beachhead on D-Day plus one, June 7.

"Fresh, spirited American troops, flushed with victory, are bringing in thousands of hungry, ragged, battle-weary prisoners . . ."
(News item)

Bill Mauldin, *Stars and Stripes* cartoonist, championed the American dogface against the romanticizers of war. This Pulitzer Prize-winning cartoon gives the soldier's view of daily life at the front.

British soldiers approach the ruins of Sant' Angelo south of Rome.

	World Affairs	European War Zone	Pacific War Zone	The Americas	Other Countries & Territories
Jan.		Russian forces lift the German blockade of Leningrad .... U.S. forces in Italy establish a beachhead behind German lines at Anzio.	U.S. air and naval forces raid the Marshall Islands preparatory to invasion.	Argentina moves against domestic Axis groups and severs diplomatic relations with Germany and Japan.	
Feb.	U.N. Food Commission completes plans for postwar food production and distribution.	U.S. forces hold their beachhead at Anzio against strong German counterattacks.	U.S. forces clear Japanese from the Marshall Islands, capturing Kwajalein and Eniwetok atolls.	An Army coup in Argentina gives General Edelmiro Farrell executive powers.	American companies announce plans to increase Saudi Arabian oil production to meet war needs.
March		British and U.S. air forces begin a concentrated attack on Berlin .... U.S. and German forces battle indecisively for control of Cassino on the Gustav line .... Russian spring offensive drives the Germans from the Ukraine .... German forces occupy Hungary.	Chinese and U.S. troops link up to battle the Japanese in Burma.	Hemispheric nations divide in their decisions to recognize the new Argentine military regime.	Arab statesmen protest the anticipated creation of a Jewish state in Palestine.
Apr.		Russian advance reaches the Czech and Rumanian frontiers and eliminates German positions in the Crimea.	British forces contain a Japanese drive into Manipur State, India .... MacArthur's naval, air and ground forces wipe out the Japanese base at Hollandia, New Guinea.	Attempted political revolts are smashed in Bolivia and El Salvador.	
May		British and U.S. air forces begin an attack on the German oil industry .... Fighting on the Eastern front subsides temporarily as Russian forces prepare for their summer offensive .... Germans begin deportation of Hungarian Jews to Auschwitz.	U.S. and Australian forces continue to advance in New Guinea .... Japanese and Chinese troops battle indecisively for control of the Peking-Hankow rail line in central China.	Argentina tightens censorship on pro-Allied radio and press.	
June		U.S. and British forces invade France and consolidate their position on the Normandy coast .... Germans begin bombardment of London with pilotless flying bombs.	U.S. Marines invade the Marianas, establishing a foothold on Saipan. U.S. Navy wins the Battle of the Philippine Sea .... MacArthur's forces complete the conquest of New Guinea, isolating the Japanese garrison at Rabaul.	Guatemalan President Jorge Ubico places the country under military rule because of threatened Nazi activities.	
July	Representatives of Allied nations confer in Bretton Woods, N.H. on the postwar world economic system and agree to establish a World Bank and International Monetary Fund.	German Army Group Center disintegrates in White Russia under Soviet attacks, with the loss of 350,000 men. Russian forces advance to the outskirts of Warsaw .... U.S. forces under Gen. Patton break out of the Normandy area in France.	U.S. forces complete the conquest of Saipan and establish footholds on Guam and Tinian in the Marianas .... Chinese forces gain against the Japanese in Hunan and Yunnan provinces.	Juan Peron becomes Argentina's vice president .... Frederico Ponce becomes president of Guatemala.	Gandhi and Indian Moslem leader Mohammed Ali Jinnah discuss the creation of separate Hindu and Moslem states in India.
Aug.	Allied representatives attend a World Security Conference at the Dumbarton Oaks mansion in Washington to formulate plans for a postwar United Nations organization.	Allied forces invade the French Mediterranean coast, pushing up the Rhone River .... Allies win undisputed control of the air over Germany .... Polish underground forces rise unsuccessfully against the Germans in Warsaw .... German forces occupy Slovakia following an unsuccessful partisan rising .... Germans complete the liquidation of the Lodz ghetto, the last major Jewish settlement in Poland.	U.S. forces clear the Japanese from the Marianas, capturing Guam and Tinian .... British forces drive the Japanese from India.	Argentina is ostracized by a few Latin American nations and the U.S. freezes Argentine assets for its failure to cooperate in hemispheric defense.	Britain refuses to grant India immediate independence in return for war cooperation.
Sept.	FDR and Churchill hold the "Octagon" conference in Quebec, discussing war strategy and postwar occupation plans for Germany.	Russia forces Bulgaria and Rumania out of the war .... U.S. forces breach the Gothic line north of Rome, while British forces overrun Belgium and enter Holland .... U.S. and British troops unsuccessfully attempt a quick penetration of Germany near the Dutch border (Operation Market Garden) .... German rocket attacks on England begin.	U.S. carrier-based planes raid the Philippines, while Marines establish a foothold on Peleliu.	Argentina continues to come under attack for its "pro-Axis" neutrality stand.	Gandhi and Ali Jinnah fail to settle Hindu-Moslem differences in India.
Oct.	Dumbarton Oaks Conference ends with the Big Four in agreement on the United Nations' framework.	U.S. troops move slowly into Germany, taking Aachen .... British forces occupy Greece .... Russian armies invade Hungary, Czechoslovakia and East Prussia, while German troops withdraw from the Riga area on the Baltic.	U.S. carrier-based planes attack Japanese bases on Formosa .... U.S. forces under MacArthur establish a foothold on Leyte Island in the Philippines, while the U.S. Navy wins the Battle of Leyte Gulf .... Japanese kamikaze attacks on U.S. naval vessels begin.	Military governments are formed in El Salvador and Guatemala.	
Nov.	International Aviation Conference meets in Chicago to formulate regulations for postwar commercial flying.	U.S. forces continue to advance in Germany, while Allies resume their offensive in Italy.	U.S. forces occupy most of Leyte Island .... Japanese kamikaze attacks on U.S. vessels supporting the Leyte operation continue .... U.S. bombers based on Saipan begin to attack Tokyo.	Protests against the sending of additional troops abroad create a political crisis in Canada.	
Dec.		U.S. forces contain the German offensive in the Battle of the Bulge .... Communist and royalist partisans clash in Athens.	U.S. forces complete the conquest of Leyte and establish a foothold on Mindoro Island in the Philippines .... British units based in India invade Burma.		Iranian parliament moves to prevent the granting of oil concessions to foreign nations.
	A *Includes developments that affect more than one world region, international organizations and important meetings of major world leaders.*	B *Includes all developments in European countries and military engagements between Allied and Axis powers in Africa and at sea.*	C *Includes all developments in Japan and China, Japanese foreign policy and military actions in the Pacific region.*	D *Includes all domestic and regional developments in Latin America, the Caribbean and Canada.*	E *Includes developments in those independent nations and colonial possessions not covered in Columns B, C and D.*

U.S. Politics & Social Issues	U.S. Foreign Policy & Defense	U.S. Economy & Environment	Science, Technology & Nature	Culture, Leisure & Life Style	
Several Democratic groups come out in favor of a fourth term for FDR.		A House special committee begins to study the problem of postwar economic reconversion.	British medical researchers report the successful use of blood from cattle as a substitute for human plasma.		Jan.
					Feb.
FDR begins to enter state presidential primaries and wins in New Hampshire, though he is not an announced candidate.	FDR supports establishment of a Jewish state in Palestine.	Wartime shortages bring further restrictions on civilian alcohol and gasoline consumption.	Several penicillin manufacturers agree to exchange information in an effort to increase production.		March
Supreme Court rules an end to racial discriminatory practices in Florida and Texas.	Army reaches its maximum strength of 7.7 million men, and plans are made to meet replacement requirements.	NWLB opens hearings on a labor dispute resulting from attempted unionization of Montgomery Ward workers.	Tornadoes sweep Arkansas, Georgia and South Carolina.	New York's Metropolitan Museum of Art reveals the return of valuable art objects which were hidden after Pearl Harbor.	Apr.
FDR and N.Y. Gov. Thomas Dewey gain the lead in delegate strength for the Democratic and Republican presidential nominations.	Navy admirals from the Pacific theater gather in San Francisco, and FDR meets with Ambassadors Harriman and Winant in Washington for war strategy talks.	Federal government control of Montgomery Ward's Chicago operations ends after a CIO affiliate wins election there.		Television stations reach an estimated 22 million viewers.	May
Dewey wins the GOP presidential nomination and Norman Thomas the Socialist Party candidacy.				Ball-point pens hit the U.S. market and rapidly become the nation's favorite writing implement.	June
FDR accepts re-nomination as Democratic candidate for President.	After meeting with de Gaulle, FDR extends de facto recognition to the Free French government.	Politicians and economists begin debating proposals on tax programs, materials allocation and employment guidelines for postwar economic reconversion.		On Broadway, *Othello* and *Ziegfeld Follies* close after lengthy performances.	July
Both major party presidential candidates prepare for the campaign as surveys already proclaim FDR the winner.	Debate over the size and scope of the postwar Army begins.	Because of labor disputes, federal authorities temporarily seize and operate the Philadelphia Transportation Company, 103 Midwestern motor freight lines and over 100 West Coast machinery plants.			Aug.
Dewey begins his presidential campaign, describing FDR's New Deal policies as failures.	House Naval Affairs Comm. asks for an immediate investigation of the Pearl Harbor attack.		A hurricane along the Atlantic Coast causes $100 million in property damage.		Sept.
	Army and Navy state that their Pearl Harbor investigations will be kept secret because of classified materials.	With the easing of war demands, the WPB permits the expansion of civilian goods production.			Oct.
FDR wins an unprecedented fourth presidential term, and Democrats retain control of Congress.					Nov.
Army liquidates most internment camps for Japanese-Americans, allowing them to return to the West Coast.	Stimson and Forrestal announce that Army and Navy investigations of Pearl Harbor preclude the court-martialing of Adm. Kimmel and Gen. Short.	Material and manpower shortages limit civilian goods production to their present levels.			Dec.
F	G	H	I	J	
Includes elections, federal-state relations, civil rights and liberties, crime, the judiciary, education, health care, poverty, urban affairs and population.	*Includes formation and debate of U.S. foreign and defense policies, veterans affairs and defense spending. (Relations with specific foreign countries are usually found under the region concerned.)*	*Includes business, labor, agriculture, taxation, transportation, consumer affairs, monetary and fiscal policy, natural resources, pollution and accidents.*	*Includes worldwide scientific, medical and technological developments, natural phenomena, U.S. weather and natural disasters.*	*Includes the arts, religion, scholarship, communications media, sports, entertainment, fashions, fads and social life.*	

	World Affairs	European War Zone	Pacific War Zone	The Americas	Other Countries & Territories
Jan. 1	FDR says the U.N. should continue after the war to deal with problems of social and economic distress.	Soviet offensive west of Kiev moves to within 27 miles of the Polish border .... Polish Pres. Wladislaw Raczkiewicz says Poland's borders must be respected after the war .... Lt. Gen. Ira C. Eaker says American planes made 64,000 offensive sorties over Europe in 1943, dropping 55,000 tons of bombs .... Foreign Economic Administration reports Germany "cannot possibly meet the increasing strength and pressures" of the U.N. offensives in 1944.	In an attack on Keviang, New Ireland Island, Allied planes leave two Japanese cruisers and one destroyer afire as a result of repeated torpedo and bomb hits.		
Jan. 2		Canadian troops take a strongly defended peak three miles beyond Ortona on the Italian Adriatic coast .... On the Kiev front Soviet troops take Poyaski, within 14 miles of the Polish border .... Moscow discloses the new national anthem, which replaces the *Internationale*, is the *Hymn of the Soviet Union.*	U.S. Marines move 1½ miles beyond the Cape Gloucester airport on New Britain, counting 1,000 Japanese slain .... U.S. forces land at Saidor on the north coast of New Guinea, 55 miles southeast of the Japanese airbase at Madang .... Chiang Kai-shek claims FDR approved his suggestions at the Cairo Conference "that all Japanese militarists be wiped out and that Japanese police be purged of every vestige of aggressive elements."		
Jan. 3		Advance units of the Soviet Army west of Kiev reach the old Polish border after capturing Olevsk .... In their second attack within 24 hours, British planes drop 1,100 tons of bombs on Berlin, reporting the Chancellery building virtually destroyed .... British troops improve their positions along the Adriatic coast and link the cities of Villa Grande and Miglianico.	U.S. planes complete two days of raids on the oil center of Yenangyaung, Burma, dropping more than 130 tons of bombs.	Argentine Foreign Office announces the recognition of the revolutionary government of Bolivia.	
Jan. 4		Soviet troops capture the Nazi defense base and railway junction of Belaya Tserkov, 50 miles south of Kiev.	U.S. Marines begin a drive against Japanese positions at Borgen Bay in the Cape Gloucester area of New Britain .... U.S. planes raid the Jaluit and Mili atolls of the Marshall Islands.		
Jan. 5	AFL Vice Pres. Matthew Woll announces the union's refusal to send delegates to the British-sponsored international meeting of trade union representatives in June because of Russian participation.	Russian 2nd Ukranian Army army opens a new offensive and forces a breakthrough on a front 62 miles long to a depth of 25 miles .... After five days of fighting, Russian troops take Berdichev, an important rail center 100 miles west-southwest of Kiev .... U.S. forces gain approximately one mile along a 10-mile front between Venafro and Rocca d' Evandro and extend their holdings in San Vittore.	Chinese troops reportedly advance on the suburbs of Owchihkow, Yangtze River port north of Tungting Lake, after capturing all surrounding villages.	Argentina establishes strict control of the press and forbids publication of news "contrary to the general interests of the nation."	
Jan. 6		Union of Polish Patriots announces in Moscow a proposal to cede sections of eastern Poland to Russia and extend Poland's westward borders into Germany as compensation .... First Ukrainian Army captures Rakitno, 10 miles inside the prewar Polish border .... In its drive on Cassino, American troops take the village of San Vittore after a desparate German house-to-house stand.	U.S. bombers raid the Japanese bases at Wotje and Taroa in the Marshall Islands.		
Jan. 7		Chief of the U.S. Army Air Forces Gen. Henry H. Arnold says three-quarters of Berlin is already destroyed .... Second Ukrainian Army encircles the important base at Kirovograd in the upper part of the Dnieper bend.	Allies claim that through Jan. 4 600 Japanese have been killed in the Marines' offensive toward Bogen Bay on New Britain Island.	Secy. of State Hull says he has information which "strengthens the belief that forces outside of Bolivia .... inspired and aided the Bolivian revolution."	

A	B	C	D	E
Includes developments that affect more than one world region, international organizations and important meetings of major world leaders.	*Includes all developments in European countries and military engagements between Allied and Axis powers in Africa and at sea.*	*Includes all developments in Japan and China, Japanese foreign policy and military actions in the Pacific region.*	*Includes all domestic and regional developments in Latin America, the Caribbean and Canada.*	*Includes developments in those independent nations and colonial possessions not covered in Columns B, C and D.*

U.S. Politics & Social Issues	U.S. Foreign Policy & Defense	U.S. Economy & Environment	Science, Technology & Nature	Culture, Leisure & Life Style	
	Lt. Gen. Alexander A. Vandegrift takes over as new commandant of the Marine Corps.	Labor Dept. reports retail prices of staple articles rose 3½% in 1943, the smallest yearly advance since 1940 .... Theodore W. Kheel is named executive director of the NWLB.		Sir Edward Luytens, reputed to be Great Britain's greatest architect since Sir Christopher Wren and president of the Royal Academy since 1938, dies at 74 in London .... Major bowl scores: Rose — USC 29, Washington 0; Sugar — Georgia Tech. 20, Tulsa 18; Orange — LSU 19, Texas A&M 14; Cotton — Randolph Field 7, Texas 7..	Jan. 1
	United Jewish Appeal for Refugees. Overseas Needs and Palestine announces in New York it has raised approximately $75,000,000 since 1939 to help almost 2,000,000 Jews.				Jan. 2
Rep. James M. Curley (D, Mass.) and five associates of the Engineers' Group Inc. are indicted by a Washington federal grand jury for fraud .... FDR names Walter Stacy chairman of a committee to study alleged racial discrimination against Negroes by Southern railroads and three unions.	Unexplained explosions sink the destroyer *Turner* in N.Y. Bay, with 163 survivors rescued .... Supreme Court rules that a draftee who objects to his classification must report for duty before taking court action .... A federal grand jury in Washington indicts 30 persons on charges of attempting to incite mutiny in the armed forces and set up a Nazi regime in the U.S.			FDR deeds his Hyde Park home and 30 acres of land to the government as a national historic site, retaining the right of occupancy during the lifetimes of his immediate family.	Jan. 3
Sen. Clyde Reed (R, Kans.) and Reps. Andrew May (D, Ky.) and Charles Plumley (R, Vt.) agree with an anonymous statement of Dec. 31, since attributed to Army Chief of Staff George Marshall, that the threatened steel and railroad strikes might be used as Axis propaganda.	It is announced in San Francisco that Vice Adm. John Greenslade will retire Feb. 1 as commander of the Western Sea Frontier and commandant of the 12th Naval District.			Walter Bronson (Bide) Dudley, dramatic critic, playwright and radio commentator, dies at 66 in New York.	Jan. 4
U.S. Army and Navy outline a soldier vote plan to Frank Bane, executive director of the Council of State Governments, covering the physical details of distribution and return of ballots .... Rep. Jessie Sumner (R, Ill.) says she will not be a candidate for reelection because "practically all the major questions of policy are now decided in the White House rather than by Congress."		WPB recommends to the Defense Plant Corp. in Washington further cutbacks in the steel production expansion program.		Doubleday, Doran announces a prize of $20,000 for the best novel submitted by any writer on any theme in a contest to run from June 1, 1944 to Jan. 1, 1945.	Jan. 5
	Navy Secy. James Forrestal says 65 aircraft carriers were completed in 1943 .... FDR reports Lend-Lease aid to American allies totaled $18.6 billion through Dec. 1, 1943.	Justice Dept. files suit in a N.Y. federal court, charging four corporations with conducting an international cartel in the chemical industry.	U.S. Army discloses the development of a propellerless fighter plane capable of flying at speed of 500 to 600 mph powered by jet propulsion.	Ida M. Tarbell, biographer of Lincoln and author who won fame for her "expose" of the Standard Oil "trust," dies at 86 in Bridgeport, Conn. .... OWI discloses Arturo Toscanini has completed making a film presentation of Verdi's *Hymn of the Nations* for the U.S. government.	Jan. 6
	WPB announces American factories produced 85,946 planes in 1943, an increase of 80% over 1942 .... Selective Service announces that as of Feb. 1 local draft board screening examinations will be eliminated and draftees will be given military physical tests at least 21 days before induction .... Three German-born naturalized citizens—Fritz Schroeder, Hans P. Koenig and Carl C. Kranz—are sentenced to eight years in prison for violation of the 1917 Espionage Act.	American Iron & Steel Institute reports steel production for 1943 reached an all-time high of 88,872,598 net tons .... Justice Dept. issues subpoenas for the records of 85 more distillers, vintners, processers and wholesalers of liquor in connection with a federal grand jury investigation of the industry.			Jan. 7

F	G	H	I	J
Includes elections, federal-state relations, civil rights and liberties, crime, the judiciary, education, health care, poverty, urban affairs and population.	*Includes formation and debate of U.S. foreign and defense policies, veterans affairs and defense spending. (Relations with specific foreign countries are usually found under the region concerned.)*	*Includes business, labor, agriculture, taxation, transportation, consumer affairs, monetary and fiscal policy, natural resources, pollution and accidents.*	*Includes worldwide scientific, medical and technological developments, natural phenomena, U.S. weather and natural disasters.*	*Includes the arts, religion, scholarship, communications media, sports, entertainment, fashions, fads and social life.*

	World Affairs	European War Zone	Pacific War Zone	The Americas	Other Countries & Territories
Jan. 8	State Dept. adviser on European political affairs James Dunn says agreements concluded in Moscow averted "the dread certainty" of a third world war.	Second Ukrainian Army captures more than 80 inhabited places, including Kirovograd, 130 miles west of Dniepropretrovsk .... The German General Staff is reportedly speeding defense preparations in France and the Low Countries and is bringing its estimated 45 divisions there to full strength .... American troops mop up the remaining German resistance in San Giusta, as Allied forces press their attack on Cassino.			
Jan. 9		Allied units reach to within 4½ miles of Cassino on the northern end of their 10-mile line .... Germans add large reinforcements to their units in an effort to eliminate the Yugoslavian partisans in western and central Bosnia .... Russian offensives continue in the Ukraine with more than 110 localities being captured, including Polonnoye and Alexandrovka .... Antanas Smetona, first president of Lithuania and head of its exiled government, dies at 69 in a fire in Cleveland, Ohio.			Iraq and Syria announce an agreement on questions of unity.
Jan. 10		Berne sources report an Italian Fascist tribunal in Verona has condemned Count Ciano and 17 other members of the Fascist Grand Council to death for treason .... American and British units seize new heights on both sides of the road leading to Cassino .... Russia reaffirms claims to eastern Poland through the official news agency Tass.			
Jan. 11		Count Ciano and four others convicted of treason in Verona are executed by firing squad .... First Ukrainian Army advances 39 miles inside the prewar Polish borders .... U.S. planes bomb Piraeus, Greece, port of Athens .... More than 700 Flying Fortresses and Liberators raid three of Germany's most important fighter assembly plants at Oschersleben, Halberstadt and Brunswick.	In the face of strong Japanese opposition, Allied troops take Maungdaw and continue down the Mayu Peninsula in Burma.		
Jan. 12		On the second day of a new offensive in southern White Russia, Soviet troops advance nine miles along a 19-mile front .... German forces lose Cervaro, four miles east of the Allied drive on Cassino .... French troops take two heights in the northern sector of the Cassino front and advance more than half a mile.	U.S. planes bomb Takao, Formosa in their second raid on the Japanese-held island.	All political activity in Argentina is outlawed by a decree.	
Jan. 13		Churchill and de Gaulle complete two days of military and political talks in Marrakesh, Morocco .... American troops move beyond Cerfaro to threaten the northern edge of Mt. Trocchio, three miles from Cassino.	Allied troops pressing toward Borgen Bay, east of Cape Gloucester, New Britain, count another 500 Japanese dead, bringing the total to 2,975.	U.S. Foreign Economic Administration notifies exporters that it will pass on all applications for exports to Bolivia.	
Jan. 14		Polish government-in-exile in London asks the U.S. and Britain to act as intermediaries in discussions with Russia .... In their White Russia drive, Soviet forces push westward 20 miles beyond Mozyr to take Skrygalovo on the south bank of the Pripet River .... French units capture Acquafondata and three nearby heights in the Allied drive on Cassino.	American forces take the important hill 660 in the Borgen Bay area of New Britain.		

	A	B	C	D	E
	Includes developments that affect more than one world region, international organizations and important meetings of major world leaders.	*Includes all developments in European countries and military engagements between Allied and Axis powers in Africa and at sea.*	*Includes all developments in Japan and China, Japanese foreign policy and military actions in the Pacific region.*	*Includes all domestic and regional developments in Latin America, the Caribbean and Canada.*	*Includes developments in those independent nations and colonial possessions not covered in Columns B, C and D.*

U.S. Politics & Social Issues	U.S. Foreign Policy & Defense	U.S. Economy & Environment	Science, Technology & Nature	Culture, Leisure & Life Style	
	Selective Service announces that no further occupational deferments will be granted to men in the 18-21 age group, with a few exceptions.	FDR offers three operating railroad brotherhoods the same terms granted to the Railroad Trainmen and Locomotive Engineers, provided they definitely cancel their strike call and sign contracts with the carriers .... Maury Maverick is named vice chairman of the WPB in charge of the Smaller War Plants Corp. .... William K. Vanderbilt, former president of the New York Central Railroad and a great-grandson of the founder of the Vanderbilt fortune, dies at 65 in New York.		Bill Terry, former N.Y. Giant great, announces his retirement to go into the cotton business.	Jan. 8
Claude A. Watson is nominated as the presidential candidate of the Prohibition Party and calls for a fight against "governmental bureaucracy and extravagance and the strongly entrenched liquor power."		AFL Pres. Green and the CIO's Postwar Planning Comm. urge the creation of centralized agencies to plan reconversion of industry to peacetime activities.			Jan. 9
FDR says Atty. Gen. Francis Biddle has notified him that it is unconstitutional for members of Congress to hold their seats while serving in the armed forces .... The 78th Congress reconvenes for its second session .... CP General Secy. Earl Browder says the American organization is abandoning its function as a political party and will not raise the issue of socialism in the postwar period "in such a form .... as to weaken national unity." .... U.S. Court of Appeals in Washington affirms the conviction of George Sylvester Viereck for violation of the Foreign Agents Registration Act.					Jan. 10
GOP National Comm. announces its 1944 presidential nominating convention will open June 26 in Chicago .... Census Bureau announces that the 1943 birth rate was the greatest in U.S. history with 3.2 million births.		FDR asks Congress for a national service law "to prevent strikes" and to make available for essential war service "every able-bodied adult in the nation."			Jan. 11
		AFL and CIO presidents Green and Murray tell FDR that labor will strongly oppose a compulsory labor system .... FDR submits plans to Congress for a 34,000-mile federally aided road program, costing an estimated $750,000,000 for 10 to 20 years and employing an estimated two million .... A federal court jury in Providence, R.I. finds the Anaconda Wire & Cable Co. guilty of conspiracy to defraud the government with defective wire and cable.		The film Lifeboat, directed by Alfred Hitchcock and featuring Tallulah Bankhead, opens in New York.	Jan. 12
Rep. Albert Gore (D, Tenn.) says he will resign from the Army to resume his seat in Congress.		FDR presents Congress with a $99.769 billion budget outlining the requirements for victory and a demobilization plan .... Atty. Gen. Biddle orders an investigation of a charge that the $750,000 CIO political fund violates the Connally-Smith anti-strike law provisions forbidding political contributions by labor organizations .... N.J. Atty. Gen. David Wilentz rules that the state and its political subdivisions have no legal authority to enter into bargaining agreements with trade unions.		FCC votes against barring newspapers from acquiring radio stations .... Final judgement is filed in a N.Y. federal court enjoining the AP from rejecting membership applications on the grounds of competition between the applicant and members.	Jan. 13
New Hampshire Democrats name a slate of presidential delegates who support a fourth term for FDR .... WRA announces the Army has restored the Tule Lake, Calif. Japanese Segregation Center to full civil administration.	Selective Service says an additional 700,000 recruits must be called up in the first six months of 1944 to meet armed forces requirements.	The three railroad brotherhoods covering firemen, enginemen, conductors and switchmen accept wage terms suggested by FDR.	*British Medical Journal* reports the successful use of blood from bullocks and heifers as a substitute for human plasma.		Jan. 14

F	G	H	I	J
Includes elections, federal-state relations, civil rights and liberties, crime, the judiciary, education, health care, poverty, urban affairs and population.	*Includes formation and debate of U.S. foreign and defense policies, veterans affairs and defense spending. (Relations with specific foreign countries are usually found under the region concerned.)*	*Includes business, labor, agriculture, taxation, transportation, consumer affairs, monetary and fiscal policy, natural resources, pollution and accidents.*	*Includes worldwide scientific, medical and technological developments, natural phenomena, U.S. weather and natural disasters.*	*Includes the arts, religion, scholarship, communications media, sports, entertainment, fashions, fads and social life.*

	World Affairs	European War Zone	Pacific War Zone	The Americas	Other Countries & Territories
Jan. 15		American troops take Mt. Trocchio, the last mountain obstacle before Cassino .... In a three-way drive on the Nazi lines before the Baltic states, Russian troops open a new offensive in the Leningrad and Lake Ilmen areas and near Nevel.		Puerto Rico completes its program of purchase of electric power utilities and becomes the first U.S. territory or state with public ownership in this field.	
Jan. 16		Eisenhower arrives in London to take command of the Allied forces to invade the European continent .... Russian government rejects the Polish bid to discuss boundary issues and ignores its plea for resumption of diplomatic relations .... Moscow announces that in the Dec. 24-Jan. 13 period Russian forces alone killed more than 100,000 Germans west and south of Kiev .... American troops reach the east bank of the Rapido River, two miles east of Cassino.		Severe earthquakes virtually destroy the Andes Mountain town of San Juan in western Argentina and cause heavy damage to others.	
Jan. 17	Colombia becomes the 34th nation to adhere to the U.N. agreement.	An American patrol crosses to the west bank of the Rapido River just north of Cassino and penetrates 100 yards into German defenses .... Russian troops in Poland seize Tuchin, 40 miles northeast of Rovno.	Navy planes attack installations on Kusaie Island, easternmost of Japan's Caroline Islands, including the base on Truk.		
Jan. 18	Dir. Herbert H. Lehman announces the appointment of Alexeyovich Menshikov, a member of the Soviet delegation, as deputy director of UNRRA.	Churchill returns to London after an 11-week absence during which he traveled 10,000 miles. He discloses he has been convalescing from pneumonia at Marrakesh, French Morocco since Dec. 27 .... In two new northern offensives, Russian troops break the Nazi lines 25 miles west of Leningrad and on the Volkhov front north of Novgorod .... British troops cross the Garigliano River at the southern end of the Italian front and despite strong opposition manage to establish bridgeheads at three points .... Leader of the United Irish opposition party in the Dail Eireann, William T. Cosgrove, announces his retirement due to poor health; Thomas O'Higgins will succeed him.	Allied forces open a new offensive in northern Burma in the Kyankshaw area .... Australia and New Zealand conclude an agreement for cooperative action in the South Pacific.		
Jan. 19		British forces along the Tyrrhenian coast drive into the outskirts of Minturno after capturing Sujo, Tufo and Argento .... Russian troops occupy new positions in the Novosokolniki area opposite Latvia and capture Goshcha, 17 miles east of Rovno, in fighting along Polish frontier .... British Foreign Secy. Eden tells the Commons he has advised Spain "of the serious effect" that "continuing unneutral assistance to our enemies" must have on Anglo-Spanish relations.	China-based U.S. planes bomb the dock area at Campha and barracks at Moncay in French Indochina.	A spokesman for the Inter-American Emergency Comm. for the Political Defense of the Continent discloses in Montevideo that Bolivian revolutionaries were in touch with Nazi agents in Argentina prior to the Dec. 20, 1943 Bolivian coup .... Venezuelan Pres. Gen. Isaias Medina is received by FDR at the White House.	
Jan. 20		Russian forces west of Leningrad cut off the German corridor to the Gulf of Finland .... British units take Minturno, two miles inland from the Gulf of Gaeta, and advance to a point five miles northwest .... Berlin radio says all civilians have been removed from Helgoland, the German North Sea naval base and island fortress.		Argentina decrees the Army may expropriate privately owned materials and equipment because of shortages reportedly due to U.S. refusal to extend Lend-Lease aid.	
Jan. 21		Russian offensive in the Leningrad area brings the capture of Mga, Vitino and Mutakyuya .... U.S. and Britain reach an agreement with the Norwegian government in exile in London on terms of restoring civil administration once the Germans are driven out.	Gen. Tojo says air power will decide the Pacific war, in which there is "only a hair's breadth between victory and defeat." .... Australian troops advance to the watershed of the Faria River in Ramu Valley, New Guinea, while Allied planes attack Japanese positions on the upper reaches of the river .... Aleutian-based bombers raid Japan's Paramushiro Island in the Kuriles twice today.	Bolivian Pres. Gualberto Villarroel says his regime is not sympathetic to fascism and that State Secy. Hull does not understand the reasons for its revolution.	

	A	B	C	D	E
	Includes developments that affect more than one world region, international organizations and important meetings of major world leaders.	*Includes all developments in European countries and military engagements between Allied and Axis powers in Africa and at sea.*	*Includes all developments in Japan and China, Japanese foreign policy and military actions in the Pacific region.*	*Includes all domestic and regional developments in Latin America, the Caribbean and Canada.*	*Includes developments in those independent nations and colonial possessions not covered in Columns B, C and D.*

U.S. Politics & Social Issues	U.S. Foreign Policy & Defense	U.S. Economy & Environment	Science, Technology & Nature	Culture, Leisure & Life Style	
	Under Secy. of State Edward B. Stettinius Jr. says "anything other than complete cooperation with Soviet Russia after the war would be blundering."	WPB reports 1943 war expenditures as $85.135 billion.			Jan. 15
Vermont Democratic state convention endorses FDR for a fourth term and wires a request that he accept the nomination.					Jan. 16
Joseph Savage is elected national chairman of the MacArthur Clubs to seek the GOP presidential nomination for the General . . . . Atty. Gen. Biddle announces Louis (Lepke) Buchalter will be surrendered to N.Y. State, where he is scheduled to be executed for murder.		The fourth War Loan drive is launched in a national radio broadcast seeking $14 billion.		Byron Nelson wins the $10,000 San Francisco open golf tournament with a 13 under par 275.	Jan. 17
	FEA reports American Lend-Lease shipments to Russia reached a record $338,000,000 in November.	Secy. Stimson returns the railroads to private operation after FDR announces agreements calling for wage increases of one to five percent.			Jan. 18
Mayors of 250 American and 19 Canadian cities meet in Chicago to discuss postwar public works programs.	House passes and sends to the Senate a bill providing mustering-out pay of $100 to $300 for war veterans.	Stimson says he favors immediate enactment of a national service act because "industrial unrest and lack of a sense of patriotic responsibility" has angered men in the armed forces . . . . AFL metal trades division Pres. John Frey urges that some 25 federal agencies now dealing with labor problems be merged into the Labor Dept.		Leopold Stokowski accepts an invitation to organize and conduct a 30-piece orchestra for the N.Y.C. Center of Music and Drama, to be known as the N.Y.C. Symphony.	Jan. 19
Sen. Wallace White Jr. (R, Me.) is named acting minority leader by a caucus of GOP senators to serve during the illness of Charles McNary.	Army announces that loyal Japanese-Americans will henceforth be accepted for military duty . . . . Stimson says Gen. MacArthur will not be retired when he reaches the retirement age of 64 on Jan. 26.	Senate confirms the renomination of Marriner S. Eccles to a 14-year term as a governor of the Federal Reserve System.			Jan. 20
Democratic national committeemen from 12 Midwestern states adopt a resolution endorsing FDR for a fourth term.		Senate passes a tax bill to raise an estimated $2.275 billion in new revenue and sends it to conference.	Stevens Inst. of Technology Pres. Harvey Davis announces plans to establish the Stevens Research Foundation for postwar work on new products, uses for old ones and better manufacturing methods.	The magazine *Esquire* sues in federal district court to restrain Postmaster General Walker from revoking its second class mailing privileges . . . . Boston Braves are sold to Joseph Maney, Guido Rugo and Louis Perini . . . . James Harper, one-time mayor of New York and founder of Harper & Brothers publishers, dies at 64 in Pelham, N.Y.	Jan. 21

F	G	H	I	J
Includes elections, federal-state relations, civil rights and liberties, crime, the judiciary, education, health care, poverty, urban affairs and population.	*Includes formation and debate of U.S. foreign and defense policies, veterans affairs and defense spending. (Relations with specific foreign countries are usually found under the region concerned.)*	*Includes business, labor, agriculture, taxation, transportation, consumer affairs, monetary and fiscal policy, natural resources, pollution and accidents.*	*Includes worldwide scientific, medical and technological developments, natural phenomena, U.S. weather and natural disasters.*	*Includes the arts, religion, scholarship, communications media, sports, entertainment, fashions, fads and social life.*

	World Affairs	European War Zone	Pacific War Zone	The Americas	Other Countries & Territories
Jan. 22		In a surprise landing, Lt. Gen. Mark Clark's 5th Army establishes beachheads at Anzio, Italy, south of Rome, and encounter almost no immediate opposition. Called Operation Shingle, the landing is made to outflank the German front and move to take Rome. Allied troops involved number 50,000 .... On the Leningrad front, Soviet troops take 70 localities, with the Leningrad-Mga-Kirishi railroad falling into complete Russian control .... Soviet Col. Gen. Alexander Scherbakoff says Germany's efforts to split the Allies have failed and "confidence and unity are growing among the members of the anti-Hitler coalition."		Cuban CP changes its name to the Popular Socialist Party.	
Jan. 23		Allies announce Gen. Dwight D. Eisenhower will command U.S. forces in the European theater, as well as being the supreme Allied commander .... Russian-sponsored All-Slav Comm. issues a warning to Bulgaria that the war's end is approaching, and urges unity to expel the Nazis .... Russian troops wipe out a strong German bridgehead on the east bank of the Volkhov River .... Yugoslavian partisans claim the annihilation of a strong German force and throw back other enemy units with heavy losses in the Livno-Grachovo sector of western Bosnia.	Tojo says an Axis conference to counter Allied conferences would be "devoid of merit."		Portuguese liner *Nyassa* sails from Lisbon with 180 Jewish refugees and will pick up 650 more at Cadiz en route to Palestine.
Jan. 24	UNRRA Dir. Lehman appoints Sir Frederick Leith-Ross as deputy director general with headquarters in London.	Allied forces capture Neturno, south of Rome, and nearby Anzio .... Russian advances on the Leningrad front take Smolkovo, thus severing the rail line to Narva, Estonia.	Allied bombers and fighters attack Japanese installations in the Admiralty Islands, 240 miles north of New Guinea.	U.S. announces official recognition will not be given to the Bolivian revolutionary government and recalls Amb. Pierre de Lagarde Boal.	
Jan. 25		American units reach the outskirts of Cassino, encountering light opposition .... Russian troops on the Leningrad front cut the railroad at Vladimir, leaving the Nazis below Leningrad without a lateral railroad.		Argentine Foreign Min. Alberto Gilbert says Allied charges of German espionage there are correct and that the government is determined to end such activities .... Foreign Secy. Anthony Eden announces that Britain will not recognize the Bolivian government.	
Jan. 26		Allied forces make some progress in their assault below Rome. Two infantry battalions supported by tanks attack German Panzer forces, putting the Allies three miles from Cisterna .... Secy. Hull states Russia has declined American good offices to settle Russian-Polish differences .... With the capture of Mednikovo, Russian troops reach 42 miles inside the Estonian border .... The Duke of Alba, Spanish ambassador to London, informs Foreign Secy. Eden that Spain is taking stringent measures to prevent sabotage of shipments to England.	Chinese forces driving across the Hukawng Valley in Burma reportedly make new gains as Allied units in the upper Chindwin Valley inflict heavy casualties on an ambushed Japanese force.	Argentina breaks diplomatic relations with Germany and Japan .... Cuban Pres. Batista resigns as leader of the Socialist-Democratic coalition in a move to placate the opposition.	Britain reports Liberia has declared war on Japan and Germany.
Jan. 27		Russians celebrate the liberation of Leningrad after a 2½-year German siege, while other Russian forces west of Leningrad capture Volosovo and Zakornovo .... Allied troops continue to advance south of Rome, capturing Velletri, while reinforcements are landed on the beachheads .... Yugoslavian partisans claim the liberation of 70% of central Bosnia from the Germans.	Army and Navy issue a joint report charging the Japanese with starving and murdering more than 5,200 American soldiers captured on Corregidor and Bataan Peninsula.		
Jan. 28		Allied beachhead south of Rome is again enlarged, this time to about 24 miles in length .... Soviet troops extend their Estonian line by 36 miles with a 13-mile advance south from Volosovo to Repolka .... Russian troops are reported in control of all but 11 miles of the Moscow-Leningrad railway.	On New Guinea, Australian troops advance up the coast beyond Sio to narrow the gap between them and the Americans in the Saidor area to 40 miles.		

A	B	C	D	E
Includes developments that affect more than one world region, international organizations and important meetings of major world leaders.	*Includes all developments in European countries and military engagements between Allied and Axis powers in Africa and at sea.*	*Includes all developments in Japan and China, Japanese foreign policy and military actions in the Pacific region.*	*Includes all domestic and regional developments in Latin America, the Caribbean and Canada.*	*Includes developments in those independent nations and colonial possessions not covered in Columns B, C and D.*

U.S. Politics & Social Issues	U.S. Foreign Policy & Defense	U.S. Economy & Environment	Science, Technology & Nature	Culture, Leisure & Life Style	
Democratic National Comm. meets in Washington and names Robert Hannegan its chairman, selects Chicago as its convention site and lauds FDR's work .... A one-man grand jury in the circuit court in Lansing, Mich. returns indictments charging conspiracy and bribery against 13 members and seven former members of the state legislature and six automobile finance company executives.	FDR establishes a War Refugee Bd. to take action for immediate rescue of as many as possible of Europe's persecuted .... AFL Executive Council's postwar planning committee suggests that labor be represented on all diplomatic delegations dealing with postwar problems, and that labor attaches be added to U.S. diplomatic staffs.				Jan. 22
Willkie says he will not enter the California GOP primary, where Gov. Earl Warren is a "nominal" candidate.	Sen. Harold H. Burton (R,O.) proposes the U.S. call an early U.N. meeting to discuss postwar problems.		Dr. Luke J. Fleming, inventor of the gas mask used in WW I, dies at 75 in Tarrytown, N.Y.	Edvard Munch, Norway's most distinguished painter and founder of the modern expressionist school, dies at 80 in Norway.	Jan. 23
				U.S. District Court of Appeals in Cincinnati rules that newspaper reporters are not "professional" workers and are covered by the Fair Labor Standards Act.	Jan. 24
Sen. Frederick Van Nuys (D, Ind.) dies at 69 at his home near Vienna, Va.	House passes and sends to the Senate a bill providing $1.35 billion for U.S. participation in UNRRA.	Federal court rules against local UMW unions, declaring operators do not have to pay workers for travel time.			Jan. 25
FDR sends a message to Congress calling the "states rights" soldier-vote bill a fraud on servicemen and endorses the Green-Lucas federal ballot bill.	Senate and House pass and send to the White House a bill providing veterans' mustering out pay of $100 to $300.	WPB says war needs will absorb all of the estimated 593,000,000 gallons of alcohol to be produced in 1944 .... The chairman of the House committee investigating government agencies, Howard Smith (D, Va.), files a report charging that the NWLB has exceeded its authority .... House Speaker Sam Rayburn names a bipartisan committee of 18 chaired by William Colmer (D, Miss.) to study postwar economic problems.	Gen. William E. Mitchell Memorial Award for 1943 for "the outstanding individual contribution to aviation progress" is given to Igor I. Sikorsky for his work with helicopters.	*An American Dilemma*, a penetrating analysis of American race problems by Gunnar Myrdal, is published .... *Variety* reports the most popular songs are: (1) *Shoo Shoo Baby*, (2) *People Will Say We're In Love* and (3) *Oh, What a Beautiful Morning*.	Jan. 26
	Stimson says two-thirds of the Army will be overseas by the end of the year.	CIO Executive Committee adopts a resolution opposing the Austin-Wadsworth bill for a national service act.		National Institute of Arts and Letters awards its gold medal for "distinguished achievement" to Willa Cather for her "sustained contribution to American fiction." .... *The Lost Weekend*, the story of a confirmed drunk and a study of alcoholism by Charles Jackson, is published.	Jan. 27
	State Dept. discloses it is reviewing policy towards Spain and that oil shipments to Spain have been stopped.			David Nederlander of Lafayette Dramatic Productions, Inc., Detroit, files suit for $500,000 in damages in N.Y. State Supreme Court against James Petrillo, charging conspiracy to force the Lafayette Theatre to hire six musicians at $500 a week although its productions do not require music.	Jan. 28
F	G	H	I	J	
Includes elections, federal-state relations, civil rights and liberties, crime, the judiciary, education, health care, poverty, urban affairs and population.	*Includes formation and debate of U.S. foreign and defense policies, veterans affairs and defense spending. (Relations with specific foreign countries are usually found under the region concerned.)*	*Includes business, labor, agriculture, taxation, transportation, consumer affairs, monetary and fiscal policy, natural resources, pollution and accidents.*	*Includes worldwide scientific, medical and technological developments, natural phenomena, U.S. weather and natural disasters.*	*Includes the arts, religion, scholarship, communications media, sports, entertainment, fashions, fads and social life.*	

	World Affairs	European War Zone	Pacific War Zone	The Americas	Other Countries & Territories
Jan. 29		American troops fight their way to a point one mile north of Cassino .... The last German hold on the Moscow-Leningrad railway is broken by the capture of Chudovo.		Mexico and Canada announce they will establish diplomatic relations and exchange ministers in the near future .... Brazilian Foreign Min. Oswaldo Aranha says air bases built by the U.S. in Brazil "are ours 100% and will always be ours."	
Jan. 30		Allied troops beat back a German counterattack three miles southwest of Cisterna in their drive on Rome .... Polish government in exile in London asks the U.S. and Britain to define the boundaries they think Poland should have at the war's end .... As Soviet troops make further advances into Estonia, German colonists are reported fleeing from the Baltic area.	U.S. landing forces are put ashore in the Marshall Islands at Roi and Kwajalein. .... Chinese troops reportedly capture the Tanai River ferry station of Taro in northern Burma.		
Jan. 31		American troops enter the suburbs of Cisternia, Italy .... Russian troops fight their way into the suburbs of Kingisepp, an important communications point only eight miles east of the Estonian frontier.	U.S. troops establish beachheads in the Marshall Islands, first territory held by Japan before Pearl Harbor to be invaded, and meet strong opposition .... George Adams, secretary of the American Advisory Comm. for Southeast China, arrives in Chungking from Kwangtung Province and says 1,000,000 have died there of starvation and cholera, which have wiped out 80% of the population of some villages .... State Secy. Hull reveals that 89 specific protests against mistreatment of U.S. war prisoners and war internees were made to Japan from Jan. 13, 1942 through Jan. 27, 1944 without result.		
Feb. 1		Allied troops north and west of Cassino breach the Nazi Gustav Line over several miles, while Americans push to within a mile of Cassino from the rear .... Soviet units take the communications center of Kingisepp. .... An earthquake destroys most of Gerede, Turkey and causes heavy damage elsewhere in the Ankara area .... Soviet newspaper *Izvestia* says the Vatican's foreign policy has disillusioned Catholics throughout the world and "earned the hatred and contempt of the Italian masses for supporting Fascism."	Chinese troops capture the village of Taihpa Ga in the Hukawng Valley of northern Burma.		
Feb. 2		Russian troops penetrate one-half mile inside Estonia, 11 miles north of Narva, and capture Vanakula.	U.S. Marines capture Roi Island at the northern end of Kwajalein atoll in the Marshalls.	Pres. Pedro Ramirez decrees that radio stations in Argentina must be wholly owned and managed by citizens who have resided in the country for at least 18 years.	
Feb. 3		The 1st and 2nd Ukrainian Russian armies in a five-day, 100-mile advance trap 10 German divisions in the region of Zvenigorodka and Shpola .... President Eduard Benes tells the Czech state council in London that the Czech-Soviet treaty of friendship guarantees his country's future security .... Spanish cabinet ratifies a policy of "strict neutrality" and announces it will enforce conformity by foreign subjects as well as its own nationals.	American troops on Bougainville Island extend their perimeter east of the Torokina River.		Lebanese Pres. Bechera el Khoury says Lebanon will not join a "Greater Syria" movement to restore the Arab empire of the the pre-1918 era .... American-owned Arabian-American Oil Co. announces plans to begin immediately the construction of a refinery in Saudi Arabia to supply petroleum products to U.N. nations.
Feb. 4		German troops open a fierce counteroffensive north of the Anzio beachhead, 20 miles south of Rome, but are thrown back by the British .... Soviet troops report tightening their grip on the 10 trapped German divisions in the Ukraine and destroying 70 Junkers transport planes attempting to supply Nazi forces .... Latvian Min. to the U.S. Dr. Alfred Bilmanis says the inclusion of Latvia in Russia's list of 16 autonomous republics is "a violation of free people."	American troops land on and take control of half of Ebeye Island north of Kwajalein .... In the first foray of its kind against the Japanese homeland, U.S. naval surface units shell installations on the south and east coasts of Paramushiro Island at the northern end of the Kuriles .... Capt. Edward W. Rickenbacker says it will take 20 years to clear the Pacific islands of Japanese soldiers.	Argentina severs diplomatic relations with Bulgaria, Vichy France, Rumania and Hungary.	
Feb. 5		Moscow reports that Soviet troops in the past several days have penetrated into Poland up to 85 miles, taking some 200 inhabited places.	U.S. forces complete their occupation of Kwajalein, Ebeye and Loi Islands in the Marshalls.		Petroleum Reserves Corp. of the U.S. announces it will build a pipeline across Arabia from the Persian Gulf to the Mediterranean.
	A *Includes developments that affect more than one world region, international organizations and important meetings of major world leaders.*	B *Includes all developments in European countries and military engagements between Allied and Axis powers in Africa and at sea.*	C *Includes all developments in Japan and China, Japanese foreign policy and military actions in the Pacific region.*	D *Includes all domestic and regional developments in Latin America, the Caribbean and Canada.*	E *Includes developments in those independent nations and colonial possessions not covered in Columns B, C and D.*

U.S. Politics & Social Issues	U.S. Foreign Policy & Defense	U.S. Economy & Environment	Science, Technology & Nature	Culture, Leisure & Life Style	
American Legion commander Warren Atherton says in a Boston speech that all Japanese nationals in the U.S. should be deported "as soon as possible" because "50 years of trial has proved that they can never be assimilated." .... Dies Committee reports the Japanese have been carrying out an organized and systematic espionage plan in the U.S. since WW I .... Wayne L. Morse resigns his post on the NWLB and announces his candidacy for the Oregon GOP Senate nomination.	The world's most powerful battleship, the 45,000-ton *Missouri*, is launched at the N.Y. Navy Yard.	R.J. Thomas and George Meany, CIO and AFL members of the Presidential Comm. on the Cost of Living, issue a statement claiming that living costs have gone up 43.5% since Jan. 1, 1941, instead of the 23.4% reported by the government.		Internationally famous editor of the *Emporia Gazette* William A. White dies at 75 at his home in Emporia, Kansas.	Jan. 29
CP Secy. Browder urges the Democratic and Republican parties to "explore the possibility of a single presidential ticket in 1944."	U.S. Supreme Court Justice Frank Murphy announces the formation of the National Comm. Against Nazi Persecution and Extermination of the Jews.				Jan. 30
N.J. Supreme Court upholds the right of two Negro children to attend a public school near their home instead of being forced to go 16 blocks to an all-Negro school.		Federal Works Admin. Maj. Gen. Fleming announces the WPA, which ended eight years of operations June 30, 1943, expended $10.1 billion in federal funds .... Senate and House conferees agree on a tax measure that will raise an estimated additional $2.3 billion in revenue.		Jean Giraudoux, French playwright, author, diplomat and Vichy government official, dies at 62 in Paris.	Jan. 31
				Piet Mondrian, a Hollander and leading exponent of non-objective painting, dies at 71 in New York .... *New York Times* announces it has made an arrangement to buy the Interstate Broadcasting Co., New York, which operates station WQXR, subject to FCC approval.	Feb. 1
Sen. Harry Byrd (D, Va.) tells the Senate that 41 states will make adequate provisions for absentee voting by armed forces members.		In a *New York Times* conference, Willkie says the U.S. should tax itself $16 billion this year in support of the war effort .... American Iron & Steel Institute reports 1943 steel production as 88,872,598 tons with 98.1% of capacity at work.			Feb. 2
House passes and sends to the Senate the Eastland-Rankin "states rights" soldier-vote bill.	Army announces the discontinuance of seven of the 26 officers' training schools in the U.S. and a general reduction in the program.			It is announced that newspaper columnist Raymond Clapper, 51, was killed during the Allied invasion of the Marshall Islands when a plane in which he was an observer collided with another and plunged into a lagoon.	Feb. 3
Senate rejects the "states rights" soldier-vote bill as a substitute for the Green-Lucas measure .... Anti-New Deal Democrats from 14 states organize the American Democratic Comm. with Harry H. Woodring as chairman and propose State Secy. Hull as its presidential candidate .... Gov. Dewey of N.Y. grants a fifth stay of the execution of Louis (Lepke) Buchalter, Louis Capone and Emanuel Weiss.	FDR signs the bill providing $100 to $300 mustering-out pay for war veterans .... Secy. Hull advises a "wait and see" attitude on the Russian grant of diplomatic and military autonomy to its 16 constituent republics.				Feb. 4
	Several hundred Lithuanian descendents petition FDR to restore Lithuania to its independent status.			Gil Dodds wins the mile run at the Melrose Games in N.Y., beating Bill Hulse by three yards in 4:10.6.	Feb. 5
F	G	H	I	J	
Includes elections, federal-state relations, civil rights and liberties, crime, the judiciary, education, health care, poverty, urban affairs and population.	*Includes formation and debate of U.S. foreign and defense policies, veterans affairs and defense spending. (Relations with specific foreign countries are usually found under the region concerned.)*	*Includes business, labor, agriculture, taxation, transportation, consumer affairs, monetary and fiscal policy, natural resources, pollution and accidents.*	*Includes worldwide scientific, medical and technological developments, natural phenomena, U.S. weather and natural disasters.*	*Includes the arts, religion, scholarship, communications media, sports, entertainment, fashions, fads and social life.*	

	World Affairs	European War Zone	Pacific War Zone	The Americas	Other Countries & Territories
Feb. 6		Moscow radio attacks the Polish government-in-exile for "imperialistic and pro-Fascist tendencies which preclude possibility of friendly agreement" with Russia, but intimates an accord will be reached with "a new, democratic Poland." .... Russians trap five more Nazi infantry divisions in the Dnieper bend and Nikopol .... In bitter street fighting American troops attempt to dislodge the Germans from Cassino.	U.S. forces take Gugewe, Bigej and Eller Islands, bringing a total of some 700 square miles in the Marshall Islands under Allied control.		
Feb. 7		Plans for rebuilding historic Coventry Cathedral, destroyed in the 1940 German blitz, are announced in London.	Japanese Information Bd. spokesman Sadao Iguchi charges that Japanese war prisoners and civilian internees have been grossly mistreated by the Americans.		
Feb. 8		Russian forces take the manganese center of Nikopol on the Dnieper River bend, completing a four-day offensive that clears the enemy from a 700-mile stretch of the east bank of the lower Dnieper River .... Britain and the French Comm. of National Liberation agree to fix the exchange rate at 200 francs to a pound and provide for mutual military assistance for the war's duration .... Yugoslavian partisans report their forces have been driven from Perusic in a growing battle for vital communication lines in western Croatia.	Australian and U.S. troops link up 14 miles east of Saidor, ending an 18-week campaign for control of of the Huon Peninsula on New Guinea.	Argentina announces the arrest of German military attache Gen. Friedrich Wolf and Japanese naval attache Rear Adm. Katsumi Yukishita for directing espionage activity. .... U.S. discontinues its activities in the development of Brazilian rubber production.	
Feb. 9		German authorities rebuff Helsinki's offer to withdraw from the war and threaten opposition to any peace efforts .... Soviet units seize Brovakhi, Vygrayev and Gorodishche to further tighten their ring around the Germans on the middle Dnieper .... Allied planes bomb German positions in Cassino and installations and reinforcements near the Anzio beachhead .... Berne reports that influential circles in northern Italy are proposing establishment of a republic with orchestra conductor Arturo Toscanini as its first president .... Tito's Yugoslavian partisan group announces adoption of a resolution forbidding the return of King Peter II.	Japanese troops advance towards British supply lines in the Arakan district of southwestern Burma.		
Feb. 10		Repeated German counterattacks slow the Allied advance in heavy fighting 18 miles south of Rome .... Allies announce civil control of Sardinia, Sicily and southern Italy will revert to the government of Premier Marshal Pietro Badoglio on Feb. 11.	As a result of daily bombing by Allied planes, all Japanese warships are withdrawn from Rabaul, New Britain.	Colombian government releases Sen. Laureano Gomez, who was arrested for refusing to testify in a case involving the Conservative Party's manifesto claiming the country was on the brink of a revolution.	Frenchmen in the pay of the Nazis are reported to have parachuted into Morocco with the intention of stirring up an Arab rebellion.
Feb. 11		Red Army troops capture Shepetovka, junction of five railways 25 miles east of the Polish border.	Japanese government extends labor conscription to include males from 12 to 60 and unmarried females from 12 to 40.	Three reported pro-Axis members of the Bolivian cabinet—Alberto Taborga, Augusto Cespedes and Carlos Montenegro—are dismissed in La Paz.	
Feb. 12		Lt. Gen. Mark Clark expresses optimism that his troops with the aid of reinforcements will overcome Nazi resistance on the Anzio beachhead .... Moscow declares a National Council representing all Polish political groups has been established inside Poland by the Union of Polish Patriots .... Leningrad dispatches report that more than a fifth of the city's buildings were destroyed and many more heavily damaged during the 27-month siege.	U.S. forces occupy Rooke (Umboi) Island in the middle of the Vitiaz Strait between New Britain and New Guinea.	Bolivia announces a decree expropriating all Axis-owned firms.	
Feb. 13		Germans at Cassino are reported using the sixth century Abbey of Mt. Cassino as a fortress, and the Allies claim it might be necessary to demolish it .... In a new drive on the northern front, Soviet troops take the rail center of Luga.			

A	B	C	D	E
Includes developments that affect more than one world region, international organizations and important meetings of major world leaders.	*Includes all developments in European countries and military engagements between Allied and Axis powers in Africa and at sea.*	*Includes all developments in Japan and China, Japanese foreign policy and military actions in the Pacific region.*	*Includes all domestic and regional developments in Latin America, the Caribbean and Canada.*	*Includes developments in those independent nations and colonial possessions not covered in Columns B, C and D.*

U.S. Politics & Social Issues	U.S. Foreign Policy & Defense	U.S. Economy & Environment	Science, Technology & Nature	Culture, Leisure & Life Style	
Willkie announces he will enter the presidential primaries in Nebraska and Wisconsin.	House members demand an investigation of costs of the Army's Pentagon building, for which $35 million has been appropriated but for which the War Dept. reports a cost of $63,645,954 plus some $10 million for special equipment and roads . . . . Army Air Force announces that improvements in the Lockhead P-38 give it a ceiling of over 40,000 ft. and a speed of over 300 mph.	U.S. Bureau of Mines estimates 46,000 of 73,000 men in the anthracite fields answered the call of Interior Secy. Ickes for Sunday work to make up coal shortages.		Academy of Motion Picture Arts and Sciences announces its nominations for 1943 awards, which include Humphrey Bogart in *Casablanca* and Gary Cooper and Ingrid Bergman in *For Whom the Bell Tolls* . . . . Baseball's postwar committee votes to recommend major and minor league measures to protect players in service, including return to their clubs at their previous salaries.	Feb. 6
A ticket of 56 national convention delegates supporting FDR's renomination is filed in California.		Congress completes action on the $2.3-billion tax bill and sends it to the White House . . . . Agriculture Dept. reports that January food prices were 37% above prewar levels.		*A Bell for Adano* by John Hershey is published.	Feb. 7
Senate passes both Soldier-vote bills—the Green-Lucas and Eastland-Rankin bills—sending the controversy to conference . . . . Mass. Gov. Leverett Saltonstall appoints Sinclair Weeks to succeed Henry Cabot Lodge Jr., who resigned his Senate seat Feb. 4 to enter the armed forces.				A seven-year-old boy is installed as the 10th Panchen Lama, spiritual leader of Tibet, in ceremonies at Hsunhwa, Chinghai Province . . . . Violinist Fritz Kreisler reverses a previous stand and agrees to appear in a series of five NBC radio programs.	Feb. 8
National Urban League reports 253 war plants are satisfied with Negro labor performance and express confidence in postwar employment opportunities.		FDR names Lloyd Garrison to replace Wayne Morse as a public member of the NWLB.		The will of Samuel Fleisher leaves his entire estate, estimated at $1 million, to the Graphic Arts Club of Philadelphia, which he founded 45 years ago . . . . Gil Dodds wins the mile run at Boston A.A. games in 4:09.5—the fastest indoor time in Boston history.	Feb. 9
U.S. Chamber of Commerce Pres. Eric Johnston says that Vice President Henry A. Wallace's charge of Fascism against American businessmen is "name-calling and the wrong way to get national unity." . . . . Gov. John W. Bricker (R, O.) says he is only interested in ending the New Deal and restoring a sound government in Washington.		Local 56, Amalgamated Meat Cutters and Butchers Workers of North America asks 25¢ weekly dues from 165 German war prisoners working under Army guard at the Seabrook Farms, Bridgeton, N.J. . . . . Joseph Nunan, Jr. is nominated by FDR to be U.S. Commissioner of Internal Revenue.		Motion picture comedian Charlie Chaplin, two friends and four Beverly Hills, Calif. public officials are indicted on charges growing out of his association with Joan Berry, who brought a paternity suit against him . . . . John P. Marquand's *So Little Time* and Wendell Willkie's *One World* lead the fiction and non-fiction lists of the Book of the Month Club's poll of outstanding books of 1943.	Feb. 10
Robert McCormick withdraws his name from the Illinois GOP primary, leaving only MacArthur on the Republican ballot . . . . Democratic committees in Neb., N.H. and Wisc. announce FDR will be entered as a candidate in those states' presidential primaries.	Navy reports that the 29,000-ton battleship *Oklahoma*, capsized at Pearl Harbor, has been repaired, modernized and set afloat.	Senate votes to end most food subsidies Europe, June 30.			Feb. 11
N.Y. Gov. Thomas E. Dewey (R) assails FDR as a self-willed executive, and charges that the New Deal "seeks power for the sake of power."		WPB Chmn. Nelson says smaller plants will have priority in the postwar reconversion program.			Feb. 12
AFL Brotherhood of Carpenters and Joiners, representing some 600,000 workers, adopts a resolution calling for an end fo the New Deal.		Deputy Food Admin. C.W. Kitchen announces civilian allotments of canned fruits and vegetables will be cut 43% and 19% in 1944 . . . . RFC announces it will make loans for postwar reconversion of industry in cooperation with private funding.			Feb. 13

F	G	H	I	J
Includes elections, federal-state relations, civil rights and liberties, crime, the judiciary, education, health care, poverty, urban affairs and population.	*Includes formation and debate of U.S. foreign and defense policies, veterans affairs and defense spending. (Relations with specific foreign countries are usually found under the region concerned.)*	*Includes business, labor, agriculture, taxation, transportation, consumer affairs, monetary and fiscal policy, natural resources, pollution and accidents.*	*Includes worldwide scientific, medical and technological developments, natural phenomena, U.S. weather and natural disasters.*	*Includes the arts, religion, scholarship, communications media, sports, entertainment, fashions, fads and social life.*

	World Affairs	European War Zone	Pacific War Zone	The Americas	Other Countries & Territories
Feb. 14		Commander of Nazi defense forces in western Europe, Field Marshal Karl von Rundstedt, says there will be no evasive or withdrawal action in the face of an Allied coastal invasion . . . . Russian forces take the main German stronghold in the Cherkassy pocket in the middle Dnieper area.	The Japanese position in the Arakan sector of western Burma deteriorates in the face of heavy Allied pressure . . . . U.S. and N.Z. troops with naval and air support meet little enemy resistance in occupying the Green Islands at the northern end of the Solomons.	Administration candidate Teodoro Picado wins the Costa Rican presidential election.	
Feb. 15		In an Allied effort to rout German troops, 228 heavy and medium American bombers blast into ruins the historic Benedictine monastery and its abbey atop Mt. Cassino, Italy . . . . British Admiralty reports that the 150,000-square-mile sea area of the Bay of Biscay bordering France and northern Spain is blockaded and that ships entering it do so at their own peril . . . . U.S. completes agreements with the Belgian and Dutch governments covering civilian administration following Allied occupation after invasion.		A group of junior Army officers forcibly occupies the Argentine Foreign Ministry and ousts Foreign Min. Alberto Gilbert. The group is led by Col. Juan D. Peron . . . . Senate passes and sends to the House a bill providing for an elective government for Puerto Rico and granting the island territory a greater degree of self-determination.	
Feb. 16		U.S. bombers complete two days of bombing raids against the Cassino monastery . . . . In the heaviest attack made to date on Berlin, nearly 1,000 RAF planes unload 2,500 tons of bombs in 30 minutes . . . . Russians occupy more than 35 localities today in their advance on the German-held rail center of Pskov.	A MacArthur statement says Japan will be defeated only by ground forces destroying the Japanese Army as a result of ground, sea and air cooperation.	The government of Ecuador grants an oil concession of one million acres to the International Petroleum Co.	
Feb. 17		Allied planes engage in record operations on the Anzio beachhead to aid in breaking German counterattacks . . . . Italian Premier Badoglio reorganizes his cabinet . . . . Russian troops liquidate the remnants of 10 Nazi divisions trapped in the Ukraine west of Cherkassy, bringing the totals after two weeks to 52,000 killed and 11,000 captured . . . . Netherlands government in London reports 180,000 Jews have been killed in Holland by the Nazis . . . . Health Minister Henry Willink presents a White Paper proposing legislation be enacted providing every Briton with health care.	U.S. forces invade Eniwetok Atoll, westernmost of the Marshall Islands, and establish beachheads . . . . A U.S. naval task force strikes at the Japanese base on Truk in the Caroline Islands, destroying 19 ships and 201 planes.	Parliament receives an order in council providing for compulsory collective bargaining for Canadian workers for the war's duration . . . . The dominant Liberal Radical Party names Miguel Angel Albornez as its presidential candidate in Ecuador.	Viceroy of India Viscount Wavell warns Indian leaders that self-government depends on the ability of rival forces to settle their differences.
Feb. 18		Russian units capture Staraya Russa, 10 miles south of Lake Ilmen and the most eastern point held by the Germans in northern Russia.		In an attack upon a delivery truck of the pro-Axis newspaper *Federal* in Buenos Aires, one person is killed and several are injured.	
Feb. 19		*London Observer* reports Stalin has given assurances to a Moscow diplomat that "Russia has no intention whatsoever of expanding into central or western Europe." . . . . Reinforcements reaching the Allies enable new progress to be made against the Germans on the Cassino line . . . . The three-pronged Russian drive on Pskov results in the occupation of 130 communities.	Marines capture the Japanese airbase at the northern end of the Engebi Island in the Marshalls.		
Feb. 20	UNRRA Dir. Herbert H. Lehman appoints Soviet trade expert Nicolai Feonov as a deputy director general in charge of the regional supply office in London.	An all-out effort by six German divisions to eliminate the Allied beachhead at Anzio is thrown back . . . . In their continued drive on Pskov, Russian troops push back the Germans along a 100-mile front . . . . U.S. Rear Adm. Alan Kirk is named commander of the combined Allied naval force in the coming invasion of Europe.			
Feb. 21		Russian troops fight their way to the outskirts of the iron ore city of Krivoi Rog in the Dnieper bend.	Japanese Army Chief of Staff Field Marshal Sugiyama and Navy Chief of Staff Adm. Osami Nagano are dismissed; Tojo assumes Army control, and Adm. Shigetaro Shimade is assigned Nagano's duties . . . . U.S. forces eliminate all but a few pockets of Japanese resistance on Eniwetok and Parry Islands . . . . British forces in the Arakan area continue to disperse Japanese troops and regain high ground overlooking Ngakyedauk Pass, Burma.		

A	B	C	D	E
Includes developments that affect more than one world region, international organizations and important meetings of major world leaders.	*Includes all developments in European countries and military engagements between Allied and Axis powers in Africa and at sea.*	*Includes all developments in Japan and China, Japanese foreign policy and military actions in the Pacific region.*	*Includes all domestic and regional developments in Latin America, the Caribbean and Canada.*	*Includes developments in those independent nations and colonial possessions not covered in Columns B, C and D.*

U.S. Politics & Social Issues	U.S. Foreign Policy & Defense	U.S. Economy & Environment	Science, Technology & Nature	Culture, Leisure & Life Style	
Willkie formally announces he will seek the GOP presidential nomination.	Senate Foreign Relations Comm. votes to approve U.S. participation in UNRRA and to establish a $1.3-billion appropriation for it.	FDR signs a bill appropriating $36.5 million to the War Food Administration for its farm labor recruiting programs.		American Academy of Arts and Letters announces the award of its medal for stage diction to Paul Robeson.	Feb. 14
					Feb. 15
A Dies Committee report charges the Peace Now movement with seditious and treasonable activities in attempting to persuade U.S. servicemen to "lay down their arms."	Army purchases director Gen. Albert Browning says equipment contracts have been reduced an average of 20%, resulting in a two-year savings of $9 billion .... Senate's Truman Committee files a report recommending "a positive vigorous American policy" to assure the U.S. a proper share of the world's oil reserves.		Miller Reese Hutchison, inventor of the Acousticon, the Klaxon horn and dictograph, dies at 67 in N.Y.	The will of Mrs. George Bernard Shaw leaves an estimated $400,000 trust fund to be used to "teach" the Irish "self-control, deportment, elocution and the art of personal behavior and social intercourse."	Feb. 16
	Army says 200,000 men besides sick and wounded have returned stateside on furloughs and that rotation furloughing is in "full swing." .... Senate passes the UNRRA bill carrying an appropriation of $1.3 billion with restrictions on fund uses.	House passes and sends to FDR a bill extending the life of the CCC with a rider ending consumer food subsidies after June 30.	U.S. Army fliers locate the headwaters of the 1,500-mile Orinoco River in a jungle mountain gorge separating Brazil and Venezuela.		Feb. 17
Charles E. Bedeaux, 58, French-born naturalized American citizen, friend of the Duke and Duchess of Windsor and international "mystery man," dies of an overdose of sleeping tablets as a federal grand jury was about to inquire into his relations with high German and Vichy France officials.		Bernard Baruch presents his report on postwar reconversion, which emphasizes the coordination of existing agencies through the Office of War Mobilization .... FDR vetoes the CCC bill, and is sustained by the House. Rep. Brent Spence (D, Ky.) immediately introduces a bill extending the CCC's life to June 1945, without the rider ending food subsidies.	Hungarian scientist Albert Szent-Gyorgyi discovers a hitherto unknown element in the blood that causes hemophilia.		Feb. 18
				Gil Dodds wins the Baxter mile at the NYAC games in 4:08.	Feb. 19
Former Gov. Joseph Ely announces his candidacy for the Democratic presidential nomination in Massachusetts.					Feb. 20
Oklahoma Democratic state committee endorses FDR for a fourth term.			Canadian Army medical officer Brig. Gen. Frank Lott says war experience suggests that plastic may replace glass for artificial eyes after the war.		Feb. 21
F	G	H	I	J	
Includes elections, federal-state relations, civil rights and liberties, crime, the judiciary, education, health care, poverty, urban affairs and population.	*Includes formation and debate of U.S. foreign and defense policies, veterans affairs and defense spending. (Relations with specific foreign countries are usually found under the region concerned.)*	*Includes business, labor, agriculture, taxation, transportation, consumer affairs, monetary and fiscal policy, natural resources, pollution and accidents.*	*Includes worldwide scientific, medical and technological developments, natural phenomena, U.S. weather and natural disasters.*	*Includes the arts, religion, scholarship, communications media, sports, entertainment, fashions, fads and social life.*	

	World Affairs	European War Zone	Pacific War Zone	The Americas	Other Countries & Territories
Feb. 22		Churchill tells the House of Commons the U.S., Britain and Russia are united as ever against the common foe despite whatever interpretation might be put on recent events in Poland .... Red Army captures Krivoi Rog .... In the first such coordinated attack, U.S. planes from Britain and Italy simultaneously bomb targets in central and southern Germany.	Several hundred carrier-based planes attack Japanese bases on Saipan and Tinian Islands of the lower Marianas group.	Chile announces the arrest of 14 alleged Axis spies operating under the direction of Ludwig von Bohlen, German air attache.	
Feb. 23		British Foreign Secy. Eden tells the House of Commons that Britain reserves the right to intervene in the settlement of political affairs in any part of Europe and denies any reported agreement on spheres of influence .... Front reports indicate the Nazis are regrouping for another assault aimed at wiping out the Allied beachhead near Anzio .... Russian troops driving westward on Pskov fight their way into Dno .... Greek guerrillas led by a British officer kill 400 German soldiers, blowing up a troop train in the vicinity of Mt. Olympus.	Under the pressure of several days of air and ground assaults by the Allies, the Japanese are forced to retreat in northern Burma and on the Arakan front.		
Feb. 24		In a three-day-old offensive, Soviet troops advance 12-15 miles along a 30-mile front in White Russia and capture the large railway junction of Rogachev .... In their second coordinated attack, U.S. planes from Britain and Italy strike at targets in Germany.	Allies announce that the western end of New Britain Island from Rottock Bay to Arawe is now completely in American hands .... Allies clear the Japanese from Ngakyedauk Pass on the Arakan front.	Argentine Pres. Gen. Pedro Ramirez resigns because of "ill health," but Montevideo reports it is due to an Army coup .... Chilean government smashes a Nazi espionage ring with the arrest of scores of alleged Nazi agents.	
Feb. 25		Polish government-in-exile in London notifies the British it will not accept the Curzon Line as a basis for border discussions with Russia .... CP newspaper *Pravda* denounces "assistants of Wm. Randolph Hearst" for "spilling poisoned ink to wreck the anti-Hitler coalition." *Pravda* refers to specific editorials which outline supposed Soviet plans to annex the Balkan countries.	British troops capture the town of Kyauktaw in the Kaladan Valley of western Burma .... Tokyo radio reports a cabinet decision to restructure national life for the war effort, which means a belt-tightening process.	Gen. Edelmiro Farrell is named "vice president in exercise of the executive power" and assumes functions as acting president in Argentina.	
Feb. 26		London diplomatic quarters report Franco has assured Allied governments that Spain will follow a course of "honorable neutrality." .... Churchill's son Randolph is reported in Yugoslavia with Marshal Tito in an effort to further British efforts to effect closer cooperation between Tito and King Peter in exile.			
Feb. 27	Interim U.N. food commission, meeting in Hot Springs, Va., completes plans for a permanent organization to guide production and distribution of food in the postwar period.	A convoy carrying one of the largest contingents of American troops ever to cross the Atlantic arrives in England .... Soviet troops reach two points within 15 miles of Pskov with the capture of Zamelnichye and Zakhodtsy.			
Feb. 28		A Soviet commission investigating German atrocities during the occupation of Kiev reports that 195,000 persons there were "tortured to death, shot or poisoned in murder vans."	In two weeks of fighting in the jungles of western Burma around Arakan, the Allies reportedly disperse some 8,000 Japanese.		
Feb. 29		Soviet government offers peace terms to Finland if she will break with Germany, withdraw her troops to the 1940 borders and intern Nazi troops and equipment .... In their drive on Pskov, Soviet troops capture 250 more inhabited places and move to within six miles of the city with the capture of Pogorelka and Podlipye .... In a new offensive designed to wipe out the Anzio beachhead, German units attack between Aprilia and Cisterna.	U.S. troops land on Los Negros Island of the Admiralty group, some 330 miles northwest of Rabaul; they quickly secure Momote airfield.		
March 1		Allied troops drive the Germans back between Aprilia and Cisterna .... As the result of a newly announced offensive, Russian troops have swung south of the Narva River in Estonia and are now blocking the Nazis' only railway escape route to Tallinn.	Japanese counteroffensive to retake Momote airfield on Los Negros Island is repulsed.	An attempted coup by Argentine Army and Navy elements opposed to the Farrell regime fails.	Cairo reports Egypt, Saudi Arabia, Syria and Lebanon have made protests to American ministers against the creation of a national Jewish homeland in Palestine.

A	B	C	D	E
Includes developments that affect more than one world region, international organizations and important meetings of major world leaders.	*Includes all developments in European countries and military engagements between Allied and Axis powers in Africa and at sea.*	*Includes all developments in Japan and China, Japanese foreign policy and military actions in the Pacific region.*	*Includes all domestic and regional developments in Latin America, the Caribbean and Canada.*	*Includes developments in those independent nations and colonial possessions not covered in Columns B, C and D.*

U.S. Politics & Social Issues	U.S. Foreign Policy & Defense	U.S. Economy & Environment	Science, Technology & Nature	Culture, Leisure & Life Style	
Dem. National Chmn. Robert Hannegan says he thinks FDR will be renominated.		FDR vetoes the tax bill and scores Congress for passing a "wholly ineffective revenue measure." . . . . Mayor Bowson of Los Angeles says Army troops will take over the municipal power system Feb. 23 to end a nine-day strike which has halted production in 150 war plants.	French army medical officers announce the development of an anti-typhus and anti-smallpox serum.		Feb. 22
Senate Majority Leader Alben Barkley (D, Ky.) breaks with FDR over his veto of the tax bill and resigns his leadership in protest . . . . Dewey announces he has asked his supporters not to enter his name in the Wisconsin GOP presidential primary . . . . House rejects a bill under which past expressions of disloyalty to the U.S. would be grounds for withdrawal of citizenship of Japanese-Americans and then passes a bill providing expatriation of native-born citizens of foreign ancestry who refuse to pledge allegiance to the U.S.		Senate votes to extend the life of the CCC through June 30, 1945 without banning consumer food subsidies . . . . Army takes over operation of the Los Angeles water and power system to end a strike of 3,000 employes over wage demands.	Inventor of the plastic bakelite, Leo H. Baekeland, dies at 80 in Beacon, N.Y.		Feb. 23
New York Court of Appeals refuses a rehearing for Louis (Lepke) Buchalter, Emanuel Weiss and Louis Capone, under sentence of death for the murder of Joseph Rosen in Brooklyn in 1936 . . . . Former War Secy. Harry Woodring says his stop-FDR group, the American Democratic Comm., plans to raise a $1.5-million campaign fund.	Army and Navy report total U.S. casualties of 157,865 through Feb. 7, including 36,005 killed, 54,867 wounded, 35,830 missing and 31,163 captured . . . . Rep. John Coffee (D, Wash.) asks Congress to sever diplomatic relations with Franco's Spain and give support to anti-Fascist forces there.	House overrides FDR's veto of the tax bill, and a Democratic Senate caucas reelects Barkley as leader after accepting his resignation.			Feb. 24
Sen. Charles McNary (R, Ore.), minority leader, dies at 69 in Fort Lauderdale, Fla. . . . . Special counsel to the House committee investigating the FCC, Eugene Carey, resigns, charging the investigation "has degenerated into a whitewashing affair." . . . . Seventeen of the 24 delegates pledged to Dewey in the Wisconsin GOP primary refuse to withdraw.	Selective Service Dir. Hershey tells the Senate Agricultural Comm. that the bottom of the manpower barrel has been reached.		James Reid Moir, British archaeologist who established the existence of man in the Pliocene period, dies at 64 in London.		Feb. 25
	FDR orders the WMC and Selective Service Commission to review draft deferments of some five million registrants.	CIO-UAW Pres. R.J. Thomas announces local unions responsible for unauthorized work stoppages will be disciplined . . . . Criminal charges of violating the Sherman Antitrust Act are filed against the A&P Co.		Gil Dodds wins the AAU mile at Madison Square Garden in 4:07.4, while the NYAC wins the team title, with Michigan second and Dartmouth third.	Feb. 26
	Foreign Economic Admin. Crowley reports Lend-Lease shipments to Russia from October 1941 to December 1943 totaled 8,400,000 tons valued at $4,243,804,000.			Gil Dodds is awarded the James E. Sullivan Award as "the amateur athlete who did the most to advance the cause of sportsmanship in 1943."	Feb. 27
		UMW Pres. Lewis says the CIO is dominated by Communists and that its leaders "are prisoners of the Communists and can't do a thing about it."		Univ. of Chicago Pres. Robert Hutchins announces organization of a commission to make a two-year study of "the nature, duties and responsibilities of the press in America".	Feb. 28
Senate and House conferees reach a compromise on soldier-vote legislation which would permit use of a federal ballot for residents of states that have not provided for absentee voting . . . . South Carolina House adopts and sends to the Senate a resolution reaffirming "belief and allegiance to established white supremacy" and warning "damned agitators of the North to leave the South alone." . . . . Mrs. Dorothy E. Vredenburgh is named secretary of the Democratic National Comm. She is the first woman to hold the post.		Commerce Dept. reports one of every three American families now has an income of more than $3,000, as compared with only one of ten between 1935 and 1940.		*Strange Fruit*, a story of inter-racial predjudice in Georgia by Lillian Smith, is published.	Feb. 29
FDR's name is entered in the presidential primaries in Nebraska and Wisconsin.	Foreign Economic Admin. Leo T. Crowley urges the House Foreign Affairs Comm. to extend Lend-Lease, which expires June 30.			Henry Sleeper Harper, director of Harper & Brothers and last family member in the publishing firm, dies at 79 in N.Y.	March 1
F *Includes elections, federal-state relations, civil rights and liberties, crime, the judiciary, education, health care, poverty, urban affairs and population.*	G *Includes formation and debate of U.S. foreign and defense policies, veterans affairs and defense spending. (Relations with specific foreign countries are usually found under the region concerned.)*	H *Includes business, labor, agriculture, taxation, transportation, consumer affairs, monetary and fiscal policy, natural resources, pollution and accidents.*	I *Includes worldwide scientific, medical and technological developments, natural phenomena, U.S. weather and natural disasters.*	J *Includes the arts, religion, scholarship, communications media, sports, entertainment, fashions, fads and social life.*	

	World Affairs	European War Zone	Pacific War Zone	The Americas	Other Countries & Territories
March 2		Soviet forces drive to within 24 miles of Latvia with the capture of Soshikhino.	West African troops continue to drive southward in the Kaladan Valley of western Burma and are about 40 miles north of Akyab . . . . Washington reports Lt. Gen. Stilwell has complained of the failure to launch a full-scale attack against the Japanese in Burma . . . . Navy planes bomb targets on Paramushiro and Shimushu Islands in the Kuriles.	Acting Argentine Pres. Farrell says his country's foreign policy will not be modified and that he will work closely with other American nations.	
March 3	FDR says the U.S., Britain and Russia have agreed to divide the Italian naval fleet equally.	Red Army units take Maloye Fomkino, five miles east of Pskov. Markovo, seven miles northwest, and Pokhvalshchina, seven miles southeast . . . . Stockholm newspaper *Dagen Nyheter* says the Finnish parliament has voted to reject the Russian demand that internment of German troops be a condition for peace . . . . Yugoslavian partisans capture Lastya, southern Bosnia, 20 miles east of Dubrovnik.	Americans continuously assault the Japanese on Los Negros Island, inflicting an estimated 3,000 casualties.	Chile announces recognition of the Farrell regime in Argentina . . . . A delegation of senators asks the Puerto Rican Congress to remove Gov. Rexford Tugwell because "he has built up a vast bureaucracy seeking government control."	
March 4		One group of Flying Fortresses from a large force attacking targets in eastern Germany today bombs the Berlin district, the first American bomber attack on the German capital . . . . Allies repulse a German assault at Cisterno . . . . Russian troops force the Ingulets River south of Krivoi Rog in the Ukraine to capture seven places and break the last natural German defense line before the Black Sea port of Nikolayev.	Tokyo decrees the mobilization of all high school students, use of school buildings as military storehouses and their yards for vegetable gardens.	Acting State Secy. Stettinius says the U.S. will not recognize the Farrell regime until it takes steps to bring Argentina "fully and completely into the realm of hemispheric solidarity."	Iraq tells Vice Pres. Wallace that a U.S. resolution favoring a Jewish Palestine "would be tantamount to the United States declaring war on the Arabs." . . . . Sen. Gerald P. Nye reports that Gen. Marshall told the Senate Foreign Relations Comm. that he favors a postponement of Jewish immigration into Palestine.
March 5		In a new offensive in the southwestern Ukraine, Russian forces route 12 German divisions and gain 15 to 31 miles on a 112-mile front in two days.	Leapfrogging along the north coast of New Guinea, a small U.S. amphibious force lands behind the Japanese lines at Yaula Point.	Sergei Orloff, Russian minister to Uruguay, arrives in Montevideo following the restoration of diplomatic relations.	
March 6		The second attack on Berlin by U.S. bombers occurs today, with some 850 Flying Fortresses and Liberators involved dropping more than 2,000 tons of bombs . . . . Russian forces take more than 200 inhabited places and cut the vital Odessa-Lwow rail line in the Ukraine.	U.S. Marines land on the west coast of the Willaumez Peninsula of New Britain Island.		
March 7		Russian forces repulse strong German counterattacks in the western Ukraine and advance to a point 10 miles above the railroad town of Tarnopol.	American and Chinese forces in northern Burma link up in an effort to wipe out some 2,000 Japanese in the Hukawng Valley.	El Salvador announces it will abstain from relations with Argentina "to fortify continental solidarity."	
March 8	ILO reports that jobs for 130 million throughout the world will have to be found in the shift back to a peacetime economy.	Russia rejects the Polish exile government's suggestion of a temporary boundary and insists upon the acceptance of the Curzon Line . . . . London Missionary Society reports almost 4,000 British churches have been destroyed or damaged by German bombings.	Japanese planes attack U.S. installations on Engebi Island in the Marshalls for the first time . . . . American and Chinese forces in northern Burma fight side-by-side against some 2,000 Japanese trapped in the Hukawng Valley.	Argentine Acting Foreign Min. Diego Mason says Paraguay will continue diplomatic relations with Buenos Aires.	
March 9		King Peter of Yugoslavia arrives in London for talks with British leaders on differences between his government and the partisan regime of Marshal Tito . . . . Churchill says units of the Italian fleet for the present will operate "where they now operate" and that Italian ships are unsuitable for Russia's northern waters . . . . On the third Ukrainian front, Russian troops advance 18 to 38 miles along a 105-mile front southwest of Krivoi Rog.	U.S. Marines cut the Willaumez Peninsula of New Britain in taking the village of Talasea.	Mexican Pres. Manuel Avila Camacho puts all railroads under government control and curtails the power of railroad unions.	American Zionist Emergency Council cochairmen Drs. Stephen Wise and Abba Silver announce after a White House visit that FDR supports the establishment of a national Jewish homeland in Palestine.
	A *Includes developments that affect more than one world region, international organizations and important meetings of major world leaders.*	B *Includes all developments in European countries and military engagements between Allied and Axis powers in Africa and at sea.*	C *Includes all developments in Japan and China, Japanese foreign policy and military actions in the Pacific region.*	D *Includes all domestic and regional developments in Latin America, the Caribbean and Canada.*	E *Includes developments in those independent nations and colonial possessions not covered in Columns B, C and D.*

U.S. Politics & Social Issues	U.S. Foreign Policy & Defense	U.S. Economy & Environment	Science, Technology & Nature	Culture, Leisure & Life Style	
Sidney Alderman, attorney for 10 railroads dealing with the FEPC, tells a House committee that the railroads have no intention of following a FEPC order to hire an increased number of Negroes . . . . Gov. Dewey of N.Y. grants another stay of execution to Louis (Lepke) Buchalter and two others convicted of murder shortly before they are to die in the Sing Sing prison's electric chair.	Lend-Lease aid to Turkey is halted because of Turkish unwillingness to enter the war or give the Allies air bases for use in the Mediterranean . . . . Fifty-five oil companies of the Petroleum Industry War Council approve a resolution assailing the proposed Arabian oil project of the Petroleum Reserves Corp. as a postwar rather than a war enterprise . . . . Sen. Mon Wallgren (D, Wash.) tells the Senate's Truman Committee that Liberty ships have developed defects in such numbers that it is unsafe to use them for troop or hospital ships . . . . U.S. Army announces plans to expand its training program for boys aged 17, who were not affected in the recent curtailment of the program.	Navy Secy. Knox says a national service act is needed to maintain war production schedules.			March 2
	FDR announces Edward Stettinius will attend the London conferences on war and postwar problems.		U.S. Bureau of Mines announces the discovery of new steel manufacturing processes that will permit production of high grade steel in 25 states . . . . The magazine *Air Force* reports that the drug benzedrene has been used with good results to help weary pilots fight off sleepiness and fatigue on return trips of combat missions.	Bob Montgomery outpoints Beau Jack in a 15-round bout in N.Y., regaining the state's lightweight title.	March 3
Buchalter is put to death in the electric chair at Sing Sing after receiving six reprieves . . . . Oregon Gov. Earl Snell appoints Guy Gorden to the seat of the late Sen. Charles McNary. . . . . The opening of President Roosevelt's 12th year in the White House is marked by special religious services attended by more than 200 officials.				Paul Lukas and Jennifer Jones win Academy Awards for best individual performances in 1943. *Casablanca* is named best picture of the year . . . . Federal Judge George More rules that the 20th Century-Fox Film Corp. picture *Alexander's Ragtime Band* was based on the unpublished novel *Love Girl* and says he will appoint a commision to set damage awards for the author, Mrs. Marie Dieckhaus.	March 4
	Rep. Andrew May (D, Ky.) says the Army has abandoned plans to distribute the pamphlet *The Races of Mankind* following a House Military Affairs Committee threat "to expose the motives behind this book". He says it describes Northern Negroes as equal in intelligence to Southern whites.				March 5
FEPC Chmn. Malcolm Ross says the Chicago & Northwestern Railway will upgrade Negroes, promoting car cleaners to helpers and dining car waiters to stewards as recommended by the FEPC.		Willard H. Dow tells the Senate Truman Committee that government charges linking Dow Chemical Co. with a German cartel are wrong.			March 6
Senate and House conferees adopt a soldier-vote bill limiting a federal ballot to citizens of states that have no absentee voting laws and then only if valid under state laws . . . . U.S. Office of Education makes public a survey on Negro education with recommendations that facilities of all colleges and universities in the South be opened to Negroes.					March 7
				Superior Court Judge Stanley Mosk rules in Los Angeles that Charlie Chaplin must stand trial in the suit of Joan Berry, who charges he is the father of her child. The decision holds that blood tests are not reliable evidence of parentage.	March 8
					March 9
F	G	H	I	J	
Includes elections, federal-state relations, civil rights and liberties, crime, the judiciary, education, health care, poverty, urban affairs and population.	*Includes formation and debate of U.S. foreign and defense policies, veterans affairs and defense spending. (Relations with specific foreign countries are usually found under the region concerned.)*	*Includes business, labor, agriculture, taxation, transportation, consumer affairs, monetary and fiscal policy, natural resources, pollution and accidents.*	*Includes worldwide scientific, medical and technological developments, natural phenomena, U.S. weather and natural disasters.*	*Includes the arts, religion, scholarship, communications media, sports, entertainment, fashions, fads and social life.*	

	World Affairs	European War Zone	Pacific War Zone	The Americas	Other Countries & Territories
March 10		Moscow reports a new Soviet breakthrough in the Ukraine after five days of fighting which has resulted in the defeat of 14 German divisions on a 110-mile front southwest of Cherkassy .... FDR backs Churchill's statement concerning the Italian fleet, and says that U.S. and British warships will be transferred to the Russians.	U.S. and Chinese forces advance three to four miles in northern Burma against heavy Japanese resistence.	Argentine Pres. Ramirez resigns and acting Pres. Farrell assumes full powers.	
March 11		Ankara sources report Rumania is regrouping its army for a desperate defense against the Russians, that the evacuation of Bucharest is under way and that efforts to reach Russian diplomats in Ankara to arrange a peace settlement have been fruitless .... Red Army establishes a new bridgehead on the west bank of the lower Dnieper River by capturing Berislav, only 40 miles northeast of the river seaport of Kherson .... U.S. planes hit the historic Italian art center of Florence, aiming at the destruction of rail yards.	Americans turn back an assault by 3,000 Japanese upon their positions on Empress Augusta Bay, Bougainville .... British and Indian troops take Buthedaung in western Burma and gain control of both ends of the east-west Maungdaw-Buthedaung road.		
March 12		Pope Pius XII calls on the belligerents to avoid making Rome a battleground .... British Home Office bans travel between Britain and Ireland effective tomorrow, except in rare emergencies and on official business .... For the first time since 1940, Hitler does not speak at the observance of Heroes' Day ceremonies in Berlin.	Americans take Wotho Atoll in the Marshalls, the fourth island in the group to be captured by U.S. forces.		
March 13		Climaxing a week's drive, Russian forces take Kherson, 15 miles up the Dnieper River from the Black Sea .... Badoglio's Italian government announces that Russia has agreed to a resumption of diplomatic relations and an exchange of ambassadors.	American troops make a new landing on New Britain at the base of Willaumez Peninsula.		
March 14		Russian troops close a trap on several German divisions on the third Ukrainian front .... Stockholm reports that the Soviet reply to Finland's counter-peace proposals reiterates Russia's original demands and insists on compliance .... State Secy. Hull expresses the hope that Finland will "withdraw from its association with Germany in the war."	The fighting on Bougainville Island reaches a climax, with the Japanese failing to break the Allied beachhead on the Empress Augusta Bay.	Cuban President Batista appoints Cuban Communist leader Carlos Rodriguez as a cabinet minister without portfolio.	
March 15		Russian troops force the Bug River along a 62-mile front and advance 12 to 19 miles..... In a five-hour air attack, Allied planes virtually level the Italian town of Cassino .... Yugoslavian partisans announce the smashing of a German attempt to break into liberated Slovenian territory.	Land-based planes make the first Allied attack on Japanese-held Truk in the Carolines .... American troops land on the northeastern tip of Manus Island, largest of the Admiralty group.	Dr. Carlos Saladrigas is nominated presidential candidate by the Cuban government coalition of the Liberal, Democratic, ABC and Popular Socialist parties.	
March 16		Allied infantrymen occupy three-quarters of Cassino, but the Nazis hold stubbornly to a corner of the leveled Italian town .... Russian troops sever the Odessa-Zhmerinka railroad at Vapnyarka, 28 miles north of Bessarabia, thus splitting the German front in the Ukraine .... FDR expresses the hope that Finland will "withdraw from her hateful partnership with Germany."	American troops take the airfield near Lorengau on Manus Island in the Admiralties .... U.S. bombers make the deepest penetration yet of Japan's Kurile Islands, bombing Matsuwa, less than 500 miles from the Japanese mainland at Hokkaido.	Canadian P.M. W.L. Mackenzie King announces the renewal of mutual aid pacts with Australia, Britain and Russia.	
March 17		Russian troops in the central Ukraine gain 19 miles, capturing Klembovka and Olshanka, only 10 miles above the Dniester River.		Government employes in Cuba demonstrate in Havana in support of a 20% wage increase.	
March 18		Russian troops fight their way to the west bank of the Dniester River and take Yampol on the Bessarabian boundary .... In the Polish offensive Soviet units reach Khotyn, 60 miles northeast of Lwow.	American troops take the town of Lorengau on the eastern end of Manus Island in the Admiralties.	Argentine government closes the UP's news gathering and distribution facilities and charges violation of terms of its concessions.	

A	B	C	D	E
Includes developments that affect more than one world region, international organizations and important meetings of major world leaders.	*Includes all developments in European countries and military engagements between Allied and Axis powers in Africa and at sea.*	*Includes all developments in Japan and China, Japanese foreign policy and military actions in the Pacific region.*	*Includes all domestic and regional developments in Latin America, the Caribbean and Canada.*	*Includes developments in those independent nations and colonial possessions not covered in Columns B, C and D.*

U.S. Politics & Social Issues	U.S. Foreign Policy & Defense	U.S. Economy & Environment	Science, Technology & Nature	Culture, Leisure & Life Style	
Maryland and Virginia legislatures adopt bills authorizing absentee voting by members of the armed services . . . . FDR approves recommendations of the Army and Navy permitting political nominations of officers of the armed services provided they come without solicitation or direct effort.		WPB announces that imports of alcoholic beverages derived from cane sugar in Cuba and other Latin American countries will be put on a strict quota basis beginning March 5 to prevent further excessive diversion from wartime needs.			March 10
Minnesota legislature adopts a bill permitting absentee balloting by service men and women.		Sen. Patrick McCarren (D, Nev.), chairman of the Senate Judiciary subcommittee investigating the alcoholic beverage industry, says he will ask the WPB to permit manufacture of beverage alcohol for a limited time "to prevent a return to bootleg conditions."		An NWLB panel directs members of the American Federation of Musicians to resume recording for subsidiaries of RCA and CBS, rejecting the AFM charge that radio and phonograph recordings have caused unemployment among musicians . . . . Gil Dodds set a new world indoor record of 4:07.3, winning the mile at the K of C games in N.Y. . . . . Michigan wins the Big Ten indoor track and field championships in Chicago with 75 1/4 points. Illinois is second and Purdue third.	March 11
		House GOP leader Joseph Martin announces the formation of a 25-member committee to make a study of the tax field and "prepare a postwar revenue program."			March 12
House passes a resolution calling for an investigation of the status of the American Indian.	Army announces it will cancel draft deferments for all except a few of its 8,500 civilian workers in the 22-25 age bracket "as an example to Selective Service boards."				March 13
Senate passes and sends to the House the "states' rights" soldier-vote bill, which sharply restricts use of the short federal ballot . . . . Willkie wins the GOP and FDR the Democratic N.H. presidential primary.	Selective Service Dir. Hershey orders local boards to end deferments for men 18-25 years of age in industry unless they are certified "as key men" in war industry by state draft directors.	OPA announces gasoline allotments to holders of "A" coupons will be cut to two gallons weekly throughout the nation effective Mar. 22.			March 14
House passes the "states' rights" soldier-vote bill and sends it to FDR, who telegraphs all state governments asking whether the federal ballot can legally be used . . . . Sens. Robert Taft (O.), Wallace White (Me.) and Arthur Vandenberg (Mich.) are named members of the GOP Congressional steering committee.	Selective Service Dir. Hershey says farm workers' deferments must be cancelled to meet armed service requirements of 1.1 million men by July 1 . . . . North American Aviation Inc. announces its P-51 Mustang fighter has a speed of 425 m.p.h. in level flight, a radius of more than 500 miles and a ceiling of 40,000 feet.	NWLB rejects a petition of the AFL to modify the Little Steel wage formula limiting wage increases to 15%.		Manuel Ortiz, world bantamweight champion, outpoints Ernesto Aguilar in a 15-round bout in Los Angeles.	March 15
North Carolina GOP state convention unanimously adopts a resolution favoring the drafting of Dewey as the party's presidential candidate.	WPB Chmn. Nelson and Selective Service Dir. Hershey tell steel industry representatives that they must reconcile themselves to losses of workers under 26 to the armed services . . . . U.S. War and Navy Depts. announce that 23 Army transport planes were shot down over Sicily in July 1943 by "friendly naval and ground gunfire" as well as enemy fire, with a loss of 410 American lives.	Justice Dept. files a suit charging Imperial Chemical Industries, Ltd., two U.S. export associations and other concerns with conspiracy to operate a cartel in alkalis.	Representatives of 21 penicillin producers meet with the WPB and other government agencies and organize a committee to work out agreements for exchange of technical information and other measures to increase the output of the drug.	Mrs. Ruth Googins Roosevelt, second wife of Col. Elliot Roosevelt, files suit for divorce, charging "unkind, harsh and tyrannical conduct."	March 16
Dies Committee announces it will investigate the radio activities of Walter Winchell, who Chmn. Dies accuses of personal attacks and attacks upon Congress.	Senate Finance Comm. approves the "GI Bill of Rights" - an omnibus measure providing for hospitalization, education, vocational training, unemployment benefits and loans for war veterans . . . . House Foreign Affairs Comm. votes to defer action on a resolution recommending continued Jewish immigration to Palestine.	House Ways and Means Comm. approves a tax plan that would relieve 30 million individual taxpayers from filing returns and would simplify forms for others.		Brother Clement Frischauf, O.S.B., who laid the mosaics in the crypt of the bombed Monastery of Mt. Cassino, Italy, dies at 74 in Minnesota.	March 17
				Gil Dodds breaks the world's indoor record for the mile at 4:06.4 in Chicago.	March 18

F	G	H	I	J
Includes elections, federal-state relations, civil rights and liberties, crime, the judiciary, education, health care, poverty, urban affairs and population.	*Includes formation and debate of U.S. foreign and defense policies, veterans affairs and defense spending. (Relations with specific foreign countries are usually found under the region concerned.)*	*Includes business, labor, agriculture, taxation, transportation, consumer affairs, monetary and fiscal policy, natural resources, pollution and accidents.*	*Includes worldwide scientific, medical and technological developments, natural phenomena, U.S. weather and natural disasters.*	*Includes the arts, religion, scholarship, communications media, sports, entertainment, fashions, fads and social life.*

	World Affairs	European War Zone	Pacific War Zone	The Americas	Other Countries & Territories
March 19		Red Army sweeps across the Dniester River on a 31-mile front and captures more than 40 localities in Bessarabia.	Japanese troops from Chindwin River, Burma open a major offensive towards India's Manipur State .... After five days of air attacks, an entire Japanese convoy of three corvettes and two transports is destroyed off the northeast coast of New Guinea.		
March 20		German troops complete their move into Hungary, as Hitler summons Regent Adm. Nicholas Horthy and his aides to Nazi headquarters .... Russian units in the western Ukraine capture the industrial and railroad center of Vinnitsa and the Dniester River city of Mogilev-Podolski.	Chinese-American forces smash Japanese resistance in the Hukawng Valley of northern Burma .... U.S. Marines land on Emirau Island of the St. Matthias group and occupy it against light opposition.		
March 21		German troops consolidate their hold on Hungary, where a puppet regime is reported established under pro-Nazi Bela Imredy .... Finnish government announces the rejection of the Russian armistice terms as being "harsh" and unclear .... Eruptions of Mount Vesuvius force the evacuation of three Italian towns.	Japanese offensive against Manipur State is reported 15 miles west of the border.		Premier Ali Scheily of Iran resigns and Shah Mohammed Reza Pahlevi asks former Foreign Min. Mohammed Saed Maraghei to form a new cabinet.
March 22		Imredy is unable to form a new Hungarian government and a new cabinet is appointed with Field Marshal Doeme Sztojay as premier and foreign minister .... U.S. and Britain inform Russia that they will not extend recognition to the Italian government of Badoglio .... In the bitter struggle for Cassino, the Germans throw new units into battle .... After two days of fighting Soviet troops capture the fortified Bug River rail center of Pervomaisk in the northeastern Ukraine.	New Delhi reports Japanese troops have crossed India's border into Manipur state .... Tojo tells the Japanese Diet that the Empire "is now facing battles which will decide its fate."		
March 23		After three days of fighting, Russian troops in the western Ukraine advance 25 to 37 miles from Tarnopol to Proskurov .... Provisional Consultative Assembly of French Comm. of National Liberation approves an article in the provisional government code extending the franchise to women.	A second Japanese unit enters Manipur State, advancing some 25 miles south of Imphal.		In a series of gunfights and bombings in Jerusalem, Tel Aviv and Haifa by political terrorists, six British constables are killed and 12 injured.
March 24		Churchill says the invasion of Europe will occur "soon." .... FDR appeals to the people of Germany and Nazi-subjugated nations to aid Jews and other victims of persecution to escape and asks free nations to open their borders to the refugees .... Nazi troops regain one-fourth of the ruins of Cassino and are now strongly entrenched on the west side of the town .... Russian troops reach the Dniester River at Zaleshchiki, on the Bukovina border in the southwestern Ukraine.		Colombian government press office reports it has interned 150 Japanese and German nationals and says others will be taken into custody.	
March 25		Russian forces make new gains in the Ukraine, reaching the outskirts of of the Black Sea port of Nikolayev and the Dniester River along a 50-mile front north of Cernauti and Proskurov.	American and Chinese troops take Shaduzup in northern Burma in a blow at the east flank of Japanese forces now cut off in the Mogaung Valley.		
March 26		Churchill in a radio broadcast says that the Allies' "hour of greatest effort and action is approaching." .... Russian forces drive the Germans back to the Rumanian border along a 53-mile front .... Greek government-in-exile rejects suggestions of the National Liberation Front to broaden the government to include the guerrilla group.	British commandos reach a point 147 miles from Myitkyina, the main Japanese base above the Burma Road.		

A	B	C	D	E
Includes developments that affect more than one world region, international organizations and important meetings of major world leaders.	*Includes all developments in European countries and military engagements between Allied and Axis powers in Africa and at sea.*	*Includes all developments in Japan and China, Japanese foreign policy and military actions in the Pacific region.*	*Includes all domestic and regional developments in Latin America, the Caribbean and Canada.*	*Includes developments in those independent nations and colonial possessions not covered in Columns B, C and D.*

	U.S. Politics & Social Issues	U.S. Foreign Policy & Defense	U.S. Economy & Environment	Science, Technology & Nature	Culture, Leisure & Life Style
March 19	White House makes public the responses from governors of 41 states concerning their positions on the soldier-vote legislation. The responses indicate 5 states will accept, 14 are likely to, while 18 propbably will refuse it .... William Hale (Big Bill) Thompson, three times mayor of Chicago who once threatened King George V of England "with a punch in the snoot," dies at 74 in Chicago.				
March 20	House passes and sends to the Senate a bill making it a criminal offense to publish or distribute anonymous statements regarding candidates for federal office.				Boston Bd. of Retail Merchants bans the sale of the novel *Strange Fruit*, which deals with love between a white man and Negro woman.
March 21	Sen. Edwin Johnson (D, Colo.) charges the third term of FDR has been a great failure and that should he gain a fourth, it will be one of "defeat and frustration."	State Secy. Hull states U.S. foreign policy is based upon winning the war, international cooperation and the Atlantic Charter .... Naples announces that Lt. Gen. George S. Patton Jr. has been replaced as commander of the U.S. 7th Army by Maj. Gen. Alexander M. Patch .... U.S. State Dept. denies Algiers reports that it may deal with the Vichy government as well as the French Comm. of National Liberation in liberated France.			
March 22		House passes the conference-approved bill establishing UNRAA and sends it to the White House.	NWLB instructs its panel considering United Steel Workers wage demands to take union testimony supporting the 17¢ hourly increase request.		*Variety* reports the most popular songs are: (1) *Mairzy Doats*, (2) *Besame Mucho* and (3) *I Couldn't Sleep a Wink Last Night*.
March 23	N.J. Gov. Walter Edge signs an absentee-voting bill for distribution of federal and state ballots to servicemen and women .... The governor of South Carolina reports that the federal ballot is unacceptable in that state.	House Foreign Affairs Comm. approves an amendment to the bill extending Lend-Lease for another year, which prohibits the President from settling Lend-Lease obligations in the postwar period "except by constitutional procedure."	Treasury Secy. Morgenthau announces the fifth war loan goal will be $16 billion .... WPB announces the armed services have approved a plan to exempt men 22-26 from the draft in several vital war industries.		Myron Selznick, the actors' agent who represented more than 300 performers and directors and whose 1939 payroll was estimated at more than $10,000,000, dies at 45 in Santa Monica, Calif.
March 24	Senate passes the independent offices appropriations bill, with drastic restrictions on executive agencies, and sends it to conference.	Senate approves and sends to the House the "GI Bill." .... Selective Service Dir. Hershey orders state directors to call all deferred registrants under 26 for pre-induction physical examinations.			
March 25		Sen. Tom Connally (D, Tex.) reveals that State Secy. Hull has suggested that a congressional committee be established to consult with the State Dept. on a postwar peace organization.	CIO United Steel Workers present a brief to the NWLB demanding a fixed annual wage based upon a 40-hour week.		
March 26	Martin Dies assails Walter Winchell as the "tool" of an organized movement to undermine the prestige of Congress; in response, Winchell challenges Dies to take the case to court.				
	F	G	H	I	J
	Includes elections, federal-state relations, civil rights and liberties, crime, the judiciary, education, health care, poverty, urban affairs and population.	*Includes formation and debate of U.S. foreign and defense policies, veterans affairs and defense spending. (Relations with specific foreign countries are usually found under the region concerned.)*	*Includes business, labor, agriculture, taxation, transportation, consumer affairs, monetary and fiscal policy, natural resources, pollution and accidents.*	*Includes worldwide scientific, medical and technological developments, natural phenomena, U.S. weather and natural disasters.*	*Includes the arts, religion, scholarship, communications media, sports, entertainment, fashions, fads and social life.*

	World Affairs	European War Zone	Pacific War Zone	The Americas	Other Countries & Territories
March 27		Polish Telegraph Agency announces underground leaders in Poland have been instructed to get in touch with Russian military leaders "to coordinate military operations against the Germans." .... Three German attacks on the Allied beachhead at Anzio are repulsed.	A fourth Japanese column enters Manipur State, India from the Sumra jungle area on the Burmese border.		
March 28		Soviets capture Nikolayev on the Black Sea.	Heavy fighting breaks out on the Manipur plain as British forces seek to throw back the Japanese invasion force, 35 miles northeast of Imphal.		The Jewish military organization Irgun Zvai Leumi admits responsibility for the March 23 bombings in Jerusalem, Jaffa and Haifa.
March 29		Allied forces withdraw from the eastern slopes of Mt. Cassino, leaving the Nazis in control of all heights dominating the highway entering the Liri Valley .... Nazi assaults at the Anzio beachhead are driven off .... *Izvestia* warns Rumania and Bulgaria to break with Germany "or share Germany's fate." .... Russian troops cross the Prut River and reach the outskirts of Cernauti, capital of northern Bukovina.	U.S. Pacific fleet attacks Japanese positions on the Palau Islands, 550 miles east of the Philippines, and Woleai and Yap Islands, east of the Palaus, destroying all enemy ships.		
March 30		Soviet forces capture Cernauti, northern Bukovina .... Churchill wins a vote of confidence in the House of Commons, 425 to 23, on a motion to remove an amendment from an educational bill granting equal pay to men and women teachers.	American troops occupy Pityilu Island in the Admiralties.		
March 31		Nazi raids on the Anzio beachhead force U.S. troops to retreat 1½ miles southwest of Aprilia .... Allied troops advance about one mile and seize Mt. Marrone, 13 miles northeast of Cassino .... RAF's bomber command suffers its heaviest loss when 94 bombers of about 1,000 that raid Nuremburg, Germany fail to return .... The Black Sea port of Ochakov falls to the Russians, placing them 38 miles east of Odessa.	Soviet government announces the cancellation of Japanese oil concessions in northern Sakhalin, 26 years in advance of treaty expiration, in view of "operations of our Allies in the Pacific." .... British abandon their foward Burmese base of Tiddim, 100 miles south of Imphal, Manipur State in the face of Japanese assaults.	Colombian government announces that "concerted revolutionary activity" has been suppressed in the town of Purification with the arrest of 75 persons.	
Apr. 1		An article in the *Hamburger Fremdenblatt* quotes Benito Mussolini as always confident that he would be rescued by Hitler. He charges that the Allies planned to take him to the U.S. "to put him on exhibition as a war criminal and charge a fee to see him." .... With the capture of Kablevo, Russian forces reach a point 24 miles northeast of Odessa.			
Apr. 2		Russian troops enter Rumania, the first time in the war the Soviets have stepped on soil not claimed by Moscow.	An Army spokesman claims 100,000 Japanese troops are trapped in the Marshalls, Bismarck Archipelago, northern Solomons and parts of New Guinea.	An uprising in El Salvador aimed at overthrowing Pres. Maximiliano Hernandez-Martinez is crushed.	
Apr. 3		Greek P.M. Tsouderos resigns after a session of the Greek cabinet in Cairo and suggests to King George II, now in London, that Sophocles Venizelos be named as his successor .... Russian drive across the Prut River into Rumania establishes two bridgeheads, one at Carpiti and the second between Dangeni and Saveni.	U.S. Army forces complete the occupation of 10 more atolls in the Marshalls .... Japanese forces cut the main road supplying Imphal in Manipur State, India.		

A	B	C	D	E
Includes developments that affect more than one world region, international organizations and important meetings of major world leaders.	*Includes all developments in European countries and military engagements between Allied and Axis powers in Africa and at sea.*	*Includes all developments in Japan and China, Japanese foreign policy and military actions in the Pacific region.*	*Includes all domestic and regional developments in Latin America, the Caribbean and Canada.*	*Includes developments in those independent nations and colonial possessions not covered in Columns B, C and D.*

U.S. Politics & Social Issues	U.S. Foreign Policy & Defense	U.S. Economy & Environment	Science, Technology & Nature	Culture, Leisure & Life Style	
Supreme Court refuses to review the conviction of George S. Viereck under the Foreign Agents Registration Act.		Supreme Court sustains the power of the OPA to fix ceiling prices on meats and rents and rules that miners must be paid for time spent going from the face of the mine to working places.		American Academy of Arts and Letters announces that its Award of Merit and $1,000 cash prize will go to novelist Theodore Dreiser .... A $90,000 suit against James C. Petrillo, president of the American Federation of Musicians, by Opera on Tour, Inc., is disclosed in N.Y. The suit alleges that Petrillo interfered with the plaintiff's efforts to present grand opera through recordings.	March 27
	FDR says his declaration favoring a Jewish state in Palestine and disapproving of the British White Paper referred to future settlements and is not in conflict with the War Dept.'s desire that no action be taken now on a Senate resolution on the Jewish-Palestine question.			Utah Univ. defeats Dartmouth, 42-40, to win the NCAA basketball title in N.Y.	March 28
A Dies Committee report says the CIO's Comm. for Political Action is Communist-dominated and that Sidney Hillman has replaced Earl Browder "as the Communist political leader in the United States."	FDR signs a bill authorizing American participation in UNRRA.	Montgomery Ward & Co. labor relations manager John Barr tells the NWLB that the firm will not obey a board directive to renew a contract with the CIO United Retail, Wholesale and Warehouse Workers Union because it has pending a court decision to declare the directive illegal .... OPA announces all frozen fruits and vegetables will be ration-free as of April 2.			March 29
		GM announces that 1943 sales were a record $3,796,115,800, with 93.3% of the production in munitions.		Utah Univ. defeats St. John's Univ., 43-36, to win the unofficial national college title .... Montreal and Chicago win the semi-finals of the Stanley Cup hockey playoffs by defeating Toronto and Detroit.	March 30
Soldier-vote bill becomes law without the signature of FDR, who calls the "states' rights" measure "inadequate" and asks its amendment to provide wider and freer use of the short federal ballot .... Dewey telegraphs his supporters in Oregon to withdraw his name from the May 19 primary there .... Rep. John M. Coffee (D,Wash.) charges in the House that Connecticut industrialist Vivien Hellems has been guilty of treasonable and seditious conduct in urging businessmen not to pay income taxes.					March 31
Vivien Kellems says in Toronto that Rep. Coffee "is a coward" and dares him to make his charges "outside of the House so I can hale you into court and put you in prison where you belong." .... Sen. Robert Wagner (D, N.Y.) urges FDR's renomination because "the people do not want to turn the Presidency over to some untried novice in the critical days ahead."	Army reports that 1,058,000 enlisted men were discharged from Dec. 1, 1941 to Jan. 31, 1944.			Bill Smith wins three titles in the two-day AAU indoor swimming championships in Ann Arbor, taking the 100, 220 and 440-yard freestyle events.	Apr. 1
Harry Woodring resigns as chairman and withdraws from the American Democratic National Comm., saying that many anti-FDR people are too timid "to stand up and be counted."	FEA reports Lend-Lease munitions and supplies to Russia in January and February exceeded 1,000,000 tons and that total shipments since October 1941 were 9,500,000 tons.	NWLB denies a 15% wage increase to 9,000 Alcoa workers, saying they have received all increases allowed under the Little Steel formula.		Dmitri Shostakovich's *Symphony No. 8*is presented for the first time in the U.S. by the N.Y. Philharmonic Symphony in Carnegie Hall.	Apr. 2
Supreme Court rules that Negroes cannot be barred from voting in the Texas Democratic primaries on the grounds of race and, in an 8 to 1 decision, repudiates the contention that political parties are private associations free of constitutional regulation. Applying equally to other states with "white primaries," the decision holds that discrimination against Negroes by a political party violates the 15th amendment and that political parties function as state agencies in primary elections.					Apr. 3

F	G	H	I	J
Includes elections, federal-state relations, civil rights and liberties, crime, the judiciary, education, health care, poverty, urban affairs and population.	*Includes formation and debate of U.S. foreign and defense policies, veterans affairs and defense spending. (Relations with specific foreign countries are usually found under the region concerned.)*	*Includes business, labor, agriculture, taxation, transportation, consumer affairs, monetary and fiscal policy, natural resources, pollution and accidents.*	*Includes worldwide scientific, medical and technological developments, natural phenomena, U.S. weather and natural disasters.*	*Includes the arts, religion, scholarship, communications media, sports, entertainment, fashions, fads and social life.*

	World Affairs	European War Zone	Pacific War Zone	The Americas	Other Countries & Territories
Apr. 4		French Comm. of National Liberation announces that a National Defense General Staff has been established under de Gaulle with complete authority over the Army, Navy and Air Force . . . . After three days of street fighting, Russian forces gain control of Tarnopol, Poland.	Because of jungle fires set by the Japanese, British troops are forced back into the Manipur plain, east of Imphal.		
Apr. 5		Russian troops capture Kubanka, 17 miles north of Odessa, and also take Razdelnaya and Kuchurgan, thus cutting the last major rail and highway escape route for an estimated 100,000 Germans in the Odessa area . . . . Crown Prince Humbert of Italy says he is prepared to act as deputy for King Victor Emmanuel, who has agreed to name him his lieutenant with authority to exercise the prerogatives of the crown . . . . British government ends public telephone service to Ireland and halts export of newspapers and most other printed matter to Ireland and Gibraltar as a safety measure.	Japanese invasion forces seize a 15-mile stretch of the Imphal-Kohima highway in Manipur State and push to a point 80 miles east of Dimapur, which is the Allied lifeline to northern Burma.		
Apr. 6		Yugoslavian partisans report a Nazi armored force has smashed to within five miles of Tito's headquarters at Jajce . . . . Russian troops capture Skala, north of Cernauti, northern Bukovina . . . . Istanbul Observatory reports violent earthquake shocks in the Balikisri area of Anatolia.	Indian troops reach Imphal, after they were held up for three weeks by the Japanese.		
Apr. 7		Russian troops trap five or six German divisions north of Razdelnaya, 40 miles above Odessa . . . . American troops on the Anzio beachhead gain a new strongpoint northwest of Padiglione in small-scale action.	A Japanese advance unit penetrating the outskirts of Kohima, Manipur State is repulsed.		Former Premier Rashid Ali el Gailani of Iraq is arrested along with 19 associates and is held prisoner in Baghdad.
Apr. 8		Red Army reaches the Czech frontier at Zhabye just east of the Tartar Pass . . . . In their drive on Odessa, Russian units take another 30 places including Gildendorf, only eight miles northeast of the Black Sea port.	Allied forces drive the Japanese from one vital point north of Imphal and generally improve their positions in Manipur State.		
Apr. 9		Red Army continues its advance inside Rumania with the capture of 200 more localities, mostly between the Prut and Siretul Rivers . . . . By taking the railroad junction of Sortirovochnaya the Russians move to within three miles of Odessa.	Japanese pressure continues in Manipur State with patrols infiltrating across the Tiddem Road only 18 miles southwest of Imphal.		
Apr. 10		Odessa, which has been under Nazi control since October 1941, falls to the Russians . . . . Two small Nazi thrusts are repulsed on the British beachhead south of Rome and by the Italians holding Mt. Marrone.		Ten army officers are executed as ringleaders of last week's abortive revolt in El Salvador . . . . Ottawa announces that Canadian armed forces will be increased by 98,000 during the next 12 months.	Liberia becomes the 35th member of the U.N.
Apr. 11		Hungarian exiles in England form a government under the leadership of former President Count Michael Karolyi . . . . German reinforcements break into the Russian ring around Nazi forces in the Skala region and join their comrades.	Japanese troops swing around north of Kohima in an effort to encircle the Indian city.		
Apr. 12		King Victor Emmanuel announces he will "irrevocably" withdraw from public affairs in favor of his son, Crown Prince Humbert, on the day Allied troops enter Rome.	Allied counterattacks relieve the Japanese pressure on Kohima, Manipur State.		

A	B	C	D	E
Includes developments that affect more than one world region, international organizations and important meetings of major world leaders.	*Includes all developments in European countries and military engagements between Allied and Axis powers in Africa and at sea.*	*Includes all developments in Japan and China, Japanese foreign policy and military actions in the Pacific region.*	*Includes all domestic and regional developments in Latin America, the Caribbean and Canada.*	*Includes developments in those independent nations and colonial possessions not covered in Columns B, C and D.*

U.S. Politics & Social Issues	U.S. Foreign Policy & Defense	U.S. Economy & Environment	Science, Technology & Nature	Culture, Leisure & Life Style	
Delegates pledged to Dewey win the Wisconsin GOP presidential primary over Harold Stassen, Willkie and MacArthur.				Charlie Chaplin is acquitted of charges of a Mann Act violation by a federal court jury in Los Angeles. The trial opened March 21 on charges that Chaplin had transported Joan Berry on a round trip from Hollywood to New York for immoral purposes .... Marshall Field transfers 10,000 shares of Marshall Field & Co. stock and the 38-story Pittsfield Building to the Chicago Natural History Museum.	Apr. 4
Willkie says the results of the Wisconsin primary convince him he cannot win the GOP presidential nomination and announces his withdrawal from the race .... Committee on Fair Employment Practices reveals that the Pennsylvania Railroad Co. has agreed to employ qualified dining car stewards without regard to race, creed, color or national origin .... Board of Immigration Appeals announces it has withdrawn a 1940 deportation order against the Russian-born wife of CP chief Earl Browder.				Rose O'Neill, creator of the Kewpie Doll, which brought her $1,400,000 in royalties, dies at 69 in Springfield, Mo.	Apr. 5
	OWI reports the Army has reached its planned strength of 7.7 million but will require 75,000 to 100,000 monthly replacements.	Standard Oil Co. of N.J. Vice President Eugene Holman says the nation's oil reserves are "sufficient for a thousand years." .... NWLB orders Montgomery Ward to continue its contract with the CIO Mail Order, Warehouse and Retail Employes Union until an election determines whether workers want union representation .... Solid Fuels Admin. Ickes predicts tighter restrictions on use of coal during the coming winter because of shortages due to the drafting of young miners.			Apr. 6
Southern senators disclose that "more than 1,000 amendments" have been prepared to delay and prevent action on the anti-poll tax bill approved by the House and sent to the Senate .... Nebraska legislature ends its special session by passing a bill to liberalize voting laws for persons in the armed forces and absentees working in war industries outside the state.	FDR says no further action has been taken by the U.S. to recognize de Gaulle's French Comm. and adds that the matter is one of self-determination for the French people .... Stettinius arrives in London for conferences with Foreign Secy. Anthony Eden.				Apr. 7
Sidney Hillman is elected state chairman of the American Labor Party in N.Y.	Selective Service Dir. Hershey instructs local draft boards to complete action on registrants under 26 before calling older men.				Apr. 8
Col. Robert McCormick's *Chicago Tribune* backs Gen. Douglas MacArthur in the April 11 Illinois presidential primary, saying that a vote for him "will be a vote for the return of stalwart Americanism to the White House."					Apr. 9
Supreme Court holds that Florida's "peonage" law is unconstitutional, saying that "involuntary servitude" cannot be enforced "even if voluntarily contracted for."		Supreme Court sustains an NLRB decision finding the Medo Supply Co. of N.Y. guilty of unfair practices in dealing individually with employes who abandoned membership in a union.	The annual report of the National Foundation for Infantile Paralysis expresses regret at the publicity given the Kenny method for treating the disease.	*The First Lady Chatterly*, by D.H. Lawrence (first version of *Lady Chatterly's Lover*), is published in New York.	Apr. 10
	Vice Pres. Wallace announces plans to visit China in the late spring or early summer as a representative of FDR.		Thirty-four persons are killed and more than 100 injured in a tornado which causes heavy damage at several points in Arkansas.	Dodd, Mead & Co. and *Red Book* magazine announce that Dorothea Cornwell is the winner of their joint $10,000 fiction prize for her novel *They Dare Not Go A'Hunting*.	Apr. 11
		An estimated 1,000 employes of a Montgomery Ward & Co. CIO union strike in Chicago against the company's refusal to accept an NWLB order to recognize the union .... National Industrial Conference Bd. makes public a report on living costs, putting the rise at 20.8% since 1941.			Apr. 12

F	G	H	I	J
Includes elections, federal-state relations, civil rights and liberties, crime, the judiciary, education, health care, poverty, urban affairs and population.	*Includes formation and debate of U.S. foreign and defense policies, veterans affairs and defense spending. (Relations with specific foreign countries are usually found under the region concerned.)*	*Includes business, labor, agriculture, taxation, transportation, consumer affairs, monetary and fiscal policy, natural resources, pollution and accidents.*	*Includes worldwide scientific, medical and technological developments, natural phenomena, U.S. weather and natural disasters.*	*Includes the arts, religion, scholarship, communications media, sports, entertainment, fashions, fads and social life.*

	World Affairs	European War Zone	Pacific War Zone	The Americas	Other Countries & Territories
Apr. 13		Russians capture Simferopol, capital of the Crimea, and the ports of Feodosia and Yevpatoria.	Australian forces occupy Bogadjim on the north coast of New Guinea and make contact with enemy patrols along the road to the larger base of Madang .... Soviet Union and New Zealand agree to establish diplomatic relations and exchange ministers.		
Apr. 14		In forming a new Greek cabinet, Premier Sophocles Venizelos takes the war, navy, air and justice portfolios .... George Papandreou, leader of the Socialist-Democratic Party who escaped from German imprisonment in Athens, arrives in Cairo to serve in the Venizelos cabinet .... Turkish Foreign Min. Numan Menemencioglu says "we will, in the general direction of our foreign policy, aid the Allies to the limit of our material possibilities." .... Only a 1,000-square-mile area at the southern end of the Crimean Peninsula is reported still in German hands.	A Japanese force reaches the the Bishenpur-Silchar trail southwest of Imphal, threatening to cut the last land supply line to the capital of Manipur State.		
Apr. 15		A conference of leaders of six opposition parties in Naples votes, 4 to 1, to cooperate with the government of Badoglio upon retirement of King Victor Emmanuel .... Russians take Lyubimovka, only three miles north of Sevastopol.		Brazilian Pres. Getulio Vargas says that after the war democracy will be restored.	
Apr. 16		Soviet Commissar of Foreign Affairs Andrei Vishinsky says Moscow and Washington have agreed to create a new Italian government representing all democratic elements .... Soviet troops advance more than 30 miles along the southeast coast of the Crimea and capture 40 localities, including the port of Yalta.	Mountbatten announces that the Imphal plain is firmly in Allied hands with the pressing of a new offensive.		
Apr. 17		Italian Marshal Badoglio's government resigns and King Victor Emmanuel asks Badoglio to form a new ministry representing all parties .... To prevent leakage of invasion plans, Britain imposes unprecedented restrictions on all foreign envoys save those of Russia and the U.S. .... Russian troops sweep another 12 miles across the Crimea, taking the highway junction of Varnutka.	Allied forces cut a Japanese road block on the Kohima-Dimapur road, four miles north of Kohima.	Mexican labor leader Vicente Lombardo Toledano says the assassination attempt on President Avila Camacho April 12 was plotted by a Fascist group hoping to establish an Argentine-model government.	
Apr. 18	Churchill tells the House of Commons that something may be salvaged out of the League of Nations in the plans for postwar machinery to maintain peace.	BBC broadcasts a warning to French citizens telling them "that the time is very short" and to prepare for an Allied invasion .... About 2,000 U.S. planes raid Germany, striking at military targets in the Berlin area .... Russian troops capture historic Balaklava, Crimea, some nine miles southeast of Sevastopol.	Chungking radio reports a "county system" of democratic local government has been established in 21 provinces—"the greater part of unoccupied China." .... Japanese open a new drive in Honan Province, China, advancing 23 miles from Chungmow .... Allies report gains in several parts of the Imphal plain against the Japanese.		
Apr. 19		FDR says the fate of Rome rests with the Germans, who are using the city for purely military reasons .... More than 1,000 Allied planes attack French railway junctions at Noisy-le-Sec, Juvisy, Rouen and Tergnier .... Nazi troops launch strong counterattacks in the southeastern corner of Poland.	After breaking down the Japanese roadblocks, Allied forces drive Japanese troops beyond the Imphal plain.	Bolivian Labor Min. Victor Andarade says that the failure of the U.S. to recognize Bolivia has nullified plans to increase tin production .... Panama City reports all newspapers in El Salvador except *Diario Nuevo*, the government organ, have been suspended.	
Apr. 20	ILO opens its conference in Philadelphia and elects Walter Nash president.	Russian air and sea forces sink 18 Nazi ships off Sevastopol, disrupting enemy evacuation efforts .... London reports that the Turkish government will end exports of chrome to Germany.	Chinese troops encircle a Japanese division in the Mansum area of northern Burma.	Haitian General Assembly extends the term of President Elie Lescot to May 15, 1951 and suspends elections of senators, deputies and mayors until one year after the war .... A general strike closes all Bolivian tin mines in protest against a writ of habeas corpus granted to government officials charged with shooting workers.	
Apr. 21	Treasury Secy. Morgenthau says representatives of some 30 Allied nations have agreed in principle on a plan for establishment of an $8-billion currency stabilization fund to be administered by the World Bank .... Churchill says the Atlantic Charter reserves the right of Britain to maintain her empire.	Marshal Badoglio announces a new Italian cabinet in which he will serve as premier and foreign minister, with representatives of opposition parties which have been critical of his government .... Lt. Gen. George S. Patton is assigned to an undisclosed European command.	With the aid of reinforcements from Manchukuo, the Japanese are reported quickly encircling the northern Honan town of Chengchow.		

	A	B	C	D	E
	Includes developments that affect more than one world region, international organizations and important meetings of major world leaders.	*Includes all developments in European countries and military engagements between Allied and Axis powers in Africa and at sea.*	*Includes all developments in Japan and China, Japanese foreign policy and military actions in the Pacific region.*	*Includes all domestic and regional developments in Latin America, the Caribbean and Canada.*	*Includes developments in those independent nations and colonial possessions not covered in Columns B, C and D.*

U.S. Politics & Social Issues	U.S. Foreign Policy & Defense	U.S. Economy & Environment	Science, Technology & Nature	Culture, Leisure & Life Style	
Sen. Burnet Maybank (D, S.C.) says the South will resist the Supreme Court decision opening primary elections to Negroes.	Judge Delbert Metzger rejects testimony of Adm. Chester Nimitz and Lt. Gen. Robert Richardson that martial law is still necessary and rules that military government in the Hawaiian Islands is invalid.			Montreal Canadiens defeat the Chicago Black Hawks for the fourth successive time in the Stanley Cup playoffs to win the NHL title.	Apr. 13
	Navy Secy. Knox says court martial of Lt. Gen. Walter Short and Adm. Husband Kimmel will not be held at this time.	Interior Secy. Ickes proposes that government-owned war plants be turned over to veterans to be operated in competition with private industry after the war.		CBS gets the 1944 award of the Socieda Gombasta Panamericana for its contributions to hemispheric solidarity through its Latin American network .... Mrs. Helen G. Carlisle files suit for $300,000 damages, charging that Warner Bros. Pictures, Inc. pirated the picture *Princess O'Rourke* from a novelette she wrote.	Apr. 14
	Lt. Gen. George S. Patton Jr. says in a talk at the opening of a soldier's club in England that "it is the destiny" of the U.S. and Great Britain "to rule the world." .... Vice Pres. Wallace will reportedly go to China to reassure Chiang Kai-shek that the delay of an all-out Allied effort to take Burma is only temporary.	Civil Service Commission reports that 72% of the 2,797,000 federal employes within the U.S. in October 1943 were on war agency rolls.			Apr. 15
MacArthur denies he is a presidential candidate.		In an unprecedented decision, the NLRB rules that the American News Co. was justified in discharging nine workers who struck to compel payment of wage increases that had not been approved by the NWLB.	A tornado sweeps through northeastern Georgia and western South Carolina, killing 39 and injuring more than 500 persons and causing heavy property damage.		Apr. 16
South Carolina General Assembly passes hundreds of bills repealing laws governing primary elections in order to remove such elections from Supreme Court jurisdiction .... Trial of 30 alleged seditionists, who are charged with plotting to establish a Nazi government in the U.S., opens in Washington, D.C.	War Secy. Stimson says the Army will need a minimum of 750,000 men during the remainder of 1944.	Henry Ford says the Ford company will give employment preference to war veterans as they are demobilized.	A Lockheed Constellation transport plane piloted by Howard Hughes and Jack Frye flies from Burbank, Calif. to Washington in the record time of six hours, 58 minutes at an average speed of 355 mph.		Apr. 17
				American and National Leagues open the 1944 baseball season in seven cities .... Mrs. Elliot Roosevelt is granted a divorce in Fort Worth, Tex. from Col. Elliot Roosevelt. She receives custody of the three children and is awarded half the communal property.	Apr. 18
Maine Gov. Sumner Sewall signs a soldier-vote bill permitting use of the federal ballot and liberalizing sections of the absentee voting law.	A special court commission in Chicago finds Hans Max Haupt sane. Federal Judge Barnes orders the father of the executed Nazi saboteur to stand trial May 15 on charges of treason .... House votes to extend Lend-Lease until June 30, 1945.	Representatives of 14 state alcohol control commissions meeting in N.Y.C. urge a resumption of alcoholic beverage production.			Apr. 19
		War Secy. Stimson, Navy Secy. Knox and Maritime Commission Chmn. Adm. Emory S. Land send a joint message to the House Military Affairs Comm. urging some form of labor draft to man war plants depleted by inductions into the armed services.	Dr. James L. Gamble reports that experiments show glucose prevents excretions of body water and energy and should be useful in sustaining castaways at sea.	W. Somerset Maugham's novel *The Razor's Edge* is published in N.Y.	Apr. 20
Sen. Clyde Reed (R, Kan.) introduces a resolution in the Senate for an investigation of "unauthorized disclosures of information obtained through censorship channels."		Maritime Commission announces in Washington it has completed negotiations with Henry Kaiser's Oregon Shipbuilding Corp., reducing its profits by $6,322,954.		Adriano Lopez, internationally known artist and director of the Lisbon Museum of Modern Painting, dies at 65 in Lisbon.	Apr. 21
F	G	H	I	J	
Includes elections, federal-state relations, civil rights and liberties, crime, the judiciary, education, health care, poverty, urban affairs and population.	*Includes formation and debate of U.S. foreign and defense policies, veterans affairs and defense spending. (Relations with specific foreign countries are usually found under the region concerned.)*	*Includes business, labor, agriculture, taxation, transportation, consumer affairs, monetary and fiscal policy, natural resources, pollution and accidents.*	*Includes worldwide scientific, medical and technological developments, natural phenomena, U.S. weather and natural disasters.*	*Includes the arts, religion, scholarship, communications media, sports, entertainment, fashions, fads and social life.*	

	World Affairs	European War Zone	Pacific War Zone	The Americas	Other Countries & Territories
Apr. 22	Labor delegates to the ILO convention vote to exclude Luis Girola, Argentina's representative, on the grounds he was named "by a fascist government which favors the Axis."	Moscow announces peace negotiations with Finland have collapsed with the rejection of Soviet demands .... German attempts to attack Russian positions at Narva, Estonia and around Stanislav, Poland are repulsed .... Long-range Nazi artillery engages in heavy shelling of the Anzio beachhead.	Supported by large forces of the Pacific fleet, American troops land at points in northern New Guinea .... Japanese troops enter Chengchow.		
Apr. 23	The national executive committee of the British Labor Party proposes a single international armed force to maintain order throughout the post-war world.	Greek Premier Sophocles Venizelos and his cabinet resign and King George II asks George Papandreou to form a new government .... Hitler and Mussolini complete two days of conferences at Hitler's headquarters and reach "an unshakable decision .... to bring the war against the Bolshevists .... the Jews .... and the plutocrats .... to a successful conclusion."	Allied troops occupy Hollandia, Dutch New Guinea .... U.S. forces occupy Ujelang Atoll of the Marshall Islands.		
Apr. 24		American troops advance more than a mile on the east flank of the Anzio beachhead, reaching a point two miles from the vital Appian Way southeast of Cisterna .... Britain announces a ban on overseas travel effective April 28 except on business of national importance.	Japanese start a new spring offensive in Anhwei Province in China.		
Apr. 25			Allied forces continue to push back Japanese troops within the Imphal and Kohima areas in India .... Allied forces capture Sentani and Cyclops airfields on Hollandia, Dutch New Guinea.		
Apr. 26		British planes sink three German convoy ships off Norway .... The Russians sink five more German transport ships off Sevastopol.	Chinese and American forces in northern Burma make a six-mile advance through the Mogaung Valley to a point 10 miles from Kamaing.		The Archbishop of York defends British policy in India and Palestine, indicating that without previous Hindu-Moslem agreement independence for India would be meaningless. He says that the Balfour Declaration did not intend for all of Palestine to be a Jewish home.
Apr. 27	ILO conference receives a request from the Italian government for readmission. It quit in 1937.	U.S. planes make morning and afternoon raids on railyards and airfields in France.	Allied operations end on Hollandia, Dutch New Guinea as two Allied columns join forces .... Completion of MacArthur's talks with Adm. Chester Nimitz to integrate operations against the Japanese is announced.	Nicaraguan Congress approves a constitutional revision to permit the president to run for reelection in 1946 .... The federal commissioner in Entre Rios Province, Argentina warns newspapers in his jurisdiction that they will be closed if they editorially discuss such subjects as freedom.	
Apr. 28		At least 2,000 U.S. planes of all types smash at Nazi targets in northern France.	Japanese troops take Hulao Pass, gateway to Loyang in Honan Province, China.	Bolivian government announces a "revolutionary plot" has been broken up with the arrest of several plotters.	
Apr. 29			Mountbatten states that the Japanese invasion of India has not upset the Allied strategic schedule and that owing to the terrain the battles in India could last several weeks.		
Apr. 30		Soviet planes make a mass raid on the old Polish fortress city of Brest-Litovsk .... Britain reaches an agreement with Tito which permits cooperation between air forces .... About 3,000 Allied planes attack Nazi targets in France.			
May 1		A sharp German attack against the British at Anzio beachhead results in a slight advance.		Puerto Rican resident commissioner in Washington denounces the administration of Rexford Tugwell and compares him "to Hitler and Mussolini."	

A	B	C	D	E
Includes developments that affect more than one world region, international organizations and important meetings of major world leaders.	*Includes all developments in European countries and military engagements between Allied and Axis powers in Africa and at sea.*	*Includes all developments in Japan and China, Japanese foreign policy and military actions in the Pacific region.*	*Includes all domestic and regional developments in Latin America, the Caribbean and Canada.*	*Includes developments in those independent nations and colonial possessions not covered in Columns B, C and D.*

U.S. Politics & Social Issues	U.S. Foreign Policy & Defense	U.S. Economy & Environment	Science, Technology & Nature	Culture, Leisure & Life Style	
Kentucky GOP convention endorses Dewey as the party's presidential nominee.	Chmn. Tom Connally appoints himself and seven other members of the Senate Foreign Relations Comm. to a special group to confer with State Secy. Hull on the establishment of a postwar organization to maintain world peace.	House Ways and Means Comm. approves a simplified tax bill to apply to income after Jan. 1, 1945, relieving an estimated 30 million taxpayers from filing returns .... SEC announces completion of a study of corporate profits for the 1936-42 period which shows drops in profits due to higher taxation and costs.		Metropolitan Museum of Art discloses that 15,000 of its most valuable art objects, removed shortly after Pearl Harbor, have been returned to the museum .... The $50,000 Wood Memorial is run in two sections at Jamaica, N.Y., with Stir Up and Lucky Draw the winners.	Apr. 22
					Apr. 23
	Selective Service Dir. Hershey says large numbers of the 3.6 million rejected registrants in the 18-36 age group will be re-examined.				Apr. 24
Delegates favoring FDR's renomination are elected in primaries in Massachusetts and Pennsylvania.	War Secy. Stimson tells the House Postwar Comm. on Military Policy he favors "a single authority in planning, supervision and control" of the armed forces.	Montgomery Ward telegraphs FDR that the company will not recognize the CIO union until elections are held.			Apr. 25
	War Secy. Stimson says the statement of Lt. Gen. Patton that the U.S. and Britain are destined to rule the world "represents Patton's personal views" and not that of the War Dept. .... Army service forces chief Lt. Gen. Brehon Somervell says that unity of command of U.S. armed forces should begin now.	U.S. Army troops take possession of the Chicago plant of Montgomery Ward, which has rejected FDR's order to recognize a CIO union. Ward board chairman Sewell Avery is carried out of his office by U.S. soldiers.			Apr. 26
	Dewey advocates solid relationships with Britain, Russia and China in the postwar period.	A special Senate committee studying wages of white collar workers reports that 20 million are receiving substandard pay.		Jim Tobin, Boston Braves pitcher, holds the Brooklyn Dodgers hitless in the first major league no-hitter since 1941.	Apr. 27
	Navy Secy. Frank Knox dies in Washington at 70. Under Secy. James V. Forrestal takes charge temporarily .... Forrestal says any move to unify Army and Navy commands during the war "is unthinkable." .... Sen. Arthur Vandenberg (R, Mich.) says that, if in power, the GOP would be committed to postwar cooperative organizations.	Under Secy. of Commerce Wayne Taylor, operating the Chicago Montgomery Ward plant, ejects Pres. Clement Ryan for refusing to cooperate.		James McLean of GE announces nine television stations are currently operating, covering an area with a population of 22 million .... St. Louis Browns win their ninth straight game, tying a major league record for most consecutive victories from a season's opening day.	Apr. 28
MacArthur announces from New Guinea that he will not accept nomination as a presidential candidate.		As the NWLB opens hearings to determine whether a CIO union represents the workers, Army troops leave the Montgomery Ward plant.			Apr. 29
					Apr. 30
In overruling a Pennsylvania court decision, the Supreme Court rules that government property is not taxable by states.				NWLB rejects the contention of the American Federation of Musicians that radio station musicians are not in a war industry and orders strikes ended at stations WJJD, Chicago, and KSTP, Minneapolis .... *Journey in the Dark*, by Martin Flavin, is awarded the Pulitzer Prize for fiction.	May 1
F *Includes elections, federal-state relations, civil rights and liberties, crime, the judiciary, education, health care, poverty, urban affairs and population.*	G *Includes formation and debate of U.S. foreign and defense policies, veterans affairs and defense spending. (Relations with specific foreign countries are usually found under the region concerned.)*	H *Includes business, labor, agriculture, taxation, transportation, consumer affairs, monetary and fiscal policy, natural resources, pollution and accidents.*	I *Includes worldwide scientific, medical and technological developments, natural phenomena, U.S. weather and natural disasters.*	J *Includes the arts, religion, scholarship, communications media, sports, entertainment, fashions, fads and social life.*	

	World Affairs	European War Zone	Pacific War Zone	The Americas	Other Countries & Territories
May 2	U.S. delegates to the ILO conference submit a program calling for agreement by the U.N. on postwar labor and production problems.	Red Army ends a three-week lull on the Rumanian front by opening an offensive along the middle Siret River.			Egyptian Minister of Education Naguib el Hilaly Pasha says that postwar plans for sending students to the U.S. have been developed .... A U.S. technical mission headed by James M. Landis arrives in Addis Ababa to study postwar economic possibilities in Ethiopia.
May 3	U.S. and British oil experts end "exploratory conversations" on postwar oil development and reportedly recommend equal opportunity for the U.S. and Britain in the development of world sources.	The Germans flood large portions of the Pontine Marshes between the Anzio and Cassino fronts.	Japanese drive along the Peking-Hankow railway from Chengchow is complemented by a new offensive northward along the route from Sinyang in southern Honan Province .... British armored columns take several points from the Japanese around Kohima in eastern India.	Mexico issues a decree ending the siesta—the custom of stopping work at midday for a nap.	
May 4	U.S. delegates submit a plan to the ILO conference calling for expeditious handling of demobilization, termination of war contracts and adjustment of tax rates to encourage postwar production.	Eleven Nazi ships are sunk by a Russian air assault on Sevastopol.	Japanese clear all but a 65-mile gap along the Peking-Hankow railroad.		
May 5		Allied fliers breach the Pescara dam on Italy's Adriatic coast in three attacks.	American forces in Dutch New Guinea expand their holdings westward along the coast in the Humboldt Bay area with new landings at Torare Bay and Demta .... A Japanese communique discloses Adm. Mineichi Koga, commander of the combined fleet, was killed in March.		Gandhi is released from detention in the Aga Khan's Palace "unconditionally" for "medical reasons."
May 6	An ILO subcommittee votes to recommend that the organization adopt a "hands off" policy towards U.N. administration of Germany.	Nazi assaults on the Anzio beachhead and in the upper Garigliano Valley are repulsed by the Allies .... U.S. Maj. Gen. John Cannon, chief of the Allied Tactical Air Force in the Mediterranean area, says that railyards below Florence are out of commission due to air attacks .... Icelandic cabinet and leaders of all prominent political parties join in a statement urging voters to ratify a decision of parliament to break ties with Denmark.	Japanese forces reach the outskirts of Loyang in Honan Province, China.		
May 7		De Gaulle says France wants to be a center of cooperation in western Europe and a permanent ally of Russia .... Father Stanislaus Orlemansky, American Catholic priest, leaves Russia by plane for the U.S. after a 12-day visit in which he twice saw Premier Joseph Stalin and visited Polish troops serving with the Red Army .... Yugoslavian partisans report the capture of Kladanj, Bosnia, 30 miles east of Sarajevo.	Japanese gain control of all but 14 miles of the Peking-Hankow railroad .... British withdraw from their western Burma base of Buthedaung.		
May 8		After an 18-day lull, the Russians smash the main German defense belt around Sevastopol .... Americans and British consent to the signing of a Russian-Czech agreement, granting the Soviets supreme authority in a liberated Czechoslovakia, with Czech administrators assuming jurisdiction as the fighting ends.	British turn back a new Japanese offensive in the Manipur hills.	Pres. Maximiliano Hernandez Martinez resigns as unrest sweeps El Salvador because of a general strike.	
May 9		The Russians capture the Black Sea port of Sevastopol .... More than 4,000 Allied planes of all types raise the Allied air offensive to a new peak in Europe .... British troops occupy the villages of Gamberale, Fallascosa and Palena on the Maiella Plateau in central Italy.	Crossing the Yellow River in the vicinity of Yuanchu, the Japanese move south, posing a new threat to the important Honan Province base of Loyang .... Japanese gain full control of the north-south Peking-Hankow railway in Honan Province.		
May 10				El Salvador government announces the appointment of a new cabinet with Enrique Avila as foreign minister.	
	A	B	C	D	E
	Includes developments that affect more than one world region, international organizations and important meetings of major world leaders.	*Includes all developments in European countries and military engagements between Allied and Axis powers in Africa and at sea.*	*Includes all developments in Japan and China, Japanese foreign policy and military actions in the Pacific region.*	*Includes all domestic and regional developments in Latin America, the Caribbean and Canada.*	*Includes developments in those independent nations and colonial possessions not covered in Columns B, C and D.*

U.S. Politics & Social Issues	U.S. Foreign Policy & Defense	U.S. Economy & Environment	Science, Technology & Nature	Culture, Leisure & Life Style	
		NLRB orders an election to determine whether 6,000 employes of Montgomery Ward in Chicago want the CIO union .... Indictments charging conspiracy to sell whiskey above OPA ceiling prices are returned against the Schenley Distillers Corp., Benjamin F. Pross, an official of the AFL Wine, Liquor and Distillery Workers Union, and 16 others.			May 2
	House World War Veterans Comm. approves the "GI Bill" with only minor changes from the Senate version.	OPA announces that all meats will be ration-free effective tomorrow, except for steaks and roast beef .... Senate approves without opposition a resolution by Sen. Harry Byrd (D. Va.) for an investigation by the Judiciary Committee of government seizure of the Montgomery Ward & Co. plant in Chicago and of the dispute between the company and its employes.	Polaroid Corp. announces that synthetic quinine has been produced from coal tar products by Drs. Robert Woodward and William Doering.	General Conference of the Methodist Church in Kansas City rejects a resolution to admit women to full rights of ministers.	May 3
	In compliance with the Hatch Act, the Army announces that all commanders must practice strict impartiality in the dissemination of political information .... Stettinius returns to Washington from Britain, where he has conferred with the British on war and postwar problems .... Legislation to draft one million 4-F registrants not in essential jobs and assign them to special work units is endorsed before the Senate Military Affairs Comm.	FBI agents arrest Paul Sowell, assistant manager of Montgomery Ward & Co., when he removes a placard posted by the governement in the Chicago plant .... WPB Director Nelson says proposals to allocate "a small percentage" of beverage alcohol to distillers "appear to have merit" but that there will be no releases for three or four months.			May 4
		Eric A. Johnston is elected to a third term as president of the U.S. Chamber of Commerce.			May 5
				Pensive, ridden by Conn McCreary, wins the Kentucky Derby at Churchill Downs.	May 6
	U.S. Army discloses that there are 183,618 war prisoners in the U.S.—133,155 Germans, 50,136 Italians and 347 Japanese.			*New York Herald Tribune*'s best-selling book list includes *A Tree Grows in Brooklyn* by Betty Smith and *Good Night, Sweet Prince* by Gene Fowler .... Arnold Denker defeats Reuben Fine to win the national chess title in N.Y.	May 7
Supreme Court denies a request of Texas Atty. Gen. Grover Sellers for a rehearing on the decision voiding the Texas "white primary." .... Washington's 16 GOP delegates endorse Dewey. Delaware leaders say their six votes also will go to Dewey .... Democratic National Chmn. Robert E. Hannegan says the people are determined to reelect FDR.	Senate passes and sends to conference the Lend-Lease extension bill.	A federal court in Philadelphia orders Pullman, Inc. to separate its railroad car building business from its sleeping car operation .... House Ways and Means Comm. approves a bill raising the public debt to $240 billion, $20 billion less than the Treasury's request.			May 8
	Adms. Chester Nimitz, Ernest J. King and William F. Halsey Jr. complete talks in San Francisco on the Pacific War .... Army reports total strength of 7,481,925 as of Jan. 1.	The government ends its control of the Montgomery Ward & Co. Chicago plant shortly before the NLRB announces that the CIO United Mail Order Warehouse and Retail Employes Union won today's election to represent the firm's Chicago workers.			May 9
	FDR names James V. Forrestal as secretary of the Navy.	House passes and sends to the Senate a bill increasing the national debt limit to $240 billion.		Prof. Howard Mumford Jones of Harvard is elected president of the American Academy of Arts and Sciences.	May 10
F	G	H	I	J	
Includes elections, federal-state relations, civil rights and liberties, crime, the judiciary, education, health care, poverty, urban affairs and population.	*Includes formation and debate of U.S. foreign and defense policies, veterans affairs and defense spending. (Relations with specific foreign countries are usually found under the region concerned.)*	*Includes business, labor, agriculture, taxation, transportation, consumer affairs, monetary and fiscal policy, natural resources, pollution and accidents.*	*Includes worldwide scientific, medical and technological developments, natural phenomena, U.S. weather and natural disasters.*	*Includes the arts, religion, scholarship, communications media, sports, entertainment, fashions, fads and social life.*	

	World Affairs	European War Zone	Pacific War Zone	The Americas	Other Countries & Territories
May 11	ILO conference adopts a resolution urging member governments to establish programs of state medical care.	Allies open their spring Italian offensive, striking at Cassino and the Gustav Line . . . . Russians throw back a German tank-supported attack on their bridgehead on the western bank of the Dniester River above Tiraspol.	More than 20,000 Chinese troops cross the Salween River in China's western Yunnan Province along a 100-mile front in a drive aimed at linking the Burma and Ledo roads.	Canadian P.M. Mackenzie King says he opposes changes in the existing organization of the British Commonwealth.	
May 12	ILO conference ends in Philadelphia after adopting a proposal to include a world social and employment program in the peace treaty.	A joint Allied statement to Finland, Hungary, Rumania and Bulgaria warns them to "get out of the war" and "cease aiding Germany." . . . . More than 1,000 U.S. planes bomb five synthetic oil plants at Merseburg Lutzendorf and Halle, Germany, and Zeitz and Bruex, Czechoslovakia.	Japanese cut the Chinese retreat route by slicing the east-west Lung-Hai railway 48 miles west of Loyang.		
May 13	ILO governing body names a committee of nine and instructs it to present the ILO viewpoint to any international conferences prior to the next general ILO meeting.	Allied troops advance up to six miles along the Gustav Line in Italy.	Chinese troops capture Suiping on the Peking-Hankow railway, cutting the Japanese hold on that line . . . . Chinese forces launch a new drive on the Japanese bases of Kamaing, Mogaung and Myitkyina in northern Burma.	Argentine province of Entre Rios expropriates the Compania de Electricidad del Este Argentina, a subsidiary of the American & Foreign Power Co.	
May 14		French troops cut the Cassino-Formia road, a vital highway linking the two main north-south routes out of Rome . . . . Yugoslavian partisans report the breaking of the enemy ring in Macedonia and the capture of the Starigrad harbor in Dalmatia.			
May 15		French Comm. of National Liberation repudiates all agreements made by the Darlan regime and recommends changing its name to the Provisional Government of the French Republic.		Colombia's Senate rejects the resignation of Pres. Alfonso Pumarejo Lopez, offered after strikes were called to force him from office.	
May 16		American troops pursue the Germans fleeing up the Tyrrhenian coast . . . . U.S. and Britain sign agreements with the exiled governments of Norway, Belgium and the Netherlands defining terms of civil administration during liberation of these countries.	A new Japanese thrust at India is thrown back southwest of Imphal and Kohima.		
May 17	Prime ministers of Australia, Britain, Canada and New Zealand announce in London their agreement on war and postwar policies, favoring a world organization with power to prevent aggression.	American and French troops reach the outposts of the Germans' Hitler Line at the southern end of their offensive between Cassino and the sea . . . . Spain announces the closing of the Japanese and German consulates in Tangiers, Spanish Morocco.	American amphibious forces, leapfrogging 125 miles up the Dutch New Guinea coast from Hollandia, land unopposed at Tum and Arara, establishing a 7½-mile beachhead . . . . American troops gain control of the airstrip on Insumuar, the main island of the Wakde group . . . . American and Chinese troops capture the main airport of Myitkyina in northern Burma.	Argentine government tightens censorship on radio broadcasts and bans programs sponsored by firms and organizations friendly to the U.N. . . . . WPB Chmn. Nelson urges a program of American aid to industrialize Latin American countries.	Gov.-Gen. of French Equatorial Africa Felix Eboue, the first African to hold high rank in French colonial administration, dies at 56 in Cairo.
May 18	Sumner Welles urges immediate organization of the U.N. to deal with war plans and postwar peace measures.	British and Polish troops capture Cassino and Monastery Hill, and the Allies claim that the Gustav Line south of the Apennines is destroyed . . . . German forces at the southern end of the front retreat in disorder after losing the port of Formia on the Gulf of Gaeta, and abandon Gaeta as indefensible . . . . Field Marshal Karl Rudolf Gerd von Rundstedt is named chief of the German anti-invasion forces in western Europe.		Mexican appeals court upholds a 20-year sentence for Ramon Mercader for the murder of Leon Trotsky and directs him to pay a $7,000 indemnity to the slain man's widow.	
May 19			American troops complete the capture of the Wakde Islands, as the Japanese fight until wiped out.		
May 20		Yugoslavian King Peter II removes Minister of War Gen. Draja Mikhailovich from his cabinet post . . . . A record force of about 6,000 British-based planes drop a least 8,000 tons of explosives on targets in a 150-mile strip between Brittany and Belgium . . . . Germans set up a new defense line anchored at Pico in the north and at Terracina on the Tyrrhenian seacoast.		Ecuador and Peru accept the recommendations of a joint U.S., Brazilian and Argentine committee to settle their border dispute.	Commission on Palestine Surveys discloses plans for a $150-million postwar irrigation and hydro-electric development in Palestine.
	A *Includes developments that affect more than one world region, international organizations and important meetings of major world leaders.*	B *Includes all developments in European countries and military engagements between Allied and Axis powers in Africa and at sea.*	C *Includes all developments in Japan and China, Japanese foreign policy and military actions in the Pacific region.*	D *Includes all domestic and regional developments in Latin America, the Caribbean and Canada.*	E *Includes developments in those independent nations and colonial possessions not covered in Columns B, C and D.*

U.S. Politics & Social Issues	U.S. Foreign Policy & Defense	U.S. Economy & Environment	Science, Technology & Nature	Culture, Leisure & Life Style	
	Selective Service announces an easing of demands for registrants over 25 as a result of decreased demands by the armed forces.	U.S. Commissioner Edwin Walker dismisses charges against Montgomery Ward & Co. manager Paul Sowell, who was arrested on charges of removing a government poster from the company's Chicago plant, and rebukes the government agent who brought the charges . . . . Henry J. Kaiser says production of the Brewster Aeronautical Corp. has increased 344% in the seven months since he took over the management.		Herbie Kay, band leader and former husband of actress Dorothy Lamour, dies at 40 in Dallas, Tex.	May 11
Rep. Martin Dies (D,Tex.) announces he will not be a candidate for reelection because of illness and a desire to return to private life.	House passes the bill extending the Lend-Lease operation through June 1945 after accepting Senate amendments and sends it to the White House.	Packard Motor Co. shuts down its Detroit plants because of a strike of foremen and refusal of the armed forces to accept products "in absence of inspection supervision."			May 12
				Pensive takes the Preakness and $60,075 in prize money in Pimlico, Md.	May 13
Harold R. Mason, 37, frequently a conductor on FDR's special trains, is indicted by a federal grand jury in Washington on charges of threatening the President.				Post Office bans Lillian Smith's novel *Strange Fruit* from the mails.	May 14
Senate votes to reject cloture in debate on the House bill to repeal poll taxes in federal elections in eight Southern states and then votes to delay action on the bill.	Ambassadors John Winant and Averell Harriman arrive in Washington from London and Moscow for consultations with FDR and the State Dept.	Supreme Court rules that a state may assess personal property taxes on the entire fleet of airplanes operated by an airline having its "home port" within that state.		Metropolitan Sergius, Patriarch of Moscow and head of the Russian Orthodox Church, dies of a brain hemorrhage at 78 in Moscow . . . . Clyde Shoun of the Cincinnati Reds pitches a no-hitter against the Boston Braves.	May 15
FDR and Dewey gain more delegates in state primaries and conventions in Calif., N.J., Mont. and Del.		After the Navy refuses to accept work without supervision, the foremen's strike at the Briggs Mfg. plant in Detroit idles 10,000 workers . . . . NWLB upholds the right of the Borg Warner Corp. to discharge 41 employes who quit work last December without following grievance procedures specified in their union contract.		George Ade, creator of *Fables in Slang*, playwright and one of America's foremost humorists, dies at 78 in Indiana.	May 16
	Selective Service announces revised regulations deferring students preparing for the ministry and priesthood . . . . FDR signs the bill extending Lend-Lease and reports expenditures of $24.2 billion through March 1944.	Foremen's Assn. of America orders 3,300 members to return to work in Detroit war plants.		Greta Palmer tells the House committee investigating the FCC that Chmn. James Ely tried to persuade *The Reader's Digest* not to publish a critical article she had been assigned to write . . . . *Variety* reports the most popular songs are: (1) *I Love You*, (2) *Long Ago and Far Away*, and (3) *Love, Love, Love.*	May 17
	Navy Secy. Forrestal urges the Senate Military Affairs Comm. to pass legislation to force able-bodied persons into war plant jobs or into labor units of the armed forces.				May 18
Members of the right-wing faction of the American Labor Party, who lost control of the organization in the recent N.Y. state primary, meet in N.Y.C. and form the Liberal Party.		NWLB approves a wage agreement between the UMW and operators representing 70% of the country's soft coal production . . . . Secy. Hull asks American business to avoid postwar production that calls for heavy tariff protection or government subsidies.		American Academy of Arts and Letters and the National Institute of Arts and Letters present their 1944 awards to Willa Cather, S.S. McClure, Theodore Dreiser and Paul Robeson.	May 19
Dewey gains the GOP convention delegates from Utah and Oregon . . . . Sen. Burnet R. Maybank (D, S.C.) says Southern Democrats are prepared to fight for "white supremacy" at the party's national convention . . . . National convention of the CP votes to disband as a separate political unit but to continue as the Communist Political Assn.	Vice Pres. Wallace leaves for Asia as FDR's messenger to Chiang and to report on transport problems in Siberia and China.			Salt Lake City court convicts 15 Utah polygamists of "unlawful cohabitation." The defendants, with two to six wives each, offer no defense and announce plans to appeal to the U.S. Supreme Court.	May 20
F	G	H	I	J	
Includes elections, federal-state relations, civil rights and liberties, crime, the judiciary, education, health care, poverty, urban affairs and population.	*Includes formation and debate of U.S. foreign and defense policies, veterans affairs and defense spending. (Relations with specific foreign countries are usually found under the region concerned.)*	*Includes business, labor, agriculture, taxation, transportation, consumer affairs, monetary and fiscal policy, natural resources, pollution and accidents.*	*Includes worldwide scientific, medical and technological developments, natural phenomena, U.S. weather and natural disasters.*	*Includes the arts, religion, scholarship, communications media, sports, entertainment, fashions, fads and social life.*	

	World Affairs	European War Zone	Pacific War Zone	The Americas	Other Countries & Territories
May 21		Greek Premier Papandreou returns to Cairo from Beirut, where he agreed to fuse with Greek guerrillas to form a representative government .... Advance American elements enter Terracina, but are forced to pull out and set up a line three miles south of the city.	Chinese troops capture Sinantien, Honan Province, the fifth town they have regained along the Peking-Hankow railway.		
May 22			Chinese forces in Yunnan Province cut the Burma Road at Chefang, 28 miles east of the Burma border.		
May 23		British and American troops on the Anzio beachhead start a drive on all sides of the perimeter, gaining four miles and extending the length of the beachhead to 24 miles .... The final returns of the Icelandic referendum favor creation of a republic June 17, when the country will sever ties with Denmark established in 1381.			
May 24		American troops capture Terracina, a key German strongpoint in Italy .... Churchill opens parliamentary debate on British foreign policy, announcing the single aim is to defeat the Axis at the least cost.	Chinese troops smash the second Japanese attempt in two days to reinforce their besieged troops in Myitkyina, Burma .... American troops reach the Maffin Bay airfield in New Guinea.		
May 25		German paratroops and glider-borne infantry capture Marshal Tito's headquarters near Drvar, Bosnia; Tito and Maj. Randolph Churchill (son of the British prime minister) escape .... Advance elements of U.S. forces link the Anzio beachhead with the main front when they meet in the vicinity of Borgo Grappa .... On the main Italian front U.S. and French troops take Sonnino and Roccasecca de Volsci, while Canadian units clean out Pontecorvo .... Ankara reports indicate that German forces are taking over strategic points in Bulgaria.	After a 20-day battle Loyang, Honan Province, falls to the Japanese.		
May 26	FDR issues invitations to 41 governments and the French Liberation Comm. to send delegates to a U.N. monetary conference to open July 1 at Bretton Woods, N.H.				
May 27		American troops fight their way into Artena, two miles below Valmontone, and the Via Casilina, which is the Germans' main escape route from the Liri Valley .... A British broadcast by Eisenhower to the people of occupied countries stresses that civilians should not impede Allied military traffic during the invasion.	American troops, in another leapfrogging attack, invade Biak Island, Dutch New Guinea and establish a beachhead.		
May 28		British troops take Aprilia and Carreceto as pressure on the Nazi line at Rome increases.	Japanese troops begin a drive down the Hankow rail route in northern Hunan Province from the area of Yochow.		
May 29		Allies advance to within 16 miles of Rome .... Berne dispatches report that Bulgarian Regent Bogdan Philov has returned to Sofia after receiving an ultimatum from Hitler at Berchtesgaden to sever relations with Russia.	American and Chinese troops penetrate the southern portion of Myitkyina, Burma, blocking one of the last escape routes of the Japanese garrison.	A military junta seizes control in Guayaquil, Ecuador, forcing the resignation of the Carlos Arroyo del Rio government, and names Dr. Fausto Navarro Allende provisional president.	
	A *Includes developments that affect more than one world region, international organizations and important meetings of major world leaders.*	B *Includes all developments in European countries and military engagements between Allied and Axis powers in Africa and at sea.*	C *Includes all developments in Japan and China, Japanese foreign policy and military actions in the Pacific region.*	D *Includes all domestic and regional developments in Latin America, the Caribbean and Canada.*	E *Includes developments in those independent nations and colonial possessions not covered in Columns B, C and D.*

U.S. Politics & Social Issues	U.S. Foreign Policy & Defense	U.S. Economy & Environment	Science, Technology & Nature	Culture, Leisure & Life Style	
		Army seizes the Hummer Manufacturing Co., Springfield, Ill., subsidiary of Montgomery Ward & Co. Hummer has been strikebound since May 5 because of company refusal to include a union maintenance clause in its contract with the workers.		Alexei, 67-year-old Metropolitan of Leningrad and Novgorod, is named acting Patriarch of the Russian Orthodox Church with the announcement of the Holy Synod that the late Patriarch Sergius had directed "in his last will" that Alexei succeed him.	May 21
Earl Browder is chosen president of the Communist Political Assn.	FDR's 15th Lend-Lease report to Congress discloses that from March 1941 through March 1944 U.S. expenditures were $24,224,806,000.	Former Maritime Commission Chmn. Joseph P. Kennedy says the U.S. should maintain a postwar fleet of 10,000,000 tons of fast, long-range merchant ships, transfer needed excess ships to the Army and Navy and to friendly nations and scrap the rest .... Presidential authority to issue suspension orders through the OPA against firms violating rationing rules is upheld by the Supreme Court .... NWLB Chmn. Davis tells the special House committee investigating the government seizure of Montgomery Ward that if the NWLB cannot have jurisdiction over labor disputes in the distribution field, 15.5 million workers could strike without hindrance.			May 22
Delegates to the Texas Democratic convention split over instructing delegates to the national convention on FDR's nomination, and his supporters bolt.		House accepts the Senate amendments to the tax bill and sends it to FDR.		Chicago Univ. notifies the Big Ten that it is withdrawing from all athletic competition .... The 1944 Churchmen Award for "promotion of good will and better understanding of all people" is presented to Bernard M. Baruch.	May 23
Rep. Will Rogers Jr. (D, Calif.) resigns from Congress to resume active service with the Army.	Senate Military Affairs Comm. denies Lt. Gen. George S. Patton promotion to a permanent rank of major general.	Atty. Gen. Francis Biddle tells the House committee investigating the seizure of Montgomery Ward's mail order plant that the action was within the President's powers as commander-in-chief .... CIO-UAW announce that its executive committee has removed Pres. William Jenkins and 14 others of Chrysler Local 390 for calling an unauthorized strike.			May 24
	Army and Navy announce creation of a committee to investigate proposals for unification of the armed forces and report to the joint chiefs of staff .... The board of managers of the National Congress of Parents and Teachers announces that the organization opposes the drafting of 17 year olds.				May 25
		A Senate Judiciary subcommittee report investigating FDR's decision to seize the Montgomery Ward & Co. Chicago plant is called absurd by Atty. Gen. Biddle, who says the report fails to take into account court decisions supporting his advice to the President .... Army says 100,000 war prisoners will be available for farm work and as laborers on projects not in war production.		Sir Herbert Thompson, Egyptologist and a leading authority on hieroglyphics, dies at 85 in London.	May 26
California Gov. Earl Warren announces he has written all the state's delegates pledged to him "not to nominate him or vote for him for any position." .... WRA reports 22,000 Japanese-Americans have been transferred from camps to private homes and hostels countrywide, "with only a few instances of local opposition or discrimination."	Senate Foreign Relations postwar subcommittee accepts in principle U.S. participation in the U.N. organization.	WPB reports April munitions output was 3% below schedule and 2% behind March production.		Michigan track team wins the Western Conference outdoor championship with 50 points. Illinois is second, Purdue third.	May 27
	Army reveals plans to curtail air defense installations in the U.S. to obtain personnel and equipment for service overseas.				May 28
	Sen. Lister Hill (D, Ala.) introduces a bill which would provide for the postwar consolidation of the Army, Navy and Air Force in one department under a civilian secretary .... Dewey says the U.S. "must not again sit on the sidelines as mere observers" in world affairs.			N.Y. Magistrate Charles G. Keutgen finds D.H. Lawrence's novel *The First Lady Chatterly* obscene and orders a trial of the publisher, Dial Press, Inc.	May 29

	World Affairs	European War Zone	Pacific War Zone	The Americas	Other Countries & Territories
May 30	Secy. Hull invites the governments of Britain, Russia and China to designate representatives to open conversations on postwar security plans.	U.S. planes attack targets in Germany, Belgium and France, striking at airports and railroads .... British troops seize the small Tyrrhenian port of L'Americano and the town of Ardea, four miles northeast.	Chinese troops in northern Burma capture Malakawng on the Mogaung Valley road, 15 miles north of Kamaing .... Japanese forces land on the southeastern shore of Lake Tungting, breaching the Chinese second line of defense at the Milo River.	Quito reports that Gen. Luis Larrea Alba is now in control of the Ecuadorian revolutionary government.	
May 31		A false report that Allies have launched the invasion of Europe with landings in France is sent by the London office of the AP to the U.S. and Latin America, and in five minutes before the error is killed it is broadcast by all the major American networks .... American troops pierce the Germans' Alban Hills defenses, swinging east around Velletri and seizing Mt. Peschio.		Dr. Jose Maria Velasco Ibarra accepts the presidency of Ecuador, offered to him by the military junta.	
June 1	State Secy. Hull says the postwar international organization will give small nations "equality with all others in every practicable way."	King Peter II announces that Dr. Ivan Subasitch will form a new government representing all Yugoslavian elements resisting the enemy .... Generalissimo Francisco Franco of Spain is denounced by the Soviet newspaper *Izvestia* as "the sick devil turned monk."	The Japanese defense of Biak Island is reported unusually strong .... Japanese units driving south through Hunan Province take Ansiang and Pingkiang.		
June 2		A Nazi offensive in Rumania drives a wedge into the Russian lines northwest of Jassy .... American troops capture the key German defense points of Velletri and Valmontone in Italy .... French Comm. of National Liberation approves the suggestion of the Consultative Assembly to change its name to the Provisional Government of the French Republic .... New Bulgarian cabinet of Premier Ivan Bagrianov meets to discuss German demands for breaking Soviet relations and raising an army to aid the Nazis.	Navy planes bomb Shimushu and Paramushiro Islands in the Kuriles, while Army bombers strike at Matsuwa in the same chain.	Ramon Grau San Martin is elected president of Cuba over the administration's candidate, Dr. Carlos Saladrigas.	
June 3		American troops move to within 15 miles of Rome as they push through the Alban Hills in the wake of collapsing German defenses.	American troops start a fresh drive on the three Biak Island airports .... British airborne Chindits cross the Irrawaddy River and cut the last escape route of the Japanese garrison cornered in the northern half of Myitkyina, Burma.	Argentine "nationalists" call for attacks on Jews, whom they consider responsible for the proposed day of civil disobedience June 7.	
June 4		American soldiers fight their way into Rome. Weak German resistence is ended by 9:45 p.m. .... Germans announce Rome has been abandoned because Hitler did not wish it to be destroyed.		A state of siege is declared in Honduras "to preserve public peace" and the government bans all public meetings and demonstrations.	
June 5		Allied troops pour through Rome and across the Tiber River in pursuit of the fleeing Germans .... King Victor Emmanuel III announces his retirement and yields power to Crown Prince Humbert .... Polish Premier Mikolajczyk arrives in Washington at the invitation of the U.S. for conversations with FDR and State Secy. Hull concerning the boundary dispute with Russia.			
June 6		Eisenhower states the hour of liberation has arrived as Operation Overlord begins. Allied units consist of 6,939 naval vessels, 15,040 aircraft, and 156,000 troops (132,000 seaborne, 23,500 airborne). British planes drop 5,000 tons of bombs on 10 coastal-defense batteries; other forces distract the Germans with dummy paratroops, strips of metallized paper and fireworks to give the impression of wide-front airborne landings in Normandy. The only German panzer division in Normandy checks Allied progress as the day unfolds .... Allied forces sweep forward along a 70-mile front in an effort to smash German armies fleeing northward from Rome.			
	A	B	C	D	E
	Includes developments that affect more than one world region, international organizations and important meetings of major world leaders.	*Includes all developments in European countries and military engagements between Allied and Axis powers in Africa and at sea.*	*Includes all developments in Japan and China, Japanese foreign policy and military actions in the Pacific region.*	*Includes all domestic and regional developments in Latin America, the Caribbean and Canada.*	*Includes developments in those independent nations and colonial possessions not covered in Columns B, C and D.*

U.S. Politics & Social Issues	U.S. Foreign Policy & Defense	U.S. Economy & Environment	Science, Technology & Nature	Culture, Leisure & Life Style	
	FDR says Spain is still exporting too much to Germany and that U.S. dissatisfaction with the Franco government has not changed.				May 30
National Governors' Conference adopts a resolution demanding postwar return to the states of powers yielded to the federal government in the war emergency . . . . Sen. Hugh A. Butler (R, Neb.) calls for an investigation of the CIO's political committee and charges that Atty. Gen. Biddle "has gone out of his way" to forgive violations of the Corrupt Practices Act.	A committee of Protestant laymen and ministers issues a report warning against impoverishment of Germany after the war.	Solid Fuels Admin. Harold Ickes returns most of 3,000 bituminous coal mines to their owners after seven months of government operation . . . . Officers of the Chicago local of the CIO United Retail, Wholesale and Department Store Employes of America threaten another strike against Montgomery Ward & Co. unless the NWLB orders the company to continue the contract which expired last December.	Univ. of California announces production of synthetic sugar by Profs. H. Barker, Michael Doudoroff and W.Z. Hassid.		May 31
					June 1
		U.S. Court of Appeals in Washington holds that orders of the NWLB are not subject to court review . . . . WMC Chmn. Paul McNutt announces that the WMC will take over "absolute control of male workers over 17 years old" to maintain essential labor needs . . . . House Roads Comm. approves a bill providing $1.5 billion for construction of roads, bridges and railroad crossings after the war.			June 2
	House passes and sends to the Senate a bill appropriating $3.9 billion for foreign economic operations for fiscal 1945 . . . . U.S. Interdepartmental Proclaimed List Comm. lists 84 Finnish firms and individuals to be deprived of U.S. trade rights without explanation.			Bounding Home wins the Belmont Stakes in N.Y., earning $55,070.	June 3
Socialist Party nominates Norman Thomas for the presidency and Darlington Hoopes as his running mate at its Reading, Pa. national convention . . . . *The Atlanta Georgian* reports the KKK has disbanded and that Imperial Wizard James Colescott has left Atlanta.					June 4
		Senate approves a bill extending wartime price, wage and rent controls through 1945 . . . . Supreme Court holds that insurance companies are engaged in interstate commerce and subject to the Sherman Antitrust Law and federal regulation.			June 5
		Sewell Avery, chairman of Montgomery Ward & Co., tells a special House committee investigating government seizure of the firm's Chicago plant that he let himself be carried from the property by soldiers to "make the public aware of the situation."			June 6

F	G	H	I	J
Includes elections, federal-state relations, civil rights and liberties, crime, the judiciary, education, health care, poverty, urban affairs and population.	*Includes formation and debate of U.S. foreign and defense policies, veterans affairs and defense spending. (Relations with specific foreign countries are usually found under the region concerned.)*	*Includes business, labor, agriculture, taxation, transportation, consumer affairs, monetary and fiscal policy, natural resources, pollution and accidents.*	*Includes worldwide scientific, medical and technological developments, natural phenomena, U.S. weather and natural disasters.*	*Includes the arts, religion, scholarship, communications media, sports, entertainment, fashions, fads and social life.*

	World Affairs	European War Zone	Pacific War Zone	The Americas	Other Countries & Territories
June 7		Reinforcements are landed on the French Channel beachheads as the Allies expand their lines .... Nazi military commentators say that Field Marshal Gerd von Rundstedt's counterattack will take place once he is sure of the real focal point of the invasion .... Allied troops capture the seaport of Civitavecchia, 38 miles northwest of Rome .... Vatican announces its determination to maintain neutrality no matter who controls Rome.	American troops capture an airfield less than 900 miles from the southern tip of the Philippines and also take the Mokmer field on Biak Island .... Japanese troops reach a point in the Laotao River Valley only four miles from Changsha, Hunan Province.	Cuba announces its recognition of the new Ecuadorian government.	
June 8	Representatives of 32 U.N. countries adopt a resolution in Frederick, Md. favoring higher education standards, with the establishment of world school systems.	Allies capture Bayeux, five miles inland from Normandy and report hand-to-hand combat on the Cherbourg Peninsula.	American and Australian ships thwart another Japanese effort to reinforce Biak Island.		
June 9		In the Caen area the Germans continue strong resistance, throwing in armored units to save the town from British and Canadian assaults .... American troops capture Ste. Mere-Eglise and push to within 17 miles of Cherbourg .... In their rapid advance above Rome, U.S. troops take Viterbo, Vetralla and Tarquinia .... Prince Humbert names Ivanoe Bonomi as head of a new Italian government after Badoglio declines an attempt to form a new cabinet.	Allied forces seize the northern end of the airstrip north of Myitkyina and occupy several more villages around Kamaing, Burma.		
June 10		American forces capture Isigny and Trevieres on the Cherbourg Peninsula .... De Gaulle issues a statement criticizing the failure of Allied governments to come to agreement with his French provisional government for civil administration of liberated areas .... U.S. forces take Tuscania as the pace of the offensive north of Rome is maintained .... U.N. Committee for the Investigation of War Crimes finds seven German officials responsible for the Lidice massacre in 1942.	A U.S. Pacific fleet task force begins carrier-raids on Saipan, Tinian and Guam in the Marianas.		French provisional government closes the frontier between Spanish and French Morocco.
June 11		U.S. units take Lison and fight across flooded country to the edge of Cerisy Forest in an advance on the German communications center of St. Lo .... As the Germans continue to withdraw along the Adriatic, British troops enter Francaville, Pescara and Chieti .... In a day-old offensive against Finland in the Karelian Isthmus, Russian troops take 80 localities, including the coastal city of Terijoki.	For the second consecutive day, U.S. naval units assault the Marianas Islands, with blows covering a distance of 120 miles and destroying 140 Japanese planes and 13 vessels.		
June 12		P.M. Churchill, Field Marshal Jan Christian Smuts and Gen. Sir Alan Brooke, chief of the Imperial General Staff, spend three hours on the Normandy beachhead as Allied ships bombard German positions .... American troops capture Carentan, 30 miles southeast of Cherbourg .... FDR says Allied forces firmly established on the shores of France "are now ready to meet the inevitable counterattack of the Germans with power and confidence." .... Vichy radio reports that German military authorities are in control of many government functions due to uprisings by patriots throughout France .... Greek cabinet votes the ban of the return of King George II to Greece until a plebiscite determines whether his return is desired by the people.		Hull says that postwar use by the U.S. of bases in Latin America "must depend on developments" but that arrangements will be based upon mutual consent.	
June 13		Allied troops deepen the beachhead on Normandy in a drive south of Bayeux that takes them behind Tilly-sur-Seulles .... Lt. Gen. Mark W. Clark reports U.S. forces are 70 miles north of Rome.	Naval units attack the southern Marianas Islands, bombarding Saipan and Tinian Islands .... Japanese troops near the gates of Changsha, Hunan Province, on three sides.		

A	B	C	D	E
Includes developments that affect more than one world region, international organizations and important meetings of major world leaders.	*Includes all developments in European countries and military engagements between Allied and Axis powers in Africa and at sea.*	*Includes all developments in Japan and China, Japanese foreign policy and military actions in the Pacific region.*	*Includes all domestic and regional developments in Latin America, the Caribbean and Canada.*	*Includes developments in those independent nations and colonial possessions not covered in Columns B, C and D.*

U.S. Politics & Social Issues	U.S. Foreign Policy & Defense	U.S. Economy & Environment	Science, Technology & Nature	Culture, Leisure & Life Style	
	U.S. Army discloses that Maj. Gen. J.F. Miller, former commander of the 9th Air Force Service Command in Great Britain, has been demoted to his permanent rank of lieutenant colonel for careless talk about the invasion date at a London cocktail party .... Senate and House adopt and send to the White House a compromise bill extending the statute of limitations for six months in the trials of Adm. Kimmel and Gen. Short.			NBC says that the contract for Leopold Stokowski to share direction of its Symphony Orchestra with Arturo Toscanini has not been renewed.	June 7
James Farley, chairman of the N.Y. State Democratic Comm. since 1930, announces his resignation effective July 11.	U.S. State Dept. Bulletin refers to the government of Generalissimo Francisco Franco of Spain as "a dictatorship under debt to Hitler."				June 8
An estimated 30 leaders of the Democratic forces in six Southern states opposed to FDR's renomination meet in Shreveport, La. and name Eugene Germany leader of an anti-fourth term coalition .... Hans Max Haupt, father of executed Nazi saboteur Herbert Haupt, is convicted in Chicago a second time for treason .... North Carolina Board of Education votes to grant equal pay for Negro and white teachers.	FDR discloses de Gaulle has been invited to meet with him in Washington at the General's convenience.	NWLB says its docket has been cleared of strike cases for the first time since its establishment in January 1942 .... WPB announces an end to the importation of Mexican workers to relieve labor shortages in foundries and forge shops.			June 9
Senate subcommittee on appropriations eliminates $500,000 for the FEPC.	Sen. Robert Taft (R, O.) says Treasury plans for an $8-billion world stabilization currency fund mean "that we put up all of the money and someone else disperses it."			Illinois Univ. wins the NCAA track and field championships in Milwaukee, with Notre Dame second and Michigan third.	June 10
Willkie publishes the first of eight articles on campaign issues and warns the Republicans not to make an issue of states' rights.					June 11
Supreme Court reverses convictions under the Espionage Act of 1917, limiting its application to "willful or specific intent to promote insubordination, disloyalty or unrest in the armed forces."	Senate passes a modified "GI Bill," costing an estimated $3 to 6.5 billion.				June 12
Chairman of the CIO political action committee, Sidney Hillman, tells the Senate Comm. on Campaign Expenditures that "we have no purge list, either public or secret, which we seek to impose on local members of the CIO from our offices in N.Y."			Newly elected president of the AMA, Dr. Herman Kretschmer, condemns widespread use of vitamins as extravagant and useless.		June 13
F	G	H	I	J	
Includes elections, federal-state relations, civil rights and liberties, crime, the judiciary, education, health care, poverty, urban affairs and population.	*Includes formation and debate of U.S. foreign and defense policies, veterans affairs and defense spending. (Relations with specific foreign countries are usually found under the region concerned.)*	*Includes business, labor, agriculture, taxation, transportation, consumer affairs, monetary and fiscal policy, natural resources, pollution and accidents.*	*Includes worldwide scientific, medical and technological developments, natural phenomena, U.S. weather and natural disasters.*	*Includes the arts, religion, scholarship, communications media, sports, entertainment, fashions, fads and social life.*	

	World Affairs	European War Zone	Pacific War Zone	The Americas	Other Countries & Territories
June 14		The largest armored battle of the war is fought in an area bounded by Caumont, Villers-Bocage, Tilly-sur-Seulles and Ballroy, France .... Gen. Charles de Gaulle spends part of today in Normandy, receiving enthusiastic welcomes in several liberated French towns .... Allied troops break through a makeshift German defense line above Rome, arching from the Tyrrhenian Sea to the top of Lake Bolsena .... Russian units drive on the Karelian Isthmus, engulfing Kuuterselkae as four columns advance along a 28-mile front.	American troops land on Saipan in the Marianas, and beachheads are quickly secured.		
June 15		Allied forces continue their advance all along the Italian line and on the Cherbourg Peninsula in France .... Turkish Foreign Min. Numan Menemencioglu resigns because of a cabinet dispute involving the passage of German ships through the Dardenelles.	American troops on Saipan advance a half mile .... For the first time B-29 Superfortresses are used in a strike on Japan.		
June 16		London reveals that small pilotless German planes have been used against the English coast .... American troops cut the next-to-the-last line in front of Cherbourg by capturing St. Sauveur-le-Vicomte .... Allied forces gain as much as 25 miles, reaching points less than 70 miles from the enemy's Pisa-Florence-Rimini defense line .... Russian troops advance to within 28 miles southeast of Viborg by taking Luonatjoki in Finland.	Chinese troops capture Kamaing, Burma and later in the day take Parentu to the southeast and Mogaung to the north .... U.S. forces advance more than half way to the east coast across the southern half of Saipan.	U.S. Civil Aeronautics Administration announces that 147 men from 11 Latin American nations will receive aviation training in the U.S. .... Canadian Socialist party, the Cooperative Commonwealth Federation, wins 43 of the 52 seats in the Saskatchewan provincial election.	
June 17		American troops cut off Cherbourg by pushing across the isthmus and establishing a seven-mile position on the west coast between Barneville and St. Lo d'Ourville .... American troops pushing up the Italian west coast advance beyond Grosseto .... French troops invade Napoleon's exile island of Elba off the Italian coast .... Icelandic Parliament, after proclaiming itself a republic, elects Regent Sveinn Bjoernsson as the country's first president.			
June 18		Russian troops make a 15-mile advance on the Karelian Isthmus .... British troops reach the outskirts of Perugia in central Italy, 110 miles north of Rome .... Tito announces agreement on several points between the National Liberation Comm. and Dr. Ivan Subasitch of the royal Yugoslavian government.	American naval units supporting the invasion of Saipan report shooting down more than 300 Japanese aircraft off the Marianas.		
June 19		U.S. planes strike the Pas-de-Calais area of the French coast to knock out more launching bases used for the robot bombs being directed against England .... American troops capture Bricquebec and reach a point only eight miles south of Cherbourg .... British troops enter Perugia, Italy .... German forces holding Porto Longone on the west coast of Elba surrender to French troops .... Russian offensive against Finland gains up to 14 miles.	Battle of the Philippine Sea begins as Admiral Spruance's 5th Fleet engages the Japanese fleet of Admiral Toyoda. In the greatest aircraft carrier battle of the war, American carriers number 15 as against nine Japanese.		
June 20		American troops press through the outer perimeter of the Cherbourg defenses and hold positions only four to seven miles from the port .... Russian troops take the ancient fortress city of Viborg in their Karelian Isthmus drive.	Battle of the Philippine Sea ends with the Japanese losing three aircraft carriers and 480 aircraft, after sending four waves of air attacks on American vessels. U.S. losses are 130 aircraft and one sustained hit on the battleship *South Dakota* .... American troops on Saipan hold the entire southern portion of the island .... American troops capture the last two airfields on Biak Island in the Schoutens .... Vice Pres. Wallace arrives in Chungking for talks with Chiang Kai-shek.		

A	B	C	D	E
Includes developments that affect more than one world region, international organizations and important meetings of major world leaders.	*Includes all developments in European countries and military engagements between Allied and Axis powers in Africa and at sea.*	*Includes all developments in Japan and China, Japanese foreign policy and military actions in the Pacific region.*	*Includes all domestic and regional developments in Latin America, the Caribbean and Canada.*	*Includes developments in those independent nations and colonial possessions not covered in Columns B, C and D.*

U.S. Politics & Social Issues	U.S. Foreign Policy & Defense	U.S. Economy & Environment	Science, Technology & Nature	Culture, Leisure & Life Style	
Hans Max Haupt is fined $10,000 and sentenced to life imprisonment by Federal Court Judge John Barnes in Chicago.	U.S. officials end talks with Polish Premier Stanislaw Mikolajczk, who announces that Poland can count on U.S. support .... House Military Affairs Comm. files a report charging that Col. Theodore Wyman, the Army's engineer in Hawaii, was negligent and permitted a work lag which contributed to the Japanese success at Pearl Harbor.				June 14
	FDR confers with State Dept. officials and later issues a statement endorsing a postwar international organization .... FDR and Premier Mikolajczyk meet; FDR says it is Churchill who is insisting on the Curzon Line as a Polish boundary and not Stalin.	A U.S. district court in Washington denies a government motion to dismiss an injunction filed by Montgomery Ward to restrain the NWLB from enforcing any penalties for violation of its orders.	A committee of orthopedic physicians of the AMA files a report criticizing the Kenny method of treating infantile paralysis.	NWLB orders the American Federation of Musicians to end its ban on transcriptions and phonograph recordings.	June 15
The first CIO political committee conference adopts a resolution urging the Democrats to renominate FDR .... Federal judge orders the American citizenship of eight leaders of the German-American Bund revoked on the grounds that they obtained naturalization by falsely swearing allegiance to the U.S.	State Dept. orders Finnish Minister Hjalmar Procope and three legation counselors to leave the U.S. for advancing propaganda favorable to the Axis.	A UMW district conference in Hazelton, Pa. approves a contract covering wages and working conditions for some 80,000 anthracite coal miners.			June 16
		WPB Chmn. Nelson announces plans to help industry prepare for peacetime production through the purchase of materials and tools not essential for current war production.		*Arsenic and Old Lace* closes on Broadway after 1,444 performances. *Tomorrow the World* closes after 499 performances.	June 17
				Francisco Segura of Ecuador defeats Billy Talbert in Detroit to win the national clay court tennis title.	June 18
	U.S. House approves a Philippines independence bill and returns it to the Senate for concurrence with an amendment to grant independence as soon as constitutional processes are restored .... Rep. John Coffee (D, Wash.) introduces a House resolution to have the U.S. sever diplomatic relations with Spain .... Secy. Morgenthau says any agreements reached at the forthcoming Bretton Woods monetary conference will not be binding on the U.S. without congressional approval.				June 19
		WPB advises the distilling industry that beverage alcohol can be produced throughout August because the need for alcohol in the synthetic rubber program has declined.	National Foundation for Infantile Paralysis announces grants totaling $1.12 million will be made to 27 universities and other institutions to aid studies of the disease.		June 20
F	G	H	I	J	
Includes elections, federal-state relations, civil rights and liberties, crime, the judiciary, education, health care, poverty, urban affairs and population.	*Includes formation and debate of U.S. foreign and defense policies, veterans affairs and defense spending. (Relations with specific foreign countries are usually found under the region concerned.)*	*Includes business, labor, agriculture, taxation, transportation, consumer affairs, monetary and fiscal policy, natural resources, pollution and accidents.*	*Includes worldwide scientific, medical and technological developments, natural phenomena, U.S. weather and natural disasters.*	*Includes the arts, religion, scholarship, communications media, sports, entertainment, fashions, fads and social life.*	

	World Affairs	European War Zone	Pacific War Zone	The Americas	Other Countries & Territories
June 21		American forces reach points three to five miles from Cherbourg on the southwest and west, and begin a siege of the city .... Some 2,200 U.S. bombers attack Berlin, with many continuing eastward to land in Russia .... Russian forces open new drives in Finland, advancing north and southwest of Lake Onega .... Vatican announces that the archives and art treasures of the Abbey of Mt. Cassino had been removed to the Vatican prior to the Abbey's destruction by Allied planes.	Chinese troops win control of the Kaolikung mountain range in western Yunnan Province, which the Japanese have used to guard the eastern Burmese frontier.		
June 22		More than 1,000 Allied planes blast Cherbourg's defenses for 80 minutes and then American troops begin an assault at 12:40 p.m. .... In making a stand against the Allies in central Italy, the Germans retake Chiusi and counterattack above Perugia .... U.S. troops take Paganico on the Tyrrhenian coast, while British units on the Adriatic enter Fermo.	British troops clear the Japanese from the Manipur Road in eastern India.	Guatemalan Pres. Jorge Ubico suspends five constitutional provisions guaranteeing civil rights, including freedom of press and assembly, because of "Nazi-Fascist agitation."	
June 23	FDR names Secy. Morgenthau chairman of the U.S. delegation to the upcoming Bretton Woods Conference.	American troops fight their way through the outer Cherbourg defenses against fierce opposition .... Red Army opens its summer offensive on the main eastern front with an attack upon Vitebsk.	U.S. carrier-based planes attack Iwo Jima in the Volcano Islands, shooting down 116 enemy aircraft at a loss of five.		
June 24		American troops trap a large German force on the Tyrrhenian coast between Grosseto and Follonica .... Two Russian army units close pincers from the north and south on Vitebsk.	U.S. Marines scale Mt. Topatchau on Saipan, while the west coast town of Garapan and the Kagman Peninsula are also brought under Allied control .... Allied troops break into Mogaung, Burma and fight their way to the center of town .... Vice Pres. Wallace ends his talks with Chiang in Chungking with an agreement on war policies towards Japan and her disarmament at the war's end.		
June 25		American troops fight their way into Cherbourg from the east, south and west. The Germans concede loss of the port later in the day .... U.S. units in Italy take Follonica and move further northward and inland, nearing the highway center of Massa .... Russians close the Vitebsk trap and push into the city, where street fighting erupts.		With stores and theaters closed, police use smoke bombs to disperse student demonstrations against the suspension of civil rights in Guatemala City.	
June 26		Russian forces take Vitebsk and Zhlobin and then push to within 35 miles of the Polish border in western Russia .... American troops mop up the remaining German resistance in Cherbourg.			
June 27		British units on the left flank of the Normandy beachhead launch an offensive that gains more than five miles southeast of Tilly-sur-Seulles .... British troops recapture Chiusi, Italy .... Russian troops capture Orsha, halfway between Vitebsk and Mogilev.	American troops push two miles north of Kagman Point on the eastern shore of Saipan.	Guatemalan Pres. Ubico issues a decree placing all personnel of railroads, health, light and water organizations under military laws and regulations until further notice.	
June 28		British infantry and armor units close in on Caen from three sides .... Americans capture Castagneto, Italy .... Russian troops take Mogilev, 110 miles east of Minsk.	Japanese launch a general offensive northward from Canton with the aim of joining forces with troops pushing southward from Hunan Province.	U.S. Amb. to Argentina Norman Armour is recalled to Washington for immediate consultation.	
June 29		German forces open fierce counterattacks against the British at Caen .... Allied troops make gains of up to nine miles along 100-mile front in Italy .... Russian units report the liberation of 1,050 localities in White Russia, including Bobruisk.		Argentine government seizes all properties of the "House of Bemberg", reportedly worth more than $1 billion, for allegedly falsifying inheritance tax reports.	
June 30		Russian troops outflank Minsk, capital of White Russia.			

	A	B	C	D	E
	Includes developments that affect more than one world region, international organizations and important meetings of major world leaders.	*Includes all developments in European countries and military engagements between Allied and Axis powers in Africa and at sea.*	*Includes all developments in Japan and China, Japanese foreign policy and military actions in the Pacific region.*	*Includes all domestic and regional developments in Latin America, the Caribbean and Canada.*	*Includes developments in those independent nations and colonial possessions not covered in Columns B, C and D.*

U.S. Politics & Social Issues	U.S. Foreign Policy & Defense	U.S. Economy & Environment	Science, Technology & Nature	Culture, Leisure & Life Style	
	Senate passes the Army appropriations bill of $49,107,735,795 and sends it to the White House.	Senate and House approve extension of the Price Control Act for one year beyond June 30 and send it to the White House.		*Variety* reports the most popular songs are: (1) *I'll be Seeing You,* (2) *Long Ago and Far Away,* and (3) *I'll Get By.*	June 21
Texas Supreme Court rules that only electors named by the anti-FDR regular convention can appear on the ballot for the Democratic primary.	FDR signs the "GI Bill" to aid veterans in the transition from military to private life at the war's end.	House passes and sends to the Senate a bill exempting insurance firms from the Sherman and Clayton Antitrust acts.			June 22
	Senate Truman Committee calls the Liberty ship "the truck horse of the sea" but opposes its use as a troop or hospital ship because of slow speed and possible structural defects.	Jones & Laughlin Steel Corp. asks the NWLB to name a permanent arbitrator to enforce the contract with the CIO United Steel Workers.	A tornado sweeps parts of Pennsylvania, West Virginia and Maryland, leaving 146 dead and over 1,000 injured.	Novelist Thomas Mann and his wife become U.S. citizens in Los Angeles. The former German writer predicts the Nazis will be defeated within a year . . . . Mrs. Ruth Goggins Roosevelt, recently divorced from Col. Elliot Roosevelt, is married in Fort Worth, Tex. to Col. Harry T. Edison, an Army Air Force pilot from Indianapolis.	June 23
			American Physical Society reveals a motor operated by magnetic current from a permanent magnet developed by Felix Ehrenhaft.	Babe Didrikson Zaharias wins the Women's Western Golf Open in Chicago.	June 24
				Gunder Haegg runs two miles in 8:46.4 at Ostersund, Sweden, breaking his own two-year-old world record.	June 25
Gov. Earl Warren delivers the keynote speech at the opening of the GOP national convention in Chicago, pledging the party to cooperation in international affairs and internal reconstruction.				It is announced that the total estate of Simon Guggenheim, who died in 1941, is $16,557,291.	June 26
GOP platform pledges old age and unemployment insurance extension, promises labor freedom from "political trickery," offers farmers reorganization of the Agriculture Dept. and approves U.S. participation in a postwar organization to prevent the rise of militarism.				*Ten Little Indians* by Agatha Christie opens on Broadway.	June 27
Thomas E. Dewey and John W. Bricker win the GOP presidential and vice presidential nominations on the first ballot.	FDR signs a bill giving government employment preference to war veterans.				June 28
Dewey meets leaders of 32 states to work out campaign plans.	White House publishes a joint statement by service chiefs Gen. George C. Marshall, Gen. Henry H. Arnold and Adm. Ernest J. King warning against optimism over an early military victory.	An estimated 10,000 workers strike at the Timken Roller Bearing Co. plant in Canton, O. due to a breakdown in labor relations and the company's plans to close down its furnaces.	American Red Cross announces development of a serum to prevent measles . . . . Dr. Charles G. Abbot, secretary of the Smithsonian Institution and one of the world's leading authorities on solar radiation, resigns.	Margaret Landon's *Anna and The King of Siam* is published in N.Y.	June 29
Herber Brownell, Jr. is named chairman of the GOP National Comm.	State Secy. Hull announces an end of diplomatic relations with Finland because of its partnership with Nazi Germany . . . . FDR signs the congressional resolution granting the Philippines independence as soon as the Japanese are ejected.	The WPA officially ends. During its eight years it gave employment to nearly 8.5 million persons, spending almost $13 billion . . . . FDR signs the OPA extension bill.			June 30

F	G	H	I	J
Includes elections, federal-state relations, civil rights and liberties, crime, the judiciary, education, health care, poverty, urban affairs and population.	*Includes formation and debate of U.S. foreign and defense policies, veterans affairs and defense spending. (Relations with specific foreign countries are usually found under the region concerned.)*	*Includes business, labor, agriculture, taxation, transportation, consumer affairs, monetary and fiscal policy, natural resources, pollution and accidents.*	*Includes worldwide scientific, medical and technological developments, natural phenomena, U.S. weather and natural disasters.*	*Includes the arts, religion, scholarship, communications media, sports, entertainment, fashions, fads and social life.*

	World Affairs	European War Zone	Pacific War Zone	The Americas	Other Countries & Territories
July 1	An international monetary conference opens in Bretton Woods, N.H., with 44 nations represented.	Despite repeated German armored attacks, the British units around Caen stand fast .... Copenhagen is paralyzed by a general strike in protest against Nazi curfew orders. An estimated 15,000 Danish underground members attack German troops in the city .... Russian troops capture Borisov, 45 miles northwest of Minsk, and approach to four miles of Polotsk at the northern end of the White Russian front .... Allied troops gain along the Italian front, with U.S. forces reaching Cecina.	On the east coast of Saipan, U.S. troops advance to a point within 5½ miles of the northern tip.	Guatemalan Pres. Ubico resigns in favor of a military junta headed by Gens. Eduardo Villagran, Ariza Buenaventura Pineda and Federico Ponce.	
July 2		Minsk is taken by storm by Russian troops, who also enter Polotsk, 122 miles to the north .... American troops take Cecina, as three French columns close in on Siena.	American soldiers invade Numfor Island off the northwest coast of Dutch New Guinea and within three hours control the Kamiri airport.		
July 3		American troops open a new drive southward along a 30-mile front below the base of the Cherbourg Peninsula .... On the Finnish front, Russian units drive eight miles across the pre-1940 border to take Varpaselkae .... French and American troops take Siena, 31 miles south of Florence.			
July 4		In their advance on La Haye du Puits at the western end of the front, U.S. troops take La Broquiere, St. Remy des Landes and Baudreville, while Canadian and British forces press closer to Caen from the west .... After an agreement with the Germans, including their withdrawal from Copenhagen, the Danish Freedom Council orders an end to the general strike.	U.S. forces capture Garapan, capital of Saipan, and Tanapag on the west coast .... American troops take the Kornasoren airfield on the north coast of Numfor Island .... Chinese troops open a counterattack in the Hengyang area of Hunan Province.	Federico Ponce is elected Guatemalan president by the National Assembly .... Maj. Gaulberto Villarroel is elected president of Bolivia.	
July 5		Greek cabinet rejects terms of EAM, the left-wing guerrilla organization, for its collaboration with the government-in-exile .... About 200 U.S. planes return to England after bombing Germany, with refueling stops in Russia and Italy. .... In a move to shorten their lines, the Germans abandon Kovel, 175 miles southeast of Warsaw.	American troops on Numfor Island occupy Manim Islet, three miles off the west coast .... Navy Secy. Forrestal claims that since Pearl Harbor, U.S. submarines have sunk 640 Japanese ships. He puts the total Japanese merchant ships sunk by all means at 985.		
July 6		Nazi commander-in-chief in France, Field Marshal Gen. Karl von Rundstedt, resigns and is replace by Gen. Guenther von Kluge .... American troops advance southward on both sides of La Haye du Puits, but are forced to quit the town itself .... Churchill says that since June 15 Nazi robot bombs have killed 2,752 and injured nearly 8,000 in London .... Russian troops gain 24 miles to reach within 32 miles of Vilna, Lithuania.		Honduran troops machine-gun demonstrators in Ocotepeque, killing several and wounding many.	
July 7	UNRRA Dir. Gen. Lehman announces the appointment of Dr. Eduardo Santos, former Colombian president, as deputy director general for liaison with American republics.	Georges Mandel, former French cabinet minister and opponent of collaboration, is shot to death in a forest at Fontainbleau on orders of Joseph Darnand, police head of the Vichy government .... U.S. forces cross the Vire River north of St. Lo to establish a bridgehead threatening the encirclement of the Germans in St. Jean de Daye .... American troops capture Rosignano, Italy .... Russian forces capture Losha, Lithuania .... Two followers of Tito are placed in the new Yugoslavian cabinet of Premier Ivan Subasitch. The two are Sreten Vukosavylyevitch and Drago Marusitch.	Japanese Vice Adm. Chuichi Nagumo, commander in the central Pacific theater and leader of the Pearl Harbor attack in December 1941, and Rear Adm. Yano are reported killed on Saipan .... U.S. planes raid the Japanese naval base at Sasebo and industrial objectives at Yawata, both on Kyushu.	War Min. Juan Peron is named vice president to fill a vacancy in Argentina.	
July 8		Russian units fight their way into the streets of Vilna, Lithuania .... British and Canadian troops launch an all-out attack against Caen.	U.S. troops complete the capture of Saipan Island after defeating a Japanese effort to break out of their penned-in position on the northern end of the island. U.S. casualties total 15,053 with 2,359 dead; Japanese dead number 11,948, many of them committing suicide by jumping off cliffs.	Amb. Boaz Long announces U.S. recognition of the Guatemalan government of Gen. Federico Ponce.	
	A *Includes developments that affect more than one world region, international organizations and important meetings of major world leaders.*	B *Includes all developments in European countries and military engagements between Allied and Axis powers in Africa and at sea.*	C *Includes all developments in Japan and China, Japanese foreign policy and military actions in the Pacific region.*	D *Includes all domestic and regional developments in Latin America, the Caribbean and Canada.*	E *Includes developments in those independent nations and colonial possessions not covered in Columns B, C and D.*

U.S. Politics & Social Issues	U.S. Foreign Policy & Defense	U.S. Economy & Environment	Science, Technology & Nature	Culture, Leisure & Life Style	
Sen. Samuel Jackson (Ind.) is named permanent chairman of the Democratic National Convention.		U.S. Circuit Court in Sioux Falls, S.D. upholds a state law requiring labor unions to file annual financial statements.		Carl Mayer, Austrian-born film writer who wrote the script for *Sunrise* and produced *Dr. Caligari* and *The Last Laugh* and who refused all Hollywood offers, dies at 49 in London .... *Othello* closes after setting a record of 296 consecutive Broadway performances — the longest run by any Shakespearian play.	July 1
	An appeal to FDR by 25 Western senators asks the inclusion of silver as a media of exchange in the post-war world monetary program .... Norman H. Davis, chairman of the American Red Cross since 1938 and ambassador-at-large representing FDR on many special missions, dies at 65 in Hot Springs, Va.				July 2
FDR signs a bill withdrawing citizenship of disloyal Japanese-Americans after the Attorney General's office says the legislation is needed to deal with them under the enemy alien statutes.		Alabama's labor department tells the NWLB it will not sanction a board order that Ingalls Iron Works suspend employes who are delinquent in union dues because to do so would violate state law .... Treasury reports that in the year ending June 30, war expenditures were $87 billion. Total national debt was over $201 billion.			July 3
Negroes are prevented from voting in today's Georgia Democratic primary election.					July 4
Federal Judge Edward Eicher dismisses James Laughlin, the attorney for two of the 29 defendants in a D.C. sedition trial, after Laughlin files a petition of impeachment against Eicher in the House.				Harry Friedgut resigns as managing director of the N.Y.C. Center of Music and Drama.	July 5
Harry Hopkins, special assistant to FDR, returns to work after a six-month absence due to illness.	De Gaulle arrives in Washington for meetings with FDR, Hull and U.S. military leaders .... Army and Navy statements disclose that in 31 months of war, total casualties are 261,541, including 56,772 dead, 55,903 missing, 107,938 wounded and 40,928 prisoners.			Fire destroys the Ringling Bros. Barnum & Bailey Circus main tent in Hartford, Conn., causing 163 deaths, mostly women and children, and some 200 injuries.	July 6
		Teasury Secy. Morgenthau announces that the fifth war loan quota of $16 billion has been oversubscribed by $500 million.		Five officials of the Ringling Bros. Barnum & Bailey Circus are arrested on charges of manslaughter after yesterday's fire. Authorities charge the management was negligent in providing fire protection and that the tent was waterproofed with a paraffin-gasoline mixture .... Gunder Haegg sets a new world record of 3:43 for the 1,500 meters in Goteborg, Sweden.	July 7
Virginia Democratic convention adopts a resolution instructing delegates to the National Convention to oppose the renomination of Vice Pres. Wallace.					July 8

F	G	H	I	J
Includes elections, federal-state relations, civil rights and liberties, crime, the judiciary, education, health care, poverty, urban affairs and population.	*Includes formation and debate of U.S. foreign and defense policies, veterans affairs and defense spending. (Relations with specific foreign countries are usually found under the region concerned.)*	*Includes business, labor, agriculture, taxation, transportation, consumer affairs, monetary and fiscal policy, natural resources, pollution and accidents.*	*Includes worldwide scientific, medical and technological developments, natural phenomena, U.S. weather and natural disasters.*	*Includes the arts, religion, scholarship, communications media, sports, entertainment, fashions, fads and social life.*

	World Affairs	European War Zone	Pacific War Zone	The Americas	Other Countries & Territories
July 9		After capturing Caen, British and Canadian units move southward toward the confluence of the Odon and Orne Rivers .... Russian troops reach the Latvian border at Druya .... American forces take Volterra, Italy.			Gandhi submits to Mohammed Ali Jinnah a plan for the division of India into Hindu and Moslem states.
July 10		British troops moving south of Caen take Eterville and Maltot .... French troops drive to within 20 miles of Florence, Italy.	Chinese troops in Yunnan Province fight their way to the walls of Tenguyueh, the Japanese base blocking the Chinese from Allied forces in Burma.		
July 11		German troops counterattack against the British effort to break across the Orne River but lose heavily in both men and materials.	Chinese troops take Yungfeng, Hunan Province.	Loyal troops rescue Colombian Pres. Alfonso Pumarejo Lopez from rebel troops at Pasto.	
July 12		In a drive near Latvia, the Russians advance along a 93-mile front with the aim of pushing the Germans from their last stand in prewar Russia .... American troops approach to within 1½ miles of St. Lo.		U.S. and Mexico agree on plans for U.S. economic aid with emphasis on Mexican transportation systems.	
July 13		American troops take 11 villages in their drive on St. Lo on the western end of the front .... After five days of street fighting, Russian forces take Vilna, Lithuania .... Brig. Gen. Theodore Roosevelt, son of former President Theodore Roosevelt, dies at 56 from a heart attack at his division command post in Normandy.		The last German diplomatic and consular agents leave Argentina for Lisbon, where they will be exchanged for Argentine nationals.	
July 14		Russian troops capture Pinsk, in the heart of the Pripet Marshes.	Reinforced Japanese troops encircle Hengyang, Hunan Province .... Allied bombers raid the great petroleum center of Bula, Ceram, NEI.	Brazilian Pres. Vargas issues a decree ordering industrial mobilization for military purposes, including a 10-hour workday.	
July 15	Bretton Woods Conference proposes an international stabilization currency fund of $8.8 billion .... UNRAA announces the recognition of the French provisional government.	Russian units outflank Grodno and Kaunas, bastions guarding the way to East Prussia .... U.S. forces enter the outskirts of Lessay, western anchor of the German defense line in France..... British troops overcome the last defenses of Arezzo, a key central Italian city in the German defense line .... Berlin radio confirms reports that Nazi ambassador Franz von Papen has left Istanbul; reports that the Turkish government plans to break diplomatic relations with the Axis are not confirmed.	Japanese effort to smash through the American lines at Aitape, New Guinea fails at the Driniumor River.	Dr. Arturo Romero of El Salvador proposes that the five Central American nations form a federation for mutual benefit.	
July 16		British push forward on a six-mile front between the Odon and Orne Rivers in France .... Russian troops capture Grodno, 45 miles east of the border of prewar East Prussia .... British troops cross the Arno River in the center of Italy and establish a bridgehead just south of Castiglion Fibocchi .... Polish government in London publishes a pamphlet summing up claims to East Prussia, Danzig and the Polish Corridor, which it says must become part of postwar Poland.	U.S. planes and ships complete 13 days of consecutive attacks on Japanese-held Guam.		
July 17		U.S. troops establish themselves in the outskirts of St. Lo, while advance units push into the city itself.	Japanese Navy Min. Adm. Shigetaro Shimada is replaced by Adm. Naokuni Nomura.		

A	B	C	D	E
Includes developments that affect more than one world region, international organizations and important meetings of major world leaders.	*Includes all developments in European countries and military engagements between Allied and Axis powers in Africa and at sea.*	*Includes all developments in Japan and China, Japanese foreign policy and military actions in the Pacific region.*	*Includes all domestic and regional developments in Latin America, the Caribbean and Canada.*	*Includes developments in those independent nations and colonial possessions not covered in Columns B, C and D.*

U.S. Politics & Social Issues	U.S. Foreign Policy & Defense	U.S. Economy & Environment	Science, Technology & Nature	Culture, Leisure & Life Style	
	Arriving in Seattle from China, Vice Pres. Wallace predicts a period of prosperity in Asia after the war ends.	OPA begins establishing Regional Verification Centers to count ration coupons and check returns for dealers and shortages, counterfeit coupons and other irregularities.		Cairo reports the discovery of a buried city at nearby Helwan, indicating it predates the first dynasty.	July 9
Sen. Guy M. Gillette (D, Ia.) says he cannot support FDR for a fourth term and withdraws as a delegate to the National Convention.	President J. Carlton Ward Jr. of the Fairchild Engine & Aircraft Co. tells the Senate Military Affairs Comm. that Germany planned to invade the U.S. in 1940 through Newfoundland and Mexico after bombing England out of the war.				July 10
FDR tells his press conference that although "All that is within me cries out to go back to my home on the Hudson River, to avoid responsibilities and to avoid also the publicity . . . . of the nation's Chief Executive . . . . If the people command me to continue in office . . . . I have as little right to withdraw as a soldier has to leave his post in the line." He says he will run if nominated.	FDR announces de facto recognition of de Gaulle's French provisional government.	Washington reports WPB Chmn. Nelson has won his fight to release materials for reconversion planning and limited civilian production.		National League defeats the American League at the All Star Game in Pittsburgh.	July 11
Census Bureau reports a population increase from 131,699,275 in 1940 to 133,942,410 in 1943.	State Dept. announces British-American talks will be held shortly to fix joint policies on world oil resources.			Mrs. Betty Compton Knappen, former musical comedy actress and the second wife of Mayor James J. Walker, dies at 37 in New York.	July 12
	Washington reports an agreement between FDR and de Gaulle provides that Eisenhower can ask removal of any French civilian officer appointed by the Provisional Government of the French Republic in liberated France who does not cooperate with Allied military authorities . . . . State Dept. announces an agreement with Spain to permit U.S. commercial airplanes to land on Spanish fields.	U.S. Chamber of Commerce Pres. Eric Johnston, after six weeks in Russia, says in Washington that he expects increased U.S.-Soviet trade after the war.	Investigators at the Mayo Clinic say cigarettes may injure wounded men by constricting blood vessels.	NBA lists its ranking of fighters. First in each category are: Joe Louis, heavyweight; Gus Lesnivich, lightheavyweight; Tony Zale, middleweight; Freddie Cochrane, welterweight; Juan Zurita, lightweight; and Sal Bartolo, featherweight.	July 13
James Byrnes calls Truman from Washington and asks him to nominate him at the Democratic convention in Chicago, claiming that FDR has decided on him as the new nominee for vice president.	Army and Navy name "boards of investigation" to inquire into responsibility for negligence during the Japanese attack on Pearl Harbor.	Representatives of the major auto makers tell the WPB that they are too busy with war work to plan for reconversion at an early date.		A Hartford, Conn. superior court order gives Ringling Bros. Barnum & Bailey Circus permission to leave Hartford after it deposits $1,005,000 in cash and insurance policies to cover $1,000,000 in damage claims filed by relatives of the victims of the recent fire.	July 14
	Navy says it has reached its manpower goal of 3,650,000 and is accepting 10,000 men monthly as replacements.				July 15
		U.S. Chamber of Commerce publishes its reconversion program which, among other things, calls for government aid to industry.			July 16
FDR declines to dictate the renomination of Wallace for vice president, leaving the choice to convention delegates . . . . *United Mine Workers Journal* endorses Dewey for the presidency . . . . War Dept. says 20 states have authorized the use of the federal ballot by their citizens in the armed services.					July 17
F *Includes elections, federal-state relations, civil rights and liberties, crime, the judiciary, education, health care, poverty, urban affairs and population.*	G *Includes formation and debate of U.S. foreign and defense policies, veterans affairs and defense spending. (Relations with specific foreign countries are usually found under the region concerned.)*	H *Includes business, labor, agriculture, taxation, transportation, consumer affairs, monetary and fiscal policy, natural resources, pollution and accidents.*	I *Includes worldwide scientific, medical and technological developments, natural phenomena, U.S. weather and natural disasters.*	J *Includes the arts, religion, scholarship, communications media, sports, entertainment, fashions, fads and social life.*	

	World Affairs	European War Zone	Pacific War Zone	The Americas	Other Countries & Territories
July 18		British troops break the German defense line at Caen, moving into open country east of the Orne River .... U.S. troops reach the Arno River between Pisa and Florence at the town of Pontedera .... War Dept. announces that a Brazilian expeditionary force is in Italy .... In a three-day-old offensive Russian forces advance up to 31 miles along a 125-mile front between Tarnopol and Kovel.	Japanese Premier Hideki Tojo and his cabinet resign because it "was not able to achieve its objectives."		
July 19		American troops capture the Italian west coast port of Livorno, while Polish forces take the east coast port of Ancona .... British advance another five miles south of Caen and capture 12 towns and villages .... Russian forces advance to within 8½ miles of Lwow, Poland.			London announces the appointment of Field Marshal Viscount Gort as commander in chief for Palestine and high commissioner for Transjordan.
July 20		An unsuccessful assassination attempt on Hitler at Wolf's Lair, East Prussia is made by Col. Count Claus Schenck von Stauffenberg. Stauffenberg places a bomb under a meeting-room table. When it explodes at 12:42 p.m., four Nazi officials are killed. Hitler's right ear is deafened and his legs are burned .... Allied forces push through the Arno River valley on a 25-mile line, as the Germans retreat toward the Gothic Line .... British forces widen the 11-mile front south and east of Caen despite strong German resistance.	American troops storm ashore on Guam on either side of Port Apra .... Chinese relief forces make deep penetrations of the Japanese siege lines around Hengyang, Hunan Province.	Mexico City says 300 airmen will leave this week for training in the U.S. and after six months will be ready for overseas combat.	Bombay announces a cholera epidemic in four districts of Bihar Province has taken 34,808 lives in three months.
July 21		Field Marshals Walther von Brauchitsch, Karl Rudolf Gerd von Rundstedt and Fedor von Bock and Gens. Franz Halder and Alexander von Falkenhausen are reported to have been arrested in Berlin in connection with the attack upon Hitler .... Russians envelop Ostrov in their drive towards the Latvian border.	American troops on the west coast of Guam repulse two Japanese attacks and take Mt. Alifan, more than a mile inland.		
July 22	Bretton Woods Conference ends with agreement to establish an international loan fund of $8.8 billion to stabilize world currencies and a World Bank with $9.1 billion in capitalization to help needy nations with loans.	Russian troops break into the streets of Pskov, the last prewar Russian city in German hands .... Three Allied columns menace Florence, while patrols on the west coast pierce the German lines less than four miles from Pisa.	Gen. Kuniaki Koiso and Adm. Mitsumasa Yonai, named by Emperor Hirohito to form a new cabinet with "joint responsibility for government leadership," become premier and deputy premier, respectively, and announce they will "work for thoroughgoing realization of the principles of the Greater East Asia Declaration, thereby carrying the sacred war to complete victory, setting the Imperial mind at rest." .... Chindits in northern Burma capture Pungan and Ngusharawng, 17 miles west of Mogaung.	Argentine government lifts censorship of outgoing news dispatches filed by accredited correspondents.	
July 23		Russian units enter Lublin, Poland, 85 miles southeast of Warsaw .... Moscow radio announces establishment of a Polish Comm. of National Liberation to take over administration of liberated areas of Poland .... American troops fight their way into Pisa, taking the part of the city south of the Arno River.	U.S. Marines land on Tinian Island, 2½ miles southwest of Saipan, against light opposition. .... U.S. forces cross the base of Orote Peninsula on Guam's west coast, cutting off the island's largest airfield.		
July 24		Russian troops capture Lublin, splitting the German armies in Poland east of the Vistula and San Rivers by cutting their north-south communications.	Japanese troops retreat from the Driniumor River valley in the Aitape-Wewak area of Dutch New Guinea.	State Secy. Hull says the U.S. stand towards Argentina remains unchanged.	
July 25		American troops begin a strong offensive from St. Lo west to the sea .... An American bomb drops short of German lines and kills Lt. Gen. Lesley J. McNair near St. Lo .... Russian troops encircle Lwow, Poland and fight their way into the southern suburbs.	Two thousand Japanese are reported killed making a strong counterattack on the Orote Peninsula, Guam .... British forces capture seven hill positions east of Palel on the Imphal-Tamu road in Manipur State, India.		

A	B	C	D	E
Includes developments that affect more than one world region, international organizations and important meetings of major world leaders.	*Includes all developments in European countries and military engagements between Allied and Axis powers in Africa and at sea.*	*Includes all developments in Japan and China, Japanese foreign policy and military actions in the Pacific region.*	*Includes all domestic and regional developments in Latin America, the Caribbean and Canada.*	*Includes developments in those independent nations and colonial possessions not covered in Columns B, C and D.*

U.S. Politics & Social Issues	U.S. Foreign Policy & Defense	U.S. Economy & Environment	Science, Technology & Nature	Culture, Leisure & Life Style	
				Arne Andersson runs the mile in 4:01.6 in Malmo, Sweden, cutting a full second off the world record.	July 18
Democratic National Convention opens in Chicago. In his keynote address, Gov. Robert Kerr (Okla.) asks for continued support of FDR. Truman is named chairman of the Missouri delegation.		U.S. Court of Appeals in Washington upholds the NWLB's contention that its directives are not subject to court review .... N.Y. Court of Appeals rules that the Railway Mail Assn. is a labor union and cannot bar Negroes from membership .... Pullman, Inc. announces that its directors have voted to give up operation of its sleeping car business and to retain its manufacturing units.		*Variety* reports the most popular songs are: (1) *I'll Be Seeing You* (2) *Long Ago and Far Away* and (3) *Amor*.	July 19
FDR is renominated by the Democratic Party, receiving 1,086 votes to 89 for Sen. Harry F. Byrd (Va.) and one for James Farley.					July 20
In a surprise move FDR selects Sen. Harry S. Truman as his running-mate for the general election. The final ballot gives Truman 1,031 votes and Wallace 105.					July 21
	A U.S. appellate court in Chicago reverses convictions of five persons found guilty of treason for harboring German spy Herbert Haupt. The reversal is based on a U.S. Supreme Court decision prohibiting use of statements by the defendants before their formal arraignment. The death sentence of Hans Haupt, the spy's father, is changed to life imprisonment.			*Ziegfeld Follies* closes after 553 performances on Broadway .... Archbishop Francis J. Spellman is received by Pope Pius XII .... Count Fleet, 1943 "Horse of the Year," is retired after failing to recover from an injury in last year's Belmont Stakes.	July 22
Indictments against 26 Japanese-American internees in California on charges of draft evasion are dismissed under a ruling that they "are in custody and are not free agents."		The National Planning Assn. in Washington publishes a tax program prepared by Beardsley Ruml and H. Christian Sonne which recommends a balanced budget and abolition of income tax on corporations. The plan argues that corporation taxes are passed on to the public and that relief would result in lower prices and increased production and employment.			July 23
American Democratic Comm. Chmn. Gleason Archer announces the group will support Dewey for the presidency.		VFW Commander Carl J. Schoeninger says he has agreements with the AFL and CIO pledging preferential treatment for war veterans.			July 24
	War Secy. Henry L. Stimson, after returning to Washington from the French and Italian battle fronts, says that the "end of the war is not yet apparent."			American Fed. of Musicans Pres. James C. Petrillo orders 16 musicians of radio station KSTP Minneapolis to strike despite a court injunction.	July 25

F	G	H	I	J
Includes elections, federal-state relations, civil rights and liberties, crime, the judiciary, education, health care, poverty, urban affairs and population.	*Includes formation and debate of U.S. foreign and defense policies, veterans affairs and defense spending. (Relations with specific foreign countries are usually found under the region concerned.)*	*Includes business, labor, agriculture, taxation, transportation, consumer affairs, monetary and fiscal policy, natural resources, pollution and accidents.*	*Includes worldwide scientific, medical and technological developments, natural phenomena, U.S. weather and natural disasters.*	*Includes the arts, religion, scholarship, communications media, sports, entertainment, fashions, fads and social life.*

	World Affairs	European War Zone	Pacific War Zone	The Americas	Other Countries & Territories
July 26		Led by tanks, U.S. forces advance all along their 40-mile front in France .... Russian troops reach the Vistula River, taking Deblin, 55 miles southeast of Warsaw .... British troops reach a point eight miles south of Florence.	Chungking reports a "partial agreement" with the Communist Chinese but indicates that it is "too much to expect a total accord." Chiang Kai-shek has offered the Communists free participation in politics after the war in return for wartime acceptance of control by the Chungking regime .... Chinese troops recapture Leiyang, Hunan Province, 40 miles south of besieged Hengyang .... U.S. Marines gain control of the northern third of Tinian Island.	U.S. State Secy. Hull makes public a memorandum to American nations recommending continued refusal to recognize the Argentine government .... Colombian government seizes property of German nationals to cover damage by German war measures.	
July 27		The Russians advance from the Baltic to the Carpathian foothills, taking several Polish, Latvian and Lithuanian localities .... Polish Premier Stanislaw Mikolajczyk heads a committee from the London government to Moscow for talks with Stalin .... German Propaganda Min. Goebbels issues his first orders in a program for total mobilization, which cancels vacations for women workers and directs the army to use frontline troops as labor battalions.	U.S. planes make their first large-scale raid on Halmahera Island in the Moluccas, west of Dutch New Guinea.		
July 28		Russian units take Brest-Litovsk and Przemysl, Poland.		Crowds of nationalist demonstrators in Buenos Aires stone British-owned commercial establishments and are held off from the U.S. embassy by the police.	
July 29		The east bank suburbs of Warsaw come under Russian artillery attack .... U.S. troops take Coutances and push to reach the sea at Montmartin-sur-Mer.	FDR completes a strategy conference in Hawaii with Nimitz, MacArthur and other Pacific military officers .... Thai Premier Luang Pibul Songgram and his cabinet resign as a result of the National Assembly's rejection of proposals to build a new capital at Pechabun.		
July 30		Americans register large gains on the western front in France .... Russian troops push 6½ miles into the Suwalki triangle in East Prussia .... Yugoslavian partisans report their flank attacks against Germans in Serbia are breaking through the enemy's lines in Toplica and Jablanica .... Istanbul reports that the Turkish government has ordered all Turkish ships in Rumanian and Bulgarian ports to return home at once "with or without cargo."	U.S. troops make another amphibious leap along the northern coast of New Guinea, seizing the Sansapor coastal area and the nearby islands of Amsterdam and Middelburg.		All-India Moslem League authorizes Mohammed Ali Jinnah to meet with Gandhi on a plan to establish separate Moslem and Hindu states in India.
July 31		American units in France sweep down the west coast of the Cotentin Peninsula and capture the important town of Avranches .... Russian troops begin outflanking Warsaw on the northeast, approaching within 10 miles of the city .... German Amb. Franz von Papen warns Premier Sukru Saracoglu that a break with the Axis would have "grave consequences" for Turkey .... Rumanian peace terms submitted to Allied representatives are rejected because of Russian objections.	American troops on New Guinea cross the lower portion of the Driniumor River below Aitape and then begin moving eastward.	Ecuadorian Pres. Jose Velasco Ibarra names Alfreda Vera, a Communist, as education minister.	
Aug. 1		Warsaw uprising begins as Soviet troops approach the city but do not enter. Polish partisans loyal to the Polish government-in-exile in London engage German forces in fierce fighting. .... American forces cross the Selune River on a wide front and drive from Normandy into Brittany .... Russian forces take Klapkalns on the Gulf of Riga, Latvia .... Pres. Risto Ryti of Finland resigns and Field Marshal Carl Gustav Mannerheim is appointed to succeed him.	Philippine Pres. Manuel Quezon dies at 65 from tuberculosis in Saranac Lake, N.Y. Vice Pres. Sergio Osmena assumes the presidency .... Allies report that organized resistance on Tinian has ended.	Canadian P.M. Mackenzie King says Canada is taking over the two chains of airfields built in Canada by or in conjunction with the U.S. for continental defense.	
Aug. 2	Churchill reviews the progress of the war in an address to the House of Commons and predicts that "victory may perhaps come soon," with no great lapse between the defeat of Germany and that of Japan.	Turkish government severs diplomatic relations with Germany .... American drive into Brittany continues, with one column moving towards St. Malo and Brest and another towards Rennes.	American forces on Guam make gains averaging two miles .... Japanese troops fail in four attempts to break out of the Allied encirclement at Aitape, Dutch New Guinea.	Octavio Vejar Vazquez, head of the Mexican Comm. for Postwar Problems, says the Pan-American Union has failed to cement hemispheric relations and proposes replacing it with an Inter-American Union.	

A	B	C	D	E
Includes developments that affect more than one world region, international organizations and important meetings of major world leaders.	*Includes all developments in European countries and military engagements between Allied and Axis powers in Africa and at sea.*	*Includes all developments in Japan and China, Japanese foreign policy and military actions in the Pacific region.*	*Includes all domestic and regional developments in Latin America, the Caribbean and Canada.*	*Includes developments in those independent nations and colonial possessions not covered in Columns B, C and D.*

U.S. Politics & Social Issues	U.S. Foreign Policy & Defense	U.S. Economy & Environment	Science, Technology & Nature	Culture, Leisure & Life Style	
Rep. J.W. Fulbright wins the Arkansas Democratic senatorial primary over Gov. Homer Adkins.	Army Service Forces commander Lt. Gen. Brehon B. Somervell cancels leaves of Army civilian workers in arsenals and depots and orders a 54-hour work week.			Minneapolis Judge W.W. Bardwell issues a warrant for the arrest of Petrillo for ordering musicians of radio station KSTP to strike.	July 26
				Betty Jane Vallee, wife of Rudy Vallee, is granted a divorce in Los Angeles.	July 27
Dewey says he opposes the renomination of Rep. Hamilton Fish because Fish charged that "Jews are more or less for the New Deal, unfortunately."					July 28
Willkie offers to appear as an unpaid counsel for author Maxwell Anderson in libel suits against him by Rep. Fish.		OPA cancels ration certificates for heavy-duty rubber tires due to shortages.			July 29
Socialist Party presidential candidate Norman Thomas says that peace terms must be based on reason and that plans should be made for improving Germany and Japan.		National Housing Agency says plans are being shaped for sale of $1 billion worth of permanent housing projects.		Ann Curtiss breaks the world record for the women's 880 free-style swim with a mark of 11:08.6 . . . . Ringling Bros. Barnum & Bailey Circus, whose main tent was destroyed by fire in Hartford, Conn. July 6, leaves Sarasota, Fla. quarters to resume its tour in outdoor arenas.	July 30
					July 31
Senate and House reconvene, but both bodies lack a quorum to conduct business.	Selective Service Dir. Hershey orders local draft boards to proceed with the induction of men over 25 who are not making a contribution to the war effort . . . . Lt. Gen. Joseph W. Stilwell is nominated to the rank of full general.	Distilleries throughout the country resume production of beverage alcohol.			Aug. 1
Dewey and Bricker meet with 24 state GOP governors in St. Louis to unify party policy.		Following riots, the NWLB refers the strike of 6,000 Philadelphia Transportation Co. workers to FDR for "appropriate action," and the NAACP asks the President to order the Army to take over the transit system. The strike followed a move by the company to upgrade eight Negro workers by order of the Committee on Fair Employment Practices. Eleven persons are injured in the rioting and 300, mostly Negroes, are arrested.		Gen. Mgr. Edward Johnson of the Metropolitan Opera Assn. signs a six-year contract with the Blue Network to continue the Saturday afternoon opera broadcasts.	Aug. 2
F	G	H	I	J	
Includes elections, federal-state relations, civil rights and liberties, crime, the judiciary, education, health care, poverty, urban affairs and population.	*Includes formation and debate of U.S. foreign and defense policies, veterans affairs and defense spending. (Relations with specific foreign countries are usually found under the region concerned.)*	*Includes business, labor, agriculture, taxation, transportation, consumer affairs, monetary and fiscal policy, natural resources, pollution and accidents.*	*Includes worldwide scientific, medical and technological developments, natural phenomena, U.S. weather and natural disasters.*	*Includes the arts, religion, scholarship, communications media, sports, entertainment, fashions, fads and social life.*	

	World Affairs	European War Zone	Pacific War Zone	The Americas	Other Countries & Territories
Aug. 3		An intensive German V-1 rocket attack on southern England lasts a record 14 hours .... American drive into Brittany sweeps through Rennes .... Russian forces cross the Vistula River in Poland along a 19-mile front 110 miles south of Warsaw .... Polish Premier Mikolajczyk meets with Stalin for more than two hours..... Germans begin evacuation of the Lodz ghetto, the largest concentration of Jews left in Poland.	FDR visits the Aleutians on return from his Honolulu military conference, stating that Japan will never again be able to invade the Alaskan Islands .... U.S. troops take possession of Mt. Barrigada, dominating the northern plateau of Guam.		
Aug. 4		Berlin says Hitler has established "a court of honor" at the request of the Army and that 12 officers held for complicity in the July 20 bombing will be tried .... American units continue their quick advance in Brittany, with columns reaching to within 75 miles of Brest .... Allied patrols enter Florence, Italy.	A U.S. carrier task force attacks a large Japanese convoy in the Bonin and Volcano Islands, reportedly sinking 17 and damaging at least 23 enemy ships .... The last organized Japanese resistance is crushed at Myitkyina, Burma.		
Aug. 5		As Allied tanks cut off Brittany from the remainder of France, U.S. units reach the outskirts of Brest .... The Germans are reportedly making a strong stand and holding the Russians eight miles from the East Prussian border .... Britain proposes to the USSR an arrangement whereby Rumania and Bulgaria should be Soviet zones of operation and Greece and Yugoslavia British zones.	Japanese troops begin to flee south and west from all strongpoints on Geelvink Bay and the Upper Vogelkop Peninsula on Dutch New Guinea .... Japanese open a new drive in the southwestern part of Kwangtung Province, China on the Luichow Peninsula.	Argentine government releases a number of political prisoners, including Juan Antonio Solari, Americo Ghildi, Ernesto Sammartino and Federico Pinedo Argentina.	
Aug. 6		British troops cross the Arno River into the northern section of Florence and fight German troops in the streets .... American units sweep east from Brittany towards Le Mans in the direction of Paris.	British forces capture the Japanese base of Tamu in western Burma.	Maj. Gualberto Villarroel is sworn in for a four-year term as president of Bolivia.	
Aug. 7	Acting State Secy. Edward Stettinius says preliminary Allied postwar talks have been postponed until Aug. 31 at Russia's request.	Russian troops reportedly complete the seizure of 2,000 oil wells in Polish Galicia.	One-third of the remaining enemy-held territory on Guam is taken by the Americans.	The governments of Brazil, Colombia and Venezuela say they will not recognize the Argentine government because it is not cooperating with hemispheric solidarity.	
Aug. 8	Representatives of the U.S. and Britain sign an agreement establishing principles for future development of world petroleum resources.	British and Canadian troops southeast of Caen gain four to six miles in a new drive .... The Germans make desperate counterattacks along most of the 1,000-mile Russian front, but are being "bled white," Moscow reports .... Eight German Army officers are hanged after a "people's tribunal" finds them guilty of treason in connection with the July 20 bomb plot.	Japanese forces occupy Hengyang, Hunan Province after a siege of more than six weeks.		
Aug. 9		American armored forces enter Le Mans and push beyond toward Paris .... In a joint announcement, FDR and Churchill claim that 500 German subs have been sunk since the war's start.	After 20 days of fighting, organized Japanese resistence on Guam ends .... American troops take control of Baker Island, 2,000 miles southeast of Honolulu.		
Aug. 10	UNRRA's Displaced Persons Bureau estimates that the war's end will leave two million refugees, causing a major resettlement problem.	Polish patriots in Warsaw plea for outside help, indicating they face extinction unless assisted .... Russian units drive south and northeast of Warsaw in an effort to outflank the city and drive a wedge between it and Cracow .... Premier Mikolajczyk of the London Polish government and his party leave Moscow after inconclusive talks with the Polish Comm. of National Liberation .... Polish troops on the Adriatic advance to the Cesano River, only 17 miles from the eastern end of the German Gothic Line in northern Italy.	U.S. planes strike at two widely separated targets: Nagasaki, an industrial center on Kyushu Island, and the oil refinery at Pladju, Palembang, Sumatra.	Ecuador's Constituent Assembly confirms the tenure of Pres. Jose Maria Velasco Ibarra, after he settled a strike yesterday of 8,000 railway workers by meeting their demands to dismiss Public Works Min. Julio Teodoro Salem.	

	A	B	C	D	E
	Includes developments that affect more than one world region, international organizations and important meetings of major world leaders.	*Includes all developments in European countries and military engagements between Allied and Axis powers in Africa and at sea.*	*Includes all developments in Japan and China, Japanese foreign policy and military actions in the Pacific region.*	*Includes all domestic and regional developments in Latin America, the Caribbean and Canada.*	*Includes developments in those independent nations and colonial possessions not covered in Columns B, C and D.*

U.S. Politics & Social Issues	U.S. Foreign Policy & Defense	U.S. Economy & Environment	Science, Technology & Nature	Culture, Leisure & Life Style	
Truman submits his resignation as chairman and member of the Senate Investigating Comm. due to campaign commitments and politics.	Selective Service notifies local draft boards to review the cases of all registrants in the 18-25 age bracket who have been disqualified for either educational or mental reasons.	FDR orders the Army to take control of the Philadelphia Transportation Co. because of the strike by 6,000 workers . . . . A Senate committee investigating the liquor shortage charges that four firms control 70% of the national supply and are charging excessive prices by flooding the market with new brands not subject to price control.			Aug. 3
		War Mobilization Dir. James F. Byrnes announces that labor ceilings will be imposed in nonessential industries in labor-shortage areas.		Gunder Haegg sets a new world record of 8:42.8 for the two-mile run in Stockholm . . . . Prof. Albert Einstein says the biography *Einstein—An Intricate Study of a Great Man,* written by his former son-in-law, Dimitri Marianoff, is "generally unreliable."	Aug. 4
	Rear Adm. Don Pardee Moon, 50, who commanded a task force in the Normandy invasion, commits suicide in Washington, "apparently as a result of combat fatigue."				Aug. 5
Rep. Martin Dies (D, Tex.) asks Atty. Gen. Francis Biddle to prosecute leaders of the "Communist-dominated" CIO Political Action Comm.		Transit service is restored in Philadelphia as most of the 6,000 workers return to work following orders by Maj. Gen. Philip Hayes that the leaders of the unauthorized strike be arrested.	Harvard Univ. discloses that Comdr. Howard Aiken in collaboration with IBM has developed an automatic calculator capable of solving any mathematical problem. This sequence-controlled calculator is the largest and most completely automatic calculator in operation. Multiplication and division with 23 significant figures are possible, and mathematical tables are used in the form of punched tapes. It will be used by the U.S. Navy for the duration of the war.	Theological Institute of the Russian Orthodox Church is opened in the Novodevichy Monastery, Moscow for the first time since 1917.	Aug. 6
			U.S. Public Health Service says gonorrhea can be cured in 7½ hrs. with penicillin.	Justice Dept. files a suit ordering motion picture producers to end theater ownership in order to restore competition in communities where they now have monopolies . . . . Boston bans the sale of Lt. Joseph Stanley Pennell's novel *The History of Rome Hanks and Kindred Matters* because "it is more improper" than Lillian Smith's *Strange Fruit.*	Aug. 7
					Aug. 8
Newsweek reports that 50 political writers believe FDR will win the 1944 election but are split on the question of whether it is good for the country.	Selective Service Dir. Hershey says the end of the European war will not end the draft, as both the Army and Navy will need replacements.	Atty. Gen. Biddle reports the Justice Dept. will bring suit against 12 Western railroads for violations of the Sherman Antitrust Act.	A Colombian newspaper reports that Abjon Jaramillo, 75, the father of 43 children, became the father of quadruplets today.	Yankee Maid, with Henry Thomas up, wins the $34,427 Hambletonian Stakes, the richest harness racing stake, at Goshen, N.Y. . . . . Antoine de St. Exupery, French pilot and author, age 44, is reported missing and presumed dead on a flight over France.	Aug. 9
American Labor Party pledges support to the Roosevelt-Truman ticket.	Army discloses plans for cutbacks in many types of planes except heavy bombers.		One of America's first woman doctors, Annie Surgis Daniel, dies at 85 in N.Y.C.	Samuel Reshevsky wins the U.S. Chess Federation title, beating Anthony E. Santasiere.	Aug. 10

F	G	H	I	J
Includes elections, federal-state relations, civil rights and liberties, crime, the judiciary, education, health care, poverty, urban affairs and population.	*Includes formation and debate of U.S. foreign and defense policies, veterans affairs and defense spending. (Relations with specific foreign countries are usually found under the region concerned.)*	*Includes business, labor, agriculture, taxation, transportation, consumer affairs, monetary and fiscal policy, natural resources, pollution and accidents.*	*Includes worldwide scientific, medical and technological developments, natural phenomena, U.S. weather and natural disasters.*	*Includes the arts, religion, scholarship, communications media, sports, entertainment, fashions, fads and social life.*

	World Affairs	European War Zone	Pacific War Zone	The Americas	Other Countries & Territories
Aug. 11		American forces move north from Le Mans to link up with British and Canadian troops in the Caen-Vire sector and close a trap on part of the German 7th Army .... Russians renew their Estonian offensive, advancing 16 miles along a 43-mile front.		Canadian P.M. Mackenzie King says Canada will take an appropriate part in the war against Japan.	
Aug. 12	Sir Alexander Cadogan heads the British delegation that arrives in Washington for postwar security talks with U.S. and Russian officials.	Allied forces take control of Florence, Italy as the city is spared destructive fighting .... Russian troops widen their front northeast of Warsaw .... Joseph P. Kennedy, Jr., son of former U.S. ambassador to Britain, is lost in action while on a special mission in the European war theater.			
Aug. 13		As American units pass Argentan, German forces are limited to an 18-mile wide escape gap in the Caen-Vire area .... British units capture the mountain town of Frontone, Italy .... Russian troops smash to within 11 miles northeast of Warsaw by taking Moskowka.	Pacific Fleet Commander Adm. Chester Nimitz says that a combination of a sea blockade and aerial bombardments may force Japan to surrender before an invasion of the home islands takes place.		
Aug. 14	Russian delegation in Washington rejects a postwar police force and instead proposes an international police air force made up of volunteers from all nations, subject to the authority of the Big Four.	Allied forces close the German escape route to 12 miles between Argentan and Falaise, and subject the gap to artillery fire, slowing escape for an estimated 100,000 Nazi troops .... Almost 3,000 U.S. and British planes attack German targets.			
Aug. 15		Allied troops invade southern France between Marseilles and Nice, meeting little concentrated opposition.			
Aug. 16		Russian troops enter Ossow, seven miles northeast of Warsaw, but retreat in the face of strong German counterattacks .... Allied troops are reported firmly entrenched on France's southern coast, penetrating up to eight miles at various points.		U.S. State Dept. orders the freezing of Argentine gold stocks.	
Aug. 17	FDR returns to Washington and tells a press conference that Germany and Japan will be occupied by Allied forces.	In one of the war's greatest fire raids, nearly 1,200 RAF planes drop 70,000 incendiary bombs on Kiel and Stettin .... As American troops push towards Paris on a 70-mile front, the cities of Orleans, Dreux, Chartres and Chateaudun are freed .... In southern France, Allied units advance up to 35 miles with the capture of Draguigan .... Russian forces reach the frontier of East Prussia along the Sesupe River in western Lithuania .... U.S. War Dept. reports American casualties for the first two months of fighting in France through Aug. 6 totaled 16,434 dead, 76,535 wounded, 19,704 missing.	British drive the Japanese out of eastern India and move two miles south of the Burmese border along the Tiddim Road.		Indian Viceroy Viscount Wavell rejects a request of Gandhi to discuss war support in return for immediate independence.
Aug. 18		American troops drive to within 12 miles of Paris as they reach the suburbs of Versailles .... In southern France, U.S. forces take Sollies-Pont and approach Brignoles in a drive for Marseilles .... Red Army storms and takes Sandomierz south of Warsaw.		Ecuadorian Assembly votes to deny the U.S. bases or other privileges in the Galapagos Islands.	British authorities in Palestine fine residents of a Jerusalem suburb $2,000 for the attempted assassination of High Commissioner Sir Harold MacMichael.
Aug. 19		More than 20,000 members of the French Forces of the Interior revolt against the rear-guard German garrison in Paris. Eisenhower moves to their support .... U.S. 3rd Army tanks reach the Parisian suburbs .... In the drive on Marseilles the towns of St. Maximin and La Roquebrussanne are freed by Allied forces .... Russian troops take Kolomiya, principal German bulwark defending the southern approaches to East Prussia.	Japanese are driven from Assam, northeastern India, after Stilwell's air-supported British troops and Chindits lead a successful offensive against them .... Chinese troops in Hupeh Province along the Yangtze River gain to the north in the direction of Kiangling and south towards Hwajung and Owchikhow.		

A	B	C	D	E
Includes developments that affect more than one world region, international organizations and important meetings of major world leaders.	*Includes all developments in European countries and military engagements between Allied and Axis powers in Africa and at sea.*	*Includes all developments in Japan and China, Japanese foreign policy and military actions in the Pacific region.*	*Includes all domestic and regional developments in Latin America, the Caribbean and Canada.*	*Includes developments in those independent nations and colonial possessions not covered in Columns B, C and D.*

U.S. Politics & Social Issues	U.S. Foreign Policy & Defense	U.S. Economy & Environment	Science, Technology & Nature	Culture, Leisure & Life Style	
		Senate passes the George demobilization and reconversion bill, which establishes federal agencies to direct reconversion and contract settlements.		A Hartford, Conn. court charges five officials of Ringling Bros. Barnum & Bailey Circus with manslaughter for the death of 167 persons in the July 6 fire.	Aug. 11
	Speaking in Bremerton, Wash., FDR says the U.S. must control the "great circle" route across the Pacific to guard against future "sneak attacks."				Aug. 12
		Petroleum War Council announces a new gasoline known as "100 octane plus," which surpasses all other fuels in volatility and performance, is ready for production.			Aug. 13
		An estimated 25,000 drivers and handlers return to work in eight Midwestern states, following government seizure of 103 motor freight lines which refused a NWLB directive to give them a 7 cent hourly wage increase . . . . WPB Chmn. Nelson orders production of civilian goods resumed "where local conditions" permit to utilize manpower and plants where war production has been reduced.		MGM announces that the winner of its first annual prize novel competition is *Green Dolphin Street*, by Elizabeth Goudge.	Aug. 14
About 500 of 1,800 German prisoners of war employed at the Army Ordnance Depot in Stockton, Calif. call off a strike begun yesterday in protest against the War Dept.'s order increasing the work day to nine hours.		AFL Pres. Green announces the International Typographical Union has completed the process of reaffiliation with the AFL after a four-year absence.	American Red Cross announces in Washington that it is equipping 10 hospitals of 500 beds each for the civilian population of freed areas in Russia.		Aug. 15
House approves and sends the the White House an amendment to the Soldier Vote Act ending censorship of reading matter . . . . House Comm. on Education names Dr. Francis Brown to head a committee of 12 educators to survey the needs of American colleges and recommend legislation to provide aid.	Dewey says the Russian plan for postwar world domination by the Big Four is one of "imperialism which would coerce smaller nations."			*Variety* reports the most popular songs as (1) *Swinging on a Star*, (2) *I'll Be Seeing You* and (3) *I'll Walk Alone*.	Aug. 16
	War Secy. Stimson says "the present war will not end wars" and proposes universal military training.	OPA Dir. Chester Bowles says prices will be held in tight check in the reconversion and postwar periods "to prevent the mistakes of 1918-1919."	National Foundation for Infantile Paralysis says outbreaks of the disease have reached epidemic proportion in five states: N.Y., N.C., Ky., Pa. and Va.		Aug. 17
Dewey names John Foster Dulles as his representative to meet with State Secy. Hull for discussions on postwar security plans.	Rep. Clare Boothe Luce (R, Conn.) disagrees with FDR's proposals that the U.S. take Pacific island bases for postwar security "because seizure of these lands would be called imperialism, and we can get all necessary bases from the British Empire."			Film actress Lillian Arch files suit for divorce in Los Angeles from Bela Lugosi, screen "horror man," charging that he is cruel and inhuman.	Aug. 18
	FDR announces that WPB Chmn. Nelson and Maj. Gen. Patrick Hurley will leave for China soon on special missions.	FDR orders 99 more West Coast machine plants seized when workers persist in refusing to work 48 hours per week.		Sir Henry Wood, for 50 years a British conductor who worked to "democratize" music, dies at 75 in London.	Aug. 19

F	G	H	I	J
Includes elections, federal-state relations, civil rights and liberties, crime, the judiciary, education, health care, poverty, urban affairs and population.	*Includes formation and debate of U.S. foreign and defense policies, veterans affairs and defense spending. (Relations with specific foreign countries are usually found under the region concerned.)*	*Includes business, labor, agriculture, taxation, transportation, consumer affairs, monetary and fiscal policy, natural resources, pollution and accidents.*	*Includes worldwide scientific, medical and technological developments, natural phenomena, U.S. weather and natural disasters.*	*Includes the arts, religion, scholarship, communications media, sports, entertainment, fashions, fads and social life.*

	World Affairs	European War Zone	Pacific War Zone	The Americas	Other Countries & Territories
Aug. 20		American troops cross the Seine River above Paris, as armored units strike northwest and southeast of the city .... Allied troops reach the outskirts of Aix-en-Province, 13 miles northeast of Marseilles .... Two Russian armies launch an offensive in Rumania and Bessarabia .... Russian troops achieve a 16-mile breakthrough in central Latvia and drive to within 55 miles of Riga.	Two flights of B-29's make day and night assaults on the Yawata industrial district of Kyushu Island .... British troops break into Burma in pursuit of Japanese troops retreating from Manipur State, India.		Kamil Shabi, leader of Iraq's May 1941 revolt, is sentenced to death by a court martial in Baghdad and is immediately hanged.
Aug. 21	Dumbarton Oaks Conference convenes in Washington to lay out the various proposals and plans for a permanent U.N. organization. Representatives of the four powers are Edward R. Stettinius of the U.S., Sir Alexander Cadogan of Britain, Andrei Gromyko of Russia and V.K. Wellington Koo of China.	American armored forces turn the left flank of the German 15th Army by thrusting across the Seine southeast of Paris .... French troops reach the Toulon suburbs in southern France .... Tito and Yugoslavian Premier Ivan Subasitch sign an agreement for collaboration in freeing the country of Germans and letting the question of the monarchy rest until liberation is acheived.			
Aug. 22		Bulgarian Foreign Min. Parvan Dragnov says he is seeking peace with the Allies and that Bulgarian troops have been withdrawn from Yugoslavia .... Allied forces besiege Bordeaux on the French west coast as an American and French volunteer force lands by sea.	Japan begins a compulsory labor draft for women and girls from 12 to 40.	Mexican Pres. Avila Camacho decrees all literate citizens in the 18-60 age bracket must teach at least one illiterate from 14 to 60 to read and write.	
Aug. 23	FDR says the Big Four can maintain the postwar peace "if we remain friends."	Russian forces seize Vaslui and two Bessarabian towns, Bendery and Akkerman, in Rumania .... King Michael announces Rumania's unconditional surrender and the dismissal of Premier Marshal Ion Antonescu .... American forces drive 140 miles into France from the south coast to capture Grenoble, as French troops gain control of Marseilles.	Japanese open a new drive in southern China, moving northward from the neck of Luichow Peninsula opposite Hainan Island.	Brazilian Foreign Min. Oswaldo Aranha resigns and is succeeded by Pedro Leao Veloso.	
Aug. 24	Britain proposes at the Dumbarton Oaks Conference that a U.N. Military Staff Comm. be set up to prevent and repel aggression.	Russian drives in Rumania bring the Moldavian capital of Kishinev under control, while other units reach the Black Sea at Zolokary .... The new Rumanian government of Marshal Constantin Senatescu is reported in firm control of the country, save a few scattered areas where there are concentrations of Nazi troops .... Navy Secy. Forrestal quotes Eisenhower as warning against expectations of collapse on the German home front.	British troops clear more than 10 miles of the Tiddim Road inside western Burma.	Pro-Axis Argentine Min. of Justice and Education Alberto Baldrich resigns following Buenos Aires demonstrations celebrating the liberation of Paris .... Argentine government announces it has placed 100,000 tons of wheat and 5,000 tons of beef at the disposal of French authorities as a gift.	
Aug. 25		Nazi Gen. Dietrich von Choltitz signs an unconditional surrender of Paris. At 2 p.m. French Gen. LeClerc, speaking in a baggage room at the Gare Montparnasse, announces the surrender of the German garrison of 10,000 and the liberation of Paris .... U.S. and Britain conclude agreements with de Gaulle's provisional government for administration of areas of liberated France pending establishment of a permanent government .... Rumania declares war on Germany after the Nazis bomb Bucharest, attack Rumanian troops and strafe civilians .... King Peter of Yugoslavia signs a decree ending official connections with Gen. Draja Mikhailovich, who had headed the Yugoslavian high command since June 1942.			
Aug. 26		Moscow reports that Bulgaria has agreed to proclaim neutrality and disarm German troops within its borders, and another source says Bulgaria is asking the Allies for peace terms .... Russian troops complete the reconquest of Bessarabia .... In southern France, Allied troops capture Arles, Tarascon and Avignon and advance closer to Lyon and the Italian frontier in the vicinity of Nice .... Icelandic Foreign Min. Vilhjalmur Thor says he expects American armed forces to withdraw from Iceland at the end of the war and that he sees no necessity for granting the U.S. peacetime military bases.			

	A	B	C	D	E
	Includes developments that affect more than one world region, international organizations and important meetings of major world leaders.	*Includes all developments in European countries and military engagements between Allied and Axis powers in Africa and at sea.*	*Includes all developments in Japan and China, Japanese foreign policy and military actions in the Pacific region.*	*Includes all domestic and regional developments in Latin America, the Caribbean and Canada.*	*Includes developments in those independent nations and colonial possessions not covered in Columns B, C and D.*

U.S. Politics & Social Issues	U.S. Foreign Policy & Defense	U.S. Economy & Environment	Science, Technology & Nature	Culture, Leisure & Life Style	
	Adm. Husband Kimmel disputes statements by Harry Truman that Kimmel refused to cooperate with the Army in Hawaii and was not on speaking terms with Maj. Gen. Short.			Bob Hamilton wins the PGA title in Spokane, Wash., defeating Byron Nelson in the 36-hole final.	Aug. 20
Sen. Ellison D. ("Cotton Ed") Smith (D, S.C.) says he will support Southern Democratic electors who will vote against a fourth term for FDR.					Aug. 21
		Walter Reuther of the UAW asks the NWLB to order GM to set up an employe postwar security fund.			Aug. 22
FDR wins 28 states to Dewey's 20 in a preliminary Gallup Poll and leads by 286 to 245 in electoral votes.	FDR tells Congress that Lend-Lease expenditures through June 30 totaled $28.37 billion and asks that the program be extended through the defeat of Germany and Japan.	Justice Dept. files suit against 47 Western railroads, charging violations of the Sherman Antitrust Act by rate fixing and failure to improve service and equipment.			Aug. 23
	FDR submits to the Senate an Anglo-American agreement on world petroleum resources for ratification.	WPB Vice Chmn. Charles E. Wilson quits his post, charging that his usefulness has been impaired by press attacks by aides of Chmn. Nelson	*Science* magazine says a mold of the penicillin group inhibits the growth of tuberculosis germs.		Aug. 24
Hull and John Foster Dulles complete three days of talks on American postwar security and in a joint statement say they "are trying to keep the subject out of politics."		Senate passes and sends to conference the House war-surplus disposal bill, to be administered by an eight-man board.		American artist Paul Ullman is killed while leading a French underground force in France . . . . Viljo Heino, Finnish track star, sets a new world record in the 10,000-meter run with a mark of 29:35.4.	Aug. 25
			N.Y. State Hospital Commission reports insulin shock treatment for dementia praecox patients has enabled 55% of those treated to become useful members of society.		Aug. 26

F	G	H	I	J
Includes elections, federal-state relations, civil rights and liberties, crime, the judiciary, education, health care, poverty, urban affairs and population.	*Includes formation and debate of U.S. foreign and defense policies, veterans affairs and defense spending. (Relations with specific foreign countries are usually found under the region concerned.)*	*Includes business, labor, agriculture, taxation, transportation, consumer affairs, monetary and fiscal policy, natural resources, pollution and accidents.*	*Includes worldwide scientific, medical and technological developments, natural phenomena, U.S. weather and natural disasters.*	*Includes the arts, religion, scholarship, communications media, sports, entertainment, fashions, fads and social life.*

	World Affairs	European War Zone	Pacific War Zone	The Americas	Other Countries & Territories
Aug. 27		American troops reach the Marne River at Lagny, 15 miles east of Paris .... Russian forces take Galati, Rumania, while other units push through Foscani to take Ramnicul-Sarat.	Chinese troops in Hunan Province occupy Chuting on the Siang River, some 45 miles north of enemy-held Hengyang .... Japanese troops open a new drive in Honan Province, moving westward from the Peking-Hankow railroad.		
Aug. 28		American troops cross the Marne at Meaux and drive into Chateau-Thierry .... Russian forces drive 10 miles inside Transylvania.			
Aug. 29	Dumbarton Oaks Conference reaches agreement on (1) an assembly of sovereign nations, (2) a smaller council of "principal states" supplemented by rotating representation of other states and (3) an international court of justice and "other means" to maintain world order.	Polish and Soviet authorities report that about 1.5 million persons have been systematically murdered at the Maidanek concentration camp at Lublin .... Russian forces combine a 65-mile overland drive with an 82-mile amphibious operation to capture the Rumanian Black Sea port of Constanta .... U.S. forces close in on Reims, north of Pons, and capture Cuvergnon and Soissons.			
Aug. 30		Russian troops capture the Rumanian oil center of Ploesti, cutting Germany's last major source of natural oil .... A French provisional government under de Gaulle is set up in Paris.	Moving from Hengyang, two Japanese columns advance 11 miles towards the Kwangsi Province airbase at Kweilin.	Gen. Arturo Rawson is put under house arrest in Buenos Aires for participation in demonstrations following the liberation of Paris.	
Aug. 31		Polish Premier Stanislaw Mikolajczyk says the London exiles have forwarded to Moscow proposals for a settlement of the Polish problems .... Russian troops enter Bucharest, Rumania .... British forces seize Amiens and cross the Somme, as U.S. units bridge the Meuse River and storm Mezieres, Charleville and Sedan .... Polish troops capture Pesaro on the Adriatic.			
Sept. 1		U.S. forces advancing from Sedan reach the Belgian border .... U.S. forces take Verdun, St. Mihiel, Joinville and Commercy as they push eastward towards Metz and the German Saar .... British troops smash into a section of the German Gothic Line near the Adriatic.	U.S. Naval task force operating against the Bonin and Volcano Islands reports sinking 13 Japanese ships and destroying 85 planes .... U.S. bombers make their heaviest raid on the Philippines, hitting the Davao airfields and the principal port of Mindanao Island.	The president of the Mexican Chamber of Deputies, Herminio Ahumada, is voted out of office after attacking the annual report to the Chamber by Pres. Avila Camacho .... Cuban Pres.-elect Dr. Ramon Grau San Martin arrives in Washington for meetings with State Secy. Hull.	
Sept. 2		Finnish Premier Hackzell says the country will quit the war against Russia and that Germany has agreed to withdraw its troops by Sept. 15 .... Shortly before noon U.S. troops enter Belgium, taking Tournai, some 43 miles from Brussels .... In four columns, Allied armor makes a 34-mile advance up both sides of the Rhone River to a point 14 miles from Lyon .... U.S. forces move across the Arno River in a new offensive, capturing Pisa.		Prof. Juan Jose Arevalo, exiled by the Guatemalan government, returns to the country from Argentina.	
Sept. 3		Helsinki reports an agreement with Russia to cease fighting at 8 a.m. tomorrow .... American troops occupy Lyons and push 36 miles beyond .... As British troops enter Brussels, U.S. forces reach the Luxembourg border .... Cairo reports five representatives of the Communist-led EAM and other Greek guerrillas are sworn in as members of the Greek cabinet-in-exile.	Indian troops advancing along the Lyitkyina-Mandalay railroad occupy the village of Kyagyigon, while British troops close in on Tiddim in western Burma.		
Sept. 4		As Belgium is being cleared of Nazi troops, British units enter the Netherlands and capture Breda, 25 miles southeast of Rotterdam .... Finnish-Soviet ceasefire becomes effective along a 500-mile front from Viborg to Salla at 7:59 a.m.	Allied planes sink or damage nearly 40 Japanese barges and cargo ships in attacks against the Philippines, Halmahera and NEI targets.		
Sept. 5		Russia notifies Bulgaria at 7 p.m. that a state of war exists between the two countries because of Bulgaria's failure to sever relations with Germany.			

A	B	C	D	E
Includes developments that affect more than one world region, international organizations and important meetings of major world leaders.	*Includes all developments in European countries and military engagements between Allied and Axis powers in Africa and at sea.*	*Includes all developments in Japan and China, Japanese foreign policy and military actions in the Pacific region.*	*Includes all domestic and regional developments in Latin America, the Caribbean and Canada.*	*Includes developments in those independent nations and colonial possessions not covered in Columns B, C and D.*

U.S. Politics & Social Issues	U.S. Foreign Policy & Defense	U.S. Economy & Environment	Science, Technology & Nature	Culture, Leisure & Life Style	
National Urban League announces plans for community projects to combat racial friction by organizing and educating civic leadership to recognize and eliminate its causes . . . . Army announces that beginning in September short wave radio facilities will be available on an equal basis to presidential candidates to speak to overseas troops.				Keo Nakama, OSU's Hawaiian swim star, wins the 400, 800 and 1,500-meter freestyle events at the AAU indoor championships in Great Lakes, Ill.	Aug. 27
CIO Political Action Comm. and National PAC Chmn. Sidney Hillman tells the House Campaign Expenditures Comm. that both groups are functioning legally, contemplate no third party movement and "have no plans to capture any political party."		Most of 8,000 workers of the Ford Motor Co. Highland Park Plant in Detroit, on strike since Aug. 24 over wages and seniority rights, return to work. CIO-UAW officials call the walkout unauthorized.		Byron Nelson wins the All-American golf tourney at the Tam O'Shanter Club in Chicago, winning a record $13,462 in war bonds.	Aug. 28
GOP opens its presidential campaign with national radio broadcasts by Govs. Earl Warren (Calif.), Dwight Green (Ill.) and Raymond Baldwin (Conn.).					Aug. 29
National convention of the America First Party nominates Gerald Smith as presidential candidate and Harry Romer as his running mate.	Navy says 65,000 ships have been built since Sept. 1, 1939, with nearly 36% of the total 9 million tons being combatant ships.			Chicago Bears win the annual football all-star game against the collegians, 24-21, in Evanston, Ill.	Aug. 30
Harry S. Truman accepts the vice presidential nomination in a Lamar, Mo. speech, saying that the voters "should trust experienced leaders."		House passes and returns to the Senate a revised version of the George reconversion bill, calling for an office of War Mobilization and Reconversion to replace the present OWM . . . . FDR orders the takeover of 10 Pennsylvania coal mines closed by strikes.		P.G. Wodehouse, British humorist who made a series of broadcasts from Berlin urging Allied capitulation, is discovered in Paris and says he "made a terrible mistake."	Aug. 31
	Gen. George C. Marshall advises subordinates working on postwar plans that he favors a small professional army supported by trained citizen reserves chosen by a draft system . . . . Selective Service tells the Senate and House Military Affairs Committees that few men beyond the age of 26 will be drafted during the rest of 1944.			*Arsenic and Old Lace*, a Warner Bros. film featuring Cary Grant, opens in New York . . . . Helsinki reports the manuscripts of Finnish composer Jean Sibelius were destroyed during an Allied bombing raid on Leipzig, Germany.	Sept. 1
Former Sen. George Norris, defeated in 1942 after 40 years in Congress, dies at 83 in McCook, Neb.		War Mobilization Dir. Byrnes creates a War Plants Utilization Comm. to direct reconversion of an estimated $15 billion worth of government-owned war plants.	National Foundation for Infantile Paralysis says more than a million dollars has been spent this year fighting the spreading polio epidemics.		Sept. 2
				Pauline Betz wins the women's national tennis title, defeating Margaret Osborne at Forest Hills, N.Y.	Sept. 3
In a Labor Day speech in Detroit, Harry S. Truman says future prosperity depends upon the reelection of FDR.		AFL Pres. Green and CIO Pres. Murray call for government-controlled reconversion of industry to peacetime production.		Frank Parker wins the national tennis title at Forest Hills, N.Y., defeating William Talbert.	Sept. 4
		WPB releases plans for shifting production from war to civilian output when Germany is defeated . . . . FDR orders the Army to seize and operate two strikebound plants of the Cleveland Graphite Bronze Co.	An earthquake at 12:40 is felt throughout the Eastern seaboard, with only minor damage in the U.S. but with about $1 million worth in Cornwall, Ont., Canada.		Sept. 5
F	G	H	I	J	
Includes elections, federal-state relations, civil rights and liberties, crime, the judiciary, education, health care, poverty, urban affairs and population.	*Includes formation and debate of U.S. foreign and defense policies, veterans affairs and defense spending. (Relations with specific foreign countries are usually found under the region concerned.)*	*Includes business, labor, agriculture, taxation, transportation, consumer affairs, monetary and fiscal policy, natural resources, pollution and accidents.*	*Includes worldwide scientific, medical and technological developments, natural phenomena, U.S. weather and natural disasters.*	*Includes the arts, religion, scholarship, communications media, sports, entertainment, fashions, fads and social life.*	

	World Affairs	European War Zone	Pacific War Zone	The Americas	Other Countries & Territories
Sept. 6		American troops fight their way across the Moselle River between Metz and Nancy, making progress toward the German border .... Russian troops capture Turnu Severin, Rumania at the Danube River's Iron Gate pass .... U.S. State Dept. announces recognition of the Czech and Slovak resistance forces and warns Germany to treat them according to the rules of war.	WPB Dir. Nelson and Patrick Hurley arrive in Chungking on a mission "to lay the groundwork for postwar industrialization of China."		
Sept. 7		Russian troops close in on the Polish fortress city of Lomzha just south of the East Prussian border .... Americans capture Sedan.	Allied amphibious units land on Supiori Island, in Geelvink Bay at the northwestern end of Dutch New Guinea .... Japanese capture Lingling, Hunan Province, former site of a U.S. airbase .... Japanese forces capture the Chekiang seaport of Wenchow, giving them control of approximately two-thirds of the province .... Emperor Hirohito and Premier Gen. Kuniaki Koiso report to the Diet on increased Allied pressure and warn that consideration of a mainland invasion must be considered.	U.S. State Secy. Hull says Argentina is headquarters for a Fascist movement in the Americas .... Nicaraguan Congress repeals a Chinese exclusion law and authorizes limited immigration.	
Sept. 8		Russian units begin crossing the Bulgarian border, gaining 18-41 miles and occupying Varna on the Black Sea and Ruschuk on the Danube .... Dr. Karl Goerdeler is sentenced to death for participation in the assassination attempt against Hitler.	Adm. Halsey commands a naval assault on Mindanao Island in the Philippines, sinking scores of Japanese vessels and destroying many enemy planes .... U.S. planes operating from China make a daylight attack upon Anshan, Manchuria.		
Sept. 9		Russia grants Bulgaria's request for an armistice, as Moscow claims that Bulgaria is no longer "a center of German influence in the Balkans." .... Col. Kimon Georgiev is installed as premier of Bulgaria .... German troops make strong counterattacks along the Siegfried Line in the Metz-Nancy region.	British planes make 21 attacks within 23 hours after sighting a convoy of about 15 Japanese ships in the Andaman Sea, dispersing the ships over hundreds of miles.	Argentina announces it will withdraw from the Inter-American Emergency Advisory Comm. because of criticisms of Argentina.	Gandhi and Mohammed Ali Jinnah open talks in Bombay in an effort to resolve political differences between Hindus and Moslems.
Sept. 10	Churchill arrives in Halifax en route to Quebec, where he will confer with FDR.	Russian forces advance 18 miles into the part of Transylvania annexed by Hungary, capturing nearly 60 localities. .... For the first time U.S. shells strike at Germany, hitting Bildchen on the Siegfried Line.			
Sept. 11	FDR and Churchill arrive in Quebec and open discussions on ways to speed the defeat of Germany and Japan .... State Dept. sends invitations to 50 nations for an international civil air conference in the U.S. starting Nov. 1.	U.S. troops push five miles into German territory northwest of Trier at 6:11 p.m. .... British troops enter the Netherlands above Neerpelt after crossing the Schelde-Meuse Canal .... Greek Premier Papendreou and most of his ministers arrive in Naples to await the liberation of Greece.			
Sept. 12		Marshal Rodion Y. Malinovsky signs on behalf of Russia, Britain the U.S. and all U.N. countries an armistice with Rumania .... Gen. de Gaulle pledges again to turn over the government to an elected national assembly "as soon as France reestablishes her sovereignty." .... American 1st Army penetrates the German border again, crossing at the Belgian frontier town of Eupen.			
Sept. 13	FDR says the aim of the Quebec Conference is to bring maximum effort to all war theaters and coordinate Allied war efforts.	Allied troops reach the vicinity of two passes above Florence leading through the Apennines to the Po Valley .... Russia announces the terms of its armistice with Rumania, which include a $300-million war reparation, the ceding of Bessarabia and northern Bukovina to Russia and the return of Transylvania to Rumania .... Russian forces break through the German defenses on a 35-mile front in southern Poland and reach the Czech border at Ciechania, 80 miles southeast of Cracow .... After seizing Rotgen, U.S. forces dig into the heights above Aachen, Germany.		Between 80 and 100 persons are reported killed in a Mexican cyclone and cloudburst covering nine states a week ago.	
Sept. 14		Antwerp is captured by the Allies .... U.S. forces take six German towns south of Aachen and shell the city from a mile's distance .... Polish and Russian troops capture the Warsaw suburb of Praga, saving it from total destruction.	U.S. Army troops and Marines invade Peleliu Island of the Palau group in the western Carolines .... Chinese troops recapture the fortress city of Tengyueh in Yunnan Province.		

	A	B	C	D	E
	Includes developments that affect more than one world region, international organizations and important meetings of major world leaders.	*Includes all developments in European countries and military engagements between Allied and Axis powers in Africa and at sea.*	*Includes all developments in Japan and China, Japanese foreign policy and military actions in the Pacific region.*	*Includes all domestic and regional developments in Latin America, the Caribbean and Canada.*	*Includes developments in those independent nations and colonial possessions not covered in Columns B, C and D.*

U.S. Politics & Social Issues	U.S. Foreign Policy & Defense	U.S. Economy & Environment	Science, Technology & Nature	Culture, Leisure & Life Style	
	Army says it will demobilize about one million soldiers when the war with Germany ends.	Comm. for Economic Development recommends postwar tax reductions, equalization on ability to pay, a flat corporation tax and sufficient revenue to provide national debt reduction.			Sept. 6
Dewey opens his presidential campaign in a broadcast blasting the New Deal as "inept, quarrelsome and inefficient," with 10 million still unemployed in 1940.					Sept. 7
Dewey says that he favors force to maintain world peace and that the U.S. cannot isolate itself from world affairs.					Sept. 8
		War Mobilization Dir. Byrnes denies that the government plans to operate its war plants in competition with private industry after the war . . . . Commerce Dept. reports that July income payments to individuals increased 9% over July 1943 to $12.892 billion.	Harvard Medical School reports a synthetic skin or membrane useful in healing burns has been developed from fractionation of blood plasma.	FCC says it will build and operate a frequency modulation (FM) radio station to obtain technical data.	Sept. 9
		A special House Economic Planning Comm. issues a postwar economic program calling for reduced taxation and measures to maintain high peacetime production.			Sept. 10
A GOP landslide in Maine elects Horace Hildreth governor and reelects three GOP congressmen: Robert Hale, Margaret Smith and Frank Fellows.	Navy Secy. Forrestal says he favors a year's military training for American youth . . . . State Secy. Hull says time has almost run out for Austria to demonstrate fitness for independence when Germany is defeated.				Sept. 11
		UMW Pres. Lewis tells the union convention in Cincinnati that FDR "kicked every coal miner in the face" during the 1943-44 wage negotiations.		Gus Sonnenberg, former Dartmouth football star who introduced "the flying tackle" into professional wrestling, dies at 44 of leukemia.	Sept. 12
Dewey says "greater scope and recognition" should be granted to MacArthur "now that he is no longer a political threat to the New Deal." . . . . Senate confirms the renomination of Leland Olds as chairman of the FPC for a five-year term.	Senate approves a House bill permitting Waves to be sent to U.S. stations outside continental America.			*Variety* reports the most popular songs are (1) *I'll Walk Alone*, (2) *Swingin' on a Star* and (3) *I'll Be Seeing You*.	Sept. 13
ABA convention rejects a resolution critical of the Supreme Court for "reflecting New Deal political purposes in its decisions."		CIO-UAW votes to retain its no strike pledge pending a mail referendum of union members . . . . Two NWLB panels report that Labor Dept. cost-of-living reports do not reflect actualities, claiming that there has been a 5% rise over the 24.5% reported by the Labor Dept.	In the worst storm since 1938, a hurricane sweeps the Atlantic Coast from the Carolinas to Canada, causing 40 deaths and at least $100 million in property damage.		Sept. 14
F	G	H	I	J	
Includes elections, federal-state relations, civil rights and liberties, crime, the judiciary, education, health care, poverty, urban affairs and population.	*Includes formation and debate of U.S. foreign and defense policies, veterans affairs and defense spending. (Relations with specific foreign countries are usually found under the region concerned.)*	*Includes business, labor, agriculture, taxation, transportation, consumer affairs, monetary and fiscal policy, natural resources, pollution and accidents.*	*Includes worldwide scientific, medical and technological developments, natural phenomena, U.S. weather and natural disasters.*	*Includes the arts, religion, scholarship, communications media, sports, entertainment, fashions, fads and social life.*	

	World Affairs	European War Zone	Pacific War Zone	The Americas	Other Countries & Territories
Sept. 15		American troops breach the Siegfried Line at its strongest point east of Aachen and move eastward toward Cologne .... Russian artillery hits Warsaw steadily, while infantrymen drive the Germans back toward the Vistula River on a 14-mile front north of captured Praga .... British commando troops begin landing on the Greek island of Cythera .... French Justice Commissioner Francois de Menthon orders the arrest of Marshal Henri-Phillippe Petain and all Vichy cabinet members.	MacArthur's troops invade Morotai Island, northernmost of the Halmahera group.	An earthquake destroys the Ecuadorian village of Pastocalle and shakes five nearby towns.	
Sept. 16	Second Quebec Conference ends with FDR and Churchill secretly agreeing to the "Morgenthau Plan" for converting Germany into an agricultural nation, and approving Eisenhower's plan to attack Germany in the north with a subsidiary attack in the south. Churchill also agrees to supply more troops for the capture of Rangoon, Burma and asks for air and naval tasks in the U.S. plan for defeating Japan .... At the opening session of the second meeting of UNRRA, Lester Pearson of Canada is elected chairman.	Allied breach in the Siegfried Line southeast of Aachen is widened by some 14 miles .... An Allied invasion of the Albanian and Yugoslavian Adriatic Islands begins.	U.S. forces land on Angaur, southernmost of the Palau Islands, and quickly gain control of one-third of it.		
Sept. 17		Operation Market-Garden begins as 4,700 aircraft and 2,500 gliders carry Lt. Gen. Lewis H. Brereton's 1st Allied Airborne Army to Arnhem, Holland. It is the largest airborne invasion in history and is designed to sprint troops and tanks through Holland, bridge the Rhine and penetrate Germany to bring a quick end to the war.	All Allied objectives on the perimeter of Morotai Island are taken as the Japanese are pursued into the surrounding hills .... The 14th U.S. Army Air Force destroys its bases at Kweilin, Kwangsi Province, because of the Japanese threat to the city.	U.S. Amb. Jefferson Caffrey leaves Brazil for Washington for consultations with the State Dept.	Cairo announces the Jebel Druz cabinet has voted to relinquish autonomy and merge with Syria to restore the Arab empire of the pre-1918 era.
Sept. 18	UNRRA Dir. Herbert H. Lehman says only Britain and Canada have paid their obligations to the agency in full.	Allied airborne troops link up with British units in the Netherlands and move towards the Rhine .... Russians and Germans engage in a major battle in the forest and lake regions of Estonia and Latvia, with the Russians attempting to crush Nazi armies on the flank of a Soviet salient aimed at East Prussia .... Allied Headquarters in France says Germany will be ruled by an Allied Military Government representing Britain, Russia and the U.S. .... Donato Carreta, former Regina Coeli prison director, is beaten in a Rome courtroom while on trial for crimes during the Fascist regime and thrown into the Tiber by a mob of 7,000.	Army troops on Angaur Island take control of another third of the island, while Marines on Peleliu to the north make slight gains.		
Sept. 19		Acting Finnish Premier Ernst von Born discloses an outline of armistice terms signed today by Finland with Russia and Great Britain. The terms include: payment of $300,000,000 reparations to Russia over a six-year period and recognition of the 1940 borders, giving Russia Karelia and the Arctic port of Petsamo .... British troops and Allied airborne units cross the Meuse River in the Netherlands, but surrounded advance units at Arnhem meet stiffening opposition .... In four days of fighting in Estonia and Latvia the Russians take 2,800 towns, advancing on a curving 200-mile front.	U.S. troops complete occupation of Angaur Island in the Carolines.	El Salvador's Unionist Party convention adopts a resolution proposing immediate federation with Guatemala as a first move in unification of the five Central American republics.	British announce the formation of a Jewish brigade from battalions recruited in Palestine for use in the European theater .... U.S. recognizes the independence of Syria, and FDR nominates George Wadsworth to be minister to Syria and Lebanon.
Sept. 20		Port of Brest falls to American troops .... U.S. Army troops cut a six-mile gap in the Gothic Line north of Florence, Italy .... Allied forces are locked in battle with the Germans at Nijmegen in the Netherlands.	Japanese cavalry reaches to within 19 miles north of Kweilin, Kwangsi Province.		
Sept. 21		American and British troops cross the Rhine at Nijmegen .... Russian forces reach points only 17 miles from Hungary's prewar border with Rumania and are now 138 miles from Budapest .... Greek units attached to the British Army enter Rimini, Italy .... Urho Castren is named to succeed the stricken Finnish Premier Antii Hackzell.	Wuchow and Jungyung in southeastern Kwangsi Province, China fall to the Japanese.	Argentine government closes the pro-Nazi newspaper *Momento Argentino* and arrests its editor for publishing anti-U.S. statements originating in Berlin.	

A	B	C	D	E
Includes developments that affect more than one world region, international organizations and important meetings of major world leaders.	*Includes all developments in European countries and military engagements between Allied and Axis powers in Africa and at sea.*	*Includes all developments in Japan and China, Japanese foreign policy and military actions in the Pacific region.*	*Includes all domestic and regional developments in Latin America, the Caribbean and Canada.*	*Includes developments in those independent nations and colonial possessions not covered in Columns B, C and D.*

U.S. Politics & Social Issues	U.S. Foreign Policy & Defense	U.S. Economy & Environment	Science, Technology & Nature	Culture, Leisure & Life Style	
		Senate and House conferees agree on a surplus property bill providing for a three-man administrative board . . . . UMW convention adopts a resolution condemning FDR for regimenting the U.S. labor movement.			Sept. 15
Arkansas Democratic convention amends party rules to permit Negroes to vote in primaries "if they meet party loyalty requirements."		OPA orders sharp increases in the point values of processed foods remaining on the rationed list.		*Double Indemnity*, a Paramount film starring Barbara Stanwyck, Fred MacMurray and Edward G. Robinson, opens in New York . . . . Ted Atkinson rides five straight winners at Aqueduct Race Track in New York.	Sept. 16
		CIO-UAW convention reelects Pres. R.J. Thomas, Vice Presidents Richard Frankensteen and Walter Reuther and Secy.-Treas. George Addis.			Sept. 17
Dewey attacks FDR's administration for "forcing labor leaders to go to the White House with their hats in their hands to get their rights."					Sept. 18
Earl Browder announces the Communist Political Assn. will work for the reelection of FDR.					Sept. 19
	A House Naval Affairs subcommittee asks an immediate investigation of the Pearl Harbor attack.				Sept. 20
Speaking in San Francisco, Dewey outlines a plan for a peacetime economy halfway between New Deal regimentation and uncontrolled business.		FDR urges Congress to consider legislation which would set up federal establishments patterned after the TVA throughout most of the country west of the Mississippi.		St. Louis Cardinals clinch their eighth NL pennant and third in a row by winning a double-header from Boston, 5-4 and 6-5.	Sept. 21

F	G	H	I	J
Includes elections, federal-state relations, civil rights and liberties, crime, the judiciary, education, health care, poverty, urban affairs and population.	*Includes formation and debate of U.S. foreign and defense policies, veterans affairs and defense spending. (Relations with specific foreign countries are usually found under the region concerned.)*	*Includes business, labor, agriculture, taxation, transportation, consumer affairs, monetary and fiscal policy, natural resources, pollution and accidents.*	*Includes worldwide scientific, medical and technological developments, natural phenomena, U.S. weather and natural disasters.*	*Includes the arts, religion, scholarship, communications media, sports, entertainment, fashions, fads and social life.*

	World Affairs	European War Zone	Pacific War Zone	The Americas	Other Countries & Territories
Sept. 22	UNRRA's policy committee adopts three resolutions providing for $50 million for "limited" help to Italy and aid for Allied nationals, German Jews and other anti-Nazis found in enemy territory.	German defenses stiffen along the front in Western Europe .... Helsinki reports that 11 Russian members of the Allied Armistice Commission arrived there today .... Russians capture Tallinn, Estonia's capital and Gulf of Finland port.	After several days of stalemate, U.S. Marines continue their advance on Peleliu Island in the Palau group.		
Sept. 23		Transport planes and gliders deliver reinforcements to the trapped airborne troops in the Arnhem area of the Netherlands .... Allied Military Government (AMG), following the combat troops, is reported to have begun operations in Germany .... Russian troops reach the Gulf of Riga at Paernu, Estonia .... Finnish troops attack the Germans in northern Finland after the Nazis fail to withdraw as required by the Russian armistice.	Tokyo reports Premier Joseph Laurel of the Philippines has declared war on the U.S. and Britain as a result of air attacks on the islands.		
Sept. 24		British patrols establish contact with besieged Allied forces in the Arnhem area .... Following conferences with the Council of National Resistance, French Forces of the Interior are incorporated into the regular army by a decree of the War Ministry .... Russian minitry .... Russian forces take the Estonian Baltic port of Paldiski.			
Sept. 25		Soviet troops sweep down the northwestern Estonian coast and capture the port of Haapsalu, leaving Virtsu the only Estonian port open to the Germans .... Yugoslavian partisans take the vital Bosnian center of Banja Luka on the outskirts of Belgrade.			
Sept. 26		German forces evacuate Riga, Latvia as four Russian columns converge on the city .... In the nine days since the beginning of Operation Market-Garden in Holland, Allied troops are reported to have suffered more than 17,000 casualties, more than the 10-12,000 suffered on the first day of the Normandy invasion.	U.S. Marines control all but a small portion of Palau, where they have isolated the enemy in the Umurgrogol Mountains.	Argentina informs Britain that war criminals will be barred from the country and prohibited from depositing funds or acquiring property .... Hull states that effective Oct. 1 U.S. ships will no longer pick up cargoes in Argentine ports.	
Sept. 27		More than 1,100 U.S. bombers attack railway and industrial targets in Germany at Cologne, Mainz, Ludwigshafen and Kassel .... Under Secy. of Foreign Affairs Visconti Giovanni Venosti says in Rome that Italy considers itself at war with Japan although no formal declaration has been made .... Allied assault in the Adriatic results in the German evacuation of the Albanian coastal road, and the Yugoslavian partisan occupation of Paga Island.		Ecuador cancels the oil concessions to the German-controlled company known as Ecuapetrol and transfers the concession to an Anglo-American group.	Gandhi-Jinnah talks aimed at settling Hindu-Moslem differences break down, although both say they will meet again.
Sept. 28		Canadian forces take the citadel at Calais, France .... Russian units take more than 50 localities—including Lode—in their drive on the Latvian capital of Riga .... Churchill tells the House of Commons that several months of fighting in 1945 will be needed to defeat the Germans.	In two days of air attacks, Allied planes reportedly sink or damage 12 Japanese ships and five barges in the Philippines, Macassar Strait and the NEI.		The Jewish extremist group Irgun Zvai Leumi attacks several police stations in various parts of Palestine.
Sept. 29	Russian phase of the Dumbarton Oaks Conference ends with agreements on recommendations for the general framework of the organization and peace-keeping operations. China opens discussion with the British and Americans.	German forces are pushed back at opposite ends of the 460-mile western front — at Arnhem, Netherlands and Belfort, France .... Russian troops extend their front along the Czech border to 170 miles and open a new drive against the Tatar Pass through the Carpathian Mountains.	Japanese troops land on the coast of Fukien Province and advance on Foochow, the last big seaport in Chinese hands.	Mexican Senate approves a pact with the U.S. to settle the expropriation of U.S. oil property in Mexico in 1938, providing for a $23.9 million settlement to the companies.	Asst. Police Superintendent T.J. Wilkin is assassinated in Jerusalem, allegedly by the Jewish extremist group Irgun Zvai Leumi.
Sept. 30		Russia reveals that Red Army troops have crossed into Yugoslavia and hold a 60-mile-wide bridgehead on the south side of the Danube River .... U.S. forces advance to within nine miles of Belfort.	Allied heavy bombers, in one of their longest missions, raid the oil center of Balikpapen, Borneo, leaving large fires raging .... U.S. 14th Army Air Force destroys its base at Tanchuk, southeastern Kwangsi Province, before the Japanese occupation of it today.		Jewish commercial and residential districts of Jerusalem are placed under curfew following yesterday's violence.
Oct. 1		De Gaulle says he favors state control of the economy for the betterment of all French people after the war .... Canadian troops complete the conquest of Calais.	Allied troops secure four Palau Islands: Angaur, Peleliu, Ngesebus and Kongauru.		
	A	B	C	D	E
	Includes developments that affect more than one world region, international organizations and important meetings of major world leaders.	*Includes all developments in European countries and military engagements between Allied and Axis powers in Africa and at sea.*	*Includes all developments in Japan and China, Japanese foreign policy and military actions in the Pacific region.*	*Includes all domestic and regional developments in Latin America, the Caribbean and Canada.*	*Includes developments in those independent nations and colonial possessions not covered in Columns B, C and D.*

U.S. Politics & Social Issues	U.S. Foreign Policy & Defense	U.S. Economy & Environment	Science, Technology & Nature	Culture, Leisure & Life Style	
Anti-FDR Democrats organize a National Agricultural Comm. chaired by Sen. Ellison D. (Cotton Ed) Smith (S.C.) to fight a fourth term for FDR.	FDR indicates he will not attempt to have Adm. Husband Kimmel and Maj. Gen. Walter Short court martialed for their role at Pearl Harbor before the election . . . . Lt. Gen. Brehon Somervell orders a relaxation of the 54-hour week in Army arsenals and depots because the backlog of military work has been reduced.				Sept. 22
FDR opens his campaign with a speech to the AFL Teamsters and charges that the GOP is attempting "to pass itself off as the New Deal."		U.S. Chamber of Commerce sends a letter to local chambers warning against "bringing pressure on the federal government to continue operation of war plants beyond the time needed for the war program."			Sept. 23
			Dr. Clarence Cook Little of the Roscoe B. Jackson Memorial Laboratory for Cancer Research says cancer is acquired by humans through a combination of hereditary and environmental conditions.	The board of directors of Freedom House in New York announces that its annual Freedom Award goes to Sumner Welles, former under secretary of state, "for his constructive liberalism and internationalsim, and his contribution to the concept of a world organization."	Sept. 24
In closing his western tour in Oklahoma City, Dewey claims FDR has resorted to mudslinging tactics to cover "a desperately bad record" for which America had to pay "a desperately high price." . . . . Harvard University Medical School announces women will be accepted as students beginning in the fall of 1945.				*Film Daily* announces that a poll of the country's newspaper, magazine, syndicate and radio movie critics and editors resulted in Henry King being chosen the best director of 1943-44 for the film *The Song of Bernadette.*	Sept. 25
					Sept. 26
		War Mobilization Dir. Byrnes says government control of prices, wages and rationing must remain until after total defeat of the enemy, otherwise rampant inflation will ruin plans for postwar recovery.		Aimee Semple McPherson, famed Los Angeles evangelist, dies at 53 in Los Angeles . . . . French newspaper *Resistance* says the noted French film star Harry Bauer has died as a result of torture inflicted when the Germans held him for four months in 1942.	Sept. 27
Pres. Earl Browder of the Communist Political Action Comm. endorses FDR because he claims Dewey would permit Europe to plunge itself into civil war after defeat of the Axis.		Labor Dept. reports a total of 485 strikes in August, the highest in five years for any one month.		The Most. Rev. Richard Cushing is appointed Archbishop of Boston, succeeding the late William Cardinal O'Connell . . . . *The Seventh Cross,* an MGM film about a German anti-Nazi who escapes from a prison camp and starring Spencer Tracy, opens in New York.	Sept. 28
Sen. Joseph Ball (R. Minn.) says he will not support Dewey because the GOP candidate has not been convincing in his support of a U.S. foreign policy aimed at preventing WW III.		FDR makes public a Victory in Europe Day program, which will relax export controls after Germany's defeat, curtail the foreign procurement program, ease preclusive buying, speed reconstruction and promote foreign trade . . . . The Fisher Brothers, who recently quit GM, file for incorporation in Michigan and Delaware.		Willie Pep retains his world featherweight title by outpointing Chalky Wright in N.Y.	Sept. 29
		FDR accepts the resignation of WPB Chmn. Nelson and appoints acting Chmn. Julius Krug to succeed him . . . . Krug announces a tentative program whereby the WPB will revoke 350 of its 500 control orders on VE Day.			Sept. 30
				St. Louis Browns defeat N.Y. Yankees, 5-2, to win the AL pennant on the last day of the season.	Oct. 1

F	G	H	I	J
Includes elections, federal-state relations, civil rights and liberties, crime, the judiciary, education, health care, poverty, urban affairs and population.	*Includes formation and debate of U.S. foreign and defense policies, veterans affairs and defense spending. (Relations with specific foreign countries are usually found under the region concerned.)*	*Includes business, labor, agriculture, taxation, transportation, consumer affairs, monetary and fiscal policy, natural resources, pollution and accidents.*	*Includes worldwide scientific, medical and technological developments, natural phenomena, U.S. weather and natural disasters.*	*Includes the arts, religion, scholarship, communications media, sports, entertainment, fashions, fads and social life.*

	World Affairs	European War Zone	Pacific War Zone	The Americas	Other Countries & Territories
Oct. 2	At the Dumbarton Oaks Conference the Chinese propose establishment of six committees — social, economic, territorial, law codification, labor and culture — as a means to ensure world peace after the current war.	Warsaw uprising ends as Polish patriots in Warsaw are forced to surrender to the Germans. A total of 100,000 persons were murdered by German S.S. troops. Russian troops have been in the suburbs since Aug. 1 and reportedly encouraged the uprising but then refused to aid it .... Yugoslavian Comm. of National Liberation refuses the UNRRA offer of food and supplies because of the agency's plans for distribution .... After saturation bombing, U.S. troops advance two miles inside Germany north of Aachen.	Four and one-half months of negotiations between the Chinese Communists and Nationalists end in failure in Chungking.		
Oct. 3		American troops continue a slow advance through the Siegfried Line inside Germany .... Russian troops enter Yugoslavia at two new points, outflanking Belgrade 38 miles to the north and at a point within 27 miles of the last railroad escape route for the Germans.	Japanese invading Fukien Province reportedly are six miles east of Foochow.		
Oct. 4		With tank and mobile artillery support, the American advance north of Aachen moves ahead slowly against stiff German resistance .... Russian forces reach within 14 miles of Belgrade .... British troops in Greece take Patras, the country's third largest city .... A French military court permits the Paris police to gather information concerning the activities of Marshal Petain, accused of treason.	Japanese capture Foochow.		
Oct. 5		Goebbels orders new cuts in food for German civilians to follow last week's cut in bread and sugar rations .... American troops exploiting the Siegfried Line breakthrough north of Aachen gain one mile.	It is reported today that Mitsuru Toyama, head of Japan's Black Dragon Society, a terrorist patriotic organization, has died at 90.	Mexican Economics Min. Gustavo Serrano announces the government will invest $20 million in cooperation with private enterprise to electrify Mexico over a 15-year period.	
Oct. 6		Russian troops invade Hungary on a 73-mile front, driving as much as 12 miles inside the country .... Netherlands P.M. Pieter Gerbrandy says in London his country faces the greatest disaster by flood and famine it has ever known as a result of the prolongation of fighting there .... American troops gain southeast of Aachen with a thrust of about a mile through the forest of Hurtgen.			
Oct. 7	Dumbarton Oaks Conference concludes with a 5,000-word document in the name of the four powers represented and proposes a U.N. organization to (1) maintain international peace and security, (2) develop friendly relations among nations and take other measures to strengthen peace, (3) achieve international cooperation in the solution of economic, social and humanitarian problems, (4) afford a center for harmonizing the actions of nations in the achievement of these ends.	Russian forces take nine major Hungarian towns and 300 other localities as they advance from Gyula to Gyoma and reach to within 83 miles of Budapest .... In the largest U.S.-coordinated air assault in the European theater, more than 3,400 planes strike at Nazi targets in Germany and Austria .... U.S. troops take Alsdorf and Baesweiler north of Aachen.	For the first time since March, Japanese troops penetrate the Indian state of Bengal.		
Oct. 8		American forces northeast and southeast of Aachen close the German escape gap to about three miles .... In the face of resistance from Russian and Finnish troops, the Nazis claim military occupation of northern Finland .... After four days of fighting the Russians advance 62 miles along a 175-mile front in Lithuania, reaching to within 30 miles of the Baltic Sea .... As the British approach, the Germans are reportedly fleeing Corinth, Greece.	U.S. ships bombard the coastal defense barriers on Marcus Island, 1,150 miles from Tokyo.		A preliminary pan-Arab conference ends in Alexandria, Egypt with representatives of Syria, Transjordan, Iraq, Lebanon and Egypt signing a protocol providing for creation of an Arab League .... King Farouk dismisses the cabinet of Mustafa Nahas Pasha and asks Ahmed Maher Pasha to form a new Egyptian government.
Oct. 9	Churchill and Foreign Secy. Eden arrive in Moscow for talks with Stalin.	In the Netherlands, Canadian and British paratroopers land behind the German lines at Hoofdplatt.	U.S. ships attack the Ryukyu Islands, the closest penetration to the Japanese home islands.		Amid minor disturbances in Cairo, Ahmed Maher Pasha installs a new 13-man cabinet.

U.S. Politics & Social Issues	U.S. Foreign Policy & Defense	U.S. Economy & Environment	Science, Technology & Nature	Culture, Leisure & Life Style	
				International Arts Guild is formed in London to encourage interaction among artists of all nations.	Oct. 2
Dewey offers a tax program which includes (1) elimination of income taxes on those making less than $11 weekly, (2) reduction of personal income tax rates, (3) revision of corporation income taxes and (4) elimination of excise taxes.		FDR signs the industrial reconversion and surplus war property disposal bills.			Oct. 3
Alfred E. Smith, 70, former N.Y. governor and Democratic presidential candidate in 1928, dies in N.Y.		A Philadelphia grand jury indicts 30 employes of the Philadelphia Transportation Co. on charges of violating the Smith-Connally Anti-Strike Act in connection with a six-day walkout in August . . . . WPB announces it has authorized seven manufacturers to produce 664,500 pieces of aluminum household utensils during the fourth quarter.	The governing council of the American Public Health Assn. adopts an outline of a program to make available to the entire population all preventative and diagnostic services.	FDR wire urges James Petrillo to comply with a NWLB order and lift the Music Federation's ban on making recordings.	Oct. 4
FDR says he does not want the political support of any person or group associated with Communism, fascism or any other ideology committed to the undermining of the U.S.					Oct. 5
			GE researcher Dr. Ernest Charlton says a two-million volt mobile X-ray machine, which will take pictures through a foot of steel, has been perfected.	Twenty men and 11 women, all Mormons, are convicted in Salt Lake City of conspiring to preach and practice polygamy.	Oct. 6
Dewey charges the Communists are supporting FDR because he is forming his own corporate state.				Dir. Francis Taylor of the N.Y. Metropolitan Museum of Art announces upon his return from Europe that the continent's fine art collections and historic landmarks escaped with little damage except in Britain.	Oct. 7
Former GOP presidential candidate Wendell L. Willkie dies at age 50 of coronary thrombosis in N.Y. . . . . Dewey urges all Americans of Polish descent to do everything possible to bring the Polish question into the open forum.		AFL reports its membership as of Aug. 31 totaled 6,806,913, its highest in history.		The *New York Herald Tribune* best-seller list includes *Strange Fruit* by Lillian Smith, *The Razor's Edge* by W. Somerset Maugham and *A Time for Decision* by Sumner Welles.	Oct. 8
	Selective Service directs local boards to abolish the limited service classification of 1-A(L) because the armed services no longer want men qualified for limited duty only.			Winning 3-1 in the sixth game, the St. Louis Cardinals take the World Series from the St. Louis Browns four games to two.	Oct. 9

F	G	H	I	J
Includes elections, federal-state relations, civil rights and liberties, crime, the judiciary, education, health care, poverty, urban affairs and population.	*Includes formation and debate of U.S. foreign and defense policies, veterans affairs and defense spending. (Relations with specific foreign countries are usually found under the region concerned.)*	*Includes business, labor, agriculture, taxation, transportation, consumer affairs, monetary and fiscal policy, natural resources, pollution and accidents.*	*Includes worldwide scientific, medical and technological developments, natural phenomena, U.S. weather and natural disasters.*	*Includes the arts, religion, scholarship, communications media, sports, entertainment, fashions, fads and social life.*

	World Affairs	European War Zone	Pacific War Zone	The Americas	Other Countries & Territories
Oct. 10	Third Moscow Conference begins with British P.M. Churchill and For. Secy. Anthony Eden conferring with Stalin on zones of British and Russian operations in Greece and Yugoslavia.	Russian troops reach the Baltic Sea at Palanga, Lithuania .... British troops enter Corinth and find it evacuated by the Germans .... U.S. forces deliver a 24-hour surrender ultimatum to the Germans in Aachen.	After securing Garakayo Island in the Palaus, U.S. forces land on Bairakaseru Islet without meeting opposition.	Dr. Ramon Grau San Martin is sworn in as president of Cuba in Havana.	
Oct. 11		After the Germans refuse to capitulate in Aachen, the U.S. troops begin the bombardment of the city .... Russian troops reach the northeastern border of Prussia by seizing Ponove, Lithuania .... Moscow radio announces Bulgaria has accepted pre-armistice terms that provide for evacuation of all Bulgarian troops and officials from Greece and Yugoslavia within 15 days .... The director of the Museum Les Invalides announces today that the Germans looted it of 1,800 pieces, including antique weapons, before leaving Paris.		Mexican Chamber of Deputies defeats a measure which would prohibit the press and theater from "ridiculing members of Congress."	
Oct. 12	FDR in an address to the heads of 19 American Republics urges establishment of the U.N. organization agreed upon at Dumbarton Oaks.	American troops fight their way into Aachen, which has been 85% destroyed by planes and artillery .... Russian troops reach to within 12 miles of Tilsit, East Prussia, as they drive the Nazis back across the frontier on a 110-mile front .... Premier Mikolajczyk of the Polish government-in-exile and Chmn. Edward Osubka-Morawski of the Polish Comm. Of National Liberation arrive in Moscow for talks.	Adm. William F. Halsey's 3rd Fleet completes two days of attacks on Japanese installations on Formosa, reportedly destroying 396 enemy aircraft and 27 ships .... Australia announces Sir Frederick Eggleston will succeed Min. Sir Owen Dixon in Washington.	Former Argentine Pres. Ramon S. Castillo dies at 70 in Buenos Aires.	
Oct. 13		Russian troops capture Riga, the Latvian capital .... American troops fight their way through the eastern section of Aachen while a German attack northwest of the city is repelled.	Japanese reportedly kill the entire Chinese garrison in capturing Kweiping in southern Kwangsi Province .... U.S. ships continue their attacks on Formosa and the Philippines.		
Oct. 14		Greek and British troops occupy Athens after converging by sea and air on the city, which the Germans have held since April 1941 .... Yugoslavian partisans and Russian troops fight their way into the streets of Belgrade .... Moscow announces that the Polish government-in-exile and the Polish Comm. of National Liberation have agreed to reopen formal negotiations to form a single government .... Field Marshal Gen. Erwin Rommel, 52, is forced to commit suicide by German authorities for plotting against Hitler.	The largest number of B-29 bombers ever used in a single raid strike Okayama on Formosa .... Chinese troops turn back a Japanese drive on Kweilin, Kwangsi Province, less than 17 miles northeast of the city.		
Oct. 15		Regent Adm. Nicholas Horthy asks the Allies for armistice terms for Hungary .... Russian troops, assisting the Finns in clearing northern Finland of Germans, capture the Arctic Finnish port and naval base of Petsamo.			FDR tells the Convention of the Zionist Organization of America he will use his efforts to effect "establishment of Palestine as a free and democratic Jewish commonwealth."
Oct. 16		British forces land on Lemnos Island, which guards the entrance to the Dardanelles .... Despite five German attacks outside the city, the Americans complete their encirclement of Aachen.	U.S. planes blast Formosa, concentrating on Okayama and Heito on the west coast.		
Oct. 17	FDR says the Dumbarton Oaks security proposals can serve to safeguard peace in our time.	German forces remaining in Aachen are mopped up as attacks outside the city cease .... Russian troops push to within two miles of the southern Czech border by taking Visau-Bistra in Transylvania.	In its ninth day of activities in the western Pacific, the U.S. 3rd Fleet sinks seven more Japanese ships and destroys 19 planes in an attack on Luzon, Philippines.	Argentine government bans Nazi and Fascist propaganda in the country.	Iranian government turns down a Soviet request for the immediate granting of a concession for exploitation of oil in northern Iran.

A	B	C	D	E
Includes developments that affect more than one world region, international organizations and important meetings of major world leaders.	*Includes all developments in European countries and military engagements between Allied and Axis powers in Africa and at sea.*	*Includes all developments in Japan and China, Japanese foreign policy and military actions in the Pacific region.*	*Includes all domestic and regional developments in Latin America, the Caribbean and Canada.*	*Includes developments in those independent nations and colonial possessions not covered in Columns B, C and D.*

U.S. Politics & Social Issues	U.S. Foreign Policy & Defense	U.S. Economy & Environment	Science, Technology & Nature	Culture, Leisure & Life Style	
				Music Federation Pres. Petrillo tells FDR the union will not grant his request that it permit its members to make phonograph recordings for commercial use unless all recording companies pay royalties on each record to the union treasury .... *Sporting News* names Martin Marion of the St. Louis Cardinals (NL) and Bobby Doerr of the Boston Red Sox (AL) MVPs in their respective leagues for 1944.	Oct. 10
		Agriculture Secy. Wickard discloses that the REA has a three-year postwar plan for spending $585 million on rural electrification .... NWLB refuses to recommend that FDR modify the "Little Steel" wage formula on the ground that it could not say what effect it would have on the price structure.		Archbishop Francis Spellman is received by Pope Pius XII at the Vatican .... *Variety* reports the most popular songs are (1) *I'll Walk Alone*, (2) *Is You Is or Is You Ain't* and (3) *Dance with a Dolly*.	Oct. 11
		The Treasury reveals that movie executive Louis B. Mayer drew $1,138,992 in salary, the nation's highest, through Aug. 31.			Oct. 12
Rep. Clare Boothe Luce (R, Conn.) charges FDR is "not only untrustworthy but also incompetent."					Oct. 13
White House issues a statement charging Dewey with distortion, dishonesty and playing "fast and loose with the American people" in charges he has leveled against FDR.					Oct. 14
	Sen. Robert La Follette (P, Wisc.) demands that American foreign policy depart from the "imperial designs of Mr. Churchill."				Oct. 15
Dewey charges that FDR plans to keep men in the armed services because he does not have peacetime jobs for them.					Oct. 16
		WPB and National Housing Agency announce removal of certain restrictions on home design and construction that will make possible the building of houses to prewar standards.			Oct. 17

F	G	H	I	J
Includes elections, federal-state relations, civil rights and liberties, crime, the judiciary, education, health care, poverty, urban affairs and population.	*Includes formation and debate of U.S. foreign and defense policies, veterans affairs and defense spending. (Relations with specific foreign countries are usually found under the region concerned.)*	*Includes business, labor, agriculture, taxation, transportation, consumer affairs, monetary and fiscal policy, natural resources, pollution and accidents.*	*Includes worldwide scientific, medical and technological developments, natural phenomena, U.S. weather and natural disasters.*	*Includes the arts, religion, scholarship, communications media, sports, entertainment, fashions, fads and social life.*

	World Affairs	European War Zone	Pacific War Zone	The Americas	Other Countries & Territories
Oct. 18		Russian troops cross into Czechoslovakia along a 171-mile front in the east and join forces with troops in Transylvania .... Trades Union Congress, representing some 10,000,000 British workers, votes to adopt the Anglo-Soviet Trade Union Comm. report that says the German people cannot be absolved from all responsibility for crimes committed by their leaders .... American troops push to within seven miles of Bologna, Italy .... Hitler decrees the organization of a Volkssturm, or "Home Army," to include men aged 16-60 not already engaged in military activities.		San Salvador reports a revolt against Honduran Pres. Tiburcio Carias Andino.	
Oct. 19		Russian troops invade East Prussia, capturing Eydtkau, a half-mile inside the border.	British Indian troops take the important Japanese base of Tiddim in northwestern Burma.		Palestine government announces the banishment of 251 persons detained as terrorists or for complicity.
Oct. 20	Churchill-Stalin talks end in Moscow after a three-hour conference in which they discuss the former Greek and Yugoslavian agreement, modifying it to grant Soviet preponderance in Rumania, Bulgaria and Hungary, British preponderance in Greece and equal Soviet and British influence in Yugoslavia.	Russian and Yugoslavian troops capture Belgrade and Hungary's third largest city, Debrecen .... A special court of justice in Marseilles sentences Pierre Laval to death in absentia.	MacArthur's troops invade the Philippines, landing on the east coast of Leyte Island. Forces consist of four U.S. Army divisions. Strong opposition is met at only one of the four beaches as an American armada of battleships, carriers, cruisers and destroyers pound the area with shells before the landing and during its early stages .... FDR pledges that, once the Japanese are driven from the islands, the Philippines will be given their independence.	The government of Gen. Federico Ponce is overthrown in Guatemala by young army officers, who form a triumverate headed by Capt. Jacobo Arbenz, Maj. Francisco Javier Arana and Jorge Toriella.	
Oct. 21		American troops capture Aachen .... Russian units in Hungary reach the Danube River and advance 24 miles towards the Czech border .... Russians in East Prussia reportedly reach a point 15 miles from the rail center of Insterburg.	American troops move inland from the beachhead on Leyte Island, meeting increased Japanese opposition.	El Salvador Pres. Andres Ignacio Menendez resigns under pressure; Col. Osmin Aguirre y Salinas assumes control.	
Oct. 22		In the Netherlands, the British and Canadians advance against the Germans, taking Breskens and Esschen .... Russian troops reach the Norwegian border along an 80-mile front, and are only three miles from the Norwegian base at Kirkeres, used by the Germans as a submarine base.	U.S. forces capture Tacloban, capital of Leyte Island. MacArthur arrives on Leyte Island accompanied by Philippine Pres. Sergio Osmena and announces that he has returned to the Philippines.		
Oct. 23		U.S., Russia, Britain, Canada, Australia, Brazil, Peru and Venezuela accord official recognition of the French government of Charles de Gaulle .... In the face of Canadian and British pressure, the German line between Nijmegen and the North Sea deteriorates .... British troops reach Lamia, 11 miles northwest of Athens .... Olafurs Thors, leader of the Icelandic Independent Party, forms a cabinet with himself as premier and minister of foreign affairs.	Battle of Leyte Gulf begins with the first two stages: the Battle of Sibuyan Sea and the Battle of Surigao Strait. In the Sibuyan Sea battle the Japanese lose two cruisers and one battleship; the Americans, 30 aircraft. In the Surigao Strait battle the Japanese lose three cruisers, two destroyers and two battleships; no American ships are lost .... American troops are reported firmly established on the east coast of Leyte and driving the Japanese into the hills.	Maj. Francisco Javier Arana forms a new Guatemalan cabinet as Gen. Federico Ponce arrives in Mexico as an exile.	
Oct. 24		Premier George Papandreou forms a new Greek cabinet with himself holding war and foreign affairs portfolios.	The second half of the Battle of Leyte Gulf takes place with battles off Samar and Cape Engano. In the battle off Samar American losses are two destroyers, one destroyer escort and two carrier escorts; no Japanese vessels are sunk. In the battle off Cape Engano the Japanese lose four aircraft carriers and one destroyer as opposed to no American ship losses. Called "the greatest sea battle in history," the total number of participating ships is 282 .... U.S. troops on Leyte capture 12 towns and the San Pablo airstrip, only $17\frac{1}{2}$ miles from the west coast .... U.S. planes attack strategic targets on the Japanese island of Kyushu.		

A	B	C	D	E
Includes developments that affect more than one world region, international organizations and important meetings of major world leaders.	*Includes all developments in European countries and military engagements between Allied and Axis powers in Africa and at sea.*	*Includes all developments in Japan and China, Japanese foreign policy and military actions in the Pacific region.*	*Includes all domestic and regional developments in Latin America, the Caribbean and Canada.*	*Includes developments in those independent nations and colonial possessions not covered in Columns B, C and D.*

U.S. Politics & Social Issues	U.S. Foreign Policy & Defense	U.S. Economy & Environment	Science, Technology & Nature	Culture, Leisure & Life Style	
Dewey charges FDR's "secret diplomacy" threatens to block efforts for a lasting peace.		WPB reveals it has permitted 1,110 manufacturers to resume civilian production.		Charles Sessler pays $34,000 in a N.Y. auction for the original manuscript of Edgar Allen Poe's *Murders in the Rue Morgue.*	Oct. 18
	Rep. Melvin Maas (R, Minn.) declares he will press for release of the report of the Navy Court of Inquiry on Pearl Harbor.	CAB approves acquisition of control of TWA by the Hughes Tool Co., owned by Howard Hughes.	A hurricane sweeps Florida, causing an estimated $20-million in damage to the citrus crop.	*I Remember Mama,* a play by John Van Druten, opens in New York. The play is adapted from the novel *Mama's Bank Account* by Kathryn Forbes . . . . Kathleen Windsor's novel *Forever Amber* is removed from Boston book stores due to the protest of the Watch and Ward Society.	Oct. 19
Dewey charges FDR plays with rights of labor to gain his own ends and to further "one-man rule."	Navy Secy. Forrestal says the report of the Naval Court of Inquiry on Pearl Harbor will be kept secret for the time being because parts of it are classified "top secret."	Explosions in a liquid gas storage plant in Cleveland start a fire that spreads over a 50-block east side area, causing 121 deaths and injuring at least 200. An explosion in the testing laboratory of the American Gas Assn. is the primary cause of the disaster.			Oct. 20
	In a N.Y. campaign speech FDR asks Congress to permit U.S. participation in a world security organization, which he believes should be put in operation before the war's end . . . . Amb. to Moscow Averell Harriman arrives in Washington for consultations.				Oct. 21
	Maj. Gen. Bennett Meyers reveals that at least 10 war plants have been engaged in producing replicas of the German V-1 rocket.				Oct. 22
Sen. Joseph Ball (R, Minn.) announces his support for FDR because he believes the President can best harmonize domestic and foreign policies.	War Dept. reveals that the investigation of Pearl Harbor prepared by an Army board has been turned in and has been marked "top secret" pending reviews by competent authorities.	NLRB orders seven collective bargaining elections within 90 days among 60,000 Western Union workers to determine whether the AFL or CIO will represent them.			Oct. 23
	Dewey says the U.S. delegate to the proposed U.N. should not have to consult Congress every time he has to make a decision . . . . FDR announces the end of martial law in Hawaii and restoration of habeas corpus.		Census Bureau reports that infant deaths in the U.S. for 1943 were 118,484, an increase of some 5,000 over 1942.		Oct. 24

F	G	H	I	J
Includes elections, federal-state relations, civil rights and liberties, crime, the judiciary, education, health care, poverty, urban affairs and population.	*Includes formation and debate of U.S. foreign and defense policies, veterans affairs and defense spending. (Relations with specific foreign countries are usually found under the region concerned.)*	*Includes business, labor, agriculture, taxation, transportation, consumer affairs, monetary and fiscal policy, natural resources, pollution and accidents.*	*Includes worldwide scientific, medical and technological developments, natural phenomena, U.S. weather and natural disasters.*	*Includes the arts, religion, scholarship, communications media, sports, entertainment, fashions, fads and social life.*

	World Affairs	European War Zone	Pacific War Zone	The Americas	Other Countries & Territories
Oct. 25		Britain, the U.S. and other American republics announce the resumption of diplomatic relations with Italy . . . . Russian forces outflank Warsaw on the northwest and advance towards the confluence of the Vistula and Narew Rivers . . . . Russian troops enter northern Norway and liberate the Barents Sea port of Kirkenes and 30 other villages . . . . British forces in Greece enter Dhomokos, making their greatest one-day advance in pursuit of the fleeing Germans.	A Chinese government spokesman charges that Red Chinese troops attacked Nationalist forces in northern China because of remarks by Marshal Yen Hsishan.	Guatemalan government blocks the funds and attaches the property of former Pres. Jorge Ubico, Federico Ponce and Alfred Denby, an American.	In a radio broadcast Iranian Premier Mohammed Said says his government refused to grant oil concessions to the Russians because to do so would have the appearance of yielding to the pressure of foreign troops in Iran . . . . Inner Zionist General Council and the National Council of Palestine Jews adopt resolutions scoring recent acts of violence by small Jewish political extremist groups in Palestine.
Oct. 26		Russian troops capture the rail center of Mukacevo in eastern Czechoslovakia.	Chinese troops score a "major victory" over the Japanese at Sungkiangkou, 22 miles northeast of Kweilin.	Guatemalan junta dissolves the legislature and calls for new elections Nov. 3-5.	
Oct. 27	Churchill tells the House of Commons he hopes to meet with FDR and Stalin this year to settle issues discussed at his recent Moscow conference.	Greek CP leader George Siantos visits British Foreign Secy. Eden in Athens and pledges Communist and EAM (National Liberation Front) cooperation with Britain . . . . Russian forces take the Ruthenian capital of Uzhorod, virtually freeing Hungarian-annexed Ruthenia in eastern Czechoslovakia . . . . British troops take Tilburg and Hertogenbosch and drive towards the mouth of the Meuse River in the Netherlands.		Argentine government asks the Pan-American Union to call a foreign ministers meeting to consider Argentina's foreign relations.	
Oct. 28		RAF bombers drop a record 4,000 tons of explosives on Cologne, Germany . . . . Canadian units capture the ancient seacoast fortress of Bergen op Zoom in the Netherlands . . . . Russian troops enter Slovakia on a broad front west of Ruthenia . . . . Bulgaria signs an armistice with the U.N., which includes provisions that Bulgaria give up portions of Greece and Yugoslavia acquired in 1941, immediately make available foodstuffs for relief of the people of Greek and Yugoslavian territories that suffered from Bulgarian occupation, and release Allied prisoners.	American troops and Philippine guerrillas overrun and complete the occupation of Samar Island . . . . Gen. Joseph W. Stilwell is removed from his Far Eastern posts as chief of staff to Chiang Kai-shek, deputy to Lord Mountbatten and U.S. commander in the China-Burma-India theater. Lt. Gen. Daniel I. Sultan is given command of the Burma-India front and Maj. Gen. A.C. Wedemeyer the China front.		
Oct. 29	Russia announces it will not attend the International Aviation Conference in Chicago Nov. 1 because certain pro-fascist countries have been invited.	Polish troops capture Breda and advance west to cut the Breda-Rosendaal road in the Netherlands.	American troops control 67 miles of the Leyte coastline and push west and south against deteriorating Japanese defenses.	Panamanian Democratic Party convention approves the extension of President Ricardo de la Guardia's presidential term until 1947.	
Oct. 30		Allied troops push some 40,000 Nazis towards the Meuse River on a 50-mile front in the Netherlands . . . . Greek patriots claim the liberation of Salonika, as British units catch up with the fleeing Germans in Greece some 40 miles from the Yugoslavian border.	With two-thirds of Leyte Island controlled by the Americans, the Japanese begin escape operations on the west coast.	Members of the cabinet of Gov. Rexford Tugwell of Puerto Rico spend an hour in jail for contempt of court for continuing to spend the $16-million fund of the war emergency program.	Tass reports demonstrations in Teheran and other cities against Iranian Premier Mohammed Maraghei Said because of his refusal to grant the Soviets oil concessions.
Oct. 31		Russian troops seize more than 200 towns as they advance to within 44 miles of Budapest, Hungary . . . . Allies report the taking of 637,544 German prisoners on the western front since June 6.	After taking the Japanese stronghold of Jaro in the center of Leyte, U.S. forces push a spearhead across the northern end of the island . . . . Three Japanese columns close on Kweilin, Kwangsi Province, advancing to within six miles of the city.		
Nov. 1	International Civil Aviation Conference opens in Chicago to seek agreements on postwar air travel.	The Yugoslavian exile government in London and Tito's National Comm. of Liberation agree to form a "united national government" within the shortest time . . . . The Germans are reported cleared from the entire Petsamo nickel region of northern Finland . . . . In a drive across the Hungarian plains between the Danube and Tisza Rivers, Russian troops reportedly are within 32 miles of Budapest . . . . British commandos go ashore at Weskapelle and Flushing on Walcheren Island in an attack upon the last German defenses around Antwerp.		Canadian Defense Min. Col. J.L. Ralston resigns, reportedly over the issue of sending reinforcements overseas.	
Nov. 2	Adolf A. Berle, Jr. is elected permanent chairman of the Chicago aviation conference.	The political bureau of the French CP refuses "to associate itself in any way" with the government's decision to disarm and disolve the so-called Patriotic Guard.	FDR says the advance on Japan is "many months ahead of our own optimistic schedule." . . . . U.S. infantry reaches to within six miles of the Japanese retreat route to Ormoc on Leyte's west coast . . . . FDR asks Donald Nelson to return to China to organize a WPB for that country to increase its war productivity.		
	A	B	C	D	E
	Includes developments that affect more than one world region, international organizations and important meetings of major world leaders.	*Includes all developments in European countries and military engagements between Allied and Axis powers in Africa and at sea.*	*Includes all developments in Japan and China, Japanese foreign policy and military actions in the Pacific region.*	*Includes all domestic and regional developments in Latin America, the Caribbean and Canada.*	*Includes developments in those independent nations and colonial possessions not covered in Columns B, C and D.*

U.S. Politics & Social Issues	U.S. Foreign Policy & Defense	U.S. Economy & Environment	Science, Technology & Nature	Culture, Leisure & Life Style	
Dewey charges FDR sponsored a fund-raising idea known as the One Thousand Club, whose members would contribute $1,000 each for the Democratic campaign.	Sun Oil Pres. J. Howard Pew attacks the British-American oil pact as a "blank check" to the government that would involve the domestic oil industry in a "vicious cartel system."	FDR directs the Maritime Commission to prepare a plan for improving the U.S. merchant marine with modern cargo and passenger ships at the war's end.		Blue Network files applications with the FCC requesting permission to change its name to the American Broadcasting Co., Inc.	Oct. 25
	War and Navy Depts. announce a policy of removing from combat duty all men who may be the sole surviving sons of parents who have lost two or more sons in the war.		Stockholm announces the first Nobel Prizes since the war's start. The physiology and medicine awards go to Joseph Erlanger and Herbert Spencer Gasser.	Archbishop of Canterbury and Primate of all England Dr. William Temple dies at 63 of a heart attack in Westgate-by-the-Sea.	Oct. 26
				Allied Artists of America make 14 awards at the opening of their annual exhibition in N.Y., giving gold medals to Ogden M. Pleissner and Richard J. Crocker.	Oct. 27
Three Mississippi Democratic electors announce they will vote for Sen. Harry F. Byrd (D, Va.) for president .... Speaking in Syracuse, N.Y., Dewey says that if elected he would end all farm controls established by the New Deal .... FDR pledges himself to a postwar program of high pay and adequate return for farm and factory products.					Oct. 28
					Oct. 29
					Oct. 30
Dewey labels FDR's pledge of postwar prosperity as ridiculous.					Oct. 31
Rep. Richard Kieberg (D, Tex.) casts his absentee ballot for Dewey because he opposes a fourth term for FDR. .... Dewey charges that the Communists through Sidney Hillman's Political Action Comm. are trying to gain control of the government but that a GOP victory will thwart that aim .... Board of Regents of the Univ. of Texas ousts President Homer Rainey after charging that Rainey refused to conform to their regulations and made statements "reflecting on the motives and good faith of the board."		Marshall Field discloses the book publishing houses of Pocket Books, Inc. and Simon & Schuster will become part of Field Enterprises.	Quadruplets, three girls and a boy, are born to Mrs. Kathleen Cirminello by a Caesarian operation in Philadelphia, the first time the procedure has been used for such a multiple birth.	Branch Rickey, along with Walter F. O'Malley and Andrew J. Schmitz, purchase 25% of the Brooklyn Dodgers stock .... N.Y.C. Public Library reveals the return from a wartime hideout in Saratoga Springs, N.Y. of 27,000 of its most valuable books, prints and manuscripts .... Justices Nathan D. Perman and George R. DeLucca rule in N.Y. that the novel *The First Lady Chatterley* by D.H. Lawrence is not obscene.	Nov. 1
James L. Fly announces his resignation as chairman of the FCC effective Nov. 15 to resume his law practice.			Thomas Midgley, Jr., the inventor of ethyl gasoline and a pioneer researcher in synthetic rubber, dies at 55 in Columbus, O.		Nov. 2

F	G	H	I	J
Includes elections, federal-state relations, civil rights and liberties, crime, the judiciary, education, health care, poverty, urban affairs and population.	*Includes formation and debate of U.S. foreign and defense policies, veterans affairs and defense spending. (Relations with specific foreign countries are usually found under the region concerned.)*	*Includes business, labor, agriculture, taxation, transportation, consumer affairs, monetary and fiscal policy, natural resources, pollution and accidents.*	*Includes worldwide scientific, medical and technological developments, natural phenomena, U.S. weather and natural disasters.*	*Includes the arts, religion, scholarship, communications media, sports, entertainment, fashions, fads and social life.*

	World Affairs	European War Zone	Pacific War Zone	The Americas	Other Countries & Territories
Nov. 3	Aviation conference adopts a resolution accepting the principle of international cooperation in postwar commercial aviation.	Franco says in an interview that Spain has never been fascist or Nazi and never has been allied secretly or otherwise with Axis powers .... Russians capture Alsonemedi and are within six miles of Budapest .... Allies occupy the Belgian port of Antwerp.	U.S. troops overrun Carigara on the north coast of Leyte .... Chinese troops capture Lungling, Yunnan Province, the last major Allied objective in the drive to open the Burma Road .... Japanese forces surround Kweilin.		
Nov. 4		Remaining German troops are driven out of Greece and into Yugoslavia .... After the Germans force a U.S. withdrawal from Schmidt, 15 miles southeast of Aachen, Allied bombing attacks level the city .... Bucharest radio reports that Rumanian Premier Gen. Constantin Sanatescu has reshuffled his cabinet, assuming the war ministry portfolio himself.	Japanese reinforcements are landed in the Ormoc Bay area on the west coast of Leyte .... American forces open a new drive for Pinamopoan, a key highway terminus on Carigara Bay, Leyte .... Carrier-based planes blast Manila Harbor, reportedly destroying almost 200 Japanese planes.		
Nov. 5	Latin American representatives at the aviation conference support the U.S. plan for an international body but oppose the Washington plan for a 15-man committee to direct postwar civil aviation.	Allied troops drive the Germans beyond the Meuse River and hold a 50-mile front from Hertogenbosch to the North Sea .... Soviet units take Andrassy, Taksony and Uelloe around Budapest and open artillery fire on the Hungarian capital .... Greek government decides to call up on Nov. 24 all Greek males aged 27 to begin service Dec. 1 as members of a provisional home guard which will replace the temporary National Militia Corps.			
Nov. 6		Stalin announces the restoration of the Soviet frontier along its 1,800-mile length from the Barents Sea to the Black Sea.			Two gunman kill Lord Moyne, the British resident minister in Cairo.
Nov. 7		British Navy announces the Aegean Sea is clear of German shipping.	In the second attack on Manila Bay, U.S. planes reportedly destroy another 249 enemy aircraft and sink three cargo ships and an oil tanker .... Japanese reach within 20 miles of the important railway center of Liuchow in southern Kwangsi Province.	U.S. and other American republics extend recognition to the new Guatemalan government.	
Nov. 8		American Army troops open a drive in the Metz-Nancy sector of the French front along a 27-mile line.		Argentine government issues a decree establishing strict control of Axis-owned firms.	Cairo police announce the capture of Moshe Cohen and Itzchak Salzman, members of the extremist Jewish group the Stern Gang, for the murder of Lord Moyne.
Nov. 9		Russians cross the Tisza River northeast of Budapest, Hungary and establish a west bank bridgehead of 45 miles .... American troops cross the Moselle River, taking Konigsmacher and Ham and outflanking Metz.	Chinese troops open a new drive in northern Burma by crossing the Irrawaddy River between Bhamo and Katha, threatening to outflank both of those Japanese strongholds .... Japanese open an all-out attack upon the encircled city of Kweilin, while to the south the enemy converges on the last U.S. air base at Liuchow in Kwangsi Province.		Iranian cabinet of Premier Mohammed Maraghei Said resigns.
Nov. 10	Some 500 delegates and assistants from 52 countries open an international business conference in Rye, N.Y., sponsored by the American Section of the International Chamber of Commerce, the Chamber of Commerce of the U.S., the National Foreign Trade Conference and the NAM. The aim of the meeting is to get back export capital in the shape of goods and services and provide raw materials to countries to promote world industrialization.	In a speech to the British House of Commons, Churchill confirms the use against Britain of the German V-2 rocket. Saying that the rockets have been in use for the past few weeks, he notes that they contain about the same amount of explosive as the V-1 but penetrate more deeply before exploding, and that they fly through the stratosphere at heights of 60 to 70 miles and at a speed faster than sound, making it impossible to give adequate public warning .... U.S. forces in the Metz-Nancy area drive to within 2½ miles of the German frontier north of Thionville .... Russian troops expand their bridgehead across the Tisza River, gaining up to seven miles and cutting the railroad linking Budapest with eastern Slovakia.	Japan claims the capture of both Kweilin and Liuchow in Kwangsi Province .... Wang Ching-wei, the Japanese puppet leader at Nanking, dies at 62 of diabetes .... Seven Japanese destroyers and three transports are sunk in the Ormoc Bay by Allied planes and a PT boat.		
Nov. 11		U.S. and Russia invite the French provisional government to participate in the European Advisory Commission in London .... U.S. forces cut enemy communications with Metz, as infantrymen come within five miles of the city.			

A	B	C	D	E
Includes developments that affect more than one world region, international organizations and important meetings of major world leaders.	*Includes all developments in European countries and military engagements between Allied and Axis powers in Africa and at sea.*	*Includes all developments in Japan and China, Japanese foreign policy and military actions in the Pacific region.*	*Includes all domestic and regional developments in Latin America, the Caribbean and Canada.*	*Includes developments in those independent nations and colonial possessions not covered in Columns B, C and D.*

U.S. Politics & Social Issues	U.S. Foreign Policy & Defense	U.S. Economy & Environment	Science, Technology & Nature	Culture, Leisure & Life Style	
		WPB authorizes the production of 12,400 domestic electric ranges .... Officials of all major CIO unions in Alameda, Calif. issue a statement calling members of Local 1304 who are abstaining from machinist work on 82 ships in San Francisco "enemies of labor and of the nation."	Army Surgeon General Maj. Gen. Norman Kirk says the incidence of malaria has been reduced by one-fourth since the early part of the war.		Nov. 3
In his last campaign speech, FDR says in Boston that Dewey has revealed "a shocking lack of trust in America."		At FDR's direction, the Army takes over seven war plants in the Toledo, O. area because of a strike by the Mechanics Educational Society of America.			Nov. 4
	U.S. State Dept. announces the French government has invited FDR and State Secy. Hull to make an official visit to Paris at their convenience. The invitation is meant as a cordial gesture thanking the Americans for their war efforts.				Nov. 5
Dewey says an argument for retention of an administration during an ordeal simply amounts to "the bald plea for the reelection .... of whoever happens to be President." .... In a radio address, FDR asks all citizens to vote tomorrow in a practical demonstration to the world of American democracy.		The government drops import controls on 38 food items and shifts administrative functions connected with importation of certain other items from the WPB to the War Food Administration.			Nov. 6
FDR wins the presidential election against Dewey, taking 36 states and 432 electoral votes with 53% of the popular vote. For the House of Representatives, 243 Democrats, 190 Republicans, 1 Progressive and 1 American Laborite win election.					Nov. 7
		Commerce Dept. reports an 8% increase in retail sales for September over the same month of 1943.		The Most Rev. Richard Cushing is installed as Archbishop of Boston, becoming the world's youngest archbishop at age 49.	Nov. 8
			The 1944 Nobel Prize for physics goes to Dr. Isidor Isaac Rabi for research on the resonance method of registering the magnetic moments of atomic particles.	Danish author Dr. Johannes Jensen wins the 1944 Nobel Prize for literature for his novels *The Fall of the King* and *Long Journey.*	Nov. 9
		Distillers are informed by the WPB that they may take a holiday from production of industrial alcohol in January to make liquor.		Eleven women and 20 men convicted of polygamous marriage charges are sentenced in Salt Lake City to jail sentences of one year each after they are denied motions for a new trial.	Nov. 10
	State Dept. announces that civilian travel without military approval is now possible in Morocco, Algeria, Tunisia, Libya, Syria, Lebanon, Turkey, Cyprus and that part of France not involved in fighting.	NWLB rules that no wartime strike is legal even though the employes involved have observed the 30-day notice and election provisions of the War Labor Disputes Act. An opinion rendered by public member Edwin Witte says that whether the act was "wise or unwise legislation, it is clear that Congress did not place its stamp of approval on strikes in wartime."		RCA and CBS sign a contract with American Fed. of Musicians Pres. Petrillo calling for royalty payment to the union treasury for recordings.	Nov. 11
F	G	H	I	J	
Includes elections, federal-state relations, civil rights and liberties, crime, the judiciary, education, health care, poverty, urban affairs and population.	*Includes formation and debate of U.S. foreign and defense policies, veterans affairs and defense spending. (Relations with specific foreign countries are usually found under the region concerned.)*	*Includes business, labor, agriculture, taxation, transportation, consumer affairs, monetary and fiscal policy, natural resources, pollution and accidents.*	*Includes worldwide scientific, medical and technological developments, natural phenomena, U.S. weather and natural disasters.*	*Includes the arts, religion, scholarship, communications media, sports, entertainment, fashions, fads and social life.*	

	World Affairs	European War Zone	Pacific War Zone	The Americas	Other Countries & Territories
Nov. 12		Russian forces seize more than 30 Hungarian towns and advance up to 13 miles in a flanking movement east of Budapest . . . . Only 12½ miles reportedly separate American troops attempting to encircle Metz . . . . Heinrich Himmler gives a radio address on behalf of Hitler, who claims he is too busy leading the war effort to speak to the people.	Carrier planes reportedly wipe out four Japanese convoy ships attempting to land an estimated 8,000 troops on Leyte Island as other U.S. aircraft inflict severe damage on the harbors of Manila and Cavite.	Miguel Tomas Molina establishes an El Salvadorean government in exile in Guatemala City.	
Nov. 13		American troops occupy the first group of 22 forts defending Metz as the Nazis flee.	Americans destroy and abandon their airbase at Liuchow . . . . Chungking announces the establishment of a War Production Bd. under Economic Affairs Min. Wong Wen-hao.		
Nov. 14		Russians reportedly wipe out the last enemy bridgehead on the east bank of the Danube south of Budapest . . . . U.S. forces fight their way into the western and eastern suburbs of Metz.	MacArthur's troops threaten both flanks of the Japanese lines in Ormoc Valley on Leyte.		
Nov. 15		De Gaulle announces his acceptance of an invitation to visit Moscow at an undisclosed date . . . . Russian troops capture Jaszbereny, 31 miles east of Budapest . . . . Germany issues a new decree whereby all German officers and non-commissioned officers who are members of the Nazi Party must "educate their men in the Nazi philosophy" both on duty and off, "to form a closer link between the armed forces and the party."			
Nov. 16		American 9th and 1st Armies launch a main offensive in Germany and France as an air bombardment prepares the way. Dueren, Eschweiler and Juelich are levelled. Two German divisions in the process of shifting positions are severely hit . . . . Brussels radio announces Allied forces will support the government of Premier Hubert Pierlot.	Japanese troops capture the walled city of Ishan in Kwangsi Province . . . . British African troops capture Kalemyo and join Indian soldiers who had fought over the Chin Hills from Tiddim, Burma . . . . Australian Min. to the U.S. Sir Frederic Eggleston says Australian troops will clear islands bypassed in the main Allied offensive in the Pacific.		
Nov. 17		Soviet troops capture the key Hungarian rail junction of Fuezesabony, 60 miles northeast of Budapest, giving them control of a 27-mile stretch of the Budapest-Miskok trunk line.	U.S. troops envelop the Japanese at the northern end of the front in the western part of Leyte Island.	Argentine government issues a decree ordering all persons over 12, regardless of sex, to prepare themselves for the defense of the country.	Churchill warns the Jewish community of Palestine to destroy terrorist elements, implying that he might withdraw support from the Zionist cause.
Nov. 18		Gen. Enver Hoxha leads his troops in driving the Germans out of the Albanian capital of Tirana . . . . Russian units tear three new holes in the German-Hungarian defense line running northeast from Budapest to Miskolc . . . . British troops cross the Zig Canal and seize Helden, 7½ miles from the German stronghold of Venlo in Holland.		Nicaragua announces its recognition of the Soviet Union.	
Nov. 19		British and American units capture Geilenkirchen, northern pivot of the German line across the Cologne plain.	Japanese troops attack U.S. positions, trying to break the hold in the Limon area on Leyte.	El Salvador government places five of its 14 provinces under a state of siege because of terrorist activities.	
Nov. 20	U.S., Britain and Canada submit a plan for postwar control of commercial aviation to the international conference in Chicago.	All resistance to U.S. troops at Metz ceases.	Chiang Kai-shek replaces War Min. Gen. Ho Ying-chen with Gen. Chen Cheng and Finance Min. H.H. Kung with O.K. Yui.		
Nov. 21		Germans stiffen their defense against U.S. forces along an 11-mile front east of Luxembourg.	Americans repulse another Japanese attempt to break their roadblock south of Limon on Leyte.		
Nov. 22		U.S. troops reach the Germans' Roer River line in the battle of the Cologne plain . . . . British troops advancing toward Faenza, Italy cross the Cosina River and establish five bridgeheads . . . . Russian troops push to within 18 miles of Budapest.	U.S. troops smash through Limon, practically destroying the Japanese 1st Division.	A committee is formed to work for a union of Central American republics in Managua, Nicaragua.	

U.S. Politics & Social Issues	U.S. Foreign Policy & Defense	U.S. Economy & Environment	Science, Technology & Nature	Culture, Leisure & Life Style	
	Eisenhower appeals for support of the sixth war loan drive to begin Nov. 20, stating it is essential to the final victory cause.	Chmn. Davis of the NWLB offers his resignation to FDR effective Jan. 1.	Public Health Institute in N.Y. reports on a new method of immunization against malaria, which promises to lead to a vaccine for human protection.		Nov. 12
		Supreme Court rules NWLB orders are not subject to federal court review .... NWLB members George Taylor and Dr. Frank Graham submit their resignations to FDR.			Nov. 13
Congress reassembles after an eight-week recess.		Officials of the Wright Aircraft Supervision Assn. agree to send delegates to the NWLB in Washington for consultations on ending a strike by 1,800 workers.	GE demonstrates a radically new type of synthetic rubber in which silicon takes the place of carbon.		Nov. 14
		Striking supervisory employes of Wright Aircraft in Paterson, N.J. vote to end their strike and return to work .... War Food Administrator Marvin Jones says the 1945 food production program should equal that of 1944 .... Atty. Gen. Francis Biddle announces that 18 steel companies and six of their officers have been indicted in Trenton, N.J. on charges that since 1944 they have been engaged in a conspiracy to fix prices.			Nov. 15
		White House announces that NWLB members William Davis, George Taylor and Frank Graham will not press their resignations, which have been rejected by FDR .... War Mobilzation Dir. Byrnes warns that unless manpower shortages are remedied in war producing areas he will be forced to suspend authorization for new civilian production.			Nov. 16
Sen. Ellison D. (Cotton Ed) Smith (D. S.C.), dean of the Senate, dies at 80 near Lynchburg, S.C.					Nov. 17
	Fifty Negro seamen are sentenced to eight to 15 years in prison and given dishonorable discharges for mutiny when refusing to load ammunition at Port Chicago .... U.S. Coast Guard announces that general recruiting of Spars will end Nov. 23.	FDR's special committee to survey the cost of living reports a rise from January 1941 to September 1944 of 23.4%.			Nov. 18
					Nov. 19
Gov. Olin Johnston of S.C. appoints Wilton Hall as U.S. senator to fill out the term of the late Ellison Smith .... A special House committee recommends the modernization of Congress with a legislative staff of unbiased experts, an expenditure investigating committee and an agency to determine whether laws are being administered according to congressional intent.	Senate Judiciary Comm. agrees to postpone for another six months the Short-Kimmel trial concerning Pearl Harbor.				Nov. 20
Donald Nelson becomes a "personal representative" of FDR, giving him the right to sit in on cabinet meetings.				Baseball writers announces their choice of Marty Marion, St. Louis Cardinal shortstop, as the MVP in the NL for 1944.	Nov. 21
		CIO national convention in Chicago approves continuation of the Political Action Committee as its permanent political instrument .... Pacific Mills of Lawrence, Mass. pays the OPA $2,165,842.02 for charging more than the ceiling price on more than 20 million yards of cloth .... Ohio Fed. of Telephone Workers calls off its week-old strike of operators in Dayton after conferences with the NWLB in Washington.			Nov. 22

F	G	H	I	J
Includes elections, federal-state relations, civil rights and liberties, crime, the judiciary, education, health care, poverty, urban affairs and population.	*Includes formation and debate of U.S. foreign and defense policies, veterans affairs and defense spending. (Relations with specific foreign countries are usually found under the region concerned.)*	*Includes business, labor, agriculture, taxation, transportation, consumer affairs, monetary and fiscal policy, natural resources, pollution and accidents.*	*Includes worldwide scientific, medical and technological developments, natural phenomena, U.S. weather and natural disasters.*	*Includes the arts, religion, scholarship, communications media, sports, entertainment, fashions, fads and social life.*

	World Affairs	European War Zone	Pacific War Zone	The Americas	Other Countries & Territories
Nov. 23	The technical committees of the aviation conference adopt a code of common practices involving worthiness of craft, identification markers, weather reporting procedures, scales, symbols and customs procedures.	Russian troops renew their drive in the eastern end of Slovakia, capturing Cop .... Tito announces plans for a federal democratic government in Yugoslavia .... French troops enter Strasbourg against light German opposition.	American planes destroy or damage four troop-laden Japanese ships heading for Ormoc.	Canada issues an order-in-council making 16,000 drafted men eligible for immediate overseas duty as reinforcements.	
Nov. 24		Polish Premier Stanislaw Mikolajczyk resigns after a cabinet disagreement over methods of negotiating with Russia .... U.S. forces in Germany reach a line from Kesselingen to Remering, thus threatening the Saar Basin.	U.S. planes destroy three transports and a destroyer escort carrying Japanese reinforcements to Leyte .... Pacific Fleet planes strike at Luzon Island, sinking 20 Japanese ships .... U.S. planes bomb industrial targets in Tokyo for the second time.		
Nov. 25		War Refugee Bd. reveals the first details of Nazi atrocities at Birkenau and Auschwitz in Poland, stating that nearly 1.7 million Jews were murdered there .... Russian units capture Hatvan, 30 miles northeast of Budapest, and other units land on Csepel Island in the Danube.		Nearly 1,000 Canadian Home Defense troops protest against the government policy of conscription for overseas service.	
Nov. 26		Italian Premier Ivanoe Bonomi and his cabinet resign .... Americans split the Maginot Line in gains of five miles on the Saar Basin front.			
Nov. 27		U.S. troops move up another six miles on the Saar Basin, capturing Merten.	All Britons and Americans in Kweichow Province are directed to leave as Japanese forces advance .... FDR announces his appointment of Maj. Gen. Patrick Hurley as ambassador to China.		
Nov. 28		Russian troops join to force the Tisza River on a wide front in northern Hungary .... Americans continue to advance on the Saar Basin along a 26-mile front.		Canadian House of Commons meets secretly on the crisis over sending drafted men abroad.	
Nov. 29		U.S. troops advance on the left flank in Germany, taking Beeck and Lindern .... Russian troops capture the ancient fortress city of Pecs as they force the Danube River 100 miles south of Budapest.	B-29s from Saipan make their first night attack upon Tokyo's industrial targets .... U.S. fliers in China reveal the Japanese have made startling gains in Kweichow Province, outflanking some Chinese units expected to defend the provincial capital of Kweiyang .... Americans repulse another Japanese effort to reinforce Leyte.		
Nov. 30		U.S. troops establish a seven-mile front along the Roer River in Germany just west of Duren .... Russian troops surround Miskolc in northeastern Hungary with the capture of Eger and Szikszo .... Polish government in London forms a new cabinet headed by socialist Tomasz Arciszewski.			
Dec. 1		Russian drive through southwestern Hungary gains 15 miles, placing Soviet troops within 91 miles of the Austrian border .... U.S. forces driving at the Saar Basin engage the main German defenses in this region .... Former Italian Premier Bonomi announces he will try to form another government.	Chinese Communist leader Chou En-lai leaves Chungking for Yenan with Chiang's suggestions for solving political differences .... Japanese fall back toward Mandalay, yielding the railroad town of Pinwe without resistance to the British.	Brazil reports 19 persons will receive a total of 254 years at hard labor upon conviction for being Nazi spies.	
Dec. 2		U.S. troops fight their way into Saarlautern on the Saar front .... Russian offensive in southwestern Hungary gains another 15 miles, putting it 75 miles from the Austrian border.			

A	B	C	D	E
Includes developments that affect more than one world region, international organizations and important meetings of major world leaders.	*Includes all developments in European countries and military engagements between Allied and Axis powers in Africa and at sea.*	*Includes all developments in Japan and China, Japanese foreign policy and military actions in the Pacific region.*	*Includes all domestic and regional developments in Latin America, the Caribbean and Canada.*	*Includes developments in those independent nations and colonial possessions not covered in Columns B, C and D.*

U.S. Politics & Social Issues	U.S. Foreign Policy & Defense	U.S. Economy & Environment	Science, Technology & Nature	Culture, Leisure & Life Style	
			AMA Journal publishes a Duke Univ. study claiming that Americans with a normal diet do not benefit from vitamins.	British novelist P.G. Wodehouse is released by Paris police today after being arrested two days ago with the provision that he report at intervals to French authorities . . . . U.S. celebrates Thanksgiving Day quietly with prayers for a quick victory in the war.	Nov. 23
	U.S. casualties through Nov. 7 are reported to be 528,795, including 162,860 killed . . . . Annual convention of the Middle States Assn. of Colleges and Secondary Schools urges a delay in universal military training legislation until war emotions subside.	CIO criticizes NWLB for poor administration and unfortunate policies and asks for an immediate upward revision of the Little Steel wage formula.			Nov. 24
		NWLB agrees to permit some adjustments in the steel wage formula but rejects a CIO demand for a guaranteed annual wage.		Baseball Commissioner Kenesaw Mountain Landis dies at 78 in Chicago.	Nov. 25
	The 17,000-ton aircraft carrier *Bonhomme Richard* is commissioned at the New York Navy Yard in Brooklyn in the presence of 10,000 invited guests.			Trustees of Ohio Univ. in Athens, O. announce the election of Dr. John Baker, assistant dean of Harvard Univ., as O.U.'s next president . . . . In his first big tournament since being mustered out of the Navy, Sam Snead wins the Portland Open.	Nov. 26
	FDR accepts State Secy. Hull's resignation and names Edward Stettinius to succeed him.	FTC charges the National Lead Co. and other companies with a conspiracy to maintain "monopolistic and non-competitive" prices for white lead.		The 16th season of the N.Y. Metropolitan Opera opens with the presentation of *Faust* . . . . Plans are announced in Chicago for the debut in 1945 of the new U.S. Football League with eight teams and Red Grange as president.	Nov. 27
Asst. Atty. Gen. Norman Littell, whose resignation has been demanded by Atty. Gen. Francis Biddle, tells the Senate War Investigating Comm. that Biddle intervened improperly in a Justice Dept. case on behalf of Thomas Corcoran, former New Deal "braintruster" now in private law practice. Littell says he refused "to cooperate with conduct of the Attorney General which was contrary to basic principles of good government."	National Planning Assn. announces a report of its Committee on International Policy which says the U.S. must completely reverse its attitude on imports if it is to make the most of postwar trade opportunities and fulfill its obligations as the principal creditor nation.			Baseball writers name Detroit pitcher Hal Newhouser as the AL's MVP for 1944.	Nov. 28
		Pres. Green tells the AFL convention in New Orleans there must be amendments to the Wagner Act to maintain craft union integrity.	Carl Norden, inventor of the bombsight and automatic pilot bearing his name, receives the Holley Medal from the American Society of Mechanical Engineers.		Nov. 29
FDR dismisses Asst. Atty. Gen. Norman Littell, saying his actions have substantiated charges of Atty. Gen. Francis Biddle that Littell was insubordinate . . . . Albert Fall, former U.S. senator and Secretary of the Interior in the Harding cabinet who served a prison term for his part in the Teapot Dome oil scandal, dies at 83 in El Paso, Tex.	U.S. and Britain reach a new Lend-Lease agreement providing for a 43% reduction in assistance to England . . . . Senate approves the appointment of Edward Stettinius as Secretary of State . . . . Senate confirms Patrick Hurley as ambassador to China . . . . FDR nominates Alexander Kirk as ambassador to Italy.				Nov. 30
	War. Secy. Stimson and Navy Secy. Forrestal announce the Army and Navy investigations of Pearl Harbor have disclosed no evidence to justify court martials of Adm. Kimmel and Gen. Short.	Reconversion to civilian production in 126 cities is halted by production and manpower officials for 90 days.		World Jewish Congress ends in Atlantic City with the adoption of a program calling for the Jewish people to seek peace, freedom and equality . . . . Utah Supreme Court upholds the convictions of 15 Mormon polygamists, who say they will appeal to the U.S. Supreme Court . . . . Leslie Horvath of Ohio State wins the Heisman Trophy as the outstanding college football player of 1944.	Dec. 1
		WPB discloses that it has approved a $500-million building program to increase facilities for mortar ammunition.		Joseph Lhevinne, noted pianist who won wide acclaim as a soloist and in recitals with his wife, dies at 69 in N.Y.	Dec. 2

F	G	H	I	J
Includes elections, federal-state relations, civil rights and liberties, crime, the judiciary, education, health care, poverty, urban affairs and population.	*Includes formation and debate of U.S. foreign and defense policies, veterans affairs and defense spending. (Relations with specific foreign countries are usually found under the region concerned.)*	*Includes business, labor, agriculture, taxation, transportation, consumer affairs, monetary and fiscal policy, natural resources, pollution and accidents.*	*Includes worldwide scientific, medical and technological developments, natural phenomena, U.S. weather and natural disasters.*	*Includes the arts, religion, scholarship, communications media, sports, entertainment, fashions, fads and social life.*

	World Affairs	European War Zone	Pacific War Zone	The Americas	Other Countries & Territories
Dec. 3		Twenty-one persons are killed and 140 wounded when members of EAM stage a demonstration in Athens, Greece contrary to government orders .... Russian troops capture Miskolc and Satoraljaujhely, last Nazi strongholds northeast of Budapest .... Americans drive the Germans from Inden, Lucherberg, Luchem and Brandenberg on the Cologne plain .... U.S. units cross the Saar River and establish a foothold on the east bank.	American forces turn back a Japanese tank-supported attack on the roadblock outside Limon on Leyte.		Iranian parliament approves a bill prohibiting any official from negotiating or signing any oil agreement with a foreign nation.
Dec. 4		Civil war breaks out in Greece as members of the EAM and government troops engage in fighting. Martial law is imposed .... U.S. armored and infantry divisions begin drives towards Saarbrucken and Saareguemines.	Chinese Foreign Min. T.V. Soong assumes duties as Chinese premier, thus paving the way for an agreement with the Communists.		
Dec. 5		Russian drive in western Hungary reaches the southern shore of Lake Balaton .... British tanks and Greek mountain troops disperse bands of armed ELAS (militia arm of the EAM) members laying siege to police barracks in Athens .... U.S. units establish another bridgehead on the east bank of the Saar River south of Saarlautern .... Stettinius states the U.S. maintains that the composition of the Italian government is strictly an Italian matter.	Chinese troops rushed to Kweichow Province regain the town of Pachai .... U.S. forces cross the Palanas River about 10 miles south of Ormeo on Leyte.		
Dec. 6		British and Greek regulars battle left-wing ELAS forces in Athens .... Russian drive in western Hungary sweeps to within 44 miles of the Austrian border .... U.S. forces establish three more bridgeheads on the east bank of the Saar River .... A new Rumanian cabinet is sworn in with Gen. Nicolai Radescu as premier.		Nicaraguan Congress passes labor legislation providing for collective bargaining, illness pay, an 8-hour work day and vacation pay.	
Dec. 7	International Aviation Conference ends in Chicago with agreements setting up a permanent committee to regulate international air traffic. The interim agreement is to become effective for three years once it is accepted by 26 nations.	On the Saar front, the Americans enter Forback; the Saarbrucken and Saarlautern bridgeheads are merged; other units move into the Pachtener-Buchwald woods .... Ivanoe Bonomi forms a new Italian cabinet .... Stettinius states the U.S. is in agreement with Churchill that the Greek people should determine their own form of government .... British and Greek forces clear ELAS resistance from about three square miles of Athens, and British naval units shell ELAS positions at Piraeus.	U.S. forces split the Japanese on the west coast of Leyte with an amphibious landing three miles south of Ormoc .... As Saipan-based B-29s strike at Tokyo, other U.S. planes based in China strike at Mukden, Manchuria .... Chou En-lai reports Chiang Kai-shek has turned down the Communist proposal for a coalition government.		
Dec. 8		German forces make strong counter-attacks and hold on the Saar front at Dillingen and Saarlautern .... Army reveals U.S. motorized columns had to stop at Metz due to a lack of gasoline .... ELAS snipers continue to infiltrate areas of Athens from which they had been previously cleared by British and Greek troops .... Churchill receives a vote of confidence from the House of Commons on his foreign policy.			
Dec. 9		U.S. forces crack the Maginot Line near Aachen and join forces with units on the Saar front on the east bank of the Saar River .... A spokesman for EAM in Athens says the present struggle will continue until Papandreou quits .... Russian troops tighten their circle around Budapest with the capture of Vac.	Chinese War Min. Gen. Chen Cheng says the Japanese attack on Kweiyang, capital of Kweichow Province, has been repulsed.	A Peruvian cabinet crisis ends with Finance Min. Julio East assuming the premiership and Manuel Gallagher becoming foreign minister.	
	A	B	C	D	E
	Includes developments that affect more than one world region, international organizations and important meetings of major world leaders.	*Includes all developments in European countries and military engagements between Allied and Axis powers in Africa and at sea.*	*Includes all developments in Japan and China, Japanese foreign policy and military actions in the Pacific region.*	*Includes all domestic and regional developments in Latin America, the Caribbean and Canada.*	*Includes developments in those independent nations and colonial possessions not covered in Columns B, C and D.*

U.S. Politics & Social Issues	U.S. Foreign Policy & Defense	U.S. Economy & Environment	Science, Technology & Nature	Culture, Leisure & Life Style	
				Warner Brothers purchases the film rights to the Russel Crouse-Howard Lindsay play *Life With Father* for a $500,000 down payment against royalties.	Dec. 3
	FDR nominates Joseph Grew as undersecretary of state.	Railroad Express Agency suspends acceptance of express shipments for 12 states and 13 cities as a wartime measure.			Dec. 4
		WPB announces the release of cellophane for packaging of small articles such as cigarettes, chewing gum and bakery products . . . . House passes a bill freezing the Social Security tax at its present level of 1% on both worker and employer.			Dec. 5
	Petroleum Industry War Council offers its substitute for the British-American oil agreement, which provides that no provision in the agreement should be construed to require a signatory government to act upon a suggestion made by the International Petroleum Commission, nor any provision be applied to the operation of the domestic petroleum industry within either country . . . . Senate votes to send back to the Foreign Relations Comm. the nominations of Joseph Grew, William Clayton, Nelson Rockefeller and Archibald MacLeish to State Dept. posts pending a hearing on their views of international affairs.		GE announces its development of a sheet of plastic two-millionths of inch thick to be used in making electron microscope pictures.	*A Bell for Adano*, a play by Paul Osborn based on the novel of the same title by John Hershey, opens on Broadway.	Dec. 6
	War Dept. discloses revised plans that now permit 18-year-olds to enter combat zones.	WPB orders civilian production for the first quarter of 1945 to be held at present levels.		Maxwell Memorial Football Club in Philadelphia elects Glenn Davis of West Point as the outstanding football player of 1944.	Dec. 7
FDR instructs the Army to seize and operate the plant of Cudahy Brothers Co., meat packers, Cudahy, Wisc., after the company's refusal to obey an NWLB directive granting maintenance of membership and checkoff union dues.	FDR vetoes a bill which would change the date of the end of the Philippine Insurrection to 10½ years after the recognized date of 1902.	Senate approves the freezing of the Social Security tax at 1% for 1945 . . . . A U.S. court in Cincinnati, O., affirms the conviction of three of the country's largest tobacco companies on charges of violating antitrust laws. They are the American Tobacco Co. Liggett and Myers Tobacco Co. and R.J. Reynolds Tobacco Co.			Dec. 8
	Selective Service announces the renewed induction of men aged 26-37 who are needed as replacements.				Dec. 9
F *Includes elections, federal-state relations, civil rights and liberties, crime, the judiciary, education, health care, poverty, urban affairs and population.*	G *Includes formation and debate of U.S. foreign and defense policies, veterans affairs and defense spending. (Relations with specific foreign countries are usually found under the region concerned.)*	H *Includes business, labor, agriculture, taxation, transportation, consumer affairs, monetary and fiscal policy, natural resources, pollution and accidents.*	I *Includes worldwide scientific, medical and technological developments, natural phenomena, U.S. weather and natural disasters.*	J *Includes the arts, religion, scholarship, communications media, sports, entertainment, fashions, fads and social life.*	

	World Affairs	European War Zone	Pacific War Zone	The Americas	Other Countries & Territories
Dec. 10		At the conclusion of de Gaulle's Moscow visit a treaty of alliance is signed between France and Russia providing for both sides to continue the war until full victory, for neither side to conclude a separate peace with Germany, for each to take in all common measures intended to oppose a new German threat and for both to join the U.N. The treaty is valid for 20 years .... U.S. troops renew their assault on Duren on a 10-mile front .... Russian threat to Budapest increases as a tank unit drives down the east bank of the Danube River to within 7½ miles of the city .... ELAS forces shell Omonia Square in Athens, while RAF bombers drop explosives on ELAS establishments for the first time.	U.S. forces in the Ormoc area eliminate all Japanese opposition in the area and capture the city itself.		
Dec. 11		The greatest single fleet of bombers in the war, 1,600 Fortresses and Liberators, attack German military targets .... Under steady American pounding, the Germans evacuate several defense positions on the west bank of the Roer River .... Germans throw in fresh troops south of Faenza in an effort to check the British .... British Labor Party decides its ministers should remain in Churchill's coalition government until the war is won but that the party should fight as a political entity again in the next general election.	Japanese are reported completely cleared from Kweichow Province.		
Dec. 12		U.S. troops gain seven miles between the Rhine and Hagenau Forest as the Germans are driven from 10 localities .... British present terms for cessation of hostilities to Greek Communists, which provide for the evacuation of the Attic peninsula, cessation of all resistance and surrender of all arms .... With the capture of Goedoelloe by the Russians, only nine miles north of Budapest, the last major fort guarding the Hungarian capital falls.	U.S. planes smash another convoy seeking to land Japanese reinforcements on Leyte.		
Dec. 13		Russians close in on Budapest, taking Kisalag, six miles north, and Isaszeg, eight miles east .... ELAS forces increase their attacks in Athens .... U.S. troops make small gains at several points of a 30-mile line in Germany from Julich to Monschau.	American Army and Navy commanders of the central Pacific and Aleutian areas conclude secret conferences at which plans for the war against Japan are laid .... Carrier-based planes strike at Japanese installations in the northern Philippines, destroying nearly 100 enemy aircraft.	El Salvadorean rebels begin an uprising against the provisional regime of Col. Osmin Aguirre y Salinas.	
Dec. 14		American forces reach Scheibenhard and Eberbach close to the southern Franco-German border .... Russian troops make gains along a 50-mile front in Hungary.	Chinese troops in Burma capture Tonkwa, 129 miles north of Mandalay.	Navy reports the Coast Guard dispersed during the past four months three German expeditions to establish weather reporting stations on Greenland's northeastern coast.	
Dec. 15		U.S. troops reach the German border along a 17-mile front from the Vosges Mountains to the Rhine .... Churchill backs Russian demands for the part of Poland east of the Curzon Line, including Vilna and Lwow .... Russian troops capture the Czech stronghold of Sahy after a five-day battle.	Chinese troops capture Bhamo after the failure of an attempt by the Japanese garrison to fight its way south along the Irrawaddy River .... U.S. forces land on Mindoro Island without any losses.		

U.S. Politics & Social Issues	U.S. Foreign Policy & Defense	U.S. Economy & Environment	Science, Technology & Nature	Culture, Leisure & Life Style	
	War Dept. says Negroes in the Army as of Sept. 30 numbered 701,678.			N.Y. Giants win the eastern title of the NFL by defeating Washington, 31-0, and will meet Green Bay for the championship .... A committee of major league baseball owners and writers announces the selection of late commissioner Kenesaw Mountain Landis to the Hall of Fame.	Dec. 10
FDR accepts the resignation of REA Admin. Harry Slattery, which resulted from his feud with Agriculture Secy. Wickard.	Senate passes and sends to FDR a bill authorizing the appointment of four five-star generals and four five-star admirals .... A delegation representing many Greek-American organizations visits the State Dept. to protest British intervention in Greece and to urge American mediation.				Dec. 11
	Stettinius tells the Senate Foreign Relations Comm. he has confidence in the men appointed to new posts in the reorganized State Dept.: Grew, Rockefeller and MacLeish.	NWLB orders the CIO United Mail Order, Warehouse and Retail Employes union to appear before the Board and explain why it has not ended its Detroit strike against Montgomery Ward.			Dec. 12
James F. Roe, for 20 years holder of an exclusive contract with the government to provide bonds for immigrants and deportees on Ellis Island, is sentenced in N.Y. to a prison term of four to eight years for having defrauded deportees and war internees of $200,000 in 10 years.		Solid Fuels Administration announces that due to manpower shortages and strikes, stocks of bituminous coal will be reduced to a real danger point by next April .... National Labor Conference in Washington adopts a resolution recommending that all states establish a minimum wage of 65 cents hourly .... ICC votes to postpone for another year the freight rate increase granted in 1942.		*Variety* reports the most popular songs are: (1) *The Trolley Song*, (2) *Together* and (3) *I'm Making Believe*.	Dec. 13
	Senate Foreign Relations Comm. approves and sends to the Senate the nominations of six men as aides to State Secy. Stettinius.	NWLB orders Montgomery Ward to comply with its wage directives at the company's four Detroit area stores .... FDR appoints a three-man board under the Railway Labor Act to investigate a dispute involving the Seaboard Air Line Railway and 800 firemen threatening to strike.		MGM release of *National Velvet*, featuring Elizabeth Taylor, opens in New York.	Dec. 14
	Senate votes the new five-star rank to Gens. MacArthur, Eisenhower and Henry H. Arnold and to Adms. Leahy, King and Nimitz .... A federal grand jury in Newark, N.J. returns indictments charging Carl Emil Ludwig Krepper with conspiring to aid the eight Nazi saboteurs rounded up in 1942 .... Selective Service announces that manpower needs after next Feb. 1 cannot be met by men in the 18-25 age bracket and that a larger proportion of older men will be taken after that time.	NWLB notifies Montgomery Ward to comply with its orders in San Rafael, Calif., St. Paul, Chicago, Portland, Denver and Jamaica, N.Y. by Dec. 18.		Director of the U.S. Air Force band and popular orchestra leader Maj. Glenn Miller is lost on a flight from England to Paris.	Dec. 15

F	G	H	I	J
Includes elections, federal-state relations, civil rights and liberties, crime, the judiciary, education, health care, poverty, urban affairs and population.	*Includes formation and debate of U.S. foreign and defense policies, veterans affairs and defense spending. (Relations with specific foreign countries are usually found under the region concerned.)*	*Includes business, labor, agriculture, taxation, transportation, consumer affairs, monetary and fiscal policy, natural resources, pollution and accidents.*	*Includes worldwide scientific, medical and technological developments, natural phenomena, U.S. weather and natural disasters.*	*Includes the arts, religion, scholarship, communications media, sports, entertainment, fashions, fads and social life.*

Dec. 16		German counter-offensive begins, opening the Battle of the Bulge, at 5:30 a.m. German artillery fire pounds American positions near Bastogne. The Nazis attack with three armies (some 19 divisions) and five in reserve. By nightfall the American VII Corps line (1st Army) on the south flank is broken . . . . Russian troops drive from three sides on the important railway center of Kosice, seized by Hungary from Czechoslovakia. . . . . Moscow radio announces the postponement until December 1945 of elections to the Supreme Soviet because of the war . . . . New Zealand troops capture Faenza, Italy.	U.S. troops on Mindoro Island occupy San Jose and its adjacent airfield five miles in from the coast.	Lester Pearson is appointed Canadian ambassador to the U.S.	
Dec. 17		In a day-old offensive, the Germans gain against the southern flank of U.S. troops, moving through Belgium and Luxembourg . . . . Germans massacre 115 American prisoners of war near Malmedy, Belgium. Fifteen escape to freedom . . . . ELAS troops renew their shelling of Athens . . . . Russia and Finland sign an agreement on Finnish deliveries to fulfill Russian demands for $300 million in war damages.	For the first time since May, U.S. troops are reported active in Burma, fighting the Japanese northeast of Mandalay.		
Dec. 18		The large-scale German offensive into Belgium and Luxembourg picks up, driving at Consdorf and St. Vith. U.S. 1st Army is supported by 60,000 men and 11,000 vehicles of the 3rd Army. U.S. 9th Army takes Wurm and Muellendorf . . . . Russians take more than 40 towns in a 12-mile advance on a 68-mile front aimed at Slovakia . . . . State Secy. Stettinius issues a statement on Poland, reiterating the U.S. desire to defer border settlements to after the war.	U.S. forces on Mindoro Island fan out six miles from San Jose.		
Dec. 19		Americans strike back at the German offensive and take Stavelot, Belgium and are engaged in bitter fighting at Malmedy . . . . UNRRA Dir. Lehman announces the withdrawal from Greece of most of the UNRRA staff due to military conditions in the country . . . . Russian forces drive to within nine miles of the Kosice rail junction in Czechoslovakia.	In wide-ranging attacks, Allied planes hit Omura on Kyushu Island, Japan and Shanghai and Nanking, China.		British Information Service announces in Washington that under the terms of an interim agreement Britain will withdraw all its forces, save a few border patrols, from Ethiopia.
Dec. 20		American forces are holding on the flanks of the German offensive into Belgium. U.S. 1st Army's VII Corps resumes its attack toward the Roer, blocking the Winden-Untermanbach highway and pushing into Schneidhausen . . . . British Foreign Secy. Eden tells the House of Commons that Britain wants only to feed the starving Greeks and ensure a stable democratic government in Greece and is not trying to force a regency or unwelcome king on the populace.	U.S. troops capture Valencia, Leyte and its airfield, recent headquarters for the Japanese 35th Army . . . . MacArthur claims that the Allies have won the battle for Ormoc.		
Dec. 21		In their pincer movement to trap the last German troops in Hungary, the Russians close the gap between their armies to 22 miles . . . . British troops use tanks and rocket-firing planes against ELAS in Greece . . . . Canadian troops take Bagnacavallo and advance on the eastern front to the Senio River in Italy.		FDR signs a bill authorizing a $10,000,000 public works program for the Virgin Islands . . . . Juan Jose Arevalo is elected president of Guatemala.	
Dec. 22		N.Y. Federal Reserve transfers $223,292,833 in fine gold to the National Bank of Belgium from the Bank of France, ending a dispute dating to the Nazi occupation of France . . . . Churchill's office announces that 250,000 more fighting men will have to be found for Britain's armies in 1945 . . . . Russians throw about 240,000 troops into battle in Latvia as their winter offensive opens.	Japanese troops retreating through Kwangsi Province stiffen their resistance at Hochih, 95 miles northwest of Liuchow.		
	A	B	C	D	E
	Includes developments that affect more than one world region, international organizations and important meetings of major world leaders.	*Includes all developments in European countries and military engagements between Allied and Axis powers in Africa and at sea.*	*Includes all developments in Japan and China, Japanese foreign policy and military actions in the Pacific region.*	*Includes all domestic and regional developments in Latin America, the Caribbean and Canada.*	*Includes developments in those independent nations and colonial possessions not covered in Columns B, C and D.*

	F	G	H	I	J
Dec. 16			FDR signs the bill freezing Social Security taxes for 1945 at their present 1% level.		Boston police announce proceedings against a bookseller for selling Erskine Caldwell's latest novel, *Tragic Ground*, to an agent of the Watch and Ward Society, which previously had noted 20 allegedly obscene pages in the book.
Dec. 17	Western Defense Command chief Maj. Gen. H. Conger Pratt proclaims that effective Jan. 2 all persons of Japanese ancestry who have been proved loyal to the U.S. may return to their former homes on the Pacific Coast.				Wassily Kandinsky, dean of non-objective painters, dies at 78 in Paris .... Green Bay Packers win the NFL title by defeating the N.Y. Giants, 14-7.
Dec. 18	Members of the Electoral College meet in state capitols to cast 432 ballots for FDR and 99 for Dewey .... Supreme Court upholds the constitutionality of wartime regulations under which Americans of Japanese desent were removed from West Coast areas .... Supreme Court rules that Negro employes on American railroads are protected by the Railway Labor Act against management-union pacts seeking to oust them from jobs and deny them promotions.				As a result of a nationwide poll, the AP names Ann Curtis and Byron Nelson the outstanding athletes of 1944.
Dec. 19	The 77th Congress expires at 8:22 p.m. with adjournment sine die of the Senate.	A N.Y. federal grand jury indicts Carl L. Norden, Inc., Theodore Barth and Ward Marvelle, officials of the organization, and Comdr. John Corrigan, USNR, on charges of conspiring to defraud the government by restricting production of the famous Norden bombsight to the Norden firm .... Senate confirms all six of FDR's State Dept. nominees as assistants to Secy. Stettinius.	Montgomery Ward announces a basic minimum wage plan, approved by the NWLB, for its Detroit-area stores.		
Dec. 20			FDR signs the measure appropriating $1.5 billion in federal aid for building state highways.		*Winged Victory*, a 20th Century-Fox film featuring the Army Air Corps cast of the stage production, opens in New York.
Dec. 21	James Allen files a $75 million suit against FDR, Atty. Gen. Francis Biddle, FBI Dir. J. Edgar Hoover and others on charges that they "conspired" to injure his reputation and property, deprive him of his liberty and use of freedom of the press and intimidate him into submission. He was convicted of conspiracy to obstruct drafting of men into the armed services and his case was turned down by the Supreme Court four times .... FDR appoints Paul Porter as chairman of the FCC .... GOP leaders meet in N.Y. to make plans to function as a vigorous opposition party.				National Institute of Arts and Letters announces election to membership of composer Jerome Kern and artists Frank Benson and Edward Hopper.
Dec. 22					Harry Langdon, one of the highest-paid comedians of the silent movie days, dies at 60 in Los Angeles.

F
Includes elections, federal-state relations, civil rights and liberties, crime, the judiciary, education, health care, poverty, urban affairs and population.

G
Includes formation and debate of U.S. foreign and defense policies, veterans affairs and defense spending. (Relations with specific foreign countries are usually found under the region concerned.)

H
Includes business, labor, agriculture, taxation, transportation, consumer affairs, monetary and fiscal policy, natural resources, pollution and accidents.

I
Includes worldwide scientific, medical and technological developments, natural phenomena, U.S. weather and natural disasters.

J
Includes the arts, religion, scholarship, communications media, sports, entertainment, fashions, fads and social life.

	World Affairs	European War Zone	Pacific War Zone	The Americas	Other Countries & Territories
Dec. 23		Exiled Basque, Catalan and Galician leaders sign a pact of solidarity in Mexico City, pledging to overthrow the Spanish regime of Francisco Franco .... Fighting between left-wing ELAS and right-wing EDES guerrillas breaks out in northwestern Greece .... Moscow announces Premier Gen. Bela Miklos has formed a Hungarian provisional government in Debrecen.	U.S land-based planes attack Grace Park Field in the Manila area and destroy about 25 enemy aircraft.		
Dec. 24		With the largest tactical air assault to date, involving some 6,500 planes, the Allies momentarily check the Nazi advance into Belgium. U.S. 9th Army's V Corps repels a German attack on Butgenbach. Americans take La Gleize. Fierce fighting continues in Bastogne .... ELAS forces attacking the EDES guerrilla army in northeastern Greece force the latter to evacuate Yanina and Arta.			
Dec. 25		Americans attack toward Grandmeuil and establish a defensive line in the Werpin-Armonines area. Verdenne is recovered and Celles is seized .... Churchill and Eden arrive in Athens in an effort to settle the civil war .... Russians cut the last westward rail lines from Budapest as they close their arc to nine miles.	U.S. forces take the last Japanese stronghold on Leyte Island, Palompon, ending the Leyte-Samar operation.		
Dec. 26		U.S. 1st Army halts the German westward drive short of Meuse. U.S. 7th Army seizes Grandmeuil. Army units break through to Bastogne .... Russians complete their encirclement of Budapest and break into the city streets .... Churchill confers with Greek leaders, including those of ELAS, in an effort to unify the government there .... Canadian troops capture Rosetta, Italy.	A Japanese task force including a battleship attacks the American positions on Mindoro Island, resulting in minor damage to the Americans.		
Dec. 27		Patton's armored forces cut a northward path through the Nazi salient in Belgium to relieve troops surrounded at Bastogne. Manhay, Humain, Surre, Boluide and Boschleiden are taken by the Americans .... Nazi elite troops are ordered to fight to the last man in house-to-house combat against the Russians in Budapest .... A conference of Greek political leaders in Athens agrees to a regency under Archbishop Damaskinos.	U.S. air strikes drive off the Japanese task force at Mindoro Island.		
Dec. 28		The German offensive stands still as Americans register gains in counter-drives at several points along the perimeter in Belgium, and successfully repel the final German effort to take Elsenborn .... On the western front of the Italian line, the Germans force an American retreat of three miles and take the villages of Barga and Gallicano .... Russian troops move westward along a 90-mile front from Budapest towards Austria.		U.S. and Brazil agree that the U.S. will supply 2,500 tons of synthetic rubber annually, in return for Brazil's reduction of natural rubber by a similar amount.	
Dec. 29		The point of the German salient in Belgium is driven back to Rochefort. U.S. 3rd Army prepares for a drive on Houffalize, and other American troops move toward Neufchateau. The Arlon-Bastogne highway is opened .... Americans halt the German drive on the Italian west coast south of Gallicano .... Bitter street fighting continues as the Russians attempt to complete control of Budapest .... UNRRA Dir. Lehman reports after his six-week European tour that the Allies have promised all available shipping to take relief supplies to Europe.		Panamanian Pres. Ricardo Adolfo de la Guardia suspends the 1941 constitution and dissolves the National Assembly.	
Dec. 30		Three American divisions launch attacks on both sides of the Bastogne corridor and thrust into the German Belgium salient. Moircy is taken but lost to a German counterattack later in the day .... King George II of Greece issues a royal proclamation in London appointing Archbishop Damaskinos as his regent.	U.S. planes make their deepest penetration of the Japanese-held Philippines, sinking eight ships at Lingayen Gulf, Luzon.		

A	B	C	D	E
Includes developments that affect more than one world region, international organizations and important meetings of major world leaders.	*Includes all developments in European countries and military engagements between Allied and Axis powers in Africa and at sea.*	*Includes all developments in Japan and China, Japanese foreign policy and military actions in the Pacific region.*	*Includes all domestic and regional developments in Latin America, the Caribbean and Canada.*	*Includes developments in those independent nations and colonial possessions not covered in Columns B, C and D.*

U.S. Politics & Social Issues	U.S. Foreign Policy & Defense	U.S. Economy & Environment	Science, Technology & Nature	Culture, Leisure & Life Style	
	James Byrnes says he finds it difficult to understand how men can be physically unfit for military service but yet still participate in professional sports.	FDR signs the bill providing for post-war flood control projects estimated at $1 billion and authorizing a $400,000 multipurpose project in the Missouri Valley.		Charles Gibson, one of America's best known artists, whose *Gibson Girl* was symbolic of an era, dies at 77 in N.Y.C. . . . . War Mobilization and Reconversion Dir. James Byrnes bans horse racing and all other types of animal racing, effective Jan. 3, to save labor and critical materials.	Dec. 23
		OPA announces new ration quotas, putting all beef back on the list.		In his Christmas message, Pope Pius XII expresses support for an international organization to keep world peace.	Dec. 24
Six of twenty-five escaped German prisoners from the Papago Park Prison in Arizona are recaptured.		OPA announces January allocations of tires for civilian passenger cars and small buses and trucks. There will be 1,800,000 new passenger tires available and 216,000 small truck and bus tires.			Dec. 25
	Byrnes orders that the re-examination of professional athletes classified 4-F be extended to college athletes with the same classification.	Up to 35% of New York City's retail meat stores remain closed today as many butchers carry out their plan not to open until a ceiling is put on livestock prices so they can operate legally at a profit.		Negro composer William Grant Still wins the $1,000 war-bond prize offered for a jubilee overture celebrating the Cincinnati Symphony Orchestra's 50th anniversary.	Dec. 26
		Pres. Harry Bridges of the CIO International Longshoremen's Union asks the Supreme Court for a final adjudication of the order to deport him to Australia . . . . WPB orders a reduction in the use of lead for civilian production in 1945 because of war needs.		N.Y. film critics select *Going My Way* as the year's best picture.	Dec. 27
		FDR orders the Army to seize the executive offices and other facilities of Montgomery Ward in Chicago and Detroit for its refusal to obey NWLB orders.		Judge Elijah Adlow in Boston rules Erskine Caldwell's *Tragic Ground* is not obscene and dismisses police charges against a bookseller for distributing the work . . . . *Motion Picture Herald* announces announces that Bing Crosby was the top 1944 box office attraction.	Dec. 28
		FDR kills by "pocket veto" a bill that would have abolished the 221,610-acre Jackson Hole National Monument in Wyoming, established by executive order March 15, 1943 after Congress had refused to approve this extension of Teton National Park because of opposition to government acquisition of grazing areas . . . . Montgomery Ward officials refuse to cooperate with FDR by making the company's books and other data available to the Army.			Dec. 29
	Sen. Burton Wheeler (D, Mont.) proposes the Senate proclaim its own peace aims "in the absence of the President taking a stand."	Army authorities in control of the Montgomery Ward & Co. offices in Chicago seize the firm's books and set their accountants to study them . . . . Stabilization Dir. Fred Vinson approves the NWLB adjustments in the "Little Steel" wage formula.		Romain Rolland, noted French novelist, Nobel Prize winner in 1915 and author of *Jean-Christophe*, dies at 78 in Vezelay, France.	Dec. 30
F	G	H	I	J	
Includes elections, federal-state relations, civil rights and liberties, crime, the judiciary, education, health care, poverty, urban affairs and population.	*Includes formation and debate of U.S. foreign and defense policies, veterans affairs and defense spending. (Relations with specific foreign countries are usually found under the region concerned.)*	*Includes business, labor, agriculture, taxation, transportation, consumer affairs, monetary and fiscal policy, natural resources, pollution and accidents.*	*Includes worldwide scientific, medical and technological developments, natural phenomena, U.S. weather and natural disasters.*	*Includes the arts, religion, scholarship, communications media, sports, entertainment, fashions, fads and social life.*	

	A	B	C	D	E
Dec. 31		Polish Comm. of National Liberation, operating from Lublin with the cooperation of Russia, proclaims itself Poland's provisional government .... After a 48-hour battle the Americans seize Rochefort on the western end of the German salient in Belgium. U.S. troops attack north of Bastogne, while other units advance against the Germans between Bastogne and St. Hubert. Remagen is captured .... Archbishop Damaskinos is sworn in as Regent of Greece, with ELAS forces accepting this as the basis for truce negotiations. Papandreou's government leaves office .... American forces on the Italian west coast advance one-and-a-half miles north of Barga and capture Sommocolonia.	MacArthur's aircraft make their first daylight raid on Formosa .... In his New Year's message to the Chinese people, Chiang Kai-shek promises them a constitutional government before the war's end.		

Dec. 31

Dr. Nicholas Murray Butler, president of Columbia Univ., says in a year-end message in N.Y. that unless the world is rebuilt on a moral foundation the end of all that has been accomplished in 5,000 years will not be far off . . . . Forty-eight persons are killed and more than 80 injured when the second section of the Southern Pacific Railroad's Pacific Limited rams into the rear of the first section 18 miles west of Ogden, Utah.

KITES
POULTRY-STO

1945

Standing among his co-defendants at the Nuremberg war crimes trial, former Gestapo chief Ernst Kaltenbrunner addresses the International Military Tribunal. Second from left in the first row is Rudolf Hess, Hitler's former deputy; beside Hess sit former Foreign Min. Joachim von Ribbentrop and Field Marshal Wilhelm Keitel. Third from right in the second row is former Armaments Min. Albert Speer.

Women auto workers in Detroit protest being laid off in November to make room for returning war veterans.

Meeting of friends: A U.S. and Russian soldier embrace after their armies link up at Torgau in central Germany, April 15.

U.S. congressmen view the bodies of concentration camp inmates at Buchenwald. Standing beside the officer on the right is Sen. Alben Barkley (D, Ky.); beside Barkley is Sen. Kenneth Wherry (R, Neb.).

A British Army bulldozer pulls down a bombed-out building in Berlin shortly after the war's end.

A Japanese POW on Guam weeps as he listens to Emperor Hirohito's surrender announcement, Aug. 15.

Preceding page: Wartime scarcities did not end with the defeat of Germany, as these disappointed Atlanta residents learn in front of a closed poultry shop on May 19.

Braving Japanese sniper fire, Marine Lt. Col. R. P. Ross, Jr. plants the American flag on the parapet of Shuri Castle on Okinawa, June 10.

Navy patrol planes circle over the U.S. task force preparing to invade the Philippine island of Luzon at Lingayen Gulf, Jan. 9.

Col. Paul Tibbets, pilot of the *Enola Gay,* gives last-minute instructions to his crew before takeoff on the first nuclear bombing run over Hiroshima.

Troops and supplies move towards China in January along the Stilwell Road, the last link of the reopened Burma Road.

A view of the Clinton Engineering Works in Oak Ridge, Tenn., where the first atomic bombs were produced.

Army quarterback Felix (Doc) Blanchard weaves to avoid three Michigan Wolverines closing in for the kill, Oct. 13.

Crouching to avoid Japanese fire, U.S. Marines inch up the beach on Iwo Jima. Mt. Suribachi is in the background.

The Big Three in 1945: Stalin, Truman and Churchill pose uneasily for photographers at the start of the Potsdam conference in July. Churchill was soon replaced by Clement Attlee .

	World Affairs	European War Zone	Pacific War Zone	The Americas	Other Countries & Territories
Jan.	FDR and Churchill meet on Malta, reviewing plans for a final thrust at Germany and preparing for meeting with Stalin at Yalta.	U.S. forces eliminate the German salient in Belgium .... Russian armies overrun Poland and East Prussia, reaching the Oder River.	U.S. forces under MacArthur establish positions on Luzon, chief island of the Philippines .... Supplies to China begin flowing on the Ledo Road through Burma.		
Feb.	FDR, Churchill and Stalin meet at Yalta, arriving at secret agreements on Poland's postwar borders and compensation for Soviet participation in the Pacific war.	Russian advance overruns Hungary, Slovakia and Silesia.	U.S. forces continue to advance on Luzon, while Marines gain a foothold on Iwo Jima.	Representatives of all American states but Argentina meet in Mexico City to discuss hemispheric security.	Arab leaders meet in Cairo to discuss formation of a pan-Arab federation.
March	Thirty-seven nations accept an American invitation to meet in San Francisco and draw up a United Nations Charter.	U.S. and British forces cross the Rhine, envelop the Ruhr and enter southwestern Germany .... Russian troops advance through Austria past Vienna.	U.S. Marines complete the conquest of Iwo Jima .... British forces advance through central Burma .... U.S. bombers step up their attacks on Japanese cities .... British Pacific Fleet begins joint operations with U.S. naval units near Japan.	Mexico City Conference ends with endorsement of Dumbarton Oaks proposals and an agreement (the Act of Chapultepec) for mutual consultation should be a hemispheric nation be attacked.	Cairo conference ends with formation of an Arab League.
Apr.	United Nations Conference opens in San Francisco. International jurists, educators and air transportation officials hold separate meetings, agreeing on the need for postwar cooperation.	U.S. and British armies overrun the Ruhr and central and southern Germany .... Russians launch their final drive on Berlin, occupying the city and linking up with U.S. forces on the Elbe.	U.S. Marines invade Okinawa and overrun four-fifths of the island .... Japanese kamikaze aircraft begin intensive attacks on U.S. and British naval units supporting the Okinawa invasion (Operation Floating Chrysanthemum).	Argentina moves its foreign policy into line with that of other American states, declaring war on the Axis and signing the Act of Chapultepec.	Government crises errupt in Iran and Syria.
May	Delegates to the San Francisco Conference reach agreement on several aspects of the postwar U.N. organization, including Security Council membership.	Allies mop up German resistance and force unconditional German surrender.	U.S. bombers continue to intensify their attacks on Japanese cities .... British forces occupy southern Burma, including Rangoon.		Violence erupts in Syria and Lebanon as nationalists protest continued French presence there.
June	San Francisco Conference ends with agreement on colonial trusteeships, the role of the General Assembly and Big Five veto rights in the postwar U.N. organization.	Moscow establishes a provisional Polish government with representatives of the Polish exile government in London and the Polish Committee of National Liberation in Lublin .... Expulsion of Germans from Silesia, the Sudetenland and other parts of Central Europe begins.	U.S. forces complete the occupation of Okinawa and Luzon .... Australian forces advance along the coast of northern Borneo, occupying Brunei.		
July	Big Three meet at Potsdam, with Clement Attlee replacing Churchill after Labor's victory in the British elections.	National elections bring changes of government in Britain, Belgium and Sweden.	U.S. vessels begin naval shelling of Japan .... Australian forces invade eastern Borneo, occupying the oil refinery center of Balik Papen.	El Salvador and Nicaragua ratify the U.N. Charter.	British and Indian political leaders meeting in Simla fail to devise a plan for an Indian government.
Aug.	Big Three end their Potsdam discussions on Russian participation in the Pacific war, Poland's postwar boundaries, denazification of Germany and other questions. Little substantive agreement is reached .... Russian push to achieve nuclear capability begins on Stalin's direct orders.	Allies begin planning for the trial of German war criminals .... French government tries Gen. Henri Petain, leader of the Vichy state, for treason.	Two U.S. atomic bombs force Japan's unconditional surrender .... Russian forces occupy Manchuria and northern Korea.		International debate on the fate of Palestine intensifies as British authorities attempt to prevent increased Jewish immigration .... Vietnamese nationalists under Ho Chi Minh occupy Tonkin and Annam .... Indonesian nationalists begin to organize a government on Java and Sumatra.

A	B	C	D	E
Includes developments that affect more than one world region, international organizations and important meetings of major world leaders.	*Includes all developments in European countries and military engagements between Allied and Axis powers in Africa and at sea.*	*Includes all developments in Japan and China, Japanese foreign policy and military actions in the Pacific region.*	*Includes all domestic and regional developments in Latin America, the Caribbean and Canada.*	*Includes developments in those independent nations and colonial possessions not covered in Columns B, C and D.*

U.S. Politics & Social Issues	U.S. Foreign Policy & Defense	U.S. Economy & Environment	Science, Technology & Nature	Culture, Leisure & Life Style	
Congress blocks the nomination of Henry A. Wallace as commerce secretary.	House debates a bill authorizing limited national service for all men aged 18 to 45.	Justice Dept. charges companies in the electric, steel and diamond industries with monopolistic practices.		Although FDR encourages major league baseball to continue, a wartime order ends horse racing.	Jan.
	Because of military replacement needs, the Selective Service places more rigid restrictions on occupational deferments.		Dr. Raymond Libby develops a method for taking penicillin orally.	A nationwide midnight curfew on entertainment is imposed.	Feb.
Senate confirms Henry A. Wallace as commerce secretary but rejects Aubrey Williams as REA administrator.	Government officials, including FDR, endorse U.S. involvement in postwar organizations.	Government intervention ends a wage dispute affecting Pennsylvania coal miners . . . . Federal agencies announce plans for increased civilian goods production.	Ohio River floods cause extensive damage in Ohio.		March
FDR dies and is succeeded by Vice Pres. Harry S Truman.	As new President, Truman reaffirms FDR's policies of committing the U.S. to postwar international involvement.	Labor and management negotiators conclude wage agreements for coal miners and steel, textile and auto workers.	Natural disasters cause heavy damage in Louisiana, Oklahoma, Arkansas, Missouri and Illinois.		Apr.
Truman reorganizes his cabinet.	War Department enacts plans for releasing some men from military service, while transfering others to the Pacific.		Several new drugs, including streptomycin, corticin and pleurotin, enter the market in the U.S.	Horse racing reopens across the country.	May
Congress debates extension of the Fair Employment Practices Commission.		Congress completes action and sends to Truman legislation extending OPA for another year.			June
Congress votes to extend the FEPC for another year, but with a reduced budget.	The atomic bomb is successfully tested, and Truman decides that the weapon will be used against Japan.	Congressional liberals introduce bills for a 65¢ hourly minimum wage rate.	Senate takes up the issue of creating a National Science Foundation.	Methodists in Britain and Ireland agree to permit single women to serve as ordained ministers.	July
	Truman signs the U.N. Charter and Bretton Woods agreement, making the U.S. the first nation to accept both documents.	Federal agencies begin to lift controls over materials essential for civilian goods production . . . . Labor and management representatives promise cooperation in postwar economic reconversion.	Planning for the Sloan-Kettering Cancer Research center begins in N.Y.	Branch Rickey and two associates gain control of the Brooklyn Dodgers.	Aug.

F	G	H	I	J
Includes elections, federal-state relations, civil rights and liberties, crime, the judiciary, education, health care, poverty, urban affairs and population.	*Includes formation and debate of U.S. foreign and defense policies, veterans affairs and defense spending. (Relations with specific foreign countries are usually found under the region concerned.)*	*Includes business, labor, agriculture, taxation, transportation, consumer affairs, monetary and fiscal policy, natural resources, pollution and accidents.*	*Includes worldwide scientific, medical and technological developments, natural phenomena, U.S. weather and natural disasters.*	*Includes the arts, religion, scholarship, communications media, sports, entertainment, fashions, fads and social life.*

	World Affairs	Europe	Africa & the Middle East	The Americas	Asia & the Pacific
Sept.	Allied Council of Foreign Ministers begins discussions in London on peace treaties with Italy, Rumania and Finland.	Norwegian government tries wartime collaborationist leader Vidkun Quisling for treason.			Japanese forces surrender to the Allies throughout the Pacific and Southeast Asia. MacArthur begins to direct Japanese government functions .... U.S. troops under Gen. John Hodge occupy southern Korea .... British forces under the Allied Southeast Asia command begin to occupy Indonesia for the Dutch .... Vietnamese nationalists in Cochin China clash with returning French colonial troops.
Oct.	Allies trade accusations on responsibility for failure to reach agreement on Axis peace treaties.	French government tries collaborationist politician Pierre Laval for treason.	Several Arab nations threaten war should a separate Jewish state be created.	Political crises in Argentina and Venezuela bring new governments to power.	British forces on Java clash with Indonesian nationalists.
Nov.	Organization of U.N. offices begins. U.S., Britain and Canada agree not to place the atomic bomb under international control.	Allied military tribunal at Nuremberg begins trial of major German war criminals.	Azerbaijani separatists revolt in Iran as the Iranian government clashes with Russia over the timetable for the withdrawal of Russian forces from the northern and central parts of the country.		Civil war erupts in China between Nationalists and Communists .... Warfare on Java between British forces and Indonesian nationalists continues.
Dec.					MacArthur orders the arrest of Japanese military and civilian leaders for possible war crimes trials .... Clashes between British troops and Indonesian nationalists continue on Java.

A	B	C	D	E
Includes developments that affect more than one world region, international organizations and important meetings of major world leaders.	*Includes all domestic and regional developments in Europe, including the Soviet Union, Turkey, Cyprus and Malta.*	*Includes all domestic and regional developments in Africa and the Middle East, including Iraq and Iran and excluding Cyprus, Turkey and Afghanistan.*	*Includes all domestic and regional developments in Latin America, the Caribbean and Canada.*	*Includes all domestic and regional developments in Asian and Pacific nations, extending from Afghanistan through all the Pacific Islands, except Hawaii.*

U.S. Politics & Social Issues	U.S. Foreign Policy & Defense	U.S. Economy & Environment	Science, Technology & Nature	Culture, Leisure & Life Style	
House Un-American Activities Comm. questions the reorganization of the Communist Party.	Army and Navy enact demobilization plans amidst widespread demands for rapid discharge of overseas troops.	Postwar strike wave begins with walkouts by miners and oil, steel, construction and other workers.		Negroes in Connecticut protest to showing of *Uncle Tom's Cabin.*	Sept.
	Heated debate arises in the U.S. over the question of submitting the atomic bomb to international control.	Congress completes action on a $5.9-billion tax program.	CBS and NBC research improves the quality of television transmission.		Oct.
Truman urges congressional action on a far-reaching social reform program, later called the "Fair Deal."		Truman's labor-management conference ends in Washington, issuing a call for the use of arbitration in contract settlements.			Nov.
Truman reluctantly signs a government reorganization bill after his own proposals are rejected by Congress.	Former Amb. Patrick Hurley causes debate over U.S. policy in China by charging that State Dept. officials have "sold out" the country to the Communists.	In response to labor's demand for wage increases, Truman proposes the use of fact-finding boards to facilitate wage settlements.	An influenza epidemic grips the nation.		Dec.

F	G	H	I	J
Includes elections, federal-state relations, civil rights and liberties, crime, the judiciary, education, health care, poverty, urban affairs and population.	*Includes formation and debate of U.S. foreign and defense policies, veterans affairs and defense spending. (Relations with specific foreign countries are usually found under the region concerned.)*	*Includes business, labor, agriculture, taxation, transportation, consumer affairs, monetary and fiscal policy, natural resources, pollution and accidents.*	*Includes worldwide scientific, medical and technological developments, natural phenomena, U.S. weather and natural disasters.*	*Includes the arts, religion, scholarship, communications media, sports, entertainment, fashions, fads and social life.*

	World Affairs	European War Zone	Pacific War Zone	The Americas	Other Countries & Territories
Jan. 1	France becomes a member of the U.N.	Hitler tells the German people in a radio broadcast that the war will not end until 1946 unless "by German victory," because Germany will never capitulate .... After taking another 200 blocks on both sides of the Danube, Russian troops now claim to control about 35 square miles of Budapest .... Germans reportedly lose 208 planes in attacks upon Allied positions in Belgium, France and the Netherlands.	U.S. forces land unopposed on the east coast of Mindoro Island in the Phillippines.		
Jan. 2	FDR says he is not worried over Allied "differences" as he prepares for a meeting with Churchill and Stalin in the near future.	More than 1,000 RAF heavy bombers strike Ludwigshafen, Nuremberg and Berlin.	U.S. troops land unopposed on the west coast of Mindoro Island .... British troops occupy the Mu River town of Kabo, 75 miles northwest of Mandalay.	Mexico completes payment of installments on American claims of damage incurred in the Mexican Revolution by turning over a check for $448,000 to the State Dept.	
Jan. 3		U.S. troops open a drive against the northern flank of the German salient in Belgium .... German counterattacks northwest of Budapest wrest several towns on the south bank of the Danube River from the Russians .... Gen. Nicholas Plastiras forms a new Greek cabinet with himself as premier.	Carrier-based U.S. planes make simultaneous attacks on Formosa and Okinawa, sinking 25 Japanese ships and destroying 111 enemy aircraft .... American troops land unopposed at Buenavista on the southwest coast of Marinduque Island in the Philippines. .... British and Indian troops occupy the west coast island port of Akyab, Burma without opposition .... Chinese troops capture the Burma Road town of Wanting on the Chinese-Burmese border.		
Jan. 4		Athens says Premier Plastiras today appealed to the leftist ELAS organization to lay down its arms, pledging his new government will eliminate their fear of dictatorship .... In the offensive against the northern German flank in Belgium, U.S. forces gain up to 3½ miles.			
Jan. 5		Soviet Union extends diplomatic recognition to the provisional government of Poland set up under Russian sponsorship .... U.S. and British forces advance another one to three miles against the northern German flank in Belgium.			
Jan. 6		Hungarian sources report German troops have penetrated 12 to 15 miles into Russian positions northwest of Budapest .... U.S. forces extend the front line against the Nazi bulge in Belgium to 25 miles .... Athens reports that ELAS forces left the capital yesterday and that there was no fighting today.			Egyptian officials report that Saudi Arabian King Ibn Saud has agreed to participate with other Moslem states in a pan-Arab federation.
Jan. 7		Germans open a new counteroffensive against the U.S. 7th Army along the French-German border .... German forces capture the key Danube River fortress city of Esztergom, 19 miles northwest of Budapest.	Maj. Thomas B. McGuire, Jr., the leading U.S. air ace with 38 Japanese planes to his credit, is killed in action off the coast of Luzon in the Philippines.		
Jan. 8		Germans fall back in Belgium, the Saar and in Alsatian border areas .... Soviet troops stave off German attacks northwest and west of Budapest.		Pan-American Union indefinitely postpones consideration of Argentina's request to call a foreign ministers' meeting to consider Argentine foreign policy.	
Jan. 9		German bulge in Belgium is further compressed along its perimeter as the Americans move close to La Roche .... Retreating German forces in the extreme eastern end of the Italian front halt and dig in on the southern bank of the Reno River .... Russian troops drive to within 3½ miles of the Czech supply and transportation center of Komarno near the Hungarian border.	American troops invade Luzon, largest of the Philippine Islands, at Lingayen Gulf, establishing five beachheads. The town of Lingayen and adjoining airstrip are captured .... Chinese troops capture Yamhsien and Limchow on the Kwangtung Province coast .... Australian and New Zealand troops relieve U.S. soldiers on by-passed islands in the Southwest Pacific to mop up Japanese remnants.		

A	B	C	D	E
Includes developments that affect more than one world region, international organizations and important meetings of major world leaders.	*Includes all developments in European countries and military engagements between Allied and Axis powers in Africa and at sea.*	*Includes all developments in Japan and China, Japanese foreign policy and military actions in the Pacific region.*	*Includes all domestic and regional developments in Latin America, the Caribbean and Canada.*	*Includes developments in those independent nations and colonial possessions not covered in Columns B, C and D.*

	U.S. Politics & Social Issues	U.S. Foreign Policy & Defense	U.S. Economy & Environment	Science, Technology & Nature	Culture, Leisure & Life Style
Jan. 1		State Secy. Edward Stettinius announces the U.S. will continue to recognize the Polish government in London.	Dir. Byrnes of the Office of War Mobilization and Reconversion suggests legislation to increase the authority of the WMC and the NWLB so that decisions can be enforced without making property seizures by the military necessary.		Major college bowl scores: Rose, USC 25-Tenn. 0; Sugar, Duke 29-Ala. 26; Orange, Tulsa 26-Ga. Tech. 12; and Cotton, Okla. A&M 34-TCU 0.
Jan. 2	California Supreme Court rules the AFL Boilermakers Union must admit Negroes under the same conditions as whites .... Supreme Court approves new uniform rules for procedures in federal district courts.		Maj. Gen. Joseph Byron, in charge of the Army's seizure of Montgomery Ward & Co., reveals in Chicago that he is displacing key employees who refuse to cooperate with the Army.		In compliance with the government's wartime order, horse racing ends in the U.S. .... John Steinbeck's *Cannery Row* is published.
Jan. 3	The 76th Congress convenes with Sam Rayburn (D, Tex.) reelected as House Speaker .... In an unexpected maneuver, the House votes to make permanent the House Un-American Activities Comm. Seventy Democrats join 137 Republicans in supporting the measure .... Democratic and GOP National Committees report to Congress that they spent $2,056,121.58 and $2,828,651.56, respectively, in the 1944 campaign.	Russian Foreign Secy. Molotov formally hands Amb. Averell Harriman a request for a $6-billion postwar loan in the form of credit for manufactured goods.			A majority of the House committee investigating the FCC issues a report passing favorable judgment on the agency. It urges revision of the Communications Act of 1934 "to meet the developing needs of the radio industry."
Jan. 4					A mistrial is declared in the Los Angeles paternity case against Charlie Chaplin .... Rt. Rev. Dr. Geoffrey Francis Fisher, Bishop of London, is named Archbishop of Canterbury, the 98th to head the Church of England .... Women's swim star Ann Curtis wins the James E. Sullivan Award as the outstanding amateur athlete of 1944.
Jan. 5			Montgomery Ward & Co. files court papers charging the Army's seizure of company property is unconstitutional.	American Section of the Society of Chemical Industry awards the Perkin Medal for applied chemistry to Dr. Elmer Bolton for his work with synthesis of neoprene, the first general purpose synthetic rubber.	
Jan. 6	FDR delivers his "State of the Union" message to Congress and asks passage of a National Service Act to ensure full production for the country's war effort. He also asks for (1) legislation to make use of 4,000,000 4-F's, (2) an amendment to the Selective Service Act providing for the induction of nurses, (3) universal military training after the war to preserve peace, (4) revision of the tax program when the war ends.	Selective Service announces that men up to 38 who leave jobs for which they were deferred without draft board consent will be inducted into the armed services.	War Mobilization Dir. Byrnes submits an affidavit for the Chicago court fight over the seizure of Montgomery Ward & Co. in which he says the firm's conduct, "if allowed to continue, will seriously interfere with the successful prosecution of the war."		
Jan. 7					
Jan. 8		Adm. Jonas Ingram, new chief of the Atlantic fleet, says German robot bombing of New York or Washington within 30 to 60 days is not only "possible but probable."	Government and Montgomery Ward & Co. begin their battle in Chicago federal court to test the power of the President to seize private property .... U.S. Supreme Court rules unconstitutional a Texas law requiring labor organizers to obtain registration cards before soliciting members. The decision reverses the contempt of court conviction of R.J. Thomas, president of the CIO-UAW.		
Jan. 9			In his budget message to Congress, FDR sets expenditures for the 1946 fiscal year at $83 billion, almost $17 billion under 1945 .... Federal Judge Philip Sullivan gives Montgomery Ward & Co. seven days in which to file its answer in the government's suit to establish legality of its seizure of the firm's property.		Internationally known sportsman and former president of the AAU Lord Desborough dies at 89 in Hertfordshire, England.
	F	G	H	I	J
	Includes elections, federal-state relations, civil rights and liberties, crime, the judiciary, education, health care, poverty, urban affairs and population.	*Includes formation and debate of U.S. foreign and defense policies, veterans affairs and defense spending. (Relations with specific foreign countries are usually found under the region concerned.)*	*Includes business, labor, agriculture, taxation, transportation, consumer affairs, monetary and fiscal policy, natural resources, pollution and accidents.*	*Includes worldwide scientific, medical and technological developments, natural phenomena, U.S. weather and natural disasters.*	*Includes the arts, religion, scholarship, communications media, sports, entertainment, fashions, fads and social life.*

	World Affairs	European War Zone	Pacific War Zone	The Americas	Other Countries & Territories
Jan. 10		British report that the Greek National Liberation Front (EAM) has asked for a truce . . . . Russian troops now control three-fourths of Budapest with the capture of 1,000 more blocks, while to the northwest German counterattacks are smashed . . . . Allied pressure on three sides further reduces the German bulge in Belgium with indications that Nazi troops are retreating eastward.	U.S. forces link beachheads at Lingayen Gulf and advance inland.	Argentina announces it will no longer participate in the Pan-American Union as long as it disregards Argentine rights . . . . Mexico announces an Inter-American Foreign Ministers Conference will convene in Mexico City Feb. 15 . . . . FDR nominates Adolf A. Berle, Jr. to be ambassador to Brazil.	Cairo announces Eliahu Bet-Tsouri, 23, and Eliahu Hakim, 20, Jews from Tel Aviv and Haifa, Palestine, go on trial and admit the premeditated murder last Nov. 6 of Lord Moyne, British minister resident in the Middle East.
Jan. 11		Allied troops further reduce the German bulge in Belgium and U.S. forces destroy Nazi units on the Luxembourg border. Hill positions overlooking the Kall River and the Haies-de-Tillet woods are cleared, and Bonnerue, Pironpre, Vesqueville and St. Hubert are occupied. Germans withdraw from the pocket southeast of Bastogne.	American forces extend their line on Luzon to 22 miles and push inland up to nine miles . . . . U.S. carrier aircraft attack Japanese positions along the French Indochina coast, destroying ships and aircraft . . . . British forces take Shwebo, 54 miles north of Mandalay, Burma.		
Jan. 12		As Allied armies push in on all sides the Germans are in full retreat from their Belgian bulge, abandoning some 100 square miles . . . . Terms of the British-ELAS truce are announced. They provide for cessation of hostilities in Greece at 1 a.m., Jan. 15.	U.S. advance on Luzon continues unchecked with the capture of San Carlos and Malasiqui . . . . Philippine Pres. Sergio Osmena arrives in the U.S. for conferences on relief and rehabilitation measures.		
Jan. 13		In an effort to cut off the western Nazi forces from Germany, U.S. troops open a drive on the northern flank in Belgium . . . . Russian troops open a winter offensive in south-central Poland under the command of Marshal Ivan Konev.	U.S. forces on Luzon advance another 20 miles inland against little enemy opposition . . . . Allied forces land on the Burmese west coast some 32 miles below Akyab, getting behind Japanese retreating down the coast.		
Jan. 14		Red Army advances to within 65 miles of southeastern Germany as it gains up to 17 miles in south-central Poland . . . . U.S. forces take Nadrin, Filly, Petite Mormont, Grande Mormont, Wibrin, Cheveoumont, Wilogne and Dinez in Belgium. Germans are cleared from Cobru.	With the capture of Wetlet, British commando units are only 30 miles north of Mandalay.		
Jan. 15		The ceasefire between British and ELAS goes into effect at 12:01 a.m. . . . . American troops enter Houffalize and drive to within six miles of St. Vith, further reducing the German salient. Allied forces seize Bakenhoven, Holland and clear Achouffe, Mont and Tavernaux . . . . Russian troops reach 21 miles northeast of Cracow, Poland.	American troops are reported 28 miles inland from their Luzon beachhead, driving into Tarlac Province, and meeting little Japanese resistance . . . . U.S. announces the Burma-China supply road is complete but not yet operable as the Japanese still hold Wanting on the border.		
Jan. 16		British troops strike at the Maeseyck salient in the Netherlands, 18 miles northeast of Aachen, Germany . . . . Russian troops take Radom in a new offensive in central Poland that outflanks Warsaw on the south.	U.S. troops continue to expand their beachhead on Luzon, pushing 30 miles inland. A Japanese attack on the central part of the beachhead is repulsed.	Gen. Salvador Castaneda Castro is elected president of El Salvador without opposition.	
Jan. 17		Marshal Gregory Zhukov's White Russian Army and forces of the Lublin Poles capture Warsaw five years, three months and 20 days after the Germans marched into the city. Russians sweep around the city on both flanks and penetrate west almost to Lodz . . . . In new gains in the Maeseyck sector of the Netherlands, the British take Dieteren. Americans seize Petit Thier and Vielsalm . . . . A French decree nationalizes the huge Renault automobile works, which will be under "national management" with the workers participating through an "enterprise committee."		Nearly 1,500 persons perish in a sudden flood of the Mosna River in Peru.	
Jan. 18		Berlin radio reports Russian troops have reached the German Silesian border . . . . British forces widen their front in the Netherlands to more than seven miles and gain up to 2½ miles . . . . Churchill tells the House of Commons the Allies still insist on unconditional surrender.	American troops in Luzon, expanding inland from their beachhead, take the town of Urdaneta, an important road center . . . . Japanese launch an attack at both ends of the Canton-Hankow railroad.		A military tribunal in Cairo pronounces the death sentence for Eliahu Hakim and Eliahu Bet-Tsouri, confessed slayers of Lord Moyne, British resident minister in the Middle East.
	A *Includes developments that affect more than one world region, international organizations and important meetings of major world leaders.*	B *Includes all developments in European countries and military engagements between Allied and Axis powers in Africa and at sea.*	C *Includes all developments in Japan and China, Japanese foreign policy and military actions in the Pacific region.*	D *Includes all domestic and regional developments in Latin America, the Caribbean and Canada.*	E *Includes developments in those independent nations and colonial possessions not covered in Columns B, C and D.*

U.S. Politics & Social Issues	U.S. Foreign Policy & Defense	U.S. Economy & Environment	Science, Technology & Nature	Culture, Leisure & Life Style	
	Sen. Arthur Vandenberg (R, Mich.) proposes the U.S., Britain, France, Russia and China immediately sign a treaty to keep Germany and Japan demilitarized . . . . FDR asks the Senate to return the Anglo-American petroleum agreement with a view to drafting a new pact "to remove grounds for misunderstanding."	War Mobilization Dir. Byrnes orders as a fuel conservation measure a ban on ornamental and display lighting, except where excess gas and hydroelectric power is available without drawing on the coal supply.		*Variety* reports the most popular songs are: (1) *Don't Fence Me In*, (2) *There Goes That Song*, and (3) *I'm Making Believe.*	Jan. 10
State Sen. Warren Hooper (R) is found shot to death north of Springport, Mich. He was a principal witness in a special grand jury case against three men charged with conspiracy to bribe legislators.	War Secy. Stimson instructs the Selective Service to raise its March quotas from 80,000 to 100,000 to meet replacement needs.				Jan. 11
Frank Briggs (D) is appointed a U.S. senator from Missouri to serve the remaining two years of the term of Vice President-elect Harry S. Truman.	FDR issues an order placing Nazi saboteurs in the U.S. under the jurisdiction of military tribunals, to be tried by military commissions.				Jan. 12
Atty. Gen. Biddle says 5,000 Japanese in the Tule Lake, Calif. relocation camp have applied for repatriation to Japan.		FDR orders the Army to seize the plants and facilities of the Cleveland Illuminating Co. to end a strike of 400 coal passers and maintenance men that has hampered war production in the area.			Jan. 13
		NWLB reports it closed approximately 362,000 voluntary and dispute cases affecting 24 million employes since its founding three years ago.	U.S. Army research reveals that jaundice is a disease transferred from person to person through flies, polluted water and other means in much the same way as dysentery.		Jan. 14
	War Dept. announces that stern measures have been taken to wipe out Gestapo-like terrorism in prison camps in the U.S. housing German war prisoners.	War Mobilization Dir. Byrnes calls on Selective Service Dir. Hershey to apply a priority system to control inductions of war workers in order to give the maximum protection to war production . . . . WPB announces that effective Feb. 1 outdoor illumination for advertising and the like will be ended to save an estimated two million tons of coal annually.			Jan. 15
		Commerce Dept. reports that Americans in 1944 spent more than $7 billion for alcoholic beverages, an increase of 18% over the 1943 spending.		FDR says he favors continuation of baseball this season if it can be done without interfering with war production and without using healthy young men . . . . U.S. Jr. Chamber of Commerce announces its selection of Asst. Secy. of State Nelson Rockefeller as the "nation's outstanding young man" of 1944 . . . . George W. (Gilbert) Patten, who used the pen name of Burt L. Standish in writing the "Frank Merriwell" stories, dies at 78 in Vista, Calif.	Jan. 16
	In a letter to Chmn. Andrew May of the House Military Affairs Comm., FDR appeals for quick enactment of "work-or-fight" legislation for men 18 to 45.				Jan. 17
	WPB reports U.S. war expenditures in 1944 totaled $94.174 billion, a 7.1% increase over 1943.	NWLB rules that an employe who leaves his regular job for another at the request or order of the WMC accumulates seniority in his original job as though he never left it . . . . Federal government files suit in Newark, N.J. against General Electric, charging conspiracy with foreign manufacturers, including German and Japanese concerns, to divide world markets for electrical goods.			Jan. 18

F	G	H	I	J
Includes elections, federal-state relations, civil rights and liberties, crime, the judiciary, education, health care, poverty, urban affairs and population.	*Includes formation and debate of U.S. foreign and defense policies, veterans affairs and defense spending. (Relations with specific foreign countries are usually found under the region concerned.)*	*Includes business, labor, agriculture, taxation, transportation, consumer affairs, monetary and fiscal policy, natural resources, pollution and accidents.*	*Includes worldwide scientific, medical and technological developments, natural phenomena, U.S. weather and natural disasters.*	*Includes the arts, religion, scholarship, communications media, sports, entertainment, fashions, fads and social life.*

	World Affairs	European War Zone	Pacific War Zone	The Americas	Other Countries & Territories
Jan. 19	FDR announces the U.S., Britain and Canada have agreed to continue the Combined Production and Resources Bd., the Combined Raw Materials Bd. and the Combined Food Bd. until Japan is defeated.	Russian armies capture Lodz and Cracow, Poland .... Russia notifies UNRRA that its port and inland transportation systems needed to take relief supplies to Poland and Czechoslovakia are now available .... As the British make further advances in the Netherlands, the Americans tighten pressure on the German salient in the Ardennes.			
Jan. 20		Hungarian provisional government established at Debrecen signs an agreement with the Allies in Moscow providing for unconditional surrender, a declaration of war against Germany and reparations of $300 million .... In a surprise offensive French troops move forward from the Vosges Mountains to the Rhine in the Alsace sector of Mulhouse .... East Prussian stronghold of Tilsit is taken by the Russians.	The important communications center and provincial capital of Tarlac, 65 miles north of Manila, is taken by the Americans .... American carrier-based planes attack Formosa, the Pescadores and Sakishima island groups, reportedly destroying 140 enemy aircraft .... Chinese troops capture Wanting, eliminating the last enemy resistance along the old land route to India through northern Burma.		
Jan. 21		Russian troops invade German Silesia on a 56-mile front, driving 19 miles beyond the border between Reinersdorf and Guttentag .... Germans abandon 22 square miles in the Ardennes bulge.	Japanese Premier Kuniaki Koiso announes a drastic manpower mobilization law and tells the Diet that the U.S. offensive has brought the country to the brink of life or death.		
Jan. 22		Russian troops sweep through East Prussia, taking Insterburg in the east and Allenstein, Osterode and Deutsch Eylau in the south .... U.S. planes unleash a merciless assault on the Germans retreating from the Ardennes.	British commando forces carry out their fourth amphibious operation in Burma, landing on the Arakan coast four miles southwest of Kangaw to cut the enemy's Myohaung-Taungup escape route.		
Jan. 23	FDR secretly leaves Newport News, Va. aboard the *U.S.S. Quincy* to attend the Yalta Conference with Churchill and Stalin.	Russian units reach the Oder River in Silesia along a 37-mile front in the vicinity of Breslau. The capture of Tost and Bischofstal to the south cuts off the Silesian coal basin .... American troops take St. Vith, Belgium, as the German salient in the Ardennes is compressed to a five-mile strip.		Guatemala severs diplomatic relations with Spain on the grounds that the Spanish Falange is a threat to the Americas.	
Jan. 24		British troops take Weerd, Aandenberg and Montfort in the Netherlands and Heinsberg in Germany. Americans take Aldringen and Moderscheid .... Russian units take Oppeln, Silesia and advance to within four miles of Breslau.			
Jan. 25		Germans increase their threat to Strasbourg with a 2,000-yard advance in the Hagenau Forest and a crossing of the Moder River. British take Linne, Putbrock and Kirchhoven. Americans take Wallerode, Medel, Ambleve and Mirfeld .... Russian forces advance to within four miles of Posen and cut the Nazis' escape corridor in East Prussia to 11 miles.	MacArthur's troops capture the Clark Field airstrips and nearby Fort Stotsenburg on Luzon.	Russian Amb. to Mexico Constantine Oumansky and his wife are killed in a plane crash outside Mexico City.	
Jan. 26		Russian troops reach the Baltic Sea at Tolkemit, thus cutting East Prussia off from the rest of Germany .... U.S. Army troops join the attack north of Aachen, supporting the British against the German salient west of the Roer River.	Japanese drive against U.S. airbases in southeastern China continues to progress in Hunan, Kiangsi and Kwangtung provinces.		
Jan. 27		Russian armies surround Posen and Torun, Poland and push within four miles of Koenigsberg, East Prussia .... As the remainder of the bulge in Belgium and the Netherlands is nearly wiped out, the Germans retreat to near the Siegfried Line .... FDR's assistant Harry Hopkins arrives in Paris to confer with de Gaulle.	Allied planes from the Marianas attack Tokyo, destroying 31 enemy planes, while India-based planes bomb Saigon for the first time .... Japanese shell Clark Field from well-prepared hill positions .... Allied forces land on Cheduba Island, 32 miles off the Burmese coast.		

	A	B	C	D	E
	Includes developments that affect more than one world region, international organizations and important meetings of major world leaders.	*Includes all developments in European countries and military engagements between Allied and Axis powers in Africa and at sea.*	*Includes all developments in Japan and China, Japanese foreign policy and military actions in the Pacific region.*	*Includes all domestic and regional developments in Latin America, the Caribbean and Canada.*	*Includes developments in those independent nations and colonial possessions not covered in Columns B, C and D.*

U.S. Politics & Social Issues	U.S. Foreign Policy & Defense	U.S. Economy & Environment	Science, Technology & Nature	Culture, Leisure & Life Style	
	State Secy. Stettinius announces he will accompany FDR to the meeting with Churchill and Stalin and that he will also attend the Inter-American Conference in Mexico City.	Federal government files suit in Trenton, N.J., charging 18 steel concerns, including Carnegie, Republic and Bethlehem, with conspiring to fix prices and restrain trade since 1934.			Jan. 19
FDR is sworn in at the White House for his fourth term in the simplest and smallest inauguration on record. Truman is sworn in as vice president by retiring Henry A. Wallace. In his inaugural address, FDR pledges to work for victory and a secure and durable peace . . . . A 24-hour guard is put on the farm of a Japanese-American in Placer County, Calif. to protect the alien's property against vigilantes.	FDR nominates former Sen. Guy Gillette as chairman of the Surplus War Property Administration.			Gil Dodds announces his retirement from track to devote full time to gospel work in Los Angeles after winning the two-mile run in the Boston YMCA games.	Jan. 20
Commerce Secy. Jones reveals correspondence from FDR asking him to surrender his posts to Henry A. Wallace.					Jan. 21
FDR nominates Aubrey Williams to head the REA and Henry Wallace as Secretary of Commerce . . . . In a move against the Wallace nomination, Sen. Walter George, (D, Ga.), introduces a bill to remove from the Commerce Department all lending agencies and return them to their status as of September 1940 . . . . GOP National Comm. adopts a program to establish a fulltime national headquarters in Washington to prepare for the 1946 and 1948 campaigns and names Mrs. Dudley Hay as secretary.					Jan. 22
					Jan. 23
FDR asks Labor Secy. Frances Perkins to remain in her post, scotching rumors she would quit the cabinet . . . . Commerce Secy. Jones announces his support of the separation of the RFC from the Commerce Dept. because of Wallace's "untried ideas and idealistic schemes."	May-Bailey bill providing "limited national service" for men in the 18-45 age group is approved and reported out by the House Military Affairs Comm.				Jan. 24
	A survey by Selective Service reveals that 40.3% of the men called for the draft at age 28 are rejected as physically unfit.	NLRB announces the collective bargaining elections for Western Union resulted in AFL victories in all sections of the country save metropolitan N.Y., which chose the CIO . . . . Assn. of American Railroads orders a 72-hour freight embargo effective Jan. 27 on everything but war material.			Jan. 25
Former Missouri Democratic political boss Thomas Pendergast dies at 72 in Kansas City . . . . Senate Commerce Comm. turns down Henry A. Wallace as Secretary of Commerce and approves the George bill to separate federal lending agencies from the Department.	Herbert Pell reportedly will not return to London as the American commissioner of the U.N. War Crimes Commission because of the congressional failure to appropriate $30,000 for his salary and expenses.			A syndicate consisting of Larry MacPhail, Dan Topping and Del Webb buys 96.88% of the N.Y. Yankees and its minor league properties for $2.8 million from the hiers of the late Col. Jacob Ruppert.	Jan. 26
		Federal Judge Philip Sullivan rules in Chicago that the FDR-directed Army seizure of Montgomery Ward property in seven localities was illegal.			Jan. 27

F	G	H	I	J
Includes elections, federal-state relations, civil rights and liberties, crime, the judiciary, education, health care, poverty, urban affairs and population.	*Includes formation and debate of U.S. foreign and defense policies, veterans affairs and defense spending. (Relations with specific foreign countries are usually found under the region concerned.)*	*Includes business, labor, agriculture, taxation, transportation, consumer affairs, monetary and fiscal policy, natural resources, pollution and accidents.*	*Includes worldwide scientific, medical and technological developments, natural phenomena, U.S. weather and natural disasters.*	*Includes the arts, religion, scholarship, communications media, sports, entertainment, fashions, fads and social life.*

	World Affairs	European War Zone	Pacific War Zone	The Americas	Other Countries & Territories
Jan. 28		Russians take Memel in Lithuania and clear the Germans from southern German-Polish Silesia, areas that produce 20% of Germany's coal supply .... In a sudden attack U.S. troops move northeast of St. Vith and gain up to two miles, while the French to the south threaten to outflank Colmar.	The first convoy of American supplies from India arrives at Wanting .... Japanese troops capture Kukong, Kwangtung Province, the last Chinese strongpoint on the Hankow-Canton railway, thus cutting the eastern section of the country to the coast from the rest of China .... American troops take Angeles in Pampanga Province, only 44 air miles northwest of Manila.		
Jan. 29		American troops break into Germany from the Ardennes bulge, crossing at the Our River near Oberhausen and Peterskirsche, and capture Schlierbach, Setz, Welchenhausen and Stupbach .... Russian troops invade Germany's northeastern province of Pomerania on a 30-mile front, driving to Woldenberg, only 93 miles from Berlin .... Yugoslavian King Peter II abandons his stand against plans for a regency.	American troops take Rosario in northeastern Luzon after two weeks of fighting. Other forces land on the island's west coast, establishing beachheads in Zambales Province.	Argentine government decrees drastic penalties for almost every form of treason, espionage and sabotage.	
Jan. 30	FDR and Churchill meet at Malta for discussions preparatory to the Yalta meeting.	A strong American push into Germany develops on a broad front directed at the Siegfried Line .... Russian drive on Berlin goes unchecked with a 21-mile gain .... In a radio broadcast Hitler tells the German people that there is still hope for victory by maintaining unity.	Japanese advance on the Hankow-Canton railroad reduces the line to a 20-mile section in Hunan Province .... American rangers and Filipino guerrillas free 513 prisoners from the Cabanatuan prison camp near Cabu.		
Jan. 31		Russians capture Beyersdorf and are within 63 miles of Berlin .... U.S. forces drive into the Monschau Forest in Germany and complete the capture of Rocherath, Andler, Schonberg, Amelscheid, Heuem and Alzerath .... U.N. War Crimes Commission elects Lord Wright of Australia as chairman.	American forces go ashore on the west coast of Batangas Province, thus outflanking Manila to the south.	U.S. and Canada reach an agreement whereby Ottawa will pay for defense facilities established in Canada that will not be removed at the war's end.	
Feb. 1		Sofia radio announces that death sentences have been pronounced for "treason" upon three former Bulgarian regents—Prince Cyril, former Premier Bodgan Philov and Lt. Gen. Nikola Mikhov—22 former cabinet ministers and nine king's counselors .... Americans find little German resistance on the Siegfried Line, recording advances of up to two miles .... Russian troops gain 12 miles in eastern Germany, reaching Liebenow.			
Feb. 2	Malta Conference ends after FDR and Churchill discuss Eisenhower's plans for driving up to and across the Rhine and agree to withdraw two divisions from Greece and three from Italy to reinforce northwest Europe. They proceed to the Crimea for the Yalta Conference with Stalin .... At its London meeting, the general council of the International Fed. of Trade Unions shelves future consideration of a report proposing the entry of the CIO and Russian trade unions.	Dr. Karl Goerdeler is hanged at Plotzensee prison for plotting against Hitler .... In East Prussia the Russians take Petershagen, Domnau and Germau, gaining control of most of the province.	Establishing a bridgehead across the Angat River at Bustos, U.S. forces push to within 15 miles of Manila, as other units advance halfway across the Bataan Peninsula.	A commission investigating utility company concessions in Argentina recommends the dissolution of virtually all the Argentine subsidiaries of the American & Foreign Power Co.	
Feb. 3		American bombers drop 2,266 tons of bombs on Berlin in the most concentrated attack on the city to date .... U.S. forces clear Belgium of last Germans with the capture of Krewinkel .... Russian forces reach a point six miles west of Kuestrin and 11 miles west of Frankfurt an der Oder in their drive on Berlin .... Peace talks between the Greek government and EAM-ELAS factions open in Athens.	Forces of U.S. 6th Army break into the suburbs of Manila. They liberate over 5,000 Allied prisoners held at the Manila General Hospital, the University of Manila and other locations.		
Feb. 4	Yalta Conference opens with FDR, Churchill and Stalin conferring principally on the problem of the Polish government. Other matters include Soviet participation in the Far Eastern war.	Russian units make a 19-mile advance on the Oder River front and outflank Kuestrin on the north, driving a wedge between it and Stettin on the Baltic .... U.S. troops continue their advance with the capture of Ruhrberg, Einruhr, Urft, Morsbach and Gerhahn.			

A	B	C	D	E
Includes developments that affect more than one world region, international organizations and important meetings of major world leaders.	*Includes all developments in European countries and military engagements between Allied and Axis powers in Africa and at sea.*	*Includes all developments in Japan and China, Japanese foreign policy and military actions in the Pacific region.*	*Includes all domestic and regional developments in Latin America, the Caribbean and Canada.*	*Includes developments in those independent nations and colonial possessions not covered in Columns B, C and D.*

U.S. Politics & Social Issues	U.S. Foreign Policy & Defense	U.S. Economy & Environment	Science, Technology & Nature	Culture, Leisure & Life Style	
	The 27,000-ton aircraft carrier *Antietam* is commissioned in Philadelphia.			Sammy Byrd wins the Texas Open Golf Tournament, beating Byron Nelson by one stroke.	Jan. 28
Harry Bridges wins a U.S. Supreme Court petition for a review of the government's deportation order.		Justice Dept. files a suit against seven companies and nine individuals, charging a conspiracy to restrict production, monopolize sales and arbitrarily inflate prices of 95% of the world's diamond output.			Jan. 29
		Gov. Dewey proclaims a statewide emergency affecting transportation and delivery of coal and livestock feed in New York due to drastically bad weather tying up transportation.	*Medical Press and Circular* announces in London the discovery of a new drug called hypholin which is made from penicillin notatum. It has been successfully used in cases of meningitis, osteomyelitis, pneumonia, impetigo and staphylococcale.	Football coach William Alexander—at Ga. Tech since 1920—announces his resignation. Bobby Dodd is named his successor.	Jan. 30
		U.S. government carries its case against the Montgomery Ward & Co. to the Circuit Court of Appeals . . . . Commerce Dept. reports that exports in 1943, including Lend-Lease, broke all records with a value of $14.065 billion.		Five Brooklyn College basketball players—Robert Leder, Lawrence Pearlstein, Stanley Simon, Jerome Greene and Bernard Barret—admit accepting a $1,000 bribe to "throw" a game with Akron Univ. in Boston tonight.	Jan. 31
Senate passes the George bill separating lending agencies from the Commerce Dept.	House passes and sends to the Senate the May-Bailey bill providing "limited national service" for men 18-45 . . . . Acting State Secy. Grew says in a Washington statement there is no question that Germans responsible for war crimes within the Reich will be punished.			*The Thurber Carnival* by James Thurber is published.	Feb. 1
		Due to the tight fuel situation the WPB orders the cutting off of natural gas in amusement places in N.Y., Pa., Ohio, D.C. and parts of Md. and Va.	American Institute of Chemists reports the awarding of its gold medal to John M. Thomas for his contributions to synthetic rubber.		Feb. 2
	New York Times says 50 senators favor Sen. Vandenburg's proposal for immediate Allied pacts to keep Germany and Japan demilitarized.			Club owners of the American and National League baseball teams adopt a new charter with only one major change, whereby the owners cannot appeal decisions of the commissioners to the courts.	Feb. 3
	American Bankers Assn. announces a proposal for an international financial organization that would include the International Bank for Reconstruction and Development but would eliminate the International Monetary Fund.				Feb. 4

F	G	H	I	J
Includes elections, federal-state relations, civil rights and liberties, crime, the judiciary, education, health care, poverty, urban affairs and population.	*Includes formation and debate of U.S. foreign and defense policies, veterans affairs and defense spending. (Relations with specific foreign countries are usually found under the region concerned.)*	*Includes business, labor, agriculture, taxation, transportation, consumer affairs, monetary and fiscal policy, natural resources, pollution and accidents.*	*Includes worldwide scientific, medical and technological developments, natural phenomena, U.S. weather and natural disasters.*	*Includes the arts, religion, scholarship, communications media, sports, entertainment, fashions, fads and social life.*

	World Affairs	European War Zone	Pacific War Zone	The Americas	Other Countries & Territories
Feb. 5	De Gaulle lists minimum French terms for peace in Europe and serves notice that France will not be bound by any U.S.-British-Russian decisions until it is treated as an equal partner.	The first concentrated Allied offensive in Italy against the Germans in more than three months opens 10 miles below Bologna .... White Russian troops line up along the Oder River on a 75-mile front, pushing to within 33 miles of Berlin with the capture of Zellin .... U.S. forces take the important communications center of Brandscheid on the Siegfried Line.			
Feb. 6		Russians break across the Oder River and establish a 50-mile-long bridgehead on the western bank .... Americans reach to within less than three miles of the largest of five dams controlling the level of the Roer River.	Japanese take the abandoned U.S. airbase sites at Namyung, Kwangtung Province and Kanhsien, Kiangsi Province.		
Feb. 7		Four U.S. divisions cross the German frontier opposite Luxembourg at 10 places, bridging the Our and Sauer Rivers .... Russian troops extend their hold on the east bank of the Oder River, capturing Zaeckerick, 31 miles from the capital .... Belgian Premier Pierlot resigns with his cabinet in anticipation of an unfavorable vote in parliament.	U.S. forces close in on downtown Manila. Much of the old city, dating from Spanish colonial period, is destroyed by American artillery fire and Japanese demolitions.	Paraguayan Council of State approves a declaration of war against the Axis.	
Feb. 8		British and Canadian troops open an offensive against the northern end of the Siegfried Line southeast of Nijmegen, Netherlands .... Premier Pieter S. Gerbrandy of the Netherlands government-in-exile and his cabinet resign .... Russian forces take Bernstein and Reetz in their drive on Stettin on the Baltic.			
Feb. 9		Canadian drive on the Siegfried Line overruns six villages and spreads out along a 10-mile front .... Stockholm reports German authorities in Norway executed a total of 34 Norwegians yesterday and today in reprisal for growing sabotage and for the assassination yesterday of Maj. Gen. Carl Martinsen, commander of Quisling's elite guards .... With the capture of Brallentin, the Red Army moves to within 29 miles southeast of Stettin.	In fierce fighting, the Japanese offer bitter resistance in southern Manila.	American & Foreign Power Co. announces an agreement with Chile for the latter's purchase of properties in Santiago, Valparaiso and San Bernardo.	Three days of rioting for food and clothing subside in Cairo after one student is killed.
Feb. 10	London Poles present a list of 29 proposals to the U.S. and Britain for amending the Dumbarton Oaks world security program, including the denial of veto rights in aggression cases and enlargement of the security council to 15 members.	FDR's special assistant Samuel Rosenman arrives in London with his advisers to study the economic problems of the liberated countries and the occupation of Germany .... After the Germans blast open the flood gates of the main Roer River dam at Schwammenauel, the Americans take control of it .... Russian forces capture the East Prussian port of Elbing.	An earthquake described as "fairly severe" strikes the main Japanese island of Honshu. Among the cities affected are Tokyo and Yokohama, the country's largest. Damage is not reported, but American sources estimate that it is extensive.		
Feb. 11	Yalta Conference ends with a secret agreement on Poland providing for the inclusion of non-Communist representatives in the Lublin Committee and non-recognition of the Polish government-in-exile in London. The question of Poland's western boundary is left to future negotiations. It is agreed that Germany will be divided into occupation zones—the Soviets to control up to 200 miles west of Berlin, the British to administer the northwest, and the U.S. the remainder, south of the Saar and the Palatinate. They agree to eliminate all German industry that could be used for military production, try war criminals and impose reparations to be paid by Germany. A secret agreement is also made that Russia will enter the Pacific War two or three months after the surrender of Germany in return for the annexation of territory lost to Imperial Russia during the 1904-5 Russo-Japanese War. The U.N. charter and voting format of the Security Council are also agreed to.	British troops enter Cleve, Germany on the northern end of the Siegfried Line .... After a four-day offensive the Russians move 37 miles west of the Oder River along a 100-mile front, resulting in the virtual encirclement of Breslau .... A new Belgian government is formed with Socialist Achille van Acker as premier and with participation by all four political parties.			

A	B	C	D	E
Includes developments that affect more than one world region, international organizations and important meetings of major world leaders.	*Includes all developments in European countries and military engagements between Allied and Axis powers in Africa and at sea.*	*Includes all developments in Japan and China, Japanese foreign policy and military actions in the Pacific region.*	*Includes all domestic and regional developments in Latin America, the Caribbean and Canada.*	*Includes developments in those independent nations and colonial possessions not covered in Columns B, C and D.*

U.S. Politics & Social Issues	U.S. Foreign Policy & Defense	U.S. Economy & Environment	Science, Technology & Nature	Culture, Leisure & Life Style	
Legislative action on the repeal of the Georgia poll tax law is completed in Atlanta when the state Senate passes a bill restoring permanent registration.		Supreme Court denies the right of the Treasury Dept. to order that only an "official" rate be used in converting British pounds into dollars for customs duty purposes.			Feb. 5
					Feb. 6
				NYSE and the Philadelphia Stock Exchange announce they will report daily sales in round totals in an effort to deprive numbers game operators of the basis for their gambling activities . . . . AFL American Fed. of Musicians notifies the four radio networks that the National Music Camp at Interlochen, Mich. has been placed on its "unfair list," which bars musicians there from commercial employment.	Feb. 7
Conn. Gov. Raymond E. Baldwin names Adm. Thomas Hart (R) to fill the unexpired U.S. Senate term of the late Francis Maloney (D).	State Dept. completes a Lend-Lease and reciprocal trade agreement with Jean Monnet of France . . . . First private bank loan to be made by N.Y. banks to a foreign country outside of Lend-Lease is made to the Netherlands by a group of 14 banks headed by Chase Manhattan for $100 million . . . . N.Y. Gov. Dewey urges a strong role for the U.S. in world affairs and backs Sen. Vandenberg's demand for an immediate Allied pact on postwar treatment of the Axis.			Lt. Paul Brown is signed to a five-year contract as coach, effective when he leaves the service, with the newly proposed Cleveland team of the All-American Football Conference.	Feb. 8
House Rules Comm. adjourns without approving submission to the House of the Senate-passed George bill, divorcing lending agencies from the Commerce Dept. This also holds up the vote on Wallace's nomination as Commerce Secretary.		Without public explanation, the Army releases control of two Chicago Montgomery Ward properties.			Feb. 9
		Government officials warn that meat may virtually disappear from civilian markets by mid-summer.		*Carmen Jones* and *One Touch of Venus* close on Broadway.	Feb. 10
		AFL makes public a housing program designed to provide 19 million post-war jobs through construction of 15 million homes in the 10 years after the war.		Publication of the newspaper, *The Flat Hat*, at the College of William & Mary is suspended due to an editorial by Marily Kaemmerle, which suggests the time will come for interracial education, social contacts and marriage . . . . Al Dubin, lyricist of scores of popular songs, including *Among My Souvenirs* and *Tip-Toe Through the Tulips*, dies at 54 in New York.	Feb. 11

F	G	H	I	J
Includes elections, federal-state relations, civil rights and liberties, crime, the judiciary, education, health care, poverty, urban affairs and population.	*Includes formation and debate of U.S. foreign and defense policies, veterans affairs and defense spending. (Relations with specific foreign countries are usually found under the region concerned.)*	*Includes business, labor, agriculture, taxation, transportation, consumer affairs, monetary and fiscal policy, natural resources, pollution and accidents.*	*Includes worldwide scientific, medical and technological developments, natural phenomena, U.S. weather and natural disasters.*	*Includes the arts, religion, scholarship, communications media, sports, entertainment, fashions, fads and social life.*

	World Affairs	European War Zone	Pacific War Zone	The Americas	Other Countries & Territories
Feb. 12		Greek government reaches agreement with EAM-ELAS calling for an end to hostilities there .... Soviet forces reach the Bober River with a 16-mile advance in Silesia that includes the occupation of Bunzlau .... British units capture Cleve and with Canadian forces push south through Reichswald, while further south on the Siegfried Line U.S. units take Pruem.	American armored units split Luzon from coast to coast, reaching the east coast at Dingalan Bay.	Peru announces it is in a "state of belligerency" with Germany and Japan.	
Feb. 13		London Poles reject the Yalta proposals on Poland, claiming they provide for the fifth partition of the country and that they violate the principles of the Atlantic Charter .... The Russians complete the conquest of Budapest after a 50-day siege which cost the Axis 159,000 troops—the largest single loss since Stalingrad in 1943 .... U.S. troops create a 10-mile bridgehead across the Our and Sauer Rivers near Echternach with a depth of up to two miles.	U.S. forces occupy Nichols Airfield and the Cavite Naval Base in the outskirts of Manila.		French cabinet announces it will create a large military base at Dakar, French West Africa to guarantee the communications of the French Empire and contribute to collective security.
Feb. 14		British P.M. Churchill and Foreign Secy. Eden arrive in Athens as martial law in Greece ends and all sentences passed by military courts in their trials of ELAS supporters are annulled .... About 8,000 Allied planes make day and night attacks on Germany .... In their drive on Berlin and Dresden, the Russians take seven major German strongholds—Neustaedtel, Neusalz, Freystadt, Sprottau, Goldberg, Jauer and Striegau .... London says German radio today urged the Germans to "cast overboard our last scruples" and "kill, murder and poison" Allied troops.	Forces of U.S. 6th Army attack the Japanese garrison of Fort McKinley in southeastern Manila. Other American units begin clearing operations on the Bataan peninsula, the first of moves intended to reopen Manila Bay .... Chinese forces break the Japanese hold on the Canton-Hankow railroad with the capture of Pingshek, 165 miles north of Canton .... Chinese Nationalists and Communists meet to negotiate their differences with the aid of U.S. Amb. Patrick Hurley.		A conference of Arab leaders opens in Cairo to consider a federation plan including Egypt, Arab Palestine, Iraq, Syria, Transjordan and Saudi Arabia.
Feb. 15	Washington reports that the U.N. membership has reached 40 nations with the addition of Peru, Paraguay, Chile, and Ecuador.	Russian troops cross from Silesia into Brandenburg to threaten Berlin from the south and to drive a wedge between Berlin and Dresden.	U.S. troops land at several places around Mariveles Bay on the southern side of Bataan, seven miles from Corregidor .... Chungking announces plans to draft 500,000 men into its army.	Jeptha Duncan is sworn in as president of Panama by Alfredo Aleman, president of the National Assembly in exile at Curundu, Canal Zone. He says he was designated first vice president by the Assembly and that he is the legal successor to President Ricardo Adolfo de la Guardia today under the 1941 Constitution. He also names a cabinet.	
Feb. 16	World Trade Union Congress in London adopts a program for participation in the peace settlement, including these points: (1) authorities occupying Germany shall recognize the voice of labor, (2) the trade union movement should be consulted on the use of material and manpower for restoration of Germany, (3) that Dumbarton Oaks is obligated to put an end to international cartels and monopolies, and (4) that provision should be made for labor representation in the U.N.	European director of the American Jewish Joint Distribution Comm., Dr. Joseph Schwartz, estimates that only one to one-and-a-half million of six million Jews are still alive on the European continent .... In a 17-mile gain on the Oder River, the Russians come to within 62 miles southeast of Berlin.	U.S. paratroopers and sea assault units invade Corregidor, making quick advances against little Japanese resistance.	Argentina closes the newspapers *Cabildo* and *Pampero*, both anti-U.S., on the grounds that they were printed on imported newsprint and that this was protested by several foreign ministers.	
Feb. 17	World Trade Union Congress in London ends today after an 11-day session which failed to bring establishment of a new world labor organization to replace the International Federation of Trade Unions.	British and Canadian troops divide the German lines in the West by cutting the Goch-Calcar highway .... Russian troops breach the Germans' Queis River defenses, reaching Rauscha some 60 miles northeast of Dresden.	Two days of assaults on the Tokyo area by U.S. planes result in the loss of 177 Japanese planes and the sinking of 14 ships. Americans lose 49 planes.	Ambassadors of Peru and Ecuador sign an agreement ending the 120-year-old border dispute between the two countries.	
Feb. 18		Americans expand their bridgehead over the Our and Sauer Rivers north of Echternach to five miles .... Russians move to 16 miles east of city of Goerlitz, which guards Dresden, and complete mop-ups in Pomerania and Brandenburg.	Japanese retake the town of Pingshek, again regaining control of the Canton-Hankow railway .... *Pravda* charges that China is not giving its full effort to the war.		
Feb. 19			Iwo Jima, 750 miles south of Tokyo, is invaded by 30,000 U.S. Marines at 9 a.m. Intense resistance from the 20,000-man Japanese garrison causes 2,400 American casualties on invasion day. By nightfall Marines have advanced across southern part of the island, cutting off Japanese defenders on Mt. Suribachi from forces in the north .... American troops take Fort McKinley and force the Japanese into a one-square-mile pocket in southern Manila.	Declaring the present government has fulfilled requirements of international law, the U.S. announces recognition of the new El Salvador regime.	

A	B	C	D	E
Includes developments that affect more than one world region, international organizations and important meetings of major world leaders.	*Includes all developments in European countries and military engagements between Allied and Axis powers in Africa and at sea.*	*Includes all developments in Japan and China, Japanese foreign policy and military actions in the Pacific region.*	*Includes all domestic and regional developments in Latin America, the Caribbean and Canada.*	*Includes developments in those independent nations and colonial possessions not covered in Columns B, C and D.*

U.S. Politics & Social Issues	U.S. Foreign Policy & Defense	U.S. Economy & Environment	Science, Technology & Nature	Culture, Leisure & Life Style	
	FDR urges Congress to take prompt action on the Bretton Woods proposals, declaring that U.S. participation in a world fund and bank are essential for a peaceful and prosperous world.	Commerce Dept. reports that personal income reached a record high in 1944, totaling $157 billion.	A tornado sweeps through Meridian, Miss. eastward to Montgomery, Ala., taking 43 lives and causing heavy property damage.		Feb. 12
				National Institute of Arts and Letters awards its 1945 gold medal to sculptor Paul Manship for his achievements.	Feb. 13
	A military commission at Governors Island finds William Colepaugh and Erich Gimpel guilty of espionage and sentences them to death.	Justice Dept. files a petition asking the Supreme Court to assume jurisdiction in the Montgomery Ward case .... Stabilization Dir. Vinson orders the Army and Navy to cancel contracts with E.A. Laboratories, Inc. because it failed to comply with an NWLB order.		The students of William and Mary College accept a proposal for partial faculty supervision of their newspaper, *The Flat Hat*.	Feb. 14
N.J. Atty. Gen. Walter Van Riper is indicted by a Trenton federal grand jury on black market charges involving gasoline.	Bills are introduced in both Houses of Congress seeking approval of the Bretton Woods financial and monetary agreements .... Treasury Dept. announces that the Baltic zone is no longer under German control and thus will not be considered "enemy territory," thus ending bans on business and communications in that area.	AFL Executive Council announces that negotiations with the CIO-UMW remain stalemated because of John L. Lewis's demand for a Council seat.	Lederle Laboratories in New York announces Dr. Raymond Libby of the American Cyanamid Co. has developed a method for administering penicillin by mouth. The medicine is suspended in cottonseed oil and placed in a gelatin capsule for consumption.		Feb. 15
House passes the George bill divorcing lending agencies from the Commerce Dept.	War Dept. announces draft registrants under 38 who are not physically qualified for general military service but who have left essential war jobs are being inducted into the Army.			Drew Pearson, author of the newspaper column *Washington Merry-Go-Round*, starts a suit for libel in N.Y. against columnist Westbrook Pegler, charging Pegler with writing that Pearson is "a miscalled news broadcaster specializing in falsehoods and smearing people with political and personal motivation." .... Minneapolis radio station KSTP ends an 11-month fight against American Fed. of Musicians Pres. James Petrillo and gives in to union demands to employ an additional eight musicians 22 hours weekly at $52 each.	Feb. 16
		S.D. Gov. M.Q. Sharpe (R) signs a bill ending the closed shop in that state.			Feb. 17
					Feb. 18
				War Mobilization Dir. Byrnes "requests" all places of entertainment in the country to observe a midnight curfew beginning Feb. 26 for an indefinite period to conserve energy .... Willie Pep successfully defends his featherweight title with a 15-round decision over Phil Terranova in Madison Sq. Garden.	Feb. 19

F	G	H	I	J
Includes elections, federal-state relations, civil rights and liberties, crime, the judiciary, education, health care, poverty, urban affairs and population.	*Includes formation and debate of U.S. foreign and defense policies, veterans affairs and defense spending. (Relations with specific foreign countries are usually found under the region concerned.)*	*Includes business, labor, agriculture, taxation, transportation, consumer affairs, monetary and fiscal policy, natural resources, pollution and accidents.*	*Includes worldwide scientific, medical and technological developments, natural phenomena, U.S. weather and natural disasters.*	*Includes the arts, religion, scholarship, communications media, sports, entertainment, fashions, fads and social life.*

	World Affairs	European War Zone	Pacific War Zone	The Americas	Other Countries & Territories
Feb. 20		Russian troops battle to within eight miles of Guben, an outer fortress of Berlin . . . . Soviet units push into the Polish Corridor to within 40 miles of Danzig.	Marines advance against the Japanese central airfield on Iwo Jima, while other units advance yard-by-yard up the slopes of Mt. Suribachi . . . . MacArthur announces that the remaining Japanese in southern Manilla have been compressed into an area approximately 1,200 by 800 yards.	Venezuela formally adheres to the U.N. declaration.	FDR meets at Great Bitter Lake with King Farouk of Egypt, Emperor Haile Selassie of Ethiopia and King Ibn Saud of Saudi Arabia. Progress of the war and politics of the Middle East are discussed.
Feb. 21		Russians reach the confluence of the Oder and Neisse Rivers, 45 miles southeast of Berlin . . . . American troops regain Mt. Belvedere on the Bologna front in Italy . . . . Twenty-nine former Greek cabinet ministers go on trial for collaboration with the enemy.	Japanese planes made seven direct bomb hits on the aircraft carrier *Saratoga* off Iwo Jima, killing 123 and wounding 192. The carrier makes for Puget Sound Navy Yard for repairs.	Inter-American Conference to discuss problems of war and peace opens in Mexico City with Argentina absent.	
Feb. 22		As infantry units cross the Saar River in assault boats south of Saarburg, U.S. troops clear the Germans from the triangle between the Saar and Moselle Rivers . . . . More than 3,000 American planes take part in an assault on German transportation systems, bombing Lueneburg, Steudal, Haldenstadt and Nordheim in western, central and southern Germany . . . . Stalin claims that the Germans have lost 1.15 million men in the 40-day-old Soviet offensive and that "full victory is near."	Remaining Japanese forces in Manila are trapped in the ancient walled sector of the city . . . . American forces land on Capul Island, at the mouth of San Bernardino Strait off the northwest coast of Samar Island, and occupy it by nightfall.	State Secy. Edward R. Stettinius, speaking at the Inter-American Conference in Mexico City, reaffirms the Good Neighbor Policy towards Latin America and promises the U.S. will provide economic assistance to help Latin American countries adjust to postwar economic conditions.	
Feb. 23	Turkish National Assembly votes a declaration of war against Germany and Japan.	Russian troops complete the conquest of by-passed Posen, reporting 84,000 German troops killed there in the month-long siege . . . . U.S. forces cross the Roer River and fight their way to Juelich and Dueren . . . . Netherlands Premier Pieter Gerbrandy completes formation of a new Dutch cabinet, except for two positions to be filled shortly . . . . Alberto Tarchiani, the new Italian ambassador to the U.S., arrives in Washington to assume his duties.	U.S. Marines storm Mt. Suribachi volcano and plant the American flag on its rim.		
Feb. 24		In two days of fighting across the Roer River, the Americans report the capture of 21 towns and the taking of 4,000 prisoners . . . . Hitler says in a radio speech that after the blows already taken "there is no greater terror in store" for Germany and predicts a turning point in the war this year.	Fight for Manila ends with complete destruction of the Japanese garrison, which made a last stand in the fortress of Intramuros.	Uruguay becomes a member of the U.N., leaving Argentina as the only Latin American Republic not yet a member.	Egyptian Premier Ahmed Maher Pasha is fatally shot in Cairo after reading a royal decree declaring war against Germany and Japan.
Feb. 25		U.S. 1st Army takes Dueren, while the 9th Army reports the capture of 15 other German towns . . . . Russians take the Pomeranian stronghold of Preussisch Friedland and send tank spearheads to within 60 miles of the Baltic coast . . . . Rome reports an announcement issued today by Harold Macmillan saying the Allied Control Comm. has relinquished control over liberated Italian territory and that Italy can now appoint its own functionaries without committee approval except in cases of military necessity, which must be approved by the Supreme Allied Commander.	Marianas-based U.S. bombers attack Tokyo, destroying 240 square blocks of the city.		
Feb. 26	Syrian Chamber of Deputies votes approval of a declaration of war against Germany and Japan.	American troops reach 10½ miles west of Cologne and open artillery barrages against the city.	Marine observation planes begin operating from the southern airfield on Iwo Jima.	U.S. proposes to the Inter-American Conference an "economic charter" designed to help in the conversion to peacetime economies and raise living standards in the Hemisphere.	Allies return the Algerian supply center of Oran to the French.
Feb. 27			Gen. MacArthur turns over control of the civil government of the Philippines to Pres. Sergio Osmena.		
	A *Includes developments that affect more than one world region, international organizations and important meetings of major world leaders.*	B *Includes all developments in European countries and military engagements between Allied and Axis powers in Africa and at sea.*	C *Includes all developments in Japan and China, Japanese foreign policy and military actions in the Pacific region.*	D *Includes all domestic and regional developments in Latin America, the Caribbean and Canada.*	E *Includes developments in those independent nations and colonial possessions not covered in Columns B, C and D.*

U.S. Politics & Social Issues	U.S. Foreign Policy & Defense	U.S. Economy & Environment	Science, Technology & Nature	Culture, Leisure & Life Style	
Maj. Gen. Edwin M. "Pa" Watson, secretary and military aide to FDR, dies at 61 aboard a U.S. warship en route home from Yalta.	Harold Stassen accepts nomination as one of the U.S. delegates to the U.N. conference in San Francisco.	Senate Military Affairs Comm. puts aside consideration of the May-Bailey bill and begins consideration of a substitute that would drop all "labor draft" aspects of war worker mobilization .... NWLB orders a minimum wage 55¢ an hour for 50,000 textile workers to correct substandard wages.			Feb. 20
	Carl Emil Ludwig Krepper is convicted on two counts of conspiring to "obstruct, interfere with and injure the defense of the United States" as the contact man for submarine-landed Nazi saboteurs.	Wrigley gum company is forced to discontinue the manufacture of trade brand gums due to ingredient shortages.		Baseball officials cancel the 1945 All-Star Game as a travel conservation measure .... After pleading *nolo contendere* to manslaughter charges connected with last July's disastrous fire, six key men of Ringling Barnum & Bailey Circus receive jail terms ranging from six months to seven years.	Feb. 21
Reps. John Rankin (D, Miss.) and Frank Hook (D, Mich.) grapple and exchange blows on the House floor after verbal exchanges over whether the CIO's PAC is Communist-influenced .... House Military Affairs Comm. names a subcommittee to investigate charges that Communists receive Army commissions.		Senate Military Affairs Comm. reports out a "no-labor-draft" substitute for the House May-Bailey bill for "limited national service." The Senate measure would cover all workers, rather than those aged 18 to 45 .... Public members of the NWLB report to FDR that wages on the average are surpassing prices and that it is essential to maintain the "Little Steel" formula for the time being .... House passes the Senate-approved postwar rivers and harbors bill authorizing nearly $500 million in projects and sends it to the White House.			Feb. 22
	Under Secy. of War Robert Patterson says the Army and Navy will need 900,000 more men and that war industries will need 700,000 in the first six months of 1945.			Alexei Tolstoy, regarded as one of the greatest contemporary Russian novelists, dies at 62 in Moscow.	Feb. 23
FDR signs the George bill, which strips the Commerce Dept. of control over federal lending agencies.	Selective Service announces that men up to age 34 will have to meet more rigid specifications to be eligible for occupational deferments.	Interior Secy. Harold Ickes announces the return to owners of 72 bituminous coal mines in W. Va., Ky. and Pa.		N.Y. Athletic Club retains its team title in the AAU track and field championships in N.Y., with West Point second and Annapolis third. .... A nationwide Gallup Poll of movie magazine readers determines that Greer Garson is the most popular star in the U.S.	Feb. 24
Democratic National Chmn. Robert Hannegan says the Party will scrap its traditional Jackson Day dinners for Jefferson dinners on April 13, with funds contributed to be used solely for the 1946 elections.		Pan American Airways signs a contract in San Diego, Calif. for 15 giant six-engined clippers from Consolidated Vultee Aircraft Corp. for postwar travel abroad. The planes weight 160 tons, have a range of 4,200 miles, carry 204 passengers and 15,300 pounds of baggage, fly at 310 to 342 mph, and can travel between London and N.Y. in a little over nine hours.			Feb. 25
	Sen. Hugh Butler (R, Neb.) accuses FDR of "secrecy" and demands that he give Congress a full account of his conduct of foreign policy, particularly at the Yalta Conference .... Gen. H.H. Arnold, Army Air Force commanding general, warns in his annual report that the U.S. will be the first target in the next war and that air power will be the next weapon.	In accordance with the Smith-Connally Act, UMW files formal notice of a possible strike when contracts expire March 31.		The nationwide midnight curfew on entertainment goes into effect. In N.Y.C. police are instructed to take the names and addresses of all persons violating the curfew.	Feb. 26
Maj. Gen. Clayton Bissel, in charge of Army intelligence, and Asst. War Secy. John McCloy testify at a House Military Affairs investigation that they know of no Communists who have been given commissions in the Army .... Senate Judiciary Comm. decides to shelve all proposed constitutional amendments for the duration of the war.		NWLB announces authorization of regional loans to permit payment of a 55 cent hourly wage to eliminate rates that result in a low standards of living.			Feb. 27
F ***Includes elections, federal-state relations, civil rights and liberties, crime, the judiciary, education, health care, poverty, urban affairs and population.***	G *Includes formation and debate of U.S. foreign and defense policies, veterans affairs and defense spending. (Relations with specific foreign countries are usually found under the region concerned.)*	H *Includes business, labor, agriculture, taxation, transportation, consumer affairs, monetary and fiscal policy, natural resources, pollution and accidents.*	I *Includes worldwide scientific, medical and technological developments, natural phenomena, U.S. weather and natural disasters.*	J *Includes the arts, religion, scholarship, communications media, sports, entertainment, fashions, fads and social life.*	

	World Affairs	European War Zone	Pacific War Zone	The Americas	Other Countries & Territories
Feb. 28	Egyptian and Turkish representatives sign the U.N. declaration in Washington .... Korean provisional government in Chungking, not yet recognized by any nation, declares war on Germany in order to participate in the San Francisco Conference.	British House of Commons approves the decisions taken on Poland at the Yalta Conference .... U.S. troops cross the Erft River, the last natural obstacle before the Rhine, in the vicinity of Sindorf .... Russian troops seize the Pomeranian rail center of Neustettin.	American forces land on Palawan, the fifth largest and westernmost island in the Philippines, and quickly seize control of vital points without much opposition .... On Iwo Jima, U.S. Marines push forward, reaching the uncompleted northern airstrip.	U.S. proposes to the Inter-American Conference a plan to guarantee Hemispheric boundaries and an assurance that it would take action with Latin American states against any nation attacking their territorial integrity.	George Atcheson, U.S. charge d'affaires in Chungking, sends a telegram to the State Dept. criticizing the Chinese Nationalist government as ineffectual and urging more even-handed treatment of the Communists. The cable provokes a bitter conflict between the State Department's "China hands" and Gen. Patrick Hurley, U.S. adviser to the Nationalist government.
March 1	Saudi Arabia and Iran notify Washington of their declarations of war against the Germans and Japanese.	U.S. troops clear the Germans from the twin cities of Muenchen-Gladbach and Rheydt, 15 miles west of Duesseldorf .... British House of Commons gives unanimous approval to the Yalta Declaration.	MacArthur reports American troops have practically completed the destruction of about 6,000 Japanese troops on Corregidor Island .... American forces land on the island of Lubang, which commands the western exit of Verde Passage leading from the Sibuyan Sea into the China Sea.	Organization Comm. of the Inter-American Conference approves a suggestion that the next conference of American Republics be held in Bogota, Colombia .... Canada reaches an agreement with Czechoslovakia to provide the latter with $15 million in credits to purchase Canadian goods to be used in reconstruction.	
March 2		U.S. troops take the Dutch cities of Venlo and Roermond. Neuss on the Rhine River opposite Duesseldorf is also captured.	U.S. Marines drive a 700-yard salient into the Japanese defense lines on the northern part of Iwo Jima .... U.S. troops land on Ticao and Burias islands off the west side of the long southeast extension of Luzon in a move to eliminate the Japanese in southern Luzon.	El Salvador decrees a general amnesty, adding that political exiles may now return home.	
March 3		Russian drive toward the Baltic through Pomerania results in the capture of Dargen, Pollnow and Rummelsburg .... American and Canadian units effect a junction between Kevelaer and Geldern and drive eastward in the direction of the Rhine River city of Wesel.	A British motorized force completes an 11-day drive through central Burma to take the communications center of Meiktila, 80 miles south of Mandalay.	Organization Comm. of the Inter-American Conference adopts the Act of Chapultepec, which guarantees mutual aid of American nations against aggressors who impede the war effort by attacking the territorial integrity or political independence of any of these nations. It provides for a treaty to be drafted extending the guarantee into the postwar period.	At the meeting of Arab states in Cairo, representatives agree upon a draft constitution of the proposed Arab Federation .... The first Syrian diplomatic delegation since the country's recent independence arrives in N.Y.C. en route to Washington.
March 4	U.S. invites 39 nations to attend the April San Francisco conference to draw up a charter for an international organization.	Reaching to within two miles of Cologne, U.S. troops seize Koenigsdorf and enter Widdersdorf and Loevenich .... Russian troops reach the Baltic coast of Pomerania in the vicinity of Kolberg.	U.S. 6th Army completes clearing of Manila one month after entering city. Japanese garrison consisting originally of 20,000 naval soldiers is eliminated.	Inter-American Conference approves eight resolutions concerning economic problems of the war.	
March 5		Three U.S. troop columns smash into Cologne, pushing towards the city's center .... Russian forces take Stettin's outer bastions of Stargard and Naugard .... Some 7,000 London dock workers, who struck two days ago because they were asked to report for work at an outside rather than an inside place, refuse to follow the orders of their union leaders to resume work.		Inter-American Conference decides that Argentina must adhere to the Act of Chapultepec, declare war on the Axis and sign the declaration of the U.N. before it can be restored to the American family of nations.	
March 6		Cologne, Germany's fourth largest city, falls to the Americans .... After a two-day advance of 29 miles the Russians enter Cammin, 36 miles northeast of Stettin .... Dr. Petre Groza forms a new Rumanian cabinet with himself as premier.	Marines on Iwo Jima make small gains on the left and center flanks of their lines.		
March 7	In a letter to *The Times* of London Sir William Beveridge denounces the proposed voting procedure in a new international security organization as "a short way to a third World War," arguing that it would place the Big Five powers above the law established for other nations.	U.S. troops establish a bridgehead on the east bank of the Rhine by a surprise crossing at the Ludendorff railroad bridge at Remagen. Erpal (near the eastern end of the bridge) is captured and German counterattacks are repulsed. On the west side of the Rhine the U.S. 1st and 3rd Armies effect a junction between Remagen and Coblenz, trapping five or six German divisions. The 1st Army completes the capture of Bonn, 12 miles north of Remagen .... Russians launch seven armies in an all-out offensive toward Berlin from the Oder River, 40 miles eastward .... Marshal Tito completes the formation of a new Yugoslavian cabinet of 28 members with himself as premier and minister of national defense.	Chinese troops seize both New and Old Lashio, where the railroad from Rangoon joins the old Burma Road.		

U.S. Politics & Social Issues	U.S. Foreign Policy & Defense	U.S. Economy & Environment	Science, Technology & Nature	Culture, Leisure & Life Style	
	FDR returns to Washington from his 14,000-mile round trip to the Yalta Conference .... Head of the Army Air Force Gen. H.H. Arnold reveals that the Army's first jet-propelled combat plane, the P-80 Shooting Star, is in production .... State Dept. reaches a Lend-Lease agreement with France to provide the latter with immediate and postwar reconstruction aid.	NWLB grants an increase of $2 to $4 a week to 21,250 telephone employes in N.Y., Louisville, Washington and Memphis.		*Black Boy* by Richard Wright, the autobiography of the youthful years of the author of *Native Son*, is published .... Twentieth Century Fox release of *A Tree Grows in Brooklyn*, featuring Joan Blondell, Peggy Ann Garner and James Dunn, premiers in New York.	Feb. 28
Wallace is confirmed as Secretary of Commerce by the Senate.	FDR tells a joint session of Congress that the Yalta Conference was a success and that the U.S. will have to take responsibility for world collaboration or bear the responsibility for another world war.	RFC announces it will take up to 75% of loans made by the more than 100 regional credit pools formed by commercial banks to aid small business. The RFC rate will be 4%, while the pools may charge up to 6% for their portion of loans .... UMW submits demands for a wage settlement to coal operators, including a proposal for a 10¢-a-ton royalty to be used for medical insurance for the miners.		Representatives of theatrical organizations in N.Y. adopt resolutions that include proposed legislation to prevent censorship by administrative officials in reaction to the closing of the play *Trio* by License Commissioner Paul Moss.	March 1
	FDR expresses the idea that some German ex-soldiers be used in the reconstruction of Russia, although he claims the subject did not come up at Yalta.	FDR signs the bill for postwar rivers and harbors projects.			March 2
	Acting State Secy. Grew says an international organization as proposed at Dumbarton Oaks is the only alternative to world anarchy. He also says that the U.S. still accredits and recognizes the representatives of Estonia, Latvia and Lithuania stationed in Washington.	NWLB denies a blanket wage increase to GM employes, granting only a 2½% rise in differentials for those working the third shift.		Famous Swedish distance runner Gunder Haegg loses the first race of his second U.S. visit after a delayed arrival two days ago, finishing last in a field of five in the Louis Zamperini Mile, a feature of the Intercollegiate AAAA indoor championship meet at Madison Square Garden, N.Y. .... Reginald Marsh wins the first W.A. Clark Prize and the Corcoran Gold Medal in the Corcoran Gallery of Art's 19th biennial exhibition of contemporary American paintings.	March 3
					March 4
FDR nominates Fred M. Vinson to succeed Jesse Jones as Federal Loan Administrator in charge of the RFC .... N.Y. State Senate completes action on the Ives-Quinn anti-discrimination bill and sends it to Gov. Dewey.					March 5
	House Foreign Affairs Comm. recommends the extension of the Lend-Lease Act another year beyond its June 30th expiration date.	Montgomery Ward & Co. files a brief with the Supreme Court asking a review of the decision handed down by the U.S. District Court in Chicago in January .... ICC rules illegal the Alleghany Corp's. control of the Chesapeake & Ohio Railroad, the New York, Chicago & St. Louis Railroad and the Pere Marquette Railroad.		Paris reports French police have released from "preventive detention" P.G. Wodehouse, The British novelist who made broadcasts while a captive of the Nazis .... Notre Dame Univ. names Hugh Devore as acting head football coach and athletic director.	March 6
	House Banking and Currency Comm. opening hearings on the Bretton Woods Conference hears Treasury Secy. Morgenthau call the monetary proposals "the first practical test of our willingness to cooperate in the work of world reconstruction and stabilization." .... House passes and sends to the Senate a bill which would draft all nurses 20 through 44 who are not married before March 15 and have no dependents.	NWLB Chmn. Davis is named by FDR to be economic stabilization director. NWLB Vice Chmn. Dr. George Taylor is named to succeed Davis .... Revercomb-Robertson bill providing for "voluntary" mobilization and deployment of manpower is killed in the Senate.	WPB announces that after March 15 more than three times the former supply of penicillin for public use will be available to hospitals and physicians.	American Academy of Arts and Letters announces that its Howells Medal, awarded every fifth year for excellence in fiction writing, goes to novelist Booth Tarkington. Tarkington is the first man to receive the medal since its inception in 1921.	March 7
F *Includes elections, federal-state relations, civil rights and liberties, crime, the judiciary, education, health care, poverty, urban affairs and population.*	G *Includes formation and debate of U.S. foreign and defense policies, veterans affairs and defense spending. (Relations with specific foreign countries are usually found under the region concerned.)*	H *Includes business, labor, agriculture, taxation, transportation, consumer affairs, monetary and fiscal policy, natural resources, pollution and accidents.*	I *Includes worldwide scientific, medical and technological developments, natural phenomena, U.S. weather and natural disasters.*	J *Includes the arts, religion, scholarship, communications media, sports, entertainment, fashions, fads and social life.*	

	World Affairs	European War Zone	Pacific War Zone	The Americas	Other Countries & Territories
March 8		Russians throw a 40-mile siege arc around Stettin and drive to within six miles of the port.		Inter-American Conference on Problems of War and Peace closes in Mexico City after approving 60 resolutions strengthening the Western Hemisphere. These include endorsement of Dumbarton Oaks and passage of the Act of Chapultepec, guaranteeing hemispheric cooperation in the war against the Axis.	
March 9	The ministers to London of Syria and Lebanon file protests with Foreign Secy. Eden over the failure to invite their countries to the forthcoming San Francisco Conference.	Russians drive from three directions at Danzig and reach to within nine miles of the port .... A British Foreign Office spokesman says the British embassy in Bucharest is sheltering Gen. Nicolai Radescu, the former Rumanian premier .... Italian Premier Ivanoe Bonomi and chief of UNRRA's mission to Italy Spurgeon Keeny sign an agreement governing the use of $50 million worth of relief to the country.	The 19th British Indian Division drives its way into Mandalay, breaking out of its bridgehead on the east bank of the Irrawaddy River. The Japanese put up fierce resistance .... American troops drive 12 miles north along the west coast of Luzon, seizing the town of Aringay.		
March 10		German defense of Wesel, the last Nazi bridgehead west of the Rhine River, collapses .... Soviet troops capture Lauenburg and Kartuzy on the road to Danzig and split the enemy lines on the city's outskirts.	More than 300 Marianas-based Superfortresses drop 2,000 tons of incendiary bombs on Tokyo in the heaviest raid on the city to date. Casualties are estimated at 125,000, with 40% of the city destroyed and one million residents made homeless .... Japanese forces occupying French Indochina seize control of the country, placing Gov. Gen. Hean Decoux and other French leaders in "protective custody." .... Lord Louis Mountbatten completes three days of talks in Chungking, where complete agreement on cooperation of the various commands is reportedly reached .... U.S. troops enter Antipolo, southern anchor of the Japanese defense line east of Manila.		
March 11		American bridgehead opposite Remagen on the Rhine is expanded to a length of nine miles and a depth of three miles.	U.S. troops land secretly on Romblon and Simara Islands in the central part of the Philippines .... U.S. forces capture Zamaboanga on Mindanao Island and occupy San Rocque airfield four miles from the town .... Chinese troops recapture Suichwan, Kiangsi Province, the first former U.S. airbase in China to be retaken.		
March 12		Russian forces capture Kuestrin, the Oder River fortress 38 miles east of Berlin.			
March 13		American bridgehead on the eastern side of the Rhine opposite Remegen is extended to points five miles beyond the river.	U.S. forces on Mindanao Island push on from Zamboanga to capture the villages of Santa Maria, Canelar, Sinung and Pitogo.	Gen. Eurico Dutra is nominated to run against Maj. Gen. Eduardo Gomes for the Brazilian presidency.	
March 14		U.S. troops expand their bridgehead up to 10½ miles on the east bank of the Rhine.	U.S. Marines formally raise the American flag at 9:30 a.m. atop Mt. Suribachi on Iwo Jima. Japanese resistance continues on slopes of the mountain .... U.S. Superfortresses drop more than 2,000 tons of fire bombs on Osaka, Japan.		
March 15		U.S. troops net gains of up to three miles in new operations in the Saar Basin and the Palatinate .... Russian forces make a seven-mile breakthrough to the coast of the Frisches Haff southwest of Koenigsberg, isolating the city from the main German forces .... Three of the liberated Dodecanese Islands—Simi, Nisiro and Stampalia—unanimously request a union with Greece .... Churchill tells the Conservative Party convention that the war will end "before summer ends or even sooner."	American troops repulse a Japanese attempt to land from barges 4½ miles northwest of Batangas, Luzon.	Dr. Juan Jose Arevalo is sworn in as president of Guatemala.	

A	B	C	D	E
Includes developments that affect more than one world region, international organizations and important meetings of major world leaders.	*Includes all developments in European countries and military engagements between Allied and Axis powers in Africa and at sea.*	*Includes all developments in Japan and China, Japanese foreign policy and military actions in the Pacific region.*	*Includes all domestic and regional developments in Latin America, the Caribbean and Canada.*	*Includes developments in those independent nations and colonial possessions not covered in Columns B, C and D.*

U.S. Politics & Social Issues	U.S. Foreign Policy & Defense	U.S. Economy & Environment	Science, Technology & Nature	Culture, Leisure & Life Style	
		Senate passes the O'Mahoney-Kilgore bill, a committee substitute for the May-Bailey bill, which gives the WMC power to mobilize workers for war production.	The flood-swollen Ohio River causes 10 deaths and millions of dollars in damage in Ohio, Pa., W. Va., Ky and Ind.		March 8
Gov. Fred Aandahl (R, N.D.) names State Sen. Milton Young (R) to the U.S. Senate seat vacated by the death of John Moses (D) . . . . Census Bureau reports the population of the South and West increased by nearly four million between 1940 and 1944.		FDR tells his press conference that a voluntary system is inadequate to supply the manpower needed to carry on war production . . . . Southern Coal Producer's Assn. petitions the NWLB to abandon plans for a strike poll of soft coal miners scheduled for March 28.			March 9
	State Secy. Stettinius returns from Mexico City and says Americans must share in the responsibility of establishing and maintaining world peace.	Due to low civilian supplies of meats, sugar, butter and canned fruits and vegetables, the OPA announces reduced allotments of rationed foods for industrial users.			March 10
		Mobilization Dir. Byrnes announces the formation of an interagency committee to coordinate foreign shipments under the direction of Leo T. Crowley.		*New York Herald Tribune* reports the bestselling books to be *Cannery Row* by John Steinbeck and *Great Son* by Edna Farber (fiction) and *Brave Men* by Ernie Pyle and *The Thurber Carnival*by James Thurber (non-fiction).	March 11
N.Y. becomes the first state to set up a permanent commission to eliminate racial discrimination in employment as Gov. Dewey signs the Ives-Quinn Act . . . . Supreme Court dismisses the suit of the Shoshone Indians for $15 million in damages because of occupation by white settlers of lands in Idaho, Utah, and Nevada on grounds that the Box Elder Treaty left them no cause for claiming the land.		Supreme Court rules against the government's appeal for any early review of the Montgomery Ward case, pending circuit court action . . . . Three judges of the U.S. Circuit Court in N.Y. declare Alcoa to be a participant in a monopolistic aluminum conspiracy violating the Sherman Antitrust Act.			March 12
	House votes to extend the life of the Lend-Lease Act until June 30, 1946 but directs that it not be used for postwar reconstruction.				March 13
	Army and Navy announce that starting tomorrow all enlisted men 18-20 years old, except radio technicians, will be assigned to the Army as combat replacements.	House and Senate go to conference over the House's May-Bailey "limited national service" bill and the Senate's "voluntary" manpower measure.			March 14
	War Dept. reveals U.S. ground forces casualties in Europe from D-day through March 1 totaled 425,007, including 70,414 killed.	Senate votes to increase by $100 million an authorization for FHA insurance on privately financed war housing . . . . Stabilization Dir. Davis writes other department heads that the defeat of Germany will bring shock waves to the economy and that it would be advisable to maintain controls for some time after the war.		Academy Awards go to *Going My Way* as the best film, Bing Crosby as the best actor and Ingrid Bergman as the best actress for 1944.	March 15
F *Includes elections, federal-state relations, civil rights and liberties, crime, the judiciary, education, health care, poverty, urban affairs and population.*	G *Includes formation and debate of U.S. foreign and defense policies, veterans affairs and defense spending. (Relations with specific foreign countries are usually found under the region concerned.)*	H *Includes business, labor, agriculture, taxation, transportation, consumer affairs, monetary and fiscal policy, natural resources, pollution and accidents.*	I *Includes worldwide scientific, medical and technological developments, natural phenomena, U.S. weather and natural disasters.*	J *Includes the arts, religion, scholarship, communications media, sports, entertainment, fashions, fads and social life.*	

	World Affairs	European War Zone	Pacific War Zone	The Americas	Other Countries & Territories
March 16		British censorship permits revelation that giant German V-2 rocket bombs have been hitting the London area and southern England recently .... French officials announce that purge courts have handed down 679 death sentences against war criminals. They include Jacques Schweitzer, a close associate of Otto Abetz (former German ambassador), and writer Drieu La Rochelle, who committed suicide last night rather than face trial .... U.S. troops begin closing pincers on the Germans in the Saar Basin .... Russian troops fight their way to within 4½ miles of Stettin and within six miles of Danzig and Gdynia, all Baltic ports.	Maj. General Harry Schmidt, commander of U.S. Marines on Iwo Jima, announces the island is secure.	A plot to overthrow the Cuban government is broken up with the arrest of 40 conspirators, including Col. Jose Pedraza, former army chief of staff.	
March 17		Russians pierce Stettin's outer defenses, while in Prussia they capture Brandenburg .... Coblenz falls to the Americans .... The center span of the Ludendorff Bridge at Remagen collapses at 3 p.m., causing some loss of life among the 200 engineering troops working on it. American Army troops first crossed the Rhine using this bridge.	The battle for Iwo Jima officially ends as Marines reach Kitano Point at the northern end of the island.		
March 18		More than 1,300 U.S. bombers drop 12,400 high explosives and 650,000 fire bombs on Berlin in the heaviest assault on that city to date, leaving massive fires blazing .... Russian forces capture the Pomeranian port of Kolberg, clearing the northern flank along a 175-mile stretch of the Baltic coast from the Polish Corridor to Stettin Bay.	American units land on Basilan, the northernmost island in the Sulu archipelago .... Tokyo radio reports all schools ordered closed for one year starting April 1 to mobilize students for food and munitions production, air raid defense and other war support activities.		
March 19		American bridgehead on the east bank of the Rhine near Remagen is expanded to a depth of eight miles and a length of 18 miles .... Red Army drives to within one to three miles of the East Prussian cities of Braunsberg and Heiligenbeil.	U.S. carrier *Franklin* is hit by two 500 lb. bombs off the Japanese coast, killing 832 crewmen and wounding 270. It is the largest casualty toll suffered by any American warship in a single engagement. The vessel is not sunk .... U.S. carrier planes attack Kobe and Kure, Japan, and the Japanese fleet in the Inland Sea. Americans shoot down 200 enemy planes and sink six small freighters in addition to destroying shore installations.	An attempt by two Peruvian noncommissioned officers and a small group of men to seize Air Min. Gen. Fernando Melgar at the Ancon air base is stopped.	
March 20		German defense of the Saar collapses as Nazi troops flee from the converging U.S. 3rd and 7th Armies .... Russian troops capture Alt-Dam, a Stettin outpost, wiping out the Germans' strong bridgehead on the east bank of the Oder River 70 miles northeast of Berlin.	British complete the conquest of Mandalay, two years, 10 months and 12 days after the Japanese occupation. The 19th Indian Division drives home the attack as remaining Japanese defenders abandon their lost defense posts .... American forces take Iloilo, capital of Panay Island in the southern Philippines, 24 hours after invading the island. The 2,000-man Japanese garrison withdraws into the interior of the island with little resistance.		
March 21	UNRRA Dir. Lehman asks for 938,000 tons of food for 1945's second quarter.	Under the blows of U.S. troops, the Germans fall back seven to 12 miles in the Palatinate.	Japanese Premier Kuniaki Koiso asks for new and sweeping powers for the Army which would place virtually all Japan under military law in preparation for an invasion .... Japanese open a 60,000-man, tank-led offensive in central China north of Hankow against the Chinese threat to the Hankow-Canton railroad.	Guatemalan Assembly votes to reestablish diplomatic relations with Russia.	
March 22		Some 20 divisions of the U.S. 3rd and 7th Armies make progress in clearing the remaining Germans from the west side of the Rhine, taking the area between Bingen and Mainz. The Americans also enter Boehl, reach Gommersheim, seize Annweiler and establish a new bridgehead across the Rhine east of Frankenthal .... Russians claim their offensive in Upper Silesia has trapped or liquidated 45,000 German troops.		U.S. State Dept. notifies 14 Latin American countries that the request for a rise in the ceiling price of green coffee cannot be granted because it is necessary to hold the line against inflation.	Two Jewish assassins of Lord Moyne—Eliahu Bet-Tsouri and Eliahu Hakim—are hanged at the Cairo jail .... Delegates of six Arab nations sign the final draft of the constitution of an Arab League.
March 23		Russians reach the Baltic coast between Danzig and Gdynia, splitting the Germans defending the two ports.	French cabinet says French Indochina will get partial self-government after the war and that its citizens will be declared citizens of the "French Union," which will include France and all parts of "the imperial community." .... Americans advance to within 10 miles of Baguio, the summer capital of Luzon.		

A	B	C	D	E
Includes developments that affect more than one world region, international organizations and important meetings of major world leaders.	*Includes all developments in European countries and military engagements between Allied and Axis powers in Africa and at sea.*	*Includes all developments in Japan and China, Japanese foreign policy and military actions in the Pacific region.*	*Includes all domestic and regional developments in Latin America, the Caribbean and Canada.*	*Includes developments in those independent nations and colonial possessions not covered in Columns B, C and D.*

U.S. Politics & Social Issues	U.S. Foreign Policy & Defense	U.S. Economy & Environment	Science, Technology & Nature	Culture, Leisure & Life Style	
	War Dept. says U.S. citizens of Japanese ancestry will take a special oath foreswearing "allegiance or obedience to the Japanese Emperor" before acceptance into the Army.	UMW rejects a contract offer by soft coal operators that would raise basic earnings by $1.69 weekly.			March 16
	Selective Service announces deferment of some 145,000 younger men in steel, coal mining, synthetic rubber and non-ferrous mining industries.	OWI announces that meat available for civilian consumption will be 12% less for the next three months than for the same period last year.			March 17
National Lawyer's Guild petitions FDR to cancel the deportation proceedings against Harry Bridges, saying it would "jeopardize" the "unified functioning of democratic world forces."	In his annual report to Congress Atty. Gen. Biddle asks for new legislation classifying conscientious objectors and for new sabotage laws to include conspiracy and to make aid to escaped prisoners of war a treasonable offense.			N.Y. Mayor Fiorello La Guardia announces immediate extension of the city's curfew from midnight to 1 a.m.	March 18
	Comm. for Economic Development, a national postwar planning group, endorses the Bretton Woods financial plan.	OPA announces retailers' markups for clothing, textiles, furniture and house furnishings will be frozen at March 19, 1945 levels.		Mayor Fiorello La Guardia's unauthorized curfew extension from midnight to 1 a.m. draws sharp criticism today from Mobilization Dir. Byrnes and from other mayors and several congressmen.	March 19
		FDR orders a study of a guaranteed annual wage by the advisory board of OWM in the light of "reconversion and the transition from a war economy to a peace economy."		Lord Alfred Douglas, British author, poet and lover of Oscar Wilde, dies at 74 in Sussex, England.	March 20
		Sen. Warren Austin (R, Vt.) proposes a compromise bill to the Senate-House conference committee on manpower bills. It would draft 18-45-year-old men for war and farm work . . . . American Meat Institute and two GOP senators blame the OPA for meat shortages, alleging it does not allow the packers a reasonable margin of profit.		WMC rules baseball players may return to the game from any off-season employment, provided the sport constitutes their "principle business."	March 21
Joint Comm. on Reduction of Nonessential Federal Expenditures reports to Congress and FDR that the country has saved more than $3 billion in three years through its recommendations.	American Labor Conference on International Affairs issues a report urging Congress to approve the Bretton Woods agreements for international financing.	OPA announces a rise of subsidy payments to cattle slaughterers by 50¢ per 100 lbs. in an effort to get more beef to consumers.			March 22
Senate rejects the nomination of Aubrey Williams as REA administrator after heatedly debating his alleged Communist connections.	House passes and sends to the Senate a bill to extend the Selective Service Act for one year beyond May 15.		Census Bureau reports that the death rate from cancer in the U.S. has more than doubled since 1900 . . . . Dr. Norbert Fell of Parke, Davis & Co. secures a patent on a method to control hay fever, asthma and similar allergies by use of an antigen for building resistance to allergic reactions.		March 23
F *Includes elections, federal-state relations, civil rights and liberties, crime, the judiciary, education, health care, poverty, urban affairs and population.*	G *Includes formation and debate of U.S. foreign and defense policies, veterans affairs and defense spending. (Relations with specific foreign countries are usually found under the region concerned.)*	H *Includes business, labor, agriculture, taxation, transportation, consumer affairs, monetary and fiscal policy, natural resources, pollution and accidents.*	I *Includes worldwide scientific, medical and technological developments, natural phenomena, U.S. weather and natural disasters.*	J *Includes the arts, religion, scholarship, communications media, sports, entertainment, fashions, fads and social life.*	

	World Affairs	European War Zone	Pacific War Zone	The Americas	Other Countries & Territories
March 24	Spanish government orders its diplomats to stop representing Japanese interests in countries with which Japan has no diplomatic relations because of the war.	American and British troops cross the Rhine to establish beachheads on the east bank between Rees and Duisburg . . . . A new Russian offensive in western Hungary gains 43 miles along a 62-mile front, placing Soviet troops only 40 miles from Austria . . . . Moscow reports the enactment two days ago of a new agrarian reform law in Rumania for expropriation of properties of absentees, traitors and Germans and division of estates of more than 50 hectares among poor peasants.	Japanese Premier Kuniaki Koiso calls on the nation's "100,000,000 people" to join a volunteer army ordered established by the cabinet . . . . U.S. forces take Nagulian and its airport, 12 miles northwest of Baguio, against light Japanese opposition.	FDR appoints Wallace Harrison to head the Office of Inter-American Affairs.	
March 25		A U.S. armored division sweeps ahead 27 miles east of the Rhine and crosses the Main River, while bridgeheads on the east bank of the Rhine are expanded by Allied troops . . . . New Russian forces join the Vienna offensive, gaining 28 miles along the Danube while further south other Russian troops reach to within 72 miles of the Austrian capital.	MacArthur reports that the shores of Batangas Bay on Luzon are completely cleared of the Japanese.		
March 26		Lloyd George, Britain's Prime Minister during WW1, dies at 82 at his home in Llanystumdwy, Wales . . . . Seven Allied armies advance east of the Rhine as German resistance becomes increasingly disorganized.	American troops land on the east coast of Cebu Island in the central Visayan group and, facing only moderate opposition, reach within 2½ miles of Cebu City.	Argentine government decree puts all Axis firms under military control.	
March 27		British units break through German defenses around Brunen at the northern end of the front and plunge eastward across the Westphalian front . . . . Russian troops drive to within 58 miles of Vienna and within 20 miles of the Austro-Hungarian border.	U.S. troops capture Cebu City and its port facilities.	Argentina declares war on Japan and Germany.	
March 28		In northern Germany, the British reach the city of Borken and push on to Muenster, while further south the Americans take Kirchellen, Sterkrade and Ruhrort . . . . Russians capture Gdynia on the Baltic and Gyoer and Komarno at the Czech-Hungarian border . . . . Reykjavik reports that Pres. Sveinn Bjoernsson will have no opposition in Iceland's first presidential election in June.	Japanese drive on the U.S. airbase at Laohokow reaches a point 25 miles northeast of the Chinese city.	Buenos Aires says staff members of the Japanese embassy have been confined to their homes under police guard.	State Dept. announces an invitation to Syria and Lebanon to attend the San Francisco Conference.
March 29	A White House announcement says the U.S. and Russia will seek three votes each instead of one in the assembly of the proposed world security organization to equalize the votes of the "Big Three," since the British Empire will have six votes, including those of her dominions. Russia raised the question at the Yalta Conference.	Russian troops reach the Austrian border at a point 52 miles south of Vienna . . . . Allies drive to within 10 miles of Paderborn in an effort to isolate the Ruhr.	U.S. troops land on the east coast of Negros Island in the central Visayan group and quickly push to the outskirts of its capital, Bacolod.		Palestinian Arab leaders reject a proposal which would rotate the office of mayor of Jerusalem among Moslem, Jewish and Christian officials. The proposal, advocated by British High Commissioner Viscount John V. Gort, was accepted with reservations by Jewish leaders.
March 30	State Dept. announces that to date 37 nations have accepted invitations to the San Francisco Conference.	Russian units take the Baltic city of Danzig, hoisting a Polish flag, thus supporting that country's claim to the former internationalized city . . . . Russian forces invade Austria north of Koeszeg . . . . U.S. troops enter Paderborn . . . . Marshal Tito announces recognition and establishment of diplomatic relations with the Moscow-backed provisional Polish government.	American forces land on Cauit and Mactan Islands, less than a mile from Cebu . . . . American troops occupy Bacolod, the capital of Negros Island . . . . Political Assn. of Great Japan is inaugurated in an effort to unify the country for a defense against an anticipated invasion.		
March 31		U.S. and British reject a Soviet appeal that the Polish provisional (Lubin) government be invited to the San Francisco Conference . . . . U.S. and French troops join seven other Allied armies in the drive into Germany, as Eisenhower asks German soldiers to surrender to avoid futile bloodshed . . . . Russians drive 17 miles inside Austria, capturing 70 towns.		Pan-American Union authorizes Argentina to sign the Mexico City Pact (Act of Chapultepec) after Argentina declares war on Germany and Japan.	
	A *Includes developments that affect more than one world region, international organizations and important meetings of major world leaders.*	B *Includes all developments in European countries and military engagements between Allied and Axis powers in Africa and at sea.*	C *Includes all developments in Japan and China, Japanese foreign policy and military actions in the Pacific region.*	D *Includes all domestic and regional developments in Latin America, the Caribbean and Canada.*	E *Includes developments in those independent nations and colonial possessions not covered in Columns B, C and D.*

U.S. Politics & Social Issues	U.S. Foreign Policy & Defense	U.S. Economy & Environment	Science, Technology & Nature	Culture, Leisure & Life Style	
FDR names Jonathan Daniels as White House secretary in charge of press relations to replace Stephen Early, who is expected to return to private employment.	State Dept. reiterates that the U.S. is "definitely committed to the policy of unconditional surrender" of both Germany and Japan.	Senate-House conferees vote for a job bill compromise that would vest in War Mobilization Dir. Byrnes power to use any government agencies to administer the act.		Cairo reports say archaeologists have located the sacred city of Heliopolis, an Egyptian capital that was obliterated over 6,000 years ago.	March 24
				Byron Nelson takes the Greensboro, N.C. Open Golf Tournament, defeating Sam Byrd by eight strokes.	March 25
		Opening its food inquiry, the Senate Agricultural Comm. hears representatives of the meat packing industry charge OPA with being largely responsible for meat shortages because it follows "a social philosophy which regards profit as a sin." . . . . Senate votes to raise the national debt limit $40 billion to $300 billion and sends the measure to FDR . . . . Supreme Court agrees to hear arguments on the charge that 20 railroads have conspired to maintain freight rates discriminating against the state of Georgia as alleged by Gov. Ellis Arnall.		De Paul Univ. wins the NIT basketball tournament in N.Y., defeating Bowling Green (O.), 71-54.	March 26
		House approves the compromise job bill giving extensive power to War Mobilization Dir. Byrnes and sends it to the Senate.			March 27
		U.S. Chamber of Commerce Pres. Eric Johnston, AFL Pres. Green and CIO Pres. Murray sign a charter for postwar industrial relations, calling for mutual recognition, social security measures, increased foreign trade and the establishment of a national business-labor committee . . . . FDR makes a fourth appeal for enactment of a manpower bill, urging the Senate to adopt the conference report . . . . Soft-coal miners vote to authorize UMW Pres. Lewis to call a strike.	IT&T announces the formation of International Telecommunications Laboratories Inc. to coordinate the parent firm's worldwide electronic research on radio, television and aerial navigation . . . . Dr. Katherine Blodgett of General Electric is chosen by the AAUW for its annual achievement award for inventing "invisible gas" and developing a method of preventing wasteful loss of light by depositing a non-reflecting film on glass.	American Academy of Arts and Letters announces that Wystan Hugh Auden is the winner of the Academy's annual poetry prize.	March 28
	FDR says Maj. Gen. Lucius Clay is resigning as deputy war mobilization director to become Eisenhower's deputy in charge of civilian affairs in occupied Germany.	UMW accepts and the coal operators reject a compromise suggested by Labor Secy. Perkins calling for a seven-hour work-day, time-and-a-half for overtime and $75 yearly vacation pay.		Oklahoma A&M upsets DePaul Univ., 52-44, in N.Y. to win the national basketball championship.	March 29
		Montgomery Ward & Co. refuses to pay a bill for $350,966 presented by the Army to cover merchandise the company received when the Army took control of its properties last December.			March 30
				The Glass Menagerie by Tennessee Williams opens on Broadway . . . . War Mobilization Dir. Byrnes says that after V-E Day emergency measures such as the horse racing ban, the brownout and midnight curfew will be ended.	March 31

F	G	H	I	J
Includes elections, federal-state relations, civil rights and liberties, crime, the judiciary, education, health care, poverty, urban affairs and population.	*Includes formation and debate of U.S. foreign and defense policies, veterans affairs and defense spending. (Relations with specific foreign countries are usually found under the region concerned.)*	*Includes business, labor, agriculture, taxation, transportation, consumer affairs, monetary and fiscal policy, natural resources, pollution and accidents.*	*Includes worldwide scientific, medical and technological developments, natural phenomena, U.S. weather and natural disasters.*	*Includes the arts, religion, scholarship, communications media, sports, entertainment, fashions, fads and social life.*

	World Affairs	European War Zone	Pacific War Zone	The Americas	Other Countries & Territories
Apr. 1		Allied forces encircle the Ruhr, where an estimated 30,000 German troops are trapped .... Red Army troops capture Sopron, Hungary, and drive on across the border into Austria to take Trauersdorf.	In the largest amphibious operation of the Pacific war, U.S. forces land on Okinawa in the Ryukyu Island group, 360 miles south of Japan. By the end of the day 50,000 troops have landed on an eight-mile stretch of the island's southwest coast and penetrated three miles inland, capturing two airfields. Japanese resistance is unexpectedly light .... Sailing under a safe conduct guarantee, the liner *Awa Maru* is accidentally sunk in the Pacific by an American submarine. State Dept. later accepts full responsibility.	Argentina decrees all Japanese and German residents must register with the police and will be restricted.	
Apr. 2		British and Canadian gains in both the Netherlands and Germany threaten to topple the whole German position in the region.	U.S. forces cut across Okinawa to the east coast at Tobara on Awase Harbor, thus spliting the island in half. Resistance is still reported as relatively light.	Brazil resumes diplomatic relations with Russia.	Iranian Foreign Min. Nasrullah Entezan resigns.
Apr. 3	State Secy. Stettinius says the U.S. will not ask for three votes in the assembly of the proposed international organization but will continue to back the Russian request for separate votes for White Russia and the Ukraine.	Russian troops smash ahead 21 miles in Austria to reach a point six miles south of Vienna .... Russians reportedly take Bratislava, Czechoslovakia, which the Germans had used as capital of their "Slovak" republic .... Canadian troops take Huissen, Netherlands, as British units roll into Germany and move toward the North Sea and eastward to enter Osnabrueck.	Marines reach the east coast of Okinawa in a drive that cuts off the Katachin Peninsula.		
Apr. 4		Allied troops capture Osnabrueck, Siegen, Gotha, Suhl, Wuerzburg, Karlsruhe and Bruchsal in advances along the western front.	U.S. Amb. to China Patrick Hurley arrives in London for talks with British and American officials on Far Eastern war policy .... U.S. troops are reportedly in secure control of about 80 square miles of Okinawa .... U.S. troops make a 200-mile amphibious movement from Zamboanga, Mindanao Island, to seize the islands of Sanga Sanga and Bongao in the Tawi Tawi group at the southernmost point of the Philippines. There is little opposition.	Argentina signs the Act of Chapultepec, providing for cooperation among Western Hemisphere nations in the war against the Axis, after declaring war on Japan and Germany .... Canadian P.M. W.L. Mackenzie King says Canadian troops will go to fight in the Pacific on a voluntary basis only.	
Apr. 5	Russian denounces its neutrality pact with Japan, ostensibly because of the latter's aid to Germany.	Russian units reach the southern city limits of Vienna .... British troops advancing from the south reach within about 30 miles of Bremen .... American troops attack below German-held Massa on the Italian Tyrrhenian coast and gain two miles .... Britain publishes a secret protocol to the Polish treaty of 1939 in which Britain pledged Poland assistance against German aggression only.	Premier Kuniaki Koiso's Japanese cabinet resigns, and Emperor Hirohito orders Adm. Baron Kantaro Suzuki to form a new government .... Joint Chiefs of Staff announce that Gen. Douglas MacArthur and Adm. Chester Nimitz will lead all Army and Navy forces respectively against Japan.	New police chief of Rio de Janeiro promises to permit legitimate strikes and respect religious freedom in the city.	
Apr. 6	Tokyo says it is prepared to meet the consequences of Russia's denunciation of the neutrality pact but adds that the pact must remain in force until April 1946, because one year's termination notice is required.	State Secy. Stettinius says the U.S. is doing all it can to assist the establishment of a new Polish government of unity so that the country can be represented at the San Francisco conference .... Allied left flank moves forward between five and 30 miles on the western front.	Japanese initiate Operation Ten-Go, a series of massed kamikaze attacks aimed at destroying the U.S. 5th Fleet off Okinawa. 355 Kamikaze planes participate in first attack, sinking six American vessels and damaging 17.		
Apr. 7		Russian troops sweep around Vienna, encircling most of the city .... A new Czech cabinet with Col. Zdenek Fierlinger as premier takes office, pledging itself to maintaining good relations with Russia .... U.S. troops discover a hoard of German gold and currency, along with numerous art treasures, stored in a 2,100-foot-deep salt mine at Merkers, Germany.	Carrier planes of the U.S. 5th Fleet sink the 45,000-ton Japanese battleship *Yamato* 60 miles southwest of Kyushu Island .... Premier Baron Kantaro Suzuki's new government is sworn in at Tokyo .... SEA Headquarters reports the end of organized Japanese resistance in central Burma, opening way to the invasion of Rangoon.		
Apr. 8		London reports that the German V-2 rocket campaign against Britain has ended. It has killed 8,436 and wounded an estimated 25,000 since it began on June 15, 1944 .... British advance to within seven miles of Bremen, cutting off thousands of Germans to the southwest between the Ems and Weser Rivers.		Guatemalan Congress suspends constitutional guarantees in the country for six months following the crushing of an alleged plot to stage a revolution.	Syrian Premier Fayez el Khoury forms a new cabinet.
Apr. 9	Jurists from 38 countries assemble in Washington to draft a statute for the proposed International Court of Justice .... A world committee to promote forest conservation and replenishment is formed in London by representatives of 18 countries.	Russian forces take the heart of Vienna and begin a quick mop-up campaign .... Germany's pocket battleship *Admiral Scheer* is sunk by British planes in Kiel harbor .... Last land escape routes for the Nazis in the Netherlands are cut as Canadian troops take Meppel.	Shigenori Togo is installed as foreign minister and Kiichiro Hiranuma as president of the privy council in the new Japanese cabinet .... U.S. troops land at Jolo, old capital of the sultans, in the Sulu Archipelago at the southernmost end of the Philippines .... All Japanese escape routes on the Bicol Peninsula of southern Luzon are cut.	U.S. resumes diplomatic relations with Argentina, and Spruille Braden is named ambassador.	
	A	B	C	D	E
	Includes developments that affect more than one world region, international organizations and important meetings of major world leaders.	*Includes all developments in European countries and military engagements between Allied and Axis powers in Africa and at sea.*	*Includes all developments in Japan and China, Japanese foreign policy and military actions in the Pacific region.*	*Includes all domestic and regional developments in Latin America, the Caribbean and Canada.*	*Includes developments in those independent nations and colonial possessions not covered in Columns B, C and D.*

U.S. Politics & Social Issues	U.S. Foreign Policy & Defense	U.S. Economy & Environment	Science, Technology & Nature	Culture, Leisure & Life Style	
		UMW Pres. Lewis agrees to urge miners to keep the mines open for a 30-day extension of the present contract on condition that any wage adjustments be retroactive to April 1.		Robert Merrill and Thomas Hayward win first awards in "*The Metropolitan Opera Presents*" auditions.	Apr. 1
		James Byrnes resigns as war mobilization director because victory "is not far distant."		Joe F. Carr Trophy, for the NFL's most valuable player, goes to Frank Sinkwich of the Detroit Lions.	Apr. 2
		Senate rejects a compromise manpower control bill and insists on its own "voluntary" bill, calling for a new conference with the House.	Mississippi River spills over its banks in one of Louisiana's worst floods, forcing 10,000 persons to evacuate their homes.		Apr. 3
	Adm. Ernest King says the U.S. must maintain a large postwar Navy and keep its new Pacific bases safe from future aggression .... London dispatches reveal extensive use of new U.S. warplane, the P-38, equipped with a bombsight that permits greater accuracy at high speeds.	UMW asks hard coal operators for a 25% wage increase and a 10¢-a-ton welfare fund royalty for 72,000 miners .... Senate confirms Fred Vinson as war mobilization director.			Apr. 4
	John Foster Dulles accepts appointment as an adviser to the U.S. delegation to the San Francisco security conference.	NWLB warns UMW coal miners that unless work stoppages are halted at some 200 mines the government will seize the operations.		The 1945 Nicholas Butler Gold Medal, awarded every five years, goes to George Santayana for his contribution to philosophy in his new book *The Realm of Being* .... *The Collected Poetry of W.H. Auden* is published.	Apr. 5
				Board of Motion Picture Censors in Memphis, Tenn. bans the movie *Brewster's Millions*, calling it "inimical to the friendly relations" between blacks and whites.	Apr. 6
		Stabilization Dir. Davis, Price Admin. Bowles and War Food Admin. Jones report to FDR that the dangers of inflation are apparent and call for continuation of controls into the postwar period.			Apr. 7
	War Secy. Stimson endorses a proposal for a postwar merger of the Army and Navy into a single department headed by a Secretary of the Armed Forces.			Senate's Small Business Comm. begins investigation of charges that major motion picture chains are forcing small independent houses out of business .... Byron Nelson sets a new PGA record for 72 holes as he wins the Iron Lung Open Golf Tournament in Atlanta with a 263.	Apr. 8
	Sen. Arthur Vandenberg (R, Mich.) asks that the Administration provide a survey of prospective postwar commitments.				Apr. 9
F	G	H	I	J	
Includes elections, federal-state relations, civil rights and liberties, crime, the judiciary, education, health care, poverty, urban affairs and population.	*Includes formation and debate of U.S. foreign and defense policies, veterans affairs and defense spending. (Relations with specific foreign countries are usually found under the region concerned.)*	*Includes business, labor, agriculture, taxation, transportation, consumer affairs, monetary and fiscal policy, natural resources, pollution and accidents.*	*Includes worldwide scientific, medical and technological developments, natural phenomena, U.S. weather and natural disasters.*	*Includes the arts, religion, scholarship, communications media, sports, entertainment, fashions, fads and social life.*	

	World Affairs	European War Zone	Pacific War Zone	The Americas	Other Countries & Territories
Apr. 10	U.S. delegates to the World Security Conference agree to decide on questions of policy by majority rule, support the Security Council voting procedure and Russia's claim to three votes .... International jurists agree that The Hague be the seat of the new World Court.	Americans take Hanover, as the British reach Bremen's outskirts .... U.S. troops capture former Nazi Vice Chancellor Franz von Papen .... All of Vienna west and south of the Danube except the island between the river and the Danube Canal is seized by the Russians .... British open an offensive across the Senio River in the general vicinity of Lugo in the southeastern corner of the Po Valley.	U.S. Marines clear most of Motobu Peninsula on the northern half of Okinawa, capturing the naval base at Unten Harbor.		
Apr. 11	International Education Assembly of the U.N. opens in N.Y., hearing plans for postwar exchanges of students and teachers .... Spain severs relations with Japan because of Japanese mistreatment of Spanish nationals in Manila.	In a sweep into Saxony, U.S. troops reach the Elbe River at Magdeburg, 63 miles from Berlin .... British troops cross the Santerno River and advance along a 30-mile front towards Bologna.	American troops land on Bohol Island in the Visayan group of the southern Philippines and overcome enemy resistance.	Chilean Congress approves the cabinet's decision to enter the war against Japan.	
Apr. 12		Yugoslavia and Russia conclude a 20-year friendship and military treaty, providing for mutual aid against attack and abstinence from alliances against each other .... Russian troops enter Moravia and cut the last serviceable communications in an eight-mile Nazi escape corridor from Vienna .... U.S. troops take Weimar and Erfurt and capture Schweinfurt and Heilbronn .... UNRAA reaches an agreement with Czechoslovakia for relief aid.	Japanese launch a second massed kamikaze attack against U.S. 5th Fleet off Okinawa. 185 kamikaze planes participate, sinking two U.S. ships and damaging nine.		Moscow reports armed clashes between right and left-wing factions in Iran over Iranian policy towards the USSR .... Saudi Arabia, Syria and Lebanon sign the U.N. Declaration, bringing total membership to 47 countries.
Apr. 13		Soviets complete the conquest of Vienna, seven years, one month and one day after the 1938 German "Anschluss." .... U.S. troops cross the Mulde River to reach a point 38 miles west of Dresden and 98 miles from the Russians.		Canadian P.M Mackenzie King announces in Ottawa that general elections will be held June 11.	
Apr. 14		German reports place American forces only 21 miles from Berlin .... Russians advance to a point 63 miles from Linz, Austria .... Polish troops fighting with the British in Italy capture Imola, 20 miles southeast of Bologna .... Stalin names Foreign Affairs Commissar Vyacheslav M. Molotov as Russia's representative to the San Francisco Conference.	Superfortresses drop thousands of incendiary bombs on Tokyo, starting large fires, including some within the Imperial Palace.		
Apr. 15		Tito says the people of Istria and Trieste "desire to be incorporated into the new Yugoslavia." .... Germans destroy one of two U.S. 9th Army bridgeheads across the Elbe River near Magdeburg.	Japanese launch a third massed kamikaze attack against the U.S. 5th Fleet off Okinawa. 165 kamikaze planes participate, sinking one American vessel and damaging six.		
Apr. 16	At its closing session the International Education Assembly adopts a resolution calling for the San Francisco Conference to establish a permanent International Office of Education.	U.S. troops enter Nuremberg as Eisenhower announces that victory will be announced when "all important enemy pockets on the western front" are destroyed .... Although Moscow remains silent, the Germans report an all-out Russian drive for Berlin.	British and Indian troops occupy the Burmese port of Taungup, encountering little Japanese opposition .... Tokyo is again hit with incendiary bombs by Mariannas-based Superfortresses.		
Apr. 17		After capturing Halle, U.S. troops enter Leipzig's outskirts.	Allies report one-half of Tokyo's useful military and industrial targets have been wiped out.		Gandhi says the delegation named to represent India at San Francisco is "worse than no representation."
Apr. 18		Germany is divided in two as spearheads of the U.S. 3rd Army drive into Czechoslovakia near Asch .... German broadcasts say Russian troops are within 14 miles of Berlin and are moving southward to outflank the city.	Ernest (Ernie) Pyle, 44, the most famous war correspondent of World War II, is killed on Ie Jima when he is hit by a machine gun bullet .... MacArthur reports his forces have rescued about 7,000 civilians, mostly Filipinos but including Americans, Britons and others, from the Japanese cornered at Baguio, Luzon since March 28 .... British troops capture Chauk, center of one of Burma's richest oil producing areas.	U.S. Senate ratifies the Mexican water pact guaranteeing Mexico 1.5 million acre-feet of water annually from the Colorado River and giving the U.S. about 350,000 acre-feet from the Rio Grande .... Brazilian Communist Luis Carlos Prestes is released after nine years in prison under a general amnesty signed by Pres. Getulio Vargas.	
	A *Includes developments that affect more than one world region, international organizations and important meetings of major world leaders.*	B *Includes all developments in European countries and military engagements between Allied and Axis powers in Africa and at sea.*	C *Includes all developments in Japan and China, Japanese foreign policy and military actions in the Pacific region.*	D *Includes all domestic and regional developments in Latin America, the Caribbean and Canada.*	E *Includes developments in those independent nations and colonial possessions not covered in Columns B, C and D.*

U.S. Politics & Social Issues	U.S. Foreign Policy & Defense	U.S. Economy & Environment	Science, Technology & Nature	Culture, Leisure & Life Style	
	Senate votes to extend the Lend-Lease Act another year after June 30.	Agriculture Dept. forecasts a record winter wheat crop of about 862,515,000 bushels.	Prof. Albert Einstein retires from the faculty of the Institute for Advanced Study at Princeton Univ. and receives the title of professor emeritus.	N.Y. Drama Critics select Tennessee Williams' *The Glass Menagerie* as the season's best American play.	Apr. 10
	Army Air Force announces that most of its air strength will be redeployed to the Pacific after V-E Day, with only a small force remaining in Europe.	UMW and soft coal operators sign a new contract that increases pay for travel and lunch time by $6.44 for a six-day week and provides time-and-a-half pay for work over 35 hours a week . . . . WPB announces preparatory steps toward providing $50 million in machinery and equipment for auto industry reconversion.		*Variety* reports the most popular songs are: (1) *My Dreams Are Getting Better All the Time*, (2) *A Little On the Lonely Side*, and (3) *Rum and Coca-Cola*.	Apr. 11
FDR dies of a cerebral hemorrhage at the "Little White House" in Warm Springs, Ga. after 12 years, one month and eight days in the presidency. Harry S Truman is sworn in as president by Chief Justice Harlan Stone at the White House.	War Secy. Stimson informs Pres. Truman of the secret Manhattan Project to develop an atomic bomb . . . . Adm. Nimitz suggests the U.S. keep Iwo Jima Island and the Marianas Islands after the war because they would be vital for future defense.	Bethlehem Steel and the CIO-USW sign a new wage pact covering 17,000 workers and including 6¢ night shift premiums and vacation provisions . . . . U.S. government files a civil antitrust suit in Newark, N.J. against Westinghouse, accusing it of being in conspiracy with two German concerns to restrict production and trade.	A tornado hits parts of Okla., Ark., Mo. and Ill., killing more than 100 persons . . . . Organization of The Eye Bank for Sight Restoration is announced in N.Y. for the collection of healthy cornea tissue for grafting operations.		Apr. 12
The body of the late President Roosevelt leaves the Warm Springs Foundation in a hearse at 9:25 a.m., accompanied by Mrs. Roosevelt and troops from Ft. Benning, Ga. President Truman proclaims April 14 the day of the funeral and a day of mourning and prayer throughout the nation. He says of FDR: "His fellow countrymen will sorely miss his fortitude and faith and courage in the time to come." . . . . With Truman becoming president, Sen. Kenneth McKellar (D, Tenn.) becomes the regular presiding officer of the Senate.					Apr. 13
Simple funeral services attended by members of the family, close friends, Truman, British Foreign Secy. Eden and other officials are held at 4 p.m. in the White House for FDR. Some 500,000 people line the streets leading to the White House during the day in solemn tribute. Businesses of all types are suspended for the entire day throughout the country.		Army authorizes a $200-million cutback in artillery orders, which will affect 75 plants.			Apr. 14
FDR is buried at Hyde Park after an austere military ceremony.					Apr. 15
In an address to a joint session of Congress, President Truman asks for continuation of FDR's policies and promises prosecution of the war to its conclusion, punishment of war criminals and creation of United Nations organization for "just settlement of international differences."	Truman meets with British Foreign Secy. Eden.	Cattle feeders and packers tell a congressional food investigation committee that the OPA is to blame for meat shortages . . . . U.S. government starts an antitrust suit in Danville, Ill. against the A&P Co., charging it has conspired to control food prices in restraint of trade and to gain a monopoly.			Apr. 16
	Truman signs the bill extending Lend-Lease through June 1946 . . . . Truman endorses the Bretton Woods financial plan, continuation of the reciprocal trade policy and the San Francisco Conference.	Truman names John Snyder to be federal loan administrator.		Actor Charlie Chaplin is found to be the father of Carol Ann, the 18-month-old daughter of Joan Berry, in a Los Angeles court . . . . The baseball season opens with a full schedule being played.	Apr. 17
					Apr. 18

F	G	H	I	J
Includes elections, federal-state relations, civil rights and liberties, crime, the judiciary, education, health care, poverty, urban affairs and population.	*Includes formation and debate of U.S. foreign and defense policies, veterans affairs and defense spending. (Relations with specific foreign countries are usually found under the region concerned.)*	*Includes business, labor, agriculture, taxation, transportation, consumer affairs, monetary and fiscal policy, natural resources, pollution and accidents.*	*Includes worldwide scientific, medical and technological developments, natural phenomena, U.S. weather and natural disasters.*	*Includes the arts, religion, scholarship, communications media, sports, entertainment, fashions, fads and social life.*

	World Affairs	European War Zone	Pacific War Zone	The Americas	Other Countries & Territories
Apr. 19	International Air Transport Conference ends in Havana after deciding on a policy of widespread competition for world air transportation and electing H.J. Symington as president.	For the first time Moscow reveals its offensive against Berlin as Berlin radio reports the Soviets to be 10 miles east of the city .... U.S. forces under Gen. George Patton liberate the Buchenwald concentration camp, freeing 21,000 inmates. Evidence of atrocities, including crematoria and mass graves, are discovered on the camp grounds .... U.S. troops capture Leipzig .... War Secy. Stimson says that since D-day the Allies have taken 2.1 million German prisoners on the western front.	U.S. forces reach northern tip of Okinawa and begin an assault on Japanese defenders on southern part of the island, estimated at 77,000.	Insurgent Honduran forces in Coban State are reported defeated by three government units .... Guatemala establishes diplomatic relations with Russia.	Iranian Premier Morteza Quilikhan Bayat's cabinet resigns after failure to obtain the approval of parliament.
Apr. 20	Jurists of 44 United Nations member states sign a preliminary draft of a plan for the International Court of Justice, which will be submitted to the San Francisco Conference.	Units of the U.S. 7th Army take Nuremberg, the main city of northern Bavaria and site of Nazi party rallies .... The High Court of Justice in Paris sentences Gen. Henri-Fernand Dentz, former high commissioner of Syria, to death with military degradation and property confiscation, as a traitor to France .... Berlin radio reports Soviet troops at Werneuchen, 7½ miles north of the city .... Allies break through the last mountain barriers southwest of Bologna and advance in the Po Valley.	A British month-long drive on Rangoon places them 220 miles north of the city.		
Apr. 21		Russia and Polish provisional government sign a treaty of friendship, mutual assistance and postwar collaboration .... Russian troops are three to four miles inside of Berlin's city limits, according to German broadcasts .... British capture Bologna.	American troops seize Iegusugu Peak on Ie Island, ending organized Japanese resistance there .... More than 200 U.S. Marianas-based bombers carry out assaults on nine Japanese airfields on Kyushu.		
Apr. 22	Hundreds of delegates and advisers to the U.N. Conference on International Organization arrive in San Francisco and express hope and confidence in constructive results .... Molotov arrives in Washington and confers with Truman.	Soviet troops reportedly take 16 suburbs and five towns on the outskirts of Berlin .... French troops capture Stuttgart and Sigmaringen, cross the Danube and reach the Swiss border 20 miles west of Lake Constance.		Argentina lifts its censorship on outgoing news.	Indian government announces it will take over development of major industries, such as automobile and steel production, if private capital is not available.
Apr. 23	Truman greets Molotov at Blair House and although he expresses a commitment to FDR's policies, he indicates concern over the Polish question .... Truman and de Gaulle meet in Washington to discuss the French role in Allied diplomacy; no agreement is reached .... Molotov confers with State Secy. Stettinius, Foreign Secy. Eden and Amb. T.V. Soong, discussing the Polish question inconclusively, and other matters relative to the San Francisco Conference.	Polish exile government in London asks the British and Americans again to have it represent Poland at San Francisco .... Soviet troops drive deeper into Berlin, swing north to cross the Havel River and seize Oranienburg, Frankfort-on-Oder and Cottbus, according to reports from Moscow .... U.S. troops seize Modena, near the center of Italy, and on the west coast seize the naval base of La Spezia .... U.S. 3rd Army plunges south towards Regensburg, its columns reaching to points 13 and 25 miles from the city.	Americans win the high ground west of Ishin in southern Okinawa, and first real gain in four days.		
Apr. 24		Two Russian Armies link up inside Berlin, giving the Russians control over at least a quarter of the city .... Heinrich Himmler meets Sweden's Count Bernadotte in Luebeck, asking Bernadotte to arrange a meeting with Eisenhower for capitulation on the entire western front .... Eisenhower asks the U.N. War Crimes Commission to send investigators to German concentration camps to make an official survey of the situation .... Marshal Henri-Philippe Petain arrives in Switzerland from southern Germany on his way to France to face treason charges.	In substantial gains on Okinawa, Americans retake Kakuzu in the center of the line after days of very strong Japanese resistance .... Chinese counterattacks against a Japanese drive into western Hunan Province in an effort to keep the enemy from reaching the U.S. airbase at Chihkiang, 250 miles southeast of Chungking.		
Apr. 25	Via a telephone hookup, Truman appeals to delegates at the opening session of the San Francisco Conference to achieve a just and lasting peace .... De Gaulle says the U.N. Conference cannot deal with world problems until it deals with France .... Labor delegates from the U.S., Britain, Russia and France meet at the opening of the World Trade Union Conference in Oakland, Calif. to make relevant suggestions to the nearby U.N. conference.	Truman confers with his military leaders, cables Churchill and informs Stalin of the Himmler offer; all agree that only unconditional surrender will be accepted .... American congressmen who visited the Buchenwald concentration camp report that the daily death quota was 80 and that Russian officers were burned alive.			

A	B	C	D	E
Includes developments that affect more than one world region, international organizations and important meetings of major world leaders.	*Includes all developments in European countries and military engagements between Allied and Axis powers in Africa and at sea.*	*Includes all developments in Japan and China, Japanese foreign policy and military actions in the Pacific region.*	*Includes all domestic and regional developments in Latin America, the Caribbean and Canada.*	*Includes developments in those independent nations and colonial possessions not covered in Columns B, C and D.*

U.S. Politics & Social Issues	U.S. Foreign Policy & Defense	U.S. Economy & Environment	Science, Technology & Nature	Culture, Leisure & Life Style	
Truman tells congressional leaders that he supports pending legislation sponsored by FDR, which includes reciprocal trade agreements, the OPA and Stabilization Act, drafting of 18-year-olds and the Bretton Woods proposals.		Stabilization Dir. Davis approves a NWLB-sponsored wage increase of 5¢ an hour for about 55,000 textile workers.	Lord & Taylor presents the 1945 American Design Award and $25,000 to the National Academy of Sciences for the collective acheivements of American scientists in creating weapons of war.	Rodgers and Hammerstein's *Carousel* opens on Broadway .... Most Rev. Geoffrey Francis Fisher is enthroned as Archbishop of Canterbury and Primate of all England.	Apr. 19
Truman designates Charles Ross of the *St. Louis Post Dispatch* as his press secretary.		NWLB approves an increase of 5¢ an hour for 30,000 maintenance workers at five auto manufacturers.			Apr. 20
				Gloria Vanderbilt di Cicco marries orchestra conductor Leopold Stokowski in Mexico following her divorce in Reno yesterday from Pasquale de Cicco.	Apr. 21
		Stabilization Dir. Davis announces a 10-point plan to give civilians more meat without raising ceiling prices.		Toronto Maple Leafs win the NHL Stanley Cup, defeating the Detroit Red Wings, 2-1, in the seventh game in Detroit.	Apr. 22
		NWLB approves the soft coal wage contract.		Dr. Nicholas Murray Butler, president of Columbia Univ. for 44 years, sends in his resignation to take effect Oct. 1. He will become president emeritus.	Apr. 23
	Senate votes in favor of an amendment to prohibit the Army's use of 18-year-old soldiers in combat until they have at least six months training .... House Foreign Affairs Comm. asks the government to use arms and ignore treaties if necessary to track down German war criminals.			The 16 major league baseball clubs elect U.S. Sen. Albert Chandler (D, Ky.) as commissioner.	Apr. 24
		WPB Chmn. Krug says that the board is ready to end controls as soon as possible and that probably one-third of them will be removed in the next four months .... RFC announces removal of Army and Navy restrictions on disposal of surplus equipment and machinery.	National Foundation for Infantile Paralysis Pres. Basil O'Connor says the organization will continue despite the death of its founder, FDR.		Apr. 25
F	G	H	I	J	
Includes elections, federal-state relations, civil rights and liberties, crime, the judiciary, education, health care, poverty, urban affairs and population.	*Includes formation and debate of U.S. foreign and defense policies, veterans affairs and defense spending. (Relations with specific foreign countries are usually found under the region concerned.)*	*Includes business, labor, agriculture, taxation, transportation, consumer affairs, monetary and fiscal policy, natural resources, pollution and accidents.*	*Includes worldwide scientific, medical and technological developments, natural phenomena, U.S. weather and natural disasters.*	*Includes the arts, religion, scholarship, communications media, sports, entertainment, fashions, fads and social life.*	

	World Affairs	European War Zone	Pacific War Zone	The Americas	Other Countries & Territories
Apr. 26	At the first plenary session in San Francisco, State Secy. Stettinius says the world body should work out only a charter. Molotov says the lessons of the League of Nations must be remembered. Foreign Secy. Eden asks that a charter be drafted by May. 24.	Italian partisans capture Benito Mussolini in northern Italy as he tries to escape to Switzerland .... Elements of the U.S. 1st Army and the 1st Ukrainian Army make contact at Torgau on the Elbe River, 75 miles south of Berlin .... British capture Bremen, while to the south Allied forces advance towards the German redoubt in Bavaria .... Allied forces capture Verona and Parma in Italy .... Marshal Petain is arrested at the French border and taken to Paris to await trial.		Brazilian Communist Luis Prestes says he will be a candidate in forthcoming presidential elections.	
Apr. 27	U.N. Conference agrees to give one vote each to White Russia and the Ukraine but denies representation to the Polish provisional government .... Truman names Edwin Pauley as the U.S. member of the Allied Reparation Commission.	Bernadotte delivers the Allied reply to the German surrender offer to Himmler at Flensburg .... Russian troops overwhelm the southern half of Berlin, capturing four city districts including Tempelhof airport .... American troops enter Genoa, Italy's greatest port .... Acting State Secy. Grew condemns German atrocities and says there must be effective punishment of those responsible.	American troops take the summer Philippine capital of Baguio.		
Apr. 28	Russian Foreign Commissar Molotov demands that White Russia and the Ukraine be given their seats at the San Fransisco Conference at once, before working committees start deliberations.	Mussolini is executed by Italian partisans near Dongo after a brief trial along with his mistress Clara Petacci and several of his followers .... An AP dispatch quoting Sen. Tom Connally (D, Tex.) says Germany has surrendered unconditionally, but Truman denies the report .... Russian forces drive the remaining Nazi elements in Berlin into an area of 25 square miles in the city's center .... U.S. Brig. Gen. Eric Wood calls Buchenwald concentration camp an "extermination factory" which has deprived Europe of its best democratic personnel.	U.S. hospital ship *Comfort* is damaged when attacked by Japanese planes, and 29 persons are killed. The ship was properly designated as a hospital ship and was attacked 50 miles south of Okinawa .... Amb. Hurley says in Chungking that the Allies are in agreement about China, favoring its unification.		
Apr. 29	U.S. proposes four changes in Dumbarton Oaks agreement: (1) that the charter written now be subject to future revision, (2) that members settle disputes with justice, (3) that the assembly have the right to recommend revision of treaties, and (4) that the organization assume the functions of the League and establish a trusteeship system.	The U.S. 7th Army enters Munich, the birthplace of the Nazi Party, against slight resistance after freeing the 30,000 inmates of nearby Dachau concentration camp .... Russian occupation forces set up an Austrian provisional government in Vienna under the premiership of Dr. Karl Renner .... U.S. troops enter Milan as the British take Venice, Padua, Mestre, Vicenza and Como.	Americans take the Machinato airfield on the west coast of Okinawa.		
Apr. 30	Argentina is invited to the U.N. Conference.	Hitler and Eva Braun commit suicide in the early afternoon. Their bodies are burned outside the Reich Chancellery bunker in Berlin .... Russian flag is raised over the ruins of the Reichstag .... Munich is secured by American troops, who receive cooperation from the freedom movement within the city.			
May 1	Big Four set up working committees to draft a U.N. Charter.	Hamburg radio says Hitler died in the battle of Berlin while at his command post in the Chancellery. Grand Adm. Karl Doenitz proclaims himself the country's new leader .... As the Russians continue to diminish the German hold on Berlin, the British and Americans link up northwest of the city .... British troops make contact with Yugoslavian units at Monfalcone, eight miles northwest of Trieste.	An Allied invasion opens on Borneo with landings on Tarakan Island, just off the northeast corner of Netherlands Borneo.	Brazilian Pres. Vargas announces his support for Gen. Eurico Gaspar Dutra for the presidency.	
May 2	World Trade Union Conference demands official recognition from the U.N. meeting for consultative purposes.	The war in Italy and part of Austria ends at noon under terms of a German unconditional surrender signed April 29 in Caserta .... Germans surrender Berlin to the Russians at 3 p.m. after 12 days of intense street fighting in which much of the German capital has been destroyed .... British troops capture Wismar on the Baltic, cutting off the Kiel area and the Danish peninsula .... Truman names Associate Justice Robert Jackson of the U.S. Supreme Court as chief U.S. counsel on the international military tribunal to be set up by the Allies to try war criminals .... Former French Premier Pierre Laval arrives in Barcelona on a Luftwaffe plane and is interned by the Spanish government pending a decision on turning him over to the Allies.	British forces land on both sides of the Rangoon River, 20 miles south of Rangoon .... American troops enter Davao on Mindanao Island.		

A	B	C	D	E
Includes developments that affect more than one world region, international organizations and important meetings of major world leaders.	*Includes all developments in European countries and military engagements between Allied and Axis powers in Africa and at sea.*	*Includes all developments in Japan and China, Japanese foreign policy and military actions in the Pacific region.*	*Includes all domestic and regional developments in Latin America, the Caribbean and Canada.*	*Includes developments in those independent nations and colonial possessions not covered in Columns B, C and D.*

U.S. Politics & Social Issues	U.S. Foreign Policy & Defense	U.S. Economy & Environment	Science, Technology & Nature	Culture, Leisure & Life Style	
	U.S. carrier *Franklin,* hit by Japanese bombs on March 19, arrives for repairs at the Brooklyn Navy Yard. It is described as the most damaged ship ever to make port.	Stabilization Dir. Davis grants NWLB discretionary authorization to set rigid standards on "fringe" wage adjustments . . . . Truman asks Commerce Secy. Henry Wallace to investigate alleged misuse of patents to support monopolies.			Apr. 26
	House accepts the Senate bill to prevent 18-year-olds from going to battle without six months training and sends it to Truman.				Apr. 27
		WPB revokes 40 lesser controls over industry covering a variety of consumer goods . . . . Senate Agriculture Comm. votes to remove the REA from the Agriculture Dept.		Michigan captures the team title at the Penn Relays in Philadelphia . . . . Illinois wins the team title at the Drake Relays.	Apr. 28
	The aircraft carrier *Franklin D. Roosevelt* is launched at Brooklyn.			Pope Pius forecasts that the late Mother Frances Cabrini will be proclaimed a saint after the war.	Apr. 29
	U.S. and the Netherlands sign Lend-Lease agreements in Washington with a total value of $242,000,000 . . . . Acting State Secy. Grew says the U.S. does not recognize the new Austrian government.	Because sugar reserves "are at rock bottom" the OWI announces a 25% cut in sugar rations . . . . NWLB orders Lewis and the UMW to extend the hard coal contract until a new agreement is reached.			Apr. 30
		About 72,000 anthracite miners walk out after their contract expires.			May 1
Truman announces the resignation of Postmaster Gen. Frank Walker and appointment of Robert Hannegan as his successor, effective June 30.		Because of changing war conditions, Truman asks Congress to reduce the 1946 federal budget accordingly . . . . OPA files suit in N.Y. against the Dairymen's League Cooperative Assn. to restrain it from violating ceiling price regulations.			May 2
F	G	H	I	J	
Includes elections, federal-state relations, civil rights and liberties, crime, the judiciary, education, health care, poverty, urban affairs and population.	*Includes formation and debate of U.S. foreign and defense policies, veterans affairs and defense spending. (Relations with specific foreign countries are usually found under the region concerned.)*	*Includes business, labor, agriculture, taxation, transportation, consumer affairs, monetary and fiscal policy, natural resources, pollution and accidents.*	*Includes worldwide scientific, medical and technological developments, natural phenomena, U.S. weather and natural disasters.*	*Includes the arts, religion, scholarship, communications media, sports, entertainment, fashions, fads and social life.*	

	World Affairs	European War Zone	Pacific War Zone	The Americas	Other Countries & Territories
May 3	The four main committees start work on the U.N. Charter in San Francisco.	Hamburg is surrendered to the British without battle, as they link up with the Russians on a 65-mile front south of the city . . . . British forces occupy Trieste and Gorizia, formerly Italian cities claimed by Yugoslavia.	Japanese begin fifth massed kamikaze attack on U.S. 5th Fleet off Okinawa. 125 kamikaze planes participate, sinking six American vessels and damaging six others . . . . Rangoon is secured by the British 14th Army, with most of the Japanese forces fleeing. Its fall virtually brings the Burma campaign to its end.	Brazilian War Minister Eurico Gaspar Dutra says national troops in Italy will return home immediately.	
May 4	UNRRA Dir. Lehman announces reorganization of his office, setting up a director general's office in London.	All German forces in the Netherlands, northwest Germany, Denmark, Helgoland and the Frisian Islands surrender unconditionally to Field Marshal Montgomery . . . . American units occupy Innsbruck, Salzburg and Berchtesgaden, while elements drive into Italy, joining with U.S. troops at Vipiteno . . . . Russian troops complete the liberation of Slovakia and move towards a link-up with U.S. forces in Austria near Linz.	The Chinese claim to have halted a four-pronged Japanese drive towards the U.S. airbase at Chihkiang, 250 miles south of Chungking.		
May 5	Big Four powers propose 22 amendments to Dumbarton Oaks plan at the U.N. Conference in San Francisco. Proposals concern statement of principles for charter of future world organization . . . . World Trade Union Conference, with representatives from 35 countries, ends in Oakland, publishing an agreed-upon charter calling for free labor movements in member states.	Russian Foreign Commissar Molotov tells the U.S. and Britain that 16 Polish underground leaders connected with the Polish government-in-exile in London have been arrested by Russia on charges of diversionist activities against the Red Army. Britain and the U.S. request an explanation and break off negotiations with Russia on the Polish provisional government pending receipt of the facts . . . . Eighteen American editors who toured German prison camps issue a statement condemning the Nazi plan of calculated brutality and urging punishment of war criminals . . . . German Army Group G, comprising between 200,000 and 400,000 men, surrenders to the Americans, ending resistance in Bavaria and western Austria.	Planes from Okinawa sink five Japanese ships and damage 16 others in the Tsushima and Korean Straits, according to Navy reports.		
May 6	Big Four nations agree on two amendments to Dumbarton Oaks plan, allowing the General Assembly to recommend action against conditions threatening peace and giving the future world organization jurisdiction over alliances not directed against Axis powers.	U.S. Agriculture Dept. says European food production is expected to drop 5-10% and that 12 million tons of food must be imported for the year starting this August . . . . U.S. 3rd Army, advancing along a 130-mile front in Czechoslovakia, takes Karlsbad and Pilsen . . . . Portugal severs relations with Germany.		Women vote for the first time in a special election for members to a new constitutional convention in Panama.	
May 7	Molotov tells a San Francisco news conference that the Big Four have reached agreement on the world security organization.	AP reporter Edward Kennedy reports from Riems that Germany has signed an unconditional surrender at Eisenhower's headquarters there . . . . Spain and Sweden sever diplomatic relations with Germany.			Haj Amin el Husseini, Grand Mufti of Jerusalem, arrives by German plane in Berne, Switzerland and is deported to France.
May 8	U.S. delegation asks the San Francisco Conference to accept the formula for relating the Pan-American security system to the U.N., which would permit the Western Hemisphere to deal with its own disputes.	Unconditional surrender of Germany is ratified and confirmed in Berlin at 11:01 p.m., local time. V-E Day is proclaimed by the Allies and greeted with enormous celebrations in Moscow, London and New York; but observers note that the mood of Americans is muted by the continuing war against Japan.			
May 9	Molotov leaves the U.N. conference for Moscow with the Polish question still unresolved . . . . Smaller nations attack the single-vote veto of the Big Five at the U.N. Conference and suggest a three-vote veto in its place.	Amidst mass surrender of German forces to the Allies, scattered fighting is still reported . . . . Reich Marshal Hermann Goering, Field Marshal Gen. Albert Kesselring and Gen. Franz Ritter von Epp surrender to the U.S. 7th Army . . . . Norwegian puppet Premier Vidkun Quisling is arrested along with various officials of his government . . . . King Christian X of Denmark opens parliament in Copenhagen and pays tribute to the Allies.	Japanese offer their first serious resistance on Mindanao Island north of the captured town of Davao.		Arab agitators massacre over 50 Europeans and pillage houses during V-E Day celebrations in Algeria's Constantine Dept.

	A	B	C	D	E
	Includes developments that affect more than one world region, international organizations and important meetings of major world leaders.	*Includes all developments in European countries and military engagements between Allied and Axis powers in Africa and at sea.*	*Includes all developments in Japan and China, Japanese foreign policy and military actions in the Pacific region.*	*Includes all domestic and regional developments in Latin America, the Caribbean and Canada.*	*Includes developments in those independent nations and colonial possessions not covered in Columns B, C and D.*

U.S. Politics & Social Issues	U.S. Foreign Policy & Defense	U.S. Economy & Environment	Science, Technology & Nature	Culture, Leisure & Life Style	
		Solid Fuels Admin. Ickes seizes 363 Pennsylvania coal mines on a presidential order and tells miners to return to work by May 7.			May 3
Truman and former FDR adviser Harry Hopkins confer for the first time at the White House.	Army Chief of Staff Gen. George C. Marshall warns that it is "urgently necessary" to increase Army replacements in the Pacific over and above battle losses.	Ickes seizes 33 more coal mines in Pennsylvania .... A.P. Giannini, chairman of the of the Bank of America National Trust and Savings Assn., Los Angeles, says he will retire on May 8 and plans to form a non-profit foundation for humanitarian purposes.	What scientists describe as an exploding bolide, the largest type of meteor, awakes many in eastern Pa., Md., N.J., and Del. by a series of shocks and explosions following a blue-white flash in the sky.		May 4
	A Japanese balloon bomb kills a woman and five children near Lakeview, Ore., the first recorded war victims of an enemy attack upon the U.S. mainland .... War Dept. announces that two million overseas veterans will be discharged after V-E Day and about six million will be sent to the Pacific .... The 27,000-ton aircraft carrier *Kearsarge* is launched in N.Y.			The arrest near Genoa of poet Ezra Pound, who espoused Fascism and made Axis radio broadcasts, is announced by U.S. officials in Italy.	May 5
N.Y. Mayor Fiorello La Guardia announces that he will not seek a fourth term.		Nine Pennsylvania UMW locals defy the government's order to return to work tomorrow.			May 6
Truman family moves into the White House.		Supreme Court upholds portal-to-portal pay for bituminous coal miners.		John Hershey's *A Bell for Adano*, Mary Coyle Chase's play *Harvey* and James Reston's national affairs reporting receive Pulitzer Prizes .... Mass. Gov. Maurice Tobin signs a bill aimed at ending unofficial book censorship in the state .... Branch Rickey announces the formation of the United Negro Baseball League with six teams: Brooklyn, Hilldale, Pa., Detroit, Chicago, Toledo and Pittsburgh.	May 7
Jersey City, N.J. Mayor Frank Hague is reelected for his eighth successive term.	Navy Secy. James Forrestal names Adm. Henry K. Hewitt to conduct further Pearl Harbor investigations .... War Dept. indefinitely suspends a regulation requiring review of all cases of professional athletes.	Treasury Secy. Henry Morgenthau says U.S. costs for WWII have reached $276 billion.		The national brownout of non-essential lighting is lifted by the WPB.	May 8
	Army Service Forces Chief Gen. Brehon B. Somervell says that about 3.1 million U.S. troops will be withdrawn from Europe within a year .... Truman signs the bill extending the Selective Service Act to May 15, 1946 "reluctantly" because of restrictions on 18 and 19-year-olds.	War Mobilization Dir. Vinson says unemployment may increase by 1.5 million over the next six months .... Associated General Contractors of America and the AFL make public their pact for postwar working relations, including a joint committee to deal with industry problems without recourse to government.		War Mobilization Dir. Vinson announces the immediate lifting of the midnight curfew and ban on horse racing .... Henry Rosen and Harvey Stemmer, who bribed five Brooklyn College basketball players, are convicted in N.Y.	May 9

F	G	H	I	J
Includes elections, federal-state relations, civil rights and liberties, crime, the judiciary, education, health care, poverty, urban affairs and population.	*Includes formation and debate of U.S. foreign and defense policies, veterans affairs and defense spending. (Relations with specific foreign countries are usually found under the region concerned.)*	*Includes business, labor, agriculture, taxation, transportation, consumer affairs, monetary and fiscal policy, natural resources, pollution and accidents.*	*Includes worldwide scientific, medical and technological developments, natural phenomena, U.S. weather and natural disasters.*	*Includes the arts, religion, scholarship, communications media, sports, entertainment, fashions, fads and social life.*

	World Affairs	European War Zone	Pacific War Zone	The Americas	Other Countries & Territories
May 10		Churchill tells the House of Commons that conscription of men for the war against Japan must continue .... The first German submarine to surrender after the Nazi capitulation, the *U-249*, arrives in Plymouth under escort .... OWI announces that all newspapers and periodicals originating in foreign countries will be barred from Germany and that the Allied government information offices will be the German source for news.	The largest number of Superfortresses to date, 400, is sent against Japan in a one-day strike at Kyushu, Honshu and Shikoku.	State Dept. opens Bermuda to travel under limited conditions.	
May 11	Russian delegation at the U.N. parley demands the Soviets be given a permanent seat on the proposed Trusteeship Council and a larger role in the Security Council.	American and Russian forces link up in Czechoslovakia, where some Germans continue to fight .... War Secy. Stimson says that the American zone in Germany will be administered in a "tough" and "ruthless" manner.	Two Japanese suicide planes crash into the aircraft carrier *Bunker Hill* off Okinawa, causing 373 deaths and heavy fire .... American troops seize high ground on Okinawa commanding the main point in the Japanese defense line .... Chinese fight their way into the east coast port of Foochow and also take the airfield south of the city .... Australian troops capture Wewak Peninsula, clearing all Japanese from the north coast of New Guinea.		
May 12	Security Committee of the United Nations Conference on International Organization agrees on 11-member Security Council, with non-permanent members chosen by General Assembly.	Acting State Secy. Grew opposes Marshal Tito's claims to Trieste and the surrounding area, saying Tito had previously agreed to Allied military control of the region .... U.N. War Crimes Commission indicts Goering on eight counts of being a war criminal .... Truman names Lt Col. Joseph V. Hodgson as U.S. commissioner to the U.N. War Crimes Commission.			
May 13		Netherlands' Queen Wilhelmina arrives home after five years of exile in England .... Crown Prince Olaf returns to Oslo and says the Norwegian high court will demand the death sentence for all traitors.	American forces take the Maramag airfield in central Mindanao, as other units reach to within one mile of the Del Monte airfields .... Tokyo shakes up its puppet government in Manchukuo because of reputed Communist threats. Sun Pei-fong becomes governor.		
May 14	Truman confers separately with Chinese Amb. T.V. Soong and British Foreign Secy. Eden on Lend-Lease and other matters.	Americans and Britons propose to Tito that Trieste remain under Allied control until its future is determined at a peace conference .... Dr. Karl Renner's provisional government declares Austrian independence, abolishes all Nazi laws and dissolves the Nazi Party.	U.S. carrier-based planes complete three days of assaults on Kyushu and Shikoku, reportedly destroying 284 Japanese aircraft with a U.S. loss of about 10.		
May 15		Moscow reports Russian troops found Nazi Propaganda Min. Paul Joseph Goebbels and his family dead of suicide in bunkers beneath the Tiergarten in Berlin .... Yugoslavian partisans establish their own military government in Klagenfurt, capital of the province of Carinthia, Austria, side by side with the British military government.	Marines capture Chocolate Drop Hill after a five-day struggle on Okinawa's southern front .... Americans take Balete Pass in northern Luzon, gaining the only road entrance to the Cagayan Valley, where the main Japanese forces are concentrated .... Chinese troops in Foochow are forced out in the face of large Japanese reinforcements.	Truman proposes that a postwar security treaty be negotiated for all American republics.	
May 16		Churchill tells the House of Commons that it is the Allied intention to have the Germans rule themselves under Allied directions .... Yugoslavian troops continue occupation of Trieste, imposing military rule and a curfew and renaming streets, although Allied troops patrol the city and Allied headquarters in Rome announces that "an Allied naval force is now operating in Trieste." .... Paal Berg, Norwegian chief justice, says Quisling will be tried by a special jury of three judges and four laymen .... U.N. War Crimes Commission calls a meeting of member governments for May 31 in London to set up procedures and begin substantive operations.	Chinese claim they have smashed the Japanese effort to take the U.S. air-base at Chihkiang, Hunan Province.		
May 17		American troops capture Lt. Col. Otto Skorzeny, suspected of being a leader of German guerrilla forces and the man who liberated the late Benito Mussolini from the Allies in 1943.	U.S. Marines gain positions inside Naha, Okinawa, as other units advance to Ishimmi, close to the central anchor of the Japanese defense line, but further advances are stalled by stiffening Japanese resistance.		A British White Paper discloses three steps in a plan to provide Burma "full self-government within the British Commonwealth." .... Truman addresses a message of friendship to Emperor Haile Selassie in opening the first direct radio-telegraphic circuit between the U.S. and Ethiopia.

A	B	C	D	E
Includes developments that affect more than one world region, international organizations and important meetings of major world leaders.	*Includes all developments in European countries and military engagements between Allied and Axis powers in Africa and at sea.*	*Includes all developments in Japan and China, Japanese foreign policy and military actions in the Pacific region.*	*Includes all domestic and regional developments in Latin America, the Caribbean and Canada.*	*Includes developments in those independent nations and colonial possessions not covered in Columns B, C and D.*

U.S. Politics & Social Issues	U.S. Foreign Policy & Defense	U.S. Economy & Environment	Science, Technology & Nature	Culture, Leisure & Life Style	
	War Dept. announces a system for determining soldier release based on a point system giving priority credit for service overseas and in combat.	WPB Chmn. Krug announces the immediate revocation of 73 orders prohibiting or limiting manufacture of civilian goods . . . . NWLB announces a system for setting up new wage rates without the board's approval for plants shifting to consumer goods production.			May 10
	Eisenhower instructs his officers on reassignment of American forces to the Pacific, ordering them not to send men who have fought in both Africa and Europe.	Truman gives tentative approval to a program of tax concessions which is designed to make an estimated $5.7 billion in cash available to business for reconversion . . . . WMC Chmn. Paul McNutt announces limited relaxation of manpower controls between now and July 1.			May 11
	Foreign Economic Administration announces suspension of Lend-Lease shipments to Russia, as such aid was a war measure only.			Achmed Abdullah, author and playwright, noted for his stories of adventure and romance, reputed son of a Russian grand duke and an Afghan princess, dies at 64 in N.Y. . . . . Horse racing reopens at Narragansett Park, Pawtuckett, R.I. as the $3,000 Inaugural Purse draws 25 entries overnight.	May 12
		CIO Pres. Murray urges an immediate wage increase of 17¢ an hour for steel and other industrial workers.			May 13
	Senate Appropriations Comm. reveals the Navy is planning on a postwar force of 50,000 officers and 500,000 men.	WPB announces a 50% increase in the amount of passenger car tires that will be available for rationing in May.		Latter-Day Saints Church President Heber Grant dies at 88 in Salt Lake City.	May 14
		Truman says the government will take whatever steps are necessary to obtain coal, as Ickes presses for an agreement between miners and operators.		Santa Anita racetrack reopens in Arcadia, Calif. after a long war idleness.	May 15
	U.S. Army discloses that soldiers over 42 are being sent home from the European front.	WPB revokes controls on 1,200 common civilian items, permitting their production but not supplying the necessary iron and steel. . . . . House Ways and Means Comm. approves a three-year extension of the Reciprocal Trade Agreements Act and sends it to the floor for debate.			May 16
		Senate passes a bill granting increases in basic and overtime pay for 1,225,000 federal employes.			May 17
F *Includes elections, federal-state relations, civil rights and liberties, crime, the judiciary, education, health care, poverty, urban affairs and population.*	G *Includes formation and debate of U.S. foreign and defense policies, veterans affairs and defense spending. (Relations with specific foreign countries are usually found under the region concerned.)*	H *Includes business, labor, agriculture, taxation, transportation, consumer affairs, monetary and fiscal policy, natural resources, pollution and accidents.*	I *Includes worldwide scientific, medical and technological developments, natural phenomena, U.S. weather and natural disasters.*	J *Includes the arts, religion, scholarship, communications media, sports, entertainment, fashions, fads and social life.*	

	World Affairs	European War Zone	Pacific War Zone	The Americas	Other Countries & Territories
May 18		Truman expresses a desire to meet de Gaulle and a willingness to give France an occupation zone in Germany.	Chinese forces regain Foochow, as independent sources indicate that the Japanese are abandoning the city without a fight . . . . U.S. Army forces take the northern anchor of the Shimbu line east of Manila at the Ipo dam . . . . Washington reports indicate a scandal involving gold loaned to China by the U.S. is developing in Chungking.		
May 19	Commission on Judical Organization meets in San Francisco for the first time to consider creation of a new world court.	U.S 15th Army is temporarily controlling 14,000 square miles of Germany, as the Russians announce for their zone a variety of measures including free trade and food rationing . . . . In a message to Allied troops in the Mediterranean theater, Field Marshal Sir Harold R.L.G. Alexander compares Marshal Tito's seizure of Trieste to methods "reminiscent of Hitler, Mussolini and Japan."	After taking Sugar Loaf Hill for the fifth time, U.S. Marines advance in the center of the Japanese lines on Okinawa . . . . Gen. MacArthur announces that Allied forces have secured all major installations and objectives on Tarakan Island near Borneo . . . . The Sixth National Kuomintang Congress approves a resolution calling for legalization of political groups aside from the government party.		
May 20	The Big Five at the San Francisco Conference agree on the rights of regional groups within the context of the new league. The league will have paramount authority in enforcement against aggressors.	Yugoslavian troops withdraw from Carinthia, Austria while at the same time local committees of national liberation are established . . . . Russian newspapers *Izvestia* and *Red Star* condemn the Allied use of German military officers for administrative functions . . . . Edward Leo Delaney, an American who broadcast for the Nazis from Berlin, is captured in Prague after being indicted by the U.S. for high treason.	Chinese government announces the arrest of two officers of the Central Trust, the Chinese banking agency, on charges of speculating with gold as part of the "gold scandal."		
May 21		British Labor Party rejects Churchill's invitation to remain in the coalition cabinet until the end of the war with Japan.		Canadian Naval Ministry announces that 60 warships will be sent to the Pacific for the battle against Japan.	Syria and Lebanon break off negotiations with France and protest the arrival of additional French troops without their consent, asking withdrawl of all foreign troops.
May 22		Churchill states that the conditions for a coalition cabinet no longer exist.	Chinese troops fanning out from captured Hochih drive 21 miles into the Japanese corridor above French Indochina . . . . U.S. troops enter the ruins of Yonabaru on Okinawa as the Japanese apparently have abandoned the town.	U.S. Amb. to Argentina Spruille Braden says it was necessity and not choice that forced the U.S. recognize the Buenos Aires government.	
May 23	United Nations Conference on International Organization in San Francisco approves veto right of Big Five powers on the Security Council.	Churchill resigns as prime minister in a move to prepare for general elections; but he is named by King George VI to form a government to serve until after elections . . . . Allies dissolve the remnants of the Third Reich and arrest Grand Adm. Karl Doenitz and other leaders.	Japanese begin seventh massed kamikaze attack on the U.S. 5th Fleet off Okinawa. 165 kamikaze planes participate, sinking three American vessels and damaging six.		Syria and Lebanon issue statements in Paris condemning stationing of French troops in their countries and say they will do everything possible to resist a return to colonial status . . . . French war office reports a revolt of Berber tribesmen in Algeria has resulted in 1,300 casualties.
May 24	United Nations Conference discusses status of trusteeship territories. The U.S., China, Britain and France agree that such territories should eventually become independent but that "self-government" should be the objective for British colonies . . . . White House Press Secy. Charles Ross says a "Big Three" meeting is being planned now and hopefuly will be held soon.	Heinrich Himmler, former head of Nazi SS and police forces, commits suicide with a cyanide capsule while being examined by British authorities in Luneburg . . . . A British-American occupation government is established for Austria.	Philippine President Sergio Osmena tells the press in Manila the U.S. will get military bases in the islands with the "full support of the Filipino people" when the islands become independent sometime before July 4, 1946.	Chile and the U.S. sign a three-year agreement providing for a U.S. naval mission to Chile.	
May 25	At San Francisco, committee action decides that the Economic and Social Council shall have 18 members elected by the General Assembly.	Foreign affairs committee of the French Consultative Assembly proposes that the Allies jointly ask Franco to abdicate immediately in favor of a democratic government in Spain and that if he does not do this France will break off relations . . . . Churchill names a new cabinet with himself as prime minister, first lord of the treasury and defense minister . . . . Hopkins arrives in Moscow and Davies in London.	Two columns of U.S. forces meet in Mindanao north of Malaybalay, clearing the island's main highway and forcing the Japanese into the southeastern corner.		Iraqi Regent Prince Abdul Illah arrives in N.Y. on an official visit to the U.S.

A	B	C	D	E
Includes developments that affect more than one world region, international organizations and important meetings of major world leaders.	*Includes all developments in European countries and military engagements between Allied and Axis powers in Africa and at sea.*	*Includes all developments in Japan and China, Japanese foreign policy and military actions in the Pacific region.*	*Includes all domestic and regional developments in Latin America, the Caribbean and Canada.*	*Includes developments in those independent nations and colonial possessions not covered in Columns B, C and D.*

U.S. Politics & Social Issues	U.S. Foreign Policy & Defense	U.S. Economy & Environment	Science, Technology & Nature	Culture, Leisure & Life Style	
Justice Dept. announces former German-American Bund leader Fritz Kuhn will be deported to Germany as an undesirable alien .... Byron Price, director of censorship, lifts many restrictions on dissemination of news by press and radio in the U.S., Europe and Atlantic area, but announces a new code for the Pacific and Asian areas.		War Mobilization Dir. Vinson announces a program designed to give civilians more beef and pork but warns that the effects will not be felt for some time.			May 18
		Anthracite coal operators and the UMW agree on a compromise offered by Interior Secy. Ickes providing for a wage increase of $1.37½ per day .... ICC orders 10% cuts in basic railroad freight rates in southern, western and southwestern states and a 10% increase in the East, pending preparation of permanent freight rates.		Naval Academy retains the IC 4-A track and field team title at West Point.	May 19
					May 20
Supreme Court rules each state may decide whether six weeks' residence required by Nevada divorce laws establishes a legal domicile.		Only seven of the 333 anthracite mines remain idle under government jurisdiction as 64,000 workers end a 20-days strike .... WPB announces that 700,000 washing machines may be produced during the last half of 1945 .... OPA announces increases of $2 to $7 a ton in basic steel prices to cover increased production costs .... Senate confirms the reappointment of David Lilienthal as TVA chairman.		Lauren Betty Bacall and Humphrey Bogart are married in Mansfield, Ohio .... Horse-racing is resumed in N.Y. with the opening of the Jamaica track.	May 21
Census Bureau estimates that as of last Jan. 1 U.S. population was 138,955,469 .... Senate Appropriations Comm. approves a recent House bill to grant $2,500 annually in tax-free expenditure money for congressmen.	Selective Service announces that a reduction of 25% in manpower needs of the armed services and a need for younger men will enable local boards to grant indefinite deferments to men over 30 in essential jobs.				May 22
Truman reorganizes his cabinet, accepting resignations from Atty. Gen. Francis Biddle, Labor Secy. Frances Perkins and Agriculture Secy. Claude Wickard, replacing them respectively with Thomas C. Clark, Lewis B. Schwellenbach and Clinton P. Anderson .... Senate Comm. on Education and Labor approves a bill to establish a permanent Fair Employment Practices Commission.	Washington announces that Harry L. Hopkins and Joseph E. Davies are to go on special missions for Truman to Moscow and London, respectively .... U.S. government formally takes over the German embassy and property in Washington as a trustee until a responsible German government is formed.	OPA announces that ration coupons will allow purchase of 50% more gas after June 22 .... U.S. files suit in Toledo accusing 10 companies, including Pittsburgh Plate Glass, of conspiring to monopolize production, distribution and sale of flat glass.	*AMA Journal* reveals that five typhoid patients have been treated successfully with a new drug called streptomycin.		May 23
Sens. Robert Wagner (D, N.Y.) and James Murray (D, Mont.) and Rep. John Dingell (D, Mich.) offer identical bills to Congress calling for broader coverage by Social Security.	Commerce Secy. Wallace asks for lower U.S. tariffs and trade with other countries on a "live and let live basis."		Dr. William Robbins reveals his discovery of six new antibiotic drugs: pleurotin, grisic acid, pleurin, irpexin, obtusin and corticin.		May 24
	Pres. Earl Browder of the Communist Political Assn. says the U.S. delegates at San Francisco have deviated from FDR's policy of U.S.-Soviet amity.	NWLB says employers may increase wages to 55¢ an hour without board approval.			May 25

F	G	H	I	J
Includes elections, federal-state relations, civil rights and liberties, crime, the judiciary, education, health care, poverty, urban affairs and population.	*Includes formation and debate of U.S. foreign and defense policies, veterans affairs and defense spending. (Relations with specific foreign countries are usually found under the region concerned.)*	*Includes business, labor, agriculture, taxation, transportation, consumer affairs, monetary and fiscal policy, natural resources, pollution and accidents.*	*Includes worldwide scientific, medical and technological developments, natural phenomena, U.S. weather and natural disasters.*	*Includes the arts, religion, scholarship, communications media, sports, entertainment, fashions, fads and social life.*

	World Affairs	European War Zone	Pacific War Zone	The Americas	Other Countries & Territories
May 26	United Nations Conference widens the powers of the proposed General Assembly by requiring the Security Council to report to the Assembly on all matters of peace and international security .... Churchill says he may have to leave Britain for a "Big Three" meeting before the elections.	Vidkun Quisling is arraigned in Oslo, Norway and pleads "not guilty" to charges of treason .... Eisenhower moves his headquarters from Reims to an office building in Frankfurt, Germany.	About 500 Marianas-based Superfortresses drop 4,000 tons of incendiary bombs on Tokyo. Japanese radio broadcast reports that the city has been "scorched to the ground" by the raid and subsequent firestorm .... Chinese troops north of Foochow drive towards Saipu to check Japanese who landed there.		
May 27		UNRRA Dir. Lehman says 1.25 million tons of relief supplies will have to be shipped to Europe by the end of June.	American troops capture Sante Fe, mountain key to Japanese positions defending the entrance to the Cagayan Valley in northern Luzon .... Chinese forces take Nanning, 470 miles south of Chungking.		
May 28	Hopkins and Stalin meet alone in Moscow, each expressing concerns over the other country's policies: Soviet actions in Poland and U.S. termination of Lend-Lease.	Nobel prize winner in literature Knut Hamsun and his wife are arrested in Grimstad, Norway for allegedly having made pro-Nazi statements during the German occupation .... U.S. State Dept. removes from "enemy territory" category Albania, Austria, Czechoslovakia, Danzig, Denmark, Netherlands, Norway and Yugoslavia, permitting resumption of commercial relations.	Superfortresses make their first raid on Yokohama, dropping 3,200 tons of incendiary bombs. The Japanese report some 60,000 homes are destroyed in the attack .... American troops capture the remaining fortifications of the Shimbu Line east of Manila.	Brazilian Pres. Vargas sets general elections for Dec. 12, 1945.	Street fighting between French and Syrians breaks out in Hama and spreads to Homs, 30 miles to the south .... Egyptian P.M. Mahmoud Fahmy Nokrashy says his country supports the Syrian and Lebanese independence movements.
May 29	Big Five at San Francisco agree that when the question of using a country's forces against an aggressor arises that country shall have a vote on the issue.		Commander of the Japanese Fleet Adm. Soemu Toyada is replaced by Vice Adm. Jisaburo Ozawa.		British Foreign Secy. Eden tells the House of Commons that Britain is greatly concerned over the crisis in the Levant because it is "liable to affect our lines of communications with the Far East."
May 30	U.S. delegation agrees to some type of interim machinery to deal with functions of the old League until a new world body is in operation .... American Univ. researchers estimate the total expenditures of WWII exceed $1 trillion thus far.		Marines take Shuri Castle, the key defense point in the center of the Japanese line on southern Okinawa.		Iran asks that British, Russian and American troops leave the country now that the European War is over .... French troops take over parliament building in Damascus as street fighting continues.
May 31		De Gaulle announces that the French people will vote later this year to determine what type of government they want .... Norwegian government of P.M. Johann Nygaardvold arrives in Oslo after five years of operation in Britain .... Representatives of 16 nations gather in London for the first meeting of the U.N. War Crimes Commission.	Chiang Kai-shek resigns as premier of Nationalist China and is succeeded by Acting Premier T.V. Soong.	Argentine government proclaims its "Organic Statute of Political Parties," which lays down rules for approval of parties and makes voting compulsory. Observers charge the document is an abridgement of domestic political freedom.	French troops in Syria and Lebanon agree to a cease-fire at demand of British government. Big Four powers in San Francisco warn France that its continued conflict with Syria jeopardizes its request for changes in the security charter .... Churchill orders his commander-in-chief in the Middle East, Gen. Sir Bernard Paget, to intervene in Syria to halt the bloodshed there.
June 1	Truman says he will meet soon with Churchill and Stalin .... Russia backs the French contention that the Franco-Russian alliance and other alliances directed against Germany should be completely independent of the new world organization.		More than 450 U.S. planes drop 3,000 tons of incendiary bombs on Osaka .... U.S. troops take the town of Shuri and move along the north bank of the Kokuba River in Okinawa .... U.S. claims up to 30,000 Japanese troops are trapped between American forces moving north through the Cagayan Valley on Luzon and powerful guerrilla units to the north.		Moscow sends a note to the French, British, Chinese and American governments asking that France's Middle East activities cease because they are contrary to U.N. principles.
June 2	Big Five are reportedly divided over a Russian demand for a veto right over discussion of international disputes.				De Gaulle issues a statement blaming the British for the Middle East trouble and saying that he will not negotiate directly with Syria and Lebanon.
June 3	Small and medium sized nations describe as "outrageous" the Russian proposal that the Big Five have veto right over discussion of international disputes.	Poland orders that Germans not engaged in reconstruction work must leave the country along with those in the "newly liberated western territories."	Chinese claim the capture of the important railroad junction town of Tsinkong, some 30 miles south of Liuchow.		Lebanese Premier Abdel Hamid Karamah and President of the Syrian Chamber of Deputies Saadullah el Gabry charge the French are using Lend-Lease materials in the Syrian fighting.
June 4	U.S. and Britain appeal directly to Stalin on the issue of the Big Five veto power in the U.N.	U.N. War Crimes Commission ends its London meeting, promising "harmony and reciprocal help" among national offices investigating Axis war crimes.	U.S. troops reach the southeast coast of Okinawa and on the west make an amphibious crossing of Naha harbor to seize half of the airfield there.		
	A *Includes developments that affect more than one world region, international organizations and important meetings of major world leaders.*	B *Includes all developments in European countries and military engagements between Allied and Axis powers in Africa and at sea.*	C *Includes all developments in Japan and China, Japanese foreign policy and military actions in the Pacific region.*	D *Includes all domestic and regional developments in Latin America, the Caribbean and Canada.*	E *Includes developments in those independent nations and colonial possessions not covered in Columns B, C and D.*

U.S. Politics & Social Issues	U.S. Foreign Policy & Defense	U.S. Economy & Environment	Science, Technology & Nature	Culture, Leisure & Life Style	
	House votes to extend and broaden the reciprocal trade program, defeating all GOP amendments.		A Royal Air Force exploration group reports finding the true magnetic North Pole in the Sverdrup Islands of the Soviet Union.	Illinois Univ. wins the Western Conference track and field championship in Champaign, Ill.	May 26
		WPB outlines a policy for "partial reconversion" of the U.S. in the midst of "partial demobilization," which includes an end to production restrictions . . . . Commerce Secy. Wallace approves a department report recommending increased exemption from the excess profits tax and total repeal soon after victory in the Pacific.			May 27
Senate rejects an annual $2500 expense account for its members, but votes to let the House do as it will in the matter.	State Secy. Stettinius outlines the major aims of U.S. policy, which include preventing Germany and Japan from being able to wage another war and helping remove the economic and social causes of war . . . . A Senate committee postpones until six months after Japan's defeat courts-martial on the Pearl Harbor disaster.				May 28
U.S. government sues in Los Angeles federal court to determine whether it or California owns petroleum deposits beyond the low waterline and the three-mile limit.					May 29
		OPA estimates that the civilian meat supply will be 7% less in June than it was in May.			May 30
	In a memorandum to Truman, Bernard M. Baruch says the most important factor in making peace is the "earliest definite settlement of what is to be done with Germany and Japan," saying both must be kept from reestablishing themselves as industrial nations capable of mass production of military arms . . . . Sen. Robert M. La Follette (P. Wisc.) criticizes Dumbarton Oaks plan for creation of a United Nations organization, attacking the veto right of Big Five powers in the Security Council . . . . Under War Secy. Robert Patterson says lowering the Army discharge age further would increase front line service of men in the Pacific.				May 31
	Truman tells Congress says that fighting forces in the Pacific will be doubled with the addition of 3.5 million men from Germany.	OPA Chief Bowles orders all commercial slaughterers to follow the geographical pattern of meat distribution used in 1944 to bring some relief from the meat shortage.		Louis Fischer, noted author and foreign correspondent, resigns from editorial board of *The Nation* after protesting the magazine's favorable view of Soviet foreign policy.	June 1
Leaders of U.S. Communist Party, meeting in New York, adopt a new policy that ends the period of "popular front" cooperation with other political groups.				Pope Pius XII defends the Church's 1933 concordat with the Reich as a "stronghold behind which to shield" its opposition to Nazism.	June 2
		War Mobilization Dir. Fred Vinson gives support to the "full employment" bill due for hearings soon in Congress . . . . IRS says a total of $76 million in refund checks for overpayment of withholding taxes is being returned to taxpayers.			June 3
		Supreme Court upholds the OPA's method of determining maximum prices for building materials and other durable goods.		U.S. Court of Appeals in Washington voids Postmaster Gen. Walker's revocation of *Esquire* magazine's second class mailing privileges because of the alleged impropriety of some of its contents.	June 4

F	G	H	I	J
Includes elections, federal-state relations, civil rights and liberties, crime, the judiciary, education, health care, poverty, urban affairs and population.	*Includes formation and debate of U.S. foreign and defense policies, veterans affairs and defense spending. (Relations with specific foreign countries are usually found under the region concerned.)*	*Includes business, labor, agriculture, taxation, transportation, consumer affairs, monetary and fiscal policy, natural resources, pollution and accidents.*	*Includes worldwide scientific, medical and technological developments, natural phenomena, U.S. weather and natural disasters.*	*Includes the arts, religion, scholarship, communications media, sports, entertainment, fashions, fads and social life.*

	World Affairs	European War Zone	Pacific War Zone	The Americas	Other Countries & Territories
June 5	U.N. Conference formally admits Denmark to membership as the technical committees complete their work.	Supreme Allied Headquarters announces American ground force casualties on the Continent from the Normandy invasion to V-E Day totaled 514,534 .... Allied Control Commission meets for the first time in Berlin, proclaiming its assumption of the government of the Reich.	About 500 U.S. planes drop 3,000 tons of fire bombs on Kobe, Japan .... U.S. troops gain two miles on the east coast of Okinawa and cut off the Chinen Peninsula .... Japanese troops have quit Hoiping, Szetsin, Sunwui and Toishan in a 55-mile area west of Hong Kong, according to Chinese reports.		Churchill charges French provocations have caused the Middle East flareup and hopes that U.S.-British-French conferences can settle the issue.
June 6		Berlin reports a high Russian military official as claiming that the charred remains of Hitler were found in the Reich Chancellery bunker .... Moscow newspapers publish a map delineating Russia's version of the part of Germany it will occupy, roughly one-half of the country.	On Okinawa, U.S. forces take the Naha airfield and overrun the Chinen Peninsula .... With the capture of the border town of Chugching, Chinese troops report reaching the French Indochina border.	Brazil declares war on Japan, leaving Colombia as the only Latin American nation still at peace with Tokyo.	
June 7	Stalin instructs the Soviet delegation at San Francisco to drop its request for a Big Five veto over discussion of international disputes .... U.S. State Dept. announces acceptance by 30 nations of the Interim Agreement on International Civil Aviation, enough to permit its coming into force.	Churchill turns down a demand from the House of Commons to reveal all that was discussed at Yalta but says there were no secret agreements.	U.S. Marines clear Oroku Peninsula in the southwestern section of Okinawa .... The first important settlement north of the mountains of Balete Pass on Luzon, Bayombong, falls to the Americans.		Council of the Arab League adopts a resolution demanding complete evacuation of French troops from the Levant.
June 8	Big Five report to the "Little 45" their agreement on the veto right over virtually all issues except discussion of international disputes .... World Court Comm. completes a draft for an International Court of Justice, with rotating members and provisions for amendment .... Acting State Secy. Grew denies reports of a secret pledge at Yalta to concede Korea to Russia for Soviet entry into the Pacific war.	Marshal Petain tells Paris high court commissioners that he was having a secret treaty negotiated with Great Britain at the same time he was meeting with Hitler in 1940.	Tokyo radio reports new economic controls for Japan aimed at increasing war production, to be carried out "forcibly if necessary."		
June 9		Delayed dispatches from Frankfurt on the Main say the Nazis exterminated at least 80% of the Reich's Jews and that their program called for killing every remaining Jew in occupied Europe before the summer of 1946. Allied authorities estimate that about 150,000 German Jews survived .... U.S., Britain and Yugoslavia reach an agreement for a temporary Allied military administration of the Italian province of Venezia Giulia, including Trieste.	Premier Kantaro Suzuki tells the Diet that Japan will "fight to the last." .... Philippine Congress meets in Manila in its first session since the islands' liberation .... After capturing Ishan on the outskirts of Liuchow, Chinese forces storm the city's suburbs in Kwangsi Province.	Argentina announces the release of all political prisoners except "extreme rightists."	
June 10	Forty-five smaller countries at the United Nations Conference, led by Herbert Evatt of Australia, seek to restrict veto right of Big Five powers on Security Council. Evans suggests that the veto be inapplicable in Council decisions dealing with peaceful settlement of disputes.	Eisenhower and Montgomery receive Russia's highest award, the jeweled Order of Victory, from Marshal Gregory K. Zhukov .... A joint U.S-British statement lists 713 German U-boats destroyed between Sept. 3, 1939 and May 8, 1945.	American and Australian forces make a new invasion thrust at Borneo, landing on the main island as well as on Labuan and Muara islands.	Peru holds elections to choose a new president, two vice presidents, 49 senators and 152 deputies. Dr. Jose Luis Bustamante Rivero, a liberal candidate, wins the presidential race.	
June 11	Big Five agree to record in the minutes that nations have the right to withdraw from the U.N. in case amendments are passed which violate their constitutions .... U.N. Economic and Social Council is approved with a membership of 18. It will report directly to the Security Council.		In a nine-mile gain, U.S. troops capture the cross-roads town of Bagabag on Luzon, the Philippines.	Canadian P.M. W.L. Mackenzie King is defeated in seeking reelection to his old House of Commons seat in the Prince Albert, Sask., riding. But Mackenzie King's Liberal Party wins the nationwide general election.	
June 12	U.N. Comm. of Jurists approve a revised statute of the World Court, calling for 15 members to be elected by the General Assembly and the Security Council.	Polish leaders of various factions agree to meet in Moscow June 15 in an effort to revise the Polish provisional government to conform to the Yalta Conference formula .... Italian Premier Ivanoe Bonomi and his cabinet resign but remain in office pending agreement on a new government.	U.S. troops take the Yaeju Dake escarpment on Okinawa, breaching the last defense line of the island's Japanese garrison .... In a drive on Japanese mountain positions in the Philippines, U.S. units take Santa Ines, 23 miles northeast of Manila.		

A	B	C	D	E
Includes developments that affect more than one world region, international organizations and important meetings of major world leaders.	*Includes all developments in European countries and military engagements between Allied and Axis powers in Africa and at sea.*	*Includes all developments in Japan and China, Japanese foreign policy and military actions in the Pacific region.*	*Includes all domestic and regional developments in Latin America, the Caribbean and Canada.*	*Includes developments in those independent nations and colonial possessions not covered in Columns B, C and D.*

U.S. Politics & Social Issues	U.S. Foreign Policy & Defense	U.S. Economy & Environment	Science, Technology & Nature	Culture, Leisure & Life Style	
Truman asks the House Rules Comm. to vote out the Fair Employment Practices Commission (FEPC) bill .... N.Y.C. Democratic leaders choose Dist. Atty. William O'Dwyer as their mayoral candidate.					June 5
	FBI arrests six persons on charges of conspiring to violate a law dealing with unauthorized possession or transmittal of defense data: Lt. Andrew Roth, USNR; Emmanual Larsen and John Service, both of the State Dept.; Philip Jaffe and Kate Mitchell of *Amerasia* magazine; and free-lance writer Mark Gayn.	NWLB approves the new wage contract between the UMW and anthracite coal operators.	National TB Assn. awards the 1945 Trudeau Medal to Dr. Florence Sabin for her work on TB pathology.		June 6
House votes to keep the $2,500 tax-free annual expense account for members.	House approves U.S. participation in the IMF and Bank for Reconstruction and Development as planned at Bretton Woods .... Acting State Secy. Grew says the arrest of six persons yesterday is only part of a "comprehensive security program" designed to halt leaks of confidential information.	Truman names Paul Herzog as chairman of the NLRB, succeeding H.A. Hollis, who resigned.		*Peter Grimes*, first opera by Benjamin Britten, premiers at the Sadler's Wells theater, London .... The 1945 Catholic Directory reveals an increase of 543,970 in the number of Roman Catholics in the U.S. over 1944.	June 7
A bill is introduced into the Senate to increase the $10,000 yearly salary of congressmen by 100%.	Senate Finance Comm. votes down the House-approved Administration bill for extension of the Reciprocal Trade Agreements Law .... Navy Secy. James Forrestal announces the establishment of an Office of Research and Inventions for research in naval weapons.	U.S. Circuit Court of Appeals in Chicago rules that the Army seizure of Montgomery Ward & Co. under FDR was unconstitutional.			June 8
		Army announces plans to enforce the NWLB's directive to Montgomery Ward to grant its employes back pay and union dues check-off and maintenance of membership privileges .... Truman authorizes Alien Property Custodian James Markham to seize liquid assets of German and Japanese nationals in the U.S. and turn the proceeds over to the U.S. Treasury.		Hoop Jr., with Eddie Arcaro up, wins the Kentucky Derby .... Navy scores 62 points over Illinois's $57\frac{3}{4}$ to win the NCAA track and field championship in Milwaukee.	June 9
				Representing the American Society of Newspaper Editors, Wilbur Forrest, Ralph McGill and Carl Ackerman tell Truman that their objective in peace treaties is a pledge not to censor news and to permit the free flow of information. .... *New York Herald Tribune* reports the best-selling fiction book to be *Captain from Castile*, by Samuel Shellabarger, and non-fiction to be *Brave Men*, by Ernie Pyle .... Byron Nelson wins the $10,000 Canadian Professional Golfers Assn. Open in Montreal.	June 10
		Senate votes to extend the OPA another year but outlaws price ceilings that fail to give meat processers and farmers a "reasonable" profit .... Supreme Court invalidates a Florida law requiring the licensing of union business agents and the filing of information about both the union and its officers.			June 11
House passes a bill to ban a poll tax requirement for voting in federal elections in Tex., Tenn., Va., S.C., Ala., Miss. and Ark.					June 12
F	G	H	I	J	
Includes elections, federal-state relations, civil rights and liberties, crime, the judiciary, education, health care, poverty, urban affairs and population.	*Includes formation and debate of U.S. foreign and defense policies, veterans affairs and defense spending. (Relations with specific foreign countries are usually found under the region concerned.)*	*Includes business, labor, agriculture, taxation, transportation, consumer affairs, monetary and fiscal policy, natural resources, pollution and accidents.*	*Includes worldwide scientific, medical and technological developments, natural phenomena, U.S. weather and natural disasters.*	*Includes the arts, religion, scholarship, communications media, sports, entertainment, fashions, fads and social life.*	

	World Affairs	European War Zone	Pacific War Zone	The Americas	Other Countries & Territories
June 13	Yalta voting procedure for the Security Council is adopted by a 40-2 vote with 15 abstensions at San Francisco .... Truman announces that plans for a Big Three summit are complete and that the objective of the meeting will be to prepare for a peace conference .... A joint U.S.-British statement says the U.N. and neutral countries lost 4,770 merchant ships aggregating 21.14 million tons from Sept. 3, 1939 to May 8, 1945.				French troops evacuate Syria as the Damascus government requests a conference, sponsored by U.S. and Britain, to settle the dispute between France and the Levantine countries.
June 14		Nazi Foreign Min. Joachim von Ribbontrop is caught while sleeping in a Hamburg rooming house by American troops.	Americans take the highest point on Okinawa, Yaeju Hill, and open a pincer movement at both ends of the Japanese defense lines .... In their continued advance in northern Borneo, Australian troops take Brunei.	Pres. Getulio Vargas is accused in Brazil's highest court of seizing power illegally on Nov. 10, 1937.	A British White Paper presented in the House of Commons proposes that the Viceroy's Executive Council be reconstituted as a completely representative all-Indian body.
June 15	Official British sources report the Big Three meeting will be held in Berlin, probably from July 5 through July 26 .... San Francisco conference adopts an amendment to prevent the U.N. from interfering in a state's domestic jurisdiction.	King George VI dissolves Parliament after its longest session since 1679. It will reconvene Aug. 1, five days after election results are revealed .... Swedish and Norwegian governments sign three financial pacts in Oslo.	A force of 444 Superfortresses makes the 75th American air raid on Japan, attacking Osaka and neighboring Amagasaki. Most of Osaka's industry is destroyed by the 3,157 tons of bombs dropped in the raid.	Panama's Constitutional Assembly elects Enrique Jimenez as provisional president .... U.S. and Argentina conclude an oil agreement, whereby Buenos Aires will receive heating oil in return for vegetable oils.	
June 16	Because of the urgent health problems resulting from the war, the U.S. delegation at San Francisco pushes for immediate establishment of an international health organization.	British Air Ministry says the RAF lost 16,385 planes in the European and Mediterranean theatres through V-E Day.		Haitian government establishes censorship in all internal communications "for reasons of a political nature."	
June 17	Gromyko asks that the U.N. General Assembly be limited in its discussions to issues of "maintenance of international peace and security" rather than having the right to discuss any matter of international relations.	Italian Comm. of National Liberation agrees that Ferruccio Parri lead the formation of a new government.			
June 18	Big Five agree on a charter provision stating that colonial trusteeships must provide for eventual self-government and social, economic and educational advancement of the people involved.	William Joyce (Lord Haw Haw) is charged with high treason before London's chief metropolitan magistrate .... Moscow reports that 16 Polish underground leaders have confessed to the alleged murders of 594 Russian officers and terroristic propaganda activities behind Soviet lines.	Lt. Gen. Simon Bolivar Buckner Jr., 58, commander of the 10th Army and of all land forces on Okinawa, is killed at a forward observation post when hit by a Japanese shell. He is replaced by Maj. Gen. Roy Geiger, commander of the 3rd Marine Amphibious Corps.		
June 19	Big Five agree that enemy nations of WWII may not participate in the U.N. until a Security Council vote invites them.		At the southern tip of Okinawa, American troops pushing to the sea cut the Japanese forces into two groups.		
June 20	U.N. Conference settles its last major controversy when the Big Five agree to let the General Assembly have the right to discuss "any matters within the scope of the charter."	British, Americans and Yugoslavs sign an agreement partitioning the Venezia Giulia area of Italy, pending a final peace conference settlement .... Former Italian Army Chief of Staff Marshal Rudolfo Graziani and Gen. Gastone Gamberra and five other generals are indicted in Rome for high treason .... A German policeman tells U.S. authorities that he saw the bodies of Hitler and Eva Braun burning at the Berlin Chancellery.			
June 21	San Francisco Conference chooses London as interim location for the world organization.	London says Moscow radio has reported that 12 of the 16 accused Polish underground leaders on trial in the Russian capital were found guilty early today and given prison sentences ranging from 10 years to four months .... Ferruccio Parri forms a new Italian cabinet and is sworn in by Crown Prince Humbert in Rome.	U.S. 10th Army reaches southernmost point of Okinawa, ending Japanese resistance after 82 days of battle .... Australian troops land on the northern head of Brunei Bay, Borneo and gain control of both sides of the entrance to the bay.	Guatemalan government exiles 19 persons and holds 30 under arrest without explanation.	Lebanese and Syrian governments announce an agreement on policy for winning independence which includes the elimination of all French personnel.

A	B	C	D	E
Includes developments that affect more than one world region, international organizations and important meetings of major world leaders.	*Includes all developments in European countries and military engagements between Allied and Axis powers in Africa and at sea.*	*Includes all developments in Japan and China, Japanese foreign policy and military actions in the Pacific region.*	*Includes all domestic and regional developments in Latin America, the Caribbean and Canada.*	*Includes developments in those independent nations and colonial possessions not covered in Columns B, C and D.*

U.S. Politics & Social Issues	U.S. Foreign Policy & Defense	U.S. Economy & Environment	Science, Technology & Nature	Culture, Leisure & Life Style	
				Billboard reports the most popular songs are: (1) *Sentimental Journey,* (2) *Bell-Bottom Trousers* and (3) *There! I've Said It Again.*	June 13
	Truman expresses hope that the U.N. charter can be completed and ratified by the U.S. Senate in time for the Big Three conference.	OPA reveals that nine rings of racketeers in the East have issued fraudulant ration stamps, most of which have been traced to 600 N.Y.C. food merchants.			June 14
	Eisenhower writes the House that even in peacetime there should be military training required of all able-bodied men . . . . Senate agrees to limit debate on the reciprocal trade agreements bill.	Truman orders the Office of Defense Transportation to seize the entire trucking industry in Chicago, involving 80,000 workers who are voting on a strike.			June 15
	Gen. George Marshall, Navy Secy. Forrestal and Fleet Adm. Ernest King tell the House Comm. on Postwar Military Policy that universal military training in peacetime should be implemented.	Over 6,000 truck drivers ignore government orders and strike in Chicago.		Truman names Luther Evans as Librarian of Congress.	June 16
	The 86th Infantry Division arrives in N.Y. as the first unit to come home *in toto* from Europe. It will be the first full unit sent to the Pacific.	Army calls 5,000 more troops to Chicago to keep trucks moving.			June 17
Supreme Court upholds the New York Civil Rights Law in ruling that the Railway Mail Assn. cannot limit its labor union to white personnel only.	Gen. Eisenhower returns home and receives the greatest reception ever accorded a hero in Washington.	Supreme Court rules "it is not a violation of the Sherman Act for laborers in combination to refuse to work."		Supreme Court rules that the AP bylaws violate the Sherman Act in restraint of commerce in news.	June 18
Truman arrives at McChord Field, in the state of Washington, before addressing the final session of the international conference in San Francisco. This is the first time a U.S. president has used air transportation to travel within the country . . . . Truman asks Congress to pass a bill changing the Presidential Succession Act of 1886 to make the Speaker of the House next in line after the vice president . . . . Senate Appropriations Comm. votes to raise congressional salaries from $10,000 to $15,000.					June 19
	Senate votes to extend the Reciprocal Trade Agreements Law for three years, including the presidential power to reduce tariffs.	A new federal labor relations bill is introduced into the Senate to replace the Wagner Act. It calls for the creation of two boards, one an unfair labor practices tribunal and the other to mediate labor disputes . . . . WPB authorizes production by 10 manufacturers of 691,018 passenger cars from July 1, 1945 to March 31, 1946, to be used primarily for war or essential civilian transportation . . . . A Newark, N.J. federal court jury acquits E.I. du Pont Co. and the Rohm and Haas Co. on charges of conspiracy under the Sherman Act to monopolize international production and fix prices for acrylic products.			June 20
An equal pay bill to protect women workers from wage discrimination when the war is over is introduced into the Senate.		An AFL-CIO jurisdictional dispute idles 21,000 workers at Packard Motors and 1,400 at Ford's River Rouge plant . . . . Senate confirms Claude Wickard as REA administrator . . . . Commerce Dept. estimates American businessmen plan to spend a record high of $4.5 billion for plants and equipment in the next fiscal year.		Motion picture producers and the Screen Actors Guild conclude contract talks, increasing salaries for day workers to $35, freelance players to $115 weekly and stock contracts to $60 weekly.	June 21

F	G	H	I	J
Includes elections, federal-state relations, civil rights and liberties, crime, the judiciary, education, health care, poverty, urban affairs and population.	*Includes formation and debate of U.S. foreign and defense policies, veterans affairs and defense spending. (Relations with specific foreign countries are usually found under the region concerned.)*	*Includes business, labor, agriculture, taxation, transportation, consumer affairs, monetary and fiscal policy, natural resources, pollution and accidents.*	*Includes worldwide scientific, medical and technological developments, natural phenomena, U.S. weather and natural disasters.*	*Includes the arts, religion, scholarship, communications media, sports, entertainment, fashions, fads and social life.*

	World Affairs	European War Zone	Pacific War Zone	The Americas	Other Countries & Territories
June 22		Czech government seizes more than 270,000 farms and corporations of Germans, Hungarians and "traitors and Nazi collaborationists."	Chinese troops enter the Kwangsi Province city of Liuchow, while other units attack the nearby former U.S. airbase . . . . Australian troops participating in the invasion of Borneo capture the oil refinery at Lutong on the island's west coast and Seria oil fields on the north coast.	Argentine newspapers begin printing news cabled from the U.S. in line with the government's promise not to interfere with incoming or outgoing news.	British government issues a statement saying that its intervention in the Levant was only to halt events that threatened the Allied war effort.
June 23		Moscow announces formation of compromise Polish government, including representatives of exiled London Poles and the Soviet-supported Lublin regime. Big Four powers in San Francisco agree to allow the new Polish government to sign world charter . . . . French announce that their occupation zone in Germany includes the southern half of the Saar, the Rhineland Palatinate and most of Baden Province.	Emperor Hirohito tells the Japanese people that the present crisis is the worst in the nation's history . . . . Using glider planes for the first time in the Southwest Pacific, the 11th Airborne Division lands near Aparri, Luzon to move against 20,000 trapped Japanese in the Cagayan Valley.		
June 24			The first American newspaper published in Free China, the *Shanghai Evening Post and Mercury*, announces its suspension because it is hampered by "wartime censorship restrictions."		France appeals to State Secy. Stettinius to appoint a commission to investigate the Levant crisis . . . . Gandhi rejects an invitation to the conference for revision of India's government but says he will be available in an advisory capacity.
June 25	The last plenary session of the San Francisco Conference meets and members receive the final draft of the U.N. charter.	Moscow reports that the German CP issued a manifesto in Berlin today which barred a soviet system for the Reich and asked for a coalition parliamentary government and development of private enterprise and the profit system.	U.S. naval units make their first foray past the Kurile islands into the Sea of Okhotsk north of Japan, sinking three Japanese ships . . . . In the pincer movement in the Cagayan Valley on Luzon, the 37th Infantry Division reaches to within 11 miles of the 11th Airborne group.		Simla Conference opens to consider British proposals for revising India's government.
June 26	Delegates from 50 U.N. countries meet in their last session at San Francisco and hear China's Dr. V.K. Wellington Koo compare the charter to the Magna Carta and the U.S. Constitution.		A force of 510 Superfortresses and 148 fighter escorts attacks industrial targets on Japan's Honshu and Shikoku islands, including the cities of Nagoya and Osaka.		
June 27			Tokyo radio says all Japanese communications were put under government control tonight to prepare against an invasion.		Simla Conference adjournes until June 29 after a conflict of views between the All-India Congress group and the Moslem League over cabinet makeup.
June 28		New Polish unity government takes office in Warsaw . . . . War Dept. designates Gen. Mark W. Clark as head of the U.S. forces that will occupy Austria.	MacArthur announces the liberation of Luzon, largest island of the Philippine group, at 6:30 a.m., five months and 19 days after its invasion began.	A day-long countrywide student strike is reported in Argentina.	
June 29		Czechs and Russians sign an agreement calling for the cession of Ruthenia to Russia, a population exchange in the area and a commission to fix the new boundary.	Chinese Communists approve visit of a seven-member, non-partisan commission to Yenan for purpose of discussing Communist-Nationalist differences . . . . U.S. bombers attack the Japanese naval base at Sasebo on Kyushu Island. The port of Shiogama is closed by mines dropped from the air.	Panamanian cabinet approves a break in relations with Spain, effective for as long as the Franco regime continues.	After failing to agree on a list of ministers for the new cabinet, the All-India Congress and Moslem League notify Viscount Wavell to recess the Simla Conference until July 14.
June 30			Chinese troops capture the burning city of Liuchow in Kwangsi Province . . . . A Tokyo broadcast says the Japanese have changed the name of Annam, French Indochina, to Vietnam . . . . American patrols complete their occupation of Kume Island, westernmost of the Okinawa group . . . . Chinese Premier T.V. Soong arrives in Moscow to confer with Stalin.		

A	B	C	D	E
Includes developments that affect more than one world region, international organizations and important meetings of major world leaders.	*Includes all developments in European countries and military engagements between Allied and Axis powers in Africa and at sea.*	*Includes all developments in Japan and China, Japanese foreign policy and military actions in the Pacific region.*	*Includes all domestic and regional developments in Latin America, the Caribbean and Canada.*	*Includes developments in those independent nations and colonial possessions not covered in Columns B, C and D.*

U.S. Politics & Social Issues	U.S. Foreign Policy & Defense	U.S. Economy & Environment	Science, Technology & Nature	Culture, Leisure & Life Style	
Eisenhower says he has "no political ambitions at all."					June 22
	Truman commutes to life imprisonment the death sentences of recently convicted spies Erich Gimpel and William Colepaugh.	House passes the OPA bill with amendments giving power over food to the Secretary of Agriculture — including OPA ceilings and regulations.	Simon Lake, inventor and father of the modern submarine, dies at 78 in Bridgeport, Conn.	Babe Didrikson Zaharias takes her third Western Women's Open Golf Title with a victory over Dorothy Germain in Indianapolis .... The play *Kiss and Tell* closes after 962 performances on Broadway.	June 23
		Labor Secy. Frances Perkins reports a .07% increase in the cost of living for May, which raises the index to 128% of the 1935-39 average.			June 24
	American Banker's Assn. reverses its previous stand and endorses the Bretton Woods monetary proposals.	Independent Truck Drivers Union orders its 6,000 striking members in Chicago to return to work since present "facts" make it "impossible to gain anything by this unprovoked .... walkout." .... U.S. Emergency Appeals Court in Washington rules that OPA ceiling rents for luxury apartments in N.Y.C. are too low but upholds ceilings for substandard and medium-size dwellings.			June 25
Congress approves retention of 3¢ first-class postage for another two years .... Justice Dept. says 12 of the 24 German-American Bundists freed by the Supreme Court will now be held as dangerous enemy aliens.					June 26
Gov. Ellis Arnall of Georgia announces his opposition to the FEPC as "unworkable" and adds, "We in the South do not believe in social equality with the Negro."	Truman accepts the resignation of State Secy. Stettinius and then appoints him as chairman of the U.S. delegation to the U.N. .... Secy. Stettinius expresses hope that the U.S. will be the first nation to ratify the U.N. Charter .... House Military Affairs Comm. says points for Army discharge will be lowered from 85 to 78 or 80 in a few weeks.	Senate and House agree in conference to a compromise on the OPA bill, which gives the Secretary of Agriculture power over food at the processing level.		To make FM more free from interference the FCC orders frequency modulation broadcasting changed from between 42 and 50 megacycles to between 88 and 106.20 channels, of which the segment from 88 to 92 megacycles will be for non-commercial educational FM.	June 27
House Rules Comm. tables a proposal appropriating $125,000 to the FEPC, leaving the agency with no funds to operate after June 30.	Sen. Tom Connally (D, Tex.) urges speedy ratification of the U.N. Charter .... Business and Industry Comm. for Bretton Woods adopts a resolution at its N.Y. meeting endorsing the monetary proposals .... The Office of Scientific and Research Development is established by executive order to direct the development of atomic energy.	Senate votes to extend the OPA another year, accepting the conference committee compromise .... WMC Commissioner McNutt estimates that employment in munitions plants declined by 600,000 between March 15 and June 1 and that unemployment in the industry will rise to 1,800,000 by June 1946.	AT&T announces plans to install a mobile radio-telephone system in motor vehicles and principal cities which will enable citizens to have two-way communications similar to walkie-talkies.	Nicholas Tcherepnine, the Russian composer, dies at 72 in Paris.	June 28
House passes and sends to the Senate Truman's presidential succession bill.	Sen. Vandenburg (R, Mich.) asks Congress for early ratification of the U.N. Charter in the "self-interest of the United States." .... Acting State Secy. Grew reveals the U.S. leased bases in Newfoundland in June 1941 for 99 years.	House Ways and Means Comm. approves a tax bill increasing the excess profits tax exemption from $10,000 to $25,000 .... OPA says used 1942 autos can be sold on an unrationed basis beginning July 2.			June 29
Clinton Anderson, Lewis Schwellenbach, Thomas Clark and Robert Hannegan are sworn in respectively as secretaries of agriculture and labor, attorney general and postmaster general .... House Comm. on Un-American Activities member John Rankin charges that Hollywood "is the greatest hotbed of subversive activities" in the U.S. .... Senate passes the bill to continue the FEPC, allocating it $250,000.	Truman names James F. Byrnes to be Secretary of State.	House passes the compromise OPA bill for another year and sends it to Truman.			June 30

F	G	H	I	J
Includes elections, federal-state relations, civil rights and liberties, crime, the judiciary, education, health care, poverty, urban affairs and population.	*Includes formation and debate of U.S. foreign and defense policies, veterans affairs and defense spending. (Relations with specific foreign countries are usually found under the region concerned.)*	*Includes business, labor, agriculture, taxation, transportation, consumer affairs, monetary and fiscal policy, natural resources, pollution and accidents.*	*Includes worldwide scientific, medical and technological developments, natural phenomena, U.S. weather and natural disasters.*	*Includes the arts, religion, scholarship, communications media, sports, entertainment, fashions, fads and social life.*

	World Affairs	European War Zone	Pacific War Zone	The Americas	Other Countries & Territories
July 1		British and American troops begin to withdraw from German zones which are to be occupied by Russians. Advance representatives of the Western Allies reach Berlin.	Australian troops under MacArthur land on the east coast of Borneo at Balik Papan, the second largest oil refinery area in the Dutch East Indies. A beachhead is established against initially light Japanese resistance .... Chinese forces capture Weichow Island off the south coast in the Gulf of Tonkin.		
July 2	Russia notifies the French Foreign Ministry that it wishes to participate in the international conference that will consider the provisional status of the port of Tangier.		The largest number of Superfortresses ever sent aloft, nearly 600, bomb Kure, Shimonoseki and Ube on Honshu Island and Kumamoto on Kyushu Island.		
July 3		American and British troops begin moving into Berlin, but traffic and other problems hold the entry to a trickle .... New Polish government assures Britain and the U.S. that "free and unfettered elections" will be held as soon as possible.	More than 450 Superfortresses drop 3,000 tons of incendiary bombs on Tokushima, Takamatsu and Kochi on Shikoku Island and Himeji on Honshu Island, destroying 48-78% of the target areas.		
July 4	U.S. delegation to the Tangier Conference informs the French government that it has no objection to the Russians participating.	U.S. troops formally establish themselves in Berlin under commander Maj. Gen. Floyd Parks.	Australian troops enter the Borneo oil refining center of Balik Papan and capture the most important air field in the area at Sepingang.	Commander of the U.S. Atlantic Fleet Adm. Jonas Ingram says several U.S. naval ships will be turned over to the Brazilian Navy after the war.	U.S. Foreign Economic Administration announces resumption of trade between the U.S. and French North Africa, Algeria, French Morocco and Tunisia.
July 5		U.S. and British announce recognition of the Polish regime in Warsaw; Arthur Bliss Lane will be the U.S. ambassador there .... U.S. military government in Germany seizes the management, assets and 24 plants of I.G. Farben, the chemical industry combine.	War Dept. announces that Gen. Carl Spaatz will be commander of a newly created U.S. Army Strategic Air Force in the Pacific to direct the Superfortress attacks against Japan .... MacArthur reports that all of the Philippine Islands are now liberated .... Japanese troops retake the city of Tinpak, 170 miles southwest of Canton .... Australian P.M. John Curtin dies at his official residence in Canberra from heart disease.	Censorship of the Argentine press is reestablished.	
July 6	Truman's invitation to de Gaulle to visit Washington is accepted.	U.S., Britain and Russia agree upon three principles governing war crimes trials: (1) the accused shall have a fair hearing, (2) they can develop their own defense, and (3) the trials shall not be subjected to obstructionist tactics by the defense .... London Polish leaders say they will not surrender documents or Polish property to anyone .... London radio says the Norwegian government announced in Oslo tonight that it has been in a state of war with Japan since Dec. 7, 1941 but that formal announcement was withheld until the government returned to home soil.	Superfortresses drop 4,000 tons of incendiary bombs on targets at Kofu, Chiba, Shimizu and Akashi on Honshu Island, destroying 43-65% of the target areas .... Speaking on the eighth anniversary of the war, Chiang Kai-shek says the coming year will bring great results, including a landing in Japan.	Pres. Edelmiro Farrel calls elections for Argentina before the year's end, promising they will be absolutely free .... Adm. Ingram tells Brazil that by July 8 all naval bases occupied by the U.S. will be returned to Brazil .... Nicaragua officially ratifies the U.N. Charter.	All-India Congress submits to Viceroy Wavell 15 candidates from which its representatives to the proposed reorganized Indian government are to be chosen.
July 7	Truman sails from Newport News, Va. aboard the *U.S.S. Augusta* to the Potsdam conference.		Fourth People's Political Council opens in Chungking without the Communists, who refuse to participate .... The 10 p.m. curfew that has prevailed in Hawaii since Pearl Harbor is lifted.		France yields to Syrian and Lebanese demands that native troops recruited into the French Army be released to become part of their states' national armies.
July 8		British military governor in Berlin, Brig. Gen. W.R.M. Hinde, says "the Russians are running all Berlin" as a result of the stalemate over supplying food and fuel to the American and British sectors .... Marshal Tito charges Greek citizens with firing morters across the Yugoslavian frontier.	Japanese stiffen their resistance to the Australian advance up the coast of Borneo northeastward from Manggar.		
July 9		U.S. authorities in Germany announce a three-point plan for the I.G. Farben chemical plants seized, including transfer to the U.N. of assets that might be used for reconstruction.	Chinese forces report retaking two former U.S. airbases at Sincheng, Kiangsi Province and Tanchuk, Kwangsi Province. Nanking, the main city of Kiangsi Province, is also taken.		Moscow radio, quoting *Pravda*, demands the ouster of "reactionary forces" from Iran and drastic economic and political reforms.

A	B	C	D	E
Includes developments that affect more than one world region, international organizations and important meetings of major world leaders.	*Includes all developments in European countries and military engagements between Allied and Axis powers in Africa and at sea.*	*Includes all developments in Japan and China, Japanese foreign policy and military actions in the Pacific region.*	*Includes all domestic and regional developments in Latin America, the Caribbean and Canada.*	*Includes developments in those independent nations and colonial possessions not covered in Columns B, C and D.*

U.S. Politics & Social Issues	U.S. Foreign Policy & Defense	U.S. Economy & Environment	Science, Technology & Nature	Culture, Leisure & Life Style	
	N.Y. Gov. Dewey, speaking "as titular leader" of the GOP Governor's Conference, calls for speedy ratification of the U.N. Charter.	Truman tells War Petroleum Admin. Ickes to seize and operate the Texas Co.'s plants at Port Arthur, Tex. because of a work stoppage by 175 employes.		Welby Van Horn wins the national professional tennis championship over John Nogrady in N.Y.	July 1
House committees refuse to accept the Senate appropriation of $250,000 for the FEPC.	Truman presents the U.N. Charter to the Senate, urging rapid ratification .... Senate confirms James F. Byrnes as Secretary of State.				July 2
Special adviser to the President Harry L. Hopkins resigns because of ill health .... Truman signs a bill to pay $101,630 to Sioux Indians for ponies the Army took from them after the Custer massacre in 1876.	After being sworn in as Secretary of State, Byrnes states there will be no change in U.S. foreign policy and no personnel changes until he returns from the upcoming Big Three conference .... Navy ends segregation of Negroes from whites in training .... Sen. Harlan Bushfield (R, S.D.) withdraws his opposition to the U.N. Charter.	Federal Reserve raises margin requirements from 50% to 75%, the highest ever, to cut down on speculation in the stock market .... Truman orders all but six federal agencies to reduce their work week from 48 to 44 hours, affecting 2.5 million employes.			July 3
	Governor's Conference on Mackinac Island, Mich. adopts a resolution urging the ratification of the U.N. Charter.	WPB orders the use of some synthetic rubber in all future tires, regardless of size, to save about 1,300 tons of natural rubber per year .... FTC orders the Book Paper Mfg. Assn. of N.Y. and 42 member manufacturers to stop fixing "uniform prices."		The U.S. is praised and congratulated in worldwide Independence Day celebrations. Thomas Paine, who lost the right to vote in New Rochelle, N.Y. 139 years ago, has his franchise posthumously "restored."	July 4
Associate Justice Owen J. Roberts resigns from the U.S. Supreme Court effective July 31 .... Thurman Arnold resigns as associate justice of the U.S. District Court of Appeals to resume his private law practice and work for "liberalism in business."	House Comm. on Postwar Military Policy recommends that Congress adopt universal military training, stating the program is essential to world security .... Truman signs the Reciprocal Trade Agreement Act, extending it to June 12, 1947.	Henry Morgenthau, Jr. announces his resignation as Secretary of the Treasury effective upon Truman's return from the Potsdam Conference.			July 5
		White House announces that Fred M. Vinson will succeed Morgenthau as Secretary of the Treasury .... House passes and sends to the Senate the tax relief bill for business.		Boston Braves outfielder Tommy Holmes hits safely in his 34th consecutive game, a new National League record .... Vatican excommuncates the Most. Rev. Don Carlos Duarte da Costa, bishop of Maura in Brazil, for preaching revolutionary practices.	July 6
	NAACP Secy. Walter White says "a few Marines have been throwing bricks, empty beer bottles .... hand grenades and smoke bombs into camps occupied by Negro Navy men" on an important Pacific island recently, resulting in riots and several deaths.	OPA announces counterfeit coupons valued at eight million points passed over national meat counters in the last month .... House Small Business Comm. reports the Diamond Match Co. and Swedish Match Co. "apparently control" the world market in a cartel arrangement.			July 7
Rep. Joseph Martin, Jr. (R, Mass.) urges an amendment to the Constitution to limit the tenure of any president to two terms.	MacArthur says national defense has become international defense and no nation in the future can rely only upon its own capabilities.				July 8
	Stettinius presents the U.N. Charter to the Senate Foreign Relations Comm. at its opening of hearings on the subject.		Americans witness their first total eclipse of the sun in 15 years. Beginning at sunrise in Idaho, the eclipse is visible in Montana and eastern Canada before extending to Greenland, Scandanavia and Russia. A partial eclipse of the sun is visible in most of the Northern Hemisphere.		July 9

F	G	H	I	J
Includes elections, federal-state relations, civil rights and liberties, crime, the judiciary, education, health care, poverty, urban affairs and population.	*Includes formation and debate of U.S. foreign and defense policies, veterans affairs and defense spending. (Relations with specific foreign countries are usually found under the region concerned.)*	*Includes business, labor, agriculture, taxation, transportation, consumer affairs, monetary and fiscal policy, natural resources, pollution and accidents.*	*Includes worldwide scientific, medical and technological developments, natural phenomena, U.S. weather and natural disasters.*	*Includes the arts, religion, scholarship, communications media, sports, entertainment, fashions, fads and social life.*

	World Affairs	European War Zone	Pacific War Zone	The Americas	Other Countries & Territories
July 10			In the greatest coordinated air assault on Japan to date, 600 Superfortresses, 1,000 carrier-based craft and 300 planes from Okinawa hit several cities on Honshu . . . . Australian and Dutch troops in Borneo occupy Teloktebang and Kariango peninsulas along Balik Papan Bay near the mouth of the Sumber River . . . . Counterattacking Japanese force the British from Nyaungkasho, an outpost on the lower Sittang River bend 70 miles northeast of Rangoon, Burma.	El Salvador's Constitutional Assembly ratifies the U.N. Charter.	U.S. Army relinquishes operation of the Iranian state railway to the government.
July 11		In the first formal meeting of the inter-Allied city council for Berlin, Russia agrees to turn over both military and civilian administration to U.S. and British zones tomorrow . . . . P.M. Eamon de Valera causes a sensation in the Eire Parliament when he says that Eire, part of the British Commonwealth, is a republic.	Allied forces complete capture of Balik Papan, Borneo.	Mexican Foreign Min. Ezequil Padilla resigns as his international policies come under attack.	Viceroy Wavell and President Mohammed Ali Jinnah of the Moslem League fail to reach agreement on the question of Moslem seats in the proposed Indian government.
July 12		U.S. War Dept. announces the Army will cease supplying food to civilians in liberated European countries as of Sept. 1.	After taking Tangkiang and Fengkang, Chinese troops report capture of Kanhsien, Kiangsi Province.	Brazil tightens import controls on machinery, rubber, chemicals and several other products.	
July 13			Chinese claim recapture of another former U.S. airbase near Kanhsien, Kiangsi Province.		
July 14	Russia and China reach an understanding on important questions after discussions between Stalin and T.V. Soong.	Eisenhower announces the end of SHAEF. The organization's headquarters in Frankfurt, Germany will be turned over to the newly formed United States Force, European Theater . . . . American occupation authorities permit U.S. troops to converse in public places with adult Germans.	U.S. carrier planes raid military facilities on Honshu and Hokkaido islands, claiming destruction of 108,000 tons of shipping and 28 airplanes.	Venezuelan cabinet resigns and Pres. Isaias Medina Angarita makes five changes in the reorganized body.	Viceroy Wavell announces the end of the Simla Conference in failure and accepts responsibility for the lack of results.
July 15	Truman and Churchill arrive in Berlin for the Big Three Conference.	Gen. Mark W. Clark eases the non-fraternization ban between Austrians and his troops.	U.S. warships continue their attack on Japan's home islands with the shelling of steel and iron works at Muroran, Hokkaido Island, causing damage equivalent to 2½ months' production.		U.S. Foreign Policy Assn. suggests the internationalization of Palestine as part of a long-range program to settle Middle Eastern problems . . . . Lebanese government reaches an agreement for construction and operation of two oil refineries near Tripoli with the Mediterranean Refining Co. and the Mediterranean Standard Oil Co.
July 16	Big Three Conference is delayed one day because of Stalin's failure to appear.	British Foreign Office issues a statement denying that Churchill ever made a "gentleman's agreement" with Marshal Petain.	British troops take five villages in the Sittang River bend north of Rangoon and close in on the enemy at Myitko in central Burma.		

A	B	C	D	E
Includes developments that affect more than one world region, international organizations and important meetings of major world leaders.	*Includes all developments in European countries and military engagements between Allied and Axis powers in Africa and at sea.*	*Includes all developments in Japan and China, Japanese foreign policy and military actions in the Pacific region.*	*Includes all domestic and regional developments in Latin America, the Caribbean and Canada.*	*Includes developments in those independent nations and colonial possessions not covered in Columns B, C and D.*

U.S. Politics & Social Issues	U.S. Foreign Policy & Defense	U.S. Economy & Environment	Science, Technology & Nature	Culture, Leisure & Life Style	
	Acting State Secy. Joseph Grew denies rumors that the U.S. has received peace feelers from Japan .... Five German soldiers are hanged in Fort Leavenworth, Kan., for the slaying of a fellow prisoner, Johannes Kunze, on Nov. 4, 1943 at Tonkawa, Okla. Kunze had been accused of writing a "traitorous" note and was beaten to death. The five executed men were sentenced to death by a court martial on Jan. 25, 1944, and FDR approved the death sentences on Oct. 5, 1944 .... Senate Foreign Relations Comm. debates whether the U.S. representative to the Security Council shall have the right to vote on the use of U.S. troops against an aggressor.	The 16,000 striking employes of the Firestone Tire & Rubber Co., Akron, Ohio, refuse an NWLB request to return to work.			July 10
	House Veterans Comm. approves a liberalized "GI Bill of Rights" but strips it of a bonus provision to give each veteran $1,040 .... Sixteen opponents of the U.N. Charter register their complaints before the Senate Foreign Relations Comm.	The government wins its antitrust suit against the Du Pont Co., National Lead Co. and the Titan Co. when a N.Y. federal court rules that the three have a world monopoly on titanium.	Cheplin Laboratories says penicillin will be released to the public as tablets, ointment and eyedrops starting Aug. 1.		July 11
Congress passes compromise legislation to extend the FEPC another year with a $250,000 appropriation .... House names Rep. John Wood (D, Ga.) to chair the Un-American Activities Comm.	Sen. Robert Taft (R, O.) attacks the Bank for Reconstruction and Development as a guise to "lend our people's and government's money abroad."	NWLB warns the 16,600 striking Firestone employes that they will be denied contract benefits if they do not return to work by July 16.			July 12
House Un-American Activities Comm. assigns an agent to discover whether there is any basis for rumors of subversive activities in Hollywood.	Senate Foreign Relations Comm. approves the U.N. Charter without reservation or amendment .... House approves the expansion of the Import-Export Bank's lending authority to $3.5 billion and sends the measure to the Senate.	The executive board of the CIO adopts a resolution asking Truman to revise the national wage policy to eliminate wages below 65¢ hourly .... WPB relaxes its restrictions on sheet and strip steel for the third quarter to facilitate the reconversion of small businesses.			July 13
	GOP Sens. Taft, Butler, Millikin and Thomas issue a minority report against the Bretton Woods proposals, charging that they are "merely a waste of money." .... Sen. Hiram Johnson (R, Calif.) announces he will vote against the U.N. Charter .... Maj. Gen. Chennault announces he is quitting as commander of the U.S. 14th Army Air Force and will retire from the Army.	NWLB suspends adjustment of all grievances raised by the AFL International Typographical Union in response to the union's demand that its bylaws be written into wage agreements without recourse to collective bargaining or arbitration.			July 14
		A subcommittee of the Senate Labor Comm. recommends that Congress direct the NWLB and the NMB to increase the minimum hourly wage to 65¢.			July 15
The nomination of Fred Vinson to be Secretary of the Treasury is sent to the Senate after Secy. Henry Morgenthau, Jr. asks Truman to be relieved as soon as possible.	The first secret testing of the atomic bomb takes place at Alamagordo Air Force Base, New Mexico. It is equivalant to 15,000-20,000 tons of TNT. Its flash and explosion can be seen and heard up to 180 miles away .... Senate Foreign Relations Comm. submits its official report on the U.N. Charter, asking unreserved ratification and saying that any attempt to give Congress power to decide every time the new world organization could use U.S. troops against a recalcitrant country would violate both the Charter and the U.S. Constitution .... Minority House Leader Joseph Martin (Mass.) announces he will introduce a resolution asking Truman to work for the abandonment of universal military training by all nations.	Agriculture Secy. Clinton Anderson tells the nation it must consume 5% less food this year than during "last year's eating spree" and that fats and oils, sugar, condensed and evaporated milk and canned fruits and vegetables will remain in short supply.			July 16

F	G	H	I	J
Includes elections, federal-state relations, civil rights and liberties, crime, the judiciary, education, health care, poverty, urban affairs and population.	*Includes formation and debate of U.S. foreign and defense policies, veterans affairs and defense spending. (Relations with specific foreign countries are usually found under the region concerned.)*	*Includes business, labor, agriculture, taxation, transportation, consumer affairs, monetary and fiscal policy, natural resources, pollution and accidents.*	*Includes worldwide scientific, medical and technological developments, natural phenomena, U.S. weather and natural disasters.*	*Includes the arts, religion, scholarship, communications media, sports, entertainment, fashions, fads and social life.*

	World Affairs	European War Zone	Pacific War Zone	The Americas	Other Countries & Territories
July 17	Truman, Stalin and Churchill begin the Potsdam Conference near Berlin, with Truman presiding.	Belgian Chamber of Deputies votes to continue Prince Charles' regency and to bar King Leopold from returning without Parliament's permission . . . . Franco indicates he expects his regime to be succeeded eventually by a traditional monarchy . . . . Explaining his statement that Eire is a republic, de Valera tells Parliament that this status was achieved Dec. 29, 1937 when the Constitution became operative, but that Eire still is "associated as a matter of our external policy with the British Commonwealth."			
July 18		Belgian Senate approves the action of the Chamber of Deputies in extending indefinitely the regency of Prince Charles, thus virtually exiling King Leopold III.	U.S. naval units carry out the third shelling of the Japanese home islands with an attack on large war plants in Hitachi, 80 miles northeast of Tokyo. Production in the target plants is halted almost entirely . . . . Samboja oil fields and refinery on Borneo are taken by the Australians.	Brazilian Expeditionary Force that fought in Italy receives a great reception upon arriving in Rio de Janeiro.	
July 19			Marianas-based Superfortresses strike at several industrial cities on Honshu Island, destroying 65-85% of the target areas.	Pres. Alfonso Lopez Pumarejo submits his resignation to the Colombian Senate.	
July 20	Truman says in Berlin that the U.S. seeks no monetary or territorial gains from the war.	World Jewish Congress in London appeals to the Big Three to remedy treatment of Jewish displaced persons in Europe.		Leaflets are distributed in Buenos Aires attacking U.S. Amb. Spruille Braden.	
July 21		Premier Edward Osubka-Morawski says in a Warsaw broadcast that there will be an amnesty for Polish political prisoners.	An official U.S. spokesman, Capt. E.M. Zacharias, broadcasts to Japan an appeal to surrender unconditionally or face total destruction and a dictated peace . . . . Australian troops make shore-to-shore movement to seize the southwestern head of Balik Papan Bay, gaining control of all entrances to the harbor.		
July 22			The first U.S. troops to reach the Philippines from Germany arrive in Manila, 5,000 strong . . . . Japanese forces, moving 83 miles in the last 22 days, make a 25-mile breakthrough along the South China Sea opposite Formosa.	Dr. Jose Luis Bustamente y Rivero is proclaimed president of Peru.	
July 23		Marshal Petain goes on trial in Paris, maintaining that he is not a traitor . . . . Frankfurt dispatches reveal that U.S. occupation forces carried out mass raids from sunrise July 21 until sunrise today throughout the American zone. Some 80,000 Germans are taken into custody for suspected membership in the SS or other criminal organizations.	U.S. destroyers break up a four-ship Japanese convoy in Sagami Bay near Tokyo, sinking two vessels and damaging one . . . . Chinese retake the former U.S. airbase at Namyung, Kwangtung Province.		
July 24		Former French Premiers Paul Reynaud and Edouard Daladier testify that Petain plotted with Nazi Germany.	U.S. and British naval planes attack Japan's largest naval base at Kure, Honshu island, claiming damage to two battleships, two heavy cruisers, one aircraft carrier, one light cruiser and one escort carrier.	Mexican government announces its suit against the American firm Palomas Land & Cattle Co. to recover about 400 million acres of land it contends the company holds illegally.	
	A	B	C	D	E
	Includes developments that affect more than one world region, international organizations and important meetings of major world leaders.	*Includes all developments in European countries and military engagements between Allied and Axis powers in Africa and at sea.*	*Includes all developments in Japan and China, Japanese foreign policy and military actions in the Pacific region.*	*Includes all domestic and regional developments in Latin America, the Caribbean and Canada.*	*Includes developments in those independent nations and colonial possessions not covered in Columns B, C and D.*

U.S. Politics & Social Issues	U.S. Foreign Policy & Defense	U.S. Economy & Environment	Science, Technology & Nature	Culture, Leisure & Life Style	
		ODT orders all railway coaches, combination passenger and baggage cars and express cars pooled for military purposes.		Gunder Haegg sets a new mile mark of 4:01.4 in Malmo, Sweden.	July 17
A subcommittee of the House Military Affairs Comm. releases the names of 16 commissioned and non-commissioned Army officers with backgrounds which "reflect Communism." .... House moves to adjourn July 21 until Oct. 8 after passing a bill extending the time in which veterans may take advantage of the "GI Bill." .... AMA offers a 14-point program to provide medical care for all people without increased taxation.	A State Dept. spokesman says it has no knowledge of a reported peace offer submitted by the Japanese through Stalin .... Forty-four prominent Americans, including Herbert Hoover, Alf Landon, John Dewey and George Creel, sign a petition to Truman to use his influence at the Potsdam conference to have the Yalta agreement for free elections in Poland carried out .... Senate votes for immediate consideration of the Bretton Woods proposals, defeating Sen. Taft's proposal to delay consideration until Nov. 15 .... WPB reports that munitions production for the remainder of the year will drop to about 70% of the March peak.	Bills are introduced in the House and Senate proposing that legal minimum wages start at 65¢ hourly for an estimated 10 million workers.	Office of Scientific Research and Development Dir. Vannevar Bush suggests that Congress establish a National Research Foundation to promote a national policy for scientific research and education.		July 18
	Senate approves the Bretton Woods Agreement and sends it back to the House for concurrence in several amendments .... Sen. Arthur Vandenberg makes public a communication from Undersecy. of State Joseph Grew that the U.S. will insist on being a full and equal partner in supervising free elections in Poland.	OPA reveals part of its program to put ceiling prices on civilian goods made in the reconversion period, assuring industry reasonable profits to get production rolling .... Army again seizes five Chicago units of Montgomery Ward because of the firm's failure to obey NWLB directives .... Senate passes the new tax bill designed to provide relief for business.			July 19
	House approves changes in the Bretton Woods legislation, and the bill is dispatched to Truman in Germany for his signature .... Senate approves the House version of a bill to increase the lending power of the Export-Import Bank by $2.8 billion .... Interior Secy. Ickes says he has decided it is imperative that the U.S. send 6,000,000 tons of coal to Europe because the "race" in Europe today is between coal and anarchy."	House completes action on the tax bill by approving Senate changes and sends it on to Truman .... Labor Dept. says that non-agricultural employment dropped in June for the first time in seven years, to 37,495,000.	American Cyanamid Co. announces its discovery of the synthesis of a new vitamin, folic acid, in the Vitamin B class.	Paul Valery, noted poet, author and member of the French Academy, dies at 73 in Paris.	July 20
	Senate vote backs U.S. membership in the U.N. Food and Agriculture Organization .... The 72½-ton *Hawaii Mars*, Navy cargo carrier and the world's largest flying boat, is launched at Baltimore, Md.			A conference of Methodists of Britain and Ireland resolves that women may now become fully ordained ministers but that they must retire when married.	July 21
Communist Political Assn. of N.Y. votes to return to its status as a political party.	War Dept. says discharge points for soldiers will be reduced from the present 85 by the month's end.	NWLB announces an order for Montgomery Ward officials to come to Washington for an Aug. 3 hearing on charges of ignoring a board closed-shop order in seven cities.	Pres. Reginald Coombe of the Memorial Hospital for the Treatment of Cancer and Allied Diseases, N.Y.C., announces plans to expand the hospital into the largest cancer research center in the world.		July 22
Sen. Theodore Bilbo (D, Miss.) refuses the demand of Rep. Vito Marcantonio (ALP, N.Y.) that he apologize to Miss Josephine Piccolo for addressing her as "my Dear Dago" in a letter, after she had written Bilbo about his opposition to FEPC legislation.	With the approval of Truman, Gen. Groves secretly directs that the 509 Composite Group of the 20th Air Force prepare to drop the atomic bomb on Japan .... Sen. Tom Connally presents the U.N. Charter to the full Senate for discussion.	Fred Vinson takes office as the 53rd Secretary of the Treasury. John Snyder takes over as director of the Office of War Mobilization and Reconversion.	A bill to establish a National Science Foundation is introduced into the Senate .... Northern N.J. and the Berkshire area of Massachusetts suffer $4 million in damage from floods following eight days of heavy rain.		July 23
E.P. Carville (D) resigns as governor of Nevada and is named by his successor Lt. Gov. Vail Pittman as U.S. senator.	Truman secretly decides to use the atomic bomb on a Japanese city if Japan does not surrender by July 30 .... Sen. Burton K. Wheeler (D, Mont.) attacks the U.N. Charter as incapable of dealing with Europe's "rampant totalitarian tyranny."				July 24

F	G	H	I	J
Includes elections, federal-state relations, civil rights and liberties, crime, the judiciary, education, health care, poverty, urban affairs and population.	*Includes formation and debate of U.S. foreign and defense policies, veterans affairs and defense spending. (Relations with specific foreign countries are usually found under the region concerned.)*	*Includes business, labor, agriculture, taxation, transportation, consumer affairs, monetary and fiscal policy, natural resources, pollution and accidents.*	*Includes worldwide scientific, medical and technological developments, natural phenomena, U.S. weather and natural disasters.*	*Includes the arts, religion, scholarship, communications media, sports, entertainment, fashions, fads and social life.*

	World Affairs	European War Zone	Pacific War Zone	The Americas	Other Countries & Territories
July 25	Big Three Conference recesses so that Churchill may return to England for election results . . . . Russia asks the UNRRA for $700 million in supplies.	Petain refuses to answer when asked at his Paris trial whether he congratulated Hitler on the British defeat at Dieppe and asked Hitler's permission for French troops to fight beside the Germans.	Tokyo radio says Japanese government might be inclined to end the war if punitive measures of the U.S. terms were softened . . . . About 2,500 Japanese troops attempting to escape across the Sittang River in lower Burma are wiped out by British forces.		An accord between British Gen. Sir Bernard C. Paget and French Gen. Paul Etienne Beynet provides that French troops will remain along the Levant coast but will withdraw from eastern Syria.
July 26	Truman releases the Potsdam ultimatum, assented to by Churchill and Chiang Kai-shek, demanding that Japan immediately surrender or face utter destruction.	British Labor Party wins a landslide victory, resulting in the resignation of Churchill and the naming of Clement Attlee as prime minister . . . . Premier Achille van Acker's Belgian government, which maintains that King Leopold III should not resume the throne, wins a vote of confidence in the Chamber of Deputies . . . . Swedish wartime coalition cabinet resigns, and Premier Per Albin Hannsson forms a new one, made up completely of Social Democratic Party members.	Gen. Jacob Devers, chief of U.S. ground forces, says about seven million men will be used for the invasion of Japan.		
July 27		Attlee announces he will concurrently hold the posts of first lord of the treasury and minister of labor in his new cabinet and names Ernest Bevin his foreign secretary.	Chinese troops report the capture of a Japanese supply base at Pinglo and the recapture of a former U.S. airbase near Kweilin, both in Kwangsi Province.		
July 28	Attlee arrives at Potsdam to participate in the Big Three Conference.	Mrs. Herbert H. Asquith, Countess of Oxford and Asquith and widow of the former prime minister, dies at 81 in London.	U.S. planes attack six Japanese cities that had been forewarned by leaflets dropped the previous night. (According to Japanese officials interviewed after the war, the measure persuades many civilians of America's good intentions and causes many to lose faith in the ability of the Japanese Army to defend the homeland.)	Dr. Jose Luis Bustamente Rivero takes office as Peru's president.	An Egyptian military court sentences Mahmud Issawy to hang for the assassination of former Premier Ahmed Maher Pasha.
July 29			Japanese Premier Kantaro Suzuki says the Imperial government will take no notice of the Potsdam ultimatum, claiming it is no different from previous Allied statements.	Col. Osmin Aguirre y Salinas is reportedly being held in El Salvador as leader of a plot to overthrow the government.	
July 30			U.S. cruiser *Indianapolis* is sunk by a Japanese submarine in the Philippine Sea. Of the 1,199 men on board, 316 are rescued days later after drifting in the sea. The vessel is sunk after making a high speed run from San Francisco to Guam, where it delivered atomic bomb materials . . . . Premier T.V. Soong relinquishes his post as China's foreign minister and is named vice-chairman of the joint administration office of the four government banks.		
July 31	U.N. educational organization draft proposals are revealed by the State Dept. Their objectives will be to facilitate consultation among educators, permit the free flow of ideas and foster support for international peace.	Pierre Laval is flown from Barcelona, Spain to Linz, Austria, where he surrenders to American troops, who in turn hand him over to the French at Innsbruck.		King George VI appoints Field Marshal Sir Harold R.L.G. Alexander as governor-general of Canada.	
Aug. 1	Albania signs an agreement to receive UNRRA aid.	In a readjustment of the Austrian occupation zones, the Russians hold all territory north of the Danube River with the Americans on the south bank . . . . At Petain's trial, a letter from former U.S. Amb. to Vichy William Leahy is introduced in which the ambassador indicates Petain hoped the Nazis would be destroyed but at times refused to oppose them . . . . Pierre Laval and his wife reach Paris by plane from Austria, and he is lodged in the Fresnes prison.			At the opening of the first Zionist Conference since 1939 in London, President Chaim Weizmann asks the U.N. to recognize the establishment of a Jewish state in Palestine.

U.S. Politics & Social Issues	U.S. Foreign Policy & Defense	U.S. Economy & Environment	Science, Technology & Nature	Culture, Leisure & Life Style	
	Senate discussion of the U.N. Charter centers on the use of U.S. troops under the authority of the Security Council.	Henry Kaiser and Joseph Frazer announce the formation of the Kaiser-Frazer Corp. to produce two postwar autos bearing their names . . . . Packard Motor Co. and the CIO-UAW reach a truce, with the existing contract remaining in effect during negotiations.			July 25
Malcolm Ross, chairman of the Fair Employment Practices Commission, announces that the FEPC staff will be cut from 117 to 51 and five branch offices will be closed due to lack of funds . . . . Communist Political Assn. opens its national convention in N.Y. with attacks on Earl Browder and his "opportunistic errors."		OPA officially lowers meat ration values for beef, lamb and veal and allocates about 80 million more pounds of sugar to the East by September.			July 26
Florida Supreme Court upholds a lower court decision that Negroes may vote in the Democratic Party primaries in the state . . . . Communists vote to reorganize the CP and warn Earl Browder he will be expelled if he tries to split the party.		IRS says government income from taxes in the 1945 fiscal year reached a new high of $43.8 billion.			July 27
CP formally deposes Browder and names William Z. Foster as its new head.	Senate, with only William Langer and Henrik Shipstead dissenting, votes 89-2 for the U.N. Charter . . . . A B-25 bomber crashes into the Empire State Building in New York City at a point 915 feet above the street, killing 13 and injuring 25 persons and causing $500,000 damages.				July 28
	Truman says he opposes sending the wives and families of U.S. occupation troops to Germany because he doesn't want Americans to settle in Europe.		American Society of Mechanical Engineers Medal is awarded to Dr. William Durand for his work in hydro-dynamic and aerodynamic science, particularly in the area of jet propulsion.		July 29
	Senate Foreign Relations Comm. chairmen Tom Connally and Arthur Vandenberg disagree as to whether the President can act alone in appointing the U.S. delegate to the Security Council.	ODT says the 1,700 seized Chicago truck lines will be returned to their owners Aug. 1.		Byron Nelson wins the All American Open Golf Tournament in Chicago.	July 30
In the N.Y.C. primary, William O'Dwyer becomes the mayoral candidate of both the Democratic Party and the American Labor Party.		Solid Fuels Admin. Ickes tells the Mead War Investigating Comm. this country faces its "coldest" winter of the war because of lack of manpower in the coal mines.		U.S. Circuit Court of Appeals in N.Y. rules that NBC and ABC must bargain collectively with their disc jockeys through the National Assn. of Broadcast Engineers and Technicians, rather than James C. Petrillo's American Fed. of Musicians . . . . Australian Customs Min. Richard Keane bans the book *Forever Amber* as an "undesirable book and not an acquisition to Australian literature."	July 31
Anticipating its longest recess since 1938, the Senate adjourns until Oct. 8.	Gen. Henry Arnold says the U.S. must maintain its position with the most powerful air force in the world during peacetime.	Labor Dept. says the cost-of-living index, as of June 15, stood at 129% of the 1935-39 average, the highest since the spring of 1921 . . . . Agriculture Secy. Anderson says that due to a cut in government needs, the civilian butter supply for August will be increased to 100 million lbs.			Aug. 1

F	G	H	I	J
Includes elections, federal-state relations, civil rights and liberties, crime, the judiciary, education, health care, poverty, urban affairs and population.	*Includes formation and debate of U.S. foreign and defense policies, veterans affairs and defense spending. (Relations with specific foreign countries are usually found under the region concerned.)*	*Includes business, labor, agriculture, taxation, transportation, consumer affairs, monetary and fiscal policy, natural resources, pollution and accidents.*	*Includes worldwide scientific, medical and technological developments, natural phenomena, U.S. weather and natural disasters.*	*Includes the arts, religion, scholarship, communications media, sports, entertainment, fashions, fads and social life.*

	World Affairs	European War Zone	Pacific War Zone	The Americas	Other Countries & Territories
Aug. 2	Stalin, Truman and Attlee end the Potsdam Conference with a declaration praising the session as an important step towards "the creation of a just and lasting peace." The declaration also provides for: (1) creation of a Council of Foreign Ministers of the major Allied powers to conclude peace treaties with former Axis countries; (2) destruction of Nazism and the reconstruction of German life "on a democratic and peaceful basis;" (3) international trial of major European war criminals; (4) regulation of reparations to be taken by Russia from both its own occupation zone and Western zones of Germany; (5) Allied recognition of the Polish government in Warsaw and provisional extension of Poland's western frontier to the Oder-Neisse line; and (5) an "orderly transfer" of Germans from Poland, Czechoslovakia and Hungary into Germany . . . . Truman departs from the Potsdam Conference by plane to Plymouth, England where he boards the cruiser *Augusta* for his trip to the U.S.		About 800 U.S. planes bomb the Japanese cities of Hachioji, Toyama, Nagaoka and Mito and the petroleum installations at Kawasaki in the greatest single bombing effort in history.	U.S. State Dept. reports that Argentine labor leaders told Amb. Spruille Braden that the majority of the people there are in sympathy with Braden and are against Peron . . . . Ecuadorean government suppresses an army revolt at Loja and imprisons two leaders . . . . Guatemala reports that the volcano Fuego is erupting for the first time since 1932.	Arab leaders cable Attlee that any solution to the Palestine problem not acceptable to the Arabs will threaten Middle East peace.
Aug. 3	Truman tells reporters on the *Augusta* that he made no secret agreements at Potsdam.	An announcement from Nuremberg reports that the war crimes trials will start there Sept. 1 . . . . Laval acknowledges at Petain's trial in Paris that in a June 22, 1942 broadcast to the French people he did say he "hoped for a German victory."	The 20th Air Force at Guam reports that a mine-planting operation, under way since March 27, has effectively blockaded shipping to and from Japan . . . . Chinese troops capture Sinin, Hunan Province and drive northward towards Tungan.	Brazilian War Min. Eurico Dutra resigns to seek the presidency.	
Aug. 4		Laval claims at Petain's trial that at the time of the Allied landing in North Africa the latter secretly instructed French commanders to aid the invaders.	MacArthur announces extension of his Army military command to the Ryukyu Islands.		
Aug. 5		Yugoslavian Parliament passes a far-reaching amnesty law, pardoning thousands held on collaboration charges. War criminals and members of certain fascist groups are not included in the measure.	Chungking reports claim that 50,000 Chinese were killed or are missing in recently liberated Kiangsi Province.		
Aug. 6			The Superfortress *Enola Gay* drops the atomic bomb on Hiroshima, causing 78,150 instant deaths and destroying 60% of the city. The crew of *Enola Gay* includes Col. Paul W. Tibbets, Jr. (pilot), Maj. Thomas W. Ferebee (bombardier) and Capt. William S. Parsons (who armed the device in flight). U.S. military authorities announce that the bomb, a uranium fission device, had the force of 20,000 tons of TNT.	Canadian government discloses plans for a full-scale postwar employment program, which includes a proposal that the provinces relinquish their taxes to the central government for three years . . . . Argentine Interior Min. Dr. Hortensio Quijano reports the lifting of the state of siege in effect since December 1941.	
Aug. 7		Frankfurt dispatches report that former Nazi leaders to be tried for war crimes include Hermann Goering, Joachim von Ribbentrop, Franz von Papen, Arthur Seyss-Inquart and Gustav Jodl . . . . Tito says that a monarchy is "incompatible with democracy in Yugoslavia" and indicates that there will be legislation to bar the return of King Peter II.		Alberto Llevas Camargo is inaugurated as president of Colombia for the remaining term of former Pres. Alfonso Lopez Pumarejo.	
Aug. 8		U.N. War Crimes Commission announces an agreement establishing an International Military Tribunal to try the major European Axis criminals . . . . State Dept. announces a Four-Power Agreement for Austria, providing for an Allied Council of four military commanders to govern Austria as a whole and confining the country to its 1937 frontiers.	Russia declares war against Japan, citing Japanese rejection of the Allied call for unconditional surrender contained in the Potsdam declaration. The state of war will begin Aug. 9.		Iranian Foreign Office reports that British and Russian troops will be withdrawn at once from Teheran but that no decision on their leaving the rest of the country has been reached . . . . A five-point plan for the future of the Jewish state is submitted to the World Zionist Conference in London.
	A *Includes developments that affect more than one world region, international organizations and important meetings of major world leaders.*	B *Includes all developments in European countries and military engagements between Allied and Axis powers in Africa and at sea.*	C *Includes all developments in Japan and China, Japanese foreign policy and military actions in the Pacific region.*	D *Includes all domestic and regional developments in Latin America, the Caribbean and Canada.*	E *Includes developments in those independent nations and colonial possessions not covered in Columns B, C and D.*

U.S. Politics & Social Issues	U.S. Foreign Policy & Defense	U.S. Economy & Environment	Science, Technology & Nature	Culture, Leisure & Life Style	
		Sen. Vandenberg asks Labor Secy. Lewis Schwellenbach to call a labor-industry-government conference to work towards industrial peace in the postwar period . . . . Agriculture Dept. member W.R. Arnold submits a farm relief program to Secy. Anderson, suggesting elimination of the FCA, FSA and Soil Conservation Service, which would save about $500 million yearly.		Pietro Mascagni, the Italian composer noted for his opera *Cavalleria Rusticana*, dies at 81 in Rome.	Aug. 2
		NWLB turns over the Montgomery Ward case to Stabilization Dir. William Davis.		Memphis, Tenn. Board of Censors bans the eight-year-old movie *Dead End* because it "might influence boys to be gangsters."	Aug. 3
CP warns Earl Browder that until he publicly accepts the national convention's decisions his "future work" with the Party will not be discussed.	Truman signs the Bretton Woods legislation, making the U.S. the first country to so do . . . . Truman signs bills approving U.S. membership in the U.N. Food and Agriculture Organization and authorizing an increase in the Export-Import Bank lending capability to $3.5 billion.	Solid Fuels Administration reports 14 more wildcat coal mine strikes and says that coal losses due to strikes since April 1 total 12,445,920 tons . . . . Truman approves the Reconversion Tax bill raising excess-profits tax exemptions.			Aug. 4
	Sen. Vandenberg recommends to State Secy. Byrnes that the Western Hemisphere be left outside the peace-keeping functions of the U.N., giving the American republics continued responsibility for policing the area . . . . Assn. of American Physicians & Surgeons asks Truman to investigate rumors of a doctor surplus in the armed forces and to release immediately those not needed.				Aug. 5
Former GOP presidential candidate Alf Landon predicts that "left-wing New Dealers" will seek more power in the Truman Administration and possibly form a third party in 1948 . . . . Sen. Hiram Johnson (R, Calif.) dies at 79 in Washington. He served in Congress since 1917 and opposed both the League of Nations and the U.N.					Aug. 6
Georgia votes to adopt a new constitution, replacing the current one, which dates from 1877.	Truman arrives at the White House from the Potsdam Conference and immediately confers with his cabinet.	WPB announces a new plan to speed reconversion involving the transfer of some cancelled war contracts to other government buying agencies that need the items being produced.	GM Chmn. Alfred P. Sloan announces a $4 million grant financed by the Alfred P. Sloan Foundation for a Sloan-Kettering Institute for Cancer Research in N.Y.C.		Aug. 7
	Truman signs the U.N. Charter, making the U.S. the first nation to complete such action . . . . Censorship Dir. Byron Price lifts the ban on individual mailing of books, magazines, newspapers, catologues and other printed matter to neutral European countries.	Senate ICC Comm. Chmn. Burton Wheeler charges that officials of the RFC are speculating in B&O Railroad securities.			Aug. 8

F	G	H	I	J
Includes elections, federal-state relations, civil rights and liberties, crime, the judiciary, education, health care, poverty, urban affairs and population.	*Includes formation and debate of U.S. foreign and defense policies, veterans affairs and defense spending. (Relations with specific foreign countries are usually found under the region concerned.)*	*Includes business, labor, agriculture, taxation, transportation, consumer affairs, monetary and fiscal policy, natural resources, pollution and accidents.*	*Includes worldwide scientific, medical and technological developments, natural phenomena, U.S. weather and natural disasters.*	*Includes the arts, religion, scholarship, communications media, sports, entertainment, fashions, fads and social life.*

	World Affairs	European War Zone	Pacific War Zone	The Americas	Other Countries & Territories
Aug. 9	Reaction to use of the A-bomb varies: Truman hails the release of atomic energy as "a new era in man's understanding of nature's forces." But the Vatican condemns the bomb as "a temptation, if not for horrified contemporaries then for posterity, to whom .... history teaches very little."	Former Vichyites Fernand de Brinon and Joseph Darnand testify that Petain favored collaboration with Germany.	A second atomic bomb is dropped on Nagasaki, causing 40,000 deaths and destroying one-third of the city. U.S. military authorities announce that the bomb, a plutonium fission device, has already made the uranium device dropped earlier on Hiroshima "obsolete." .... Russian troops plunge into Manchuria from the east, north and west in a giant pincer move, advancing from nine to 14 miles .... Japanese military and political leaders meet in Tokyo to discuss surrender. War Minister Anami, speaking for the military command, urges continued resistance; Premier Suzuki and Foreign Min. Shigenori Togo favor peace. The deadlocked conference requests an "Imperial decision," allowing Emperor Hirohito to cast his vote for surrender.		
Aug. 10	Tangier Conference opens in Paris, with Russian representatives joining the U.S., Britain and France.	British give the French two of their Berlin boroughs for occupation.	Japanese cabinet ratifies Hirohito's surrender decision of yesterday, with the provision that the Emperor be allowed to remain in power. A message to this effect is sent to Washington .... Russians advance 105 miles into Manchuria from the west along the Chinese Eastern Railroad.		
Aug. 11	UNRRA chief Lehman says the agency needs another $500 million to meet increased relief demands next year.	French public prosecutor demands the death penalty for Petain, although the charge against him has been reduced from treason to "intelligence with the enemy."	Truman replies to Japan that the Allies will accept Japan's surrender, with Emperor Hirohito on the throne for the time being but subject to the decisions of the Allied command .... The Russians continue their rapid advance in Manchuria, reaching into the Great Hingan Mountain valleys leading to Harbin, while in the east they report reaching Matita and to the north enter Mulingchen, Lishuchen and Pankiehhotze.	Brazilian Pres. Vargas amends the country's 1941 press laws to permit publication there of newspapers in English, Spanish, Portuguese and French.	
Aug. 12		Attlee issues a statement pledging British cooperation in keeping the secret of the atomic bomb as a peacekeeping measure.	Soviet Marines invade Korea with support of the Red Fleet, capturing the naval base of Rashin and nearby port of Yuki .... Chiang Kai-shek orders Chinese Communists never again to take independent action after learning Red leaders ordered the disarmament of Japanese troops and occupation of Japanese territory.		
Aug. 13			Chinese Communist broadcast charges that Chiang Kai-shek is plotting a civil war in China.		World Zionist Conference in London discloses that the five-point program laid before the British government last May by the Jewish Agency includes: (1) creation of a Jewish state in Palestine and (2) permission for the Agency to settle as many Jews as possible in Palestine and develop resources.
Aug. 14	Moscow radio says Russia and China have reached an agreement on all questions of common interest.	France ratifies the U.N. Charter.	A tearful Emperor Hirohito tells his cabinet that Japan must publicly accept Truman's peace terms of Aug. 11. He declares he can no longer "endure to see [my] subjects killed in the fire of battle." .... A Japanese broadcast announces Japan's acceptance of Allied demand for unconditional surrender, setting off worldwide celebration of V-J Day. Official U.S. announcement of surrender comes from Truman at 7 p.m.	Ecuadorean Pres. Jose Velasco Ibarra grants a general amnesty to members of the former administration.	
Aug. 15		Marshal Petain is condemned to death by the Paris jury hearing his case, but he expresses hope that because of his age, 89, the sentence will not be carried out .... Soviet Union announces resumption of diplomatic relations with Bulgaria.	Emperor Hirohito's surrender message is broadcast to the Japanese people at 12 noon. Premier Kantaro Suzuki and his cabinet resign in Tokyo, claiming that "the new situation created by Japan's acceptance of the Potsdam Declaration requires a new cabinet of men with fresh ideas." .... MacArthur directs the Japanese to send emissaries to discuss peace terms at Manila .... Russian units continue to fight in Manchuria, reportedly because the Japanese there have not been ordered to lay down their arms.		
	A *Includes developments that affect more than one world region, international organizations and important meetings of major world leaders.*	B *Includes all developments in European countries and military engagements between Allied and Axis powers in Africa and at sea.*	C *Includes all developments in Japan and China, Japanese foreign policy and military actions in the Pacific region.*	D *Includes all domestic and regional developments in Latin America, the Caribbean and Canada.*	E *Includes developments in those independent nations and colonial possessions not covered in Columns B, C and D.*

U.S. Politics & Social Issues	U.S. Foreign Policy & Defense	U.S. Economy & Environment	Science, Technology & Nature	Culture, Leisure & Life Style	
	In a radio address Truman threatens Japan with obliteration by atomic bombing unless Allied demands for unconditional surrender are accepted, and says the U.S. will not reveal its A-bomb secret until an international arms control plan is formulated .... Truman appoints Edward J. Stettinius as U.S. representative on the Preparatory Commission of the U.N.	Truman requests WPB Chmn. Krug to carry out a five-point reconversion program, including a drive to manufacture short-supply material, a limit on the manufacture of goods using scarce resources, imposition of effective inventory controls and a priority system to break bottlenecks through allocation of scarce materials.	Westinghouse Co. and Glenn L. Martin Co. announce a plan for TV and frequency modulation broadcasting from airplanes flying in the stratosphere.		Aug. 9
		WPB authorizes six companies to begin production of civilian electronic equipment, including radios .... Pres. Roy White of the B&O Railroad denies Wheeler's charges and demands an investigation .... Agriculture Dept. predicts that the 1945 food crops will be the third largest in the nation's history.		Richard Muckerman becomes president of the St. Louis Browns baseball team with the purchase of stock from Don Barnes.	Aug. 10
Sen. Alben W. Barkley announces that Congress will heed Truman's request that it return to work Sept. 4 .... Interior Secy. Ickes proposes that Alaska become the forty-ninth state of the union and share the "American right of self-government."		Social Security Bd. reports on 10 years of the program. Nearly $8.75 billion has been paid, with 1,285,000 recipients on Social Security rolls as of July 1 .... WMC Dir. John W. Snyder calls on labor and industry to cooperate in reconversion.			Aug. 11
				Michigan State Univ. captures the National AAU swimming team title in Akron, Ohio, with the Great Lakes Naval Training Center placing second.	Aug. 12
		OPA establishes rules for determination of reconversion price ceilings on building materials, plant machinery and rubber.		Branch Rickey and two associates purchase 50% of the Brooklyn Dodgers stock from the estate of Charles Ebbetts, giving them 75% control of the club.	Aug. 13
		Navy announces that nearly $6 billion worth of prime contracts are being canceled as a result of Japan's surrender .... WMC abolishes all manpower controls over employers and workers.	U.S. War and Navy Depts. tell for the first time the full story of radar, and in London Sir Stafford Cripps says radar played a greater role in winning the war than the atom bomb itself.		Aug. 14
	War Dept. announces it will release five million men within the next year and discharge immediately all those over 38 and the 78,000 high-point men in the states.	WPB Chmn. Krug reports that only 30 or 40 controls on allocation of materials will remain in effect by the week's end, including tin, crude rubber, some textiles, lumber and hard fibers .... OPA Administrator Chester Bowles frees gasoline from rationing .... WMC predicts over 5,000,000 unemployed during the next three months and possibly 6,200,000 by mid-December.	Illinois Univ. Prof. Dr. H.W. Anderson says the drug streptomycin may surpass penicillin in effectiveness.	A.L. umpire Ernest Stewart is fired by league president Will Harridge for asking for higher salaries for umpires .... *Billboard* reports the most popular songs are: (1) *On the Atchison, Topeka and Santa Fe*, (2) *Sentimental Journey* and (3) *Bell-Bottom Trousers*.	Aug. 15
F	G	H	I	J	
Includes elections, federal-state relations, civil rights and liberties, crime, the judiciary, education, health care, poverty, urban affairs and population.	*Includes formation and debate of U.S. foreign and defense policies, veterans affairs and defense spending. (Relations with specific foreign countries are usually found under the region concerned.)*	*Includes business, labor, agriculture, taxation, transportation, consumer affairs, monetary and fiscal policy, natural resources, pollution and accidents.*	*Includes worldwide scientific, medical and technological developments, natural phenomena, U.S. weather and natural disasters.*	*Includes the arts, religion, scholarship, communications media, sports, entertainment, fashions, fads and social life.*	

	World Affairs	European War Zone	Pacific War Zone	The Americas	Other Countries & Territories
Aug. 16	Chinese Premier T.V. Soong arrives in Washington for conferences with Truman and State Secy. Byrnes.	Russia and Poland sign a treaty in Moscow fixing the post-World War I Curzon Line as the basis of their new frontier. Russia also agrees to give Poland 15% of the German reparations she receives.	Hirohito orders all Japanese forces to cease fire at 6 p.m., but the Japanese government estimates that it will take 2-12 days for word to reach all front-line troops .... Prince Naruhiko Higashi-Kuni, cousin of Emperor Hirohito, today completes formation of a new Japanese cabinet with himself as premier and war minister .... Truman says U.S. authorities alone will be responsible for ruling Japan, although troops of all Allied nations in the Pacific will occupy the country .... Russian Field Marshal Alexander Vasilevski tells the Japanese Kwantung Army to cease operations and surrender by Aug. 20 .... Chinese Communist Gen. Chu Teh asks the Allies for Communist participation in the Japanese surrender and requests a halt in Lend-Lease aid to Chiang because of the possibility of civil war.	Buenos Aires says several hundred uniformed soldiers committed deliberate violence today upon individuals who oppose their cries of "long live Peron." .... Nicaraguan Pres. Anastasio Somoza decrees the end of martial law.	Truman calls for free settlement of Palestine by Jews to a point consistent with civil peace.
Aug. 17		De Gaulle commutes Petain's death sentence to life imprisonment.	Premier Higashi-Kuni orders all Japanese soldiers to observe Hirohito's cease-fire order after an attempt by hardline militarists to assassinate leading peace advocates in the government and prevent the Emperor from delivering his peace message to the Japanese people .... The Thai cabinet of Premier Kuang Kovid Aphaiwong resigns.	U.S. Amb. Spruille Braden says a self-respecting world can no longer accept dictatorships, thus implying a denunciation of the Argentine government.	Indonesian nationalist leader Ahmed Sukarno begins formation of a native government on Java.
Aug. 18		U.S. State Dept. informs the Bulgarian government that it does not feel the regime of Premier Kimon Georgiev fully represents the Bulgarian people or has taken steps to ensure proper elections.	Japanese Foreign Min. Mamoru Shigemitsu tells his people the nation has been defeated and urges all Japanese to understand the terms of the Potsdam Declaration. "Any wishful thinking should be avoided and the nation should calmly face realities," he says .... Mao Tze-tung advises Chiang Kai-shek that he will consider a conference only after the Communists participate in the Japanese surrender .... Indian politician Subhas Chandra Bose, leader of pro-Japanese Indian National Army, dies in airplane crash during an attempted escape to Formosa.		
Aug. 19	Thirty-four clergymen ask Truman to order the immediate discontinuation of atomic bomb production and urge all nations to outlaw its use.	Moscow dispatches disclose that Russia plans a new five-year plan for 1946-50 to create a greater industrial base than existed before the war.	Japanese armistice commission arrives in Manila, headed by Lt. Gen. Torashiro Kawabe .... A rescue team of Americans parachuted into Manchuria finds Lt. Gen. Jonathan M. Wainwright and Marine Lt. Col. James P.S. Devereux in Japanese POW camps .... Moscow reports that Japan's Kwantung Army is virtually destroyed .... Gen. Chu Teh warns Chiang Kai-shek in a note today to act quickly to avert the "grave threat" of civil war between the Communist and government forces in China.		
Aug. 20		Making his first speech in Parliament as Britain's new foreign secretary, Ernest Bevin aligns the labor government with the former Churchill government on matters of foreign policy and says the present Greek government should continue pending an election .... U.S. announces agreement with Britain and France on sending commissioners to Greece to assist in assuring free elections there .... Vidkun Quisling goes on trial in Oslo on treason charges, and he repeatedly shouts that he was "the savior of Norway." .... Russian Presidium ratifies the U.N. Charter.	MacArthur reports the Manila conference with Japanese peace emissaries is over. They have returned to Japan with instructions for preparing the surrender .... Russian troops enter Manchurian cities of Mukden, Harbin and Changchun .... France accepts a U.S. invitation to take part in the signature of the Japanese surrender and to participate with the British and Chinese in the Indochina surrender.		
Aug. 21			Japanese Domei news agency announces that Allied occupation troops will begin landing on Aug. 26 and asks the populace to remain calm and to avoid contact with the troops.		New Delhi announces that general elections will be held in British India as soon as possible .... Lebanese cabinet resigns, and former Premier Sami el Solth is asked to form a new government.
	A *Includes developments that affect more than one world region, international organizations and important meetings of major world leaders.*	B *Includes all developments in European countries and military engagements between Allied and Axis powers in Africa and at sea.*	C *Includes all developments in Japan and China, Japanese foreign policy and military actions in the Pacific region.*	D *Includes all domestic and regional developments in Latin America, the Caribbean and Canada.*	E *Includes developments in those independent nations and colonial possessions not covered in Columns B, C and D.*

U.S. Politics & Social Issues	U.S. Foreign Policy & Defense	U.S. Economy & Environment	Science, Technology & Nature	Culture, Leisure & Life Style	
	Undersecy. of State Grew resigns and is succeeded by Dean Acheson .... After investigating the Army bomber-Empire State Building crash, the War Dept. finds the pilot guilty of "misjudgment" and blames the accident on "unfavorable flying conditions."	Truman says he will call an industry-labor conference and orders continuation of the NWLB to handle disputes until the conference ends .... Defense Transportation Dir. J. Monroe Johnson removes controls on taxicab mileage, the operation of trucks and starting or extending commercial services.			Aug. 16
	Army Air Force Gen. Henry Arnold reveals the existence of new weapons, some not yet completed, such as a monster bomber surpassing the B-29 and robot jet-propelled atomic bombs guided by television and radar. He warns that "this thing is so terrible in its aspects that there may not be any more wars." .... Sen. David I. Walsh (R, Mass.) asks Navy Secy. Forrestal to submit to the Senate Naval Affairs Comm. the Navy investigation of Pearl Harbor .... Archibald MacLeish and Gen. J.C. Holmes resign as assistant secretaries of state.	WPB cancels virtually all allotments of steel, copper and aluminum and all preference ratings except for the military.		Defense Transportation Dir. Johnson ends curbs on travel to professional and amateur sporting meets.	Aug. 17
	A House Naval Affairs subcommittee urges the U.S. to claim full title to Pacific islands where U.S. bases are now located.	Truman directs the OPA and the Secretary of Agriculture to take necessary steps to keep down prices and the cost of living .... Defense Transportation Dir. Johnson ends the nationwide 35-mile-an-hour speed limit.			Aug. 18
		Comm. for Economic Development estimates on the basis of an 18-month survey among manufacturers in 20 leading industries that 54,448,000 workers will be employed by September 1946.			Aug. 19
		WPB cancels 210 production controls, leaving only 130 in effect, and releases a wide range of consumer goods and necessary materials .... Montgomery Ward files a $1.3-million libel suit against the CIO United Retail, Wholesale and Dept. Store Employes union, charging the union with injuring the company's good name and credit.			Aug. 20
	Truman orders a halt to all further Lend-Lease operations and notifies those Allied governments interested to take over the $2 billion in goods already contracted for in this country.	WPB ends the ban against industrial construction.			Aug. 21
F	G	H	I	J	
Includes elections, federal-state relations, civil rights and liberties, crime, the judiciary, education, health care, poverty, urban affairs and population.	*Includes formation and debate of U.S. foreign and defense policies, veterans affairs and defense spending. (Relations with specific foreign countries are usually found under the region concerned.)*	*Includes business, labor, agriculture, taxation, transportation, consumer affairs, monetary and fiscal policy, natural resources, pollution and accidents.*	*Includes worldwide scientific, medical and technological developments, natural phenomena, U.S. weather and natural disasters.*	*Includes the arts, religion, scholarship, communications media, sports, entertainment, fashions, fads and social life.*	

	World Affairs	European War Zone	Pacific War Zone	The Americas	Other Countries & Territories
Aug. 22	Paris conference on Tangier announces that the Moroccan port will be under a provisional international regime based on the 1923 convention .... Truman meets in Washington with Gen. de Gaulle, who presses for creation of a separate Rhenish state in Germany and American support for French reoccupation of Indochina. Truman remains non-committal on the German question but agrees to continued French possession of Indochina .... UNRRA Council in London approves aid to Italy and Austria.	King Michael of Rumania asks the Big Three to assist in forming a new Rumanian government that they could recognize.	Russian airborne troops occupy Shimushu, northernmost island of the Kuriles, while others occupy Dairen and Port Arthur, two ports on the Yellow Sea.	Truman proposes early congressional action to allow Puerto Rico to settle by free elections its future status .... Argentine Finance Min. Ceferino Alonso Irigoyen resigns.	Iranian general staff reports killing of seven rebellious officers and men who were planning to lead an attack on the Russian-garrisoned city of Meshed.
Aug. 23		American, British and French forces move into their occupation zones in Vienna .... Both houses of the British Parliament ratify the U.N. Charter .... Leo Borchard, conductor of the Berlin Philharmonic Orchestra, is shot to death just before midnight by an American sentry in Berlin when the automobile in which he is riding fails to stop at the order of the guards.	Stalin proclaims complete Russian victory in Manchuria and occupation of the entire territory .... MacArthur orders Japanese airplanes grounded, removal of all explosives from ships and clearance of mine fields .... Tokyo radio claims that Allied bombing wiped out 44 cities with nearly 10 million killed .... Attlee tells the House of Commons that arrangements are complete for a British commander to accept the Japanese surrender in Hong Kong.		
Aug. 24			Russia agrees to respect the sovereignty and territorial integrity of China and to avoid interference in Chinese internal affairs.	Nelson A. Rockefeller charges that the Argentine government has failed to carry out pledges as a signatory to the Act of Chapultepec.	
Aug. 25	Truman and de Gaulle end their talks, expressing fundamental harmony and agreement to establish closer co-operation. They agree that they will, with the British, supervise Greek elections.	Bulgaria announces the indefinite postponement of general elections upon the recommendation of the Allied Control Commission.	Due to typhoons, MacArthur says that the formal Japanese surrender will be delayed until Sept. 2 .... Chiang Kai-shek says he will yield to the British occupation of Hong Kong and hopes that the status of the city can be resolved through legal means.	Jose Ismael Herrera and Luis Ochoa del Cid are sentenced to death in Guatemala for assassinating Guatemalan Congressman Alejandro Cordova on Oct. 2, 1944. Former Pres. Federico Ponce Vaides and Moises Evaristo Orozco, now in Mexico, are charged with complicity and their arrest is ordered.	
Aug. 26			MacArthur informs the Japanese that U.S. fleet units are moving into Sagami Bay, just south of Tokyo .... Chiang's troops win the race with Communist forces to enter Shanghai and Nanking .... Moscow announces Russian troops have completed occupation of the 32-island Kurile chain, stretching from the northern tip of Japan to the Kamchatka peninsula in the sea of Okhotsk.		
Aug. 27		A psychiatric examination of Quisling reveals that he is sane.	American troops will occupy a part of Korea, Manila reports.	Colombia and Costa Rica abolish all forms of censorship.	Premier Fayez el Khoury forms a new Syrian cabinet, using only members of the Liberal Party.
Aug. 28			The first U.S. soldiers to enter Japan arrive at Atsugi airport near Yokohama after successful efforts by Prince Takamatsu, Hirohito's brother, to avert a threatened kamikaze attack on occupation forces .... Japanese envoys sign a preliminary surrender to the British in Rangoon for troops in Southeast Asia .... Escorted by U.S. Amb. Hurley, Mao Tse-tung arrives in Chungking and says he hopes that Chinese unity can be attained.	Braden accuses the Argentine government of brutality and intimidation against its citizens.	

A	B	C	D	E
Includes developments that affect more than one world region, international organizations and important meetings of major world leaders.	*Includes all developments in European countries and military engagements between Allied and Axis powers in Africa and at sea.*	*Includes all developments in Japan and China, Japanese foreign policy and military actions in the Pacific region.*	*Includes all domestic and regional developments in Latin America, the Caribbean and Canada.*	*Includes developments in those independent nations and colonial possessions not covered in Columns B, C and D.*

U.S. Politics & Social Issues	U.S. Foreign Policy & Defense	U.S. Economy & Environment	Science, Technology & Nature	Culture, Leisure & Life Style	
	State Secy. Byrnes reinstates John S. Service, exonerated by a grand jury of removing confidential government documents . . . . Army Air Force says it will discharge between 1.4 and 2.3 million men during the next year.	WPB drops the priority system and sets Sept. 30 for cessation of the "controlled materials plan." . . . . Commissioner Joseph Nunan of the IRS says employers may increase salaries immediately without government approval . . . . ODT Dir. Johnson says wartime curbs on wholesale and retail truck deliveries will be lifted Nov. 1.		FCC allows amateur radio operators to go on the air again.	Aug. 22
	Truman says he is awaiting advice from the war and navy secretaries before deciding on public trial to fix responsibility for the Pearl Harbor disaster.	RFC Chmn. Henderson absolves Roy White of the B O Railroad from responsibility for loans made by the RFC . . . . OPA Chief Bowles suspends price controls on mercury, aluminum and magnesium.			Aug. 23
	Despite British protests, the U.S. announces it will remain firm against continuing Lend-Lease aid . . . . Truman directs his administrative assistant, Samuel I. Rosenman, to study the proposal to merge the War and Navy Depts.	WPB removes all controls on automobile output and lifts restrictions on the use of paper by all branches of the publishing industry except newspapers.		Arturo Toscanini agrees to return to Italy from the U.S. in February 1946 to conduct the opening performance at La Scala Opera House in Milan . . . . Because of needs in the populous northeast, the FCC revises its rules for frequency modulation, increasing from 70 to 80 the channels originally allocated to FM.	Aug. 24
	Nelson A. Rockefeller resigns as assistant secretary of state in charge of American republic affairs, and is succeeded by Spruille Braden.	Truman orders that 24 firms seized by the government to avert work stoppages be returned to their owners "as soon as possible." . . . . Foreign Economic Administration says most export curbs will end about Sept. 1 . . . . ODT says all wartime controls over local bus, trolley, coach and streetcar service will be lifted Aug. 31.			Aug. 25
	War Dept. says that for the present it will draft 50,000 men monthly.				Aug. 26
	Truman tells Congress that because of "elements of danger" in the Pacific, the need for 1.2 million servicemen in disorganized Europe and the feeling that veterans should return home, the Selective Service should continue to draft men 18-25 . . . . Navy speeds up demobilization, planning now to discharge 2.9 million men in the next year and reducing enlisted personnel to about 500,000 . . . . Dean Acheson is sworn in as under secretary of state . . . . Two million New Yorkers cheer de Gaulle along a 62-mile tour of the city as he stresses U.S.-French unity.	OPA says rent controls will remain in effect until June 30, 1946 and probably will be "a little tighter."			Aug. 27
	War Dept. tells a House committee it will reduce its personnel from the present 8.05 million to 2.5 million men by July 1, 1946.				Aug. 28
F	G	H	I	J	
Includes elections, federal-state relations, civil rights and liberties, crime, the judiciary, education, health care, poverty, urban affairs and population.	*Includes formation and debate of U.S. foreign and defense policies, veterans affairs and defense spending. (Relations with specific foreign countries are usually found under the region concerned.)*	*Includes business, labor, agriculture, taxation, transportation, consumer affairs, monetary and fiscal policy, natural resources, pollution and accidents.*	*Includes worldwide scientific, medical and technological developments, natural phenomena, U.S. weather and natural disasters.*	*Includes the arts, religion, scholarship, communications media, sports, entertainment, fashions, fads and social life.*	

	World Affairs	European War Zone	Pacific War Zone	The Americas	Other Countries & Territories
Aug. 29		A total of 24 German leaders are indicted as major war criminals to be tried at Nuremberg, including Goering, Hess, von Ribbentrop, Funk, Schacht and Seyss-Inquart .... U.S. military authorities in Germany announce that American civilians will assume the duties and responsibilities now held by military and government personnel in the U.S. zone of occupation .... Hungary postpones general elections until the last Sunday of next October.	MacArthur leaves Manila by plane for Okinawa, en route to Japan .... Soviet fleet units enter Port Arthur.	Pan American Union announces the formation of an Inter-American Economic and Social Council .... Guatemala ends all forms of wartime censorship.	
Aug. 30	Gen. de Gaulle and his party return to Paris, and the French officials disclose that while in Washington the mission asked the U.S. for more than $1,000,000,000 in loans.	U.S. resumes diplomatic relations with Finland.	American and British Marines and sailors go ashore at Yokosuka naval base on Honshu, while airborne troops land at Atsugi airfield, preparing for the arrival of MacArthur.		Syria ratifies the U.N. Charter .... Egyptian government announces an end of personal and business letter censorship and says that all censorship will end Sept. 30.
Aug. 31	UNRRA Deputy Dir. Hendrickson says that relief supplies are going to the liberated European countries at the rate of 300,000-400,000 tons monthly.	Public prosecutor in Oslo asks for the death penalty for Quisling on three counts.	MacArthur establishes his headquarters in the New Grand Hotel in Yokohama, Japan .... Nai Thawi Bunyakat forms a new Thai cabinet with himself as premier and foreign minister.	Argentine Supreme Court voids the government's conviction of Gen. Adolfo Espindola and all other retired officers on conspiracy charges passed last June.	

A	B	C	D	E
Includes developments that affect more than one world region, international organizations and important meetings of major world leaders.	*Includes all developments in European countries and military engagements between Allied and Axis powers in Africa and at sea.*	*Includes all developments in Japan and China, Japanese foreign policy and military actions in the Pacific region.*	*Includes all domestic and regional developments in Latin America, the Caribbean and Canada.*	*Includes developments in those independent nations and colonial possessions not covered in Columns B, C and D.*

	U.S. Politics & Social Issues	U.S. Foreign Policy & Defense	U.S. Economy & Environment	Science, Technology & Nature	Culture, Leisure & Life Style
Aug. 29		Truman releases the Army and Navy reports on Pearl Harbor, which place responsibility upon Gen. Walter E. Short and Adm. Husband E. Kimmel for unpreparedness and cites the failure of the State Dept. to keep the commanders adequately informed on the status of Japanese negotiations.	WMC reports that since the surrender of Japan two million war workers have been dismissed from their jobs .... WPB lifts restrictions on the sale of domestic wool.		
Aug. 30		Truman warns any effort to collect the $42 billion in Lend-Lease supplies to the Allies will sow the seeds for "a new world conflagration." .... Truman says the nation as much as any individual can be blamed for Pearl Harbor, because FDR's repeated efforts to increase preparedness were villified.	Truman abolishes the 48-hour minimum work week in war plants and orders time-and-a-half for overtime .... Brooklyn Federal Court Judge Matthew Abruzzo holds that a veteran of WW II is entitled to the job he held prior to entering the service even if it means dismissal of a worker with more seniority.		Barbara Hutton wins her divorce in Los Angeles from actor Cary Grant .... The NFL champion Green Bay Packers win the annual game against the College All-Stars in Chicago, 19-7.
Aug. 31		OWI is abolished by Truman and its foreign information functions and those of the Office of Inter-American Affairs are transferred to a temporary International Information Service under the State Dept.	John Green, president of the CIO Industrial Union of Marine and Shipbuilding Workers of America, announces that the union will appeal a Brooklyn federal court ruling that veterans have top priority in postwar job assignments. Green contends that job seniority should determine order of assignment .... Treasury Secy. Vinson says the Murray "full employment" bill is essential to postwar prosperity .... Stabilization Dir. Davis approves the return of 10 plants seized by the Army or Navy to their private owners.		

F	G	H	I	J
Includes elections, federal-state relations, civil rights and liberties, crime, the judiciary, education, health care, poverty, urban affairs and population.	*Includes formation and debate of U.S. foreign and defense policies, veterans affairs and defense spending. (Relations with specific foreign countries are usually found under the region concerned.)*	*Includes business, labor, agriculture, taxation, transportation, consumer affairs, monetary and fiscal policy, natural resources, pollution and accidents.*	*Includes worldwide scientific, medical and technological developments, natural phenomena, U.S. weather and natural disasters.*	*Includes the arts, religion, scholarship, communications media, sports, entertainment, fashions, fads and social life.*

	World Affairs	Europe	Africa & the Middle East	The Americas	Asia & the Pacific
Sept. 1	Stettinius says the U.S. will give the problem of the atomic bomb to the U.N. Security Council . . . . OWI publishes a report predicting a world-wide coal shortage.				The main forces of the U.S. 8th Army begin landing at Yokohama . . . . British troops land in the naval yard at Hong Kong and raise the British flag.
Sept. 2					Japanese Foreign Min. Mamoru Shigemitsu and Gen. Yoshiro Umezu sign the unconditional surrender document on the battleship *Missouri* in Tokyo Bay. The 20-minute ceremony, presided over by Gen. MacArthur, officially ends World War II . . . . Stalin states in a radio broadcast that the Soviet Union intends to retain the southern half of Sakhalin Island and the Kurile Islands . . . . Vietnamese nationalist leader Ho Chi-minh proclaims the Democratic Republic of Vietnam in Hanoi.
Sept. 3				Brazilian Pres. Vargas lets the deadline pass without filing his intention to run for reelection.	Allied occupation troops begin taking control of military facilities in Japan. U.S. military authorities report 25,000 Allied troops are on the main island of Honshu, centering on Yokohama . . . . Units of the British East Indies Fleet enter Singapore harbor preparatory to occupying the city . . . . In a victory message to the Chinese people, Chiang Kai-shek promises a democratic form of government for China and warns against taking vengeance on innocent Japanese civilians.
Sept. 4	A new Tangier agreement is announced providing for a control commission comprised of Russia, Spain, the U.S., France and Britain, but most of the administrative burdens will fall to the Netherlands, Belgium, Portugal and Sweden.	Polish government denounces its concordat with the Holy See, charging that the Church turned over administration of Polish dioceses to German bishops in 1940.		Argentina recalls its ambassador to the U.S., Dr. Oscar Ibarra Garcia, to take over duties in the foreign ministry.	Allied occupation zone in Japan spreads to over 720 square miles, as the U.S. 8th Army crosses the Tama River outside Tokyo . . . . MacArthur issues directions for the complete occupation of Japan, indicating that Tokyo will be occupied Sept. 8. He orders all Japanese POW camps turned over to the highest-ranking Allied officer among the prisoners . . . . Emperor Hirohito opens the first postwar session of the Japanese Diet in Tokyo with a speech urging "reconstruction in every field" and a rehabilitation policy designed to "win the confidence of the world, establish . . . . a peaceful state and contribute to the progress of mankind."
Sept. 5					British Imperial Forces go ashore at Singapore to reclaim the city and naval base . . . . Japanese Premier Prince Naruhiko Higashi-Kuni tells the Diet that Japan was losing the war before the atom bomb was dropped and Russia began hostilities.
Sept. 6		Berlin newspapers report that Russian authorities in Saxony have broken up large German estates and sold them to poor farmers . . . . British Control Commission arrests 40 German industrialists in the Ruhr in a move to de-Nazify industry . . . . U.S. military authorities break up a German underground resistance ring which had plotted to blow up Allied installations in Thuringia. A ringleader and 40 would-be saboteurs are arrested.	Ethiopian government grants the Sinclair Oil Co. of the U.S. a 50-year concession for the development of oil resources in the country.	State Dept. removes all passport and visa restrictions for tourist travel to Bermuda.	In a ceremony on a British aircraft carrier, Japanese Southwest Pacific commander Gen. Hitoshi Inamura surrenders 85,000 men on New Guinea, the Solomons and lesser islands bypassed by the Allied island-hopping campaign.
Sept. 7		Britain and the Netherlands sign an agreement fixing the exchange rate at 10.691 guilders to the pound sterling for the next three years.		Argentine Foreign Min. Juan Cooke reports satisfactory conversations with U.S. Assistant State Secy. Spruille Braden, and pledges he will use his influence to carry out the Act of Chapultepec . . . . Cuba announces that U.S. citizens no longer need passports to visit the country.	
Sept. 8			Ethiopian Foreign Office reaches an agreement with the French on border issues concerning French Somaliland and the jointly owned railroad from Djibouti to Addis Ababa.	Argentine government ratifies the U.N. Charter.	American troops enter Tokyo and raise the U.S. flag on the American embassy . . . . After a three-day voyage from Okinawa, U.S. forces go ashore at Jinsen, Korea . . . . Some 23,000 Japanese troops surrender to the Australians at Bougainville, Solomon Islands.
	A *Includes developments that affect more than one world region, international organizations and important meetings of major world leaders.*	B *Includes all domestic and regional developments in Europe, including the Soviet Union, Turkey, Cyprus and Malta.*	C *Includes all domestic and regional developments in Africa and the Middle East, including Iraq and Iran and excluding Cyprus, Turkey and Afghanistan.*	D *Includes all domestic and regional developments in Latin America, the Caribbean and Canada.*	E *Includes all domestic and regional developments in Asian and Pacific nations, extending from Afghanistan through all the Pacific Islands, except Hawaii.*

U.S. Politics & Social Issues	U.S. Foreign Policy & Defense	U.S. Economy & Environment	Science, Technology & Nature	Culture, Leisure & Life Style	
	Truman declares tomorrow will be VJ Day	Truman hails Labor Day as one of peace and assures the nation that the government is committed to every worker earning a wage sufficient to sustain a decent standard of living.			Sept. 1
	War Dept. cuts the discharge points for enlisted men to 80 points and to 41 for WAC's.	N.Y. Mayor Fiorello La Guardia urges the CIO and AFL to merge into one organization along "vertical" lines.		Sarah Palfrey Cooke beats Pauline Betz to win the women's national tennis title at Forest Hills, N.Y.	Sept. 2
		In a Labor Day address, Labor Secy. Schwellenbach appeals to workers for restraint in wage demands, threatening government intervention if unions do not observe their "responsibilities to the common good." . . . . Comm. for Economic Development reports industry is reconverting much more quickly than anticipated and unemployment is smaller than expected . . . . AFL Pres. William Green denounces "prophets of gloom" and predicts that "we stand on the threshold of a new industrial revolution."	California Institute of Technology announces that work will resume in November on a 200-inch telescope to be installed in a Mt. Palomar observatory. The project, scheduled for completion in 1947, was postponed during the war.	Frank Parker defeats Bill Talbert to win the men's national amateur tennis title at Forest Hills, N.Y.	Sept. 3
	War Dept. announces further liberalization of service rules that will keep 665,000 from going overseas.	Stabilization Dir. Davis says he favors permitting substantial wage increases without affecting price levels, which must be maintained if the nation is to pay its $275-billion public debt.			Sept. 4
Congress reconvenes for its first peacetime session in almost four years.	Resolutions are introduced calling for a joint House-Senate investigation of the Pearl Harbor attack . . . . Navy recommends that the U.S. keep 15 major bases in the Atlantic and Pacific to support its expanded fleet and keep aggressors from U.S. shores . . . . State Dept. reveals that during the war it made 240 protests to Japan through the Swiss government concerning POWs and civilian internees, but to no avail.	Truman recommends a 37% cut of $3.5 billion in congressional appropriations for 1946 to 28 war agencies . . . . Office of Defense Transportation says most passenger rail travel curbs will end by Sept. 16 and promises increased train service.		Titan Hanover, driven by Harry Pownall, completes a Detroit horse-trotting exhibition in a new world record for three-year olds of 1:58 minutes.	Sept. 5
Atty. Gen. Tom C. Clark says the President's wartime powers do not end with the battlefield victories and that he has the authority to redistribute functions among government agencies . . . . Clark orders former German-American Bund leader Fritz Kuhn deported to Germany.	War Dept. puts out a new point system for commissioned officers which will make 200,000 eligible for immediate discharge and another 600,000 eligible by July 1946 . . . . Latest Army and Navy figures place overall U.S. casualties at 1,070,452 . . . . The Army successfully test flies its 77-ton Douglas C-74 "Globemaster," the world's largest plane, with a speed of over 300 mph and a maximum range of 7,800 miles.	Truman sends a 21-point reconversion plan to Congress, which includes $25 weekly unemployment compensation, an increase in minimum wages and a call for full employment legislation.	Bills are introduced into the Senate calling for government control of atomic power.	James Caley and Edward Versteeg, two Ringling Brothers Barnum and Bailey workers serving prison terms for a July 1944 circus tent fire in Hartford, Conn., are released.	Sept. 6
		RFC ends its lease of government-owned Alcoa plants in a move to "create competition in the aluminum industry."		National Hockey League ends many wartime restrictions on players in the armed services or in essential war work.	Sept. 7
	Navy Secy. Forrestal tells Sen. David Walsh (D, Mass.) that publication of certain Pearl Harbor facts would "compromise sources of information . . . . of great value to our national security."		MIT reveals a new radar net which can detect vessels 25 miles out to sea at an accuracy of five yards in any direction . . . . Interior Secy. Harold Ickes directs that the Alamogordo Bombing Range be reserved for a new national monument.		Sept. 8

F	G	H	I	J
Includes elections, federal-state relations, civil rights and liberties, crime, the judiciary, education, health care, poverty, urban affairs and population.	*Includes formation and debate of U.S. foreign and defense policies, veterans affairs and defense spending. (Relations with specific foreign countries are usually found under the region concerned.)*	*Includes business, labor, agriculture, taxation, transportation, consumer affairs, monetary and fiscal policy, natural resources, pollution and accidents.*	*Includes worldwide scientific, medical and technological developments, natural phenomena, U.S. weather and natural disasters.*	*Includes the arts, religion, scholarship, communications media, sports, entertainment, fashions, fads and social life.*

	World Affairs	Europe	Africa & the Middle East	The Americas	Asia & the Pacific
Sept. 9					MacArthur states that the Japanese economy will be controlled to achieve U.N. objectives and that civilians will be expected to obey all laws but will be free from unwarranted interference in their individual liberty and property rights . . . . Lt. Gen. John R. Hodge, commander of the U.S. occupation forces in South Korea, says the area will be administered by the Americans through Japanese officials already in office . . . . Gen. Yasuji Okamura signs the formal surrender of about one million Japanese troops in China at Nanking ceremonies.
Sept. 10		A tribunal of the Norwegian Superior Court finds Vidkun Quisling guilty of high treason and sentences him to death . . . . Chairman of Britain's Labor Party Prof. Harold Laski says "the age of capitalism is drawing to a close, and it rests upon us now to inaugurate with this government the age of democratic socialism in Britain."		Bolivia and the U.S. Foreign Economic Administration reach an agreement for U.S. purchase of tin through 1946.	MacArthur orders Hirohito to abolish the Japanese Imperial General Headquarters and establishes censorship over the Japanese radio and press.
Sept. 11	Council of Foreign Ministers of Britain, Russia, France, China and the U.S. convenes in London, beginning work on the peace treaty with Italy. British Foreign Secy. Ernest Bevin presides.	*Osservatore Romano* warns Italian Catholics who become Communists that they will be guilt of deserting the Catholic faith.			After former Japanese Premier Hideki Tojo fails in a suicide attempt, he and 39 other high officials are ordered arrested by MacArthur . . . . Chinese Nationalist troops occupy Hanoi, French Indochina, and are reported in full force in Hankow, China.
Sept. 12		Russia and Rumania reach an economic agreement including the return of several ships to Rumania, Rumanian control of railroads and reduction in indebtedness to Russia . . . . Truman names Francis J. Biddle the U.S. judge on the International Tribunal to try Axis war criminals . . . . Russians establish a civilian government for their occupation zone in Germany, with 11 departments functioning under Soviet "advisers." Departments have few initial tasks, but are intended to secure Russian influence in the future government of a reunited Germany.		Mexican government nationalizes all deposits of uranium, actinium and other radioactive minerals that can be used in atomic bombs . . . . Export-Import bank approves a $20-million loan to Chile for construction of a steel mill.	MacArthur orders the arrest of seven leaders of the Black Dragon Society, including Koki Hirota, Kingoro Hashimoto and Taketora Ogata . . . . Former Japanese War Min. Gen. Sugiyama and his wife commit suicide, although he was not on the list of 40 Japanese officials to be tried as war criminals . . . . Chinese government takes control of Shanghai, and Nationalist troops complete the occupation of Canton . . . . Allied SEA Chief Mountbatten accepts the formal Japanese surrender of its southern armies from Lt. Gen. Seishiro Itagaki at Singapore . . . . Truman says occupation policy in Korea is entirely up to the theater commander and promises the Japanese will be removed from there as soon as possible.
Sept. 13		Lord Keynes presents the British case to the U.S. for financial aid, which is deemed essential for Britons to maintain a decent standard of living in the immediate postwar period.		Four persons are killed and at least 25 injured by an earthquake in central Chile.	Japanese government dissolves the Imperial General Staff . . . . Last Japanese troops in Burma formally surrender to the British in Rangoon.
Sept. 14				Braden says that the "Nazi element" in the Argentine government seeks to undermine friendly relations with the U.S.	Red Chinese Army troops claim sweeping territorial gains during the last week from the Yangtze River Valley to areas north and west of Peking . . . . Japanese Premier Higashi-Kuni asks that the U.S. "forget Pearl Harbor" as the Japanese will forget the devastation of their homeland by U.S. bombers.
Sept. 15	U.S. submits to the Council of Foreign Ministers a plan to strip Italy of its colonies.	Spain and France sign a new trade agreement, with France receiving Spanish credits.			Dissatisfied with the way his Sept. 10 directive is being enforced, MacArthur places 100% censorship on Japanese press and radio . . . . In response to American pressure for sterner action against guerrilla groups, the Philippine government announces postponement of the election scheduled for early 1946.
Sept. 16					MacArthur orders Japanese Premier Higashi-Kuni to impound and report to him within 15 days all property, assets and records controlled wholly or in part by the Japanese government and Axis nationals in Japan . . . . British Rear Adm. Cecil H.J. Harcourt formally accepts from Japan the surrender of Hong Kong.

A	B	C	D	E
Includes developments that affect more than one world region, international organizations and important meetings of major world leaders.	*Includes all domestic and regional developments in Europe, including the Soviet Union, Turkey, Cyprus and Malta.*	*Includes all domestic and regional developments in Africa and the Middle East, including Iraq and Iran and excluding Cyprus, Turkey and Afghanistan.*	*Includes all domestic and regional developments in Latin America, the Caribbean and Canada.*	*Includes all domestic and regional developments in Asian and Pacific nations, extending from Afghanistan through all the Pacific Islands, except Hawaii.*

U.S. Politics & Social Issues	U.S. Foreign Policy & Defense	U.S. Economy & Environment	Science, Technology & Nature	Culture, Leisure & Life Style	
	Sixty-four University of Chicago scientists petition Truman to share knowledge of the atomic bomb with other nations, claiming that this will bring "a new basis of confidence and real security" for the U.S. . . . . Navy liberalizes its point system, making 430,000 servicemen and women eligible for discharge Sept. 15.	Comm. for Economic Development reports a survey indicating that total employment after reconversion should be 24% higher than 1940 but 12½% lower than at the wartime peak.		Sam Snead defeats Harold McSpaden to win the Dallas Open Golf Tournament.	Sept. 9
	Truman presents Gen. Jonathan Wainwright with the Congressional Medal of Honor for "intrepid and determined leadership" of U.S. troops in the Philippines and later in POW camps.	Chmn. Sewell L. Avery of Montgomery Ward protests to War Secy. Stimson that the Army's continued occupation of company property is illegal.			Sept. 10
	House votes to adopt a Senate resolution setting up a joint 10-man committee to investigate the Pearl Harbor disaster.	Senate Finance Comm. opposes a federal guarantee of $25 maximum weekly unemployment compensation . . . . Foreign Economic Administration lifts about 80% of its controls over exports, leaving less than 1,000 items in need of special permit.			Sept. 11
	Undersecy. of War Robert Patterson says that the Army is demobilizing men at the rate of 10,000 men a day.	SEC reports that the combined assets of 199 leading gas and electric companies were $12.8 billion in 1944, or 80% of the total assets of all registered holding companies.		The original Japanese surrender documents are put on public exhibition in the National Archives Building in Washington . . . . Arthur M. Schlesinger Jr's. *The Age of Jackson* is published by Little, Brown & Co. . . . . House of Representatives passes a resolution to return the country to standard time effective Sept. 30.	Sept. 12
	Truman withdraws from private sale all public lands in the U.S. "which contain deposits of radioactive mineral substances," reserving their use for the government.	RFC announces a new seven-point program to aid banks and industry in reconversion . . . . Senate Finance Comm. approves a rewritten unemployment compensation bill, which rejects the $25 weekly maximum payment for 26 weeks.		Anton von Webern, 62, seminal composer of the second Viennese school and pupil of Arnold Schoenberg, is accidentally shot and killed by a soldier of the U.S. occupation forces.	Sept. 13
	Congress names a 10-man committee of lawyers to investigate the Pearl Harbor attack . . . . Army announces plans to release 13,000 doctors, 3,500 dentists, 25,000 nurses and other medical personnel by Jan. 1.	Ford Motor Co. shuts down all of its automobile plants, laying off 50,000 workers, due to "crippling and unauthorized strikes" against companies supplying it with parts. The lockout is directed against the UAW and other unions demanding a 30% wage raise in the auto industry.			Sept. 14
		CIO-UAW sets aside a $4-million strike fund and decides to go all out to obtain a 30% wage increase and full employment in the auto industry.	A tropical hurricane with peak winds of 143 mph sweeps inland from Miami, causing an estimated $50 million damage.		Sept. 15
	U.S. Navy announces plans to tow the Japanese battleship *Nagoto* 500 miles to sea and test the effect of an atomic bomb on it.	To support their demand for a 25% pay increase, the CIO Steel Workers claim that the industry's war profits after taxes rose 113% in the 1940-1944 period . . . . Officials of the CIO United Retail, Wholesale & Dept. Store Employes Union threaten Montgomery Ward & Co. in Chicago with a strike unless it agrees to bargain with the union after the return of the company's property by the Army.		FCC Chmn. Paul Porter officially opens a new nationwide radio network, the Associated Broadcasting Co., with 19 affiliated stations . . . . John McCormack, world famous Irish tenor, dies at 61 in Dublin, Ireland . . . . *New York Herald Tribune* reports the best selling fiction and non-fiction books, respectively, as James Hilton's *So Well Remembered* and Bill Mauldin's *Up Front*.	Sept. 16

F	G	H	I	J
Includes elections, federal-state relations, civil rights and liberties, crime, the judiciary, education, health care, poverty, urban affairs and population.	*Includes formation and debate of U.S. foreign and defense policies, veterans affairs and defense spending. (Relations with specific foreign countries are usually found under the region concerned.)*	*Includes business, labor, agriculture, taxation, transportation, consumer affairs, monetary and fiscal policy, natural resources, pollution and accidents.*	*Includes worldwide scientific, medical and technological developments, natural phenomena, U.S. weather and natural disasters.*	*Includes the arts, religion, scholarship, communications media, sports, entertainment, fashions, fads and social life.*

	World Affairs	Europe	Africa & the Middle East	The Americas	Asia & the Pacific
Sept. 17	Council of Foreign Ministers in London announces its inability to draft a peace treaty for Italy in the current session, due to continued disagreement among the Allies over the fate of former Italian colonies.	British begin the trial of concentration camp director Josef Kramer and 44 of his SS staff for conspiring to commit mass murder at Auschwitz.		In return for a $20 million Import-Export Bank loan, Ecuador grants the U.S. one of the Galapagos islands for defense of the Panama Canal.	MacArthur says the "smooth progress" of the occupation of Japan will allow a "drastic cut" in the number of troops originally estimated as needed for the occupation . . . . Gen. Wainwright urges a 20-year occupation of Japan . . . . Vietnamese Nationalists loyal to Ho Chi-minh declare a general strike in Saigon to protest the allegedly pro-French policies of the Allied Southeast Asia Command . . . . Philippine Pres. Sergio Osmena promises there will be quick prosecution of Filipinos guilty of collaboration with Japan.
Sept. 18	Soviet Foreign Commissar Molotov tells the Council of Foreign Ministers that Russia believes in individual rather than collective trusteeship for Italian colonies and that the Russians would like Tripolitania in North Africa.	Yugoslavia formally presents its demands on Italy, asking sovereignty over the disputed province of Venezia Giulia, which includes the city of Tureste.			Premier Higashi-Kuni says the Japanese War and Navy ministries will be abolished and the democratic process broadened, with the influence of the House of Peers being curtailed . . . . Truman says the Allies have agreed "that Korea shall become free and independent."
Sept. 19	After Molotov claims that Trieste should go to Yugoslavia, the Council of Foreign Ministers appoints a committee of experts to study the whole Yugoslav-Italian boundary question.	Marshal Zhukov, Russian administrator in Germany, announces that Poland's new western frontier will include several hundred additional square miles of territory west of Stettin on the lower Oder River . . . . Franco says that a change in Spain's present regime "will take place how and when I choose." . . . . A London court sentences William Joyce (Lord Haw Haw) to die for treason.			British P.M. Attlee says elections of legislators in India this winter will be followed by the establishment of a constituent assembly to frame a new constitution . . . . MacArthur announces formation of an economic and scientific section of his headquarters to investigate every aspect of Japanese business and science and make recommendations . . . . U.S. occupation forces in Korea revoke Japanese laws preventing freedom of religious worship, speech and press and freedom from persecution for political activity.
Sept. 20	Council of Foreign Ministers begins a review of proposals for peace treaties with Rumania and Finland.	Allied Control Commission lifts, effective Oct. 1, ban on fraternization between troops and Germans except for reservations on billeting and intermarriage . . . . British officials present the U.S. with statistics on depletion of British resources during the six years of war in support of their request for financial aid.		Chilean cabinet resigns to permit Pres. Juan Antonio Rios to choose a government to function while he is abroad.	Allied command in southern Indochina declares virtual martial law to prevent clashes between Annamites and the French . . . . Tokyo reports that about 75% of the Japanese Army has been demobilized in half the alloted time.
Sept. 21					Working Committee of the All-India Congress adopts a resolution demanding independence for India, Burma, Malaya, Indochina and the Indonesian Islands . . . . MacArthur orders the arrest of Lt. Gen. Kenji Doihara, who is known as the "Lawrence of Manchuria" for his reputed undercover work preparatory to Japanese conquest.
Sept. 22	U.S. delegation to the Council of Foreign Ministers requests that no reparation demands be made on Italy and that the so-called Wilson Line be the basis for establishing an Italian-Yugoslav frontier.				White House reveals the directives under which MacArthur is working, which call for complete elimination of Japan as a military threat to the world . . . . All-India Congress Party rejects demands for a revolutionary program to win Indian independence from Britain and expresses its willingness to negotiate . . . . Philippine Pres. Sergio Osmena signs the ratification of the U.N. Charter.
Sept. 23			London announces the British government has decided to refer the problem of Palestine and Jewish immigration to the U.N. . . . . Egyptian cabinet calls for withdrawal of British troops from Egypt and for incorporation of Anglo-Egyptian Sudan into Egypt.	Former Amb. to Argentina Spruille Braden leaves Buenos Aires for Washington to assume duties as assistant secretary of state for American republic affairs.	Japanese government turns over urns containing the ashes of 2,600 Allied war prisoners who died in camps.
	A *Includes developments that affect more than one world region, international organizations and important meetings of major world leaders.*	B *Includes all domestic and regional developments in Europe, including the Soviet Union, Turkey, Cyprus and Malta.*	C *Includes all domestic and regional developments in Africa and the Middle East, including Iraq and Iran and excluding Cyprus, Turkey and Afghanistan.*	D *Includes all domestic and regional developments in Latin America, the Caribbean and Canada.*	E *Includes all domestic and regional developments in Asian and Pacific nations, extending from Afghanistan through all the Pacific Islands, except Hawaii.*

U.S. Politics & Social Issues	U.S. Foreign Policy & Defense	U.S. Economy & Environment	Science, Technology & Nature	Culture, Leisure & Life Style	
	Truman says the U.S. is now in a position to supply Europe with subsistence levels of several basic foodstuffs.	Atty. Gen. Clark recommends that Alcoa be split into several competing companies to facilitate and aid competition in the aluminum industry .... West coast labor leader Harry Bridges becomes an American citizen in San Francisco.		Massachusetts Supreme Court upholds the conviction of bookseller Abraham Einsenstadt on charges of possessing with intent to sell an obscene book, Lillian Smith's *Strange Fruit.*	Sept. 17
Truman nominates Sen. Harold Burton (R, O.) as Supreme Court justice to succeed Owen Roberts.	Henry L. Stimson resigns as Secretary of War, and Truman names Robert C. Patterson to succeed him.	Truman orders reorganization of government labor functions, including the merger of the NWLB and WMC into the Labor Dept.			Sept. 18
	Navy Secy. Forrestal advocates a postwar Navy unmatched by any possible combination of other naval countries .... Truman assures the country that the troops are coming home from service duty as fast as possible.	Senate rejects efforts to restore the $25 weekly maximum unemployment benefit .... A House committee reports out a bill authorizing Truman to reorganize the executive agencies of the government, excluding the ICC, the FTC and the SEC .... Transcontinental & Western Air, Inc., Pan American Airways, Eastern Airlines and American Export Airlines announce they have purchased large fleets of Lockheed Constellation planes, which will carry 43 to 51 passengers at 340 mph and provide 11-hour service between N.Y. and London.		Eric A. Johnston becomes president of the Motion Picture Producers & Distributors of America, Inc.	Sept. 19
House passes and sends to the Senate a bill guaranteeing the states sovereign title to tidelands.	Truman ends the OSS effective Oct. 1 and orders a permanent foreign intelligence division to be created under the State Dept. .... Army cuts its service points for discharge to 60. Within a month it says it expects to discharge men who have no useful job in service .... Writing in *Life*, John Chamberlain says the U.S. had broken the Japanese "ultra" code and that 15 hours before Pearl Harbor FDR knew the Japanese were going to sever diplomatic relations .... Former French liner *Normandie*, which the Navy took over and renamed the *USS Lafayette*, is declared surplus by the Navy and turned over to the Maritime Commission for disposal.	Senate passes a compromise unemployment compensation bill and sends it to the House; it establishes payments up to 26 weeks at state-established rates of $15-$25 weekly .... Strike of 20,000 oil workers threatens shutdown of refineries, storage plants and pipelines in Texas, Indiana and Michigan .... NWLB Chmn. Dr. George W. Taylor announces his resignation effective no later than Oct. 15 .... OPA raises the price of foreign silver imported into the U.S. from 45¢ to 71.111¢ per fine ounce.	Washington reveals that during the war Germany developed a synthetic blood plasma substitute called periston.		Sept. 20
	A purported suggestion by Commerce Secy. Wallace that the atomic bomb secret be given to Russia is said to have been discussed by the cabinet.	Social Security Bd. reports that claims for unemployment insurance reached 1,479,606 in the week ending Sept. 15.			Sept. 21
	Sen. Kenneth Wherry (R, Neb.) submits 10 questions on MacArthur's policy in Japan to Undersecy. of State Dean Acheson and demands they be answered publicly by Sept. 24.	About 34,000 coal miners strike for higher wages in the Pittsburgh area, closing nine mines .... CIO-UAW petitions the NWLB for a strike vote at 96 GM plants, affecting about 350,000 workers .... Washington announces the War Production Board will be dissolved Oct. 31 and its functions turned over to the Office of War Mobilization and Reconversion .... Sen. Walter George (D, Ga.) proposes a 50% cut in federal taxes on personal incomes.			Sept. 22
House Committee on Un-American Activities says it will investigate the recent reorganization of the CP to determine whether its aims now are "dangerous to the country."	Truman says he will take full responsibility for future development of the atomic bomb and atomic energy.	Bureau of Selective Service rules that returning veterans are entitled to first priority in reemployment at their old jobs, regardless of union protests.			Sept. 23
F	G	H	I	J	
Includes elections, federal-state relations, civil rights and liberties, crime, the judiciary, education, health care, poverty, urban affairs and population.	*Includes formation and debate of U.S. foreign and defense policies, veterans affairs and defense spending. (Relations with specific foreign countries are usually found under the region concerned.)*	*Includes business, labor, agriculture, taxation, transportation, consumer affairs, monetary and fiscal policy, natural resources, pollution and accidents.*	*Includes worldwide scientific, medical and technological developments, natural phenomena, U.S. weather and natural disasters.*	*Includes the arts, religion, scholarship, communications media, sports, entertainment, fashions, fads and social life.*	

	World Affairs	Europe	Africa & the Middle East	The Americas	Asia & the Pacific
Sept. 24	Molotov asks Council of Foreign Ministers for an Allied control commission in Japan as he critcizes U.S. actions there, citing alleged irregularities in demobilization of Japanese soldiers .... Interior Secy. Harold Ickes and British Fuel Min. Emanuel Shinwell sign a new Anglo-American oil pact, forming the basis of a multilateral agreement which other nations may sign.	Acting head of the Russian embassy in Washington says Franco has put himself on the same level with Hitler and Mussolini and should be tried as a war criminal.			MacArthur orders the Japanese government to establish controls over prices and wages; he also prohibits import or export of foreign exchange by Japanese without Allied approval.
Sept. 25		Allied authorities in Berlin issue a 48-point proclamation that formally ends the war-making power of the Reich and emphasizes the totality of Germany's defeat .... Eisenhower issues a new order making any German corporation employing members of the Nazi party or its affiliates in any capacity liable to closure by the military government .... Hungarian government expresses willingness to meet American conditions for diplomatic recognition, including a democratic political structure and free elections.		Argentine government reports thwarting of an attempted coup led by Gen. Arturo Rawson and Gen. Osvaldo Martin.	In his first interview with a foreign correspondent since the beginning of the war, Emperor Hirohito tells Frank Kluckhohn of the *New York Times* that he favors constitutional reform along British lines in Japan. He also claims that former Premier Tojo misused his powers in attacking Pearl Harbor without a formal declaration of war .... Saigon reports that British troops today fired on Annamite demonstrators seeking immediate independence from French rule in Indochina.
Sept. 26	France gains agreement by the Council of Foreign Ministers on quick consideration of the Rhineland and Ruhr problems. Byrnes, Eden and Molotov hold a private session on the Balkans, but reach no accord.	Eisenhower reprimands Gen. Patton for the latter's remarks of Sept. 22, suggesting that the Allies should strive for popularity among Germans and downplay denazification .... Representatives of Austria's provinces give approval to the Renner government as the provisional regime for all Austria, after removing control of elections and police from Communist Interior Min. Franz Khonner .... Soviet Presidium orders the demobilization of soldiers and officers between 32 and 42 .... Paris reports the French government has exonerated singing star Maurice Chevalier of suspicion of wartime collaboration with the Germans.	Arab League Secy. Gen. Abdul Rahman Azzam Bey arrives in London for conferences on the Palestine question.	Argentine government reimposes a state of siege, lifted last month after the failure of a coup attempt.	Emperor Hirohito visits Gen. MacArthur for a two-hour conversation at the U.S. embassy in Tokyo. Hirohito compliments MacArthur on the smoothness of the U.S. occupation, and MacArthur invites Hirohito's future "suggestions" on the reconstruction of Japan .... Hindu and Moslem rioting in Bombay results in 17 deaths and 75 injured .... Annamite revolt grows in Saigon, with reports of widespread street fighting. Lt. Col. A. Peter Dewey, senior American officer of the Office of Strategic Services in Saigon, is killed by Annamite rebels .... Shanghai reports that U.S. Army officials have discovered records that reveal three of the U.S. fliers who participated in the Doolittle raid on Tokyo in 1942 were given perfunctory trials and shot.
Sept. 27		U.N. War Crimes Commission sends a new, secret list of German war criminals to the Allied governments for immediate arrest .... U.S., Russia, Britain, France, Yugoslavia, Norway, the Netherlands, Belgium, Luxembourg, Greece and Czechoslovakia sign a two-year pact for joint control and allocation of civil transport on the European continent .... White House announces that German art objects will be removed to the U.S. for safekeeping, pending return to their rightful owners.			Nehru announces a plan for a free India that would include state ownership of key industries and a reorganization of the land system .... Domei announces its impending dissolution as the executive heads of Japan's three leading newspapers reveal they are sponsoring formation of an independent news agency to furnish world news to the Japanese.
Sept. 28		Sir Geoffrey Lawrence is named the British member of the international court to try European war criminals.		Spruille Braden arrives by plane in Washington from his post as U.S. envoy to Argentina and expresses confidence in the "genuinely democratic" Argentine people .... Bolivia breaks off diplomatic relations with Spain.	Lord Mountbatten sends British troops to Java, where Indonesian groups armed and trained by the Japanese have revolted against Dutch colonial rule .... Supreme Allied Command denies Japan the use of its merchant fleet to repatriate Japanese soldiers from other Pacific areas.
Sept. 29		Eisenhower recommends that the U.S., Britain, Russia and France take action to bring the German economy to solvency at the subsistence level .... Truman asks Eisenhower to investigate reports that Jews in western Germany and Austria are being kept by Allied authorities in unsanitary camps with inadequate food and medical treatment.			British accept a U.S. proposal for establishing a Far Eastern Commission to formulate a policy for carrying out the Japanese surrender terms .... Moscow announces the beginning of partial Russian troop withdrawal from Manchuria .... Truman names Edwin Locke to go to China as his personal representative to aid in industrialization of China .... British troops land on Java to begin the Allied reoccupation of the Dutch East Indies.
Sept. 30		Eisenhower claims that reports of Allied mistreatment of Jews in Germany are outdated and that displaced persons are now well treated.			American troops occupy 21 of Japan's largest banks, which had been used in the Japanese effort to secure economic control over Asia .... Chungking says the Nationalists and Communists have agreed to submit their outstanding differences to a political council whose decision will be binding.

A	B	C	D	E
Includes developments that affect more than one world region, international organizations and important meetings of major world leaders.	*Includes all domestic and regional developments in Europe, including the Soviet Union, Turkey, Cyprus and Malta.*	*Includes all domestic and regional developments in Africa and the Middle East, including Iraq and Iran and excluding Cyprus, Turkey and Afghanistan.*	*Includes all domestic and regional developments in Latin America, the Caribbean and Canada.*	*Includes all domestic and regional developments in Asian and Pacific nations, extending from Afghanistan through all the Pacific Islands, except Hawaii.*

U.S. Politics & Social Issues	U.S. Foreign Policy & Defense	U.S. Economy & Environment	Science, Technology & Nature	Culture, Leisure & Life Style	
	Senate confirms Acheson as undersecretary of state, with only Sen. Kenneth Wherry voting in opposition.	Some 60,000 AFL lumber workers strike for a minimum wage of $1.10 an hour, closing about 500 Pacific northwest logging camps, sawmills and woodworking plants.		Argentinita, world famous Spanish dancer, known in private life as Encarnacion Lopez, dies at 47 in N.Y.	Sept. 24
Census Bureau reports that U.S. births fell to 2,794,800 in 1944, 140,000 below 1943.	Chmn. Tom Connally of the Senate Foreign Relations Comm. says Acheson's role as under secretary of state will be limited to administrative management and exclude policy determination .... Adm. Thomas C. Kinkaid says the U.S. 7th Fleet is scheduled to assume the functions of the old U.S. Asiatic Fleet.	Over 28,000 miners and foremen are idled and 67 soft coal mines closed in Pennsylvania and West Virginia as a result of strikes by supervisory employes demanding the right to organize .... The mediation conference between representatives of nine leading oil firms and 30,000 striking members of the CIO-United Oil Workers opens in Chicago. Subject of the conference is union demand for a 30% wage increase .... NLRB fixes Oct. 25 for the strike vote in 20 Chrysler plants with about 120,000 workers .... Federal Reserve announces all restrictions over credit used for home repairs will be relaxed Oct. 15.		New Haven, Conn. officials ban the musical version of *Uncle Tom's Cabin* due to the protests of Negro and citizen groups. Similar action has already been taken in Bridgeport .... Dr. Julius Korngold, retired Viennese music critic, dies at 84 in Hollywood.	Sept. 25
House Comm. on Un-American Activities opens its inquiry on the new U.S. CP.	Former Treasury Secy. Henry Morgenthau says in N.Y.C. "I don't know why so little has been done by us in Germany since Hitler's defeat." .... He says he believes there can be no peace in Europe until the Saar and Ruhr are internationalized .... Truman rejects a suggestion that the U.S. is pursuing an isolationist trend again .... Senate passes and returns to the House the voluntary enlistment bill .... Under Secy. of State Acheson makes public a letter written March 10 by FDR to Amb. Armour in Madrid saying that Spain cannot expect economic aid or friendship from the U.S. as long as Franco is in power.	Ten more mines are closed as more supervisory workers in Pennsylvania and West Virginia bituminous coal fields walk out.		Hungarian composer Bela Bartok, a leader in the "neoclassical" school of modern music and one of the first composers to adopt the 12-tone scale, dies at 64 in New York.	Sept. 26
	Herbert Hoover urges that the U.S. and Britain maintain the secret of the atomic bomb .... Robert P. Patterson is sworn in as Secretary of War.	Truman accepts the resignation of FDIC Chmn. Leo Crowley and also abolishes the Foreign Economic Administration.	A new radio-telegraphy and broadcast transmission system is demonstrated in N.Y.C.; this wartime secret permits 24 or more simultaneous telephone conversations.	Bridgeport, Conn. lifts its ban on *Uncle Tom's Cabin*.	Sept. 27
Truman proclaims the exclusive right of the U.S. to all mineral resources in the 759,600 square miles of the continental shelf, running out to an offshore depth of 600 feet from the mainland.	Marine Corps Commandant A.A. Vandergrift suggests that the Marines become "trouble shooters" for the U.N. to enforce world peace.	Senate passes the Murray "full employment" bill, which emphasizes the government's intention to stimulate the economy during the transition from wartime to peacetime production.			Sept. 28
		Labor Secy. Schwellenbach opens the Washington session of a conference between oil industry, union and government representatives .... AFL Longshoremen and N.Y. shipowners sign a contract calling for a 10¢-an-hour straight time increase, a 15¢-an-hour overtime increase and a 40-hour work week.		Chicago Cubs win National League pennant, their 16th, an all-time high.	Sept. 29
				Detroit Tigers beat the St. Louis Browns, 6-3, in St. Louis to win the American League pennant .... War time ends in the U.S. at 2 a.m. today.	Sept. 30

F	G	H	I	J
Includes elections, federal-state relations, civil rights and liberties, crime, the judiciary, education, health care, poverty, urban affairs and population.	*Includes formation and debate of U.S. foreign and defense policies, veterans affairs and defense spending. (Relations with specific foreign countries are usually found under the region concerned.)*	*Includes business, labor, agriculture, taxation, transportation, consumer affairs, monetary and fiscal policy, natural resources, pollution and accidents.*	*Includes worldwide scientific, medical and technological developments, natural phenomena, U.S. weather and natural disasters.*	*Includes the arts, religion, scholarship, communications media, sports, entertainment, fashions, fads and social life.*

	World Affairs	Europe	Africa & the Middle East	The Americas	Asia & the Pacific
Oct. 1		A royal proclamation is issued as exiled King Leopold of Belgium arrives in Switzerland defending his policies during the German occupation.		Wartime controls, in effect since June 1, 1942, end in Mexico.	
Oct. 2	Council of Foreign Ministers ends a 22-day London session without agreement on signing of peace treaties with former Axis powers. U.S. State Secy. Byrnes reveals that differences arose over a Russian demand that participation in treaty discussions be limited to Allied signatories of surrender terms.	Eisenhower announces that Gen. Patton has been relieved as Army commander and military governor of Bavaria and made head of a unit compiling a military history of the war in Germany.		Guatemala suspends constitutional guarantees for one month because of the belief that an armed revolt is brewing.	The Allied Southeast Asia Command announces that the French and Annamese rebels have reached a ceasefire agreement effective tonight.
Oct. 3	Molotov says that the refusal of the other foreign ministers to accept the Russian proposals to continue discussions has resulted in their collapse. Molotov's proposals would exclude China from signing the Italian pact and China and France from the Balkan and Finnish pacts .... U.N. Executive Comm. votes to recommend that the U.N. permanent headquarters be in the U.S., with San Francisco as the most favored site .... World Trade Union Conference in Paris proclaims the formation of the new World Federation of Trade Unions.	Gen. Patton defends his administration of Bavaria, saying that he carried out his orders "with vigor and loyalty."	Iraq informs the U.S. that "any support given Zionism is deemed an act directed against Iraq in particular and the Arab people in general."	In opposition to alleged government terror, 30,000 Argentine university students go on a nationwide strike .... Mexico ratifies the U.N. Charter .... Truman urges Congress to speed authorization of the U.S.-Canadian St. Lawrence Seaway and power project .... Brazilian Pres. Vargas reaffirms his decision not to be a candidate for reelection.	MacArthur prohibits all financial, business or commercial communications from Japan except with Allied permission .... Chungking reports street fighting in Kunming between Nationalist and Communist forces.
Oct. 4		Eisenhower instructs U.S. troops not to force Russian nationals to return home, temporarily suspending one part of the Yalta agreement in the American zone of Germany .... Pierre Laval goes on trial in Paris, and is ejected from the High Court of Justice after a tumultuous session which his attorneys refuse to attend.		Police rout students at the University of La Plata, Argentina.	In restoring full civil liberties to the Japanese, MacArthur demands the resignation of Home Min. Iwao Yamazaki as the person responsible for infringement of such liberties .... Indonesian nationalists revolting against Dutch rule take control of some of Java's principal cities, including Surabaya and Bandung.
Oct. 5	Izvestia charges that State Secy. Byrnes and British Foreign Secy. Ernest Bevin attempted to break the Potsdam accord by insisting on French participation in peace treaty negotiations with Rumania, Bulgaria, Hungary and Finland. In a broadcast from Washington, Byrnes stresses he will continue to work for a general peace conference because all countries involved in a war should make peace.	Spanish government assumes provisional control of all areas in Spain where there are presumed to be deposits of uranium-bearing minerals.		Police rout some 1,000 women gathered in Buenos Aires to protest jailing of students, provoking serious rioting in which police use firearms on the crowd.	Japanese Premier Naruhiko Higashi-Kuni and his cabinet resign, noting that the first phase of occupation and demobilization in Japan is completed.
Oct. 6	John Foster Dulles, adviser to the U.S. delegation at the Council of Foreign Ministers, says the Russian attempt to exclude France and China was made to test how firmly the U.S. would back its own principles.	Police in Paris arrest 20 Indochinese, including Prof. Tran Duc Thao, vice president of a delegation which claims to represent 25,000 Indochinese laborers and several hundred students in France.			Baron Kijuro Shidehara is named the new Japanese premier. He pledges complete cooperation with Allied authorities .... Chinese Communists accuse central government troops of attacking Communist forces in Red-controlled areas of central China.
Oct. 7		Gen. Patton surrenders his 3rd Army command to Lt. Gen. Lucian Truscott at Bad Tolz, Germany.		Argentine government arrests more students, bringing the total to 2,100, and also occupies four universities.	
Oct. 8		U.S. authorities announce that by Nov. 15, AMG detachments will be withdrawn from county and city governments, which will revert to German control.	Jews in Palestine protest for five hours against British immigration restrictions.	Washington says an Argentine bid for diplomatic recognition has been rejected by Russia .... Pres. Salvadore Castaneda Castro names a new El Salvadorean cabinet with Dr. Hector Escobar Serrano as minister of foreign affairs.	
Oct. 9		Paris High Court of Justice finds Pierre Laval guilty of plotting against the state and intelligence with the enemy and sentences him to death .... Eight judges from Allied countries meet in Berlin for the first time to plan the trials of Nazis accused of war crimes .... Greek Premier Petros Voulgaris and his cabinet resign as a result of developing opposition to election plans.		A military group headed by Gen. Eduardo Avalos forces the resignation of Vice President Juan Peron in Argentina.	
	A *Includes developments that affect more than one world region, international organizations and important meetings of major world leaders.*	B *Includes all domestic and regional developments in Europe, including the Soviet Union, Turkey, Cyprus and Malta.*	C *Includes all domestic and regional developments in Africa and the Middle East, including Iraq and Iran and excluding Cyprus, Turkey and Afghanistan.*	D *Includes all domestic and regional developments in Latin America, the Caribbean and Canada.*	E *Includes all domestic and regional developments in Asian and Pacific nations, extending from Afghanistan through all the Pacific Islands, except Hawaii.*

U.S. Politics & Social Issues	U.S. Foreign Policy & Defense	U.S. Economy & Environment	Science, Technology & Nature	Culture, Leisure & Life Style	
Truman sets a precedent by appearing in the Supreme Court chambers as Harold H. Burton takes the oath of office as an associate justice.	Truman authorizes a broad reorganization of the Navy, abolishing the job of commander-in-chief and transferring principal command to the chief of naval operations . . . . Top Army Air Force generals urge that the Air Force be given full parity with land and sea commands . . . . Acting State Secy. Dean Acheson confers with French Amb. to the U.S. Henri Bonnet, reaffirming U.S. support for French occupation of Indochina.	Treasury Secy. Vinson proposes to Congress a tax reduction program for 1946 affecting 12 million taxpayers and cutting revenues by $5 billion . . . . War Mobilization and Reconversion Dir. John Snyder reports to Truman that unemployment may rise to eight million by next spring . . . . OPA Chief Chester Bowles says rent controls will be maintained as long as necessary in all congested areas, while being lifted where not needed.			Oct. 1
		House Way & Means Comm. votes for a plan providing $435 million additional tax relief above the Administration's proposal.			Oct. 2
Senate confirms R.I. Gov. J. Howard McGrath's nomination as solicitor general.		Oil conference collapses as 10 of 12 participating oil companies reject mediation proposal for a 15-30% wage increase . . . . A wildcat strike, started two days ago by N.Y.C. AFL International Longshoremen, spreads until 30,000 New York dockworkers are out . . . . GM rejects the 30% wage increase demanded by the CIO-UAW.	Truman urges immediate congressional legislation to create an "atomic energy commission" and determine national policy on nuclear power.	Betty MacDonald's *The Egg and I* and Sinclair Lewis's *Cass Timberlane* are published.	Oct. 3
House passes and sends to the Senate Truman's proposed legislation to reorganize the executive agencies for "greater efficiency and harmony."	State Secy. Byrnes arrives back in Washington from the Council of Foreign Ministers Conference in London . . . . U.S. Treasury unblocks about $1.4 billion in French government assets in the U.S.	House Ways & Means Comm. votes to give $5.3 billion in tax relief to individuals and corporations in 1946 . . . . Truman orders the Navy to seize 26 struck oil producing and refining companies and operate them under employment conditions now in effect.	A second day of dispute over creation of a federal atomic energy commission holds up Senate action on U.S. nuclear policy . . . . A C-54 Douglas Skymaster lands in Washington after completing its first round-the-world trip of 23,279 miles in 149 hours and 44 minutes, a world record . . . . A *New York Times* survey of 25 colleges and universities reveals that they will spend over $50 million to build science labs and to buy equipment and technical material.		Oct. 4
		Employes of the National Federation of Telephone Workers disrupt national telephone service for four to six hours and vote to authorize a strike vote.			Oct. 5
Post Office resumes limited mail service between the U.S. and Europe.	Adm. Nimitz says that unnecssary Pacific naval bases are being closed more quickly than anticipated, thus enabling the Navy to reduce points necessary for a discharge . . . . Navy reveals that the Mark-18, a wakeless torpedo driven by electric power, was used to destroy 300 Japanese ships during the war.	John L. Lewis refuses to order striking coal miners back to work at the operators' request, arguing that he has not called them out.			Oct. 6
Ohio Gov. Frank Lausche (D.) appoints James Huffman as U.S. senator, succeeding Harold Burton.					Oct. 7
Virginia Supreme Court of Appeals rejects a petition to remove Carter Glass from the U.S. Senate on the grounds that his two years of absence due to illness constitutes a vacancy.	Truman announces the U.S. will retain the atomic bomb secret, with only Canada and Britain sharing its knowledge.		Dr. Irvin Langmuir warns that Soviet science is progressing so rapidly that within 10-20 years it will be far ahead of the U.S. He urges the establishment of a National Science Foundation.	Austrian writer Felix Salten, the author of *Bambi*, dies at 75 in Zurich, Switzerland.	Oct. 8
Sen. Albert Chandler (D, Ky.) resigns his seat under pressure from major league baseball club owners after being elected to the $50,000-a-year post of baseball commissioner.	Army Chief of Staff Gen. George C. Marshall warns that "the only effective defense a nation can now maintain is the power to attack" and goes on to urge universal conscription.	Negotiations to end the coal strike collapse as the operators reject a compromise offered by Labor Secy. Schwellenbach . . . . In its final report the WPB discloses that the nation produced $186 billion in war material and more than doubled its productivity in a five-year period.			Oct. 9

F	G	H	I	J
Includes elections, federal-state relations, civil rights and liberties, crime, the judiciary, education, health care, poverty, urban affairs and population.	*Includes formation and debate of U.S. foreign and defense policies, veterans affairs and defense spending. (Relations with specific foreign countries are usually found under the region concerned.)*	*Includes business, labor, agriculture, taxation, transportation, consumer affairs, monetary and fiscal policy, natural resources, pollution and accidents.*	*Includes worldwide scientific, medical and technological developments, natural phenomena, U.S. weather and natural disasters.*	*Includes the arts, religion, scholarship, communications media, sports, entertainment, fashions, fads and social life.*

	World Affairs	Europe	Africa & the Middle East	The Americas	Asia & the Pacific
Oct. 10	State Secy. Byrnes announces invitations to Allied nations primarily concerned with the Far East to send representatives to Washington for an Oct. 23 conference to establish an Allied Advisory Commission on Japan.	House of Commons receives a bill to nationalize the Bank of England.	British Foreign Secy. Bevin reveals a recent exchange of letters with Russia in which each agrees to withdraw its troops from Iran by March 2, 1946.	Peron speaks to 10,000 workers in Buenos Aires, asking their support in his fight against "the oligarchy of capitalism."	A typhoon strikes the southern section of Okinawa island, causing heavy damage to dock facilities and preventing ships from landing supplies. Losses among U.S. servicemen are 28 dead and 70 missing .... Japanese troops, serving as a police force for French authorities, clash with Indochinese nationalists near Saigon, with 80 Indochinese killed and 150 wounded .... House of Commons is informed of the British government's plan for a Malayan Union consisting of the Straits Settlements and Malay States.
Oct. 11	British and American finance negotiators agree on three basic points: (1) nations in the planned International Trade Organization will keep members informed of domestic programs that will affect international trade, (2) private and public traders will be subject to the same rules and (3) export and import duties will be submitted to international negotiation .... Spanish administrators hand over control of Tangier to a commission of French, British, U.S., Russian and Spanish officials, created by international agreement on Aug. 22 .... U.N. Executive Comm. bows to Russian insistance that its report contain "observations" rather than recommendations concerning prewar specialized agencies of the old League.	Yugoslavian radio announces resignations of Foreign Min. Ivan Subasitch and Minister without Portfolio Juraj Sutej, effective Oct. 8. Both officials, representatives of the royalist faction in the Tito regime, denounced illegal government property seizures and claimed that the election laws are biased in favor of the Communists.	A Jewish force overpowers Jewish guards at the Palestine training depot at Rehobeth and escapes with a large quantity of arms and ammunition.	Army garrison headed by War Minister Gen. Eduardo J. Avalos demands the resignation of the Argentine cabinet .... Truman welcomes Chilean Pres. Juan Antonio Rios to the U.S.	MacArthur presents a five-point reform program to the Japanese government: (1) Women are to obtain voting rights; (2) labor unions are to be encouraged; (3) education system is to be liberalized; (4) control over citizens' thoughts and actions is to be abolished; and (5) economic institutions are to be democratized .... Chinese central government and Communist negotiators issue a joint declaration announcing a limited agreement to cooperate in forming a government under the leadership of Chiang Kai-shek.
Oct. 12		Norwegian Supreme Court upholds the sentence of death imposed on Vidkun Quisling .... Eisenhower tells a news conference that the U.S. Army will "uproot Nazism in every shape and form." .... Five U.S. Army officers comprising a military court in Rome sentence German Gen. Anton Dostler to die before a firing squad for ordering the shooting of 15 Americans without trial after they were captured in Italy in March 1944.	Washington legations of Egypt, Iraq, Lebanon and Syria present State Secy. Byrnes a note warning that war will result if efforts are made to set up a separate Jewish state in Palestine.	Pres. Edelmiro J. Farrell and his cabinet resign in Argentina, and Col. Peron is reportedly arrested by the Army .... The first postwar Canadian budget presented in Ottawa provides for five tax reductions, including a 16% cut in personal income taxes.	
Oct. 13					Indonesian People's Army issues a proclamation calling for all-out guerrilla warfare against the Dutch .... Allies order the dissolution of three large semi-official Japanese organizations which controlled the silk industry and direct the Japanese government to supply figures on present silk stocks and estimated production.
Oct. 14					British Maj. Gen. D.C. Hawthorn proclaims in Batavia in the Dutch East Indies that looting, sabotage, the bearing of arms or refusal to surrender arms are punishable by death .... MacArthur orders all Japanese stocks of petroleum products to be made available immediately to essential civilian industries and consumers .... Hirohito officially dissolves the headquarters of the Japanese Imperial General Staff.
Oct. 15	ILO opens its 27th conference in Paris with a renewed invitation for Russian membership.	Pierre Laval dies before a firing squad at Fresnes prison in Paris .... Polish Foreign Min. Wicenti Rzymowski signs the U.N. Charter for Poland in Washington.	Syrian government closes Catholic schools and imposes travel restrictions on Jews .... Sen. Ralph Brewster (R, Me.) blames Britain's imperialist policy for the Jewish-Arab problem in the Middle East.	Gen. Avalos of Argentina annuls the Peronist "Organic Statute of Political Powers" and allows elections to be held under laws passed by Congress .... Peruvian Congress ratifies the U.N. Charter.	MacArthur announces that Japanese armed forces throughout the country have been completely demobilized.
Oct. 16	Delegates of 30 out of 45 eligible nations sign the constitution of the U.N. Food and Agriculture Organization in Quebec.	London says Budapest radio tonight reported establishment of a state of siege in Hungary "because murder and robbery are spreading throughout the country."		Gen. Avalos says Peron has not been and will not be arrested.	Dutch minister of overseas territories says his government is willing to discuss the granting of self-government within the Netherlands Commonwealth to Indonesia.

A	B	C	D	E
Includes developments that affect more than one world region, international organizations and important meetings of major world leaders.	*Includes all domestic and regional developments in Europe, including the Soviet Union, Turkey, Cyprus and Malta.*	*Includes all domestic and regional developments in Africa and the Middle East, including Iraq and Iran and excluding Cyprus, Turkey and Afghanistan.*	*Includes all domestic and regional developments in Latin America, the Caribbean and Canada.*	*Includes all domestic and regional developments in Asian and Pacific nations, extending from Afghanistan through all the Pacific Islands, except Hawaii.*

U.S. Politics & Social Issues	U.S. Foreign Policy & Defense	U.S. Economy & Environment	Science, Technology & Nature	Culture, Leisure & Life Style	
Managing editor Louis Budenz of *The Daily Worker*, the CP organ in N.Y., renounces Communism because "it aims to establish tyranny over the human spirit" and returns to the Catholic Church.	Army orders deactivation of 32 of its 89 divisions.	As the coal negotiations in Washington fail, 82 additional mines are shut down . . . . At the last reservoir to be completed in the TVA chain, Kentucky Dam, Truman says he hopes this model project will "result in the development of our other river valleys."	CBS executive Paul W. Kesten reports a successful transmission of color television to the FCC . . . . Aviation executives recommend that a special board be created to work out a long-range national policy for aeronautical development, atomic energy and jet propulsion.	Detroit Tigers win the World Series from the Chicago Cubs, 4 games to 3, with a 9-3 victory in Chicago.	Oct. 10
DAR refuses to permit Negro pianist Hazel Scott to use Constitution Hall in Washington.		House votes to reduce federal taxes by $5.35 billion in 1946, eliminating about 12 million taxpayers . . . . N.Y.C. Mayor La Guardia announces he will attempt to negotiate a settlement of the longshoremen's strike.			Oct. 11
Truman condemns the DAR, comparing their refusal to permit Hazel Scott use of Constitution Hall to Nazi "racial discrimination." . . . . Federal Judge T. Hoyt Davis upholds the right of Negroes to vote in Georgia's Democratic primary elections . . . . A Senate subcommittee backs a government agency reorganization bill to permit wider presidential powers than those in the House version.		N.Y.C. longshoremen refuse La Guardia's plea to return to work.	Senate Interstate Commerce Comm. approves a resolution to create a special congressional committee of nine to have charge of all bills on atomic energy.		Oct. 12
	Assn. of Los Alamos Scientists, some 400 experts who worked on the atomic bomb, decry the U.S. decision to keep the bomb secret for itself.	Some striking members of the Longshoremen's Assn. begin to return to work in N.Y.C. . . . . NLRB says petitions for strike votes reached a record 307 in September.			Oct. 13
		Rank and-file ILA members accept Mayor La Guardia's proposal to return to work, as shipowners indicate they will resume negotiations with a committee elected by workers.		Louisville Colonels of the American Assn. defeat the Newark Bears of the International League, 5-3, to win the "Little World Series" in the sixth game in Louisville . . . . Byron Nelson breaks his own world record for par-70 golf courses by shooting 66 to win the Seattle Open.	Oct. 14
	Truman opens files from FDR's Administration to the congressional committee investigating the Pearl Harbor disaster.	Labor Secy. Schwellenbach says the Washington coal talks have collapsed, as John L. Lewis places blame on the operators for not wanting to negotiate issues . . . . NWLB announces a $4 weekly pay increase for 10,000 N.Y. Telephone Co. employes . . . . NWLB urges the creation of a federal "blue-ribbon" commission to formulate postwar wage and price policy.			Oct. 15
	Thirty prominent Americans meeting at Dublin, N.H., sign the Declaration of the Dublin Conference urging creation of a world federal government to prevent atomic war.	Solid Fuels Admin. Ickes warns that the nation is in for serious trouble unless 200,000 striking miners return to work . . . . More than 7,000 ILA members return to work at N.Y.C. docks, defying pickets.			Oct. 16
F *Includes elections, federal-state relations, civil rights and liberties, crime, the judiciary, education, health care, poverty, urban affairs and population.*	G *Includes formation and debate of U.S. foreign and defense policies, veterans affairs and defense spending. (Relations with specific foreign countries are usually found under the region concerned.)*	H *Includes business, labor, agriculture, taxation, transportation, consumer affairs, monetary and fiscal policy, natural resources, pollution and accidents.*	I *Includes worldwide scientific, medical and technological developments, natural phenomena, U.S. weather and natural disasters.*	J *Includes the arts, religion, scholarship, communications media, sports, entertainment, fashions, fads and social life.*	

	World Affairs	Europe	Africa & the Middle East	The Americas	Asia & the Pacific
Oct. 17		U.S. military authorities in Berlin report the seizure of the Nazi Party master files, listing nearly eight million members, two million names of those rejected for membership and a blacklist of expelled party members .... Russia signs an agreement with the U.S. purchasing up to $400 million in Lend-Lease goods, payable in 30 years at $2\frac{3}{8}$% interest .... Greek Regent Archbishop Damaskinos personally takes over the government as premier after failure of other efforts to solve the crisis resulting from a dispute over national elections.		In a coup d'etat aided by widespread strikes, Col. Juan Peron overthrows the Argentine government of Gen. Eduardo Avalos. Peron himself does not take office, but installs his supporters in key positions.	State Secy. Byrnes says Russia has reiterated its desire for an Allied Control Council in Tokyo similar to the one in Berlin .... Hirohito grants an amnesty to nearly one million Japanese held in prisons and concentration camps for various reasons .... Indonesian nationalists kill 15 persons in Depok, Java.
Oct. 18	U.S. State Dept. reveals that the interim agreement on Tangier provides that, if the Franco regime is still in power in Spain six months hence, Spain will be barred from the Paris conference to establish a permanent international organization for control of the North African city .... Against Russian opposition the U.N. Executive Comm. establishes a trusteeship committee to administer territory taken from enemy nations .... At the World Air Conference in Montreal, 57 airlines agree to establish nine regional traffic conferences to prevent rate wars.	An indictment presented to the International Military Tribunal in Berlin charges 24 high Nazis with plotting against world peace.	State Secy. Byrnes states the U.S. will make no final decisions on proposals to change the basic Palestinian situation without "full consultation with Jewish and Arab leaders."	General Confederation of Labor calls a general strike in Argentina in support of Peron, resulting in a nationwide paralysis.	Indonesian nationalists reject Dutch overtures for partnership in the empire and instead demand independence .... MacArthur's Tokyo headquarters forbids the Japanese from cultivating the opium poppy and orders the freezing of all existing narcotics stocks.
Oct. 19	Truman names Archibald MacLeish chairman of the U.S. delegation to the Educational, Scientific & Cultural Organization of the U.N. to meet in London.	International War Crimes Tribunal announces in Nuremburg that trials of accused Nazi leaders will open the Palace of Justice there Nov. 20.		An Army revolt ousts Venezuelan Pres. Isaias Medina Angarita, and a seven-man junta is named to rule the country.	Japanese Foreign Min. Shigeru Yoshida says two groups are studying ways to liberalize the nation's constitution in accordance with Allied orders.
Oct. 20	UNRRA Dir. Lehman warns that unless $1.8 billion is forthcoming in support, the agency will have to end its operations .... U.S. delegation to the U.N. Food and Agriculture Organization proposes a world agency to control the flow and use of agricultural products.	Allied Council for Austria gives de facto recognition to the Austrian government of Premier Karl Renner .... Eisenhower recommends measures to break up the I.G. Farben combine and reports that its key personnel are under arrest and that three plants will be destroyed.			Indonesian nationalist leader Ahmed Sukarno cables Truman, asking that he halt the use of U.S. equipment against the independence movement.
Oct. 21		U.S. and Britain protest to Moscow against the proposed Russian-Hungarian trade pact, which would tie up 50% of Hungary's industry and transportation.		Army garrisons support the Venezuelan revolutionary government of Provisional Pres. Romulo Betancourt .... President Juan Antonio Rios of Chile dedicates the Avenue of the Americas, formerly Sixth Ave., in N.Y.C.	Communist New 4th Army begins withdrawal from strategic points in east central China in connection with an agreement with the Nationalists.
Oct. 22		U.S. State Dept. reveals that Moscow has not yet replied to its "presentation of views" on the proposed Hungarian-Russian economic pact .... Franco issues a decree in Madrid instituting a "bill of rights," which provides liberties so long as they do not run contrary to the "fundamentals of the state."		Venezuelan rebel junta names a provisional cabinet, dominated by members of the Democratic Action Party .... U.S. Senate confirms the appointment of Spruille Braden as assistant secretary of state for Latin American affairs.	A program for liberalizing the Japanese school system is presented to the government by Allied authorities. It calls for abolition of military instruction and ultra-nationalistic ideologies .... MacArthur orders the family-owned monopolies of Japan to disclose their financial and manufacturing records for the years 1935-44.
Oct. 23		Vidkun Quisling, Norwegian premier during the Nazi occupation, dies before a firing squad in Oslo.			Japanese newspaper *Asahi* reveals partial plans for removing the top layer of Mitsui officials and divorcing ownership and management in moves to secure more democratic control of the company.
Oct. 24	At 4:50 p.m. EST the U.N. Charter goes into force, with Russian ratification bringing the total number of signers to 29.	Czech Pres. Eduard Benes signs a decree nationalizing commercial banks, insurance companies and 27 other industries.	Cairo dispatches say Arab states are threatening economic sanctions against American oil companies in their campaign against opening up Palestine to Jewish immigration .... Iranian Parliament elects Abrahim Hakimi as premier to succeed Muhsin Sadr.	Venezuelan Provisional Pres. Romulo Betancourt pledges no cancellations of U.S. business concessions in the country.	Tokyo reports indicate that on Jan. 1, 1946 a contingent of 40,000 British Empire troops will arrive in Japan to assist in the country's occupation .... Indonesian nationalist leader Ahmed Sukarno invites U.S. and British committees to visit Indonesia to observe the situation there.
	A *Includes developments that affect more than one world region, international organizations and important meetings of major world leaders.*	B *Includes all domestic and regional developments in Europe, including the Soviet Union, Turkey, Cyprus and Malta.*	C *Includes all domestic and regional developments in Africa and the Middle East, including Iraq and Iran and excluding Cyprus, Turkey and Afghanistan.*	D *Includes all domestic and regional developments in Latin America, the Caribbean and Canada.*	E *Includes all domestic and regional developments in Asian and Pacific nations, extending from Afghanistan through all the Pacific Islands, except Hawaii.*

U.S. Politics & Social Issues	U.S. Foreign Policy & Defense	U.S. Economy & Environment	Science, Technology & Nature	Culture, Leisure & Life Style	
	Three atomic bomb experts tell a Senate committee that the bomb is so dangerous it requires international control .... War Secty. Robert P. Patterson urges a single Defense Dept. with a cabinet-level head.	John L. Lewis calls for an end to the coal strike in the "public interest," ordering miners back to work Oct. 22 and temporarily suspending negotiations.		Composer of numerous hit tunes, James V. Monaco, dies at 60 in Hollywood, Calif.	Oct. 17
	A group of atomic scientists appears before a House committee to protest the Administration's atomic energy bill, claiming that it would prevent international control over nuclear power and hinder scientific research in the area .... Gen. Marshall tells a Senate committee that a single defense unit of the Army, Navy and Air Force is essential for future peace efforts.	Senate Finance Comm. votes to repeal wartime excess profits taxes, to reduce tax rolls 12 million, to freeze social security at 1% for another year and to reduce other individual and business taxes .... The 18-day longshoremen's walkout ends in N.Y.C. as all dockers return to their jobs .... Army relinquishes control of the properties of Montgomery Ward & Co. in Chicago and six other cities.		Count Leo Tolstoy, son of the noted Russian novelist and a sculptor and writer in his own right, dies at 76 in Sweden .... Billy Conn signs to fight heavyweight champ Joe Louis for the title next June.	Oct. 18
		Senate Finance Comm. approves bigger tax cuts to give $2.6 billion in relief to individuals and $2.8 billion to businesses .... House passes and sends to the Senate a bill giving control of the Employment Service back to the states, refusing Truman's request to keep it under federal control until 1947 .... NAM calls the "full employment" bill defeatist and says it does nothing to accomplish its goal.			Oct. 19
War Relocation Authority reports that all Japanese relocation centers are closed with only 12,000 Japanese aliens and 16,000 "disloyal" persons left in the Tule Lakes segregation center.	War Dept. announces that nearly half the soldiers from both the Atlantic and Pacific theaters have returned home.		GE makes public details of the world's largest "electron accelerator," which hurls an electron stream at the speed of light.		Oct. 20
	Columbia Univ. Prof. Harold C. Urey, who aided in development of the A-bomb, says the only way to avoid an atomic war is to prevent the bomb's manufacture.	AFL Pres. William Green says labor cannot go back to a longer work week when there is going to be widespread unemployment.			Oct. 21
	Navy Secy. Forrestal says the unification of the three military branches under one person would put too much power in the hands of a single individual.	CIO Fed. of Glass, Ceramic and Silica Sand Workers halts operations at 12 Libbey-Owens-Ford and Pittsburgh Plate Glass Company plants in seven states due to the firms' refusal to continue contract negotiations .... NAM says that, although industry believes in high wages, increasing minimum wages will cause either "serious inflation" or be very "deflationary."	Senate adopts a resolution authorizing a special congressional committee to study the development, use and control of atomic energy .... Western Union announces plans to construct thousands of super high-frequency, radio-beam stations across the country to replace the current 2.3 million miles of wire channels.		Oct. 22
	At a joint congressional session Truman asks for enactment of a program of universal military training .... Fleet Adm. Ernest J. King calls the military merger bill "revolutionary, dangerous and unnecessary."	U.S. Steel Corp. rejects the CIO-USW demand for a $2-a-day wage increase.		Jackie Robinson becomes the first Negro player admitted to organized professional baseball as he signs with Montreal of the International League, a Brooklyn Dodgers farm team.	Oct. 23
	Marine Corps cuts its discharge score from 60 to 50 points for men and from 25 to 20 for women.	Senate passes and sends to conference a $5.7-billion tax reduction bill .... N.Y.C. longshoremen vote overwhelmingly against a revised contract proposal by shipowners.	An American Airlines plane arrives at Hurn Airfield, England from N.Y.C. in 14 hours, 5 minutes flying time, to complete the first land plane commercial flight from North America to Europe.		Oct. 24

	World Affairs	Europe	Africa & the Middle East	The Americas	Asia & the Pacific
Oct. 25		Gen. de Gaulle commutes the death sentence of Gen. Dentz for ordering resistance to the Allies in Syria to life imprisonment.	Truman and Attlee are reportedly in agreement on the Palestine issue.	Paraguay, Ecuador and Cuba extend recognition to the new Venezuelan government.	Allied headquarters orders Japan to sever all diplomatic relations, recall all diplomatic representatives stationed overseas and turn over all diplomatic materials throughout the world to Allied powers.
Oct. 26	In an *Atlantic Monthly* article, Albert Einstein says the secret of the atom bomb should be given to a world government as a means of preventing atomic war.				British Indian troops repulse a heavy attack by Annamese forces on Saigon.
Oct. 27	Executive Comm. of the U.N., in its last formal act, sets Nov. 23 for convening the full preparatory commission in London . . . . British MP Sir John Boyd Orr is elected director general of the U.N. Food and Agriculture Organization in Quebec.				Dutch government orders Acting Gov. Gen. Hubertus van Mook of the NEI to begin negotiations with Indonesian independence leaders.
Oct. 28			British government appoints Maj. Gideon Brand van Zyl to be governor general of the Union of South Africa, effective Jan. 1, 1946.		A Chinese Communist spokesman says that fighting with Nationalist troops has spread to 11 of the country's 28 provinces.
Oct. 29	FAO Dir. Orr asks that his agency be allowed to set up a commodity pool to stabilize prices and supplies of the expected world wheat surplus.			Brazilian Pres. Vargas resigns, turning over the office to Supreme Court Chief Justice Jose Linhares until a new president is elected.	War crimes trial of Japanese Gen. Tomoyuki Yamashita opens in Manila . . . . British Brig. A.W. Mallaby, commanding troops at Surabaya, is killed there in fighting between British Indian troops and Indonesian nationalists . . . . Communist troops are reported entrenched in Manchuria along rail lines and near three ports where U.S. warships are scheduled to land Chinese government troops.
Oct. 30				Secy. Byrnes announces full U.S. recognition of the new Venezuelan government . . . . Chief Justice Linhares is sworn in as president of Brazil and appoints a new cabinet.	Allied Far Eastern Advisory Commission assembles in Washington. Russia refuses to join unless U.S. agrees to share occupation of Japan with other Allied powers.
Oct. 31	In a major foreign policy address, State Secy. Byrnes says he recognizes Russia's special interests in eastern and central Europe but that a world divided "into spheres of exclusive influence" is more dangerous than national isolation . . . . Because their government is deemed fascist, Argentina's representative, Juan Rodriguez, and his adviser, Manuel Pichel, are barred by the ILO.	In his third report as military governor, Eisenhower declares that the terms of the Potsdam Declaration are being carried out in the American zone of Germany . . . . Moscow reports indicate that Russia wants Italy to pay $300 million in reparations, a third to Russia and the rest to Greece, Yugoslavia and Albania.		Venezuelan Provisional Pres. Betancourt promises free elections in six months for a new president and National Assembly to rewrite the nation's constitution . . . . New Brazilian government pledges to eliminate all traces of the previous "dictatorship." Gen. Getulio Vargas leaves Rio de Janeiro by plane for his ranch, promising to "harbor no hatred or personal animosities."	Truman reports that Stalin has informed him of Russia's willingness to join the Far Eastern Advisory Commission meeting in Washington . . . . Allied headquarters orders the Japanese Education Ministry to investigate 400,000 teachers in 39,000 schools and to eliminate all militarists . . . . Shansi Province Gov. Gen. Yen Hsi-shan reports 100,000 Chinese Communist troops are attacking Tatung.
Nov. 1	U.N. education conference opens in London, with 42 nations represented. The Soviet Union is not present . . . . U.N. FAO conference ends in Quebec with an appeal that constructive world action be taken to escape "atomic obliteration."	British Labor government reveals plans to nationalize civil aviation and the communications industry . . . . British on the Allied Control Council in Berlin report that on the basis of all available evidence Adolf Hitler and Eva Braun committed suicide on April 30 . . . . Twenty-one German bankers are arrested in the American zone for investigation as war criminals.	Palestine's transportation system is paralyzed by Zionist terrorist activities, which include the sabotaging of railroads at 50 points from Acre to Gaza and damage to police launches at Jaffa.		Tass reports Russia favors a four-power control council for Japan, with an American as chairman . . . . Dutch government orders Gen. Hubertus J. van Mook not to negotiate with Sukarno in the NEI.

	A	B	C	D	E
	Includes developments that affect more than one world region, international organizations and important meetings of major world leaders.	*Includes all domestic and regional developments in Europe, including the Soviet Union, Turkey, Cyprus and Malta.*	*Includes all domestic and regional developments in Africa and the Middle East, including Iraq and Iran and excluding Cyprus, Turkey and Afghanistan.*	*Includes all domestic and regional developments in Latin America, the Caribbean and Canada.*	*Includes all domestic and regional developments in Asian and Pacific nations, extending from Afghanistan through all the Pacific Islands, except Hawaii.*

U.S. Politics & Social Issues	U.S. Foreign Policy & Defense	U.S. Economy & Environment	Science, Technology & Nature	Culture, Leisure & Life Style	
Truman unfurls a new presidential flag and exhibits a new seal of the president of the U.S.	American Assn. for an International Office of Education urges State Secy. Byrnes to call a U.S. conference for creation of a national commission to cooperate with the Educational and Cultural Organization .... GOP leader Alf Landon criticizes the administration's foreign policy for being vindictive and suggests Germany be made self-sufficient.	Truman releases agenda of the proposed labor-management-government conference in Washington, scheduled for Nov. 5 to deal with problems of industrial conflict and collective bargaining .... Members of the CIO-UAW at GM vote by a 6 to 1 margin for strike action to obtain a 30% wage increase .... Executive board of the United Retail, Wholesale & Department Store Employes union votes to call a strike at plants of Montgomery Ward.	Dr. Karl Compton, president of MIT, and three other physicists who helped develop the A-bomb tell a Senate committee scientists must have freedom to exchange information with colleagues in other nations .... Nobel prizes for physiology and medicine are awarded to Sir Alexander Fleming, Sir Howard Florey and Dr. Ernest Chain for their work on penicillin .... NBC demonstrates a new TV camera more than 100 times as sensitive as any previously used, permitting greater depth of view and stability of operation.	ABC joins CBS and NBC in announcing discontinuation of FM music as of Oct. 29 because of demands for double crews by Pres. Petrillo of the musicians' union.	Oct. 25
	House conferees agree to accept the Senate provisions exempting service pay of enlisted men in the armed forces from income tax and giving them and officers three years to pay deferred taxes .... Assn. of Colleges & Universities of N.Y. asks Truman for selective service deferment for science and engineering students to alleviate shortages.	CIO-USW Pres. Philip Murray says the union will file petitions with the NLRB for strike votes among steel, aluminum and iron ore workers.			Oct. 26
	In Navy Day ceremonies, Truman commissions the 45,000-ton aircraft carrier *Franklin D. Roosevelt* in N.Y.C. He states that U.S. military strength will be used to maintain world peace, establish "peaceful, democratic governments" in the former Axis states and ensure equal access for all countries to "the trade and raw materials of the world."	Congressional conferees agree on a tax reduction bill of $5.9 billion, repealing the excess profits tax and the automobile use tax and reducing corporate and individual income taxes .... GM asks the CIO to join in petitioning Congress to extend the work week from 40 to 45 hours, assuring a general wage increase of 6%.			Oct. 27
	Both GOP and Democratic congressional leaders acclaim Truman's foreign policy speech and urge full support by Congress .... A group of House GOP members urges that UNRRA receive an appropriation of $550 million in order for the agency to complete its job.	CIO United Electrical, Radio & Machine Workers union announces the filing of a petition for a strike vote with the NLRB at 54 GE plants in an attempt to overcome the company's refusal to grant a $2-a-day increase .... WPB places lumber under inventory control to prevent hoarding and speed expansion of industry.			Oct. 28
Labor Secy. Lewis Schwellenbach tells a Senate committee the payment of "uniformly lower wages" to women "depresses the whole wage structure," and urges legislation banning wage differentials because of sex.	Gen. Marshall warns that if the U.N. is to have any chance at success, the U.S. must remain strong and demobilization must not become military "disintegration." .... Assn. of Manhattan District Scientists, whose members worked on the A-bomb, criticzes the May-Johnson bill because it aims to maintain an American monopoly on the bomb.	ILA and shipowners' representatives agree to accept arbitrators named by Labor Secy. Schewellenbach .... OPA Chief Bowles and WPB Chmn. Krug announce the end of automobile rationing.	Census Bureau reports maternal and infant mortality deaths were 6,139 and 111,127 respectively in 1944, the lowest on record.		Oct. 29
	In its plan submitted to the Senate Military Affairs Comm., the War Dept. calls for the merger of the Armed Forces into one agency under a cabinet-level secretary .... A House committee supports congressional appropriations of $550 million for UNRRA.	House approves the $5.9 billion tax reduction bill .... In an executive order amending his Aug. 18 policy statement, Truman recommends higher wages in order for workers to catch up with the cost of living.	House Military Affairs Comm. approves a bill establishing a strong atomic energy commission.		Oct. 30
		Truman says that no maximum percentage for wage increases can be set on a nationwide or industry-wide basis .... Bureau of Labor Statistics reports 550 strikes and lockouts in September, involving 455,000 workers and 3,650,000 man-days of idleness.		Booker T. Washington becomes first Negro elected to the NYU Hall of Fame. Also chosen are Revolutionary War hero Thomas Paine, Army doctor Walter Reed and Southern poet Sidney Lanier.	Oct. 31
	Truman directs U.S. Reparations Commission representative Edwin Pauley to go to Japan to work out a reparations program .... Senate Military Affairs Comm. makes public a statement by Eisenhower favoring the merger of the armed forces into a single government branch.	Senate passes and sends to the President the $5.9-billion tax reduction bill, relieving 12 million individuals from tax payment and repealing excess profits taxes and the automobile use tax .... Former NWLB Chmn. Davis is named to arbitrate the AFL-ILA — N.Y. shipowners dispute.	Iraq's top antiquities official, Dr. Naji al Asil, says archeologists have discovered evidence that human civilization existed near Ur in Iraq 8,000 years ago, 2,000 year earlier than previously believed.	Robert E. Burns, 55, convicted in 1922 for a $5.85 hold-up of an Atlanta grocer and author of the best-selling *I Am A Fugitive From a Georgia Chain Gang*, surrenders to Gov. Ellis Arnall, and the Georgia parole board commutes his 23-year sentence to time served.	Nov. 1

F	G	H	I	J
Includes elections, federal-state relations, civil rights and liberties, crime, the judiciary, education, health care, poverty, urban affairs and population.	*Includes formation and debate of U.S. foreign and defense policies, veterans affairs and defense spending. (Relations with specific foreign countries are usually found under the region concerned.)*	*Includes business, labor, agriculture, taxation, transportation, consumer affairs, monetary and fiscal policy, natural resources, pollution and accidents.*	*Includes worldwide scientific, medical and technological developments, natural phenomena, U.S. weather and natural disasters.*	*Includes the arts, religion, scholarship, communications media, sports, entertainment, fashions, fads and social life.*

	World Affairs	Europe	Africa & the Middle East	The Americas	Asia & the Pacific
Nov. 2		Forty-two members of the Dachau concentration camp staff are indicted in Nuremberg for trial Nov. 15 .... Belgian government publishes the official German version of King Leopold's conversation with Adolf Hitler in November 1940, saying the two men agreed on linking their countries' fortunes.		Secy. Brynes directs the U.S. embassy in Rio de Janeiro to carry on normal relations with the new Brazilian government of Jose Linhares as official recognition is extended .... Cuban Pres. Ramon Grau San Martin places the 1946 national budget at a record high of $163,880,000.	Arab nationalists call a one-day strike in Egypt, Lebanon, Syria and Palestine in protest against Zionism and the Balfour Declaration .... British Colonial Secy. George Hall announces the resignation of Viscount Gort as high commissioner for Palestine and Transjordan because of ill health .... The 43-party central committee of the Korean provisional parliament, meeting in Seoul, calls on the U.N. to end the Soviet-U.S. division of Korea and to grant the nation independence .... Chungking reports 20,000 Communists are attacking Kwisui, Suiyuan Province's capital.
Nov. 3	ILO votes in Paris to admit Argentina.				Nationalist Chinese Information Min. K.C. Wu reports a four-point peace plan sent to the Communists at Yenan, including a halt to all attacks .... Russian government praises the Indonesian nationalist revolt against Dutch control, the first instance of postwar Soviet support for a "war of national liberation."
Nov. 4		The conservative Small Landowners Party wins the national and municipal elections in Hungary, capturing 59% of the votes cast. Communists gain 17% of the vote .... Allied Control Council in Berlin promulgates a law designed to force neutral nations to give up any property owned by German nationals in their territory.			While Communists attack cities in northern Hupeh, Nationalist Gen. Ho Ying-chin indicates his government's determination to reopen rail lines through Communist areas .... British commander in northern Palestine orders a 5:30 p.m. to 5:30 a.m. curfew for the coastal region around Haifa .... Soviet publication *New Times* hails the national liberation movements in the NEI and French Indochina.
Nov. 5		Lt. Gen. Lucius Clay says in Washington there is no food in any substantial amount in Europe. U.S. military authorities in Germany have asked the War Dept. for 300,000 tons of food to supply civilians in the U.S. zone.			Chinese Communists charge that U.S. troops helped Nationalist forces at Hayiyang, Pehtaiho and near Chinwangtao and that U.S. planes attacked Red-held Antze.
Nov. 6	ILO elects Guildhaume Myrddin-Evans of Britain as its new chairman, replacing Carter Goodrich of the U.S.	Molotov declares the atomic bomb cannot be kept secret and promises that Russians will develop atomic energy.			Japanese government orders the dissolution of the Mitsui, Mitsubishi, Yasuda and Sumitomo holding companies, which comprise the group of wealthy families known as Zaibatsu .... Gen. Hubertus van Mook reiterates Queen Wilhelmina's 1942 offer of home rule in a Netherlands Commonwealth for the Indonesians.
Nov. 7	Churchill and Foreign Secy. Bevin tell the House of Commons that the U.S. and Britain should keep the atomic secret until the U.N. can be entrusted with it.	In her Mediterranean proposals, Italy suggests that Fiume and Zara be given to Yugoslavia and that Trieste become a free city.	In riots since Nov. 4 more than 100 Jews have been slain in Tripoli, and more than 550 Arabs have been arrested by the British .... Rome and Washington report that Italy has requested she be allowed to keep her African territories, including Ethiopia, Tripolitania and Somaliland.	Eleven persons are arrested in Asuncion, Paraguay as a precaution against a possible attempt to overthrow dictator Higinio Morinigo .... Brazil reports that 7.5 million have registered for the Dec. 2 presidential election.	Allied headquarters in Tokyo announces that all incoming news dispatches must be approved by Russian, Chinese and British missions, as well as the American mission before publication.
Nov. 8	British reportedly approve a U.S. proposal for the creation of an International Trade Organization to investigate all private cartels.	Rumanian troops fire into a crowd of rioting Communists and supporters of King Michael before the royal palace, killing 13 and wounding 80 .... Field Marshal August von Mackensen, last surviving leader of the Imperial German Army, dies at 95 in the British zone of Germany.	British appoint Lt. Gen. Sir Alan Cunningham as high commissioner for Palestine and Transjordan .... Iranian deputy claims that the Russians have stationed 12,000 troops at Bandar Shak on the Caspian Sea and two new divisions in Azerbaijan.	Splitting from the radicals, Peronistas set up a new political party in Buenos Aires in support of Peron.	British commander in eastern Java, Maj. Gen. E.C. Mansergh, issues an ultimatum to the Indonesians at Surabaya and other areas to surrender their arms by 6 a.m., Nov. 10 or face all-out attack .... Chinese Communists report that Chungking has massed 90 divisions for a drive into Manchuria.
Nov. 9	Before departing for the U.S., Attlee says he will discuss with Truman "not so much how to control atomic energy as what kind of world society is necessary."	Czechoslovakian Premier Zdenek Fierlinger tells Parliament that Russia and the U.S. have agreed to withdraw their troops from Czechoslovakia.			Communist Chinese cancel peace talks with the Nationalists and announce their intention to oppose Nationalist efforts to enter Manchuria and other "liberated areas." .... Japanese cabinet ends conscription.
	A *Includes developments that affect more than one world region, international organizations and important meetings of major world leaders.*	B *Includes all domestic and regional developments in Europe, including the Soviet Union, Turkey, Cyprus and Malta.*	C *Includes all domestic and regional developments in Africa and the Middle East, including Iraq and Iran and excluding Cyprus, Turkey and Afghanistan.*	D *Includes all domestic and regional developments in Latin America, the Caribbean and Canada.*	E *Includes all domestic and regional developments in Asian and Pacific nations, extending from Afghanistan through all the Pacific Islands, except Hawaii.*

U.S. Politics & Social Issues	U.S. Foreign Policy & Defense	U.S. Economy & Environment	Science, Technology & Nature	Culture, Leisure & Life Style	
Civil Service Commission, backed by Truman, recommends to a Senate committee a salary increase of about $10,000 annually for almost all top federal officials. The program would add $415,570,000 annually to the budget.	Gen. George Kenney, commander of the Far East Air Forces, asks for Senate approval of a bill to merge the armed forces.	About 18,500 members of the Textile Workers Union in 21 New England textile mills strike for a union shop and wage increase .... UAW airline mechanics vote to end their two-week strike against the American Export Airlines and return to work Nov. 3 .... NWLB returns 1,000 pending disputes to the parties concerned for further collective bargaining, clearing its dockets.	At the final Senate committee hearing on the projected National Science Foundation, Harvard Univ. Pres. James Conant endorses the project.	Archbishop Joseph Schrembs of the Roman Catholic diocese of Cleveland dies at 79 in Cleveland.	Nov. 2
Irvin Mollison, Republican of Chicago, is sworn in as U.S. Customs Court judge in N.Y.C., becoming the first Negro on the federal bench within the continental U.S.	Petroleum Industry War Council approves the revised Anglo-U.S. oil agreement and urges prompt Senate ratification.	WPB winds up its business and is disbanded.			Nov. 3
			Eastman Kodak announces a new color printing process, the dye transfer method, which reduces printing time by two-thirds to three-fourths.	Ben Hogan wins the Richmond Golf Tournament over Dick Metz.	Nov. 4
		Truman opens the labor-management conference in Washington with a plea to end industrial strife and formulate a broad foundation for industrial peace and progress .... Supreme Court refuses a plea by Montgomery Ward for a decision on whether the government was right or wrong in its seizure of the company's property in seven cities last December.	Bell Aircraft Corp. releases details of its new twin-jet fighter plane, the XP-83, for long-range use, with a speed of 500 mph.		Nov. 5
		An executive committee for the Washington labor-management conference is formed, composed of eight labor and eight management representatives.	Sen. Joseph Ball (R, Minn.) introduces a substitute for the May-Johnson atomic energy bill to create a nine-man control commission including the secretaries of War, Navy, State, Interior and Commerce. Ball denounces the other bill as monopolistic and undemocratic.		Nov. 6
	Senate Foreign Relations Comm. approves full U.S. participation in the U.N., with its Security Council representative able to vote the use of American troops to secure the peace .... War Dept. announces that enlisted men with 50 points on duty in the U.S. or on leave will be discharged by the month's end.	Truman asks the House to act on his recommendation for a $107.5-million public works fund .... UAW rejects a GM offer to raise wages 8-10% for all workers whose salaries have lagged behind the cost of living, charging it is an effort to "sandbag" the public into higher auto costs .... Washington AFL transit workers accept a 30¢ hourly wage increase and agree to end their walkout.	RAF pilot Capt. Hugh J.. Wilson flies the Gloster Meteor jet plane at a word record speed average of 606 mph over Herne Bay, England .... Army announces the development of a new vaccine effective against two types of influenza.		Nov. 7
	Senate passes and sends to the House a revised "GI Bill," which would cost $9 billion .... As Truman orders all government departments to give any information they have on the Pearl Harbor attack to congressional investigators, the GOP charges that records are missing or have been destroyed .... Harold E. Stassen proposes that atomic bomb production be outlawed and its control be given to the U.N. Security Council.	UAW files complaints of unfair labor practices against GM with the NLRB, charging the company with refusing to bargain collectively.	Bell Aircraft reports the successful testing of remote-controlled jet planes .... MIT President Karl Compton, who recently returned from Japan, says Japanese scientists tried to split uranium atoms to make a substitute for coal after deciding that an atomic bomb was not feasible .... Bell Labs demonstrates a new "visual" language of phonetic sounds for the deaf, which are projected through microphones on screens that the deaf can read.		Nov. 8
National Housing Admin. John Blandford, Jr. urges mayors of all cities with more than 25,000 people to organize local committees to help alleviate crowded housing conditions.	Lt. Gen. James Doolittle tells a Senate committee that he favors a merger of the armed forces, stressing the need for an air command.	NLRB reports that Ford Motor Co.'s UAW workers have voted to strike in support of their 30% wage increase demand .... NAM urges an end to all OPA controls, except on rents, because the controls retard production.		John Marquand's *Repent in Haste* and Jessamyn West's *The Friendly Persuasion* are published.	Nov. 9
F *Includes elections, federal-state relations, civil rights and liberties, crime, the judiciary, education, health care, poverty, urban affairs and population.*	G *Includes formation and debate of U.S. foreign and defense policies, veterans affairs and defense spending. (Relations with specific foreign countries are usually found under the region concerned.)*	H *Includes business, labor, agriculture, taxation, transportation, consumer affairs, monetary and fiscal policy, natural resources, pollution and accidents.*	I *Includes worldwide scientific, medical and technological developments, natural phenomena, U.S. weather and natural disasters.*	J *Includes the arts, religion, scholarship, communications media, sports, entertainment, fashions, fads and social life.*	

	World Affairs	Europe	Africa & the Middle East	The Americas	Asia & the Pacific
Nov. 10	Attlee and Mackenzie King arrive in Washington for talks with Truman about the atomic bomb.			Ruling Mexican Revolutionary Party refuses to support any reforms in the electoral law, which now empowers the Chamber of Deputies to count votes in national elections.	Chinese Nationalists report their troops have made progress against Communist forces along the Great Wall and are driving on Chinhsien. Communist and Nationalist forces clash near the coastal anchor of the Great Wall at Shanhaikwan . . . . After the Indonesians reject the British ultimatum, British troops attack the port of Surabaya.
Nov. 11					Chinese Nationalists report that efforts to obtain Russian permission to let their forces be flown into Manchuria are under way.
Nov. 12					British destroyers shell Indonesian positions in Surabaya as Indian troops occupy the northern half of the city.
Nov. 13	In addressing the U.S. Congress, British P.M. Attlee asserts that "man's material discoveries have outpaced his moral progress" and world cooperation is necessary for man to survive the atomic bomb.		U.S. and British agree to create a joint committee of inquiry to examine the problem of European Jews and Palestine.		Socialist leader Sutan Sjahrir is appointed premier of the "Indonesian Republic," leaving Pres. Sukarno with little power.
Nov. 14		Harold Laski, British Labor Party's executive committee chairman, denounces the Labor government's "criminal policy" towards Java, Indochina and India.	Riots break out in Tel Aviv in protest against the U.S.-British statement on Palestine, killing two and wounding 57.	Asst. Secy. of State Spruille Braden says that with one exception — Argentina — every American republic has a fine record of economic cooperation.	British Indian troops battle against an estimated 15,000 Indonesians in their attempt to occupy Surabaya . . . . Molotov demands that the unanimity rule be adopted on the Far Eastern Advisory Commission, which would give any member veto power over decisions affecting Japan.
Nov. 15	Truman, Attlee and Mackenzie King announce their joint decision to share the atomic secret with other U.N. members "as soon as effective enforceable safeguards against its use for destructive purposes can be devised." . . . . The 44-nation conference in London establishes the U.N. Economic, Social and Cultural Organization.	In Dachau, Germany 40 elite guard members, including camp commander Martin Gottfried Weiss, go on trial in a military court.	British troops restore order in Tel Aviv after another outburst of rioting.		Chinese Communists close in on the Changchun airfield to prevent Nationalist landings as Soviet troops withdraw from the area.
Nov. 16	U.N. Educational, Scientific and Cultural Organization adopts a constitution in London at its closing session signed by 44 nations. Educational equality, regardless of sex, race or other distinctions is stressed.	U.S. informs Bulgaria that as a result of Mark Ethridge's report that only a single list of candidates will appear in the Nov. 18 elections and that "threats of coercion and later reprisals" are being used, it will not consider the election fair or free.	Led by the Communist Party, rebels revolt in Russian-occupied Azerbaijan, and the Teheran government charges the Russians with supporting the move.	The Mexican government settles the strike on the Southern Pacific Railroad, granting wage increases of 20¢ a day.	U.S. reports ongoing conferences with the Russians on Korea and hopes communications, trade and travel will be resumed between the northern and southern zones . . . . Lt. Gen. Albert Wedemeyer orders Marines in North China to carry out an air strafing mission against a Communist-held village on the Tangshan-Chinwangtao railway unless Red troops stop firing upon Americans.
Nov. 17		British military court at Luneberg sentences 11 to death and 19 to prison terms in the Belsen-Auschwitz concentration camp case. Among those to be executed is Josef Kramer, head of the Auschwitz camp . . . . Britain announces it will accept Hungary's diplomatic representative but without ambassadorial rank.			Nationalist delegation returns to Peking from Changchun, Manchurian capital, after failing to arrange for the landing of government troops . . . . The first peace conference between Premier Sutan Sjahrir, Acting Gov. Gen. Hubertus van Mook and Lt. Gen. Sir Philip Christison ends without result.
Nov. 18		British House of Lords approves the Bretton Woods monetary stabilization agreement . . . . Swiss major banks and Foreign Office deny charges of Nazi collaboration and defend the Bundesrat's refusal to recognize the rights of Allied control over German property in Switzerland . . . . Portuguese Premier Antonio de Oliveira Salazar's National Union Party wins elections for a new National Assembly, which is boycotted by the opposition.		Argentina's Catholic bishops issue a pastoral letter urging all Catholics to vote but not to support parties advocating religious discrimination.	Allied headquarters in Tokyo orders Japan to abolish all aviation personnel training, dissolve all civil airlines and dismantle airports throughout the nation . . . . British troops occupy Semarang in central Java.

A	B	C	D	E
Includes developments that affect more than one world region, international organizations and important meetings of major world leaders.	*Includes all domestic and regional developments in Europe, including the Soviet Union, Turkey, Cyprus and Malta.*	*Includes all domestic and regional developments in Africa and the Middle East, including Iraq and Iran and excluding Cyprus, Turkey and Afghanistan.*	*Includes all domestic and regional developments in Latin America, the Caribbean and Canada.*	*Includes all domestic and regional developments in Asian and Pacific nations, extending from Afghanistan through all the Pacific Islands, except Hawaii.*

U.S. Politics & Social Issues	U.S. Foreign Policy & Defense	U.S. Economy & Environment	Science, Technology & Nature	Culture, Leisure & Life Style	
		UAW authorizes a special board headed by R.J. Thomas to act "as it may see fit" in negotiations with GM, Ford and Chrysler.	Dr. Samuel N. Kramer of the Pennsylvania Museum announces discovery of a previously unknown heroic age in Sumer, lower Babylonia, that flourished some 5,000 years ago.		Nov. 10
	In his last report to War Secy. Patterson on the Army Air Force, Gen. Henry H. Arnold predicts that any future war will see the use of robot planes launched from space vehicles and that the U.S. should begin appropriate military defense measures . . . . House Colmer Committee recommends the reorganization of U.S. foreign economic policy directed by an under secretary for economic affairs; it adds that Russia should disclose production statistics and trade pact details before receiving U.S. aid.	Labor Secy. Schwellenbach is told by U.S. Steel head Benjamin Fairless that the OPA must permit higher ceiling prices for the steel industry.		Metropolitan Museum of Art Dir. William C. Osborn announces plans for a $10,240,000 construction program in the museum's diamond jubilee year . . . . Jerome Kern, noted song writer for stage and screen, dies at 60 in N.Y.	Nov. 11
		Senate Appropriations subcommittee votes to return U.S. Employment Service facilities to the states within 120 days after passage of legislation.		Norwegian Parliament's Nobel committee awards its 1945 Peace Prize to Cordell Hull . . . . American League announces a record paid attendance for the 1945 season of 5,580,420.	Nov. 12
Nearly 1,000 petitions are filed in San Francisco federal district court by American-born Japanese to regain their U.S. citizenship, forfeited during the war, and to bar their deportation to Japan as aliens . . . . Special counsel and a member of FDR's original "brain trust" Samuel Rosenman submits his resignation to Truman, effective Dec. 31.	Truman asks Congress for an additional $1.35 billion for UNRRA.				Nov. 13
Sen. Robert F. Wagner (D, N.Y.) introduces a new compromise housing bill, combining the FHLB, FHA and the NHA into a single unit and reducing required down payments to 5%.	Army Ground Forces Commander Gen. Jacob Devers tells a Senate committee that merging the armed forces would help eliminate competition detrimental to the services' functioning.	Maritime Commission announces plans to start construction of 11 superliners, costing nearly $25 million each and about one-third faster than present U.S. merchant ships.	*AMA Journal* reports successful treatment of scarlet fever by injecting penicillin into the muscles every three hours for seven days . . . . *Izvestia* reports Russian scientists have discovered that cosmic rays knocked protons out of lead, which may have a direct bearing on Soviet atomic research.	Baseball writers vote Chicago Cub first baseman Phil Cavarretta as the NL's most valuable player . . . . According to *Billboard*, the most popular songs are: (1) *It's Been a Long, Long Time*, (2) *Till the End of Time* and (3) *It Might as Well Be Spring*.	Nov. 14
Senate votes amendments to the agency reorganization bill, exempting 14 agencies from presidential trimming.	Joint congressional committee investigating Pearl Harbor begins hearings in Washington with the introduction of 379 pages of Japanese messages intercepted prior to the attack . . . . Eisenhower tells a House committee universal military training is "essential" to meet any "threat of aggression" and to assure "keeping the peace for which we fought."	Ford joins GM and Chrysler in opposing the UAW demand for a 30% wage increase and asks for 31 modifications in the current contract.	Nobel Prizes are awarded to Prof. Wolfgang Pauli for physics and Artturi Wirtanen for chemistry.	Nobel Prize for literature is awarded to Chilean poet Gabriela Mistral.	Nov. 15
	Eisenhower tells a Senate committee that a single defense command is essential to prevent another Pearl Harbor and effect a 25% savings in service personnel and expenses . . . . UNRRA Dir. Lehman warns a House committee that unless $1.35 billion is appropriated for the agency a new social disaster will arise on the international scene.		Escorted by a military guard, 88 German scientists arrive in N.Y.C. to work on secret national scientific projects . . . . Dr. Glenn Seaborg, a Univ. of California chemistry professor, announces the discovery of two new elements — 95 and 96 — as a result of bombarding U-238 and Plutonium 239 with high energy ions of 40 million electron volts.		Nov. 16
	Fleet Adm. Chester W. Nimitz reverses his position and now opposes a merger of the military services . . . . Chief of Naval Intelligence Rear Adm. Thomas Inglis tells the Pearl Harbor committee that on Oct. 5, 1941 Yamamoto briefed pilots on the planned attack.				Nov. 17
Upon his arrival in Washington, Ezra Pound denies he "betrayed his country" and is turned over to the Justice Dept.	Japanese special envoy to Washington prior to Pearl Harbor, Saburo Kurusu, says in Japan that a U.S. cabinet member and another influential American worked closely with Japanese diplomats in an effort to prevent war.	Price Admin. Chester Bowles announces price ceilings for 1946 model passenger cars which on the average are higher than the January 1942 levels. A Ford model which sold at $850 now has a ceiling of $882.			Nov. 18

F	G	H	I	J
Includes elections, federal-state relations, civil rights and liberties, crime, the judiciary, education, health care, poverty, urban affairs and population.	*Includes formation and debate of U.S. foreign and defense policies, veterans affairs and defense spending. (Relations with specific foreign countries are usually found under the region concerned.)*	*Includes business, labor, agriculture, taxation, transportation, consumer affairs, monetary and fiscal policy, natural resources, pollution and accidents.*	*Includes worldwide scientific, medical and technological developments, natural phenomena, U.S. weather and natural disasters.*	*Includes the arts, religion, scholarship, communications media, sports, entertainment, fashions, fads and social life.*

	World Affairs	Europe	Africa & the Middle East	The Americas	Asia & the Pacific
Nov. 19		French Constituent Assembly upholds de Gaulle's mandate to form a new government and votes that the cabinet should be made up of the three leading parties — the Socialists, Communists and Popular Republicans .... Herbert Morrison, lord president of the council, tells British Parliament that the British gas and electricity industries, transport services (except shipping) and coal mines will be nationalized during the life of the present Parliament.			MacArthur orders the arrest of 11 Japanese war leaders, including ex-Foreign Minister Yosuke Matsuoka, former Amb. to Rome Gen. Shigeru Honjo, and the "brains" of the military regime, Gen. Sadao Araki.
Nov. 20		International War Crimes Tribunal opens with the reading of indictments against 20 Nazi war leaders .... Greek Premier Panayotis Canellopoulos resigns and Regent Archbishop Damaskinos appoints Themistocles Sophoulis to form a new cabinet.	Teheran protests to Britain and the U.S. that a battalion of gendarmes sent to relieve besieged garrisons in Azerbaijan Province was turned back by the Russians at Kazvin. Russian troops are also reported moving from Kazvin towards Teheran.	Brazilian Pres. Jose Linhares suspends the mayors of all municipalities until Dec. 3 to ensure free elections scheduled for Dec. 2.	
Nov. 21		Chief American prosecutor at Nuremberg, Robert H. Jackson, makes a four-hour opening statement charging the Nazi defendants with responsibility for the war .... De Gaulle creates a coalition cabinet with the three major parties each obtaining five posts .... State Secy. Byrnes and Maurice Couve de Murville, director of the French Foreign Ministry, conclude their talks on French plans to internationalize the Ruhr and form a "sovereign" state in the Rhineland.			Defense of Gen. Tomoyuki Yamashita opens in Manila with an explanation that he commanded only 120,000 of the 300,000 troops on Luzon and a denial that he knew of any atrocities .... Chinese Nationalist troops drive 30 miles deeper into Manchuria, claiming Hingcheng and threatening the port of Hulutao .... Along with the banning of the classical Japanese masterpiece *The Forty-Seven Ronin*, which glorifies death and revenge, Allied headquarters begins screening other plays and music scores.
Nov. 22	U.S. and British Commonwealth nations open a conference on telecommunications in Hamilton, Bermuda.	An affidavit signed by former German Interior Min. Wilhelm Frick implicating Goering and the late Heinrich Himmler in the 1934 "blood purge" is presented at the Nuremberg trials .... Premier Sophoulis forms a new cabinet in Greece.	Palestinian Arab leaders form a 12-man committee to present their views to the Arab League.		Nationalist troops capture Lienshan, 10 miles from the Manchurian port of Hulutao, while other units lift the two-week Communist siege of Paotow, Suiyuan Province in northeastern China.
Nov. 23		Secret documents at Nuremberg reveal Hitler's plans to invade the U.S., to crush the Russians, and to exterminate the Poles. They also disclose how he derided Italy and Japan as allies .... State Dept. obtains confidential correspondence between Franco, Hitler and Mussolini revealing Spain's close collaboration with the Axis.		State Dept. reveals that Uruguay has proposed collective intervention by American nations to curb "violation by any republic of the elementary rights of man."	Anti-British riots continue for the third day in Calcutta in protest against the trial of Indian Army officers organized by the late Subhas Chandra Bose to help the Japanese .... In their drive on Mukden, Nationalist troops advance 35 miles and surround communist-held Chinhsien in Manchuria.
Nov. 24	U.N. 51-nation Preparatory Commission meets in London to arrange the first sessions of the General Assembly, Security Council, Economic & Social Council, Trusteeship Council, Secretariat and International Court of Justice.	After three rightist parties — the Christian Democrats, Democratic Laborites and Liberals — withdraw from his cabinet, Italian Premier Ferruccio Parri resigns.	U.S. and British send a note to Russia pointing out it has violated the Teheran Declaration by not permitting Iranian forces into Azerbaijan.	Peron supporters raid Jewish quarters of Buenos Aires, assaulting several residents and smashing shop signs without police interference.	MacArthur orders the Japanese government to abolish the military pension system and to impose a 100% war profits tax on all war industries, taxes of up to 100% in other industries and a graduated capital tax of up to 70% .... President Kim Koo of the provisional Korean government arrives in Seoul "as a private citizen to cooperate" with American military authorities in establishing order in Korea .... Nationalists capture Hulutao, their first Manchurian port .... Gen. Wedemeyer reports that U.S. troops in Manchuria to aid the Nationalists have been withdrawn at Russia's request.
Nov. 25			"National Congress" in Azerbaijan demands autonomy for the province but disclaims any intention of dividing Iran.	Women vote for the first time in Ecuador's municipal elections, in which conservatives capture most posts.	After a 35-mile advance, the Nationalists claim the capture of the Communist strongpoint of Chinhsien in Jehol Province.
Nov. 26		Results of yesterday's elections for an Austrian National Assembly give Leopold Figl's rightist Catholic People's Party at least 85 seats, the Social Democrats 77 and the Communists three. Communist press says, "We are just at the beginning of the war for Austria, and this war we will win."	In clashes with 10,000 British troops, at least nine Jews are killed and 75 injured in the Sharon Valley .... Russia proposes that the Arab-Jewish problem be submitted to the Big Five.		

A	B	C	D	E
Includes developments that affect more than one world region, international organizations and important meetings of major world leaders.	*Includes all domestic and regional developments in Europe, including the Soviet Union, Turkey, Cyprus and Malta.*	*Includes all domestic and regional developments in Africa and the Middle East, including Iraq and Iran and excluding Cyprus, Turkey and Afghanistan.*	*Includes all domestic and regional developments in Latin America, the Caribbean and Canada.*	*Includes all domestic and regional developments in Asian and Pacific nations, extending from Afghanistan through all the Pacific Islands, except Hawaii.*

U.S. Politics & Social Issues	U.S. Foreign Policy & Defense	U.S. Economy & Environment	Science, Technology & Nature	Culture, Leisure & Life Style	
Truman asks Congress for a wide-ranging national health program, including compulsory health insurance, hospital aid, maternal and child care and greater medical research .... Senate passes and sends to conference the agency reorganization bill .... Kentucky Gov. Simeon Willis appoints William Stanfill (R) to succeed A.B. Chandler as U.S. senator .... John L. Green, GOP treasurer of Arlington County, Va., appeals to the Supreme Court to declare vacant the Senate seat of ailing Carter Glass.	Zionist Organization of America approves a $51.7 million budget for 1946 to be used for immigration, land acquisition and settlement programs supported through the United Palestine Appeal.				Nov. 19
	Truman names Eisenhower as Army Chief of Staff and Adm. Chester A. Nimitz as Chief of Naval Operations to succeed Gen. Marshall and Adm. King, respectively.	UAW orders a nationwide strike against GM starting Nov. 21, charging GM with refusing arbitration of the auto industry dispute .... Senate votes against a compromise proposal to return the U.S. Employment Service to the states on June 30, 1946, a year earlier than asked by Truman.		Harvard Univ. receives a gift of $1.5 million from alumnus Thomas Lamont to build an undergraduate library.	Nov. 20
	At its closing session in Chicago the American Legion recommends a unified defense and universal military training .... Lt. Gen. Alexander M. Patch, Jr., commander of the U.S. 7th Army in Europe during WW II, dies at 56 in San Antonio.	About 180,000 UAW members strike at 80 GM plants in 20 states .... House releases two bills for floor action to restrict unions. One would bar union political activity, release companies from contracts violated by a union strike and allow companies to sue unions for damages suffered during strikes. The other bill would prevent labor interference with interstate transport.	Head of the Micro-Biological Institute of the Academy of Sciences in Moscow, Nikolai Krassilnikov, reports the development of a new drug, "aspergillin," useful in treating diphteria.	Novelist Ellen Glasgow, who won the 1942 Pulitzer Prize for *In This Our Life*, dies at 71 in Richmond, Va. .... Robert Benchley, humorist and screen actor, dies at 56 in N.Y. .... Baseball writers elect Detroit Tiger pitcher Hal Newhouser as the AL's most valuable player for 1945.	Nov. 21
	Eisenhower pleads to a House committee for an appropriation of $1.35 billion to UNRRA if "our military victory is to have lasting significance."		Northrop Aircraft reveals its JBIA, a jet-propelled buzz bomb with a 30-foot wing spread, which when catapulted can travel at 220 m.p.h. carrying two tons of explosives inside its wings.	Americans celebrate their first peacetime Thanksgiving in four years.	Nov. 22
	Former State Secy. Cordell Hull tells the Pearl Harbor Committee that on Nov. 7, 1941 he warned FDR that the nation should be prepared for a Japanese attack anytime and anyplace.	Agriculture Secy. Clinton Anderson announces the end of rationing of meat, fats and oils, canned fish and other red-point foods. He says that sugar will probably have to remain under control into 1946.			Nov. 23
	Sumner Welles reveals at the Pearl Harbor inquiry that Churchill twice urged FDR to warn the Japanese that further Pacific aggression would mean war.	NAM's representative to the labor-management conference in Washington says industry is ready to forego lockouts and unfair labor practices but charges that labor is unwilling to forego strikes, boycotts and other "weapons of industrial warfare."	Navy reports a "complete cure" for cholera through the proper use of blood plasma and sulfadiazine and saline solution.		Nov. 24
					Nov. 25
Atty. Gen. Clark says Ezra Pound has been indicted a second time on 19 counts for treason on charges of receiving payment from fascist Italy for propaganda broadcasts during the war .... House Appropriations Comm. omits flood control and navigation funds from the current spending bill, recommending "further investigation."	Senate opens debate on the U.N. Participation Act, whereby the U.S. would become an active member .... A House committee reports out a $1.35 million UNRRA bill .... Former U.S. Amb. to Japan Joseph Grew tells the Pearl Harbor inquiry that Hull's Nov. 26, 1941 message to Japan "touched the button that started the war." .... Navy Secy. Forrestal urges adoption of a universal military training bill .... Rep. Hugh De Lacy (D. Wash.) introduces a resolution asking Truman to recall all U.S. aid from China immediately.	Retail Workers union's "national demonstration" against Montgomery Ward begins in branches throughout the country, and the union claims 75-80% effectiveness, while the company reports that 92% of its employes are at work.		Mrs. Bess Truman and daughter Margaret attend the season's opening of the Metropolitan Opera to hear Wagner's *Lohengrin*.	Nov. 26
F *Includes elections, federal-state relations, civil rights and liberties, crime, the judiciary, education, health care, poverty, urban affairs and population.*	G *Includes formation and debate of U.S. foreign and defense policies, veterans affairs and defense spending. (Relations with specific foreign countries are usually found under the region concerned.)*	H *Includes business, labor, agriculture, taxation, transportation, consumer affairs, monetary and fiscal policy, natural resources, pollution and accidents.*	I *Includes worldwide scientific, medical and technological developments, natural phenomena, U.S. weather and natural disasters.*	J *Includes the arts, religion, scholarship, communications media, sports, entertainment, fashions, fads and social life.*	

	World Affairs	Europe	Africa & the Middle East	The Americas	Asia & the Pacific
Nov. 27		Due to leftist opposition, WWI Italian Premier Vittorio Emanuel Orlando fails to form a new cabinet.			
Nov. 28		Austrian Chancellor Karl Renner's provisional government resigns.		Panamanian National Assembly approves a resolution to begin inter-American discussions on breaking relations with the "authoritarian" governments of Nicaragua, Honduras and the Dominican Republic.	
Nov. 29	Truman tells reporters he does not favor further Big Three conferences, since the U.N. will soon be in a position to take over issues growing out of the war .... International Women's Congress in Paris establishes the Women's International Democratic Federation with permanent headquarters there .... Attlee reports that British Empire battle casualties during the war totaled 1,246,025 with 353,652 killed .... The radio-cable conference in Bermuda agrees on a 30¢-a-word ceiling on cables to all points in U.S. and British territory, effective April 1, 1946.	Constituent Assembly proclaims the "Federal People's Republic of Yugoslavia" and abolishes the Karageorgevitch monarchy headed by King Peter II .... Films of 12 concentration camps are shown to the Nazi defendants at Nuremberg.	Truman modifies his earlier support for a Palestine Jewish commonwealth, favoring formation of an Anglo-American fact-finding commission to study the Palestinian question .... Iranian Amb. to the U.S. Hussein Ala says Russia has rejected Iran's request to send troops into Azerbaijan to put down the rebellion.		Gen. Yamashita denies he knew of the atrocities committed under his command and says he would have punished the perpetrators had he known .... Moscow radio reports that Russia has agreed to the Chinese request that Russian troop withdrawals from Manchuria be deferred until Nationalist forces are able to take over.
Nov. 30		Rudolf Hess announces that he is sane, saying that he has been faking amnesia and that he is ready to go on trial .... Allied Control Council bans military training, war veterans' organizations and parades in Germany .... Alcide de Gasperi, Christian Democrat, is chosen premier in Italy by the six-party National Liberation Comm.			Field Marshal Count Juichi Terauchi, Japanese commander in Southeast Asia, surrenders to Mountbatten in Rangoon .... An earthquake and tidal wave cost 400 lives in Pasni, India.
Dec. 1		German Gen. Anton Dostler is executed by a U.S. Army firing squad in Aversa, Italy .... British arrest 76 German steel industrialists for investigation and possible trial.			Russia rejects Iranian charges of interference in Azerbaijan as its troops complete evacuation of Teheran. .... Gen. Wedemeyer reveals Chinese Nationalists are still receiving U.S. arms under Lend-Lease .... Liu Shao-chi, Chinese CP Politiburo member, tells reporters that the party's program is one of democratic capitalism .... American Military Government's department of investigation reveals that Japanese officials took millions of dollars from the Koreans towards the end of the war.
Dec. 2		French Constituent Assembly votes to nationalize the Bank of France and four other major banks .... Albanian Premier Enver Hoxha's Democratic Front Party, the only slate in the election, wins all 32 seats and 95% of the vote for a Constituent Assembly.			MacArthur's headquarters orders arrest of 59 Japanese generals, admirals and government figures as war criminal suspects. Among those arrested is Prince Morimasa Nashimoto, brother of former Premier Higashi-Kuni and a relative of the Emperor.
Dec. 3	Dr. Vannevar Bush tells a Senate committee that the A-bomb "means the end of world war."	Britain proposes that the four armies occupying Austria sharply reduce their forces and recognize the country's 1937 frontiers.	Arab League announces its seven member states will boycott all Jewish-produced goods from Palestine beginning Jan. 1 .... State Dept. discloses Russia has rejected a U.S. proposal for the Allies to withdraw their troops from Iran by Jan. 1.	A bill to increase Export Credit Act loans from $100 to $750 million is introduced in the Canadian House of Commons; most of the loans are for war-ravaged Europe.	Japanese CP completes its first national congress in 19 years and urges an end to the monarchy.

U.S. Politics & Social Issues	U.S. Foreign Policy & Defense	U.S. Economy & Environment	Science, Technology & Nature	Culture, Leisure & Life Style	
	Patrick J. Hurley resigns as ambassador to China, charging that U.S. global policy is failing due to weak foreign service officers; Truman names Gen. George C. Marshall as Hurley's replacement . . . . Sen. Burton Wheeler (D, Mont.) argues against the U.N. Participation Act, charging the organization's principles have been compromised by appeasement of Russia.			World famous Spanish mural painter Jose Maria Sert dies at 69 in Barcelona.	Nov. 27
	Resolutions are introduced in both houses of Congress to investigate Hurley's charges that some State Dept. officials sought to undermine U.S. policy in China . . . . Navy Secy. Forrestal offers a substitute merger plan providing for a National Security Council, Joint Chiefs of Staff and a "Chief of Staff" to the president, along with centralized research and intelligence agencies . . . . Telegrams from U.S. diplomats in Latin America are introduced at the Pearl Harbor hearings, showing that Japanese representatives there were predicting war with the U.S. between April and December 1941.	CIO-USW members vote to strike the steel industry to enforce their demand for a $2 daily wage increase.			Nov. 28
	Pearl Harbor inquiry learns that Hawaiian commanding Gen. Walter G. Short did not receive intercepted Japanese messages bearing on the Pearl Harbor attack.			*Strange Fruit*, a play adapted by Lillian and Esther Smith from the former's novel, opens in N.Y.	Nov. 29
	Evidence is introduced at the Pearl Harbor hearings that Adm. Harold R. Stark, then Chief of Naval Operations, sent two warnings to Adm. Kimmel regarding possible Japanese actions on Nov. 27 and Dec. 3.	Labor-management conference ends in Washington with agreement on the use of arbitration in contracts with no-strike, no-lockout clauses and the strengthening of the U.S. Conciliation Service . . . . House passes a deficiency appropriations bill of $1,435,267,312, adding $122,275,000 for flood control and navigation projects.	A two-day storm in New England causes 34 deaths and heavy property damage.		Nov. 30
				Glenn Davis and 'Doc' Blanchard lead Army to a 32-13 victory over Navy before 102,000 football fans, including Truman . . . . Paramount release of *The Lost Weekend*, featuring Ray Milland, premiers in New York.	Dec. 1
Alabama Public Service Commission orders 15 railroads to post segregation laws in every passenger car following complaints against non-segregation . . . . Twenty-five state medical societies reveal a voluntary health insurance program as an alternative to the compulsory federal plan proposed by Truman.			Dr. Ernest O. Lawrence says the Berkeley cyclotron will be converted to produce radioactive substances for use in treatment of cancer and other diseases.		Dec. 2
Charles Houston, Negro member of the FEPC, resigns to protest Truman's refusal to allow issuance of a decision ordering Capitol Transit Co. to stop anti-Negro discrimination.	Navy opens the court-martial of Capt. Charles B. McVay 3rd, charged with "culpable negligence" for not zigzagging the cruiser *Indianapolis* through an enemy submarine area and failure to issue an abandon-ship order.	Truman proposes legislation empowering him to name fact-finding boards to investigate important labor disputes and to bar strikes and lockouts for up to 30 days in vital industries.		Felix 'Doc' Blanchard, Army's fullback, is awarded the Heisman Memorial Trophy as 1945's outstanding football player.	Dec. 3

F	G	H	I	J
Includes elections, federal-state relations, civil rights and liberties, crime, the judiciary, education, health care, poverty, urban affairs and population.	*Includes formation and debate of U.S. foreign and defense policies, veterans affairs and defense spending. (Relations with specific foreign countries are usually found under the region concerned.)*	*Includes business, labor, agriculture, taxation, transportation, consumer affairs, monetary and fiscal policy, natural resources, pollution and accidents.*	*Includes worldwide scientific, medical and technological developments, natural phenomena, U.S. weather and natural disasters.*	*Includes the arts, religion, scholarship, communications media, sports, entertainment, fashions, fads and social life.*

	World Affairs	Europe	Africa & the Middle East	The Americas	Asia & the Pacific
Dec. 4	Eight countries sign an executive pact cutting international communications rates at the radio-cable conference in Bermuda.	Sir Hartley Shawcross, chief British prosecutor at Nuremberg, opens the British case against the Nazis, charging the defendants with planning and waging wars of aggression .... Norwegian court convicts Albert Hagelin, Quisling's interior minister, of treason and sentences him to be shot .... Berlin city government bans several books and works of specific authors as Nazi propaganda; U.S. military government protests that the list is incomplete .... Austrian Political Council elects Leopold Figl, whose Catholic People's Party won the election of Nov. 25, as chancellor to succeed Karl Renner .... Anti-Communist rioters wreck two newspaper plants and two book stores in Istanbul, Turkey.			British government announces its decision to send an all-party parliamentary group to discuss an offer of dominion status with Indian leaders .... U.S. Marines shell a village near Anshan, China after villagers refuse to surrender two Chinese gunmen who killed a Marine and wounded another.
Dec. 5	A U.S.-British agreement is reported on a $375 one-way plane fare between New York and London. (Pan Am has already cut its fare from $572 to $275.)	Byrnes says U.S. may urge Big Three to centralize administration in their German zones without the French if France continues to insist on a permanent separation of the Ruhr, Saar and Rhineland as a precondition to German reunification. .... French Constituent Assembly's constitution commission votes, 22 to 18, for a single-house legislature for the Fourth Republic .... British Foreign Secy. Bevin is cheered in the House of Commons when he says "we detest the regime" of Generalissimo Franco in Spain.		Pan American Union elects Brazilian Amb. Carlos M. Pereria de Souza as chairman of its governing board .... State Dept. discloses that representations have been made to Argentina on its failure to deport 71 Nazi agents as promised to the U.S.	
Dec. 6		Truman and Attlee announce a $4.4-billion loan agreement under which the U.S. waives repayment of $25 billion in Lend-Lease .... Actor Maurice Chevalier is acquitted of charges of collaborating with the Germans by the National Committee of the Theatrical Purge.	Iranian troops in Tabriz radio that rebels have surrounded the Azerbaijan capitol.	Ninety-four Axis agents are reported to have evaded deportation from Argentina through court action, illness, escape or government negligence.	MacArthur orders the arrest of Prince Fumimaro Konoye, former Japanese premier, and eight others as war criminals .... Nationalist troops halt within 25 miles of Mukden after advancing from the Chinese border opposed, and wait for negotiations with the Russians to be completed before proceding.
Dec. 7	State Dept. announces the Big Three foreign ministers will meet in Moscow on Dec. 15 to discuss atomic energy and other international issues.	State Dept. announces plans to resettle 6.6 million Germans from eastern Europe in the U.S. and Soviet zones of Germany within the next eight months .... According to evidence introduced at the war crimes trial, Hitler planned a full-scale campaign in the West through the Low Countries to start Nov. 7, 1939 but was delayed until May by bad weather.		Brazilian President Jose Linhares orders all publications under federal and state control sold at public auction within 30 days.	Gen. Tomoyuki Yamashita, Japanese commander in the Philippines, is convicted by a U.S. Military Commission of condoning atrocities and is sentenced to death; he immediately appeals to the U.S. Supreme Court .... U.S. Reparations Commissioner Pauley recommends that Japan be stripped of all assets abroad and most domestic heavy industry.
Dec. 8				Peronistas fire into a mass meeting of the Democratic Union in Buenos Aires, Argentina, killing four and wounding 40.	MacArthur orders trial of Lt. Gen. Masaharu Homma, who oversaw the "Death March" from Bataan, and four other Japanese commanders in the Philippines.
Dec. 9		Gen. George S. Patton Jr. suffers a fractured vertabra when an Army truck crashes into his car near Mannheim, Germany .... A Rumanian court sentences former Education Minister Ferenc Rainess to death for treason.		Peron is reported to have protected important Argentine businessmen suspected of being enemy agents .... Argentine Army-Navy court sentences former President Arturo Rawson and Gen. Osvaldo Martin to prison for inciting the Sept. 25 Cordoba rebellion.	A British female Red Cross worker and an Army major are reportedly killed by Indonesians near Padang, Sumatra.
Dec. 10		Italian Premier Alcide de Gasperi and his six-party cabinet, the sixth since the Allied invasion, are sworn in .... Allied Control Council allots 26 industrial plants in western Germany (value $92 million) to 19 Allied nations as reparations.	Truman names six U.S. members to the British-American committee of inquiry on Palestine, and London announces the six British members.	Peron is married to Eva Duarte in a La Plata church; they were wed civilly Oct 18 .... Argentine appeals court upholds the dismissal of a government suit against *New York Times* correspondent Arnaldo Cortesi, which charged him with writing insulting articles about Peron.	MacArthur orders the Japanese government to submit a land reform plan before March 15, 1946 .... RAF planes destroy the village of Chibadak, Java, where a convoy was ambushed by Indonesians the night before with 20 killed and 65 wounded .... Chungking reports 120,000 Communists have been attacking Lincheng on the Tientsin-Pukow railroad for 13 days.

A	B	C	D	E
Includes developments that affect more than one world region, international organizations and important meetings of major world leaders.	*Includes all domestic and regional developments in Europe, including the Soviet Union, Turkey, Cyprus and Malta.*	*Includes all domestic and regional developments in Africa and the Middle East, including Iraq and Iran and excluding Cyprus, Turkey and Afghanistan.*	*Includes all domestic and regional developments in Latin America, the Caribbean and Canada.*	*Includes all domestic and regional developments in Asian and Pacific nations, extending from Afghanistan through all the Pacific Islands, except Hawaii.*

U.S. Politics & Social Issues	U.S. Foreign Policy & Defense	U.S. Economy & Environment	Science, Technology & Nature	Culture, Leisure & Life Style	
	Senate passes, 65-7, the U.N. participation bill . . . . House passes a bill authorizing a postwar Navy of 666,000; Navy Secy. Forrestal announces a naval reorganization stressing aviation . . . . FDR's message to Philippine High Commissioner Francis Sayre, dated Nov. 26, 1941, is introduced at the Pearl Harbor inquiry. The message warns of war and indicates possible Japanese movement into Southeast Asia.	CIO President Murray charges Truman has "appeased" industry and opposes his fact-finding proposal because it aims at weakening unions and curtailing the right to strike.	TWA Lockheed Constellation sets a commercial aviation record of 12 hrs., 57 mins. on its first flight from Washington to Paris . . . . Dr. Thomas Hunt Morgan, biologist and winner of the 1933 Nobel Prize, dies at 79 in Pasadena, Calif.	Friends of the World Council of Churches receives a $1 million gift from John D. Rockefeller, Jr. to help finance "religious reconstruction" in Europe.	Dec. 4
	Gen. Patrick Hurley appears before the Senate Foreign Relations Comm., accusing the State Department's "China hands" of "sabotaging" his work with the Chinese Nationalist government . . . . U.S. Treasury lifts curbs on financial transactions with all foreign countries except enemy states and six former neutrals . . . . Twenty-seven Navy airmen in six planes disappear in the Bermuda Triangle area off the Florida coast. The Navy begins a major search.	OPA Chief Bowles predicts inflation "followed by a shattering smash-up" if price controls are not maintained and extended to 1947 . . . . Ira Mosher, NAM president, supports Truman's new labor policy with reservations.		Former Archbishop of York and Canterbury, Lord Cosmo Gordon Lang, dies at 81 in London.	Dec. 5
	Gen. Hurley charges Dean Acheson, now under secretary of state, with responsibility for "defeating" and "destroying" U.S. policy toward Iran but refuses to offer specific evidence . . . . Gen. Marshall testifies at the Pearl Harbor hearings that he did not anticipate an attack on Pearl but that an "alert" defense would have prevented all but "limited harm."	GM renews its offer of a 10% wage increase, and the UAW rejects it at resumption of negotiations in Detroit.	U.S. intelligence expert tells a Senate committee that German scientists were trying to build a "uranium machine" for power generation purposes and not for an atomic bomb.		Dec. 6
	Byrnes tells a Senate committee U.S. policy is to encourage Chinese Nationalists to broaden their government to include "so-called Communists" and defends career officials against Hurley's charges.				Dec. 7
	Adm. Ernest J. King asserts that a service merger under a single chief of staff would ruin the Navy's effectiveness.	UAW rejects Truman's appeal to end its 18-day GM strike and denounces his legislative proposals . . . . Sidney Hillman, president of the Amalgamated Clothing Workers, announces union ratification of a contract with shirt manufacturers for a 20% wage increase plus benefits affecting workers in 32 states.			Dec. 8
			Dr. Ernest O. Lawrence says a new 4,000-ton supercyclotron is being built at Berkeley to be ready in 1946, which will permit artificial production of cosmic rays and production of atomic energy from iron and other sources cheaper than uranium.	Network Hooper Rating reports Bob Hope, Fibber McGee and Molly, Radio Theater and Walter Winchell lead the list of popular shows.	Dec. 9
	Dean Acheson denies Hurley's charges of wrecking U.S. policy in Iran . . . . Reps. May and Vinson introduce bills to create a separate Air Force with cabinet-level civilian secretary and a U.S. Aviation Academy . . . . Gen. Marshall gives evidence of Japanese troop movement via ships into the South China Sea at the end of November 1941 during the Pearl Harbor hearings.	UMW President John L. Lewis criticizes Truman's proposal for government fact-finding commissions in important labor disputes, calling it "the first step" towards an "absolute state to regulate the liberties of all citizens." . . . . UAW offers Ford a no-strike, no lock-out "security" plan.			Dec. 10

F	G	H	I	J
Includes elections, federal-state relations, civil rights and liberties, crime, the judiciary, education, health care, poverty, urban affairs and population.	*Includes formation and debate of U.S. foreign and defense policies, veterans affairs and defense spending. (Relations with specific foreign countries are usually found under the region concerned.)*	*Includes business, labor, agriculture, taxation, transportation, consumer affairs, monetary and fiscal policy, natural resources, pollution and accidents.*	*Includes worldwide scientific, medical and technological developments, natural phenomena, U.S. weather and natural disasters.*	*Includes the arts, religion, scholarship, communications media, sports, entertainment, fashions, fads and social life.*

	World Affairs	Europe	Africa & the Middle East	The Americas	Asia & the Pacific
Dec. 11	Byrnes says he will urge calling a general peace conference and creation of a U.N. commission on atomic energy at the Moscow foreign ministers meeting.	Byrnes outlines U.S. German occupation aims: increase coal exports to liberated countries, prevent mass starvation, reach agreement on industrial reparations and speed up organization of German administration in production and trade .... A memorandum from Rosenberg's files introduced at the Nuremberg trial shows Hitler ordered the seizure of 40,000 to 50,000 Polish and Russian youths between 10 and 14 in 1944 for shipment to Germany to work as apprentices.		Attlee tells British House of Commons that Newfoundland, which lost dominion status in 1933 when it failed to meet debts, has regained the right of self-rule and a national assembly will be elected soon .... The election of Gen. Eurico Gaspar Dutra as Brazil's new president is announced.	All-Indian Congress working committee adopts resolutions reiterating its faith in non-violence and praising the pro-Japanese "Indian National Army." .... Nationalist radio station of Java declares "we are determined to annihilate" all Dutch troops "even if we have to poison them to death."
Dec. 12		According to evidence introduced at the Nuremberg trials, Himmler ordered political prisoners to be "worked to death" in September 1942 .... Dutch fascist leader Anton Mussert is convicted of treason and sentenced to death in the Netherlands .... Lazio Budinszy, justice minister in Szalasi's cabinet, is sentenced to death as a war criminal in Hungary.	Iranian Premier Hakimi tells Parliament he plans to go to Moscow soon to discuss the Azerbaijan revolt.	Venezuelan President Romulo Betancourt says 168 Venezuelan millionaires will be tried and deprived of their property if it is found they obtained it through "dictatorial" means.	Chinese Nationalist troops move into Manchurian cities of Mukden and Changchun under an agreement with the Russians.
Dec. 13	State Dept. is reported to have invited 14 countries to a preliminary meeting for the International Trade Conference to discuss reciprocal lowering of tariffs.	British House of Commons approves the Anglo-American loan agreement and Bretton Woods Monetary Stabilization Agreement .... Thirty-six convicted yesterday for atrocities at the Dachau concentration camp are sentenced to death and four are given long prison terms by a U.S. military court .... Gen. Henri-Fernand Dentz, French collaborationist whose death sentence was recently commuted to life by de Gaulle, dies at 74 in Paris.	Britain and France sign an agreement to withdraw their troops from Lebanon and Syria and to collaborate in the Near East.		Australian military court convicts 11 Japanese for crucifying three Australian airmen and one American. Three Japanese officers are sentenced to death by a U.S. military court at Kwajalein for killing U.S. airmen.
Dec. 14	Byrnes arrives in Moscow for the foreign ministers meeting .... CAB approves British restrictions on U.S.-London flights to 14 weekly by American lines.	An affidavit introduced at Nuremberg trials claims the Nazis had killed 6,000,000 Jews by August 1944.		Peron officially declares himself a candidate for the presidency at a mass meeting in Buenos Aires .... Colombian President Alberto Lleras Camargo is reported to have freed 25 army officers and officials serving prison terms for the July 1944 revolt.	
Dec. 15	U.N. Preparatory Commission votes 80 to 14 to establish U.N. headquarters in the U.S.	Abel Hermant, 83, a member of the French Academy, is sentenced to life imprisonment in Paris for collaboration .... Count Fidel Palfy, Szalasi's agriculture minister, is sentenced to death in Hungary.			Truman bars U.S. military intervention in Chinese internal strife and urges an end to hostilities between Nationalists and Communists and a national conference of major political elements to bring about "the unification of China."
Dec. 16	Byrnes, Bevin and Molotov hold their first conference in Moscow.		Moscow radio announces a revolutionary "National Government of Iranian Azerbaijan" has been established in Tabriz.	Venezuelan President Betancourt promises "audacious" development of the oil industry .... Reports indicate that more than 100 persons were arrested in Asuncion, Paraguay to stem a revolt against the Morinigo regime.	MacArthur orders the Japanese government to end all financial support of state Shinto and abolish the teaching of Shinto in state schools; he also forbids the propagation of the doctrine that the Emperor is of divine origin .... Prince Konoye commits suicide at home during the night by taking poison; he was to be tried as a war criminal.
Dec. 17	In a Washington speech, Charles A. Lindbergh urges "a world organization backed by military power" and guided by "Christian ideals" to prevent the misuse of power as exemplified by Nazi Germany.	Nuremberg prosecution asks the Tribunal to declare the entire Nazi leadership corps guilty of war crimes and its 500,000 members subject to punishment.		Mackenzie King says Canada has protested against being excluded from peace talks.	Maj. Gen. Archer Lerch, newly appointed military governor of Korea, declares he will continue the U.S. program of establishing a free Korean government and then withdrawing troops.
Dec. 18		Allied Council approves the new Austrian coalition cabinet after Chancellor Figl drops three members accused by the Russians of having fascist connections .... House of Lords dismisses William (Lord Haw Haw) Joyce's appeal of his death sentence for treason.		U.S. Ambassador to Mexico is ordered to investigate charges by a Mexican labor leader that certain U.S. companies have smuggled arms to a rival union.	State Dept. admits the decision to send British troops to Java was made by the Anglo-American combined chiefs of staff.

A	B	C	D	E
Includes developments that affect more than one world region, international organizations and important meetings of major world leaders.	*Includes all domestic and regional developments in Europe, including the Soviet Union, Turkey, Cyprus and Malta.*	*Includes all domestic and regional developments in Africa and the Middle East, including Iraq and Iran and excluding Cyprus, Turkey and Afghanistan.*	*Includes all domestic and regional developments in Latin America, the Caribbean and Canada.*	*Includes all domestic and regional developments in Asian and Pacific nations, extending from Afghanistan through all the Pacific Islands, except Hawaii.*

U.S. Politics & Social Issues	U.S. Foreign Policy & Defense	U.S. Economy & Environment	Science, Technology & Nature	Culture, Leisure & Life Style	
Senate votes for a $700,000,000 federal aid bill for hospital and health center construction in the next five years .... U.S. Education Commissioner John Studebaker reports college and university enrollment this fall reached 950,000, up 200,000 from 1944, compared to with the 1,400,000 peak in 1939.	Senate Foreign Relations Committee concludes investigation of Gen. Hurley's charges without making any recommendations.	House blocks, 200 to 182, consideration of a bill to penalize unions for violating no-strike contracts and barring unions from contributing to political activities .... Steel workers union threatens a nationwide strike if its $2-a-day wage demand is not met.		Pacific Coast League's demand that it be recognized as a third major baseball circuit is rejected at the Chicago major league meeting.	Dec. 11
Truman adopts a housing program prepared by Reconversion Director John Snyder and appoints Wilson Wyatt as housing expeditor.	Senate Foreign Relations Committee approves a resolution urging U.S. aid in opening Palestine to the Jews.	Atty. Gen. Tom Clark opens a new drive to smash the nationwide black market in clothing, textiles and allied products .... Truman names a fact-finding board for the GM-UAW dispute despite labor opposition .... Treasury reports the top incomes in the 1944 fiscal year, with Louis Mayer again heading the list with $908,070. Others include: Charles Wilson (GM) with $459,041; Thomas Watson with $425,548, Fred MacMurray with $419,166, and Walter Wanger with 409,928.		Baseball Commissioner Chandler votes with the National League against the American League not to restrict night games .... Tommy Manville Jr., 51, weds Georgina Campbell, 27, in Larchmont, N.Y. It is his eighth marriage and her first.	Dec. 12
Senate and House pass a compromise government reorganization bill, exempting many federal regulatory agencies from restructuring by the President.			Public Health Service reports 49,694 new influenza cases for the week ending Dec. 8, compared with 13,220 the week before.	Pope Pius XII, in a letter commemorating the 400th anniversary of the Council of Trent, urges non-Catholic Christians to return to the Roman Catholic faith .... Chief Justice Harlan Stone accepts custody of some 200 paintings brought to the U.S. from German museums on behalf of the National Gallery of Art.	Dec. 13
Senate defeats a temporary 33% salary increase for members of Congress.	Adm. Halsey parades through New York and calls for a "strong, healthy national defense," but he insists the "merger [of armed service commands] will not achieve it." .... Four staff members of the Pearl Harbor congressional committee announce their resignations because of the slow pace of the investigation.	House passes, 254 to 126, a less sweeping version of the Senate's "full employment" bill; the House version deletes the statement that the government will "assure" jobs for all.		American Society of Newspaper Editors creates a standing committee on world freedom of news .... *Dream Girl*, a play by Elmer Rice, featuring Wendell Corey and Betty Field, opens to favorable reviews in New York.	Dec. 14
	Gen. Marshall leaves Washington for his post in China in an effort to bring the Nationalists and Communists together in a viable government .... Senate passes a $2.4-billion emergency appropriation bill providing funds for UNRRA and expanded veterans housing.	U.S. District Court in Trenton, N.J. fines a group of drug and chemical companies and executives $52,000 for violating the Sherman Antitrust Act.		The top three songs based on sales and broadcasts are: (1) *It's Been a Long, Long, Time*, (2) *Chickery Chick* and (3) *It Might As Well Be Spring*, according to *Billboard*.	Dec. 15
		Navy announces that Sinclair Oil Co. has granted an 18% wage increase with a 40-hour week to the CIO United Oil Workers; the Navy will return the company's 11 properties, seized Oct. 5, on Dec. 17.	American Chemical Society reports discovery of a new sulfa drug, metachloride, which may surpass atabrine and quinine in treating malaria.	*New York Herald Tribune* reports *The Black Rose* by Thomas Costain and *Up Front* by Bill Mauldin are, respectively, the best-selling fiction and nonfiction books .... Cleveland Rams defeat the Washington Redskins, 15-14, in Cleveland to win the NFL title.	Dec. 16
Truman orders FEPC to investigate discrimination against displaced war workers seeking peacetime jobs, following a report by FEPC Chairman Malcolm Ross of widespread racial and religious discrimination.	Senate passes the UNRRA fund bill and the Wagner-Taft resolution urging free entry of Jews into Palestine and establishment of a Jewish Commonwealth .... The AAF reveals details of its six-engine Consolidated-Vultee XB-36, which will weigh over 125 tons and have a 5,000-mile radius and a 3,650 hp engine.			*New York World Telegram* selects, via a poll, Bo McMillin of Indiana Univ. as college football coach of 1945.	Dec. 17
Senate passes a bill providing an 11% pay increase, totaling $200 million, for more than 1,000,000 federal employes.	Sumner Welles tells the Pearl Harbor hearings that FDR agreed with Churchill on warning Japan against further aggression in August 1941 in hopes of gaining 30 days' time.	UAW rejects a Ford offer of a 15¢ hourly increase, in return for which the union would have to guarantee elimination of work stoppages, reduction in the number of union committeemen and other concessions.	A total lunar eclipse, visible to North America for the first time since 1942, occurs at 8:40 p.m. EST.	Boxing Writers Assn. at N.Y. announces its selection of Joe Lewis as world heavyweight champion and Billy Conn as the number one challenger in the 1945 rankings.	Dec. 18

F	G	H	I	J
Includes elections, federal-state relations, civil rights and liberties, crime, the judiciary, education, health care, poverty, urban affairs and population.	*Includes formation and debate of U.S. foreign and defense policies, veterans affairs and defense spending. (Relations with specific foreign countries are usually found under the region concerned.)*	*Includes business, labor, agriculture, taxation, transportation, consumer affairs, monetary and fiscal policy, natural resources, pollution and accidents.*	*Includes worldwide scientific, medical and technological developments, natural phenomena, U.S. weather and natural disasters.*	*Includes the arts, religion, scholarship, communications media, sports, entertainment, fashions, fads and social life.*

	World Affairs	Europe	Africa & the Middle East	The Americas	Asia & the Pacific
Dec. 19	Byrnes and Bevin confer separately with Stalin after meeting with Molotov .... Soviet press urges the creation of an international tribunal to judge "internationally dangerous newspaper crimes" such as slandering "peace-loving" states.	House of Commons passes the third reading of the bill nationalizing the Bank of England and receives a bill nationalizing coal mines .... John Amery, 33, son of Leopold S. Amery, former state secretary for India, is hanged as a traitor in London.			State Dept. urges all parties in the NEI to resume peace negotiations and reach a settlement based on the Charter and Declaration of the U.N. .... French colonial troops land at Haiphong, Indochina.
Dec. 20	The Netherlands, Costa Rica and Belgium approve the Bretton Woods agreement.	Moscow newspapers publish articles demanding that Turkey relinquish a 180-mile strip of Black Sea coast below Batum, held by Russia from 1878 to 1921. Turkish leaders declare they will fight if Russia tries to take the Dardanelles or the Kars Plateau by force .... Austrian National Assembly elects Karl Renner, a Socialist, as president of the second Austrian republic.		Argentine government orders a general 10-25% wage increase and year-end bonus for lower-bracket workers, as press dispatches call the action a Peron election move.	Gen. Marshall arrives in Shanghai and confers with Gen. Wedemeyer.
Dec. 21		Gen. George S. Patton Jr., former commander of the U.S. 3rd Army who led his troops to victory in North Africa and Sicily and who was described by Nazi generals as the field commander they feared most, dies at 60 in Heidelberg from complications following an automobile accident .... Inter-Allied Reparations Commission completes plans for payment of reparations by Germany, with the U.S. receiving 28% of German assets abroad and 11.8% of German assets at home .... Army Inspector Gen. Jean de Lattre de Tassigny reports that the French postwar army will total 500,000 men.			MacArthur announces that further directives to the Japanese government will probably be limited to implementing reforms already ordered.
Dec. 22		Britain and the U.S. recognize the new Yugoslavian Republic and the ending of King Peter's reign.		Panamanian government arrests former Pres. Arnulfo Arias on charges of instigating a revolt in Colon.	
Dec. 23	State Secy. Byrnes, Amb. Harriman and Charles Bohlen confer with Stalin in Moscow and then with Molotov and Bevin.		Sumner Welles says the U.N. Trusteeship Council should be given responsibility for establishing a Jewish Commonwealth in Palestine.	Clashes between Padillistas and supporters of government-sponsored presidential candidate Miguel Aleman in Cuernavaca, Mexico and nearby towns result in three deaths and 86 injuries.	Gen. Marshall confers with Communist leaders Chou En-lai, Yeh Chieh-ying and Tung Pih-wu .... Indonesians agree to help the British disarm the Japanese and get them to Javanese ports for evacuation.
Dec. 24	Big Three Foreign Ministers agree, subject to French and Chinese approval, on drawing up peace treaties with Italy, Rumania, Bulgaria, Hungary and Finland.				War Crimes Investigation Commission compiles a list of Japanese atrocities in Java, resulting in the arrest of 43 persons .... New Zealand P.M. Peter Fraser tells reporters in Washington that the U.S. should surrender ultimate authority over Japan to a commission representing all nations that fought in the Pacific.
Dec. 25	Chinese give their assent to the proposed peace treaties with Axis states as suggested at the Moscow Conference.	French finance ministry announces a devaluation of the franc to a rate of 119.107 to the dollar.		Gen. Damaso Arenas is named commander in chief of the Bolivian Army.	A U.S. Naval court condemns 11 Japanese officers to hang for the mass execution of 96 U.S. airmen on Kwajalein in October 1943 .... Nationalist Gen. Tu Li-ming begins a drive to clear Jehol Province west of Lianoning of Communist troops and is moving in on Mukden.
Dec. 26		French Constituent Assembly votes approval of the Bretton Woods Agreements, the U.S. Import-Export Bank credit and devaluation of the franc.		Truman names Fiorello H. La Guardia as his personal representative with ambassadorial rank at Gen. Eurico Dutra's inauguration as Brazilian president.	A delegation of the 10-nation Far Eastern Commission leaves Washington for Japan .... A Netherlands Eurasian soldier fails in an assassination attempt upon Indonesian Republic Premier Sutan Sjahrir.
Dec. 27	Representatives of the U.S., Britain and Russia, meeting in Moscow, conclude an agreement providing for establishment of an Allied Council in Japan, democratic government in Korea and unification of China under the Nationalist regime .... Bretton Woods agreements to set up the IMF and Bank for Reconstruction and Development are formally signed by 28 nations in Washington.	Turkish National Assembly votes confidence in Premier Sukru Saracoglu after he declares that Turkey will follow a policy of international independence .... Greece rejects as inadequate the reparations award proposed for it by the Allied Reparations Commission.	Jewish terrorists kill eight persons in bomb blasts and gun battles in Jaffa and Tel Aviv .... Mulla Mustafa Al-barazani, his brother Sheikh Ahmad Albarazani and 33 of their followers are sentenced to death in absentia in Baghdad for the Kurdish revolt in northern Iraq last August.	The campaign manager for Miguel Aleman says there never has been any U.S. support, private or official, for Mexican opposition candidate Ezequiel Padilla.	Big Three announce a series of agreements calling for a Far Eastern Commission, a Four-Power Allied Council for Japan and a provisional Korean democratic government .... Chou En-lai submits a written proposal for an immediate truce in the Chinese civil war.

A	B	C	D	E
Includes developments that affect more than one world region, international organizations and important meetings of major world leaders.	*Includes all domestic and regional developments in Europe, including the Soviet Union, Turkey, Cyprus and Malta.*	*Includes all domestic and regional developments in Africa and the Middle East, including Iraq and Iran and excluding Cyprus, Turkey and Afghanistan.*	*Includes all domestic and regional developments in Latin America, the Caribbean and Canada.*	*Includes all domestic and regional developments in Asian and Pacific nations, extending from Afghanistan through all the Pacific Islands, except Hawaii.*

U.S. Politics & Social Issues	U.S. Foreign Policy & Defense	U.S. Economy & Environment	Science, Technology & Nature	Culture, Leisure & Life Style	
	Both houses of Congress accept the conference report on the U.N. participation bill voted yesterday in the House . . . . Truman nominates Stettinius as chief U.S. representative to the U.N. . . . . Truman asks Congress for unification of the nation's armed services under a single civilian secretary of defense . . . . Capt. McVay of the cruiser *Indianapolis* is acquitted by a court martial of a charge that he failed to give timely abandon ship orders.		Council of the American Geographical Society of New York exhibits its 107-sheet map of Hispanic America on the 1:1,000,000 scale after 25 years in preparation . . . . American Institute of Electrical Engineers awards the 1945 Edison Medal to Philip Sporn for his power generation work.		Dec. 19
Truman signs the Government Reorganization Act passed seven days ago by Congress, commenting that it will not save 25% as the bill suggests . . . . Sen. Bilbo (D, Miss.) criticizes Eleanor Roosevelt for her pro-Negro statements . . . . Kings County (N.Y.) grand jury charges mayor-elect William O'Dwyer with failure to indict and convict Albert Anastasia for the murder of a longshoreman when he possessed evidence of Anastasia's guilt in 1940.	Truman signs the U.N. participation bill as the Senate confirms his nominations to the U.S. delegation in the U.N. Assembly . . . . Truman says he knows nothing to support an ABC broadcast saying MacArthur threatened to resign if Russia was allowed any further participation in the Japanese occupation.	OPA orders the end of tire rationing Jan. 1.	Assn. of American Railroads is reported to have halted rail traffic to Buffalo, N.Y. after a blizzard deposits 73 inches of snow there; N.Y.C. gets 8½ inches.		Dec. 20
On the basis of reports of four psychiatrists, a district judge in Washington, D.C. rules that Ezra Pound is insane . . . . U.S. Office of Education and the Surplus Property Admin. announce completion of plans to supply schools and colleges with educational equipment from federal surplus property stocks . . . . Congress adjourns the first meeting of its 79th session, having enacted some 640 laws.		The United Electrical, Radio and Machine Workers of America rejects a 10% wage increase offered by GE.	Pioneer in radiophoto and phototelegraphy Dr. Arthur Korn dies at 75 in Jersey City, N.J.	AP names Byron Nelson the best male athlete for 1945 and Babe Didrickson Zaharias as the best women athlete . . . . Author Ernest Hemingway receives a divorce in Havana from Martha Gellhorn for abandonment . . . . National Board of Motion Pictures announces the selection of *The True Glory* as the best 1945 film and Ray Milland and Joan Crawford the best actor and actress . . . . FCC assigns TV channels to several licensees, including CBS and NBC in N.Y.C. and Radio Corp. of America in Camden, N.J.	Dec. 21
Truman orders key U.S. officials to cooperate to facilitate immigration of some 3,900 refugees monthly . . . . Interior Secy. Ickes proposes that Hawaii be admitted to statehood because of its excellent war record.		Ford lays off 80,000 workers, Packard 10,000 and Briggs Mfg. Co. 2,000 because of parts shortages . . . . Bureau of Labor Statistics reports 335 new strikes in November, involving 405,000 workers and 6.1 million man-hours lost.	War Dept. reveals the "static finder," a weather detector based on electronics which can detect a thunderstorm at a 2,000-mile range within two degrees of accuracy.		Dec. 22
		Truman vetoes a $51-billion bill canceling certain war funds because of a rider transferring the U.S. Employment Service to the states within 100 days.		Pope Pius XII names 32 prelates from 19 countries to become members of the Sacred College of Cardinals.	Dec. 23
		U.S. Conciliation Dir. Edgar L. Warren invites representatives of GE, Westinghouse and the United Electrical, Radio and Machine Workers of America to Washington for a post-Christmas conference to avert a threatened strike . . . . U.S. reports that 1944 per capita income reached a new high of $1,117.		AFM Pres. Petrillo bars American radio stations from broadcasting musical programs originating in any foreign country except Canada, beginning Dec. 31 . . . . Truman lights the National Community Christmas tree at the White House for the first time since 1941.	Dec. 24
				World authority on card games Robert Foster dies at 92 in Eastham, Mass.	Dec. 25
				George Bernard Shaw proposes a new phonetic English alphabet with only one sign for each sound . . . . *The Ring* selects featherweight champ Willie Pep as fighter of the year.	Dec. 26
		Wage Stabilization Bd. approves an average 25¢ hourly wage increase for some 200,000 building trades union members in the N.Y.C. area . . . . Truman abolishes the Smaller War Plants Corp. as of Jan. 28, 1946 and transfers its functions to the RFC.		National Institute of Arts & Letters announces selection of 15 artists, writers and musicians for works that "survive temporary appeal," including Lillian Hellman, Wallace Stevens, James Thurber and Charles Ives . . . . Annual poll of the *Motion Picture Herald* chooses Bing Crosby as the top box office attraction of 1945.	Dec. 27

F	G	H	I	J
Includes elections, federal-state relations, civil rights and liberties, crime, the judiciary, education, health care, poverty, urban affairs and population.	*Includes formation and debate of U.S. foreign and defense policies, veterans affairs and defense spending. (Relations with specific foreign countries are usually found under the region concerned.)*	*Includes business, labor, agriculture, taxation, transportation, consumer affairs, monetary and fiscal policy, natural resources, pollution and accidents.*	*Includes worldwide scientific, medical and technological developments, natural phenomena, U.S. weather and natural disasters.*	*Includes the arts, religion, scholarship, communications media, sports, entertainment, fashions, fads and social life.*

	World Affairs	Europe	Africa & the Middle East	The Americas	Asia & the Pacific
Dec. 28	U.N. interim committee narrows choice for its permanent headquarters to Boston and New York.	Paul Joseph Hoffmann, former commandant of the Maidanek concentration camp who was convicted of ordering the deaths of two million prisoners, is hanged outside the camp crematorium .... A Canadian military court in aurich sentences former SS Hitler Youth Division Commander Maj. Gen. Kurt Meyer to be shot for killing prisoners.	Lebanese Premeir Sami Solh says the U.N. will be pressed to ask that British and French troops be removed from the country.	Panama's Constitutional Congress votes a budget of over $30 million, the highest in the country's history.	British-Dutch Conference on Indonesia ends in London with a statement that the situation there should be settled, but there is no agreement on how this should be done .... More than 10,000 holdout Japanese troops surrender to Gen. Li Yen-nien in the Shantung area of China.
Dec. 29	American Assn. of Scientific Workers issues a statement supporting the Moscow Agreement for U.N. control of atomic energy.			President-elect Eurico Dutra pledges to restore full democracy, maintain close ties with the U.S., ease immigration laws and encourage the flow of foreign capital into Brazil.	Lt. Gen. Wedemeyer announces that U.S. troops will help Nationalist forces move into Manchuria .... British troops disarm all Indonesian police on the ground that they have not been able to maintain law and order.
Dec. 30	State Secy. Byrnes says the decisions at the Moscow conference have furthered world peace .... League of Nations acting Secy.-Gen. Sean Lester issues the final report of that body and states that the U.N. is in many respects a continuation of the League.	U.S. 3rd Army headquarters releases to the Nuremberg trial Hitler's "political testament," which names Adm. Karl Doenitz head of the German state and predicts that Nazism will be reborn.	Egyptian cabinet approves a boycott of goods produced by Zionists in Palestine.	The Argentinian Radical Party names Dr. Jose Tamborini as its presidential candidate, and gets pledges of support from the Socialists, Communists and Progressive Democrats.	Mayor Shichiro Kihara tells Allied reporters that Americans should rebuild Hiroshima because "we were sacrificed to end the war." He lists casualties at 139,000 killed out of a population of 310,000 .... Secy. Byrnes says MacArthur's authority in Japan will not be obstructed in any way by the Far Eastern Commission.
Dec. 31	Russia relinquishes its rights to original membership in the International Monetary Fund by failing to sign the Bretton Woods agreements on time.	British and American intelligence officers declare that they are convinced Hitler and Eva Braun died in the Chancellery bunker on April 30, 1945 .... Tass reports the Polish Council in Warsaw has ratified the pact establishing the Russo-Polish border along the old Curzon line with a few deviations "in Poland's favor." .... France officially recognizes the Yugoslavian republic.		Bermuda Legislative Council votes to end curbs on automobile use .... Mexico signs the Bretton Woods agreement.	MacArthur orders the suspension of all courses in Japanese history, geography and morals after a survey shows them interwoven with state Shinto and militarism .... Chungking responds to the Communist truce proposal with a plan of its own, proposing Marshall as mediator .... New Zealand P.M. Fraser offers to place the country's mandate of western Samoa under U.N. trusteeship.

A	B	C	D	E
Includes developments that affect more than one world region, international organizations and important meetings of major world leaders.	*Includes all domestic and regional developments in Europe, including the Soviet Union, Turkey, Cyprus and Malta.*	*Includes all domestic and regional developments in Africa and the Middle East, including Iraq and Iran and excluding Cyprus, Turkey and Afghanistan.*	*Includes all domestic and regional developments in Latin America, the Caribbean and Canada.*	*Includes all domestic and regional developments in Asian and Pacific nations, extending from Afghanistan through all the Pacific Islands, except Hawaii.*

U.S. Politics & Social Issues	U.S. Foreign Policy & Defense	U.S. Economy & Environment	Science, Technology & Nature	Culture, Leisure & Life Style	
OPA Chief Bowles protests to the White House for a second time that certain officers in federal agencies discriminate against Negroes seeking employment.	Truman signs the liberalized GI Bill of Rights.	GM officials walk out of Truman's fact-finding board hearing, objecting to union demands that wages be related to prices and company profits .... OPA raises the retail price ceilings 10¢-a-ton on coal, coke and other solid fuels as of Jan. 2 .... A Chicago federal district court enters a decree enjoining further monopoly, restraint of competition and rate fixing by Allied Van Lines.		Noted American author Theodore Dreiser dies at 74 in Hollywood.	Dec. 28
	Army and Navy create a joint advisory board to work with Maj. Gen. Leslie Groves on the atomic bomb.	National Federation of Telephone Workers Pres. Joseph Beirne appeals to Truman to intervene in the dispute between Western Electric and its Employes Assn. to avert a strike by Jan. 3 .... NWLB recommends $3 and $4 weekly wage raises to 11,500 employes of the Northwestern Bell Telephone Co. in five states.	Sydney, Australia records a large earthquake centered within 1,000 miles of the South Pole.	Northern All-Stars beat the South, 26-0, in the eighth annual Blue-Gray game in Montgomery, Ala.	Dec. 29
			Republic Aviation Corp. reveals development of a four-engine flying photographic laboratory, named the XF-12, for the Air Technical Service.	Noted French novelist and Nobel Prize winner Romain Rolland, author of *Jean-Christophe*, dies at 78 in Vezelay, France.	Dec. 30
	Adm. Harold R. Stark testifies at the Pearl Harbor hearings that 11 "specific warnings" of possible hostile Japanese actions were sent to the Pacific commanders between Oct. 16 and Dec. 6, 1941.	Truman terminates the NWLB by executive order and creates a National Wage Stabilization Board to succeed it .... Arbitrator William Davis announces a 20% wage increase to $1.50 an hour, a work week reduction to 40 hours and a week's vacation pay for the N.Y.C. longshoremen .... Truman names a three-man fact-finding board to avert the scheduled Jan. 14 steel strike and orders the OPA to review ceiling prices for steel.			Dec. 31

F	G	H	I	J
Includes elections, federal-state relations, civil rights and liberties, crime, the judiciary, education, health care, poverty, urban affairs and population.	*Includes formation and debate of U.S. foreign and defense policies, veterans affairs and defense spending. (Relations with specific foreign countries are usually found under the region concerned.)*	*Includes business, labor, agriculture, taxation, transportation, consumer affairs, monetary and fiscal policy, natural resources, pollution and accidents.*	*Includes worldwide scientific, medical and technological developments, natural phenomena, U.S. weather and natural disasters.*	*Includes the arts, religion, scholarship, communications media, sports, entertainment, fashions, fads and social life.*

1946

Milton Berle, the "Laff King of America," proclaims National Laff Week on April Fool's Day in a New York ceremony.

Italian soldiers move up in Rome to control a demonstration protesting the internationalization of Trieste, July 7.

Ships of Adm. Richard E. Byrd's naval expedition penetrate the Antarctic ice pack.

Vietnamese nationalist leader Ho Chi Minh arrives in Paris on June 22 for talks with French Colonial Min. Marius Moutet, standing to his left. Behind Ho is Pham Van Dong, later premier of North Vietnam.

Berlin's bombed-out Potsdamer Platz was the scene of clashes between U.S. and Russian troops in 1946, the first stirrings of the Cold War.

Preceding page: Germany, Anno Zero. Two women walk past piles of rubble cleared from a road in bombed-out Essen.

Equipped with cane and cigar, Winston Churchill flashes his "V" sign as he arrives in New York on the last leg of his U.S. tour, March 11.

An Office of Price Administration poster warns against "under-the-counter" food purchases. Price ceilings and shortages of consumer goods continued to arouse controversy months after the war ended.

"Wanna Go Home": GIs (plus one officer) demonstrate in Chicago on Jan. 2, demanding faster demobilization.

Mushroom cloud rises from the first underwater atomic test off Bikini Island, July 24. Eighty-three warships, obsolete U.S. vessels and captured Axis ships, are anchored around the blast to test its effect.

Even at the start of his political career, John F. Kennedy had strong appeal for the female vote. Here he poses with a group of Boston women during his successful 1946 campaign for the House of Representatives.

	World Affairs	Europe	Africa & the Middle East	The Americas	Asia & the Pacific
Jan.	United Nations convenes in London amidst controversy over atomic controls and the presence of British troops in Greece and the Dutch East Indies.	Allied prosecutors at Nuremberg continue to introduce evidence charging German defendants with war responsibility and extermination of Jews.	Iran seeks U.N. assistance in forcing Russian withdrawal from Azerbaijan.	Political unrest breaks out in Argentina and Chile.	Chinese Nationalists and Communist representatives meet in Nanking to discuss formation of a coalition government.
Feb.	General Assembly adjourns after refusing to investigate the Greek and Indonesian situations.	Britain's House of Commons accepts the Labor Party's socialist reform program . . . . Belgian political parties debate the return of King Leopold, accused of wartime collaboration with the Germans.	U.N. considers Syrian and Lebanese demands for removal of British and French troops from their countries.	Juan Peron wins the Argentine presidential election, despite U.S. efforts to discredit him as a wartime supporter of Nazism.	Negotiations between U.S. and Russian military authorities in Korea fail to produce agreement on creation of a single Korean government.
March	Gromyko boycotts the Security Council as it considers the issue of Soviet presence in Iran.	Hermann Goering and Rudoff Hess take the stand at Nuremburg and justify their acts as Nazis . . . . Western Allies speak out against the Franco regime but oppose strong international sanctions.	U.S. becomes involved in the Iranian controversy, threatening U.N. action against Russia if Soviet troops do not withdraw from Iran.	Canadian government breaks up a spy ring directed from the Soviet embassy in Ottawa.	Japanese political leaders complete work on a new "peace" constitution . . . . Nationalists and Communists in China negotiate a truce agreement under the mediation of Gen. George Marshall.
Apr.	Big Four Foreign Ministers meet in Paris in a effort to conclude European Peace treaties.	U.S. and Soviet occupation authorities clash on the question of German political parties as the U.S. refuses to recognize creation of the Socialist Unity Party in the eastern zone.	Anglo-American Palestine Inquiry Commission ends its lengthy consideration of the Palestine question with a recommendation for creation of a U.N. trusteeship.		Civil war again erupts in China, with Communists registering gains in Manchuria.
May	Paris conference ends without agreement on European Peace Treaties . . . . A U.N. subcommittee conducts hearings on the Franco regime in Spain.	Trials of secondary German war leaders begin in the U.S. occupation zone.	Arab states intensify their expressions of opposition to the creation of a Jewish state in Palestine . . . . Russian troops withdraw from Iran.	Political and labor violence in Bolivia results in the declaration of a state of siege.	An Allied military tribunal begins the trial of Japanese war leaders in Tokyo . . . . British government decides on independence for India despite unresolved Hindu-Moslem conflicts.
June	Allied Foreign Ministers reconvene in Paris to discuss peace treaties.	French and Italians elect constituent assemblies to begin the formation of postwar governments.	Iran negotiates a settlement providing for "home rule" in Azerbaijan.		British and Indian political leaders negotiate fruitlessly on the composition of an Indian interim government.
July	Russia and the Western powers fail to conclude European peace treaties and remain split over atomic control.	A Yugoslavian court in Belgrade tries wartime Chetnik leader Draja Mikhailovich for treason.	Palestinian Jewish groups continue to protest against British restrictive immigration policies and failure to create an independent Jewish state in Palestine.		Chinese Nationalist forces begin a successful drive to clear Communists from the Yangtze River valley.
Aug.	Care and repatriation of European war refugees becomes a major U.N. problem.	A U.S.-Yugoslavian diplomatic clash results from alleged U.S. violations of Yugoslavian air space . . . . Closed shop dispute begins in British transport industry.	British authorities divert thousands of Jewish immigrants to Cyprus from Palestine.		
Sept.		U.S. and British authorities in Germany take initial steps to unify their occupation zones as the Russians establish Communist primacy in their zone . . . . Greek monarchy is restored following a plebiscite.	Arab representatives meet with British leaders in London to discuss the Palestine question. Zionists boycott the conference.	Panama pressures the United States to relinquish wartime military bases outside the Canal Zone.	U.S.-sponsored negotiations for an end to the Chinese civil war break down as Nationalist forces resume their offensive against the Communists, taking several cities in Manchuria and northern China.
Oct.	U.N. debates proposals for atomic control, but remains deadlocked on the issue of inspection . . . . Paris Peace Conference ends after reaching agreement on Axis satellite peace treaties.	Nuremburg trial ends with 19 top Nazis found guilty of war crimes and sentenced to death.	Iranian government moves to subdue rebellious Ghashghai tribesmen . . . . Arab-British discussions on Palestine continue in London.	A month-long political crisis ends in Chile as Communists join the cabinet.	
Nov.	Big Four Foreign Ministers meet in New York to resolve remaining peace treaty problems.	Communists win electoral contests in France, Italy and Bulgaria.	Terrorist acts sweep Palestine as militant Zionists attempt to change British policy towards Jewish immigration and creation of a Jewish state.		French Navy shells the Tonkinese port of Haiphong, killing thousands . . . . Negotiations between Dutch officials and Indonesian nationalists result in agreement on creation of an Indonesian Republic on Java and Sumatra, with eventual formation of a United States of Indonesia.
Dec.	U.N. General Assembly debates proposals for international action against Spain's Franco government.		World Zionist Congress meets in Basel, Switzerland to consider means of creating a Jewish state in Palestine.		Fighting between French forces and Vietnamese nationalists spreads throughout Indochina.

A	B	C	D	E
Includes developments that affect more than one world region, international organizations and important meetings of major world leaders.	*Includes all domestic and regional developments in Europe, including the Soviet Union, Turkey, Cyprus and Malta.*	*Includes all domestic and regional developments in Africa and the Middle East, including Iraq and Iran and excluding Cyprus, Turkey and Afghanistan.*	*Includes all domestic and regional developments in Latin America, the Caribbean and Canada.*	*Includes all domestic and regional developments in Asian and Pacific nations, extending from Afghanistan through all the Pacific Islands, except Hawaii.*

U.S. Politics & Social Issues	U.S. Foreign Policy & Defense	U.S. Economy & Environment	Science, Technology & Nature	Culture, Leisure & Life Style	
Congress begins consideration of Truman's "Fair Deal" legislative proposals . . . . College enrollments soar as returning veterans begin or resume their higher education. Educators begin pressing for increased federal aid to colleges and universities to accommodate the sudden influx of students.	GIs in Europe and the Pacific stage massive "Wanna Go Home" demonstrations, protesting a slowdown in the Army's demobilization schedule.	Organized labor strikes electronic, meat-packing and steel industries, demanding high hourly wage increases.	British and American jet planes with improved design and engine performance set several new speed records.	Bob Hope's radio show continues to top the Hooper ratings of radio programs.	Jan.
	A congressional inquiry commission concludes public hearings on the responsibility of Adm. Kimmel and Gen. Short for lack of U.S. preparedness at Pearl Harbor.	As Congress debates anti-strike legislation, organized labor continues its demands for wage increases and a shorter work week.	New developments in television transmission and use of computors highlight advances in electronics.	World Council of Churches, meeting in Geneva, issues a call for world order and justice . . . . NBC begins Washington-New York television transmission.	Feb.
Congressional hearings on Truman's nomination of Edwin Pauley as Navy under secretary bring out information that discredits Pauley and forces Truman to withdraw the nomination.	Congress debates issues of atomic control and war preparedness amidst controversy over Soviet foreign policy following Churchill's "Iron Curtain" speech in Fulton, Mo.	Electronics, rubber, garment and auto industries conclude wage agreements with striking workers.			March
Democrats debate the issue of party loyalty as Southern congressmen resist Truman's proposed civil rights legislation.	A Senate Military Affairs Comm. recommendation for merger of the armed forces under a civilian chief causes controversy in Congress and the military.	A soft coal miners' strike drastically reduces the nation's fuel reserves.		The world's first television network begins operation in New York, Philadelphia and Washington.	Apr.
Congress balks at efforts to revive the Fair Employment Practices Commission.		Congress completes action on anti-strike legislation following the end of strikes by railroad workers and soft coal miners.	The flooding Susquehanna River causes $3 million in damage in New York and Pennsylvania.	Mexican Baseball League attempts to lure major league stars out of the U.S.	May
	Congress completes action on a bill continuing conscription for another year.	Congress sustains Truman's veto of the Case anti-strike bill.	Tornadoes, electrical storms and earthquakes strike various regions of the U.S.	After a record 713 performances, *I Remember Mama* closes on Broadway.	June
	Congress debates the status of the military on the proposed Atomic Energy Commission.	Wholesale and retail inventories reach record levels of $4.6 billion and $7.4 billion, respectively, as industry shifts to peacetime production. Civilian employment increases to 58.1 million, up 1.4 million from last month.			July
Several states initiate action against the Ku Klux Klan.	Government begins stockpiling of critical war materials.	Labor disputes filed with the NLRB reach a record monthly high of 1,651.	U.S. experiences its worst infantile paralysis epidemic since 1916.		Aug.
Civic and professional groups express increasing concern over alleged Communist influence in the U.S.	Controversy over U.S. foreign policy intensifies following Truman's dismissal of Commerce Secy. Wallace for a N.Y. speech advocating cooperation with Russia.	A truckers' strike paralyzes New York City.	Continued improvements permit electronic transmission of color television.	Frederic Wakeman's *The Hucksters* and Betty MacDonald's *The Egg and I* continue to be the best selling books in the U.S.	Sept.
House Un-American Activities Comm. moves to investigate Communist espionage.		Factory production and employment hit record peacetime levels, with output at 182% of the prewar average and employment at 146%.			Oct.
Republicans gain control of Congress in mid-term elections.		The year's second coal strike, affecting 300,000 miners, begins in defiance of a court order.	Plans for construction of several nuclear research facilities are announced.		Nov.
A struggle erupts in Georgia to name a successor to the late Governor-elect Eugene Talmadge.	U.S. Mediterranean Fleet undertakes a "goodwill" visit of European and Middle Eastern ports.				Dec.

F	G	H	I	J
Includes elections, federal-state relations, civil rights and liberties, crime, the judiciary, education, health care, poverty, urban affairs and population.	*Includes formation and debate of U.S. foreign and defense policies, veterans affairs and defense spending. (Relations with specific foreign countries are usually found under the region concerned.)*	*Includes business, labor, agriculture, taxation, transportation, consumer affairs, monetary and fiscal policy, natural resources, pollution and accidents.*	*Includes worldwide scientific, medical and technological developments, natural phenomena, U.S. weather and natural disasters.*	*Includes the arts, religion, scholarship, communications media, sports, entertainment, fashions, fads and social life.*

	World Affairs	Europe	Africa & the Middle East	The Americas	Asia & the Pacific
Jan. 1		French Constituent Assembly approves the 1946 national budget after Gen. Charles de Gaulle threatens to resign over proposed cuts in defense spending .... At his Nuremberg trial, Nazi Foreign Min. von Ribbentrop reveals that a week before committing suicide Hitler said that his spirit would again rise and "one will see that I have been right." .... Britain's King George makes Field Marshal Bernard Montgomery, British victor in North Africa and Germany, a viscount, and awards the Order of Merit to Winston Churchill.			In elections to India's Central Legislative Assembly, the All-India Congress Party captures 59.6% of the vote to 27.6% for the Moslem League .... Britain and India sign a peace treaty with Siam, ending the state of war that existed since Jan. 25, 1942 .... In a New Year's Day rescript, Emperor Hirohito tells the Japanese he is not a god.
Jan. 2	Russian Amb. to the U.S. Andrei Gromyko is appointed Russian representative on the Far Eastern Commission.	Gestapo leader Ernst Kaltenbrunner is charged at Nuremberg with witnessing gas executions at Mauthausen and ordering the slaughter of camp inmates in the path of advancing Allied armies .... Lt. Gen. Sir Frederick Morgan, UNRRA chief in Germany, declares he is unimpressed "by all the talk about pogroms in Poland" and claims that Polish Jews are entering the American sector with a "well-organized, positive plan" to leave Europe.	Commercial life in Damascus, Aleppo and Beirut is paralyzed by a strike protesting continued British-French occupation .... Chief Secy. of the Palestine Administration J.V.W. Shaw discloses that all immigration permits issued under the 1939 White Paper, some 75,000, have been used and no more are available.	U.S. State Dept. proposes an Inter-American military defense treaty conference, to be held in Brazil this March .... Forty persons are killed and 300 wounded in rioting during the inauguration of the mayor of Leon, Mexico.	U.S. War Dept. releases MacArthur's occupation report, which says the Communist Party is coming to life in Japan and younger Japanese are beginning to question whether Japan's future lies in Communism or democracy .... Japanese are astonished by publication of two photographs of Emperor Hirohito and his family, one showing him in civilian dress for the first time .... Nationalist troops enter Jehol Province in northeastern China to take it over from the Communists, who announce they will resist such efforts.
Jan. 3	French government accepts the Big Three proposal to hold the European peace conference in Paris but asks how much authority France will have at the conference.	At Nuremberg former Nazi police general Otto Ohlendorf testifies that his mobile unit entered Poland and Russia, executing some 90,000 Jewish men, women and children between June 1941 and June 1942 .... Gen. Morgan of the UNRRA denies that his Jan. 2 remarks were "an attack on the motives of European Jewry." Simon Rifkind, adviser to the U.S. military government in Germany, claims Jews are leaving Poland "under a sense of compulsion." .... France and Russia sign a five-year agreement in Moscow for the resumption of trade on a most-favored-nation basis .... William Joyce (Lord Haw Haw) is hanged as a traitor at Wandsworth Prison after issuing a statement attacking Jews and Russians and praising Nazism.		The Mexican government sends a draft of an inter-American defense pact, calling for peaceful settlement of disputes, to all American states.	UP reports reveal that insurgent Vietnamese have suffered more than 4,000 casualties since the "shooting war" with French forces started last September .... Chinese Communists accept Chiang Kai-shek's proposal that Gen. George C. Marshall serve as mediator in their dispute.
Jan. 4		The American prosecution begins its presentation of evidence to prove that the German general staff and high command were criminal organizations that plotted war .... Polish Parliament nationalizes industry, banks and public utilities, recognizes Austria and Hungary and ratifies the Bretton Woods agreement .... After refusing to resign, Gen. Morgan is dismissed from his UNRRA post in Germany for his allegedly anti-semitic remark of two days ago .... Nobel Prize winner Frederic Joliot-Curie is appointed French high commissioner for atomic energy.		Ignacio Quiroz, newly-elected mayor of Leon, is dismissed by the Guanajuato State government of Mexico, and a provisional governing board is appointed pending investigation of the Jan. 2 riots in Leon.	MacArthur directs the Japanese government to remove from office all "active exponents" of military nationalism, bar them from coming elections, and abolish 27 nationalist societies .... Lt. Col. Michio Kitayama testifies in Manila that Gen. Masaharu Homma ordered the Bataan death march .... In an Australian inquiry into the conduct of British Gen. Henry Bennett, who escaped from Singapore shortly after the city's surrender to the Japanese in 1942, Justice George Ligertwood declares that Bennett was not justified in leaving his command when he did.
Jan. 5	A seven-nation U.N. subcommittee lands in New York to inspect sites for the organization's headquarters.	Moscow radio reports that eight Germans tried for atrocities in Leningrad have been sentenced to be hanged.	Palestine High Commissioner Lt. Gen. Sir Alan Cunningham asks several members of the Palestine Arab Higher Comm. in Jerusalem to consent to the monthly admission of 1,500 European Jews while the Anglo-American Commission of Inquiry studies the Palestinian problem.	Truman names Judge William Hastie to be Virgin Island governor. If confirmed he will be the first Negro governor there.	Former head of the Japanese "thought control" police in the Philippines, Lt. Col. Seichi Ohta, is sentenced by a U.S. military commission in Manila to be hanged for crimes at Fort Santiago .... U.S. Joint Chiefs of Staff direct MacArthur to arrange a conference between U.S. and Soviet authorities in Korea for the purpose of coordinating economic and administrative policies .... State Dept. resumes diplomatic relations with Siam after a break of nearly four years.
Jan. 6		European Coal Organization announces that the U.S., Britain, France, Belgium, the Netherlands, Luxembourg, Norway, Denmark, Greece and Turkey have agreed to make it a permanent body .... Premier Sukru Saracoglu declares Russia has no right to the Turkish border provinces of Kars and Ardahan because they voted to return to Turkey in a plebescite after WWI.	Nationalist activity is reported near Maragheh, Mianeh and Malik Kandi in Iran against the autonomous Azerbaijan regime .... Cairo students demonstrate against Premier Nokrashy Pasha's government during the funeral of assassinated Wafdist Amin Osman Pasha.	Ecuador proposes a permanent conciliation commission to handle disputes in the Western Hemisphere.	Combined Chiefs of Staff announce the end of U.S. participation in the Allied Southeast Asia Command.
	A *Includes developments that affect more than one world region, international organizations and important meetings of major world leaders.*	B *Includes all domestic and regional developments in Europe, including the Soviet Union, Turkey, Cyprus and Malta.*	C *Includes all domestic and regional developments in Africa and the Middle East, including Iraq and Iran and excluding Cyprus, Turkey and Afghanistan.*	D *Includes all domestic and regional developments in Latin America, the Caribbean and Canada.*	E *Includes all domestic and regional developments in Asian and Pacific nations, extending from Afghanistan through all the Pacific Islands, except Hawaii.*

U.S. Politics & Social Issues	U.S. Foreign Policy & Defense	U.S. Economy & Environment	Science, Technology & Nature	Culture, Leisure & Life Style	
Census Bureau reports birth rates tend to decline with the advance in the educational status of husband or wife.	Upon return from his fact-finding trip for Truman, Mark Ethridge says Russia "made great concessions to the American viewpoint at Moscow" but that neither Bulgaria or Rumania have representative governments in "the Yalta sense." . . . . At the Pearl Harbor investigation, Maj. Gen. Walter Short, U.S. commander in Hawaii at the time of the Pearl Harbor attack, reveals that he expected the War Dept. to "let me know of a crisis." . . . . The Senate ratifies extension of the U.S.-Mexican sanitation and coffee pacts.		The Sun Oil Co. and the Houdry Process Corp. announce plans for quantity production of the rare Carbon 13, an isotope which can trace "intricate chemical reactions" in the body.	Results of today's Bowl games: Rose, Ala. 34-USC 14; Sugar, Okla. A & M 33 - St. Mary's 13; Cotton, Tex. 40 - Mo. 27; and Orange, Miami 13-Holy Cross 6 . . . . N.Y. Film Critics choose *The Lost Weekend* as the best film of 1945, its lead actor Ray Milland best actor, and its director Billy Wilder as top director.	Jan. 1
Supreme Court rules that Mormon fundamentalists William Chatwin, Charles Zitting and Edna Christensen are not guilty of breaking the Lindbergh kidnapping law in taking Dorothy Wyler to Mexico to become Chatwin's second wife, since the girl was not forced into the marriage . . . . The Court also rejects John Green's suit to oust Virginia's Sen. Carter Glass, who has been absent from the Senate since 1942 due to illness.	Adm. Harold R. Stark tells the Pearl Harbor committee he thought the Hawaiian command had adequate warning to prepare for war.	Three thousand CIO-American Communications Assn. members employed by Western Union vote in N.Y. to strike Jan. 8 against an NWLB decision reducing wage increases.			Jan. 2
Truman asks the public to spur congressional action on domestic problems, where legislative progress "has been distressingly slow."	U.S. War Dept. reveals that the Allies had surpassed the Axis in biological warfare research and would have used these methods if the enemy had resorted to them first . . . . Adm. Stark tells the Pearl Harbor committee that U.S. ships served with British convoys in the North Atlantic after August 1941, with "shoot on sight orders."	A strike by 17,200 employes shuts down 27 Western Electric plants in N.Y. and N.J.	The U.S. Office of Scientific Research & Development reports discovery of a new synthetic drug, SN 7618, which relieves malarial attacks three times as quickly as atabrine or quinine.	Publisher of the *New York Sun*, William Dewart, dies at 36 in an airplane crash near Reno, Nev. . . . . Evelyn Waugh's novel *Brideshead Revisited* is published in N.Y.	Jan. 3
Sen. Robert A. Taft (R, O.) calls some of Truman's proposed legislation (including national health insurance and full employment measures) "leftwing" inspired.	War Dept. says that because of overseas requirements and demobilization the return of overseas GIs the next six months must be cut down . . . . Pearl Harbor inquiry releases former Navy Secy. Frank Knox's secret report on the Japanese attack, blaming Gen. Short and Adm. Kimmel for lack of preparedness but admitting that they did not have all available information on Japanese intentions.		A tornado in northeast Texas kills 29 persons, injures several hundred and causes heavy property damage . . . . British geographer Dr. Herbert Fleure writes in the *Geographical Review* that variations in skin pigmentation are caused by climate, solar radiation, geographical location and prehistoric racial migration.	All-America Football Conference votes to start the 1946 season with an eight-club league: N.Y., Brooklyn, Chicago, Los Angeles, Buffalo, Miami, San Francisco and Cleveland . . . . Sportswriters in Chicago vote quarterback Bob Waterfield of the champion Cleveland Rams the 1945 most valuable player in the NFL . . . . N.Y. State Bd. of Censors bans the film *Scarlet Street*, a story of illicit love.	Jan. 4
Sen. Wayne Morse (Ore.) assails Sen. Taft and other Republican "reactionaries" and asks progressive GOP members to support liberal legislation.		CIO United Electrical, Radio and Machine Workers of America calls a strike of 200,000 workers at General Electric, Westinghouse Electric and General Motors electrical division for Jan. 15 after rejecting a second offer to raise wages . . . . Surplus Property Administrator Stuart Symington accuses Alcoa of obstructing disposal of government-owned aluminum plants to competitors.			Jan. 5
			Federation of American Scientists, a merger of individual atomic scientist organizations with 2,500 members, holds its first meeting in N.Y.	Arthur Devlin wins the 148-foot Torger Tokle Memorial jump at Bear Mountain, N.Y. with 231.1 points.	Jan. 6

F	G	H	I	J
Includes elections, federal-state relations, civil rights and liberties, crime, the judiciary, education, health care, poverty, urban affairs and population.	*Includes formation and debate of U.S. foreign and defense policies, veterans affairs and defense spending. (Relations with specific foreign countries are usually found under the region concerned.)*	*Includes business, labor, agriculture, taxation, transportation, consumer affairs, monetary and fiscal policy, natural resources, pollution and accidents.*	*Includes worldwide scientific, medical and technological developments, natural phenomena, U.S. weather and natural disasters.*	*Includes the arts, religion, scholarship, communications media, sports, entertainment, fashions, fads and social life.*

	World Affairs	Europe	Africa & the Middle East	The Americas	Asia & the Pacific
Jan. 7	American Society of Newspaper Editors and UP Pres. Hugh Baillie ask Edward Stettinius, acting head of the U.S. delegation to the U.N., to work for the free exchange of international news.	U.S., Britain, Russia and France formally recognize Austria .... Rumanian cabinet is reformed in line with Russian directives with the appointment of Mihai Romniceanu and Emil Hatsieganu as ministers without portfolio .... In his summation of the case against the German general staff and high command, Col. Telford Taylor declares its plans for conquest "turned Europe into a charnel house."	Economist Robert Nathan tells the Anglo-American Comm. of Inquiry on Palestine at its opening session in Washington that Palestine could absorb 615,000 to 1,125,000 displaced Jews within 10 years.	A petition signed by 77 prominent Argentinians urges the U.N. to intervene against undemocratic governments and destroy "the Nazi redoubt installed in Argentina."	
Jan. 8		British and American prosecutors close their case against six of the 21 Nazi defendants at Nuremberg.			British troops attack Indonesians in the Semarang area after evacuating the town of Ungaran under Indonesian shelling.
Jan. 9	Britain's King George VI welcomes U.N. delegates at a state dinner in St. James's Palace, asking them to place the community of nations above selfish interests.	Evidence introduced at the Nuremberg trials reveals Ribbentrop told Japanese Amb. Hiroshi Oshima that Hitler had ordered "the entire German Navy to attack American ships" three days before Germany declared war on the U.S.	Arab Higher Comm. rejects a British proposal for interim Jewish immigration and demands that Palestine be given independence and the Grand Mufti be allowed back into Jerusalem .... American Jewish Comm. President Joseph Proskauer urges the Anglo-American Comm. of Inquiry on Palestine to recommend that the country be placed under U.N. trusteeship.		The Japanese cabinet approves a reform plan for the Japanese House of Peers, reducing the membership from 418 to 300.
Jan. 10	The first session of the 51-nation U.N. General Assembly opens in the Central Hall of Westminster with a welcoming address by P.M. Clement Attlee.	Evidence against Hjalmar Schacht, Hans Frank and Julius Streicher is summarized at the Nuremberg trials .... The diary of former Italian Foreign Min. Count Galeazzo Ciano, covering the years 1939-1943, is published after being introduced at Nuremberg as evidence against Nazi Foreign Min. von Ribbentrop .... London announces that Dr. Otto Hahn, German nuclear scientist captured by the British in 1944, has been released and is returning to Germany .... Former Hungarian Premier Laszlo de Bardossy is hanged for treason in Budapest.			At the opening session of the Political Consultative Conference between Chinese Nationalist and Communist leaders, Chiang Kai-shek announces that both sides have agreed to a truce and promises that all parties will enjoy equal status in the future.
Jan. 11	U.N. General Assembly selects chairmen of the following committees: political and security, economic and financial, social, humanitarian and cultural, trusteeship, administrative and budget and legal.	Export-Import Bank grants a $25 million loan to Greece to buy essential supplies .... Allied Control Council fixes German steel production at 5.8 million tons a year .... Albanian Constituent Assembly proclaims a republic under Premier Enver Hoxha, without mentioning King Zog in London.	Prof. Albert Einstein tells the Anglo-American Comm. of Inquiry on Palestine he prefers U.N. trusteeship to British colonial policy and sees no need for a Jewish commonwealth advocated by the Zionist organizations.	Haitian President Elie Lescot is ousted by a coup led by Army Chief of Staff Col. Frank Levaud, Maj. Antoine Levelt and Maj. Paul Magloire.	Vietnamese nationalist leader Ho Chi Minh claims in Hanoi that an undisclosed source offered him $285,000 to give up his fight for Indochinese independence. French officials deny any bribe attempt.
Jan. 12	U.N. General Assambly chooses six temporary members of the Security Council: Australia, Brazil and Poland (two years each) and Holland, Egypt and Mexico (one year each).		Iranian government announces that national gendarmerie repulsed armed Iraqi nomads invading Khorramshahr under the Sheik of Khazal.	Assembly of Argentine Industry, Commerce and Production announces a nationwide three-day lockout beginning Jan. 14 to protest the government's wage-bonus decree of Dec. 20, 1945.	Japanese Premier Kijuro Shidehara reorganizes his cabinet for the fourth time since last August .... Korean National Mobilization Comm. Against Trusteeship stages large demonstrations in Seoul, demanding immediate creation of a national government to direct the country "without further outside interference."
Jan. 13		Greek Premier George Papandreou denounces fascism and demands the return of the Dodecanese Islands and Northern Epirus as six major political parties meet in Athens .... Ante Pavelich, leader of the Croation fascist organization Ustashe, goes on trial in Yugoslavia as a war criminal with 27 Germans and 14 Croatians.			MacArthur orders the Japanese government to hold elections for the new House of Representatives "not earlier" than March 15 so that approximately 1,000 candidates can be investigated.
Jan. 14	U.S. State Secy. Byrnes tells the General Assembly the U.N. should move "immediately" to give the Security Council "the military force it needs to maintain peace" and urges creation of an international commission to control the atomic bomb.	British prosecution at Nuremberg charges that Adm. Doenitz instructed German submarines to kill Allied crews as well as sink their ships .... Rumanian Justice Min. Lucretiu Patrascanu, a Communist, says that no foreign observers of proposed elections will be permitted.	Anglo-American Comm. of Inquiry on Palestine ends its Washington hearings and prepares to move to London.	The nationwide three-day lockout ordered by Argentine industry goes into effect, paralyzing all activities .... A joint Anglo-American policy statement on the Caribbean promises financial aid to expand food and industrial production and trade in territorial and colonial possessions.	Mayor of Tokyo Histada Hirose resigns under MacArthur's Jan. 4 purge order.

A	B	C	D	E
Includes developments that affect more than one world region, international organizations and important meetings of major world leaders.	*Includes all domestic and regional developments in Europe, including the Soviet Union, Turkey, Cyprus and Malta.*	*Includes all domestic and regional developments in Africa and the Middle East, including Iraq and Iran and excluding Cyprus, Turkey and Afghanistan.*	*Includes all domestic and regional developments in Latin America, the Caribbean and Canada.*	*Includes all domestic and regional developments in Asian and Pacific nations, extending from Afghanistan through all the Pacific Islands, except Hawaii.*

U.S. Politics & Social Issues	U.S. Foreign Policy & Defense	U.S. Economy & Environment	Science, Technology & Nature	Culture, Leisure & Life Style	
J. Edgar Hoover says the American Youth for Democracy reflects "all the sinister purposes of the Communist Party in the U.S." .... House Territorial Affairs Subcommittee begins hearings in Honolulu for Hawaiian statehood.	GIs in Manila, Guam, Camp Boston (France) and Andrews Field (Md.) demonstrate against a reported demobilization slowdown .... State Secy. Byrnes states U.S. interests in the atomic issue will not be jeopardized by any U.N. commission and denies that atomic secrets will be given up without congressional approval.	The UAW and the Kaiser-Frazer Co. reach a wage agreement giving the union a $1.20 average hourly wage.		Supreme Court rules that members of Jehovah's Witnesses have the right to distribute their literature in company-owned or federal towns.	Jan. 7
	Truman states at a press conference that he reserves the right to withdraw even conditional recognition of Rumania, Bulgaria and Yugoslavia if they fail to guarantee the democratic rights agreed upon at Yalta .... Truman announces that "the critical need for troops overseas has begun to slow down" and that demobilization is proceeding with efficiency.	N.Y.C.'s commercial and financial life is paralyzed and international cable and radio messages affected by a strike of some 7,000 Western Electric employes associated with the CIO American Communications Assn. .... Truman says the government will allow a steel price increase, reported to be about $4 a ton.	Dr. Cornelius Rhoads announces the organization of the Committee on Growth to promote and coordinate cancer research.	*Film Daily's* poll of movie reviews cites Alexander Knox, Ingrid Bergman and Greer Garson as best male and female performers of 1945 .... Lt. Col. Gregory Boyington, Marine air ace in the Pacific, weds former actress Frances Baker in Las Vegas.	Jan. 8
	During a visit to Canada, Gen. Eisenhower orders all U.S. overseas commanders to send home "without delay" all soldiers "for whom there is no military need." .... The Navy reveals its first fighter plane exclusively powered by jet engines, the *FD-1 Phantom*, with a 1,000-mile range and a more than 500 mph speed .... At the Pearl Harbor inquiry, an FDR letter of Dec. 5, 1941 to Wendell Willkie indicates the President expected a Japanese attack on "the Philippines, Dutch Indies, Malaya or Borneo," but not Hawaii.	Demanding a 5-7¢ hourly wage increase, 7,704 telephone mechanics at Western Electric go on strike in 44 states.	Dr. John van Neumann and Dr. Vladimir Kosma Zworykin submit plans to the Army, Navy and Weather Bureau for development of a new electronic computer which may enable long-range weather forecasting.	Negro poet Countee Cullen dies at 42 in N.Y.	Jan. 9
A Washington U.S. District Court acquits James Underwood and Bert Hall of mail fraud charges, but continues the trial of three other officials of Engineers Group, Inc.: James Curley, James Fuller and Donald Smith.	Manila-based GIs draft a protest note to the War Dept., asking explanation of the Army's mission in the Philippines and the number of troops needed.	The GM-UAW fact-finding board reports to Truman, recommending a 19½¢ hourly wage increase .... Alcoa grants the government free use of its patents for aluminum production and the right to license them to competitors acquiring government-owned plants.	The Army makes the first radar contact with the moon, "bouncing back" a signal in 2.4 seconds.	AAU and NCAA enter formal partnership in St. Louis, sharing Olympic selectors and agreeing for the first time to respect each other's rights, rules and territories.	Jan. 10
	Pearl Harbor inquiry learns of a charge made by Adm. Kimmel in 1944 that he and Gen. Short were targets of a "deliberate smear campaign."	GM rejects the government fact-finding board's recommendation for a 19½¢ hourly increase for UAW workers.		Bert Bell succeeds Elmer Layden as NFL commissioner, and the league's office is transferred from Chicago to New York.	Jan. 11
Alabama Democratic Executive Comm. votes to open party primaries to qualified Negro voters for the first time .... Truman accepts Abe Fortas's resignation as undersecretary of the Interior Department.		A government fact-finding board recommends an 18% wage increase in the oil industry to settle a three-month old dispute involving 141,147 workers .... Pan American Airways announces daily air service to France via Newfoundland, Ireland and Portugal. One-way fare is $295.		NFL grants the Cleveland Rams a franchise in Los Angeles.	Jan. 12
	GI protests against the demobilization slowdown are held in Paris, Frankfurt and Calcutta .... Fleet Adm. Chester W. Nimitz announces plans for a postwar Navy of seven fleets.	UAW accepts the fact-finding committee's recommendation of a 17.5% raise and urges Truman to persuade GM to do likewise .... The Texas Co. and the United Oil Workers agree on an 18% pay raise package recommended by the government fact-finding board.		*N.Y. Herald Tribune* reports the best-selling fiction and non-fiction books to be *The Black Rose* by Thomas Costain and *The Egg and I* by Betty MacDonald.	Jan. 13
The 79th Congress reconvenes, and House members indicate they are ready to push measures curbing labor.		Truman asks Congress to repeal $5.75 billion in appropriations for the War Shipping Administration, Federal Works Administration, Maritime Commission, Lend-Lease and the Agriculture, Interior, Labor, War and Navy Depts. ... Supreme Court rejects the N.Y. State claim for immunity from U.S. excise taxes on bottled water sold from Saratoga Springs.		Interior Secy. Harold Ickes announces publication of the first book on the native Aleutian tongue, *The Aleut Language*, compiled over 12 years.	Jan. 14
F	G	H	I	J	
Includes elections, federal-state relations, civil rights and liberties, crime, the judiciary, education, health care, poverty, urban affairs and population.	*Includes formation and debate of U.S. foreign and defense policies, veterans affairs and defense spending. (Relations with specific foreign countries are usually found under the region concerned.)*	*Includes business, labor, agriculture, taxation, transportation, consumer affairs, monetary and fiscal policy, natural resources, pollution and accidents.*	*Includes worldwide scientific, medical and technological developments, natural phenomena, U.S. weather and natural disasters.*	*Includes the arts, religion, scholarship, communications media, sports, entertainment, fashions, fads and social life.*	

	World Affairs	Europe	Africa & the Middle East	The Americas	Asia & the Pacific
Jan. 15	The first chairman of the U.N. Security Council, Norman J.O. Makin of Australia, says that the atomic bomb should be placed at the U.N.'s disposal to maintain peace.	German physicist Wilhelm Westphall says two groups of German scientists have been settled by the Russians on the Black Sea to work on military applications of electronics and atomic energy.		Argentine Labor Party elects Juan D. Peron as its presidential candidate .... Canadian government names Gordon MacDonald governor of Newfoundland to succeed Sir Humphrey Walwyn.	At the Manila trial of Gen. Masaharu Homma, witnesses describe Japanese brutality at Camp O'Donnell, where about 30,500 inmates died .... Chinese Communists on the Political Consultative Comm. agree on retaining President Chiang Kai-shek as head of the proposed all-party government.
Jan. 16		Allied Control Council reports that 19 of the 42 I.G. Farben chemical plants in the U.S. occupation zone have been set aside for reparations .... Dr. Robert Kempner of the American prosecution staff at Nuremberg introduces documents showing that Nazi Interior Min. Wilhelm Frick ordered the killing of 275,000 insane, crippled and old persons and that he made it possible for Hitler to obtain German citizenship.	Iranian government instructs its U.N. delegation to request the organization's assistance in expediting the Russian withdrawal from Iran, scheduled for March 2 .... The kings of Saudi Arabia and Egypt insist that Palestine remain an Arab country.	U.S. State Dept. reports that a majority of the 21 American republics have responded negatively to the Uruguayan proposal for collective intervention to protect individual rights in the Western Hemisphere.	An Australian commission at Labuan sentences 28 Japanese to death for war crimes .... Former Buddhist priest Hiromichi Kumazawa petitions MacArthur to confirm his claim that he is the legitimate emperor of Japan and that Hirohito is "illegal." .... Soviet and U.S. military missions begin talks on the Korean problem in Seoul .... Chinese Nationalist and Communist delegates to the Political Consultative Conference agree on a mutual reduction of military forces within the next six months.
Jan. 17	British Foreign Secy. Bevin announces to the U.N. General Assembly that Britain will place its mandated territories of Tanganyika, the Cameroons and Togoland under U.N. Trusteeship. The Assembly also approves a motion urging member nations to sever ties with Franco Spain.			Chilean Pres. Rios steps down temporarily due to ill health and is replaced by Alfredo Duhalde.	Dr. Ba Maw, Burmese premier during the Japanese occupation, surrenders at Allied headquarters in Tokyo .... Export-Import Bank approves a $33 million credit grant to China to help finance the import of U.S. raw cotton and speed reconversion of China's cotton industry.
Jan. 18		Lt. Gen. Sir Frederick E. Morgan appeals his dismissal as director of UNRRA activities in Germany to his chief, Herbert H. Lehman .... U.S. military government in Munich provisionally licenses the Communist Party of Bavaria in a step towards the destruction of German National Socialism.		Mexican Revolutionary Party (PRM) votes its dissolution and reorganizes under the name of Party of Revolutionary Institutions (PRI).	MacArthur orders the arrest of 100 more Japanese, including seven generals, for trial as war criminals.
Jan. 19	Anglo-American Civil Aviation Congress in Bermuda agrees upon mutual commercial use of nine military airfields built during the war in British Caribbean and North Atlantic posessions.	UNRRA and Italy sign a 1946 contract for $375,000,000 in vital imports .... Austrian Archdukes Karl Ludwig and Rudolf Hapsburg are expelled from Innsbrueck after the banning of the Austrian monarchist party.	Zionist terrorists blow up a power sub-station and a wall of the central prison in Jerusalem .... Syria and Lebanon repeat their demand that British and French troops leave the Levant area .... Iran charges Russia with interference in its internal affairs and asks the U.N. Security Council to intervene.		MacArthur announces the establishment of an international military tribunal for the Far East to try top Japanese war criminal suspects.
Jan. 20		The first free elections in Germany since 1933 are held in U.S.-occupied Hesse. The Social Democrats win with 146,508 votes, followed by the Christian Social Union with 99,591 votes .... Russians take over the Hungarian oilfields at Lispe .... French Pres. de Gaulle resigns for the third time in three months, on this occasion over a Communist-Socialist demand that the Army budget be cut 20% .... Belgian Premier Achille van Acker rejects a request of exiled King Leopold that a national plebiscite be held on the question of his return to Belgium.			MacArthur orders 394 Japanese aircraft plants, arsenals and war laboratories seized and kept intact for possible use in reparations payments.
Jan. 21	Deputies of the Allied Council of Foreign Ministers meet in London to discuss the proposed peace treaties .... Russia's acting U.N. delegate Andrei Gromyko and chief Ukrainian representative Dmitry Z. Manuilsky urge the Security Council to investigate the presence of British troops in Greece and the Dutch East Indies .... The U.N. General Assembly's Political and Security Comm. adopts a resolution to create an atomic energy commission.	Greek government proclaims martial law in the southern Peloponnesus and sends troops and a warship to quell royalist uprisings in Kalamata.		Cuban Pres. Grau San Martin appoints Dr. Joaquin Martinez Saenz as minister without portfolio.	Clashes are reported in eastern Java and street barricades are thrown up by Dutch authorities in Bandung to repel attacks by Indonesian nationalists.
	A *Includes developments that affect more than one world region, international organizations and important meetings of major world leaders.*	B *Includes all domestic and regional developments in Europe, including the Soviet Union, Turkey, Cyprus and Malta.*	C *Includes all domestic and regional developments in Africa and the Middle East, including Iraq and Iran and excluding Cyprus, Turkey and Afghanistan.*	D *Includes all domestic and regional developments in Latin America, the Caribbean and Canada.*	E *Includes all domestic and regional developments in Asian and Pacific nations, extending from Afghanistan through all the Pacific Islands, except Hawaii.*

U.S. Politics & Social Issues	U.S. Foreign Policy & Defense	U.S. Economy & Environment	Science, Technology & Nature	Culture, Leisure & Life Style	
South Carolina's House of Representatives votes against a bill to abolish the poll tax.	In his first public testimony, Adm. Husband E. Kimmel tells the Pearl Harbor committee the government had withheld information from him and led him to believe the Japanese would attack elsewhere .... Eisenhower announces that by April 30 all enlisted Army men with 45 points or 30 months service will be released .... Truman says the U.S. will insist upon retention of Pacific Islands considered essential for national defense, but will turn others over to the U.N. for trusteeship.	Westinghouse Electric, GE and GM electrical plants in 16 states are closed as 200,000 United Electrical, Radio and Machine Workers union members strike for a $2 daily wage increase .... CIO United Packing House Workers and AFL Amalgamated Meat Cutters & Butcher Workmen call a strike of 125,000 meat industry workers after labor negotiations break down .... Agriculture Dept. re-establishes wartime control over distribution of protein feed for livestock and poultry to correct the growing shortage in some areas and oversupply in others.		Felix A. (Doc) Blanchard, Army fullback, is awarded the James E. Sullivan Trophy for 1945 as the year's outstanding amateur athlete.	Jan. 15
	AP news service stops providing news to the State Dept. for dissemination abroad, stating that this practice creates "the fear of propaganda." United Press announces it is contemplating similar action .... Adm. Kimmel tells the Pearl Harbor inquiry that he had doubted the Japanese could stage an attack on Pearl Harbor .... U.S. intelligence sources report that Japan launched 9,000 bomb-carrying silk and paper balloons against the U.S. in 1944 and 1945, with about 10% reaching their target.	The strike of meat packers and butchers cuts U.S. meat output 75%, as the AFL Amalgamated Meat Cutters and Butchers union reduces its wage demand from a 25¢ hourly increase to 15¢.			Jan. 16
American Association of Junior Colleges holds its first meeting in Chicago and reports that 300-500 junior colleges will be opened in the U.S. during the next 10 years, with facilities for 500,000 students .... Sen. Homer Ferguson (R, Mich.) and Sen. Ralph Brewster (R, Me.) offer a motion at the Pearl Harbor inquiry to call Winston Churchill as a witness on British policy towards Japan in 1941.		Truman proposes an 18.5¢ hourly wage increase to avert a strike in the steel industry, while Labor Secy. Schwellenbach appoints a fact-finding board to settle the meat industry dispute.	At the Soviet Academy of Sciences in Moscow, Prof. A.A. Lebedev demonstrates a six-foot electronic microscope capable of 50,000 power magnification .... The Navy and Coast Guard demonstrate the Loran, an electronic instrument that determines the position and windspeed of ships, measuring the difference in arrival time of two radio signals.	The Lincoln Cathedral copy of the *Magna Charta* which has been in the U.S. Library of Congress since August 1939 is turned over to the liner *Queen Elizabeth*'s master for return to England .... A *Life* magazine article reports the growing popularity of Jean-Paul Sartre's philosophy of existentialism, which "sweeps aside the moral and ethical values of all past philosophies and takes as its departure the brute fact of man's existence."	Jan. 17
Boston Mayor James Curley, Donald Smith and James Fuller are convicted by a Washington District Court of using the mails to defraud .... Southern Democrats start a filibuster in the Senate to delay FEPC action.	Pearl Harbor inquiry committee rejects demands that Churchill be called as a witness.	Truman announces the USW's acceptance and the steel industry's rejection of his 18.5¢ pay raise proposal .... Civilian Production Administration orders distributors to set aside 60-70% of their bathtubs, cast iron radiators and cast iron soil pipes to maintain adequate stocks for the government's reconversion program .... All 17 persons aboard an Eastern Air Lines plane are killed when the plane catches fire in midair and crashes near Cheshire, Conn.		Network Hooper ratings list the most popular radio shows as: *Bob Hope*, *Fibber McGee and Molly*, *Radio Theater* and *Charlie McCarthy*.	Jan. 18
Hon. Adam Clayton Powell Jr.'s *Marching Blacks*, a program for Negro political action, is published.		Steel magnate Kaiser and the USW sign an agreement providing for an 18½¢ hourly wage increase .... CIO Federation of Glass, Ceramic & Silica Glass Workers and the Pittsburgh Plate Glass and Libbey-Owens-Ford companies settle a three-month-old strike with a 10.7¢ hourly wage increase.		*Billboard* reports the most popular songs are: (1) *Symphony*, (2) *I Can't Begin to Tell You* and (3) *Let It Snow! Let It Snow! Let It Snow!*	Jan. 19
	Truman issues an executive order establishing the Control Intelligence Group, later to become the CIA.		A Pan Am Constellation Clipper sets a commercial plane record for the New York-Lisbon flight by covering the 3,425 miles in 9:58 hours .... Agriculture Dept. reports the development of a new weed killer—2, 4 Di—which does not harm grass, hastens the ripening of fruit and makes apples cling to the tree longer for harvest .... The Navy reveals development of an underwater sound system to locate survivors at sea as far as 2,000 miles from shore stations .... Dr. Don Gudakunst, director of National Foundation for Infantile Paralysis, dies at 51 in Chicago.		Jan. 20
Truman sends a 25,000-word State of the Union Message and 1974 Budget Message to Congress, demanding full legislative support of his programs.	Truman appoints Vice Adm. Alan Kirk as ambassador to Belgium and minster to Luxembourg.	Steel plants throughout the nation shut down as 750,000 USW members go on strike for wage increases .... Federal Reserve issues a 100% margin ruling for the NYSE to check inflation, as Truman names James Vardaman, Jr. to a 14-year term on the Fed's board of governors.			Jan. 21

F	G	H	I	J
Includes elections, federal-state relations, civil rights and liberties, crime, the judiciary, education, health care, poverty, urban affairs and population.	*Includes formation and debate of U.S. foreign and defense policies, veterans affairs and defense spending. (Relations with specific foreign countries are usually found under the region concerned.)*	*Includes business, labor, agriculture, taxation, transportation, consumer affairs, monetary and fiscal policy, natural resources, pollution and accidents.*	*Includes worldwide scientific, medical and technological developments, natural phenomena, U.S. weather and natural disasters.*	*Includes the arts, religion, scholarship, communications media, sports, entertainment, fashions, fads and social life.*

	World Affairs	Europe	Africa & the Middle East	The Americas	Asia & the Pacific
Jan. 22	Britain announces it would welcome a U.N. inquiry into its activities in Greece and Indonesia.	U.S., Britain and Russian reveal an agreement to divide main units of the German fleet equally among themselves .... An explosion of 20 carloads of surplus ammunition destroys a large section of Torre Annunziata, Italy, killing 13 persons.			
Jan. 23	U.N. Economic and Social Council elects Sir H. Ramaswami Mudaliar of India as president.	British Foreign Secy. Bevin charges the Polish government with murdering political prisoners and challenges it to implement provisions of the Yalta agreement calling for "free and unfettered elections." .... Socialist Felix Gouin is elected president of the French provisional government by the Constituent Assembly.		A statement by 500 prominent Catholics in Buenos Aires denounces Peron as a totalitarian.	Followers of the late Subhas Chandra Bose, leader of the pro-Japanese Indian National Army during World War II, stage anti-British demonstrations in Bombay. Two are killed and 300 injured in clashes with police.
Jan. 24	U.N. General Assembly votes to establish a commission to study the control of atomic energy.	Britain and Greece sign an agreement giving Greece a 10 million pound loan to stabilize the drachma and $500,000 pounds in direct assistance .... French prosecution at Nuremberg charges that at least 29,660 French hostages were executed by the Nazis .... Franco denies he shared the views of Hitler and Mussolini and says Spain will become a democracy when the people are fully prepared.		National Democratic Front leader Julio Ernesto Portugal heads a new Peruvian cabinet which for the first time includes three members of the Aprista movement.	Allied headquarters orders the Japanese government to stop deficit financing or printing additional banknotes and directs the government to try to balance the budget .... The first American war crimes trial in China begins with 18 Japanese charged with the torture and execution of U.S. airmen.
Jan. 25	Sir Archibald Clark Kerr is appointed British ambassador to the U.S. to succeed Earl Halifax, whose resignation is effective May 1.		Soviet delegate Andrei Vishinsky tells the Security Council that Russia opposes any U.N. inquiry into the Iranian situation .... Anglo-American Comm. of Inquiry begins hearings in London on the Palestine issue.		Rioting by followers of Subhas Chandra Bose continues for the third day in Bombay, with casualties mounting to 22 dead and over 600 wounded.
Jan. 26		French President Gouin forms a new cabinet consisting of six Socialists, six Communists, six Popular Republican Movement members and one independent.	Iranian Parliament elects Ahmed Ghavam Saltaneh to head the government for a fourth term.		Moscow claims that secret clauses of the Yalta agreement promise Russia permanent possession of the Kurile Islands, southern Sakhalin and adjacent islands.
Jan. 27		Gen. Georg Thomas of the German General Staff charges at Nuremberg that Reinhard Heydrich staged the 1939 Munich beer cellar explosion to break up a peace movement in the Army.	The ruler of Transjordan, Emir Abdullah Ibn Hussein, hails the British independence plan as putting an end to a Zionist plot to take over his country .... King Farouk intervenes to prevent a dissolution of the Egyptian cabinet after Premier Mahmoud Fahmy Nokrashy Pasha threatens to resign over a dispute on the right to appeal to the U.N. against Britain.		
Jan. 28	U.N. Social, Humanitarian and Cultural Comm. begins debate on the refugee problem .... Thirty-four members of the International Monetary Fund and International Bank for Reconstruction and Development are invited by the State Dept. to a March 3 conference at Wilmington Island, Ga.	Former French Premier Leon Blum is appointed special ambassador to foreign countries on the problems of finance, economics and food.	High Commissioner Sir Alan Cunningham decrees the death penalty for terrorists attacking British military facilities in Palestine .... Iranian delegate to the U.N. Security Council Seyed Hassan Taquzadeh charges that Russia has been violating the 1942 Treaty of Alliance and the Teheran Declaration by aiding the Azerbaijan rebels.	A 60-day state of siege is declared in Chile as a result of a clash between police and members of the Workers Federation in Santiago.	Gen. Homma's defense counsel argues in Manila that the defendant never ordered atrocities and files an appeal to the U.S. Supreme Court for a writ of certiorari .... Chinese Communist, Democratic League and Youth Party representatives at the Political Consultative Conference reject a Nationalist offer to share seven or eight seats on a proposed cabinet, with the Kuomintang holding 10-12 seats for itself .... Korean Communists refuse to participate on the 35-man, all-party unification committee being organized under U.S.-Russian sponsorship.
Jan. 29	Norwegian Foreign Min. Trygve Lie is nominated by the Security Council as the first U.N. Secretary-General after Russia threatens to veto the U.S. choice, Lester Pearson of Canada .... UNRRA Director Lehman reinstates Gen. Morgan as German chief after several "long and searching" talks .... British Overseas Airways announces plans for world-wide service with daily flights to N.Y.	At Nuremburg, secret documents reveal that FDR, Churchill and Vatican officials knew in advance of the 1944 bomb plot against Hitler .... French Pres. Gouin receives a vote of confidence from the Constituent Assembly after he outlines a severe austerity program to check inflation.		Chilean Ministers Eduardo Frei and Enrique Arraigada resign when Adm. Vincente Merino Bielich orders the arrest of all Federation of Labor leaders after yesterday's clash .... Canadian Supreme Court establishes a formula, binding on Ford Motor Co. of Canada Ltd. and the UAW, requiring each employe to vote before the union may call a strike.	State Secy. Byrnes confirms Soviet claims that FDR and Churchill agreed to let the Russians have the Kuriles, southern Sakhalin and a small adjacent island at Yalta.

	A	B	C	D	E
	Includes developments that affect more than one world region, international organizations and important meetings of major world leaders.	*Includes all domestic and regional developments in Europe, including the Soviet Union, Turkey, Cyprus and Malta.*	*Includes all domestic and regional developments in Africa and the Middle East, including Iraq and Iran and excluding Cyprus, Turkey and Afghanistan.*	*Includes all domestic and regional developments in Latin America, the Caribbean and Canada.*	*Includes all domestic and regional developments in Asian and Pacific nations, extending from Afghanistan through all the Pacific Islands, except Hawaii.*

U.S. Politics & Social Issues	U.S. Foreign Policy & Defense	U.S. Economy & Environment	Science, Technology & Nature	Culture, Leisure & Life Style	
	Gen. Walter Short tells the Pearl Harbor committee that the War Dept. made him a "scapegoat" instead of admitting its failure to supply him with real information.	The UP reports that current strikes are costing the 1.65 million workers involved about $13.5 million a day in wages .... Acting on a Supreme Court mandate, Federal Judge Philip Sullivan of Chicago dismisses the government suit against Montgomery Ward & Co.			Jan. 22
	Truman names Rear Adm. Sidney Souers as director of the CIA, an agency which will coordinate all U.S. intelligence activities overseas .... Navy Secy. Forrestal urges that the vice president and State, War and Navy Dept. secretaries be placed on the proposed Atomic Energy Commission, and opposes giving the President power to remove Commission members .... State Dept. bars American-flag vessels from carrying troops or ammunition for use in suppressing anti-colonial revolts in French Indochina and the Dutch East Indies .... Maj. Gen. Short tells the Pearl Harbor inquiry that Army-Navy liaison in Hawaii was poor in 1941.	AFL Amalgamated Meat Cutters and Butchers union orders its striking members to return to work Jan. 26 to avert a threatened government seizure of meat-packing plants .... House Interstate & Foreign Commerce Comm. approves a bill aimed at AFL American Federation of Musicians President James Petrillo, who has barred the broadcast of records and programs originating outside the U.S.	Civilian Production Administration reveals the development of a "motion transformer," a new means of mechanical movement eliminating crankshafts and other conventional parts.	Bobby Riggs retains his world's professional tennis title by defeating Don Budge in Los Angeles.	Jan. 23
	U.S. Joint Chiefs of Staff announce that airborne atom bomb tests against warships will be held in May and July at Bikini Atoll in the Marshall Islands .... Gen. Carl A. Spaatz is named AAF chief by Truman and calls for a peacetime air force of 400,000 men and 6,000 planes .... U.S. State Dept. reports Siam has agreed to respect U.S. treaties made before the war.	Truman orders the Agriculture Dept. to seize and operate 134 plants of 17 meat packing companies at midnight Jan. 25 if striking workers do not resume their jobs by then.		N.Y. State Bd. of Censors lifts its ban on *Scarlet Street* after reviewing the film and persuading producer Walter Wanger to revise and delete some portions.	Jan. 24
		AFL Executive Council votes to readmit the UMW and elects John L. Lewis vice president of the AFL.		Dr. Max Euwe wins Section B of the International Chess Masters tournament in London.	Jan. 25
		Ford and Chrysler settle with the UAW for an hourly pay increase of 18½¢ .... CIO Packinghouse Workers vote to resume work in government-operated plants pending rulings by fact-finding boards.	Col. William Councill shatters the transcontinental record when he flies an Army Lockheed P-80 jet-propelled "Shooting Star" from Long Beach, Calif. to La Guardia in N.Y. in 4:13:26 .... The important cosmic ray component, meson, is isolated artificially for the first time at the GE labs in Schenectady, N.Y. .... The third earthquake in 24 hours hits Switzerland, causing damage in St. Moritz and the Canton of Valais.	Louis B. Mayer's Honeymoon wins the $28,705 Santa Maria Stakes in Calif. .... Herman Steiner wins Section A of the International Chess Masters tournament in London.	Jan. 26
		RCA signs with the CIO United Electrical Radio and machine Workers union for a 17½¢ hourly wage increase for 8,000 workers in Camden, N.J. .... OPA gives the Federal Housing Adminstration power to set rent ceilings on housing built with priority aid under the veterans' preference system and on FHA-insured homes.	Russia's Stalin Prize goes to Sergei Vavilov, Igor Tamm, Pavel Cherenkov and Alya Frank for their work with radiation electrons, and to Konstantin Petrozhak and Georgi Floryov for bringing about the spontaneous fission of uranium in 1943.	World Conference of Churches Provisional Comm. reveals it will meet in Geneva Feb. 20-24 to draft plans for a world assembly of Protestant church representatives.	Jan. 27
	Assistant Secy. of State William Benton protests the refusal of Associated Press and United Press to supply the State Dept. with news releases, claiming it is the result of rivalries between the news services.	260,000 striking butchers and meat packers return to work at 134 plants seized by the Department of Agriculture .... Supreme Court rules that owners of oil lands leased to producing companies are entitled to deductions for depletions in figuring federal income tax on their share of net profits.		Ben Hogan defeats Herman Keiser in the Phoenix Open by scoring 68 in a playoff.	Jan. 28
Harry L. Hopkins, former FDR adviser and confidant, dies at 55 in N.Y.	At the Pearl Harbor inquiry, evidence from MacArthur's headquarters is introduced stating no Japanese witness had confirmed that a "winds code" message had been sent prior to the surprise attack to indicate war with the U.S. .... Retiring Army Ordnance Chief Lt. Gen. Levin H. Campbell Jr. says the Army now has a rocket which reaches a height of 50 miles.	Rep. Francis Case (R., N.D.) introduces a new labor bill to set up mediation boards, enforce "cooling-off" periods, outlaw boycotts and sympathy strikes and authorize court injunctions .... House votes to return the U.S. Employment Service to the states by June 30.	An Australian government scientist reports that noise waves generated by the sun have been recorded with radar.		Jan. 29
F	G	H	I	J	
Includes elections, federal-state relations, civil rights and liberties, crime, the judiciary, education, health care, poverty, urban affairs and population.	*Includes formation and debate of U.S. foreign and defense policies, veterans affairs and defense spending. (Relations with specific foreign countries are usually found under the region concerned.)*	*Includes business, labor, agriculture, taxation, transportation, consumer affairs, monetary and fiscal policy, natural resources, pollution and accidents.*	*Includes worldwide scientific, medical and technological developments, natural phenomena, U.S. weather and natural disasters.*	*Includes the arts, religion, scholarship, communications media, sports, entertainment, fashions, fads and social life.*	

	World Affairs	Europe	Africa & the Middle East	The Americas	Asia & the Pacific
Jan. 30		British House of Commons passes a bill nationalizing the coal industry and creating a nine-man board within the Fuel and Power Ministry to manage it.	British authorities in Palestine announce that pending the Anglo-American Inquiry Committee's decisions 1,500 Jewish immigrants a month may enter Palestine .... Security Council votes to return the Iranian dispute to Iran and Russia for settlement by direct negotiation, but "retains the right to request information on [their] progress." .... Iraqi cabinet of Hamdi el Pacchechi resigns as a result of Regent Prince Abdul Illah's demand for social reforms.	Presidential candidate Juan Peron says in Buenos Aires he will not attempt a coup and charges that the U.S. embassy is involved in smuggling arms into Argentina.	
Jan. 31		Yugoslavian Assembly passes a new constitution making Yugoslavia a republic and asks Tito to form a new government .... Secy. Byrnes instructs the U.S. embassy in Warsaw to ask the Polish government to take steps to ensure political rights and free elections.		Gen. Eurico Gaspar Dutra is inaugurated president of Brazil at ceremonies in Rio de Janeiro .... Chilean Federation of Labor ends a 24-hour general strike after moderate Alfredo Duhalde is installed as acting president with a promise to form a new cabinet.	Truman acknowledges in a press conference that the agreement giving southern Sakhalin and the Kuriles to Russia was a secret part of the Yalta pact, and promises that other secret Allied agreements will be disclosed "at the proper time." .... At the final session of the Chinese Political Consultative Conference, Nationalists and Communists approve plans to set up a coalition government, to draft a constitution and to reorganize the National Assembly .... Arrangements for British troops to enter Japan are announced in London and Washington; the force is to be composed of men from Australia, the U.K., N.Z. and India .... Kuang Aphaiwong succeeds Seni Pramoj as premier of Siam.
Feb. 1	At the U.N. Security Council, Russian delegate Vishinsky demands the withdrawal of British troops from Greece.	The National Assembly passes a bill making Hungary a republic and elects Premier Zoltan Tildy its first president.	Arab League spokesman Faiz al-Khoury tells the Palestine Inquiry in London that Arabs will not accept Palestine partition or continued Jewish immigration.	On instructions from Secy. Byrnes, U.S. Charge d'Affairs John Moors Cabot asks Argentine Foreign Min. Juan Cooke to repudiate Peron's charges of U.S. arms smuggling.	In Manila, Japanese Gen. Hikotaro Tajima is sentenced to hang for the execution of American fliers on Bataan.
Feb. 2	Trygve Lie is installed by the General Assembly as the first U.N. secretary-general .... The U.N. site subcommittee chooses the North Stamford-North Greenwich area containing 42 square miles in Westchester County, N.Y. and Fairfield County, Conn. as first choice for a permanent U.N. headquarters.	Allied Control Council orders the elimination of nine key German industries, including synthetic gasoline, rubber, aluminum, magnesium, and heavy machine tools.		Venezuelan government grants all political parties the right to hold public meetings and announces that a constitutional assembly will soon be called to draw up new election laws.	
Feb. 3	Residents of Westchester and Fairfield Counties protest to Truman and N.Y. and Conn. governors against plans to locate the U.N. in their communities.	Greek Public Order Minister Stamatis Mercuris denies Russian charges of right-wing excesses in Greece .... Heinrich Himmler's secret papers, cited at Nuremberg, reveal that he ordered his former sweetheart and her doctor husband murdered to conceal medical experiments on Jews and Catholic priests.		Chilean Acting Pres. Alfredo Duhalde forms a new middle-of-the-road cabinet, which legalizes two unions in an attempt to avert a renewed general strike called by the Labor Federation.	MacArthur names Mass. Chief Justice John Higgins as the U.S. representative on the International Military Tribunal for the Far East .... British special envoy Sir Archibald Clark Kerr confers with Indonesian Premier Sjahrir and Dutch governor van Mook in Batavia.
Feb. 4	Threatening to invoke his veto power, Soviet delegate Vishinsky prevents the Security Council from passing a resolution stating British troops in Greece are not endangering world peace.	Testimony at Nuremberg reveals that German counter-intelligence chief Adm. Wilhelm Canaris refused to carry out Gen. Keitel's orders to seize and immobilize the French fleet six months before the Allied landing in North Africa. In other testimony, Belgian Professor Leon van der Essen claims that two German batteries destroyed the famous Univ. of Louvain library in May 1940, an incident the Nazis later tried to blame on the British.		Argentine Foreign Office reports ratification of the Bretton Woods agreement, and informs the U.S. it has no evidence substantiating Peron's claim that the U.S. embassy engaged in arms smuggling.	Supreme Court upholds the legality of the U.S. military tribunal which sentenced Japanese Gen. Tomoyuki Yamashita to death.
	A *Includes developments that affect more than one world region, international organizations and important meetings of major world leaders.*	B *Includes all domestic and regional developments in Europe, including the Soviet Union, Turkey, Cyprus and Malta.*	C *Includes all domestic and regional developments in Africa and the Middle East, including Iraq and Iran and excluding Cyprus, Turkey and Afghanistan.*	D *Includes all domestic and regional developments in Latin America, the Caribbean and Canada.*	E *Includes all domestic and regional developments in Asian and Pacific nations, extending from Afghanistan through all the Pacific Islands, except Hawaii.*

U.S. Politics & Social Issues	U.S. Foreign Policy & Defense	U.S. Economy & Environment	Science, Technology & Nature	Culture, Leisure & Life Style	
Sen. James Mead (D, N.Y.) fails in an effort to break the anti-FEPC fillibuster.	Truman urges Congress to approve a $4.4-billion credit to Britain for post-war economic adjustments .... Capt. A.H. McCollum tells the Pearl Harbor committee that as head of Navy intelligence in 1941 he never saw a Japanese "winds code" message, signifying war with the U.S. .... Sen. Harry Byrd (D, Va.) says the U.S. should follow the Russian example of control over the Kuriles and oppose any U.N. trusteeship of vital islands captured by the U.S.				Jan. 30
	War Dept. announces the creation of the First Experimental Guided Missiles Group to perfect robot bombs and aerial guided missles .... Adm. P.N.L. Bellinger, naval air wing commander at Pearl Harbor in 1941, testifies that he had not been ordered to carry out reconnaissance to the north by Adm. Kimmel the week before the Japanese attack.			The Washington home of M. Robert Guggenheim is swept by fire, bringing an estimated $1 million in damage to his art collections .... Jean Renoir's film *Diary of a Chambermaid*, describing a servant girl's search for wealth, opens in N.Y. .... Eisenhower receives an honorary Doctor of Laws degree from Boston University.	Jan. 31
Testifying before the Senate Naval Affairs Comm. on Truman's nomination of Edwin Pauley as under secretary of the Navy, Interior Secy. Harold Ickes claims that Pauley urged him in 1945 to cancel a government suit for title to tidelands oil fields in order to help raise Democratic campaign funds from oilmen.	American Legion National Commander John Stelle claims that the Veterans Administration has suffered a "tragic breakdown" and must be headed by "a seasoned businessman, not a soldier." VA Administrator Gen. Omar Bradley defends the agency and claims that Stelle's criticism does not represent general opinion in veterans organizations .... MIT Pres. Karl Compton urges the Senate Atomic Energy Comm. to set up separate policy-making and administrative bodies for atom control .... Capt. L.F. Stafford, assistant director of naval communications for cryptography in 1941, tells the Pearl Harbor committee that a Japanese "winds code" message was deciphered in Washington on Dec. 4, 1941.		A TWA Lockheed Constellation sets a N.Y.-L.A. commercial record of 10 hours 49 minutes .... Dr. Nicholas Wagman announces he has used a new photographic filter to locate a star similar to the sun, previously hidden by the brilliant Ophiucus constellation.		Feb. 1
GOP chairmen of 14 Midwestern states issue a 14-point "declaration of principles" to be included in the party platform, calling for a drastic change in Truman's foreign and domestic policies.			A magnetic storm on the sun covering 3.5 billion square miles disrupts short-wave communications between the U.S. and Europe .... German physicists Otto Hahn and Werner Heisenberg claim they had completed an "atomic energy machine" in Leipzig at the end of 1941 but could not produce a bomb because of lack of money and facilities.	L.E. Huston's Nanby Pass wins the $50,000 Santa Catalina Handicap.	Feb. 2
			Air Force reveals development of a plane with automatic devices controlling take-off, flight and landing, leaving the crew only to monitor equipment .... A TWA Constellation sets a commercial record by flying from Burbank, Calif. to N.Y. in 7 hours and 52 minutes .... CBS demostrates color television broadcasting, and claims that the system will be available to the public in 1947 .... The *AMA Journal* charges that indiscriminate use of foot remedies results in "chemical abuse" and that most are worthless.	Bob Fitzgerald captures the national men's senior speed skating championship and Elaine Gordon takes the women's title in St. Paul, Minn. .... Jimmy Demaret wins the Tucson open golf championship .... Edward Phillips Oppenheim, author of 150 suspense novels, dies at 79 on the Island of Guernsey.	Feb. 3
Sen. Alben W. Barkley (D, Ky.) fails to invoke cloture to end a filibuster against the FEPC.	War, Navy and State Depts. announce organization of a college for high-ranking officials in Washington to emphasize problems of national security.	About 3,500 tugboat workers of the AFL International Longshoremen's Assn. strike in N.Y. for a 40-hour work week.		*Born Yesterday*, featuring Judy Holliday and Paul Douglas, opens on Broadway to favorable reviews.	Feb. 4
F	G	H	I	J	
Includes elections, federal-state relations, civil rights and liberties, crime, the judiciary, education, health care, poverty, urban affairs and population.	*Includes formation and debate of U.S. foreign and defense policies, veterans affairs and defense spending. (Relations with specific foreign countries are usually found under the region concerned.)*	*Includes business, labor, agriculture, taxation, transportation, consumer affairs, monetary and fiscal policy, natural resources, pollution and accidents.*	*Includes worldwide scientific, medical and technological developments, natural phenomena, U.S. weather and natural disasters.*	*Includes the arts, religion, scholarship, communications media, sports, entertainment, fashions, fads and social life.*	

	World Affairs	Europe	Africa & the Middle East	The Americas	Asia & the Pacific
Feb. 5	U.S. and Britain recognize Rumania in accordance with the Big Three Moscow agreement .... The 18-nation U.N. Headquarters interim committee approves the subcommittee report recommending the Greenwich-North Stamford site .... Mrs. Eleanor Roosevelt introduces a resolution before the U.N. Social, Economic and Humanitarian Comm. recommending that the refugee problem be referred to the Economic and Social Council and that refugees not be forced to return to their homelands against their will.		In a note to the Security Council, Syria and Lebanon demand the total evacuation of British and French troops from their territory.		At his Manila trial, Gen. Homma admits witnessing part of the Bataan "death march" but denies he saw any bodies .... A joint Russian-U.S. communique indicates an agreement permitting railroad, motor and water transportation between the two Korean zones, exchange of mail, establishment of radio broadcasting frequencies within the country and return of refugees to their homes.
Feb. 6	The U.N. Security Council closes the Greek issue after Vishinsky withdraws the Russian charge that British troops are endangering world peace there, and Bevin withdraws his request that the Council acquit Britain of the accusation .... General Assembly and Security Council elect 15 jurists to serve on the new International Court of Justice .... All 18 nations attending a United Maritime Authority conference in London agree on cooperative action to meet the shipping needs of UNRRA.				Japanese Gen. Homma admits "moral" responsibility for the acts of his subordinates and for giving the order for the Bataan "death march." .... Sarawak, a privately-owned dominion in northern Borneo rich in oil and other raw materials, is ceded to Britain by "White Rajah" Sir Charles Brooke.
Feb. 7	Ukrainian delegate Dmitri Manuilsky charges at the Security Council that British troops in Indonesia are suppressing legitimate nationalist aspirations in violation of the U.N. Charter .... William McChesney Martin succeeds Wayne C. Taylor as president of the Export-Import Bank.	The British prosecution at Nuremberg declares that Rudolf Hess organized German fifth columns throughout the world	After eight years of exile, head of the Palestine Arab Party Jamal el Husseini returns to Jerusalem.	Mexican Foreign Ministry opens negotiations with Britain and the Netherlands to settle payments for oil lands expropriated in 1938.	War Dept. orders a stay of execution for convicted Gen. Yamashita, pending Truman's action on his clemency appeal .... U.S. Secy. of War Phillip Mason reveals that about 6,000 pro-Japanese Indian National Army members are imprisoned in India and 2,000 in Asia.
Feb. 8	In a meeting of the U.N. Social, Humanitarian and Cultural Comm., Mrs. Eleanor Roosevelt successfully opposes a Russian proposal restricting aid given to refugees who refuse to return to their homelands.	Lt. Gen. Roman A. Rudenko opens the Russian case against the 21 Nazi defendents at Nuremberg by reading a 79-page document recounting German atrocities.		Adolf A. Berle, Jr. resigns as U.S. ambassador to Brazil.	Truman refuses the clemency appeal of Gen. Yamashita.
Feb. 9		Speaking at a Communist Party Congress, Stalin predicts future conflict with the West and announces a new five-year plan to put Russia on a war footing.		Peron releases a 4,000-word document calling for closer relations with the U.S. and invites U.S. capital investments in Argentina.	Japanese cabinet, on MacArthur's directive, bars nearly nine-tenths of the current Parliament members from the March 31 elections.
Feb. 10		The Soviet Communist Party wins the first general elections held in Russia since 1937, facing opposition only in the recently annexed Baltic states.		Congressional elections in Costa Rica give the government 11 seats, with Communists winning two and other opposition parties 10.	Nearly 100,000 demonstrators protest a 50% reduction in the wheat ration in Cawnpore, India .... Dutch negotiators offer the right of self-determination within the Netherlands commonwealth to Indonesian nationalist leaders in Batavia.
Feb. 11	At the U.N. Security Council, the U.S. leads successful opposition to a Soviet proposal for an international investigation of the Indonesian problem .... Uruguay's proposal that the International Military Tribunal at Nuremberg be urged not to sentence Nazi defendants to death is defeated unanimously by the U.N. General Assembly .... Washington and London publish the secret text of the Yalta agreement .... An Anglo-American air travel treaty is signed in Bermuda for cooperation in the development of international airlines.	British House of Commons approves a Labor Party "cradle to grave" security bill providing for sickness, unemployment and retirement benefits .... Testifying at Nuremberg, German Stalingrad commander Friedrich von Paulus charges Goering, Keitel and Jodl with planning the attack on Russia .... The Allied Control Council in Berlin enacts a 1946 tax program for Germany designed to raise 15-20 billion marks .... U.S. combat engineers and intelligence officers recover the complete records of the German occupation of Czechoslovakia .... The smallest French military force in recent history, with an army of only 400,000 men, is agreed on by the country's military leaders.	Arab Higher Comm. decides to allow Palestinian Arabs to appear before the Palestine inquiry hearings in Jerusalem.		Japanese Gen. Homma is convicted by a U.S. military tribunal in Manila of ordering the "Bataan Death March" and is sentenced to death.
Feb. 12	Secy. Byrnes reveals that Russia demanded sole trusteeship of the former Italian colony of Tripolitania at the Allied Council of Foreign Ministers.			State Dept. issues a Blue Book accusing the Argentine government of complicity with Germany during the war and continued protection of Nazi interests.	Russian military authorities announce formation of an all-Korean Central Government of North Korea .... Japanese home office announces that 1,931 candidates are seeking election to the reformed House of Representatives
	A	B	C	D	E
	Includes developments that affect more than one world region, international organizations and important meetings of major world leaders.	*Includes all domestic and regional developments in Europe, including the Soviet Union, Turkey, Cyprus and Malta.*	*Includes all domestic and regional developments in Africa and the Middle East, including Iraq and Iran and excluding Cyprus, Turkey and Afghanistan.*	*Includes all domestic and regional developments in Latin America, the Caribbean and Canada.*	*Includes all domestic and regional developments in Asian and Pacific nations, extending from Afghanistan through all the Pacific Islands, except Hawaii.*

U.S. Politics & Social Issues	U.S. Foreign Policy & Defense	U.S. Economy & Environment	Science, Technology & Nature	Culture, Leisure & Life Style	
Truman puts Civil Service on a peacetime basis, ordering competitive exams for 1.6 million war service appointees .... Testifying before the Senate Naval Affairs Comm., Interior Secy. Ickes calls Pauley's attempt to stop a government suit for oil lands "the rawest proposition ever made to me."		Truman orders the Office of Defense Transportation to seize 91 struck towboat companies in N.Y.C. .... A month-old strike against Cleveland's three daily newspapers ends as the publishers and the AFL Pressmen's union agree to arbitration of their wage dispute.		Actor George Arliss, star of *Disraeli* and *The Green Goddess*, dies at 77 in London.	Feb. 5
National Board of the Communist Party recommends the expulsion of Earl Browder for conducting a publishing business "along a political line that coincides with the interest of .... American imperialism."		House ends its deliberations on the Case anti-strike bill, and passes and sends to the Senate the compromise full employment bill .... In putting into effect a food conservation program, Truman warns that the world faces a food crisis unprecedented in modern times.	Reuters reports from Rome that astronomers at Castel Gandolfo Observatory have discovered a new comet twice as big as the sun.		Feb. 6
		House passes and sends to the Senate the Case strike-control bill, calling for arbitration, cooling-off periods, penalties for boycotts and jurisdictional strikes and court action for breach of contract and violent picketing .... A government fact-finding board investigating the meat industry dispute recommends a 16¢ hourly wage increase for workers, to be met largely through price increases or government subsidies.		French National Radio Director Claude Bourdet is dismissed for permitting a Feb. 4 broadcast which caused widespread panic through a realistic description of the world's atomic destruction.	Feb. 7
Senate unanimously completes action on the compromise full employment bill, before Southern Democrats resume their anti-FEPC filibuster.	After its European tour, the House Colmer committee reports Russia has drawn Poland, the Baltic and Balkan states into its economic and political orbit to the point where trade with them is practically impossible .... A joint Army-Navy report reveals that the bomb-carrying balloons released by the Japanese cost about $18,000,000 and caused six deaths in Oregon and a few small forest fires.	The month-old strike of N.Y.C. communications workers against Western Union ends with an agreement to submit the wage dispute to arbitration .... Truman asks prompt congressional action on a two-year emergency housing plan calling for 2.7 million new homes.	Government scientists disclose a process of "printing" wiring circuits on a ceramic plate, making possible the production of miniature radios and other electronic equipment.		Feb. 8
Senate rejects a cloture motion in the 23-day filibuster against the FEPC and moves on to the Independent Offices Appropriations bill.		CIO Union of Electrical, Radio and Machine Workers settles with GM for an 18½¢ hourly increase.	Astronomers at Yerkes Observatory (Wisc.) announce they have observed the explosion of a nova—a star which flares suddenly, then returns to its original magnitude—at the western edge of Corona Borealis, trillions of miles from earth.	Ken Bartholomew wins the Eastern States speed skating championship in Saratoga Springs, N.Y. and Norma Davis takes the women's senior title .... Dr. Ludwig Schopp announces that 72 scholars under his direction are preparing a 72-volume edition of the writings of the Catholic Church fathers.	Feb. 9
Mafia leader Charles (Lucky) Luciano is deported to Italy.	The *Queen Mary* docks in N.Y. with 1,666 war brides and 668 children, the largest over-water movement of women and children in history.	CIO Transport Workers Union calls a strike of 9,606 employes of the Philadelphia Transportation Co. to gain a $2 daily wage increase.	War Dept. reveals the development of the "*Eniac*," an electronic numerical integrator and computer which solves mathematical problems 1,000 times faster than human computation.	Ben Hogan beats Sam Byrd and Byron Nelson to win the Texas open in San Antonio.	Feb. 10
	U.S. Navy Capt. R.H. Lavender discloses that the government has a patent on the atomic bomb filed in a special safe in the Patent Office.	N.Y.C. virtually shuts down when tugboat operators vote to continue their strike. With fuel supplies low, Mayor William O'Dwyer orders closing of most schools and places of business .... AFL Building and Construction Trades Council signs a five-year contract in N.Y., stabilizing wages for at least 1½ years .... Supreme Court rules that newspapers are engaged in interstate commerce and are subject to the Wage-Hour Law .... Commerce Dept. reports 1945 income payments to individuals hit an unprecedented high of $160.7 billion.			Feb. 11
Reps. Hugh De Lacy (D, Wash.) and John Rankin (D, Miss.) are ruled off the House floor after a dispute over Rankin's reference to newsman Walter Winchell as "a little slime-mongering kike."	U.S. Treasury releases Dutch assets of $1.8 billion, which were frozen when Germany overran Holland.	UAW rejects the GM offer of an 18½¢-an-hour wage increase and breaks off negotiations.	A N.Y. State Senate committee kills two bills outlawing the use of dogs for medical experiments.	Lauren Bacall and Humphrey Bogart are scheduled for the leads in *Stallion Road*, replacing Ronald Reagan and Alexis Smith.	Feb. 12

	World Affairs	Europe	Africa & the Middle East	The Americas	Asia & the Pacific
Feb. 13	U.N. General Assembly adopts a resolution rejecting Russian demands for forced repatriation of refugees. Russia also loses bids to gain Albania's admission to the U.N. and to have the Security Council examine the Indonesian situation .... U.N. Permanent Headquarters Comm. vote to locate the organization in N.Y. and names a nine-man commission to choose a final site.	The Russian prosecution at Nuremberg accuses the Germans of murdering and mistreating uncounted Soviet prisoners .... According to an official census taken by the Vienna Jewish Community Organization, 3,028 Jews remaining in the city intend to leave Europe and 1,065 wish to go to Palestine. More than half are willing to go anywhere .... British House of Commons repeals the 1927 Trade Disputes Act, which banned general strikes .... U.S. military authorities in Germany announce that Yugoslavian nationals employed by the Army will be dismissed immediately, after raids on refugee camps uncover documents of an underground "Royal Yugoslav Army."	Earthquakes cause 276 deaths in Algeria.	Asst. State Secy. Spruille Braden says evidence captured in Germany indicates Argentina had been guilty of supporting the Nazi cause.	
Feb. 14			U.N. Security Council takes up the Syrian and Lebanese appeal for withdrawal of British and French troops from the Levant; British Foreign Secy. Bevin urges that all countries involved in the dispute begin negotiations in Paris next week.	Peron charges that Spruille Braden heads a spy ring covering all of Latin America and is financing a political campaign against him.	Korean nationalists under Kim Koo and Syngman Rhee form the Korean Democratic Representative Council in Seoul .... In a new treaty, Cambodia gains autonomy within French Indochina.
Feb. 15	U.N. General Assembly adjourns until Sept. 3.	At Nuremberg Russian prosecutor Smirnov says defendant Hans Frank was responsible for the deaths of at least three million Jews.	The Security Council agrees that British and French troops should leave Syria and Lebanon, but fails to settle on a timetable .... After a week of anti-British student demonstrations in Cairo, Premier Mahmoud Fahmy Nokrashy Pasha and his cabinet resign.	Canadian Royal Mounted Police seize 22 members of a spy ring which allegedly transmitted atomic and radar secrets to Russia.	Anti-British demonstrations in India spread to Meerut, after three days of rioting in Calcutta, Bombay and New Delhi kill 45 and injure 400 .... Chinese Communists demand joint control of Manchuria with the Kuomintang and other parties.
Feb. 16	Russia uses its Security Council veto for the first time when rejecting a U.S. motion that Britain and France negotiate withdrawal from the Levant states.			Argentine Foreign Office affirms the government's loyalty to the American republics, calling U.S. accusations of wartime collaboration with Germany "unjustified and inexact."	In an anti-inflation move, the Japanese government limits incomes to 500 yen monthly, cuts bank withdrawals to 300 yen for family heads, restricts food distribution and calls for conversion of currency into new bank notes .... Viscount Wavell cuts the basic cereal ration from 16 to 12 ounces daily in India after declaring a three-million ton food shortage .... Forty left-wing Korean parties form the Korean Democratic People's Front in Seoul.
Feb. 17	Adrian Pelt of the Netherlands is appointed assistant secretary of the U.N. in charge of conferences and services; Russia's Arkady Sobolev will head the department of Security Council affairs.	Polish emigre army commander Wladyslaw Anders denies Russian-Yugoslav charges that his troops are menacing the peace .... Belgian parliamentary elections give Socialists and Communists a majority in the Chamber of Deputies and right-wing parties a majority in the Senate.	Ismail Sidky Pasha forms a new Egyptian cabinet, composed of five liberals and seven independents.		Chungking reports the resumption of warfare between Nationalists and Communists in Manchuria.
Feb. 18	U.N. Economic and Social Council creates five commissions: Narcotic Drugs, Economic and Employment, Social and Statistical, Human Rights and a 20-man committee to study the refugee problem.	Russian prosecution at Nuremberg charges that the Germans, in an effort to conceal mass killings, burned bodies.		Gov. Sir John Higgins declares a state of emergency as strikes sweep Jamaica after a weekend of unrest in Kingston.	MacArthur announces the nine judges who will sit on the international military tribunal for the Far East, including jurists from Australia, Canada, China, Holland, Russia, Britain, France and the U.S.
Feb. 19		Hungarian Primate Joseph Cardinal Mindszenty, who had denounced both German and Russian occupation of his country, arrives in Rome from Budapest .... The Anglo-American Committee of Inquiry on Jewish problems announces in Vienna that it has been refused permission to enter Hungary and Rumania.		Army, Navy and Air Force take over the task of preserving order in Argentina until after the presidential elections .... Brazilian government refuses to accept newly appointed Spanish ambassador Eduardo Aunos, charging him with Nazi ties.	Kim Il Sung is named chairman of the North Korean People's Government in Pyongyang, while the Democratic People's Front claims sole authority to form an interim government in Seoul .... British Prime Minister Attlee appoints a commission of three cabinet members to negotiate with Indian leaders on creation of a constituent assembly and executive council as a step towards self-government for India.
	A	B	C	D	E
	Includes developments that affect more than one world region, international organizations and important meetings of major world leaders.	*Includes all domestic and regional developments in Europe, including the Soviet Union, Turkey, Cyprus and Malta.*	*Includes all domestic and regional developments in Africa and the Middle East, including Iraq and Iran and excluding Cyprus, Turkey and Afghanistan.*	*Includes all domestic and regional developments in Latin America, the Caribbean and Canada.*	*Includes all domestic and regional developments in Asian and Pacific nations, extending from Afghanistan through all the Pacific Islands, except Hawaii.*

U.S. Politics & Social Issues	U.S. Foreign Policy & Defense	U.S. Economy & Environment	Science, Technology & Nature	Culture, Leisure & Life Style	
Interior Secy. Ickes resigns in his dispute with Truman over the appointment of Edwin Pauley as under secretary of the Navy .... Communist Party expels Earl Browder for factional activity and violation of party discipline and warns members against "Browderism." .... A Washington federal court rules that Ezra Pound is mentally unsound and cannot stand trial on treason charges.		The 10-day old strike of N.Y.C. tugboat operators ends as International Longshoremen's Assn. workers agree to arbitration of their dispute, permitting normal fuel supplies to reach N.Y.C.	A tornado hits Ardmore, Okla., injuring 15 people and leaving 200 homeless.		Feb. 13
	Navy Secy. Forrestal and Adm. Chester Nimitz tell the Senate Naval Affairs Comm. that a strong Navy with widespread bases is the surest defense against atomic attack .... W. Averell Harriman resigns as ambassador to Russia, and Truman names Gen. Walter Bedell Smith to be his replacement.	Truman announces a new policy allowing wage increases consistent with the general wage pattern set in industry since August 1945 and permitting price adjustments without a six-month wait.		London is chosen as the site of the 1948 Summer Olympics.	Feb. 14
	Army and Navy sources reveal that robot aircraft called "drones" will be used to gather data during the atomic bomb tests at Bikini atoll .... Former White House naval aide Lester Schulz testifies at the Pearl Harbor inquiry that FDR said "This means war" after reading the decoded Japanese message of Dec. 6, 1941, but did not mention Pearl Harbor.	U.S. Steel and the CIO-USW agree on an $18\frac{1}{2}$¢ hourly wage increase, ending a four-week strike by 150,000 steel workers.	John J. Brown, developer of hydraulic machinery and oil distilling processes, dies at 73 in N.Y.C.		Feb. 15
	VA announces a two-year plan to build 183 hospitals with 151,500 beds in 39 states .... The White House announces Truman was informed of the Canadian spy ring several months ago.	Strikes of 67,000 Republic Steel and 75,000 Bethlehem Steel workers are settled by an agreement providing for an $18\frac{1}{2}$¢-hourly wage increase.	Austrian-born chemist Ernst Berl, who developed a process for converting vegetation into coal and oil, dies at 68 in Pittsburgh.		Feb. 16
			The 1945 Fawcett Award for "the greatest scientific contribution to the progress of aviation" is given to Fred E. Weick, designer of the Ercoupe "spinproof" plane.		Feb. 17
Boston Mayor James Curley is sentenced to 6-18 months in prison and fined $1,000 for mail fraud.	Former Asiatic Fleet Commdr. Thomas Hart tells the Pearl Harbor committee that the Nov. 27, 1941 war warning from Washington was enough to prepare him for war .... W. John Kenney is confirmed by the Senate as assistant secretary of the Navy.	Jones & Laughlin Steel Corp. and other firms throughout the U.S. settle with the CIO-USW for an $18\frac{1}{2}$¢ hourly wage increase .... OPA Dir. Bowles urges extension of price controls and says that the government's new wage-price policy will prevent price increases on food, rent and clothing .... Senate confirms George E. Allen as Reconstruction Finance Corp. director and Horace Chapman as Contract Settlements director .... John J. Raskob resigns as director and vice president of E.I. duPont de Nemours & Co., where he began to work as a stenographer in 1902.		Thirty-two cardinals nominated by Pope Pius XII, among them Francis Spellman of New York, are approved by a secret consistory of the Sacred College of Cardinals .... Patriarch Benjamin, supreme leader of the Greek Orthodox Church, dies at 78 in Istanbul .... *Antigone*, a play by Jean Anouilh based on Sophocles' tragedy, opens in N.Y.	Feb. 18
	American Council on Education reveals in Washington that one million veterans have applied for educational and vocational courses under the GI Bill of Rights .... Secy. Byrnes says there have been no leaks of U.S. atom information and that the U.S. has exclusive knowledge of the methods of atomic bomb manufacture .... Gen. Short's chief of staff in 1941, Col. Walter Phillips, tells the Pearl Harbor inquiry that the Army-Navy Joint Planning Comm. never met between Nov. 27 and Dec. 7 despite Washington's war warning.	In what analysts say is a reaction to Bowles' price-control statements, prices on the NYSE drop two to seven points, the sharpest decline since 1940 .... Truman appoints O. Max Gardner to succeed Daniel W. Bell as Treasury under secretary.	Dr. I.M. Rabinowitch reports that a 15-year test of a high carbohydrate diet on 5,000 diabetics shows diabetics may eat an ordinary amount of sweets and starches but must avoid fats.	International Amateur Athletic Federation lists Gunder Haegg's world mile record of 4:01.4 despite charges he is a pro.	Feb. 19
F *Includes elections, federal-state relations, civil rights and liberties, crime, the judiciary, education, health care, poverty, urban affairs and population.*	G *Includes formation and debate of U.S. foreign and defense policies, veterans affairs and defense spending. (Relations with specific foreign countries are usually found under the region concerned.)*	H *Includes business, labor, agriculture, taxation, transportation, consumer affairs, monetary and fiscal policy, natural resources, pollution and accidents.*	I *Includes worldwide scientific, medical and technological developments, natural phenomena, U.S. weather and natural disasters.*	J *Includes the arts, religion, scholarship, communications media, sports, entertainment, fashions, fads and social life.*	

	World Affairs	Europe	Africa & the Middle East	The Americas	Asia & the Pacific
Feb. 20		Spanish Pretender Don Juan's spokesman in Lisbon says that negotiations for Franco's surrender of power have ended in failure . . . . Chancellor Leopold Figl promises Austrian Jews full citizenship rights and restitution of their property stolen by the Nazis . . . . Allied Control Council drafts a new marriage law repealing the Nazi law which banned "interracial" marriages and permitted political divorces.	Zionist terrorists attack police headquarters in Haifa and Tel Aviv and blow up an RAF radar station at Mount Carmel.	Soviet government admits gaining atomic information from Canadian citizens but adds it has been insignificant.	
Feb. 21		Russians charge at Nuremberg that Heinrich Himmler decided only 30,000,000 persons should be left alive in Russia after Germany won the war . . . . Eight wartime Finnish leaders are sentenced to prison in Helsinki for leading Finland into war on Germany's side.	At least 14 persons are killed and 123 wounded as anti-British riots sweep Egypt.		In Bombay, India, British troops fire on mobs as they loot and set up barricades after a mutiny of Indian sailors.
Feb. 22		Russians introduce evidence at Nuremberg that Russian civilians shipped to Germany in 1942 were sold at $4-6 a head for slave labor . . . . Norwegian government drops treason charges against Nobel Prize novelist Knut Hamsun, 86, because of "mental deficiencies" due to old age.		Peron issues a 127-page "Blue and White Book" accusing U.S. embassy officials of espionage and denying charges of wartime Argentine collaboration with Germany.	British authorities impose a 9 p.m. curfew in Bombay as rioting and looting continue for the second day.
Feb. 23		Records of the Nazi occupation of Czechoslovakia, found by U.S. combat engineers near Prague, are given to the Czech government following a Czech protest . . . . Moscow announces the death of Vladimir Potemkin, 66, former vice commissar for foreign affairs and a member of the Communist Party Central Comm.	Tewfiq Suweidy forms a new cabinet in Iraq, with himself as premier and foreign minister.		Japanese Gen. Yamashita, Lt. Col Ohta and Takuma Higashiga are hanged as war criminals near Los Banos, southeast of Manila . . . . The mutiny of Indian sailors in Bombay ends after British authorities promise that strikers will not be punished for pressing reasonable grievances.
Feb. 24		A committee of U.S., British and French experts reports in Frankfurt on the basis of a 10-day survey that German workers are showing evidence of physical deterioration from lack of enough food.		Argentina's presidential election is held without major incident and results in the victory of Juan Peron over centrist-liberal candidate Jose Tamborini.	MacArthur limits Japan's 1946 exports to 25% of the 1934-39 average . . . . Chinese Communists open a seven-pronged drive in Manchuria to cut the Nationalists' communications between Sinmin and Mukden.
Feb. 25		Dr. Wilhelm Furtwaengler's invitation to conduct the Vienna Philharmonic is withdrawn by an Austrian investigating committee on the grounds of possible Nazi affiliation.	Iranian Premier Ahmad Gavam Saltaneh is told in Moscow that Russian troops will remain in northwestern Iran "until the situation has been elucidated."		A long-debated agreement to unify the Communist and Nationalist armies is signed in Chungking . . . . Japanese cabinet postpones Diet elections to April 10 to enable closer screening of the 2,850 candidates.
Feb. 26		French cabinet orders the Franco-Spanish border closed and commercial relations virtually suspended in protest against the Franco government's execution of 10 Spanish veterans of the French resistance movement.	British troops in Palestine seize 5,000 Jews in a search for terrorists who wrecked 22 RAF planes at Quastina, Petah Tikvah and Lydda last night.	Canadian government names Finance Minister J.L. Ilsley as its representative in the IMF and International Bank for Reconstruction and Development.	With Russia represented for the first time, the Allied Far Eastern Commission meets in Washington, D.C. at its permanent headquarters in the Japanese embassy . . . . Nehru tells a Bombay rally that every Indian in the armed forces should refuse to shoot or harm fellow Indians on British orders.
Feb. 27		Spain closes part of the Franco-Spanish border and sends up a contingent of Moorish troops in response to French action yesterday . . . . U.S. sends a note to Britain and France calling for cooperation in ousting Franco from Spain . . . . U.S. authorities in Frankfurt announce the arrest of Friedrich Flick, 62, head of a $400-million armaments combine called the "greatest single power behind the Nazi war machine."			Russia and Mongolia sign a military alliance in Moscow.

A
Includes developments that affect more than one world region, international organizations and important meetings of major world leaders.

B
Includes all domestic and regional developments in Europe, including the Soviet Union, Turkey, Cyprus and Malta.

C
Includes all domestic and regional developments in Africa and the Middle East, including Iraq and Iran and excluding Cyprus, Turkey and Afghanistan.

D
Includes all domestic and regional developments in Latin America, the Caribbean and Canada.

E
Includes all domestic and regional developments in Asian and Pacific nations, extending from Afghanistan through all the Pacific Islands, except Hawaii.

U.S. Politics & Social Issues	U.S. Foreign Policy & Defense	U.S. Economy & Environment	Science, Technology & Nature	Culture, Leisure & Life Style	
	Pearl Harbor committee ends its hearings after accumulating nearly 15,000 pages of testimony, and promises to report to Congress by June 1.	Stabilization Administrator John C. Collet issues an order permitting wage increases without government approval until March 15, after which they must be submitted to the National Wage Stabilization Board .... U.S. Employment Service begins a nationwide canvass to find jobs for more than six million veterans and others expected to seek employment through June.		World Council of Churches conference convenes in Geneva, with representatives of nearly 100 Protestant and Orthodox church organizations in 32 countries present .... DAR bars Eddie Condon's jazz band from Constitution Hall "because of the type of audience" which would attend the concert.	Feb. 20
House passes the national school lunch bill and the Lea bill, aimed at curbing "coercive" labor practices in the communications industry.	Navy reveals that it will send a task force to the Arctic next month to test the operation of carrier planes in cold regions .... Truman says plans to outlaw peacetime military training throughout the world are impractical.	Senate confirms FCC Chairman Paul A. Porter as head of the OPA.			Feb. 21
					Feb. 22
	Navy high command confirms the court martial ruling that Capt. Charles McVay 3rd was guilty of negligence in the loss of the cruiser *Indianapolis* last July, but remits his sentence and returns him to active duty. McVay was earlier acquitted on charges of failing to give a timely "abandon ship" order.			N.Y.A.C. wins the national AAU indoor track and field title in N.Y.	Feb. 23
Herbert Brownell tells GOP leaders he will resign as national chairman because the party's success in the 1946 congressional elections is assured.		U.S. Labor Dept. names five representatives each from the CIO and the AFL to a Labor Education Advisory Comm. to help plan a long-range program for industrial peace.		Provisional Comm. of the World Council of Churches establishes a Commission of International Relations to stimulate a "vigorous expression" of Christian demands for justice and world order .... *New York Herald Tribune* reports Daphne du Maurier's *The King's General* and Betty MacDonald's *The Egg and I* as the best-selling fiction and non-fiction books.	Feb. 24
Supreme Court rules that military courts set up under martial law in Hawaii have no power to try civilians.		Truman issues a directive re-establishing the Office of Economic Stabilization with former OPA director Chester W. Bowles as its head.		Pope Pius XII tells diplomats and Church officials he refrained from approving the war against Russia in 1941 in the hope that it could be stopped.	Feb. 25
State militia seize 300 weapons in a house-to-house search in Columbia, Tenn. after 10 persons are injured in race riots .... Truman nominates Julius Krug to be Interior secretary... passes a $100-million national school lunch bill and also approves a $250 million emergency housing bill for veterans.	War and Navy Depts. asks Congress for a 20% pay increase for all men in the armed services to meet higher living costs and provide recruitment incentive.	Ford and the UAW sign an agreement calling for an 18¢ hourly wage increase and stringent action against workers who begin wildcat strikes .... Wage Stabilization Bd. orders a 16¢ hourly wage increase for packing house workers and the OPA approves a 1½% retail price rise for meat after March 11 .... House passes the ships sale bill giving U.S. shipping lines priority in the purchase or leasing of 50 million tons of shipping built during the war .... Mediation efforts by CIO President Philip Murray and RCA chief David Sarnoff avert a strike by transport workers in N.Y.C.			Feb. 26
Univ. of Texas bars Negroes from its law school.	Manhattan Project Dir. Gen. Leslie Groves tells the Senate Atomic Energy Comm. that he favors a federal nuclear control commission of nine members, including several assigned by the military.	Senate cuts OPA funds for the next four months to $927,000 and votes to cut Civilian Production Admin. funds to $750,000.			Feb. 27

F	G	H	I	J
Includes elections, federal-state relations, civil rights and liberties, crime, the judiciary, education, health care, poverty, urban affairs and population.	*Includes formation and debate of U.S. foreign and defense policies, veterans affairs and defense spending. (Relations with specific foreign countries are usually found under the region concerned.)*	*Includes business, labor, agriculture, taxation, transportation, consumer affairs, monetary and fiscal policy, natural resources, pollution and accidents.*	*Includes worldwide scientific, medical and technological developments, natural phenomena, U.S. weather and natural disasters.*	*Includes the arts, religion, scholarship, communications media, sports, entertainment, fashions, fads and social life.*

	World Affairs	Europe	Africa & the Middle East	The Americas	Asia & the Pacific
Feb. 28		French government accepts the U.S. proposal to condemn Franco but reveals it has asked for Big Three support of its plan to submit the Spanish issue to the U.N. Security Council March 21 . . . . Chief U.S. Prosecutor Robert H. Jackson demands at Nuremberg that 2,040,155 members of six Nazi organizations be found guilty of war crimes . . . . Former Hungarian Premier Bela Imredy is executed in Budapest for collaboration with the Nazis . . . . Former governor of Bessarabia Gen. Constantin Voiculescu and 10 Rumanian officers are sentenced to life imprisonment for crimes against Jews.			France signs a treaty with Chungking ending French extraterritorial rights in Peking, Amoy, Shanghai, Tientsin, Hankow and Canton.
March 1		Ferenc Szalasy, leader of the Hungarian fascist "Arrow Cross" movement, is sentenced to death for treason in Budapest with six of his former cabinet members . . . . U.S. State Dept. reveals Britain has accepted its proposals on Spain.	Russian forces prevent Iranian troops from occupying three towns in eastern Iran supposedly evacuated by the Soviets.	Panama adopts a new constitution, replacing the one introduced by former President Arnulfo Arias.	Indonesian Nationalist Premier Sutan Sjahrir resigns in a dispute with President Sukarno over broadening the cabinet but is renamed by the central committee to form a new one.
March 2	Voters of Greenwich, Conn. reject locating U.N. headquarters in or near the town.	French Foreign Min. Georges Bidault calls for a four-power conference on Germany to consider permanent separation of the Ruhr and the Rhineland . . . . The Franco government denounces French closing of the Pyrenees border as a result of Pyrenees pressure.	Secy.-Gen. Abdul Rahman Assam Pasha of the Arab League tells the Anglo-American Comm. of Inquiry on Palestine the League will oppose creation of a Jewish state in Palestine with every means at its disposal.	Puerto Rican Gov. Rexford G. Tugwell vetoes bills authorizing a plebiscite to determine the island's political status and giving voters the right to recommend gubernatorial candidates.	
March 3		Swiss officials agree to confer with the U.S., Britain and France on the disposal of German assets in Switzerland.			Left and right-wing Koreans protest a U.S. military government ordinance requiring all political parties to register with American authorities . . . . Soviet ambassador to China Appolon Petrov protests over anti-Russian demonstrations in many Chinese cities, aimed at the allegedly slow withdrawal of Russian forces from Manchuria.
March 4	Trygve Lie names four assistant secretaries: benjamin Cohen, Chile; Henry Laugier, France; Ivan Kerno, Czechoslovakia; and Victor Hoo, China.	London, Paris and Washington issue a statement declaring that "so long as Gen. Franco continues in control of Spain, the Spanish people cannot expect full and cordial association" with other nations . . . . Field Marshal Baron Carl Gustav Mannerheim, 78, who fought the Russians in World Wars I and II, resigns as president of Finland due to ill health . . . . At Nuremberg, defense lawyers for Ernst Kaltenbrunner, Alfred Rosenberg, Hans Frank and Wilhelm Frick declare that their clients were pro-Jewish humanitarians who resisted Nazi excesses.	Britain and France announce an agreement to begin withdrawing their troops from Syria, with complete evacuation by April 30 . . . . Seventeen Egyptians and two British soldiers are killed and 299 civilians and two British soldiers are wounded in Alexandria riots protesting continued British presence in Egypt . . . . Iranian Premier Ahmad Gavam Saltaneh protests Russia's decision to keep troops in Iran.	Canadian government reports that a network of undercover agents was operating through the Russian embassy in Ottawa under direct Moscow instructions to obtain atomic secrets . . . . Puerto Rican legislature overrides Gov. Tugwell's veto of bills giving the island a voice in choosing its governor and calling for a political status plebiscite.	Adm. Mountbatten deactivates Indochina as a territory within the Allied Southeast Asia Command, ending British military assistance to French forces in the area . . . . U.S. military police in Tokyo arrest four Americans and seven Japanese, alleged operators of a 13 million-yen black market ring.
March 5	In a speech at Westminster College in Mo., Churchill says an "iron curtain" has descended across Europe and urges a close U.S.-British alliance to combat world Communism . . . . State Dept. protests Russia's continued presence in Iran and Soviet claims to all Japanese enterprises in Manchuria as war booty.	Eugene Cardinal Tisserant of France claims that a secret clause of the Yalta agreement provides for repatriation of Russians who fled the Soviet Union after 1929 and that thousands of refugees are being forcibly returned to Russia by Britain and the U.S. . . . . U.S. military government presents a "definitive" denazification law to German officials from the U.S. occupation zone meeting in Munich. The law provides penalties ranging from property confiscation and disenfranchisement to forced labor abroad for convicted Nazis . . . . Dr. Alan May, British nuclear scientist, is taken into custody after being arraigned in London on charges of disclosing official secrets.			

A	B	C	D	E
Includes developments that affect more than one world region, international organizations and important meetings of major world leaders.	*Includes all domestic and regional developments in Europe, including the Soviet Union, Turkey, Cyprus and Malta.*	*Includes all domestic and regional developments in Africa and the Middle East, including Iraq and Iran and excluding Cyprus, Turkey and Afghanistan.*	*Includes all domestic and regional developments in Latin America, the Caribbean and Canada.*	*Includes all domestic and regional developments in Asian and Pacific nations, extending from Afghanistan through all the Pacific Islands, except Hawaii.*

U.S. Politics & Social Issues	U.S. Foreign Policy & Defense	U.S. Economy & Environment	Science, Technology & Nature	Culture, Leisure & Life Style	
	Secy. Byrnes tells the Overseas Press Club that the U.S. wants Russian friendship but warns that it "cannot allow aggression to be accomplished by coercion or pressure or by subterfuge." . . . . Air Force reveals it is experimenting with radar detection of captured German V-2 bombs to find a defense against atom bomb raids.	Bureau of Labor Statistics reveals that 1.4 million workers were on strike in January, a record high for any single month.	United Air Lines reveals it has ordered a jet plane for commercial use.	*Road to Utopia* sets a $15,565 opening day paid attendance record for films at New York's Paramount Theater.	Feb. 28
	U.S. delegate to the U.N. John Foster Dulles says in a Philadelphia speech, "It is particularly hard to find ways of working together with the Soviet Union, for it seems not to want cooperation".			N.Y. State Supreme Court awards Donald Flamm $350,000 for being coerced by the Commerce Dept. to sell a radio station.	March 1
	Gen. Carl A. Spaatz orders the reorganization of the AAF into Strategic, Tactical and Continental Defense Commands.	On the 102nd day of the UAW strike at GM, union leaders propose that work be resumed while demands are submitted to an arbitrator appointed by Truman . . . . Goodyear, Goodrich, Firestone and U.S. Rubber companies sign a contract with the CIO Rubber Workers Union calling for an 18¢ hourly wage increase for 100,000 workers . . . . The government charges the A&P food chain with monopoly.		White House Correspondents Assn. gives the Raymond Clapper Memorial Award for reporting to Bert Andrews of the *New York Herald Tribune* . . . . Richard Button takes the men's national figure skating title in Philadelphia and Gretchen Merrill takes the women's senior title . . . . Logan Piersall Smith, British essayist and critic and author of *All Trivia*, dies in London at 80.	March 2
	War Dept. announces a new plan limiting the size of Negro units in the postwar Army to infantry regiments and calling for creation of composite Negro and white units.	GM rejects the UAW proposal for resumption of work while a contract is being arbitrated . . . . An American Airlines plane crashes against a fog-shrouded peak of the Laguna Mountains, Calif., killing 27 persons.		Ben Hogan wins the St. Petersburg, Fla. Open Golf Tournament, with Sam Snead second.	March 3
Senate-House committee on legislative reorganization recommends a 37-point program calling for restrictions on deficit financing, curbs on lobbies, a congressional pay raise and a cut in the number of committees.		N.Y. garment industry mediator Arthur Meyer grants 400,000 ILGWU members a $2-5 weekly pay increase . . . . Justice Dept. asks the Supreme Court to bar the sale of the Pullman Co. to 43 railroads on the grounds that this would perpetuate a monopoly.			March 4
The Rev. Dr. John M. Coleman becomes the first Negro appointed to the N.Y.C. Board of Higher Education.	House Military Affairs Comm. votes to place the controversial May-Johnson atom control bill before the full House . . . . Eisenhower declares that Army efficiency is low and that it will take at least a year to restore the service to prewar status.	Office of Economic Stabilization Director Chester Bowles assails "greedy, reckless lobbies" in a Topeka, Kan. speech and proclaims the next several weeks vital in "our fight to maintain a stabilized economy."		A 21-man special commission of the Federal Council of Churches of Christ in America presents a report condemning the atomic bombing of Japan and urging that the U.S. abandon the bomb pending international control.	March 5

F	G	H	I	J
Includes elections, federal-state relations, civil rights and liberties, crime, the judiciary, education, health care, poverty, urban affairs and population.	*Includes formation and debate of U.S. foreign and defense policies, veterans affairs and defense spending. (Relations with specific foreign countries are usually found under the region concerned.)*	*Includes business, labor, agriculture, taxation, transportation, consumer affairs, monetary and fiscal policy, natural resources, pollution and accidents.*	*Includes worldwide scientific, medical and technological developments, natural phenomena, U.S. weather and natural disasters.*	*Includes the arts, religion, scholarship, communications media, sports, entertainment, fashions, fads and social life.*

	World Affairs	Europe	Africa & the Middle East	The Americas	Asia & the Pacific
March 6	N.Y.C. signs a contract leasing part of Hunter College to the U.N. from March 1 to May 15 for $9,333.34 monthly . . . . Atlantic Traffic Conference of the International Air Transport Assn., meeting in N.Y., sets Atlantic fares at about 10.4¢ per passenger mile.	Spain issues regulations barring all French nationals from its possessions and suspending mail, telegraphic communications and trade between the two countries . . . . In messages to Britain and the U.S., Russia demands the Turkish Kars-Ardahan area as the price of a defense treaty with Turkey.	Iranian War Ministry charges that Iranian troops were stopped by Russian forces 60 miles east of Teheran as they moved to occupy towns which the Russians had promised to evacuate.	Nearly 23,000 Chilean miners strike against coal companies and the government, demanding "fulfillment of their economic aspirations" and a diplomatic break with Spain.	Japanese government publishes a new constitution, approved by MacArthur, which renounces war, prohibits maintenance of an army, navy or air force, subjects the Emperor to constitutional checks and establishes a "Bill of Rights." . . . . French officials reach a tentative agreement with Vietnamese nationalists under Ho Chi-minh, recognizing the Democratic Republic of Vietnam as "a free state . . . . forming part of the Indochinese Federation of the French Union."
March 7		U.S., Russia and Britain announce a three-way division of 500 German merchant ships, leaving Germany with some 100 vessels . . . . Socialist Paul-Henri Spaak is charged by the Regent to form a new Belgian government . . . . Conductor Wilhelm Furtwaengler, barred from performing under a denazification statute, protests to the mayor of Berlin that he has not been given an opportunity to defend himself.	Teheran reports that the Azerbaijan rebels have incorporated a 60-mile stretch of the northern Gilan Province extending from the Soviet border to Shafarud into their autonomous region.		
March 8		Hermann Goering begins his Nuremberg defense by claiming that he loved peace, befriended Jews and regarded Allied airmen as brother fliers . . . . Russia rejects a U.S. request that the Bulgarian cabinet include two ministers "who would really represent the opposition parties." . . . . Greek Foreign Min. Constantine Rendis asks the world powers to help Greece protect its frontiers against Bulgaria, Albania and Italy.	Dr. Chaim Weizmann, president of the Jewish Agency for Palestine, presents the Zionist case before the Anglo-American Commission of Inquiry, urging the creation of a Jewish state in Palestine.	Venezuela confiscates the fortune of Julio Medina Angarita for misusing public funds while his brother was president.	
March 9	Truman tells the 34-nation International Monetary Conference at Wilmington Island, Ga. that the Bretton Woods Agreement is the cornerstone of a sound new economic world.	Pro-Russian Premier Juho K. Paasikivi is elected president of Finland by Parliament.			Chungking reports that Russian troops are evacuating Mukden, turning over their garrison duties to Chinese Nationalist forces . . . . Three Dutch battalions arrive in Batavia to relieve British and Indian troops fighting Indonesian nationalists.
March 10		Karl Haushofer, Hitler's political adviser and originator of the term *Lebensraum*, commits suicide with his wife in Frankfurt.		A 24-day strike of municipal workers in Kingston, Jamaica is reported over.	Japanese government bars from public life all writers, artists, publishers and editors who promoted military aggression, all businessmen who helped finance it and all diplomats who had anything to do with the Axis pact.
March 11	U.S. Treasury Secy. Fred Vinson is elected chairman of the Boards of Governors of both the World Bank and the International Monetary Fund . . . . Soviet newspaper *Pravda* denounces Churchill's March 6 proposal for an Anglo-American alliance as an attempt to dominate the world and "liquidate" the U.N. . . . . The 18 nations of the United Maritime Executive Bd. end wartime controls of international shipping.	Secy. Byrnes deplores Russia's refusal to permit opposition members in the Bulgarian cabinet, claiming that such participation had been agreed upon by Allied foreign ministers . . . . The U.S. rejects the French proposal to join in bringing the Spanish situation before the U.N.	David Ben Gurion, chairman of the Jewish Agency for Palestine, tells the Anglo-American Commission of Inquiry that Palestine's Jews can and will defend themselves if British troops are withdrawn . . . . Iranian Premier Ahmad Ghavam Saltaneh returns to Teheran from Moscow as left-wing members of parliament prevent the legislature from extending its session, leaving Ghavam virtual dictator of the country.		Shortly before leaving China for consultations in the U.S., Gen. Marshall persuades the Nationalists and Communists to extend the authority of the Peking truce board to parts of Manchuria not held by the Russians.
March 12	Membership Comm. of the IMF extends for six months the opportunity for Russia and eight other nations to ratify the Bretton Woods Agreement . . . . Because of ill health, Herbert H. Lehman resigns as director-general of the UNRRA.	Hungarian fascist leader Ferenc Szalasy is executed in Budapest along with four aides.	State Dept. reveals it has sent Russia a second note inquiring about the southward and westward movement of Soviet troops in Iran . . . . Palestinian Arab leader Jamal el Husseini states that "we are willing to shed our own blood" to gain British evacuation from Palestine.		

A	B	C	D	E
Includes developments that affect more than one world region, international organizations and important meetings of major world leaders.	*Includes all domestic and regional developments in Europe, including the Soviet Union, Turkey, Cyprus and Malta.*	*Includes all domestic and regional developments in Africa and the Middle East, including Iraq and Iran and excluding Cyprus, Turkey and Afghanistan.*	*Includes all domestic and regional developments in Latin America, the Caribbean and Canada.*	*Includes all domestic and regional developments in Asian and Pacific nations, extending from Afghanistan through all the Pacific Islands, except Hawaii.*

U.S. Politics & Social Issues	U.S. Foreign Policy & Defense	U.S. Economy & Environment	Science, Technology & Nature	Culture, Leisure & Life Style	
	Domestic reaction to Churchill's "iron curtain" speech varies: Rep. Eugene Cox (D, Ga.) agrees that Russia seeks to "communize the world," but Sens. Claude Pepper (D, Fla.), Harley Kilgore (D, W. Va.) and Glen Taylor (D, Idaho) claim that Churchill's proposal for an Anglo-American alliance would "cut the throat of the United Nations." . . . . The Air Force discloses plans for tactical air games in Alaska and reveals the aircraft carrier *Midway* is en route to the Davis Strait to participate in "Expedition Frostbite," a test of planes and armament in subfreezing temperatures.	The city of Detroit asks Truman's personal intervention in the UAW strike against GM.			March 6
Truman orders the reopening of homesteading on all public lands in the U.S. and Alaska except those containing deposits of fissionable minerals.		House passes and sends to the Senate the weakened Patman bill on housing.		Academy Awards go to Ray Milland and Joan Crawford as best actor and actresses, and *The Lost Week-End* is named best picture for 1945 . . . . Edmund Wilson's novel *Memoirs of Hecate County* is published.	March 7
	Army bars Communists and personnel judged "subversive or disaffected" from sensitive assignments, including radar, cryptography and atomic research.	The 65-day strike of 17,500 Westinghouse Electric workers in N.Y. and N.J. ends when the workers and company agree on an 18.2% pay raise . . . . OPA authorizes increases in cotton textile prices, some as high as 15%.	Researchers at Johns Hopkins Univ. reveal the development of an infrared "eye" known as a super-conducting bolometer which can "see" 10-15 miles in the dark.	In a letter to Stalin, the Uniate Church Assembly of the Western Ukraine announces its decision to abolish the 1596 Brest Union with the Vatican and return to the Russian Orthodox Church. The letter thanks Stalin for "reuniting" the Ukrainians.	March 8
Rep. Hatton Sumners (D, Tex.), in Congress for 33 years, announces he will not seek reelection.			Western Union Telegraph Co. reveals development of the "concentrated arc lamp," which will be used for optical devices, photography and medical research.	Robert Grant 3rd takes the national amateur court tennis crown over Robert Gerry Jr.	March 9
		Stabilization Director Bowles presents a "blueprint" to clarify government policy, stating that wage increases will be based on area and industrial patterns.		Independent Citizens Comm. of the Arts, Sciences and Professions in N.Y. names former Interior Secy. Harold Ickes as executive chairman.	March 10
	House Appropriations Comm. reveals Truman has proposed a $4.2-billion Navy budget for 1947.	House approves by voice vote a $1.1-billion appropriation for the Agriculture Dept.	Univ. of Calif. chemist Dr. Melvin Calvin discloses a new method of obtaining oxygen from the air based on the process used by the human body.		March 11
	Senate Foreign Relations Comm. Chmn. Tom Connally (D, Tex.) declares in a report to the Senate that Russia does not want war but "those who want peace must not commit acts that tend to provoke war." . . . . Gen. Carl A. Spaatz reveals plans to equip the Air Force almost exclusively with jet planes and to bring it to combat strength by the year's end . . . . The House passes and sends to the Senate a bill permitting Truman to send technical advisers and lease or give 271 naval vessels to China . . . . The Senate Atomic Energy Comm. approves the Vandenberg proposal setting up a military board to review decisions of the Atomic Energy Control Council.	The Bureau of Labor Statistics states that the new government wage policy will permit a general increase of 12½% over last October's wage rates . . . . OPA grants a 4½% raise on prices of steel castings and railroad specialties . . . . Samuel Gompers, son of the AFL founder and former chief clerk of the Labor Dept., dies at 78 in Washington.		Shooting of *Forever Amber* begins in Hollywood with a record-breaking $3 million budget.	March 12

F	G	H	I	J
Includes elections, federal-state relations, civil rights and liberties, crime, the judiciary, education, health care, poverty, urban affairs and population.	*Includes formation and debate of U.S. foreign and defense policies, veterans affairs and defense spending. (Relations with specific foreign countries are usually found under the region concerned.)*	*Includes business, labor, agriculture, taxation, transportation, consumer affairs, monetary and fiscal policy, natural resources, pollution and accidents.*	*Includes worldwide scientific, medical and technological developments, natural phenomena, U.S. weather and natural disasters.*	*Includes the arts, religion, scholarship, communications media, sports, entertainment, fashions, fads and social life.*

	World Affairs	Europe	Africa & the Middle East	The Americas	Asia & the Pacific
March 13	In an interview published in *Pravda*, Stalin calls Churchill a "firebrand of war" and compares him with Hitler, further denying that eastern Europe is under Soviet control . . . . The site committee of the World Bank and IMF chooses Washington, D.C. for the permanent headquarters.	Speaking at his Nuremberg trial, Goering defends Nazism, Hitler, concentration camps, the Gestapo and the 1933 seizure of power and suppression of opposition parties . . . . Yugoslavian government forces capture royalist Chetnik leader Draja Mikhailovich, wanted for wartime collaboration with the Germans, in a mountain cave.	Russian forces in Iran enter Karaj, 20 miles from Teheran.	Pan-American Union votes for indefinite postponement of the Inter-American Conference on Peace and Security, scheduled to begin in Rio de Janeiro March 15.	Dutch and Indonesian leaders begin formal negotiations for a peace settlement in Batavia . . . . Nationalist commander Gen. Chao Kung-wu enters Mukden as Soviet troops leave.
March 14		Goering proudly assumes "full responsibility" at Nuremberg for the seizure of Austria, the invasion of Norway and the sending of German fliers to Spain during its Civil War, although he says Hitler alone decided on the invasion of Czechoslovakia . . . . Paul-Henri Spaak completes formation of his predominantly socialist Belgian cabinet.			Chang Kai-ngau, head of the Chinese Economic Commission to Manchuria, reports that Russia demanded war booty and economic concessions as the price of complete withdrawal from Manchuria, preventing any agreement.
March 15	Speaking in New York, Churchill denies that he proposed a military alliance in his March 5 speech but reiterates his plea for an Anglo-American "fraternal association."	Supreme Soviet adopts a new five-year plan designed to increase production 50% over the prewar level and votes to change the administrative title "Commissar" to "Minister." . . . . Gen. J.M. Bevans of the U.S. GIs government in Germany says GIs are forbidden to marry Germans because the latter are "still our enemies."	Iranian Premier Ghavam announces he will appeal to the U.N. Security Council against Russia's continued occupation of Iran.	Dr. Jose P. Tamborini concedes the Argentine presidential election to Peron . . . . Communist M.P. Fred Rose is arrested in Ottawa and arraigned in Montreal on a charge of violating the official secrets act by turning over secret information to Russia.	
March 16		Goering attempts to exonerate seven of his fellow defendants at Nuremberg by picturing them as "yes" men and lackeys of the real top Nazi leaders, Hitler and himself . . . . Dutch Nazi broadcaster Maximillien Blokziji is shot as a traitor in The Hague, the first execution in Holland since 1854.			Vietnamese President Ho Chi-minh requests American recognition of his government in a message addressed to Truman.
March 17	Combined Food Board submits a report to the UNRRA stating that the world food supply is down 40% from prewar years and that the grain crisis will continue into 1947.	*London Observer* reports that 75% of the Russian occupation forces in Eastern Europe have been replaced by a small Soviet military police force and that the rest are to leave soon.			
March 18	International Monetary Conference ends with the election of seven executive directors each for the World Bank and IMF . . . . Retiring UNRRA chief Herbert Lehman calls for creation of an international food control board, including Russia, and urges the World Bank to take over relief costs when UNRRA ends.	BBC announces plans to start daily Russian-language broadcasts to the Soviet Union due to Soviet censorship and curtailment of British news.	Iraqi politician Majid Bey Mustafa says that Kurds in southern Azerbaijan, Iran have established an "independent Kurdish state."	Canadian Prime Minister Mackenzie King tells the House of Commons a former Russian clerk in the Soviet embassy, Igor Gouzenko, disclosed that Canada was "being used" to gather intelligence for Russia.	Chou En-lai denounces the Kuomintang as seeking to retain one-party rule of China, contrary to the decisions of the Political Consultative Conference . . . . French colonial forces occupy Hanoi, capital of the newly-recognized Democratic Republic of Vietnam.
March 19	Following a formal Iranian appeal, Secy. Gen. Trygve Lie puts the Iranian-Russian dispute on the Security Council agenda.	U.S. authorities in Berlin report Russian reactivation of the Buchenwald and Sachsenhausen concentration camps to house Germans who oppose the Communist-Social Democratic Party merger . . . . Mikhail Ivanovich Kalinin, president of Russia since 1919, retires due to ill health and the Supreme Soviet elects Nikolai Mikhailovich Shvernik to succeed him . . . . In London, Dr. Alan Nunn May pleads not guilty to charges that he disclosed atomic bomb information to the Russians. . . . . Switzerland resumes diplomatic relations with Russia, which were severed in 1924.			
March 20		U.S. military authorities in Berlin announce the capture of Mildred E. Gillars of Portland, Me., known as "Axis Sally" for her radio broadcasts from Germany.		The derailing of a train near Aracaju, Brazil results in the death of 185 persons.	
March 21	Security Council rejects Russia's request for a delay in considering Iran's appeal . . . . The UNRRA Central Comm. nominates former N.Y.C. Mayor Fiorello La Guardia to be the organization's director-general, replacing Lehman . . . . Ending his U.S. tour, Churchill sails from N.Y. on the *Queen Mary*.	In his Nuremberg defense, Goering admits ordering the burning of villages in reprisal for partisan attacks and says he knew slave laborers were forced to work in Germany . . . . Labor Health Min. Aneurin Bevan introduces the national health service bill in Parliament, aimed at providing every Briton with medical care "from birth to death." . . . . Belgian Premier Spaak submits his resignation after the centrist Christian Socialist Party refuses to support his government, attacking it as "excessively socialist" in character.		State Dept. notifies all Latin American nations the U.S. will not sign a hemispheric pact to maintain peace and security if the Peron government of Argentina participates.	
	A *Includes developments that affect more than one world region, international organizations and important meetings of major world leaders.*	B *Includes all domestic and regional developments in Europe, including the Soviet Union, Turkey, Cyprus and Malta.*	C *Includes all domestic and regional developments in Africa and the Middle East, including Iraq and Iran and excluding Cyprus, Turkey and Afghanistan.*	D *Includes all domestic and regional developments in Latin America, the Caribbean and Canada.*	E *Includes all domestic and regional developments in Asian and Pacific nations, extending from Afghanistan through all the Pacific Islands, except Hawaii.*

U.S. Politics & Social Issues	U.S. Foreign Policy & Defense	U.S. Economy & Environment	Science, Technology & Nature	Culture, Leisure & Life Style	
Truman "reluctantly" withdraws his nomination of Edwin Pauley for Navy under secretary, defending his integrity in spite of "misrepresentations" and "vicious attacks." .... Former GOP Sen. Gerald Nye fails to gain his party's senatorial nomination in a N.D. comeback try.	Speaking at a secret session of the House Military Affairs Comm., Secy. Byrnes outlines a "pessimistic" picture of world conditions, while Secy. of War Patterson and Gens. Eisenhower and Spaatz urge extension of the draft to ensure an Army of over one million men.	GM and the UAW end a 113-day strike of 175,000 auto workers with an agreement providing for an 18½¢ hourly wage increase .... N.Y. dress industry mediator Harry Uviller grants an 8% pay increase to 75,000 AFL-ILGWU workers.		Bennett Cerf agrees to include 12 poems by Ezra Pound in the new edition of *An Anthology of Famous English and American Poetry*, after omitting them from the first edition as works of a proclaimed fascist .... George C. Tyler, veteran theatrical producer, dies at 78 in Yonkers, N.Y.	March 13
	Former Interior Secy. Harold Ickes assails "sniping at Russia" and urges Truman to "stand up aggressively for the foreign policies of President Roosevelt."	House votes an additional $250 million for temporary veterans' housing.		Ernest Hemingway marries Mary Welsh in Havana.	March 14
	Senate Atomic Energy Comm. votes for a nine-man advisory board with military participation to assist the civilian control commission.	House votes to extend until March 31, 1947 the second War Powers Act, which gives the president authority over rationing and production priorities.	A series of earthquakes shakes southern California from the San Joaquin Valley to Mexico, damaging the L.A. aqueduct.		March 15
Texas Atty. Gen. Grover Sellers rules that Texas Univ. may bar Negroes so long as adequate training is provided at public expense elsewhere in the state.	Senate Atomic Energy Comm. votes to give the president direct control over the production of atomic bombs.			Francisco Segura of Ecuador wins the U.S. indoor tennis title over Don McNeill in N.Y.	March 16
Wisconsin Progressive Party votes to rejoin the GOP.	Navy cancels plans for a Mediterranean cruise by the 8th Fleet at the request of the State Dept., which explains it might be construed as anti-Russian.	A U.S. Federal Reserve Bd. report says production is now above the level of any previous peacetime period.	Seven persons are killed as tornadoes sweep Ala., Miss. and Ga.	George Foster Peabody Awards in radio drama go to Edgar Bergen and Arch Obeler; for education, to *The Town Meeting of The Air*, for news, to CBS and Paul White .... Gunder Haegg and Arne Andersson, the world's fastest milers, are ruled professionals and barred from amateur competition for life by the Swedish Athletic Assn.	March 17
	Truman asks extension of the Selective Service Act for one year and names Bernard Baruch U.S. representative on the U.N. Atomic Energy Commission.	National Assn. of Manufacturers Pres. Robert Wason charges that the OPA is inflationary and urges its termination June 30.	Drs. Phyllis Harroun and F.E. Beckert of the Univ. of California Medical School report that a combination of nitrous oxide and curare has made possible the use of the electric knife chest operations without the danger of sparks causing explosions in the patient's lungs.	Winston Churchill receives an honorary LL.D. degree from Columbia University.	March 18
Democrats and Republicans in the Senate and House attack Henry Wallace for proposing that congressmen who defy the party line on major issues be refused party support in elections .... Former War Production Bd. aide Edwin Locke, Jr. is named a special presidential assistant to plan reorganization of the government.	Selective Service Commissioner Lewis B. Hershey calls for indefinite extension of the draft, with service limited to 18 months.	UAW notifies GM that 154,400 members have ratified the wage agreement, but the company says it will remain closed and assume that the strike is continuing until 20 more locals vote to return .... House passes and sends to the Senate a bill taking all farm credit agencies from the Agriculture Dept. and placing them under a seven-man independent board.	Senate Military Affairs Comm. approves a bill for federal funds for scientific research.		March 19
				Dr. Frederick Madison Smith, president of the Reorganized Church of Jesus Christ of Latter Day Saints and son of its founder, dies at 72 in Independence, Mo.	March 20
	Secy. Byrnes tells the Senate Military Affairs Comm. that failure to extend the draft will result in a critical manpower shortage in U.S. occupation forces .... Senate confirms the appointment of Gen. Walter Bedell Smith as ambassador to Russia .... Truman meets with French emissary Leon Blum on a proposed loan to France.	After six years on the Securities and Exchange Commission, Sumner T. Pike resigns.	Geologist Vladimir Vize announces in Moscow plans for an oceanographic and geophysical survey of the unexplored part of the central Arctic.	Kenny Washington becomes the first Negro in the NFL since 1933 when he signs with the Los Angeles Rams .... Van Wyck Brooks wins the National Institute of Arts and Letters Gold Medal for essays and criticism, awarded once every 10 years.	March 21
F	G	H	I	J	
Includes elections, federal-state relations, civil rights and liberties, crime, the judiciary, education, health care, poverty, urban affairs and population.	*Includes formation and debate of U.S. foreign and defense policies, veterans affairs and defense spending. (Relations with specific foreign countries are usually found under the region concerned.)*	*Includes business, labor, agriculture, taxation, transportation, consumer affairs, monetary and fiscal policy, natural resources, pollution and accidents.*	*Includes worldwide scientific, medical and technological developments, natural phenomena, U.S. weather and natural disasters.*	*Includes the arts, religion, scholarship, communications media, sports, entertainment, fashions, fads and social life.*	

	World Affairs	Europe	Africa & the Middle East	The Americas	Asia & the Pacific
March 22	With Soviet support, the French Foreign Office again urges the U.S. and Britain to take a joint stand against Franco before the U.N. . . . . U.S. and Britain take the lead in blocking a Soviet move to have Albania admitted to UNRRA, while Turkey is admitted without dissent . . . . In an interview with AP correspondent Eddy Gilmore, Stalin calls the U.N. "a serious instrument for the preservation of peace," based on "the principle of equality of states."	Rudolf Hess begins his Nuremberg defense by challenging the jurisdiction of the Tribunal and accepting full responsibility for his official acts as Hitler's deputy . . . . In Hamburg tool plants 33 workers collapse from hunger as mobs try to loot food shops for the fourth day after British authorities cut the ration to 1,000 calories daily . . . . U.S. sends the Russian commander in Hungary a note requesting removal of Soviet personnel from American-owned oil fields and return of the wells to American management . . . . Soviet Council of Ministers issues a decree unifying the Army, Navy and Air Force, with Stalin as minister of armed forces and supreme commander . . . . Pro-Nazi Hungarian Premier Marshal Doeme Sztojay and three of his ministers are condemned to death in Budapest.			
March 23	U.N. Secy. Gen. Trygve Lie names John B. Hutson of the U.S. as assistant secretary general in charge of administrative and financial services.	Francisco Largo Caballero, left socialist who served as premier and war minister of the Spanish Republic in 1936, dies at 76 in Paris.			
March 24			Moscow radio announces that the withdrawal of Soviet troops from Meshed, Shanrud and Semnan is complete and that remaining troops will be evacuated from Iran in five or six weeks . . . . Truman threatens to send American naval forces to the Mediterranean if the Soviets do not remove troops from Iran as agreed at the Potsdam Conference.		Bangkok high court orders the release of Luang Pibul Songgram, premier during the Japanese occupation, and all other prisoners held on war crimes charges.
March 25	U.N. Security Council convenes in the Hunter College gymnasium . . . . U.N. Military Staff Comm., composed of the U.S., Russia, Britain, China and France, holds its first session.	U.S. charges before the UNRRA council that Russian occupation armies in Austria have seized land upon which the population's food supply depends.		Canadian government reports that Soviet agents were seeking atomic information five months before the first nuclear explosion . . . . Argentine Pres. Edelmiro Farrell decrees the nationalization of the central bank, part of whose stock is held by U.S. banks.	MacArthur suspends the repatriation of about 500,000 Koreans from Japan to Russian-occupied North Korea because of lack of transportation.
March 26	U.N. Security Council defeats a Russian proposal to keep the Iranian issue off the agenda, resulting in a threat by Russian delegate Gromyko to boycott sessions.	UNRRA Council approves a resolution urging occupation armies to refrain from requisitioning land and consuming indigenous food supplies . . . . Speaking at the Nuremberg trial of Nazi Foreign Min. Joachim von Ribbentrop, defense witness Adolf von Steengracht says Ribbentrop was a "powerless puppet of the Fuehrer."	Anglo-American Commission of Inquiry on Palestine concludes its hearing in Jerusalem.	McGill University chemistry professor Raymond Boyer admits in Montreal that he gave details of the new explosive RDX to Fred Rose "to help the Soviet Union."	
March 27	Gromyko walks out of a Security Council session after his motion to postpone the Iranian issue until April 10 is defeated . . . . Provisional International Aviation Organization ends its 23-day Dublin conference on North Atlantic air routes after establishing procedures for trans-Atlantic travel.				
March 28	Russia supports a UNRRA Council vote to continue aid to refugees without the consent of their governments in return for a UNRRA commitment to facilitate repatriation.				
March 29	Fiorello La Guardia accepts appointment as director-general of UNRRA.	French Constituent Assembly votes to nationalize the electric and gas industries . . . . Deputy Military Gov. Gen. Lucius Clay cuts the food ration in the U.S. zone of Germany to 1,275 calories daily.	Under a new constitution, the Gold Coast becomes Britain's first African colony to have a majority of elected Africans in its legislature.	Royal Canadian Commission names five more suspects detained in the espionage case and charges that Vitali Pavlov, Soviet consul in Ottawa, is a leading NKVD agent there . . . . Argentine Foreign Office appeals to the U.S. for harmony and cites the recent presidential election as "the best reply to charges of totalitarianism."	UNRRA officials in Shanghai report epidemics of cholera, bubonic plague, small pox and meningitis and mass hunger in China.
	A *Includes developments that affect more than one world region, international organizations and important meetings of major world leaders.*	B *Includes all domestic and regional developments in Europe, including the Soviet Union, Turkey, Cyprus and Malta.*	C *Includes all domestic and regional developments in Africa and the Middle East, including Iraq and Iran and excluding Cyprus, Turkey and Afghanistan.*	D *Includes all domestic and regional developments in Latin America, the Caribbean and Canada.*	E *Includes all domestic and regional developments in Asian and Pacific nations, extending from Afghanistan through all the Pacific Islands, except Hawaii.*

U.S. Politics & Social Issues	U.S. Foreign Policy & Defense	U.S. Economy & Environment	Science, Technology & Nature	Culture, Leisure & Life Style	
	Truman postpones the atomic bomb tests originally scheduled for May 15 for about six weeks, enabling congressmen to witness the event during a legislative recess.				March 22
Speaking at the Democratic Party's annual Jackson Day Dinner, Truman calls for "party unity and responsibility" in support of his legislative program.	Truman names W. Averell Harriman ambassador to Britain.	Walter Reuther announces he will run for the UAW presidency against R.J. Thomas.	Gilbert Lewis, co-author of the Lewis-Langmuir atomic theory and a member of the team which developed the cyclotron, dies at 70 in Berkeley, Calif.		March 23
		A committee of 39 Democratic and four GOP representatives is formed to press for passage of the minimum wage bill.	*Izvestia* reports that Russia will spend hundreds of millions of rubles in a five-year scientific program, including the study of atomic energy and cosmic rays.	Sam Snead ties the tourney record of 270 to win the Greensboro Open.	March 24
Supreme Court agrees to review the case of Robert Lovett, Goodwin Watson and William Dodd, Jr., who challenged the constitutionality of a law ousting them from government jobs for alleged subversive activities.	Under Secy. of State Dean Acheson presents before a secret session of the Senate Atomic Energy Comm. the Administration's international nuclear control plan, putting radioactive materials under U.N. ownership but leaving the operation of nuclear facilities to the individual states.	With some local disputes still pending, GM ends its lockout of auto workers and resumes production in Detroit .... OPA allows a 4% rise on all machinery, parts and industrial equipment where the percentage of steel costs in sale prices is over 40% .... Supreme Court rules that the federal anti-kickback law does not apply to unions demanding initiation fees from workers in closed shops.		Cellist Pablo Casals cancels his English concert tour in protest against the country's recognition of the Franco government.	March 25
	Gen. Leslie Groves, head of the Army's atomic research program, tells a Senate Appropriations subcommittee that the U.S. is still producing atomic bombs.	Civilian Production Admin. John Small and National Housing Expediter Wilson Wyatt order a halt to all general building construction and repairs in order to speed construction of veterans' housing.		Okla. A&M takes the NCAA basketball crown with a 43-40 victory over North Carolina Univ.	March 26
		Walter P. Reuther is elected president of the UAW by 124 votes at the union's Atlantic City convention .... A report of the U.S. Chamber of Commerce urges gradual elimination of price controls .... Senate Banking and Currency Comm. approves the nomination of James J. Vardaman to the Federal Reserve Bd.			March 27
House approves a resolution to start contempt proceedings aginst Dr. Edward Barsky, chairman of the Joint Anti-Fascist Refugee Comm., for refusing to testify before the Un-American Activities Comm.	Truman expresses unequivocal support of Secy. Byrnes' actions in the Iranian dispute at the U.N. .... Truman sets up a 10-man military brain trust to plan national defense and nominates Gens. Marshall, MacArthur, Eisenhower and Arnold and Adms. Leahy, Nimitz, King and Halsey for permanent five-star rank.	Bureau of Labor Statistics reports that a record 21.5 million man-days were lost in February because of strikes.		The Right Rev. William Manning, Episcopal Bishop of N.Y. for 25 years, announces his retirement.	March 28
		House passes and sends to the Senate the conference-approved version of the Lea "anti-Petrillo" bill, aimed at curbing labor practices in the communications industry .... Senate approves the Russell amendment to the minimum wage bill, calling for the inclusion of farm labor costs in computing parity prices for farm products.			March 29
F	G	H	I	J	
Includes elections, federal-state relations, civil rights and liberties, crime, the judiciary, education, health care, poverty, urban affairs and population.	*Includes formation and debate of U.S. foreign and defense policies, veterans affairs and defense spending. (Relations with specific foreign countries are usually found under the region concerned.)*	*Includes business, labor, agriculture, taxation, transportation, consumer affairs, monetary and fiscal policy, natural resources, pollution and accidents.*	*Includes worldwide scientific, medical and technological developments, natural phenomena, U.S. weather and natural disasters.*	*Includes the arts, religion, scholarship, communications media, sports, entertainment, fashions, fads and social life.*	

	World Affairs	Europe	Africa & the Middle East	The Americas	Asia & the Pacific
March 30		U.S. headquarters in Frankfurt announces the arrest of 800 Germans in the American and British zones of Austria and Germany in "Operation Nursery," a campaign against efforts to revive the Hitler Youth organization.		Ecuador suppresses a revolutionary plot believed to be led by former dictator Gen. Alberto Enriquez.	Batavia announces that Dutch and Indonesian leaders are close to agreement on Indonesian demands and that negotiations will be transferred to The Hague.
March 31	Russia pays the U.N. $1.7 million, its share of the organization's $25 million working capital fund.	Social Democrats in the Western zones of Berlin reject a merger with the Communists but vote for continued cooperation, while Russian authorities prevent a vote in their zone .... Right-wing Greek Populist Party wins a majority of 200 seats as leftists boycott the country's first parliamentary elections in 10 years .... Former Italian premiers Vittorio Orlando, Ivanoe Bonomi and Francesco Nitti and philosopher Benedetto Croce announce formation of the right-wing Democratic Union .... Socialist Premier Achille van Acker's moderate leftist cabinet takes office in Belgium, with former Premier Paul-Henri Spaak as foreign minister .... Hero of Dunkerque and fomer commander of British forces in France and Belgium, Field Marshal Viscount Gort, dies at 59 in London.			
Apr. 1	Russia rejects an invitation to join 18 nations in an emergency conference on cereal supplies in London April 3.			Secy. Byrnes informs Cuba that on May 20 the U.S. will give up its wartime Cuban bases.	Chiang Kai-shek says Chinese Communist demands for control of Manchuria will not be considered until the government completes occupation of the area .... Gen. Albert Wedemeyer announces U.S. forces in the China theater will disband May 1.
Apr. 2		At his Nuremberg trial, Ribbentrop admits supporting Hitler's repressive policy against the Jews but says he did so in order not to upset the Fuehrer.			
Apr. 3			Gromyko claims that Russia has negotiated a troop withdrawal agreement with Iran, but the Iranian government denies this.	Argentine government says it will approve George Messersmith as the U.S. ambassador.	Japanese Gen. Homma is executed by a 12-man U.S. Army firing squad at Los Bancos, south of Manila .... Discussions between French officials and Vietnamese nationalists begin in Dalat on the status of Vietnam within the French Union.
Apr. 4	U.N. Security Council accepts Byrnes's resolution to postpone consideration of the Iranian issue until May 6 .... David Sarnoff, Radio Corp. of America president, urges the U.N. to establish an international broadcasting system.	Greek Archbishop Damaskinos swears in State Council Pres. Panayotis Poulitsas and his cabinet to serve as an interim government until the Populist Party can choose its own leader .... Dr. Marcel Petiot, 49, the "Bluebeard of Paris," is convicted of robbing and killing 24 persons and is condemned to death.		Brazilian Foreign Min. Joao Neves de Fontoura says his country will continue friendly relations with Peron's government in Argentina.	
Apr. 5	Secy. Byrnes urges a new conference of U.S., British, Russian and French foreign ministers in Paris to work for some agreement on European peace treaties.	Rumania breaks off diplomatic relations with Spain, while Poland establishes relations with the Spanish Republican exile government .... German Field Marshal Gen. Wilhelm Keitel admits in his Nuremberg trial that the March 1939 attack on Czechoslovakia was an act of treachery, but says it was necessary to keep the Poles from seizing Czech coal mines and steel mills.	Premier Ghavam and Soviet Amb. Ivan Sadchikov complete an agreement in Teheran promising withdrawal of Russian troops by May 6.	Workers' delegates at an International Labor Organization conference in Mexico City expel the Argentine representative, claiming he does not come from a "free and independent labor movement."	
Apr. 6	A 17-nation emergency food conference in London ends after appealing to Argentina to increase wheat exports and urging creation of a single international agency to meet the world food crisis .... International Court of Justice elects Jose Gustavo Guerrero of El Salvador to be its president.			U.S. informs Ecuador it will evacuate its military bases in the Galapagos Islands by July 1.	

A	B	C	D	E
Includes developments that affect more than one world region, international organizations and important meetings of major world leaders.	*Includes all domestic and regional developments in Europe, including the Soviet Union, Turkey, Cyprus and Malta.*	*Includes all domestic and regional developments in Africa and the Middle East, including Iraq and Iran and excluding Cyprus, Turkey and Afghanistan.*	*Includes all domestic and regional developments in Latin America, the Caribbean and Canada.*	*Includes all domestic and regional developments in Asian and Pacific nations, extending from Afghanistan through all the Pacific Islands, except Hawaii.*

U.S. Politics & Social Issues	U.S. Foreign Policy & Defense	U.S. Economy & Environment	Science, Technology & Nature	Culture, Leisure & Life Style	
		AFL reports a membership of 6,931,221 and a treasury of $2,087,021 as of last Aug. 31.	Dr. Donald Menzel of Harvard presents a theory explaining the energy production of giant red stars in terms of nuclear fusion.	Ohio State Univ. wins the NCAA swimming title in New Haven, Conn. .... Oxford beats Cambridge by three lengths in the first official Thames River crew race since 1939 .... Metropolitan Opera Guild announces that a poll of 123,000 radio listeners shows their favorite operas to be *Aida*, *Carmen*, *La Traviata*, *Hansel and Gretel* and *Boris Goudenov*.	March 30
	State, War and Navy Depts. announce that the Army and Navy Staff College will be reorganized as the National War College and will give courses in civilian subjects pertinent to national defense.		American Chemical Society awards the Priestly Medal to Sir Ian Morris Heilbron of Britain for his work with penicillin and vitamins .... American Geographical Society announces plans for the compilation of an Atlas of Diseases to aid in the study of the relationship between environment and health.	World Council of Churches in Geneva establishes a loan fund to help rebuild churches destroyed in the war.	March 31
Supreme Court refuses to review a lower court ruling sustaining the right of Negroes to vote in Georgia's primary elections .... Tennessee Rep. B. Carroll Reece is elected GOP national chairman .... Truman selects James Landis as CAB chairman to succeed L. Welch Pogue, whose resignation will take effect June 8.	House passes a bill for a peacetime Navy of 500,000 men and 100,000 Marines and also calls for burial of an unknown soldier of World War II at Arlington National Cemetery.	A nationwide strike of 400,000 UMW soft coal miners begins after failure of Labor Dept. mediation in a wage dispute .... Supreme Court upholds a controversial clause of the 1935 utility holding company act which compels public utilities to confine themselves to a single, integrated system.	An underwater earthquake near Dutch Harbor, Alaska causes huge seismic waves to sweep Hawaii, leaving $10 million in damages and 205 persons killed or missing.	The auction of the late FDR's stamp collection is concluded with total sales estimated at $211,000 .... The eight-team Mexican Baseball League, backed by the $60 million fortune of the Pasquel brothers, signs Brooklyn Dodger catcher Mickey Owen, who joins other Americans in Mexico — George Hausmann, Roy Zimmerman and Sal Maglie.	Apr. 1
	Senate Atomic Energy Comm. approves the revised Vandenberg amendment, calling for a military committee appointed by the Navy and War secretaries which will have jurisdiction over military applications of atomic energy.		Dr. John Enders reports isolation of the virus which causes mumps, making serums and vaccines possible.		Apr. 2
		Two railroad arbitration boards in Chicago grant a 16¢ hourly wage increase to 1.22 million railroad employes .... Senate confirms the appointment of James Vardaman Jr. for a 14-year term on the Federal Reserve Bd. of Governors.			Apr. 3
	A Senate Military Affairs subcommittee sends Truman the draft of a bill calling for a single Dept. of National Defense .... Truman names Capt. Clark M. Clifford, former assistant to James Vardaman, as his naval aide.	Senate Banking & Currency Comm. approves the Wagner-Ellender-Taft bill, providing federal aid for construction of one million homes a year during the next 10 years.			Apr. 4
		Senate passes and sends to the House a bill raising the minimum wage to 65¢ hourly.		Mary Jane Ward's *The Snake Pit*, a novel about a sane woman in a mental hospital, is published by Random House and is named a Book of The Month Club selection .... Vincent Youmans, noted popular song composer, dies at 47 from tuberculosis in Denver, Colo.	Apr. 5
Arkansas Gov. Ben Laney says Negroes will not be permitted to vote in the state's Democratic primary despite a declaration by U.S. Solicitor Gen. J. Howard McGrath that he will prosecute any official who keeps a person from voting because of race .... Truman tells a meeting of student editors he advocates giving the vote to 18-year-olds but says repeal of the poll tax is a state matter.	In an Army Day speech in Chicago, Truman warns that Anglo-Russian rivalry in the Middle East "might erupt into conflict" and pledges that the U.S. will remain strong to support U.N. peace-keeping efforts and retain its leadership in world affairs.	UMW leader John L. Lewis rejects U.S. Steel's offer to operate its mines on a retroactive wage basis while contract negotiations are going on.	Oklahoma City residents turn out for VD tests as preachers, teachers and socialites back the nation's first citywide rapid-treatment drive against VD .... U.S. Navy reveals that sonar was the most effective single weapon used against enemy submarines in World War II.	Senate passes and sends to the White House the "anti-Petrillo" bill curbing coercive labor practices in radio broadcasting.	Apr. 6
F *Includes elections, federal-state relations, civil rights and liberties, crime, the judiciary, education, health care, poverty, urban affairs and population.*	G *Includes formation and debate of U.S. foreign and defense policies, veterans affairs and defense spending. (Relations with specific foreign countries are usually found under the region concerned.)*	H *Includes business, labor, agriculture, taxation, transportation, consumer affairs, monetary and fiscal policy, natural resources, pollution and accidents.*	I *Includes worldwide scientific, medical and technological developments, natural phenomena, U.S. weather and natural disasters.*	J *Includes the arts, religion, scholarship, communications media, sports, entertainment, fashions, fads and social life.*	

	World Affairs	Europe	Africa & the Middle East	The Americas	Asia & the Pacific
Apr. 7	International Labor Organization conference in Mexico City rejects a proposal presented by employer delegates to ban union participation in politics.	Social Democrats of Berlin's western zones vote to expel Otto Grotewohl as party chairman for favoring a merger with the Communists .... U.S. District Judge Simon Rifkind, adviser on Jewish affairs to the U.S. military government in Germany, concludes a report on the problems of concentration camp survivors and urges the immediate settlement of 100,000 Jews still in German and Austrian refugee camps .... In an agreement announced in Prague, Hungary promises to pay $300 million in reparations, with two-thirds going to Russia.	Premier Ghavam discloses a Soviet-Iranian agreement giving Russia a 51% share of the Russian-Iranian Oil Co. for 25 years, and 50% for the next 25.		Communists lead 10,000 demonstrators to the Tokyo residence of Japanese Premier Kijuro Shidehara, demanding his resignation .... The schedule for the Russian evacuation of Manchuria, to be completed by April 16, is announced in Chungking.
Apr. 8	Secy. Byrnes announces Russia and Britain have agreed to meet in Paris April 25 for a foreign ministers' meeting prepatory to a general peace conference .... Hector McNeil of Britain is elected chairman of the 20-nation U.N. Special Comm. on Refugees and Displaced Persons at its opening session held in London .... Asst. Secy.-Gen. Victor Hoo reports that negotiations have begun to bring the British mandated areas of Tanganyika, Togoland and the Cameroons and Belgian mandated Ruanda-Urundi under U.N. trusteeship .... The 21st League of Nations Assembly convenes in Geneva to end the organizations. superceded by the U.N.	Chmn. Harold Laski of the British Labor Party's National Executive Comm. issues a pamphlet opposing a proposed Labor-Communist merger on the grounds that the Communists want a one-party system .... Greek Populist Party leader Constantin Tsaldaris says he favors continued cooperation with the Western Allies and promises to hold a plebiscite on the return of King George II to Greece.		State Dept. says Argentina will be welcomed as a signatory of the proposed hemispheric defense treaty if it eliminates "Axis influences."	A Yenan-bound U.S. Army plane crashes in northwestern Shansi Province, killing the American crew and four prominent Chinese Communists: Gen. Yeh Ting, Gen. Teng Fa, Wang Jo-fei and Pang-hsien.
Apr. 9		British Exchequer Chancellor Hugh Dalton presents the House of Commons with a $15-billion budget for 1946-47, down 31% from the previous year.		Canada grants France a $242.5 million credit at 3% annual interest.	
Apr. 10	Polish delegate Oscar Lange asks the U.N. Security Council to place the case of Franco Spain on its agenda, charging that it is a danger to international peace.	Andrei Gromyko becomes Russia's permanent U.N. delegate and Nikolai Novikov is named ambassador to the U.S., while Gen. Vassily Sokolovsky is appointed Soviet member of the Allied Control Council in Berlin, succeeding Marshal Georgi Zhukov .... French Salvation Army official Charles Pean discloses in New York that he has been empowered to liquidate Devil's Island off the coast of French Guiana, the world's most notorious prison colony, over the next three years.			Japan's moderate liberal and progressive parties win a majority of 230 seats in parliamentary elections .... Chungking announces that Communist troops have begun an offensivie in Manchuria to cut the Peking-Mukden railway and stop Nationalist reinforcements.
Apr. 11	Russia, France and Mexico side with Poland on placing the Spanish issue before the U.N. Security Council, while Britain and the U.S. are opposed .... U.N. Secy. Gen. Trygve Lie announces that next September's session of the General Assembly will be held in the New York City Building of the World's Fair site at Flushing Meadow, N.Y.			U.S. Commerce Dept. removes export restrictions on trade with Argentina.	
Apr. 12					After three days of talks in the Netherlands, Dutch and British officials reach substantial agreement on the withdrawal of British troops from Indonesia .... President of the Japanese Nanking puppet government Chen Kung-po is condemned to death in Soochow.
	A *Includes developments that affect more than one world region, international organizations and important meetings of major world leaders.*	B *Includes all domestic and regional developments in Europe, including the Soviet Union, Turkey, Cyprus and Malta.*	C *Includes all domestic and regional developments in Africa and the Middle East, including Iraq and Iran and excluding Cyprus, Turkey and Afghanistan.*	D *Includes all domestic and regional developments in Latin America, the Caribbean and Canada.*	E *Includes all domestic and regional developments in Asian and Pacific nations, extending from Afghanistan through all the Pacific Islands, except Hawaii.*

U.S. Politics & Social Issues	U.S. Foreign Policy & Defense	U.S. Economy & Environment	Science, Technology & Nature	Culture, Leisure & Life Style	
A group of liberal farm and labor leaders meeting in Chicago sets up a provisional committee headed by union leader A. Philip Randolph to explore possibilities of a third political party .... Sen. James Mead (D, N.Y.) announces he will not press charges against his former partner, Edward O'Dea, who was arrested in Buffalo after allegedly assaulting the Senator in a hotel lobby.	The "Win the Peace" conference ends its three-day Washington meeting after registering opposition to military service, production of atomic bombs, the Franco government and the granting of loans which may be used for "oppression of colonial peoples."	A White House report urges Congress to extend price controls until June 30, 1947, claiming the danger of inflation will be over by then .... FHA restores its prewar Title I, Class 3 program to finance construction of homes in the $3,000-$5,000 price range .... A seven-day Detroit transit strike ends as 5,200 members of the Amalgamated Assn. of Electric Street, Railway and Motor Coach Operators accept a 15¢-hourly wage increase.	Physicists H.W. Wells, J.W. Watts and D.E. George of the Carnegie Institution reveal the discovery of clouds of electrically charged gases that speed from the sun into the upper layers of the earth's atmosphere, disrupting radio communications .... A tornado kils four persons and causes heavy damage in Anniston, Ala.	Joseph Verdeur of Philadelphia sets new world records in swimming: 2:19.5 min. for the 200-yard breast stroke and 2:35.6 min. for 200 meters.	Apr. 7
	Washington reports the U.S. is still spending about $500 million yearly on the development of atomic energy and the atomic bomb.	Wage Stabilization Board approves an 18½¢-an-hour increase for 110,000 GE employes.			Apr. 8
	Lt. Nikolai Redin of the Russian Purchasing Commission in Seattle, arrested by the FBI on March 26, is indicted on charges of espionage .... Senate Military Affairs Comm. submits to the full Senate a bill to unify the armed forces into a Dept. of Common Defense under a civilian head .... House Military Affairs Comm. votes to extend the draft of men 18-30 until Feb. 15, 1947, with fathers and farmers exempted.	CIO-United Farm and Metal Workers settle an 80-day strike of 30,000 International Harvester Co. workers with agreement on an 18¢ hourly wage increase .... House passes and sends to Truman the veterans temporary housing bill .... Kansas City, Mo. wheat market receives the smallest amount of grain in 43 years as growers hold back wheat in the hope of higher prices .... A consent decree signed in a U.S. District Court in N.Y. ends U.S. participation in what the Justice Dept. charges was a world match cartel formed by Swedish, British and American producers.		Montreal Canadians beat the Boston Bruins, 6-3, in Montreal, capturing the NHL's Stanley Cup with 4 games to 1 .... American Fed. of Musicians Pres. James C. Petrillo demands in contract negotiations with major film companies that they virtually triple their staffs of musicians and increase the annual wage by 100% to $10,400.	Apr. 9
	Senate Banking and Currency Comm. approves a $3.75 billion loan to Britain while French envoy Leon Blum tells the Senate Foreign Relations Comm. France needs a $4 million U.S. loan .... In a radio interview, Adm. Aaron Merrill attacks plans to unify the armed forces commands, stating that the next war will be fought on American shores because of a "greatly weakened Navy, submerged under Army control." .... Truman issues an executive order dissolving the Office of Coordinator of Inter-American Affairs and transferring its functions to the State Dept.	Senate passes and returns to the House an emergency $600 million housing bill.	Dr. Glen Seaborg and other scientists who worked on the atom bomb reveal that atomic research has resulted in isolation of elements 43 and 61 and production of pure, non-active carbon by radiation.		Apr. 10
	Senate Atomic Energy Comm. approves the McMahon bill, which calls for the President to name a five-man civilian atomic energy control commission .... National Conference on the Education of Veterans in Colleges and Universities reveals VA figures showing 695,000 vets will seek college enrollment next fall .... Asst. Secy. of State William Clayton backs the proposed loan to Britain, saying U.S. foreign economic policy is based on the fostering of world trade and democracy .... Adm. J.R. Beardall, FDR's naval aide in 1941, testifies to the Pearl Harbor committee that the President showed no special alarm when he read the conclusion of Japan's last diplomatic note to the U.S. on the morning of Dec. 7, 1941.				Apr. 11
	Senate confirms the appointment of William Pawley as ambassador to Brazil.		Evidence is presented to an American Chemical Society meeting that submicroscopic, virus-like substances are among the causes of cancer.	On the first anniversary of FDR's death, Truman dedicates the Roosevelt home in Hyde Park, N.Y. as a national shrine.	Apr. 12

F	G	H	I	J
Includes elections, federal-state relations, civil rights and liberties, crime, the judiciary, education, health care, poverty, urban affairs and population.	*Includes formation and debate of U.S. foreign and defense policies, veterans affairs and defense spending. (Relations with specific foreign countries are usually found under the region concerned.)*	*Includes business, labor, agriculture, taxation, transportation, consumer affairs, monetary and fiscal policy, natural resources, pollution and accidents.*	*Includes worldwide scientific, medical and technological developments, natural phenomena, U.S. weather and natural disasters.*	*Includes the arts, religion, scholarship, communications media, sports, entertainment, fashions, fads and social life.*

	World Affairs	Europe	Africa & the Middle East	The Americas	Asia & the Pacific
Apr. 13		Otto Grotewohl and his followers among Berlin's Social Democrats merge with the Communists to form the Socialist Unity Party (SED) .... Gen. Joseph McNary of the U.S. military government in Germany says there is not enough food in the U.S. zone to sustain life.		Foreign Min. Juan Cooke announces that Argentina will turn over most of its 150,000-ton wheat contribution to the UNRRA by May 31.	Prince Morimasa Nashimoto and Mitsubishi official Kiyoshi Goko are released from prison in Tokyo for lack of war crimes evidence.
Apr. 14		Meeting in the Russian zone of Berlin, 1,200 delegates of the Socialist and Communist Parties approve their merger into the Socialist Unity Party .... World Jewish Congress officials protest Czechoslovak acceptance of Russian demands that 40,000 refugees from the Carpatho-Ukraine, including 10,000 Jews, be returned without their consent to Soviet control .... Foreign Min. Albert Martin Artajo issues an order forbidding 330 German firms in Spain from engaging in capital transactions without government permission.			Chou En-lai declares that because of Nationalist attacks on Communists in Manchuria, all-out hostilities have begun there.
Apr. 15	Iran withdraws its complaint against Russia at the Security Council, but Soviet efforts to have the problem stricken from the agenda meet strong opposition from Britain and the U.S. .... UNRRA director La Guardia discloses a survey showing that 30 million Chinese are facing starvation.	Rudolf Hoess, who has admitted supervising the extermination of three million inmates at Auschwitz, asserts at his Nuremberg trial that Ernst Kaltenbrunner or his deputy signed the orders.			Chinese Central News Agency claims capture of the Manchurian city of Szepingkai by Nationalist troops, as Communist forces attack Changchun .... A U.S. military court in Shanghai sentences four Japanese involved in the execution of Doolittle fliers to prison terms of three to nine years.
Apr. 16	U.S. Famine Emergency Commision chief Chester Davis says the world food situation is worsening, while former UNRRA head Herbert Lehman accuses the U.S. of "faulty planning" for famine relief and urges reimposition of rationing.	Holland, Belgium and Luxembourg form a customs and economic union at a meeting in The Hague .... British Food Min. Sir Ben Smith announces a sharp cut in the export of food products containing sugar or grain as a step to aid the home market.	British High Commissioner Sir Alan Gordon Cunningham promises that the 1,014 Jewish refugees detained in Italy will be permitted to enter Palestine under the 1,500 monthly quota system.	A conference of trade union representatives from American states ends in Mexico City after adopting resolutions to improve industrial relations and rejecting government control of industry.	
Apr. 17	Polish delegate Oscar Lange asks that all U.N. members break diplomatic relations with Spain.	British Supply Min. John Wilmot announces a plan to establish a government control board for iron and steel production, followed by nationalization of a good portion of the industry.		Argentina decrees control of wheat exports and subsidies to growers to stop hoarding.	
Apr. 18	U.N. Security Council Comm. of Experts votes that the Council has the right to keep the Iranian dispute on the agenda, despite Russian objections .... British, Brazilian, Chinese and Australian delegates to the Security Council express opposition to breaking with Spain .... League of Nations expires at midnight, turning over its property to the U.N.	Former Nazi Governor of Poland, Hans Frank, admits at Nuremberg that he ordered the extermination of Jews and the introduction of forced labor .... U.S. grants full diplomatic recognition to the Tito government in Yugoslavia.	Iran announces that taxes will be collected on any oil shipped to the country from the British-protected island of Bahrain in the Persian Gulf.		Communist forces capture the Manchurian city of Changchun, taking U.S. military attache Robert Rigg and five American correspondents into custody .... Gen. Marshall arrives in Chungking after visiting MacArthur in Tokyo .... A U.S. military tribunal in Manila sentences Gen. Shiyoku Kuo, former head of Japanese prison camps in the Philippines, to hang for war crimes.
Apr. 19		French Constituent Assembly adopts a new constitution establishing the Fourth Republic, subject to approval in a national referendum .... U.S. military headquarters in Frankfurt reveals that 1,900 German prisoners in a U.S.-run camp were poisoned, none fatally, by arsenic sprinkled on bread in a local bakery.	Saudi Arabian King Ibn Saud says that Australia, N.Z. and the two Americas could easily absorb all Jewish refugees, ending the Palestine problem.		
Apr. 20					Gen. Rikichi Ando, wartime Japanese governor of Taiwan brought to Shanghai to stand trial, poisons himself in his cell.

	A	B	C	D	E
	Includes developments that affect more than one world region, international organizations and important meetings of major world leaders.	*Includes all domestic and regional developments in Europe, including the Soviet Union, Turkey, Cyprus and Malta.*	*Includes all domestic and regional developments in Africa and the Middle East, including Iraq and Iran and excluding Cyprus, Turkey and Afghanistan.*	*Includes all domestic and regional developments in Latin America, the Caribbean and Canada.*	*Includes all domestic and regional developments in Asian and Pacific nations, extending from Afghanistan through all the Pacific Islands, except Hawaii.*

U.S. Politics & Social Issues	U.S. Foreign Policy & Defense	U.S. Economy & Environment	Science, Technology & Nature	Culture, Leisure & Life Style	
		Stabilization Dir. Bowles admits the existence of a national clothing shortage, which he blames on both government and industry policies.	Bell Telephone Labs reveals the wartime development of a metal "lens" that focuses radio waves on the antenna of a distant station, increasing sending power and freedom from static.		Apr. 13
Communist Party expells William Browder from the party for being identified with his brother Earl's "anti-party, anti-working class program."	Army and Navy announce safety measures for the 37,000 men participating in the Bikini Atoll nuclear tests; most ships will be kept 20 miles away from the bomb site.			The first film to have a world premiere aboard a scheduled airliner, *So Goes My Love*, is shown on a Pan Am Clipper en route from N.Y. to Ireland.	Apr. 14
	House passes and sends to the Senate a bill extending the Selective Service Act for nine months beyond May 15.	U.S. railroads ask the ICC for a 25% rise in freight rates because of declining revenues and higher costs .... Senate passes and sends to the House the Wagner-Ellender-Taft housing bill to help build and finance 12.5 million homes during the next 10 years .... OPA and the Agricultural Dept. reinstate wartime controls to channel livestock to legitimate slaughterers.	Army reveals development of the sniper-scope, an infra-red sighting device small enough to be used by individual soldiers.	The world's first permanent television network, linking N.Y., Philadelphia and Washington, begins operation .... Victor Kravchenko's *I Chose Freedom*, describing the decision of a Soviet official to flee to the West, is published.	Apr. 15
House votes to cite for contempt 17 officials of the Joint Anti-Fascist Refugee Comm. in N.Y. for refusing to produce records demanded by the Un-American Activities Comm.	Eleven Democratic congressmen and Laborite Vito Marcantonio ask Truman to sever relations with Spain.	Arthur Chevrolet, auto pioneer and racer who helped found the Chevrolet Motor Co., is found hanged in his Slidell, La. home.	Scientists at the Wister Institute of Anatomy and Biology in Philadelphia disclose the development of an alcoholic extract which destroys tumors and cancers in albino rats.	Truman opens the baseball season by tossing out the first ball of a Red Sox-Senators game in Griffith Stadium, Washington .... Baseball Commissioner Albert Chandler rules that players who jump to foreign leagues are automatically suspended for five years .... Truman signs without comment the Lea "anti-Petrillo" bill .... Major film studios in Hollywood offer an 18½¢ hourly wage increase to 17,000 workers as union leaders confer on a possible strike.	Apr. 16
House Democrats, disturbed at what they consider threats by the party's National Comm. to "purge" congressmen who do not follow the party line, create an 11-man liaison committee to prevent "misunderstandings."	Reacting to the April 10 remarks of Adm. Merrill, Truman enjoins active Navy officers from public discussion of the armed forces unification plan.	U.S. Famine Emergency Comm. urges further government regulations to save food, warning that voluntary measures will not produce enough for export.	American Cancer Society reveals that isotopes, radioactive elements produced in research on the atom bomb, will be used in a proposed $3-million cancer research program.		Apr. 17
	U.S. sources in Berlin reveal plans to rebuild the American Air Force in Europe, which will consist of 500 B-29s plus A-26 and P-80 jet aircraft.	House passes and sends to the Senate a much-amended price control bill extending the OPA for nine months after June 30.	A method of telephoning using microwave radar pulses is demonstrated in Paris.		Apr. 18
	Secy. Byrnes confirms that the U.S. has sent a new note to Moscow inviting the Russians to begin discussions on their request for a billion-dollar loan .... In a special radio broadcast, Truman urges Americans to eat less so that the U.S. can help overcome the world food crisis. Agriculture Secy. Clinton Anderson orders a 25% cut in production of flour for domestic use.		Dr. Walter Dandy, known as the foremost neurosurgeon of his time, dies at 60 in Baltimore.	German-born conductor Bruno Walter files a citizenship petition in N.Y.	Apr. 19
N.Y. Gov. Thomas Dewey signs a bill fixing a 50-mph speed limit on state highways.	Gen. Curtis LeMay announces plans for an AAF air engineering center for research on supersonic craft, missiles, space ships, interplanetary bases and atomic energy.	Truman confers with John L. Lewis and Labor Secy. Lewis Schwellenbach on the coal strike, but reports "no conclusive result."		Ilya Ehrenburg and two other Soviet writers visiting the U.S. say they favor greater interchange of correspondents between the U.S. and Russia, but warn U.S. papers to refrain from "malice or slander" against the Soviet state .... Pope Pius XII urges the Italian Catholic Action Youth to fight "anti-Christian forces" in politics as well as in private life.	Apr. 20
F *Includes elections, federal-state relations, civil rights and liberties, crime, the judiciary, education, health care, poverty, urban affairs and population.*	G *Includes formation and debate of U.S. foreign and defense policies, veterans affairs and defense spending. (Relations with specific foreign countries are usually found under the region concerned.)*	H *Includes business, labor, agriculture, taxation, transportation, consumer affairs, monetary and fiscal policy, natural resources, pollution and accidents.*	I *Includes worldwide scientific, medical and technological developments, natural phenomena, U.S. weather and natural disasters.*	J *Includes the arts, religion, scholarship, communications media, sports, entertainment, fashions, fads and social life.*	

	World Affairs	Europe	Africa & the Middle East	The Americas	Asia & the Pacific
Apr. 21	Big Four foreign ministers' deputies, meeting in London, end attempts to draw up draft peace treaties for Italy and the Balkan states without reaching agreement on major issues.	Two thousand Communist and Socialist delegates, claiming to represent one million party members in the Soviet zone of Germany, approve the merger of their parties into the Socialist Unity Party. . . . . John Maynard Keynes, world-reknowned and controversial economist, dies at 63 in Sussex, England.	Cairo reports that 60,000 British troops have evacuated Egypt in the past month, leaving about 100,000.		
Apr. 22	U.S. State Dept. joins the British Foreign Office in criticizing a TWA contract for air service to Italy as "monopolistic" and a violation of the Bermuda air agreement.	French political campaign for the May 5 constitutional referendum begins, with Socialists and Communists supporting the proposed constitution and right-wing Popular Republican leaders claiming it could result in a dictatorship . . . . U.S. military headquarters in Frankfurt reports evidence indicating that the recent poisoning of German POWs in a U.S.-operated camp was the result of a plot against 15,000 German SS prisoners held there . . . . Addressing Tyrolese refugees in Innsbruck, Chancellor Leopold Figl urges that the Tyrol be returned to Austria.	Iranian Premier Ghavam Saltaneh announces a seven-point proposal to Azerbaijan under which the autonomous province may return to central government control.		Communists in Chungking announce their refusal to participate in the central government or the proposed constitutional assembly so long as the "civil war" continues . . . . Japanese Premier Kijuro Shidehara and his cabinet resign, but he continues his efforts to form a coalition cabinet . . . . Japanese Gen. Masataka Kaguragi and four others are hanged by U.S. authorities in Shanghai for ordering the death of three American airmen from the 1942 Doolittle expedition.
Apr. 23	U.N. Security Council votes to keep the Iranian question on the agenda until May 6, defeating a French proposal to drop this question . . . . UNRRA head La Guardia warns that "have countries" must "come down in their reserve stocks" of food or he will "take such action as may be necessary." . . . . Conference of British Dominions Foreign Ministers opens in London, with P.M. Attlee presiding.	Members of the Italian "Democratic Fascist Party" steal Mussolini's body from his unmarked pauper's grave in Maggiore Cemetery.	A strike of 50,000 government employes in which Jews and Arabs cooperated is called off after the British Palestine administration raises wages.		
Apr. 24		Poland receives a $40 million U.S. loan through the Export-Import Bank . . . . French Constituent Assembly votes to nationalize 50 large insurance companies, with shareholders receiving 3% government bonds.		Argentine government places all banks including private deposits under its control . . . . Brazilian Foreign Min. Joao Neves da Fontura announces that the Pan American Peace and Security Conference will be held in Rio de Janeiro Sept. 7.	Chiang Kai-shek indefinitely postpones the Chinese constitutional assembly scheduled to convene May 5 due to Communist refusal to participate.
Apr. 25	Big Four Foreign Ministers Conference opens in Paris, as Molotov accepts French participation but opposes French voting on peace treaties with Rumania, Bulgaria, Hungary, Finland and Italy.				Chinese Communist troops enter the Manchurian city of Harbin as the Russians leave.
Apr. 26	Big Four agree on the preamble to the Italian peace treaty and on a committee to discuss Italian reparations.	Allied Control Council in Berlin fails to agree on recognition of the new Socialist Union Party as requested by the Russians . . . . Former Gestapo agent Hans Bernd Gisevius says at Nuremberg, after implicating most of the Nazi defendants in war crimes, that he was in contact with the U.S. OSS in Switzerland and Germany since 1943.		A conference of Venezuela, Colombia and Ecuador in Caracas agrees on an initial investment of $20 million in a joint merchant marine.	
Apr. 27	Big Four agree on a strict limitation of the Italian fleet, with Britain, Russia, the U.S., Yugoslavia and Greece sharing in the division of ships exceeding the limit.	Italy's strongest party, the Christian Democrats, votes at a Rome congress to favor a republic against a monarchy . . . . Icelandic Premier Olafur Thors rejects a U.S. bid for long-term leases of military bases there.			
Apr. 28		More than 4,000 Germans engage in a four-hour riot after an attack on civilians in Landsberg by Jews of the nearby displaced persons camp . . . . Francois de la Rocque, Petain supporter and founder of the fascist *Croix de Feu* movement, dies at 60 in Paris.	Azerbaijani leader Mir Sayid Jafar Pishevari arrives in Teheran to discuss Premier Ghavam's seven-point peace proposal of April 22.		The important Manchurian railway center of Tsitsihar is seized by the Chinese Communists.
Apr. 29	Italian Premier Alcide de Gasperi telegraphs a plea to the Big Four in Paris that Italy be heard before any final decision is taken on the Italian peace treaty . . . . Secy. Byrnes urges the peace conference to consider a U.S. proposal for a four-power treaty to keep Germany disarmed for 25 years, but he gains no support from Britain or Russia . . . . With Russia abstaining, the Security Council adopts an Australian resolution to investigate whether Spain is a menace to world peace . . . . Mrs. Franklin D. Roosevelt is elected to lead the U.N. Commission on Human Rights, with Mrs. Bodil Begtrup chairperson of the Subcommission on the Status of Women.	British government reports that nearly two million soldiers have been demobilized since the end of the war.		Argentine Chamber of Deputies meets for the first time since its dissolution after the 1943 revolution.	Headed by former Japanese Premier Hideki Tojo, 28 officials are indicted in Tokyo on 55 counts of crimes against peace, "conventional war crimes" and "crimes against humanity." . . . . Chiang Kai-shek rejects Marshall's proposal that the Chinese Communists keep the city of Changchun and almost 90% of Manchuria, bringing an end to talks between the two factions . . . . Gen. Manuel Acuna Roxas' election as Philippine president is conceded by Pres. Sergio Osmena.

A	B	C	D	E
Includes developments that affect more than one world region, international organizations and important meetings of major world leaders.	*Includes all domestic and regional developments in Europe, including the Soviet Union, Turkey, Cyprus and Malta.*	*Includes all domestic and regional developments in Africa and the Middle East, including Iraq and Iran and excluding Cyprus, Turkey and Afghanistan.*	*Includes all domestic and regional developments in Latin America, the Caribbean and Canada.*	*Includes all domestic and regional developments in Asian and Pacific nations, extending from Afghanistan through all the Pacific Islands, except Hawaii.*

U.S. Politics & Social Issues	U.S. Foreign Policy & Defense	U.S. Economy & Environment	Science, Technology & Nature	Culture, Leisure & Life Style	
Truman leaves Washington for a vacation cruise aboard the yacht *Williamsburg.*	Truman refuses to endorse any position on the Palestine question, preferring to wait for U.N. action on the matter.		An Army P-80 jet fighter piloted by Capt. Martin Smith flies from N.Y. to Washington in 29.15 minutes, averaging over 450 mph to set a new world speed record . . . . CBS discloses that tests of color television over coaxial cables between N.Y. and Washington have proved successful.	Crowds throng churches and one million persons parade on N.Y.'s Fifth Ave., setting a new Easter Sunday record.	Apr. 21
Commerce Secy. Wallace says Democrats in Congress should discipline any member violating party policy by denying him committee appointments . . . . Chief Justice Harlan Stone of the U.S. Supreme Court dies at 73 in Washington, while the Court rules that an alien seeking U.S. citizenship need not pledge to bear arms in defense of the U.S.	Sen. Arthur Vandenberg (R, Mich.) approves of the loan to Britain on the basis of "intelligent American self interest," warning that refusal of aid might force the British into "unintended socialization." . . . . Army announces it has discharged seven million men since the start of demobilization May 12, 1945.	AFL announces plans for an organizing drive in the South with a goal of one million new members . . . . Supreme Court rules that OPA pricing regulations may be challenged after they are rewritten.			Apr. 22
	Senate Military Affairs Comm. votes to report in favor of the Administration's bill for unification of the armed services.	CIO United Federal Workers and the State, County and Municipal Workers merge, forming the United Public Workers of America with 103,000 members.		Joseph Tinker, Johnny Evers, Frank Change, Jack Chesbro, Clark Griffith, Joseph McGinnity, Edward Waddell, Eddie Plank, Ed Walsh, Jesse Burkett and Tom McCarthy are elected to baseball's Hall of Fame.	Apr. 23
			National Academy of Sciences elects 29 U.S. scientists to membership and names Russian physicist Peter Kapitza a foreign associate.	Harper & Bros. publishes Leon Trotsky's biography of Joseph Stalin, his rival for leadership of Soviet Russia.	Apr. 24
		The Railroad Trainmen and Locomotive Engineers Brotherhoods reject a fact-finding board's 16¢ hourly wage increase recommendation and call a strike of 300,000 members for May 18.			Apr. 25
		Agriculture Dept. calls all loans on the 1945 corn crop as of May 1 to stop hoarding.	U.S. Navy reveals development of an aircraft rocket engine which generates 6,000 pounds of thrust but weighs only 210 lbs.		Apr. 26
	Air Force reveals the XB-35 flying wing bomber, with no fuselage, a wing span of 172 feet and a range of over 10,000 miles.			*Billboard* reports the most popular songs are: (1) *Oh! What It Seemed To Be,* (2) *Shoo-Fly Pie and Apple Pan Dowdy,* and (3) *One-zy, Two-zy.*	Apr. 27
Truman returns to the White House after completing his vacation cruise on the *Williamsburg*. . . . Russell Sage Foundation reports that low interest rates are reducing funds available to the nation's 505 social welfare foundations, which have an estimated $1.8 billion in capital assets.	Army-Navy Munitions Bd. announces plans for a survey of the nation's caverns for underground military and industrial installations in the event of an atomic war.	Senate Education and Labor Comm. approves a compromise bill returning the U.S. Employment Service to the states on Dec. 31, 1946.		The Alliance for the Preservation of American Reform Judaism, opposed to Zionism and Jewish nationalism, is formed in Baton Rouge, La.	Apr. 28
Jouett Ross Todd resigns as treasurer of the GOP National Committee.		John L. Lewis and soft coal operators meet in Washington at the request of Labor Secy. Schwellenbach as the nation's coal reserves drop to 31 million tons . . . . Agriculture Dept. reports that prices received by farmers as of April 15 are at the highest level since July 1920 and that U.S. corn supplies are 19% above last year's level.			Apr. 29

F	G	H	I	J
Includes elections, federal-state relations, civil rights and liberties, crime, the judiciary, education, health care, poverty, urban affairs and population.	*Includes formation and debate of U.S. foreign and defense policies, veterans affairs and defense spending. (Relations with specific foreign countries are usually found under the region concerned.)*	*Includes business, labor, agriculture, taxation, transportation, consumer affairs, monetary and fiscal policy, natural resources, pollution and accidents.*	*Includes worldwide scientific, medical and technological developments, natural phenomena, U.S. weather and natural disasters.*	*Includes the arts, religion, scholarship, communications media, sports, entertainment, fashions, fads and social life.*

	World Affairs	Europe	Africa & the Middle East	The Americas	Asia & the Pacific
Apr. 30	Big Four in Paris agree to Italy's retention of the southern Tyrol, claimed by Austria.	At his Nuremberg trial, former Reichsbank head Hjalmar Schacht claims that he aided the Nazis because he thought their sole motive was national defense.	The Anglo-American Commission of Inquiry issues its report, recommending the termination of the British mandate in Palestine and its transfer to a U.N. trusteeship. It also calls for admission of 110,000 European Jews into Palestine and creation of a binational state. Both Jews and Arabs reject the plan . . . . Britain and France complete their evacuation from Syria 15 days ahead of schedule.		Allied headquarters in Tokyo announces discovery of a plot to assassinate MacArthur, headed by former Kamikaze pilot Hideo Tokayama.
May 1	Molotov rejects proposals at the Paris conference for a quadripartite military commission to enforce armistice terms in Italy, claiming Britain and the U.S. might seek to send similar commissions to the Balkan states.	Physicist Alan Nunn May, convicted of giving atomic research information to the Russians, is sentenced in London to 10 years imprisonment.	British P.M. Attlee tells the House of Commons that Britain will not carry out the recommendations of the Palestine Inquiry Commission "single-handed," and asks what share of responsibility the U.S. is willing to take.	Senate confirms William Hastie as governor of the Virgin Islands.	
May 2	British Chancellor of the Exchequer Hugh Dalton is named a governor of the IMF and World Bank, succeeding the late John Maynard Keynes.		Arab Higher Comm. sends a letter described as "the next thing to an ultimatum" to the British cabinet, warning of a national struggle against the recommendations of the Palestine Inquiry Commission.	Argentine government takes over six universities, placing them under federal directors, after anti-Peron demonstrations break out among students.	Dutch Overseas Territories Min. J.H.A. Logemann announces that a tentative agreement for an Indonesian Republic under Netherlands sovereignty has been reached at The Hague.
May 3	Delegates to the U.N. Atomic Energy Commission are announced, including Bernard Baruch of the U.S. and Andrei Gromyko of Russia.	Yugoslavian Vice Premier Eduard Kardelj rejects four Yugoslav-Italian border proposals and warns that Yugoslavia will not accept any solution which leaves Slavs under Italian control.		Brazil ousts Communists from government posts, charging that Red leader Luis Carlos Prestes is inciting civil war . . . . Kathleen Mary Willsher, involved in the Soviet embassy spy ring, is sentenced in Ottawa to three years in prison.	
May 4	Secy. Byrnes suggests at the Paris Foreign Ministers Conference that a plebiscite be held in the disputed Yugoslav-Italian border region.		Iranian Army officers report in Teheran that the Red Army has completed its evacuation of Iran.		Nationalist Gen. Tu Yu-ming says his troops have "smashed" a surprise Communist attack against the Manchurian city of Mukden.
May 5		French voters reject a proposed constitution, supported by Communists and socialists, by a small margin in a national referendum.	Arab opposition to the Anglo-American report urging increased Jewish migration to Palestine heightens with a call by Arab Higher Comm. Chmn. Jamal el Husseini urging Palestinian Arabs to resist "external enemies."	Juan Peron notifies UNRRA that Argentina will ship 500,000 tons of wheat and corn to Europe before June . . . . Former dean of the Dominican Univ. Law Dept. Jose Antonio Bonilla seeks sanctuary in the Mexican embassy as Dominican Republic dictator Rafael Trujillo cracks down on "subversive" elements.	Chiang Kai-shek proclaims Nanking the capital of China, as Nationalist-Communist clashes are reported in Shansi and Hupeh provinces and in Manchuria.
May 6	At the Paris conference, Molotov offers to modify the Russian stance on Italian colonies and reparations in return for the awarding of Trieste to Yugoslavia, but Britain and the U.S. reject the proposal.	British House of Commons passes the second reading of a bill to nationalize the civil aviation industry, while the government announces plans to build up Stevenage, one hour by train from London, as the first of 10 "satellite towns" to relieve congestion in the capital . . . . At his Nuremberg trial, former Economics Min. Walther Funk claims to have signed anti-Jewish decrees "to protect Jews from arbitrary violence." . . . . Marshal Ion Antonescu, wartime Rumanian dictator and Iron Guard leader, goes on trial for treason in Bucharest with three of his former ministers.	Iranian Ambassador Hussein Ala reports to the Security Council that Iranian officials are not able to verify that Soviet troops have left Azerbaijan.	Mariano Ospina Perez is elected president of Colombia, the first conservative to win the post since 1930.	Australian government announces plans to establish a national medical service despite opposition from the medical profession.
May 7	Foreign ministers in Paris agree on Balkan boundaries for Rumania, Hungary, Bulgaria and Russia . . . . Security Council subcommittee investigating Spain asks the 51 member nations of the U.N. to submit evidence on the Spanish threat to world peace.	Hermann Dietrich is appointed food commissioner by the minister-presidents of the three states in the U.S. zone of Germany . . . . Anton Mussert, 52, Hitler's "leader of the Netherlands people," is executed in The Hague.	A British delegation in Cairo announces plans to withdraw all British forces from Egypt as part of a proposed Anglo-Egyptian military alliance.		
May 8	Gromyko boycotts the U.N. Security Council for the second time when the Council again takes up the Iranian issue . . . . Secy. Byrnes proposes that the Big Four Foreign Ministers postpone their negotiations until the start of a 21-nation general peace conference, scheduled for June 15.		Arab Higher Comm. asks Russia for help to prevent implementation of the Palestine Inquiry Commission report.		U.S.-Soviet talks in Seoul on establishment of an interim Korean government, in progress since March 20, adjourn indefinitely due to Russian refusal to permit participation of the U.S.-sponsored Representative Democratic Council, headed by Syngman Rhee.
May 9	In response to Byrnes's proposal for adjournment of the Foreign Ministers Conference, Molotov urges that agreement on all peace treaties be reached before a general peace conference . . . . UNRRA Council demands improvement of international food allocation machinery, after criticizing the Combined Food Bd.	King Victor Emmanuel III, who has ruled Italy since July 1900, abdicates in favor of his son Crown Prince Humbert and leaves for exile in Egypt . . . . Adm. Karl Doenitz claims at his Nuremberg trial that "millions of German lives" were saved because the war was prolonged until last spring so they could flee from the Russians.			Eisenhower concludes an inspection trip through China by visiting Gen. Marshall in Nanking.

A	B	C	D	E
Includes developments that affect more than one world region, international organizations and important meetings of major world leaders.	*Includes all domestic and regional developments in Europe, including the Soviet Union, Turkey, Cyprus and Malta.*	*Includes all domestic and regional developments in Africa and the Middle East, including Iraq and Iran and excluding Cyprus, Turkey and Afghanistan.*	*Includes all domestic and regional developments in Latin America, the Caribbean and Canada.*	*Includes all domestic and regional developments in Asian and Pacific nations, extending from Afghanistan through all the Pacific Islands, except Hawaii.*

U.S. Politics & Social Issues	U.S. Foreign Policy & Defense	U.S. Economy & Environment	Science, Technology & Nature	Culture, Leisure & Life Style	
Florida State Supreme Court rules against Dade County zoning laws barring Negroes from certain areas of Miami.		Senate passes and sends to the White House a bill providing $523 million for aid in the development of municipal airports.	Physicist Ernest Lawrence of the University of California, Berkeley reveals development of the synchrotron, a new atom smasher which can accelerate electrons to energies of 300 million volts.	Cleveland Indians pitcher Bob Feller hurls the season's second no-hitter against the New York Yankees in N.Y., as the Indians win, 1-0.	Apr. 30
	Navy Secy. Forrestal says that the pending bill for armed services unification would give too much power to a supreme chief of staff .... Truman asks Congress to appropriate $600 million already authorized for UNRRA for the 1946 fiscal year.	Bureau of Labor Statistics reports that 1.66 million strikers caused a record loss of 54.7 million man-days in the first quarter of 1946.			May 1
An attempted jail break by 16 Alcatraz convicts is foiled after a battle in which 80 Marines aid in storming the prison.		Office of Defense Transportation orders an embargo on all non-essential rail freight and a 25% reduction in passenger service in order to conserve coal during the miners' strike .... Truman asks Congress to vote funds for 34 government corporations, including the Reconstruction Finance Corp., promising to discontinue them as soon as inflationary pressures ease.			May 2
		Office of Defense Transportation decrees a further 25% reduction in passenger service on coal-burning railroads, effective May 15. .... Truman signs a bill appropriating $330 million for navigation, hydro-electric and flood control programs.		*The Postman Always Rings Twice*, a film based on the thriller by James M. Cain, opens in N.Y.	May 3
Fair Employment Practices Commission shuts down after Congress refuses liquidation funds.				Warren Mehrtens rides Assault to victory in the Kentucky Derby.	May 4
Wisconsin GOP State Convention nominates Joseph R. McCarthy for the U.S. Senate over Sen. Robert M. La Follette.					May 5
	Truman requests a $7.25-billion appropriation for the War Dept. in fiscal 1947 and sends Congress the Inter-American Military Cooperation Act, calling for U.S. aid in the training, organization and equipment of Latin American armed forces .... Gen. Alexander Vandegrift tells the Senate Naval Affairs Comm. that unification of the armed forces will probably "spell extinction" for the Marine Corps, which he says the Army is determined to reduce.	A strike of 35,000 members of the CIO Industrial Union of Marine and Shipbuilding Workers against the Bethlehem Steel Co. is called off when a contract is signed providing an 18¢ hourly wage increase .... Truman confers with advisers on the coal situation, while AFL Pres. William Green backs the stand of John L. Lewis.		Pulitzer Prize in drama goes to Russell Crouse and Howard Lindsay for their play *State of the Union;* in history to Arthur M. Schlesinger, Jr. for his *Age of Jackson;* and in music to Leo Soweby for *Canticle of the Sun* .... A federal court in St. Louis issues an injunction temporarily restraining the Pasquel brothers of the Mexican Baseball League from persuading Brooklyn Dodger players to break their contracts .... The New York Yankees will become the first club to travel by air for a full season when they sign a contract with UAL for 1946.	May 6
		Lewis and the UMW policy committee stand firm in their demand that mine operators set up a health and welfare fund as a prerequisite to discussion of wages and hours in the coal dispute.	Office of Scientific Research and Development reveals that wartime researchers in Germany and Japan developed telephones of limited range which sent signals on beams of infra-red light.		May 7
	An Army-Navy study reveals that 295,867 members of the armed forces were killed during World War II.	Civilian Production Admin. orders a "dimout" in 22 Eastern states as the emergency coal supply dwindles to less than enough for a normal 12-hour period.	American Museum of Natural History's first overseas expedition since 1939 flies to Africa to collect small mammals and poisonous plants that may be used in infantile paralysis treatment.		May 8
		Senate unanimously extends the Selective Service Act for possible use in the coal strike, and empowers the President to seize strike-bound plants .... A 115-day strike of 75,000 United Electrical, Radio and Machine Workers against Westinghouse Electric is settled with an agreement calling for an 18¢ hourly wage increase .... House votes $400 million for housing subsidies.	U.S. Army Commission on Neurotropic Diseases discloses the development of a vaccine against dengue fever.		May 9

F	G	H	I	J
Includes elections, federal-state relations, civil rights and liberties, crime, the judiciary, education, health care, poverty, urban affairs and population.	*Includes formation and debate of U.S. foreign and defense policies, veterans affairs and defense spending. (Relations with specific foreign countries are usually found under the region concerned.)*	*Includes business, labor, agriculture, taxation, transportation, consumer affairs, monetary and fiscal policy, natural resources, pollution and accidents.*	*Includes worldwide scientific, medical and technological developments, natural phenomena, U.S. weather and natural disasters.*	*Includes the arts, religion, scholarship, communications media, sports, entertainment, fashions, fads and social life.*

	World Affairs	Europe	Africa & the Middle East	The Americas	Asia & the Pacific
May 10	Molotov supports a French proposal that the Italian African colonies of Libya and Eritrea be placed under Italian trusteeship within the U.N., and Byrnes accepts the compromise.	The U.S. military government dissolves the Bavarian monarchist "King and Fatherland" Party under Soviet prodding.	An Arab League message to the U.S. warns that Arab states will consider any support of the Palestine Inquiry Commission's report "hostile to the Arab people."		
May 11	Byrnes agrees at the Paris Peace Conference to the award of $100 million in Italian reparations to Russia, provided it comes from assets abroad, surplus war industrial machinery and specified warships.	Representatives of German Social Democrats in the U.S., British and French zones re-establish their party with Kurt Schumacher as chairman.		Nazi agent Joaquin Watjen, wanted by the U.S., is released by the Argentine Supreme Court, which rules that Nazis must have a hearing before deportation.	A truce is signed in Tsinan to end the fighting between Chinese Communist and government forces in Shantung Province.
May 12		Aroused by rumors that Jews were kidnapping and killing Hungarian children, mobs lynch three workmen in the suburbs of Budapest.		Police patrol the port of Santos, Brazil and the Labor Ministry closes the dock workers' union for six months after stevadores refuse to load Spanish ships .... Venezuelan Democratic Action Party turns down a Communist proposal for a common front against possible counter-revolutionary moves by former Pres. Eleazar Lopez Contreras.	A seven-day conference between British, Moslem and Indian Congress Party representatives ends in Simla without agreement on the composition of an independent Indian government .... UNRRA engineers announce plans to direct 100,000 workers in repairing a mile-long break in dikes of China's Yellow River to reclaim two million acres of flooded land.
May 13	Britain and the U.S. agree to accept a French proposal for the Yugoslav-Italian boundary, which is closer to Soviet and Yugoslavian views but still leaves Trieste to the Italians .... Concluding a worldwide food survey, Herbert Hoover states that the world grain shortage has been reduced from 11 million to 3.6 million tons within the past two months.	A U.S. military court in Dachau sentences 58 Germans to hang and three to life imprisonment for murder of 70,000 inmates in the Mauthausen concentration camp .... U.S. Military authorities order all German military and Nazi memorials destroyed and all books glorifying war and Nazism confiscated.	Negotiations between Iranian Premier Ahmad Ghavam Saltaneh and Azerbaijani leader Mir Sayid Jafar Pishevari end in failure.	Brazilian Foreign Min. Joao Neves da Fontoura proposes that the U.S. and all other American nations settle their differences with Peron in order to present a united front against Russia.	Allied Far Eastern Commission issues an interim reparations plan for MacArthur, specifying that Japanese arsenals, the aircraft industry and light metals industry should be made available for reparations .... Japanese Defense Counsel Ichiro Kiyose challenges the legality of the International Military Tribunal, declaring Japan's surrender affected the armed forces but not the government .... Afghanistan's King Zahir Shar dismisses his cabinet and asks Sha Mahmoud Khan to form a new one.
May 14	Subcommittee on the Status of Women recommends a 13-point program to the U.N. Commission on Human Rights, declaring that "democracy is now the only social order in which women can enjoy full rights."				Maj. Bruce Blakeney, U.S. defense counsel at the Tokyo war crimes trial, opens his argument by claiming that the atomic bombing of Japan was as murderous as the attack on Pearl Harbor, and that the Allies are setting a precedent under which "our own leaders may be on trial after the next war."
May 15	Council of Foreign Ministers votes to adjourn until June 15 after failing to agree on major issues in the Italian and Balkan peace treaties.	German Social Democratic leader Kurt Schumacher charges that most of the police in the British zone are former Nazi Party members.	Arab Higher Comm. demands dissolution of the Jewish Agency, which it holds responsible for illegal immigration to Palestine.		Chiang Kai-shek shakes up his cabinet in an effort to gain leftist support, but the Kuomintang remains in control.
May 16	Gromyko ends his boycott of the U.N. Security Council as members convene again to debate rules of procedure .... Commission on Human Rights adopts a recommendation for a U.N. agency to enforce worldwide observance of an International Bill of Rights.	Gen. Josef (Sepp) Dietrich and 73 other German SS men go on trial before an American military court in Dachau for the murder of more than 500 American prisoners and 90 Belgian civilians near Malmedy, Belgium.			In the face of a Hindu-Moslem deadlock, the British cabinet issues a White Paper recommending independence for a unified India and immediate convocation of a constitutional assembly .... Emperor Hirohito appoints conservative politician and former Foreign Min. Shigeru Yoshida as premier.
May 17	U.S. and Britain agree to export 10 million tons of cereals to famine-stricken nations through September .... Security Council defers consideration of applications for U.N. membership until August, while a Council subcommittee considers evidence submitted by Russia and Belgium that Franco Spain is a fascist state and a menace to world peace.	Rumania's wartime dictator Marshal Ion Antonescu and 12 of his cabinet members are sentenced to death in Bucharest for war crimes .... The Dutch Labor government of Willem Schermerhorn is defeated in parliamentary elections, yielding its position as largest party to the Catholic People's Party.	Truman sends telegrams to the heads of Arab states assuring them that the U.S. will not take any independent action concerning the settlement of the Palestine question.		The International Military Tribunal in Japan dismisses defense motions challenging its authority to try civilians.
May 18	U.N. Refugee Comm. in London votes against Russian-bloc opposition to accord "political emigres" the same rights and treatment as other refugees.	U.S. military sources reveal in Frankfurt that American forces captured more than eight million of the 17 million soldiers listed in the German Army.			
May 19			British authorities permit 1,014 Jewish refugees from La Spezia, Italy to disembark in Haifa.	La Paz reports indicate that Bolivian Pres. Gualberto Villarroel's dictatorial government, having failed to win popular support in May 5 elections, is waging a campaign of political terror to stay in power.	Gen. Tu Li-ming announces that Nationalist forces have recaptured the Manchurian city of Szepingkai from the Chinese Communists .... A Manila newspaper announces the Communist Hukbalahap movement has established a "state within a state" in central Luzon, resulting in 600 dead in clashes with Philippine military police.
	A	B	C	D	E
	Includes developments that affect more than one world region, international organizations and important meetings of major world leaders.	*Includes all domestic and regional developments in Europe, including the Soviet Union, Turkey, Cyprus and Malta.*	*Includes all domestic and regional developments in Africa and the Middle East, including Iraq and Iran and excluding Cyprus, Turkey and Afghanistan.*	*Includes all domestic and regional developments in Latin America, the Caribbean and Canada.*	*Includes all domestic and regional developments in Asian and Pacific nations, extending from Afghanistan through all the Pacific Islands, except Hawaii.*

U.S. Politics & Social Issues	U.S. Foreign Policy & Defense	U.S. Economy & Environment	Science, Technology & Nature	Culture, Leisure & Life Style	
	Senate approves and sends to the House the $3.75 billion loan to Britain.	Soft coal operators accept a two-week truce offered by Lewis, who orders 400,000 miners back to work May 13.			May 10
		In response to the truce in the coal industry, the government orders cancellation of freight and passenger rail curbs . . . . Delegates of seven maritime unions end their San Francisco meeting after electing a committee to plan a national federation of 214,000 maritime workers.		Arturo Toscanini reopens Milan's La Scala opera house, conducting an orchestra in his native Italy for the first time in 15 years . . . . Assault, with Warren Mehrtens up, takes the $100,000 Preakness at Pimlico, Md.	May 11
	Emergency Food Collection Comm., headed by Commerce Secy. Henry Wallace, begins a nationwide drive to aid famine-struck countries.		AT&T begins service in St. Louis between regular phone outlets and vehicles equipped with radiophone installations.	Byron Nelson defeats Ben Hogan by two strokes in the Houston Golf Tournament.	May 12
	Army reveals a "major reorganization" plan to save manpower and money, eliminate nine service commands, give Eisenhower broader powers, strengthen research and grant "increased autonomy" to the AAF . . . . Truman confers with War Secy. Robert Patterson and Navy Secy. James Forrestal on unification of the armed forces . . . . House passes and returns to the Senate a resolution extending Selective Service until July 1, exempting fathers and all 18-19 year olds.	John L. Lewis changes his proposal for financing a $470-million miners' health and welfare fund, asking a 7% payroll levy instead of a 10¢-per-ton royalty . . . . A federal fact-finding board in Washington recommends a 20% pay increase for 16,000 CIO International Longshoremen's and Warehousemen's Union members on the Pacific Coast.			May 13
	Senate passes and sends to Truman the House-approved resolution extending the life of Selective Service.		Russian physicist Peter Kapitza says in Moscow that it will be 100 years before atomic energy fundamentally changes the world economic structure.		May 14
South Carolina lowers the voting age from 21 to 18 in the coming primaries.		Coal operators "unequivocally" reject Lewis's demand for a 7% payroll levy to finance a miners' health and welfare fund.		American Baseball Guild informs the Pittsburgh Pirates that a majority of its players are union members and wish to discuss collective bargaining.	May 15
Truman submits a government reorganization plan to Congress, involving consolidation of some federal agencies and reform of the welfare system.			In a Pittsburgh speech, physicist J. Robert Oppenheimer urges creation of an international atomic development authority which might serve as the start toward the setting up of a world government.	Amory Houghton is named president of the Boy Scouts of America, succeeding Walter Head.	May 16
Georgia Gov. Ellis Arnall calls for the end of poll taxes and the lowering of the voting age to 18.		Truman seizes the nation's railroads and directs the Office of Defense Transportation to operate them 24 hours before a scheduled strike by the Locomotive Engineers and Railroad Trainmen Brotherhoods.	Navy scientists reveal the discovery of a 300-mile wide layer of colloidal particles or minute marine life in the Pacific Ocean off the coast of lower California.	*Annie Get Your Gun*, produced by Rogers and Hammerstein and featuring Ethel Merman and Ray Middleton, opens on Broadway to favorable reviews.	May 17
		Truman announces that the scheduled nationwide strike of railroad workers has been called off by union leaders at his request.			May 18
War Reconversion Dir. Snyder reports to Truman that of 2,080,000 persons who will seek admission to colleges next fall, only one million can be accommodated.	Sen. David Walsh (D. Mass.) and Rep. Carl Vinson (D. Ga.) state in a letter to Navy Secy. Forrestal that Congress will not approve unification of the armed forces.	OPA estimates that since July it has lifted price ceilings on 3,000 commodities with an annual sales volume of $10 million.		Playwright and novelist Booth Tarkington dies at 76 in Indianapolis, Ind.	May 19
F *Includes elections, federal-state relations, civil rights and liberties, crime, the judiciary, education, health care, poverty, urban affairs and population.*	G *Includes formation and debate of U.S. foreign and defense policies, veterans affairs and defense spending. (Relations with specific foreign countries are usually found under the region concerned.)*	H *Includes business, labor, agriculture, taxation, transportation, consumer affairs, monetary and fiscal policy, natural resources, pollution and accidents.*	I *Includes worldwide scientific, medical and technological developments, natural phenomena, U.S. weather and natural disasters.*	J *Includes the arts, religion, scholarship, communications media, sports, entertainment, fashions, fads and social life.*	

	World Affairs	Europe	Africa & the Middle East	The Americas	Asia & the Pacific
May 20	Representatives of 21 nations in the U.N. Food and Agriculture Organization hold an emergency meeting in Washington to deal with world food shortages.	British House of Commons passes the coal industry nationalization bill on its third reading .... U.S. State Dept. sends Premier Tito a note charging Yugoslavia with seeking to discredit the Anglo-American administration of Venezia Giulia and listing nine incidents of alleged Yugoslav provocation.		The government assumes control of the Argentine Industrial Union, a manufacturers' group which opposed Peron's election.	MacArthur bans demonstrations in Japan after 125,000 protesters marched on the royal palace yesterday, demanding increased food rations and the resignation of Premier Yoshida.
May 21	U.S. informs the Security Council subcommittee on Spain it has no evidence that Spain is working on the atomic bomb or deploying troops for offensive purposes.	Despite Russian objections, former German Foreign Office Secy. Baron Ernst von Weizsaecker testifies at Nuremberg that the 1939 Russian-German pact placed Finland, Estonia, Latvia, eastern Poland, parts of Rumania and Lithuania within the Soviet sphere .... U.S. troops search 397 Danube River boats in Bavaria in an effort to break up smuggling and an underground railway for escaping SS men .... Switzerland agrees informally with 18 Allied nations to give up half the German capital in the country and $58 million in looted gold shipped there by Germany.	Iranian Propaganda Min. Mouzaffar Firouz reports that there is no evidence of Soviet troops or supplies in Azerbaijan.		
May 22	Gromyko boycotts the Security Council for the third time as other members vote to keep the Iranian issue on the agenda.	British Foreign Secy. Ernest Bevin announces plans to demobilize 200,000 Polish troops under British control in Britain, Germany and Italy .... Karl Hermann Frank, Nazi administrator of Bohemia-Moravia, is hanged in Prague as a war criminal.		Former Canadian National Research Council engineer Edward Wilfred Mazerall is found guilty in Ottawa of revealing secret information to Russia.	Premier Shigeru Yoshida completes his new conservative cabinet and takes office with Allied approval.
May 23	Former Spanish Republican Premier Jose Giral y Pereira warns the U.N. Security Council subcommittee on Spain that Franco has authorized all Spanish citizens to bear arms on the pretext of a possible Soviet attack.			Argentinian President-elect Peron announces the merger of all parties supporting him into a single National Revolutionary Party.	U.S. government officials disclose that only 10% of relief food sent to China is reaching famine zones .... Nationalist forces recapture the Manchurian city of Changchun from the Communists, as Chiang Kai-shek leaves Nanking for Mukden in Gen. Marshall's plane.
May 24			Soviet Ambassador Ivan Sadchikov officially notifies Iran that the Red Army completed its evacuation May 6 .... Arab Higher Comm. in Jerusalem submits three demands to the U.S. and Britain: (1) abrogation of the British mandate and cessation of Jewish immigration, (2) establishment of an Arab Palestine and (3) withdrawal of all foreign troops .... Churchill accuses Egypt of ingratitude and urges it be held to the 1936 treaty permitting British troops in the country.		
May 25	The second UNESCO session convenes in N.Y. with Sir Ramaswami Mudaliar of India presiding.		Transjordan's newly-crowned king, Abdullah Ibn El-Hussein, offers his throne as a "rallying point" for an Arab federation to include Syria, Lebanon and Iraq.		Indonesian Premier Sutan Sjahrir calls the latest proposal of Dutch administrator Van Mook "a definite step backward" from earlier Dutch willingness to recognize Indonesian control over Sumatra.
May 26		Nearly complete returns in municipal elections in the U.S. zone of Germany give the Christian Social Union 484 council seats, Social Democrats 421, the Communists 47 and the Liberal Democrats 34 .... Communists win 114 of 300 assembly seats in Czechoslovakia to become the country's strongest party .... An investigation commission of the Austrian government rules conductor Wilhelm Furtwaengler eligible to perform in Austria.			

	A	B	C	D	E
	Includes developments that affect more than one world region, international organizations and important meetings of major world leaders.	*Includes all domestic and regional developments in Europe, including the Soviet Union, Turkey, Cyprus and Malta.*	*Includes all domestic and regional developments in Africa and the Middle East, including Iraq and Iran and excluding Cyprus, Turkey and Afghanistan.*	*Includes all domestic and regional developments in Latin America, the Caribbean and Canada.*	*Includes all domestic and regional developments in Asian and Pacific nations, extending from Afghanistan through all the Pacific Islands, except Hawaii.*

U.S. Politics & Social Issues	U.S. Foreign Policy & Defense	U.S. Economy & Environment	Science, Technology & Nature	Culture, Leisure & Life Style	
A group of 795 immigrants, the first to enter the U.S. under Truman's 1945 refugee admission order, arrives in N.Y.	Reporting in Washington on the Paris Foreign Ministers Conference, Secy. Byrnes blames Russia for the "disappointingly slow" progress made at the conference and criticizes the veto rule in the Council of Foreign Ministers for permitting one power to "stop all efforts towards peace."				May 20
DAR Continental Congress in Atlantic City votes for "immediate dissolution" of Rep. Clare Booth Luce's Comm. Against Racial Discrimination in Constitution Hall, but Mrs. Luce refuses to comply.		Truman orders Interior Secy. Julius Krug to take over operation of soft coal mines at midnight as the UMW-management deadlock continues.			May 21
House blocks efforts to revive the Fair Employment Practices Commission.	Chmn. Tom Connally (D, Tex.) of the Senate Foreign Relations Comm. protests the efforts of Big Four foreign ministers to write peace treaties before convocation of a general peace conference.	Truman signs the emergency housing bill, providing $400 million in subsidies for building materials.			May 22
	The joint Pearl Harbor investigation committee closes its inquiry.	Transportation across the nation is paralyzed as 250,000 members of the Railroad Trainmen and Locomotive Engineers Brotherhoods strike, rejecting Truman's proposal for an 18½¢ hourly wage increase. In response, Truman places all transportation under the ODT and ICC, which will determine freight priorities .... Truman asks the Senate to extend the OPA for a year without crippling amendments, and signs a bill continuing government export controls until July 1947.			May 23
		Truman threatens to call out the Army to run the nation's railroads if striking workers do not return to work by 4 p.m. tomorrow. Skeleton crews maintain rail service at only 1% of normal, threatening many areas with a food shortage.		Rev. Dr. Harry E. Fosdick, leading spokesman of liberal Protestantism in the U.S., retires as a Baptist minister.	May 24
		Before a joint congressional session, Truman asks for the right to use court injunctions against labor leaders who urge workers to stay away from their jobs after the government has taken over an industry. During his address, he is given a note stating that leaders of the striking rail unions have settled with railroad operators for an 18½¢ hourly wage increase.		Navy wins the Intercollegiate 4-A track and field meet over 30 colleges in Annapolis.	May 25
Rep. Zebulon Weaver (D, N.C.), in Congress since 1917 save for one term, is defeated in the primaries.	Agriculture Secy. Clinton Anderson states the U.S. will ship a record 74 million bushels of wheat to famine areas by June 30.	The government relinquishes control of the nation's railroads as normal service is resumed.		Joseph Patterson, founder and publisher of the first successful tabloid in the U.S., the *N.Y. Daily News*, dies at 67 in N.Y.C. .... Garson Kanin and Arthur Laurents share the Playwrights Co. $1,500 Sidney Howard Memorial Award for "new American playwrights."	May 26

F	G	H	I	J
Includes elections, federal-state relations, civil rights and liberties, crime, the judiciary, education, health care, poverty, urban affairs and population.	*Includes formation and debate of U.S. foreign and defense policies, veterans affairs and defense spending. (Relations with specific foreign countries are usually found under the region concerned.)*	*Includes business, labor, agriculture, taxation, transportation, consumer affairs, monetary and fiscal policy, natural resources, pollution and accidents.*	*Includes worldwide scientific, medical and technological developments, natural phenomena, U.S. weather and natural disasters.*	*Includes the arts, religion, scholarship, communications media, sports, entertainment, fashions, fads and social life.*

	World Affairs	Europe	Africa & the Middle East	The Americas	Asia & the Pacific
May 27	UNESCO approves plans to call a World Health Conference and to establish a World Health Organization .... Former Spanish Republican leader Giral y Pereira tells the Security Council subcommittee that civil war will break out in Spain if the U.N. does not take measures to remove Franco.	Molotov tells *Pravda* that the British and Americans attempted to impose their will on Russia at the Paris Foreign Ministers' Conference .... Gen. Lucius Clay of the U.S. military government in Germany confirms reports that dismantling of factories for reparations had been halted in the U.S. zone until Germany is treated as a single economic unit .... A British government committee reports that Britain must train 5,000 scientists yearly to maintain the country's economic progress.		Haitian government orders an 8 p.m. curfew after 30 defeated parliamentary candidates urge a general strike, overthrow of the provisional government and new elections.	Fighting breaks out along the Indochinese-Siam border in an area ceded by Vichy France to Siam in 1941 but claimed by the present French government.
May 28		Rumanian police enter the U.S. military mission in Bucharest and arrest three Rumanians employed there .... British House of Commons approves the government's notice of its intention to nationalize parts of the iron and steel industry.	Rulers of seven Arab states meet on the estate of Egypt's King Farouk to discuss the Palestine problem.	Eisenhower and Adm. Chester W. Nimitz urge military collaboration with Latin American nations and possibly Canada before the House Foreign Affairs Comm.	Philippine Pres. Manuel Roxas is inaugurated in Manila.
May 29	UNESCO drafts an agreement with the International Labor Organization under which the latter will become a specialized U.N. agency .... Montreal Assembly of the Provisional International Civil Aviation Organization votes to offer the seat held open for Russia to another country.	British Ministry of Supply reveals the development of the de Haviland Swallow, the world's first jet-propelled flying wing fighter plane.	Representatives of seven Palestinian Arab parties form the Arab Higher Front in Jerusalem, led by Hussein Khalidi and Auni Bey Abdul Hadi. The new group differs from the existing Arab Higher Comm. in favoring submission of the Palestine dispute to the U.N. .... Iranian embassy in Washington discloses that Premier Ghavam has ordered Amb. Hussein Ala not to make any more statements to the Security Council following Ala's contention that Soviet forces remain in Azerbaijan.		Nationalist troops report capturing the Manchurian city of Kirin from the Chinese Communists.
May 30			Arab League announces in Cairo that its members have agreed on rejection of further Jewish immigration to Palestine and freedom for Libya and other Arab countries in North Africa.	Bolivian government declares a state of siege after making many arrests on charges of plotting revolution .... Argentine Pres. Edelmiro Farrell places the stock and commodity exchanges and export and insurance businesses under government control.	Gen. Marshall in Nanking appeals to both sides in the Chinese civil war to stop fighting.
May 31	Soviet delegate Nikolai Feonov protests a proposal before UNESCO to create a subcommission on freedom of the press and information.			President-elect Peron is reinstated on the Argentinian Army's active list and promoted to brigadier general.	
June 1	The five-power Security Council subcommittee investigating Franco reports that the Spanish regime is a potential menace to peace but not yet an "existing threat."	Moscow calls Gen. Clay's decision to halt reparations from Germany a "violation of the Potsdam decisions." .... Former Rumanian Premier Ion Antonescu and three aides are executed in Bucharest .... Pope Pius XII warns Italian and French voters that Communism is incompatible with Catholicism, and urges them to choose "the firm rock of Christianity." .... An earthquake strikes eastern Turkey, causing about 1,400 deaths.		Edward Mazerall is sentenced in Ottawa to four years in prison on Soviet spy charges.	The Philippine government announces that 11,000 Hukbalahap guerrilla fighters in central Luzon have agreed to surrender their arms by July 4 .... France asks U.S. and British support for its demand that Siam return 25,000 square miles ceded from Indochina by the Vichy regime in 1941.
June 2		The conservative Popular Republican Movement gains the largest number of seats in elections for France's new Constituent Assembly, with the Communist Party placing second .... U.S. military government turns over denazification of the clergy and church employes in Hesse to the state ministry of cults.	American Council for Judaism, the American Zionist Emergency Council and the Zionist Federation of Britain and Ireland urge the U.S. and Britain to carry out the recommendations of the Palestine Inquiry Commission.		Gen. Marshall proposes a new truce to stop fighting in Manchuria between Nationalists and Communists.
June 3		Italians end a two-day referendum on their form of government, voting by a small majority to replace the monarchy with a republic .... British Foreign Office announces that Portugal has agreed to continued use of air bases in the Azores by Britain and the U.S. .... A U.S.-British nutrition committee reports after a survey of the three Western German zones that the civilian population is showing signs of hunger edema .... U.S. Army arrests Col. Jack Durant and his wife, Capt. Kathleen Nash Durant, on charges of stealing the crown jewels of the House of Hesse from Kronberg Castle near Frankfurt .... Recently-retired Soviet President Mikhail Kalinin dies at 70 in Moscow.	Haj Amin el Husseini, exiled Grand Mufti of Jerusalem, appeals from Paris for Arabs to stand firm against Zionism.	U.S. Communist leader William Foster agrees to leave Canada at the request of the Canadian government after a one-day stay in which he addressed a Labor-Progressive Party convention.	Terunori Arai, arrested in connection with the Japanese May Day plot to assassinate MacArthur, admits planning to kill the General but denies contact with other plotters.
	A *Includes developments that affect more than one world region, international organizations and important meetings of major world leaders.*	B *Includes all domestic and regional developments in Europe, including the Soviet Union, Turkey, Cyprus and Malta.*	C *Includes all domestic and regional developments in Africa and the Middle East, including Iraq and Iran and excluding Cyprus, Turkey and Afghanistan.*	D *Includes all domestic and regional developments in Latin America, the Caribbean and Canada.*	E *Includes all domestic and regional developments in Asian and Pacific nations, extending from Afghanistan through all the Pacific Islands, except Hawaii.*

U.S. Politics & Social Issues	U.S. Foreign Policy & Defense	U.S. Economy & Environment	Science, Technology & Nature	Culture, Leisure & Life Style	
	War Dept. board investigating the Army's "caste" system says it found many "injustices" and that there is a "need for a new philosophy."	Soft-coal miners renew their strike as the two-week truce ends .... CIO Pres. Murray and AFL Pres. Green denounce Truman's strike control proposals as violating fundamental constitutional guarantees .... National Maritime Union members in N.Y. reject $12.50 monthly wage increase offer by 39 shipping companies, already accepted by a union negotiating committee .... Supreme Court rules that the Selective Service Act does not give veterans "super-seniority" in their prewar jobs.			May 27
Sen. Carter Glass (D, Va.) dies at 88 in Washington.	Secy. Byrnes and Leon Blum of France sign agreements in Washington settling Lend-Lease accounts and extending two credits totaling $137 billion to France.		Flooding along the Susquehanna River and its tributaries leaves 20 dead or missing and $3 million in damage in Pennsylvania, Ohio and southern N.Y.	American Federation of Musicians Pres. Petrillo tells reporters he is ready to test the Lea Act after station WAAF, Chicago refuses to hire more musicians.	May 28
	Secy. Byrnes tells the House Foreign Affairs Comm. that the U.S. favors the regulation of armaments to allow nations no more than is necessary to maintain internal order and international peace and security.	The 59-day soft coal strike ends as UMW Pres. Lewis signs a government-sponsored contract providing for an 18½¢ hourly raise and a miner's "welfare and retirement fund" financed by a 5¢-per-ton levy .... House passes and sends to Truman the Case strike control bill, calling for a 60-day cooling off period before strikes, increased federal mediation and union and management liability for breach of contract .... A 22-hour general strike of 26,000 union members ends in Rochester, N.Y. after the city agrees to allow its workers to join any organization "which does not claim the right to strike against the public."			May 29
Georgia Gov. Ellis Arnall orders legal action to revoke the state charter of the KKK.		A strike of 75,000 hard coal miners begins as negotiations continue in N.Y.C., with UMW leaders demanding the same terms as those recently granted to soft coal miners.	Canadian scientist Dr. Louis Slotin dies from exposure to radiation after a Los Alamos accident that occured May 21.	George Robson wins the Indianapolis 500, averaging 114.82 mph.	May 30
	Truman discloses that Edward Stettinius has submitted his resignation as U.S. delegate to the U.N. Security Council.	Senate passes and returns to the House Truman's strike control bill, empowering the government to seek injunctions against workers who leave their jobs.			May 31
	Senate votes and sends to the House the McMahon bill, providing for civilian government control of atomic energy under a five-man Atomic Energy Commission.			Assault with Warren Mehrtens up wins the $100,000 Belmont Stakes, becoming the seventh horse to win the triple crown.	June 1
National Negro Congress ends its Detroit convention after condemning Truman's administration, opposing a third political party and voting not to affiliate with any single party.		CIO Pres. Murray urges Truman to veto the Case strike-control bill, calling it aggressively anti-labor.		*New York Herald Tribune* reports *This Side of Innocence* by Taylor Caldwell and *The Egg and I* by Betty MacDonald as the best-selling fiction and nonfiction books, respectively.	June 2
Supreme Court rules that the dismissal of Robert Lovett, Goodwin Watson and William Dodd Jr., from government service for alleged subversive actions was punishment by administrative act without judicial trial and therefore unconstitutional. The Court also rules racial segregation of passengers on interstate buses unconstitutional.	Truman receives newly-appointed Soviet ambassador Nikolai V. Novikov, who says good U.S.-Soviet relations are essential for world peace.	Soft coal miners resume work under their new contract .... U.S. Chamber of Commerce Pres. W.E. Jackson asks approval of the Case anti-strike bill as "definitely in the public interest." .... Senate passes and sends to the House the Byrd bill, cutting the federal debt limit from $300 billion to $275 billion.		Supreme Court reverses a contempt conviction against the *Miami Herald* and its associate editor, John Pennekamp, for publishing articles and cartoons critical of Florida's state judicial system.	June 3
F	G	H	I	J	
Includes elections, federal-state relations, civil rights and liberties, crime, the judiciary, education, health care, poverty, urban affairs and population.	*Includes formation and debate of U.S. foreign and defense policies, veterans affairs and defense spending. (Relations with specific foreign countries are usually found under the region concerned.)*	*Includes business, labor, agriculture, taxation, transportation, consumer affairs, monetary and fiscal policy, natural resources, pollution and accidents.*	*Includes worldwide scientific, medical and technological developments, natural phenomena, U.S. weather and natural disasters.*	*Includes the arts, religion, scholarship, communications media, sports, entertainment, fashions, fads and social life.*	

	World Affairs	Europe	Africa & the Middle East	The Americas	Asia & the Pacific
June 4		British Foreign Secy. Bevin tells the House of Commons that Russia appears to feel secure only "when every country of the world has adopted the Soviet system."		Juan Peron is inaugurated as Argentine president in Buenos Aires, and hints in his address that his government may not accept the Act of Chapultepec and the U.N. Charter.	Chief Prosecutor Joseph Keenan declares before the International Military Tribunal for the Far East that the 28 Japanese defendants are "murderers, pirates [and] plunderers" and that their prosecution "will be no ordinary trial."
June 5	In a note to the U.N., Franco calls its Spanish inquiry "an intrusion into national sovereignty."	Speaking before the House of Commons, Churchill charges that "the seeds of a new world war . . . . are being sown" behind Russia's "iron curtain," while P.M. Attlee warns against "the counsel of despair that would divide Europe into two separate camps." . . . . Reports from Bratislava indicate that more than 100,000 Ukrainians and Jews have fled from the Carpatho-Ukraine into Czechoslovakia rather than accept Soviet rule.		Former Argentinian Chief of Staff Gen. Carlos von der Becke visits Eisenhower in Washington to discuss possible military aid.	
June 6	Security Council gives Secy. Gen. Trygve Lie power to intervene in any of its debates . . . . Australian U.N. delegate Herbert Evatt urges the U.N. to adopt the Security Council subcommittee report condemning Franco Spain . . . . A 32-nation International Labor Organization Conference opens in Seattle to consider establishment of an international minimum wage for maritime workers.	Soviet occupation zone commander Marshal Vassily Sokolovsky asserts his troops have stopped all dismantling of German factories as of May 1.		Argentina resumes relations with Russia, which had been broken in 1918.	Moslem League's executive council votes to accept the British cabinet plan for a free India . . . . Chiang Kai-shek orders a 15-day truce in Manchuria starting at noon tomorrow.
June 7	U.N. Economic and Social Council refuses to accept a subcommittee recommendation limiting the right of the World Federation of Trade Unions to attend Council sessions and present its views.	Russian authorities arrest Franz Neumann, chairman of the German Social Democratic Party in Berlin, and three of Neumann's aides for attempting to reorganize the party in the eastern sector of Berlin.			In Rangoon 50,000 Burmese demand independence in demonstrations staged by Gen. Aung Sang's Anti-Fascist League . . . . Chinese Premier T.V. Soong tells UNRRA delegates on the Far East committee that food shipments to China have fallen "far short of the allocation."
June 8		Representatives of the Soviet-sponsored Free German Youth Movement meet in Brandenburg to hear speakers criticize Western zone policy . . . . U.S. troops lead a gigantic parade in London celebrating the first anniversary of victory in World War II. Russia, Poland and Yugoslavia are invited to participate but refuse.	Haj Amin el Husseini, exiled Grand Mufti of Jerusalem, disappears from France, causing an international controversy over his whereabouts.		A Nationalist spokesman charges that Communist troops attacked four strategic points in Manchuria after agreeing to a 15-day truce . . . . President Sukarno of the Indonesian Republic broadcasts an appeal to his followers to mobilize against the Dutch after the outbreak of renewed fighting between nationalists and colonial forces.
June 9		U.S. Army Maj. David Watson is arrested in Frankfurt in connection with the $1.5-million Hesse jewel theft case.		Geological studies in Peru reveal that the Andes foothills may hold one of the richest oil deposits in the world.	Siamese King Ananda Mahidol, 20, is found dead of a bullet wound in his Bangkok palace . . . . UNRRA Council Comm. for the Far East adopts a resolution in Nanking asking the Chinese government to make adequate local currency available for the distribution of relief supplies.
June 10		The dominant Popular Republican Movement endorses Foreign Min. Georges Bidault for the French premiership . . . . British Labor Party's 45th annual conference begins in Bournemouth, with Chmn. Harold Laski pleading for an understanding with Russia . . . . At Nuremberg, former Nazi Netherlands Commissioner Arthur Seyss-Inquart testifies that he objected to Gestapo shootings but could not prevent them . . . . Gen. Draja Mikhailovich, Chetnik leader, and 23 others go on trial in Belgrade on charges of treason and collaboration with the Germans and Italians during the war.		Brazil reports that of 50,000 men who were sent to the upper Amazon to extract rubber for the Allies during the war, only 3,000 have returned, with the fate of the others unknown.	
June 11		Yugoslavian Chetnik leader Mikhailovich takes the stand to declare his innocence, although he admits contact with the Germans.			Allied headquarters in Japan forbids any aircraft to land in or to fly over Japanese territory without its specific approval.

A	B	C	D	E
Includes developments that affect more than one world region, international organizations and important meetings of major world leaders.	*Includes all domestic and regional developments in Europe, including the Soviet Union, Turkey, Cyprus and Malta.*	*Includes all domestic and regional developments in Africa and the Middle East, including Iraq and Iran and excluding Cyprus, Turkey and Afghanistan.*	*Includes all domestic and regional developments in Latin America, the Caribbean and Canada.*	*Includes all domestic and regional developments in Asian and Pacific nations, extending from Afghanistan through all the Pacific Islands, except Hawaii.*

U.S. Politics & Social Issues	U.S. Foreign Policy & Defense	U.S. Economy & Environment	Science, Technology & Nature	Culture, Leisure & Life Style	
Calif. Gov. Earl Warren wins the nomination for re-election of both major parties in the state's primary .... Rep. Andrew May (D, Ky.), chairman of the House Military Affairs Comm., admits to the Senate War Investigating Comm. that he acted as an agent for the Cumberland Lumber Co. during the war .... Truman signs a bill setting up a permanent school lunch program with annual appropriations of $75 million.	U.S. Military Academy graduates its largest class in history, with 875 members .... War Dept. announces that GE will succeed Du Pont as operator of the $347 million plutonium plant in Hanford, Wash.				June 4
	Senate passes and sends to the House a bill extending the draft until May 15, 1947 .... Truman appoints Sen. Warren Austin (R, Vt.) to succeed Stettinius as permanent U.S. representative at the U.N. He also greets newly-appointed British ambassador Sir Archibald Clark Kerr.	Senate Banking and Currency Comm. approves a bill to extend the OPA after including provisions to allow price rises on autos, farm machinery, refrigerators and other consumer goods.	A fire in Chicago's La Salle Hotel causes 61 deaths.		June 5
Truman names Treasury Secy. Vinson to be Chief Justice of the Supreme Court and War Reconversion Dir. John Snyder to be Treasury Secretary.	A U.S. government White Paper lists American World War II casualties as: armed forces, 916,699 (357,116 killed, 6,244 missing, 369,267 wounded and 184,072 imprisoned or interned); civilians, 60,595 killed.		*N.Y. Academy of Medicine Bulletin* reveals that a German refugee, Dr. Walter Loewe, has developed a drug called anthallan which relieves hay fever and other allergies.		June 6
House Un-American Activities Comm. issues a report assailing the Joint Anti-Fascist Refugee Comm. and the Army's wartime indoctrination course.	Lt. Gen. Hoyt Vandenberg is appointed by Truman to succeed Adm. Sidney Souers as director of the CIA.	An eight-day strike of hard coal miners ends with an 18.5¢ hourly wage increase and creation of a health and welfare fund for the miners, to be administered by one union and one management trustee .... The International Longshoremen's and Warehousemen's Union rejects a 22¢ hourly wage increase offered by a government fact-finding board in San Francisco.		A majority of the Pittsburgh Pirates team votes to strike for recognition of the American Baseball Guild. The vote is less than the two-thirds required for strike authorization, however .... N.Y. recognized featherweight champ Willie Pep KOs Sal Bartolo, NBA title holder, to gain undisputed possession of the title.	June 7
			In the *Journal of the AMA*, Col. Paul Keller reports that primary results of the radiation disease suffered by Hiroshima and Nagasaki survivors are suppression of the blood formation system and disturbed liver function.	Gerhart Hauptmann, German dramatist, novelist and poet, dies at 83 in Agnetendorf, Germany .... Bob Fitch, Univ. of Minn., sets a new world discus mark of 180 ft. 2$\frac{3}{4}$ in.	June 8
	Speaking to graduates of Norwich Univ. in Vt., Eisenhower asserts there is "an obvious limit to our unilateral disarmament," and urges support of the U.N.		An electrical storm in Massachusetts takes 10 lives and causes heavy damage.		June 9
Senate passes and sends to the House a bill reorganizing the congressional committee system, requiring the registration of lobbyists and raising the salaries of congressmen to $15,000 .... Supreme Court votes 4-3 against an appeal for reapportionment of Illinois congressional districts, ruling that "it is hostile to democracy to involve the judiciary in the politics of the people." The Court also rules that a naturalized citizen may be deprived of his citizenship if he violates the oath of allegiance .... Justice Robert Jackson, chief U.S. prosecutor at Nuremberg, charges that Supreme Court Justice Hugo Black participated in decisions involving a former law partner.		Supreme Court upholds fines totalling $225,000 against the R.J. Reynolds Tobacco Co, the Ligget & Myers Tobacco Co. and the American Tobacco Co. for violation of antitrust laws .... William A. Whitcomb, president of the Great Northern Paper Co., is shot dead in his Boston office.		Former world heavyweight champion Jack Johnson dies of injuries received from an auto accident in Raleigh, N.C.	June 10
John Snyder is confirmed by the Senate as Treasury Secretary.	Truman creates a special cabinet committee of the secretaries of State, War and Treasury to advise him on the Palestine problem.	Truman vetoes the Case anti-strike bill, claiming that none of the recent major strikes would have been affected by it. The House immediately upholds the veto .... Five thousand CIO Mine, Mill and Smelting Workers end a 2½-month strike against the American Smelting and Refining Co. with an agreement providing for an 18½¢ hourly wage increase.			June 11

F	G	H	I	J
Includes elections, federal-state relations, civil rights and liberties, crime, the judiciary, education, health care, poverty, urban affairs and population.	*Includes formation and debate of U.S. foreign and defense policies, veterans affairs and defense spending. (Relations with specific foreign countries are usually found under the region concerned.)*	*Includes business, labor, agriculture, taxation, transportation, consumer affairs, monetary and fiscal policy, natural resources, pollution and accidents.*	*Includes worldwide scientific, medical and technological developments, natural phenomena, U.S. weather and natural disasters.*	*Includes the arts, religion, scholarship, communications media, sports, entertainment, fashions, fads and social life.*

	World Affairs	Europe	Africa & the Middle East	The Americas	Asia & the Pacific
June 12		Speaking at the British Labor Party's conference in Bournemouth, Foreign Secy. Bevin wins overwhelming support for a resolution opposing increased Jewish immigration into Palestine and favoring continued ties with Franco Spain .... Hungarian Premier Ferenc Nagy arrives in Washington for discussions with U.S. officials and announces his support of Secy. Byrnes's plan to internationalize the Danube River.	Representatives of 10 Arab League states end a four-day meeting in Syria with a resolution urging a strengthened boycott of Jewish goods from Palestine and punishment of the sale of land to Jews.		Allied Control Council doubles the area southwest of Kyushu allowed to Japanese fishing boats .... Field Marshal Juichi Terauchi, Japanese war minister in 1936-37 and commander of forces in southern Asia during World War II, dies of a cerebral hemorrhage in Johore, Malaya.
June 13	Soviet U.N. delegate Andrei Gromyko refuses to accept a Security Council subcommittee resolution urging the General Assembly to recommend that member nations sever diplomatic relations with Spain. He claims the resolution is not strong enough and does not view the Franco government as a "threat to peace."	Italian King Humbert leaves Rome by plane for Barcelona as Christian Democratic Premier Alcide de Gasperi becomes head of state, bringing an end to the monarchy.	*New York Post* offers a $5,000 reward for the indictment of the Grand Mufti of Jerusalem, Haj Amin el Husseini, as a war criminal, claiming that he collaborated with the Germans in the extermination of European Jews.	Five persons are killed as the Bolivian government puts down an uprising by Army Air Force members who attempted to bomb La Paz.	At the Tokyo war crimes trial, the prosecution charges the Japanese defendants with violation of nearly 100 treaties and agreements .... In an agreement signed in Moscow, Afghanistan obtains water rights on the Kushka River and in exchange gives up claims to the Kushka district in the Turkmen Soviet Republic.
June 14	At the first meeting of the U.N. Atomic Energy Commission, Bernard Baruch outlines the U.S. plan for international control, calling for an independent authority to supervise all nuclear projects.	French Constituent Assembly elects Socialist Vincent Auriol as its president .... British Zone Deputy Military Gov. Sir Brian Robertson reports the release of German prisoners in his zone is almost complete.	Iran announces a 10-point agreement ending its eight-month dispute with Azerbaijan, providing "home rule" for the province and integrating its troops into the national army .... The Grand Mufti of Jerusalem, Haj Amin el Husseini, is reported near Damascus at the home of former Syrian Premier Jamil Mardam.		All-India Congress Party rejects the British cabinet mission's plan for an interim Indian government with equal Congress-Moslem League representation.
June 15	Paris Conference of Allied Foreign Ministers reconvenes in Luxembourg Palace after a one-month recess.	Yugoslavian Chetnik leader Draja Mikhailovich retracts an admission of collaboration with the Germans which he made yesterday, claiming he was too exhausted to know what he was saying.		Fred Rose, the only Communist in the Canadian Parliament, is convicted by a Montreal jury of conspiring to communicate wartime secrets to the Russians.	Communist representatives in Nanking announce the signing of a new agreement with the Nationalists for establishment of a truce executive headquarters in Changchun, the Manchurian capital.
June 16		British Food Min. John Strachey says Britain has reached "the limit" in aiding starving nations .... At his Belgrade trial, Mikhailovich denies all personal responsibility for the 23,000 murders charged by the prosecution against the Chetniks.	The Jewish Agency for Palestine declares that the Palestine Inquiry Commission's plan for Jewish immigration should be implemented immediately but that creation of a Jewish state is the only "just" solution to the Palestine problem.		British Viceroy Wavell invites 14 Indian leaders representing all groups to serve in an interim government, as further negotiations for Indian independence break down.
June 17	Secy. Byrnes proposes at the Paris Foreign Ministers Conference that the Big Four withdraw all financial claims against Italy .... Australian External Affairs Min. Herbert Evatt appeals to Gromyko not to veto the Security Council subcommittee report on Spain.	Mrs. Maria Quisling, widow of Norwegian fascist leader Vidkun Quisling, is acquitted of collaboration with the Nazis.	Fighting between Zionists and British troops results in the death of nine Jews and the destruction of the Palestine Railway's central workshops in Haifa .... Iranian government appoints a Communist, Salamollah Javid, as governor of Azerbaijan Province.	Panamanian high school and university students strike, demanding educational reforms and the resignation of Education Min. Jose Crespo.	U.S. Prosecutor Joseph Keenan of the International Military Tribunal for the Far East says a "high political level" decision has been made not to try Hirohito as a war criminal .... Allied Control Council agrees on a rural land reform program for Japan under which surplus lands will be made available to small farmers .... Siam's Parliament authorizes the government to take the border dispute with French Indochina to the U.N. Security Council.
June 18	Gromyko casts the second Soviet veto on the U.N. Security Council when he votes against a subcommittee recommendation that the General Assembly urge member states to sever diplomatic relations with Spain .... British Foreign Secy. Bevin supports Secy. Byrnes at the Paris Peace Conference in urging that the Big Four drop claims to Italian reparations .... AFL Secy.-Treasurer George Meany tells a Calif. Federation of Labor convention that the WFTU is a Communist "worldwide fifth column organization."	Italian authorities release final results of the June 3 referendum on the country's form of government, showing that 12,717,923 voters favored a republic, vs. 10,719,284 for contintuation of the monarchy .... Former German Vice Chancellor Franz von Papen's defense counsel introduces evidence at Nuremberg to show that von Papen took part in the 1944 bomb plot against Hitler.	Jewish extremists kidnap five British officers from a Tel Aviv club and hold them as hostages to prevent the execution of two Irgun Zvai Leumi members condemned for attacking a British camp.		
June 19	Gromyko presents Russia's plan for nuclear arms control to the U.N. Atomic Energy Commission, calling for the destruction of all existing bombs but rejecting proposals to strip the Big Five of their Security Council veto power in the field of atomic energy .... U.S. leads successful opposition at the U.N. to a Lebanese attempt to prevent the proposed International Refugee Organization from aiding immigration of Jews to Palestine .... International Health Conference opens in N.Y. and hears Truman pledge U.S. support for proposals to coordinate worldwide medical research .... U.S. Budget Bureau Dir. Harold Smith accepts the vice-presidency of the International Bank for Reconstruction and Development.	French Constituent Assembly elects centrist leader Georges Bidault president of the provisional government .... U.S. announces it will return to Hungary $32 million in gold plundered by Germany and recovered by Army engineers.			Chinese Premier T.V. Soong says in Nanking that his government is spending 80% of its revenues on its huge army, estimated at 250-300 divisions.

A	B	C	D	E
Includes developments that affect more than one world region, international organizations and important meetings of major world leaders.	*Includes all domestic and regional developments in Europe, including the Soviet Union, Turkey, Cyprus and Malta.*	*Includes all domestic and regional developments in Africa and the Middle East, including Iraq and Iran and excluding Cyprus, Turkey and Afghanistan.*	*Includes all domestic and regional developments in Latin America, the Caribbean and Canada.*	*Includes all domestic and regional developments in Asian and Pacific nations, extending from Afghanistan through all the Pacific Islands, except Hawaii.*

U.S. Politics & Social Issues	U.S. Foreign Policy & Defense	U.S. Economy & Environment	Science, Technology & Nature	Culture, Leisure & Life Style	
Sen. John Bankhead (D, Ala.), a member of Congress since 1926, dies at 73 in Washington.	Navy reveals plans to train reserve officers in 52 civilian schools.	House Ways and Means Comm. votes to raise the Social Security tax from 1% to 1.5% for five years beginning January 1947.	Mayo Clinic Drs. H. Corwin Hinshaw and William Feldman report at the National TB Assn. meeting that streptomycin seems to check TB but is too toxic for wide use.		June 12
		Senate passes and sends to conference a bill extending the OPA to June 30, 1947 but curtailing its powers .... Chicago Bd. of Trade halts all trading in wheat and rye futures, stating that government shipments to famine areas prevent a "free, open and orderly market."		A consistory in Rome votes to canonzie Mother Frances Xavier Cabrini, who only 27 years after her death will become the second American to achieve sainthood .... Edward E. Bowes, American entertainer famous for his radio amateur hour, dies at 72 in Rumson, N.J.	June 13
After losing his party's senatorial nomination, Rep. Charles La Follette (R, Ind.) says he will leave the GOP when his congressional term is ended.	In a report to Congress, Truman estimates Lend-Lease aid from March 11, 1941 to Dec. 31, 1945 at $30,753,304,000.	A nationwide strike of maritime workers is averted when union leaders reach an agreement with the American Ship Owners Assn. and the Waterfront Employers Assn., granting wage increases and a limitation of the work week for several categories of workers.	John L. Baird, noted as the "father of television," dies at 58 in London.	Mexican tennis team defeats Canada in Montreal, eliminating it from the Davis Cup, while Sweden advances to the European finals by beating Belgium.	June 14
	Truman submits to Congress a 12-point plan to unify the armed services into one department under a civilian secretary.			American Federation of Musicians Pres. James Petrillo is arraigned in Chicago's U.S. District Court on charges of violating the Lea Act by attempting to force station WAAF to hire additional employes .... The Norwegian Lutheran Church of America changes its name to the Evangelical Lutheran Church.	June 15
Pres. Alexander Whitney of the Brotherhood of Railroad Trainmen discloses he has hired an investigator to look into "Pendergast politics" in Missouri and uncover information to be used against the re-election of Truman.		Ford Motors ends a five-week shutdown in Detroit, recalling 65,000 workers .... Atty. Gen. Tom Clark approves the sale of a $200-million government steel plant in Geneva, Utah to U.S. Steel for about $47.5 million.	The Federation of American Scientists announces formation of a "Committee for Foreign Correspondence" to promote "worldwide exchange of information."	Lloyd Mangrum wins the National Golf Open in Cleveland by a single stroke over Byron Nelson and Vic Ghezzi.	June 16
A Texas court orders the Univ. of Texas to admit Herman Sweatt, a black, as a law student but suspends action for six months to allow the state to create a law school in the state-owned Negro university.		House passes and sends to the Senate bills extending the sugar quota act for one year and reducing the national debt limit to $275 billion.	A tornado in the Detroit-Windsor area causes 14 deaths and wrecks homes and factories.		June 17
	A four-member subcommittee of the House Foreign Affairs Comm. which toured Europe last fall recommends "immediate abandonment of any semblance of appeasement" in U.S. relations with Russia .... Truman calls for improvement of veterans' medical care, rehabilitation and pension policies in accordance with recommendations of his Presidential Commission on Integration of Government Medical Services.				June 18
	Truman urges Congress to appropriate the remaining $465 million in funding already authorized for UNRRA.			Joe Louis knocks out Billy Conn in the eighth round to retain his world heavyweight championship before 45,266 in New York's Yankee Stadium.	June 19

F	G	H	I	J
Includes elections, federal-state relations, civil rights and liberties, crime, the judiciary, education, health care, poverty, urban affairs and population.	*Includes formation and debate of U.S. foreign and defense policies, veterans affairs and defense spending. (Relations with specific foreign countries are usually found under the region concerned.)*	*Includes business, labor, agriculture, taxation, transportation, consumer affairs, monetary and fiscal policy, natural resources, pollution and accidents.*	*Includes worldwide scientific, medical and technological developments, natural phenomena, U.S. weather and natural disasters.*	*Includes the arts, religion, scholarship, communications media, sports, entertainment, fashions, fads and social life.*

	World Affairs	Europe	Africa & the Middle East	The Americas	Asia & the Pacific
June 20	A 19-nation conference in Washington terminates the Combined Food Board and replaces it with an International Emergency Food Council to allocate supplies "for the duration of the shortage." .... Big Four conference in Paris appoints a four-man committee to study proposals to postpone the Italian colonial question for a year.			Canadian Communist M.P. Fred Rose is sentenced to six years in prison by a Montreal court for giving state secrets to the Russians.	Chou En-lai rejects the Nationalist proposal that Gen. Marshall be given supreme arbitration power in the truce negotiations .... Jawaharlal Nehru, president-elect of India's Congress, is arrested by Kashmiri authorities for refusing to obey an order banning him from the state.
June 21	U.S. State Dept. discloses the draft text of a Japanese peace treaty proposed by Byrnes at Paris, under which the U.S. would share control of Japan with Russia, Britain and China for 25 years .... International Chamber of Commerce Council in Paris calls for the establishment of a peaceful Germany as vital to the world economy.			Peron promises to ask the Argentine Congress to act on the Mexico City and San Francisco agreements but claims that he cannot legally recommend approval.	Chiang Kai-shek extends the Nationalist-Communist truce until June 30.
June 22		Italian cabinet formally abolishes the Senate, whose members were appointed by the King for life .... Former Nazi Foreign Min. Constantin von Neurath declares at his Nuremberg trial that the Versailles Treaty and the League of Nations were responsible for the war.		Representatives of the American republics sign a convention for uniform copyright protection of literary, scientific and artistic works.	At the request of U.S. authorities, Russia withdraws its consul from Seoul, Korea .... Returning from a tour of Korea, U.S. Reparations Commissioner Edwin Pauley reports to Truman that "Communism in Korea could get off to a better start than practically anywhere else in the world" and warns that "the U.S. should not waive its ... claim to Japanese assets located in Korea until a democratic form of government is assured." .... Nehru returns to New Delhi after his release by Kashmiri authorities, prompted by strikes and disturbances in Bombay, Calcutta and other cities.
June 23	India appeals to the U.N. to place its dispute with South Africa on the General Assembly's agenda, charging South Africa with discrimination against 250,000 Indians there.	U.S. Army authorities report that 10,000 East European Jews are entering the U.S. German Zone every month.			A crowd of 100,000 protesters carrying anti-American signs greets a U.S. truce inspection team in Shanghai.
June 24	Foreign Ministers Conference in Paris adopts a Soviet resolution rejecting Austria's claim to a portion of South Tyrol .... *Pravda* rejects the Baruch international atomic control plan as reflecting "an obvious tendency toward world domination." .... A Polish resolution urging the U.N. Security Council to recommend a worldwide diplomatic break with Franco Spain is defeated.	George Bidault forms a new French cabinet with his own Popular Republican Party getting nine posts, Socialists six and Communists seven .... Britain and Poland sign a financial agreement settling most of the Polish war debts to Britain and transferring the former Polish exile government's assets to the current Polish provisional government .... Truman charges that the Soviets are censoring U.S. correspondents covering UNRRA operations in the Ukraine and White Russia.		Peron says his government will try Nazis who took refuge in Argentina .... Canadian government takes over inland freighters idled by a one month old strike of the Canadian Seamen's Union.	Mao Tse-tung charges that U.S. military aid to the Koumintang has intensified the civil war.
June 25	U.N. Atomic Energy Commission sets up a 12-member committee to draft a plan for atomic control and development.	Italian Constituent Assembly elects Socialist Guiseppe Saragat as chairman at its first session.		U.S. unfreezes $700 million in gold held by Argentina in the N.Y. Federal Reserve Bank .... One person is killed and a number are arrested in San Jose as the Costa Rican government puts down an alleged coup attempt.	All-India Congress Party working committee accepts Viceroy Wavell's long-range proposals for Indian independence, after rejecting his plan for an interim government .... Massachusetts Chief Justice John Higgins resigns from the International Military Tribunal for the Far East.
June 26	Gromyko uses his Security Council veto twice on the Spanish issue, defeating censure proposals which he considers too weak.	Soviet State Control Ministry announces widespread dismissals and fining of factory directors, engineers and accountants for falsifying production figures, distributing bonuses illegally and misappropriating funds .... Constantin von Neurath says at Nuremberg he opposed some of Hitler's policies and does not know why he was not liquidated.			The three-man British negotiating team in India announces it will suspend further negotiations on an interim government and return to England.

A	B	C	D	E
Includes developments that affect more than one world region, international organizations and important meetings of major world leaders.	*Includes all domestic and regional developments in Europe, including the Soviet Union, Turkey, Cyprus and Malta.*	*Includes all domestic and regional developments in Africa and the Middle East, including Iraq and Iran and excluding Cyprus, Turkey and Afghanistan.*	*Includes all domestic and regional developments in Latin America, the Caribbean and Canada.*	*Includes all domestic and regional developments in Asian and Pacific nations, extending from Afghanistan through all the Pacific Islands, except Hawaii.*

U.S. Politics & Social Issues	U.S. Foreign Policy & Defense	U.S. Economy & Environment	Science, Technology & Nature	Culture, Leisure & Life Style	
Senate confirms the nomination of Fred Vinson as Chief Justice of the Supreme Court . . . . State of Georgia begins court proceedings to revoke the charter of the KKK, charging it with a conspiracy to seize key government agencies and issuing propaganda advocating violence.	A Senate-House Conference votes to extend the draft nine months after July 1, setting induction ages at 19-45 years . . . . Truman urges that nuclear research and development in the U.S. be placed in the hands of a civilian commission, and supports Bernard Baruch's plan for international control of atomic energy.		Jordanian scientist Djamil Pasha Tutunji urges increased study of birth control, saying that within 100 years the world will be too small for its population "and war would be inevitable."		June 20
Senate completes action on the Hobbs anti-racketeering bill, which provides for up to 20 years imprisonment and up to $10,000 in fines for interference by "robbery or extortion" or threats of violence with the movement of interstate goods.	House passes and sends to the Senate a bill giving the Army $7.091 billion for fiscal 1947, the largest peacetime military appropriation in U.S. history.	OPA grants a 40½¢-a-ton price rise on soft coal to offset wage increases . . . . Senate raises the price of silver from 71.1¢ to 90.3¢ an ounce on July 1 as part of an appropriations bill for the Treasury and Post Office.		American Library Assn. elects Mary Rothrock as president after hearing Rep. Emily Douglas (D, Ill.) assert that 35 million Americans lack adequate library service.	June 21
		Stabilization Dir. Bowles forecasts an increase in meat supplies within six months and alleviation of bread shortages within 30 days . . . . Bureau of Labor Statistics reports that the Cumulative Price Index rose .5% in the month ending May 15 to reach 131.5% of the 1935-39 index.		A syndicate including Bob Hope and headed by Bill Veeck buys the Cleveland Indians.	June 22
	Eisenhower releases his official report on Allied operations in Europe from D-Day to VE Day, stating that the war was won due to material superiority and spirit of the fighting men.		An earthquake along the coasts of Ore., Wash., and British Columbia causes minor property damage and no casualties.	Don Budge beats Bobby Riggs to capture the world professional clay courts tennis crown in Richmond, Va. . . . . Univ. of Ill. wins the NCAA track and field championship at Minneapolis . . . . William Hart, cowboy idol of silent films, dies at 75 in Los Angeles.	June 23
	A Superfortress drops a dummy flash bomb on the battleship *Nevada* off Bikini Atoll in a full dress rehearsal of the atom bomb test . . . . Truman signs a bill providing that the body of an unknown service man of World War II be placed beside the first Unknown Soldier in Arlington National Cemetery.	Former AFL leaders Martin Parkinson and William McGeory are sentenced in N.Y. to prison terms of three to six years for extortion.			June 24
Former North Dakota Sen. Gerald Nye loses to Sen. Milton Young (R, N.D.) in a special primary held to fill a 4½-year Senate term, while Sen. William Langer (R, N.D.) is renominated for a regular six-year term.	Congress passes a bill extending the Selective Service until March 31, 1947, requiring childless men 18-44 years of age to serve for 18 months.	OPA grants a 91¢-a-ton increase on the price of hard coal . . . . Truman breaks precedent by attending swearing-in ceremonies for Treasury Secy. John Snyder, who promises to balance the fiscal 1947 budget . . . . Bureau of Labor Statistics reports that average hourly wages for production workers in manufacturing hit a record high of $1.06 in April, with weekly earnings averaging $42.92 weekly . . . . First Boston Corp. and the Mellon Corp. merge, creating a capital fund of $25 million, the largest of any investment banking firm in the U.S.	Curtiss-Wright Corp. donates to Cornell Univ. a $4.5 million aeronautical research laboratory built during the war.	Catholic Theological Society of America is formed in N.Y., with Dr. Francis Connell of Catholic University as president.	June 25
House votes to cite for contempt Corliss Lamont, chairman of the National Council of American-Soviet Friendship, for refusing to produce records demanded by the Un-American Activities Comm.	Responding to the May 27 "caste" report, War Secy. Patterson promises to work for improved social relations between officers and enlisted men in the armed forces.				June 26

F	G	H	I	J
Includes elections, federal-state relations, civil rights and liberties, crime, the judiciary, education, health care, poverty, urban affairs and population.	*Includes formation and debate of U.S. foreign and defense policies, veterans affairs and defense spending. (Relations with specific foreign countries are usually found under the region concerned.)*	*Includes business, labor, agriculture, taxation, transportation, consumer affairs, monetary and fiscal policy, natural resources, pollution and accidents.*	*Includes worldwide scientific, medical and technological developments, natural phenomena, U.S. weather and natural disasters.*	*Includes the arts, religion, scholarship, communications media, sports, entertainment, fashions, fads and social life.*

	World Affairs	Europe	Africa & the Middle East	The Americas	Asia & the Pacific
June 27	Molotov agrees at the Paris Foreign Ministers Conference to the awarding of the Dodecanese Islands to Greece and the cession of Mont Cenis and the Tenda and Briga regions of northern Italy to France .... World Federation of Trade Unions executive committee adopts resolutions demanding a voice in U.N. decisions and the restoration of democracy in Spain.	British Food Min. Strachey announces that bread, flour and cake will be rationed for the first time in British history starting July 21.	Thirty members of the Zionist organization Irgun Zvai Leumi are sentenced by a British court in Jerusalem to 15 years in prison for unlawfully carrying firearms.	Juan Antonio Rios, president of Chile since 1942, dies at 58 in Santiago.	Ken Inukai, son of murdered Japanese Premier Tsuyoshi Inukai, testifies at the Tokyo war crimes trial that Emperor Hirohito opposed but could not halt the invasion of Manchuria .... Yosuke Matsuoka, former Japanese foreign minister on trial as a war criminal, dies at 66 of tuberculosis in Tokyo.
June 28		Former Liberal Party member Enrico de Nicola is elected provisional president of the Italian Republic by the Constituent Assembly .... Allied Council of Foreign Ministers removes zonal restrictions on the movement of Austrian citizens and goods.			Acting Secy. of State Dean Acheson restates U.S. policy barring foreign interference in China's internal affairs and helping the nation to recover its strength .... The memoirs of former Japanese Foreign Min. Yosuke Matsuoka, released at the Tokyo war crimes trial, state that Japan signed the Axis Pact and the prewar Russian agreement to avoid a Pacific war.
June 29	International Labor Organization maritime conference in Seattle adopts an international convention setting a $64 minimum monthly wage for seamen.	At Nuremberg, the defense says it cannot prove the death of Nazi Party deputy leader Martin Bormann, who is being tried in absentia.	British authorities raid Jewish communities throughout Palestine, searching for the leadership of the Jewish underground group Hagana.		Viceroy Wavell names an executive council consisting of six Britons, one Hindu and one Moslem to serve as a "caretaker" government in India until a Constituent Assembly is elected .... The unrecognized Indonesian government announces that President Sukarno has declared martial law and assumed all executive powers following the kidnaping of Premier Sutan Sjahrir and other government officials by an armed band at Surakarta.
June 30		Christian Social Union wins over the German Social Democratic Party in state assembly elections in U.S.-occupied Bavaria, Baden-Wuerttemberg and Hesse. In Russian-occupied Saxony, a 77% majority approves a referendum for nationalization of large industrial plants .... Chief of UNRRA German operations Sir Frederick Morgan announces that 714,187 refugees in the western occupation zone will be rescreened to eliminate those ineligible for aid .... Lord Woolton succeds Ralph Assheton as chairman of the British Conservative Party.		Mexico's Supreme Court rules that no U.S. company can sue directly for reimbursement for the expropriation of oil properties .... Elections in Ecuador for a national constituent assembly give conservatives 33 seats, independents 6, dissident liberals 20, dissident leftists 2, and democrats 1.	Nationalist forces are ordered to retaliate against Communist moves as the Manchurian truce expires .... Gandhi and his party escape injury when their train rams into boulders placed across the tracks near Poona.
July 1	At the Paris Conference of Foreign Ministers, Molotov agrees to the French proposal for a Yugoslav-Italian boundary already accepted by Britain and the U.S. .... Chmn. Herbert Evatt of the U.N. Atomic Energy Commission appoints a subcommittee to draft an international nuclear control plan.	U.S. and British troops quell disturbances in Trieste after three days of Yugoslav-Italian rioting leave two dead and 60 injured .... Despite Soviet objections, defense witnesses at Nuremberg testify on the Katyn massacre of 11,000 Polish officers, which they blame on the Russians .... Soviet authorities cut prices on consumer goods by an average of 40%.	British authorities in Palestine discover a Zionist arms cache at Meshek Yagur after a three-day search of 27 settlements.	Uruguay announces it has put down a plot against the government led by former Air Force chief Col. Esteban Christi.	
July 2	Byrnes and Bevin abandon their fight for Italian control of Trieste and agree to the city's internationalization but insist that the zone be administered by the U.N. Security Council.	Gen. Lucius Clay of the U.S. military government announces a general political amnesty for all German war criminals up to 27 years old except active Nazi Party members and supporters .... London extends the BBC charter for five years, reaffirming its determination not to allow commercial programs on the air.	Truman confers with four Jewish Agency leaders, including Rabbi Stephen Wise, who protests against Britain's "brutal aggression" in Palestine.		Hindu-Moslem riots in Ahmadabad, India result in 33 dead and several hundred injured .... Adm. Keisuke Okada, former premier and commander of the Japanese Navy, testifies at the Tokyo war crimes trial that Japan had a "gentlemen's agreement" with the U.S. permitting Japanese forces to move into Manchuria in 1931.
July 3		Czech Pres. Eduard Benes names Communist leader Klement Gottwald as premier .... Belgrade court trying Draja Mikhailovich refuses to allow American or British witnesses to appear for the defendant or to admit a statement from German Gen. Alfred Jodl that Mikhailovich was regarded by the Germans as an enemy.	Palestine High Commissioner Sir Alan Cunningham commutes to life imprisonment the death sentences of Joseph Simkhon and Isaac Ashbel, members of the Irgun Zvai Leumi captured in a raid on a British Army camp.		
July 4	Allied foreign ministers meeting in Paris reach a compromise giving Russia $100 million in Italian reparations and setting July 29 for the start of a 21-nation general peace conference.	With defense testimony concluded, attorneys for the 21 Nazi defendants at Nuremberg blame Hitler for the war and ask for acquittal .... Moscow radio attacks the U.S. atomic test at Bikini as "atomic diplomacy."	Irgun Zvai Leumi releases three British officers kidnaped June 18 in Jerusalem in response to the commutation of sentences of Simkhon and Ashbel.		Philippine Republic is born at 10 a.m. after 48 years of U.S. sovereignty.

A	B	C	D	E
Includes developments that affect more than one world region, international organizations and important meetings of major world leaders.	*Includes all domestic and regional developments in Europe, including the Soviet Union, Turkey, Cyprus and Malta.*	*Includes all domestic and regional developments in Africa and the Middle East, including Iraq and Iran and excluding Cyprus, Turkey and Afghanistan.*	*Includes all domestic and regional developments in Latin America, the Caribbean and Canada.*	*Includes all domestic and regional developments in Asian and Pacific nations, extending from Afghanistan through all the Pacific Islands, except Hawaii.*

U.S. Politics & Social Issues	U.S. Foreign Policy & Defense	U.S. Economy & Environment	Science, Technology & Nature	Culture, Leisure & Life Style	
House Ways and Means Comm. votes to increase federal aid to the needy, aged and blind to $60 monthly and to increase old age and survivors insurance by 50% . . . . Truman signs a $7-million bill to make up teacher salary deficits in "war-impacted" communities.			Russian Prof. Alexander Zhdanov receives the 100,000 ruble Stalin Prize for discovering "new ways of splitting atomic nuclei with cosmic rays." . . . . Dr. William Stone, pioneer in the use of radium in cancer treatment, dies at 79 in Norwalk, Conn.		June 27
House defeats Truman's plan for reorganization of federal agencies and reform of the welfare and housing programs.	Herbert Kennedy admits at the espionage trial of Russian Lt. Col Nicolai Redin that he was an FBI contact and that data he sold to Redin was available to the public . . . . House passes an appropriations bill including $465 million for UNRRA operations, but a rider aimed at Russia denies funds to countries that censor news of the UNRRA.	Senate completes action on the OPA bill, extending the agency for one year but weakening its powers. Bowles charges that the price control measures favored by Congress make stabilization "flatly impossible," and resigns as Office of Economic Stabilization director.	Dr. Bertram Lou-Beer of the University of California reports the successful use of a byproduct of atomic research, radioactive phosphorus, in the treatment of superficial skin cancers.		June 28
	Truman signs a bill extending the draft and raising Army pay.	Truman vetoes the OPA extension bill, saying it will only contribute to inflation; the House sustains the veto.		The Broadway play *I Remember Mama* closes after a record 713 performances.	June 29
As its annual convention closes in Cincinnati, the NAACP votes to promote the economic goals of Negroes as well as civil rights.	State Dept. reveals it is transferring control of cultural affairs in Germany, Japan, Austria and Korea to the War Dept.	After Truman's veto of the extension bill, OPA expires and food subsidies end at midnight.			June 30
FEPC Chmn. Malcolm Ross gives his final report to Truman, stating that only the force of law can stop job discrimination against minorities, as the FEPC goes out of existence.	A Nagasaki-type atom bomb is exploded over Bikini atoll, sending a cloud 30,000 feet into the air and destroying five test ships, including a Japanese cruiser. Ten percent of the experimental animals exposed to radiation from the bomb die immediately . . . . At the espionage trial of Soviet Lt. Nikolai Redin, Navy Commdr. John McQuilkin says the U.S. has withheld latest types of radar and gun-fire control equipment from Russia.	House passes a resolution continuing OPA for 20 days after Truman's veto of the extension bill, but a similar measure in the Senate is blocked by W. Lee O'Daniel (D, Tex.).	IBM demonstrates an electrically operated Chinese typewriter that types 5,400 characters horizontally or vertically.	George Fazio wins the Canadian Open Golf Tournament by one stroke over Dick Metz . . . . *Oklahoma* breaks the longest run record for Broadway musicals with its 1,405th N.Y. performance.	July 1
		A wildcat strike of 5,000 UAW members hits the Plymouth Division plant in Detroit after 93 workers are required to take an extra half-hour for lunch without pay.			July 2
American Bar Assn. meeting in Chicago sets up a committee to pass on the qualifications of candidates for the federal bench and to take action to oust unfit justices.		Truman signs the Hobbs anti-racketeering bill, which bars labor interference with interstate commerce.	Senate passes the Kilgore-Magnuson bill, creating the National Science Foundation.		July 3
		Dun & Bradstreet reveals that its food commodity index July 2 was $4.54, the highest since July 29, 1920.			July 4
F *Includes elections, federal-state relations, civil rights and liberties, crime, the judiciary, education, health care, poverty, urban affairs and population.*	G *Includes formation and debate of U.S. foreign and defense policies, veterans affairs and defense spending. (Relations with specific foreign countries are usually found under the region concerned.)*	H *Includes business, labor, agriculture, taxation, transportation, consumer affairs, monetary and fiscal policy, natural resources, pollution and accidents.*	I *Includes worldwide scientific, medical and technological developments, natural phenomena, U.S. weather and natural disasters.*	J *Includes the arts, religion, scholarship, communications media, sports, entertainment, fashions, fads and social life.*	

	World Affairs	Europe	Africa & the Middle East	The Americas	Asia & the Pacific
July 5	U.N. Secretary General Trygve Lie announces that applications from Afghanistan, Albania, Siam and Mongolia will be considered by the Security Council Aug. 1.	Polish mobs in Kielce beat 36 Jews to death and injure 40 in the worst pogrom since the German defeat. A Polish Army officer and policeman attempting to quell the riot are also killed.		Finance Min. J.L. Ilsley raises the Canadian dollar from 90¢ to parity with the U.S. dollar after abandonment of price controls by the U.S.	
July 6		Soviet occupation authorities in eastern Austria order the confiscation of all German assets in their zone.			Jawaharlal Nehru is chosen president of the All-India Congress Party in Bombay, succeeding Dr. Maulana Abul Kalam Azad .... Gen. Ryukichi Tanaka testifies at the Tokyo war crimes trial that Japan seized Manchuria in 1931 in order to train its Kwantung Army for an expected war with Russia .... Dr. Cheng Tien-hsi is appointed Chinese ambassador to Britain, replacing Dr. Wellington Koo, who becomes ambassador to the U.S.
July 7		Russian journal *Culture and Life* reveals that part two of the Sergei Eisenstein's film *Ivan the Terrible* has been banned for being "contrary to historical truth."		Presidential elections in Mexico result in the victory of Miguel Aleman Valdes of the Party of Revolutionary Institutions.	All-India Congress Party approves the British cabinet mission's long-term independence plan despite opposition from the socialists and Gandhi .... Communist Central Committee charges the U.S. is "fostering civil war in China" by Lend-Lease aid to the Nationalists.
July 8	Australian Foreign Min. Herbert Evatt urges the U.N. Atomic Energy Commission to support creation of a strong international arms control agency not subject to a Big Five veto .... U.S., Britain and Canada abolish their blacklists of firms and individuals who aided the Axis .... Representatives of 51 nations attend the opening session of the League of Red Cross Societies in Oxford, England.				Nationalist forces occupy the transportation center of Hsuanhuatien, threatening to trap 60,000 Communist troops in Hupeh Province .... Hukbalahap leader Luis Taruc charges that Philippine Pres. Manuel Roxas' "reactionary policies" prevent peace in Luzon.
July 9	At the Paris Conference of Foreign Ministers, Molotov rejects as "wholly inadequate" the U.S. proposal for a 25-year period of disarmament for Germany, insisting on 40 years with $10 billion in reparations.	British Colonial Secy. George Hall tells the House of Commons the government will administer the colonies so that they may attain self-government "as soon as practicable."	Jewish Agency Pres. Chaim Weizmann appeals to Britain to abandon its course in Palestine and says Hagana will not obey British demands that it surrender its weapons.	Paraguayan Pres. Higinio Morinigo repeals the 1940 press control law.	UNRRA Director Fiorello La Guardia cuts off relief shipments to China due to Nationalist "misuse" of food supplies.
July 10	At the Paris Conference of Foreign Ministers, Molotov opposes dismemberment, federalization or "agrarianization" of Germany and rejects French proposals for the separation of the Ruhr and Rhineland .... In a policy statement submitted to the U.N. Atomic Energy Commission, U.S. representative Bernard Baruch says that unless war is abolished the U.S. will have no alternative but to develop more and bigger atomic bombs.	Germany's Thuringian state government, acting on a Russian directive, orders the restoration of property taken from Jews after 1933 .... Austrian Parliament votes to define "German assets" in Austria, liable to be taken for reparations, as property owned by Germans before the 1938 annexation.	Egyptian police seize 1,000 political suspects as the government bans an anti-British general strike scheduled for tomorrow.		
July 11		A U.S. military court in Dachau convicts 73 SS soldiers, including Gen. Joseph (Sepp) Dietrich, for slaying American prisoners and Belgian civilians during the Battle of the Bulge .... King George VI attends a service of thanksgiving for the preservation of Canterbury Cathedral, becoming the first English king since 1660 to visit the Cathedral.		Peron government delays 167 food ships in Argentine ports when it demands higher prices for its exports .... Carlos C. Arosemena, leader of Panama's independence movement, dies at 78 in N.Y.	
July 12	Paris Council of Foreign Ministers ends with an agreement on the division of 125,000 tons of Italian shipping between Greece and Yugoslavia, but fails to reach accord on Germany and Austria.	Yugoslavian patrols clash with U.S. forces on the Yugoslav-Italian border, resulting in the death of two Yugoslavs .... The trial of Yugoslavian Chetnik leader Mikhailovich ends as Mikhailovich and 23 co-defendants make their final speeches .... Mauro Rana confesses in Rome that he led the group which stole Mussolini's body from a Milan graveyard, but refuses to disclose its present location.	Iraqi police kill five persons and wound 14 when they fire on striking oil workers at Kirkuk .... Cairo reports that Egyptian police have made 220 arrests in nationwide anti-Communist raids.		

A	B	C	D	E
Includes developments that affect more than one world region, international organizations and important meetings of major world leaders.	*Includes all domestic and regional developments in Europe, including the Soviet Union, Turkey, Cyprus and Malta.*	*Includes all domestic and regional developments in Africa and the Middle East, including Iraq and Iran and excluding Cyprus, Turkey and Afghanistan.*	*Includes all domestic and regional developments in Latin America, the Caribbean and Canada.*	*Includes all domestic and regional developments in Asian and Pacific nations, extending from Afghanistan through all the Pacific Islands, except Hawaii.*

U.S. Politics & Social Issues	U.S. Foreign Policy & Defense	U.S. Economy & Environment	Science, Technology & Nature	Culture, Leisure & Life Style	
AMA convention ends in San Francisco after voting to establish a $500,000 loan fund to help finance voluntary medical care plans . . . . Senate passes and sends to the House a bill providing $30.35 million for vocational training and education.				Sam Snead captures the British Open Golf Tournament in St. Andrews, Scotland.	July 5
Truman assails *N.Y. Daily News* correspondent John O'Donnell for reporting that he asked Supreme Court justices to resign, labeling the story a lie.			Russian scientist A. Izatov reports in Leningrad that the earth has three axes and three equators and that its radius is 850 meters greater than the currently accepted measurement.	Pauline Betz wins the women's tennis crown at Wimbledon, Louise Brough and Margaret Osborne capture the women's doubles title; Tom Brown and Jack Kramer take the men's doubles crown.	July 6
			Airplane producer and test pilot Howard Hughes is critically injured when an experimental XF-11 Army plane he is piloting crashes in Beverly Hills, Calif.	Pope Pius XII canonizes Mother Frances Xavier Cabrini, the first U.S. citizen to become a Roman Catholic saint . . . . Frankie Parker beats Billy Talbert to win the national clay court tennis title at River Forest, Ill.	July 7
Rep. Andrew May (D, Ky.) publicly repudiates his earlier admission of procuring government orders for the Cumberland Lumber Co., claiming he is a victim of "sinister attacks."	Truman signs a $4,119,659,300 Navy appropriations bill.		National Foundation for Infantile Paralysis announces it has granted $1,648,559 this year for poliomyelitis research.	N.Y.C. police seize 130 copies of Edmund Wilson's *Memoirs of Hecate County*, condemned as obscene by the New York Society for the Suppression of Vice . . . . Moscow reports the death of Alexander Alexandrov, composer of the Soviet National Anthem.	July 8
	Truman appoints John Leighton Stuart, director of Yenching University in Peking, to succeed Gen. Patrick Hurley as ambassador to China.			Powered by Ted Williams' three home runs, the A.L. defeats the N.L., 12-0, in the 13th annual All-Star Game in Boston.	July 9
		President Sidney Hillman of the Amalgamated Clothing Workers union, dies at 59 in Point Lookout, N.Y.		Hessketh Pearson's biography *Oscar Wilde, His Life and Wit* is published by Harper.	July 10
House Un-American Activities Committee makes public a report by Chief Counsel Ernie Adamson charging that physicists at the government's Oak Ridge, Tenn. nuclear facility are guilty of subversive activities . . . . National Farmers Union President James Patton discloses that his organization has broken with the Administration in a dispute over agricultural subsidies . . . . N.Y. Liberal Party nominates Sen. James Mead (D, N.Y.) for the governorship and former governor and UNRRA director Herbert Lehman for U.S. senator.	A Joint Chiefs of Staff evaluation board and a presidential commission report that the Bikini atom bomb damaged more vessels than any previous single explosion and conclude that ships' superstructures must be redesigned . . . . War. Dept. announces plans for a National Guard of 682,114 men in mobile units, twice the prewar force.	Office of War Mobilization and Reconversion director John Steelman states in his agency's seventh quarterly report that the country must choose between high inflation or government control of the economy.		Cagney Productions announces in Hollywood the signing of World War II hero Audie Murphy as an actor.	July 11
	Truman releases Agriculture Secy. Clinton Anderson's report on American food shipments, stating that the U.S. exported 16.5 million tons of food relief in 1945-46.			Ray S. Baker, author of *Woodrow Wilson—Life and Letters* and muckraking magazine articles, dies at 76 in Amherst, Mass.	July 12

F	G	H	I	J
Includes elections, federal-state relations, civil rights and liberties, crime, the judiciary, education, health care, poverty, urban affairs and population.	*Includes formation and debate of U.S. foreign and defense policies, veterans affairs and defense spending. (Relations with specific foreign countries are usually found under the region concerned.)*	*Includes business, labor, agriculture, taxation, transportation, consumer affairs, monetary and fiscal policy, natural resources, pollution and accidents.*	*Includes worldwide scientific, medical and technological developments, natural phenomena, U.S. weather and natural disasters.*	*Includes the arts, religion, scholarship, communications media, sports, entertainment, fashions, fads and social life.*

	World Affairs	Europe	Africa & the Middle East	The Americas	Asia & the Pacific
July 13	Bernard Baruch supports Australia's Herbert Evatt in proposing that the Big Five renounce their veto right in matters pertaining to atomic energy.		Egypt's cabinet dissolves 11 educational, cultural, scientific, social and labor organizations for propagating "subversive" ideas.		Nationalist commanders report that 20,000 Communist troops are attacking near Tientsin, Paoting and Tsingtao in northern China. Communist troops seize seven U.S. Marines in a village along the Peking-Mukden railroad, claiming they were aiding Nationalist forces.
July 14		Italian Provisional Pres. Enrico de Nicola swears in the first Italian Republican government under Christian Democratic Premier Alcide de Gasperi . . . . Parades and street dancing mark the 157th anniversary of Bastille Day in France.			India gives Siam a 20-year, $13 million credit to increase export of Siamese rice.
July 15	State Secy. Byrnes, commenting on the just-concluded Paris Conference of Foreign Ministers, acknowledges "tremendous difficulties" in concluding peace treaties with former Axis powers and complains that Russian conduct raises "doubts and suspicions" among the other Allies . . . . In a N.Y. radio broadcast, Australian Foreign Min. Herbert Evatt says that the smaller nations will not act as "rubber stamps" at the forthcoming Paris peace conference.	Military Section of the People's Supreme Court in Belgrade finds Gen. Mikhailovich and 23 co-defendents guilty of treason and sentences Mikhailovich to death by shooting . . . . The Spanish Cortes votes $100 million in loans to aid small farmers.	Over 4,000 Jewish war veterans end a two-day demonstration in Washington, demanding that 100,000 European Jews be admitted to Palestine.	Concluding a five-month study of espionage in Canada, Supreme Court Justices R. Tachereau and R. Kellock charge that several parallel spy networks have been operating under members of the Soviet embassy . . . . Venezuela orders the heirs of former Pres. Antonio Pimentel to surrender their entire fortune, estimated at $15 million, to a special graft investigating tribunal . . . . Britain, France, Holland and the U.S. agree to formation of the Caribbean Commission, an advisory body intended to promote cooperative planning and economic development among colonies and independent states in the area.	Fighting between Communists and Nationalists intensifies at numerous points in Manchuria and north China . . . . Siam formally submits its border dispute with French Indochina to the U.N. Security Council.
July 16		Russian authorities release U.S. Warrant Officer Samuel Harrison and his wife, imprisoned two weeks ago for entering the Russian occupation zone without orders, after U.S. authorities agree to release three Russians held for one month on suspicion of espionage . . . . An American military court in Dachau sentences Col. Joachim Peiper and 42 other SS soldiers to death for killing U.S. prisoners during the Battle of the Bulge . . . . U.S. military governor Gen. Mark Clark turns over the Hermann Goering iron works in Linz to the Austrian government.	Over 100,000 oil workers in Iran end a three-day strike against the Anglo-Iranian Oil Co., protesting company interference in Iranian politics.	U.S. signs a contract to purchase most of Cuba's 1946 and 1947 sugar crops.	
July 17		Yugoslavian Chetnik leader Mikhailovich and eight co-defendants are executed by a firing squad in Belgrade.			Owners of the Mitsui economic combine vote in Tokyo to break their company up into its component industrial branches.
July 18	International Health Assembly meeting in N.Y. creates an interim commission to prepare for the establishment of the World Health Organization . . . . Control Comm. of the U.N. Atomic Energy Commission unanimously elects Capt. Alvara Alberto da Motta Silva of Brazil as chairman.	British House of Commons upholds bread rationing, after Churchill accuses the government of being "panic stricken" and describe the move as "futile." . . . . Belgian Premier Achille van Acker refuses to form a new government when Socialists reject a cabinet coalition.	Palestine Jews end a 15-hour general strike protesting alleged police brutality in the Rafa and Latrun detention camps.		Parliament approves the British cabinet mission report on India, but Churchill says that the mission went too far in offering India independence outside of the Commonwealth.
July 19	Bernard Baruch tells the U.N. Scientific and Technical Commission that the U.S. does not intend to reveal any atomic energy secrets at present.	French Constituent Assembly votes to seat former Premier Edouard Daladier, elected on the Popular Republican ticket, over Communist objections.			

A	B	C	D	E
Includes developments that affect more than one world region, international organizations and important meetings of major world leaders.	*Includes all domestic and regional developments in Europe, including the Soviet Union, Turkey, Cyprus and Malta.*	*Includes all domestic and regional developments in Africa and the Middle East, including Iraq and Iran and excluding Cyprus, Turkey and Afghanistan.*	*Includes all domestic and regional developments in Latin America, the Caribbean and Canada.*	*Includes all domestic and regional developments in Asian and Pacific nations, extending from Afghanistan through all the Pacific Islands, except Hawaii.*

U.S. Politics & Social Issues	U.S. Foreign Policy & Defense	U.S. Economy & Environment	Science, Technology & Nature	Culture, Leisure & Life Style	
A federal district court in Atlanta issues an injunction to stop the purging of names of Negroes from voter registration lists in Atkinson County, Ga. . . . . Truman names a 30-member commission under American Council on Education director George Zook to see how the nation's overburdened college system can be improved . . . . Ingram Stainback is confirmed by the Senate as governor of Hawaii.	House passes and sends to the White House the Anglo-American Trade and Financial Agreement, extending a $3.75-billion credit to Britain . . . . War Dept. announces creation of the Army Air Forces Univ. at Maxwell Field, Ala. to provide career training for Air Force officers.	Senate approves a bill to revive the OPA with limited powers for one year and sends the measure to House conference.	Russian Prof. Gavril Tikhov says that astrobotanical studies show there is vegetation on Mars.	Photographer Alfred Stieglitz, husband of painter Georgia O'Keefe, dies at 72 in New York . . . . Cosmic Bomb with Shelby Clark up wins the Arlington Futurity, Chicago, earning $65,875.	July 13
Arthur Capper (R, Kan.), oldest U.S. senator, celebrates his 81st birthday in Washington . . . . House Ways and Means Committee reverses its decision to increase the Social Security tax, voting to retain the 1% levy another year.		Jacob Potofsky is elected president of the CIO Amalgamated Clothing Workers Union, succeeding the late Sidney Hillman.		Joyce McRae sets three new U.S. swim marks: 100-yd. breast-stroke in 1:51.1; 50-meter breast-stroke in 0:37.1, and the 150-meter medley in 2:05.1.	July 14
	Truman signs the $3.75-billion British loan bill.	The Treasury announces it will cut the national debt $1.25 billion on Aug. 1 by retiring short-term loans.		GM research head Charles Kettering is elected president of the newly-established Thomas Alva Edison Foundation, whose aim is to promote "educational advancement" in the sciences.	July 15
	War Dept. suspends Army enlistment of Negroes, which has recently exceeded the Negro-white ratio of 1:10 maintained by the Army . . . . Truman directs that only men aged 19-29 be inducted when the draft is resumed in September.	La. Gov. James Davis signs a bill making unions and employers responsible for fulfillment of contracts, banning "violence or threats" in labor relations and prohibiting unions from conspiring to restrain trade.		Leopold Stokowski signs a contract with Boris Morros and William LeBaron to appear in the movie *Carnegie Hall*, which will be filmed in N.Y.	July 16
Sen. Burton Wheeler (D, Mont.) loses his party's senatorial nomination to Leif Ericson.	Soviet Lt. Redin is acquitted in Seattle of espionage and conspiracy charges by a federal court jury, which he thanks for "this fair trial."	Waterfront Employers Assn. signs a contract with the International Longshoremen's and Warehousemen's Union, effective to Sept. 30, setting up arbitration machinery and raising basic hourly pay to $1.37.		Musical producer Busby Berkeley is arrested after failing in a suicide attempt.	July 17
Although trailing in popular votes, Eugene Talmadge wins enough electoral votes to clinch the Georgia Democratic gubernatorial nomination despite the opposition of 100,000 newly registered Negro voters . . . . Truman promises his aid to Democratic nominees in November elections but opposes the renomination of Rep. Roger Slaughter (D, Mo.), who voted against all Administration measures in the last session of Congress.	Sen. Warren Austin (R, Vt.) is appointed to head the five-man U.S. delegation to the U.N. General Assembly.	CIO executive board names Jack Kroll to succeed Sidney Hillman as head of the organization's Political Action Comm.	N.Y. State Bd. of Regents announces that a federally financed nuclear physics lab will be set up in N.Y. with participation of nine universities under the supervision of Manhattan Project physicists . . . . Univ. of Illinois announces development of a 22-million volt betatron, capable of producing an electron beam which can "penetrate the core of an atom."	American fashion critics vote their annual award for outstanding fashion work to designers Clare Potter, Omar Kiam and Vincent MonteSano.	July 18
An Equal Rights Amendment to the Constitution, banning sex discrimination in all jobs, fails to gain the required two-thirds majority for passage in the Senate . . . . House sets up a five-man board to investigate this year's congressional primaries after widespread charges of vote fraud . . . . Senate War Investigating Comm. subpoenas Rep. Andrew May (D, Ky.) to testify on alleged bribe-taking in connection with war contracts, but May claims congressional immunity.		House completes action on a $2.7-billion deficiency funds bill, providing $460 million for the UNRRA, and also passes a bill allowing the Treasury to sell silver at 90.5¢ per ounce . . . . CIO asks Truman and the Labor Dept. to seize nine Allis-Chalmers and J.I. Case plants, closed by a wildcat strike, "in the interest of producing needed farm equipment" to relieve the world food shortage.		Network Hooperatings list most popular radio shows as: *Mr. District Atty., Walter Winchell, Screen Guild Players* and *Kay Kaiser.*	July 19
F *Includes elections, federal-state relations, civil rights and liberties, crime, the judiciary, education, health care, poverty, urban affairs and population.*	G *Includes formation and debate of U.S. foreign and defense policies, veterans affairs and defense spending. (Relations with specific foreign countries are usually found under the region concerned.)*	H *Includes business, labor, agriculture, taxation, transportation, consumer affairs, monetary and fiscal policy, natural resources, pollution and accidents.*	I *Includes worldwide scientific, medical and technological developments, natural phenomena, U.S. weather and natural disasters.*	J *Includes the arts, religion, scholarship, communications media, sports, entertainment, fashions, fads and social life.*	

	World Affairs	Europe	Africa & the Middle East	The Americas	Asia & the Pacific
July 20		Gen. Joseph McNary of the U.S. military government in Germany tells the Allied Control Council in Berlin that the U.S. will join any other occupying power in treating their zones as a single economic unit . . . . U.S. military authorities in Frankfurt reveal they are investigating two more cases of art looting by American officers in Germany, one involving a Rubens painting valued at $20,000 . . . . A cyclone strikes the Rimini beach area in Italy, causing 33 deaths.		Bolivian Pres. Gualberto Villarroel names a military cabinet after a three-day rising of students and workers in which 100 are reported killed.	
July 21		In Turkey's first multiparty parliamentary elections, the ruling Republican People's Party gains a large majority of seats.			
July 22	Delegates of 60 nations sign the World Health Organization charter in N.Y. . . . . U.N. Secretariat announces that the next General Assembly meeting will be postponed to Sept. 23 to avoid conflict with the Paris peace conference.	Gen. Joseph-Pierre Koenig, French military governor in Germany, announces the incorporation of 79 Rhineland districts covering over 600 square miles into the Saar.	Zionist terrorists of the Irgun Zvai Leumi explode land mines in the west wing of the King David Hotel in Jerusalem, which houses British military headquarters for Palestine. British authorities announce a preliminary toll of 79 dead, 46 wounded and 26 missing.	Bolivian Pres. Gualberto Villarroel is killed and hung from a lamppost in La Paz as an armed revolt of students and workers sweeps the government out of power; Supreme Court Justice Nestor Guillen is named to head a provisional government.	Mme. Sun Yat-sen, widow of the founder of the Chinese Republic, urges the U.S. to withdraw its forces from China and refuse to aid the Nationalist government until it is reorganized and is "truly representative."
July 23		Austrian cabinet protests the Red Army's seizure of property that does not meet the government's definition of "German assets." . . . . James Maxton, Independent Labor Party leader in Britain, dies at 61 in Largs, Scotland.		Paraguayan Pres. Higinio Morinigo accepts the resignation of his entire cabinet after reaching a power-sharing agreement with the recently legalized Colorado and Febrerista parties.	UNRRA sources estimate that 16 million people in the Chinese provinces of Kwangsi and southern Hunan are victims of "acute starvation."
July 24	Gromyko tells the U.N. Atomic Energy Commission that Russia will not accept the U.S. international atomic control plan, declaring that the Security Council must retain full authority over nuclear power . . . . UNRRA recommends creation of a permanent international agency to oversee relief operations, estimating that only $750 million in food assistance will be available to fill a $1.1-billion need in 1947.		A British White Paper accuses Hagana, Irgun Zvai Leumi and the Stern group of planned sabotage in Palestine under direction of the Jewish Agency.		Chinese Communist forces release seven U.S. Marines seized in Manchuria July 13.
July 25		Turkish government imposes press restrictions to maintain internal "amity."	An Anglo-American cabinet committee proposes a division of Palestine into Jewish and Arab sectors, with over-all control resting with British authorities, which would directly administer Jerusalem, Bethlehem and the Negev.	Canada and Great Britain announce a trade agreement calling for the sale of 600 million bushels of Canadian wheat to Britain during the next four years . . . . Truman names Jesus Pinero governor of Puerto Rico, succeeding Rexford G. Tugwell.	MacArthur approves a plan to decentralize economic power in Japan by liquidating the *zaibatsu* combines . . . . Chinese Nationalists drive the Communists northward from the Nanking-Shanghai area in Kiangsu Province.
July 26	Washington reports that the U.S., Britain and Canada will recommend ending the UNRRA.	In his summation of the prosecution case at Nuremberg, U.S. Chief Prosecutor Robert Jackson calls for the conviction of the 22 Nazi defendants for subjugating Germany to a police state, waging wars, disregarding international law in warfare, enslaving populations and exterminating Christians and Jews . . . . Former French Premier and Vichy cabinet member Pierre-Etienne Flandin is sentenced in Paris to five years of national dishonor, but the court annuls the penalty due to his long imprisonment.	State Secy. Byrnes distances the U.S. from the Palestine division plan proposed yesterday by the Anglo-American cabinet committee.		
	A *Includes developments that affect more than one world region, international organizations and important meetings of major world leaders.*	B *Includes all domestic and regional developments in Europe, including the Soviet Union, Turkey, Cyprus and Malta.*	C *Includes all domestic and regional developments in Africa and the Middle East, including Iraq and Iran and excluding Cyprus, Turkey and Afghanistan.*	D *Includes all domestic and regional developments in Latin America, the Caribbean and Canada.*	E *Includes all domestic and regional developments in Asian and Pacific nations, extending from Afghanistan through all the Pacific Islands, except Hawaii.*

U.S. Politics & Social Issues	U.S. Foreign Policy & Defense	U.S. Economy & Environment	Science, Technology & Nature	Culture, Leisure & Life Style	
	House passes and sends to the Senate the amended version of the MacMahon atomic energy control bill, which provides for military representation on the proposed control commission and allows the Army and Navy to manufacture nuclear weapons without supervision . . . . In their final report to Truman, members of the Strategic Bombing Survey suggest the creation of an air arm having equal status with the Army and Navy . . . . The report of the Pearl Harbor investigation is released, with the Democratic majority section accusing Gen. Walter Short and Adm. Husband Kimmel of errors of judgment and the Republican minority section blaming members of FDR's cabinet for failing "to perform the responsibilities . . . . essential to the defense of Pearl Harbor."	After five days of sessions, a House-Senate conference committee agrees to a compromise OPA bill, extending the agency's life until June 30, 1947.		Four Winds with Ovie Scurlock up wins the $62,250 Arlington Lassie Stakes in Chicago.	July 20
Columnist Drew Pearson denounces the Ku Klux Klan from the steps of the Georgia capitol, while in Alabama the Klan files for incorporation.				Elbert Booker sets a big-car world speed record of 21.35 seconds on a half-mile track in Dayton, Ohio . . . . *New York Herald Tribune* lists Frederic Wakeman's *The Hucksters* and Betty MacDonald's *The Egg and I* as best-selling fiction and non-fiction books.	July 21
		National Mediation Bd. certifies the CIO Transport Workers Union as bargaining agent for 3,400 mechanics at American Airlines.			July 22
Ambrose Kennedy is found guilty by the U.S. Civil Service Commission of violating the Hatch Act by taking part in political campaigns in 1943 and 1944 while employed by the Maryland Unemployment Compensation Bd.	Commerce Secy. Wallace writes an unpublicized letter to Truman urging a shift in U.S. foreign policy to avert a war with Russia. Among the changes he advocates are U.S. destruction of its atomic bombs and recognition of Russia's right to maintain "friendly" regimes in states along its borders . . . . In a note to Russia, the State Dept. accuses the Soviets of stripping Hungary of food and industrial materials.	Truman reluctantly signs a bill providing for government stock-piling of strategic and critical materials, but condemns its "buy American" clause . . . . James L. Caffrey is named head of the Securities and Exchange Commission . . . . Order of Railway Conductors calls a strike of its 40,000 members for Aug. 7 against Pullman Co., demanding a 19¾¢ hourly wage increase.	Biologist F.L. Vanderplank announces a method of preventing sleeping sickness by disturbing the tsetse fly's sex life.		July 23
House approves and sends to the Senate Social Security legislation freezing the 1% tax, increasing federal dependency benefits and aid to the blind and aged and granting survivors insurance to relatives of World War II veterans.		GE signs a contract with the CIO United Electrical, Radio and Machine Workers providing for an 18½¢ hourly wage increase, improved job security, vacations and higher starting pay for 100,000 workers . . . . Truman names Sperry Gyroscope Vice President James Webb as director of the budget, and signs a $2-billion bill for river and harbor improvement and flood control.	Pres. Willard Dow of the Dow Chemical Co. receives the 1946 Chemistry Industry Medal from the Society of the Chemical Industry.		July 24
A congressional reorganization bill, with provisions for the registering of lobbyists and reduction of the number of standing committees, is passed by the House and sent to the Senate . . . . Rep. Andrew May claims he is unable to attend the Senate war profits inquiry due to a heart attack, after agreeing previously to testify . . . . A band of 20 white men force four Negroes out of a car near Monroe, Ga. and kill them for allegedly stabbing a white man.	The first atomic bomb detonated under water is dropped from a plane near Bikini atoll, falling in the midst of 75 warships and sinking 10 . . . . War Dept. report affirms that defective mortar shells killed U.S. combat soldiers but denies that faulty parts were made by the armaments firm under investigation in the Senate.	Truman "reluctantly" signs the House and Senate-approved bill which extends the OPA through June 30, 1947, stating he will call a special session of Congress if this new law fails to stem inflation . . . . By executive order Truman shifts the Office of Economic Stabilization to the Office of War Mobilization and Reconversion, making John Steelman temporary stabilization chief.			July 25
	House and Senate pass and send to Truman a version of the disputed MacMahon atomic energy bill, which provides for a five-man control commission without military representation and allows the Army and Navy to manufacture atomic weapons with presidential approval.	Truman signs the Labor Security-NLRB bill, which returns the U.S. Employment Service to the states Nov. 15.			July 26

F	G	H	I	J
Includes elections, federal-state relations, civil rights and liberties, crime, the judiciary, education, health care, poverty, urban affairs and population.	*Includes formation and debate of U.S. foreign and defense policies, veterans affairs and defense spending. (Relations with specific foreign countries are usually found under the region concerned.)*	*Includes business, labor, agriculture, taxation, transportation, consumer affairs, monetary and fiscal policy, natural resources, pollution and accidents.*	*Includes worldwide scientific, medical and technological developments, natural phenomena, U.S. weather and natural disasters.*	*Includes the arts, religion, scholarship, communications media, sports, entertainment, fashions, fads and social life.*

	World Affairs	Europe	Africa & the Middle East	The Americas	Asia & the Pacific
July 27		Drafts of tentative peace treaties prepared at the Paris Conference of Foreign Ministers are published, showing that Italy, Rumania, Bulgaria, Hungary and Finland will be stripped of war-making potential, Italy will lose her colonies and Finland will cede territory to the Soviet Union . . . . London announces that Prime Minister Attlee will represent Britain at the Paris Peace Conference during the illness of Foreign Secy. Bevin.	Arab Higher Comm. rejects a British proposal for a Jewish-Arab conference, calling for an independent Arab Palestine with no Jewish immigration.		Nanking government rejects Chinese Communist proposals for a ceasefire, stating questions of the control of Manchuria, reorganization of the armies and the reopening of communications must be settled first.
July 28		De Gaulle calls for an Anglo-French entente to "re-establish equilibrium" between the U.S. and Russia, the world's leading postwar powers . . . . UNRRA Director La Guardia charges that millions of dollars of supplies are being stolen by soldiers in the Trieste area.	British Palestine Commander Sir Evelyn Barker bans fraternization of British troops with Palestinian Jews.	Jamaica announces settlement of a dock workers' strike with an agreement dividing waterfront work between two unions.	Nationalist and Communist representatives in Changchun accept a U.S. proposal to form a no-man's land along the Sungari River in Manchuria, while Nationalist forces advance along the Lung Hai railway on the Yellow River.
July 29	French Premier Georges Bidault opens the 21-nation Paris Peace Conference in Luxembourg Palace and is chosen temporary chairman of the conference.	French government decrees a general wage increase for public servants averaging 18%.		A Panamanian court acquits former President Arnulfo Arias of charges of participating in an abortive armed revolt in December 1945.	Chinese Communist troops attack a U.S. Marine convoy between Tientsin and Peking, killing three Marines and wounding 12 . . . . India's Moslem League withdraws its acceptance of British independence proposals, accusing Britain and the Congress Party of going back on their original pledge to guarantee Moslems certain posts in the new government.
July 30		Paris Peace Conference releases draft peace treaties for Italy, Finland, Rumania, Bulgaria and Hungary without reaching agreement on Danube River navigation rights.	Tel Aviv is placed under a 22-hour-a-day curfew as 20,000 British troops begin a house-to-house search for terrorists.		
July 31	Gromyko tells the U.N. Atomic Energy Commission that the U.S. proposal for international inspection of atomic energy developments is an infringement of national sovereignty.	U.S. Army Capt. Harold Cobin and Lt. George Wyatt are released by the Russians in Berlin after being held 26 days on spy charges.	An arms cache, counterfeiting equipment and almost a million dollars in forged government bonds are discovered by the British in Tel Aviv's largest synagogue.		
Aug. 1		Speaking at the Paris Peace Conference, Yugoslav Vice Premier Edward Kardelj rejects the French recommendation for the Yugoslav-Italian boundary and internationalization of Trieste . . . . Russia rejects a U.S. protest note concerning Soviet policies in Hungary, calling "absolutely groundless" the charge that it took reparations amounting to 24% of Hungary's national income in 1945 . . . . French Constituent Assembly approves agreements with the U.S. for the settlement of French war debts, disposal of war surplus and liquidation of Lend-Lease.	Churchill tells Commons that Britain should turn over its Palestine mandate to the U.N. if the U.S. will not "share the burden of the Zionist cause." . . . . Iranian Premier Ahmed Ghavam presents his new cabinet to the Shah, including three members of the leftist Tudeh Party.	Juan Peron says Argentina would fight on the side of the U.S. in the event of another war . . . . Paraguay legalizes the Communist Party, outlawed under previous regimes.	
Aug. 2	Cuba requests a special U.N. conference to discuss eliminating the veto power of the major Security Council members.	Camille Huysmans forms a provisional Belgian cabinet composed of Socialists, Liberals and Communists . . . . Moscow reports the execution of Gen. Andrei Vlassov and 10 subordinates who formed a Russian "army of liberation" under German control during World War II.	British authorities in Palestine reveal that the Zionist bombing of Jerusalem's King David Hotel resulted in 91 deaths and 45 injuries . . . . Steamer *Vitya* sinks in Lake Nyassa, Tanganyika, drowning 295 followers of the Aga Khan traveling to a celebration of the Khan's golden jubilee.	Bermuda drops its 38-year ban on private autos.	

A	B	C	D	E
Includes developments that affect more than one world region, international organizations and important meetings of major world leaders.	*Includes all domestic and regional developments in Europe, including the Soviet Union, Turkey, Cyprus and Malta.*	*Includes all domestic and regional developments in Africa and the Middle East, including Iraq and Iran and excluding Cyprus, Turkey and Afghanistan.*	*Includes all domestic and regional developments in Latin America, the Caribbean and Canada.*	*Includes all domestic and regional developments in Asian and Pacific nations, extending from Afghanistan through all the Pacific Islands, except Hawaii.*

U.S. Politics & Social Issues	U.S. Foreign Policy & Defense	U.S. Economy & Environment	Science, Technology & Nature	Culture, Leisure & Life Style	
		Truman invokes the Railway Labor Act to gain a two-month delay of the Pullman strike called July 23 . . . . House completes action on a Senate-approved bill giving the states title to submerged oil lands.		Gertrude Stein, American expatriate writer noted for her emphasis on sound rather than meaning in her works, dies at 72 in Paris . . . . *Billboard* reports the most popular songs are: (1) *The Gypsy*, (2) *They Say It's Wonderful*, and (3) *Doin' What Comes Natur'lly*.	July 27
Negroes vote for the first time in the Texas Democratic primary, which results in the renomination of Sen. Tom Connally and Reps. Wright Patman, Sam Rayburn and Lyndon Johnson.	Asst. War Secy. Howard Petersen reports that Japanese war crimes accounted for 142,076 U.S. and Filipino deaths.	AFL and CIO announce formation of a National Maritime Council of seven unions to eliminate jurisdictional disputes.		Pope Pius XII appoints the Most Rev. Paul Schulte Archbishop of Indianapolis and the Most Rev. Joseph Ritter Archbishop of St. Louis . . . . World Lutheran Convention executive committee ends a three-day meeting in Uppsala, Sweden after drafting a constitution and electing Swedish Archbishop Erling Eidem as president.	July 28
U.S. Controller General Lindsay C. Warren tells the Senate War Investigating Comm. that loopholes in war contracts have cost the government "untold millions." . . . . N.Y. State revokes the state KKK charter, while the Justice Dept. reveals it is investigating Klan activities in seven states.		Brookings Institution Vice President Edwin G. Nourse is named chairman of the Economic Advisory Council administering the Full Employment Act . . . . Senate passes and sends to Truman a bill extending the Reconstruction Finance Corp. to June 30, 1947 . . . . United Aircraft Corp. makes history's first commercial helicopter sale, a $48,500-delivery to Helicopter Air Transport Inc.	Bahaman subsidiary of Standard Oil of N.J. announces it will use radar and a diving chamber to search for oil under the Caribbean ocean floor.	British heavyweight champ Bruce Woodcock KO's French challenger Albert Renet in the sixth round to win the European championship.	July 29
Attorney Gen. Tom Clark reports Truman has ordered a Justice Dept. investigation of the July 25 murder of four Negroes in Georgia . . . . Mississippi arrests six white men on charges of flogging a Negro, Leon McTatie, to death July 22.	Truman signs a joint congressional resolution authorizing the U.S. to join UNESCO.				July 30
Senate kills an anti-poll tax bill by refusing to limit debate on the measure.	Senate ratifies a treaty establishing relations with the Philippine Republic.	Senate-House conference committee sends Truman the Wheeler-Reed railroad bill, which would allow termination of bankruptcy proceedings against seven major railroads, including the Missouri Pacific and the New Haven & Rock Island, showing specific improvements in their financial position . . . . Truman signs bills authorizing the Treasury to sell silver at 90.5¢ an ounce and liberalizing railroad unemployment compensation and retirement benefits.	Curtiss-Wright Corp. demonstrates a new million-dollar pilot training device capable of simulating all flight conditions.		July 31
	Truman signs the McMahon atomic energy control bill.	Truman vetoes the tidelands oil bill, pointing out that the question of ownership of offshore deposits is now before the Supreme Court "and should be decided there." . . . . GM, Chrysler and Ford reject a UAW invitation to a joint conference on means to increase auto production.	Manhattan Project director Leslie R. Groves says Camp Upton on Long Island will be the site of the first of three federally-financed nuclear research centers in N.Y.	Salzburg Music Festival, suspended since the annexation of Austria by Germany in 1938, is revived . . . . Dodger outfielder Pete Reiser suffers a concussion while chasing a ball when he strikes his head against a wall in Ebbetts Field, Brooklyn.	Aug. 1
Truman signs the congressional reorganization bill, which reduces House standing committees, requires lobbyists to register and provides that four major committees will meet each year to draw up a national budget . . . . A group of Georgia citizens file a federal suit attacking the constitutionality of the unit election system under which Eugene Talmadge won the Democratic gubernatorial nomination . . . . Athens, Tenn. Sheriff Pat Mansfield surrenders impounded ballot boxes to armed war veterans in a ballot count dispute following a Democratic primary contest between a GI reform slate and the local entrenched political machine. The vote count shows a large victory for the veterans . . . . The 79th Congress adjourns.	By a 60-2 vote, the Senate ratifies and sends to the President the Morse resolution, giving the World Court jurisdiction in international disputes involving the U.S. . . . . House and Senate leaders appoint an 18-member Permanent Joint Congressional Comm. on Atomic Energy . . . . Truman appoints William Clayton under secretary of state for economic affairs.	House sustains Truman's veto of the tidelands oil bill.	U.S. nuclear plant at Oak Ridge, Tenn. sells one millicurie of Carbon 14 to the Barnard Free Skin and Cancer Hospital in St. Louis for use in cancer research. It is the first sale of radioactive isotopes to a private institution.		Aug. 2
F	G	H	I	J	
Includes elections, federal-state relations, civil rights and liberties, crime, the judiciary, education, health care, poverty, urban affairs and population.	*Includes formation and debate of U.S. foreign and defense policies, veterans affairs and defense spending. (Relations with specific foreign countries are usually found under the region concerned.)*	*Includes business, labor, agriculture, taxation, transportation, consumer affairs, monetary and fiscal policy, natural resources, pollution and accidents.*	*Includes worldwide scientific, medical and technological developments, natural phenomena, U.S. weather and natural disasters.*	*Includes the arts, religion, scholarship, communications media, sports, entertainment, fashions, fads and social life.*	

	World Affairs	Europe	Africa & the Middle East	The Americas	Asia & the Pacific
Aug. 3	Procedure Comm. of the Paris Peace Conference votes to rotate the chairmanship of the conference among the Big Four and China .... Belgian delegate Henri-Spaak says at the Paris Peace Conference that the rights of small nations must be respected and urges Britain, France and Russia to support recommendations made by a two-thirds majority of the conference.			Brazil appropriates $10 million for its second UNRRA contribution.	Komakichi Matsuoka, leader of the conservative bloc within the Japanese Social Democratic Party, is elected president of the Japanese Federation of Labor Unions .... Chinese Communists sources say the Nationalist government has begun an offensive in Shantung Province south of Peking.
Aug. 4		*Tass* reveals that Russia has increased its reparation demands on Hungary by $19.8 million, raising the total to $219.8 million.		One of the most violent earthquakes ever recorded strikes the Dominican Republic, causing 73 deaths and "innumerable" injuries according to the Dominican government.	Twelve French soldiers are killed and 41 wounded when Vietnamese nationalists ambush a French truck convoy in Bac Ninh near Hanoi.
Aug. 5	UNRRA Director La Guardia opens the fifth UNRRA Council in Geneva, as Soviet delegate Nikolai Feonov reports that Russia is prepared to continue its contributions through 1947.	Ismet Inonu is re-elected by the Turkish National Assembly for his fourth term as president over Marshal Fevzki Cakmak.	British authorities place a security blackout on Haifa, where 2,250 illegal Jewish immigrants are being held aboard ships .... Jewish Agency executive committee in Paris condemns Anglo-American Palestine federalization plan.	Guatemala grants the Standard Oil Co. a 50-year petroleum products concession in the port of San Jose .... A five-day railway strike in Sao Paulo, Brazil ends with a 20% wage increase for workers.	Nationalist and Communist sources report clashes across China, from Kiangsi Province in the south to Manchuria.
Aug. 6	State Secy. Byrnes accuses Russia of attempting to dictate the Paris Peace Conference and says he will let world opinion decide the issue. He challenges Russia to allow his statement to be printed in Soviet newspapers .... U.S. delegate John Hancock tells the U.N. Atomic Energy Commission the U.S. will consider nuclear control measures short of an international control authority, as proposed by Russia .... Security Council committee on membership meeting in N.Y. postpones action on the admission of Albania until it can study a protest submitted yesterday by Greece, which accuses Albania of holding Greek territory.	Britain introduces a "bonuses for babies" program under the Family Allowance Act, designed to increase the birth rate at a weekly cost of $4 million.			Nationalist and Communist representatives at the Truce Executive headquarters in Peking agree to a truce in the western provinces of Hupeh, Honan and Shansi.
Aug. 7	Allied foreign ministers at the Paris Peace Conference agree to invite five former Axis countries to attend plenary sessions of the conference. The Procedure Committee approves a British proposal allowing the conference to recommend treaty amendments by either a two-thirds vote (as demanded by the Russians) or a simple majority .... U.N. Food and Agriculture Organization proposes creation of a World Food Board to establish an emergency world food reserve, stabilize world agricultural prices and finance the purchase of surplus food by needy countries.	Inaugurating a campaign to increase industrial efficiency, Soviet trade union newspaper *Trud* attacks some union leaders for allowing low job standards and poor living conditions among workers.		Colombia inaugurates Mariano Ospina Perez as president.	
Aug. 8	U.S. urges the U.N. General Assembly to promote the development of international law in matters of atomic energy .... Russia assails Greek charges that Albania is holding Greek territory in northern Epirus as irrelevant to the question of Albania's admission to the U.N.	In retaliation to a U.S. order halting reparations deliveries to Russia from western Germany, Soviet authorities announce that they will seize and operate 200 key industries in their own occupation zone.	Arab Higher Comm. leader Jamal el Husseini rejects the British Palestine federalization proposal and refuses to attend a conference to be held in London on the Palestine problem.		
Aug. 9	Paris Peace Conference adopts the majority rule for treaty amendments over the opposition of Russia, Czechoslovakia, Yugoslavia and Poland.	Allied commanders in Berlin agree on a constitution restoring political freedom and self-government to the city .... Yugoslavian fighter planes force down a U.S. Army C-47 transport with 10 passengers near Ljubljana.			After fruitless efforts to mediate the Nationalist-Communist dispute, Gen. Marshall and U.S. Amb. John Stuart state that a settlement seems impossible and that civil war "threatens to engulf the country." .... British Viceroy Lord Wavell renews his efforts to persuade the All-India Congress Party to enter a coalition central government.
Aug. 10	In a heated plenary session of the Paris Peace Conference, Russia and Yugoslavia argue for the admission of Albania to the conference, finally accepting a Czechoslovakian proposal that Albania be heard on the Italian peace treaty.	Testifying at Nuremberg, Field Marshal Erich von Mannstein claims that Hitler attacked Russia to forestall a Soviet invasion of Germany.		Ecuadorian Pres. Jose Maria Velasco Ibarra resigns as the National Assembly meets to restore constitutional order after an attempted left-wing coup.	Indian government lifts a four-year ban on the "All-India Forward Bloc" composed of the late Subhas Chandra Bose's followers.
Aug. 11	U.S. delegate Col. Tyler Wood tells the UNRRA Council in Geneva the U.S. does not believe that the 1974 world food situation will require "the vast machinery of UNRRA."	Communist leader Gustav Husak is named head of a new Slovakian cabinet in Czechoslovakia.		Ecuador's National Assembly reelects Velasco Ibara as president.	

A	B	C	D	E
Includes developments that affect more than one world region, international organizations and important meetings of major world leaders.	*Includes all domestic and regional developments in Europe, including the Soviet Union, Turkey, Cyprus and Malta.*	*Includes all domestic and regional developments in Africa and the Middle East, including Iraq and Iran and excluding Cyprus, Turkey and Afghanistan.*	*Includes all domestic and regional developments in Latin America, the Caribbean and Canada.*	*Includes all domestic and regional developments in Asian and Pacific nations, extending from Afghanistan through all the Pacific Islands, except Hawaii.*

U.S. Politics & Social Issues	U.S. Foreign Policy & Defense	U.S. Economy & Environment	Science, Technology & Nature	Culture, Leisure & Life Style	
		Truman announces that the 1947 fiscal year budget deficit will be reduced to $1.9 billion due to increased revenues.			Aug. 3
Kentucky primaries result in the nomination of Democrat John Brown and Republican John Cooper to compete for the Senate seat vacated by Baseball Commissioner Albert Chandler.	Bernard Baruch, architect of the U.S. international atomic control plan, is named recipient for the 1946 Freedom House Award for "outstanding service to peace."	Reconstruction Finance Corp. releases enough woolen fabrics from military stockpiles to make one million men's suits and coats.			Aug. 4
		Packard Motor Co. closes down in Detroit as 7,500 UAW members walk out in a dispute over the layoff of foundry workers .... American Railroads Assn. denies charges by Sen. Glenn Taylor (D, Ida.) that U.S. railroads overcharged the government millions of dollars for war shipments .... OPA approves price increases of 8% for cotton textiles and 17% for sheets and towels.	Univ. of Pennsylvania receives a small amount of carbon 14 from the government nuclear facility at Oak Ridge, Tenn., the first radioactive substance to be used in medical research.	Major League Policy Committee meets with player representatives to discuss baseball contract reforms.	Aug. 5
Rep. John Sparkman (D, Ala.) is chosen in the state Democratic primary to complete the term of the late Sen. John H. Bankhead .... Virginia Democrats renominate Sen. Harry Byrd in the state primary and name Porter Hardy, Jr. and Thomas Stanley candidates for the House.		National Safety Council announces that 18 U.S. airlines completed 1945 schedules with no fatal accidents.		Benjamin Britten's opera *Peter Grimes* receives its American premiere at the Berkshire Music Center in Lenox, Mass.	Aug. 6
Truman signs a bill authorizing the coining of five million half dollars in honor of Negro educator Booker T. Washington.				Former Yankee second baseman Tony Lazzeri dies at 42 in Milbrae, Calif.	Aug. 7
	Air Force successfully tests the world's largest land-based bomber, the XB-36, with a bomb-carrying capacity of 30 tons.	Truman signs a bill extending the life of the Reconstruction Finance Corp. through June 1947.	Temple Univ. Medical School announces development of the electrokymograph by Dr. Bert Boone, allowing doctors to detect heart disease in early stages by photographing heart motion.		Aug. 8
Truman accepts the resignation of Mrs. Lucille Foster McMillin as U.S. Civil Service Commissioner .... State attorney's offices of N.J. and Georgia agree to trade evidence on KKK activities.			U.S. Public Health Service reports 5,622 persons have been stricken and 154 killed in 1946 by the worst infantile paralysis outbreak since 1916.		Aug. 9
Truman signs bills freezing Social Security taxes at 1% and permitting non-quota immigration of Chinese wives of U.S. citizens .... Fifty to 100 Negroes are injured in an Athens, Ala. race riot touched off by a fistfight between white war veterans and a Negro.	In accordance with the stockpiling bill signed by Truman July 23, Under Secy. of War Kenneth Toyall reports the U.S. is accumulating a $2.1-billion reserve of critical war materials.		Truman congratulates the Smithsonian Institution on its 100th anniversary.	Ben Hogan wins the Canadian Professional Golfers Assn. Tournament in Winnipeg.	Aug. 10
		A CIO United Radio, Electrical and Machine Workers union regional convention in Pittsburgh passes a resolution calling for removal of Communist union officials.	Albert Einstein and a group of nuclear researchers form the Emergency Committee of Atomic Scientists to advance the peacetime uses of atomic energy.	Six-week Berkshire Music Festival at Tanglewood ends with a record audience of 12,000 at the final concert.	Aug. 11
F	G	H	I	J	
Includes elections, federal-state relations, civil rights and liberties, crime, the judiciary, education, health care, poverty, urban affairs and population.	*Includes formation and debate of U.S. foreign and defense policies, veterans affairs and defense spending. (Relations with specific foreign countries are usually found under the region concerned.)*	*Includes business, labor, agriculture, taxation, transportation, consumer affairs, monetary and fiscal policy, natural resources, pollution and accidents.*	*Includes worldwide scientific, medical and technological developments, natural phenomena, U.S. weather and natural disasters.*	*Includes the arts, religion, scholarship, communications media, sports, entertainment, fashions, fads and social life.*	

	World Affairs	Europe	Africa & the Middle East	The Americas	Asia & the Pacific
Aug. 12	UNRRA Council creates a committee to establish future world food policy as Director-General La Guardia points out that the organization has no funds to continue in 1947 .... In accordance with a U.S.-Russian agreement, the Paris Peace Conference invites Albania, Mexico, Cuba and Egypt to present their views on the Italian treaty.	Yugoslavia admits it is holding eight U.S. soldiers and two civilians after Yugoslavian fighter planes forced down their C-47 transport Aug. 9 .... In Berlin the Army Criminal Investigation Division announces it has arrested former Navy Lt. Oscar Warner and former Air Force Lt. Lewis Warner, who with their father and two other brothers operated a world-wide black market ring .... The body of Benito Mussolini is found in a trunk in the Pavia Monastery near Milan.	Britain announces a halt to unscheduled immigration into Palestine and states that Jews seeking entry will be sent to Cyprus or elsewhere for detention .... Six South African gold mines shut down as 50,000 workers strike for a daily wage of two dollars, four times their present wage.	Minor tremors continue in the Dominican Republic after a week of serious earthquakes, as malaria and intestinal diseases sweep through camps set up to house those made homeless by the disaster.	Viceroy Lord Wavell reveals that the All-India Congress Party has accepted an invitation to form a government pending the drawing up of a new constitution.
Aug. 13	Speaking at the Paris Peace Conference, Molotov criticizes an Italian plea for a more lenient peace treaty and asserts that Italy must introduce radical reforms to eliminate the remnants of fascism .... Rumanian Foreign Min. George Tatarescu asks that his nation be granted the status of a co-belligerent at the Peace Conference and attacks the military, economic and political provisions of the Rumanian treaty.	Russia releases the text of a note to Turkey protesting the 1936 Montreaux Convention on the Black Sea Straits and proposing joint Russo-Turkish defense of the straits.	Two British transports leave Haifa for Cyprus with 1,300 illegal Jewish immigrants, while a ship carrying 600 more immigrants is captured and detained in Haifa. British troops kill three Jews and wound seven when they fire on a crowd of 1,000 trying to break into the city's harbor area .... Seven Arab League states and the Arab Higher Comm. announce their acceptance of a British invitation to a Palestine conference.		
Aug. 14	Bulgarian Foreign Min. Georgi Kulishey requests co-belligerent status for his country at the Paris Peace Conference and cancellation of all or part of its reparation obligations.	A Czechoslovakian court sentences Vojtech Tuka, Slovakian premier and foreign minister under the Nazis, to death in Bratislava.		Argentine Migration Director Santiago Peralta reports that under a 50-year program to raise the population he is permitting 1,000 Norwegian collaborationists to settle in the country and is negotiating the entry of 200,000 followers of the Polish exile government and their families.	Chiang Kai-shek promises to end Kuomintang rule of China and institute constitutional government "without delay" in return for Communist assurances that they will observe the truce agreement, restore communications and integrate their forces into the Chinese National Army .... UNRRA announces that Communist attacks on Taiyuan in Shansi Province and Kaifeng in Honan Province are forcing the virtual suspension of relief activities in those areas.
Aug. 15	Speaking at the Paris Peace Conference, State Secy. Byrnes denies Russian charges that the U.S. seeks to exploit former enemy states for "selfish advantage."	U.S. State Dept. sends Premier Tito a note charging that Yugoslavian troops violated the U.S. zone in Venezia Giulia when they clashed with U.S. forces July 12 .... U.S. Army authorities in Frankfurt announce the arrest of three Americans and 22 Germans suspected of leading a European counterfeiting ring.		Argentine Pres. Peron announces that future food exports will be limited to countries supplying Argentina with manufactured goods.	Chinese prosecutor Che Chun-hsiang accuses the Japanese on trial in Tokyo of responsibility for 95,000 atrocities in China between 1937 and 1945.
Aug. 16	UNRRA Council adjourns after establishing an international fund to care for children in liberated countries.	Russia demands that France be denied the right to vote on commissions of the Paris Peace Conference dealing with the Rumanian, Bulgarian, Hungarian and Finnish treaties .... U.S. and Britain reject a French proposal to create special offices under the Allied Control Council in Berlin for coordination of economic activities in the four zones of Germany.		Democratic candidate Dumarsais Estime is elected president of Haiti by the country's General Constituent Assembly.	A Moslem League protest in Calcutta against the British independence plan for India sparks a Hindu-Moslem riot, resulting in 270 deaths and 1,600 injuries .... Former Emperor Henry Pu Yi testifies at the Tokyo war crimes trials that he became the puppet ruler of Manchuria because of Japanese threats against his life.
Aug. 17		Russia and Denmark sign a five-year trade and navigation treaty.			Communist headquarters in Yenan reports that 8,000 Nationalist troops have been killed in fighting along the Lunghai railroad south of the Yellow River during the past week.
Aug. 18	Australian Foreign Min. Herbert Evatt proposes to the Paris Conference that all pending treaties provide for an International Court of Human Rights.		British troops use tear gas and fire hoses to force 640 Jewish refugees aboard the troopship *Empire Heywood* for transport to internment camps on Cyprus.	Ecuador ends all political and military restrictions imposed after the 1944 revolution.	
Aug. 19		Allied headquarters in Caserta announces that a U.S. transport plane has been downed by Yugoslavian fighters near the Italian border, the second such incident in 10 days .... Gen. Lucius Clay of the U.S. military government in Germany announces that 70% of the war plants in the U.S. zone have been or are being destroyed .... Rita Zucca, American-born "Axis Sally" who made German propaganda broadcasts from Italy during the war, is granted amnesty by an Italian court in Rome.	South Africa Communist leader Daniel Duplessis is arrested in Johannesburg for allegedly instigating last week's four-day strike of gold miners.	Argentine Senate ratifies the Chapultepec solidarity pact and the San Francisco U.N. agreement.	Communist headquarters in Yenan broadcasts a call for mobilization of militiamen in Communist-controlled areas "to shatter Generalissimo Chiang Kai-shek's offensive." .... Chinese government sets a new exchange rate of $3,350 Chinese to $1 American.
	A *Includes developments that affect more than one world region, international organizations and important meetings of major world leaders.*	B *Includes all domestic and regional developments in Europe, including the Soviet Union, Turkey, Cyprus and Malta.*	C *Includes all domestic and regional developments in Africa and the Middle East, including Iraq and Iran and excluding Cyprus, Turkey and Afghanistan.*	D *Includes all domestic and regional developments in Latin America, the Caribbean and Canada.*	E *Includes all domestic and regional developments in Asian and Pacific nations, extending from Afghanistan through all the Pacific Islands, except Hawaii.*

U.S. Politics & Social Issues	U.S. Foreign Policy & Defense	U.S. Economy & Environment	Science, Technology & Nature	Culture, Leisure & Life Style	
AFL Executive Council condemns the record of the 79th Congress and plans expansion of union political education activity aimed at bringing about a "sweeping congressional house-cleaning."				Truman signs bills to convert N.Y.'s Aquarium into the Castle Clinton National Monument and to establish a national air museum in Washington under Smithsonian Institution supervision.	Aug. 12
		Truman vetoes the Wheeler-Reed railroad bill, claiming it does not affect excessive interest rates on railroad loans and may permit "improper control of railroads after their reorganization." .... AFL's Executive Council says it will back American Federation of Musicians Pres. Petrillo's fight to have the Lea Act ruled unconstitutional.		British novelist and historian Herbert George Wells, author of 76 books including *The Time Machine* and *The Outline of History*, dies at 79 in London.	Aug. 13
Wisconsin Circuit Court Judge Joseph McCarthy defeats Sen. Robert La Follette Jr. for the state's GOP senatorial nomination.		Truman signs a bill establishing the Farmers Home Corp. to administer agricultural loans.			Aug. 14
		OPA ends three days of hearings on reimposing grain, livestock and milk price controls while granting price increases on many durable goods including radios, vacuum cleaners, washing machines and clocks. The agency also files complaints in N.Y. courts against Armour, Swift and two other meat packing firms for black market practices.	Raytheon Mfg. Co. and Radion Inventions reveal development of a new microwave relay communications system, capable of sending facsimile messages at 2,000 words per minute.		Aug. 15
Truman boards his yacht *Williamsburg* for his first extended vacation, 18 days, since taking office.	Truman says he may ask Congress to pass legislation admitting more Jewish refugees and European displaced persons as permanent U.S. residents. He also emphasizes the U.S. has no solution of its own to the Palestine problem.		Heaviest rainfall recorded in St. Louis in 109 years floods the city, making 2,000 families homeless and causing two deaths and an estimated $2 million in property damage.	Women's swimming records are set by Suzanne Zimmerman (48.7 sec. in the 200-meter backstroke) and Nancy Merki (29.9 sec. in the 300-meter individual medley) at Shakamak State Park, Ind.	Aug. 16
		Reconversion Director John Steelman authorizes the Commodities Credit Corp. to subsidize sugar beet processors, guaranteeing them a return of 35¢ more per 100 lbs. than on 1945 crops.		Education, with Johnny Adams up, takes the $80,024 Washington Park Futurity, earning $65,125.	Aug. 17
			American chemistry's highest award, the Priestly Medal, is presented to Dr. Roger Adams of Illinois Univ. for his work in inorganic chemistry .... A tornado in Mankato, Minn. causes seven deaths and injures 50.	A world conference of the teaching profession, meeting in Endicott, N.Y., advocates introduction of universal history and geography textbooks to eliminate national bias .... Crystal Plunge team retains its national women's swimming and diving championship at Shakamak State Park, Ind.	Aug. 18
In a letter to Senate War Investigating Committee Chmn. James Mead, the War Contracts Price Adjustment Board denies charges that slipshod renegotiation practices have cost the government billions.	U.S. Dept. of Agriculture announces that Undersecy. Norris Dodd has gone to Europe to head a survey studying methods of rehabilitating European agriculture.	OPA permits price increases of 12-26.8% on automotive parts, 6% on refrigerators and 1-7¢ on canned fruits and juices.	MIT physics proffessor Philip Morse is named scientific research director of the government-sponsored nuclear research center at Camp Upton, N.Y.		Aug. 19

	World Affairs	Europe	Africa & the Middle East	The Americas	Asia & the Pacific
Aug. 20	UNRRA Director-Gen. La Guardia dismisses Gen. Frederick Morgan as director of UNRRA operations in Germany, claiming he has found no evidence to support Morgan's charges that Russia has used U.N. refugee camps for espionage .... U.N. Secretariat completes its move from Hunter College to the former Sperry Gyroscope Co. building at Lake Success, Long Island.	U.S. State Dept. protests "emphatically" against recent Yugoslavian attacks on U.S. transport planes. A Yugoslavian reply criticizes U.S. "violations of state sovereignty" through "unauthorized flights" over Yugoslavia .... Poland receives a U.S. and British note charging repression of political activity and calling for free participation of all democratic parties in national elections scheduled for November.	Anglo-Egyptian treaty negotiations in Alexandria are broken off by the Egyptians, who reject British compromise proposals.		Calcutta slowly returns to normal after three days of Hindu-Moslem riots cause an estimated 3,000 deaths.
Aug. 21		U.S. issues an ultimatum to the Yugoslav government demanding that it release the occupants of the two planes forced down in Yugoslavia within 48 hours and threatening otherwise to bring the matter before the U.N. Security Council .... Yugoslavian Pres. Tito denies over Belgrade radio that the U.S. plane forced down Aug. 9 was lost in the clouds, claiming witnesses attest to the fact that the weather was clear .... Albanian Premier Enver Hoxha assails Italy and Greece at the Paris Peace Conference and pleads for greater curtailment of Italy's armed forces .... U.S. State Dept. objects to a Soviet proposal for joint Russo-Turkish control of the Dardanelles, stating that defense of the straits should be left to Turkey.			Nationalist sources report that Communist forces are retreating along the Lunghai railway in central China after the launching of a government counteroffensive.
Aug. 22		Responding to the U.S. ultimatum, Yugoslavia releases seven Americans and two Hungarians who were aboard the U.S. plane forced down Aug. 9 .... Moscow announces a campaign to rid Leningrad's literature, theater, movies and radio of foreign "decadence."			Communist headquarters at Yenan announces the establishment of a Communist government in Manchuria under the provisional administration of 86 elected officials.
Aug. 23	U.N. and UNRRA officials, meeting in N.Y., recommend creation of an interim commission to care for refugees in the period between the ending of UNRRA and establishment of the International Refugee Organization.	Belgrade reports there were no survivors of the second U.S. plane forced down on Aug. 19 and calls the incident "regrettable." .... Moscow announces start of a large-scale purge of state officials, including Foreign Min. Maxim Litvinov and P.V. Smirnov, head of Soviet meat and milk production. The housing situation and conditions in hospitals are sharply criticized in government reports.			Adm. Thawan Dhamrong Navaswat is named Siamese premier to succeed Nai Pridi Phanamjong, who recently resigned.
Aug. 24		Turkey sends a note to Russia turning down its proposal for joint control of the Dardanelles and suggesting an international convention to bring the Montreaux agreement up to date .... Speaking at the U.N. Security Council, Ukrainian Foreign Min. Dmitri Manuilski charges Greece with attempting to provoke war with Albania and endangering peace in the Balkans.			Japanese House of Representatives approves the proposed new constitution, proclaiming popular sovereignty and renouncing war as an instrument of national policy, by a large margin .... MacArthur orders 505 Japanese plants in eight industries set aside as potential war reparations .... Viscount Wavell announces the appointment of a Hindu-Moslem Executive Council headed by Nehru, to take office Sept. 2 and govern India until a new constitution is drawn up by the Assembly.
Aug. 25		Belgrade charges that British and American military planes violated Yugoslavian air space 110 times between Aug. 10 and 20 .... London *Sunday Observer* reports that Russian authorities have confiscated over 200 industrial works in their German zone, employing over 300,000 workers, as "Soviet state property."			Moslem extremists attempt to assassinate Shafaat Ahmad Khan, a Moslem official who violated Moslem League policy by accepting a post in India's interim government.
Aug. 26	At the Paris Peace Conference, Australian delegate E.R. Walker urges creation of an inter-Allied commission to regulate reparations, but Molotov insists on bilateral reparations agreements between the Allies and former Axis powers .... U.S. joins Britain and Holland in accepting the compulsory jurisdiction of the International Court of Justice in disputes over the interpretation of treaties and international law.	British Foreign Office admits sending radar equipment to Turkey "for civil purposes" but denies Russian charges that Britain has established a radar post on the Turkish coast to spy on Black Sea submarines.			
	A	B	C	D	E
	Includes developments that affect more than one world region, international organizations and important meetings of major world leaders.	*Includes all domestic and regional developments in Europe, including the Soviet Union, Turkey, Cyprus and Malta.*	*Includes all domestic and regional developments in Africa and the Middle East, including Iraq and Iran and excluding Cyprus, Turkey and Afghanistan.*	*Includes all domestic and regional developments in Latin America, the Caribbean and Canada.*	*Includes all domestic and regional developments in Asian and Pacific nations, extending from Afghanistan through all the Pacific Islands, except Hawaii.*

U.S. Politics & Social Issues	U.S. Foreign Policy & Defense	U.S. Economy & Environment	Science, Technology & Nature	Culture, Leisure & Life Style	
Physicians attending a National Negro Medical Assn. meeting sign petitions to oust Sen. Theodore Bilbo (D. Miss.) and outlaw lynchings and the KKK. A special Senate committee probing 1946 campaign expenditures promises to investigate Bilbo .... Acting Chmn. John Rankin (D. Miss.) of the House Un-American Activities Committee orders a probe of the CIO Political Action Comm., which he charges is engaged in subversive activities.		OPA's Price Decontrol Bd. restores ceiling prices on meat, cottonseed and soybeans but exempts milk, dairy products and grain.		Pittsburgh Pirates players reject the American Baseball Guild in baseball's first collective bargaining election.	Aug. 20
Returning to Washington from a tour of Alaska, Interior Secy. Julius Krug suggests that the territory be granted statehood.	Bartley Crum, former member of the Anglo-American Commission of Inquiry on Palestine, charges that "middle-level" State Dept. officials are sabotaging U.S. policy in the Middle East and calls for the resignation of Loy Henderson, head of the Near Eastern and African Affairs Office .... Navy announces completion of the first four-engine Lockheed Constitution, the Navy's largest transport, capable of carrying 69,000 lbs.	Federal Budget Director James Webb orders that civil service be reduced by 104,400 employes.			Aug. 21
		Delegates at an American Federation of Teachers convention in Miami Beach vote to reconsider the organization's no-strike policy, claiming "the strike may well be a desperate but indispensable means for rescuing American children from an intolerable situation." .... Bureau of Labor Statistics reports that wholesale food prices rose 31.3% since June 30, the day OPA controls ended.			Aug. 22
	War Dept. discloses that some officers in specialist categories are being recalled to active duty "without their consent" because of poor response to the Army's request for volunteers.	The AFL International Typographical Union ends a seven-day Miami conference after rejecting proposals to merge with the CIO and engage in unified political action .... CIO National Maritime Union reaches an agreement with Standard Oil Co. of Indiana establishing a 48-hour week at sea and 44 hours in port for crews of oil tankers .... Agriculture Dept. eases some grain controls, permitting whiter bread, greater whiskey and beer production and higher wheat exports.			Aug. 23
James Clark McReynolds, former Supreme Court justice who opposed FDR's New Deal, dies at 84 in Washington.	Air Force announces that all states have accepted their force allotments in the newly created Air National Guard, which will number 72 fighter and 12 light bomber squadrons.				Aug. 24
	Army Ground Forces Commander Gen. Jacob Devers authorizes creation of 315 Negro reserve units.			Ben Hogan wins the Professional Golfers Assn. title in Portland, Ore.	Aug. 25
U.S. District Court in Atlanta rejects a citizens' petition to void Georgia's unit-vote system.		OPA orders the arrest of six men in Leesville, S.C. in a drive against automobile black markets.		George Orwell's *Animal Farm* is published in N.Y. and becomes a Book of the Month Club selection .... *Brief Encounter*, a film based on Noel Coward's play *Still Life*, opens in N.Y.	Aug. 26
F *Includes elections, federal-state relations, civil rights and liberties, crime, the judiciary, education, health care, poverty, urban affairs and population.*	G *Includes formation and debate of U.S. foreign and defense policies, veterans affairs and defense spending. (Relations with specific foreign countries are usually found under the region concerned.)*	H *Includes business, labor, agriculture, taxation, transportation, consumer affairs, monetary and fiscal policy, natural resources, pollution and accidents.*	I *Includes worldwide scientific, medical and technological developments, natural phenomena, U.S. weather and natural disasters.*	J *Includes the arts, religion, scholarship, communications media, sports, entertainment, fashions, fads and social life.*	

	World Affairs	Europe	Africa & the Middle East	The Americas	Asia & the Pacific
Aug. 27	Molotov charges at the Paris Peace Conference that Australia is acting as a front for other Western nations in proposing numerous treaty amendments, while Australian delegate J.A. Beasely accuses Russia of attempting to thrust its views "down the throats" of other delegates .... International Education Conference ends in Endicott, N.Y., after approving the constitution of a World Organization of the Teaching Profession intended to improve the professional status of teachers and make "full and free education available to all without discrimination."	Gen. Robert McClure of the U.S. military government in Germany threatens to bar all Soviet-licensed newspapers and reporters from the U.S. zone unless Russia agrees by Sept. 16 to permit free exchange of German publications among the four occupation zones .... De Gaulle charges that the draft constitution now being debated by the French Constituent Assembly would create a weak state and empire .... In the opening session of the Hesse jewel theft trial, Army prosecutors in Frankfurt introduce Capt. Kathleen Nash Durant's confession that she and her husband, Col Jack Durant, collaborated with Maj. David Watson and Sgt. Roy Carlton in stealing the $1.5-million Hesse family jewels and smuggling them into the U.S.		Peron establishes the Argentine Foreign Trade Institute as the sole sales agent for the nation's meat exports.	Moslem League Pres. Mohammed Ali Jinnah orders all members to boycott Indian government meetings, including those of the new interim regime.
Aug. 28	U.S. representatives at the Paris Peace Conference defend Australia's right to present reparations demands against Yugoslavian charges that "big Western countries" seek to interfere in the "home affairs of small European nations." .... Acting U.S. delegate Herschel Johnson warns the U.N. Security Council that the U.S. will veto the Soviet-sponsored membership applications of Albania and Outer Mongolia.	Yugoslavian authorities deliver the bodies of five American soldiers killed in the Aug. 19 crash to the U.S. Army .... Moscow announces that food rationing will continue in Russia into 1947.			
Aug. 29	U.N. Security Council votes to admit Afghanistan, Iceland and Sweden to U.N. membership, while a Russian veto excludes Eire, Portugal and Transjordan .... In an effort to speed the work of the Paris Peace Conference, delegates of the Big Four meet at the French Foreign Office and promise to vote jointly on "the agreed articles of the draft treaties."	U.S. Army intelligence authorities in Stuttgart announce they have broken a pro-Soviet German spy ring.	British government reveals it has decided against inviting Jamal Amin el Husseini, Grand Mufti of Jerusalem, to a Sept. 9 conference on Palestine in London.		MacArthur bans strikes of Japanese workers "inimical to the objectives of the military occupation." .... Documents are introduced at the Tokyo war crimes trial to show that Japanese troops killed 280,000 Chinese in the 1937 "rape of Nanking." .... Nationalist forces report the capture of Chengte, a key transport junction northeast of Peking.
Aug. 30	World Bank reports that 32 of its 38 members have made their first capital payments, but that Norway, China, Greece, Poland, Czechoslovakia and Yugoslavia have requested postponements.	Speaking at the Paris Peace Conference, Molotov accuses the U.S. and Britain of interfering with Greek internal affairs and of supporting the present royalist government in an effort to influence the Sept. 1 plebiscite .... In a note to the U.S., Belgrade charges that since Aug. 19, 11 U.S. bombers, 14 fighters, and 7 transports have deliberately flown over Yugoslav territory.		Argentine Chamber of Deputies follows the Senate in approving the Act of Chapultepec and the U.N. Charter .... Brazil imposes an export embargo on grain, fertilizers, cotton and cottonseed, shoes, meat, scrap metal, leather and vegetable and animal oils.	MacArthur's headquarters reports the destruction of the Japanese military machine after one year of occupation .... Nationalist sources report that the Communists have taken Tatung, 100 miles southwest of Nanking on the Yangtze River, after a 25-day siege.
Aug. 31	Molotov leaves the Paris Peace Conference after being summoned to Moscow without explanation.	The nine-month Nuremberg war crimes trial ends after the 21 defendants make their final pleas. The judges announce that a verdict will be handed down Sept. 23 .... Greek government announces 31 arrests have been made in two days of clashes between Communists and royalists.			Chinese Premier T.V. Soong and U.S. Foreign Liquidation Commissioner Thomas McCabe announce the conclusion of a surplus property agreement which will give the Nationalist government more than $800 million in U.S. war goods.
Sept. 1		In a plebiscite on the Greek form of government, 70% of the electorate rejects a republic and votes to retain King George II .... Municipal elections in Russian-occupied Saxony give the Socialist Unity Party 56% of the vote .... Soviet Communist Party organ *Culture & Life* reports that the party's Central Committee has ordered a purge of Western and domestic plays that preach "bourgeois" ideology and anti-Soviet ideas .... French Socialist Party congress ends in Paris with an address by Leon Blum, after passing resolutions calling for continued independence from the Communists and condemning domination of the U.N. by the Big Four.		Brazilian government imposes martial law in Rio de Janeiro after four days of anti-inflation riots.	Japanese government Liquidation Commission sets Sept. 30 for the dissolution of Japan's five largest Zaibatsu holding companies: Mitsui, Mitsubishi, Sumitomo, Yasuda and Fuji Industrial .... Riots break out in Bombay as Moslems protest installation of the Hindu-dominated Indian interim government .... Communist leader Chou En-lai assails the U.S. surplus property deal with the Nationalist regime, saying "it is inconceivable that American peace envoys can mediate in China while the U.S. government [aids] the Kuomintang in waging war."
	A	B	C	D	E
	Includes developments that affect more than one world region, international organizations and important meetings of major world leaders.	*Includes all domestic and regional developments in Europe, including the Soviet Union, Turkey, Cyprus and Malta.*	*Includes all domestic and regional developments in Africa and the Middle East, including Iraq and Iran and excluding Cyprus, Turkey and Afghanistan.*	*Includes all domestic and regional developments in Latin America, the Caribbean and Canada.*	*Includes all domestic and regional developments in Asian and Pacific nations, extending from Afghanistan through all the Pacific Islands, except Hawaii.*

U.S. Politics & Social Issues	U.S. Foreign Policy & Defense	U.S. Economy & Environment	Science, Technology & Nature	Culture, Leisure & Life Style	
Roswell Biggers is arrested by the FBI on charges of holding five Negroes at forced labor on his farm near Atlanta, Ga.	War. Secy. Robert Patterson begins a series of secret atomic energy lectures before key Army personnel, claiming the U.S. must proceed "on the basis that there is and will be no adequate [international nuclear] control." . . . . Cpl. Harry J. Brickheimer successfully demonstrates an automatic ejection parachute device which catapults him from a speeding P-81.				Aug. 27
	Jewish National Fund of America forwards $5 million to Palestine, the largest single contribution ever made to the Zionist cause . . . . Former OSS Chief Gen. William Donovan is named to head the American Institute of International Information, a new nonprofit organization that will seek information on world problems.	Agriculture Secy. Clinton Anderson orders an increase in meat prices over OPA objections.	A long distance call between Milwaukee and an auto 135 miles away inaugurates the world's first highway mobile radio-telephone system . . . . Dr. Charles Coale Price, chemistry department head at the Univ. of Notre Dame, is awarded the American Chemical Society Prize in Pure Chemistry for 1946.	A joint meeting of American and National League owners in Chicago votes to give players representation in formulating rules and policies and agrees to set a minimum salary and establish a pension fund.	Aug. 28
Pennsylvania Gov. Edward Martin orders state police to probe KKK activities and asks the Justice Dept. for FBI assistance.	Grand Army of the Republic ends its 80th encampment in Indianapolis, attended by 11 former Union civil war soldiers who vote to continue their annual meetings.				Aug. 29
	Acting State Secy. Dean Acheson announces the U.S. will claim indemnity from Yugoslavia for damages and lives lost in the downing of two U.S. planes.			Paul Mantz wins the Bendix trophy air race, averaging 435.604 mph in a P-51 for the 2,048 miles from California to Cleveland.	Aug. 30
	U.S. Navy ends its demobilization program reporting 3,070,581 discharges since V-J Day.	N.Y.C. trucking halts as 12,000 members of the AFL Teamsters union strike in a dispute over wage, hour, and vacation demands . . . . Agriculture Dept. lifts price controls on all fruits and vegetables except oranges and bananas . . . . In a Labor Day statement released by the White House, Truman praises U.S. workers and says the country can "maintain and increase" production and employment "if we carry on together as we did during wartime." . . . . Senate War Investigating Committee issues its annual report, recommending an industrial mobilization plan kept up to date with technological developments and a clear government production control system.		*New Yorker* devotes its entire issue to novelist John Hersey's account of the nuclear destruction of Hiroshima, emphasizing "the terrible implications" of the atom bomb.	Aug. 31
	U.S. Naval Academy reports that only 879 midshipmen have entered the class of 1950, the lowest number since 1939.	CIO Longshoremen's and Warehousemen's Union calls a strike of its 25,000 Hawaiian sugar plantation workers for a 15¢ hourly wage increase.			Sept. 1

F	G	H	I	J
Includes elections, federal-state relations, civil rights and liberties, crime, the judiciary, education, health care, poverty, urban affairs and population.	*Includes formation and debate of U.S. foreign and defense policies, veterans affairs and defense spending. (Relations with specific foreign countries are usually found under the region concerned.)*	*Includes business, labor, agriculture, taxation, transportation, consumer affairs, monetary and fiscal policy, natural resources, pollution and accidents.*	*Includes worldwide scientific, medical and technological developments, natural phenomena, U.S. weather and natural disasters.*	*Includes the arts, religion, scholarship, communications media, sports, entertainment, fashions, fads and social life.*

	World Affairs	Europe	Africa & the Middle East	The Americas	Asia & the Pacific
Sept. 2	U.N. Food and Agricultural Organization opens its annual conference in Copenhagen. A world food survey shows a continued gap of eight million tons between world food needs and supplies .... Britain files a $11.2-billion reparations claim against Italy at the Paris Peace Conference, reportedly hoping the move will force a study of Italy's capacity to pay.	*Pravda* announces that the Soviet Communist Party has ordered Ukrainian authors to stop trying to spread Ukrainian nationalism.		Panama's National Assembly passes a resolution calling on the U.S. to relinquish immediately the 131 defense bases in the country granted during the war .... Praising ratification of the Act of Chapultepec and the U.N. Charter by the Argentine Congress, Peron tells diplomats that misunderstandings between Argentina and other Western Hemisphere nations are now at an end.	MacArthur warns that the customary regimentation of the Japanese people may make them "easy prey" for Communism. His statement is criticized as "unwarranted" by middle-level State Dept. officials in Washington .... Philippine government begins a drive against Hukbalahap guerrillas in central Luzon who failed to surrender their arms by Sept. 1 .... India's first all-Indian Executive Council, composed of Hindu and Moslem representatives, assumes office in New Delhi.
Sept. 3	After 18 hours of debate, the U.N. Security Council votes to consider Ukrainian charges that the Greek royalist government is endangering peace in the Balkans .... Paris Peace Conference Military Commission fixes Italy's armed forces at 297,500 men and adopts a British proposal permitting former fascist officers to serve in the new army providing they have been "exonerated by the appropriate body under Italian law."	Acting State Secy. William Clayton denies Tito government charges that the U.S. has repeatedly violated Yugoslavian airspace, noting that U.S. Air Force records indicate no flights near Yugoslavian territory.	Cairo reports that Syria has refused to discuss oil and transport agreements with the U.S. because of American sympathy towards Zionism.		
Sept. 4		French Constituent Assembly approves a two-house parliament consisting of a National Assembly with legislative powers and an Advisory Council.		Leftist Gabriel Gonzalez Videla defeats Conservative Eduardo Cruz Coke in Chile's presidential election but does not win a majority in the four-way race, leaving Congress to chose from the two candidates.	China's Foreign Ministry discloses the country has suffered $30-40 billion in damage during eight years of war and claims 40% of Japanese reparations.
Sept. 5	Soviet Deputy Foreign Min. Andrei Vishinsky urges the Italian Political and Territorial Commission of the Paris Peace Conference to support Yugoslavia's claim to the whole of Istria and Trieste. The Rumanian Commission awards the predominantly Hungarian area of Transylvania to Rumania .... British U.N. delegate Sir Alexander Cadogan lables Ukrainian charges against Greece "unbridled propaganda."	Gen. Lucius Clay of the U.S. military government in Germany announces plans for the economic unification of the British and U.S. zones, involving the creation of German bizonal agencies responsible for finance, food and agriculture, economics and transport.			
Sept. 6	U.S. State Secy. Byrnes tells the Paris Peace Conference that the current Polish-German border is not final but is subject to future revision .... In a major policy address before German officials in Stuttgart, Byrnes urges that Germany be reunited under a provisional government, opposes French proposals to sever the Rhineland and Ruhr and rejects Russian demands for $10 billion in reparations.	Italy and Austria announce a compromise on South Tyrol allowing the territory to remain Italian but giving regional autonomy to its German-speaking inhabitants.			U.S. forces in Seoul, Korea close three leftist newspapers, including the local Communist organ, for encouraging unrest against the occupation authorities.
Sept. 7	Italian Political and Territorial Commission of the Paris Peace Conference rejects a Brazilian proposal that the questions of Trieste and the Italian-Yugoslav frontier be postponed for one year.	Greek Acting Premier Stylianos Gonatas reinstates martial law due to internal disorders following the popular plebiscite on the Greek monarchy Sept. 1.			Jawaharlal Nehru, head of the interim Indian government, says in a radio address that free India will stand aside from "power politics" and continue working against "the curse of untouchability." Hindu-Moslem riots continue for the seventh day in Bombay and spread to Calcutta and other cities, leaving 220 dead and 659 injured.
Sept. 8		Bulgarian voters approve a referendum to replace their country's monarchy with a republic, the sixth European nation to do so since the end of the war .... Communist-organized "squatters," protesting an acute housing shortage in Britain, seize the Duchess of Bedford's house and nine other luxury buildings in London .... Protesting a statement by Secy. Byrnes that the Polish-German frontier is not final, Polish Communists demonstrate before the U.S. ambassador's residence in Warsaw.	Explosives planted by the Zionist Irgun Zvai organization cut the Palestine railway in 50 places. Irgun leaders say the action is a protest against the upcoming London conference on Palestine.		Communist leader Chou En-lai says his party will not seek any Russian aid in order to preserve its own independence.
Sept. 9	U.N. Secy. Gen. Lie approves postponement of the scheduled Sept. 23 General Assembly meeting for one month after a request from Russian, French, Chinese and Belgian delegations at the Paris Peace Conference .... Speaking at the U.N. Security Council, U.S. delegate Herschel Johnson and Australian delegate Paul Hasluck reject Ukrainian charges of Greek aggression in the Balkans on grounds of insufficient evidence.	Yugoslavian Deputy Foreign Min. Alesh Bebler begins a filibuster before the Paris Peace Conference's Italian Political and Territorial Commission to avert a showdown on Yugoslavia's demand for more Italian territory.		Caribbean Regional Air Navigation Conference meeting in Washington proposes setting up nine Caribbean air control centers.	

U.S. Politics & Social Issues	U.S. Foreign Policy & Defense	U.S. Economy & Environment	Science, Technology & Nature	Culture, Leisure & Life Style	
Truman returns to Washington after his 18-day Atlantic cruise.		OPA authorizes price increases of 10% on wool fabrics.		Alvin Johnston wins the Thompson Trophy Race in Cleveland, averaging 373.908 mph over the 300-mile course in a Bell Airacobra for $19,200 in prizes.	Sept. 2
J. Strom Thurmond wins the South Carolina gubernatorial nomination in a Democratic run-off election .... Charles Falconer Stearns, Supreme Court Chief Justice from 1929 to 1935, dies at 80 in Providence, R.I.	National War College opens in Washington with a student body of 100 State Dept., Army and Navy officers.	Leading stocks fall 2 to 17 points on the N.Y. Stock Exchange, the biggest drop in 16 years.			Sept. 3
N.Y. Democrats nominate Sen. James Mead for governor to oppose the GOP incumbent, Thomas Dewey.		Ten thousand New Jersey truck drivers begin a sympathy strike to support the wage demands of 15,000 striking N.Y. Teamsters.		Ben Hecht's and Charles MacArthur's newspaper melodrama *The Front Page* opens on Broadway to favorable reviews.	Sept. 4
Virginia's Democratic State Convention names Rep. Willis Robertson to succeed the late Sen. Carter Glass .... Indiana Gov. Ralph Gates demands an investigation of possible subversive influences in the faculties of Indiana Univ. and Indiana State Teachers College.	Despite pleas from UNRRA director La Guardia, N.Y. longshoremen refuse to load a freighter with relief supplies for Yugoslavia due to Yugoslavian attacks on U.S. aircraft.	More than 60,000 members of the AFL Seafarers Union and the AFL Sailors Union tie up Atlantic, Pacific and Gulf shipping in a dispute over the Wage Stabilization Board's rejection of a wage raise won through collective bargaining.	Speaking at the American Congress of Physical Medicines in N.Y., Dr. Russell Reynolds of Britain describes a method of making X-ray motion pictures without harm to the patient.	Formation of Alaska's first radio network, the Alaska Broadcasting System, is announced in Anchorage.	Sept. 5
		A presidential emergency board considering the wage demands of Pullman porters and conductors recommends a $44.40 monthly increase.			Sept. 6
	Truman announces his decision to suspend further atomic testing, claiming that tests already conducted are sufficient for "a proper evaluation" of the bomb .... Navy reveals that the new battleship *Kentucky* and battlecruiser *Hawaii* are being redesigned as "guided missile warships."	CIO United Electrical, Radio and Machine Workers union ends an eight-month strike against Phelps-Dodge Copper Products in New Jersey with an agreement providing for an 18½¢ hourly wage increase.	British Group Capt. E.M. Donaldson sets a world speed record of 616 mph in a Gloster Meteor jet over Littlehampton, England.		Sept. 7
Senate War Investigating committee discloses Henry Garsson's testimony that Rep. Andrew May (D, Ky.) received no pay from Garsson armaments firms.		CIO Pres. Murray withdraws the CIO from the International Labor Organization after a Labor Dept. decision making the AFL sole U.S. representative at the upcoming Montreal ILO conference.		John Kramer defeats Tom Brown to win the national singles amateur tennis title at Forrest Hills, N.Y.; Pauline Betz tops Doris Hart for the women's crown.	Sept. 8
Sen. James Mead announces he will resign as chairman of the Senate War Investigating committee because of his nomination for the N.Y. governorship. He also repudiates Communist support he has been offered in the election .... Republicans win all major offices in Maine elections, re-electing Gov. Horace Hildreth, Sen. Owen Brewster, and Reps. Robert Hale, Frank Fellows and Margaret C. Smith.	Pres. Joseph Ryan of the International Longshoremen's Assn. says union members will not load any relief ships destined for Yugoslavia until proper action is taken against those responsible for shooting U.S. planes down.		IT&T demonstrates a new radio broadcasting method which sends eight programs from one transmitter and unscrambles them in a single receiver.		Sept. 9
F	G	H	I	J	
Includes elections, federal-state relations, civil rights and liberties, crime, the judiciary, education, health care, poverty, urban affairs and population.	*Includes formation and debate of U.S. foreign and defense policies, veterans affairs and defense spending. (Relations with specific foreign countries are usually found under the region concerned.)*	*Includes business, labor, agriculture, taxation, transportation, consumer affairs, monetary and fiscal policy, natural resources, pollution and accidents.*	*Includes worldwide scientific, medical and technological developments, natural phenomena, U.S. weather and natural disasters.*	*Includes the arts, religion, scholarship, communications media, sports, entertainment, fashions, fads and social life.*	

	World Affairs	Europe	Africa & the Middle East	The Americas	Asia & the Pacific
Sept. 10		U.S. Under Secy. of State William Clayton says Yugoslavia tentatively agrees to indemnify families of five downed American airmen but objects to paying for the two planes . . . . Russian members of the Allied command in Berlin protest the U.S. Army's sports program, in which German children are taught baseball and football, and the sending of U.S. food packages to Berliners . . . . Russia agrees to pay about $140 million for the $160 million worth of non-consumer civilian goods contracted for with the British government in 1941.	British P.M. Attlee opens the Palestine Conference in London, with 15 Arab delegates present but no Jewish organizations represented. Attlee calls for compromise in Palestine on both sides and says Britain is not committed to any existing federalization plan.	U.S. State Dept. announces Brazil will receive only $50 million of the $350 million it requested for transportation improvement from Export-Import Bank.	
Sept. 11	Russian Security Council delegate Gromyko assails the presence of U.S. warships and British troops in Greece as an "insult to the Greek people" and a "threat to peace." Greek delegate Vassili Dendramis replies that his government invited the British force.	U.S. Commander in Austria Gen. Mark Clark charges the Russians in eastern Austria "take almost everything on the ground that it is a German asset." . . . . Albania announces the signing of an Albanian-Yugoslav naval pact, while a Rome report says Albania has concentrated two large forces on the Greek border.			Five thousand Japanese march on the Russian embassy in Tokyo to demand repatriation of Japanese prisoners still held by Russia . . . . In an effort to reopen peace negotiations in China, Gen. Marshall confers with Chiang Kai-shek in Kuling and then with Chou En-lai in Nanking.
Sept. 12		Oscar Wilhelm, government-appointed administrator of Jewish properties in Austria, is reportedly sentenced to two years imprisonment by Soviet authorities for resisting Russian seizure of Jewish property.	Egyptian Premier Ismail Sidky Pasha forms a new three-party cabinet with Ibrahim Abdul Hadi Pasha as foreign minister.	Panama and the U.S. agree to negotiate the return of 131 military bases held by the U.S.	
Sept. 13	U.N. Subcommission on Economic Reconstruction of Devastated Areas adopts its final report, urging creation of an economic commission in Europe to supervise reconstruction . . . . A U.N. Food and Agriculture Organization meeting in Copenhagen ends after passing a resolution supporting proposals for a world food board and an international price stabilization program . . . . White Russian Foreign Min. K.V. Kisselev walks out on a meeting of the Bulgarian Political and Territorial Commission at the Paris Peace Conference to prevent a vote on Greek frontier claims against Bulgaria.	About 300,000 public workers end a six-day strike in northern Italy after the government promises partial fulfillment of their demands for a 100% wage increase and price control enforcement.			
Sept. 14	After returning to the Paris Peace Conference from Moscow, Molotov assails the U.S. and Britain for attempting "to form another bloc directed against peace-loving countries," and warns that continuation of this policy will bring another world war.	Britain commemorates the defeat of the Luftwaffe in the Battle of Britain with a London air show including 300 British and U.S. planes.			Vietnamese nationalist leader Ho Chi Minh and French Colonial Min. Marius Moutet sign an accord in Paris after two months of negotiation, recognizing French property and business interests in Vietnam and the right of France to conduct French education. One important issue, the Vietnamese claim to Cochin China, remains unresolved.
Sept. 15		German Socialist Unity Party wins large victories in communal elections in Soviet-occupied Mecklenburg and Brandenburg provinces, but Social Democrats carry elections in the British zone . . . . Bulgaria is officially proclaimed a People's Republic . . . . Russia's secret police organization, the People's Commissariat of Internal Affairs (NKVD), is renamed Ministry of Internal Affairs (MGB).			
Sept. 16	Responding to Secy. Byrnes' Sept. 6 statement on the Polish-German border, Molotov states at the Paris Peace Conference that the Oder-Neisse line is final and awaits only formal confirmation.		British Foreign Secy. Bevin attempts to convince Arab delegates at the Palestine conference of the viability of a binational state in Palestine . . . . Arab Party in Jerusalem announces it is organizing a militia to defend Arabs against Zionist terrorism.		

A	B	C	D	E
Includes developments that affect more than one world region, international organizations and important meetings of major world leaders.	*Includes all domestic and regional developments in Europe, including the Soviet Union, Turkey, Cyprus and Malta.*	*Includes all domestic and regional developments in Africa and the Middle East, including Iraq and Iran and excluding Cyprus, Turkey and Afghanistan.*	*Includes all domestic and regional developments in Latin America, the Caribbean and Canada.*	*Includes all domestic and regional developments in Asian and Pacific nations, extending from Afghanistan through all the Pacific Islands, except Hawaii.*

U.S. Politics & Social Issues	U.S. Foreign Policy & Defense	U.S. Economy & Environment	Science, Technology & Nature	Culture, Leisure & Life Style	
		N.Y. Mayor William O'Dwyer charges that Communist agitators are behind the 10-day trucking strike which has tied up the city, and demands that Teamsters President Daniel Tobin come to New York to "take control" of the local union organization . . . . OPA re-establishes meat price ceilings, but no meat is available in cities as farmers withhold steers from the market . . . . CIO National Maritime Union Pres. Joseph Curran warns Truman and Labor Secy. Schwellenbach that CIO maritime workers expect wage parity with AFL workers in the current maritime contract dispute.		At their 55th triennial convention in Philadelphia, deputies of the Episcopal Church elect former Supreme Court Justice Owen Roberts as the church's first lay president and Mrs. Randolph Dyer as the first woman deputy.	Sept. 10
	Sen. Robert Taft (R, O.) says Truman's policy towards Russia has "only helped to build up the greatest totalitarian state the world has ever seen."		U.S. Navy announces it plans to construct the "world's largest centrifuge" for human use to test the effects of supersonic speed on the human body.	Brooklyn Dodgers and Cincinnati Reds battle to the longest scoreless tie (19 innings) in baseball history.	Sept. 11
Ex-Labor Secy. Frances Perkins is appointed Civil Service Commissioner by Truman.	In a controversial N.Y. speech, Commerce Secy. Henry Wallace warns against growing "get tough with Russia" sentiment in the U.S., saying "the tougher we get, the tougher the Russians will get." He also attacks British "imperialism" in the Middle East and urges U.N. control of atomic bombs and military bases "with which the U.S. and Britain have encircled the world." Truman in Washington says he has read and endorsed the speech, and does not think it contradicts Secy. Byrnes's policy at the Paris Peace Conference.	OPA permits a 15% price increase on some small electrical appliances and clothing items.		A group of prominent authors, including John Erskine, Benjamin Stolberg and Katherine Bush, form an American Writers Assn. to counteract alleged Communist efforts to gain "monopoly control" over U.S. literary output . . . . Babe Ruth sells screen rights to his life story to Howard Hughes Productions.	Sept. 12
FBI Dir. J. Edgar Hoover reports that juvenile crime in the U.S. is on the wane, down almost 3% over the first six months of 1945.	Republicans and Southern Democrats attack Truman's endorsement of Wallace's N.Y. speech, claiming the President has "betrayed" Secy. Byrnes in Paris. Byrnes himself is reported to be "deeply disturbed" by the speech.		American Chemical Society ends its Chicago convention after appropriating $25,000 to enable foreign chemists to study in the U.S.		Sept. 13
	In response to growing controversy over Wallace's N.Y. speech, Truman says he supports the Commerce Secretary's right to speak but did not intend to indicate approval of the speech as a statement of U.S. foreign policy.	CIO National Maritime Union extends its strike on the East and Gulf coasts to include coal carriers and foreign flag ships under NMU contract and withdraws security watches from ships with perishable goods.			Sept. 14
		AFL Upholsterers' International Union announces it will admit 5,000 workers who left the CIO United Furniture Workers union due to alleged Communist domination.	CBS demonstrates a color TV which is "suitable for commercial manufacture."	The Very Rev. John Baptist Janssens is elected General of the Society of Jesus in Rome by representatives of the order from 33 countries . . . . Federal Security Agency reports that the U.S. divorce rate rose in 1945 to one-third the total number of marriages.	Sept. 15
	Responding to criticism of his Sept. 12 speech, Commerce Secy. Wallace reiterates his support for friendship with Russia.	OPA orders restaurant prices on meals and food items that have meat as the major ingredient set back to June 30 levels.		A baseball policy committee adjourns in N.Y. after setting a major league minimum salary of $5,000 and limiting pay cuts to 25%.	Sept. 16

	World Affairs	Europe	Africa & the Middle East	The Americas	Asia & the Pacific
Sept. 17		Reports from Greece indicate widespread fighting between royalist troops and Communists in the mountains of Thessaly and Macedonia. Royalists are charged with using "brutal and inhumane" methods against insurgents and manipulating the UNRRA relief program to gain support for the monarchy . . . . A revised Anglo-French debt settlement is signed in Paris, allowing France to repay its 110-million pound debt to Britain at ½% interest starting in 1950.		Argentina and Britain conclude a trade and investment agreement . . . . Brazil's National Assembly approves a new constitution to replace the charter adopted under former dictator-president Getulio Vargas in 1937.	Nationalist forces claim the capture of Tsing Kiang, the main Communist base in northern Kiangsu Province near Nanking.
Sept. 18	Russia and the U.S. clash at the Paris Peace Conference over Russian unwillingness to submit treaty disputes to the International Court of Justice.	Archbishop Aloysius Stepinac, Catholic primate of Yugoslavia, is arrested and charged with "crimes against the people" for allegedly collaborating with Croatian fascists during the war.			
Sept. 19	International Labor Organization opens its 29th conference in Montreal with Canadian Labor Min. Humphrey Mitchell as president.	U.S. military authorities in Germany announce a land reform project which will break up estates larger than 250 acres in the American zone into small farm holdings . . . . Speaking at the University of Zurich, Churchill calls for a "partnership" between France and Germany as the first step in the creation of a "United States of Europe."			Chou En-lai breaks off peace negotiations in Nanking, charging the Nationalists and Americans with basing their policies on the assumption of war with Russia.
Sept. 20	U.N. Committee on Refugees votes for a Russian proposal to repatriate displaced children to their countries of origin and to permit such countries the right to control propaganda in refugee camps . . . . British Transport and General Workers Union Secy. Arthur Deakin is elected provisional president of the World Federation of Trade Unions . . . . After 12 meetings and eight ballots the U.N. Security Council votes to drop the Greek issue.	Yugoslavian Deputy Premier Edward Kardelj notifies the Italian Political and Territorial Commission of the Paris Peace Conference that Yugoslavia "will not be bound by any decisions of this conference" after the commision rejects all Yugoslavian amendments to the Trieste and Italian border agreements . . . . British government brings an end to the "squatter" movement by agreeing to house 20,000 homeless in 718 unused Army camps . . . . Britain reports 12 killed in its worst floods in 30 years, caused by torrential rains and gales.	A nine-man committee is appointed at the Palestine Conference in London to study Arab proposals for an independent Palestine in which Jewish rights would be guaranteed.		Japanese Diet passes laws introducing popular election of prefectural officials.
Sept. 21		French Constituent Assembly passes the new constitution on its first reading.		Bolivian government removes all Supreme Court justices for "collaboration" with the ousted Villarroel regime.	
Sept. 22		A Soviet-licensed German newspaper, the *Berliner Zeitung*, charges American authorities are sanctioning the secret manufacture of munitions in their zone.	Fars Province tribesmen revolt against the Iranian government, demanding autonomy, and capture the Persian Gulf port of Ganaveh.		Chou En-lai says American mediation of the China dispute is "neither fair nor impartial," and accuses the U.S. of violating the Big Three Moscow pledge to withdraw from China.
Sept. 23	Gromyko charges before the Security Council that continued presence of U.S. troops in China, Brazil, Iceland and Panama and British troops in Egypt, Greece and Indonesia are a possible threat to world peace . . . . Russia's delegate to UNESCO, Nikolai Feonov, charges the U.N. has failed to solve the refugee problem and that the Anglo-American delegations have rejected almost all of Russia's proposals for the International Refugee Organization.	U.S. embassy in Belgrade is notified that Roy Stoeckel, an American civilian, is being held on charges of entering Yugoslavia illegally and photographing "prohibited objects." . . . . U.S. and British authorities increase the basic German ration in their zone by 340 calories, to 1,550 calories per person per day . . . . British newsprint restrictions are partially lifted, allowing London newspapers to issue 6-12 page editions.			
	A *Includes developments that affect more than one world region, international organizations and important meetings of major world leaders.*	B *Includes all domestic and regional developments in Europe, including the Soviet Union, Turkey, Cyprus and Malta.*	C *Includes all domestic and regional developments in Africa and the Middle East, including Iraq and Iran and excluding Cyprus, Turkey and Afghanistan.*	D *Includes all domestic and regional developments in Latin America, the Caribbean and Canada.*	E *Includes all domestic and regional developments in Asian and Pacific nations, extending from Afghanistan through all the Pacific Islands, except Hawaii.*

U.S. Politics & Social Issues	U.S. Foreign Policy & Defense	U.S. Economy & Environment	Science, Technology & Nature	Culture, Leisure & Life Style	
In discussions with Democratic candidates and campaign managers from five states, Truman expresses his hope for election of a Democratic Congress that will carry out his recommendations . . . . Conn. Democrats nominate Lt. Gov. Wilber Snow for governor over Chester Bowles.	Commerce Secy. Wallace releases a letter to Truman charging "there is a school of military thinking [which] advocates a 'preventive' war" on Russia before the Soviets acquire the atomic bomb.	Teamsters union members end the 2½-week N.Y. trucking strike by ratifying an agreement for a 31¢ hourly wage increase and a 40-hour week with vacation and overtime adjustments . . . . A 15-day strike against 41 N.Y. hotels by the American Federation of Musicians ends with agreement on a 20% wage increase . . . . Following an AFL threat to cross waterfront picket lines, CIO unions withdraw pickets from East and Gulf Coast ships under contract to the AFL.			Sept. 17
Charles Andrews, Democratic Senator from Florida, dies at 69 in Bethesda, Md.	After a 2½-hour conference with Truman, Wallace says he will not make public speeches until the Paris conference ends and he will not resign as Commerce Secretary . . . . State Dept. announces formation of a 100-member U.S. National Commission on Educational, Scientific and Cultural Cooperation to serve as a link with UNESCO.	Wildcat UAW strikes at Chrysler and Briggs Mfg. Co. plants in Detroit idle more than 50,000 workers.		Joe Louis successfully defends his heavyweight title for the 23rd time with a first round knockout of Tami Mauriello in Yankee Stadium in N.Y. . . . . Network Hooperatings list as most popular shows: *Mr. District Attorney, Charlie McCarthy Show, Screen Guild Players,* and *Walter Winchell* . . . . *Film Daily*'s poll of the nation's screen critics names Alfred Hitchcock as the best director of 1945-46 for his film *Spellbound.*	Sept. 18
	State Dept. releases a proposal for a world trade charter detailing a code of practices and proposing creation of an International Trade Organization.		Physicist J.A. Van Allen of Johns Hopkins University reveals that tests of German V-2 rockets have disclosed a belt of cosmic rays 20 miles above the earth with a radiation level 300 times greater than that found on the surface . . . . Army Chemical Corps Chief Gen. Alden Waitt reports the development of an unnamed bacteria toxin, "perhaps the most highly toxic substance known," but says it has been isolated only in minute quantities . . . . Dutch paleontologist G.H.R. von Koenigswald, held for 30 months in Japanese prison camps, arrives in N.Y. with the bones of Java Man, the earliest known human being who lived 500,000 years ago.	Univ. of Chicago Chancellor Robert Hutchins announces he is taking a leave of absence to direct the adult education program of Encyclopedia Brtiannica, Inc.	Sept. 19
	After conferring with Secy. Byrnes in Paris, Truman asks for and receives the resignation of Secy. Wallace. The President attributes the move to a "fundamental conflict" between the foreign policy views of Wallace and the Administration. In a radio address following his dismissal, Wallace declares that "winning the peace is more important than high public office," and urges his listeners to work for a peaceful U.S. foreign policy as "a holy duty."	CIO National Maritime Union ends its strike against Atlantic and Gulf shipping owners, who agree to FCC Chmn. James Fly's arbitration award giving the NMU wage parity with AFL maritime unions.	A 100-mile-an-hour typhoon sweeps the Marianas, causing $1.5-million in damage to the U.S. naval base at Guam.	First National Youth Convention of the Protestant Episcopal Church adjourns in Philadelphia after passing resolutions urging friendship with Russia and endorsing the U.N.	Sept. 20
	A Senate Military Affairs subcommittee charges that favoritism and "lax, incompetent practices" are prevalent in the War Assets Admin.	A federal court in Danville, Ill. convicts 16 officers of the A&P food chain for conspiring to restrain trade and "to monopolize a substantial part of [food] products in interstate commerce."		Father Manuel Suarez of Spain is named master general of the Order of Preaching Friars (Dominicans) in Rome.	Sept. 21
Truman names W. Averell Harriman, U.S. ambassador to Britain, to succeed Wallace as Commerce Secretary.	A group of 139 American writers headed by Dorothy C. Fisher petitions Truman to free 1,500 conscientious objectors still in prison . . . . Columnist Drew Pearson reports that the men behind Truman's dismissal of Wallace were Sens. Tom Connally (D, Tex.) and Arthur Vandenberg (R, Mich.), presidential adviser James Farley and John Foster Dulles, adviser to Gov. Thomas Dewey.	Detroit firms recall workers as strikes end at the Briggs and Chrysler plants.			Sept. 22
An American Crusade to End Lynching delegation led by singer Paul Robeson warns Truman that if the government does not take steps to halt mob violence "the Negroes will." . . . . Champlain College, the first "GI university" in America, opens in Plattsburg, N.Y. with state and private support.		GAO accountant Ralph Casey declares before the House Merchant Marine Committee that 19 firms operating government-built shipyards during the war made estimated profits of $356 million on capital investments of $23 million, a profit ratio which he calls a "gift."			Sept. 23

F	G	H	I	J
Includes elections, federal-state relations, civil rights and liberties, crime, the judiciary, education, health care, poverty, urban affairs and population.	*Includes formation and debate of U.S. foreign and defense policies, veterans affairs and defense spending. (Relations with specific foreign countries are usually found under the region concerned.)*	*Includes business, labor, agriculture, taxation, transportation, consumer affairs, monetary and fiscal policy, natural resources, pollution and accidents.*	*Includes worldwide scientific, medical and technological developments, natural phenomena, U.S. weather and natural disasters.*	*Includes the arts, religion, scholarship, communications media, sports, entertainment, fashions, fads and social life.*

	World Affairs	Europe	Africa & the Middle East	The Americas	Asia & the Pacific
Sept. 24	Answering questions submitted by Alexander Werth of the London *Sunday Times*, Stalin says he does not feel the danger of war exists at present, but he claims that U.S. monopoly on atomic weapons is a threat to peace. He also reaffirms "unconditionally" his desire for "friendly and lasting collaboration" with the West.	Following Turkish rejection of a Soviet demand for joint defense of the Dardanelles, Russia warns Turkey against organizing "military measures" in the Straits with any non-Black Sea power.		Martial law is decreed in El Salvador as opposition parties call a general strike to force cabinet and police reorganization.	
Sept. 25	U.N. Secy. Gen. Lie complains at the Montreal International Labor Organization conference that the Security Council veto rule prevents the U.N. from acting as a referee among the Big Five . . . . Russian delegate Nikolai Feonov rejects a UNESCO subcommission's recommendation for creation of a central coordinating committee for European reconstruction, objecting to U.S. membership on the proposed body . . . . A meeting of the 13-nation Provisional International Civil Aviation Organization in London agrees to operate 13 weather ships along North Atlantic air routes.	Greek Premier Constantin Tsaldaris blames "foreign influences" for disorders in the country and says that fighting between royalists and Communists has reached civil war intensity . . . . Italy's Christian Democratic Premier Alcide de Gasperi receives a vote of confidence in parliament after a long debate on financial and economic problems.	A council of Zionist organizations in Jerusalem votes not to let the Jewish Agency for Palestine take part in the London Conference until interned Zionist leaders are released.		Jawaharlal Nehru resigns as president of the Congress Party's executive committee so he can devote more time to India's interim government.
Sept. 26		Soviet Council of Ministers orders eight Communist Party leaders and collective farm officials in the Ukraine dismissed and prosecuted for graft . . . . U.S. Information Service operations in Belgrade are halted by U.S. Amb. Richard Patterson at the demand of the Yugoslav government.	Teheran reports that Moslem religious leaders in Persian Gulf ports have demanded autonomy for their areas.		Following British policy in India, Gov. of Burma Sir Hubert Rance forms an executive council with representatives of all parties to prepare for independence . . . . Japanese Education Ministry reports that 743 teachers have been dismissed out of 80,508 screened under MacArthur's purge directive.
Sept. 27	Despite Soviet bloc opposition, the Italian Political and Territorial Commission of the Paris Peace Conference adopts a U.S.-British-French proposal that disputes arising from the Italian treaty be submitted to the International Court of Justice . . . . Governors of the World Bank and International Monetary Fund hold their first business meeting in Washington.			A mob in La Paz hangs former Lt. Oblitas Bustamente after he tries to assassinate Bolivian Pres. Tomas Monje Guitierrez.	Renewed Hindu-Moslem rioting in India, continuing for five days, results in 23 deaths and 80 injuries in Agra, Calcutta, Bombay and Dacca . . . . Prosecutors at the Tokyo war crimes trial introduce 170 documents to show that Germany encouraged Japan to strike at Britain and the U.S. in the Pacific.
Sept. 28	Italian Political and Territorial Commission of the Paris Peace Conference approves the French-proposed Italian-Yugoslav border, providing for internationalization of Trieste as a free city. Yugoslavian Deputy Premier Kardelj says Yugoslavia will refuse to sign any treaty containing the proposed border, nor will it withdraw its forces from northwest Istria.	King George II returns to Greece after 5½ years of exile . . . . A week-old strike of bank personnel ends in France when union leaders win a 25% wage increase.	Premier Ghavam rejects demands for regional autonomy in Iran, while the Iranian ambassador in London asks the British government to investigate charges that British diplomatic officials in southern Iran have encouraged autonomy movements . . . . Ismail Sidky Pasha resigns as Egyptian premier after failing to reach agreement with Britain on an Anglo-Egyptian military pact.		
Sept. 29	A British-U.S. proposal to include most-favored-nation trade provisions in the Italian and Rumanian treaties is adopted over Russian opposition by the Economic Commissions for Italy and the Balkans at the Paris Peace Conference . . . . Soviet organ *Pravda* comments that U.S. Army training activities in the Arctic "do not assist toward strengthening peace and trust among peoples."				
Sept. 30	At the Paris Peace Conference, Britain and the U.S. drop their demand that specific measures guaranteeing nondiscriminatory administration of Danube River traffic be written into the Rumanian treaty, supporting a French proposal which affirms free navigation in principle. The Economic Commission for the Balkans and Finland approves the proposal over Soviet opposition.	Yugoslav Archbishop Stepinac goes on trial in Zagreb for treason . . . . A U.S. court martial in Frankfurt sentences WAC Capt. Kathleen Durant to dishonorable discharge and five years hard labor for her part in the Hesse jewel robbery.			U.S. Army announces termination of its China Command in Shanghai.

A	B	C	D	E
Includes developments that affect more than one world region, international organizations and important meetings of major world leaders.	*Includes all domestic and regional developments in Europe, including the Soviet Union, Turkey, Cyprus and Malta.*	*Includes all domestic and regional developments in Africa and the Middle East, including Iraq and Iran and excluding Cyprus, Turkey and Afghanistan.*	*Includes all domestic and regional developments in Latin America, the Caribbean and Canada.*	*Includes all domestic and regional developments in Asian and Pacific nations, extending from Afghanistan through all the Pacific Islands, except Hawaii.*

U.S. Politics & Social Issues	U.S. Foreign Policy & Defense	U.S. Economy & Environment	Science, Technology & Nature	Culture, Leisure & Life Style	
		A common pleas court in Pittsburgh sentences Pres. George Mueller of the independent Duquesne Light Co. workers union to one year in jail when the union strikes despite an anti-strike injunction issued Sept. 9 . . . . Appearing before the House Merchant Marine Comm., Henry Kaiser states that shipyard operations of four of his companies showed a net loss of $13 million because of ventures in steel and magnesium but admits that these companies brought his family $16,362,000 after taxes.			Sept. 24
	Army begins to assemble 1,500 men in Fairbanks, Alaska for Task Force Frigid, which will test the operation of personnel and equipment in arctic conditions.				Sept. 25
Clarence Norris, a defendant in the "Scottsboro Case" 15 years ago, is paroled in Montgomery, Ala. after serving nine years of a life sentence. Only one of the defendants, Haywood Patterson, remains in prison . . . . An estate tax return filed in Poughkeepsie, N.Y. values FDR's estate at $1,085,486.		Despite reports of a "meat famine" in many cities caused by widespread withholding of livestock from the market, Truman refuses to raise or lift price ceilings on meat . . . . Pittsburgh common pleas court revokes its injunction against a strike of Duquesne Light Co. workers and orders the release of union leader George Mueller in the face of CIO and AFL strike threats . . . . Trucks begin operating again in northern New Jersey after a four-day strike when employers sign a contract with the Teamsters union . . . . Production stops at seven Hollywood film studios as the AFL Conference of Studio Unions calls a strike of carpenters and other technicians in a jurisdictional dispute with the AFL International Alliance of Theatrical Stage Employes.			Sept. 26
U.S. Communist Party reveals it has expelled one of its founders, William Dunne, because of "factional activity."		A&P food chain is fined $175,000 on a monopoly charge in Danville, Ill. after the conviction of 16 of its executives.	British test pilot Geoffrey De Havilland is killed when his experimental jet explodes over the Thames estuary . . . . A flash flood in San Antonio, Texas causes six deaths and extensive damage.	Tony Zale retains his middleweight title when he KO's Rocky Graziano in the sixth round at Yankee Stadium.	Sept. 27
					Sept. 28
Progressive Conference, composed of representatives of the National Citizens Political Action Comm., the CIO Political Action Comm. and the Independent Citizens Comm. of the Arts, Sciences and Professions, ends in Chicago after calling for continued adherence to FDR's economic "bill of rights" and a foreign policy based on "world good neighborliness."	U.S. National Commission for UNESCO submits a report to Secy. Byrnes calling for a UNESCO budget of $1.5 billion.			For the first time in baseball history the National League season ends with two teams tied for first place: Brooklyn and St. Louis . . . . Cleveland Indians pitcher Bob Feller sets a new strikeout mark of 348 for the season as Cleveland defeats Detroit, 4-1 . . . . The *New York Herald Tribune* reports the best selling books to be: fiction, *The Hucksters* by Frederic Wakeman and non-fiction, *The Egg and I* by Betty MacDonald.	Sept. 29
Speaking at an American Legion convention in San Francisco, FBI director J. Edgar Hoover claims that at least 100,000 Communists are operating in the U.S., in "some newspapers, magazines, books, radio and the screen . . . . some churches, schools, colleges and even fraternal orders."	Truman confers with Navy Secy. Forrestal and Navy Pacific commanders on plans to convert Guam into a major U.S. base in the Pacific . . . . Forrestal states that U.S. naval forces will not be withdrawn from the Mediterranean but denies any U.S. intention of acquiring European shore bases.				Sept. 30
F	G	H	I	J	
Includes elections, federal-state relations, civil rights and liberties, crime, the judiciary, education, health care, poverty, urban affairs and population.	*Includes formation and debate of U.S. foreign and defense policies, veterans affairs and defense spending. (Relations with specific foreign countries are usually found under the region concerned.)*	*Includes business, labor, agriculture, taxation, transportation, consumer affairs, monetary and fiscal policy, natural resources, pollution and accidents.*	*Includes worldwide scientific, medical and technological developments, natural phenomena, U.S. weather and natural disasters.*	*Includes the arts, religion, scholarship, communications media, sports, entertainment, fashions, fads and social life.*	

	World Affairs	Europe	Africa & the Middle East	The Americas	Asia & the Pacific
Oct. 1		International Military Tribunal at Nuremberg hands down verdicts on the 22 Nazi defendants. Nineteen are found guilty of war crimes and 12 (including Goering, Keitel and Streicher) are sentenced to hang. Hjalmar Schacht, Franz von Papen and Hans Fritzsche are acquitted.	Egyptian King Farouk asks Premier Ismail Sidky Pasha to form a new cabinet despite his recent resignation.	U.S. returns the $1-million Chorrera Air Base to Panama .... Argentina's meat packing industry shuts down after workers stage an 18-day "slow-down" strike to enforce wage demands.	Chou En-lai says in a letter to Gen. Marshall that the Nationalist drive on Kalgan, a Communist stronghold in northern China, may cause a "total national split."
Oct. 2	Mexican delegate Luis Padilla Nervo urges the U.N. Atomic Energy Commission to recommend that plants producing nuclear fuel be placed under U.N. authority in a closely guarded international zone .... U.N. creates permanent commissions with Big Five membership: Economic and Employment, Fiscal, Transport and Communications, Human Rights, Population, Social, Statistical and Status of Women .... International Monetary Fund governors admit four countries to membership: Italy, Turkey, Syria and Lebanon .... International Labor Organization votes in Montreal to associate itself with the U.N. on a partnership basis.	World reaction to the Nuremberg verdicts: The London *Times* declares that "one of the purposes for which the Allies went to war has been accomplished"; the *Christian Science Monitor* says the verdict "should arouse all people .... to take a larger individual share in keeping the peace"; the Russian newspaper *Izvestia* charges the court showed "amazing mildness to those four hardened criminals," Hess, Schacht, von Papen and Fritzsche .... Defense attorneys for 11 Nazis condemned to death at Nuremberg appeal to the Allied Control Council for clemency, asking also that their clients be shot rather than hanged if the appeal is denied .... King George II approves Premier Constantin Tsalaris' new Greek cabinet, with no Communist or Liberal participation .... Reversing its earlier position, Russia agrees to Western proposals on the Allied Control Council for demilitarization surveys to be conducted by four-power commissions in all German occupation zones.	London Conference on Palestine adjourns until Dec. 16 after Arab delegates present a plan for an independent Palestine to include an interim government of Arabs and Jews.		In a note to Gen. Marshall, the Chinese Nationalist government says it will agree to a ceasefire only if the Communists begin integrating their forces into the National Army and participate in the proposed State Council and National Constituent Assembly .... Gen. Kuzma Derevyanko, Russian member of the Allied Control Council in Japan, charges that former Japanese General Staff members continue to exert influence by taking refuge in the demobilization boards."
Oct. 3	At the Paris Peace Conference, Secy. Byrnes says he hopes that Stalin's statement of Sept. 24 will put an and to "unwarranted charges that any nation or group of nations is seeking to encircle the Soviet Union." .... Italian Political and Territorial Commission of the Paris Peace Conference adopts a French proposal for international control of Trieste, putting the city under Security Council authority .... U.N. Security Council adjourns for the year after voting to call a conference on Danube navigation rights, adopting a draft constitution for the International Refugee Organization and shelving proposals for coordinated economic reconstruction of Europe due to Soviet dissent.	Yugoslavian Pres. Tito demobilizes several large army units and most partisan units remaining from the war.			
Oct. 4		British government announces plans to create a Ministry of Defense to coordinate the policies of the three fighting services.	Truman issues a statement on the Palestine Conference urging Britain to permit "substantial immigration" of Jews into Palestine and supporting the Zionist plan for establishment of a "viable Jewish state."		
Oct. 5	Italian Economic Commission of the Paris Peace Conference ends a recrimination-filled debate by voting to fix Italian reparations at $225 million in addition to the $100 million previously awarded to Russia.	Swedish Premier Per Hansson dies at 60 in Stockholm.	Iranian General Staff orders government forces to subdue rebellious Ghashghai tribesmen in Fars Province.		
Oct. 6		Italian crowds shouting "Duce" and giving the Fascist salute attack a Communist-organized Slovene demonstration in Gorizia.			
Oct. 7		Hjalmar Schacht is arrested by German police after his release from prison in Nuremberg for trial before a denazification court. Similar action is started against acquitted defendants Franz von Papen and Hans Fritzsche .... Russia and Sweden sign a trade treaty providing a $2.8-billion Swedish credit to Russia for 15 years at 3% interest and a $2.8 million barter arrangement for five years.		Chilean Communists protest the forthcoming visit of five U.S. warships for Chile's Nov. 4 presidential inauguration.	Truce negotiations between Dutch administrators and Indonesian nationalist leaders begin in Batavia under British chairmanship.
	A *Includes developments that affect more than one world region, international organizations and important meetings of major world leaders.*	B *Includes all domestic and regional developments in Europe, including the Soviet Union, Turkey, Cyprus and Malta.*	C *Includes all domestic and regional developments in Africa and the Middle East, including Iraq and Iran and excluding Cyprus, Turkey and Afghanistan.*	D *Includes all domestic and regional developments in Latin America, the Caribbean and Canada.*	E *Includes all domestic and regional developments in Asian and Pacific nations, extending from Afghanistan through all the Pacific Islands, except Hawaii.*

U.S. Politics & Social Issues	U.S. Foreign Policy & Defense	U.S. Economy & Environment	Science, Technology & Nature	Culture, Leisure & Life Style	
Air mail stamp goes up to 5¢.	In a telegram to Henry Morgenthau and other speakers at a CIO rally in Chicago, Bernard Baruch denies Wallace's charge that the U.S. atomic energy control plan would prevent other countries from engaging in nuclear research while leaving the U.S. free to continue . . . . Truman receives Rumanian Minister Mihail Ralea, officially resuming diplomatic relations with Rumania.	CIO Maritime Engineers Beneficial Assn. and AFL Organization of Masters, Mates and Pilots begin a national strike for wage increases of 30-35%.	Navy Lockheed Neptune twin-engine patrol bomber *Truculent Turtle* lands in Columbus, Ohio after an 11,236-mile flight from Perth, Australia, a non-stop distance record.	Soviet music critic I. Nestiev attacks Dmitri Shostakovich's Ninth Symphony as bitter, ironic and "not expressive of modern ideas," while Shostakovich declines an invitation from Serge Koussevitzky to appear as guest conductor of the Boston Symphony Orchestra . . . . Elliot Roosevelt's *As He Saw It*, an account of FDR at international wartime conferences with a forward by Mrs. Eleanor Roosevelt, is published.	Oct. 1
J. Howard McGrath submits his resignation as U.S. solicitor general.	Bernard Baruch releases four documents on his controversy with Wallace over the U.S. atomic energy control plan, attacking Wallace's views as "gravely dangerous to the delicate negotiations now under way" and creating "confusion and division among our people." . . . . War Dept. discloses a plan for one year of compulsory military training for youths between 18 and 20.	Thirty-four union leaders in N.Y. form the CIO Committee for Democratic Trade Unionism to combat Communist activities in the CIO.. Leaders of the group are Jack Altman, vice president of the Retail, Wholesale and Dept. Store Clerks Union, and Charles Kerrigan, regional UAW director . . . . U.S. Maritime Commission sells the one-time luxury liner *Normandie* as junk for $161,680.	Assn. for the Advancement of Research on Multiple Sclerosis is formed in N.Y.		Oct. 2
House Campaign Expenditures Committee votes to send investigators to Missouri and Florida to look into charges of irregularities in primaries.		An American Overseas Airlines Douglas DC-4 en route to Berlin from N.Y. explodes east of Stephenville, Newfoundland, killing all 39 aboard, in the worst accident in the history of commercial airlines . . . . Truman predicts there will be no "meat famine" and says he is watching the situation in the meat industry carefully.		With an 8-4 win against Brooklyn, the St. Louis Cardinals take two of three games in the National League playoff to capture the pennant.	Oct. 3
Former Gov. of Pennsylvania and Interior Secy. Gifford Pinchot dies at 81 in N.Y.		United Mine Workers union ends its Atlantic City convention after lauding John L. Lewis (absent due to a recent appendicitis operation) and voting its top officials pay raises.		Barney Oldfield, pioneer auto racer and developer, dies at 68 in Beverly Hills, Calif. . . . . Montreal defeats Louisville to win the Little World Series, 4 games to 2.	Oct. 4
		OPA head Paul Porter urges continuation of price controls for the sake of stabilization, while War Mobilization and Reconversion adviser Eric Johnston calls for an end to "the fiction of controls," claiming they lack public support and constitute "an open invitation" to the growth of black markets.			Oct. 5
			Army B-29 *Pacusan Dreamboat* arrives in Cairo from Honolulu, completing what Air Force Gen. Carl Spaatz calls an "epochal" flight of 8,750 miles over the North Pole in 39 hrs., 36 mins. . . . . A group of Univ. of Chicago scientists headed by Dr. Andrew Ivy reports isolating a hormone called enterogastrone, which may be a permanent chemical cure for peptic ulcers.	Cannes International Film Festival names Billy Wilder's *The Lost Week-End* the the best U.S. film for 1945.	Oct. 6
Ben Fishel, head of an auto black market ring with a $3-million turnover, is fined $65,000 and given two years imprisonment in Cairo, Ill.					Oct. 7

F	G	H	I	J
Includes elections, federal-state relations, civil rights and liberties, crime, the judiciary, education, health care, poverty, urban affairs and population.	*Includes formation and debate of U.S. foreign and defense policies, veterans affairs and defense spending. (Relations with specific foreign countries are usually found under the region concerned.)*	*Includes business, labor, agriculture, taxation, transportation, consumer affairs, monetary and fiscal policy, natural resources, pollution and accidents.*	*Includes worldwide scientific, medical and technological developments, natural phenomena, U.S. weather and natural disasters.*	*Includes the arts, religion, scholarship, communications media, sports, entertainment, fashions, fads and social life.*

	World Affairs	Europe	Africa & the Middle East	The Americas	Asia & the Pacific
Oct. 8	U.N. Atomic Energy Commission adopts a Canadian resolution to enlist the world's top physicists in an investigation of the international safeguards needed in every phase of atomic development .... France submits a trusteeship proposal for the U.N.-mandated territories of Cameroons and Togoland to the General Assembly.	British Fuel and Power Min. Emanuel Shinwell warns Britain will face a grave fuel shortage and possible industrial breakdown if fuel consumption is not reduced by 10% .... Inter-Allied Reparations Agency in Brussels votes to urge the speed-up of German industrial and capital reparations.		The opposition Socialist Worker's Party and Patriotic Junta are legalized in Venezuela.	Soviet prosecution begins its case at the Tokyo war crimes trial, charging that Japan hoped to use the German invasion of Russia as an opportunity to seize Russian Far Eastern territory .... Gen. Marshall and Amb. John Stuart report that the Communists have rejected a proposed 10-day truce in northern China.
Oct. 9		Angered by the announcement of layoffs in public works projects, over 20,000 Italian workers riot and storm government offices in Rome. One demonstrator is killed by police .... U.S. State Dept. reports that Yugoslavia has paid a $150,000 indemnity to the families of five slain American fliers but refuses to pay for the planes .... A Council for Collective Farm Affairs, headed by A.A. Andreev, is created in Moscow to remedy abuses and speed up production on collective farms.			
Oct. 10		Italian peace treaty draft is approved at the Paris Peace Conference despite Molotov's warning that Russia will not accept the Western solution for Trieste .... Allied Control Council in Berlin rejects appeals for clemency from 16 of the 19 Nazis, convicted at Nuremberg, and upholds the death ruling for 11 .... Icelandic Premier Olafur Thors and his cabinet resign in a controversy with the Communists over U.S. air rights in the country.			
Oct. 11	Paris Peace Conference approves the Rumanian peace treaty, including U.S.- and British-sponsored provisions for freedom of navigation on the Danube and convocation of a Danubian conference six months after the treaty goes into effect.	A Zagreb court finds Yugoslavian Archbishop Stepinac guilty of aiding Croatian Premier Ante Pavelich's wartime Ustashi regime, provoking racial hatred and forcibly converting Serbs to Catholicism, and sentences him to 16 years hard labor and loss of property .... U.S. Amb. to Britain W. Bedell Smith states in a note to the Foreign Office that the U.S. stands by its position on the Dardanelles, favoring revision of the Montreux Convention but rejecting the Soviet view that the straits question concerns only Turkey and Russia. Smith joins Britain in warning that the U.N. Security Council would be called into action if the straits were threatened "by an aggressor." .... An attempted military revolt against Portuguese Premier Antonio de Oliveira Salazar's dictatorship is put down in Estarreja, with 900 arrests reported by Lisbon.			Nationalist forces claim capture of the major Communist base of Kalgan in northern China.
Oct. 12		Paris Peace Conference approves the Bulgarian peace treaty but leaves the Bulgarian-Greek border question unresolved.	Teheran reports the Ghashghai tribes of southern Iran are suing for peace after a three-week revolt against the central government.		Japan's first postwar Diet adjourns after approving a record peacetime budget of $8 billion.
Oct. 13		Paris Peace Conference approves the Hungarian peace treaty after an unsuccessful U.S. attempt to reduce Hungarian reparations .... In a national referendum, the French electorate accepts the new constitution establishing the Fourth Republic .... Rural district elections are held in the British zone of Germany, giving a majority of votes to the Social Democrats but more district council seats to the Christian Democrats.	Meyer Weisgal, American director of the Jewish Agency for Palestine, charges in London that British policy and the British Army are contributing to the growth of terrorism in Palestine.	Campaigning in parliamentary elections, Venezuelan Communists urge nationalization of the nation's oil industry.	
Oct. 14	U.N. Atomic Energy Commission's political committee begins hearings at Lake Success on how to implement international inspection of nuclear production plants.	Paris Peace Conference approves the peace treaty for Finland after an unsuccessful U.S. attempt to reduce Finnish reparations .... Vatican's Sacred Congregation of the Council excommunicates all Catholics, including Marshal Tito, who "concurred physically or morally" in the conviction of Yugoslavian Archbishop Stepinac.			Indonesian Premier Sutan Sjahrir and Netherlands officials sign a truce in Batavia .... Allied headquarters in Tokyo approves new Japanese history textbooks, eliminating militarism and ancestor worship.
	A	B	C	D	E
	Includes developments that affect more than one world region, international organizations and important meetings of major world leaders.	*Includes all domestic and regional developments in Europe, including the Soviet Union, Turkey, Cyprus and Malta.*	*Includes all domestic and regional developments in Africa and the Middle East, including Iraq and Iran and excluding Cyprus, Turkey and Afghanistan.*	*Includes all domestic and regional developments in Latin America, the Caribbean and Canada.*	*Includes all domestic and regional developments in Asian and Pacific nations, extending from Afghanistan through all the Pacific Islands, except Hawaii.*

U.S. Politics & Social Issues	U.S. Foreign Policy & Defense	U.S. Economy & Environment	Science, Technology & Nature	Culture, Leisure & Life Style	
Chmn. J. Percy Priest (D, Tenn.) of the House Campaign Expenditures Comm. reveals that 135 organizations (including the AFL, CIO and KKK) have not responded to a questionnaire on political spending sent out by the Committee.	Atty. Gen. Tom Clark reveals a presidential directive requiring all agents of former Allied governments to register with the Justice Dept. . . . . Accepting the 1946 Freedom House Award from Mrs. Eleanor Roosevelt at a N.Y. dinner, Bernard Baruch rejects "unilateral disarmament in the cause of international good will."			Brian Hooker's version of *Cyrano De Bergerac* opens on Broadway to favorable reviews . . . . Michele Morgan is named best actress of the year at the Cannes Film Festival.	Oct. 8
			Dr. R.F. Loeb reveals the development of pentaquine, a drug which can cure malaria instead of suppressing it.	*The Iceman Cometh*, Eugene O'Neill's first play in 12 years, opens in New York.	Oct. 9
N.J. Supreme Court files a judgment outlawing the KKK in the state . . . . Elections to the Alaskan territorial legislature result in GOP gains, while an advisory referendum shows that Alaskan voters favor statehood by a 2-1 margin.		Negotiations on the strike of maritime engineers and pilots break down in Washington due to CIO refusal to deal separately with Gulf and East Coast shipping lines . . . . OPA Advisory Bd. files a petition with Agriculture Secy. Anderson for removal of meat price controls, stating that no livestock shortage exists . . . . CIO Amalgamated Clothing Workers union signs with the Clothing Manufacturers Assn. for a $5 weekly cost-of-living increase, covering 150,000 workers.		A national television conference and exhibit opens in New York, with sets on display ranging from $250 to $2,000.	Oct. 10
	FBI arrests ex-servicemen George Comer, Miles Daubenheyer and James Rike for an alleged attempt to sell photographs of atomic bomb material and equipment to the *Baltimore News Post* . . . . Army cancels all draft calls for the rest of 1946 due to increased voluntary enlistments.				Oct. 11
	Hero of the Burma campaign Gen. Joseph W. Stilwell dies at 63 in San Francisco of carcinoma of the liver.			Former Commerce Secy. Henry Wallace accepts the editorship of the *New Republic* . . . . *Billboard* reports the most popular songs are: (1) *To Each His Own*, (2) *Five Minutes More* and (3) *Rumors Are Flying*.	Oct. 12
		Detroit UAW members end a 13-day wildcat strike protesting lack of safety measures in the Ford open hearth plant.		St. Louis Cardinals win the seventh game of the World Series against the Boston Rex Sox, 4-1, taking the baseball crown four games to three.	Oct. 13
House Campaign Expenditures Comm. hears CIO Political Action Director Jack Kroll and National Citizens Political Action Vice Chairman C.B. Baldwin deny that their organizations have prepared national "purge" lists of candidates for the coming elections.		Responding to congressional pressure and a continuing meat shortage, Truman removes price controls from livestock and meat . . . . Production in 10 major Hollywood studios halts as film-processing technicians refuse to cross picket lines in a jurisdictional dispute between two AFL unions.			Oct. 14
F	G	H	I	J	
Includes elections, federal-state relations, civil rights and liberties, crime, the judiciary, education, health care, poverty, urban affairs and population.	*Includes formation and debate of U.S. foreign and defense policies, veterans affairs and defense spending. (Relations with specific foreign countries are usually found under the region concerned.)*	*Includes business, labor, agriculture, taxation, transportation, consumer affairs, monetary and fiscal policy, natural resources, pollution and accidents.*	*Includes worldwide scientific, medical and technological developments, natural phenomena, U.S. weather and natural disasters.*	*Includes the arts, religion, scholarship, communications media, sports, entertainment, fashions, fads and social life.*	

	World Affairs	Europe	Africa & the Middle East	The Americas	Asia & the Pacific
Oct. 15	Paris Peace Conference ends after 79 days. Yugoslavia boycotts the final session to protest the conference's Trieste decision .... U.N. Security Council rejects a Polish resolution to bar Spain from appearing before the International Court of Justice .... Central Committee of the International Emergency Food Council names a six-nation subcommittee in Washington to study bilateral and barter pacts which may interfere with food allocation.	A U.S. Reconstruction Finance Corp. mission in Berlin announces it will help finance limited revival of German industry in order to enable the Germans to increase exports, and thus cut cost of U.S. occupation forces. .... Papal Nuncio Bishop Joseph Patrick Hurley charges six bishops have been prevented from touring their Yugoslavian dioceses.			Viceroy of India Viscount Wavell names five Moslem members to the Indian Executive Council after the Moslem League announces its decision to participate in the government .... V. Acharya Kripalani becomes president of the All-India Congress Party following Nehru's resignation as Maulana Abul Kalam Azad withdraws as a candidate .... Siam's parliament approves the cabinet's decision to return to French Indochina four border areas transferred to Siam by the Vichy regime.
Oct. 16		Ten Nazi war criminals are hanged in the Nuremberg prison: von Ribbentrop, Keitel, Kaltenbrunner, Rosenberg, Frank, Frick, Streicher, Sauckel, Jodl, Seyss-Inquart. Hermann Goering, scheduled to hang with the others, commits suicide in his cell by taking potassium cyanide two hours before his execution .... Soviet Budget Commission Chmn. L.R. Kornietz scores five industrial ministries for losing money, misuse of machinery, lagging output and falsifying production statistics.			Chiang Kai-shek offers an eight-point truce proposal to the Communists, including a redisposition of troops in Manchuria.
Oct. 17			Saudi Arabian King Ibn Saud tells Truman that his request for more Jewish immigration into Palestine violates "previous promises" made to the Arabs .... Egyptian Premier Ismail Sidky Pasha and Foreign Min. Ibrahim Abdul Hadi Pasha arrive in London to reopen Anglo-Egyptian military talks.	Acting Chilean Pres. Alfredo Duhalde resigns and is succeeded by Interior Min. Juan Irabarren.	
Oct. 18	U.N. Inter-Governmental Committee for Refugees announces that "travel documents" similar to passports will be issued to displaced persons starting Jan. 15 .... U.N. Secy. Gen. Lie rejects a new membership application from Albania.				Communist Central Executive Committee rejects Chiang Kai-shek's Oct. 16 truce proposal.
Oct. 19		Italian Deputy Premier Pietro Nenni is named foreign minister, he is the first Socialist to hold the post .... Bombings attributed to Nazis damage U.S. military government buildings and denazification headquarters in Stuttgart and nearby Backnang.	British authorities impose a night curfew on Jerusalem due to intensified sniping and land mine-laying by Zionist terrorists .... Iranian Premier Ghavam reshuffles his cabinet, dropping three left-wing members and appointing Prince Mozzafar Firouz as ambassador to Russia.		
Oct. 20		Berlin's first postwar city council elections result in a large victory for the Social Democrats over the Christian Democrats and Socialist Unity Party .... August Cardinal Hlond of Poland issues a pastoral letter criticizing the Communist government and urging Catholics to support the conservative Peasant Party in coming elections .... *Pravda* charges that Turkey's rejection of of a Soviet request for joint defense of the Dardanelles resulted from American pressure.			
Oct. 21	International Telecommunications Conference ends in Moscow after recommending another meeting in the U.S. in 10 months, creation of an international board to register radio frequencies and establishment of relations between the U.N. and the International Telecommunications Union.		British authorities arrest members of the Arab Boycott Committee in Haifa for bombing Arab shops that refuse to boycott Jews .... Zionist Stern Group distributes handbills in Palestine containing threats to kill British soldiers and policemen.	A special session of Argentina's Congress hears a message from Pres. Peron outlining a five-year plan for industrialization and economic development.	Communist, Nationalist and Democratic League representatives resume truce negotiations in Nanking after the return of Communist leader Chou En-lai .... UNRRA director La Guardia partially lifts the embargo on shipments to China as relief supplies begin to move from harbor warehouses into the countryside.

A	B	C	D	E
Includes developments that affect more than one world region, international organizations and important meetings of major world leaders.	*Includes all domestic and regional developments in Europe, including the Soviet Union, Turkey, Cyprus and Malta.*	*Includes all domestic and regional developments in Africa and the Middle East, including Iraq and Iran and excluding Cyprus, Turkey and Afghanistan.*	*Includes all domestic and regional developments in Latin America, the Caribbean and Canada.*	*Includes all domestic and regional developments in Asian and Pacific nations, extending from Afghanistan through all the Pacific Islands, except Hawaii.*

U.S. Politics & Social Issues	U.S. Foreign Policy & Defense	U.S. Economy & Environment	Science, Technology & Nature	Culture, Leisure & Life Style	
CIO Pres. Philip Murray announces formation of the Coordinating Comm. of the Conference of Progressives, which will set policy for a number of liberal groups.		OPA estimates that only 15% of the family food budget is still under price restraints as director Paul Porter orders a list of items drawn up for decontrol next month . . . . Striking Duquesne Light Co. employes vote for an independent company union by an overwhelming majority over AFL and CIO unions in an NLRB election.	Dr. Glen Seaborg of the Univ. of California Berkeley reveals the discovery of a new chemical element — neptunium 237 — which can be split like uranium 235 and plutonium.		Oct. 15
A Gallup Poll reports that 54% of the nation's voters now prefer the GOP and disapprove of Truman's performance as President.	A group of 36 Protestant ministers picket the White House asking amnesty for 1,200 conscientious objectors still in prison . . . . U.S. cancels the remaining $40 million of a $50 million credit to Czechoslovakia for purchase of surplus Army equipment because of Czech plans to sell $10 million of the material to Rumania at a profit.	In the aftermath of price decontrol, Chicago cattle prices hit a record high of $35.25 per 100 lbs.	Dentist William T.G. Morton completes the first public demonstration of ether anesthesia at the Mass. General Hospital, Boston.	Pauline Betz of the U.S. and Philippe Washer of Belgium win the Pan American mixed doubles tennis title in Mexico City.	Oct. 16
Former Communist Louis Budenz names Gerhard Eisler as a Kremlin agent who directs all Communist activities in the U.S.	Army reveals that by Jan. 1 it will release all 1945 draftees and reduce its strength to 1.31 million men . . . . Lend-Lease Admin. discloses that up to V-J Day it furnished the Allies with $49,096,125,000 in munitions.	A four-day AFL convention concludes in Chicago after re-electing William Green as president, revealing plans to aid in the re-establishment of German trade unions and passing a resolution calling for a 30-hour workweek.		American Fed. of Musicians Pres. Petrillo announces a national agreement for a 37½% wage raise for musicians who make recordings.	Oct. 17
	German-born Argentine citizen Teodoro Erdmann Lau is charged in N.Y. with espionage and identified as the paymaster of German spies in the U.S. during World War II.				Oct. 18
		Civilian Production Admin. cancels all limitations on manufacture of women's clothes and children's coats and dresses . . . . N.Y., New Orleans and Chicago Cotton Exchanges suspend trading after cotton futures on the N.Y. Exchange plunge the maximum daily limit of $10 a bale for the third successive day.		Princeton University celebrates its 200th anniversary, awarding 23 honorary degrees to scholars and statesmen from 11 nations.	Oct. 19
	National Conference on China and the Far East, representing some 300 foreign affairs groups, ends a San Francisco meeting after passing resolutions urging the withdrawal of U.S. troops from China and the Philippines, termination of U.S. aid to the Nationalist Chinese government and greater emphasis on the establishment of democratic governments in the Far East.	Duquesne Light Co. workers end their 27-day strike in Pittsburgh by voting to submit their wage demands to arbitration . . . . Seventy-two war veterans end a 23-hour sit-down strike in the N.Y. State Senate Chamber after unsuccessfully demanding a special legislative session to appropriate $800 million for housing.			Oct. 20
		U.S. aviators call their first strike when 1,400 members of the AFL Air Line Pilots Assn. walk out against Transcontinental & Western Air Inc. in a wage dispute . . . . U.S. cotton exchanges re-open as cotton operator Thomas Johnson admits in New Orleans that the Oct. 19 "break" resulted from his attempts to liquidate his large cotton holdings in a declining market.		Network Hooperatings list the most popular radio shows as: *Fred Allen*, *Fibber McGee & Molly*, *Bob Hope*, *Charlie McCarthy Show* and *Jack Benny*.	Oct. 21
F	G	H	I	J	
Includes elections, federal-state relations, civil rights and liberties, crime, the judiciary, education, health care, poverty, urban affairs and population.	*Includes formation and debate of U.S. foreign and defense policies, veterans affairs and defense spending. (Relations with specific foreign countries are usually found under the region concerned.)*	*Includes business, labor, agriculture, taxation, transportation, consumer affairs, monetary and fiscal policy, natural resources, pollution and accidents.*	*Includes worldwide scientific, medical and technological developments, natural phenomena, U.S. weather and natural disasters.*	*Includes the arts, religion, scholarship, communications media, sports, entertainment, fashions, fads and social life.*	

	World Affairs	Europe	Africa & the Middle East	The Americas	Asia & the Pacific
Oct. 22		Two British destroyers are damaged, with 40 sailors killed or missing, when they strike mines off the coast of Albania .... Soviet authorities in the eastern sector of Berlin round up about 400 German engineers, their families and furniture and ship them to Russia for five years of work. The German Social Democratic Party protests the deportations, but the Russians claim the engineers have signed contracts to work in Russia .... *Pravda* announces the appointment of Georgi Malenkov as one of eight vice chairmen of the Council of Ministers, the main Soviet executive organ .... Meeting for the second day, the annual convention of the British Trades Union Congress adopts a report urging a goal of 100% union membership in all industries and barring jurisdictional disputes within factories.			U.S. tanks patrol Seoul, Korea after a mob protesting the arrest of left-wing leader Moon Eun-chong tries to kill Seoul's chief of police.
Oct. 23	Truman greets delegates at the new session of the U.N. General Assembly and says the U.S. is "troubled by the failure of the Allied nations to make more progress in their common search for lasting peace."	British P.M. Attlee charges in the House of Commons that the use of the veto power is reducing "to a nullity the usefulness of the Security Council." Churchill supports Attlee and says Soviet troops in Eastern Europe "may constitute a positive danger to peace." .... Gen. Kurt Daluege, former head of the German gendarmerie who ordered the destruction of Lidice in 1942, is hanged in Prague.			
Oct. 24	At the first business meeting of the General Assembly's current session, Secy. Gen. Lie denounces Franco Spain, and smaller nations criticize the Big Five veto power on the Security Council .... Sir Carl August Berendsen of New Zealand is elected chairman of the Social and Humanitarian Affairs Commission.	Brig. Gen. Telford Taylor, new U.S. chief prosecutor in Germany, says that 250-500 top German industrialists and others will be tried as war criminals within three months.	Manilal Gandhi, son of Mohandas Gandhi, chooses to spend 30 days in jail with 357 other passive resisters rather than pay a $12 fine after refusing to observe a housing segregation law in Pretoria, South Africa.	A joint session of the Chilean Congress chooses Radical Party candidate Gabriel Gonzales Videla as president.	Chinese Communists in Yenan radio an appeal to the U.N. General Assembly to investigate U.S. involvement in Chinese affairs.
Oct. 25	Soviet delegate Vishinsky drops his fight in the U.N. General Assembly to keep the veto question off the agenda but calls a Cuban proposal to eliminate the veto "very dangerous."	Twenty-three German physicians accused of concentration camp atrocities go on trial in Nuremberg. Among them is Karl Brandt, Hitler's personal physician .... U.S. Army announces suspension of the military government officer of Nuremberg pending investigation of an alleged anti-German demonstration in the city Sept. 30 by U.S. soldiers and Jewish and Polish refugees.		Cuban Premier Carlos Prio Socarras announces the suppression of an anti-government plot.	Iva Toguri D'Aquino, one of the radio Japan workers who broadcast as "Tokyo Rose" during the war, is released from prison in Tokyo.
Oct. 26		French Premier Georges Bidault warns of panic buying and inflation and urges farmers to stop withholding food from the market in order to get higher prices.	Egyptian Premier Ismail Sidky Pasha returns to Cairo after further treaty discussions with British Foreign Secy. Bevin.		Continued Hindu-Moslem violence results in 27 deaths in Calcutta. Civil strife is also reported in Bombay and eastern Bengal, with thousands of refugees fleeing to Calcutta .... Nationalist forces report capturing the Manchurian port of Antung on the Korean border.
Oct. 27		Elections to the Bulgarian National Assembly give the Communists 277 of the total 465 seats.		Democratic Action Party gains an overwhelming victory in Venezuela's Constitutional Congress elections.	MacArthur reports that U.S.-Russian negotiations to unify Korea have broken down because of the Soviet refusal to tolerate opposition political parties in their zone.
Oct. 28	In his first interview with an American correspondent since the end of the war, Stalin tells UP President Hugh Baillie that he hopes for a relaxation of East-West tensions, is still interested in a loan from the U.S. and desires the political and economic reunification of Germany. He claims that Russia will reduce its armed strength of 60 divisions in Europe, and denies that Russia has the A-bomb secret .... Kuzma Kisselev, White Russian delegate to the General Assembly, accuses the U.S. and Britain of violating the U.N. Charter by maintaining troops in non-enemy territories.		Responding to criticism from Saudi Arabian King Ibn Saud, Truman reiterates his plea for the establishment of a Jewish national home in Palestine and immediate admission of 100,000 Jews on humanitarian grounds.		Dutch forces land in Sumatra to relieve Japanese troops guarding U.S., British and Dutch oil installations.

U.S. Politics & Social Issues	U.S. Foreign Policy & Defense	U.S. Economy & Environment	Science, Technology & Nature	Culture, Leisure & Life Style	
House Un-American Activities Committee subpoenas Gerhard Eisler, charged by former Communist Louis Budenz with being a Soviet agent.	War Dept. reveals that MacArthur has been asked for a report on the morale of troops in the Pacific after numerous complaints of clashes between U.S. soldiers and civilians in Europe and Asia.	Agriculture Dept. reports 265 million pounds of meat were produced in the first week of decontrol, a 134% increase over the previous week.		Mendel Najdorf of Poland wins the international chess competition in Prague.	Oct. 22
		OPA lifts controls from all foods and beverages except rice, sugar, syrups and molasses . . . . U.S. Circuit Court of Appeals in St. Louis upholds the right of Montgomery Ward & Co., Kansas City to present its views to employes before an NLRB collective bargaining election.	A three-day meeting of the National Academy of Sciences ends in Philadelphia after scientists from 25 nations hear pleas for international cooperation in research and reports on nuclear physics, meteorology and other subjects.		Oct. 23
		Truman discloses that funds for civilian public works during the present fiscal year will be $165 million more than his Aug. 1 estimate of $900 million.	A German V-2 rocket packed with scientific instruments rises 65 miles into the air at White Sands, N.M.		Oct. 24
Special Asst. to the U.S. Atty. Gen. O. John Rogge is dismissed for indicating in a speech that Nazi Germany favored the election of Republican presidential candidate Thomas Dewey in 1944.	In response to a War Dept. request for a report on the morale of U.S. forces in the Pacific, MacArthur blames military-civilian clashes in the Philippines on Filipino nationalism and the "irresponsibility" of some U.S. recruits.	Truman proclaims a state of emergency in housing and orders the lifting of import duties from lumber and lumber products.			Oct. 25
		AFL National Organization of Masters, Mates and Pilots ends its 26-day strike against East and Gulf Coast ship operators with an agreement calling for a 15% pay increase.			Oct. 26
			American Social Hygiene Assn. announces that reported cases of syphilis increased 42% in the 12 months ended June 30.		Oct. 27
Supreme Court refuses to hear two suits protesting the unit rule in Georgia Democratic primary elections . . . . Senate Campaign Expenditures Investigating Committee dismisses for lack of evidence charges of excessive spending against Sen. Kenneth McKellar (D, Tenn.)	Truman names David Lilienthal, former chairman of the Tennessee Valley Authority, to head the newly created Atomic Energy Commission. Lilienthal is replaced as TVA head by Gordon Clapp . . . . U.S. Agriculture Under Secy. Norris Dodd tells a U.N. Food and Agriculture Organization meeting in Washington that the U.S. will not support the proposed World Food Board, stating that international pooling and price regulation of food commodities is not practicable . . . . Zionist Organization of America convention ends in Atlantic City, after resolving to boost its enrollment to a million calling on American Jews to provide a market for Palestine products and re-electing Rabbi Abba Hillel Silver president.	New York's two-month trucking strike ends as truck operators sign individual contracts granting 31¢ hourly wage increases and a 40-hour week.		Charles Despiau, noted French sculptor and a pupil of Rodin, dies at 72 in Paris.	Oct. 28

F	G	H	I	J
Includes elections, federal-state relations, civil rights and liberties, crime, the judiciary, education, health care, poverty, urban affairs and population.	*Includes formation and debate of U.S. foreign and defense policies, veterans affairs and defense spending. (Relations with specific foreign countries are usually found under the region concerned.)*	*Includes business, labor, agriculture, taxation, transportation, consumer affairs, monetary and fiscal policy, natural resources, pollution and accidents.*	*Includes worldwide scientific, medical and technological developments, natural phenomena, U.S. weather and natural disasters.*	*Includes the arts, religion, scholarship, communications media, sports, entertainment, fashions, fads and social life.*

	World Affairs	Europe	Africa & the Middle East	The Americas	Asia & the Pacific
Oct. 29	Molotov urges the General Assembly to recommend a general reduction of armaments, including the banning of the atomic bomb but demands continuation of the great power veto in nuclear matters . . . . Baruch tells the U.N. Atomic Energy Commission the U.S. is ready to accept the Russian proposal to outlaw the atom bomb and destroy its own stockpiles, but only if the agreement provides "full compulsion to obey it."	France refuses to approve an Allied Control Council proposal backed by the Big Three to permit amalgamation of German political parties on a national basis.			Moslem-Hindu violence continues in India as Gandhi's train is stoned at Aligarh.
Oct. 30	U.S. delegate Warren Austin tells the General Assembly that the U.S. is just as eager as Russia is for world disarmament but demands inspection to ensure compliance.	U.S. Reparations Commissioner Edwin Pauley rejects Russian demands for 25% of the current production of the Ruhr-Rhineland area in return for Soviet cooperation in the economic unification of Germany . . . . Gen. Lucius Clay of the U.S. military government in Germany approves a draft constitution for the state of Hesse approved yesterday by the state assembly. The constitution, which provides for nationalization of important raw materials and industries, must be approved by popular referendum . . . . Albanian Pres. Enver Hoxha appeals to the General Assembly against alleged violations of his country's territorial integrity by British and Greek forces.		U.S. objects to some sections of a British-Argentine trade pact as violating promises made by Britain in obtaining its U.S. loan.	
Oct. 31	U.N. General Assembly's plenary session ends with agreement to place the Russian disarmament proposal, Franco Spain and a Danish declaration on women's rights on the agenda of the Assembly's six main committees, which will meet at Lake Success . . . . La Guardia says he will resign as UNRRA director at the end of the year and announces transfer of $1.5 million in UNRRA funds to the World Health Organization.	Maj. David Watson is sentenced in Frankfurt to three years in prison and dismissal from service for conspiracy and receiving stolen property in the Hesse jewel theft.	Zionist squad damages the Ras El Ain airfield near Jerusalem and kills two British soldiers in a gun battle, while the National Council of Palestine Jews condemns political terrorism.	Three Communists join the Chilean cabinet, the first official Communist participation in a Latin American government.	Nationalist forces in Manchuria are reported advancing towards the Russian-held port of Darien . . . . Australia's Labor Party chooses a new cabinet, renominating Prime Minister Joseph Chifley and External Affairs Min. Herbert Evatt.
Nov. 1	Secy. Gen. Trygve Lie presents the General Assembly with budget estimates of $19,627,964 for 1946 and $23,790,008 for 1947 to cover U.N. administrative costs . . . . International Air Transport Assn. sets up a financial clearing house to handle all international airline transactions on a sterling and dollar basis.		Two British ships leave Haifa for Cyprus with 1,279 illegal Jewish immigrants captured yesterday on board their vessel . . . . Reporting on his treaty negotiations with Britain, Egyptian Premier Ismail Sidky Pasha tells his cabinet that British Foreign Secy. Bevin has agreed to recognize Egyptian sovereignty over the Sudan and withdraw British forces from Egypt in three years.		Chinese negotiators in Nanking reject truce proposals which would give them military control of only three northern Manchurian provinces.
Nov. 2		Municipal and borough elections in Britain give a net gain of 159 seats to the Labor Party.	Arabs stage a one-day general strike in Palestine against Jewish immigration.		India's Congress Party and Moslem League send representatives to Calcutta for discussions on means of ending the latest wave of Hindu-Moslem violence.
Nov. 3	U.N. delegates, including Molotov and General Assembly Pres. Paul-Henri Spaak, pay tribute to FDR's memory at Hyde Park, N.Y.			Chilean Pres. Gabriel Gonzalez Videla is inaugurated in Santiago . . . . Sir John Shaw is named governor of Trinidad and Tobago.	Hirohito reads an Imperial Rescript officially promulgating Japan's new constitution . . . . Jawaherlal Nehru and three other Hindu and Moslem leaders appeal from Calcutta for an end to civil strife in India.
Nov. 4	Allied Council of Foreign Ministers holds its first meeting in N.Y. to deal with unresolved questions from the Paris Peace Conference, including the Trieste issue . . . . Field Marshal Jan Christiaan Smuts defends South Africa's proposal to annex Southwest Africa as the General Assembly's Trusteeship Committee begins its debates on dependent territories . . . . U.N. Security Council accepts Poland's motion to remove the Spanish question from its agenda so that the General Assembly may discuss it.	Boycotted by the opposition, Greek Premier Constantin Tsaldaris forms a new cabinet but does not follow U.S. and British suggestions for a broadened government coalition . . . . American Fed. of Labor announces it will set up a permanent office in Germany to help in the reconstruction of German trade unions.			Dutch, Indonesian and British authorities meeting in Batavia issue ceasefire orders to their forces throughout the Dutch East Indies . . . . China and the U.S. sign a five-year Treaty of Friendship, Commerce and Navigation in Nanking, providing for most favored nation treatment but not affecting current U.S. restrictions on Chinese immigration.

A	B	C	D	E
Includes developments that affect more than one world region, international organizations and important meetings of major world leaders.	*Includes all domestic and regional developments in Europe, including the Soviet Union, Turkey, Cyprus and Malta.*	*Includes all domestic and regional developments in Africa and the Middle East, including Iraq and Iran and excluding Cyprus, Turkey and Afghanistan.*	*Includes all domestic and regional developments in Latin America, the Caribbean and Canada.*	*Includes all domestic and regional developments in Asian and Pacific nations, extending from Afghanistan through all the Pacific Islands, except Hawaii.*

U.S. Politics & Social Issues	U.S. Foreign Policy & Defense	U.S. Economy & Environment	Science, Technology & Nature	Culture, Leisure & Life Style	
					Oct. 29
	MacArthur names Gen. George Moore as commander of U.S. Western Pacific forces, most of which are stationed in the Philippines.		RCA demonstrates a color television system in which colors are transmitted electronically rather than mechanically, as in previous systems.		Oct. 30
California State Supreme Court upholds a law giving the state title to lands operated by aliens ineligible for citizenship.		OPA abolishes its 1,642 local price control boards and dismisses half of its 20,000 employes, effective Nov. 4 .... A 20-day strike of Washington hotel employes ends with wage increases of up to 7½¢ per hour.	Indiana Univ. Prof. Herman Muller is awarded the Nobel Prize in medicine and physiology for his discovery of mutations caused by X-rays.		Oct. 31
			Univ. of California, Berkeley announces completion of its 184-inch cyclotron the most powerful atom smasher in the world.	Basketball Assn. of America, a new pro league, opens its season .... British film *A Matter of Life and Death* is shown in London in the first Royal command performance of a motion picture.	Nov. 1
White House announces that 48 Estonians who recently entered the country without papers will not be deported and will be eventually given immigration visas.		A 50-day United Parcel Service strike in N.Y. ends with Teamster union members winning a 33½¢ hourly wage increase and a 40-hour week.	Dr. Forest Huddleson of Michigan State College announce development of a new vaccine for undulant fever in cattle.		Nov. 2
			Navy airship XM1 lands in Glynco, Ga. after setting a record of 170.3 hours in the air without refueling.	Arlene Rogers, wife of actor Roy Rogers, dies in Hollywood after giving birth to a son.	Nov. 3
Concluding this year's congressional campaign, Democratic National Chmn. Robert Hannegan calls voters to give the party a big mandate while GOP campaign director Clarence Brown predicts the election of a Republican Congress.	War and Navy Depts. name a military liaison committee headed by Gen. Lewis Brereton and Adm. Thorvald Solberg to work with the newly formed Atomic Energy Commission.			New York newspaper *PM* gives up its policy of relying on circulation income and announces that it will accept paid advertising. Editor Ralph Ingersoll resigns in protest of the decision and is replaced by John P. Lewis.	Nov. 4
F	G	H	I	J	
Includes elections, federal-state relations, civil rights and liberties, crime, the judiciary, education, health care, poverty, urban affairs and population.	*Includes formation and debate of U.S. foreign and defense policies, veterans affairs and defense spending. (Relations with specific foreign countries are usually found under the region concerned.)*	*Includes business, labor, agriculture, taxation, transportation, consumer affairs, monetary and fiscal policy, natural resources, pollution and accidents.*	*Includes worldwide scientific, medical and technological developments, natural phenomena, U.S. weather and natural disasters.*	*Includes the arts, religion, scholarship, communications media, sports, entertainment, fashions, fads and social life.*	

	World Affairs	Europe	Africa & the Middle East	The Americas	Asia & the Pacific
Nov. 5		Gen. Clay of the U.S. military government in Germany tells 200 German officials in Stuttgart that they have not proceeded thoroughly enough with denazification and threatens to place the program in American hands if there is not rapid improvement.	British authorities release eight Jewish Agency leaders from the Latrun detention camp in Palestine, where they have been held since June 29. Over 2,000 Haganah suspects are also released.		
Nov. 6	Speaking before the U.N. Social, Humanitarian and Cultural Commission, Soviet Deputy Foreign Min. Andrei Vishinsky reiterates his criticism of U.S. and British-operated refugee camps in Central Europe, claiming that fascist war criminals are hiding there . . . . In a trusteeship plan submitted to the U.N. Security Council, Truman demands sole authority for the U.S. over the Marshalls, Carolines and Marianas, island chains taken from Japan during World War II.	A meeting of state assembly representatives in the U.S. zone of Germany adopts a law guaranteeing freedom of the press . . . . Austrian Chancellor Leopold Figl announces that food rations will be increased from 1,200 to 1,550 calories daily due to a rise in UNRRA shipments.		Meeting in Washington, the Pan American Union elects Antonio Rocha, Colombian ambassador to the U.S., chairman of the governing board.	
Nov. 7	U.S. delegate John Foster Dulles tells the U.N. Trusteeship Comm. that the U.S. will retain "de facto control" over islands taken from Japan even if its trusteeship proposals are rejected . . . . At the N.Y. Council of Foreign Ministers, Italy rejects a Yugoslavian offer to let Italy keep Trieste in return for the town of Gorizia.	The 29th anniversary of the October Revolution is observed throughout the Soviet Union with parades and speeches, but Stalin is absent from the main celebration in Moscow.	Railroad traffic in Palestine halts for 21 hours following the fourth Zionist attack on railway installations and trains in two days.	Argentine Pres. Peron suspends all the country's newspapers for one day in an effort to eliminate criticism of his government.	Japan's national trade union organization joins the Social Democrats and Communists in demanding that the conservative Yoshida cabinet resign.
Nov. 8	Switzerland agrees to give the U.N. the 144-acre former League of Nations site in Geneva . . . . Socialists from 18 countries meet in Bournemouth under the chairmanship of British Labor Party leader Harold Laski to discuss possible formation of a new Socialist International.				Chiang Kai-shek orders troops to cease hostilities on Nov. 11 and invites the Communists to participate in a constitutional assembly meeting Nov. 12.
Nov. 9	A plenary session of the General Assembly admits Afghanistan, Iceland and Sweden as members, bringing total U.N. membership to 54 nations.				Vietnamese nationalists under Ho Chi Minh approve a new constitution for the Democratic Republic of Vietnam, not mentioning Vietnamese membership in the French Union and claiming Cochin China as an integral part of Vietnam.
Nov. 10		Elections for the first French National Assembly under the new constitution give the Communists the largest number of seats, 163 out of 619 . . . . Municipal elections in Rome and four other Italian cities result in large victories for the Socialist and Communist parties against the Christian Democrats.			Twenty thousand Moslems flee Bihar Province in northeastern India as Hindu-Moslem riots break out again following the departure of Viscount Wavell to New Dehli . . . . Pres. Nguyen Van Thinh of the French-supported provisional government for Cochin China commits suicide in Saigon. Local sources attribute the death to pressure among Thinh's associates for a union with the neighboring Democratic Republic of Vietnam.
	A *Includes developments that affect more than one world region, international organizations and important meetings of major world leaders.*	B *Includes all domestic and regional developments in Europe, including the Soviet Union, Turkey, Cyprus and Malta.*	C *Includes all domestic and regional developments in Africa and the Middle East, including Iraq and Iran and excluding Cyprus, Turkey and Afghanistan.*	D *Includes all domestic and regional developments in Latin America, the Caribbean and Canada.*	E *Includes all domestic and regional developments in Asian and Pacific nations, extending from Afghanistan through all the Pacific Islands, except Hawaii.*

U.S. Politics & Social Issues	U.S. Foreign Policy & Defense	U.S. Economy & Environment	Science, Technology & Nature	Culture, Leisure & Life Style	
Midterm elections give Republicans a landslide victory as they gain control of both houses of Congress and win a majority of state governorships. N.Y. Gov. Thomas Dewey emerges as a Republican presidential possibility when he wins re-election by 680,000 votes and becomes the first Republican in recent history to carry New York City. Among the winners in congressional elections are Senator-elect Joseph McCarthy (R, Wisc.), Representative-elect Richard Nixon (R, Calif.) and Representative-elect John F. Kennedy (D, Mass.) .... A measure requiring registered voters to "understand and explain" any part of the U.S. Constitution to the satisfaction of county registrars, aimed at barring Negro voters from the polls, is approved in Alabama .... District of Columbia residents vote overwhelmingly for the right to participate in national elections, but the referendum has no official standing.		Constitutional amendments outlawing the closed (or union) shop are adopted in Neb., S.D., and Ariz., while Mass. adopts a proposal requiring unions to publish financial statements.		Joseph Stella, American artist and innovator in visual arts, dies at 70 in N.Y.	Nov. 5
Truman returns to the White House after visiting Independence, Mo. He refuses to comment on yesterday's elections.	Air Force announces the start of production on its new B-36 bomber, which can carry nuclear weapons to any inhabited region in the world and return home without refueling.	Wage Stabilization Board approves wage increases of 10-16½¢ an hour for Western Union Telegraph workers in N.Y.C.		Mexico wins permanent possession of the International Military Special Challenge Trophy at the first full-scale National Horse Show in N.Y.	Nov. 6
		GM announces it will float a $100-million stock issue.	Navy Dept., Univ. of Michigan and the Johns Hopkins Univ. Applied Physics Lab announce construction of a 15-ton, 300 million volt synchrotron to produce energy for the study of subnuclear particles.	Dr. Allan Nevins of Columbia Univ. is awarded the $10,000 Scribner prize in American history for his forthcoming work *Ordeal of the Union* .... Ben Hogan captures the North & South Open Golf Tourney at Pinehurst, N.C.	Nov. 7
	State Dept. recalls the U.S. mission to Albania because the Hoxha regime "has failed to affirm its recognition of the validity" of treaties and agreements between the two countries .... Navy discloses that strong fleet units will visit ports in Turkey, Greece, Lebanon, Egypt, Saudi Arabia and Crete in late November and early December "incident to training exercises." Plans for an Antarctic expedition are also revealed, involving 5,000 Navy personnel under Adm. Richard Byrd to study weather conditions, test equipment and search for uranium deposits.				Nov. 8
		Truman removes all price, wage and salary controls except ceilings on rents, sugar and rice.	War Dept. announces plans for construction of a $20-million nuclear research laboratory in Schenectady, N.Y. to study use of atomic energy in power generation. The facility will be operated by General Electric.		Nov. 9
			Dr. Sanford Moss, inventor of the turbosupercharger for planes, dies at 74 in Lynn, Mass.		Nov. 10

F	G	H	I	J
Includes elections, federal-state relations, civil rights and liberties, crime, the judiciary, education, health care, poverty, urban affairs and population.	*Includes formation and debate of U.S. foreign and defense policies, veterans affairs and defense spending. (Relations with specific foreign countries are usually found under the region concerned.)*	*Includes business, labor, agriculture, taxation, transportation, consumer affairs, monetary and fiscal policy, natural resources, pollution and accidents.*	*Includes worldwide scientific, medical and technological developments, natural phenomena, U.S. weather and natural disasters.*	*Includes the arts, religion, scholarship, communications media, sports, entertainment, fashions, fads and social life.*

	World Affairs	Europe	Africa & the Middle East	The Americas	Asia & the Pacific
Nov. 11	UNRRA Director La Guardia urges that the U.N. establish a $400-million emergency food fund to take over the food allocation program when UNRRA ends Dec. 31.	U.S. military authorities announce a plan to break up the I.G. Farben chemical combine in the U.S. zone of Germany into 30 independent companies. Four hundred Danube barges and ships held by U.S. forces are also ordered returned to Yugoslavia and other owners .... Albanian Premier Enver Hoxha protests to the U.N. against a British decision to begin mine-clearing operations between Corfu and Albania. He also decries entry of a U.S. ship into the Albanian port of Durazzo to remove the American mission in Albania.			
Nov. 12	U.N. Social, Humanitarian and Cultural Commission resumes debate on the charter of the proposed International Refugee Organization, with agreement only on special arrangements for Spanish Republican refugees.	Moscow announces a drive to mobilize boys and girls of 14 for labor reserve and training in industrial schools as part of the five-year plan goal of increasing the work force by 1.2 million workers each year .... Franco announces that Spain will not seek U.N. membership at this time in order to avoid "disunion among nations," which its application might provoke .... British Parliament's second session under the Labor government is convened by King George VI.	British authorities in Palestine announce that 1,050 Jewish refugees now held in Cyprus will be admitted to Palestine under quotas until the middle of January.	Mexican government reveals discovery of uranium in Chihuahua Province .... Brazil's Supreme Electoral Tribunal raises the House of Deputies membership to 306.	U.S. prosecution at the Tokyo war crimes trial introduces evidence to show that Tojo was responsible for the July 1941 decision to go to war with Britain and the U.S. .... A typhoon strikes Negros Island in the Philippines, causing 260 deaths.
Nov. 13	South African Premier Jan Smuts tells the U.N. Trusteeship Council his country rejects any trusteeship plan for Southwest Africa and will continue to administer the territory even if the General Assembly votes against the proposed annexation.	U.S. and Britain begin talks in Washington on unified economic administration of their German occupation zones .... Swedish parliament ratifies the Russian trade and credit agreements concluded Oct. 7.	Bombs planted by Zionist terrorists in railway stations and streetcars kill 19 soldiers and policemen in Palestine in the fourth day of intensified violence.	Earthquakes continuing for the third day in the mountainous area of northern Peru cause over 500 deaths, the total destruction of two towns and extensive damage in more than 20.	
Nov. 14	U.S. delegate John Foster Dulles rejects South African annexation of Southwest Africa at the U.N. Trusteeship Council, virtually assuring rejection of the plan by the General Assembly. At the Economic and Financial Council, U.S. delegate Adlai Stevenson rejects La Guardia's proposal for an interim international relief fund, stating the U.S. prefers "direct" relief to needy countries.		In a speech opening the current session of the Egyptian parliament, King Farouk says the British have promised to withdraw their forces from Egypt by March 31 of next year.		
Nov. 15				Colombia's five Conservative ministers resign when the Liberal majority in Congress fails to agree on a proposal for cooperation with the administration.	Dutch and Indonesian negotiators meeting near Batavia sign the Linggadjati Agreement, providing for creation of a United States of Indonesia, including Sumatra, Java, Celebes and most of Borneo, within a Netherlands Union. Holland promises to sponsor Indonesia for U.N. membership .... China's Constitutional Assembly convenes in Nanking despite a boycott by Communists, the Democratic League and Social Democrats. Addressing the opening session, Chiang Kai-shek calls the Assembly the beginning of constitutional government in China.
Nov. 16	U.N. Social, Humanitarian and Cultural Commission unanimously adopts a Danish resolution urging all U.N. members to grant equal political rights to women.	U.S. and Britain warn Rumania that they expect upcoming parliamentary elections to be "free and fair."	Eight Communist leaders are arrested in Capetown, South Africa, on charges on inciting last August's gold mine strike.		Chou En-lai says in Nanking that the government's unilateral action in convening the Constitutional Assembly means the complete termination of peace negotiations.
Nov. 17		U.S. officials reveal in Washington that 18 Allied nations will receive an estimated $450 million from the liquidation of German assets in neutral countries.			Following termination of Communist-Nationalist negotiations, prices rise in Shanghai and Nanking as householders and businessmen buy up commodities and foreign currency in anticipation of full-scale civil war.
	A *Includes developments that affect more than one world region, international organizations and important meetings of major world leaders.*	B *Includes all domestic and regional developments in Europe, including the Soviet Union, Turkey, Cyprus and Malta.*	C *Includes all domestic and regional developments in Africa and the Middle East, including Iraq and Iran and excluding Cyprus, Turkey and Afghanistan.*	D *Includes all domestic and regional developments in Latin America, the Caribbean and Canada.*	E *Includes all domestic and regional developments in Asian and Pacific nations, extending from Afghanistan through all the Pacific Islands, except Hawaii.*

U.S. Politics & Social Issues	U.S. Foreign Policy & Defense	U.S. Economy & Environment	Science, Technology & Nature	Culture, Leisure & Life Style	
In his first public comment on the GOP election victories, Truman asks both parties to exercise "wisdom and restraint" and avoid the "serious difficulties" of divided government control.				Manuscript of a previously unknown string quartet by Benjamin Franklin is found in Paris .... Pre-war glitter marks the opening of the 62nd season of the Metropolitan Opera with Lily Pons singing the Leo Delibe's *Lakme.*	Nov. 11
Treasury Dept. announces that Robert Linville, "the most important international trafficker in narcotics known to the Narcotics Bureau at this time," has been arrested in Phoenix, Ariz.	Navy announces a reorganization of its operating forces effective January 1947, including elimination of the 3rd and 4th Fleets.	Federal Reserve Board permits corporate stockholders to buy new issues on 50% margin .... Chicago Bd. of Trade restores prewar daily price limits for grain futures.	*AMA Journal* reports that three doctors at Chicago's Children's Memorial Hospital have successfully operated on "blue babies" whose malformed hearts cannot pump sufficient blood to their lungs.	For the first time in history, Negro and white Baptists meet together in Georgia, as the General Missionary Baptists Convention holds a joint "good will" session in Savannah.	Nov. 12
		Mediator Charles Poletti grants weekly wage increases of $3-7 to 42,000 members of the International Ladies Garment Workers Union in N.Y.			Nov. 13
GOP House and Senate steering committees meet to set policy for the new Congress approving proposals for a 20% income tax cut, a decrease in government agency funds and reorganization of Congress .... Charges against three Army veterans accused of attempting to sell photographs of atom bomb equipment to a Baltimore newspaper, are dismissed by a federal court due to insufficient evidence.	Annual convention of Hadassah, the American Women's Zionist Organization, ends in Boston after hearing David Ben Gurion and others attack British policy in the Middle East and voting $1.5 million for medical work in Palestine during the next year.		Nobel Prize in chemistry is awarded to Prof. James Sumner of Cornell Univ. for enzymes research and Profs. Wendel Stanleu and John Northrop of Rockefeller Institute for Medical Research for work on viruses. The Nobel Prize in physics goes to Prof. Percy Bridgman of Harvard for atmospheric pressure studies.	German writer Hermann Hesse wins the Nobel Prize for literature, while the Nobel Peace Prize goes to Florida evangelist John Mott and Prof. Emily Greene of Wellesley, Mass., honorary president of the Women's International League for Peace and Freedom .... Manuel de Falla y Mateu, Spanish composer best known for his ballets, dies at 70 in Buenos Aires .... Maynard Dixon, American artist who spent more than 50 years interpreting the American West, dies at 71 in Tucson, Ariz. .... Samuel Reshevsky regains the U.S. chess title in N.Y. by defeating a field of competitors led by Isaac Kashdan.	Nov. 14
Rep. John Rankin (D, Miss.) requests that Harvard astronomer Harlow Shapley be cited for contempt of Congress, claiming that Shapley showed "utter disrespect" during testimony before the House Un-American Activities Comm.		United Mine Workers leader John Lewis notifies Interior Secy. Julius Krug that the UMW will terminate the collective contract for the soft coal industry in five days .... In a move to curb left-wing union affiliates, the annual CIO convention in Atlantic City adopts a rule threatening local councils with expulsion for actions opposed to CIO policy .... U.S. Employment Service, with 1,800 field offices and 24,000 employes, returns to state control after nearly five years of federal operation.		James Kendis, song writer and co-composer of *I'm Forever Blowing Bubbles*, dies at 63 in N.Y.	Nov. 15
Senate Campaign Investigating Committee votes to investigate the fitness of Sen. Theodore Bilbo (D, Miss.) to hold a Senate seat.	VA announces that 1,958,033 veterans have enrolled in college or on-the-job training courses under the GI bill.	TWA flights are resumed after the Air Line Pilots Assn. calls off its strike and agrees to submit the wage dispute to an arbitration board .... CIO Amalgamated Clothing Workers union announces establishment of a $1-million Sidney Hillman Foundation to foster work in the field of labor-management relations.			Nov. 16
Truman flies to Key West, Fla. for a week's vacation at the Navy submarine base.	Albert Einstein, head of an Emergency Committee of Atomic Scientists, opens a drive to raise one million dollars for public education on the atomic bomb menace.	Truman orders Attorney Gen. Tom Clark to obtain a court order preventing the United Mine Workers union from striking against government-operated plants.			Nov. 17
F *Includes elections, federal-state relations, civil rights and liberties, crime, the judiciary, education, health care, poverty, urban affairs and population.*	G *Includes formation and debate of U.S. foreign and defense policies, veterans affairs and defense spending. (Relations with specific foreign countries are usually found under the region concerned.)*	H *Includes business, labor, agriculture, taxation, transportation, consumer affairs, monetary and fiscal policy, natural resources, pollution and accidents.*	I *Includes worldwide scientific, medical and technological developments, natural phenomena, U.S. weather and natural disasters.*	J *Includes the arts, religion, scholarship, communications media, sports, entertainment, fashions, fads and social life.*	

	World Affairs	Europe	Africa & the Middle East	The Americas	Asia & the Pacific
Nov. 18	Big Four foreign ministers meeting in N.Y. reach a compromise on the powers of the governor of Trieste, who will control police and have emergency powers to suspend legislation under the city's international statute .... U.N. Political and Security Comm. concludes debate on the great power veto in the Security Council, with most small nations urging its elimination.	British House of Commons defeats a left-wing Laborite proposal for a "review and recast" of the government's foreign policy, stressing a loosening of ties with the U.S. British Fuel and Power Minister Emanuel Shinwell announces the government will take over ownership of coal mines Jan. 1, 1947 .... Marshal Ivan Konev succeeds Marshal Georgi Zhukov as commander of all Russian ground forces .... Gens. Eberhard von Mackensen and Kurt Maelzer, former German commanders in Italy, plead not guilty before a British military court in Rome trying them on charges of ordering the 1944 killing of 335 Italian civilians at the Ardeatine caves.	Reacting to recent assassinations of policemen and British soldiers, Tel Aviv police riot against Jews, firing into houses and attacking passers-by. Twenty Jews are injured in clashes with British troops.	Former Canadian Army officer David Lunan is sentenced to five years in prison for transmitting information to Russian agents.	French and Siamese negotiators agree to create a commission with French, Siamese and neutral representatives to study the dispute over the Siamese-French Indochina border.
Nov. 19	Afghanistan, Iceland and Sweden sign brief proclamations of adherence to the U.N. Charter and take their seats in the General Assembly .... Belgium, Colombia and Syria are elected to the Security Council for two-year terms .... French Premier Georges Bidault opens the first general UNESCO conference in Paris.	Russian Foreign Ministry abolishes broadcasts from Moscow by foreign correspondents, claiming they were a "temporary measure" resulting from wartime communications difficulties .... Parliamentary elections in Rumania give a two-thirds majority to the government bloc of Communists, Socialists, Ploughmen's Front and dissident Liberals .... Twenty students are injured as leftists battle conservatives at the Univ. of Vienna following a conservative victory in the election of Austrian student confederation leaders .... Municipal elections in the central Italian port of Leghorn give the Communists a 59% majority, the first undivided Communist victory in a Western European city.			
Nov. 20	Speaking before the U.N. Political and Security Comm., Molotov accuses U.S. and British troops of interfering in the internal affairs of countries in which they are stationed and urges all U.N. members to report to the Security Council on their military strength abroad.	Gen. William Draper, head of the economics division of the U.S. military government in Germany, issues his report *A Year of Potsdam*, stating that Germany faces economic collapse and demanding uniform application of the Potsdam agreement to revive the country .... U.S. State Dept. reaches an agreement with Czechoslovakia guaranteeing the U.S. most-favored-nation treatment.			Vietnamese nationalists set up barricades in Haiphong, killing 23 French soldiers, after Vietnamese militia units open fire on a French ship in the harbor .... Communists bar foreign newsmen from Yenan as the city prepares to defend itself against an anticipated Nationalist attack.
Nov. 21		At the N.Y. Council of Foreign Ministers, Molotov drops his demand for a customs union between Yugoslavia and Trieste but urges that British and U.S. forces be withdrawn from the city before local elections to avoid "external pressure" on voters .... Twenty-three German doctors plead not guilty before an American court in Nuremberg to charges of torturing thousands of concentration camp inmates in medical "experiments." .... Greek government announces that Communist guerrillas have been defeated in a nine-day battle at Skra near the Yugoslav border.	Gen. Nuri Pasha as Said becomes premier of Iraq.		Moslem League leader Mohammed Ali Jinnah reveals in New Delhi that the League will not participate in the Constituent Assembly to meet Dec. 9 due to continued killing of Indian Moslems in clashes with Hindus.
Nov. 22		Bulgarian Communist leader Georgi Dimitrov becomes premier and names a cabinet that includes 10 Communists, five Peasant Party members and two Socialists.		Bolivia's ruling Liberal Party nominates Luis Gernando Guachalla, former ambassador to the U.S., as president.	
Nov. 23	Negotiations on the great power veto in the Security Council end unsuccessfully when Britain, France, China and the U.S. reject a resolution proposed by Molotov opposing any modification of veto rights.	Polish Pres. Boleslaw Bierut says in Warsaw that the Catholic Church must "accept the new state of affairs" in Poland if it is to continue to enjoy its present privileges.	Fawzi Husseini, cousin of the Palestine Arab High Committee chairman, is murdered in Jerusalem, reportedly for selling land to Jews.		French cruiser *Suffren* shells Haiphong, reportedly killing 6,000 civilians, in continued fighting between Vietnamese nationalists and French forces.
Nov. 24		Voters in U.S.-occupied Wuerttemberg-Baden approve a new constitution and give the Christian Democrats a plurality of seats in the new state assembly .... Denmark reintroduces fuel rationing and France, the Netherlands, Sweden and Switzerland study methods of conserving fuel as Britain cuts coal exports from the Ruhr area .... Twelve Americans, stranded for five days in the Bernese Alps after the crash of their Army transport plane, are rescued by Swiss pilots.		Thomas Berreta, candidate for the pro-U.S. Colorado Party, is elected president of Uruguay.	Sydney, Australia reports plans to establish a 3,000-mile rocket testing range for Britain and the Commonwealth countries in western Australia and the Indian Ocean.

A	B	C	D	E
Includes developments that affect more than one world region, international organizations and important meetings of major world leaders.	*Includes all domestic and regional developments in Europe, including the Soviet Union, Turkey, Cyprus and Malta.*	*Includes all domestic and regional developments in Africa and the Middle East, including Iraq and Iran and excluding Cyprus, Turkey and Afghanistan.*	*Includes all domestic and regional developments in Latin America, the Caribbean and Canada.*	*Includes all domestic and regional developments in Asian and Pacific nations, extending from Afghanistan through all the Pacific Islands, except Hawaii.*

U.S. Politics & Social Issues	U.S. Foreign Policy & Defense	U.S. Economy & Environment	Science, Technology & Nature	Culture, Leisure & Life Style	
James J. ("Jimmy") Walker, mayor of New York from 1926 to 1932, dies at 65 in New York .... Senate War Investigating Committee orders a subcommittee to begin hearings on the dealings of Sen. Theodore Bilbo (D, Miss.) with war contractors in 1942.		Justice Dept. obtains a nine-day restraining order from federal district court in Washington, requiring UMW leader John Lewis to revoke his contract termination notice. Preparing for a possible coal strike, the Office of Defense Transportation orders a 25% cut in passenger train service and halts the movement of all trains not required as common carriers.			Nov. 18
		CIO International Longshoremen's and Warehousemen's union ends a 2½-month strike by Hawaii sugar plantation workers.			Nov. 19
	Navy Dept. reveals plans for the development of nuclear submarines capable of carrying atomic weapons.	Truman orders the Justice Dept. to press contempt charges against John L. Lewis if he disobeys the Nov. 18 court order against termination of the coal industry contract.		Western and Pacific Coast Football Conferences sign an agreement eliminating outside teams from Rose Bowl competition for five years .... Lillian Hellman's play *Another Part of the Forest* opens in N.Y. to favorable reviews.	Nov. 20
		A strike of 400,000 soft coal miners begins when UMW leader John Lewis refuses to obey a court order for postponement of the contract termination date. Lewis is ordered to appear at federal district court in Washington and "show cause" why he should not be prosecuted for contempt of court.		North Carolina Baptist Convention in Ashville defeats a resolution banning racial segregation in churches.	Nov. 21
U.S. district court in Washington dismisses charges against 26 surviving defendants of the 1942 mass sedition indictments, saying another trial would be a "travesty on justice."		UMW President Lewis returns to Washington to appear before U.S. district court in the current mining dispute, while 3,000 striking hard coal miners resume work .... Annual CIO convention ends in Atlantic City after re-electing Philip Murray president and UAW leaders Walter Reuther and R.J. Thomas vice presidents.		Baseball Writers Assn. votes St. Louis Cardinal Stan Musial the National League's most valuable player.	Nov. 22
Oscar Ewing of N.Y. is named Democratic national chairman, succeeding Robert Hannegan, who is reportedly on leave "for reasons of health."	Truman directs his personal representative to the Vatican, Myron Taylor, to return to Rome after a three-month absence.	Truman returns to Washington from Florida to confer on the coal strike with Labor Secy. Schwellenbach, Atty. Gen. Clark, Interior Secy. Krug and Special Counsel Clark Clifford.		Arthur Dove, American artist noted for his abstract paintings, dies at 66 in Centerport, N.Y.	Nov. 23
		OPA's Consumer Price Division ends its operations.	Dr. Robert Williams of N.Y. is awarded the 1946 Perkin Medal of the American chemical industry for his research on Vitamin B-1.	Orthodox Church of Serbia, with 100,000 members in the U.S., celebrates its 600th anniversary in services at the Cathedral of St. Sava, N.Y. .... Laszlo Moholy-Nagy, noted designer and director of the Institute of Design in Chicago, dies at 51.	Nov. 24

F	G	H	I	J
Includes elections, federal-state relations, civil rights and liberties, crime, the judiciary, education, health care, poverty, urban affairs and population.	*Includes formation and debate of U.S. foreign and defense policies, veterans affairs and defense spending. (Relations with specific foreign countries are usually found under the region concerned.)*	*Includes business, labor, agriculture, taxation, transportation, consumer affairs, monetary and fiscal policy, natural resources, pollution and accidents.*	*Includes worldwide scientific, medical and technological developments, natural phenomena, U.S. weather and natural disasters.*	*Includes the arts, religion, scholarship, communications media, sports, entertainment, fashions, fads and social life.*

	World Affairs	Europe	Africa & the Middle East	The Americas	Asia & the Pacific
Nov. 25		Britain agrees to release 45,000 Italians remaining in British prison camps by the end of January 1947.			
Nov. 26	Preparatory Committee of the International Conference on Trade and Employment ends its six-week London meeting with adoption of a draft world trade charter aimed at expanding employment through reduction of trade barriers .... Haiti is admitted to UNESCO, bringing the total number of voting nations to 29.	British P.M. Attlee blames delays in demobilization of the armed forces on slow progress with the European peace treaties.	A British soldier and a Jew are reported killed and 21 soldiers wounded as 3,375 Jewish refugees resist transfer to Cyprus from Haifa .... Egyptian Chamber of Deputies gives a vote of confidence to Premier Ismail Sidky Pasha, enabling him to sign the proposed security pact with Britain.		
Nov. 27	Council of Foreign Ministers reaches an agreement on Trieste after three weeks of negotiation, providing for a governor appointed by the Security Council, reduction of Allied troops and election of a local assembly.	U.S., Britain and France advise Berlin's City Assembly to elect 16 aldermen despite Russian insistence that each candidate have prior Allied approval.	Azerbaijan Province threatens to declare independence as Iranian troops enter the area to supervise upcoming elections.	Argentine Pres. Peron tells a meeting of industrial leaders "you must either accept a system of state intervention and controls or lose everything by way of Communism." .... Wartime controls on wages and salaries are removed in Canada, but price controls are retained .... Brazil completes plans for transferring the capital to a specially designed city in the central plateau.	MacArthur orders the freezing of all assets of Japan's 10 wealthiest families, which will be placed under supervision of the Holding Co. Liquidation Commission .... Russia and U.S. sign an interim agreement permitting the repatriation of 25,000 Japanese prisoners now in Soviet-held territory .... Parliamentary elections in New Zealand result in a victory for the governing Labor Party over the minority National Party.
Nov. 28	At the N.Y. Council of Foreign Ministers, Byrnes accepts Molotov's proposal for a Big Four declaration recognizing the principle of free trade and free navigation on the Danube .... Relief and Rehabilitation Committee of UNESCO approves a plan to raise $100 million in 1947 for reconstruction of schools and educational equipment in war-devasted areas.	British Labor government makes public the text of its transportation nationalization bill under which most of the road, rail and inland waterway transport systems will be taken over by the state on Jan. 1, 1948 and placed under a transport commission .... French National Assembly meets for the first time in the old Chamber of Deputies as the cabinet and Premier Georges Bidault resign to permit selection of a new government by the Assembly.			French forces battling Vietnamese nationalists in Tonkin report capturing the Haiphong airfield .... Claiming that he has "no more political ambition," Chiang Kai-shek presents the Chinese Constitutional Assembly with a draft of a new constitution providing for a system of checks and balances and limitations upon the president .... Congress Party leader Nehru agrees to accompany Viscount Wavell to London to take part in an emergency meeting of the British cabinet on India.
Nov. 29		Communist and Socialist parties agreee to unite in Poland as two socialists are named to the government .... Greek Premier Constantin Tsaldaris calls his cabinet into an extraordinary session as fighting between government forces and guerrillas is reported in various parts of the country .... Gustav Noske, former German defense minister under the Weimar Republic who was imprisoned by the Nazis, dies at 78 in Hanover.	Palestine's Supreme Court rejects a habeas corpus petition to prevent the deportation of Jewish refugees.	Ecuador's Constitutional Congress votes to retain Dr. Jose Maria Velasco Ibarra as president until Sept. 1, 1948.	French cabinet decides to send reinforcements to Tonkin, where fighting between French forces and Vietnamese nationalists continues .... All British and Indian troops are withdrawn from newly independent Indonesia.
Nov. 30	U.N. General Assembly approves an Indian-sponsored resolution urging South Africa to improve its policies towards Indians and other "colored" residents of the country. Britain, Australia, Canada and the U.S. oppose the resolution .... A revised U.N. emblem is adopted and legal steps recommended to protect it against commercialization.	British military court in Rome sentences Gens. Eberhard von Mackensen and Kurt Maelzer to death for the 1944 shooting of Italian hostages in the Ardeatine caves.			Social Democrats and Youth Party boycott today's Assembly session in Nanking to avoid taking an oath binding them to obey the Kuomintang.
Dec. 1	Sen. Tom Connally, U.S. delegate to the U.N. Political and Security Comm., says the U.S. will not accept any veto arrangement in an international arms control agreement.	Legislative elections in Bavaria result in a victory for the conservative Christian Social Union, while voters in Hesse approve the new state constitution and give Social Democrats a majority in the state assembly .... Rumanian's King Michael affirms a policy of friendship with Russia and announces that the state will take over the national bank.		Miguel Aleman Valdes is inaugurated as Mexico's president.	
Dec. 2	U.S. delegate Connally presents a resolution to the U.N. Political and Security Comm. barring Spain from all U.N. activities until a "new and acceptable government" is formed. The action follows a Polish demand that all U.N. members sever relations with Spain.	U.S. and Britain sign an agreement for the economic merger of their German occupation zones, effective Jan. 1, 1947 .... Rev. Joseph Tiso, president of the wartime collaborationist Slovak Republic, goes on trial for war crimes in Czechoslovakia.		Panama's cabinet resigns after the public works and education ministers clash over the site of a trade school.	

A	B	C	D	E
Includes developments that affect more than one world region, international organizations and important meetings of major world leaders.	*Includes all domestic and regional developments in Europe, including the Soviet Union, Turkey, Cyprus and Malta.*	*Includes all domestic and regional developments in Africa and the Middle East, including Iraq and Iran and excluding Cyprus, Turkey and Afghanistan.*	*Includes all domestic and regional developments in Latin America, the Caribbean and Canada.*	*Includes all domestic and regional developments in Asian and Pacific nations, extending from Afghanistan through all the Pacific Islands, except Hawaii.*

U.S. Politics & Social Issues	U.S. Foreign Policy & Defense	U.S. Economy & Environment	Science, Technology & Nature	Culture, Leisure & Life Style	
Truman sets up a Temporary Commission on Employe Loyalty to study ways of barring "disloyal or subversive" persons, particularly Communists, from the government payroll .... Supreme Court supports a claim by the Tillamook Indians of Oregon for payment for lands taken from them by the U.S.		Justice T. Alan Goldsborough of U.S. district court in Washington orders UMW Pres. Lewis to stand trial on contempt charges for disobeying a court order to postpone termination of the coal industry contract .... Supreme Court upholds a clause of the 1935 Public Utility Holding Co. Act that calls for the dissolution of holding companies whose existence "unduly" complicates a corporate structure or causes unfair distribution of voting power among security holders .... St. Paul, Minn. schools are closed as 1,160 teachers strike for $2,400-$3,600 yearly wages.	Dorothy Burns sues Westinghouse Electric for $200,000, charging she became ill through exposure to uranium and other fissionable materials while working at the company's Newark, N.J. plant.		Nov. 25
House Campaign Expenditures Committee announces it will conduct an investigation of the 18th Congressional District of N.Y., home of Rep. Vito Marcantonio (American Labor Party), to determine if voters were intimidated or coerced.	President and Mrs. Truman hold a diplomatic dinner for representatives of 30 nations, the first since 1939.			*No Exit*, a play by Jean-Paul Sartre staged by John Huston, opens in N.Y.	Nov. 26
			Allen Dumont Labs in Washington demonstrates a new method of transmitting pictures and sound by light beams instead of radio.	A New York special sessions court finds Edmund Wilson's *Memoirs of Hecate County* obscene and fines the publisher, Doubleday, $1,000.	Nov. 27
			Theodore Miller, pioneer in the development of international telephone communications, dies at 66 in San Antonio, Tex.		Nov. 28
		OPA Dir. Paul Porter resigns for personal reasons.			Nov. 29
		Continuing coal strike causes unemployment in steel and related industries to rise to 100,000, while 175,000 auto workers are given weekend layoffs .... CIO officials reveal in Pittsburgh that steps are being taken to remove Communists and "fellow travelers" from positions of influence within the CIO.			Nov. 30
Veterans who occupied 50 homes in Chicago as "squatters" begin to move out after the Chicago Housing Authority promises not to prosecute.	U.S. Mediterranean Fleet under Adm. Bernard Bieri anchors in Beirut for a "goodwill" visit.				Dec. 1
		Federal Judge Walter La Guy in Chicago strikes down the Lea Act, aimed at restricting labor practices in the communications industry, as unconstitutional .... A UP survey finds 13 of 14 leading U.S. economists think the country faces a depression in the near future.	Eight Navy ships leave Norfolk, Va., to be joined by four more from San Diego and Port Hueneme, Calif., in the largest Antarctic expedition in history .... Dr. Enrico Fermi reveals in Chicago that the U.S. now has five controlled nuclear chain reaction piles in operation.	France's top literary prize, the Goncourt, is won by Jean Jacques Gautier for his first novel, *Histoire d'un Faitdivers*.	Dec. 2

F	G	H	I	J
Includes elections, federal-state relations, civil rights and liberties, crime, the judiciary, education, health care, poverty, urban affairs and population.	*Includes formation and debate of U.S. foreign and defense policies, veterans affairs and defense spending. (Relations with specific foreign countries are usually found under the region concerned.)*	*Includes business, labor, agriculture, taxation, transportation, consumer affairs, monetary and fiscal policy, natural resources, pollution and accidents.*	*Includes worldwide scientific, medical and technological developments, natural phenomena, U.S. weather and natural disasters.*	*Includes the arts, religion, scholarship, communications media, sports, entertainment, fashions, fads and social life.*

	World Affairs	Europe	Africa & the Middle East	The Americas	Asia & the Pacific
Dec. 3		Socialist Vincent Auriol is elected president of the French National Assembly.		Argentine Pres. Peron names Jose Figuerola administrator of his five-year social-military development program.	
Dec. 4	In the first Soviet concession on the veto issue, Molotov tells the General Assembly that the veto need not apply to proposed international arms control commissions . . . . U.N. General Assembly turns over all resolutions on Spain to an 18-nation subcommittee for consideration . . . . Greek delegate Vassili Dendramis submits to the Security Council charges of border violations by Yugoslavia, Albania and Bulgaria, asking an investigation commission be sent to Greece.	Gen. Joseph McNarey orders the U.S. military government in Germany to drop its policy of hostility towards Germans and help in the country's reconstruction.			Australian Labor Party refuses to approve the Bretton Woods Agreement, preventing Australia from joining the World Bank by year's end.
Dec. 5	Despite an impassioned appeal from UNRRA director LaGuardia to the U.N. Economic and Financial Comm., the U.S. and Britain refuse to join any new international relief agency.	Elections to the Berlin City Council give Social Democrats the largest number of seats (seven of 14), allowing Socialist Otto Ostrowski to become Lord Mayor of Berlin.			
Dec. 6	Council of Foreign Ministers in N.Y. completes negotiation on all questions relating to the Italian, Rumanian, Hungarian and Finnish peace treaties and decides to present the treaties for signature in early February . . . . British biologist Julian Huxley is elected UNESCO director-general for a two-year term . . . . A subcommittee of the U.N. Trusteeship Council over-rides Russian objections and assigns control of Western Samoa to New Zealand, Ruanda-Urundi to Belgium, New Guinea to Australia, Tanganyika and the British Cameroons to Britain and French Togoland and the French Cameroons to France.	Russian military authorities forbid meetings of the Berlin Council of Aldermen, claiming it must first be approved by all Allied commanders . . . . Yugoslavia's National Assembly approves a law nationalizing 42 industries with owners paid in state bonds.			British cabinet conference on India breaks down in London as Moslem League leader Mohammed Ali Jinnah refuses to change his stand on the Moslem boycott of the forthcoming Indian Constituent Assembly . . . . Chinese Communists notify Gen. Marshall they will not resume negotiations with the Nationalists until the dissolution of the "illegal" Constitutional Assembly in Nanking.
Dec. 7	U.S. tells the U.N. Political and Security Comm. it will not observe a U.N. decision to break off diplomatic relations with Spain.		Britain postpones the reopening of the London Palestine Conference until January to allow delegates from the World Zionist Congress to attend after their forthcoming meeting.		
Dec. 8	U.N. General Assembly adopts a resolution noting India's charge of racial discrimination against South Africa and calling for a report on the situation in the next Assembly session.				
Dec. 9		Britain sends Albania a note protesting the laying of mines in the Corfu channel as a "deliberately hostile act."	World Zionist Congress convenes in Basel, Switzerland and hears its president, Chaim Weizmann, reiterate his demand for a Jewish state in Palestine . . . . Egypt's King Farouk names Mahmoud Fahmy Nokrashy Pasha of the Saasist Party as premier after Ismail Sidky Pasha resigns due to ill health.		India's Constituent Assembly opens in New Delhi despite a Moslem League boycott.

A	B	C	D	E
Includes developments that affect more than one world region, international organizations and important meetings of major world leaders.	*Includes all domestic and regional developments in Europe, including the Soviet Union, Turkey, Cyprus and Malta.*	*Includes all domestic and regional developments in Africa and the Middle East, including Iraq and Iran and excluding Cyprus, Turkey and Afghanistan.*	*Includes all domestic and regional developments in Latin America, the Caribbean and Canada.*	*Includes all domestic and regional developments in Asian and Pacific nations, extending from Afghanistan through all the Pacific Islands, except Hawaii.*

U.S. Politics & Social Issues	U.S. Foreign Policy & Defense	U.S. Economy & Environment	Science, Technology & Nature	Culture, Leisure & Life Style	
An all-white jury in Atlanta acquits Roswell Biggers on charges of holding five Negroes in involuntary servitude.	Republican members of the Senate War Investigating Comm. publish a report which criticizes the U.S. military government in Germany for supporting Eastern European refugees who refuse to return to their home countries and alleges that migration of Jews from Poland to Western Europe is part of an "organized and well-financed plan." .... United Jewish Appeal ends a four-day conference in Atlantic City after hearing War. Secy. Robert Patterson urge that the U.S. admit European refugees and approving a fund-raising goal of $170 million for refugee aid in 1947.	Justice T. Alan Goldsborough of U.S. District Court in Washington convicts UMW Pres. Lewis of civil and criminal contempt for violating an order to revoke the union's notice of contract termination. Lewis admits the violation but condemns the order for forcing miners into "involuntary servitude." .... Oakland, Calif. is tied up by a general strike of more than 100,000 union members protesting police action in breaking up a department store clerks' picket line.		AP sports writers choose Notre Dame as the best college football team, while Army receives the Lambert Trophy for being the best Eastern team.	Dec. 3
	Army announces creation of a commission of five generals to study defense against atomic and other modern weapons.	After convicting UMW leader Lewis for contempt, Judge Goldsborough fines the UMW $3.5 million and Lewis $10,000.			Dec. 4
Senate Campaign Investigating Committee ends a four-day probe into the campaign tactics of Sen. Theodore Bilbo (D, Miss.) after hearing testimony of over 50 Negroes who charged they were prevented from voting in the Mississippi Democratic primary .... Truman establishes a 15-man Committee on Civil Rights with GM Pres. Charles Wilson as chairman.	Despite a drop in enlistments, the War Dept. extends the draft suspension through January.	Little Inch pipeline, operated by the Tennessee Gas and Transmission Co., begins moving natural gas from the Southwest to the Northeast at a daily rate of 50 million cubic feet .... Civilian Production Administrator John Small resigns.			Dec. 5
	Fleet Adm. William Halsey, hero of Guadalcanal and Leyte Gulf, retires from the Navy.	After UMW leader Lewis appeals his contempt conviction and fine to the circuit court of appeals in Washington, the Justice Dept. asks the Supreme Court to try the case .... Interstate Commerce Commission raises rail and water freight rates an average of 17.6%.			Dec. 6
		Lewis ends the 17-day national coal strike, claiming the Supreme Court must be allowed to judge the union-government dispute "free from public pressure induced by the hysteria and frenzy of an economic crisis." .... Atlanta's Winecoff Hotel is swept by fire, causing 119 deaths — the highest toll in any U.S. hotel fire.		Football Writers Assn. names Notre Dame tackle George Connor winner of the Outland Trophy.	Dec. 7
	Acting State Secy. Dean Acheson says the U.S. will not give free relief to nations which have not proved their need or which maintain large armies after UNRRA's end.	N.J. CIO approves a strong resolution opposing Communist "interference in the affairs of the CIO." .... Despite the end of the coal strike, the Solid Fuels Admin. announces that coal controls will be continued to ensure deliveries to essential users until stocks are replenished.		Sam Snead wins the Miami Open Golf Tourney.	Dec. 8
Supreme Court upholds the 1928 murder conviction of Leroy Carter of Illinois, despite evidence that Carter had no lawyer at his trial.	Carnegie Endowment for International Peace in New York elects State Dept. official Alger Hiss as president.	Supreme Court agrees to hear the Lewis-UMW contempt appeal.	Univ. of Minnesota's Mayo Clinic receives the American Pharmaceutical Manufacturers Assn. award for public health work.		Dec. 9

F	G	H	I	J
Includes elections, federal-state relations, civil rights and liberties, crime, the judiciary, education, health care, poverty, urban affairs and population.	*Includes formation and debate of U.S. foreign and defense policies, veterans affairs and defense spending. (Relations with specific foreign countries are usually found under the region concerned.)*	*Includes business, labor, agriculture, taxation, transportation, consumer affairs, monetary and fiscal policy, natural resources, pollution and accidents.*	*Includes worldwide scientific, medical and technological developments, natural phenomena, U.S. weather and natural disasters.*	*Includes the arts, religion, scholarship, communications media, sports, entertainment, fashions, fads and social life.*

	World Affairs	Europe	Africa & the Middle East	The Americas	Asia & the Pacific
Dec. 10	Molotov agrees in the General Assembly to a British proposal for creation of a veto-free international commission to inspect troops and armaments of all nations .... Director La Guardia addresses the opening session of the Sixth UNRRA Council in Washington, denying charges of "politics" in the UNRRA and warning that no nation can be allowed to interfere with the organization's plan to distribute $662 million in aid .... General Assembly approves a draft constitution for the International Refugee Organization despite Soviet bloc opposition.	Allied commanders in Berlin approve the 14 new members of the city's council of aldermen.	World Zionist Congress meeting in Basel re-elects Chaim Weizmann president and hears Rabbi Abba Hillel Silver oppose partition of Palestine into Jewish and Arab states.		
Dec. 11	U.N. General Assembly adopts a resolution urging wealthy nations to establish individual relief programs and recommending creation of a 10-nation committee to report on relief needs after the end of UNRRA.	A four-day All-Slav Congress ends in Belgrade after adopting a resolution to create a cultural alliance of five-Slavic nations: Russia, Bulgaria, Czechoslovakia, Poland and Yugoslavia .... U.S. Army announces lifting of the ban against marriage of American soldiers to German girls.	Speaking at the World Zionist Congress meeting in Basel, Vice Pres. Emanuel Neumann of the Zionist Organization of America rejects negotiations with Britain and says Zionists must depend on U.S. influence and the armed strength of Palestinian Jews .... Iranian troops occupy Mianeh in Azerbaijan, ending the province's autonomy. Azerbaijani nationalist leader Jaafar Pishevari orders his forces to surrender and flees to Russia.	Venezuelan Pres. Betancourt announces that a day-old military revolt against the government is crushed and says there will be no executions.	
Dec. 12	U.N. General Assembly passes a compromise resolution on Spain, urging member nations to recall their ministers from Spain, barring the country from participation in U.N. agencies and calling on the Security Council to take up the issue again if Spain does not establish a democratic government "within a reasonable time." .... Council of Foreign Ministers ends its N.Y. meetings after agreeing to set up special committees to study the Austrian and German peace treaties.	Socialist Leon Blum is elected by the French National Assembly to serve as interim premier .... Greek Premier Constantin Tsaldaris accuses Yugoslavia, Bulgaria and Albania of creating a state of "undeclared war" in border clashes against Greece.		Guatemala temporarily bans strikes and slowdowns in the face of threatened protests against United Fruit Co. and International Railways of Central America .... Canadian Prime Minister W. Mackenzie King announces cabinet changes involving the Defense, Foreign Affairs, Finance and National Health and Welfare ministries.	South Korea's first occupation legislature opens in Seoul, boycotted by the rightist Han Kook Party because of invalidation of elections in two provinces .... Allied authorities in Tokyo issue requirements for the licensing of news media in Japan to control "propaganda" from Soviet and other sources.
Dec. 13		British House of Commons ends a two-day debate on India by endorsing the government policy on Indian independence.			U.S. Reparations Commissioner Edwin Pauley charges that Russian forces did $850 million in damage by dismantling industrial facilities during their occupation of Manchuria.
Dec. 14	U.N. General Assembly unanimously approves a disarmament proposal calling for prohibition of nuclear weapons, international control of atomic energy and creation of an arms control agency not limited by great power veto .... General Assembly accepts an offer by John D. Rockefeller, Jr. to buy and turn over to the U.N. an $8.5-million property on the east side of Manhattan between 42nd and 48th Streets. The area will be the site of the U.N. general headquarters .... General Assembly rejects South Africa's plan to annex Southwest Africa and requests that a trusteeship plan be drawn up for the territory.	Greek Acting Foreign Min. Stephanos Stefanopoulos protests to the Big Four concerning "unjust" Greek-Bulgarian frontier provisions contained in the Bulgarian peace treaty.		Chile lays claim to parts of Antarctica "between the 53rd and 90th meridians west of Greenwich."	Chinese Nationalist troops claim the capture of Yengcheng, one of the last Communist centers in the economically crucial coastal province of Kiangsu .... Moslem League leader Mohammed Ali Jinnah rejects a British proposal that the Federal Court of India rule on Moslem-Hindu differences on the British plan for drafting an Indian constitution.
Dec. 15	U.N. General Assembly holds its final meeting until September 1947 after passing a budget and a constitution for the International Refugee Organization and admitting Siam as 55th U.N. member.	U.S. officials in Vienna complete a proposed four-year economic reconstruction plan for Austria.	Executive committee of the World Zionist Congress suspends six members of the Zionist Revisionist Union of America for requesting U.N. discussion of the Palestine problem and appealing for funds to support "underground fighters." .... Kurdish nationalist leader Ghazi Mohammed surrenders to Iranian forces after the capture of Mehabad, capital of Kurdistan Province.		Nationalist sources report strong Communist attacks on the fortress city of Yulin in northern Shensi province.
	A	B	C	D	E
	Includes developments that affect more than one world region, international organizations and important meetings of major world leaders.	*Includes all domestic and regional developments in Europe, including the Soviet Union, Turkey, Cyprus and Malta.*	*Includes all domestic and regional developments in Africa and the Middle East, including Iraq and Iran and excluding Cyprus, Turkey and Afghanistan.*	*Includes all domestic and regional developments in Latin America, the Caribbean and Canada.*	*Includes all domestic and regional developments in Asian and Pacific nations, extending from Afghanistan through all the Pacific Islands, except Hawaii.*

U.S. Politics & Social Issues	U.S. Foreign Policy & Defense	U.S. Economy & Environment	Science, Technology & Nature	Culture, Leisure & Life Style	
	Air Force discloses that its first rocket plane, the Bell XS-1, capable of 1,700 mph at an 80,000-ft. altitude, has been successfully flown at Muroc Lake, Calif.	GM Pres. Charles Wilson, head of Truman's civil rights commission, proposes a five-point labor law program which would outlaw industry-wide bargaining and compulsory unionization as well as sympathy strikes and boycotts.	CBS announces development of a television receiver capable of handling either black and white or color images.	Hall of Fame baseball pitcher Walter Johnson dies at 59 in Washington .... Damon Runyon, columnist and widely read short story author, dies at 62 in New York.	Dec. 10
	Former OPA head Paul Porter is named leader of a State Dept. economic mission to Greece.	CIO releases a market analysis report stating that "total corporate business can support a 25% increase in wages" without raising prices. CIO Pres. Murray says unions will use the report as a "guidepost" in wage talks .... CIO Textile Workers Union Pres. Emil Rieve announces agreement with New England and Middle Atlantic state cotton manufacturers on a 10¢ hourly wage increase for 90,000 textile workers .... House Special Committee on Post-War Economic Policy and Planning issues its final report, recommending lower income taxes, continued rent controls and "constructive but not punitive" labor legislation.			Dec. 11
Senate War Investigating committee hears Army engineers testify that Sen. Theodore Bilbo (D, Miss.) was active in securing over $25-million in contracts to build war installations in his state.	Truman names nine scientists as advisers to the Atomic Energy Commission, including Manhattan Project workers Enrico Fermi, Glenn Seaborg and J. Robert Oppenheimer.	Truman creates an office of Temporary Controls headed by Gen. Philip Fleming to take over and liquidate the OPA, Civilian Production Administration, Office of Economic Stabilization and Office of War Mobilization and Reconversion.	Robert J. Collier Aviation Trophy goes to Dr. Luis W. Alvarez for his work on radar .... Physicist Charles B. Thwing, author of Thwing's law of inductivity, dies at 86 in Philadelphia.		Dec. 12
An Atlanta grand jury indicts Pres. Emory Burke and Secy. Homer Loomis of the white supremacist Columbians, Inc. on charges of conspiring to riot and illegal possession of dynamite.	Speaking before the U.N. General Assembly, State Secy. Byrnes reveals that the U.S. has 550,000 troops stationed abroad, mainly in Germany, Austria, Japan and Korea .... Abilene, Kan. announces that the Eisenhower home will be preserved as the center of a million-dollar memorial to him and the armed forces.			National Negro Congress in N.Y. pickets Walt Disney's *Song of the South* as "an insult to the Negro."	Dec. 13
		Truman drops building materials priorities and the $10,000 limit on new homes, allowing greater participation in the housing market.	Columbia Univ. announces it will build a 2,500-ton cyclotron as part of a research center being set up in cooperation with the Navy in Irvington, N.Y.		Dec. 14
Maud Nathan, women's suffrage pioneer and social reformer, dies at 85 in N.Y.				Alvin Paris is arrested in N.Y. on charges of trying to bribe N.Y. Giant players Merle Hapes and Frank Filchock to throw the NFL championship game.	Dec. 15
F *Includes elections, federal-state relations, civil rights and liberties, crime, the judiciary, education, health care, poverty, urban affairs and population.*	G *Includes formation and debate of U.S. foreign and defense policies, veterans affairs and defense spending. (Relations with specific foreign countries are usually found under the region concerned.)*	H *Includes business, labor, agriculture, taxation, transportation, consumer affairs, monetary and fiscal policy, natural resources, pollution and accidents.*	I *Includes worldwide scientific, medical and technological developments, natural phenomena, U.S. weather and natural disasters.*	J *Includes the arts, religion, scholarship, communications media, sports, entertainment, fashions, fads and social life.*	

	World Affairs	Europe	Africa & the Middle East	The Americas	Asia & the Pacific
Dec. 16		French socialist Premier Leon Blum forms an all-Socialist interim cabinet with Guy Mollet as minister of state .... Reports from Irkutsk reveal that three million German and Japanese POWs are building railways and highways in Siberia.	Egyptian Premier Mahmoud Fahmy Nokrashy Pasha receives a vote of confidence from parliament on his intention to bring about a union with the Sudan.	Argentine Pres. Peron announces the liberalization of credit, allowing the government to make home and business loans at 2-5% interest.	
Dec. 17		An electoral commission in Warsaw approves the candidacy of 110 conservative Peasant Party members in upcoming parliamentary elections .... Turkey arrests 44 "Marxists" and suspends two Socialist parties, the Union of Istanbul Workers Syndicates and the Istanbul Workers Club, charging them with activities aimed at "reversing the economic and social order." .... German conductor Wilhelm Furtwaengler is cleared and allowed to resume his career by a denazification tribunal in Berlin.		Venezuela's new Constituent Assembly officially assumes power.	Fighting between French troops and Vietnamese nationalists spreads from Tonkin to Annam, as French Minister for Overseas Territories Marius Moutet leaves Paris for Hanoi to investigate the situation .... Japan's House of Representatives defeats a Socialist motion for immediate dissolution of the Diet, while 150,000 demonstrators in Tokyo demand the resignation of the Yoshida cabinet.
Dec. 18		A bill to nationalize all of Britain's transport is approved by the House of Commons on its second reading .... U.S. military authorities in Berlin ban the use of cigarettes for trading in the officially approved barter markets.	Sir William Fitzgerald, British chief justice of Palestine, recommends the division of Jerusalem into Jewish and Arab sectors.		Allied Far Eastern Commission in Washington eases Japan's reparations schedule to help the government combat inflation.
Dec. 19	U.N. Security Council accepts a U.S. proposal to set up a commission to investigate border strife in Greece.	Britain's National Coal Board orders a five-day week for workers in state-owned mines beginning May 5.		Ricardo Guardo and Silvio Pontieri resign as president and vice president of the Argentine Chamber of Deputies.	Vietnamese nationalists attack French districts in Hanoi and seize French civilians as hostages in the current conflict .... Russia signs a pact with the U.S. to repatriate Japanese prisoners now in the Soviet-held areas at the rate of 50,000 a month.
Dec. 20	U.N. Atomic Energy Commission votes to accept the Baruch nuclear control plan "on principle."	British authorities in Hamburg order immediate trials for 27,000 members of the SS and other Nazi organizations condemned for war crimes at Nuremberg.			French forces recapture parts of Hanoi seized yesterday by Vietnamese nationalists, who take refuge west of the city near Ha Dong .... Russian occupation authorities order a U.S. courier ship out of the Manchurian port of Dairen after a two-day stay, creating an international incident .... Britain offers Burma independence on the same terms extended to India and invites a Burmese delegation to London for negotiations.
Dec. 21		In accordance with the Dec. 9 U.N. decision on Spain, Britain recalls its ambassador to Spain, Sir Victor Mallet .... Bavarian State Assembly elects Christian Social Unionist Hans Ehard as minister president of Bavaria.	Arab Higher Executive Comm. announces that Palestinian Arabs will refuse to pay taxes if the money is used to support Jewish immigration.	Mexican Pres. Miguel Aleman supports the state oil agency in dismissing 50 leaders of the national oil workers' union for a Dec. 19 strike.	A major subterranean earthquake followed by six tidal waves strikes 60,000 square miles of southern Japan, causing more than 1,000 deaths and leaving 100,000 homeless.
Dec. 22		British and Soviet officials in Germany sign a three-month agreement by which the Russian zone will furnish grain, forage, fuel and wood pulp to the British zone in return for iron, steel and tires .... Warsaw reports the Peasant Party has been allowed to file candidates for the forthcoming elections in all 52 electoral districts.			British Viceroy of India Viscount Wavell returns to New Delhi from conferences in London.
Dec. 23	A U.N. Food and Agricultural Organization report issued today that a food crisis still confronts the world, with food production still below prewar levels.	Gen. Lucius Clay, deputy U.S. military governor in Germany, protests a French decision to set up a customs barrier between the Saar and the rest of Germany .... Britain rejects a Soviet request for a "further exchange of views" on control of the Dardanelles.			French Premier Blum reiterates France's recognition of Vietnam's independence within the French Union but insists that order be restored before negotiations can begin on the composition of the Vietnamese government .... Britain announces it will send a Treasury delegation to India to negotiate the settlement of India's wartime sterling debt of $5.2 billion.
Dec. 24		French Fourth Republic officially comes into existence as the Council of the Republic, the upper legislative house, holds its first session .... U.S. military authorities in Frankfurt announce a Christmas amnesty for more than 800,000 Germans in the U.S. zone facing prosecution under denazification laws.	World Zionist Congress ends its 16-day meeting in Basel after adopting a resolution to boycott the London Palestine conference in January.	Mexican Oil Workers union votes not to fight the dismissal of 50 union leaders from their jobs in the government-owned oil industry.	Vietnamese nationalist leader Ho Chi Minh claims in a Christmas message that current fighting with French forces was precipitated by a French demand for control of the police in Hanoi .... A committee representing Britain, native Sultans and the United Malaya nationalist organization proposes a new constitution for an independent "Federation of Malaya."
	A *Includes developments that affect more than one world region, international organizations and important meetings of major world leaders.*	B *Includes all domestic and regional developments in Europe, including the Soviet Union, Turkey, Cyprus and Malta.*	C *Includes all domestic and regional developments in Africa and the Middle East, including Iraq and Iran and excluding Cyprus, Turkey and Afghanistan.*	D *Includes all domestic and regional developments in Latin America, the Caribbean and Canada.*	E *Includes all domestic and regional developments in Asian and Pacific nations, extending from Afghanistan through all the Pacific Islands, except Hawaii.*

U.S. Politics & Social Issues	U.S. Foreign Policy & Defense	U.S. Economy & Environment	Science, Technology & Nature	Culture, Leisure & Life Style	
N.Y. Court of Appeals upholds the government's right to discharge employes suspected of disloyalty by rejecting the reinstatement plea of Morton Friedman, a War Manpower Commission employe dismissed for associating with a Communist-controlled group . . . . Mississippi contractors tell the Senate War Investigating Committee that they gave Sen. Bilbo a Cadillac and other gifts in the hope of gaining government contracts.	Truman approves a directive placing all U.S. armed forces under a single commander in each overseas theater.	CIO-United Office and Professional Workers union announces a policy to eliminate "Communist interference" in its affairs.		Bert Bell signs a new five-year contract as NFL Commissioner.	Dec. 16
Former Minnesota Gov. Harold Stassen declares his candidacy for the GOP presidential nomination in Washington.	House Military Affairs Comm. recommends creation of an intelligence corps for continuous military espionage abroad, the first such organization in U.S. history.		A German V-2 rocket sets a new record by flying 114 miles into the air at 5,450 ft. a second above White Sands Proving Grounds . . . . U.S. Antarctic Expedition discovers a submarine mountain range which apparently connects Easter Island with the South American mainland.		Dec. 17
	Father of Henry Stewart files suit in Pittsburgh to stop further enlistment in the Army until segregation is banned. Stewart, a Negro, was allegedly refused enlistment on racial grounds.		Nobel Prize Winner Carl Anderson and Dr. Robert Brode report the discovery of new high-energy cosmic rays.	National Bd. of Review of Motion Pictures lists the best films of 1946 as *Henry V, Open City, The Best Years of Our Lives* and *Brief Encounter* . . . . *British Kinematograph Weekly* reports James Mason was the most popular British film star of 1946.	Dec. 18
In the final session of a Senate investigation of his conduct, Sen. Bilbo testifies for six hours and denies all charges of accepting bribes and other wrongdoing . . . . A federal grand jury in Atlanta ends a three-week inquiry into the July 25 murder of four Negroes without being able to identify any of the guilty.	Truman announces that he is not satisfied with the execution of his December 1945 directive on refugee immigration and sets aside four ships to transport refugees to the U.S.	Coal operators from the Northern states, meeting in Washington, offer to negotiate with the UMW on wages and other issues, while Southern operators insist on waiting until Supreme Court resolution of the Lewis-UMW case . . . . CIO United Chemical Workers in Oak Ridge, Tenn. win a 10% wage increase from the Carbide and Carbon Chemicals Corp.	American Chemical Society elects Dr. Charles Thomas of the nuclear research center at Oak Ridge, Tenn. as president . . . . Roland Collier of the Chicago Natural History Museum announces that the relics of eight separate Indian civilizations, the oldest dating back almost 2,000 years, have been found in the Viru Valley of Peru.	"Sugar" Ray Robinson outpoints Tom Bell in 15 rounds in N.Y. to earn undisputed title to the welterweight boxing crown.	Dec. 19
	Commanding general of U.S. ground forces Gen. Jacob Devers announces plans for an increase in the size and firepower of fighting units to meet the requirements of the "atomic age."				Dec. 20
Eugene Talmadge, Georgia's governor-elect and champion of "white supremacy," dies at 62 in Atlanta.	War Department Advisory Comm. on Military Justice issues a report detailing seven basic defects in the Army court martial system, including domination of courts by commanders and excessive sentences. Among the changes recommended is inclusion of enlisted men on courts martial.			A 14th-century manuscript of Petrarch's *De Africa*, a Latin poem missing from the Trieste Library since the end of the war, turns up in Union City, N.J., in the possession of a former GI, who says he bought it from an Italian in Naples. The library says it was stolen by the Italian.	Dec. 21
	National Advisory Comm. for Aeronautics reveals the development of "Tiamat," an experimental winged rocket missile with a speed of 600 mph.			Warner Bros. sign Humphrey Bogart to a record 15-year contract.	Dec. 22
Supreme Court refuses to review a suit on the constitutionality of Tennessee's poll tax on the grounds that Congress has jurisdiction in such matters. The Court also rules that collection of federal social security taxes from bankrupt companies has priority over state taxes . . . . Three men are indicted in Atlanta for arson in the Dec. 7 Winecoff Hotel fire.	Truman sets up a three-man board to review the cases of draft violators and make recommendations for executive clemency . . . . Supreme Court orders new trials for two Jehovah's Witnesses sentenced to five years in prison as conscientious objectors, stating that they were not allowed to challenge draft classifications which barred their deferment as ministers.		U.S. Office of Temporary Controls drops distribution control of penicillin.	Mrs. Mildred (Babe) Didrikson Zaharias of Denver, winner of the 1946 women's golf championship, is chosen outstanding woman athlete of the year in an AP poll of sportswriters.	Dec. 23
Following the death of Georgia Governor-elect Eugene Talmadge, Gov. Ellis Arnall announces he will turn over his post to Lt. Governor-elect M.E. Thompson, while supporters of Talmadge lobby to have his son Herman declared governor by the State Assembly.		Pres. Joseph Curran of the CIO National Maritime Union resigns as co-chairman of the Comm. for Maritime Unity, ending AFL-CIO cooperation in the maritime industry.			Dec. 24
F	G	H	I	J	
Includes elections, federal-state relations, civil rights and liberties, crime, the judiciary, education, health care, poverty, urban affairs and population.	*Includes formation and debate of U.S. foreign and defense policies, veterans affairs and defense spending. (Relations with specific foreign countries are usually found under the region concerned.)*	*Includes business, labor, agriculture, taxation, transportation, consumer affairs, monetary and fiscal policy, natural resources, pollution and accidents.*	*Includes worldwide scientific, medical and technological developments, natural phenomena, U.S. weather and natural disasters.*	*Includes the arts, religion, scholarship, communications media, sports, entertainment, fashions, fads and social life.*	

	World Affairs	Europe	Africa & the Middle East	The Americas	Asia & the Pacific
Dec. 25		Britain and France sign an agreement eliminating visa requirements and other restrictions on citizens of one country travelling in the other.	Arab landowner Emir Mohammed Zeinati is slain in Haifa by unknown assassins, apparently for selling land to Jews.	Chile's Socialist Party rejects a proposed alliance with the Communists.	French High Commissioner for Indochina Adm. Thierry d'Argenlieu issues a Christmas message stating, "France does not intend in the present stage of evolution of the Indochinese people to give them total and unconditional independence." . . . . Boycotted by Communists, China's Constitutional Assembly passes a new constitution, based on British and American models, which will go into effect Jan. 1. Communist spokesmen call the charter "illegal" and say it will not be recognized in Communist-held areas . . . . Queen Wilhelmina proclaims the Provisional State of East Indonesia, including all of the former Dutch East Indies east of Java and Borneo except New Guinea.
Dec. 26		French cabinet raises telephone tolls, subway fares and other public service charges by up to 150% in an anti-inflation move . . . . Former German banker and philanthropist Max M. Warburg dies at 79 in N.Y.	Arabian-American Oil Co., controlled by Standard Oil of California, announces it will sell 30% of its Saudi Arabian holdings to Standard Oil of N.J. and 10% to the Socony-Vacuum Oil Co. . . . . Commander Mohammed Nimer el Huwari of the Arab underground army Najada announces the merger of his forces with the Arab youth organization Futuwah for joint operations under the Arab Higher Comm. in Palestine.	Colombia becomes the 39th nation to join the World Bank.	State Dept. spokesman Lincoln White affirms that Russian authorities in Manchuria were within their rights in ordering a U.S. ship out of Dairen harbor Dec. 20.
Dec. 27		Albania and Yugoslavia ratify a pact providing for economic collaboration.		Cuba's cabinet raises wages of all public employes $5-10 monthly.	Fighting between French forces and Vietnamese nationalists spreads to Cochin China, where 24 civilians are killed.
Dec. 28		Charles de Gaulle refuses to run for the French presidency, declaring he cannot be a "guarantor" of the present constitution . . . . Soviet Council of Ministers orders increased concentration on production of consumer goods, especially clothing.	A new Syrian cabinet is named by Jamil Mardam Bey, with Naim Antaki as foreign minister.	Venezuela's National Constituent Assembly passes a bill providing for a progressive tax on corporate profits up to 28%.	
Dec. 29		Italian Confederation of Labor calls off a general strike in the southern Italian city of Bari after the government agrees to a 3,000-lira weekly subsidy for the unemployed . . . . Russia returns Helsinki's Malm airport, occupied since the 1944 armistice, to Finland.	Irgun members kidnap and flog four British soldiers in retaliation for the British flogging of an imprisoned Zionist arrested for bank robbery.		
Dec. 30	Despite Russian objections, U.N. Atomic Energy Commission approves a U.S.-sponsored nuclear control plan recommending creation of a strong international inspection agency not subject to a great power veto.	Allied Control Council in Berlin announces adoption of a law forbidding Germany to manufacture, possess, import or export any equipment that may be used to wage war.		Venezuela becomes the 40th nation to join the World Bank and International Monetary Fund . . . . Argentina and Uruguay sign a pact allowing Argentina to receive electric power from the Uruguay River power project.	After conferring with French officials in Indochina, Overseas Territories Min. Moutet reiterates France's determination to reestablish "order" in the territory before resuming negotiations with nationalist guerrillas.
Dec. 31		Soviet newspaper *Izvestia* assails the merger of the U.S. and British occupation zones in Germany as a violation of the Potsdam agreement . . . . Yugoslavia releases Roy Stoeckel, an American jailed on espionage charges.		Mexican cattle, sheep, goats and hogs are banned from the U.S. because of an epidemic of hoof and mouth disease.	Gen. MacArthur states in Tokyo that Japan has made "major advances" towards establishing a democratic social and political system.

A	B	C	D	E
Includes developments that affect more than one world region, international organizations and important meetings of major world leaders.	*Includes all domestic and regional developments in Europe, including the Soviet Union, Turkey, Cyprus and Malta.*	*Includes all domestic and regional developments in Africa and the Middle East, including Iraq and Iran and excluding Cyprus, Turkey and Afghanistan.*	*Includes all domestic and regional developments in Latin America, the Caribbean and Canada.*	*Includes all domestic and regional developments in Asian and Pacific nations, extending from Afghanistan through all the Pacific Islands, except Hawaii.*

U.S. Politics & Social Issues	U.S. Foreign Policy & Defense	U.S. Economy & Environment	Science, Technology & Nature	Culture, Leisure & Life Style	
		Gas for industrial use is cut off in six N.J. counties following a strike at the Jersey City and Piscataway Township plants of the Public Service and Electric Co.	Nuclear scientist C. Rogers McCullough reveals that researchers are constructing the world's first atomic power pile for peacetime use at Oak Ridge, Tenn.	Screen actor and comedian W.C. Fields dies at 66 in Pasadena, Calif.	Dec. 25
Counsel to the House Un-American Activities Committee Ernie Adamson issues an unauthorized report claiming that 17 CIO unions are dominated by Communists, that Communists are plotting a general strike to provoke revolution and that the Library of Congress is a "haven for foreign-minded Americans." . . . . Truman returns to Washington after a Christmas holiday in Independence, Mo.			Norwegian anthropologist Thor Heyerdahl announces he will sail 4,000 miles in a wooden raft from Peru to Tahiti in an attempt to prove that Polynesia was settled by inhabitants of South America.	*Motion Picture Herald's* poll indicates 1946 top box office attractions are: Bing Crosby, Ingrid Bergman, Van Johnson, Gary Cooper, Bob Hope, Humphrey Bogart and Greer Garson.	Dec. 26
	U.S. State Dept. announces it will release $9.3 million in Polish assets frozen in the U.S. and $27.5 million in gold to the current Polish government.	FCC authorizes a 10% rate rise by the Western Union Telegraph Co. . . . . St. Paul, Minn. public school teachers end a 27-day strike after gaining wage increases of $1,100-1,600 a year . . . . Reconstruction Finance Corp. Director George Allen resigns after urging that the agency be reduced to a lending institution for banks and small businesses.		With Jack Kramer and Ted Schroeder taking the doubles in Melbourne, the U.S. wins the Davis Cup for the first time since 1938.	Dec. 27
				Carrie Jacobs Bond, composer of *I Love You Truly* and other songs, dies at 84 in Hollywood.	Dec. 28
Delegates from 10 liberal political action groups vote in N.Y. to merge into a new organization, the Progressive Citizens of America, with Frank Kingdon and Jo Davidson as co-chairmen.	Navy announces development of the "Mark 3 Toss Director," a new bombsight which permits dive-bombers to project bombs after they have pulled out of their dives.			*Ring* Magazine names Tony Zale as fighter of the year.	Dec. 29
GOP congressional leadership fills majority posts in the new Senate: Arthur Vandenberg, (Mich.), president pro-tempore; Wallace White, Jr. (Maine), majority floor leader; Robert Taft (Ohio), steering committee chairman; Kenneth Wherry (Neb.), majority whip; and Eugene Milliken (Colo.), Republican conference chairman.		Chicago federal circuit court of appeals upholds the right of a union in a closed shop to force the discharge of a member for joining a rival union.	Univ. of California physicist Glenn Seaborg, co-discoverer of plutonium, americium and curium, is selected "chemist of the year" in an American Chemical Society poll.	N.Y. Film Critcs vote *The Best Years of Our Lives* the best 1946 motion picture and Laurence Olivier and Celia Johnson best actor and actress.	Dec. 30
GOP steering committee votes to oppose the seating of Sen. Theodore G. Bilbo (D, Miss.) in the next Congress.	Truman declares an official end to World War II hostilities, terminating his emergency powers and 20 wartime control laws. He admits the move is an effort to cooperate with the new Republican Congress . . . . Truman signs an executive order turning over the Army's atomic energy facilities to the Atomic Energy Commission.	NLRB recognizes the right of supervisory workers to organize when it orders Jones and Laughlin Steel Corp. to bargain with a United Mine Workers affiliate that accepts foremen as members.			Dec. 31
F	G	H	I	J	
Includes elections, federal-state relations, civil rights and liberties, crime, the judiciary, education, health care, poverty, urban affairs and population.	*Includes formation and debate of U.S. foreign and defense policies, veterans affairs and defense spending. (Relations with specific foreign countries are usually found under the region concerned.)*	*Includes business, labor, agriculture, taxation, transportation, consumer affairs, monetary and fiscal policy, natural resources, pollution and accidents.*	*Includes worldwide scientific, medical and technological developments, natural phenomena, U.S. weather and natural disasters.*	*Includes the arts, religion, scholarship, communications media, sports, entertainment, fashions, fads and social life.*	

1947
III

Fortifications and Nationalist soldiers guard the strategic Peking-Tientsin rail line from attack by Communist guerrillas in China's expanding civil war.

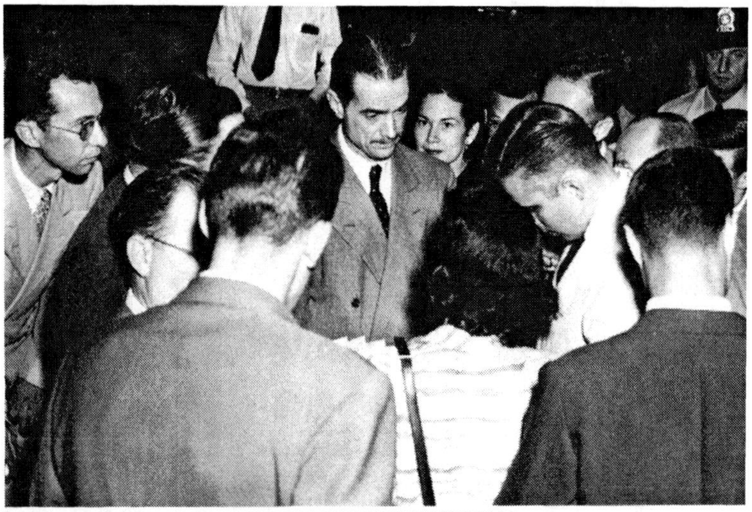

Reporters crowd around aircraft manufacturer Howard Hughes as he emerges from Senate War Investigating Committee hearings on Aug. 11.

House-Un-American Activities Committee Chairman J. Parnell Thomas (R, N.J.) points a questioning finger at Victor Kravchenko, former Soviet government employe and author of *I Chose Freedom*.

Members of the Joint Congressional Atomic Energy Committee question David Lilienthal on his fitness for the new post of Atomic Energy Commission director. Sen. Kenneth McKellar (D, Tenn.), Lilienthal's chief adversary, sits second from left on the dais.

Dutch forces, attempting to reoccupy the East Indies, land on Sumatra shortly before a truce temporarily ended fighting with Indonesian nationalists.

UMW leader John L. Lewis, whose craggy face was a familiar landmark of the forties, orders 400,000 soft coal miners to strike for two weeks on April 1 in memory of the Centralia, Illinois, mine disaster.

Preceding page: Moslem refugees fleeing India take up every inch of space, including the roof, on a train bound for Pakistan, Sept. 26.

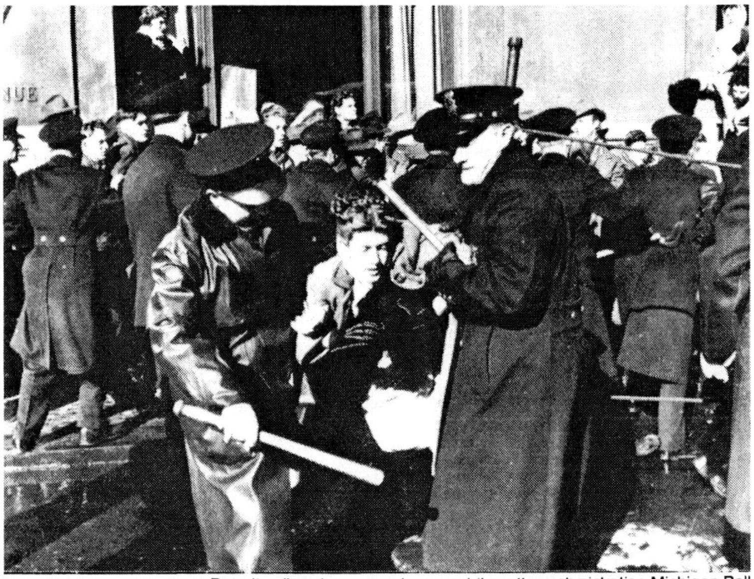

Detroit police clear a way for non-strikers through picketing Michigan Bell workers, part of a nationwide strike of telephone workers which began on April 7.

Abandoned cars choke the Grand Central Parkway in Queens on Dec. 27 as a record-breaking 25.8-inch snowfall brought New York City to a virtual standstill.

Greek government soldiers smoke their cigarette ration as they head for action against Communist guerrillas in northern Greece, Dec. 5.

Jewish militiamen evacuate residents of the Jaffa-Tel Aviv border area on Dec. 7 as fighting with the Arabs spreads following the U.N. decision to partition Palestine.

Britain's Princess Elizabeth and Prince Philip, Duke of Edinburgh, leave Westminster Abbey Nov. 20 following their marriage.

	World Affairs	Europe	Africa & the Middle East	The Americas	Asia & the Pacific
Jan.	Allied deputy foreign ministers, meeting in London, discuss German and Austrian peace treaties.	Communists gain a dominating position in the Polish government despite Western protests.		Paraguay is placed under a state of siege as guerrilla activities against the government break out.	Clashes between Vietnamese nationalist guerrillas and French colonial forces spread and increase in intensity.
Feb.	U.S. and Russia carry their disagreement over atomic energy controls to the U.N. General Assembly.	Britain restricts energy use as severe cold weather grips the nation.	Unable to reach an agreement with Arabs and Jews, Britain prepares to turn the Palestinian question over to the U.N.		
March	Allied foreign ministers, convening in Moscow, discuss German and Austrian peace treaties.	Intensifying Greek civil war forces Britain to announce the forthcoming withdrawal of its troops from the country.	Zionist terroists increase their violence against British installations in Palestine.	Rebels continue hostilities against Paraguayan government forces.	Chinese Communists begin a counterattack against Nationalist forces in Manchuria and northern China. Communists rapidly overrun the countryside and rail lines, isolating the Nationalists in the cities .... Civil unrest erupts on Taiwan, bringing extensive repression by Nationalist authorities.
Apr.	Allied foreign ministers fail to reach agreement on German and Austrian peace treaties.	Fuel crisis eases in Britain.	Special session of U.N. General Assembly hears testimony on Palestine question .... Nationalist guerrillas on Madagascar clash with French colonial forces.		Hindu-Moslem strife continues throughout India.
May		Food riots and strikes erupt in France and western Germany.	French colonies in Africa protest a return to stringent colonial rule.	Former Nicaraguan president Anastasio Somoza returns to power in a bloodless coup.	Anti-government demonstrations in China spread and increase in violence.
June		Communist Party consolidates its control in Hungary .... British, French and Russian representatives discuss participation in the proposed Marshall Plan for Europe.	U.N. Palestine Commission conducts hearings in Jerusalem.	Mexican government takes steps to increase the nation's industrial output and limit foreign investment.	Indians debate British plan for partitioning of Pakistan and India.
July	After four months of futile debate, U.N. terminates discussion of atomic energy controls.	Representatives of Western European nations meet in Paris to devise a recovery program under the Marshall Plan .... U.S. sources in Germany report a mass flight of Germans from the Soviet zone to escape forced labor.	Zionist terrorism against the British continues in Palestine.		Dutch military action against Indonesian nationalists brings critical worldwide reaction .... Gen. Albert Wedemeyer begins a two-month fact-finding tour of China and Korea for Truman.
Aug.	U.S. and Russia clash in the U.N. over admission of new members.	British, French and U.S. occupation authorities discuss means of raising German industrial production .... British government invokes an austerity economic program.	Egypt presents its case for independence from Britain at the U.N.		Hindu-Moslem strife intensifies following India's independence .... Indonesians present their independence demands before the U.N.
Sept.		European Communist Party representatives, meeting in Poland, discuss possible responses to the Marshall Plan.	French colonial forces suppress the nationalist revolt on Madagascar.	Inter-American Defense Conference in Rio de Janeiro negotiates a Western Hemisphere defense treaty.	
Oct.	Representatives of 53 nations gather in Geneva to discuss international trade problems.	British government imposes additional austerity economic measures .... French and low country delegates discuss a mutual currency agreement.	Arab states threaten military action should Palestine be partitioned .... A two-month cholera epidemic strikes Egypt.	Labor unrest in Chile brings government action against the Communist Party.	Chinese Communists continue to gain territory from the Nationalists in Manchuria and northern China .... India and Pakistan clash over control of Kashmir.
Nov.	General Assembly debates the Big Five veto power, as small nations demand a greater voice in U.N. affairs.	Labor and political unrest, resulting from inflation and food shortages, erupts in France and Italy.	U.N. and Zionist groups take initial steps to create a separate Jewish state in Palestine, despite repeated Arab protests.		U.N. General Assembly take steps to supervise Korean elections scheduled for 1948.
Dec.	Allied foreign ministers, meeting in London, again fail to agree on German and Austrian peace treaties.	Greek civil war continues to intensify as United States military observers enter the country.	Following the U.N. decision to partition Palestine, Arab-Jewish violence intensifies.	U.S.-Panamanian negotiations fail to bring agreement on use of military installations outside the Canal Zone.	

A	B	C	D	E
Includes developments that affect more than one world region, international organizations and important meetings of major world leaders.	*Includes all domestic and regional developments in Europe, including the Soviet Union, Turkey, Cyprus and Malta.*	*Includes all domestic and regional developments in Africa and the Middle East, including Iraq and Iran and excluding Cyprus, Turkey and Afghanistan.*	*Includes all domestic and regional developments in Latin America, the Caribbean and Canada.*	*Includes all domestic and regional developments in Asian and Pacific nations, extending from Afghanistan through all the Pacific Islands, except Hawaii.*

U.S. Politics & Social Issues	U.S. Foreign Policy & Defense	U.S. Economy & Environment	Science, Technology & Nature	Culture, Leisure & Life Style	
Lt. Governor-elect Melvin Thompson and Herman Talmadge, son of deceased Governor-elect Eugene Talmadge, struggle for the Georgia governorship.		Steel and rubber industries avert strikes as labor and management negotiators conclude contract settlements.	Medical researchers report progress in finding causes of infantile paralysis.		Jan.
Congress debates Truman's presidential succession bill.		Truman seeks continuation of some wartime price and production controls to restrict inflation.	A U.S. Naval expedition under Adm. Richard E. Byrd completes a three-month exploration of Antarctica.	Bob Hope and Fibber McGee and Molly continue to be radio's most popular shows.	Feb.
House Un-American Activities Comm. conducts hearings on Communist activities in the U.S.	Congress debates President Truman's request for $400 million in aid to Greece and Turkey.	Congressional committees hear testimony on proposals to restrict labor union activities.			March
	Henry Wallace criticizes Truman's foreign policy while on a speaking tour of Europe.	Debate emerges over safety conditions in the nation's coal mines as UMW leader Lewis accuses Interior Secy. Krug of laxity in enforcing government regulations.			Apr.
House Un-American Activities Comm. charges rampant Communist influence in Hollywood after conducting hearings on the film industry.	Congress completes action on the Greek and Turkish aid bill.	A nationwide telephone workers' strike against AT&T crumbles as local unions reach contract agreements.	Congress considers legislation establishing a National Science Foundation.		May
	National debate opens over State Secy. George Marshall's proposal that the U.S. commit itself to European economic recovery.	Congress completes action on the controversial Taft-Hartley labor bill, which becomes law when the Senate overrides Truman's veto.			June
Congress considers legislation permitting loyalty investigations of federal government employes.	Congress completes action on a bill to unify the armed services under one cabinet secretary.	AFL and CIO leaders explore possible merger of the two organizations.		Laura Hobson's *Gentlemen's Agreement* becomes the best selling fiction book in the U.S.	July
	Senate War Investigating Committee conducts hearings over alleged profiteering by aircraft producer Howard Hughes.	Several large labor unions, including the UAW, attempt to safeguard their closed-shop contracts against the Taft-Hartley Act by signing special agreements with employers.	Construction begins on the first non-military atomic stockpile at Brookhaven, N.Y.	Hit tune *Peg O' My Heart* sweeps the country.	Aug.
Georgia Democrats debate the exclusion of Negroes from state primary elections.	After James Forrestal is sworn in as defense secretary, plans are implemented to unify the armed forces.	A number of labor leaders, primarily in the CIO, reject NLRB orders to sign affidavits asserting they are not Communists, as required by the Taft-Hartley Act.	A hurricane causes heavy damage along the Gulf Coast.		Sept.
Actors ban together to challenge House Un-American Activities Comm. allegations of Communist influence in Hollywood.	Public debate over the extent of American aid to Europe continues.	NLRB attempts to force labor leaders to comply with Taft-Hartley Act requirements by refusing to hear complaints brought by recalcitrant unions.			Oct.
Civil Service Commission opens its loyalty investigation of federal employes.	Congress receives several requests from Truman for stop-gap aid to Western European nations.	Truman again presses Congress to enact anti-inflation measures.			Nov.
	Special congressional session completes action on emergency aid to needy nations.	A new round of wage demands hits industry as prices continue to rise rapidly.	A second U.S. Naval force under Commodore Finn Ronne completes an 11-month mapping expedition in Antarctica.	Fibber McGee and Molly becomes the top radio show in America.	Dec.

F	G	H	I	J
Includes elections, federal-state relations, civil rights and liberties, crime, the judiciary, education, health care, poverty, urban affairs and population.	*Includes formation and debate of U.S. foreign and defense policies, veterans affairs and defense spending. (Relations with specific foreign countries are usually found under the region concerned.)*	*Includes business, labor, agriculture, taxation, transportation, consumer affairs, monetary and fiscal policy, natural resources, pollution and accidents.*	*Includes worldwide scientific, medical and technological developments, natural phenomena, U.S. weather and natural disasters.*	*Includes the arts, religion, scholarship, communications media, sports, entertainment, fashions, fads and social life.*

	World Affairs	Europe	Africa & the Middle East	The Americas	Asia & the Pacific
Jan. 1		French Premier Leon Blum imposes a 5% price reduction on all goods in an effort to control inflation .... British government takes over management of the nation's 1,500 coal mines, with 692,000 miners, under the nationalization control act .... British War Office announces the forced retirement of Gen. Frederick Morgan, former UNRRA director in Germany.		A new Mexican voting law goes into effect, giving women the right to vote in municipal elections and to hold municipal posts.	Five thousand university students demonstrate in Shanghai against the U.S. military presence in China and the alleged rape of a Chinese girl by a U.S. Marine .... French reinforcements land in Cochin China near Saigon as French sources report that a rebellion of Cambodian nationalists has been suppressed after three weeks of fighting.
Jan. 2		American Fed. of Labor protests against a decision of the World Fed. of Trade Unions tolerating forced labor in Ruhr coal mines, while AFL European representative Irving Brown announces the AFL will not open its European office in Paris due to "mudslinging" by the Communist-dominated French General Confederation of Labor.	A wave of violence sweeps Palestine as Zionist extremists stage bombings and machine gun attacks on British troops in five cities.		Gandhi begins a walking tour of Indian villages in eastern Bengal to improve Hindu-Moslem relations.
Jan. 3		Eleven former SS members go on trial before a U.S. military court in Stuttgart on charges of plotting terrorism in the U.S. zone of Germany.	N.Y. Rabbi Stephen Wise resigns as vice president of the Zionist Organization of America and condemns the World Zionist Congress for boycotting the London Conference on Palestine .... British authorities in Jerusalem threaten "drastic action" against the entire Jewish population of Palestine unless Zionist terrorism is halted.		U.S. sends a note to Russia urging that the Manchurian port of Dairen be reopened to world trade, as stipulated in the Chinese-Russian agreement of August 1945.
Jan. 4		Hungary's Interior Ministry announces it has made 55 arrests in breaking up a plot to overthrow the government and restore the regime of Adm. Nicholas Horthy .... Austrian government orders a two-week shutdown of heavy industry to conserve coal.			French Overseas Min. Marius Moutet says a "military decision" is a prerequisite to negotiations with Ho Chi Minh's Vietnamese government, despite nationalist pleas for talks .... Chinese Premier T.V. Soong forbids anti-U.S. demonstrations in Chinese cities and universities.
Jan. 5		U.S. asks Britain and Russia to join in demanding that upcoming Polish parliamentary elections be "free and unfettered." .... A British parliamentary delegation, reporting on its visit to Greece last August, urges that British troops be withdrawn from the country "at an early date."	Haganah's secret radio condemns terrorists and calls for an end to violence in Palestine.	Presidential elections are held in Bolivia, resulting in a victory for Socialist Republican Union candidate Enrique Hertzog over Liberal Party candidate Luis Fernando Guachalla.	Japanese Adm. Osami Nagano, who ordered the attack on Pearl Harbor, dies at 65 in Tokyo of pneumonia. He was standing trial as a war criminal.
Jan. 6	N.Y. architect Wallace Harrison is named director of planning for construction of U.N. headquarters.	Three Serbs are sentenced to death in Yugoslavia for participating in a spy ring allegedly organized by the U.S. embassy in Belgrade .... Truck drivers halt food distribution in London when they strike in a wage dispute.			India's Congress Party approves a resolution submitted by Nehru urging compulsory formation of provincial delegations to draft a constitution according to British proposals.
Jan. 7		French Planning Council adopts economist Jean Monnet's four-year plan for modernization of the country's basic industries .... Britain's Labor government reveals its town-and-country planning bill, designed to give the state control over land development and encourage the reconstruction of old towns.			Completing his duties as U.S. envoy to China, Gen. Marshall assails "extremists" in both the Communist and Nationalist camps and asserts that China's salvation lies in a liberal coalition government under Chiang Kai-shek's guidance .... Forces of the Indonesian Republic accept a Dutch demand that they withdraw from the oil center of Palembang in Sumatra after two days of street fighting in the city.
Jan. 8		Poland's conservative Peasant Party drops its threat to boycott forthcoming parliamentary elections and announces that it will "actively" participate .... British forces complete the evacuation of Alexandria by turning over the Ras El Tin Citadel to Egypt.			French Defense Ministry places all regular army and air force troops on call for service in Indochina.
	A *Includes developments that affect more than one world region, international organizations and important meetings of major world leaders.*	B *Includes all domestic and regional developments in Europe, including the Soviet Union, Turkey, Cyprus and Malta.*	C *Includes all domestic and regional developments in Africa and the Middle East, including Iraq and Iran and excluding Cyprus, Turkey and Afghanistan.*	D *Includes all domestic and regional developments in Latin America, the Caribbean and Canada.*	E *Includes all domestic and regional developments in Asian and Pacific nations, extending from Afghanistan through all the Pacific Islands, except Hawaii.*

U.S. Politics & Social Issues	U.S. Foreign Policy & Defense	U.S. Economy & Environment	Science, Technology & Nature	Culture, Leisure & Life Style	
	U.S. and Britain agree to standardize armed forces training and certain items of military equipment.		American Foundation for Tropical Medicine announces that industrialist Harvey Firestone Jr. has given the Liberian government $250,000 to build an international institute for tropical diseases.	College Bowl Scores: Rose Bowl—Illinois 45, UCLA 14; Cotton Bowl—Ark. 0, LSU 0; Orange Bowl—Rice 8, Tenn. 0; and Sugar Bowl—Georgia 20, N.C. 10.	Jan. 1
GOP announces following chairmen of Senate committees: Judiciary, Alexander Wiley (Wisc.); Labor and Public Welfare, Robert A. Taft (Ohio); Armed Services, Chan Gurney (S.D.); Foreign Relations, Arthur H. Vandenberg (Mich.); and Interstate and Foreign Commerce, Wallace White, Jr. (Me.) .... House Un-American Activities Comm. issues a report recommending restriction of mailing privileges of "subversive" groups and creation of a bureau empowered to discharge government employes "whose loyalty to the U.S. is found to be in doubt."	House Military Affairs Comm. issues a report criticizing U.S. occupation forces in Germany for black market activities and a lax denazification record.	Rockwell Mfg. Co., sued for $3 million in back wages by its employes, files a $15-million counter-suit against four AFL unions in Pittsburgh for production lost during worker slowdowns last year.	Adm. Richard Byrd sails from Norfolk, Va. to join the Navy's Antarctic expedition.		Jan. 2
After electing its new officers, the House adopts the changes in committee structure provided for in the Legislative Reorganization Act.				AFL American Federation of Radio Artists in Chicago signs a one-year contract with four major studios granting 20-30% wage and fee increases to about 20,000 communications workers..... Ogden Mills Reid, owner and editor of the New York *Herald-Tribune*, dies at 64 in N.Y.	Jan. 3
Americans for Democratic Action is founded in Washington to encourage the spread of liberal and anti-Communist ideas .... Swearing in of new senators is delayed by a controversy over the seating of Sen. Theodore Bilbo (D, Miss.), declared unfit for office by Senate Republicans. The conflict ends when Bilbo temporarily steps aside to undergo urgent surgery on his jaw .... Georgia Attorney Gen. Eugene Cook rules that Lt. Governor-elect Melvin Thompson should succeed to the governorship following the death of Governor-elect Eugene Talmadge Dec. 21.	Bernard Baruch and other U.S. delegates to the U.N. Atomic Energy Commission resign their posts, stating that work on an international nuclear control plan has been completed and that remaining problems can be handled in the General Assembly. Baruch urges Truman to continue production of nuclear weapons "at least until ratification of the treaty."	N.Y. Stock Exchange registers its largest single corporate bond transaction in history with the sale of $6.8 billion in AT&T debentures .... A N.Y. tugboat strike is averted by agreement on a one-year pact granting an 11¢ hourly wage increase and a 40-hour week to N.Y. tug operators.	Physicist J. Robert Oppenheimer is elected chairman of the General Advisory Comm. of Scientists for the U.S. Atomic Energy Commission.		Jan. 4
				Film Daily poll lists *The Lost Week-End* as the best picture of 1946.	Jan. 5
Truman delivers a 48-minute State of the Union address to Congress, urging the GOP-dominated legislature to cooperate with him in labor, housing, health and welfare and other fields. Republican congressmen view the speech as conciliatory, but several criticize Truman's labor proposals as not going far enough in curbing union power .... Alphonse Rocco, who attempted to murder his former wife with a "camera-gun" apparatus, is killed in a gun battle with police in the Catskills near Gilboa, N.Y.	Gen. Lucius Clay succeeds Gen. Joseph McNary as commander of U.S. forces in Europe, following McNary's appointment as U.S. Air Force representative on the U.N. Military Staff Comm.	Supreme Court upholds rent controls by refusing to review a test case brought by N.Y. landlords seeking to raise rents.	Bacteriologist Harry Plotz, discoverer of the typhus bacillus and the measles virus, dies at 55 in N.Y.	Ben Hogan captures the Los Angeles Golf Open with a record score of 280 .... Violinist Jascha Heifetz marries Frances Spiegelberg in Beverley Hills, Calif.	Jan. 6
Reps. John McCormick (D, Mass.) and Leslie Arends (R, Ill.) are elected House Democratic and GOP whips.	State Secy. James Byrnes, Truman's trusted adviser and U.S. representative at the Paris Peace Conference, resigns due to ill health. Truman names Gen. George Marshall, U.S. envoy to China, as Byrnes' successor .... Treasury Dept. releases Poland's blocked accounts in the U.S.	Charles Sumner Woolworth, co-founder of the Woolworth retail store chain, dies at 90 in Scranton, Pa.	Harvard Univ. reveals development of the Mark II, the world's largest computer, capable of solving multi-digit multiplication problems in one second .... Spring Grove State Hospital in Md. announces the release of several "incurable" psychiatric patients who had undergone a prefontal lobotomy, separating the emotional and action centers of the brain.	Horald Dade takes the bantamweight boxing title from Manuel Ortiz in 15 rounds of a San Francisco match.	Jan. 7
		In his first economic report to Congress, Truman recommends government action to ensure the lowering of prices, maintenance of present wage levels and extension of rent controls.	M.I.T. Prof. Norbert Wiener refuses to address a Harvard symposium on computers because they are used "for war purposes" and announces he will not publish work "which may do damage in the hands of irresponsible militarists."	A N.Y. jury convicts Alvin Paris of trying to bribe two N.Y. Giant football players to throw the NFL championship game Dec. 23 .... N.Y. Yankees chairman Edward Barrow announces his retirement after 51 years as a baseball executive.	Jan. 8
F	G	H	I	J	
Includes elections, federal-state relations, civil rights and liberties, crime, the judiciary, education, health care, poverty, urban affairs and population.	*Includes formation and debate of U.S. foreign and defense policies, veterans affairs and defense spending. (Relations with specific foreign countries are usually found under the region concerned.)*	*Includes business, labor, agriculture, taxation, transportation, consumer affairs, monetary and fiscal policy, natural resources, pollution and accidents.*	*Includes worldwide scientific, medical and technological developments, natural phenomena, U.S. weather and natural disasters.*	*Includes the arts, religion, scholarship, communications media, sports, entertainment, fashions, fads and social life.*	

	World Affairs	Europe	Africa & the Middle East	The Americas	Asia & the Pacific
Jan. 9	U.N. Asst. Gen. Secy. John Hutson of the U.S. resigns, reportedly because Secy. Gen. Trygve Lie is dissatisfied with his work.	State Dept. sends a note to the Polish government claiming that Poland has violated "the letter as well as the spirit of the Yalta and Potsdam agreements" by engaging in "suppression, coercion and intimidation" of political opposition during the current election campaign .... Gen. Robert Harper of the U.S. military government in Germany reports that the country's "physical disarmament ... is now virtually complete."		Nelson Rockefeller sets up a $3-million International Basic Economy Corp. in N.Y. to aid Brazilian agriculture.	French forces in Indochina report driving Vietnamese guerrillas away from the perimeter of Hanoi and clearing the Hanoi-Haiphong highway.
Jan. 10		British Labor government reveals a bill nationalizing the electrical industry and announces it has added the domestic oil market to its nationalization program .... Britain files a complaint against Albania on the mining of Corfu Channel, asking the Security Council to review the case .... Gen. Lucius Clay of the U.S. military government in Germany orders all military power sources diverted to civilian use in the U.S. zone to overcome the effects of a coal shortage.			French forces report capturing the transportation center of Son La in the northern Vietnamese highlands northwest of Hanoi.
Jan. 11		Italy's Socialist Party splits into three factions on the issue of collaboration with the Communists, with two groups opposed to Communist ties seceding from the party.	Transjordan's King Abdullah Ibn El-Hussein signs a pact of friendship with Turkey in Ankara.	Price controls are removed from many items in Canada, including household articles and fresh vegetables, fruit and fish.	
Jan. 12			A Jewish terrorist drives an explosive-laden truck into the Haifa central police station, killing four and wounding 140. In the confusion of the blast, the terrorist escapes.	Mexico announces that four U.S. fishing vessels have been impounded for netting shrimp in the Bay of Campeche.	
Jan. 13		SS Gen. Oswald Pohl, former head of all German concentration camps, is indicted with 17 other SS officers by U.S. authorities in Nuremberg .... Guiseppe Saragat, leader of an anti-Communist faction which left the Italian Socialist Party, resigns as president of Italy's Constituent Assembly.		Pres. Higinio Morinigo declares a 30-day state of siege in Paraguay to suppress an "anarcho-communist" plot against the government.	Mt. Mayon volcano on the Philippine island of Luzon blows off its top in a great explosion. No casualties are reported due to the evacuation of nearby towns.
Jan. 14	British Foreign Secy. Bevin welcomes Big Four deputy foreign ministers meeting in London to negotiate on German and Austrian peace treaties in preparation for an upcoming foreign ministers' conference in Moscow.	Polish Pres. Bierut rejects Anglo-American charges of political oppression in Poland as "without evidence," while military tribunals hand down death sentences for eight Poles convicted of plotting to overthrow the government .... Russia and Norway sign a two-year renewable trade treaty as Moscow denounces the 1920 treaty giving Norway sovereignty over the Spitzbergen islands. Tass claims the treaty was signed without Russia's knowledge and "totally disregards" Soviet interests.			
Jan. 15		Socialist Unity Party in Berlin announces that Russian occupation authorities have promised to stop dismantling German factories, limit reparations from current production in the Soviet zone and increase industrial output by 200-300% .... Britain and France agree to conclude a military alliance within the framework of the U.N. Charter, aimed at preventing future German aggression .... A committee of Italy's Constituent Assembly approves a Christian Democrat-supported measure making divorce illegal .... U.S. State Dept. claims Russia and Norway cannot modify the 1920 pact regulating sovereignty over the Spitsbergen islands without consulting the U.S., which was a treaty signatory.		Paraguay, under a state of siege for three days, outlaws the Communist Party.	A truce between French forces and Vietnamese nationalists permits several thousand Vietnamese, Chinese and Indians trapped in Hanoi's native quarter since Dec. 19 to leave the city. AP reports that French authorities have imposed complete censorship on news broadcasts.

A	B	C	D	E
Includes developments that affect more than one world region, international organizations and important meetings of major world leaders.	*Includes all domestic and regional developments in Europe, including the Soviet Union, Turkey, Cyprus and Malta.*	*Includes all domestic and regional developments in Africa and the Middle East, including Iraq and Iran and excluding Cyprus, Turkey and Afghanistan.*	*Includes all domestic and regional developments in Latin America, the Caribbean and Canada.*	*Includes all domestic and regional developments in Asian and Pacific nations, extending from Afghanistan through all the Pacific Islands, except Hawaii.*

U.S. Politics & Social Issues	U.S. Foreign Policy & Defense	U.S. Economy & Environment	Science, Technology & Nature	Culture, Leisure & Life Style	
			Chemist Claude Zobell of UCLA reports discovery of a bacterium that makes previously unreachable oil available for exploitation by modifying the chemical composition of imprisoned oil deposits.		Jan. 9
Sens. Harley Kilgore (D, W. Va.) and William Fulbright (D, Ark.) introduce legislation on presidential succession, giving the vice president the right to appoint his own successor.	Truman names Warren Austin, U.S. representative in the General Assembly, to succeed Bernard Baruch on the U.N. Atomic Energy Commission.	Truman presents Congress with a fiscal 1948 balanced budget of $37.528 billion and asks for a one-year extension of excise taxes.	Dr. Hubert Loring and Dr. C.E. Schwerdt of Stanford Univ. announce they have isolated the polio virus, opening the way to work on prevention of the disease .... Dr. Hanns Sachs, psychoanalyst and one of Freud's earliest students, dies at 66 in Boston.	E.Y. Harburg's musical *Finian's Rainbow* opens on Broadway.	Jan. 10
	Retiring State Secy. Byrnes states in a valedictory address that the U.S. will maintain its military strength and accept its responsibility in helping to shape world politics.				Jan. 11
			An Eastern Air Lines plane bound from Detroit to Miami crashes in a rainstorm near Galax, Fla., killing 18 of 19 on board.	National Boxing Assn. rates as champions: Heavyweight, Joe Louis; Light Heavyweight, Gus Lesnevich; Middleweight, Tony Zale; Welterweight, Ray Robinson; Lightweight, Ike Williams; Featherweight, Willie Pep; Bantamweight, Harold Dade; and Flyweight, Jackie Paterson.	Jan. 12
Supreme Court rules, 5-4 that Louisiana may order another execution for convicted murderer Willie Francis, who survived one attempted execution due to mechanical defects in the electric chair .... GOP names 280 congressmen to House committees, leaving the Democrats with 205 places.		National Maritime Union asks Labor Secy. Lewis Schwellenbach to name an arbitrator in a dispute with 39 Atlantic and Gulf Coast shipping firms over the union's demand for a 25% wage increase .... AFL National Farm Labor Union convention in Washington hears a pledge from the AFL to support its goal of organizing three million U.S. farm workers.		Whitelaw Reid is named to succeed his late father Ogden Reid as editor of the *New York Herald Tribune*.	Jan. 13
Assn. of American Colleges meeting in Boston ends after hearing Gen. Omar Bradley disclose that the VA is working out a plan to pay 75% of GI tuition in advance.	Gen. Daniel Sultan, U.S. Army inspector-general and commander of the Burma-India theater during World War II, dies at 61 in Washington.	Supreme Court hears arguments from the government and the defense on the contempt conviction of John L. Lewis and the UMW.		Former boxer Barney Ross is released from a U.S. Public Health Service hospital in Lexington, Ky. after being cured of his drug habit.	Jan. 14
Georgia's General Assembly ignores a previous ruling in favor of Lt. Governor-elect Melvin Thompson and names Herman Talmadge, son of the late governor-elect, to be governor. Talmadge sets up office in the outer rooms of Atlanta's executive mansion when Gov. Arnall refuses to vacate for him .... Rep. Vito Marcantonio (ALP, N.Y.) is left without a committee post as both the GOP and Democrats say that responsibility for assigning him to a committee rests with the other party.		Ford Motors Pres. Henry Ford II announces a $15-50 cut in prices of passenger cars to halt the "insane spiral of mounting costs and rising prices." .... CIO Textile Workers union announces it has won 10-15¢ hourly wage increases for 200,000 northern textile workers.			Jan. 15

F	G	H	I	J
Includes elections, federal-state relations, civil rights and liberties, crime, the judiciary, education, health care, poverty, urban affairs and population.	*Includes formation and debate of U.S. foreign and defense policies, veterans affairs and defense spending. (Relations with specific foreign countries are usually found under the region concerned.)*	*Includes business, labor, agriculture, taxation, transportation, consumer affairs, monetary and fiscal policy, natural resources, pollution and accidents.*	*Includes worldwide scientific, medical and technological developments, natural phenomena, U.S. weather and natural disasters.*	*Includes the arts, religion, scholarship, communications media, sports, entertainment, fashions, fads and social life.*

	World Affairs	Europe	Africa & the Middle East	The Americas	Asia & the Pacific
Jan. 16	London conference of deputy foreign ministers agrees to invite Poland, the Netherlands, Yugoslavia, Australia, South Africa and Canada to present their views on the German and Austrian peace treaties.	A joint session of the French Parliament elects Socialist leader Vincent Auriol first president of the Fourth Republic .... Socialist Victor Agartz is named chairman of the new Economic Executive Council, created to coordinate economic development in the British and U.S. zones of Germany .... Leaders of Britain's Transport and General Workers Union end a 10-day strike of London truckers by agreeing to let the government-sponsored Joint Industrial Council mediate the dispute.			
Jan. 17		French Pres. Auriol names Socialist Paul Ramadier to form a new cabinet after Leon Blum refuses to continue as premier due to his advanced age .... Polish Commissioner for Elections Kazimierz Bzowski rules that voters may cast their ballots openly in coming parliamentary elections despite constitutional guarantees of a secret ballot.		Cuba requisitions 50% of all beef cattle as livestock owners refuse to sell at the official price of 8¢ per lb. on the hoof.	In an interview with UP correspondents, Vietnamese nationalist leader Ho Chi Minh emphasizes his intention of fighting until complete independence is achieved. He charges that France has made no effort to negotiate an end to the current conflict.
Jan. 18		First intra-German trade pact is concluded between the Soviet and U.S.-British zones, calling for a 1947 exchange of goods valued at 210 million marks.			French forces begin offensive operations against Vietnamese nationalist guerrillas, attacking the former imperial city of Hue.
Jan. 19		In Poland's first parliamentary elections since 1935, the Communist-socialist government bloc captures 383 of 444 seats. The largest minority vote goes to the conservative Peasant Party, with 27 seats .... Greek steamer *Himara* sinks after it strikes a mine in the Gulf of Petalia, resulting in the drowning of some 392 out of 637 persons aboard.			
Jan. 20	Norwegian representative Ragnar Frisch is elected chairman of the U.N. Economic and Employment Commission, while Czech representative Fratisek Kraus becomes chairman of the Social Commission.	Britain's Labor government issues a White Paper urging workers to increase production without asking for higher wages in order to save Britain from an "extremely serious" economic situation .... Britain grants Malta internal self-government under a new constitution.			A British commission investigating the Royal Indian Navy mutiny of February 1946 issues a report criticizing racial discrimination by British officers towards Indian enlisted men.
Jan. 21	*Look* Magazine publishes an interview with Stalin in which the Russian Premier says "the danger of a new war is not real" and admits that Russia "should be subject to the same rules of [nuclear] inspection ... as any other nation."	French Premier Paul Ramadier obtains a vote of confidence from the National Assembly, which elects Edouard Herriot as its speaker .... Former Hitler Youth member Siegfried Kabus is sentenced to death by a U.S. military court in Stuttgart for the bombing of denazification offices last October. He is the first underground Nazi terrorist to be condemned.		Leaders of the Puerto Rican independence movement, jailed in the U.S. since 1936, appeal to Secy. Gen. Trygve Lie to bring the question of the island's independence before the U.N.	Chinese Nationalist government issues a four-point peace bid to the Communists but rejects their demands that the new constitution be annulled and troops withdrawn from contested areas .... Demonstrators supporting Vietnamese independence riot in Calcutta, resulting in one death and 100 arrests.
Jan. 22	Oswaldo Aranha is named Brazil's representative to the U.N. Security Council to succeed the late Pedro Leao Velloso.	Poland's delegation to the London conference demands ratification of the Polish-German frontier and $20 billion in German reparations as part of the German peace treaty .... French Premier Ramadier announces formation of a five-party coalition cabinet, including nine Socialists, five Left Republicans, five Popular Republicans, five Communists and two Independent Republicans .... U.S. authorities re-arrest Mildred Gillars, the American "Axis Sally," released from prison in a Christmas amnesty Dec. 24.			India's Constituent Assembly adopts Nehru's resolution declaring its intention "to proclaim India as an independent sovereign republic" incorporating British India, the Indian States and parts of India outside these territories as "autonomous units" in an Indian union .... Chinese Foreign Min. Wang Shih-chieh protests the landing of French troops in the Chinese-administered Parcel Islands off the Indochinese coast.
Jan. 23		Chmn. J. Eaton Griffith of the European Coal Organization announces that the organization's program of voluntary coal distribution to needy countries will continue for another year.			
	A	B	C	D	E
	Includes developments that affect more than one world region, international organizations and important meetings of major world leaders.	*Includes all domestic and regional developments in Europe, including the Soviet Union, Turkey, Cyprus and Malta.*	*Includes all domestic and regional developments in Africa and the Middle East, including Iraq and Iran and excluding Cyprus, Turkey and Afghanistan.*	*Includes all domestic and regional developments in Latin America, the Caribbean and Canada.*	*Includes all domestic and regional developments in Asian and Pacific nations, extending from Afghanistan through all the Pacific Islands, except Hawaii.*

U.S. Politics & Social Issues	U.S. Foreign Policy & Defense	U.S. Economy & Environment	Science, Technology & Nature	Culture, Leisure & Life Style	
Using state troopers, Herman Talmadge takes possession of the executive mansion in Atlanta. Gov. Ellis Arnall accuses him of engineering a "military coup d'etat" with "storm troopers."	Truman announces that the Army and Navy have reached agreement on merger of the armed forces into a Defense Department, with separate secretaries of the Army, Navy and Air Force. The agreement also provides for creation of a War Council, a Council of National Defense and a National Security Resources Board.		National Foundation for Infantile Paralysis reveals development of a new method of infecting white mice with the human polio virus, enabling scientists to speed research on the disease.	Tennis star William Tilden is sentenced in Los Angeles to nine months in prison for having sexual relations with a 14-year-old boy.	Jan. 16
Former State Dept. employe Carl Marzani is indicted in Washington on charges of concealing his membership in the Communist Party while holding his job .... House Ways and Means Comm. approves bills freezing postal rates and excise taxes on luxury goods.		Easing its anti-inflation policy, the Federal Reserve Bd. cuts margin requirements for security purchases on the N.Y. Stock Exchange from 100% to 75%.			Jan. 17
Melvin Thompson is sworn in as governor of Georgia following the resignation of Ellis Arnall.				Home-run leader Hank Greenberg is sold by the Detroit Tigers to the Pittsburgh Pirates.	Jan. 18
Common Cause, a liberal anti-Communist organization, is formed in N.Y. with Mrs. Natalie Wales Latham as chairwoman.	Navy discloses the successful flight testing of the XF2R-1, a mixed propulsion system plane with a gas turbine-driven propeller and a jet tail boost.			U.S. Junior Chamber of Commerce names 10 outstanding young men of 1946, including boxer Joe Louis, historian Arthur Schlesinger Jr., cartoonist Bill Mauldin and Rep. John F. Kennedy (D, Mass.).	Jan. 19
Judge Marvin Jones is named by Truman to be Chief Justice of the U.S. Court of Claims following the resignation of Justice Richard Whaley .... Sen. Theodore Bilbo (D, Miss.) undergoes oral surgery at the Trouro Infirmary in New Orleans .... Former Rep. Andrew Volstead (R, Minn.), sponsor of the 1919 Prohibition Act, dies at 87 in Granite Falls, Minn.		Supreme Court rules that N.Y. tenants have the right to challenge an OPA order for their eviction after their apartment building was turned into a cooperative.		Roland Raymond is named president of the Metropolitan Museum of Art in N.Y. to succeed William Osborn.	Jan. 20
Georgia's Gov. Melvin Thompson rejects a proposal of Herman Talmadge that he resign and "let the white people of Georgia determine their choice" in a new election .... N.Y. State legislature approves an emergency $300 yearly pay increase for 77,000 public school teachers.	Gen. Marshall is sworn in as secretary of state after James Byrnes performs his last official act by signing the Italian, Hungarian, Rumanian and Bulgarian peace treaties.			N.Y. Giants pitcher Carl Hubbell, St. Louis Cardinals second baseman Frank Frisch, Detroit Tigers catcher Mickey Cochrane and Philadelphia Athletics pitcher Lefty Grove are elected to the Baseball Hall of Fame by the Baseball Writers Assn.	Jan. 21
U.S. Conference of Mayors ends in Washington after passing resolutions urging passage of the Wagner-Ellender-Taft housing bill and continuation of rent controls.	Herbert Hoover accepts a request from Truman to study food conditions in Germany and Austria "to relieve some of the burden on the American taxpayer."	Sen. Robert Taft (R, O.) is named chairman of the joint Senate-House Economic Committee .... A Chicago arbitration board grants TWA pilots flying DC-4 Skymasters and Constellations on transworld routes a pay increase of about $1,200. Co-pilots get a yearly increase of $720.			Jan. 22
A federal grand jury in Washington indicts former Rep. Andrew May (D., Ky.) and arms manufacturers Henry Garsson, Murray Garsson and Joseph Freeman on charges of bribery and conspiracy to defraud the government, arising from the Senate War Investigating committee hearings .... Harvard Pres. James B. Conant urges a program of federal and state aid for two-year colleges to meet the growing demand for higher education.			Rockefeller Foundation contributes $10 million to the China Medical Bd. to aid the Peking Union Medical College.		Jan. 23
F	G	H	I	J	
Includes elections, federal-state relations, civil rights and liberties, crime, the judiciary, education, health care, poverty, urban affairs and population.	*Includes formation and debate of U.S. foreign and defense policies, veterans affairs and defense spending. (Relations with specific foreign countries are usually found under the region concerned.)*	*Includes business, labor, agriculture, taxation, transportation, consumer affairs, monetary and fiscal policy, natural resources, pollution and accidents.*	*Includes worldwide scientific, medical and technological developments, natural phenomena, U.S. weather and natural disasters.*	*Includes the arts, religion, scholarship, communications media, sports, entertainment, fashions, fads and social life.*	

	World Affairs	Europe	Africa & the Middle East	The Americas	Asia & the Pacific
Jan. 24	Prepatory Commission of the U.N. Food and Agriculture Organization proposes in its final report that an 18-nation World Food Council be created under the FAO as an advisory group to help draw up a world food program for needy nations.	In notes to Britain and the U.S., France proposes a federal structure for a reunited Germany, with a weak central parliament and strong states exercising police power and authority over foreign policy .... Greek Populist leader Demetrios Maximos forms a coalition cabinet to succeed the government of Constantin Tsaldaris, who resigned Jan. 22.			
Jan. 25		First postwar pact permitting direct trade between German and foreign businesses is signed by Dutch, American, and British representatives in The Hague .... National Democratic Party of Germany, a right-wing group advocating vigorous opposition to Communism and creation of a United States of Europe, is organized in the U.S. zone with banker Heinrich Leuchtgens as president.		Argentine Pres. Peron issues a decree empowering the government to purchase all businesses in the country that formerly belonged to Axis nationals.	Adm. George Thierry d'Argenlieu, French high commissioner for Indochina, charges in Saigon that Pres. Ho Chi Minh's Vietnam government is patterned after the Soviets, and claims that the war in Vietnam is a struggle between Western democracy and Marxism.
Jan. 26		A KLM airliner crashes and explodes in Copenhagen while taking off for Stockholm. All 22 passengers are killed, including American opera star Grace Moore and Prince Gustav Adolf of Sweden.	Egypt breaks off treaty negotiations with Britain for the second time in five months, objecting to British insistence on self-determination for the Sudan.	Nelson Rockefeller reveals he will establish a project to aid agriculture in Venezuela, financed by private U.S. and Venezuelan capital.	
Jan. 27	Fiodor Gusev, Russian delegate to the London conference, demands that the German and Austrian peace treaties be drawn up by the Big Four, with smaller nations restricted to ratification of the treaties .... U.S. delegate Eleanor Roosevelt is elected chairman of the U.N. Economic and Social Council's Human Rights Commission.		London Palestine Conference reconvenes without Jewish representation, as Palestine Arab leader Jamal el Husseini declares the Arab world is unalterably opposed to partition as a solution to the Palestine problem.	Canadian P.M. Mackenzie King announces the Chinese immigration act will be repealed, eliminating special restrictions on the entry of Chinese into the country.	
Jan. 28	U.S., Britain and France agree at the London conference to a Russian demand that smaller nations be excluded from full participation in the German peace treaty discussions .... UNESCO launches a campaign to raise $100 million for restoration of schools, libraries and museums devastated by war.	U.S. State Dept. charges the Polish government with exercising "coercion and intimidation against democratic elements" in the Jan. 19 parliamentary elections. The State Dept. note says the U.S. reserves "full liberty of action" in determining its future attitude towards Poland, but denies that an immediate diplomatic break is planned .... London reports that the Labor government has decided to admit 500,000 displaced persons, including 80,000 Jews, to relieve Britain's manpower shortage.		Several Bolivian soldiers and policemen are wounded when members of the opposition National Revolutionary Movement attack a police barracks in the Potosi region.	After confering with Burmese leaders, British P.M. Clement Attlee announces a plan for Burma's independence which calls for election of a constituent assembly in April to pave the way for a permanent government .... Australia's External Affairs Min. Herbert Evatt is elected president of the six-nation South Pacific Regional Conference in Canberra.
Jan. 29		Poland's Communist-socialist government bloc issues a statement promising a new constitution with guarantees for civil rights and improved social services. The statement also attacks the conservative Peasant Party as "the legal superstructure of the reactionary underground." .... Molotov signs the Italian, Bulgarian, Rumanian, Hungarian and Finnish peace treaties in Moscow.	British Foreign Secy. Bevin confers with David Ben-Gurion and other Jewish leaders on long-term policy in Palestine amid reports that the Labor government has decided to partition the country.		U.S. State Dept. abandons its year-long effort to mediate the Chinese civil war, withdrawing from the Committee of Three and its executive headquarters in Peking. Military spokesmen announce that most of the 15,000 Marines stationed in China will be withdrawn.
Jan. 30		Security Council's Balkan Inquiry Commission holds its first meeting in Athens amid charges that the Greeks purposely delayed issuing visas to the Yugoslav delegation .... Irish labor leader James Larkin dies at 69 in Dublin.			Wang Ping-nan, Communist representative in Nanking, affirms his confidence in the Communists' ability to defeat the Kuomintang and declares that "the only way out is to fight."
Jan. 31	Research director for *American Cyanimid Co.*, Dr. M.L. Crossley, is named winner of the *American Institute of Chemistry's* gold medal for his work that led to discoveries in the fields of dyes and pharmaceuticals.	Allied Control Commission for Italy ceases functioning and is absorbed by the Italian Military Affairs Section of Allied Force Headquarters in Europe .... A German denazification court in Nuremberg sentences Hans Fritzsche, Nazi propagandist acquitted by the International War Crimes Tribunal, to nine years imprisonment. Hitler's photographer, Heinrich Hoffmann, is sentenced to 10 years.	Churchill urges Britain to turn over its Palestine mandate to the U.N. if the U.S. refuses to share responsibility in the Middle East.		Acceding to an order from MacArthur, Japanese labor leader Yashiro Ii cancels a threatened strike of government and utilities workers .... French liner *Ile de France* arrives in Indochina with 8,000 French troops.
Feb. 1		France urges the London conference to support international ownership and control of basic German industries in the Ruhr .... A cold wave grips western Europe for the 10th consecutive day, disrupting transportation and causing numerous deaths.		Rafael Gonzalez Monoz is named Cuba's foreign minister.	
	A	B	C	D	E
	Includes developments that affect more than one world region, international organizations and important meetings of major world leaders.	*Includes all domestic and regional developments in Europe, including the Soviet Union, Turkey, Cyprus and Malta.*	*Includes all domestic and regional developments in Africa and the Middle East, including Iraq and Iran and excluding Cyprus, Turkey and Afghanistan.*	*Includes all domestic and regional developments in Latin America, the Caribbean and Canada.*	*Includes all domestic and regional developments in Asian and Pacific nations, extending from Afghanistan through all the Pacific Islands, except Hawaii.*

U.S. Politics & Social Issues	U.S. Foreign Policy & Defense	U.S. Economy & Environment	Science, Technology & Nature	Culture, Leisure & Life Style	
		GOP succeeds in re-establishing the Senate Comm. on Small Business for eight months and names Kenneth Wherry (R., Neb.) as chairman.		Sixty British painting masterpieces worth $5 million, on loan from King George VI to British museums, go on display at the Metropolitan Museum in N.Y. . . . . Noted French artist Pierre Bonnard dies at 79 in Cannot, France.	Jan. 24
Former gangster of the prohibition era Al Capone dies at 48 in Miami Beach, Fla. . . . . Fulton National Bank of Atlanta obtains a court order preventing both Melvin Thompson and Herman Talmadge from drawing on state funds deposited in the bank by former Gov. Ellis Arnall.		United Steel Workers Union and the U.S. Steel Corp. announce an agreement on job reclassification which will give workers in six of the company's subsidiaries $32 million in back pay and wage increases of about $17 million.			Jan. 25
Paul Robeson announces he will halt his singing career for two years to embark on a campaign against racial discrimination in the U.S.			Navy Antarctic expedition finds a new mountain range and five uncharted islands off the coast of the continent.	Ben Hogan wins the Phoenix Open Golf Tournament with a record score of 270.	Jan. 26
Chief Justice Grafton Green of the Tennessee Supreme Court, who wrote the opinion in the Scopes evolution case, dies at 74 in Nashville.		The first nationwide contract in the rubber industry is signed in Cincinnati by the U.S. Rubber Co. and the CIO United Rubber Workers, affecting 30,000 workers . . . . Senate confirms W. Averell Harriman as commerce secretary.		Middleweight boxer Rocky Graziano admits to N.Y. District Atty. Frank Hogan that he was offered $100,000 to throw a bout (later cancelled) with "Cowboy" Reuben Shank.	Jan. 27
Arkansas legislature repeals a 1945 bill intended to prevent Negroes from voting on state and local issues by separating state and federal primaries.	Former War. Secy. Henry Stimson reveals in a *Harper's Magazine* article that Truman made the final decision to drop the atomic bomb on Japan. He was supported by several members of the Advisory Comm. on Atomic Policy, including physicists Enrico Fermi, Ernest Lawrence and J. Robert Oppenheimer.		Dr. Lee de Forest, who invented the electron tube in 1906, is awarded the Edison Medal for "pioneering achievement in radio."	Dr. A.S.W. Rosenbach buys the Bay Psalm Book, the first book printed in England's American colonies, at a N.Y. auction for a record $151,000.	Jan. 28
		House passes and sends to the Senate a bill to extend indefinitely wartime excise taxes on luxuries and transportation . . . . Labor Department's Meat Packing Commission concludes a two-year study by recommending a $5 million annual wage increase for 100,000 workers in the industry.	Seaplanes of the Navy Antarctic expedition complete the charting of 800 unexplored miles of coastline . . . . Lewis Chubb, director of the Westinghouse Research Laboratories in Pittsburgh, is awarded the John Fritz Medal for notable scientific achievement in 1946.	Arthur Miller's play *All My Sons* opens in N.Y. to favorable reviews . . . . Noted philosopher and author Morris Raphael Cohen dies at 66 in Washington.	Jan. 29
		House Speaker Joseph Martin (R, Mass.) says that Republican support for a tax cut will depend on the Administration's ability to balance the budget and begin repayment of the national debt.	Tornadoes sweep five Southern and border states, causing 20 deaths and extensive damage.		Jan. 30
Senate Campaign Investigating Committee issues a report calling for repeal of the Corrupt Practices and Hatch acts as "utterly inadequate." . . . . Truman nominates Philip Perlman as U.S. Solicitor General.	U.S. Atomic Energy Commission files its first semiannual report, listing current activities, and names Col. James McCormack, Jr. as its director of military research and applications.	AFL Executive Council proposes a merger with the CIO and names a five-man committee to discuss the matter with a similar CIO committee. The move is a response to CIO Pres. Philip Murray's request for unified labor action to meet the "ferocious attacks" of anti-union politicians . . . . A special Senate committee on oil resources warns that the continental oil reserves now known would not meet requirements in case of a large-scale war.		War Dept. rejects the requests of Felix Blanchard, Glen Davis and Barney Poole for leave from the armed forces to play pro football.	Jan. 31
		Truman reveals that the Associated General Contractors of America and the AFL Building and Construction Trades Dept. have agreed to government suggestions for a national labor-management committee to settle disputes in the construction industry.		Network Hooperatings list the most popular radio shows as: Bob Hope, Fibber McGee and Molly, Charlie McCarthy Show, Jack Benny and Fred Allen.	Feb. 1

F	G	H	I	J
Includes elections, federal-state relations, civil rights and liberties, crime, the judiciary, education, health care, poverty, urban affairs and population.	*Includes formation and debate of U.S. foreign and defense policies, veterans affairs and defense spending. (Relations with specific foreign countries are usually found under the region concerned.)*	*Includes business, labor, agriculture, taxation, transportation, consumer affairs, monetary and fiscal policy, natural resources, pollution and accidents.*	*Includes worldwide scientific, medical and technological developments, natural phenomena, U.S. weather and natural disasters.*	*Includes the arts, religion, scholarship, communications media, sports, entertainment, fashions, fads and social life.*

	World Affairs	Europe	Africa & the Middle East	The Americas	Asia & the Pacific
Feb. 2		Italian Premier Alcide de Gasperi announces formation of a new cabinet consisting of seven Christian Democrats, three Communists, three Socialists, and two independents .... Athens reports renewed fighting between Communist and royalist bands in the northern provinces of Macedonia, Thrace and Thessaly.		Liberal Party candidate Leonardo Arguello wins the Nicaraguan presidential elections, defeating Conservative candidate Enoc Aguardo Farfan .... Opposition parties in Guatemala charge voting irregularities in Jan. 24 congressional elections, which resulted in victory for all candidates of the ruling Revolutionary Action Party.	Gen. Hodge of the U.S. military government in Korea issues a statement attacking Syngman Rhee and other South Korean politicians for planning "widespread demonstrations .. against the so-called trusteeship, coupled with attempts to discredit the American effort in Korea." .... A nationwide poll taken by the Tokyo newspaper *Asahi* indicates that 48.7% of Japanese voters oppose the conservative Yoshida government, while only 26.4% support it.
Feb. 3		British embassy in Athens announces plans to withdraw half of the 40,000 British troops stationed in Greece .... An Allied court in Hamburg hands down death sentences for 11 Ravensbrueck concentration camp guards (five women and six men) who participated in the murder of 80,000 female camp inmates.	British authorities in Palestine demand that the Jewish Agency and the Palestinian Jewish Council mobilize the Jewish community against Zionist terrorists.		
Feb. 4	UNESCO and the Food and Agriculture Organization officially become specialized U.N. agencies with the signing of protocols at Lake Success.	British House of Commons approves a bill nationalizing the electric power industry, while a national coal shortage causes factory shutdowns affecting 50,000 British workers .... Fritz Kuhn, former German-American Bund leader deported to Germany after the war, is cleared by a denazification court in Munich because he was not in Germany during the Third Reich.	London Conference on Palestine adjourns after Arab representatives categorically reject any British plan for partition of Palestine.		France recognizes the provisional government of Cochin China, under Pres. Levan Hoach, as a "free state within the French Union." .... Anti-Fascist People's Freedom League, Burma's majority party, accepts Britain's proposal for Burmese independence in Rangoon.
Feb. 5		Inter-Allied Reparations Agency ends its seventh session in Brussels after reporting that in 1946 it received 122 German plants and 227 ships for distribution as reparations .... In an effort to ensure that the 1947 crop fulfills production goals, Russia's Council of Ministers merges three ministries concerned with agricultural affairs into a single Agriculture Ministry under Ivan Benedictov .... Boleslaw Bierut, provisional president of Poland since 1945, is re-elected to a seven-year presidential term by parliament.	Palestine's Jewish Council rejects British demands for Jewish support in combatting terrorism, while the Irgun Zvai Leumi asserts it will continue to fight against British authority in Palestine .... South African P.M. Jan Smuts establishes an Indian Advisory Board to help the government deal with Indian nationals.		French forces break the siege of Hue, former imperial city in central Vietnam, after a two-week campaign.
Feb. 6		Austria's parliament approves a denazification law requiring the registration and penalization of 536,000 Austrian Nazis.	Samir Pasha Rifai succeeds Ibrahim Pasha Hashin as premier of Transjordan.		
Feb. 7	A U.N. Security Council committee on disarmament deadlocks over a U.S. proposal barring it from atomic energy matters .... UNRRA Director Lowell Rooks announces establishment of a $35-million emergency food relief fund for the world's neediest nations, intended to last until creation of other international relief arrangements.	Socialist leader Josef Cyrankiewicz forms Poland's first official postwar cabinet, with 10 key posts (including foreign affairs, labor and industry) held by Communists or socialists .... British Military Government in Berlin announces it will clear 1-1.5 million Nazi suspects in its occupation zone under a new and more lenient denazification procedure.	Zionist and Arab leaders reject the latest British plan for partition of Palestine into Jewish and Arab areas.		
Feb. 8		U.S. authorities in Frankfurt indict Friedrich Flick, Germany's most powerful steel industrialist, for war crimes arising from the exploitation of slave labor in his factories .... Franz Ritter von Epp, German World War I general and leader of right-wing militarists in Bavaria during the Weimar years, dies at 78 in Munich.			
Feb. 9		London increases subway, bus and trolley fares in an effort to add $23 million yearly to the city treasury.			Indonesian Republic announces it will sponsor the migration of more than 15 million inhabitants of Java to underpopulated Sumatra.
Feb. 10	Twenty Allied nations participate in ceremonies at the Galerie de la Paix of the French Foreign Office marking the official acceptance of the Italian, Bulgarian, Hungarian and Rumanian peace treaties.	Drastic power conservation measures are imposed in England to alleviate the country's fuel shortage. All industries but those classified as essential are closed in central and northwest England and Wales .... Col. Frak Howley of the U.S. military government in Berlin charges that Russian authorities have failed to deliver a promised 100,000 tons of coal for home heating in the city.			Shanghai department store employes riot, causing one death, after a mass meeting urging a boycott of U.S. goods to protest American import restrictions.

A	B	C	D	E
Includes developments that affect more than one world region, international organizations and important meetings of major world leaders.	*Includes all domestic and regional developments in Europe, including the Soviet Union, Turkey, Cyprus and Malta.*	*Includes all domestic and regional developments in Africa and the Middle East, including Iraq and Iran and excluding Cyprus, Turkey and Afghanistan.*	*Includes all domestic and regional developments in Latin America, the Caribbean and Canada.*	*Includes all domestic and regional developments in Asian and Pacific nations, extending from Afghanistan through all the Pacific Islands, except Hawaii.*

U.S. Politics & Social Issues	U.S. Foreign Policy & Defense	U.S. Economy & Environment	Science, Technology & Nature	Culture, Leisure & Life Style	
					Feb. 2
Supreme Court unanimously orders a new trial for Rene de Meerleer, who in 1932 received a life sentence in Michigan for murder after a one-day trial without a lawyer.	Armed Forces Staff College opens in Norfolk, Va. with a class of 150 Navy and Army officers .... Adm. Marc Mitscher, commander of the Navy's Atlantic Fleet and wartime chief of a carrier task force which led the attack on Japan, dies at 60 in Norfolk, Va.	Truman asks Congress for a one-year extension of wartime presidential authority to regulate imports and control the distribution of scarce raw materials, in order to assure "the effective completion of reconversion." .... Reconstruction Finance Corp. allows U.S. firms to deal directly with German manufacturers in purchasing German goods.		James Michener's *Tales of the South Pacific* is published in N.Y.	Feb. 3
Largest narcotics seizure in nine years is reported as federal agents in N.Y. find $250,000 worth of heroin in the possession of a seaman on a U.S. ship returning from France.	Gerhard Eisler, German Communist accused of being a Russian spy, is arrested in N.Y. and held as an enemy alien, while convicted German spy Teodoro Lau is sentenced to 10 years imprisonment .... Truman accepts the credentials of Polish Amb. Josef Winiewicz in Washington but tells him that Poland has violated its pledge to hold free elections.			American financier Thomas Lamont donates $500,000 toward a $1.2 million fund to restore England's bomb-damaged Canterbury Cathedral.	Feb. 4
Truman asks Congress to change the line of presidential succession so that the speaker of the House rather than the secretary of state follows the vice president.	Douglas Aircraft Co. completes work on the Navy's D-55 Skystreak, a supersonic experimental plane.	AFL Executive Council ends a Miami meeting after expressing opposition to universal military service and creating a three-man committee to fight labor curbs pending in Congress.			Feb. 5
House approves and sends to the Senate a Republican-backed resolution calling for a constitutional amendment limiting the presidential tenure to two terms.	Accused Soviet spy Eisler appears before the House Un-American Activities Comm. and is charged with conspiracy to overthrow the U.S. government.		Adm. Byrd and 197 men of the Navy's Antarctic expedition remain at Little America while three ships sail to seek safe passage through the Ross Sea ice pack.	Hans Fallada, popular German novelist and author of *Little Man, What Now?*, dies at 53 in Berlin.	Feb. 6
Georgia Superior Court Judge Claude Porter rules that the State General Assembly did not have the right to declare Herman Talmadge governor and that Melvin Thompson's claim to the governorship is constitutionally valid.	State Secy. Marshall tells his first press conference that the U.S. will not disarm until peace problems have been solved, collective security arrangements organized and atomic energy put under effective international control.	Truman asks Congress to pass legislation supporting the synthetic rubber industry and extending controls on rubber allocation one year in the interests of national security.			Feb. 7
	Senate Foreign Affairs Comm. Chmn. Arthur Vandenberg tells the Michigan State Republican Convention the U.S. will not "abandon the advantage of the atomic bomb" until a foolproof international control system is in operation.			American Federation of Musicians Pres. Petrillo announces the union will finance a program of free public concerts in the U.S. and Canada with $2.5 million in royalties collected yearly from record companies.	Feb. 8
		Executive board of the Committee for Maritime Unity recommends the committee's dissolution due to the resignation of its chairman, National Maritime Union Pres. Joseph Curran.		*New York Herald Tribune* lists *Lydia Bailey* by Kenneth Roberts and *Peace of Mind* by Joshua Liebman as best-selling fiction and non-fiction books.	Feb. 9
Supreme Court upholds the Hatch Act, forbidding political activity by federal workers and state employes paid from federal funds. The Court also rules that the cost of transporting children to parochial schools in N.J. may be paid out of state tax funds .... A federal grand jury in Washington indicts Kenneth Romney, former House sergeant at arms, on charges of seeking to "swindle or defraud" the government by concealing a $143,863 shortage in his accounts.	State Secy. George Marshall names William Eddy head of the State Department's intelligence unit.		Planned Parenthood Federation of America announces that a recent poll of 15,000 U.S. doctors shows 97.8% in favor of birth control.		Feb. 10

F	G	H	I	J
Includes elections, federal-state relations, civil rights and liberties, crime, the judiciary, education, health care, poverty, urban affairs and population.	*Includes formation and debate of U.S. foreign and defense policies, veterans affairs and defense spending. (Relations with specific foreign countries are usually found under the region concerned.)*	*Includes business, labor, agriculture, taxation, transportation, consumer affairs, monetary and fiscal policy, natural resources, pollution and accidents.*	*Includes worldwide scientific, medical and technological developments, natural phenomena, U.S. weather and natural disasters.*	*Includes the arts, religion, scholarship, communications media, sports, entertainment, fashions, fads and social life.*

	World Affairs	Europe	Africa & the Middle East	The Americas	Asia & the Pacific
Feb. 11	International Labor Organization's 12-nation oil committee, meeting in Los Angeles, recommends regional minimum wages, free unionization and collective bargaining in the oil industry . . . . First postwar International Shipping Conference opens in London and elects Sir Joseph Maclay chairman.	Greek Air Min. Themistocles Tsatsos announces completion of a contract for British planes and supplies to aid Greek armed forces . . . . Military authorities in the U.S. and British zones issue laws forbidding German participation in international or domestic cartels.			Cambodian King Norodom Sihanouk declares in Pnompenh that, although he would prefer independence, the inability of Cambodia to support or defend itself means that it must continue under French protection.
Feb. 12	After two days of debate the U.N. Security Council adopts a U.S. resolution prohibiting the Council's Disarmament Commission from infringing on nuclear arms questions within the authority of the U.N. Atomic Energy Commission.	British government extends restrictions on power use to all of England, while the House of Commons passes a Polish resettlement bill allowing 65,000 of the 127,000 Poles still in England to become permanent residents . . . . Britain recognizes Bulgaria's Communist-dominated coalition government . . . . Polish Pres. Bierut announces an amnesty effective Feb. 18 which will free most political prisoners and enable members of the anti-government underground to come out of hiding.	Sir Evelyn Barker, outgoing British commander in Palestine, confirms the death sentences of three Irgun Zvai members condemned for carrying firearms.	U.S. and Canada announce a defense accord continuing wartime military collaboration, with provisions for personnel exchange and "mutual and reciprocal availability of military, naval and air facilities in each country." . . . . Argentina buys the country's British-owned railway system for $150 million.	
Feb. 13	U.N. Security Council creates a Commission for Conventional Armaments, empowered to prepare a plan for international regulation of non-nuclear weapons . . . . Architects Howard Robertson of Britain, Charles Le Corbusier of France, Oscar Niemeyer of Brazil, Nikolai Bassov of Russia and Liang Ssu-chang of China are appointed to a board to design the future U.N. headquarters in N.Y.				Premier Paul Ramadier announces he will not negotiate with Ho Chi Minh's Vietnam government, which he accuses of committing "massacres and atrocities."
Feb. 14	Speaking before the U.N. Security Council, Gromyko reiterates Russia's argument against the U.S. atomic energy control plan and the Russian demand for immediate outlawing of the atomic bomb.	British cabinet rejects military cutbacks in a White Paper on defense and asks Parliament for a $3.6-billion armed forces appropriation . . . . Five million public employes strike for four hours throughout France to protest a government wage-freezing decree.	London Conference on Palestine ends as British Foreign Secy. Bevin informs Arab delegates that the cabinet has decided to refer the Palestine problem to the U.N.		
Feb. 15		U.S. Amb. Arthur Lane informs Polish Premier Cyrankiewicz that he has been recalled indefinitely from Warsaw by the State Dept.			Nationalist forces report capturing Communist New 4th Army headquarters at Lini in Shantung Province.
Feb. 16		A Yugoslavian court hands down a death sentence for Gen. Alexander Loehr, wartime German commander in southeastern Europe, and six other German officers convicted of war crimes.			Chiang Kai-shek introduces a series of economic measures to deal with China's runaway inflation, restoring wartime business controls and banning strikes and lockouts.
Feb. 17	U.S. delegate Warren Austin asks the Security Council to consider the U.S. trusteeship plan for the 650 formerly Japanese-controlled islands in the Marianas, Marshalls and Carolines.	A British military tribunal in Venice begins the trial of Field Marshall Albert Kesselring, German commander in Italy charged with responsibility for the slaying of 1,413 hostages and prisoners of war.			
Feb. 18		Sir Alexander Cadogan, British delegate to the U.N. Security Council, accuses Albania of illegally laying mines in the Corfu Channel.	Faris el Khouri, Syrian delegate to the U.N. Security Council, accuses Britain of being too "humane" to Zionist terrorists and claims the U.S. government "favors the Jews."		
Feb. 19		Albanian delegate Hysni Kapo denies British charges of mine laying at the U.N. Security Council, accusing British ships of "provocative" actions against Albania's sovereignty . . . . Poland and France sign a five-year cultural relations pact in Paris.		Fifteen U.S. congressmen arrive in San Juan to investigate conditions in Puerto Rico.	After three months of fighting, French forces claim that they have eliminated the last Vietnamese nationalist resistance in Hanoi.
Feb. 20		French Premier Paul Ramadier wins a vote of confidence in the National Assembly after announcing a second series of 5% price reductions scheduled for Feb. 24 . . . . British zone commander Sir Sholto Douglas announces a new policy requiring employable refugees in Germany to work or leave the country.	British government issues a White Paper on Palestine containing several partition plans which it will refer to the U.N.	Mexico announces that it will accept the jurisdiction of the International Court of Justice for a five-year trial period.	Admitting failure to solve India's internal strife, P.M. Attlee tells the House of Commons that Britain will withdraw from the former colony by June 1948 . . . . Japanese government orders the liquidation of the personal fortunes of 56 Japanese families (estimated at $80 million) in its drive to break up the Zaibatsu combines.
	A *Includes developments that affect more than one world region, international organizations and important meetings of major world leaders.*	B *Includes all domestic and regional developments in Europe, including the Soviet Union, Turkey, Cyprus and Malta.*	C *Includes all domestic and regional developments in Africa and the Middle East, including Iraq and Iran and excluding Cyprus, Turkey and Afghanistan.*	D *Includes all domestic and regional developments in Latin America, the Caribbean and Canada.*	E *Includes all domestic and regional developments in Asian and Pacific nations, extending from Afghanistan through all the Pacific Islands, except Hawaii.*

U.S. Politics & Social Issues	U.S. Foreign Policy & Defense	U.S. Economy & Environment	Science, Technology & Nature	Culture, Leisure & Life Style	
		Kenneth Hogate, chairman of Dow-Jones and president of the *Wall Street Journal*, dies at 49 in Palm Springs, Calif.			Feb. 11
Henry County Superior Court in Georgia rules that the state General Assembly was within its rights in naming Herman Talmadge governor and dismisses a suit brought against Talmadge by Gov. Melvin Thompson.		Addressing a Lincoln Day dinner in N.Y., Harold Stassen urges Republicans to abandon their high-tariff policy and support reciprocal trade agreements with safeguards against abuses.	A 1,000-ton meteorite falls to earth in Siberia with a shock recorded on seismographs in the eastern U.S.		Feb. 12
U.S. Circuit Court of Appeals in Chicago orders a trial in a $6 million libel suit by A.N. Spanel against columnist Westbrook Pegler, who called Spanel a Communist. The court rules that such labels are "libelous per se," placing the accused "beyond the pale of respectability."		CIO Textile Workers Union announces agreement on a 10% wage increase for 15,000 workers at the Dan River Cotton Mills in Virginia and the Marshall Field Mills In N.C. The agreement is expected to set a pattern for the industry in the South.		Radio Corp. of America and the National Broadcasting Co. oppose the commercial introduction of color television as premature at FCC hearings .... National Institute for Arts and Letters awards its gold medal for distinguished services in music to composer John Alden Carpenter.	Feb. 13
		Joint Congressional Committee on the Budget votes to cut Truman's $37-billion budget for fiscal 1948 by $6 billion.			Feb. 14
Secy. Homer Loomis, Jr. of the anti-Negro, anti-Jewish Colombians is sentenced in Atlanta to one year in a public works camp for inciting to riot.				CBS Hit Parade presents *For Sentimental Reasons* as the most popular song.	Feb. 15
Rep. Allen Treadway (R., Mass.) dies at 79 in Washington.				Finland's Lasse Parkkinen wins the world speed skating title in Oslo .... Ralph Townsend gains the U.S. national skiing championship at Lake Placid, N.Y.	Feb. 16
Senate Judiciary Comm. approves a proposed constitutional amendment limiting presidential tenure to two terms.	State Dept's. International Broadcasting Division begins a one-hour daily Russian program of news and music transmitted from N.Y. and relayed to the Soviet Union via Munich.	Supreme Court rules that apprentices receiving job training are not employes and not entitled to pay and other benefits called for in the Fair Labor Standards Act .... Senate approves the indefinite continuation of wartime excise taxes on luxury items and sends the bill to conference.		John Steinbeck's novel *The Wayward Bus* is published in N.Y. by Viking.	Feb. 17
	W. Bedell Smith, U.S. ambassador to Russia, proposes a nine-point program of improved U.S.-Russian cultural and scientific relations.	House turns down an OPA request for $5.9 million to maintain current operations, despite a warning from OPA head Max McCullough that the action will end rent controls and sugar rationing .... Following similar AFL action on Feb. 5, CIO Pres. Philip Murray names a five-man commission to discuss unification of the U.S. labor movement.			Feb. 18
Time publisher Henry Luce is named chairman of the National Urban League's 1947 drive to raise funds for Negro economic self-help projects.				Malcolm Lowry's novel *Under the Volcano* is published in London by Reynal and Hitchcock.	Feb. 19
Herman Talmadge, claimant to Georgia's governorship, signs a bill establishing all-white primaries in the state by allowing the Democratic Party to function as a private "political club."	War Secy. Patterson asks Congress to approve changes in the Articles of War which would end discrimination between officers and enlisted men in military courts and allow enlisted men to serve on courts-martial .... Truman says he will again ask Congress for a universal military training law.	Wage Stabilization Board issues its final report and goes out of existence.	Navy surveyors in Antarctica reach the camp site of Capt. Robert Scott's unsuccessful 1912 expedition.		Feb. 20
F	G	H	I	J	
Includes elections, federal-state relations, civil rights and liberties, crime, the judiciary, education, health care, poverty, urban affairs and population.	*Includes formation and debate of U.S. foreign and defense policies, veterans affairs and defense spending. (Relations with specific foreign countries are usually found under the region concerned.)*	*Includes business, labor, agriculture, taxation, transportation, consumer affairs, monetary and fiscal policy, natural resources, pollution and accidents.*	*Includes worldwide scientific, medical and technological developments, natural phenomena, U.S. weather and natural disasters.*	*Includes the arts, religion, scholarship, communications media, sports, entertainment, fashions, fads and social life.*	

	World Affairs	Europe	Africa & the Middle East	The Americas	Asia & the Pacific
Feb. 21		In his last press conference as U.S. military governor of Germany, Gen. McNarney declares that the Allied Control Commission is failing to govern the country effectively because it did not establish the central agencies specified by the Potsdam Agreement.	Arab Higher Commission in Jerusalem announces a tax assessment on all Palestine Arabs to raise 220,000 Palestinian pounds, which will be used to buy Arab land that might otherwise be sold to Jews . . . . King George VI becomes the first British monarch to open a Dominion parliament as he addresses the South African legislature in Capetown.	Argentina and Italy sign a pact under which Argentina will accept an unlimited number of Italian immigrants.	
Feb. 22	London conference of deputy foreign ministers completes most work on the Austrian peace treaty, agreeing to limit the country's armed forces to 50,000 men and to withdraw all occupation troops within 90 days after the treaty takes effect.			Charles (Lucky) Luciano, former N.Y. underworld leader deported to Italy in 1946, is arrested in Havana, where he recently settled.	
Feb. 23		U.S. and British authorities round up several hundred former German officers who claim possession of bacteriological warfare secrets . . . . Commemorating the Red Army's 29th anniversary, *Pravda* claims that Russia won World War II single-handedly, with no "decisive" help from the Western Allies.	Cairo reports that five U.S. engineering firms have been awarded the contract to construct the Saudi Arabian section of a pipeline from the Arabian oilfields to the Mediterranean Sea.		
Feb. 24		Britain secretly informs the U.S. it can no longer afford to maintain present levels of military and economic aid to Greece and Turkey, and urges the U.S. to assume the burden . . . . A denazification court in Nuremberg sentences former German vice chancellor Franz von Papen to eight years in labor camp as a "major offender." . . . . Sicily's Mt. Etna erupts, sending streams of lava as far as 10 miles. No loss of life is reported due to evacuation of villages in the area.		In a speech marking the first anniversary of his election, Argentine Pres. Peron attacks Communism and outlines 10 "essential rights" for workers, including the right to jobs, adequate pay and safe working conditions.	Gen. John Hodge, U.S. commander in Korea, charges that Russia is forming a large army in its zone with Korean conscripts aged 17-25 . . . . A British military court in Hong Kong hands down a death sentence for Col. Noma Kennosuke, commander of wartime Japanese occupation forces on the island, as a war criminal.
Feb. 25	London conference of Allied deputy foreign ministers ends with a partial draft of the Austrian peace treaty but little agreement on the German treaty. Disputed points are forwarded to the foreign ministers for the forthcoming Moscow conference.	Marshal Vassily Sokolovsky, Russian representative on the Allied Control Council in Berlin, charges that the U.S.-British zone merger violates the Potsdam accord and is an attempt to create a West German state that can secede from the rest of the country . . . . French National Assembly continues the cabinet's wartime powers for another year.	British Foreign Secy. Bevin charges that London's Palestine negotiations were "spoiled" last autumn when Truman issued a campaign statement urging the immediate admission of 100,000 Jews to Palestine.		Peking sources report that Kuomintang police have made over 1,500 arrests in the past week searching for suspected liberals and Communists.
Feb. 26	Speaking before the Security Council, Gromyko approves U.S. control over former Japanese Pacific islands, but offers amendments to the trusteeship plan allowing the U.N. to change or cancel it.	Bela Kovacs, former leader of the Hungarian Peasant Party and anti-Communist member of parliament, is arrested by Russian soldiers in Budapest on charges of plotting to overthrow the government . . . . Supreme Soviet adopts a proposal of Deputy Foreign Min. Andrei Vishinsky to write the principle of the eight-hour day for workers into the Russian constitution.	Truman issues a statement denying that U.S. Palestine policy "is motivated by partisan and local politics," as charged yesterday by British Foreign Secy. Bevin.		Punjab's Hindu-dominated provincial government agrees to release 1,500 Moslems from jail and lift a ban on political meetings, ending a 34-day mass civil disobedience campaign by India's Moslem League . . . . French authorities in Saigon report receiving an appeal from nationalist leader Ho Chi Minh for an Indochina truce and return to the Dec. 19 status quo.
Feb. 27	Australia, Colombia and Poland are named to a special Security Council commission investigating British charges of Albanian mine-laying in the Corfu Channel.		Commenting on his conflict with Truman over Palestine policy, British Foreign Secy. Bevin denies that the problem will "drive any wedge ... between our two countries."		
Feb. 28	N.Y. attorney John McCloy is elected president of the International Bank for Reconstruction and Development.	French cabinet approves a $59 monthly minimum wage demanded by the country's labor unions . . . . With the improvement of weather and coal reserves, British P.M. Attlee announces that the end of Britain's worst economic crisis is in sight.		Truman signs a bill calling for cooperation with Mexico in ending the epidemic of hoof-and-mouth disease attacking U.S. and Mexican cattle.	India's Executive Council submits a budget abolishing the "salt tax," raising income tax exemptions in the lowest bracket, doubling the corporation tax and levying a 25% tax on incomes over $30,000.
March 1	International Monetary Fund begins operations in Washington with a potential reserve of $7.5 billion from its 40 members.	Allied Control Council in Berlin dissolves the State of Prussia, an important factor in Germany's unification and subsequent militarism.	In a new escalation of violence in Palestine, Zionist terrorists stage 16 attacks on British personnel and installations, causing 22 deaths and 27 injuries.		Chinese Premier T.V. Soong resigns due to the failure of his anti-inflation program, as Communist forces begin a large-scale offensive against Nationalist positions in Manchuria.
	A *Includes developments that affect more than one world region, international organizations and important meetings of major world leaders.*	B *Includes all domestic and regional developments in Europe, including the Soviet Union, Turkey, Cyprus and Malta.*	C *Includes all domestic and regional developments in Africa and the Middle East, including Iraq and Iran and excluding Cyprus, Turkey and Afghanistan.*	D *Includes all domestic and regional developments in Latin America, the Caribbean and Canada.*	E *Includes all domestic and regional developments in Asian and Pacific nations, extending from Afghanistan through all the Pacific Islands, except Hawaii.*

U.S. Politics & Social Issues	U.S. Foreign Policy & Defense	U.S. Economy & Environment	Science, Technology & Nature	Culture, Leisure & Life Style	
Emory Burke, president of the white supremacist Columbians, Inc., is sentenced in Atlanta to three years in prison for usurping police powers by establishing an anti-Negro patrol last year.	Truman asks Congress to appropriate $350 million for distribution of relief supplies in countries which suffered under Axis occupation.		Polaroid Corp. Pres. Edwin Land demonstrates a new camera which produces a developed negative and positive print in one minute after the picture is taken.		Feb. 21
	Speaking at Princeton, State Secy. Marshall warns against the American public's indifference to international affairs, which he claims is a danger to the nation's security.	Reversing an earlier ruling, the NLRB declares that workers who participate in an unlawful strike are not entitled to protection of the Wagner Act.	*Oak Ridge Journal* reports the start of government experiments in the use of atomic energy for aircraft propulsion.	New York Univ. takes the AAU senior indoor track title in N.Y. . . . . Harry Thaw, N.Y. playboy who shot architect Stanford White in 1906, dies at 76 in Miami Beach, Fla.	Feb. 22
	United World Federalists, an organization advocating world government, is formed by the merger of six national groups after a three-day convention in Asheville, N.C.		Rear Adm. Byrd and his 197-man Navy crew sail from Little America, Antarctica to Wellington, N.Z. to avoid being trapped by the freezing of the Ross Sea ice pack.	Czechoslovakia wins the world amateur ice hockey title in Prague.	Feb. 23
	Truman asks Congress to authorize U.S. participation in the International Refugee Organization, pointing out that two-thirds of the one million refugees in Central Europe are under U.S. care.	In the largest teachers' strike in U.S. history, 2,400 members of the Buffalo Teachers' Federation walk out demanding pay increases.			Feb. 24
	Truman issues an executive order calling for "escape clauses" in all reciprocal trade agreements, allowing the revocation of concessions if they work "serious injury" to domestic industry . . . . An Army C-54 transport piloted by Lt. Bobbie Cavnar lands at Westover Field, Mass. after rescuing the 11-man crew of a photo reconnaissance plane which crashed in northern Greenland Feb. 21. Cavnar and his crew receive Air Medals for a daring landing and takeoff on a frozen lake.	In a letter to CIO Pres. Murray, AFL Pres. William Green rejects proposals for united union political action, stating the two union groups must merge before this would be possible.			Feb. 25
A group of anti-Talmadge Democrats calling themselves the "Aroused Citizens of Georgia" opens a drive in Atlanta to oust Herman Talmadge's faction from the state Democratic Party.	Truman sends Congress the draft of a bill unifying the armed services under a civilian secretary.	Senate votes to cut Truman's proposed $37.5-billion budget by $4.5 billion and sends the measure to conference.		N.Y.C. Bd. of Education bans Howard Fast's *Citizen Tom Paine* from school libraries because of alleged "objectionable passages." . . . . Retired Adm. Jonas Ingram is named commissioner of the All-American Football Conference.	Feb. 26
	Truman discusses "the European problem" with State Dept. officials and congressional leaders, urging that funds be approved to aid Greece, Turkey and other countries threatened by Communist pressure . . . . Reporting on his European food mission, Herbert Hoover recommends that the U.S. and Britain each spend $475.5 million through June 1948 for civilian food needs in their German zones.			Foreign Correspondents' Assn. cites Rosalind Russell and Gregory Peck for top acting honors in 1946 and names *The Best Years of Our Lives* best picture . . . . Laura Hobson's *Gentlemen's Agreement*, an account of anti-Semitism in the U.S., is published in N.Y. by Simon and Schuster.	Feb. 27
	Appearing before the House Foreign Affairs Comm., Herbert Hoover urges that foreign countries be required to repay American food relief and that the level of relief be no higher than that proposed for Germany.	Reversing previous House action, the Appropriations Comm. votes to restore $9 million in current OPA funds and grants over $7 million to maintain rent and sugar controls until June 30.	Army P-82 *Betty Jo*, piloted by Col. Robert Thacker, lands in N.Y. to complete a record non-stop 4,798-mile flight from Honolulu in 14 hrs., 33 mins.		Feb. 28
	U.S. asks Britain to continue its aid to Greece and Turkey while the Americans consider ways to help Britain carry out its commitments.		Scientists confer at Brookhaven National Laboratory in N.Y. on plans to make the facility the largest center for nuclear research in the U.S.	Columnist Thomas Stokes receives the Raymond Clapper journalism award.	March 1
F	G	H	I	J	
Includes elections, federal-state relations, civil rights and liberties, crime, the judiciary, education, health care, poverty, urban affairs and population.	*Includes formation and debate of U.S. foreign and defense policies, veterans affairs and defense spending. (Relations with specific foreign countries are usually found under the region concerned.)*	*Includes business, labor, agriculture, taxation, transportation, consumer affairs, monetary and fiscal policy, natural resources, pollution and accidents.*	*Includes worldwide scientific, medical and technological developments, natural phenomena, U.S. weather and natural disasters.*	*Includes the arts, religion, scholarship, communications media, sports, entertainment, fashions, fads and social life.*	

	World Affairs	Europe	Africa & the Middle East	The Americas	Asia & the Pacific
March 2			Following yesterday's outbreak of violence in Palestine, British High Commissioner Gen. Alan Cunningham declares martial law in Tel Aviv, the Mea Shearim district of Jerusalem and the towns of Ramat Gan, Petah Tikva and Benei Beraq .... National Administrative Council of the Zionist Organization of America adopts a resolution in Pittsburgh pledging every resource to aid Jewish immigration to Palestine "in defiance of the British blockade."		Korean nationalist leader Kim Koo proclaims a provisional Korean government in Seoul, but U.S. military authorities rule the move illegal.
March 3		Stalin resigns as Soviet armed forces minister due to the "excessive pressure of his main work," leaving the post to Gen. Nikolai Bulganin .... After a three-week shutdown, electric power is restored to idle sectors of British industry.	Criticizing British Palestine policy in the House of Commons, Churchill urges that the issue be submitted immediately to the U.N.	Truman reaffirms U.S. non-intervention commitments towards other Western Hemisphere nations at a dinner in his honor in Mexico City.	Reports from Nanking and Shanghai indicate that civil unrest has prevailed on Taiwan for several days due to widespread discontent with administrative corruption and the government monopoly on salt and tobacco sales. Drastic police action has caused up to 3,000 deaths.
March 4	Gromyko announces Russia's rejection of the U.S. atomic control plan at a meeting of the U.N. Security Council, charging it is designed to secure an American monopoly over atomic energy.	France and Britain sign a pact providing for mutual military aid, economic coordination and delivery to France of a large part of the coal produced in the British zone of Germany .... Soviet Construction Industry Min. Lazar Kaganovich is named Communist Party secretary in the Ukraine, succeeding Nikita Khrushchev, who remains Ukrainian premier.		Continuing his Mexican visit, Truman wins popular acclaim by visiting the Child Heroes shrine in Chapultepec, commemorating the U.S.-Mexican War. The monument has never before been decorated by an American .... Canadian Finance Min. Douglas Abbott submits a $2-billion budget to Parliament, $906 million lower than the current one.	Nationalist Manchurian commander Gen. Tu Yu-ming claims the Communist offensive has been broken and the attackers driven back to the Lesser Sungari River in central Manchuria.
March 5		A British White Paper on defense reports that armed forces spending for fiscal 1948 will be less than half of last year's total. Britain also announces that all British troops will be withdrawn from Greece by the end of the summer and promises cooperation in assisting the U.S. to assume primary responsibility in the area.	Zionist underground stages raids in Jerusalem and Haifa, dynamiting the Haifa tax office.		Emile Bollaert is appointed French high commissioner for Indochina, succeeding Adm. Georges Thierry d'Argenlieu.
March 6		Auguste Champetier de Ribes, president of the Council of the Republic and chief French prosecutor at the Nuremberg war crimes trial, dies at 64 in Paris.			Despite conservative opposition, British House of Commons approves the Labor government proposal to end Britain's presence in India by June 1948.
March 7			U.N. Security Council tentatively approves Secy. Gen. Trygve Lie's plan to create a special committee to investigate the Palestine issue and report to the General Assembly in September.	Paraguayan troops suppress a revolt of Communists and other opposition groups in Asuncion, killing six .... Brazil revives the Central Price Commission in a new campaign against high prices, black markets and food speculators.	British and Indian troops quell widespread Hindu-Moslem rioting in the province of Punjab, which has caused 192 deaths in the past three days.
March 8		Soviet commander in Germany Gen. F. Kominsky announces that his occupation forces have been cut 75% because of Russian demobilization.	Zionist terrorists attack British operational headquarters in Tel Aviv, an army camp in Sarona and the Jaffa police headquarters.	Peru acquires the El Pato air base and 56 warplanes from the U.S. for $714,000.	
March 9	*Chicago* section of the *American Chemical Society* awards its *Gibbs Medal* to Dr. *William H. Stanley* for his wartime development of an influenza vaccine.	Speaking for the first time in western Germany, Socialist Unity Party Chmn. Otto Grotewohl tells a Frankfurt audience that "no one but the Germans can solve their problems" and pleads for "German unity."		AFL delegates returning to the U.S. from a tour of Argentina charge that Peron is using force, bribery and favoritism to make the Argentine General Labor Confederation his political tool.	Native chiefs of Western Samoa appeal to the U.N. Trusteeship Council for union of Western and American Samoa and urge self-government
March 10	Fifth conference of the Allied Council of Foreign Ministers opens near Moscow to discuss the German and Austian peace treaties .... Following Russian refusal to accept a Security Council resolution on international nuclear energy control, the Council adopts a U.S. proposal to refer the problem to the U.N. Atomic Energy Commission, with instructions to report in the next General Assembly session in September.	Poland and Czechoslovakia sign a 20-year mutual defense treaty in Warsaw, aimed against potential German aggression.		Enrique Hertzog is inaugurated as president of Bolivia.	A Chinese military court in Nanking sentences Japanese Gen. Hisao Tani to death for the 1937 "rape of Nanking."

A	B	C	D	E
Includes developments that affect more than one world region, international organizations and important meetings of major world leaders.	*Includes all domestic and regional developments in Europe, including the Soviet Union, Turkey, Cyprus and Malta.*	*Includes all domestic and regional developments in Africa and the Middle East, including Iraq and Iran and excluding Cyprus, Turkey and Afghanistan.*	*Includes all domestic and regional developments in Latin America, the Caribbean and Canada.*	*Includes all domestic and regional developments in Asian and Pacific nations, extending from Afghanistan through all the Pacific Islands, except Hawaii.*

U.S. Politics & Social Issues	U.S. Foreign Policy & Defense	U.S. Economy & Environment	Science, Technology & Nature	Culture, Leisure & Life Style	
			Dr. James Hoffman of the National Bureau of Standards wins the Hillebrand Award of the Chemical Society of Washington for developing a method of purifying uranium for nuclear reactors.	Pope Pius XII celebrates his 71st birthday.	March 2
	Truman recommends that Congress discontinue Selective Service on March 31 to determine if voluntary enlistments can meet Army and Navy manpower needs. War Dept. orders domestic and overseas commanders to prepare for the release of all draftees by June 30.	Senate votes to limit fiscal 1948 government spending to $33 billion and apply $3.7 billion to the national debt, sending the measure to conference .... Treasury Dept. eliminates licensing requirements for U.S. firms doing business with Germany and Japan.	An American Geographical Society expedition exploring the unmapped Venezuelan rain forest is attacked by Indians, and two members are killed.		March 3
	State Secy. Marshall urges prompt Senate ratification of the European peace treaties completed at the Paris Peace Conference.	House votes to extend the farm labor import program to Dec. 31.			March 4
	State Secy. Marshall leaves Washington for the Moscow Foreign Ministers Conference after protesting the arrest of anti-Communist Hungarian politician Bela Kovacs, calling it "an unjustified interference in Hungarian internal affairs." .... Fleet Adm. William F. Halsey, hero of the World War II Pacific theater, retires from active naval service at 64.				March 5
National Education Assn. convention closes in Atlantic City after voting for a national teachers' pay scale of $2400 to $5000 and urging increased state aid to schools .... House votes overwhelmingly to rename Colorado's Boulder Dam Hoover Dam.		Supreme Court rules, 7-2, that John L. Lewis and the United Mine Workers were in civil and criminal contempt of court when they struck government-operated coal mines last November against a court injunction .... A private arbitrator awards the CIO National Maritime Union a 6% basic wage increase in its dispute with 39 Atlantic and Gulf coast shipping lines and agents.	Arriving in Wellington, N.Z., Adm. Byrd says his airmen mapped 845,000 square miles of Antarctica, nearly one-third of which is newly discovered.		March 6
Interior Secy. Julius Krug recommends statehood for Hawaii in hearings before the House Public Lands Comm.		Senate-House Conference Comm. agrees on a final OPA allocation of $14 million, ensuring that agency operations will end by June 30 .... In hearings before the House Labor Comm., National Association of Manufacturers Pres. Ira Mosher urges government action against industry-wide collective bargaining, closed shop contracts, secondary boycotts and mass picketing.			March 7
				David Krakauer, Jerry Zarowitz and Harvey Stemmer are convicted of conspiring to bribe pro football players in N.Y. .... Wisconsin takes the Big Nine basketball championship, and Illinois wins the track title.	March 8
Women's suffrage crusader and peace militant Mrs. Carrie Chapman Catt dies at 88 in New Rochelle, N.Y.				Gretchen Merrill takes the U.S. women's figure skating title in Berkeley, Calif.	March 9
	After extensive debate, the Joint Congressional Atomic Energy Comm. votes 8-1 to recommend David Lilienthal's confirmation as U.S. Atomic Energy Commission chairman .... Reporting to Truman on his European food mission, Herbert Hoover recommends that the U.S. spend $155 million on Austrian relief from April 1, 1947 to July 1, 1948 .... In an effort to crack down on counterfeiters, U.S. occupation authorities in Germany and Japan issue new military scrip without notice.	Supreme Court upholds collective bargaining rights of foremen's unions under the Wagner Act in a suit brought by the Foremen's Assn. of America against Packard Motors .... A new Taft-Ellender-Wagner bill is offered in the Senate to provide 15 million new homes in the next decade through slum clearance and low-rent housing.		Mass. Superior Court rules that Kathleen Winsor's *Forever Amber* is not obscene and restore it to sale in the state .... French entertainer Maurice Chevalier opens a one-month revue in N.Y.C.	March 10

F	G	H	I	J
Includes elections, federal-state relations, civil rights and liberties, crime, the judiciary, education, health care, poverty, urban affairs and population.	*Includes formation and debate of U.S. foreign and defense policies, veterans affairs and defense spending. (Relations with specific foreign countries are usually found under the region concerned.)*	*Includes business, labor, agriculture, taxation, transportation, consumer affairs, monetary and fiscal policy, natural resources, pollution and accidents.*	*Includes worldwide scientific, medical and technological developments, natural phenomena, U.S. weather and natural disasters.*	*Includes the arts, religion, scholarship, communications media, sports, entertainment, fashions, fads and social life.*

	World Affairs	Europe	Africa & the Middle East	The Americas	Asia & the Pacific
March 11		At the second session of the Moscow Foreign Ministers Conference, Molotov denounces the slow progress of demilitarization in western Germany and demands that all German war material and installations be completely destroyed by 1949 .... Council of German States in the U.S. zone, meeting in Stuttgart, approves a law to restore an estimated $125 million in identifiable property to religious and political victims of the Nazis.			Indonesian Republic announces an "open door" policy towards foreign trade and investment.
March 12		Belgian cabinet of Camille Huysmans resigns in a dispute over coal prices.		J.A. Sullivan resigns as Canadian Seamen's Union president after charging that Communists control the union.	
March 13		Britain's Conservative Party elects Harold Macmillan president and demands protection of "the freedom and rights of the individual against the Labor government's encroachments."			A Taiwanese delegation in Nanking charges that Kuomintang police have created a "reign of terror" on the island during the past two weeks in an effort to suppress popular unrest.
March 14	Senate confirms Eugene Black as U.S. representative on the Executive Bd. of the World Bank.	French National Assembly concludes three days of acrimonious debate on Indochina, with Radical and Republican Party deputies accusing the Communists of aiding rebellion in the colony.	Egyptian Premier Mahmoud Fahmy Nokrashy Pasha declares that the Anglo-Egyptian treaty talks will not be resumed due to disagreement on the question of Sudanese independence .... Zionist terrorists blow up part of an oil pipeline in Haifa and a section of rail line near Beer Yaacov.		U.S. and Philippine governments sign a 99-year treaty guaranteeing the U.S. military and naval bases in the islands.
March 15		Molotov criticizes the Western powers at the Moscow Foreign Ministers Conference for a "tendency toward federalization" in their occupation zones of Germany .... Italian Constituent Assembly votes to make Italy a party to the Bretton Woods pact .... Gen. Lucius Clay officially assumes command of U.S. forces in Europe, succeeding Gen. Joseph McNarey.			Indian troops fire on rioters in the Punjabi city of Kanoni, bringing the death total in the area's Hindu-Moslem-Sikh disturbances to 1,036.
March 16	State Secy. Marshall rejects Molotov's request for three-power talks on China at the Moscow Foreign Ministers Conference.	U.S. War Secy. Robert Patterson announces that soup kitchens will be set up in Germany to feed 3.5 million children and one million aged persons in the U.S. and British zones.	Egyptian cabinet approves the appointment of Sir Robert Howe to succeed Sir Hubert Huddleston as governor-general of Anglo-Egyptian Sudan.	Congressional elections in Colombia give a continued majority to the ruling Liberal Party.	Chinese Central News Agency announces that government forces have successfully diverted the Yellow River to its pre-1938 course.
March 17		Molotov urges Britain and the U.S. to annul the economic merger of their German zones at the Moscow Foreign Ministers Conference .... Paris newspaper workers end a 32-day strike after failing to win their demand for a 25% wage increase.	British authorities in Palestine end a 16-day period of martial law that tied up economic activity in several Jewish cities and districts.		Nationalist Army forces arrive in Taiwan to reinforce police attempting to put down civil unrest on the island. Reports from travellers charge the Nationalists with continued massacre of Taiwanese civilians.
March 18		Radical Socialist Gaston Monnerville is elected president of France's upper legislative house, the Council of the Republic, defeating Communist Henri Martel.		Paraguayan government declares a state of siege in an effort to put down a six-day old military revolt in Concepcion.	
March 19	U.N. Atomic Energy Commission resumes discussion of international arms control.	Socialist Premier Paul Henri Spaak forms a new Belgian cabinet, taking the post of foreign affairs minister for himself.			Chinese Nationalist forces take Yenan, site of the Communist headquarters since 1936 .... Japanese Premier Yoshida urges continued U.S. military presence in Japan after the signing of a peace treaty, claiming "we have our battles with the Communists, too."
	A	B	C	D	E
	Includes developments that affect more than one world region, international organizations and important meetings of major world leaders.	*Includes all domestic and regional developments in Europe, including the Soviet Union, Turkey, Cyprus and Malta.*	*Includes all domestic and regional developments in Africa and the Middle East, including Iraq and Iran and excluding Cyprus, Turkey and Afghanistan.*	*Includes all domestic and regional developments in Latin America, the Caribbean and Canada.*	*Includes all domestic and regional developments in Asian and Pacific nations, extending from Afghanistan through all the Pacific Islands, except Hawaii.*

U.S. Politics & Social Issues	U.S. Foreign Policy & Defense	U.S. Economy & Environment	Science, Technology & Nature	Culture, Leisure & Life Style	
	Senate Foreign Relations Comm. approves Truman's request for U.S. participation in the International Refugee Organization but stipulates that the move will not result in an easing of U.S. immigration laws.	Appearing before the House Labor Comm., Labor Secy. Schwellenbach approves the outlawing of Communists from public or union office because "their purpose is to destroy the government." He also says employers "theoretically" should have the right to fire Communists .... Truman signs a bill to extend wartime excise taxes to July 1948.			March 11
Supporters of Herman Talmadge fail to gain a two-thirds majority in the Georgia House for a constitutional amendment applying the county unit voting system to general elections.	In a major foreign policy address before a joint congressional session, Truman asks for a $400 million aid package for Greece and Turkey in order to prevent Soviet expansion in the Near East and Balkans. Many Republicans and Southern Democrats criticize the proposal as an attempt to increase U.S. foreign involvement and bypass the U.N. Charter. Soviet ambassadors Georgi Zarubin and Nikolai Novikov leave London and Washington for "consultations" with their government .... Alleged Communist agent Gerhard Eisler loses his habeas corpus plea against deportation when a N.Y. Federal Court rules him an enemy alien.	Senate completes passage of the House bill to liquidate OPA by June 30 .... U.S. government wins an antitrust suit in N.Y. against General Electric and Westinghouse, which it charges with forming an international electrical equipment cartel with German, English and Swiss manufacturers.		Manuel Ortiz wins a 15-round decision over Harold Dade for the world bantamweight title in Los Angeles .... Novelist Winston Churchill, known in the U.S. for *Richard Carvel* and *The Crisis*, dies at 75 in Winter Park, Fla.	March 12
	State Dept. establishes a Foreign Service Institute, headed by William Maddox, to train diplomatic personnel.			Oscars go to Frederic March and Olivia De Havilland as best actor and actress, and *The Best Years of Our Lives* is named best picture by the Academy of Motion Picture Arts and Sciences .... Pittsburgh Steeler halfback Bill Dudley, now coach at Virginia Univ., is named the NFL's most valuable player for 1946.	March 13
		N.Y. State legislature passes bills outlawing strikes by public employes, raising teachers' salaries and extending rent control one year.		Lord Tyrrell of Avon, British Board of Film Censors president, dies at 80 in London.	March 14
	State Dept. announces plans to send specialists in agriculture, internal revenue, budget control, civil service and public health as well as highway, transportation and bridge engineers to Greece as part of the government's aid program.	AFL and CIO maritime unions create a commission in Washington to combat Communist influence on union policy.		*Anniversary Waltz*, by Al Jolson and Saul Chaplin, ranks first on CBS's *Your Hit Parade*.	March 15
					March 16
Supreme Court turns down an appeal request from Morton Friedman, a government employe dismissed for belonging to a Communist organization.		William Durant, founder of General Motors, dies at 85 in N.Y.			March 17
	Chmn. Charles Eaton (R, N.J.) of the House Foreign Affairs Comm. introduces the Administration's bill giving Truman blanket powers to distribute $400 million in aid to Greece and Turkey .... In his third report to Truman following his European food inspection tour, Herbert Hoover urges the U.S. and Britain to restore German industry in their occupation zones to save taxpayers the $600-million yearly cost of feeding Germany.	Brotherhood of Locomotive Engineers convention in Cleveland bars Communists from membership in the union.	N.Y. authorities report that 17 children have died recently from overdoses of the suppository drug Analbis, a tonsilitis treatment now under a nationwide ban.	FCC rules against immediate commercial use of the CBS mechanical color television system, favoring initial introduction of black and white TV.	March 18
Georgia's State Supreme Court rules, 5-2, that Melvin Thompson is legal governor, ending Herman Talmadge's claim to the office .... House Public Lands Comm. approves a Hawaiian statehood bill.	House Foreign Affairs Comm. approves Truman's request for $350 million in food relief for Italy, Greece, Poland, Hungary, Austria and China .... U.S. Atomic Energy Commission introduces strict licensing requirements for uranium and thorium production, halting the use of fissionable materials in glass, ceramics and photographic film.	John L. Lewis lifts the threat of a coal strike set for April 1 by withdrawing a contract cancellation notice to the government, which will operate the mines until June 30 under the Smith-Connally Act.	Charles Sumner Beach, inventor of automatic devices including the typewriter, cartridge loader and industrial knitting machine, dies at 94 in Bennington, Vt.		March 19
F *Includes elections, federal-state relations, civil rights and liberties, crime, the judiciary, education, health care, poverty, urban affairs and population.*	G *Includes formation and debate of U.S. foreign and defense policies, veterans affairs and defense spending. (Relations with specific foreign countries are usually found under the region concerned.)*	H *Includes business, labor, agriculture, taxation, transportation, consumer affairs, monetary and fiscal policy, natural resources, pollution and accidents.*	I *Includes worldwide scientific, medical and technological developments, natural phenomena, U.S. weather and natural disasters.*	J *Includes the arts, religion, scholarship, communications media, sports, entertainment, fashions, fads and social life.*	

	World Affairs	Europe	Africa & the Middle East	The Americas	Asia & the Pacific
March 20		At the Moscow Conference of Foreign Ministers, French representative Bidault drops his country's objection to an increased level of German industrial output but opposes German economic unity without treaty provisions guaranteeing France adequate coal supplies .... U.S. military authorities in Berlin say they will not permit an extension of the Soviet-sponsored Socialist Unity Party into the U.S. zone.		Cuban authorities deport former U.S. gangster Charles (Lucky) Luciano to Italy.	India announces that 11,414 Indian occupation troops will be withdrawn from Japan as soon as transportation becomes available.
March 21		Supreme Soviet of the USSR issues a decree forbidding marriages between Russian citizens and foreigners .... France signs an agreement with Italy providing for the immigration of 200,000 Italian workers and their families within the next year .... A U.S. military court in Dachau hands down a death sentence for SS Gen. Juergen Stroop, head of the German forces that suppressed the Warsaw Ghetto rising in 1943.			U.S. Army announces plans to withdraw from Guadalcanal, Fiji and Espiritu Santo in the Southwest Pacific .... Australia's House of Representatives ratifies the Bretton Woods Pact.
March 22		French National Assembly gives Premier Paul Ramadier a unanimous vote of confidence on the government's Indochina policy .... Spring floods burst the Norfolk fenland dikes in England, damaging 25,000 acres of farmland.			Kuomintang Central Executive Comm. calls for the dismissal of Taiwan's Gov. Gen. Chen Yi, who is blamed for unrest and repression on the island .... Philippine government troops report capture of the secret Hukbalahap headquarters in central Luzon.
March 23		U.N. Balkan Inquiry Commission completes nearly two months of inquiries in Greece and leaves for Bulgaria.	Jewish Agency leaders end a 10-day emergency meeting in Jerusalem after directing the organization's U.S. section to present the Zionist case to the U.N.		First Inter-Asian Relations Conference opens in New Delhi, attended by 250 delegates of 25 Far Eastern nations.
March 24	U.N. Commission on Conventional Armaments begins deliberations on international control and reduction of non-nuclear weapons.	U.N. Secy.-Gen. Trygve Lie reveals a March 5 letter from five Greek leftist parties protesting U.S. and British "intervention" in Greece.	Syrian Premier Jamil Mardam Bey warns the country's Jews that pending legislation will impose a death penalty on Jewish refugees trying to reach Palestine and persons helping them.		Viscount Mountbatten takes the oath of office in New Delhi as Britain's last viceroy of India.
March 25	Gromyko casts Russia's 10th veto on the U.N. Security Council when he rejects a resolution stating that the mines in the Corfu Channel, which damaged two British destroyers in October 1946, could not have been laid without Albania's knowledge.	Elections for trade union representatives in the Russian and U.S. zones of Berlin result in a victory for the Socialist Unity Party, which wins 361 of the 436 contested seats .... Flooding from a broken dam on the Oder River near Kustrin causes several deaths and makes more than 17,000 Germans and Poles homeless.			Indonesian and Dutch representatives in Batavia sign the Cheribon Agreement, which grants de facto recognition to the Indonesian Republic and provides for Indonesian sovereignty by Jan. 1, 1949 .... U.S. State Dept. reports that Russia has indicated willingness to hand over the port of Dairen to Nationalist forces as provided for in the Sino-Soviet treaty of Aug. 14, 1945.
March 26		Italy's Constituent Assembly approves a constitutional provision making the Roman Catholic Church the tax-supported state religion of the Republic.		Paraguay's Morinigo government ends martial law to deny military rebels belligerent status in the eyes of other countries .... Canada ends meat rationing but retains price controls on meat products.	
March 27		Italy establishes its first postwar tie with Germany by signing a $4-million trade agreement with the French zone .... U.S. State Dept. announces a worldwide search for Hitler's deputy Martin Bormann amid rumors that he escaped Berlin at the war's end .... Sweden accuses Russia of violating the two countries' mutual trade agreement by demanding payment in dollars for Russian goods.			Nanking reports that the Chinese Communists have established their headquarters in the Shansi city of Kolan following the Nationalist capture of Yenan.
March 28		Britain, France and the U.S. reject Russia's proposed definition of German assets in Austria at the Moscow Foreign Ministers Conference, claiming that no property taken from Austrians by "force or duress" during the Nazi occupation should be used for reparations .... Over 50,000 Germans demonstrate against food shortages in British-occupied Duesseldorf, Solingen, Essen and Wetter.		Argentina's Chamber of Deputies passes a new budget providing for a 29% increase in defense spending and approves Peron's five-year plan for industrial development.	
	A *Includes developments that affect more than one world region, international organizations and important meetings of major world leaders.*	B *Includes all domestic and regional developments in Europe, including the Soviet Union, Turkey, Cyprus and Malta.*	C *Includes all domestic and regional developments in Africa and the Middle East, including Iraq and Iran and excluding Cyprus, Turkey and Afghanistan.*	D *Includes all domestic and regional developments in Latin America, the Caribbean and Canada.*	E *Includes all domestic and regional developments in Asian and Pacific nations, extending from Afghanistan through all the Pacific Islands, except Hawaii.*

U.S. Politics & Social Issues	U.S. Foreign Policy & Defense	U.S. Economy & Environment	Science, Technology & Nature	Culture, Leisure & Life Style	
	Army Air Force announces introduction of daily weather flights over the North Pole and says it plans to abandon its base in Iceland.	A California state court of appeals rules against a Los Angeles police union, claiming it would divide policemen's allegiance.		Pope Pius XII issues an encyclical asking for worldwide contributions to rebuild the Monte Cassino monastery, destroyed during World War II.	March 20
House approves a constitutional amendment limiting presidents to two terms or 10 years maximum. The proposal goes to the states for ratification.		House Ways and Means Comm. sends the House a revised bill to cut personal income taxes 30% for 20 million taxpayers who have less than $1,000 net income .... Philip Lehman, founder of the N.Y. investment banking firm Lehman Bros., dies at 85 in N.Y.	Sir Joseph Barcroft, eminent physiologist and a leader in poison gas research, dies at 74 in Cambridge, England.		March 21
Truman issues an executive order barring from federal employment anyone belonging to or sympathizing with Communist, fascist or other organizations that advocate the overthrow of the U.S. government.		Truman signs a bill ending the OPA as of June 30 but urges quick congressional action to save sugar and rent controls.		Bobby Riggs takes the singles and, with Don Budge, the doubles title in the world professional indoor tennis championship contest in Philadelphia .... Phillips Oilers defeat Oakland Bittners, 62-41, in Denver to capture the AAU basketball title.	March 22
	State Dept. charges in documents submitted to the House Foreign Affairs Comm. that Russia is waging a "war of nerves" against Turkey but claims the Turks "are united ... in resisting outside pressure."	UAW Vice Pres. Walter Reuther attempts unsuccessfully to oust the union's national legislative representative, Irving Richter, whom Reuther criticizes as a "leftist influence."			March 23
House Un-American Activities Comm. starts hearings on proposals to restrict Communist activities in the U.S. and hears former Amb. to Russia William Bullit charge that the Communist Party seeks to prepare for a Russian attack on the U.S.	Acting State Secy. Acheson, War Secy. Patterson and Navy Secy. James Forrestal testify in favor of Greek and Turkish aid before the Senate Foreign Relations Comm.	Truman confers with congressional leaders to urge extended war controls over certain scare goods, including sugar and rice.		Utah beats Kentucky, 49-45, to win the National Invitation Tournament basketball finals in N.Y.	March 24
	Sen. Claude Pepper (D. Fla.) charges that the "Truman Doctrine" of aid to countries threatened by totalitarianism will lead to a struggle with Russia for global power .... Senate passes a bill authorizing U.S. membership in the International Refugee Organization.	In the worst U.S. mine disaster since 1928, 111 miners are killed in an explosion in Centralia, Ill.	Atomic Bomb Casualty Comm. reports some abnormalities among children recently born to atomic bomb victims in Hiroshima and Nagasaki.	Holy Cross topples Oklahoma, 58-47, to win the NCAA Basketball Tournament in N.Y.	March 25
FBI director J. Edgar Hoover states before the House Un-American Activities Comm. that U.S. Communists are "a fifth column if there ever was one" but advises against outlawing the party .... Senate Rules Comm. issues a favorable report on Truman's request that the speaker of the House follow the vice president in the presidential succession.					March 26
Georgia's Gov. Melvin Thompson vetoes the Talmadge-sponsored "white primary" law, which he had earlier promised to support.	Navy reports that only Britain, Mexico and Panama have returned any of the 4,795 naval vessels sent under Lend-Lease to U.S. allies.	House passes an income tax reduction bill and sends it to the Senate .... Despite AFL and CIO protests, N.Y. Gov. Thomas Dewey signs a state law barring strikes by public employes.			March 27
	Senate passes and sends to Truman a bill ending Selective Service March 31 but preserving draft records through an Office of Selective Service Records .... Returning from a two-month economic mission to Greece, former OPA head Paul Porter urges that an American administrator be placed in charge of the country's foreign trade.	A United Steel Workers convention in Pittsburgh re-elects Philip Murray union president, while Harry Lundeberg is re-elected president of the AFL Seafarers International Union.		Former Chicago White Sox second baseman Johnny Evers, part of the famous "Tinker-to-Evers-to-Chance" double-play combination, dies at 65 in Albany, N.Y.	March 28
F	G	H	I	J	
Includes elections, federal-state relations, civil rights and liberties, crime, the judiciary, education, health care, poverty, urban affairs and population.	*Includes formation and debate of U.S. foreign and defense policies, veterans affairs and defense spending. (Relations with specific foreign countries are usually found under the region concerned.)*	*Includes business, labor, agriculture, taxation, transportation, consumer affairs, monetary and fiscal policy, natural resources, pollution and accidents.*	*Includes worldwide scientific, medical and technological developments, natural phenomena, U.S. weather and natural disasters.*	*Includes the arts, religion, scholarship, communications media, sports, entertainment, fashions, fads and social life.*	

	World Affairs	Europe	Africa & the Middle East	The Americas	Asia & the Pacific
March 29	U.N. Economic and Social Council completes its fourth session after creating economic commissions for both Europe and Asia, establishing a committee to draft an international bill of rights and forming two subcommittees on freedom of information and on prevention of discrimination.		Nationalist guerrillas on Madagascar begin attacks on French colonial forces, killing 20 soldiers in the Moramanga garrison and five other posts.		
March 30		Former French Pres. Charles de Gaulle creates a domestic furor when he criticizes the constitution of the Fourth Republic at a reunion of resistance leaders in Bruneval .... After winning elections for trade union representatives in Berlin, the Socialist Unity Party gains a majority of 37 seats on the city's Free Trade Union Organization managing board.		Paraguayan rebel planes attack Campo Grande barracks outside Asuncion.	
March 31		Britain returns the 12 Dodecanese Islands to Greek control .... Spanish Premier Franco announces the formation of a Regency Council under a new law which provides for the enthronement of a Spanish king if Franco dies or becomes incapacitated .... In response to widespread anger over his criticism of the French constitution, de Gaulle agrees to avoid discussing politics when he appears in public as a war hero.	Zionist terrorists dynamite the British-owned Shell-Mex oil tanks in Haifa, causing over one million dollars in damage .... Iran executes Ghazi Mohammad, president of the outlawed Kurdish Republic.		Japan's 92nd Diet, the last under the prewar constitution, adjourns after passing a government plan for parliamentary elections April 25.
Apr. 1	Big Four Foreign Ministers meeting in Moscow issue a formal statement admitting failure to agree on the level of German reparations or the degree to which German industry should be allowed to rebuild.	House of Commons passes Britain's peacetime conscription bill .... Greek King George II dies in Athens, seven months after returning to the throne, and is succeeded by his brother Prince Paul.			Preparing for independence, Burma drops its currency link with India.
Apr. 2	Security Council approves U.S. trusteeship over the formerly Japanese-mandated Caroline, Marshall and Mariana Islands.	A Yugoslavian delegation arrives in Moscow to present the Foreign Ministers Conference with Yugoslavia's claim to Austrian Carinthia and $150 million in German reparations .... Former Auschwitz commandant Rudolf Hoess is sentenced to death in Warsaw for supervising the extermination of concentration camp inmates .... British House of Commons ratifies the Italian, Bulgarian, Hungarian and Finnish peace treaties.	British representative Sir Alexander Cadogan formally requests a special U.N. General Assembly session on Palestine.	Argentina's Marine Ministry lays claim to the Melchior Archipelago in Antarctica.	Hindu-Moslem warfare continues in India's main cities, with 10 deaths in southwestern Punjab Province and the imposition of curfews in three towns .... Ten-day Inter-Asian Relations Conference ends in New Delhi after voting to create an Asian Relations Organization with a 30-man General Council headed by Jawaharlal Nehru .... Nationalist troops report capturing Taian, the last big Communist base on the southern Shantung section of the Tientsin-Pukow railroad.
Apr. 3		Following the example of France, Italy's government orders a 5% cut in the prices of all unrationed goods.	A Jerusalem court sentences two members of the terrorist Irgun Zvai Leumi, Daniel Azulai and Meyer Feinstein, to die for an attack on the Jerusalem railway station .... King Farouk raises the Egyptian flag over the Kasr el Nil barracks in Cairo to mark the evacuation of British troops.		Despite Russian objections, the U.S. authorizes MacArthur to make advance reparations payments from Japan to China, Indonesia, the Philippines and other East Asian countries.
Apr. 4		Rumanian opposition parties protest to King Michael concerning the arrest last month of 263 conservative politicians.	French reinforcements are flown to Madagascar to help suppress a nationalist revolt.		
Apr. 5		British authorities in Germany report the end of a two-day strike by 300,000 Ruhr coal miners demanding larger food rations.		Paraguayan government claims the capture of a military rebel strongpoint at Ybaspobo near Concepcion.	Local elections in Japan result in a victory for the conservative Liberal and Democratic parties, with the Socialists and Communists together polling 25% of the vote .... Five U.S. Marines are killed and 16 wounded when Chinese Communists raid a Marine ammunition dump near Tangku in the Peking region.
Apr. 6				Municipal elections in Chile result in a victory for the Anti-Communist Front, which gains 834 city council seats to 568 for the leftist Democratic Alliance.	
	A *Includes developments that affect more than one world region, international organizations and important meetings of major world leaders.*	B *Includes all domestic and regional developments in Europe, including the Soviet Union, Turkey, Cyprus and Malta.*	C *Includes all domestic and regional developments in Africa and the Middle East, including Iraq and Iran and excluding Cyprus, Turkey and Afghanistan.*	D *Includes all domestic and regional developments in Latin America, the Caribbean and Canada.*	E *Includes all domestic and regional developments in Asian and Pacific nations, extending from Afghanistan through all the Pacific Islands, except Hawaii.*

U.S. Politics & Social Issues	U.S. Foreign Policy & Defense	U.S. Economy & Environment	Science, Technology & Nature	Culture, Leisure & Life Style	
House Un-American Activities Comm. ends its hearings on Communist organizations in the U.S. without recommending the banning of the Communist Party .... Americans for Democratic Action, meeting in Washington, elects Wilson Wyatt president and Leon Henderson vice president and bans Communists from membership in the organization .... National Education Association launches a nationwide drive aimed at obtaining $2 billion for U.S. schools.				*Anniversary Song* again leads the CBS *Hit Parade;* other favorites include: *How Are Things in Glocca Morra, Managua, Nicaragua,* and *Heartaches.*	March 29
	Americans for Democratic Action ends its Washington conference with an endorsement of the "Truman Doctrine" and U.S. aid to Greece and Turkey.			CBS commentator and war correspondent William Shirer resigns in a dispute over the amount of editorial opinion to be included in his broadcasts .... Washington Capitols and Chicago Bruins win, respectively, the Eastern and Western Division titles of the American Basketball Assn.	March 30
N.Y.C. Mayor William O'Dwyer submits a record $1-billion budget for fiscal 1948, the largest in the U.S. aside from the federal budget .... A Washington federal grand jury returns a contempt of Congress indictment against 16 Anti-Fascist Refugee Comm. officials for failing to supply the House Un-American Activities Comm. with requested records .... Supreme Court upholds the life sentence of Max Haupt, convicted Nazi agent whose son was executed as a saboteur in 1942.	Former Commerce Secy. Henry Wallace, speaking at a N.Y. Progressive Citizens of America rally, accuses the Truman Administration of heading towards war with Russia for the sake of Middle Eastern oil.	Truman signs two control bills passed by Congress, one extending sugar controls to Oct. 31, the other renewing controls on scarce commodities deemed essential to U.S. foreign commitments .... Sale of the Pullman sleeping car business to 43 railroads, previously challenged by the government, is upheld by the Supreme Court.	General Electric begins shipping the first commercially produced betatron to Oak Ridge.		March 31
House Un-American Activities Comm. asks Atty. Gen. Tom Clark to start prosecuting Communists as unregistered foreign agents .... In a record voter turnout, Democratic candidate Martin Kennelly is elected mayor of Chicago over Republican Russell Root.		UMW soft coal miners begin a six-day work stoppage in a mine safety campaign memorializing the accident victims in Centralia, Ill.	A new comet entering the solar system is discovered by the Harvard Observatory at Mazelspoort, South Africa.		Apr. 1
Senate Rules Comm. rejects a proposal to end filibusters with a simple majority instead of a two-thirds vote.					Apr. 2
After a two-day White House meeting, the President's Committee on Civil Rights asks for a federal law against employment discrimination.	Senate Foreign Relations Comm. votes to approve Truman's aid program for Greece and Turkey, adopting a resolution giving the U.N. power to stop such aid or take over the program if it feels able to do so.	Following the Centralia mining disaster, Interior Secy. Krug orders the indefinite closing of 518 of the 2,531 government-operated soft coal mines until safety hazards are removed. UMW leader Lewis calls the measure inadequate and demands Krug's dismissal.		National Football League Commissioner Bert Bell indefinitely suspends N.Y. Giants backfielders Merle Hapes and Frank Filchock for failing to report an attempted bribe last December before the team's championship playoff with the Chicago Bears. Neither player accepted the bribe.	Apr. 3
	Acting State Secy. Acheson names veteran diplomat Henry Grady first U.S. ambassador to India.		Dr. Edward Bortz of Philadelphia is named acting president-elect of the American Medical Assn. following the resignation of Dr. Olin West.		Apr. 4
	Truman tells a Jefferson Day dinner audience of Washington Democrats that increased foreign responsibilities require the U.S. to aid "peoples whose freedoms are endangered by foreign pressures" and act "to stamp out the smoldering beginnings of any conflict" that threatens to spread.	Delaware Gov. Walter Bacon signs a law banning mass picketing and secondary boycotts and restricting closed shop demands and union initiation fees.	Portland, Ore. meteorologist E.S. Ellison changes snow to rain by sowing ice pellets from a plane.	Retired Supreme Court Chief Justice Charles Evans Hughes is named head of the newly created World Council of Christians and Jews .... Play verson of Lewis Carroll's story *Alice in Wonderland* receives favorable reviews following opening night in N.Y.C.	Apr. 5
	Gallup Poll reports that 56% of U.S. voters support aid to Greece, 49% aid to Turkey.		Easter Day floods and heavy winds cause 15 deaths and heavy damage in the East and Midwest, with the Flint-Lansing area of Michigan hardest hit.	German conductor Wilhelm Furtwaengler, recently cleared by a denazification court, makes his first postwar concert appearance in Rome.	Apr. 6
F *Includes elections, federal-state relations, civil rights and liberties, crime, the judiciary, education, health care, poverty, urban affairs and population.*	G *Includes formation and debate of U.S. foreign and defense policies, veterans affairs and defense spending. (Relations with specific foreign countries are usually found under the region concerned.)*	H *Includes business, labor, agriculture, taxation, transportation, consumer affairs, monetary and fiscal policy, natural resources, pollution and accidents.*	I *Includes worldwide scientific, medical and technological developments, natural phenomena, U.S. weather and natural disasters.*	J *Includes the arts, religion, scholarship, communications media, sports, entertainment, fashions, fads and social life.*	

	World Affairs	Europe	Africa & the Middle East	The Americas	Asia & the Pacific
Apr. 7		De Gaulle tells a Strasbourg audience that retaining French independence in face of U.S.-Russian rivalry is a "ticklish problem" and that Europe must reorganize to create a balance between the two superpowers .... Bavarian Communist leader Fritz Sperling announces that his party will merge with the Soviet-sponsored Socialist Unity Party .... Swedish Commerce Min. Gunnar Myrdal is named executive secretary of the U.N. Economic Commission for Europe.			In a letter to State Secy. Marshall, Molotov accuses the U.S. of violating its 1945 pledge to withdraw its troops from China, pointing out that Russian forces have already been withdrawn and charging that the presence of foreign soldiers "can but lead to the fanning of the civil war."
Apr. 8		At the Moscow Conference of Foreign Ministers, Molotov drops Russian demands for creation of a central German police force and agrees with a Western proposal to leave police and security matters to the individual German states. Discussion on the Austrian treaty ends without agreement on German assets, frontiers or Yugoslavian reparations demands.		Cuban Interior Ministry bans all political meetings that may provoke disorders after a series of killings due to labor strife.	Countering Russian criticism of U.S. China policy, State Secy. Marshall charges that Russian authorities in Korea have caused economic distress by refusing to cooperate in the nation's unification.
Apr. 9	In a 90-minute interview with Republican politician Harold Stassen, Stalin expresses hope for U.S.-Russian cooperation, defends each country's right to its own economic system and claims that "things are leading up to" a solution of the nuclear arms problem .... With Russia and Poland abstaining, the U.N. Security Council recommends that Albania and Britain take the Corfu Channel dispute to the International Court of Justice.	Big Three foreign ministers clash in Moscow over Poland's western frontier, with State Secy. Marshall and Foreign Secy. Bevin demanding that some Polish-occupied territory be returned to Germany. Molotov reiterates the Russian position that the existing Polish-German boundary is final and awaits only formal confirmation .... British Supply Ministry discloses that Britain has sold 350 fighter planes to Turkey and will sell another 150 under a new accord .... French cabinet authorizes a 220,000-man increase in the Army due to disorders in French overseas possessions.			Elections to Burma's Constituent Assembly result in a majority for the centrist Anti-Fascist People's Freedom League.
Apr. 10		French Foreign Min. Bidault, supported by Marshall and Bevin, urges the Moscow Foreign Ministers Conference to approve a French plan to detach the Saar from Germany and incorporate it economically into France. Molotov refuses to commit himself on the proposal.	Britain urges France and Italy to prevent Jews from embarking for Palestine from Mediterranean ports.	Paraguayan government promises free elections as soon as the current military revolt is crushed.	
Apr. 11			Asher Eskovitch, a Jew, is beaten to death by Moslems as he enters the sacred Mosque of Omar in Jerusalem.		U.S. State Dept. announces that 239 Japanese surface warships in American custody will be divided equally among the U.S., Britain, Russia and China.
Apr. 12		Moscow Conference of Foreign Ministers agrees that land reform and redistribution of large estates should be completed in all zones of Germany by the end of 1947.		Haitian Pres. Dumarsais Estime swears in a new cabinet.	
Apr. 13	N.Y. Mayor William O'Dwyer officially turns over seven acres of city property to the U.N., rounding out the East River site of the world organization's proposed headquarters.		U.N. Secy. Gen. Trygve Lie calls a special General Assembly session for April 28 to consider the Palestine issue.	Venezuelan government arrests 11 alleged conspirators and accuses former Pres. Eleazar Lopez Contreras of plotting to return from exile.	New Delhi reports an agreement establishing diplomatic relations between India and Russia.
	A	B	C	D	E
	Includes developments that affect more than one world region, international organizations and important meetings of major world leaders.	*Includes all domestic and regional developments in Europe, including the Soviet Union, Turkey, Cyprus and Malta.*	*Includes all domestic and regional developments in Africa and the Middle East, including Iraq and Iran and excluding Cyprus, Turkey and Afghanistan.*	*Includes all domestic and regional developments in Latin America, the Caribbean and Canada.*	*Includes all domestic and regional developments in Asian and Pacific nations, extending from Afghanistan through all the Pacific Islands, except Hawaii.*

U.S. Politics & Social Issues	U.S. Foreign Policy & Defense	U.S. Economy & Environment	Science, Technology & Nature	Culture, Leisure & Life Style	
	Agriculture Dept. announces an emergency allocation of 296,000 long tons of grain for shipment to France, Italy, Norway, Germany, Belgium, Egypt and Latin America.	AT&T employes begin the first nationwide strike against the Bell System, stopping work in all states except New England, Montana, Virginia and Indiana with demands for a $12 weekly wage increase and better fringe benefits. Unions sponsoring the strike are the National Federation of Telephone Workers and several local unions .... Automobile tycoon Henry Ford dies at 83 of a cerebral hemorrhage in Dearborn, Mich. His will leaves controlling stock of the Ford Motor Co. to his four grandchildren and divides his estate (estimated at $200 million) between his family and the Ford Foundation.		Track Writers Assn. votes miler Gil Dodds as the indoor season's top athlete.	Apr. 7
Gallup Poll reports Truman's popularity is rising due to his coal and foreign policies, registering 60% approval of his conduct in office.	Opening Senate debate on the Greek-Turkish aid bill, Sen. Arthur Vandenberg (R, Mich.) urges prompt passage and calls on Russia to prove by deeds as well as by words that the program is not necessary .... A War Dept. study warns that U.S. atomic superiority will be gone in six years and urges creation of a worldwide intelligence network to prevent an "atomic Pearl Harbor."	Senate authorizes extension of the Commodity Credit Corp. to June 30, 1948 .... Texas Gov. Beauford Jester signs a state law prohibiting employment discrimination because of union membership or nonmembership.			Apr. 8
	Beginning a speaking tour of Western Europe, Henry Wallace tells a London press conference that Truman's interventionist foreign policy is establishing "a pattern which ... will lead to war." .... Senate confirms David Lilienthal as chairman of the U.S. Atomic Energy Commission.		Civil Aeronautics Admin. approves use of the Army wartime GCA radar device in commercial planes .... Night tornadoes tear a path 225 miles long and 50 miles wide through the Texas panhandle and Oklahoma, killing at least 138 and injuring 1,305.	Baseball Commissioner Albert Chandler suspends Brooklyn Dodger manager Leo Durocher for the 1947 season because of "an accumulation of unpleasant incidents ... detrimental to baseball," including association with gamblers.	Apr. 9
		Interior Secy. Krug tells a Senate committee investigating the Centralia mining disaster that UMW leaders have refused to cooperate with the Interior Dept. on mine safety measures since the government took over operation of coal mines .... Alcoa grants a 10¢ hourly raise to its employes in the AFL Aluminum Workers Union.		Infielder Jackie Robinson becomes the first Negro in major league baseball as the Dodgers purchase his Montreal contract .... National Catholic Education Assn. ends its Boston conference after rejecting public school monopoly of tax-derived education funds.	Apr. 10
	Henry Wallace continues his speaking tour in London by criticizing Truman's Greek-Turkish aid program as a "political maneuver" to take the anti-Communist initiative from the Republicans and says he "cannot guarantee" that he will support the Democrats in 1948.		Univ. of Chicago researchers report that a commercial dye, toludine blue, counteracts destruction of blood corpuscles resulting from exposure to radioactivity.		Apr. 11
		Spurred by the telephone strike, the House Labor Comm. passes a sharp anti-union bill which bans the closed shop, Communist union leadership and most industry-wide collective bargaining and authorizes government injunctions against critical strikes .... UMW leader Lewis authorizes all soft coal miners to return to work April 14, ending a two-week protest against mine safety hazards.			Apr. 12
Sen. Claude Pepper (D, Fla.) rejects suggestions that he lead a third party, stating he will remain a Democrat as long as the party is "truly liberal."	A Gallup Poll reports that 63% of the American public favors turning over the Greek and Turkish problems to the U.N.			*New York Herald Tribune* lists Kenneth Roberts' *Lydia Bailey* as the best-selling fiction book and Joshua Liebman's *Peace of Mind* as the nonfiction bestseller.	Apr. 13
F	G	H	I	J	
Includes elections, federal-state relations, civil rights and liberties, crime, the judiciary, education, health care, poverty, urban affairs and population.	*Includes formation and debate of U.S. foreign and defense policies, veterans affairs and defense spending. (Relations with specific foreign countries are usually found under the region concerned.)*	*Includes business, labor, agriculture, taxation, transportation, consumer affairs, monetary and fiscal policy, natural resources, pollution and accidents.*	*Includes worldwide scientific, medical and technological developments, natural phenomena, U.S. weather and natural disasters.*	*Includes the arts, religion, scholarship, communications media, sports, entertainment, fashions, fads and social life.*	

	World Affairs	Europe	Africa & the Middle East	The Americas	Asia & the Pacific
Apr. 14	Archibald MacLeish resigns as U.S. representative on the UNESCO executive council, criticizing the organization for substituting "broad generalizations for specific actions" in its programs. He is replaced by Milton Eisenhower, president of Kansas State College.	State Secy. Marshall presents the Moscow Foreign Ministers Conference with a U.S. proposal for a four-power treaty to guard against German rearmament, but Molotov counters with numerous controversial amendments, including four-power control of the Ruhr .... Former French Pres. Charles de Gaulle announces in Paris that he will lead a new party founded by his followers, the Reunion of the French People .... Warning that U.S. aid to refugees "cannot continue indefinitely," Gen. Clay of the U.S. military government in Germany offers a 60-day ration supply to all displaced persons in the U.S. zone who volunteer to return to their homes. He also announces that "new applicants" to U.S. refugee camps will be barred after April 21.		U.S. surrenders control over all wartime air bases in Brazil.	
Apr. 15		British Exchequer Chancellor Hugh Dalton presents the House of Commons with a $14-billion anti-inflation budget with a $1-billion revenue surplus for 1947-48 .... Auschwitz commandant Rudolf Hoess is hanged on the site of the former extermination camp in Poland.		Brazilian Pres. Eurico Gaspar Dutra orders a six-month suspension of the Young Communist League and directs his attorney general to seek its permanent dissolution in the courts.	Mohandas Gandhi and Moslem League leader Mohammed Ali Jinnah issue a joint declaration calling on their followers to end India's civil strife.
Apr. 16		Moscow Foreign Ministers Conference resumes consideration of the Austrian peace treaty, debating a Russian demand that Austrian war guilt be mentioned in the preamble .... Pressed by Premier Alcide de Gasperi, Italy's parliament gives a vote of confidence to two ministers accused of corruption, but warns that the government must "keep itself free of leftover fascist habits."	Despite threatened reprisals, British authorities in Palestine hang Dov Bela Gruner and three other Irgun Zvai members, convicted of terrorist acts. Jewish communities in Palestine are held under curfew during the executions.	Chilean Pres. Babriel Bonzales Videla swears in a new cabinet consisting of one Democrat and 11 Radicals.	Chiang Kai-shek appoints Gen. Chang Chun to succeed T.V. Soong as Chinese premier.
Apr. 17		A U.S. court in Nuremberg sentences Field Marshal Erhard Milch, deputy commander of the Luftwaffe, to life imprisonment for extensive use of slave labor in aircraft construction.			U.S. grants de facto recognition to the Indonesian Republic.
Apr. 18		With Russia and Poland abstaining, U.N. Security Council approves a U.S. resolution ordering the Balkan Inquiry Commission to maintain observers in the Balkans pending Council action. The Council rejects a Polish amendment requiring that U.S. aid to Greece be distributed without prejudice "because of race, creed or political belief." .... British authorities use 3,500 tons of explosives to raze German fortifications and naval facilities on the North Sea island of Helgoland .... Msgr. Joseph Tiso, former head of the German puppet state of Slovakia, is hanged in Prague.	In response to the execution of three Zionist terrorists, Irgun Zvai members attack a field dressing station near Nathanya and an armored car in Tel Aviv, causing two deaths.		
Apr. 19		Britain, France and the U.S. oppose Yugoslavia's claim to southern Carinthia at the Moscow Foreign Ministers Conference, insisting that the 1920 plebiscite that awarded the territory to Austria was fair.			
Apr. 20		State Assembly elections in the British zone of Germany result in a victory for the Social Democrats, who gain 173 seats to the opposition Christian Democrats' 144 and the Communists' 36 .... First elections to Sicily's regional legislative assembly give a substantial plurality to the Communist-Socialist bloc .... Danish King Christian X dies in Copenhagen and is succeeded by his son, who becomes King Frederick X.			Elections to Japan's House of Councilors, the legislative upper house, give the Social Democrats a plurality of 44 seats, although unaffiliated Independents take 96 seats.

A	B	C	D	E
Includes developments that affect more than one world region, international organizations and important meetings of major world leaders.	*Includes all domestic and regional developments in Europe, including the Soviet Union, Turkey, Cyprus and Malta.*	*Includes all domestic and regional developments in Africa and the Middle East, including Iraq and Iran and excluding Cyprus, Turkey and Afghanistan.*	*Includes all domestic and regional developments in Latin America, the Caribbean and Canada.*	*Includes all domestic and regional developments in Asian and Pacific nations, extending from Afghanistan through all the Pacific Islands, except Hawaii.*

U.S. Politics & Social Issues	U.S. Foreign Policy & Defense	U.S. Economy & Environment	Science, Technology & Nature	Culture, Leisure & Life Style	
Segregation of children of Mexican descent in Southern California schools is ruled unconstitutional by a San Francisco U.S. Appeals Court.		Supreme Court rules that the Selective Service Act does not guarantee a veteran's work seniority after he has been back on the job more than one year.	Returning to Washington from his Antarctic expedition, Adm. Byrd reports that Antarctica has large coal deposits and could be used to store world food supplies, but doubts its military value.		Apr. 14
House Un-American Activities Comm. denounces American Youth for Democracy as a Communist "training school for violence" and demands that colleges and state governors deny it recognition as a student organization.	State Dept. reports that Russia has agreed to negotiate settlement of $11.1 billion in wartime Lend-Lease aid . . . . Truman presents the Medal of Merit with Oak Leaf Clusters to former State Secy. Cordell Hull, whom he calls "the father of the United Nations."	AT&T and the National Federation of Telephone Workers reject Labor Secy. Schwellenbach's offer of federal mediation in the nationwide telephone strike . . . . Missouri Supreme Court collects $2.09 million in fines from 122 fire insurance companies, ending a rate fraud case that began in 1922 and involved former Kansas City political boss Thomas Pendergast.	Physicist J. Robert Oppenheimer, wartime director of the Los Alamos atom bomb project, is named director of the Princeton Institute for Advanced Study . . . . American Chemical Society President-elect Charles Thomas reports that the Oak Ridge nuclear laboratory is producing new atomic isotopes up to one million times faster than formerly could be produced by cyclotron.		Apr. 15
	Truman signs a bill creating a permanent Army-Navy Nurse Corps, while the War Dept. asks Congress to make the WAC a permanent part of the regular Army.	Texas City, Texas is totally destroyed in one of the greatest industrial disasters on record when a freighter explodes in the harbor, setting docks and oil tanks on fire and causing 468 deaths and 3,000 injuries.	Converted A-26 *Reynolds Bombshell* lands in N.Y. after a 20,000-mile round-the-world flight in a record time of 78 hrs., 55 mins. . . . . American Chemical Society's Priestly Medal is conferred on MIT Prof. Warren Lewis for petroleum research.		Apr. 16
		Despite Democratic threats of a presidential veto, the House passes and sends to the Senate a labor bill containing numerous restrictions on union activity and collective bargaining . . . . Interior Secy. Krug issues a report condemning most company-owned bituminous coal mining towns as "a menace to healthful living" and urging government-company-labor cooperation in their improvement.		Winners of Peabody radio awards are named, including commentator William Shirer, CBS's *Columbia Workshop* and NBC's *Orchestras of the Nation*.	Apr. 17
				Burt Shotton succeeds suspended Leo Durocher as Brooklyn Dodger manager.	Apr. 18
	In speeches before the American Society of Newspaper Editors in Washington, Atomic Energy Commission head David Lilienthal and physicist Vannevar Bush claim that U.S. atomic research has lagged since the war, but Gen. Eisenhower says the Army Atomic Warfare Bd. has power to demand any measures it considers necessary to U.S. security.	Truman reports a $1.25-billion budget surplus for fiscal 1947 but says it should be applied to the national debt rather than a tax reduction . . . . Western Union grants the AFL Commercial Telegraphers Union a 5¢ hourly wage increase retroactive to April 1, ending the threat of a second nationwide communication workers' strike.		Toronto Maple Leafs capture the Stanley Cup hockey playoffs over Montreal, 4 games to 2 . . . . C.V. Whitney's Phalanx and Jaclyn Stable's I Will, both with Eddie Arcaro up, take the two-part Wood Memorial race at Jamaica, N.Y., each winning $31,625.	Apr. 19
	Continuing his European speaking tour in Oslo, Wallace says "it would be unfortunate for world peace" if Russia's current system of government is upset and denies contentions that "heavy armaments are the road to peace."				Apr. 20
F	G	H	I	J	
Includes elections, federal-state relations, civil rights and liberties, crime, the judiciary, education, health care, poverty, urban affairs and population.	*Includes formation and debate of U.S. foreign and defense policies, veterans affairs and defense spending. (Relations with specific foreign countries are usually found under the region concerned.)*	*Includes business, labor, agriculture, taxation, transportation, consumer affairs, monetary and fiscal policy, natural resources, pollution and accidents.*	*Includes worldwide scientific, medical and technological developments, natural phenomena, U.S. weather and natural disasters.*	*Includes the arts, religion, scholarship, communications media, sports, entertainment, fashions, fads and social life.*	

	World Affairs	Europe	Africa & the Middle East	The Americas	Asia & the Pacific
Apr. 21		Britain and the U.S. agree to an increase in coal shipments from the Ruhr and Saar areas to France . . . . Italian Premier Alcide de Gasperi agrees to allow separate legislative representation for German-speaking inhabitants of the northern Italian provinces of Trento and Bolzano.	Meir Feinstein and Moshe Barazani, Irgun Zvai members condemned to death by British authorities for terrorism, commit suicide with explosives smuggled into their cells several hours before their scheduled execution.	Ottawa reports that the new Canadian budget allows a 10% income tax cut and increased tax exemptions.	U.S. Marines report the end of last-ditch Japanese resistance on the Pacific island of Peleliu with the surrender of 33 soldiers.
Apr. 22	International Civil Aviation Organization announces creation of a new worldwide rescue and search system to minimize aircraft losses.	A special train dispatched by U.S. authorities arrives in Budapest, returning $25 million in silver and art treasures looted from Hungary by the Nazis.	Jewish Agency for Palestine and the Hebrew Comm. of National Liberation request that they be allowed to send nonvoting delegates to the upcoming General Assembly session on Palestine as representatives of the Jewish people.		Former ambassador to the U.S. Wai Tao-ming is named Nationalist governor of Taiwan as the island officially becomes a Chinese province.
Apr. 23	International Wheat Conferece ends a five-week session in London without agreement after Britain rejects a five-year price stabilization plan.	Big Four reach an agreement to devalue the reichsmark 90%, cancelling most of the currency now in circulation.			Chinese Premier Chang Chun announces his new cabinet, drawing 16 of its 26 members from the Kuomintang.
Apr. 24	Moscow Foreign Ministers Conference adjourns after 46 days without agreement on the German or Austrian peace treaties. Participants agree to reduce occupation forces in Germany by Sept. 1 and appoint a four-power commission which will meet in Vienna to negotiate disputed points of the Austrian treaty.	Announcing a 200,000-ton wheat shortage, the French government reduces the daily bread ration from 300 to 250 grams . . . . Britain's Fuel and Power Ministry proclaims a five-month ban on the use of gas or electricity for home heating starting May 5 . . . . Yugoslavia announces a five-year electrification and agricultural improvement plan costing $5.6 billion.	Palestine High Commissioner Sir Alan Cunningham flies to Egypt to ask for more troops from the British Middle East command.	Argentine government announces that all its Central American diplomatic missions will be raised to embassy rank.	Chinese Communist forces release two U.S. Army officers captured March 1 in Manchuria.
Apr. 25		Greek government orders the disarming and disbanding of royalist groups terrorizing the Laconia area of the Peloponnesus.	Non-Zionist American Council for Judaism announces its opposition to the seating of special Jewish representatives in the upcoming General Assembly session on Palestine.		Elections to Japan's House of Representatives result in a victory for the Social Democrats, who gain 142 of the chamber's 466 seats although the conservative Liberal Party wins the largest number of popular votes.
Apr. 26			A week of reprisals for the recent execution of Dov Gruner ends in Palestine with the assassination of Haifa's deputy police chief A.E. Conquest by Zionist terrorists.		Vietnam radio announces that an envoy of Ho Chi Minh has arrived in Saigon to open truce negotiations with French High Commissioner Emile Bollaert . . . . Truman orders the transfer of an unspecified number of surplus ships together with naval personnel to the Chinese Nationalists.
Apr. 27		A Polish court martial sentences five Ukrainian nationalists to death in Przemysl.			Pres. Le Van Hoach of Cochin China suspends 13 Vietnamese nationalist newspapers in southern Vietnam.
Apr. 28		London shipping is paralyzed by an unauthorized strike of 10,000 dockworkers supporting striking Glasgow harbor workers.	First special session of the U.N. General Assembly meets in Flushing Meadows, N.Y. to consider the Palestine question. Oswaldo Aranha of Brazil is chosen chairman of the session.		Third session of the Indian Constituent Assembly opens in New Dehli as Congress Party leaders admit that partition of India into Hindu and Moslem sections may be the only solution to the country's civil strife.
Apr. 29			Arab delegates to the General Assembly demand immediate debate on Palestine, opposing a British proposal for creation of a special U.N. commission to study the problem. Jewish Agency for Palestine protests lack of Jewish representation at the session.	Mexican Pres. Miguel Aleman receives an all-out official reception as he arrives in Washington for a nine-day visit . . . . Canadian Finance Min. Douglas Abbott presents his budget for the 1947-48 fiscal year, recommending a 29% average income tax cut and estimating a $190 million surplus from total revenues of $2.45 billion.	India's Assembly abolishes untouchability, making its observance a penal offense.
Apr. 30		A U.S. Army court-martial in Frankfurt finds Col. Jack Durant guilty of the Hesse jewel theft, sentencing him to 15 years imprisonment and dismissal from the Army . . . . Bank of England issues its first annual report in its 235-year history, revealing that deposits grew by $364 million since nationalization last year.		Argentina's Congress votes Peron summary powers to reduce living costs by decree.	

	A	B	C	D	E
	Includes developments that affect more than one world region, international organizations and important meetings of major world leaders.	*Includes all domestic and regional developments in Europe, including the Soviet Union, Turkey, Cyprus and Malta.*	*Includes all domestic and regional developments in Africa and the Middle East, including Iraq and Iran and excluding Cyprus, Turkey and Afghanistan.*	*Includes all domestic and regional developments in Latin America, the Caribbean and Canada.*	*Includes all domestic and regional developments in Asian and Pacific nations, extending from Afghanistan through all the Pacific Islands, except Hawaii.*

U.S. Politics & Social Issues	U.S. Foreign Policy & Defense	U.S. Economy & Environment	Science, Technology & Nature	Culture, Leisure & Life Style	
		Intensifying his anti-inflation campaign, Truman says in a nationwide radio broadcast that a tax cut and continued price increases will bring an "economic cloudburst." He praises labor for moderation in wage policy but accuses some businesses of unjustified price hikes.		N.Y. Drama Critics Circle names Arthur Miller's *All My Sons* the season's best play and *Brigadoon* the best musical.	Apr. 21
House issues a contempt citation for Communist Party Secy. Eugene Dennis, who failed to answer an April 9 subpoena from the House Un-American Activities Comm .... Former Rep. Andrew May goes on trial in Washington's Federal District Court with three businessmen connected with the Garsson munitions firm on charges of war contract fraud and bribery .... Gallup Poll reports that 79% of Democratic voters favor Truman as the party's 1948 presidential candidate against 9% for Wallace.	After two weeks of debate, the Senate votes approval of Truman's $400 million aid package to Greece and Turkey, 67-23 .... Continuing his European speaking tour, Wallace arrives in Paris and is greeted by French Communist leaders Jaques Duclos and Marcel Cachin. He urges the U.S. to prove its peaceful intentions by granting a "non-political" loan to help rebuild Russia's war-devastated areas.			Basketball Assn. of America's first playoff championship goes to the Philadelphia Warriors, who defeat the Chicago Stags, 4 games to 1.	Apr. 22
Senate passes a bill changing the name of Colorado's Boulder Dam to Hoover Dam in honor of former Pres. Herbert Hoover .... A N.Y. federal court sentences multimillionaire international financier Serge Rubinstein to 2½ years in prison and a $50,000 fine for wartime draft evasion.	War Secy. Robert Patterson orders elimination of the distinction between officers and enlisted men on national cemetary grave markers.	USW Pres. Philip Murray promises "peace in the [steel] industry for two years" as he signs a contract with U.S. Steel providing for a 12½¢ hourly wage increase plus a 2½¢ hourly increase in fringe benefits .... Iowa's legislature passes a law banning the closed shop, union shop and dues checkoff.		John Fischer's influential study of the Soviet Union, *Why They Behave Like Russians*, is published by Harpers and becomes a Book-of-the-Month Club selection.	Apr. 23
		UAW approves a one-year contract providing for an 11½¢ hourly wage increase for 220,000 General Motors workers .... General Electric Pres. Charles Wilson announces a 7% price increase to cover the cost of a $40 million wage raise recently granted to the company's employes .... Senate confirms Gordon Clapp as TVA chairman.		Pulitzer Prize-winning novelist Willa Cather, author of *Death Comes for the Archbishop*, dies at 70 in N.Y.	Apr. 24
	House Foreign Affairs Comm. formally approves Truman's Greek-Turkish aid bill, calling the measure "a positive move for the preservation of world peace."	AT&T refuses a National Federation of Telephone Workers offer to end the three-week national strike for an immediate $6 weekly raise for all Bell workers.			Apr. 25
					Apr. 26
					Apr. 27
	Truman issues an executive order creating a U.S. Mission to the U.N. headed by Warren R. Austin.				Apr. 28
	John Foster Dulles, Republican adviser to State Secy. Marshall at the Moscow Foreign Ministers Conference, says in N.Y. that Russia's foreign policy depends less on diplomacy than on "penetrating into the political parties and labor organizations of other countries."	Government-sponsored collective bargaining talks between coal companies and the UMW begin in Washington. Most Southern operators refuse to participate .... Continuing his anti-inflation campaign, Truman appeals to the U.S. Chamber of Commerce to encourage businessmen to cut prices "wherever possible at all levels."	Norwegian archaeologist Thor Heyerdahl sets sail from Peru in his balsa raft Kon Tiki, heading for the Marquesas islands and Tahiti in an attempt to prove that Polynesia could have been settled by pre-Inca Indians from South America .... Town of Worth, Mo. is destroyed by a tornado, with 14 deaths reported.		Apr. 29
A group of Georgia Democrats headed by Gov. Melvin Thompson sets up an anti-Talmadge organizing committee, promising to support Truman for president in 1948.	Soviet Amb. Nikolai Novikov and Asst. State Secy. Willard Thorp begin negotiations in Washington for settlement of Russia's $11-billion Lend-Lease account.	USW signs contracts with Bethlehem, Republic and Crucible Steel and the Colorado Fuel and Iron Co. containing the U.S. Steel settlement of a 12½¢ hourly wage increase plus increased fringe benefits.	U.S. Atomic Energy Commission offers heavy water for research purposes at $15 an ounce .... National Academy of Sciences elects Univ. of Pennsylvania Vice President Alfred Ricards as president.	Harvard's Faculty of Arts and Sciences votes to make the university coeducational by admitting women students from Radcliffe .... A.B. Guthrie's western novel *The Big Sky* is published by William Sloane Associates.	Apr. 30

F	G	H	I	J
Includes elections, federal-state relations, civil rights and liberties, crime, the judiciary, education, health care, poverty, urban affairs and population.	*Includes formation and debate of U.S. foreign and defense policies, veterans affairs and defense spending. (Relations with specific foreign countries are usually found under the region concerned.)*	*Includes business, labor, agriculture, taxation, transportation, consumer affairs, monetary and fiscal policy, natural resources, pollution and accidents.*	*Includes worldwide scientific, medical and technological developments, natural phenomena, U.S. weather and natural disasters.*	*Includes the arts, religion, scholarship, communications media, sports, entertainment, fashions, fads and social life.*

	World Affairs	Europe	Africa & the Middle East	The Americas	Asia & the Pacific
May 1	May Day is celebrated with large demonstrations in most important cities, including Moscow, Paris, New York and Tokyo. Violence breaks out in Sicily, where armed rightists attack a procession of agricultural workers, and in Trieste, where police disperse anti-British crowds demanding Italian possession of the city.	Gen. Lucius Clay revises U.S. military government regulations in Germany to conform with new War Dept. policy, which calls for encouragement of the country's economic reconstruction and gives Germans "primary responsibility" for their own affairs .... After three days of debate, British House of Commons approves a government-sponsored bill nationalizing all inland transport.	General Assembly session considering the Palestine question approves a British request for a special U.N. commission to study and report on Palestine by September.	Leonard Arguello begins a six-year term as Nicaraguan president.	
May 2		In a *N.Y. Times* interview, Polish Communist leader Jakob Berman asserts that capitalism and Communism can coexist and predicts that Poland will follow a "separate evolution" differing from both systems.	Gromyko urges the General Assembly's special session to hear Jewish Agency representatives, pointing out that the Arab viewpoint has already been presented. U.S. delegate Warren Austin and Secy. Gen. Trygve Lie counter that only national representatives can be heard by the full Assembly.	Addressing a Pan American Society dinner in N.Y., Mexican Pres. Aleman says U.S. investment is welcome in Mexico so long as it is "satisfied with a fair profit, without selfish greed or the illusion of becoming a law unto itself." .... Paraguayan Pres. Higinio Morinigo claims that the military revolt in Asuncion has been suppressed.	Marshall and Molotov agree on the resumption of U.S.-Russian negotiations for the establishment of a provisional Korean government.
May 3	U.N. Security Council's Military Staff Comm. issues its first report on an international police force, showing wide disagreement between the U.S. and Russia on the proposed force's size, composition and powers.	U.S. Prosecutor Telford Taylor files a five-point indictment in Nuremberg against 24 officials of the I.G. Farben chemical combine, accusing them of fomenting aggressive war and using slave labor .... U.S. military government in Berlin rejects a request from the Bavarian Communist Party to merge with the Soviet-zone Socialist Unity Party.			Japan's new constitution goes into effect as MacArthur restores the right to fly the national flag without special permission.
May 4		French Premier Paul Ramadier ousts four Communist members of his cabinet, including Deputy Premier Maurice Thorez, after the Communists vote against the government's wage-freezing program in the National Assembly .... Italian Premier Alcide de Gasperi grants a 15% wage increase to one million government workers threatening a half-day strike for tomorrow.	An Irgun Zvai bomb squad breaches the walls of Acre prison, allowing 251 Jewish and Arab prisoners to escape.	Havana Mayor Manuel Fernandez commits suicide after failing to obtain a new waterworks system for the city.	A Sundanese separatist group in Indonesia proclaims the independence of West Java and offers to return Dutch property in return for military protection.
May 5		Yugoslavia and Albania refuse to allow the U.N. Security Council's Balkan Inquiry Commission to enter their territory while investigating Greek complaints .... Czechoslovakia abolishes its revolutionary People's Courts, becoming the first country in Eastern Europe to resume normal trial by jury.	General Assembly's special session on Palestine rejects a Polish-Czech resolution to permit the Jewish Agency to present its case before the full Assembly, restricting Jewish representatives to the Assembly's Political and Social Comm.	U.S. submits a proposed agreement to Panama allowing continued American control and modernization of military bases there.	
May 6		A British military court in Venice condemns German Field Marshal Albert Kesselring to death for war crimes.	U.N. General Assembly's Political and Social Comm. votes to hear both the Jewish Agency and Arab Higher Comm. in the current Palestine debate.	Canada ratifies a trade pact with Mexico.	
May 7		Austria's parliament passes a resolution urging the Allies to end their occupation of the country before the signing of the peace treaty and to give up control over the civil administration.		Brazil's Supreme Electoral Tribunal outlaws the Communist Party, charging it with unconstitutional aims against democracy. Pres. Eurico Gaspar Dutra simultaneously suspends the Brazilian Confederation of Workers for six months for spreading "friction and agitation" in the labor force .... Mexican Pres. Miguel Aleman returns to Mexico City, completing a nine-day U.S. tour.	After meeting yesterday with Moslem League leader Mohammed Ali Jinnah, Mohandas Gandhi denounces proposals for the partition of India into Hindu and Moslem sections.
May 8		Exchequer Chancellor Hugh Dalton announces that Britain will freeze its war debts until its creditors agree to reductions .... Berlin's City Council elects Social Democrat Luise Schroeder acting mayor following the resignation of Otto Ostrowski.	General Assembly's Political and Social Comm. hears Cleveland Rabbi Abba Hillel Silver, head of the Jewish Agency in the U.S., urge the creation of an independent Jewish state in Palestine.	Cuban Pres. Ramon Grau San Martin lifts all duties on imports of beef after 56 meatless days during which cattlemen refused to sell at official prices.	
May 9	International Bank for Reconstruction and Development makes its first loan, a $250-million credit to France for 30 years at 3¼% interest.	120,000 Hamburg workers stage the largest food demonstration to date in the British occupation zone as Allied authorities confirm reports of a mounting food crisis throughout Germany .... French Premier Ramadier appoints three Socialists and one Popular Republican to fill cabinet vacancies caused by the ouster of Communist ministers five days ago.	Henry Cattan, spokesman for the Arab Higher Comm., urges the General Assembly's Political and Social Comm. to end Britain's "illegal" Palestine mandate and establish majority Arab rule in the country.		
	A	B	C	D	E
	Includes developments that affect more than one world region, international organizations and important meetings of major world leaders.	*Includes all domestic and regional developments in Europe, including the Soviet Union, Turkey, Cyprus and Malta.*	*Includes all domestic and regional developments in Africa and the Middle East, including Iraq and Iran and excluding Cyprus, Turkey and Afghanistan.*	*Includes all domestic and regional developments in Latin America, the Caribbean and Canada.*	*Includes all domestic and regional developments in Asian and Pacific nations, extending from Afghanistan through all the Pacific Islands, except Hawaii.*

U.S. Politics & Social Issues	U.S. Foreign Policy & Defense	U.S. Economy & Environment	Science, Technology & Nature	Culture, Leisure & Life Style	
	Adm. Roscoe Lillenkoetter succeeds Gen. Hoyt Vandenberg as director of central intelligence.	House passes and sends to the Senate a bill to continue rent controls with no general increase until at least Dec. 31.			May 1
	Following his European trip, Wallace begins a national speaking tour with a Cleveland speech attacking Truman's Greek-Turkish aid program as an "anti-Soviet crusade."	A two-day AFL-CIO conference ends in Washington after agreeing on the need for "organic union" of the U.S. labor movement.	N.Y.C. ends a three-week campaign against smallpox after dispensing six million vaccinations.	Drama League of N.Y. gives its award for best performance of the season to actress Ingrid Bergman, who starred in *Joan of Lorraine*.	May 2
	Military police quell an all-night riot by 700 inmates of the Army disciplinary barracks at Ft. Leavenworth, Kan. The disturbance, which caused one death and 11 injuries, began when white prisoners refused to share a mess hall with Negroes.			Jet Pilot, ridden by Eric Guerin, noses out favorite Phalanx to win the Kentucky Derby.	May 3
				San Francisco's Crystal Plunge team wins the national women's AAU swimming title in Seattle.	May 4
In a 5-4 decision on a draft evasion case, the Supreme Court widens police search powers and permits law officers to seize any evidence of crime they discover during a legal search . . . . Urging the House Appropriations Comm. to approve the FBI's $35-million budget request, Director J. Edgar Hoover reports that Communists have penetrated "every field of endeavor in this country."				Columbia Univ. trustees announce the awarding of Pulitzer Prizes for Letters to Robert Penn Warren and Robert Lowell in literature, James Baxter in history and Charles Ives in music. Pulitzer Prizes for Journalism go to Howard Norton, Frederick Woltman, Edward Folliard, Brooks Atkinson, Eddy Gilmore and William Grimes.	May 5
N.Y. State Supreme Court strikes down an Albany school board order forbidding controversial Negro singer Paul Robeson from performing in a school auditorium.	Adm. Ernest J. King, retired wartime naval operations chief, opposes the armed forces merger bill in testimony before the Senate Armed Services Comm.	National Federation of Telephone Workers gives up its demand for a national collective contract after N.Y. and Northwest Bell workers end their strike and settle separately with AT&T . . . . Chicago U.S. Circuit Court of Appeals rules that a returned veteran is entitled to regain his specific prewar job regardless of interim company reorganization or the job's increased income value.	An outbreak of infant diarrhea in Philadelphia is checked after causing 27 deaths among children less than a year old.		May 6
	Navy announces the creation of three new sections in the Bureau of Ships to speed development of atomic power for warships.	Inland Steel conforms to the industry wage pattern by granting its workers a 12½¢ hourly wage increase with increased fringe benefits, ending a seven-day strike in its Chicago area plants . . . . Missouri's legislature passes a state law banning public utility strikes.		Archaeologist Nelson Glueck is named to succeed Julian Morgenstern as president of Cincinnati's Hebrew Union College, oldest Jewish seminary in the U.S.	May 7
	On his 63rd birthday and second VE Day anniversary, Truman says he is optimistic on prospects for a lasting peace and the eventual success of the U.N.	CIO United Packinghouse Workers union ends its Cleveland convention after voting to exclude Communists from leadership positions and demanding a 15¢ hourly pay increase and a 30-hour week in upcoming wage negotiations.		National League Pres. Ford Frick reports that the St. Louis Cardinals management has squelched a players' strike against the signing of Negro infielder Jackie Robinson with Brooklyn. Cardinals players deny the incident occurred.	May 8
Truman asks Congress for $24 million to finance an investigation of the loyalty of federal employes.	After four days of debate, the House approves Truman's $400-million aid package for Greece and Turkey by a 287-107 vote . . . . Senate Foreign Relations Comm. unanimously approves immediate ratification of the peace treaties with Italy, Bulgaria, Hungary and Rumania.				May 9

F	G	H	I	J
Includes elections, federal-state relations, civil rights and liberties, crime, the judiciary, education, health care, poverty, urban affairs and population.	*Includes formation and debate of U.S. foreign and defense policies, veterans affairs and defense spending. (Relations with specific foreign countries are usually found under the region concerned.)*	*Includes business, labor, agriculture, taxation, transportation, consumer affairs, monetary and fiscal policy, natural resources, pollution and accidents.*	*Includes worldwide scientific, medical and technological developments, natural phenomena, U.S. weather and natural disasters.*	*Includes the arts, religion, scholarship, communications media, sports, entertainment, fashions, fads and social life.*

	World Affairs	Europe	Africa & the Middle East	The Americas	Asia & the Pacific
May 10		An international tribunal in Nuremberg indicts 10 German generals for war crimes committed in Norway, Greece, Yugoslavia and Albania.	France outlaws the Malagasy Renovation Party, a nationalist group accused of organizing the revolt in Madagascar.		
May 11		French government introduces a series of breadless Sundays to cope with the country's critical wheat shortage.	Iraq declares martial law on the Iranian frontier, where Kurdish guerrilla chief Mulla Mustafa Barazani is being hunted.	In a move to increase the country's population, Venezuela announces 740,000 acres of public land will be distributed to landless persons and European immigrants.	
May 12		Pres. Ismet Inonu says Turkey will use the $100-million grant from the U.S. for military purposes and seek a World Bank loan for economic development. He denies that Turkey will grant a base in the Dardanelles to any power.	General Assembly's Political and Social Comm. adopts a Zionist proposal that the proposed Palestine inquiry commission be allowed to visit European refugee camps and assess the need for free immigration to Palestine. The Committee also hears testimony from Zionist leader David Ben Gurion and Arab Higher Comm. representative Emile Ghouri.	Consumers' strikes, denounced by business leaders as "Communist-inspired," begin in several western Canadian cities to protest high prices.	Chinese Communists announce the creation of an Inner Mongolian autonomous government in Wangyehmiao, Manchuria.
May 13		Italian Premier Alcide de Gasperi resigns with his coalition cabinet after failing to replace left-wing ministers with conservatives .... Hjalmar Schact is convicted by a Stuttgart denazification court as a major Nazi offender and sentenced to eight years imprisonment.	General Assembly's Political and Social Comm. votes to create an 11-nation Palestine inquiry commission, barring Big Five membership over Soviet objections.		
May 14		Speaking in London at the first meeting of the United Europe Comm., Churchill urges Britain and France to take the lead in European unification, a step he calls essential to the development of world government.	Speaking before the General Assembly, Gromyko urges creation of a binational Jewish-Arab state in Palestine. He also urges the Assembly to consider the Palestine question in connection with the European refugee situation .... U.N. Secy.-Gen. Trygve Lie names Victor Hoo of China to head the U.N. staff accompanying the Palestine investigation commission.		
May 15		U.N. Economic Comm. on Europe ends a two-week conference in Geneva after agreeing to take over the European Coal Organization later this year.	General Assembly's special session on Palestine ends after approving creation of a U.N. Palestine inquiry commission and appealing for a truce in Palestine fighting during the commission's investigation .... Paris reports an intensification of insurgent activity on Madagascar as Gen. Marcel Pellet temporarily replaces Marcel de Coppet as governor of the island.		Chinese Communist forces open a new offensive in Manchuria, aimed at taking the regional capital of Changchun .... Burmese Communist leader U Seinda and 12 of his followers are arrested in an alleged anti-government plot.
May 16	Italy is granted membership in the International Civil Aviation Organization, filling Russia's vacant seat.	Strikes and hunger demonstrations spread throughout western Germany in response to the country's food crisis despite warnings from U.S. military authorities that the death penalty will be imposed for offenses against the occupation.		Presidential elections in the Dominican Republic result in a victory for incumbent Rafael Trujillo.	
May 17		Gen. Clay of the U.S. military government in Germany announces formation of a council for the British and U.S. zones to deal with the food crisis .... Yugoslavian opposition leader and National Presidium member Dragoljub Jovanovic is arrested on espionage charges.			Japan's Central Screening Comm. disqualifies three cabinet members from public service for promoting militarism and foreign conquest during the war.
May 18		State Assembly elections in the French zone of Germany result in a victory for the Christian Democratic Union, which gains 52% of the votes to 26% for the Social Democrats and 8% for the Communists.			Vietnamese nationalist forces supported by artillery strike a surprise blow against French military headquarters in Saigon.
	A	B	C	D	E
	Includes developments that affect more than one world region, international organizations and important meetings of major world leaders.	*Includes all domestic and regional developments in Europe, including the Soviet Union, Turkey, Cyprus and Malta.*	*Includes all domestic and regional developments in Africa and the Middle East, including Iraq and Iran and excluding Cyprus, Turkey and Afghanistan.*	*Includes all domestic and regional developments in Latin America, the Caribbean and Canada.*	*Includes all domestic and regional developments in Asian and Pacific nations, extending from Afghanistan through all the Pacific Islands, except Hawaii.*

U.S. Politics & Social Issues	U.S. Foreign Policy & Defense	U.S. Economy & Environment	Science, Technology & Nature	Culture, Leisure & Life Style	
		N.J. Bell workers settle with AT&T for a $4.79 weekly wage increase, ending the telephone strike in most major urban centers.		Southern Baptists end a four-day convention in St. Louis after voting to oppose aid to parochial schools and creation of a U.S. diplomatic mission to the Vatican .... Faultless with Doug Dodson up earns $98,005 by winning the Preakness at Pimlico, Md.	May 10
				South African champion Bobby Locke wins the $10,000 Houston golf open.	May 11
N.Y. Liberal Party elects former Asst. State Secy. Adolf Berle chairman.		N.Y. Stock Exchange names investment banker Robert P. Boylan chairman.			May 12
	State Under Secy. Dean Acheson resigns to enter private law practice; Truman nominates former Asst. War Secy. Robert Lovett to succeed him.	Senate passes the Taft labor bill, containing a number of restrictions on unions, including a ban on the union shop and Communists in union leadership positions. The measure also provides for 80-day government injunctions against "public interest" strikes.			May 13
		AFL Brotherhood of Railway and Steamship Clerks bans segregated union locals.			May 14
Former House Sergeant-at-Arms Kenneth Romney is convicted in Washington of concealing a $143,863 shortage in funds under his control.	House and Senate conferees complete action on the Greek-Turkish aid bill and send it to Truman.	House passes and sends to the Senate an appropriations bill for major executive and judicial agencies that is 25% less than Truman's budget request .... Americans for Democratic Action proposes a nine-point anti-inflation program in Washington, calling for a 65¢ minimum hourly wage and tax relief for lower income groups.			May 15
House Un-American Activities Comm. Chmn. J. Parnell Thomas says the committee has "hundreds of names" of Communists who have infiltrated the Hollywood film industry after a week of testimony by actors Robert Taylor, Adolphe Menjou and others .... Austin District Judge Roy Archer dismisses the suit of Negro Herman Sweatt for admission to the Univ. of Texas law school, claiming that racial segregation of state schools is required by the Texas constitution .... Former Rep. Andrew J. May testifies at his Washington trial that money he received from the Garsson munitions firm was repayment of loans and investments and not a bribe.	Senate and House conferees agree to authorize Truman's $350-million foreign aid request, including $15-40 million for the U.N. International Children's Emergency Fund.		Sir Frederick Gowland Hopkins, British biochemist credited with discovering vitamins in 1906 and winner of the 1929 Nobel Prize for psychology and medicine, dies at 86 in Cambridge.	Most Rev. Michael J. Curley, Catholic Archbishop of Baltimore and Washington, dies at 67 in Baltimore.	May 16
		N.Y. stocks end a week of heavy selling at the lowest point since January 1945, reflecting a general slackening of business activity and consumer resistance to high prices .... Last striking telephone workers return to work as Southwestern Bell, Michigan and Ohio Bell and Chesapeake and Potomac Bell announce settlements.		U.S. regains the Walker Cup in golf competitions at St. Andrews, Scotland.	May 17
	American Assn. of Scientific Workers issues a study of germ warfare technology, warning that bacterial weapons rival the atom bomb as "one of the most important hazards to humanity which could result from the misuse of science."				May 18

F	G	H	I	J
Includes elections, federal-state relations, civil rights and liberties, crime, the judiciary, education, health care, poverty, urban affairs and population.	*Includes formation and debate of U.S. foreign and defense policies, veterans affairs and defense spending. (Relations with specific foreign countries are usually found under the region concerned.)*	*Includes business, labor, agriculture, taxation, transportation, consumer affairs, monetary and fiscal policy, natural resources, pollution and accidents.*	*Includes worldwide scientific, medical and technological developments, natural phenomena, U.S. weather and natural disasters.*	*Includes the arts, religion, scholarship, communications media, sports, entertainment, fashions, fads and social life.*

	World Affairs	Europe	Africa & the Middle East	The Americas	Asia & the Pacific
May 19	Italy formally applies for U.N. membership.	Yugoslavia and the U.S. begin negotiations in Washington for settlement of $32 million in wartime lend-lease aid .... U.S. military government in Munich approves revival of the Oberammergau Passion Play, but stipulates that the cast must be free of Nazi connections and avoid anti-Semitic references.	Britain protests to the U.S. against American fund-raising drives for Palestine resistance groups.	Interior Secy. Krug urges Congress to let Puerto Rico elect its own governor.	Navy announces plans for a scientific survey of 1,400 islands and atolls under U.S. control in the Marshalls, Carolines and Marianas.
May 20		Greek Premier Demetrios Maximos accepts U.S. suggestions of an amnesty for Communist guerrillas to help end the country's civil strife.	An Anglo-French-Belgian conference begins in Paris to coordinate medical, agricultural, reforestation and irrigation activities in the three countries' African colonies.		Allied Far Eastern Commission announces that Japanese reparations will be taken from the country's current industrial production, reversing a principle of the Potsdam declaration opposing such practices in the case of Germany .... Hindu priests and holy men gather in New Delhi to protest plans for the partition of India, the ban on untouchability and other legislation against Hindu religious practices.
May 21		France signs trade agreements in Paris with the British and U.S. zones of Germany .... Strikes and riots break out in Lyons, Lille and other French cities as workers demand more bread, higher wages and an end to government economic controls.		Presidents Eurico Gaspar Dutra of Brazil and Juan Peron of Argentina exchange friendship pledges as they dedicate a new Uruguay River bridge linking the two countries.	A 10-man U.S.-Soviet commission meets in Seoul to renew talks on establishment of a provisional Korean government.
May 22		European Coal Organization ends a two-day meeting in London after allocating 600,000 tons of coal to Britain.		A Brazilian mission arrives in Austria to select 150,000 refugee camp residents for immigration to southern Brazil .... Confederation of Colombian Workers is banned for alleged Communist connections.	
May 23		Security Council's Balkan Inquiry Commission concludes its four-month study of the area by charging that Yugoslavia, Bulgaria and Albania have supported guerrilla units fighting the Greek government, and recommends creation of a neutral commission to supervise the Greek frontier for two years .... Speaking in London, German Nobel Prize-winning author Thomas Mann deplores the Allies' "race for Germany's love" and urges creation of a federation of German states.	Sultan Sidi Mohammed of Morocco refuses to sign the French colony's budget in protest against a clause giving France increased economic control over Moroccan industries.		Student demonstrations for higher subsistence payments turn into anti-government rallies at 43 Chinese universities and high schools, as Chiang Kai-shek charges that Communists are behind student unrest.
May 24		Italian Pres. Enrico de Nicola asks ex-Premier Alcide de Gasperi to form his fourth Cabinet.	U.S. and Yemen sign an agreement granting the Arab kingdom a $1-million credit for the purchase of surplus U.S. Army equipment.	Jamaican government declares a state of emergency, banning public meetings and parades, after a large opposition demonstration in Kingston.	Socialist leader Tetsu Katayama is installed as Japan's new premier following the Socialist victory in last month's parliamentary elections.
May 25		Finland announces an experimental collective farm program along Soviet lines.		Canadian coal miners end a three-month strike in Nova Scotia after accepting a $1 daily wage increase from the Dominion Steel and Coal Corp. .... Clashes between Communists and Peron supporters in Buenos Aires during Argentina's Liberty Day celebrations result in eight casualties.	Vietnamese nationalists reject a truce offer from French High Commissioner Emile Bollaert as "tantamount to surrender."
May 26		British Labor Party opens its 46th annual conference in London with resolutions approving government conscription and colonial policies.	Eleven-nation U.N. Palestine Inquiry Commission holds its first meeting at Lake Success, N.Y. and agrees to begin hearings in Palestine in mid-June.	Truman presents Congress with a plan to standardize the armed forces of all Western Hemisphere nations, including Canada, with U.S. training and equipment .... Units of the Nicaraguan National Guard under former Pres. Anastasio Somoza take over the government and oust Pres. Leonardo Arguello in a bloodless coup.	
May 27			Jewish underground leaders in Frankfurt, Germany declare they hope to transport one million European Jews to Palestine but deny reports that non-Jewish Slavs in refugee camps are being recruited for the Palestine army.	Nicaraguan Chamber of Deputies Pres. Benjamin Lacayo Sacasa, a supporter of dictator Anastasio Somoza, is named provisional president.	Nanking reports an incipient famine in the southern Chinese provinces of Kwangsi and Hunan, despite stockpiles of undistributed UNRRA food in Chinese warehouses.

	A	B	C	D	E
	Includes developments that affect more than one world region, international organizations and important meetings of major world leaders.	*Includes all domestic and regional developments in Europe, including the Soviet Union, Turkey, Cyprus and Malta.*	*Includes all domestic and regional developments in Africa and the Middle East, including Iraq and Iran and excluding Cyprus, Turkey and Afghanistan.*	*Includes all domestic and regional developments in Latin America, the Caribbean and Canada.*	*Includes all domestic and regional developments in Asian and Pacific nations, extending from Afghanistan through all the Pacific Islands, except Hawaii.*

U.S. Politics & Social Issues	U.S. Foreign Policy & Defense	U.S. Economy & Environment	Science, Technology & Nature	Culture, Leisure & Life Style	
Truman urges Congress to pass legislation expanding public health services, claiming that protection against sickness is "the major missing element in our national social insurance program." .... House Post Office Comm. recommends general postal rate increases, including a permanent 3¢ rate for first-class mail and 6¢ for airmail.				Supreme Court cites constitutional guarantees of press freedom in reversing a Texas contempt conviction of three journalists for editorial criticism of a county judge in the Corpus Christi *CallerTimes*.	May 19
		Last major strike of telephone workers ends as Western Electric employes accept an 11½¢ hourly pay increase as part of a two-year, no-strike contract.	Senate approves creation of a National Science Foundation and sends the measure to the House .... Scientists from 20 nations observe a 3:48 min. total eclipse of the sun in Brazil.		May 20
An all-white jury in Greenville, S.C. acquits 28 white men accused of participating in the Feb. 17 lynching of Negro Willie Earle .... Controller Gen. Lindsay Warren warns that federal employes who strike against the government will forfeit their jobs and undelivered pay.	House Foreign Affairs Comm. approves the Mundt bill authorizing creation of a State Dept. Office of Information and Education Exchange to continue U.S. overseas cultural programs and broadcasts.	Four thousand foremen strike at the Ford River Rouge plant in Detroit, demanding that the Foremen's Assn. of America be made sole bargaining agent for all supervisory workers .... Interstate Commerce Commission grants 60 Eastern railroads a 10% basic fare increase.			May 21
	Truman signs the $400-million Greek-Turkish aid bill in Kansas City.			American Academy of Arts and Letters inducts historian Charles A. Beard, landscape architect Gilmore Clark and poet Archibald MacLeish.	May 22
Former House Sergeant-at-Arms Kenneth Romney draws a one to three year sentence in Washington for embezzlement of House funds.				Light-heavyweight champion Gus Lesnevich KOs Melio Bettina in 59 secs., a speed record for New York's Madison Square Garden.	May 23
Attacking the May 21 acquittal of 28 accused lynchers as an "outrage," Atty. Gen. Tom Clark says he will ask the Supreme Court if federal lynching prosecutions are possible under the civil rights code .... Rep. Fred Bradley (R, Mich.), chairman of the House Merchant Marine and Fisheries Comm., dies at 49 of a heart attack in New London, Conn.	Navy announces it will buy the new twin-jet, 600 mph McDonnell Banshee, to be used as a carrier-based fighter.				May 24
					May 25
	War Secy. Patterson and Gen. Eisenhower announce plans to organize 2,500 specialized reserve units to provide medical and scientific skills in a national emergency.	National Federation of Telephone Workers Pres. Joseph Beirne rejects an invitation to affiliate with the CIO.		Dr. Nellie Neilson, Mt. Holyoke College professor and first woman president of the American Historical Assn., dies at 74 in South Hadley, Mass.	May 26
Harvard recognizes American Youth for Democracy as a campus student organization despite congressional condemnation of the group as Communist-oriented.		In a mesage to Congress, Truman announces plans to create a permanent Housing and Home Finance Agency to succeed the wartime National Housing Agency, scheduled to cease operations June 30. Real estate interests oppose continued existence of a central housing authority.		Montreal Canadien right wing Maurice Ricard wins the National Hockey League's most valued player award.	May 27

F	G	H	I	J
Includes elections, federal-state relations, civil rights and liberties, crime, the judiciary, education, health care, poverty, urban affairs and population.	*Includes formation and debate of U.S. foreign and defense policies, veterans affairs and defense spending. (Relations with specific foreign countries are usually found under the region concerned.)*	*Includes business, labor, agriculture, taxation, transportation, consumer affairs, monetary and fiscal policy, natural resources, pollution and accidents.*	*Includes worldwide scientific, medical and technological developments, natural phenomena, U.S. weather and natural disasters.*	*Includes the arts, religion, scholarship, communications media, sports, entertainment, fashions, fads and social life.*

	World Affairs	Europe	Africa & the Middle East	The Americas	Asia & the Pacific
May 28		U.S. authorities in Landsberg hang 26 Mauthausen concentration camp guards, the largest single execution of Nazi war criminals. Twenty-two Mauthausen guards were executed yesterday.	Fawzi el-Kawukji, leader of the 1936-39 revolt of Palestinian Arabs, threatens war against the Jews of Palestine if the U.N. Palestine Inquiry Commission makes recommendations unfavorable to the Arabs.	Nicaraguan dictator Somoza, who seized power two days ago, assumes control of the country's armed forces.	A bill giving U.S. citizenship to the inhabitants of Guam is endorsed by the Interior, State, War and Navy secretaries and submitted to the House Public Lands Comm.
May 29		Hungarian Premier Ferenc Nagy, on vacation in Switzerland, resigns in response to Russian charges that he plotted with Bela Kovacs and other Peasant Party leaders to overthrow "Hungarian democracy." .... U.S. and British authorities consolidate economic agencies in their zones of Germany into a bi-zonal Economic Council, empowered to formulate "general policies for the ... economic reconstruction of both zones as an integrated economic area." .... Under Russian pressure, Denmark demands renegotiation of a 1941 agreement allowing the U.S. to construct and maintain weather stations, air fields and a Navy refueling station in Greenland.	Speaking on Palestine to the British Labor Party congress in London, Foreign Secy. Bevin says that neither the Balfour Declaration nor Britain's League of Nations mandate justifies depriving Palestinian Arabs of their rights or sanctions unlimited Jewish immigration.		A U.S. Army court martial in Yokohama sentences Col. Edward Murray to 10 years imprisonment for stealing $92,000 in diamonds while serving as custodian of the Bank of Japan vaults.
May 30		French General Confederation of Labor urges a relaxation of the government's wage-freezing policy as workers stage short strikes in five industries to enforce wage demands .... British Labor Party congress ends in London after approving the government's housing, education, insurance and health programs and Foreign Secy. Bevin's foreign policy.	French forces in Madagascar capture Samuel Rakotondrabe, alleged leader of the colony's nationalist rebellion.		
May 31		Lajos Dinnyes, a Peasant Party leader acceptable to Russia, becomes Hungarian premier .... Italian Premier de Gasperi presents his fourth cabinet, the first postwar government without Communist representation.			Student disturbances and anti-government demonstrations continue in China, resulting in five deaths among Sun Yat-sen University students in Canton .... Japanese Premier Tetsu Katayama presents his new cabinet, with Socialists and conservative Democrats filling most positions.
June 1		New Hungarian Premier Lajos Dinnyes says his government will seek "peaceful cooperation ... especially with our great neighbor the Soviet Union." .... British Labor Min. George Isaacs begins a drive to bring more women into the industrial work force for the duration of the country's economic crisis.			
June 2		Forty thousand Communists and Socialists demonstrate in Rome against the lack of leftist representation in the new government of Premier de Gasperi.	Emil Sandstroem, Swedish representative on the Permanent Court of Arbitration in The Hague, is chosen chairman of the U.N. Palestine Inquiry Commission .... American, British, French and Dutch interests in the internationally owned Iraq Petroleum Co. agree to unrestricted expansion of Middle Eastern operations.	Kent Federation of Agriculture in Ontario announces arrangements for the immigration of 1,000 Dutch farm workers to Canada to help relieve the country's labor shortage.	China's three-year-old People's Political Council goes out of existence in Nanking, with Communists still refusing to participate.
June 3		Hungarian Justice Min. Istvan Ries announces a new electoral law which will deprive all "enemies of democracy" of the franchise, affecting about 10% of Hungary's voters .... British House of Commons passes an industrial organization and development bill, which provides for state supervision of private industry.		Following talks with Argentine Amb. Oscar Ivanissevich, the White House announces that Truman is ready to resume consultations with Argentina and other American republics on a Western Hemisphere defense treaty.	P.M. Attlee and Viscount Mountbatten jointly announce a British plan to partition India into Hindu and Moslem states. The plan calls for British withdrawal as early as this summer, if the Indian provinces act swiftly in forming their own governments.
June 4		British Defense Min. A.V. Alexander announces that the Royal Army and Navy have dropped their peacetime ban on enlistment of "colored" minorities.	Zionist Stern Gang sends letter bombs to British Foreign Secy. Bevin, Anthony Eden and other officials in London. No casualties are reported.	Asst. State Secy. for American Republic Affairs Spruille Braden resigns in opposition to Administration policy towards Argentina .... Chilean Pres. Gabriel Gonzales Videla opposes joint Western Hemisphere action against Communism, stating that each country should deal with the problem in its own way.	Canton reports the arrest of more than 1,000 students and professors as anti-government and anti-war demonstrations continue in Chinese universities .... Mohandas Gandhi reluctantly accepts the British plan for partition of India but predicts that "the Moslem League will ask to come back" to the Hindu provinces .... Australian Defense Min. John J. Dedman announces a five-year, $807.5-million defense program emphasizing naval buildup, while the ruling Labor Party approves a bill penalizing union boycotts of defense projects.

A	B	C	D	E
Includes developments that affect more than one world region, international organizations and important meetings of major world leaders.	*Includes all domestic and regional developments in Europe, including the Soviet Union, Turkey, Cyprus and Malta.*	*Includes all domestic and regional developments in Africa and the Middle East, including Iraq and Iran and excluding Cyprus, Turkey and Afghanistan.*	*Includes all domestic and regional developments in Latin America, the Caribbean and Canada.*	*Includes all domestic and regional developments in Asian and Pacific nations, extending from Afghanistan through all the Pacific Islands, except Hawaii.*

U.S. Politics & Social Issues	U.S. Foreign Policy & Defense	U.S. Economy & Environment	Science, Technology & Nature	Culture, Leisure & Life Style	
	Monsanto Chemical Co., operator of the Oak Ridge nuclear facility, terminates its contract with the U.S. Atomic Energy Commission after the AEC refuses its request to move some operations to other plants.	Week-old strike of Ford supervisory workers demanding representation by the Foremen's Assn. of America spreads to the company's Buffalo, N.Y. plant .... Housing Expediter Frank Creedon ends federal construction permit requirements for veterans and home-builders who plan to occupy their dwellings.		General Assembly of the Presbyterian Church ends in Grand Rapids, Mich. after passing resolutions against ordination of women ministers, peacetime military conscription and federal aid to education .... John Gunther's *Inside U.S.A.* is published in N.Y. by Harper.	May 28
		House and Senate conferees agree on a bill providing a 30% tax reduction for low incomes and a 20% reduction for middle and upper incomes. A labor bill is also approved containing most of the union restrictions of the Senate's Taft bill.	A United Air Lines DC-4 crashes during takeoff from La Guardia airport in N.Y., killing 42 passengers.		May 29
			Crash of an Eastern Air Lines DC-4 near Ft. Deposit, Md. kills all 53 passengers, the worst U.S. air disaster on record.	Mauri Rose of Chicago wins the 31st annual Indianapolis 500-mile racing classic in 4 hrs., 17 mins., 52.17 secs. .... Baron Georg von Trapp, head of the Trapp Family Singers who fled from Austria in 1938, dies at 67 in Stowe, Vt.	May 30
	Truman signs the $350-million foreign aid bill for Europe and Asia, delegating its administration to State Secy. Marshall.			Phalanx, ridden by Ruperto Donosco, wins the $100,000 Belmont Stakes at Belmont Park, N.Y.	May 31
	Truman's civilian Advisory Comm. on Universal Training issues a report urging immediate unification of the armed forces and reintroduction of conscription, claiming that the alternative is "extermination" of the U.S. in a surprise attack.		A tornado causes 35 deaths in a heavily settled farming district near Pine Bluff, Ark.		June 1
House unanimously passes a bill, aimed at Communists and other "subversives," authorizing the State Dept. to fingerprint all applicants for U.S. passports .... Supreme Court upholds the mail fraud conviction of former Boston Mayor James Curley.	State Secy. Marshall suspends the remaining half of a $30-million loan to Hungary "pending clarification" of events in the country. Marshall also praises and promises further aid to the anti-Communist government of Italian Premier Alcide de Gasperi .... A U.S.-German Chamber of Commerce is formed in N.Y. to promote trade between the two countries.			In his semi-annual address on world events, Pope Pius XII implicitly condemns Russia when he says that "millions of human beings continue to live under oppression and despotic rule."	June 2
	State Secy. Marshall urges the House Armed Services Comm. to approve legislation authorizing the President to send peacetime U.S. military missions to any foreign country requesting them.	Senate passes a compromise tax bill, approved yesterday by the House, reducing income taxes by 10½-30%.			June 3
	A House Judiciary subcommittee begins hearings on a bill by Rep. William Stratton (R, Ill.) permitting non-quota entry of 400,000 European refugees to the U.S. in the next four years.	House passes the Taft-Hartley labor bill, containing numerous restrictions on union activity and collective bargaining, by a 320-79 vote .... Contract talks between the UMW and coal mining firms deadlock in Washington as employers refuse to accept the union's demand for a 35¢ hourly wage increase.			June 4

	World Affairs	Europe	Africa & the Middle East	The Americas	Asia & the Pacific
June 5		French Premier Paul Ramadier accuses Communists of instigating recent strikes of bakers and oil workers and says he will not grant wage demands he considers inflationary.		In a move to improve the foreign image of his government, Argentine Pres. Peron ousts federal police chief Filomena Velcazo, who earlier organized and commanded strong-arm Peronist squads .... U.S. withholds recognition of the new Somoza regime in Nicaragua "pending further developments."	
June 6		Bulgarian Agrarian Party leader Nikola Petkov, leader of opposition forces in parliament, is arrested in Sofia on charges of plotting to overthrow the government .... Five German representatives from the Russian zone withdraw from a Munich conference on German economic problems when they fail to have political questions placed on the agenda .... Britain signs a three-year, $240-million trade pact with Poland providing for importation of 250,000 tons of coal during the first year.			Indonesian nationalist leaders accept a Dutch proposal for an interim National Government of the Dutch East Indies, charged with preparing for establishment of the promised Indonesian Republic.
June 7		Hungarian government releases an alleged confession of Peasant Party Secy. Bela Kovacs, admitting to plotting with former Premier Nagy and others to establish a fascist regime. Premier Dinnyes renews his pledge of close cooperation with Russia.			
June 8			Stern Gang member Ami Kam declares in Genoa that he is responsible for mailing letter bombs to prominent Britons, including King George VI.		
June 9		Soviet Gen. V.P. Sviridov, chairman of the Allied Control Commission for Hungary, rejects British and U.S. requests for information on events leading to the Hungarian change of government .... French Foreign Office announces introduction of a new Saar currency to replace the German mark preparatory to the area's economic union with France .... European Socialist parties end a three-day meeting in Zurich without agreement on revival of the Socialist International or admission of the German Social Democratic Party.	Palestine Supreme Court upholds the 1939 British White Paper ban on transferring land to Jews in most of Palestine.	Canadian Finance Min. Douglas Abbott announces removal of rationing and price controls on most dairy, textile and leather products.	Moslem League Council in New Delhi accepts the British plan for partition of India .... U.S. State and War Depts. announce that limited private international trade with Japan will resume Aug. 15.
June 10		Hungarian Premier Dinnyes announces a purge of "anti-democratic elements" from the army and says that most of the officer corps has already fled to the West .... Bizonal Economic Council begins functioning in the U.S. and British areas of Germany, with authority over most financial and economic public services.		Canadian Reconstruction Min. C.D. Howe announces a government order authorizing immediate entry of 5,000 European refugees under a new policy admitting all immigrants suitable for employment in labor-short industries.	
June 11		Bulgaria's National Assembly expels 23 Agrarian Party deputies, charging them with being "tools" of arrested Agrarian leader Nikola Petkov .... Britain's Exchequer Chancellor Hugh Dalton rejects legislation guaranteeing equal pay for women, claiming it may prove inflationary.		Truman begins a state visit to Canada with a speech before Parliament in Ottawa, defending his policy of providing U.S. aid for "those who seek to live at peace with their neighbors." He strongly endorses U.S.-Canadian joint defense and the St. Lawrence Seaway project.	Japanese Premier Katayama announces emergency rules to combat the nation's economic crisis, including tighter food control, more extensive rationing, price revision and promotion of foreign trade .... Moslem League chooses Karachi as temporary capital of the Moslem state of Pakistan.
June 12		French railroad workers end a six-day nationwide rail strike after Premier Ramadier signs a compromise agreement providing a total $82-million increase in wages and benefits .... Former Austrian Foreign Min. Guido Schmidt is acquitted in Vienna of charges that he helped the Nazis to annex Austria in 1938.		Argentine government seizes factory stocks of clothing and shoes and introduces retail price controls in an effort to lower inflated living costs.	
June 13		Hungarian Liberal Party leader Dezso Sulyok threatens to boycott upcoming parliamentary elections unless Russian troops are withdrawn from Hungary and freedom of speech and assembly is restored. Communist newspapers demand Sulyok's ouster from parliament.		Chilean capital of Santiago is placed under a state of emergency following clashes yesterday between striking bus drivers and soldiers called out to man the city's transportation system.	
	A *Includes developments that affect more than one world region, international organizations and important meetings of major world leaders.*	B *Includes all domestic and regional developments in Europe, including the Soviet Union, Turkey, Cyprus and Malta.*	C *Includes all domestic and regional developments in Africa and the Middle East, including Iraq and Iran and excluding Cyprus, Turkey and Afghanistan.*	D *Includes all domestic and regional developments in Latin America, the Caribbean and Canada.*	E *Includes all domestic and regional developments in Asian and Pacific nations, extending from Afghanistan through all the Pacific Islands, except Hawaii.*

U.S. Politics & Social Issues	U.S. Foreign Policy & Defense	U.S. Economy & Environment	Science, Technology & Nature	Culture, Leisure & Life Style	
Democratic National Comm. officially recognizes Georgia's Democratic State Comm., controlled by Gov. Melvin Thompson.	In a major foreign policy address before Harvard students, State Secy. Marshall proposes a comprehensive U.S. foreign aid program, planned in cooperation with European governments, to speed European economic recovery. Newspaper reports dub Marshall's aid proposals the "Marshall Plan." . . . . Truman denounces the Communist coup in Hungary as an "outrage" and dismisses Republican criticism of his foreign aid program as "fallacious and dangerous." . . . . Senate ratifies the Italian, Hungarian, Rumanian and Bulgarian peace treaties.		Dr. Eben Carey, famous anatomist and dean of the Marquette Univ. medical school, dies at 57 in Milwaukee.	N.Y. Music Critics Circle names Aaron Copland's Third Symphony the best orchestral work and Ernst Bloch's Second Quartet the best chamber music work of the past season.	June 5
		Senate passes the Taft-Hartley labor bill by a 54-17 vote, sending it to the President . . . . CIO International Longshoremen's and Warehousemen's Union agrees in San Francisco to a one-year contract extension, ending the threat of a West Coast shipping strike.			June 6
			Tornadoes cause five deaths in Sharon, Pa. and extensive damage in Youngstown, Ohio.		June 7
		Members of the CIO Food, Tobacco and Agricultural Workers union end a five-week strike against the R.J. Reynolds Tobacco Co. in N.C. after accepting a 12¢ hourly wage increase.			June 8
	Truman nominates veteran diplomat Norman Armour to succeed Spruille Braden as assistant secretary of state.	National Federation of Telephone Workers is reorganized in Miami as the Communications Workers of America, combining 41 unions with 161,000 members.	Mississippi River floods lowland areas of Missouri, Illinois and southern Iowa, forcing evacuation of 22,240 residents.		June 9
Accused Communist agent Gerhard Eisler is convicted in Washington federal court of contempt of Congress for refusing to appear as a witness before the House Un-American Activities Comm.		CIO Pres. Philip Murray urges Truman to veto the Taft-Hartley labor bill as a measure for "smashing unions and wrecking collective bargaining," while 180,000 demonstrators in N.Y. hear veto appeals from Mayor William O'Dwyer and Henry Wallace.		Farrar & Strauss publishes G.M. Gilbert's *Nuremberg Diary*, an account of conversations with major Nazi war criminals by a U.S. Army prison psychologist.	June 10
	Former Sen. David Walsh (D, Mass.), wartime chairman of the Senate Naval Affairs Comm., dies at 74 in Boston.	Agriculture Secy. Clinton Anderson ends household and institutional sugar rationing, but industrial rationing and price controls will continue.			June 11
	U.S. Atomic Energy Commission refuses to fill foreign requests for radioactive isotopes until American demand is fully met and legal problems are worked out.	Fifteen thousand soft coal miners end a week-long unauthorized strike in western Pennsylvania protesting the Taft-Hartley labor bill.	American Medical Association's centennial meeting in Atlantic City names Dr. Roscoe Sensenich of South Bend, Ind. president-elect of the organization.		June 12
Knights of the Ku Klux Klan voluntarily surrenders its Georgia charter in Atlanta, but Klan officials say the organization will continue to operate in Georgia without corporate privileges.	Responding to State Secy. Marshall's suggestion for a comprehensive European aid program, Sen. Arthur Vandenberg (R, Mich.) urges establishment of a bipartisan committee to advise the President and Congress on European reconstruction.	American Federation of Musicians ends its annual convention in Detroit after electing James Petrillo to his eighth term as union president.			June 13
F	G	H	I	J	
Includes elections, federal-state relations, civil rights and liberties, crime, the judiciary, education, health care, poverty, urban affairs and population.	*Includes formation and debate of U.S. foreign and defense policies, veterans affairs and defense spending. (Relations with specific foreign countries are usually found under the region concerned.)*	*Includes business, labor, agriculture, taxation, transportation, consumer affairs, monetary and fiscal policy, natural resources, pollution and accidents.*	*Includes worldwide scientific, medical and technological developments, natural phenomena, U.S. weather and natural disasters.*	*Includes the arts, religion, scholarship, communications media, sports, entertainment, fashions, fads and social life.*	

	World Affairs	Europe	Africa & the Middle East	The Americas	Asia & the Pacific
June 14		Russian authorities in Germany announce the formation of a German Economic Commission to advise existing economic agencies in the Soviet zone.			
June 15		Soviet Gen. V.P. Sviridov rejects an American request for a three-power inquiry into the Hungarian coup, calling the proposal a "rude interference in Hungarian affairs."			Congress Party's Executive Comm. in New Delhi accepts Britain's plan for the partition of India but bars independence for any princely state.
June 16		*Pravda* rejects French and British suggestions that Russia participate in formulating a joint plan for European reconstruction, as proposed by State Secy. Marshall. The newspaper denounces the Marshall Plan as a "program for interference in the internal affairs of other states." .... Macedonian Communist leader Pendelis Goussides is sentenced to death in Salonika for supporting guerrillas.	U.N. Palestine Inquiry Commission holds its first session in Jerusalem, hearing secret testimony from British authorities. The city's Arabs observe a one-day general strike to protest the British mandate.		
June 17		British Foreign Secy. Bevin arrives in Paris to confer with French Foreign Min. Georges Bidault on European recovery needs to be filled through U.S. Marshall Plan aid .... Germany's I.G. Farben chemical industry combine is officially divided into 47 separate firms under the authority of the Allied Control Council.	Jewish Agency representative Moshe Shertok testifies before the U.N. Palestine Inquiry Commission in Jerusalem, claiming that Arab-Jewish cooperation exists in Palestine on the economic level but cannot be extended to politics until the Arabs accept increased Jewish immigration.		Chinese Communist forces establish a beachhead near Tientsin as the U.S. Marine detachment stationed there withdraws to nearby Tangku harbor .... Burma's Constituent Assembly votes to establish a Union of Burma as an independent republic.
June 18		Concluding their Paris talks, Bevin and Bidault urgently request Soviet Foreign Min. Molotov to join them for discussions on European recovery based on American aid.		Argentine Pres. Peron confers the Order of the Grand Cross of the Liberator on retiring U.S. Amb. George Messersmith as a "symbol of closer relations" with the U.S.	U.S-Soviet Trusteeship Commission in Seoul agrees to meet with Koreans for the first time after major Korean parties promise not to attack the trusteeship plan .... British Colonial Secy. Arthur Creech Jones promises Ceylon dominion status within the Empire but refuses to allow the island an independent defense policy.
June 19		Returning to London from his Paris visit, British Foreign Secy. Bevin warns that British "appeasement" of Russia is at an end and indicates that Britain will accept Marshall Plan aid as quickly as possible, with or without Russian participation .... Seventy thousand French bank employes strike for productivity bonuses, bringing most financial operations in the country to a halt.			
June 20		U.S. Amb. Lincoln MacVeigh and Greek Foreign Min. Constantin Tsaldaris sign an agreement in Athens formally transferring $300 million in U.S. aid to Greece and allowing the U.S. to supervise the use to which the money is put .... French cabinet approves Premier Paul Ramadier's emergency fiscal program, which abolishes bread, milk and farm subsidies, increases rates on government services and raises taxes in an effort to eliminate a growing budget deficit.	Iran and the U.S. sign an agreement in Washington giving Iran a $25-million loan over 15 years to buy surplus U.S. military equipment.		Hindu and Moslem delegates to the Bengal Provincial Assembly in Calcutta vote to partition the area between India and Pakistan.
June 21				Nelson Rockefeller signs an agreement in Caracas providing capital for Venezuelan agricultural and industrial development.	
June 22		Hungarian government issues a 150-page White Book on the alleged plot of former Peasant Party leaders to overthrow the republic and establish a fascist regime. The document charges the plotters had British help.	U.N. Palestine Inquiry Commision passes a resolution opposing the scheduled execution of three condemned terrorists, claiming it would have "unfavorable repercussions" in Palestine.		
June 23		British authorities in Dortmund order a one-month suspension of the Communist newspaper *Westdeutsches Volksecho* for "malicious" criticism of the occupation.		Mexican Pres. Miguel Aleman creates a committee to supervise foreign investments and decrees that foreign investors may not hold more than a 49% interest in any Mexican enterprise.	Punjab's Legislative Assembly in Lahore votes for partition between India and Pakistan.

	A	B	C	D	E
	Includes developments that affect more than one world region, international organizations and important meetings of major world leaders.	*Includes all domestic and regional developments in Europe, including the Soviet Union, Turkey, Cyprus and Malta.*	*Includes all domestic and regional developments in Africa and the Middle East, including Iraq and Iran and excluding Cyprus, Turkey and Afghanistan.*	*Includes all domestic and regional developments in Latin America, the Caribbean and Canada.*	*Includes all domestic and regional developments in Asian and Pacific nations, extending from Afghanistan through all the Pacific Islands, except Hawaii.*

U.S. Politics & Social Issues	U.S. Foreign Policy & Defense	U.S. Economy & Environment	Science, Technology & Nature	Culture, Leisure & Life Style	
House Un-American Activities Comm. denounces the Southern Conference for Human Welfare, which has invited Henry Wallace to speak in Washington, as a "deviously camouflaged Communist front."				Broadway play *Life with Father* sets a N.Y. record with 3,183 consecutive performances.	June 14
	In a letter to Senate Appropriations Comm. Chmn. Styles Bridges (R, N.H.), Herbert Hoover opposes State Secy. Marshall's plan for European reconstruction, stating the U.S. should limit its foreign aid and "bluntly insist [on a] return for our sacrifices" in terms of foreign cooperation with U.S. policy.				June 15
	Completing his nationwide speaking tour with an address in Washington's Watergate Amphitheater, Wallace urges a meeting between Truman and Stalin to counteract "the present suicidal course toward war and depression." He indicates he is willing to participate in a third party in the next election.	Truman vetoes the $4-billion congressional tax reduction bill as inflationary, claiming that surplus revenues should be used to fund the national debt.			June 16
		House unexpectedly sustains Truman's veto of the congressional tax reduction bill when its vote to override falls two votes short of the required two-thirds majority.	Harvard chemist Robert Woodward announces he has synthesized a new protein from amino acids which can be used in the production of synthetic textiles and plastics.	Maxwell Perkins, Scribners & Sons editor, dies at 62 in Stamford, Conn.	June 17
A Phenix City, Ala. court hands down a 20-year prison sentence for Jimmy Harris, a Negro rescued from a lynch mob at Hurtsboro, Ala. June 11. Harris was convicted of attempting to rape a white woman.	War Dept. issues an anti-Communist pamphlet to all Army personnel, stating that Communists "seek the downfall of the American system of government" and "hate our American Army in particular."	House passes and sends to the Senate bills extending the 1% Social Security payroll tax until 1950 and rejecting Truman's plan for a permanent federal Housing and Home Finance agency.		Cincinnati Reds pitcher Ewell Blackwell pitches the season's first no-hit game to beat the Boston Braves, 6-0.	June 18
		CIO National Maritime Union ends a four-day national strike after agreeing to accept a one-year extension of the 48-hour week and resume wage negotiations with employers . . . . Senate approves and sends to Truman a rent control bill extending modified controls through early 1948 but exempting new or newly remodelled houses from all controls.	Col. Albert Boyd pilots a Lockheed P-80R jet to a new world speed record of 623.8 mph at Muroc, Calif.		June 19
Benjamin (Bugsie) Siegel, reputed West Coast chief of "Murder, Inc.," is shot to death in Beverly Hills, Calif.		Truman vetoes the Taft-Hartley labor bill, but the House immediately votes to override.			June 20
		Senate opponents of the Taft-Hartley labor bill end a 28-hour filibuster, agreeing to let the Senate vote on the bill June 23.	War Dept. announces plans to build a $40-million medical research center, reportedly the world's largest, at Forest Glen, Md.	King Ranch's Assault becomes an all-time high money-winner when it earns $38,100 in the Brooklyn Handicap at Aqueduct, N.Y., with Eddie Arcaro up.	June 21
N.Y. Gov. Thomas Dewey wins a GOP presidential preference poll in Wisconsin, with Harold Stassen and Gen. Douglas MacArthur trailing.	Following the suggestions of Sen. Arthur Vandenberg (R, Mich.) and Herbert Hoover, Truman establishes three bipartisan committees to study the relationship between the U.S. foreign aid program and the domestic economy.		Extensive flooding along the Missouri and Mississippi rivers causes 11 deaths and $160 million in damage . . . . Annual Daniel Guggenheim Medal for advancement of aeronautics goes to Lester Gardner, founder of the Institute of Aeronautical Sciences in N.Y.	Bobby Riggs defeats Don Budge to retain the national professional tennis title at Forest Hills, N.Y.	June 22
Supreme Court rules that California's tidal oil lands belong to the federal government.	State Secy. Marshall and War Secy. Patterson testify before the House Foreign Affairs Comm. in favor of the inter-American military cooperation bill, which permits the shipment of U.S. weapons and ships to 20 American states.	Taft-Hartley labor bill becomes law after being passed by the Senate over Truman's veto . . . . Supreme Court upholds the constitutionality of the Lea Act, restricting labor practices in the communications industry.		U.S. files an antitrust suit in N.Y. against the American Society of Composers, Authors and Publishers, charging that it is engaged in in a world-wide cartel and conspiracy to monopolize music performing rights.	June 23

	World Affairs	Europe	Africa & the Middle East	The Americas	Asia & the Pacific
June 24		Polish Amb. Josef Winiewicz informs the U.S. State Dept. that Poland is eager to participate in the Marshall Plan . . . . French National Assembly approves Premier Ramadier's 135 billion franc austerity budget . . . . Berlin's City Council names Ernst Reuter as permanent mayor, while British and U.S. authorities reject a proposed economic merger of their Berlin sectors.	Baghdad court hands down a death sentence for Iraqi Communist leader Yusuf Salman and two of his followers.		
June 25	Drafting committee of the U.N. Human Rights Commission completes work at Lake Success on an international bill of rights.	Bizonal German Economic Council holds its first meeting in Frankfurt, as British and U.S. authorities announce plans to create an "exporters' fund" which will aid German firms engaged in foreign trade . . . . Former SS Col. Otto Skorzeny, leader of a daring German raid which rescued Mussolini from Allied captivity in 1943, goes on trial in Dachau on charges of murdering U.S. prisoners during the Battle of the Bulge.	British Colonial Secy. Arthur Creech Jones announces establishment of a Colonial Development Corp. to foster export trade in Britain's African colonies.	A seven-man Newfoundland delegation meets with a cabinet committee in Ottawa to begin discussions on possible union with Canada.	Chinese Foreign Office protests to Russia that Soviet obstruction has prevented government forces from taking control of Dairen and Port Arthur in Manchuria.
June 26				Mexican government announces a national development program aimed at creating new industrial centers.	
June 27		Molotov begins discussions in Paris with British Foreign Secy. Bevin and French Foreign Min. Bidault on proposed Russian participation in the Marshall plan . . . . Gen. Alexander Kotikov, Russian representative on the Allied command in Berlin, vetoes the June 24 election of Ernst Reuter as the city's mayor.	Sheik Hassan Abu el Seoud, leader of the 1939 Arab revolt against Britain and the 1941 Iraqi uprising, returns from Cairo to Jerusalem with permission of British authorities.	Peru lifts import restrictions on all items except certain foods, drugs and industrial machinery.	Pres. Ahmed Sukarno of the Indonesian Republic accepts the resignation of Premier Sutan Sjahrir and assumes executive control of the state . . . . A five-nation mediation commission in Washington concludes six weeks of deliberations by rejecting Siamese claims to territory in French Indochina.
June 28		Yugoslavia rejects the U.N. Balkan Inquiry Commission request for permission to investigate charges of Greek guerrilla encampments on Yugoslavian territory.	A document submitted to the U.N. Palestine Inquiry Commission in Jerusalem by the Irgun Zvai Leumi demands creation of a Jewish state covering Palestine and Transjordan. Stern Gang gunmen fire on British soldiers outside a Tel Aviv theater, killing three and wounding two.		
June 29			U.N. Palestine Inquiry Commission votes unanimously to condemn continued Zionist terrorism as a "flagrant disregard" of the U.N. appeal for a temporary truce.		Representatives of British Baluchistan meeting in Quetta vote to join Pakistan.
June 30	UNRRA officially ends its operations after spending $3 billion in four years to maintain refugee camps in 17 countries.	French Interior Min. Edouard Depreux announces that government agents have broken up a rightist plot to overthrow the Fourth Republic and set up a military dictatorship . . . . German administrators take over control of the port of Bremerhaven from U.S. military authorities.	Egypt and Britain reach an agreement permitting Egypt to leave the sterling bloc in return for a temporary moratorium on Britain's war debt to Egypt.	Canadian House of Commons approves the peace pacts with Italy, Rumania, Hungary and Finland.	
July 1		Hungary's National Assembly passes a three-year economic plan with provisions for nationalization of the country's industry and a $54-million capital levy.			Viscount Mountbatten announces immediate division of India's armed forces into Moslem and Hindu sections.
July 2		Big Three Paris conference on the Marshall Plan ends with Russian rejection of the Anglo-French proposal for European reconstruction. Britain and France announce their intention of proceeding with their economic plans in cooperation with the U.S.	South African P.M. Jan Smuts, a cosigner of the Balfour Declaration, denies that the promise of a "national home" for the Jews applies to the whole of Palestine and urges partition of the country into Arab and Jewish areas.		

	A	B	C	D	E
	Includes developments that affect more than one world region, international organizations and important meetings of major world leaders.	*Includes all domestic and regional developments in Europe, including the Soviet Union, Turkey, Cyprus and Malta.*	*Includes all domestic and regional developments in Africa and the Middle East, including Iraq and Iran and excluding Cyprus, Turkey and Afghanistan.*	*Includes all domestic and regional developments in Latin America, the Caribbean and Canada.*	*Includes all domestic and regional developments in Asian and Pacific nations, extending from Afghanistan through all the Pacific Islands, except Hawaii.*

U.S. Politics & Social Issues	U.S. Foreign Policy & Defense	U.S. Economy & Environment	Science, Technology & Nature	Culture, Leisure & Life Style	
	House passes the Mundt bill giving permanent status to the State Department's international cultural, education and information programs, including Voice of America broadcasts.	CIO Industrial Union of Marine and Ship Building Workers calls a strike of 35,000 East Coast shipyard workers whose contract has expired, halting work on 79 major merchant and naval vessels.		Gen. Eisenhower accepts the presidency of Columbia Univ., promising to assume the post after retiring as Army chief of staff . . . . Jim Ferrier of Australia wins the Professional Golfers Assn. Championship in Chicago.	June 24
Georgia dedicates FDR's "Little White House" in Warm Springs as a state shrine.		AFL building trades unions in N.Y. pledge to avoid strikes and maintain full production through 1950 to accelerate the city's construction program.		Boxer Jimmy Doyle dies of a cerebral hemorrhage in Cleveland after a TKO by welterweight champion Sugar Ray Robinson in a title bout last night.	June 25
Communist Party Secy. Eugene Dennis is convicted in Washington federal court of contempt of Congress and posts $10,000 appeal bond . . . . A Washington federal court denies a probation plea from Boston Mayor James Curley, forcing him to begin a 6-8 month prison term in Danbury, Conn. The Mass. legislature names City Clerk John Hynes acting mayor of Boston.		AFL Pres. William Green calls the Taft-Hartley labor bill a "tragic mistake," but dismisses proposals for a general strike against the new law. U.S. Chamber of Commerce Pres. Earl Shreve threatens to press for still more labor legislation . . . . Truman vetoes a congressional wool price support bill, claiming that its tariff restrictions "would have an adverse affect on our international relations:"			June 26
Federal district court in Washington gives accused Communist agent Gerhard Eisler a maximum one year jail sentence and $1,000 fine for contempt of Congress. Sixteen members of the Joint Anti-Fascist Refugee Comm. are also convicted of contempt of Congress for refusing to turn over organization records to the House Un-American Activities Comm.	Senate and House complete action on a measure providing $73.5 million for U.S. participation in the International Refugee Organization . . . . State Dept. announces the dismissal of 10 unidentified employes for Communist affiliations or suspected disloyalty.	Ford Motors grants the UAW the auto industry's first pension plan, costing an initial $200 million and $15 million yearly.			June 27
Chicago meeting of the Progressive Citizens of America approves a resolution stating that a third party may be required in the 1948 elections to give U.S. voters a political choice . . . . Former Baltimore journalist Douglas Chandler is convicted in Boston on 10 counts of treason for wartime activity as a Nazi broadcaster.				Central Conference of American Rabbis, a reform group, votes in Montreal to retain a 1909 resolution opposing marriages between Jews and unconverted non-Jews.	June 28
Addressing the final session of the National Assn. for the Advancement of Colored People convention in Washington, Truman calls for an intensified attack on racial discrimination and says the federal government must be the "vigilant defender of the rights and equalities of all Americans."				Betty Jameson takes the U.S. Women's Open Golf Title in Greensboro, N.C.	June 29
House approves an Administration-backed Hawaiian statehood bill, 196-133, and sends it to the Senate.		Truman signs the congressional modified rent control bill, indicating that he would prefer stronger and more comprehensive controls. He also signs bills establishing a permanent 3¢ postage rate for first-class mail and extending the Reconstruction Finance Corp. through mid-1948.	A Pan American Constellation completes the first globe-circling commercial flight, landing in N.Y. after travelling 25,003 miles in 13 days.	World Film Festival in Brussels selects *Silence Est d'Or*, starring Maurice Chevalier, as the world's best film in 1946. Acting awards go to Gerarde Philippe for *Diable au Corps* and Myrna Loy for *The Best Years of Our Lives*.	June 30
	Navy announces discovery of oil near Point Barrow in the arctic region of northern Alaska.	Week-old strike of CIO shipyard workers extends to eight more East Coast yards, bringing the number of striking workers to 60,000 . . . . Michigan and Pennsylvania put into effect laws banning public utility strikes.	Mississippi River at St. Louis reaches its highest crest in 104 years, causing $12 million damage in the area . . . . Reporting from a research station on Stonington Island, Antarctica, meteorologists H.C. Peterson and H.H. Thompson claim there is a definite correlation between low-pressure storms and earth vibrations.		July 1
		USW Executive Bd. rejects no-strike clauses in future contracts and votes to boycott the NLRB due to changes in the agency's procedures mandated by the Taft-Hartley Act . . . . Responding to recent disastrous floods in the Midwest, the House passes and sends to the Senate a $339-million omnibus flood control bill . . . . Sens. Claude Pepper (D, Fla.) and Wayne Morse (R, Ore.) introduce a bill mandating equal pay for male and female factory workers.			July 2

F	G	H	I	J
Includes elections, federal-state relations, civil rights and liberties, crime, the judiciary, education, health care, poverty, urban affairs and population.	*Includes formation and debate of U.S. foreign and defense policies, veterans affairs and defense spending. (Relations with specific foreign countries are usually found under the region concerned.)*	*Includes business, labor, agriculture, taxation, transportation, consumer affairs, monetary and fiscal policy, natural resources, pollution and accidents.*	*Includes worldwide scientific, medical and technological developments, natural phenomena, U.S. weather and natural disasters.*	*Includes the arts, religion, scholarship, communications media, sports, entertainment, fashions, fads and social life.*

	World Affairs	Europe	Africa & the Middle East	The Americas	Asia & the Pacific
July 3		Following Molotov's departure from Paris, Britain and France invite 22 European nations to a second Paris conference for discussion of a coordinated European recovery plan in cooperation with the U.S. .... U.S. Commerce Secy. Averell Harriman and Agriculture Secy. Clinton Anderson arrive in Berlin to examine Germany's economic and food situation.	U.N. Palestine Inquiry Commission completes an 11-day inspection tour of Palestine .... French forces repulse an attack by Madagascar nationalists on the capital city of Tananarive, reporting the surrender of 3,000 insurgents.		Socialist Amir Sjahrifoeddin is named premier of the Indonesian Republic.
July 4		French National Assembly gives Premier Ramadier a vote of confidence on new anti-inflation measures, including drastic anti-black market laws .... British authorities in Rome commute the death sentences of Gen. Albert Kesselring and two other German officers to life imprisonment.		Laborite politician Cipriano Reyes, leader of the anti-Peron bloc in the Argentine Chamber of Deputies, survives an assassination attempt in La Plata.	Chinese Council of State in Nanking orders total mobilization of manpower and resources in Nationalist-controlled areas to combat the Communist "rebellion." .... British P.M. Attlee presents the government's Indian independence bill, accepted by Hindu and Moslem leaders, to Parliament .... Japan's Economic Stabilization Bd. announces new industrial "standard wages" ranging from 2,441 yen a month ($17) to 1,124 yen ($8).
July 5	International Postal Union signs an agreement establishing close ties (but not affiliation) with the U.N.	Danish newspapers resume publication as printers end a four-month strike for increased pay and benefits.		Venezuela's National Assembly approves a new constitution, giving the government a large role in economic planning but subjecting political arrests to congressional approval.	
July 6		Spanish voters ratify Franco's proposed law of succession by a 12-1 majority in a national referendum, the first election held in 11 years.	Moslem and Christian Arabs meeting in Haifa adopt a resolution to ostracize any Palestinian Arab who sells land to a Jew.		
July 7		French Socialist Party's National Council, meeting in Paris, votes to support the Marshall Plan and approves exclusion of Communists from the Ramadier cabinet .... Austria applies for U.N. membership.			
July 8	Work begins on the N.Y. site of future U.N. headquarters.	Lord President of the Council Herbert Morrison warns the House of Commons that Britain faces a 25% reduction in living standards in the absence of Marshall Plan aid.	U.N. Palestine Inquiry Commission votes not to visit British internment camps on Cyprus, where 17,000 illegal Jewish immigrants are held.	Argentina lifts all limitations on foreign investment.	Indonesian Republic leaders reject Dutch demands for a joint Dutch-Indonesian police force during the interim government period preceeding Indonesian independence.
July 9	U.S. delegate Frederick Osborn urges the U.N. Atomic Energy Commission to impose limitations on nuclear research aimed at preventing the accumulation of "dangerous and therefore militarily useful quantities" of fissionable materials by individual states.	Britain's King George VI announces the engagement of his daughter Princess Elizabeth Alexandra Mary Windsor, presumptive heiress to the British throne, to Lt. Philip Mountbatten, former Prince of Greece .... Greek police arrest 2,800 political suspects as the government suppresses an alleged Communist coup plot and breaks off recently opened negotiations with Communist guerrillas.			
July 10		After initially agreeing to attend the European economic conference in Paris, Czechoslovakia withdraws from participation as Czech Premier Klement Gottwald confers in Moscow with Stalin.		Mexico and Cuba sign a cultural relations treaty providing for exchange of teachers, students and art exhibits. Mexico also announces a temporary ban on luxury imports to conserve foreign exchange reserves.	British House of Commons passes the Indian independence bill on its second reading.
July 11	International Labor Conference in Geneva adopts a resolution demanding world recognition of the right to organize and bargain collectively.	Czech Premier Gottwald and Foreign Min. Jan Masaryk sign a five-year trade agreement with Russia in Moscow .... Hungarian police break up a conservative Freedom Party rally in Budapest, arresting 100 participants.	Egyptian Premier Mahmoud Fahmy Nokrashy Pasha complains to the U.N. Security Council that continued presence of British troops in Egypt endangers world peace and demands termination of the British administration in the Sudan.		Russia denies that China's Nationalist government has any right to garrison Port Arthur as Russian forces begin to construct fortifications in the city.
July 12	Thirty-three nation International Cereals Conference concludes a four-day Paris meeting by adopting resolutions calling for world cooperation in rationing, grain collection and anti-black market operations.	Sixteen-nation European economic conference opens in Paris to formulate a recovery program using Marshall Plan aid. Russia and other Eastern European states boycott the meeting .... Bulgaria's cabinet approves an $87-million trade agreement with Russia for 1947-48.	Irgun Zvai Leumi kidnaps two British soldiers in Nathanya in retaliation for death sentences imposed on three Irgun members convicted of leading the May 4 raid on Acre prison.		Fighting between Nationalist and Communist forces continues in Manchuria and northern China, with both sides claiming victories.
July 13		Switzerland signs a one-year trade pact with the Soviet zone of Germany.		Nicaraguan government threatens all Communists and other political suspects with summary execution.	Communists Sukeji Yoshida and Togo Kameda are elected secretary-general and vice chairman of Japan's 1.25-million-member Congress of Industrial Unions in Tokyo.
	A *Includes developments that affect more than one world region, international organizations and important meetings of major world leaders.*	B *Includes all domestic and regional developments in Europe, including the Soviet Union, Turkey, Cyprus and Malta.*	C *Includes all domestic and regional developments in Africa and the Middle East, including Iraq and Iran and excluding Cyprus, Turkey and Afghanistan.*	D *Includes all domestic and regional developments in Latin America, the Caribbean and Canada.*	E *Includes all domestic and regional developments in Asian and Pacific nations, extending from Afghanistan through all the Pacific Islands, except Hawaii.*

U.S. Politics & Social Issues	U.S. Foreign Policy & Defense	U.S. Economy & Environment	Science, Technology & Nature	Culture, Leisure & Life Style	
A Washington jury convicts former Rep. Andrew May and munitions manufacturers Murray and Henry Garsson on bribery and conspiracy charges.			A tornado takes 11 lives on the U.S.-Canadian border near Grand Forks, N.D.		July 3
	Navy announces the scrapping of the 36-year-old *Wyoming,* oldest active U.S. battleship.		A United Air Lines plane flying over Idaho reportedly is passed by nine "flying discs," described as "flat and round" and "bigger than aircraft." The Air Force disclaims knowledge of the craft, saying they may be weather phenomena.	Fred Daly of Belfast, Ireland wins the British Open Golf Championship at Hoylake, England.	July 4
				First baseman Larry Doby becomes the first Negro player in the American League as he signs a contract with the Cleveland Indians.	July 5
			Army aircraft fruitlessly search the West Coast states for widely reported "flying discs."		July 6
	Truman sends Congress a special message urging admission of a "substantial number" of Eastern European refugees to the U.S. He does not endorse specific immigration measures pending in Congress.	St. Louis-San Francisco Railroad returns to private control after 14 years in receivership.	A presidential board of inquiry examining recent airline disasters recommends that commercial planes be required to carry radar and maintain an altitude of 2,000 feet above mountainous terrain.		July 7
A Washington court sentences Communist Party Secy. Eugene Dennis to one year in prison and a $1,000 fine for contempt of Congress after he again refuses to obey a House Un-American Activities Comm. subpoena.		U.S. soft coal mines revert to private operation as the UMW signs a one-year contract covering most of the industry, with provisions for an eight-hour day and a 44.4¢ hourly wage increase.		American League wins its 10th victory in 14 All-Star baseball games, defeating the National League, 2-1 .... South African Bobby Locke wins the $36,000 Tam O'Shanter Golf Open in Chicago.	July 8
	Senate passes and sends to the House a bill to place the armed forces under a single cabinet-level secretary of national security.	A Washington meeting of 200 AFL officials issues a policy statement pledging to fight the Taft-Hartley Act in court, work for the defeat of congressmen who supported the bill and omit no-strike clauses from all future AFL contracts .... Pennsylvania Gov. James Duff signs laws banning jurisdictional strikes and secondary boycotts.	Public Health Service makes a record $14-million grant to the National Cancer Research Center in Bethesda, Md.		July 9
House passes and sends to Truman a bill placing the speaker of the House after the vice president in the line of presidential succession.					July 10
Senate approves the appointment of Robert Jones as federal communications commissioner.	House unanimously passes and sends to the Senate a measure enabling the U.S. to assume trusteeship over formerly Japanese-mandated Pacific islands .... House Armed Services Comm. ends hearings on universal military training.	House and Senate complete action on a compromise bill extending export-import controls on oil and other scarce commodities until March 1, 1948 .... Radio Corp. of America Pres. David Sarnoff succeeds retiring James Harbord as chairman of the board.	Univ. of California announces the first extensive nuclear fission attempt in its Berkeley cyclotron, which has released 22-30 particles from the arsenic atom under a force of 200 million electron volts. Previous man-made fission attempts released only 2-5 nuclear particles .... Biochemist Rene Dubos of the Rockefeller Institute for Medical Research in N.Y. announces development of a method for laboratory cultivation of tuberculosis bacilli, speeding efforts to find a cure for the disease.	National Education Assn. ends a five-day convention in Cincinnati after passing resolutions opposing teacher strikes and urging greater federal aid to education.	July 11
A federal court in Charleston, S.C. rules that the Democratic Party has no right to bar Negroes from voting in state primaries .... Sen. John Bricker (R, Oh.) escapes an assassination attempt when former Capitol policeman William Kaiser shoots at him in the Capitol Building subway. Kaiser is held for trial .... Oldest member of the House, Rep. Joseph Mansfield (D, Tex.), dies at 86 in Bethesda, Md.				Broadway play *Life with Father* closes after a record 3,213 performances.	July 12
			A Douglas DC-3 flying to Puerto Rico crashes near Melbourne, Fla., killing 21 passengers.	New York *Herald Tribune* reports *Gentlemen's Agreement* by Laura Z. Hobson and *Inside U.S.A.* by John Gunther as best selling fiction and non-fiction books.	July 13

F	G	H	I	J
Includes elections, federal-state relations, civil rights and liberties, crime, the judiciary, education, health care, poverty, urban affairs and population.	*Includes formation and debate of U.S. foreign and defense policies, veterans affairs and defense spending. (Relations with specific foreign countries are usually found under the region concerned.)*	*Includes business, labor, agriculture, taxation, transportation, consumer affairs, monetary and fiscal policy, natural resources, pollution and accidents.*	*Includes worldwide scientific, medical and technological developments, natural phenomena, U.S. weather and natural disasters.*	*Includes the arts, religion, scholarship, communications media, sports, entertainment, fashions, fads and social life.*

	World Affairs	Europe	Africa & the Middle East	The Americas	Asia & the Pacific
July 14			British authorities in Palestine impose martial law on Nathanya, where two British soldiers were kidnapped by the Irgun Zvai Leumi July 12 . . . . Iraqi Supreme Court commutes Communist leader Yusuf Salman's death sentence to life imprisonment.		
July 15	Security Council debate on a proposed international police force ends in deadlock after Russia and the U.S. fail to agree on the size of contingents to be contributed by participating states.	Paris Economic Conference ends after establishing a 16-member Committee of European Economic Recovery to formulate a four-year recovery program in cooperation with the U.S. Russia warns that participation in the Marshall Plan will mean the subordination of Europe to the U.S. . . . . U.S. Joint Chiefs of Staff issue a new directive to American authorities in Germany ordering them to foster German economic recovery and promising financial aid towards this goal. The directive replaces the anti-German JCS 1067 of May 1945 and marks the end of the Morgenthau plan to transform Germany into an agricultural area . . . . Rumanian police arrest six parliamentary deputies belonging to the National Peasant Party on charges of plotting to overthrow the government.			
July 16		Hungarian Interior Min. Laszlo Rajk presents Parliament with a new election law containing several provisions that favor the Communists in coming legislative elections. The law extends the life of the Communist-dominated National Election Comm., which has authority to decide what parties can participate in the election and what politicians can run as candidates . . . . France and Poland sign a four-year economic agreement providing for French participation in construction of Poland's hydroelectric power system.			
July 17		Gromyko rejects a U.S. proposal for a permanent Security Council Balkan commission as a "sharp breach" of the U.N. Charter.	U.N. Palestine Inquiry Commission ends its Jerusalem hearings after 31 sessions and prepares to move to Beirut, where it will hear Arab testimony.		Indian coastal vessel *Ramdas* sinks during a storm in Bombay harbor, killing an estimated 570 passengers.
July 18		France protests to the U.S. over British and American plans to increase German industrial production without the consent of other Allies.	British warships capture the American-manned Haganah refugee ship *Exodus 1947*, sailing for Palestine from Sete, France with 4,554 passengers, the largest number of illegal immigrants on a single ship.		Shafa'at Ahmad Khan, Indian Moslem leader who defied Moslem League policy by joining the Indian provisional government, dies at 54 in Simla, India.
July 19		Anglo-American talks on German economic recovery are stopped in Berlin following a sharp French protest.	British authorities in Palestine issue a memo to the U.N. Palestine Inquiry Commission charging that a Jewish "campaign of lawlessness, murder and sabotage" has cost 70 lives and $6 million in damage since 1940.		British Viceroy Viscount Mountbatten announces the division of India's provisional government into two cabinets, one for India and one for Pakistan . . . . Terrorists belonging to a conservative political faction assassinate eight members of Burma's Executive Council in Rangoon, including Premier U Aung San.
July 20		Poland joins France in protesting U.S. plans to speed German economic recovery, claiming that countries which suffered at Germany's hands should have priority in reconstruction.			Dutch forces attack Indonesian Republic installations on Java and Sumatra and arrest Indonesian officials in Batavia, including Deputy Premier A.K. Gani. Dutch officials deny any "designs on the integrity" of Indonesia, justifying the action as a response to alleged truce violations by Indonesian nationalists . . . . Burmese police arrest conservative politician and former Premier U Saw with 19 aides in Rangoon on charges of planning yesterday's assassination of eight Executive Council members.
	A	B	C	D	E
	Includes developments that affect more than one world region, international organizations and important meetings of major world leaders.	*Includes all domestic and regional developments in Europe, including the Soviet Union, Turkey, Cyprus and Malta.*	*Includes all domestic and regional developments in Africa and the Middle East, including Iraq and Iran and excluding Cyprus, Turkey and Afghanistan.*	*Includes all domestic and regional developments in Latin America, the Caribbean and Canada.*	*Includes all domestic and regional developments in Asian and Pacific nations, extending from Afghanistan through all the Pacific Islands, except Hawaii.*

U.S. Politics & Social Issues	U.S. Foreign Policy & Defense	U.S. Economy & Environment	Science, Technology & Nature	Culture, Leisure & Life Style	
	State Secy. Marshall urges the Governors' Conference in Salt Lake City to support extensive economic aid to Europe, stating that the U.S. has "an incalculable stake in the preservation of European civilization."	Truman appeals to coal and steel industry leaders to refrain from raising prices until the effect of recent mining wage increases on profits can be determined.		Jean Paul Sartre's *The Age of Reason* is published in N.Y. by Knopf .... Banker Orval Overall, who pitched for the World Series-winning Chicago Cubs before World War I, dies at 66 in Fresno, Calif.	July 14
House votes, 319-61, for a bill which orders a loyalty investigation of federal employes and permits dismissal without the right of court appeal.		Truman signs a Decontrol Act which continues wartime import-export controls and government power to allocate scarce raw materials . . . . First $250-million issue of World Bank bonds offered on the N.Y. Stock Exchange is oversubscribed in less than three hours.		Walter Winchell tops the Hooper ratings, followed by *Crime Doctor, Take it or Leave It, Mr. District Attorney, Screen Guild Players* and *Life of Riley.*	July 15
A Washington federal court sentences 16 members of the Joint Anti-Fascist Refugee Comm. to prison terms and fines for contempt of Congress after they refuse to provide documents to the House Un-American Activities Comm.	State Secy. Marshall appears before a House Judiciary subcommittee on immigration to urge passage of the Stratton bill, permitting 400,000 European refugees to enter the U.S. .... Governors' Conference in Salt Lake City ends with a resolution supporting a bipartisan foreign policy but not specifically endorsing the Truman Doctrine or the Marshall Plan.	International Longshoremen's and Warehousemen's Union ends a five-day strike against the Hawaiian pineapple industry after agreeing to continue wage negotiations.		Rocky Graziano wins the world middleweight title with a TKO over Tony Zale in the sixth round at Chicago Stadium.	July 16
Truman appoints a 12-man Commission on the Organization of the Executive Branch, to be chaired by Herbert Hoover.	House Foreign Affairs Comm. approves Truman's bill providing $50 million for military cooperation with Canada and Latin America.	In a letter to CIO Pres. Philip Murray, AFL Pres. William Green urges a rapid organizational merger of the two labor groups, rejecting CIO proposals for immediate unification of political activities .... Truman names Maryland Republican Robert Denham general counsel of the NLRB, newly reorganized under the Taft-Hartley Act.		Archbishop Gregory, Metropolitan of Leningrad and Novgorod, arrives in N.Y. on a mission to unite the U.S. Russian Orthodox church with the mother church in Russia.	July 17
Truman signs a bill changing the line of presidential succession.	War. Secy. Robert Patterson resigns to return to private law practice; Truman nominates War Under Secy. Kenneth Royall to succeed him .... Gen. Eisenhower names Florence Blanchfield, superintendent of Army nurses, as the first regularly commissioned woman officer in Army history.	Truman vetoes a revised version of the congressional income tax reduction bill. His veto is sustained by the Senate.	Norwegian archaeologist Thor Heyerdahl reports by radio that his balsa raft *Kon Tiki* is nearing the Marquesas Islands in the Pacific after an 84-day voyage from Peru.	Detroit Tigers stop the New York Yankees, 8-0, ending a 19-game Yankee winning streak which ties the American League record set by Chicago in 1906.	July 18
California Democrats led by former State Atty. Gen. Robert Kenny organize a Wallace for President faction at a meeting in Fresno .... A San Diego court convicts Mrs. Alfred Wesley Ingalls of enslaving Negro maid Dora Jones with threats of punishment for an affair with Mrs. Ingall's husband 40 years ago .... Former Sen. Robert Owen of Oklahoma, a leading liberal Democrat who helped draft the Federal Reserve and Farm Loan acts, dies at 91 in Washington.	Truman eliminates military government in all Pacific islands under U.S. trusteeship and names Adm. Louis Denfeld high commissioner pending creation of a civilian administration.		Univ. of Illinois announces plans to begin first large-scale manufacture of a tuberculosis vaccine, known as BCG.	Stymie wins the first running of the $100,000 Empire Gold Cup at Belmont Park, N.Y., with Conn McCreary up.	July 19
					July 20
F	G	H	I	J	
Includes elections, federal-state relations, civil rights and liberties, crime, the judiciary, education, health care, poverty, urban affairs and population.	*Includes formation and debate of U.S. foreign and defense policies, veterans affairs and defense spending. (Relations with specific foreign countries are usually found under the region concerned.)*	*Includes business, labor, agriculture, taxation, transportation, consumer affairs, monetary and fiscal policy, natural resources, pollution and accidents.*	*Includes worldwide scientific, medical and technological developments, natural phenomena, U.S. weather and natural disasters.*	*Includes the arts, religion, scholarship, communications media, sports, entertainment, fashions, fads and social life.*	

	World Affairs	Europe	Africa & the Middle East	The Americas	Asia & the Pacific
July 21					Dutch planes continue to attack Indonesian airfields on Java and Sumatra as the Netherlands government declines a British offer to mediate the conflict.
July 22		Hungary's Liberty Party, the largest remaining conservative opposition group, dissolves in protest against government restrictions on political activity and free speech. The cabinet imposes a special $15-million tax on the Hungarian-American Oil Co. . . . . U.S. and British authorities in Berlin announce agreement on a new plan to increase coal production in the Ruhr, including a profit-sharing plan and food premiums for the miners.			Gen. Albert Wedemeyer, wartime U.S. liaison officer with the Nationalist Chinese government, arrives in Nanking on a fact-finding mission for Truman.
July 23	U.N. Atomic Energy Commission drops discussion of nuclear arms control after four months of debate.	Albania accepts a U.N. request that the Corfu Channel dispute with Britain be referred to the International Court of Justice . . . . British Bd. of Trade Pres. Sir Stafford Cripps calls for greater production and fewer imports to meet the country's economic crisis.	U.N. Palestine Inquiry Commission ends its Middle Eastern hearings with a session of testimony from Arab spokesmen in Amman, Transjordan.	A general strike called by opponents of the government disrupts business and transport in Costa Rica, while political riots cause eight deaths and 56 injuries in several cities . . . . A French-Argentine trade pact is signed in Paris by Eva Peron, wife of the Argentine president.	Dutch Premier Louis Beel rejects arbitration of the current conflict in Indonesia, claiming that the 1946 Linggadjati agreement gave Holland sovereignty over the islands during the interim period preceding independence . . . . Russia rejects a U.S. invitation to an 11-power conference on the Japanese peace treaty.
July 24		Britain and France accept a U.S. invitation to a Washington conference on the level of German industry to be permitted by the Allies . . . . Greek government orders the arrest of Communist Party leader Nicolas Zachariades and former Labor Min. Militadas Porphyrogenis on charges of plotting a revolt.			British Colonial Office issues a White Paper proposing a Federation of Malaya governed by a British high commissioner.
July 25		Hungarian Pres. Zoltan Tildy dissolves the National Assembly and sets elections for Aug. 31.			
July 26		France's National Assembly approves French participation in the Marshall Plan after a two-day debate.			
July 27					
July 28		Rumanian government dissolves the conservative Peasant Party for allegedly conspiring with foreign interests against Rumanian sovereignty.			Worldwide protests against the Dutch campaign in Indonesia grow as Dutch troops continue to advance in Java and Sumatra. Indian Congress Party leader Jawaharlal Nehru calls the attack a threat to world peace, while 19 unions and political parties in Singapore agree to organize a volunteer force to fight the Dutch.
July 29	Russia casts its 11th veto in the U.N. Security Council when it rejects a U.S. resolution to establish a two-year frontier commission for the Balkans.	Russian announces the signing of a trade and credit agreement with Yugoslavia.	British authorities in Palestine hang three Irgun Zvai members convicted of leading the May 4 raid on Acre prison . . . . Refugees from the *Exodus 1947*, returned to France by British authorities, refuse to disembark from British transports at Port de Bouc.	U.S. objects to the recently concluded Argentine-French trade pact, claiming it discriminates against merchant shipping of other countries.	An Indian-owned transport plane piloted by two Britons is shot down by Dutch fighters as it flies from Singapore to Jakarta with a load of medical supplies.
July 30	Russia proposes in the Security Council that the U.N. applications of Austria, Hungary, Italy and Rumania be held up until their respective peace treaties go into effect.	British P.M. Attlee gains solid Labor support in Parliament for a new program of drastic cuts in foreign spending scheduled to take effect next week . . . . U.N. Palestine Inquiry Commission votes in Geneva to visit refugee camps in Central Europe and examine the situation of stateless Jews . . . . Socialist Unity Party leader Max Seydewitz is elected president of Saxony in Soviet-occupied Germany.	Irgun Zvai Leumi hangs two British soldiers kidnapped July 12 in retaliation for yesterday's execution of three Irgun members by British authorities.		Australia and India appeal to the U.N. to halt the Dutch campaign in Indonesia, while British Foreign Secy. Bevin announces that Britain will refuse to supply Holland with weapons and material for use in Indonesia . . . . UNRRA suspends relief shipments to northern China until it can arrange for distribution of a "fair share" of the shipments to Communist-controlled areas.

U.S. Politics & Social Issues	U.S. Foreign Policy & Defense	U.S. Economy & Environment	Science, Technology & Nature	Culture, Leisure & Life Style	
House passes a bill to outlaw the poll tax in voting for federal offices, but the Senate postpones action on the measure until 1948.	Truman delivers his mid-year economic report to Congress, stressing that the Marshall Plan is "at the core" of U.S. foreign policy.	Sen. Joseph Ball (R, Minn.) and Rep. Fred Hartley (R, N.J.) are named to top positions on the newly created Joint Congressional Labor-Management Comm.		Baseball's Hall of Fame inducts fifteen former players, including Philadelphia Athletics pitcher Eddie Plank, Chicago White Sox pitcher Ed Walsh and Chicago Cubs infielders Joe Tinker, Johnny Evers and Frank Chance.	July 21
	Navy cuts 1,000 of its 47,000 officers to conform to budget requirements.	Florida State Supreme Court rules that state laws barring the closed shop are unconstitutional.	Congress completes action on a bill establishing a National Science Foundation to coordinate U.S. scientific research .... Torrential rains sweep Erie, Pa., causing $1 million in damage as the Midwest experiences its coldest summer weather in 72 years.		July 22
	In its second report to Congress, the Atomic Energy Commission reveals plans to set up proving grounds in the Pacific "for routine experiments and tests of atomic weapons."	Vice Pres. Joseph Fay of the AFL International Union of Operating Engineers begins serving an 8½-16 year prison term in N.Y. for extortion and conspiracy after the State Supreme Court denies his appeal for a suspended or reduced sentence .... Wisconsin Gov. Oscar Rennebohm signs a law banning public utilities strikes.			July 23
Utah celebrates the 100th anniversary of the entry of Brigham Young's Mormons into Salt Lake Valley.		An 18-man committee headed by Commerce Secy. Averell Harriman begins hearings in Washington on U.S. capacity to aid other nations .... Twenty-seven coal miners die in an explosion at the Old Ben Mine near West Frankfort, Ill.		Republican politician Harold Stassen is re-elected president of the International Council of Religious Education at a Des Moines convention.	July 24
Andrew May and Murray and Henry Garsson are given prison sentences of eight months to two years for war contract bribery.	Congress passes and sends to the White House the armed forces unification bill, while Truman signs a Senate joint resolution ending 60 wartime emergency laws.				July 25
Mrs. Martha Truman, the President's mother, dies at 94 in Grandview, Mo.	Truman signs the armed forces unification bill and nominates Navy Secy. James Forrestal as defense secretary.	Retiring Federal Bureau of Mines director R.R. Sayers is named chairman of the UMW medical board, established under the union's welfare fund.	International Congress for Microbiology in Stockholm condemns bacterial warfare and urges elimination of all secret research .... Library of Congress opens 18,350 papers of Abraham Lincoln for public use.	But Why Not wins $71,500 in Chicago's Arlington Classic, while the $100,000 Hollywood Gold Cup goes to Jack Addington's Cover Up.	July 26
Gallup Poll indicates that Truman would defeat leading Republican presidential contender Thomas Dewey in a current election with 51% of the vote .... California's State Democratic Comm. refuses to support the Wallace for President faction led by Robert Kenny.		AFL and CIO announce a united drive to force down retail prices by organizing more consumer cooperative stores.			July 27
Truman and 35 members of his family attend funeral services for Mrs. Martha Truman at her home in Grandview, Mo. .... N.Y. State Supreme Court confirms the Metropolitan Life Insurance Company's right to bar Negroes from its Stuyvesant Town development in Manhattan .... Joseph Brodsky, Communist attorney and defense counsel in the Scottsboro case, dies at 57 in N.Y.	A Senate War Investigating subcommittee opens hearings on two government contracts with the Howard Hughes aircraft firm for planes that never saw wartime service .... House Majority Leader Charles Halleck (R, Ind.) says the GOP-controlled House wants to be recognized by Truman as a "full-fledged partner" in conducting foreign affairs.	Agriculture Dept. ends industrial sugar rationing and institutes inventory controls to prevent "a mad scramble for sugar." .... Former National Housing Agency administrator Raymond Foley is named temporary head of the new Housing and Home Finance Agency.			July 28
Mrs. Elizabeth Ingalls, convicted of enslaving her Negro maid Dora Jones, is fined $2,500 and ordered to pay $6,000 in damages to Jones.				Evangelical Lutheran Synod of Missouri and Ohio, meeting in Chicago, passes a resolution calling for unity with the American Lutheran Church.	July 29
	Sen. Chapman Revercomb (R, W. Va.) is named chairman of a Senate Judiciary subcommittee to study the possible immigration of European refugees to the U.S.				July 30

F	G	H	I	J
Includes elections, federal-state relations, civil rights and liberties, crime, the judiciary, education, health care, poverty, urban affairs and population.	*Includes formation and debate of U.S. foreign and defense policies, veterans affairs and defense spending. (Relations with specific foreign countries are usually found under the region concerned.)*	*Includes business, labor, agriculture, taxation, transportation, consumer affairs, monetary and fiscal policy, natural resources, pollution and accidents.*	*Includes worldwide scientific, medical and technological developments, natural phenomena, U.S. weather and natural disasters.*	*Includes the arts, religion, scholarship, communications media, sports, entertainment, fashions, fads and social life.*

	World Affairs	Europe	Africa & the Middle East	The Americas	Asia & the Pacific
July 31		Italy's parliament ratifies the country's peace treaty after a seven-day debate . . . . U.S. Export-Import Bank approves a $13-million loan to Austria.	Enraged by yesterday's execution of two British soldiers by Irgun Zvai Leumi terrorists, British troops riot in Tel Aviv, killing five Jews.		Dutch authorities in Batavia establish autonomous areas in the tin-producing islands of Billiton and Bangka and the bauxite-rich Riow Archipelago, formerly considered part of Indonesia . . . . Princely states of Hyderabad and Travancore announce they will join the Dominion of India.
Aug. 1		Italian cabinet devalues the lira by 55%, establishing an official dollar exchange rate of 350:1 . . . . Continuing his conferences with U.S. military government leaders in Germany, War Secy. Kenneth Royall denies reports that the U.S. has agreed to consult with France before raising the level of German industry.	Anti-British riots in Tel Aviv result in 33 injuries during the funeral processions of five Jews killed yesterday by British troops.		U.N. Security Council calls on Dutch and Indonesian forces to cease hostilities immediately and settle their dispute by arbitration or other peaceful means. Belgium, Britain and France abstain in voting on the resolution . . . . British Viceroy Viscount Mountbatten announces that units of the British Army will begin withdrawing from India Aug. 17.
Aug. 2	*New York* section of the *American Chemical Society* awards its William H. *Nichols Medal* to Berkeley nuclear chemist Glenn T. *Seaborg*, co-discoverer of plutonium.	Soviet authorities in Austria seize the Lobau oil refinery near Vienna, owned by the Socony Vacuum Oil Co. and the Shell Petroleum Co. . . . . Spanish Premier Franco issues an amnesty decree to celebrate recent popular approval of the Law of Succession, but bars the release of political prisoners.		Chilean Pres. Gonzalez Videla forms a new "non-political" cabinet.	
Aug. 3		Bulgarian Premier Georgi Dimitrov returns to Sofia after concluding agreements with Yugoslavia for a customs union, abolition of visas and co-ordination of foreign policy.		Nicaraguan voters choose a 49-man Constituent Assembly to name a new president and revise the constitution.	Acting on orders from The Hague, Dutch Gov. Gen. Hubertus van Mook orders his forces in Indonesia to cease fire in compliance with the U.N. Security Council resolution. He also expresses willingness to accept U.S. mediation of the conflict . . . . *Pravda* demands full veto power for Russia in formulation of the Japanese peace treaty.
Aug. 4		Greek cabinet urges the U.S. to speed delivery of arms and other equipment to help government forces battling guerrillas along the border.		Argentina and Eire establish full diplomatic relations.	Indonesian Pres. Ahmed Sukarno complies with the Security Council resolution by ordering his troops to cease fire.
Aug. 5	Australia formally joins the World Bank and International Monetary Fund, becoming the 45th member.	Rumanian Parliament votes to expel 33 conservative Peasant Party deputies due to the banning of their party . . . . Russia signs a one-year trade agreement with Poland.	British authorities in Palestine arrest 35 leading Zionists, including Tel Aviv Mayor Israel Rokach, and send them to the Latrun detention camp in an attempt to wipe out the Irgun Zvai Leumi leadership . . . . Egyptian Premier Mahmoud Fahmy Nokrashy Pasha appears before the U.N. Security Council to request assistance in evicting British troops from Egypt and the Sudan.	Truman signs a bill providing for popular election of the governor of Puerto Rico beginning in 1948.	
Aug. 6		British P.M. Attlee presents the House of Commons with an austerity economic program calling for a 40% reduction in food imports, demobilization of skilled workers in the armed forces and a drive to increase British imports to 150% of the 1939 level by 1948 . . . . U.S. and British representatives on the Allied Co-ordinating Comm. in Berlin declare that they will list no more plants as available for reparations until the level of the German industry is raised and Russia cooperates in the country's economic unification.	Tunisian labor leaders end a three-day general strike protesting French refusal to grant the colony self-government.		Bells in Hiroshima toll for one minute at 8:14 a.m., the second anniversary of the city's atomic destruction.
Aug. 7		British House of Commons approves the government's emergency economic program.		Colombia's Council of State invalidates the government's suspension of the Colombian Federation of Labor.	Deputy Indonesian Premier A.K. Gani cables the Security Council that his government will accept any decision made by the Council to settle the dispute with Holland, while Premier Amir Sjarifoeddin urges U.N. mediation of the conflict.
Aug. 8	U.N. Security Council's Comm. on New Members ends debate on 11 membership applications, agreeing unanimously only to admit Yemen.	A subcommittee of the U.N. Palestine Inquiry Commission leaves Geneva for a tour of refugee camps in Germany and Austria . . . . Gen. Anton Denikin, former Imperial Russian Army chief of staff who led a White Russian army against the Bolsheviks in 1918, dies at 76 in Ann Arbor, Mich.	South Africa rejects a U.N. General Assembly resolution calling for a trusteeship arrangement for South-West Africa, but promises not to annex the territory.	Paraguayan civil war continues despite government victory claims, with both sides reporting heavy fighting north of Asuncion.	Japan provides Allied headquarters in Tokyo with its first postwar list of goods available for export, including 26 million yards of silk fabrics.

A	B	C	D	E
Includes developments that affect more than one world region, international organizations and important meetings of major world leaders.	*Includes all domestic and regional developments in Europe, including the Soviet Union, Turkey, Cyprus and Malta.*	*Includes all domestic and regional developments in Africa and the Middle East, including Iraq and Iran and excluding Cyprus, Turkey and Afghanistan.*	*Includes all domestic and regional developments in Latin America, the Caribbean and Canada.*	*Includes all domestic and regional developments in Asian and Pacific nations, extending from Afghanistan through all the Pacific Islands, except Hawaii.*

U.S. Politics & Social Issues	U.S. Foreign Policy & Defense	U.S. Economy & Environment	Science, Technology & Nature	Culture, Leisure & Life Style	
Sen. Robert A. Taft (R, Ohio.) launches a campaign for the GOP presidential nomination in a speech to 1,300 Ohio Republican leaders in Columbus.		CIO Pres. Philip Murray writes to AFL Pres. William Green, reiterating his proposal that the two labor groups take common action on economic and political problems without waiting for a complete merger.			July 31
N.Y. Gov. Thomas Dewey returns to Albany after a week-long campaign trip in Michigan, where he refused Sen. Taft's challenge to "speak out" on foreign and domestic issues.		General Motors announces automobile price increases of 2-6% for next year, a move denounced by UAW Pres. Walter Reuther as inflationary and "unjustified."	Anthropologists in South Africa discover remains of a man-ape known as Australopithecus, an important advance in the study of human evolution . . . . B-29 *Pacusan Dreamboat* sets a world non-stop distance record of 8,854.8 miles in two trips on a triangular course from MacDill Field, Fla. to Tucson, Ariz. and Washington.		Aug. 1
		Federal Works Agency approves a 37,681-mile national highway system, to be built by the states with federal aid in a $3-billion program. The completed system will connect 182 of the 199 U.S. cities with more than 50,000 residents.	Iraqi archaeologists uncover ruins of a temple indicating the Babylonians of 4,000 B.C. had devised a system of architecture and religious ritual.	*Peg O'My Heart* tops the CBS *Your Hit Parade*, with *That's My Desire* and *I Wonder, I Wonder* following.	Aug. 2
				A World Baptist Alliance congress in Copenhagen ends with a manifesto on religious freedom and a promise to support the U.N.	Aug. 3
	Former Air Force Gen. Elliott Roosevelt appears before the Senate War Investigating committee to testify on his role in recommending the Hughes aircraft firm for wartime government contracts. He denies any improper activity, attacking the investigation as a Republican attempt to "smear" the reputation of his father, FDR.	Truman signs a bill providing for stricter safety regulations in coal and lignite mines.		Ike Williams knocks out Bob Montgomery in the sixth round in Philadelphia to become world lightweight boxing champ.	Aug. 4
A county jury in Jackson, N.C. acquits seven white men accused of attempting to lynch Negro Godwin Bush. Gov. R. Gregg Cherry orders the State Superior Court to investigate.	AFL Pres. William Green and CIO Pres. Philip Murray enthusiastically endorse U.S. aid to Greece at a N.Y. luncheon honoring Clinton Golden, a CIO official recently appointed labor adviser to the American mission to Greece.	AFL International Ladies Garment Workers Union breaks with AFL policy by refusing to boycott the NLRB and renounce no-strike clauses in future contracts as a result of the Taft-Hartley Act.			Aug. 5
William Callahan, presiding judge in the Scottsboro case, dies at 83 in Montgomery, Ala.	Aircraft manufacturer Howard Hughes makes his first appearance before the Senate War Investigating Comm. and charges that committee chairman Owen Brewster (R, Me.) offered to call off the investigation if Hughes agreed to merge his Trans World Airlines with Pan American Airways, in which Brewster has part interest . . . . State Under Secy. William Clayton concludes a three-day conference in Paris on European economic problems with U.S. ambassadors to Britain and France, who emphasize that U.S. aid is urgently required.		Truman vetoes a bill for a 24-member National Science Foundation, claiming that it sets up a cumbersome organization and deprives the President of necessary administrative power . . . . Lloyd George Mountains Exploration Expedition announces that its members have scaled the 9,800-foot peaks of the Lloyd George group, the last unclimbed group in the Canadian Rockies.		Aug. 6
	U.S. Atomic Energy Commission appoints Adm. John Gingrich director of its Division of Security and Intelligence, responsible for coordinating work with the CIA and FBI.		Thor Heyerdahl reports the landing of the *Kon Tiki* on the Raroia Reef of the Tuamotu Archipelago, ending a 4,000-mile journey from Peru that lasted 15 weeks.		Aug. 7
		Labor Secy. Schwellenbach rules that financial reports which unions must file under the Taft-Hartley Act will be kept confidential and opened only to "proper" government officials and union members, pointing out that knowledge of a union's financial situation might give an employer the advantage in a labor dispute.			Aug. 8

F	G	H	I	J
Includes elections, federal-state relations, civil rights and liberties, crime, the judiciary, education, health care, poverty, urban affairs and population.	*Includes formation and debate of U.S. foreign and defense policies, veterans affairs and defense spending. (Relations with specific foreign countries are usually found under the region concerned.)*	*Includes business, labor, agriculture, taxation, transportation, consumer affairs, monetary and fiscal policy, natural resources, pollution and accidents.*	*Includes worldwide scientific, medical and technological developments, natural phenomena, U.S. weather and natural disasters.*	*Includes the arts, religion, scholarship, communications media, sports, entertainment, fashions, fads and social life.*

	World Affairs	Europe	Africa & the Middle East	The Americas	Asia & the Pacific
Aug. 9		U.S. State Secy. Marshall invites France to participate in a London conference on German economic reconstruction, promising that French views will be taken into consideration before the U.S. and Britain reach any final decisions.	A mine planted by the Irgun Zvai Leumi derails a Cairo-Haifa troop train as the organization launches a campaign to disrupt all rail transport in Palestine.	Argentine Central Bank restricts credit on speculative ventures to curb inflation.	
Aug. 10		Gen. Clay of the U.S. military government in Germany reports the release of the last of eight million German war prisoners in U.S. custody and the complete destruction or conversion of all armaments plants in the U.S. zone.			
Aug. 11	In his annual report to the General Assembly, U.N. Secy. Gen. Trygve Lie says there has been no improvement in the world political situation and urges the General Assembly to take up deadlocked disputes in the Balkans and other areas. He also suggests establishment of a subsidiary U.N. headquarters at the former League of Nations office in Geneva.	French Foreign Min. Georges Bidault accepts an American invitation to meet in London with the U.S. and Britain to discuss raising the level of German industrial production .... Russia rejects a U.S. proposal for issue of a new German currency under four-power supervision in Berlin.		Argentine government orders a general wage increase for the federal police force.	
Aug. 12		British House of Commons passes an emergency powers bill called for in P.M. Attlee's economic program, giving the government broad authority to "ensure that the whole resources of the community are used in a manner best calculated to serve the interests of the community." .... U.S. and Britain begin a Washington conference on means of doubling Ruhr coal production to a daily quota of 400,000 tons. At British insistence, U.S. negotiators agree to discuss political issues and socialization as well as technical matters .... Greek Reconstruction Min. Stylianos Gonatas claims in Athens that future U.S. troop presence in Greece is "a strong probability." .... Yugoslavia signs a four-year, $100-million trade agreement with the U.S.-British zone of Germany.			U.N. Security Council votes to hear representatives of the Indonesian Republic, while Holland calls for a conference of all Indonesian states and ethnic minorities to discuss creation of a United States of Indonesia. Dutch officials in Batavia reject U.N. arbitration of the current dispute, demanded by Indonesian nationalists .... Siam abandons its claim to territory in French Indochina.
Aug. 13		Gen. Clay of the U.S. military government in Germany testifies before the U.N. Palestine Inquiry Commission in Berlin, claiming that anti-Semitism in Europe is growing and that increasing numbers of refugees want to settle in Palestine.	British authorities in Palestine impose curfews on settlements between Tel Aviv and Jaffa in an effort to curb mounting Jewish-Arab violence .... Speaking before the U.N. Security Council, British delegate Lord Cadogan questions whether the majority of Sudanese want union with Egypt. Sudanese National Front leader Ismail Al Azhary states at Lake Success that most Sudanese political groups do favor a merger with Egypt, but proposes separate Egyptian and Sudanese legislatures.		In a letter to Molotov, State Secy. Marshall threatens to act without Russia in establishing a united Korean government and calls for a report by Aug. 21 on deadlocked U.S.-Soviet Joint Comm. talks in Seoul.
Aug. 14		Soviet command refuses to permit its Austrian occupation zone to receive any U.S. aid, claiming that the right of inspection demanded by the U.S. violates Austrian sovereignty .... U.S. military tribunal in Dachau hands down death sentences for 22 Buchenwald concentration camp officials convicted of war crimes. The condemned include Ilse Koch, wife of a camp commandant singled out as the perpetrator of extreme cruelties .... U.N. Palestine Inquiry Commission concludes its tour of Central European refugee camps and returns to Geneva.		Nicaragua's Constituent Assembly elects Victor Manuel Roman y Reyes the country's president.	Indonesian nationalist leader Sutan Sjahrir addresses the U.N. Security Council, requesting that all Dutch forces be withdrawn from islands claimed by the Indonesian Republic and that a U.N. commission be created to supervise the current ceasefire.
	A	B	C	D	E
	Includes developments that affect more than one world region, international organizations and important meetings of major world leaders.	*Includes all domestic and regional developments in Europe, including the Soviet Union, Turkey, Cyprus and Malta.*	*Includes all domestic and regional developments in Africa and the Middle East, including Iraq and Iran and excluding Cyprus, Turkey and Afghanistan.*	*Includes all domestic and regional developments in Latin America, the Caribbean and Canada.*	*Includes all domestic and regional developments in Asian and Pacific nations, extending from Afghanistan through all the Pacific Islands, except Hawaii.*

U.S. Politics & Social Issues	U.S. Foreign Policy & Defense	U.S. Economy & Environment	Science, Technology & Nature	Culture, Leisure & Life Style	
In a newly issued campaign pamphlet entitled "Republican Congress Delivers," House Majority Leader Charles Halleck claims that the Republican-controlled Congress has reversed the "ruinous New Deal trend" towards regimentation, bureaucracy, machine politics and vote-buying. Democratic National Comm. counters that Republicans have catered to business interests with a "soak-the-poor, coddle-the-rich tax reduction bill," weakened labor unions and fostered inflation.	Appearing again before the Senate War Investigating Comm., Howard Hughes attacks Army procurement methods, claiming that contracts are assigned to firms that provide the most lavish entertainment for procurement officers.	International Longshoremen's and Warehousemen's Union signs a no-strike, no-lockout agreement for the Hawaiian pineapple industry giving 24,000 workers a 10¢ hourly wage increase.		With Pleasure, with Jack Westrope up, takes the $36,650 Sheridan Handicap in Chicago.	Aug. 9
			William Odom lands in Chicago after a record 73-hour solo flight around the world in a converted A-26 bomber, the *Reynolds Bombshell.*	Howard Candler, son of the Coca-Cola founder, presents Emory Univ. with a $5-million grant in Asa G. Candler, Inc. stock.	Aug. 10
	Republicans on the Senate War Investigating Comm. suspend their investigation of Howard Hughes' government contracts, reportedly advised by Senate President Pro Tempore Arthur Vandenberg (R, Mich.) to drop the open hearings due to unfavorable publicity. Hughes claims that the move is a "vindication" of his conduct forced by public opinion.	Truman issues an executive order eliminating the National Railroad Labor Panel, established in 1942 as an emergency wartime agency .... Pearl Bergoff, known as "King of the Strike Breakers" while heading the Bergoff Service Bureau, dies at 68 in N.Y.	Construction begins on the first nonmilitary atomic energy pile in Brookhaven, N.Y. .... Dr. William C. White, a leading tuberculosis researcher, dies at 72 in Washington.		Aug. 11
		CIO Federation of Dyers, Finishers, Printers and Bleachers signs a closed shop agreement with 385 garment industry employers in N.Y., N.J. and Pennsylvania giving 30,000 workers a 5¢ hourly wage increase.		Hugh Trevor-Ropers' *The Last Days of Hitler,* a British intelligence agent's report on his investigation of the Nazi dictator's life in his Berlin bunker, is published in N.Y. by Macmillan.	Aug. 12
	Grand Army of the Republic begins its 81st encampment in Cleveland, with five Civil War veterans participating.	Rep. Fred Hartley (R, N.J.) discloses plans to conduct a congressional investigation of alleged labor racketeers in Detroit .... B.F. Goodrich averts a strike by 21,000 CIO United Rubber Workers union members when it agrees to negotiate its first company-wide contract.		Former heavyweight boxer George Godfrey, who won 72 of his 81 matches, dies at 50 in Los Angeles.	Aug. 13
	In a move to bolster the Italian economy and check Communist gains, the U.S. cancels $1 billion in war claims against Italy .... State Dept. announces the dismissal of 10 employes for disloyalty, raising total dismissals since the start of 1946 to 20.	UAW ends a 17-day strike against the Clinton Machine Co. in Michigan after clashes between pickets and police cause Gov. Kim Sigler to alert the National Guard. Settlement terms include a 10¢ hourly wage increase.		League of New York Theaters accepts an Actor's Equity Assn. contract ban on performances in Washington's National Theater if it continues to bar Negroes .... Golf star Mildred Didrikson Zaharias announces she will relinquish her amateur status and accept $300,000 for a series of golf movies.	Aug. 14
F	G	H	I	J	
Includes elections, federal-state relations, civil rights and liberties, crime, the judiciary, education, health care, poverty, urban affairs and population.	*Includes formation and debate of U.S. foreign and defense policies, veterans affairs and defense spending. (Relations with specific foreign countries are usually found under the region concerned.)*	*Includes business, labor, agriculture, taxation, transportation, consumer affairs, monetary and fiscal policy, natural resources, pollution and accidents.*	*Includes worldwide scientific, medical and technological developments, natural phenomena, U.S. weather and natural disasters.*	*Includes the arts, religion, scholarship, communications media, sports, entertainment, fashions, fads and social life.*	

	World Affairs	Europe	Africa & the Middle East	The Americas	Asia & the Pacific
Aug. 15		A U.S. court in Nuremberg indicts 12 Krupp munitions executives as war criminals, including Alfried Krupp von Bohlen und Halbach, head of the firm .... Former Hungarian Premier Ferenc Nagy appeals by radio from Washington for Hungarians to boycott forthcoming parliamentary elections, charging that electoral changes have eliminated one million voters from the ballot lists .... Rumania introduces a new and devalued currency, imposing exchange limits which virtually eliminate the savings of wealthy families.		Twenty American nations, Nicaragua excluded, convene at Petropolis, Brazil, to draft a Western Hemisphere defense pact implementing the Act of Chapultepec.	Britain gives up its 346-year rule in India, which is officially partitioned into Hindu and Moslem states. Britain's Viscount Mountbatten becomes the first governor-general of the new Dominion of India, with Jawaharlal Nehru as premier. Moslem League Pres. Mohammed Ali Jinnah is sworn in as governor-general of Pakistan .... AP reports from West Java call the Indonesian ceasefire truce a "mockery," with "more men dying now than when the war was officially on." .... State Secy. Marshall rejects a Soviet proposal that the Japanese peace treaty be written by the Big Four foreign ministers, with each power possessing a veto .... Burmese police stage a nationwide roundup of Communist suspects.
Aug. 16		Greek guerrilla leader Markos Vafiades proclaims establishment of a "Free Greek Government," calling for the overthrow of King Paul and expulsion of "all foreigners and their agents." .... A Sofia court convicts Agrarian Party leader Nikola Petkov of plotting to overthrow the government and sentences him to death.		Rafael Trujillo begins his fourth term as president of the Dominican Republic.	George Atcheson Jr., chairman of the Allied Control Commission in Japan and author of a controversial 1945 memorandum on China, is killed when his Army B-17 crashes in the Pacific west of Honolulu.
Aug. 17	U.N. Economic and Social Council ends its fifth session after recommending that the General Assembly make the International Monetary Fund and World Bank specialized U.N. agencies.	Soviet authorities in Germany decree an amnesty for all Nazis except important party officials.		Quebec Premier Maurice Duplessis announces discovery of a clandestine Communist radio station in the Abitibi region of northwestern Quebec.	India and Pakistan announce agreement on borders running through the divided provinces of Punjab and Bengal.
Aug. 18	A Soviet veto denies U.N. membership to Transjordan, Eire and Portugal after the Security Council turns down membership applications from Albania and Outer Mongolia.	An explosion at a naval torpedo and mine factory in Cadiz, Spain causes 300 deaths and demolishes shipyards, factories, houses and an orphanage .... A French Socialist Party congress in Lyons passes a resolution urging Premier Ramadier to press harder for socialist economic measures and a more liberal colonial administration in Algeria .... U.S. demands a stay of execution for condemned Bulgarian Agrarian Party leader Nikola Petkov, calling his death sentence "a gross miscarriage of justice."			
Aug. 19		U.N. Security Council Chairman Faris el Khouri of Syria declares that the Council has failed to end the Greek dispute after Russia vetoes U.S. and Australian resolutions for a negotiated settlement of the conflict.		Paraguayan government reports the surrender of most insurgent troops assaulting Asuncion, and claims that rebel leader Rafael Franco has fled to Argentina.	
Aug. 20		A U.S. court in Nuremberg sentences Karl Brandt, Hitler's personal physician, and six other German doctors to death for performing medical "experiments" on concentration camp inmates .... U.S. military government in Germany dismisses Communist publisher Emil Carlebach from his post on the *Frankfurter Rundschau*, leaving two Communists among the 80 licensed newspaper publishers in the U.S. zone .... Under U.S. pressure, Britain temporarily ends free convertibility of pounds sterling into U.S. dollars, interrupting a rapid flow of dollars into several European and Latin American countries .... France and Poland reach a provisional four-year trade agreement to exchange French autos for Polish coal, if French claims on nationalized Polish industry can be settled.		Speaking at the Inter-American Defense Conference in Brazil, State Secy. Marshall turns aside proposals for a Latin American "Marshall Plan," warning that Europe's economic needs are temporarily more urgent and must take priority.	
Aug. 21	Russia vetoes U.N. membership for Italy and Austria after the Security Council turns down membership applications of Hungary, Rumania and Bulgaria.			Chile's Chamber of Deputies authorizes the government to suspend individual liberties to deal with a series of Communist-led strikes.	Sikhs and Hindus begin driving Moslems out of eastern Punjab, depriving Jullundar and other cities of nearly half of their population.

A	B	C	D	E
Includes developments that affect more than one world region, international organizations and important meetings of major world leaders.	*Includes all domestic and regional developments in Europe, including the Soviet Union, Turkey, Cyprus and Malta.*	*Includes all domestic and regional developments in Africa and the Middle East, including Iraq and Iran and excluding Cyprus, Turkey and Afghanistan.*	*Includes all domestic and regional developments in Latin America, the Caribbean and Canada.*	*Includes all domestic and regional developments in Asian and Pacific nations, extending from Afghanistan through all the Pacific Islands, except Hawaii.*

U.S. Politics & Social Issues	U.S. Foreign Policy & Defense	U.S. Economy & Environment	Science, Technology & Nature	Culture, Leisure & Life Style	
Gerhard Eisler is convicted in a Washington federal court on charges of hiding his Communist affiliations when he applied for a 1945 visa to leave for Germany.	Army's Manhattan Engineer District, which spent $2 billion to develop the atomic bomb, officially goes out of existence.	Daniel Tobin is re-elected president of the International Brotherhood of Teamsters in San Francisco.		*Life With Father*, produced by Warner Bros. and starring William Powell and Irene Dunne, opens in N.Y. The film version of James Thurber's *The Secret Life of Walter Mitty*, starring Danny Kaye and Boris Karloff, also premiers.	Aug. 15
					Aug. 16
			A Canadian Mines and Resources Dept. expedition reports that the North magnetic pole has moved 200 miles north since 1904, with probable present location on Somerset Island.	*Billboard* poll of theater professionals chooses *All My Sons* as the best play and *Finian's Rainbow* the best musical of the 1946-47 season.	Aug. 17
Federal agencies begin filling out loyalty check forms for 1.9 million government workers under an $11-million congressional appropriation.		Justice Dept. sues the eight-firm Rubber Manufacturers Assn., which produces 90% of U.S. tires and inner tubes, for price conspiracy.			Aug. 18
	U.S. withdraws its offer to mediate the Dutch-Indonesian dispute when nationalist leaders refuse to drop their demand for U.N. arbitration .... Oscar Ewing, former Democratic National Comm. assistant chairman, succeeds Watson Miller as head of the Federal Security Agency.			American Federation of Musicians Pres. James Petrillo rejects a plan of four radio networks to broadcast music simultaneously on AM and FM stations without double pay for musicians .... Daniel Ashley, *U.S. News and World Report* publisher, dies at 63 in Darien, Conn.	Aug. 19
N.J. State Constitutional Convention, meeting in New Brunswick, adopts a ban on racial or religious segregation in the state National Guard and public schools.	Library of Congress issues a special report for the Senate Foreign Relations Comm., noting that U.S.-Russian relations have "deteriorated seriously" since the war's end and blaming this development on Russian aggression and intolerance.	Truman's mid-year review of the budget predicts a record $4.7-billion revenue surplus for the current fiscal year but cautions that most of the surplus will be used to fund the national debt .... James Guthrie Harbord, Gen. Pershing's chief of staff in 1917 and Radio Corp. of America president for 17 years, dies at 81 in Rye, N.Y.	Univ. of Chicago Chancellor Robert Hutchins announces a privately funded $12-million research program on peacetime atomic energy uses.		Aug. 20
Sen. Theodore Bilbo (D, Miss.), champion of white supremacy, dies at 69 in New Orleans after undergoing several unsuccessful mouth cancer operations.	Truman names Kenneth Royall as Army secretary, John Sullivan as Navy secretary and William Symington as secretary for air. All are non-cabinet posts under Defense Secy. James Forrestal.	Dun & Bradstreet reports that wholesale prices of 30 basic commodities have hit a post-war record of 274% of the 1930-32 average .... International Typographical Union convention in Cleveland approves a decision to combat the Taft-Hartley Act by refusing to sign contracts with employers in the U.S. The meeting also urges a merger of the AFL, CIO and railroad brotherhoods in a Taft-Hartley repeal campaign.			Aug. 21
F *Includes elections, federal-state relations, civil rights and liberties, crime, the judiciary, education, health care, poverty, urban affairs and population.*	G *Includes formation and debate of U.S. foreign and defense policies, veterans affairs and defense spending. (Relations with specific foreign countries are usually found under the region concerned.)*	H *Includes business, labor, agriculture, taxation, transportation, consumer affairs, monetary and fiscal policy, natural resources, pollution and accidents.*	I *Includes worldwide scientific, medical and technological developments, natural phenomena, U.S. weather and natural disasters.*	J *Includes the arts, religion, scholarship, communications media, sports, entertainment, fashions, fads and social life.*	

	World Affairs	Europe	Africa & the Middle East	The Americas	Asia & the Pacific
Aug. 22	Preparatory Comm. of the International Trade Organization, meeting in Geneva, approves the draft of an ITO charter which commits signatory members to a policy of eliminating trade barriers.	European Economic Conference in Paris issues a proposed reconstruction program for Europe, calling for $29.2 billion in Marshall Plan aid over the next four years .... Britain, France and the U.S. begin talks in London on means of raising the level of German industrial production, despite Russian objections that the sessions violate the Potsdam Agreement.	British transport ships with 4,500 *Exodus 1947* refugees leave Port de Bouc, France bound for Hamburg following the passengers' refusal to disembark.	Inter-American Conference in Brazil adopts a Mexican proposal referring Latin American economic problems to a Buenos Aires conference scheduled for 1948.	U.S. military authorities in Korea admit arresting many political suspects recently to curb "widespread" revolutionary activity, blamed by Gen. John Hodge on "agitators" from the Russian zone.
Aug. 23		Seven-month-old coalition cabinet of Greek Premier Demetrios Maximos falls when three ministers resign, demanding a broadening of the government's political base to deal with economic problems and continued guerrilla warfare.		A five-day strike of Chilean coal miners ends as the government puts the country's mines under military control .... Defense Min. Carlos Mancheno seizes control of Ecuador's government in a bloodless revolt, overthrowing Pres. Jose Velasco Ibarra.	American negotiators on the U.S.-Russian Joint Trusteeship Comm. in Seoul propose an internationally supervised plebiscite in Korea to decide the type of unified government to be created for the country.
Aug. 24			Jamal el Husseini of the Arab Higher Comm. threatens to open a flood of Arab immigration to Palestine if unauthorized Jewish immigrants continue to arrive.		Gen. Albert Wedemeyer concludes his fact-finding mission in China with a statement criticizing both the Nationalist government for allowing "incompetent and corrupt officials [to] occupy many positions" and the Communists for attempting to "impose ideologies" by force .... Indian Premier Jawaharlal Nehru flies to East Punjab and pleads for an end to communal strife in the province, which has resulted in an estimated 20,000 deaths and one million refugees since Indian independence.
Aug. 25	Annual meeting of the U.N. Food and Agriculture Organization convenes in Geneva to discuss creation of a world food council.	Former Liberty Party leader Dezso Sulyok leaves Hungary on the "advice" of Deputy Premier Matyas Rakosi .... Bulgarian Parliament unanimously ratifies the country's peace treaty, while a bill outlawing the conservative Agrarian Party is introduced in the National Assembly .... Yugoslavia ratifies the Italian, Hungarian and Bulgarian peace treaties.			U.N. Security Council offers to mediate the Indonesian dispute, stopping short of the arbitration requested by nationalist leaders. France vetoes a Russian resolution for creation of a special U.N. commission to investigate the ceasefire violations in Indonesia.
Aug. 26		Russia rejects a U.S. appeal for a review of Agrarian Party leader Nikola Petkov's death sentence by the Allied Control Commission in Bulgaria .... U.S. Army in Italy ends its ban on marriages between GIs and Italian girls.			British Commonwealth Conference on Japan, meeting in Canberra, endorses the U.S. position that Japan's peace treaty should by decided by a two-thirds majority of the nations that fought Japan, with no veto right .... U.N. Security Council passes a Polish resolution calling on Dutch and Indonesian nationalist forces to observe the U.N. ceasefire order of Aug. 1, while Holland recognizes East Borneo as a self-governing territory within the planned United States of Indonesia.
Aug. 27	U.N. Security Council debates the Big Five veto power, referring the question to a committee of experts .... U.N. legal and financial experts propose that the U.S. pay $26 million of the $65 million needed to construct the permanent U.N. headquarters in N.Y.	Making use of emergency powers recently granted by Parliament, the British Labor government introduces a series of economic restrictions, including reduction of the individual meat allotment, elimination of pleasure motoring and a ban on vacations outside the sterling area .... London conference on German economic reconstruction ends with a British-U.S. promise not to give Germany priority over "the democratic countries of Europe" and to prevent the Ruhr area "from again becoming an instrument of aggression." .... Trial of 24 I.G. Farben industrialists opens in Nuremberg, as U.S. Prosecutor Telford Taylor charges that the defendants were "master builders of the Wehrmacht."	French National Assembly passes a new Algerian statute creating a legislative assembly for the colony that gives disproportionate representation to Algerians of European descent.		
Aug. 28				Ecuadorian dictator Carlos Mancheno abolishes the country's 1944 constitution and proclaims himself president under the 1905 charter, which gives the chief executive sweeping powers.	Nanking reports that Gen. Chen Cheng, Nationalist chief of staff, will take command of nine Manchurian armies to guard against a predicted Communist offensive.
Aug. 29		U.S. and British authorities in Berlin announce a plan to restore German industry in their zones to its 1936 level .... Greek Populist Party leader Constantin Tsaldaris is sworn in by King Paul as head of an all-Populist cabinet .... Soviet Presidium ratifies the Italian, Rumanian, Hungarian, Bulgarian and Finnish peace treaties.	Three British transports carrying *Exodus 1947* refugees sail from Gibraltar for Hamburg as the passengers maintain their refusal to disembark.		Dutch officials in Batavia outlaw the Indonesian Republic in all parts of Java under Dutch control, about two-thirds of the island .... Admitting deadlock of U.S.-Soviet Joint Comm. talks in Seoul, the U.S. proposes a Big Four conference to discuss creation of a unified provisional Korean government under U.N. supervision.
	A	B	C	D	E
	Includes developments that affect more than one world region, international organizations and important meetings of major world leaders.	*Includes all domestic and regional developments in Europe, including the Soviet Union, Turkey, Cyprus and Malta.*	*Includes all domestic and regional developments in Africa and the Middle East, including Iraq and Iran and excluding Cyprus, Turkey and Afghanistan.*	*Includes all domestic and regional developments in Latin America, the Caribbean and Canada.*	*Includes all domestic and regional developments in Asian and Pacific nations, extending from Afghanistan through all the Pacific Islands, except Hawaii.*

U.S. Politics & Social Issues	U.S. Foreign Policy & Defense	U.S. Economy & Environment	Science, Technology & Nature	Culture, Leisure & Life Style	
		Taft-Hartley Act officially goes into effect, two months after its passage .... Wholesale prices of 30 basic commodities hit a postwar peak of 275.64% of the 1930-32 average.		College All Stars upset the Chicago Bears in Chicago, 16-0, the first college victory over a professional football team in 14 years.	Aug. 22
				Fervent, with Douglas Dodson up, takes the American Derby at Washington Park, Chicago, winning $93,250.	Aug. 23
Prominent U.S. liberals commemorate the 20th anniversary of the Sacco-Vanzetti execution with a manifesto warning against tyranny. Signers include Rep. Helen Gahagan Douglas (D, Calif.), Univ. of Chicago Chancellor Robert Hutchins and Eleanor Roosevelt.			National Bureau of Standards announces the creation of National Applied Mathematics laboratories, equipped with computers to help in atomic and aeronautical research.	Crystal Plunge swim team of San Francisco captures the AAU outdoor championships in Chicago.	Aug. 24
			Maj. Marion Carl sets a 650.6 mph world speed record in a D-558 Skystreak at Muroc Lake, Calif. .... Anthropologist Clark Wissler, an authority on American Indians, dies at 76 in N.Y.		Aug. 25
Disabled veteran Charles Potter wins a special election for the House seat of the late Fred Bradley (R, Mich.), defeating Democrat Harold Beaton.	War and Navy Depts. announce construction of a research laboratory for the Armed Forces Special Weapons Project, successor to the Manhattan Project, at Sandia base near Albuquerque, N.M. .... Navy reports that voluntary enlistments are growing but still below the 15,000 monthly goal needed to maintain authorized naval strength of 400,000 by July 1948.	NLRB General Counsel Robert Denham reorganizes his 600-man Washington staff, creating four divisions to enforce rulings and investigate disputes coming before the new five-man NLRB.	Univ. of California's Lick Observatory on Mount Hamilton announces discovery of a new minor planet called "Wirtanen's Object," less than 10 miles in diameter in an orbit about 156 million miles from the sun.		Aug. 26
	Ten Republican and eight Democratic members of the House Foreign Affairs Comm. leave the U.S. to study reconstruction needs in England and European continental countries.	Assn. of Colored Railway Trainmen and Locomotive Firemen files suit in St. Louis against the St. Louis-San Francisco Railway and four railroad workers' unions to annul a 1928 agreement barring Negroes from all jobs except train porters.	Truman releases a report by John Steelman, chairman of the President's Scientific Research Bd., calling for expenditure of 1% of the national income to increase the number of scientists available for basic and medical research.	*Kiss of Death*, written by Ben Hecht and starring Victor Mature and Coleen Gray, is released by 20th Century - Fox.	Aug. 27
	American Legion convention opens in N.Y. and hears messages from Truman, Navy Secy. Forrestal and N.Y. Gov. Thomas Dewey urging the introduction of universal military service.				Aug. 28
			U.S. Atomic Energy Commission announces development of a new atomic power plant known as a "fast reactor," using plutonium rather than uranium as fuel.	Manuel Rodriguez (Manolete), Spain's most famous bullfighter, dies at 30 in Linares after being gored by a bull.	Aug. 29
F *Includes elections, federal-state relations, civil rights and liberties, crime, the judiciary, education, health care, poverty, urban affairs and population.*	G *Includes formation and debate of U.S. foreign and defense policies, veterans affairs and defense spending. (Relations with specific foreign countries are usually found under the region concerned.)*	H *Includes business, labor, agriculture, taxation, transportation, consumer affairs, monetary and fiscal policy, natural resources, pollution and accidents.*	I *Includes worldwide scientific, medical and technological developments, natural phenomena, U.S. weather and natural disasters.*	J *Includes the arts, religion, scholarship, communications media, sports, entertainment, fashions, fads and social life.*	

	World Affairs	Europe	Africa & the Middle East	The Americas	Asia & the Pacific
Aug. 30		Sir George Higgins, chairman of Lloyd's Register of Shipping from 1929 to 1943, dies at 80 in London.		Inter-American Defense Conference in Brazil concludes by approving a joint defense treaty for the entire Western Hemisphere.	
Aug. 31		Hungary's second parliamentary elections since the war result in a victory for the Communists, who gain 21.6% of the vote and emerge as the largest single party, followed by the Democratic People's Party and the Peasant Party .... British Food Min. John Strachey announces temporary suspension of British food purchases in the U.S. due to high prices and the American tariff system, which limits U.S. buying overseas.	U.N. Palestine Inquiry Commission issues a report recommending independence for Palestine with Jewish and Arab zones and some form of U.N. help for 250,000 European refugees. The report's majority section recommends separate Jewish and Arab states, while the minority section favors a single binational government.		
Sept. 1		U.S. assumes responsibility from Britain for supplying all Greek armed forces and gendarmerie personnel with food .... Turkey's National Assembly ratifies the U.S. aid pact.	Zionist leaders express support for the U.N. Palestine Inquiry Commission's report, but Arabs denounce its "astonishing" proposal to include the predominantly Arab port of Jaffa in the Jewish area of settlement .... Syrian Premier Jamil Mardam Bey signs an agreement with the Trans-Arabian Pipe Line Co. for construction of a 1,100-mile pipeline from Saudi Arabia to the Mediterranean, to pass through Syrian territory.	Arriving in Rio de Janeiro on a state visit to Brazil, Truman is greeted by Brazilian Pres. Eurico Gaspar Dutra and a welcoming throng of one million .... Mexican Pres. Miguel Aleman announces an agreement to pay $21.25 million to British and Dutch firms whose oil-bearing properties were expropriated.	
Sept. 2		French-Spanish border is re-opened to travel for the first time in 17 months.		Nineteen American states sign the Inter-American Treaty of Reciprocal Assistance in Rio de Janeiro, concluding the Inter-American Defense Conference. The treaty provides for peaceful settlement of disputes in the Western Hemisphere and common action against aggressors. Canada, Ecuador and Nicaragua do not sign. Truman addresses the final session of the conference, criticizing Soviet foreign policy and praising the treaty as a sign of "fidelity to the U.N." .... An Army counter-revolt led by Col. Angel Baquero Davila topples the nine-day-old regime of Ecuadorian dictator Carlos Mancheno.	Nationalist Chinese Premier Chang Chun says his government's domestic and foreign policy will not be altered as a result of Gen. Albert Wedemeyer's critical fact-finding report .... Australia announces a $35-million cut in imports from North America to reduce the nation's expected $85-million deficit this year.
Sept. 3	India asks the General Assembly to take action on South Africa's refusal to comply with an Assembly resolution on treatment of Indian nationals.	A British military court in Hamburg sentences 14 former Gestapo officials to death for killing 50 Allied airmen who attempted to escape from a Silesian prison camp in 1944.		Ecuador's Vice President Mariano Suarez Veintimilla proclaims himself acting president and forms a conservative government in Quito, while Maj. Sergio Enrique Giron forms a "Junta of National Concentration" in Guayaquil, representing the military units which overthrew Mancheno. Ecuador's Council of State calls a special congress session to name a new president.	
Sept. 4		Hungarian cabinet of Premier Lajos Dinnyes resigns, but Pres. Zoltan Tildy asks it to continue until the newly elected parliament holds its first session in mid-September .... Greek government averts a strike by 72,000 Athens civil servants by granting a 25-50% wage increase.			
Sept. 5		Britain and the U.S. agree in Washington on a plan for joint operation of Ruhr coal mines .... French Premier Ramadier wins a vote of confidence in the National Assembly on a controversial price control subsidy for the nation's coal industry .... British Trades Union Congress ends a five-day conference in Southport by voting to postpone nationalization of the iron and steel industry and supporting close British-U.S. ties.			
Sept. 6		Hungarian Deputy Premier Matyas Rakosi announces an income limitation of 3,000 florins ($273) per month and says the assets of wealthy Hungarians who have fled abroad will be confiscated.		Two-week Canadian National Exposition in Toronto ends with a record total attendance of 2,250,000.	
Sept. 7		Greek Liberal leader Themistocles Sophoulis becomes premier as head of a new Liberal-Populist coalition cabinet .... Moscow residents stage a large celebration to mark the city's 800th anniversary.		Truman sails from Rio de Janeiro to Washington on the battleship *Missouri*, ending a seven-day Brazilian visit.	Russia refuses to participate in a Big Four conference on Korea proposed by the U.S.

A	B	C	D	E
Includes developments that affect more than one world region, international organizations and important meetings of major world leaders.	*Includes all domestic and regional developments in Europe, including the Soviet Union, Turkey, Cyprus and Malta.*	*Includes all domestic and regional developments in Africa and the Middle East, including Iraq and Iran and excluding Cyprus, Turkey and Afghanistan.*	*Includes all domestic and regional developments in Latin America, the Caribbean and Canada.*	*Includes all domestic and regional developments in Asian and Pacific nations, extending from Afghanistan through all the Pacific Islands, except Hawaii.*

U.S. Politics & Social Issues	U.S. Foreign Policy & Defense	U.S. Economy & Environment	Science, Technology & Nature	Culture, Leisure & Life Style	
A House Un-American Activities Comm. report charges that the U.S. Civil Rights Congress is a "Communist front organization" set up to protect members in trouble with the law.		In his annual Labor Day message, Truman urges an increase in the minimum wage, broadening of the Social Security system and introduction of national health insurance.	Paul Mantz wins the Bendix Trophy air race for the second time, flying in a P-51 from Van Nuys, Calif. to Cleveland in 4 hrs., 27 mins. at an average speed of 460.4 mph.		Aug. 30
	American Legion concludes its N.Y. convention with resolutions supporting the Marshall Plan and universal military training and opposing international control or inspection of atomic weapons . . . . Gen. Jonathan Wainwright, commander of U.S. forces which surrendered on Bataan in 1942, retires from the Army after a 45-year career.	CIO National Maritime Union signs a contract with four Great Lakes carriers guaranteeing a 40-hour week and an 11% wage increase.	U.S. Atomic Energy Commission reveals plans to continue studying the medical and biological effects of the atomic bomb on the Hiroshima and Nagasaki survivors.	184-year-old Touro Synagogue, the oldest Jewish temple in the U.S., is dedicated as a national religious shrine in Newport, R.I.	Aug. 31
		Speaking at a Labor Day rally in Kansas City, CIO Pres. Philip Murray asserts that organized labor is "determined to change the anti-labor complexion of Congress" and wipe out the "infamous Taft-Hartley law." AFL Pres. William Green tells a Chicago audience that his organization will defeat congressmen responsible for "the new wave of hostile, anti-labor legislation."	Cook Cleland wins the $40,000 Thompson Trophy Air Race in Cleveland in a converted Vought Corsair, averaging a closed-course record of 396.1 mph.	U.S. players retain the Davis Cup in tennis competition at Forest Hills, N.Y., with Jack Kramer taking the singles title.	Sept. 1
		Wholesale prices of 30 basic commodities again hit a postwar record of 276.26% of the 1930-32 average.		White House is re-opened to the public after a series of repairs and improvements costing $130,000.	Sept. 2
			Truman sends a message to the fourth International Cancer Research Congress in St. Louis announcing that the U.S. will distribute radioactive isotopes to foreign scientists for "medical and biological research." . . . . Returning from an Arctic expedition, Canadian geologist J.L. Robinson reports locating the North Magnetic Pole on Prince of Wales Island and says it shifts constantly in a 50-mile ellipse.		Sept. 3
	A Charleston, W.Va. U.S. district court voids the court martial conviction of WAC Capt. Kathleen Nash Durant in the Hesse jewel case, ruling she was a civilian at the time of her arrest.	Top CIO officials including Pres. Philip Murray refuse to file affidavits verifying that they are not Communists with the NLRB, violating the Taft-Hartley Act and jeopardizing CIO cases pending before the NLRB.			Sept. 4
Civil Service Commissioner Arthur Fleming announces that membership in a Communist front organization is in itself not cause for dismissal from federal employment.		Executive Bd. of the AFL International Ladies Garment Workers Union votes to establish a $1.8-million special fund to meet emergencies arising from the Taft-Hartley Act during the next three years.		Daniel Carpio of Peru becomes the 24th person to swim the English Channel.	Sept. 5
A federal jury in Kansas City convicts three local Democratic officials in a 1946 primary election vote fraud case.	Navy successfully fires a German V-2 rocket from the carrier *Midway* in the Atlantic, the first missile launching from a moving platform.				Sept. 6
		Officials of the 650,000-member AFL United Brotherhood of Carpenters and Joiners file affidavits verifying that they are not Communists with the NLRB.			Sept. 7
F	G	H	I	J	
Includes elections, federal-state relations, civil rights and liberties, crime, the judiciary, education, health care, poverty, urban affairs and population.	*Includes formation and debate of U.S. foreign and defense policies, veterans affairs and defense spending. (Relations with specific foreign countries are usually found under the region concerned.)*	*Includes business, labor, agriculture, taxation, transportation, consumer affairs, monetary and fiscal policy, natural resources, pollution and accidents.*	*Includes worldwide scientific, medical and technological developments, natural phenomena, U.S. weather and natural disasters.*	*Includes the arts, religion, scholarship, communications media, sports, entertainment, fashions, fads and social life.*	

	World Affairs	Europe	Africa & the Middle East	The Americas	Asia & the Pacific
Sept. 8					An Australian arbitration court awards the country's workers a 40-hour week, while Australian delegate Patrick Kennelley tells the Commonwealth Conference of Labor Parties in Toronto that Australia "will never allow colored peoples" to enter the country.
Sept. 9		British cabinet approves Bd. of Trade Pres. Sir Stafford Cripps' plan for raising exports next year and obtaining skilled labor for industry by reducing armed forces strength . . . . A U.S. military court in Dachau acquits former SS Col. Otto Skorzeny and seven aides of war crimes charges for sending German troops in U.S. uniforms behind American lines during the Battle of the Bulge.	British troops complete the forced evacuation of 4,311 *Exodus 1947* refugees from three transport ships in Hamburg, bringing the last passengers ashore after a three-hour struggle which results in 27 injuries.		Speaking before the Kuomintang Central Executive Comm., Chiang Kai-shek attacks "low morale and corruption" in the Nationalist government and says his 20-year leadership has been a "failure."
Sept. 10		U.S. and Britain approve a Ruhr agreement aimed at raising coal production in the British zone of Germany to 300,000 tons a day. The agreement gives the U.S. equal voice with Britain in the operation of Ruhr mines, provides for new mine equipment from the U.S. and transfers local mine operation to German management . . . . Britain concludes an agreement with Yugoslavia providing for screening of 20,000 Yugoslav refugees in Austria, who will either be returned to Yugoslavia or sent to Germany.	Security Council tables the Egyptian complaint against Britain after failing to adopt a Chinese proposal for direct Anglo-Egyptian negotiations.		French cabinet makes a "last appeal" to Vietnamese nationalists to accept autonomy within the French Union, leaving France in control of foreign affairs and defense policy.
Sept. 11	Concluding a Geneva conference, the U.N. Food and Agriculture Organization re-elects Sir John Boyd Orr director general and names an 18-nation World Food Council to act as a liaison among nations affected by the international food crisis . . . . U.N. Atomic Energy Commission adopts a U.S. recommendation for international operation of nuclear facilities.	British tanks and troops break up a strike of 60,000 German workers in Kiel and enforce an order for the dismantling of a large machinery plant for reparations . . . . Russian authorities in Berlin announce completion of the land reform program in the Soviet zone of Germany . . . . British Exchequer Chancellor Hugh Dalton urges the World Bank and International Monetary Fund to prevent "economic catastrophe" in Europe by granting immediate assistance until the Marshall Plan can be put into effect . . . . Labor Party wins a parliamentary by-election in Liverpool, remaining undefeated in postwar by-elections during the past two years.			Gen. Arthur Lerch, U.S. military governor of Korea, dies of a heart attack at 53 in Seoul.
Sept. 12		Polish government ends its third annual Congress of the Recovered Territories in Stettin after reporting that resettlement of areas taken from Germany is nearly complete.		Venezuela reports suppression of an armed coup attempt in Caracas.	
Sept. 13		Greek Parliament votes an unconditional amnesty for guerrillas who surrender within 30 days . . . . French Communist Party calls for a popular front of leftist groups to defeat Gaullist political forces in upcoming parliamentary elections.			
Sept. 14		Polish government denounces the country's concordat with the Catholic Church . . . . Moscow consumer cooperatives introduce food price reductions of 15-25%.			
Sept. 15		U.N. Security Council turns the Balkan dispute over to the General Assembly after Russia vetoes a U.S. proposal to keep the matter on the Council's agenda . . . . World War II officially ends for Italy, Bulgaria, Finland, Hungary and Rumania, whose peace treaties are formally deposited in Paris and Moscow . . . . Poland and Rumania sign a $1.2-million trade agreement in Bucharest.			A typhoon strikes Japan's main island of Honshu, causing 1,000 deaths and 1,616 injuries, with another 1,000 missing . . . . Gen. William Dean is appointed U.S. military governor for South Korea to succeed the late Gen. Archer Lerch.
	A *Includes developments that affect more than one world region, international organizations and important meetings of major world leaders.*	B *Includes all domestic and regional developments in Europe, including the Soviet Union, Turkey, Cyprus and Malta.*	C *Includes all domestic and regional developments in Africa and the Middle East, including Iraq and Iran and excluding Cyprus, Turkey and Afghanistan.*	D *Includes all domestic and regional developments in Latin America, the Caribbean and Canada.*	E *Includes all domestic and regional developments in Asian and Pacific nations, extending from Afghanistan through all the Pacific Islands, except Hawaii.*

U.S. Politics & Social Issues	U.S. Foreign Policy & Defense	U.S. Economy & Environment	Science, Technology & Nature	Culture, Leisure & Life Style	
A federal court in San Francisco orders that 330 Japanese-Americans who allegedly renounced their U.S. citizenship during the war be released from internment camps.	Pres. David Dubinsky of the AFL International Ladies Garment Workers Union announces plans to sponsor the immigration of 10,000 refugee tailors to the U.S. from Europe.	AFL Pres. William Green advises member unions to obey the Taft-Hartley Act by filing affidavits attesting that their leaders are not Communists .... A federal court in Ft. Worth, Tex. rules that anti-Communist provisions of the Taft-Hartley Act are legal in dismissing a case brought by the CIO Oil Workers International Union against the NLRB .... Civil Aeronautics Bd. approves the nation's first helicopter service, to be operated by the Yellow Cab Co. of Cleveland.			Sept. 8
Harold Stassen officially opens his campaign for the Republican presidential nomination by announcing plans to enter the April 6 Wisconsin GOP primary .... Edward Everett Blake, national chairman of the Prohibition Party, dies at 72 in Chicago.	Veterans of Foreign Wars ends a six-day convention in Cleveland after passing resolutions supporting universal military training and opposing open immigration of refugees.		Univ. of California physicist Isadore Perlman reports that the Berkeley cyclotron has produced high energy fission in light elements such as platinum, lead and bismuth.		Sept. 9
	State Secy. Marshall tells a news conference that Europe's declining economic condition will require immediate "interim" as well as "long-term" aid from the U.S. .... State Dept. announces that all nations depending on U.S. agricultural exports have been warned to expect a 10% reduction this fiscal year due to drought damage to the U.S. corn crop.	Interstate Commerce Commission approves a 15-25% increase in commuter fares charged by 13 Eastern railroads.			Sept. 10
Speaking at a Progressive Citizens of America rally in N.Y., Henry Wallace attacks the Democrats as a "war party" and urges creation of a third party in 1948 if the Truman Administration's foreign policy remains unaltered.	Commerce Secy. Averell Harriman, reporting on a study of U.S. economic capacity to help Europe, says the Marshall Plan will involve additional government controls over exports.			*The Outlaw*, directed and produced by Howard Hughes and staring Jane Russell, opens in N.Y.	Sept. 11
		Heeding the advice of UMW leader John Lewis, the AFL Executive Council in Chicago votes to boycott the NLRB by refusing to submit affidavits verifying that union leaders are not Communists .... Brotherhoods of Locomotive Engineers and Railroad Trainmen win a 15¢ hourly wage increase and end their eight-day strike against U.S. Steel's Union Railroad.	American College of Surgeons ends a five-day meeting in N.Y. after hearing a report on the discovery of heparin, a blood clot preventive, and witnessing a demonstration of surgery instruction by television.	Pittsburgh Pirate outfielder Ralph Kiner sets a major league record of eight home runs in four consecutive games when he hits his 48th and 49th homers of the season against the Boston Braves .... *Sporting News* names Brooklyn Dodgers infielder Jackie Robinson as baseball's rookie of the year.	Sept. 12
			Sailing ship *Atlantis* returns to Woods Hole, Mass. after completing an eight-week study of the mid-Atlantic mountain ridge.	Robert Riegel wins the U.S. Amateur Golf Championship in Pebble Beach, Calif.	Sept. 13
		Rep. Adolph Sabath (D, Ill.) urges the attorney general to launch price inquiries into alleged price-fixing by food industries as food prices continue to rise to record levels.		Jack Kramer and Louise Brough take the national men's and women's tennis titles in competition at Forest Hills, N.Y.	Sept. 14
Seven hundred white Catholics in St. Louis vote to seek a court order if necessary to bar Negroes from the city's white parochial schools.		Atty. Gen. Tom Clark orders district attorneys to begin local action against price conspiracies .... Teamsters Union Pres. Daniel Tobin files an affidavit with the NLRB verifying that he is not a Communist.	MIT Prof. Warren Lewis wins the American Chemical Society's Priestly Medal for his work in oil production and refining.	N.Y. Metropolitan Museum of Art announces an agreement to purchase part of the late art collector and antiquarian Joseph Brummer's collection, consisting mostly of medieval works, for $1 million.	Sept. 15

F	G	H	I	J
Includes elections, federal-state relations, civil rights and liberties, crime, the judiciary, education, health care, poverty, urban affairs and population.	*Includes formation and debate of U.S. foreign and defense policies, veterans affairs and defense spending. (Relations with specific foreign countries are usually found under the region concerned.)*	*Includes business, labor, agriculture, taxation, transportation, consumer affairs, monetary and fiscal policy, natural resources, pollution and accidents.*	*Includes worldwide scientific, medical and technological developments, natural phenomena, U.S. weather and natural disasters.*	*Includes the arts, religion, scholarship, communications media, sports, entertainment, fashions, fads and social life.*

	World Affairs	Europe	Africa & the Middle East	The Americas	Asia & the Pacific
Sept. 16	U.N. General Assembly re-elects Oswaldo Aranha of Brazil president as it opens its second regular session in Flushing Meadows, N.Y.	Citing Big Four failure to agree on an Austrian peace treaty, Britain formally ends its state of war with Austria to permit commercial dealings .... Yugoslavian forces occupy the Isonzo River north of Trieste and move up to the new Italian-Yugoslavian border immediately after the Italian peace treaty takes effect .... Hungary's newly elected parliament holds its first session and elects Communist Imre Nagy as house speaker.		Anti-Peron newspaper *Vanguardia* appears in Buenos Aires in an underground edition after being suspended Aug. 28.	Chinese Nationalist Vice Pres. Sun Fo indicates that China may seek an alignment with Russia unless greater U.S. economic aid is forthcoming.
Sept. 17	Appearing for the first time before the U.N. General Assembly, U.S. State Secy. George Marshall attacks Russia's "frustration of the general will" in major international disputes and urges measures to curb "abuse" of the Security Council veto. Marshall later confers in N.Y. with French Foreign Min. Bidault on economic problems .... World Bank and International Monetary Fund meetings end in London after the Bank admits Finland, approves an agreement on its U.N. relations and establishes a 10-man advisory board.			Ecuador's Congress elects Carlos Julio Arosemena acting president to replace temporary president Mariano Suarez Veintimilla.	Former Chinese Nationalist Premier T.V. Soong is named governor of rice-rich Kwangtung Province.
Sept. 18	Soviet Deputy Foreign Min. Andrei Vishinsky addresses the U.N. General Assembly, attacking the U.S. for attempting to propagate "a crazy idea of [American] world domination" and obstructing Russia's "work of peaceful reconstruction."	Bulgarian Supreme Court rejects Agrarian Party leader Nikola Petkov's appeal for commutation of his death sentence.			U.N. Security Council forms a committee consisting of the U.S., Belgium and Australia to mediate the conflict in the Netherlands East Indies .... Burmese State Secy. Lord Listowel announces Burma will receive its independence next January, to be followed by immediate withdrawal of British troops.
Sept. 19		Poland and Russia conclude an agreement giving Poland full control over the Baltic port of Stettin .... One million farm workers in northern Italy end a 12-day strike after being awarded pay increases and a reduction in work hours by the government.			Representatives of seven Vietnamese political parties reject the French offer of internal autonomy for Indochina after conferring in Hong Kong with deposed Emperor Bao Dai.
Sept. 20		Hungary concludes a trade agreement with the British and U.S. zones of Germany .... Cabinet reshuffle in Bavaria results in a state government composed entirely of Christian Social Union ministers.	British cabinet accepts the majority recommendations of the U.N. Palestine Inquiry Commission but urges the U.N. to share responsibility for putting them into effect.		Prime Ministers Jawaharlal Nehru of India and Nawabzada Liaqat Ali Kahn of Pakistan issue a joint statement renouncing war between their two states as "repugnant" to both.
Sept. 21		Representatives of nine European Communist parties (Russia, Eastern European states, France and Italy) meet in the Polish resort town of Mis-zlawkowice to develop a common response to the Marshall Plan and other U.S. foreign policy initiatives .... Gen. Lucius Clay of the U.S. military government in Germany reports a 22% reduction in hydroelectric power and a prospective 20-40% crop loss in the U.S. zone as a result of severe drought.			
Sept. 22		Sixteen-nation Comm. of European Economic Cooperation issues its report on European recovery, calling for $22.4 billion in American aid to Europe. The report also urges domestic reforms in European states, including balanced budgets and increased exports .... International Transport Workers Federation votes in Washington to admit German unions organized in the U.S., British and French zones.			

	A	B	C	D	E
	Includes developments that affect more than one world region, international organizations and important meetings of major world leaders.	*Includes all domestic and regional developments in Europe, including the Soviet Union, Turkey, Cyprus and Malta.*	*Includes all domestic and regional developments in Africa and the Middle East, including Iraq and Iran and excluding Cyprus, Turkey and Afghanistan.*	*Includes all domestic and regional developments in Latin America, the Caribbean and Canada.*	*Includes all domestic and regional developments in Asian and Pacific nations, extending from Afghanistan through all the Pacific Islands, except Hawaii.*

U.S. Politics & Social Issues	U.S. Foreign Policy & Defense	U.S. Economy & Environment	Science, Technology & Nature	Culture, Leisure & Life Style	
		CIO United Rubber Workers union, meeting in Boston, refuses to authorize money for court tests of the Taft-Hartley Act .... Wholesale prices of 30 basic commodities again hit a record high of 287% of the 1930-32 average.			Sept. 16
	James Forrestal is sworn in as defense secretary, with orders from Truman to complete armed forces unification immediately.	AFL International Brotherhood of Electrical Workers files the first test case against the NLRB's right under the Taft-Hartley Act to require affidavits from union leaders affirming that they are not Communists.	Warm Springs Foundation ends a three-day conference on infantile paralysis after hearing reports emphasizing lack of current medical knowledge on polio's diagnosis and treatment.		Sept. 17
		CIO Industrial Union of Marine and Shipbuilding Workers ends an 85-day strike of 3,800 drydock workers against the N.Y. Shipbuilding Co., accepting a 12¢ hourly wage increase and an 8½¢ increase for piece-rate workers.			Sept. 18
	Gen. Albert Wedemeyer submits a report on his China trip to Truman, recommending a five-year U.S. military aid program for China and encouragement of internal reforms in the Nationalist government.	Four thousand N.Y. and N.J. Teamsters union members strike against the Railway Express Agency in a pay dispute.		National Assn. of Broadcasters, meeting in Atlantic City, adopts a code which reduces broadcast advertising, bans dramatic presentation of "controversial issues" and sets standards for treatment of religion, race, marriage and other topics .... John Cosgrave, former managing editor of *Everybody's Magazine* and *Collier's Weekly*, dies at 83 in N.Y.	Sept. 19
Former N.Y.C. Mayor and UNRRA Director-General Fiorello La Guardia dies at 64 of cancer of the pancreas in N.Y. The U.N. pays tribute to him when his death is announced in the General Assembly .... House Un-American Activities Comm. subpoenas 43 prominent entertainment industry figures, including Walt Disney and Charlie Chaplin, for hearings on Communism in Hollywood.	Wallace declares in a Trenton, N.J. speech that he is willing to cooperate with Communists or "any [other] group that wants to promote understanding with Russia."	Sen. Robert Taft, speaking in Reno, Nev., defends congressional cuts in reclamation projects and cautions against "spending money too lavishly on public works in general."	A violent hurricane begins to disintegrate in Arkansas after cutting through the Gulf states in the past three days, causing over $26 million in damage and 90 reported deaths.		Sept. 20
St. Louis Archbishop Joseph Ritter warns the city's Catholics that they face excommunication if they continue to oppose the admission of Negroes to white parochial schools.					Sept. 21
Communist Party Secy. Eugene Dennis expresses preference for Henry Wallace among prospective presidential candidates .... Georgia Democratic Party's Rules Comm. adopts a "white primary" measure imposing racial segregation in primary voting.		A Cleveland federal court imposes $5,000 maximum fines on General Motors, SKF Industries and four other ball bearing firms convicted on price-fixing charges.	An Air Force C-54 completes the first transatlantic robot flight, touching down near London on a course from Newfoundland directed by ground controllers.		Sept. 22

F	G	H	I	J
Includes elections, federal-state relations, civil rights and liberties, crime, the judiciary, education, health care, poverty, urban affairs and population.	*Includes formation and debate of U.S. foreign and defense policies, veterans affairs and defense spending. (Relations with specific foreign countries are usually found under the region concerned.)*	*Includes business, labor, agriculture, taxation, transportation, consumer affairs, monetary and fiscal policy, natural resources, pollution and accidents.*	*Includes worldwide scientific, medical and technological developments, natural phenomena, U.S. weather and natural disasters.*	*Includes the arts, religion, scholarship, communications media, sports, entertainment, fashions, fads and social life.*

	World Affairs	Europe	Africa & the Middle East	The Americas	Asia & the Pacific
Sept. 23		Bulgaria's Agrarian Party leader Nikola Petkov, convicted of plotting to overthrow the government, is hanged in Sofia. Britain and the U.S. immediately protest the execution .... Hungarian Premier Lajos Dinnyes announces formation of a new cabinet, with five posts (including the ministries of defense and finance) going to Communists .... U.S. aid mission in Greece announces a $9-million grant to increase the size of the Greek Army.		Argentine Pres. Peron signs a statute giving women the right to vote.	Dutch Premier Louis Beel announces plans for an interim government preparatory to creation of a United States of Indonesia.
Sept. 24	Geneva Trade Conference approves a General Agreement on Tariffs and Trade to govern trade relations until adoption of the International Trade Organization's charter.		Transjordan bans Syrian newspapers and forbids listening to the Damascus radio due to tension over a Transjordanian proposal to unite the two countries.		Former Burmese Premier U Saw and nine associates are formally charged with the July 19 cabinet murders in Rangoon.
Sept. 25		Austrian Treaty Commission in Vienna rejects a Soviet proposal that food and other aid be denied to refugees who refuse to return to their native countries .... Slovak cabinet head Gustav Husak rejects Czech Communist demands for a political investigation of all Slovak citizens.			Pakistan announces that 4,000 Moslem refugees aboard a train leaving East Punjab are dead, missing or wounded after an attack by a Hindu-Sikh mob .... Chief Tokyo war crimes prosecutor Joseph Keenan announces that "thorough investigation" has convinced Allied authorities not to bring charges against Emperor Hirohito .... Burma's Constituent Assembly elects Sao Shwe Thaik provisional president and Thakin Nu provisional premier of the Burmese Union.
Sept. 26			British Colonial Secy. Arthur Creech Jones tells the General Assembly's Comm. on Palestine that Britain will relinquish its Palestine mandate at an early date regardless of the U.N.'s ability to reach a settlement of the Jewish-Arab dispute .... Jewish terrorists kill four British constables in a $180,000 Tel Aviv bank robbery .... Former State Secy. Edward Stettinius and the Liberian government announce plans to establish a private company which will develop the country's natural resources.		Russian representatives on the deadlocked U.S.-Soviet Joint Trusteeship Comm. in Seoul propose that both sides withdraw their troops from Korea by 1948 and allow establishment of a native government.
Sept. 27		Yugoslavian Pres. Tito invites seven prominent Americans, including former State Secy. James Byrnes and author John Gunther, to visit Yugoslavia and "see for themselves" that the country is not menacing Greece.		Colombia cedes to Ecuador the 772-square-mile San Miguel Triangle, which the two countries have disputed for 25 years .... Former Nicaraguan President and Conservative Party leader Emiliano Chamorro is exiled to El Salvador on subversion charges.	
Sept. 28		Rumanian Communist and Socialist Democratic parties announce plans to merge into a United Workers Party.			
Sept. 29		British P.M. Attlee creates a Ministry of Economic Affairs, appointing Bd. of Trade Pres. Sir Stafford Cripps to direct it as minister without portfolio.	An Irgun Zvai Leumi squad bombs the Haifa police station in retaliation for the deportation of the *Exodus 1947* refugees, causing 10 deaths and 46 injuries.	Cuban government announces the suppression of a revolutionary plot on Cuban soil against Pres. Raphael Trujillo of the Dominican Republic.	Nationalist government files embezzlement charges in Shanghai against 13 officials of the Chinese National Relief Administration.
Sept. 30	U.N. General Assembly votes to seat Yemen and Pakistan, raising U.N. membership to 57 nations. Argentina and Canada are named temporary members of the Security Council, but the Council deadlocks on the choice of a third temporary member, with Russia favoring the Ukraine and the U.S. favoring India.	Bizonal Economic Council in Frankfurt enacts a law for confiscating livestock and meat products required to sustain the population of the U.S. and British zones through the winter.		Mexican government completes payment of a $29-million settlement for expropriated American oil property.	
Oct. 1	Russia's 21st and 22nd vetoes block the admission of Italy and Finland to the U.N. after the membership applications of Hungary, Rumania and Bulgaria fail to gain a two-thirds majority in the Security Council.	British government's new austerity measures take effect, including increased railroad fares and coal prices and a reduction in the clothing ration .... U.S. resumes full diplomatic relations with Bulgaria to "keep itself informed concerning developments" there .... Dragoljub Yovanovich, leader of the Serbian Peasant Party, goes on trial in Belgrade on charges of espionage and treason.			Gen. Nguyen Van Xuan becomes Premier of the Republic of Cochin-China following the resignation of Le Van Hoach .... Nationalist forces report capturing the Communist-held port of Chefoo on the Shantung Peninsula.
	A	B	C	D	E
	Includes developments that affect more than one world region, international organizations and important meetings of major world leaders.	*Includes all domestic and regional developments in Europe, including the Soviet Union, Turkey, Cyprus and Malta.*	*Includes all domestic and regional developments in Africa and the Middle East, including Iraq and Iran and excluding Cyprus, Turkey and Afghanistan.*	*Includes all domestic and regional developments in Latin America, the Caribbean and Canada.*	*Includes all domestic and regional developments in Asian and Pacific nations, extending from Afghanistan through all the Pacific Islands, except Hawaii.*

U.S. Politics & Social Issues	U.S. Foreign Policy & Defense	U.S. Economy & Environment	Science, Technology & Nature	Culture, Leisure & Life Style	
				Ingrid Bergman's performance in *Spellbound* wins top European honors at the Venice Film Festival.	Sept. 23
				Pulitzer Prize-winning historian Andrew Cunningham McLaughlin, author of *Constitutional History of the U.S.*, dies at 86 in Chicago.	Sept. 24
	Truman names Gen. Carl Spaatz, wartime commander of the Army Strategic Air Force, chief of staff of the newly independent Air Force.	Truman announces a nationwide "waste less" campaign to conserve food products that will affect the nation's grain supplies and ability to aid European states. . . . A joint congressional panel ends four days of price hearings in N.Y. as its chairman, Sen. Ralph Flanders (R, Vt.), declares no evidence of profiteering has been uncovered.		Cannes Film Festival names *Crossfire, Ziegfeld Follies of 1946, Dumbo, Antoine and Antoinette, The Hated* and *Storms in Poland* as the best films of 1947.	Sept. 25
House Un-American Activities Comm. recommends deportation, perjury and illegal entry proceedings against former German Communist Johannes Eisler, a Hollywood writer and brother of Gerhard Eisler.		Ford Motors announces that UAW members have rejected the company's proposed pension plan, preferring an 11½¢ hourly wage increase . . . . CIO United Electrical Workers union ends its Boston convention after passing resolutions attacking the Administration's foreign policy and demanding a boycott of the NLRB.	Canadian Radium and Uranium Corp. announces development of a radioactive compound capable of stimulating food plants to 20-50% higher yield.	Baseball Commissioner Albert Chandler announces that the Gillette Safety Razor Co. and Ford Motors will pay $65,000 for joint sponsorship of the first televised World Series . . . . Hugh Lofting, author of the *Dr. Doolittle* series and other children's books, dies at 61 in Los Angeles.	Sept. 26
Postmaster Gen. Robert Hannegan announces his resignation as Democratic National Chairman for medical reasons.	Commerce Secy. Averell Harriman's committee investigating U.S. capacity to aid Europe urges a program of "voluntary self-rationing" in the U.S. to help the country export 500 million bushels of wheat this year to Marshall Plan nations.	NLRB rules that employers cannot use their new right to demand bargaining elections under the Taft-Hartley Act if the unions involved have not filed affidavits attesting that their leaders are not Communists.	Harvard Observatory in Cambridge announces the discovery of a new comet, Eridanus, by astronomer M.J. Bester.	Armed wins over Assault in a $100,000 two-horse special at Belmont Park, N.Y.	Sept. 27
Senate Finance Comm. appoints a 17-man commission, headed by former State Secy. Edward Stettinius, to study social legislation.					Sept. 28
Truman appoints former Pres. Herbert Hoover chairman of a 12-man board assigned to study simplification and economy in the federal government.	Truman and cabinet members confer with congressional leaders in the White House, urging approval of a $580-million emergency aid grant for France and Italy to prevent imminent economic collapse and a possible Communist takeover in either of the two countries. Truman asks the congressional appropriations and foreign relations committees to meet as soon as possible and consider the aid request.	U.S. appeals court rules in Washington that under the Taft-Hartley Act employers do not have to bargain with foremen's unions.	Fire destroys the $5-million Grace Lines Pier 57 in N.Y., injuring 144 firemen.	Memphis bans the musical *Annie Get Your Gun* due to its use of an integrated cast.	Sept. 29
Alexander Chambliss, Tennessee Supreme Court justice who wrote the only dissenting opinion in the Scopes "monkey trial," dies at 83 in Jacksonville, Fla.		Chicago Transit Authority takes control of the city's surface and elevated transit lines with payment of $93 million to private companies.		New York Yankees top the Brooklyn Dodgers, 5-3, before a record crowd of 73,365 in the World Series opener . . . . Henry Kallem wins first prize in the $35,590 Pepsi-Cola "Painting of the Year" contest for his painting *Country Tenement.*	Sept. 30
	The 45,000-ton aircraft carrier *Coral Sea* is commissioned in Portsmouth, Va.	West Coast Waterfront Employers Assn. closes the ports of Los Angeles and Long Beach in a dispute over union recognition with the CIO International Longshoremen's and Warehousemen's Union.		William Haines' war drama *Command Decision* opens to favorable reviews on Broadway.	Oct. 1

F	G	H	I	J
Includes elections, federal-state relations, civil rights and liberties, crime, the judiciary, education, health care, poverty, urban affairs and population.	*Includes formation and debate of U.S. foreign and defense policies, veterans affairs and defense spending. (Relations with specific foreign countries are usually found under the region concerned.)*	*Includes business, labor, agriculture, taxation, transportation, consumer affairs, monetary and fiscal policy, natural resources, pollution and accidents.*	*Includes worldwide scientific, medical and technological developments, natural phenomena, U.S. weather and natural disasters.*	*Includes the arts, religion, scholarship, communications media, sports, entertainment, fashions, fads and social life.*

	World Affairs	Europe	Africa & the Middle East	The Americas	Asia & the Pacific
Oct. 2		Yugoslavian Amb. Sava Kosanovich reports in Washington that private Americans invited to make an inspection tour of Yugoslavia have declined the offer.	Jewish Agency for Palestine officially accepts U.N. plans for the partitioning of Palestine into Jewish and Arab states.		
Oct. 3	A Big Four deputy foreign minister's conference on disposition of former Italian colonies opens in London.	U.S. military government in Germany approves a revised denazification law for the U.S. zone which will exempt an estimated 500,000 former Nazis from trial and hasten the end of denazification proceedings .... Slovakian State Defense Ministry in Bratislava announces the arrest of 55 political suspects in an inquiry into an alleged plot against the government.	Palestinian Arabs stage a peaceful one-day general strike to protest plans to partition the country.		
Oct. 4		Danish Premier Knud Kristensen resigns in the midst of a controversy over his criticism of a government-approved plebiscite plan for South Schleswig, which is to be allowed to choose between German and Danish nationality .... Annual British Conservative Party conference ends in Brighton as Winston Churchill challenges the Labor government to hold a new general election.			Renewed Communist offensive in Manchuria cuts the Peking-Mukden railway at many points and penetrates to within 10 miles of the Manchurian capital of Changchun.
Oct. 5		Representatives of nine European Communist parties conclude a secret conference in Poland by establishing a Communist Information Bureau (Cominform) in Belgrade to "organize and exchange experiences and ... coordinate the activity of Communist parties." In addition to Russia and its Eastern European neighbors, France and Italy are represented in the organization .... State Assembly elections in the Saar result in a large victory for candidates favoring economic affiliation with France .... Italy's Constituent Assembly gives Premier de Gasperi a vote of confidence after debate over the country's economic condition.			
Oct. 6		Portugese Premier Antonio Salazar reports suppression of a monarchist coup attempt with the arrest of six leading conspirators, including five generals.		Chilean government orders troops to take over operation of coal mines and arrests 30 suspected Communists in a two-day-old miner's strike .... Canadian Resources Min. J.A. Glen announces a decision to double the country's annual refugee immigration quota to 20,000.	Indian armed forces surround the princely state of Junagadh between Bombay and Karachi after its ruler decides to affiliate with Pakistan against the wishes of his predominantly Hindu subjects.
Oct. 7		British P.M. Attlee completes a cabinet reshuffle designed to bring younger men into the government, replacing Emanuel Shinwell with Hugh Gaitskell as fuel and power minister .... Rumanian government relaxes price controls on most foods to persuade peasants to stop withholding their products from the cities.			In a visit to the White House, Australian External Affairs Min. Herbert Evatt urges the U.S. to call an early conference of the Far Eastern Commission on a Japanese peace treaty despite Russian opposition.
Oct. 8		U.N. General Assembly's Political and Security Comm. approves creation of a 15-nation commission to supervise Greece's northern border .... French Economic Affairs Director Herve Alphand says France will discontinue U.S. food and fuel purchases within a week for lack of dollars .... Serbian Peasant Party leader Dragoljub Yovanovich is convicted on espionage charges in Belgrade and sentenced to nine years in prison .... Britain and the U.S. begin talks in Washington on reducing Britain's share of the $700-million yearly cost of administering the U.S.-British zone of Germany.		Chilean government deports two Yugoslavian diplomats as Communist agitators, charging them with provoking the recent coal miners' strike .... Canadian Chamber of Commerce ends its 18th annual meeting in Quebec by recommending creation of a national immigration ministry, a general taxation settlement with all provinces and laws equalizing labor-management responsibility for observance of contracts.	Allies order the elimination of two Japanese demobilization offices, the last remnants of the Imperial Army and Navy.
Oct. 9		Rumanian Socialist Party congress in Bucharest unanimously approves a merger with the Communists to form a single working-class party .... Agricultural experts from Albania, Bulgaria, Czechoslovakia, Hungary and Rumania confer in Belgrade on coordinating Eastern European wheat production.	Arab League Council, meeting in Lebanon, urges member states to station troops on Palestine's borders, to be used against Jews in the event of a Jewish-Arab conflict after termination of the British mandate.		MacArthur approves a 25% increase in the size of the Japanese police force but forbids a centralized police administration.

A	B	C	D	E
Includes developments that affect more than one world region, international organizations and important meetings of major world leaders.	*Includes all domestic and regional developments in Europe, including the Soviet Union, Turkey, Cyprus and Malta.*	*Includes all domestic and regional developments in Africa and the Middle East, including Iraq and Iran and excluding Cyprus, Turkey and Afghanistan.*	*Includes all domestic and regional developments in Latin America, the Caribbean and Canada.*	*Includes all domestic and regional developments in Asian and Pacific nations, extending from Afghanistan through all the Pacific Islands, except Hawaii.*

U.S. Politics & Social Issues	U.S. Foreign Policy & Defense	U.S. Economy & Environment	Science, Technology & Nature	Culture, Leisure & Life Style	
House Un-American Activities Comm. announces that the Immigragion and Naturalization Service has issued deportation warrants for Johannes Eisler and his wife.	Columnist Walter Lippman concludes a series of *New York Herald Tribune* articles criticizing the concepts of "cold war" and "containment" of Russia and proposing a "policy of settlement" aimed at getting foreign troops out of Europe.	NLRB issues its first temporary restraining order under the Taft-Hartley Act, ordering the AFL to end a 10-day strike in Albany, N.Y.			Oct. 2
		CIO National Maritime Union convention, meeting in N.Y., adopts a resolution to boycott the NLRB and Federal Conciliation Service.	Physicist Max Planck, Nobel Prize-winning originator of the Quantum Theory of radiation, dies at 89 in Goettingen, Germany . . . . American Assn. of Scientific Workers urges the U.N. to begin a study of bacteriological warfare, which it calls the world's "pre-eminent terror weapon."	Yankee Bill Bevens sets a World Series record by pitching a no-hitter for $8\frac{2}{3}$ innings in the fourth series game against Brooklyn. The Yankees lose the game, 3-2, in the ninth inning.	Oct. 3
NAACP convention in Montgomery, Ala. formulates plans to fight the Boswell amendment to the Alabama constitution, designed to restrict Negro registration in state primaries.	Senate inquiry into Howard Hughes' government aircraft contracts is resumed in secret session.				Oct. 4
		In the first televised broadcast from the White House, Truman urges Americans to observe a voluntary food conservation program, including meatless and eggless days, to help the U.S. increase its food exports to Europe.			Oct. 5
				New York Yankees take their 11th World Series title with a 5-2 victory over the Brooklyn Dodgers in the seventh game.	Oct. 6
	State Dept. announces a policy of dismissing as a "security risk" any employe who associates with suspected Communists, fascists or subversive "front" members.	NLRB rules that top AFL and CIO officials do not have to file affidavits under the Taft-Hartley Act verifying that they are not Communists. Leaders of individual unions must still file, however . . . . Interstate Commerce Commission grants U.S. railroads an emergency 10% increase in freight rates.		Larry MacPhail sells his share of the world champion New York Yankees to Dan Topping and Del Webb for an estimated $2 million.	Oct. 7
AFL announces its support of Hubert Humphrey, Democratic mayor of Minneapolis, for the Senate seat of Joseph Ball (R, Minn.), a Taft-Hartley backer.		National Maritime Workers Pres. Joseph Curran wins a fight for a change in the union's constitution giving the membership a deciding voice on policy and procedure. He still urges a stronger anti-Communist program for the union.			Oct. 8
	Defense Secy. Forrestal appears before the Senate Small Business Comm., testifying that development of Saudi Arabian oil and pipeline facilities is in the U.S. national interest and should be given priority over construction of facilities in the U.S. or Western Hemisphere . . . . U.S. Atomic Energy Commission tightens controls on the export of nuclear research equipment.		U.S. Public Health Service director Thomas Parran tells the American Public Health Assn., meeting in Atlantic City, that the nation needs 50% more doctors than now graduate from medical schools.	*High Button Shoes*, staged by Jerome Roberts and featuring Phil Silvers, Joey Faye, and Nanette Fabray, opens in New York to favorable reviews.	Oct. 9

F	G	H	I	J
Includes elections, federal-state relations, civil rights and liberties, crime, the judiciary, education, health care, poverty, urban affairs and population.	*Includes formation and debate of U.S. foreign and defense policies, veterans affairs and defense spending. (Relations with specific foreign countries are usually found under the region concerned.)*	*Includes business, labor, agriculture, taxation, transportation, consumer affairs, monetary and fiscal policy, natural resources, pollution and accidents.*	*Includes worldwide scientific, medical and technological developments, natural phenomena, U.S. weather and natural disasters.*	*Includes the arts, religion, scholarship, communications media, sports, entertainment, fashions, fads and social life.*

	World Affairs	Europe	Africa & the Middle East	The Americas	Asia & the Pacific
Oct. 10	Allied deputy foreign ministers, meeting in London, agree on formation of a commission to investigate conditions in Italy's former colonies.	Italy signs a protocal with the U.S. and Britain for return of $25 million in gold captured by the U.S. 5th Army, in northern Italy .... Russia announces resumption of production at the world's second-largest synthetic rubber plant in Voronezh.		Canadian Congress of Labor elects A.R. Mosher, head of the Canadian Brotherhood of Railway Employes and a strong anti-Communist, to his eighth term as president.	
Oct. 11		U.S. agrees in the General Assembly's Political and Security Comm. to drop charges of war guilt against Yugoslavia, Albania and Bulgaria in the Balkans dispute .... Austrian Peace Commission adjourns in Vienna after failing to reach agreement on any major issue in 85 sessions .... Sir Thomas Inskip (Viscount Caldecote), Britain's lord chief justice until 1946 and wartime defense coordination minister, dies at 71 in Godalming, England.	U.S. announces its support for the partition of Palestine as proposed by the U.N. Palestine Inquiry Commission but suggests territorial changes giving the port of Jaffa to the Arab sector.	Yugoslavia severs diplomatic ties with Chile in retaliation for the expulsion of two Yugoslavian diplomats.	Chinese Communist forces surround government troops at Tiehling, 40 miles northeast of Mukden, after cutting rail lines between Nationalist-held centers in Manchuria.
Oct. 12	Members of the International Air Transport Assn. agree in Rio de Janeiro on uniform passenger and cargo rates for world airlines.	Municipal elections in Rome result in continued leadership of the Communist-led People's Bloc, which polls 33.4% of the vote to the Christian Democrats' 32.8% .... German Social Democrats win State Assembly elections in U.S.-occupied Bremen with 41.5% of the vote to 22.3% for the Christian Democrats and 8.7% for the Communists .... Baron Henri de Rothschild, French financier and playwright (under the penname Andre Pascal), dies at 75 in Jouxetons, Switzerland .... Sir Ian Standish Monteith Hamilton, British commander at Gallipoli during World War I, dies at 94 in London.			
Oct. 13		U.S. and British occupation officials urge German food ministers meeting in Frankfurt to increase food collections and act against black market operations, estimated to absorb 30% of German food production .... Greek Premier Themistocles Sophoulis announces a new austerity program including strict price controls, elimination of luxury imports and special exchange rates favoring exporters .... Sidney James Webb, British socialist and author of the 1930 White Paper restricting Jewish immigration to Palestine, dies at 88 in Liphook, England.	Russia endorses Palestine's partition into Jewish and Arab states .... A bomb attributed to Arab terrorists damages the U.S. consulate in Jerusalem, injuring two employes.	Argentina grants Italy a $175-million loan for food and raw materials purchases.	
Oct. 14	U.S. delegate John Foster Dulles urges the U.N. General Assembly to establish an Interim Comm. on Peace and Security, authorized to consider world issues when the Assembly is not in session. Soviet delegate Vishinsky criticizes the plan as an attempt to bypass the Security Council and avoid the veto .... General Assembly's Economic and Financial Comm. rejects a Polish resolution to ban the Marshall Plan and other international economic projects conducted outside the U.N.				A joint report from the consular officials of six nations in Batavia informs the Security Council that Dutch forces have continued military operations in Indonesia despite the U.N. ceasefire order .... Allied authorities in Tokyo decree the breakup of any firm controlling more than 5% of a critical commodity and most companies formed by mergers since 1941.
Oct. 15		France, Italy, Belgium, the Netherlands and Luxembourg begin talks in Paris on establishing free convertability of their currencies to stimulate trade .... Russia announces completion of the 1947 grain harvest, which it claims is 58% larger than last year's harvest .... Opening the second post-war session of Rumania's parliament, King Michael proclaims good relations with Russia "the foundation of our foreign policy."	General Assembly's Trusteeship Comm. passes a resolution calling on South Africa to submit a trusteeship plan for South-West Africa by 1948.		French forces begin a drive to close the northern Indochinese frontier to arms smuggling by Vietnamese nationalists.
Oct. 16		U.S. and British authorities in Germany announce a 60% reduction in the number of plants in their zones to be dismantled and shipped for reparations .... A chartered French airliner crashes into the Mediterranean near Cartagena, Spain, killing 41 passengers.	British Colonial Secy. Arthur Creech Jones warns the U.N. General Assembly that Britain will not assume responsibility for enforcing the partition of Palestine and urges the U.N. to prepare to assume transitional authority .... Jewish Agency for Palestine Chmn. David Ben-Gurion urges the extremist Irgun Zvai Leumi to disband and join the official Zionist militia.	Chilean government announces the end of the 13-day coal miners' strike as 8,000 of 20,000 miners return to work.	
	A *Includes developments that affect more than one world region, international organizations and important meetings of major world leaders.*	B *Includes all domestic and regional developments in Europe, including the Soviet Union, Turkey, Cyprus and Malta.*	C *Includes all domestic and regional developments in Africa and the Middle East, including Iraq and Iran and excluding Cyprus, Turkey and Afghanistan.*	D *Includes all domestic and regional developments in Latin America, the Caribbean and Canada.*	E *Includes all domestic and regional developments in Asian and Pacific nations, extending from Afghanistan through all the Pacific Islands, except Hawaii.*

U.S. Politics & Social Issues	U.S. Foreign Policy & Defense	U.S. Economy & Environment	Science, Technology & Nature	Culture, Leisure & Life Style	
		Justice Dept. announces the results of an investigation of interlocking directorates, showing that the heads of 60 major companies were found to be on the boards of competing firms. The department threatens to prosecute those who refuse to resign from one of their positions.			Oct. 10
		Teamsters union members call off a 23-day strike against the American Express Agency in N.Y. and N.J. after N.Y. Mayor William O'Dwyer promises to work for creation of a special mediation board.			Oct. 11
		Federal Power Commission approves a permanent contract for the Texas Eastern Transmission Corp. to operate two pipelines feeding natural gas to Appalachia and the Northeast.		*New York Herald Tribune* reports Thomas B. Costain's *The Moneyman* and John Gunther's *Inside U.S.A.* as the best selling fiction and non-fiction books, respectively.	Oct. 12
				Allan Nevins' *Ordeal of the Union*, winner of the $10,000 Scribner Prize in U.S. history, is published in N.Y. by Scribners.	Oct. 13
	William Clayton resigns as under secretary of state for economic affairs.	NLRB opens its first hearing on an unfair labor practices charge against a union, brought by the Baltimore Graphic Arts League against the International Typographical Union for refusing to bargain collectively .... CIO International Longshoremen's and Warehousemen's Union ends a two-month West Coast strike for union organization of supervisory workers.	U.S. Coast and Geodetic Survey announces discovery of an 11,500-foot submarine peak 800 miles west of Seattle.	AP reports that major league baseball drew an all-time record total attendence of 19,954,832 in 1947.	Oct. 14
Draft Eisenhower for President League in Washington announces its slogan: "I Like Ike."	Former State Secy. James Byrnes' memoirs, *Speaking Frankly*, are published in N.Y. by Harper. Byrnes warns of Russia's intention "to dominate all of Europe" and urges increased nuclear weapons production in the U.S. to counter this threat.		Univ. of California Physicist Ernest Lawrence announces the first experimental evidence of nuclear forces that bind together subatomic particles, the result of research in the Berkeley cyclotron.		Oct. 15
N.Y. State Court of Appeals rules that falsely accusing a person of being a Communist or Communist sympathizer is grounds for a libel suit.	U.S. Atomic Energy Commission establishes a raw materials division to locate sources of uranium .... A Brooklyn federal court sentences former Army Sgt. Arnold Kivi to 18 months in jail for stealing atomic bomb photos from Los Alamos, N.M.	AFL convention in San Francisco reelects William Green president for his 24th term as UMW leader John L. Lewis loses his place on the AFL Executive Council .... U.S. brewers agree to cut their grain consumption by 25% in response to Truman's appeal for greater food exports to Europe.		Gitz Rice, composer of *Mademoiselle from Armentiers* and other World War I song hits, dies at 56 in N.Y.	Oct. 16
F *Includes elections, federal-state relations, civil rights and liberties, crime, the judiciary, education, health care, poverty, urban affairs and population.*	G *Includes formation and debate of U.S. foreign and defense policies, veterans affairs and defense spending. (Relations with specific foreign countries are usually found under the region concerned.)*	H *Includes business, labor, agriculture, taxation, transportation, consumer affairs, monetary and fiscal policy, natural resources, pollution and accidents.*	I *Includes worldwide scientific, medical and technological developments, natural phenomena, U.S. weather and natural disasters.*	J *Includes the arts, religion, scholarship, communications media, sports, entertainment, fashions, fads and social life.*	

	World Affairs	Europe	Africa & the Middle East	The Americas	Asia & the Pacific
Oct. 17				Cuban government arrests 700 political suspects when Communists call a four-hour general strike to protest their expulsion from leadership positions in the Confederation of Cuban Workers.	U.S. submits a proposal to the General Assembly's Political and Security Comm. calling for legislative elections in Korea by March 1948, followed by formation of a national government for the entire country .... British P.M. Attlee and Burmese Premier Thakin Nu sign a treaty granting Burma independence outside the British Commonwealth, effective Jan. 6, 1948.
Oct. 18		Athens Court of Appeals suspends the Communist newspapers *Rizospastis* and *Eleftheri Ellada* for the duration of the country's civil war.	British authorities in Palestine announce that Palestine Arab units have begun to replace British forces on the country's borders.		Chinese Communist radio announces the start of a land reform program abolishing landlord holdings and cancelling all debts in the countryside.
Oct. 19		Municipal elections in France result in a victory for the Gaullist Reunion of the French People, which gains 40% of the popular vote to 30% for the Communists .... Czech Social Democratic Party rejects a proposed merger with the Communists, uniting instead with the Slovak Social Democrats to form a national Socialist organization.			
Oct. 20		Polish Peasant Party leader Stanislaw Mikolajczyk flees Warsaw after being informed of government plans to arrest and try him on treason charges .... Soviet Foreign Ministry dissolves the Anglo-American Assn. of Correspondents in Moscow, formed in 1942 .... Conservative leader Alfred "Duff" Cooper resigns as British ambassador to France and is succeeded by Sir Oliver Charles Harvey.	Arab Youth Organization in Jerusalem urges young Palestinian Arabs to register for possible military service.	Brazil severs diplomatic relations with Russia due to "slanderous" attacks on Pres. Eurico Gaspar Dutra in the Soviet press.	Soviet delegates on the Joint Trusteeship Comm. for Korea leave Seoul as the State Dept. informs Russia that it regards Korean independence as an issue for the U.N. to consider .... State Dept. bans publication of the Wedemeyer report on China because it contains information "harmful to the interests of the countries concerned".
Oct. 21	Over a Russian protest, the General Assembly passes a U.S. resolution to set up a permanent Balkan Commission to watch Greece's northern frontier and conciliate or recommend Assembly action in any border dispute.	Princess Elizabeth, heiress presumptive to the British Throne, formally accompanies the King and Queen to the opening of Parliament for the first time as the Labor government announces it will seek to halve the length of time the House of Lords can delay measures passed by the House of Commons .... U.S. Aid Mission in Greece discovers supplies worth $75 million in warehouses and docks, kept off the market to maintain high prices.		Chile severs diplomatic relations with Russia and Czechoslovakia, accusing both nations of instigating recent unrest among coal miners .... Canadian government removes price ceilings on most meat products coincident with announcement of wage raises at two major meat-packing firms, Swift Canadian Co. and Burns and Co.	
Oct. 22		French Premier Ramadier dissolves and reorganizes his cabinet, reducing it from 24 to 13 ministers.	Iranian Parliament rejects Russia's demand for an oil concession in Iran and approves Premier Ghavam's bill for a five-year oil exploration program barring all foreign capital .... Jewish National Council in Jerusalem begins recruitment of a militia to protect Jewish urban centers.	Chilean government places four nitrate and copper-producing provinces under military control to prevent renewed unrest among miners and arrests the staff of the Communist daily *Siglo*.	Chinese Nationalist sources report a revolt of Turkic tribes in the northwestern province of Sinkiang.
Oct. 23	National Assn. for the Advancement of Colored People files a formal protest with the U.N. against racial discrimination in the U.S., including poll taxes, lynching, job bias and school segregation. The petition will be considered by the U.N. Human Rights Commission.	British Economic Affairs Min. Sir Stafford Cripps orders new curtailments in housing construction and announces a $100-million reduction in U.S. imports during the next year .... Rumanian government orders leaders of the Social Democratic Party, the last active anti-government political group, to appear before court on subversion charges .... Hungarian Parliament approves the death penalty for black market activity.	Iraqi P.M. Salih Jabur threatens to move troops into Palestine if the U.N. adopts a partition.	Argentine Pres. Peron and Bolivian Pres. Enrique Hertzog meet in the Bolivian frontier town of Yacuiba to sign a trade agreement.	
Oct. 24		Alexander Panyushkin succeeds the ailing Nikolai Novikov as Russian ambassador to the U.S.			

A	B	C	D	E
Includes developments that affect more than one world region, international organizations and important meetings of major world leaders.	*Includes all domestic and regional developments in Europe, including the Soviet Union, Turkey, Cyprus and Malta.*	*Includes all domestic and regional developments in Africa and the Middle East, including Iraq and Iran and excluding Cyprus, Turkey and Afghanistan.*	*Includes all domestic and regional developments in Latin America, the Caribbean and Canada.*	*Includes all domestic and regional developments in Asian and Pacific nations, extending from Afghanistan through all the Pacific Islands, except Hawaii.*

U.S. Politics & Social Issues	U.S. Foreign Policy & Defense	U.S. Economy & Environment	Science, Technology & Nature	Culture, Leisure & Life Style	
		CIO convention in Boston re-elects Philip Murray to his eighth term as president. Murray promises to make any merger with the AFL contingent on protection of CIO affiliate jurisdiction . . . . American Bakers Assn. and Associated Retail Bakers of America join the national drive to save food by agreeing to halt consignment selling and take other steps expected to save three million bushels of wheat monthly.		Mildred "Babe" Zaharias sets a women's world record score of 293 on a 72-hole course to win the Ft. Smith, Ark., Golf Open.	Oct. 17
	Interior Secy. Julius Krug issues a report on U.S. resources showing that the country can furnish up to $20 billion in Marshall Plan aid to Europe without damaging its own security or standard of living . . . . Nine members of the House Appropriations and Armed Forces committees, returning to Washington from a European inspection trip, assert that an aid program must be considered immediately to forestall the "complete downfall of Europe."				Oct. 18
			Air Force reports the discovery of three magnetic North Poles during its year-long polar exploration and research project.	New York City dedicates a memorial to the victims of the Nazi holocaust.	Oct. 19
Hollywood producers Jack Warner, Sam Wood and Louis Mayer testify before the House Un-American Activities Comm., accusing 14 film writers and four directors of Communist or other "un-American" sympathies.		A joint congressional housing inquiry begins in Pittsburgh, where committee members hear labor and management representatives from the construction industry testify on the causes of the current housing shortage.		Rinty Monaghan of Ireland wins the world's flyweight title in London with a 15-round decision over Dado Mariano of Hawaii.	Oct. 20
Actor Adolphe Menjou appears before the House Un-American Activities Comm., accusing the Screen Actors Guild of being "Communist-dominated" and citing *Mission to Moscow* and *North Star* as examples of Communist propaganda in Hollywood.		Dun and Bradstreet daily wholesale commodity price index reaches a new record high of 191% of the 1930-32 level.		Thirteen Southern governors end an Asheville, N.C. conference after approving plans for regional professional schools separating Negroes and whites.	Oct. 21
MGM script supervisor James McGuinness charges before the House Un-American Activities Comm. that "an active fifth column" in Hollywood wants to "destroy our government in the service of foreign ideology."	Maxwell Hamilton, U.S. minister to Finland, is appointed assistant to State Secy. Marshall to conduct preliminary negotiations for a Japanese peace conference.	U.S. circuit appeals court in Baltimore rules that a union is liable for damages if it fails to protect a worker against racial discrimination in collective bargaining . . . . Standard Oil of N.J. imposes a 15% reduction in gasoline deliveries to its service stations in the Eastern states due to a gas shortage.		Otto Preminger's *Forever Amber*, adapted from Kathleen Winsor's novel, opens in N.Y. Francis Cardinal Spellman and the Catholic Legion of Decency condemn the film, which brings a record first-day box office gross of $25,308.	Oct. 22
Screen Actors Guild Pres. Ronald Reagan and actor George Murphy testify before the House Un-American Activities Comm., defending the Guild against charges of Communist infiltration. John Garfield and several other actors form the Comm. for the First Amendment of the Constitution to defend entertainment figures accused of Communist affiliation . . . . Truman calls a special session of Congress for mid-November to deal with domestic economic problems and "the crisis in Western Europe."			Nobel Prize in Medicine goes to Carl and Gerty Cory of Washington Univ. for discovery of catalytic metabolism of glycogen and to Bernardo Houssay of the Buenos Aires Institute of Biology for work on the hormone produced by the frontal lobe of the pituitary gland.		Oct. 23
Sen. Robert Taft formally announces his candidacy for the GOP presidential nomination . . . . Producer Walt Disney appears before the House Un-American Activities Comm., attacking Conference of Studio Unions Pres. Herbert Sorrell as a Communist and calling the League of Women Voters a Communist front group.	Commodore George Seitz, U.S. military governor of the Marshall Islands, dies at 50 of a heart ailment in Honolulu.	Thirty-six U.S. distillers representing more than 90% of the domestic alcohol industry begin a 60-day shutdown to help save grain for export to Europe.	Crash of a United Air Lines plane in Utah kills 52 passengers, including Jack Guenther, managing editor of *Look* Magazine, and Chicago Cardinals football player Davis Burkett . . . . Roy Hopkins, camera designer and inventor of microfilm, dies at 66 in Rochester, N.Y.		Oct. 24
F *Includes elections, federal-state relations, civil rights and liberties, crime, the judiciary, education, health care, poverty, urban affairs and population.*	G *Includes formation and debate of U.S. foreign and defense policies, veterans affairs and defense spending. (Relations with specific foreign countries are usually found under the region concerned.)*	H *Includes business, labor, agriculture, taxation, transportation, consumer affairs, monetary and fiscal policy, natural resources, pollution and accidents.*	I *Includes worldwide scientific, medical and technological developments, natural phenomena, U.S. weather and natural disasters.*	J *Includes the arts, religion, scholarship, communications media, sports, entertainment, fashions, fads and social life.*	

	World Affairs	Europe	Africa & the Middle East	The Americas	Asia & the Pacific
Oct. 25		Victor Alexander George Robert, Lord Lytton, former British Viceroy of India and head of the League of Nations commission that investigated Japanese aggression in Manchuria in 1932, dies at 71 in Knebworth, England.			
Oct. 26		A leftist Peasant Party faction headed by Czeslaw Wycech takes over party headquarters in Warsaw following the flight of Stanislaw Mikolajczyk . . . . A Swedish Air Lines Skymaster crashes on Mount Hymettos, Greece, killing 45 passengers.		Argentina and Bolivia sign an agreement in La Paz providing for arbitration of all disputes between the two states.	Maharajah Hari Singh, ruler of Kashmir, unites his land with India despite a pro-Pakistani rising among his predominantly Moslem subjects. British Viscount Mountbatten accepts the move as a temporary measure, promising a plebiscite when peace is restored . . . . Japanese government publishes a revised code of justice which abolishes *lese majesty* and adultery as criminal offenses.
Oct. 27		Commenting on the Oct. 19 election victory of his Reunion of the French People, Charles de Gaulle demands changes in the French constitution giving the executive branch greater power and replacing proportional representation with a direct majority voting system.			
Oct. 28		France, Italy, Belgium, Holland and Luxembourg sign an accord in Paris for free exchange of their currencies, allowing any participant to use a trade surplus with one member state to cover a trade deficit with another . . . . Lord Mountbatten, last British Viceroy of India, is given the title Baron Romsey by King George VI.	American women's Zionist organization, Hadassah, votes "reluctantly" to accept Palestine partition.	Chilean government arrests 170 Communist union leaders in the Antofagasta and Iquique mining areas.	U.N. General Assembly's Political and Security Comm. begins debate on Korea, with Gromyko demanding immediate withdrawal of occupation troops from both zones and settlement of the Korean question in direct U.S.-Soviet negotiations.
Oct. 29		Belgium, Holland and Luxembourg formally ratify the Benelux Customs Union, due to go into effect Jan. 1 . . . . Rumanian National Peasant Party leader Juliu Maniu goes on trial in Bucharest with 14 aides on charges of treason and espionage.			
Oct. 30	Twenty-three-nation Geneva Trade Conference ends with the signing of a general agreement to reduce tariffs, import quotas and other barriers to international trade. The accord affects over half the world's trade, about $10 billion yearly.	French National Assembly gives Premier Ramadier's center-left government a vote of confidence after conservative gains in recent municipal elections . . . . Czech Vice Premier Jan Ursiny, chief representative of the Slovak Democratic Party in Prague, resigns at the urging of Premier Klement Gottwald.			U.N. General Assembly's Political and Security Comm. approves a U.S. plan for creation of a temporary U.N. commission to supervise election of representatives in Korea, who will then negotiate with the U.N. on terms of Korean independence.
Oct. 31	U.N. General Assembly approves a headquarters agreement with the U.S. which gives U.N. delegates diplomatic immunity in N.Y. but allows the U.S. to deport delegates and U.N. employes who break American laws outside their official duties. The Assembly rejects a Soviet proposal giving colonial territories associate membership on the U.N. Economic Commission for Asia and the Far East . . . . 1947 Nobel Peace Prize goes to the American Friends Service Comm. and the British Society of Friends Service Council for humanitarian work.	Rumanian National Peasant Party leader Juliu Maniu denies at his Bucharest trial that he plotted to overthrow the state but admits giving information to U.S. and British agents while seeking their aid in removing Rumania's Communist-dominated government . . . . Slovak National Council, dominated by the centrist Democratic Party, is dissolved by its Communist chairman, Gustav Husak . . . . Greek government announces a $120-million program of emergency taxes on business, property and luxury goods for military and relief purposes.		A predominantly military cabinet headed by Navy Min. Adm. Roque Saldias takes office in Peru.	
	A *Includes developments that affect more than one world region, international organizations and important meetings of major world leaders.*	B *Includes all domestic and regional developments in Europe, including the Soviet Union, Turkey, Cyprus and Malta.*	C *Includes all domestic and regional developments in Africa and the Middle East, including Iraq and Iran and excluding Cyprus, Turkey and Afghanistan.*	D *Includes all domestic and regional developments in Latin America, the Caribbean and Canada.*	E *Includes all domestic and regional developments in Asian and Pacific nations, extending from Afghanistan through all the Pacific Islands, except Hawaii.*

U.S. Politics & Social Issues	U.S. Foreign Policy & Defense	U.S. Economy & Environment	Science, Technology & Nature	Culture, Leisure & Life Style	
			Truman proclaims Maine a disaster area as forest fires sweep extensive timberlands, causing 17 deaths and an estimated $30 million in damage.		Oct. 25
A group of 25 entertainment figures, led by Humphrey Bogart and Lauren Bacall, flies to Washington to protest violations of personal freedom by the House Un-American Activities Comm.				Catholic Interracial Council presents the 1947 James J. Hoey Award for Interracial Justice to financier Julian Reiss and banker Clarence Hunter.	Oct. 26
House Un-American Activities Comm. Chmn. J. Parnell Thomas (R, N.J.) orders writer John Lawson removed from the witness stand when he refuses to testify whether he is or was a Communist. Thomas and two other Committee members recommend that Lawson be cited for contempt of Congress .... Twenty-one Negro locomotive firemen file suit in Washington against 20 Southern railroads and the Independent Brotherhood of Locomotive Firemen, charging them with violating two 1944 Supreme Court decisions banning racial discrimination in railway employment .... Federal district court in Washington drops treason charges against Edward Delaney, Jane Anderson and Max Koischwitz for insufficient evidence. All were accused of making wartime broadcasts for the Axis.	A White House meeting of 100 business, labor and industrial leaders hears State Secy. Marshall and other Administration officials review the European aid problem.	General Electric announces an employe pension plan to replace its 13-year-old profit-sharing plan, which terminated yesterday.			Oct. 27
House Un-American Activities Comm. recommends contempt of Congress citations for writers Dalton Trumbo, Albert Maltz and Alvah Bessie when they refuse to testify on whether they are Communists .... Oregon Gov. Earl Snell is killed with State Senate Pres. Marshall Cornett and State Secy. Robert Farrell, Jr. when their private plane crashes on Dog Lake Mt. in Oregon.				Mexican Baseball League promises to desist from player raids on U.S. teams.	Oct. 28
President's Committee on Civil Rights, headed by General Electric Pres. Charles Edward Wilson, submits a 178-page report on racial discrimination in the U.S. to Truman. Among the report's recommendations are creation of special federal and state investigative units for civil rights cases, elimination of poll taxes and specific laws against bias in housing, education, health and public services.		NLRB rules that a union failing to file affidavits required by the Taft-Hartley Act cannot appear on a collective bargaining election ballot with a complying union.	Rains help quench Maine forest fires, as damage estimates reach $40 million.	Baseball Commissioner Chandler suspends the Chicago White Sox and general manager Leslie O'Connor from professional baseball for refusing to pay a $500 fine for signing high school student George Zoeterman.	Oct. 29
German playwright Bertold Brecht testifies before the House Un-American Activities Comm., denying that he is or was a Communist.	Gen. Leslie Groves, head of armed forces special weapons research, claims that Russia will need 15-20 years to develop the atomic bomb without outside help .... House Agriculture Comm. members returning from a four-week tour of 22 states report that many U.S. farmers oppose the Marshall Plan and other foreign aid.	Justice Dept. files an antitrust suit in N.Y. against 17 investment banking firms controlling 69% of the securities issued over the past nine years. Among the firms named are Morgan Stanley and Co. and Lehman Bros.		French singer Edith Piaf begins a variety revue at the N.Y. Playhouse.	Oct. 30
	Navy accepts delivery of its first transport helicopter, the Piasecki HRP 1 Rescuer, capable of carrying a one-ton load and eight passengers at more than 100 mph .... American Legion executive committee in Indianapolis reverses its position on refugee immigration and approves limited entry into the U.S.	AFL Secy.-Treasurer George Meany signs an NLRB affidavit affirming that he is not a Communist.			Oct. 31
F	G	H	I	J	
Includes elections, federal-state relations, civil rights and liberties, crime, the judiciary, education, health care, poverty, urban affairs and population.	*Includes formation and debate of U.S. foreign and defense policies, veterans affairs and defense spending. (Relations with specific foreign countries are usually found under the region concerned.)*	*Includes business, labor, agriculture, taxation, transportation, consumer affairs, monetary and fiscal policy, natural resources, pollution and accidents.*	*Includes worldwide scientific, medical and technological developments, natural phenomena, U.S. weather and natural disasters.*	*Includes the arts, religion, scholarship, communications media, sports, entertainment, fashions, fads and social life.*	

	World Affairs	Europe	Africa & the Middle East	The Americas	Asia & the Pacific
Nov. 1		Local elections in England and Wales result in a victory for Conservatives and independent candidates, who gain 600 local council seats at the expense of the Labor Party. Cities where Labor loses control include Birmingham, Manchester and York.		An earthquake in the Peruvian Andes causes 233 deaths .... Office of Price Stablization ends rationing and distribution controls in Guatemala.	U.N. Security Council rejects a Polish resolution calling for immediate Dutch withdrawal from Indonesia and adopts a compromise motion again urging both sides in the conflict to take advantage of the U.N. mediation offer.
Nov. 2					
Nov. 3		A U.S. court in Nuremberg hands down death sentences for four SS leaders, including Oswald Pohl, head of the German concentration camp administration .... Polish Peasant Party leader Stanislaw Mikolajczyk arrives in London from the British zone of Berlin as a political refugee.	U.N. General Assembly's Committee on Palestine considers transfer of power provisions, with the U.S. urging a direct transfer from British authority to the Jewish and Arab governments. Russia demands a seven-month interim period of Security Council supervision following British withdrawal from Palestine.	Canadian government ends wartime distribution controls on sugar and molasses, the last distribution controls still in effect.	
Nov. 4		Austrian government charges Soviet authorities in the Russian zone with seizing property in an unauthorized land reform project .... Greek General Confederation of Labor calls off a general strike in Athens when the government authorizes wage raises of up to 30% .... Local elections in Scotland result in a net gain of 62 seats for the Conservatives.			India and Pakistan exchange notes charging each other with neutrality violation in the Kashmir dispute as Indian troops invade the territory.
Nov. 5		Polish government announces the capture of three Peasant Party officials attempting to flee the country, including party treasurer Wincenty Bryja .... French cabinet ends coal subsidies and raises the price of coal in an effort to reduce the budget deficit.			U.N. General Assembly's Political and Security Comm. approves a U.S. plan for creation of a nine-nation commission to supervise free national elections in Korea by the end of March 1948 .... British House of Commons passes the Burmese independence bill on the second reading despite bitter criticism from Churchill and other Conservatives.
Nov. 6	U.N. General Assembly's Political and Security Comm. passes a modified U.S. proposal for creation of an Interim Comm. on Peace and Security, empowered to consider urgent international problems when the General Assembly is not in session .... Allied deputy foreign ministers meet in London to discuss German peace terms in preparation for the next session of the Foreign Ministers Conference, scheduled for Nov. 25.			Canada formally invites Newfoundland to join the Dominion as a province.	
Nov. 7		Communist leader Ana Pauker succeeds National Liberal George Tatarescu as Rumanian foreign minister after Tatarescu loses a vote of confidence in parliament.			
Nov. 8		British government imposes potato rationing for the first time since World War I, allowing a weekly quota of three lbs. per person.			
Nov. 9				Ecuadorian Army reports suppression of an armed revolt in Quito.	Former Siamese dictator Luang Pibul Songgram overthrows Premier Luang Dhamrong Nawasawat's government in a bloodless coup in Bangkok .... China signs an educational exchange pact with the U.S., promising an annual payment of $1 million for 20 years to cover the cost of educating Chinese and American students in universities of both countries.
	A	B	C	D	E
	Includes developments that affect more than one world region, international organizations and important meetings of major world leaders.	*Includes all domestic and regional developments in Europe, including the Soviet Union, Turkey, Cyprus and Malta.*	*Includes all domestic and regional developments in Africa and the Middle East, including Iraq and Iran and excluding Cyprus, Turkey and Afghanistan.*	*Includes all domestic and regional developments in Latin America, the Caribbean and Canada.*	*Includes all domestic and regional developments in Asian and Pacific nations, extending from Afghanistan through all the Pacific Islands, except Hawaii.*

U.S. Politics & Social Issues	U.S. Foreign Policy & Defense	U.S. Economy & Environment	Science, Technology & Nature	Culture, Leisure & Life Style	
A Philadelphia rally staged by the Progressive Citizens of America to protest the current hearings of the House Un-American Activities Comm. is broken up by angry war veterans.	Truman's Council of Economic Advisers reports that the U.S. can support a $22.3-billion foreign aid program over the next four years and recommends restoration of some wartime controls to check waste and inflation .... Joint Chiefs of Staff announce creation of a unified command for the Caribbean under Gen. Willis Crittenberger.	UAW Vice Pres. R.J. Thomas refuses to sign an NLRB affidavit affirming that he is not a Communist despite a majority vote for compliance by the union's executive board.		Foremost U.S. racing thoroughbred, Man o' War, dies of a heart attack in Lexington, Ky.	Nov. 1
U.S. Communist Party announces it will not join the Cominform in Belgrade for fear of intensified repression.				Editors of *Musical Digest* name Leroy Robertson, professor of music at Brigham Young Univ., winner of the $25,000 Henry H. Reichhold Symphonic Award for his composition "Trilogy."	Nov. 2
	Former U.S. ambassador to Britain and career diplomat John G. Winant dies at 58 in Concord, N.H.				Nov. 3
State and local voting results in the election of Democrat Earle Clements as Kentucky governor, while Judge John Stennis wins the race to fill the vacant Mississippi Senate seat of the late Theodore Bilbo. N.Y.C. voters discard a proportional representation system under which two Communists won City Council seats last year .... A Brunswick, Ga. jury acquits former prison warden H.G. Worthy and four guards of unnecessarily killing eight Negro convicts.	Returning from a European visit, Columnist Walter Lippman writes in the *New York Herald Tribune* that Russia has lost the "cold war" and urges the U.S. to "push toward a settlement which permits the recovery of Europe and the world."	A 10-man tax advisory committee set up by the House urges the Ways and Means Comm. to initiate large cuts in personal and corporate income taxes.		Abandoning plans for a court test of their expulsion from the American League, the Chicago White Sox and general manager Leslie O'Connor win reinstatement from Commissioner Chandler by paying a $500 fine for signing a high school player .... Gen. George Patton's wartime memoirs, *War As I Knew It*, are published by Houghton Mifflin.	Nov. 4
	State Secy. Marshall refuses to order departmental hearings for 10 State Dept. employes dismissed as "potential security risks," claiming he cannot issue a full statement of charges "for security reasons." .... Senate War Investigating Comm. resumes its public hearings on the government contracts awarded to Howard Hughes' aircraft firm.	AFL Pres. William Green files an NLRB affidavit verifying he is not a Communist.			Nov. 5
Peter Cacchione, Communist member of the N.Y. City Council, dies at 50 of a heart attack.		NLRB bars the CIO National Maritime Union and the Retail, Wholesale and Department Store Clerks union, which have refused to file affidavits required by the Taft-Hartley Act, from union elections.			Nov. 6
A New Orleans federal court rules that equally qualified Negro and white teachers must receive the same pay.		A federal district court in Delaware dismisses a Justice Dept. complaint that purchase of the Consolidated Steel Corp. by the Columbia Steel Co., a U.S. Steel subsidiary, violates antitrust laws.			Nov. 7
U.S. Civil Service Commission names a 20-man Loyalty Review Bd. headed by Washington attorney Seth Richardson as the highest administrative appeal panel for dismissed federal employes.	President's Committee on Foreign Aid, headed by Commerce Secy. Averell Harriman, issues a report urging Congress to appropriate $12.7-17.2 billion over the next four years for Marshall Plan aid to Europe. The report also recommends expansion of the World Bank's lending operations and encouragement of private loans to Europe.				Nov. 8
		UAW Pres. Walter Reuther, speaking at a union convention in Atlantic City, charges UMW leader John Lewis with attempting to influence UAW politics in favor of leftist Vice Pres. R.J. Thomas.		United Artists releases Abraham Polansky's *Body and Soul*, starring John Garfield and Lili Palmer.	Nov. 9

F	G	H	I	J
Includes elections, federal-state relations, civil rights and liberties, crime, the judiciary, education, health care, poverty, urban affairs and population.	*Includes formation and debate of U.S. foreign and defense policies, veterans affairs and defense spending. (Relations with specific foreign countries are usually found under the region concerned.)*	*Includes business, labor, agriculture, taxation, transportation, consumer affairs, monetary and fiscal policy, natural resources, pollution and accidents.*	*Includes worldwide scientific, medical and technological developments, natural phenomena, U.S. weather and natural disasters.*	*Includes the arts, religion, scholarship, communications media, sports, entertainment, fashions, fads and social life.*

	World Affairs	Europe	Africa & the Middle East	The Americas	Asia & the Pacific
Nov. 10		U.S. military government in Germany proclaims a restitution law allowing original owners to file claims for property seized by the Nazis.			Siamese military dictator Luang Pibul Songgram names a new cabinet, promises legislative elections within three months and introduces constitutional changes restoring some powers to the monarchy .... India takes over the administration of the predominantly Hindu state of Junagadh on the subcontinent's western coast pending a plebiscite.
Nov. 11		British House of Commons passes a government bill reducing the length of time the House of Lords can delay a measure passed by Commons, while the cabinet announces a decree requiring 500,000-750,000 persons in non-productive occupations to register for work in essential occupations .... Rumanian Peasant Party leader Juliu Maniu is sentenced to life imprisonment in Bucharest for treason .... Italian Communist leader Palmiro Togliatti urges his party to "intensify agitation" against the cabinet of Premier Alcide de Gasperi as anti-government strikes and demonstrations sweep major cities in northern Italy.			Australia's House of Representatives passes a bank nationalization bill.
Nov. 12		Marseille trade unions call a general strike to protest a rise in public transit fares, while crowds storm the city hall and Palace of Justice. French General Confederation of Labor adopts a manifesto demanding that the monthly minimum wage be increased from $59 to $90 .... France and Poland sign an agreement giving French owners of nationalized property in Poland $57 million, about one-seventh the real value .... British Exchequer Chancellor Hugh Dalton introduces an interim budget to the House of Commons aimed at checking inflation and raising $832 million in additional revenue next year by sharply raising sales taxes and doubling taxes on profits.			
Nov. 13	Ukraine is chosen a temporary member of the U.N. Security Council after India drops its challenge, while the General Assembly approves a U.S. proposal for creation of an Interim Comm. on Peace and Security.	British Exchequer Chancellor Dalton resigns at P.M. Attlee's request, allegedly for disclosing budget data to the press. He is succeeded by Economic Affairs Min. Sir Stafford Cripps.	Britain rejects a U.S.-Russian plan calling for British troops to maintain order in Palestine during the transition period following the end of the British mandate. British delegate Sir Alexander Cadogan informs the U.N. of Britain's decision to withdraw all troops from Palestine by Aug. 1, 1948.	Some 140,000 members of Argentina's Metal Workers Union strike for higher wages at the largest plants of the nation's metal industry.	
Nov. 14	Allied deputy foreign ministers meeting in London fail to agree on an agenda for discussion of the German and Austrian peace treaties.	Britain's National Coal Bd. grants the country's 700,000 coal miners wage increases of up to $3 a week .... French cabinet increases public transit fares and gas and electricity rates in an effort to preserve the value of the franc.			U.N. General Assembly approves the U.S. proposal for creation of a U.N. commission to supervise elections in Korea. A Russian proposal for withdrawal of all U.S. and Soviet troops from the country by the end of the year is defeated.
Nov. 15		Poland's Parliament finds exiled Peasant Party leader Stefan Mikolajczyk guilty of treason and deprives him of his parliamentary seat .... Week-long civil unrest directed against the government of Italian Premier de Gasperi spreads to Apulia and Cerignola in southern Italy.			Nationalist leaders call U.S. State Secy. Marshall's proposal for $300 million in aid to China "a drop in the bucket" and urge a $3-billion program over three years.
Nov. 16		Polish Peasant Party, the government's last opposition, is reorganized under Joseph Niecko and other officials opposed to former party leader Mikolajczyk.		Striking Argentine metal workers vote to return to work after the government "strongly suggests" that employers grant a 36% wage increase.	
	A	B	C	D	E
	Includes developments that affect more than one world region, international organizations and important meetings of major world leaders.	*Includes all domestic and regional developments in Europe, including the Soviet Union, Turkey, Cyprus and Malta.*	*Includes all domestic and regional developments in Africa and the Middle East, including Iraq and Iran and excluding Cyprus, Turkey and Afghanistan.*	*Includes all domestic and regional developments in Latin America, the Caribbean and Canada.*	*Includes all domestic and regional developments in Asian and Pacific nations, extending from Afghanistan through all the Pacific Islands, except Hawaii.*

U.S. Politics & Social Issues	U.S. Foreign Policy & Defense	U.S. Economy & Environment	Science, Technology & Nature	Culture, Leisure & Life Style	
	State Secy. Marshall appears before a joint session of the Senate and House foreign relations committees to urge immediate authorization of $597 million in stop-gap aid to help France and Italy survive the winter. Sen. Robert Taft (R, Ohio) rejects the amount, claiming it would prolong inflation, high taxes and government regulation of production.	UAW convention in Atlantic City approves union Pres. Walter Reuther's decision to file an NLRB affidavit attesting he is not a Communist.		*Boxoffice* poll rates Ingrid Bergman and Bing Crosby the year's most popular performers .... Jean-Paul Sartre's *The Reprieve*, the second novel in an existentialist trilogy, is published by Knopf.	Nov. 10
	State Secy. Marshall appears before the Senate Foreign Relations Comm., urging a $300-million authorization for economic aid to China over a 15-month period.	UAW convention in Atlantic City re-elects Walter Reuther union president, while Reuther candidate Emil Mazey is chosen secretary-treasurer.	American, United, National and Braniff Airlines ground all DC-6 planes pending investigation of fire hazards after an American DC-6 catches fire in mid-air and makes an emergency landing near Gallup, N.M.	Darryl F. Zanuck's production of *Gentlemen's Agreement*, based on Laura Hobson's novel about anti-Semitism, is released by 20th Century Fox .... U.S. riders win permanent possession of Bowman Challenge Cup and International Championship Challenge Trophy at the National Horse Show in N.Y.	Nov. 11
		UAW convention in Atlantic City elects Richard Gosser and John Livingston union vice presidents, replacing leftists R.J. Thomas and Richard Leonard.	A total solar eclipse passes over the Pacific Ocean, the Aleutian Islands and the northern tip of South America, while a partial eclipse is visible along the West Coast of the U.S.	Columnist Walter Lippmann's study of U.S. foreign policy, *The Cold War*, is published in N.Y. .... Mrs. Montague Barstow (Baroness Orczy), author of the *Scarlet Pimpernel* series, dies in London.	Nov. 12
California Gov. Earl Warren authorizes his supporters to enter his name in the state Republican presidential primary but says he will seek no delegates in other states.	AFL International Labor Relations Comm. pledges support for the Marshall Plan after voting to create a "Democratic Information Bureau" to counter Communist propaganda in Europe .... House Select Comm. on Foreign Aid, headed by Rep. Christian Herter (R, Mass.), warns that serious domestic shortages in steel, gasoline and oil will result from State Secy. Marshall's long-range foreign aid program.		Nobel Prize in physics goes to Britain's Sir Edward Appleton for his discovery of the Appleton layer in the ionosphere, while Sir Robert Robinson wins the Nobel Prize in chemistry for research in alkaloids and other plant substances.	French author Andre Gide wins the Nobel Prize for literature.	Nov. 13
Truman assures federal employes that the Civil Service Loyalty Review Bd. will provide political suspects with a list of charges against them, which they will be allowed to answer. He denies that the board was created to conduct a "witch hunt" in the civil service.		UAW convention in Atlantic City ends after electing three Reuther supporters union trustees and naming 14 Reuther-backed candidates to the union's executive board .... Brotherhood of Railroad Trainmen and the Order of Railway Conducters sign with the nation's 132 Class A railroads for a 15½¢ hourly wage increase, affecting 200,000 workers .... Sen. Ralph Flanders (R, Vt.), who headed the Congressional Joint Economic Committee's Eastern state price investigation, urges "serious consideration" of meat, butter and egg rationing to halt rising prices.			Nov. 14
Cincinnati's City Council elects Albert Cash mayor. He is the first Democrat in the post since 1913.	A House Foreign Affairs subcommittee headed by Rep. James Fulton (R, Pa.) urges the U.S. to allow refugee immigration and deny aid to European states which bar refugees .... Henry Stimson and former War Secy. Robert Patterson form a Comm. for the Marshall Plan to Aid European Recovery, with 200 members drawn from business, labor, education and religious groups.	Truman releases the report of his Merchant Marine Advisory Comm. which recommends a $600-million program to build 46 passenger ships in four years.			Nov. 15
		CIO Amalgamated Clothing Workers union and the Clothing Manufacturers Assn. sign a pact in N.Y. giving 150,000 men's clothing workers a 12½¢ hourly wage increase.			Nov. 16
F	G	H	I	J	
Includes elections, federal-state relations, civil rights and liberties, crime, the judiciary, education, health care, poverty, urban affairs and population.	*Includes formation and debate of U.S. foreign and defense policies, veterans affairs and defense spending. (Relations with specific foreign countries are usually found under the region concerned.)*	*Includes business, labor, agriculture, taxation, transportation, consumer affairs, monetary and fiscal policy, natural resources, pollution and accidents.*	*Includes worldwide scientific, medical and technological developments, natural phenomena, U.S. weather and natural disasters.*	*Includes the arts, religion, scholarship, communications media, sports, entertainment, fashions, fads and social life.*	

	World Affairs	Europe	Africa & the Middle East	The Americas	Asia & the Pacific
Nov. 17	U.N. General Assembly passes a compromise resolution on Spain's Franco government calling on the Security Council to take "any action required," after rejecting stronger proposals due to U.S. opposition. The Assembly also recommends Austria, Finland, Ireland, Italy, Portugal and Transjordan for U.N. membership over Soviet opposition.	Banker Pierre de Gaulle, brother of Charles de Gaulle, is president of the Paris municipal council, defeating a Communist candidate.		Canada receives a $300-million loan from the Import-Export Bank for U.S. equipment and raw materials, while Finance Min. Douglas Abbott bans most luxury imports and urges an increase in the automobile excise tax to preserve the country's dollar reserves.	India's Constituent Assembly begins its first session as a temporary parliament, electing G.V. Mavalankar as speaker.
Nov. 18		Bratislava police arrest 206 political suspects in an alleged conspiracy to revive a separate Slovak state, while the Czech government reorganizes the Slovak Administrative Cabinet with a plurality of Democratic Party ministers.			
Nov. 19		French Premier Paul Ramadier resigns under attack from Communists and Gaullists for his failure to lessen the country's economic problems .... U.S. and British military authorities in Germany turn over management of the Ruhr coal industry to a German board responsible to a U.S.-British control group .... Austrian Parliament passes a bill introducing a new currency at one-third the value of the current schilling.	Nine-nation partition subcommittee presents its complete plan for the partition of Palestine to the U.N. General Assembly's Palestine Comm. The Plan provides for British withdrawal by Aug. 1, 1948, progressive turning over of civil authority to separate Jewish and Arab states and U.N. administration of Jerusalem and Bethlehem.	Mexico pays the U.S. a second installment of $2.5 million for settlement of property claims by U.S. citizens.	
Nov. 20		Britain's Princess Elizabeth marries Lt. Philip Mountbatten in a Westminster Abbey ceremony.			
Nov. 21	U.N. General Assembly passes a U.S. resolution urging the Big Five to discuss revision of the veto rule and empowering the newly created Interim Comm. on Peace and Security to consider the problem .... Delegates from 63 nations participating in the U.N. Trade and Employment Conference meet in Havana to establish an International Trade Organization.	Hungarian Parliament adjourns after voting bills to nationalize banks and eliminate opposition parties .... U.N. Balkan Commission meets in Paris and votes to establish its headquarters in Salonika.			A U.S. military court in Yokohama sentences Japanese Capt. Yoshio Tsuneyoshi to life imprisonment for the death of 1,400 U.S. prisoners held at Camp O'Donnell in the Philippines.
Nov. 22	Allied deputy foreign ministers end their London meeting after failing to agree on an agenda for the forthcoming Foreign Ministers Conference.	Popular Republican Movement leader Robert Schuman receives a vote of confidence from the French National Assembly as he succeeds Paul Ramadier as premier. Communist-led political strikes, continuing for a week, idle nearly 500,000 French workers .... Strikes and anti-government demonstrations begin to subside in Italy after 1½ weeks, during which 22 persons were killed and 154 wounded.		Argentine government announces a system of bonuses for farmers and higher agricultural prices to speed marketing of grain.	
Nov. 23					Chinese Nationalist government concludes a National Assembly election, the first secret ballot vote in the country's history, with an estimated 20 million voters participating.
Nov. 24		French Premier Robert Schuman forms a centrist-conservative cabinet, excluding Communists and Gaullists.	Jewish Agency for Palestine begins registering Jewish young people for militia or labor service in the proposed new Jewish state.	Canada restores price ceilings on canned fruits and vegetables following a U.S. decision to restrict their export.	
Nov. 25	Big Four Council of Foreign Ministers begins its fifth session in London, meeting to discuss the German and Austrian peace treaties.	Mikhail Suslov succeeds Georgi Alexandrov as Soviet propaganda minister and becomes a Central Committee secretary.			Japanese House of Representatives passes the government's coal nationalization bill after raising the 1947-48 budget to $103.3 million .... Siam's Premier Khuang Aphaiwong extends the army's power to suppress anti-government elements until Feb. 12.
	A *Includes developments that affect more than one world region, international organizations and important meetings of major world leaders.*	B *Includes all domestic and regional developments in Europe, including the Soviet Union, Turkey, Cyprus and Malta.*	C *Includes all domestic and regional developments in Africa and the Middle East, including Iraq and Iran and excluding Cyprus, Turkey and Afghanistan.*	D *Includes all domestic and regional developments in Latin America, the Caribbean and Canada.*	E *Includes all domestic and regional developments in Asian and Pacific nations, extending from Afghanistan through all the Pacific Islands, except Hawaii.*

U.S. Politics & Social Issues	U.S. Foreign Policy & Defense	U.S. Economy & Environment	Science, Technology & Nature	Culture, Leisure & Life Style	
	Truman addresses the special congressional session which he requested, urging immediate approval of the $597-million emergency aid program for France, Italy and Austria.	Addressing the special session of Congress which he requested, Truman urges immediate passage of a 10-point anti-inflation program and asks for authority to impose rationing and price and wage controls. Republicans immediately score the anti-inflation proposals, called "the end of economic freedom" by Sen. Robert Taft (R, Ohio).			Nov. 17
		Senate Appropriations Comm. orders a thorough inventory of U.S. food resources and crop prospects to provide a basis for estimation of U.S. aid capacity.		Dartmouth, Mass. home of Richard Coffin is robbed of $200,000 in jewelry, including the 31.31 carat Amati diamond, 11th largest in the world . . . . Novelist Victor Serge, a Russian Communist Party member before being forced into emigration, dies at 58 of a heart attack in Mexico City.	Nov. 18
	Senate Foreign Relations Comm. unanimously approves Truman's $597-million emergency aid bill for France, Italy and Austria.	Dun & Bradstreet's commodity price index reaches another record high of 293.94% of the 1930-32 index.			Nov. 19
	N.Y. Gov. Thomas Dewey charges Truman with abandoning China to "Communist conquest" and criticizes the President's address to Congress for not dealing with the Far East.	Truman accepts Charles Luckman's resignation as chairman of the Citizens Food Comm. and transfers the group's food conservation activities to the Cabinet Food Comm., consisting of the state, agriculture and commerce secretaries.		Baseball Writers Assn. names Boston Braves third baseman Bob Elliott the National League's most valuable player of 1947.	Nov. 20
	Truman appoints Gen. Omar Bradley as chief of staff of the Army to succeed Eisenhower when he retires.				Nov. 21
James Davis, former secretary of labor and Republican senator from Pennsylvania, dies at 74 in Takoma Park, Md. . . . . Federal Council of Churches of Christ executive committee urges revision of U.S. immigration and naturalization laws to give equality to Orientals.		NLRB dismisses petitions for hearings filed by 14 unions that have refused to submit information required by the Taft-Hartley Act.	U.S. Commodore Finn Ronne's South Polar expedition reports that it has mapped 100,000 miles of hitherto unexplored territory in the vicinity of the Filchner Ice Shelf.	New York Yankees demand an investigation of the sale of seven St. Louis Browns players to three other American League clubs, netting $390,000 for the Browns.	Nov. 22
	World's largest transport plane, the six-engine Consolidated Vultee XC-99, is successfully test flown at San Diego, Calif.	CIO Amalgamated Clothing Workers union gains a 10% raise for 18,000 workers in 107 eastern Pennsylvania shirt factories.			Nov. 23
House votes overwhelmingly to cite 10 film writers and executives, including Ring Lardner and Robert Scott, for contempt of Congress as recommended by the Un-American Activities Comm. . . . . *Chicago Tribune* publisher Robert McCormick announces his support for Sen. Robert Taft as Republican presidential candidate.	Truman asks Congress for a $490-million supplementary appropriation for occupied areas, necessitated by Britain's withdrawal of dollar support payments in the U.S.-British zone of Germany . . . . Speaking in N.Y., Gov. Thomas Dewey urges a "two-ocean foreign policy," including military aid for the Chinese Nationalist government.	AFL International Typographical Union's Chicago local strikes against the city's six daily newspapers for wage increases.	Southern Medical Assn., meeting in Baltimore, drops its ban on attendance of Negro physicians at its scientific sessions.	John Steinbeck's novel *The Pearl* is published in N.Y.	Nov. 24
U.S. Motion Picture Assn. Pres. Eric Johnston announces that the 10 film writers and producers indicted yesterday for contempt of Congress will be ousted from their jobs, and asks for laws enabling the entertainment industry "to rid itself of subversive, disloyal elements." . . . . Federal district court in Washington issues a temporary order barring the Brotherhood of Locomotive Firemen and Enginemen from racial discrimination in promotions . . . . Postmaster Gen. Robert Hannegan resigns to become president of the St. Louis Cardinals. Truman nominates Asst. Postmaster Gen. James Donaldson to succeed him.		Top officials of the UAW Allis Chalmers local in Milwaukee resign in protest against signing NLRB affidavits as required by the union's Atlantic City convention.		St. Louis syndicate headed by Postmaster Gen. Hannegan buys Sam Breadon's 75% interest in the Cardinals and their 16-team minor league farm system for an estimated $3 million.	Nov. 25

F	G	H	I	J
Includes elections, federal-state relations, civil rights and liberties, crime, the judiciary, education, health care, poverty, urban affairs and population.	*Includes formation and debate of U.S. foreign and defense policies, veterans affairs and defense spending. (Relations with specific foreign countries are usually found under the region concerned.)*	*Includes business, labor, agriculture, taxation, transportation, consumer affairs, monetary and fiscal policy, natural resources, pollution and accidents.*	*Includes worldwide scientific, medical and technological developments, natural phenomena, U.S. weather and natural disasters.*	*Includes the arts, religion, scholarship, communications media, sports, entertainment, fashions, fads and social life.*

	World Affairs	Europe	Africa & the Middle East	The Americas	Asia & the Pacific
Nov. 26		French labor leaders reject a government plea to end extensive walkouts in return for a $12 monthly cost-of-living increase.			
Nov. 27	Allied Foreign Ministers Conference in London agrees on an agenda for discussion of the German and Austrian peace treaties . . . . International Civil Aviation Conference ends a 24-day Geneva meeting without reaching an agreement on commercial air rights.	Yugoslavian Pres. Tito and Bulgarian Premier Dimitrov sign a mutual assistance pact in Sofia . . . . Italian government devalues the lira 68% in an effort to end black market trading of dollars.			Australian Governor Gen. W.J. McKell signs the recently passed bank nationalization bill following P.M. Joseph Chifley's announcement of drastic restrictions on dollar imports.
Nov. 28	World Sugar Workers Congress in Havana demands a $5 daily minimum wage for sugar workers in Cuba, Puerto Rico, the U.S., Hawaii and the Philippines.	Former Free French leader Jacques-Philippe Leclerc is killed in a plane crash on the Moroccan-Algerian border.		Canadian Seamen's Union cancels strike plans after winning a $20 Federation raise from the Shipping Federation of Canada.	
Nov. 29	Seventeen-nation International Socialist Conference opens in Antwerp, with a U.S. delegation seated with observer status.	French Premier Schuman submits a "national defense" bill to the National Assembly, intended to curb strikes by nationalizing key industries and penalizing agitators. Paris police seize the plates of the Communist newspapers *L'Humanite* and *Ce Soir* for allegedly publishing "mobilization" orders against government anti-strike moves.	U.N. General Assembly formally approves the partition of Palestine into Jewish and Arab states by Oct. 1, 1948. Six Arab delegations walk out of the session, declaring they will not be bound by the decision. Jewish Agency leader Abba Hillel Silver hails the vote as "a turning point in Jewish history."		
Nov. 30		Bavarian government invalidates Hitler's will as it applies to his Bavarian property, which is made subject to seizure under denazification law.	Jewish-Arab strife begins in the aftermath of the U.N. decision on Palestine, resulting in the deaths of seven Jews. The Arab mayor of Nablus proclaims a *Jihad* (holy war) against Palestinian Jews.		Chinese Communists take the Manchurian rail center of Changtu.
Dec. 1	Four-day International Socialist Conference ends in Antwerp, after voting to create a permanent "Committee for the International Socialist Conference" (COMISCO) to offset the Cominform.	U.S., Canada and Holland agree to accept conciliation of conflicting claims to $500 million in Nazi assets left in 18 countries . . . . A hurricane off the Portuguese coast near Oporto kills 165 fishermen.	Egyptian Chamber of Deputies votes to help keep Palestine a totally Arab state.		Eldest son of Chiang Kai-shek, Gen. Chiang Ching-kuo, is named supervisor of an anti-inflation drive in Shanghai . . . . Britain, India and Nepal reach an agreement allowing Ghurka troops from Nepal to continue serving in the British Army.
Dec. 2		Gen. William Livesay, head of the U.S. military mission to Greece, announces plans to station 14 American officers in the field with the Greek Army as observers and advisers.	Palestinian Arabs begin a three-day general strike against partition and destroy a three-block Jewish business district in Jerusalem . . . . U.N. Trusteeship Council sets up a six-nation working committee to draft a constitution for the proposed Jerusalem international zone.		
Dec. 3	UNESCO ends its second general assembly in Mexico City after adopting a $7.7-million budget for 1948.		Palestinian Arabs clash with Haganah units in a six-hour battle on the Jaffa-Tel Aviv border, causing 12 deaths and 75 injuries.		
Dec. 4		French National Assembly passes Premier Schuman's strike control bill after five days of debate . . . . Russia and Czechoslovakia sign a trade agreement providing for annual exchange of $110 million worth of goods on each side, 17% of Czechoslovakia's foreign trade.	Egyptian government bans public demonstrations in Cairo after police clash with 15,000 anti-Zionist marchers.		
Dec. 5		Italian Republican party and rightist Socialists agree to enter an enlarged anti-Communist coalition cabinet headed by Premier Alcide de Gasperi.	British troops are flown into the protectorate of Aden to end Jewish-Arab strife which has caused 75 deaths in the past four days.	Chilean government breaks a 24-hour strike of railroad workers demanding a cost-of-living bonus by threatening to fire "undesirable" workers.	

	A	B	C	D	E
	Includes developments that affect more than one world region, international organizations and important meetings of major world leaders.	*Includes all domestic and regional developments in Europe, including the Soviet Union, Turkey, Cyprus and Malta.*	*Includes all domestic and regional developments in Africa and the Middle East, including Iraq and Iran and excluding Cyprus, Turkey and Afghanistan.*	*Includes all domestic and regional developments in Latin America, the Caribbean and Canada.*	*Includes all domestic and regional developments in Asian and Pacific nations, extending from Afghanistan through all the Pacific Islands, except Hawaii.*

U.S. Politics & Social Issues	U.S. Foreign Policy & Defense	U.S. Economy & Environment	Science, Technology & Nature	Culture, Leisure & Life Style	
Truman commutes the mail fraud sentence of Boston Mayor James Curley to the five months already served.	In a test vote on stop-gap aid to Western Europe, the Senate rejects a proposed $197-million cut in the $597-million French-Italian-Austrian aid bill .... Air Force Secy. Stuart Symington tells the President's Air Policy Comm. that the U.S. must have at least 630 heavy bombers and complains that current air strength is far below this level.	Commerce Secy. Harriman testifies before the Congressional Joint Economic Comm., claiming that allocation controls sought by the Administration would be applied to steel and "a very few" other commodities.	Army Signal Corps Laboratories reports development of the fastest known refracting photographic lens, with a speed of f/0.6.		Nov. 26
			Commodore Finn Ronne's South Polar Expedition maps 100,000 miles of the Palmer Peninsula.	Baseball Writers Assn. names N.Y. Yankee centerfielder Joe DiMaggio the American League's most valuable player for 1947.	Nov. 27
Federal Communications Commission authorizes the recording of interstate telephone conversations with the knowledge of all participants .... James Curley returns to Boston and resumes his duties as mayor, welcomed by a cheering crowd after his release from federal prison.					Nov. 28
Arthur Hill, Boston attorney who served as defense counsel in the Sacco-Vanzetti case, dies at 78 in Port Chester, N.Y.				Pope Pius XII issues an encyclical urging bishops to admit modern art and music to their churches .... CBS's *Your Hit Parade* names *Near You* as the most popular song, followed by *You Do, I Wish I Didn't Love You So* and *And Mimi*.	Nov. 29
				Ernst Lubitsch, German-born film director and producer, dies at 55 in Bel Air, Calif.	Nov. 30
	Senate passes the $597-million European stop-gap aid appropriation requested by Truman .... U.S. Atomic Energy Commission announces plans to construct a nuclear testing ground on Eniwetok Atoll in the Marshall Islands.			American Jewish Congress, representing 62 major U.S. Jewish groups, is reorganized as a permanent agency .... Rebecca West's *The Meaning of Treason*, a report on the British treason trials, is published in N.Y.	Dec. 1
Truman urges Congress to approve emergency aid for 61,000 Navajo Indians in four Western states who face hunger and cold this winter.		CIO Pres. Philip Murray announces his organization will seek another round of wage increases, the third this year, due to continuing inflation.		Notre Dame quarterback Johnny Lujack is named winner of the Heisman Trophy as the best college football player of 1947.	Dec. 2
	Adm. Louis E. Denfeld announces forthcoming cuts in Navy personnel at shore bases to maintain fighting strength due to a manpower shortage.	Dun & Bradstreet wholesale commodity price index reaches a record 298% of the 1930-32 average .... Agriculture Secy. Anderson tells the House Banking Comm. that price controls will be required on meat by next spring to avoid runaway prices.		U.S. Motion Picture Assn. votes stronger regulations to prevent glorification of crime on the screen, while the Screen Directors Guild bars Communists from holding office .... Tennessee Williams' play *A Streetcar Named Desire*, starring Marlon Brando and Kim Hunter, opens in N.Y. to favorable reviews .... Pope Pius XII appoints Bishop Francis Keough Archbishop of Baltimore and Msgr. Patrick O'Boyle Archbishop of Washington.	Dec. 3
Federal Loyalty Review Bd. announces the names of 90 organizations, including the Joint Anti-Fascist Refugee Comm. and the American League Against War and Fascism, listed by Atty. Gen. Tom Clark as "totalitarian, fascist, Communist or subversive."		NLRB rules that employers are not obliged to recognize or bargain with unions which refuse to file affidavits required by the Taft-Hartley Act.			Dec. 4
A federal grand jury in Washington indicts 10 film writers and executives for contempt of Congress for refusing to tell the House Un-American Activities Comm. whether they are Communists .... Atty. Gen. Tom Clark and Solicitor Gen. Philip Perlman file a Supreme Court brief arguing that real estate agreements designed to exclude racial or religious minorities are illegal.	U.S. State Dept. announces an embargo on all U.S. arms shipments to the Middle east.	AFL local presidents meeting in Washington approve creation of an $8-million political fund, to be financed through voluntary contributions by union members. Pres. William Green bars cooperation with the CIO in political affairs .... National Assn. of Manufacturers concludes a three-day N.Y. convention after presenting its own anti-inflation program, including reduced government spending, lower taxes and a wage freeze except in cases of higher production.	MIT radiologist Richard Dresser tells a Radiological Society of North America meeting in Boston that a three million-volt X-ray machine has been used successfully in treatment of cancer.	Joe Louis successfully defends his world heavyweight title for the 24th consecutive time with a split decision over Jersey Joe Walcott in N.Y.	Dec. 5

F	G	H	I	J
Includes elections, federal-state relations, civil rights and liberties, crime, the judiciary, education, health care, poverty, urban affairs and population.	*Includes formation and debate of U.S. foreign and defense policies, veterans affairs and defense spending. (Relations with specific foreign countries are usually found under the region concerned.)*	*Includes business, labor, agriculture, taxation, transportation, consumer affairs, monetary and fiscal policy, natural resources, pollution and accidents.*	*Includes worldwide scientific, medical and technological developments, natural phenomena, U.S. weather and natural disasters.*	*Includes the arts, religion, scholarship, communications media, sports, entertainment, fashions, fads and social life.*

	World Affairs	Europe	Africa & the Middle East	The Americas	Asia & the Pacific
Dec. 6	U.N. Human Rights Subcommittee on Minorities and Discrimination adjourns a two-week meeting in Geneva after drafting part of a U.N. declaration on human rights, including provisions for free travel within states and educational freedom for minorities.	U.N. Balkan Commission, meeting in Salonika, votes to establish observers only on the Greek side of the northern frontier after being denied access to Yugoslavia, Albania and Bulgaria .... Greek cabinet adopts and Parliament approves a decree prohibiting strikes "for the duration of the rebellion." The measure carries the death penalty .... British government introduces rationing of oats, barley and canned meat products.			Chinese Nationalist Navy begins evacuating the trapped 54th Army from the port of Haiyang on the Shantung Peninsula, while Communist forces attack Shantung railroads between Tsingtao and Tsinan.
Dec. 7		Local elections in Wuerttemberg-Baden result in a victory for the Christian Democrats, who gain 39% of the vote to 32% for the Social Democrats and 10% for the Communists.			
Dec. 8	Molotov presents Russia's economic demands on Germany to the London Foreign Ministers Conference, including four-power control of the Ruhr and abolition of the U.S.-British zone merger.	Yugoslavian Pres. Tito and Hungarian Premier Lajos Dinnyes sign a 20-year mutual assistance pact in Budapest similar to the recent Yugoslav-Bulgarian treaty.	Nations of the Arab League, meeting in Cairo, promise "immediate measures" to help Palestinian Arabs resist partition .... A two-month cholera epidemic begins to subside in Egypt after causing an estimated 13,000 deaths.		Dutch and Indonesian representatives open direct negotiations under U.N. auspices aboard the U.S. transport *Renville* in Batavia harbor.
Dec. 9		French General Confederation of Labor calls off a month-long strike wave which cost the country an estimated $500 million in lost production and 42 deaths from sabotage and disorders .... Russia breaks off negotiations for emergency shipment of grain to France.			
Dec. 10			Iranian Premier Ahmad Ghavam resigns after failing to receive a vote of confidence in Parliament on issues of domestic reform .... Jewish and Arab farmers in the Jaffa-Tel Avia area arrange a truce in civil strife, which has claimed 30 lives in the past three days, to save the orange harvest.	U.S. and Panama sign an agreement for a five-year American lease on the Rio Hato air base and 13 other military installations outside the Canal Zone.	Japanese Diet passes the government-sponsored economic decentralization bill, which allows the government to split corporations into smaller units.
Dec. 11		Bulgarian cabinet reorganization gives 13 of 23 ministerial posts to Communists, with Georgi Dimitrov continuing as premier.	South African P.M. Jan Smuts abandons an unpopular plan to import Italian farm workers, saying he will seek Dutch and Scandinavian workers instead.		
Dec. 12		200,000 workers end a one-day general strike in Rome after the Italian government agrees to provide an additional $18 million for public works and release 400 strikers arrested for disorder.	U.N. Trusteeship Council subcommittee on Jerusalem reaches agreement on a police force for the city and a legislative body preserving a balance of power between Jewish and Arab factions.	Police clash with students in Panama City demonstrating against the recent agreement on defense installations concluded between the U.S. and Panama.	India and Pakistan reach an agreement on the division of British India's assets, giving Pakistan $227 million of the colony's treasury balance, 17.5% of its liabilites and one-third of its military supplies.
Dec. 13		Stanley Baldwin, three-time Prime Minister of Britain before World War II, dies at 80 in Stourport-on-Severn, England.	Bombings attributed to the Irgun Zvai Leumi cause 16 deaths and 67 injuries in Jaffa and Arab sectors of Jerusalem.		
Dec. 14		Italian cabinet of Premier de Gasperi is expanded to include Right Socialists and Republican Party members .... Soviet government introduces several anti-inflation measures, including a 90% revaluation of the ruble, elimination of food rationing and introduction of price ceilings on food and consumer goods.	United Jewish Appeal, meeting in Atlantic City, sets a record goal of $250 million to be raised for Palestine and refugee aid.	Democratic Action Party candidate Romulo Gallegos is elected president of Venezuela in the nation's first popular presidential election.	
Dec. 15	Allied Conference of Foreign Ministers ends in London after failing to agree on terms of the German and Austrian peace treaties. No new meeting date is set.	Russia announces the withdrawal of its troops from Bulgaria under the peace treaty.		Leonardo Arguello, former president of Nicaragua overthrown last May, dies at 72 in Mexico City.	Japanese cabinet announces a 40% cost-of-living increase in the wages of government workers, effective Jan. 1.
	A *Includes developments that affect more than one world region, international organizations and important meetings of major world leaders.*	B *Includes all domestic and regional developments in Europe, including the Soviet Union, Turkey, Cyprus and Malta.*	C *Includes all domestic and regional developments in Africa and the Middle East, including Iraq and Iran and excluding Cyprus, Turkey and Afghanistan.*	D *Includes all domestic and regional developments in Latin America, the Caribbean and Canada.*	E *Includes all domestic and regional developments in Asian and Pacific nations, extending from Afghanistan through all the Pacific Islands, except Hawaii.*

U.S. Politics & Social Issues	U.S. Foreign Policy & Defense	U.S. Economy & Environment	Science, Technology & Nature	Culture, Leisure & Life Style	
				Brooklyn Dodgers reinstate Leo Durocher as manager for 1948 after his one-year suspension and appoint current manager Burt Shotton supervisor of the team's farm club network.	Dec. 6
		Eighteen railroad brotherhoods set up a Railway Labor Political League in Washington to cooperate with the AFL in political actions.		Nicholas Murray Butler, former president of Columbia Univ. and winner of the 1931 Nobel Peace Prize, dies at 85 in N.Y.	Dec. 7
Supreme Court unanimously sets aside the conviction of Eddie Patton, a Mississippi Negro sentenced to death for murder, on the grounds that Negroes were excluded from the jury which tried him.	Army Secy. Kenneth Royall, testifying before the Senate Appropriations Comm., announces Truman's intention to include western Germany in the European Recovery Plan .... Senate ratifies the inter-American defense treaty.		Truman issues an executive order reserving government ownership of uranium or other fissionable ore deposits in future sale or lease of public lands.		Dec. 8
House unanimously votes $2 million in aid to the Navajo and Hopi Indians .... State Dept. announces it reserves the right to dismiss employes as "bad security risks" even if they have been cleared by the Loyalty Review Bd.	Truman receives Herman Eriksson, Sweden's first ambassador to the U.S.				Dec. 9
			National Aeronautic Assn. awards the Collier Trophy, highest U.S. aviation award, to Lewis Robert for his work on ice-prevention systems.		Dec. 10
	House passes a $590-million stop-gap foreign aid appropriation, cutting $7 million from Truman's request and including a $60-million grant to China in the total amount.			Major league baseball teams reject the Pacific Coast League's request for major league status .... Washington and Jefferson College in Washington, Pa. severs its ties with the Presbyterian Church.	Dec. 11
		UMW Pres. John L. Lewis withdraws his union from the AFL in a dispute over observance of the Taft-Hartley Act (which Lewis opposes) and influence on the AFL executive board.			Dec. 12
	Senate-House conference committee agrees on the bill authorizing $597 million in emergency aid to France, Italy, Austria and China.	Senate Republicans issue an anti-inflation manifesto written primarily by Sen. Robert Taft, calling for increased production, reduced government spending and taxes, export restrictions, reduction of bank credit and consumer credit controls .... Justice Dept. sues the Du Pont Co. on charges of monopolizing the cellophane industry, claiming the firm handled over two-thirds of all U.S. cellophane sales in 1946.		Missouri Valley Conference, meeting in Kansas City, votes to ban all racial bias in its athletic affairs by September 1950.	Dec. 13
	Sen. Homer Ferguson (R, Mich.) is chosen to head the expenditures subcommittee which will continue the work of the War Investigating Comm. after its expiration Jan. 31.		Commodore Finn Ronne's South Polar expedition concludes an aerial mapping program covering 230,000 squre miles of hitherto unexplored territory.	Jimmy Demaret wins the Miami golf open and brings his tournament earnings for 1947 to $26,556, highest of professional golfers.	Dec. 14
Progressive Citizens of America executive council calls on Henry Wallace to become a third-party candidate for president .... Truman's 28-man Committee on Higher Education submits a report urging the immediate abandonment of racial segregation and racial and religious quotas in U.S. colleges. The report also proposes increased federal aid to double college enrollment by 1960 and establish a network of community colleges.	Adm. Louis Denfeld becomes chief of naval operations as Adm. Chester Nimitz retires.	Pres. Amos Ignacio of the CIO International Longshoremen's and Warehousemen's Sugar Workers Union in Hawaii announces his withdrawal from the CIO due to alleged Communist leadership. He and 4,000 followers plan to form a Union of Hawaiian Workers.			Dec. 15
F	G	H	I	J	
Includes elections, federal-state relations, civil rights and liberties, crime, the judiciary, education, health care, poverty, urban affairs and population.	*Includes formation and debate of U.S. foreign and defense policies, veterans affairs and defense spending. (Relations with specific foreign countries are usually found under the region concerned.)*	*Includes business, labor, agriculture, taxation, transportation, consumer affairs, monetary and fiscal policy, natural resources, pollution and accidents.*	*Includes worldwide scientific, medical and technological developments, natural phenomena, U.S. weather and natural disasters.*	*Includes the arts, religion, scholarship, communications media, sports, entertainment, fashions, fads and social life.*	

	World Affairs	Europe	Africa & the Middle East	The Americas	Asia & the Pacific
Dec. 16				Argentine delegation to the U.N. Trade and Employment Conference in Havana offers to lend "deserving" countries up to $5 billion for long-term recovery projects to supplement the Marshall Plan . . . . Honduras ratifies the Inter-American Defense Treaty.	
Dec. 17	U.N. Commission on Human Rights completes work on a Declaration of Rights for member states to consider.	In an agreement with Britain concluded in Washington, the U.S. undertakes to pay for most imports needed in the U.S.-British zone of Germany in return for control over their distribution and use . . . . New Italian cabinet of Premier de Gasperi wins its first test of strength when the National Assembly approves its dismissal of Socialist Mayor Antonio Giovanucci of Pescara, accused of incompetence and favoring Communists in the municipal administration . . . . Bulgaria and Albania conclude a friendship treaty obliging both countries to boycott the U.N. Balkan Commission.	Premiers of seven Arab League states conclude a secret conference in Cairo by calling on their peoples to "prepare for a struggle" over Palestine.		
Dec. 18				Holland agrees to build 30 ships over a five-year period for Argentina in return for food and raw materials.	
Dec. 19		Leon Jouhaux and other non-Communist labor leaders leave the French General Confederation of Labor in a disagreement over strike policy and establish a rival organization, the Workers Force . . . . Yugoslavian Pres. Tito and Rumanian Premier Petru Groza sign a Yugoslav-Rumanian mutual assistance pact in Bucharest . . . . Nobel Prize-winning Norwegian novelist Knut Hamsun is fined $85,000 in Oslo for writing articles favorable to the German occupation during World War II.			
Dec. 20			Haganah forces conduct a reprisal raid against the Arab village of Qazaza near Rehovoth, killing one inhabitant and wounding two.		
Dec. 21		First postwar election of deputies to local Soviets is held in the Soviet republics of Russia, the Ukraine, Moldavia, Armenia and Karelia, with Communists running unopposed.	Jewish Agency for Palestine officially approves Haganah reprisal raids on Arab villages.		
Dec. 22		Italy's Constitutent Assembly approves a new constitution for the Republic, with provisions for a seven-year presidency, universal suffrage, compulsory military service, equal rights for women in industry and prohibition of the Fascist Party . . . . Greek Army calls up new troops and forms a 50,000-man home guard to prevent a new guerrilla offensive . . . . German industrialist Friedrich Flick receives a seven-year prison sentence and five associates draw lesser terms in Nuremberg for using slave labor in their munitions factories.	Ibrahim Hakimi Al-Molk is named to succeed Ahmad Ghavam as premier of Iran.	Panamanian National Assembly votes unanimously against ratifying the Dec. 10 agreement allowing continued American use of defense bases in Panama . . . . Canada's AFL Seafarers International Union wins a basic $15.79 monthly raise from three West Coast shipping lines.	U.S. and Burma agree to a 15-year educational exchange program, to be financed by a $3-million U.S. grant.
Dec. 23		Catholic political leader Jakob Kaiser resigns as chairman of the Christian Democratic Union in the Soviet zone of Germany and sets up an "exile" political headquarters in the British sector of Berlin.		Following Panamanian repudiation of the Dec. 10 agreement on military installations, the U.S. announces it will begin immediate evacuation of all bases in Panama outside the Canal Zone.	
Dec. 24		Communist guerrillas in northern Greece proclaim a Provisional Democratic Government of Free Greece, with an all-Communist cabinet headed by Gen. Markos Vafiades . . . . Communist leader Emil Bodnaras becomes Rumania's National Defense minister, giving Communists control of all key cabinet posts . . . . Bulgarian National Assembly nationalizes most mines and factories.		Mexico announces a record federal budget of 2.3 billion pesos for 1948.	Burma's government outlaws private military forces.

	A	B	C	D	E
	Includes developments that affect more than one world region, international organizations and important meetings of major world leaders.	*Includes all domestic and regional developments in Europe, including the Soviet Union, Turkey, Cyprus and Malta.*	*Includes all domestic and regional developments in Africa and the Middle East, including Iraq and Iran and excluding Cyprus, Turkey and Afghanistan.*	*Includes all domestic and regional developments in Latin America, the Caribbean and Canada.*	*Includes all domestic and regional developments in Asian and Pacific nations, extending from Afghanistan through all the Pacific Islands, except Hawaii.*

U.S. Politics & Social Issues	U.S. Foreign Policy & Defense	U.S. Economy & Environment	Science, Technology & Nature	Culture, Leisure & Life Style	
	Truman announces that tariff reductions for Australia, Canada, France, Britain and the Benelux customs union agreed to at Geneva will go into effect Jan. 1.	A federal grand jury in Boston indicts the Boston Fruit and Produce Exchange and 12 egg dealers for alleged conspiracy to fix New England egg prices.		California Supreme Court rules against Hollywood producer Cecil B. de Mille in his effort to reverse his suspension from the AFL Federation of Radio Artists for refusing to pay a $1 political assessment.	Dec. 16
	Gen. Albert Wedemeyer appears before the Senate Appropriations Comm. to urge increased aid to the Chinese Nationalist government.	James Caffrey resigns as chairman of the Securities and Exchange Commission.	Benjamin Talbot, originator of the continuous basic open-hearth process of steel-making, dies at 83 near Northallerton, England.	Pulitzer Prize-winning novelist Esther Forbes receives the $150,000 MGM Novel Award for her forthcoming *The Running of the Tide.*	Dec. 17
	Reps. Andrew Somers (D, N.Y.) and Hugh Scott, Jr. (R, Pa.) introduce resolutions in the House calling on the U.S. to pay the transportation costs of 210,000 Jewish refugees in U.S.-occupied Europe to Palestine.	Senate passes a compromise anti-inflation bill which extends export and transportation controls for one year, authorizes Truman to introduce food conservation programs and permits voluntary agreements in industry and agriculture concerning allocation of scarce raw materials .... Truman names a 12-man National Labor-Management Panel, as required by the Taft-Hartley Act.		National Board of Motion Pictures names Charlie Chaplin's *Monsieur Verdoux* the year's best picture.	Dec. 18
	Special session of Congress adjourns after voting a compromise $540-million bill for stop-gap aid to France, Italy, Austria and China and hearing Truman's request for $17 billion to finance the full four-year European Recovery Program .... State Secy. Marshall reports on the London Conference of Foreign Ministers in a Washington broadcast, saying no peace settlement is possible until the struggle between the U.S. and Russia over the European Recovery Plan is resolved. He charges Russia with attempting to extend its control to all of Germany through its reparations demands.	House accepts the Senate version of the anti-inflation bill voted yesterday .... Truman signs a joint congressional resolution directing Agriculture Secy. Clinton Anderson to give Congress the names of all commodity exchange traders in an effort to prevent "profiteering" in commodity futures by government officials.		Sugar Ray Robinson retains his world welterweight boxing title with a sixth-round TKO over Chuck Taylor in Detroit.	Dec. 19
	Sen. Robert Taft attacks the proposed European Recovery Program, claiming it will intensify inflation and is not needed in Europe.				Dec. 20
	Gen. Claire Chennault, wartime leader of the Flying Tigers, marries Chinese Central News Agency reporter Anna Chan in Shanghai.	CIO Textile Workers of America ratify a wage agreement granting a 10% increase to 75,000 union members in Northern cotton and rayon mills.			Dec. 21
	Physicist Darol Froman is named scientific director of the Eniwetok atomic proving ground.	Agriculture Secy. Anderson releases to Congress the names of 711 individuals and firms listed as "big" traders on the commodity markets. The list includes only one Washington official, Edwin Pauley.			Dec. 22
	On the recommendation of his three-man Amnesty Board, Truman grants pardons to 1,523 men convicted during the war of violating the Selective Service Act. All but three have already served their prison sentences.	CIO United Shoe Workers union drops its demand for a 15¢ hourly wage increase for 12,000 workers due to the depressed condition of the shoe industry.			Dec. 23
			Truman issues an executive order creating the Interdepartmental Committee for Scientific Research and Development to coordinate federal scientific activities.		Dec. 24
F *Includes elections, federal-state relations, civil rights and liberties, crime, the judiciary, education, health care, poverty, urban affairs and population.*	G *Includes formation and debate of U.S. foreign and defense policies, veterans affairs and defense spending. (Relations with specific foreign countries are usually found under the region concerned.)*	H *Includes business, labor, agriculture, taxation, transportation, consumer affairs, monetary and fiscal policy, natural resources, pollution and accidents.*	I *Includes worldwide scientific, medical and technological developments, natural phenomena, U.S. weather and natural disasters.*	J *Includes the arts, religion, scholarship, communications media, sports, entertainment, fashions, fads and social life.*	

	World Affairs	Europe	Africa & the Middle East	The Americas	Asia & the Pacific
Dec. 25		Athens police begin a roundup of political suspects, arresting over 500 alleged supporters of the Free Greek Government.			
Dec. 26		Greek Army repels an attack by 2,000 guerrillas on the road center of Konitsa near the Albanian border, wanted as a capital by the Communist provisional government .... Ukrainian Premier Nikita Khrushchev is renamed to his former post of Ukrainian Communist Party secretary, succeeding Lazar Kaganovich, newly appointed deputy chairman of the Soviet Council of Ministers .... Bulgarian National Assembly extends its nationalization decree to banks and other financial institutions.		Argentine Supreme Court rules that Communist Party membership is not sufficient reason for canceling naturalized citizenship.	Speaking in his own defense at the Tokyo war crimes trial, former Japanese Premier Hideki Tojo claims that war was justified in 1941 because U.S. and British military and economic pressure had brought Japan "to the point of annihilation." He accepts responsibility for Japan's defeat but denies any war guilt .... A typhoon strikes Manila and eastern Luzon in the Philippines, causing 49 deaths.
Dec. 27		France's Popular Republican Movement, led by Robert Schuman and Georges Bidault, formally joins with Socialists, Radicals and moderate independent parties to form the "third force," a political alignment aimed at blocking capture of the government by the Communists or Gaullists .... Greek government bans the Communist Party and the Communist militia organization E.A.M. (National Liberation Front) .... A Warsaw court hands down death sentences for Waclaw Lipinski and Wlodzimierz Narszewski, leaders of underground resistance to the Communist-dominated government .... Britain signs a trade agreement with Russia, providing for exchange of Russian grain and British machinery and reduction of interest on Russia's $216-million wartime debt to Britain.			Pakistani U.N. representative Mohammed Khan is appointed foreign affairs and commonwealth relations minister .... Nationalist Gen. Feng Yu-hsiang rejects an order from Chiang Kai-shek to return to China from a tour of the U.S., charging that Chiang plans to have him killed.
Dec. 28		Former Italian King Victor Emmanuel III dies of pneumonia in Cairo, Egypt.	Jewish Agency for Palestine leader Moshe Sneh resigns from the organization's executive board, complaining of undue emphasis on relations with the Western powers and insufficient attention to Russia.		
Dec. 29		French Interior Min. Jules Moch cuts off the Communist Party's gasoline ration.	A bomb planted by the Irgun Zvai Leumi at the Damascus Gate in Jerusalem kills 11 Arabs and two British soldiers.		Communist forces take the rail center of Yuncheng in north-central China.
Dec. 30		Rumania's King Michael, last remaining monarch in eastern Europe, abdicates, claiming the monarchy "does not correspond to the conditions of our state's life" and represents "a serious impediment to Rumania's development." Parliament immediately votes to abolish the monarchy and proclaims a "People's Republic." .... Spanish government announces the execution of Augustin Zoroa Sanchez and Lucas Nunez Baos, Communist leaders accused of illegal underground activity .... Gen. Lucius Clay of the U.S. military government in Germany urges elimination of trade and travel barriers between the U.S. and French zones.	Palestinian Arabs kill 41 Jews in retaliation for an Irgun Zvai Leumi bombing of a Haifa oil refinery, which left six Arabs dead.	Brazilian Pres. Eurico Dutra signs a measure fixing the number of enlisted personnel in the peacetime armed forces at 172,000.	Former Burmese Premier U Saw and eight associates are convicted in Rangoon and sentenced to death for the July 19 assassination of Premier U Aung San and six cabinet members.
Dec. 31		French National Assembly completes work on a $7-billion anti-inflation budget for 1948, while the government raises the national minimum wage by 23.5% .... Albert Grzesinski, former Prussian interior minister and a strong opponent of the Nazis in the last years of the Weimar Republic, dies at 68 in N.Y.			Nationalist forces battle Communists in an effort to retain control over the Manchurian industrial city of Mukden and its rail link with the south, while Communist troops attack opposite ends of the vital Peking-Hankow railroad.

A	B	C	D	E
Includes developments that affect more than one world region, international organizations and important meetings of major world leaders.	*Includes all domestic and regional developments in Europe, including the Soviet Union, Turkey, Cyprus and Malta.*	*Includes all domestic and regional developments in Africa and the Middle East, including Iraq and Iran and excluding Cyprus, Turkey and Afghanistan.*	*Includes all domestic and regional developments in Latin America, the Caribbean and Canada.*	*Includes all domestic and regional developments in Asian and Pacific nations, extending from Afghanistan through all the Pacific Islands, except Hawaii.*

U.S. Politics & Social Issues	U.S. Foreign Policy & Defense	U.S. Economy & Environment	Science, Technology & Nature	Culture, Leisure & Life Style	
	Members of the Committee for Amnesty picket the White House demanding that Truman extend pardons to 12,764 draft law violators.				Dec. 25
	Truman names State Secy. Marshall to supervise the administration of $522 million appropriated for aid to France, Italy and Austria.		A heavy snowstorm sweeps the Eastern Seaboard and New England, paralyzing N.Y.C. with a record 25.8 inches in 16 hrs. . . . . An Australian Antarctic expedition sets up a base and weather station on Heard Island.		Dec. 26
Civil Service Loyalty Review Bd. announces its standards for testing federal employes, promising to avoid a "witch hunt" but denying political suspects the right to confront their accusers, cross-examine witnesses or inspect FBI reports.					Dec. 27
				Ring Magazine and Boxing Writers Assn. name light-heavyweight champion Gus Lesnevich "Fighter of the Year."	Dec. 28
In a speech before a Chicago rally of the Progressive Citizens of America, Henry Wallace announces his intention to run for president in 1948 as a third party candidate, charging that both major parties "stand for a policy which opens the door to war in our lifetime."	U.S.-Bulgarian relations are formally restored as Truman receives the new Bulgarian minister, Nissim Mevorah . . . . N.Y. Mayor William O'Dwyer gives a formal reception in City Hall for Tel Aviv Mayor Israel Rokach.	Agriculture Dept. releases further names of grain traders and speculators, including Utah Gov. Herbert Maw and Truman's personal physician, Gen. Wallace Graham.		New York Film Critics Assn. votes *Gentleman's Agreement* the year's best American picture and *To Live In Peace* the best foreign film . . . . National Institute of Arts and Letters in N.Y. inducts 11 new members, including composer Virgil Thomson and British poet W.H. Auden . . . . National Boxing Assn. ranks Joe Louis as top fighter in the heavyweight class, Gus Lesnevich as the best light-heavyweight and Rocky Graziano as the best middleweight.	Dec. 29
Fourth U.S. Circuit Court of Appeals in Richmond upholds a district court ruling barring all-white primaries in South Carolina.	Speaking in Milwaukee, Wallace calls the Marshall Plan "insane" and proposes an alternative arrangement which would place U.S. aid funds under U.N. administration.	SEC orders the reorganization and ultimate dissolution of the Public Service Corp. of N.J., one of the nation's largest energy and transportation holding companies. The Commission also approves construction of a $104-million pipeline to carry natural gas from Texas to the Midwest . . . . Building Trades Employers Assn. and the AFL Building and Construction Trades Council of Greater N.Y. agree to stablize wages and conditions for most of the 250,000 workers in the N.Y. area until mid-1949 with a 5% pay increase . . . . Interstate Commerce Commission grants railroads, water carriers and freight forwarders a 20% freight rate increase, superceding a 10% increase granted in October.		Alfred North Whitehead, British-born philosopher and mathematician, dies at 86 in Cambridge, Mass . . . . Hooperatings list *Fibber McGee & Molly* as the most popular radio show, followed by *Jack Benny*, *Fred Allen*, *Charlie McCarthy*, *Radio Theater* and *Red Skelton*.	Dec. 30
	Gen. Clifton Cates takes office as Marine Corps commandant, succeeding Gen. Alexander Vandegrift.		American Assn. for the Advancement of Science gives its annual $1,000 award to Prof. Harrison Brown of the Univ. of Chicago for an analysis of meteorites indicating that most extraterrestrial matter that lands on earth was once part of a planet orbiting between Mars and Jupiter.	AAU presents the James E. Sullivan Trophy for the year's outstanding amateur athlete to sculls champion John Kelly, Jr.	Dec. 31
F	G	H	I	J	
Includes elections, federal-state relations, civil rights and liberties, crime, the judiciary, education, health care, poverty, urban affairs and population.	*Includes formation and debate of U.S. foreign and defense policies, veterans affairs and defense spending. (Relations with specific foreign countries are usually found under the region concerned.)*	*Includes business, labor, agriculture, taxation, transportation, consumer affairs, monetary and fiscal policy, natural resources, pollution and accidents.*	*Includes worldwide scientific, medical and technological developments, natural phenomena, U.S. weather and natural disasters.*	*Includes the arts, religion, scholarship, communications media, sports, entertainment, fashions, fads and social life.*	

1948

Residents of Troy, N.Y. picket a grocery store, protesting high meat prices. The incident was part of a nationwide series of consumer protests against inflation.

Communist coup in Czechoslovakia: A crowd of 250,000 gathers in Prague on Feb. 25 to hear Premier Klement Gottwald announce cabinet changes ensuring Communist domination of the government.

Harry Truman gives 'em hell as he accepts the Democratic presidential nomination on July 15 at the party's National Convention. Attacking the Republican-dominated Congress for failing to act on important legislation, he announces that he will call a special session of Congress on July 26.

Preceding page: West Berlin children perch on a fence around Tempelhof airport to watch U.S. cargo planes fly in supplies for their city, isolated by the Russian blockade.

Sen. Robert Taft (R, Ohio), "Mr. Republican" to many in his party, led the conservative bloc which dominated the 80th Congress. Taft's presidential ambitions were frustrated by his stiff, colorless public image.

Shanghai police break up a demonstration of students protesting the alleged rape of a Chinese woman by U.S. soldiers.

Paris police close in on a striking aircraft worker as they break up a Communist demonstration, Sept. 15.

Communists arrive in Washington's Union Station on Aug. 6 to demonstrate for civil rights and protest the sedition trial of U.S. Communist leaders.

Brooklyn Dodgers second baseman Jackie Robinson, the first Negro in major league baseball, steals home in a game against the Boston Braves.

West Berliners gather in front of the bombed-out Reichstag building on Aug. 29 to protest the Russian blockade and Communist efforts to split the city government.

An Arab soldier guards the Wailing Wall in the Old City of Jerusalem. Jews were barred from the holy place after the outbreak of Palestine fighting.

Alger Hiss studies a photograph of Whittaker Chambers in testimony before the House Un-American Activities Committee on Aug. 5. Standing over Hiss is committee investigator Robert Stripling.

	World Affairs	Europe	Africa & the Middle East	The Americas	Asia & the Pacific
Jan.		Widespread strikes break out in western Germany as workers protest food shortages.	Protest against defense pact with Great Britain erupts in Iraq		Assassination of Mohandas Gandhi intensifies unrest in India.
Feb.		A coup brings Communists to power in Czechoslovakia.	Zionist terrorists intensify violence against British authorities in Palestine.	Rival claims in Antarctica cause a diplomatic feud between Argentina, Chile and Britain.	Communists advance in Manchuria and northern China, isolating Nationalist forces in major cities.
March		Western European states negotiate defense and economic agreements with U.S. encouragement .... U.N. Security Council hears testimony concerning the Communist coup in Czechoslovakia.	U.N. Security Council debates proposed Palestine partition plan.	Civil strife erupts in Costa Rica between government and rightest rebel forces.	North Koreans begin to organize political opposition against U.N.-sponsored elections in the South.
Apr.		U.S. and Britain begin airlifting supplies into western Berlin, isolated by a Soviet blockade .... A purge of liberals and "bourgeois" elements from the Rumanian armed forces, industry and government results in the arrest of 2,000 political suspects in the Bucharest area.	Arab-Jewish strife intensifies as the British withdraw from Palestine.	Representatives of the American republics, meeting in Bogota, Colombia, negotiate a hemispheric solidarity pact which establishes the Organization of American States .... Rightist rebel forces under Jose Figueres win the civil war in Costa Rica.	Civil strife envelops much of Burma as government forces battle in Communist guerrillas and Karen nationalists.
May	Truman and Acheson reject a peace conference proposal from Stalin, ending rumors of an impending general agreement between the two superpowers.	Allied representatives fail to agree on Austrian peace treaty terms .... A cabinet crisis in Finland reduces the power of the country's Communists.	Proclamation of the State of Isreal touches off the first Arab-Jewish war.		U.S.-Soviet split in Korea moves towards establishment of separate governments .... Philippine security forces begin a campaign to eradicate the Hukbalahap guerrilla movement.
June		Russia and its eastern European satellites openly attack the Yugoslavian government for "nationalist deviation" from the Cominform line.	Negotiations for an end to the Arab-Israeli conflict begin under U.N. auspices on Rhodes.	Political tension in Peru rises due to alleged military pressures on the government.	Floods on the southern Chinese coast near Foochow drown 1,000 inhabitants and leave 200,000 homeless.
July		German political leaders and western Allied governors agree on formation of a West German state.		Enrique Jimenez battles political opposition to retain Panama's presidency.	
Aug.	Allied representatives begin discussion of the Berlin dispute in Moscow.	U.S. and Russian troops clash in Berlin as tension increases .... Danubian Conference approves Soviet proposals for creation of an Eastern European commission to regulate river traffic.	Arab and Israeli representatives on Rhodes discuss the problem of Palestinian refugees, but reach no agreement.	Argentine Pres. Peron seeks to increase his power with proposals for constitutional change.	Communist guerrilla insurgencies continue in Burma and the Philippines.
Sept.	After failing to resolve the Berlin problem in direct negotiations with the Soviets, the Western Allies take the issue to the U.N.	Western European states begin to discuss formation of a European parliamentary assembly and a North Atlantic security system.	Continued violence in Jerusalem results in the death of U.N. mediator Count Folke Bernadotte.		Indian forces complete the occupation of Hyderabad.
Oct.		Greek government forces begin to restrict Communist guerrillas to an area near the Albanian frontier .... Communist-led strikes shut down French coal mines.	Arab-Israeli conflict breaks out again as both sides reject the Bernadotte peace plan.		Continued Communist gains in northern China result in the capture of Changchun, capital of Manchuria.
Nov.			Arabs and Israelis renew their cease-fire under U.N. pressure.		Chinese Communists consolidate their hold on northern China and begin to drive on the Nationalist capital of Nanking.
Dec.		Berlin city government moves towards a split as Communists establish their own agencies for the eastern sector.	Arab states dispute Transjordanian King Abdullah's proclamation of sovereignty over Arab Palestine.	OAS seeks to end Costa Rican civil turmoil caused by the invasion of forces loyal to former Pres. Rafael Calderon Guardia.	Mme. Chiang Kai-shek visits the U.S., appealing for aid to the Nationalists .... Dutch forces violate their truce with the Indonesian Republic, invading Java and Sumatra and capturing nationalist leaders. Most nations, including the U.S. and Russia, strongly condemn the action.

A	B	C	D	E
Includes developments that affect more than one world region, international organizations and important meetings of major world leaders.	*Includes all domestic and regional developments in Europe, including the Soviet Union, Turkey, Cyprus and Malta.*	*Includes all domestic and regional developments in Africa and the Middle East, including Iraq and Iran and excluding Cyprus, Turkey and Afghanistan.*	*Includes all domestic and regional developments in Latin America, the Caribbean and Canada.*	*Includes all domestic and regional developments in Asian and Pacific nations, extending from Afghanistan through all the Pacific Islands, except Hawaii.*

U.S. Politics & Social Issues	U.S. Foreign Policy & Defense	U.S. Economy & Environment	Science, Technology & Nature	Culture, Leisure & Life Style	
State of Oklahoma attempts to maintain segregation in its higher education system following a court ruling ordering the admission of Negro students.	House and Senate Committees begin hearing testimony on the proposed European Recovery Program.	Truman begins consideration of possible anti-inflation measures.	A four-day cold wave sweeps the U.S., leaving 21 dead and a record accumulation of snow in N.Y.C. . . . . U.S. Atomic Energy Commission begins a program designed to increase the availability of nuclear research and materials to non-military institutions.		Jan.
Southern Democrats come out strongly against any national party platform favoring civil rights, threatening to create their own party.	Truman seeks congressional approval for aid to Greece, Turkey and China.			Winter Olympics conclude in St. Moritz, Switzerland.	Feb.
Several ranking Democrats speak out against Truman's renomination for the presidency, claiming that he has antagonized too many important groups.	Senate completes action on the European Recovery Program, while the House continues to debate the measure.	A miners' strike resulting from a pension fund dispute causes rail tieups and layoffs of steel and auto workers.		College basketball season comes to an end, with Kentucky capturing the NCAA and St. Louis the NIT championship.	March
Harold Stassen and Thomas Dewey battle for the GOP presidential nomination in state primaries.	Implementation of the Marshall Plan begins, with Paul Hoffman taking control as Economic Cooperation Administrator.			*Now is the Hour* sweeps the nation to become number one song.	Apr.
National debate over Communist influence in government intensifies as Congress considers the Mundt-Nixon Communist Control bill.			Severe flooding in the Northwest causes heavy damage and loss of life.	*Oklahoma!* closes on Broadway after a record four-year run.	May
Dewey wins the GOP presidential nomination . . . . Truman completes a political campaign trip through Midwest and Western states.	Congress completes action on several defense measures, including one for peacetime military conscription.	CIO locals representing more than 100,000 union members withdraw from the Greater New York CIO Council, charging that the Council is Communist-controlled.		Columbia Records introduces long-playing records and turntables designed to play at $33\frac{1}{3}$ rpm.	June
Democrats nominate Truman for president on a strong civil rights platform, as Southerners split from the national party.					July
Celebrated confrontation between Whittaker Chambers and Alger Hiss begins before the House Un-American Activities Comm.	State Dept. and Soviet diplomats debate the status of two Russian consular officials, Mikhail Samarin and Oksana Kosenkina, who defected to the U.S.	Administration seeks emergency powers, including price and wage controls, to deal with continued inflation.		Fourteenth Summer Olympiad concludes in London.	Aug.
Presidential campaign opens, as Truman undertakes a "whistle stop" tour of farm states.	Administration considers proposals for elimination of segregation in the armed forces.	A longshoremen's strike ties up West Coast shipping.			Sept.
House Un-American Activities Comm. Chmn. J. Parnell Thomas comes under attack for accepting salary kickbacks from his congressional employes . . . . Public opinion surveys unanimously predict a Dewey presidential victory.					Oct.
Truman confounds pollsters by winning the presidential election, while Democrats regain control of Congress.		West Coast dock workers end their strike after obtaining a favorable contract.	A blizzard causes heavy damage in the Midwest.		Nov.
Southern states formulate plans for a segregated regional higher education system.	Defense Secy. Forrestal implements armed forces unification, eliminating overlapping agencies and increasing the power of his own office.	Congress debates labor legislation as the Administration begins its effort to repeal the Taft-Hartley Act . . . . U.S. industrial output begins to drop for the first time since the end of the war, signifying the start of a deflationary economic trend.		Duke Ellington's band sweeps the nation in musical popularity . . . . RCA Victor introduces the 45 rpm record.	Dec.

F	G	H	I	J
Includes elections, federal-state relations, civil rights and liberties, crime, the judiciary, education, health care, poverty, urban affairs and population.	*Includes formation and debate of U.S. foreign and defense policies, veterans affairs and defense spending. (Relations with specific foreign countries are usually found under the region concerned.)*	*Includes business, labor, agriculture, taxation, transportation, consumer affairs, monetary and fiscal policy, natural resources, pollution and accidents.*	*Includes worldwide scientific, medical and technological developments, natural phenomena, U.S. weather and natural disasters.*	*Includes the arts, religion, scholarship, communications media, sports, entertainment, fashions, fads and social life.*

	World Affairs	Europe	Africa & the Middle East	The Americas	Asia & the Pacific
Jan. 1		Benelux customs union goes into effect . . . . Greek Communist guerrillas withdraw from Konitsa after a one-week siege.		Canada establishes diplomatic relations with Yugoslavia, appointing Emile Vaillancourt minister to Belgrade.	India complains to the U.N. Security Council that Pakistani forces are raiding Kashmir . . . . Emperor Hirohito opens the Imperial Palace grounds to visitors for the first time in Japanese history.
Jan. 2		Josef Orlopp, head of the Central Administration for Foreign Trade in the Soviet Zone of Germany, announces that eastern Germany will direct its trade primarily towards eastern and southeastern Europe.		Vicente Huidobro, Chilean poet and author, dies at 54 in Santiago.	Indian P.M. Jawaharlal Nehru threatens Indian action to stop alleged Pakistani raids into Kashmir.
Jan. 3		France grants self-government to the Saar after signing a treaty with the Saarland government extending French economic and financial control in the area . . . . Russian government forbids the use of low-paid home labor by plant managers attempting to turn out extra goods.			
Jan. 4			Stern Gang terrorists bomb the Arab National Comm. headquarters in Jaffa, causing 14 deaths and 100 injuries.		Burma officially becomes an independent republic.
Jan. 5	U.N. General Assembly's Interim Comm. on Peace and Security opens its first session at Lake Success, boycotted by the Soviet bloc.	Yugoslavian Pres. Tito demands the release of $70 million in gold deposited in the N.Y. Federal Reserve Bank by the National Bank of Yugoslavia in 1941.			
Jan. 6		U.S. aid mission to Greece reallocates $15 million from civilian needs to the Greek Army and national guard, whose manpower strength is to be increased . . . . French National Assembly passes an anti-inflation income tax measure designed to remove 125 billion francs from circulation . . . . U.S. tribunal in Nuremberg begins the war crimes trial of 21 Nazi diplomats and economic administrators, including Baron Ernst von Weiszaeker and Otto Meissner, former chief of the presidential chancellery . . . . German workers strike in Hamburg, Essen, Munich and other western cities to protest continuing food shortages.	Exiled Riff leader Abd el Krim proclaims a Comm. for the Liberation of Northwest Africa in Cairo.	Haiti raises its daily minimum wage from 40¢ to 70¢.	Former Japanese Premier Hideki Tojo completes his testimony at the Tokyo war crimes trial, refusing to admit either personal or national war guilt . . . . Nationalist Chinese government commits 1.25 million troops to battle Communists north of the Yangtze River.
Jan. 7	U.N. Secy. Gen. Trygve Lie appoints Robert G.A. Jackson of Australia as assistant secretary general.	French cabinet establishes eight civil defense "security districts" to guard against labor unrest . . . . Soviet Council of Ministers condemns the Tatar Autonomous Republic for failing to meet production goals and demands a reorganization of the region's administration.		Brazilian Chamber of Deputies votes to oust Communist legislators on all levels of government . . . . Leftist Vicente Lombardo Toledano is expelled from Mexico's Federation of Labor, which he helped establish in 1936.	
Jan. 8		U.S., British and German officials conclude a two-day meeting in Frankfurt with an agreement providing for creation of a German government in the Anglo-American occupation zone. The government, consisting of executive, legislative and judicial branches, is denied the right to raise armed forces and conduct its own foreign relations. Russian authorities immediately object to the agreement, but the U.S. military government announces plans to shift its operations from Berlin to Frankfurt.		Rio de Janeiro police forcibly close the Communist newspaper *Imprensa Popular* in the current Brazilian anti-Communist drive . . . . Export-Import Bank grants Canada a $300-million loan for purchase of U.S. cotton, coal and other raw materials.	
	A *Includes developments that affect more than one world region, international organizations and important meetings of major world leaders.*	B *Includes all domestic and regional developments in Europe, including the Soviet Union, Turkey, Cyprus and Malta.*	C *Includes all domestic and regional developments in Africa and the Middle East, including Iraq and Iran and excluding Cyprus, Turkey and Afghanistan.*	D *Includes all domestic and regional developments in Latin America, the Caribbean and Canada.*	E *Includes all domestic and regional developments in Asian and Pacific nations, extending from Afghanistan through all the Pacific Islands, except Hawaii.*

U.S. Politics & Social Issues	U.S. Foreign Policy & Defense	U.S. Economy & Environment	Science, Technology & Nature	Culture, Leisure & Life Style	
A federal court in Roanoke, Va. upholds segregation in public transportation.	U.S. Navy completes evacuation of Port Lyautey, Morocco, the last U.S. military base in French North Africa.			U. of Michigan defeats USC, 49-0, in the Rose Bowl game. Other bowl scores: U. of Texas 27, U. of Alabama 7 in the Sugar Bowl; SMU 13, Penn State 13 in the Cotton Bowl; Georgia Tech 20, U. of Kansas 14 in the Orange Bowl . . . . Communist weekly *New Masses* announces suspension of publication after 37 years for financial reasons . . . . A *Motion Picture Herald* survey names Bing Crosby as the top money-making star for the fourth straight year.	Jan. 1
Plans are announced for a $15,000 second story balcony on the White House south portico for presidential family use.		A federal court in Utica, N.Y. issues the first injunction against a secondary strike under the Taft-Hartley Act, barring a strike by an Albany Teamsters union local.	Univ. of Chicago announces formation of a partnership with seven corporations to link pure atomic research with industrial development.		Jan. 2
Gallup presidential poll shows Truman leading Taft, 55-33%, with 12% undecided . . . . Edwin Pauley resigns as California's Democratic national committeeman in a leadership dispute with James Roosevelt.		Truman assigns the Agriculture, Commerce and Interior secretaries and the Office of Defense Transportation to negotiate voluntary industry price agreements under provisions of the Republican-sponsored, anti-inflation law.		Professional Golfers Assn. awards Jimmy Demaret the 1947 Vardon Trophy as the best U.S. tournament golfer.	Jan. 3
			Univ. of California announces development of the world's first supersonic wind tunnel, capable of duplicating pressure conditions up to an altitude of 250,000 feet.		Jan. 4
Supreme Court rules that a warrant is necessary to arrest and search a criminal suspect, reversing the conviction of a Buffalo man found in possession of counterfeit gasoline ration coupons . . . . N.Y. State CIO votes to condemn Henry Wallace's third-party presidential candidacy.		Truman and Treasury Secy. John Snyder endorse the American Banker's Assn. plan for voluntary restriction of bank credit to help curb inflation.		Ross Lockridge's *Raintree County*, a fictional portrait of the post-Civil War U.S., is published by Houghton, Mifflin . . . . Oliver Cox's *Caste, Class and Race*, winner of the George Washington Carver Award for its analysis of racial antagonism, is published by Doubleday.	Jan. 5
AFL Pres. William Green denounces Henry Wallace's third-party presidential candidacy following a meeting with the AFL Labor League for Political Education.	House Foreign Affairs Comm. Chmn. Charles Eaton (R, N.J.) introduces Truman's European Recovery Program, requesting $6.8 billion for the plan's first 15 months . . . . Retiring Fleet Adm. Chester Nimitz issues his final report, claiming that the U.S. has complete mastery of the seas.				Jan. 6
Truman delivers his annual State of the Union Address before a joint session of Congress, urging an immediate income tax cut of $40 per person, passage of the European Recovery Program bill and rapid action on anti-inflation measures. Republicans react angrily to the speech, claiming Truman's tax bill has no chance of passage in its present form . . . . Twenty-four CIO leaders resign from the N.Y. State executive committee of the American Labor Party, leaving the party under Communist domination. The state executive committee elects Rep. Vito Marcantonio chairman and endorses Wallace for president.				Screen writer Ring Lardner, Jr. sues 20th Century Fox for $1.4 million and Edward Dmytryk sues RKO for $1.8 million for dismissal after their convictions on contempt of Congress charges . . . . *United States News* magazine announces its merger with *World Report*.	Jan. 7
	Senate Foreign Relations Comm. begins hearings on the European Recovery Program, calling State Secy. Marshall as its first witness.	Harry Ferguson, former business partner of Henry Ford, files a $251-million suit against Ford Motors and Henry Ford II in N.Y. federal court, charging patent infringement and violation of antitrust laws . . . . Agriculture Dept. announces sugar quotas of 7.8 million tons, 3 million tons to come from Cuba.	National Foundation for Infantile Paralysis announces allocation of $1.18 million to U.S. and Canadian universities for polio research and training.	Austrian-born tenor Richard Tauber dies at 55 in London.	Jan. 8

F	G	H	I	J
Includes elections, federal-state relations, civil rights and liberties, crime, the judiciary, education, health care, poverty, urban affairs and population.	*Includes formation and debate of U.S. foreign and defense policies, veterans affairs and defense spending. (Relations with specific foreign countries are usually found under the region concerned.)*	*Includes business, labor, agriculture, taxation, transportation, consumer affairs, monetary and fiscal policy, natural resources, pollution and accidents.*	*Includes worldwide scientific, medical and technological developments, natural phenomena, U.S. weather and natural disasters.*	*Includes the arts, religion, scholarship, communications media, sports, entertainment, fashions, fads and social life.*

	World Affairs	Europe	Africa & the Middle East	The Americas	Asia & the Pacific
Jan. 9		U.S. Navy transfers four submarines and 11 other ships to Turkey and promises to train Turkish submarine crews under the Truman Doctrine aid program . . . . Poland's Foreign Ministry issues a list of objectives for 1948 emphasizing stronger ties with other Slav states.	U.N. Palestine Comm. holds its first meeting at Lake Success, electing Karel Lisicky of Czechoslovakia chairman . . . . Syrian forces crossing into Palestine from Lebanon attack the Jewish settlements of Kfar Szold and Dan in the Upper Galilee, killing two Jews before being repulsed by British forces . . . . Lebanon bans all Communist activity.		China's Nationalist government announces a record budget of 96 trillion Chinese dollars ($427 million) for the first half of 1948.
Jan. 10					French cabinet urges former Vietnamese Emperor Bao Dai to call a conference of Vietnamese leaders interested in reestablishing peace in Indochina.
Jan. 11					
Jan. 12		Peter de Rochegune Munch, former Danish foreign minister and head of the interwar League of Nations Disarmament Commission, dies at 77 in Copenhagen.			Despite a Russian and Ukrainian boycott, the UN Security Council's Temporary Commission on Korea convenes in Seoul to prepare for national elections.
Jan. 13		Italian bank employes end a two-week nationwide strike after gaining a 15% salary increase . . . . Norwegian King Haakon VII opens Parliament in Oslo by urging nationalization of the Bank of Norway.	Anton Gemayel Pasha, Egyptian official and editor of Cairo's *Al Ahram*, the largest newspaper in the Middle East, dies at 61 in Cairo.	Western Hemisphere labor groups, including the AFL, end a four-day conference in Lima by establishing an International American Labor Confederation to rival the leftist World Federation of Trade Unions.	Mohandas Gandhi begins fasting for a "reunion of hearts" among Hindus, Moslems and Sikhs on the strife-torn Indian subcontinent.
Jan. 14		A Dutch firing squad executes Gestapo agent Ans van Dijk, the first execution of a woman in Holland in this century.	Iranian Premier Ibrahim Hakimi cancels a $25-million purchase of surplus U.S. war materiel and a $250-million International Bank loan for oil field development, claiming Iran can finance the project from its own resources.	Colombian Pres. Mariano Ospina Perez completes formation of a new cabinet, headed by Conservative Jose Antonio Montalvo.	A Chinese Communist broadcast predicts that all of northeastern China will be taken from the Nationalists this year.
Jan. 15			Arab League headquarters in Cairo announces plans to occupy all of Palestine immediately after British withdrawal . . . . Britain signs a 20-year military agreement with Iraq, allowing British forces to remain in two Iraqi air bases.	Canada reimposes price ceilings on meat and butter.	
Jan. 16		Bulgaria and Rumania sign a friendship treaty . . . . German unions in Duisburg, Muelheim and Dinslaken begin a 24-hour strike to protest inadequate food rations in the British zone.			
Jan. 17			Palestinian Arabs kill 35 Haganah soldiers attempting to reach the Jewish settlement of Kfar Etzion south of Jerusalem.		U.N. Security Council concludes three days of hearings on the Indian-Pakistani conflict over Kashmir by calling for a ceasefire and negotiations on the territory's status . . . . Dutch officials and Indonesian nationalist leaders sign a new ceasefire agreement under U.N. auspices aboard a U.S. transport ship off the Java coast.
	A *Includes developments that affect more than one world region, international organizations and important meetings of major world leaders.*	B *Includes all domestic and regional developments in Europe, including the Soviet Union, Turkey, Cyprus and Malta.*	C *Includes all domestic and regional developments in Africa and the Middle East, including Iraq and Iran and excluding Cyprus, Turkey and Afghanistan.*	D *Includes all domestic and regional developments in Latin America, the Caribbean and Canada.*	E *Includes all domestic and regional developments in Asian and Pacific nations, extending from Afghanistan through all the Pacific Islands, except Hawaii.*

U.S. Politics & Social Issues	U.S. Foreign Policy & Defense	U.S. Economy & Environment	Science, Technology & Nature	Culture, Leisure & Life Style	
		House group headed by August Andresen (R, Minn.) begins hearings on commodity market transactions by government officials, calling Harold Stassen as the first witness .... Attempting to restrict the expansion of credit, the Federal Reserve Bd. raises the rediscount rate from 1% to $1\frac{1}{2}$% in nine of 12 Federal Reserve banks.			Jan. 9
	State Dept. puts radar equipment on its list of militarily sensitive items which require a license for export to Russia and Eastern Europe.			Gallup Poll issues an 11-nation survey of religious belief, showing Brazil with the highest proportion of believers (96%) and France with the lowest (66%). Of U.S. respondents, 94% claimed to believe in God.	Jan. 10
		In response to congressional disclosures, Edwin Pauley admits making $932,703 in three years of commodity trading while holding various government jobs.	American Univ. in Beirut announces development of a new cholera serum, considered the most effective to date.	*Film Daily* poll of film critics selects *The Best Years of Our Lives* as the best picture of 1947 .... Lloyd Mangrum wins the $10,000 Bing Crosby Open golf title in Del Monte, Calif.	Jan. 11
Supreme Court unanimously orders Oklahoma to provide the same law education to Negro students as to whites. The ruling is a response to a suit brought by Ada Fisher, who was denied admission to the Univ. of Oklahoma law school after graduating from a Negro college in Langston, Okla. .... President's Commission on Higher Education recommends a federal aid program to help establish a system of free junior colleges.		Truman presents Congress with a $39.7-billion budget proposal, the second largest peacetime budget in U.S. history. Congressional reaction divides along party lines, with Republicans attacking the budget as extravagant and irresponsible .... A federal grand jury in Los Angeles indicts General Electric, Westinghouse and eight smaller firms for fixing prices of electrical equipment sold to West Coast public utilities.			Jan. 12
Truman begins planning his strategy for the upcoming presidential campaign by conferring with Adolph Berle, chairman of the N.Y. State Liberal Party, on means of keeping the Liberal vote away from third-party candidate Henry Wallace.	Truman's five-man Air Policy Comm. concludes a study of U.S. air power by warning that the Air Force is "hopelessly inadequate" and has only five years to prepare for an atomic attack. The report recommends a $1.3-billion increase in Air Force spending for 1948 .... Army permits Negroes to enlist in all ground forces, including airborne and technical units.		French High Commissioner for Atomic Energy Frederic Joliot-Curie announces discovery of a new nuclear particle, the mesotron lambda, responsible for some cosmic rays.		Jan. 13
Two Communist rallies in N.Y., called to mark the anniversary of Lenin's death, urge support for Henry Wallace's third-party presidential campaign .... Screen Writers Guild votes against extending financial support to six members indicted for contempt of Congress .... Assn. of American Colleges concludes a three-day meeting in Cincinnati by creating a commission to combat discrimination against minority groups in college admissions.	U.S. refuses to release Yugoslavian funds frozen in N.Y. until the Tito government agrees to settle $42 million in American business claims on nationalized property.	Truman issues his annual economic report to Congress, urging immediate enactment of credit restraints and other anti-inflation measures to prevent an economic downturn .... Rep. John Dingell (D, Mich.) introduces Truman's tax bill in the House, calling for an income tax reduction of $40 per person and a compensatory increase in corporate taxes.		American Fed. of Musicians Pres. James Petrillo is cleared in Chicago of government charges that he violated the Lea Act by ordering a strike to force a radio station to hire three unneeded musicians.	Jan. 14
Alexander Bittelman, Russian-born national committeeman of the U.S. Communist Party, is arrested for deportation in Miami .... Screen Actors Guild votes to require affidavits from all officials affirming that they are not Communists.	House passes a bill revising the Articles of War to permit enlisted men to serve on military courts trying other enlisted men .... Josephus Daniels, former navy secretary and ambassador to Mexico, dies at 85 in Raleigh, N.C.	Interior Secy. Julius Krug confers with representatives of 24 states complaining of fuel shortages and calls on the nation to reduce its consumption of gasoline and fuel oil by 15% to relieve a "critical" supply situation.		A Detroit syndicate headed by Lyle Fife buys the NFL Lions for $200,000 .... U.S. edition of Hermann Hesse's novel *Demian*, with a foreword by Thomas Mann, is published in N.Y. by Holt.	Jan. 15
N.Y. Gov. Thomas Dewey formally enters the presidential race, announcing through an aide that he will run as the Republican candidate "if nominated."	Justice Dept. tightens restrictions on foreign visitors, reducing the validity of visas to six months and requiring aliens to register with authorities after three months.				Jan. 16
		UAW's GM national council votes to accept a 20¢ increase in upcoming wage negotiations if the company offers an "acceptable" pension plan.		Negro professional golfers Bill Spiller, Ted Rhodes and Madison Gunter sue the Richmond (Va.) Golf Club and the Professional Golfers Assn. for $105,000, charging they were barred from a Richmond golf tournament on racial grounds.	Jan. 17
F *Includes elections, federal-state relations, civil rights and liberties, crime, the judiciary, education, health care, poverty, urban affairs and population.*	G *Includes formation and debate of U.S. foreign and defense policies, veterans affairs and defense spending. (Relations with specific foreign countries are usually found under the region concerned.)*	H *Includes business, labor, agriculture, taxation, transportation, consumer affairs, monetary and fiscal policy, natural resources, pollution and accidents.*	I *Includes worldwide scientific, medical and technological developments, natural phenomena, U.S. weather and natural disasters.*	J *Includes the arts, religion, scholarship, communications media, sports, entertainment, fashions, fads and social life.*	

	World Affairs	Europe	Africa & the Middle East	The Americas	Asia & the Pacific
Jan. 18					Mohandas Gandhi ends a five-day fast in New Delhi when Hindu, Moslem and Sikh leaders promise to guarantee peace among their followers.
Jan. 19		A Franco-Italian commission meeting in Paris recommends that the two countries form a customs union.		Chilean steamship *Cautin* sinks in the Imperial River, drowning 150 passengers.	Japan's Socialist Party reelects Premier Tetsu Katayama as its chairman but votes for greater emphasis on socialist programs in the government.
Jan. 20		Seventeen Rumanian Peasant Party officials are convicted of sedition in Bucharest and sentenced to prison terms of up to 10 years.		William Mackenzie King announces his upcoming retirement as Canadian prime minister and Liberal Party leader.	U.N. Security Council establishes a three-member commission to mediate the Indian-Pakistani conflict in Kashmir.
Jan. 21		British Admiralty announces the scrapping of five outmoded capital ships: the battleships *Queen Elizabeth, Valiant, Nelson* and *Rodney* and the battle cruiser *Renown*.	Britain refuses to comply with a General Assembly request that a port and inland area in Palestine be opened to increased Jewish immigration by Feb. 1.		
Jan. 22		In a major foreign policy address before the House of Commons, British Foreign Secy. Ernest Bevin announces a shift from Britain's traditional balance of power politics to support for a "western union" of European states working in close cooperation with the U.S.	Iraqi students protesting their country's recently concluded treaty with Britain end three days of riots in Baghdad, with 11 demonstrators dead.		
Jan. 23		One million workers strike in 26 Bavarian cities to protest continuing food shortages, forcing enactment of a stern food collection measure in the U.S.-British zone of Germany .... Italian Socialist Party congress in Rome votes to cooperate with Communists in upcoming legislative elections.		Nicaragua's National Assembly completes work on a new constitution, outlawing the Communist Party.	Russian authorities refuse to allow the U.N. Security Council's Korean Commission to consult with political leaders in the northern zone on upcoming elections.
Jan. 24		Moscow sources report the dismissal of Russia's leading economist, Eugen Varga, from the Soviet Academy of Sciences for advocating Russian cooperation with the U.S. and Western Europe .... Sir George Alan Powell, retired BBC chairman, dies at 69 in Gerrard's Cross, England.			China's Nationalist government concludes parliamentary elections, which return 200 Kuomintang representatives from districts earlier promised to the minority Young China and Social Democratic parties.
Jan. 25		French cabinet devalues the franc, eliminating the old exchange rate of 119 francs to the dollar and allowing free market trading in currency. Britain and the International Monetary Fund issue statements condemning the move as a threat to the financial stability of other countries.			

A	B	C	D	E
Includes developments that affect more than one world region, international organizations and important meetings of major world leaders.	*Includes all domestic and regional developments in Europe, including the Soviet Union, Turkey, Cyprus and Malta.*	*Includes all domestic and regional developments in Africa and the Middle East, including Iraq and Iran and excluding Cyprus, Turkey and Afghanistan.*	*Includes all domestic and regional developments in Latin America, the Caribbean and Canada.*	*Includes all domestic and regional developments in Asian and Pacific nations, extending from Afghanistan through all the Pacific Islands, except Hawaii.*

U.S. Politics & Social Issues	U.S. Foreign Policy & Defense	U.S. Economy & Environment	Science, Technology & Nature	Culture, Leisure & Life Style	
Committee of One Thousand establishes Washington headquarters to work for abolition of the House Un-American Activities Comm. Among the group's sponsors are Albert Einstein, Archibald MacLeish and Rexford G. Tugwell . . . . Progressive Citizens of America ends a two-day convention in Chicago by establishing committees to create a third party supporting the presidential candidacy of Henry Wallace . . . . Joseph Freeman, co-defendant in the May-Garsson munitions fraud case, dies at 50 of a heart attack in Los Angeles.			Czech astronomer Antonin Mrkos discovers a new comet, which will bear his name.	*New York Herald Tribune* reports the best-selling fiction and non-fiction books as Ben Ames Williams' *House Divided* and John Gunther's *Inside U.S.A.*	Jan. 18
Oklahoma's Bd. of Regents establishes a Negro School of Law with three teachers in Oklahoma City to comply with the recent Supreme Court order demanding equal education for Negro students. The plaintiff in the case, Mrs. Ada Fisher, says she will not attend . . . . Supreme Court rules that Fred Oyama, a U.S. citizen of Japanese descent, owns land in California purchased by his Japanese father despite the state's Alien Land Law.	House passes and sends to Truman a Senate-approved measure giving legal authority to a permanent State Dept. international information and cultural program . . . . Testifying before the Senate Foreign Relations Comm., financier Bernard Baruch urges U.S. sponsorship of a strong European federation covering economic, political and military affairs as "the best guarantee against a third world war." He also urges massive purchase of non-perishable goods by the U.S. with the aim of spurring world production and stockpiling scarce raw materials . . . . National Council Against Conscription hears Albert Einstein and 20 other prominent figures denounce plans for universal military training.	Republicans introduce legislation in both Houses authorizing the Administration to prepare a standby meat rationing system but allowing Congress to determine when it should be used.		NFL Chicago Bears sign two Notre Dame All-Americans, quarterback Johnny Lujack and tackle George Connor.	Jan. 19
	John Foster Dulles appears before the Senate Foreign Relations Comm. to support the Administration's European Recovery Program, claiming the alternative would be a vast armaments effort.		A severe cold wave begins to lift after gripping the U.S. for five days and causing 21 reported deaths.	Delegates to an Anti-Saloon League convention in Pittsburgh vote to change the organization's name to Temperance League of America.	Jan. 20
U.S. Junior Chamber of Commerce honors 10 young men for outstanding achievement in 1947, including nuclear chemist Glen Seaborg and Rep. Richard Nixon (R, Calif.).	Herbert Hoover attacks the European Recovery Program in a letter to Sen. Arthur Vandenberg of the Senate Foreign Relations Comm., urging a one-third reduction in proposed European aid expenditures to avoid endangering the U.S. economy . . . . State Dept. releases a volume, *Nazi-Soviet Relations 1939-1941*, containing captured German Foreign Office records concerning the German-Russian alliance of 1939 and other dealings between the two countries before Hitler's invasion of Russia.			Opera composer Ermanno Wolf-Ferrari dies at 72 in Venice.	Jan. 21
CIO Executive Council votes, 33-11, against supporting the third-party presidential candidacy of Henry Wallace.	Adm. Louis Denfeld announces that improvements in V-2 rocket weapons allow them to be installed on ships for use against trans-oceanic targets.	State and federal officials participating in the Missouri Basin Inter-Agency Commission agree to a six-year program committing $2.4 billion to development of land and water resources in the 10 Missouri basin states . . . . N.Y. State Labor Relations Bd. bars the R.H. Macy Co. from fulfilling its promise of triple pay for employes who crossed picket lines during a 1946 delivery drivers' strike.		Hooperatings list *Bob Hope, Radio Theater, Jack Benny, Fibber McGee & Molly* and *Fred Allen* as the top radio programs.	Jan. 22
Army Dept. releases a statement from Gen. Eisenhower renouncing any intention of entering the upcoming presidential campaign . . . . Three local Democratic committeemen are indicted in St. Louis on charges of vote-buying in the 1946 election.	AFL Pres. William Green and representatives of the National Assn. of Manufacturers appear before the Senate Foreign Relations Comm. to support the European Recovery Program.	Harold Stassen appears again before Senate Appropriations Comm. investigators, renewing charges that Edwin Pauley and other government "insiders" have made profits of more than $5 million in commodity speculation since the war.		*Treasure of the Sierra Madre*, directed by John Huston and starring Humphrey Bogart, premiers in N.Y.	Jan. 23
AFL International Ladies Garment Workers Union executive board, meeting in Miami, denounces Henry Wallace's third-party presidential candidacy as "Communist-inspired."		United Air Lines signs a contract with the AFL Air Line Pilots Assn., giving a top pay of $1,266 monthly to senior pilots.			Jan. 24
Former Gov. Philip La Follette of Wisconsin begins campaigning in Madison for Gen. Douglas MacArthur as a Republican presidential candidate.				Bobby Locke wins the $10,000 Phoenix Open Golf Tournament.	Jan. 25

F	G	H	I	J
Includes elections, federal-state relations, civil rights and liberties, crime, the judiciary, education, health care, poverty, urban affairs and population.	*Includes formation and debate of U.S. foreign and defense policies, veterans affairs and defense spending. (Relations with specific foreign countries are usually found under the region concerned.)*	*Includes business, labor, agriculture, taxation, transportation, consumer affairs, monetary and fiscal policy, natural resources, pollution and accidents.*	*Includes worldwide scientific, medical and technological developments, natural phenomena, U.S. weather and natural disasters.*	*Includes the arts, religion, scholarship, communications media, sports, entertainment, fashions, fads and social life.*

	World Affairs	Europe	Africa & the Middle East	The Americas	Asia & the Pacific
Jan. 26		Sixteen European states participating in the Marshall Plan begin a conference in Rome to coordinate use of their resources . . . . Poland and Russia sign a five-year trade agreement providing for exchange of goods worth $1 billion.	A hurricane strikes Reunion Island in the Indian Ocean, causing 300 deaths.		Renewing their Manchurian offensive, Communist forces take the rail junction of Sinlitun west of Mukden. The attacks leave Communists in control of 95% of Manchuria's food-producing land and 85% of its population.
Jan. 27		Soviet Council of Ministers decrees criminal penalties for Russians attempting to communicate with foreigners without official authorization . . . . Yugoslavia complains to the UN Economic and Social Council against U.S. refusal to surrender $43.2 million in Yugoslavian gold held in N.Y. . . . . Thomas Theodor Heine, German political cartoonist and founder of the satirical magazine *Simplicissimus*, dies at 80 in Stockholm.	Iraqi cabinet resigns in the face of protests over the recently concluded defense pact with Britain.	Bolivian government imposes a state of siege to frustrate an alleged military coup plot.	
Jan. 28		Soviet military government in Berlin announces plans to take over direction of industry in the Soviet zone, claiming that German officials are unable or unwilling to meet requirements.	Britain threatens to withdraw its annual two million pound subsidy from the Transjordanian Arab Legion if the Legion attacks Jewish settlements following the British withdrawal from Palestine.	Newfoundland's advisory national convention votes against union with Canada, forcing a referendum on the issue . . . . Argentine government imposes censorship on all radio speeches in the current congressional campaign.	
Jan. 29		French cabinet invalidates all 5,000-franc banknotes, reducing currency circulation by 35%.	Mohammed el Sadr, an opponent of the recently concluded defense pact with Britain, becomes premier of Iraq.		
Jan. 30		British Air Marshal Sir Arthur Coningham, commander of the 2nd Tactical Air Force in the Normandy invasion, is presumed killed in the crash of a British South American Airways plane between the Azores and Bermuda.	Britain rejects a resolution of the U.N. Security Council's Palestine Comm. urging establishment of a Jewish militia in Palestine before the end of the British mandate . . . . State Secy. Marshall threatens to revoke the passports of Americans fighting on either side in the Palestine conflict.	Former McGill Univ. professor Raymond Boyer receives a two-year prison sentence in Montreal for conspiring to reveal Canadian war secrets to Russia.	Indian leader Mohandas Gandhi is shot and killed by Hindu nationalist Narayan Vinayak Gadse at 5:10 p.m. in New Delhi. News of the assassination sets off riots in Bombay and Calcutta, where crowds ransack offices of the militant Hindu Mahasabha Society. The U.N. begins a three-day period of mourning for Gandhi, while the Security Council suspends debate on the Indian-Pakistani conflict in Kashmir.
Jan. 31		Greek government removes Gen. Constantin Ventiris as commander-in-chief of army units fighting Communist guerrillas and places all military forces under the general staff . . . . Russian Finance Min. Arzeny Zverev submits a record budget of 387.9 billion rubles ($77.58 billion) to the Supreme Soviet.			Gandhi's body is cremated on the bank of the Jumna River in a funeral ceremony attended by one million mourners . . . . Indonesian nationalists form a new cabinet for the Indonesian Republic in Jakarta, with Mohammed Hatta as premier.
Feb. 1					Britain establishes the Federation of Malaya under a constitution giving the nine Malay states local self-government, with Britain retaining control of defense and foreign affairs. Singapore remains a crown colony.
Feb. 2		U.S. and Italy sign a friendship treaty granting reciprocal use of seaports.			Acting to prevent further unrest in the wake of Gandhi's assassination, the Indian government outlaws all private armies as well as militant Hindu, Moslem and Sikh organizations, including the Mahasabha society.

A	B	C	D	E
Includes developments that affect more than one world region, international organizations and important meetings of major world leaders.	*Includes all domestic and regional developments in Europe, including the Soviet Union, Turkey, Cyprus and Malta.*	*Includes all domestic and regional developments in Africa and the Middle East, including Iraq and Iran and excluding Cyprus, Turkey and Afghanistan.*	*Includes all domestic and regional developments in Latin America, the Caribbean and Canada.*	*Includes all domestic and regional developments in Asian and Pacific nations, extending from Afghanistan through all the Pacific Islands, except Hawaii.*

U.S. Politics & Social Issues	U.S. Foreign Policy & Defense	U.S. Economy & Environment	Science, Technology & Nature	Culture, Leisure & Life Style	
Mrs. Ada Fisher returns her case to the Supreme Court after refusing to accept admission to an all-Negro law school established for her by the Univ. of Oklahoma .... Alabama's Democratic Executive Comm. adopts a resolution warning national party leaders not to support anti-segregation policies in the coming presidential campaign.	Truman nominates Gen. Omar Bradley to succeed Eisenhower as Army chief of staff following Eisenhower's retirement .... State Dept. resumes negotiations in Washington on settlement of Russia's Lend-Lease account.	NLRB rules that it has sole jurisdiction in unfair labor practice complaints under the Taft-Hartley Act, challenging the right of federal courts to consider such cases .... International Ladies Garment Workers Union Pres. David Dubinsky announces the expulsion of union officials who refuse to sign affidavits required by the Taft-Hartley Act.			Jan. 26
Alabama Gov. James Folsom announces he will challenge Truman's renomination by the Democratic Party, claiming the President is dominated by "monopolists."	House Select Comm. on Foreign Aid urges continued U.S. support of the Greek government despite its shortcomings.	Truman nominates Thomas McCabe as chairman of the Federal Reserve Bd., succeeding Marriner Eccles, who is demoted to vice-chairman. Observers view the move as a victory for the conservative monetary views of Treasury Secy. John Snyder .... Detroit auto plants lay off 200,000 workers due to gas shortages as a severe cold wave strikes the Midwest.	A TWA Constellation flies from Chicago to N.Y. in 1 hr. 40 mins. at a 482 mph cruising speed, a commercial record.		Jan. 27
Henry Wallace names a six-member National Wallace for President Comm., including singer Paul Robeson and economist Rexford G. Tugwell.	Senate confirms Truman's nomination of Gen. Omar Bradley to succeed Eisenhower as Army chief of staff.	Gallup Poll reports that 51% of the U.S. public favors rationing and price controls to stop inflation, with farmers the only significant group opposed.	U.S. Atomic Energy Commission establishes a $1-million fellowship fund to train biologists and physicians in applications of atomic energy to the life sciences.	Marshall Field's Chicago *Sun* merges with the Chicago *Daily Times* to form the Chicago *Daily Sun and Times.*	Jan. 28
Sen. James Eastland (D, Miss.) urges Southerners to protest "anti-Southern legislation" sponsored by the national Democratic Party, while 48 Democratic legislators in South Carolina protest that the national party no longer represents the South.				American Fed. of Musicians withdraws its ban on FM radio duplication of AM musical programs .... Tarzan hero Johnny Weismuller divorces Beryl Scott in Reno and marries Allene Gates.	Jan. 29
	Congressional Joint Comm. on Atomic Energy approves priority of weapons development over civilian research in the U.S. atomic energy program.		Orville Wright, who with his brother Wilbur built and tested the first successful airplane in 1903, dies at 76 in Dayton, Ohio.	Fifth Winter Olympiad opens in St. Moritz, Switzerland, with 27 nations participating .... Herbert Pennock, general manager of the Philadelphia Phillies and former star baseball pitcher, dies at 53 in N.Y.	Jan. 30
Univ. of Delaware follows the Univ. of Arkansas law school in allowing Negro students to enter graduate courses which are unavailable in state Negro schools.				Dr. L.D. Reddick resigns as head of the Schomburg Collection of Negro History in N.Y., charging neglect by the city's public library officials .... Flashco, with Jack Westrope up, wins the $128,500 Santa Anita Maturity Stakes in Arcadia, Calif.	Jan. 31
Truman's Committee on Higher Education urges larger federal appropriations for colleges and universities, starting at $450 million annually and reaching $850 million by 1960.				George Fischer of Chicago and Loraine Sabbe of Detroit take the men's and women's speed skating titles in St. Paul, Minn.	Feb. 1
Truman sends Congress a 10-point civil rights program, with measures against lynching, poll taxes and segregation in interstate transport. The President's message also urges home rule for the District of Columbia and creation of a permanent Fair Employment Practices Commission. Southern Democrats immediately attack the proposals, accusing Truman of "stabbing the South in the back." .... AFL Executive Council announces its opposition to Henry Wallace's presidential candidacy, charging that he is a "front, spokesman and apologist" for the Communist Party .... Supreme Court upholds a Michigan anti-discrimination statute under which the Bob-Lo Excursion Co. of Detroit was fined for refusing a Negro passage to Canada .... Federal immigration officials arrest accused Communist agent Gerhard Eisler in N.Y. on a deportation warrant.	Gen. Leslie Groves, head of wartime atomic bomb development, accuses Russia of attempting to use U.S. Communists and supporters of the "third party ticket" to gain secret nuclear information.	House passes and sends to the Senate the Knutson bill, which lowers 1948 income taxes by $6.3 billion .... Thomas W. Lamont, board chairman of J.P. Morgan & Co., dies at 77 in Boca Grande, Fla. His will bequeaths $5 million to Harvard, $1 million to the Metropolitan Museum of Art and $4 million to other educational institutions.		Alan Paton's *Cry, the Beloved Country,* a story of racial discrimination in South Africa, is published in N.Y. by Scribners.	Feb. 2
F *Includes elections, federal-state relations, civil rights and liberties, crime, the judiciary, education, health care, poverty, urban affairs and population.*	G *Includes formation and debate of U.S. foreign and defense policies, veterans affairs and defense spending. (Relations with specific foreign countries are usually found under the region concerned.)*	H *Includes business, labor, agriculture, taxation, transportation, consumer affairs, monetary and fiscal policy, natural resources, pollution and accidents.*	I *Includes worldwide scientific, medical and technological developments, natural phenomena, U.S. weather and natural disasters.*	J *Includes the arts, religion, scholarship, communications media, sports, entertainment, fashions, fads and social life.*	

	World Affairs	Europe	Africa & the Middle East	The Americas	Asia & the Pacific
Feb. 3		Food demonstrations in western Germany continue as 1.5 million workers strike to protest the ration administration in Wuerttemberg-Baden, Hamburg and Hanover .... U.S. and Portugal agree to a three-to-five year extension of American use of a military airfield in the Azores.		Brazil's Sao Paulo Univ. announces plans to install the world's second largest cyclotron, built in the U.S.	
Feb. 4		Supreme Soviet ends its winter session after approving the dismissal of Justice Min. Nikolai Rychkov for tolerating laxity and graft among his subordinates. Arts Comm. Chmn. Mikhail Khrapchenko is also removed for approving art and music works that lack the "correct direction" determined by the Communist Party .... Bulgaria's ruling Fatherland Front, consisting of Communists and four other groups, is merged into a single party .... Russia and Rumania sign a 20-year friendship and mutual aid treaty in Moscow .... British government calls on unions to accept a voluntary wage freeze, warning that prices must be kept down for the sake of exports .... Former German-American Bund leader Fritz Kuhn escapes from an internment camp in Dachau.	Iraq denounces its recently concluded defense treaty with Britain.		Ceremonies held in Colombo, capital of Ceylon, mark the island's change in status from a British colony to a dominion.
Feb. 5					
Feb. 6		U.S. and British military authorities in Germany authorize creation of a German "Bizonal Economic Administration," headed by an executive committee responsible to the bizonal parliament. Allied military governors retain a veto right over all decisions of German officials .... Paris newspaper *Figaro* reports that a Soviet factory in the Urals built an atomic bomb which failed to explode last August.			Indian troops report killing 1,900 Moslems in the heaviest battle of the Kashmir conflict near Naoshera.
Feb. 7		Poland's Peasant Party abandons its role as a legal opposition and joins the Communist-dominated government coalition .... France and Spain agree to reopen their frontier, officially closed for two years.	U.N. Palestine Commission urges Britain to allow militia training among Palestinian Jews and Arabs, so that both groups will have defense forces when the British mandate ends.	Argentina signs a trade agreement with Britain, assuring Britain of an uninterrupted monthly supply of 10,000 tons of beef and formalizing an earlier Argentine commitment to purchase the country's British-owned railroads.	U.S. authorities in southern Korea report on an outbreak of Communist-led sabotage and strikes against transit lines and communications, resulting in 27 deaths, 150 arrests and 50 damaged locomotives. A "General Strike Comm. of South Korea" demands immediate evacuation of U.S. troops and creation of a "People's Republic" in Korea .... Chinese Nationalist forces report continuing Communist attacks in the Mukden area and other parts of southern Manchuria .... Indian government seizes the administration of Alwar State near New Delhi, a stronghold of radical Hindu nationalists.
Feb. 8				National Unionist candidate Otilio Ulate defeats government-endorsed National Republican Calderon Guardia in Costa Rican presidential elections.	
	A *Includes developments that affect more than one world region, international organizations and important meetings of major world leaders.*	B *Includes all domestic and regional developments in Europe, including the Soviet Union, Turkey, Cyprus and Malta.*	C *Includes all domestic and regional developments in Africa and the Middle East, including Iraq and Iran and excluding Cyprus, Turkey and Afghanistan.*	D *Includes all domestic and regional developments in Latin America, the Caribbean and Canada.*	E *Includes all domestic and regional developments in Asian and Pacific nations, extending from Afghanistan through all the Pacific Islands, except Hawaii.*

U.S. Politics & Social Issues	U.S. Foreign Policy & Defense	U.S. Economy & Environment	Science, Technology & Nature	Culture, Leisure & Life Style	
Silas Hunt of Texarkana becomes the first Negro student accepted by the Univ. of Arkansas law school.	House passes two bills increasing educational benefits to war veterans by more than $350 million.		August Klein, designer of the Oak Ridge electromagnetic uranium separation plant, dies at 60 in Jamaica.	National Institute of Arts and Letters awards its gold medal "for distinguished achievement" to historian Charles Beard.	Feb. 3
	Defense Secy. James Forrestal consolidates the Navy and Air Force air transport systems into the Military Air Transport Service, under the command of Air Force Gen. Laurence Kuter.	Prices of wheat and other grains begin a sharp plunge on U.S. commodity markets, attributed by observers to the decreasing world cereal shortage .... Arizona's Supreme Court upholds an amendment to the state constitution banning the closed shop.			Feb. 4
Testifying before a House Un-American Activities subcommittee, Atty. Gen. Tom Clark opposes outlawing the U.S. Communist Party but urges that Communists be required to register as foreign agents.	A subcommittee of the House Select Comm. on Foreign Aid issues a report on occupation policy in Germany, calling for an immediate halt to the dismantling of war plants, a general amnesty for unimportant Nazis and creation of a West German government in the U.S., British and French zones.				Feb. 5
	Army announces the first successful use of an electronic guidance system to determine the course of a V-2 rocket fired from White Sands, N.M.	Joint Congressional Budget Comm. votes to trim at least $2.5 billion from Truman's $39.7 billion fiscal 1949 budget.	British Squadron Leader W.A. Waterton sets a world speed record of 542.9 mph in a two-engine Gloster Meteor jet over Moreton Valence Airdrome in England.		Feb. 6
Southern Governors Conference urges Southern Democrats to study Truman's civil rights proposals during a 40-day "cooling-off period." The conference rejects a proposal of Mississippi Gov. Fielding Wright that Southerners leave the Democratic Party .... Governors of Iowa, Kansas, South Dakota and Michigan end a conference in Des Moines by voting to form a Midwestern Governors Conference of 12 states.	Gen. Eisenhower officially turns over command of the Army to Gen. Omar Bradley in a Pentagon ceremony and receives his third Distinguished Service Medal oakleaf cluster from Truman .... Edwin Pauley resigns as special assistant to Army Secy. Kenneth Royall following disclosures of his commodity exchange speculations.			Gil Dodds runs the fastest indoor mile ever timed, 4 mins., 8.1 secs., in Boston.	Feb. 7
Southern Governors Conference names a committee headed by South Carolina Gov. Strom Thurmond to formulate plans for maintaining "white supremacy" in the South. The conference also approves a plan to establish a regional system of segregated colleges and universities .... Harvard astronomer Harlow Shapley is named third-party candidate for Massachusetts governor by the state's Progressive Citizens of America chapter in Boston .... Joseph Frelinghuysen, former Republican Senator from N.J. and board chairman of the J.S. Frelinghuysen Insurance Corp., dies at 78 in Tucson.			Internationally known botanist Burton Livingston dies at 72 in Baltimore.	Sweden captures the Winter Olympics at St. Moritz, Switz., with 82 team points vs. 77 for second-place Switzerland .... Book publisher Julian Messner dies at 62 in N.Y.	Feb. 8

F	G	H	I	J
Includes elections, federal-state relations, civil rights and liberties, crime, the judiciary, education, health care, poverty, urban affairs and population.	*Includes formation and debate of U.S. foreign and defense policies, veterans affairs and defense spending. (Relations with specific foreign countries are usually found under the region concerned.)*	*Includes business, labor, agriculture, taxation, transportation, consumer affairs, monetary and fiscal policy, natural resources, pollution and accidents.*	*Includes worldwide scientific, medical and technological developments, natural phenomena, U.S. weather and natural disasters.*	*Includes the arts, religion, scholarship, communications media, sports, entertainment, fashions, fads and social life.*

	World Affairs	Europe	Africa & the Middle East	The Americas	Asia & the Pacific
Feb. 9	Karl Burkhardt of Switzerland resigns as International Red Cross president, to be succeeded by Paul Ruegger.	French government freezes wholesale meat prices and increases food imports in an effort to check a sharp rise in food prices .... Sixteen European states participating in the Marshall Plan end a Rome conference after approving creation of a permanent agency to train professional workers and promote exchange of skilled workers within Europe .... Western sources report the dismissal of geneticist Anton Zhebrak as president of the White Russian Academy of Science for challenging the genetic theories of Trofim Denisovich Lysenko.			
Feb. 10		Greek Army units conduct their first operation planned by U.S. field advisers, defeating guerrilla bands on the Albanian border .... Soviet Information Bureau issues *Falsifiers of History—A Historical Note,* attacking State Dept. publication of German Foreign Office documents as an attempt to undermine Russia's international standing by portraying prewar events from Hitler's standpoint.	Jewish terrorists execute 10 Arabs near an RAF base in central Palestine, while British authorities report that they have prevented Arabs from smuggling firebombs into Jerusalem's Old City in an effort to destroy the Jewish quarter.		Japanese cabinet of Premier Tetsu Katayama resigns due to dissension between left- and right-wing socialists over cooperation with Communists.
Feb. 11		Soviet Communist Party's Central Committee criticizes composers Dmitri Shostakovich, Sergei Prokofiev and Aram Katchaturian for writing "anti-democratic" music and abandoning Russian traditions of melody .... Danish, Norwegian and Swedish airlines merge to form the Scandinavian Airlines System.			
Feb. 12		British Exchequer Chancellor Sir Stafford Cripps announces a price freeze and asks industry to submit plans for voluntary price and profit reduction.			The ashes of Gandhi are scattered into the sacred waters of the Ganges River in a ceremony attended by Indian P.M. Jawaharlal Nehru.
Feb. 13		Russian authorities in Germany revise the economic administration of their occupation zone, adding more German members to the existing economic advisory commission and giving the commission greater authority to determine production schedules.		Chile rejects a British protest against establishment of a Chilean base on Greenwich Island in Antarctica, 800 miles south of Chile.	Chinese Communists report capturing five U.S. Marines near Tsingtao, charging them with interfering in the civil war.
Feb. 14		Some 100,000 Belgian coal miners, textile workers and gas and electric works employes strike for higher wages. The government blames the outbreak on Communist agitation .... U.S. and British military governors in Germany decide to allow production of aluminum in their zones, an activity forbidden by the Potsdam agreement.			
Feb. 15		Greek government expands its National Defense Council to include U.S. Gen. James Van Fleet and British Gen. E.E. Downs, commanders of the two countries' military forces in Greece.		Romulo Gallego is inaugurated as Venezuela's first popularly elected president in Caracas, succeeding Romulo Betancourt .... Running unopposed, economist Juan Natalicio Gonzalez is elected to succeed Higinio Morinigo as president of Paraguay.	
Feb. 16	UN Secy. Gen. Trygve Lie selects Paris to host the General Assembly's next regular session this September.	Russian composers Sergei Prokofiev and Aram Katchaturian, recently attacked for their music, thank the Communist Party for its criticism and promise to correct their mistakes.	In a report to the Security Council, the U.N. palestine Commission urges creation of a special U.N. military force to save the Palestine partition plan from "catastrophic" failure after the end of the British mandate.	Quebec police close two leftist weeklies, *Le Combat* and *Le Progress de Villeray,* charging that both publications served as centers of Communist activity .... Britain warns Chile against "acts of trespass" in parts of the Palmer Peninsula in Antarctica claimed by both countries.	North Korean People's Council in Pyongyang announces plans to establish a 200,000-man army and draw up a Democratic People's Republic constitution.
Feb. 17		Soviet Council of Ministers names Alexei Kosygin to replace Arseny Zverev as finance minister.		Chilean Pres. Gonzalez Videla lands at Discovery Bay in Antarctica, claimed by Chile and Britain, to visit a Chilean base established last year.	

A	B	C	D	E
Includes developments that affect more than one world region, international organizations and important meetings of major world leaders.	*Includes all domestic and regional developments in Europe, including the Soviet Union, Turkey, Cyprus and Malta.*	*Includes all domestic and regional developments in Africa and the Middle East, including Iraq and Iran and excluding Cyprus, Turkey and Afghanistan.*	*Includes all domestic and regional developments in Latin America, the Caribbean and Canada.*	*Includes all domestic and regional developments in Asian and Pacific nations, extending from Afghanistan through all the Pacific Islands, except Hawaii.*

U.S. Politics & Social Issues	U.S. Foreign Policy & Defense	U.S. Economy & Environment	Science, Technology & Nature	Culture, Leisure & Life Style	
Sen. James Eastland (D, Miss.) calls in a Senate speech for Southern secession from the Democratic Party, attacking Truman's civil rights program as an effort of "mongrel Northern minority groups" to eliminate "the pure blood of the South."		Commerce Dept. suspends oil exports from Atlantic ports until the end of March to ease a fuel oil shortage on the East Coast . . . . Truman urges Congress to approve a two-year continuation of federal aid for highway construction, currently running at $500 million per year.			Feb. 9
CIO Pres. Philip Murray orders CIO regional directors and industrial union council officials to follow national union policy in opposing Wallace's candidacy and supporting the Marshall Plan . . . . Federal agents arrest John Williamson, U.S. Communist Party labor secretary, on a deportation warrant in N.Y.	Battleship *Pennsylvania*, which survived Pearl Harbor and the Bikini nuclear tests, is scuttled near Kwajalein in the Marshall Islands.			Sergei Eisenstein, influential Russian film director, dies at 49 in Moscow . . . . Gallup poll shows *The Jolson Story* as the most popular film of 1947 and Ingrid Bergman and Bing Crosby the most popular performers.	Feb. 10
		A federal grand jury in Washington indicts the CIO and its president, Philip Murray, on charges of violating the Taft-Hartley Act's ban on political expenditures by labor and employer organizations.		A five-man Latin American team scales Argentina's 23,081-ft. Mt. Aconcagua, highest peak in the Western Hemisphere.	Feb. 11
Four thousand Mississippi Democrats meeting in Jackson endorse Gov. Fielding Wright's demand that "all true white Jeffersonian Democrats" unite against the national party leadership.	Nancy Leftenant of Amityville, N.Y. becomes the first Negro admitted into the Army Nurse Corps.		Truman appoints Dr. Leonard Scheele to succeed Dr. Thomas Parran as surgeon general of the U.S. Public Health Service.	British composer Benjamin Britten's opera *Peter Grimes* premiers in N.Y. at the Metropolitan Opera.	Feb. 12
	Senate Foreign Relations Comm. votes unanimously to cut the initial appropriation for the European Recovery Program to $5.3 billion for 12 months beginning April 1.		Science Museum of South Kensington, London announces plans to return the original Wright plane *Kitty Hawk* to the U.S., in accordance with wishes expressed by Orville Wright in a December 1943 letter.	Pope Pius XII names Francis McIntyre Archbishop of Los Angeles and Gerald Bergan Archbishop of Omaha . . . . Mordecai "Three-fingered" Brown, one of baseball's great pitchers, dies at 71 in Terre Haute, Ind.	Feb. 13
		Wholesale commodity prices begin to level off after 10 days of heavy trading on U.S. exchanges, averaging 12% less than Feb. 4 levels.	Floods in the Midwest and South cause seven deaths as a cold wave begins to break.	Joe Verdeur of LaSalle College sets a new world 200-meter breast stroke record of 2:35 in a Yale swimming meet . . . . Winthrop Rockefeller, heir to the Rockefeller oil fortune, marries actress Barbara Sears in Palm Beach, Fla.	Feb. 14
			Engineers meeting in N.Y. award the John Fritz Medal to Theodore von Karman for his work in jet and supersonic flight engineering.	Joseph Hitree wins the $10,000 Harper Prize novel contest with his first novel, *Son of the Moon*.	Feb. 15
Supreme Court rejects an appeal of Mrs. Ada Fisher for admission to the all-white Univ. of Oklahoma law school . . . . Federal agents in N.Y. arrest Ferdinand Smith, a Communist and secretary of the National Maritime Union, on charges of being an illegal alien.	Truman presents Congress with his second report on the $400-million Greek-Turkish aid program and announces that he will seek more military aid for the two countries.	Supreme Court refuses to hear a case brought by the Foremen's Assn. of America challenging the constitutionality of the Taft-Hartley Act, while the NLRB rules that employers can require foremen to leave unions of rank-and-file workers.		Gennaro Cardinal Granito Pignatelli di Belmonte, dean of the Sacred College of Cardinals since 1930, dies at 96 in Vatican City.	Feb. 16
American Labor Party candidate Leo Isacson wins election to Congress from the traditionally Democratic 24th district of the Bronx in N.Y., gaining 55.9% of the vote.	Senate Foreign Relations Comm. unanimously approves the European Recovery Program, voting to finance the program's first year in part with $3 billion from the current Treasury surplus.			Film version of John Steinbeck's *The Pearl* premiers in N.Y.	Feb. 17
F	G	H	I	J	
Includes elections, federal-state relations, civil rights and liberties, crime, the judiciary, education, health care, poverty, urban affairs and population.	*Includes formation and debate of U.S. foreign and defense policies, veterans affairs and defense spending. (Relations with specific foreign countries are usually found under the region concerned.)*	*Includes business, labor, agriculture, taxation, transportation, consumer affairs, monetary and fiscal policy, natural resources, pollution and accidents.*	*Includes worldwide scientific, medical and technological developments, natural phenomena, U.S. weather and natural disasters.*	*Includes the arts, religion, scholarship, communications media, sports, entertainment, fashions, fads and social life.*	

	World Affairs	Europe	Africa & the Middle East	The Americas	Asia & the Pacific
Feb. 18		Hungary and Russia sign a 20-year mutual defense agreement, completing a series of military treaties linking Russia with her western neighbors .... British Trades Union Congress agrees to accept the government's request for a wage freeze, provided that British industries reduce prices and profits .... Belgian Premier Paul-Henri Spaak ends a strike of coal miners and other workers by threatening to draft strikers .... Ireland's Parliament elects Finn Gael moderate John Costello as prime minister, ending the 16-year leadership of Eamon de Valera.	Arab League Secretariat announces the assassination of Imam Yahya, King of Yemen. Yahya's son, Abdullah Ibn Ahmed el Wazir, takes the throne and a new government is formed under Emir Saif el Hak Ibrahim.	Argentina adds its claims in Antarctica to those of Britain and Chile, disputing possession of the Palmer Peninsula and nearby islands. Pres. Gonzalez Videla orders construction of a second Chilean base in Antarctica on the Palmer Peninsula.	
Feb. 19		French National Assembly votes to freeze prices at the Jan. 15 level .... A Nuremberg court sentences Field Marshal Wilhelm List and Gen. Walter Kuntze, German commanders in the Balkans, to life imprisonment for ordering execution of hostages in their theater of operations.			U.N. General Assembly's Interim Comm. on Peace and Security begins debate on the Korean question.
Feb. 20		Eleven non-Communist ministers resign from the Czech cabinet in protest against the recent assignment of important police offices to Communists .... Britain and the U.S. formally approve France's efforts to integrate the Saar into the French economy.		Truman begins a Caribbean tour with a visit to Puerto Rico.	
Feb. 21		Charging a rightist plot to bring Czechoslovakia into the Western sphere of influence, Czech Premier Klement Gottwald demands that Pres. Eduard Benes agree to a reorganization of the government .... U.N. Food and Agriculture Organization opens a permanent European office in Rome following a conference of food experts from 17 European states.	Britain drops Palestine and Transjordan from the sterling bloc as a preliminary step to ending the British mandate.		Japan's House of Representatives elects Democratic Party leader Hitoshi Ashida premier .... China's Nationalist government reports losing the Manchurian steel center of Anshan to the Communists.
Feb. 22		U.S. and British diplomats walk out on a Red Army anniversary celebration in Vienna when Gen. L.V. Kurasov, Soviet high commissioner for Austria, accuses the West of planning a new war against Russia.	Palestinian Arabs plant two truckloads of explosives in the Jewish sector of Jerusalem, destroying a three-block area with 54 deaths and 200 injuries.	Truman continues his Caribbean tour with a visit to the U.S. Virgin Islands, where he promises "an increased measure of self-government and better living conditions."	
Feb. 23		Czech Interior Min. Vaclev Nosek, a Communist, announces that police have uncovered a coup plot by the conservative National Socialist Party and forbids any Czech citizen from leaving the country without special permission. Police raid the National Socialists' Prague headquarters, while members of the majority Democratic Party of Slovakia are ousted from the Slovak provincial cabinet .... U.S., British and French experts meet in London to discuss French demands for internationalization of the Ruhr and other German economic problems.			
Feb. 24	U.N. Headquarters Advisory Comm. accepts a $65-million, interest-free U.S. loan for construction of the Manhattan U.N. building.	Czech Communists begin forming "action committees" to oust anti-Communist officials on all levels of government, while leftist Zdenek Fierlinger takes control of the Czech Social Democratic Party from conservative socialist Bohumil Lauschmann. Prague workers hold large pro-Communist demonstrations as the Czech Federation of Labor begins seizing factories for nationalization .... British government freezes the prices of 9,000 consumer goods at their midwinter levels, effective March 15.	U.S. delegate Warren Austin addresses the U.N. Security Council on the Palestine question, avoiding firm commitment to partition or the sending of a U.N. peace-keeping force to the area.		
	A *Includes developments that affect more than one world region, international organizations and important meetings of major world leaders.*	B *Includes all domestic and regional developments in Europe, including the Soviet Union, Turkey, Cyprus and Malta.*	C *Includes all domestic and regional developments in Africa and the Middle East, including Iraq and Iran and excluding Cyprus, Turkey and Afghanistan.*	D *Includes all domestic and regional developments in Latin America, the Caribbean and Canada.*	E *Includes all domestic and regional developments in Asian and Pacific nations, extending from Afghanistan through all the Pacific Islands, except Hawaii.*

U.S. Politics & Social Issues	U.S. Foreign Policy & Defense	U.S. Economy & Environment	Science, Technology & Nature	Culture, Leisure & Life Style	
	Truman urges Congress to appropriate $570 million for economic aid to the Chinese Nationalist government.	Nine thousand N.Y. bakery workers end a 13-day strike when employers agree to contribute to the welfare funds of the AFL Bakers and Confectionary Workers union and the Retail Clerks Protective Assn.	Legal executors of Orville Wright's estate announce that the Wright brothers' airplane *Kitty Hawk* will be permanently displayed at the Smithsonian Institution in Washington.	*Mister Roberts*, a comedy about noncombat shipboard life during the war, opens on Broadway to favorable reviews .... Thorton Wilder's *The Ides of March*, a historical novel of ancient Rome, is published by Harper and becomes a Book-of-the-Month-Club selection for March .... *Road to Rio*, starring Bing Crosby and Bob Hope, premiers in N.Y.	Feb. 18
Southern Democrats, led by the wife of South Carolina Sen. Olin Johnston, boycott a Jefferson-Jackson Day speech by Truman in Washington's Mayflower Hotel due to the unsegregated attendance of Negroes.		Robert Lamont, former Commerce Secretary and American Iron and Steel Institute president, dies at 80 in N.Y.			Feb. 19
Fifty-two Southern Democratic congressmen meeting in Washington adopt a resolution warning national party leaders against incorporating a strong civil rights plank in the 1948 platform .... CIO leaders order Harry Bridges, president of the International Longshoremen's and Warehousemen's Union, to stop supporting Henry Wallace and opposing the Marshall Plan, threatening otherwise to suspend him from his post as regional CIO director in northern California.		Commerce Dept. imposes licensing requirements on all crude oil exports in an effort to ease the domestic oil shortage.		Lightweight boxer Terry Young defeats former champion Beau Jack by a split 10-round decision in Madison Square Garden, N.Y.	Feb. 20
Wallace supporters establish the Progressive Party of Michigan at a meeting in Lansing.		House and Senate GOP leaders agree to a 30-day extension of the current rent-control law, giving Congress more time to work on a long-term bill.		James McGraw, founder of the McGraw-Hill Publishing Co., dies at 87 in San Francisco.	Feb. 21
					Feb. 22
Sen. Glen Taylor (D, Ida.) announces his withdrawal from the Democratic Party to campaign with Henry Wallace as vice presidential candidate on the third party ticket .... Five Southern governors meet with Sen. J. Howard McGrath (D, R.I.), Democratic National Comm. chairman, to protest Truman's civil rights program. The governors warn after the meeting that "the South is no longer 'in the bag'" for the national party .... Americans for Democratic Action, meeting in Philadelphia, refuse to endorse Truman for re-election but vote to support liberal congressional candidates "regardless of party."					Feb. 23
Earl Long defeats Sam Houston Jones in the Louisiana Democratic gubernatorial run-off primary, virtually assuring his election in November.				Willie Pep retains his world featherweight boxing title in Miami with a 10th-round knockout of Humberto Sierra.	Feb. 24

F	G	H	I	J
Includes elections, federal-state relations, civil rights and liberties, crime, the judiciary, education, health care, poverty, urban affairs and population.	*Includes formation and debate of U.S. foreign and defense policies, veterans affairs and defense spending. (Relations with specific foreign countries are usually found under the region concerned.)*	*Includes business, labor, agriculture, taxation, transportation, consumer affairs, monetary and fiscal policy, natural resources, pollution and accidents.*	*Includes worldwide scientific, medical and technological developments, natural phenomena, U.S. weather and natural disasters.*	*Includes the arts, religion, scholarship, communications media, sports, entertainment, fashions, fads and social life.*

	World Affairs	Europe	Africa & the Middle East	The Americas	Asia & the Pacific
Feb. 25		Czech Pres. Eduard Benes agrees to P.M. Klement Gottwald's demand for creation of a Communist-dominated cabinet after the Czech Social Democratic Party signs an agreement to cooperate with the Communists. Large crowds of workers in Prague celebrate the change of government .... A nine-member group of Western European states begins work in Rome on a tariff agreement for nations participating in the Marshall Plan.			
Feb. 26		U.S., Britain and France issue a joint protest against the Communist coup in Czechoslovakia, engineered "by means of a crisis artificially and deliberately instigated."			U.N. General Assembly's Interim Comm. on Peace and Security votes to advise the U.N. Korean Commission to proceed with plans for elections in Korea despite Soviet refusal to cooperate.
Feb. 27		Czech Pres. Eduard Benes swears in Klement Gottwald's new cabinet, with eight Communists and two Social Democrats among 17 ministers.			Chinese Communist forces report capturing the Manchurian port of Yingkow, frustrating Nationalist plans to land relief units in Manchuria.
Feb. 28		Czech Communist leader Rudolf Slansky is named head of a government committee authorized to purge all parties of "reactionaries." .... Greek police arrest 800 suspected Communists and other "subversives" in Athens and Piraeus.	Rioting by demobilized British colonial troops causes 16 deaths and 100 injuries in Accra on the West African Gold Coast.	Argentina and Uruguay announce an agreement to submit all future disputes to arbitration .... Peruvian Pres. Jose Bustamante Rivero appoints an all-military cabinet.	
Feb. 29		Czech P.M. Klement Gottwald announces plans to break up estates of more than 125 acres, but denies that a collective farm system on the Soviet model will be established.	Stern Gang members blow up a Haifa-bound British train near Rehoveth, killing 28 British soldiers and wounding 35.		
March 1				Costa Rica's Congress annuls the election of Otilio Ulate as president, charging vote fraud. Ulate disappears immediately after the decision.	Gen. John Hodge announces in Seoul that U.N.-supervised elections will be held May 9 in the U.S. zone of Korea, as recommended by the Interim Comm. on Peace and Security.
March 2		Christian Democrat Hermann Puender, mayor of Cologne, is elected head of the Executive Committee, highest organ of the German bizonal administration in Frankfurt .... First Leipzig Trade Fair opens in the Russian zone of Germany, managed by three Soviet export agencies.	U.S. delegate Warren Austin and Soviet delegate Andrei Gromyko inform the U.N. Security Council that their governments favor the partition of Palestine but dislike forcing the plan on the Arabs .... Marquis Louis de Vogue, president of the Suez Canal Co., dies at 80 in Paris.		
March 3		Juraj Slavik and Frantisek Nemec, Czech envoys to the U.S. and Canada, resign with several staff members in protest against the Communist coup in Czechoslovakia.	Leaders of 11 Christian communities in Palestine urge suspension of partition plans to preserve peace.		Vietnamese nationalist guerrillas attack two French convoys moving between Saigon and Dalat in southern Vietnam, killing 175 colonial troops .... Chinese Nationalist government files treason charges against Henry Pu-Yi, former Japanese puppet emperor of Manchuria now in Russian custody.
March 4	International Maritime Conference in Geneva establishes the 35-nation Intergovernmental Maritime Consultative Organization to advise on technical problems in international shipping.	Former King Michael of Rumania issues a statement in London repudiating his abdication, which he claims was "imposed on me by force" by Communist leaders.		Argentina and Chile agree to act jointly in their dispute with Britain over territory in Antarctica.	
	A *Includes developments that affect more than one world region, international organizations and important meetings of major world leaders.*	B *Includes all domestic and regional developments in Europe, including the Soviet Union, Turkey, Cyprus and Malta.*	C *Includes all domestic and regional developments in Africa and the Middle East, including Iraq and Iran and excluding Cyprus, Turkey and Afghanistan.*	D *Includes all domestic and regional developments in Latin America, the Caribbean and Canada.*	E *Includes all domestic and regional developments in Asian and Pacific nations, extending from Afghanistan through all the Pacific Islands, except Hawaii.*

U.S. Politics & Social Issues	U.S. Foreign Policy & Defense	U.S. Economy & Environment	Science, Technology & Nature	Culture, Leisure & Life Style	
U.S. Court of Appeals in Austin rules that Negro student Heman Sweatt cannot be admitted to the Univ. of Texas law school because the state provides equal segregated facilities.				John Sorrells, executive editor of the Scripps-Howard newspaper chain, dies at 51 in N.Y.	Feb. 25
Southern congressmen block House action on an anti-lynching law, already approved by the House Judiciary Comm.				Gertrude Berg's play *Me and Molly* opens on Broadway to mixed reviews.	Feb. 26
	Commenting on the Communist coup in Czechoslovakia, Henry Wallace states that "the men in Moscow, from their viewpoint, would be utter morons if they failed to respond [to U.S. foreign policy] with acts of pro-Russian consolidation."	House passes the Senate-approved $2.5-billion cut in Truman's budget request.			Feb. 27
American Assn. of University Professors, meeting in St. Louis, announces it will defend college teachers accused of being Communists.	Senate Foreign Relations Comm. Chmn. Arthur Vandenberg declares that the Communist coup in Czechoslovakia and Russian pressure on Finland necessitate rapid action on the Marshall Plan. He sets March 15 as the deadline for Senate consideration of foreign aid measures.	Truman signs bills extending wartime export-import controls on scarce raw materials and increasing the pensions of 1.5 million federal employes.		Talon, with Eddie Arcaro up, wins the Santa Anita Handicap in Arcadia, Calif., earning $102,500 .... Eight-year-old Ferruccio Burco makes his American conducting debut in Carnegie Hall.	Feb. 28
Campaigning in Cleveland, Sen. Robert Taft promises Republican support for Truman's civil rights program.	Col. Kenneth Nichols is appointed head of the Armed Forces Special Weapons Project following the retirement of Gen. Leslie Groves.			French entertainer Maurice Chevalier opens a revue of songs and skits in N.Y.	Feb. 29
A House Un-American Activities subcommittee charges National Bureau of Standards director Edward Condon with being "one of the weakest links" in the U.S. nuclear security system, claiming that he associated with "alleged Soviet espionage agents." Condon immediately denies all charges of disloyalty .... State Democratic committees in Tennessee and South Carolina announce their opposition to Truman's reelection.	Sen. Arthur Vandenberg (R, Mich.) opens Senate debate on the European Recovery Program, urging quick passage to prevent the spread of "aggressive Communism."		Dr. Abraham Brill, the psychiatrist who first translated Freud's work into English, dies at 73 in N.Y.		March 1
House Judiciary Comm. passes an anti-lynching measure, bringing Southern warnings that the Republican-dominated Congress has lost its first chance to "make friends with the South." .... N.Y. State CIO executive board approves creation of a state-wide political action committee to oppose Henry Wallace's presidential candidacy .... Christine Johnston asks a Cullman, Ala. circuit court to declare Alabama Gov. James Folsom her common-law husband and father of her 22-month old son, charging that Folsom broke a promise to marry her.		Wholesale food prices begin rising after a six-week decline which brought them to 282% of the 1930-32 average.			March 2
Memoirs of Democratic leader James Farley are published in N.Y. by Whittlesey under the title *Jim Farley's Story: The Roosevelt Years.*	State Secy. Marshall and Defense Secy. Forrestal appear before the House Foreign Affairs Comm. to urge authorization of an additional $275 million in military aid to Greece and Turkey.	CIO United Office and Professional Workers union, meeting in N.Y., defies CIO policy by voting against requiring its officials to sign affidavits required by the Taft-Hartley Act.			March 3
Interstate Commerce Commission dismisses a $15,000 suit brought by three Negroes against the Southern Railway Co. for maintaining segregated passenger accommodations, stating that the cars reserved for Negroes were "not substantially different" from others .... Southern Regional Council on Education, meeting in Gainesville, Fla., approves participation of Negroes in educational policy planning and asks all Southern governors to assign a Negro educator to work with the Council.	Testifying before the House Foreign Affairs Comm., Gen. Albert Wedemeyer urges increased military aid for the Chinese Nationalist government, claiming that "dollars alone will [not] stop Communism."			Mark Hellinger's *Naked City,* a film about the N.Y. underworld, premiers in N.Y.	March 4
F *Includes elections, federal-state relations, civil rights and liberties, crime, the judiciary, education, health care, poverty, urban affairs and population.*	G *Includes formation and debate of U.S. foreign and defense policies, veterans affairs and defense spending. (Relations with specific foreign countries are usually found under the region concerned.)*	H *Includes business, labor, agriculture, taxation, transportation, consumer affairs, monetary and fiscal policy, natural resources, pollution and accidents.*	I *Includes worldwide scientific, medical and technological developments, natural phenomena, U.S. weather and natural disasters.*	J *Includes the arts, religion, scholarship, communications media, sports, entertainment, fashions, fads and social life.*	

	World Affairs	Europe	Africa & the Middle East	The Americas	Asia & the Pacific
March 5		Greek government forces take the guerrilla outpost of Kakavi near the Albanian border after a five-day battle.		Guatemala closes its border with British Honduras in a territorial dispute with the colony.	Indian P.M. Nehru announces creation of an interim "popular" Kashmiri government under Sheik Mohammed Abdullah.
March 6		U.S., British and French negotiators meeting in London report progress towards an economic merger of the French and Anglo-American zones and agree that Germany should be given "a federal form of government."			Philippine Pres. Manuel Roxas outlaws the Hukbalahap guerrillas of Central Luzon, charging they are Communists.
March 7				Congressional elections in Argentina result in a victory for Pres. Peron's party, which increases its share of the popular vote by 10% over the 1946 election.	Chinese Communists claim victory over Nationalist forces in a three-day battle near Yenan in Shensi Province.
March 8		Hungarian Social Democrats vote to merge with the Communist Party .... French National Assembly passes Premier Schuman's income tax program.	Zionist militia Haganah and the extremist Irgun Zvai Leumi agree to coordinate their actions, though maintaining separate commands.		
March 9		Finnish Pres. Juho Paasikivi names a seven-member commission to negotiate a mutual security agreement with Russia.	First U.S.-Russian differences over U.N. policy in Palestine appear when Soviet officials criticize the U.S. for weakening in its support of the partition plan.	Chilean cabinet removes all Communists from government jobs.	Japanese Premier Hitoshi Ashida announces formation of a new cabinet drawn mainly from the Democratic and right Socialist parties .... Dutch officials in Batavia install a new interim government for the Netherlands East Indies under Acting Gov. Gen. Hubertus Van Mook.
March 10		Czech Foreign Min. Jan Masaryk dies in a fall from a window of the Foreign Ministry building in Prague, shortly before a scheduled appearance before Parliament as part of the new Communist-dominated cabinet. His death, reported as a suicide, rouses widespread indignation in the West, where it is viewed as a result of despondency over the Communist coup .... Labor groups from countries participating in the Marshall Plan, including the AFL and CIO, set up a committee in London to advise on labor participation in the aid program.			
March 11		Czech Parliament begins its first session since the Communist coup by passing a vote of confidence in the Gottwald cabinet. It also approves nationalization of all factories with more than 50 workers and a 123.5-acre limit on the size of farms .... U.S. Aid Mission to Greece criticizes government forces for failing to start a major offensive against Communist guerrillas despite superiority in manpower and weapons.			Burmese police arrest Communist leader Thakin Soe on charges of plotting against the government.
March 12	Chile formally charges Russia with threatening world peace in a complaint to the U.N. Security Council occasioned by the Communist coup in Czechoslovakia.	Britain, France, Belgium, Holland and Luxembourg establish a Union of Western Europe in Brussels, covering defense, trade and cultural matters .... Gen. Lucias Clay of the U.S. military government in Germany announces a halt to the dissolution of German industrial monopolies in the face of U.S.-Russian tension .... Coal miners in northern France and Alsace-Lorraine strike for higher wages .... Irish Republican Movement leader George Noble dies at 96 in Dublin.			
March 13		Speaking at a state funeral for Jan Masaryk, Czech Premier Klement Gottwald attacks Western press criticism of the Czech government as responsible for the Foreign Minister's suicide.			
	A *Includes developments that affect more than one world region, international organizations and important meetings of major world leaders.*	B *Includes all domestic and regional developments in Europe, including the Soviet Union, Turkey, Cyprus and Malta.*	C *Includes all domestic and regional developments in Africa and the Middle East, including Iraq and Iran and excluding Cyprus, Turkey and Afghanistan.*	D *Includes all domestic and regional developments in Latin America, the Caribbean and Canada.*	E *Includes all domestic and regional developments in Asian and Pacific nations, extending from Afghanistan through all the Pacific Islands, except Hawaii.*

U.S. Politics & Social Issues	U.S. Foreign Policy & Defense	U.S. Economy & Environment	Science, Technology & Nature	Culture, Leisure & Life Style	
N.Y. Gov. Thomas Dewey enters the Wisconsin Republican presidential primary, running against Harold Stassen and Gen. Douglas MacArthur . . . . CIO Pres. Philip Murray suspends Harry Bridges, head of the International Longshoremen's and Warehousemen's Union, as CIO regional director in northern California for supporting Henry Wallace and opposing the Marshall Plan.	Gen. Uzal Ent, Leader of the Ploesti bombing raid in August 1943, dies at 48 in Denver.		A Navy rocket sets U.S. speed and altitude records at White Sands, N.M., flying to 78 miles at 3,000 mph.	Gus Lesnevich retains his world light-heavyweight title in N.Y. by knocking out Billy Fox during the first round.	March 5
			U.S. Atomic Energy Commission announces free distribution of certain radioactive isotopes for use in cancer treatment.	Ross Lockridge, author of the best-selling novel *Raintree Country*, commits suicide in Bloomington, Ind. . . . . Johnny Longden rides Salmagundi to victory in the Santa Anita Derby, earning $79,800.	March 6
James McConaughy, Republican governor of Connecticut and former president of Wesleyan Univ., dies at 60 in Hartford.					March 7
Democratic National Chmn. J. Howard McGrath announces Truman's intention to run for President, ending rumors that dissatisfaction over the Administration's civil rights program and foreign policy would force his withdrawal from the race.		Supreme Court upholds the convictions of U.S. Gypsum, The National Gypsum Co. and four other firms for price-fixing.		Supreme Court rules that public school teaching of religion is unconstitutional in a case brought by an atheist parent against the school board of Champaign, Ill.	March 8
N.Y. Gov. Thomas Dewey defeats Harold Stassen in the New Hampshire Republican presidential primary, winning six delegates to Stassen's two . . . . Gen. Douglas MacArthur declares in Tokyo that he will accept a Republican presidential draft but has "no plans for leaving my post in Japan." . . . . House votes a $200,000 appropriation for the Un-American Activities Comm.				National Hockey League Pres. Clarence Campbell suspends N.Y. Ranger player Billy Taylor indefinitely for gambling on a hockey game.	March 9
	Testifying before the House Foreign Affaris Comm., Gen. Claire Chennault urges a $1.5-billion military aid program for China over the next three years . . . . Two FJ-1 North American Fury fighters become the first jet planes to land on an aircraft carrier, setting down on the U.S.S. *Boxer* off the California coast.		Harvard Univ. Observatory reports discovery of a new satellite of Uranus.		March 10
United Electrical, Radio and Machine Workers union leaves the CIO Political Action Comm. in protest against CIO opposition to the presidential candidacy of Henry Wallace.	House Foreign Affairs Comm. concludes its hearings on foreign aid by voting to include Greek, Turkish and Chinese assistance with the European Recovery Program in a single bill.	Leaders of 19 AFL building trades unions, meeting in Washington, approve the creation of an arbitration board to settle jurisdictional disputes.		Zelda Fitzgerald, novelist and widow of author F. Scott Fitzgerald, is killed with eight other psychiatric patients in a hospital fire in Asheville, N.C. . . . . *I Remember Mama*, the film version of John Van Druten's play, premiers in N.Y.	March 11
	Senate defeats a foreign aid amendment proposed by Sen. Robert Taft (R, Ohio) limiting Marshall Plan funds for the first year to $4 billion.			Edgar Sisson, former editor of *Cosmopolitan* Magazine, dies at 72 in N.Y.	March 12
Six Southern governors and Sen. Harry Byrd (D, Va.) announce in Washington that they will resist the nomination of any presidential candidate advocating a civil rights program.	Former State Secy. James Byrnes, speaking in Charleston, S.C., warns of an impending international crisis and urges a U.S. military buildup to meet any Russian threat to France, Greece, Italy or Turkey.			Harrison Dillard of Baldwin-Wallice College sets U.S. records of 7.7 secs. in 70 yd. low hurdles and 8.4 secs. in 70 yd. high hurdles in Chicago.	March 13
F	G	H	I	J	
Includes elections, federal-state relations, civil rights and liberties, crime, the judiciary, education, health care, poverty, urban affairs and population.	*Includes formation and debate of U.S. foreign and defense policies, veterans affairs and defense spending. (Relations with specific foreign countries are usually found under the region concerned.)*	*Includes business, labor, agriculture, taxation, transportation, consumer affairs, monetary and fiscal policy, natural resources, pollution and accidents.*	*Includes worldwide scientific, medical and technological developments, natural phenomena, U.S. weather and natural disasters.*	*Includes the arts, religion, scholarship, communications media, sports, entertainment, fashions, fads and social life.*	

	World Affairs	Europe	Africa & the Middle East	The Americas	Asia & the Pacific
March 14					
March 15	U.N. General Assembly's Interim Comm. for Peace and Security establishes a subcommittee to study plans for curbing use of the Security Council veto.	British government bars Communists and suspected sympathizers from civil service positions affecting national security.			Japanese rightist groups merge into a single conservative party, the Democratic Liberals, with 251 members in Parliament. Former Premier Shigeru Yoshida is named party president .... Nationalist forces report losing Kirin and Szepingkai in Manchuria and the former Communist capital of Yenan in Shensi Province.
March 16		Comm. on European Economic Cooperation concludes a two-day session in Paris by agreeing to admit Allied representatives of the three western German zones to Marshall Plan discussions.			
March 17	U.N. Security Council votes to hear Chile's complaint against Russia in connection with the Communist coup in Czechoslovakia.	Britain, Belgium, Holland, France and Luxembourg sign a 50-year defense, economic and cultural treaty in Brussels, formalizing the Union of Western Europe .... Greek government imposes general national mobilization, denying government employes the right to strike, following a one-day walkout of civil servants protesting non-payment of Christmas bonuses.		Canada announces a plan to ease restrictions on private prospecting for uranium and other nuclear materials.	Indian Socialists vote in Bombay to withdraw from the All-India Congress Party.
March 18		Russian authorities sponsor creation of a German People's Congress in Berlin, intended as "the first step towards a constitutional assembly for Germany." .... Bulgaria and Russia sign a 20-year mutual defense and friendship treaty in Moscow .... Premiers Einar Gerhardsen of Norway, Hans Hedtoft of Denmark and Tage Erlander of Sweden confer in Stockholm on Scandinavian cooperation with Western Europe and warn against Communist bids for power in their countries.			
March 19		Former Deputy Foreign Min. Vladimir Clementis, a Communist, replaces the late Jan Masaryk as Czech foreign minister .... French National Assembly passes a bill giving the Army special powers to help the Interior Ministry curb disorders.	Speaking before the U.N. Security Council, U.S. delegate Warren Austin announces a shift in American policy on Palestine, urging that partition be abandoned in favor of a U.N. trusteeship under which Jews and Arabs could negotiate a compromise settlement.		
March 20		Soviet Communist Party Central Comm. sends a secret message to the Yugoslavian Communist Party, accusing it of deviating from the "internationalist" line laid down for European Communists in Moscow and attempting to follow a separate path of economic and political development for Yugoslavia .... Russian representatives walk out of the Allied Control Council in Berlin for the first time when Western members refuse to discuss decisions of the London conference of experts on Germany .... U.S., Britain and France jointly propose abandoning U.N. trusteeship of Trieste and returning the city to Italian control. The three-power statement cites difficulties in choosing a governor for the international zone and frequent clashes between Yugoslavian and Allied troops as reasons for the change.	Rabbi Abba Hillel Silver, director of the Jewish Agency's U.S. office, attacks the "shocking reversal" in American policy on Palestine announced yesterday. Jewish Agency Chmn. David Ben-Gurion rejects "any sort of trusteeship, permanent or temporary." State Secy. Marshall discloses that he originated the U.S. shift in Palestine policy, recommending trusteeship to Truman as the best way to preserve peace in the area.		
March 21					
	A *Includes developments that affect more than one world region, international organizations and important meetings of major world leaders.*	B *Includes all domestic and regional developments in Europe, including the Soviet Union, Turkey, Cyprus and Malta.*	C *Includes all domestic and regional developments in Africa and the Middle East, including Iraq and Iran and excluding Cyprus, Turkey and Afghanistan.*	D *Includes all domestic and regional developments in Latin America, the Caribbean and Canada.*	E *Includes all domestic and regional developments in Asian and Pacific nations, extending from Afghanistan through all the Pacific Islands, except Hawaii.*

U.S. Politics & Social Issues	U.S. Foreign Policy & Defense	U.S. Economy & Environment	Science, Technology & Nature	Culture, Leisure & Life Style	
	Senate ends 13 days of foreign aid debate by passing the Economic Co-operation Act, authorizing $5.3 billion in Marshall Plan assistance to 16 European states over the next year .... Army Secy. Kenneth Royall announces plans to reorganize the Army for faster mobilization, giving Chief of Staff Omar Bradley direct command over forces stationed in the continental U.S.			*New York Herald Tribune* lists *Eagle in the Sky* by F. Van Wyck Mason and *Peace of Mind* by Joshua Liebman as best-selling fiction and non-fiction books.	March 14
A Washington federal court rules the Taft-Hartley Act's ban on union political activity unconstitutional, dismissing charges against CIO Pres. Philip Murray for violating the ban.	A federal court in Washington sentences Gen. Bennett Meyers, second-ranking Air Force procurement officer during the war, to 20 months to five years in prison for persuading an employe to lie in testimony before the Senate War Investigating Committee .... State Secy. Marshall testifies before the Senate Foreign Relations Comm., urging an additional $275 million in military aid to Greece and Turkey.	Some 206,000 coal miners in 11 states strike in a dispute with operators over the miners' welfare fund.	Paul Goedrich, Austrian-born chemist and developer of sulfa drugs, dies at 61 in Newark, N.J.	Toronto Univ. defeats Darmouth, 5-0, to win the Alexis Thompson international collegiate ice hockey trophy.	March 15
FBI reports clearing 1,005,944 federal employes in the loyalty review program.		Some 100,000 members of the CIO United Packinghouse Workers union strike throughout the nation, demanding a 29¢ hourly wage increase .... The number of striking coal miners increases to 360,000, reducing the nation's coal output by 90% .... House votes to extend rent control through March 31, 1949.		*Miracle of the Bells,* starring Frank Sinatra and Fred MacMurray, premiers in N.Y.	March 16
	Speaking before a joint session of Congress, Truman attacks Soviet foreign policy and urges rapid passage of the European Recovery Program and a universal military training bill to halt Russian expansion in Europe .... House Foreign Aid Comm. approves the full $5.3-billion European Recovery Program bill.	Senate rejects the House rent control bill and returns the measure to joint conference.		Phillips 66 Oilers take the AAU basketball title in Denver, defeating the Denver Nuggets, 62-48. St. Louis Univ. beats New York Univ., 65-52, to capture the National Invitation Basketball Tournament in N.Y.	March 17
Florida's Gov. Millard Caldwell and three-fourths of Alabama's electoral college candidates announce they will not support Truman .... U.S. Court of Appeals in Washington upholds contempt convictions of Edward Barsky and 15 other members of the Joint Anti-Fascist Refugee Comm. for refusing to give organization records to the House Un-American Activities Comm.		Office of Defense Transportation orders a 25% mileage reduction for coal-burning passenger trains to maintain reserves during the current coal strike.		American Fed. of Musicians reaches a three-year agreement with four major networks in N.Y., permitting live broadcast of music on television.	March 18
Fed. of American Societies for Experimental Biology ends a four-day convention in Atlantic City after passing a resolution against the "actions and procedures" of the House Un-American Activities Comm.	State Secy. Marshall threatens to end European Recovery Program aid to Italy if Communists win upcoming elections.	Justice Dept. obtains a court order preventing a strike by 800 technicians of the Oak Ridge nuclear laboratory in a contract dispute with the Carbon and Carbide Corp., operator of the facility.	A series of tornadoes striking nine states from Texas to central New York causes 42 deaths and at least 300 injuries.	Doris Hart and Barbara Scofield, both of Miami, win the national indoor women's doubles tennis title in N.Y.	March 19
				Academy of Motion Picture Arts and Sciences awards an Oscar to Elia Kazan's *Gentleman's Agreement* as the best film of 1947. Loretta Young and Ronald Colman take awards for best performances .... Billy Talbert of Brooklyn wins the national indoor men's singles tennis championship in N.Y., while Pat Todd of La Jolla, Calif. takes the women's singles title.	March 20
Truman's Committee on Higher Education issues its final report, urging a federal aid program aimed at increasing the number of college students to 4.6 million by 1960.		Minneapolis teachers end a 27-day strike by accepting a monthly wage increase of $40.		Lloyd Mangrum wins the $10,000 Greensboro Open Golf Tournament in N.C.	March 21

F	G	H	I	J
Includes elections, federal-state relations, civil rights and liberties, crime, the judiciary, education, health care, poverty, urban affairs and population.	*Includes formation and debate of U.S. foreign and defense policies, veterans affairs and defense spending. (Relations with specific foreign countries are usually found under the region concerned.)*	*Includes business, labor, agriculture, taxation, transportation, consumer affairs, monetary and fiscal policy, natural resources, pollution and accidents.*	*Includes worldwide scientific, medical and technological developments, natural phenomena, U.S. weather and natural disasters.*	*Includes the arts, religion, scholarship, communications media, sports, entertainment, fashions, fads and social life.*

	World Affairs	Europe	Africa & the Middle East	The Americas	Asia & the Pacific
March 22	British delegate Sir Alexander Cadogan urges the U.N. Security Council to investigate the Communist coup in Czechoslovakia and states that Communism in Europe must be "dammed back" even at the risk of war.	Italian government agrees to discuss the Western proposal for return of Trieste but rejects a Yugoslavian offer to give up claims to Trieste in return for the Italian border city of Gorizia .... European socialists from 14 states end a two-day London conference by agreeing to support the Marshall Plan as Europe's only hope of avoiding "economic misery and political disorder." .... U.S. military authorities in German issue a new occupation currency.		Colombian Pres. Mariano Ospina Perez appoints a new all-Conservative cabinet following the resignation of Liberals from the previous coalition government.	
March 23	International Conference on Freedom of Information and of the Press opens in Geneva, attended by 57 U.N. members and 13 non-member states.	U.N. Balkan Commission unanimously condemns Yugoslavia for permitting Greek guerrillas to operate across its borders.	Jewish Agency and the Jewish Council of Palestine agree to establish a Jewish provisional government on May 16, the day after termination of the British mandate.	Canadian authorities in Ontario arrest U.S.-born Reid Robinson, vice president of the International Union of Mine, Mill and Smelter Workers, as a Communist alien.	
March 24	International Conference on Trade and Employment in Havana completes work on an International Trade Organization Charter, emphasizing principles of global free trade. The conference also establishes an interim committee of the International Trade Organization, to function until enough nations ratify the charter to make the ITO a specialized U.N. agency.	Belgian Senate ratifies the 50-year treaty establishing the Union of Western Europe.			Chinese Nationalist forces report the loss of Fusin and Tzuchuan in southern Manchuria.
March 25		State Secy. Marshall warns Russia against breaking up the Allied Control Council in Berlin, stating that the U.S. will continue as a "joint occupant" of the city regardless of Soviet actions.	Truman issues a statement urging U.N. trusteeship for Palestine as an "emergency action" aimed at preserving peace, rather than a definitive solution. The Arab Office in Washington rejects trusteeship, calling Truman's plea a delaying tactic intended to give the Jews time to increase their military strength.	Nicaraguan troops are flown out of Costa Rica after Panama publicly demands that Nicaragua stop aiding Costa Rican Pres. Teodor Picado against rightist rebels.	Chinese Communist forces capture the mining center of Tatung in northern Shansi Province.
March 26		Soviet officials indicate that their recent withdrawal from the Allied Control Council in Berlin is not permanent.			North Korean People's Comm. announces plans for a conference in Pyongyang, to include all Korean political groups opposed to separate U.N.-sponsored elections in the U.S. zone .... Indian state of West Bengal outlaws the Communist Party and begins arresting leftist political suspects.
March 27		Gen. Lucius Clay of the U.S. military government in Germany approves dismissal of denazification cases against 300,000 "lesser" party members.	Hagannah uses aircraft for the first time in Palestine fighting against Arabs raiding a Jewish truck convoy near Bethlehem. A second Arab attack on a Jewish convoy results in 45 Jewish casualties at Kabiri in northern Palestine. The raids are part of an Arab effort to disrupt movement of food and supplies between Jewish communities .... Iraqi Foreign Min. Hamdi Pachachi dies at 65 of a heart attack in Baghdad.		Chinese Pres. Chiang Kai-shek orders 300 Kuomintang members elected to the National Assembly as independents to give up their seats, which were promised to lesser parties. He also orders the removal of 400 independents who defeated regular Kuomintang nominees.
March 28		Parliamentary elections in Rumania result in a victory for the Communist-dominated Popular Democratic Front, which gains 405 of 414 seats in the National Assembly.	Easter observances in Palestine are sharply curtailed by Jewish-Arab fighting in the Jerusalem and Bethlehem areas.	Rightist rebels in Costa Rica advance against government forces, taking the San Isidro del General airfield near the capital.	
March 29					China's National Assembly convenes in Nanking as 60 dissident Kuomintang members refuse Chiang Kai-shek's demand that they yield their seats to representatives of smaller parties.
	A *Includes developments that affect more than one world region, international organizations and important meetings of major world leaders.*	B *Includes all domestic and regional developments in Europe, including the Soviet Union, Turkey, Cyprus and Malta.*	C *Includes all domestic and regional developments in Africa and the Middle East, including Iraq and Iran and excluding Cyprus, Turkey and Afghanistan.*	D *Includes all domestic and regional developments in Latin America, the Caribbean and Canada.*	E *Includes all domestic and regional developments in Asian and Pacific nations, extending from Afghanistan through all the Pacific Islands, except Hawaii.*

U.S. Politics & Social Issues	U.S. Foreign Policy & Defense	U.S. Economy & Environment	Science, Technology & Nature	Culture, Leisure & Life Style	
A civil rights delegation headed by A. Philip Randolph visits Truman and declares that American Negroes will not "shoulder a gun to fight for democracy abroad unless they get democracy at home."		Senate approves a Republican-backed $4.7-billion individual income tax reduction for 1948 and sends the measure to the House.			March 22
A Washington federal court hands down a contempt conviction for Richard Morford of the National Council for American-Soviet Friendship, who refused to surrender the group's records to the House Un-American Activities Comm. . . . . Boston's school board bars the Daughters of the American Revolution from sponsoring contests in the public schools because of the group's anti-civil rights stand.	Truman annuls plans to give the State Dept. authority over occupation matters in Germany, allowing the Army to keep control . . . . Senate approves a $275-million supplementary military aid grant for Greece and Turkey.		British test pilot John Cunningham sets a world altitude record of 59,492 feet in a De Havilland Vampire jet fighter.	Univ. of Kentucky defeats Baylor, 58-42, to win the NCAA basketball title in N.Y.	March 23
A Washington federal court sentences Gerhart Eisler to one-to-three-years imprisonment for concealing his Communist affiliations while applying for a passport.	Testifying before the Senate Foreign Relations Comm., State Secy. Marshall defends U.S. opposition to the partition of Palestine by noting the possibility of a Russian military presence in the Middle East as part of a U.N. unit enforcing partition.	House approves and sends to Truman the Republican-sponsored, $4.7-billion income tax cut . . . . Truman names a three-man board to investigate the 10-day-old strike of 400,000 coal miners, while the Interstate Commerce Commission orders a 25% reduction in coal-burning rail freight traffic to conserve coal during the strike.	Physicist Glenn Martin reveals development of a radioactive cloud with an effective lethal area greater than that of the atom bomb.		March 24
	Defense Secy. James Forrestal, the three service secretaries and other military officials appear before the Senate Armed Services Comm. to urge passage of a universal military training bill and temporary restoration of the draft.	House and Senate give final approval to a bill extending rent controls for one year . . . . A federal court in Cleveland orders the A.B. Dick Co. and four other firms to end their domination of the U.S. mimeographing industry, fining the defendants $99,000.	American Academy of Arts and Sciences awards Rumford Medals to Edwin Land for work in polarized light and photography and to E. Newton Harvey for bioluminescence research.		March 25
Franklin D. Roosevelt, Jr. and Elliott Roosevelt, sons of the former President, issue statements urging a Democratic presidential draft of Gen. Eisenhower.	Senate Foreign Relations Comm. passes a one-year, $463-million aid appropriation for the Chinese Nationalist government but refuses to authorize the use of U.S. combat troops in China . . . . Truman tightens restrictions on the sale of aircraft to Eastern Europe, adding pleasure and commercial planes to the list of war goods requiring State Dept. export licenses.		Storms and tornadoes in eight Midwestern states cause 23 deaths.	Jacob Klatzkin, philosopher and editor of the *Encyclopedia Judaica*, dies at 66 in Vevey, Switzerland.	March 26
A federal jury in Kansas City acquits eight defendants on charges of vote fraud in the 1946 congressional election.	Adm. Ernest Gunther, wartime air commander of the Pacific Fleet, dies at 60 in Menlo Park, Calif.	A presidential board recommends a 15½¢ hourly raise for 125,000 locomotive engineers, firemen and switchmen, retroactive to Nov. 1.		*All My Sons*, a film adaptation of Arthur Miller's play, premiers in N.Y. . . . . Univ. of Michigan wins the NCAA swimming title in Ann Arbor.	March 27
				Second annual Antoinette Perry Award for the season's outstanding play goes to *Mister Roberts*.	March 28
Gen. Eisenhower announces through the Army Public Information office that he will not accept a Democratic presidential draft.				Supreme Court rules a N.Y. State ban on publications devoted to "bloodshed, lust or crime" unconstitutional, calling it too vague . . . . *New York Herald Tribune* wins the N.W. Ayer & Son typography award as the best-looking U.S. newspaper.	March 29

F	G	H	I	J
Includes elections, federal-state relations, civil rights and liberties, crime, the judiciary, education, health care, poverty, urban affairs and population.	*Includes formation and debate of U.S. foreign and defense policies, veterans affairs and defense spending. (Relations with specific foreign countries are usually found under the region concerned.)*	*Includes business, labor, agriculture, taxation, transportation, consumer affairs, monetary and fiscal policy, natural resources, pollution and accidents.*	*Includes worldwide scientific, medical and technological developments, natural phenomena, U.S. weather and natural disasters.*	*Includes the arts, religion, scholarship, communications media, sports, entertainment, fashions, fads and social life.*

	World Affairs	Europe	Africa & the Middle East	The Americas	Asia & the Pacific
March 30	Control Comm. of the U.N. Atomic Energy Commission adjourns indefinitely after failing to agree on basic principles of an international nuclear control plan.	Russia moves to restrict ground traffic to the western zones of Berlin, announcing plans to inspect all motor vehicles and trains moving between Berlin and western Germany. The action is justified as a hunt for spies and "illegal" shipments of machinery to the West .... U.S. and British military authorities in Germany suspend most price controls in their zones and fix the Reichsmark at U.S. 30¢ for most foreign trade. The order is seen as a forerunner of bizonal currency reform .... Italian government puts its security forces on alert to prevent a breakdown of the ban on campaign violence after political riots cause seven deaths in 24 hours.	Jewish Agency and Arab Higher Comm. agree to adhere to the Geneva conventions on treatment of wounded and prisoners in Palestine fighting and to let the International Red Cross work in war-damaged areas.	International Conference of American States meets in Bogota, Colombia for a detailed review of hemispheric problems .... Canada's Bd. of Transport Commissioners authorizes a general 21% increase in rail freight rates.	
March 31			Land mines destroy an Arab train near Haifa, killing 40 and injuring 60.		Chinese Nationalist forces announce plans to withdraw from all ports on the Shantung peninsula except Chefoo.
Apr. 1		U.S. begins airlifting supplies to Berlin as Russian forces tighten their ground blockade of the city .... British government takes over operation of the country's electrical industry.	U.N. Security Council passes U.S. resolutions calling for a truce in Palestine fighting and a special session of the General Assembly to "consider further the question of the future government of Palestine."	State Secy. Marshall addresses the International Conference of American States in Bogota, emphasizing that European recovery must temporarily take precedence over U.S. aid to Latin America .... Brazilian government reports supression of an attempted leftist coup and the arrest of several Communist leaders in Sao Paulo state.	South Korean rightist political leaders Kim Koo and Kimm Kiu Sic accept a North Korean invitation to participate in a Pyongyang political conference, charging that U.N.-sponsored elections in the U.S. zone will lead to the permanent division of Korea. Both oppose Syngman Rhee, the political leader considered most likely to win a U.N.-sponsored election.
Apr. 2		Russian representatives quit six of 18 committees of the Allied command in Berlin.			Russian troops maneuver and begin digging fortifications along the U.S.-Soviet demarcation line in Korea .... Indian police arrest Communist leader S.A. Dange in Bombay.
Apr. 3		U.S. authorities close the American sector of Berlin to Russian officials traveling from Potsdam to the center of the city.			
Apr. 4			Algeria's first legislative elections as a French colony result in a victory for pro-French and Gaullist candidates.		
Apr. 5	Working Committee of the U.N. Atomic Energy Commission adjourns indefinitely after voting to stop discussion of Russia's nuclear control plan.	A British transport plane flying to Berlin collides with a Russian fighter and crashes near the Gatow airport in the British sector of Berlin, killing 14 passengers and the Russian pilot. Russia apologizes for the incident and promises not to violate air corridores to Berlin in the future .... A U.S. court in Nuremberg acquits Alfried Krupp von Bohlen und Halbach and 11 other Krupp directors of conspiring with the German government to wage wars of aggression. The defendants remain on trial on charges of abusing slave labor and plundering occupied territories.	U.S. delegate Warren Austin presents the American Palestine trusteeship plan to the U.N. Security Council, indicating that the U.S. will seek to exclude Russia from administration of the trusteeship.		
Apr. 6		Finland and Russia sign a 10-year friendship treaty in Moscow, guaranteeing Finnish neutrality in event of an East-West conflict .... British Exchequer Chancellor Sir Stafford Cripps presents the House of Commons with the government's budget for the coming fiscal year, calling for reduced income and sales taxes, a new capital gains levy and higher luxury taxes .... Former Soviet official Victor Kravchenko brings a one-million franc libel suit against the Paris Communist journal *Les Lettres Francaises* for charging him with embezzling funds from a Russian factory.	Palestinian Jews seeking arms raid a British Army camp near Pardes Hannah south of Haifa, killing seven British soldiers.		
	A	B	C	D	E
	Includes developments that affect more than one world region, international organizations and important meetings of major world leaders.	*Includes all domestic and regional developments in Europe, including the Soviet Union, Turkey, Cyprus and Malta.*	*Includes all domestic and regional developments in Africa and the Middle East, including Iraq and Iran and excluding Cyprus, Turkey and Afghanistan.*	*Includes all domestic and regional developments in Latin America, the Caribbean and Canada.*	*Includes all domestic and regional developments in Asian and Pacific nations, extending from Afghanistan through all the Pacific Islands, except Hawaii.*

U.S. Politics & Social Issues	U.S. Foreign Policy & Defense	U.S. Economy & Environment	Science, Technology & Nature	Culture, Leisure & Life Style	
	Senate approves a $463-million appropriation for aid to the Chinese Nationalist government, substituting a laudatory Foreign Relations Comm. report on China for an earlier report criticizing Nationalist "inefficiency, corruption and bureaucratic maladies." . . . . House votes to make Spain eligible for Marshall Plan aid, but State Dept. spokesmen immediately attack the move.				March 30
		Presidential inquiry board investigating the current miners' strike issues a report pinning responsibility for the walkout on UMW leader John Lewis.		New York Drama Critics Circle names Tennessee Williams' *A Streetcar Named Desire* the best new American play shown in N.Y. during the past year . . . . Max Eastman's autobiography, *Enjoyment of Living*, is published in N.Y. by Harper.	March 31
Senate passes a $300-million aid-to-education bill sponsored by Sen. Robert Taft (R, O.), intended to ensure a yearly expenditure of at least $50 per student in every state.	White House announces the upcoming retirement of Air Force Chief of Staff Carl Spaatz and his replacement by Gen. Hoyt Vandenberg.				Apr. 1
	Congress completes action on the $6.1-billion Foreign Assistance Act of 1948, including the first-year authorization for the European Recovery Program, military aid to Greece and Turkey, aid to China and a grant to the U.N. International Children's Fund.	Truman vetoes the $4.7-billion income tax reduction bill but is immediately overridden by Congress.			Apr. 2
		A federal court in Washington issues a 10-day restraining order against the UMW, calling on striking miners to return to work and resume negotiations with employers. U.S. steelmakers begin to curtail production due to shortages resulting from the strike.		Ohio State Univ. takes team honors at the men's national AAU swimming competition in New Haven, Conn. The women's national AAU swimming championship goes to San Francisco's Crystal Plunge team in Daytona Beach, Fla.	Apr. 3
N.Y. Gov. Thomas Dewey signs a bill establishing a state university system.				Dick Button and Gretchen Merrill retain their national figure skating champion titles in competition at Colorado Springs, Colo.	Apr. 4
N.J. Democratic boss Frank Hague begins campaigning actively for Truman.	Truman names Paul Hoffman, a Republican and president of the Studebaker Corp., to supervise the European Recovery Program as economic cooperation administrator.	Mrs. John D. Rockefeller, Jr., wife of the oil millionaire, dies at 73 in N.Y.		Former federal District Attorney Maurice Milligan's *Missouri Waltz: The Inside Story of the Pendergast Machine* is published N.Y. by Scribners . . . . Revisionist historian Charles Beard's *President Roosevelt And The Coming of The War* is published in New Haven by Yale University.	Apr. 5
Wisconsin's Republican presidential primary results in a victory for Harold Stassen, who wins 19 delegate votes to Gen. Douglas MacArthur's eight. N.Y. Gov. Thomas Dewey wins all 90 delegate votes in the New York Republican primary.	Senate Armed Services Comm. delays action on universal military training pending consideration of Administration requests for funds to increase the size of the Air Force.			U.S. Golf Assn. bars Mildred (Babe) Zaharias from the National Golf Open in Los Angeles, ruling that the tournament is restricted to men.	Apr. 6

F	G	H	I	J
Includes elections, federal-state relations, civil rights and liberties, crime, the judiciary, education, health care, poverty, urban affairs and population.	*Includes formation and debate of U.S. foreign and defense policies, veterans affairs and defense spending. (Relations with specific foreign countries are usually found under the region concerned.)*	*Includes business, labor, agriculture, taxation, transportation, consumer affairs, monetary and fiscal policy, natural resources, pollution and accidents.*	*Includes worldwide scientific, medical and technological developments, natural phenomena, U.S. weather and natural disasters.*	*Includes the arts, religion, scholarship, communications media, sports, entertainment, fashions, fads and social life.*

	World Affairs	Europe	Africa & the Middle East	The Americas	Asia & the Pacific
Apr. 7	World Health Organization becomes a specialized U.N. agency following ratification of its charter by the Ukraine, White Russia and Mexico.		U.N. Security Council Pres. Alfonso Lopez of Colombia opens Palestine truce negotiations in N.Y. with the Arab Higher Comm. and the Jewish Agency.		Chinese Communist forces take the rail center of Loyang in Honan Province and approach Chenghsien, the crossroads of China's north-south and east-west railroads.
Apr. 8					Burmese government announces the start of military operations against Communist guerrillas in central and southern Burma .... Siam's Supreme State Council calls on Field Marshal Pibul Songgram to form a new government after military pressure forces the resignation of Premier Kuang Aphaiwong.
Apr. 9		Soviet Council of Ministers decrees price reductions of 10-20% on many consumer items, including bicycles, radios and cameras .... Minister-Pres. Hans Ehard of Bavaria proposes creation of an interim West German federation from the occupation zones of the Western Allies.	Stern Gang and Irgun Zvai Leumi units attack the Jerusalem suburb of Deir Yashin, killing 250 Arabs.	International Conference of American States is disrupted by rioting in Bogota following the assassination of Colombian Liberal Party leader Jorge Eliecer Gaitan. Mobs searching for Conservative Party leader Laureano Gomez invade the Capitol Building, site of the conference, while the Communist-led Colombian Confederation of Labor calls a general strike .... Argentina grants a $437-million loan to Spain.	Chinese Pres. Chiang Kai-shek announces that the focus of military operations against Communist forces will be shifted from northern to central China, promising to "annihilate all Communists below the Yellow River" within six months.
Apr. 10	Security Council unanimously approves Burma's admission to the U.N., but a Russian veto denies admission to Italy for the third time.	Czech Social Democratic leaders announce plans to merge their party with the Communists .... A U.S. court in Nuremberg hands down death sentences for 14 SS officers, including Gen. Otto Ohlendorf, convicted of carrying out mass executions of Russian Jews.		Colombian Pres. Ospina Perez announces a new cabinet consisting of six Conservatives, six Liberals and one independent.	
Apr. 11		Russia ends an agreement permitting U.S. and British forces to maintain service stations along highways connecting Berlin to western Germany.		Colombian government reports suppression of domestic unrest and imposes martial law to prevent fresh outbreaks.	
Apr. 12				Colombian police arrest Communist leader Gilberto Viera and 18 other Communists, charging them with unlawful assembly under martial law. Speaking at the International Conference of American States, State Secy. Marshall accuses Communists of instigating the Colombian disturbances.	
Apr. 13		Russia rejects the Western proposal for Italian control of Trieste .... Rumania's National Assembly re-elects Petru Groza as premier and adopts a constitution modeled on that of the Soviet Union .... J. Christmans Moeller, wartime leader of the Free Danes organization and Danish foreign minister in 1945, dies at 54 in Copenhagen.			Delegates to the Chinese National Assembly from Manchuria and northern China criticize the Nationalist government's conduct of the civil war, accusing army commanders of withholding weapons and supplies from potentially strong local militia units.
Apr. 14		British House of Commons passes a bill eliminating the death penalty in murder cases for a trial period of five years.		International Conference of American States resumes in a school building on the outskirts of Bogota following suppression of the recent disorders.	
Apr. 15				Brazil begins a roundup of Communists after an explosion at the Villa Militar ammunition depot causes at least 34 deaths near Rio de Janeiro.	Manuel Acuna Roxas, first president of the Philippine Republic, dies of a heart attack at 56. He is succeeded by Vice Pres. Elpidio Quirino.

	A	B	C	D	E
	Includes developments that affect more than one world region, international organizations and important meetings of major world leaders.	*Includes all domestic and regional developments in Europe, including the Soviet Union, Turkey, Cyprus and Malta.*	*Includes all domestic and regional developments in Africa and the Middle East, including Iraq and Iran and excluding Cyprus, Turkey and Afghanistan.*	*Includes all domestic and regional developments in Latin America, the Caribbean and Canada.*	*Includes all domestic and regional developments in Asian and Pacific nations, extending from Afghanistan through all the Pacific Islands, except Hawaii.*

U.S. Politics & Social Issues	U.S. Foreign Policy & Defense	U.S. Economy & Environment	Science, Technology & Nature	Culture, Leisure & Life Style	
Rep. Orville Zimmerman (D, Mo.) dies at 67 in Washington.		Justice Dept. charges John Lewis and the UMW with contempt of court for attempting to void an injunction ordering miners to return to work .... Civil Aeronautics Bd. grants a $5.3-million yearly increase to major air mail carriers, including American, Eastern and United Air Lines.			Apr. 7
	Truman urges Congress to increase the Export-Import Bank's loan authority by $500 million to finance development in Latin American countries.				Apr. 8
House Un-American Activities Comm. approves a bill imposing $10,000 in fines and 10-year prison terms for Communists found guilty of "criminal conspiracy" to overthrow the U.S. government by force .... N.Y. State Democratic presidential primary gives Truman 89 of 90 delegate votes.	Economic Cooperation Admin. Paul Hoffman orders $21 million in supplies sent immediately to Western Europe, the first foreign aid disbursements under the European Recovery Program.	Office of Defense Transportation orders a second 25% reduction in coal-burning passenger rail service to conserve coal during the current miners' strike.		George Lyndon Carpenter, former international commander of the Salvation Army, dies at 75 in Sydney, Australia.	Apr. 9
Gen. Eisenhower holds a Washington news conference to reiterate his unavailability for a presidential nomination.		UMW leader John Lewis and mine operators reach a compromise in their dispute over the miners' welfare fund, agreeing to accept Sen. Styles Bridges (R, N.H.) as a neutral member of the fund's board of directors.			Apr. 10
Midwest Democratic Conference in Des Moines endorses Truman's candidacy .... Communist Party announces a drive for 15,000 new members, focusing on labor groups, Negroes, veterans and Wallace supporters.				Claude Harmon wins the $10,000 Master's Golf Tournament in Augusta, Ga. .... Pittsburgh Steelers coach John Sutherland dies at 59 of a brain tumor in Pittsburgh.	Apr. 11
Mrs. May Broadhead Wallace, mother of Henry Wallace, dies at 80 in Des Moines, Iowa.	Fifteen senators led by Homer Ferguson (R, Mich.) introduce a bi-partisan resolution calling on Truman to propose changes in the U.N. Charter, including abolition of the Security Council veto under certain conditions and creation of an international police force.	Coal miners begin returning to work following agreement on administration of their welfare fund, ending a 28-day strike. Some 175,000 miners remain away from work pending the outcome of contempt charges against UMW leader Lewis .... Senate confirms Truman's appointment of Thomas McCabe to the Federal Reserve Bd. chairmanship despite strong Southern opposition.		Eleanor Roosevelt unveils a 10-foot bronze statue of FDR in London's Grosvenor Square on the third anniversary of her husband's death.	Apr. 12
Nebraska's Republican presidential primary results in a victory for Harold Stassen, who gains 13 of 15 delegate votes.		A Washington federal court upholds the constitutionality of provisions of the Taft-Hartley Act requiring the filing of union financial statements and affidavits affirming that union leaders are not Communists.	Commodore Finn Ronne's Antarctic expedition returns to N.Y. and reports that Antarctica is a single continent rather than two islands, as previously believed .... Ohio River overflows its banks, forcing the evacuation of 3,000 families along the river's course.	First volume of Dumas Malone's biography *Jefferson and His Times* is published by Little, Brown.	Apr. 13
	Truman urges Congress to appropriate $4.2 billion for the first year of the European Recovery Program, while Economic Cooperation Admin. Paul Hoffman authorizes an additional $16.9 million in emergency aid .... Senate War Investigating Comm. issues its final report on wartime military aircraft purchases, charging that Howard Hughes maintained an "obviously corrupt" association with Gen. Bennett Meyers, wartime assistant head of Air Force procurement.			Toronto Maple Leafs defeat the Detroit Red Wings in four straight games to take the National Hockey League's Stanley Cup .... *On Active Service*, Henry Stimson's account of his wartime years as War Secretary and Secretary of State, is published in N.Y. by Harper.	Apr. 14
Tennessee's Democratic Convention defeats an anti-Truman resolution and votes to send its 40-man delegation to the National Convention without instructions.	House authorizes $822 million to increase the size of the Air Force, despite pleas from Truman and Defense Secy. Forrestal for greater balance between the services in defense expenditures. The House also rejects a bill sponsored by Rep. Adam Clayton Powell (D, N.Y.) banning racial segregation in the Air Force .... *Toward World Peace*, Henry Wallace's statement on international politics, is published in N.Y. by Harcourt, Brace.				Apr. 15
F	G	H	I	J	
Includes elections, federal-state relations, civil rights and liberties, crime, the judiciary, education, health care, poverty, urban affairs and population.	*Includes formation and debate of U.S. foreign and defense policies, veterans affairs and defense spending. (Relations with specific foreign countries are usually found under the region concerned.)*	*Includes business, labor, agriculture, taxation, transportation, consumer affairs, monetary and fiscal policy, natural resources, pollution and accidents.*	*Includes worldwide scientific, medical and technological developments, natural phenomena, U.S. weather and natural disasters.*	*Includes the arts, religion, scholarship, communications media, sports, entertainment, fashions, fads and social life.*	

	World Affairs	Europe	Africa & the Middle East	The Americas	Asia & the Pacific
Apr. 16		Seventeen European states, including Allied representatives for western Germany, sign an agreement establishing the Organization for European Economic Cooperation. Belgian Premier Paul-Henri Spaak is chosen chairman of the organization, with a headquarters to be located in Paris .... Greek Army begins its spring offensive with attacks on guerrilla forces in central Greece .... A Sofia court sentences Bulgarian Peasant Party leader Dimiter Gichev to life imprisonment on charges of inciting peasants to sabotage and destruction of food supplies.	U.N. General Assembly begins a special session devoted to the Palestine problem, electing Jose Arce of Argentina to preside over the conference.	Colombian Confederation of Labor calls off its general strike.	Prosecution and defense attorneys end their arguments in the Tokyo war crimes trials.
Apr. 17		Britain, France, Belgium, Holland and Luxembourg establish a permanent committee in London to coordinate security measures .... Russian authorities order a halt to further nationalization of industry in their zone of Germany and stop efforts to restrict traffic to U.S. and British airports in Vienna .... Italian security forces mass 100,000 men in northern Italy to guard against alleged Communist coup plans during upcoming parliamentary elections.	U.N. Security Council passes a formal request for a truce in Palestine fighting .... Haganah forces claim victory in the heaviest fighting of Palestine's partition war, repulsing a three-day Arab attack on the Jewish fortress of Mishmar Haemek south of Haifa.		Baron Kantaro Suzuki, Japanese premier at the time of Japan's surrender in 1945, dies at 79 of a liver ailment in Tokyo.
Apr. 18			Syria's Chamber of Deputies reelects Shukri al-Kuwatly president.		
Apr. 19	U.N. General Assembly unanimously votes to admit Burma as the organization's 58th member.	Parliamentary elections in Italy result in victory for Premier Alcide de Gasperi's Christian Democrats, who win 49% of the popular vote and 53.5% of the legislative seats. Communists and left socialists gain 31% of the popular vote and 30% of the seats.		Costa Rica's five-week-old civil war ends with the victory of rightist rebels under Col. Jose Figueres over the government of Pres. Teodoro Picado Michalski. U.S. State Dept. protests last-minute intervention by Nicaraguan forces on the side of Michalski.	China's National Assembly re-elects Chiang Kai-shek president, disregarding Chiang's disclaimer of candidacy.
Apr. 20		British authorities in Germany announce the suspension of water transport between Berlin and the British occupation zone, accusing the Russians of attempting to impose new restrictions .... A Munich denazification court convicts former German-American Bund leader Fritz Kuhn as a major Nazi offender and sentences him in abstentia to 10 years imprisonment and confiscation of property.	Speaking before the U.N. General Assembly's Political Comm., U.S. delegate Warren Austin urges that plans for a U.N. trusteeship over Jerusalem be extended temporarily to all of Palestine.	Funeral of assassinated Colombian Liberal leader Jorge Eliecer Gaita is held in Bogota without incident.	Adm. Mitsumasa Yonai, Japanese premier in 1940 and an opponent of the Tojo militarist clique, dies at 68 of pneumonia in Tokyo.
Apr. 21	Conference on Freedom of Information and of the Press in Geneva adopts three resolutions, opposed by Russia, urging free access to all sources of information and elimination of censorship.				U.N. Security Council approves a plan for a U.N.-supervised plebiscite in Kashmir to determine whether the territory will join India or Pakistan. The Council also establishes a five-nation commission to mediate Hindu-Moslem conflict in Kashmir.
Apr. 22	International Civil Aviation Organization Council in Montreal adopts rules on technical procedures to be observed by the airlines of 51 nations.	Some 130,000 French coal miners end a three-day strike for better safety regulations following a mine explosion in Sallaumines which caused 13 deaths .... A U.S. court in Nuremberg clears 23 I.G. Farben officials of crimes against humanity but continues to try them on charges of plundering occupied countries.	Haganah forces defeat Arab resistance and occupy Haifa as British troops withdraw to the harbor area. Arabs surrender their arms and begin a mass exodus from the city.	International Conference of American States in Bogota passes a resolution urging participating countries to exchange information on subversive activities and work against "agents in the service of international Communism."	Twenty-two Indian princely states merge to form the Malwa Union.
Apr. 23			U.N. Security Council votes to establish a Palestine truce commission consisting of the U.S., France and Belgium.		All-Korea Joint Political Conference opens in Pyongyang to press for suspension of U.N.-supervised elections in the U.S. zone. The conference is attended by Soviet zone Communists and rightist politicians from southern Korea.
	A *Includes developments that affect more than one world region, international organizations and important meetings of major world leaders.*	B *Includes all domestic and regional developments in Europe, including the Soviet Union, Turkey, Cyprus and Malta.*	C *Includes all domestic and regional developments in Africa and the Middle East, including Iraq and Iran and excluding Cyprus, Turkey and Afghanistan.*	D *Includes all domestic and regional developments in Latin America, the Caribbean and Canada.*	E *Includes all domestic and regional developments in Asian and Pacific nations, extending from Afghanistan through all the Pacific Islands, except Hawaii.*

U.S. Politics & Social Issues	U.S. Foreign Policy & Defense	U.S. Economy & Environment	Science, Technology & Nature	Culture, Leisure & Life Style	
		N.Y.C. Mayor William O'Dwyer ends a 10-day bus strike by promising to support an increase in the city's 5¢ transit fare and a wage raise for transit workers.	Alfred Church Lane, geologist and pioneer nuclear physicist, dies at 85 in Cambridge, Mass.	George Foster Peabody radio awards go to CBS *View of the Press* for news, *Theater Guild of the Air* for drama, ABC's Boston Symphony Orchestra series for music, *CBS Is There* for education and Washington station WOQW's *The Children's Hour* for children's programming.	Apr. 16
				Minneapolis Lakers defeat the Rochester Royals in the National Basketball League finals .... Harrison Dillard sets a new world record of 13.6 secs. in the 120-yard high hurdles, and Charles Fonville sets a world shotput mark of 58 ft. ¼ in. at the Kansas Relays in Lawrence, Kan. .... NBC's *Your Hit Parade* lists *Now Is The Hour* as most popular song, followed by *I'm Looking Over a Four-Leaf Clover* and *Beg Your Pardon.*	Apr. 17
					Apr. 18
A federal district court in Washington convicts film writer John Lawson of contempt of Congress for refusing to tell the House Un-American Activities Comm. whether he is a Communist .... Supreme Court refuses to review a South Carolina circuit court decision banning the practice of viewing a political party as a "private club" in order to exclude Negroes from primary elections.	U.S. Atomic Energy Commission announces the successful testing of an atomic bomb on Eniwetok Atoll in the Marshall Islands.	Interstate Commerce Commission approves a 5% increase in rail freight rates.		Truman opens the baseball season by throwing the first ball in a game between the Washington Senators and N.Y. Yankees at Washington's Griffith Stadium.	Apr. 19
Michael Quill, co-founder of the American Labor Party, quits the party in N.Y., charging that it is Communist-dominated.	Truman names David Lilienthal to a five-year term as permanent U.S. Atomic Energy Commission chairman.	UAW Pres. Walter Reuther is badly wounded in the arm and chest by an unidentified assailant firing a shotgun through a window of Reuther's Detroit home .... A Washington federal court fines the UMW $1.4 million and UMW Pres. Lewis $20,000 in a contempt of court conviction resulting from the recent miners' strike.			Apr. 20
	Truman names Commerce Secy. Averell Harriman special U.S. representative to the 16 European states participating in the Marshall Plan .... House passes and sends to Truman a bill increasing veterans' educational benefits.		U.S. Atomic Energy Commission reports the successful use of irradiated cobalt in cancer treatment.	Baltimore Bullets defeat the Philadelphia Warriors to capture the Basketball Assn. of America title .... *The Goebbels Diaries, 1942-43,* edited and translated by Louis Lochner, is published in N.Y. by Doubleday and named a Book-of-the-Month-Club selection.	Apr. 21
House passes a resolution demanding that the Commerce Dept. surrender the full text of the FBI's loyalty report on Bureau of Standards Director Edward Condon, accused of being a potential security risk by the House Un-American Activities Comm.		U.S. Steel Corp. rejects a USW demand for increased wages and promises to reduce prices in an effort to start a trend towards lower living costs .... Senate passes and sends to the House the Taft-Ellender-Wagner housing bill, designed to encourage the construction of 15 million new homes by 1958 .... Truman names Cincinnati lawyer Charles Sawyer to succeed Averell Harriman, newly appointed U.S. envoy to Marshall Plan nations, as Commerce Secretary.			Apr. 22
Minneapolis Mayor Hubert Humphrey announces plans to run for the Senate as a Democratic Farm-Labor Party candidate.		Club-swinging police break up a United Packinghouse Workers picket line in front of a Kansas City factory and wreck the city's union hall, causing 45 injuries.	American Chemical Society awards the Priestly Medal to Edward Weidlein, director of the Mellon Institute for Industrial Research in Pittsburgh.		Apr. 23

F	G	H	I	J
Includes elections, federal-state relations, civil rights and liberties, crime, the judiciary, education, health care, poverty, urban affairs and population.	*Includes formation and debate of U.S. foreign and defense policies, veterans affairs and defense spending. (Relations with specific foreign countries are usually found under the region concerned.)*	*Includes business, labor, agriculture, taxation, transportation, consumer affairs, monetary and fiscal policy, natural resources, pollution and accidents.*	*Includes worldwide scientific, medical and technological developments, natural phenomena, U.S. weather and natural disasters.*	*Includes the arts, religion, scholarship, communications media, sports, entertainment, fashions, fads and social life.*

	World Affairs	Europe	Africa & the Middle East	The Americas	Asia & the Pacific
Apr. 24		Gen. Lucius Clay of the U.S. military government in Germany says the U.S. will ignore Russian efforts to impose restrictions on Western air traffic to Berlin.		Brazilian police stage a nationwide roundup of leading Communists after Pres. Eurico Gaspar Dutra urges Congress to pass "preventive and repressive" anti-Communist laws . . . . Victorious Costa Rican rebel leader Jose Figueres assumes control of the ministries of Justice, Foreign Affairs and Public Security in an interim cabinet appointed by acting Pres. Leon Herrera.	U.S. and Japanese forces suppress rioting by Korean emigres in Osaka and Kobe. Although the immediate cause of the unrest is Japanese control over Korean emigre schools, U.S. authorities connect it with Communist attempts to prevent U.N.-supervised elections in Korea.
Apr. 25	Russia ends its year-long boycott of the U.N. Trusteeship Council.	Communal elections in the U.S.-occupied states of Hesse and Bavaria result in gains for the moderate Liberal Democrats, the conservative National Democrats and the separatist Bavarian People's Party . . . . Congress of Soviet Composers concludes a Moscow conference after criticizing six Russian composers, including Sergei Prokofiev and Aram Katchaturian, for following an "individualistic" line in their music opposed to the Communist Party's "collective" line . . . . British government offers citizenship to all Polish exiles living in Britain for at least five years.	Irgun Zvai Leumi attacks the Arab city of Jaffa, claiming that it serves as a base for Arab raids on Jewish settlements.		
Apr. 26		A Ljubljana court sentences 11 Yugoslavian officials to death and four others to imprisonment as Anglo-American spies . . . . First Germans to take part in a postwar international conference arrive in Paris to advise the Organization of European Economic Cooperation on German participation in the Marshall Plan.	Jewish National Council in Tel Aviv announces creation of a provisional cabinet, to assume control over Jewish areas of Palestine following British withdrawal. David Ben-Gurion is designated premier and defense minister and Moshe Shertok foreign minister . . . . Transjordan's King Abdullah Ibn el Hussein claims control of all Palestine after British withdrawal, offering Jews a national area as part of their citizenship rights.		
Apr. 27			Zionist military organizations Haganah and Irgun Zvai Leumi agree to operate jointly in the future under the Haganah command and to avoid conflicting fund-raising drives.		Chinese Communist forces advance along the Shantung Peninsula, capturing the rail center of Weihsien.
Apr. 28		Finland's Parliament approves the Russo-Finnish defense treaty.	British forces in Jaffa attack Irgun Zvai Leumi troops to keep them from invading the city's port area, needed for the British evacuation from Palestine.		
Apr. 29		A Bratislava court hands down a seven-year prison sentence for former Czech Deputy Premier Jan Ursiny, convicted of treason for alleged participation in a Slovak separatist plot . . . . A Polish court in Gdansk (formerly Danzig) sentences former Nazi Gauleiter Albert Foerster to death for planning the German seizure of the city in 1939.	Haganah and Irgun Zvai Leumi forces complete the encirclement of Jaffa following the flight of most of the city's Arab inhabitants.	Colombian Superior Court in Bogota orders the release of 12 Communists for lack of evidence linking them to April 9 disorders following the assassination of Jorge Eliecer Gaitan.	Conservative supporters of former Vietnamese Emperor Bao Dai, meeting in Hong Kong, decide to form a provisional central government in Vietnam under French protection, liquidating the separate state of Cochin China. The projected central government is a rival to the Democratic Republic of Vietnam proclaimed by nationalist leader Ho Chi Minh . . . . China's National Assembly elects Li Tsung-jen, a liberal Kuomintang critic of Chiang Kai-shek, vice president.
Apr. 30		Union of Western Europe establishes a permanent military committee in London to handle "common defense problems." . . . . Greek government forces claim a major victory over Communist guerrillas in the Mt. Parnassus-Mt. Ghiona area northwest of Athens, eliminating an important rebel stronghold . . . . Gen. Wilhelm Ritter von Thoma, commander of the German Afrika Korps at the time of the Korps' surrender in 1943, dies at 56 in Soecking, Germany.	Haganah forces overrun the Christian Arab quarter of southwestern Jerusalem and take the Greek Orthodox St. Simon Monastery, an Arab strongpoint.	International Conference of American States in Bogota approves an agreement establishing the Organization of American States, a permanent agency supervising conduct of hemispheric affairs. Participating countries also sign the Pact of Bogota, committing themselves to try measures of conciliation within the hemisphere before seeking U.N. assistance in settling hemispheric disputes . . . . Temporary Costa Rican government of Col. Jose Figueres announces plans to form a junta after the retirement of interim Pres. Santos Leon Herrera.	
	A *Includes developments that affect more than one world region, international organizations and important meetings of major world leaders.*	B *Includes all domestic and regional developments in Europe, including the Soviet Union, Turkey, Cyprus and Malta.*	C *Includes all domestic and regional developments in Africa and the Middle East, including Iraq and Iran and excluding Cyprus, Turkey and Afghanistan.*	D *Includes all domestic and regional developments in Latin America, the Caribbean and Canada.*	E *Includes all domestic and regional developments in Asian and Pacific nations, extending from Afghanistan through all the Pacific Islands, except Hawaii.*

U.S. Politics & Social Issues	U.S. Foreign Policy & Defense	U.S. Economy & Environment	Science, Technology & Nature	Culture, Leisure & Life Style	
Acting Commerce Secy. William Foster, following Truman's orders, rejects a House resolution demanding the FBI loyalty report on Bureau of Standards Director Edward Condon .... Washington's Democratic convention instructs its delegates to support Truman, while Idaho names an uninstructed delegation.				My Request wins the $49,150 Wood Memorial race in Jamaica, N.Y.	Apr. 24
					Apr. 25
Supreme Court Justice Felix Frankfurter names William T. Coleman to serve as his law clerk, the first Negro lawyer to be awarded such a post.	Senate confirms Averell Harriman as U.S. special envoy to European states participating in the Marshall Plan .... Truman orders the release of Ernest Burger and George Dasch, Nazi saboteurs who landed in the U.S. in 1942 and subsequently offered information on fellow conspirators to U.S. authorities. The two are to be deported to Germany .... Truman names Gen. Francis Newcomer governor of the Panama Canal Zone.		U.S. Atomic Energy Commission announces plans to construct a new $9-million cyclotron, the world's largest, at the Univ. of California, Berkeley.		Apr. 26
Harold Stassen defeats N.Y. Gov. Thomas Dewey by a narrow margin in the Pennsylvania Republican presidential primary, while Truman wins the state's Democratic primary.		Bethlehem, Jones & Laughlin and Republic Steel join U.S. Steel in rejecting USW wage demands and promising future price reductions .... William Knudsen, former president of General Motors and wartime director of Army production, dies at 69 in Detroit .... Louis Hill, Sr., former chairman of the Great Northern Railway and son of railroad baron James Hill, dies at 75 in St. Paul, Minn.			Apr. 27
House Un-American Activities Comm. approves a bill sponsored by Reps. Karl Mundt (R, S.D.) and Richard Nixon (R, Calif.), denying Communists non-elective federal jobs and passports and requiring them to register with the Justice Dept. .... A Washington federal court imposes three-month prison sentences and $500 fines on Ernestina Fleischmann and Helen Bryan of the Joint Anti-Fascist Refugee Comm. for refusing to divulge their group's records to the House Un-American Activities Comm.		Two railway workers brotherhoods schedule a national railroad strike for May 11 following the end of a mandatory 30-day cooling-off period in a wage dispute with employers.	Air France Constellation makes the first non-stop commercial flight between Paris and New York in 16 hours .... National Academy of Sciences awards the Charles Doolittle Walcott bronze medal for 1947 to Russian geologist Alexander Vologdin for his work on cambrian fossils.	Speaking before the Quadrennial General Conference of the Methodist Church in Boston, Bishop G. Bromley Oxnam of N.Y. urges a union of U.S. Protestant churches.	Apr. 28
A federal court in San Francisco restores U.S. citizenship to 2,700 Japanese-Americans who signed statements renouncing their citizenship in wartime internment camps.		AFL United Financial Employes union ends a 31-day strike against the N.Y. Stock Exchange by accepting a $3-5 weekly wage increase.		American Fed. of Musicians signs an interim agreement with four major networks permitting studio musicians to play for lower wages on television than on radio .... Hooperatings name *Fibber McGee and Molly* the most popular radio show, followed by *Jack Benny, Radio Theater of the World, Bob Hope* and *Amos and Andy.*	Apr. 29
				Musical review *Inside U.S.A.*, featuring Beatrice Lillie, Jack Haley and Estelle Loring, opens in N.Y. to favorable reviews.	Apr. 30

F	G	H	I	J
Includes elections, federal-state relations, civil rights and liberties, crime, the judiciary, education, health care, poverty, urban affairs and population.	*Includes formation and debate of U.S. foreign and defense policies, veterans affairs and defense spending. (Relations with specific foreign countries are usually found under the region concerned.)*	*Includes business, labor, agriculture, taxation, transportation, consumer affairs, monetary and fiscal policy, natural resources, pollution and accidents.*	*Includes worldwide scientific, medical and technological developments, natural phenomena, U.S. weather and natural disasters.*	*Includes the arts, religion, scholarship, communications media, sports, entertainment, fashions, fads and social life.*

	World Affairs	Europe	Africa & the Middle East	The Americas	Asia & the Pacific
May 1		Greek Justice Min. and Liberal Party leader Christos Ladas is killed in Athens by a hand grenade thrown at his car. The government charges that the assassin, Evstratos Moutsoyannis, belongs to a Communist "execution squad."			Russian-sponsored People's Committee of North Korea proclaims a People's Republic and adopts a Soviet-type constitution, claiming authority over all Korea .... General Padma Shum Shere Jung Bahadur Rana, premier of Nepal since 1945, resigns due to illness and is succeeded by Maharajah Chandra Shum Shere Jung Bahadur Rana.
May 2		German auto manufacturer Wilhelm von Opel, known as the "Henry Ford of Germany," dies at 76 in Wiesbaden.	Britain reinforces its Palestine garrison with Royal Marine commandos and army troops in an effort to limit Jewish-Arab fighting during the British withdrawal.	Municipal elections in Panama result in a victory for the governing Liberal Party, which gains 40% of the popular vote.	Gen. MacArthur declares on the first anniversary of the enactment of Japan's postwar constitution that the country "is now fully oriented" towards democracy and has become "a land of relative calm and purposeful effort."
May 3		British government freezes prices of most manufactured goods at the midwinter level.		Colombia severs diplomatic relations with Russia, citing ideological differences between the two countries.	King George VI names West Bengal Gov. Chakravarthi Rajagopalachari to succeed Earl Mountbatten as governor general of the Dominion of India.
May 4		Soviet Communist Party reiterates its charges of Yugoslavian "deviation" from Russian leadership in a secret letter to European Communist leaders .... Greek government begins executing 213 prisoners convicted on murder charges stemming from a 1944 leftist revolt against the German occupation.	Irgun Zvai Leumi captures the Arab town of Yehudia, commanding the road between Tel Aviv and Lydda airfield.		
May 5		Russia tightens restrictions on the movement of food parcels and precious metals between Berlin and the western occupation zones .... British Medical Assn. announces that it will cooperate with the government's socialized medicine program, despite a membership poll indicating 64% opposition to the plan .... Belgian cabinet of Premier Paul-Henri Spaak resigns in a dispute over the issue of higher state subsidies to Roman Catholic schools.	Haganah forces begin clearing Arab resistance from the Upper Galilee.		Conservative Korean political leaders Kim Koo and Kimm Kiu Sic return to Seoul from a meeting with Communist leaders in Pyongyang and call for a boycott of upcoming U.N.-sponsored elections in the U.S. zone .... Eight Sikh princely states in East Punjab form the Phulkian Union as part of India.
May 6		Allied deputy foreign ministers in London suspend negotiations on the Austrian peace treaty after the U.S., Britain and France attack Yugoslavian reparations and territorial claims against Austria .... Yugoslavian Pres. Tito dismisses Finance Min. Streten Zujovich and Light Industry Min. Andrija Hebrang, charging both with sabotaging the country's five-year economic plan and pushing socialization measures too rapidly .... An investigating committee of the French High Court of Justice clears Gen. Maxim Weygand of charges of collaboration with the Nazis and restores his civil rights.	Zionist militia Haganah is redesignated the Jewish State Army .... Jews take control of Safad, capital of the Upper Galilee, after Arab residents desert the city.		India rejects the U.N. Security Council's plebiscite plan for Kashmir, but offers to negotiate with the U.N. Kashmir Commission on the territory's future status.
May 7	U.S., Britain and France urge the U.N. Atomic Energy Commission to abandon its efforts to devise an international nuclear control plan, blaming Russia for the impasse.	European federalists convene a Congress of Europe in The Hague and hear Winston Churchill urge creation of an assembly representing all European states.			
	A *Includes developments that affect more than one world region, international organizations and important meetings of major world leaders.*	B *Includes all domestic and regional developments in Europe, including the Soviet Union, Turkey, Cyprus and Malta.*	C *Includes all domestic and regional developments in Africa and the Middle East, including Iraq and Iran and excluding Cyprus, Turkey and Afghanistan.*	D *Includes all domestic and regional developments in Latin America, the Caribbean and Canada.*	E *Includes all domestic and regional developments in Asian and Pacific nations, extending from Afghanistan through all the Pacific Islands, except Hawaii.*

U.S. Politics & Social Issues	U.S. Foreign Policy & Defense	U.S. Economy & Environment	Science, Technology & Nature	Culture, Leisure & Life Style	
				Citation, with Eddie Arcaro up, wins the 74th Kentucky Derby over his stablemate Coaltown, taking $83,400 of the $111,450 purse.	May 1
	Gen. Eisenhower formally retires from the Army in ceremonies at Ft. Meyer, Va.				May 2
Missouri's Democratic convention instructs its 34 delegates to support Truman's renomination at the National Convention.	House Armed Services Comm. approves a bill providing for two-year conscription of men 19-25 years old .... Adm. John H. Newton, wartime deputy commander of Allied forces in the South Pacific, dies at 66 in Fort Ord, Calif.		Univ. of Minnesota announces isolation of human poliomyelitis virus in concentrated form for the first time .... A tornado devastates McKinney, Tex., killing three residents and injuring 300.	Columbia Univ. awards Pulitzer Prizes to Tennessee Williams' *A Streetcar Named Desire* (drama), James Michener's *Tales of the South Pacific* (fiction), Bernard De Voto's *Across the Wide Missouri* (history), W.H. Auden's *The Age of Anxiety* (poetry) and the *St. Louis Post-Dispatch* (public service reporting of the Centralia mine disaster) .... J.B. Priestley's *The Linden Tree* wins the annual Ellen Terry Award in London as the best British play for 1948.	May 3
Ohio's Republican presidential primary gives 14 delegate votes to Sen. Robert Taft and nine votes to Harold Stassen. Taft also receives 30 uncontested delegates. Alabama's Democratic primary results in the election of 11 delegates pledged to oppose any candidate advocating a civil rights program .... House Rules Comm. approves a bill requiring the Administration to hand over confidential data demanded by congressional committees and providing jail sentences for anyone who makes such information public .... House approves and sends to the Senate a measure authorizing Southern states to operate segregated regional universitites .... A Birmingham, Ala. police court convicts third party vice-presidential candidate Glen Taylor of disorderly conduct for attempting to use the Negro entrance to a meeting Hall May 1. Taylor is fined $50 and receives a 180-day suspended sentence.	A federal appeals court in Richmond, Va. orders former WAC Capt. Kathleen Nash Durant returned to prison to complete a five-year term for her part in the Hesse jewel theft.	Matthew Woll, head of the AFL international relations committee, praises CIO Pres. Philip Murray for his anti-Communist policy and expresses hope for an AFL-CIO merger.			May 4
A Washington federal court convicts film writer Dalton Trumbo of contempt of Congress for refusing to tell the House Un-American Activities Comm. whether he was a Communist.	Testifying before the House Foreign Affairs Comm., State Secy. Marshall and U.N. delegate Warren Austin warn that efforts to alter the U.N. Charter and limit the great power veto might destroy the world organization.	Government mediation efforts fail to end a railroad wage dispute as union negotiators reject a 15½¢ hourly wage increase offer. Union leaders reaffirm their intention to strike U.S. railroads on May 11.	Senate passes and sends to the House a bill establishing a National Science Foundation with a director appointed by the President and confirmed by the Senate.	Soviet Press Day announcements hail Mikhail Sholokov, author of *Quiet Flows the Don*, as Russia's leading contemporary author.	May 5
	Senate passes a bill providing funds for expansion of the Air Force, allowing for construction of 2,911 planes in 1949.	UAW negotiators break off talks with Chrysler after refusing to modify demands for a 30¢ hourly wage increase and improved benefits.		Norman Mailer's *The Naked and the Dead* is published in N.Y. by Rinehart.	May 6
		Atty. Gen. Tom Clark informs Truman that the government can seize the nation's railroads in event of a strike by railroad workers.			May 7
F *Includes elections, federal-state relations, civil rights and liberties, crime, the judiciary, education, health care, poverty, urban affairs and population.*	G *Includes formation and debate of U.S. foreign and defense policies, veterans affairs and defense spending. (Relations with specific foreign countries are usually found under the region concerned.)*	H *Includes business, labor, agriculture, taxation, transportation, consumer affairs, monetary and fiscal policy, natural resources, pollution and accidents.*	I *Includes worldwide scientific, medical and technological developments, natural phenomena, U.S. weather and natural disasters.*	J *Includes the arts, religion, scholarship, communications media, sports, entertainment, fashions, fads and social life.*	

	World Affairs	Europe	Africa & the Middle East	The Americas	Asia & the Pacific
May 8		Strikes against special meat and fat rations for Ruhr miners spread through the U.S. and British zones of Germany, idling 90,000 workers in Hanover and 3,000 transit workers in Munich . . . . Conservative leaders Ivanoe Bonomi and Giovanni Gronchi are elected presidents of the Italian Senate and Chamber of Deputies over Communist opposition.	Arab commanders order a ceasefire in Jerusalem.	An 11-man junta headed by Jose Figueres, victorious leader of right-wing forces in the recent civil war, takes control of Costa Rica . . . . Student rioting against Chancellor Jaime Benitez forces Puerto Rico Univ. in San Juan to close for the remainder of the term.	Former Burmese Premier U Saw and five associates are hanged in Rangoon for the assassination of Premier U Aung San and six cabinet members last July 19.
May 9		Czech Parliament passes a new constitution, modelled on that of the Soviet Union.		Presidential elections in Panama end in a contested result, with Arnulfo Arias of the Revolutionary Party claiming a narrow victory over Domingo Diaz Arosemena of the ruling Liberal Party.	
May 10		Congress of Europe ends in The Hague after delegates unanimously pass a resolution urging European governments to establish a European Deliberative Assembly to advise on the economic and political union of Europe.		A 10-nation agreement on regional development of the Amazon River basin is signed in Iquitos, Peru. The signatories, who agree to participate in a new International Institute of the Amazon Forests, include Bolivia, Brazil, Colombia, Ecuador, Peru, Venezuela and the U.S.	U.N.-supervised elections in the U.S. zone of Korea result in victory for Syngman Rhee's conservative National Society for the Rapid Realization of Independence, which wins a slight majority of the 192 representatives chosen.
May 11	Truman and State Secy. Marshall deny rumors of a forthcoming U.S.-Russian "peace conference," attributing them to a false interpretation of an exchange of notes between Russian Foreign Min. Molotov and U.S. Amb. Walter Bedell Smith. In a N.Y. speech, Henry Wallace urges an "open, fully reported" great power meeting for discussion of armaments and other cold war issues.	Italy's National Assembly elects Liberal Sen. Luigi Einaudi to a seven-year term as president of the Italian Republic.			
May 12		Holland's Queen Wilhelmina announces her abdication, effective Sept. 6, due to ill health. Her daughter Princess Juliana will succeed her.			
May 13			Arab League in Damascus declares war on Palestine's Jewish community . . . . U.N. Secy. Gen. Trygve Lie names Philadelphia lawyer Harold Evans neutral mayor of Jerusalem under a U.N. trusteeship plan for the city, which will go into effect after the end of the British mandate.		Chinese Communist forces renew their attacks around the Manchurian industrial city of Mukden after a 10-week lull.
May 14		Allied military governors in the western zones of Germany establish a trizonal Bank of German States in Frankfurt, while U.S. and British authorities eliminate restrictions on the entry and movement of foreign businessmen in the Anglo-American zone . . . . Belgian cabinet of Premier Paul-Henri Spaak withdraws its resignation after coalition parties reach a compromise on the issue of state aid to religious schools . . . . Lady Kathleen Hartington, daughter of Joseph P. Kennedy, is killed with her husband, Lord Fitzwilliam, in an airplane crash near Valence, France.	Jewish National Council in Tel Aviv proclaims the state of Israel as Britain's Palestine mandate comes to an end. In a surprise move, Truman announces U.S. recognition of Israel as de facto authority in Palestine, while the U.N. General Assembly ends its special session by approving a plan to send a U.N. mediator to Palestine.		North Koreans cut off hydroelectric power supplied to the U.S. zone after U.S. authorities insist on dealing with their Russian counterparts rather than the Soviet-sponsored People's Republic.
	A	B	C	D	E
	Includes developments that affect more than one world region, international organizations and important meetings of major world leaders.	*Includes all domestic and regional developments in Europe, including the Soviet Union, Turkey, Cyprus and Malta.*	*Includes all domestic and regional developments in Africa and the Middle East, including Iraq and Iran and excluding Cyprus, Turkey and Afghanistan.*	*Includes all domestic and regional developments in Latin America, the Caribbean and Canada.*	*Includes all domestic and regional developments in Asian and Pacific nations, extending from Afghanistan through all the Pacific Islands, except Hawaii.*

U.S. Politics & Social Issues	U.S. Foreign Policy & Defense	U.S. Economy & Environment	Science, Technology & Nature	Culture, Leisure & Life Style	
Supreme Court rules that covenants barring racial minority groups from owning or living on property are legally unenforceable .... Agriculture Secy. Anderson announces his resignation to seek the Democratic senatorial nomination in New Mexico .... Senate Comm. on Public Lands blocks action on Hawaiian statehood during the current session of Congress.	House Armed Services Comm. issues a majority report stating that Russia may risk war with the U.S. even before it produces an atomic bomb. The report urges reintroduction of military conscription .... Three thousand paratroopers in Camp Campbell, Ky. begin Operation Assembly, the largest U.S. military exercise since World War II .... Naval Ordnance Test Station for secret weapons at Inyokern, Calif. officially opens the $8-million Michelson physics lab.			Methodist Church ends its Quadrennial General Convention in Boston after authorizing its Committee on Church Union to consider a merger with the Protestant Episcopal and Evangelical churches.	May 8
Socialist Party names Norman Thomas as its presidential candidate for the sixth time at its Reading, Pa. convention.			Eclipse of the sun is visible along a 5,320-mile path from the Aleutian Islands to the Indian Ocean.	Russian Mikhail Botvinnik captures the world chess championship in Moscow .... *New York Herald Tribune* reports *Pilgrim's Inn*, by Elizabeth Gould, and *Peace of Mind*, by Joshua Liebman, as the nation's best-selling fiction and non-fiction books.	May 9
Democrats from seven southern states meet in Jackson, Miss. to plan a separate Southern Democratic convention, to be held if the national party renominates Truman or refuses to repudiate his civil rights program .... Supreme Court rules for the second time that real estate agreements aimed at excluding racial minorities are unenforceable.		Three U.S. railroad brotherhoods call off a scheduled national strike after Truman orders the Army to seize the railroads "for the protection of our citizens."		Basketball Assn. of America expands to 12 teams when Minneapolis, Rochester, Indianapolis and Fort Wayne jump from the National League.	May 10
	Senate Armed Services Comm. passes a bill reviving military conscription for men 19-25 years old. A Southern-sponsored amendment authorizing racial segregation in the armed forces is defeated before approval .... Both Houses of Congress approve and send to Truman a bill appropriating $3.2 billion for expansion of the Air Force and naval aviation .... Sen. Arthur Vandenberg (R, Mich.) submits a proposal for revision of the U.N. Charter to the Senate Foreign Relations Comm., urging elimination of the great power veto on questions of international conciliation but not on military or economic sanctions.	House rejects a TVA request for $4 million to start construction on a power generation plant.		New York Comm. Against War Propaganda members picket New York's Roxy Theater to protest the forthcoming premier of *The Iron Curtain*, a 20th Century Fox film about Russian espionage in Canada .... Howard Hughes buys 929,000 shares of RKO Studios stock in Los Angeles, enough to give him control of the firm .... New York Ranger center Buddy O'Connor wins the David A. Hart Trophy as the National Hockey League's most valuable player and the Lady Byng Trophy for sportsmanship in Montreal.	May 11
		Seventy-five thousand Chrysler Corp. workers strike 19 plants in Michigan, Indiana and California in a wage dispute .... House approves a measure extending the Reconstruction Finance Corp. through mid-1954 but reducing its lending powers from $2 billion to $1.5 billion.		American Academy of Arts and Sciences names 71 new fellows, including Gen. Dwight Eisenhower, European Cooperation Administration head Paul Hoffman and Atomic Energy Commissioner David Lilienthal .... Attorneys for Russian composers Dmitri Shostakovich, Sergei Prokofiev, Aram Katchaturian and Nikolai Miaskovsky sue 20th Century Fox for allegedly unauthorized use of the composers' music in *The Iron Curtain*.	May 12
Despite a threatened presidential veto, the House passes and sends to the Senate a bill to jail or fine executive branch employes, including cabinet members, who withhold information demanded by Congress .... Senate shelves a House-approved resolution favoring creation of a segregated regional university system in the South.					May 13
Sen. John Overton (D, La.) dies at 72 following an abdominal operation in Bethesda, Md.		Truman presents Congress with a farm program involving "flexible price supports" for agricultural products and other measures intended to raise farmers' living standards .... Minnesota Gov. Luther Youngdahl sends the National Guard into south St. Paul to halt three days of picket line violence in the current meatpackers' strike .... CIO Amalgamated Clothing Workers ends its five-day convention in Atlantic City after condemning Wallace's third party movement and re-electing Jacob Potofsky president .... Traders on the N.Y. Stock Exchange buy and sell 3,840 million shares of stock, the most for any day since May 21, 1940.			May 14

F	G	H	I	J
Includes elections, federal-state relations, civil rights and liberties, crime, the judiciary, education, health care, poverty, urban affairs and population.	*Includes formation and debate of U.S. foreign and defense policies, veterans affairs and defense spending. (Relations with specific foreign countries are usually found under the region concerned.)*	*Includes business, labor, agriculture, taxation, transportation, consumer affairs, monetary and fiscal policy, natural resources, pollution and accidents.*	*Includes worldwide scientific, medical and technological developments, natural phenomena, U.S. weather and natural disasters.*	*Includes the arts, religion, scholarship, communications media, sports, entertainment, fashions, fads and social life.*

	World Affairs	Europe	Africa & the Middle East	The Americas	Asia & the Pacific
May 15			Arab armies of Transjordan, Egypt, Syria, Iraq and Lebanon invade Palestine, taking Gaza and Jericho. Egyptian fighters attack Tel Aviv. An Israeli government headed by David Ben-Gurion takes power, while Israel's first 1,700 new Jewish immigrants land at Tel Aviv and Haifa.		Philippine government orders its security forces to halt offensive operations against Hukbalahap guerrillas in central Luzon . . . . Japanese government suspends war bond interest payments for one year effective July 1 in order to gain $54 million for reconstruction and aid to repatriates.
May 16		CBS Middle East correspondent George Polk is found shot in the Greek port of Salonika, where he attempted to arrange an interview with guerrilla leader Markos Vafiades.	Chaim Weizmann is named president of Israel, as the new country applies for admission to the U.N.		
May 17	Responding to a campaign proposal of Henry Walace, Stalin suggests a great power conference devoted to "peaceful settlement of differences between the USSR and the U.S." . . . . U.N. Atomic Energy Commission votes to suspend negotiations on international nuclear control.		Russia recognizes Israel as the legal authority in Jewish Palestine . . . . Supported by Russia, U.S. delegate Warren Austin charges that Palestine fighting is a "threat to peace" under the U.N. Charter and demands Security Council action to separate Jewish and Arab forces.		
May 18	U.S. State Dept. rejects Stalin's proposal for a U.S.-Soviet peace conference, claiming that Russia shows no greater willingness than before to negotiate on important issues.	U.S. Supreme Court refuses to review the convictions of 74 Germans for the massacre of U.S. prisoners during the Battle of the Bulge, claiming it has no jurisdiction over the tribunal that tried the case.	Typhoid-ridden Arab garrison of Acre surrenders to Israeli forces.		
May 19		Big Four talks on the Austrian peace treaty break down in London when Russia refuses to modify its support of Yugoslavian territorial and reparations demands against Austria . . . . U.S. military authorities ban all Russian-authorized publications from the U.S. zone of Germany in retaliation for a similar ban on U.S.-authorized publications in the Russian zone.	British and Belgian delegates to the Security Council oppose U.S. and Russian proposals for U.N. action to stop Palestine fighting between Arabs and Jews.		
May 20			Big Five Security Council powers unanimously choose Count Folke Bernadotte, head of the Swedish Red Cross, to serve as U.N. mediator in Palestine . . . . Arab forces led by Transjordan's Arab Legion gain control over most of Jerusalem despite U.N. truce efforts.		
May 21		Greek government forces report defeating a 2,000-man guerrilla army northeast of Salonika after a two-day battle . . . . Britain's Labor Party ends its six-day annual convention in Scarborough by endorsing eventual European unification and rejecting proposals to condemn the Marshall Plan as an "imperialistic" plot . . . . Yugoslavian government nationalizes all retail stores in Belgrade except cafes, pharmacies and shops producing their own goods.		Brazil signs a $400-million, one-year trade agreement with Britain.	
May 22		Finland's Pres. Juho Paasikivi dismisses Communist Interior Min. Yrjo Leino, recently censured by Parliament for surrendering 20 internees to Russia in 1945 without formal extradition proceedings . . . . Communists and socialists split in Berlin's Federation of Free Trade Unions, the socialists announcing plans to establish a rival labor group.	U.N. Security Council passes a compromise resolution on Palestine, urging Arabs and Jews to stop fighting but avoiding any reference to the situation as a "threat to peace." . . . . Egyptian forces continue their advance in Palestine, taking Bethlehem and moving beyond Gaza on the Mediterranean coast . . . . British Foreign Secy. Bevin discusses Middle Eastern policy with U.S. Amb. Lewis Douglas, urging the U.S. not to lift its embargo on shipment of arms to the area . . . . U.S. Counsel General Thomas Wasson is fatally wounded by a sniper's bullet in Jerusalem.	James L. Ralston, Canada's wartime defense minister, dies at 66 in Montreal.	
	A	B	C	D	E
	Includes developments that affect more than one world region, international organizations and important meetings of major world leaders.	*Includes all domestic and regional developments in Europe, including the Soviet Union, Turkey, Cyprus and Malta.*	*Includes all domestic and regional developments in Africa and the Middle East, including Iraq and Iran and excluding Cyprus, Turkey and Afghanistan.*	*Includes all domestic and regional developments in Latin America, the Caribbean and Canada.*	*Includes all domestic and regional developments in Asian and Pacific nations, extending from Afghanistan through all the Pacific Islands, except Hawaii.*

U.S. Politics & Social Issues	U.S. Foreign Policy & Defense	U.S. Economy & Environment	Science, Technology & Nature	Culture, Leisure & Life Style	
		Federal efforts to mediate a wage dispute at the Oak Ridge, Tenn. nuclear laboratory end in failure as negotiations are indefinitely suspended .... United Steelworkers union ends a five-day convention in Boston after voting to bar Communists from union office and fight affidavit requirements of the Taft-Hartley Act.		Citation, with Eddie Arcaro up, captures the Preakness Crown in Baltimore, earning $91,870 .... James West, former head of the Boy Scouts of America and editor of *Boy's Life*, dies at 71 in New Rochelle, N.Y. .... Msgr. Edward Flanagan, founder of Boys Town in Nebraska, dies at 61 in Berlin while making a tour of youth facilities abroad.	May 15
					May 16
	White House announces the successful testing of three atomic bombs on Eniwetok Atoll in the Marshall Islands. Truman authorizes further development of the nuclear weapons program based on information gained from the tests .... National Advisory Council suggests to Truman and Congress that countries participating in the Marshall Plan be required to reduce high exchange rates that impede foreign trade .... Joint Congressional Atomic Energy Comm. votes to extend terms of present Atomic Energy Commission to mid-1950.	NLRB rules that under the Taft-Hartley Act an employer may require workers to listen to anti-union talks on company time and property during a union campaign.		Igor Gouzenko's *The Iron Curtain*, the story of a Russian espionage ring in Canada, is published in N.Y. by Dutton .... N.Y. lawyer Thomas Finletter is elected president of the Woodrow Wilson Foundation.	May 17
Medical Society of the State of New York adopts a resolution urging elimination of racial discrimination in admission to the American Medical Assn.		UMW Pres. John Lewis and mine operators begin negotiations in Washington on a new contract for the coal industry. A Washington federal court drops contempt convictions against Lewis and the UMW.			May 18
House passes and sends to the Senate the Mundt-Nixon Communist control bill, requiring Communist groups to register with the Justice Dept. and establishing penalties for any effort to create a "totalitarian dictatorship" in the U.S. The bill also denies passports and federal jobs to Communists .... South Carolina Democratic convention commits its 20 national convention votes to the anti-Truman Southern bloc, while Montana Democrats pledge their 12 delegates to Truman.	State Secy. Marshall holds a press conference to reaffirm the U.S. position that major disputes between the U.S. and Russia can be settled through existing international agencies .... Truman urges Congress to approve $150 million in economic aid to Japan, Korea and the Ryukyu Islands for the coming fiscal year.	Coal contract negotiations in Washington break down after one day when UMW leader Lewis walks out to protest the seating of a Southern mine operators' representative.		Former N.Y.C. Mayor Fiorello La Guardia's autobiography, *The Making of an Insurgent*, is published in N.Y. by Lippincott.	May 19
Senate refuses to consider a House-approved bill granting statehood to Hawaii .... Democratic National Committee selects Kentucky's Sen. Alben Barkley as keynote speaker for the National Convention.			American Psychiatric Assn. ends a four-day convention in Washington after hearing reports on the prevention of epilepsy seizures through use of dilantin and mesantoin.	RKO-Radio releases the film *Berlin Express*, starring Merle Oberon, Robert Ryan, Charles Korvin and Paul Lukas.	May 20
U.S. district court in Washington convicts film writers John Lawson and Dalton Trumbo of contempt of Congress and imposes $1,000 fines and one-year prison sentences on both for refusing to tell the House Un-American Activities Comm. whether they were Communists .... Oregon's Republican presidential primary results in a victory for N.Y. Gov. Thomas Dewey over Harold Stassen, giving Dewey 12 additional convention delegates. Truman wins the state's Democratic primary unopposed .... Truman urges Congress to make Alaska a state and outlines a program for settlement and economic development of the territory, emphasizing its "strategic importance."	Truman names veteran diplomat Henry Grady to succeed Lincoln MacVeagh as U.S. ambassador to Greece and administrator of the U.S. aid program there .... Truman signs the $3.2-billion Air Force and Navy procurement bill.	CIO United Packinghouse Workers union ends its 67-day strike against all meatpacking firms except Wilson & Co., as workers accept a 9¢ hourly wage increase .... Contract discussions in the railroad industry, renewed after railroad brotherhoods called off a scheduled strike May 11, collapse in Washington.		Speaking before the International College of Surgeons in Rome, Pope Pius XII declares that sterilization, birth control and childbirth operations in which the mother's life is saved at the expense of the child's are not permissible for Catholics.	May 21
AFL United Hatters, Cap and Millinery Workers International Union ends a six-day convention in N.Y. after voting to "do everything possible" to defeat Wallace, while the CIO International Fur and Leather Workers Union convention in Atlantic City endorses Wallace's candidacy.			Defense and Commerce secretaries announce plans for development of a nationwide aircraft navigation system, including a radar network, for military and civilian use.	Claude McKay, Jamaican-born novelist and poet, dies at 58 in Chicago.	May 22

F	G	H	I	J
Includes elections, federal-state relations, civil rights and liberties, crime, the judiciary, education, health care, poverty, urban affairs and population.	*Includes formation and debate of U.S. foreign and defense policies, veterans affairs and defense spending. (Relations with specific foreign countries are usually found under the region concerned.)*	*Includes business, labor, agriculture, taxation, transportation, consumer affairs, monetary and fiscal policy, natural resources, pollution and accidents.*	*Includes worldwide scientific, medical and technological developments, natural phenomena, U.S. weather and natural disasters.*	*Includes the arts, religion, scholarship, communications media, sports, entertainment, fashions, fads and social life.*

	World Affairs	Europe	Africa & the Middle East	The Americas	Asia & the Pacific
May 23		Primate of Hungary, Josef Cardinal Mindszenty, issues a pastarol letter condemining a government proposal to nationalize the nation's schools .... Italian Premier Alcide de Gasperi announces his sixth cabinet since 1945, consisting mainly of Christian Democrats and Right Socialists.			
May 24		Allied deputy foreign ministers in London formally suspend Austrian peace treaty discussions indefinitely .... Russia vetoes a resolution establishing a U.N. Security Council subcommittee to hear Czech refugees testify on the Communist coup in Czechoslovakia .... U.N. Balkan Commission in Salonika supports Greek government charges that Communist guerrillas have transported Greek children to Albania, Bulgaria and Yugoslavia.	South Africa grants *de facto* recognition to Israel.		Chinese Pres. Chiang Kai-shek names Wong Wen-hao premier, succeeding Gen. Chang Chun, who declined reappointment .... Tatsukichi Minobe, former Japanese privy councilor and prominent Liberal politician, dies at 75 in Tokyo.
May 25					Chinese Communists report establishment of a unified "administrative region" in the "North China Liberated Area," with a population of 40 million.
May 26		Finnish cabinet crisis is resolved when Pres. Juho Paasikivi names leftist Eino Kilpi to replace Yrjo Leino as interior minister and appoints Communist Hertta Kuusinen minister without portfolio. Communist union leaders cancel a general strike called May 22, at the start of the crisis.	Arab League in Amman rejects the U.N. Security Council's appeal for a truce in Palestine fighting .... Parliamentary elections in South Africa result in victory for the Nationalist-Afrikaaner coalition over the ruling United Party of Premier Jan Smuts, who fails to gain reelection from his home district of Standerton, Transvaal.		
May 27		Maj. Augustin Sram, a leading strategist of the Czech Communist Party, is assassinated in Prague by an unknown assailant.	Lebanon's Parliament reelects Pres. Bechara el-Khoury for a six-year term.		Philippine security forces resume their attack on Hukbalahap guerrillas in central Luzon after Huk leader Luis Taruc rejects a government peace offer .... Narayan Vinayak Godse and eight co-defendants are formally charged in New Dehli with the murder of Gandhi.
May 28	International Court of Justice in The Hague rules that Russia acted illegally in vetoing the U.N. membership requests of five countries. The ruling is advisory and not binding on the U.N.	Rumania establishes state monopolies for oil exports and all imports, completing nationalization of the country's commerce .... U.S. authorities in Germany lift their ban on Russian-authorized publications after Soviet authorities promise a free inter-zonal flow of information .... Twenty-four exiled members of the Czech parliament, meeting in London, denounce upcoming legislative elections in their country and resolve to fight for restoration of political freedom.	Arab Legion forces the surrender of 2,500 Jews in the Old City of Jerusalem after a 10-day siege. Surrender terms provide for the imprisonment of 500 Jewish fighters outside Palestine and the evacuation of other Jewish inhabitants. Jews remain in control of Jerusalem's New City .... Jan Smuts resigns as South African premier following his party's defeat in parliamentary elections.		
May 29		Bulgaria and Poland sign a 20-year mutual assistance pact in Warsaw .... Unity Freeman-Mitford, sister-in-law of British fascist leader Oswald Mosley and a former associate of Adolf Hitler, dies at 33 of meningitis in Oban, Scotland.	U.N. Security Council passes a resolution calling again for a truce in Palestine fighting and a worldwide embargo of arms shipments to the Middle East, threatening to take police action under the U.N. Charter if Arabs and Jews ignore the appeal .... Arab and Jewish forces clash near Latrun on the Tel Aviv-Jerusalem highway in the heaviest battle of the Palestine war, with indecisive results.		
	A *Includes developments that affect more than one world region, international organizations and important meetings of major world leaders.*	B *Includes all domestic and regional developments in Europe, including the Soviet Union, Turkey, Cyprus and Malta.*	C *Includes all domestic and regional developments in Africa and the Middle East, including Iraq and Iran and excluding Cyprus, Turkey and Afghanistan.*	D *Includes all domestic and regional developments in Latin America, the Caribbean and Canada.*	E *Includes all domestic and regional developments in Asian and Pacific nations, extending from Afghanistan through all the Pacific Islands, except Hawaii.*

U.S. Politics & Social Issues	U.S. Foreign Policy & Defense	U.S. Economy & Environment	Science, Technology & Nature	Culture, Leisure & Life Style	
				Belgian Cyrille Delannoit wins the European middleweight boxing crown from Marcel Cerdan of French Morocco.	May 23
Truman names N.Y. lawyer Frieda Hennock the first woman member of the Federal Communications Commission.	Senate Armed Services Comm. agrees to eliminate compulsory military training of 18-year-olds from its military conscription bill.	Truman urges Congress to increase social security and survivor pensions by "at least 50%." He also requests an extension of unemployment insurance to federal employes and workers in small firms . . . . Truman names Charles Brannan to succeed Clinton Anderson as Agriculture Secretary . . . . AT&T signs 13 contracts containing no general wage increase for 54,000 Bell Telephone workers . . . . AFL International Printing Pressmen's Union and the Printing Industry of America sign a five-year industry-wide agreement barring strikes and lockouts.		Oldest continuously run race in North America, the 89th annual King's Plate in Toronto, is won by Last Mark, with Howard Bailey up . . . . Memoirs of former State Secy. Cordell Hull are published in two volumes by Macmillan.	May 24
Texas Democratic convention directs its national convention delegates to fight Truman's civil rights program, but pledges its 23 presidential electors to vote for the party nominee . . . . Harold Stassen declares that three-fourths of the Oregon delegates chosen in the state's presidential primary are his supporters, despite his second-place showing in the popular vote. Voting at the Texas Republican convention results in a victory for Sen. Robert Taft, who gains 30 delegates.	Israeli Pres. Chaim Weizmann visits Truman at the White House and later expresses hope that the U.S. will lift its arms embargo and grant Israel a $90-100 million loan.	GM averts a threatened strike of UAW members by granting workers an 11¢ hourly wage increase in a contract providing for an automatic cost-of-living increase, the first such provision in the auto industry . . . . Railway Labor Executives Assn., representing 20 unions, and the Brotherhood of Locomotive Engineers urge nationalization of the nation's railroads following the breakdown of industry contract negotiations.		Ben Hogan takes the Professional Golfers Assn. title in St. Louis, winning $3,500 . . . . *The Stilwell Papers*, Gen. Joseph Stilwell's wartime memoirs edited by Theodore White, are published in N.Y. by Sloane.	May 25
Oklahoma and New Mexico Apaches file an $8-million claim against the U.S. government, charging that the tribe was imprisoned by the Army in Florida, Alabama and Oklahoma from 1886 to 1913 and that Apache lands in New Mexico were given to whites in 1877.	House approves and sends to the Senate a bill extending the Reciprocal Trade Agreement for one year, with provisions giving Congress power to veto any tariff concession exceeding limits set by the U.S. Tariff Commission.			A *Variety* poll of drama critics names Judith Anderson and Paul Kelly best actress and actor for the 1947-48 theater season.	May 26
In a letter to the President's Loyalty Review Bd., Atty. Gen. Tom Clark rules that the Communist Party advocates violent overthrow of the U.S. government and that party members can be dismissed from federal employment under the Hatch Act.	Senate Foreign Relations Comm. unanimously recommends that the U.S. support regional defense arrangements like the Union of Western Europe to remove "dangerous uncertainties that might mislead potential aggressors."			Rudolph Wurlitzer, former president of the musical instrument company, dies at 74 in Cincinnati.	May 27
President's Loyalty Review Bd. releases a list of 32 organizations described as subversive, including the Young Communist League, the Civil Rights Congress (Michigan and Milwaukee chapters), the German-American Republican League and the United Harlem Tenants and Consumers Organization.	U.S. Treasury ends a seven-year freeze on $60 million in Spanish assets in the U.S.	Chrysler Corp. workers end their 17-day strike after accepting a 13¢ hourly wage increase in a contract with no cost-of-living escalator.	Lewis Allen, nationally known radiologist and teacher at the Univ. of Kansas medical school, dies at 75 in Kansas City.		May 28
Kansas Democratic convention in Wichita instructs its 16 delegates to vote for Truman.				*Oklahoma!* closes on Broadway after a world record 2,246 performances, grossing $7 million on an $80,000 investment.	May 29

F	G	H	I	J
Includes elections, federal-state relations, civil rights and liberties, crime, the judiciary, education, health care, poverty, urban affairs and population.	*Includes formation and debate of U.S. foreign and defense policies, veterans affairs and defense spending. (Relations with specific foreign countries are usually found under the region concerned.)*	*Includes business, labor, agriculture, taxation, transportation, consumer affairs, monetary and fiscal policy, natural resources, pollution and accidents.*	*Includes worldwide scientific, medical and technological developments, natural phenomena, U.S. weather and natural disasters.*	*Includes the arts, religion, scholarship, communications media, sports, entertainment, fashions, fads and social life.*

	World Affairs	Europe	Africa & the Middle East	The Americas	Asia & the Pacific
May 30		Parliamentary elections in Czechoslovakia result in a 90% vote for Communists and their coalition partners in the absence of significant opposition .... Pope Pius XII broadcasts an appeal to Hungarian Catholics to resist "bolshevization" of their country through nationalization of religious schools .... Municipal elections in Bavaria result in a 15.6% vote for the new rightist Bavarian Party, which gains most of its support from the previously dominant Christian Social Union.	U.N. mediator Folke Bernadotte arrives in the Middle East and begins ceasefire negotiations with rival leaders in Egypt, Transjordan and Palestine.		A meeting of Peking University students approves a resolution charging the U.S. with supporting the military and economic revival of Japan in violation of the Potsdam Agreement, creating a renewed threat to Chinese independence.
May 31	Britain's Overseas Development Corp. begins a 100-million pound program to encourage the economic growth of British colonies, concentrating on power and agricultural industries.	Negotiators for the U.S., Britain, France, Holland, Belgium and Luxembourg, meeting in London, agree to allow creation of a West German government with limited sovereignty within the next year.	Arab and Jewish forces continue their indecisive struggle for the Jerusalem-Tel Aviv road around Latrun.		South Korea's newly elected National Assembly convenes in Seoul and elects Syngman Rhee chairman .... Chinese Premier Wong Wen-hao forms the country's first constitutional cabinet, consisting of 18 Kuomintang, four Young China and two nonparty members.
June 1		French Premier Robert Schuman wins a vote of confidence in the National Assembly on government plans to dismiss 150,000 civil servants in an economy move.	Israel and the Arab League inform U.N. mediator Folke Bernadotte that they are willing "in principle" to accept a truce in Palestine fighting.	Presidential elections in Cuba result in victory for government-supported Republican Alliance candidate Carlos Prio Socarras. Former Pres. Fulgencio Batista is elected senator in Santa Clara Province .... Mexico City's government-built Hotel del Prado is forced to open without the blessing of Archbishop Luis Maria Martinez due to a controversial mural by artist Diego Rivera containing the inscription "God does not exist."	Gen. MacArthur announces a currency agreement between Japan and the British sterling area providing for increased trade .... Australia inaugurates a free medical care plan despite a physicians' boycott.
June 2		U.S. Army's European Command transfers its headquarters from Frankfurt to Heidelberg .... British House of Lords rejects the five-year trial abolition of capital punishment approved earlier by the House of Commons .... Seven SS physicians convicted of conducting medical "experiments" on concentration camp prisoners, including Karl Brandt and Karl Gebhardt, are hanged in Landsberg prison.			
June 3		Polish government begins sale of homes and businesses seized from Germans to settlers in Poland's new western territories .... Yugoslavian government orders pre-military training for all young people under military service age and more military courses in schools and colleges.	Britain extends its arms embargo to all Arab states fighting Israel .... Nationalist leader Daniel Malan announces his first cabinet as South Africa's new premier, consisting of 11 Nationalists and one Afrikaaner.	A plebiscite in Newfoundland and Labrador results in a slight majority in favor of self-government, but a second vote is called for July to decide between autonomy and federation with Canada .... A bloodless military coup staged by followers of President-elect Juan Natalico Gonzalez forces Gen. Higinio Morinigo to resign as Paraguay's chief executive.	
June 4		International Socialist Conference meeting in Vienna suspends Italy's Left Socialists, led by Pietro Nenni, for cooperating with the Communists .... Russia orders a 15-20% wage increase for workers in its Berlin sector, despite British complaints that the move violates a Big Four agreement to maintain equal wage scales .... Sir Brian Robertson, British military governor in Germany, announces a new policy of encouraging contacts between British officials and Germans, whom he describes as "civilized people whose interests converge with ours."	South Africa refuses to account for its administration of South-West Africa, a former League of Nations mandate territory, to the U.N. Trusteeship Council.	Colombia, Ecuador, Panama and Venezuela give preliminary approval to a customs union in a Quito meeting.	
June 5					French Indochina High Commissioner Emile Bollaert and conservative Vietnamese political leader Nguyen Van Xuan sign the Bay of Along agreement, establishing a provisional Vietnamese government in Tonkin, Annam and Cochin China. France retains control over the new state's foreign and military affairs.
June 6		Josef Cardinal Mindszenty urges Hungarian Catholics to boycott pro-government newspapers, which he denounces for "falsehood, deceit and terror."		Presidential elections in Ecuador result in victory for National Democratic Movement candidate Galo Plaza Lasso over Manuel Elicio Flor Torres of the Conservative Party and Socialist-Liberal Gen. Alberto Enriquez.	
	A	B	C	D	E
	Includes developments that affect more than one world region, international organizations and important meetings of major world leaders.	*Includes all domestic and regional developments in Europe, including the Soviet Union, Turkey, Cyprus and Malta.*	*Includes all domestic and regional developments in Africa and the Middle East, including Iraq and Iran and excluding Cyprus, Turkey and Afghanistan.*	*Includes all domestic and regional developments in Latin America, the Caribbean and Canada.*	*Includes all domestic and regional developments in Asian and Pacific nations, extending from Afghanistan through all the Pacific Islands, except Hawaii.*

U.S. Politics & Social Issues	U.S. Foreign Policy & Defense	U.S. Economy & Environment	Science, Technology & Nature	Culture, Leisure & Life Style	
		Federal Power Commission authorizes construction of a 1,840-mile pipeline to carry natural gas from Texas to the Middle Atlantic states.	Armenian physicists Abram and Artemy Alikhanov win the Stalin Prize for work in cosmic ray research.		May 30
			Truman declares parts of Washington, Oregon and Idaho disaster areas after a week of flooding along the Columbia River causes 23 deaths and over $100 million in property damage, making 50,000 residents homeless.	Mauri Rose wins the 32nd 500-mile Memorial Day race in Indianapolis with a record average speed of 119.813 mph, earning $28,000.	May 31
Senate unanimously approves and sends to the House a bill authorizing the dismissal of "indiscreet or disloyal" government employes by "sensitive" departments .... State Democratic conventions in California and Maryland pledge a total of 74 delegates to Truman.	Senate approves and sends to the House a bill allowing the Export-Import Bank to lend an additional $500 million to Latin American states.	Supreme Court unanimously rules that veterans holding Civil Service jobs have "absolute preference" over non-veteran government employes in job retention.			June 1
Senate passes and sends to the House a bill authorizing the immigration of 200,000 European refugees over the next two years, stipulating that half of the quota must come from Baltic states overrun by Russia and that all immigrants must have spent time in Central European refugee camps.		White House talks aimed at settling the railroad industry's contract dispute end in failure .... AFL Atomic Trades and Labor Council rejects a "final" wage offer by the Carbon and Carbide Chemical Corp. in the Oak Ridge nuclear laboratory dispute .... Truman appoints Herbert Bergson head of the Justice Department's antitrust division.		Pope Pius XII proclaims 1950 a Holy Year and urges Catholics to visit Rome as a "shining example" of international and interracial unity.	June 2
Truman leaves Washington aboard a special train for an officially "unpolitical" trip through the Midwest and West.	House appropriates $10.2 billion of the Administration's $11-billion request for military spending in the coming fiscal year.		California Institute of Technology astronomers dedicate the world's largest telescope, with a 200-inch mirror, at the Mt. Palomar Observatory.		June 3
Senate Judiciary Comm. suspends hearings on the Mundt-Nixon Communist control bill after 3,000 Progressive Party protesters arrive in Washington to lobby for the bill's defeat .... Ohio bars the Progressive Party from the state ballot on the grounds that the group's original affidavit omitted a statement that it is not directed by a foreign government.	House votes a 26% cut in foreign aid expenditures, including a $1.3-billion reduction in Marshall Plan aid. The move is a victory for House Appropriations Comm. Chmn. John Taber (R, N.Y.), a critic of "extravagance" in foreign aid .... Senate eliminates compulsory military training for 18-year-olds from its conscription bill.	Congress passes a bill blocking Administration plans to extend social security coverage to 500,000 sales personnel and other exempt workers but grants an additional $184 million in benefits to dependent children and aged and handicapped pensioners .... A Washington federal court issues an injunction ordering UMW Pres. Lewis to bargain with representatives of Southern mine operators. Lewis agrees to do so.			June 4
Speaking in Omaha, Truman criticizes congressional Republicans for inaction on farm legislation and urges a program of price supports and other federal aid measures to increase farmers' living standards .... Massachusetts Democratic convention gives 36 delegate votes to Truman.		United Packinghouse Workers union ends its 82-day strike against Wilson and Co., where a standard meatpacking industry contract goes into effect .... Ford Motor Co. announces price increases averaging 8.7% on its 1949 models .... Joint Congressional Labor-Management Comm. ends 11 days of hearings on the Taft-Hartley Act by voting not to recommend any changes in the law this year.		My Love, with William Johnstone up, wins the 169th English Derby at Epsom downs, earning $49,736.	June 5
Roper Poll survey indicates that Eisenhower would defeat Truman 53% to 26% in a current election if he ran as a Republican and would beat any Republican candidate if he ran as a Democrat.					June 6
F	G	H	I	J	
Includes elections, federal-state relations, civil rights and liberties, crime, the judiciary, education, health care, poverty, urban affairs and population.	*Includes formation and debate of U.S. foreign and defense policies, veterans affairs and defense spending. (Relations with specific foreign countries are usually found under the region concerned.)*	*Includes business, labor, agriculture, taxation, transportation, consumer affairs, monetary and fiscal policy, natural resources, pollution and accidents.*	*Includes worldwide scientific, medical and technological developments, natural phenomena, U.S. weather and natural disasters.*	*Includes the arts, religion, scholarship, communications media, sports, entertainment, fashions, fads and social life.*	

	World Affairs	Europe	Africa & the Middle East	The Americas	Asia & the Pacific
June 7		Eduard Benes resigns as president of Czechoslovakia, officially for reasons of health. He does not sign the new Czech constitution .... London conference of U.S., British and Western European representatives publishes its recommendations on Germany, including creation of a West German federal state and stationing of Western troops in Germany "until the peace of Europe is secured."	U.N. mediator Bernadotte offers Palestinian Jews and Arabs a truce based on the following terms: limited Jewish immigration and no movement of fresh Arab troops into Palestine, access to Jerusalem and Jaffa for Red Cross relief teams and a ban on the stockpiling of military supplies.		
June 8					Gen. MacArthur approves a $60-million U.S. credit to finance Japanese purchases of raw cotton.
June 9		British House of Lords rejects a government bill halving the time period during which the Lords can veto legislation.	Israel and the Arab League announce unconditional acceptance of Bernadotte's truce terms.		
June 10	Speaking at Harvard commencement exercises, U.N. Secy. Gen. Trygve Lie urges creation of a small "guard" force to "back up" Security Council decisions.	Turkish Premier Hasan Saka reorganizes his cabinet following parliamentary criticism of the government for food shortages and other economic difficulties. The new cabinet includes more politicians from the "progressive" wing of the governing Republican People's Party.			
June 11		British and American authorities in Germany authorize the formation of cartels in their occupation zones to speed German economic recovery .... Prosecution and defense attorneys end their summations at the war crimes trial of I.G. Farben directors in Nuremberg .... Rumania's National Assembly approves a sweeping nationalization measure affecting most manufacturing and service industries.	U.N.-sponsored ceasefire goes into effect in Palestine, ending 28 days of open warfare between Jews and Arabs. Col. David Marcus, former member of the U.S. Army Judge Advocate's Office who participated in the Teheran, Yalta and Potsdam conferences, is killed fighting on the side of Israeli forces shortly before the start of the truce.	Argentine government decrees that employers must pay all future wage increases out of profits without raising prices.	
June 12		Russian authorities in Germany end a 22-hour embargo on U.S. and British rail freight traffic to Berlin .... Greece accepts a Bulgarian offer to begin negotiations for restoration of "normal diplomatic relations" between the two countries .... Hungary's Socialists and Communists merge into the Hungarian Workers' Party.			
June 13			Iranian Parliament elects former Finance Min. Abdul Hussein Hajir to succeed Ibrahim Hakimi as premier following the latter's resignation .... First Jewish immigrant ship to arrive in Israel since the truce lands in Tel Aviv. Men of military age are ordered sent to a refugee camp.		
June 14		Russian authorities in Germany halt shipment of coal from the British occupation zone to Berlin and close the Elbe River bridge on the main Berlin-Helmstedt highway, allegedly for "repairs." .... Czech Parliament elects Communist leader Klement Gottwald to succeed Eduard Benes as president of Czechoslovakia. Vice Premier Antonin Zapotocky, head of the General Confederation of Labor, succeeds Gottwald as premier.			
June 15		Russia accepts a U.S. proposal for a conference on Danube River navigation.	Secret Zionist organization Irgun Zvai Leumi establishes itself as a political party in Israel, the Jewish Freedom Movement, under Menahem Begin.		
	A	B	C	D	E
	Includes developments that affect more than one world region, international organizations and important meetings of major world leaders.	*Includes all domestic and regional developments in Europe, including the Soviet Union, Turkey, Cyprus and Malta.*	*Includes all domestic and regional developments in Africa and the Middle East, including Iraq and Iran and excluding Cyprus, Turkey and Afghanistan.*	*Includes all domestic and regional developments in Latin America, the Caribbean and Canada.*	*Includes all domestic and regional developments in Asian and Pacific nations, extending from Afghanistan through all the Pacific Islands, except Hawaii.*

U.S. Politics & Social Issues	U.S. Foreign Policy & Defense	U.S. Economy & Environment	Science, Technology & Nature	Culture, Leisure & Life Style	
Republican National Comm. names Massachusetts Sen. Henry Cabot Lodge, Jr. chairman of the party's resolutions committee, which will write the party platform for the National Convention .... Supreme Court hands down two decisions upholding the legality of "quick" Florida and Nevada divorces in other states.		Supreme Court rejects a Justice Dept. charge that purchase of Columbia Steel Co. by the Consolidated Steel Corp. violates antitrust laws .... Charles Warren Nash, who founded the Nash Motors Co. in 1916, dies at 84 in Beverly Hills, Calif.		Dwight Eisenhower takes office as the 13th President of Columbia Univ. .... Former actor Harry Browne is elected president of the First Church of Christ, Scientist in Boston .... Louis Lumiere, co-inventor (with his brother Auguste) of motion pictures in 1894, dies at 84 in Bandol, France.	June 7
Senatorial primaries in New Mexico result in victory for former Agriculture Secy. Clinton Anderson on the Democratic side and former War Secy. Patrick Hurley on the Republican side.					June 8
Speaking in Spokane, Wash., Truman sets off a barage of Republican criticism by attacking the Republican-dominated 80th Congress as "the worst ... we have had."				Rabbi Joshua Liebman, author of the best-seller *Peace of Mind*, dies at 41 of a heart attack in Boston.	June 9
	Senate passes and sends to the House a peacetime draft bill authorizing the annual induction of 250,000 men 19 to 25 years old for two-year terms of service.	Labor Secy. Lewis Schwellenbach dies at 53 in Washington .... Federal Judge T. Alan Goldsborough signs a preliminary injunction against a nationwide railroad strike by three unions, replacing a temporary restraining order which expires tomorrow .... USW Pres. Philip Murray files a petition in a Chicago federal court challenging the constitutionality of the Taft-Hartley Act provision requiring union officials to file affidavits certifying they are not Communists.	Air Force Secy. Stuart Symington announces that Capt. Charles Yeager has repeatedly broken the sound barrier in a rocket-powered Bell X-1 at 35,000 feet .... In an article in the *British Medical Journal*, Dr. R.C. Brock reports the first successful operation within the human heart to relieve pulmonary stenosis.	Tony Zale regains the world middleweight boxing title by knocking out Rocky Graziano in the third round in Newark, N.J.	June 10
Southern Democrats meeting in Jackson, Miss. announce that they will choose their own presidential candidate to run against Truman .... House approves and sends to joint conference a bill authorizing the admission of 202,000 European refugees to the U.S. during the next two years.	Senate passes a resolution sponsored by Foreign Relations Comm. Chmn. Arthur Vandenberg, urging Truman to give military aid to defensive alliances of non-Communist nations.	CIO United Furniture Workers union ends a five-day convention in Chicago after endorsing Henry Wallace's presidential candidacy and re-electing Morris Pizer union president.			June 11
Democratic executive committee of Greenville County, S.C. announces that Negroes will be permitted to vote in primary elections. It is the first such action in the state.	Speaking at Univ. of California commencement exercises in Berkeley, Truman delivers an important foreign policy address accusing Russia of "obstruction and aggression" in its "attitude" towards the U.S. .... Senate Appropriations Comm. restores most of the $1.3 billion cut by the House from the European Recovery Program by shortening the period to be covered by the House-approved funds.	Truman vetoes a bill permitting rate agreements among major railroads, claiming it would allow "an important segment of the economy to obtain immunity from antitrust laws."		Ben Hogan captures the national open golf championship in Los Angeles with 278 strokes, a tournament record .... Citation, with Eddie Arcaro up, takes the $117,300 Belmont Stakes in N.Y. to win racing's triple crown.	June 12
		A threatened strike at the Oak Ridge nuclear laboratory is averted when the AFL Atomic Trades and Labor Council accepts an average 15½¢ hourly wage increase for the facility's 875 employes.			June 13
Democratic National Comm. names Sen. Francis Myers of Pennsylvania head of a committee which will make the preliminary draft of the party's 1948 platform .... Supreme Court refuses to review the contempt of Congress convictions of 11 Joint Anti-Fascist Refugee Comm. leaders, while a Washington federal court upholds the contempt of Congress conviction of Gerhard Eisler.	Senate passes a measure reviving the Reciprocal Trade Act for one year and increasing the role of the U.S. Tariff Commission in determining tariff concessions.	Federal judges in N.Y., Cleveland and San Francisco avert a nationwide maritime strike by seven unions scheduled for tomorrow by issuing a 10-day restraining order. At issue in the dispute is the unions' insistence on retaining union hiring halls, banned by the Taft-Hartley Act .... Truman vetoes a social security bill passed by Congress on the grounds that it excludes the self-employed from pension coverage. Senate and House immediately vote to override.		Gertrude Franklin Horn Atherton, novelist and early supporter of equal rights for women, dies at 90 in San Francisco.	June 14
		Representatives of Northern and Western mine operators walk out on negotiations with UMW leader Lewis in a disagreement over use of 1947 contributions to the miners' welfare and pension fund.	Air Force Capt. Charles Yeager receives the 1947 Mackay Air Trophy for his flights in the Bell X-1, the first manned vehicle to break the sound barrier.		June 15
F	G	H	I	J	
Includes elections, federal-state relations, civil rights and liberties, crime, the judiciary, education, health care, poverty, urban affairs and population.	*Includes formation and debate of U.S. foreign and defense policies, veterans affairs and defense spending. (Relations with specific foreign countries are usually found under the region concerned.)*	*Includes business, labor, agriculture, taxation, transportation, consumer affairs, monetary and fiscal policy, natural resources, pollution and accidents.*	*Includes worldwide scientific, medical and technological developments, natural phenomena, U.S. weather and natural disasters.*	*Includes the arts, religion, scholarship, communications media, sports, entertainment, fashions, fads and social life.*	

	World Affairs	Europe	Africa & the Middle East	The Americas	Asia & the Pacific
June 16		Hungarian Parliament adopts a bill nationalizing the country's Catholic schools . . . . Former German-American Bund leader Fritz Kuhn is recaptured by Allied authorities while applying for a permit to operate a chemist's laboratory in the French occupation zone.		Mexico cancels concessions of all foreign communications companies of mid-1949.	British authorities in Malaya impose emergency measures to suppress a wave of strikes and violence, allegedly instigated by Communists.
June 17	International Labor Conference convenes in San Francisco, attended by 51 nations.	French Chamber of Deputies narrowly approves the London agreement on West Germany but demands stronger guarantees of international control over Ruhr mines and industry.	U.N. Secy. Gen. Trygve Lie recruits a 50-man volunteer force from U.N. personnel in N.Y. to supervise the Palestine truce.	Peruvian Pres. Jose Luis Bustamante Rivero names a new cabinet of six civilians and five military men to replace an all-military ministry.	India and Hyderabad break off merger negotiations after the Moslem ruler of Hyderabad refuses to promise majority rule for the state's predominantly Hindu population.
June 18	Eighteen-nation U.N. Commission on Human Rights completes two years of work on a draft declaration on human rights, to be submitted to the Economic and Social Council for consideration by the autumn session of the General Assembly.	U.S., British and French authorities in Germany introduce a currency reform, replacing the devalued Reichsmark with a new Deutsche Mark. The move leaves western and eastern Germany with different currency systems. Russian authorities halt all ground passenger traffic from West Germany to Berlin, allegedly to prevent a mass transfer of Reichsmarks to the Soviet zone . . . . Greek government announces the start of a major offensive intended to encircle the main Communist guerrilla force in the stronghold of Mt. Grammos near the Albanian-Yugoslavian border.	U.N. mediator Bernadotte arrives on the Island of Rhodes to begin negotiations with Jewish and Arab delegations for a permanent peace settlement in Palestine.		
June 19				Costa Rican Pres. Jose Figueres suspends constitutional guarantees for 30 days and levies a 10% tax on private capital to raise reconstruction funds.	
June 20		U.S. halts movement of rail freight from western Germany to Berlin rather than grant Russian demands for inspection of transports.			
June 21		Western Allies begin distribution of the Deutsche Mark in their zones of Germany.			Philippine government grants Hukbalahap guerrillas an unconditional amnesty and admits Huk leader Luis Taruc to Congress in an effort to end unrest in central Luzon . . . . Chakravarthi Rajagopalachari takes office as governor general of India in New Delhi, replacing Lord Louis Mountbatten.
June 22		Allied representatives end a Berlin meeting without agreement on a common currency for the city as Russian authorities decree a separate currency reform in their occupation zone. Western representatives also refuse to accept the Russian claim that Berlin is a Soviet zone city in which U.S., British and French troops are guests.	Haganah forces attack an Irgun Zvai Leumi ammunition dump near Natanya when the Irgun refuses to observe the ceasefire ban on importation of foreign arms.		
June 23		U.S., British and French authorities announce plans to introduce the new West German Deutsche Mark into their sectors of Berlin . . . . Vatican charges that the Albanian government is suppressing the country's Catholic Church by murdering or jailing its members.	Irgun Zvai Leumi leader Menahem Begin withdraws recognition from the Israeli government and denounces Premier David Ben-Gurion as a "lunatic dictator" following a second attack by Haganah forces on an Irgun supply dump.		

A	B	C	D	E
Includes developments that affect more than one world region, international organizations and important meetings of major world leaders.	*Includes all domestic and regional developments in Europe, including the Soviet Union, Turkey, Cyprus and Malta.*	*Includes all domestic and regional developments in Africa and the Middle East, including Iraq and Iran and excluding Cyprus, Turkey and Afghanistan.*	*Includes all domestic and regional developments in Latin America, the Caribbean and Canada.*	*Includes all domestic and regional developments in Asian and Pacific nations, extending from Afghanistan through all the Pacific Islands, except Hawaii.*

U.S. Politics & Social Issues	U.S. Foreign Policy & Defense	U.S. Economy & Environment	Science, Technology & Nature	Culture, Leisure & Life Style	
Fortieth annual Governors' Conference ends in Portsmouth, N.H. after passing resolutions urging reduction of federal taxes and statehood for Alaska and Hawaii.		N.Y. State Supreme Court reverses a State Labor Relations Bd. ruling against payment of triple wages to Macy Co. employes who crossed picket lines during a 1946 strike. The court rules that the strike was illegal, making extra wage payments a "lawful countermeasure."		Hebrew Union College of Cincinnati and the Jewish Institute of Religion in N.Y., Reform Judaism's two rabbinical schools, announce their merger . . . . Rufus Matthew Jones, co-founder of the American Friends Service Comm., dies at 85 in Philadelphia.	June 16
		Congress overrides Truman's veto of the Reed-Bulwinkle bill, making railroad freight rate agreements approved by the Interstate Commerce Commission immune to antitrust laws.	A N.Y.-bound United Airlines DC-6 crashes near Mt. Carmel, Pa., killing all 43 passengers, including actress Beryl Wallace and "Vanities" showman Earl Carroll.		June 17
Truman returns to Washington after completing his 16-day tour of 18 Midwestern and Western states, covering 9,504 miles and making 73 speeches. Observers credit the trip with bringing about a sharp increase in Truman's popularity.	Senate approves a $65-million loan for construction of U.N. headquarters in Manhattan.	Alvah Curtis Roebuck, cofounder of Sears Roebuck & Co., dies at 84 in Chicago.			June 18
Congress completes work on a compromise bill allowing the admission of 205,000 European refugees to the U.S. during the next two years . . . . Progressive Party of Ohio is founded in Cleveland in an effort to put the Wallace ticket back on the state ballot.	Congress completes work on a compromise peacetime draft bill following an unsuccessful 17-hour filibuster by Sens. Glen Taylor (D, Ida.) and William Langer (R, N.D.) . . . . Truman names a 12-member advisory board representing labor, industry, agriculture and other groups to assist Economic Cooperation Admin. Paul Hoffman.	Truman appoints a three-man, fact-finding board to investigate deadlocked contract talks in the mining industry after the UMW threatens to call a strike for July 6.	A committee of experts advises an American Heart Assn. meeting in Chicago that use of drugs against blood clotting significantly reduces deaths from coronary thrombosis.	Univ. of Minnesota captures the NCAA track and field title in Minneapolis.	June 19
Congress adjourns after a 43-hour marathon session . . . . Rhode Island Democratic convention gives 12 delegate votes to Truman.				Jack Kramer defeats Bobby Riggs for the U.S. professional tennis singles title in Forest Hills, N.Y., while Kramer and Pancho Segura beat Riggs and Don Budge for the doubles title.	June 20
Republican National Convention, the first in U.S. history to be televised, opens in Philadelphia.		Supreme Court completes its term after ruling that the Taft-Hartley Act does not prevent unions from endorsing political candidates and upholding the provision of the Act that requires union officials to submit affidavits certifying they are not Communists . . . . Chrysler Corp. follows Ford in announcing price increases for its 1949 models.		Winston Churchill's *The Gathering Storm*, the first volume of a projected series on World War II, is publishhed in N.Y. by Houghton Mifflin and becomes a July Book-of-the-Month-Club selection.	June 21
Mississippi Democrats elect 30 anti-Truman delegates to the National Convention.	Truman names James McDonald, an expert on refugee problems who served on the Palestine Inquiry Commission in 1946, as U.S. special representative to Israel.	A Cleveland federal court extends its restraining order against a maritime workers' strike to July 2.			June 22
Republican National Convention adopts a party platform favoring a strong anti-Communist foreign policy and reduction of federal government initiative in domestic affairs.		A federal court in San Francisco extends its restrainting order against a maritime workers' strike to July 12, while a N.Y. federal court replaces its earlier restraining order with an 80-day, anti-strike injunction.		Evelyn Waugh's *The Loved One*, a satire on the mortuary business, is published by Little, Brown.	June 23
F	G	H	I	J	
Includes elections, federal-state relations, civil rights and liberties, crime, the judiciary, education, health care, poverty, urban affairs and population.	*Includes formation and debate of U.S. foreign and defense policies, veterans affairs and defense spending. (Relations with specific foreign countries are usually found under the region concerned.)*	*Includes business, labor, agriculture, taxation, transportation, consumer affairs, monetary and fiscal policy, natural resources, pollution and accidents.*	*Includes worldwide scientific, medical and technological developments, natural phenomena, U.S. weather and natural disasters.*	*Includes the arts, religion, scholarship, communications media, sports, entertainment, fashions, fads and social life.*	

	World Affairs	Europe	Africa & the Middle East	The Americas	Asia & the Pacific
June 24		Russian authorities halt all land transport between West Germany and Berlin and cut off electric power to the city's western sectors, claiming "technical difficulties." Britain retaliates by banning the shipment of Ruhr coal and steel to the Soviet occupation zone .... Representatives of Russia and seven other Eastern European states conclude a two-day conference in Warsaw by issuing a five-point proposal for a German settlement, including withdrawal of all occupation forces from Germany and creation of a "provisional democratic German government" representing all political parties and trade unions .... Italian Chamber of Deputies passes a 12-month extension of the ban on possession of weapons, aimed primarily at Communist partisans .... Hungarian Catholic Church announces the excommunication of all Catholic members of Parliament who voted to nationalize religious schools.	Israeli government announces the suppression of the Irgun Zvai Leumi "rebellion" and the arrest of 400 insurgents.		
June 25		Extending their blockade of Berlin, Russian authorities halt food and fuel deliveries from the Soviet zone to the city's western sectors .... Greek government forces take the guerrilla stronghold of Mt. Boufos after a week-long battle.	U.N. mediator Bernadotte charges Egyptian forces with violating the Palestine truce and sanctions Israeli defensive actions in the Negev desert .... Golda Myerson, former head of the Jewish Agency's political department in Jerusalem, is named Israeli minister to Russia.		
June 26		U.S. authorities double daily cargo flights to Berlin in an effort to keep the city's western sectors supplied despite the Russian blockade .... Western Allies fix the value of the new Deutsche Mark at 10 old Reichsmarks, leaving the currency's foreign exchange rate to float.	Iraq's cabinet is reorganized, with Muzahim al Pachachi as new premier and foreign minister.		
June 27		Czech Social Democratic Party officially merges with the Communist Party.			Indian forces begin deploying around the Moslem-ruled state of Hyderabad in an effort to force the territory to unite with India.
June 28		Communist Information Bureau (Cominform) publicly charges Yugoslavian Pres. Tito with deviation from the "internationalist" Moscow line in a statement published in the Prague Communist newspaper *Rude Pravo*. Yugoslavian Communists are urged to repudiate their party leadership, which is accused of retreating from Marxism-Leninism in foreign and domestic policy and attempting to secure the favors of imperialist states. The statement expels Yugoslavia from the Cominform .... Britain's King George VI proclaims a state of emergency and authorizes soldiers to move cargoes immobilized on London docks by a 15-day wildcat strike of 19,000 London longshoremen.	Bernadotte submits a proposal for a permanent Palestine settlement to the Arab League and Israel, calling for a union of Arab Palestine with Transjordan, free Jewish immigration for a trial period of two years and territorial readjustments (the Negev desert going to the Arabs and the western Galilee to the Jews).	Peruvian Pres. Jose Luis Bustamente imposes emergency rule by decree to avert an "acute national crisis" caused by the "dangerous" growth of political tension and unrest within the armed forces.	A series of earthquakes followed by fires destroys most of the Japanese industrial city of Fukui and surrounding towns on Honshu, killing over 3,200 residents.
June 29		Yugoslavian Pres. Tito replies to Cominform charges against his government, calling them "slanders" and "fabrications" and accusing Russia of suppressing criticism among European Communists. He urges Yugoslavian Communists to "close their ranks" around the party leadership .... In an interview with Homer Bigart of the *New York Herald Tribune*, Greek guerrilla leader Markos Vafiades offers to discuss peace with any "sincere" Athens government. He admits that his forces cannot hold out indefinitely in their Mt. Grammos redoubt .... London longshoremen vote to end their 16-day dock strike after employers promise to review contract penalty clauses condemned by workers as unfair.			Communist forces establish a blockade of Mukden and Changchun, the main Nationalist-held cities of Manchuria .... Japanese Gen. Yoshitaka Kawane and Col. Kurataro Hirano are sentenced to death by a U.S. military tribunal in Yokohama for ordering the 1942 Bataan "death march." .... Indian troops report capturing the Kashmiri transport center of Gurais.

	A	B	C	D	E
	Includes developments that affect more than one world region, international organizations and important meetings of major world leaders.	*Includes all domestic and regional developments in Europe, including the Soviet Union, Turkey, Cyprus and Malta.*	*Includes all domestic and regional developments in Africa and the Middle East, including Iraq and Iran and excluding Cyprus, Turkey and Afghanistan.*	*Includes all domestic and regional developments in Latin America, the Caribbean and Canada.*	*Includes all domestic and regional developments in Asian and Pacific nations, extending from Afghanistan through all the Pacific Islands, except Hawaii.*

U.S. Politics & Social Issues	U.S. Foreign Policy & Defense	U.S. Economy & Environment	Science, Technology & Nature	Culture, Leisure & Life Style	
Republican National Convention nominates N.Y. Gov. Thomas Dewey for president on the third ballot, following the withdrawal of Harold Stassen and Sen. Robert Taft.	Truman signs the peacetime selective service bill, providing for induction of 200,000 men during the system's first year of operation.				June 24
Republican National Convention names California Gov. Earl Warren as Dewey's running mate in this year's presidential election .... Truman signs a bill authorizing the admission of 205,000 European refugees to the U.S. over the next two years, but criticizes the measure as "flagrantly discriminatory" against Jews and Catholics.	Gen. William Lee, organizer of the first U.S. paratroop forces, dies at 53 in Dunn, N.C.	UMW ends the threat of a July coal strike by accepting a one-year contract providing a 12½¢ hourly wage increase and doubling the employer contribution to the miners' welfare fund .... Harry Millis, former NLRB chairman and a prominent labor arbitrator, dies at 75 in Chicago.		Joe Louis retains his world heavyweight title with an 11th-round knockout of Jersey Joe Walcott in Yankee Stadium, then announces his retirement from boxing.	June 25
Pennsylvania Rep. Hugh Scott, a Dewey supporter, is elected chairman of the Republican National Comm. .... American Medical Assn. ends a seven-day meeting in Chicago after rejecting a proposal of the N.Y. State delegation to bar racial discrimination in accepting members.	Civil rights leader A. Philip Randolph calls for a nationwide campaign of resistance to the new draft law until segregation is eliminated in the armed forces.				June 26
NAACP ends a six-day convention in Kansas City after adopting resolutions praising Truman's civil rights program but demanding the resignation of Army Secy. Kenneth Royall for maintaining segregation in the armed forces.			Army researchers report that chloromycetin, a new drug, can cure typhoid fever within three days.	Bob Mathias, leader of the U.S. Olympic track team, wins the national AAU decathlon title in Bloomfield, N.J.	June 27
	Truman signs the $6.03-billion foreign aid bill, providing funds for the Marshall Plan, U.S. aid to Greece, Turkey and China and U.S. participation in the International Children's Fund and the International Relief Organization.			Sugar Ray Robinson successfully defends his welterweight crown with a 15-round decision over Bernard Docusen in Chicago.	June 28
John Studebaker resigns as U.S. Education Commissioner to join *Scholastic Magazine* .... Republican candidates Dewey and Warren meet in Pawling, N.Y. to coordinate campaign strategy.				Audience Research, a branch of the Gallup Poll, reports that 354,000 television sets are in use in the U.S.	June 29

F	G	H	I	J
Includes elections, federal-state relations, civil rights and liberties, crime, the judiciary, education, health care, poverty, urban affairs and population.	*Includes formation and debate of U.S. foreign and defense policies, veterans affairs and defense spending. (Relations with specific foreign countries are usually found under the region concerned.)*	*Includes business, labor, agriculture, taxation, transportation, consumer affairs, monetary and fiscal policy, natural resources, pollution and accidents.*	*Includes worldwide scientific, medical and technological developments, natural phenomena, U.S. weather and natural disasters.*	*Includes the arts, religion, scholarship, communications media, sports, entertainment, fashions, fads and social life.*

	World Affairs	Europe	Africa & the Middle East	The Americas	Asia & the Pacific
June 30		U.S. State Secy. Marshall and British Foreign Secy. Bevin announce their determination to resist Russian efforts to force Western withdrawal from Berlin . . . . Responding to Soviet charges of nationalism, Yugoslavia's Communist Party releases a statement calling for a Balkan federation of Bulgaria, Yugoslavia and Albania. It also announces plans to modernize the 800,000-man Yugoslavian Army.	Last British troops leave Palestine.	Cuban sugar workers end strike threats when Pres. Ramon Grau San Martin promises to maintain their wages at 1947 levels and reduce their work week from 48 to 44 hours.	
July 1		Russian representatives begin to boycott the four-power Allied Berlin command . . . . U.S., British and French military governors present plans for creation of a West German state to a conference of western German political leaders in Frankfurt . . . . Britain's Town and Country Planning Act goes into effect, giving local authorities power to direct all building and land development . . . . Italian Socialist Party concludes a four-day conference in Genoa by repudiating Pietro Nenni and other advocates of cooperation with the Communists.			
July 2		Italian Labor Confederation calls a 12-hour strike of three million industrial workers demanding a general wage increase. Government spokesmen and conservative parties charge that the strike is politically motivated, a Communist attempt to prevent Marshall Plan aid from becoming effective . . . . Parliamentary elections in Finland result in a setback for the Communist-led Popular Democratic Union, which loses 13 of its 51 seats.	U.N. Trusteeship Council completes five days of hearings on complaints against British administrative practices in the trust territory of Tanganyika, including use of compulsory labor on government projects.		Chinese Communist forces in Haiyang release four U.S. Marine fliers held since April 5.
July 3		Albania severs trade relations with Yugoslavia and expels Yugoslav military, political and cultural missions.	Transjordan's King Abdullah rejects U.N. mediator Bernadotte's peace proposals, insisting that the Arabs will "rely on our arms" in Palestine.		
July 4		French Socialist Party congress ends in Paris after passing resolutions permitting the party to support the cabinet of Premier Robert Schuman . . . . Sir Edward Gent, British high commissioner for Malaya, is killed with 39 other passengers in an air crash near London.		Panamanian Pres. Enrique Jimenez declares a state of siege after clashes erupt between police and supporters of former Pres. Arnulfo Arias, who claims he won last May's presidential election.	
July 5		British Labor government's social security and national health care plans, covering 27.5 million people, go into effect.	Bernadotte appeals for Security Council action to prevent renewal of Middle East hostilities following the failure of Arabs and Jews to agree on a permanent Palestine peace settlement.	Truman joins Venezuelan Pres. Romulo Gallegos Friere to dedicate a $100,000 statue of Simon Bolivar in Bolivar, Mo.	Peking Univ. students riot, with five deaths, following a government attempt to impose military training on students from Communist-held areas . . . . Japanese Diet concludes a record 209-day session after adopting a 414-billion yen budget, a new criminal code and measures decentralizing public schools and strengthening antitrust laws.
July 6		Britain, France and the U.S. jointly protest the Russian blockade of Berlin, reasserting their right to maintain troops in the city . . . . U.S., Canada, Britain, France, Belgium, and Holland begin talks in Washington on U.S. political and military support for the Union of Western Europe . . . . European Communist leaders reject a Yugoslavian invitation to attend an upcoming party congress in Belgrade . . . . Czech police break up a crowd of 3,000 anti-Communist demonstrators in Prague.	American Independent Oil Co. Pres. Ralph Davies announces that his company, a combination of 10 U.S. oil firms, has won a concession to drill in the oil-rich neutral zone between Kuwait and Saudi Arabia.		
July 7	U.N. General Assembly's Interim Comm. on Peace and Security urges elimination of the Security Council veto in cases involving peaceful settlement of disputes, U.N. membership applications and certain procedural questions.	Parliamentary elections in Holland result in victory for the Catholic Party, which maintains its position as the country's largest political group.	U.N. Security Council begins debate on the Middle East situation and sends an "urgent appeal" to Arabs and Jews to extend the Palestine truce.	Chilean Pres. Gabriel Gonzalez Videla reorganizes his cabinet to include Radical, Liberal and Conservative ministers . . . . Peruvian Col. Alfonzo Llosa Gonzalez flees to Bolivia after failing in an attempted military coup.	British and Ghurka forces begin operations in Malaya against Communist-led insurgents attempting to take control of rubber plantations and urban centers.
	A *Includes developments that affect more than one world region, international organizations and important meetings of major world leaders.*	B *Includes all domestic and regional developments in Europe, including the Soviet Union, Turkey, Cyprus and Malta.*	C *Includes all domestic and regional developments in Africa and the Middle East, including Iraq and Iran and excluding Cyprus, Turkey and Afghanistan.*	D *Includes all domestic and regional developments in Latin America, the Caribbean and Canada.*	E *Includes all domestic and regional developments in Asian and Pacific nations, extending from Afghanistan through all the Pacific Islands, except Hawaii.*

U.S. Politics & Social Issues	U.S. Foreign Policy & Defense	U.S. Economy & Environment	Science, Technology & Nature	Culture, Leisure & Life Style	
Robert Best, a U.S. citizen convicted of broadcasting Nazi propaganda during the war, is sentenced to life imprisonment for treason in Boston.	Economic Cooperation Admin. Paul Hoffman threatens to cut off U.S. aid to any country exporting war materials to Russia.	Truman signs a bill authorizing $126.5 million over five years for research on means of combatting water pollution . . . . Illinois, Indiana, Ohio, Kentucky, New York, Pennsylvania, Virginia and West Virginia sign an agreement establishing a joint sanitation authority for the streams of the Ohio River Valley.		Cleveland Indian Bob Lemon pitches the first major league no-hitter of 1948, beating the Detroit Tigers, 2-0, in Detroit.	June 30
N.Y.C. Mayor William O'Dwyer splits with Tammany Hall in a dispute over appointments and says he will form a new Democratic organization for New York County.		Truman signs a compromise housing bill but criticizes it for not including slum clearance and public housing funds . . . . Washington federal district court grants a government request to extend an injunction against a strike of railroad workers for the duration of government operation of the nation's railroads . . . . New York International Airport opens at Idlewild.			July 1
	Truman approves a Senate resolution urging U.S. support for regional anti-Communist military pacts, and authorizes the State Dept. to begin negotiations on a defense agreement with western European states.	Mine-owning steel firms reject the national contract negotiated by the UMW and other mine operators, accusing the union of attempting to introduce a union shop without an election . . . . Treasury Secy. John Snyder announces a budget surplus of $8.4 billion for fiscal 1948, the largest in U.S. history.		Bob Falkenburg of the U.S. beats John Bromwich of Australia to win the men's singles championship in the Wimbledon tennis competition.	July 2
Nineteen Democratic leaders, including N.Y.C. Mayor O'Dwyer and National Committeeman James Roosevelt, issue a statement urging Democrats to choose "the ablest and strongest man" as their candidate in the coming election. The statement refrains from endorsing Truman.		Anthracite mine operators sign a national contract with the UMW covering 78,000 workers.		Louise Brough of the U.S. wins the women's singles championship in the Wimbledon tennis competititon.	July 3
N.J. Democratic boss Frank Hague announces his willingness to support a draft Eisenhower movement at the party's national convention.					July 4
Eisenhower issues a statement through the Columbia Univ. press office reiterating his refusal to accept a presidential draft.				Film actress Carole Landis, 29, commits suicide in her Hollywood home with an overdose of sleeping pills.	July 5
A Kansas City court dismisses charges against the last five defendants in the 1946 vote fraud case.	Adm. Russell Willson, wartime deputy commander of the U.S. fleet and a participant in the Dumbarton Oaks and San Francisco conferences, dies at 64 in Bethesda, Md.	Forty thousand coal miners strike in mines operated by steel firms following the owners' refusal to sign a union shop contract with the UMW.	Dr. Eli Burton, Toronto scientist who helped develop the electron microscope and the colloidal arsenic treatment for cancer, dies at 69 in Toronto.	World Jewish Congress ends a 10-day convention in Montreux, Switz., after urging all countries to support Israel and work against anti-Semitism.	July 6
State and Interior departments urge Congress to transfer U.S Pacific possessions and trusteeships from military to civilian control . . . . A House Labor subcommittee opens hearings in N.Y. on alleged Communist infiltration of the city's labor unions.	Six women, the first to enlist under the Women's Armed Services Integration Act, are inducted into the Navy.		Bethlehem Steel announces a $100,000 grant for the Univ. of Chicago's atomic and metal research program.	Cleveland Indians sign Negro pitching star Satchel Paige, who started in baseball in 1925.	July 7

F	G	H	I	J
Includes elections, federal-state relations, civil rights and liberties, crime, the judiciary, education, health care, poverty, urban affairs and population.	*Includes formation and debate of U.S. foreign and defense policies, veterans affairs and defense spending. (Relations with specific foreign countries are usually found under the region concerned.)*	*Includes business, labor, agriculture, taxation, transportation, consumer affairs, monetary and fiscal policy, natural resources, pollution and accidents.*	*Includes worldwide scientific, medical and technological developments, natural phenomena, U.S. weather and natural disasters.*	*Includes the arts, religion, scholarship, communications media, sports, entertainment, fashions, fads and social life.*

	World Affairs	Europe	Africa & the Middle East	The Americas	Asia & the Pacific
July 8	Britain quits the International Wheat Agreement after the U.S. Congress fails to ratify it.	Western Allies order drastic energy conservation measures in their sectors of Berlin, including closing of the elevated railway and limitation of electricity consumption by homes and small factories .... British Foreign Office announces suspension of all reparations deliveries from western Germany to the Soviet occupation zone due to the Berlin blockade .... Socialist leader Willem Drees forms a new Dutch cabinet consisting mainly of Socialist and Catholic People's Party representatives.	U.S. delegate Philip Jessup tells the U.N. Security Council the U.S. will support international economic or military sanctions against the Arabs if they renew Palestine warfare.		Chinese Nationalist troops claim victory in an eight-day battle with Communists in eastern Honan province .... A five-man U.N. commission lands in Karachi to mediate Indian-Pakistani differences over Kashmir.
July 9		Leaders of 11 western German states end a two-day conference in Coblenz after considering proposals for creation of a West German government. They urge that greater power be given to German administrators but refrain from referring to the proposed government as a "state." .... Russians order the Berlin city treasury to stop payment of occupation costs totaling 22 million Reichsmarks a month to the Western Allies .... Rumania announces suspension of all oil deliveries to Yugoslavia.	Arab League rejects proposals for extension of the Palestine truce, accusing Israel of "flagrant [truce] violations" and demanding creation of a provisional unitary government in Palestine dominated by the Arab majority. Arab-Jewish fighting begins again on all fronts as the truce expires.		
July 10	International Labor Conference ends in San Francisco after passing resolutions affirming the right of workers and employers to form and join professional organizations.	Russian authorities protest alleged safety violations by U.S. and British cargo planes flying to Berlin and announce that Soviet fighters will conduct instrument tests along the Berlin air corridors .... Greek government leaders confer with U.S. aid officials in Athens, asking for more military assistance to revive the stalled offensive against guerrilla forces in the Grammos mountains .... Turkish Parliament passes a new election law, which guarantees a secret ballot and open vote-counting procedures.	Tanks appear for the first time in Palestine fighting as an Israel armored force captures the Lydda airfield, the largest in Palestine.		
July 11		Gen. Norton de Matos announces his candidacy for president of Portugal against incumbent Pres. Oscar de Fragoso Carmona, a supporter of Premier Antonio de Oliveira Salazar.			
July 12		Britain settles its Lend-Lease account with the U.S. by agreeing to repay the $615-million balance in 50 annual installments after 1950.	Israeli forces take Lydda and Ramle on the Tel Aviv-Jerusalem road, while Bernadotte returns to N.Y. to report on his unsuccessful efforts to reach a Palestine peace agreement.	Panamanian National Assembly votes to oust Pres. Enrique Jimenez, electing Controller Gen. Enrique Obarrio to replace him. Jimenez denounces the action as illegal and remains in control with the support of the National Police.	South Korean National Assembly adopts a constitution for the Democratic Republic of Korea, establishing a single-house parliament and a strong presidency.
July 13		Polish Communists approve a program of "voluntary" socialization of agriculture, urging peasants to join farm cooperatives.			
July 14		Russia responds to Western protests over the Berlin blockade, claiming that Western troops have no right to remain in Berlin and that the blockade is necessary to protect "the economy of the Soviet zone." .... Italian Communist leader Palmiro Togliatti is shot and seriously wounded in Rome by a Sicilian law student, Antonio Pallante. The General Confederation of Labor immediately calls a general strike to protest the assassination attempt and force the resignation of Premier Alcide de Gasperi.		Canadian Labor Min. Humphrey Mitchell averts a threatened nationwide rail strike by obtaining agreement on a 17¢ hourly wage increase for the nation's 150,000 railroad workers.	

A	B	C	D	E
Includes developments that affect more than one world region, international organizations and important meetings of major world leaders.	*Includes all domestic and regional developments in Europe, including the Soviet Union, Turkey, Cyprus and Malta.*	*Includes all domestic and regional developments in Africa and the Middle East, including Iraq and Iran and excluding Cyprus, Turkey and Afghanistan.*	*Includes all domestic and regional developments in Latin America, the Caribbean and Canada.*	*Includes all domestic and regional developments in Asian and Pacific nations, extending from Afghanistan through all the Pacific Islands, except Hawaii.*

U.S. Politics & Social Issues	U.S. Foreign Policy & Defense	U.S. Economy & Environment	Science, Technology & Nature	Culture, Leisure & Life Style	
A South Carolina federal district court forbids state Democratic leaders from interfering with Negro participation in primary elections . . . . A Cullman, Ala. court dismisses Christine Johnston's paternity suit against Gov. James Folsom.		Threat of a nationwide railroad strike ends when three railroad brotherhoods accept a 15½¢ hourly wage increase and contract rule changes in a White House bargaining session.			July 8
In a letter to Sen. Claude Pepper (D, Fla.), Eisenhower again rebuffs efforts to draft him as a Democratic presidential candidate . . . . House Labor subcommittee in N.Y. votes to recommend contempt of Congress charges for nine department store union officials who refused to testify whether they were Communists . . . . National Education Assn. ends a six-day convention in Cleveland after voting its support of the $300-million Taft aid-to-education bill . . . . Seymour Stedman, co-founder of the U.S. Socialist Party, dies at 76 in Chicago.				A Nevada court declares prostitution legal in Reno.	July 9
Supreme Court Justice William Douglas tells supporters he is not available for a Democratic presidential draft.				Marcel Cerdan of French Morocco regains the European middleweight boxing title with a 15-round decision over Cyrille Delannoit in Brussels.	July 10
	Economic Cooperation Admin. Paul Hoffman urges U.S. firms to invest in countries receiving Marshall Plan aid, promising a guaranteed return on investments in U.S. dollars.		Franz Weidenreich, anthropologist who discovered the skull of Peking Man in 1937, dies at 75 in N.Y.		July 11
Democratic National Convention opens in Philadelphia.				Ike Williams successfully defends his world lightweight title with a sixth-round TKO over Beau Jack in Philadelphia . . . . Graham Greene's novel *The Heart of the Matter* is published by Viking and becomes a Book-of-the-Month-Club selection.	July 12
Democratic National Convention votes to seat Mississippi delegates despite Northern objections that they were instructed to vote against Truman and the party's civil rights program. The convention also defeats a Southern motion to restore the two-thirds voting rule on nominations . . . . Judge P. James Pellecchia, chief police court magistrate in Newark, N.J., confesses to embezzling $657,000 from his family's Columbus Trust Co. and losing it gambling during the past three years.		UMW ends a seven-day strike against coal mines owned by steel firms after accepting a contract providing for a wage increase and an employers' contribution to the miners' welfare fund. Employer charges that the contract's union shop provision violates the Taft-Hartley Act are referred to the NLRB.		American League All Stars defeat the National League, 5-2, in St. Louis for the fourth straight AL victory.	July 13
Truman is nominated at the Democratic National Convention as his party's presidential candidate by Missouri Gov. Phil Donnelly; Will Rogers makes the first seconding speech. The Convention also passes a strong platform statement on civil rights, urging rapid elimination of poll taxes, lynching, segregation and job discrimination. Mississippi and Alabama delegates walk out of the Convention in protest. Other parts of the platform passed by the Convention call for full recognition of Israel, curtailment of the U.N. Security Council veto, U.S. support of regional anti-Communist military pacts and repeal of the Taft-Hartley Act.	Army announces plans to eliminate mandatory death sentences for murder and rape and to introduce a new grading system for non-commissioned officers.			*The Street with No Name*, a 20th Century Fox gangster film, premiers in N.Y. . . . . French actress Marguerite Moreno dies at 77 in Touzac, France.	July 14
F	G	H	I	J	
Includes elections, federal-state relations, civil rights and liberties, crime, the judiciary, education, health care, poverty, urban affairs and population.	*Includes formation and debate of U.S. foreign and defense policies, veterans affairs and defense spending. (Relations with specific foreign countries are usually found under the region concerned.)*	*Includes business, labor, agriculture, taxation, transportation, consumer affairs, monetary and fiscal policy, natural resources, pollution and accidents.*	*Includes worldwide scientific, medical and technological developments, natural phenomena, U.S. weather and natural disasters.*	*Includes the arts, religion, scholarship, communications media, sports, entertainment, fashions, fads and social life.*	

	World Affairs	Europe	Africa & the Middle East	The Americas	Asia & the Pacific
July 15			U.N. Security Council adopts a U.S.-sponsored resolution calling the Palestine war a threat to peace and ordering Arabs and Jews to resume their truce within three days, threatening otherwise to impose economic or military sanctions on the side determined to be the aggressor.		Allied headquarters in Tokyo ends pre-publication censorship of the Japanese press.
July 16		Italy's General Confederation of Labor calls off the general strike protesting the attempted assassination of Communist leader Togliatti. Three days of demonstrations and riots in major Italian cities end after causing 21 deaths and 200 injuries .... Andrei Gromyko leaves his U.N. post in N.Y., returning to Russia to assume full-time duties as deputy foreign minister. He is replaced at the U.N. by Jacob Malik.	Arab League and Israel agree to a renewed truce in Jerusalem, to go into effect tomorrow. Israel offers to extend the truce to all of Palestine with Arab agreement .... Israeli forces take the Arab city of Nazareth in the western Galilee.	Chilean Congress passes a bill guaranteeing workers a full week's wages regardless of days absent.	British police in Kuala Lumpur claim that they have killed the alleged leader of the Malayan Communist insurgents, Lau Yew.
July 17		Czech government announces the arrest of 84 Western spies in an alleged plot to assassinate Defense Min. Ludovic Svoboda.	Bernadotte leaves N.Y. for Rhodes to resume his role as U.N. mediator and truce overseer in Palestine.		
July 18			Arab League reluctantly accepts the U.N. Security Council demand for an indefinite truce in Palestine fighting.	Costa Rican Pres. Jose Figueres outlaws the Communist Party for "opposing representative democratic government."	
July 19		French cabinet of Premier Robert Schuman resigns after Socialists split from the ruling coalition in a disagreement over the arms budget.		John Bracken resigns as leader of Canada's Progressive Conservative Party after recent electoral losses in provincial and parliamentary by-elections.	Japanese Communist leader Kyuichi Tokuda is wounded by a home-made bomb while addressing a party rally. Ichiro Koga, leader of an anti-Communist war veterans' league, is arrested as the would-be assassin.
July 20		Russian authorities in Germany introduce Soviet zone exit permits for all land travel between Berlin and West Germany .... Consultative Council of the Union of Western Europe ends a two-day meeting in The Hague after agreeing to press for caution in handling the Berlin situation.			South Korean National Assembly elects Syngman Rhee president of the Democratic Republic of Korea in Seoul .... Chen Li-fu, vice president of the Chinese National Assembly, visits Truman to ask for "immediate military aid" against the Communists.
July 21		Yugoslavian Pres. Tito opens a Yugoslavian Communist Party congress in Belgrade with a speech attacking Cominform charges against him but reaffirming his "agreement with the policy of Soviet Russia." .... Russian authorities in Germany offer to supply the western sectors of Berlin with food if residents register their ration cards in the eastern sector and purchase their food with Soviet-zone currency .... Rumania and Czechoslovakia sign a two-year friendship and mutual aid treaty in Bucharest .... French Pres. Vincent Auriol names Radical Socialist leader Andre Marie premier.		Colombian Pres. Mariano Ospina Perez issues an executive decree granting workers a share in industrial and agricultural profits exceeding 12%.	
July 22			Israeli forces seize the Haifa oil refinery, idle for seven months, and put it back into operation.	A runoff referendum on the status of Newfoundland results in a narrow majority for federation with Canada.	
	A	B	C	D	E
	Includes developments that affect more than one world region, international organizations and important meetings of major world leaders.	*Includes all domestic and regional developments in Europe, including the Soviet Union, Turkey, Cyprus and Malta.*	*Includes all domestic and regional developments in Africa and the Middle East, including Iraq and Iran and excluding Cyprus, Turkey and Afghanistan.*	*Includes all domestic and regional developments in Latin America, the Caribbean and Canada.*	*Includes all domestic and regional developments in Asian and Pacific nations, extending from Afghanistan through all the Pacific Islands, except Hawaii.*

U.S. Politics & Social Issues	U.S. Foreign Policy & Defense	U.S. Economy & Environment	Science, Technology & Nature	Culture, Leisure & Life Style	
Democratic National Convention chooses Truman and Kentucky Sen. Alben Barkley as the party's presidential and vice presidential candidates. Truman promises in his acceptance speech to summon a special session of Congress for consideration of badly needed legislation in housing, civil rights, education and other areas .... Roper poll reports that 50.5% of voters questioned after the Republican convention favored Dewey for president, vs. 28.2% for Truman and 4% for Wallace .... A five-man committee appointed by the U.S. Atomic Energy Commission clears National Bureau of Standards director Edward Condon of disloyalty charges raised by the House Un-American Activities Comm.	Gen. John Pershing, commander of the American Expeditionary Force in Europe during World War I, dies at 87 in Washington.				July 15
Federal district court in Charleston, S.C. orders the state's Democratic Party to keep its enrollment books open two weeks longer than usual to facilitate the registration of Negroes.		U.S. Steel and the USW sign a contract giving 170,000 workers wage increases averaging 9%.		Leo Durocher replaces Mel Ott as manager of the New York Giants, while Burt Shotton succeeds Durocher at the Brooklyn Dodger helm .... *Key Largo*, a Warner Bros. film starring Humphrey Bogart, Edward G. Robinson and Lauren Bacall, premiers in N.Y.	July 16
Southern Democrats from 13 states meet in Birmingham, Ala. in a move to defeat the party's national ticket and platform. South Carolina Gov. Strom Thurmond is elected Southern Democratic presidential candidate, with Mississippi Gov. Fielding Wright as his running mate. The convention's platform stresses states' rights and segregation.	U.S. Air Force begins transferring 60 B-29s to Britain for a month of "long-range flight training" in Europe.		First international poliomyelitis conference ends in N.Y. after voting to set up a permanent World Congress on Poliomyelitis.	With Johnny Adams up, Shannon wins the $100,000 Hollywood Gold Cup in Inglewood, Calif. .... Developer of the human cannonball circus act, Ildebrando Zacchini, dies at 79 in Tampa, Fla.	July 17
				New York Herald Tribune lists Norman Mailer's *The Naked and The Dead* and Joshua Liebman's *Peace of Mind* as best-selling fiction and nonfiction books.	July 18
Elmer Irey, former head of the Treasury Department's law enforcement division who helped convict Al Capone and Tom Pendergast, dies at 60 in Shadyside, Md.	Truman meets with State Secy. Marshall and military leaders to discuss the Berlin situation .... U.S. Treasury agrees to return $30 million in Yugoslavian funds held in N.Y. after the Tito government promises to pay $17 million in private claims on nationalized property in Yugoslavia.			Eastern Orthodox Church leaders meeting in Moscow agree to work for closer ties with Protestants but reject any resumption of relations with the Roman Catholic Church.	July 19
A federal grand jury in N.Y. indicts 12 U.S. Communist leaders on charges of advocating the violent overthrow of the U.S. government in violation of the 1940 Alien Registration Act. Among those indicted are party chairman William Foster, general secretary Eugene Dennis, CIO International Fur and Leather Workers Union leader Irving Potash and Ohio Communist leader Gus Hall.	Truman issues a proclamation ordering all men between 18 and 25 to register for military service .... Truman calls Gen. Clay of the U.S. military government in Germany to Washington for consultations on the Berlin situation.	U.S. Steel raises its steel prices by an average of $9.34 a ton, claiming the increase is necessary to meet recently granted wage increases .... A federal grand jury in Pittsburgh indicts Du Pont, Sherwin-Williams, Glidden and 11 other companies on charges of fixing prices of paint and related products.		Poet Percy McKaye wins the $5,000 1948 fellowship award of the Academy of American Poets for his dramatic tetralogy *Hamlet, King of Denmark*.	July 20
FBI director J. Edgar Hoover announces that over two million federal employes have been screened in the loyalty investigation program.	State Secy. Marshall issues a statement on the Berlin situation, reaffirming U.S. refusal to be "coerced" by the blockade but emphasizing that confrontation can still be avoided through "negotiation and diplomatic procedure."	A federal district court in Trenton, N.J. orders the U.S. Pipe and Foundry Co. to release 50 patents and stop monopolizing the cast iron pressure pipe trade .... William D'Arcy, founder of the D'Arcy Advertising Co. and a leading innovator in U.S. advertising, dies at 74 in St. Louis.			July 21
Progressive Party national convention opens in Philadelphia.		Threat of a UAW strike against Ford Motors ends when the union and company agree on a 13¢ hourly wage increase with improved fringe benefits.			July 22

F	G	H	I	J
Includes elections, federal-state relations, civil rights and liberties, crime, the judiciary, education, health care, poverty, urban affairs and population.	*Includes formation and debate of U.S. foreign and defense policies, veterans affairs and defense spending. (Relations with specific foreign countries are usually found under the region concerned.)*	*Includes business, labor, agriculture, taxation, transportation, consumer affairs, monetary and fiscal policy, natural resources, pollution and accidents.*	*Includes worldwide scientific, medical and technological developments, natural phenomena, U.S. weather and natural disasters.*	*Includes the arts, religion, scholarship, communications media, sports, entertainment, fashions, fads and social life.*

	World Affairs	Europe	Africa & the Middle East	The Americas	Asia & the Pacific
July 23		Russian authorities in Germany announce plans to issue a new currency for their occupation zone, called (like the West German currency) the Deutsche Mark . . . . Gen. Clay of the U.S. military government in Germany announces plans to double the size of the Berlin airlift by assigning more large-capacity U.S. C-54 transport planes to Germany . . . . Financial experts from countries represented in the Organization for European Economic Cooperation, meeting in Paris, announce a plan for mutual convertability of European currencies to facilitate trade within Europe.	Egyptian government imposes a state of emergency on Cairo to prevent anti-American and anti-British outbreaks following the stoning and death of tourist Stephen Haas, a Philadelphia realtor.	Hoping to attract more tourists and foreign sales, Mexico devalues the peso from 4.85 to 5.75-6 pesos to the U.S. dollar.	British authorities in Kuala Lumpur and Singapore outlaw the Malayan Communist Party as the "directing force" of recent nationalist disturbances.
July 24	World Health Organization's first annual assembly ends in Geneva after voting to make its permanent headquarters in the city. Dr. Brock Chisholm of Canada is elected director-general.				
July 25		Col. Otto Skorzeny, SS officer who rescued Mussolini from imprisonment in 1943, escapes from a Darmstadt detention camp.			
July 26		Leaders of 11 western German states, meeting in Frankfurt, agree to supervise creation of a West German government, with a constituent assembly elected by the state parliaments . . . . U.S. and Britain retaliate against the Berlin blockade by imposing an embargo on all Russian rail traffic moving across western Germany to France, Italy, Switzerland, Holland and Scandinavia . . . . Berlin's Deputy Mayor Ferdinand Friedensberg dismisses Communist-sponsored police chief Paul Markgraf, who remains in control of police in the Soviet sector of the city.			
July 27		French Premier Andre Marie names his new cabinet, with Robert Schuman as foreign minister, Paul Reynaud as finance minister, Leon Blum as vice premier and Paul Ramadier as minister without portfolio . . . . Communist majority of the Italian General Confederation of Labor expels Christian Democratic members from the organization's executive committee.			
July 28		Explosions and fire wreck an I.G. Farben chemical complex in Ludwigshafen, Germany, causing 184 deaths, 2,500 injuries and about $15 million in damages.		Peruvian Congress fails to convene when 19 conservative senators refuse to attend in protest against the program of the ruling Socialist People's Party.	
July 29		Yugoslavian Communists end their party congress in Belgrade after reelecting Tito head of the party and rejecting Cominform charges against the government . . . . A U.S. tribunal in Nuremberg acquits 23 I.G. Farben officials of charges of committing crimes against peace and conspiring to wage aggressive war but convicts four defendants of using slave labor from the Auschwitz concentration camp and nine others of plundering property in occupied territories . . . . Communist delegates walk out of the Berlin City Assembly as it prepares to pass a resolution condemning the Soviet blockade . . . . Finnish Social Democratic leader Karl Fagerholm forms an all-socialist cabinet in Helsinki, excluding Communists.			
	A	B	C	D	E
	Includes developments that affect more than one world region, international organizations and important meetings of major world leaders.	*Includes all domestic and regional developments in Europe, including the Soviet Union, Turkey, Cyprus and Malta.*	*Includes all domestic and regional developments in Africa and the Middle East, including Iraq and Iran and excluding Cyprus, Turkey and Afghanistan.*	*Includes all domestic and regional developments in Latin America, the Caribbean and Canada.*	*Includes all domestic and regional developments in Asian and Pacific nations, extending from Afghanistan through all the Pacific Islands, except Hawaii.*

U.S. Politics & Social Issues	U.S. Foreign Policy & Defense	U.S. Economy & Environment	Science, Technology & Nature	Culture, Leisure & Life Style	
N.Y.C. Mayor William O'Dwyer is reconciled with the Tammany Hall Democratic organization after both agree to support Judge John Mullen as Democratic candidate for the post of N.Y. County surrogate .... Ohio state police kill ex-convict John West and capture Robert Davis, ending a two-week crime spree in which the two killed six people.		Truman names Paul Porter, last head of the OPA, as his special assistant in anti-inflation matters.		David W. Griffith, pioneer film producer and originator of the full-length feature in the U.S., dies at 73 in Hollywood.	July 23
Progressive Party convention in Philadelphia chooses Henry Wallace and Sen. Glen Taylor (D, Ida.) as its presidential and vice presidential candidates .... Leading anti-Truman Southern Democrats, including presidential candidate Strom Thurmond, meet in Atlanta and adopt the name "States' Rights Democrats" for their party.	Republican presidential candidate Thomas Dewey completes two days of consultations on the Berlin situation with Gen. Eisenhower, Sen. Arthur Vandenberg and Republican foreign affairs adviser John Foster Dulles.	General Motors announces an 8% price increase for its 1949 models.		Eleanor Medill Patterson, editor and publisher of the Washington *Times-Herald*, dies at 63 in Marlboro, Md.	July 24
Progressive Party convention in Philadelphia adopts a platform calling for full racial equality, repeal of the Taft-Hartley Act, strengthening of the U.N., complete recognition of Israel and an end to the Marshall Plan and the Truman Doctrine, which it alleges is a policy of confrontation with Russia .... Gallup Poll reports that 42% of voters questioned nationally favor racial segregation in public transportation, while 49% oppose it. In the South, 84% favor segregation, vs. 12% opposed.					July 25
Congress begins a special session called by Truman to consider inflation control, civil rights and other legislation .... Truman issues two executive orders banning racial discrimination in the armed forces and federal civil service.		National Maritime Union re-elects Joseph Curran president and defeats Communist candidates for the union's executive board.		*The Babe Ruth Story*, film version of the baseball star's autobiography starring William Bendix, premiers in N.Y. .... Freddie Mills of England takes the world light-heavyweight crown from Gus Lesnevich in a 15-round decision in London.	July 26
Truman addresses the special session of Congress, proposing an eight-point program to control inflation and urging passage of an increased minimum wage, civil rights guarantees and other measures. Republican congressional leaders reject most of Truman's proposals and condemn the special session as a "political maneuver."	Selective Service director Lewis Hershey announces plans to start conscription with the oldest men eligible for the draft.	International Assn. of Machinists ends a six-month strike of National Airlines office workers after the company agrees to rehire all strikers and negotiate a new contract.	Univ. of California's Lick Observatory announces discovery of the sixth asteroid to be found within the earth's orbit.	Joseph Tinker, former Chicago Cubs shortstop and part of the "Tinker-to-Evers-to-Chance" double-play combination, dies at 68 in Orlando, Fla. .... Susan Cook, Pulitzer Prize-winning playwright and first producer of Eugene O'Neill's work, dies at 66 in Provincetown, Mass.	July 27
A federal district court in New Haven upholds the constitutionality of the Taft-Hartley Act's ban on union political expenditures.	State Secy. Marshall appoints a three-man committee to investigate congressional charges that foreign intelligence agents have gained entry to the U.S. through the U.N. and other international organizations.	AFL International Ladies Garment Workers Union signs a three-year contract with 600 N.Y. clothing manufacturers, tying future wage increases to living costs.			July 28
Sen. John Stennis (D, Miss.) and other Southern senators begin a filibuster to prevent passage of Administration-sponsored anti-poll tax legislation .... Harold Stassen accepts appointment as president of the Univ. of Pennsylvania in Philadelphia, with the understanding that he is free to campaign for Republican presidential candidate Thomas Dewey .... James Watson, former Republican senator from Indiana and Senate Republican leader during the Hoover Administration, dies at 84 in Washington.		Truman aides testifying before the House and Senate Banking and Currency committees urge a rollback of prices to late 1947 levels, reimposition of consumer credit controls and an increase in bank reserve requirements as part of the Administration's anti-inflation program .... Interstate Commerce Commission grants U.S. railroads increased freight rates amounting to $67.4 million a year.		Britain's King George VI formally opens the summer Olympics in London .... Sidney Hanover wins the $25,000 American Trotting Championship in Westbury, N.Y.	July 29
F *Includes elections, federal-state relations, civil rights and liberties, crime, the judiciary, education, health care, poverty, urban affairs and population.*	G *Includes formation and debate of U.S. foreign and defense policies, veterans affairs and defense spending. (Relations with specific foreign countries are usually found under the region concerned.)*	H *Includes business, labor, agriculture, taxation, transportation, consumer affairs, monetary and fiscal policy, natural resources, pollution and accidents.*	I *Includes worldwide scientific, medical and technological developments, natural phenomena, U.S. weather and natural disasters.*	J *Includes the arts, religion, scholarship, communications media, sports, entertainment, fashions, fads and social life.*	

	World Affairs	Europe	Africa & the Middle East	The Americas	Asia & the Pacific
July 30	Big Four representatives meet in Moscow to begin discussions on settlement of the Berlin situation.	Ten-nation Danube River Conference opens in Belgrade to discuss navigation rights on the international waterway .... British House of Commons passes the British Citizenship Act, conferring the status of British subjects on all Commonwealth citizens .... Hungarian Pres. Zoltan Tildy resigns following the arrest of his son-in-law on charges of espionage and treason .... Russia establishes a Greater Berlin Trading Corp. to handle the city's trade with the rest of Germany and foreign countries .... Trade union representatives from the U.S. and western Europe end a two-day conference on the Marshall Plan in Paris by voting to establish a liaison office with the Organization for European Economic Cooperation and defend the Marshall Plan from Communist attack.			
July 31		A U.S. tribunal in Nuremberg hands down prison sentences for 11 officials of the Krupp munitions firm, convicted on charges of using slave labor and plundering occupied territories. Among those sentenced is Alfried Krupp von Bohlen und Halbach, owner of the firm, who receives a 12-year term.			
Aug. 1					
Aug. 2	U.S., British and French representatives meet in Moscow with Soviet Premier Stalin and Foreign Min. Molotov to discuss settlement of the Berlin situation. Stalin offers to lift the blockade in exchange for uniform use of Soviet-zone currency in Berlin.	Soviet Deputy Foreign Min. Andrei Vishinski presents the Danube conference in Belgrade with the Russian plan for control of traffic on the river, calling for creation of a navigation commission representing Russia, the Ukraine, Rumania, Bulgaria, Yugoslavia, Hungary and Czechoslovakia, with Austria eventually to join.		Willem Huender takes office as governor of Dutch Guiana under a new constitution that reduces the governor's powers in favor of the all-native legislature and cabinet.	
Aug. 3		Hungarian Parliament elects Deputy Premier Arpad Szakasits, former Social Democratic leader, to succeed Zoltan Tildy as president .... Communist-led People's Council in Berlin approves a draft constitution for a German People's Republic providing for a coalition government and two-house parliament.			
Aug. 4		Greek government troops report clearing Communist guerrillas from the Smolika area in northeastern Greece, restricting main guerrilla forces to a 30-mile front on the Albanian border .... U.N. Economic and Social Council instructs the Economic Commission for Europe to work for expansion of trade between eastern and western Europe.			South Korean National Assembly approves Pres. Syngman Rhee's appointment of Gen. Lee Bum Suk as premier and defense minister. Other cabinet appointments are also announced.
	A *Includes developments that affect more than one world region, international organizations and important meetings of major world leaders.*	B *Includes all domestic and regional developments in Europe, including the Soviet Union, Turkey, Cyprus and Malta.*	C *Includes all domestic and regional developments in Africa and the Middle East, including Iraq and Iran and excluding Cyprus, Turkey and Afghanistan.*	D *Includes all domestic and regional developments in Latin America, the Caribbean and Canada.*	E *Includes all domestic and regional developments in Asian and Pacific nations, extending from Afghanistan through all the Pacific Islands, except Hawaii.*

U.S. Politics & Social Issues	U.S. Foreign Policy & Defense	U.S. Economy & Environment	Science, Technology & Nature	Culture, Leisure & Life Style	
Elizabeth Bentley, a confessed Communist spy, testifies before a Senate Expenditures subcommittee to receiving classified information during the war from 40-50 government officials. Among those she names is William Remington, an important member of the Commerce Department's Office of International Trade.		Truman submits his mid-year economic report to Congress, warning that only rapid enactment of an anti-inflation program can prevent an impending "business collapse."			July 30
Testifying before the House Un-American Activities Comm., Elizabeth Bentley accuses wartime presidential aide Lauchlin Currie and former Asst. Treasury Secy. Harry Dexter White of indirectly furnishing her with classified information. Both deny the charge. Former Commerce Dept. official William Remington also denies furnishing Bentley with classified information in testimony before a Senate Expenditures subcommittee .... States' Rights presidential candidate Strom Thurmond opens his campaign in Cherryville, N.Y. by denouncing Truman, Dewey and Wallace for their support of civil rights .... Truman and Dewey share the platform in ceremonies marking the opening of New York's Idlewild International Airport.	Mikhail Samarin, mathematics and arts teacher at a Soviet consular school in N.Y., goes into hiding with his wife following the school's closing to avoid being returned to Russia.			Washington's National Theater ends live performances when the Actors Equity Assn. demands an end to the traditional exclusion of Negroes from the audience .... Papa Redbird, with R.L. Baird up, wins $66,000 in Chicago's Arlington Classic.	July 31
		John McHugh, former president of Chase National Bank of N.Y., dies at 82 in Chappaqua, N.Y.	A Latecoere 631 flying boat disappears over the Atlantic and is presumed to have crashed with 52 passengers.		Aug. 1
Testifying before a Senate Expenditures subcommittee, former Communist editor Louis Budenz warns that "possibly thousands" of Communists have infiltrated the federal civil service and urges Congress to outlaw the Communist Party .... U.S. Communist Party opens its first national convention since 1945 in N.Y. as party chairman William Foster promises Communist support of the Progressive Party in upcoming elections .... An Oklahoma state court in Norman rejects an appeal by three Negro students for admission to the Univ. of Oklahoma law school because the state maintains a separate Negro law school. Texas Atty. Gen. Price Daniel rules that the Texas State Univ. for Negroes must reject white student Jack Coffman's application for admission because the state constitution requires segregation of educational facilities .... Truman appoints a three-man Displaced Persons Commission to supervise the admission of 205,000 European refugees to the U.S.				Albert Camus' *The Plague* is published in N.Y. by Knopf.	Aug. 2
House Un-American Activities Comm. hears testimony from *Time* editor Whittaker Chambers, who claims that he served as a Communist underground courier during the 1930s. Among those implicated by Chambers as part of his underground "ring" is Alger Hiss, president of the Carnegie Endowment for International Peace and former State Dept. director of special political affairs.			Charles Hubbard, U.S. Weather Bureau chief of Arctic operations, discovers a cache of documents left by Adm. Robert Perry on Ellesmere Island, Canada during a polar expedition in 1905-06. The documents include copies of records left by British explorer Sir George Nares.	International Film Festival in Marienbad names the Polish entry *Oswiecim* the year's best film and lauds William Wyler as best director for *The Best Years of Our Lives.*	Aug. 3
Senate Republican leaders drop anti-poll tax legislation from the current session's order of business, bowing to a filibuster by Southern senators .... Navy and Commerce departments refuse to supply files on William Remington to the Senate Expenditures subcommittee.		Republican congressional leaders agree to kill the Taft-Ellender-Wagner housing bill following the refusal of the House to accept the bill's slum clearance and public housing provisions .... Price of hogs rises to a record $31.50 per hundredweight on Chicago's livestock market.	Public Health Service reports new polio outbreaks in North Carolina, Texas and California and reveals that incidence of the disease is increasing in other states as well.	New York's Metropolitan Opera cancels its 1948-49 season after three of 12 unions representing the organization's employes refuse to accept contracts on last season's terms.	Aug. 4

	World Affairs	Europe	Africa & the Middle East	The Americas	Asia & the Pacific
Aug. 5	U.N. Interim Commission on Peace and Security ends its first session in Lake Success, N.Y. Though boycotted by Russia, the Commission unanimously votes to continue its operations.	U.S., British and French authorities in Germany agree to formulate common export-import policies for their zones and maximize West German trade with France.	Israel urges the Arab League to begin direct negotiations for a Palestine settlement in an invitation submitted through U.N. mediator Folke Bernadotte . . . . Bernadotte urges the Security Council to work for the return of Arab refugees to their former homes in Israeli territory, despite Israeli objections.		
Aug. 6		U.S. and Britain renounce four-power control of the I.G. Farben chemical combine and announce plans to sell plants of the concern located in their occupation zones.	Egypt rejects Israeli proposals for direct negotiations on the Palestine situation.	Forty-two members of the anti-Peronist Radical Party resign from Argentina's Parliament in protest against the expulsion of a deputy for a speech critical of Peron.	
Aug. 7	U.N. Secy. Gen. Trygve Lie releases his third annual report to the General Assembly, calling Germany the most troublesome international problem and warning that the Marshall Plan may "block coordinated [economic] action within Europe as a whole."	U.S. forces in Berlin open the Spandau airport to augment the Berlin airlift . . . . Polish-Czech Economic Cooperation Council announces plans to develop a new industrial center in the Katowice area of southwestern Poland and the adjoining Ostrava area of Czechoslovakia.		Canadian Liberal Party convention in Ottawa elects External Affairs Secy. Louis St. Laurent to succeed William Mackenzie King as party leader . . . . Panama's national elections board rules that Domingo Diaz Arosemena defeated Arnulfo Arias in last May's disputed presidential election.	Nanking officials estimate that more than three million Chinese are homeless and one million tons of rice destroyed as a result of severe flooding along the Yangtze and Yellow rivers.
Aug. 8		Greek Army reports advancing to the Albanian frontier at both ends of the semi-circular Grammos front . . . . Russian authorities in Berlin act against food hoarding and black market traders in an effort to prevent the growth of food shortages . . . . Russian biologist Trofim Denisovich Lysenko announces re-affirmation of his environmentalist view of genetics by the Soviet Communist Party's Central Comm. Lysenko denounces Mendelian genetics as an "alien foreign bourgeois biology."			
Aug. 9		Berlin's City Assembly authorizes a separate food administration for West Berlin to thwart Communist efforts to win city-wide control of food supplies.		Ecuador, Colombia, Venezuela and Panama sign the Charter of Quito, providing for creation of a customs union.	
Aug. 10		Christian Socialist leader Gaston Eyskens forms a coalition cabinet in Belgium with Liberal support.		Bolivian Pres. Enrique Hertzog appoints a new cabinet to replace one that resigned last week.	
Aug. 11		Greek government forces report capturing a major guerrilla stronghold on Mt. Alevista near the Albanian border.			

A	B	C	D	E
Includes developments that affect more than one world region, international organizations and important meetings of major world leaders.	*Includes all domestic and regional developments in Europe, including the Soviet Union, Turkey, Cyprus and Malta.*	*Includes all domestic and regional developments in Africa and the Middle East, including Iraq and Iran and excluding Cyprus, Turkey and Afghanistan.*	*Includes all domestic and regional developments in Latin America, the Caribbean and Canada.*	*Includes all domestic and regional developments in Asian and Pacific nations, extending from Afghanistan through all the Pacific Islands, except Hawaii.*

U.S. Politics & Social Issues	U.S. Foreign Policy & Defense	U.S. Economy & Environment	Science, Technology & Nature	Culture, Leisure & Life Style	
Alger Hiss appears before the House Un-American Activities Comm. and denies under oath that he ever knew Whittaker Chambers or belonged to the Communist Party .... Truman denounces congressional hearings on alleged Communist connections of high government officials, calling the charges a "red herring" that allows Republican leaders to ignore pressing legislatives matters. Truman orders all executive departments to refrain from providing congressional committees with "information of any sort relating to [a federal] employe's loyalty or other aspects of the individual's record." .... Rep. Estes Kefauver and former Gov. Gordon Browning win the Democratic senatorial and gubernatorial nominations in Tennessee over candidates backed by the state's powerful Crump machine .... Delegates to the Communist Party's national convention unanimously reject former chairman Earl Browder's application for readmission to the party.	House passes and sends to Truman a Senate-approved resolution authorizing a $65-million, interest-free loan for construction of U.N. headquarters in N.Y.	Ford Motors announces a 5% average price increase on new models, its third increase in the past year .... N.Y. State Federation of Labor amends its constitution to bar Communists from office, reelects Thomas Murray president and names Thomas Young its first Negro vice president.			Aug. 5
Senate Expenditures subcommittee suspends public hearings on the loyalty of federal officials after Chmn. Homer Ferguson (R, Mich.) threatens impeachment proceedings against Truman if the Administration continues to withhold information on officials under congressional investigation .... U.S. Communist Party ends its five-day national convention in N.Y. after adopting a platform similar to that of the Progressive Party.	Army Engineer Corps announces a $3.5-million plan to expand the White Sands rocket testing ground in New Mexico .... Two B-29s land at Davis-Monthan Air Force Base in Arizona after completing the bomber's first round-the-world flight. Another B-29 sets a long-distance record for the plane by completing a 5,120-mile flight from Fuerstenfeldbruck, Germany to Marshall Field, Kansas.	Senate Republicans defeat final attempts to pass the Taft-Ellender-Wagner housing bill, substituting a compromise measure that provides federal loan guarantees for private construction of low-cost housing.	Dr. Dorman Lichty of Ann Arbor, Mich. demonstrates a new lightweight respirator for polio victims.	Bob Mathias, leader of the U.S. track and field Olympic team, takes the Olympic decathlon title in London with 7,139 points .... Veteran pitcher Bucky Walters is named manager of the seventh-place Cincinnati Reds.	Aug. 6
Congress ends its two-week special session after completing action on three of 11 measures considered urgent by Truman .... NAACP Executive Secy. Walter White refuses to support a civil disobedience campaign advocated by other civil rights leaders to protest armed forces segregation.		Congress passes a compromise anti-inflation program, restricting bank and consumer credit but rejecting Truman's request for price, wage and rent controls and standby rationing authority .... Truman nominates former Massachusetts Gov. Maurice Tobin to succeed the late Lewis Schwellenbach as labor secretary.	Sidney Brown, inventor of the drum cable relay and other communications devices, dies at 75 in Sidmouth, England.		Aug. 7
	Soviet consular employe Mikhail Samarin contacts the FBI from hiding and denounces "the party, police and government machinery of the Soviet Union."	NLRB issues its first ruling against "featherbedding," ordering a Los Angeles local of the AFL Plasterers and Cement Finishers International Assn. to refund wages paid to four employes for work not done.		Protestant clergymen represented in the National Council Against Conscription call on U.S. churches to observe a day of "mourning and repentance" to protest the peacetime draft .... Anglican Church ends a five-week conference in Lambeth, England after hearing Cyril Garbett, Archbishop of York, urge a union of all Christian churches.	Aug. 8
Appearing before the House Un-American Activities Comm., former Treasury Dept. official Victor Perlo and engineer Alexander Koral refuse to answer questions on their alleged participation in a wartime Communist spy ring.				Lloyd Mangrum wins the Tam O'Shanter golf tournament in Chicago, ending four days of tournament victories with $22,500 in prizes.	Aug. 9
	House Un-American Activities Comm. subpoenas Mikhail Samarin, giving him immunity from a search warrant issued by N.Y. police at the request of the Soviet consulate.	Truman signs the congressional housing bill but denounces it as "emasculated" for ignoring the needs of Americans living in "disgraceful urban and rural slums."	American Cancer Society announces an expanded program of cancer research awards, amounting to $3.5 million in the coming year.		Aug. 10
South Carolina Gov. Strom Thurmond formally accepts the presidential nomination of the States' Rights Democrats in Houston and attacks Truman's civil rights program as a call for "a police state in this country."	Soviet Foreign Min. Molotov accuses the U.S. of "kidnapping" Russian consular employes in N.Y. and demands their return to Russian custody .... Truman signs a joint congressional resolution authorizing a $65-million loan to build the U.N. headquarters in N.Y.	Bethlehem Steel signs the biggest passenger ship contract ever negotiated in the U.S., guaranteeing to build two 20,000-ton luxury liners at a cost of $46,830,000 for American Export Lines' Mediterranean service.		Harrison Hoyt drives Demon Hanover to victory in the 23rd Hambletonian Stakes in Goshen, N.Y., winning $32,500.	Aug. 11

F	G	H	I	J
Includes elections, federal-state relations, civil rights and liberties, crime, the judiciary, education, health care, poverty, urban affairs and population.	*Includes formation and debate of U.S. foreign and defense policies, veterans affairs and defense spending. (Relations with specific foreign countries are usually found under the region concerned.)*	*Includes business, labor, agriculture, taxation, transportation, consumer affairs, monetary and fiscal policy, natural resources, pollution and accidents.*	*Includes worldwide scientific, medical and technological developments, natural phenomena, U.S. weather and natural disasters.*	*Includes the arts, religion, scholarship, communications media, sports, entertainment, fashions, fads and social life.*

	World Affairs	Europe	Africa & the Middle East	The Americas	Asia & the Pacific
Aug. 12		Anglo-American airlift to Berlin achieves its goal of transporting 4,500 tons of supplies a day . . . . Gen. Arso Jovanovich, wartime Yugoslav partisan chief of staff, is killed on the Yugoslavian frontier while attempting to escape to Rumania. The Yugoslavian government accuses him of working with the Cominform against Pres. Tito.		Mexican government fixes retail prices of rice, flour, lard, beans and salt to curb rising living costs.	
Aug. 13		Russia formally quits the four-power Allied Berlin command . . . . Danubian Conference in Belgrade rejects a U.S. proposal to give the U.S., Britain and France places on a new international commission to control navigation on the river.			India issues a White Paper attacking the government of Hyderabad as feudal and demanding the territory's absorption into the Indian federation.
Aug. 14			In a message to U.N. mediator Bernadotte, Egypt reiterates its refusal to negotiate directly with Israel on a Palestine settlement. Israel demands immediate U.N. action to stop alleged Arab violations of the Palestine truce.	Argentine Chamber of Deputies calls a national assembly to consider government requests for revision of the constitution. The proposed changes will give the government greater power over the economy and allow Pres. Peron to succeed himself at the end of his six-year term. The opposition Radical Party calls for impeachment of Peron on charges of attempting to establish a totalitarian state.	Burmese government forces report suppressing a four-day mutiny of Burma Rifles units in the Irrawaddy delta region. The government charges the mutinous troops with attempting to establish a military dictatorship.
Aug. 15				Defense Secy. Forrestal begins a two-day conference with Canadian officials in Ottawa on U.S.-Canadian military cooperation . . . . Paraguay's new president, Juan Natalicio Gonzalez, is inaugurated for a five-year term.	Democratic Republic of Korea is formally proclaimed in Seoul ceremonies addressed by Pres. Syngman Rhee and Gen. MacArthur. Truman immediately recognizes the South Korean government and orders an end to the U.S. military administration in Korea . . . . Philippine government's amnesty offer for Hukbalahap guerrillas expires after attracting little response.
Aug. 16		In an effort to stimulate trade, Poland makes Gdynia a duty-free port for U.S., Czech, Rumanian and Yugoslavian shipping.			
Aug. 17	U.N. Security Council's Commission on Conventional Armaments concludes 18 months of work with a report admitting failure to achieve agreement on regulation of non-nuclear weapons.	French National Assembly enacts an economic plan sponsored by Finance Min. Paul Reynaud, giving the government sweeping economic powers to control inflation and balance the budget.	Israeli government issues a new national currency, the Israeli pound, valued at $4 U.S.	Canadian Defense Min. Brooks Claxton and U.S. Defense Secy. Forrestal meet in Ogdensburg, N.Y. to pledge continued military cooperation between their two countries.	Burmese Pres. Saw Shwe Thaik authorizes military officials to proclaim martial law in any part of the country after Communist-led guerrillas kidnap Rangoon's police chief near the city.

U.S. Politics & Social Issues	U.S. Foreign Policy & Defense	U.S. Economy & Environment	Science, Technology & Nature	Culture, Leisure & Life Style	
	Soviet consular employe Oksana Kosenkina jumps from a third-floor window of the Russian consulate in N.Y., injuring herself critically. She charges that consular officials were holding her prisoner and preparing to return her to Russia after she attempted last week to escape from the consulate. A second escaped consular employe, Mikhail Samarin, appears in Washington to testify before a closed session of the House Un-American Activities Comm. . . . . State Secy. Marshall refuses to open confidential visa files to a Senate Immigration subcommittee investigating charges that Communist spies have entered the U.S. as U.N. representatives.	Truman orders the Reconstruction Finance Corp. to study the critical financial situation of the nation's airlines and recommend means of obtaining funds for their immediate operations and long-term development.			Aug. 12
Five former government officials, including former presidential aide Lauchlin Currie and former Asst. Treasury Secy. Harry Dexter White, appear before the House Un-American Activities Comm. to deny charges of participating in a wartime Communist spy ring.		Truman signs a bill appropriating $10 million for the Housing and Home Finance Agency to use in establishing a housing investment insurance fund . . . . Maurice Tobin is sworn in as Labor Secretary.			Aug. 13
Former OPA director Chester Bowles wins the Democratic gubernatorial nomination for Connecticut at the party's state convention in Hartford.		NLRB finds the AFL International Typographical Union in violation of the Taft-Hartley Act for insisting on closed-shop conditions in unionized plants.		Fourteenth Olympiad ends in London after 16 days of games drawing 1.5 million spectators. The U.S. leads in gold medals with 38, followed by Sweden and France.	Aug. 14
		In his mid-year budget review, Truman predicts that the federal government will end the 1949 fiscal year with a $1.54-billion operating deficit as a result of the Republican-sponsored tax cut.		Donald Strub, 13, of Warren, Ohio wins the 11th All-American Soap Box Derby in Akron . . . . *New York Herald Tribune* reports Evelyn Waugh's *The Loved One* and Winston Churchill's *The Gathering Storm* as best-selling fiction and non-fiction books.	Aug. 15
Alger Hiss appears before a secret session of the House Un-American Activities Comm. in Washington. Although continuing to deny any knowledge of Whittaker Chambers under that name, he states that he may have been briefly acquainted with Chambers as "George Crosley." . . . . Former Treasury Dept. and International Monetary Fund official Henry Dexter White, under investigation for alleged wartime Communist spy activities, dies of a heart attack at 56 in Fitzwilliam, N.H. Friends attribute his death in part to strain resulting from the spy hearings . . . . Atty. Gen. Clark asks the Army to arrest Iva Toguri D'Aquino in Tokyo for immediate transfer to San Francisco on charges of broadcasting Japanese propaganda during the war.		Truman signs the Anti-Inflation Control Act, authorizing him to restrict bank credit and reimpose wartime consumer credit controls.		Home run king George Herman (Babe) Ruth, N.Y. Yankees outfielder who tied or set 76 baseball hitting records, dies at 53 of cancer of the throat in N.Y.	Aug. 16
Hiss and Chambers confront each other at a closed House Un-American Activities Comm. hearing in N.Y. Hiss continues to deny any association with Chambers.	Soviet Consul Gen. Jacob Lomakin charges that Russian consular employe Oksana Kosenkina is being held prisoner by police in a N.Y. hospital following her jump from a third-floor window of the Soviet consulate . . . . Campaigning in Albany, N.Y., Republican presidential candidate Dewey advocates returning former Italian colonies to Italian control under a U.N. trusteeship.			Anglican Church issues a report on the Lambeth conference, condemning Communism and urging closer ties with other Christian churches.	Aug. 17
F	G	H	I	J	
Includes elections, federal-state relations, civil rights and liberties, crime, the judiciary, education, health care, poverty, urban affairs and population.	*Includes formation and debate of U.S. foreign and defense policies, veterans affairs and defense spending. (Relations with specific foreign countries are usually found under the region concerned.)*	*Includes business, labor, agriculture, taxation, transportation, consumer affairs, monetary and fiscal policy, natural resources, pollution and accidents.*	*Includes worldwide scientific, medical and technological developments, natural phenomena, U.S. weather and natural disasters.*	*Includes the arts, religion, scholarship, communications media, sports, entertainment, fashions, fads and social life.*	

	World Affairs	Europe	Africa & the Middle East	The Americas	Asia & the Pacific
Aug. 18	Russia vetoes Ceylon's U.N. membership application in the Security Council, claiming that the country is still dominated by Britain.	Danubian Conference in Belgrade ends with passage of a Russian-sponsored agreement for exclusive Eastern European control of the Danube waterway. U.S. representatives abstain in the final vote but attack the agreement as a Russian attempt to impose "political and economic enslavement" on the Danube region .... French cabinet asks Britain, Belgium, Holland and Luxembourg to participate in a conference on creation of a European parliament .... Marie Provaznikova, leader of the Czech women's Olympic team, seeks asylum in the U.S. and denounces Czech government purges of the national youth organization.			
Aug. 19	U.S. State Dept. declares Jacob Lomakin, Soviet consul general in N.Y., persona non grata for attempting to regain custody of consular employes seeking asylum in the U.S. The State Dept. note demands that Lomakin leave the U.S. "within a reasonable time," the first expulsion of a high Russian diplomat in the history of U.S.-Soviet relations.	Greek Premier Themistocles Sophoulis claims victory for government forces in the "battle of Grammos" along the Albanian frontier.			Chinese Nationalist government announces a program of price controls and currency reform, establishing a new gold yuan at 25¢ U.S.
Aug. 20		Russian military police enter the U.S. zone of Berlin in a raid on black market traders which ends with the arrest of 2,500 suspects.			
Aug. 21		U.S. authorities in Berlin station 600 soldiers at the Potsdamer Platz, on the border between the U.S. and Soviet sectors, to prevent further Russian incursions into the U.S. sector.			
Aug. 22		Russian military police in Berlin arrest Thomas Headen, deputy chief of the U.S. military government's information division, for carrying a camera in the Potsdamer Platz area. Headen is released after a short imprisonment in the Soviet sector .... Polish Communist Party announces plans to push nationalization of agriculture in conformity with the Cominform line.	Israel proposes separate direct peace negotiations with every Arab state engaged in Palestine fighting.		
Aug. 23	Soviet Premier Stalin and Foreign Min. Molotov meet with Western envoys in Moscow and agree to continue Berlin talks despite failure to reach agreement on the city's status in seven negotiating sessions.		Syrian Premier Jamil Mardam Bey forms a new cabinet, shifting Moshen el-Barazi from the Interior to the Foreign Ministry.		
Aug. 24		Russian and U.S. authorities in Berlin agree to inform one another before making anti-black market raids, ending a series of arrests and counter-arrests of Allied personnel .... Communist Party of Trieste ends a special congress by resolving to support the Cominform against Yugoslavia and to oppose the Marshall Plan through the city's labor unions.			Gen. John Hodge and South Korean Pres. Syngman Rhee sign an agreement in Seoul providing for continued training of South Korean troops by the U.S. .... Princely state of Hyderabad formally petitions the U.N. Security Council to consider its demand for continued independence from India .... Philippine government reports a new outbreak of Hukbalahap guerrilla attacks in central Luzon.

U.S. Politics & Social Issues	U.S. Foreign Policy & Defense	U.S. Economy & Environment	Science, Technology & Nature	Culture, Leisure & Life Style	
Civil rights leader A. Philip Randolph quits the League for Non-Violent Civil Disobedience Against Military Segregation after Truman promises to end segregation in the armed forces. Bayard Rustin and other civil rights leaders vow to continue their civil disobedience campaign.		NLRB rules that hiring halls operated by the National Maritime Union in the Great Lakes region are illegal under the Taft-Hartley Act. The ruling invalidates a provisional agreement between the NMU and Atlantic and Gulf coast shippers allowing continued operation of union hiring halls .... War Assets Administration announces an agreement to sell one of the world's largest blast furnace and coke oven facilities in Cleveland to the Kaiser-Frazer Corp. for $14.2 million.	Republic Steel Corp. announces development of a machine which casts molten steel into semi-finished shapes, shortening the steel-making process and saving $3 a ton in production.		Aug. 18
Charles Fitzmorris, gang-busting Chicago police chief of the early 1920s, dies at 64 in Chicago.		Federal Reserve Bd. publishes "Regulation W," to go into effect Sept. 20 under a bill giving the Administration power to restrict consumer credit. The regulation requires increased down payments and shortened repayment periods on most small and medium credit purchases.		A high mass is chanted in New York's St. Patrick's Cathedral for baseball star Babe Ruth, who is then buried in Valhalla, N.Y. .... International Council of Christian Churches, an organization of fundamentalist Protestant groups, ends its founding assembly in Amsterdam after electing Rev. Carl McIntyre of Collingswood, N.J. president.	Aug. 19
	Truman issues regulations for the peacetime draft, exempting men with dependents and those engaged in essential duties. He also bans racial or political discrimination in administration of the draft .... Disabled American Veterans concludes a five-day convention in N.Y. after electing Gen. Jonathan Wainwright president.	NLRB regional office in San Francisco issues a complaint charging the International Longshoremen's and Warehousemen's Union with maintaining illegal hiring halls on the West Coast .... AFL International Typographical Union ends a national convention in Milwaukee after supporting Pres. Woodruff Randolph's refusal to file affidavits required by the Taft-Hartley Act.	International Congress on Mental Health in London forms a World Federation for Mental Health, with Dr. J.R. Reese of Britain as president. Purpose of the group is to promote world peace by curbing individual aggressiveness.		Aug. 20
Wallace formally opens his presidential campaign in Bridgeport, Conn. with a speech accusing both major parties of responsibility for the nation's domestic and international problems .... Christian National Crusade nominates its leader, Gerald L.K. Smith, to run for president on a platform of racial segregation and curtailment of immigration of Jews and non-whites .... Mildred Gillars, the wartime "Axis Sally," arrives in Washington to face trial for treason.	Alfons Vogel, press attache of the Rumanian mission in Washington, seeks U.S. asylum and denounces his country's Communist government .... Gen. Carl Spaatz issues his final report before retiring as Air Force chief of staff, announcing plans to develop a supersonic guided missile capable of carrying an atomic warhead 5,000 miles.	A federal district court in N.Y. issues a temporary injunction against a strike of AFL International Longshoremen's Union members in northern Atlantic ports in a dispute over overtime payments.	Golden Jubilee Exposition opens in N.Y., with scientific exhibits including a display of the transmutation of metals through atomic radiation .... Astronomers Willem Luyten of the Univ. of Minnesota and David MacLeish of Argentina's Cordoba Observatory announce discovery of nine new white dwarf stars, bringing to 100 the number found.	Ray Sprigle, Pulitzer-Prize-winning reporter who spent a month disguised as a Negro in the South, concludes a 12-day series of articles published in the Pittsburgh *Post-Gazette* and other papers. He reports that Southern Negroes want "as little contact with the white world as possible" but demand the right to vote and equal economic and educational opportunity.	Aug. 21
Oregon Republican leaders John Snellstrom, Earle Johnson, H.H. Evans and William Fluhrer are killed in the crash of a private plane near Lake of the Woods, Ore.	Defense Secy. Forrestal reports progress towards ending an Air Force-Navy dispute over control of airborne weapons following a Joint Chiefs of Staff meeting in Newport, R.I.	International Longshoremen's and Warehousemen's Union opens a new hiring hall in San Francisco despite recent NLRB rulings against union hiring halls.		World Council of Churches opens its first assembly in Amsterdam, attended by 450 delegates and 1,000 officials of Protestant and Orthodox churches from 42 countries. The assembly is boycotted by the Roman Catholic and Russian Orthodox churches.	Aug. 22
Rev. Archie Ware, a Negro minister in Columbia, S.C., charges that he was beaten by white men in the presence of two policemen after voting in the state's Aug. 10 Democratic primary .... Univ. of Arkansas medical school announces admission of its first Negro student, Edith Irby.			I.G. Farben laboratories in Hamburg report development of Supronalum, a drug that combats diseases due to infections, including pneumonia, peritonitis and blood poisoning.	After 12 unions agree to work for last year's wages, New York's Metropolitan Opera announces it will perform during the 1948-49 season.	Aug. 23
In a letter to the House Un-American Activities Comm., Alger Hiss accuses committee members of prejudging his guilt and offers the names of several prominent officials as references, including Senate Foreign Affairs Comm. Chmn. Arthur Vandenberg and Republican foreign affairs adviser John Foster Dulles. Former Communist editor Louis Budenz testifies at a secret session of the Un-American Activities Comm. that he regarded Hiss during the war as "the equivalent to" a Communist Party member .... Speaking in Cincinnati, Wallace denies that he has ever been a Communist or that Communists dominate his campaign. His statement is intended to retain the support of economist Rexford G. Tugwell, anti-Communist former co-chairman of the Wallace-for-President Comm.	Navy Secy. John Sullivan announces plans to deactivate the battleship *Iowa*, leaving the *Missouri* the only U.S. dreadnought in active service.	CIO Retail, Wholesale and Dept. Store Union Pres. Samuel Wolchok announces the suspension of officers and executive boards of four leftist N.Y. department store locals for refusing to file affidavits required by the Taft-Hartley Act .... AFL International Molders and Foundry Workers Union Pres. Harry Stevenson dies at 69 in Manchester, England.			Aug. 24

F	G	H	I	J
Includes elections, federal-state relations, civil rights and liberties, crime, the judiciary, education, health care, poverty, urban affairs and population.	*Includes formation and debate of U.S. foreign and defense policies, veterans affairs and defense spending. (Relations with specific foreign countries are usually found under the region concerned.)*	*Includes business, labor, agriculture, taxation, transportation, consumer affairs, monetary and fiscal policy, natural resources, pollution and accidents.*	*Includes worldwide scientific, medical and technological developments, natural phenomena, U.S. weather and natural disasters.*	*Includes the arts, religion, scholarship, communications media, sports, entertainment, fashions, fads and social life.*

	World Affairs	Europe	Africa & the Middle East	The Americas	Asia & the Pacific
Aug. 25	Russia breaks off consular relations with the U.S. in retaliation for the expulsion of Soviet Consul Gen. Jacob Lomakin. The action means the closing of Soviet consulates in N.Y. and San Francisco and the U.S. consulate in Vladivostok and suspension of plans to open a new U.S. consulate in Leningrad.	Yugoslavia threatens to break off diplomatic relations with Rumania, which it charges with leading Cominform attacks on Pres. Tito.		Chilean Interior Min. Alfonso Quintana Burgos resigns after admitting failure in his conciliatory policy toward the Communist Party. He is succeeded by anti-Communist Adm. Immanuel Holger.	Burmese government forces report suppression of Communist-led guerrilla bands in the Rangoon area.
Aug. 26		Berlin Communists occupy the City Hall in the Soviet sector to prevent the predominantly non-Communist City Assembly from meeting.			Burmese government forces report renewed attacks by Communist-led guerrillas in the Karenni Hill area of eastern Burma.
Aug. 27		Russian Academy of Sciences dismisses biologists L.A. Orbeli and I.I. Schmalhausen, promising to correct "mistakes" in its work which clash with the officially accepted environmentalist genetics of T.D. Lysenko.			
Aug. 28	Jacob Lomakin, the expelled Soviet consul general in N.Y., leaves the city with his family on a Swedish ship.	Communist-dominated Socialist Unity Party demands creation of an 18-member special committee to take control of Berlin's civil government from the "bankrupt" City Assembly .... Czech government announces discovery of a Western espionage plot, resulting in the arrest of Dutch embassy official Leonardus Bartolomeous van Dam and a group of Czechs .... French cabinet of Premier Andre Marie resigns after socialists withdraw from the governing coalition in a dispute over cost-of-living raises.	Two French U.N. Palestine truce observers die when their plane is fired on near an Egyptian base in Gaza.		India challenges the right of the U.N. to intervene in the Hyderabad dispute, claiming that the territory is not a sovereign country.
Aug. 29	Communist-dominated World Congress of Intellectuals concludes a five-day meeting in Wroclaw (formerly Breslau), Poland with a strong condemnation of U.S. foreign policy. Henry Wallace and Albert Einstein send messages to the congress deploring the postwar growth of international tensions.	Greek government forces open a new offensive against Communist guerrillas in the Vitsi Mountain area of northwestern Greece.			
Aug. 30	Soviet Foreign Min. Molotov, meeting with Western envoys in Moscow, agrees to shift talks on a Berlin settlement to Allied military governors in the city .... International Refugee Organization becomes an official U.N. specialized agency after Denmark ratifies the IRO charter, the 15th nation to do so .... International Red Cross ends a 10-day conference in Stockholm after appealing for a ban on nuclear weapons and revision of the rules of war to emphasize protection of civilians.	Former Czech U.N. delegate Jan Papanek claims knowledge of a medical report which shows that Jan Masaryk was murdered before being thrown through a window of the Foreign Ministry building in Prague.			
Aug. 31	Allied military governors begin negotiations on a Berlin settlement, holding the first session of the Allied Control Council since Russia's withdrawal on March 20 .... Allied deputy foreign ministers end a year of discussions on disposition of Italy's former colonies without agreement.	Andrei Zhdanov, secretary of the Soviet Communist Party's Central Comm. and leader of the Cominform, dies of a heart attack at 52 near Moscow .... Yugoslavian Pres. Tito eliminates all non-Communists from his cabinet, with the exception of Justice Min. Frane Frol. Deputy Premier Eduard Kardelj replaces Stanoje Simich as foreign minister .... French National Assembly gives Robert Schuman a vote of confidence following his appointment as premier by Pres. Vincent Auriol.			
	A *Includes developments that affect more than one world region, international organizations and important meetings of major world leaders.*	B *Includes all domestic and regional developments in Europe, including the Soviet Union, Turkey, Cyprus and Malta.*	C *Includes all domestic and regional developments in Africa and the Middle East, including Iraq and Iran and excluding Cyprus, Turkey and Afghanistan.*	D *Includes all domestic and regional developments in Latin America, the Caribbean and Canada.*	E *Includes all domestic and regional developments in Asian and Pacific nations, extending from Afghanistan through all the Pacific Islands, except Hawaii.*

U.S. Politics & Social Issues	U.S. Foreign Policy & Defense	U.S. Economy & Environment	Science, Technology & Nature	Culture, Leisure & Life Style	
Hiss and Chambers testify jointly before the House Un-American Activities Comm., upholding their contradictory versions of their past association .... AFL Executive Council concludes a three-day meeting in Chicago by announcing that an independent committee of affiliated union presidents will actively support Truman's presidential candidacy.	Former Soviet consular employe Oksana Kosenkina holds a press conference in her N.Y. hospital room, stating that she intended to seek U.S. asylum ever since her transfer two years ago to the Russian consulate in N.Y.	A federal district court in N.Y. extends a temporary injunction against a strike by 45,000 East Coast longshoremen following failure to agree on overtime contract provisions.	World Health Organization announces development of a chemical dehydration process for extracting insulin, simplifying production of the drug and raising hopes of alleviating the drastic world insulin shortage .... Lederle Laboratories in N.Y. announces discovery of APF (animal protein factor), a vitamin that builds red corpuscles in pernicious anemia sufferers.		Aug. 25
			Brookhaven National Laboratory in N.Y. announces development of a short strain of field corn which is less vulnerable to weather and produces more stalks per acre than standard strains.		Aug. 26
In secret testimony before the House Un-American Activities Comm., Chambers names Noel Field, former official in the State Department's Western Europe Division, as a member of a Communist cell attempting to infiltrate the federal government during the 1930s .... Charles Evans Hughes, former governor of New York, State Secretary and Chief Justice of the Supreme Court, dies at 86 in Osterville, Mass.	State Dept. issues a statement which "strongly favors" French proposals for creation of a European parliament.			International Congress on Population and World Resources in Relation to the Family, meeting in Cheltenham, England, establishes a four-nation committee (with U.S., British, Dutch and Swedish representation) to promote birth control in all countries .... Howard Wheeler takes the National Negro Golf Title in Indianapolis .... Oley Speaks, composer of *On the Road to Mandalay* and other popular songs, dies at 74 in N.Y.	Aug. 27
House Un-American Activities Comm. issues a preliminary report on its spy hearings, stating that it has "definitely established" the existence of espionage by domestic and foreign Communists, urging the Administration to cooperate with the investigation and calling on Congress to pass the Mundt-Nixon Communist control bill .... Texas Democratic senatorial primary results in a narrow victory for Rep. Lyndon Johnson over former Gov. Coke Stevenson.	State Dept. proposes creation of an international agency to control Antarctica.	UAW Pres. Walter Reuther announces plans to raise a $1-million political fund, financed by voluntary contributions from union members, to help pro-labor candidates.		Citation, with Eddie Arcaro up, wins the American Derby in Chicago, taking $66,450. The victory brings the horse's all-time earnings to $651,750.	Aug. 28
			A five-day heat wave ends after bringing record high temperatures to most of the U.S. and causing 218 deaths and extensive crop damage.	City of Frankfurt gives the $3,000 Goethe Prize to novelist and playwright Fritz von Unruh, whose writings were banned by the Nazis.	Aug. 29
Former Asst. State Secy. Adolf Berle tells the House Un-American Activities Comm. that Alger Hiss advocated a "pro-Russian" policy while serving in the State Dept. during the war but was investigated and cleared of charges of being a Communist agent .... Alexander Stevens, a Czech national and alleged Communist spy, appears before a House Un-American Activities subcommittee while in N.Y. to face deportation hearings. Although he refuses to answer the subcommittee's questions, Whittaker Chambers identifies him as head of the Communist espionage network in the U.S. during the 1930s .... New York's American Labor Party endorses the Wallace-Taylor ticket.	Registration begins for the peacetime draft, the second in U.S. history.	Kaiser-Frazer Corp. announces plans to enter the low-price auto field in competition with Chevrolet, Ford and Plymouth.		Hooperatings report *Take It or Leave It, Stop The Music* and *Horace Heidt* as the most popular evening radio programs.	Aug. 30
AFL International Ladies Garment Workers Union Pres. David Dubinsky announces formation of an ILGWU Political Campaign Comm. to support Truman and congressional candidates opposed to the Taft-Hartley Act. The CIO Executive Bd. also promises to back Truman .... Illinois bars the Progressive Party from the state ballot in coming elections.				Herman Steiner of Los Angeles becomes U.S. chess champion at the conclusion of U.S. Chess Federation competition in South Fallsburg, N.Y.	Aug. 31

F	G	H	I	J
Includes elections, federal-state relations, civil rights and liberties, crime, the judiciary, education, health care, poverty, urban affairs and population.	*Includes formation and debate of U.S. foreign and defense policies, veterans affairs and defense spending. (Relations with specific foreign countries are usually found under the region concerned.)*	*Includes business, labor, agriculture, taxation, transportation, consumer affairs, monetary and fiscal policy, natural resources, pollution and accidents.*	*Includes worldwide scientific, medical and technological developments, natural phenomena, U.S. weather and natural disasters.*	*Includes the arts, religion, scholarship, communications media, sports, entertainment, fashions, fads and social life.*

	World Affairs	Europe	Africa & the Middle East	The Americas	Asia & the Pacific
Sept. 1		West Germany's 65-member Parliamentary Assembly, appointed by the western-zone state governments, convenes in Bonn to begin deliberations on a constitution. Christian Democratic leader Konrad Adenauer is chosen Assembly president . . . . A German appeals court in Stuttgart acquits former Reichsbank president Hjalmar Schacht of war crimes charges and orders him released from a Ludwigsburg internment camp.	Sidi Mohammed al-Moncef Pasha Bey, former ruler of Tunis imprisoned by the Free French for supporting the Axis, dies at 67 in Pau, France.	Maritime Federation leader Juan Arevalo y Veitia, Cuba's chief anti-Communist union official, is shot to death by unknown assailants in a Havana suburb . . . . In his second annual report to Congress, Mexican Pres. Miguel Aleman promises to push industrial expansion and anti-inflation programs and defends the recent revaluation of the peso . . . . Galo Plaza Lasso is inaugurated for a four-year term as president of Ecuador.	Communist radio in Shensi Province announces formation of a North China People's Government, with a 528-member Assembly and a Council of People's Commissioners . . . . Mt. Hibok Hibok volcano on Camiguin Island in the Philippines erupts, forcing evacuation of most of the island's inhabitants.
Sept. 2		Berlin's City Assembly suspends meetings until conclusion of Allied negotiations on the city's status . . . . Soviet Communist leader Andrei Zhdanov is buried in the Kremlin near Lenin's tomb after an elaborate state ceremony.			Rebellious Karen tribesmen demanding creation of a separate state seize Moulmein and Thaton in southeastern Burma.
Sept. 3		Polish Deputy Premier and Communist Party Secy. Wladislaw Gomulka announces his decision to remain at his posts despite his opposition to the party's new policy of nationalizing agriculture and "suppressing" rich peasants . . . . Berlin Communists occupy the City Hall, announcing that they will hold regular meetings and act on matters within the jurisdiction of the City Assembly . . . . Former Czech Pres. Eduard Benes dies at 64 of a paralytic stroke at his Sezimovo Usti country home.	Export-Import Bank postpones action on a $100-million loan to Israel due to "unsettled political conditions" in the Middle East.	Chile's Congress passes a measure outlawing the Communist Party.	
Sept. 4		European Parliamentary Congress ends a five-day meeting in Interlaken, Switz. by calling on western European countries to confer on proposals for creation of a European parliament with a federal constitution . . . . Pres. Hermann Puender of the Bizonal Economic Council appeals for a halt to the dismantling of factories in the French zone of Germany . . . . Queen Wilhelmina ends her 50-year reign over the Netherlands as she abdicates in favor of her daughter, Juliana.	Jews and Arabs establish a second neutral zone in southern Jerusalem between the new and old cities . . . . U.S. State Dept. refuses to permit unlimited immigration of 18-45 year old men to Israel from U.S.-controlled refugee camps in Central Europe.		
Sept. 5		Polish Deputy Premier Gomulka is dismissed as secretary of the Communist Party for supporting Yugoslavia in its dispute with the Cominform. Pres. Boleslaw Bierut succeeds Gomulka . . . . French Premier Robert Schuman announces his new cabinet, composed of Radicals, Socialists and Popular Republicans. The cabinet immediately begins deliberations on union demands for wage increases and a cost-of-living bonus . . . . British cabinet votes to curtail demobilization due to the Berlin crisis and conflict in Malaya.			
Sept. 6		Polish Deputy Premier Gomulka issues a public apology for his "errors" in opposing Cominform policy and is permitted to remain in the cabinet . . . . Communist disorders disrupt a meeting of the Berlin City Assembly in the Soviet sector, forcing the Assembly's non-Communist majority to move to the British sector . . . . Juliana of Orange and Nassau takes her oath as Queen of the Netherlands in a ceremony in Amsterdam's 500-year-old Nieuwe Kerk.			

A	B	C	D	E
Includes developments that affect more than one world region, international organizations and important meetings of major world leaders.	*Includes all domestic and regional developments in Europe, including the Soviet Union, Turkey, Cyprus and Malta.*	*Includes all domestic and regional developments in Africa and the Middle East, including Iraq and Iran and excluding Cyprus, Turkey and Afghanistan.*	*Includes all domestic and regional developments in Latin America, the Caribbean and Canada.*	*Includes all domestic and regional developments in Asian and Pacific nations, extending from Afghanistan through all the Pacific Islands, except Hawaii.*

U.S. Politics & Social Issues	U.S. Foreign Policy & Defense	U.S. Economy & Environment	Science, Technology & Nature	Culture, Leisure & Life Style	
	A three-man citizens' committee reports to State Secy. Marshall that there is no basis for charges that Communist agents have infiltrated the U.S. on U.N. passports.	In his annual Labor Day message, Truman calls for repeal of the Taft-Hartley Act, expansion of the Social Security System and an enlarged Labor Dept. . . . . N.Y. teamsters strike in a dispute over wages and welfare benefits, tying up freight traffic as the American Assn. of Railroads imposes an embargo on the city.	Dr. Murray Sanders of Columbia Univ. announces the first successful use of the drug phenosulfazole, of the sulfa group, to cure infantile paralysis in mice . . . . Air Force XR-1 reconnaisance plane photographs a 2,700-mile strip of the U.S. during a flight from California to New York, a photographic record.	American historian Charles Beard dies at 73 in New Haven, Conn.	Sept. 1
Truman rejects House Un-American Activities Comm. charges that he is protecting Communist elements in the government by refusing to disclose the contents of loyalty investigation files. He calls the charges "a plain lie out of the whole cloth." . . . . Testifying before a House Labor subcommittee, CIO Secy.-Treas. James Carey charges that the United Electrical, Radio and Machine Workers of America is a "Communist front on many questions." He claims that Westinghouse, RCA and other companies have dismissed anti-Communist workers to appease UE leaders . . . . Truman reveals details of a proposed 10-year public health program, committing $4.3 billion in federal, state and local funds to medical insurance, research and education.		Twelve thousand members of the CIO International Longshoremen's and Warehousemen's Union strike West Coast ports in a dispute over union hiring halls, creating a large freight tieup as the Assn. of American Railroads imposes an embargo on the affected areas.			Sept. 2
Democratic National Comm. asks States' Rights presidential candidate Strom Thurmond to resign as South Carolina Democratic national committeeman.	Veterans of Foreign Wars concludes a five-day convention in St. Louis after rejecting a resolution by Negro delegates barring future conventions from cities which practice racial segregation. The convention also endorses the Mundt-Nixon Communist control bill and refuses to support Truman's civil rights program.	NLRB asks a circuit court of appeals in N.Y. to direct the National Maritime Union to stop insisting on union hiring hall provisions in its Great Lakes contract. It is the NLRB's first attempt to enforce one of its orders through the courts.			Sept. 3
Senate Expenditures subcommittee investigating the loyalty of federal employes issues a report criticizing Truman's loyalty review program as inadequate, demanding faster and standardized loyalty checks and recommending creation of an independent board to handle loyalty cases in all executive departments . . . . Wallace completes a seven-day campaign tour of seven Southern states, during which hostile crowds attempted to disrupt 30 of his appearances.		Sixteen thousand CIO Oil Workers Union members strike in a West Coast wage dispute, shutting down nine major California oil refineries.	Eugene Ford, IBM engineer and business machine inventor, dies at 82 in Endicott, N.Y. . . . . Paul Mantz becomes the first pilot to take the Bendix Air Trophy three times as he wins the 2,080-mile air race from Long Beach, Calif. to Cleveland, Ohio, earning $10,000.	World Council of Churches ends a two-week assembly in Amsterdam with resolutions opposing both Communism and "laissez-faire capitalism" and denouncing anti-Semitism as "a sin against God and man."	Sept. 4
			Richard Chase Tolman, a leading mathematical physicist, adviser to the Manhattan Project and originator of the "undying universe" theory, dies at 67 in Pasadena, Calif.		Sept. 5
Truman launches his re-election campaign with a speech before a joint AFL-CIO rally of 125,000 workers in Detroit's Cadillac Square. He charges Republicans with attempting to dismantle the American labor movement and urges workers to preserve "our democratic institutions of free labor and free enterprise." . . . . A group of eight atomic scientists, including MIT Pres. Karl Compton, issues a statement denouncing House Un-American Activities Comm. spy investigations as "an imminent threat to our national security and the entire governmental atomic research program."				U.S. defeats Australia, 5-0, in Davis Cup tennis matches at Forest Hills, N.Y. Ted Schroeder wins the singles competition, William Talbert and Gardnar Mulloy the doubles competition.	Sept. 6

F	G	H	I	J
Includes elections, federal-state relations, civil rights and liberties, crime, the judiciary, education, health care, poverty, urban affairs and population.	*Includes formation and debate of U.S. foreign and defense policies, veterans affairs and defense spending. (Relations with specific foreign countries are usually found under the region concerned.)*	*Includes business, labor, agriculture, taxation, transportation, consumer affairs, monetary and fiscal policy, natural resources, pollution and accidents.*	*Includes worldwide scientific, medical and technological developments, natural phenomena, U.S. weather and natural disasters.*	*Includes the arts, religion, scholarship, communications media, sports, entertainment, fashions, fads and social life.*

	World Affairs	Europe	Africa & the Middle East	The Americas	Asia & the Pacific
Sept. 7	Canadian External Affairs Min. Louis St. Laurent endorses a "North Atlantic security system" including the U.S., Canada and western Europe.	French Premier Robert Schuman's cabinet resigns after 64 hours, a record short tenure, when socialists and moderate conservatives in the National Assembly refuse to support Schuman's compromise proposals on wages and food prices.			
Sept. 8	Allied military governors suspend their Berlin negotiations as Russian planes begin holding maneuvers in Western air corridors to Berlin.	Socialist Unity Party refuses to recognize actions taken by the Berlin City Assembly in the British sector, effectively dividing the city government .... Radical Socialist Henri Queuille accepts a request from Pres. Vincent Auriol to form a new French cabinet .... Greek and Yugoslav troops clash briefly in the Kaimakchalan border area.			
Sept. 9		Russian guards fire on an anti-Communist rally of 250,000 West Berliners outside the Reichstag building in the British sector, killing one demonstrator and wounding 22 .... U.S. and British forces in Germany hold mixed maneuvers for the first time near Grafenwoehr.			
Sept. 10		French National Assembly confirms Henri Queuille as Premier, heading a cabinet composed of Radicals, Socialists, Republican Liberals and Popular Republicans. Former Premier Schuman remains as foreign minister .... British Trades Union Congress ends a five-day convention in Margate after voting conditional support for the government's anti-inflation drive .... U.S. authorities establish a military court of appeal as the highest tribunal in the U.S. zone of Germany .... Former Bulgarian ruler Ferdinand I dies at 87 in Coburg, Germany.		Argentine government issues a general organization law giving Pres. Peron sweeping emergency powers .... Lester Pearson is appointed Canadian state secretary for external affairs, succeeding current Acting Premier Louis St. Laurent.	Indian P.M. Nehru demands that Indian troops be admitted to Hyderabad as a "peace-keeping force" following the outbreak of disorders in the princely state.
Sept. 11	Congress of World Government Federalist Movements completes a meeting in Luxembourg by adopting a declaration holding that only a world government can avert a catastrophic war.	Organization for European Economic Cooperation Council in Paris agrees on division of Marshall Plan aid for the coming fiscal year, increasing funds for Germany at the expense of French, Italian and Dutch aid.			Kim Il Sung becomes premier in a North Korean cabinet claiming sovereignty over the entire country .... Mohammed Ali Jinnah, founder of Moslem Pakistan and the country's first governor general, dies at 71 in Karachi of a heart attack.
Sept. 12					
Sept. 13					Indian forces invade Hyderabad after the territory's ruler refuses them permission to enter as a "peace-keeping force."
Sept. 14	Western envoys return to the Kremlin to confer with Molotov on resumption of Berlin talks.				Kwaja Nazimuddin, premier of East Bengal, is appointed acting governor of Pakistan following the death of Mohammed Ali Jinnah.
Sept. 15	Big Four refer their dispute over disposition of former Italian colonies to the U.N. following a three-day conference in Paris.	British Foreign Secy. Bevin tells the House of Commons that the government intends to "stamp out" Communist-led revolts wherever they occur in the British Empire.			

A	B	C	D	E
Includes developments that affect more than one world region, international organizations and important meetings of major world leaders.	*Includes all domestic and regional developments in Europe, including the Soviet Union, Turkey, Cyprus and Malta.*	*Includes all domestic and regional developments in Africa and the Middle East, including Iraq and Iran and excluding Cyprus, Turkey and Afghanistan.*	*Includes all domestic and regional developments in Latin America, the Caribbean and Canada.*	*Includes all domestic and regional developments in Asian and Pacific nations, extending from Afghanistan through all the Pacific Islands, except Hawaii.*

U.S. Politics & Social Issues	U.S. Foreign Policy & Defense	U.S. Economy & Environment	Science, Technology & Nature	Culture, Leisure & Life Style	
Harold Stassen opens the Republican presidential campaign in Detroit with a speech charging Truman with attempting "to set class against class" and scoring the Administration's postwar policies as "a record of failures." . . . . Defense Secy. James Forrestal releases a report on the armed forces' racial policies by civil rights leaders, who urge abolition of segregation in all branches and the ending of racial quotas for enlistments.	Truman calls the National Security Council together to survey the Berlin situation.			CBS buys the rights to Freman Gosden's and Charles Correll's *"Amos 'n Andy"* radio characterizations for $2 million.	Sept. 7
"White supremacy" champion Herman Talmadge wins the Georgia Democratic gubernatorial primary, defeating Gov. Melvin Thompson in a campaign directed against Truman's civil rights program.		Federal Reserve Bd. orders member banks to increase reserves on demand deposits by 2% and on time deposits by 1½%, an anti-inflationary move designed to take $2 billion out of the economy.	Yale medical school reports development of a rubberized nylon respirator to replace the iron lung for polio victims.		Sept. 8
Pollster Elmo Roper states that "Thomas E. Dewey is almost as good as elected to the presidency," citing a recent *Fortune* poll giving Dewey 44.2% of the vote, vs. 31.4% for Truman.		Justice Dept. files antitrust charges against International Harvester, J.I. Case Co. and Deere Co. in Minneapolis for allegedly combining to fix prices of farm equipment.			Sept. 9
House Un-American Activities Comm. holds a secret session to question wartime atomic research director Leslie Groves on possible security leaks in the Manhattan Project . . . . An Indianapolis court permanently bans the States' Rights ticket from the Indiana ballot because of a suit charging that the party's paltform "seeks to discriminate against minority groups." . . . . Louisiana's Democratic Central Comm. votes to support States' Rights candidates in coming elections, denying Truman a place on the state ballot . . . . A federal grand jury in Washington indicts Mildred Gillars on 10 counts of treason for wartime Axis propaganda broadcasts.	Senate Foreign Affairs Comm. Chmn. Arthur Vandenberg states after conferring with Dewey that U.S. actions in Berlin represent bipartisan foreign policy and will not be affected by the presidential campaign.	Aeronautical Mechanics Union ends a 140-day strike by 14,800 Boeing Aircraft workers in Seattle after failing to gain satisfaction of demands for a 30¢ hourly wage increase . . . . International Longshoremen's and Warehousemen's Union Pres. Harry Bridges announces a recent poll of union members directing union officials not to file affidavits required by the Taft-Hartley Act.	Walther Mayer, Austrian-born mathematician who collaborated with Albert Einstein on the theory of relativity, dies at 61 in Princeton, N.J.		Sept. 10
				Sporting News names Philadelphia Phillies outfielder Richie Ashburn rookie of the year . . . . Beatrice Shopp of Hopkins, Minn. is crowned 1948 "Miss America" in Atlantic City, N.J.	Sept. 11
Virginia Negro leaders form a Comm. for the Reelection of Truman in Richmond.				Literary historian Samuel Sukel identifies 18 anonymous short stories published in 1840 as works of Nathaniel Hawthorne.	Sept. 12
Speaking before the American Assn. for the Advancement of Science, Truman endorses the protest of eight atomic scientists against House Un-American Activities Comm. spy hearings, which he claims promote "the public airing of unfounded rumors, gossip and vilification." . . . . Rep. Margaret Chase Smith (R, Me.) is elected to the Senate by a record majority of 92,850 votes, becoming the first Republican woman to win a full Senate term.				Mohandas Gandhi's autobiography, *The Story of My Experiments with Truth,* is published by Public Affairs Press.	Sept. 13
Gerald Ford defeats incumbent Rep. Bartel Jonkman in the Michigan GOP primary.			British Assn. for the Advancement of Science ends its annual convention in Brighton after hearing a report on a diffraction microscope with which viruses and molecules can be seen.		Sept. 14
		Justice Dept. files an antitrust suit against the Armour, Swift, Dudahy and Wilson meat-packing firms, accusing them of suppressing competition in their business and demanding that they be split into 14 separate companies.		National Council of Catholic Women concludes a five-day convention in New Orleans after urging the Supreme Court to reconsider its ruling against religious education in the public schools and denouncing the Kinsey sex report as an "insult" to Americans.	Sept. 15
F *Includes elections, federal-state relations, civil rights and liberties, crime, the judiciary, education, health care, poverty, urban affairs and population.*	G *Includes formation and debate of U.S. foreign and defense policies, veterans affairs and defense spending. (Relations with specific foreign countries are usually found under the region concerned.)*	H *Includes business, labor, agriculture, taxation, transportation, consumer affairs, monetary and fiscal policy, natural resources, pollution and accidents.*	I *Includes worldwide scientific, medical and technological developments, natural phenomena, U.S. weather and natural disasters.*	J *Includes the arts, religion, scholarship, communications media, sports, entertainment, fashions, fads and social life.*	

	World Affairs	Europe	Africa & the Middle East	The Americas	Asia & the Pacific
Sept. 16	*Pravda* attacks U.N. Secy. Gen. Trygve Lie for siding with the "Anglo-American bloc" on most issues and failing to serve "the interests of peace."	Judge Advocate General's Dept. of the U.S. Army reduces the life prison sentence of Ilse Koch, wife of a Buchenwald concentration camp commandant, to four years. The decision, based on lack of proof of atrocity charges, evokes widespread protest in Germany and the U.S.	Arab-Jewish artillery duel breaks out in Jerusalem after several days of intermittent small arms and mortar exchange. U.N. mediator Bernadotte leaves Rhodes for Jerusalem in an attempt to preserve the city's ceasefire.		
Sept. 17		Czechoslovakia demands the recall of five members of the Yugoslavian embassy in Prague for "disturbing public order." . . . . Catholic Assn. of Italian Workers is formed in Rome as a rival to the Communist-led General Confederation of Labor.	Jewish extremists in Jerusalem assassinate U.N. mediator Folke Bernadotte and Col. Andre Serot, leader of French troops in the U.N. truce observer force. The Israeli government condemns the killings and orders a roundup of Stern Gang suspects.		Indian forces complete their invasion of Hyderabad as the territory's Moslem ruler surrenders, promising not to press his case in the U.N. . . . . Communist forces capture Suichung in southern Manchuria, severing Nationalist connections to the rich Hulatao agricultural area.
Sept. 18		U.S. and British transport planes fly a record 7,000 tons of supplies into Berlin in celebration of U.S. Air Force Day . . . . Col. Sergei Tulpanov, director of German Political Affairs for the Soviet military government, tells German Communists that the existing Polish-German frontier is "unchangeable."	Former U.S. State Dept. official Ralph Bunche, Bernadotte's chief U.N. aide, succeeds Bernadotte as U.N. mediator in Palestine. A group calling itself *Hazit Hamoledet* (Fatherland Front) claims credit for Bernadotte's assassination, charging that he "worked for the British and carried out their orders." Israeli government charges that the group is a cover for the Stern Gang.		Communist guerrillas seize the town of Madiun in central Java and proclaim a "Soviet" government for Indonesia.
Sept. 19		First postwar legislative elections in Sweden result in gains for the Liberal Party against the ruling Social Democrats, who lose their absolute majority in parliament.	Stern Gang disbands as a military force, ordering its members to join the regular Israeli Army. The group continues to disclaim responsibility for Bernadotte's assassination.		Russia announces plans to withdraw its troops from Korea by the start of 1949 at the request of the North Korean government.
Sept. 20	U.S. State Secy. Marshall, British Foreign Secy. Bevin and French Foreign Min. Robert Schuman meet in Paris to plan Berlin strategy after failure to reach agreement with Russia in Moscow talks.	A Danish court hands down a death sentence for Werner Best, Gestapo official and head of the German occupation of Denmark.	Bernadotte's Palestine peace plan, drawn up shortly before his assassination, is issued by the U.N. in Paris. It calls for admission of Israel to the U.N., territorial readjustments in the western Galilee and Negev desert and internationalization of Jerusalem, Haifa and Lydda airport . . . . Arab League in Amman announces formation of an Arab government for Palestine in Gaza. Transjordan's King Abdullah denounces the plan as de facto recognition of the partition of Palestine . . . . Israel enacts an "emergency regulation" banning terrorist organizations and imposing fines and prison sentences on members. Irgun Zvai Leumi begins surrendering its arms to the Israeli Army.		Indonesian Republic's Parliament votes to give Pres. Ahmed Sukarno emergency powers for suppression of the Communist revolt in central Java.
Sept. 21	U.N. General Assembly begins its third annual session in Paris's Palais de Chaillot, electing Australian Foreign Affairs Min. Herbert Evatt president.	Britain suspends commercial work in the royal dockyards to begin refitting 100 warships for service by next April.	Arab League leaders reject the Bernadotte plan for Palestine, claiming they will never recognize the country's partition. State Secy. Marshall announces U.S. support for the plan.		
Sept. 22	In identical notes to Russia, the Western Allies demand an immediate end to the Berlin blockade and four-power control over the city's currency before resumption of Moscow negotiations.	Soviet-zone German Economic Comm. bans direct dealings between business firms in eastern and western Germany.	Israel indicates willingness to discuss a permanent Palestine settlement on the basis of the Bernadotte peace plan, while British Foreign Secy. Bevin declares Britain's "wholehearted and unqualified support" for the plan.		
Sept. 23					
Sept. 24		French National Assembly passes Premier Henri Queuille's anti-inflation plan, which calls for higher taxes and reduced government spending in an effort to balance the budget. Dissatisfied with the cabinet's wage increase proposals, French workers stage a two-hour general strike . . . . Negotiators in Paris announce agreement on the first multilateral East-West transaction, an $80-million lumber purchase by six Western European countries from five Eastern European states.		Argentine Pres. Peron touches off widespread anti-U.S. demonstrations when he charges former U.S. cultural attache John Griffith with participating in a plot to assassinate him and seize the government for the opposition Labor Party.	Chinese Communist forces capture Tsinan, capital of Shantung Province and a major rail and industrial center, after a nine-day siege.
	A *Includes developments that affect more than one world region, international organizations and important meetings of major world leaders.*	B *Includes all domestic and regional developments in Europe, including the Soviet Union, Turkey, Cyprus and Malta.*	C *Includes all domestic and regional developments in Africa and the Middle East, including Iraq and Iran and excluding Cyprus, Turkey and Afghanistan.*	D *Includes all domestic and regional developments in Latin America, the Caribbean and Canada.*	E *Includes all domestic and regional developments in Asian and Pacific nations, extending from Afghanistan through all the Pacific Islands, except Hawaii.*

U.S. Politics & Social Issues	U.S. Foreign Policy & Defense	U.S. Economy & Environment	Science, Technology & Nature	Culture, Leisure & Life Style	
		Army hires longshoremen to load military vessels during the current West Coast dock strike. The move brings charges of strikebreaking from the International Longshoremen's and Warehousemen's Union.	Seventy-nine seamen are rescued from three foundering vessels in a North Atlantic hurricane.		Sept. 16
Truman begins a whistlestop campaign tour of the Midwest and West, vowing to give the Republicans "hell" in his speeches.			Cultural anthropologist Ruth Benedict dies at 61 in N.Y.	Emil Ludwig, German biographer who published 115 books, dies at 67 in Ascona, Switz.	Sept. 17
Democratic vice presidential candidate Alben Barkley begins a campaign tour of eight Eastern states.	Air Force celebrates its first anniversary as an independent service by conducting mock bombing raids on 25 U.S. cities with B-29s based in Japan, Germany and Alaska. Air Force spokesmen stress the ease with which such attacks can be made and urge the strengthening of air defenses .... Truman appoints a seven-man Commission on Equality of Treatment and Opportunity in the Armed Services to recommend means of ending military racial discrimination.			*Sporting News* names St. Louis Cardinal outfielder Stan Musial and Cleveland Indian manager-shortstop Lou Boudreau as outstanding baseball players of 1948 .... A House select committee investigating the Federal Communications Commission denounces an agency decision permitting atheists radio time to answer religious programs.	Sept. 18
Atty. Gen. Tom Clark attacks congressional investigators for betraying confidential information on the loyalty of government workers and spreading "incorrect and misleading statements." .... Dewey begins a 13-state campaign tour of the Midwest and West.		CIO International Longshoremen's and Warehousemen's Union agrees to load military cargoes during the current West Coast dock strike at prestrike wages.		Pancho Gonzales wins the U.S. men's amateur singles tennis title and Margaret Osborne duPont the women's singles title in Forest Hills, N.Y.	Sept. 19
	Gen. Curtis LeMay, wartime head of the bomber offensive against Japan, becomes chief of the Strategic Air Command, succeeding Gen. George Kenney.	Strike of N.Y. teamsters ends as most trucking employers sign individual contracts with the Teamsters Union locals involved in the dispute .... Armed thugs attack the N.Y. headquarters of the International Ladies Garment Workers Union and an ILGWU picket line in the city's garment district, injuring three union organizers and seven members. Union officials blame the violence on attempts of underworld elements to enter the garment shipping business.		Mexican Baseball League is disbanded after taking reported losses of $362,000 in the past three years.	Sept. 20
			Stanford Univ. announces development of an X-ray microscope able to penetrate hard body structures and examine live specimens.	Marcel Cerdan defeats Tony Zale to gain the world middleweight boxing title in Jersey City, N.J.	Sept. 21
Speaking in Oakland, Calif., Truman attacks Republican policies for catering to the "selfish men" of big business and labels his campaign a "crusade of the people against the special interests."		Treasury Secy. John Snyder, speaking at a meeting of the National Assn. of Supervisors of State Banks, warns against the current expansion of consumer credit, which he views as an important inflationary factor.	A hurricane strikes Florida with winds up to 160 mph, leaving three dead and $25 million in damage.	Eugene Cowles, dean of American light opera, dies at 88 in Boston.	Sept. 22
Wallace leaves N.Y. for a 15-day campaign trip through the Midwest, Texas and the West Coast .... Communist Party opens its election campaign with a rally in New York's Madison Square Garden.			Bell and Howell announces development of the Foton, a $700, 35 mm. still camera which takes 15 pictures at five per second.	Ike Williams retains his world lightweight boxing title by knocking out Jesse Flores in the 10th round in N.Y. .... E. Eastman Irvine, editor of *The World Almanac*, dies at 65 in N.Y.	Sept. 23
Mildred Gillars pleads not guilty in Washington to charges that she committed treason by broadcasting wartime Axis propaganda.		Bolstered by a record $3.4 million congressional appropriation, the Justice Department's Antitrust Div. announces plans to investigate the du Pont industrial empire. The Justice Dept. also files a petition in N.Y. to break up the Aluminum Co. of America.			Sept. 24
F	G	H	I	J	
Includes elections, federal-state relations, civil rights and liberties, crime, the judiciary, education, health care, poverty, urban affairs and population.	*Includes formation and debate of U.S. foreign and defense policies, veterans affairs and defense spending. (Relations with specific foreign countries are usually found under the region concerned.)*	*Includes business, labor, agriculture, taxation, transportation, consumer affairs, monetary and fiscal policy, natural resources, pollution and accidents.*	*Includes worldwide scientific, medical and technological developments, natural phenomena, U.S. weather and natural disasters.*	*Includes the arts, religion, scholarship, communications media, sports, entertainment, fashions, fads and social life.*	

	World Affairs	Europe	Africa & the Middle East	The Americas	Asia & the Pacific
Sept. 25	Responding to Western demands for an end to the Berlin blockade, Russia insists on control over all traffic between Berlin and western Germany and a veto over the city's economic affairs.	Italy and France agree to abolish customs barriers at the start of 1950 .... U.S. and British military governors in Germany propose a halt to the dismantling of German factories for reparations in exchange for a reduction in Marshall Plan aid to Germany.		Argentina's pro-U.S. Navy Minister and acting Foreign Minister Adm. Fidel Anadon resigns from the Peron cabinet.	
Sept. 26	U.S., Britain and France break off Moscow talks on Berlin, claiming the Russians have gone back on an earlier agreement to lift the blockade in exchange for use of Soviet-zone currency in the city. The Western Allies announce that they will place the Berlin dispute before the U.N. Security Council.	Yugoslavian sources report the execution of seven Albanian officials during a purge of pro-Tito elements in Albania .... Hungary expels two officials of the Hungarian-American Oil Co., a Standard Oil of N.J. subsidiary, on charges of sabotaging oil production.			New Zealand abolishes meat rationing, retaining restrictions on butter and gasoline.
Sept. 27	U.N. General Assembly begins debate on nuclear arms control as British Foreign Secy. Bevin denounces Russia for blocking disarmament proposals favored by the U.N. majority.				A typhoon sinks a fleet of fishing boats off the Chinese coast near Leichow, causing 800 deaths.
Sept. 28		Defense ministers of Britain, France, Belgium, Holland and Luxembourg agree in Paris to establish a Permanent Defense Organization for Western Europe .... International Monetary Fund approves a $6-million loan to Czechoslovakia for food purchases, the first IMF loan made to a Communist government.			Pakistani government begins a round-up of all Communist leaders.
Sept. 29	U.S., Britain and France formally request the U.N. Security Council to consider the Berlin situation "at the earliest possible moment," calling the Russian blockade a "threat to peace."				
Sept. 30		Berlin Communists establish a separate City Assembly in the Soviet sector following the refusal of the regular City Assembly to resume its meetings in the City Hall.	Israeli police report the capture of Sternist leader Nathan Friedman Yellin and an aide, Matityahu Schmulewitz, in Tel Aviv.		Indonesian Republic forces report capturing the town of Madiun in central Java from Communist insurgents .... Afghanistan and Russia sign an agreement in Tashkent delineating their border.
Oct. 1		U.S. and Britain protest against continued buzzing of airlift transports by Soviet fighters in the Berlin air corridors .... U.S. and British bizonal authorities eliminate special incentive rations for Ruhr coal miners, a long-standing object of resentment among other German workers. Basic food rations are increased to compensate for the change.	Haj Amin el Husseini, Grand Mufti of Jerusalem, is elected president of the Arab Palestine National Assembly in Gaza and returns to Palestine after an 11-year exile .... U.N. truce commission in Palestine complains of frequent violations of the Jerusalem ceasefire by Jewish forces under Bernard Joseph, Israeli military governor of the city.		
	A *Includes developments that affect more than one world region, international organizations and important meetings of major world leaders.*	B *Includes all domestic and regional developments in Europe, including the Soviet Union, Turkey, Cyprus and Malta.*	C *Includes all domestic and regional developments in Africa and the Middle East, including Iraq and Iran and excluding Cyprus, Turkey and Afghanistan.*	D *Includes all domestic and regional developments in Latin America, the Caribbean and Canada.*	E *Includes all domestic and regional developments in Asian and Pacific nations, extending from Afghanistan through all the Pacific Islands, except Hawaii.*

U.S. Politics & Social Issues	U.S. Foreign Policy & Defense	U.S. Economy & Environment	Science, Technology & Nature	Culture, Leisure & Life Style	
	Air Force Secy. Stuart Symington reveals at a N.Y. convention of the Air Force Assn. that a U.S. military plane has flown "hundreds of miles faster than the speed of sound."			Blue Peter, with Eric Guerin up, wins the Belmont Futurity in N.Y., earning $88,410 of the $113,110 purse.	Sept. 25
Dewey leaves San Francisco on a campaign tour of the Pacific and Mountain states . . . . Louisiana state legislature approves the inclusion of Truman's name on the state ballot but refuses to allow him to be listed as a Democrat.	Air Force Assn. ends its second annual convention in N.Y. after demanding unification of the Air Force and naval aviation under a single command and criticizing Navy plans for a carrier-based strategic bomber force.			Boston Braves capture the National League baseball pennant with a 3-2 victory over the New York Giants.	Sept. 26
House Un-American Activities Comm. issues a report claiming widespread Communist infiltration of the wartime atom bomb project and demanding prosecution of five scientists associated with nuclear weapons development . . . . Alger Hiss files a $50,000 libel suit against Whitaker Chambers in N.Y., charging that Chambers slandered him by calling him a former Communist . . . . A federal district court in Baltimore rules that segregation on southern railroad diners is permissible under federal law if Negroes are given the same service as white passengers . . . . Sen. Harlan Bushfield (R, S.D.), an opponent of the New Deal and the U.N. dies at 66 in Miller, S.D.				James Thurber's *The Beast in Me and Other Animals* is published by Harcourt, Brace. William Faulkner's *Intruder in the Dust* is published by Random House.	Sept. 27
				Robert Flaherty's *Louisiana Story* premiers in N.Y.	Sept. 28
Justice Dept. refuses to prosecute five scientists accused of wartime espionage by the House Un-American Activities Comm., claiming there is "absolutely no competent proof" of committee charges . . . . U.S. Atomic Energy Commission orders General Electric and the Univ. of Chicago, which operate atomic reactors under government contract, not to recognize the CIO United Electric Workers Union or the United Public Workers of America due to the "alleged Communist affiliation" of officials of both unions . . . . Supreme Court Justice Hugo Black stays a temporary injunction barring Rep. Lyndon Johnson from the ballot in the Texas senatorial election following Johnson's narrow victory in the Democratic runoff primary.				Lawrence Olivier's film of *Hamlet*, starring Olivier in the title role, premiers in N.Y.	Sept. 29
Progressive Party headquarters in Washington withdraws 13 Progressive candidates in five states from congressional races against Democrats, claiming the Democratic candidates in question "have turned to a much more constructive liberal path." . . . . Mrs. Edith Kermit Roosevelt, widow of former Pres. Theodore Roosevelt, dies at 87 in Oyster Bay, N.Y.	Senate Armed Forces Comm. Chmn. Chan Gurney (R, S.D.) urges resumption of "complete relations between Spain and the other great powers" following a conference with Franco in Madrid . . . . Speaking in Salt Lake City on the 10th anniversary of the Munich agreement, Dewey calls for national unity and vigilance against Russian efforts to "enslave mankind." . . . . Grand Army of the Republic completes its five-day national encampment in Grand Rapids, Mich., attended by six of the 43 surviving Civil War Union veterans.	Charles Swift, board chairman of Swift & Co. meat packers, dies at 75 in Chicago.		Federal Communications Commission suspends licensing of television stations pending a review of broadcasting rules to determine how many new stations should be allowed. Thirty-seven stations are now operating and 86 others have been granted construction permits . . . . Hooperratings list *Walter Winchell*, *Radio Theatre* and *Arthur Godfrey's Talent Scouts* as top radio shows . . . . James Gould Cozzens' *Guard of Honor* is published in N.Y. by Harcourt, Brace.	Sept. 30
California State Supreme Court declares the state's 98-year-old ban on interracial marriages unconstitutional.				British rules requiring film theaters to devote 45% of their first-feature screen time to British films go into effect. The American Motion Picture Assn. retaliates by banning mixed British-American billings in U.S. theaters . . . . Irwin Shaw's *The Young Lions* is published in N.Y. by Random House.	Oct. 1

F	G	H	I	J
Includes elections, federal-state relations, civil rights and liberties, crime, the judiciary, education, health care, poverty, urban affairs and population.	*Includes formation and debate of U.S. foreign and defense policies, veterans affairs and defense spending. (Relations with specific foreign countries are usually found under the region concerned.)*	*Includes business, labor, agriculture, taxation, transportation, consumer affairs, monetary and fiscal policy, natural resources, pollution and accidents.*	*Includes worldwide scientific, medical and technological developments, natural phenomena, U.S. weather and natural disasters.*	*Includes the arts, religion, scholarship, communications media, sports, entertainment, fashions, fads and social life.*

	World Affairs	Europe	Africa & the Middle East	The Americas	Asia & the Pacific
Oct. 2	Responding to Western charges of Russian obstruction in Berlin negotiations, Marshal Sokolovsky of the Soviet military government claims that plans for creation of a West German government are the "fundamental" cause of the Berlin crisis.		Palestine National Assembly in Gaza proclaims Palestine's independence as an Arab state, denouncing the Jews as "aggressive intruders."	Canada's Conservative Party elects Ontario Premier George Drew as its leader in an Ottawa convention .... Domingo Diaz Arosemena is inaugurated president of Panama and pledges cooperation with the U.S. in defending the Canal .... Argentine government revokes the press privileges of five foreign correspondents in the aftermath of an alleged plot to assassinate Pres. Peron.	
Oct. 3	Russia proposes an Allied foreign ministers conference on Berlin and the question of Germany as an alternative to U.N. consideration of the dispute.	French coal miners strike against government plans for a 10% wage cut in the nationalized coal industry.	Israel sends a note to the U.N. rejecting provisions of the Bernadotte peace plan calling for surrender of the Negev desert to the Arabs.	Peruvian government forces suppress a revolt in the port of Callao staged by the leftist Apra Party and mutinous naval troops.	
Oct. 4		British Field Marshal Viscount Montgomery is named head of the Western European Permanent Defense Organization, with two French officers and one British officer as his aides.			
Oct. 5	U.N. Security Council votes over Russian objections to put the Berlin dispute on its agenda.	Soviet-zone German officials announce formation of a 400,000-man militia force to resist "alarming civil war preparations" in the West .... Earthquakes wreck Ashkhabad, capital of the Soviet Turkmen Republic, causing about 200 deaths and 6,000 injuries.		Peruvian Pres. Jose Luis Bustamante y Rivero outlaws the Apra Party following suppression of the Callao revolt.	
Oct. 6	U.N. Security Council begins discussion of the Berlin dispute, with Russian and Ukrainian representatives refusing to participate. U.S. delegate Philip Jessup reiterates the U.S. offer to attend an international conference on "all questions related to Germany" as soon as the Berlin blockade is lifted.		Israeli Foreign Min. Moshe Shertok sends the U.N. General Assembly a memorandum stating Israel's territorial demands: the western Galilee, the new city of Jerusalem and a land corridor connecting Jerusalem with the rest of Israel. Arab League states reiterate their refusal to accept the partition of Palestine.	Argentina and the U.S. agree on a four-year U.S. military mission to advise the Argentine Army.	
Oct. 7	General Assembly's Political Comm. establishes an 11-nation subcommittee to help the U.N. Atomic Energy Commission resume operations. Western delegates to the Political Comm. reject Russian proposals for gradual nuclear disarmament without specific provisions for arms control and inspection.				Japanese cabinet of Premier Hitoshi Ashida resigns in the midst of a bribery scandal involving upper-level government officials and Showa Denko, Japan's largest chemical and fertilizer company.

U.S. Politics & Social Issues	U.S. Foreign Policy & Defense	U.S. Economy & Environment	Science, Technology & Nature	Culture, Leisure & Life Style	
Truman returns to Washington after a two-week campaign trip through the Midwest and West, vowing "I have only begun to fight."			Columbia Univ. geologists announce discovery of a new uranium-bearing mineral, sengierite, in the Belgian Congo.	American League baseball season ends with the Boston Red Sox and Cleveland Indians tied for first place .... *Finian's Rainbow* closes on Broadway after 723 performances.	Oct. 2
Dewey returns to Albany from his 14-day Western tour.	A House Foreign Affairs subcommittee on world Communism headed by Rep. Frances Bolton (R, Ohio) urges that the U.S. give the Chinese Nationalist government increased economic aid and a "guarantee of territorial and political integrity" against Communist incursions.			Cleveland Indians beat the Boston Red Sox, 8-3, to take the American League pennant for the first time since 1920.	Oct. 3
Truman orders careful screening of immigrant refugees by the Army, FBI, State Dept. and Displaced Persons Comm. to prevent entry of Communist agents.	Army, Navy and Air Force begin extensive war games on both coasts, practicing coordination of surprise attack procedures.	U.S. railroads grant a 10¢ hourly wage raise to 175,000 members of the Order of Railway Conductors and the Brotherhood of Railroad Trainmen.		American Municipal Assn. reports that laws in 50 cities ban comic books dealing with crime or sex.	Oct. 4
In a speech opening the annual UMW convention in Cincinnati, union leader John Lewis attacks Truman as "totally unfitted" to be President.	Truman calls State Secy. Marshall, Sen. Tom Connally and other advisers to the White House and proposes sending Supreme Court Chief Justice Frederick Vinson to Moscow for a conference on major East-West differences. Marshall strongly opposes the project, claiming that it might be misunderstood by America's allies as a ploy in the presidential campaign .... Senate Armed Forces Comm. Chmn. Chan Gurney says Spain's Franco government deserves recognition because it "has been fighting Communists since 1936." He urges a military alliance of the U.S., Spain and the five Union of Western Europe nations .... Truman appoints MIT Pres. Karl Compton to succeed Vannevar Bush as Research and Development Bd. chairman of the Defense Dept.		Pittsburgh immunologist Bettina Carter announces development of a blood extract, RH hapten, which can save the lives of rh babies whose blood type is different from that of the mother .... A hurricane causes 11 deaths and $10 million damage in Cuba, and $6 million in crop damage near Miami.		Oct. 5
Justice Dept. asks the FBI to investigate charges by columnist Drew Pearson that House Un-American Activities Comm. Chmn. J. Parnell Thomas has added unnecessary employes to his congressional staff and taken kickbacks from their salaries .... A House Education and Labor subcommittee concludes hearings on alleged Communist domination of N.Y. department store unions by recommending that 13 union officials and attorneys, mainly from the CIO Retail, Wholesale and Department Store Workers Union, be cited for contempt of Congress .... Univ. of Oklahoma's board of regents orders the University to teach Negro student George McLaurin on an individual basis following a federal court ruling barring exclusion of McLaurin on racial grounds.	Former Democratic leader James Farley visits Franco in Madrid and expresses hope for closer U.S.-Spanish relations .... United Confederate Veterans hold their 58th reunion in Montgomery, Ala., attended by only three former rebels.		Westinghouse reveals that it has formed the country's first atomic power division to produce commercial energy from nuclear sources.		Oct. 6
Brandeis Univ. is officially inaugurated in Boston ceremonies attended by the school's first president, Dr. Abram Sacher .... Federal circuit court of appeals in Atlanta sets aside Justice Hugo Black's stay of an injunction barring Rep. Lyndon Johnson from the Texas ballot as Democratic nominee for the Senate.					Oct. 7

F	G	H	I	J
Includes elections, federal-state relations, civil rights and liberties, crime, the judiciary, education, health care, poverty, urban affairs and population.	*Includes formation and debate of U.S. foreign and defense policies, veterans affairs and defense spending. (Relations with specific foreign countries are usually found under the region concerned.)*	*Includes business, labor, agriculture, taxation, transportation, consumer affairs, monetary and fiscal policy, natural resources, pollution and accidents.*	*Includes worldwide scientific, medical and technological developments, natural phenomena, U.S. weather and natural disasters.*	*Includes the arts, religion, scholarship, communications media, sports, entertainment, fashions, fads and social life.*

	World Affairs	Europe	Africa & the Middle East	The Americas	Asia & the Pacific
Oct. 8	U.N. General Assembly elects Norway, Cuba and Egypt to replace Belgium, Colombia and Syria as temporary members of the Security Council.	Gen. Sir William Slim, hero of the Burma campaign against the Japanese, is appointed to succeed Field Marshal Montgomery as Britain's Imperial chief of staff.	Israel announces the signing of agreements with the Shell and Socony Vacuum oil companies, guaranteeing it an adequate oil supply.		
Oct. 9	In his strongest foreign affairs statement since the war, Winston Churchill tells the Conservative Party's annual conference in Llandudno, Wales that the West should "bring matters to a head" with Russia while the Soviets still lack an atomic bomb.		British leaders conclude a 10-day conference with political leaders from British Africa after agreeing on common action against Communists and increased British economic aid for Africa.		
Oct. 10		Yugoslavian Pres. Tito accuses Cominform nations of withholding shipments of oil and other raw materials, forcing Yugoslavia to seek new and higher-priced sources of supply .... Greek government forces begin a new offensive in northwestern Greece intended to wipe out the remnants of guerrilla forces on the Albanian border.		Carlos Prio Socarras is inaugurated Cuba's 17th president .... Pro-U.S. Nationalist Party candidate Juan Manuel Galvez is elected president of Honduras without formal opposition.	
Oct. 11					
Oct. 12	General Assembly's Political and Security Comm. endorses the majority nuclear arms control plan of the U.N. Atomic Energy Commission, opposed by Russia. The committee also urges the Big Five and Canada to renew nuclear arms control talks whenever a basis of agreement is felt to exist.		Egypt and Iraq recognize the Palestinian Arab government in Gaza.		Burmese Parliament passes a land nationalization bill placing all arable land in Burma under government ownership for redistribution to farmers.
Oct. 13		Berlin City Assembly formally moves its meetings from the Soviet to the British sector.	U.S. refuses to recognize the Palestinian Arab government in Gaza, citing Transjordanian opposition.		
Oct. 14		Constituent Assembly meeting in Bonn votes to name the new West German state the Federal Republic of Germany.			Indonesian Republic Premier Mohammed Hatta announces suppression of the Communist revolt in central Java, blaming it on unrest caused by the Dutch blockade of Indonesia .... Japanese Diet names Shigeru Yoshida, leader of the Democratic Liberal Party, to succeed Hitoshi Ashida as premier.
Oct. 15	U.N. Trusteeship Commission defeats a Soviet resolution requiring colonial powers to give annual reports and permit U.N. inspection of local self-government provisions .... General Assembly's Legal Comm. excludes a provision against the extermination of political groups from a draft convention against genocide, ruling that the provision would hamper action against domestic revoluntionaries.	Norway, Sweden and Denmark establish a defense ministers' committee to coordinate defense plans.	U.N. mediator Ralph Bunche appears before the General Assembly to plead for adoption of the Bernadotte peace plan for Palestine.	Nicaraguan War Min. Anastasio Somoza charges that Cuba, Costa Rica, Guatemala and Venezuela are providing arms to revolutionaries in Nicaragua, Honduras and El Salvador.	North Korea establishes diplomatic relations with Poland and Mongolia. Russia names its former military commander in Korea, Terenti Shtikov, to serve as ambassador to the North Korean government .... Siam announces an agreement with British Malaya allowing troops of either country to penetrate 10 miles beyond the border in pursuit of Communist guerrillas.
Oct. 16		France announces a partial devaluation of the franc, setting dollar exchange rates at the median between the fixed official rate (214 francs per U.S.$) and the free market rate (313 francs per U.S.$) .... Finland eliminates the political police established by former Interior Min. Yrjo Leino.	Israeli-Egyptian clashes over Jewish road communications in the Negev flare into open fighting in violation of the U.N.-supervised ceasefire.	Canadian Congress of Labor concludes a six-day convention in Toronto by reelecting anti-Communist A.R. Mosher as president.	Philippine Justice Dept. outlaws the Communist Party.
	A *Includes developments that affect more than one world region, international organizations and important meetings of major world leaders.*	B *Includes all domestic and regional developments in Europe, including the Soviet Union, Turkey, Cyprus and Malta.*	C *Includes all domestic and regional developments in Africa and the Middle East, including Iraq and Iran and excluding Cyprus, Turkey and Afghanistan.*	D *Includes all domestic and regional developments in Latin America, the Caribbean and Canada.*	E *Includes all domestic and regional developments in Asian and Pacific nations, extending from Afghanistan through all the Pacific Islands, except Hawaii.*

U.S. Politics & Social Issues	U.S. Foreign Policy & Defense	U.S. Economy & Environment	Science, Technology & Nature	Culture, Leisure & Life Style	
UMW convention in Cincinnati indirectly endorses Dewey for president by adopting a resolution condemning Truman and stating that "the other major party candidate" has never acted against the UMW .... Alger Hiss files a second libel suit for $25,000 against Whittaker Chambers in Baltimore, charging further slanderous remarks concerning Hiss' alleged Communist connections .... Iva Toguri D'Aquino is charged with treason in San Francisco for wartime Japanese propaganda broadcasts .... House Post Office and Civil Service Comm. announces that a 1950 legislative reapportionment will give seven additional House seats to California and one seat each to Florida, Indiana, Michigan, Oregon, Texas and Washington.		A federal district court in N.Y. fines the CIO Retail, Wholesale and Department Store Workers Union $20,000 for picketing two department stores in violation of an anti-strike injunction. It is the first such ruling under the Taft-Hartley Act.			Oct. 8
	Navy announces conversion of the seaplane tender *Norton Sound* into a seagoing rocket launcher, the first ship specially equipped for this task.				Oct. 9
				Ted Schroeder wins the men's singles title and Gertrude Moran the women's singles title in the first national hard court tennis competition in San Francisco.	Oct. 10
Dewey begins an eight-day campaign tour of nine Midwestern and border states.			*Gulfhawk II*, a famous test plane and the last biplane fighter in operation, is sent to the Smithsonian Institution following a final exhibition flight.	Cleveland Indians win the World Series, four games to two, with a 4-3 victory over the Boston Braves .... Former Brooklyn Dodgers and Boston Braves manager Casey Stengel signs as manager of the New York Yankees .... Los Angeles *Mirror*, owned by the publisher of the morning *Times*, begins publication.	Oct. 11
Federal court of appeals in Washington upholds the contempt of Congress conviction of Communist Party Secy. Eugene Dennis .... Gen. Dwight Eisenhower is formally installed as 13th president of Columbia Univ. .... Dewey wins the support of the San Francisco Democratic Club, the group's first endorsement of a Republican candidate.	Speaking in Louisville, Ky., Dewey claims credit for originating the Administration's bipartisan foreign policy and states that Republicans first suggested a number of the U.N.'s present features. He blames current international problems on Truman's failure to consult with the GOP on foreign policy issues.				Oct. 12
					Oct. 13
A Brooklyn grand jury indicts former Air Force Lt. Martin Monti on treason charges for making wartime Nazi propaganda broadcasts after flying a stolen fighter plane into German-held territory.		A federal court in Indianapolis finds the AFL International Typographical Union guilty of contempt for insisting on closed shop clauses in union contracts despite a temporary injunction barring such provisions.		United Lutheran Church in America ends a nine-day convention in Philadelphia after voting to negotiate on unification with seven other groups in the National Lutheran Council .... Kay Summersby's *Eisenhower Was My Boss*, a portrait of the Allied commander by his British chauffeur, is published by Prentice-Hall .... Raphael Gleitsmann's *Medieval Shadows* wins first prize at the Carnegie Institute's art exhibition in Pittsburgh.	Oct. 14
Earl Warren ends a 31-day, coast-to-coast campaign in Eugene, Ore., declaring that the GOP is the only party that can unite America.			U.S. Public Health Service announces that a five-minute test for diabetes will be used in a nationwide effort to find an estimated one million hidden diabetes cases.		Oct. 15
Truman returns to the White House after a seven-day campaign tour through the Midwest.	Truman orders an increase in the strength of U.S. military reserves.			Citation ups his career winnings to $820,000 by taking the $111,700 International Gold Cup at Belmont Park, N.Y.	Oct. 16
F	G	H	I	J	
Includes elections, federal-state relations, civil rights and liberties, crime, the judiciary, education, health care, poverty, urban affairs and population.	*Includes formation and debate of U.S. foreign and defense policies, veterans affairs and defense spending. (Relations with specific foreign countries are usually found under the region concerned.)*	*Includes business, labor, agriculture, taxation, transportation, consumer affairs, monetary and fiscal policy, natural resources, pollution and accidents.*	*Includes worldwide scientific, medical and technological developments, natural phenomena, U.S. weather and natural disasters.*	*Includes the arts, religion, scholarship, communications media, sports, entertainment, fashions, fads and social life.*	

	World Affairs	Europe	Africa & the Middle East	The Americas	Asia & the Pacific
Oct. 17		Italian Communists begin a month-long series of anti-American rallies, charging the U.S. with attempting to bring Italy into a military alliance directed against Russia . . . . Greek government announces that Greek Communist Party Central Comm. member Adam Mouzenides killed CBS correspondent George Polk in Salonika last May.			Chinese Nationalist 60th Army, attempting to fight its way from Changchun to Mukden, mutinies and surrenders to Communist forces.
Oct. 18		Russian authorities in Germany begin organizing a German "People's Police" force and impose new traffic restrictions to prevent the smuggling of supplies into West Berlin . . . . Western Allies in Germany sign an agreement joining the foreign trade of the French zone to that of the British-American zone . . . . Gen. William Donovan, who investigated the murder of CBS correspondent George Polk for the Overseas Writers Assn., announces in N.Y. that he is sceptical of Greek efforts to place the responsibility on a local Communist leader . . . . Field Marshal Walther von Brauchitsch, commander-in-chief of the German Army from 1938 to 1941, dies at 67 of coronary thrombosis in Hamburg, where he was awaiting trial by a British tribunal as a war criminal.	Israeli forces consolidate control over major transport routes in the Negev desert and isolate Egyptian bases in Gaza, Hebron and Faluja.	Canadian Trades and Labor Congress ends a six-day convention in Victoria, B.C. by reelecting Percy Bengough president and defeating anti-Communist efforts to purge the organization of Communists . . . . Spanish Foreign Min. Alberto Martin Artajo signs an agreement in Buenos Aires providing for increased Spanish immigration to Argentina, exchange of literature and reciprocal recognition of university degrees . . . . Mexico breaks off its agreement with the U.S. on migrant labor, charging that the U.S. has violated it by permitting massive illegal entry of Mexicans at El Paso, Texas.	
Oct. 19		Western Allies agree to lend the West Berlin city government 150 million West German marks during the next three months to meet expenses.	U.N. Security Council unanimously calls for a new Palestine truce to stop fighting between Israeli and Egyptian forces.		Japan's first single-party cabinet since the war takes office as Shigeru Yoshida and his Democratic Liberal ministers are sworn in by Emperor Hirohito . . . . Chinese Nationalist sources report the loss of the Shantung port of Chefoo to the Communists.
Oct. 20	Six neutral members of the U.N. Security Council propose a Berlin compromise to the U.S. and Russia, calling for an immediate end to the blockade, adoption of Soviet-zone currency for the entire city and a Big Four conference to discuss all German questions . . . . General Assembly's Political and Security Comm. rejects Russia's latest nuclear arms control proposal and sends the General Assembly a resolution favoring new discussions based on the U.S. plan.				Communist forces take the Manchurian capital of Changchun after a year-long siege . . . . Communist soldiers and civilians stage a revolt in the South Korean port of Yosu and nearby Sunchon, gaining control over the surrounding area.
Oct. 21	U.S., Britain and France accept the Berlin compromise proposed by neutral members of the U.N. Security Council. Russia agrees to consider the proposals.	Crash of a KLM airliner in Scotland kills 39 passengers, including KLM managing director Hendrik Veendendaal.			
Oct. 22	Western delegates to the U.N. Security Council reject a Russian proposal for simultaneous lifting of the Berlin blockade and introduction of Soviet-zone currency throughout the city. They demand an end to the blockade before the start of currency negotiations . . . . British Commonwealth countries end a two-week conference in London after endorsing Britain's association with the Western European Union.	August Cardinal Hlond, Polish church leader and a leading opponent of the government's education and marriage policies, dies at 67 in Warsaw.	Israeli and Egyptian forces stop fighting in accordance with the new U.N. ceasefire order, with Israel claiming control over the entire Negev desert.		
Oct. 23		French troops seize seven of the nation's largest coal mines after a week of riots between Communist-led striking workers and nonstrikers.	Pope Pius XII issues an encyclical letter calling for internationalization of Jerusalem and appealing for preservation of all Christian shrines in Palestine.		South Korean officials claim suppression of the Communist rising in Yosu and Sunchon with 1,500 arrests . . . . Chinese Communists claim capture of the Honan rail junction of Chengchow and the western terminus of the Peking-Suiyuan rail line at Paotow.

	A	B	C	D	E
	Includes developments that affect more than one world region, international organizations and important meetings of major world leaders.	*Includes all domestic and regional developments in Europe, including the Soviet Union, Turkey, Cyprus and Malta.*	*Includes all domestic and regional developments in Africa and the Middle East, including Iraq and Iran and excluding Cyprus, Turkey and Afghanistan.*	*Includes all domestic and regional developments in Latin America, the Caribbean and Canada.*	*Includes all domestic and regional developments in Asian and Pacific nations, extending from Afghanistan through all the Pacific Islands, except Hawaii.*

U.S. Politics & Social Issues	U.S. Foreign Policy & Defense	U.S. Economy & Environment	Science, Technology & Nature	Culture, Leisure & Life Style	
	Air Force urges 10,000 air veterans to volunteer for duty in the Berlin airlift and on European B-29 bases.	Ruling on a Chicago strike by the United Electrical Workers Union, an NLRB trial examiner concludes that mass picketing is "intimidatory and coercive" and violates the Taft-Hartley Act . . . . David Kerr, partner of Andrew Carnegie and former vice president of U.S. Steel, dies at 84 in Pittsburgh.		*New York Herald Tribune* lists Norman Mailer's *The Naked and the Dead* and Dale Carnegie's *How to Stop Worrying and Start Living* as best-selling fiction and non-fiction books.	Oct. 17
A *New York Times* survey asserts that Dewey is sure of 333 electoral votes and Truman of only 82.			New York City begins a flouridation program by coating the teeth of 50,000 children with sodium flouride to prevent decay.	Maximos V resigns as Patriarch of the 140 million-member Greek Orthodox Church due to a nervous disorder.	Oct. 18
					Oct. 19
				Robert Sherwood's *Roosevelt and Hopkins*, a history of the war years reconstructed from the private notes of presidential aide Harry Hopkins, is published in N.Y. by Harper . . . . *Life with Mother*, by Howard Lindsay and Russel Crouse, opens on Broadway to favorable reviews.	Oct. 20
Supreme Court upholds the Illinois law which bars Wallace from the state ballot . . . . Heads of 17 Negro land-grant colleges conclude a three-day meeting in Washington by objecting to the proposed creation of a segregated regional university for the South.	Gen. Lucius Clay of the U.S. military government in Germany visits Washington to confer on the Berlin situation with Truman and the National Security Council. He is promised an additional 66 C-54 transport planes for the airlift . . . . American Legion ends a four-day convention in Miami after demanding the outlawing of the Communist Party and government pensions for all veterans over 55.	A federal court in N.Y. fines the Rubber Manufacturers Assn. and eight corporations $50,000 for restraining competition in tire sales.	Ultrafax, a radio device developed by RCA and Eastman Kodak for transmitting still and moving pictures, is publicly demonstrated for the first time in Washington.		Oct. 21
A federal grand jury in Washington begins investigation of columnist Drew Pearson's charges that House Un-American Activities Comm. Chmn. J. Parnell Thomas (R, N.J.) received salary kickbacks from employes of his congressional office who did no work.		A Pittsburgh federal court fines five paint and varnish firms and six officers $42,500 for conspiring to fix prices.	Xerography, an inkless printing reproduction process invented by Chester Carlson, is publicly demonstrated for the first time in N.Y.	*The Red Shoes*, a ballet film directed by Michael Powell and Emeric Pressburger, premiers in N.Y.	Oct. 22
				Emile Bruneau and Louis Saen of Belgium win the 68th international six-day bicycle race in N.Y.	Oct. 23

F	G	H	I	J
Includes elections, federal-state relations, civil rights and liberties, crime, the judiciary, education, health care, poverty, urban affairs and population.	*Includes formation and debate of U.S. foreign and defense policies, veterans affairs and defense spending. (Relations with specific foreign countries are usually found under the region concerned.)*	*Includes business, labor, agriculture, taxation, transportation, consumer affairs, monetary and fiscal policy, natural resources, pollution and accidents.*	*Includes worldwide scientific, medical and technological developments, natural phenomena, U.S. weather and natural disasters.*	*Includes the arts, religion, scholarship, communications media, sports, entertainment, fashions, fads and social life.*

	World Affairs	Europe	Africa & the Middle East	The Americas	Asia & the Pacific
Oct. 24		A Russian military court convicts six Berlin anti-Communist leaders, including City Assembly Pres. Otto Suhr and Assembly member Franz Neumann, of agitating for war and a revival of fascism . . . . German People's Council of the Russian zone adopts a constitution based on that of the Soviet Union, to be enacted after the end of the occupation.	Focus of Palestine fighting shifts to the country's northern half, with Israelis checking Syrian advances in the northern Galilee and Iraqi forces attacking in the Nablus area southeast of Haifa . . . . Truman issues a statement calling the Bernadotte Palestine plan "a basis for" new negotiations.		
Oct. 25	Russia vetoes the Berlin compromise proposed by neutral U.N. Security Council members . . . . A subcommittee of the General Assembly's Political and Security Comm. rejects a Russian proposal for gradual reduction of conventional arms and a ban on nuclear weapons. The subcommittee accepts a Belgian proposal to refer the disarmament question back to the Conventional Armaments Comm.		U.N. mediator Ralph Bunche orders Israel to give up all territory gained in the Negev desert during the past 10 days.	Former Panamanian Pres. Harmodio Arias is among 27 suspects arrested for allegedly plotting to overthrow Pres. Domingo Diaz Arosemena.	Chinese Communist forces report capturing Kaifeng, the capital of Honan Province.
Oct. 26	Foreign ministers of the Western European Union nations, meeting in Paris, announce plans to form a North Atlantic defense alliance with the U.S. and Canada.	Russian military authorities in Germany charge that safety rules for the Berlin air corridors are invalid because they have never been approved by the Allied Control Council.		Paraguayan government announces suppression of a military revolt in Asuncion.	
Oct. 27			Iraqi troops in Palestine open a drive in the Nablus area southeast of Haifa.		
Oct. 28	In a *Pravda* interview, Stalin accuses the Western Allies of violating an earlier Berlin understanding by submitting the Berlin dispute to the U.N., where Security Council neutrals "are obviously lending their support to a policy of aggression."	A U.S. tribunal in Nuremberg convicts 11 high German commanders of crimes against humanity after acquitting them of plotting a war of aggression. Among the convicted is Gen. Walter Warlimont, Hitler's former general staff aide . . . . Forty thousand Stuttgart workers demonstrating against high prices are dispersed by U.S. tanks and cavalry after some protestors begin to attack shops.			
Oct. 29		Greek government imposes martial law on the entire country as government forces and guerrillas battle indecisively in the Vitsi mountain area . . . . British government proposes a steel nationalization bill bringing 107 iron and steel firms under state control by mid-1950.	Truman orders U.S. representatives at the U.N. to oppose British and Chinese proposals for sanctions against Israel if the Jews refuse to give up recent gains in the Negev desert.	Peru's Pres. Jose Luis Bustamante y Rivero is overthrown in a military coup led by Gen. Manuel Odria.	
Oct. 30		Non-Communist French coal miners resume work after accepting government terms for settlement of the coal strike, including a 15-25% pay raise and increased family benefits. Miners belonging to the Communist-led General Confederation of Labor remain on strike.	Israeli forces open a drive to capture the Galilee from Fawzi el-Kawukji's Palestinian Arab Army.	Gen. Manuel Odria becomes head of a military junta in Peru, promising to retire after election of a "truly democratic government."	Chinese Nationalist forces report the loss of Mukden to the Communists, leaving the government in control only of the southern coastal sector of Manchuria.
Oct. 31		Irving Ross, a U.S. employe of the Economic Cooperation Administration, is murdered in the Soviet sector of Vienna, allegedly by men in Russian uniforms. Russian military authorities claim jurisdiction over the investigation.	Israel completes its conquest of the Galilee, gaining control over all of northern Palestine.		Chinese Nationalist government urges Americans to leave Peking, Tientsin and other northern cities threatened by Communists. The government also abandons its program of price restraints after merchants refuse to sell at money-losing ceiling prices . . . . Indonesian Communist leader Muso Suparto is killed near Madiun by Republic of Indonesia troops, while Dutch Foreign Min. D.U. Stikker arrives in Batavia to negotiate a general settlement of Indonesian issues.
Nov. 1					Chinese Communist leader Mao Tzetung claims that his forces control 24.5% of China's territory and 35% of its population. The U.S. approves a $5-million Nationalist arms purchase and promises a speedup of shipments to the government.

A	B	C	D	E
Includes developments that affect more than one world region, international organizations and important meetings of major world leaders.	*Includes all domestic and regional developments in Europe, including the Soviet Union, Turkey, Cyprus and Malta.*	*Includes all domestic and regional developments in Africa and the Middle East, including Iraq and Iran and excluding Cyprus, Turkey and Afghanistan.*	*Includes all domestic and regional developments in Latin America, the Caribbean and Canada.*	*Includes all domestic and regional developments in Asian and Pacific nations, extending from Afghanistan through all the Pacific Islands, except Hawaii.*

U.S. Politics & Social Issues	U.S. Foreign Policy & Defense	U.S. Economy & Environment	Science, Technology & Nature	Culture, Leisure & Life Style	
States' Rights Party leaders, meeting in Memphis, promise to keep the movement alive after the election "within the framework of the national Democratic Party."		Edward Yancey, du Pont vice president who built and operated an atomic energy plant in Hanford, Wash. during World War II, dies at 60 in Wilmington, Del.		Franz Lehar, Austrian composer of more than 30 operettas including *The Merry Widow*, dies at 78 in Bad Ischl, Austria . . . . Patty Berg defeats Mildred Didrikson Zaharias to win the Hardscrabble Women's Golf Open in Ft. Smith, Ark. . . . . Frederic Logan Paxson, Pulitzer Prize-winning historian of the American West, dies at 71 in Berkeley, Calif.	Oct. 24
		A federal court in Trenton, N.J. issues a consent judgment against 18 stainless steel manufacturers representing 90% of the industry, ordering the defendants to desist from price fixing and restraint of trade.		Supreme Court upholds a New York obscenity ban on Edmund Wilson's *Memoirs of Hecate County* . . . . Benito Mussolini's memoirs are published by Farrar, Straus under the title *The Fall of Mussolini: His Own Story*.	Oct. 25
		Dun & Bradstreet's wholesale food price index drops to a 15-month low at $6.47.		FDR's "Little White House" in Warm Springs, Ga. is dedicated as a national shrine.	Oct. 26
		CIO Oil Workers Union and the Shell Oil Co. sign an agreement providing for a 12½% wage increase, the first break in the 53-day strike of West Coast oil refinery workers.		Judah Leon Magnes, founder and president of Hebrew University in Jerusalem, dies at 71 in N.Y.	Oct. 27
	Addressing a Liberal Party rally N.Y., Truman promises to ensure that Israel will be "large enough and strong enough to make its people self-supporting and secure."		Nobel Prize in medicine goes to Dr. Paul Mueller of Switzerland for his 1939 discovery of the insect-killing properties of DDT.		Oct. 28
An *Editor and Publisher* survey reports that 65% of the nation's daily newspapers support Dewey, vs. 15% for Truman.	Army Secy. Kenneth Royall announces a reorganization of the top command, creating the post of vice chief of staff, to be filled by Gen. J. Lawton Collins. Gens. Wade Haislip and Albert Wedemeyer become new deputy chiefs of staff.	CIO Maritime Engineers Beneficial Assn. signs an agreement with the Pacific American Shipowners Assn. calling for a 5.3% wage increase, the first break in the 57-day West Coast dockworkers strike.		Sandy Sadler wins the world's featherweight crown in N.Y. with a fourth-round KO of Willie Pep . . . . Thomas Mann's novel *Doktor Faustus* is published by Knopf and becomes a November Book-of-the-Month-Club selection.	Oct. 29
Dewey ends his presidential campaign with an address in New York's Madison Square Garden, attacking Truman's "desperate tactics." Truman, speaking in St. Louis, contrasts his "positive position" on problems to Dewey's failure to talk about issues . . . . An Army transport lands in N.Y. with 813 European refugees, the first to arrive in the U.S. under the Displaced Persons Admissions Act of 1948 . . . . Tennessee Gov. Jim McCord calls out the National Guard to protect Loudon Sheriff Henry McDonald from angry mountaineers following the death of country singer Ray Brewster, killed in a car accident while fleeing arrest on a theft charge.		A federal district court in Toledo approves an out-of-court antitrust settlement ordering the dissolution of the National Glass Distributors Assn. and banning restraint of trade practices by the Libby-Owens-Ford, Pittsburgh Plate Glass, American Window Glass plate Fourco Glass companies.		American Council of Christian Churches, representing 15 fundamentalist Protestant denominations in the U.S., concludes a three-day convention in Philadelphia after denouncing the World Council of Churches as a "co-operating front for world socialism" and urging a "complete and frank showdown with Russia." . . . . RKO agrees to separate its film production and distribution section from its theater holdings in compliance with a Justice Dept. antitrust suit. Howard Hughes becomes a member of the company's board of directors.	Oct. 30
				Mary Nolan, film actress and famous Ziegfeld Follies performer, dies at 42 in Hollywood.	Oct. 31
Gallup Poll predicts a Dewey presidential victory with 49.5% of the popular vote vs. 44.5% for Truman.				Archbishop Spyrou Athenagoras of N.Y. is elected Patriarch of the Greek Orthodox Church in Istanbul, the first U.S. citizen named to the post.	Nov. 1

F	G	H	I	J
Includes elections, federal-state relations, civil rights and liberties, crime, the judiciary, education, health care, poverty, urban affairs and population.	*Includes formation and debate of U.S. foreign and defense policies, veterans affairs and defense spending. (Relations with specific foreign countries are usually found under the region concerned.)*	*Includes business, labor, agriculture, taxation, transportation, consumer affairs, monetary and fiscal policy, natural resources, pollution and accidents.*	*Includes worldwide scientific, medical and technological developments, natural phenomena, U.S. weather and natural disasters.*	*Includes the arts, religion, scholarship, communications media, sports, entertainment, fashions, fads and social life.*

	World Affairs	Europe	Africa & the Middle East	The Americas	Asia & the Pacific
Nov. 2				First elections for Puerto Rico's governor result in a victory for Popular Democratic Party candidate Luis Munoz Marin. The Popular Democrats also gain control over both houses of the territory's legislature.	
Nov. 3	U.N. General Assembly chooses a 15-member International Law Comm. to codify international law.	Russia and Hungary conclude a one-year, $150-million trade agreement for exchange of Russian raw materials for Hungarian industrial goods and food products.			Narayan Vinayak Godse, assassin of Mohandas Gandhi, claims in his New Delhi trial that he killed Gandhi "for the benefit of humanity" to frustrate reconciliation between Hindus and Moslems.
Nov. 4	General Assembly approves a Canadian resolution endorsing the U.S. nuclear arms control plan and calling for a resumption of U.N. Atomic Energy Commission sessions.		U.N. Security Council passes a British-Chinese resolution threatening sanctions against Israel if Israeli forces do not give up gains made in the Negev desert since Oct. 14 and negotiate a new ceasefire line.		Chinese Communist forces take the Manchurian port of Yingkow, leaving the southern port of Hulutao as the only Nationalist escape route from Manchuria.
Nov. 5		U.S. authorities in West Berlin open Tegel airfield, the third in use for airlift operations . . . . Italy and Greece sign a trade and friendship treaty, providing for creation of a permanent commission to conciliate disputes between the two countries.			Americans are advised to leave Nanking, the Chinese Nationalist capital, following the advance of Communist forces in the area . . . . South Korean government begins a roundup of all Communist suspects to forestall a new rising.
Nov. 6		Italy and France eliminate visa requirements for citizens of both countries on trips of less than three months . . . . Actress and film director Leni Riefenstahl is acquitted by a denazification court in Villingen on charges of collaborating with the Nazi government.	Egyptian troops abandon the Negev desert, withdrawing southward along the Mediterranean coast to the Gaza area.		
Nov. 7		Gaullist candidates win 107 of 264 seats in elections to France's upper legislative house, the Council of the Republic . . . . Russia celebrates the 31st anniversary of the Bolshevik revolution with a military parade in Moscow stressing air strength. Stalin is not present.			
Nov. 8		Britain's Field Marshal Montgomery meets with British, U.S. and French military governors in Germany to coordinate Western European defense plans.	Mohammed Maraghei Said becomes premier of Iran following the resignation of Abdul Hussein Hajir.		

U.S. Politics & Social Issues	U.S. Foreign Policy & Defense	U.S. Economy & Environment	Science, Technology & Nature	Culture, Leisure & Life Style	
Presidential election results in an upset victory for Truman, who gains 50% of the popular vote, 304 electoral votes and 28 states. Dewey takes 45.5% of the popular vote, 189 electoral votes and 16 states. Congressional elections give control in both houses to the Democrats, who gain 75 seats in the House and nine in the Senate. Among the newly-elected congressmen are Sens. Hubert Humphrey (D, Minn.), Lyndon Johnson (D, Tex.) and Paul Douglas (D, Ill.) and Reps. Abraham Ribicoff (D, Conn.) and Gerald Ford (R, Mich.). Democrats also net six victories in gubernatorial races, controlling 30 governorships vs. 18 for the Republicans. Among the newly elected Democratic governors are Adlai Stevenson of Illinois and former OPA head Chester Bowles of Conn. . . . . In other election issues, Massachusetts voters reject a measure legalizing distribution of birth control information, while Kansas repeals its 68-year-old prohibition statute and Washington approves the sale of liquor in bars and restaurants.		Measures banning the union shop are defeated in Massachusetts and New Mexico but win in Arizona.			Nov. 2
U.S. Atomic Energy Commission orders General Electric to withdraw recognition from the United Electrical Workers union as a bargaining agent for workers in restricted nuclear projects due to "alleged Communist affiliation" of some union officials.		Truman's unexpected reelection causes a sharp drop on the N.Y. Stock Exchange, where prices fall one to six points in heavy trading.			Nov. 3
House Un-American Activities Comm. Chmn. J. Parnell Thomas refuses to testify before a federal grand jury in Washington on charges of padding his congressional payroll and accepting kickbacks.	Air Force announces formation of the Rand Corp., a non-profit military research organization.		Nobel Prize in physics goes to British nuclear physicist Patrick Blackett for his work in cosmic radiation and the photography of radioactive particles. Swedish biochemist Arne Tiselius wins the Nobel Prize in chemistry for isolating a polio virus in mice and developing an electrical measurement of organic substances.	Nobel Prize in literature goes to British-American poet Thomas Stearns Eliot . . . . Film version of Mary Jane Ward's novel *The Snake Pit* premiers in N.Y. . . . . Former N.Y. Yankee baseball star Jake Powell kills himself in Washington police headquarters after being arrested for passing bad checks.	Nov. 4
Truman returns to Washington from Missouri, receiving a tumultuous welcome from 750,000 well wishers		War Assets Admin. announces the sale of a $5-million government aluminum plant in Massena, N.Y. to Alcoa, giving the company control over 50% of the nation's aluminum production.			Nov. 5
					Nov. 6
		In their first policy statements since the election, Administration spokesmen stress the importance of anti-inflation legislation and repeal of the Taft-Hartley Act.		Management engineer Lillian Gilbreth wins the "Woman of the Year" award of the American Women's Assn. for her studies on human motion and industrial efficiency.	Nov. 7
A federal grand jury in Washington indicts House Un-American Activities Comm. Chmn. J. Parnell Thomas on charges of conspiring to defraud the government by padding his congressional payroll . . . . Democratic National Comm. Chmn. J. Howard McGrath announces that he will bar all active States' Rights Party supporters from party leadership positions. Birmingham, Ala. Internal Revenue Collector Mortimer Jordan is dismissed for practicing racial discrimination in federal employment . . . . A Republican-controlled Senate Campaign Investigating subcommittee votes to refer the cases of three Democratic senators, including Senator-elect Lyndon Johnson of Texas, to the new Congress for investigation of possible vote fraud.			A new comet, 1948 K, is sighted from observatories in South Africa and Argentina.		Nov. 8
F *Includes elections, federal-state relations, civil rights and liberties, crime, the judiciary, education, health care, poverty, urban affairs and population.*	G *Includes formation and debate of U.S. foreign and defense policies, veterans affairs and defense spending. (Relations with specific foreign countries are usually found under the region concerned.)*	H *Includes business, labor, agriculture, taxation, transportation, consumer affairs, monetary and fiscal policy, natural resources, pollution and accidents.*	I *Includes worldwide scientific, medical and technological developments, natural phenomena, U.S. weather and natural disasters.*	J *Includes the arts, religion, scholarship, communications media, sports, entertainment, fashions, fads and social life.*	

	World Affairs	Europe	Africa & the Middle East	The Americas	Asia & the Pacific
Nov. 9			Israel reports capturing the Iraq Suweidan police fortress at the northern end of the Negev desert from Egyptian troops.		Food riots break out in Shanghai following the abandonment of price controls by the Nationalist government.
Nov. 10		Russian military authorities threaten to force down Western airlift planes found outside the 20-mile-wide corridors to Berlin, regardless of weather conditions .... U.S. and British military governors in Germany issue a decree giving control over Ruhr heavy industry to a German board of trustees pending election of a German government able to determine ultimate ownership of the area's industry. France immediately protests renewed German authority in the Ruhr .... General Assembly's Political and Security Comm. ends a two-week debate on Greece by passing a resolution to retain the Special U.N. Balkan Commission another year. The resolution charges Yugoslavia, Albania and Bulgaria with endangering peace in the Balkans .... German authorities arrest Hjalmar Schacht near Hamburg for retrial on charges of collaborating with the Nazi government after an appeals court reverses his earlier acquittal.	U.S. Securities and Exchange Commission authorizes a stock issue permit for the Israel Corp. of America, formed in N.Y. to raise funds for housing construction in Israel.		Chinese Nationalist government places Nanking and Shanghai under martial law as Communist forces threaten the nearby rail junction of Suchow.
Nov. 11		In an interview with *New York Times* correspondent C.L. Sulzberger, Generalissimo Francisco Franco expresses hope for closer Spanish ties with the U.S. and a $200-million economic development loan. He expresses willingness to join an "alliance of the Occident" against Russia.			
Nov. 12		Eight million German workers in the U.S. and British zones stage a 24-hour general strike to protest high food prices.	Israeli Premier David Ben-Gurion reports that Israel has begun talks with two Arab governments on a Palestine peace settlement.		International Military Tribunal for the Far East finds former Japanese Premier Hideki Tojo and 24 co-defendants guilty of war crimes and planning aggressive war. Tojo and six co-defendants receive death sentences, while 16 others are given life prison terms. The tribunal exonerates Emperor Hirohito, ruling that he opposed militarist policies and was deceived by cabinet members. Gen. MacArthur gives all defendants one week to appeal their sentences .... Chinese Amb. to the U.S. Wellington Koo warns that "the whole of Asia" may fall under Communist control unless the U.S. increases its aid to the Nationalist government.
Nov. 13	U.N. Secy. Gen. Trygve Lie and General Assembly Pres. Herbert Evatt urge a resumption of Big Four Berlin talks despite U.S. and British objections to negotiating with Russia while the blockade is still in effect.		U.N. Security Council adopts Palestine mediator Ralph Bunche's proposal for a renewed truce, calling on Israeli forces to withdraw from recent gains in the Negev desert and Egyptian troops to remain in their present positions.		South Korea imposes martial law in its southern provinces to suppress alleged revolutionary plots.
Nov. 14		Britain's Princess Elizabeth gives birth to a son in Buckingham Palace, inspiring celebrations throughout the British Empire.			
Nov. 15	U.N. Food and Agriculture Organization begins its fourth annual meeting in Washington, where British Agriculture Min. Tom William recommends a global food price control plan.		Israel rejects a U.N. Security Council call for demilitarization of the Negev desert. Speaking before the General Assembly's Political Comm., Israeli Foreign Min. Moshe Shertok lists his government's peace terms, including a corridor linking the Jewish-controlled section of Jerusalem to the rest of Israel and no readmission of Arab refugees to Palestine until conclusion of a general peace.	William Mackenzie King resigns as Canada's prime minister after 21 years in office, the longest tenure of any government head in the British Commonwealth. He is succeeded by Louis St. Laurent.	

A	B	C	D	E
Includes developments that affect more than one world region, international organizations and important meetings of major world leaders.	*Includes all domestic and regional developments in Europe, including the Soviet Union, Turkey, Cyprus and Malta.*	*Includes all domestic and regional developments in Africa and the Middle East, including Iraq and Iran and excluding Cyprus, Turkey and Afghanistan.*	*Includes all domestic and regional developments in Latin America, the Caribbean and Canada.*	*Includes all domestic and regional developments in Asian and Pacific nations, extending from Afghanistan through all the Pacific Islands, except Hawaii.*

U.S. Politics & Social Issues	U.S. Foreign Policy & Defense	U.S. Economy & Environment	Science, Technology & Nature	Culture, Leisure & Life Style	
	Defense Secy. Forrestal asks the service secretaries to submit proposals for an Air Force Academy similar to the Army and Navy institutions.	International Longshoremen's Assn. Pres. Joseph Ryan announces a contract agreement for East Coast dock workers raising the guaranteed work period two to four hours and increasing hourly wages by 10¢.		Oveta Culp Hobby, wartime WAC director, becomes the first woman president of the Southern Newspaper Publishers Assn. . . . . Edgar Kennedy, film comedian and one of the original "Keystone Kops," dies at 58 in San Fernando, Calif.	Nov. 9
Democratic House leaders announce plans to kill the House Un-American Activities Comm. and supplant it with a Committee on Civil Liberties.		N.Y. dockworkers refuse to ratify a contract negotiated by the International Longshoremen's Assn. and begin an unauthorized walkout.			Nov. 10
Herbert Hoover, head of the Commission on Organization of the Executive Branch, unofficially proposes several reforms, including elimination of Senate control over postmaster appointments and transfer of responsibility for federal appointments from the Civil Service Commission to individual government departments.		Maritime unions resume negotiations with employers in San Francisco to end the West Coast dock workers' strike.	American Public Health Assn. presents seven Lasker awards for contributions to the medical profession at its Boston convention; among the recipients are Selman Waksman, discoverer of streptomycin, and biochemist Rene Dubos.	*Joan of Arc*, starring Ingrid Bergman, premiers in N.Y.	Nov. 11
		International Longshoremen's Assn. Pres. Joseph Ryan authorizes the wildcat walkout of N.Y. dockworkers and orders all East Coast ILA members to strike in a wage dispute with employers . . . . A Cleveland grand jury indicts General Electric, Westinghouse and four other street lighting equipment manufacturers on charges of monopolizing the $10-million-a-year industry.	Col. James Cooney, head of the Army Surgeon General's special projects division, claims at the American Public Health Assn. convention in Boston that the atomic bomb leaves little radiation and kills primarily with its blast.		Nov. 12
	Defense Secy. James Forrestal releases a civil defense plan prepared by the Defense Dept., calling for creation of a permanent national civil defense agency. The plan estimates that a nuclear attack would cause 40,000 deaths and 60,000 injuries for each atomic bomb used.				Nov. 13
		CIO Retail, Wholesale and Department Store Workers union begins its fifth biennial convention in Grand Rapids, Mich., considering means of winning back 30,000 members of left-wing New York department store locals which have seceded from the union.			Nov. 14
House Un-American Activities Comm. Chmn. J. Parnell Thomas is arraigned before a Washington federal court on payroll padding charges, pleading not guilty.					Nov. 15
F	G	H	I	J	
Includes elections, federal-state relations, civil rights and liberties, crime, the judiciary, education, health care, poverty, urban affairs and population.	*Includes formation and debate of U.S. foreign and defense policies, veterans affairs and defense spending. (Relations with specific foreign countries are usually found under the region concerned.)*	*Includes business, labor, agriculture, taxation, transportation, consumer affairs, monetary and fiscal policy, natural resources, pollution and accidents.*	*Includes worldwide scientific, medical and technological developments, natural phenomena, U.S. weather and natural disasters.*	*Includes the arts, religion, scholarship, communications media, sports, entertainment, fashions, fads and social life.*	

	World Affairs	Europe	Africa & the Middle East	The Americas	Asia & the Pacific
Nov. 16	Responding to letters from Trygve Lie and Herbert Evatt, Russia agrees to "immediate conversations" on the Berlin problem but refuses to lift the blockade as a precondition. Truman reiterates Western refusal to negotiate on Berlin while the blockade remains in effect.	Russian authorities in Berlin dismiss the non-Communist directors of the municipal economics and public utilities departments, establishing separate agencies for the Soviet sector.	U.N. Security Council passes a resolution demanding that Israel and Egypt negotiate an armistice, either directly or through U.N. mediator Ralph Bunche, to end fighting in the Negev desert.		
Nov. 17		British House of Commons passes the government's steel industry nationalization bill over strong conservative opposition .... Russian authorities order East Berlin residents to obtain new police identity cards, a move to reduce contacts between the two sectors of the city.			
Nov. 18	U.N. General Assembly passes 1949 budget assessments, assigning 40% of the U.N. budget to the U.S., 11.3% to Britain and 6.3% to Russia. The Assembly also approves the International Refugee Organization as a specialized U.N. agency over Soviet bloc opposition.	Themistocles Sophoulis becomes Greek premier as head of a Liberal-Populist cabinet which includes former Premier Constantin Tsaldaris as foreign minister.	In response to U.N. Security Council pressure, Israel offers to withdraw forces sent to the Negev desert since Oct. 14 without giving up recently acquired territory.		Nationalist leader Chiang Kai-shek appeals directly to Truman for increased military aid, technical advice and a firm declaration of support.
Nov. 19	U.N. General Assembly makes its final disarmament decision by adopting a Belgian plan for renewal of work by the Committee on Conventional Armaments. Russia's proposal for prohibition of atomic weapons and a one-third of the great powers' conventional arms is rejected .... Trusteeship Commission urges the General Assembly to insist that South Africa submit a trusteeship plan for its League of Nations mandate territory in South-West Africa.	U.S. and British military governors drop most export licensing restrictions on German businessmen. France signs the first combined trade agreement with the western zones of Germany, providing for a $300-million exchange of industrial goods and raw materials .... Belgian cabinet of Premier Paul-Henri Spaak resigns when Justice Min. Paul Struye is attacked for commuting the death sentences of two Belgian war criminals.	U.N. mediator Ralph Bunche accepts Israel's offer to withdraw some troops from the Negev desert, while Egypt agrees to establish contact with Israeli negotiators though the U.N. truce mission. The General Assembly establishes a $30-million fund to aid Palestine war refugees .... King Farouk of Egypt and Mohammed Reza Pahlevi, the Shah of Iran, announce they have divorced their wives, who have failed to bear male heirs.		
Nov. 20			U.S. Gen. William Riley, head of the U.N. truce observation force, meets in Tel Aviv with Israeli officials and in Gaza with Egyptian officers to arrange preliminary armistice talks.		Chinese Communist and Nationalist forces battle indecisively around Suchow, northwest of Nanking.
Nov. 21					
Nov. 22		A Bulgarian court hands down 10 to 15-year prison sentences for nine non-Communist members of parliament charged with pro-Western activities.			Nationalist forces abandon Paoting, capital of Hopeh Province in northeastern China, to concentrate on the defense of Peking.
Nov. 23		U.S. Army Corps of Engineers announces the completion of Greece's 430-mile Athens-Salonika highway.			
Nov. 24		French National Assembly gives the government of Premier Henri Queuille a vote of confidence on its use of troops to protect non-striking coal miners and dock workers .... State Secy. Marshall seeks to assuage French objections to U.S. and British policy in the Ruhr by inviting France to participate in bizonal boards supervising German coal and steel production.	U.N. truce mission in Palestine announces a provisional Arab-Jewish truce line for the Bethlehem area.	A military coup ousts liberal Venezuelan Pres. Romulo Gallegos. He is replaced by a three-man military junta led by former Defense Min. Col. Carlos Delgado Chalbaud.	Gen. MacArthur upholds sentences passed on all 25 defendants at the Tokyo war crimes trial.

A	B	C	D	E
Includes developments that affect more than one world region, international organizations and important meetings of major world leaders.	*Includes all domestic and regional developments in Europe, including the Soviet Union, Turkey, Cyprus and Malta.*	*Includes all domestic and regional developments in Africa and the Middle East, including Iraq and Iran and excluding Cyprus, Turkey and Afghanistan.*	*Includes all domestic and regional developments in Latin America, the Caribbean and Canada.*	*Includes all domestic and regional developments in Asian and Pacific nations, extending from Afghanistan through all the Pacific Islands, except Hawaii.*

U.S. Politics & Social Issues	U.S. Foreign Policy & Defense	U.S. Economy & Environment	Science, Technology & Nature	Culture, Leisure & Life Style	
In his first post-election press conference, Truman promises to work for repeal of the Taft-Hartley Act, civil rights legislation and tax revision.	Navy commissions the 17,000-ton *Des Moines*, the largest heavy cruiser in the world.	A House Investigating subcommittee headed by W. Kingsland Macy (R, N.Y.) ends two days of hearings on the auto sales business by charging that customers were cheated of $450 million during the first part of 1948 through special charges for prompt delivery, required purchase of accessories and other illegal arrangements.	Frederick Cottrell, chemist who invented a commercially viable process for isolating helium, dies at 71 in Berkeley, Calif.		Nov. 16
		Agriculture Dept. announces a one-third reduction in potato price supports and a 200,000-acre cut in potato acreage for the coming year following a $100-million loss in the 1948 potato support program.			Nov. 17
	Air Force creates a Continental Air Command, headed by Gen. George Stratemeyer, to take charge of the nation's air defense . . . . Truman appoints John Foster Dulles acting head of the U.S. delegation at the U.N. as Warren Austin takes leave for medical reasons.		*American Review of Soviet Medicine*, the only permanent organ for exchange of medical information between the U.S. and Russia, suspends publication . . . . Belgium announces construction of the world's largest uranium processing plant near the Shinklobwe uranium mine in the southern Belgian Congo.	Nobel Comm. of the Norwegian Parliament announces that the Nobel Peace Prize will not be awarded this year due to absence of suitable candidates. Most of the award money will go to organizations working for peace.	Nov. 18
		International Longshoremen's Assn. demands a 25¢ hourly wage increase, working rule changes and an employer-financed welfare and pension fund as 45,000 East Coast dock workers continue their strike, paralyzing eastern shipping.			Nov. 19
CIO National Executive Bd. ends a four-day session in Portland, Ore. after revoking the charter of the Greater New York CIO Council for "slavish adherence" to Communist tactics.			First major blizzard of the season ends after sweeping through the Midwest, causing 13 deaths and heavy livestock losses.		Nov. 20
Truman returns to Washington from a two-week vacation in Key West, Fla.	Gen. John Weir, head of the Allied commission which investigated European war crimes after World War II, dies at 57 of a heart attack in Washington.			*New York Herald Tribune* lists Carl Sandburg's *Remembrance Rock* and Dale Carnegie's *How to Stop Worrying and Start Living* as best-selling fiction and non-fiction books.	Nov. 21
A federal court in Oklahoma City rejects a plea by Negro student George McLaurin that he be allowed to attend classes at Oklahoma Univ. on a non-segregated basis.		AFL ends an eight-day national convention in Cincinnati after passing resolutions against creation of a new labor party, for re-affiliation of the United Mine Workers union and for U.S. aid to Israel. William Green is re-elected AFL president . . . . Securities and Exchange Commission approves a plan for dissolution of the Commonwealth and Southern Corp. of Deleware, one of the nation's largest holding companies.		*Crusade in Europe*, Gen. Eisenhower's story of World War II, is published in N.Y. by Doubleday . . . . *Box Office* poll names Bing Crosby, Ingrid Bergman and Gary Cooper as the nation's favorite actors in 1948.	Nov. 22
	Gen. Bryant Moore is appointed to succeed Gen. Maxwell Taylor as superintendent of the U.S. Military Academy in West Point.			American Academy of Arts and Letters names novelists William Faulkner and John Steinbeck, artist Leon Kroll and poet Mark Van Doren to membership . . . . Lewis Wilson, former Chicago Cubs outfielder and National League home run king, dies at 48 in Baltimore.	Nov. 23
	State Secy. Marshall confers with Truman on the Chinese situation, commenting afterwards that the U.S. must consider ways of helping the Nationalist government without crippling America's ability to fulfill its commitments in other parts of the world.	Eastman Kodak agrees to refrain from monopolozing color motion picture film production in a consent decree issued by a Los Angeles federal court.		Anna Jarvis, founder of Mother's Day, dies at 84 in West Chester, Pa.	Nov. 24
F	G	H	I	J	
Includes elections, federal-state relations, civil rights and liberties, crime, the judiciary, education, health care, poverty, urban affairs and population.	*Includes formation and debate of U.S. foreign and defense policies, veterans affairs and defense spending. (Relations with specific foreign countries are usually found under the region concerned.)*	*Includes business, labor, agriculture, taxation, transportation, consumer affairs, monetary and fiscal policy, natural resources, pollution and accidents.*	*Includes worldwide scientific, medical and technological developments, natural phenomena, U.S. weather and natural disasters.*	*Includes the arts, religion, scholarship, communications media, sports, entertainment, fashions, fads and social life.*	

	World Affairs	Europe	Africa & the Middle East	The Americas	Asia & the Pacific
Nov. 25		France accepts Marshall's invitation to participate in supervision of Ruhr industrial production.		Venezuela's military junta installs a non-party cabinet, promising to protect U.S. oil investments and other foreign property.	
Nov. 26	U.N. General Assembly adopts a compromise resolution expressing "regret" that South Africa has failed to present a trusteeship plan for South-West Africa. The resolution falls short of Trusteeship Comm. recommendations on the situation .... U.S. announces ratification of a world whale conservation agreement with Russia, Australia, Britain, Norway, South Africa and Holland.	Unity Comm. of the Western European Union convenes in Paris to discuss plans for a European federation. French National Assembly Pres. Edouard Herriot is elected chairman .... Yugoslavian Pres. Tito charges that Cominform countries have reduced trade with Yugoslavia to such an extent that the country must revise its five-year economic plan, eliminating a number of secondary projects .... Irish Parliament passes the Republic of Ireland Bill, severing Ireland's ties with the British crown .... Belgian Premier Paul-Henri Spaak revives his Socialist-Social Christian coalition government.	Israeli-Egyptian armistice negotiations bog down over U.N. mediator Ralph Bunche's demand for complete Israeli withdrawal from the Negev desert.		China's Legislative Assembly names Sun Fo to succeed Wong Wen-hao as premier following the latter's resignation. Sun Fo is the son of Sun Yat-sen, founder of the Chinese republic .... Chinese Nationalist government announces that Mme. Chiang Kai-shek will visit the U.S. to make a personal appeal for aid against the Communists. The State Dept. says the trip is not at U.S. government request, but puts a military plane at Mme. Chiang's disposal.
Nov. 27		U.N. General Assembly approves the report of the Special Balkan Commission and passes a resolution charging Albania, Bulgaria and Yugoslavia with aiding Communist guerrillas in Greece .... French General Confederation of Labor ends the eight-week strike of coal miners in northern France after most miners return to work .... Hungarian Deputy Premier Matyas Rakosi announces a program of farm collectivization .... Russian authorities in Germany order a sharp reduction in electric power due to a coal shortage caused by cut-off of British shipments from the Ruhr .... British P.M. Attlee appoints a special tribunal headed by Justice George Lynskey to investigate charges of corruption in the Bd. of Trade and other government agencies.			
Nov. 28					Former Japanese Premier Hitoshi Ashida resigns as Democratic Party president following discovery of his involvement in a bribery scandal.
Nov. 29	Russia and the Western powers approve a plan for study of the Berlin currency problem by experts from neutral Security Council member states.		Israel formally applies for admission to the U.N.		Indian's Constituent Assembly adopts a constitutional clause prohibiting the practice of untouchability "in any form." .... Nationalist forces abandon the north Chinese port of Chinwangtao to the Communists.
Nov. 30		Communist members of the Berlin City Assembly and delegates of other leftist parties meet in East Berlin to establish a separate government for the city's Soviet sector. Friedrich Ebert, Brandenburg State Assembly president and son of the Weimar Republic's first president, is named mayor. Soviet Marshal Vasily Sokolovsky sends U.S. Gen. Lucius Clay a note justifying the move as a reaction to "persecution" of "democratic elements" in the western zones of Berlin.	Col. Moshe Dayan of Israel and Col. Abdullah el Tell of the Transjordanian Arab Legion sign a ceasefire agreement for Jerusalem.		Japanese Diet passes a measure barring strikes and collective bargaining by government employes.
Dec. 1	U.N. General Assembly's Legal Comm. completes work on a draft convention making genocide a crime under international law.	Berlin's regular City Assembly, meeting in the British sector, proclaims a state of emergency after East Berlin police bar Acting Mayor Ferdinand Friedenburg from entering his office in City Hall.	A meeting of Palestinian Arab leaders in Jericho proclaims Transjordan's King Abdullah "King of all Palestine." The move sets off riots in Damascus, forcing the resignation of Premier Jamil Mardam Bey's Syrian cabinet.		Mme. Chiang Kai-shek arrives in Washington as a private guest of State Secy. Marshall.
	A *Includes developments that affect more than one world region, international organizations and important meetings of major world leaders.*	B *Includes all domestic and regional developments in Europe, including the Soviet Union, Turkey, Cyprus and Malta.*	C *Includes all domestic and regional developments in Africa and the Middle East, including Iraq and Iran and excluding Cyprus, Turkey and Afghanistan.*	D *Includes all domestic and regional developments in Latin America, the Caribbean and Canada.*	E *Includes all domestic and regional developments in Asian and Pacific nations, extending from Afghanistan through all the Pacific Islands, except Hawaii.*

U.S. Politics & Social Issues	U.S. Foreign Policy & Defense	U.S. Economy & Environment	Science, Technology & Nature	Culture, Leisure & Life Style	
	B-36-B, the most powerful propeller-driven plane in the world, is delivered to the Eighth Air Force in Ft. Worth, Tex.	Seventy-five thousand dock workers on both coasts end their strikes after reaching contract agreements with employers. The International Longshoremen's and Warehousemen's Union gains its demand for a 15¢ hourly wage increase after an 85-day strike, while the International Longshoremen's Assn. ends a 16-day strike with agreement on a 13¢ hourly increase. The ILWU contract permits continued operation of union hiring halls pending court review, and the ILA contract provides for further negotiation on pension and welfare fund provisions .... National Airlines settles a 10-month strike by members of the AFL Air Line Pilots Assn., promising to reinstate all union members at the expense of non-union pilots hired during the strike.			Nov. 25
A federal district court in Charleston, S.C. rules that Negroes are entitled to belong to the state Democratic Party and vote in its primaries .... House Labor and Un-American Activities committees drop contempt charges against 60 witnesses who refused to testify if they were Communists.		CIO ends a five-day national convention in Portland, Ore after reelecting Philip Murray president and passing a resolution attacking Russia for its opposition to the Marshall Plan and veto "abuses" in the U.N. Murray criticizes leaders of leftist CIO affiliates, including the United Office and Professional Workers of America and the United Public Workers union, stating that he will "never permit Communist infiltration into the national CIO movement."		Baseball Writers Assn. poll names Cleveland Indians manager-shortstop Lou Boudreau as the American League's most valuable player for 1948 .... National Boxing Assn. suspends Rocky Graziano following his withdrawal from a scheduled fight with Fred Apostoli .... Jack Benny sells his NBC radio program to CBS for a reported $2-3 million.	Nov. 26
				Bob Black of Rhode Island State Univ. captures the 10,000-meter National AAU senior cross country title in Detroit.	Nov. 27
National Executive Council of Phi Kappa Psi upholds suspension of the fraternity's Amherst chapter for admitting a Negro.					Nov. 28
	American Veterans Comm. ends a four-day convention in Cleveland after voting to bar Communists from membership, opposing a federal bonus for veterans and supporting Marshall Plan aid to Europe.			N.Y.'s Metropolitan Opera opens its 64th season with standing room only crowds hearing Verdi's *Otello*. The performance is televised for the first time on ABC .... Univ. of Pennsylvania's All-American center Chuck Bednarik wins the Maxwell Club Trophy as the top college football player of 1948.	Nov. 29
	Army halves its draft quotas for early 1949 to keep under the $15 billion defense budget ceiling set by Truman.	Justice Dept. files an anti-trust complaint in Cleveland charging the Republic Steel Corp. and 19 other culvert pipe manufacturers with monopolizing the corrugated sheet metal industry .... NLRB orders the Goodyear Rubber Footwear Corp. to pay back wages to 50 employes for a nine-month layoff intended to "discourage union activity."	Curtiss-Wright Corp. demonstrates a new reversible propeller that enables a four-engine plane to make a rapid, direct ascent and descent.	Negro National League is dissolved in Chicago, leaving the 10-team Negro American League the only segregated baseball association .... Southern Michigan Univ. halfback Doak Walker wins the Heisman Trophy as the year's top college football player .... Hooperatings list *Walter Winchell*, *Jack Benny* and *Radio Theater* as most popular radio shows.	Nov. 30
				Frank Brett Noyes, former president of the Associated Press and board chairman of the Washington *Evening Star*, dies at 85 in Washington.	Dec. 1
F *Includes elections, federal-state relations, civil rights and liberties, crime, the judiciary, education, health care, poverty, urban affairs and population.*	G *Includes formation and debate of U.S. foreign and defense policies, veterans affairs and defense spending. (Relations with specific foreign countries are usually found under the region concerned.)*	H *Includes business, labor, agriculture, taxation, transportation, consumer affairs, monetary and fiscal policy, natural resources, pollution and accidents.*	I *Includes worldwide scientific, medical and technological developments, natural phenomena, U.S. weather and natural disasters.*	J *Includes the arts, religion, scholarship, communications media, sports, entertainment, fashions, fads and social life.*	

	World Affairs	Europe	Africa & the Middle East	The Americas	Asia & the Pacific
Dec. 2		Russia officially recognizes the separate Communist government in East Berlin, promising to give it all necessary "help and support." . . . . French National Assembly approves a resolution condemning U.S. and British plans to put Ruhr industry under German control.		Anti-Communist Canadian union leaders organize the Canadian Assn. of International Union Representatives, with Vice Pres. Frank Hall of the Brotherhood of Railway Clerks as chairman.	Chinese Nationalist forces abandon the rail junction of Suchow to Communists, retreating southward to reinforce the defense of Nanking . . . . India's Constituent Assembly adopts a Charter of Liberty guaranteeing freedom of speech, assembly, property ownership and work.
Dec. 3	U.N. General Assembly approves continuation of the Interim Commission on Peace and Security.		John Hofmeyr, South African liberal leader and deputy head of the Union Party, dies at 54 in Pretoria.	Treaty of Rio de Janeiro, providing for mutual defense of Western Hemisphere countries, goes into effect as Costa Rica deposits the 14th ratification with the Pan American Union in Washington.	Chinese streamer *Kiangya*, filled with refugees bound for southern China, explodes and sinks near Shanghai, killing 1,100 passengers and crew members.
Dec. 4	U.N. General Assembly's Political Comm. passes a Western resolution urging the great powers to refrain from using their Security Council veto on a number of problems, including U.N. membership requests and mediation of disputes.		U.N. General Assembly's Political and Security Comm. passes a British and Canadian proposal for creation of a conciliation commission to work with Jews and Arabs on a final Palestine peace settlement.		Chinese Nationalist representatives in Washington urge the U.S. to approve a $3-billion emergency program of military and economic aid to China for the next three years.
Dec. 5		City Assembly elections in the western sectors of Berlin result in a large victory for the Social Democrats, who gain 64.5% of the popular vote. Despite a Communist boycott of the election, an 86.2% voter turnout is recorded . . . . Social Democratic and trade union leaders in Schleswig-Holstein refuse to cooperate with British authorities until plant dismantling is halted in the British zone.	Stern Gang leader Nathan Yellin and his aide, Matityahu Shmulevitz, go on trial before an Israeli military court in Acre for terrorist activity.	Elections to Argentina's constitutional assembly result in a victory for Peronist candidates, who gain 65% of the seats.	
Dec. 6		In a report to Congress, Truman criticizes the Greek government for permitting a "military stalemate" to develop in its war against the Communist guerrillas. He claims the Greek Army has failed to follow its summer victories with a "determined effort" to eliminate remaining guerrilla resistance . . . . British House of Commons passes the National Service Bill, lengthening the term of compulsory military service from 12 to 18 months . . . . Weston Hall, soldier of fortune and founder of the World War I Lafayette Escadrille, dies at 62 in Fremont, Ohio.	Israel and Iraq sign a ceasefire for northern Palestine.		Chinese Pres. Chiang Kai-shek requests the U.S. to divert all military shipments bound for China to the island of Taiwan . . . . U.S. Supreme Court agrees to hear the appeals of two former Japanese officials, Kenji Doihara and Koki Hirota, sentenced to death by the Tokyo war crimes tribunal . . . . Allied Far Eastern Commission instructs MacArthur to remove all limits on the number of foreign businessmen who can enter Japan.
Dec. 7		West Berlin's current City Assembly names Social Democratic leader Ernst Reuter to serve as mayor of Berlin until the first session of the newly elected Assembly in January . . . . Russian authorities ban all mail deliveries from West Berlin to Soviet-occupied areas . . . . Eight hundred workers and technicians strike in East Berlin power plants over political grievances and are given jobs in the city's western sectors.			
Dec. 8			Egypt orders dissolution of the Moslem Brotherhood, a fanatical nationalist organization held responsible for a six-month series of bombings, assassinations and riots.	Elections for the Costa Rican Constituent Assembly result in an overwhelming victory for supporters of Pres. Jose Figueres.	General Assembly's Political Comm. overrides Soviet bloc opposition to pass a U.S. resolution granting U.N. recognition to the South Korean government and prolonging the U.N. Korean Commission, boycotted by Russia . . . . Former Japanese Premier Hitoshi Ashida is arrested on charges of accepting a bribe after the Diet waives his parliamentary immunity.
Dec. 9	U.N. General Assembly unanimously adopts a convention making genocide a crime in international law.	John Belcher, parliamentary secretary to the British Bd. of Trade, announces his intention to resign after admitting that he solicited gifts from businessmen dealing with his agency.			

A	B	C	D	E
Includes developments that affect more than one world region, international organizations and important meetings of major world leaders.	*Includes all domestic and regional developments in Europe, including the Soviet Union, Turkey, Cyprus and Malta.*	*Includes all domestic and regional developments in Africa and the Middle East, including Iraq and Iran and excluding Cyprus, Turkey and Afghanistan.*	*Includes all domestic and regional developments in Latin America, the Caribbean and Canada.*	*Includes all domestic and regional developments in Asian and Pacific nations, extending from Afghanistan through all the Pacific Islands, except Hawaii.*

U.S. Politics & Social Issues	U.S. Foreign Policy & Defense	U.S. Economy & Environment	Science, Technology & Nature	Culture, Leisure & Life Style	
Whittaker Chambers leads House Un-American Activities Comm. investigators to a microfilmed cache of secret State, War and Navy department documents on his farm in Westminster, Md. Journalists dub the microfilms, hidden in a hollowed-out pumpkin, the "pumpkin papers." After inspecting the material, committee member Karl Mundt (R, S.D.) declares that it reveals the existence of "a vast network of Communist espionage in the State Dept." Chambers claims he received the documents from a secret contact in the State Dept. . . . . Truman holds his first post-election White House press conference, announcing that all cabinet members will remain in office at his request.				Baseball Writers Assn. poll names St. Louis Cardinals outfielder Stan Musial the National League's most valuable player for the second straight year . . . . Lambert Trophy for Eastern college football supremacy goes to Army.	Dec. 2
American Medical Assn. ends a four-day meeting in St. Louis after formulating plans to raise a $3.5-million fund to fight Truman's national health insurance program . . . . Florida's Gov. Millard Caldwell reports plans to run the projected Southern regional university system without federal aid in order to ensure segregation.		National Assn. of Manufacturers ends a three-day convention in N.Y. after passing resolutions opposing government business controls, warning of inflation and urging reduction of government expenditures . . . . CIO American Radio Assn. accepts a 10% wage increase from West Coast shippers, the last of five striking unions to reach a settlement.		Federal Council of Churches in America ends a three-day national convention in Cincinnati after passing a strong civil rights resolution urging members to work for an end to segregation in all walks of life.	Dec. 3
House Un-American Activities Comm. issues a pamphlet, *100 Things You Should Know About Communism and Education*, charging American Communists with forming a "secret army" to subvert the U.S. government and seeking "new recruits" from the Progressive Party.		George Berry, leader of the AFL International Printing Pressmen's and Assistants' Union and former Democratic senator from Tennessee, dies in Pressmen's Home, Tenn.		Jean-Paul Sartre's *Red Gloves* opens in N.Y. to mixed reviews. Sartre charges in Paris that the play's American producers made unauthorized changes to give it an anti-Soviet slant.	Dec. 4
				Songwriter Frederick Mills, who wrote the music for *Meet Me in St. Louis, Louis*, dies at 79 in Hawthorne, Calif.	Dec. 5
A House Un-American Activities subcommittee travels to N.Y. to hear further testimony from Whittaker Chambers on Communist spy activity in the State Department. Chambers accuses Alger Hiss, former State Dept. economist Henry Wadleigh and chemist William Pigman of transmitting secret documents to him for delivery to Col. Boris Bykov, head of Russian espionage in the U.S. during the late 1930s . . . . American Dental Assn. Pres. Clyde Minges announces his group's opposition to Truman's proposed national health insurance program.	Arthur Hill resigns as chairman of the National Security Resources Bd. following rejection of his demand for extensive authority over defense-related actions of other government agencies.			Maurice Druon, author of *Les Grandes Familles*, wins the Goncourt Prize for the best novel by a young Frenchman.	Dec. 6
U.S. Fourth Circuit Court of Appeals in Richmond upholds the right of an interstate bus company to segregate Negro passengers "providing there is no discrimination in the arrangement."	Truman approves a new manual for Army courts-martial allowing enlisted men to sit as court members.				Dec. 7
Justice Dept. asks the House Un-American Activities Comm. to drop its separate investigation of Communist spy activity and to refrain from calling witnesses scheduled to appear before a N.Y. federal grand jury hearing testimony on allegedly subversive acts of U.S. Communist leaders.	Philip Jessup, acting chief of the permanent U.S. mission to the U.N., is given ambassadorial rank . . . . A four-engine B-50 refuels in mid-air to complete a 9,400-mile, non-stop flight from Ft. Worth, Tex. to Hawaii.			Maxwell Anderson's *Anne of The Thousand Days*, based on Henry VIII's marriage to Anne Boleyn, opens to favorable reviews on Broadway.	Dec. 8
House Un-American Activities Comm. rejects a Justice Dept. request to drop its investigation of Communist spy activities in the State Dept.		CIO Transport Workers Union ends a four-day convention in Chicago by re-electing anti-Communist Pres. Michael Quill and ousting several leftist union officials. A measure is also adopted barring Communists and their supporters from office.			Dec. 9
F *Includes elections, federal-state relations, civil rights and liberties, crime, the judiciary, education, health care, poverty, urban affairs and population.*	G *Includes formation and debate of U.S. foreign and defense policies, veterans affairs and defense spending. (Relations with specific foreign countries are usually found under the region concerned.)*	H *Includes business, labor, agriculture, taxation, transportation, consumer affairs, monetary and fiscal policy, natural resources, pollution and accidents.*	I *Includes worldwide scientific, medical and technological developments, natural phenomena, U.S. weather and natural disasters.*	J *Includes the arts, religion, scholarship, communications media, sports, entertainment, fashions, fads and social life.*	

	World Affairs	Europe	Africa & the Middle East	The Americas	Asia & the Pacific
Dec. 10	U.N. General Assembly adopts a Declaration on Human Rights guaranteeing freedom of employment, education, opinion, movement and national identification and freedom from discrimination, cruel and inhuman punishment and arbitrary deprivation of property. A preamble holds that the declaration is a "standard of achievement" for U.N. member states. South Africa, Saudi Arabia and Soviet bloc countries abstain from voting on the declaration .... U.S., Canada and the five Western European Union states begin discussions in Washington on a North Atlantic security pact .... Winston Churchill urges that Spain be admitted to the U.N., praising the Franco regime for refusing to help the Germans take Gibraltar during the war.	West German Parliamentary Council in Bonn, working on a West German constitution, urges that Germans assume full responsibility for domestic affairs in the future state. The recommendation conflicts with earlier directives of Western Allied authorities, warning against giving too much authority to German officials .... Hungarian Premier Lajos Dinnyes resigns following the defection of Finance Min. Miklos Nyaraddy to Switzerland. He is replaced by Agriculture Min. and Peasant Party leader Istvan Dobi.			Chinese Pres. Chiang Kai-shek extends martial law to all Nationalist-controlled areas of southern and eastern China. Truman holds a brief private interview with Mme. Chiang in Washington, but refuses to commit himself on her request for military and economic aid .... South Korean government signs an agreement with the U.S. providing for $300 million in economic aid during the next three years.
Dec. 11	U.N. General Assembly approves a record $38.7-million budget for 1949.		U.N. General Assembly establishes a Conciliation Commission for Palestine, consisting of France, Turkey and the U.S. Function of the commission is to work for a permanent Palestine peace settlement, safeguard religious shrines and arrange for the repatriation of Palestinian refugees. All references to the Bernadotte Palestine peace plan, calling on Israel to give up the Negev desert, are eliminated from the resolution establishing the commission .... Egypt and Syria warn Transjordan's King Abdullah against any attempt to annex Arab Palestine.	Canada and Newfoundland sign an agreement in Ottawa providing for Newfoundland's admission to the Dominion as the 10th province .... Forces loyal to former Costa Rican Pres. Rafael Calderon Guardia invade Costa Rica from Nicaragua, causing Pres. Jose Figueres to order a nationwide mobilization.	Economic Cooperation Admin. Paul Hoffman arrives in Shanghai on an inspection trip after stating that the U.S. will no longer "finance" the Nationalist government.
Dec. 12	U.N. General Assembly ends its Paris session after 618 plenary and committee meetings.	Russia and Italy sign a one-year trade agreement providing for a $50-million exchange of goods and Russian confiscation of Italian property in Eastern Europe as part of Italy's reparations debt to Russia .... Russian authorities allow partial resumption of mail deliveries between West Berlin and Soviet-occupied Germany .... Pope Pius XII bestows his "affectionate blessing" on the Spanish government of Francisco Franco as he receives Joaquin Ruiz Jimenez Cortes, the new Spanish ambassador to the Vatican.	Council of Scholars of Cairo's El Azhar University, the highest spiritual authority in the Moslem world, warns Transjordan's King Abdullah against taking control of Arab Palestine.		U.N. General Assembly accepts the recommendation of its Political Comm. by voting to recognize South Korea as the legitimate Korean government, declaring that last May's U.N.-observed election was free and democratic .... Chinese Communists drive on the Nationalist capital of Nanking, approaching within 50 miles of the city.
Dec. 13		Greek Communist guerrillas are driven from the Thessalian town of Karditsa by government forces after occupying it for 36 hours.	Transjordanian Parliament unanimously authorizes King Abdullah to accept sovereignty over Arab Palestine.	Costa Rican government forces report checking the invasion of former Pres. Rafael Calderon Guardia's supporters after a single skirmish.	
Dec. 14				A military revolt in El Salvador deposes Pres. Salvador Castaneda Castro, who hoped to revise the country's constitution to allow himself a second four-year term.	
Dec. 15	Russia casts its 29th Security Council veto to prevent Ceylon's admission to the U.N.	Poland's Socialist and Communist parties merge into a United Workers Party .... Russia and Czechoslovakia announces a $360-million trade agreement for 1949, increasing trade between the two countries by 45%.	Israel breaks off local truce talks with its Arab neighbors, demanding negotiations for a comprehensive Palestine peace settlement.		South Korean government formally celebrates its recognition by the U.N. as political leaders claim the country will soon be unified.
	A *Includes developments that affect more than one world region, international organizations and important meetings of major world leaders.*	B *Includes all domestic and regional developments in Europe, including the Soviet Union, Turkey, Cyprus and Malta.*	C *Includes all domestic and regional developments in Africa and the Middle East, including Iraq and Iran and excluding Cyprus, Turkey and Afghanistan.*	D *Includes all domestic and regional developments in Latin America, the Caribbean and Canada.*	E *Includes all domestic and regional developments in Asian and Pacific nations, extending from Afghanistan through all the Pacific Islands, except Hawaii.*

U.S. Politics & Social Issues	U.S. Foreign Policy & Defense	U.S. Economy & Environment	Science, Technology & Nature	Culture, Leisure & Life Style	
National Comm. on Segregation in the Nation's Capital issues a report charging that discrimination against Negroes has become more prevalent in Washington during the past 50 years and is "planned as a matter of good business" by government and commercial leaders.					Dec. 10
House Un-American Activities Comm. begins to release State Dept. documents surrendered by Whittaker Chambers, most concerning U.S. relations with Germany, Japan and China during the late 1930s.	Defense Secy. James Forrestal orders creation of a Weapons Systems Evaluation Group, composed of military and civilian specialists, to study armaments in light of "probable future combat conditions."				Dec. 11
				Michigan State is admitted to the Western Collegiate Athletic Conference, which becomes the "Big 10."	Dec. 12
Supreme Court hands down three decisions giving increased protection to defendants against police abuses. The Court reverses the convictions of Andrew Upshaw, who confessed to a theft while being held illegally, and Earl McDonald and Joseph Washington, who were convicted of gambling on evidence obtained without a warrant. The Court also agrees to review the case of Elmer Uveges, who was convicted of burglary after being denied counsel .... Southern Governors Conference in Savannah, Ga. adopts an "action program" to establish a segregated regional university system, costing $1.7 million during the first two years .... Truman's election becomes official as the electoral college meets and casts 303 of a total 531 votes for him.			Guggenheim Foundation officials announce creation of two centers for rocket and jet propulsion research at Princeton Univ. and the California Institute of Technology.	American Fed. of Radio Artists, American Guild of Musical Artists, Chorus Equity and Actors Equity merge in Hollywood in an effort to strengthen the position of labor in the television industry .... AFL American Federation of Musicians' 11-month ban on phonograph recording by members ends when Atty. Gen. Tom Clark agrees that the AFM's proposed welfare-fund contract with the nation's 13 major record makers does not violate the Taft-Hartley Act .... Professional Golfers Assn. announces that the year's top tournament winners are Lloyd Mangrum ($45,898) and Ben Hogan ($36,812).	Dec. 13
House Un-American Activities Comm. claims that Soviet agents in the U.S. government had access to military secrets at the Army's Aberdeen, Md. testing ground, including the famed Norden bombsight, during the late 1930s.				Ike Williams, world lightweight champion, earns the Edward J. Neil Memorial Plaque as the year's outstanding boxer.	Dec. 14
A N.Y. federal grand jury indicts Alger Hiss on two counts of perjury, charging that he lied in swearing he had never given State Dept. documents to Whittaker Chambers and had not seen Chambers after entering State Dept. service in 1936.	Defense Secy. James Forrestal introduces a number of efficiency measures in the armed forces, including consolidation of all military sea transport under the Navy and common use of recruiting facilities by the Army, Navy and Air Force .... State Dept. announces Russian agreement to return 28 frigates and three icebreakers borrowed under Lend-Lease during the war.	CIO Pres. Philip Murray asks the CIO Amalgamated Clothing Workers union to take responsibility for organizing the field controlled by the Retail, Wholesale and Department Store Union due to factionalism in the latter organization.	First known chain reacting uranium pile in a non-English speaking nation begins operation at Ft. Chatillon near Paris.		Dec. 15

F	G	H	I	J
Includes elections, federal-state relations, civil rights and liberties, crime, the judiciary, education, health care, poverty, urban affairs and population.	*Includes formation and debate of U.S. foreign and defense policies, veterans affairs and defense spending. (Relations with specific foreign countries are usually found under the region concerned.)*	*Includes business, labor, agriculture, taxation, transportation, consumer affairs, monetary and fiscal policy, natural resources, pollution and accidents.*	*Includes worldwide scientific, medical and technological developments, natural phenomena, U.S. weather and natural disasters.*	*Includes the arts, religion, scholarship, communications media, sports, entertainment, fashions, fads and social life.*

	World Affairs	Europe	Africa & the Middle East	The Americas	Asia & the Pacific
Dec. 16		French authorities destroy two Russian radio towers in the French sector of Berlin, claiming they endangered airlift operations .... U.S. and French military officials in Frankfurt deadlock in negotiations on an occupation statute for West Germany, with U.S. representatives favoring delegation of most economic controls to the new German government. The problem is referred to the U.S., British and French governments .... Swiss Federal Assembly elects Finance Min. Ernst Nobs president of Swiss Federation, the first socialist to hold the post.			Pvt. Stratman Armistead is hanged in Yokohama for killing four Japanese last October, the first member of the occupation forces to be executed for a crime in Japan.
Dec. 17	Israel's U.N. membership application is voted down in the Security Council.		A Syrian cabinet crisis caused by public dissatisfaction over events in Palestine ends when former Foreign Min. Khaled el-Azem forms a new cabinet, appointing himself foreign and defense minister.		U.S. State and Army departments order Japan to adopt a new stringent austerity program to stablize its economy and check inflation, including a balanced budget, improved tax collection and more effective price controls.
Dec. 18		Finland and Russia announce a barter agreement covering $100 million in trade for 1949.		An Organization of American States commission opens an inquiry in San Jose on Costa Rican charges that the recent invasion by supporters of former Pres. Rafael Calderon Guardia was planned by neighboring Nicaragua .... Heavy rains and flooding in southeastern Brazil end after causing 600 deaths in 17 days.	Dutch forces based in Java attack the Indonesian Republic, ending an 11-month truce following the refusal of Indonesian nationalists to recognize temporary continuation of Dutch sovereignty over Indonesia .... Chinese Communist forces under Gen. Lin Piao surround Peking.
Dec. 19					In a quick attack Dutch troops capture Jakarta, capital of the Indonesian Republic, and intern Pres. Ahmed Sukarno and other Republican leaders .... Gen. MacArthur issues a directive ordering the Japanese government to implement the State Department's austerity recommendations, stating that Japan must temporarily surrender "some of the privileges and immunities inherent in a free society."
Dec. 20		British government issues a White Paper calling for four more years of economic austerity to increase foreign trade and industrial investment.	In an attempt to assert his authority over Arab Palestine, Transjordan's King Abdullah appoints Sheikh Hussan Meddin Jarallah as Mufti of Jerusalem, displacing Haj Amin el Husseini .... Stern Gang leader Nathan Yellin, on trial before an Israeli military court in Acre, denies any connection with the assassination of U.N. mediator Folke Bernadotte.		U.N. Security Council votes to consider the Indonesian Republic's appeal for help against Dutch attacks after U.N. observers in Java report that Holland violated last January's truce agreement. Most U.N. member states condemn the invasion and demand the release of interned Indonesian leaders .... U.S. Supreme Court refuses to reverse the death sentences imposed by the Tokyo war crimes tribunal, ruling it has no authority over the tribunal's decisions .... Chinese Premier Sun Fo announces a new Kuomintang cabinet, indicating that the Nationalist government is willing to negotiate with the Communists but will continue fighting to secure an "honorable peace."
Dec. 21		U.S., British and French military authorities re-establish the Berlin city command, boycotted by Russia since July 1, for their sectors of the city .... Irish Pres. Sean O'Kelly signs the Republic of Ireland bill, severing relations with the British crown.			A China National Airlines Skymaster crashes near Hong Kong, killing 35 passengers. Among the dead are airline executive Quentin Roosevelt, grandson of Theodore Roosevelt, and Chinese U.N. delegate Peng Hsueh-pei.
	A	B	C	D	E
	Includes developments that affect more than one world region, international organizations and important meetings of major world leaders.	*Includes all domestic and regional developments in Europe, including the Soviet Union, Turkey, Cyprus and Malta.*	*Includes all domestic and regional developments in Africa and the Middle East, including Iraq and Iran and excluding Cyprus, Turkey and Afghanistan.*	*Includes all domestic and regional developments in Latin America, the Caribbean and Canada.*	*Includes all domestic and regional developments in Asian and Pacific nations, extending from Afghanistan through all the Pacific Islands, except Hawaii.*

U.S. Politics & Social Issues	U.S. Foreign Policy & Defense	U.S. Economy & Environment	Science, Technology & Nature	Culture, Leisure & Life Style	
Hiss pleads not guilty to perjury charges in a N.Y. federal court and is freed on $5,000 bail.	Acting State Secy. Robert Lovett states that none of the Nationalist government's recent appeals have caused the U.S. to change its "hands off" policy towards China's civil war .... A 14-member bipartisan committee headed by Ferdinand Eberstadt, part of the Hoover Commission of Reorganization of the Executive Branch, issues a report on the nation's military establishment criticizing the armed forces for inefficiency and overlapping functions. Among the report's recommendations are greater military cost-consciousness, closer coordination between scientific research and strategic planning, an end to interservice rivalries and greater concentration on methods of "unconventional" warfare such as chemical and biological weapons.	Justice Dept. files charges in Cleveland against the U.S. Rubber Co., Consolidated Rubber, Dunlop and 13 foreign firms for allegedly operating an international rubber cartel.			Dec. 16
Lester Cole, a Hollywood screen writer fired last year by MGM for refusing to testify before the House Un-American Activities Comm., wins his reinstatement suit in Los Angeles. The verdict is a setback for the film industry's anti-Communist drive .... Georgia House Speaker Fred Hand, a supporter of Gov. Herman Talmadge, announces plans to reduce the state's Negro vote by raising educational requirements for registration .... Edward Alexander, constitutional lawyer prominent in the drive to repeal Prohibition, dies at 75 in N.Y.		A presidential emergency board recommends that one million members of 16 non-operating rail unions have their work week cut from 48 to 40 hours with a 7¢ hourly raise.	Truman participates in ceremonies marking the formal installation of the Wright brothers' airplane *Kitty Hawk* in the Smithsonian Institution. He presents the Robert J. Collier Aviation Trophy to aircraft designer Lawrence Bell, research engineer John Stack and test pilot Charles Yeager for their contributions to supersonic flight.		Dec. 17
			Philip Winnek, a biochemist who pioneered in the development of sulfa drugs, dies at 40 in Morristown, N.J.	William Fisher, composer of *Swing Low, Sweet Chariot* and other popular songs, dies at 87 in Brookline, Mass.	Dec. 18
				Philadelphia Eagles defeat the Chicago Cardinals in the National Football League playoff, while the Cleveland Browns defeat the Buffalo Tigers to win the All-American Conference title .... *Film Daily's* annual survey of the nation's film reviewers names *Gentlemen's Agreement* as the best film of 1948 .... *New York Herald Tribune* reports Lloyd Douglas's *The Big Fisherman* and Dwight Eisenhower's *Crusade in Europe* as the best-selling fiction and non-fiction books .... National Conference of Christians and Jews names actress Irene Dunne as the person "who has done most in 1948 to promote better understanding of people of all faiths."	Dec. 19
Institute of International Education director and former State Dept. official Laurence Duggan commits suicide in N.Y. shortly before Acting Chmn. Karl Mundt of the House Un-American Activities Comm. reveals testimony linking Duggan with the alleged Communist spy ring in the State Dept.		Members of the Joint Congressional Labor-Management Relations Comm. release a series of proposed amendments to the Taft-Hartley Act, including provisions for injunctions against "national emergency" strikes, tightened restrictions against mass picketing, elimination of the union shop election and requirements for employers to file affidavits attesting they are not Communists.	Researchers at several nuclear laboratories in the U.S. report that five scientists are going blind from cataracts as a result of their work with cyclotrons .... A heavy snowstorm passes through the Northeastern states, causing 17 deaths and leaving 19½ inches of snow in N.Y., the third largest accumulation on record.	Officials of the National Football League and All-American Football Conference meet in Philadelphia to discuss merger of their organizations, but fail to reach an agreement.	Dec. 20
Whittaker Chambers denies knowing Laurence Duggan or naming him as a Communist spy in the State Dept.	Economic Cooperation Admin. Paul Hoffman suspends $70 million in long-term reconstruction loans to the Nationalist Chinese government due to the civil war situation.		Prof. H.L. Johnston of Ohio State Univ. reports the development of a hydrogen-based liquid rocket fuel under Air Force contract and predicts the construction of rockets capable of sending men to the moon at 30,000 mph.		Dec. 21
F *Includes elections, federal-state relations, civil rights and liberties, crime, the judiciary, education, health care, poverty, urban affairs and population.*	G *Includes formation and debate of U.S. foreign and defense policies, veterans affairs and defense spending. (Relations with specific foreign countries are usually found under the region concerned.)*	H *Includes business, labor, agriculture, taxation, transportation, consumer affairs, monetary and fiscal policy, natural resources, pollution and accidents.*	I *Includes worldwide scientific, medical and technological developments, natural phenomena, U.S. weather and natural disasters.*	J *Includes the arts, religion, scholarship, communications media, sports, entertainment, fashions, fads and social life.*	

	World Affairs	Europe	Africa & the Middle East	The Americas	Asia & the Pacific
Dec. 22					Speaking before the Security Council, Dutch delegate Jan Herman van Royan calls the invasion of the Indonesian Republic an internal "police action" over which the U.N. has no jurisdiction. U.S. delegate Philip Jessup condemns the invasion as lacking "any justification," while the State Dept. suspends $14.1 million in Marshall Plan aid to the Dutch East Indies .... Japanese miners', textile workers', maritime and electrical workers' unions obey a U.S. order to end major strikes in connection with the newly proclaimed austerity program.
Dec. 23		Yugoslavia signs a one-year, $120-million trade agreement with Britain after promising to compensate British owners of nationalized Yugoslavian factories.	Israeli-Egyptian truce in the Negev desert breaks down as Israeli forces attack Egyptian positions near Gaza and other coastal cities.		Hideki Tojo and six other Japanese war leaders are hanged at Sugamo prison in Tokyo .... Japanese Diet passes a vote of no confidence in the rightist Yoshida cabinet, forcing the government to dissolve parliament and call new elections for early 1949.
Dec. 24		Greek Communist guerrillas shell the port of Salonika.	Egyptian warplanes attack Nazareth, Tel Aviv and Haifa following the renewal of fighting in the Negev desert.	Organization of American States in Washington calls on Costa Rica and Nicaragua to refrain from hostile acts against one another after an OAS investigating commission reports that Nicaragua did not aid but could have stopped the invasion of Costa Rica by exiled supporters of former Pres. Rafael Calderon Guardia.	U.N. Security Council passes a cease-fire resolution calling on Holland to halt offensive operations in Indonesia and release imprisoned Indonesian Republic leaders. Indonesian Republic spokesmen attack the resolution as "meaningless" in the absence of demands for Dutch withdrawal from captured territory .... Allied headquarters in Tokyo dismisses war crimes charges against 16 Japanese war leaders, ruling that their cases are similar to those of defendants acquitted by the International War Crimes Tribunal.
Dec. 25					Chinese Nationalists abandon Changkiakow, one of their few remaining industrial centers in northern China, to the Communists .... Last Russian occupation troops leave North Korea.
Dec. 26			Jewish immigration to Israel since the end of the British mandate passes 100,000.		
Dec. 27		Hungarian government arrests Joseph Cardinal Mindszenty, leader of the country's Catholic church and a strong anti-Communist, with 13 other church officials on charges of espionage, treason and black market currency dealings .... Yugoslavia and Russia sign a commercial agreement in Moscow providing for a sharp reduction in trade between the two countries.			Guerrilla resistance to the Dutch occupation of the Indonesian Republic begins with scattered attacks on Dutch outposts near Jakarta .... U.N. Security Council rejects a Russian proposal that Holland be given a 24-hour ultimatum to halt all military operations in Indonesia.

A	B	C	D	E
Includes developments that affect more than one world region, international organizations and important meetings of major world leaders.	*Includes all domestic and regional developments in Europe, including the Soviet Union, Turkey, Cyprus and Malta.*	*Includes all domestic and regional developments in Africa and the Middle East, including Iraq and Iran and excluding Cyprus, Turkey and Afghanistan.*	*Includes all domestic and regional developments in Latin America, the Caribbean and Canada.*	*Includes all domestic and regional developments in Asian and Pacific nations, extending from Afghanistan through all the Pacific Islands, except Hawaii.*

U.S. Politics & Social Issues	U.S. Foreign Policy & Defense	U.S. Economy & Environment	Science, Technology & Nature	Culture, Leisure & Life Style	
A Senate Civil Service subcommittee approves a bill increasing the president's annual salary from $75,000 to $100,000 and giving him a larger expense account. The measure also raises the salaries of the vice president, speaker of the House and cabinet members.				John Randall Dunn, editor of the *Herald of Christian Science* and former president of the Mother Church, dies at 70 in Centerville, Mass.	Dec. 22
House Un-American Activities Comm. issues a pamphlet, *100 Things You Should Know About Communism in Labor,* attacking 20 CIO unions as Communist-controlled. Among the unions listed are the International Longshoremen's and Warehousemen's Union, the National Maritime Union, the United Public Workers of America and the United Electrical, Radio and Machine Workers of America. ILWU Pres. Harry Bridges is criticized with 13 other CIO officials as a Communist.	A four-man civilian commission recommends military pay increases for officers and top-grade enlisted men to make salaries comparable with civilian pay.				Dec. 23
Atty. Gen. Tom Clark announces the results of an FBI investigation clearing former State Dept. official Laurence Duggan of any connection with Communist espionage.				J. Gilmour Dobie, one of college football's best-known coaches, dies at 69 in Hartford, Conn.	Dec. 24
Federal Security Agency revives the National Advisory Comm. on the Education of Negroes, appointing Ambrose Caliver of the U.S. Office of Education to head the agency .... Medical committee of Hoover's Commission on Reorganization of the Executive Branch issues a report criticizing federal medical care programs as extravagant and inefficient, claiming that "the government is moving into uncalculated obligations without an understanding of their ultimate cost."				A *Down Beat* poll lists Duke Ellington's band as the nation's most popular music group.	Dec. 25
Former State Undersecy. Sumner Welles, a close friend of Laurence Duggan and a figure in the House Un-American Activities Comm. investigation of Communist espionage, is found unconscious and frozen in a field near his Oxen Hill, Md. home after suffering a heart attack while taking a walk .... A nine-man investigating committee of the Social Science Research Council reports in N.Y. that political pollsters "acted in good faith but used poor judgment" during the 1948 presidential campaign.		Rocco Franceschini, president of the CIO United Shoe Workers of America (one of the unions accused of being Communist-dominated by the House Un-American Activities Comm.), dies at 50 in N.Y.			Dec. 26
					Dec. 27

F	G	H	I	J
Includes elections, federal-state relations, civil rights and liberties, crime, the judiciary, education, health care, poverty, urban affairs and population.	*Includes formation and debate of U.S. foreign and defense policies, veterans affairs and defense spending. (Relations with specific foreign countries are usually found under the region concerned.)*	*Includes business, labor, agriculture, taxation, transportation, consumer affairs, monetary and fiscal policy, natural resources, pollution and accidents.*	*Includes worldwide scientific, medical and technological developments, natural phenomena, U.S. weather and natural disasters.*	*Includes the arts, religion, scholarship, communications media, sports, entertainment, fashions, fads and social life.*

	World Affairs	Europe	Africa & the Middle East	The Americas	Asia & the Pacific
Dec. 28		Representatives of the U.S., Britain, France, Holland, Belgium and Luxembourg, meeting in London, agree on formation of an international Ruhr Authority (excluding Russia) to supervise much of West Germany's heavy industry. France gains a British and American guarantee that Germany's industrial potential will never be allowed to threaten French security .... Yugoslavia's first postwar trade delegation to Italy begins discussions in Rome on a commercial treaty.	Egyptian Premier and Saadist Party leader Mahmoud Fahmy Nokrashy Pasha is assassinated in Cairo by a member of the outlawed Moslem Brotherhood, angered over Egyptian military reverses in Palestine. King Farouk names Ibrahim Abdel Hadi Pasha to succeed Nokrashy Pasha as premier.		
Dec. 29			U.N. Security Council passes a British resolution demanding an immediate ceasefire in the Negev desert and establishment of a no-man's land between Israeli and Egyptian forces. Israeli troops continue their advance along the Mediterranean coast, crossing into Egyptian territory at El Arish.		
Dec. 30		Spanish government establishes a 14-member Council of the Kingdom as an advisory board representing all administrative and legislative agencies .... Vatican announces the excommunication of all Catholics who had a hand in the arrest of Hungary's Cardinal Mindszenty.			Chinese Communist forces reach the Yangtze River east of Nanking.
Dec. 31					China's Pres. Chiang Kai-shek issues a peace proposal to the Chinese Communists, offering to resign and allow formation of a coalition government based on the Nationalist constitution. Communist leaders immediately reject any compromise with the Nationalist regime .... Holland declares its "police action" on Java at an end, with all objectives taken.

A	B	C	D	E
Includes developments that affect more than one world region, international organizations and important meetings of major world leaders.	*Includes all domestic and regional developments in Europe, including the Soviet Union, Turkey, Cyprus and Malta.*	*Includes all domestic and regional developments in Africa and the Middle East, including Iraq and Iran and excluding Cyprus, Turkey and Afghanistan.*	*Includes all domestic and regional developments in Latin America, the Caribbean and Canada.*	*Includes all domestic and regional developments in Asian and Pacific nations, extending from Afghanistan through all the Pacific Islands, except Hawaii.*

U.S. Politics & Social Issues	U.S. Foreign Policy & Defense	U.S. Economy & Environment	Science, Technology & Nature	Culture, Leisure & Life Style	
		House Small Business Comm. urges a tightening of antitrust laws, with provisions for mandatory suspension of business executives convicted of antitrust violations and revisions of tax laws advantageous to large companies.		Hooperatings list *Jack Benny*, *Radio Theater* and *Walter Winchell* as the nation's most popular radio programs. Milton Berle's *Texaco Star Theater* leads the New York Hooper television rating.	Dec. 28
	Defense Secy. James Forrestal issues his first annual report on the national defense establishment, urging introduction of universal military training, increased military aid to anti-Communist governments and greater power for the Defense Secretary over the separate service secretaries. Forrestal reveals that Defense Dept. researchers are studying an "earth satellite vehicle program" for military use . . . . Navy reports the successful testing of the heaviest armed single-engine carrier-based aircraft, the Martin M-1 Mauler.				Dec. 29
House Un-American Activities Comm. issues a pamphlet, *100 Things You Should Know About Communism and Government*, charging that Communist spy operations continue in the State Dept. and other agencies despite Truman's loyalty check program. The report urges restrictions on Communist activity and increased penalties for contempt of Congress.			U.N. Food and Agriculture Organization and the World Health Organization announce plans for joint campaigns in 1949 against malaria, tuberculosis, venereal disease and malnutrition.	Internal Revenue Service forces comedian Jack Benny to pay a 75% personal income tax instead of a 25% capital gains tax on his profit from the sale of his Amusement Enterprises, Inc. to CBS . . . . Musical comedy *Kiss Me Kate*, with music and lyrics by Cole Porter, opens in N.Y. to favorable reviews . . . . Bertrand Russell's *Human Knowledge: Its Scope and Limits* is published in N.Y. by Simon and Schuster.	Dec. 30
Democratic congressional leaders agree to continued operation of the House Un-American Activities Comm., but promise that witnesses will have greater protection . . . . Republican-controlled 80th Congress adjourns as Senate Democrats choose Kenneth McKellar of Tennessee as president pro tempore and Scott Lucas of Illinois as majority leader for the 81st Congress.			Heavy precipitation followed by floods strikes the Northeast, causing four deaths and isolating many towns in Connecticut and Massachusetts.		Dec. 31

F	G	H	I	J
Includes elections, federal-state relations, civil rights and liberties, crime, the judiciary, education, health care, poverty, urban affairs and population.	*Includes formation and debate of U.S. foreign and defense policies, veterans affairs and defense spending. (Relations with specific foreign countries are usually found under the region concerned.)*	*Includes business, labor, agriculture, taxation, transportation, consumer affairs, monetary and fiscal policy, natural resources, pollution and accidents.*	*Includes worldwide scientific, medical and technological developments, natural phenomena, U.S. weather and natural disasters.*	*Includes the arts, religion, scholarship, communications media, sports, entertainment, fashions, fads and social life.*

1949

Justice Dept. employe Judith Coplon is escorted from New York federal court on March 5 following her arraignment on charges of conspiracy to commit espionage. She was convicted after a highly publicized trial.

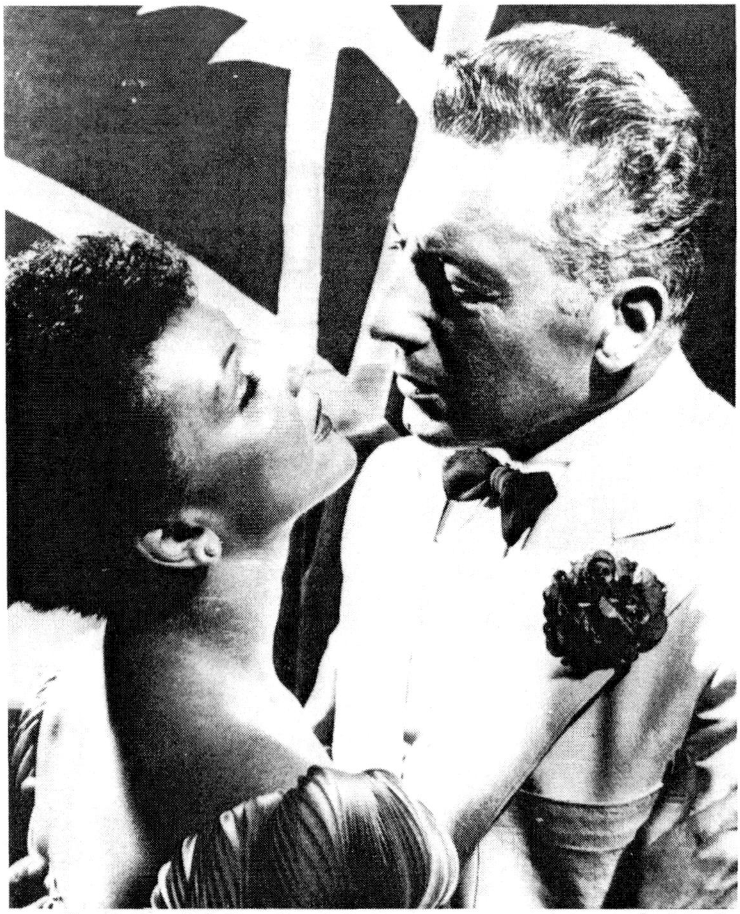

Mary Martin and Ezio Pinza starred in the Rodgers and Hammerstein musical *South Pacific*, which began its Broadway run on April 7 with record advance sales.

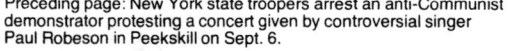

Preceding page: New York state troopers arrest an anti-Communist demonstrator protesting a concert given by controversial singer Paul Robeson in Peekskill on Sept. 6.

Jakarta residents celebrate Indonesian independence from Holland on Aug. 17. Susanto Tirtodiprodje, who represented Indonesia in negotiations with the Dutch, addresses the crowd.

New York Catholics gather on the steps of St. Patrick's Cathedral to protest the imprisonment of Hungary's Josef Cardinal Mindszenty.

U.S. airmen in Frankfurt celebrate the end of the Berlin blockade, May 10.

Nationalist soldiers seek refuge in French Indochina on Dec. 21 after the Communist conquest of the Chinese mainland.

Albert Einstein propounded a theory of gravitation in 1949 which reduced the basic physical laws of the universe to four equations. Even fellow physicists failed to understand the new hypothesis.

Eating in front of the television became a common feature of daily life in 1949, as TV invaded the homes of millions of Americans with the advent of cheap sets.

International Longshoremen's Union leader Harry Bridges talks to reporters in New York on Sept. 10 after discussing the 133-day-old strike of Hawaiian dock workers with federal mediator Cyrus Ching.

War in Vietnam: French paratroopers hunting Viet Minh guerrillas cross a stream on the Plain of Jars near Giong Dinh, Nov. 4.

	World Affairs	Europe	Africa & the Middle East	The Americas	Asia & the Pacific
Jan.		Russia responds to the Marshall Plan with measures increasing its economic control over Eastern Europe, including formation of CEMA (Council for Economic Mutual Assistance).	Israel and Egypt conduct armistice talks, but reach no agreement.	Military officers increase their influence over government in Peru and El Salvador.	Chiang Kai-shek resigns the Nationalist Chinese presidency as Communist forces continue their drive on Nanking.
Feb.		Eastern European governments begin a campaign against Catholic church leaders, highlighted by the espionage conviction of Hungary's Josef Cardinal Mindszenty.	Chaim Weizmann becomes president of Israel, as Israel and Egypt conclude an armistice agreement.		World pressure forces Holland to resume negotiations with Indonesian nationalist leaders on formation of an independent Indonesian state.
March	Twelve Western nations negotiate a North Atlantic security pact, forming the basis for NATO .... U.S. and Russian representatives conduct negotiations on the Berlin problem, the U.S. offering to convene a conference on all German questions in exchange for immediate lifting of the Soviet blockade.		Lebanon, Syria and Transjordan begin armistice negotiations with Israel, as Britain protests the alleged Israeli threat to the British-garrisoned port of Aqaba.	Argentine Pres. Peron increases his power as the country's new constitution goes into effect.	Communists begin organizing a civil administration in central China.
Apr.	U.N. General Assembly debates excessive use of veto power by permanent members of the Security Council.	German political leaders begin arrangements for creation of a West German state.	Israel successfully completes armistice negotiations with Syria and Transjordan.		Chinese Communist forces capture Nanking and trade fire with British ships on the Yangtze River.
May	Allied foreign ministers meet in Paris to discuss the status of Germany as Russia ends the Berlin blockade.	French and Russian protests fail to prevent establishment of a West German state .... Ten Western European states form an advisory Council of Europe.		Argentine government completes nationalization of important foreign-owned industries.	Communists consolidate their hold on central China and advance southward, capturing Shanghai, Wuhan and Hangchow.
June		Eastern European governments begin show trails of conservative political leaders accused of espionage.			France attempts to establish a conservative Vietnamese state in Indochina, ruled by political figures opposed to Ho Chi Minh.
July		Britain consults with other Western nations on means of easing its acute balance of payments difficulties .... Continuing conflict between Eastern European governments and the Catholic Church results in excommunication of all active Communists.	U.N. mediator Ralph Bunche proclaims a successful conclusion to months of Middle Eastern peace efforts.		Dutch forces complete their evacuation of Indonesian Republic territory .... Communist forces penetrate the "rice bowl" of southern China in their drive on Canton.
Aug.		First postwar election campaign in West Germany results in victory for the conservative Christian Democrats .... Greek government forces continue to restrict the guerrilla-controlled area near the Albanian border.		Civil unrest, attributed to Communists, breaks out in Bolivia and Chile.	Chiang Kai-shek attempts to form an anti-Communist Pacific alliance with other Asian governments as Communist forces continue their drive through southern China.
Sept.	Britain sets off a wave of currency devaluations among Western states by devaluing the pound to reduce its critical balance of payments deficit.	Political tensions rise in Eastern Europe as Russia and its satellite states cancel trade, transport and mutual aid and friendship agreements with Yugoslavia. The U.S. begins restoration of commercial ties with the Tito government.		Argentine government further limits public criticism of the Peron regime .... Bolivian government suppresses a rightist revolt.	Chinese Communists organize a national government, known as the People's Republic of China.
Oct.	Defense ministers of North Atlantic Treaty states meet in Washington to formulate alliance defense plan.	Russia establishes a separate state in its occupation zone of Germany .... Czech government moves to restrict freedom of Catholic clergy.			Communist forces overrun the South China coast, capturing the port cities of Canton and Amoy.
Nov.	U.N. General Assembly debates nuclear arms control without reconciling Russian and U.S. viewpoints.			A struggle over the presidency develops in Panama, where National Police head Jose Remon ousts Pres. Daniel Chanis.	Communist forces push inland in southern China, taking the temporary Nationalist capital of Chungking.
Dec.	Representatives of anti-Communist labor groups meet in London to form an organization which will rival the Communist-dominated World Confederation of Trade Unions.	Debate over West German rearmament begins in Europe and the U.S. after Chancellor Konrad Adenauer offers to help the West defend itself against Russia .... Yugoslavia strengthens its commercial ties with Britain and the U.S.	Israeli government transfers most of its ministries to Jerusalem in an effort to thwart U.N. plans to internationalize the city.		Western nations begin to debate the recognition of Communist China as Nationalist troops abandon the mainland. U.S. State Dept. urges postponement of recognition .... Holland withdraws from the East Indies as the United States of Indonesia comes into existence.

A	B	C	D	E
Includes developments that affect more than one world region, international organizations and important meetings of major world leaders.	*Includes all domestic and regional developments in Europe, including the Soviet Union, Turkey, Cyprus and Malta.*	*Includes all domestic and regional developments in Africa and the Middle East, including Iraq and Iran and excluding Cyprus, Turkey and Afghanistan.*	*Includes all domestic and regional developments in Latin America, the Caribbean and Canada.*	*Includes all domestic and regional developments in Asian and Pacific nations, extending from Afghanistan through all the Pacific Islands, except Hawaii.*

U.S. Politics & Social Issues	U.S. Foreign Policy & Defense	U.S. Economy & Environment	Science, Technology & Nature	Culture, Leisure & Life Style	
Trial of 11 U.S. Communist leaders, charged with advocating violent overthrow of the government, opens in New York.	Navy and Air Force adjust to lower budgets, eliminating some weapons systems.	Deflationary economic trend continues, indicated by a 1% drop in the consumer price index and a decline in individual incomes and corporate profits.	Heavy snowfalls cause severe damage to agriculture in Western states.		Jan.
Truman begins a conflict with the American Medical Assn. and private insurance companies over the Administration's proposed national health insurance plan .... Hoover Commission on Reorganization of the Executive Branch, headed by former Pres. Herbert Hoover, begins issuing a series of reports criticizing bureaucratic inefficiency and recommending elimination of overlapping federal functions.		Deflationary economic trend depresses farm prices, bringing them to their lowest level since 1946.	As temperatures reach record highs in the East, rail traffic between the Midwest and the West Coast is disrupted by snow.	American Catholics protest the controversial conviction of Hungarian prelate Cardinal Mindszenty.	Feb.
Several state governments move to restrict Communist political activities .... Hoover Commission on Reorganization of the Executive Branch concludes its review of the federal bureaucracy.	U.S. initiates a joint radar defense program with Canada.	Economic indicators point downward at the end of the year's first quarter, with industrial production falling $9 billion.		College basketball season concludes as Kentucky captures the NCAA and San Francisco the NIT championship.	March
	Congress completes action on the $5.4 billion Marshall Plan program for Europe.	Government action against the deflationary economic trend begins as the Federal Reserve Bd. lowers credit restrictions.	Pacific Northwest cleans up following the region's most damaging earthquake on record.	Roger and Hammerstein's *South Pacific* begins a long-term Broadway performance.	Apr.
Controversy over segregated higher education surfaces in several Southern states.	Congress takes action to strengthen the Defense Dept. and Central Intelligence Agency.	CIO moves to take disciplinary action against Communists within its organization.			May
Judith Coplon's espionage trial and Alger Hiss' perjury trial focus public attention on alleged Communist subversion.		Sustained selling drives down prices on the N.Y. Stock Exchange, a reflection of the continued deflationary economic trend.			June
National attention focuses on the loyalty of American Negroes as singer Paul Robeson and baseball player Jackie Robinson make conflicting statements on civil rights and Communism.	Senate completes consideration of the North Atlantic security pact, overriding the opposition of Robert Taft and other conservative Republicans.		Leading American scientists speak out against FBI loyalty checks of atomic researchers.		July
Senate begins investigation of alleged influence-peddling by Administration officials.	House completes its investigation of the Air Force's B-36 bomber procurement program, clearing participants of charges of favoritism and influence-peddling.	Government spokesmen announce that the deflationary economic trend has bottomed out .... UAW presses for introduction of company-financed worker pensions in the auto industry.	U.N. Scientific Conference on Conservation and Utilization of Resources meets in N.Y. to consider problems in the supply of oil and other raw materials.		Aug.
	Congress completes work on a $1.3 billion measure providing military aid to Western European states and other friendly governments.	Miners strike again in a dispute over company contributions to the UMW welfare fund.	Senate completes action on a measure providing federal aid for medical training and facilities.	National tennis tournaments are played on both the East and West coasts.	Sept.
N.Y. conspiracy trial of U.S. Communist leaders ends with guilty sentences for all defendants.	Controversy over the Administration's defense policies erupts as Navy officers accuse the Army and Air Force of underrating sea power.	Steel workers strike in a pension plan dispute .... Congress debates proposed changes in agricultural price supports without result.		Major League baseball ends as the New York Yankees sweep the World Series from the Brooklyn Dodgers.	Oct.
Second N.Y. perjury trial of Alger Hiss and San Francisco perjury trial of union leader Harry Bridges again focus public attention on the question of domestic Communism.	Truman takes steps to halt the leaking of atomic energy information to the public.	Coal and steel strikes end, permitting U.S. industry to return to capacity production.			Nov.
	Navy begins to shift its focus of strength from the Pacific to the Atlantic to meet the Soviet military challenge.	Labor groups continue to demand pension-welfare benefits from employers.	A water shortage plagues northern New Jersey and adjacent areas of New York.	Milton Berle's *Texaco Star Theater* is the most-viewed television program at year's end, attracting three-fourths of the nation's TV audience.	Dec.

F	G	H	I	J
Includes elections, federal-state relations, civil rights and liberties, crime, the judiciary, education, health care, poverty, urban affairs and population.	*Includes formation and debate of U.S. foreign and defense policies, veterans affairs and defense spending. (Relations with specific foreign countries are usually found under the region concerned.)*	*Includes business, labor, agriculture, taxation, transportation, consumer affairs, monetary and fiscal policy, natural resources, pollution and accidents.*	*Includes worldwide scientific, medical and technological developments, natural phenomena, U.S. weather and natural disasters.*	*Includes the arts, religion, scholarship, communications media, sports, entertainment, fashions, fads and social life.*

	World Affairs	Europe	Africa & the Middle East	The Americas	Asia & the Pacific
Jan. 1		Poland eliminates all rationing.	Egyptian ships bombard Tel Aviv in an unsuccessful attempt to impose a blockade on Israel . . . . Heavy snowfall in Iran causes 60 deaths as earthen houses collapse in Teheran and other cities.		India and Pakistan order a ceasefire in Kashmir after agreeing to a U.N.-sponsored plebiscite on the territory's future status . . . . New Zealand takes possession of the formerly British Tokelau (Union) Islands 300 miles north of Somoa . . . .
Jan. 2		Vatican rejects a Hungarian government offer to negotiate an agreement on the status of the country's Catholic church.			
Jan. 3		Russian authorities in Germany enact a two-year economic plan aimed at achieving 81% of the Soviet zone's 1936 production . . . . A cold wave in Western Europe causes 39 deaths with high gales and floods.	Egypt accepts the U.N. Security Council's ceasefire demand as Israeli forces advance into the Egyptian Sinai desert.		Philippine government establishes a central bank similar to the U.S. Federal Reserve System.
Jan. 4		U.N. Security Council committee of experts issues a plan for settlement of the Berlin currency control dispute, calling for creation of separate banking systems for East and West Berlin and a new bank of issue for the entire city under Big Four supervision.			Dutch Premier Willem Drees leaves Holland on a peace mission to Indonesia.
Jan. 5			South African Negroes break off all political relations with whites due to government plans to disband the advisory Negroes' Representative Council and refusal to restore the Negro franchise.	Maj. Oscar Osorio succeeds Col. Manuel de Jesus Cordova as head of El Salvador's five-man military junta.	Dutch forces declare their "police action" in Sumatra at an end . . . . Nationalist Gen. Pai Chung-hsi withdraws his troops from a defense perimeter around the central Chinese industrial city of Wuhan without government authorization.
Jan. 6			Gen. Nuri as-Said, a supporter of Transjordanian King Abdullah's claim to sovereignty over Arab Palestine, becomes Iraqi premier.		Congressional investigator William Bullitt reports to the Joint Congressional Comm. on Foreign Cooperation that only direct U.S. intervention in the Chinese civil war and $800 million in military aid a year can save the Nationalist government. U.N. Secy. Gen. Trygve Lie refuses to support Nationalist requests for U.N. intervention in China.
Jan. 7		British press king Lord Beaverbrook quits the Conservative Party, charging that party leaders seek to foster Britain's economic dependence on the U.S.	Israeli-Egyptian ceasefire takes effect in the Negev desert, shortly after Israeli forces down five British reconnaisance planes near the Egyptian border.		Chinese Communist forces enter Tientsin, North China's leading industrial city, in heavy fighting . . . . Dutch authorities release nine interned Indonesian leaders but restrict four, including Pres. Ahmed Sukarno and Premier Mohammed Hatta, to the island of Banka . . . . New clashes between Karen nationalists and government forces break out in southern Burma.
Jan. 8		Soviet troops and East German police begin digging trenches across main roads to West Berlin to tighten their blockade of the city.	Britain announces plans to station British troops in the Transjordanian Red Sea port of Aqaba to prevent further Israeli incursions into Arab territory.	Peru's 13-man military junta assumes legislative powers for the country.	Gen. Yoshijiro Umezu, wartime head of the Japanese General Staff recently sentenced to life imprisonment by the Tokyo war crimes tribunal, dies at 67 of cancer in Tokyo.
Jan. 9			Britain puts its Mediterranean forces on alert and threatens to take military action against Israel to prevent further downings of RAF planes in the Negev desert.		
Jan. 10		Gen. Lucius Clay of the U.S. military government warns of a revival of extreme nationalism in Germany, citing the activities of the National Democratic Party and former Nazi Otto Strasser's Black Front.	U.N. Secy. Gen. Trygve Lie and the U.S. State Dept. press Britain to de-emphasize its dispute with Israel over the downing of RAF planes.		Chinese Communists announce the start of a renewed drive on Nanking following the elimination of two Nationalist army groups south of Suchow . . . . Malayan government issues emergency regulations against aiding Communist insurgents, threatening to arrest all residents of an area harboring guerrillas.

A	B	C	D	E
Includes developments that affect more than one world region, international organizations and important meetings of major world leaders.	*Includes all domestic and regional developments in Europe, including the Soviet Union, Turkey, Cyprus and Malta.*	*Includes all domestic and regional developments in Africa and the Middle East, including Iraq and Iran and excluding Cyprus, Turkey and Afghanistan.*	*Includes all domestic and regional developments in Latin America, the Caribbean and Canada.*	*Includes all domestic and regional developments in Asian and Pacific nations, extending from Afghanistan through all the Pacific Islands, except Hawaii.*

U.S. Politics & Social Issues	U.S. Foreign Policy & Defense	U.S. Economy & Environment	Science, Technology & Nature	Culture, Leisure & Life Style	
				Major college bowl scores: Rose, Northwestern 20—California 14; Sugar, Oklahoma 14—North Carolina 6; Orange, Texas 41—Georgia 28; Cotton, SMU 21—Oregon 13; and Gator, Clemson 24—Missouri 23.	Jan. 1
	United Jewish Appeal announces in N.Y. that it collected over $150 million in 1948, the largest relief fund ever raised by a private agency.			An AP poll names the world champion Cleveland Indians the best sports team of 1948 .... Reuben Fine wins the International Chess Masters tournament in N.Y.	Jan. 2
Democratic-controlled 81st Congress convenes. Rep. Sam Rayburn (D, Tex.) is elected Speaker of the House and John McCormack (D, Mass.) House majority leader, while Sen. Robert Taft (R, Ohio) defeats a moderate Republican challenge to his leadership of the Senate Republican Policy Comm. .... Administration supporters in the House gain passage of a measure curbing the power of the House Rules Comm. to block legislation.		Supreme Court upholds the right of states to ban the closed shop in decisions sustaining the anti-closed shop laws of Nebraska, North Carolina and Arizona.	A tornado destroys most of Warren, Ark., causing at least 51 deaths and 275 injuries.	Frank Gilbreth's and Ernestine Carey's *Cheaper by the Dozen* is published by Crowell and becomes a January Book-of-the-Month-Club selection .... Former St. Louis Browns manager Luke Sewell signs as Cincinnati Reds coach .... Monument sculptor Robert Ingersoll Aitken dies at 70 in N.Y.	Jan. 3
		A special House investigating committee clears high Adminstration officials of charges that they used confidential government information to speculate on the commodity markets.	Physicist August Pfund, an authority on optics, dies at 69 in Baltimore.		Jan. 4
Truman delivers his State of the Union message to Congress, urging enactment of a comprehensive legislative program which he labels the "Fair Deal." Among the measures which he advocates are repeal of the Taft-Hartley Act, a higher minimum wage, increased taxes, public housing funds, a national health insurance program, continued agricultural price supports and universal military service.		Bell & Howell Pres. Joseph McNabb dies at 61 in Chicago.			Jan. 5
			National Bureau of Standards reports development of an "atomic clock" so accurate that it will take three million years to gain or lose a second.	An AP poll of sports writers names Cleveland Indians manager-shortstop Lou Boudreau as best male athlete of 1948 and Dutch Olympic track star Fanny Blankers-Koen as best female athlete .... Victor Fleming, director of *Joan of Arc* and other films, dies at 60 in Cottonwood, Ariz.	Jan. 6
A federal court in Mobile strikes down an Alabama state law seeking to limit the Negro vote by requiring registered voters to "understand and explain" the Constitution.	State Secy. George Marshall retires for reasons of health. Truman nominates former State Undersecy. Dean Acheson to succeed him.	Truman submits his annual economic report to Congress, urging enactment of the economic legislation advocated in his State of the Union address to ensure a 3-4% growth rate and one million more jobs for the coming year.		Elin Wagner, Swedish novelist and only woman in the Swedish Academy, dies at 66 in Berglund, Sweden.	Jan. 7
		CIO inaugurates a Southern organizing "crusade" with a convention in Atlanta.		Fordham Univ. takes team honors in the Knights of Columbus track games in N.Y.	Jan. 8
			William Kelley, inventor of the Kelley automatic printing press, dies at 79 in Summit, N.J.		Jan. 9
Truman presents Congress with a record peacetime budget of $41.9 billion, projecting an $873-million deficit unless his tax program is passed. The largest part of the budget ($14.3 billion) is devoted to defense costs, followed by $6.7 billion for foreign aid and "cold war" expenditures .... Sens. J. Howard McGrath (D, R.I.) and Matthew Neely (D, W. Va.) introduce amendments to the refugee immigration act liberalizing non-quota entry provisions.				Lloyd Mangrum wins the $10,000 Los Angeles Open golf tournament.	Jan. 10

F	G	H	I	J
Includes elections, federal-state relations, civil rights and liberties, crime, the judiciary, education, health care, poverty, urban affairs and population.	*Includes formation and debate of U.S. foreign and defense policies, veterans affairs and defense spending. (Relations with specific foreign countries are usually found under the region concerned.)*	*Includes business, labor, agriculture, taxation, transportation, consumer affairs, monetary and fiscal policy, natural resources, pollution and accidents.*	*Includes worldwide scientific, medical and technological developments, natural phenomena, U.S. weather and natural disasters.*	*Includes the arts, religion, scholarship, communications media, sports, entertainment, fashions, fads and social life.*

	World Affairs	Europe	Africa & the Middle East	The Americas	Asia & the Pacific
Jan. 11		U.S. refuses a Hungarian request to return the 950-year old Crown of St. Stephen, held by American authorities in Germany after being recovered from the Nazis.		Argentina issues the draft of a revised constitution favored by Pres. Peron, allowing Peron to succeed himself at the end of his term.	U.S. delegate Philip Jessup attacks Dutch policy in Indonesia before the U.N. Security Council, demanding that Holland withdraw its forces from the Indonesian Republic and call free elections for an Indonesian government.
Jan. 12		Russian authorities issue stringent penalties for economic offenses in their zone of Germany, including 10 years' imprisonment for violation of price laws . . . . French cabinet freezes prices and wages at their levels of Dec. 31, 1948.	Acting State Secy. Robert Lovett meets with Israeli, British and Transjordanian diplomats in Washington in an effort to prevent extension of Palestine fighting.		Chinese Nationalist cabinet urges all important government officials to leave Nanking for Canton or Taiwan.
Jan. 13		British authorities order West German Communist leader Max Reimann to stand trial on charges of threatening German politicians who cooperate with Western Allies on international control of the Ruhr.	U.N. Mediator Ralph Bunche begins Israeli-Egyptian armistice talks at his headquarters on the island of Rhodes.		Communist forces shell Peking for the first time in the Chinese civil war . . . . MacArthur issues a directive to the Japanese government easing restrictions on foreign business investments in Japan . . . . A Philippine electoral tribunal annuls the House of Representatives mandate of Hukbalahap guerrilla leader Luis Taruc.
Jan. 14		French Foreign Min. Robert Schuman and British Foreign Secy. Ernest Bevin complete two days of talks in London after agreeing to support creation of new political institutions for the Western European Union and insisting on the continued dismantling of German factories for reparations . . . . West Berlin City Assembly convenes and reelects Mayor Ernst Reuter and Assembly Pres. Otto Suhr . . . . An Oslo meeting of Swedish, Danish and Norwegian defense ministers ends without agreement on proposals to join the projected North Atlantic defense organization . . . . Britain and Poland sign a trade agreement providing for a $1-billion exchange of goods over the next five years, the largest deal made by an Eastern European state since the war.			Chinese Communist leader Mao Tze-tung broadcasts his conditions for peace over the North Shensi radio, demanding abolition of the Nationalist government, punishment of Chiang Kai-shek and other leading Nationalists, introduction of a land reform program and election of a Political Consultative Conference to create a new government . . . . U.N. observers in Batavia report the outbreak of large-scale guerrilla resistance in northern and central Java and claim that Dutch forces are not strong enough to maintain order on the island.
Jan. 15		Greek Premier Themistocles Sophoulis resigns as a result of cabinet disputes over social reforms, military appointments and composition of the governing coalition. Government forces drive guerrillas from the Macedonian town of Maoussa after a two-day battle.			Chinese Communist forces complete their conquest of the northern industrial city of Tientsin, leaving Peking and Taiyuan as the only cities north of the Yangtze still in Nationalist hands . . . . U.S. Army 24th Corps, the occupation force in South Korea since the Japanese surrender, is deactivated in Seoul.
Jan. 16		Russia and Poland announce the signing of a commercial agreement calling for a 35% increase in trade between the two countries . . . . Shemsettin Gunaltay becomes premier of Turkey following the resignation of Hasan Saka, under criticism for rising living costs.	Four days of rioting between Zulu natives and Indians around Durban, South Africa ends with 137 deaths and 1,883 injuries. Race riots are also reported in the Rand mining district of the Transvaal . . . . Israel announces the withdrawal of its forces from four Lebanese villages in an effort to stimulate armistice talks with Lebanon and Transjordan.		Chinese Nationalist government moves its capital from Nanking to Canton . . . . U.S. cuts off wheat and flour shipments to China pending civil war developments . . . . Leon Pignon, French High Commissioner for Indochina, holds talks in Cannes with former Vietnamese Emperor Bao Dai, urging him to return to Vietnam as head of a French-sponsored provisional government.
Jan. 17					

A	B	C	D	E
Includes developments that affect more than one world region, international organizations and important meetings of major world leaders.	*Includes all domestic and regional developments in Europe, including the Soviet Union, Turkey, Cyprus and Malta.*	*Includes all domestic and regional developments in Africa and the Middle East, including Iraq and Iran and excluding Cyprus, Turkey and Afghanistan.*	*Includes all domestic and regional developments in Latin America, the Caribbean and Canada.*	*Includes all domestic and regional developments in Asian and Pacific nations, extending from Afghanistan through all the Pacific Islands, except Hawaii.*

U.S. Politics & Social Issues	U.S. Foreign Policy & Defense	U.S. Economy & Environment	Science, Technology & Nature	Culture, Leisure & Life Style	
An all-white jury in Lyons, Ga. clears William Howell of murder charges in the death of Robert Mallard, a local Negro.	Air Force announces cancellation of $300 million in orders for jet fighters and other light planes in favor of long-range B-29 bombers.		San Diego, Calif. is blanketed with its first snowfall in history as a two-week cold wave grips the West Coast, causing extensive damage to citrus crops.	Publisher Nelson Doubleday dies at 59 in Oyster Bay, N.Y. . . . . Cunard liner *Caronia*, the largest passenger ship built since the war, completes its maiden voyage from Southampton to New York.	Jan. 11
Sen. Hubert Humphrey (D, Minn.) succeeds Leon Henderson as national chairman of Americans for Democratic Action . . . . Radio commentator Fulton Lewis, Jr. accuses the U.S. Atomic Energy Commission of giving secret nuclear information to Univ. of North Carolina Pres. Frank Porter Graham after Graham was declared a security risk by the AEC security advisory board.				Willie Howard, comedian and Broadway musical star, dies at 62 in N.Y.	Jan. 12
Senate approves and sends to the House a bill authorizing a presidential pay raise to $100,000 annually and a $50,000 tax-free expense account.	Truman meets with British Amb. Sir Oliver Franks to discuss Middle East problems, later denying any strain on U.S.-British relations . . . . Army temporarily suspends conscription due to a high voluntary enlistment rate and anticipated financial curtailments resulting from Truman's budget request . . . . Truman appoints Gens. Omar Bradley and Carl Spaatz and Adm. Raymond Spruance to permanent four-star rank.				Jan. 13
Atty. Gen. Tom Clark urges Congress to enact new anti-espionage laws introducing penalties for unauthorized possession of official secrets, allowing wiretapping in investigation of such cases and cancelling the statute of limitations in espionage prosecutions . . . . N.Y. federal Judge Harold Medina refuses a request by 12 top U.S. Communists that their trial be postponed for 90 days due to the continued illness of William Foster.	Senate Foreign Relations Comm. unanimously recommends Dean Acheson's confirmation as State Secretary after two days of hearings on Acheson's views . . . . State Dept. issues a policy statement reaffirming U.S. willingness to join a North Atlantic security alliance to defend Marshall Plan gains in Western Europe from Communist attempts at subversion.	Justice Dept. files an antitrust suit in Newark, N.J. demanding that the Western Electric Co. be separated from AT&T and split into three competing firms.			Jan. 14
Air Force submits a personnel policy statement to Defense Secy. Forrestal, promising elimination of segregation and discrimination against Negro airmen . . . . Charles Ponzi, con artist who engineered a multi-million dollar fraud in 1920 by promising investors he could "double your money in 90 days" by purchasing International Postal Union coupons, dies at 71 in Rio de Janeiro.	Navy Secy. John Sullivan reveals in his annual report that the Navy has exceeded its budget since the end of the war, maintaining its strength by using up war reserves and carry-over funds.			Broadway comedy *Harvey* closes after 1,775 performances.	Jan. 15
				Marshall Teague wins the National Stock Car championship in a 100-mile race at Daytona Beach, Fla.	Jan. 16
Trial of 11 U.S. Communist leaders on charges of advocating the violent overthrow of the U.S. government begins in N.Y. . . . . House passes a Senate-approved measure increasing the salaries of the president, vice president and speaker of the House . . . . Truman asks Congress for permanent power to reorganize executive departments and agencies . . . . Former U.S. Army aviator Martin Monti pleads guilty to treason and is sentenced to 25 years imprisonment in N.Y. for defecting to the Axis during World War II . . . . Supreme Court rules that August Klapprott, jailed former German-American Bund leader, did not get a fair trial in 1941 and must be retried on charges leading to revocation of his citizenship.				Grenville Baker, heir to the George Baker banking fortune, is shot to death on the family's palatial Horseshoe Plantation near Tallahassee, Fla.	Jan. 17

F	G	H	I	J
Includes elections, federal-state relations, civil rights and liberties, crime, the judiciary, education, health care, poverty, urban affairs and population.	*Includes formation and debate of U.S. foreign and defense policies, veterans affairs and defense spending. (Relations with specific foreign countries are usually found under the region concerned.)*	*Includes business, labor, agriculture, taxation, transportation, consumer affairs, monetary and fiscal policy, natural resources, pollution and accidents.*	*Includes worldwide scientific, medical and technological developments, natural phenomena, U.S. weather and natural disasters.*	*Includes the arts, religion, scholarship, communications media, sports, entertainment, fashions, fads and social life.*

	World Affairs	Europe	Africa & the Middle East	The Americas	Asia & the Pacific
Jan. 18			Bowing to U.S. pressure, British Foreign Secy. Bevin agrees to release 11,000 Jewish immigrants interned on Cyprus and urges Arab nations to negotiate a permanent peace settlement with Israel.	Britain, Argentina and Chile agree to refrain from naval maneuvers in Antarctica below 60' S latitude.	Russia rejects a Nationalist appeal for Big Four mediation of the Chinese civil war.
Jan. 19	U.S., British and Dutch labor representatives withdraw from the World Federation of Trade Unions in Paris, charging that the organization has become a Communist front.	Hungarian government publishes an alleged confession by Josef Cardinal Mindszenty admitting to cooperating with Western agents in an attempt to overthrow the government . . . . RAF Lt. Josef Horak dies at 33 in Bristol, England of injuries sustained in a plane crash. Horak, a native of Lidice, was mistakenly tied to the 1941 assassination of Reinhard Heydrich by the Nazis, who destroyed the Czech town in retaliation.	Export-Import Bank authorizes a $35-million loan to Israel for agricultural development.		China's Nationalist cabinet adopts a statement calling for an immediate ceasefire and the start of peace negotiations with the Communists.
Jan. 20		Themistocles Sophoulis forms a new five-party Greek cabinet, naming Field Marshal Alexander Papagos commander-in-chief of government forces with full power to conduct operations against Communist guerrillas . . . . Former Hungarian War Min. Albert Bartha charges in a Vienna interview that Hungary's Russian-controlled army exceeds its peace treaty limit by 5,000 men . . . . Spain devalues its currency from 16.4 to 25 pesetas per U.S. dollar.			
Jan. 21		Polish government demotes Deputy Premier Wladyslaw Gomulka to assistant budget director for deviating from the Communist Party line on farm collectivization and Yugoslavia, while Socialist leader Edward Osubka-Morawski resigns as public administration minister for opposing the recent merger of the Communist and Socialist parties . . . . James Thomas, former railway labor leader and member of five British cabinets, dies at 74 in London.		U.S. grants diplomatic recognition to the military governments of Venezuela and El Salvador, emphasizing that the action does not "imply any judgment whatsoever as to the domestic policies" of either regime.	Chinese Pres. Chiang Kai-shek resigns, turning over leadership of the Nationalist government to Vice Pres. Li Tsung-jen. Chiang immediately leaves Nanking by plane for his home in Fenghwa. T.V. Soong, Chiang's brother-in-law, resigns as governor of Kwangtung Province in southern China . . . . U.S., China, Cuba and Norway offer a Security Council resolution on Indonesia, urging a ceasefire in Sumatra and Java, gradual withdrawal of Dutch troops from Indonesia and formation of an Indonesian federation . . . . South Korean government reports an anti-Communist rising in the North Korean town of Haeju near the 38th parallel boundary.
Jan. 22			Israeli-Egyptian armistice negotiations in Rhodes are suspended due to disagreement over the extent of Israeli withdrawal to be required in the Negev desert.	Huron Indian Jules Sioui receives a two-year prison sentence in Quebec for conspiracy to incite Canadian Indians to rebellion through his activities as secretary-treasurer of the "Government of the North American Indian Nation."	Nationalist forces in Peking surrender the city to the Communists, while Acting Pres. Li Tsung-jen appoints a five-man delegation to negotiate an end to the civil war in the Communist capital of Yenan . . . . Dutch Foreign Min. Derek Stikker rejects U.N. Security Council demands for a ceasefire on Java and Sumatra, claiming that it would result in "chaos." . . . . Nineteen-nation Asian Conference on Indonesia, meeting in New Delhi, demands Dutch withdrawal from Indonesia by March 15 and creation of an independent Indonesian state. The conference also recommends creation of regional consultative agencies for Asia and Africa . . . . Rebellious Karen nationalists isolate Rangoon from railroad connections with the rest of Burma by cutting the Rangoon-Mandalay line near Toungoo.
Jan. 23					Japan's third postwar parliamentary election gives an absolute majority in the Diet to Premier Shigeru Yoshida's Democratic Liberal Party. Communists also score large electoral gains, mostly at the expense of Social Democrats.
	A *Includes developments that affect more than one world region, international organizations and important meetings of major world leaders.*	B *Includes all domestic and regional developments in Europe, including the Soviet Union, Turkey, Cyprus and Malta.*	C *Includes all domestic and regional developments in Africa and the Middle East, including Iraq and Iran and excluding Cyprus, Turkey and Afghanistan.*	D *Includes all domestic and regional developments in Latin America, the Caribbean and Canada.*	E *Includes all domestic and regional developments in Asian and Pacific nations, extending from Afghanistan through all the Pacific Islands, except Hawaii.*

U.S. Politics & Social Issues	U.S. Foreign Policy & Defense	U.S. Economy & Environment	Science, Technology & Nature	Culture, Leisure & Life Style	
House Democrats approve new committee chairmen, including Emanuel Celler of N.Y. for the Judiciary Comm. and John Wood of Georgia for the Un-American Activities Comm. .... N.Y. federal Judge Harold Medina severs the trial of U.S. Communist Party Chmn. William Foster from that of 11 other leading Communists due to Foster's poor health.	Senate confirms Dean Acheson as State Secretary .... Paul Alling, U.S. ambassador to Pakistan, dies at 52 of amoebic dysentery in Bethesda, Md.				Jan. 18
Truman signs a bill raising his annual salary to $100,000.	Defense Secy. Forrestal reports that the armed services have reached the personnel goals set by Truman for fiscal 1950, eliminating the need for conscription in the near future.	An NLRB trial examiner invalidates union shop provisions in the UMW contract with coal mines owned by steel firms .... Trenton, N.J. federal Judge Phillip Forman finds GE, Westinghouse, Corning Glass and six other manufacturers guilty of violating antitrust laws by conspiring to monopolize the incandescent electric lamp industry in the U.S.	Gulf Oil tanker *Gulfstream* rams into the Coast Guard icebreaker *Eastwind* near Barnegat, N.J., resulting in 13 deaths and 18 injuries.	MGM's war drama *Command Decision* premiers in N.Y.	Jan. 19
Truman is sworn in as president by Chief Justice Frederick Vinson. His inaugural address stresses continued U.S. support for the U.N., the Marshall Plan and anti-Communist military alliances.	State Secy. George Marshall formally relinquishes his office to Dean Acheson.	George Mead, aircraft engine designer and a co-founder of Pratt & Whitney, dies at 57 in West Hartford, Conn.			Jan. 20
South Dakota becomes the 22nd state to ratify a proposed constitutional amendment limiting a president to two terms.				Unable to reach an agreement on merger with the National League, the All-American Football Conference announces plans to operate as a seven-team league this year .... National Football League directors approve the transfer of the Boston Yanks to New York.	Jan. 21
Univ. of Washington Bd. of Regents dismisses Professors Herbert Philipps and Joseph Butterworth for membership in the Communist Party and Prof. Ralph Gundlach for refusing to state his position on Communism. The three immediately ask the American Assn. of University Professors to intervene on their behalf .... Detroit Police Commissioner Harry Toy orders newspaper reporters seeking unrestricted police and fire press cards to sign an anti-Communist loyalty oath.				Jamaican runner Herb McKenley sets a new world record for the 220-yd. dash in Sydney, Australia at 21 secs.	Jan. 22
Joe Blythe, treasurer of the Democratic National Committee, dies at 58 in Washington.		Air Force inaugurates "Operation Haylift" to drop feed to livestock cut off as a result of a series of blizzards over the West Central and Mountain states.		Jacob Blaustein is elected president of the American Jewish Comm. in N.Y., succeeding Joseph Proskauer .... Patty Berg of Minneapolis wins the Women's Golf Open in Tampa, Fla. .... Frank Kovacs takes the men's singles title and Welby Van Horn and Jim Evert the men's doubles title in the National Professional Clay Court Tennis meet in St. Augustine, Fla.	Jan. 23
F	G	H	I	J	
Includes elections, federal-state relations, civil rights and liberties, crime, the judiciary, education, health care, poverty, urban affairs and population.	*Includes formation and debate of U.S. foreign and defense policies, veterans affairs and defense spending. (Relations with specific foreign countries are usually found under the region concerned.)*	*Includes business, labor, agriculture, taxation, transportation, consumer affairs, monetary and fiscal policy, natural resources, pollution and accidents.*	*Includes worldwide scientific, medical and technological developments, natural phenomena, U.S. weather and natural disasters.*	*Includes the arts, religion, scholarship, communications media, sports, entertainment, fashions, fads and social life.*	

	World Affairs	Europe	Africa & the Middle East	The Americas	Asia & the Pacific
Jan. 24					
Jan. 25		Russia announces creation of a Soviet-bloc counterpart to the Organization for European Economic Cooperation. Called the Council for Economic Mutual Assistance (CEMA), the new organization includes all Eastern European states except Yugoslavia.	Israel's first parliamentary election results in a large plurality for Premier David Ben-Gurion's moderate Socialist (Mapai) Party, which gains 35.8% of the popular vote.		Count Nobuaki Makino, Emperor Hirohito's political adviser and keeper of the privy seal, dies at 88 in Tanaka, Japan.
Jan. 26		Former German diplomat Franz von Papen is freed by a German denazification court in Nuremberg, which reclassifies him as a secondary Nazi offender.			U.S. formally terminates its Army Advisory Group in China.
Jan. 27		Greek Communist guerrillas offer to discuss peace if the government agrees to a ceasefire and promises to release political prisoners and stop taking U.S. aid . . . . Russia and Rumania sign a commercial agreement providing for a 150% increase in trade between the two countries.			Passenger liner *Taiping*, carrying refugees from the Chinese mainland to Taiwan, collides with the freighter *Kienyuan* near Shanghai, causing 600 deaths.
Jan. 28	N.Y. architect firm of Fuller, Turner, Walsh & Slattery, Inc. receives a $23.8-million contract to build a 39-story U.N. headquarters in Manhattan.	Foreign ministers of Britain, France, Holland and Luxembourg conclude a London conference by announcing plans to form a Council of Europe as the political basis of a European federation. The organization will consist of a committee of ministers delegated by member states and an advisory parliament which will consider matters referred to it by the ministerial committee.			U.N. Security Council passes a U.S.-sponsored resolution calling for a ceasefire in Indonesia, release of Indonesian Republic leaders and creation of a U.N. Commission for Indonesia to mediate Dutch-Indonesian differences. Although the plan does not call for withdrawal of Dutch troops from Indonesia, it is rejected by Holland . . . . Sen. Patrick McCarran (D, Nev.), chairman of the Joint Congressional Comm. on Foreign Cooperation, urges a $1.5-billion U.S. loan to the Chinese Nationalist government for military and economic aid, to be accompanied by U.S. supervision of Nationalist armies.
Jan. 29		Greek government rejects the peace discussion offer of Communist guerrillas.			
Jan. 30	Responding to questions sent by the International News Service, Stalin offers to meet with Truman to discuss a non-aggression declaration. He also promises to lift the Berlin blockade if the Western Allies postpone creation of a separate West German state, omitting mention of the Berlin currency dispute as an obstacle to settlement.			A dissident faction of Paraguay's Colorado Party, led by Raimondo Rolon, forces the five-month old government of Pres. Juan Natalicio Gonzales to resign. The National Assembly elects Rolon president and schedules new elections for April.	
Jan. 31					
	A	B	C	D	E
	Includes developments that affect more than one world region, international organizations and important meetings of major world leaders.	*Includes all domestic and regional developments in Europe, including the Soviet Union, Turkey, Cyprus and Malta.*	*Includes all domestic and regional developments in Africa and the Middle East, including Iraq and Iran and excluding Cyprus, Turkey and Afghanistan.*	*Includes all domestic and regional developments in Latin America, the Caribbean and Canada.*	*Includes all domestic and regional developments in Asian and Pacific nations, extending from Afghanistan through all the Pacific Islands, except Hawaii.*

U.S. Politics & Social Issues	U.S. Foreign Policy & Defense	U.S. Economy & Environment	Science, Technology & Nature	Culture, Leisure & Life Style	
Treason trial of Mildred Gillars on charges of making wartime "Axis Sally" broadcasts opens in Washington.	House Ways and Means Comm. opens hearings on the Administration's proposal to extend the Reciprocal Trade Agreement Act.	Rep. Brent Spence (D, Ky.) and Sen. Burnet Maybank (D, S.C.) introduce bills in Congress supporting Truman's proposal to extend rent controls until March 31, 1951 .... Orlando Miller, leading paper merchant and co-founder of the National Assn. of Manufacturers, dies at 89 in Columbus, Ohio.			Jan. 24
					Jan. 25
Former Newark, N.J. Police Judge P. James Pellecchia is sentenced to 10-15 years imprisonment by a Newark court for embezzling $663,850 to cover gambling losses.		AFL International Brotherhood of Teamsters takes over a 6,000-member CIO United Distribution Workers local in St. Louis in an attempt to begin organization of department store workers .... Dun & Bradstreet wholesale food price index drops to $5.91, the lowest level since price controls ended in October 1946.			Jan. 26
Pennsylvania Rep. Hugh Scott, Jr. narrowly retains his position as GOP National Committee chairman, defeating a challenge by supporters of Harold Stassen, Robert McCormick and Sen. Robert Taft .... House Republican conference replaces the House GOP Steering Comm. with a Policy Comm. chosen on a geographical basis. The measure reduces the policy-making influence of senior Republicans and gives greater weight to "progressives" within the party .... Sen. Richard Russell (D, Ga.) introduces a measure providing federal aid to encourage the migration of Southern Negroes to the North .... Sam Carr, wanted in Canada on Soviet espionage charges, is arrested by the FBI in N.Y. and taken to Ellis Island for deportation.	Lewis Hershey gains Senate confirmation as Selective Service director.	Truman nominates Export-Import Bank Chmn. William McChesney Martin, Jr. as assistant Treasury secretary .... Truman allotts $300,000 in disaster funds to snowbound West Central and Mountain states.		Athenagoras I is formally installed in Istanbul as Patriarch of the Greek Orthodox Church .... Former Postmaster-Gen. Robert Hannegan sells his interest in the St. Louis Cardinals to Fred Saigh, Jr. for about one million dollars.	Jan. 27
	Gen. Bryant Moore succeeds Gen. Maxwell Taylor as superintendent of West Point. Taylor becomes chief of staff of U.S. forces in Europe.			New York *Star* ceases publication.	Jan. 28
	Navy's fastest and most powerful cruiser, the *Newport News*, is commissioned in Newport News, Va.	Administration issues its proposed National Labor Relations Act of 1949, to replace the Taft-Hartley Act. The measure eliminates several provisions of the existing law, including prohibition of the closed shop and affidavit requirements for union officials.		Ace Admiral, with Johnny Gilbert up, wins the $137,200 Santa Anita Maturity Stakes in Arcadia, Calif.	Jan. 29
		Brotherhood of Locomotive Engineers suspends a strike scheduled for tomorrow against 15 Western railroads following creation of an emergency board by Truman to investigate union demands for a second engineer on diesel locomotives.		Sverre Kongsgaard of Norway sets a North American competitive ski jump record of 290 feet at Olympian Hill near Hyak, Wash. .... *New York Herald Tribune* lists Lloyd Douglas' *The Big Fisherman* and Dwight Eisenhower's *Crusade in Europe* as the best-selling fiction and non-fiction books.	Jan. 30
Supreme Court rejects former Texas Gov. Coke Stenson's plea for a review of his 1948 primary election dispute with Sen. Lyndon Johnson (D, Tex.).	Truman grants full U.S. recognition to Israel and Transjordan .... Dean Rusk, director of the State Department's Office of U.N. Affairs, is named assistant state secretary.	Senate confirms Truman's appointment of Maurice Tobin as Labor secretary .... Senate Small Business Comm. issues a report on its 1½-year study of the U.S. oil industry, charging that 20 "large, integrated oil companies" dominate domestic petroleum production and marketing. The report claims that the 1947 oil shortage was induced by companies to increase prices.		Paul Brown signs a five-year contract to coach the Cleveland Browns .... Fleming Newbold, president of the Washington *Star*, dies at 75 in Washington.	Jan. 31
F *Includes elections, federal-state relations, civil rights and liberties, crime, the judiciary, education, health care, poverty, urban affairs and population.*	G *Includes formation and debate of U.S. foreign and defense policies, veterans affairs and defense spending. (Relations with specific foreign countries are usually found under the region concerned.)*	H *Includes business, labor, agriculture, taxation, transportation, consumer affairs, monetary and fiscal policy, natural resources, pollution and accidents.*	I *Includes worldwide scientific, medical and technological developments, natural phenomena, U.S. weather and natural disasters.*	J *Includes the arts, religion, scholarship, communications media, sports, entertainment, fashions, fads and social life.*	

	World Affairs	Europe	Africa & the Middle East	The Americas	Asia & the Pacific
Feb. 1		In a diplomatic note to Russia, Norway announces it must seek the protection of the projected North Atlantic security alliance following the breakdown of Scandinavian regional defense negotiations .... A British military court in Duesseldorf sentences Communist leader Max Reimann to three months in prison for encouraging Germans to ostracize those cooperating with the Western Allies.	Israeli cabinet announces plans to incorporate the new city of Jerusalem into Israel despite U.N. efforts to make Jerusalem an international city .... Transjordan's King Abdullah agrees to join the Israeli-Egyptian armistice conference on Rhodes.		Acting Nationalist Pres. Li Tsung-jen names an eight-man civilian delegation to arrange for an official peace conference in Peking .... Philippine security forces report capturing the Sierra Madre headquarters of the Hukbalahap guerrillas in central Luzon.
Feb. 2	State Secy. Dean Acheson holds a press conference to give the U.S. response to Stalin's peace conference proposal. He states that the U.S. will not engage in bilateral negotiations on matters affecting other nations, and claims that "normal [diplomatic] channels" should be adequate to resolve the Berlin dispute and other East-West difficulties.	Hungarian opposition leader Istvan Barankovics dissolves the Catholic People's Democratic Party in protest against government policies.			South Korea formally applies for admission to the U.N.
Feb. 3	Truman tells a White House press conference that he will not meet alone with Stalin unless the Soviet Premier comes to Washington as his personal guest.	Treason trial of Hungarian Primate Josef Cardinal Mindszenty and six co-defendants opens in Budapest. Mindszenty reads a statement admitting to most of the prosecution's charges that he engaged in illegal currency dealings and plotted with Western agents to overthrow the government and restore the Hungarian monarchy .... Western Allies impose a blockade on truck traffic between Western Europe and the Soviet zone of Germany .... Russian authorities in Berlin force a division of the city's court system between eastern and western sectors.			Burmese government forces report defeating Karen nationalists at Insein near Rangoon, removing the rebel threat to the capital.
Feb. 4		Testifying at his Budapest trial, Cardinal Mindszenty denies that his confession was forced by torture or drugs and retracts a pre-trial statement repudiating any confession he might make. Britain and the U.S. protest the exclusion of their observers from the trial, claiming this violates the Hungarian peace treaty .... Greek Communist radio announces the replacement of Gen. Markos Vafiades as guerrilla leader by Party Gen. Secy. Nicholas Zachariades.	Iranian Shah Mohammed Riza Pahlevi is shot and wounded by reporter Fakhr Raiee, who is beaten to death by the crowd and the Shah's guards.		
Feb. 5		Three-day trial of Cardinal Mindszenty ends as Mindszenty expresses regret for acting against the government and declares that he is not an enemy of the Hungarian people.	Lebanon and Syria agree to enter the Rhodes peace conference on condition that Israeli troops leave Lebanese soil .... Iranian government outlaws the leftist Tudeh political party following the attempted assassination of the Shah and student demonstrations against foreign oil concessions in Iran.		
Feb. 6					
Feb. 7		British P.M. Attlee and French Foreign Min. Robert Schuman declare that they oppose further Big Four meetings on any level until Russia lifts the Berlin blockade or makes some other gesture of cooperation.			
Feb. 8		A Budapest court sentences Cardinal Mindszenty to life imprisonment for treason and other crimes against the state. Mindszenty's six co-defendants also receive prison sentences ranging from life to three years .... Poland reports the arrest of 20 Catholic priests for reading a forbidden pastoral letter charging government officials with anti-religious actions .... Chase National Bank of N.Y. announces a $25-million, short-term private loan to Spain.			U.S. Army Dept. releases details of a report on a wartime Russian espionage network in the Far East. Headed by Richard Sorge, German press attache in Tokyo, the ring informed Moscow of German plans to invade Russia, Japan's intention to strike at Southeast Asia rather than Siberia and other important developments. The report was prepared by Gen. MacArthur's staff.
	A *Includes developments that affect more than one world region, international organizations and important meetings of major world leaders.*	B *Includes all domestic and regional developments in Europe, including the Soviet Union, Turkey, Cyprus and Malta.*	C *Includes all domestic and regional developments in Africa and the Middle East, including Iraq and Iran and excluding Cyprus, Turkey and Afghanistan.*	D *Includes all domestic and regional developments in Latin America, the Caribbean and Canada.*	E *Includes all domestic and regional developments in Asian and Pacific nations, extending from Afghanistan through all the Pacific Islands, except Hawaii.*

U.S. Politics & Social Issues	U.S. Foreign Policy & Defense	U.S. Economy & Environment	Science, Technology & Nature	Culture, Leisure & Life Style	
Displaced Persons Commission issues its first semi-annual report, complaining that restrictive provisions of the 1948 immigration law have severely hampered its ability to bring refugees into the U.S. The report urges elimination of provisions of the law discriminating against Jews and Catholics .... N.Y. Gov. Thomas Dewey submits a record $936.2-million state budget for fiscal 1949-50, to be financed in part by a two-thirds increase in the state income tax.	Veterans Admin. Carl Gray, Jr. announces Administration opposition to a bill sponsored by Rep. John Rankin (D, Miss.) providing pensions for all disabled or aged war veterans.			Olympic skater Barbara Ann Scott is named winner of the Lou Marsh Memorial Trophy as Canada's outstanding 1948 athlete.	Feb. 1
				Bill and Charles DeWitt acquire control of the St. Louis Browns baseball team from Richard Muckerman for an estimated $1 million.	Feb. 2
Independence, Mo. Mayor Roger Sermon announces plans for a $3½-million library and museum to honor Truman.	Enlisted men sit on an Army court martial for the first time in Heidelberg, convicting two privates of manslaughter and sentencing them to seven years in prison.			An *Editor & Publisher* survey reports that U.S. newspaper circulation in 1948 hit a new record for the eighth straight year: daily 52,285,297 and Sunday 46,308,081.	Feb. 3
Judge Harold Medina charges defense lawyers for 11 Communist leaders with deliberate "stalling" and attempting to wear him down, as the third week of the N.Y. trial ends without a jury being chosen.			Civil Aeronautics Admin. authorizes commercial planes to use ground-controlled approach radar as a "primary aid" for landings in bad weather.		Feb. 4
		AFL Executive Council concludes a seven-day meeting in Miami after unanimously approving the Administration's proposed revision of the Taft-Hartley Act.	A four-day blizzard centered in Nebraska, Colorado and Wyoming ends after disrupting Chicago-California rail traffic.	General Council of the Congregational Christian Churches votes to merge with the Evangelical and Reformed Church to form a new two-million-member United Church of Christ.	Feb. 5
	Speaking to a graduating class at Lehigh Univ. in Bethlehem, Pa., U.S. Atomic Energy Commission Chmn. David Lilienthal claims that most developments in nuclear research "can with safety be publicly reported and publicly discussed."			Francis Cardinal Spellman leads nationwide Catholic protests against the trial of Hungary's Cardinal Mindszenty, preaching a sermon on Mindszenty's "martyrdom" and denouncing Communists as "men of slaughter." .... Francis Snow, linguist and former managing editor of *Current History*, dies at 72 in N.Y.	Feb. 6
House passes and sends to the Senate a bill giving the President permanent power to reorganize government agencies.	Senate approves Truman's nomination of MIT Pres. Karl Compton as chairman of the Defense Department's Research and Development Bd. Dean Rusk is also confirmed as assistant secretary of state.	The greaest influx of livestock to U.S. markets in a year causes a drastic decline in meat prices on livestock exchanges .... Senate confirms Truman's appointment of William McChesney Martin, Jr. as assistant Treasury secretary.		New York Yankee outfielder Joe DiMaggio signs for the coming season at a $90,000 salary.	Feb. 7
N.Y. Gov. Thomas Dewey complains at a Lincoln Day dinner in Washington that the GOP is "split wide open" by reactionaries "who want to turn the clock back" and by "liberals" who try to "outpromise the Democrats."		Farm commodity prices begin a rapid drop as the Dun & Bradstreet wholesale food price index falls to $5.66, its lowest level since late 1946.	A test tube containing one ounce of uranium oxide is discovered missing from a U.S. Atomic Energy Commission laboratory in Palos Park, Ill., setting off an intensive search.	Cleveland *Press* editor Louis Seltzer and three *Press* staff members are fined $1,000 for arranging and publicizing a false divorce in an effort to demonstrate that divorces are easy to obtain in Cleveland.	Feb. 8
F *Includes elections, federal-state relations, civil rights and liberties, crime, the judiciary, education, health care, poverty, urban affairs and population.*	G *Includes formation and debate of U.S. foreign and defense policies, veterans affairs and defense spending. (Relations with specific foreign countries are usually found under the region concerned.)*	H *Includes business, labor, agriculture, taxation, transportation, consumer affairs, monetary and fiscal policy, natural resources, pollution and accidents.*	I *Includes worldwide scientific, medical and technological developments, natural phenomena, U.S. weather and natural disasters.*	J *Includes the arts, religion, scholarship, communications media, sports, entertainment, fashions, fads and social life.*	

	World Affairs	Europe	Africa & the Middle East	The Americas	Asia & the Pacific
Feb. 9		U.S. State Secy. Dean Acheson attacks the Budapest trial of Cardinal Mindszenty as a "conscienceless attack upon religious and personal freedom," while the Hungarian government expels Robin Steussy, U.S. deputy consul in Budapest, for helping Hungarians to flee the country. The U.S. House of Representatives passes a resolution urging the State Dept. to take the Mindszenty case before the U.N.	Israel announces completion of negotiations with five Eastern European states for the immigration of 60-80,000 Jews to Palestine.		
Feb. 10	U.N. Security Council rejects a Russian resolution urging gradual disarmament and a report on arms stockpiled by the great powers. Truman refuses to consider disclosing the number of nuclear weapons in the U.S. arsenal.	Fifteen Protestant church leaders are indicted in Bulgaria on charges of espionage and black market dealings .... Legislative elections in Northern Ireland result in a large majority for the Protestant, pro-British Unionist Party .... French Foreign Min. Robert Schuman receives West Berlin Mayor Ernst Reuter in Paris, the first official visit of a leading German to France since the end of the war.	An Israeli military court in Acre sentences Stern Gang leaders Nathan Yellin and Matityahu Shmulevitz to prison terms of eight and five years for terrorist activities.		North Korea formally applies for U.N. membership .... A special New Delhi court hands down a death sentence for Nathuram Vinayak Godse, confessed assassin of Mohandas Gandhi.
Feb. 11		Norwegian Foreign Min. Halvard Lange completes six days of discussions in Washington on possible Norwegian participation in the North Atlantic security pact .... Portuguese Gen. Jose Norton de Mattos withdraws as opposition candidate for president, charging that the government has not guaranteed a fair election.	Britain completes the release of Jewish immigrants interned on Cyprus to Palestine.	Canadian P.M. Louis St. Laurent arrives in Washington to confer with Truman on the North Atlantic Security pact, integration of U.S. and Canadian radar defenses and the proposed St. Lawrence waterway .... Accused Soviet spy Sam Carr and his wife are deported from the U.S. to Canada, where he is jailed in Ottawa.	
Feb. 12		Switzerland and the Benelux Customs Union sign an agreement in Brussels for mutual reduction of customs charges March 1.		Twenty persons die in a riot in Quito, Ecuador following a radio broadcast based on *War of the Worlds*, depicting a Martian invasion of Quito. After discovering the broadcast is fictional, a mob sacks and burns the building housing the radio station.	
Feb. 13		Presidential elections in Portugal result in an unopposed victory for Gen. Antonio de Fragoso Carmona, a supporter of Premier Antonio Salazar.		Canadian P.M. Louis St. Laurent ends three days of talks in Washington on defense and economic problems.	
Feb. 14	Australia becomes the first country to ratify the International Labor Organization convention on wages and hours of seamen drawn up in 1946.	Russian authorities arrest Anna Strong, pro-Soviet author and publisher of the former English-language *Moscow Daily News*, on charges of espionage .... U.S. demands that the U.N. Economic and Social Council investigate Russian labor camps, claiming that eight to 14 million prisoners are held there under conditions of slavery.	Israel's Constituent Assembly is sworn in by Acting Pres. Chaim Weizmann in Jerusalem. Western states boycott the ceremony, protesting that Jerusalem is an international city by U.N. declaration.		
Feb. 15					Chinese Acting Pres. Li Tsung-jen appeals for an end to embezzlement of public funds by government officials and army officers, claiming that the Nationalist regime will otherwise be "ruined."
Feb. 16	Russia, the Ukraine and White Russia withdraw from the World Health Organization, charging that its work in disease control and dissemination of medical knowledge is unsatisfactory.	Gen. Lucius Clay of the U.S. military government in Germany orders the Russian refugee repatriation mission to leave the U.S. zone, claiming it has had enough time to process all refugees who want to return to Russia.	Rabbi Abba Hillel Silver resigns as American section head of the Jewish Agency for Palestine and Emanuel Neumann resigns as president of the Zionist Organization of America in a dispute over the right of the United Jewish Appeal to supervise the use of funds donated to Israel by American Jews .... Leaders from Southern Rhodesia, Northern Rhodesia and Nyasaland meet in Livingston, Northern Rhodesia to plan creation of a South-Central African federation within the British Commonwealth.	Canadian Parliament approves a bill accepting Newfoundland as a new province.	U.N. Security Council refuses to consider North Korea's membership application after agreeing to consider the application of South Korea .... Dutch government announces its acceptance "in principle" of the U.N. plan for granting independence to Indonesia .... Japanese Premier Shigeru Yoshida names his third cabinet following his party's victory in parliamentary elections, appointing himself foreign minister.
Feb. 17			Israeli Constituent Assembly adopts an interim constitution limiting presidential authority and making the prime minister and his cabinet answerable to the Parliament. The Assembly also confirms Pres. Chaim Weizmann in his office .... Egyptian and Israel negotiators reach a tentative agreement on Rhodes to demilitarize Auja, a transit center near the Egyptian border.		Siam declares a state of emergency and closes its Malayan border to hinder the movement of Communist guerrillas.
	A *Includes developments that affect more than one world region, international organizations and important meetings of major world leaders.*	B *Includes all domestic and regional developments in Europe, including the Soviet Union, Turkey, Cyprus and Malta.*	C *Includes all domestic and regional developments in Africa and the Middle East, including Iraq and Iran and excluding Cyprus, Turkey and Afghanistan.*	D *Includes all domestic and regional developments in Latin America, the Caribbean and Canada.*	E *Includes all domestic and regional developments in Asian and Pacific nations, extending from Afghanistan through all the Pacific Islands, except Hawaii.*

U.S. Politics & Social Issues	U.S. Foreign Policy & Defense	U.S. Economy & Environment	Science, Technology & Nature	Culture, Leisure & Life Style	
House votes the Un-American Activities Comm. $200,000 for its operations this year.	U.S. Atomic Energy Commission announces plans to sponsor Westinghouse in construction of an experimental nuclear engine for warships.	House passes and sends to the Senate a measure extending the Reciprocal Trade Agreements Act of 1934 through mid-1951 and eliminating trade curbs imposed by the 80th Congress .... Congressional leaders cite falling food prices as justification for delaying action on Truman's request for a tax increase.		Actor Robert Mitchum receives a 60-day prison sentence in Los Angeles for possession of marijuana.	Feb. 9
Federal Loyalty Review Bd. clears Commerce Dept. official William Remington, accused by Elizabeth Bentley of participating in a Communist spy ring during the 1930s. The board's finding permits Remington's reinstatement in the Commerce Dept.		A clash between UAW organizers and CIO United Farm Equipment Workers union members in Moline, Ill. results in 22 injuries following the UFE's refusal to merge with the UAW in accordance with CIO orders .... Henry Atherton, board chairman of Allied Chemical Corp., dies at 65 in Boca Grande, Fla.		Arthur Miller's *Death of a Salesman*, staged by Elia Kazan, opens on Broadway to favorable reviews .... Joe Fulks scores 63 points for the Philadelphia Warriors, setting a Basketball Assn. of America individual game scoring record .... Former world tennis champion William Tilden is convicted in Los Angeles on a morals charge involving a 14-year-old boy and is sentenced to a year in prison.	Feb. 10
	Truman appoints Gen. Eisenhower temporary non-voting chairman of the Joint Chiefs of Staff. Eisenhower will also serve as principal military adviser to Truman and Defense Secy. Forrestal.			Willie Pep regains the world featherweight boxing title with a 15-round decision over Sandy Saddler in N.Y. .... Axel Munthe, author of the best-selling *Story of San Michele* and house physician of Sweden's late Queen Victoria, dies at 91 in Stockholm.	Feb. 11
	State Dept. orders John Florian, first secretary of the Hungarian legation in Washington, to leave the country in retaliation for Hungary's expulsion of U.S. diplomatic personnel.			Hit musical *Annie Get Your Gun* closes on Broadway after 1,147 performances.	Feb. 12
American Medical Assn. presents a national health care proposal stressing expansion of voluntary medical plans and greater state aid to the indigent. The proposal is intended as an alternative to Truman's compulsory medical insurance plan.		CIO Transport Workers Union ends a four-day strike against the Hudson and Manhattan Railroad, an important commuter line, after failing to gain union recognition.		Dave Douglas wins the Texas Open golf tournament in San Antonio .... World women's speed skating title is retained by Maria Isakova of Russia in Kongsberg, Norway.	Feb. 13
				British physicist P.M. Blackett's *Fear, War and the Bomb*, a study of the military and political consequences of nuclear weapons, is published in London by Whittlesey.	Feb. 14
		Rep. Brent Spence (D. Ky.) introduces the Administration's anti-inflation bill, which increases the President's power to regulate bank and consumer credit, prices and wages and other economic factors.	Thermometers in N.Y. soar to 71 degrees, a record for this date.		Feb. 15
		House passes and sends to the Senate a $471-million deficiency appropriation bill to carry 35 federal agencies through the rest of the current fiscal year.			Feb. 16
Mildred Gillars, on trial in Washington for wartime "Axis Sally" broadcasts, opens her defense with a plea that treason cannot be committed by "mere words." .... Truman asks Congress for $5.4 million to strengthen and rebuild the White House interior.					Feb. 17
F *Includes elections, federal-state relations, civil rights and liberties, crime, the judiciary, education, health care, poverty, urban affairs and population.*	G *Includes formation and debate of U.S. foreign and defense policies, veterans affairs and defense spending. (Relations with specific foreign countries are usually found under the region concerned.)*	H *Includes business, labor, agriculture, taxation, transportation, consumer affairs, monetary and fiscal policy, natural resources, pollution and accidents.*	I *Includes worldwide scientific, medical and technological developments, natural phenomena, U.S. weather and natural disasters.*	J *Includes the arts, religion, scholarship, communications media, sports, entertainment, fashions, fads and social life.*	

	World Affairs	Europe	Africa & the Middle East	The Americas	Asia & the Pacific
Feb. 18		First president of the Spanish Republic, Niceto Alcala Zamora, dies in exile at 71 in Buenos Aires.			
Feb. 19		Bulgaria publishes a confession attributed to arrested Protestant church leader Vassil Ziapkov, accusing himself and other Protestant leaders of cooperating with Western espionage agents .... Norway's governing Labor Party endorses Norwegian participation in the North Atlantic security pact at its Oslo convention .... East European and Western nations agree in Geneva to draw up lists of desired export and import items to facilitate a revival of trade between the two areas.			Indian government begins a roundup of leading Communists following suppression of an alleged Communist plot to seize power .... Burmese government announces that it is ready to grant the Karen ethnic minority a separate state within the Union of Burma.
Feb. 20			U.N. mediator Ralph Bunche submits the text of a proposed armistice agreement to Egyptian and Israeli negotiators on Rhodes. The agreement gives Israel temporary control over Beersheba and the Negev desert pending negotiation of a permanent peace settlement.		
Feb. 21		Norwegian Foreign Min. Halvard Lange announces Norway's decision to join the proposed North Atlantic security pact .... Greek Foreign Min. Constantin Tsaldaris meets in London with British Foreign Secy. Bevin to discuss a proposed Mediterranean defense alliance.		Costa Rica and Nicaragua sign a friendship agreement sponsored by the Pan American Union in Washington, ending their dispute over an invasion of Costa Rica by exiles from Nicaragua last December.	
Feb. 22		French Communist Party Secy. Maurice Thorez leads off a series of loyalty statements by world Communist leaders by declaring that French workers would aid the Soviet Army in the event of a war between Russia and the West .... Albania joins the Russian-sponsored Council for Economic Mutual Assistance .... Former German-American Bund leader Fritz Kuhn is freed by a German appeals court in Munich, which reduces his 10-year sentence as a major Nazi offender to the two years already served.			
Feb. 23		J.R. Campbell is appointed editor of London's Communist *Daily Worker* following the death of William Rust.	Saudi Arabia indicates willingness to accept any agreement with Israel negotiated by other Arab states.		
Feb. 24		Yugoslavian Deputy Foreign Min. Ales Beber offers to reduce his country's demands on Austria at a London conference on the Austrian peace treaty .... Pro-Soviet American writer Anna Strong arrives in N.Y. after being deported from Russia on espionage charges.	Israel and Egypt sign the armistice agreement proposed by Bunche in negotiations on Rhodes .... U.S. Commerce Dept. lifts a 10-month restriction against export of steel for completion of the 1,067-mile Trans-Arabian oil pipeline from Saudi Arabia to the Mediterranean .... South Africa discontinues annual reports to the U.N. on its Southwest Africa trust territory.		Nationalist peace envoys meet with Chinese Communist leaders Mao Tze-tung and Chou En-lai at Communist field headquarters near Peking.
Feb. 25		Fifteen Bulgarian Protestant leaders go on trial before a Sofia court on charges of espionage and currency speculation. Three defendants read confessions in the opening session .... German Economic Admin. of the U.S.-British zone nominates 12 management trustees to direct the heavy industry of the Ruhr. The nominees must be approved by Western Allied military governors .... Wuerttemberg-Baden Denazification Review Bd. nullifies the eight-year prison sentence of former Reichsbank director Hjalmar Schacht.	Truman appoints James McDonald first U.S. ambassador to Israel, while Eliahu Elath becomes Israeli ambassador to the U.S.		
	A	B	C	D	E
	Includes developments that affect more than one world region, international organizations and important meetings of major world leaders.	*Includes all domestic and regional developments in Europe, including the Soviet Union, Turkey, Cyprus and Malta.*	*Includes all domestic and regional developments in Africa and the Middle East, including Iraq and Iran and excluding Cyprus, Turkey and Afghanistan.*	*Includes all domestic and regional developments in Latin America, the Caribbean and Canada.*	*Includes all domestic and regional developments in Asian and Pacific nations, extending from Afghanistan through all the Pacific Islands, except Hawaii.*

U.S. Politics & Social Issues	U.S. Foreign Policy & Defense	U.S. Economy & Environment	Science, Technology & Nature	Culture, Leisure & Life Style	
	State Secy. Dean Acheson testifies before the Senate Foreign Relations Comm. on the proposed North Atlantic security pact, reporting that the U.S. is seeking an agreement which will imply but not promise U.S. action in the event of an attack on Western Europe.		Food and Drug Admin. orders lithium chloride, a salt substitute, withdrawn from the market after four deaths are traced to its use.		Feb. 18
Georgia legislature passes a voter registration bill imposing a literacy test and other measures intended to limit the Negro vote.	Truman reactivates the United Service Organizations to provide entertainment for a "large peacetime defense establishment."			Poet Ezra Pound receives the Bollingen Prize of the U.S. Library of Congress for his *Pisan Cantos*.	Feb. 19
		Eleven thousand Philadelphia Transit Co. workers end a 10-day strike by accepting an 8¢ hourly wage increase.			Feb. 20
	Hoover Commission on Reorganization of the Executive Branch issues a report on the conduct of foreign affairs, recommending clearer delineation of lines of authority within the State Dept. and closer coordination between the State Dept. and other government agencies concerned with foreign operations.	Truman formally presents his social security reform program to Congress asking for an increase in benefits, a reduction of the women's eligibility age, addition of disability insurance to present old age and survivors' insurance, an increase in payroll taxes and expansion of the categories of workers covered by social security .... NLRB rules that any labor action in support of a secondary boycott is illegal, including posting of boycott notices in union headquarters .... Senate passes a House-approved measure continuing Administration authority to control exports through mid-1951.			Feb. 21
Speaking at a Reserve Officers Assn. dinner in Arlington, Truman stirs up controversy by calling columnist Drew Pearson an "s.o.b." for suggesting that presidential military aide Harry Vaughn resign after accepting a military decoration from Argentine Pres. Peron.		Hoover Commission on Reorganization of the Executive Branch issues a report on agricultural policy, calling present levels of price supports and conservation payments unjustified and making recommendations for resolution of jurisdictional disputes between the Agriculture and Interior Departments.	Russell Porter, an expert on optics and builder of Mt. Palomar's 200-inch telescope, dies at 77 in Pasadena, Calif.		Feb. 22
Oregon State Univ. in Corvallis dismisses chemist Ralph Spitzer and economist L.R. La Vallee, both members of the Progressive Party, from its faculty.	House Armed Services Comm. passes a measure authorizing construction of a $161-million radar warning screen, to be linked with a similar facility in Canada.				Feb. 23
	State Secy. Acheson meets with 30 Republican congressmen demanding greater U.S. aid to China's Nationalist government. He refuses to promise any change in U.S. policy towards China .... Air Force displays its newest jet fighter, the Republic XF-91, designed to fly at 700-900 mph for high-altitude interception.	Senate Banking Comm. passes a bipartisan bill providing $1.8 billion in grants, loans and direct contributions for construction of low-cost public housing.		Sir Laurence Olivier's *Hamlet* wins the British Film Academy's top award as the best picture released in Britain during 1948.	Feb. 24
	A 20,000-man Navy task force returns to the U.S. after completing Operation Micowex, a month of amphibious maneuvers in the North Pacific.	GM announces that wages of 341,000 employees will be cut March 7 under its cost-of-living contract with the UAW due to falling living costs. The company also promises a price cut of $10-40 on new cars .... Civil Aeronautics Bd. grants a $7.8-million increase in airmail subsidies to seven U.S. airlines in an attempt to offset 1948 airline losses .... Eastern and National Airlines agree to interchange traffic between Florida and Texas.	A two-stage rocket soars to a record 250 miles at 5,000 mph above the White Sands proving grounds in New Mexico.		Feb. 25
F *Includes elections, federal-state relations, civil rights and liberties, crime, the judiciary, education, health care, poverty, urban affairs and population.*	G *Includes formation and debate of U.S. foreign and defense policies, veterans affairs and defense spending. (Relations with specific foreign countries are usually found under the region concerned.)*	H *Includes business, labor, agriculture, taxation, transportation, consumer affairs, monetary and fiscal policy, natural resources, pollution and accidents.*	I *Includes worldwide scientific, medical and technological developments, natural phenomena, U.S. weather and natural disasters.*	J *Includes the arts, religion, scholarship, communications media, sports, entertainment, fashions, fads and social life.*	

	World Affairs	Europe	Africa & the Middle East	The Americas	Asia & the Pacific
Feb. 26				Dissident Colorado Party members in Paraguay remove Provisional Pres. Raimundo Rolon in favor of former Education Min. Felipe Molas Lopez.	Dutch government promises to free all interned Indonesian Republic leaders and calls a conference of Indonesian political groups in The Hague . . . . Pakistan incorporates Baluchistan, a territory bordering on Iran and Afghanistan, as the country's fifth province.
Feb. 27				Luis Manuel Rojas Arreola, president of the 1916-17 congress which framed Mexico's constitution, dies in Mexico City.	Chinese Nationalist peace mission returns from Peking after conferring with Mao Tze-tung . . . . A two-day battle between Siamese Army and Navy forces ends in Bangkok with 50 soldiers dead. Government spokesmen blame the incident on agitation by dissident politicians.
Feb. 28		Russia reduces prices of clothing, food and other consumer goods by 10-30%.	Israeli troops occupy the fortress of Faluja in the Negev desert following withdrawal of the Egyptian garrison.		Indonesian Republic refuses to attend a Dutch-sponsored conference on Indonesia in The Hague, charging the Dutch with bypassing U.N. Security Council recommendations.
March 1			Israel opens direct armistice negotiations with Lebanon in the frontier town of Ras en Naqura.		Mrs. Sarojini Naidu, Indian independence leader and former president of the Indian National Congress, dies at 70 in Lucknow, India.
March 2		Rumanian government completes confiscation of large private landholdings.	Nahum Goldmann is named acting chairman of the Jewish Agency for Palestine's American section.	British House of Commons passes a bill authorizing Newfoundland's union with Canada.	
March 3		Norway requests and receives an invitation to attend North Atlantic treaty discussions in Washington and rejects Russia's offer of a non-aggression pact.			Truman meets with the National Security Council and top Treasury, State and Commerce Department officials to discuss extending aid to China beyond present April 3 deadline. Former Amb. to China Patrick Hurley charges in a Washington speech that the Yalta agreement undermined the Nationalist government by giving Russia Port Arthur and partial interest in China's Manchurian railways.
March 4	Security Council approves Israel's application for U.N. membership and passes it on to the General Assembly for final action.	Russia's Supreme Soviet announces replacement of Viacheslav Molotov by Andrei Vishinsky as foreign minister. Former Russian U.N. delegate Andrei Gromyko is promoted to first deputy foreign minister, while Molotov remains deputy premier and a member of the Communist Party Politburo . . . . Danish Foreign Min. Gustav Rasmussen announces plans to visit Washington and "investigate" the proposed North Atlantic security pact . . . . Italian Socialist Party directorate passes a resolution opposing Italian membership in the proposed North Atlantic security pact.			
March 5		Bulgarian trial of 15 Protestant ministers ends as defendants make final pleas for mercy, all but one admitting the charges against them . . . . A Budapest court hands down prison sentences for 13 small businessmen and church officials accused of complicity in the alleged black market dealings of Cardinal Mindszenty.	Jewish National Fund ends a six-day meeting in N.Y. after revealing plans to reclaim 25,000 acres of neglected Arab-owned land in Israel during the next three years.	Mexico's government oil monopoly, Pemex, signs a 12-year drilling contract with a U.S. group headed by Edwin Pauley.	
	A *Includes developments that affect more than one world region, international organizations and important meetings of major world leaders.*	B *Includes all domestic and regional developments in Europe, including the Soviet Union, Turkey, Cyprus and Malta.*	C *Includes all domestic and regional developments in Africa and the Middle East, including Iraq and Iran and excluding Cyprus, Turkey and Afghanistan.*	D *Includes all domestic and regional developments in Latin America, the Caribbean and Canada.*	E *Includes all domestic and regional developments in Asian and Pacific nations, extending from Afghanistan through all the Pacific Islands, except Hawaii.*

U.S. Politics & Social Issues	U.S. Foreign Policy & Defense	U.S. Economy & Environment	Science, Technology & Nature	Culture, Leisure & Life Style	
	Sen. Robert Taft opposes sending military equipment to Western European states under the proposed North Atlantic security pact, claiming it might goad Russia into a preventive attack.			Michigan State wins the intercollegiate 4-A indoor track and field title in N.Y., where West Point cadet James Sholtz throws the 35 lb. weight to a world shot put record of 60 ft. $7\frac{3}{4}$ in. . . . . Vulcan's Forge with Dave Gorman up wins the $139,100 Santa Anita Handicap in Arcadia, Calif.	Feb. 26
	Navy begins its largest postwar maneuvers to date with a simulated nuclear attack on surface ships in the Caribbean.		A joint meeting of the American Cancer Society and National Cancer Institute in Memphis ends after hearing a report linking increased cigarette smoking to the rapid rise in incidence of lung cancer during the last 25 years.		Feb. 27
Senate opens debate on an Administration-sponsored proposal to limit the filibuster. Southern Democrats filibuster against the measure . . . . N.Y. County Medical Society, the largest member group of the American Medical Assn., refuses to support the AMA's fight against Truman's compulsory medical insurance proposal.		Agriculture Dept. reports February farm prices at their lowest levels since September 1946.		Books published in N.Y. today include war hero Audie Murphy's memoirs, *To Hell and Back*, by Holt; English version of Sigmund Freud's *An Outline of Psychoanalysis*, by Norton; and Truman Capote's *A Tree of Night and Other Stories*, by Random House.	Feb. 28
Hoover Commission on Reorganization of the Executive Branch ends its last session in Washington after completing work on 18 reports intended to cut government costs, define lines of authority in the executive branch and free important officials from matters of minor detail . . . . House passes and sends to the Senate a measure ending the ban on naturalization of resident Asians.				World heavyweight champion Joe Louis announces his retirement from boxing to become director of a new fight promotion syndicate . . . . AT&T announces plans to add 13 cities to the Eastern-Midwestern television network during the coming year.	March 1
Illinois House of Representatives votes to investigate alleged Communist influences among the students of Roosevelt Univ. and the Univ. of Chicago . . . . American Assn. of School Administrators ends a five-day regional conference in St. Louis after urging construction of 2,500 two-year colleges throughout the U.S. to provide some higher education for all high school graduates.	Air Force B-50 *Lucky Lady II* lands at Carswell Air Force Base in Texas after completing the first non-stop around-the-world flight, travelling 23,452 miles in 94 hours. Strategic Air Command chief Curtis LeMay, greeting the plane at its landing, states the flight proves that a B-50 based in the U.S. can drop an atomic bomb "any place in the world."	Federal Reserve Bd. eases its curbs on installment credit following a January drop in installment sales.		Theologian Thomas Merton's *Seeds of Contemplation* is published by New Directions.	March 2
	Defense Secy. James Forrestal resigns. Truman nominates lawyer Louis Johnson to succeed him . . . . State Dept. dissolves its Office of Occupied Areas and announces plans to create an Office of German and Austrian Affairs.	A federal court in Cleveland convicts the Timkin Roller Bearing Co. of participating in a worldwide roller-bearing cartel.		A N.Y. federal court issues a consent decree separating the theater holdings of Paramount Pictures from the company's production and distribution enterprises . . . . Olympia with Ted Atkinson up wins the $67,100 Flamingo Stakes in Hialeah, Fla. . . . . T.S. Eliot's *Notes Toward The Definition of Culture* is published in N.Y. by Harcourt, Brace.	March 3
FBI agents in N.Y. arrest Justice Dept. employe Judith Coplon and Valentin Gubitchev, a Russian engineer employed by the U.N., on charges of conspiring to steal government documents . . . . N.Y. federal Judge Harold Medina rejects defense demands for proportional representation of ethnic and political minorities on the jury which will try 11 U.S. Communist leaders on charges of conspiring to overthrow the government . . . . Testimony ends at the six-week "Axis Sally" treason trial of Mildred Gillars.	Truman assigns civil defense planning tasks to the National Security Resources Bd., rejecting proposals for creation of a separate civil defense office.	Senate Labor Comm. approves the Administration-sponsored labor bill intended to replace the Taft-Hartley Act.		Sinclair Lewis' 21st novel, *The God-Seeker*, is published in N.Y. by Random House.	March 4
	Truman urges Congress to increase the defense secretary's authority over the three services and create the post of permanent chairman of the Joint Chiefs of Staff to reduce inter-service rivalries . . . . Piasecki Helicopter Corp. announces development of the world's fastest helicopter, the XHJP-1, on a Navy contract.			Univ. of Kentucky defeats Tulane, 68-52, in Louisville to take the Southeastern Conference basketball title.	March 5
F	G	H	I	J	
Includes elections, federal-state relations, civil rights and liberties, crime, the judiciary, education, health care, poverty, urban affairs and population.	*Includes formation and debate of U.S. foreign and defense policies, veterans affairs and defense spending. (Relations with specific foreign countries are usually found under the region concerned.)*	*Includes business, labor, agriculture, taxation, transportation, consumer affairs, monetary and fiscal policy, natural resources, pollution and accidents.*	*Includes worldwide scientific, medical and technological developments, natural phenomena, U.S. weather and natural disasters.*	*Includes the arts, religion, scholarship, communications media, sports, entertainment, fashions, fads and social life.*	

	World Affairs	Europe	Africa & the Middle East	The Americas	Asia & the Pacific
March 6				Congressional elections in Chile result in a victory for the supporters of Pres. Gabriel Gonzales Videla, who gain two-thirds of the contested seats.	
March 7		Rumania suspends operations of the Joint Distribution Comm., a Jewish welfare agency.	Egyptian government signs an agreement with the Suez Canal Co. giving Egypt control over the canal's administration and 7% of the canal's profits.		
March 8		A Sofia court convicts and sentences four Bulgarian Protestant ministers to life imprisonment on charges of treason and black market dealings. Eleven other defendants are given lesser prison sentences.	Israeli Premier David Ben-Gurion announces his first cabinet, a four-party coalition dominated by Ben-Gurion's Mapai Party. Ben-Gurion also presents his government's program to the Israeli Constituent Assembly, proposing a policy of neutrality in the Cold War and vigorous economic expansion.		Chinese Nationalist Premier Sun Fo resigns in favor of Gen. Ho Ying-chin, a strong peace advocate .... Japan's Democratic Party, the nation's second largest political group, splits into leftist and conservative factions.
March 9			Provincial council elections in South Africa result in a victory for the white supremacist Nationalist Party, which gains 86 seats vs. 78 for the moderate United Party.		
March 10		Russian Finance Min. Arseny Zverev presents the Supreme Soviet with a 1949 budget of 415.4 billion rubles, including a 79 billion-ruble military expenditure.			
March 11	Representatives of the U.S., Canada, Britain, France, Belgium, Holland, Norway and Luxembourg complete negotiations in Washington on a North Atlantic security pact. Italian Premier Alcide de Gasperi announces that his cabinet favors Italian participation in the alliance.	Gen. Henri Giraud, de Gaulle's wartime rival for Free French leadership, dies at 70 in Dijon.	Israel and Transjordan sign a cease-fire agreement on Rhodes .... Financier James Menhall announces agreement with the Syrian government on a $100-million oil concession in Syria.	Argentina's Constituent Assembly, boycotted by the opposition Radical Party, unanimously passes a new constitution which permits Pres. Peron to succeed himself and greatly enlarges his cabinet.	
March 12		Berlin airlift completes its record week to date with 45,683 tons of supplies flown in seven days.			French National Assembly approves a government plan to establish a territorial government in Cochin China .... Gen. MacArthur orders the Japanese government to work for greater productivity in the nation's coal mines without permitting any cost increases.
March 13		Belgium, Holland and Luxembourg sign a protocal in The Hague making their economic union effective in mid-1950 .... U.N. Economic Comm. for Europe announces a 14-nation agreement for construction of a modern network of European highways, including an Italian-French tunnel under Mont Blanc.			South Korean security forces begin a spring campaign against Communist-led guerrilla bands.
March 14		Russia's Supreme Soviet approves further reshuffling of top administrative officials, with Maxim Saburov appointed chairman of the State Planning Commission and Anatoli Kostusov promoted to minister of machine tool construction. The Supreme Soviet also approves a 415.4 billion-ruble budget for 1949.			Chinese Communists announce formation of a Central Plains Provisional People's Government for Kiangsu, Anhwei and Honan Provinces in Central China. Communist spokesmen also promise to take Taiwan, charging that the U.S. plans to use the island as a "springboard for future aggression" against China .... Burmese government offers Karen nationalists an autonomous state following capture of Mandalay, Burma's second largest city, by Karen forces and Communist guerrillas.
	A	B	C	D	E
	Includes developments that affect more than one world region, international organizations and important meetings of major world leaders.	*Includes all domestic and regional developments in Europe, including the Soviet Union, Turkey, Cyprus and Malta.*	*Includes all domestic and regional developments in Africa and the Middle East, including Iraq and Iran and excluding Cyprus, Turkey and Afghanistan.*	*Includes all domestic and regional developments in Latin America, the Caribbean and Canada.*	*Includes all domestic and regional developments in Asian and Pacific nations, extending from Afghanistan through all the Pacific Islands, except Hawaii.*

U.S. Politics & Social Issues	U.S. Foreign Policy & Defense	U.S. Economy & Environment	Science, Technology & Nature	Culture, Leisure & Life Style	
Sen. Joseph Broughton (D, N.C.), former governor of North Carolina and a civil rights advocate, dies at 60 in Bethesda, Md.			British government announces construction of the country's first atomic reactor capable of producing plutonium .... Edwin Colpitts, inventor whose work made long-distance wire and radio communications and the transatlantic telephone possible, dies at 77 in Orange, N.J.	National Ski Championships end at Big Mountain, Montana, with Yves Latreille and Andrea Mead holding the men's and women's titles.	March 6
Rep. Sol Bloom (D, N.Y.), House Foreign Affairs Comm. chairman and millionaire businessman, dies at 78 in Bethesda, Md. He is succeeded on the Foreign Affairs Comm. by Rep. John Kee (D, W. Va.) .... Jury selection begins in the N.Y. trial of U.S. Communist leaders.	House passes and sends to the Senate a measure giving the Central Intelligence Agency permanent status and exempting it from regular auditing and civil service procedures. The measure is considered under suspension of rules without debate or explanation.	Supreme Court upholds state laws imposing tighter restrictions on "union security" contracts than those provided by federal law. The specific case involves a Wisconsin measure banning maintenance-of-membership contract clauses.		Boston Red Sox outfielder and American League batting champion Ted Williams signs a 1949 contract for $100,000, the highest salary of any baseball player.	March 7
Sens. Karl Mundt (R, S.D.) and Homer Ferguson (R, Mich.) and Rep. Richard Nixon (R, Calif.) introduce Communist-control measures requiring Communist and "front" organizations to register with the government and label their statements as propaganda. The measures also deny passports to Communists, bar them from federal jobs and provide fines and prison sentences for conspiring to establish a totalitarian dictatorship in the U.S. .... N.Y. State Assembly passes a bill barring Communists from civil service and teaching positions .... House Public Lands Comm. approves bills granting statehood to Hawaii and Alaska.	Republican foreign affairs adviser John Foster Dulles, addressing a Federal Council of Churches of Christ meeting in Cleveland, warns that Scandinavian participation in the North Atlantic security pact might unnecessarily alarm Russia and "carry an offensive threat that is disproportionate to [its] defensive value."	Railway Express Agency employes in N.Y. begin a series of slowdowns and work stoppages in a dispute over wages and work hours.			March 8
	Bills authorizing $161 million for a joint U.S.-Canadian radar warning screen and $200 million for a 3,000-mile guided missile test range pass the House and are sent to the Senate.	House Labor Comm. approves a compromise measure increasing the hourly minimum wage from 40¢ to 75¢, maintaining the exemption of farm workers and other groups.			March 9
A federal grand jury in N.Y. indicts Judith Coplon and Valentin Gubitchev on espionage charges .... A federal jury in Washington convicts Mildred Gillars of treason for wartime Nazi propaganda broadcasts .... Truman appoints John Nichols to succeed William Brophy as Commissioner of Indian Affairs.		Hoover Commission on the Reorganization of the Executive Branch issues a report on government financial agencies, recommending that the Treasury Dept. take over operation of the largest federal lending and loan guarantee organizations, including the Export-Import Bank and the Reconstruction Finance Corp.			March 10
California State Commission on Organized Crime charges that N.Y. gambler Frank Costello heads a national "slot machine racket" that nets $2 billion a year and spends extensively to bribe public officials.		UMW Pres. John L. Lewis orders 400,000 Eastern coal miners to stop work for two weeks to protest the alleged incompetence of Director of Mines James Boyd.		CBS announces acquisition of NBC's George Burns and Gracie Allen show beginning this autumn.	March 11
Administration supporters in the Senate concede defeat in their efforts to restrict filibusters following a successful three-week Southern filibuster.		Railroad unions and employers, meeting in Chicago, agree to accept the recommendation of a presidential commission for a 7¢ hourly wage increase and an eight-hour reduction in the work week of non-operating railroad workers.		Hamline College defeats St. Regis, 57-46, to take the National Assn. of Intercollegiate Basketball crown in Kansas City.	March 12
				Dick Button and Yvonne Sherman win North American figure skating solo titles in Ardmore, Pa.	March 13
		Supreme Court upholds lower court rulings that three Southern railroads and the Brotherhood of Locomotive Firemen and Enginemen have illegally denied promotion rights to Negro firemen.			March 14

F	G	H	I	J
Includes elections, federal-state relations, civil rights and liberties, crime, the judiciary, education, health care, poverty, urban affairs and population.	*Includes formation and debate of U.S. foreign and defense policies, veterans affairs and defense spending. (Relations with specific foreign countries are usually found under the region concerned.)*	*Includes business, labor, agriculture, taxation, transportation, consumer affairs, monetary and fiscal policy, natural resources, pollution and accidents.*	*Includes worldwide scientific, medical and technological developments, natural phenomena, U.S. weather and natural disasters.*	*Includes the arts, religion, scholarship, communications media, sports, entertainment, fashions, fads and social life.*

	World Affairs	Europe	Africa & the Middle East	The Americas	Asia & the Pacific
March 15		Foreign and defense ministers of the Western European Union states complete a two-day London meeting with agreement on unifying and expanding their defense forces.			
March 16			Israel and Transjordan agree on Jerusalem armistice lines based on the city's existing truce, giving Israel control over modern Jerusalem and Arabs control over the old city.	Peron takes an oath of allegiance to the new Argentine constitution.	
March 17	Bolivia requests the U.N. General Assembly to take up the case of Hungary's Cardinal Mindszenty at its next session.	North Atlantic Treaty nations formally invite Denmark, Iceland and Portugal to join the security pact . . . . Truman issues a quarterly report to Congress on U.S. aid to Greece, claiming increased "discouragement and dissension within the Communist guerrilla leadership."	Transjordan announces establishment of a civil administration in the part of Arab Palestine it controls.	Costa Rica's Constituent Assembly votes to extend the Figueres junta government through mid-1950.	A North Korean delegation to Moscow led by Premier Kim Il Sung signs a commercial agreement with Russia providing for increased trade, Soviet technical assistance and cultural exchanges.
March 18	North Atlantic Treaty nations issue details of the proposed security pact, promising mutual defense in case of an unprovoked attack on any member and providing for creation of a North Atlantic Council to consult on threats to regional security. It is the first agreement in which the U.S. commits itself in advance to the defense of foreign countries. The 12 member states include Italy and Norway . . . . International Wheat Conference in Washington approves a 46-nation agreement regulating world wheat trade for the next four years. Russia refuses to accept the agreement, demanding a larger export quota.				
March 19		East German People's Council in Berlin adopts a constitution providing for creation of a strong central government in a unified Germany after the end of the Allied occupation . . . . Adm. Sir James Somerville, wartime commander of British naval forces in the Pacific and a participant in the sinking of the *Bismarck*, dies at 66 in Wells, England.			
March 20		Western Allies declare the Soviet-zone mark invalid in their sectors of Berlin . . . . Western military governors approve 12 German trustees for the heavy industry of the Ruhr.		Dutch colony of Curacao holds its first legislative elections, with victory going to the conservative National Party and the Aruban People's Party.	
March 21	Jacob Malik and Philip Jessup, Russian and U.S. delegates to the U.N., hold informal discussions in N.Y. on the Berlin situation. Malik indicates that Russia is prepared to lift the Berlin blockade if the Western Allies end their counter-blockade and set a date for a foreign ministers conference on all German questions.				Nationalist Premier Ho Ying-chin names a new cabinet, with former Amb. to Russia Fu Ping-chang as foreign minister . . . . Truman names John Muccio first U.S. ambassador to South Korea . . . . U.N. Secy. Gen. Trygve Lie names U.S. Adm. Chester Nimitz to head the Commission for India and Pakistan and supervise the plebiscite which will decide the future status of Kashmir.
March 22		Gen. Lucius Clay of the U.S. military government in Germany rules that Ilse Koch cannot be retried by a U.S. court for Buchenwald crimes but can still be tried under German law.		Canadian Finance Min. Douglas Abbott submits the 1949-50 budget to Parliament, proposing a $368.8-million reduction in income and other taxes.	
March 23		Articles in the Leningrad *Pravda* and the Moscow *New Times* warn Finland against aligning itself with the North Atlantic treaty powers in violation of the Russo-Finnish non-aggression pact . . . . Rumanian government cancels the ration cards of all non-workers, forcing them to buy food at high free-market prices.	Lebanon and Israel sign an armistice agreement in Ras en Naqura.	Argentine Pres. Peron signs a decree placing all raw materials under control of the commerce and industry ministry.	
	A	B	C	D	E
	Includes developments that affect more than one world region, international organizations and important meetings of major world leaders.	*Includes all domestic and regional developments in Europe, including the Soviet Union, Turkey, Cyprus and Malta.*	*Includes all domestic and regional developments in Africa and the Middle East, including Iraq and Iran and excluding Cyprus, Turkey and Afghanistan.*	*Includes all domestic and regional developments in Latin America, the Caribbean and Canada.*	*Includes all domestic and regional developments in Asian and Pacific nations, extending from Afghanistan through all the Pacific Islands, except Hawaii.*

U.S. Politics & Social Issues	U.S. Foreign Policy & Defense	U.S. Economy & Environment	Science, Technology & Nature	Culture, Leisure & Life Style	
	In a private letter to Senate Foreign Relations Comm. Chmn. Tom Connally, State Secy. Acheson opposes requests for further military aid to the Chinese Nationalist government.	House passes and sends to the Senate a bill extending rent control for 15 months beyond the March 31 expiration date but giving states, counties and cities authority to drop the curbs at will.		Motion Picture Export Assn. signs an agreement with Yugoslavia permitting entry of U.S. films for the first time since World War II. . . . . West Virginia State defeats North Carolina College, 60-53, to win the colored intercollegiate basketball title in Washington.	March 15
Maryland House of Delegates approves a bill outlawing all organizations judged to be subversive and providing for loyalty checks on all public employes . . . . Jury selection is completed in the N.Y. trial of U.S. Communist leaders . . . . N.J. state legislature strengthens a law against racial discrimination in education, recreation and places of public accommodation . . . . N.Y. state legislature passes a record $937 million budget, raising income taxes 50%.	House passes a Senate-approved bill allotting $16 million to aid Arab and Jewish refugees uprooted in recent Palestine fighting . . . . Russia officially returns the U.S. cruiser *Milwaukee*, loaned to the Soviet Navy during World War II.				March 16
Administration opponents in the Senate pass a measure which limits efforts to curb the filibuster, reducing chances of passing civil rights legislation during the current session . . . . South Carolina becomes the last state to legalize divorce.	Defense Secy. Forrestal orders a merger of the three armed services' public information offices to end news leaks and inter-service rivalry.	Senate Banking Comm. passes a rent control bill extending curbs for 12 months, permitting 5% increases at six-month intervals and authorizing state legislatures to drop the controls at will.			March 17
Clendenin Ryan, leader of a "clean government" movement in New York, testifies before a N.Y. grand jury that he has privately urged indictment of Mayor William O'Dwyer for fraud. Ryan claims that O'Dwyer is linked to gambler Frank Costello, whom he calls "the real boss of New York City."	House-approved bill for a joint U.S.-Canadian radar warning system passes the Senate and is sent to Truman.	Railway Express Agency sues the AFL Brotherhood of Railway Clerks for $5 million in damages suffered during the 10 day-old N.Y. slowdown strike.	Senate passes and sends to the House a bill creating a National Science Foundation to make scientific grants and loans, award scholarships, develop a national research policy and direct exchange of scientific information with other countries.		March 18
	Navy announces the first successful launching of a long-range bomber capable of carrying an atomic bomb from an aircraft carrier.		Nuclear facilities at Oak Ridge, Tenn. are opened to the public.	San Francisco Univ. defeats Chicago's Loyola Univ., 48-47, to win the National Invitational Basketball tournament in N.Y.	March 19
					March 20
Hoover Commission on Reorganization of the Executive Branch issues a report on federal social security and welfare functions, recommending creation of a separate department to handle old age and survivors' insurance, public assistance, aid to dependent children, educational grants and related matters.				Samuel McClure, founder of the nation's first newspaper syndicate and the popular magazine *McClure's*, dies at 92 in N.Y.	March 21
N.C. Gov. W. Kerr Scott appoints Univ. of North Carolina Pres. Frank Porter Graham to the Senate seat of the late Joseph Broughton.	House passes and sends to the Senate a bill authorizing an increase in Air Force strength to 70 groups with 502,000 men.	NLRB rules that lists of "unfair employers" maintained by the AFL Building and Construction Trades Council are illegal.		Edward Krause becomes athletic director of Notre Dame Univ., succeeding Frank Leahy.	March 22
National Security Council establishes an Interdepartmental Comm. on Internal Security to coordinate policy against subversive activity within the U.S.	Senate confirms Truman's nomination of Louis Johnson as Defense Secretary . . . . State Secy. Acheson denies Russian charges that the U.S. has established military bases in Iran but reaffirms America's "continuing interest" in Iranian security.	Senate passes a bill extending rent control through mid-1950, with limited opportunity for decontrol by local authorities.			March 23

F	G	H	I	J
Includes elections, federal-state relations, civil rights and liberties, crime, the judiciary, education, health care, poverty, urban affairs and population.	*Includes formation and debate of U.S. foreign and defense policies, veterans affairs and defense spending. (Relations with specific foreign countries are usually found under the region concerned.)*	*Includes business, labor, agriculture, taxation, transportation, consumer affairs, monetary and fiscal policy, natural resources, pollution and accidents.*	*Includes worldwide scientific, medical and technological developments, natural phenomena, U.S. weather and natural disasters.*	*Includes the arts, religion, scholarship, communications media, sports, entertainment, fashions, fads and social life.*

	World Affairs	Europe	Africa & the Middle East	The Americas	Asia & the Pacific
March 24		Marshal Alexander Vasilevsky succeeds Nikolai Bulganin as Soviet defense minister. Bulganin remains deputy premier and a member of the Communist Party's Politburo .... A series of five espionage trials in Munich ends with 17 defendants convicted of spying for Czechoslovakia and Poland.			
March 25		Danish Parliament approves Denmark's participation in the North Atlantic security pact as the Danish government formally accepts a U.S. invitation to sign the agreement .... Negotiations between Western military governors and representatives of the West German Constituent Assembly break down in disagreement over the strength of the proposed West German central government .... Prince August Wilhelm of Hohenzollern, the only child of Kaiser Wilhelm II to become a Nazi, dies at 62 in Stuttgart.			Chinese Communists designate Peking as their headquarters city.
March 26		France and Italy agree to eliminate tariff duties on mutual trade within one year and establish economic unity by 1955.	Iran accuses Soviet troops of raiding Iranian territory on the disputed Russian-Iranian frontier east of the Caspian Sea.		Chinese Communist Central Comm. announces its willingness to begin peace negotiations with the Nationalist government and names a five-member delegation headed by Chou En-lai to conduct talks.
March 27		Italian Senate approves "in principle" Italy's participation in the North Atlantic security system as Foreign Min. Carlo Sforza arrives in Washington to sign the agreement .... Gaullists gain 223 seats and Communists lose 147 seats in special district council run-off elections in France.			
March 28	Switzerland joins the International Refugee Organization, increasing membership to 18.				
March 29		Marshal Vasili Sokolovsky, head of the Soviet military administration in Germany, is named first deputy armed forces minister. He is succeeded in his German position by Gen. Vasili Chuikov, leader of the defense of Stalingrad and Russian military governor in Thuringia .... Czechoslovakia announces the conviction of two U.S. soldiers, George Jones and Clarence Hill, on espionage charges following a secret trial. Jones receives a 10-year and Hill a 12-year prison sentence.			
March 30	Portugal and Iceland agree to participate in the North Atlantic security system, the last of the 12 member states to give their formal consent.		Syrian Army seizes power following a wave of demonstrations protesting armistice negotiations with Israel. Army Chief of Staff Husni Zayim is named temporary head of state and promises to continue armistice talks.		Fifteen Indian princely states merge to form the Union of Greater Rajastan, a new state in the Indian Dominion.

A	B	C	D	E
Includes developments that affect more than one world region, international organizations and important meetings of major world leaders.	*Includes all domestic and regional developments in Europe, including the Soviet Union, Turkey, Cyprus and Malta.*	*Includes all domestic and regional developments in Africa and the Middle East, including Iraq and Iran and excluding Cyprus, Turkey and Afghanistan.*	*Includes all domestic and regional developments in Latin America, the Caribbean and Canada.*	*Includes all domestic and regional developments in Asian and Pacific nations, extending from Afghanistan through all the Pacific Islands, except Hawaii.*

U.S. Politics & Social Issues	U.S. Foreign Policy & Defense	U.S. Economy & Environment	Science, Technology & Nature	Culture, Leisure & Life Style	
	House narrowly votes to kill the veterans' pension bill sponsored by John Rankin (D, Miss.).	House Labor Comm. approves the Administration-sponsored labor bill intended to replace the Taft-Hartley Act.	Dr. Selman Waksman reports in *Science* magazine that neomycin, a new antibiotic, is as effective in treatment of tuberculosis as streptomycin.	Academy of Motion Picture Arts and Sciences presents Oscars to Laurence Olivier and Jane Wyman as best actor and actress and names Olivier's *Hamlet* the year's best picture.	March 24
	Cultural and Scientific Conference for World Peace opens in N.Y. with a banquet at the Waldorf-Astoria hotel attended by 2,000 American guests and 26 foreign delegates. One thousand demonstrators picket the event, charging it is Communist-dominated.			Jack Kapp, founder of Decca Records, dies at 47 in N.Y. of a cerebral hemorrhage.	March 25
A Washington federal court sentences Mildred Gillars to 10-30 years in prison and finds her $10,000 for her Nazi propaganda broadcasts.	Henry Wallace, novelist Norman Mailer and columnist I.F. Stone are among the participants in discussions at Carnegie Hall sponsored by the Cultural and Scientific Conference for World Peace. Americans for Intellectual Freedom, organized by New York Univ. Prof. Sidney Hook, holds a counter-rally to protest the conference.		Three days of tornadoes and gales in the South and Southwest end with 26 deaths.	Pancho Gonzales and Gertrude Moran win the men's and women's singles titles at U.S. indoor tennis competition in N.Y. . . . . Kentucky defeats Oklahoma A & M, 46-36, in Seattle to win the national collegiate basketball title.	March 26
	Cultural and Scientific Conference for World Peace ends its three-day N.Y. session after passing resolutions for the strengthening of the U.N. and creation of a permanent committee to work for world peace.	CIO United Farm Equipment Workers union ends a three-day convention in Cedar Rapids, Iowa after rejecting CIO demands that it merge with the UAW.			March 27
Supreme Court invalidates the Boswell Amendment to the Alabama constitution, aimed at preventing Negroes from registering to vote . . . . Betty Gannett, Polish-born director of Communist youth activities in the U.S., is arrested in N.Y. for deportation.	House Foreign Affairs Comm. approves a measure granting Nationalist China $56 million in economic aid for the coming year with funds left over from the last China aid appropriation.	Some 463,000 Eastern coal miners return to work at the order of UMW leader Lewis, ending a two-week "memorial" walkout . . . . Kaiser-Frazer Corp. announces the biggest cuts in auto prices to date, ranging from $196 to $300. The Kaiser family assumes complete control over the firm as Edgar Kaiser succeeds Joseph Frazer as president . . . . Federal Reserve Bd. cuts stock market margin requirements from 75% to 50% due to the decline in inflationary pressures.	U.S. Atomic Energy Commission notifies the FBI that most of the uranium oxide discovered missing from an Illinois laboratory last month has been recovered from wastes sent to Oak Ridge, Tenn. . . . . American Chemical Society awards the 1949 Priestly Medal to Arthur Lamb of Harvard.	Sam Snead beats Lloyd Mangrum to win the $10,000 Greensboro, N.C. open golf tournament.	March 28
	State Dept. denies permission for a U.S. tour to 18 Russian and Eastern European delegates to the Cultural and Scientific Conference for World Peace, directing them to leave the U.S. within a "reasonable time." . . . . Defense Secy. Louis Johnson names Gen. Joseph McNarney as his chief assistant in supervising armed forces unification.	House and Senate approve a compromise rent control bill extending controls through mid-1950 but permitting state and local authorities to end them sooner . . . . House Rules Comm. begins hearings on the Administration-sponsored labor bill . . . . Westinghouse announces a 20-50% decrease in its radio prices, while Jones & Laughlin and Inland Steel drop prices of several semi-finished products.	Univ. of Rochester dedicates the world's second-largest cyclotron, costing $1.5 million and capable of accelerating protons to speeds of 250 million volts.	Second volume of Winston Churchill's war memoirs, *Their Finest Hour*, is published by Houghton Mifflin and becomes a Book-of-the-Month-Club selection . . . . David Selznick's production *Portrait of Jenny*, starring Jennifer Jones, Joseph Cotton and Ethel Barrymore, premiers in N.Y.	March 29
Former Communist Louis Budenz completes eight days of testimony as the first prosecution witness in the N.Y. trial of U.S. Communist leaders. He charges that American Communists are directed from Moscow and dedicated to overthrowing the U.S. government . . . . House Un-American Activities Comm. Chmn. John Wood introduces a bill barring federal employes and defense workers from belonging or contributing to the Communist Party or front groups.	Truman signs a bill authorizing construction of a U.S.-Canadian radar system to protect North America from air attack.		Friedrich Bergius, Nobel Prize-winning German chemist who pioneered the development of substitute foods and fuels, dies at 65 in Buenos Aires.		March 30
F *Includes elections, federal-state relations, civil rights and liberties, crime, the judiciary, education, health care, poverty, urban affairs and population.*	G *Includes formation and debate of U.S. foreign and defense policies, veterans affairs and defense spending. (Relations with specific foreign countries are usually found under the region concerned.)*	H *Includes business, labor, agriculture, taxation, transportation, consumer affairs, monetary and fiscal policy, natural resources, pollution and accidents.*	I *Includes worldwide scientific, medical and technological developments, natural phenomena, U.S. weather and natural disasters.*	J *Includes the arts, religion, scholarship, communications media, sports, entertainment, fashions, fads and social life.*	

	World Affairs	Europe	Africa & the Middle East	The Americas	Asia & the Pacific
March 31	In identical notes to the seven sponsoring nations of the North Atlantic security pact, Russia charges them with forming an "openly aggressive" alliance in violation of the U.N. Charter .... Speaking in Boston at the MIT Mid-Century Convocation, Winston Churchill praises the U.S. for preventing Russian conquest of Western Europe and calls for expansion of the North Atlantic pact into a "world instrument capable of ... giving security against aggression."	Moscow announces appointment of *Pravda* editor D.T. Shepilov to replace Mikhail Suslov as head of the Communist Party Central Committee's Propaganda and Agitation Section.		Canadian Seamen's Union strikes against East Coast seagoing shippers after the latter sign contracts with the rival AFL Seafarer's International Union.	
Apr. 1				Argentina revokes its agreement to supply most of Britain's meat imports, demanding higher prices .... Newfoundland becomes the 10th province of Canada.	
Apr. 2	Foreign ministers of the 12 North Atlantic Treaty nations, meeting in Washington, reject Russian protests against the alliance and reaffirm its "completely defensive nature."	Electric signs are turned on at full brightness in London for the first time since 1939 as all restrictions on outdoor electric lighting are ended.			Peace talks between Chinese Communists and Nationalists begin in Peking, as Communist leader Mao Tze-tung indicates his willingness to work in a coalition government with former Nationalist "war criminals" who have "repented" their past actions.
Apr. 3			Israel and Transjordan sign an armistice on Rhodes covering Jerusalem and most of Palestine. The agreement allows continued division of Jerusalem between Jews and Arabs and Transjordanian occupation of central Palestine.	Costa Rican Defense Min. Edgar Cardaona Quiros surrenders to government forces following an unsuccessful attempt to seize power.	
Apr. 4	Foreign ministers of 12 nations sign the North Atlantic Treaty in a Washington ceremony.	Bulgarian government announces the dismissal and arrest of Deputy Premier Traicho Kostov for espousing "nationalistic" policies similar to those of Yugoslavian Pres. Tito .... A Paris court awards anti-Communist author Victor Kravchenko 150,000 francs plus court costs in a libel suit against the French Communist journal *Lettres Francaises.*			
Apr. 5	Philip Jessup and Jacob Malik hold a second informal Berlin discussion in N.Y. following consultations between the Western Allies. Jessup reads Malik a statement tentatively approving the Russian offer to lift the Berlin blockade in return for a German conference and an end to Western traffic restrictions .... U.N. General Assembly reconvenes in Flushing Meadows, N.Y. to complete its first regular 1948 session.		Israel and Syria begin armistice talks in the Upper Galilee.		
Apr. 6		British Exchequer Chancellor Sir Stafford Cripps presents Parliament with a severe austerity budget, calling for reduced food subsidies and maintenance of sales and income taxes at their existing levels.			
Apr. 7		County council elections in Britain result in heavy losses for the Labor Party, which loses its majority in the London County Council. The results are interpreted as a protest against Labor's austerity budget .... Portuguese Premier Antonio Salazar urges Spain's admission to the North Atlantic security pact .... Santiago Alba, leading Spanish liberal and president of the pre-Franco Spanish Parliament, dies at 76 in San Sebastian, Spain.			Chinese Communists launch a new attack in the Nanking area, capturing the Yangtze River port of Yicheng.
	A *Includes developments that affect more than one world region, international organizations and important meetings of major world leaders.*	B *Includes all domestic and regional developments in Europe, including the Soviet Union, Turkey, Cyprus and Malta.*	C *Includes all domestic and regional developments in Africa and the Middle East, including Iraq and Iran and excluding Cyprus, Turkey and Afghanistan.*	D *Includes all domestic and regional developments in Latin America, the Caribbean and Canada.*	E *Includes all domestic and regional developments in Asian and Pacific nations, extending from Afghanistan through all the Pacific Islands, except Hawaii.*

U.S. Politics & Social Issues	U.S. Foreign Policy & Defense	U.S. Economy & Environment	Science, Technology & Nature	Culture, Leisure & Life Style	
A Birmingham, Ala. jury convicts Sen. Glen Taylor (D, Ida.) of disorderly conduct and sentences him to a 180-day jail term and a $50 fine. The conviction resulted from Taylor's refusal to obey the city's segregation laws during his campaign for vice president.		An agreement to merge the 110,000-member Brotherhood of Locomotive Firemen and Enginemen with the 80,000-member Brotherhood of Locomotive Engineers is signed in Cleveland by representatives of both unions .... Willard Dow, president of the Dow Chemical Co., is killed with his wife and three others when their private plane crashes in a storm near London, Ontario.		Herman Wouk's *The Traitor*, a dramatic treatment of a college professor's decision to give atomic secrets to Soviet spies, opens in N.Y. to favorable reviews.	March 31
N.Y. Gov. Thomas Dewey signs a bill ordering the State Bd. of Regents to eliminate "subversive" employes from public schools.	Gen. Alexander Vandegrift, former Marine Corps commandant, retires from service.	Hoover Commission on Reorganization of the Executive Branch issues its last report, attacking inefficiency in the administration of government business enterprises and urging elimination of the Reconstruction Finance Corp., the Farmers Home Admin. and other agencies .... United Construction Workers union calls a strike of N.Y. taxi drivers in a dispute over union recognition and wages, idling most of the city's 11,510 cabs .... Senate passes a House-approved bill providing $45.6 million in loans to farmers and ranchers in storm-stricken Western states.			Apr. 1
	Truman signs a bill creating a new permanent under secretary position in the Defense Dept., while Defense Secy. Johnson eliminates nine "superfluous" military boards.			James Killian is formally installed as president of MIT, succeeding Karl Compton.	Apr. 2
		Ford Motors cuts prices on its new models by $12 to $120.			Apr. 3
N.J. State Senate completes action on a series of bills requiring loyalty oaths from all public employes and elected officials.			National Bureau of Standards reports the development of a non-magnetic compass for polar navigation.		Apr. 4
N.J. Gov. Charles Driscoll signs a bill strengthening bans against racial and religious employment discrimination.					Apr. 5
Herbert Philbrick, an undercover Communist Party member and FBI informant, appears as a surprise prosecution witness in the N.Y. trial of U.S. Communist leaders. He testifies that the Party has planned "violent revolution" since 1945 and that Boston Communists were instructed to infiltrate key industries in Massachusetts .... Rep. Andrew Somers (D, N.Y.), chairman of the House Public Lands Comm., dies at 54 in N.Y. He is succeeded on the Public Lands Comm. by J. Hardin Peterson (D, Fla.).	In a speech to new members of Congress, Truman says he will not hesitate to order use of the atomic bomb under circumstances similar to those in which it was dropped on Japan .... Navy announces plans to shift its focus of strength from the Pacific to the Atlantic Fleet in line with postwar strategy changes .... Last Army Day is observed throughout the nation as Defense Secy. Louis Johnson orders Army, Navy and Marine Corps days to be merged into a single Armed Forces Day.		Curtiss-Wright Corp. announces that its X-1 rocket plane has achieved speeds of 1,100 mph, the fastest by a piloted aircraft .... Seventy-four patients die in a fire at St. Anthony's Hospital in Effingham, Ill., the second-worst hospital fire in U.S. history.		Apr. 6
		Agriculture Secy. Charles Brannan presents Congress with a plan to replace existing agricultural price supports with a farm income supplement program, to be used if free market prices fall below a certain level. The plan is endorsed by the National Farmers Union and the American Farm Bureau.		Rodgers and Hammerstein's musical *South Pacific*, starring Mary Martin and Ezio Pinza, opens on Broadway with record advance sales of $500,000 .... Musical version of Mark Twain's novel *A Connecticut Yankee in King Arthur's Court* premiers in N.Y. .... Ezra Winter, painter of murals for the Library of Congress and New York's Radio City Music Hall, commits suicide at 63 near Canaan, Conn.	Apr. 7
F *Includes elections, federal-state relations, civil rights and liberties, crime, the judiciary, education, health care, poverty, urban affairs and population.*	G *Includes formation and debate of U.S. foreign and defense policies, veterans affairs and defense spending. (Relations with specific foreign countries are usually found under the region concerned.)*	H *Includes business, labor, agriculture, taxation, transportation, consumer affairs, monetary and fiscal policy, natural resources, pollution and accidents.*	I *Includes worldwide scientific, medical and technological developments, natural phenomena, U.S. weather and natural disasters.*	J *Includes the arts, religion, scholarship, communications media, sports, entertainment, fashions, fads and social life.*	

	World Affairs	Europe	Africa & the Middle East	The Americas	Asia & the Pacific
Apr. 8		State Secy. Acheson announces plans to provide military aid to North Atlantic Treaty partners at the request of Western European foreign ministers .... Western Allies announce agreement on a plan for merging their German zones and dissolving their military governments in conjunction with creation of a West German state .... Britain bans export of goods of "potential military value" to Russia and Eastern Europe .... Gen. Lucius Clay of the U.S. military government in Germany completes his review of the Malmedy massacre cases, pardoning 37 of the 43 Germans sentenced to death for the killing of American prisoners.		Guatemalan government announces suppression of a two-day guerrilla uprising near the Mexican border.	Russia vetoes South Korea's request for admission to the U.N. .... Fighting is renewed in Burma as a surrender of rebellious Karen forces in the Rangoon area fails to take place as scheduled.
Apr. 9		International Court of Justice in The Hague orders Albania to pay damages to Britain for the destruction of two British destroyers by mines off Corfu Channel in 1946.	U.N. General Assembly completes three days of debate on disposition of Italy's former African colonies, with Russia urging a five-power U.N. trusteeship and the U.S. advocating division of the colonies among Britain, Italy and other countries.		
Apr. 10	International Radio Conference in Mexico City ends after the U.S. and Russia refuse to sign a proposed agreement on use of short-wave radio frequencies.	Western Allies present their proposed German occupation statute to the West German Parliamentary Council in Bonn, which objects to provisions for continued Allied supervision of German foreign trade and industrial research.			
Apr. 11			South Africa's Parliament passes a constitutional amendment granting parliamentary representation to South-West Africa, a step towards incorporation of the territory into South Africa.	Freda Linton, the last of 20 suspects sought in connection with the 1946 Soviet espionage case, surrenders in Montreal.	
Apr. 12		British Labor Party's Executive Comm. approves a platform for the 1950 national elections, calling for a substantial increase in the government's economic role and nationalization of monopoly industries .... U.N. General Assembly votes to debate alleged human rights violations in the trials of Bulgarian and Hungarian church leaders.		U.S. and Canada establish a Joint Industrial Mobilization Comm. to coordinate plans for maintaining industrial production during an emergency.	
Apr. 13	In debate on a General Assembly resolution urging the great powers to modify their use of the Security Council veto, Russian Deputy Foreign Min. Andrei Gromyko attacks the North Atlantic security pact as an aggressive conspiracy against Russia and defends the veto as an instrument of self-defense.	Western Allies announce their willingness to let West Germany keep most factories currently marked for dismantling as reparations.	General Assembly's Steering Comm. delays a final decision on Israel's admission to the U.N. to indicate disapproval of Israeli opposition to internationalization of Jerusalem .... Israel and Syria agree to a ceasefire pending continued armistice talks.		
Apr. 14	U.N. General Assembly approves a resolution for modification of the Security Council veto, urging the great powers not to use their veto in cases involving requests for U.N. membership, peaceful settlement of international disputes and appointment of inquiry commissions.	U.S. war crimes tribunal in Nuremberg hands down prison sentences of four to 25 years for 19 former German officials convicted of planning aggressive war and crimes against humanity. Included among the convicted are former Foreign Office Secy. Ernst von Weizsaecker, Deputy Chancellor Heinrich Lammers, SS intelligence chief Walter Schellenberg and Nazi press chief Otto Dietrich. The sentencing ends the last trial scheduled for the tribunal.			Chinese Communist and Nationalist forces halt fighting around Nanking as the Nationalist government considers a Communist demand for unopposed crossing of the Yangtze River .... Dutch and Indonesian representatives meet under U.N. auspices in Batavia and begin negotiations on Dutch withdrawal from Jakarta, capital of the Indonesian Republic.
Apr. 15			Pope Pius XII issues an encyclical urging Catholic nations in the U.N. to support the internationalization of Jerusalem and other sacred places in the Holy Land.		
Apr. 16		U.S. and British crews establish a new Berlin airlift record by flying 12,941 tons of supplies into the city .... Czechoslovakia and Hungary sign a friendship and mutual security treaty in Budapest.	Gen. Husni Zayim forms a new Syrian cabinet, appointing himself premier and interior and defense minister.		
	A	B	C	D	E
	Includes developments that affect more than one world region, international organizations and important meetings of major world leaders.	*Includes all domestic and regional developments in Europe, including the Soviet Union, Turkey, Cyprus and Malta.*	*Includes all domestic and regional developments in Africa and the Middle East, including Iraq and Iran and excluding Cyprus, Turkey and Afghanistan.*	*Includes all domestic and regional developments in Latin America, the Caribbean and Canada.*	*Includes all domestic and regional developments in Asian and Pacific nations, extending from Afghanistan through all the Pacific Islands, except Hawaii.*

U.S. Politics & Social Issues	U.S. Foreign Policy & Defense	U.S. Economy & Environment	Science, Technology & Nature	Culture, Leisure & Life Style	
Senate confirms Truman's appointment of Ernest Gruening to a third term as governor of Alaska.		Eight-day strike of N.Y. taxi drivers ends in failure .... Commerce Dept. lifts export quotas on copper, brass and other nonferrous metals, minerals and manufactured items.		Gene Fowler's *Beau James: The Life and Times of Jimmy Walker*, a biography of New York's former mayor, is published by Viking.	Apr. 8
					Apr. 9
		Rivalry between leftist and conservative factions at an International Longshoremen's and Warehousemen's Union convention in San Francisco results in the nomination of Thomas George to challenge leftist Harry Bridges as union president. It is the first attempt in eight years to unseat Bridges.	Stalin prizes for scientific research go to physicists Sergei Vernov of Moscow Univ. and George Latyshev of Leningrad Univ. and to Trofim Lysenko, leader of the officially-favored environmentalist school of genetics.	Sam Snead wins the $10,000 Master golf tournament in Augusta, Ga..... *New York Herald Tribune* lists Lloyd Douglas' *The Big Fisherman* and Frank Gilbreth's and Ernestine Carey's *Cheaper by the Dozen* as the best-selling fiction and non-fiction books.	Apr. 10
	Senate passes a House-approved measure authorizing $75 million for construction of an Air Force rocket-testing range.	House Rules Comm. clears the Administration's labor bill for House action but rejects a request for a "closed" rule barring amendments not approved by the Labor Comm.			Apr. 11
	Truman submits the North Atlantic Treaty to the Senate for ratification. He also issues a protocol by State Secy. Acheson emphasizing that the pact does not infringe on the right of Congress to declare war.		Astronomers in North and South America observe the first total eclipse of the moon since 1945.	New York Drama Critics Circle chooses Arthur Miller's *Death of A Salesman* as the best new American play of the 1948-49 season .... Robert Sherwood receives the first $1,000 Gutenberg award of the Book Manufacturers Institute for his *Roosevelt and Hopkins*.	Apr. 12
Frank Meyer, former director of Communist educational activities in Chicago, appears as a prosecution witness in the N.Y. trial of U.S. Communist leaders and testifies that Party courses advocate the violent overthrow of American democracy.	House approves and sends to the Senate a $15-billion defense budget for fiscal 1950, including funds for a 70-group Air Force.	Truman urges Congress to authorize creation of a Columbia Valley Admin., modelled on the TVA, to provide federal power, irrigation and flood control programs for the Pacific Northwest .... Montgomery Ward board chairman Sewell Avery gains control over the company following the resignation of four vice presidents in a management dispute.	Pacific Northwest's worst recorded earthquake strikes a 150,000-square-mile area in Washington, Oregon and British Columbia, causing eight deaths.	Minneapolis beats Washington, 4 games to 2, in Basketball Assn. of America playoffs.	Apr. 13
Senate Republicans introduce a health care program intended to rival the Administration-sponsored plan, providing $1.25 billion in federal health care assistance but leaving primary responsibility for planning and construction of facilities to the states.	Senate and House complete action on a bill authorizing $5.4 billion in Marshall Plan expenditures for the next 15 months.				Apr. 14
U.S. court of appeals in Washington rules that U.S. citizens and aliens held by the federal government abroad have the right to seek habeas corpus writs in the U.S.				Screen star Wallace Beery dies at 64 in Beverly Hills, Calif.	Apr. 15
		A five-week Railway Express Agency strike in N.Y. ends after the company agrees to restore 10,000 abolished jobs in return for acceptance of terms that prevailed before the strike by the AFL Brotherhood of Railway Clerks.		Toronto beats Boston in four straight games to win the National Hockey League's Stanley Cup .... Eleanor Roosevelt is named winner of the Woman of the Year Award by the Women's National Press Club for her work on the U.N. Human Rights Commission.	Apr. 16
F	G	H	I	J	
Includes elections, federal-state relations, civil rights and liberties, crime, the judiciary, education, health care, poverty, urban affairs and population.	*Includes formation and debate of U.S. foreign and defense policies, veterans affairs and defense spending. (Relations with specific foreign countries are usually found under the region concerned.)*	*Includes business, labor, agriculture, taxation, transportation, consumer affairs, monetary and fiscal policy, natural resources, pollution and accidents.*	*Includes worldwide scientific, medical and technological developments, natural phenomena, U.S. weather and natural disasters.*	*Includes the arts, religion, scholarship, communications media, sports, entertainment, fashions, fads and social life.*	

	World Affairs	Europe	Africa & the Middle East	The Americas	Asia & the Pacific
Apr. 17		Italian Premier Alcide de Gasperi issues a land reform program calling for redistribution of three million acres among landless peasants.		Paraguay's Acting Pres. Felipe Molas Lopez is elected to a full term as president.	Chinese Communists issue an ultimatum to the Nationalist government demanding unopposed crossing of the Yangtze River, formation of a Communist-dominated coalition government, integration of Nationalist forces into the Communist army and punishment of Chiang Kai-shek and other Nationalist leaders.
Apr. 18		Eire officially ends its allegiance to the British Crown and becomes the Republic of Ireland.			
Apr. 19				An earthquake strikes central Chile, causing 62 deaths.	Chinese Nationalist government rejects the Communist ultimatum but asks for a ceasefire and further negotiations.
Apr. 20	World Congress of Fighters for Peace, a conference of pro-Soviet intellectuals and artists, opens in Paris. Among the first speakers are U.S. Negro singer Paul Robeson and Frederic Joliot-Curie, a Communist and head of the French Atomic Energy Commission.	German Socialist leaders, meeting in Hanover, demand a strong central government for the proposed West German state, with no Allied veto over the decisions of Parliament . . . . Antonio Fragoso Carmona is inaugurated for his fourth term as Portuguese president.			Chinese Communist forces exchange fire with British ships on the Yangtze River near Chinkiang, disabling the sloop *Amethyst.*
Apr. 21		A Greek court in Salonika hands down a life prison sentence for former Communist Gregory Staktopoulos, convicted of complicity in the murder of CBS correspondent George Polk.			Chinese Communist forces cross the Yangtze River at four points near Nanking, facing little Nationalist resistance. Exchange of fire between Communists and British ships on the Yangtze continues as the heavy cruiser *London* attempts unsuccessfully to reach the disabled *Amethyst.*
Apr. 22		U.N. General Assembly's Political and Security Comm. votes to postpone action on protests against trials of Hungarian and Bulgarian church leaders following four days of bitter debate between Russian and Western representatives.			Nationalist military forces and police abandon Nanking in the face of the Communist assault, giving rise to widespread looting in the city.
Apr. 23			Israeli Pres. Chaim Weizmann, speaking in N.Y., reiterates Israel's refusal to permit internationalization of Jerusalem but agrees to international control over holy places in the city.		Nationalist Pres. Li Tsung-jen flies to Canton in southern China, promising to coordinate resistance for "fight to the end" against the Communists. In Nanking, Communist underground members join with students in attempting to maintain public order and prevent looting . . . . Cochin China's Territorial Assembly votes for union with Vietnam, repudiating French plans for a semi-autonomous Cochinchinese state.
Apr. 24					Communist forces occupy the Nationalist capital of Nanking without opposition and advance towards Shanghai. The Shansi Province capital of Taiyuan, the only northern Chinese city remaining to the Nationalists, surrenders to the Communists.
Apr. 25	World Congress of Fighters for Peace ends in Paris after issuing a manifesto attacking U.S. foreign policy and the North Atlantic security pact.	U.N. General Assembly approves a resolution charging that Russia violates human rights by refusing to allow Russians married to foreigners to leave the Soviet Union.		Panamanian government imposes a state of siege, charging opposition politicians with plotting a coup.	
Apr. 26		German Council of States in the U.S. zone passes a law compensating Nazi victims for losses suffered through confiscation of property or expulsion from professions.	Transjordan's name is officially changed to Jordan, reflecting incorporation of the Arab areas of central Palestine.		Chinese Communist forces occupy the rail junction of Soochow in their drive on Shanghai. U.S. and British ships based in the city's harbor leave their berths to avoid entrapment by the Communists.
	A *Includes developments that affect more than one world region, international organizations and important meetings of major world leaders.*	B *Includes all domestic and regional developments in Europe, including the Soviet Union, Turkey, Cyprus and Malta.*	C *Includes all domestic and regional developments in Africa and the Middle East, including Iraq and Iran and excluding Cyprus, Turkey and Afghanistan.*	D *Includes all domestic and regional developments in Latin America, the Caribbean and Canada.*	E *Includes all domestic and regional developments in Asian and Pacific nations, extending from Afghanistan through all the Pacific Islands, except Hawaii.*

U.S. Politics & Social Issues	U.S. Foreign Policy & Defense	U.S. Economy & Environment	Science, Technology & Nature	Culture, Leisure & Life Style	
Catholic welfare agencies attack the Administration's proposed national health insurance system as "practically a government monopoly" and urge federal aid to expand voluntary insurance programs.				Rabbi Meyer Berlin (Bar Ilan), head of the World Mizrachi Union of Religious Zionists, dies at 68 in Jerusalem . . . . Bernard Pares, British historian and an authority on Russia, dies at 82 in N.Y.	Apr. 17
U.S. court of appeals in Washington upholds Gerhart Eisler's conviction on passport fraud charges . . . . Supreme Court invalidates "quick" Nevada divorces in which the couple involved are not personally involved in the proceedings.		Special presidential commission on labor relations in nuclear facilities recommends creation of a three-man board to mediate atomic energy labor disputes.		Truman throws out the first ball to open the major league baseball season as the Washington Senators beat the Philadelphia Athletics.	Apr. 18
	Truman signs the $5.4-billion authorization for the Marshall Plan's second year.			Rabbi Stephen Wise, leader of U.S. Reform Judaism and co-founder of the Zionist Organization of America and other Jewish groups, dies at 75 in N.Y.	Apr. 19
Defense Secy. Johnson orders the armed services to end racial discrimination but permits continued segregation of Negro units. . . . . Rep. Robert Coffey (D, Pa.) dies at 30 in an air crash near Albuquerque, N.M.	Truman nominates Adm. Alan Kirk to succeed Gen. Walter Bedell Smith as U.S. ambassador to Russia.		Mayo Clinic researchers report isolation of a hormone from the adrenal gland effective in relieving rheumatoid arthritis.	Paul Blanshard's *American Freedom and Catholic Power*, a critique of the Catholic church in the U.S., is published by Beacon Press.	Apr. 20
City College of New York students end an unsuccessful five-day strike aimed at forcing the removal of two faculty members accused of anti-Semitism and discrimination against Negroes.	State Secy. Acheson and Defense Secy. Johnson ask Congress to provide $1.13 billion in military aid to Western Europe under the North Atlantic security pact and $320 million to Greece and Turkey . . . . Army Secy. Kenneth Royall resigns.	Senate passes a public housing bill providing $1 billion in federal loans and $500 million in federal grants for a five-year slum clearance program.		General Synod of the Evangelical and Reformed Church, meeting in Cleveland, approves a merger with the Congregational Christian Churches to form a new, two million-member United Church of Christ . . . . A new U.S. Catholic catechism, the first major revision in 60 years, is issued. It denies that "everyone who is not a Catholic will be condemned."	Apr. 21
Former FBI informant Garfield Herron testifies at the N.Y. trial of U.S. Communist leaders that party schools view the U.S. as the chief postwar target of a Communist revolution . . . . Truman again urges Congress to enact the Administration's comprehensive health care program.	Foy D. Kohler succeeds Charles Thayer as head of the international broadcasting division in the State Department's Office of International Information. The position includes supervision of Voice of America programs.	Former Civil Aeronautics Bd. Chmn. James Landis tells a Senate Commerce subcommittee that too many U.S. airlines exist and many require an "unreasonable [government] subsidy" to survive . . . . Federal Reserve Bd. eases credit controls for the third time in seven weeks to combat the current deflationary trend.	Dr. Garwood Richardson of Northwestern Univ. reports development of an accurate urine test for pregnancy.		Apr. 22
Illinois Seditious Activities Investigation Comm. completes three days of hearings on alleged subversive activities at the Univ. of Chicago and Roosevelt Univ. Univ. of Chicago Chancellor Robert Hutchins criticizes the inquiry for attempting to establish "guilt by association" and contributing to the "miasma of thought control that is now spreading over the country."	House Un-American Activities Comm. releases testimony and documents provided by Izydor Modelski, former Polish military attache in Washington, describing Poland's U.S. embassy as a spy headquarters directed by a Russian general . . . . Seventy thousand U.S. troops end six days of maneuvers in Bavaria, practicing defense of the area against an invasion from Czechoslovakia.			Eddie Arcaro rides Olympia to victory in the $46,400 Wood Memorial race in Jamaica, N.Y.	Apr. 23
Republicans form a 21-man committee in Washington to plan strategy for the 1950 campaign.				Multnomah Club of Portland, Ore. takes the women's AAU national indoor swimming crown in Daytona Beach, Fla.	Apr. 24
Espionage trial of Justice Dept. employe Judith Coplon opens in Washington.		A New York City CIO Council is formed to replace the Greater New York CIO Council, disbanded by the national CIO leadership due to its Communist leanings. Transport Workers Union Pres. Michael Quill heads the new organization.		English version of Jean-Paul Sartre's first novel, *Nausea*, is published by New Directions.	Apr. 25
A N.Y. federal grand jury investigating subversive activities issues a report charging that current public inquiries are alerting offenders and recommending secret inquiries and elimination of the statute of limitations for espionage . . . . St. Louis-San Francisco Railway and four rail unions announce cancellation of an agreement to bar Negroes from train crews.	Navy Secy. John Sullivan resigns in protest against Defense Secy. Johnson's cancellation of plans to complete the proposed super-carrier *United States*.		William Barris and Richard Reidel land their single-engine *Sunkist Lady* in Fullerton, Calif. after setting a world flight endurance record of 1,008 hrs., 1:50 mins. . . . . Merle Tuve of the Carnegie Institution wins the National Academy of Science's $3,500 Comstock Prize in Washington for development of the proximity fuse and work in nuclear physics.	Former middleweight champion Tony Zale retires from boxing at 35.	Apr. 26
F	G	H	I	J	
Includes elections, federal-state relations, civil rights and liberties, crime, the judiciary, education, health care, poverty, urban affairs and population.	*Includes formation and debate of U.S. foreign and defense policies, veterans affairs and defense spending. (Relations with specific foreign countries are usually found under the region concerned.)*	*Includes business, labor, agriculture, taxation, transportation, consumer affairs, monetary and fiscal policy, natural resources, pollution and accidents.*	*Includes worldwide scientific, medical and technological developments, natural phenomena, U.S. weather and natural disasters.*	*Includes the arts, religion, scholarship, communications media, sports, entertainment, fashions, fads and social life.*	

	World Affairs	Europe	Africa & the Middle East	The Americas	Asia & the Pacific
Apr. 27	Russian Deputy Foreign Min. Andrei Gromyko and U.N. delegate Jacob Malik meet with U.S. delegate Philip Jessup in N.Y. and agree that Russia will no longer demand cancellation of plans for a West German government as a precondition to an Allied foreign ministers meeting on Germany.		U.N. Palestine Conciliation Commission opens a general peace settlement conference in Lausanne, Switzerland, attended by Israel, Egypt, Syria, Lebanon and Jordan.		
Apr. 28	Berlin sources report Russian plans to submit a draft German peace treaty to the proposed Allied foreign ministers conference, including demands for withdrawal of all Allied occupation forces from Germany and creation of a unified central government.	Western Allies establish a Western Ruhr authority to allocate the Ruhr's industrial production and prevent revival of German war industry.	Three electric trains collide near Johannesburg, South Africa, killing 74 passengers.	Canadian Parliament completes ratification of the North Atlantic Treaty.	Former Vietnamese Emperor Bao Dai arrives in Dalat to head a new French-sponsored Vietnam Union .... A conference of British Commonwealth prime ministers meeting in London reaches an agreement allowing India to remain in the Commonwealth after it becomes a republic.
Apr. 29		Italy establishes formal trade relations with West Germany by signing a one-year, $60-million commercial agreement .... Maier Bobrovsky, the first Soviet Jew to be granted an emigration visa to Israel, arrives in Prague on his way to the Middle East.			
Apr. 30	Anti-Communist leftist intellectuals stage an International Day of Resistance to Dictatorship and War in Paris to counter the recently-concluded World Congress of Fighters for Peace. Participants include American physicist Karl Compton and Sidney Hook of New York Univ.			Canadian Parliament is dissolved pending new elections on June 27.	
May 1				Argentina's new Congress holds its opening session as Pres. Peron announces that all public services still in private hands, including transportation, communications and power, will be nationalized .... Congressional elections in Bolivia result in a victory for the governing Republican Socialist Union.	Princely state of Baroda, the largest in western India, merges with Bombay Province.
May 2		U.S. Supreme Court refuses to intervene in cases of Germans convicted of war crimes by U.S. military tribunals at Nuremberg.		Bolivian government declares a state of siege due to disorders resulting from yesterday's elections.	Chiang Kai-shek flies from Shanghai to Taiwan.
May 3			Syrian government lifts restrictions on travel and business and property transactions by Jews.		Chinese Nationalist forces abandon the port of Hangchow near Shanghai to the Communists .... World Bank and the International Monetary Fund admit Thailand as their 48th member.
May 4	Russia, Britain, France and the U.S. formally agree to convene a foreign ministers conference on Germany in return for lifting of the Berlin blockade on May 12.	Belgian Chamber of Deputies ratifies the North Atlantic Treaty .... Italy's champion Turin soccer team is killed in a plane crash near Turin that takes 28 lives.			
May 5		Representatives of 10 Western European states sign an agreement in London establishing a two-part Council of Europe, with a Committee of Ministers and a parliamentary Consultative Assembly.		Asbestos, Quebec, the world's chief center of asbestos production, is seized by 4,000 workers in a three-month-old strike for union recognition and a wage increase.	Chinese Communists announce conclusion of a mutual defense treaty with North Korea .... British Defense Minister A.V. Alexander announces plans to reinforce Hong Kong with infantry, anti-aircraft and anti-tank units.
	A	B	C	D	E
	Includes developments that affect more than one world region, international organizations and important meetings of major world leaders.	*Includes all domestic and regional developments in Europe, including the Soviet Union, Turkey, Cyprus and Malta.*	*Includes all domestic and regional developments in Africa and the Middle East, including Iraq and Iran and excluding Cyprus, Turkey and Afghanistan.*	*Includes all domestic and regional developments in Latin America, the Caribbean and Canada.*	*Includes all domestic and regional developments in Asian and Pacific nations, extending from Afghanistan through all the Pacific Islands, except Hawaii.*

U.S. Politics & Social Issues	U.S. Foreign Policy & Defense	U.S. Economy & Environment	Science, Technology & Nature	Culture, Leisure & Life Style	
A Senate Labor and Public Welfare subcommittee defers consideration of the Administration's proposed national health insurance program until next year .... Atty. Gen. Tom Clark adds 37 organizations to the Justice Department's subversive list, including the Assn. of Georgia Klans and the Industrial Workers of the World .... Former Sen. Frederic Wallcott (R, Conn.), principal author of the bill creating the Reconstruction Finance Corp., dies at 80 in Stamford, Conn.		New York City adopts a record $1.197-billion budget for fiscal 1950, more than requested by Mayor William O'Dwyer.		George Howe receives the largest literary award in the U.S., the $15,000 Christophers Prize, for his forthcoming novel *Call It Treason.*	Apr. 27
Sen. J. Howard McGrath (D, R.I.) presents Truman's civil rights program to Congress in a four-bill package, including an omnibus Civil Rights Act of 1949 .... Truman stirs heated controversy in Congress when he threatens to deprive Democrats opposing the Administration's labor bill of their right to distribute federal jobs.	Defense Secy. Johnson appoints James Evans as his civilian assistant for racial problems.	Rep. John Wood (D, Ga.) introduces a labor bill upholding the main features of the Taft-Hartley Act in opposition to the Administration-sponsored bill .... Federal Reserve Bd. continues its anti-deflationary moves by reducing reserve requirements of 7,000 member banks by $1.2 billion.		Leonard Bernstein wins the $1,000 Boston Symphony Orchestra merit award for his symphony *The Age of Innocence.*	Apr. 28
		Civil Aeronautics Bd. issues the nation's first four charters for regular air freight service.			Apr. 29
				Steve Brooks rides Coaltown to victory in the $56,700 Gallant Fox Handicap in Jamaica, N.Y.	Apr. 30
	Catholic Association for International Peace attacks "abdication of American principles" in U.S. policy towards China, demanding more aid for the Nationalist government.				May 1
		Housing Expediter Tighe Woods issues rules to govern "fair income" rent increases under the new rent control law .... Singer Manufacturing Co. experiences its first strike when 7,000 United Electrical Workers union members stop work at the Elizabeth, N.J. sewing machine plant in a dispute over wages, hours and work standards .... Packard announces price cuts of 4½% to 8½% on its new model cars.		Columbia Univ. awards Pulitzer Prizes to Arthur Miller's *Death of a Salesman* (drama), Robert Sherwood's *Roosevelt and Hopkins* (biography), Virgil Thompson's score for *Louisiana Story* (music), Peter Viereck's *Terror and Decorum* (poetry) and Roy Nichols' *The Disruption of American Democracy* (American history) .... Supreme Court upholds the 1947 convictions of Harvey Stemmer and David Krakower on charges of trying to bribe two New York Giants pro football players.	May 2
	Truman announces Gen. Lucius Clay's forthcoming retirement as head of the U.S. military government in Germany and commander of U.S. forces in Europe .... Air Force Gen. Clair Chennault, testifying before the Senate Armed Services Comm., urges the U.S. to provide $700 million in military aid to remaining Nationalist forces in southern China.			Baseball Commissioner Albert Chandler reinstates New York Giants manager Leo Durocher after a five-day suspension for assaulting a spectator at the N.Y. Polo Grounds.	May 3
	House passes a Senate-approved measure authorizing $75 million for construction of a 3,000-mile guided missile test range based in Florida.	Administration supporters in the House succeed in recommitting the Wood labor bill, frustrating the first challenge to Administration attempts to repeal the Taft-Hartley Act.		MGM musical comedy *The Barkleys of Broadway* premiers in N.Y. .... Allen Stack sets two new U.S. swim records in New Haven, Conn.: 200 meter backstroke in 2:18.5 and 220 yard backstroke in 2:19.4.	May 4
Senate passes and sends to the House a bill authorizing $300 million yearly in federal aid to education, with the largest appropriations going to poorer states. Use of the funds to aid private and parochial schools is left up to the states .... House Judiciary Comm. approves amendments to the Displaced Persons Act of 1948 liberalizing entry requirements and eliminating discrimination against Jewish refugees.	House passes and sends to the Senate a uniform code of military justice for all the services .... Henry Wallace testifies against the North Atlantic Treaty before the Senate Foreign Relations Comm., claiming that U.S. and British business interests seek to block U.S.-Russian cooperation.	Ford Motor Company's River Rouge and Lincoln-Mercury plants are closed down by a strike of 62,250 UAW members protesting alleged management efforts to increase the pace of work .... U.S. Chamber of Commerce ends a four-day conference in Washington after adopting resolutions against Truman's tax, labor, housing, health and farm programs.	Dr. Selman Waksman, discoverer of streptomycin, contributes the patent royalties from his drug to Rutgers Univ. for establishment of a $1-million microbiology institute .... Dr. Oswald Avery of Nashville receives the $5,000 Passano Prize for isolating pneumonia germs and classifying the disease into four types.	German novelist Thomas Mann receives the Award of Merit Medal of the American Academy of Arts and Letters, one of the nation's highest literary honors .... Baseball Writers Assn. votes former Detroit Tigers second baseman Charlie Gehringer into the baseball Hall of Fame.	May 5
F *Includes elections, federal-state relations, civil rights and liberties, crime, the judiciary, education, health care, poverty, urban affairs and population.*	G *Includes formation and debate of U.S. foreign and defense policies, veterans affairs and defense spending. (Relations with specific foreign countries are usually found under the region concerned.)*	H *Includes business, labor, agriculture, taxation, transportation, consumer affairs, monetary and fiscal policy, natural resources, pollution and accidents.*	I *Includes worldwide scientific, medical and technological developments, natural phenomena, U.S. weather and natural disasters.*	J *Includes the arts, religion, scholarship, communications media, sports, entertainment, fashions, fads and social life.*	

	World Affairs	Europe	Africa & the Middle East	The Americas	Asia & the Pacific
May 6					U.S. State Dept. endorses greater independence for Japan in trade, cultural relations and technical and scientific exchanges.
May 7	Voice of America and BBC combine efforts to break through Soviet jamming of Western broadcasts to Russia.	U.N. General Assembly's Political and Security Comm. approves a resolution allowing member states to resume full diplomatic relations with Spain.	Jordan revises its cabinet to admit three Palestinian Arabs, including Abdil Hadi as foreign minister.		Chinese Communists take the rail junction of Kashing, depriving the Nationalist defenders of Shanghai of land contact with the rest of China .... Dutch and Indonesian negotiators in Batavia agree on a ceasefire providing for Dutch evacuation of Jakarta and release of political prisoners. Withdrawal of Dutch troops from the Indonesian Republic is to be settled in future negotiations.
May 8		Parliamentary Council in Bonn adopts a "Basic Law" as the constitution of the new West German state, vesting power in a two-house parliament with a president as nominal head of state .... Local elections in Sardinia result in drastic losses for the Christian Democrats, who nevertheless remain the island's strongest party.			
May 9	Eleanor Roosevelt is reelected chairwoman of the U.N. Economic and Social Council's Committee on Human Rights.	British House of Commons completes action on a bill to nationalize most of the nation's steel industry by May 1, 1950 .... Prince Louis II, ruler of Monaco, dies in Monaco and is succeeded by his grandson, Prince Ranier III.	Iranian constitution is amended to give the Shah power to dissolve parliament.	Colombian Pres. Mariano Ospina Perez appoints a new cabinet of seven Conservatives and six Liberal Party members due to Conservative objections to the composition of the previous cabinet.	
May 10	Allied representatives suspend their London talks on Austrian peace treaty terms pending the prospective foreign ministers conference on Germany.	German Parliamentary Council selects Bonn over Frankfurt as capital of the West German state.		Former Polish military attache Izydor Modelski, testifying before a Senate Judiciary subcommittee, charges that Polish agents were "deeply involved" in the riots which disrupted last year's Conference of American States in Bogota, Colombia.	
May 11			U.N. General Assembly votes, 37-12, to admit Israel as the organization's 59th member.		Siamese Premier Phibun Songgram officially changes the country's name to Thailand (Land of the Free).
May 12		Russia's Berlin blockade ends after 328 days, along with the Western counter-blockade of movement of goods to and from the Soviet zone of Germany. The U.S.-British airlift to Berlin continues with the objective of building up a 200,000-ton supply reserve .... British House of Commons votes for ratification of the North Atlantic Treaty.			U.S. vetoes payment of further war reparations by Japan as detrimental to Japanese economic recovery. MacArthur authorizes the reopening of stock exchanges in major Japanese cities.
May 13					
May 14	U.N. General Assembly adopts a "Convention on the International Transmission of News and the Right of Correction," giving journalists the right to move freely between signatory countries and have equal access to the news.	Italian government bans mass political demonstrations in an effort to reduce neo-Fascist and Communist activity .... Western Allies issue a new occupation statute for their sectors of Berlin, giving the City Council greater administrative authority .... Britain's Scotland Yard arrests Gerhard Eisler in Southampton after the accused Communist spy flees the U.S. to escape serving a one-year jail sentence for contempt of Congress.		Argentine government takes over the Buenos Aires central railroad, the last foreign-owned line in the nation .... Felipe Moas Lopez is inaugurated president of Paraguay.	Communist forces battling around Shanghai pierce the city's outer defenses .... Britain grants Malaya $80 million to cover war damages.
	A	B	C	D	E
	Includes developments that affect more than one world region, international organizations and important meetings of major world leaders.	*Includes all domestic and regional developments in Europe, including the Soviet Union, Turkey, Cyprus and Malta.*	*Includes all domestic and regional developments in Africa and the Middle East, including Iraq and Iran and excluding Cyprus, Turkey and Afghanistan.*	*Includes all domestic and regional developments in Latin America, the Caribbean and Canada.*	*Includes all domestic and regional developments in Asian and Pacific nations, extending from Afghanistan through all the Pacific Islands, except Hawaii.*

U.S. Politics & Social Issues	U.S. Foreign Policy & Defense	U.S. Economy & Environment	Science, Technology & Nature	Culture, Leisure & Life Style	
		Leaders of the 230,000-member Communications Workers of America announce plans to affiliate with the CIO .... Senate Executive Expenditures Comm. passes a measure creating a General Services Agency to centralize federal purchasing, as recommended by the Hoover Commission.		Count Maurice Maeterlinck, Belgian poet and dramatist, dies at 86 in his Chateau d'Orlamonde near Nice, France.	May 6
Truman presents 1948 Collier's Congressional Awards for distinguished service to Sen. Arthur Vandenberg (R, Mich.) and House Speaker Sam Rayburn (D, Tex.).				Steve Brooks rides 16-1 shot Ponder to victory at the 75th Kentucky Derby in Louisville.	May 7
		A one-week strike of 6,500 United Electrical Workers union members at 21 Philco plants in the Philadelphia area ends after the union drops demands for a 15¢ hourly raise and pension plan .... William Luden, originator of the menthol candy cough drop, dies at 90 in Atlantic City, N.J.	Bureau of Mines opens the nation's first factory for extracting oil and gasoline from coal in Louisiana, Missouri.	Early-day National League pitchers Mordecai Brown and Charles Nichols are voted into baseball's Hall of Fame .... *New York Herald Tribune* lists John Marquand's *Point of No Return* and Frank Gilbreth's and Ernestine Carey's *Cheaper by the Dozen* as the best-selling fiction and non-fiction books.	May 8
		William Lurye, special organizer for the International Ladies Garment Workers Union, is fatally stabbed in a N.Y. building where the ILGWU recently conducted four strikes. Union Pres. David Dubinsky charges that an anti-union dress manufacturer arranged the killing.			May 9
A House Labor subcommittee headed by Adam Clayton Powell, Jr. (D, N.Y.) begins hearings on proposals to restore the Fair Employment Practices Commission .... Frank Hague, Democratic boss of Jersey City, N.J., is defeated for the first time in 32 years by a reform slate led by John Kenny.	Former German Communist Ruth Fischer, sister of Gerhart Eisler, charges before a Senate Judiciary subcommittee that the U.N. delegations of Russia and other Eastern Euopean states "reinforce" Soviet espionage in the U.S. She also attacks the Women's International Democratic Federation, a U.N. consultative body, as "the principal Stalinist front in the women's field."			Sam Breadon, former president of the St. Louis Cardinals, dies at 72 in St. Louis.	May 10
Defense Secy. Johnson approves an Air Force proposal to eliminate segregated Negro units and open "key" positions to qualified Negroes.	Former Yugoslav information officer Bogdan Raditsa testifies before a Senate Judiciary subcommittee that Russian and Eastern European diplomacy "is nothing but a legalized espionage and subversive network." .... Truman signs the bill authorizing $75 million for a guided missile test range.	American Federation of Hosiery Workers, with 50,000 members, votes to leave the CIO and reaffiliate with the AFL.	Polaroid Land camera, which can produce a photo 60 seconds after it is snapped, goes on sale in N.Y. for $89.75.		May 11
U.S. Atomic Energy Commission sets off a heated debate in Congress when it announces the award of a $1,600 government fellowship for advanced study in nuclear physics to Hans Freistadt, a naturalized U.S. citizen and member of the Communist Party .... Levi Jackson, Negro captain of the Yale football team, is offered membership in the school's three oldest secret societies.		Truman reiterates his support of a $4-billion tax increase despite the growing deflationary trend .... House Banking and Currency Comm. approves the Administration's slum clearance bill.		Britain's Princess Margaret Rose visits Pope Pius XII despite protests by English Protestants .... Stanley Kramer's *Home of the Brave*, the story of a Negro soldier's struggle against racism, premiers in N.Y.	May 12
Univ. of Florida rejects the admissions applications of five Negroes after all reject an offer of state scholarships to study at out-of-state institutions.	Truman nominates Omaha lawyer Francis Matthews to succeed John Sullivan as Navy Secretary .... Office of the Defense Secretary establishes a Medical Services Division as the first step toward unifying military medicine.	General Electric reduces prices of television tubes by $3-10, while the price of Wyoming crude oil drops 23¢ a barrel.	A truck carrying carbon disulphide explodes in New York's Holland Tunnel, causing 26 injuries and extensive damage, including a communications tieup resulting from destruction of telephone and telegraph cables. The tunnel itself remains sound.		May 13
	State Dept. urges Congress to give Truman increased power to meet "changing situations" in the Cold War through military aid grants and other measures short of war .... Navy commissions the 17,000-ton heavy cruiser *Salem* in Boston.			New York Giants retain Leo Durocher as manager through 1951 after assault charges against him are dropped .... Ted Atkinson rides Capot to victory in the $110,879 Preakness Stakes at Pimlico, Md. Ponder, the Kentucky Derby winner, finishes fifth.	May 14
F	G	H	I	J	
Includes elections, federal-state relations, civil rights and liberties, crime, the judiciary, education, health care, poverty, urban affairs and population.	*Includes formation and debate of U.S. foreign and defense policies, veterans affairs and defense spending. (Relations with specific foreign countries are usually found under the region concerned.)*	*Includes business, labor, agriculture, taxation, transportation, consumer affairs, monetary and fiscal policy, natural resources, pollution and accidents.*	*Includes worldwide scientific, medical and technological developments, natural phenomena, U.S. weather and natural disasters.*	*Includes the arts, religion, scholarship, communications media, sports, entertainment, fashions, fads and social life.*	

	World Affairs	Europe	Africa & the Middle East	The Americas	Asia & the Pacific
May 15		A week of local elections in Britain ends with large gains for Conservatives at the expense of the Labor Party.			
May 16	General Assembly defeats a resolution permitting U.N. member states to resume diplomatic relations with Spain.	Elections for the East German People's Congress result in a two-to-one victory for the Socialist Unity Party slate and the Communist program of German reunification .... Gerhart Eisler is taken from Southampton to London and held without bail for a hearing on U.S. demands for his extradition.	Syria signs an agreement with the U.S.-owned Trans-Arabian Pipeline Co. permitting construction of the last link of an oil pipeline linking the Persian Gulf and the Mediterranean.		
May 17		British House of Commons passes a bill allowing the Ulster counties of Ireland to remain in the United Kingdom .... U.N. General Assembly defeats a Polish resolution demanding return of all Eastern European refugees to their native countries.	Israel and Syria break off armistice negotiations in a deadlock over Syria's refusal to withdraw its troops from northeastern Galilee.		India's Constituent Assembly approves Indian membership in the British Commonwealth.
May 18		Truman appoints World Bank Pres. John McCloy first civilian U.S. high commissioner for Germany, succeeding U.S. Military Gov. Lucius Clay.	U.N. General Assembly postpones a decision on disposition of Italy's former African colonies before adjourning until next September.	Truman welcomes Brazilian Pres. Eurico Dutra in Washington for a 10-day U.S. visit.	Chinese Communist forces complete the encirclement of Shanghai and continue a southward push towards the port of Foochow, opposite Taiwan.
May 19					
May 20		U.S. and Britain reject a Russian offer to negotiate an end to the Greek civil war, claiming that any settlement must come through the U.N. with the concurrence of the Greek government .... Bavarian parliament refuses to ratify the West German Basic Law, but agrees to join the new state if other state legislatures approve the constitution.	France extends formal recognition to Israel as Poland concludes a trade agreement with the Jewish state.	Bolivian Acting Pres. Mamerto Urriolagoitia names a new cabinet dominated by the Republican Socialist Union Party.	Burmese Karen nationalists proclaim a separate state in central Burma between Daiku and Toungoo.
May 21		Sixteen-thousand Berlin railway workers, residents of the western sectors who work in the Russian zone, strike for payment of their wages in West German currency .... Wuerttemberg-Hohenzollern ratifies the West German Basic Law, the last state aside from Bavaria to do so .... National Council of the Gaullist French People's Union opposes the new West German constitution, charging that it permits revival of a centralized German state.		White House announces an agreement between Truman and visiting Brazilian Pres. Dutra for U.S. economic aid to Brazil and negotiation of a cultural treaty.	French National Assembly approves a measure changing the status of Cochin China from a French colony to an autonomous member of the Indochinese group within the French Commonwealth .... Communist forces report the occupation of Sian, the largest city in northwest China.
May 22				Colombian Pres. Mariano Ospina Perez reorganizes his cabinet for the second time in two weeks, increasing the number of Conservatives and including three army officers.	Burmese troops retake the communications center of Insein, 10 miles north of Rangoon, from Karen forces.

A	B	C	D	E
Includes developments that affect more than one world region, international organizations and important meetings of major world leaders.	*Includes all domestic and regional developments in Europe, including the Soviet Union, Turkey, Cyprus and Malta.*	*Includes all domestic and regional developments in Africa and the Middle East, including Iraq and Iran and excluding Cyprus, Turkey and Afghanistan.*	*Includes all domestic and regional developments in Latin America, the Caribbean and Canada.*	*Includes all domestic and regional developments in Asian and Pacific nations, extending from Afghanistan through all the Pacific Islands, except Hawaii.*

U.S. Politics & Social Issues	U.S. Foreign Policy & Defense	U.S. Economy & Environment	Science, Technology & Nature	Culture, Leisure & Life Style	
		Paul Richter, co-founder of Trans World Airlines, dies at 53 of a cerebral hemorrhage in Berkeley, Calif.		Univ. of Southern California wins the West Coast Relays in Fresno, Calif., setting a world record of 1 min. 24.4 secs. for the 880-yard relay .... Chaim Tchernowitz, Talmudic scholar and president of the Jewish Academy of Arts and Sciences, dies at 78 in N.Y.	May 15
Senate passes and sends to House conference a bill authorizing the President to reorganize executive agencies in line with Hoover Commission recommendations .... Supreme Court voids a Chicago ordinance used to convict an anti-Semitic speaker of disorderly conduct, ruling that constitutional guarantees of free speech protect ideas that "invite dispute ... or create a disturbance."		Both houses of Congress pass a compromise $524.7-million deficiency appropriation, including $2.5 million to start construction of a controversial TVA steam plant in Johnsonville, Tenn. .... Supreme Court authorizes the federal government to file suit against Texas and Louisiana to settle the ownership of oil-rich tidelands.	Johns Hopkins Univ. physicians report that the seasickness drug dramamine relieves morning sickness in many pregnant mothers.	*The Daily Compass*, a 10¢ morning tabloid published and edited by Theodore Thackrey, appears in N.Y.	May 16
Franklin D. Roosevelt, Jr. defeats Tammany Hall candidates in a special election to fill the House seat of the late Sol Bloom (D, N.Y.).	Gen. Lucius Clay receives a hero's welcome in Washington following his retirement as head of the U.S. military government in Germany. Addressing both houses of Congress, he urges that West Germany be admitted into the alliance of Western democracies.				May 17
	Senate Foreign Relations Comm. completes hearings on the North Atlantic Treaty.			National Institute of Social Sciences presents a gold medal to former State Secy. George Marshall for "distinguished service to humanity." .... James Truslow Adams, Pulitzer Prize-winning U.S. historian, dies at 70 in Westport, Conn.	May 18
Federal prosecutors end their presentation of evidence in the N.Y. trial of U.S. Communist leaders after calling 13 witnesses during the past two months.		CIO Executive Bd. completes a three-day meeting in Washington after adopting a resolution demanding that leftist union leaders follow the CIO's anti-Communist policies or resign .... AFL Executive Council ends a four-day meeting in Cleveland after rejecting a UMW bid to re-enter the federation.		Thomas Heggan, author of the novel *Mr. Roberts* and its Broadway adaptation, commits suicide at 29 in N.Y.	May 19
Illinois' Seditious Activities Investigation Comm. clears the Univ. of Chicago and Roosevelt College of charges that they harbored subversive activities .... Responding to congressional criticism of the granting of a government fellowship to a Communist Party member, Atomic Energy Commission head David Lilienthal agrees that fellowship applicants should be required to take an oath of alliegance to the U.S. government .... Regional Council for Education, charged with carrying through the Southern plan for a segregated higher education system, begins signing contracts with universities in Virginia, Louisiana, Georgia and Tennessee for medical and dental training.				AFL International Alliance of Theatrical Stage Employes announces signing of a contract with the 10 major Hollywood film studios ending conflicts with the AFL Conference of Studio Unions .... George Papandreou (Archbishop Damaskinos), head of the autocephalous Greek Church and former Regent of Greece, dies at 58 in Athens of a heart attack.	May 20
Senate Judiciary Comm. Chmn. Patrick McCarren subpoenas Justice Dept. files on subversive activities, threatening to publish "alarming information" gathered in committee hearings if Atty. Gen. Clark fails to comply.				Klaus Mann, author and eldest son of novelist Thomas Mann, commits suicide at 42 in Cannes, France.	May 21
	Former Defense Secy. James Forrestal commits suicide at 57 by jumping from a 16th-floor window of the Bethesda Naval Hospital, where he was under treatment for "physical and mental exhaustion." .... Charging "incredible mismanagement" in the Atomic Energy Commission, Sen. Bourke Hickenlooper (R, Ia.) and other members of the Joint Congressional Atomic Energy Comm. demand the resignation of AEC head David Lilienthal and an investigation of the agency's operations.		Tornadoes sweep through the Midwest, causing 46 deaths.	Screen Directors Guild presents its first annual award for directorial achievement to Joseph Mankiewicz for "*A Letter to Three Wives*."	May 22
F	G	H	I	J	
Includes elections, federal-state relations, civil rights and liberties, crime, the judiciary, education, health care, poverty, urban affairs and population.	*Includes formation and debate of U.S. foreign and defense policies, veterans affairs and defense spending. (Relations with specific foreign countries are usually found under the region concerned.)*	*Includes business, labor, agriculture, taxation, transportation, consumer affairs, monetary and fiscal policy, natural resources, pollution and accidents.*	*Includes worldwide scientific, medical and technological developments, natural phenomena, U.S. weather and natural disasters.*	*Includes the arts, religion, scholarship, communications media, sports, entertainment, fashions, fads and social life.*	

	World Affairs	Europe	Africa & the Middle East	The Americas	Asia & the Pacific
May 23	Allied Council of Foreign Ministers convenes for the sixth time since the war in Paris and adopts an agenda including the problem of German unity, the status of Berlin and the Austrian peace treaty.	New West German constitution takes effect, formally establishing the Federal Republic of Germany.			
May 24	Speaking at the Paris Foreign Ministers Conference, Soviet Foreign Min. Andrei Vishinsky urges a return to the system of four-power Allied rule in Germany established at Potsdam, including revival of the Allied Control Council and the Allied Berlin command. State Secy. Acheson immediately rejects the proposal.	West Berlin police drive Russian-sector security forces from elevated railway stations in the western zones after violence in the current railroad workers' strike causes two deaths and 1,000 injuries . . . . A Czech Communist Party congress begins in Prague, attended by all Cominform leaders.			
May 25	U.N. Atomic Energy Commission resumes its sessions in Lake Success, N.Y. as Russia revives its demand for separate international agreements outlawing atomic weapons and establishing a nuclear control system.			Argentine government orders U.S. imports reduced to 25% of the 1947-48 average due to a shortage of dollars.	Communist forces occupy Shanghai, China's largest city and chief port. Nationalists keep a toehold in the northern part of the city and an escape route to the Yangtze port of Woosung . . . . Gen. Simon Spoor, commander of Dutch forces in the East Indies, dies at 47 of a heart attack in Batavia.
May 26				Brazilian government buys the British-owned Leopoldina and Great Western railroads for $54.7 million.	
May 27		Russian authorities again halt freight traffic from West Germany to Berlin . . . . A London court rejects a U.S. extradition request for Gerhart Eisler, ruling that he committed no crime recognized by British law.			U.S. Navy withdraws all fleet and shore units from Tsingtao in northern China, while Communist forces end fighting around Shanghai by taking the Yangtze port of Woosung with the surrender of 50,000 Nationalist soldiers.
May 28	Western Allies respond to Russian proposals at the Paris Foreign Ministers Conference by urging extension of the West German Basic Law and the Western occupation statute to all of Germany and creation of a four-power supervisory high commission which would make its decisions by majority vote. Russian Foreign Min. Vishinsky rejects the Western plan as "one-sided."	Czech Archbishop Josef Beran breaks off negotiations for a state-church agreement on Catholic schools as "vain and hopeless."		Striking Bolivian tin miners in Catavi riot when Army troops move in to operate the mines. The violence causes 52 deaths, including those of two U.S. mining engineers taken hostage by the strikers . . . . Pres. Eurico Dutra ends his U.S. visit and returns to Brazil.	Gen. Chen Yi, commander of victorious Communist forces in Shanghai, is appointed head of a military control commission established to govern the city.
May 29		Three weeks of local elections on Cyprus end with a victory for nationalist candidates who advocate a union of Cyprus with Greece and an end to the island's status as a British colony.			Communist administrators take over the Chinese Central Bank in Shanghai and declare the Nationalist gold yuan void as of June 5 . . . . Russia announces plans to close its Shanghai consulate and maintain diplomatic missions only in Nationalist China.
May 30	Vishinsky formally rejects Western proposals for German unification at the Paris Foreign Ministers Conference.	Communist-led German People's Congress ends a two-day session in East Berlin after proclaiming the German Democratic Republic in the Soviet zone and adopting a constitution providing for a parliament chosen on geographical and occupational lines.	Syrian Premier Husni Zayim abolishes political parties but promises that new parties will be permitted after upcoming legislative elections . . . . Britain signs an agreement allowing Israel to spend $28 million in Jewish assets frozen in Britain since February 1948.		
	A *Includes developments that affect more than one world region, international organizations and important meetings of major world leaders.*	B *Includes all domestic and regional developments in Europe, including the Soviet Union, Turkey, Cyprus and Malta.*	C *Includes all domestic and regional developments in Africa and the Middle East, including Iraq and Iran and excluding Cyprus, Turkey and Afghanistan.*	D *Includes all domestic and regional developments in Latin America, the Caribbean and Canada.*	E *Includes all domestic and regional developments in Asian and Pacific nations, extending from Afghanistan through all the Pacific Islands, except Hawaii.*

U.S. Politics & Social Issues	U.S. Foreign Policy & Defense	U.S. Economy & Environment	Science, Technology & Nature	Culture, Leisure & Life Style	
		General Motors announces a second 2¢ hourly wage cut for 273,000 workers under a union contract tied to the cost-of-living index.	William Hansen, Stanford Univ. atomic scientist who helped develop radar, dies at 39 of bronchitis in Palo Alto, Calif.	Ten Hollywood writers and directors dismissed from their jobs for refusing to tell the House Un-American Activities Comm. whether they were Communists file suit in Los Angeles against 10 film producers .... Joey Maxim of Cleveland wins the U.S. light-heavyweight boxing title with a 15-round decision over Gus Lesnevich in Cincinnati .... H.L. Davis' American frontier novel *Beulah Land* is published in N.Y. by Morrow.	May 23
		Victor Reuther, UAW educational director and brother of union Pres. Walter Reuther, is shot and seriously wounded by an unknown assailant in his Redford, Mich. home.	U.S. Atomic Energy Commission Chmn. Lilienthal, testifying before a Senate Appropriations subcommittee, admits that part of the uranium oxide found missing from an AEC laboratory last February has not yet been accounted for.		May 24
	State Dept. reveals that it has begun consultations with 13 Western states on means of restricting the spread of Communism in Asia and forestalling "hasty recognition" of the Chinese Communist government .... Francis Matthews is sworn in as Navy Secretary.		Dr. Benjamin Pasamanik of Kings County Hospital in Brooklyn receives the $1,500 Lester Hofheimer Research Award for a study showing that Negroes have the same mental capacity as other races.	Rabbinical Council of America ends a three-day meeting in Atlantic City after deciding that the Chief Rabbinate of Israel is now the central religious authority for all Jews .... General Assembly of the U.S. Presbyterian Church ends a seven-day Buffalo meeting after voting to reorganize into 12 synods based on population.	May 25
	Senate passes and sends to the House a bill to strengthen unification of the armed forces by increasing the Defense Secretary's authority over the three services and creating the posts of deputy defense secretary and civilian controller of military expenditures .... House passes and sends to the Senate a $5.6-billion foreign aid appropriation, including funds for the Marshall Plan and Greek-Turkish aid programs .... Truman signs a State Dept. reorganization bill, appointing George Kennan and Dean Rusk to the new posts of State Dept. counselor and deputy under secretary for substantive matters .... Truman defends Atomic Energy Commission Chmn. David Lilienthal against congressional attacks, stating "it is time people stopped getting hysterical when the word 'atom' is mentioned."	Chicago, Cleveland and St. Louis stock exchanges announce plans to merge into a single Midwestern exchange .... Justice Dept. accuses the Northern Pacific Railway Co. of violating the Sherman Antitrust Act by selling and leasing land under "traffic clauses" requiring purchasers to ship exclusively on the Northern Pacific .... N.J. Supreme Court rules that the state's no-strike law for public utility workers is unconstitutional.		Pope Pius XII issues a papal bull proclaiming 1949-50 a Holy Year.	May 26
A federal grand jury in San Francisco indicts International Longshoremen's and Warehousemen's Union Pres. Harry Bridges for perjury, accusing him of falsely denying Communist Party membership at the time of his U.S. naturalization in 1945.	Senate passes and sends to House conference a bill expanding the powers of the Central Intelligence Agency and the secrecy of its activities, personnel and expenditures.	NLRB unanimously voids the UMW's union shop contract with coal mines owned by steel companies.		American Academy of Arts and Letters presents its gold medal to Frederick Law Olmsted, the first landscape architect to win the award .... Actress Rita Hayworth marries Prince Ali Kahn, son of Indian Moslem leader Aga Kahn, on the French Riviera .... Robert Ripley, originator of *Believe It Or Not*, dies at 55 in N.Y.	May 27
Oklahoma legislature passes a bill allowing Negroes to attend state universities on a segregated basis for courses not given in the state's Negro colleges.					May 28
		A 25-day strike of Ford workers ends when both sides accept an agreement sending the dispute over work speed to arbitration .... U.S. Treasurer William Julian dies at 87 in an auto accident near Bethesda, Md.			May 29
				Bill Holland averages a record speed of 121.327 mph to win the 33rd Indianapolis 500 classic, earning $60,000.	May 30
F	G	H	I	J	
Includes elections, federal-state relations, civil rights and liberties, crime, the judiciary, education, health care, poverty, urban affairs and population.	*Includes formation and debate of U.S. foreign and defense policies, veterans affairs and defense spending. (Relations with specific foreign countries are usually found under the region concerned.)*	*Includes business, labor, agriculture, taxation, transportation, consumer affairs, monetary and fiscal policy, natural resources, pollution and accidents.*	*Includes worldwide scientific, medical and technological developments, natural phenomena, U.S. weather and natural disasters.*	*Includes the arts, religion, scholarship, communications media, sports, entertainment, fashions, fads and social life.*	

	World Affairs	Europe	Africa & the Middle East	The Americas	Asia & the Pacific
May 31		Luxembourg Chamber of Deputies ratifies the North Atlantic Treaty.		Argentina and Britain sign a five-year commercial treaty calling for at least $640 million in mutual trade each year.	Japan's Diet completes action on a 700-billion-yen balanced budget calling for the dismissal of 400,000 government employes during the next year . . . . U.S. closes its Mukden consulate but keeps its missions open in other Communist-occupied Chinese cities, including Peking and Nanking.
June 1	Allied foreign ministers in Paris begin discussions on the Berlin question but fail to reach agreement on voting in the Allied Berlin command or the right of the Western Allies to share in the occupation of Berlin.		Native Arab leaders and British administrators agree on formation of an independent government in Cyrenaica, part of the former Italian colony of Libya.	Striking Bolivian tin miners agree to return to work after the government promises to withdraw Army forces from Catavi and indemnify the families of miners killed in the disturbances . . . . Britain permits the U.S. to build radar tracking stations in the Bahamas to check guided missiles fired from Florida.	
June 2		Gerhart Eisler arrives in East Germany following his release from a London prison to assume a professorship at the Univ. of Leipzig.			
June 3		Allied military commanders in Berlin hold their first meeting since the breakup of the Berlin command last July in an unsuccessful effort to settle the strike of Berlin railway workers.		Canadian Seamen's Union, on strike against shippers in eastern Canada, is suspended from the Canadian Trades and Labor Congress due to alleged Communist leadership.	Marshal Yen Hsi-shan succeeds Ho Ying-chin as Chinese Nationalist premier . . . . Chinese Communists occupy Tsingtao following abandonment of the port and naval base by Nationalist forces.
June 4		Organization for European Economic Cooperation representatives complete two days of discussions in Paris with U.S. Special Envoy Averell Harriman with no agreement on U.S. demands for greater free trade among Western European nations.			
June 5				Canada and the U.S. conclude a commercial aviation agreement giving Canadian airlines new routes through the U.S. in return for continued American use of the Gander, Newfoundland airfield for transatlantic flights.	
June 6		Truman names John McCloy, future U.S. high commissioner for Germany, to serve as head of the Economic Cooperation Administration in Germany.			
June 7					Chinese Nationalist government prepares to transfer its capital to Chungking as Communist forces advance towards Canton.

	A	B	C	D	E
	Includes developments that affect more than one world region, international organizations and important meetings of major world leaders.	*Includes all domestic and regional developments in Europe, including the Soviet Union, Turkey, Cyprus and Malta.*	*Includes all domestic and regional developments in Africa and the Middle East, including Iraq and Iran and excluding Cyprus, Turkey and Afghanistan.*	*Includes all domestic and regional developments in Latin America, the Caribbean and Canada.*	*Includes all domestic and regional developments in Asian and Pacific nations, extending from Afghanistan through all the Pacific Islands, except Hawaii.*

U.S. Politics & Social Issues	U.S. Foreign Policy & Defense	U.S. Economy & Environment	Science, Technology & Nature	Culture, Leisure & Life Style	
Perjury trial of Alger Hiss begins in a N.Y. federal court, with Judge Samuel Kaufman presiding .... Senate passes and sends to the House a measure granting home rule to the District of Columbia.	Gen. Lucius Clay retires from the Army after 31 years of service in ceremonies at Ft. Meyer, Va.	Prices on the N.Y. Stock Exchange take their sharpest drop this year, falling one-to-three points.		Sam Snead takes the Professional Golfers Assn. championship in Richmond, Va., winning $3,500.	May 31
At Truman's direction, Atty. Gen. Clark and Asst. State Secy. John Peurifoy refuse to give the Senate Judiciary Comm. files on foreign officials suspected of subversive activity.	Joint Congressional Atomic Energy Comm. begins public hearings on operations of the Atomic Energy Commission. Citing high personnel turnover in the AEC, Sen. Bourke Hickenlooper (R, Ia.) demands David Lilienthal's resignation .... House passes and sends to the Senate a bill providing monthly pensions to low-income veterans.	International Longshoremen's and Warehousemen's Union convention in San Francisco re-elects Pres. Harry Bridges, under indictment on fraud and perjury charges.		Rudolf Bing, director of England's Glyndebourne Opera Co., is appointed to succeed Edward Johnson as general director of New York's Metropolitan Opera Assn.	June 1
House passes and sends to the Senate a measure passed by the Judiciary Comm. liberalizing provisions of the 1948 Displaced Persons Act.	Joint Congressional Atomic Energy Comm. reports discovery of the remaining uranium oxide missing since last February from an Atomic Energy Commission laboratory in Illinois. The material was found in the laboratory's "security burial ground." Continuing the committee's investigation of FBI operations, Sen. Bourke Hickenlooper scores Lilienthal for hiring nuclear weapons workers without FBI clearance.			Federal Communications Commission ends its eight-year ban on editorializing by radio stations but warns that stations must present all sides of controversial questions.	June 2
Testifying at the N.Y. trial of Alger Hiss, Whittaker Chambers admits under defense cross-examination that he lied to the FBI, the House Un-American Activities Comm. and the FBI in previous statements on Communist spy activities in the U.S. .... N.Y. Judge Harold Medina sentences three U.S. Communist leaders, including Gus Hall, to prison for contempt of court.	Wesley Brown of Washington becomes the first Negro to graduate from the U.S. Naval Academy in ceremonies in Annapolis.	Amadeo Giannini, founder and chairman of the Bank of America and the Transamerica Corp., dies at 79 in San Francisco.		Michigan State captures team honors at the intercollegiate outdoor track and field meet in N.Y.	June 3
				Jack Kramer defeats Bobby Riggs in London to take the world men's professional tennis title.	June 4
			J. Ernest Gendreau, Canadian cancer specialist and founder of Montreal's Radium Institute of Cancer Research, dies at 69 in Montreal.	Baseball Commissioner Albert Chandler permits reinstatement of 18 players suspended from U.S. baseball for jumping to the now defunct Mexican League.	June 5
Senate Judiciary Comm. passes an anti-lynching bill, the first civil rights measure to gain committee approval during the current session .... House passes and sends to the Senate a measure authorizing nationalization of 85,000 resident Asians .... Kansas' 69-year ban on sale of liquor ends.		Senate begins debate on Administration proposals to repeal the Taft-Hartley Act .... Prices on the N.Y. Stock Exchange drop to their lowest level since May 21, 1947.			June 6
Continuing his testimony at the Hiss perjury trial, Whittaker Chambers declares that he perjured himself repeatedly in earlier hearings to protect Hiss and give him a chance to quit the Communist Party .... Defense Secy. Louis Johnson accepts a Navy plan to assure racial equality for all naval and marine personnel but rejects a proposed Army plan for the second time.	Truman urges Congress to appropriate $150 million for economic aid to South Korea during the next year, calling Korea a testing ground for democracy "matched against the practices of Communism." .... House passes a compromise measure authorizing secret operation of the Central Intelligence Agency .... Senate Foreign Relations Comm. recommends prompt U.S. ratification of the North Atlantic Treaty .... Truman nominates Army Under Secy. Gordon Gray to succeed Kenneth Royall as Army Secretary.				June 7

F	G	H	I	J
Includes elections, federal-state relations, civil rights and liberties, crime, the judiciary, education, health care, poverty, urban affairs and population.	*Includes formation and debate of U.S. foreign and defense policies, veterans affairs and defense spending. (Relations with specific foreign countries are usually found under the region concerned.)*	*Includes business, labor, agriculture, taxation, transportation, consumer affairs, monetary and fiscal policy, natural resources, pollution and accidents.*	*Includes worldwide scientific, medical and technological developments, natural phenomena, U.S. weather and natural disasters.*	*Includes the arts, religion, scholarship, communications media, sports, entertainment, fashions, fads and social life.*

	World Affairs	Europe	Africa & the Middle East	The Americas	Asia & the Pacific
June 8		Demonstrating German workers prevent the dismantling of factories in Dortmund and Essen by British reparations authorities.			Communist authorities in Shanghai ban the Kuomintang and all groups affiliated with it, including the Democratic Socialists and the Young China Party.
June 9			U.S. attempts to break a six-week deadlock in U.N.-sponsored Palestine peace talks in Lausanne, Switzerland by demanding that Israel abandon its opposition to a general return of Palestinian Arab refugees and concede some land to the Arabs.		
June 10	Vishinsky urges the Paris Foreign Ministers Conference to take quick action on a German peace treaty and withdrawal of Allied occupation forces from Germany and Austria. Western delegates reject the idea of an early peace treaty in the absence of agreement on a unified German state.	Hungarian Premier Istvan Dobi announces formation of a new cabinet following Foreign Min. Laszlo Rajk's ouster for "nationalist" leanings . . . . British Labor Party's five-day annual conference ends in Blackpool after approving plans for a 1950 election campaign based on the promise of a "new social order."	Britain announces plans to resume arms shipments to Arab states with the purpose of maintaining their "internal security."		
June 11		U.S. and Russian authorities in Berlin agree on a tentative settlement of the Berlin railway workers' strike, permitting workers living in West Berlin to receive 60% of their wages in West German marks with the right to exchange a further 15% into Western currency . . . . Czech Archbishop Josef Beran orders a Catholic boycott of all government-sponsored religious groups and publications . . . . Czechoslovakia breaks off trade relations with Yugoslavia . . . . A Tirana court sentences former Albanian Deputy Premier Xoxe Koci to death for "traitorous" support of Yugoslavia.	Lebanon arrests 300 members of the Syrian National Party on charges of plotting a coup against the government in Beirut.		Chiang Kai-shek becomes head of a Supreme Policy Comm. established to advise the Nationalist cabinet . . . . Burmese government forces report taking the oil refining center of Yenangyuang on the Irrawaddy River from Communist guerrillas.
June 12					
June 13		Russia rejects Western requests for an Allied conference on alleged Bulgarian, Hungarian and Rumanian violations of human rights in trials of church officials . . . . Albania announces the execution of former Deputy Premier Kochi Rodze for collaboration with Yugoslavia . . . . Municipal elections in Trieste result in victory for parties favoring the city's return to Italy.			
June 14		Striking Berlin railway workers reject settlement terms proposed by the city's U.S. and Russian military governors . . . . Bulgarian government announces expulsion of former Deputy Premier Traicho Kostov from the Communist Party for persistently advocating "anti-Russian" and "nationalist" policies.			Bao Dai resumes the title of Emperor of Vietnam, claiming sovereignty over Annam, Tonkin and Cochin China.
	A *Includes developments that affect more than one world region, international organizations and important meetings of major world leaders.*	B *Includes all domestic and regional developments in Europe, including the Soviet Union, Turkey, Cyprus and Malta.*	C *Includes all domestic and regional developments in Africa and the Middle East, including Iraq and Iran and excluding Cyprus, Turkey and Afghanistan.*	D *Includes all domestic and regional developments in Latin America, the Caribbean and Canada.*	E *Includes all domestic and regional developments in Asian and Pacific nations, extending from Afghanistan through all the Pacific Islands, except Hawaii.*

U.S. Politics & Social Issues	U.S. Foreign Policy & Defense	U.S. Economy & Environment	Science, Technology & Nature	Culture, Leisure & Life Style	
California State Senate Comm. on Un-American Activities releases a report on Communism in California, accusing a number of prominent writers and entertainers of following "the Communist Party line .... over a long period of time." Among those listed are Pearl Buck, Charles Chaplin, Thomas Mann, Lillian Hellman, Dashiell Hammett, Rep. Helen Gahagan Douglas, Orson Welles and Frank Sinatra .... A National Education Assn. commission, including Gen. Eisenhower and Harvard Pres. James Conant, recommends exclusion of all Communists from the teaching profession.	House authorizes an Armed Services Comm. investigation of the nation's strategic air program, with emphasis on charges of irregularities in procurement of Air Force B-36 bombers.	UMW leader John Lewis orders a one-week work stoppage by 450,000 union members beginning June 13 to improve the union's bargaining position in upcoming contract talks.			June 8
	Economic Cooperation Admin. Paul Hoffman threatens to resign if Congress makes significant cuts in the Marshall Plan budget for the coming year .... A Senate Expenditures subcommittee criticizes the International Refugee Organization and member states, including the U.S., for failing to settle the more than 700,000 refugees remaining in Europe.				June 9
American Medical Assn. House of Delegates, beginning a five-day meeting in Atlantic City, bars further public statements by Morris Fishbein, editor of the AMA *Journal* and one of the most vocal opponents of the Administration's national health care plan. The move is viewed as a concession to growing public sentiment in favor of a compulsory health care program .... Southern Regional Education Program for the pooling of specialized higher education facilities is formally organized by representatives of 14 Southern states meeting in Daytona Beach, Fla.		A Chicago federal grand jury indicts Preston Tucker and seven associates for mail fraud and conspiracy after a 3½ month investigation of the defunct Tucker Auto Corp.		N.Y. Giants coach Frank Frisch is named manager of the Chicago Cubs .... Sigrid Undset, Nobel Prize-winning Norwegian novelist, dies at 67 in Lillehammer, Norway .... Sir Frederick Ogilvie, principal of Jesus College, Oxford and former head of the British Broadcasting Corp., dies at 56 in London .... H.L. Mencken's *A Mencken Chrestomathy* is published in N.Y. by Knopf.	June 10
				Ted Atkinson rides Capot to victory in the $91,500 Belmont Stakes in N.Y. .... Former dentist Cary Middlecoff captures the U.S. Open Golf Classic in Chicago.	June 11
Univ. of California, Berkeley requires its faculty to take a loyalty oath to the U.S. government and forswear membership in subversive organizations.				*New York Herald Tribune* lists John Marquand's *Point of No Return* and Frank Gilbreth's and Ernestine Carey's *Cheaper by the Dozen* as the best-selling fiction and non-fiction books.	June 12
U.S. Circuit Court of Appeals in Washington upholds the contempt of Congress convictions of film writers Dalton Trumbo and John Lawson, ruling that the House Un-American Activities Comm. has the right to ask witnesses whether they are Communists .... Government prosecutors rest their case in the espionage trial of Justice Dept. employe Judith Coplon .... Roy Wilkens becomes temporary executive secretary of the NAACP as Walter White takes a leave of absence .... In a letter to Rep. Ralph Gwinn (R, N.Y.), Eisenhower opposes Administration aid-to-education programs as encouraging "paternalism, if not outright socialism."	Senate ratifies the 41-nation International Wheat Agreement and confirms Gordon Gray as Army Secretary and John McCloy as U.S. high commissioner for Germany.	Supreme Court outlaws Standard Oil of California's "exclusive dealer" contracts, which force service station owners to obtain all their gasoline from the company .... A selling wave continues to depress N.Y. Stock Exchange prices, which drop to a five-year low.		George Orwell's *1984* is published in N.Y. by Harcourt, Brace and becomes a Book-of-the-Month-Club selection.	June 13
Frank Oppenheimer, brother of nuclear physicist J. Robert Oppenheimer and a participant in the Manhattan Project, admits to the House Un-American Activities Comm. that he and his wife belonged to the Communist Party during the late 1930s.				Philadelphia Phillies star first baseman Eddie Waitkus is shot and seriously wounded by Ruth Steinhagen, a Chicago typist who claims she loved him for two years .... Russell Doubleday, retired publisher and author, dies at 77 in Glen Cove, N.Y.	June 14
F	G	H	I	J	
Includes elections, federal-state relations, civil rights and liberties, crime, the judiciary, education, health care, poverty, urban affairs and population.	*Includes formation and debate of U.S. foreign and defense policies, veterans affairs and defense spending. (Relations with specific foreign countries are usually found under the region concerned.)*	*Includes business, labor, agriculture, taxation, transportation, consumer affairs, monetary and fiscal policy, natural resources, pollution and accidents.*	*Includes worldwide scientific, medical and technological developments, natural phenomena, U.S. weather and natural disasters.*	*Includes the arts, religion, scholarship, communications media, sports, entertainment, fashions, fads and social life.*	

	World Affairs	Europe	Africa & the Middle East	The Americas	Asia & the Pacific
June 15			Israeli Foreign Min. Moshe Sharett (formerly Shertok) rejects general readmission of Palestinian Arab refugees and territorial concessions to Arab states before conclusion of a Palestine peace settlement.		
June 16					
June 17	International Chamber of Commerce concludes a five-day meeting in Quebec after urging extension of free trade and opposing restriction on cartels and state control of business.				Chinese Communist authorities reopen the port of Shanghai to world shipping after a four-day search for Nationalist mines.
June 18		Hungarian government announces the arrest of former Foreign Min. Laszlo Rajk and 19 other officials accused of espionage and "Trotskyist" activities. A Budapest court hands down prison sentences of six months to three years for seven Zionist leaders convicted of helping Jews emigrate illegally to Israel.			
June 19		Czech government prevents Archbishop Josef Beran from issuing a pastoral letter pledging loyalty to the state but condemning its attempts to impose an "anti-Christian" ideology on the country .... German Freemasons, banned under the Nazis, meet in Frankfurt and establish a Masonic Grand Lodge for West Germany, with steel industrialist Theodor Vogel as Grand Master.			Chinese Communist leader Mao Tze-tung declares that the Communists have won the civil war and expresses willingness to establish diplomatic relations with "truly friendly" foreign countries .... French Pres. Vincent Auriol and Emperor Bao Dai sign an agreement establishing a semi-autonomous Vietnamese state .... A referendum in France's northeastern Indian territory of Chandernagore results in an overwhelming victory for union with India .... Far Eastern trade union leaders meeting in Geneva establish an Anti-Communist Asian Federation of Labor .... Prince Jagatjit Singh Bahadur, Maharajah of Kapurthala and one of the world's wealthiest men, dies at 76 in Bombay.
June 20	Paris Foreign Ministers Conference ends without accord on any important problems in Germany or Berlin. Participants agree to continue work on the Austrian peace treaty, scheduled for completion by Sept. 1 .... U.N. Human Rights Commission ends its fifth session at Lake Success after drafting a covenant guaranteeing freedom of religion, rights of assembly and association and a fair trial for all accused persons.	U.S., Britain and France sign an agreement establishing a civilian Allied High Commission to exercise supreme authority in West Germany after creation of the Federal Republic. The commission will replace separate Western Allied military governments .... Russian Amb. to Yugoslavia Anatoly Lavrentiev returns to Belgrade after a four-month absence. Hungary denounces its five-year Yugoslavian commercial agreement and Czechoslovakia bans all trade with the country.			Chinese Nationalist government bans river and sea traffic to all Communist-controlled areas and threatens to bombard Shanghai and other ports .... A typhoon accompanied by floods strikes southern Japan, causing 106 deaths.
	A	B	C	D	E
	Includes developments that affect more than one world region, international organizations and important meetings of major world leaders.	*Includes all domestic and regional developments in Europe, including the Soviet Union, Turkey, Cyprus and Malta.*	*Includes all domestic and regional developments in Africa and the Middle East, including Iraq and Iran and excluding Cyprus, Turkey and Afghanistan.*	*Includes all domestic and regional developments in Latin America, the Caribbean and Canada.*	*Includes all domestic and regional developments in Asian and Pacific nations, extending from Afghanistan through all the Pacific Islands, except Hawaii.*

U.S. Politics & Social Issues	U.S. Foreign Policy & Defense	U.S. Economy & Environment	Science, Technology & Nature	Culture, Leisure & Life Style	
	House passes and sends to the Senate a bill providing pay increases of 3-33% for all military personnel.	A Senate Banking subcommittee schedules hearings on oil industry prices and profits following criticism of continued gasoline price increases at a time of generally falling prices.		John Gunther's *Behind the Curtain*, a report on Eastern Europe, is published in N.Y. by Harper and becomes a Book-of-the-Month-Club selection.	June 15
Truman attacks current spy trials and loyalty checks for producing a nationwide hysteria. Negro singer Paul Robeson, returning from a 10-day tour of Russia, denounces the N.Y. trial of U.S. Communist leaders as "a type of domestic fascism." .... House and Senate pass a measure giving Truman authority to reorganize executive agencies in line with the recommendations of the Hoover Commission, but reserving a congressional veto over proposed changes.		CIO Textile Workers Union foregoes a raise increase this year due to poor business conditions.		Lord Derby's Alycidon wins the Gold Cup in England's Ascot race, earning $42,160 .... Jake LaMotta captures the world middleweight boxing title from Marcel Cerdan with a ninth round knockout in Detroit.	June 16
Government prosecutors rest their case in the perjury trial of Alger Hiss as Judge Samuel Kaufman denies a defense motion to dismiss Hiss's indictment .... Testifying at her Washington trial, Justice Dept. employe Judith Coplon accuses her superior of "planting" incriminating documents in her purse following discovery of her romance with Russian engineer Valentin Gubitchev .... Univ. of Kentucky announces an end to segregation of Negro students.	Economic Cooperation Admin. Paul Hoffman criticizes the Argentine-British commercial agreement for restricting free trade and threatens to cut off Marshall Plan aid to Britain if both countries adhere to the pact.				June 17
A majority of House Un-American Activities Comm. members object to the demand of Chmn. John Wood (D, Ga.) for an investigation of textbooks used by 71 U.S. colleges and 48 state education boards .... Former State Secy. James Byrnes, speaking at Washington and Lee Univ. in Virginia, warns that many Administration policies are leading to "statism" and urges a reduction in government spending programs.		Ford Motors rejects a UAW demand for wage and pension increases, declaring that "the economy is in a downward trend."		Univ. of Southern California wins the team title in NCAA track and field competition in Los Angeles.	June 18
		Sears Roebuck's new catologue appears with price cuts averaging 6½%.			June 19
Alger Hiss begins his defense in his N.Y. prejury trial with a presentation of character witnesses, including commendations from U.S. Ambassador-at-Large Philip Jessup and Supreme Court Justices Felix Frankfurter and Stanley Reed .... Truman signs a bill authorizing him to reorganize executive agencies in line with recommendations of the Hoover Commission. He immediately sends Congress the first of seven reorganization plans, providing for creation of a cabinet-level Welfare Dept. to administer most of the Federal Security Agency's programs .... Supreme Court rules that the federal government may sue itself in an attempt to recover funds paid to the Interstate Commerce Commission.		Coal miners return to work on schedule following a one-week shutdown ordered by UMW leader Lewis .... Supreme Court rules that the Federal Power Commission has no right to control a natural gas company's disposal of its gas reserves.		Vatican excommunicates the organizers and supporters of a government-sponsored Catholic Action group in Czechoslovakia.	June 20

	World Affairs	Europe	Africa & the Middle East	The Americas	Asia & the Pacific
June 21					
June 22				Dominican Republic foils an attempted airborne invasion for the second time in three days, charging Cuba and Guatemala with harboring the rebels.	Taiwan-based Nationalist planes bomb the British freighter *Anchises* near Shanghai, mistaking the ship for a Communist vessel .... Britain announces further reinforcement of its Hong Kong garrison with 2,000 troops.
June 23		Hungarian Deputy Premier Matyas Rakosi announces a purge of the country's Communist Party, involving the expulsion of 200,000 party members or 18% of the membership. Rakosi attributes the purge to discovery of a spy ring within the party.			
June 24	Security Council fails to agree on the admission of 12 new U.N. members when Britain and the U.S. refuse to approve the applications of Outer Mongolia and four Eastern European states.	Communist-led strike of one million Italian farm workers ends when the government promises the country's first national farm workers' contract .... Greek Premier Themistocles Sophoulis dies at 88 of a stroke in an Athens suburb.			Dutch troops begin evacuating the Indonesian Republic capital of Jakarta.
June 25		Western military commanders in Berlin order 15,000 striking rail workers to return to work, offering them full wage payment in Western currency and threatening to cut off their unemployment relief if they refuse to comply .... Special U.N. Balkan Commission in Athens charges Bulgaria and Albania with continuing to lend large-scale aid to Greek guerrillas.	Col. Husni Zayim, running without opposition, is elected president of Syria.		Indonesian Republic government announces the execution of four Communists who helped lead last September's Madiun revolt.
June 26	Labor delegates from 33 countries, including the U.S., vote in Geneva to set up an anti-Communist international labor organization rivalling the World Federation of Trade Unions.	Czech Catholic bishops accuse the government of mounting an anti-church campaign, with kidnapings, robbery and other measures intended to destroy religious freedom in Czechoslovakia .... Parliamentary elections in Belgium, the first in which women vote, result in gains for the conservative Christian Social Party, which narrowly fails to win a majority in the Chamber of Deputies.	Newly elected Syrian Pres. Husni Zayim names Muhsen Bey Berazi premier and head of a five-member cabinet.		South Korean rightist political leader Kim Koo is assassinated in Seoul by Lt. Ahn Do Hi following a political quarrel.
June 27		Czech government bans communications and meetings of Catholic church officials without prior state approval.		U.S. withdraws its objection to the Argentine-British trade pact after accepting Britain's explanation that its acute dollar shortage forces it to deal extensively with Argentina .... Parliamentary elections in Canada result in victory for P.M. Louis St. Laurent's Liberal Party, which gains a majority in the House of Commons.	Twenty-four thousand Australian coal miners strike for a $4.40 weekly pay raise and a 35-hour work week, forcing extensive layoffs and plant closings in other industries.
June 28		Berlin railway strike ends after 38 days as 15,000 Western-sector workers return to their jobs.			U.S. refuses to recognize the Nationalist blockade of Communist-held Chinese ports.
	A *Includes developments that affect more than one world region, international organizations and important meetings of major world leaders.*	B *Includes all domestic and regional developments in Europe, including the Soviet Union, Turkey, Cyprus and Malta.*	C *Includes all domestic and regional developments in Africa and the Middle East, including Iraq and Iran and excluding Cyprus, Turkey and Afghanistan.*	D *Includes all domestic and regional developments in Latin America, the Caribbean and Canada.*	E *Includes all domestic and regional developments in Asian and Pacific nations, extending from Afghanistan through all the Pacific Islands, except Hawaii.*

U.S. Politics & Social Issues	U.S. Foreign Policy & Defense	U.S. Economy & Environment	Science, Technology & Nature	Culture, Leisure & Life Style	
A *New York Herald Tribune* expose focuses national interest on "five percenters," influential lobbyists who obtain government contracts for private firms in return for 5% of the contract price. One lobbyist named is James Hunt, a friend of presidential aide Harry Vaughan, Defense Secy. Johnson and other officials .... St. Louis Mayor Joseph Darst revokes an order ending segregation in city swimming pools and playgrounds following a battle between white and Negro youths.	Atomic Energy Commission admits to the Joint Congressional Atomic Energy Comm. that an unspecified amount of uranium is missing from the Oak Ridge nuclear laboratory, blaming "inventory discrepancies." .... Truman appoints Washington hostess and Democratic fund-raiser Perle Mesta as U.S. minister to Luxembourg.	House Democratic caucus votes to back the Administration's housing bill after cutting maximum federal subsidies under the program from $400 million to $308 million .... CIO United Brewery Workers union ends an 82-day strike of 6,400 N.Y. beer workers by accepting an agreement providing for a wage increase and a reduction of the work week to 37½ hours .... NLRB rules that a secondary boycott against railroads does not violate the Taft-Hartley Act, which excludes rail employers and employes.			June 21
Two defense witnesses at the Hiss perjury trial testify that a Woodstock typewriter on which Hiss is alleged to have typed secret State Dept. documents during the late 1930s was in their possession at the time.	State Secy. Acheson appears before the Senate Foreign Relations Comm. to urge ratification of the North Atlantic Treaty and approval of military assistance to Western Europe, claiming that the failure of the Paris Foreign Ministers Conference emphasizes the "utmost importance" of the Atlantic alliance .... Forty-first annual National Governors Conference ends in Colorado Springs after voting unanimous support of the U.N., the Marshall Plan and the North Atlantic Treaty.	House opens debate on the Administration's public housing bill. A brief scuffle breaks out between Rep. Adolph Sabath (D, Ill.), a supporter of the bill, and Eugene Cox (D, Ga.), an opponent.	Atomic scientists Harold Urey, Herbert Anderson and Harrison Brown denounce congressional investigations of the Atomic Energy Commission for "effectively strangling" nuclear research.	Ezzard Charles wins the world heavyweight boxing title in a 15-round decision over Jersey Joe Walcott in Chicago.	June 22
Hiss takes the stand in his perjury trial to deny all charges against him .... Sen. Hugh Butler (R, Neb.) submits a report to the Senate Insular Affairs Comm. charging International Longshoremen's and Warehousemen's Union Pres. Harry Bridges with being the "unseen Communist dictator" of Hawaii's economy, and urging that statehood be withheld from the islands until Communism is suppressed there .... A federal district court in Newark, N.J. denies former German-American Bund leader August Klapprott's petition for restoration of his U.S. citizenship.		A federal court in Toledo, Ohio issues a consent judgment against price collusion in the glass fiber industry involving Owens-Corning Fiberglass, Owens-Illinois Glass and the Corning Glass Works.	Trans World Airlines Pres. Ralph Damon receives the International League of Aviators' American national trophy for 31 years of service to aviation.	Screen Writers Guild presents its first annual awards for writing excellence to Mary Jane Ward for *The Snake Pit*, B. Traven for *The Treasure of the Sierra Madre* and Sidney Sheldon, Frances Goodrich and Albert Hackett for *Easter Parade*.	June 23
Judith Coplon completes her testimony in her Washington trial by calling the charges against her "frame-ups" and charging "this whole case is so fishy that it smells to high heaven." .... Truman sends Congress a special message on Post Office reorganization, supporting the Hoover Commission's recommendation that political appointment of postmasters be eliminated.	Five Democratic and 16 Republican senators send Truman a letter demanding that the U.S. withhold recognition from the Chinese Communist regime and maintain "an affirmative friendly policy" towards the Nationalist government .... Truman presents Congress with a preliminary plan for aid to developing countries and requests $45 million for the program's first year.				June 24
House Un-American Activities Comm. issues a report attacking the American Slav Congress as a Moscow-directed Communist front.				Los Angeles Athletic Club takes the national AAU team title in track and field competition in Fresno, Calif.	June 25
			Federal Security Admin. announces grants totalling $1,504,718 for cancer research.	Bobby Riggs captures the U.S. pro tennis singles title in N.Y., while Don Budge and Frank Kovacs take the doubles title.	June 26
Supreme Court rules that state courts may consider illegally obtained evidence if permitted to do so by state law, upholding the abortion conviction of Denver physician Julius Wolf, whose records were seized without a warrant. The Court also reverses the murder convictions of three Negroes due to police coercion in obtaining confessions.					June 27
Alabama Gov. James Folsom signs a bill banning the public wearing of masks or hoods .... Sen. Robert Wagner (D, N.Y.) resigns his Senate seat due to illness.	Speaking at the Armed Forces Industrial College in Washington, Bernard Baruch accuses the Administration of "vacillation and neglect" for failing to enact a war resources mobilization plan.	Attempting to counteract the deflationary economic trend, the Federal Reserve Bd. announces plans to make more credit available to business in the purchase, sale and exchange of government securities.		William Griffin, editor-publisher of the *New York Enquirer* who was indicted in 1942 on charges of attempting to undermine armed forces morale, dies at 51 in N.Y.	June 28

F	G	H	I	J
Includes elections, federal-state relations, civil rights and liberties, crime, the judiciary, education, health care, poverty, urban affairs and population.	*Includes formation and debate of U.S. foreign and defense policies, veterans affairs and defense spending. (Relations with specific foreign countries are usually found under the region concerned.)*	*Includes business, labor, agriculture, taxation, transportation, consumer affairs, monetary and fiscal policy, natural resources, pollution and accidents.*	*Includes worldwide scientific, medical and technological developments, natural phenomena, U.S. weather and natural disasters.*	*Includes the arts, religion, scholarship, communications media, sports, entertainment, fashions, fads and social life.*

	World Affairs	Europe	Africa & the Middle East	The Americas	Asia & the Pacific
June 29			South African government imposes a ban on mixed marriages between whites and non-whites, the first step in the Nationalist Party's *apartheid* program. The South African Citizenship Act also goes into effect, suspending the automatic granting of citizenship to Commonwealth immigrants .... Israeli Parliament endorses the government's policies on boundaries, the return of Palestinian Arab refugees and the status of Jerusalem.		Last U.S. troops sail from South Korea, leaving only a military mission to advise the South Korean Army .... Three Nationalist B-24 bombers raid Shanghai, causing 155 civilian deaths and 445 injuries.
June 30	International Wheat Agreement goes into effect as India and Lebanon deposit their ratifications in Washington.	Liberal Party leader Alexander Diomedes becomes Greek premier, retaining the coalition cabinet of the late Themistocles Sophoulis with minor changes .... Baron Edouard Alphonse James de Rothschild, head of the famous banking family's French branch, dies at 81 in Paris.			Seoul police announce the arrest of seven South Korean Assembly members, including Deputy Speaker Kim Yak Soo, who were allegedly involved in a Communist plot to overthrow the government.
July 1		Yugoslavia accuses Russia and other Cominform countries of imposing an embargo on shipment of machinery and war materials .... U.S., British, French and Russian representatives resume their London negotiations on an Austrian peace treaty.		Asbestos workers in Asbestos, Quebec end their strike after accepting a 10¢ hourly wage increase negotiated by Archbishop Maurice Roy of Quebec.	In a statement celebrating the 28th anniversary of the Chinese Communist Party, Mao Tze-tung promises to establish a "people's dictatorship" in China and join with Russia in an international front of "new democratic countries." .... Vietnamese Chief of State Bao Dai appoints himself premier as he announces the composition of his first cabinet, including Nguyen Van Xuan as deputy premier and defense minister.
July 2	World Health Organization ends its second annual meeting in Rome after voting to admit Israel and South Korea as new members.	Bulgarian Premier Georgi Dimitrov, a defendant in the German Reichstag fire trial of 1933 and former leader of the Comintern, dies at 67 near Moscow.			
July 3		Yugoslavia annexes its occupation zone of the Istrian peninsula, charging "gross violation" of the Italian peace treaty by Britain, Italy and the U.S. .... Western air forces complete a nine-day mock air war over Britain to test the island's defenses against nuclear attack .... Czech government reports widespread resistance among Slovakian peasants to measures against the Catholic clergy.		Mexican Pres. Miguel Aleman's Party of Revolutionary Institutions wins a sweeping victory in elections for the Chamber of Deputies.	
July 4		Russia, Czechoslovakia, Finland and Poland sign an interlocking one-year agreement covering $56.4 million worth of trade in food, timber, coal and sugar.			
July 5		Russia, Britain, France and the U.S. order their Berlin military commanders to begin negotiations for renewal of joint four-power rule in the city.		Argentine government announces defense expenditures totalling more than one quarter of its 4.87-billion peso 1950 budget.	
July 6		British Exchequer Chancellor Sir Stafford Cripps discusses Britain's growing balance of payment difficulties before the House of Commons and calls for a halt to new imports from the U.S. except in cases of "urgent national interest." He denies any intention of devaluing the pound .... Poland joins other Cominform countries in suspending trade with Yugoslavia.			Indonesian Republic Pres. Ahmed Sukarno returns to Jakarta following Dutch withdrawal from the city.

A	B	C	D	E
Includes developments that affect more than one world region, international organizations and important meetings of major world leaders.	*Includes all domestic and regional developments in Europe, including the Soviet Union, Turkey, Cyprus and Malta.*	*Includes all domestic and regional developments in Africa and the Middle East, including Iraq and Iran and excluding Cyprus, Turkey and Afghanistan.*	*Includes all domestic and regional developments in Latin America, the Caribbean and Canada.*	*Includes all domestic and regional developments in Asian and Pacific nations, extending from Afghanistan through all the Pacific Islands, except Hawaii.*

U.S. Politics & Social Issues	U.S. Foreign Policy & Defense	U.S. Economy & Environment	Science, Technology & Nature	Culture, Leisure & Life Style	
Clashes between Negroes and whites in Washington, D.C. cause three injuries and five arrests after the Interior Dept. orders the desegregation of six government-owned swimming pools.	Joint Congressional Atomic Energy Comm. issues a report exonerating the Atomic Energy Commission of security violations, noting that none of the 4,095 researchers granted "emergency clearance" by the AEC for nuclear work were found to have engaged in espionage.	Truman wins his first major legislative victory in the current session of Congress when the House passes his public housing bill, already approved by the Senate .... Five thousand UAW members end a 71-day strike at the Bendix Aviation Corp. in South Bend, Ind. by accepting an agreement calling for a study of disputed working conditions .... Montgomery Ward's fall catalogue appears with price cuts of up to 40% over last year.			June 29
Alger Hiss and his wife complete their testimony at his perjury trial, still denying any spy activity or involvement with Whittaker Chambers .... Harvard and Brown universities announce their first Negro faculty appointments. Harvard medical school names William Hinton professor of bacteriology, while Brown appoints Jay Saunders Redding visiting professor of English .... Truman signs a bill creating an Office of General Services, as recommended by the Hoover Commission, to supervise administration of government property.		Sen. Robert Taft (R, Ohio) leads a Republican-Southern Democratic Senate coalition in passing a labor bill which preserves the main features of the Taft-Hartley Act, including prohibition of union shop elections, secondary boycotts and mass picketing .... UMW leader John Lewis orders Eastern coal miners onto a three-day work week to improve the union's bargaining position in upcoming contract talks .... Justice Dept. files an antitrust suit in Chicago aimed at breaking up the $1.6 billion du Pont industrial empire.		Bob Mathias wins the National AAU decathlon title with 7,556 points in Tulare, Calif. .... Louis de Rochemont's *Lost Boundaries*, the story of a Negro family attempting to pass as whites, premiers in N.Y.	June 30
A federal court in Washington sentences Judith Coplon to 3⅓-10 years in prison following her conviction on charges of stealing confidential government papers.	Washington and London sources report U.S. efforts to gain the support of Western European states for an embargo on shipment of strategic materials to Communist China .... Truman sends Congress two bills for aid to developing countries. One authorizes the Import-Export Bank to guarantee private American investment abroad, the other provides funds for international exchange of technical knowledge.	Treasury Secy. John Snyder reports a federal deficit of $1.8 billion for fiscal 1949, three times higher than Truman's earlier predictions .... War Assets Administration and the Office of Defense Transportation discontinue operations.			July 1
			Physicist J. Robert Oppenheimer and the Federation of American Scientists issue a statement opposing the loyalty oath requirement for Atomic Energy Commission fellowship applicants.	Americans Ted Schroeder and Louise Brough win the men's and women's singles titles in England's Wimbledon tennis championships.	July 2
			Sir Alexander Fleming, discoverer of penicillin, dedicates the new $3-million Oklahoma Medical Research Foundation in Oklahoma City.		July 3
				Double Jay, with Carroll Bierman up, wins the $56,000 American Handicap at Santa Anita Park, Calif.	July 4
Trial of Iva Toguri D'Aquino, accused of treason for wartime "Tokyo Rose" broadcasts, begins in San Francisco .... Texas legislature passes a law providing penalties ranging from imprisonment to death for members of lynch mobs .... Luther Hilton Foster, president of Virginia State College and head of the Assn. of Negro Land Grant Colleges, dies at 61 in Petersburg, Va.	Senate confirms the appointment of Perle Mesta as U.S. minister to Luxembourg.	Federal court of appeals in N.Y. upholds an NLRB ban on hiring halls of the National Maritime Union in the Great Lakes area.	William Warner Co. in N.Y. announces development of a new method for synthesizing Vitamin A on a commercial scale .... Two plagues of locusts move through Nevada, Wyoming and Montana during the past two days, stripping cattle ranches and prairies.	New York Giants buy their first Negro players, outfielder Monte Irvin and infielder Henry Thompson, from Jersey City.	July 5
Detroit Mayor Eugene Van Antwerp establishes a loyalty board to supervise the dismissal of alleged Communists on the city payroll .... Senate passes and sends to the House a bill authorizing $90 million over 10 years to aid Navajo and Hopi Indians in the Southwest.		U.S. Steel rejects union demands for a wage increase, leading USW Pres. Philip Murray to threaten a nationwide steel strike by mid-month.	A 41-day drought and heat wave in the Northeast ends.		July 6

	World Affairs	Europe	Africa & the Middle East	The Americas	Asia & the Pacific
July 7	International Refugee Organization adopts plans in Geneva for winding down operations and going out of existence by mid-1950 .... International Wheat Council, headed by F. Sheed Anderson of Britain, is established in Washington to supervise operation of the International Wheat Agreement.	British troops begin to unload food on the London waterfront to combat an unauthorized strike of dock workers supporting the striking Canadian Seamen's Union .... U.S. Treasury Secy. John Snyder concludes three days of talks with French Finance Min. Maurice Petsche on means of increasing trade among Western nations and between Eastern and Western Europe.	Reinforced by Syrian troops, the Lebanese Army puts down an attempted revolt of the right-wing Popular Syrian Party.		Tibetan State Council expels representatives of the Chinese Nationalist government from the region .... Adm. Isamu Takeshita, former commander of the Japanese fleet, is reported dead at 80 in Tokyo.
July 8		U.S. and Russian patrols clash on the border between East and West Germany near Coburg, resulting in one Russian death .... Greek government forces report capture of Mount Kaimakchalan, a guerrilla strongpoint on the Yugoslavian frontier .... U.S. Treasury Secy. John Snyder begins talks in London with British Exchequer Chancellor Cripps on solution of Britain's balance of payments problem. Britain and Russia announce a one-year trade agreement permitting Britain to avoid grain purchases in Canada and the U.S. by buying Russian wheat.			
July 9					John Cabot, U.S. consul general in Shanghai, charges the Communists with arresting and severely beating Deputy Consul William Olive.
July 10	Russian scientists set off the first Soviet nuclear explosion in the Ust-Urt desert between the Caspian and Aral seas, inaugurating the nuclear arms race.	French National Assembly approves plans for creation of a Council of Europe.			
July 11					Chiang Kai-shek concludes a two-day visit to the Philippines after obtaining agreement on Philippine participation in a proposed anti-Communist union of Pacific states. South Korea also indicates interest in the organization.
July 12					Thirteen American news correspondents returning from a tour of Indonesia are killed with 32 other passengers when a Dutch KLM Constellation crashes near Bombay, India in a blinding rainstorm.
July 13		In a move aimed against the Communist governments of Eastern Europe, Pope Pius XII orders the excommunication of all Catholics belonging to the Communist Party or otherwise helping to spread Communist ideas .... Italy's Chamber of Deputies approves Italian membership in the Council of Europe.			
July 14		British Exchequer Chancellor Sir Stafford Cripps announces a 25% cut in British dollar imports for the coming fiscal year, to be imposed in addition to the current three-month embargo on most dollar purchases .... Russian authorities end a four-day slowdown of truck traffic between West Germany and Berlin, allegedly aimed at keeping Western currency out of the Soviet zone.			

A	B	C	D	E
Includes developments that affect more than one world region, international organizations and important meetings of major world leaders.	*Includes all domestic and regional developments in Europe, including the Soviet Union, Turkey, Cyprus and Malta.*	*Includes all domestic and regional developments in Africa and the Middle East, including Iraq and Iran and excluding Cyprus, Turkey and Afghanistan.*	*Includes all domestic and regional developments in Latin America, the Caribbean and Canada.*	*Includes all domestic and regional developments in Asian and Pacific nations, extending from Afghanistan through all the Pacific Islands, except Hawaii.*

U.S. Politics & Social Issues	U.S. Foreign Policy & Defense	U.S. Economy & Environment	Science, Technology & Nature	Culture, Leisure & Life Style	
N.Y. Gov. Thomas Dewey appoints Republican foreign affairs adviser John Foster Dulles to fill the Senate seat vacated by Robert Wagner .... N.Y. espionage trial of Judith Coplon and Valentin Gubitchev, scheduled for July 11, is postponed to mid-October due to a crowded court calendar.			Senate Appropriations Comm. approves a rider to the Atomic Energy Commission supply bill calling for FBI investigation of all AEC fellowship applicants.		July 7
N.Y. perjury trial of Alger Hiss ends inconclusively as the jury fails to reach a verdict. Rep. Richard Nixon (R, Calif.) accuses Judge Samuel Kaufman of favoring the defense and demands a House Un-American Activities Comm. investigation of the trial, claiming that the truth about Hiss must "not be left in doubt because of technicalities." .... Republican national committeeman Arthur Summerfield is chosen to replace Rep. Hugh Scott, Jr. as head of the party's Strategy Comm.		Congress completes action on a compromise public housing program providing $308 million in federal subsidies for construction of 810,000 new dwelling units over six years and $325 million in loans and grants for farm housing construction .... House passes and sends to the Senate a bill raising the annual salaries of 250 high government officials, including cabinet members, from $15,000 to $20,000.	Nuclear physicist Enrico Fermi and California Institute of Technology Pres. Lee Du Bridge, testifying before the Joint Congressional Atomic Energy Comm., oppose FBI investigation of AEC fellowship applicants as a step towards a police state.	Harold Knerr, cartoonist and originator of the "Katzenjammer Kids," dies at 66 in N.Y. .... *Love in a Cold Climate* by Nancy Mitford, a member of the controversial English aristocratic family, is published in N.Y. by Random House.	July 8
National Education Assn. ends a seven-day meeting in Boston after voting overwhelmingly for a resolution urging elimination of all Communists from the teaching profession .... An Alabama grand jury investigating Ku Klux Klan terrorism indicts 17 men, including Police Chief Elmer Brock of Brookside, Ala., for participating in or aiding illegal Klan activities.		Honolulu police arrest 100 striking longshoremen for violating a newly enacted ordinance banning interference with workers going to their jobs.		Bobby Locke of South Africa wins the British Open golf tournament in Sandwich, England.	July 9
				New York Herald Tribune lists John Marquand's *Point of No Return* and Frank Gilbreth's and Ernestine Carey's *Cheaper by The Dozen* as best-selling fiction and non-fiction books.	July 10
An American Assn. of University Professors investigating committee recommends that teachers be allowed to belong to the Communist Party, as long as they do not use their classes or contacts among students to promote Communism .... Democratic Gov. Beauford Jester of Texas dies in Houston at 56 of a heart attack.	Sen. Robert Taft announces his opposition to ratification of the North Atlantic Treaty, charging that the pact will "inextricably" involve the U.S. in military aid to Europe and increase the chances of war with Russia .... Senate Appropriations Comm. cuts Truman's Marshall Plan aid request by 10% and sets aside $50 million in Marshall Plan funds for a loan to Spain outside the regular aid program .... Joint Congressional Atomic Energy Comm. ends its public hearings on charges of mismanagement and breaches of security in the Atomic Energy Commission.	Truman issues his mid-year economic report to Congress, abandoning his earlier demand for a $4-billion tax increase and urging greater federal spending to reverse the nation's deflationary economic trend .... A House Judiciary subcommittee begins hearings on possible revision of antitrust laws.		Sugar Ray Robinson retains his world welterweight boxing crown with a 15th-round decision over Kid Gavilan in Philadelphia .... Donaldson Awards for theatrical achievement go to *Death of a Salesman* as the year's best play and *South Pacific* as the best musical.	July 11
Democratic members of the House Un-American Activities Comm. decide against a committee review of the Hiss perjury trial.		UAW convention meeting in Milwaukee overwhelmingly re-elects union Pres. Walter Reuther and his slate against left-wing opposition.		American League All Stars win their 12th victory over the National League, 11-7, in N.Y.	July 12
Georgia Supreme Court rules that Negroes must be admitted to juries in counties with a substantial Negro population .... Connecticut Gov. Chester Bowles signs a law banning racial discrimination in all state and federal housing projects.		In a nationwide radio address, Truman explains his recent request for increased government spending and sets a $300-billion national income as his economic goal .... House passes and sends to the Senate a bill permitting the Rural Electrification Admin. to make low-interest loans for the purpose of extending telephone service into the countryside.		Richard Maibaum's film *The Great Gatsby*, based on F. Scott Fitzgerald's novel, premiers in N.Y. .... James McGregor Burns' *Congress on Trial*, a critique of the U.S. legislative system, is published in N.Y. by Harper.	July 13
House Un-American Activities Comm. completes two days of hearings on the loyalty of U.S. Negroes, inspired by singer Paul Robeson's statement that Negroes will not fight against Russia. Among those who appear before the committee to disavow the statement are former Communist Manning Johnson and Thomas Young, publisher of the Norfolk *Journal and Guide* .... Senate Expenditures Comm. clears Truman's plans for reorganizing the Post Office, Civil Service Commission and Maritime Commission .... Former Democratic National Comm. general counsel Edward Prichard, Jr. is convicted of vote fraud in Lexington, Ky. and sentenced to two years in prison.	On directions from Defense Secy. Johnson, the Munitions Bd. announces formation of a Military Procurement Information Center to advise businesses on bidding for government contracts without the aid of "five percenters" and influence peddlers.			Central Committee of the World Council of Churches, meeting in Chichester, England, calls on Christians living under totalitarian regimes to defend their religion regardless of the "violence or threat of any world power."	July 14

F	G	H	I	J
Includes elections, federal-state relations, civil rights and liberties, crime, the judiciary, education, health care, poverty, urban affairs and population.	*Includes formation and debate of U.S. foreign and defense policies, veterans affairs and defense spending. (Relations with specific foreign countries are usually found under the region concerned.)*	*Includes business, labor, agriculture, taxation, transportation, consumer affairs, monetary and fiscal policy, natural resources, pollution and accidents.*	*Includes worldwide scientific, medical and technological developments, natural phenomena, U.S. weather and natural disasters.*	*Includes the arts, religion, scholarship, communications media, sports, entertainment, fashions, fads and social life.*

	World Affairs	Europe	Africa & the Middle East	The Americas	Asia & the Pacific
July 15		U.S. and British military authorities give German economic administrators in their occupation zones greater control over rationing and other economic measures.			Communist authorities in Shanghai close down the city's U.S. Information Service office.
July 16		Defense ministers of Western European Union states, meeting in Luxembourg, announce an agreement to unify their arms production and military supply services . . . . Czech Communist Party issues a statement calling the Catholic church "our greatest enemy" but denying any intention of prohibiting religious observance.	Egyptian Minister of State Mahmoud Hassan Pasha dies at 78 in Alexandria.	Inter-American Press Congress concludes a six-day meeting in Quito, Ecuador after reporting that 16 American republics practice some form of censorship.	Chinese Nationalist government in Canton establishes a Supreme War Council led by Chiang Kai-shek, who effectively resumes control over the war effort.
July 17		Catholic priests in Prague issue a resolution declaring their support for Archbishop Josef Beran and other church leaders loyal to the Vatican.			
July 18	Countries in the British sterling area agree to cut their purchases of dollar goods by 25% during the current fiscal year in support of Britain's action.		Iran announces an agreement with the Anglo-American Oil Co. providing for extension of the company's oil-drilling concession through 1991 in exchange for higher royalty payments.		Chinese Communists announce the start of a new southward offensive in Kiangsi and Hunan Provinces . . . . Japan's National Railway Corp. dismisses 14 workers for their Communist affiliations.
July 19		Czech government warns that any church official seeking to implement the Vatican's order excommunicating Communists will be treated as a "high traitor." . . . . Dutch Chamber of Deputies votes for ratification of the North Atlantic Treaty.			France signs an agreement recognizing Laos as an independent member of the French Commonwealth within the Indochinese federation.

A	B	C	D	E
Includes developments that affect more than one world region, international organizations and important meetings of major world leaders.	*Includes all domestic and regional developments in Europe, including the Soviet Union, Turkey, Cyprus and Malta.*	*Includes all domestic and regional developments in Africa and the Middle East, including Iraq and Iran and excluding Cyprus, Turkey and Afghanistan.*	*Includes all domestic and regional developments in Latin America, the Caribbean and Canada.*	*Includes all domestic and regional developments in Asian and Pacific nations, extending from Afghanistan through all the Pacific Islands, except Hawaii.*

U.S. Politics & Social Issues	U.S. Foreign Policy & Defense	U.S. Economy & Environment	Science, Technology & Nature	Culture, Leisure & Life Style	
	Senate Appropriations Comm. votes to cut $1.1 billion from the fiscal 1950 military budget, including $799 million authorized by the House for an increase in Air Force strength.	A nationwide steel strike is averted when U.S. Steel and other large producers accept Truman's proposal for a 60-day extension of the current contract and creation of a three-man board to investigate the wage and pension dispute .... UAW ends its six-day Milwaukee convention after voting to continue pressing for wage increases and authorizing union leaders to raise an $8-10 million strike fund .... Sen. James Murray (D, Mont.) introduces an Administration-sponsored bill calling for federal expenditures of $11 billion over the next four or five years to aid business expansion .... Truman signs the public housing-slum clearance bill, the first major part of his legislative program passed by Congress.		Czech tennis champions Jaroslav Drbny and Vladimir Cernik defy a government order to return from a meet in Gstaad, Switz. and announce their intention of applying for entry to the U.S.	July 15
Army Secy. Gordon Gray suspends two generals, Quartermaster General Herman Feldman and Chemical Corps chief Alden Waitt, pending investigation of alleged influence peddling in the award of Army contracts. The charges result from a recent expose of "five percenter" James Hunt .... Bill of Rights Congress, called to protest FBI investigating methods, opens in N.Y. The meeting is sponsored by Henry Wallace, singer Paul Robeson and National Lawyers Guild Pres. Clifford Durr .... Central Intelligence Agency advises a Senate Judiciary subcommittee that at least 29 U.N. representatives of foreign nations are "high-ranking Communist Party officials" working against U.S. interests.		Alexander Whitney, president of the Brotherhood of Railroad Trainmen, dies at 76 in Cleveland.		Solidarity, with Ralph Neves up, wins the Hollywood Gold Cup Handicap in Arcadia, Calif., earning $101,600.	July 16
Rep. Paul Shafer (R, Mich.) demands that Truman suspend presidential military aide Harry Vaughn following reports linking Vaughn to the "five percenter" influence peddling scandal .... Bill of Rights Congress in N.Y. ends with adoption of resolutions urging an end to FBI loyalty checks and repeal of the Smith Act under which U.S. Communist leaders are being tried .... NAACP's Springarn Medal, given annually to a U.S. Negro for outstanding achievement, goes to U.N. Palestine mediator Ralph Bunche .... Freedom House presents its Freedom Awards for 1949 to Gen. Lucius Clay and Atomic Energy Commission director David Lilienthal.	American Friends Service Comm. concludes a year-long peace study by issuing a report urging the U.S. to place its nuclear weapons under U.N. supervision, ease restrictions on trade with Eastern Europe, abandon the West German government plan in favor of German reunification and work for U.N. mediation of international disputes. The report, compiled by a committee headed by Haverford College Pres. Gilbert White, is sent to State Secy. Acheson and Russian Amb. Alexander Panyushkin.			Pancho Gonzales and Magda Rurac win the men's and women's singles titles at the national clay court tennis competition in Chicago.	July 17
Brooklyn Dodgers infielder Jackie Robinson, the first Negro in major league baseball, testifies before the House Un-American Activities Comm. that U.S. Negroes will fight Russia if necessary but will remain "stirred up" until full racial equality is achieved .... Rep. Hugh Scott, Jr. announces his forthcoming resignation as Republican National Comm. chairman .... Former Capt. Kathleen Nash Durant, convicted in the Hesse jewel theft case, is freed from federal prison in Alderson, W. Va. after serving one-third of a five-year sentence.					July 18
National Guard troops restore order in Groveland, Fla. after four days of anti-Negro rioting following reports that Negroes raped a local white woman .... N.Y. State Court of Appeals upholds the right of the Metropolitan Life Insurance Co. to bar Negroes from its Stuyvesant Town housing project in N.Y. .... Americans for Democratic Action, meeting in Washington, adopts a program calling for higher wages, greater unemployment compensation and creation of another Fair Employment Practices Commission .... Associate Supreme Court Justice Frank Murphy dies at 59 in Detroit of a heart attack.	Speaking at a Shrine convention in Chicago, Truman declares that the Western democracies will win "the battle for men's minds" if the U.S. maintains a strong economy and continues to assist in European recovery.	UMW Vice Pres. Van Amberg Bittner dies at 64 in Pittsburgh.	Mt. Palomar Observatory announces discovery of a minor planet within Mercury's orbit, 22 million miles from the sun.		July 19

F
Includes elections, federal-state relations, civil rights and liberties, crime, the judiciary, education, health care, poverty, urban affairs and population.

G
Includes formation and debate of U.S. foreign and defense policies, veterans affairs and defense spending. (Relations with specific foreign countries are usually found under the region concerned.)

H
Includes business, labor, agriculture, taxation, transportation, consumer affairs, monetary and fiscal policy, natural resources, pollution and accidents.

I
Includes worldwide scientific, medical and technological developments, natural phenomena, U.S. weather and natural disasters.

J
Includes the arts, religion, scholarship, communications media, sports, entertainment, fashions, fads and social life.

	World Affairs	Europe	Africa & the Middle East	The Americas	Asia & the Pacific
July 20		Bulgarian Parliament unanimously elects Foreign Min. Vassil Kolarov to succeed the late Georgi Dimitrov as premier.	Israel and Syria sign an armistice agreement in the northern Galilee after 3½ months of negotiation.	Guatemalan government reports suppression of a three-day revolt in Guatemala City following the assassination of Col. Francisco Javier Arana, chief of the country's armed forces.	
July 21		Italian Chamber of Deputies votes for ratification of the North Atlantic Treaty despite Russian protests that the action violates the country's World War II peace treaty.			
July 22	U.N. Trusteeship Council ends its fourth regular session in Lake Success after approving U.S. administration of the Pacific trust territories.	East German People's Council calls for reunification of Berlin under a single municipal government and election of an all-German council to create a federal state superceding the West German republic .... British dock workers end their four-week wildcat strike after the Canadian Seamen's Union agrees to drop sanctions against Canadian ships in British ports .... A French military court in Paris convicts Otto Abetz, German ambassador to France during the occupation, of complicity in the deportation of French officers and sentences him to 20 years in prison.		Argentine Culture Under Secy. Antonio Castro proposes a "draft law of the intellectual worker" giving the government control over all communications media.	
July 23		Yugoslavian Foreign Min. Eduard Kardelj announces his country's withdrawal of "moral and political" support from Greek Communist guerrillas, whom he accuses of following the Cominform's anti-Tito line.			Indonesian nationalist leaders conferring in Jakarta agree on formation of a United States of Indonesia, to assume sovereignty from the Dutch government after a transitional period .... A typhoon strikes Okinawa, causing 38 deaths, 252 injuries and extensive property damage.
July 24					Typhoon which struck Okinawa sweeps into Shanghai, causing deaths and extensive flooding with 200,000 residents left homeless.
July 25	First Western press report of the Russian nuclear test appears in the Paris weekly *Samedi-Soir*.	Norwegian government clears opera singer Kirsten Flagstad of complicity in her husband's pro-Nazi wartime activities.	Egyptian and Syrian leaders opposed to Jordanian expansion meet in Lebanon and demand creation of a separate Arab Palestinian state.		
July 26		Western Allied military commanders in Berlin order restitution of all private property seized by the Nazis in excess of 1,000 marks value.	Hussein Sirry Pasha forms a new Egyptian coalition cabinet following the resignation yesterday of Saadist leader Ibrahim Abdul Hadi Pasha's cabinet.	Ecuador suppresses a revolt led by former dictator Carlos Mancheno.	India and Pakistan reach a ceasefire agreement in Kashmir through the U.N. Kashmir Commission.
July 27		French National Assembly votes for ratification of the North Atlantic Treaty after Foreign Min. Schuman assures the deputies that German participation in the pact is "unthinkable." Portugal's National Assembly also votes to ratify the treaty .... Polish government offers to negotiate an agreement on church-state relations with the Roman Catholic church.	U.N. Palestine mediator Ralph Bunche issues his final report to the Security Council, claiming that "the military phase of the [Palestine] conflict is ended" and urging elimination of the Middle East arms embargo imposed by the U.N. in 1948 .... Iran bans interference in state affairs by non-Moslem religious leaders.		South Korean forces report capturing a hill north of the 38th Parallel border to protect the frontier city of Kaesong .... Chinese Nationalist government declares martial law in Canton.
	A	B	C	D	E
	Includes developments that affect more than one world region, international organizations and important meetings of major world leaders.	*Includes all domestic and regional developments in Europe, including the Soviet Union, Turkey, Cyprus and Malta.*	*Includes all domestic and regional developments in Africa and the Middle East, including Iraq and Iran and excluding Cyprus, Turkey and Afghanistan.*	*Includes all domestic and regional developments in Latin America, the Caribbean and Canada.*	*Includes all domestic and regional developments in Asian and Pacific nations, extending from Afghanistan through all the Pacific Islands, except Hawaii.*

U.S. Politics & Social Issues	U.S. Foreign Policy & Defense	U.S. Economy & Environment	Science, Technology & Nature	Culture, Leisure & Life Style	
Bureau of Standards director Edward Condon, testifying before the Senate Rules Comm., urges Congress to pass laws guaranteeing witnesses called before congressional investigating committees an opportunity to defend themselves .... Carmine DeSapio succeeds Manhattan Borough Pres. Hugo Rogers as leader of Tammany Hall .... Hollywood underworld figure Mickey Cohen, rumored to be aiding a police vice investigation, is wounded with three companions in a shotgun ambush outside a Sunset Boulevard restaurant.		Clashes between striking CIO longshoremen and police in Honolulu result in 23 injuries and 28 arrests.		Robert McCormick announces purchase of the *Washington Times-Herald* by his *Chicago Tribune* company.	July 20
Francis Cardinal Spellman accuses Eleanor Roosevelt of participating in an "anti-Catholic campaign" for her opposition to federal aid to parochial schools.	Senate ends three weeks of debate on the North Atlantic Treaty by voting for unconditional ratification.	House defeats the Brannan farm subsidy bill and passes a measure continuing the present program of price supports for another year .... CIO National Union of Marine Cooks and Stewards ends a four-day convention in San Francisco after reaffirming its support for the World Federation of Trade Unions and calling for U.S. aid to Communist China.		Foundation for World Government Pres. Stringfellow Barr's *The Pilgrimage of Western Man* is published in N.Y. by Harcourt, Brace.	July 21
A Senate Judiciary subcommittee approves a revised Communist control bill providing 10-year jail sentences for plotting to set up a totalitarian government in the U.S.		A federal court in Trenton, N.J. issues a consent decree to restrain the American Cast Iron Pipe Co. and two other firms from alleged trade restraint in the cast iron pressure pipe industry.		Federal Communications Commission announces issuance of temporary permits to two television stations in N.Y. and Baltimore for experimental color broadcasts.	July 22
	Defense Secy. Johnson signs the final transfer order making the Air Force fully independent of the Army.			Albert Sandrin of Chicago wins the national open chess title in Omaha, Neb.	July 23
			Metallurgist Fritz Hansgirg, inventor of a commercially viable method of magnesium processing, dies at 58 in N.Y.		July 24
Atty. Gen. Tom Clark adds three allegedly Communist organizations to the Justice Department's subversive list: the American Rescue Ship Mission, the Emergency Conference to Save Spanish Refugees and the National Conference on American Policy in China and the Far East.	Truman signs the U.S. ratification of the North Atlantic Treaty and sends Congress a message urging approval of a $1.45-billion Military Assistance Program for Western Europe.	Federal Reserve Bd. reports that U.S. industrial production reached a three-year low in June, dropping for the seventh consecutive month .... A federal district court in Chicago rules that the national rent control law is unconstitutional, but rent controls remain in effect pending Supreme Court review of the decision .... Senate Banking Comm. opens an investigation of the coal industry to determine the extent of the UMW's power.		Thomas Mann accepts the Goethe Prize for Literature in Frankfurt, his first appearance in Germany in 16 years .... Professional Golfers Assn. bans South African Bobby Locke from PGA-sponsored tournaments, claiming that Locke has violated commitments to play in exhibitions.	July 25
House passes and sends to the Senate a bill outlawing poll taxes as a voting requirement for federal elections .... Ernest Thomas, one of the Negroes accused of raping a white woman in Groveland, Fla., is shot to death by vigilante whites in nearby Perry.		USW and steel company representatives begin wage negotiations in N.Y. before a presidential fact-finding board .... Hawaii's legislature convenes in special session to deal with the 87-day-old longshoremen's strike. Gov. Ingram Stainback asks for authority to seize and operate shipping facilities on the islands during the strike.	Capt. Robert Dexter Conrad, assistant director of the Brookhaven National Laboratory and a leading organizer of cancer research, dies of leukemia in N.Y.		July 26
Senate Rules Comm. votes to uphold the contested elections of Sens. Homer Ferguson (R, Mich.), Harley Kilgore (D, W. Va.), Robert Kerr (D, Okla.) and Lyndon Johnson (D, Tex.).		USW agrees to comply with the affidavit requirements of the Taft-Hartley Act despite continuing opposition to the law.	Armour Laboratories in Chicago announces development of a method for commercial production of adreno-cortico-tropic hormone (ACTH), a pituitary extract used in the treatment of arthritis, rheumatic fever and gout.		July 27

F	G	H	I	J
Includes elections, federal-state relations, civil rights and liberties, crime, the judiciary, education, health care, poverty, urban affairs and population.	*Includes formation and debate of U.S. foreign and defense policies, veterans affairs and defense spending. (Relations with specific foreign countries are usually found under the region concerned.)*	*Includes business, labor, agriculture, taxation, transportation, consumer affairs, monetary and fiscal policy, natural resources, pollution and accidents.*	*Includes worldwide scientific, medical and technological developments, natural phenomena, U.S. weather and natural disasters.*	*Includes the arts, religion, scholarship, communications media, sports, entertainment, fashions, fads and social life.*

	World Affairs	Europe	Africa & the Middle East	The Americas	Asia & the Pacific
July 28		British House of Lords vetoes the government's steel nationalization bill, ensuring that the plan will become an issue in the 1950 election.		Panamanian First Vice Pres. Daniel Chanis is sworn in as acting president following Domingo Diaz Arosemena's heart attack.	MacArthur orders the military government section of the U.S. occupation force dissolved at the end of the year, giving Japanese authorities unsupervised control over local affairs.
July 29	Anti-Communist labor leaders meeting in London, including AFL and CIO representatives, approve a draft constitution for a new international trade union organization .... U.N. Atomic Energy Commission votes again to suspend its activity pending private consultations among the Big Five and Canada on atomic control.	U.S. and Britain announce plans to phase out the Berlin airlift by Oct. 31.		Argentina's Peronista Party, meeting in Buenos Aires, nominates Juan Peron as its 1952 presidential candidate despite earlier assurances that he would not seek re-election .... Mexico signs its seventh short-term agreement with the U.S. allowing Mexican laborers to work in the U.S. harvest. The agreement ends Mexico's ban on the movement of Mexican migrant workers into Texas.	
July 30		French Council of the Republic and the Italian Senate vote approval of the North Atlantic Treaty.			British sloop *Amethyst*, trapped on the Yangtze River by Communist fire since April 20, escapes and rejoins other British ships off the Chinese coast.
July 31		West German Roman Catholic hierarchy issues a pastoral letter instructing church members to vote for Christian Democratic candidates in upcoming parliamentary elections.			Russia announces conclusion of a one-year trade agreement with Chinese Communist authorities in Manchuria.
Aug. 1		Gen. Maxwell Taylor replaces Gen. Frank Howley as commander of U.S. forces in Berlin .... Holland and East Germany conclude a one-year, $8.5-million trade agreement.		Argentina completes a one-year, $29-million trade pact with Czechoslovakia .... A Bolivian cabinet consisting entirely of Republican Socialist Union members takes office.	Dutch and Indonesian Republic commanders sign a new ceasefire agreement in Batavia.
Aug. 2				British Columbia repeals a 42-year-old ban on employment of Asian immigrants in government-connected work.	John Leighton Stuart, U.S. ambassador to China, leaves Nanking for the U.S.
Aug. 3		Holland completes ratification of the North Atlantic Treaty.			
Aug. 4		Italy and Yugoslavia sign a one-year, $94-million trade agreement.		Brazil concludes a one-year, $256.5-million trade agreement with Britain.	

A	B	C	D	E
Includes developments that affect more than one world region, international organizations and important meetings of major world leaders.	*Includes all domestic and regional developments in Europe, including the Soviet Union, Turkey, Cyprus and Malta.*	*Includes all domestic and regional developments in Africa and the Middle East, including Iraq and Iran and excluding Cyprus, Turkey and Afghanistan.*	*Includes all domestic and regional developments in Latin America, the Caribbean and Canada.*	*Includes all domestic and regional developments in Asian and Pacific nations, extending from Afghanistan through all the Pacific Islands, except Hawaii.*

U.S. Politics & Social Issues	U.S. Foreign Policy & Defense	U.S. Economy & Environment	Science, Technology & Nature	Culture, Leisure & Life Style	
Truman announces the nomination of Atty. Gen. Tom Clark to fill the Supreme Court seat vacated by the death of Frank Murphy. He asks Sen. James McGrath (D, R.I.) to replace Clark as attorney general .... Institute of Foreign Trade Pres. J. Anthony Marcus, testifying before a Senate Judiciary subcommittee, accuses the Russian foreign trade agency Amtorg of stealing technical and industrial secrets from U.S. firms.	Senate passes a compromise measure on armed forces reorganization, increasing the authority of the defense secretary over the separate services but preventing their merger.	Southern Coal Producers Assn. Pres. Joseph Moody, testifying at the Senate Banking Comm. inquiry on the coal industry, urges that the "monopoly power" of the UMW be curtailed by subjecting unions to antitrust laws.			July 28
Sen. Glen Taylor (D, Ida.) quits the Progressive Party due to the poor showing of the Wallace ticket in the last election.	Army Chief of Staff Omar Bradley and Defense Secy. Louis Johnson testify before the House Foreign Affairs Comm., urging approval of Truman's request for military aid to Western Europe.				July 29
			A collision between a Navy Hellcat fighter and an Eastern Airlines DC-3 near Ft. Dix, N.J. causes 16 deaths, the first fatal accident this year on a scheduled U.S. airline.	Ponder, with Steve Brooks up, wins the $87,750 Arlington Classic in Chicago.	July 30
				Sam Snead wins the Western Open golf tournament in St. Paul, Minn.	July 31
Massachusetts Gov. Paul Dever signs a bill barring Communists from state jobs and requiring future applicants to take loyalty oaths.	Sen. Millard Tydings (D, Md.) introduces a bill providing $171 million for construction of an Air Force Academy.	UMW Welfare Fund director Josephine Roche tells a Senate Banking subcommittee that Sen. Styles Bridges (R, N.H.) draws $35,000 a year from the fund as one of the fund's three trustees.	Truman issues his sixth semi-annual report on the U.S. Atomic Energy Commission, stating that nuclear fuels and isotopes are being produced in greater quantities and at lower costs than ever before.	San Francisco's War Memorial Opera House reverses a ban on the appearance of soprano Kirsten Flagstad, recently cleared in Norway of Nazi collaboration charges.	Aug. 1
Sen. Harry Byrd's political machine maintains its rule in Virginia as its candidate for governor, State Sen. John Battle, wins the Democratic primary .... William Morris, leader of the Alabama Ku Klux Klan, goes to jail in Birmingham for refusing to give a federal grand jury lists of Klan members.	Defense Secy. Johnson abolishes the Army's fleet and orders its 320 ocean-going ships transferred to the new Military Sea Transportation Service established by the Navy.			Sen. Kenneth McKellar (D, Tenn.), chairman of the Commission on Renovation of the Executive Mansion, announces plans to rebuild the interior of the White House, preserving the exterior walls.	Aug. 2
Sen. Homer Ferguson (R, Mich.) introduces a bill aimed against "five percenters," requiring government contractors to report commissions paid to agents. Sen. Karl Mundt (R, S.D.) introduces a measure forcing agents to register with the government .... A federal grand jury in Rome, Ga. indicts 12 white men, including Dade County Sheriff John Lynch, on charges of flogging Negro prisoners.		House passes and sends to joint conference a bill authorizing the agriculture secretary to reduce next year's cotton crop from 26.4 million to 21 million acres.	Columbia Univ. Prof. Arthur Pollister demonstrates a micro-spectro-photometer, which determines the constituents of individual cells by measuring the amount of light absorbed by different substances.	Basketball Assn. of America and the National Basketball League merge to form a new National Basketball Assn. .... Aga Khan and his wife are robbed in their car of jewels valued at $450,000 to $800,000 near Cannes, France.	Aug. 3
Francis Cardinal Spellman ends his dispute with Eleanor Roosevelt over federal aid to parochial schools by issuing a statement emphasizing that the church seeks aid only for "auxiliary services" such as transportation, text books and health equipment. Mrs. Roosevelt calls the statement "clarifying and fair." .... Guy Gabrielson, a New Jersey lawyer and Taft supporter, is elected to succeed Rep. Hugh Scott, Jr. as Republican National Comm. chairman.				MGM releases *In the Good Old Summertime*, a musical romance starring Judy Garland and Van Johnson.	Aug. 4

	World Affairs	Europe	Africa & the Middle East	The Americas	Asia & the Pacific
Aug. 5		Czech Archbishop Josef Beran charges in a letter to the state prosecutor that security agents have illegally restricted him to his Prague residence since mid-June and confiscated the funds of his archdiocese .... Italy's three union groups sign general agreements with employers providing wage increases for all categories of workers.		A severe earthquake along the eastern slope of the Andes in central Ecuador causes 6,000 deaths and $67.5 million in damages, leaving 100,000 homeless.	U.S. State Dept. issues a White Paper, *U.S. Relations with China*, justifying the Administration's decision to halt efforts to prevent a Communist victory in the Chinese civil war. The report accuses the Nationalist government of failing to introduce necessary reforms, alienating the Chinese people and Army and squandering $2 billion in U.S. aid since the end of the war. Future U.S. policy, according to the report, will concentrate on preventing extension of Communist rule to other parts of Asia. Most Republicans in Congress criticize the White Paper as an attempt to "explain and excuse past failures" in China policy .... Chinese Nationalist government reports the loss of Changsha, center of China's richest agricultural area 365 miles north of Canton .... South Korean forces repel an invasion of 6,000 North Korean troops on the Ongjin Peninsula northwest of Seoul.
Aug. 6		Polish government issues a law providing prison sentences of up to five years for Catholic priests who carry out the Pope's sentence of excommunication against Communist Party members.			Chinese Nationalist government orders the arrest of all generals suspected of planning to join the Communists following reports of the defection of 90,000 Nationalist troops in the Changsha area .... Chiang Kai-shek visits Korea for discussions with South Korean Pres. Syngman Rhee on formation of an anti-Communist Pacific Union .... A South Korean military court sentences Lt. An Du Hi to life imprisonment for assassinating conservative political leader Kim Koo.
Aug. 7					Pham Van Dong is named vice president of Ho Chi Minh's Viet Minh government in Indochina .... House Minority Leader Joseph Martin attacks U.S. China policy as revealed in the State Department's White Paper as "an Oriental Munich."
Aug. 8	U.N. Secy. Gen. Trygve Lie issues his fourth annual report to the General Assembly, predicting that the East-West ideological conflict will have less long-range importance than the emerging independence movements in Asia and Africa.	Council of Europe convenes for the first time in Strasbourg, with 10 member states. Turkey, Greece and Iceland are invited to participate.			
Aug. 9					
Aug. 10		Greece and Turkey formally join the Council of Europe .... Jewish refugees in Munich, protesting the appearance of an anti-Semitic letter in the *Sueddeutsche Zeitung*, riot when police attempt to break up their demonstration. Four protesters and 30 policemen are injured .... A new Belgian cabinet is formed under Christian Socialist leader Gaston Eyskens, with Christian Socialist and Liberal participation.			

A	B	C	D	E
Includes developments that affect more than one world region, international organizations and important meetings of major world leaders.	*Includes all domestic and regional developments in Europe, including the Soviet Union, Turkey, Cyprus and Malta.*	*Includes all domestic and regional developments in Africa and the Middle East, including Iraq and Iran and excluding Cyprus, Turkey and Afghanistan.*	*Includes all domestic and regional developments in Latin America, the Caribbean and Canada.*	*Includes all domestic and regional developments in Asian and Pacific nations, extending from Afghanistan through all the Pacific Islands, except Hawaii.*

U.S. Politics & Social Issues	U.S. Foreign Policy & Defense	U.S. Economy & Environment	Science, Technology & Nature	Culture, Leisure & Life Style	
	Truman presents Congress with a revised military aid bill, dropping his earlier request for "blank check" presidential authority to commit U.S. aid to any country deemed in need of military assistance against Communism . . . . U.S. chiefs of staff complete five days of talks with Western European military leaders on creation of a North Atlantic pact defense organization . . . . Senate cuts controversial features from the Marshall Plan aid bill passed by the Appropriations Comm., including a provision for a $50 million loan to Spain.	Ignoring UAW demands, Ford Motors imposes a one-year freeze on wages.			Aug. 5
		Hawaiian legislature passes a bill giving Gov. Ingram Stainback power to seize and operate docks during the strike of CIO longshoremen.		Chicago White Sox shortstop Luke Appling sets a new major league record by playing his 2,154th game in 19 years.	Aug. 6
Methodist Bishop Bromley Oxnam of N.Y. attacks Catholic demands for federal aid to parochial schools, accusing the church of jeopardizing the entire aid-to-education program.			A British Gloster Meteor sets a 12 hour, 3 minute endurance record for jet aircraft in a 3,600-mile flight over England . . . . Percy Newberry, British Egyptologist who helped discover and open the tomb of King Tut-ankh-Amen, dies at 80 in Hascombe, England.		Aug. 7
A Senate Investigations subcommittee headed by Clyde Hoey (D, N.C.) opens hearings on alleged influence-peddling in Washington. Defense Secy. Johnson appears before the subcommittee and pledges his department's cooperation in efforts to eliminate "five percenters." The subcommittee's first witness is Massachusetts furniture manufacturer Paul Grindle, who testifies on various influence-peddling schemes of alleged "five percenter" James Hunt . . . . Sen. Patrick McCarren (D, Nev.), chairman of a Senate Judiciary subcommittee, charges that the U.N. serves as a cover for Communist spies in the U.S. . . . . American Medical Assn. announces appointment of a Negro physician, Dr. Peter Murray, to its policy-making House of Delegates for the first time in its history.	Senate passes a $5.6-billion foreign aid bill and sends it to House conference.				Aug. 8
		Hawaii's Gov. Stainback orders seizure of shipping firms as the territorial government begins recruiting non-union dock workers in an effort to break the five-month strike of CIO longshoremen.		Lloyd Mangrum wins the All-American Golf Tournament in Chicago.	Aug. 9
Federal Housing Expediter Tighe Woods completes two days of testimony before the Senate subcommittee investigating influence-peddling. He claims that presidential military aide Harry Vaughan interceded with him in 1948 to procure scarce building materials for repair of a race track in San Bruno, Calif. . . . . A federal district court in Chicago orders the release of James Montgomery, a Waukegan, Ill. Negro who has served 26 years of a life sentence for rape. The court calls Montgomery's original trial a "sham" in which vital evidence was suppressed by the prosecution.	Truman signs a bill strengthening armed forces unification by placing the service secretaries under direct Defense Dept. authority. Defense Secy. Johnson establishes a National Defense Management Comm. to implement the bill's provisions.	UAW members employed by Ford in Michigan vote overwhelmingly to strike if necessary to enforce their demand for a $100 monthly retirement pension and a health plan.		Ezzard Charles retains the National Boxing Assn. heavyweight title with a seventh-round victory over Gus Lesnevich in N.Y. . . . . Psychologist H.A. Overstreet's *The Mature Mind* is published by Norton and becomes a Book-of-the-Month Club selection.	Aug. 10
F *Includes elections, federal-state relations, civil rights and liberties, crime, the judiciary, education, health care, poverty, urban affairs and population.*	G *Includes formation and debate of U.S. foreign and defense policies, veterans affairs and defense spending. (Relations with specific foreign countries are usually found under the region concerned.)*	H *Includes business, labor, agriculture, taxation, transportation, consumer affairs, monetary and fiscal policy, natural resources, pollution and accidents.*	I *Includes worldwide scientific, medical and technological developments, natural phenomena, U.S. weather and natural disasters.*	J *Includes the arts, religion, scholarship, communications media, sports, entertainment, fashions, fads and social life.*	

	World Affairs	Europe	Africa & the Middle East	The Americas	Asia & the Pacific
Aug. 11	Security Council votes to relieve Ralph Bunche of his duties as U.N. Palestine mediator, allowing him to resume direction of the Trusteeship Commission .... A 60-nation International Red Cross conference in Geneva adopts four new rules of war, providing greater protection for civilians and prisoners of war.	Paul Henri-Spaak of Belgium is elected president of the Council of Europe's Consultative Assembly in Strasbourg.			Philippine Pres. Elpido Quirino ends a four-day visit to Washington after failing to obtain a clear-cut U.S. commitment to participate in the proposed Pacific Union of anti-Communist states.
Aug. 12				Argentina's pro-U.S. Foreign Min. Juan Bramuglia resigns and is replace by Hipolito Jesus Paz.	India's Constituent Assembly adopts a measure conferring citizenship on Indians living abroad if they, their parents or grandparents were born in India.
Aug. 13		Organization of European Economic Cooperation approves a plan to ease trade restrictions in Western Europe by exempting certain goods from import quota limits contained in bilateral trade agreements.			
Aug. 14		West Germany's first parliamentary elections result in a victory for the conservative Christian Democrats, who gain 31% of the popular vote and 139 seats, vs. 29.4% of the vote and 131 seats for their chief rivals, the Social Democrats. Third-place Free Democrats poll 12% of the vote and 52 seats .... Greek War Min. Panayotis Kanellopoulos offers amnesty to guerrillas able to show that they were forced to join the Communists.	A military revolt in Syria overthrows Pres. Husni Zayim and his premier, Mohsen el Barazi. Both are executed as Col. Sami Hinnawi, leader of the revolt, takes power as head of the Army and Supreme War Council. Observers attribute the revolt to dissatisfaction over planned military cutbacks and Zayim's willingness to negotiate with Israel on the Palestinian refugee problem.		
Aug. 15	U.N. Economic and Social Council ends its ninth session in Geneva after approving Truman's plan for aid to developing nations.	Post-election conferences between Christian Democrats and Free Democrats in Bonn result in agreement to form a coalition government headed by Christian Democratic leader Konrad Adenauer, former mayor of Cologne. Christian Democrats agree to support Free Democratic leader Theodor Heuss for president.	Syrian military leader Sami Hinnawi appoints a new cabinet headed by former Pres. Hashem el-Atassi.		Australian coal miners end a seven-week strike after failing to achieve their demands for a 15% wage increase and a 35-hour week .... Kanji Ishiwara, former chief of staff of Japan's Manchurian army, dies at 60 in Yamagata, Japan.
Aug. 16		Anatoly Lavrentiev, Russian ambassador to Yugoslavia, is recalled to Moscow to serve as deputy foreign minister .... Greek government forces announce the end of a five-day campaign in the Vitsi border area, claiming total suppression of guerrilla resistance in the region.	Direct Arab-Israeli peace negotiations begin in Lausanne under U.N. sponsorship.		Chinese Communist forces take the transport center of Kanchow in Kiangsi Province and advance towards the Nationalist capital of Canton.
	A *Includes developments that affect more than one world region, international organizations and important meetings of major world leaders.*	B *Includes all domestic and regional developments in Europe, including the Soviet Union, Turkey, Cyprus and Malta.*	C *Includes all domestic and regional developments in Africa and the Middle East, including Iraq and Iran and excluding Cyprus, Turkey and Afghanistan.*	D *Includes all domestic and regional developments in Latin America, the Caribbean and Canada.*	E *Includes all domestic and regional developments in Asian and Pacific nations, extending from Afghanistan through all the Pacific Islands, except Hawaii.*

U.S. Politics & Social Issues	U.S. Foreign Policy & Defense	U.S. Economy & Environment	Science, Technology & Nature	Culture, Leisure & Life Style	
Former deep freezer manufacturer Albert Groos, testifying before the Hoey subcommittee on influence-peddling, reports delivery of deep freezers paid for by a perfume maker to Vaughan and other influential government officials in 1945 . . . . Federal court of appeals in Washington upholds the constitutionality of Truman's loyalty program and Atty. Gen. Clark's subversive organizations list, dismissing a suit by the Joint Anti-Fascist Refugee Comm.	Truman names Gen. Omar Bradley to serve as first permanent chairman of the Joint Chiefs of Staff, replacing temporary chairman Dwight Eisenhower.	House passes and sends to the Senate a bill raising the hourly minimun wage to 75¢ but dropping one million previously covered workers . . . . Interstate Commerce Commission authorizes a 4% increase in railroad freight rates.		British Museum displays fragments of the oldest known Bible manuscripts. Dating from the third or fourth century B.C., they were found in 1947 in a cave near the Dead Sea . . . . Screen version of Philip Yordan's play *Anna Lucasta*, starring Paulette Goddard and Oscar Homolka, premiers in N.Y.	Aug. 11
Mildred Ortmeyer, secretary of accused "five percenter" James Hunt, testifies before the Hoey subcommittee that Army Chemical Corps chief Alden Waitt wrote anonymous derogatory memos about his subordinates in an effort to prevent them from getting his job. Subcommittee member Karl Mundt (R, S.D.) calls the tactic part of an "ingenious plot" by Hunt, Waitt and Vaughan to preserve their patronage arrangements . . . . House approves a resolution establishing a seven-member committee to investigate lobbying . . . . Negro-dominated National Medical Assn. refuses to take a position on the issue of national health insurance at its Detroit convention, despite a request from the American Medical Assn. to oppose the Truman plan.	Senate passes and sends to the House a bill providing $311 million for expanded guided missile and supersonic aircraft research . . . . House Armed Services Comm. concludes a four-day session in Washington on charges of "mass dishonesty" in the B-36 bomber program after hearing Air Force Secy. Stuart Symington and other officials defend the service's procurement policies.	Federal court in N.Y. rules that the U.S. Alkali Export Assn. and 15 manufacturers, including Dow Chemical and Pittsburgh Plate Glass, violated the Sherman Antitrust Act by participating in a world-wide alkali cartel.			Aug. 12
Presidential military aide Harry Vaughan issues a statement admitting to accepting the gift of a deep freezer, but denying that this was "improper." He claims that other government officials, including Treasury Secy. John Snyder and Chief Justice Frederick Vinson, also received freezers . . . . Unknown assailants bomb the homes of two Negro ministers in sections of Birmingham, Ala. zoned for whites only.		Charles Gould, discoverer of oil and gas fields in Texas and founder of the Univ. of Oklahoma's school of geology, dies at 81 in Norman, Okla.		Curtice, with Ovie Scurlock up, wins the $72,750 Washington Park Futurity in Chicago . . . . Edward Caldwell, founder of McGraw-Hill Book Co., dies at 88 in N.Y.	Aug. 13
					Aug. 14
Advertising executive Harry Hoffman, testifying before the Hoey subcommittee, substantiates earlier statements on Vaughan's involvement with a perfume company and adds that Vaughan sponsored a trip to Europe in 1945 by the company's executives for the purpose of obtaining scarce perfume essences . . . . A Baltimore court rules that a Maryland law barring state employes from joining or aiding subversive organizations is unconstitutional.					Aug. 15
Senate defeats an Administration plan to transform the Federal Security Agency into a cabinet-level Department of Welfare with responsibility for federal education, health and social security programs . . . . Suspended Army Chemical Corps chief Alden Waitt appears before the Hoey subcommittee, admitting to charges made against him in earlier testimony but denying any illegal activity.		Galveston, Tex. becomes the first city to qualify for federal housing construction aid under the new public housing-slum clearance program . . . . Sen. Styles Bridges (R, N.H.) announces his intention to resign as trustee of the UMW Welfare Fund following criticism of his $35,000 yearly salary from the fund . . . . Senate passes and sends to the White House a bill authorizing the agriculture secretary to limit the 1950 cotton crop to 21 million acres.	U.S. Public Health Service reports that the average life span of Americans is 66.8 years, up from the prewar average of 65 . . . . Yale researchers report isolation of a "false polio" virus which produces symptoms similar to those of poliomyelitis . . . . Otis Barton makes a record 4,500-ft. deep-sea descent in the Pacific off Santa Cruz Island, Calif. in a benthoscope owned by the Univ. of Southern California.	Margaret Mitchell, author of *Gone With the Wind*, dies at 49 in Atlanta of injuries sustained in an auto accident . . . . Boston Braves manager Billy Southworth takes sick leave for the rest of the season and is replaced by coach John Cooney.	Aug. 16

F	G	H	I	J
Includes elections, federal-state relations, civil rights and liberties, crime, the judiciary, education, health care, poverty, urban affairs and population.	*Includes formation and debate of U.S. foreign and defense policies, veterans affairs and defense spending. (Relations with specific foreign countries are usually found under the region concerned.)*	*Includes business, labor, agriculture, taxation, transportation, consumer affairs, monetary and fiscal policy, natural resources, pollution and accidents.*	*Includes worldwide scientific, medical and technological developments, natural phenomena, U.S. weather and natural disasters.*	*Includes the arts, religion, scholarship, communications media, sports, entertainment, fashions, fads and social life.*

	World Affairs	Europe	Africa & the Middle East	The Americas	Asia & the Pacific
Aug. 17		U.S. Commerce Dept. announces authorization of a Yugoslavian request to buy a $3-million steel mill from Pittsburgh's Continental Foundry and Machinery Co. A World Bank mission arrives in Belgrade to study Yugoslavian requests for loans totalling $250 million . . . . Churchill urges the Council of Europe to admit West Germany in the near future.		Costa Rica outlaws the recently formed National Democratic Party, charging it is a Communist front. The country's Constituent Assembly proclaims Roman Catholicism the state religion but permits observance of other faiths.	Chinese Nationalist forces report loss of the port of Foochow to the Communists . . . . Burmese Foreign Min. U E Maung announces plans to remove restrictions against foreign investment.
Aug. 18		Gen. Frank Howley, retiring U.S. commander in Berlin, states that Western Allied representatives will only express their "points of view" on the revived Allied Berlin command and will not wait for unanimous Allied agreement before taking action . . . . Hungarian Parliament adopts a new constitution declaring the country a People's Republic . . . . Finnish government moves to suppress nationwide strikes involving 150,000 workers, putting military forces on alert and charging Communists with encouraging unrest in the hope of seizing power.		Chilean government imposes martial law in Santiago and orders the arrest of Communist labor leaders following two days of unrest resulting from a transit fare increase.	World Bank grants India a $34 million loan for railway construction.
Aug. 19		French cabinet authorizes increased imports in an effort to satisfy labor demands for lower prices.		Peru breaks off diplomatic relations with Cuba, charging that anti-government leaders sought by the police were granted asylum by the Cuban embassy in Lima.	
Aug. 20		Russia sends Yugoslavia a strong protest note, calling the Tito government a collection of "unrestrained fascist offenders" and threatening to invade the country to obtain the release of 31 Russians imprisoned in Belgrade on espionage charges . . . . Striking Finnish workers begin to return to their jobs on orders from the Central Trade Union Federation.		Chilean government extends martial law to the entire country and sends naval units to occupy copper and coal mines to forestall an alleged Communist coup plot.	
Aug. 21		John McCloy names seven assistants to help him administer the U.S. zone of Germany after creation of the Federal Republic. Among those named are Gen. James Hodges as Military Security Bd. chairman and AFL official Harvey Brown as director of the Labor Affairs Office.			
Aug. 22					Hong Kong sources report a rapid Communist advance in Yunnan Province near the Burmese and Indochinese border.
Aug. 23		Responding to the Soviet note of Aug. 20, Yugoslavia attacks Russia's attempts to "interfere in [Yugoslavia's] internal affairs" but offers to repatriate the 31 Russians held on espionage charges in return for Russian return of Yugoslavian students held in Moscow.		Panamanian Pres. Domingo Diaz Arosemena dies at 74 of a heart attack in Panama City.	Dutch-Indonesian discussions on creation of a United States of Indonesia open in The Hague . . . . South Korea joins the World Health Organization as the group's 65th member.

A	B	C	D	E
Includes developments that affect more than one world region, international organizations and important meetings of major world leaders.	*Includes all domestic and regional developments in Europe, including the Soviet Union, Turkey, Cyprus and Malta.*	*Includes all domestic and regional developments in Africa and the Middle East, including Iraq and Iran and excluding Cyprus, Turkey and Afghanistan.*	*Includes all domestic and regional developments in Latin America, the Caribbean and Canada.*	*Includes all domestic and regional developments in Asian and Pacific nations, extending from Afghanistan through all the Pacific Islands, except Hawaii.*

U.S. Politics & Social Issues	U.S. Foreign Policy & Defense	U.S. Economy & Environment	Science, Technology & Nature	Culture, Leisure & Life Style	
Truman issues a proclamation giving the Justice Dept. power to bar any alien considered dangerous to the U.S. from entering the country .... Former Agriculture Dept. official Herbert Hathorn testifies before the Hoey subcommittee that Vaughan threatened to "get my job" if he did not restore a molasses firm favored by Vaughan to the department's allocation list.		Housing Expediter Tighe Woods announces that congressional budget cuts will force him to decontrol rents in one-third of the country's rent control areas .... Senate approves an Administration plan to transfer the Bureau of Employment Security from the Federal Security Agency to the Labor Dept.	First U.N. Scientific Conference on Conservation and Utilization of Resources opens in Lake Success as N.Y. zoologist Fairfield Osborn warns of looming world overpopulation.		Aug. 17
Sen. Joseph McCarthy (R, Wisc.) demands that Truman dismiss Harry Vaughan as coordinator of veterans affairs. Truman urges the press "in common fairness" to withhold criticism of Vaughan until conclusion of hearings on influence-peddling .... Senate confirms Truman's nomination of Tom Clark as a Supreme Court justice and J. Howard McGrath as attorney general .... American Assn. for the Advancement of Science attacks Truman's loyalty check program and the security clearance requirements of the Defense Dept. and Atomic Energy Commission .... Samuel Gree, Imperial Wizard of the Georgia Ku Klux Klan, dies at 59 in Atlanta of a heart attack.	House halves the Administration request for military aid to Europe, approving $869.5 million.				Aug. 18
Six of the Administration's executive reorganization plans go into effect, including Post Office reform and creation of the post of Civil Service Commission chairman.		Striking Hawaiian longshoremen end a three-day conference with shippers after failing to reach agreement in their wage dispute.		Federal Communications Commission bans radio and television prize-giving quiz shows, charging that such audience participation programs are lotteries .... U.S. Library of Congress discontinues all prizes for art, music and literature, acting on a congressional recommendation following the award of the 1948 Bollingen poetry prize to Ezra Pound .... National AAU men's swimming and diving championships end in Los Angeles, with victory in four events going to Japanese students Hironoshin Furuhashi and Yoshihiro Hamaguchi.	Aug. 19
				Coaltown, with Steve Brooks up, sets a world record of 1 min. 34.4 secs. to win the one-mile Whirlaway Stakes in Chicago.	Aug. 20
	Sens. Patrick McCarren (D, Nev.), Kenneth Wherry (R, Neb.), William Knowland (R, Calif.) and Styles Bridges (R, N.H.) issue a statement demanding a stronger U.S. commitment to the Nationalist Chinese government and an end to State Secy. Acheson's "vacillating" Far Eastern policy.		Philadelphia engineers John Mauchly and J. Presper Eckert, Jr. demonstrate Binac, a computer capable of calculating 12,000 times faster than a human being.	Hawaiian team captures the women's national AAU swimming crown in San Antonio, Texas.	Aug. 21
Interior Dept. releases two Indian tribes, the Saginaw-Chippewas of Michigan and the Stockbridge-Munsees of Wisconsin, from government wardship. They are the first Indian tribes to be given full control over their own affairs .... Rhode Island Gov. John Pastore names lawyer Edward Leahy to complete the Senate term of newly appointed Atty. Gen. J. Howard McGrath.	Truman addresses a Veterans of Foreign Wars convention in Miami, urging congressional approval of the full $1.45-billion Military Assistance Program for Western Europe, Turkey, Greece, Iran, South Korea and the Philippines.		Geologist A.I. Levorsen of Stanford Univ., speaking at the U.N. Scientific Conference on Conservation and Utilization of Resources, estimates existing oil reserves at 70 billion barrels, a 20-year supply at present rates of consumption. He urges an intensified search for undersea deposits off continental shorelines in both hemispheres.	Mika Waltari's *The Egyptian* is published in N.Y. by Putnam and becomes a Book-of-the-Month-Club selection .... W.R. Burnett's *The Asphalt Jungle* is published in N.Y. by Knopf.	Aug. 22
Ku Klux Klan representatives from six Southern states meet in Montgomery, Ala. to form the Knights of the Ku Klux Klans of America, claiming a membership of 265,000. Lycurgus Spinks of Thomasville, Ala. is named "Imperial Emperor."		Commerce Dept. reports the first significant break in the nation's economic downturn with an 8% increase in manufacturer's orders in May and June.			Aug. 23
F *Includes elections, federal-state relations, civil rights and liberties, crime, the judiciary, education, health care, poverty, urban affairs and population.*	G *Includes formation and debate of U.S. foreign and defense policies, veterans affairs and defense spending. (Relations with specific foreign countries are usually found under the region concerned.)*	H *Includes business, labor, agriculture, taxation, transportation, consumer affairs, monetary and fiscal policy, natural resources, pollution and accidents.*	I *Includes worldwide scientific, medical and technological developments, natural phenomena, U.S. weather and natural disasters.*	J *Includes the arts, religion, scholarship, communications media, sports, entertainment, fashions, fads and social life.*	

	World Affairs	Europe	Africa & the Middle East	The Americas	Asia & the Pacific
Aug. 24	North Atlantic Treaty takes effect as all ratifications are deposited in Washington.	Bulgaria and Rumania announce integration of their electric power systems within the framework of the Council for Economic Mutual Assistance .... Finnish Federation of Labor expels the construction, transport, forestry and food workers unions for their refusal to call off strikes by their members.			French forces in Vietnam begin a drive to retake Tonkin from Vietminh guerrillas .... Chiang Kai-shek flies from Taiwan to Canton and Chungking in an effort to bolster faltering Nationalist resistance.
Aug. 25		Greek government forces begin an attack on the Mt. Grammos guerrilla stronghold .... British Bd. of Trade orders a 5% cut in retail prices of clothing, footwear and household textiles.		Dominican Republic announces construction of a state munitions plant, charging that the U.S. has refused to provide enough military equipment to meet "a threat of invasion." .... Panama's First Vice Pres. Daniel Chanis, Jr. assumes the presidency for the remainder of the late Domingo Diaz Arosemena's term. He names a new cabinet and declares an amnesty for all political prisoners.	
Aug. 26		Belgrade sources report the growth of sabotage in Yugoslavia, directed mainly against the country's rail and shipping lines.			
Aug. 27		Yugoslavia charges Russia with moving Soviet forces in Hungary and Rumania up to the Yugoslavian frontier.		Bolivian government reports a revolt by Communist and fascist groups in the country's southern provinces.	
Aug. 28	First Communist-sponsored World Youth Festival ends in Budapest as 10,000 delegates pass resolutions opposing the North Atlantic Treaty and promising to work for peace.	Greek government forces complete the conquest of the Mt. Grammos guerrilla stronghold, claiming 847 Communist casualties and an equal number of prisoners .... Albanian government removes Orthodox Archbishop Christopher Kissi from office for "activity in favor of Fascism" during the Italian occupation.			Communists take the Kansu Province capital of Lanchow in northwestern China. A People's Congress in Mukden approves creation of a "People's Government for the Northeast" to rule Manchuria.
Aug. 29		Military leaders from Russia and other Eastern European countries meet in Sofia during sessions of the Council for Economic Mutual Assistance, giving rise to rumors of an impending invasion of Yugoslavia.			
Aug. 30		Finnish metal workers end their strike to resume work on ships due to Russia as part of Finland's war reparations.			
Aug. 31		Italy signs an economic pact with Greece, agreeing to pay $101 million in war reparations during the next five years .... General Council of Britain's Trades Union Congress issues a special report urging workers to accept continuation of the government's wage freeze policy.			A typhoon strikes the heavily populated Tokyo-Yokohama area of Japan, causing 111 deaths.
	A	B	C	D	E
	Includes developments that affect more than one world region, international organizations and important meetings of major world leaders.	*Includes all domestic and regional developments in Europe, including the Soviet Union, Turkey, Cyprus and Malta.*	*Includes all domestic and regional developments in Africa and the Middle East, including Iraq and Iran and excluding Cyprus, Turkey and Afghanistan.*	*Includes all domestic and regional developments in Latin America, the Caribbean and Canada.*	*Includes all domestic and regional developments in Asian and Pacific nations, extending from Afghanistan through all the Pacific Islands, except Hawaii.*

U.S. Politics & Social Issues	U.S. Foreign Policy & Defense	U.S. Economy & Environment	Science, Technology & Nature	Culture, Leisure & Life Style	
Tom Clark is sworn in as Supreme Court justice and J. Howard McGrath as Attorney General in separate White House ceremonies .... Democratic National Comm. elects William Boyle, Jr. of Kansas City to succeed McGrath as national chairman. The committee also ousts five members who supported the States' Rights Party in the last election, including presidential candidate Strom Thurmond .... Suspended Army Quartermaster-General Herman Feldman completes two days of testimony before the Senate Hoey subcommittee, denying all charges of graft and favoritism in the assignment of Army contracts.	Defense Secy. Johnson orders the armed forces to dismiss 135,000 civilian workers, release 12,073 reserve officers from active duty and close 51 installations by mid-1950 in an effort to save $200 million .... Gen. Mark Clark is named to succeed Gen. Jacob Devers as chief of the Army Field Forces beginning Sept. 30.			Universal-International Film's *Sword in the Desert*, the story of a boatload of Jewish refugees attempting to land on the Palestinian coast, premiers in N.Y.	Aug. 24
N.Y. Judge Harold Medina refuses to declare a mistrial in the case of U.S. Communist leaders despite defense contentions that juror Russell Janney, author of *The Miracle of the Bells*, discussed the case out of court and has an anti-Communist bias.	House Armed Services Comm. clears all government officials connected with B-36 bomber procurement after learning that a civilian Navy offical made anonymous charges of fraud and favoritism in the program without evidence.	Saunders Norvell, retired hardware and small arms manufacturer, dies at 85 in Mt. Vernon, N.Y.	RCA reports development of a color television which can be adopted to existing black and white receivers through use of a converter.	Film version of Flaubert's novel *Madame Bovary*, starring James Mason and Jennifer Jones, premiers in N.Y.	Aug. 25
Federal circuit court of appeals in San Francisco upholds restoration of full U.S. citizenship to three Japanese-American women who renounced it while being held in Western internment camps during the war. The court condemns the wartime exclusion of all Japanese-Americans from the West Coast and characterizes conditions in the camps as "unnecessarily cruel and inhuman treatment." .... John Maragon, a friend of Vaughan and alleged "five percenter," refuses to testify before the Hoey subcommittee despite testimony from other witnesses implicating him in numerous cases of government graft and exercise of improper influence .... AFL American Fed. of Teachers ends a five-day Milwaukee convention after passing a resolution rejecting Communist Party membership as "sufficient grounds for the dismissal of a teacher."	In an amendment to a military appropriations bill, the Senate directs the defense secretary to appoint a special assistant to advise businessmen competing for government contracts.	General Motors accepts a UAW demand that wages be maintained at present levels despite a drop in the cost of living index.	Interior Secy. Julius Krug, speaking before the U.N. Scientific Conference on Conservation and Utilization of Resources, predicts development of atomic power generating plants within 20 years and reports progress in experiments in solar energy.		Aug. 26
War veterans break up a scheduled open-air concert by singer Paul Robeson in Peekskill, N.Y., causing eight injuries .... Accused "five percenter" James Hunt, hospitalized in N.Y., signs an affidavit for presentation to the Hoey subcommittee denying charges of influence-peddling.	Senate passes a House-approved measure permitting expansion of the Air Force to 70 groups with 24,000 aircraft.	Sixteen thousand CIO United Rubber Workers union members strike against the B.F. Goodrich Co. for a wage increase and pension plan.	Biochemist Russell Marker reports isolation of the hormone cortisone, important in the treatment of arthritis, from the tropical yam .... A hurricane completes a two-day passage through southern Florida, inflicting $40 million in property damage.	Helen Sigel captures the women's Western amateur golf crown in Chicago.	Aug. 27
					Aug. 28
		Federal district court in Honolulu upholds the legality of the government seizure of Hawaiian docks for the duration of the 121-day-old longshoremen's strike .... Truman signs a bill authorizing limitation of 1950 cotton acreage to 21 million acres.	A 22-million-volt betatron is used to treat two cancer patients at the Univ. of Illinois Chicago hospital, the first application of a nuclear device in cancer therapy.	George Howe's *Call It Treason*, winner of the Christophers Award, is published in N.Y. by Viking.	Aug. 29
		Interior Secy. Julius Krug submits a $2 billion irrigation development bill for California's Central Valley to Congress. The project would supply water for three million uncultivated acres and provide 8.1 billion kilowatt hours of electricity a year.			Aug. 30
Presidential aide Harry Vaughan completes two days of testimony before the Senate Hoey subcommittee, admitting to numerous interventions with government procurement authorities on behalf of friends but denying that any of his activities were illegal.	Grand Army of the Republic concludes its 83rd and last meeting in Indianapolis, attended by six Union veterans.	Senate approves and sends to House conference a bill raising the minimum hourly wage to 75¢ but removing 200,000 retail and service industry employes from coverage.			Aug. 31
F	G	H	I	J	
Includes elections, federal-state relations, civil rights and liberties, crime, the judiciary, education, health care, poverty, urban affairs and population.	*Includes formation and debate of U.S. foreign and defense policies, veterans affairs and defense spending. (Relations with specific foreign countries are usually found under the region concerned.)*	*Includes business, labor, agriculture, taxation, transportation, consumer affairs, monetary and fiscal policy, natural resources, pollution and accidents.*	*Includes worldwide scientific, medical and technological developments, natural phenomena, U.S. weather and natural disasters.*	*Includes the arts, religion, scholarship, communications media, sports, entertainment, fashions, fads and social life.*	

	World Affairs	Europe	Africa & the Middle East	The Americas	Asia & the Pacific
Sept. 1		Big Four representatives again suspend talks on the Austrian peace treaty due to disagreement over Russian demands for extensive economic controls in Austria.			
Sept. 2		Yugoslavia liquidates joint enterprises with Russia in Danubian shipping and Balkan civil aviation .... Gen. Sir Walter Kirke, head of the British Home Army in 1939 and 1940, dies at 72 in Carlisle, England.		Canadian Seamen's Union withdraws from the Trades and Labor Congress in a disagreement over its strike against Eastern Canadian shippers.	A fire in the Nationalist capital of Chungking causes 1,700 deaths and damages 10,000 buildings on the city's waterfront.
Sept. 3		Pope Pius XII charges the Polish government with suppressing all Catholic organizations in the country .... Rumanian government orders liquidation of all private insurance companies within six months.		Brazil's Senate refuses to ratify a commercial treaty with Czechoslovakia.	Burmese Army reports the recapture of Thawatti, former headquarters of Communist guerrillas in central Burma.
Sept. 4					
Sept. 5		Adm. Richard Conolly, U.S. naval commander in the Mediterranean and eastern Atlantic, meets Franco in La Coruna during the first official postwar visit by U.S. warships to Spain .... Council of Europe's Consultative Assembly in Strasbourg passes a resolution favoring a European union with limited power over member countries .... A gun battle in Milan between police and workers demonstrating against layoffs causes three deaths.		A leftist Continental Congress for Peace, organized by Mexican labor leader Vicente Lombardo Toledano, opens in Mexico City with 1,000 delegates attending from Western Hemisphere nations.	
Sept. 6		Finnish Trade Union Federation expels seven unions for calling strikes in violation of federation orders .... U.S. authorities in Germany order the UFA German film trust broken up and sold in separate units.		Rightist Bolivian rebels announce formation of a cabinet headed by Victor Paz Estenssoro despite reports of government gains in the southern provinces.	An Allied military court in Tokyo acquits Adm. Soemu Toyoda, last chief of staff of the Japanese Navy, of responsibility for atrocities in the Philippines. The verdict closes the last major war crimes trial in Japan .... Vietnamese Chief of State Bao Dai designates Saigon as his provisional capital.
Sept. 7	Britain, Canada and the U.S. begin talks in Washington on means of alleviating the sterling area's dollar crisis. British Exchequer Chancellor Sir Stafford Cripps emphasizes in an opening statement that Britain seeks no "charitable aid or any direct assistance other than that contemplated through the Marshall Plan."	West German Parliament officially opens in Bonn, electing Christian Democratic leader Erik Koehler president of the lower house .... Organization for European Economic Cooperation members agree in Paris to form a $284-million pool, from which countries with balance of payment difficulties can obtain extra credit.		Bolivian government charges Argentina with supporting rightist rebels in southern Bolivia.	
Sept. 8		Export-Import Bank approves a $20-million loan to Yugoslavia for mining development and other projects. Poland denounces the 1946 Polish-Yugoslavian mutual assistance treaty, accusing Yugoslavia of operating an espionage ring in Poland.		A shooting incident in the Colombian Chamber of Deputies results in the death of Liberal Deputy Gustavo Jiminez and the wounding of three other deputies.	
Sept. 9		Britain's Trades Union Congress ends a five-day conference in Bridlington, England after voting approval of the Labor government's wage freeze and the anti-Communist policy of the TUC leadership .... Vatican authorizes Catholics to pledge allegiance to the Czechoslovakian Republic without endorsing the Communist regime.		Bolivian government forces report capturing most rightist strongpoints, restricting rebel troops to a narrow strip of territory in east-central Bolivia .... Crash of a Quebec Airways DC-3 near St. Joachim, Que. causes 23 deaths, including three top executives of the Kennecott Copper Corp.: E. Tappan Stannard, Arthur Storke and R.J. Parker.	U.S. orders its consulate in Hankow closed and reduces the staffs of the Nanking embassy and Shanghai consulate, accusing the Communist government of "unwillingness or inability" to maintain normal relations.
	A *Includes developments that affect more than one world region, international organizations and important meetings of major world leaders.*	B *Includes all domestic and regional developments in Europe, including the Soviet Union, Turkey, Cyprus and Malta.*	C *Includes all domestic and regional developments in Africa and the Middle East, including Iraq and Iran and excluding Cyprus, Turkey and Afghanistan.*	D *Includes all domestic and regional developments in Latin America, the Caribbean and Canada.*	E *Includes all domestic and regional developments in Asian and Pacific nations, extending from Afghanistan through all the Pacific Islands, except Hawaii.*

U.S. Politics & Social Issues	U.S. Foreign Policy & Defense	U.S. Economy & Environment	Science, Technology & Nature	Culture, Leisure & Life Style	
Truman rejects congressional and press demands for the dismissal of Harry Vaughan from his position as presidential military aide . . . . House Education and Labor Comm. Chmn. John Lesinski (D, Mich.) dissolves his committee's four subcommittees in an effort to hurry House action on federal aid to education. Included among the dissolved bodies is Adam Clayton Powell's (D, N.Y.) fair employment practices subcommittee . . . . A federal district court in Alexandria, Va. dismisses a suit against the Washington National Airport for racial discrimination, ruling that segregation does not violate the Constitution or any congressional acts.	American Legion concludes a four-day convention in Philadelphia after passing resolutions urging curtailment of immigration, continued U.S. aid to Nationalist China and conclusion of a Pacific defense pact. George Craig becomes the first World War II veteran to be elected national commander of the organization.				Sept. 1
				Gangster film *White Heat*, starring James Cagney and Virginia Mayo, premiers in N.Y.	Sept. 2
	Gen. Walter Short, commander of Army forces in Pearl Harbor at the time of the Japanese attack, dies at 69 in Dallas.	NLRB outlaws a sympathy strike for the first time under the Taft-Hartley Act, ruling against the action of a Teamsters local in Bridgeport, Conn.	Joseph De Bona of Hollywood takes the Bendix Trophy as winner of the Los Angeles-Cleveland air race, averaging 407 mph in a modified F-51.	Charles Coe takes the U.S. amateur golf title in Rochester, N.Y.	Sept. 3
One thousand anti-Communist demonstrators picket an open-air concert by singer Paul Robeson in Peekskill, N.Y. Violence after the concert causes 145 injuries.			World's largest civilian aircraft, Britain's eight-engine Brabazon I, makes its first flight in Bristol . . . . Dr. Ralph Parker, discoverer of the vaccine for Rocky Mountain spotted fever, dies at 61 in Hamilton, Mont.		Sept. 4
Truman opens the campaign season for the 1950 congressional elections with speeches in Pittsburgh and Des Moines, Ia., promoting the farm and labor portions of his Fair Deal program.	American Veterans of World War II complete a three-day meeting in Des Moines, Ia. after passing resolutions against a Pacific defense pact and a national health insurance system and for federal bonuses for World War II veterans . . . . Guy Viskniskki, founder and first editor of the Army newspaper *Stars and Stripes* during World War I, dies at 73 in Montclair, N.J.	AFL Pres. William Green, speaking in San Diego, Calif., praises CIO efforts "to purge itself of Communist leadership" and predicts the "eventual unification" of the U.S. labor movement.	Cook Cleland wins the Thompson Trophy in Cleveland's National Air Races, flying a Vought Corsair at an average speed of 397 mph . . . . Flier William Odom, holder of the speed record for a solo round-the-world flight, dies when his plane crashes in Berea, Ohio during the Thompson Trophy race.	Pancho Gonzales and Margaret Osborne du Pont win the men's and women's singles titles at the U.S. lawn tennis championships in Forest Hills, N.Y.	Sept. 5
War veteran Howard Unruh kills 13 passers-by with a revolver in Camden, N.J. and battles police for two hours in his apartment before surrendering.			Univ. of Chicago geologist Willard Libby announces development of a means of determining the age of organic materials through measurement of radioactive carbon . . . . U.N. Conference on Conservation and Utilization of Natural Resources ends a three-week session in Lake Success.	Egypt defeats the U.S. to capture the world weightlifting championship in The Hague . . . . French author Lucien Descaves, president and last surviving founder of the Goncourt Academy, dies at 88 in Paris.	Sept. 6
Truman issues an executive order transferring the administration of Guam from the Navy to the Interior Dept.				Mexican painter Jose Clemente Orozco dies at 65 in Mexico City . . . . A six-man Egyptian team sets a relay record by swimming the English Channel in 11 hrs., 11 mins.	Sept. 7
	Senate Republicans begin a drive to block the House-approved reciprocal trade agreement bill unless Administration supporters approve a clause limiting the President's authority to make tariff concessions.	Hawaiian shippers and striking CIO longshoremen begin separate conferences with Federal Mediation Service director Cyrus Ching in an effort to end the 131-day dock strike.		German composer Richard Strauss dies at 85 in Garmisch-Patenkirchen . . . . Alfred Hitchcock's *Under Capricorn* premiers in N.Y. . . . . *The Vital Center*, an analysis of American political movements by historian Arthur Schlesinger, Jr., is published by Houghton Mifflin . . . . Nelson Algren's *The Man with the Golden Arm* is published by Doubleday.	Sept. 8
National Urban League ends a five-day convention in Denver after condemning Communists for "exploiting the issue of race for their own selfish ends."	Senate Foreign Relations and Armed Services committees approve a $75-million military aid bill for anti-Communist forces in the Far East, including Nationalist China.	A strike of 5,200 operating workers stops all service on the Missouri Pacific Railroad, the nation's ninth largest line.	World Health Organization Director-Gen. Brock Chisholm, addressing a World Union of Peace Organizations conference in Switzerland, claims that recently developed techniques of biological warfare are so lethal that "war has become an obsolete human behavior pattern."		Sept. 9

F	G	H	I	J
Includes elections, federal-state relations, civil rights and liberties, crime, the judiciary, education, health care, poverty, urban affairs and population.	*Includes formation and debate of U.S. foreign and defense policies, veterans affairs and defense spending. (Relations with specific foreign countries are usually found under the region concerned.)*	*Includes business, labor, agriculture, taxation, transportation, consumer affairs, monetary and fiscal policy, natural resources, pollution and accidents.*	*Includes worldwide scientific, medical and technological developments, natural phenomena, U.S. weather and natural disasters.*	*Includes the arts, religion, scholarship, communications media, sports, entertainment, fashions, fads and social life.*

	World Affairs	Europe	Africa & the Middle East	The Americas	Asia & the Pacific
Sept. 10		Eight high-ranking Hungarian officials, including former Foreign Min. Laszlo Rajk and Army Chief Inspector Gyorgy Palffry, are indicted in Budapest on charges of plotting with U.S. and Yugoslavian agents to overthrow the Communist government .... Henri Queuille becomes the first postwar French premier to complete a year in office.		Paraguayan Pres. Felipe Molas Lopez resigns following a decision by the Executive Bd. of the Colorado Party to make House Speaker Frederico Chavez president.	
Sept. 11				Eslanda Robeson, wife of singer Paul Robeson, tells the concluding session of the Continental Congress for Peace in Mexico City that the violence directed against her husband's audience in Peekskill, N.Y. typifies American discrimination against "Negroes, Jews and labor unions." .... Inter-American Confederation of Labor concludes a five-day conference in Havana after passing resolutions urging member states to introduce land reform programs and supporting formation of an anti-Communist world labor organization.	
Sept. 12	Britain, Canada and the U.S. end Washington talks on the British dollar crisis after the U.S. agrees to consider increasing its raw materials purchases from sterling-area countries and reducing tariffs and customs restrictions.	West German Parliament elects Free Democratic leader Theodor Heuss president of the Federal Republic.			
Sept. 13	Russia vetoes the U.N. membership applications of Austria, Ceylon, Finland, Jordan, Ireland, Italy and Portugal.		U.N. Conciliation Commission for Palestine issues a plan for internationalization of Jerusalem, calling for division of the city into demilitarized Jewish and Arab sectors under a U.N. commissioner. Israel immediately rejects the proposal.		
Sept. 14		Sen. Patrick McCarran (D, Nev.), leaving N.Y. for a visit to Spain, states that he intends to discuss possible U.S. diplomatic recognition of Spain and a loan to the Franco government.			
Sept. 15		West German Parliament chooses Christian Democratic leader Konrad Adenauer as the Federal Republic's first chancellor .... France announces plans to remove import restrictions on 15% of its foreign purchases in a move to promote European trade .... U.S. forces in Bavaria end 10 days of war games aimed at meeting an invasion from East Germany.		Rightist Bolivian revolt is suppressed after 20 days as rebel forces lose their last strongholds and flee into the jungle.	
Sept. 16	World Bank and International Monetary Fund directors end a four-day meeting in Washington with recommendations that countries suffering from a dollar shortage devalue their currencies.	Former Hungarian Foreign Min. Laszlo Rajk, testifying at his Budapest espionage trial, reads a confession admitting to charges that he collaborated with Western agents in an effort to overthrow the Hungarian government.			
Sept. 17	North Atlantic Treaty members establish a North Atlantic Council in Washington to carry out the security provisions of the pact.	Former Hungarian Gen. Gyorgy Palffy, testifying at his Budapest trial, reads a confession admitting to government charges of espionage and subversion.		Argentina suspends all imports to relieve a foreign exchange shortage .... A fire on board the Canada Steamship Lines cruise ship *Noronic*, docked in Toronto, kills 139 passengers.	British Foreign Secy. Bevin and French Foreign Min. Schuman, conferring in Washington with State Secy. Acheson, endorse the U.S. decision to restrict its support of the Nationalist Chinese government and urge aid to independent nationalist movements in Southeast Asia as the best means of containing Communism in the Far East.
Sept. 18		British government devalues the pound sterling by 30%, from $4.03 to $2.80.			
	A *Includes developments that affect more than one world region, international organizations and important meetings of major world leaders.*	B *Includes all domestic and regional developments in Europe, including the Soviet Union, Turkey, Cyprus and Malta.*	C *Includes all domestic and regional developments in Africa and the Middle East, including Iraq and Iran and excluding Cyprus, Turkey and Afghanistan.*	D *Includes all domestic and regional developments in Latin America, the Caribbean and Canada.*	E *Includes all domestic and regional developments in Asian and Pacific nations, extending from Afghanistan through all the Pacific Islands, except Hawaii.*

U.S. Politics & Social Issues	U.S. Foreign Policy & Defense	U.S. Economy & Environment	Science, Technology & Nature	Culture, Leisure & Life Style	
Associate Supreme Court Justice Wiley Rutledge dies at 55 of a cerebral hemorrhage in York, Me. . . . . Army Secy. Gordon Gray accepts the retirement request of Chemical Corps chief Gen. Alden Waitt and restores Gen. Herman Feldman to active duty as Army Quartermaster General, ending Army action on the "five percenter" case.	Navy Capt. John Crommelin publicly urges a congressional inquiry into armed forces unification, charging the Army and Air Force with working to destroy naval aviation in order to strengthen their own predominance within the military establishment.	Presidential fact-finding board on the steel industry issues a report to Truman urging that the USW drop its demand for a wage increase and employers adopt a workers' pension and welfare program.			Sept. 10
				New York Herald Tribune lists Edward Streeter's *Father of the Bride* and Frank Gilbreth's and Elizabeth Carey's *Cheaper by the Dozen* as best-selling fiction and non-fiction books.	Sept. 11
N.Y. Judge Harold Medina sentences Michigan Communist Party leader Carl Winter to jail for contempt of court when Winter refuses to answer questions regarding his father-in-law's presence at the Party's 1945 convention.		At Truman's request, the USW agrees to postpone a steel workers' strike scheduled for tomorrow in order to continue wage and pension talks with U.S. Steel.		English edition of Hermann Hesse's *Magister Ludi* is published in N.Y. by Holt . . . . Harry Thacker Burleigh, composer of Negro spirituals, dies at 82 in Stamford, Conn.	Sept. 12
		UMW leader John Lewis accuses Southern mine operators of defaulting in their contributions to the UMW welfare fund and threatens a strike if they do not resume payment. Employers respond that expiration of their contract with the UMW last June relieved them of the obligation to support the UMW fund.		Federal district court in Chicago restrains the Federal Communications Commission from enforcing its ban on radio and television give-away programs pending a federal court ruling on the ban's legality . . . . Detroit Symphony calls off its 1949-50 season because its members refuse to take a pay cut.	Sept. 13
Sen. James Eastland (D, Miss.), a prominent critic of Truman's civil rights program, becomes chairman of the civil rights subcommittee of the Senate Judiciary Comm. . . . . N.Y. Gov. Thomas Dewey orders a special grand jury investigation of recent anti-Communist riots in Peekskill, claiming that the Communists provoked the second disturbance through use of a "quasi-military [guard] force." . . . . *New York Journal American* reporter Howard Rushmore, a former Communist, testifies before a Senate Judiciary subcommittee that U.S. Communist leaders are "aliens sent here by Moscow" and urges their deportation.	Truman nominates former Sen. John Sherman Cooper to replace John Foster Dulles on the U.S. delegation to the U.N. General Assembly. He also names Gen. Anthony McAuliffe, hero of Bastogne, to succeed Gen. Alden Waitt as head of the Army Chemical Corps.	U.S. Steel Pres. Benjamin Fairless refuses to bargain with the USW on the basis of the presidential fact-finding commission report, objecting to its support for an employer-financed worker pension fund . . . . A printers' strike against five Chicago daily newspapers, in effect since November 1947, ends when the International Typographical Union settles for a $10 weekly wage increase and employer recognition of the union as sole bargaining agent . . . . NLRB rules that employes who work part-time as supervisors are ineligible to vote in union representation elections.			Sept. 14
New York Republicans nominate John Foster Dulles for election to the Senate seat he now holds by appointment. State Democrats and Liberals name former Gov. Herbert Lehman to oppose Dulles. . . . . Truman nominates Chicago federal Judge Sherman Minton to succeed the late Wiley Rutledge on the Supreme Court.	Navy Secy. Francis Matthews revokes a scheduled promotion of Capt. John Crommelin following Crommelin's controversial statements on armed forces unification . . . . Senate passes the Reciprocal Trade Agreements Act, defeating Republican efforts to limit the President's power to reduce tariffs.	Justice Dept. files an antitrust suit in N.Y. aimed at splitting the Great Atlantic and Pacific Tea Co. into seven independent retail chains and separating the firm's manufacturing and selling branches . . . . An NLRB trial examiner voids contract provisions requiring workers to pay union dues as their share of the costs of collective bargaining.	Lithomat Corp. of Cambridge, Mass. demonstrates an electronic type-composing device which reproduces type faces photographically on engraving plates without use of metal type.	Pittsburgh Pirates pitcher Tiny Bonham dies at 36 following an appendectomy in Pittsburgh.	Sept. 15
Georgia Supreme Court upholds a state law intended to curb the Negro vote by ordering all voters to re-register.		Eight thousand miners strike in Utah and Wyoming as UMW leader Lewis halts payments from the depleted union welfare fund.		A Gallup Poll lists Bob Hope, Milton Berle, Jack Benny and Red Skelton as the most popular American comedians.	Sept. 16
	Senate Foreign Relations and Armed Services committees pass a $1.3-billion military aid bill, reserving $75 million for the "general area of China."			Cannes Film Festival awards its grand prize to the British-made film *The Third Man*.	Sept. 17
			Dr. John Long, a U.S. health expert who ended plagues throughout Latin America, dies at 75 in Guayaquil, Ecuador.	U.S. Hurricanes defeat the El Trebol team of Argentina, 10-4, to win the open championship polo finals in Westbury, N.Y.	Sept. 18
F	G	H	I	J	
Includes elections, federal-state relations, civil rights and liberties, crime, the judiciary, education, health care, poverty, urban affairs and population.	*Includes formation and debate of U.S. foreign and defense policies, veterans affairs and defense spending. (Relations with specific foreign countries are usually found under the region concerned.)*	*Includes business, labor, agriculture, taxation, transportation, consumer affairs, monetary and fiscal policy, natural resources, pollution and accidents.*	*Includes worldwide scientific, medical and technological developments, natural phenomena, U.S. weather and natural disasters.*	*Includes the arts, religion, scholarship, communications media, sports, entertainment, fashions, fads and social life.*	

	World Affairs	Europe	Africa & the Middle East	The Americas	Asia & the Pacific
Sept. 19	Ten countries, including France, Sweden and Israel, follow Britain in devaluing their currencies to the free market level.				
Sept. 20	U.N. General Assembly begins its fourth annual session in Flushing, N.Y., electing Philippine delegate Carlos Romulo as session president. Yugoslavia breaks with Russia by refusing to support the Soviet-bloc candidate, Czech Foreign Min. Vladimir Clementis . . . . Four new nations, including Holland and Belgium, devalue their currencies. French Finance Min. Maurice Petsche accuses Britain of engaging in "commercial warfare" by cutting the pound without previous consultation with other states.	Gerhart Eisler is named head of the newly created Information Ministry in the Russian zone of Germany.			Two Economic Cooperation Admin. officials are taken to North Korea by the mutinous crew of a South Korean ship. North Korean authorities imprison the Americans when they refuse to acknowledge the North Korean government as the official government of Korea.
Sept. 21		West German Chancellor Konrad Adenauer names his first cabinet, a Christian Democrat-Free Democrat coalition with Ludwig Erhard as economics minister.			Chinese Communist leader Mao Tzetung proclaims the People's Republic of China at the opening session of the Chinese People's Political Consultative Conference in Peking.
Sept. 22		U.S., Britain and France formally grant the West German government sovereignty over German internal affairs . . . . Eight defendants in the Hungarian espionage trial make their final pleas, all admitting to government charges of subversion.		Argentine Congress passes a bill providing prison sentences for showing "disrespect" towards government leaders . . . . Argentine minesweeper *Fournier* sinks in the Magellan Straits with the loss of 77 crew members.	China's U.N. delegate T.F. Tsiang accuses Russia of fostering the Chinese civil war with the aim of undermining "the independence and integrity of China and the peace of the Far East."
Sept. 23	Truman, British P.M. Attlee and Canadian P.M. Louis St. Laurent report detection of a nuclear explosion in Russia, presumably an atomic bomb test. State Secy. Acheson and Joint Chiefs of Staff Chmn. Omar Bradley state that Soviet possession of a nuclear weapon will cause no changes in U.S. foreign and defense policy.				
Sept. 24		A Budapest court convicts Laszlo Rajk and seven co-defendants of subversion and espionage, sentencing Rajk and two others to death . . . . Yugoslavian Pres. Tito accuses Hungary of provoking unrest on the Hungarian-Yugoslav border with the aim of imposing a regime "servile to the Soviet Union" on Yugoslavia. He charges that the Hungarian espionage trial is part of a Russian-led "campaign and plot against Yugoslavia."		Quebec jeweler Albert Guay is charged with murdering his wife by planting a bomb in the Air Quebec airliner which crashed two weeks ago near St. Joachim, Que.	
Sept. 25	Russian news agency Tass confirms Western reports of a nuclear explosion in the Soviet Union, claiming it was part of a "large-scale blasting" operation to construct mines, canals and roads in Siberia.	Charles de Gaulle calls for initiation of a French atomic weapons program in the face of Russia's nuclear capability, claiming that the U.S. "is neither obliged nor prepared to participate in the direct and immediate defense of our continent."			
Sept. 26					
Sept. 27		Yugoslavia orders nine members of the Hungarian mission in Belgrade to leave the country within 24 hours in retaliation for similar Hungarian action yesterday against 10 Yugoslavian diplomats in Budapest . . . . British Exchequer Chancellor Sir Stafford Cripps announces a 20% profits tax increase to discourage businessmen from raising prices in the wake of devaluation . . . . Italy eliminates most restrictions on imports from other countries receiving Marshall Plan aid.			Nationalist China files a complaint against Russia in the General Assembly, accusing the Soviets of "threats to the independence and territorial integrity of China."
	A	B	C	D	E
	Includes developments that affect more than one world region, international organizations and important meetings of major world leaders.	*Includes all domestic and regional developments in Europe, including the Soviet Union, Turkey, Cyprus and Malta.*	*Includes all domestic and regional developments in Africa and the Middle East, including Iraq and Iran and excluding Cyprus, Turkey and Afghanistan.*	*Includes all domestic and regional developments in Latin America, the Caribbean and Canada.*	*Includes all domestic and regional developments in Asian and Pacific nations, extending from Afghanistan through all the Pacific Islands, except Hawaii.*

U.S. Politics & Social Issues	U.S. Foreign Policy & Defense	U.S. Economy & Environment	Science, Technology & Nature	Culture, Leisure & Life Style	
George Johnson, former U.S. district attorney who jailed Al Capone and other gangsters, dies at 75 in Chicago.		A strike of 480,000 coal miners begins when mine operators refuse to resume payments to the UMW welfare and pension fund before negotiation of a new contract . . . . U.S. Steel and USW representatives meet with Federal Mediation Service director Cyrus Ching in an attempt to settle the steel industry's pension dispute.		Roberto Rossellini's film *Germany Anno Zero* premiers in N.Y.	Sept. 19
Democratic congressional leaders from 11 Western states end a three-day meeting in San Francisco after adopting a program calling for reform of farm price supports, repeal of the Taft-Hartley Act, statehood for Hawaii and Alaska and regional reclamation and development projects modelled on the TVA.		UMW representatives meeting with Southern mine operators refuse to begin bargaining on a new contract until employers pay their back contributions to the UMW welfare fund . . . . N.Y. Stock Exchange suffers its worst price break of the year as issues slip one to three points in the face of foreign currency devaluations.	Criminologist Leonarde Keeler, developer of the lie detector, dies at 45 in Sturgeon Bay, Wisc.	Willie Pep retains his world featherweight title with a seventh-round victory over Eddie Campo in Waterbury, Conn. . . . . Veteran screen star Richard Dix dies at 54 in Hollywood.	Sept. 20
		Wildcat strikes involving 5,300 steel workers break out near Pittsburgh as a result of the current pension dispute.		Cuban Jose Cortinas swims the Straits of Gibraltar in 10 hrs., 45 mins.	Sept. 21
Nathan Leopold, jailed since 1924 for the "thrill slaying" of Bobbie Franks in Chicago, receives a reduced sentence, which leaves him eligible for parole in 1953, for participating in wartime malaria experiments . . . . Truman appoints Gen. George Marshall as president of the American Red Cross.	Senate approves and sends to House conference a $1.3-billion military aid bill for Western Europe and the Far East . . . . Commerce Dept. announces approval of the export of $500,000 worth of oil drilling machinery to Russia.	Truman persuades USW leaders to postpone a threatened steel workers' strike for the second time to allow further negotiations over pensions with U.S. Steel and other producers . . . . Sen. Guy Gillette (D, Ia.) opens a Senate Agriculture subcommittee inquiry into food prices, charging that middlemen get too large a share of agricultural profits.		Sam Wood, director of *Goodbye, Mr. Chips* and other films, dies at 66 in Hollywood.	Sept. 22
Testimony ends in the N.Y. trial of U.S. Communist leaders.		CIO United Electrical Workers union ends a five-day convention in Cleveland after re-electing leftist Pres. Albert Fitzgerald. The convention approves a resolution threatening to withdraw from the CIO unless CIO leaders stop trying to interfere in internal union affairs and cease their harrassment of the UEW for its leftist political orientation.	Senate approves a five-year, $280-million program for construction of medical schools and other health profession training facilities.		Sept. 23
				Vatican newspaper *L'Osservatore Romano* calls on Russia and the U.S. to renounce use of the atomic bomb.	Sept. 24
				Ted Schroeder and Doris Hart win the men's and women's singles titles at the national amateur hard court tennis championships in Berkeley, Calif. . . . . Charlie Lupica of Cleveland leaves his flagpole perch after setting a flagpole-sitting record of 177 days, 2 hrs. 25 mins. . . . . Louise Suggs takes the U.S. women's open golf title in Landover, Md.	Sept. 25
	Truman signs the Reciprocal Trade Agreements Act, stating that increased U.S. importation of foreign goods is necessary to solve the world economic crisis . . . . Senate confirms Warren Austin, Philip Jessup, Eleanor Roosevelt and John Sherman Cooper as U.S. delegates to the U.N. General Assembly.	CIO National Maritime Union ends a two-week convention in N.Y. after endorsing the right-wing leadership of Pres. Joseph Curran and expelling a number of leftist union officials.			Sept. 26
In a special election, Oklahoma retains its 42-year-old ban on hard liquor.	House passes a Senate-approved measure providing pay increases for armed forces personnel totalling $1.2 billion over the next four years.	Thirty-five non-union coal mines, guarded by armed private and state police, reopen in western Pennsylvania and West Virginia in defiance of UMW pickets.			Sept. 27
F	G	H	I	J	
Includes elections, federal-state relations, civil rights and liberties, crime, the judiciary, education, health care, poverty, urban affairs and population.	*Includes formation and debate of U.S. foreign and defense policies, veterans affairs and defense spending. (Relations with specific foreign countries are usually found under the region concerned.)*	*Includes business, labor, agriculture, taxation, transportation, consumer affairs, monetary and fiscal policy, natural resources, pollution and accidents.*	*Includes worldwide scientific, medical and technological developments, natural phenomena, U.S. weather and natural disasters.*	*Includes the arts, religion, scholarship, communications media, sports, entertainment, fashions, fads and social life.*	

	World Affairs	Europe	Africa & the Middle East	The Americas	Asia & the Pacific
Sept. 28		Western Allies break off talks with Russia on unifying the administration of Berlin, accusing Soviet authorities of ignoring an earlier promise to pay part of the wages of West Berlin railway workers in Western currency .... Britain and Czechoslovakia sign a five-year trade agreement.			Chinese Communists take control of Sinkiang Province in western China.
Sept. 29	A secret meeting of the Big Five and Canada in Lake Success, N.Y. fails to break the deadlock on nuclear arms control.	Russia denounces its 1945 mutual aid and friendship treaties with Yugoslavia, accusing the Tito government of cooperating with "foreign imperialist circles." .... British House of Commons passes a motion of confidence in the financial policies of the Labor government. The government also lifts half of its restrictions on importation of goods from countries outside the dollar area .... West German government devalues its currency from 33¢ to 23.8¢ U.S.		Argentine Congress deprives oppositional Radical leader Ricardo Balbin of his parliamentary immunity, allowing him to be tried under a new law for showing "disrespect" in a recent speech against Pres. Peron.	
Sept. 30		Berlin airlift ends after delivering 2.3 million tons of supplies to the city in 277,264 flights .... Poland and Hungary follow Russia in severing their mutual aid and friendship agreements with Yugoslavia.			Mao Tze-tung is named chairman of the People's Political Consultative Council, an organ supervising the government's executive functions. Deputy chairmen include Gen. Chu Teh, Liu Shao-chi and Mme. Sun Yat-sen.
Oct. 1					Mao Tze-tung appoints Chou En-lai premier as head of the State Administrative Council, chief executive organ of the Chinese Communist government. Chou sends a note to U.S. Consul Gen. O. Edmund Clubb in Peking requesting establishment of full diplomatic relations between the two countries.
Oct. 2				Congressional elections in Costa Rica result in an overwhelming victory for Otilio Ulate Blanco's National Union Party.	Chinese Communist government officially begins functioning. Russia extends diplomatic recognition to the People's Republic and breaks off relations with the Nationalist government.
Oct. 3		Yugoslavian Pres. Tito, speaking at the conclusion of large-scale military maneuvers, accuses Russia of seeking to turn Yugoslavia into a "subject region" and promises that the Army will defend the country .... A special U.N. conciliation commission begins a three-week closed session aimed at reconciling Greece with its Balkan neighbors.		Argentina devalues its currency 46%.	U.S. State Dept. and the British Foreign Office decline to take immediate action on Chinese Communist requests for diplomatic recognition.
Oct. 4		Member states of the U.N. Scientific, Educational and Cultural Organization vote in Paris to continue UNESCO cultural projects in West Germany despite Soviet bloc opposition.	Israeli cabinet orders the merging of Jaffa and Tel Aviv.		
Oct. 5	Defense ministers from the North Atlantic Treaty nations meet in Washington and establish a military committee headed by U.S. Gen. Omar Bradley to formulate a defense plan for the alliance.	French cabinet of Premier Henri Queuille resigns in a dispute over labor demands for wage increases.			
	A	B	C	D	E
	Includes developments that affect more than one world region, international organizations and important meetings of major world leaders.	*Includes all domestic and regional developments in Europe, including the Soviet Union, Turkey, Cyprus and Malta.*	*Includes all domestic and regional developments in Africa and the Middle East, including Iraq and Iran and excluding Cyprus, Turkey and Afghanistan.*	*Includes all domestic and regional developments in Latin America, the Caribbean and Canada.*	*Includes all domestic and regional developments in Asian and Pacific nations, extending from Afghanistan through all the Pacific Islands, except Hawaii.*

U.S. Politics & Social Issues	U.S. Foreign Policy & Defense	U.S. Economy & Environment	Science, Technology & Nature	Culture, Leisure & Life Style	
	House and Senate complete work on the $1.3-billion Military Assistance Program authorization bill . . . . Joint Congressional Atomic Energy Comm. begins talks with the Atomic Energy Commission and Joint Chiefs of Staff to determine means of stepping up nuclear weapons production.	USW Pres. Philip Murray rejects the final offer of U.S. Steel in contract negotiations: a 10¢ wage increase with no action on union demands for a company-financed workers' pension fund . . . . James O'Connor, member of the New Deal "brain trust" who supervised the reorganization of national banks in 1933 and helped organize the Federal Deposit Insurance Corp., dies at 63 in Los Angeles.			Sept. 28
A San Francisco jury convicts Iva Toguri D'Aquino of treason for making wartime "Tokyo Rose" broadcasts.	House and Senate pass a $5.8-billion foreign aid bill, including $4.8 billion for Marshall Plan aid.	Ford Motors averts a UAW strike by accepting union demands for a company-financed pension plan in return for union agreement to forego a wage increase . . . . Senate approves and sends to House conference a bill increasing the salaries of cabinet members and important government officials.		Isaac Deutscher's *Stalin: A Political Biography* is published by Oxford.	Sept. 29
House Un-American Activities Comm. charges that Univ. of Minnesota physics professor Joseph Weinberg passed atomic secrets to a Russian agent during World War II as a mysterious "Scientist X." Weinberg immediately denies the allegation.	Army issues a new racial equality plan, opening new training opportunities for Negroes but retaining segregated units.	UMW leader John Lewis orders 102,000 striking miners, employed in pits which produce coal for heating, to return to work . . . . CIO United Rubber Workers union ends a 35-day strike against the B.F. Goodrich Co. after accepting an increase in company contributions to existing pension and insurance plans . . . . Leaders of the CIO Farm Equipment Workers union end a four-day meeting in Chicago after agreeing to merge with the United Electrical Workers union in defiance of CIO orders to merge with the UAW . . . . Senate approves and sends to House conference bills increasing the salaries of postal workers and other civil service employes.		Eleanor Louise Patenotre pleads guilty to income tax evasion in N.Y. and pays the government $2 million in taxes owed on money she received from the sale of her interest in the *Philadelphia Inquirer* in 1930.	Sept. 30
Oswald Garrison Villard, militant liberal journalist and former editor of *The Nation* and the *New York Evening Post*, dies at 77 in N.Y.		USW begins a nationwide strike of 500,000 workers against U.S. Steel and other major steel producers in a dispute over workers' pensions.		Guillotine with Ted Atkinson up wins the $112,285 Belmont Futurity Stakes in N.Y.	Oct. 1
				On the last day of the regular baseball season the New York Yankees and the Brooklyn Dodgers capture the American and National League pennants, each by one game.	Oct. 2
House and Senate pass and send to Truman an $88-million appropriations bill establishing a 10-year rehabilitation program for the Navaho and Hopi Indians.	Navy Capt. John Crommelin, Jr. publicizes three confidential letters written to Navy Secy. Francis Matthews by Adms. Gerald Bogan, Arthur Radford and Louis Denfeld. All denounce subordination of the naval air arm to Air Force strategic planning under the armed forces unification program.	One-hundred thousand anthracite and Western soft coal miners return to work on orders of UMW leader Lewis.			Oct. 3
Senate confirms Judge Sherman Minton's nomination to the Supreme Court . . . . American Contract Bridge League refuses to admit Negro players to its tournaments.				Albert Schweitzer's *The Philosophy of Civilization* is published in N.Y. by Macmillan.	Oct. 4
	House Armed Services Comm. votes for a broad inquiry into the status of U.S. defense following revelations of widespread military dissatisfaction over armed forces unification. The committee exonerates the Air Force of charges of corruption in its B-36 procurement program.	House passes and sends to the Senate a bill extending Social Security to 11 million new recipients and increasing benefits by an average of 70% . . . . Kaiser Steel signs a contract with the USW establishing a company-financed pension plan for its 20,000 workers.			Oct. 5

F	G	H	I	J
Includes elections, federal-state relations, civil rights and liberties, crime, the judiciary, education, health care, poverty, urban affairs and population.	*Includes formation and debate of U.S. foreign and defense policies, veterans affairs and defense spending. (Relations with specific foreign countries are usually found under the region concerned.)*	*Includes business, labor, agriculture, taxation, transportation, consumer affairs, monetary and fiscal policy, natural resources, pollution and accidents.*	*Includes worldwide scientific, medical and technological developments, natural phenomena, U.S. weather and natural disasters.*	*Includes the arts, religion, scholarship, communications media, sports, entertainment, fashions, fads and social life.*

	World Affairs	Europe	Africa & the Middle East	The Americas	Asia & the Pacific
Oct. 6		Yugoslavia introduces a resolution in the General Assembly's Legal Comm. directed against the Cominform, calling for U.N. aid to countries facing economic blockades or fifth-column movements directed by foreign governments.			Communist authorities in Shanghai ban news dispatches by reporters from countries which do not recognize the People's Republic.
Oct. 7		East German People's Council transforms itself into a legislative People's Chamber and declares East Germany a separate state, the German Democratic Republic. The People's Chamber issues a 20-point manifesto calling for conclusion of a German peace treaty and German reunification.	Four private U.S. banks grant a $10-million development loan to South Africa.		Adm. Alan Kirk, U.S. ambassador to Russia, urges U.S. recognition of the Chinese Communist government as a means of countering "Soviet imperialism" in Manchuria and China.
Oct. 8		East and West German trade organizations sign a trade agreement for exchange of $112.8 million in industrial goods over the next year.			
Oct. 9	A trade conference of 33 nations meeting in Annecy, France concludes a series of tariff reduction agreements covering about 80% of the world's trade.	Legislative elections in Austria result in a victory for moderates and rightists, with the conservative People's Party of Chancellor Leopold Figl gaining the largest share (44%) of the popular vote.			
Oct. 10		International Monetary Fund grants Yugoslavia a $3-million loan for trade with the U.S. . . . . Legislative elections in Norway result in victory for Premier Einar Gerhardsen's Labor Party, which retains its parliamentary majority.			Nationalist Gen. Pai Chung-hsi retreats with his 200,000-man army from the Canton defense area to Kwangsi Province in southwestern China . . . . French government cancels the diplomatic status of eight members of the Chinese embassy staff in Paris after they announce their allegiance to the Communists.
Oct. 11		Russia formally recognizes the German Democratic Republic as the "sovereign" authority in Germany, giving it the administrative powers of the Soviet military government and the Russian-sector Berlin command. The East German People's Chamber meets in East Berlin and unanimously elects Communist leader Wilhelm Pieck president of the new government . . . . Western Allied High Commissioners for Germany approve West German membership in the Organization for European Economic Cooperation.			
Oct. 12	Norwegian Parliament awards the Nobel Peace Prize, the first given since 1947, to British nutrition expert and former U.N. Food and Agriculture Organization Director-Gen. Lord Boyd Orr.	East German Socialist leader Otto Grotewohl becomes Minister-President of the German Democratic Republic at the head of an 18-member cabinet. Communist leader Walter Ulbricht is named deputy minister-president. Grotewohl's government issues a program stressing friendship with Russia, increased trade with Eastern Europe and recognition of the Oder-Neisse border with Poland.			Chinese Nationalist government leaders flee Canton for Chungking as Communist forces approach the city . . . . U.S. State Dept. sends a circular telegram on China to U.S. diplomatic missions, emphasizing the "need for full exchange of views prior [to] any definitive or independent steps" towards recognition of the Communist government.
Oct. 13		British P.M. Attlee announces he will not call a national election this year.			Indian P.M. Jawaharlal Nehru, addressing Congress during his first visit to the U.S., asserts his country will remain neutral in the East-West conflict.

	A	B	C	D	E
	Includes developments that affect more than one world region, international organizations and important meetings of major world leaders.	*Includes all domestic and regional developments in Europe, including the Soviet Union, Turkey, Cyprus and Malta.*	*Includes all domestic and regional developments in Africa and the Middle East, including Iraq and Iran and excluding Cyprus, Turkey and Afghanistan.*	*Includes all domestic and regional developments in Latin America, the Caribbean and Canada.*	*Includes all domestic and regional developments in Asian and Pacific nations, extending from Afghanistan through all the Pacific Islands, except Hawaii.*

U.S. Politics & Social Issues	U.S. Foreign Policy & Defense	U.S. Economy & Environment	Science, Technology & Nature	Culture, Leisure & Life Style	
A federal court in San Francisco hands down a 10-year prison sentence for Iva Toguri D'Aquino, convicted of treason for her wartime "Tokyo Rose" broadcasts . . . . Robert Hannegan, former Postmaster General and Democratic National Comm. chairman, dies at 46 in St. Louis of a heart ailment.	Truman signs the $1.3-billion Military Assistance Program bill and the $5.8-billion economic aid bill for Western Europe and other strategic areas . . . . Navy Secy. Matthews suspends Capt. Crommelin from active duty and restricts him to Washington following his unauthorized release of letters protesting alleged de-emphasis of the naval air arm . . . . Joint Congressional Atomic Energy Comm. votes to end its investigation of charges of mismanagement in the Atomic Energy Commission.	Strike of CIO longshoremen in Hawaii ends after 159 days when the International Longshoremen's and Warehousemen's Union accepts a settlement providing an immediate hourly wage increase of 14¢, with a smaller increase to follow next year.		*The Heiress*, starring Olivia de Havilland and Montgomery Clift, premiers in N.Y.	Oct. 6
	Adm. Arthur Radford, commander of the Pacific Fleet, criticizes the Defense Dept. in testimony before the House Armed Services Comm., accusing Defense Secy. Johnson of withholding Navy funds already approved by Congress. He also attacks Air Force concentration on heavy bombers at the expense of tactical aircraft.	UMW and employer representatives meet with Federal Mediation Service director Cyrus Ching in Washington in an unsuccessful effort to settle the 19-day-old coal strike.		General Convention of the Protestant Episcopal Church ends in San Francisco after passing resolutions urging international control of Jerusalem and formation of a world government to keep peace.	Oct. 7
Sen. Bert Miller (D, Ida.), a strong Administration supporter, dies at 72 of a heart attack in Washington.	House Armed Services Comm. Chmn. Carl Vinson (D, Ga.) accuses Truman and Defense Secy. Johnson of secretly ordering that Naval and Marine aviation strength be reduced by half.	William Mellon, eldest surviving member of the banking family and founder of Gulf Oil, dies at 81 in Pittsburgh.	Reed Research Co. announces development of a portable earth shock detector capable of measuring earthquakes and powerful explosions from a distance of 10,000 miles . . . . Army announces development of a lightweight "radiac" (radioactivity detection) set, for use in determining areas that can be safely entered after an atomic explosion.		Oct. 8
				With a 10-6 victory, the New York Yankees win the World Series, defeating the Brooklyn Dodgers four games to one . . . . Walt Disney's feature-length cartoon *The Adventures of Ichabod and Mr. Toad* premiers in N.Y. . . . . *New York Herald Tribune* lists Mika Waltari's *The Egyptian* and Clare Barnes' *White Collar Zoo* as best-selling fiction and non-fiction books.	Oct. 9
		AFL ends an eight-day national convention in St. Paul, Minn. after passing resolutions urging U.S. aid to Nationalist China and threatening a membership raid on the leftist International Longshoremen's and Warehousemen's Union in Hawaii.	Univ. of Chicago physicist Gerard Kuiper propounds the condensation theory of the solar system, postulating that the planets were formed from a nebula of gas and dust rotating around the sun some three billion years ago . . . . Former Navy pilots Woody Jongeward and Bob Woodhouse land their two-place Aeronca in Yuma, Ariz. after setting an air endurance record of 1,124 hrs. 14 mins.	George Parker, chief editor of the Scripps-Howard newspaper chain and winner of the 1936 Pulitzer Prize for editorial writing, dies at 63 in Washington . . . . A.B. Guthrie's *The Way West*, a story of the Oregon Trail, is published by Sloane and becomes a Book-of-the-Month-Club selection.	Oct. 10
			World Medical Assn., meeting in London, adopts the first international code of medical ethics and medical care standards.		Oct. 11
House Un-American Activities Comm. investigator Robert Stripling's *The Red Plot Against America* is published by Bell.	Truman names Mrs. Eugenie Anderson U.S. envoy to Denmark, the first woman appointed to an ambassadorial post.	Senate passes and sends to House conference a bill providing for reduced farm price supports after 1950 despite Truman's warning that the measure may cost Democrats the farm vote . . . . International Longshoremen's and Warehousemen's Union agrees with West Coast shippers on a jointly financed welfare and insurance fund, with employers paying 55% and workers 45%.		Terence Rattigan's *The Browning Version* premiers with *A Harlequinade* on Broadway.	Oct. 12
Sen. Harry Cain (R, Wash.) forces postponement of Senate action on a House-approved liberalized displaced persons bill with a six-hour filibuster.	High-ranking Navy officers complete four days of testimony before the House Armed Services Comm. on U.S. military strategy, scoring the Air Force strategic bomber program and recent cuts in naval expenditures . . . . Joint Congressional Atomic Energy Comm. issues a majority report clearing Atomic Energy Commission Chmn. David Lilienthal of mismanagement charges.	Senate rejects Truman's nomination of Leland Olds for a third term on the Federal Power Commission following heated debate over allegedly radical articles written by Olds during the 1920s. Administration supporters claim that opposition to Olds is actually an attack on regulation of the natural gas industry.		Carnegie Institute's "Painting in the U.S. 1949" contest in Pittsburgh presents its $1,500 first prize to Max Beckmann for his *Fisherwoman*.	Oct. 13
F *Includes elections, federal-state relations, civil rights and liberties, crime, the judiciary, education, health care, poverty, urban affairs and population.*	G *Includes formation and debate of U.S. foreign and defense policies, veterans affairs and defense spending. (Relations with specific foreign countries are usually found under the region concerned.)*	H *Includes business, labor, agriculture, taxation, transportation, consumer affairs, monetary and fiscal policy, natural resources, pollution and accidents.*	I *Includes worldwide scientific, medical and technological developments, natural phenomena, U.S. weather and natural disasters.*	J *Includes the arts, religion, scholarship, communications media, sports, entertainment, fashions, fads and social life.*	

	World Affairs	Europe	Africa & the Middle East	The Americas	Asia & the Pacific
Oct. 14	General Assembly's Economic and Financial Comm. approves a program of technical assistance to developing countries based on Truman's proposals. The committee also votes to double the U.N. technical aid budget.	Czech National Assembly passes laws giving the government control over all church administration and making priests state employes .... French Chamber of Deputies approves Socialist leader Jules Moch as premier by a narrow margin.	Israel reopens the oil refineries of Haifa after a two-year shutdown, using Venezuelan crude oil.	Speaking in Troy, N.Y., Canadian P.M. Louis St. Laurent urges standardization of Canadian and U.S. military equipment.	
Oct. 15		Czech security forces complete a 10-day campaign to "liquidate hostile elements and imperialist agents," arresting an estimated 50,000 suspects from the clergy and middle class .... Laszlo Rajk and two co-defendants sentenced to death for espionage are hanged in Budapest.	South African government retires Field Marshal Jan Smuts, commander of the country's defense forces since 1940, from military service.		Chinese Communist forces occupy Canton, capital of the Nationalist government for six months.
Oct. 16		Greek Communist guerrillas announce a halt to their military operations "to avoid the total destruction of Greece." .... Russia establishes formal diplomatic relations with East Germany .... Belgium, Holland and Luxembourg postpone plans for economic unification due to Holland's unfavorable trade balance.			Chinese Communist forces launch an amphibious attack on the Nationalist naval base in the Chu Shan Archipelago near Shanghai.
Oct. 17		World Bank grants Yugoslavia a $2.7-million loan for timber development .... Jules Moch gives up his mandate to form a new French cabinet after Socialists, Radicals and Popular Republicans fail to agree on ministerial assignments .... German authorities arrest Ilse Koch upon her release from a U.S. military prison in Landsberg, charging her with ordering the death of German citizens imprisoned in the Buchenwald concentration camp.		Canada ends all price controls on food .... Colombia and the U.S. end their 14-year-old tariff agreement following failure to negotiate new terms.	Chinese Nationalist forces evacuate the port cities of Amoy and Swatow, their last coastal outposts between Korea and Hong Kong .... Australian Communist leader Laurence Sharkey is sentenced to three years in prison on sedition charges for stating that Russian troops would be welcomed in Australia in the event of war.
Oct. 18		Special conciliation commission of the General Assembly's Political and Security Comm. reports failure in its efforts to promote a settlement between Greece and neighboring countries due to disagreement on the issues of amnesty for Greek guerrillas and Greek territorial claims in southern Albania .... Czech government demands loyalty oaths from all Catholic priests .... Exiled Belgian King Leopold III agrees to a plebiscite on his return to Belgium, promising to remain in Switzerland if he receives less than 55% of the vote.			
Oct. 19				Torrential rains and flooding in Guatemala end after two weeks, leaving 60,000 villagers homeless and causing $50 million in damage.	
Oct. 20	U.N. General Assembly chooses Yugoslavia to replace the Ukraine as non-permanent Eastern European representative on the Security Council despite strong Russian opposition.			Canadian Seamen's Union calls off its 6½-month-old strike against East Coast shippers, charging the government with "persecuting" strikers by refusing to pay them unemployment insurance.	South Korean forces report loss of an important hilltop on Ongjin Peninsula north of the partition boundary after a five-day battle with North Korean troops.
Oct. 21		West German Chancellor Konrad Adenauer claims that the German Democratic Republic is illegal and the Federal Republic has "responsibility" for all Germans .... Czech police in Prague arrest a U.S. embassy clerk and expel a U.S. attache, accusing both of attempting to organize a spy ring last year.			
Oct. 22		An express train bound for Warsaw from Gdansk derails near Nowy Dwor in Poland, killing 200 passengers.		Colombian Pres. Mariano Ospina Perez bans all political and labor demonstrations for the duration of the current presidential campaign.	Japan's Agriculture Ministry reports a record postwar rice crop of 325 million bushels.
	A *Includes developments that affect more than one world region, international organizations and important meetings of major world leaders.*	B *Includes all domestic and regional developments in Europe, including the Soviet Union, Turkey, Cyprus and Malta.*	C *Includes all domestic and regional developments in Africa and the Middle East, including Iraq and Iran and excluding Cyprus, Turkey and Afghanistan.*	D *Includes all domestic and regional developments in Latin America, the Caribbean and Canada.*	E *Includes all domestic and regional developments in Asian and Pacific nations, extending from Afghanistan through all the Pacific Islands, except Hawaii.*

U.S. Politics & Social Issues	U.S. Foreign Policy & Defense	U.S. Economy & Environment	Science, Technology & Nature	Culture, Leisure & Life Style	
A N.Y. jury finds 11 U.S. Communist leaders guilty of criminal conspiracy against the U.S. government under the 1940 Smith Act. Judge Harold Medina cites the five defense attorneys and defendant Eugene Dennis for contempt of court, sentencing them to one-to-six month jail terms.		House-Senate conference deadlocks over the issue of farm price supports as House conferees insist on retention of existing support levels (at 90% of parity price) beyond 1950 .... Senate and House complete action on a measure increasing the salaries of 253 important government officials .... UMW leader John Lewis proposes creation of a strike fund for the USW in the current steel industry dispute, to be financed by weekly $250,000 contributions from the UMW and large AFL unions.		Ezzard Charles retains the National Boxing Assn. heavyweight crown with an eight-round knockout of Pat Valentino in San Francisco .... Philippine Archbishop Michael O'Doherty dies at 75 in Manila. His successor, Archbishop Gabriel Reyes, becomes the first native-born Filipino to hold the post.	Oct. 14
Truman nominates U.S. Atty. John McGohey, prosecutor in the trial of U.S. Communist leaders, to a federal judgeship.					Oct. 15
		Strike of 7,500 Singer Mfg. Co. workers in Elizabeth, N.J. ends in failure after 168 days.	Dr. Arne Frantzell of Upsala Univ. in Sweden demonstrates a new X-ray technique capable of producing clear pictures of body tissue.		Oct. 16
Truman vetoes a bill authorizing funds for the Navaho and Hopi Indian tribes after Indian groups criticize the measure for transferring jurisdiction over Indian affairs from federal and tribal to state courts.		Sixteen thousand USW members strike against the Aluminum Co. of America in a dispute over pension and welfare payments .... AFL Pres. William Green rejects John Lewis' proposal for a pooling of union funds to aid the steel workers' strike.	First transcontinental dial telephone call is made from Oakland, Calif. to N.Y.	Harold Robbins' novel about Hollywood, *The Dream Merchants*, is published in N.Y. by Knopf.	Oct. 17
	Congress completes action on a compromise $15.6-billion defense appropriation bill, providing funds for a 58-group Air Force .... U.S. Atomic Energy Commission announces plans for a major expansion of its uranium and plutonium production facilities in Oak Ridge, Tenn. and Hanford, Wash.	House and Senate complete action on bills increasing the minimum hourly wage from 40¢ to 75¢ and providing salary raises for postal workers and other civil service employes .... UAW ends a 128-day strike against the Bell Aircraft Corp. in Buffalo after agreeing to arbitration of all disputed issues.			Oct. 18
Eighty-first Congress adjourns after completing the longest peacetime session in 27 years .... N.J. State Superior Court in Trenton voids a state law requiring political candidates, elected officials and state employes to take a loyalty oath .... Pennsylvania Railroad abolishes segregation on its East Coast passenger routes.		House and Senate complete action on a compromise farm price support bill retaining high support levels through 1951 .... Truman accepts the resignation of Edwin Nourse, chairman of the Council of Economic Advisers and a strong opponent of the Administration's deficit financing policy.		Oksana Kosenkina's autobiography, *Leap to Freedom*, is published in N.Y. by Lippincott .... Bucky Harris signs a three-year contract to manage the Washington Senators.	Oct. 19
	Gen. Omar Bradley completes two days of testimony before the House Armed Services Comm., attacking Navy criticism of U.S. military strategy and accusing high Navy officers of causing "infinite harm" to America's world position.			John Trever of the International Council of Religious Education reports discovery of a scroll from the Book of Lamech, a previously little-known section of the Bible, in a cave near the Dead Sea.	Oct. 20
N.Y. Judge Harold Medina sentences 11 U.S. Communist leaders convicted of subversion to $10,000 fines and prison terms of three to five years.	Defense Secy. Johnson and Gen. George Marshall testify before the House Armed Services Comm., pleading for an end to the current dispute over U.S. military strategy .... A federal grand jury in Washington indicts Amtorg, a Soviet trade agency, and six of its Russian officials for failing to register as foreign agents.	East Coast longshoremen ratify a contract establishing an employer-financed pension fund.			Oct. 21
House Un-American Activities Comm. issues a report charging that the Congress of American Women is a Communist front group.					Oct. 22
F *Includes elections, federal-state relations, civil rights and liberties, crime, the judiciary, education, health care, poverty, urban affairs and population.*	G *Includes formation and debate of U.S. foreign and defense policies, veterans affairs and defense spending. (Relations with specific foreign countries are usually found under the region concerned.)*	H *Includes business, labor, agriculture, taxation, transportation, consumer affairs, monetary and fiscal policy, natural resources, pollution and accidents.*	I *Includes worldwide scientific, medical and technological developments, natural phenomena, U.S. weather and natural disasters.*	J *Includes the arts, religion, scholarship, communications media, sports, entertainment, fashions, fads and social life.*	

	World Affairs	Europe	Africa & the Middle East	The Americas	Asia & the Pacific
Oct. 23		French Pres. Vincent Auriol names Popular Republican leader Georges Bidault premier following the failure of Socialist and Radical leaders to form a new cabinet.		Emilio Jaramillo, Colombian Liberal Party leader and publisher of Bogota's *El Diario*, dies in Medellin, Colombia.	
Oct. 24	U.N. Secy.-Gen. Trygve Lie dedicates the organization's permanent N.Y. headquarters site in a cornerstone-laying ceremony addressed by Truman, who stresses the need for international atomic control.	British P.M. Attlee announces an austerity program aimed at reducing government spending by $784,000 a year and cutting dollar imports by 25% .... Four Hungarian officers convicted of espionage, including Gen. Georgy Palffy, are hanged in Budapest.			
Oct. 25		A meeting of Czech Catholic bishops agrees to permit a government loyalty oath for the country's Catholic priests with the provision that the oath not require acts that violate "the laws of God and the Church and the rights of man."			
Oct. 26		Russia announces the expulsion of the Yugoslavian ambassador to Moscow, Karl Mrazovic, for "spying and subversive activities." .... Adm. Sir Lionel Halsey, commander of the British fleet in the World War I Battle of Jutland, dies at 77 in Biggleswade, England.	British Colonial Secy. Arthur Creech Jones rejects West African nationalist demands for self-government for Britain's Gold Coast colony.		An investigating committee of the Japanese Diet charges Japanese Communists with promoting labor violence in the hope of provoking a revolution.
Oct. 27	General Assembly's Political Comm. votes to establish a 300-member U.N. guard force.	East German government formally asks West Germany to begin reunification talks, but West German political leaders reject negotiations with the Communist state .... Poland orders the International Red Cross, CARE and Foster Parents Plan for War Children to cease operations and withdraw foreign staff members .... Francisco Franco concludes a six-day visit to Portugal, his first state visit to a foreign country since becoming Spanish chief of state in 1939 .... Belgian Senate approves a plebiscite on the return of King Leopold III.			State Secy. Acheson completes a two-day meeting with his Far Eastern advisers in Washington, agreeing to withhold further military aid from the Nationalist government on Taiwan and adopt a "wait-and-see" attitude with respect to events on the Chinese mainland .... Chinese Nationalist forces report defeating a Communist attempt to invade Quemoy Island near the port of Amoy .... A cyclone strikes the southeast Indian coast, causing 1,000 deaths.
Oct. 28		French Popular Republican leader Georges Bidault wins parliamentary approval for a new cabinet with Socialist, Radical and Popular Republican representation. Most of the new ministers served in the previous Queuille cabinet .... Former world middleweight boxing champion Marcel Cerdan dies with 47 others in the crash of an Air France Constellation on Sao Miguel Island in the Azores.	Israel demands that Arab states deal directly with its representatives in peace negotiations, threatening otherwise to quit the U.N. Palestine Conciliation Commission.		MacArthur announces plans to return Japan's export trade, currently handled by Allied authorities, to private hands.
Oct. 29					Chinese Communist authorities in Mukden announce the arrest of U.S. Consul Gen. Angus Ward, charged with beating a servant .... U.N. Economic Commission for Asia and the Far East completes a 10-day session in Singapore after approving plans for a Far Eastern economic survey and participation in the U.N. technical assistance program.
Oct. 30					Chikuhei Nakajima, leading Japanese aviation industrialist and commerce and industry minister in Japan's first postwar cabinet, dies at 65 of a cerebral hemorrhage in Tokyo.
Oct. 31	U.S. delegate Warren Austin urges the Big Five to hold regular sessions before Security Council meetings with the purpose of reaching prior agreement on controversial issues and avoiding vetoes.	Organization for European Economic Cooperation begins a Paris meeting with West Germany represented for the first time .... Economic Cooperation Admin. Paul Hoffman threatens to cut off Marshall Plan aid to Europe in the absence of more rapid progress towards "integration of the Western European economy." .... Britain announces plans to withdraw 3,000 British troops remaining in Greece "in the near future." .... British House of Commons passes a government-sponsored measure halving the time in which the House of Lords can block legislation. It is the third time in the past two years such legislation has been passed.			
	A *Includes developments that affect more than one world region, international organizations and important meetings of major world leaders.*	B *Includes all domestic and regional developments in Europe, including the Soviet Union, Turkey, Cyprus and Malta.*	C *Includes all domestic and regional developments in Africa and the Middle East, including Iraq and Iran and excluding Cyprus, Turkey and Afghanistan.*	D *Includes all domestic and regional developments in Latin America, the Caribbean and Canada.*	E *Includes all domestic and regional developments in Asian and Pacific nations, extending from Afghanistan through all the Pacific Islands, except Hawaii.*

U.S. Politics & Social Issues	U.S. Foreign Policy & Defense	U.S. Economy & Environment	Science, Technology & Nature	Culture, Leisure & Life Style	
				A *Sporting News* poll of baseball writers names Brooklyn Dodger pitcher Don Newcombe and St. Louis Browns outfielder Roy Seivers as rookies of the year .... Former St. Louis Browns manager Luke Sewell signs to manage the Cincinnati Reds for two years.	Oct. 23
	Republican members of the Joint Congressional Atomic Energy Comm. issue a minority report charging the Atomic Energy Commission with a "leisurely" approach to military uses of atomic energy and a "loosely administered" security system.	Strike of 5,200 Missouri Pacific Railroad workers ends with settlement of most work rule disagreements.		William Wilgus, civil engineer who designed New York's Grand Central Terminal, dies at 83 in Claremont, N.H.	Oct. 24
	Army Secy. Gordon Gray announces plans to release 30,000 conscripts with one year's service due to military budget cuts.		Britain's De Haviland Comet, the first jet passenger liner, flies 2,980 miles from London to Tripoli and back in a record time of 6 hrs. 38 mins.	Vatican announces appointment of Bishop Aloysius Muench as Papal Nuncio in West Germany with ecclesiastical jurisdiction over all Germany.	Oct. 25
		Truman signs the Fair Labor Standards Amendment for 1949, raising the hourly minimum wage to 75¢ .... N.Y. milk distributors accept a Teamsters union contract proposal calling for creation of an employer-financed pension and welfare fund covering 15,000 workers.			Oct. 26
	Adm. Louis Denfeld, a prominent critic of U.S. defense policy, is dismissed as chief of naval operations by Truman at the request of Navy Secy. Francis Matthews .... Truman signs legislation authorizing $165.5 million for defense construction in Alaska and Okinawa and $7.7 million for expansion of military communications in Alaska .... Soviet trade agency Amtorg registers in Washington as an agency of the Russian government.		Nobel Prize in medicine goes to Walter Hess of Switzerland and Antonio Caetano de Abreu Moniz of Portugal for work in brain functions.		Oct. 27
	Eugenie Anderson, the nation's first woman ambassador, is sworn in as envoy to Denmark.	Federal Reserve Bd. reports industrial production at its lowest level in four years due to the coal and steel strikes .... Leftist CIO United Farm Equipment and Metal Workers Union announces its merger with the CIO United Electrical Workers union .... NLRB rules the International Typographical Union in violation of the Taft-Hartley Act for attempting to impose a closed-shop contract provision on Chicago newspaper publishers.			Oct. 28
	Truman signs the $15.5-billion military appropriations bill, the largest in peacetime history, but places $615 million earmarked for Air Force expansion "in reserve." .... Foy Kohler is named to succeed Charles Thayer as operating director of the Voice of America.				Oct. 29
	Defense Dept. announces forthcoming reduction of the Navy by 77 ships due to budget cuts.		Charles Kerr, mechanical engineer who invented the first steam turbine used in merchant ships, dies at 88 in Los Angeles.	*Lost in the Stars*, a musical drama based on Alan Paton's novel *Cry, the Beloved Country* with music by Kurt Weill, opens on Broadway to favorable reviews.	Oct. 30
	U.S. expels Ervin Munk, Czech consul general in N.Y., and a staff member of the Czech embassy in Washington in retaliation for Czech actions against U.S. diplomatic personnel in Prague .... Edward Stettinius, former Secretary of State and U.S. delegate to the U.N., dies at 49 in Greenwich, Conn. of coronary thrombosis.	Bethlehem Steel settles with the USW for a company-financed pension plan and an insurance program financed jointly by workers and management .... William Mahon, co-founder of the AFL and former president of the Assn. of Street, Electric Railway and Motor Coach Employes, dies at 88 in Detroit.		*Regina*, a musical drama by Marc Blitzstein based on Lillian Hellman's play *The Little Foxes*, opens on Broadway to favorable reviews.	Oct. 31
F	G	H	I	J	
Includes elections, federal-state relations, civil rights and liberties, crime, the judiciary, education, health care, poverty, urban affairs and population.	*Includes formation and debate of U.S. foreign and defense policies, veterans affairs and defense spending. (Relations with specific foreign countries are usually found under the region concerned.)*	*Includes business, labor, agriculture, taxation, transportation, consumer affairs, monetary and fiscal policy, natural resources, pollution and accidents.*	*Includes worldwide scientific, medical and technological developments, natural phenomena, U.S. weather and natural disasters.*	*Includes the arts, religion, scholarship, communications media, sports, entertainment, fashions, fads and social life.*	

	World Affairs	Europe	Africa & the Middle East	The Americas	Asia & the Pacific
Nov. 1			A subcommittee of the General Assembly's Political and Security Comm. concludes three weeks of debate on disposition of Italy's former African colonies by recommending independence for Libya by 1952 and a 10-year Italian trusteeship over Italian Somaliland .... Britain's Overseas Food Corp. reports the failure of an attempt to encourage peanut cultivation in British East Africa with the aim of satisfying British demand for edible oils.		British government sends a note to the U.S. State Dept. urging early recognition of the Chinese Communist government.
Nov. 2		Yugoslavia charges Albania with frontier violations and attempts to stir unrest among ethnic minorities in Yugoslavian border areas .... Following U.S. demands for greater economic integration, the Organization for European Economic Cooperation urges its member states to halve their import quota restrictions by midDecember.			Dutch and Indonesian representatives conclude 10 weeks of negotiations in The Hague with agreement on formation of a United States of Indonesia as sovereign power in all the Dutch East Indies except Dutch New Guinea. The new state promises to protect Dutch commercial investments in Indonesia in return for withdrawal of Dutch troops.
Nov. 3	U.N. General Assembly Pres. Carlos Romulo urges the Big Five and Canada to accept a temporary ban on the use and production of nuclear weapons to allow "a breathing space for calmer consideration" of permanent atomic controls.	U.S. eases its restrictions on trade with Eastern Europe to permit Yugoslavia to purchase commercial aircraft .... Norway, Sweden and Denmark announce plans to form a Scandinavian customs union .... British Labor Party regains its majority on the London County Council, lost last April to the Conservatives, in a North Kensington by-election.	Egyptian cabinet resigns in a dispute over election district boundaries and is replaced by a non-party cabinet governing by royal decree.		Dutch authorities in Indonesia grant amnesty to most political prisoners.
Nov. 4		U.N. General Assembly's Political and Security Comm. recommends an arms embargo against Bulgaria and Albania, intended to force the two countries to stop aiding Greek guerrillas.			
Nov. 5		Hungary annuls an agreement with Yugoslavia for joint investigation of frontier incidents, charging Yugoslavian forces with attempting to cross the Hungarian border.	Former Iranian Premier Abdul Hussein Hajir is shot to death in Teheran during a religious ceremony.	Argentina resumes imports after a 1½-month suspension.	Dutch forces begin to withdraw from the remaining territory which they occupy in Java.
Nov. 6			Addressing a Tel Aviv convention of the Palestine Foundation Fund, Israeli P.M. David Ben-Gurion warns foreign Zionists that they cannot influence Israeli policy through control of Zionist funds or organizations.		
Nov. 7		Polish government names Russian Marshal Konstantin Rokossovsky defense minister and marshal of the Polish Army .... Austrian Chancellor Leopold Figl forms a new cabinet based on a People's Party-Socialist coalition.		Paraguay devalues its currency on a sliding scale based on demand for the country's exports.	
Nov. 8		Polish Parliament amends the constitution to include Defense Min. Rokossovsky in the policy-making State Council .... Czech police release U.S. embassy clerk Samuel Meryn after 2½ weeks of detention on espionage charges.		Costa Rican junta headed by Jose Figueres steps aside as National Union Party leader Otilio Ulate Blanco is inaugurated president.	Presidential elections in the Philippines result in a victory for incumbent Elpidio Quirino over Jose Laurel, an anti-American candidate favored by the Hukbalahap guerrillas.

A	B	C	D	E
Includes developments that affect more than one world region, international organizations and important meetings of major world leaders.	*Includes all domestic and regional developments in Europe, including the Soviet Union, Turkey, Cyprus and Malta.*	*Includes all domestic and regional developments in Africa and the Middle East, including Iraq and Iran and excluding Cyprus, Turkey and Afghanistan.*	*Includes all domestic and regional developments in Latin America, the Caribbean and Canada.*	*Includes all domestic and regional developments in Asian and Pacific nations, extending from Afghanistan through all the Pacific Islands, except Hawaii.*

U.S. Politics & Social Issues	U.S. Foreign Policy & Defense	U.S. Economy & Environment	Science, Technology & Nature	Culture, Leisure & Life Style	
	Truman appoints Adm. Forrest Sherman to succeed Adm. Louis Denfeld as chief of naval operations.	CIO national convention, meeting in Cleveland, passes a resolution barring Communists, fascists and other adherents of "totalitarian" movements from high union office. The move permits the expulsion of leftist CIO Executive Bd. members, including Harry Bridges of the International Longshoremen's and Warehousemen's Union . . . . Virginia Gov. William Tuck orders seizure of strip mining operations in the southwestern part of the state to relieve a fuel crisis caused by the current miners' strike . . . . Budget director Frank Pace releases an annual review of the federal budget predicting a $5.5-billion deficit for the current fiscal year in the absence of a tax increase . . . . Gulf Coast shippers avert a strike of AFL longshoremen by accepting a contract providing for an employer-financed union benefit fund.	Fifty-five passengers and crew members die in the worst air accident to date when a P-38 fighter crashes into an Eastern Airlines DC-4 over Washington's National Airport.		Nov. 1
		CIO national convention in Cleveland expels the leftist United Electrical, Radio and Machine Workers of America and the United Farm Equipment and Metal Workers of America from the congress. A new International Union of Electrical, Radio and Machine Workers, under former UEW Pres. James Carey, is established to rival the two unions.		An AP poll of baseball writers chooses Casey Stengel of the New York Yankees as manager of the year . . . . Winston Churchill wins the London *Sunday Times* gold medal for contributions to English literature for his two volumes of World War II memoirs.	Nov. 2
James Kemper resigns as treasurer of the Republican National Comm. due to policy disagreements and depletion of party funds . . . . Eleven U.S. Communist leaders are released in N.Y. on $260,000 bail pending appeal of their conspiracy convictions.	Chief of Naval Operations Sherman abolishes the Organizational Research and Policy Division office, which planned naval resistance to Army and Air Force strategy in the armed forces unification dispute . . . . Truman accepts the resignation of Karl Compton as chairman of the Defense Department's Research and Development Bd.	Solomon Guggenheim, last survivor of the famous banking family, dies at 88 in Sands Point, N.Y.	Nobel Physics Prize goes to Japanese physicist Hideki Yukawa for his mathematical prediction of the meson. American chemist William Giaque wins the chemistry prize for his thermodynamics research.	Nobel Literature Prize is withheld when the Norwegian Academy fails to choose among Winston Churchill, William Faulkner, Carl Sandburg and Benedetto Croce . . . . *Roosevelt and the Russians*, an eye-witness account of the Yalta conference by the late Edward Stettinius, Jr., is published in N.Y. by Doubleday.	Nov. 3
	Commerce Dept. expands the list of goods banned for export to the Soviet bloc by 100.	CIO concludes its five-day national conference in Cleveland after reelecting Pres. Philip Murray and other anti-Communist officials . . . . Charles Dawson replaces Ezra Van Horn as management trustee of the UMW welfare and retirement fund . . . . Harry MacDonald is elected first Republican chairman of the Securities and Exchange Commission.		Sam Snead wins the North and South open golf tournament in Pinehurst, N.C.	Nov. 4
Truman backs the N.Y. candidacies of Herbert Lehman, running for senator against John Foster Dulles, and N.Y.C. Mayor William O'Dwyer.					Nov. 5
				Pope Pius XII urges a gathering of Catholic judges in Rome to avoid granting civil divorces in valid church marriages, but admits that an "unjust law" must sometimes be applied as "the sole means to prevent much graver evil."	Nov. 6
Supreme Court agrees to hear two school desegregation cases, involving complaints by Negro students against the Univ. of Texas law school and the Univ. of Oklahoma.		Supreme Court upholds a $1.4-million fine imposed on the UMW and John Lewis for failing to end the 1948 coal strike on court order. The ruling confirms the government's right to halt national strikes through court injunctions. The Court also upholds a Washington state law requiring commercial loggers to reforest areas from which trees are removed.		Eleanor Roosevelt's *This I Remember*, a memoir of her life with FDR from 1924 to 1945, is published in N.Y. by Harper . . . . Mexican Army Capt. Ruben Uriza wins the international individual trophy at the National Horse Show in N.Y.	Nov. 7
Off-year elections result in Democratic victories in most important races. Herbert Lehman defeats John Foster Dulles in the N.Y. senatorial election, while Democrats win contested House seats in Brooklyn and San Francisco. Boston Mayor James Curley loses his bid for re-election to fellow Democrat John Hynes. In other elections, Texas and Virginia voters reject measures repealing the poll tax . . . . Sen. Clyde Reed (R, Kan.), former governor of Kansas, dies at 78 in Parsons, Kan.	Navy Capt. John Crommelin is reprimanded and transferred to San Francisco as an aviation officer for releasing confidential letters in the controversy over U.S. military strategy.	Republic Steel, the nation's third-largest steel producer, accepts USW demands for a company-financed workers' pension plan . . . . An AP survey indicates that nearly 25% of the United Electrical Workers union's 450,000 members have left the union following its expulsion from the CIO.		*All the King's Men*, film version of Robert Penn Warren's Pulitzer Prize-winning novel, premiers in N.Y.	Nov. 8

F	G	H	I	J
Includes elections, federal-state relations, civil rights and liberties, crime, the judiciary, education, health care, poverty, urban affairs and population.	*Includes formation and debate of U.S. foreign and defense policies, veterans affairs and defense spending. (Relations with specific foreign countries are usually found under the region concerned.)*	*Includes business, labor, agriculture, taxation, transportation, consumer affairs, monetary and fiscal policy, natural resources, pollution and accidents.*	*Includes worldwide scientific, medical and technological developments, natural phenomena, U.S. weather and natural disasters.*	*Includes the arts, religion, scholarship, communications media; sports, entertainment, fashions, fads and social life.*

	World Affairs	Europe	Africa & the Middle East	The Americas	Asia & the Pacific
Nov. 9		East German People's Chamber restores full civil and economic rights to former Nazis not convicted of war crimes.		Colombian Pres. Mariano Ospina Perez declares a state of siege in an effort to suppress widespread unrest over forthcoming presidential elections.	
Nov. 10	Russian Foreign Min. Andrei Vishinsky tells the U.N. General Assembly that the Soviet nuclear development program is directed towards peaceful uses of atomic energy.	French cabinet agrees to British and U.S. suggestions for a cutback in the dismantling of West German factories on the condition that German steel production be kept below the present annual limit of 11.5 million tons .... Danube River Commission is established in Galtai, Rumania, with all important posts held by Soviet-bloc states.			
Nov. 11		State Secy. Acheson, British Foreign Secy. Bevin and French Foreign Min. Schuman conclude a three-day meeting in Paris with agreement on giving the West German government greater autonomy and fostering the integration of Germany into the European community .... Russian Gen. Vasili Chuikov formally abolishes the Soviet military government in Germany, replacing it with a Control Commission to supervise the carrying out of the Potsdam Declaration in the Russian zone .... Poland's United Workers' Party begins a purge of members with nationalist and anti-Russian leanings .... British House of Commons passes a bill raising the tax on industrial profits from 25% to 30%.			
Nov. 12	Speaking before the General Assembly's Political and Security Comm., Russian Foreign Min. Vishinsky rejects permanent on-site inspection of Soviet nuclear facilities.	Czech government refuses to accept any qualification in the loyalty oaths taken by Catholic priests and decrees that only civil marriages will be recognized beginning next year .... Yugoslavia cancels its friendship pact with Albania, charging the Hoxha government with conspiring against Yugoslavian independence.			
Nov. 13		Portuguese Premier Antonio Salazar's National Union wins all 120 seats in National Assembly elections, facing little opposition.			
Nov. 14		Three Polish Communist leaders, including former Deputy Premier Wladyslaw Gomulka, are expelled from the Party's Central Comm. for advocating "nationalist-rightist deviation" from the party line .... Viscount Runciman of Doxford, former British Bd. of Trade president and head of a commission that attempted to mediate the German-Czech dispute in 1938, dies at 78 in Chatfield, England.			Chiang Kai-shek visits Chungking in an attempt to rally the Nationalist capital's defenses .... Tsuneo Matsudaira, president of Japan's upper legislative house and former diplomat, dies at 72 in Tokyo of a heart ailment.
Nov. 15		West German Chancellor Konrad Adenauer informs Parliament of Western Allied decisions to halt dismantling of German plants for reparations and permit expansion of the West German merchant fleet.		Haitian government declares a state of siege and disbands leftist political parties in an attempt to suppress a strike of 11,000 university students.	A Chinese Communist radio broadcast urges the U.N. to oust the Nationalist delegation headed by T.F. Tsiang and recognize the Communist victory in China .... A Chinese Nationalist warship shells and damages an American freighter attempting to run the Nationalist blockade of Shanghai .... Nathuram Vinayak Godse is hanged in Ambala, India for the assassination of Mohandas Gandhi.

	A	B	C	D	E
	Includes developments that affect more than one world region, international organizations and important meetings of major world leaders.	*Includes all domestic and regional developments in Europe, including the Soviet Union, Turkey, Cyprus and Malta.*	*Includes all domestic and regional developments in Africa and the Middle East, including Iraq and Iran and excluding Cyprus, Turkey and Afghanistan.*	*Includes all domestic and regional developments in Latin America, the Caribbean and Canada.*	*Includes all domestic and regional developments in Asian and Pacific nations, extending from Afghanistan through all the Pacific Islands, except Hawaii.*

U.S. Politics & Social Issues	U.S. Foreign Policy & Defense	U.S. Economy & Environment	Science, Technology & Nature	Culture, Leisure & Life Style	
		UMW leader John Lewis orders 380,000 Eastern soft coal miners back to work for the rest of November "to enhance the remote possibility of agreement" with operators.			Nov. 9
		Cleveland financier Cyrus Eaton, testifying before a House Judiciary subcommittee investigating monopolies, accuses the Securities and Exchange Commission of maintaining an "unholy alliance" with leading Wall Street investment banking firms.		Truman proclaims Nov. 24 as Thanksgiving Day.	Nov. 10
Truman accepts the resignation of Interior Secy. Julius Krug and names Interior Under Secy. Oscar Chapman to succeed him.		U.S. Steel, the nation's largest steel producer, ends the 42-day USW strike by settling with the union for a company-financed workers' pension fund and an insurance plan financed jointly by management and workers.			Nov. 11
					Nov. 12
				American Jewish Congress concludes a four-day meeting in N.Y. after choosing Rabbi Irving Miller to succeed the late Rabbi Stephen Wise as president. The meeting also confirms the expulsion from the organization of the American Jewish Labor Council and the Jewish People's Fraternal Order, included on the Justice Dept. subversive list . . . . *New York Herald Tribune* lists Mika Waltari's *The Egyptian* and Clare Barne's *White Collar Zoo* as best-selling fiction and nonfiction books.	Nov. 13
International Longshoremen's and Warehousemen's Union Pres. Harry Bridges goes on trial in San Francisco on charges of falsely denying Communist Party membership in 1945 . . . . Hawaiian Gov. Ingram Stainback issues a proclamation ordering the election of a constitutional convention preparatory to the territory's expected statehood.		Interstate Commerce Commission grants a 12½% passenger fare boost for 61 Eastern railroads.		Edwin Upjohn, magazine cover artist and former owner of *N.Y. Standard* and *Vanity Fair*, dies at 78 in Babylon, N.Y.	Nov. 14
		AFL Masters, Mates and Pilots union agrees to a 30-day extension of talks with East and Gulf Coast shippers in a dispute over union hiring halls and other issues.		Eddie Vann scores the fastest heavyweight knockout on record when he KOs George Stern in 12 seconds of the first round in London.	Nov. 15

F	G	H	I	J
Includes elections, federal-state relations, civil rights and liberties, crime, the judiciary, education, health care, poverty, urban affairs and population.	*Includes formation and debate of U.S. foreign and defense policies, veterans affairs and defense spending. (Relations with specific foreign countries are usually found under the region concerned.)*	*Includes business, labor, agriculture, taxation, transportation, consumer affairs, monetary and fiscal policy, natural resources, pollution and accidents.*	*Includes worldwide scientific, medical and technological developments, natural phenomena, U.S. weather and natural disasters.*	*Includes the arts, religion, scholarship, communications media, sports, entertainment, fashions, fads and social life.*

	World Affairs	Europe	Africa & the Middle East	The Americas	Asia & the Pacific
Nov. 16	General Assembly gives permanent status to the U.N. program of technical assistance and economic aid to developing countries.		Elections for Syria's Constituent Assembly, with women participating for the first time, result in a heavy majority for opponents of a merger with Iraq, led by Rushdi el-Kikhya's Populist Party .... Iran's Shah Mohammed Riza Pahlevi arrives in Washington on a state visit to discuss military and economic matters with Truman.		British Foreign Secy. Bevin announces plans to recognize the Chinese Communist government in the event of similar action by the U.S. and Commonwealth countries. State Secy. Acheson rejects recognition of the Communist government as long as U.S. Consul Gen. Angus Ward remains imprisoned in Mukden.
Nov. 17	International Democratic Women's Federation meets in Moscow with delegates from 46 nations, including Eslanda Robeson of the U.S. and Dolores Ibarruri (La Passionaria) of Spain.	East German government announces plans for total integration of the country's economy into the Eastern European economic zone.			
Nov. 18	North Atlantic Council in Washington establishes a financial and economic committee to keep defense planning of member states in line with economic and budgetary goals.	Yugoslavia expels three Russian diplomats in retaliation for Soviet expulsion of the Yugoslavian ambassador to Moscow .... U.N. General Assembly approves a worldwide arms embargo against Albania and Bulgaria for aiding Greek Communist guerrillas .... Maurice Golay, leading Swiss banker and industrialist, dies at 58 in Basel.	U.N. Economic Survey Mission for the Middle East issues a report urging creation of a U.N.-sponsored relief and public works program in Arab countries for Palestinian Arab refugees .... Israel recalls its minister to Rumania in protest against Rumanian refusal to permit emigration of Jews.	Panamanian Pres. Daniel Chanis fires National Police chief Jose Remon for operating illegal monopolies in the meat-packing and bus transit industries.	
Nov. 19		Prince Rainier III is crowned 30th monarch of Monaco.		Panamanian security forces loyal to National Police chief Remon begin to arrest high government officials following Remon's dismissal.	London reports that Britain and other Commonwealth countries have agreed "in principle" to recognize the Chinese Communist government.
Nov. 20		Crash of an Aero Holland DC-3 near Oslo kills 27 Jewish refugee children from North Africa travelling from Belgium to a rehabilitation camp in Norway.		Panamanian Pres. Daniel Chanis resigns to avert an open revolt of forces loyal to Remon. Vice Pres. Roberto Chiari becomes president with Remon's approval.	Chinese Nationalist Pres. Li Tsung-jen arrives in Hong Kong to undergo medical treatment for a stomach ailment .... Albania recognizes the Chinese Communist government.
Nov. 21	U.N. General Assembly approves the indefinite extension of the Interim Commission on Peace and Security.	Paris City Council re-elects Pierre de Gaulle, brother of Charles de Gaulle, to a one-year term as Council president.	U.N. General Assembly accepts a Political Comm. recommendation on disposition of Italy's former African colonies, providing for Libyan independence in 1952 and a 10-year Italian trusteeship in Italian Somaliland.		
Nov. 22		East German government announces the arrest of nine officials for sabotage and fraud in attempting to prevent nationalization of the German Continental Gas Corp.		Panamanian National Assembly votes for reinstatement of deposed Pres. Daniel Chanis.	Communist forces enter Kweilin, capital of Kwangsi Province in southwestern China.
Nov. 23	Vishinsky informs the General Assembly that Russia no longer recognizes the Nationalist government's right to represent China at the U.N., but refrains from pressing for immediate seating of a Chinese Communist delegation.	Czech government announces a drive against black market activities and other forms of alleged economic "sabotage" by prosperous farmers.			
	A *Includes developments that affect more than one world region, international organizations and important meetings of major world leaders.*	B *Includes all domestic and regional developments in Europe, including the Soviet Union, Turkey, Cyprus and Malta.*	C *Includes all domestic and regional developments in Africa and the Middle East, including Iraq and Iran and excluding Cyprus, Turkey and Afghanistan.*	D *Includes all domestic and regional developments in Latin America, the Caribbean and Canada.*	E *Includes all domestic and regional developments in Asian and Pacific nations, extending from Afghanistan through all the Pacific Islands, except Hawaii.*

Date	U.S. Politics & Social Issues	U.S. Foreign Policy & Defense	U.S. Economy & Environment	Science, Technology & Nature	Culture, Leisure & Life Style
Nov. 16		Two Air Force B-29s collide during mock bombing raids near Stockton, Calif., killing 18 crew members.	Federal Mediation Director Cyrus Ching concedes defeat in his effort to settle the soft coal dispute and turns the case over to the White House .... Aluminum Co. of America signs a contract with the AFL International Council of Aluminum Workers providing for workers' pension and insurance funds .... Leftist and rightist factions of the National Maritime Union clash in N.Y. over Pres. Joseph Curran's attempt to dismiss David Drummond, a local NMU official .... International Ladies Garment Workers Union announces plans to open a full-time "labor college" in N.Y. to train union functionaries.		A group of U.S. academics headed by Clarence Gohdes of Duke Univ. recommends a list of 20 American literary works to UNESCO for publication in an international edition of the world's great classics. Among the authors included are Nathaniel Hawthorne, Edgar Allan Poe, Herman Melville and Henry James.
Nov. 17	Alger Hiss' second perjury trial opens in N.Y. before Judge Henry Goddard .... Sen. Raymond Baldwin (R, Conn.) resigns from the Senate to serve on the Connecticut State Supreme Court.	Atomic Energy Commission Chmn. David Lilienthal urges dispersal of vital government and industrial facilities to prevent national paralysis in the event of an atomic attack.			*She Wore a Yellow Ribbon*, U.S. cavalry film directed by John Ford and starring John Wayne, premiers in N.Y.
Nov. 18	N.Y. Federal Judge Sylvester Ryan rules that the scheduled espionage trial of Judith Coplon and Valentin Gubitchev will take place despite defense objections that a new trial will place Coplon in double jeopardy .... Vice Pres. Alben Barkley marries Mrs. Carleton Hadley in St. Louis, the first V.P. to wed in office.	In a letter to Chief of Naval Operations Forrest Sherman, Navy Capt. John Crommelin demands a court martial or withdrawal of his reprimand and renews his charges that Army and Air Force leaders are attempting to usurp civilian control of the armed forces .... Navy announces plans to decommission 480 aircraft, one-fifth of its air combat strength, due to budget cuts .... Air Force grounds all B-29s which have not been modified to withstand special stress after six recent crashes.	Crucible Steel becomes the last of 19 major steel producers to sign a USW contract establishing workers' pension and insurance funds.		Right Rev. William Manning, former Bishop of the Episcopal diocese of New York, dies at 83 in N.Y.
Nov. 19		Chief of Naval Operations Sherman refuses Capt. Crommelin's request for a court martial, stating that "the case is closed."	Agriculture Secy. Charles Brannan, addressing a National Grange convention in Sacramento, warns of a continuing decline in farm prices due to rapidly increasing agricultural production.		Baseball Writers Assn. names Brooklyn Dodgers infielder Jackie Robinson as the National League's most valuable player of 1949.
Nov. 20					
Nov. 21	White House announces the forthcoming resignation of presidential assistant Clark Clifford, who will reenter private law practice .... Eisenhower supporters begin a new "Eisenhower-for-President" movement in Burlington, Vt. .... Former State Secy. James Byrnes, addressing the Southern Governors Conference in Biloxi, Miss., attacks the Truman Administration's domestic programs as "costly" and "socialistic." .... Freedoms Foundation holds its first annual awards presentation in Valley Forge, Pa., honoring achievement in fostering "a better understanding of the American way of life." Among the 121 cash prize winners is baseball player Jackie Robinson, cited for his testimony before the House Un-American Activities Comm.	David Lilienthal resigns as head of the U.S. Atomic Energy Commission.	Morris Pizer, head of the 40,000-member United Furniture Workers union, renounces his former leftist views and promises to support "the program and policies of the CIO." .... Ford Motors extends its company-financed pension program to its 25,000 white-collar workers.		A Cleveland syndicate headed by businessman Ellis Ryan buys the Cleveland Indians from Bill Veeck for $2.2 million .... Vannever Bush's *Modern Arms and Free Men* is published in N.Y. by Simon and Schuster and becomes a Book-of-The-Month-Club selection.
Nov. 22	Vincent Hallinan, chief defense attorney in Harry Bridges' San Francisco trial is found in contempt of court and sentenced to six months in prison for repeatedly attempting to introduce evidence ruled irrelevant by Judge George Harris.	Minnesota Gov. Luther Youngdahl signs an order authorizing Negroes to enlist in the state's National Guard.	Sen. Robert Taft urges the Senate Finance Comm. to study the possibility of granting $100 monthly federal pensions, modelled on recent union contract provisions, to all citizens over 65.		
Nov. 23					
	F *Includes elections, federal-state relations, civil rights and liberties, crime, the judiciary, education, health care, poverty, urban affairs and population.*	G *Includes formation and debate of U.S. foreign and defense policies, veterans affairs and defense spending. (Relations with specific foreign countries are usually found under the region concerned.)*	H *Includes business, labor, agriculture, taxation, transportation, consumer affairs, monetary and fiscal policy, natural resources, pollution and accidents.*	I *Includes worldwide scientific, medical and technological developments, natural phenomena, U.S. weather and natural disasters.*	J *Includes the arts, religion, scholarship, communications media, sports, entertainment, fashions, fads and social life.*

	World Affairs	Europe	Africa & the Middle East	The Americas	Asia & the Pacific
Nov. 24		West German government agrees to accept Allied control of the Ruhr and refrain from rearming in exchange for Western Allied concessions on reparations and the size of the German merchant fleet .... British House of Lords passes the government's steel industry nationalization bill.		Panama's National Police install Arnulfo Arias, defeated candidate in the disputed 1948 election, as president to offset support for deposed Pres. Daniel Chanis .... Argentine government closes the offices of the AP, UP and seven Buenos Aires newspapers pending investigation of charges that they took money from anti-Peronist politicians during the 1946 election .... Mexico reports discovery of a new oil field near the Gulf port of Coatzacoalcos.	
Nov. 25		West German Parliament approves the government's agreement with the Western Allies despite strong Socialist opposition to international control of the Ruhr. Adenauer indicates that West Germany will seek a gradual easing of restrictions on German steel and gasoline production in further negotiations .... Communist and non-Communist French unions join in a one-day general strike to enforce their wage demands.	Israel rejects the U.N. Palestine Conciliation Commission's plan for internationalization of Jerusalem.	U.S. suspends relations with Panama due to the overthrow of "constituted authorities."	U.S. Consul Gen. Angus Ward and four members of his staff are freed in Mukden by Chinese Communist authorities and ordered deported for allegedly beating a Chinese servant.
Nov. 26		French National Assembly votes approval of the West German-Western Allied agreement and endorses German membership in a Western European federation .... Hungarian government announces the arrest of IT&T Asst. Vice Pres. Robert Vogeler and two other company officials in Budapest on espionage charges.	Jordan joins Israel in rejecting the U.N. plan for internationalization of Jerusalem.		India's Constituent Assembly adopts a new constitution establishing a two-chamber parliament, a figurehead presidency and separate judiciary, with fundamental rights of citizens guaranteed regardless of caste.
Nov. 27		Czech Communist Party recalls membership cards and begins a purge of "unreliable" members .... Defense Secy. Johnson and Joint Chiefs of Staff Chmn. Omar Bradley deny plans to permit German rearmament in the near future.		Conservative candidate Laureano Gomez is elected President of Colombia in an election boycotted by the Liberal Party.	
Nov. 28			South Africa quits the U.N. Trusteeship Comm. for the rest of this year when the committee hears an Anglican minister describe alleged mistreatment of natives in Southwest Africa.		U.S. proposes a U.N. resolution restating the traditional "Open Door" policy on China, urging all nations to refrain from interference in Chinese internal affairs and seek no special territorial rights or concessions in China.
Nov. 29	A U.N. Food and Agriculture Organization conference in Washington chooses Rome for the group's permanent headquarters and admits Afghanistan as the 62nd member.	Cominform issues another attack on Yugoslavia, calling for the overthrow of the Tito government and suppression of nationalist tendencies in other Communist parties .... U.S. authorities in Germany eliminate the requirement of U.S. approval for German political parties operating in the U.S. zone.			
Nov. 30		Bulgarian government charges former Deputy Premier Traicho Kostov and 10 other deposed officials with espionage and sabotage on behalf of Yugoslavia and the Western powers .... Czech government forbids workers to take new jobs in private industry.			Chinese Communist forces occupy the Nationalist capital of Chungking as Nationalists fall back on Chengtu .... Parliamentary elections in New Zealand result in victory for the opposition conservative National Party.
Dec. 1		Ten Soviet citizens, former anti-Communist refugees, go on trial in Yugoslavia on charges of spying for Russia .... West German government formally applies for membership in the International Ruhr Authority .... Western European countries agree to reduce their Western Hemisphere food imports by $1.25 billion by 1956.		Brazilian government forbids meetings by Communist and Communist front groups.	Senate Foreign Relations Comm. member H. Alexander Smith (R, N.J.), returning from a trip to the Far East, demands occupation of Taiwan by U.S. forces to save the island from Communist invasion.

A	B	C	D	E
Includes developments that affect more than one world region, international organizations and important meetings of major world leaders.	*Includes all domestic and regional developments in Europe, including the Soviet Union, Turkey, Cyprus and Malta.*	*Includes all domestic and regional developments in Africa and the Middle East, including Iraq and Iran and excluding Cyprus, Turkey and Afghanistan.*	*Includes all domestic and regional developments in Latin America, the Caribbean and Canada.*	*Includes all domestic and regional developments in Asian and Pacific nations, extending from Afghanistan through all the Pacific Islands, except Hawaii.*

U.S. Politics & Social Issues	U.S. Foreign Policy & Defense	U.S. Economy & Environment	Science, Technology & Nature	Culture, Leisure & Life Style	
				Baseball Writers Assn. chooses Boston Red Sox outfielder Ted Williams as the American League's most valuable player of 1949 .... Fire destroys the outer dome of the Church of the Holy Sepulcher in Jerusalem, leaving the shrine itself undamaged.	Nov. 24
Truman presents the Distinguished Public Service Award of the U.S. Conference of Mayors to Gen. George Marshall .... J.C. Walton, impeached and removed from office as governor of Oklahoma in 1923 for declaring martial law in an attempt to establish a virtual dictatorship, dies at 68 in Oklahoma City.	Truman orders Atty. Gen. McGrath and Chmn. Brien McMahon of the Joint Congressional Atomic Energy Comm. to stop congressional leaks of secret nuclear information. He specifically criticizes Sen. Edwin Johnson (D, Colo.) for making allegedly unauthorized disclosures on U.S. atomic weapons in a televised interview.			Bill (Bojangles) Robinson, famous Negro entertainer and vaudeville star, dies at 71 in N.Y.	Nov. 25
National Interfraternity Conference, meeting in Washington, recommends that member organizations eliminate racial and religious restrictions on membership.		Labor Secy. Maurice Tobin supports congressional proposals for a federal pension system guaranteeing $100 a month to all retired citizens.			Nov. 26
	Defense Dept. establishes an Office of Military Assistance under Gen. Lyman Lemnitzer to supervise military aid programs.	AFL Building and Construction Trades Dept. files with the NLRB for exemption from the Taft-Hartley Act, claiming that high worker turnover on most construction sites prevents the holding of union representation elections required under the law.			Nov. 27
Trial of former House Un-American Activities Comm. Chmn. J. Parnell Thomas (R, N.J.) on payroll-padding charges opens in Washington .... N.Y. State Supreme Court voids a law directing the State Bd. of Regents to dismiss all Communist and other "subversive" teachers from the public school system .... N.Y. City Council votes unanimously to expel Communist leader Benjamin Davis, Jr., recently convicted of conspiracy to overthrow the U.S. government.			U.S. Atomic Energy Commission reports development of a "breeder" reactor which produces more nuclear fuel than it consumes .... Heavy winds and flooding continue for the second day in the Pacific Northwest, causing 29 deaths.	Bob Black of Rhode Island State wins the NCAA cross country track title and Michigan State the team title in East Lansing, Mich.	Nov. 28
	Defense Dept. and Atomic Energy Commission announce plans for a new series of nuclear tests on Eniwetok Atoll in the Marshall Islands.			Notre Dame end Leon Hart receives the N.Y. Athletic Club's Heisman Trophy as the top college football player of 1949.	Nov. 29
Rep. J. Parnell Thomas withdraws his not guilty plea and pleads no contest in his Washington trial on payroll-padding charges. District Judge Alexander Holtzoff dismisses charges against Helen Campbell, Thomas' administrative assistant .... Whittaker Chambers completes seven days of testimony at Alger Hiss' perjury trial, reiterating his claim that Hiss gave him 47 secret State Dept. documents for transmission to Russia in 1938.		Four hundred thousand coal miners renew their strike after expiration of a three-week truce without contract agreement. UMW leader Lewis orders miners to begin a three-day work-week Dec. 5 while the union seeks to settle with individual companies .... Atomic Energy Commission permits limited sale of uranium on the commercial market after an eight-year interval.		Army is named winner of the Lambert Trophy for Eastern football supremacy in 1949.	Nov. 30
		CIO International Union of Electrical, Radio and Machine Workers completes a four-day founding convention in Philadelphia after adopting a provisional constitution barring Communists from union office and hearing messages of support from Truman and Labor Secy. Maurice Tobin. The new union claims the support of more than half the membership of the old United Electrical, Radio and Machine Workers union .... Midwest Stock Exchange opens in Chicago .... National Conference on Labor Legislation ends a three-day Washington meeting after calling for repeal of the Taft-Hartley Act and urging a $1 hourly minimum wage.			Dec. 1

F	G	H	I	J
Includes elections, federal-state relations, civil rights and liberties, crime, the judiciary, education, health care, poverty, urban affairs and population.	*Includes formation and debate of U.S. foreign and defense policies, veterans affairs and defense spending. (Relations with specific foreign countries are usually found under the region concerned.)*	*Includes business, labor, agriculture, taxation, transportation, consumer affairs, monetary and fiscal policy, natural resources, pollution and accidents.*	*Includes worldwide scientific, medical and technological developments, natural phenomena, U.S. weather and natural disasters.*	*Includes the arts, religion, scholarship, communications media, sports, entertainment, fashions, fads and social life.*

	World Affairs	Europe	Africa & the Middle East	The Americas	Asia & the Pacific
Dec. 2		Father Alexei Krishko, Russian Orthodox priest in Sarajevo and chief defendant in the espionage trial of 11 Russian refugees, admits to government charges that he spied on Yugoslavia.	U.N. General Assembly's Political Comm. approves a $54.9-million relief program for Palestinian refugees in the Middle East.	British House of Commons completes action on a bill giving Canada sole jurisdiction over all Canadian affairs.	
Dec. 3	General Assembly approves creation of a U.N. High Commissioner's Office for Refugees to supervise the refugee aid program in place of the International Refugee Organization, scheduled to disband in 1951.	Inter-Allied Reparations Agency cuts off shipment of dismantled German plants to Russia due to Soviet failure to deliver promised food shipments to West Germany.			State Secy. Acheson protests against the Nationalist blockade of Communist-held Chinese ports but praises U.S. shipping lines that have not violated the blockade.
Dec. 4					
Dec. 5		Chancellor Konrad Adenauer indicates his willingness to form a West German military force if necessary to maintain Western European security against Russia.			
Dec. 6		Three rightist political parties, including the Socialist Reichs Party, are formed in Bavaria following the elimination of U.S. licensing requirements.	Britain rejects a proposal for the union of Southern and Northern Rhodesia and Nyasaland into a "Dominion of Capricorn."		
Dec. 7		Espionage trial of former Bulgarian Deputy Premier Traicho Kostov and 10 co-defendants begins in Sofia as Kostov maintains his innocence of all but minor charges.			
Dec. 8	U.N. Narcotics Commission establishes a special committee in Ankara to control and supervise world opium trade.	East German government expels a Yugoslavian military mission from East Berlin.	U.N. General Assembly approves a $54.9-million relief program for Palestinian refugees recommended by the Political Comm.		Chinese Nationalist government abandons the mainland for Taiwan as Communist forces approach the headquarters city of Chengtu .... U.N. General Assembly passes a U.S.-sponsored resolution urging noninterference in China's internal affairs, rejecting Nationalist demands for a strong statement barring recognition of the Communist government by U.N. member states.
Dec. 9	Anti-Communist labor representatives from 53 countries, including the AFL and CIO, conclude a 12-day meeting in London after establishing the International Confederation of Free Trade Unions to rival the leftist World Federation of Trade Unions.	A Sarajevo court convicts 10 Russian emigres on Yugoslavian government charges of espionage and sentences them to prison terms of three to 20 years.	General Assembly reaffirms its 1947 decision to place Jerusalem under U.N. administration despite Israeli and Jordanian refusal to give up parts of the city which they control.		
Dec. 10	U.N. General Assembly ends its 1949 session after approving a record $49.6-million budget for 1950.		Former Amb. to the U.S. Ali Jawdat al-Ayubi becomes premier of a new Iraqi cabinet.		Gen. Lu Han, Nationalist governor of Yunnan Province in southwestern China, surrenders to the Communists .... Parliamentary elections in Australia result in a victory for the Liberal and Country parties, ending the eight-year-old Labor government.
	A	B	C	D	E
	Includes developments that affect more than one world region, international organizations and important meetings of major world leaders.	*Includes all domestic and regional developments in Europe, including the Soviet Union, Turkey, Cyprus and Malta.*	*Includes all domestic and regional developments in Africa and the Middle East, including Iraq and Iran and excluding Cyprus, Turkey and Afghanistan.*	*Includes all domestic and regional developments in Latin America, the Caribbean and Canada.*	*Includes all domestic and regional developments in Asian and Pacific nations, extending from Afghanistan through all the Pacific Islands, except Hawaii.*

U.S. Politics & Social Issues	U.S. Foreign Policy & Defense	U.S. Economy & Environment	Science, Technology & Nature	Culture, Leisure & Life Style	
Vice Pres. Alben Barkley formally opens the 1950 congressional campaign at a $100-a-plate N.Y. dinner, assailing advocates of the "laissez faire days of antiquity." .... Sen. John Bricker (R, Ohio) urges efforts to unite Republicans and Southern Democrats into a single party opposed to the "welfare state."	Chief of Naval Operations Forrest Sherman, speaking to Annapolis midshipmen, announces that the Navy will concentrate on development of anti-submarine warfare to offset the superior size of Russia's submarine fleet .... Gen. George Moore, commander of U.S. forces on Corregidor during the Japanese siege, commits suicide at 62 near Carolands, Calif.				Dec. 2
				Philip Barry, author of *Philadelphia Story, Hotel Universe* and other plays, dies at 53 of a heart attack in N.Y.	Dec. 3
Progressive Party National Comm., meeting in N.Y., adopts a program calling for U.S.-Russian understanding, recognition of the Chinese Communist government and the major points of Truman's Fair Deal legislation .... Rep. Martin Gorski (D, Ill.) dies at 63 of a heart attack in Chicago.	U.S. names five diplomats, including Philip Jessup and Ralph Bunche, to a newly-formed U.N. panel of mediators available for work in international disputes.				Dec. 4
Connecticut Gov. Chester Bowles appoints former Asst. State Secy. William Benton, a Democrat, to serve the remainder of Raymond Baldwin's Senate term.	Former Maj. George Jordan testifies before a House Un-American Activities subcommittee that FDR presidential aide Harry Hopkins ordered him to expedite uranium shipments to Russia during the war. Radio commentator Fulton Lewis, Jr. tells reporters that Henry Wallace, as Bd. of Economic Warfare director, ordered wartime shipment of uranium compounds and heavy water to Russia over the objections of Gen. Leslie Groves.	Supreme Court upholds an Arkansas statute forbidding the use of force by striking workers to keep non-strikers from their jobs .... Justice Dept. files a civil antitrust suit against the Celanese Corp. in N.Y. for purchasing its chief rival in the rayon warp-knit fabric industry, the Tubize Rayon Corp.	National Aeronautics Assn. presents the Wright Brothers Memorial Trophy to Charles Lindbergh.	Ike Williams retains his lightweight boxing championship with a 15-round decision over Freddie Dawson in Chicago .... France's top literary prize, the Prix Goncourt, goes to Robert Merle for his first novel, *Weekend at Zuydcoote*.	Dec. 5
		UMW leader John Lewis announces the signing of collective contracts with several small mine operators, providing for a 95¢ daily wage increase and a larger employer contribution to the UMW welfare and pension fund .... CIO Amalgamated Clothing Workers union and the Clothing Manufacturers Assn. announce a $20 monthly pension increase for 150,000 workers in the men's and boys' clothing industry, raising pensions to $100 a month.		Negro folk singer Huddie Ledbetter (Leadbelly) dies at 60 in N.Y. of a bone infection.	Dec. 6
	Former Manhattan Project director Leslie Groves, testifying before a House Un-American Activities subcommittee, denies George Jordan's claim that wartime uranium shipments to Russia were made over his objections.	Seventeen thousand USW members end their 52-day strike against the Aluminum Co. of America after the firm agrees to bear the entire cost of workers' pension and insurance programs.			Dec. 7
House of Delegates of the American Medical Assn. unanimously approves a $25 levy on all AMA members to fight Truman's proposed national health insurance plan.		Workers at the Oak Ridge nuclear facility end their first strike, a four-day wildcat protest against employment of non-union labor.	N.J. Gov. Alfred Driscoll declares a state of emergency in six northern counties due to a water shortage in the New York-New Jersey area.	Musical comedy *Gentlemen Prefer Blondes*, starring Carol Channing, opens in N.Y. to favorable reviews.	Dec. 8
A federal court in Washington sentences J. Parnell Thomas to six to 18 months in prison and a $10,000 fine for congressional payroll-padding .... Hede Massing, former wife of Gerhart Eisler, testifies at the perjury trial of Alger Hiss, corroborating Chambers' claim that Hiss belonged to the Communist underground in Washington during the late 1930s.		Anthracite coal mine operators reject UMW contract terms, including doubling of employer contributions to the UMW welfare and pension fund and a 95¢ daily wage increase .... Budget Director Frank Pace urges a tax increase to avert a federal deficit in the coming fiscal year, opposing congressional proposals for reduced government spending.		National Football League and the All American Conference end their four-year rivalry as they merge into a single National-American Football League.	Dec. 9
R. Douglas Stuart, vice chairman of the Quaker Oats Co., is named treasurer of the Republican National Comm.				American Football Coaches Assn. poll names Bud Wilkinson of Oklahoma Univ. as best coach of 1949.	Dec. 10
F	G	H	I	J	
Includes elections, federal-state relations, civil rights and liberties, crime, the judiciary, education, health care, poverty, urban affairs and population.	*Includes formation and debate of U.S. foreign and defense policies, veterans affairs and defense spending. (Relations with specific foreign countries are usually found under the region concerned.)*	*Includes business, labor, agriculture, taxation, transportation, consumer affairs, monetary and fiscal policy, natural resources, pollution and accidents.*	*Includes worldwide scientific, medical and technological developments, natural phenomena, U.S. weather and natural disasters.*	*Includes the arts, religion, scholarship, communications media, sports, entertainment, fashions, fads and social life.*	

	World Affairs	Europe	Africa & the Middle East	The Americas	Asia & the Pacific
Dec. 11					North Korean authorities release two Economic Cooperation Admin. officials to U.S. representatives on the demarcation line after an 81-day imprisonment.
Dec. 12	Thirty nations, including the Big Four powers, sign the new Geneva conventions on the rules of war in Geneva.				
Dec. 13			Israeli Parliament votes to transfer all government offices except the defense and foreign ministries to the new city of Jerusalem, a move to thwart internationalization of the city .... Syrian Premier Hashem al-Atassi resigns to become provisional president until adoption of a new Syrian constitution.		
Dec. 14		A Sofia court convicts Traicho Kostov and 10 other former Bulgarian officials on government charges of espionage, sentencing Kostov to death and his co-defendants to prison terms of eight years to life.		U.S. extends diplomatic recognition to the Arias regime in Panama.	Representatives of 16 Indonesian states and territories meeting in Jakarta approve a provisional constitution for the United States of Indonesia.
Dec. 15		West German government becomes the direct recipient of Marshall Plan aid under an agreement signed by Chancellor Konrad Adenauer and U.S. High Commissioner John McCloy .... Hungarian government arrests American Joint Distribution Comm. official Israel Jacobson on unspecified charges .... International Court of Justice in The Hague sets damages owed by Albania to Britain for the 1946 Corfu Channel incident at $2.4 million .... Max Petitpierre, political leader of Switzerland's French-speaking community, is elected Swiss president by Parliament.			
Dec. 16	Trygve Lie announces that he will not seek reappointment as U.N. Secretary-General when his present term expires in 1951.	Economic Comm. of the Council of Europe approves a Western European free trade plan providing for creation of a gold or dollar fund from contributions by member states to offset trade imbalances .... Former Bulgarian official Traicho Kostov, sentenced to death for espionage, is hanged in Sofia.	David Ben-Gurion announces that Jerusalem will become Israel's capital at year's end .... Jordan abolishes its governor general's office for Palestine, permitting regular government ministries to take over administration of Arab Palestine.		Mao Tze-tung arrives in Moscow for his first visit as chief of state .... Chinese Communist radio in Peking announces that Communist forces have reached the Indochinese border at Chenankuan .... Representatives of Indonesian states elect nationalist leader Ahmed Sukarno president of the United States of Indonesia.
Dec. 17		Britain, Sweden, Norway and Denmark agree to work towards a British-Scandinavian economic union.			Burma becomes the first non-Communist nation to recognize the Chinese Communist government .... U.S. State Dept. declares Shanghai a "danger zone" due to the Nationalist blockade and warns U.S. ships to stay away from the port .... U.N. Commission for India and Pakistan reports inability to resolve disagreements between the two countries over a plebiscite to determine the status of Kashmir. The commission recommends appointment of a single U.N. arbiter to work out a settlement.
Dec. 18		Ukrainian Communist Party leader Nikita Khrushchev is appointed to the Central Comm. of the all-Union Communist Party in Moscow .... Legislative elections in Bulgaria result in a victory for the governing Fatherland Front, which faces no organized opposition.	Iraq abolishes martial law, in force since the start of the Palestine war.		Indonesian Pres. Sukarno names Mohammed Hatta, former Indonesian Republic leader, as first premier of the United States of Indonesia.
	A	B	C	D	E
	Includes developments that affect more than one world region, international organizations and important meetings of major world leaders.	*Includes all domestic and regional developments in Europe, including the Soviet Union, Turkey, Cyprus and Malta.*	*Includes all domestic and regional developments in Africa and the Middle East, including Iraq and Iran and excluding Cyprus, Turkey and Afghanistan.*	*Includes all domestic and regional developments in Latin America, the Caribbean and Canada.*	*Includes all domestic and regional developments in Asian and Pacific nations, extending from Afghanistan through all the Pacific Islands, except Hawaii.*

U.S. Politics & Social Issues	U.S. Foreign Policy & Defense	U.S. Economy & Environment	Science, Technology & Nature	Culture, Leisure & Life Style	
				Clifford Berryman, Pulitzer Prize-winning dean of American editorial cartoonists, dies at 80 in Washington .... *New York Herald Tribune* lists Sholem Ash's *Mary* and Clare Barnes' *White Collar Zoo* as best-selling fiction and non-fiction books.	Dec. 11
Illinois Gov. Adlai Stevenson is divorced by his wife, Ellen Borden Stevenson, in Las Vegas .... Internal Revenue Service revokes the tax exemption of the George W. Armstrong Trust Fund, established to foster the teaching of white supremacy.		Ten thousand USW members end a 38-day strike against the Timken Roller Bearing Co. in Canton, Ohio, after the firm agrees to creation of an employer-financed pension fund on the steel industry model .... Supreme Court upholds the constitutionality of the 1947 rent control law, reversing the decision of a Chicago district court.	John D. Rockefeller, Jr. donates $2 million to the N.Y. Memorial Cancer Center.	Fred Haas of New Orleans wins the $10,000 Miami Open Golf Tournament .... Vittorio de Sica's *The Bicycle Thief* premiers in N.Y. .... Edmund Wade Fairchild, founder of Fairchild Publications, dies at 83 in Glen Ridge, N.J.	Dec. 12
A federal district court in Birmingham, Ala. rules that the city's racial zoning laws are unconstitutional.	A four-member House Foreign Affairs subcommittee, returning to Washington after a European trip, opposes German rearmament even as part of an international force.				Dec. 13
A former U.S. Communist Party Central Comm. member, Manning Johnson, testifies at the San Francisco trial of Harry Bridges that Bridges was elected to the Central Comm. in 1936 under the name of Rossi.	Navy announces development of the first two-engine flying boat for anti-submarine duty, the Martin P5M-1.				Dec. 14
Federal Housing Admin. and the Veterans Admin. ban federal loan insurance on property made subject to racial or religious restrictions by covenants filed in court after Feb. 15, 1950. Informal restrictions are unaffected by the new policy.		Western and Northern coal producers, meeting in Pittsburgh, agree to resume payments to the UMW pension and welfare fund to avert a renewed strike. Southern Coal Producers Assn. Pres. Joseph Moody urges Truman to intervene in the coal dispute with an injunction preventing miners from continuing their three-day work week .... AFL Pres. William Green predicts eventual unification of the U.S. labor movement due to AFL-CIO cooperation in the anti-Communist International Confederation of Free Trade Unions .... U.S. Steel raises steel prices 4% to an average of $4 a ton .... American Farm Bureau Fed. ends a four-day meeting in Chicago after rejecting Agriculture Secy. Charles Brannan's plan for reform of the farm price support system.	U.S. Atomic Energy Commision announces curtailment of its research fellowship program due to widespread opposition to loyalty checks on applicants.		Dec. 15
Univ. of California dismisses physics instructor Irving Fox following his admission that he belonged to the Communist Party while working during the war in the Berkeley radiation laboratory .... N.Y. City Council approves a measure barring racial bias in city-sponsored housing, the first such municipal statute in the U.S.	Former N.Y. banker Paul Nitze is named to succeed George Kennan as head of the State Department's policy planning staff.	CIO Pres. Philip Murray threatens to expel six leftist member unions, including the United Furniture Workers union and the International Longshoremen's and Warehousemen's union, for failure to pay dues owed to the national treasury.		John D. Rockefeller, Jr. donates 35,562 acres of land to the Grand Teton National Park and Jackson Hole National Monument in Wyoming for recreational use .... New York residents take a "water holiday," skipping baths and shaving to conserve the city's critically low water supply.	Dec. 16
A federal court in Rome, Ga. declares a mistrial in the case of 10 whites, including Dade County Sheriff John Lynch, accused of arresting and beating seven Negroes without cause.	Defense Secy. Johnson urges a three-year extension of the draft, claiming that conscription boosts voluntary enlistments and helps convince allies of U.S. determination "to maintain the strength of the free world."			Tennessee Williams' *A Streetcar Named Desire* closes in N.Y. after 855 performances .... Professional Golfers Assn. awards Sam Snead the Vardon Trophy for the lowest average 18-hole score (69.37).	Dec. 17
				Women's Professional Golf Assn. chooses Marlene Bauer of Long Beach, Calif. as woman golfer of the year.	Dec. 18
F	G	H	I	J	
Includes elections, federal-state relations, civil rights and liberties, crime, the judiciary, education, health care, poverty, urban affairs and population.	*Includes formation and debate of U.S. foreign and defense policies, veterans affairs and defense spending. (Relations with specific foreign countries are usually found under the region concerned.)*	*Includes business, labor, agriculture, taxation, transportation, consumer affairs, monetary and fiscal policy, natural resources, pollution and accidents.*	*Includes worldwide scientific, medical and technological developments, natural phenomena, U.S. weather and natural disasters.*	*Includes the arts, religion, scholarship, communications media, sports, entertainment, fashions, fads and social life.*	

	World Affairs	Europe	Africa & the Middle East	The Americas	Asia & the Pacific
Dec. 19	U.S., Britain and Canada agree on standardization of their military equipment and training.	Britain cuts its purchases of U.S. oil, shifting to greater reliance on Venezuelan and Middle Eastern oil . . . . A British military court in Hamburg sentences Field Marshal Eric von Manstein, wartime German commander on the Eastern Front, to 18 years in prison for sanctioning war crimes against Russian troops and civilians.	A group of Syrian officers led by Col. Adib el-Shishikli arrests Army commander-in-chief Sami Hinnawi, accusing him of plotting to put the government in the hands of politicians who favor union with Iraq.		A Liberal-Country Party coalition government headed by Liberal Party leader Robert Gordon Menzies takes office in Australia.
Dec. 20			U.N. Trusteeship Council passes a resolution asking Israel to refrain from establishing its capital in Jerusalem.		Indonesian Premier Mohammed Hatta names his first cabinet, retaining the foreign affairs ministry for himself.
Dec. 21	State Secy. Acheson announces agreement on division of U.S. military aid to Western Europe after the U.S. reduces or abandons its original demands for supervision of the military programs of recipient states.	Russia and Soviet-bloc countries celebrate Stalin's 70th birthday as the Supreme Soviet awards him the country's highest decoration, the Order of Lenin . . . . Council of Europe's Political Comm. in Strasbourg votes against working for a close federation of Western European nations in favor of strengthening existing regional institutions.			K.C. Wu, former mayor of Shanghai, replaces Gen. Chen Cheng as Nationalist governor of Taiwan . . . . Holland's Queen Juliana approves a law transferring sovereignty over the Dutch East Indies to the United States of Indonesia . . . . Russian delegate Kuzma Derevyanko walks out of the Allied Council for Japan in Tokyo when MacArthur charges that Japanese prisoners are still being used as forced labor in Siberia.
Dec. 22				A U.S.-Mexican agricultural commission reports successful conclusion of a three-year campaign against foot and mouth disease in Mexico.	Japanese government refuses to accept the Yalta agreement as binding on Japan, maintaining its claim to southern Sakhalin, the southern Kuriles, Okinawa and Iwo Jima . . . . Japan and Britain complete a $360-million trade agreement.
Dec. 23		A Polish military court in Wroclaw convicts four French citizens, one German and one Pole of spying for French intelligence. All receive prison terms . . . . Hungarian Catholic Church permits its priests to take an oath of allegiance to the state.			U.S. State Dept. openly supports the Nationalist blockade of Communist-controlled Chinese ports, warning U.S. shippers that they face revocation of their licenses if they permit their vessels to enter Shanghai.
Dec. 24		Greek government lifts martial law in Athens, the Peloponnesus and Aegean Islands . . . . U.S. and Yugoslavia sign an air agreement permitting U.S. airlines the use of Yugoslavian air space and landing facilities. Yugoslavian airlines receive similar rights in the U.S. zones of Germany and Austria . . . . French cabinet of Premier Georges Bidault narrowly wins a vote of confidence in the National Assembly during debate over the 1950 budget.			India suspends coal deliveries to Pakistan, charging that Pakistan has fallen behind in scheduled jute shipments to Calcutta.
Dec. 25		Czech government revokes the citizenship of persons who fled the country after the Communist coup of February 1948 . . . . Austrian Interior Ministry announces the arrest of 13 youths for attempting to form a neo-Nazi organization.			
Dec. 26		Britain and Yugoslavia sign a five-year, $616-million commercial agreement, Yugoslavia's largest postwar trade pact with a Western nation.	Egypt accuses Jordan and Iraq of interfering in Syrian politics with the aim of establishing a Jordanian-Iraqi-Syrian union.		
Dec. 27				Argentine Pres. Peron sues two leading newspapers, *Prensa* and *Nacion*, for claiming that he has enriched himself through the presidency.	Ceremonies in Amsterdam and Jakarta mark formal establishment of the United States of Indonesia . . . . U.S. headquarters in Tokyo announces plans to give control over Japanese imports to private firms.

U.S. Politics & Social Issues	U.S. Foreign Policy & Defense	U.S. Economy & Environment	Science, Technology & Nature	Culture, Leisure & Life Style	
Alger Hiss begins five days of testimony at his second N.Y. perjury trial, maintaining his claim that he never belonged to the Communist Party or passed State Dept. documents to Whittaker Chambers.	Former Chief of Naval Operations Louis Denfeld rejects an appointment as U.S. naval commander in the eastern Atlantic and Mediterranean.	A CIO commission headed by Textile Workers union Pres. Emil Rieve holds a hearing in Washington on charges that the United Office and Professional Workers union follows the Communist Party line. A second CIO commission investigates the California State Industrial Council .... Supreme Court upholds a lower court ruling that the California Automobile Assn. is subject to taxation. The decision ends the tax-exempt status of all U.S. auto clubs .... A&P Pres. David Bofinger dies at 63 in N.Y.			Dec. 19
Truman appoints White House aide Charles Murphy to succeed Clark Clifford as his special assistant .... House Judiciary Comm. member Ed Gossett (D, Tex.) concludes an inspection of N.Y. immigration facilities by charging that the city is a haven for those seeking illegal entry into the U.S.	U.S. State Dept. bars visits to Hungary by Americans and demands the release of two IT&T officials held by the Hungarian government.	An attempted bombing of UAW headquarters in Detroit fails.		Notre Dame Coach Frank Leahy is named Football Man of the Year by the Football Writer's Assn. .... Margaret Truman makes her Carnegie Hall debut with a half-hour performance of Christmas music and a Puccini aria.	Dec. 20
N.Y. Gov. Thomas Dewey denies any intention of running for president in 1952 .... East St. Louis Bd. of Education announces plans to end racial segregation in public schools in order to keep $678,000 in state funds.		Jane Wallis Waldron Bancroft, chief owner of Dow-Jones, dies at 72 in Boston .... Financier Howard Hopson, who built up the Associated Gas & Electric utilities empire during the 1920s and later served three years in prison for defrauding stockholders, dies at 67 in Greenwich, Conn.		Cecil B. deMille's biblical spectacle *Samson and Delilah* premiers in N.Y. .... German soprano Helena Braun scores a personal triumph at New York's Metropolitan Opera by singing the role of Bruennhilde in Wagner's *Die Walkuere* on four hours' notice as a stand-in for Helen Traubel.	Dec. 21
Patrick Malin is chosen to succeed Robert Baldwin as director of the American Civil Liberties Union.	Commerce Dept. tightens restrictions on shipments to Communist countries containing non-secret technical information of military importance .... U.S. Public Health Service announces creation of a radiological health branch to plan for protection against atomic radiation in case of a nuclear attack.	NLRB rules that farm workers are not covered by the Taft-Hartley Act in a case involving a strike by the AFL National Farm Labor Union against the Di Giorgio Fruit Corp. in Bakersfield, Calif. .... Agricultural Dept. ends price support purchases of eggs.	National Aeronautic Association's Collier Trophy for the year's greatest aviation achievement goes to the Radio Technical Commission for its development of a bad weather flight system used in the Berlin airlift.		Dec. 22
N.Y.C. Mayor William O'Dwyer signs a measure increasing his own salary and those of other high city officials by a total of $208,100.		N.Y. Stock Exchange prices rise to the highest levels since August 1946, with the *New York Times* price average edging up 0.3 of a point.		Hooperatings name *Texaco Star Theater, Toast of the Town* and *Arthur Godfrey's Talent Scouts* the top November television shows.	Dec. 23
				Adam's Rib, a comedy starring Spencer Tracy and Katherine Hepburne, premiers in N.Y.	Dec. 24
			Air Force announces development of a highly heat-resistant ceramic, stupalith, for use in jet and rocket engines.		Dec. 25
			Columbia Univ. physicist John Dunning reports development of a new method of producing uranium which drastically reduces the cost of nuclear energy.	*Ring Magazine* names heavyweight champion Ezzard Charles boxing's fighter of the year.	Dec. 26
Pre-trial testimony in the Coplon-Gubitchev espionage case produces a statement from an FBI agent that Judith Coplon's telephone was illegally tapped, reversing earlier government contentions that all evidence was gathered legally.			Air Force ends a two-year investigation of flying saucer reports by denying their authenticity .... Andrew Johnson, Swedish-born inventor of the combine harvester and other machines, dies at 89 in Los Angeles.	New York Film Critics Society names *All the King's Men* the best film of 1949 and *The Bicycle Thief* the best foreign-language film. Broderick Crawford is named best actor of the year and Olivia de Havilland best actress .... The $10,000 Harper literary award goes to Max Steele for his first novel, *Debby*.	Dec. 27
F *Includes elections, federal-state relations, civil rights and liberties, crime, the judiciary, education, health care, poverty, urban affairs and population.*	G *Includes formation and debate of U.S. foreign and defense policies, veterans affairs and defense spending. (Relations with specific foreign countries are usually found under the region concerned.)*	H *Includes business, labor, agriculture, taxation, transportation, consumer affairs, monetary and fiscal policy, natural resources, pollution and accidents.*	I *Includes worldwide scientific, medical and technological developments, natural phenomena, U.S. weather and natural disasters.*	J *Includes the arts, religion, scholarship, communications media, sports, entertainment, fashions, fads and social life.*	

	World Affairs	Europe	Africa & the Middle East	The Americas	Asia & the Pacific
Dec. 28		France abolishes import quotas on most food and manufactured items .... Hungary frees American Joint Distribution Comm. official Israel Jacobson after questioning him for several days on suspicion of espionage.	Syrian Pres. Hashem al-Atassi appoints a new cabinet, excluding representatives of the People's Party and other politicians accused by the Army of favoring union with Iraq.		Truman announces U.S. recognition of the United States of Indonesia, appointing H. Merle Cochran first U.S. ambassador to Indonesia.
Dec. 29		Hungarian government issues a decree nationalizing all industrial firms, including foreign-owned companies, with more than 10 employes .... Rumanian Parliament approves an economic plan for 1950 calling for a 37% increase in industrial production.	Israel begins a 10-year drive to plant forests in the northern half of the country .... Sir Arthur MacMahon, Britain's first High Commissioner for Egypt who helped induce Arab nationalists to revolt against the Turkish Empire during World War I, dies at 87 in London.		Russia objects to Chinese Nationalist representation on the U.N. Security Council but refrains from demanding replacement of the Nationalists by a Communist delegation .... Nationalist forces on Hainan Island off the South China coast report defeating a Communist invasion attempt .... U.S. Navy announces plans to assign the new aircraft carrier *Boxer* to the Seventh Fleet, operating in the western Pacific.
Dec. 30		British government introduces several measures to attract more foreign capital into the country, giving investors permission to withdraw their capital at any time and allowing foreign workers to send home all of their savings .... French Premier Georges Bidault wins a second vote of confidence in the National Assembly during debate over the 1950 budget.	Shah of Iran ends a six-week visit to the U.S.		Truman and his military advisers decide against using U.S. forces to defend Taiwan against a possible Communist attack but agree to consider the possibility of sending fresh equipment and advisers to the Nationalist government on the island .... India recognizes Communist China and ends diplomatic relations with the Nationalist government .... Vietnamese Chief of State Bao Dai and French High Commissioner Leon Pignon sign an agreement in Saigon giving the French-sponsored Vietnamese state greater control over its own internal affairs, including education and local administration. Foreign and military affairs remain in French hands .... British government gives Hong Kong Gov. Sir Alexander Grantham emergency powers to deal with disorders arising from Communist efforts to organize a general strike.
Dec. 31			Israel rejects a U.N. Trusteeship Council request to remove its capital from the new city of Jerusalem.		Communist authorities order the staff of the U.N. International Children's Emergency Fund to leave China within a month .... A Russian military court in Khabarovsk sentences 12 Japanese officers to prison terms of two to 25 years for planning to wage germ warfare against the Soviet Union.

U.S. Politics & Social Issues	U.S. Foreign Policy & Defense	U.S. Economy & Environment	Science, Technology & Nature	Culture, Leisure & Life Style	
	U.S. Atomic Energy Commission announces plans for a series of one-week courses for physicians on the hazards of atomic warfare.	Southern Coal Producers Assn. files an unfair pratices suit against the UMW with the NLRB, accusing the union of violating the Taft-Hartley Act by refusing to bargain in good faith and seeking to impose union-shop conditions .... Sears, Roebuck issues its annual catalog with price cuts averaging 10%, while Proctor & Gamble reduces household soap prices by 4%.		Novelist Hervey Allen, author of best-selling *Anthony Adverse*, dies at 60 of a heart attack in Miami.	Dec. 28
	Navy Capt. Arleigh Burke, head of the office charged with planning strategy against the Army and Air Force in the debate over U.S. military strategy, is promoted to rear admiral.	President's Council of Economic Advisers issues its fourth annual report, predicting continued economic growth and urging closer cooperation between business and government.		*Time* Magazine names Winston Churchill Man of The Half-Century.	Dec. 29
		War Assets Admin. is liquidated and its remaining property turned over to the General Services Admin.		Court-ordered dissolution of Paramount Pictures, Inc. is completed with formation of Paramount Pictures Corp. and United Paramount Theaters, Inc. .... *Radio Daily* selects CBS's *Mind the Shadows*, NBC's *Living, 1949* and ABC's *The Berlin Story* as outstanding network broadcasts of 1949. Hooperatings name *Jack Benny*, *Radio Theater*, *Fibber McGee and Molly* and *Arthur Godfrey's Talent Scouts* as the most popular network shows .... *Billboard* lists *Mule Train*, by Hy Heath, Johnny Lange and Fred Glikeman, as the most popular song at year's end .... *Sands of Iwo Jima*, a war film starring John Wayne, premiers in N.Y.	Dec. 30
Judith Coplon asks the Supreme Court to order a retrial of government espionage charges against her on grounds that the FBI tapped her telephone illegally.		NLRB issues its fourth anti-closed shop ruling against the International Typographical Union, ordering the union to stop attempting to impose such conditions on commercial printing shops in Chicago, Detroit and other cities .... AT&T Board Chmn. Walter Gifford retires and is suceeded by Pres. Leroy Wilson.		*Born Yesterday* closes on Broadway after 1,643 performances.	Dec. 31

INDEX

INDEX

The index refers to all daily entries, which are keyed to dates and column letters rather than to page numbers. Headings are arranged in letter-by-letter alphabetical order. Subject headings (e.g., AGRICULTURE, ARMAMENTS) refer to events in the U.S. unless otherwise indicated by a cross-reference or relevant subhead. For subject entries in foreign countries, see country names.

A

B

C

K

N

T

V

Z

PHOTO CREDITS

Front Endpaper—Official U.S. Navy photograph
Pages 4-5—National Archives
6—All photos, Wide World
7—Upper left, Wide World; lower left, Black Star; upper right, National Archives; center right, Wide World; lower right, National Archives.
84-85—Wide World
86—Lower left, National Archives; upper right, official U.S. Navy photograph; middle and lower right, National Archives.
87—right (all photos), National Archives; upper and middle left, National Archives.
178-179—Wide World
180—Upper left, Office of War Information; lower left, National Archives; lower right, United Press International.
181—Center left, National Archives; lower left, Wide World; right (all photos), National Archives.
264-265—Official U.S. Marine Corps photograph.
266—Upper left, National Archives; center and lower left, Wide World; right (all photos), National Archives.
267—Upper left, National Archives; center left, Wide World; lower left, National Archives; upper right, Wide World; center right, United Press International; lower right (two photos), Wide World.
358-359—National Archives.
360—Left (all photos), National Archives; upper right, United Press International; center and lower right, National Archives.
361—Left (all photos), National Archives; upper right, drawings copyrighted 1944, renewed 1972, Bill Mauldin; lower right, National Archives.
454-455—Wide World.
456—Left (all photos), National Archives; upper and center right, National Archives; lower left, United Press International; bottom center, National Archives.
457—Left (all photos), National Archives; upper right, National Archives; center right, Wide World; bottom right (two photos), National Archives.
556-557—National Archives
558—Upper left, Wide World; lower left, National Archives; right (all photos), National Archives.
559—Upper left, Wide World; lower left, National Archives; upper and center right, National Archives; lower right, Wide World.
660-661—Wide World.
662—Upper and center left, Wide World; lower left, National Archives; right (all photos), Wide World.
663—All photos, Wide World.
752-753—Wide World.
754—Upper left, National Archives; center left, Wide World; lower left, United Press International; center and lower right, National Archives.
755—Upper left, National Archives; center and lower left, Wide World; upper right, National Archives; lower right, Wide World.
856-857—National Archives
858—Left (upper and lower), Wide World; upper and center right, National Archives; lower right, Wide World.
859—Upper left, National Archives; upper and center right, Wide World; lower right, National Archives.